WORLD HISTORY
VOYAGES OF EXPLORATION

KENNETH R. CURTIS

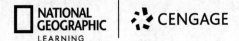

Acknowledgments

Grateful acknowledgment is given to the authors, artists, photographers, museums, publishers, and agents for permission to reprint copyrighted material. Every effort has been made to secure the appropriate permission. If any omissions have been made or if corrections are required, please contact the Publisher.

Photographic Credits

Front Cover: Atakorn/iStock/Getty Images

Back Cover: (bkgd) coolbiere photograph/Getty Images, (c) Ossiridian/Getty Images, (c) kathykonkle/DigitalVision Vectors/ Getty Images

Acknowledgments and credits continue on page R43.

For product information and technology assistance, contact us at Customer & Sales Support, 888-915-3276

For permission to use material from this text or product, submit all requests online at **www.cengage.com/permissions**

Further permissions questions can be emailed to **permissionrequest@cengage.com**

National Geographic Learning | Cengage
200 Pier 4 Blvd., Suite 400
Boston, MA 02210

National Geographic Learning, a Cengage company, is a provider of quality core and supplemental educational materials for the PreK–12, adult education, and ELT markets. Cengage is a leading provider of customized learning solutions with employees residing in nearly 40 different countries and sales in more than 125 countries around the world. Find your local representative at NGL.Cengage.com/RepFinder.

Visit National Geographic Learning online at NGL.Cengage.com

Visit our corporate website at **www.cengage.com**

ISBN: 978-0-357-36997-5

Printed in Mexico
Print Number: 3   Print Year: 2023

AUTHOR

KENNETH R. CURTIS
Professor of History
California State University Long Beach

Kenneth R. Curtis received his Ph.D. from the University of Wisconsin-Madison in African and Comparative World History. He is Professor of History at California State University Long Beach, where he has taught world history at the introductory level, in special courses designed for future middle and high school teachers, and in graduate seminars. He has worked to advance the teaching of world history at the collegiate and secondary levels in collaboration with the World History Association, the California History/Social Science Project, and the College Board's Advanced Placement World History program. He is coauthor, with Valerie Hansen of Yale University, of *Voyages in World History*, a National Geographic Learning text widely adopted by both college and AP teachers.

SENIOR CONSULTANTS

PEGGY ALTOFF
Past President
National Council for the Social Studies

Peggy Altoff's career includes teaching middle school and high school students, supervising teachers, and serving as adjunct university faculty. Peggy served as a state social studies specialist in Maryland and as a K–12 coordinator in Carrol County, Maryland, and Colorado Springs. She is a past president of the National Council for the Social Studies (NCSS) and served on the task force for the 2012 NCSS National Curriculum Standards.

FREDRIK HIEBERT
Explorer Programs
Archaeologist-in-Residence
National Geographic Society

Fred Hiebert is National Geographic's Archaeologist-in-Residence. He has led archaeological expeditions at ancient Silk Roads sites across Asia. Hiebert was curator of National Geographic's exhibition: *Afghanistan: Hidden Treasures from the National Museum, Kabul,* and its more recent exhibitions, *Tomb of Christ* and *Queens of Egypt.*

NATIONAL GEOGRAPHIC SOCIETY

The National Geographic Society contributed significantly to *World History: Voyages of Exploration.* Our collaboration with each of the following has been a pleasure and a privilege: National Geographic Maps, National Geographic Education and Children's Media, and National Geographic Missions programs. We thank the Society for its guidance and support.

NATIONAL GEOGRAPHIC EXPLORERS AND PHOTOGRAPHERS

National Geographic supports the work of a host of anthropologists, archaeologists, adventurers, biologists, educators, writers, and photographers across the world. The following individuals each contributed substantially to *World History: Voyages of Exploration.*

AZIZ ABU SARAH
Cultural Educator

LYNSEY ADDARIO
Photojournalist

SALAM AL KUNTAR
Archaeologist

ELLA AL-SHAMAHI
Paleoanthropologist and Stand-Up Comic

BUZZ ALDRIN
Astronaut and Author

JACK ANDRAKA
Inventor

ROBERT BALLARD
Oceanographer

CHRIS BASHINELLI
Cross-Cultural-Explorer

ARI BESER
Filmmaker

JIMMY CHIN
Photographer and Filmmaker

ROBERT CLARK
Photographer

KARA COONEY
Egyptologist and Author

JAGO COOPER
Archaeologist

ADJANY COSTA
Conservationist and Ichthyologist

T.H. CULHANE
Urban Ecologist

GUILLERMO DE ANDA
Underwater Archaeologist

LESLIE DEWAN
Nuclear Engineer

AMELIA EARHART
Aviator

SYLVIA EARLE
Oceanographer

STEVEN ELLIS
Archaeologist

KEOLU FOX
Human Geneticist

KEN GARRETT
Photographer

JERRY GLOVER
Agricultural Ecologist

KAVITA GUPTA
Science Educator

JEFFREY GUSKY
Photographer

DAVID GUTTENFELDER
Photographer

KEVIN HAND
Astrobiologist

PATRICK HUNT
Archaeologist

TERRY HUNT
Archaeologist

JEDIDAH ISLER
Astrophysicist

LYNN JOHNSON
Photographer

YUKINORI KAWAE
Archaeologist

KATHRYN KEANE
Vice President of Public Experiences

PEG KEINER
Educator

AMANDA KOLTZ
Biologist

KATHY KU
Engineer

LOUISE LEAKEY
Paleoanthropologist

MEAVE LEAKEY
Paleoanthropologist

NATALIA LEDFORD
Filmmaker

CHRISTINE LEE
Bioarchaeologist

DANIELLE N. LEE
Biologist

ALBERT LIN
Engineer

CARL LIPO
Archaeologist

GERD LUDWIG
Photographer

JODI MAGNESS
Archaeologist

O. LOUIS MAZZATENTA
Photographer

STEVE MCCURRY
Photographer

KAKENYA NTAIYA
Women's Advocate

SARAH PARCAK
Space Archaeologist

ALAN PARENTE
Creator of Exhibitions and Global Experiences

WILLIAM PARKINSON
Archaeologist

MATTHEW PISCITELLI
Archaeologist

KRISTIN ROMEY
Archaeologist and Writer

JEFFREY ROSE
Paleoarchaeologist

ANDRÉS RUZO
Geothermal Scientist

PARDIS SABETI
Computational Geneticist

ENRIC SALA
Marine Ecologist

PAUL SALOPEK
Writer and Journalist

MAURIZIO SERACINI
Cultural Engineer

NORA SHAWKI
Archaeologist

HAYAT SINDI
Medical Research Scientist

BRIAN SKERRY
Photographer

CHRISTOPHER THORNTON
Archaeologist

NEIL DEGRASSE TYSON
Astrophysicist

MIGUEL VILAR
Molecular Anthropologist

AMI VITALE
Photographer

GENEVIEVE VON PETZINGER
Paleoanthropologist

JON WATERHOUSE
Environmental Steward

TOPHER WHITE
Engineer and Physicist

GRACE YOUNG
Ocean Engineer

THE NATIONAL GEOGRAPHIC APPROACH

Most of us recognize that familiar magazine with the yellow border on newsstands and library shelves. You've probably come to expect from *National Geographic* engaging stories on historical and global topics, with interesting photographs. But did you know that the magazine is only one part of an institution that dates back more than 128 years—and today plays an important role in world events?

OUR PURPOSE

The National Geographic Society pushes the boundaries of exploration to further our understanding of our planet and empower us all to generate solutions for a healthier and more sustainable future.

SCIENCE AND EXPLORATION

National Geographic has become one of the largest nonprofit scientific and educational institutions in the world. NatGeo supports thousands of scientists, archaeologists, marine biologists, divers, climbers, photographers, researchers, teachers, oceanographers, geologists, adventurers, physicists, artists, curators, and writers who work on projects that add to the scientific and human record.

THE NATIONAL GEOGRAPHIC LEARNING FRAMEWORK

The Learning Framework defines and shapes National Geographic's philosophy about teaching and learning. The framework is based on the **Attitudes, Skills,** and **Knowledge** that embody the Explorer mindset. It covers diverse fields of knowledge and recognizes the core principles established at National Geographic, as well as the values held by families, communities, and cultures.

The attributes of the Learning Framework are **Attitudes**— Curiosity, Responsibility, and Empowerment; **Skills**—Observation, Communication, Collaboration, and Problem-Solving; **Knowledge**— Our Human Story, Our Living Planet, Critical Species, and New Frontiers. You will see National Geographic Learning Framework activities in each unit of this text.

NATIONAL GEOGRAPHIC LEARNING
SOCIAL STUDIES CREDO

National Geographic Learning wants students to think about the impact of their choices on themselves and others, to think critically and carefully about ideas and actions, to become lifelong learners and teachers, and to advocate for the greater good as leaders in their communities. NGL follows these guidelines:

1 Our goal is to establish relevance by connecting the physical environment and historical events to students' lives.

2 We view history as the study of identity.

3 We foster the development of empathy, tolerance, and understanding for diverse peoples, cultures, traditions, and ideas.

4 We empower students to explore their interests and strengths, find their own voices, and speak out on their beliefs.

5 We encourage students to become active and responsible citizens on local and national levels and to become global citizens.

6 We believe in the beauty and endurance of the human record and the need to preserve it.

7 We affirm the critical need to care for the planet and all of its inhabitants.

PLANNING A MUSEUM VISIT

As they study history, students learn how and where civilizations developed through the centuries. They learn how to think about the world and discover the ways in which cultures and civilizations are similar—and how they are unique. They come to understand that knowing why a civilization developed can help them interpret the past, analyze the present, and anticipate the future.

To help your students take a trip into the past, to actually immerse themselves in history, take them to a museum. Museums are like time machines. They are the keepers of our shared and collective history. Museums were created to keep track of the most special examples of human-made objects, or **material culture**. Paintings, sculpture, pottery, jewelry, clothing, furniture, cars, toys, weapons, tools, fishing lures—just about anything that humans make is a remarkable historical record of the way we live.

Some examples of material culture are featured in the Material Culture lessons in this program. Each lesson features objects that focus on a specific theme as it has been portrayed across time. Many of these examples can be found in museums or at preserved cultural sites around the world. But what do we learn from this stuff? Why is it important?

Generally, museums look for the best artifacts for their collections, the ones that helped define a people or culture. Egyptian sarcophagi, Peruvian face pots, African ceremonial masks, Native American pottery, or Cycladic figurines from the Greek islands are all examples of artifacts that help us better understand those who made them. People from thousands of miles away and hundreds of years ago feel more familiar when you observe that even in the distant past people ate on plates and drank from cups, had rugs on their floors and keys for their doors, and rocked their babies to sleep in wooden cradles. Material culture refers to what humans make—but also what makes us human. There is no better way to see this than in a museum. Use the following tips to ensure a positive museum visit for your class.

KATHRYN KEANE
Vice President, Exhibitions
National Geographic Society

Encourage students to explore the museums in their community and to check out museums when they travel. Museums can become familiar and exciting companions in studying history.

---

1. Plan ahead. Before you visit, talk about the museum and its collection. Most museums have great websites, and many even have their entire collections online. Identify the must-see artifacts and works of art—the more students know ahead of time, the better. Contact the museum to see if a docent or museum educator can accompany your group. Plan travel logistics carefully, building in frequent small breaks, snacks, and so forth.

2. Let the museum help. Once you arrive, check in with the information desk. Get maps and brochures for your students. If you haven't arranged for a docent or tour guide, ask if one might be available to accompany your class on a tour.

3. Encourage students to read, listen, and learn—and to use their imaginations. Point out that labels, maps, time lines, videos, and audio tours will give students all the information they need as "context" for the objects. Audio tours are usually narrated by a curator, or expert, and are almost like getting a private tour.

Remind students to use an artifact analysis form similar to the one shown in their History Notebook to help them analyze an artifact. Model how to think about the meaning of the objects. Ask students to imagine what it was like to live a long time ago or in a faraway place—or even in the mind of a creative artist. **ASK:** What will students 100 years from now learn about our society in a museum?

4. Remind students of dos and don'ts. Remind students to keep their voices down and leave their phones turned off and out of sight. Most important: Don't touch artifacts or lean on cases. Don't take photos unless expressly allowed, and make sure students are careful around fragile or delicate objects.

5. Take it back to the classroom. Spend some class time reviewing the visit and eliciting students' reactions to what they saw. **ASK:** What did you like best about the museum? What was your favorite artifact? What surprised you the most?

SUPPORTING YOUNG PHOTOGRAPHERS

Photography as storytelling. For 40 years, I have made photographs for *National Geographic* magazine. Do you have students who are interested in photography? Here are some ideas to discuss with them.

Help students understand how to know their subject thoroughly.
To photograph or illustrate a story, they need to think about what they want to communicate. Explain that they can follow the work of key scientists or historians in the field. It is all about being ready to photograph the moment of discovery and then to publish it in the popular media for everyone to see. Without media coverage, many great discoveries lie silent on shelves in storerooms around the world. The process is always the same. Research the subject. Know the people. Know how to be in the right place at the right time.

KENNETH GARRETT
National Geographic
Photographer

Help students practice their photographic and storytelling skills. I have held this advice close to my heart throughout my career—always working to make sure that my photographs have something to say. Assignments that can be accompanied by photographs will give students practice at explaining something with visuals. Obviously, the more practice, the better.

Explain the importance of crafting each image with intent and being prepared. I was in Guatemala working on a story about remote imaging of Maya cities, and my editor knew there was going to be a planetary alignment of Venus, Jupiter, and Mars directly over a temple in Tikal and that it would not happen again for 200 years. Of course he wanted me to get a photograph of it. I brought a portable spotlight to "paint" the temple with light and made a wonderful photo with the planets aligned over the temple. This is what I call making your own luck—being prepared and ready for what's about to happen.

Talk about customizing lighting and how to make the subject "pop." If my subject is an artifact in a museum, I study it with a flashlight until I find an angle where it "speaks" to me. Then I create a lighting setup to bring out the personality that I identified with the flashlight. Sometimes I even make the photo by painting the object with the light from the flashlight. Photographs are made up of light, so lighting the subject, whether it is an object, a landscape, or an architectural feature, is most important. The image must pop, and readers must say "wow," or they won't stop to learn. There is simply too much visual competition out there.

Emphasize that students should be adaptable but at the same time unafraid to develop their own vision. I was trained to be a generalist, flexible, able to adapt to any situation. I was identified as the photographer to send if there was nothing to photograph because I would find something to photograph. In today's world, I still believe it is important to be adaptable, but the market is often looking for photographers with an unusual specialty—a way of seeing that translates into your own unique style.

Help students develop a portfolio. Encourage students to work for the school newspaper or yearbook. Once they have built a portfolio, they can approach local newspapers. Today, with Instagram, Facebook, and other platforms, they can have their photos "out there" as soon as they shoot them. Remind students that the ownership of their photos can be compromised if they are posted online.

Remind students to follow the new technology in photography. Today's cameras have eliminated much of the technical difficulty of capturing an image. With this new technology come exciting new opportunities to push the envelope—for example, to shoot in virtual darkness, shoot remotely, shoot from a drone, or shoot underwater from a remotely operated submersible. Constantly following the new technology is a requirement of today's photography business.

Caution students to be prepared for the lifestyle of a photographer. An established photographer has to be prepared to be away from home for weeks or months at a time, living with a subject until just the right situation presents itself: until a rapport is established that allows special access to an event, until a discovery is made, or until a polar bear walks up to the camera!

INQUIRY AND THE HISTORY NOTEBOOK

The History Notebook that accompanies *World History: Voyages of Exploration* is the student's space to comment on ideas raised in the lessons in each chapter. Many lessons in the Student Edition are supported by History Notebook pages that foster inquiry by providing critical-thinking questions and writing prompts. These features and lessons include the following:

- **The Global Perspective** feature at the beginning of each unit in the Student eEdition

- **National Geographic Explorer** lessons featuring men and women doing critical research and exploration around the world

- **Material Culture** lessons featuring a collection of artifacts

- **Preserving Cultural Heritage** lessons featuring iconic places and artifacts around the world

- **A Global Commodity** lessons focusing on important commodities across time

- **Through the Lens** lessons providing a closer look at the work of National Geographic Photographers

- **Traveler** lessons featuring people across time and place who present a unique perspective

- **State of the World** lessons providing snapshots of the world at different times in history

EXAMPLE p. 62

Not all students can memorize and recite the numerous dates and facts in a world history program. However, all students are capable of reacting to events and ideas and forming solid opinions. All students can learn to use evidence to support their opinions, and all students can come to realize that their opinions count. The History Notebook is their partner in that endeavor.

Students can record their thoughts about how they see themselves fitting into the larger picture of the world and its many cultures today. The Notebook also provides a format for raising questions they want to answer as they study world history and options for student projects, such as oral history projects. The History Notebook is a key to helping students explore what it means to be a global citizen.

ASSESSMENT IN *WORLD HISTORY: VOYAGES OF EXPLORATION*

World History: Voyages of Exploration provides opportunities for two main types of assessment: formative and summative.

- **Formative assessment** is assessment for learning. Its focus is to assist in immediate learning, it is delivered from teacher to individual students, and it takes place during instruction or in the sequence of lessons.

- **Summative assessment** is assessment of learning. Its focus is to measure students' progress and inform future teaching or to evaluate educational programs. Summative assessment takes place at the end of a unit, semester, or course.

Some tests or projects may serve both a formative and a summative purpose. Effective use of both formative and summative assessment enables you to create a positive feedback loop in which you can use assessment results to differentiate instruction or determine which content or skills need to be retaught and then customize future assessments to gauge learning of new and retaught material.

It is important, too, to engage in a variety of assessment modes. Some students may better demonstrate their understanding through performance assessments, such as discussions, debates, or presentations. Others may be more accurately assessed using pencil-and-paper tests and writing assignments. Students should have chances to demonstrate their knowledge through both individual and cooperative assessments.

The activities and tests in *World History: Voyages of Exploration* offer a generous variety of opportunities for both formative and summative assessment in numerous modes. The following assessments, with examples, will enable you to support and measure learning at the lesson, chapter, and unit levels.

Albert Lin teamed up with other National Geographic Explorers as part of his Valley of the Khans Project. Here, he lays out a grid at an archaeological site in the forests of Mongolia.

NATIONAL GEOGRAPHIC EXPLORER ALBERT LIN

Searching For Genghis Khan's Tomb

Genghis Khan wanted his burial site to remain a secret, and he got his wish. That didn't stop National Geographic Explorer Albert Lin from trying to find it, though. He began his search for Genghis's tomb in 2009. But since, as Lin says, "Mongolian custom warns that disturbing Genghis Khan's burial site will unleash a curse that could end the world," he figured out how to look for the tomb without using a shovel. Instead, Lin used noninvasive computer-based technologies, such as satellite imagery, ground-penetrating radar, and remote sensors. He also tried crowdsourcing, inviting volunteers to examine satellite images online and tag anything that warranted further investigation. Lin didn't find Genghis Khan's tomb, but the explorer remains undaunted and continues to apply similar approaches in his other undertakings. As he says, "The most exciting thing about science is the unknown—anything is possible."

Historical Thinking Each lesson in the Student Edition ends with questions that assess students' understanding of the lesson's content and their ability to analyze it. You can use this quick formative assessment to help students develop their critical thinking skills and to determine whether any concepts need to be reinforced or retaught.

The skill head on each question reflects the support for historical thinking offered in *World History: Voyages of Exploration*. Practice with these social studies skills supports student comprehension and enables students to improve their writing about history.

astronomers, engineers, metallurgists, artisans, and merchants to Karakorum. In addition, the Mongols left many local governments intact and allowed conquered peoples to practice their own religions and customs. Some of the people who demonstrated great loyalty to the empire were even permitted to join the Mongol armies.

Under Ogodei's rule, the Mongol Empire expanded to its greatest extent. After his death, however, the rulers of the khanates struggled for power, and the empire began to fall apart.

HISTORICAL THINKING

1. **READING CHECK** Who were the Mongols?

2. **INTERPRET MAPS** Why do you think the Mongols made Karakorum the capital of their empire?

3. **MAKE PREDICTIONS** What might have happened if Ogodei hadn't died during the Mongol army's invasion of Europe?

4. **DRAW CONCLUSIONS** Why was it wise to allow conquered peoples to keep their local government and practice their religions?

The Mongol Empire, Ming Dynasty, and Ottoman Rise **329**

EXAMPLE SE p. 329

Guided Discussion and Active Options For each lesson, this Teacher's Edition provides Guided Discussion questions and an On Your Feet activity that requires students to engage physically by moving in the classroom and to perform collaborative activities, such as fishbowl conversations, interviews, and inside-outside circles. By observing students and providing feedback, you can use these activities for formative assessment of content mastery, critical thinking skills, and discussion skills.

Guided Discussion questions provide additional material for classroom interaction. These questions can be discussed as a whole class, used for small group work, or assigned as homework.

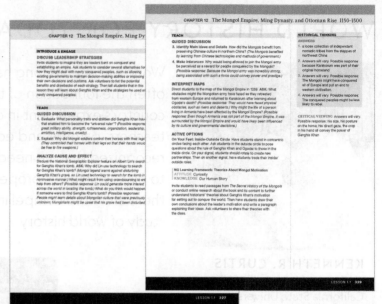

EXAMPLE TE pp. 327 & 329

Chapter Review Each chapter concludes with a review that includes a short vocabulary test and a series of constructed response items that require students to restate the main ideas in the chapter, engage in historical thinking, interpret a visual, analyze a primary source, and write a brief essay connecting the chapter topic to their lives. This summative assessment allows you to measure students' progress and give feedback in the form of a chapter grade.

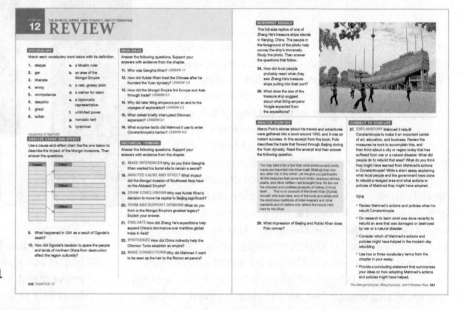

EXAMPLE SE pp. 350–351

Chapter and Unit Tests At the end of each chapter and unit, a summative assessment evaluates students' grasp of main ideas and overarching themes. In the Chapter Test, students answer historical thinking questions, interpret visuals, and analyze primary sources. In the Unit Test, students engage in comparative thinking as they compare two eras or themes in history.

Projects At the end of each unit, a Unit Inquiry Project can be used as a summative performance assessment. Teachers may use this project to assess students' research and presentation skills as well as their content knowledge. In addition, three Projects for Inquiry-Based Learning in the History Notebook can be used for both formative and summative assessment. Over the course of these long-term projects, you will have frequent opportunities to provide ongoing assessment and feedback to students, and the end products can be assessed to measure student learning.

EXAMPLE SE p. 353

WORLD HISTORY FOR TODAY'S CLASSROOMS

World history has long had its place in American schools. True, it is often the foundation of the United States and the ongoing story of our country's experiment in democracy that attracts the most attention from teachers, parents, and educational administrators. Still, we have long recognized that we need a history broader in space and deeper in time to place ourselves properly in the world. In today's globalizing society, there are more compelling reasons than ever before to prioritize the study of world history.

KENNETH R. CURTIS
Author and Professor of History
California State University
Long Beach

Knowledge for effective citizenship is one important mandate. History educators gladly take up the challenge of civics education, and world history has at least two roles to play. First, students in our classrooms come from an increasingly diverse set of world regions. It is our responsibility to help those students locate themselves in the complex story of humanity's past. In today's United States, that means a more balanced attention to the histories of various world regions. Second, forces of globalization continue apace. As I write, the coronavirus is upsetting international travel and global markets. How can we help students make sense of the very real ways events in the wider world affect their local realities? The growing importance of connecting the local and the global, and of relating past global events to contemporary ones, is certain. Knowledge of the worldwide Spanish influenza outbreak in 1918–1920 might not provide a solution to current issues, but it does allow us to put them in context.

Four decades ago, far-seeing history educators from both the K–12 and higher education communities founded the World History Association and have been working ever since to enhance not only the effectiveness of world history teaching, but also the scholarship that supports it. As an entirely new program, *World History: Voyages of Exploration* has given us the opportunity to use the latest historical research to invigorate the text. I am proud to have collaborated with a remarkable team of professionals at National Geographic Learning to create a learning program that we believe advances world history in multiple areas: up-to-date scholarship, global perspectives, civic engagement, and effective pedagogy.

EXAMPLE UNIT 1 GLOBAL PERSPECTIVE *online*

Consider the title *Voyages of Exploration.* The terms *voyages* and *exploration* indicate that **active movement in search of discovery** will be key to student learning. In fact, the title aligns beautifully with the long and distinguished heritage of the National Geographic Society. You will find that both in the text itself and in the supporting features we encourage active inquiry across both time and space. The Global Perspective feature (in the Student eEdition) that begins each unit, full of striking imagery, will alert readers to the fresh perspectives and explorations that lie ahead.

Take, for example, the inclusion of National Geographic Explorers at key points in the narrative. Here students will encounter scientists and scholars using the world as their laboratory, expanding the frontiers of knowledge. To cite just one example, we meet Dr. Albert Lin, who uses the latest technology to address an age-old question: where is the tomb of Genghis Khan? Apart from his scientific work, students will also discover that during his fieldwork Dr. Lin also enjoys learning more about Mongolians and their culture, such as their strong focus on horseback riding. We believe that explorers like Dr. Lin will give students role models for how their own curiosity might lead to voyages of exploration and discovery.

The powerful visual imagery supplied by National Geographic's world-renowned photographers brings this and other stories to life. You will find their work throughout the program, sometimes highlighted in special Through the Lens features. For visual learners, our program provides a wealth of opportunities.

We have also encouraged student engagement with Preserving Cultural Heritage and Global Commodity features. We are always in danger of losing important historical sites and artifacts due to factors such as war and climate change. Introduced by National Geographic's Archaeologist-in-Residence Fredrik Hiebert, Preserving Cultural Heritage features lead us to consider threats to historical sites that affect us all and what efforts we can make to preserve them. Global Commodity features lead students to consider their own roles as consumers of goods from across the globe. Building on the most recent research, we trace the history of commodities—both essential ones like salt and goods of consumer choice like coffee—across seas and continents. Again, visual layouts bring abstract concepts to life.

Our focus on material culture likewise makes history tangible. In seeking to understand global societies, historians analyze not only texts, but objects as well. History educators well know that material objects can stimulate the curiosity that propels learning, while world history educators find that comparing objects from diverse societies can help achieve a more balanced global perspective. Thus, our Material Culture features allow students to examine trends across cultures, such as in the feature on Renaissances around the world. Here we view the artistic achievements of 15th-century Europe in a global perspective by learning of other instances—in the Philippines, China, and Harlem—where a "rebirth" in the arts has taken place.

Because of its broad view, one of the challenges of world history is to hear individual human voices. Our strategy is to "tag along" with historical voyagers as they crossed oceans and continents, opening our eyes to how they experienced their travels and what they discovered along the way. Through his forays

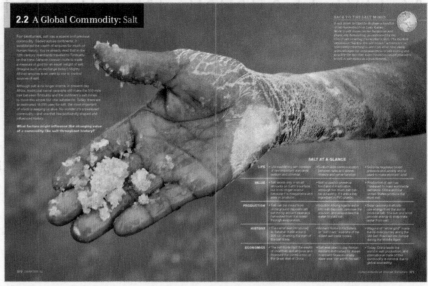

into Arab, Persian, and European lands, for example, the great Turkish Ottoman traveler Evliya Çelebi shows us just how deeply intertwined were the major Christian and Muslim empires of the 17th century. Through the travels of Olaudah Equiano we learn not only of his own bitter experience of the tragic Middle Passage during the age of the Atlantic slave trade, but also how he overcame these hardships to become a free man and active abolitionist. Then there is the story of Paul Salopek, sponsored by the National Geographic Society as he walks "Out of Eden" and around the world. Students will be able to follow Salopek's real-time story of discovery and exploration, expanding their own horizons as they learn of his travels.

Using these resources, we are confident that you as teachers will find many ways to connect students to World History in ways that go beyond mere facts to active investigation, discovery, and exploration.

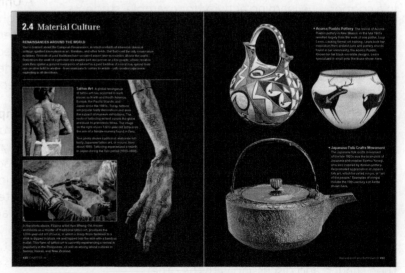

ACTIVE LEARNING IN THE HISTORY CLASSROOM

Easily influenced by peers and distracted by text messaging and social media, high school learners can be challenging. A class of high school students is a highly diverse group of learners with myriad personalities and learning styles—what's the best way to reach them?

As you know from experience, a high school teacher must be fully prepared to engage students each day and flexible enough to change plans at a moment's notice with the shifting classroom dynamic. *World History: Voyages of Exploration* contains a wealth of teaching options that are perfect for the active teacher—and active students.

PEGGY ALTOFF
Senior Consultant,
Former Teacher, and Past
President of NCSS

Variety and Flexibility An expansive repertoire of proven strategies and appropriate activities provides the best preparation for each day's teaching. The structure of the Student Edition in this program is specifically designed to provide options that engage students in meaningful learning activities. The varied lesson lengths in a chapter allow for several approaches, including:

- selecting lessons and sections that are most appropriate for any given class of learners;

- focusing on one lesson each day to provide a depth of content knowledge;

- using cooperative learning activities that allow students to teach and learn from each other.

In a cooperative learning activity, for example, students can participate in a Jigsaw strategy, in which groups of students become "experts" on one lesson in a chapter. Next, all expert groups switch into new groups with each new group having one expert on each lesson. Each expert is then responsible for teaching the others in the group about the lesson. (See **Cooperative Learning Strategies** in this Teacher's Edition for a complete explanation of the Jigsaw strategy.)

Another cooperative learning possibility involves breaking a lesson into segments by section headings. Most of the lessons in the Student Edition have two to four section headings. This makes it easy for students to work in pairs or small groups, with each student reading and learning about information in one segment and then sharing and discussing with the others.

You may also consider having students work in pairs or small groups to discuss a **Historical Thinking** question, a **Critical Viewing** question, or other text-based features. Experience suggests that each grouping strategy requires practice with students so that they can meet teacher expectations for appropriate conduct while acquiring knowledge of the content presented.

Student Edition activities are intended to address a variety of learning styles. The Historical Thinking questions at the end of each lesson provide skill practice with interpreting maps, analyzing visuals, sequencing events, and so on that can be completed individually, in small groups, or as a class. **Chapter Reviews** include an activity that requires students to demonstrate what they have learned through writing. A **Unit Wrap-Up** at the end of each unit offers students insight into the work of archaeologists, scientists, writers, and other experts. It also includes a Unit Inquiry Project that asks students to present what they've learned using many different formats, including writing, video, and multimedia.

Components for the Teacher The Teacher's Edition of *World History: Voyages of Exploration* presents many possibilities for active learning and student engagement. The **Cooperative Learning Strategies** section offers a preview of the types of strategies located throughout the Teacher's Edition with a clear explanation of how to implement each one. For the highly experienced teacher, this may offer a review of practical procedures. Those new to the profession will probably want to return to these pages frequently to plan new experiences for students.

The **Chapter Planner** in the Teacher's Edition provides an overview of the lesson support in, each chapter and lists such tools as **Reading and Note-Taking, Vocabulary Practice, Social Studies Skills Lessons, Section Quizzes, and Formal Assessment Tests**. The **Strategies for Differentiation** section that opens each Teacher's Edition chapter offers ideas that engage different groups of students under the headings Striving Readers, Inclusion, English Language Learners, Gifted & Talented, and Pre-AP. You can decide how to apply each of these strategies to individual learners.

For daily planning, refer to each lesson's **Plan, Teach, and Differentiate** sections. The Teach section includes discussion questions and activities that help students summarize and analyze the lesson. It also contains an **Active Options** component that especially engages students with **National Geographic Learning Framework** and (my personal favorite) **On Your Feet** activities. We know that high school students are constantly moving and doing, and this feature provides ways to channel that bounding energy meaningfully.

Think carefully about how to select the options that are appropriate for your students. For me, Rule No. 1 in working with high school students has always been to start simple and move toward the complex. It may not be a good idea, for example, to try to implement all of the available strategies and activities in one lesson. Start with those that make the most sense to you and gradually experiment with others. Inform students when you attempt a new strategy or activity and get their feedback on ways to improve it the next time. The activities and strategies in this program are not meant to provide a recipe for success. Instead, they form a menu of options that support daily decision-making based on your own abilities and preferences and those of your students.

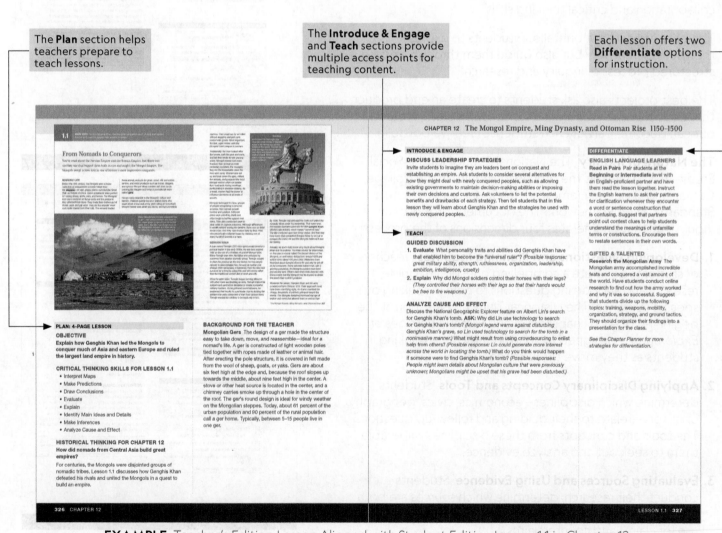

The **Plan** section helps teachers prepare to teach lessons.

The **Introduce & Engage** and **Teach** sections provide multiple access points for teaching content.

Each lesson offers two **Differentiate** options for instruction.

EXAMPLE Teacher's Edition Lesson Aligned with Student Edition Lesson 1.1 in Chapter 12

PROJECT-BASED LEARNING

Project-based learning is integral to successful history–social studies instruction. Well-designed projects allow students to

- **explore a topic in depth;**

- **hone their skills in research, analysis, and critical thinking;**

- **work collaboratively with others toward a shared goal—an ability that is highly valued in both academic circles and the professional marketplace;**

- **become engaged and enthusiastic about a social studies topic;**

- **exercise creative control over their final product.**

In addition, teachers may use projects to assess both students' grasp of content and their progress in developing collaboration and critical thinking skills.

The best projects not only allow students to express themselves creatively but also guide them through a rigorous, structured process of inquiry and research.

The best projects also ask students to create an end product that can be shared with their classmates. This project read-out can become part of each student's creative portfolio.

The Nature of Inquiry The National Council for the Social Studies (NCSS) details the process of inquiry in the College, Career, and Civic Life Framework for Social Studies State Standards, or C3 Framework. The document proposes an Inquiry Arc that enumerates four dimensions of the process:

1. **Developing Questions and Planning Inquiries** Teachers or students generate a compelling question to guide research and supporting questions to help in seeking out specific evidence. The Historical Thinking Question at the beginning of each chapter in *World History: Voyages of Exploration* is designed to spark inquiry-style thinking in students as they move through the text.

2. **Applying Disciplinary Concepts and Tools** Students determine which disciplines—economics, civics, geography, or history—relate to their guiding and follow-up questions. The tools and concepts from these disciplines will enable them to seek out and analyze evidence.

3. **Evaluating Sources and Using Evidence** Students conduct their research, determine which sources are both useful and reliable, and locate relevant evidence they can use for claims and counterclaims.

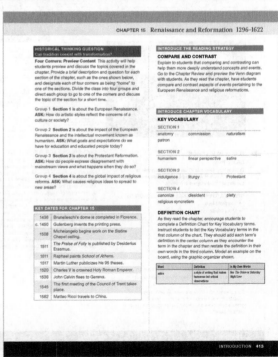

EXAMPLE TE pp. 7 & 413

4. **Communicating Conclusions and Taking Informed Action** Students shape and present their final projects, which may take a wide variety of forms, such as traditional essays, multimedia presentations, performance pieces, or virtual museum galleries. When a project relates to a present-day issue, students may also follow up on their conclusions by taking constructive action within the school or in the wider community.

Of necessity, some projects during the school year will be smaller in scope and may not emphasize all four dimensions of the Inquiry Arc. For example, the inquiry question may be determined in advance by the teacher, or students may be directed to use the textbook or other preselected sources for their research. Similarly, students' choices of methods for communicating their conclusions may be limited to a few options that take less time to produce.

World History: Voyages of Exploration offers a variety of options for inquiry and project-based learning:

- The History Notebook contains three long-term **Projects for Inquiry-Based Learning** that can be completed over a semester or a school year. Over the course of the projects, students conduct research and synthesize information from multiple sources to answer questions on broader themes.
- At the end of each unit, a **Unit Inquiry** challenges students with open-ended questions and guides them to gather evidence from the text, synthesize a response, and present their conclusion to the class in a creative, engaging format.

For example, the Unit Inquiry for Unit 2 in *World History: Voyages of Exploration* asks students to design a civilization-building game that realistically shows how and why civilizations grow or fail.

Students use a chart to record how various factors affect a civilization and create a game that they either pitch to a hypothetical game company or play with their classmates.

You may choose to expand the scope of the Unit Inquiry by having students conduct independent research using other sources or explicitly apply concepts from more than one discipline in their presentations. Alternatively, you might choose to limit the scope of the project by limiting students' options for presenting their projects.

Research Skills Developing good research skills benefits students both inside and outside the classroom. Learning how to locate and evaluate information helps them improve the critical thinking skills they need not only to make and support an argument within a social studies project but also to make well-considered decisions in their everyday lives. Students can hone their research skills through instruction, guidance, and a great deal of practice.

Before launching the first inquiry project, make sure students understand the differences between quantitative and qualitative research:

quantitative research: "hard evidence"—numbers, facts, and figures that can support an assertion

qualitative research: opinions from scholars, scientists, and other experts; firsthand accounts of events; information that provides insights into reasons or motivations

You might also explain that quantitative research answers *who, what, where,* and *when* questions. Qualitative research helps answer *why* and *how* questions.

Social studies inquiry projects should incorporate both types of research. Often, it is qualitative research that enables students to form hypotheses or outline their arguments. Both qualitative and quantitative research can be used to support claims and counterclaims.

Teachers should provide examples of sources students can use to conduct both types of research. For example, government websites, scientific articles, newspaper articles, and encyclopedia entries can be mined for quantitative information.

Qualitative information can be found in firsthand accounts of historical events and analyses of those events written by scholars. Of course, many sources contain both types of information, and students might benefit from an activity in which they review an article to distinguish the qualitative and quantitative information it contains.

Similarly, at the beginning of the year, teachers should provide numerous examples of both reliable and unreliable sources and clearly explain the characteristics of each. You might also provide a list of approved sources for students to use or have students submit their sources before they proceed to gather evidence. As students gain confidence and skill, you can gradually release to them the responsibility for finding and evaluating sources.

USING KEY INSTRUCTIONAL STRATEGIES

It is important to use a variety of instructional strategies to support students' development of reading and thinking skills for content mastery. This Teacher's Edition provides numerous activities to scaffold and advance learning. Many of these are cooperative learning strategies for partners, small groups, or the whole class. Below are some additional strategies you might implement across all units or in selected chapters to support and engage students.

BEFORE READING A CHAPTER

Vocabulary The first page of each chapter includes a list of the Key Vocabulary terms students will find as they read. Review the vocabulary terms with the class. Point out that some terms are important names, places, and events (e.g., Parliament, the Middle Passage), while others are general vocabulary words students will need to understand the chapters (e.g., patrician, amphitheater). The latter are Tier Two and Tier Three words for the most part.

Read all the Key Vocabulary terms aloud so that students can hear the pronunciation of those unfamiliar to them. Read each general vocabulary word and have students raise their hands if they understand it. Ask students to define the words or use them in sentences. Then encourage students to make as many connections as they can between the words and their own lives (e.g., "Dad says it's my duty to babysit my siblings sometimes.").

Tell students that all the vocabulary words for the entire text are gathered in a glossary in the reference section of the book. They can refer to the glossary as they read through the chapters. You can also assign the digital Vocabulary Practice page for each section of a chapter as homework.

Critical Viewing Have pairs or small groups briefly discuss the Critical Viewing question on the introductory image for each chapter. One student should record the group's answers. When the class has finished reading the chapter, tell the pairs or groups to reconvene and examine the photo again. Ask them to discuss whether they would change or expand their answers based on what they have learned. Encourage students to share their responses with the class.

Global Perspectives Some students are most comfortable working on their own and find collaborative learning activities stressful. Use the Global Perspective at the beginning of each unit in the student eEdition as an opportunity to allow students to work independently from time to time. Ask students to

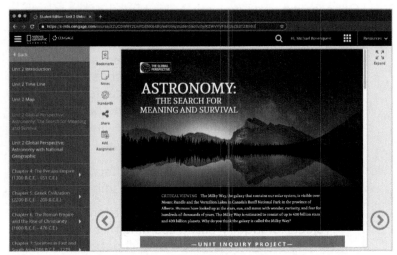

EXAMPLE Global Perspective

perform a task appropriate to the Global Perspective in question, such as

- finding connections between the topic and their own lives;
- choosing a photo or feature and explaining why they find it interesting;
- summarizing the key points.

You may have students present their answers to the class or write a short paragraph to turn in.

When students work in small groups to read a Global Perspective, you might choose one of the following strategies, depending on the format of the story:

- Give the groups a thematic question to guide their reading and to discuss after completing their reading. Group members might take turns reading aloud, or they might read independently and get together for discussion.
- Some Global Perspectives lend themselves to a Jigsaw approach. Assign individual students to read separate sections or features and then share their understanding with the group. This strategy is especially effective for English language learners or striving readers because each student can take the time to focus on understanding a shorter portion of the text.

WHILE READING A CHAPTER

Reading Strategy Assign partners to make a copy of the graphic organizer mentioned in the chapter reading strategy (visible in the review at the end of each chapter). At the end of each lesson, allow partners time to briefly discuss their reading and update the graphic organizer. You may wish to have partners compare their graphic organizers with those of other pairs before they complete the review activities at the end of the chapter.

Consider varying your pairing strategy, sometimes placing more advanced learners with students who are struggling or with English language learners at the beginning or intermediate level and sometimes pairing advanced learners and challenging them to find as many entries for their graphic organizers as possible.

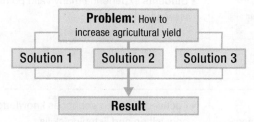

EXAMPLE Reading Strategy

Collaborative Conversations The Teach section that accompanies each lesson in this Teacher's Edition offers a variety of cooperative learning opportunities in the Guided Discussions and Active Options. Use these activities to introduce and practice the skills and concepts of collaborative conversations. The following strategies are some behaviors students should practice in order to have productive conversations. At the beginning of the year, explain these behaviors to students:

- Listen actively—Make eye contact and use body language to convey attentiveness.
- Use meaningful transitions—Make it clear to your classmates that you are reacting to their ideas by using transitions that indicate agreement or disagreement, clarification, building on an idea, and so forth.
- Be inclusive—Ensure that all members of the group participate.
- Take risks—Explore ideas that may be challenging and questions that have no easy answers.
- Focus on the prompt—Group members should help each other stay on topic.
- Use textual evidence—Cite specific evidence from the text to support your points.
- Keep an open mind—Consider all viewpoints presented in the conversation and be ready to change your opinion if someone presents solid evidence to support a claim.

Monitor conversations and provide feedback on students' use of these behaviors. As the year progresses, transfer responsibility for monitoring and rating their conversational skills to the students.

You may wish to provide sentence frames at the start of the year to help students use meaningful transitions and to support the participation of English language learners and students who feel insecure about speaking up in a group. Some states' departments of education provide an extensive list of sentence frames that you may customize for your class.

Analyze Author's Choices Engage students in discussions analyzing the choices of visuals to illustrate the regular lessons and the special features such as Material Culture and Preserving Cultural Heritage. Ask questions such as: What do these objects tell about people's attitudes during the respective time period? What other objects could have been included in this feature? Why did the author choose to use a political cartoon in this lesson? Questions like these help students reach for a deeper understanding of the material and give them practice for interrogating other texts, such as primary sources.

AFTER READING A CHAPTER

Chapter Review Use the Chapter Review to assess students' mastery of the content, and review lessons as necessary. You may wish to have students work in pairs. In particular, consider pairing English language learners the beginning or intermediate level with more proficient readers for the Analyze Sources item. Encourage English language learners to ask questions about words or structures they find difficult and tell the partners to answer to the best of their ability. This process will enable both partners to gain a deeper understanding of the primary source passage.

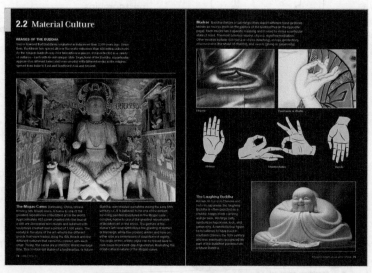

EXAMPLE Material Culture

COOPERATIVE LEARNING STRATEGIES

Cooperative learning strategies transform today's classroom diversity into a vital resource for promoting students' acquisition of both challenging academic content and language. These strategies promote active engagement and social motivation for all students.

STRUCTURE & GRAPHIC	DESCRIPTION	BENEFITS & PURPOSES
CORNERS 1's 2's 3's 4's 1 Topic A 2 Topic B 3 Topic C 4 Topic D	• Corners of the classroom are designated for focused discussion of four aspects of a topic. • Students individually think and write about the topic for a short time. • Students group into the corner of their choice and discuss the topic. • At least one student from each corner shares about the corner discussion.	• By "voting" with their feet, students literally take a position about a topic. • Focused discussion develops deeper thought about a topic. • Students experience many valid points of view about a topic.
FISHBOWL	• Part of the class sits in a close circle facing inward; the other part of the class sits in a larger circle around them. • Students on the inside discuss a topic while those outside listen for new information and/or evaluate the discussion according to pre-established criteria. • Groups reverse positions.	• Focused listening enhances knowledge acquisition and listening skills. • Peer evaluation supports development of specific discussion skills. • Identification of criteria for evaluation promotes self-monitoring.
INSIDE-OUTSIDE CIRCLE	• Students stand in concentric circles facing each other. • Students in the outside circle ask questions; those inside answer. • On a signal, students rotate to create new partnerships. • On another signal, students trade inside/outside roles.	• Talking one-on-one with a variety of partners gives risk-free practice in speaking skills. • Interactions can be structured to focus on specific speaking skills. • Students practice both speaking and active listening.
JIGSAW Expert Group 1 — A's Expert Group 2 — B's Expert Group 3 — C's Expert Group 4 — D's	• Group students evenly into "expert" groups. • Expert groups study one topic or aspect of a topic in depth. • Regroup students so that each new group has at least one member from each expert group. • Experts report on their study. Other students learn from the experts.	• Becoming an expert provides in-depth understanding in one aspect of study. • Learning from peers provides breadth of understanding of overarching concepts.

STRUCTURE & GRAPHIC	DESCRIPTION	BENEFITS & PURPOSES
NUMBERED HEADS Think Time Talk Time Share Time	• Students number off within each group. • Teacher prompts or gives a directive. • Students think individually about the topic. • Groups discuss the topic so that any member of the group can report for the group. • Teacher calls a number and the student with that number reports for the group.	• Group discussion of topics provides each student with language and concept understanding. • Random recitation provides an opportunity for evaluation of both individual and group progress.
ROUNDTABLE	• Seat students around a table in groups of four. • Teacher asks a question with many possible answers. • Each student around the table answers the question a different way.	• Encouraging elaboration creates appreciation for diversity of opinion and thought. • Eliciting multiple answers enhances language fluency.
TEAM WORD WEBBING	• Provide each team with a single large piece of paper. Give each student a different colored marker. • Teacher assigns a topic for a word web. • Each student adds to the part of the web nearest to him or her. • On a signal, students rotate the paper and each student adds to the nearest part again.	• Individual input to a group product ensures participation by all students. • Shifting points of view support both broad and in-depth understanding of concepts.
THINK, PAIR, SHARE Think A B Pair A B Share A B	• Students think about a topic suggested by the teacher. • Pairs discuss the topic. • Students individually share information with the class.	• The opportunity for self-talk during the individual think time allows the student to formulate thoughts before speaking. • Discussion with a partner reduces performance anxiety and enhances understanding.
THREE-STEP INTERVIEW A 1 → B ← 2 3 GROUP	• Students form pairs. • Student A interviews Student B about a topic. • Partners reverse roles. • Student A shares with the class information from Student B; then Student B shares information from Student A.	• Interviewing supports language acquisition by providing scripts for expression. • Responding provides opportunities for structured self-expression.

CROSS-DISCIPLINARY TEACHING

World History: Voyages of Exploration includes numerous features to support students' reading development, including explicit vocabulary instruction, text within the appropriate grade-level Lexile band, and differentiation notes in the Teacher's Edition to help teachers scaffold comprehension for striving readers.

Vocabulary support begins in the Student Edition. Striving readers will benefit from the highlighting that calls out key vocabulary, signaling each word's critical role in enhancing comprehension of content area text. In addition, a list of vocabulary and an introductory activity are included on the first page of the chapter in the Teacher's Edition.

At the beginning of the year, you can identify striving readers in the class and provide ongoing support, such as additional vocabulary help and small-group time during which students can ask questions. Advanced readers can be offered activities from the Teacher's Edition differentiation notes for gifted and talented and pre-AP students.

The Vocabulary Practice page for each section of the Student Edition (available online) reinforces students' understanding of social studies terms.

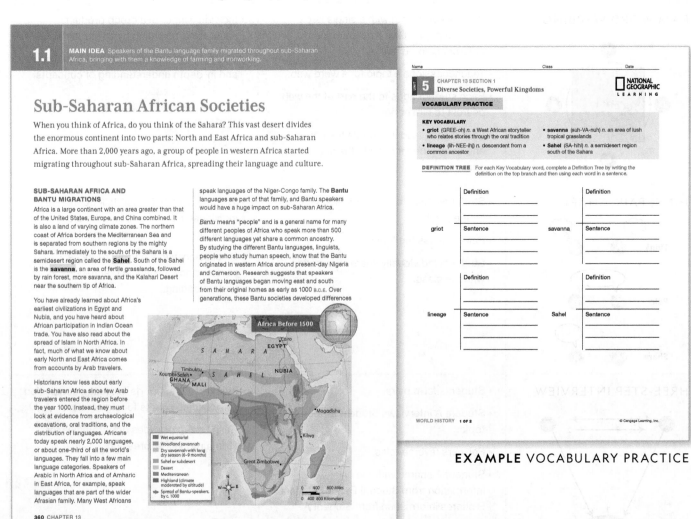

EXAMPLE SE p. 360

EXAMPLE VOCABULARY PRACTICE

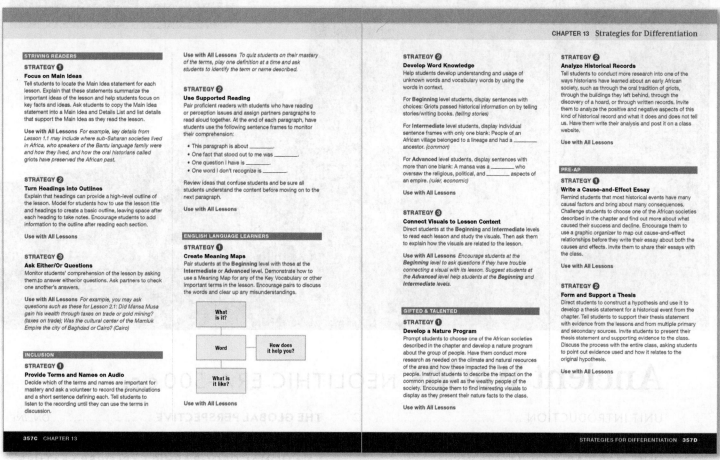

EXAMPLE Teacher's Edition Chapter 13 Strategies for Differentiation

This Teacher's Edition also provides differentiation activities to customize instruction for English language learners at the beginning, intermediate, and advanced levels. To support English language development (ELD), teachers should establish ongoing routines, such as previewing the lessons to identify language that may be challenging to English language learners and providing specific help with these passages, working with small groups of students, and occasionally pairing English language learners with more proficient readers.

You might also collaborate with the ELD teacher to incorporate content or language from the current *World History: Voyages of Exploration* lesson. Where possible, it is valuable to encourage English language learners to share the connections they can make between social studies content and their own experiences or home culture. This practice creates speaking opportunities for English language learners and allows them to experience the rewards of making a unique and useful contribution to the classroom conversation.

IN THE CONTENT AREAS

STEM History–social studies topics often lend themselves to cross-disciplinary lessons with STEM concepts. Annotations throughout this Teacher's Edition highlight opportunities to connect to STEM instruction. You can also encourage students to look for such connections on their own and point them out to the class.

Geography An obvious cross-disciplinary connection for history students is geography. The National Geographic maps in *World History: Voyages of Exploration* are created using real-time data as appropriate and are geared toward a student audience. An online National Geographic Atlas furnishes ample support for both history and geography.

In addition, a Geography Handbook in the reference section (available online) provides support and practice for analyzing maps and covers common geographic concepts.

Wadi Methkandoush
archaeological site, Libya

UNIT 1

Ancient Worlds NEOLITHIC ERA–500 C.E.

Chapter 3, Lesson 2.1

CHAPTER 3

ANCIENT SOUTH ASIA AND CHINA

UNIT 2

Far-Reaching Civilizations and Empires 2200 B.C.E.–1279 C.E.

Chapter 7, Lesson 2.4

Sheikh Lotfollah
Mosque, Isfahan, Iran

UNIT 3

Byzantine and Arab Civilizations

330–1258

Chapter 9, Lesson 1.1

CHAPTER 9
ARAB EMPIRES AND ISLAMIC EXPANSION 550–1258 242

17th-century Japanese screen depicting Japan's 12th-century Genpei War

Feudal Europe and Imperial East Asia 481–1500

Maya temple El Castillo, western Belize

Dynamics in Africa and the Americas 3100 B.C.E.–1532 C.E.

Chapter 13, Lesson 2.5

CHAPTER 14
CIVILIZATIONS IN THE AMERICAS 3100 B.C.E.–1532 C.E. 382

1719 painting by Gaspar van Wittel depicting Naples, Italy

Global Explorations and Expansions 1296–1850

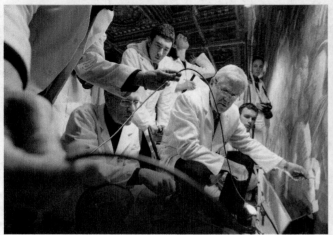

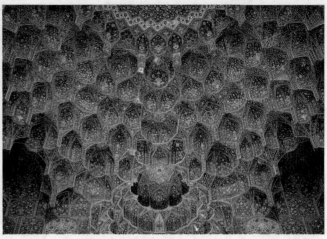

L'Arc de Triomphe, Paris, France

UNIT 7

New Ideas and Revolution 1543–1848

Chapter 20, Lesson 2.2

Chapter 21, Lesson 2.1

1801 painting by Philip James de Louterbourg depicting Shropshire, England.

UNIT 8

Industrialization and Imperialism 1615–1928

The World Wars 1870-1945

Hong Kong, China

UNIT 10

Global Challenges 1945–PRESENT

NATIONAL GEOGRAPHIC
AND SPECIAL FEATURES

MAPS

Additional maps appear online in the Student eEdition.

TIME LINES, CHARTS, MODELS, GRAPHS

Additional visuals appear online in the Student eEdition.

PRIMARY AND SECONDARY SOURCES

Additional primary and sources appear online in the Student eEdition.

DOCUMENT-BASED QUESTIONS

NATIONAL GEOGRAPHIC ADAPTED ARTICLES

NATIONAL GEOGRAPHIC EXPLORER/PHOTOGRAPHER FEATURES

Additional Explorer features appear online in the Student eEdition.

GLOBAL PERSPECTIVE FEATURES

Global Perspective features appear online in the Student eEdition.

PRESERVING CULTURAL HERITAGE FEATURES

MATERIAL CULTURE FEATURES

GLOBAL COMMODITY FEATURES

Additional Global Commodity features appear online in the Student eEdition.

STATE OF THE WORLD FEATURES

TRAVELER FEATURES

Additional features, including videos and image galleries, are available in the Student eEdition.

JIMMY CHIN AND THE TYRANNY OF PASSION

National Geographic photographer and filmmaker Jimmy Chin hangs from a rope while filming part of his Academy Award-winning documentary, *Free Solo*.

It takes a while to make textbooks. If we had been able to go to press as quickly as we would have liked, you'd have been using this book (either in print or ebook form) in February 2019. And if that had happened, you would have seen the person pictured on this page, National Geographic photographer Jimmy Chin, win an Academy Award for Best Documentary Feature.

Jimmy is a man of many talents. He won the Oscar for producing a documentary on Alex Hannold, an American professional rock climber who had completed a "free solo" climb—meaning no ropes, harnesses, or protective equipment—of El Capitan in Yosemite National Park. Jimmy himself is a professional climber, skier, photographer, and now filmmaker.

As writers and editors for a World History textbook for National Geographic, we have access to hundreds of National Geographic Explorers and photographers. All of them are completely brilliant and inspired and doing work that contributes to the common good—either by capturing ideas and images that reveal our world to us in new ways or by using their considerable knowledge and creative skills to innovate new processes and new approaches in their fields.

When several of us were in the audience at a National Geographic Explorers Symposium in 2018, we watched Jimmy Chin talk with another NatGeo photographer about the work that they both do. He used the phrase "the tyranny of passion" and explained that the words aptly describe the way he lives his life.

Jimmy has found in his work something so fundamental to who he is, something he loves so much, that he simply can't *not* do it. His work is so much a part of his thoughts, feelings, and actions that he can't imagine a different life.

The tyranny of passion. Those words have meaning for all of us.

Watch the video of Jimmy that accompanies this textbook. You'll see him talk about how he found what he wants to do with his life. You'll hear him admit that he found a direction that caught him—and his family—by surprise. He's never looked back.

Our message to you, then, is to know that there is something wonderful that you can do with your life, something that draws on your heart and your mind and that you will love to do. You have only to seek it.

Your ideas and your actions are important.

Share them with others.

Be heard.

And along the way, listen to others' voices too.

Chin heads up the side of El Capitan in Yosemite National Park. He quietly climbed alongside friend and fellow climber Alex Honnold for four hours to document Honnold's climb up the mountain without ropes.

INTRODUCE THE PHOTOGRAPH

WADI ROCK ENGRAVINGS IN LIBYA

Wadi Methkandoush, where the Messak Settafet meets the Murzuq Plateau in Libya, has one of the oldest and richest concentrations of prehistoric rock engravings in the world. A wadi is a dried riverbed or stream, many of which are found in the Sahara in North Africa. Wadi Methkandoush is known as an "open-air gallery" that showcases numerous rock carvings of animals, including wildcats, elephants, hippopotamuses, giraffes, ostriches, and crocodiles. Other engravings in Libya include Wadi Ghanjuwan (known for its elephant carvings), Wadi Wan Habeter (known for its giraffe carving), and Wadi Tiksateen (known for its carving of a woman milking a cow).

Wadi Methkandoush's rock carvings stand out in what is now a barren section of the Sahara. But the engravings, along with animal bones and preserved vegetation remains, suggest that long ago this region had an abundant amount of water that supported a lush habitat where humans and large animals once lived. Little is known about the people who created the rock carvings. However, the technical quality and the placement of the engraving of the "Fighting Cats" suggest that they have religious or cultural importance. Several engravings—perhaps serving as milestones—lead to the "Fighting Cats" that overlook the wadi below. Archaeologists believe that the carvings had a main purpose as there are several other similar catlike engravings nearby. Some suggest that the "Fighting Cats" were symbolic physical landmarks for travelers; others suggest they were religious symbols of mythological creatures that were placed in prominent locations to represent their divine powers.

CRITICAL VIEWING

These rock engravings of fighting cats at the Wadi Methkandoush archaeological site in Libya are believed to be at least 12,000 years old. Why do you think people created these carvings?

2

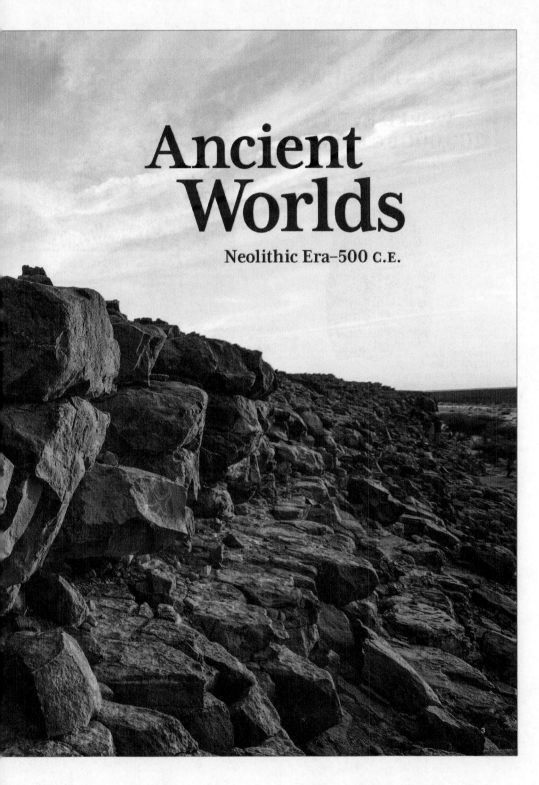

Ancient Worlds

Neolithic Era–500 C.E.

Direct students' attention to the photograph and tell them that scholars debate about what types of animals the carvings depict. **ASK:** How would you describe the two main animals in the engravings? *(Answers will vary. Possible responses: mythical beings; half man, half cat; lions; monkeys)* What other animals are engraved in the rocks? *(Possible responses: ostrich, antelope, mouse or rodent, monkey, another fighting cat or monkey)*

CRITICAL VIEWING Possible response: People might have created the carvings to warn others of animals or to tell stories about animals.

INTRODUCE TIME LINE EVENTS

IDENTIFY PATTERNS AND THEMES

Have volunteers read aloud each of the world events in the time line. **ASK:** What are some common themes or patterns that you notice with regard to these events? *(Possible response: Some common themes or patterns include exploration, settlements, architecture, art, religion, agriculture, and innovation.)* Sort the themes and patterns into categories and put them in a chart like the one shown here.

Period or Place	Exploration and Settlements	Art, Architecture, and Religion	Agriculture and Innovation
Neolithic Period			
Ancient Near East			
Kingdoms of the Nile			
Mediterranean Kingdoms			
Ancient South Asia			
Early China			

As students read the lessons for each chapter in the unit, have them add the information to the appropriate column in the chart. Advise students that they may also add or revise categories as necessary. At the end of the unit, revisit students' charts and create a final list of categories to summarize the historical themes students encountered as they read each chapter.

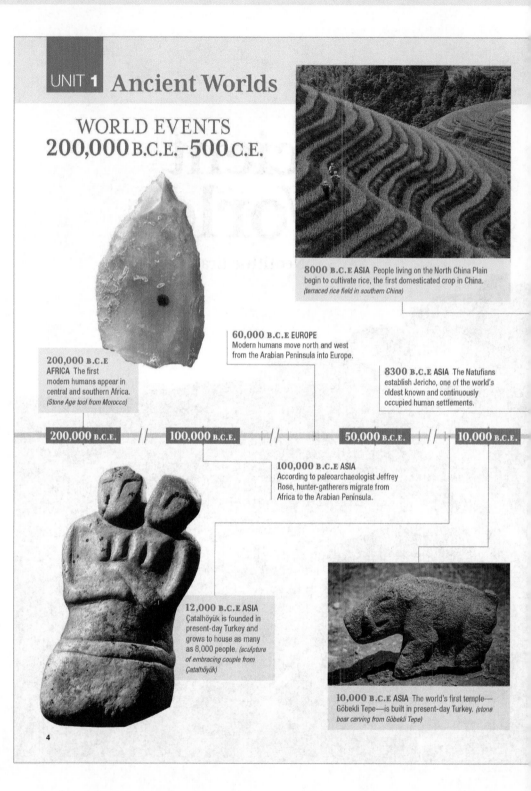

UNIT **1** **Ancient Worlds**

WORLD EVENTS
200,000 B.C.E.–500 C.E.

8000 B.C.E ASIA People living on the North China Plain begin to cultivate rice, the first domesticated crop in China. *(terraced rice field in southern China)*

60,000 B.C.E EUROPE Modern humans move north and west from the Arabian Peninsula into Europe.

8300 B.C.E ASIA The Natufians establish Jericho, one of the world's oldest known and continuously occupied human settlements.

200,000 B.C.E AFRICA The first modern humans appear in central and southern Africa. *(Stone Age tool from Morocco)*

| 200,000 B.C.E. | // | 100,000 B.C.E. | // | 50,000 B.C.E. | // | 10,000 B.C.E. |

100,000 B.C.E ASIA According to paleoarchaeologist Jeffrey Rose, hunter-gatherers migrate from Africa to the Arabian Peninsula.

12,000 B.C.E ASIA Çatalhöyük is founded in present-day Turkey and grows to house as many as 8,000 people. *(sculpture of embracing couple from Çatalhöyük)*

10,000 B.C.E ASIA The world's first temple— Göbekli Tepe—is built in present-day Turkey. *(stone boar carving from Göbekli Tepe)*

4

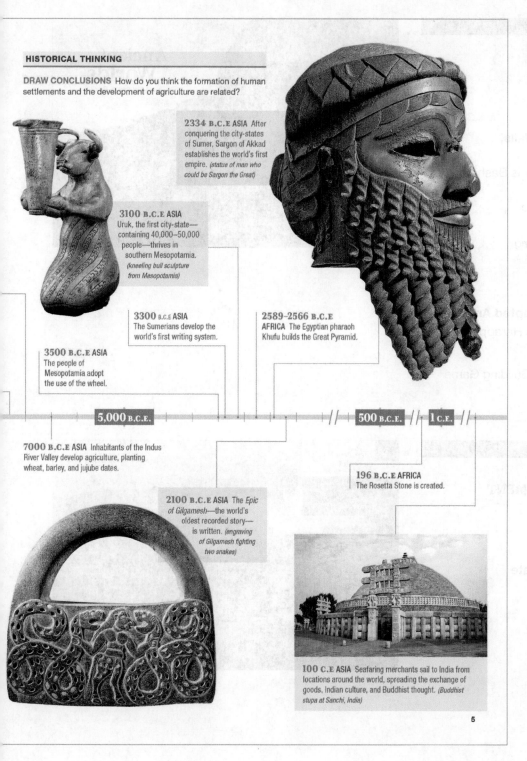

HISTORICAL THINKING
Draw Conclusions
Possible response: Once humans learned how to grow their own food, they no longer needed to continually hunt and gather, so they could settle in one place.

Student eEdition online
Additional content, including the unit map and Global Perspective feature, is available online.

HISTORICAL THINKING

DRAW CONCLUSIONS How do you think the formation of human settlements and the development of agriculture are related?

2334 B.C.E ASIA After conquering the city-states of Sumer, Sargon of Akkad establishes the world's first empire. *(statue of man who could be Sargon the Great)*

3100 B.C.E ASIA Uruk, the first city-state—containing 40,000–50,000 people—thrives in southern Mesopotamia. *(kneeling bull sculpture from Mesopotamia)*

3300 B.C.E ASIA The Sumerians develop the world's first writing system.

2589–2566 B.C.E AFRICA The Egyptian pharaoh Khufu builds the Great Pyramid.

3500 B.C.E ASIA The people of Mesopotamia adopt the use of the wheel.

5,000 B.C.E.   **500 B.C.E.**   **1 C.E.**

7000 B.C.E ASIA Inhabitants of the Indus River Valley develop agriculture, planting wheat, barley, and jujube dates.

196 B.C.E AFRICA The Rosetta Stone is created.

2100 B.C.E ASIA The *Epic of Gilgamesh*—the world's oldest recorded story—is written. *(engraving of Gilgamesh fighting two snakes)*

100 C.E ASIA Seafaring merchants sail to India from locations around the world, spreading the exchange of goods, Indian culture, and Buddhist thought. *(Buddhist stupa at Sanchi, India)*

5

UNIT 1 RESOURCES

UNIT INTRODUCTION

UNIT TIME LINE

UNIT MAP online

THE GLOBAL PERSPECTIVE: No Walls, No Borders: Nomads online

- National Geographic Explorers: Chris Bashinelli and Albert Lin
- On Your Feet: Inside-Outside Circle

| NG Learning Framework
  Discuss Challenges of Nomadic Herding

UNIT WRAP-UP

National Geographic Magazine Adapted Article
- "Cities of Silence (Thoughts on the Harappan Culture)"

Unit 1 Inquiry: Design a Civilization-Building Game

Unit 1 Formal Assessment

CHAPTER 1 RESOURCES

Available in the Teacher eEdition

TEACHER RESOURCES & ASSESSMENT

Reading and Note-Taking

Vocabulary Practice

Document-Based Question Template

Social Studies Skills Lessons
- Reading: Determine Chronology
- Writing: Explanatory

Formal Assessment
- Chapter 1 Pretest
- Chapter 1 Tests A & B
- Section Quizzes

Chapter 1 Answer Key

Cognero®

STUDENT DIGITAL RESOURCES

Available in the Student eEdition

- **eEdition** (English)
- **National Geographic Atlas**
- **Biographies**
- **Handbooks**
- **History Notebook**
- **Literature Analysis**

STRATEGY ①
Set a Purpose for Reading

Before beginning a lesson, help students set a purpose for reading by reading the titles and headings with them and then prompting them to look at the visuals and read the captions. Based on this information, instruct students to write a question they expect the lesson to answer. After they read the lesson, have students answer the question in writing.

Use with All Lessons *For example, a question for Lesson 2.1 could be "How did the earliest humans switch from hunting and gathering to agriculture?"*

STRATEGY ②
Turn Headings into Outlines

To help students organize and understand lesson content, explain that headings can provide a high-level outline of the lesson. Model for students how to use the lesson title and subheadings to create a basic outline, leaving space after each subheading to take notes. Encourage students to add information to the outline after reading each section.

Use with All Lessons

STRATEGY ③
Create Main-Idea-and-Details Diagrams

Have students read aloud the Main Idea statement at the beginning of each lesson. Explain that these statements identify and summarize the key ideas for the lessons. As students read, encourage them to find details in the text that support the Main Idea statements and write these details in a Main Idea and Details List. Explain that these diagrams will help students identify and remember the lessons' most important information.

Main Idea:
Detail
Detail
Detail
Detail
Detail

Use with All Lessons

STRATEGY ①
Preview and Predict

Pair visually impaired students with students who are not visually impaired. Instruct pairs to go through the lesson title and subheadings together. Tell sighted students to describe lesson visuals in detail to help their partners understand them. Then have pairs work together to write notes predicting what the lesson will be about. After they have finished the lesson, ask pairs to review their notes to see whether their predictions were confirmed.

Use with All Lessons *For example, in Lesson 1.5, ask sighted students to describe the photographs of Genevieve von Petzinger in front of distinct geometric shapes made on rocks as well as the cave paintings in France, Argentina, and Somaliland. Pairs will then write predictions, such as: This lesson will be about how historians study cave paintings made by early humans and what the art might mean.*

STRATEGY ②
Provide Terms and Names on Audio

Decide which terms and names are important for mastery and ask a volunteer to record each chosen term or name, its pronunciation, and a short sentence defining it. Encourage students to listen to recordings as often as needed for them to use the terms comfortably in discussion.

Use with All Lessons *You might also use the recordings to quiz students on their mastery of the terms. Play one definition at a time and ask students to identify the term or name described.*

STRATEGY ①
Create Meaning Maps

Pair students at the **Beginning** level with those at the **Intermediate** or **Advanced** level. Demonstrate how to use a Meaning Map for any of the Key Vocabulary or other important words and terms in the lesson. As students work, encourage them to discuss the words together and clear up any misunderstandings.

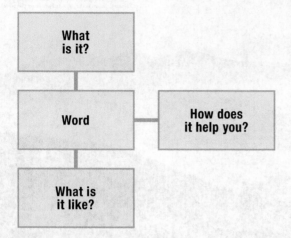

Use with All Lessons *Encourage students at the* *Beginning* *level to ask questions if they have trouble writing a definition. Students at the* *Advanced* *level could help students at the* *Beginning* *and* *Intermediate* *levels write their definitions.*

STRATEGY ❷
Look for Cognates
Suggest to students that as they read, they should look for words that are similar in spelling and meaning to words in their home language. For each word they identify, have students of **All Proficiencies** make a vocabulary card with the English word and definition on one side and the word and definition in their home language on the other side. Encourage them to note any differences in the meanings of the two words.

Use with All Lessons *For example, in Lesson 1.1, the words* expert, ancient, migrate, *and* continent *have cognates in Spanish:* experto, anciano, migrar, continente.

STRATEGY ❸
Use Paired Reading
Pair students at the **Intermediate** or **Advanced** levels and have them read passages from the text aloud.

1. Partner 1 reads a passage. Partner 2 retells the passage in his or her own words.
2. Partner 2 reads a different passage. Partner 1 retells it.
3. Pairs repeat the process, switching roles.

Use with All Lessons

STRATEGY ❶
Design an Infographic
Have students conduct online research about the discoveries of the Leakeys, Jeffrey Rose, or other paleoanthropologists regarding the earliest humans. Tell students to use the most compelling data and images from their research to create an infographic. Invite them to post their infographics on a class website or on the class bulletin board.

Use with Lessons 1.1 and 1.2

STRATEGY ❷
Present a Settlement
Tell students to choose one of the early settlements described in Lesson 2.3. Have them conduct more research as needed to be able to draw or build one of the settlements as it is described in the text and in their research. Have them present their settlements to the class and describe how the early humans lived and worked there and why the settlement was beneficial to the people.

Use with Lesson 2.3

PRE-AP

STRATEGY ❶
Explore Impacts of Geologic History
Instruct students to conduct research into their area's geologic history. Prompt them to use what they learn to write an essay describing the area in the past and how early humans lived in or migrated through the area. Then have them examine how geologic processes have changed the area, describing how it differs today from long ago.

Use with All Lessons

STRATEGY ❷
Write a Persuasive Speech
Ask students to conduct online research to find out more about a topic, a person, or a place introduced in Chapter 1. Have students consider why it is important to learn about early humans, their behavior, and their migrations. Invite students to present their findings in a persuasive speech to the class from the viewpoint of an investor who would provide the funding for continued research into the subject.

Use with All Lessons

CHAPTER
1 First Peoples
and Societies
Neolithic Era–5650 B.C.E.

HISTORICAL THINKING How do societies help
people survive?

SECTION 1 History Is Discovery
SECTION 2 The Neolithic Revolution

CRITICAL VIEWING
Abijatta-Shalla National Park in Ethiopia is part of
East Africa's Great Rift Valley. What do the physical
features shown in the photo tell you about this place?

6 CHAPTER 1

First Peoples and Societies 7

INTRODUCE THE PHOTOGRAPH

THE GREAT RIFT VALLEY

Instruct students to examine the photograph of the Great
Rift Valley in Kenya, East Africa. Explain to students that
a rift valley is created when Earth's outer layer, or crust,
has split apart. The Great Rift Valley spans 4,000 miles
from Southwest Asia to southern Africa, with valleys
ranging from 30 to 40 miles wide. Point out the large
body of water in the valley. Tell students that the Great
Rift Valley is important because many experts believe this
is the birthplace of the first humans. **ASK:** Why do you
think early humans would settle in this area? *(The area
has plants to eat and water to drink; both are needed for
human survival.)*

SHARE BACKGROUND

Few features break the flatness of Africa, and most of the
region's lakes lie in or near East Africa's Great Rift Valley.
The valley is home to Lake Tanganyika, which is the
longest (420 miles) and second deepest (4,710 feet) lake in
the world. Because humans rely on freshwater to live, it is
no surprise that the Great Rift Valley may have been home
to humanity's earliest ancestors. It is widely believed
that the first human species appeared in Africa and are
believed to have lived in Africa for millions of years before
Homo sapiens. The area has provided archaeologists
with a wealth of human fossils. The layers of sediment
from several volcanic eruptions have preserved the
early human remains and helped provide a time line for
researchers to determine when these early humans may
have lived.

CRITICAL VIEWING Answers will vary. Possible
response: The Great Rift Valley has different landforms,
including mountains, forests, and lakes. It also
looks isolated, without visible cities or modern
technology. I think this part of the world is sparsely
populated.

HISTORICAL THINKING QUESTION
How do societies help people survive?

Brainstorming Activity: Societal Survival Discuss with students the various aspects of a society that may aid in its members' survival. To help students get started, share the following ideas:

Food When people live together, they can work together to hunt or gather food. Members of a society can also share the food they have acquired with others.

Protection Living in a community can be safer than living alone. Living in a group may deter animals or other groups of people from attacking. It is also helpful to have people looking out for one another. Some societies even had towers where a designated member would keep a watchful eye on his or her people, particularly at night.

Health Care Whether it is a trained medical professional or an individual who is capable of aiding the injured or ill or caring for the old and the young, some form of health care is an essential part of any society.

Goods and Services The production of various goods and the performance of services is common in nearly every society. In modern society, goods and services are typically traded for money, which is necessary for survival.

KEY DATES FOR CHAPTER 1

300,000 years ago	Early humans use tools.
200,000 years ago	The first modern humans appear in central and southern Africa.
100,000 B.C.E.	Modern humans leave Africa.
100,000–50,000 B.C.E.	Humans begin to speak.
74,000 B.C.E.	Modern humans settle on the Indian subcontinent.
63,000 B.C.E.	Cave drawings indicate artistic desire.
50,000 B.C.E.	Modern humans reach Southeast Asia and Australia.
16,000–12,000 B.C.E.	Modern humans arrive in the Americas.
8,000 B.C.E.	Eastern Mediterranean people grow crops.

INTRODUCE THE READING STRATEGY

DETERMINE CHRONOLOGY

Explain to students that determining chronology can help them understand why and how events in history occurred. Go to the Chapter Review and preview the sequence chain with students. As they read the chapter, have students determine the chronology of the first peoples and societies.

INTRODUCE CHAPTER VOCABULARY

KEY VOCABULARY

SECTION 1

adapt	artifact	diaspora
historiography	hunter-gatherer	indigenous
migrate	mitochondrial Eve	Neanderthal

SECTION 2

agriculture	domestication	economy
Neolithic	surplus	

DEFINITION CHART

As they read the chapter, have students complete a Definition Chart for Key Vocabulary terms. Instruct students to list the Key Vocabulary terms in the left column of their chart. They should add each term's definition in the center column as they encounter the term in the chapter and then restate the definition in their own words in the right column. Model an example on the board, using the graphic organizer shown.

Word	Definition	In My Own Words
adapt	to develop characteristics that aid in survival	like chameleons changing color to hide from predators

History Joins Science

How do scholars know what happened long ago? Written sources may not exist for some events, and even when written accounts survive, the writer may not have known everything that happened or may have described only part of the story.

TELLING THE STORY OF HUMANKIND

For some world regions, historians work to establish basic facts such as the names of kings or when they reigned. However, most historians today study societies where the basic chronology, or order of events, is already known; in those cases, they bring new questions to the past that reflect the world's changing concerns. As you read, you will learn what historians and scientists think happened in the past and how they came to their conclusions. This text uses B.C.E. and C.E. (before the *Common Era* and *Common Era*) for dates before and after the year 1. Other sources or websites may use the abbreviations B.C. and A.D. for these same time periods.

Ultimately, historians rely on primary sources—documents and **artifacts**, which are objects of historical value made by human beings. Historians read their sources carefully, checking the meaning of different words and grappling with unfamiliar languages from long ago. They also mine these sources for evidence, which they weave into historical arguments. Historians consult fellow historians and other experts, such as linguists, archaeologists, anthropologists, and geographers. However, views of the past are always changing. Sometimes, researchers discover new primary sources and artifacts. Sometimes, historians return to the sources earlier researchers have examined, raise different questions about them, and revise their conclusions. These are all aspects of **historiography**, the art and science of creating a reliable and useful story from bits of information about the past.

"Examining sources" doesn't mean merely going through old documents. Today's high-tech tools can unlock the secrets of the past. For example, archaeologists use LiDAR (light-detection and ranging technology, also known as laser speed guns) to discover the sites of previously unknown ancient cities under thick rain forest vegetation. Scientists may know about

other important sites, such as the tomb of an ancient Chinese emperor, but they do not want to disturb the contents. Experts use equipment and methods such as radar, core sampling, and remote sensing to learn more about the tomb without entering it. They do the same to collect data at other fragile sites with little disruption of these sensitive locations. As the ability of scientists to collect and analyze a wider range of information progresses, the understanding of history keeps expanding and increasing.

THE EARLIEST HUMANS

Scientific advances have provided insights into human evolution as well. Scientists believe that the first modern humans appeared in central and southern Africa some 200,000 years ago. *Modern humans* is the term used for early humans who had a physical build, brain size, and appearance similar to that of present-day people. This scientific view is supported by recent research into genetic material, which supplements what historians and other experts can learn from archaeologically excavated remains.

When a woman and a man have a child, most of their DNA, or genetic code, recombines to form a new sequence unique to their baby. (DNA is short for deoxyribonucleic acid.) However, a certain type of DNA, known as mitochondrial DNA, passes directly from the mother to the child. By analyzing mitochondrial DNA, geneticists—scientists who study how the characteristics of living things are controlled by genes—have determined that human beings share a single human female ancestor, known as **mitochondrial Eve**. This woman is believed to have lived in Africa about 200,000 years ago. She was not the first or only modern human female of her time, but she was the first who had daughters who also gave birth to daughters. Every human being alive today has mitochondrial DNA passed down from this individual. We all trace our ancestry to Africa.

NATIONAL GEOGRAPHIC EXPLORERS **MEAVE AND LOUISE LEAKEY**

Family Traditions

National Geographic Explorers Meave Leakey and Louise Leakey (shown digging in Kenya above) are paleoanthropologists, scientists who study fossils of early humans and their ancestors, at the Turkana Basin Institute, a center for human origins research in northern Kenya, near the borders of Ethiopia and South Sudan. Meave, a woman who originally trained to study marine zoology, could not get a job in that field in the 1960s because of her gender. She applied for a position at the Leakey family Primate Research Centre in Kenya, where she discovered her life's work. She also met her future husband,

Richard, the son of well-known archaeologists and paleoanthropologists Louis Leakey and Mary Leaky. Working with Richard and their daughter Louise, Meave has made important discoveries about human ancestors dating back millions of years. Louise continues the work of her parents and her grandparents, and her most recent project has been the development of a virtual laboratory. At AfricanFossils.org, users can virtually explore the Lake Turkana site, lab, and fossils as well as download models for 3-D printing.

Human skull and mandible (lower jawbone) found in Morocco

EARLY HUMANS OUTSIDE EAST AFRICA While scientists have long believed that the first modern humans evolved in east Africa's Ethiopia, recent discoveries have challenged that view. Using a technique called thermoluminescence, which measures the release of energy from crystals exposed to extreme heat, scientists estimate that 300,000 years ago, humans made tools found at a site called Jebel Irhoud (JEH-buhl EE-rood), Morocco, in northwestern Africa. Prior African finds had revealed humans dating back nearly 200,000 years. The humans discovered in Morocco shared many characteristics of other modern humans. They had faces much like ours, which might mean they had developed speech; they made tools; and their brains were as large as ours, though a different shape. This discovery led some scientists to suggest that early humans continued to evolve as they spread throughout Africa.

OBJECTIVE

Explain how historians and scientists bring their knowledge and research to understand what happened in the past.

CRITICAL THINKING SKILLS FOR LESSON 1.1

- Identify
- Draw Conclusions
- Describe
- Make Connections
- Make Inferences
- Analyze Cause and Effect
- Sequence Events
- Interpret Maps

HISTORICAL THINKING FOR CHAPTER 1

How do societies help people survive?

Historians and scientists, such as geneticists, examine evidence of the earliest modern humans and their related artifacts. Lesson 1.1 discusses how groups of early humans used and improved tools to help them survive as they migrated around the world.

BACKGROUND FOR THE TEACHER

How Archaeologists Use LiDAR Through advances in modern computing technology, archaeologists have found an extraordinarily accurate tool to survey and record 3-D data of an area. Light-detection and ranging technology, or LiDAR, uses lights sensors to measure the distance between the sensor and the area being studied. A computer then assembles all the measurements into a 3-D map of the area. LiDAR can be employed both on the ground and in the air, such as in a helicopter or a twin-engine plane. Operating LiDAR in an aircraft has allowed archaeologists to study areas covered with thick vegetation that would be difficult to reach—let alone study—using traditional survey methods. LiDAR also costs much less and is much faster than traditional survey methods, and it has little to no impact on the environment.

Student eEdition online ▸

Additional content for this lesson, including a video and two sidebars, is available online.

INTRODUCE & ENGAGE

DISCUSS MIGRATION

Display the Early Human Migration map presented in the lesson. Write "Migration" at the top of a four-column chart. Then discuss the following questions:

- Why do people migrate?
- How can natural resources influence migration?
- How do environmental barriers, such as bodies of water, affect migration?
- Why might people need to modify tools when migrating?

Record students' answers to each question in each column. At the end of the lesson, revisit the chart and modify answers based on what students learned.

TEACH

GUIDED DISCUSSION

1. **Make Connections** How do today's high-tech tools help archaeologists understand the past? (*LiDAR, radar, core sampling, and remote sensing help archaeologists discover ancient cities under thick rainforest vegetation and learn about fragile sites without actually entering them.*)

2. **Describe** How have geneticists contributed to historical knowledge of the earliest humans? (*Geneticists have learned that mitochondrial DNA passes directly from mother to child, and they have used this knowledge to trace all humans living today to a single human female ancestor who lived in Africa about 200,000 years ago known as mitochondrial Eve.*)

SEQUENCE EVENTS

Discuss the Mitochondrial DNA feature (available in the Student eEdition). Emphasize how the knowledge of DNA is a recent development in the study of humans. **ASK:** When was a complete DNA sequence first decoded? *(2001)* When did the Genographic Project start? *(2005)* How many individuals' DNA have Genographic Project scientists sequenced in only a few years? *(tens of thousands)* When was a successful DNA sequence done for an ancient human? *(2009)* What does this sequence of events tell you? (*Possible response: This sequence of events occurred quickly, which tells me that people realized the importance of DNA knowledge immediately and that geneticists and anthropologists used this knowledge to understand people of today and early humans.*) Would you have your DNA tested? If so, what would you like to find out from the test? (*Possible response: Yes, because I'd like to know more about my ancestors and where I came from.*)

DIFFERENTIATE

STRIVING READERS

Create a Time Line Help students gain an understanding of the time frames within the lesson by having them tape 12 horizontal 11" x 17" sheets of paper together end to end. Tell them to draw one continuous horizontal line across all sheets of paper and make a hash mark across the line every inch, which will result in 102 hash marks. Tell them that every mark represents 1,000 years. Instruct them to put an X on the 100th hash mark and tell them that it marks the beginning of the Common Era. Encourage them to mark 100,000 B.C.E. (first hash mark), 75,000 B.C.E. (25th hash mark), 50,000 B.C.E. (50th hash mark), and 25,000 B.C.E. (75th hash mark). Then help them write the migration dates from the "Human Behavior and Migration" section on the time line.

GIFTED & TALENTED

Design a Technology Poster Direct pairs of students to choose one form of technology mentioned in the lesson and conduct online research to learn more about how this technology helps historians and scientists understand history and human behavior. Have each pair design a poster that explains the technology and what that technology has uncovered. Ask students to prepare a brief presentation to discuss their poster and explain how their researched technology is changing how people think about history.

See the Chapter Planner for more strategies for differentiation.

HUMAN BEHAVIOR AND MIGRATION

Scientists debate when members of our species first acted like modern humans. The ability to plan ahead is an important indicator of human behavior. Additional clues lie in the ability to improve tools, the existence of trade networks, the practice of making art, the ritual of burying the dead, and the ability to speak. Early humans had larynxes, or voice boxes, but they did not begin to speak until sometime between 100,000 and 50,000 B.C.E. Scientists cannot know the exact date because the act of speaking does not produce lasting evidence. Instead, paleontologists have identified certain human activities, such as organizing hunting parties to trap large game, as sufficiently complex to require speech. Speech may have begun because of a genetic mutation, or change in DNA.

Studies of mitochondrial DNA have helped determine when and where modern humans traveled as they spread over the globe. From Africa, modern humans migrated, or moved from one region to another, traveling by land and water until they had settled all over Earth. As modern humans left Africa around 100,000 B.C.E. (or perhaps even earlier), they modified tools for new environments. They built boats or rafts to cross bodies of water. Tens of thousands of years ago, water levels were much lower than they are today, so distances between some landmasses were shorter. As you will read later in the chapter, many present-day archaeologists believe that people crossed a land bridge to move from Africa to the Arabian Peninsula.

There is evidence that by 74,000 B.C.E. modern humans lived on the Indian subcontinent and by 50,000 B.C.E. had reached Southeast Asia and Australia. The earliest humans to arrive in Australia may have been people fishing from canoes or dugout boats that may have been blown off course by a storm. It's possible that some of the first settlers in South America arrived in a similar manner tens of thousands of years later.

Some early humans went north and west into Europe, starting about 60,000 years ago. Some traveled along the Danube River into eastern Europe; others moved along the coast of the Mediterranean Sea. Archaeological evidence indicates that by 38,000 B.C.E., early humans thought about the future. For example, they made bone needles, which they probably used to make warm clothing for protection in cold European winters. Making clothing out of plant fibers or animal skins is a process that requires many steps and keeps future events or conditions in mind.

The Americas were the last major landmass to be populated by modern humans. The earliest confirmed human occupation dates to about 12,000 B.C.E. One theory is that humans reached the Americas by traveling from Siberia to Alaska over **Beringia**, a land bridge that is now a series of islands in the Bering Sea because today's ocean levels are higher. The first migrations may have occurred in 16,000 B.C.E. or earlier. Part of North America was covered by a sheet of ice more than 1.75 miles thick at that time, but some scientists believe that an ice-free corridor between ice masses allowed movement through present-day Canada. Other scientists suggest that ancient settlers hugged the coast in boats made of animal skins stretched tightly over frames of wooden poles. The ancient site of Monte Verde, Chile, provides clear evidence of human occupation dating from 12,000 B.C.E. You will learn more about this site in a later chapter.

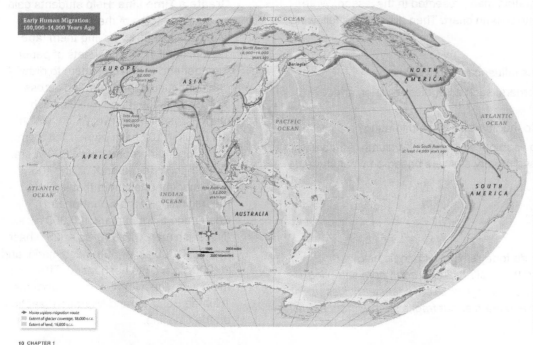

Early Human Migration: 100,000–14,000 Years Ago

→ Homo sapiens migration route
▨ Extent of glacier coverage, 18,000 B.C.E.
▨ Extent of land, 16,000 B.C.E.

HISTORICAL THINKING

1. **READING CHECK** Why does the understanding of human history keep changing?

2. **IDENTIFY** What factors led to the sequence of migration from Africa to other parts of the world?

3. **DRAW CONCLUSIONS** What can you conclude about the intelligence of early humans based on their long-distance migration?

4. **DESCRIBE** How might early humans have migrated from Beringia through the rest of the Americas?

BACKGROUND FOR THE TEACHER

Evidence of Seafaring People In 2010, archaeologists found more than 30 hand axes and hundreds of other stone tools on the island of Crete, in the Mediterranean Sea, that are at least 130,000 years old. The number of tools found at several different locations reveals that people were purposely traveling to Crete, rather than blown off course by a storm. This discovery overrides the previous evidence that people did not reach the Greek Islands until 14,000 B.C.E. The cache of tools also challenges the theory that early humans migrated throughout the world primarily by land. Additional evidence of sea travel includes early human remains and stone tools in Spain that suggest that people crossed the Straits of Gibraltar from Morocco, a distance of 12 miles. To reach Australia 50,000 years ago, early humans had to navigate a 600-mile-long string of islands and several ocean straits, the widest spanning 44 miles of open water. These discoveries support theories that early humans knew more about traveling by boat than previously believed and displayed curiosity and bravery by crossing seas and oceans.

TEACH

GUIDED DISCUSSION

3. Make Inferences Why is the ability to plan ahead an important indicator of modern human behavior? *(Possible response: The ability to plan ahead means thinking about what is needed to survive and making tools and other artifacts to address those needs especially when traveling through new environments. This takes analytical thinking, which indicates the more advanced mind of modern humans.)*

4. Analyze Cause and Effect How did much lower water levels thousands of years ago affect modern humans? *(Possible response: Lower water levels meant that there was more land and land bridges between land masses allowing modern humans to migrate more easily around the world.)*

INTERPRET MAPS

Guide students to analyze the Early Human Migration map. Discuss the chronology of events shown on the map. **ASK:** Which migration shown on the map happened first? Which migration happened next? Which migration happened last? *(The migration from Africa to the Middle East happened first. Early humans then migrated toward India and into Europe. The migration to North and South America happened last.)* What obstacle in the north made an impact on early human migration? *(Ice sheets)* Then share with students the Background for the Teacher information on the evidence of seafaring people. **ASK:** Which migrations included travel by sea? *(migrations to Australia, the Philippines, and Japan)* Which migration dates could change with more evidence of travel by sea? *(migrations to North and South America)*

ACTIVE OPTIONS

On Your Feet: Jigsaw Strategy Organize students evenly into four "expert" groups and assign each group one of the following topics: early human migration to India, early human migration to Europe, early human migration to Australia, early human migration to the Americas. Each group should research their topic and collect as much information as they can. Then rearrange students into a new group, making sure that each new group includes at least one member from each original group. Instruct experts within each new group to report on their early human migration findings. Encourage students to ask questions of the experts. Then have students compare and contrast the facts found on the four different migrations.

> **NG Learning Framework: Explore African Fossils**
> **SKILL** Communication
> **KNOWLEDGE** Our Human Story

Invite students to visit the online virtual laboratory AfricanFossils.org, where users can explore the lab, the excavation site, and the fossils of Lake Turkana. Discuss how the artifacts and fossils tell a story of early humans and how the website communicates this information to people all around the world. Tell students to write a review of AfricanFossils.org, including what they learned, what they found most interesting, and what questions they would like answered about the contents of the virtual lab.

HISTORICAL THINKING

ANSWERS

1. The understanding of human history keeps changing because researchers discover new documents or artifacts or pose new questions about existing primary sources.

2. Water levels were much lower than they are today, so distances between some landmasses were shorter. Some land bridges existed where there is now water.

3. Early humans were intelligent enough to plan and think of the future. They used tools, had trade networks, made art, buried the dead, made clothes for colder climates, and moved their communities for both shelter and food.

4. Early humans might have migrated from Beringia by an ice-free corridor between ice masses or hugged the Pacific coasts of the present-day Americas in boats.

Tracing the Paths of
Early Humans

"If you set out to prove yourself right, you won't learn anything new." –Jeffrey Rose

Jeffrey Rose holds a small stone tool in Zubara, Qatar, one of many areas in Southwest Asia where he conducts his research.

Jeffrey Rose is a paleoanthropologist, a scientist who studies the development of early humans and how this informs us about the meaning of humanity. He spends his days in the southwest Asian country of Oman with his team of experts, sifting through rocks in 100°F heat and learning about the first modern humans who migrated out of Africa. Rose shares, "The evidence from South Arabia has turned the entire story upside down, changing the route, timing, and reason for the expansion out of Africa."

MAIN IDEA National Geographic Explorer Jeffrey Rose's discoveries have changed theories about human migration from Africa.

LOOKING INTO THE PAST

Scientists such as Rose are constantly looking for answers to questions about human migration, including when, where, and why modern humans moved to different areas on Earth. They believe that determining how ancient people adapted to their environments may hold the key to solving some of today's problems, such as adjusting to climate change.

Rose, who became a National Geographic Explorer in 2012, studies the landscape to understand the geography of the world as it was in the past, a way of seeing he says is almost four-dimensional, incorporating the dimension of time into the three dimensions of length, width, and depth. "I'm looking at a sand dune, but it wasn't a sand dune 100,000 years ago," he explains. "It was a lake." Thinking about how the landscape might have looked long ago allowed Rose to make a discovery that has altered what researchers understand about human migration out of Africa.

When Rose began his work, he questioned the theory of many scientists at the time: Humans migrated from Kenya to the southeastern coast of the Arabian Peninsula about 60,000 years ago. The present-day Arabian Peninsula is a desert, and it made sense to think that people who specialized in fishing would have lived along its coast. Rose spent many fruitless months searching the coast for artifacts that would support this theory—and found nothing.

"When you don't find anything," Rose points out, "morale starts to get low, and you feel a tangible sense of despair, which can be really depressing when you're isolated out in the field." Yet not finding anything can also be valuable, as it can indicate that a researcher is looking for the wrong thing or in the wrong place.

Eventually, the missing evidence along the coast led Rose to change course and search inland, where he and his team struck gold (or flint, in this case). They uncovered stone tools made with a special technique developed and widely used by people in the Nile Valley. Never before had tools of this type been found outside of Africa.

A NEW VIEW OF HUMAN MIGRATION

More surprises awaited. To find out how old the artifacts were, Rose used a technique called optically stimulated luminescence (OSL), which measures the last time crystalline materials were exposed to light. The specialized tools he found were more than 100,000 years old—much older than the 60,000 years he expected—and Rose realized he needed to look at the land not as it is today but as it was long ago. Extreme changes in climate explain why Rose found the stone tools inland rather than along the coast. The Arabian Peninsula 100,000 years ago was a fertile grassland and a land of many lakes, an ideal environment for **hunter-gatherers**, people who survive by hunting animals and gathering wild plants.

"I had never thought about modern humans coming from the Nile Valley," Rose says, but in hindsight that seems to be the most obvious scenario. Rose's findings have completely altered claims about modern humans migrating out of Africa. He believes people probably traveled back and forth between Africa and the Arabian Peninsula for tens of thousands of years. As the climate of the peninsula became drier, large animals disappeared, and stone hunting tools became smaller as people were forced to survive on lizards, birds, and rodents. By 70,000 years ago, Rose argues, the climate in the Arabian Peninsula had become so dry that early humans contracted into specific zones called environmental refugia, where they could rely on stable sources of fresh water. Many of these pioneers were forced out of Arabia, kicking off the great human migration beyond the peninsula.

HISTORICAL THINKING

1. **READING CHECK** What did Jeffrey Rose and his team finally find, and why was this discovery important?

2. **IDENTIFY PROBLEMS AND SOLUTIONS** Why is a period of failure sometimes valuable to researchers?

PLAN: 2-PAGE LESSON

OBJECTIVE
Explore how Jeffrey Rose's discoveries have changed theories about early human migration from Africa.

CRITICAL THINKING SKILLS FOR LESSON 1.2
- Identify Problems and Solutions
- Make Inferences
- Analyze Cause and Effect
- Interpret Maps

HISTORICAL THINKING FOR CHAPTER 1
How do societies help people survive?

People in the Arabian Peninsula 100,000 years ago survived by hunting animals and gathering plants. When plants and animals were no longer available in that region, most likely due to climate changes, people needed to move to where these resources could be found. Lesson 1.2 discusses the changing theory about migration from Africa as discovered by Jeffrey Rose.

Student eEdition online
Additional content for this lesson, including a video and a map, is available online.

BACKGROUND FOR THE TEACHER

Jeffrey Rose Dr. Jeffrey Rose strives to keep his paleoanthropological discoveries relevant today through his written publications, documentary series, and presentations. He specializes in the prehistory, paleoenvironments, genetics, and religious traditions of the Middle East. Over the past 30 years, Rose has conducted fieldwork in Illinois, Wales, Ukraine, Israel, Portugal, Yemen, and Oman. His discoveries and pioneering research have been featured in documentaries aired on BBC, PBS, SBS Australia, and National Geographic Channel. While other researchers have proposed that Egyptian Nubian toolmakers moved rapidly to the Middle East, Rose argues that these early humans traveled to Arabia first, and that their Arabian descendants later developed the Emiran tools. Rose also proposes that the travelers may have been influenced by archaic people—possibly Neanderthals—who left tools behind because both sets of peoples used the same types of tools. The timing for this theory fits, but not everyone agrees with Rose's hypothesis.

History Notebook
Encourage students to complete the National Geographic Explorer page for Chapter 1 in their History Notebooks as they read.

INTRODUCE & ENGAGE

DESCRIBE HOW PALEOANTHROPOLOGISTS WORK

Write the word *paleoanthropologist* on the board. Ask students to define the term and volunteer words, phrases, or names they associate with it. Write student responses on the board. Then invite students to discuss their perceptions about what paleoanthropologists do and the tools they use. Explain that in this lesson they will learn about National Geographic Explorer Jeffrey Rose, who studies early human migration in Oman.

TEACH

GUIDED DISCUSSION

1. **Make Inferences** Why do you think Rose found artifacts far away from the southeastern coast of the Arabian Peninsula? *(With plants and animals inhabiting inland lakes and grasslands, there would be little need for early humans to live along the coast.)*

2. **Analyze Cause and Effect** According to Rose, what circumstances might have caused people to migrate from the peninsula to the Middle East? *(Possible responses: climate change; disappearance of large animals)*

INTERPRET MAPS

Have students look at the map (available in the Student eEdition). **ASK:** What does the map show about how early humans traveled to the Arabian Peninsula? *(The map shows that early humans crossed the Red Sea and then dispersed in different directions in present-day Saudi Arabia.)*

ACTIVE OPTIONS

On Your Feet: Fishbowl Have one half of the class sit in a close circle, facing inward. The other half of the class sits in a larger circle surrounding them. Remind students of the paragraph in which Rose "'reads' the landscape to understand the geography of the world as it was in the past." Pose the questions: How can we "read" the landscape around us to learn about the past? What may have changed and why? Students in the inner circle should discuss the questions for five minutes while those in the outer circle listen to the discussion and evaluate the points made. Then have the groups reverse roles and continue the discussion.

NG Learning Framework: Research Technology
ATTITUDE Curiosity
SKILL Collaboration

Show the video of Jeffrey Rose (available in the Student eEdition) and discuss the tools and technology he might use as he works in the desert. Have small groups conduct online research into the various types of technology used by today's anthropologists and archaeologists. Encourage each group to focus on a different type of technology, if possible, and gather information about who uses it and why, how it works, where it can be used, and what the benefits of its use are. Invite groups to present their researched technology with the class.

DIFFERENTIATE

STRIVING READERS

Use Reciprocal Teaching Tell partners to take turns reading each paragraph of the lesson aloud. At the end of the paragraph, the reading student asks the listening student questions about the paragraph. Students may ask their partners to state the main idea, identify important supporting details, or summarize the paragraph in their own words. Then have students work together to answer the Historical Thinking questions.

PRE-AP

Compare Desert Formations Tell students to conduct online research on a present-day desert region other than the Arabian Peninsula that used to be lush and green. Once they have chosen a region, have them answer the following questions: How does the desert today compare with the region at an earlier time? How did experts learn what the region used to be like? Then ask them to summarize their findings in a brief report comparing the desert then and now.

See the Chapter Planner for more strategies for differentiation.

HISTORICAL THINKING

ANSWERS

1. In the Arabian Peninsula, Rose and his team found stone tools made with a special technique developed and widely used by people in the Nile Valley. This discovery was important because these types of tools had never been found outside of Africa.

2. If researchers do not find what they are looking for, it can mean that they are looking in the wrong place or looking for the wrong thing.

The Earliest Migrations

For at least 100,000 years, humankind stayed in Africa. Then, sometime around 100,000 years ago, people began to migrate all over the world. By about 14,000 years ago, humans had settled every continent except Antarctica.

THE GREAT HUMAN EXPANSION

People did not start moving from place to place because of crowding. Scientists believe the size of the world's population did not change significantly during this migration. People who stayed in Africa were also on the move—spreading thousands of miles over that continent, the world's second largest after Asia.

This worldwide migration took tens of thousands of years. People moved from areas that were warm to regions that were cold and from grasslands to forests. Their only tools were made of stone, bone, and wood, but they used these tools to obtain food and to survive. There is evidence that humans spent a long time in

some areas before moving to another one. For example, modern humans most likely spent about 15,000 years in Beringia as they migrated from Asia to the Americas. Even so, while some people moved, others stayed behind, and eventually humans lived all over the planet.

When this migration began, conditions were ideal. Places that are dry desert today were grasslands with freshwater rivers and lakes and edible plants. The grasslands were home to wild animals, and the open spaces made hunting fairly easy. As modern humans flourished, they **adapted**, or developed characteristics to help them survive in this environment. Long legs were good for walking and running, and an upright posture

CRITICAL VIEWING A zebra herd crosses a savanna in Tanzania. What physical characteristics of this place in Africa would appeal to early humans?

and forward-facing eyes allowed humans to spot and gather plants and hunt game.

People did not plan to settle in distant regions. Those who left Africa and began moving into Asia and Europe had no idea of the size of the landmasses they entered, because the well-watered grasslands stretched as far as they could see. One researcher believes that as people searched for food, they saw inviting new places within a day's journey or so of their settlement. When they returned with their catch, they shared the news about the new territory. Over the course of a generation, or a period of roughly 20 years, people pushed the boundaries of settlement by an average of about 78 miles.

When early humans entered Europe 60,000 years ago, they had to adjust to colder temperatures. Although no clothing has survived from this time, researchers believe these early people made clothing out of animal skins or woven plant material to stay warm. Evidence for this comes from geneticists, who have found the DNA of clothing lice in ancient human remains. Geneticists also tell us that these early human migrants to Europe mingled with the **Neanderthals** (nee-AHN-duhr-tawls), an extinct species of early humans, who were already living there. People today who have some European ancestry may have inherited Neanderthal DNA as well.

THE STORY OF HUMAN MIGRATION

How do scientists know what these early modern humans were like? This knowledge comes from multiple experts, including archaeologists and paleontologists who analyze tools and fossils. As you read earlier, the location of tools on the Arabian Peninsula was an important discovery. Scientists can also learn a great deal from the shapes of skulls. For example, bones connecting the head to the neck reveal whether a creature walked upright or on all fours. The shape of the face, jaws, and teeth might reveal whether an individual could talk and the kind of foods he or she ate.

Apart from technologies scientists use for determining the ages of bones and artifacts, the field of linguistics, or the scientific study of language, provides valuable information about the spread of people throughout the world. By studying sounds that make up different languages, linguists can trace patterns of migration and settlement.

NATIONAL GEOGRAPHIC EXPLORER
KEOLU FOX

The Wisdom of Indigenous Peoples

National Geographic Explorer Keolu Fox (shown above) is a geneticist who is particularly interested in the ways that indigenous, or native, peoples have adapted to their environments. "There's a treasure trove of information in their DNA that could benefit all of humanity," he says. Fox, who grew up in Hawaii and whose mother is native Hawaiian, believes it is important for scientists to understand the communities that they study. Indigenous people may also offer different points of view that can cast fresh light on scientific inquiry. At the same time, Fox emphasizes that "it's the responsibility of scientific investigators to ensure that 'exploration' of indigenous people's genomes benefits that community as well, financially or otherwise."

The movement of humans from Africa to almost every corner of the globe was a long one. One theme is constant: our ancestors were always on the move. They followed herds, crossed rivers, traveled by boat, and ultimately covered enormous distances at a time when their most powerful weapon was a stone hand ax and the fastest means of moving on land was running. From their beginnings, humans have traveled the world, driven by curiosity and necessity.

HISTORICAL THINKING

1. **READING CHECK** Why did early humans migrate out of Africa?

2. **IDENTIFY MAIN IDEAS AND DETAILS** How can scientists trace early human migration?

3. **DESCRIBE** What evidence shows that early humans made clothing to stay warm after they entered Europe?

PLAN: 2-PAGE LESSON

OBJECTIVE

Identify why and when early modern humans left Africa and settled in the rest of the world.

CRITICAL THINKING SKILLS FOR LESSON 1.3

- Identify Main Ideas and Details
- Describe
- Compare and Contrast
- Make Connections
- Analyze Visuals

HISTORICAL THINKING FOR CHAPTER 1

How do societies help people survive?

Early modern humans lived in communities and shared food and water. They combined knowledge about tools made of stone, bone, and wood. They communicated information about new territory they saw as they searched for food. Some groups migrated together, while other groups stayed in one place. Lesson 1.3 explores how groups of early modern humans lived and migrated.

Student eEdition online

Additional content for this lesson, including an image gallery, is available online.

BACKGROUND FOR THE TEACHER

The Evolution of Language By examining similarities and differences in vocabulary and grammar, anthropologists can determine how languages have evolved and where they began. A study of the Indo-European language family traced the languages back 7,000 years and determined that they began in the area that is now Turkey. In their study of world languages, linguists have developed the online resource *World Atlas of Language Structures*. This atlas includes phonemes from 504 languages. A phoneme is the smallest unit of sound, such as the sound of a single vowel, a single consonant, or certain vowel and consonant combinations. Different languages use different phonemes; English has 44. By concentrating on these smallest units of sound, rather than entire words or grammar, linguists continue to trace languages back even further in time.

INTRODUCE & ENGAGE

DISCUSS RESOURCES FOR SURVIVAL

Direct students to look at the photograph in the lesson of zebras crossing a savanna in Tanzania. Encourage students to imagine that they are in this area with nothing but the clothes they are wearing. Ask them to identify resources in the photograph that they would use to survive, such as food, shelter, and tools. Discuss how they might travel to find a better place to live, which land features might restrict travel, and the challenges early humans faced.

TEACH

GUIDED DISCUSSION

1. **Compare and Contrast** How was the world tens of thousands of years ago different from today, and how did this difference affect migration? *(Areas that are desert today were grasslands with rivers that provided early humans with food and water as they migrated.)*

2. **Make Connections** Why did early humans migrate to different areas and how did they adapt to these new environments? *(Possible response: Early humans followed animal herds for food and clothing and gathered grain to eat. If their food source was depleted, they needed to move. As they moved, they learned how to find healthy food and they adapted to warm and cold climates.)*

ANALYZE VISUALS

Direct students to the look at the Neolithic tools gallery (available in the Student eEdition). **ASK:** How would these tools have helped early humans survive? *(Possible responses: The pins helped hold things together, the sickle to cut grain, and the stones to grind the grain. Arrowheads, axes, and harpoons were used to hunt animals and fish for food, shelter, and clothing.)* **ASK:** How do you think early humans made these tools? *(They probably used bones and rocks shaped in practical ways to cut and shape wood, bones, and rocks.)*

ACTIVE OPTIONS

On Your Feet: Corners Read aloud the Background for the Teacher information on the study of languages. Select four languages other than English that are pertinent to your students and their cultures. Label each corner of the room with one of the languages. Invite English Language Learners to lead the corner with their home language. If other students are fairly evenly distributed, let them choose which corner to join. Tell students to conduct online research to learn the number, pronunciation, and uniqueness of phonemes in the language. Invite a student from each corner to share the research.

NG Learning Framework: Research the Tools of Early Modern Humans
ATTITUDE Curiosity
SKILL Problem-Solving

Encourage students to use information in the lesson and from other sources to create an infographic on how early modern humans made one of the tools. Invite students to research the stones early modern humans chose and how they shaped them into spear heads and axes. Invite others to research tools made of bones and how they were shaped and polished. Have students present their infographics.

DIFFERENTIATE

ENGLISH LANGUAGE LEARNERS

Pronounce Vocabulary Words Before reading, preview with students of **All Proficiencies** the words *archaeologists*, *paleontologists*, and *linguistics*. Point out the grouping of vowels in the middle of each word. Then say each word slowly and tell students to repeat it. Preview other challenging words, such as *Beringia, edible, flourished, ancestry*, and *Arabian Peninsula*. Have students make word cards that include definitions and pronunciation hints.

PRE-AP

Analyze a Standstill Have students research and analyze a group of modern humans who spent a long time in one place before moving to another one, such as the people who spent about 15,000 years in Beringia. This stop in migration, or a standstill, helped these isolated early humans become genetically distinct from the people they had left behind. Encourage students to find possible causes for the standstill and reasons that the migration ultimately continued. Have students share their research through a poster or diagram.

See the Chapter Planner for more strategies for differentiation.

HISTORICAL THINKING

ANSWERS

1. They migrated out of Africa in search of food and because of curiosity.

2. Scientists can trace early human migration by studying tools, human skulls, and language sounds.

3. Geneticists found the DNA of clothing lice in ancient human remains.

CRITICAL VIEWING The savanna offers plants, grains, and water for people and animals. People can also hunt animals for food.

Out of Eden: Paul Salopek Walks Through Time

"Everybody has a story. They may tell it in a different language, they may whisper it, they may shout it, but they have a story." –Paul Salopek

Embarking on a historic journey, Paul Salopek and guide Ahmed Alema Hessan leave the Ethiopian village of Bouri.

10 CHAPTER 1

From the earliest moments of human history, our restless ancestors were on the move. National Geographic Fellow and Pulitzer Prize–winning journalist Paul Salopek has become a traveler himself, retracing the paths of human migration over the course of about 10 years. Starting in Africa, in Ethiopia, his 21,000-mile journey takes him through Asia and North America and ends at the tip of South America. Along the way, Salopek is practicing what he calls "slow journalism," relying on personal interaction with people who reveal compelling stories about their lives.

PRIMARY SOURCE

JANUARY 2013—ETHIOPIA: TO WALK THE WORLD

I am on a journey. I am in pursuit of an idea, a story, a chimera [something imaginary], perhaps a folly. I am chasing ghosts. Starting in humanity's birthplace in the Great Rift Valley of East Africa, I am retracing, on foot, the pathways of the ancestors who first discovered the Earth at least 60,000 years ago. This remains by far our greatest voyage. Not because it delivered us the planet. No. But because the early *Homo sapiens* who first roamed beyond the mother continent—these pioneer nomads numbered, in total, as few as a couple of hundred people—also bequeathed us the subtlest qualities we now associate with being fully human: complex language, abstract thinking, a compulsion to make art, a genius for technological innovation, and the continuum of today's many races. We know so little about them. They straddled the strait called *Bab el Mandeb*—the "gate of grief" that cleaves Africa from Arabia—and then exploded, in just 2,500 generations, a geological heartbeat, to the remotest habitable fringe of the globe.

Using fossil evidence and the burgeoning science of "genography"—a field that sifts the DNA of living populations for mutations useful in tracking ancient **diasporas** [migrations of people from an ancestral homeland]—I will walk north from Africa into the Middle East. From there my antique route leads eastward across the vast gravel plains of Asia to China, then north again into the mint blue shadows of Siberia. From Russia I will hop a ship to Alaska and inch down the western coast of the New World to wind-smeared Tierra del Fuego, our species' last new continental horizon. I will walk 21,000 miles.

If you ask, I will tell you that I have embarked on this project, which I'm calling the Out of Eden Walk, for many reasons: to relearn the contours of our planet at the human pace of three miles an hour. To slow down. To think. To write. To render current events as a form of pilgrimage. I hope to repair certain important connections burned through by artificial speed, by inattentiveness. I walk, as everyone does, to see what lies ahead. I walk to remember.

Out of Eden Walk, Planned Route

First Peoples and Societies 17

PLAN: 4-PAGE LESSON

OBJECTIVE

Explore the migration of early humans out of Africa through Paul Salopek's Out of Eden Walk.

CRITICAL THINKING SKILLS FOR LESSON 1.4

- Explain
- Make Predictions
- Identify
- Form and Support Opinions
- Analyze Primary Sources

HISTORICAL THINKING FOR CHAPTER 1

How do societies help people survive?

As our early ancestors traveled to new places to hunt animals and gather plants for food, they experienced changes in geography and climate—and sometimes discovered other people and societies as well. Lesson 1.4 discusses how the places early humans discovered along their journey reveal their values and their home societies as they settled and explored new lands.

Student eEdition online

Additional content for this lesson, including a video, is available online.

BACKGROUND FOR THE TEACHER

Paul Salopek In an age when everything is instantaneous and media is a driving force, National Geographic Explorer and journalist Paul Salopek has chosen to slow things down and fully immerse himself in his work. As he walks 21,000 miles from northern Africa to the southern tip of South America, Salopek records his observations and interactions and shares them with the world. While following the path of our early ancestors, Salopek covers major stories and gives voice to the people and issues that often go unheard. Salopek is no stranger to this immersive form of journalism. He prefers an anthropological approach and uses his experiences to collect information, such as working on a ranch in Mexico or joining fishermen in their small boats on the Congo River. Salopek's love of Africa combined with his scientific knowledge of human origins, anthropological method of writing, and interest in current events sparked the decision to retrace the footsteps of early humans out of the continent and across the world.

History Notebook

Encourage students to complete the National Geographic Explorer and Traveler page for Chapter 1 in their History Notebooks as they read.

INTRODUCE & ENGAGE

BRAINSTORM MAKING A LONG TRIP

Tell students to put themselves in the position of a person taking a long trip by foot. Ask them to think about what they would take with them and what they would leave behind. Write the categories "Need to Survive," "Want to Have," and "Should Leave Behind" on the board. Ask volunteers to share items in each category, thinking practically about what is necessary, what is nice to have, and what is unrealistic. Rearrange the items as the class agrees on the proper category for each one.

TEACH

GUIDED DISCUSSION

1. **Explain** What route is Salopek following, and how has he mapped his journey? *(Salopek is following the route of the earliest humans out of Africa, and he mapped his journey based on fossil evidence and results found through genography.)*

2. **Make Predictions** What prediction can you make about Salopek's journey? *(Possible responses: He is determined and will make it to the end. He will get sick and have to end his journey.)*

ANALYZE PRIMARY SOURCES

Discuss the first primary source with students. **ASK:** How is the trail different for Salopek than it was for the early humans? *(Possible responses: Early humans walked largely unoccupied lands. Landforms included vast, open stretches of untouched grasslands, desert, mountains, rivers, lakes, seas, and other physical characteristics. Any areas Salopek traverses could be completely different, such as a lake that has dried up and is now a desert.)* Because of these differences, what challenges could Salopek face during his walk? *(Possible response: People now inhabit the lands where Salopek is traveling, which could be dangerous as political conflicts can close borders.)* How might Salopek's journey be simpler than early humans'? *(Possible responses: The early humans were unable to ask someone for directions or readily find and buy food, water, or other necessities. If Salopek needs information or a specific item, he can ask someone, buy it as he travels, and acquire what he needs. Early humans did not have this luxury; they had to find food and make their own clothes, shoes, and shelters. Early humans could not simply "hop a ship" to cross from Russia to Alaska. And they could not ask someone for a place to sleep.)*

DIFFERENTIATE

ENGLISH LANGUAGE LEARNERS

Summarize This lesson has two primary sources—"Ethiopia: To Walk the World" and "Great Rift Valley: Baby Steps." Pair students and assign each pair a section of the text to read together. Encourage students to use a graphic organizer to make notes about their part of the lesson, including questions they have about vocabulary, descriptive language, and idioms. After answering their questions, have each pair write a one- to two-sentence summary.

GIFTED & TALENTED

Write an Article Have students read several of Salopek's articles to understand how he writes about his experiences. Students should then think of a topic from their own lives—considering personal adventures or those of family members—and write a descriptive article. For example, they may write about their observations as they walked through the Grand Canyon, something they learned about a friend's culture through food or language, or a great-grandmother who migrated from Europe during World War II. Encourage students to immerse themselves in their subject matter, just as Salopek has immersed himself in his. The articles should include accurate details from the experiences or online sources, if necessary, and visuals.

See the Chapter Planner for more strategies for differentiation.

Salopek's journey begins in Ethiopia at one of the world's oldest human fossil sites, Herto Bouri, and unspools across the scalding Afar Triangle, in the Great Rift Valley. Along this pathway our ancestors headed toward the Gulf of Aden, where they first stepped out of Africa to explore the wider world. As Salopek attests, this ancient pathway remains a conduit of opportunity—and sometimes fatal tragedy—for migrants seeking a better life today.

PRIMARY SOURCE

JANUARY 2013—GREAT RIFT VALLEY: BABY STEPS

"Where are you walking?" the Afar nomads ask.

"North. To Djibouti." (We do not say Tierra del Fuego [in South America]. It is much too far—it is meaningless.)

"Are you crazy? Are you sick?"

In reply, Ahmed Alema Hessan—wiry and energetic, the ultimate go-to man, a charming rogue, my guide and protector through the blistering Afar Triangle—doubles over and laughs. He leads our micro-caravan: two skinny camels. I have listened to his guffaw many times already. This project is, to him, a punch line—a cosmic joke. To walk for seven years! Across three continents! Enduring hardship, loneliness, uncertainty, fear, exhaustion, confusion—all for a rucksack's worth of ideas, palaver, scientific and literary conceits. He enjoys the absurdity of it. This is fitting. Especially given our ridiculous launch.

We broke camp this morning in darkness at Bouri, Alema's smoky home—a village of hackers, of coughers—at the western foot of the Great Rift Valley, in the arid northeast of Ethiopia.

I awoke and saw snow: thick, dense, choking, blinding. Like plankton at the bottom of a sea, swirling white in the beam of my headlamp. It was the dust. Hundreds of village animals churned up a cloud as fine as talc. Goats, sheep, cows, donkeys, and camels—but, sadly, not our camels.

The cargo animals I had requisitioned last October (a key arrangement in a project that has consumed thousands of hours of planning) were nowhere to be found. Their drivers were absent, too. They never showed up. So we sat in the dust, waiting. The sun rose. It began to grow hot. To the east, across the Rift, which is widening by the year by a quarter of an inch, lay our first border: Djibouti.

Are you crazy? Are you sick? Yes? No? Maybe?

The sky above is the color of polished lead.

The Afar Triangle is dreaded as a waterless death march, as a moonscape. Temperatures of 120°F. Saltpans so bright they burn the eyes out. Yet today it rained. And Alema and I have no waterproof tents. We have an Ethiopian flag, which Alema wraps himself in. We lead the two camels ourselves. (Whose are they? I'm not sure. Alema procured them Afar-style, off the cuff.) We inch across an acacia plain darkened to the color of chocolate by the warm raindrops. We tread on a photographic negative. The camels' moccasin-like feet pull up the frail crust of moisture, leaving behind white circles of dry dust.

HISTORICAL THINKING

READING CHECK How does Salopek convey both the very real details of life on foot and his thoughts and feelings about his trek?

What is a Traveler?

In this textbook, you will read about additional National Geographic Explorers who, like Paul, are on their own journeys of exploration and discovery. You will also read about historical figures whose journeys have provided us with much information about the past. Their reactions to the people they met and the places they saw on their journeys reveal much about their home societies as well as about the societies they visited.

Use your History Notebook to comment on what you've read.

18 CHAPTER 1

Camel-ology

You must allow camels a generous rest at midday. This improves their dispositions. You must avoid walking camels on stones—a camel's foot is not a hard hoof but a smooth pad, soft as a pot holder. (Our older bull, Fares, will take your shoulder between his jaws as you lead him with a rope, and squeeze gently, communicating his distress on sharp rocks.) . . .

While traveling, feed your camels twice a day, morning and night: one lozenge of alfalfa a hand-span thick and one bucket of grain when available. They also will eat orange rinds, banana peels, stale flatbread, plastic bubble wrap encasing laptop computers, the living hair off your scalp, and a thousand different varieties of grasses, thorns, shrubs, and trees.

To pack a cargo camel is to confront a daunting problem of geometry, of architecture: the hump. The placement of the saddle is critical. It cannot be an inch too far forward, or an inch too far back. The camel will complain otherwise. It will roll in the sand. No one hump is like any other hump. Thus, you must achieve loading perfection on just one. . . . It is a pleasing ritual that connects us to these large, fatalistic, self-satisfied animals through our hands.

Paul Salopek and his local guides—along with the camels he would come to know so well—walk through the Afar region of northeastern Ethiopia.

Nearly hidden in the swirling dust, goats make their way back from a day of grazing to their Ethiopian village.

First Peoples and Societies 19

BACKGROUND FOR THE TEACHER

Out of Eden Walk Paul Salopek began his Out of Eden Walk in January 2013 in Ethiopia, the birthplace of humans. Specifically, Salopek departed from Herto Bouri, the archaeological dig site where some of the oldest human bones have been found. He followed historic caravan routes across the Afar Triangle, to the Djibouti coast, and out of Africa. Despite nearly two years of planning, political conflicts derailed Salopek's route through certain areas. Approximately 3,000 miles into the journey, while attempting to cross through eastern Turkey, Salopek and his guide were detained by Kurdish villagers. The villagers thought the travelers were members of the Islamic State from Syria, trying to sneak in and infiltrate their region. After a threat on his guide's life and no option to stay the night or continue their trek, Salopek reluctantly agreed to load their mule into a truck and take a 118-mile detour around the dangerous city of Diyarbakir, where people were being killed.

Salopek and his guide encountered additional obstacles as their journey continued through Kurd territory. They were not offered shelter and could not camp in the fields, for fear of being identified as enemies and shot. Salopek was then held at gunpoint by three Kurds working for the Turkish military; luckily, Salopek and his guide diffused the situation. However, Salopek's planned route veered off track again. Iran denied his visa, and Salopek had to push north through Georgia and northeast across the Caspian Sea into Kazakhstan instead. Although his course has been carefully mapped, it is impossible to predict what other hurdles may impede Salopek's eventual arrival in Tierra del Fuego.

As Salopek continues on his journey, visit the Out of Eden Walk website to see other challenges he has faced as well as his current location.

TEACH

GUIDED DISCUSSION

3. **Identify** What words and phrases does Salopek use to help his readers visualize his experiences? *(Possible responses: wiry; energetic; blistering; hackers; dense; blinding; like plankton at the bottom of a sea; as fine as talc; polished lead; darkened to the color of chocolate by the warm raindrops; tread on a photographic negative; moccasin-like feet; frail crust of moisture)*

4. **Form and Support Opinions** What tone does Salopek use in his "Camel-ology" feature, and why do you think he chose it? *(Possible response: Salopek uses an informal, entertaining tone in "Camel-ology." I think Salopek used this tone to deliver camel facts in an interesting way. A more formal tone could have caused readers to lose interest.)*

ANALYZE PRIMARY SOURCES

Direct students' attention to the fourth paragraph in the second primary source. Read aloud: "To walk for seven years! Across three continents! Enduring hardship, loneliness, uncertainty, fear, exhaustion, confusion—all for a rucksack's worth of ideas, palaver, scientific and literary conceits." **ASK:** What effects may years of "loneliness, uncertainty, fear, exhaustion, confusion" and other hardships have on Salopek? *(Possible responses: He may suffer physically or psychologically. He may become an even stronger person after working through so many challenges.)*

ACTIVE OPTIONS

On Your Feet: Three-Step Interview Ask students to review the text and video (available in the Student eEdition), as they work in pairs to consider what they have learned. Direct one partner to interview the other by asking questions about traveling, such as: What culture interests you the most? What historic sites would you like to see? If you could go anywhere in the world, where would you go? Why? Direct the interviewer to ask follow-up questions, such as: How would you get there? Would you consider walking? How much time would you spend there? What would you hope to learn? Then have partners reverse roles, with the second interviewer asking the same questions. Encourage students to draw on information from the lesson and their own knowledge of the subject. Invite pairs to share information from their interviews with the class.

NG Learning Framework: Create an Annotated Time Line
ATTITUDE Curiosity
KNOWLEDGE Our Human Story

Invite students to visit the Out Of Eden Walk website to track Salopek's journey. Students should explore the chapters and select an article to read. Ask them to share the dates of their articles so that each article is only read by one student. Encourage them to choose articles from different months, years, and locations. While the students choose their articles and begin to read, prepare a class time line with their chosen dates. If possible, add a map, and have students provide locations as well. When students finish reading their articles, have them write a brief summary of Salopek's experience. Invite students to share their summaries with the class and add them to the time line or map.

HISTORICAL THINKING

ANSWER

1. Possible response: In his writing, Salopek describes his feelings about his trek ("I am on a journey. I am in pursuit of an idea, a story, a chimera, perhaps a folly."), but he also includes realistic details that let the reader see what he is experiencing ("I awoke and saw snow: thick, dense, choking, blinding. Like plankton at the bottom of a sea, swirling white in the beam of my headlamp. It was the dust.").

Artifacts are important sources of information for scientists who study ancient peoples. What can researchers learn from looking at an object or at paintings that have no words and no date? You've read about technology that helps date artifacts, or tell us how old things are. However, there is more to understanding an artifact than knowing when it was made. Scientists put their skills of observation and deduction to work to understand the messages in artifacts.

"There's something about caves—a shadowy opening in a limestone cliff that draws you in. As you pass through the portal between light and dark, you enter a subterranean world—a place of perpetual gloom, of earthy smells, of hushed silence," says paleoanthropologist and National Geographic Explorer Genevieve von Petzinger (shown above in a cave in western Europe). Von Petzinger has twisted and crawled into dangerous and narrow passageways as much as three-quarters of a mile deep to examine images left behind by ancient peoples. Cave drawings in these hidden chambers reveal that some people had time

and energy to create art after meeting their basic needs for survival as early as 63,000 B.C.E.—and perhaps even before.

Von Petzinger studies distinct geometric shapes—dots, lines, rectangles, triangles, ovals, circles—made by early humans. She has found many of the same 32 signs appearing in different caves, sometimes more than a thousand miles apart. The repetition of these symbols over thousands of years, from 10,000 to 40,000 years ago, is a significant forerunner of writing, which first appeared between 4,000 and 5,000 years ago.

ARTIFACT ONE
Primary Source: Ocher Cave Painting
from from Lascaux Caves in Lascaux, France

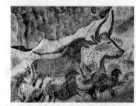

Paleolithic painters mixed ocher, a natural clay containing minerals that give it colors ranging from yellow to red, with animal fat and other liquids to make the earliest known paint. Ocher was used to paint these figures on a cave in Lascaux, France, more than 17,000 years ago. Charcoal was also used to create black outlines. Scientists believe that people used the burnt tips of long sticks to draw images on higher levels of the caves.

CONSTRUCTED RESPONSE What steps would the painter of these figures have had to follow to create this art?

ARTIFACT TWO
Primary Source: Hand Stencils
from Cueva de las Manos in Santa Cruz, Argentina

Stenciled hands are found in ancient caves in South America, Europe, Africa, Borneo, and Australia. The hands shown here were made between 9,500 and 13,000 years ago. Using data about the relative length of fingers in male and female hands, archaeologist Dean Snow, a National Geographic Explorer, examined eight cave sites in France and Spain over more than a decade. He has determined that about three-quarters of the stenciled hands in those caves belonged to women.

CONSTRUCTED RESPONSE Why are most of the hand stencils found in eight European caves believed to be made by women?

ARTIFACT THREE
Primary Source: Cave Paintings
from Laas Geel outside of Hargeisa, Somaliland

Like humanity, art itself started in Africa. Experts found an "art studio" in South Africa that contained tools dating back 100,000 years. Many millennia later in the Horn of Africa peninsula in Laas Geel, artists created these exaggerated paintings of humans and animals. The colorful ocher figures of people, cattle, giraffes, and different types of canines are more than 5,000—and may even be 10,000—years old.

CONSTRUCTED RESPONSE What are the similarities and differences between this cave painting in Africa and the art from France and Argentina?

SYNTHESIZE & WRITE

1. REVIEW Review what you have read and observed about modern humans and these cave paintings.

2. RECALL On your own paper, list two details you observed looking at each cave painting.

3. CONSTRUCT Construct a topic sentence that answers this question: How are the three cave paintings and the materials used to make them similar and different?

4. WRITE Using evidence from this chapter and the cave paintings, write an informative paragraph that supports your topic sentence in Step 3.

PLAN: 2-PAGE LESSON

OBJECTIVE
Synthesize information about cave paintings from primary source photographs.

CRITICAL THINKING SKILLS FOR LESSON 1.5
- Synthesize
- Make Inferences
- Draw Conclusions
- Evaluate

HISTORICAL THINKING FOR CHAPTER 1
How do societies help people survive?

The use of symbols and pictures that portray animals and people indicates an important stage in communication—and represents the first step in developing a writing system. Lesson 1.5 focuses on three photographs of cave art created by early modern humans dating back to the Paleolithic Era.

Student eEdition online
Additional content for this lesson, including a video, is available online.

BACKGROUND FOR THE TEACHER

Cave Art There are about 400 known cave art sites on Earth. Although the majority of this art does not show human forms, handprints appear in caves all over the world. Some human heads and other body parts also appear in isolation. Most cave art includes geometric shapes that vary by location as well as animals, including some that are extinct (mammoths, woolly rhinoceroses, cave lions, and bears) and some that live today (horses, bison, and deer).

The exact meanings of cave art remains unknown, but the images probably served as a meaningful way to depict daily life. Some experts believe the paintings represented religious practices and beliefs and were part of ceremonies contacting spirits before a hunt—or another activity—to bring about success.

Artists often chose protrusions or natural swellings in the walls of caves for their work, giving paintings a three-dimensional effect. It is reported that after influential 20th century artist Pablo Picasso viewed the paintings in Lascaux Cave in France, he remarked, "We have learned nothing in twelve thousand years."

INTRODUCE & ENGAGE

PREPARE FOR THE DOCUMENT-BASED QUESTION

Before students start the activity, briefly preview the three photographs. Remind students that a constructed response requires full explanations in complete sentences. Emphasize that students should use what they have learned about ancient artifacts in addition to the information shown in the photographs.

TEACH

GUIDED DISCUSSION

1. **Make Inferences** What do you think is the purpose of each cave painting? (*Possible response: Ocher Cave Painting—to show animals that they hunted or animals that were in the area; Hand Stencils—to record the people/women who were in the cave or some sort of a religious symbol; Cave Paintings—to show exaggerated representations of humans and animals*)

2. **Draw Conclusions** According to Petzinger's video (available in the Student eEdition), why is it important to research and understand the geometric shapes in cave paintings when learning about Paleolithic people? (*Possible response: If scientists can understand the geometric shapes, then they can follow the people, ideas, and the culture of the Paleolithic people.*)

EVALUATE

After students have completed the Synthesize & Write activity, allow time for them to exchange paragraphs and read and comment on the work of their peers. Establish guidelines for comments prior to the activity so that feedback is constructive and encouraging in nature. Comments should focus on the most significant parts that address the purpose of the activity and the audience.

ACTIVE OPTION

On Your Feet: Think, Pair, Share Ask the following question and then allow a few minutes for students to think about it: What emotions and impressions do the cave paintings inspire? Then tell students to choose partners and talk about the question for five minutes. After discussion time, invite students to share their ideas with the class.

DIFFERENTIATE

INCLUSION

Clarify Text Pair sight-impaired students with sighted students. As they read or listen to the text, have the sight-impaired students indicate if there are words or passages they do not understand. Their partner can clarify meanings by rereading passages, emphasizing context clues, and paraphrasing.

PRE-AP

Research Cave Paintings Explain to students that teenage boys, not archaeologists, discovered Lascaux Cave in France and for years experts did not believe cave paintings were created during the Paleolithic Age because the art appeared "too advanced." Invite students to research Lascaux Cave. Also, have them research the information and techniques archaeologists use to date cave paintings. Tell students they can present their findings in a written report or multimedia presentation.

SYNTHESIZE & WRITE

ANSWERS

1. Answers will vary.

2. Possible response: Ocher cave painting—detailed animal figures and red and black paint. Hand stencils—recognizable hands and red and black paint. African cave painting—abstract style and shapes, and red and white paint.

3. Possible response: Although all three cave paintings use red paint, their subjects and techniques differ.

4. Answers will vary. Students' paragraphs should include their topic sentence from Step 3 and provide several details from the cave paintings.

CONSTRUCTED RESPONSE

Artifact One: First, artists would think about what to draw. Next, they would mix ocher with animal fat and other liquids to make their paints. They would use different clays to make different colors. Then they would choose something to draw with, such as a stick. Finally, they would put the paint on the sticks and apply it to the cave walls, burning the end of a long stick to reach higher parts of the cave.

Artifact Two: Women tend to be smaller than men, so it would be easier for them to move through narrow passageways in the caves.

Artifact Three: All three paintings use red ocher, and the European and African cave art both depict animals. But the paintings in Africa use white "paint," and its figures are on a curved—not flat—surface.

Early Agriculture

You may think that farmers practice a more traditional way of life. Compared with foraging and hunting-gathering traditions, the shift to farming was remarkable. Planting seeds, harvesting crops, and using domesticated animals to help with work meant people lived more closely together in settled communities. This change was so dramatic that it is often called a revolution.

CULTIVATING PLANTS

Archaeologists use the term **Neolithic**, or new stone age, to describe societies that used stone tools and practiced **agriculture**, the cultivation of plant foods and domestication of animals as sources of food and labor. It is not clear why more and more communities chose to adopt agriculture after nearly 200,000 years of hunting and gathering, but climate change or religious beliefs may have been contributing factors. This progression between two different ways of life is sometimes called the **Neolithic Revolution**, and it had a significant impact on the way in which people lived.

The transition took place slowly, and like the process of migration out of Africa, occurred independently in several places. People did not give up hunting and gathering and become farmers in a single generation. Traces of seeds, grasses, and beans have recently been discovered on 23,000-year-old grinding stones in the Huang He region of northern China. Processing foods, or performing a series of actions to change them, was an early precursor to agriculture; people had to use and understand which plants before they could grow them. Turning foods into flour would have been one of many steps that could lead to the development of agriculture.

Agriculture appeared in northern China about 10,000 years ago, around the same time that agriculture appeared in the area known today as the Middle East. The **Natufians** (nuh-TOO-fee-uhnz)—people who lived in present-day Israel, the Palestinian territories, and southern Syria—were among the earliest people to cultivate, or plant and raise, crops. The first food they

MORTAR
This mortar for grinding materials dates back to 4,000–2,000 B.C.E.

grew was figs; they planted fig trees but did not settle near them. They hunted and gathered as before and visited the fig trees from time to time to collect the fruit. Many other people continued to forage for all their food.

The next crops the Natufians cultivated were grains—wheat and barley. At first, they gathered wild grain. The seeds of wild grain fell easily to the ground because the plants had weak stems, which meant the grain grew back year after year without being planted. Wild grains also had thick husks that protected the seed kernels, but these thick husks made it difficult for humans to remove the seeds. The Natufians chose seeds from plants that were taller and had thinner husks and planted those.

Over time, the wheat and barley the Natufians planted became quite different from the wild plants. The seeds were less likely to fall to the ground, and it was easier for people to remove the kernels. This process of choosing and planting the seeds of grains and other crops to make them more useful continued and

CRITICAL VIEWING A shepherd leads sheep between Madaba and Mount Nebo, Jordan. Why do you think the flock is moving through the area instead of stopping?

spread. By 8000 B.C.E., people throughout the eastern Mediterranean, especially those in dryer areas, were growing grain crops. Once they had begun to cultivate crops, the larger size of their villages forced them to continue farming because agriculture could support a larger population than foraging could.

DOMESTICATING ANIMALS

The second element of agriculture was the **domestication**, or taming, of wild animals. Researchers do not know a great deal about how different animals became domesticated, but it seems likely that people began to watch over herds and then feed the animals. The first animals to be domesticated were probably dogs, who are believed to have descended from wolves. In fact, people may have domesticated dogs before they domesticated grains, as there are dog fossils as old as 15,000 years. Current evidence indicates that dogs were domesticated in Asia and Europe at about the same time.

After several thousand years, goats, sheep, and cattle had been domesticated. Archaeologists believe people were riding horses by about 3500 B.C.E. Horse teeth from that era are ground in a way that might indicate

FELINE FRIENDS
While dogs were domesticated with the help of humans, cats may have decided on their own to become our furry companions. One theory is that cats domesticated themselves because their prey—rodents and small animals—lived on the grain stored in farming villages. People long believed that cats were first domesticated in Egypt about 4,000 years ago. However, the discovery of a cat buried with a human dating nearly 10,000 years ago on the Mediterranean island of Cyprus suggests humans and cats may have had close relationships long before that.

Egyptian cat mummy, 672–332 B.C.E.

PLAN: 4-PAGE LESSON

OBJECTIVE

Analyze the transition from hunting and gathering to agriculture and why this process took thousands of years.

CRITICAL THINKING SKILLS FOR LESSON 2.1

- Make Inferences
- Draw Conclusions
- Interpret Maps
- Identify Main Ideas and Details
- Determine Chronology
- Synthesize
- Analyze Cause and Effect
- Make Generalizations

HISTORICAL THINKING FOR CHAPTER 1

How do societies help people survive?

Neolithic societies chose and planted seeds of preferred plants. The increased amounts of food led to larger settled communities. People then tamed wild animals such as dogs, goats, sheep, cattle, and horses. These animals provided protection, food, and transportation. Lesson 2.1 explores these advancements.

BACKGROUND FOR THE TEACHER

Natufian Crops The first figs favored by the Natufians were sweet due to a mutation. However, these figs did not have fertile seeds. To grow the figs, people had to plant a branch from one of the fig trees in the ground to reproduce the plant. Because these fig trees continued to grow, scientists know that someone deliberately planted them and continued to do so year after year.

The Natufians started growing grain to eat, of course, but also to brew beer. Archaeologists have discovered 13,000-year-old beer-brewing resources in a Natufian cave. These materials are older than the first evidence of cultivated grains. So the question remains: Did the Natufians start planting and growing grain for bread or for beer?

INTRODUCE & ENGAGE

PREVIEW WITH VOCABULARY

Draw a Word Web on the board and write the word *revolution* in the center. Ask students what they think of when they hear the word *revolution*. Write students' answers on the outer spokes of the web. Answers will most likely include war, rebellion, or overthrow of a government. Write *agriculture* on one of the spokes. Ask students why agriculture would be considered a revolution. As needed, explain that one definition of *revolution* is "a sudden, radical, or complete change." Tell students that although agriculture was not a sudden change for early humans, it was a radical and complete change to their daily lives.

TEACH

GUIDED DISCUSSION

1. **Identify Main Ideas and Details** Why would people need to understand wild plants before they could grow them? *(Possible response: People needed to know that plants grow from seeds and which part of the plant was the seed. They needed to know about soil and that plants need water and sunlight.)*

2. **Determine Chronology** List in order the foods that Natufians grew. *(figs and then grains, such as wheat and barley)*

INTERPRET MAPS

Direct students' attention to the map of Cultural Hearths and the Spread of Agriculture. Ask students to use the map to answer the following questions:

- How much time does the map represent? *(about 7,500 years)*
- Which areas were the first to establish agriculture, and what were they called? *(Central America, along the Nile, Southwest Asia, and China; cultural hearths)*
- What plants and animals were raised in these four different areas? *(corn, beans, grains, rice, sheep, and cattle)*
- Where was agriculture established by 5000 B.C.E.? *(along the Nile, in Southwest Asia, and in China)*
- Where did agriculture spread to next? *(more of Southwest Asia, Europe, northern Africa, India, more of China, Southeast Asia, and Oceania)*
- Where was agriculture established by 500 B.C.E.? *(middle of Asia, Arabian Peninsula, middle of Africa, Central America, northern South America.)*

Discuss the different types of plants and animals raised in each of these locations and the amount of time represented by each color on the map.

DIFFERENTIATE

INCLUSION

Sequence Events Write the following events on index cards, with one event on each card.

- People began to understand plants and how they grow.
- People domesticated dogs.
- The Natufian people grew fig trees.
- The Natufian people grew wheat and barley.
- People domesticated goats, sheep, and cattle.
- With the increase in food, families and communities grew larger.
- People domesticated horses and used them for transportation and travel.

After students read the lesson, have them work with a partner to put the cards in chronological order.

GIFTED & TALENTED

Engage in a Debate Direct students to choose the domesticated animal they think would have been most important to early humans and list their reasons in a graphic organizer. Have them prepare to debate another student about why their animal was the most important by collecting evidence and anticipating a counterargument. Tell pairs that have researched two different animals to conduct a short debate for the class. Then have the class discuss the persuasiveness of each argument.

See the Chapter Planner for more strategies for differentiation.

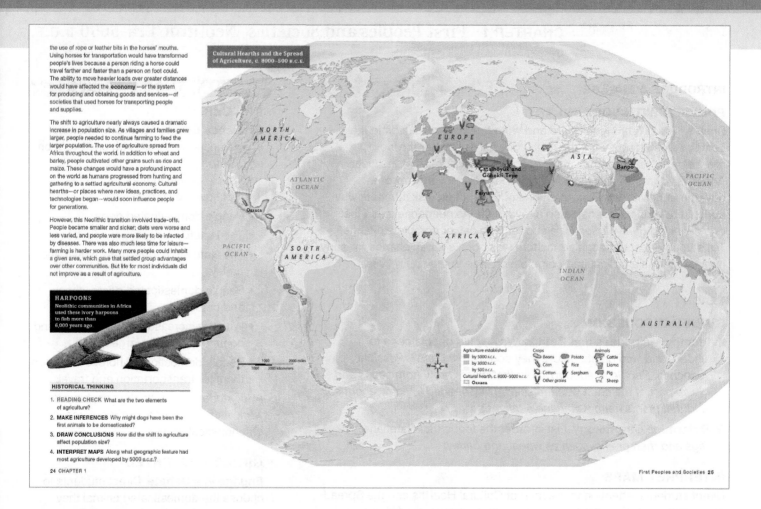

the use of rope or leather bits in the horses' mouths. Using horses for transportation would have transformed people's lives because a person riding a horse could travel farther and faster than a person on foot could. The ability to move heavier loads over greater distances would have affected the **economy**—or the system for producing and obtaining goods and services—of societies that used horses for transporting people and supplies.

The shift to agriculture nearly always caused a dramatic increase in population size. As villages and families grew larger, people needed to continue farming to feed the larger population. The use of agriculture spread from Africa throughout the world. In addition to wheat and barley, people cultivated other grains such as rice and maize. These changes would have a profound impact on the world as humans progressed from hunting and gathering to a settled agricultural economy. Cultural hearths—or places where new ideas, practices, and technologies began—would soon influence people for generations.

However, this Neolithic transition involved trade-offs. People became smaller and sicker; diets were worse and less varied, and people were more likely to be infected by diseases. There was also much less time for leisure—farming is harder work. Many more people could inhabit a given area, which gave that settled group advantages over other communities. But life for most individuals did not improve as a result of agriculture.

HARPOONS
Neolithic communities in Africa used these ivory harpoons to fish more than 6,000 years ago.

HISTORICAL THINKING

1. **READING CHECK** What are the two elements of agriculture?

2. **MAKE INFERENCES** Why might dogs have been the first animals to be domesticated?

3. **DRAW CONCLUSIONS** How did the shift to agriculture affect population size?

4. **INTERPRET MAPS** Along what geographic feature had most agriculture developed by 5000 B.C.E.?

Cultural Hearths and the Spread of Agriculture, c. 8000–500 B.C.E.

Agriculture established
by 5000 B.C.E.
by 3000 B.C.E.
by 500 B.C.E.
Cultural hearth, c. 8000–5000 B.C.E.
Oaxaca

Crops: Beans, Potato, Corn, Rice, Cotton, Sorghum, Other grains

Animals: Cattle, Llama, Pig, Sheep

BACKGROUND FOR THE TEACHER

Animals for Food The first animals to be domesticated for food were goats and sheep. They were used for their meat, milk, and hides. These herbivores grazed on nearby natural vegetation, which made them easier to tame and raise than animals that eat meat or special crops. Numerous bones of one-year-old sheep in a Middle East settlement (10,000–9,000 B.C.E.) found by scientists provide evidence that these animals were being raised for food by the people living there. Larger herbivores, such as cattle, were domesticated next. Chickens eat the same seeds and grain that people do, so they were not domesticated until a community had enough grain to feed people and chickens. Over many years, humans recognized certain traits in animals—such as a calm temperament—and decided to breed animals that had these attributes. Through careful breeding choices, people changed domestic animals from their wild ancestors.

TEACH

GUIDED DISCUSSION

3. Synthesize Why would the shift to agriculture cause "a profound impact on the world"? *(Possible response: With agriculture, people grew more food and could then domesticate goats, sheep, and cattle for food as well. With more food, children lived to become adults and had children of their own, so the population grew. These people then settled in communities and diverted water for their crops. More people meant that more land was converted to growing crops, grazing herds, and eventually building cities, which all made an impact on the world.)*

4. Analyze Cause and Effect What negative effects did agriculture have on humans? *(Possible responses: Agriculture is hard work. People lived in larger, settled groups. Disease traveled more quickly when more people lived in one area. Diets were less varied.)*

MAKE GENERALIZATIONS

Discuss the sidebar feature "Feline Friends." Instruct students to consider how the feline-human relationship was mutually beneficial. **ASK:** Why were cats attracted to areas where people lived? *(because the rodents and small animals that cats ate lived off people's grain)* How would people have felt about the presence of the cats? *(People would have been glad that cats kept the rodents' and small animals' population under control.)* What might have people done to encourage the cats to stay? *(They may have provided water and shelter. They may have spoken gently to the cats, so as not to frighten them.)* Then instruct students to consider how the relationship between felines and humans evolved over time. **ASK:** Why do you think people would bury a cat with a human? *(Possible response: The person and the cat had a special relationship or bond of friendship.)*

ACTIVE OPTIONS

On Your Feet: Think, Pair, Share Read the Background for the Teacher "Animals for Food" aloud to students. Then give students a few minutes to think about the following question: What steps might early humans have taken to domesticate animals? Then tell students to choose partners and discuss the question for several minutes. Finally, allow volunteers to share their ideas with the class.

> **NG Learning Framework: Tame Wild Horses**
> **SKILL** Communication
> **KNOWLEDGE** Our Human Story

Invite students to go online to research a story of how wild horses are tamed today. Then encourage students to think about how early humans might have tamed wild horses so that the horses could be used for transportation. Have students make inferences about the differences between current training methods and domestication during the Neolithic era. Instruct students to consider what kind of equipment early humans might have used to ride and guide the horses. Tell students to write their ideas in a brief essay to share with the class.

HISTORICAL THINKING

ANSWERS

1. cultivating plants and domesticating animals

2. Possible response: Dogs could have been helpful to hunters and also offered humans protection from other animals.

3. The greater availability of food may have also led to increased life expectancy and the birth of more children, causing the population to increase.

4. rivers

CRITICAL VIEWING The land looks sandy and dry. The sheep need grass to eat and water to drink, and neither of these needs are shown in the photograph.

2.2 Material Culture

THE POWER OF ANIMALS
You've learned that early humans domesticated, or tamed, wild animals for practical reasons, including for food, for animal fur or skin, and for the transportation of goods as well as people. And, as you've read, some experts believe that dogs were domesticated before plants were cultivated, which emphasizes their importance as beloved pets. Recall that some cave paintings featured animals as subjects. Humans also saw—and continue to see—animals as spiritual and religious symbols. These complex and varied relationships between people and animals have helped shape the human experience over thousands and thousands of years.

Imaginary Animals Early humans also imagined and depicted animals that did not exist in reality. Representations of the mythical unicorn can be found in art and literature from civilizations as diverse as Mesopotamia, India, China, Greece, and the Islamic world. This detail from a 15th-century tapestry shows the European version of the unicorn: a white horse with a single long horn emerging from its forehead. The image also alludes to the legend that only a maiden can tame this pure creature.

Animals in Religion or Mythology
The Toltec civilization, which lasted from about 950 to 1200 C.E. in what is now Mexico, is another society that blended human and animal forms in its spiritual art. This small figure is made of clay that was then covered in mother of pearl. Most experts believe it depicts a warrior wearing a coyote helmet. However, some think it represents a god's face coming out of a feathered snake's mouth.

Ancient Egypt Animals figured prominently in ancient Egyptian religious beliefs, with gods and other creatures often portrayed as part animal and part human. For example, a sphinx usually has the body of a lion and the head of a person. However, these sphinxes near the Temple of Amun—who was the king of the gods—near Thebes (now Luxor) each combine a lion's body and a ram's head. Underneath the head and between the paws of each sphinx is a small figure of Ramses II, an important Egyptian pharaoh.

Hanuman Langurs in Jodhpur, India
These animals, also known as gray langurs, are named after the monkey commander in the Hindu epic *Ramayana* who commands an army of monkeys to help save the god Rama's wife. The langurs' black faces, hands, and feet are said to reflect the burns that Hanuman suffered during the rescue. Hanuman langurs are considered sacred to Hindus, so the people of Jodhpur feed the monkeys and allow them to roam freely throughout the city.

Asian Guardian Lions *Shishi* (Chinese for "stone lions") first appeared during the Han dynasty. Lions are not native to China; many experts believe that they were introduced to the area through trade with the Persians. Initially, these sculptures were placed near temples, palaces, royal tombs, and government offices and residences as powerful symbols of strength and protection.

HISTORICAL THINKING

1. **READING CHECK** What are three relationships that people had and have with animals?

2. **COMPARE AND CONTRAST** How are the animals you read about the same and how do they differ?

3. **MAKE CONNECTIONS** What interaction do you or have you had with animals?

PLAN: 2-PAGE LESSON

OBJECTIVE
Learn how the relationships between people and animals have helped shape the human experience over thousands and thousands of years.

CRITICAL THINKING SKILLS FOR LESSON 2.2
- Analyze Visuals
- Make Connections
- Compare and Contrast
- Make Inferences

HISTORICAL THINKING FOR CHAPTER 1
How do societies help people survive?

Early humans domesticated animals to help meet their survival needs. Lesson 2.2 explores how humans learned to revere certain animals as something more than sources of food, clothing, or transportation.

Student eEdition online
Additional content for this lesson, including photos and a painting, is available online.

BACKGROUND FOR THE TEACHER
Animal Protection Animals have been protecting humans physically—and sometimes spiritually—for millennia. Today, when most people look for a guard animal, they think of a dog. However, donkeys, llamas, alpacas, ostriches, and emus are also used for protecting sheep and other farm animals. In 2011, dolphins were used in the Iraq war to detect mines and ensure safe passage for ships. Their ability to detect unfamiliar noises allowed geese to warn U.S. soldiers of enemy infiltration in their camps during the Vietnam War. Alligators have been used in moats to safeguard castles. Meanwhile, some institutions have turned to even more unusual deterrents. After animals were stolen from the Skansen Zoo in Stockholm, the zoo announced that a 14-foot king cobra, whose bite could kill a person in 15 minutes, would be released each night to discourage any would-be criminals. An international gem exhibit in Sri Lanka also used a cobra to guard the world's largest sapphire.

History Notebook
Encourage students to complete the Material Culture page for Chapter 1 in their History Notebooks as they read.

INTRODUCE & ENGAGE

PREVIEW THE VISUALS

Tell students that the photographs and artifacts in this lesson represent only a few examples of the many uses and representations of animals in humans' lives. **ASK:** What animals do you see? *(Answers may vary. Possible responses: monkeys; a unicorn; lions with ram heads)* Based on the photos and art, how do you think humans viewed these animals? *(Possible response: The animals appear to be respected by humans.)*

TEACH

GUIDED DISCUSSION

1. **Make Inferences** Why might people living during the Han dynasty have chosen the lion, an animal they had never seen before, as a symbol of strength and protection? *(Possible response: They heard stories about strong, fierce, and majestic lions and wanted to bring that sense of strength to their own culture.)*

2. **Compare and Contrast** Based on the information about sled dogs (available in the Student eEdition), how do humans view dogs today compared with how people treated dogs thousands of years ago? *(Possible responses: Dogs are typically not buried with their owners today. But some dogs are buried in pet cemeteries or special places, with an object—such as a blanket or favorite toy—that symbolizes their lives or bonds with their owners.)*

MATERIAL CULTURE

Point out that most of the animals in this lesson, real or imagined, are not essential to the physical survival of people today. Sled dogs are used more for sport than necessity, and modern Maasai people are not solely dependent on their herds. **ASK:** Based on the information and photographs presented in this lesson, what relationships—other than practical ones—have humans developed with animals over the years? *(Possible response: Humans have respected, cared for, used, and worshiped various types of animals in societies all over the world for millennia.)*

ACTIVE OPTION

On Your Feet: Jigsaw Strategy Organize students into "expert" groups and assign each group a topic from one of the photographs and artifacts, such as Shishi, Hanuman langurs, animals in religion or mythology, or Göbekli Tepe, the sphinxes of Amun, sled dogs, or the Maasai people (available in the Student eEdition). Ask each group to conduct online research and then discuss the additional information gathered, including any images. Then regroup students into new groups so that each new group has at least one member from each expert group. Students in the new groups take turns sharing the information from their expert groups.

DIFFERENTIATE

INCLUSION

Categorize Artifacts Students who are visual learners may benefit from grouping and categorizing the artifacts in the lesson, such as by type of art or artifact, type of animal, purpose or reason, or location. Have students work in pairs to make their groupings. Then have pairs compare their categories with other pairs.

GIFTED & TALENTED

Research Imaginary Animals Have students conduct online research into imaginary animals, such the unicorn or the sphinx pictured in this lesson. Students should conduct a search about different mythological animals and then choose one for further study. Their research should answer the following questions: Where and when did the imaginary animal originate? Does the animal have any religious or spiritual connections to humans? What animal or animals is the imaginary animal based on? What is the common view of this creature today? Students should develop a written report and a visual depiction of the animal, such as a drawing, painting, or sculpture.

See the Chapter Planner for more strategies for differentiation.

HISTORICAL THINKING

ANSWERS

1. Possible responses: practical companions, spiritual and religious symbols, beloved pets

2. Possible response: Many of the animals are sacred and have a role in organized religion. Others are used for practical reasons. The animals are different in that there is such a wide variety of them, reflecting the types of animals that are unique to each environment.

3. Answers will vary. Possible responses: pets, zoos, mascots

The First Large Settlements

Determining causes and effects can be difficult when historians are looking at people and events from 10,000 years ago—or more. Archaeological evidence can help. So can investigations of plant life and landforms in the areas being studied. Everyone needs food, fresh water, and safety. Insights into the ways in which people from long ago met those needs can uncover how they lived.

JERICHO AND GÖBEKLI TEPE

Researchers are not sure whether people settled in one place because they had become agricultural or whether they became agricultural because they settled in one place. What is known is that the transition to the Neolithic era brought important changes to human life wherever people adopted agriculture.

One of the world's oldest known continuously occupied human settlements is **Jericho** (JEHR-ih-koh), which began as a Natufian settlement near the Jordan River in the West Bank area of the present-day Palestinian territories. As many as 1,000 people may have lived in Jericho between 8300 and 7500 B.C.E. in mud-brick dwellings with stone foundations. These early people planted wheat and barley and perhaps figs and lentils as well, but they hunted instead of domesticating animals. They also made salt by evaporating water from the Dead Sea. This combination of activities shows the gradual nature of the Neolithic transition.

The residents of Jericho dug a wide ditch and built a wall at least 8 feet high around their settlement for protection from wild animals, human enemies, or possibly both. They also built a 28-foot tower inside the wall that may have served as a lookout post. The ditches, the wall, and the tower all show that one or more leaders coordinated workers and supplies for large-scale construction. These structures indicate a more complex political organization than a band of hunter-gatherers would have had.

The number of people living in Jericho suggests that the rise of agriculture contributed to an increase in population and thus large settlements. However, some scientists argue the opposite. They see the rise of large settlements as causing the shift to agriculture rather than being an effect of it. Evidence from a temple structure at **Göbekli Tepe** in southeastern Turkey could support this view. At least 500 people came together to build an elaborate religious structure on this site some 12,000 years ago. The need to feed this large workforce may have encouraged people in this cultural hearth to cultivate seeds and domesticate animals.

ÇATALHÖYÜK

Settlements of the eastern Mediterranean increased in size gradually. One early example is **Çatalhöyük** (chah-tahl-hoo-YOOK), a settlement in present-day Turkey that was, at its peak, home to as many as 8,000 people. This community developed around 12,000 years ago and lasted more than a thousand years. Houses were so close together that there was no room for streets—or even front doors. People used ladders to enter their homes through the roof and socialized on the flat roofs the way people in today's cities might socialize on sidewalks or in parks.

The people of Çatalhöyük hunted and fished, but most of the food in the settlement came from farming, which created **surpluses**, or supplies of goods and labor not needed for short-term survival. These surpluses allowed people to focus on other work, such as the creation of new technology and artistic expression. Researchers at the site of Çatalhöyük have discovered pottery, cloth, cups, utensils made of bone, tools, and jewelry. People who made these items could have traded them for other goods.

The dozens of limestone pillars of Göbekli Tepe measure up to 18 feet high and weigh between 7 and 10 tons. These pillars may represent dancing priests, with hands resting above a belt.

Scientists are still exploring Çatalhöyük to understand the people who built it and lived in it. One surprising feature of this community is that the settlement seems to have been located at least six miles from the fields where food crops were grown. Another feature is that the settlement is located right next to the clay soils people used to plaster the walls and floors of their houses as well as to make bowls, bins, and sculptures. Scientists speculate that it was easier for the people who lived at Çatalhöyük to carry lightweight crops over a distance than it was to carry heavy clay.

HISTORICAL THINKING

1. **READING CHECK** How did the first large settlements demonstrate a gradual transition to the Neolithic era?

2. **IDENTIFY MAIN IDEAS AND DETAILS** What are the two different theories on the emergence of large settlements?

3. **ANALYZE CAUSE AND EFFECT** What was one effect of the surpluses at Çatalhöyük?

PLAN: 2-PAGE LESSON

OBJECTIVE
Explain how elements of both hunter-gatherer and agricultural economies benefited the first large settlements.

CRITICAL THINKING SKILLS FOR LESSON 2.3
- Identify Main Ideas and Details
- Analyze Cause and Effect
- Identify Problems and Solutions
- Compare and Contrast
- Interpret Visuals

HISTORICAL THINKING FOR CHAPTER 1
How do societies help people survive?

The first large settlements provided mud-brick or clay dwellings for shelter and protection. The people grew grain and hunted and/or fished for food. Lesson 2.3 discusses the first large settlements and how a food surplus helped people develop specialized skills.

Student eEdition online
Additional content for this lesson, including an image gallery and a diagram, is available online.

BACKGROUND FOR THE TEACHER
The Salty Sea Early humans living near the Dead Sea had an abundant source of salt. Water in the Dead Sea is almost 10 times saltier than ocean water; the rocks near the sea's shore glitter with salt. Long ago, people most likely figured out that the heat of the sun had caused the water to evaporate and leave the salt behind. One quart of Dead Sea water produces eight ounces, or half a pound, of salt after evaporation.

INTRODUCE & ENGAGE

CONSIDER LEADERSHIP AND COLLABORATION

Have four or five volunteers meet for a few minutes to suggest local natural resources they could use to build walls for protection and how they would set about building these walls. Have students report to the class the results of their discussion and if they worked together to reach a consensus. Ask if a leader naturally evolved from the group. Discuss the need for a leader in large scale projects and how leaders most likely emerged in early human communities.

TEACH

GUIDED DISCUSSION

1. **Identify Problems and Solutions** How did the residents of Jericho protect themselves from wild animals and human enemies? *(They dug a wide ditch, built a wall eight feet high around the settlement, and built a 28-foot tower that may have been a lookout tower.)*

2. **Compare and Contrast** How did the distance of Çatalhöyük to its agricultural fields compare to the distance to the clay soils they used to build their houses? *(Çatalhöyük was at least six miles from its agricultural fields but right next to the clay soils.)*

INTERPRET VISUALS

Ask students to study the diagram of Çatalhöyük (available in the Student eEdition). Elicit descriptions of the structure depicted. **ASK:** What similarities and differences do you see between Çatalhöyük and modern apartment or condominium buildings? *(Possible response: The diagram shows a number of individual dwellings that share walls, like modern apartment or condominium buildings. Unlike modern dwellings, people in Çatalhöyük entered through the roofs and used the roof space as public plazas.)*

ACTIVE OPTIONS

On Your Feet: Numbered Heads Ask students to think about how the people of Jericho may have built the 28-foot tower inside the city wall without machinery. Then have them form small groups and number off within the group. Students should discuss the prompt until each one has the concept understanding and language needed to report for the group. Call a number and have students with that number give their reports.

| **NG Learning Framework: Observing Our World**
| **SKILL** Observation
| **KNOWLEDGE** Our Living Planet

Share the Background for the Teacher information. Prompt students to discuss other evidence from the lesson that early people observed the world around them and learned from nature how best to use its natural resources. Have small groups discuss local natural resources they know or have observed. Instruct them to research the history of their area to learn what natural resources first brought people to the region. Then tell them to observe whether those same resources are being used today and, if not, to observe and record how the area has changed.

DIFFERENTIATE

STRIVING READERS

Identify Cause and Effect Remind students that a cause is why something happened and an effect is what happened. Point out that a "because sentence" can help them identify cause and effect. Write the following two sentences: The population increased because people started growing their own food. People started growing their own food because there were more people to feed. Discuss the two different views and write each cause and effect. Tell students to find at least two more causes and effects in the lesson and write a "because sentence" for each. Invite students to share their sentences and record the causes and effects in a Cause and Effect graphic organizer.

GIFTED & TALENTED

Analyze Artifacts Have students research and analyze archaeological artifacts from Jericho or Çatalhöyük using online sites. Ask students to choose a few artifacts and write an analysis on how having a surplus of food from agriculture may have enabled the people to develop these artifacts.

See the Chapter Planner for more strategies for differentiation.

HISTORICAL THINKING

ANSWERS

1. The first large settlements contained elements of both hunter-gatherer and agricultural societies.

2. One theory is that the adoption of agriculture led people to build large permanent settlements; the other theory is that the creation of large settlements led people to take up agriculture.

3. Possible response: The surpluses allowed people to focus on things other than growing food.

1 REVIEW

VOCABULARY

Use each of the following vocabulary words in a sentence that shows an understanding of the term's meaning.

1. artifact
2. migrate
3. hunter-gatherer
4. adapt
5. agriculture
6. domestication
7. economy
8. surplus

READING STRATEGY
DETERMINE CHRONOLOGY

Use a sequence chain like the one below to show the order in which humans populated different regions of Earth based on our current understanding. Then answer the question that follows.

9. Which regions of Earth were last to be populated by human beings, and why?

MAIN IDEAS

Answer the following questions. Support your answers with evidence from the chapter.

10. Name three types of scientists who have contributed to understanding early modern humans and where they lived, and describe the work these scientists do. LESSON 1.1

11. What route do some scientists believe early humans used to migrate to the Americas? LESSON 1.1

12. What type of environment did early modern humans first inhabit? LESSON 1.3

13. What evidence found by geneticists could indicate that early humans in Europe wore clothes? LESSON 1.3

14. What were two characteristics of the Neolithic era? LESSON 2.1

15. Describe two actions people are believed to have taken to domesticate wheat and barley. LESSON 2.1

16. What was an important feature of the Çatalhöyük economy? LESSON 2.3

HISTORICAL THINKING

Answer the following questions. Support your answers with evidence from the chapter.

17. DESCRIBE What characteristics did early modern humans share with present-day people?

18. MAKE GENERALIZATIONS How do we know what early modern humans were like and where and how they lived?

19. DRAW CONCLUSIONS What does the domestication of plants and animals suggest about the development of humans?

20. FORM AND SUPPORT OPINIONS What do you think were some advantages and disadvantages to a more settled life over the hunter-gatherer one?

21. SUMMARIZE Briefly state two different viewpoints of the relationship between agriculture and large settlements.

INTERPRET CHARTS

Look at the chart, which shows the dates and location of the world's earliest cultivation. Then answer the questions that follow.

22. According to the chart, which crops were found in both Africa and China? What can you infer about the climate of each area?

23. Which animal was domesticated in three different places during a time span of 3,400 years? Why do you think early humans domesticated this animal?

Date of Earliest Cultivation	Place	Crops and Animals
8400 B.C.E.	West Asia	fig, barley, lentil, wheat, cattle, dog, goat, pig, sheep
8000 B.C.E.	Chang Jiang Basin, China	rice, millet, soybean, pig, dog
8000 B.C.E.	East African Highlands	finger millet, sesame, sorghum, teff grass, cattle
6000 B.C.E.	Southeast Asia	banana, rice, yam, water buffalo, chicken, zebu cattle
5000 B.C.E.	New Guinea	root crops, sugar cane, pig
5000 B.C.E.	Central Mexico	bean, maize, squash, sweet potato, turkey
4000 B.C.E.	Peruvian Andes	bean, peanut, potato, quinoa, guinea pig, llama
3000 B.C.E.	Sub-Saharan Africa	pearl millet, sorghum, rice

ANALYZE SOURCES

History professor and author Yuval Noah Harari coined the term *Cognitive Revolution* to describe humanity's development of "fictive language"—the ability to speak about fictions—that started around 70,000 B.C.E. Read the excerpt from his June 2015 TED talk and answer the question that follows.

> The real difference between us and other animals is on the collective level. Humans control the world because we are the only animal that can cooperate flexibly in large numbers. . . . Yet how come humans alone of all the animals are capable of cooperating flexibly in large numbers, be it in order to play, to trade, or to slaughter? The answer is our imagination. We can cooperate with numerous strangers because we can invent fictional stories, spread them around, and convince millions of strangers to believe in them. As long as everybody believes in the same fictions, we all obey the same laws, and can thereby cooperate effectively.

24. According to Harari, what skill separates us from animals, and how do we use this skill?

CONNECT TO YOUR LIFE

25. EXPLANATORY Think about your basic needs and the needs of others in your household or community. Then think about how much time you or others spend working for money you spend on nonessential items, such as video games or designer clothing, and what you or others do with your free time. Compare your thoughts about survival in your world with what you know about survival in the world of ancient hunter-gatherers. Write an essay presenting your thoughts, citing examples from the chapter and your own research. Use the tips below to help you plan, organize, and write your essay.

TIPS

• Define the term *survival* for yourself.

• List what is needed for survival as you have defined it.

• Describe how much time it takes to meet these needs.

• Use two or three vocabulary words from the chapter in your explanation.

• End with a comparison to the challenges faced by early modern humans.

VOCABULARY ANSWERS

1. Possible response: An **artifact** from thousands of years ago can help researchers understand how people lived during that time.

2. Possible response: Scientists know that modern humans **migrated** from one continent to another.

3. Possible response: A **hunter-gatherer** pursues wild animals and collects wild plants to survive.

4. Possible response: People found many ways to **adapt** to colder climates.

5. Possible response: **Agriculture** includes planting and raising crops for food and taming wild animals.

6. Possible response: People feeding animals led to **domestication**.

7. Possible response: People do many types of work in the **economy** of a complex society.

8. Possible response: People can store a **surplus** if there is food left after a harvest.

READING STRATEGY ANSWERS

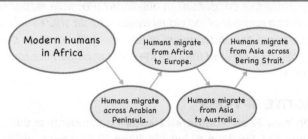

9. The Americas were the last area of Earth to be populated by human beings because early humans needed thousands of years to migrate from Africa, where all humanity began.

MAIN IDEAS ANSWERS

10. Reponses should include any three of the following: linguists study languages, archaeologists and anthropologists study fossils and other artifacts, geographers study geography, geneticists study genes.

11. Scientists believe early humans crossed from Asia to North America over the land bridge known as Beringia, which existed when sea levels were lower.

12. open grasslands with fresh water rivers and lakes, rich plant life, and plenty of game animals

13. Geneticists found the DNA of clothing lice in ancient human remains.

14. During the Neolithic era, people used stone tools and practiced agriculture.

15. They probably weeded wild grains and planted seeds they picked from plants with characteristics they wanted.

16. Surpluses were an important feature of the Çatalhöyük economy.

HISTORICAL THINKING ANSWERS

17. Early modern humans had a similar physical build, brain size, and appearance to the people of today.

18. Scientists, including archaeologists, geneticists, linguists, and anthropologists, examine fossils, artifacts, and other evidence to draw conclusions, but those ideas change as new evidence becomes available.

19. The domestication of plants and animals suggest that humans were learning how to control their environment rather than merely reacting to it.

20. Answers will vary. Possible response: Some advantages to a settled life include a higher level of safety, better access to food and animals, more permanent shelters, and opportunities to know other peoples and cultures. Some disadvantages include worse and less varied diets, a better chance of being infected by diseases, and much less time for leisure.

21. One viewpoint is that the use of agriculture led to large settlements; the other viewpoint is that large settlements led to the adoption of agriculture.

INTERPRET CHARTS ANSWERS

22. Both millet and rice were found in Africa and China. I can infer that the weather was similar in both regions, since they could grow the same crops.

23. The pig was domesticated in West Asia, China, and New Guinea. I think people domesticated the pig as a food source.

ANALYZE SOURCES ANSWER

24. According to Harari, imagination separates humans from animals. Humans use imagination to invent collective stories so that everyone can follow the same laws and cooperate.

CONNECT TO YOUR LIFE ANSWER

25. Students' essays should provide their definition of the term *survival*, a clear list of what is needed for survival, and how much time it takes to meet these needs; support their explanation with examples and evidence from their lives; compare their ideas of survival with that of survival in the world of ancient hunter-gatherers; support their comparison with examples from the chapter and additional research; and be written in a formal style.

UNIT 1 RESOURCES

UNIT INTRODUCTION

UNIT TIME LINE

UNIT MAP online

THE GLOBAL PERSPECTIVE: No Walls, No Borders: Nomads online

- National Geographic Explorers: Chris Bashinelli and Albert Lin
- On Your Feet: Inside-Outside Circle

| **NG Learning Framework**
Discuss Challenges of Nomadic Herding

UNIT WRAP-UP

National Geographic Magazine Adapted Article

- "Cities of Silence (Thoughts on the Harappan Culture)"

Unit 1 Inquiry: Design a Civilization-Building Game

Unit 1 Formal Assessment

CHAPTER 2 RESOURCES

Available in the Teacher eEdition

TEACHER RESOURCES & ASSESSMENT

Reading and Note-Taking

Vocabulary Practice

Document-Based Question Template

Social Studies Skills Lessons

- Reading: Draw Conclusions
- Writing: Informative

Formal Assessment

- Chapter 2 Pretest
- Chapter 2 Tests A & B
- Section Quizzes

Chapter 2 Answer Key

Cognero®

STUDENT DIGITAL RESOURCES

Available in the Student eEdition

- **eEdition** (English)
- **Handbooks**
- **National Geographic Atlas**
- **History Notebook**
- **Biographies**
- **Literature Analysis**

STRATEGY ❶
Read and Recall

Invite students to work in pairs. First, have each student read the lesson independently. After reading, students should meet without the book and share ideas they recall. One student takes notes. Students then review the lesson and decide what to add or change in the notes and make a copy of their notes for each to have.

Use with All Lessons

STRATEGY ❷
Ask Either/Or Questions

Monitor students' comprehension of the lesson by asking them to answer either/or questions. After students have answered the questions, ask partners to check one another's answers. Then have pairs work together to answer the Historical Thinking questions.

Use with All Lessons *For example, you may ask questions such as these for Lesson 1.1.*

- Did the first civilizations form along rivers or the seashore? *(rivers)*
- Does *division of labor* refer to a government role or the different jobs people do? *(the different jobs)*

STRATEGY ❸
Use a TASKS Approach

Have students analyze visuals to obtain information by using the following TASKS strategy.

T Look for a **title** that may give the main idea.
A **Ask** yourself what the visual is trying to show.
S Determine how any **symbols** are used.
K Look for a **key**, legend, and/or caption.
S **Summarize** what you learned.

Use with All Lessons *Students may find the TASKS strategy especially useful in analyzing the maps in Lessons 1.1, 2.1, and 3.3 as well as the header photograph in Lesson 3.2.*

STRATEGY ❶
Make Directions Clear

If you turn your back to students as you give directions to write information on the board, be aware that hearing-impaired students often rely on seeing a speaker's lips and facial expressions to help them understand. Be sure to face the class and speak clearly. Use your natural speaking voice, rather than speaking loudly, in case hearing-impaired students have hearing aids. Once you have given oral directions while facing the class, you can write important directions on the board, or have a volunteer write them as you are speaking. Then students also have a visual presentation of the directions.

Use with All Lessons

STRATEGY ❷
Create Vocabulary Cards

Encourage students to create a vocabulary card for each boldfaced vocabulary word in a section. Students may draw a picture to illustrate each word or write a definition, synonym, and/or example. Students can work in pairs to review the words when they finish reading a section. Encourage pairs to share their cards and copy any synonyms or examples that will be helpful in remembering the meaning of the words.

Use with All Lessons

STRATEGY ❶
Order Sentence Strips

Choose a key paragraph from the lesson to read aloud while students at **All Proficiencies** follow along in their books. After reading, tell students to close their books. Provide sentence strips of the paragraph and direct students to place the strips in order. Ask students to read their paragraphs aloud.

Use with All Lessons *You may wish to ask students at the Beginning level to read the sentence strips aloud and identify meaningful words before they start placing the strips in order.*

STRATEGY ②

Develop Word Knowledge

Help students develop understanding and usage of unknown words and vocabulary words by using the words in context.

For **Beginning** level students, display sentences with choices: Ancient people used irrigation to bring (water/seeds) to their farm fields.

For **Intermediate** level students, display individual sentence frames with only one blank: Ancient people used irrigation to bring _____ to their farm fields. *(water)*

For **Advanced** level students, ask a question using the word. Students will use the word in the answer: What did ancient people use irrigation for? *(They used irrigation to bring water to their fields.)*

Use with All Lessons

STRATEGY ③

Pair Partners for Dictation

After reading a section, ask students at **All Proficiencies** to write a sentence summarizing its main idea. Arrange students in pairs and ask them to dictate their sentences to each other. Then tell pairs to work together to check their sentences for spelling and accuracy.

Use with All Lessons *You might pair students at the **Beginning** level with those at the **Advanced** level and students at the **Intermediate** level with each other.*

GIFTED & TALENTED

STRATEGY ①

Create a Podcast

Allow students to choose one lesson as the basis for a history podcast. Tell them to establish a point of view that is both informative and entertaining about the group of ancient people they have chosen. Suggest that students write a script that includes appropriate sound effects. Then prompt them to present their episode live to the class or record it on a phone or other device to post on a class or school website.

Use with All Lessons

STRATEGY ②

Debate Environmental Benefits

Tell students to choose one of the early civilizations described in the chapter. Have them conduct more research as needed on the area where this civilization developed. Have them list the environmental benefits of living in this area. How did the environment provide the people with the food, water, shelter, and other resources they needed to survive? Then ask pairs to debate the merits of the areas they researched. Have the audience choose which area they think would be the best based on the debate.

Use with All Lessons

PRE-AP

STRATEGY ①

Create an Annotated Time Line of Civilizations

Direct students to look back through the chapter and organize a time line that shows the time periods when each civilization developed and how they overlapped. Remind students that the civilizations existed before the common era (B.C.E.) and that their time lines should start with the latest date and progress toward the number 1. Instruct them to include dates, locations, key events, and the impact of those events. Students should draw their own conclusions about ancient civilizations based on the information in the time line and write an explanation of their conclusions.

Use with All Lessons

STRATEGY ②

Write a Cause and Effect Essay

Remind students that most historical events have many causal factors and bring about many consequences. Challenge students to select one topic from the chapter to find out more about, such as the building/exploring of the pyramids or unlocking the meaning of Egyptian hieroglyphs. Encourage them to use a graphic organizer to map out cause-and-effect relationships pertaining to the topic. Have them use their graphic organizer to write an essay explaining the causes and effects.

Use with All Lessons

HISTORICAL THINKING How are people today linked to the first civilizations?

CRITICAL VIEWING
The Temple of Hathor is one of the best-preserved ancient temples in Egypt. Supported by large columns, its ceiling features detailed carvings. What conclusions might you draw about ancient Egyptian civilization based on artistic details in this ceiling?

INTRODUCE THE PHOTOGRAPH

TEMPLE OF HATHOR

Direct students to examine the photograph of the temple ceiling that appears at the beginning of the chapter. Tell them that this temple is located at Dandarah, Egypt, and is dedicated to Hathor, the ancient Egyptian goddess of the sky and fertility. Direct students' focus to the tops of the columns and point out that the columns are topped by carved heads. Explain that the interior of the temple is a grand hall filled with 18 columns, each of which is topped with a carving of Hathor's head. **ASK:** Why might the creators of this temple have focused so much on details far above people's heads? *(Hathor was a goddess of the sky.)* Many temples and shrines were dedicated to Hathor, and she was an important figure in Egyptian religious imagery. Tell students that in this chapter they will learn more about the religion and other cultural features of ancient Egypt and other early river valley civilizations.

CRITICAL VIEWING Answers will vary. Possible response: Ancient Egyptian rulers and religion were honored by architects who built elaborate temples, and their religion involved many ritual practices that artists wished to depict in great visual detail.

SHARE BACKGROUND

Much of what scholars know about ancient Egyptian religion comes from the monuments that were built for royal rulers and the nobility, like the temple shown in the photograph. Ancient Egyptian religion focused on not just the gods but also the king—the king was believed to operate both in the spiritual world and the physical world, of which Egypt was the center. The king was responsible for maintaining order in the relationship between the gods and his people.

Egyptians inscribed details about their religion on monuments and in formal documents written on papyrus. The inscriptions reflect a wealth of information, but only about the relationship between the king and nobility and religion. Little to nothing is known about how working-class Egyptians practiced religion, or even if they held the same religious beliefs as the king and the elite.

Other ancient peoples also built monuments and temples to reflect their religious practices. The Sumerians built a large temple complex in every city-state to worship their many gods. The Hebrews built Solomon's Temple to worship God, and later, when the temple was destroyed and the Hebrews separated from it, they constructed synagogues for worship.

HISTORICAL THINKING QUESTION
How are people today linked to the first civilizations?

Four Corners: Characteristics that Link Civilizations
Use a Four Corners activity to engage students in discussing four questions: How is work divided among people in modern times? What kinds of government exist in modern times? What is the role of religion in modern times? What technologies do we rely on the most in modern times? Assign each question to a corner of the room and ask students to go to the corner of their choice to discuss the question. Then hold a class discussion to share each group's ideas.

KEY DATES FOR CHAPTER 2

3500 B.C.E.	Many early civilizations have adopted the use of the wheel.
c. 3300 B.C.E.	The people of Sumer develop the world's first writing system.
3100 B.C.E.	Uruk, the first city of about 40,000 or 50,000 people, is thriving in southern Mesopotamia.
2500 B.C.E.	The people of Mesopotamia are making wheels with spokes.
2334 B.C.E.	Sargon of Akkad conquers all Sumerian city-states to create the world's first empire.
c. 2100 B.C.E.	The *Epic of Gilgamesh* is written.
1792 B.C.E.	Hammurabi becomes king of Babylon.
1570 B.C.E.	The New Kingdom begins in Egypt.
1285 B.C.E.	The Hittites defeat the Egyptians in the Battle of Kadesh.
700 B.C.E.	Sumerian written symbols stand for sounds rather than objects.

INTRODUCE THE READING STRATEGY

DRAW CONCLUSIONS
Explain to students that in order to fully understand a text, sometimes a reader must use details within the text to determine its overall meaning, if the meaning is not explicitly stated. Tell students they may have to "read between the lines" to gather these details and draw conclusions about the ultimate purpose of the text. Go to the Chapter Review and preview the chart with students. As they read the chapter, have students use the chart to take notes about the relationship between civilizations and rivers, and then draw a conclusion about the importance of rivers to ancient civilizations.

INTRODUCE CHAPTER VOCABULARY

KEY VOCABULARY

SECTION 1

alliance	bronze	city-state
civilization	cuneiform	division of labor
empire	epic	institution
		irrigation
polytheism	public works	silt
social class	stela	technology
ziggurat		

SECTION 2

cataract	delta	diplomacy
dynasty	hieroglyph	monarchy
		mummy
papyrus	pharaoh	pyramid
scribe		

SECTION 3

cavalry	covenant	cultural heritage
exile	human record	iron
		monotheism
refugee	relief	synagogue
theocracy	tribe	

DEFINITION CHART
As they read the chapter, encourage students to complete a Definition Chart for Key Vocabulary terms. Instruct students to list the Key Vocabulary terms in the first column of the chart. They should add each term's definition in the center column as they encounter the term in the chapter and then restate the definition in their own words in the third column. Model an example on the board, using the graphic organizer shown.

Word	Definition	In My Own Words
delta	a triangular-shaped area of low, flat land at the mouth of a river	a low area at the mouth of a river

Mesopotamia and City Life

You have likely visited large modern cities, or you may live in one. Have you ever wondered when, and why, people first started living in large groups? This development occurred further back in time than you might have imagined, and the success of farming had a lot to do with it.

CITIES ALONG RIVERS

You have read that the development of agriculture caused food surpluses, which led to a population increase in farming settlements such as Çatalhöyük. Eventually, some of these farming settlements grew into large cities. Many of these first cities formed in the southern portion of Southwest Asia—an area that historians have called **Mesopotamia** (meh-suh-puh-TAY-mee-uh). In Greek, the term *mesopotamia* means "between two rivers." It's no wonder then that this name was given to the land between the **Tigris** (TY-gruhs) **River** and the **Euphrates** (yu-FRAY-teez) **River**. Today, the country of Iraq covers much of the river valley region of Mesopotamia.

By 3100 B.C.E., **Uruk**, the first city of about 40,000 or 50,000 people, was thriving in southern Mesopotamia. At Uruk, a complex society took shape as people began to specialize in different occupations. As you will learn in this chapter and the next, complex societies arose along river valleys elsewhere in the world as well, including in Egypt, China, and India. These societies formed in river valleys where the fertile soil and available water caused agriculture to boom, producing food surpluses.

CHARACTERISTICS OF EARLY CIVILIZATIONS

Many historians refer to any advanced and complex society as a **civilization**, though scholars differ somewhat on the defining characteristics. The first civilizations typically developed in cities with populations in the tens of thousands. They arose where there was a food surplus and not everyone had to work to produce food. People started to specialize in various other kinds of work, such as making pottery, building shelters, or keeping records. They created a **division of labor**, or a system in which people perform different jobs to meet the needs of

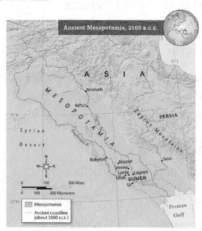

Ancient Mesopotamia, 2500 B.C.E.

a society. This division of labor led to the creation of **social classes**, in which people were grouped by what they did. Some types of work were regarded as more important than others, and the people who did those jobs were in a higher social class, which gave them higher status and more power. Such inequality in civilizations has therefore long meant that the hard work of common people has been exploited to support the power and luxury of privileged ruling classes.

The first civilizations also developed a number of **institutions**, or organizations that are established for a specific purpose and continue over time. Government and religion were the most common types of institutions in early civilizations. Both served to unify communities and provided rules to help people, who were now often strangers to one another in large cities, live together peacefully.

Other features of early civilizations included record-keeping systems for managing information and advances in **technology**, or the practical application of knowledge. The term *technology* refers to any tool or technique that helps people accomplish tasks.

MESOPOTAMIA: A CRADLE OF CIVILIZATION

In some ways, Mesopotamia was an unlikely place to become a birthplace of civilization. The region received little rainfall, which made raising crops difficult. Nor did wild grain grow naturally there.

The swift Tigris River and the slower, meandering Euphrates did bring much-needed water to the region. When the rivers flooded, they deposited **silt**, or especially fine and fertile soil, on the land. The fertile soil was good for growing crops. Yet both rivers were unpredictable, so no one knew just when or where they would overflow their banks. Unexpected floods could destroy wheat, barley, and other crops.

Instead of leaving this harsh environment, the early people of Mesopotamia adapted it to meet their needs. For example, they developed the technological innovation known as **irrigation**, or human-made systems that transport water to where it is needed. They dug canals to bring water from the rivers to their farm fields, and they found ways to store water for future use. To prevent flooding, they built dikes, or walls of dirt, along rivers.

The people of Mesopotamia also came up with the idea of using an ox-drawn plow to help them prepare the soil for planting crops. Neolithic farmers had depended on tools made from bone, wood, or stone. But Mesopotamian farmers began using a new technology—tools made of **bronze**, a mixture of the metals tin and copper—to improve the way they farmed. Bronze plow and axe blades were sharper than stone tools.

Another technological innovation on which the people of Mesopotamia depended was the wheel. Archaeologists do not know exactly when the wheel was invented. They do know that by 3500 B.C.E., many early civilizations had adopted the use of the wheel. By 3000 B.C.E., the people of Mesopotamia were using narrow carts with four wheels to move loads from place to place. By 2500 B.C.E., they were making wheels with spokes. Lighter-weight spoked wheels allowed vehicles to move faster and gave people the ability to transport scarce resources such as timber, stone, and metals over longer distances. The desire for such resources inspired the people of Mesopotamia to become skilled traders.

As the city of Uruk grew larger, it developed into a major economic, cultural, and political center. The bustling city

The development of bronze tools, such as these ax-heads, improved farming methods in ancient Mesopotamia.

PLAN: 4-PAGE LESSON

OBJECTIVE

Identify what led to the rise of a river valley civilization in Southwest Asia.

CRITICAL THINKING SKILLS FOR LESSON 1.1

- Identify Main Ideas and Details
- Identify Problems and Solutions
- Interpret Maps
- Describe
- Make Connections
- Analyze Cause and Effect
- Draw Conclusions
- Make Inferences

HISTORICAL THINKING FOR CHAPTER 2

How are people today linked to the first civilizations?

Many of the developments of early civilizations are aspects of modern-day civilization that people take for granted. Farming, wheeled vehicles, written language, record keeping, government, and irrigation all developed during ancient times. Lesson 1.1 explores the characteristics of early civilizations.

BACKGROUND FOR THE TEACHER

Mesopotamians and Clay The earth in Mesopotamia provided its residents with one of their most important raw resources—the mineral clay was used for everything from building to writing. Almost every building in ancient Mesopotamia was constructed from clay bricks. Artisans used clay to sculpt figurines and pottery. Mesopotamians stored food and other items in jars made from clay. Even the world's first system of writing involved pressing a tool into soft clay to make symbols. The earliest writings that have been found come from ancient Sumer and were lists of items to be bought or sold. The lists featured pictographs of the objects along with numbers and names. As Mesopotamians spread their influence beyond the region, so did the use of clay for many purposes.

Student eEdition online

Additional content for this lesson, including an image gallery, is available online.

INTRODUCE & ENGAGE

PREVIEW WITH VISUALS

Direct students' attention to the illustration for "Cities" in the Characteristics of Early Civilizations feature. **ASK:** What part of the illustration shows one of the single most important elements to the development of human civilization? Explain. *(Some students will understand that the river was critical to the development of civilization. Other students may point out buildings or plant life.)* Then point to the river in the illustration and tell students that one of the single most important elements to the development of civilization was the river. Settling near the river provided water and fertile land for farming, which in turn led to the development of the first civilization.

TEACH

GUIDED DISCUSSION

1. **Identify Main Idea and Details** What is the significance of the name Mesopotamia? *(It means "between two rivers" in Greek, and it refers to the fact that the region lies between the Tigris and Euphrates rivers.)*

2. **Describe** How did food surpluses affect the development of civilization? *(They allowed people to spend time on tasks other than farming, which led to specialization and the division of labor.)*

DRAW CONCLUSIONS

Point out the artwork in the Characteristics of Early Civilizations feature. **ASK:** How did the division of labor lead to the existence of these artifacts from long ago? *(The division of labor meant that some people were granted the time to contribute artistically to society. Whether they created artwork for themselves or were ordered to by a ruler, their work survives and tells us about their society.)*

DIFFERENTIATE

INCLUSION

Identify Map Details Pair students with disabilities with students who can read the lesson aloud to them. Encourage the partner without disabilities to describe the map in detail. When pairs have finished reading the lesson, you may want to have them work together to answer Historical Thinking question number four.

GIFTED & TALENTED

Research Systems of Government Direct students to conduct online research to find information on how the people of ancient Mesopotamia organized their governments. Then, ask them to diagram the structure of what they found and write a paragraph that discusses whether or not parallels can be drawn to any modern world governments.

See the Chapter Planner for more strategies for differentiation.

Characteristics of Early Civilizations

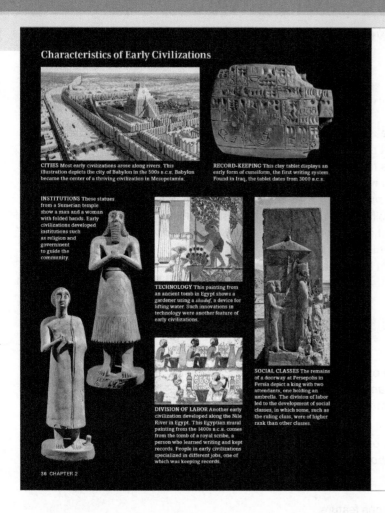

CITIES Most early civilizations arose along rivers. This illustration depicts the city of Babylon in the 500s B.C.E. Babylon became the center of a thriving civilization in Mesopotamia.

INSTITUTIONS These statues from a Sumerian temple show a man and a woman with folded hands. Early civilizations developed institutions such as religion and government to guide the community.

TECHNOLOGY This painting from an ancient tomb in Egypt shows a gardener using a *shaduf*, a device for lifting water. Such innovations in technology were another feature of early civilizations.

DIVISION OF LABOR Another early civilization developed along the Nile River in Egypt. This Egyptian mural painting from the 1400s B.C.E. comes from the tomb of a royal scribe, a person who learned writing and kept records. People in early civilizations specialized in different jobs, one of which was keeping records.

RECORD-KEEPING This clay tablet displays an early form of cuneiform, the first writing system. Found in Iraq, the tablet dates from 3000 B.C.E.

SOCIAL CLASSES The remains of a doorway at Persepolis in Persia depict a king with two attendants, one holding an umbrella. The division of labor led to the development of social classes, in which some, such as the ruling class, were of higher rank than other classes.

became a **city-state**, in which a ruler governs both the city and the surrounding countryside. In time, other city-states formed in Mesopotamia.

Each Mesopotamian city-state was ruled by a king, who claimed to have a special connection to the gods. This divine leader made most governmental decisions, but he sought the advice of temple priests and wealthy families. A group of administrators enforced laws, ensured that taxes were collected, and kept the city-state running smoothly.

The farms in the surrounding countryside provided each city-state with grain. Uruk had such a large stock of grain that leaders stored it in warehouse-like buildings. With a surplus of grain for food, inhabitants of Uruk were able to specialize in particular jobs. While city residents depended on surplus food grown on surrounding farms, the city provided residents of the farming villages with military protection from raids by neighboring cities.

Like the ancient city of Jericho, the city-state of Uruk had a protective wall, but Uruk's wall was much longer. By about 3000 B.C.E., Uruk's wall stretched about six miles and surrounded about 1,000 acres of land, much of it open farmland. The citizens used an available nearby resource to build the wall. Since the area had few trees or large rocks, they dug up the clay earth around them and crafted sun-dried mud bricks.

How do we know so much about this ancient city? The ruins of temples at the archaeological site where Uruk once prospered provide proof of the importance of religion and the belief in many gods. Large quantities of broken pottery found in one area suggest that potters lived and worked together, as did other craftworkers. The varied sizes of houses unearthed by archaeologists provide evidence of the existence of social classes. Archaeologists also rely on written primary sources to piece together the history of ancient Mesopotamia.

THE *EPIC OF GILGAMESH*

Perhaps the best-known primary source from Mesopotamia is the *Epic of Gilgamesh* (GIHL-guh-mehsh). An **epic** is a long narrative poem that relates

Written about 2100 B.C.E., the *Epic of Gilgamesh* is the oldest recorded story in the world. Historians have discovered that a real king named Gilgamesh once ruled Uruk. The epic provides insight into the way that the people of ancient Mesopotamia viewed Gilgamesh.

PRIMARY SOURCE

It was he who opened the mountain passes,

who dug wells on the flank of the mountain.

It was he who crossed the ocean, the vast seas, to the rising sun,

who explored the world regions, seeking life. . . .

Who can compare with him in kingliness?

Who can say like Gilgamesh: "I am King!"?

—from the *Epic of Gilgamesh* translated by Maureen Gallery Kovacs

the adventures of a legendary or historical hero. Like many ancient literary works, the *Epic of Gilgamesh* was first told orally and then written down in later centuries. Historians consider this epic a valuable resource for understanding ancient Mesopotamia.

Gilgamesh tells the story of the unlikely friendship between two men: Enkidu (EHN-kee-doo), who lives in the wild, and Gilgamesh, an early king of the ancient city of Uruk. While describing Enkidu and Gilgamesh's exploits, the epic reveals details about the benefits of living in a complex society.

Gilgamesh is depicted in the poem as being part god and part man, a common belief about rulers at that time. His travels include visits to the land of the gods and contact with gods and goddesses.

In the next lesson, you will learn more about ancient writing in Mesopotamia. Early writings continue to serve as a key to unraveling the mystery of what life was like long ago.

HISTORICAL THINKING

1. READING CHECK How did the development of farming in Mesopotamia lead to the rise of civilization there?

2. IDENTIFY MAIN IDEAS AND DETAILS What are some common characteristics of a civilization?

3. IDENTIFY PROBLEMS AND SOLUTIONS What problems did farmers in Mesopotamia face, and how did they solve these problems with technological innovations?

4. INTERPRET MAPS Based on the map, what natural resources made Mesopotamia a good site for human settlement?

BACKGROUND FOR THE TEACHER

The Discovery of the *Epic of Gilgamesh* During the mid-1800s, a Turkish scholar found parts of 12 tablets at Nineveh, in the library of the Assyrian king Ashurbanipal, who ruled during the 600s B.C.E. The tablets were written in the Akkadian language and told the story of Gilgamesh, who was portrayed as a ruler and warrior who was part god and part human. Though the tablets were incomplete, other fragments of writing found later filled in missing pieces of the story, as did a handful of Sumerian poems about Gilgamesh found on other ancient tablets.

The *Epic of Gilgamesh* was used as a way to train cuneiform scribes to write standard text. Interestingly, some of the episodes in the epic seem to correspond to popular Biblical stories, which include the story of Adam and Eve, Noah and the great flood, and elements of the lives of Sampson and David. Historical literature helps today's readers to understand society, culture, and values of people from earlier time periods.

TEACH

GUIDED DISCUSSION

3. **Make Connections** Why did a division of labor lead to the development of social classes? *(People were categorized by the type of work that they did. Some types of work were considered more important than other types, which gave the people who did that work more power and prestige in society.)*

4. **Analyze Cause and Effect** Why did city-states develop? *(As cities grew larger, they became important economic, cultural, and political centers. In time, they developed governments led by a powerful ruler.)*

MAKE INFERENCES

Share the Background for the Teacher information on the *Epic of Gilgamesh* with students. Then have students read the primary source from the *Epic of Gilgamesh* that appears in the lesson. **ASK:** Who do you think "he" is in the passage—Gilgamesh or Enkidu? *("He" is Gilgamesh; you know this because "he" seems to have godlike powers that allow him to travel vast distances to hard-to-reach places.)*

ACTIVE OPTIONS

On Your Feet: Debate Mesopotamia's Most Important Technology
Organize the class into groups of four and instruct members to number off from one to four. Ask each group to think about and discuss a response to the following question: Which technological development of the Mesopotamians was most important to the development of civilization? After a time, call out a number, and ask the students with that number to report their answer to the group. After each student has answered, have groups debate a final answer to the question. Have groups report on the outcome of their debates to the class.

NG Learning Framework: Create an Early Civilization STEM
SKILL Collaboration
KNOWLEDGE Our Human Story

Organize students into pairs to collaborate to create a model of an early civilization. Tell them that their models should include all of the elements they have learned about in the lesson—location, technology, buildings, and people. Their model can be three dimensional, or it can be drawn. Invite students to conduct online research for more information about early civilizations as needed. Have volunteers present their models to the class and describe their characteristics.

HISTORICAL THINKING

ANSWERS

1. The development of farming resulted in food surpluses, which led to a population increase in farming settlements. Some settlements grew into large cities, where complex societies, or civilizations, formed as people began to specialize in various occupations.

2. Civilizations typically include cities with a division of labor and social classes, complex institutions such as government and religion, technological advances, and systems of record-keeping.

3. Mesopotamian farmers faced the problems of a dry climate and unpredictable flooding; they solved these problems through irrigation. They also faced the problem of scarce resources in the immediate area; they solved this problem by using wheeled carts to transport resources.

4. flat land and water from rivers and lakes

Sumer and the Beginnings of Writing

As you have learned, historians use a wide variety of sources, artifacts, and techniques—including methods borrowed from science—to uncover the story of the human past. After written records became available, historians gained a powerful new tool. They now were able to learn about early civilizations directly through the words of the people who lived during the time.

LIFE IN SUMER

In the previous lesson, you learned about the rise of the first city-state, Uruk, in the southern part of Mesopotamia. This region of Mesopotamia is known as **Sumer.** Located along the southern portions of the Tigris and Euphrates rivers, Sumer reached all the way to the Persian Gulf. Around 3000 B.C.E., Sumer featured 12 or more independent city-states, including not only Uruk but also such kingdoms as Lagash, Nippur, Ur, and Larsa.

Like many other people of the time, the Sumerians practiced a religion based on **polytheism,** or the belief in many gods. They believed the various gods controlled different natural forces. For example, the storm-god was thought to control storms and floods.

The fact that every city-state featured a large temple complex is evidence of the strong connection the Sumerians felt to their gods. In the ancient city of Uruk, the temple to Ishtar, the goddess of love and

Dating from between 2600 and 2400 B.C.E., the Standard of Ur is a small box covered with mosaics that depict daily life in early Mesopotamia. One side of the standard depicts a time of war (shown here). The other side (not shown) depicts a time of peace.

war, towered over the city. The largest structure in each temple complex was the **ziggurat,** a mud-brick construction with as many as seven stepped stories, each smaller than the last. The top step contained a temple shrine dedicated to the city-state's most respected god or goddess.

At first, city-states operated independently, with very little close contact. For many years, each had its own ruler. As time passed, trade between city-states increased and so did conflict, including outright warfare. Archaeologists cite the building of higher city walls in the 2000s B.C.E. and a greater number of bronze weapons as evidence of such hostility.

The lack of natural barriers such as mountains made city-states in Sumer prone to attacks from outsiders. The first ruler to conquer all the city-states and unify the region was **Sargon of Akkad,** whose kingdom lay to the north of Sumer. In 2334 B.C.E., after claiming the city-states one by one, Sargon established the world's first **empire,** or rule by a single power over a diverse group of conquered peoples.

Building on Sumerian achievements, Sargon and his Akkadian descendants ruled over southern Mesopotamia for about 100 years. Trade networks expanded during this time. Based on new discoveries of obsidian, a volcanic black glass, at archaeological sites in the area, researchers believe the Akkadians had trade networks that reached as far as central Turkey.

Eventually, the Akkadians lost control of their sprawling empire, and other rulers conquered the region. But Mesopotamian civilization lasted for about 3,000 years in various forms.

THE EARLIEST WRITING SYSTEM

The people of Sumer developed the world's first writing system, known as Sumerian, sometime around 3300 B.C.E. We still have examples of this early writing system because the symbols were etched into clay, which hardened to provide a permanent record.

Some time after 4000 B.C.E., the Sumerians began using small clay objects of different shapes to keep track of merchandise, such as animals being traded or donated to a temple. Later, they placed these small objects in clay bags and marked the bags to indicate

A cuneiform tablet from about 2300 B.C.E.

their contents. But archaeologists have not been able to decipher the markings.

Sumerians later etched drawings of specific animals into clay. For the first time, a symbol clearly stood for a single object and could not be mistaken for something else. The first written documents depict an item being counted with a tally next to it to show the number of items. Temple accountants used writing to record such transactions as the number and type of animal or the amount of grain donated on successive days. By 3300 B.C.E., a complete writing system of more than 700 signs had emerged.

By 700 B.C.E., the Sumerian symbols had come to stand for sounds rather than objects. Because the Sumerians used a triangle-shaped writing tool to record symbols, this later writing is known as **cuneiform** (kyoo-NEE-uh-fawrm), meaning "wedge-shaped." From deciphering cuneiform records, historians have learned much about the Sumerian religion and economy.

In addition to a writing system, the Sumerians created a number system to solve economic and architectural problems. Their interests in engineering, astronomy, and calendars led them to develop an exceptionally complex system of mathematics.

HISTORICAL THINKING

1. **READING CHECK** What role did the ziggurat play in Sumerian culture?

2. **MAKE INFERENCES** How did physical features influence empire building in Mesopotamia?

3. **IDENTIFY** How did the Sumerian system of writing develop over time?

PLAN: 2-PAGE LESSON

OBJECTIVE

Discover how Sumer became the site of the world's first empire and how Sumerians developed the world's first writing system.

CRITICAL THINKING SKILLS FOR LESSON 1.2

- Make Inferences
- Identify
- Explain
- Draw Conclusions
- Analyze Visuals

HISTORICAL THINKING FOR CHAPTER 2

How are people today linked to the first civilizations?

Sargon of Akkad gained control of southern Mesopotamia and established an empire. Although conquered by various rulers, civilizations in Mesopotamia have endured for over 3,000 years. Lesson 1.2 discusses the achievements of the ancient Sumerians, which include the world's first writing system.

Student eEdition online

Additional content for this lesson, including a photograph, is available online.

BACKGROUND FOR THE TEACHER

Sargon of Akkadia Most of what scholars know about Sargon comes from legends written after his death, not from documents written during his life. One story about Sargon says that he was a man of humble beginnings. A gardener named Akki found him as a baby, in a basket on a river. The gardener raised him as his own child, in humble surroundings. As an adult, Sargon became part of the royal court as a "cupbearer," which is a butler to the king. He had the king's trust, until another king, Lugalzagesi of Umma, started conquering city-states in Sumer. According to legends, Sargon's king sent him as a gift to the king of Umma; however, Sargon came to power when he defeated the king of Umma, who had already united many of the city-states under his own rule. Sargon proclaimed himself the king of Kish and swiftly took over the region of Sumer. Sargon was widely known as a great military leader, but the exact dates of his life and rule are not known.

INTRODUCE & ENGAGE

ACTIVATE WARRIOR KNOWLEDGE

Draw a Word Web on the board and write the word *warrior* in the center. Ask students to associate words and phrases with the term, drawing on their knowledge of world history and how warriors and warfare affected events such as the creation of empires. Discuss with them different conquerors they may have read or learned about. Then explain that this lesson describes how Sargon of Akkadia established the world's first empire through conquest.

TEACH

GUIDED DISCUSSION

1. **Explain** How do scholars know that the Sumerians were highly religious? *(Every city-state had a large temple complex.)*

2. **Draw Conclusions** Why do you think Sumerians pressed their written symbols into clay? *(Possible response: They did not have paper at this time, and they wanted a somewhat permanent record. Clay hardens to provide a lasting material.)*

ANALYZE VISUALS

Direct students to examine the photograph of the Sumerian temple (available in the Student eEdition). **ASK:** Based on the photograph, how do you think the Sumerians were able to build this temple without modern technology? *(Possible response: It most likely required many laborers working together for years to design and build.)*

ACTIVE OPTIONS

On Your Feet: Question and Answer Tell half the class to write True-False questions based on the information about the Sumerians and their accomplishments. Tell the other half to create answer cards, with "True" written on one side and "False" written on the other. Then ask students who wrote questions to read them aloud. Direct students in the second group to respond by holding up either "True" or "False." When discrepancies occur, review the question and the text and discuss which answer is correct. After all questions are answered, if time permits, have groups reverse roles.

> **NG Learning Framework: Create a Sketch Map**
> **ATTITUDE** Empowerment
> **SKILL** Problem-Solving

Have students work in groups to sketch two maps—one of Mesopotamia as it existed during Sumerian times and one of the region as it exists today, which includes the names of modern countries. Students will most likely need to find source material online or in the library. Ask student volunteers to present their maps to the class, and then hold a class discussion about the changes in the region.

DIFFERENTIATE

STRIVING READERS

Understand Main Ideas Check students' understanding of the main ideas in the lesson by asking them to correctly complete statements such as the following:

- Sumer was located in the southern part of Mesopotamia, a land between (two mountains or two rivers). *(two rivers)*
- Sumerians practiced polytheism, or worship of many (kings or gods). *(gods)*

GIFTED & TALENTED

Create a System of Writing Direct students to conduct online research on cuneiform, finding some of the symbols. Then, have them create a simple alphabet of their own cuneiform symbols and write three short sentences. Ask them to exchange their sentences with a partner along with a key of their symbols. Partners translate the sentences and then discuss the translations. Ask volunteers to share their work with the class.

See the Chapter Planner for more strategies for differentiation.

HISTORICAL THINKING

ANSWERS

1. part of a temple complex dedicated to the city-state's god or goddess; center of Sumerian religion

2. The lack of physical barriers such as mountains made it easy for outsiders to attack the Sumerian city-states, so eventually higher city walls were built for protection. Sargon of Akkad was the first ruler to conquer all the city-states and unify them to form an empire.

3. The Sumerians first used markings to keep track of objects in bags. Then these markings evolved and became clearly recognizable symbols of objects. Finally, the symbols came to stand for sounds instead of objects.

The Babylonian Empire

How would you feel if you did not know what laws you had to follow and yet faced punishment for breaking them? For a long time, no clear, written record of laws existed for the people of Mesopotamia. Then one king decided to make a public list of the legal decisions he thought were most important.

CRITICAL VIEWING This segment of a brick wall comes from the Ishtar Gate, one of eight fortified entryways to the ancient city of Babylon. Based on this segment, how does the Ishtar Gate differ from typical gates in modern cities?

HAMMURABI RULES MESOPOTAMIA

After the fall of the Akkadian Empire, Mesopotamia again broke into several different kingdoms. In 1792 B.C.E., **Hammurabi** (ha-muh-RAH-bee) became king of **Babylon**, a city-state along the Euphrates River to the north of Uruk. Under Hammurabi's rule, Babylon grew in power.

Hammurabi focused on improving life for the citizens of the city-state. He initiated a series of **public works**, or construction projects that benefit a community, such as reinforcing city walls and rebuilding old temples and constructing new ones. He also created **alliances**, or partnerships, with other city-states, though turmoil within the region often caused these alliances to fall apart.

Early in his reign, Hammurabi fought to maintain his kingdom's control over the Euphrates River. Later, his focus shifted to threats from neighboring kingdoms, particularly Larsa in the south. Hammurabi strengthened his military, and in time he began a series of conquests. Eventually, he united much of Mesopotamia in the first Babylonian Empire, which would last until 1595 B.C.E. You will learn about the second Babylonian Empire later in this chapter.

CODE OF LAWS

Hammurabi is most remembered for the laws he established. You may have heard the expression "an eye for an eye," which means that if a person harms someone, the punishment will be the same kind of harm. This idea was just one of 282 provisions of Hammurabi's laws, commonly known as **Hammurabi's Code**. These laws encompassed such varied topics as divorce, criminal punishment, commerce, trade, and the treatment of slaves. Hammurabi was not the first ruler to establish a set of laws, but he combined existing laws with new laws of his own to create one organized, written code of laws for all the people of the empire.

Hammurabi's Code was inscribed on an eight-foot stone pillar called a **stela** for everyone to see. However, most Sumerians were not able to read it. The code tells more about the intentions of the rulers than about the actual behavior of the people. Only records of actual court cases can reveal whether people really followed all the laws.

Hammurabi's Code addressed the concept of justice, or fairness under the law. Yet the laws did not treat all people equally. The punishment for many crimes varied depending on the social classes of the people involved. Babylonian society at the time had three main classes. The upper class included the royal family, priests, merchants, and other free men and women who owned land. In the middle were commoners, and at the bottom were slaves. If a man of the upper class put out the eye of his social equal, he himself would be blinded. But if he took out the eye of a commoner, he would only pay a fine. If he put out the eye of a slave, he would compensate the slaveowner, not the slave.

Hammurabi's Code provides historians with insight into life in ancient Mesopotamia, including the roles and status of women. For example, according to the code, a woman was entitled to a share of her parents' property, either as a gift when she married or upon the death of her father. In some cases, women could initiate a divorce, something women in many other ancient societies were not allowed to do. In addition, the code made it clear that people who had been wronged had to work through the legal system. Private retribution, or personal revenge, was not acceptable.

Hammurabi's code also confirms that humankind has been using legal systems to resolve disputes for thousands of years. Although our modern legal system differs in important ways from the one described on Hammurabi's stela, the impact of law in daily life has persisted across time and cultures.

The top of the stela of Hammurabi's code (above) shows Hammurabi receiving a set of laws from the sun god Shamash. Many of the laws describe punishments for criminal offenses. This excerpt from the code concerns the "eye-for-an-eye" punishment, also known as exact retaliation.

PRIMARY SOURCE

196. If a man [of the upper class] put out the eye of another man [of the upper class], his eye shall be put out.

197. If he break another man's bone, his bone shall be broken.

198. If he put out the eye of a freed man [commoner], or break the bone of a freed man, he shall pay one gold mina.

199. If he put out the eye of a man's slave, or break the bone of a man's slave, he shall pay one-half of its [the slave's] value.

—from "The Code of Hammurabi"
translated by L. W. King

HISTORICAL THINKING

1. **READING CHECK** How did Hammurabi develop the first Babylonian Empire?

2. **ANALYZE CAUSE AND EFFECT** What were the political and legal impacts of Hammurabi's Code?

3. **COMPARE AND CONTRAST** How is the view of justice in Hammurabi's Code different from that in the laws of the United States today?

PLAN: 2-PAGE LESSON

OBJECTIVE

Learn about the ruler of the Babylonian Empire, Hammurabi, who developed the world's first written code of laws.

CRITICAL THINKING SKILLS FOR LESSON 1.3

- Analyze Cause and Effect
- Compare and Contrast
- Evaluate
- Form and Support Opinions
- Analyze Primary Sources

HISTORICAL THINKING FOR CHAPTER 2

How are people today linked to the first civilizations?

Hammurabi was the king of Babylon, a Mesopotamian city-state. Hammurabi's Code, which holds people responsible for their actions, was the first written code of laws. Lesson 1.3 focuses on Hammurabi and how he improved life for his citizens.

Student eEdition online

Additional content for this lesson, including a photograph, is available online.

BACKGROUND FOR THE TEACHER

Hammurabi's Rule Like the Sumerians before them, the Babylonians recorded information using cuneiform on clay tablets. Scribes recorded when temples, walls, and public buildings were constructed. They also recorded when wars were fought. Little is known about details of everyday life in Babylon, however.

Some experts compare Hammurabi's Code to the Hebrew law code, which includes the Ten Commandments. Hammurabi received a code of laws from a god; Moses received a code of laws from God. Both codes included rules regulating social behavior, but the Hebrew code also regulated religious behavior. Similarly, both included the attitude of "an eye for an eye" or "a tooth for a tooth," although the punishments for breaking the Ten Commandments were softened by the Hebrew expression of God's mercy.

INTRODUCE & ENGAGE

OBSERVE HAMMURABI'S CODE

Direct students to examine the stela in the lesson. Point out that the stela includes not only written laws, but also an illustration of Hammurabi receiving the code of laws from the sun god. Encourage students to discuss why the illustration might have been included with the laws. Then remind students that most Babylonians could not read. Point out that including an illustration might provide justification for the laws to those who could not read because they would believe the laws came from a higher power. Tell students that in this lesson they will learn more about Hammurabi's Code and how the leader ruled his kingdom.

TEACH

GUIDED DISCUSSION

1. **Evaluate** What are three main ways Hammurabi strengthened his kingdom? (Possible response: He made alliances, improved his people's lives, and built up his military for defense and for conquering neighboring kingdoms.)

2. **Form and Support Opinions** Why do you think that many of Hammurabi's laws dealt with matters of everyday life, such as divorce or the treatment of slaves? (Possible responses: A set of specific rules to govern these types of issues was probably needed because they were common to many and expectations had to be set.)

ANALYZE PRIMARY SOURCES

Point students' attention toward the primary source. Ask them to take note of the last two entries, 198 and 199. **ASK:** Why do you think the punishment of a person who harms a slave resulted in paying one-half of the slave's value? (Possible response: because the slave could not work at the same level if injured) Why do you think harm to commoners and slaves warranted less of a punishment than harm to members of the upper class? (Members of the upper class were considered more important and were to be respected.)

ACTIVE OPTIONS

On Your Feet: Think, Pair, Share Have students use the Think, Pair, Share strategy as they consider the following question: Was Hammurabi's Code a fair system of justice? Allow a few minutes for students to think, and then pair students to discuss their ideas for five minutes. After discussion time, invite students to share their ideas with the class.

NG Learning Framework: Document a Legal Code
ATTITUDE Curiosity
SKILL Collaboration

Tell students to collaborate in small groups to conduct online research to find more examples of laws in Hammurabi's Code. Have groups collaborate to make a chart showing the examples and their punishments and then share their work with the class. Discuss as a class what kinds of problems the laws were meant to address and whether or not governments address similar issues when making laws today.

DIFFERENTIATE

STRIVING READERS

Rewrite a Passage Instruct pairs to read the text under the heading Code of Laws and define the following words using a dictionary or online source: *provisions, encompassed, insight,* and *persisted.* Ask them to rewrite the text in conversational, or informal, English.

PRE-AP

Analyze a Paradox Instruct students to analyze the paradox of Hammurabi's Code. On the one hand, Hammurabi provided a code of laws to establish a sense of justice, or fairness, in society. However, the law did not apply to all equally and many could not read the laws to determine what was right or wrong. Have students consider paradoxes that form under systems of law and justice. Can a society be truly just? Direct students to write an essay about this question, citing examples including Hammurabi's Code and their own knowledge of modern criminal justice systems.

See the Chapter Planner for more strategies for differentiation.

HISTORICAL THINKING

ANSWERS

1. He used military means to conquer and unify much of Mesopotamia.

2. It provided an organized and written list of laws for all the peoples of the Babylonian Empire to use to resolve disputes. It made clear that people who were wronged had to seek justice through a legal system, not private revenge.

3. Hammurabi's Code prescribed different punishments for different social classes; the laws of the United States call for equal justice for all.

CRITICAL VIEWING Possible response: The Ishtar Gate is more intricate; modern gates are typically simpler without color or scenes.

African Origins of Egyptian Civilization

As in Mesopotamia, civilization in ancient Egypt developed along a river valley where people grew an abundance of crops. But life along the Nile River in Africa differed in key ways from that along the Tigris and Euphrates rivers.

WHO WERE THE EGYPTIANS?

For many years, Westerners who marveled at Egyptian achievements assumed those responsible must have come from outside the continent. Today, historians know that the ancient Egyptians were in fact Africans. Egypt remained an African civilization even as the Nile Valley region became a crossroads of interaction between peoples from Africa, Asia, and Europe. The ancient Egyptians spoke a now lost language that belonged to the Afrasian, or mixed African and Asian, language family. That family includes such modern languages as Amharic (spoken in Ethiopia), Hausa (spoken in Nigeria), and Berber (spoken in Morocco), as well as Hebrew and Arabic.

Between about 6000 and 3500 B.C.E., agriculture had developed in several places in Africa. One such place was the **Sahel**, a semiarid region south of the Sahara. There, the Sudanese people farmed and raised such livestock as goats, cattle, and sheep. At that time, regular rainfall created grasslands that were good for grazing livestock.

Over a long period of time, a decrease in rainfall caused much of the land of the Sahel to become desert. The increase in desert lands led many people to move and settle along the banks of the Nile River in what would become Egypt. They brought their agricultural practices, language, and religion with them. This congregation of a large number of Sudanese farmers along the narrow but lengthy Nile River Valley led to the development of a great civilization in Africa.

LIFE ALONG THE NILE

From its two sources in east-central Africa, the Nile River flows north for more than 4,000 miles. Near its mouth at the Mediterranean Sea, it splits into several branches and forms a triangular-shaped area of low, flat land called a **delta**. Along the course of the river are six steep, unnavigable rapids called **cataracts**.

The low land at the northern end of the Nile became known as Lower Egypt, while the higher land to the south was named Upper Egypt. The smooth flow of the Nile River enabled easy water travel and connected Egyptians living in Lower and Upper Egypt. Beyond Upper Egypt, however, the six cataracts

Ancient Egypt and Nubia, 3000–2000 B.C.E.

made travel by boat impossible. This land was known as **Nubia**, which became the home of an ancient kingdom called **Kush**.

Although rivers were the life blood of both Mesopotamia and Egypt, the geography of the two places differed dramatically. The Nile River was much more predictable than the Tigris and Euphrates rivers, so the Egyptians knew when floods would occur. Also unlike Mesopotamia, Egypt had a mild climate and was surrounded by natural barriers—deserts on three sides and the Mediterranean Sea on the fourth. These factors made the Egyptians feel more secure than the people of Mesopotamia. That sense of security even extended to the afterlife. While the less secure Sumerians regarded life after death with horror, Egyptians felt assured in their chances for everlasting life.

Because almost no rain fell anywhere along the Nile, the ancient Egyptians used irrigation to bring water to their farm fields. The area of rich soil along the banks of the Nile became known as *Kemet*, or "the Black Land." Beyond that lay an area of less fertile, red soil called *Deshret*, or "the Red Land." Beyond the red land lay uncultivable desert. Although unsuitable for farming, the desert was a source of both stone and gold.

The Egyptians created a calendar with three seasons based on the predictability of the Nile. During the season of *Inundation*, the Nile flooded. Egyptian farmers, who could not work in the fields, completed construction projects for their leaders. During the season of *Emergence of the Fields from Waters*, farmers irrigated their fields and planted wheat, barley, beans, and peas. During the season of *Drought*, farmers harvested their crops.

Civilization arose in Egypt at about the same time as in Mesopotamia, around 3100 B.C.E. Although Egypt did not have the large cities that were characteristic of Sumer, it was similar in other ways. Egyptian society was also highly stratified, with great differences between the poor and the rich. Large construction projects, like the building of monuments, required the same kind of job specialization. And ancient Egypt shared the belief that the ruler governed with the support of the gods.

Isis (center left), the Egyptian goddess of life, was often associated with the pharaohs of ancient Egypt, who would call upon her to protect them against their enemies.

During certain periods, Upper Egypt and Lower Egypt were united under a single ruler, who as time passed would be revered as the **pharaoh** (FEHR-oh). As a god-king, the pharaoh presided over rituals in honor of the Egyptian gods. Since the pharaoh was often occupied with ritual duties, his chief advisor, called the *vizier*, handled most matters of state.

Historians call the periods during which Egypt was unified under a series of strong rulers *kingdoms*. The times when no one ruler governed the entire land are called *intermediate periods*. In the next lesson, you will learn about the three main kingdoms of Egypt: The Old Kingdom (2686–2181 B.C.E.), the Middle Kingdom (2040–1782 B.C.E.), and the New Kingdom (1570–1069 B.C.E.).

HISTORICAL THINKING

1. **READING CHECK** Why did large numbers of Sudanese farmers move to the Nile River Valley?

2. **COMPARE AND CONTRAST** Identify the similarities and differences in the effects of rivers on the lives of people in ancient Mesopotamia and Egypt.

3. **INTERPRET MAPS** Describe the physical shape of ancient Egypt. What physical features influenced this shape?

PLAN: 2-PAGE LESSON

OBJECTIVE

Explain how people of African origins developed a unique civilization along the Nile River in Egypt.

CRITICAL THINKING SKILLS FOR LESSON 2.1

- Compare and Contrast
- Interpret Maps
- Describe
- Explain
- Analyze Visuals

HISTORICAL THINKING FOR CHAPTER 2

How are people today linked to the first civilizations?

The people who developed a civilization in Egypt were of African origin. They were drawn to the waters and fertile land of the Nile River. Lesson 2.1 discusses how and why Egypt became home to this great civilization.

BACKGROUND FOR THE TEACHER

The Upper and Lower Nile The Nile River flows northward for over 4,100 miles, making it the longest river in the world. The water comes from distant mountains, lakes, and plateaus in present-day Burundi, Ethiopia, Tanzania, and Uganda. Throughout history, many have worshiped the Nile as a god who gives life and seldom brings about destruction. However, there are drastic differences between the Upper and Lower Nile River Valleys. At one time, the change from fertile soil (Black Land) to desert (Red Land) was so abrupt that a person was able to stand with one foot within both types of soil.

For many years, people only settled in the lower part of the Nile because of the fertile soil. This part of the river stretches for about 750 miles north before it empties into the Mediterranean Sea. To the south, the river has large boulders and steep cliffs, making it difficult to navigate by boat. In the Upper Nile, there are narrow strips of land, and the river flows into many branches. Most people live close to the river because the valley is surrounded by desert.

INTRODUCE & ENGAGE

DISCUSS THE IMPACT OF GEOGRAPHY

Ask students to think of ways geography affects the cultural aspects of places in the modern world. Examples might include differences between communities built in arid lands, like those near Phoenix, Arizona, versus ones where rainfall is common, such as Seattle, Washington. Another example is the difference between coastal communities and those located in the mountains. **ASK:** How might people feel when their surroundings are unpredictable, such as when natural disasters like flooding occur? *(Possible responses: confusion, anger, fear, wariness)* Guide students to discuss how an ancient civilization might have reacted to environmental events and circumstances. Tell them that Lesson 2.1 explores how extremes in environment made an impact on cultural elements of ancient civilizations, such as religion.

TEACH

GUIDED DISCUSSION

1. **Describe** How did an increase in desert land lead to the settlement of Egypt? *(As the Sahel became more arid, people needed to move to find better farmland. They were drawn to the region around the Nile.)*

2. **Explain** What did Egyptians do to ensure they benefited from the flooding of the Nile? *(Possible response: They created a calendar with three seasons to ensure their farms benefited from the flooding.)*

ANALYZE VISUALS

Direct students to examine the map of Ancient Egypt and Nubia, 3000–2000 B.C.E., in the lesson. Have them take note of the labels. Ask volunteers to point out what feature might have pushed Africans to settle in Egypt. Then ask them which feature pulled Africans to this particular area of northeast Africa. *(The deserts pushed people toward sources of water. The Nile River pulled people to settle there.)*

ACTIVE OPTIONS

On Your Feet: Four Corners Arrange students into four teams and assign each team to a corner of the room for a Four Corners activity. Instruct each team to create a list of four or five questions about the development of civilization in Egypt. Start the quiz by inviting Team One to ask Team Two one of the listed questions. When Team Two gives the correct answer, invite Team Two to ask Team Three a question. Continue until all teams have exhausted their questions.

> **NG Learning Framework: Create a Web Page**
> SKILL Collaboration
> KNOWLEDGE Our Living Planet

Arrange students in small groups to create a web page about the geography of the Nile River. Instruct them to assign members of the group to each of these tasks: conduct research and choose facts and visuals to include; determine how the research, such as graphics and bulleted facts, will be presented; assemble the finished product and upload the web page to the class or school website. Have groups share their pages with the class.

DIFFERENTIATE

ENGLISH LANGUAGE LEARNERS

Use Synonyms Help students at **All Proficiencies** expand their English vocabulary by introducing familiar synonyms for unfamiliar words they encounter. For example, a synonym for the word *marveled* is wondered. Guide students in using a thesaurus when they come across unfamiliar words to find a synonym that makes sense in context.

PRE-AP

Design an Infographic Instruct students to create an infographic that uses information from the text and their own research on Egyptian religion to show the different gods and their relationship to the environment and to the daily lives of Egyptians. Invite students to compare infographics and present them to the class.

See the Chapter Planner for more strategies for differentiation.

HISTORICAL THINKING

ANSWERS

1. because decreased rainfall had turned their lands into desert and they could no longer farm or raise livestock on those lands

2. Possible response: Similarities: Rivers provided a source of water and the silt needed to produce fertile farmland. Differences: The predictability of the Nile River made the Egyptians more secure in their environment and united the people as one entity.

3. Ancient Egypt was generally long and narrow but formed a triangular shape near the Mediterranean Sea. It took this shape because it developed along the course of the Nile River where the soil was fertile and along the river's delta near the Mediterranean Sea. The land beyond the river was desert, where water was scarce and human settlement was extremely difficult.

The Old and Middle Kingdoms

If you were a farmer in ancient Egypt, you would give much of your grain to the pharaoh, who owned the land, and work periodically on one of his building projects. You could not escape these obligations. Your farming community could never survive in the desert, away from the fertile soil along the Nile.

The most famous ancient Egyptian monuments are the three pyramids at Giza (shown here) and the Great Sphinx, a large statue of a lion with a human head.

NATIONAL GEOGRAPHIC EXPLORER YUKINORI KAWAE

Strange, Unexplored Places

The desire to find answers to difficult questions came early to Yukinori Kawae, shown above at the site of the Great Pyramid. As a junior high school student in Japan, he watched a TV documentary about the Great Pyramid. The documentary posed these questions: Why are the chambers identified by archaeologists located on just one side of the pyramid? Could there be unexplored spaces on the other side? As an adult, Kawae became an archaeologist with a specialization in Egyptology and set out to find answers to such questions.

Using traditional methods at first, Kawae found his task daunting. As he said, "Discussions about pyramid construction can be likened to a crime investigation with scant evidence and insufficient onsite inspection."

Kawae now takes an interdisciplinary approach to archaeology by incorporating computer science, 3-D data surveys, and other technology to find out how the pyramids were built. He and his team of computer scientists and mathematicians rely on data collected by video cameras, scanners, laser beams, and drones at the site of the Great Pyramid. They use the data to make three-dimensional models back at Kawae's lab in Japan. Such models let him "peek" into hidden areas of the pyramid to uncover the mysteries hidden behind the thick stone walls. They may help him answer unresolved questions about the construction methods used to build the pyramids—for instance, how workers managed to raise more than three million stones.

MONUMENTAL ACHIEVEMENTS

The uniting of Upper and Lower Egypt marked the beginning of the **Old Kingdom**, which lasted from 2686 to 2181 B.C.E., or more than 500 years. During this period, the Egyptians enjoyed prosperity and a stable government. Ancient Egypt had a **monarchy**, or a government ruled by a single person. The Egyptian pharaoh exerted absolute power over all the people.

Rule over Egypt passed from generation to generation of a family. This succession of hereditary rulers, called a **dynasty**, lasted until a family line died out or another family gained power. Through its long history, Egypt had 31 dynasties. Ten different dynasties ruled during the time of the Old Kingdom. The government was based in the capital city of Memphis.

The Old Kingdom is especially remembered for its large, four-sided monuments known as **pyramids**. The pyramids were built as gigantic tombs to hold the bodies of dead pharaohs. The Egyptians believed that each person had a life force, or ka, that survived on energy from the body. When a person died, the Egyptians preserved the body with chemicals and wrapped it to form a **mummy**. They believed preserving the body this way allowed the life force to continue. They even surrounded the mummified body with food to nourish the person's spirit in the afterlife. From mummifying bodies, the Egyptians developed a detailed knowledge of anatomy and an understanding of the role of the heart in the human body.

A preserved body alone was not enough to ensure a happy afterlife, however. Egyptians believed the dead had to appear before Osiris (oh-SY-ruhs), the god of the underworld. He and other judges would decide whether a dead person deserved entrance to the realm of eternal happiness. According to the Egyptians, the gods weighed each person's heart to determine if the good within the person surpassed the bad.

A pharaoh named Djoser (JOH-sur) ordered the building of the first pyramid in preparation for his afterlife. His vizier, Imhotep, came up with a plan to carry out the pharaoh's vision. This first pyramid looked like a huge, four-sided tomb, which is why historians call it a step pyramid. Later, the architectural design would change to create pyramids with smooth sides.

PLAN: 4-PAGE LESSON

OBJECTIVE

Describe the advancements of the ancient Egyptians during the Old and Middle Kingdoms.

CRITICAL THINKING SKILLS FOR LESSON 2.2

- Make Generalizations
- Draw Conclusions
- Make Inferences
- Make Connections
- Synthesize
- Identify Problems and Solutions
- Analyze Cause and Effect
- Analyze Visuals

HISTORICAL THINKING FOR CHAPTER 2

How are people today linked to the first civilizations?

The unification of Upper and Lower Egypt marked the beginning of the Old Kingdom, which lasted more than 500 years and was followed by the Middle Kingdom. Rule by a series of dynasties began during this period and continued throughout ancient Egypt's long history. Lesson 2.2 discusses key characteristics of life in Egypt during the Old and Middle Kingdoms.

BACKGROUND FOR THE TEACHER

Egyptian Architecture Stone monuments first appeared in Egypt between 2890–2670 B.C.E. when upright, four-sided, flat-topped stone monuments called obelisks were erected. Obelisks are architectural marvels that reflect the Egyptian relationship between the gods and the people, as they were always raised in pairs. It was believed that the two created on Earth were mirrored by two identical pieces raised in the heavens at the same time. In order to construct obelisks, early Egyptians needed to quarry, carve, transport, and raise the heavy stone monuments. At times, obelisks were transported for many miles once they were built. These complex structures showed that Egyptians had mastered stonework, which led to the building of the pyramids. The pyramids of Egypt were built as tombs for royalty beginning in the Old Kingdom and continuing over a period of 2,700 years. The structures involved the triangular-sided tomb in which the body was placed, as well as a temple nearby accompanied by a road that led to a pavilion. A canal connected the entire complex to the Nile. Ancient Egyptian architecture has lasted for thousands of years, and many structures remain intact today.

Student eEdition online

Additional content for this lesson, including a video, is available online.

INTRODUCE & ENGAGE

BUILD A PYRAMID

Ask students to imagine they are in charge of the planning and construction of a pyramid that will be 50 stories high and made entirely of giant stone blocks. The blocks weigh on average around 2.5 tons. Tell students that they will not be able to use modern technology to build the pyramid. Ask students to discuss the following questions: What method will you use to move the stones? How will you ensure that the sides are geometrical? After discussing students' ideas, tell them that in this lesson they will learn how the ancient Egyptians achieved the feat of building these structures without cranes, backhoes, and other modern technology.

TEACH

GUIDED DISCUSSION

1. **Make Connections** Why might living a good life while on Earth be of concern to most ancient Egyptians? *(The Egyptians believed that the gods determined whether or not a person would have a happy afterlife based on his or her heart and actions during life.)*

2. **Synthesize** What are some of the lasting scientific contributions developed in ancient Egypt during this period? *(Possible response: a 365-day calendar and some geometric principles)*

DRAW CONCLUSIONS

Direct students' attention to the National Geographic Explorer feature "Strange, Unexplored Places." Have them read the feature and take note of how Yukinori Kawae uses modern technology in his exploration of the Egyptian pyramids. **ASK:** Why do you think Kawae uses drones and laser beams in his research? *(Possible responses: He can see areas of the pyramid that one cannot see in person and on foot.)* What "traditional methods" do you think Kawae used when starting out? *(Possible response: He probably used the tools that archaeologists have been using for centuries—drawings, digging, etc.)*

DIFFERENTIATE

ENGLISH LANGUAGE LEARNERS

Dictate Sentence Summaries Pair students at the **Beginning** level with those at the **Advanced** level. After students read the sections Monumental Achievements and Writing System, direct them to identify three sentences that contain an important idea. Then tell each student to write that idea in a summary sentence using his or her own words. Partners then take turns dictating their sentences to each other. Encourage them to work together to check each other's work for accuracy and spelling.

GIFTED & TALENTED

Create a Presentation Tell students that Egyptians mummified not just people but also some animals. Direct students to conduct online research to find out more about who and what was mummified in ancient Egypt and why, and what we know about the process of mummification. Ask students to prepare a brief presentation to discuss their findings.

See the Chapter Planner for more strategies for differentiation.

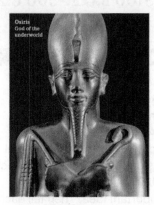

Osiris
God of the
underworld

One of the most impressive pyramids, called the Great Pyramid, still stands in Giza (GEE-zuh), near the present-day city of Cairo. The Great Pyramid was built between 2589 and 2566 B.C.E., a period of 23 years, to house the life force of the pharaoh Khufu (KOO-foo).

The building of the Great Pyramid demonstrates both the strong influence of religion and the power of the pharaoh in Egyptian society. About 15,000 to 20,000 laborers, both male and female, worked on the pyramids each year during the flood season. None of these laborers were enslaved. About 5,000 skilled workers and craftspeople worked full-time, while the rest of the laborers rotated in and out.

Using just the limited technology available at the time, the Egyptians created an architectural masterpiece covering an area of 571,211 square feet and standing 480 feet tall. That's twice the area of the U.S. Capitol Building and taller than the Statue of Liberty. The builders used a system of ramps and poles to move an estimated four million stone blocks into position. Some of the blocks weighed as much as nine tons.

Obviously, the Egyptians employed planning, mathematics, and engineering skills to determine how many blocks were required and how to produce the correct slant. The need for exact calculations led the Egyptians to formulate some of the key principles of geometry. In addition, they developed measurement

tools, including the cubit, a fixed unit of length of about 18 inches. Careful study of astronomy allowed the Egyptians to create a 365-day calendar of 24-hour days, which they used to keep track of progress on the pyramids.

The pyramid workers lived in special villages, and evidence from an ancient worker village shows that the laborers were well fed and well cared for. The pyramid workers completed other building projects as well, such as the remarkable limestone statue known as the Great Sphinx. This statue depicts a creature with the body of a lion and the head of a human and appears to be guarding three nearby pyramids. Historians now believe that the Sphinx may have been brightly painted at one time.

WRITING SYSTEM

The Egyptians kept written records of such events as the building of the pyramids using picture symbols called **hieroglyphs** (HY-uh-ruh-glihfs). Historians do not know exactly when or how hieroglyphs developed, but the Egyptians credited their god Thoth with their invention. Some of the picture symbols simply represented a single object, such as a house. But other symbols stood for one or more sounds and could be combined to express complex ideas. For this reason, hieroglyphs provided a more comprehensive form of communication than cuneiform.

The Egyptians painted and carved hieroglyphs on tombs, temples, and monuments. For important records and documents, they wrote on a paperlike material called **papyrus** (puh-PY-ruhs), named after the reeds used to make it. Only certain people gained mastery over the more than 800 hieroglyphs in the complex Egyptian writing system. The Egyptian government employed a large number of professional writers, called **scribes**, to keep detailed papyrus records of most transactions, including goods used and traded. The great demand for scribes created a rare chance for social mobility in Egyptian society.

Unlike the clay tablets of the Sumerians, most papyrus scrolls of the Egyptians did not last long. Historians rely mainly on ancient writings in stone for information about Egyptian history and ways of life. An archaeological find called the **Rosetta Stone** unlocked the meaning of Egyptian hieroglyphs. This black granite artifact, which dates to 196 B.C.E., was discovered near Rosetta, Egypt, in 1799 C.E. The stone features an ancient message written not only in Egyptian hieroglyphs but also in Greek and another type of Egyptian writing called demotic. Experts were able to use the Greek translation to decipher Egyptian hieroglyphs.

EXPANSION DURING THE MIDDLE KINGDOM

The Old Kingdom eventually broke apart into semi-independent regions ruled by rival dynasties. Egypt then entered the First Intermediate Period, which lasted about 140 years. Then in 2040 B.C.E., a ruler based in the city of Thebes reunited Egypt and began the **Middle Kingdom**, which continued until 1782 B.C.E. During this time, order returned throughout the land, agriculture expanded farther beyond the Nile, building projects resumed, and contacts with other kingdoms and city-states increased.

Like Mesopotamia, Egypt had few natural resources. The pharaohs of the Middle Kingdom increased trade with other regions to obtain scarce natural resources such as wood, gold, silver, and semiprecious stones. Egypt's main trading partners were people living in the lands that are now Syria and Lebanon to the north and in Nubia to the south.

The pharaohs of the Middle Kingdom also ventured out on a path of conquest. They took over land along the eastern Mediterranean Sea and in Nubia. Their control extended south to the area around the Third Cataract, which allowed them to engage in extensive trade with the kingdom of Kush. This connection with Kush enabled the Egyptians to gain valuable trade goods from Ethiopia and other societies to the south. Such items as panther skins, ivory from elephant tusks, and gold were carried through Nubia, overland around the cataracts, and down the Nile to Egypt.

Sometime around the 1700s B.C.E., the Middle Kingdom weakened because of invasions by the Hyksos (HIHK-sohs), a group of people from present-day Turkey. The time that followed has become known as the Second Intermediate Period. Egyptian foot soldiers proved no match against the horse-drawn chariots and the strong bows of the Hyksos. Eventually, the Hyksos claimed complete control of Egypt and ruled over it from 1650 to 1570 B.C.E.

HISTORICAL THINKING

1. **READING CHECK** What were the major achievements of the Old Kingdom and the Middle Kingdom?

2. **MAKE GENERALIZATIONS** What role did religion play in the building of the pyramids?

3. **DRAW CONCLUSIONS** Why do you think Egyptian farmers cooperated in helping construct the pyramids?

4. **MAKE INFERENCES** Why do you think the Egyptians kept so many records on papyrus even though this material was not durable?

NATIONAL GEOGRAPHIC EXPLORER
NORA SHAWKI

Looking for Everyday Life in Ancient Egypt

Since she was a little girl, Egyptian archaeologist Nora Shawki, shown above at a dig site, has been fascinated by the ancient civilization that once flourished in her homeland. After working on numerous excavations unearthing fragments of ancient Egypt, Shawki received a National Geographic Young Explorer Grant in 2015, which has permitted her to plan and direct her own dig at Tell Zuwelen, a settlement near the city of Tanis. Shawki's goal is to learn about the lives of ordinary Egyptians by tracking settlements in the Nile Delta. These settlements have the potential to tell us more about how ordinary people used to live their daily lives. "My research is focused on the ordinary Egyptians rather than the royals," she says. "It's imperative in understanding how the political and economic dynamics worked in ancient Egypt."

Settlement archaeology in the Nile Delta is extremely urgent due to the fact that the delta itself will not be there in the next 40 years due to modern encroachment and looting. Shawki believes she needs to excavate and document as much as possible because once it's gone, it's gone forever. "As an Egyptian, I aim to break boundaries as a female in a male-dominated society and make a change in the way we as the young generation of Egyptians view our own heritage and are able to access it."

BACKGROUND FOR THE TEACHER

Hieroglyphs The word *hieroglyph* comes from the Greek language. In Greek, *hiero* means "holy," and *glypho* means "writing." The Greeks who encountered Egyptian hieroglyphs, such as the historian and writer Herodotus, believed that the writings were sacred. The Egyptians themselves also called their writing "the gods' words." Egyptians believed that names had great power and if someone's name was remembered then that person would survive in the afterlife. Therefore, pharaohs' names were written in hieroglyphs within their tombs. Most experts believe there were three types of hieroglyphs. Many hieroglyphic symbols represented their picture, but a second type represented a particular sound. For instance, in Egyptian the owl represents the sound "m" and the cobra or snake represents the sound "j." Hieroglyphics contain other symbols that related to the daily lives of Egyptians; for instance a basket with folded laundry represents the sound "x" and a hand represents the sound "d." A third type was similar to a suffix for the hieroglyph before it and helped make the meaning of the previous hieroglyph clear. At one time, there were over 1,000 different types of hieroglyphs in use, but by 2055 B.C.E., it is believed that this number was reduced to 750. Egyptian hieroglyphs were read either in columns from top to bottom or in rows—from the right or the left. This made deciphering quite difficult, which is why it took until the 1820s when Frenchman Jean-François Champollion used the Rosetta Stone to make sense of the complex system of writing.

TEACH

GUIDED DISCUSSION

3. **Identify Problems and Solutions** What caused an increase in trade during the period of the Middle Kingdom? *(A scarcity of natural resources and the conquest of lands to the south led to an increase in trading partners and trade.)*

4. **Analyze Cause and Effect** Why did the Middle Kingdom decline? *(invasion and conquest by the Hyksos)*

ANALYZE VISUALS

Direct students to watch the Egyptian Hieroglyphs video from the lesson (available in the Student eEdition). Discuss the examples of the hieroglyphs from the Karnak temple complex in Luxor, Egypt. Then explain that this temple complex was larger than some ancient cities. Construction began about 4,000 years ago and was continually modified by subsequent Egyptian rulers for another 2,000 years, until the Romans took control of Egypt. **ASK:** Why might new pharaohs want to make changes to the temple complex? *(Possible response: Each would want to leave a historical mark on the buildings.)*

ACTIVE OPTIONS

On Your Feet: Numbered Heads Arrange students in groups and have students number off within each group. Provide the following prompts for them to think about and discuss: How did the Rosetta Stone change our understanding of ancient Egypt? How might modern technology continue to improve our understanding of the everyday lives of ancient peoples? After sufficient time, call a number and have each student with that number report on the group's discussion.

> **NG Learning Framework: Create Posters on Ancient Egypt**
> **SKILL** Communication
> **KNOWLEDGE** Our Human Story

Divide the class into four groups and assign each group one of the following topics: government of ancient Egypt; differences between the Old and Middle Kingdoms; architecture of ancient Egypt; religious traditions of ancient Egypt. Direct groups to research their topic and summarize their findings for the class. Have students take notes during the other groups' presentations and then work in their groups to create posters that could be used in a guide on ancient Egypt.

HISTORICAL THINKING

ANSWERS

1. During the Old Kingdom, Upper and Lower Egypt were united, workers built the pyramids and other impressive monuments, and scribes created and used the hieroglyphic writing system. During the Middle Kingdom, the pharaohs extended trade networks and expanded into the eastern Mediterranean and Nubia.

2. Egyptians believed in a life force that persisted after death, and the pyramids were built to house the life force of the pharaohs, who were revered as god-kings.

3. Possible response: Egyptians probably worked willingly for their pharaohs because they regarded them as gods. The farmers likely believed that what they were doing was good for Egypt and for ensuring their own passage into the afterlife.

4. Possible response: Papyrus was available and probably easier to write on than stone. The scribes did not see themselves as keeping records for posterity, but simply for their present-day concerns.

The New Kingdom and Nubia

The pharaoh Akhenaten (AH-keh-NAH-tehn) and his beautiful queen, Nefertiti (NEHF-ur-tee-tee), were powerful and controversial figures in the New Kingdom. They promoted the worship of Aten, a new form of sun-god, but their religious revolution died with them. When the next pharaoh ascended to the throne, Egyptians resumed worship of the former sun-god, Amun-Ra.

GROWTH DURING THE NEW KINGDOM

After 80 years of foreign rule, an Egyptian leader named Ahmose (AH-mohz) rebelled, fought the Hyksos, and defeated them. By 1570 B.C.E., Egypt was once again united under the absolute control of a strong monarch. This beginning of the **New Kingdom** ushered in another period of stability along the Nile.

Ahmose and the pharaohs who followed him vowed that, rather than be conquered again, they would be the ones to conquer. Egypt created its first full-time army and marched into Southwest Asia. It took over a swath of territory that included the present-day Palestinian territories, Lebanon, and Syria. It also advanced south into Nubia, gaining access to Nubia's most valuable resource—gold—which the Egyptians associated with immortality and the sun-god Amun-Ra. With the Nubian gold mines under their control, the Egyptians now had unlimited access to the cherished metal.

Determined to keep Nubia under their control, the pharaohs worked to transform Nubia into an Egyptian society. They brought the sons of Nubian chiefs to Egypt. In Egypt, the Nubians studied the Egyptian language and worshipped Egyptian deities. When they returned home, they served Egypt as administrators. Over time, the Nubians adopted Egyptian gods and values while adapting them to their own culture.

Egypt continued to trade with Nubia and other regions during the reign of **Hatshepsut** (haht-SHEHP-soot), the only woman pharaoh of the 18th dynasty. She gained power in 1473 B.C.E. as the guardian for her young stepson but then assumed the duties of pharaoh on her own. Ruling for 15 years, she initiated extensive trade expeditions to gain ebony, ivory, cedar, myrrh trees, and other goods.

During the New Kingdom period, Egypt established a series of alliances with the various powers in the eastern Mediterranean region and occasionally went to war with them. Letters written by the pharaoh Akhenaten, who ruled from 1352 to 1336 B.C.E., show that he communicated with rulers in the eastern Mediterranean lands of Babylonia, Assyria, and Anatolia. Over a period of 500 years, the eastern Mediterranean states engaged in both trade and **diplomacy**, or negotiation between governments.

Akhenaten moved the capital of Egypt to a new site about 200 miles north of Thebes, where he began construction on a city and temples devoted to the worship of Aten. In the past, some scholars concluded that Akhenaten worshipped Aten as the only god. But in fact, he continued to worship other gods as well, though Aten clearly ranked highest.

In the 1330s B.C.E., a nine-year-old boy named **Tutankhamen** (too-tang-KAH-muhn) followed Akhenaten as pharaoh. Tutankhamen ruled for only 10 years and might have been forgotten if not for the discovery of his lavish tomb by British archaeologist Howard Carter in 1922. Unlike most other royal tombs, this one had not been stripped of its treasures by looters. The tomb provided information about the ancient Egyptians' belief in the afterlife.

Tutankhamen's tomb was not a pyramid like the tombs of pharaohs of the Old Kingdom. Like many New Kingdom pharaohs, he was buried in a tomb cut out of rock in an area near Thebes called the Valley of the Kings. The tombs in the valley were built into the landscape to deter robbers. Even so, only Tutankhamen's tomb remained untouched for centuries.

Although New Kingdom pharaohs stopped building pyramids, they continued to construct large temples and other monuments. A long-reigning pharaoh of the 19th dynasty known as **Ramses II**, or Ramses the Great, was the most prolific builder of the New Kingdom. He commissioned hundreds of temples, monuments, and statues. Under Ramses, who ruled from 1279 to 1213 B.C.E., Egypt's power reached its peak.

The many wall paintings that graced Egyptian temples and tombs illustrate the prosperity of the Egyptians and the influence religion had on them. Some paintings show pharaohs interacting with Egyptian gods and goddesses, such as Osiris, Horus, Isis, and Anubis. Others portray leaders performing brave feats in battles or farmers at work in the fields or building pyramids. Such scenes provide historians with insight about the history of the Egyptian people as well as details about their daily lives.

NUBIAN RULE AND DECLINE

The New Kingdom began to weaken after 1200 B.C.E., and Egyptian rulers gradually lost control of Nubia. After 1069 B.C.E., torn by civil war, Egypt was once again split in two. Free of Egyptian rule, the Nubians began to rebuild an independent government based at Napata, a city along the Nile. Then around 747 B.C.E., the Nubians set their sights on the land of Egypt. Believing they were the rightful heirs to the pharaoh's throne, Nubian rulers conquered Egypt.

The high point of Nubian rule occurred under the leadership of King Taharqa (tuh-HAWR-kuh), who reigned from 690 to 664 B.C.E. He revived the practice of building pyramids, which had ended in Egypt about 1,000 years earlier, near the end of the Middle Kingdom. The first Nubian pyramid constructed under King Taharqa stood 160 feet tall and featured a flat, rather than a pointed, top. The Nubians followed other Egyptian traditions, including mummification and the worship of Egyptian gods. Not long after King Taharqa's death, the Nubians lost control of Egypt.

After 332 B.C.E., the Macedonians, who came from the Greek peninsula, gained control of Egypt. The last pharaohs of Egypt were all Macedonians, including the final one, the famous **Cleopatra VII**. Early historians and biographers, who were mostly Roman and male, tended

to depict Cleopatra as a woman who relied on her beauty and charm to win special treatment from men. Later historians have suggested that this assessment reflects bias, or prejudice, against women. Some modern historians have pointed out that Cleopatra was an intelligent, accomplished woman who spoke nine languages. They regard her as a shrewd leader whose calculated actions served to secure her power and win the allegiance of the people she ruled. She managed to delay Roman takeover of Egypt until her death in 30 B.C.E. That date marks the end of ancient Egyptian civilization, which lasted about 3,000 years. Egyptian civilization actually rose and fell over a longer period of time than the entire history of the world since then.

Ramses II ruled Egypt from c. 1279–1212 B.C.E.

HISTORICAL THINKING

1. **READING CHECK** How did Egypt increase its power during the New Kingdom period?

2. **DRAW CONCLUSIONS** How did the Egyptians' belief in immortality help shape the relationship between Egypt and Nubia?

3. **ANALYZE PERSPECTIVE** How do the past and present views of Cleopatra VII reflect the changing nature of history over time?

PLAN: 2-PAGE LESSON

OBJECTIVE

Identify details about the New Kingdom and describe its takeover by Nubia.

CRITICAL THINKING SKILLS FOR LESSON 2.3

- Draw Conclusions
- Analyze Perspective
- Identify
- Make Inferences
- Analyze Visuals

HISTORICAL THINKING FOR CHAPTER 2

How are people today linked to the first civilizations?

The New Kingdom defeated the Hyksos and reunited Egypt. To protect Egypt from future takeovers, New Kingdom rulers pursued a policy of expansion and conquest. Lesson 2.3 explores the outcome of this policy and other developments during the rule of the New Kingdom.

Student eEdition online

Additional content for this lesson, including two image galleries, is available online.

BACKGROUND FOR THE TEACHER

King Tut's Tomb The tomb of Tutankhamen, who became pharaoh after Akhenaten, lay undisturbed for thousands of years after Tutankhamen died. Presumably because Tutankhamen was a relatively unknown pharaoh—he had ruled for only nine years and had been removed from official historical records of Egypt—grave robbers had not looted the tomb's contents. British archaeologist Howard Carter combed the region for years and almost lost the funding for his exploration before he finally found the tomb's entrance. When he entered the tomb in November 1922, he saw the "glint of gold" everywhere.

INTRODUCE & ENGAGE

DISCUSS EGYPTIAN ART

Direct students to examine the photographs that appear in the lesson (available in the Student eEdition). Explain that the subject matter of Egyptian art often related to rulers and/or the gods. Hold a class discussion on how this fact illustrates the relationship that Egyptians had with their religion and with their rulers. Tell students that in this lesson they will learn more about the art, architecture, and rule of the New Kingdom in Egypt.

TEACH

GUIDED DISCUSSION

1. **Identify** What event initiated the development of the New Kingdom? *(the defeat of the Hyksos by Ahmose)*

2. **Make Inferences** What evidence suggests that Nubians identified with Egyptians after Egyptian rule came to an end? *(Possible responses: They adopted many Egyptian customs and believed the Egyptian throne belonged to them after Egypt declined.)*

ANALYZE VISUALS

Have students examine the Rulers of Egypt image gallery (available in the Student eEdition). **ASK:** Based on what you saw, how did artists typically portray the royal ruler? *(Possible response: in elaborate clothing, crown, or headdress)* What do you see on most of the faces of the rulers? *(Possible response: something that resembles a beard)* Tell students that pharaohs wore false beards, but no one is quite sure why. Historians believe the beards might have been worn to show a connection to the gods.

ACTIVE OPTIONS

On Your Feet: Three-Step Interview Direct pairs to interview each other about the rulers of Egypt. First, one student interviews the other using the following questions: Who were the most important rulers in Egypt after the beginning of the New Kingdom? What changes did each make to Egyptian government and society? Then have students reverse roles, with the following questions: How did rule over Egypt change after the decline of the New Kingdom? What contributions did the Nubians and Macedonians make to Egyptian government and society? Invite each student to share with the class the results of his or her interview.

> **NG Learning Framework: Report on an Excavation**
> ATTITUDE Empowerment
> KNOWLEDGES Our Human Story, Our Living Planet, Critical Species

Ask students to read the National Geographic Explorer feature on Nora Shawki in Lesson 2.2. Prompt them to research other regions that are threatened by overpopulation, natural disasters, climate change, or conflicts that they would like to excavate. Have them create a report detailing what they would hope to uncover, what they would try to preserve, and what would be lost if the excavation did not take place. Students' research may include human history and cultures, extinct or threatened species or destroyed lands and the need for land preservation.

DIFFERENTIATE

STRIVING READERS

Summarize Using a Concept Cluster Help pairs summarize the lesson by guiding them to create a Concept Cluster with the lesson title in the center oval and the subsection headings in the smaller ones. As students read each subsection, tell them to record key facts and ideas on the spokes. After students complete the Concept Cluster, invite volunteers to summarize the lesson and explain how New Kingdom rulers changed government and society under their rule.

PRE-AP

Analyze the Fall of a Civilization Tell students to research the fall of Egypt to Rome and then write an essay to share with the class. Tell them to include the main participants and where and when key events took place. Have them include information about the role Egypt played in the Roman Empire and how the governing of Egypt changed under Roman rule.

See the Chapter Planner for more strategies for differentiation.

HISTORICAL THINKING

ANSWERS

1. New Kingdom pharaohs began to conquer other lands to stay strong and independent and to gain access to additional natural resources.

2. To the Egyptians, gold was associated with the god Amun-Ra and the afterlife. This led the Egyptians to conquer Nubia to have access to its gold mines.

3. The Romans viewed her as a woman who used her beauty and charm to gain special treatment from men. Later historians regarded her as a shrewd leader. These differing opinions reflect the different views of women in power at different periods of time.

2.4 Preserving Cultural Heritage

Queens of Egypt

You've read about the royal tomb of Tutankhamen and that it and similar burial places for New Kingdom pharaohs are located in the Valley of the Kings. But did you know that there is also a Valley of the Queens? Most women—including royalty—in the ancient world did not hold much power, but Egypt was an exception. Women sometimes ruled with their husbands in political and social realms and sometimes on their own, for example, as the guardian of a younger male heir. And one of them even declared herself king.

In 2019, the National Geographic Society debuted a new exhibition featuring more than 300 artifacts that highlight the women of Egypt with a focus on the New Kingdom through the last queen and pharaoh, Cleopatra VII. We can use these artifacts and other evidence to speculate about what these women were like and how their leadership influenced ancient Egypt.

ABU SIMBEL, EGYPT
Ramses II commissioned two temples in what was then Nubia; the smaller temple honored his wife Nefertari and Hathor, goddess of women. At the time, it was unusual for an Egyptian king to dedicate a temple to his wife. But it was almost unthinkable for a woman to be depicted at the same size of a pharaoh, as shown here.

NEFERTITI
Nefertiti was married to Akhenaten, the 10th pharaoh of the 18th dynasty. Her name translates as "The Beautiful One Has Come" or "A Beautiful Woman Has Come," but she was more than a pretty face. Some historians believe that she co-ruled Egypt with her husband, playing important religious and political roles. Nefertiti also may have assumed some of the pharaoh's duties as he strived to reform his empire under its new religion—the worship of the sun-god Aten. In 1912, workers excavated the now famous painted limestone bust (shown here) near Amarna, Egypt, in the workshop of the court sculptor Thutmose. The personalized features and unique crown helped identify the well-preserved sculpture as Nefertiti.

NEFERTARI
Nefertari, whose name means "Beautiful Companion," was wife to the powerful Ramses II. Historians have not found many specific details of her life. But they believe that she was highly educated and participated in both state and religious business. At the main temple at Abu Simbel, one scene shows the royal couple making offerings to the sun gods. In her tomb, wall paintings depict Nefertari both in the company of the gods and as a divine figure, wearing a white gown and a golden headdress. Ramses II was devastated when she died. He said, "Just by passing, she has stolen away my heart." The wall painting shown here, in which Nefertari presents scrolls to the Egyptian god Toth, dates to about 1255 B.C.E.

50 CHAPTER 2

Early River Valley Civilizations 51

PLAN: 4-PAGE LESSON

OBJECTIVE
Identify selected female rulers from ancient Egypt and describe the political and social power these women held.

CRITICAL THINKING SKILLS FOR LESSON 2.4
- Analyze Visuals
- Make Connections
- Explain
- Identify Supporting Details
- Form and Support Opinions

HISTORICAL THINKING FOR CHAPTER 2
How are people today linked to the first civilizations?

The social and power structures of ancient Egypt provide a fascinating counterpoint to those same structures as they exist in the present day. Lesson 2.4 looks at the social and political roles female rulers played in ancient Egypt. The stories of these rulers may generate questions about female leadership and power today.

Student eEdition online
Additional content for this lesson, including photographs and artifacts, is available online.

BACKGROUND FOR THE TEACHER
Harems To ensure they had offspring who would succeed them, ancient Egyptian pharaohs took multiple wives. The pharaoh, his wives, and other people connected to the pharaoh lived in a place called a harem. A harem was overseen by the God's Wife, and below her were secondary wives and other female attendants. Some women were trained in the performing arts, including dance, music, and song. They entertained the pharaoh, dancing together or playing instruments like the harp and lute. The pharaoh's children, whether male or female, lived in the harem and were educated there. There also were male attendants who saw that the harem ran smoothly. The harem itself was an actual parcel of land on which crops were grown and livestock were raised. Textiles and crafts were made there, as well.

History Notebook
Encourage students to complete the "Queens of Egypt" Preserving Cultural Heritage page in their History Notebooks as they read.

INTRODUCE & ENGAGE

FEMALE LEADERS TODAY

Write *female world leaders* in the center of a Concept Cluster on the board and ask students to name three examples of female leaders from the present day. Encourage students to think not only of political leaders, but leaders in other areas as well, such as business or nongovernmental organizations. Record and discuss student responses and fill in the rest of the cluster. Tell students that in this lesson, they will learn about female rulers in ancient Egypt.

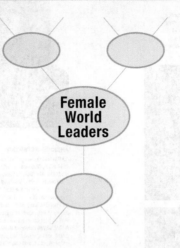

Female World Leaders

TEACH

GUIDED DISCUSSION

1. **Explain** Who held the title of "God's Wife," and what did it mean? *(A woman who was a God's Wife was from the royal family and served as a mediator between the god and the king. Some expanded the role and held great power, even attaining the authority of a high priest and receiving payments.)*

2. **Identify Supporting Details** Why was Tiye considered to be a "power behind the throne"? *(Tiye was married to the pharaoh and demonstrated a talent for diplomacy and other administrative duties. She went on to advise Akhenaten, who was her son. Foreign rulers suggested to Akhenaten that he consult his mother for advice.)*

PRESERVING CULTURAL HERITAGE

Kara Cooney's study of women leaders in Egypt is not only concerned with the physical artifacts they left behind. She is also a passionate investigator of women's roles in ancient Egypt—and what that tells her about the role of powerful women in the world today. One point she repeatedly makes is that the women who rose to power in ancient Egypt were allowed to do so mostly to protect the kingship, which was a patriarchal, authoritarian system. Cooney says, "I'm trying to wake everybody up to see that women continue to be used to protect a system that does not necessarily serve them. It's important to really understand how women are cogs in the patriarchal machine." However, Cleopatra, she says, provides an interesting counterexample: "Cleopatra is probably the only woman in our story who uses her reproductive abilities like a man, to create a legacy. The other women are either ruling on behalf of a younger child or they're ruling because there is no male offspring and are stepping in during years when they couldn't produce any children." Indeed, Cleopatra placed the children she had with the Romans Julius Caesar and Mark Antony in positions of rule as a way of ensuring her legacy.

DIFFERENTIATE

ENGLISH LANGUAGE LEARNERS

Practice Pronunciation Write the following names and terms on the board: Ahmose-Nefertari, Amenhotep, Deir el-Medina, Hatshepsut, Thutmose, Amun, Tiye, Akhenaten, Nefertiti, and Nefertari. Pronounce each name and have students repeat. Pair students at the **Beginning** level with those at the **Intermediate** or **Advanced** level and instruct them to take turns finding passages in the lesson that contain any of the names and read the passages aloud.

PRE-AP

Report on Kara Cooney's Book Direct students to read sections of Kara Cooney's book *When Women Ruled the World* to learn more about one of the six female leaders they read about in the lesson. Tell them to take a deep dive into the life and rule of the leader they select. Also encourage them to consider the issues of female power that Cooney raises and that are discussed in the Background for the Teacher sections. Students may wish to use a graphic organizer to organize their thoughts and ideas. Have students write up a brief report of their findings and present it to the entire class.

See the Chapter Planner for more strategies for differentiation.

HATSHEPSUT

You learned that Hatshepsut was the only woman pharaoh of the 18th dynasty. She seized the throne from her stepson Thutmose III by claiming that the god Amun was her father—and Amun wanted Hatshepsut to rule. She insisted, "I acted under his command; it was he who led me." Portraits of Hatshepsut after she declared herself king and consolidated her power feature inscriptions of "His Majesty" as well as the ceremonial garb of the pharaohs, including a royal headdress, kilt, and false beard. After her death, Thutmose III attempted to eradicate all evidence of his stepmother and her reign by destroying her likenesses and monuments and removing her name from the list of kings. Fortunately for us, he was unsuccessful. The limestone statue of the queen shown here dates to about 1479–1458 B.C.E.

TIYE

The daughter of a high-ranking official, Tiye grew up in the royal palace and eventually married Amenhotep III, the ninth pharaoh of the 18th dynasty. Her talent for diplomacy was a definite asset when it came to Egypt's involvement in foreign affairs. In art, Tiye and Amenhotep III are constant companions and partners, with wife and husband depicted at the same height, symbolizing their equality. Letters and inscriptions support this conclusion, as does evidence that Tiye oversaw many important administrative tasks herself. She also advised her son, Amenhotep IV, who later changed his name to Akhenaten. Surviving letters to the pharaoh from foreign rulers encourage Akhenaten to ask his mother for advice. No wonder she gained a reputation as the true power behind the throne! The realistic wood, gold, and silver portrait of Tiye shown here dates to about 1355 B.C.E. It shows the queen in her later years.

NATIONAL GEOGRAPHIC EXPLORER KARA COONEY

When Women Ruled the World

Professor, Egyptologist, and National Geographic Explorer Kara Cooney specializes in craft production, coffin studies, and economies of the ancient world. She has studied nearly 300 coffins in collections all around the world. She was originally drawn to Egyptian art and architecture for the "pretty pictures," but she moved toward the truths of the systems behind the hieroglyphics, sacred texts, and grand monuments.

"I find myself trying to pull the veils away from Egyptian society to see what was really going on," Cooney says. Her 2018 book *When Women Ruled the World* delves into the lives of the six women rulers mentioned in this lesson. "Six powerful queens, five of them becoming pharaohs in their own rights—and yet each and every one of them had to fit the patriarchal systems of power around them, rather than fashioning something new," Cooney points out. "The story of female power in ancient Egypt is a tragedy."

CLEOPATRA VII

Recall that Cleopatra was the last pharaoh to rule Egypt. Her family's claim to the throne dated back to Ptolemy, a Macedonian general who fought for Alexander the Great. (You will read about Alexander and Ptolemy in a later chapter.) Cleopatra ascended the throne at the age of 18 in 51 B.C.E. with her younger brother Ptolemy XIII. The siblings were supposed to rule their empire together, but they soon were at war. Cleopatra allied with Julius Caesar of Rome to regain her royal position. Ptolemy XIII died during the conflict. Although another brother, Ptolemy XIV, was designated as co-ruler, Cleopatra wielded all the power. Her 11-year relationship with the Roman general Mark Antony helped stave off a Roman takeover until her death. The basalt statue of Cleopatra shown here dates from the first century B.C.E.

AHMOSE–NEFERTARI

As the first queen of the New Kingdom from 1539 to 1514 B.C.E., Ahmose-Nefertari worked closely with her husband, Ahmose, to transition from war to peace and reunify Egypt. She held the title of "God's Wife of Amun" or "Wife of the God," in which a woman from the royal family served as a mediator between the god and the king. Ahmose-Nefertari increased the power of this position to gain religious influence as well as political clout and a higher social standing. A God's Wife mirrored the authority of a high priest, and she received payment in the form of property, staff, and many different material goods. Ahmose-Nefertari and her son Amenhotep I were deified after their deaths, and she was worshiped as a goddess of resurrection at the ancient Egyptian village of Deir el-Medina. The wooden statue shown here depicts the queen with braids and in a long linen robe. A vulture pelt and a partial headdress indicate her royal status.

HISTORICAL THINKING

ANALYZE VISUALS Why might the study of artifacts be a better way to learn about the women of ancient Egypt than relying on written documents from that time?

Early River Valley Civilizations 53

BACKGROUND FOR THE TEACHER

Discovering Nefertari's Tomb The temple that Ramses II had built in Abu Simbel for his wife, Nefertari, is one of the grandest and most beautiful royal tombs in all of the Valley of the Queens. It was discovered in 1904 by an Italian archaeologist named Ernesto Schiaparelli. Schiaparelli was director of the Egyptian Museum in Turin, Italy, and led the Italian Archaeological Mission to Egypt that commenced in 1903 and ended in 1920. Among his group's Egyptological achievements was the excavation of many sites in the Valley of the Queens. Among those sites were thirteen royal tombs, including those of Nefertiti and Nefertari.

Nefertari's tomb, Schiaparelli discovered, was made up of two levels of rooms connected by a staircase. He found numerous artifacts (despite the fact that looters had plundered the tomb in antiquity), including a pair of sandals and the lid to Nefertari's sarcophagus, made of pink granite. The most significant discovery, however, was the paintings that covered the plaster walls of the tomb's interior. The paintings depicted scenes of Nefertari preparing for the afterlife accompanied by hieroglyphs that were supposed to guide and protect her. The walls were in extremely poor condition when Schiaparelli found them. Not only had the plaster dehydrated, but salt crystals had formed underneath the paintings themselves. In fact, so fragile was the tomb (and so debated was the plan for refurbishing it), restoration of the tomb didn't begin until 1986, some 80 years after Schiaparelli first uncovered its hidden treasures. Conservation work on the paintings continues to this day.

TEACH

GUIDED DISCUSSION

3. **Analyze Visuals** What can be learned from the small box that belonged to Nefertari (available in the Student eEdition)? *(The cartouches of Ramses II and Nefertari likely confirm that it belonged to her; if it is true that Nefertari probably stored cosmetics in the box, then that reveals that some ancient Egyptian women (perhaps only royalty) wore makeup; that the box is made of hippopotamus ivory indicates that hippopotamuses roamed Egypt during that era and were useful to ancient Egyptians.)*

4. **Form and Support Opinions** Do you agree with Kara Cooney that "the story of female power in ancient Egypt is a tragedy"? Explain your thinking. *(Possible response: I don't agree with Cooney's statement because these particular women achieved great social and political power in ancient Egypt, which was very rare among early civilizations. That is a notable achievement, not a tragedy.)*

ANALYZE VISUALS

Ask students to reexamine the depictions of the women of ancient Egypt in the lesson. **ASK:** What do the images of the women all have in common? *(Possible response: All the images display a certain type of headdress, which means that either women in general had to cover their heads, or perhaps only women who were royalty covered their heads.)* What generalizations can archaeologists draw from the images? Provide an example. *(Possible responses: Archaeologists can discern that these women were of royal status; for example, Ahmose-Nefertari wears a partial headdress and a vulture pelt.)*

ACTIVE OPTION

NG Learning Framework: Create a Class Collage
ATTITUDE Curiosity
KNOWLEDGE Our Human Story

Have students work in small groups and conduct online research about the following ancient Egyptian goddesses: Bastet, Hathor, Mut, Sekhmet, Isis, Taweret, and Maat. Direct groups to select images they find and write one or two paragraphs about each goddess. Encourage them to look for connections between these goddesses and the female leaders they learned about in the lesson. For example, are any of the goddesses depicted on the tombs of any of the leaders? Then tell groups to assemble their photos and captions into a class collage. Have groups present their parts of the collage to the rest of the class.

HISTORICAL THINKING

ANSWER

1. Possible response: The study of artifacts is a better way to learn about the women of ancient Egypt because women were not really written about at that time. They were not considered to be as important as men and did not usually hold prominent places in Egyptian society.

The Hittites and the Assyrians

Most businesses today are quick to adopt new technology, believing they need any edge they can get to match or beat the competition. The same philosophy held true in ancient times and gave a distinct advantage to two groups—the Hittites and the Assyrians.

THE HITTITE KINGDOM

You have read that the New Kingdom pharaohs communicated and formed alliances with various powers in the eastern Mediterranean region. The **Hittites** (HIH-tyts), who were based in Anatolia, now the country of Turkey, were one of these groups.

Like Egyptian pharaohs, Hittite kings not only led the military and presided over government but also acted as high priests and directed religious practices. The Hittites erected temples to the weather-god Teshub, considered the highest god.

Unlike the Egyptian language, the language of the Hittites belonged to the Indo-European family. Its structure resembled that of Latin, Greek, and Sanskrit, the ancient language of southern Asia. While the Hittite language has not survived, many Indo-European languages are still widely spoken today, including Hindi, Farsi, Greek, Spanish, French, Italian, Irish, German, and English.

The Hittites were the first speakers of an Indo-European language to establish a complex society in western Asia. **Iron**, a heavy metal used to make steel, was the foundation of the Hittite civilization. Iron technology enabled the Hittites to create stronger tools and weapons than the bronze implements used by neighboring peoples. Iron could not be melted and poured into molds like bronze. Instead, skilled

The archaeological site of Hattusha, which was the capital of the Hittite kingdom, preserves the ruins of temples, royal residences, fortifications, gateways, and other types of construction.

metalworkers heated iron and hammered it into the desired shape. The Hittites traded their iron tools and weapons to other peoples, but they kept the process for making them secret.

Advanced iron weapons gave the Hittites an advantage in battle. An iron Hittite sword could crush the skull of an enemy whose head was protected only by a soft bronze helmet. Another new technology, the war chariot, made the Hittites victorious in battle after battle. Two horses pulled a chariot that carried a driver and two warriors into action. During the Battle of Kadesh in 1285 B.C.E., the Hittite ruler commanded 2,500 chariots to defeat the Egyptian army. Later, the two sides signed a peace treaty and promised to aid each other in time of war.

Between 1322 and 1220 B.C.E., the Hittite kingdom reached its largest size, covering all of Anatolia and Syria and the eastern edge of Mesopotamia. But in 1200 B.C.E., the Hittite capital fell to outsiders. Historians are unsure who the invaders were, but ancient Egyptian texts refer to "sea peoples" who attacked parts of the Mediterranean region.

THE ASSYRIAN EMPIRE

The homeland of the **Assyrians** (uh-SIHR-ee-uhnz) was in northern Mesopotamia. Like the Hittites, the Assyrians forged iron weapons that gave them an advantage over their enemies. The Assyrian army also had the first true **cavalry**, or group of soldiers mounted on horseback. Armed with bows and arrows, the Assyrian soldiers rode bareback since saddles and stirrups had not yet been invented.

The Assyrian leaders sought to take over land in order to control trade routes. Unlike previous conquerors in the eastern Mediterranean region, the Assyrians did not immediately take other peoples' territory by force. Because the Assyrian ruler saw himself as the representative of the gods, he believed it was his duty to convince foreign rulers to submit to him voluntarily. Those who surrendered received gentle treatment, but those who resisted were cruelly punished. Soldiers skinned captives alive, gouged out eyes, cut off hands and feet, or impaled victims on stakes. These atrocities served as a warning to those who had not yet been conquered: surrender quickly or else. The Assyrians themselves believed such treatment was justified

CRITICAL VIEWING This wall relief shows an Assyrian battle scene. What kinds of weapons and armor did the soldiers use?

because the enemy was resisting the gods, not just a human king.

Besides conquering southern Mesopotamia and Egypt, the powerful Assyrian army defeated the kingdom of Israel in 721 B.C.E., which you will learn about in the next lesson. After conquering a region, the Assyrians forced the defeated rulers and skilled craftsmen to relocate to another part of the empire. These forced migrations were originally intended to fill lightly populated parts of the empire. Later, resettlement became a method of demonstrating the ruler's power. Several hundred thousand people were resettled, including many people from Israel who were sent to Assyria.

The Assyrians built a network of roads to connect settlements and established a messenger system to relay messages. They also made the center of government, Nineveh, a showplace, with huge gates, wide streets, canals, an impressive palace, and a library containing more than 20,000 cuneiform tablets. The booming agricultural economy financed such improvements. Yet even the fearsome Assyrians were not indestructible, and their empire fell to a people known as the Chaldeans in 612 B.C.E.

HISTORICAL THINKING

1. **READING CHECK** How did technology help the Hittites and the Assyrians build empires?

2. **FORM AND SUPPORT OPINIONS** Why do you think the Hittites wanted to keep the technology of making iron a secret?

3. **EVALUATE** How would you characterize the Assyrian methods of warfare and rule?

PLAN: 2-PAGE LESSON

OBJECTIVE
Identify how the Hittites and Assyrians used their military strength to build empires in Southwest Asia.

CRITICAL THINKING SKILLS FOR LESSON 3.1
- Form and Support Opinions
- Evaluate
- Make Connections
- Compare and Contrast
- Analyze Visuals

HISTORICAL THINKING FOR CHAPTER 2
How are people today linked to the first civilizations?

The Hittites and Assyrians established empires in Southwest Asia using new military technology, including iron weapons and cavalry. Lesson 3.1 discusses how the empires rose to power and what led to their decline.

Student eEdition online
Additional content for this lesson, including a photograph, is available online.

BACKGROUND FOR THE TEACHER

The Sea Peoples No one knows for certain who the Sea Peoples were, but scholars have used Egyptian and Hittite texts, as well as archaeological artifacts, to identify some possible groups. It is believed that the invaders included groups from Sardinia, Sicily, Anatolia, and Greece. The Hittites were not the only group to face invasions by Sea Peoples. Anatolia, Syria, Palestine, and Cyprus were among the victims of the Sea Peoples' century-long attacks throughout the Mediterranean. Egyptians fought two wars against the invaders, in the 1200s and 1100s B.C.E. and have provided much of the little information about these mysterious attackers. The latter of the attacks on Egypt ended the terror of the Sea Peoples. They vanished after that, and no other information has been recorded or discovered.

INTRODUCE & ENGAGE

DISCUSS MONUMENTAL ARCHITECTURE

Direct students to examine the photograph of the capital of the Hittite kingdom that appears in the lesson. Have them study the details of the stonework. Ask volunteers to suggest ways in which the details are similar to those in Egyptian temples and tombs. (*Possible responses might include the sphinxlike figures on the columns and the flat illustrations of people marching in lines on the walls. The material used—stone—is also similar.*) Tell students that in this lesson they will learn about the similarities and differences between the Hittites and the Egyptians and other ancient civilizations.

TEACH

GUIDED DISCUSSION

1. **Make Connections** What bridges the language of the Hittites to the languages many speak today? (*The structure of the Hittite language belonged to the Indo-European family. Indo-European languages, including English, are still spoken today.*)

2. **Compare and Contrast** What are some similarities and differences between the Hittites and the Assyrians? (*Possible responses: Similarities: They both were warlike, made iron weapons, and focused on military advancements and conquests. Differences: The Hittites erected temples to weather-god Teshub, while the Assyrian king believed he was the representative of the gods.*)

ANALYZE VISUALS

Have students carefully examine the Assyrian battle scene relief. **ASK:** How does the relief illustrate the military advancements of the Assyrians? (*Possible response: It shows iron weapons and bows and arrows.*)

ACTIVE OPTIONS

On Your Feet: Create a Quiz Organize students into two teams. Instruct each team to write 10 True/False or multiple-choice questions focusing on the technologies and achievements of the Hittites and Assyrians. Have teams alternate asking one of their questions, to which the other team responds. Keep track of the number of correct answers for each team. The team with the most correct answers is the winner.

| **NG Learning Framework: Create a Model** STEM
| **ATTITUDE** Empowerment
| **SKILL** Problem-Solving

Invite pairs of students to use information from the lesson and from online resources on the architecture of the Hittites to create a scale model or drawing of a Hittite structure, such as the Lion Gate at Hattusha or the archaeological site at Alacahöyük. If students build the model, prompt them to use cardboard, glue, cotton balls, stones, and any other materials that help demonstrate the building materials of the Hittites. Encourage pairs to share their completed projects with the class.

DIFFERENTIATE

ENGLISH LANGUAGE LEARNERS

Clarify Word Meaning Explain that readers can often use context clues to figure out the meaning of unfamiliar words. Pair students at the **Beginning** level with students at the **Intermediate** or **Advanced** level. Prompt partners to find the Key Vocabulary word *cavalry* and the context clue *mounted on horseback*. Then have students look for additional Key Vocabulary words or other unfamiliar words. Prompt them to read the sentences before and after the target word to look for clues to the word's meaning. Encourage them to look up the word in a dictionary to verify its meaning.

GIFTED & TALENTED

Extend Knowledge Prompt students to gather information from a variety of sources to learn more about the process of ironworking. Have them research the differences between ironwork and other metalwork. Ask them to share their findings in an oral or written report.

See the Chapter Planner for more strategies for differentiation.

HISTORICAL THINKING

ANSWERS

1. Both peoples developed the technology of iron weapons to overpower enemies. The Hittites also developed horse-drawn chariots.

2. Iron weapons gave the Hittites an advantage in both trade and warfare.

3. Possible response: The Assyrians were gentle to those who voluntarily submitted to their rule but cruel to those who did not. Their treatment of captives in warfare was brutal. They forced conquered peoples to move from their homelands.

CRITICAL VIEWING They used iron weapons and armor, including shields, bows and arrows, spears, and chariots for speed.

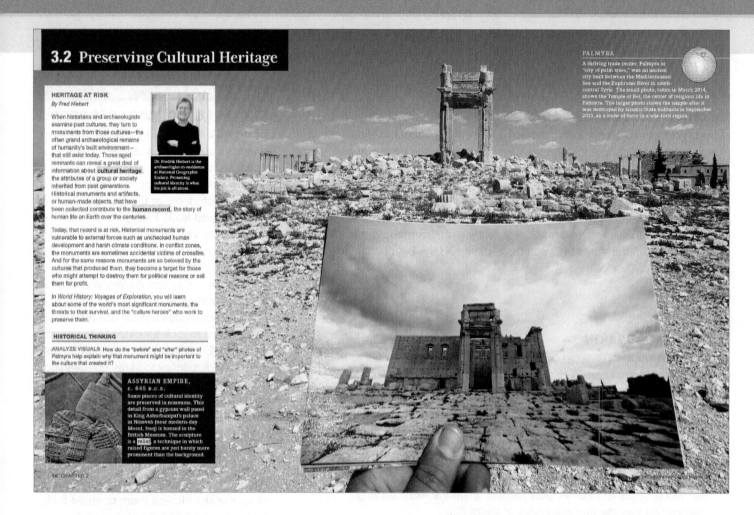

3.2 Preserving Cultural Heritage

HERITAGE AT RISK
By Fred Hiebert

When historians and archaeologists examine past cultures, they turn to monuments from those cultures—the often grand archaeological remains of humanity's built environment—that still exist today. Those aged remnants can reveal a great deal of information about **cultural heritage**, the attributes of a group or society inherited from past generations. Historical monuments and artifacts, or human-made objects, that have been collected contribute to the **human record**, the story of human life on Earth over the centuries.

Today, that record is at risk. Historical monuments are vulnerable to external forces such as unchecked human development and harsh climate conditions. In conflict zones, the monuments are sometimes accidental victims of crossfire. And for the same reasons monuments are so beloved by the cultures that produced them, they become a target for those who might attempt to destroy them for political reasons or sell them for profit.

In *World History: Voyages of Exploration*, you will learn about some of the world's most significant monuments, the threats to their survival, and the "culture heroes" who work to preserve them.

HISTORICAL THINKING

ANALYZE VISUALS How do the "before" and "after" photos of Palmyra help explain why that monument might be important to the culture that created it?

Dr. Fredrik Hiebert is the archaeologist-in-residence at National Geographic Society. Protecting cultural identity is what his job is all about.

ASSYRIAN EMPIRE, c. 645 B.C.E.
Some pieces of cultural identity are preserved in museums. This detail from a gypsum wall panel in King Ashurbanipal's palace in Nineveh (near modern-day Mosul, Iraq) is housed in the British Museum. The sculpture is a **relief**, a technique in which raised figures are just barely more prominent than the background.

PALMYRA
A thriving trade center, Palmyra or "city of palm trees," was an ancient city built between the Mediterranean Sea and the Euphrates River in south-central Syria. The small photo, taken in March 2014, shows the Temple of Bel, the center of religious life in Palmyra. The larger photo shows the temple after it was destroyed by Islamic State militants in September 2015, as a show of force in a war-torn region.

56 CHAPTER 2

PLAN: 2-PAGE LESSON

OBJECTIVE
Understand the importance of preserving cultural heritage and the impact of its loss.

CRITICAL THINKING SKILLS FOR LESSON 3.2
- Analyze Visuals
- Make Connections
- Analyze Cause and Effect
- Identify

HISTORICAL THINKING FOR CHAPTER 2
How are people today linked to the first civilizations?

Due to the impermanence of many written materials, the only traces of some civilizations are the structures built out of long-lasting resources. These structures provide us with information about what life was like in an earlier civilization. Lesson 3.2 discusses the importance of protecting historic monuments to preserve cultural heritage.

Student eEdition online
Additional content for this lesson, including a video, is available online.

BACKGROUND FOR THE TEACHER

The Islamic State The Islamic State, formerly known as ISIS, ISIL, and Daesh, is a terrorist militant group known for heinous acts of violence and the destruction of historical monuments across large areas of the Middle East. The group is driven by the desire to instill traditional Islamic rules and practices. The Islamic State is responsible for hundreds of terrorist attacks around the world and is known for videotaping brutal executions and broadcasting them online. The group believes that cultural monuments should not be worshiped and has destroyed historical sites and artifacts throughout Iraq, Syria, and Libya. Interestingly, reports show that the group has profited from the sale of these artifacts. The Islamic State has claimed responsibility for the destruction of churches, temples, mosques, shrines, museums, ancient ruins, monuments, and buildings throughout the Middle East, including the city of Palmyra, Syria. More than 150,000 tourists per year visited Palmyra before the Islamic State attacks began in 2015. Today the city is in ruins and many of its artifacts destroyed.

History Notebook
Encourage students to complete the "Heritage at Risk" Preserving Cultural Heritage page in their History Notebooks as they read.

INTRODUCE & ENGAGE

DISCUSS CULTURAL SYMBOLS

Have students think about countries and cultures across the world. Explain that buildings and structures often come to symbolize a culture, such as the Statue of Liberty in the United States. Ask volunteers to name other monuments that symbolize cultures. *(Possible responses: Mount Rushmore or the Lincoln Memorial in the United States; the Taj Mahal in India; the Colosseum or the Leaning Tower of Pisa in Italy; the Great Wall of China)* Tell students that in this lesson they will learn about the importance of preserving cultural monuments.

TEACH

GUIDED DISCUSSION

1. **Analyze Cause and Effect** What are the causes and effects of the destruction of historical monuments? *(Possible responses: Causes: weather conditions, war; Effects: loss of valuable information about a culture, devastation from the loss of a sacred building, artifact, or object)*

2. **Identify** What message is Hiebert conveying in the video (available in the Student eEdition)? *(Possible responses: The destruction of monuments and historical artifacts is not the destruction of the heritage; Everyone should care about artifacts throughout the world because artifacts are important aspects of human history, and they are important to more than just a single heritage.)*

PRESERVING CULTURAL HERITAGE

The Temple of Bel was an ancient temple consecrated to the Mesopotamian god Bel and was dedicated in 32 C.E., though architectural elements were added throughout the first and second centuries. The temple was considered an important architectural achievement and cultural center of the ancient world, as it incorporated Greco-Roman elements, among others, into its over 1,000 columns and 500 tombs. The Islamic State attacks leveled most of the Temple, leaving behind a few raised pillars and a destroyed facade of crumbling stone.

ACTIVE OPTION

NG Learning Framework: Create a Monument STEM
ATTITUDE Responsibility
SKILL Collaboration

Divide the class into four or five groups. Have each group draw plans for a monument they might construct in their town. The monument can be a statue, building, artistic sculpture, or any other structure that symbolizes something important to the students. Symbolic ideas for the monument include a person, such as an athlete, Hollywood star, politician, or community leader that has made a cultural impact; a cause, such as animal rescue or recycling; or an event, such as 9/11 or Martin Luther King, Jr. Day. After they have finished with their plans, have each group present its monument to the rest of the class. As a class, discuss each monument's significance and the responsibility to help preserve it.

DIFFERENTIATE

INCLUSION

Use Supported Reading In small groups, have the students read aloud a section of text and spend time looking at the photos. At the end of the section, have the students stop and use these sentence starters to explain what they learned from the text.

A. This text is about _____.

B. One detail that stood out to me is _____.

C. The photograph shows me _____.

D. The vocabulary word _____ means _____.

E. I don't think I understand _____.

GIFTED & TALENTED

Write a News Article Ask students to think of an important building or structure and come up with a hypothetical but realistic event that could destroy the site, either through natural forces or human impact. Have them write a news article detailing the destruction of the site and the impact it will have on people and culture today and in the future. They should consider the following questions: Why is this site significant? How old is it? How and why was it made? How might people react if the hypothetical event really occurred? What would be lost? Invite students to share their articles on a class blog or website.

See the Chapter Planner for more strategies for differentiation.

HISTORICAL THINKING

ANSWER

Possible response: Just the fact that it was targeted for destruction shows that the people who destroyed it must have believed it was important to the culture they are fighting against.

Judaism and the Israelite Kingdoms

Stories of men, women, and children forced to flee their homelands frequently appear in the news today. As these people settle in new lands, some will hold on to the traditions of their home countries for at least a generation. One group of people who had to abandon its homeland in ancient times has maintained its core traditions for thousands of years.

Today, many Jews come to pray at the Western Wall, a small remnant of an ancient wall in the Old City of Jerusalem. Some people place slips of paper containing written prayers into cracks in the wall. Jews consider the Western Wall and an elevated plaza in Jerusalem called the Temple Mount especially holy sites.

58 CHAPTER 2

ORIGINS OF JUDAISM

You have read about rulers or groups who used their military strength to build powerful empires in the Mediterranean region. Conquest is not the only way to unify people and bring change, however. In fact, the introduction of a new religious idea in the region had a powerful impact that is still felt today.

This monumental innovation took place along the eastern shore of the Mediterranean Sea where modern-day Israel, Lebanon, Jordan, and Syria are located. This lightly populated and politically weak region, sometimes called the Levant, was the homeland of the ancient Hebrews. The Hebrews were the first people from the eastern Mediterranean region to practice **monotheism**, or the belief in one God. This belief formed the basis of their religion, **Judaism**, and is explained in their holy book, the Hebrew Bible.

The current text of the Hebrew Bible dates to around 500 B.C.E. Historians regard the text of the Hebrew Bible as a rich source of information about the beliefs of the ancient Hebrews. But the historical accuracy of the stories in the Bible is questionable. By combining analysis of the Bible with archaeological findings, historians can come closer to an accurate understanding of the ancient Hebrew past.

According to the Hebrew Bible, **Abraham**, a Mesopotamian shepherd, was the first person to worship one God. The Bible says that God instructed Abraham to move his family to Canaan, a land in the southern part of the Levant, and offered him a **covenant**, or religious agreement. According to the Bible, if Abraham promised to be faithful to God, then God would grant the land of Canaan to Abraham and his descendants. In other words, Canaan was to be the Promised Land of the Hebrews. The Bible says that Abraham upheld his part of the contract and took his family to Canaan, where they lived as herders and farmers, moving frequently with their flocks.

As the Hebrew population grew, small groups built villages high atop hills. While the Hebrews followed many of the same customs as other peoples in Southwest Asia, their language and religious practices distinguished them from their neighbors.

According to the Hebrew Bible, a drought generations later led to food shortages in Canaan, and so the Hebrews, now known as the Israelites, moved to Egypt. The Bible says that the Egyptian pharaoh enslaved the Israelites and they endured a long period of suffering until God selected a man named **Moses** to lead them out of slavery. Their departure from Egypt and return to Canaan is known as the **Exodus**. According to the Bible, at one point during this 40-year journey, Moses climbed Mount Sinai, where God gave him two stone tablets with a set

The text of the Ten Commandments (shown above in a Hebrew illuminated manuscript) has been translated from its original language into many other languages, including English. Many variations in wording, and even in the way of numbering, exist. The basis of many modern laws, such as the law against stealing, date back to the Ten Commandments, as well as to Hammurabi's Code and other ancient moral and legal codes.

PRIMARY SOURCE

1. I am the Lord Your God, who brought you out of the land of Egypt, out of the house of bondage.

2. You shall have no other gods before Me. You shall not make for yourself any graven image. . . . You shall not bow down to them, nor serve them.

3. You shall not take the name of the Lord Your God in vain; for the Lord will not hold him guiltless that takes His name in vain.

4. Remember the Sabbath, to keep it holy. Six days you shall labor, and do all your work; but the seventh day is a Sabbath unto the Lord Your God. . . .

5. Honor your father and your mother. . . .

6. You shall not murder.

7. You shall not commit adultery.

8. You shall not steal.

9. You shall not bear false witness against your neighbor.

10. You shall not covet your neighbor's house . . . nor anything that is your neighbor's.

—from the JPS Tanakh, 1917

Early River Valley Civilizations 59

INTRODUCE & ENGAGE

ACTIVATE PRIOR KNOWLEDGE

Point out the map of the Jewish Diaspora in the lesson. Tell students that a diaspora is the movement of a people away from their homeland. Ask students to consider why people might leave their homeland. As part of the discussion, guide students to consider the following reasons:

- conflict over territory
- wars
- persecution
- natural disasters

TEACH

GUIDED DISCUSSION

1. **Identify Supporting Details** How were the religious beliefs of the Hebrews different from those of other peoples in the Mediterranean region? *(The Hebrews practiced monotheism; their beliefs are explained in the Hebrew Bible.)*

2. **Explain** What role does the Exodus play in Judaism? *(According to the Hebrew Bible, the Exodus is the time period when the Israelites left Canaan for Egypt, where they were enslaved by the pharaoh. During this period, Moses received the Ten Commandments from God. The Ten Commandments described how to live a righteous life according to God and renewed God's promise to the Israelites.)*

ANALYZE PRIMARY SOURCES

Direct students' attention to the primary source and have them read the list of the Ten Commandments. **ASK:** Are there any laws you think are missing from the list? Explain. *(Answers will vary but may mention some of the concerns of modern life.)* Why do you think the Ten Commandments have been translated into many other languages? *(Possible response: They are basic principles on how to live and could apply to any society.)* Are there any in the list that you think don't apply to the modern world? *(Possible response: The prohibition against graven images—this might have been more relevant in a historical era during which other civilizations worshiped multiple gods.)*

DIFFERENTIATE

STRIVING READERS

Chart Lesson Information Instruct students to draw a five-column chart and label the columns with the lesson's subsection headings. As they read, tell students to complete the chart with important details from each subsection. After reading, encourage students to compare and revise their completed charts as necessary.

PRE-AP

Create an Annotated Time Line Tell students that the city of Jerusalem is holy to all three of the world's major religions—Judaism, Christianity, and Islam. Though people of different faiths do coexist peacefully here, the city has also been the site of violent conflict throughout its history. Have each student create an annotated time line of significant events in the history of Jerusalem. Tell them to ensure that their time lines cover the significance of Jerusalem to each of the religions.

See the Chapter Planner for more strategies for differentiation.

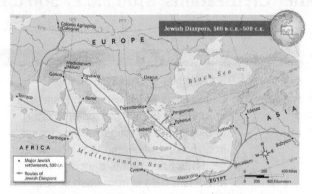

Jewish Diaspora, 586 B.C.E.–500 C.E.

EUROPE

Colonia Agrippina (Cologne)

Mediolanum (Milan)

Genoa

Ravenna

Oescus

Black Sea

Torraco

Rome

Thessalonika

Pergamum

Edessa

ASIA

Ephesus

Athens

Antioch

Carthage

AFRICA

Mediterranean Sea

Babylon

Cyrene

Jerusalem

Alexandria

EGYPT

- Major Jewish settlements, 500 C.E.
- Routes of Jewish Diaspora

0   200   400 Miles
0   200   400 Kilometers

---

of laws called the Ten Commandments. The Israelites believed that, in this way, God renewed his covenant with them and provided them with guidelines for living a righteous life.

THE ARCHAEOLOGICAL RECORD

No archaeological evidence confirms that a single migration out of Egypt took place. Many scholars think that the story of the Exodus might have grown out of a series of migrations rather than one.

Archaeological excavations have revealed that in 1300 B.C.E., approximately 12,000 to 15,000 people lived in about 300 small villages on previously unoccupied hillsides in the southern Levant. By 1100 B.C.E., the population had grown to 80,000. Most residents had tools made of bronze, flint, and occasionally iron. One piece of evidence suggests that the residents were the Israelites: the lack of pig bones at excavated sites is a sign that the people observed a religious ban on eating pork. This practice is recorded later in the Hebrew Bible.

Archaeologists believe that a complex society first took shape in the region between 1000 and 900 B.C.E. The main evidence, as in Mesopotamia, is the formation of large urban centers with massive walls. At this time, loosely united groups of people became a small kingdom run by non-elected government administrators. The population of the Levant around 1000 B.C.E. has been estimated at 150,000. About 5,000 people lived in the region's largest city, **Jerusalem**, in 700 B.C.E.

THE KINGDOMS OF ISRAEL AND JUDAH

The Israelites who returned to Canaan from Egypt consisted of 12 **tribes**, or extended family units. They had a difficult task in reclaiming Canaan because other people had settled there, including a group called the Philistines. The Israelites soon realized that the 12 tribes would have to band together under a single strong leader to win back the land.

Jerusalem was the site of a magnificent temple, which you will learn about later in this lesson.

IMPACT OF THE HEBREW BIBLE

Hebrew monotheism profoundly shaped the teachings of two other major world religions, Christianity and Islam. Today, belief in a single God forms the foundation for all three religions. For the most part, the writings in the Hebrew Bible are the same ones that make up the Old Testament of the Christian Bible. Certain stories from the Hebrew Bible and the Christian Bible also appear in the holy book of Islam, the Quran. These stories include Abraham's covenant with God and Moses' experience on Mount Sinai.

The Torah, which comprises the first five books of the Hebrew Bible, stresses the importance of accepting and honoring God, treating all people with respect and fairness, and caring for the less fortunate. The ethical principles of ancient Judaism had an enormous impact on Christianity, Islam, and later ideas of human rights to which all people are entitled.

According to the Hebrew Bible, **Saul** became the first king of the Israelites in about 1020 B.C.E. and led them in battle against the Philistines. Saul was followed by **David**, who united the 12 tribes, defeated the Philistines, and revitalized the city of Jerusalem. **Solomon**, David's son, oversaw a time of growth and built a magnificent temple in Jerusalem. According to the Bible, the temple housed the Ark of the Covenant, which held the original tablets listing God's commandments. The temple became the central location for all Jews to pray to God.

After Solomon's reign ended, tensions between the northern and southern tribes split the kingdom. The northern region took the name **Israel**, while the southern land became known as **Judah**. Both kingdoms had a form of government called a **theocracy**, in which the legal system is based on religious law.

THE SPREAD OF JUDAISM

You've read that the Assyrian army swept in to conquer Israel in 722 B.C.E. In 586 B.C.E., the Chaldean king Nebuchadnezzar conquered Judah, leaving the Temple in ruins. The people of Judah were forcibly moved to the city of Babylon, an event known as the Babylonian Exile. The word **exile** refers to a forced removal from one's homeland. The Babylonian Exile lasted until 538 B.C.E.

During the years of the Babylonian Exile, the people of Judah recorded the main part of the Hebrew Bible. The name Jew literally means a member of the nation of Judah, but it came to refer to all Hebrews.

The Jews became **refugees**, or people forced to leave their homeland because of wars, persecution, or natural disasters. The loss of their homeland led to changes in how the Jewish people practiced their religion. Unable to worship at the Temple, they built the first **synagogues**, or Jewish houses of worship. Jewish religious teachers, called rabbis, led worship services in the synagogues, a practice that continues today.

The Babylonian Exile strengthened the identity of the Jewish people and made it clear that Judaism could survive outside its birthplace. It marked the beginning of the **Diaspora**, the migration of Jews to locations far from their homeland. Over the following centuries, Jewish people would live and practice their religion in places throughout the world.

HISTORICAL THINKING

1. **READING CHECK** Where and how did monotheism develop?

2. **IDENTIFY** What ethical principles are emphasized in the Torah?

3. **IDENTIFY MAIN IDEAS AND DETAILS** How did Judaism influence other major world religions?

4. **MAKE CONNECTIONS** Give two examples of modern laws that are reflected in the Ten Commandments.

Tales Told by Mosaics

Determined to find out more about the roots of the Jewish people, archaeologists and other experts turn over every stone, so to speak. Every June, Professor Jodi Magness (left) journeys to an ancient site in Huqoq, Israel, to explore the ruins of a synagogue that dates from the fifth century, when the land was under the rule of the Roman Empire. Within these ancient ruins, Magness and her colleagues have discovered an amazing series of mosaics, artworks created using pieces of stone. Most art in synagogues illustrates biblical stories, but one mosaic discovered by Magness and her team includes pictures of elephants that Magness says represents "the first time a non-biblical story [is] depicted in an ancient synagogue."

Examining the mosaics helps Magness determine when the synagogue itself was constructed. She thinks the mosaic with the elephants might even depict a visit of the conqueror Alexander the Great to Jerusalem.

This mosaic of an elephant comes from an ancient synagogue in Huqoq, Israel.

BACKGROUND FOR THE TEACHER

Ark of the Covenant According to Jewish and Christian tradition, the tablets containing the Ten Commandments given to Moses by God were stored in a gold-plated wooden box, known as the Ark of the Covenant. The Ark was first housed in the Temple of Jerusalem and then carried during the Exodus by priests. After returning to Canaan, the Israelites often carried the Ark into battle. Tradition holds that it was eventually housed in Solomon's Temple in Jerusalem but then disappeared sometime before the destruction of Jerusalem by the Chaldeans. No one knows the fate of the Ark, but there are several theories. One is that it is held by a church in Ethiopia, which claims to house the Ark but does not allow its examination for authenticity. Another is that the Ark was hidden below the First Temple in Jerusalem before the sacking of the city and now cannot be dug up because the site of the temple is also sacred to Islam as the Dome of the Rock. Finally, an archaeologist claims to have dug up the Ark at the site believed to be where Jesus was crucified, but no proof to his claim has ever been provided. The search for the Ark of the Covenant has been the subject of movies, including *Raiders of the Lost Ark*.

TEACH

GUIDED DISCUSSION

3. **Compare and Contrast** What similarities can be found in Judaism, Christianity, and Islam? *(belief in one God, common early stories in the principal religious texts, common ethical principles)*

4. **Analyze Cause and Effect** How did conquest lead to the Jewish Diaspora? *(Possible response: The kingdom of Israel was conquered by the Assyrians, and Judah was conquered by the Chaldeans. Jews were forced to leave their homeland and became refugees who took their religion to other parts of the world.)*

EVALUATE

Direct students' attention to the National Geographic Explorer feature on Jodi Magness. Have them read the feature and examine the mosaic. Then lead a class discussion on what ancient works of art can tell scholars about a civilization. **ASK:** What might artworks be able to tell us that written works cannot? *(Possible responses: They can visually show how the people of the time viewed their world and can indicate what people believed to be significant. As many people in the past could not write, artworks might reflect more varied perspectives than written works.)*

ACTIVE OPTIONS

On Your Feet: Roundtable on Refugees Arrange students in groups of four to discuss the following question: What advice would you give to refugees on how to preserve cultural traditions, based on the story of the Jews? Provide each group with a sheet of paper. The first student in each group writes an answer, reads it aloud, and passes the paper clockwise to the next student. Each student in the group adds at least one answer. Students circulate the paper around the table until they run out of ideas. Call on volunteers from each group to share their ideas.

NG Learning Framework: Compare World Religions
SKILL Collaboration
KNOWLEDGE Our Human Story

Tell students to work in small groups to compare the beliefs of Jews, Christians, and Muslims. Have students conduct online research and interview members of each religion in their community, if possible. Ask students to consider each group's main religious beliefs, major social concerns, public actions, and visions for the future. In addition, have them share similarities between the groups. Invite students to summarize their findings in a written report, chart, or infographic. Have groups share their work with the class.

HISTORICAL THINKING

ANSWERS

1. Monotheism developed in the Levant of the eastern Mediterranean, the homeland of the ancient Hebrews, who are the first people known to have believed in one God. According to the Hebrew Bible, a Mesopotamian shepherd named Abraham was the first person to worship one God.

2. Some scholars believe that the Torah's emphasis on treating all with respect and fairness and caring for the less fortunate exemplifies the later ethical ideas of human rights to which all people are entitled.

3. The belief in monotheism is central to both Christianity and Islam. In addition, the writings in the Hebrew Bible are the same ones that make up the Old Testament of the Christian Bible. Certain stories from the Hebrew Bible and the Christian Bible also appear in the Quran.

4. Possible response: Modern laws do not allow people to steal or murder.

3.4 Comparing Flood Narratives

You may have heard or read the story of Noah and the great flood that appears in Genesis, the first book of the Hebrew Bible. But you may not know that the Hebrew Bible is not the only ancient book that tells a story about a great flood. Like the Hebrew Bible, the *Epic of Gilgamesh* describes a monstrous flood that covers all the land. Striking similarities in the two versions of the flood story suggest that the Hebrew Bible drew on the oral traditions of Mesopotamia.

Other peoples also tell stories of great floods. The early Aztec people, who lived in what is now Mexico, describe a devastating flood that lasted 55 years. There are also stories and legends about a great flood from ancient India, China, and Scandinavia.

The various accounts of floods differ most notably in their depictions of the divine powers that shaped the world. In the *Epic of Gilgamesh*, multiple gods squabble. In the Bible, there is only one God, who sends the flood to punish humanity. In the story from India, the flood is a natural phenomenon and a god saves humanity.

Despite differences among these three accounts, the people who composed them had the same purpose in writing them—to explain how the world came to be as it is and why.

CRITICAL VIEWING

The first scene in this painting depicts Noah supervising the building of the ark. The second portrays God telling Noah to board the ark with his family and animals to be saved. How does the painting convey the importance of saving animals as well as people?

DOCUMENT ONE

Primary Source: Epic Poem
from the *Epic of Gilgamesh* translated by Benjamin R. Foster, 2001

The most complete version of the *Epic of Gilgamesh* was written in 700 B.C.E., but it drew on written versions dating back to at least 2100 B.C.E. and even earlier oral traditions. According to the epic, multiple gods squabble and the god Enki warns a man named Utanapishtim that the storm god Enlil is sending the flood to destroy his home city.

CONSTRUCTED RESPONSE What image is created by the use of the words *deluge, leveled,* and *tempest?*

Six days, and seven nights

The wind continued, the deluge and windstorm leveled the land.

When the seventh day arrived,

The windstorm and deluge left off their battle,

Which had struggled . . .

The sea grew calm, the tempest stilled, the deluge ceased.

DOCUMENT TWO

Primary Source: Sacred Text
from the *Jewish Publication Society Hebrew Bible,* 1917

Like the *Epic of Gilgamesh,* the Hebrew Bible had a long history of oral transmission before being recorded in its current version around 500 B.C.E. Some of its earliest content may have circulated orally as early as 1200 B.C.E., when the ancient Hebrews first settled what is now modern Israel. According to the Bible, God decides to punish all of humanity except for a man named Noah and his family.

CONSTRUCTED RESPONSE How is the portrayal of the flood in this excerpt different from the description in the *Epic of Gilgamesh?*

17 And the flood was forty days upon the earth; and the waters increased, and bore up the ark [a ship], and it was lifted up above the earth.

18 And the waters prevailed, and increased greatly upon the earth; and the ark went upon the face of the waters.

19 And the waters prevailed exceedingly upon the earth; and all the high mountains that were under the whole heaven were covered.

20 Fifteen cubits upward did the waters prevail; and the mountains were covered.

DOCUMENT THREE

Primary Source: Epic Poem
from *The Mahabharata of Krishna-Dwaipayana Vyasa* translated by Kisari Mohan Ganguli, 1883–1896

The *Mahabharata* is an epic poem of ancient India that provides information on the development of Hinduism and on Hindu moral law. Historians believe that the complete text was written down in 400 B.C.E. but existed in oral form much earlier. According to the flood story in the Mahabharata, the god Vishnu, in the form of a fish, warns a man named Manu about an impending flood and tells him how to save himself.

CONSTRUCTED RESPONSE How is this flood narrative similar to the one in the Hebrew Bible?

And there was water everywhere and the waters covered the heaven and the firmament also. And . . . when the world was thus flooded, none but Manu . . . and the fish could be seen. And . . . the fish diligently dragged the boat through the flood for many a long year and then, . . . it towed the vessel towards the highest peak of the Himavat [Himalaya]. And . . . the fish then told those on the vessel to tie it to the peak of the Himavat.

SYNTHESIZE & WRITE

1. **REVIEW** Review what you have learned about flood narratives of various cultures.

2. **RECALL** On your own paper, make a list of the similarities and differences among the three excerpts you have read.

3. **CONSTRUCT** Construct a topic sentence that answers the following question: Based on the excerpts, what are the similarities and differences among the three flood stories?

4. **WRITE** Using evidence from this chapter and the documents, write an informative paragraph that supports the topic sentence you wrote in Step 3.

PLAN: 2-PAGE LESSON

OBJECTIVE

Synthesize information from three primary source documents of flood narratives from various cultures.

CRITICAL THINKING SKILLS FOR LESSON 3.4

- Synthesize
- Make Inferences
- Analyze Point of View
- Evaluate

HISTORICAL THINKING FOR CHAPTER 2

How are people today linked to the first civilizations?

Accounts of the great flood are distinguished by explanations of how long the flood lasted and why the flood happened. The three primary sources in Lesson 3.4 link people today with the first civilizations that had stories of a great flood that happened long ago.

BACKGROUND FOR THE TEACHER

Sea Fossils Found on Mountaintops The quest by Christians, Jews, and Muslims to find the ark that belonged to the Biblical personage Noah has been ongoing for many years. The quest started as explorers began to climb to the top mountain peaks around the world. The Himalaya are a chain of mountain ranges located north of India that stretch across the borders of China, Bhutan, Nepal, and Pakistan.

Although the Himalaya are now more than 26,000 feet (8,000 m) above sea level, fossils of marine animals, plants, and coral reef remnants have been found in large numbers in Nepal and other locations within the mountain range. Experts believe that the discovery of sea fossils and the evidence of sedimentary rock layers, which are typical in seabeds, provide proof that the Himalaya were at one time under water.

The same can be said about Turkey's Mount Ararat, which is where explorers claim to have found the remains of Noah's Ark beneath snow and volcanic debris. However, despite various claims, there is no scientific evidence at this time that supports that the wooden structure found in Turkey is indeed a wooden boat that once belonged to Noah.

INTRODUCE & ENGAGE

PREPARE FOR THE DOCUMENT-BASED QUESTION

Before students start on the activity, briefly preview the three documents. Remind students that a constructed response requires full explanations in complete sentences. Emphasize that students should use what they have learned about the great floods in addition to the information in the documents.

TEACH

GUIDED DISCUSSION

1. **Make Inferences** Based on the documents and the information about them, why do you think so many cultures have accounts of a great flood? *(Possible responses: Perhaps there was a great flood that happened on Earth, so different cultures have written about the event. OR The stories help to explain how the world came to be as it is and give each culture a way to structure their beliefs.)*

2. **Analyze Point of View** How would you describe the beliefs that ancient societies held about the great flood? *(Answers will vary. Students' answers should have analysis from all three accounts.)*

EVALUATE

After students have completed the Synthesize & Write activity, allow time for them to exchange paragraphs and read and comment on the work of their peers. Establish guidelines for comments prior to the activity so that feedback is constructive and encouraging in nature. Comments should focus on the most significant parts that address the purpose of the activity and the audience.

ACTIVE OPTION

On Your Feet: Jigsaw Strategy Organize students into "expert" groups and assign each group one of the primary source documents to analyze, and to summarize its main ideas in their own words. Then regroup students into new groups so that each new group has at least one member from each expert group. Students in the new groups take turns sharing the summaries from their expert groups.

DIFFERENTIATE

ENGLISH LANGUAGE LEARNERS

Summarize Place students at **Beginning** and **Intermediate** proficiencies in pairs and assign each pair a document. Instruct them to read the document together and then write a few sentences to summarize it. When all pairs are finished, call on them to read their summaries aloud in the order in which the material appears to provide an overview of the entire lesson.

GIFTED & TALENTED

Analyze Literature Tell students to find a flood story from a different culture. They might choose from among the following: Aztec, ancient Indian, Chinese, or Scandinavian. Have students prepare a graphic organizer or poster that displays the important elements of their story and compares and contrasts their story with the stories in the text. Have students present their visuals to the class. Afterwards, as a class, discuss the similarities and differences between the stories.

SYNTHESIZE & WRITE

ANSWERS

1. Answers will vary.

2. Answers will vary, but students should note the similarity of inundation and the differences in length of time, the presence of vessels, and fish as active agents.

3. Possible response: The three stories all describe catastrophic flooding, but they differ in their details.

4. Answers will vary. Students' paragraphs should include their topic sentence from Step 3 and provide several details from the documents to support the topic sentence.

CONSTRUCTED RESPONSE

Document One: These words create the image of a massive flood and storm that caused great devastation.

Document Two: The flood lasts much longer—40 days—and the account includes a description of an ark.

Document Three: It also includes a description of a vessel.

CRITICAL VIEWING Answers will vary. Possible response: God is guiding the animals and birds onto the ark after the people have already boarded it. There are many more animals than people. The painting shows the importance of saving the animals because God is the one making sure the animals get safely on the ark.

2 REVIEW

VOCABULARY

Match each vocabulary word with its definition.

1. silt
2. technology
3. irrigation
4. ziggurat
5. empire
6. cuneiform
7. pharaoh
8. pyramid
9. monotheism
10. covenant

a. human-made systems of transporting
b. an ancient Egyptian king
c. the belief in one God
d. Mesopotamian writing
e. an Egyptian tomb
f. a religious agreement
g. fertile soil
h. a group of nations or peoples
i. the practical application of knowledge
j. a Sumerian religious structure

READING STRATEGY
DRAW CONCLUSIONS

When you draw conclusions, you make a judgment based on what you have read. Use a chart like this one to draw a conclusion about the importance of rivers to early civilizations. Then answer the question that follows.

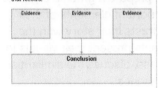

Evidence Evidence Evidence

Conclusion

11. Based on your conclusion, explain why the Babylonian and Egyptian empires were so much stronger than the Israelite kingdoms of the eastern Mediterranean.

MAIN IDEAS

Answer the following questions. Support your answers with evidence from the chapter.

12. How are aspects of the culture of ancient Mesopotamia reflected in the *Epic of Gilgamesh*? LESSON 1.1

13. How did the ancient Sumerians use cuneiform? LESSON 1.2

14. What insight into the roles and status of women can be gained from Hammurabi's Code? LESSON 1.3

15. How did the ancient Egyptians excel in mathematics, science, and technology? LESSON 2.1

16. Why did ancient Egyptians devote so much time, wealth, and energy to building pyramids? LESSON 2.2

17. Why did the pharaohs of the New Kingdom set out to conquer other lands? LESSON 2.3

18. Why were the Assyrians particularly brutal in their warfare? LESSON 3.1

19. What challenges did the Israelites face as they developed their society? LESSON 3.3

HISTORICAL THINKING

Answer the following questions. Support your answers with evidence from the chapter.

20. MAKE INFERENCES How did physical features influence the development of civilization in Mesopotamia?

21. MAKE GENERALIZATIONS What aspects of ancient Egyptian culture are reflected in its art and architecture?

22. SYNTHESIZE What methods have archaeologists used to analyze evidence from early civilizations in Southwest Asia and Egypt?

23. EVALUATE Which achievement of ancient peoples do you think had the greatest impact on the world? Explain your answer.

24. FORM AND SUPPORT OPINIONS What artistic ideal or visual principle do you think the ancient Egyptian pyramids best demonstrate? Explain your answer.

INTERPRET MAPS

Study the map below, which shows the expansion of Egypt during the New Kingdom. Then answer the questions that follow.

Expansion of Ancient Egypt, 2575 B.C.E.–1070 B.C.E.

25. Based on the map, how did physical features of the region influence the development of Egyptian civilization?

26. Based on the map, what resource was controlled by Kush? How do you think this situation might have affected interactions between Egypt and Kush?

ANALYZE SOURCES

Preparing for the afterlife was so important to the ancient Egyptians that they created a book about it. Compiled in the 1500s B.C.E. but drawing on materials dating back to 2400 B.C.E., the *Book of the Dead* contains detailed instructions for what the deceased should say upon meeting Osiris, the god of the underworld, to gain entry to the afterlife.

I have not committed evil against men.
I have not mistreated cattle.
I have not committed sin in the place of truth [that is, a temple or burial ground]. . . .
I have not blasphemed a god. . . .
I have not made (anyone) sick.
I have not made (anyone) weep.
I have not killed. . . .
I have not held up water in its season [that is, denied floodwaters to others].
I have not built a dam against running water. . . .

27. What does this passage reveal about the values and morals of the ancient Egyptians?

CONNECT TO YOUR LIFE

28. INFORMATIVE Review what you have learned about cuneiform and hieroglyphics. Then think about the kinds of images and symbols you use today to communicate, including the alphabet, emojis, memes, GIFs, and other media. Write an essay describing the similarities and differences among several of these forms of communication.

TIPS

* Review what you have read about cuneiform and hieroglyphics.

* Make a table listing the characteristics of one or two forms of modern communication.

* Draft your essay, describing the forms of communication and identifying their similarities and differences.

* Provide a conclusion that supports the information presented.

VOCABULARY ANSWERS

1. g
2. i
3. a
4. j
5. h
6. d
7. b
8. e
9. c
10. f

READING STRATEGY ANSWERS

Evidence	Evidence	Evidence
Possible response: The first civilization formed between two rivers.	Possible response: People of the Sahel settled along the Nile when the Sahel turned to desert.	Possible response: The Hebrews migrated to Egypt, along the Nile, due to drought.

Conclusion
Rivers allowed early civilizations to form and thrive.

11. Answers will vary, but students should note that the Israelite kingdoms had no major rivers to provide the water, fertile bottomland, and transportation that were available to the peoples of the Mesopotamian and Nile regions.

MAIN IDEAS ANSWERS

12. The epic depicts a friendship between an urban ruler and a man who lives in the forest, thus showing that Mesopotamians were aware of these two ways of living. It also portrays a ruler who is half god and the benefits of living in a complex society.

13. The Sumerians used cuneiform to create religious and economic records.

14. Hammurabi's Code reveals that Babylonian women could own property and initiate divorces, thus showing they had more status than women in other cultures of the time.

15. The ancient Egyptians used mathematical and engineering skills to build pyramids. The need for exact measurements caused them to formulate some of the key principles of geometry, and they developed tools for measuring objects and time.

16. The ancient Egyptians believed that pyramids were needed to help ensure safe passage of their deceased pharaohs into the afterlife.

17. The pharaohs of the New Kingdom began a path of conquest to strengthen their kingdom, avoid conquest by others, and control trade routes.

18. Because the Assyrian ruler saw himself as the representative of the gods, he believed it was his duty to convince foreign rulers to submit to him and his deities voluntarily. Those who resisted were cruelly punished to persuade others to submit voluntarily.

19. Challenges the Israelites experienced included surviving in their dry land, enslavement in Egypt, a long journey back to Canaan, attacks by enemies, internal divisions, and exile.

HISTORICAL THINKING ANSWERS

20. Possible response: A dry climate and land located between two rivers that flooded unpredictably led the people of Mesopotamia to develop irrigation systems, build dikes, and make bronze tools in order to grow crops more reliably.

21. Possible response: The Egyptian belief in the afterlife and the belief in many gods and goddesses are reflected in Egyptian art and architecture. Pyramids were elaborate tombs filled with objects for the pharaoh's afterlife. The Egyptian style in dress and the importance of certain animals are also reflected in the art.

22. Archaeologists use visual examination of archaeological sites and artifacts, computer science, 3-D data surveys, writings, and data collected by video cameras, scanners, laser beams, and drones to analyze evidence from early civilizations in Southwest Asia and Egypt.

23. Possible response: Writing had the greatest impact on the world because it allowed ancient peoples to keep permanent records and tell their history and achievements in their own words. It also allowed people to express complex ideas and share information, opinions, and demands with other societies. In addition, it provided historians with an important means of learning about the past.

24. Possible response: I believe the ancient Egyptian pyramids reflect the artistic ideal of the impact of simple, clean lines. Each of the three sides of a pyramid forms a triangle.

INTERPRET MAPS ANSWERS

25. The development of ancient Egypt followed the course of the Nile at first and then the coastline of the eastern Mediterranean Sea. As a result, the shape of ancient Egypt was elongated and narrow because settlements stayed close to the Nile.

26. Possible response: The Kingdom of Kush had much gold. The availability of gold might have encouraged trade between Egypt and Kush. It might have made Kush wealthier than Egypt and given Kush power over Egypt at times. It also may have made Egypt want to gain control of Kush.

ANALYZE SOURCES ANSWER

27. The passage shows that agriculture, irrigation, the afterlife, and living a righteous life were important to the ancient Egyptians.

CONNECT TO YOUR LIFE ANSWER

28. Students' essays should identify similarities and differences between cuneiform, hieroglyphics, and one or two forms of communication used today. For example, students might note that various symbols stand for objects, ideas, or sounds in the past, while many alphabets today do not include symbols, ideas, or objects.

UNIT 1 RESOURCES

UNIT INTRODUCTION

UNIT TIME LINE

UNIT MAP online

THE GLOBAL PERSPECTIVE: No Walls, No Borders: Nomads online

- National Geographic Explorers: Chris Bashinelli and Albert Lin
- On Your Feet: Inside-Outside Circle

| NG Learning Framework
| Discuss Challenges of Nomadic Herding

UNIT WRAP-UP

National Geographic Magazine Adapted Article

- "Cities of Silence (Thoughts on the Harappan Culture)"

Unit 1 Inquiry: Design a Civilization-Building Game

Unit 1 Formal Assessment

Ancient Worlds
Neolithic Era–500 C.E.

CRITICAL VIEWING These rock engravings of fighting cats at the Wadi Mathendous archaeological site in Libya are believed to be at least 12,000 years old. Why do you think people created these carvings?

CHAPTER 3 RESOURCES

Available in the Teacher eEdition

TEACHER RESOURCES & ASSESSMENT

Reading and Note-Taking

Vocabulary Practice

Social Studies Skills Lessons

- Reading: Determine Chronology
- Writing: Explanatory

Formal Assessment

- Chapter 3 Pretest
- Chapter 3 Tests A & B
- Section Quizzes

Chapter 3 Answer Key

Cognero®

3 Ancient South Asia and China
2600 B.C.E.–207 B.C.E.

HISTORICAL THINKING How did religious and philosophical systems support societies in ancient India and China?

SECTION 1 Foundations of Hindu Societies
SECTION 2 The Rise of Buddhism
SECTION 3 Early Dynasties of China
SECTION 4 China's First Empire

CRITICAL VIEWING Built under the rule of the Shang-di, the Great Wall defined an empire. What details in the photo show how wall would have protected China from invaders?

STUDENT DIGITAL RESOURCES

Available in the Student eEdition

- **eEdition** (English)
- **Handbooks**
- **National Geographic Atlas**
- **History Notebook**
- **Biographies**
- **Literature Analysis**

STRATEGY ❶

Make a List

Write on the board: "Five Things I Know About" and then insert the topic of the lesson. Ask students to copy what you have written on a sheet of paper. As they read the lesson, prompt students to write at least five sentences under the heading, including key people and events. Invite volunteers to share their sentences with the class.

Use with All Lessons

STRATEGY ❷

Focus on Main Ideas

Tell students to locate the Main Idea statement at the beginning of each lesson. Explain that these statements summarize the important ideas of the lessons and will help them focus on what matters most in the text.

Use with All Lessons *Throughout the chapter, help students set a purpose for reading by using the Main Idea statements.*

STRATEGY ❸

Sequence Events

To build understanding of a lesson, direct students to note critical events in a Sequence Chain, such as the one shown, including the date and a brief summary of each event. Encourage students to add circles and arrows as necessary to show the causes and effects of historical events and how they relate to each other.

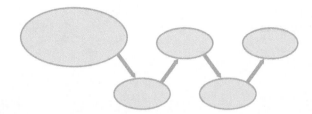

Use with All Lessons

STRATEGY ❶

Sequence Events

Write the main events of a lesson on index cards. There should be one event on each index card. Allow the student to work with another student or a teacher aide to read the section. Then have the student place the cards listing the events in the order that they occurred. Use the following main events for Lesson 2.3:

- In 320 B.C.E., Chandragupta Maurya conquered surrounding kingdoms, establishing the first great Indian empire.
- Chandragupta's grandson, Ashoka, started his reign as a brutal ruler.
- After a violent battle, Ashoka felt deep remorse, renounced war, and converted to Buddhism.
- Ashoka allowed religious freedom and contributed money for temples and hospitals open to all.
- Although the Maurya Empire broke apart, Ashoka's legacy continued through the practice of Buddhism.

Use with All Lessons

STRATEGY ❷

Provide Alternative Ways of Reporting

Instead of a written report, allow students with disabilities to report their knowledge in other ways. For example, students who are comfortable communicating orally could give an oral presentation instead of a written report. Students who struggle with writing and speaking could give a photographic essay on a chapter topic, such as where today's common spices first came from and how far people in the past traveled to get them.

Use with All Lessons

STRATEGY ❶

Pronounce Words

Before reading, preview the lesson vocabulary terms with students at **All Proficiencies**. Say each word slowly, and have students repeat, noting the pronunciation and syllable stress. Suggest students make word cards for each word, writing definitions and pronunciation hints for themselves.

Use with All Lessons

STRATEGY ❷
Develop Vocabulary

Work with students at each level to develop understanding of the lesson vocabulary words. Write the words and keep them displayed throughout the chapter, adding terms for each new lesson. Discuss each term as it comes up during reading.

- **Beginning** Use vocabulary words in yes/no questions, such as: Do **nomads** stay in one place? *(no)* Do **nomads** move from place to place? *(yes)* Does an **ascetic** choose to be poor? *(yes)* Or use vocabulary words in either/or questions, such as: Are **monsoons** strong or mild winds? *(strong)* In a **meritocracy**, are people chosen based on achievements or family background? *(achievements)*
- **Intermediate** Use sentence frames with one blank, such as: **Nomads** _____ from place to place. *(migrate/move)* An **ascetic** chooses to be _____. *(poor)* **Monsoons** are _____ winds. *(strong)*
- **Advanced** Use sentence frames with two blanks, such as: An **ascetic** _____ to be _____. *(chooses, poor)* In a **meritocracy**, people are chosen based on _____ instead of _____. *(achievements, family)*

Use with All Lessons

STRATEGY ❸
Review Sequence Words

To help students put events from the lessons in chronological order, or sequence, write these sequence words on the board: *first, second, next, then, finally, before, after, earlier, later.* Direct students at the **Beginning** and **Intermediate** levels to work together to write a series of sentences that explains what happens in each lesson. Encourage them to use a variety of sequence words and to vary sentence structure.

Use with All Lessons

STRATEGY ❶
Make a Spice Cookbook

Tell students, working in pairs, to choose one spice from the Spice Islands and conduct online research to learn how valuable it was in the past and how far people went to get it. Then have them find several recipes that use the spice. Instruct them to create a cookbook that teaches about the spice and includes the recipes. Encourage

students to share their cookbooks on a school website. Remind them to give credit to their sources.

Use with Lesson 2.4

STRATEGY ❷
Create a Photo Essay

Prompt students to research one of Shi Huangdi's enormous projects, the Great Wall or the army of terra-cotta warriors guarding his tomb. Encourage them to find visuals as well as compelling facts to present in a photo essay that conveys how amazing the project was when it was first built and still is today. Invite students to share their photo essays with the class.

Use with Lesson 4.1

STRATEGY ❶
Study Historic Travels

Direct students to conduct online research about early Indian Ocean trade. Ask how these ancient seafaring merchants were capable of traveling across the Indian Ocean. Tell students to research the merchants' boats and navigation tools, and how they used the winds to travel more quickly and safely. Allow students to decide the best way to share the information with the class.

Use with Lesson 2.4

STRATEGY ❷
Research a Religion or Philosophy

Ask students to choose one of the religions or philosophies presented in the chapter: Hinduism, Buddhism, Confucianism, or Daoism. Tell them to conduct online research to learn more about this religion or philosophy. Ask how the belief system affected early followers and how it is practiced today. Direct students to write an informative essay using what they learned.

Use with Lessons 1.2, 2.1, and 3.3

Ancient South Asia and China

2600 B.C.E.–207 B.C.E.

HISTORICAL THINKING How did religious and philosophical systems support societies in ancient India and China?

CRITICAL VIEWING
Built under the rule of Shi Huangdi, the Great Wall defined his empire. What details in the photo show how the wall would have protected China from invaders?

INTRODUCE THE PHOTOGRAPH

THE GREAT WALL OF CHINA

Tell students to examine the photograph of the Great Wall of China that appears at the beginning of the chapter. Explain to students that the Great Wall is so massive that it can even be seen by astronauts in outer space. **ASK:** How might the terrain have challenged workers during the construction of the Great Wall? *(Possible response: It would have been difficult to transport the stone and supplies up the rugged mountains. It also might have been difficult to support the wall on sloped terrain.)* Shi Huangdi, the first emperor of China, ordered the expansion and fortification of the Great Wall, which would protect China for many centuries. Shi Huangdi also unified and brought order to China through a philosophy that emphasized strong government. Tell students that this chapter will focus on how religion and philosophy shaped life in early China and ancient India.

SHARE BACKGROUND

Construction and maintenance of the Great Wall of China began in the first millennium B.C.E. and continues today. Initially, several kingdoms in the northern part of China built fortifications out of soil and stones. Passes were built into the wall along major trade routes to allow merchants to pass into and out of China. These passes had ramps for merchants' horses to cross over and ladders for humans to climb. Signal towers were built at strategic locations along the wall and were used to send fire or smoke signals, raise banners, or fire guns for military communication. The Great Wall averages about 20 feet in width and measures about 23–26 feet high in most sections.

CRITICAL VIEWING Answers will vary. Possible response: The height and width of the wall would be difficult for invaders to cross. Also, invaders would be discouraged by the fortified walls and rugged mountains and by soldiers who could fire weapons at them from openings in the Great Wall.

HISTORICAL THINKING QUESTION

How did religious and philosophical systems support societies in ancient India and China?

Four Corners: Preview Content This activity will help students preview and discuss the topics covered in the chapter. For each section of the chapter, provide a brief description and question, such as the ones shown below, and designate each of four corners as being "home" to one of the sections. Divide the class into four groups and direct each group to go to one of the corners and discuss the topic of the section for a short time. Then tell each group to share important details from their discussion with the class.

Group 1 Section 1 is about the first civilizations that rose along the banks of the Indus River. **ASK:** How can religious texts be used as communication tools between different generations?

Group 2 Section 2 is about the rise of Buddhism in India. **ASK:** How do leadership styles affect society?

Group 3 Section 3 is about early Chinese dynasties. **ASK:** How do philosophy and spirituality affect the behavior of people?

Group 4 Section 4 is about China's first empire. **ASK:** How can a civilization gain power, influence, and control over vast regions?

KEY DATES FOR CHAPTER 3

7000 B.C.E.	Agriculture begins along the Indus River.
1900 B.C.E.	Harappan society declines.
c. 1600 B.C.E.	The Shang dynasty begins.
1045 B.C.E.	The Shang dynasty is overthrown and the Zhou dynasty takes over.
c. 1000 B.C.E.	Sanskrit is written down.
551 B.C.E.	Confucius is born.
c. 500 B.C.E.	The first money circulates in China.
481–221 B.C.E.	The Warring States Period occurs.
c. 400s B.C.E.	Siddharta Gautama initiates Buddhism.
320 B.C.E.	Chandragupta conquers Pataliputra.
268 B.C.E.	Ashoka takes control of the Mauyra Empire.
221 B.C.E.	The Qin dynasty begins.
100 C.E.	Seafaring merchants use wind to carry their vessels.

INTRODUCE THE READING STRATEGY

DETERMINE CHRONOLOGY

Explain to students that determining the chronology of events can help them more deeply understand cause and effect relationships and how major historical events affect people's lives. Go to the Chapter Review and preview the time line with students. As they read the chapter, have students fill the time line with dates of events pertinent to the early history of India and China.

INTRODUCE CHAPTER VOCABULARY

KEY VOCABULARY

SECTION 1

caste system	dharma	karma
nomad	reincarnation	Sanskrit
varna	Vedic	

SECTION 2

ascetic	cultural diffusion	enlightenment
monsoon	nirvana	

SECTION 3

ancestor worship	dynastic cycle	filial piety
loess	Mandate of Heaven	oracle bone

SECTION 4

bureaucracy	meritocracy

DEFINITION CHART

As they read the chapter, encourage students to complete a Definition Chart for Key Vocabulary terms. Instruct students to list the Key Vocabulary terms in the first column of the chart. They should add each term's definition in the center column as they encounter the term in the chapter and then restate the definition in their own words in the third column. Model an example on the board, using the graphic organizer shown.

Word	Definition	In My Own Words
filial piety	respect for one's parents	doing what one's parents request, even when they are not present

Cities Along the Indus

Until the early 20th century, we knew little about the ancient cities that developed around the Indus River. That changed when archaeologists went searching for the source of a tiny artifact, a stone seal, and discovered a lost civilization.

CIVILIZATION FORMS AROUND RIVERS

The South Asian landmass is often called the Indian subcontinent and can be divided into three geographic regions. The region to the north is largely uninhabited due to the **Himalaya**, the tallest mountains in the world. In the plains, the **Indus River** flows from the Himalaya to the west, where it empties into the Arabian Sea. The **Ganges** (GAN-geez) **River** flows from the Himalaya to the east and empties into the Bay of Bengal. These river valleys make up the most densely populated region of the subcontinent. The southern peninsula isn't

as heavily populated and contains the large Deccan Plateau, a high area with a drier climate.

Like the river valleys of the Tigris and Euphrates rivers in Mesopotamia and the Nile in Egypt, the river valleys of the Indian subcontinent provided water and fertile soil—ideal conditions for agriculture. Sometime around 7000 B.C.E., people of this area began planting wheat, barley, and jujube dates. People domesticated elephants, sheep, and goats and began to build large settlements. By about 2600 B.C.E., cities emerged in the Indus River Valley.

The "Great Bath" at the Indus River Valley city of Mohenjo-Daro shows the Harappan society's sophisticated use of a grid to plan and build a public works structure. Located in present-day Pakistan, these ancient ruins are a UNESCO World Heritage Site.

THE RISE AND FALL OF THE HARAPPAN CIVILIZATION

Around the time that Egyptians were building pyramids, the people of the Indus Valley were building their first cities. At its height, the Indus Valley civilization extended over a large area that included parts of present-day Pakistan, India, and Afghanistan. Known today as the **Harappan civilization**, this complex society used a grid for planning large cities and built them with mud bricks of standardized sizes. The cities had open plazas, drainage systems, and avenues several yards wide.

Archaeological excavations of the city of Harappa reveal that it had an area of 380 acres (or 288 football fields) and a population of between 40,000 and 80,000. Archaeologists hoped to find temples or palaces that would help them understand who ruled Harappan society, such as a king or pharaoh. Instead, they found that homes were similar in style. Cities were divided into distinct communities where similar goods have been found. This discovery has led historians to believe that neighborhoods were formed based on people's various occupations.

Unlike other cities of the ancient world, **Mohenjo-Daro** (moh-HEHN-joh DAHR-oh), the second largest Indus Valley settlement, provided drinking water, in-home plumbing, and sewer drains to all its residents, not just a privileged few.

Beginning in 1900 B.C.E., the large urban communities of Harappan society declined. After a long period with little rainfall, Indus River tributaries began to change course or dry up. Many historians believe that change in climate and rainfall were major factors in the decline. They have no written evidence because the Harappan script has not been deciphered. If we ever learn how to read Harappan writing, we will learn much more about this fascinating civilization.

Indus River Valley Civilization

Extent of the Indus Valley Civilization

0 200 400 Miles
0 200 400 Kilometers

INDO-ARYAN MIGRATIONS

Sometime between 1500 and 1000 B.C.E., several hundred years after the fall of Harappan society, **nomads** arrived in the Indus Valley. The nomads migrated from place to place, using horses and carts to travel across Eurasia. Although they later began to grow crops, early arrivals tended their herds full time.

These migrants called themselves *Aryan,* meaning "noble." Today, historians refer to these people as Indo-Aryans because they spoke **Sanskrit,** an Indo-European language that developed in Central Eurasia. Sanskrit has similar grammatical structures and contains many words related to Latin, Greek, Spanish, French, and English. For example, the word *mother* in English is *mater* in Latin and *matar* in Sanskrit. The Indo-Aryans brought Sanskrit into what is today northern India, but not into southern India or East Asia. The people who live in the region today speak a range of Indo-European languages descended from Sanskrit, including Hindi and Urdu. As you continue reading, you will learn more about Sanskrit's importance in the history and culture of India.

HISTORICAL THINKING

1. **READING CHECK** What important role did rivers play in the development of civilization in the Indus River Valley?

2. **DESCRIBE** What information about the Harappan civilization did archaeologists glean from artifacts and excavations?

3. **EXPLAIN** Why do linguists think Sanskrit is related to Latin and Spanish?

PLAN: 2-PAGE LESSON

OBJECTIVE

Explain how agriculture and the domestication of animals along the Indus River led to the development of sophisticated cities and trade among ancient societies.

CRITICAL THINKING SKILLS FOR LESSON 1.1

- Describe
- Explain
- Make Inferences
- Analyze Cause and Effect
- Interpret Maps

HISTORICAL THINKING FOR CHAPTER 3

How did religious and philosophical systems support societies in ancient India and China?

The river valleys of the Indian subcontinent provided ideal conditions for agriculture. Lesson 1.1 discusses how those conditions led people to settle in the area. The development and growth of civilization along the Indus River later led to the development of Hinduism and Buddhism.

BACKGROUND FOR THE TEACHER

Harappan Script To this day, no one has succeeded in translating Harappan script, although over 2,000 inscriptions with this language have been discovered. Some of these inscriptions contain only a single character, whereas others are up to 20 characters long. From these inscriptions, linguists have identified over 500 different Harappan characters, some of which seem to be several characters combined into one. Very few of the characters are repeated, making it more difficult to find patterns and decode the language. The characters are believed to represent a combination of ideas or words and sounds, and some numerical representations have been discovered. The language was typically written from right to left, although some instances of bidirectional writing have been found. Scholars have determined that the Harappan language, unlike Sanskrit, does not have Indo-European origins. Its closest contemporary cousins are the Dravidian language in southern India and the Brahui language in Pakistan.

Student eEdition online

Additional content for this lesson, including a video and a sidebar, is available online.

INTRODUCE & ENGAGE

DISCUSS THE IMPACT OF GEOGRAPHY ON CIVILIZATIONS

Explain to students that geographic characteristics allowed the civilizations they will read about to flourish. The Indus River produced fertile soil, good for agriculture, and as the river's size and course changed, so did the societies along its banks. Have students consider how geographic characteristics have affected places they are familiar with, such as their town or one they have visited. Ask volunteers to name present-day examples of how geography affects people.

TEACH

GUIDED DISCUSSION

1. **Make Inferences** What can you infer about social status in Harappan cities based on the fact that most homes were built in a similar style with similar amenities? *(Harappan society was fairly egalitarian, without extremely wealthy people living in fancy houses.)*

2. **Analyze Cause and Effect** Why did an agricultural society give way to a nomadic society in the Indus Valley? *(The river changed course or dried up, making farming more difficult.)*

INTERPRET MAPS

Tell students to examine the map. **ASK:** What separates India from the rest of Asia? *(the Himalaya mountains)* How do you think the mountains helped the Indus Valley civilizations? *(Possible response: by creating a barrier that intruders would not be able to cross)*

ACTIVE OPTIONS

On Your Feet: Jigsaw Strategy Display a list of common words in English. Organize students into four "expert" groups to cover the languages Latin, Greek, French, and Sanskrit. Ask each group to translate the words into their assigned language, using the Internet. Regroup students so that each group has at least one person from every expert group. Have students in the new groups compare the translations in the four languages.

Sanskrit	Greek	Latin	French	English
matar	meter	mater	mére	mother
pitar	pater	pater	pére	father
bhratar	phrater	frater	frére	brother
swasar	(unrelated)	soror	sœur	sister
ma	me	me	moi	me

NG Learning Framework: Compare and Contrast Indus Valley Cities
ATTITUDE Curiosity
KNOWLEDGE Our Human Story

Show the Mohenjo-Daro video (available in the Student eEdition). Direct students to research the Indus Valley cities Harappa and Mohenjo-Daro. Have students design a diagram to compare and contrast the two cities, focusing on cultural and economic similarities and differences.

DIFFERENTIATE

STRIVING READERS

Summarize Group students in pairs and tell them to read and summarize the text by writing at least three important details from the lesson. Have partners compare notes and combine information. Then instruct students to write a summary statement for the whole lesson.

GIFTED & TALENTED

Write a Blog Post Tell students to conduct online research to further understand the day-to-day lives of people living in either Harappa or Mohenjo-Daro. Then direct students to write a blog post about daily activities and family life from the perspective of a teenager living in one of the Indus Valley cities.

See the Chapter Planner for more strategies for differentiation.

HISTORICAL THINKING

ANSWERS

1. Civilization developed in the Indus River Valley because of the important presence of water from the Indus River and the Ganges. Along with fertile land for farming, the rivers enabled the development of a sophisticated water system, home plumbing, drinking water, and travel routes for trade.

2. Stone seals with ancient text suggested that the Indus Valley civilization had a written language and traded widely with others. Excavations revealed a complex society with sophisticated city planning.

3. It has similar grammatical structures and contains words related to Latin and Spanish.

Sanskrit and Epic Texts

The Indo-European language of Sanskrit helps us gain a clearer understanding of who the Indo-Aryans were, how they lived, and how their lives changed over time.

CRITICAL VIEWING This finely detailed illustration from an 18th-century edition of the Bhagavad Gita shows Krishna, an avatar of the Hindu deity Vishnu, serving as the chariot driver for Prince Arjuna, as they head into battle. What details in the illustration convey the action that is taking place?

SANSKRIT: THE LANGUAGE OF RELIGION AND SCHOLARSHIP

As you have read, the Indo-Aryans spoke Sanskrit. Although these early migrants had no written language, they passed the language down orally until it was eventually written down around 1000 B.C.E. In time, Sanskrit became India's language of religion and scholarship with texts covering subjects as diverse as poetry, law, and medicine.

Dating back to 1500 B.C.E., Indo-Aryan priests sang hymns that were passed from generation to generation. The collective hymns are called the Rig Veda, which is Sanskrit for "knowledge of the verses." This collection of 1,028 hymns describes numerous gods including Indra,

the king of the gods, as well as the god of war, the god of fire, the sun-god, the god of death, and many other minor gods. Elaborate rituals honoring these gods could last several days. The Rig Veda has given historians a glimpse into the **Vedic** (VAY-dihk) religion as well as the everyday life of the Indo-Aryans. (The word *Vedic* can be used to describe both the religion and the society of the Indo-Aryans.)

LITERATURE REFLECTS HISTORY AND CULTURE

The Rig Veda reflects the social roles of men, women, and children in Vedic society. One early hymn shows the variety of occupations in Vedic society, such as carpenters, doctors, and priests. Through other hymns,

historians have learned that women in Vedic society shared a similar status with men. Girls could go out unsupervised in public, and, with permission from their parents, were allowed to choose their own husbands. Women could even inherit property, and widows could remarry. Both girls and boys studied the hymns, yet only men were allowed to recite them in public ceremonies.

Later hymns, composed around 1000 B.C.E., reflect changes in Vedic society. By that time, the nomads had settled down and taken up farming. Roles in the society became more fixed, and women's freedoms declined. In addition, people were classified, or organized, into four social groups, called **varna**. Ranked in order of purity, priests, called Brahmins, were at the top. Next came warriors, then farmers and merchants, and finally dependent laborers. Though these categories were flexible in the beginning, much later they developed into a **caste system**, a rigid social hierarchy that dictated the kind of work people could do, who they could marry, and what they could eat.

Another collection of texts, the Upanishads (oo-PAH-nih-shahdz), was composed between 900 and 600 B.C.E. Challenging the old order, these texts introduced new ideas and gods. The Upanishads established the ideas of **reincarnation**, or the rebirth of the soul in different life cycles, and **karma**, the idea that people's actions in this life determine how they will be reborn in the next life. Unlike the gods in the Rig Veda, gods in the Upanishads intervened in human lives and sometimes took human form.

The composition of two great works of epic literature began at approximately the same time. Both were written in Sanskrit. One of these works, the *Mahabharata* (MAH-hah-BAHR-rah-tah), describes a long feud between two clans in more than 100,000 verses. One part of the *Mahabharata*, the Bhagavad Gita (BAH-gah-vuhd GEET-ah), was often read as an independent work. Composed in 200 C.E., it tells the story of a battle between two armies and reflects a conversation between Arjuna, a great warrior, and the god Krishna, who is disguised as a chariot driver. Krishna argues that each person should fulfill his **dharma**, or the way of righteous conduct in life. Krishna urges the warrior to devote himself fully to

worshiping him. Krishna's teachings later became fundamental ideas of **Hinduism**. (You will learn more about Hinduism in a later chapter.) The second of these two great epics, the *Ramayana* (rah-MAH-yah-nah), is the tale of the great king Rama who fights to rescue his wife Sita after she is abducted.

In the centuries following their composition, many versions of the *Mahabharata* and the *Ramayana* have appeared throughout South Asia and Southeast Asia. Today these epics have been made into television series popular in those regions.

JAINISM New religious concepts emerged in succeeding centuries. Between the sixth and fourth centuries B.C.E., **Jainism** (JY-nih-zuhm) took shape. Mahavira (shown above), the founder of the Jains, took on a very simple life and traveled by foot for 12 years, debating ideas as he traveled. He was a leading opponent of the caste system that placed Brahmins at the top of the social hierarchy. He died after voluntarily giving up food and water. Jains believe in right faith, right knowledge, and right conduct. They believe that humans must not harm any living beings. For example, to avoid killing insects by mistake, Jains refrain from eating and drinking when it is dark.

HISTORICAL THINKING

1. **READING CHECK** What does the Rig Veda suggest about how women's roles changed over time? What led to the change?

2. **DESCRIBE** What is the principle of karma as introduced in the Upanishads?

3. **MAKE INFERENCES** Why do historians know so much more about the culture of the Indo-Aryans than they do about the culture of the Harappan people?

PLAN: 2-PAGE LESSON

OBJECTIVE

Describe how Sanskrit hymns and epics reflect the history and culture of ancient India.

CRITICAL THINKING SKILLS FOR LESSON 1.2

- Describe
- Make Inferences
- Make Connections
- Determine Chronology

HISTORICAL THINKING FOR CHAPTER 3

How did religious and philosophical systems support societies in ancient India and China?

Religious hymns and texts were essential for disseminating knowledge and information in ancient Indian society. Lesson 1.2 discusses the Rig Veda, Bhagavad Gita, and other religious texts that were integral to conveying the ideas and beliefs of Vedic society.

Student eEdition online

Additional content for this lesson, including a primary source excerpt and a video, is available online.

BACKGROUND FOR THE TEACHER

Contemporary Jainism Jainism is still a thriving religion today. Historically concentrated in India, Jainism spread to other parts of the world during the 20th century, notably via Indian immigrants in East Africa, the United Kingdom, and North America. Contemporary Jainism holds true the original, intertwined tenets of Right Knowledge, Right Faith, and Right Practice. For many who practice Jainism in the contemporary world, this manifests in environmentalism, vegetarianism, and nonviolence. Jain monasteries rose and then declined over the course of the 19th century, but today, many Jain religious leaders have dedicated themselves to preserving temples and texts. Contemporary Jains have also been active in disaster-relief efforts and caring for animals.

INTRODUCE & ENGAGE

DISCUSS THE IMPORTANCE OF STORYTELLING AND MUSIC

Direct students to the primary source (available in the Student eEdition) and tell them that music and storytelling passed along information orally before Sanskrit developed a written language. Ask students to list examples of how music and storytelling are still used to entertain and communicate information. *(Possible responses: jingles used in advertisements; children's books that use a story with a moral to explain a concept)*

TEACH

GUIDED DISCUSSION

1. **Make Connections** Based on the ritual in the Ganges River video (available in the Student eEdition), and the information in the text, how does the concept of karma benefit society? *(People might behave well and do good deeds in order to be rewarded in the next life.)*

2. **Make Inferences** What can you infer about the role of religion in Vedic society from the fact that the Rig Veda includes both religious hymns and descriptions of everyday life? *(Religion was a well-integrated and important part of Vedic society.)*

DETERMINE CHRONOLOGY

Discuss with students the roles women had in Vedic society. **ASK:** What freedoms did women have around 1500 B.C.E.? *(Women could inherit property. Widows could remarry. Girls were allowed to go out unsupervised in public, choose their own husbands, and study the hymns.)* Why did this change around 1000 B.C.E.? *(Possible response: The nomads settled into a society and roles became fixed.)* Direct students to the primary source (available in the Student eEdition). **ASK:** What is significant about a woman's power over her husband in early Vedic society? *(Possible response: Women have often been oppressed in societies around the world, and many still are today. It is significant that women during 1500s B.C.E. were not only equal but could be viewed as superior.)*

ACTIVE OPTIONS

On Your Feet: Think, Pair, Share Organize students into pairs. Ask students to think about how the caste system evolved and how women began to lose their rights in ancient India. Encourage students to think about what factors led to these societal changes and what outcomes these changes might have caused. Then have students discuss their thoughts with their partners. Finally, invite volunteers to share their thoughts.

| **NG Learning Framework: Research Jainism**
| **ATTITUDE** Curiosity
| **KNOWLEDGE** Our Human Story

Ask students to conduct online research to learn more about Jainism and how it influences the daily lives of those who practice the religion. Remind students to dive deeply into the subject matter and consider the practices of Jainism, the motivation and rationale behind those practices. Discuss students' findings as a class.

DIFFERENTIATE

STRIVING READERS

Set a Purpose for Reading Before reading, direct students to use the lesson subheadings and features to create purpose-setting questions, such as: Why was Sanskrit the language of religion and scholarship? After reading, let student pairs answer the questions. Then ask volunteers to share their answers.

GIFTED & TALENTED

Compose Lyrics About Daily Life Instruct students to compose song lyrics that describe their daily lives and contemporary society, just as the Rig Veda describes ancient Indian life and society. Students with musical training could write music to accompany their lyrics. All students should consider characteristics such as rhythm and melody.

See the Chapter Planner for more strategies for differentiation.

HISTORICAL THINKING

ANSWERS

1. Initially, women shared a common status with men, but over time they lost their freedoms as society became more stable and developed fixed roles.

2. people's actions in this life determine how they will be reborn in the next life

3. Sanskrit has been preserved through literature, and historians can read about Indo-Aryan cultures through the Rig Veda, the Upanishad, the *Mahabharata*, and the *Ramayana*. Archaeologists and linguists have not been able to decipher the language spoken by the Harappan people, so their culture can only be guessed at through architecture and artifacts.

The Buddha's Teachings

Do material possessions, such as the latest smartphone, bring you happiness?
Or does your desire to own things only bring you suffering? Would you be
willing to give up everything you have to find out? More than 2,500 years ago,
a man named Siddhartha Gautama did just that.

THE LIFE OF THE BUDDHA

Born along the southern edge of the Himalaya in today's
Nepal, **Siddhartha Gautama** (sih-DAR-tuh GOW-tuh-
muh) lived to almost 80 and died around 483 B.C.E. The
legend of Siddhartha Gautama's life begins with the
story of how his mother dreamed of a white elephant
with a lotus flower in its trunk. She consulted oracles,
or wise men, who predicted that she would give birth to
either a great monarch or a great teacher. Siddhartha's
parents raised him inside a walled palace so that he
would never see any signs of suffering or illness. He
grew up, married, and fathered a child.

One day, while traveling inside the palace park,
Siddhartha had four encounters. He came across an
elderly man, an extremely ill man, and a dead body
being taken away for cremation. Then Siddhartha saw
an **ascetic**, or one who chooses a life of poverty,
wearing a simple robe and looking happy. These
encounters made Siddhartha think about suffering,
old age, disease, and death. But seeing the ascetic's
happiness gave Siddhartha hope, and he decided
to follow the man's example. Siddhartha gave up
his wealth and his family to live a life of poverty.
After six years of wandering, Siddhartha sat down
to meditate under a tree, where he remained for 49
days and attained **enlightenment**, a state of deep
understanding and clarity. Through this enlightenment,
Siddhartha became the Buddha, "the enlightened or
awakened one," and his teachings became the religion
of Buddhism.

BUDDHIST BELIEFS

The Buddha's first sermon described the path to
enlightenment. He told his listeners to avoid extremes
of self-denial, such as going without food for long
periods of time. He also warned against the complete

self-gratification of those who did exactly as they
pleased. Instead, he encouraged people to follow the
Four Noble Truths: 1) All life is suffering; 2) The cause of
suffering is desire; 3) The end of desire means the end
of suffering; and 4) Following the Noble Eightfold Path
can end suffering.

According to the Buddha, following the Noble Eightfold
Path would bring suffering to an end because a person
would have attained **nirvana**, a state of blissful escape
from suffering. In Buddhism, the term also takes on the
meaning of gaining true understanding.

While the Buddha believed in the concept of
reincarnation, his teachings marked a major departure
from other aspects of the Vedic religion. As you've read,
according to the Rig Veda, people could do nothing
to change their social class. In contrast, Buddhists
suggested that salvation was the result of an individual's
actions, not his or her varna. The Buddha encouraged
people to leave their families and join him as monks in
the Buddhist order. Only those monks who joined the

The Eightfold Path

RIGHT VIEW See and understand things as they really are

RIGHT INTENTION Commit to ethical self-improvement

RIGHT SPEECH Tell the truth and speak gently

RIGHT ACTION Act kindly, honestly, and respectfully

RIGHT LIVELIHOOD Earn a living in a moral, legal, and
peaceful way

RIGHT EFFORT Focus your will onto achieving good things

RIGHT MINDFULNESS Value a good mind

RIGHT CONCENTRATION Single-mindedness

CRITICAL VIEWING In this wood carving, the Buddha sits under a bodhi tree, where,
according to Buddhist tradition, he meditated for 49 days and gained enlightenment. How
would you interpret the expression on the Buddha's face in this carving?

order could attain nirvana. The Buddha's first followers
were all men, but Buddhist sources record that the
Buddha's aunt asked to join the Buddhist order. The
Buddha refused her until his star disciple intervened
and persuaded him to change his mind. Later, women
did become Buddhist nuns, but they were always
subordinate to men. Those outside the order could
gain merit by donating food and money. A merchant,
a farmer, or even a laborer who made a donation to
the order could enhance his or her social standing.
Many kings and merchants gave large gifts in the
hope of improving their lives, either in this world or in
future rebirths.

HISTORICAL THINKING

1. **READING CHECK** Why did Siddhartha Gautama leave
his life of luxury?

2. **IDENTIFY MAIN IDEAS AND DETAILS** What are the
main ideas presented in the Four Noble Truths and the
Noble Eightfold Path?

3. **DRAW CONCLUSIONS**
Which aspects of the Buddha's teachings do you think
most appealed to people who had previously followed
the Vedic religion?

PLAN: 2-PAGE LESSON

OBJECTIVE

Explain how the origins of Buddhism grew out of the
life of Siddhartha Gautama, the Buddha, who sought
to find a cure for suffering.

CRITICAL THINKING SKILLS FOR LESSON 2.1

- Identify Main Ideas and Details
- Draw Conclusions
- Evaluate
- Analyze Cause and Effect
- Analyze Visuals

HISTORICAL THINKING FOR CHAPTER 3

How did religious and philosophical systems support
societies in ancient India and China?

The onset of Buddhism influenced many people's
attitudes towards wealth and social status. Lesson 2.1
discusses the origin of Buddhism and how early Buddhist
beliefs affected social structures.

BACKGROUND FOR THE TEACHER

The Eightfold Path The Eightfold Path was derived
from Siddhartha Gautama's first sermon. Its purpose
was to outline a "middle way" to live that was neither
a stark ascetic existence nor an indulgent life full of
pleasure. The eight parts of the path include: 1) correct
view, understanding facts accurately; 2) correct intention,
avoiding malicious motivation; 3) correct speech,
refraining from lying and slandering others; 4) correct
action, avoiding knowingly harming others; 5) correct
livelihood, avoiding trades that harm others and
earning a living in a way that benefits society; 6) correct
effort, maintaining positive states of mind; 7) correct
mindfulness, an awareness of the present moment; and
8) correct concentration, focusing on one thing at a time.
Those who follow the Eightfold Path are considered
noble.

INTRODUCE & ENGAGE

CONSIDER THE BUDDHA'S APPROACH TO SUFFERING AND DESIRE

Ask students to think about things that they currently desire, such as possessions or experiences. Then ask them to think about the possessions they currently own or recent experiences they have had. Explain that the Buddha believed that suffering is caused by desire, and the path to spiritual enlightenment and contentment involves relinquishing desire. Ask students to consider what relinquishing, or giving up, all desire might be like in contemporary society and the benefits and drawbacks of this outlook.

TEACH

GUIDED DISCUSSION

1. **Evaluate** How might Buddhist monks accepting monetary donations for favor conflict with Buddhist teaching? (*Buddhist teaching encourages followers to let go of desire, and accepting gifts could fuel desire within the monks.*)

2. **Analyze Cause and Effect** How did Siddhartha's early life influence his journey to Buddhism? (*Possible responses: Because Siddhartha's early life was very sheltered, he was shocked when he witnessed people suffering and was motivated to find an end to suffering.*)

ANALYZE VISUALS

Have students look closely at the carving of the Buddha sitting beneath the bodhi tree. **ASK:** What details did the artist include and why? (*Possible response: details in the background such as elephants, birds, and other trees show the connection between enlightenment and nature*)

ACTIVE OPTIONS

On Your Feet: Inside-Outside Circle Organize students into two concentric circles facing each other. Have students in the outside circle ask students in the inside circle about the merits and obstacles of Siddhartha's decision to leave his family and wealth behind in order to seek enlightenment. On a signal, have students rotate to create new partnerships. On another signal, students should trade roles.

NG Learning Framework: Solve Contemporary Issues Using the Noble Eightfold Path
ATTITUDE Responsibility
SKILL Problem-Solving

Share the Background for the Teacher information about the Noble Eightfold Path and discuss contemporary issues, such as government corruption, war, poverty, religious conflicts, lack of education, inequality, civil rights, animal rights, destruction of nature, and so on. Have small groups each focus on a different issue and suggest how applying the concepts laid out in the Noble Eightfold Path could help solve or address this issue. Encourage groups to share their solutions with the class.

DIFFERENTIATE

STRIVING READERS

List Details About a Topic Have pairs create a table with the lesson's section headings. Ask students to take turns reading paragraphs aloud, while their partners listen and identify details to add to the table columns.

GIFTED & TALENTED

Create a Visual Tell students to research the design of and features within ancient walled palaces, similar to that in which Siddhartha lived before he gave up his wealth and family. Instruct each student to create a poster, sketch, or infographic showing the features within a walled palace. Encourage students to include labels or text explaining the buildings, parks, or structures within the palace infrastructure. Invite students to present their visuals to the class.

See the Chapter Planner for more strategies for differentiation.

HISTORICAL THINKING

ANSWERS

1. He witnessed suffering brought on by old age, illness, and death. He also noticed that a person could be happy even without many worldly possessions. He left his previous life to search for an understanding of how to relieve suffering.

2. The Four Noble Truths described suffering, explained the cause of suffering, presented the idea that a cure existed, and introduced the Noble Eightfold Path as that cure. The Noble Eightfold Path led to nirvana by teaching people how to live a righteous life.

3. Buddhism allowed people to take more control over their own salvation. The Vedic religion taught that people could never improve the social status into which they had been born.

CRITICAL VIEWING Possible response: content, accepting, peaceful

2.2 Material Culture

IMAGES OF THE BUDDHA

You've learned that Buddhism originated in India more than 2,500 years ago. Since then, Buddhism has spread all over the world with more than 488 million adherents. As the religion made its way over time into new places, it was reflected in a variety of cultures—each with its own unique style. Depictions of the Buddha, in particular, appeared in different forms and were created with different media as the religion spread from India to East and Southeast Asia and beyond.

The Mogao Caves Dunhuang, China, once a thriving Silk Roads oasis, is home to one of the greatest repositories of Buddhist art in the world. Approximately 492 caves chiseled into the face of a cliff are decorated with murals and adorned with sculptures created over a period of 1,000 years. The variety in the style of the art reflects the different goods that were traded along the Silk Roads and the different cultures that came into contact with each other. Today, the caves are a UNESCO World Heritage Site. This 10-foot-tall statue of a bodhisattva, or future

Buddha, was created sometime during the early fifth century c.e. It is believed to be one of the earliest surviving painted sculptures in the Mogao cave complex, home to one of the greatest repositories of Buddhist art in the world. The gesture of the statue's left hand symbolizes the granting of wishes or blessings, while the crossed ankles and lions on either side are reminiscent of depictions of royalty. The origin of this artistic style can be traced back to rock caves in present-day Afghanistan, illustrating the cross-cultural nature of the Mogao caves.

Mudras Buddha statues or paintings often depict different hand gestures known as *mudras* (such as the gesture of the bodhisattva on the opposite page). Each mudra has a specific meaning and is used to evoke a particular state of mind. The most common mudra, *dhyana*, signifies meditation. Other mudras include *vyakhyana* or *vitarka* (teaching), *abhaya* (protection), *dharmachakra* (the wheel of dharma), and *varada* (giving or generosity).

Dhyana

Vyakhyana or Vitarka

Abhaya

Dharmachakra

Varada

The Laughing Buddha Known as *Budai* in Chinese and *Hotei* in Japanese, the laughing Buddha is often depicted as a chubby, happy monk carrying a large sack. His large belly symbolizes happiness, luck, and generosity. A semihistorical figure, he is believed to have lived in southern China in the 10th century and was eventually recognized as part of the Buddhist pantheon as a future Buddha.

PLAN: 4-PAGE LESSON

OBJECTIVE
Explore how the Buddha has been represented in cultures across the world.

CRITICAL THINKING SKILLS FOR LESSON 2.2
- Analyze Visuals
- Make Connections
- Make Inferences
- Compare and Contrast
- Explain

HISTORICAL THINKING FOR CHAPTER 3
How did religious and philosophical systems support societies in ancient India and China?

Buddhism originated in ancient India and spread to China and to other societies across the world. Lesson 2.2 explores various depictions of the Buddha in different forms and media as Buddhism spread throughout Asian cultures.

Student eEdition online
Additional content for this lesson, including additional images, is available online.

BACKGROUND FOR THE TEACHER
The Silk Roads A network of land and sea routes, the Silk Roads were used to trade goods—including textiles, grain, vegetables and fruit, animal hides, tools, metalwork, and much more—between China and the rest of Asia, as well as Europe, and Africa. As merchants traveled the Silk Roads into other countries, it was beneficial to learn the languages and customs of the people. This helped to spread new inventions and technologies, such as paper making, printing press technology, and irrigation. It also led to the exchange of ideas and information, such as science, philosophy, literature, arts, crafts, and religion. One such religion was Buddhism, beginning in India and spreading to Central and Southeast Asia into China, Korea, and Japan. It even spread west to Afghanistan and beyond, evidenced by the Buddhist art and shrines found throughout these regions. Travelers on the Silk Roads included Buddhist monks who brought sacred texts from India to China, helping to disseminate the newly popular religion.

History Notebook
Encourage students to complete the Material Culture page for Chapter 3 in their History Notebooks as they read.

INTRODUCE & ENGAGE

EXPLORE HISTORY USING PHOTOGRAPHS

Tell students that the photographs in this lesson are examples of the many cultural representations of the Buddha. **ASK:** What representations of the Buddha on these pages intrigue you? What about this collection do you find interesting? *(Possible responses: The details in the art and sculptures in the Mogao Caves are intriguing. I think it's interesting that there are so many variations of the Buddha.)* Where have you seen representations of the Buddha in your community? *(Possible response: My favorite restaurant has a Buddha statue by the front door.)*

TEACH

GUIDED DISCUSSION

1. **Compare and Contrast** Ask students to examine the early Indian Buddha relief (available in the Student eEdition) and the bronze Chinese Buddha sculpture. **ASK:** How are these representations similar and different? *(Possible responses: Similarities: similar appearances, hair, and clothing, both have flames coming out of their shoulders; Differences: the early Indian Buddha is standing with his hand out as a sign of protection, the Chinese Buddha is sitting with his hands together in his lap as a sign of meditation, the flames coming out of their shoulders have different meanings, the Indian Buddha has a parasol over his head and water coming out of his feet, the Chinese Buddha has a lion on either side)*

2. **Make Connections** Which Buddhist hand gestures can be used in our everyday lives? *(Possible responses: the abhaya gesture of the hand up for protection could be used to stop a person's advance, protecting someone behind you; the varada gesture of the hand out for generosity could be used in the same way, to show openness and kindness)*

MATERIAL CULTURE

Remind students of the Historical Thinking question for this chapter: How did religious and philosophical systems support societies in ancient India and China? **ASK:** How can you use the information and different depictions of the Buddha presented in this lesson to answer the question? *(Possible response: Buddhism brought people together from different cultures and allowed adaptations in each society, while still focusing on the original teachings of the Buddha.)*

DIFFERENTIATE

STRIVING READERS

Partner Read Let student pairs read each paragraph and study its accompanying depiction of the Buddha. Partners should discuss the relationship between the photograph and the text, and then write a summary statement for each paragraph.

PRE-AP

Create a Travel Brochure Direct students to research one of the locations of Buddhist art in the lesson, such as the Mogao Caves, the Hasa-dera Temple, Sichuan, Kathmandu, or Mok Khan Lan. Then tell students to create a travel brochure encouraging people to visit their location. Students should include information about Buddhism and the representation of the Buddha in the chosen location, as well as other interesting artifacts or architecture visitors may see, information about climate and currency, and an explanation of the current political climate of the region. Ask students to include photographs or illustrations and a map to guide travelers.

See the Chapter Planner for more strategies for differentiation.

▲ **Boudhanath Stupa** The Boudhanath Stupa in Kathmandu, Nepal, is the center of Tibetan Buddhism in Nepal. (A stupa is a dome-shaped structure built as a Buddhist shrine.) Built in the 14th century, the stupa remains an active sacred site today, as illustrated by the prayer flags streaming from the gold spire. The 13 steps of the spire represent the Buddhist path to enlightenment, while the all-seeing eyes of the Buddha gaze out from each of the four sides at the spire's base. Severely damaged by a massive earthquake that struck Nepal in 2015, the spire was repaired entirely with the help of private donations and local volunteers.

▶ **Chinese Buddha** This bronze sculpture depicts the Buddha seated on a rectangular throne flanked by a pair of small lions. The Buddha's hands form the *dhyana* mudra (the gesture of meditation), and the triangular points emanating from his shoulders represent flames—in this instance a visible manifestation of the body heat associated with meditation. This sculpture is one of the earliest-known iconic images of the Buddha produced in China.

Monumental Buddhist Art Large Buddha statues appear in a variety of cultures touched by Buddhism.

▲ The reclining Buddha shown above is part of the Buddhist temple complex of Mok Khan Lan in Thailand. The reclining Buddha represents the historical Buddha during his last illness as he is about to attain nirvana. To the far left of the reclining Buddha is a statue of the Hindu deity Ganesha, reflecting the overlap of Buddhist and Hindu traditions in Thailand.

◀ This 180-foot-tall Buddha statue was the larger of two monumental statues in the Bamiyan Valley in central Afghanistan. Built along the Silk Roads during the first half of the sixth century c.e., the statues were the largest examples of standing Buddha carvings in the world. Tragically, the statues were declared to be idols by the ruling Taliban and were destroyed in March 2001.

HISTORICAL THINKING

1. **READING CHECK** What are three different ways in which the Buddha has been depicted in art?
2. **ANALYZE VISUALS** How has Buddhist art evolved as it has spread across cultures and the world?
3. **MAKE INFERENCES** How has the Buddhist art you've read about reflected both religious tolerance and intolerance?

BACKGROUND FOR THE TEACHER

The Dalai Lama The Dalai Lama is the head monk of Tibetan Buddhism and belongs to the Gelugpa tradition, the largest and most influential sect. The title Dalai Lama means "Ocean of Wisdom" and is reserved for one believed to be the reincarnation of a past lama. The High Lamas of the Gelugpa tradition are responsible for finding the Dalai Lama's reincarnation by searching for a boy born around the time of the Dalai Lama's death. They rely on dreams and visions to guide their search for this boy, sometimes taking up to four years. Once a boy is found, they present him with items belonging to the late Dalai Lama. If the boy is drawn to any of the Dalai Lama's items, it is considered to be a sign that he is the reincarnation.

In 1938, the High Lamas followed the signs to a three-year-old boy who identified the previous Dalai Lama's items as his own. At five years old, the boy began his training at the local monastery and was taught by the highest monks in the land. At age 15, the 14th Dalai Lama, Tenzin Gyatso, was enthroned. The 1950s brought political changes that drove the Dalai Lama and thousands of his followers out of their homes and into India. For maintaining peace in the face of Chinese violence and oppression, he received the Nobel Peace Prize in 1989. Tenzin Gyatso is the first Dalai Lama to have traveled to the West. He has increased international support for Buddhism and the Tibetan resistance movement. However, as political conflicts have not been resolved, the Dalai Lama fears he may not be reborn and the Gelugpa tradition may end.

TEACH

GUIDED DISCUSSION

3. **Make Inferences** Why might the text include a photograph of monks playing basketball (available in the Student eEdition)? *(Possible responses: to show that Buddhism is still relevant today; to show that monks are still normal people who enjoy common activities; to help readers relate to the monks)*

4. **Explain** Direct students' attention to the monumental Buddha statue in Thailand. **ASK:** How is the Buddha depicted in this statue and why? *(Possible response: The Buddha is lying down, but he does not look like he is dying. He appears to be almost smiling in a very peaceful state. This is because he is not suffering and knows he is about to attain nirvana.)*

ANALYZE VISUALS

Direct students to the Death of the Historical Buddha painting (available in the Student eEdition). Point out that the other depictions of the Buddha do not include other people. **ASK:** Why does this painting include bystanders in the death of Buddha? *(Possible response: It is important to show how much people cared about the Buddha. The expressions on their faces show they were tormented by the grief of his passing.)*

ACTIVE OPTION

On Your Feet: Jigsaw Strategy Divide the class evenly into "expert" groups. Assign each group a branch of Buddhism to study, such as Indian, Chinese, Japanese, Thai, or Tibetan. Tell each group to conduct online research into their branch to answer the following questions: How and when did the branch of Buddhism form? What makes the branch unique? How is it different today than it was when it first formed? Has it spread? Regroup students so that each new group has at least one member from each expert group. Instruct students to share their research.

HISTORICAL THINKING

ANSWERS

1. The Buddha has been depicted as a statue, as part of a building, and in paintings.

2. Buddhist art has evolved to incorporate and reflect the cultures and places to which it has spread.

3. Examples of religious tolerance include blending elements of earlier religions such as Shinto and Hinduism with Buddhist beliefs. Examples of religious intolerance include the destruction of Buddhist art in Afghanistan.

The Maurya Empire

Imagine an experience so dramatic that it completely changes your life. For one king, this dramatic moment happened after a violent conquest. His life changed in a way that would affect his entire empire and how he ruled it.

CHANDRAGUPTA RULES THE MAURYA EMPIRE

In 320 B.C.E., approximately 150 years after the Buddha's death, a general named **Chandragupta Maurya** (chuhn-druh-GUP-tuh MOWR-yuh) defeated another general and gained control of the territory and capital Pataliputra, located along the Ganges. Chandragupta conquered many surrounding kingdoms, establishing an empire that united most of northern India and became the first great Indian empire.

Chandragupta exercised direct control over the area around the Maurya capital and the trade routes linking

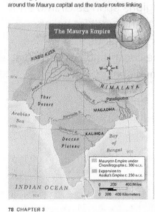

ASHOKA RULES BY EXAMPLE

Chandragupta's grandson, **Ashoka** (uh-SHOH-kuh), began his reign in 268 B.C.E. as a brutal ruler, leading armies on violent campaigns in north and central India. The attack of Kalinga in modern-day Orissa on India's eastern coast was particularly brutal. According to Ashoka's own words, "a hundred and fifty thousand people were deported, a hundred thousand were killed, and many times that number perished." After so much violence, Ashoka felt deep remorse and underwent a dramatic change. He renounced war, converted to Buddhism, and used the fundamental ideas of Buddhism to guide the way he ruled.

Committed to dharma, Ashoka turned to leading by example rather than ruling by force. He strove to demonstrate how a humane leader should rule. By adopting Buddhism as the state religion, Ashoka became a chakravartin (chuhk-ruh-VAHR-TUHN). According to Buddhist beliefs, a chakravartin is an ideal leader who does not leave his family to become a monk but does promote Buddhism. As a chakravartin, Ashoka encouraged cultural unity and strengthened his political power. However, he allowed religious freedom and tolerated other religions. Rather than forcing his subjects to convert to Buddhism, he sponsored religious observances and contributed money for the construction of Buddhist temples, monasteries, and hospitals for both humans and animals. These

Pataliputra with outlying trade centers. These trade routes allowed officials to collect taxes from markets in outer regions of the empire. However, unlike the Assyrians and ancient Egyptians, the Mauryans exercised much less direct control over their subjects. Local kings with reduced powers remained in place in many of the regions, and in some areas local assemblies made decisions.

Ashoka used stone pillars for public announcements. His proclamations were inscribed onto tall columns and erected on roads and in towns across the empire, such as the one shown here in the ancient city of Vaishali in Bihar, India.

services were available to everyone, without regard to religious faith. Ashoka hoped that his subjects would recognize his generosity and willingly acknowledge him as their divine leader. Historians call this type of rule a "ceremonial state."

After Ashoka's death in 232 B.C.E., the Maurya Empire began to break apart. The Mauryans lost control of the last remaining section, the Ganges Valley, around 185 B.C.E. However, Ashoka's legacy continued through the observance and practice of Buddhism. The religion spread throughout the Ganges, northern Indus, and Godavari river valleys. A century later, as kings in Sri Lanka and Afghanistan emulated Ashoka's example, Buddhism extended even farther. Eventually it would become a major world religion with followers in South Asia, Southeast Asia, and East Asia.

> Ashoka's inscriptions served several purposes. They showed compassion for Ashoka's subjects and encouraged them to live a life of virtue.
>
> **PRIMARY SOURCE**
>
> Through his instruction in dharma, abstention from killing and non-injury to living beings, deference to relatives, Brahmins and shramanas [non-Vedic religious followers], obedience to mother and father, and obedience to elders have all increased as never before for many centuries. These and many other forms of the practice of dharma have increased and will increase.
>
> —from the Fourth Major Rock Edict

HISTORICAL THINKING

1. **READING CHECK** How did governing by example help Ashoka build his image and protect his power?

2. **DRAW CONCLUSIONS** What do you think Ashoka hoped to accomplish by carving his beliefs into stone?

3. **EVALUATE** Do you think Ashoka's strategy of spreading Buddhism by example was more or less effective than dictating that all subjects must convert to Buddhism? Why?

PLAN: 2-PAGE LESSON

OBJECTIVE

Describe how the Maurya Empire formed from violent conquests and then spread its power by projecting an image of respect and peace.

CRITICAL THINKING SKILLS FOR LESSON 2.3

- Draw Conclusions
- Evaluate
- Make Connections
- Analyze Cause and Effect
- Analyze Primary Sources

HISTORICAL THINKING FOR CHAPTER 3

How did religious and philosophical systems support societies in ancient India and China?

Buddhism spread throughout the Maurya Empire and consequently advanced to other parts of East and South Asia. Lesson 2.3 discusses how Ashoka's devotion to Buddhism inspired him to lead by example rather than force.

BACKGROUND FOR THE TEACHER

Ashoka's Pillars Ashoka erected massive pillars and engraved them to spread dharma and encourage support for Buddhism. The pillars, of which only 19 survive, are each 40–50 feet tall and weigh 50 tons. The shaft of each pillar was usually cut from just one piece of stone. On top of each shaft sits the capital. Most of the capitals are sculptures of animals, either a seated or standing lion or bull, with an inverted lotus flower. The animals were always carved from one piece of stone. The lotus flower is a symbol of Buddhism, representing its upward growth through muddy waters to bloom flawlessly at the water's surface. The flower analogy was, and still is, used to encourage Buddhist practitioners to push through their challenges in order to attain Enlightenment. The inscriptions on the pillars are called *edicts*. Ashoka dictated these edicts as his interpretations of Buddhism. Ashoka's goal was to communicate his reforms and encourage people to lead moral lives.

INTRODUCE & ENGAGE

DISCUSS LEADERSHIP STYLES

Explain to students that Ashoka was an Indian king who led by example rather than forcing his subjects to adhere to his Buddhist beliefs. Ask students to think of various authority figures with whom they interact, including authority figures whom they respect and authority figures with whom they have clashed. Ask students what characteristics of these leaders instilled respect or what characteristics caused frustration. Then ask what characteristics a good leader should have. *(Possible responses might include respecting a teacher who asks students for their opinions and that good leaders should listen as well as instruct.)*

TEACH

GUIDED DISCUSSION

1. **Make Connections** How did Chandragupta's empire benefit from controlling trade routes? *(The empire was able to collect taxes from a larger region.)*

2. **Analyze Cause and Effect** How did Ashoka's conversion to Buddhism affect the popularity of the religion? *(Possible response: Ashoka built temples and monasteries throughout the Maurya Empire, which caused Buddhism to spread throughout the empire and eventually to farther regions.)*

ANALYZE PRIMARY SOURCES

Tell students to read the primary source of one of Ashoka's inscriptions. **ASK:** What does this inscription suggest about Ashoka's hope for the future? *(Possible response: He believes that Buddhism will continue to spread because more people were living their lives according to dharma.)*

ACTIVE OPTIONS

On Your Feet: Roundtable Seat students around a table in groups of four. Ask students to consider how Chandragupta's decision to allow local kings to continue governing their regions affected those regions as well as the Maurya Empire as a whole. Students should answer the question in their own words, taking turns going around the table.

NG Learning Framework: Research the Edicts of Ashoka
SKILL Communication
KNOWLEDGE Our Human Story

Share the Background for the Teacher and instruct students to further research the Edicts of Ashoka inscribed on pillars throughout the Maurya Empire. Tell students to write a set of guidelines, based on the edicts, describing how an ideal Mauryan citizen should behave. Encourage students to share their guidelines with the class.

DIFFERENTIATE

STRIVING READERS

Sequence Events Instruct students to work in pairs to complete a Sequence Chain detailing the major events of the Maurya Empire. Tell students to read the lesson, pausing after each paragraph to write notes in the chain. Then tell students to take turns reading the notes aloud, using transition words to introduce the contents of each link in the chain. Provide students with a list of transition words to use, such as *first, then, also, and, but, next, although,* and *however.*

PRE-AP

Connect Past and Present Tell students that Buddhism is still practiced in many parts of the world and instruct them to research where and how Buddhism is practiced today. Ask students to consider how teachings vary from region to region, and how those beliefs connect back to the teaching that influenced Ashoka's rule. After completing their research, students should write an essay evaluating how Buddhism has changed and how it has remained consistent from region to region and over time.

See the Chapter Planner for more strategies for differentiation.

HISTORICAL THINKING

ANSWERS

1. He was able to portray himself as a benevolent leader and convince people to support his rule.

2. spread his message of dharma, convert people to Buddhism, elevate his image as a virtuous leader

3. His strategy was more effective because people could see the benefits of choosing Buddhism. The religion then became a positive choice for people, rather than something imposed on them by Ashoka.

Early Indian Ocean Trade

Can you imagine math without decimals? Or food without spices? Early travel and trade in ports throughout the Indian Ocean region gave the world products and ideas that influence our lives to this day.

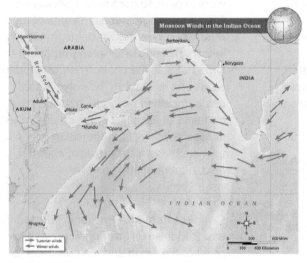

Monsoon Winds in the Indian Ocean

Summer winds
Winter winds

0   300   600 Miles
0   300   600 Kilometers

TRAVEL AND TRADE
Because of India's proximity to western Asia, travelers came to India in very early times, bringing new ideas and valuable goods to trade. These same people then carried Indian culture, including Buddhist teachings, out of India along the same paths they had used to bring ideas and products into India.

Land routes through the mountains of the Hindu Kush in the northwest allowed cultural contacts and the movement of valuable goods between South Asia and Central Asia through present-day Afghanistan. The Indo-Aryans probably used these land routes when they entered the Indian subcontinent sometime between 1500 and 1000 B.C.E.

80 CHAPTER 3

But in ancient times, the most important form of travel between South Asia and the rest of the world was by sea. For instance, people in the Harappan civilization traded with Mesopotamia as early as 2500 B.C.E. DNA evidence indicates that Harappan ships were capable of traveling not just to Mesopotamia but all the way across the Indian Ocean to Australia.

Trade rapidly grew around 100 C.E. when seafaring merchants learned how to use the wind to carry them all the way from the Persian Gulf, southern Arabia, and coastal East Africa to India and back— if they timed it right. From April to October, strong winds called **monsoons** blow northeast toward India. Between November and March, the winds reverse direction and blow southwest, away from India. If merchants caught the winds just right on a summer departure, they could avoid violent storms as they traveled west and return the following winter. By harnessing the strength of these seasonal winds, traders were able to travel more quickly and relatively safely.

THE *PERIPLUS*: AN ANCIENT GUIDEBOOK
Around 50 C.E. a merchant from Egypt wrote a book called the *Periplus*, a Greek word meaning "around the world." Written for merchants, the *Periplus* describes trading ports, distances between ports, and the products traded at each location. The book covers trade throughout the Indian Ocean, but it describes Indian ports as the most important trading destinations.

The author of the *Periplus* instructed his readers to bring money, and lots of it, to India's southwest coast because the markets were chock-full of precious and semiprecious stones, clothing, textiles, coral, pearls, ivory, raw glass, copper, tin, lead, and spices. Initially, most trade was among Indians, Mesopotamians, Persians, and Africans. However, thousands of Roman silver and gold coins have been found on India's south coast. It turns out that one of the most important commodities for Roman traders was peppercorn, which was used to conceal the taste of rancid meat. Roman traders spent so much money on this Indian spice that the Roman emperor eventually banned it as an import.

Glass, such as these jars from ancient Rome, was exported to India from Persia.

DIFFUSION OF MATH, SCIENCE, AND TECHNOLOGY
Early trade in the Indian Ocean involved more than the exchange of valuable goods. People also shared ideas in areas such as mathematics, science, technology, and religion. The spread of ideas from one culture to another is known as **cultural diffusion**. For example, the decimal system, which you'll read more about in a later chapter, was originally used in weights and measures in the Harappan civilization and spread both within India and to other parts of the globe. Traders also shared technological knowledge such as metalworking, shipbuilding, and agricultural techniques.

Medical and veterinary knowledge spread along the same trade routes, too. The holistic medical techniques of Ayurveda and yoga were first practiced in India over 2,000 years ago. Knowledge of veterinary medicine may have been shared among Mesopotamia, ancient Egypt, and India. One ancient Sanskrit text, *Shalihotra Samhita*, describes the veterinary care of horses and elephants.

Perhaps the most widely spread idea from early India, though, was Buddhism, which spread to Southeast Asia and, via land routes, to China and East Asia. In the next lessons, you will learn more about the origins of Chinese civilization.

HISTORICAL THINKING

1. **READING CHECK** What ideas spread from India through early trade in the Indian Ocean?

2. **DRAW CONCLUSIONS** Why is the *Periplus* important to historians who want to learn about trade in the Indian Ocean?

3. **INTERPRET MAPS** What effect did monsoon winds have on trade in the Indian Ocean?

Ancient South Asia and China 81

PLAN: 2-PAGE LESSON

OBJECTIVE
Explain how commodities and ideas spread across the Indian Ocean by way of an extensive trade network.

CRITICAL THINKING SKILLS FOR LESSON 2.4
- Draw Conclusions
- Interpret Maps
- Identify Problems and Solutions
- Make Inferences

HISTORICAL THINKING FOR CHAPTER 3
How did religious and philosophical systems support societies in ancient India and China?

Increased technologies in shipbuilding and a desire for exotic goods led to significant seafaring trade across the Indian Ocean. Lesson 2.4 discusses trade and the dissemination of ideas across the Indian Ocean between India, East Africa, Southwest Asia, and Europe.

Student eEdition online
Additional content for this lesson, including an image gallery and a Global Commodity feature, is available online.

BACKGROUND FOR THE TEACHER
Indian Seafaring Technology and Breadth People in ancient India developed trade partnerships not only to the west, across the Indian Ocean, but also to the east. They explored much of Southeast Asia and exported aspects of their culture to these regions. At one point, India had colonies extending as far east as Cambodia and present-day Indonesia. Records of seafaring in India date back as far as Mohenjo-Daro, where a panel showing a sea vessel was found. Another discovery was that of the Yukti Kalpa Taru, which is an ancient Indian instruction manual on shipbuilding, listing proper materials, construction techniques, and types of ships. In terms of seafaring technology, ancient Indians were ahead of other civilizations. In fact, the word *navigation* comes from the Sanskrit word *navgatih*, and the word *navy* comes from the Sanskrit word *nou*.

History Notebook
Encourage students to complete the "Spices" Global Commodity page for Chapter 3 in their History Notebooks as they read.

INTRODUCE & ENGAGE

CONSIDER TRANSPORTATION FOR INTERNATIONAL TRADE

Encourage students to discuss the means by which goods are transported around the world and imported to the United States today. Explain that the Indian Ocean was a hotbed of international trade around 2,000 years ago— and that civilizations had developed technologies to ease travel both over sea and across land. Ask students to think about what obstacles these technologies might have overcome. *(Possible responses might include roads through mountainous terrain or improvements in shipbuilding and navigation.)* Tell students that in this lesson they will learn about how international trade affected the economy and lifestyles of people in ancient India.

TEACH

GUIDED DISCUSSION

1. **Identify Problems and Solutions** Why did the Roman emperor think that banning peppercorn imports would benefit Rome? *(Possible response: The large amounts of money that Roman traders were spending on peppercorn could be spent on Roman goods instead.)*

2. **Make Inferences** Why were sea routes across the Indian Ocean used more than land routes for trading with West Africa and Southwest Asia? *(Possible response: Sea routes were used more because they were faster and more direct than traveling over land.)*

INTERPRET MAPS

Tell students to examine the map of monsoon winds in the Indian Ocean. **ASK:** If you were traveling from Rhapta to Barygaza and back, during which months should you depart from each city? *(Possible response: depart from Rhapta in May and depart from Barygaza in November)*

ACTIVE OPTIONS

On Your Feet: Research Trade Goods Direct students to the image gallery and the Global Commodity feature (available in the Student eEdition). Ask them to select a good and conduct online research about its supply, demand, and use in different regions along the Indian Ocean trade routes. Have students create a simplified summary of their chosen good and share it with the class.

| NG Learning Framework: Write a Travel Log
| ATTITUDE Curiosity
| SKILL Communication

Ask students to research details about ancient Indian Ocean trade and then imagine themselves as early traders traversing the Indian Ocean. Each student should write a brief travel log documenting a possible journey, including life on the ship as well as stops at various ports. Suggest that students consider the following questions: What types of vessels did traders use and how were they operated? How many traders were on the vessels? How did they plan for food and water for the people aboard the vessels? How far did the traders travel? What types of weather did they encounter? Have students read their completed travel logs to the class.

DIFFERENTIATE

ENGLISH LANGUAGE LEARNERS

Make Word Cards As they read the lesson, prompt students at the **Advanced** level to keep a list of unfamiliar words, such as *subcontinent, seafaring, harnessing, semiprecious, peppercorn*, and *rancid*. Direct students to look up each word in a dictionary and make a word card to help them understand and pronounce the word. Tell them to write the word on one side of a card and define the word and spell it phonetically on the other side.

PRE-AP

Extend Knowledge Prompt students to gather information from a variety of sources to learn more about one of the trading cities or ports on the western coast of India. Ask them to research the early development of the port city and how the port city functions today. Encourage students to cite primary and secondary sources, as appropriate. Invite volunteers to share their findings in an oral or written report.

See the Chapter Planner for more strategies for differentiation.

HISTORICAL THINKING

ANSWERS

1. Some of the most important ideas that spread from India because of early trade on the Indian Ocean include Buddhism; mathematics, including the decimal system; and medical knowledge.

2. The writer of the *Periplus* gave detailed descriptions of the routes, ports, and products traded along the Indian Ocean.

3. Monsoon winds helped to facilitate trade on the Indian Ocean, especially as traders learned to use the shifting summer and winter winds to their advantage to speed their travel and make their travel safer.

China's First Cities

Think about the objects you use every day. What do they reveal about you and how you live? Quite a bit, actually. From studying bronze pots, jade weapons, and carved animal bones, archaeologists have learned a lot about China's first cities and the people who lived there.

CRITICAL VIEWING In this majestic aerial photo, the Karst Mountains and Li River surround the city of Guilin in southern China. What do you think it would be like to live here?

82 CHAPTER 3

EARLY CHINESE CIVILIZATION

As you've read, early civilizations arose around fertile river valleys in Africa and Eurasia. China's civilization was no exception. The ancient people of China built their first cities around the **Huang He** (hwahng huh) and the **Chang Jiang** (chahng jyahng) in an area known as the **North China Plain**. The name *Huang*, which is the Mandarin word for "yellow," refers to the high concentration of fine yellow silt called **loess** that floats on the water and covers the entire Huang He Valley.

Sometime around 8000 B.C.E, people living in the North China Plain began to cultivate rice, the first crop to be domesticated in China. Archaeologists have traced the spread of agriculture north from the Chiang Jiang to the Huang He Valley. The earliest known appearance of ancient China's greatest commodity—silk—was around 4500 B.C.E.

THE SHANG DYNASTY

Recent archaeological evidence suggests that China's first dynasty, the Shang, emerged along the banks of the Huang He around 1600 B.C.E. Initially the Shang spread across a series of capitals, but they eventually settled in Anyang. Like the people of ancient Mesopotamia, the Shang built walled cities. They used sun-dried loess as a construction material. They also built canals to control the water flow from the Huang He into the rice, wheat, and millet fields, improving agricultural yields. These construction and farming practices supported a large population of approximately 120,000. Anyang was probably one of the largest cities in the world at its time.

During the Shang dynasty, Chinese artisans mastered the technique of working bronze and created richly decorated pots and ornaments. Many of these bronze objects and vessels were used in ceremonies to honor deceased ancestors. Shang artisans also carved jade, bone, and ivory into intricate figurines, many of which were buried in tombs with the dead.

BONES EXPOSE THE PAST

Archaeologists cannot be certain when people first spoke Chinese, but the first recognizable written Chinese characters appeared on animal bones around 1200 B.C.E. Scholars called the bones **oracle bones** because Shang rulers used them to forecast the future. First, the rulers prayed to their ancestors for advice on the outcomes of future events. Then they heated the bones to the point where they cracked and interpreted the cracks, which they believed revealed the answer. They then recorded on the bone the name of the ancestor, the topic of the question, and the outcome.

Scholars have deciphered the text on these bones to learn about Shang religion and history. The Shang believed their dead ancestors could intercede in human affairs on their behalf. They also conducted rituals in which they offered food and drink to the ancestors. This type of religion is called **ancestor worship**.

By studying oracle bones and Shang archaeological sites, historians have learned how Shang government and society functioned. For example, Shang rulers exercised direct control over a relatively small area. Their society was hierarchical with a king at the top, warlords next, and farmers at the bottom. Many oracle bones describe battles between the Shang and their enemies. When the Shang defeated an enemy, they took thousands of captives. Some captives became laborers. Others were sacrificed to appease the ancestors.

Over the past century, archaeologists have excavated more than 200,000 oracle bones. The deciphering of these bones marks one of the great breakthroughs in our understanding of ancient Chinese history.

[Map: Ancient China, c. 1300 B.C.E. — showing North China Plain, Anyang, SHANG DYNASTY, Huang He, East China Sea; scale 0–150–300 Miles, 0–150–300 Kilometers]

HISTORICAL THINKING

1. **READING CHECK** What role did the Huang He play in the development of the first Chinese cities?

2. **IDENTIFY MAIN IDEAS AND DETAILS** Why was the discovery of oracle bones so important to understanding the Shang dynasty?

3. **DESCRIBE** What were some of the religious practices of the Shang?

Ancient South Asia and China 83

PLAN: 2-PAGE LESSON

OBJECTIVE

Identify why China's first cities were built in the Huang He Valley and how this location facilitated the development of a complex culture.

CRITICAL THINKING SKILLS FOR LESSON 3.1

- Identify Main Ideas and Details
- Describe
- Make Inferences
- Form and Support Opinions
- Interpret Visuals

HISTORICAL THINKING FOR CHAPTER 3

How did religious and philosophical systems support societies in ancient India and China?

Just as in other regions of the world, civilizations grew along rivers in China, too. Lesson 3.1 discusses the origin of China's first dynasty, the Shang, and their society.

Student eEdition online

Additional content for this lesson, including a photograph and a Global Commodity feature, is available online.

BACKGROUND FOR THE TEACHER

Oracle Bones The discoveries of many oracle bones along the Huang He provided archaeologists with important clues about the existence of the Shang dynasty. Scholars have determined that in order to inscribe writing on bones and turtle shells, ancient Shang people first wrote the characters in ink, then scraped them into the bone or shell using a sharp tool. The irregular surface of shells and bones led archaeologists to believe that these early Chinese characters had some inconsistencies in their size and shape. In total, over 3,000 different characters have been discovered on oracle bones, about half of which were legible and have been interpreted. Like contemporary Chinese writing, the characters on oracle bones appeared to be written from top to bottom.

History Notebook

Encourage students to complete the "Silk" Global Commodity page for Chapter 3 in their History Notebooks as they read.

INTRODUCE & ENGAGE

DISCUSS GEOGRAPHY

Ask students to look at the map of the Shang dynasty. Discuss the geographic features they think influenced the Shang boundaries. *(Possible responses: mountains and desert to the north; mountains to the west; the Huang He and Chang Jiang flowing through the region; the sea to the east)*

TEACH

GUIDED DISCUSSION

1. **Make Inferences** What can you infer about the Shang dynasty based on the fact that many oracle bones convey information about battles? *(Possible response: The Shang were often at war.)*

2. **Form and Support Opinions** Do you think having a hierarchical society was beneficial for the Shang? Why or why not? *(Possible responses: Yes, because everyone knew their role and place in society; No, because people did not have social mobility.)*

INTERPRET VISUALS

Direct students to look at the photograph of the cracked turtle shell with the Chinese characters inscribed on it (available in the Student eEdition). Explain to students that ancient Shang people would heat the turtle shell until it cracked and then interpret the cracks to forecast the future. Ask volunteers to consider the benefits of this practice. *(Possible response: Interpreting the cracks could give someone peace of mind about an issue outside of his or her control.)*

ACTIVE OPTIONS

On Your Feet: Jigsaw Strategy Organize students into three "expert" groups and have them review the Global Commodity feature (available in the Student eEdition). Ask one group to research the details of silk production and if there have been any changes in production methods over time or in different areas. Assign another group to research what silk is used for today in different societies. Ask the third group to research the value of silk today, compare it with its value 5,000 years ago, and investigate its importance to different regions throughout history. Students should discuss their research in their groups and then rotate to form new groups that include "experts" on each topic.

| **NG Learning Framework: Draw a Diagram**
| **ATTITUDE** Curiosity
| **SKILL** Communication

Direct students to conduct online research about the layout of Shang cities. Students should examine the relationship between homes and public structures, as well as the infrastructure used by the Shang, such as walls and canals. Ask students to draw a diagram of a Shang city to communicate what they learn.

DIFFERENTIATE

STRIVING READERS

Summarize with Tweets As students read the lesson, direct them to pause after each paragraph and write a tweet summarizing the paragraph's main idea in their own words. Then place students in pairs, and have partners take turns reading their tweets aloud to each other. Ask partners to observe how their summaries differ.

GIFTED & TALENTED

Create a Podcast Prompt students to prepare a history podcast episode about a topic discussed in this lesson, such as oracle bones, the rise of Chinese civilization along the Huang He, or technology used during the Shang dynasty. Suggest that students write scripts for their podcasts, including sound effects. Invite them to present their episode to the class, either live or on a recording.

See the Chapter Planner for more strategies for differentiation.

HISTORICAL THINKING

ANSWERS

1. Loess from the river provided fertile soil for cultivating rice and a heavy clay for building walls.

2. The text on the bones revealed details about the Shang religion, structure of society, and ancient battles.

3. The Shang practiced ancestor worship. They made sacrifices for their ancestors, provided food for their ancestors, and asked their ancestors to intercede on their behalf.

CRITICAL VIEWING Possible response: Living in Guilin would inspire a deep appreciation for nature.

The Zhou Dynasty

Many rulers have told their people, and may have believed, that they were divinely chosen. In ancient China, the Zhou believed that a king could rule only as long as the gods believed he was worthy.

THE ZHOU GAIN THE MANDATE OF HEAVEN

After more than 500 years of rule, the Shang dynasty began to weaken, and people from the west overthrew the Shang in 1045 B.C.E. The Zhou (joh) dynasty took over the kingdom and became China's longest ruling dynasty, lasting about 800 years. The Zhou adopted much of the Shang culture, including ancestor worship, writing, and the production of bronze.

However, the Zhou also introduced a new concept that explained how they had been able to conquer the Shang. According to this new concept, known as the **Mandate of Heaven**, a dynasty could rule as long as Heaven believed it was worthy. Worshiped by

the Zhou ruling house but not by the previous Shang dynasty, Heaven represented the generalized forces of the cosmos, not a place where people went after death. The Zhou believed that Heaven would send signs—such as terrible storms, famines, unusual astronomical events, or peasant rebellions—before it would withdraw its mandate. After overthrowing a dynasty by force, a new dynasty could justify the actions by claiming to have gained the Mandate of Heaven.

The Mandate of Heaven led to a pattern in the rise and fall of dynasties in China called the **dynastic cycle**. In this cycle a new dynasty arises and people believe it has gained the Mandate of Heaven. Then the dynasty weakens and disasters occur, leading people to believe that the dynasty has lost the Mandate of Heaven. Finally the dynasty is overthrown and a new dynasty emerges. The cycle begins anew with the new dynasty claiming that it has been granted the mandate.

THE WARRING STATES PERIOD

The Zhou people gradually settled more and more territory, expanding their rule to nearly twice the size of the earlier Shang kingdom. The spread of iron tools enabled people to plow the land more deeply and to settle in new areas. Agricultural productivity increased, and the first money circulated around 500 B.C.E.

During the last 500 years of their rule, the Zhou divided their lands among local lords who grew powerful and independent. These local lords fought among themselves and disobeyed Zhou decrees, leading to violence in the final centuries of the dynasty. This time period from 481 to 221 B.C.E. is commonly called the Warring States Period. Armies began to fight battles farther south in different terrain where generals' skills in chariot fighting didn't apply. These generals had to abandon their horse-drawn chariots and lead large armies on foot.

THE DYNASTIC CYCLE

1. The people believe that the gods approve of the new dynasty.
2. The dynasty weakens.
3. Disasters occur.
4. The people believe that the gods no longer approve of the dynasty.
5. The dynasty is overthrown.
6. A new dynasty re-establishes order.

The dynastic cycle developed during the Zhou dynasty.

As local lords continued to gain power through battle, the Zhou king became less of an authority and more of a ceremonial figure. In 221 B.C.E. the last of the Zhou kings was overthrown.

During the violent Warring States Period, people began to think deeply about life and how to develop a more civilized society. Local lords invited philosophers to move to their cities and to discuss ideas freely with other philosophers, ushering in an era of philosophical advancement that became known as "A Hundred Schools of Thought." As you will read, one of these great thinkers, a man named Confucius, would have a profound influence on Chinese philosophy.

CHINA'S BRONZE AGE

The term Bronze Age refers to the first use of metal in tools of early societies, such as in Mesopotamia, when farmers began making tools of bronze. China's Bronze Age reached its peak during the Shang dynasty, but the Zhou created new techniques and unique decorative elements as seen in the vessels shown above. They also introduced the practice of writing inscriptions on the bronze, honoring the success of hunters or warriors in battle. Like the Shang, the Zhou used these bronze vessels in weekly ceremonies during which they offered extravagant meals to ancestors.

The process for making bronze vessels required great artistic and technical skills. Zhou artisans used a series of steps to create bronze vessels. First, they made a wax model and carved intricate designs into the wax. Next, they covered the model in clay, leaving small holes. After that, they heated the clay mold so that the wax would melt out through the holes. Once the wax was gone, they poured molten bronze made of copper, tin, and lead into the mold to take the place of the wax. Finally, when the bronze cooled, they broke the clay away from the vessel and used abrasives to sand the bronze and create a shiny surface.

HISTORICAL THINKING

1. **READING CHECK** How did the Zhou use the Mandate of Heaven to justify their rule?

2. **SYNTHESIZE** How did the Zhou build upon the culture and achievements of the Shang?

3. **MAKE INFERENCES** Why do you think people were interested in philosophical questions during the Warring States Period?

PLAN: 2-PAGE LESSON

OBJECTIVE

Explain how the Zhou overthrew the Shang and became the longest lasting dynasty in Chinese history.

CRITICAL THINKING SKILLS FOR LESSON 3.2

- Synthesize
- Make Inferences
- Make Predictions
- Sequence Events
- Analyze Visuals

HISTORICAL THINKING FOR CHAPTER 3

How did religious and philosophical systems support societies in ancient India and China?

During the Zhou dynasty, ancient Chinese people built upon the accomplishments of the Shang and developed an increased appreciation for philosophy. Lesson 3.2 discusses the rise and fall of the Zhou dynasty, the dynastic cycle, and the concept of the Mandate of Heaven.

BACKGROUND FOR THE TEACHER

The Arts in Zhou China Because Zhou China was composed of many smaller states, there was great diversity in the art, sculpture, and pottery produced during this era. In the Warring States Period, much of the artwork created during the Zhou dynasty was destroyed. Although no known paintings have survived, scholars have discovered detailed descriptions of Zhou paintings. Pottery during this period built on Shang methods, developing into new shapes. The Zhou used gold, silver, and bronze in their pottery and used jade to make highly ornamented sculptures. The Zhou also used wood to make bowls and other objects, covering these with lacquer for preservation and ornamentation.

INTRODUCE & ENGAGE

DISCUSS THE RELATIONSHIP BETWEEN CHURCH AND STATE

Remind students that the separation of church and state is established in the First Amendment of the United States Constitution, although the extent to which this separation should apply is still a hot political topic today. Explain to students that in early Chinese dynasties, citizens believed that their ruler was mandated by Heaven. Ask students to consider this approach to government and to think about the benefits and drawbacks of a governmental system that is so closely tied to religious beliefs. *(Possible responses might include that there would be little religious conflict if all citizens had the same beliefs.)* Tell students that in this lesson they will learn about the Zhou, China's longest-lasting dynasty and the first believed to be mandated by Heaven.

TEACH

GUIDED DISCUSSION

1. **Make Predictions** What do you think would happen if Zhou China experienced a series of natural disasters and diseases? *(Possible response: People would assume that government leaders had lost the Mandate of Heaven, and the dynasty could be overthrown.)*

2. **Sequence Events** How did iron tools lead to the development of a currency? *(Iron tools allowed people to farm more efficiently, which increased economic production and led to the need for money.)*

ANALYZE VISUALS

Ask students to examine the diagram of the Dynastic Cycle. **ASK:** How could a weakened dynasty lead to disasters? *(Possible response: A corrupt or poorly functioning government would not be able to provide decent relief if a disaster occurred, so the damage of the disaster would be greater than if the government were able to take swift action.)*

ACTIVE OPTIONS

On Your Feet: Team Word Webbing Organize students into teams of four and give each team a single large piece of paper. Give each team member a different colored marker. Assign the topic *Zhou dynasty* and direct students to create a word web. Each student should write an important detail about the Zhou dynasty on the part of the web nearest to him or her. On a signal, students should rotate the paper and each student should add details to the part of the word web that is now nearest to him or her.

NG Learning Framework: Research A Hundred Schools of Thought
ATTITUDE Responsibility
SKILL Problem-Solving

Organize students into groups, and have each group choose a philosophy from the Zhou dynasty's "A Hundred Schools of Thought," such as Legalism, Moism, or the School of Yin-Yang. Direct groups to focus on how their particular philosophy approached problem-solving and created a more peaceful society in Zhou China. Encourage students to share their research with the class.

DIFFERENTIATE

STRIVING READERS

Use Clarifying Questions Allow students to work with a partner who can read the lesson aloud to them. Encourage students to ask and answer clarifying questions about the diagram, photograph, and any unfamiliar text. Then instruct pairs to work together to answer the Historical Thinking questions.

PRE-AP

Write a Diary Entry Instruct students to conduct online research to learn more about daily life during the Warring States Period. Based on their research, have students write a diary entry from the perspective of a teenager during this era. Encourage students to include how the violence and increased appreciation for philosophy might have affected the daily life of the diarist. Have students present their diary entries to the class, including background information from their research.

See the Chapter Planner for more strategies for differentiation.

HISTORICAL THINKING

ANSWERS

1. The Zhou claimed that the Shang had lost the Mandate of Heaven and that Heaven had granted this mandate to the Zhou, allowing them to conquer the Shang and rule over the kingdom.

2. The Zhou continued the practice of ancestor worship, writing, working with bronze, and agriculture. However, they advanced the art of bronze work and began to use iron tools to improve agriculture.

3. Possible response: As life became violent, chaotic, and dangerous, people looked for ways to understand their situation and improve it, as well as deal with painful losses of life and property.

Confucianism and Daoism

What virtues serve as a guide for your own behavior? Kindness? Generosity? Respect for your parents and teachers? In ancient China, the virtues of respect, benevolence, and goodness served as a moral guide for millions of people during an upsetting time.

CONFUCIANISM

Confucius was born in 551 B.C.E. and lived through the Warring States Period of the Zhou dynasty. Confucius made his living by tutoring students, who knew him as Master Kong. He became China's most famous teacher. In reaction to the violence around him, Confucius advocated benevolence, goodness, and virtue, seeking to return to an earlier era, before the Zhou dynasty had fallen into disorder and conflict.

Scholars have not found any texts written by Confucius himself, as bound books did not exist during Confucius' lifetime. However, after Confucius' death, his students collected and recorded the discussions they'd had with him, and these conversations were eventually collected into a book called *The Analects*, which means "discussions and conversations." Students carefully studied *The Analects* because it was thought to be the only text that quoted Confucius directly.

Confucianism is the term used for the philosophy based on the teachings of Confucius. The main tenets, or beliefs, of Confucianism emphasize the role of ritual

The following excerpt from the first chapter of *The Analects* describes the concept of filial piety.

PRIMARY SOURCE

The Master said: "When the father is alive, watch the son's aspirations. When the father is dead, watch the son's actions. If three years later, the child has not veered from the father's ways, he may be called a dutiful son indeed."

—From *Confucius Analects with Selections from Traditional Commentaries* translated by Edward Slingerland

in bringing out people's inner humanity, or benevolence and goodness. The cornerstone of Confucianism is **filial piety**, or respect for one's parents. According to Confucianism, if children obey their parents and the ruler follows Confucian teachings, then a country in turmoil will right itself because an inspiring example will lead people toward goodness.

DAOISM

Many of Confucius' followers were also familiar with the teachings of **Daoism**, the other major philosophy that arose during the chaotic Warring States Period. The origin of Daoism is uncertain, but legend suggests that it originated with a man named Laozi (low-dzuh), meaning "old master." According to the legend, while traveling to the west on an ox, Laozi was stopped by the guardian of a mountain pass and forced to write down his beliefs. Those writings were said to be the *Dao de Jing*, or *Classic of the Way of Power*.

There are inconsistent accounts of Laozi's actual existence. Historians agree that the *Dao de Jing* is a compilation of teachings by different masters. Daoism emphasizes *Dao*, "the Way," as the path to enlightenment. It urges rulers to allow things to follow their natural course. This concept is often translated as "nonaction," but it is much more. Daoists believe that people should not strive to be in control or to change the world. A person should not boast, argue to prove a point, or try to gain attention. Instead, a person should let go of the stresses of life, live simply, and seek order and balance in his or her life by living in harmony with nature.

Daoists believe that an energy called *qi* is the origin of the cosmos. Qi is made up of yin and yang. Yin represents dark, cold, water, and the earth. Yang represents light, hot, fire, and the heavens. Every human

A woman prays at Man Mo Temple in Hong Kong. The Daoist temple is open to everyone.

and every object in nature contains both yin and yang. Harmony is achieved through the balance of these complementary forces.

LEGACY OF THE PHILOSOPHIES

Confucianism and Daoism became hallmarks of Chinese traditions and values, influencing everything from government to healthcare to familial roles. The ideals promoted in the philosophies caused leaders to embrace them or reject them wholeheartedly. Starting with the Han dynasty (which you'll learn about in a future chapter), Confucianism served as a unifying force. Confucius' teachings became required reading for all government officials, who had to pass an examination testing their knowledge. In later dynasties, astrologers consulted Daoist sages for advice and for predictions that would legitimize the emperor's decisions.

Daoists believed that meditation, breathing techniques, and special diets could lead to a long life and possibly even immortality. Today Daoists around the world use these practices as well as exercise to achieve emotional harmony and longevity.

Confucianism and Daoism are alive and well in China today, influencing millions of people. Through time, the ideas have often mingled with Buddhism to create a unique and eclectic Chinese philosophy. Thousands of years after their compilations, *The Analects* and the *Dao de Jing* have been translated into many languages and are popular around the world. Chinese medical practices, based on the principles of qi, pharmacology, as well as acupuncture, have also had a global impact.

HISTORICAL THINKING

1. **READING CHECK** How did events in Chinese history influence the development of Confucianism and Daoism?

2. **DESCRIBE** How are Chinese culture and history reflected in *The Analects*?

3. **MAKE CONNECTIONS** Which ideas in Confucianism and Daoism do you think could serve as useful advice for people living today?

Ancient South Asia and China 87

PLAN: 2-PAGE LESSON

OBJECTIVE

Explain how China's two oldest philosophies originated during a time of instability in Chinese history and helped restore order to society.

CRITICAL THINKING SKILLS FOR LESSON 3.3

- Describe
- Make Connections
- Analyze Cause and Effect
- Analyze Primary Sources

HISTORICAL THINKING FOR CHAPTER 3

How did religious and philosophical systems support societies in ancient India and China?

The instability during the Warring States Period left many Chinese people seeking spiritual and intellectual ideas that could stabilize society. Lesson 3.3 discusses the philosophies of Confucianism and Daoism and how they influenced Chinese culture.

Student eEdition online

Additional content for this lesson, including photographs, is available online.

BACKGROUND FOR THE TEACHER

The Cosmic Dao There are several interpretations of the *dao*, the most prevalent being that the Cosmic Dao is the Way of the Universe as depicted in the *Dao de Jing*, the classic text of Daoism. The Cosmic Dao is not a deity in the sense of a god or creator. Unlike many western manifestations of God, the Cosmic Dao is not a being that interacts with or looks out for humanity. Rather, it manifests in the order of nature and the universe. The Cosmic Dao is both yin and yang and is the entirety of all things in the universe. It is seen as a unifying force that maintains balance between yin and yang and harmony in the universe. Another prominent interpretation of the *dao* is that it is the way of all things. In other words, each thing and being has its own natural way of existence.

INTRODUCE & ENGAGE

PREVIEW PHOTOGRAPHS

Direct students to the photograph of the statue of Confucius (available in the Student eEdition). Explain that Confucius was a Chinese philosopher whose ideas were influential through many generations. Ask students to examine the statue and make inferences about Confucius based on how he is depicted. *(Possible responses might include that Confucius seems to have been calm and approachable.)* Tell students that in this lesson they will learn how Confucianism and Daoism, another ancient Chinese philosophy, influenced life during the late Zhou dynasty and beyond.

TEACH

GUIDED DISCUSSION

1. **Analyze Cause and Effect** What inspired Confucius to preach kindness and compassion? *(witnessing the horrors of violence during the Warring States.)*

2. **Make Connections** How would practicing Daoism help relieve stress? *(Possible response: By practicing Daoism, a person would not fixate on altering things in the world and would instead focus on living in harmony with the world, which would relieve stress.)*

ANALYZE PRIMARY SOURCES

Ask students to read the primary source excerpt from *The Analects*. **ASK:** What does the excerpt convey about filial piety and the roles of parents and children? *(Possible response: Children should respect and honor their parents by living as their parents intended even after their parents' death.)*

ACTIVE OPTIONS

On Your Feet: Three-Step Interview Organize students into pairs. Direct one student in each pair to interview the other student about Confucianism and Daoism by asking the following questions: Do you agree with one philosophy more than the other? Why or why not? Is it important for you, as part of a community, to implement these ideas? How well do you think our society applies these ideas? Then have partners reverse roles and have the second student interview the first student using the same questions. Encourage partners to ask follow-up questions as they see fit. Come together as a class, and prompt students to share key insights they gained from interviewing one another.

> **NG Learning Framework: Apply Confucianism or Daoism to a Contemporary Issue**
> **ATTITUDE** Responsibility
> **SKILL** Problem-Solving

Direct students to choose a contemporary issue and use either principles of Confucianism or Daoism to address the issue. Encourage students to think about current societal problems, such as poverty or inequality. Students should write a short essay about how the tenets of either Confucianism or Daoism could be used to solve a problem. Invite volunteers to read their essays to the class.

DIFFERENTIATE

STRIVING READERS

List Section Facts Ask students to read the lesson and write a list of facts they learned from each section. Then assign partners to compare their lists and fill in any facts that may have been missed. Direct students to explain what each section was about in their own words, using their list of facts as a memory prompt.

PRE-AP

Engage in a Debate Tell students they will debate the validity of incorporating Confucian ideals into Chinese society. Assign students to be either in favor of or against incorporating Confucian ideals. To prepare for the debate, ask students to review the text and conduct online research to further understand Confucian philosophy and how it manifested in late Zhou social norms, values, and customs. After the debate, guide a discussion about new information the class identified and how the debate deepened their understanding of Confucianism and its impact on Chinese society.

See the Chapter Planner for more strategies for differentiation.

HISTORICAL THINKING

ANSWERS

1. Both philosophies resulted from the violence and disorder experienced during the Warring States Period of the Zhou dynasty. Confucius hoped to bring order back to China.

2. In *The Analects*, Chinese rituals, family dynamics, and virtuous government are described and taught. During later dynasties, officials were required to study *The Analects* and put their teachings into practice in government and in their family relationships and lives.

3. Answers will vary.

Qin Rulers Unify China

What does it take to accomplish a lot in a short period of time? Efficiency? Focus? Force? In just 11 years, a cruel but skilled ruler built an empire by creating a system based on merit, forcing his subjects into hard labor, and stifling dissent.

CHINA UNIFIES UNDER AN EMPEROR

China's Warring States Period finally ended in 221 B.C.E. when Ying Zheng, the ruler of Qin (chin), defeated the Zhou and other kingdoms. He united the conquered kingdoms, formed an empire, and named himself **Shi Huangdi** (shee hwahng-dee), which means "first emperor."

Chinese historians portray Shi Huangdi as one of the worst tyrants in Chinese history, claiming he murdered his opponents, suppressed all learning, and forced his subjects into hard labor. This view of China's first emperor still prevails today.

Shi Huangdi, the first emperor of China, used cruel methods to bring order to China.

QIN GOVERNMENT AND LAW

Following the practices of his Qin homeland in western China, Shi Huangdi governed according to **Legalism**, a philosophy that emphasized order through strong government and strictly enforced laws. In keeping with Legalism, Qin officials recognized no hereditary titles, not even for members of the ruler's family.

Instead, Qin officials introduced a strict **meritocracy**, a system in which qualified people are chosen and promoted on the basis of their achievement rather than social position. Instead of appointing military and government officials because of their family background, officials sought the most qualified people. The idea of strict meritocracy was unique in the ancient world, and it proved very effective in creating a strong army.

Qin dynasty sources reveal that Shi Huangdi exercised far more control over his subjects than his predecessors. Shi Huangdi initiated several enormous public works projects and enlisted all able-bodied men to build them. Shi Huangdi linked different parts of his empire by building thousands of miles of new roads. He also built canals and irrigation systems. However, the most famous of his public works projects was the Great Wall. He ordered thousands of laborers to link pre-existing dirt walls across the northern border. These stronger walls were meant to protect his empire from the horse-riding nomadic invaders from Central Asia who were to threaten the security of northern China for many centuries. Thus, the wall would be expanded and fortified during the Ming dynasty, which followed the Qin by about 1,500 years.

The Qin dynasty did not last long enough to develop a governmental system for all of China, but it did create a basic **bureaucracy**, or group of administrative government officials. Shi Huangdi appointed a prime

The Great Wall as it stands today spans more than 13,000 miles in length. It is one of the largest building projects ever undertaken and was designated as a UNESCO World Heritage Site in 1987.

minister as the top official. Different departments in the capital administered the emperor's staff, the military, and revenue. The Qin divided the empire into districts headed by governors, military commanders, and magistrates.

Evidence from an official's tomb shows that Qin laws were surprisingly detailed, the product of a government concerned with following legal procedures carefully. For example, the Qin established procedures for officials to follow before reaching a judgment and provided clear instructions for investigating cases. Laws also defined fine legal distinctions among different types of crimes. Qin punishments were ruthless, such as the severing of one's foot or nose, but harsh punishments were not unusual in societies elsewhere in the world at the time.

SHORT LIFE, LONG LEGACY

Shi Huangdi lived in a state of fear, believing that his enemies would assassinate him. In preparation for his death, Shi Huangdi forced laborers to create an army of thousands of terra-cotta, or baked clay, warriors to be buried with him and to protect him after his death. You will learn more about the legacy of Shi Huangdi's burial site and the terra cotta warriors in the next lesson.

Shi Huangdi died in 210 B.C.E., just 11 years after he became emperor, and the dynasty fell soon thereafter. However, the Qin name has lived on in the country's name; we call the country "China" because of the Qin.

HISTORICAL THINKING

1. **READING CHECK** How did Shi Huangdi unify his empire?

2. **ANALYZE POINTS OF VIEW** How did Chinese historians portray Shi Huangdi?

3. **IDENTIFY** What are some of the most important accomplishments of the Qin dynasty?

PLAN: 2-PAGE LESSON

OBJECTIVE

Explain how the Qin dynasty unified the warring states of China and formed an empire.

CRITICAL THINKING SKILLS FOR LESSON 4.1

- Analyze Points of View
- Identify
- Identify Supporting Details
- Draw Conclusions
- Analyze Visuals

HISTORICAL THINKING FOR CHAPTER 3

How did religious and philosophical systems support societies in ancient India and China?

Shi Huangdi, the first emperor of China, governed according to Legalism, which was a philosophy that emphasized order through strong government and strictly enforced laws. Lesson 4.1 discusses how Shi Huangdi used this philosophical system to unite the Qin Empire.

Student eEdition online

Additional content for this lesson, including a video, is available online.

BACKGROUND FOR THE TEACHER

Chinese Characters Shi Huangdi imposed a common writing system across his empire. Chinese characters are formed by combining basic symbols called *radicals*. These radicals usually provide a clue to the word's meaning. For example, the radical for sun (*ri*) combines with the character for moon (*yue*) to create the character for bright (*ming*). Other times, a radical will provide a clue to the word's pronunciation rather than its meaning. For instance, the radical for female (*nu*) combines with the radical for horse (*ma*), creating the character for mother (*ma*). In this case, the horse character provides the sound "ma" rather than meaning.

INTRODUCE & ENGAGE

DISCUSS QUALIFICATIONS FOR GOOD LEADERS

Tell students that in many ancient societies, leaders were chosen based on family connections or triumph in war, not because they were the most qualified or experienced. Encourage students to discuss the qualifications for good leaders and how the most qualified people could be chosen based on their knowledge and achievements rather than their family or wealth.

TEACH

GUIDED DISCUSSION

1. **Identify Supporting Details** How did Shi Huangdi exercise far more control over his subjects than his predecessors? *(He forced all able-bodied men to build enormous public works projects, including roads, canals, irrigation systems, and the Great Wall.)*

2. **Draw Conclusions** How might Shi Huangdi's belief in Legalism have contributed to the dynasty falling apart after he died? *(In Legalism there is no hereditary title, and there most likely was no established way to select the next emperor when he died after just 11 years.)*

ANALYZE VISUALS

Tell students to look at the portrait of Shi Huangdi. **ASK:** How does the portrait fit the description of Shi Huangdi in the lesson? *(Possible responses: The lines in his forehead and his slanted eyebrows give the impression of someone frowning or scowling, which fits the description of a cruel tyrant. His eyes and pursed lips also look mean or cruel.)* Why do you think the artist drew the hairs in his beard and moustache so precisely? *(Possible response: Shi Huangdi was very precise in everything he did, including defeating the other kingdoms; unifying China; developing strict, detailed laws; and forcing thousands to build enormous projects.)*

ACTIVE OPTIONS

On Your Feet: Team Word Webbing Organize students into teams and provide each team with a large piece of paper and each team member with a different colored marker. Share the video about the Great Wall of China (available in the Student eEdition) and tell students to create a web about the wall with facts from the video, the text, and their background knowledge. Each student should write an important detail about the Great Wall on the part of the web nearest to him or her. On a signal, students should rotate the paper and continue to add details to the web.

> **NG Learning Framework: Does the Achievement Outweigh the Means?**
> **ATTITUDE** Empowerment
> **SKILL** Problem-Solving

Discuss how Shi Huangdi governed according to Legalism and meritocracy. Invite students to explore the link between these beliefs and the possibility that Shi Huangdi hoped that he would be remembered for his achievements rather than the means he used to achieve them. Direct students to write an opinion piece on whether a leader should be able to force people to build something for the public good and what modern leaders could learn from Shi Huangdi.

DIFFERENTIATE

INCLUSION

Provide an Oral Preview Hearing some of the main ideas of the lesson will help students begin to comprehend the lesson material before they read it. Read aloud the following preview: The ruler of the Qin defeated the other kingdoms, united the empire, and named himself Shi Huangdi, which means *first emperor*. Shi Huangdi accomplished a great deal during the 11 years he ruled. He had thousands of miles of roads built to unite the empire. He built canals and irrigation systems. He made thousands of workers build the Great Wall of China, which still stands today. However, Shi Huangdi accomplished all of this through cruel means, forcing his subjects into hard labor. He is portrayed by Chinese historians as one of the worst tyrants in Chinese history.

GIFTED & TALENTED

Create a Language Poster Share with students the Background for the Teacher information. Explain that Shi Huangdi issued this common writing system to help unify the empire. Ask students to conduct online research to find a chart of radicals for Chinese characters and to learn more about Chinese writing. Have them make a poster of some Chinese characters and the radicals that make up these characters. Invite students to share their posters with the class.

See the Chapter Planner for more strategies for differentiation.

HISTORICAL THINKING

ANSWERS

1. He defeated the different kingdoms to unite them under one dynasty, built a wall connecting different areas, and created a bureaucracy of districts.

2. as a tyrant

3. the unification of China, the Great Wall, and the road networks

4.2 Through The Lens

O. LOUIS MAZZATENTA

For over 40 years, National Geographic photographer O. Louis Mazzatenta has traveled extensively and performed many roles at *National Geographic* magazine. Though he retired in 1994, he continues to travel and take photographs. Italy and China are two of his favorite countries to work in because of the abundance of archaeological and historical subjects. "Archaeology is ancient history, but it's made new with the discovery of these things coming out of the earth," explains Mazzatenta.

One of his most thrilling assignments has been capturing the mystery of China's terra-cotta warriors, life-sized clay figures sculpted to stand guard at the tombs of China's first emperor, Shi Huangdi, and Jing Di, the fifth emperor of China's Han dynasty. "As I photographed the soldiers coming out of the ground, they seemed like real people," he says.

What details captured in this photo may have given Mazzatenta that impression?

XI'AN, CHINA
About 7,000 clay soldiers, each with unique expressions and features, have been unearthed from the tomb of Shi Huangdi. Although faded gray now, patches of paint suggest the warriors' clothing was once brightly colored. Archaeologists have also found swords, arrow tips, and other weapons.

PLAN: 2-PAGE LESSON

OBJECTIVE
Describe the details in the thousands of life-size terra-cotta warriors standing guard at the tomb of Shi Huangdi.

CRITICAL THINKING SKILLS FOR LESSON 4.2
- Analyze Visuals
- Make Connections
- Identify
- Make Inferences

HISTORICAL THINKING FOR CHAPTER 3
How did religious and philosophical systems support societies in ancient India and China?

Shi Huangdi ordered thousands of life-size terra-cotta soldiers made to stand guard around his tomb. Lesson 4.2 uses detailed photographs to show how Shi Huangdi's need for protection in the afterlife impacted the thousands of workers forced to create and arm these clay warriors.

BACKGROUND FOR THE TEACHER
O. Louis Mazzatenta Mazzatenta started working at National Geographic in 1961 as an intern in the illustrations department. After he served in the army, he returned to the magazine and worked for 30 years in various jobs that included illustrations editor, head of layout and design, and director of the control center. But his real love was photography. So after he "retired," he took assignments doing what he loved to do best. When he was photographing the terra-cotta warriors, he treated them with such respect and reverence that the Chinese archaeologists, in return, respected him. They allowed him to get up close and personal with the soldiers, which other foreign photographers were not allowed to do. He took close-up photographs of many parts of the warriors including their arms, hands, and heads. These photographs reveal brightly painted armor, hands molded to hold real weapons, and heads made unique through the careful sculpting of facial features and hair.

History Notebook
Encourage students to complete the Through the Lens page for Chapter 3 in their History Notebooks as they read.

INTRODUCE & ENGAGE

DISCUSS FACIAL EXPRESSIONS AND EMOTIONS

Invite volunteers to quickly draw a few different emojis with fierce-looking expressions. Discuss the details they use to show this expression and how many different fierce-looking emojis they think they could make before they started repeating the same details. Then have students look at the terra-cotta warriors in the lesson photos. Discuss the challenge the creators had in making unique expressions on the thousands of faces.

TEACH

GUIDED DISCUSSION

1. **Identify** What are two of O. Louis Mazzatenta's favorite places to photograph? Why? *(Italy and China because of the many historical and archaeological and historical subjects)*

2. **Make Inferences** Why do you think historians estimate that more than 700,000 laborers worked for 38 years to complete the warriors? *(Possible response: The detail included in each warrior's face, clothes, hands, and weapons would have taken much planning and hard work. Digging out the ground around the tomb and erecting the thousands of warriors would have taken many laborers a great deal of time, too.)*

THROUGH THE LENS

Share the Background for the Teacher information with students. Then have them study the photos in the lesson. **ASK:** Where do you see evidence that the terra-cotta warriors were once brightly painted? *(red paint on their armor)* Explain that real warriors of the Qin dynasty wore brightly painted leather armor fashioned in a similar manner. When archaeologists started excavating the terra-cotta warriors, they found more of this paint but it quickly flaked off when exposed to air. Over the years, archaeologists developed methods to preserve more of this paint. **ASK:** How do the photos reveal the unique features of the warriors? *(Possible responses: The faces show different eyes, eyebrows, mouths, and hair. The fallen warrior in the first photo has his arm and hand at his side; those in the second photo have their arms bent and hands extended. Some of their heads are turned; some are looking straight on.)*

ACTIVE OPTION

NG Learning Framework: A Photo Is Worth a Thousand Words
ATTITUDE Responsibility
SKILL Communication

From Background for the Teacher, share Mazzatenta was allowed to get up close when photographing the soldiers because he was respectful. Discuss the responsibility writers and photographers have to treat historical and archaeological artifacts and subjects with respect, as they tell the artifacts' story and create a new understanding for the reader and viewer. Have students research other photos by O. Louis Mazzatenta, choose one or two, and write descriptions of what the photos communicate and how they reveal Mazzatenta's respect for the subject.

DIFFERENTIATE

ENGLISH LANGUAGE LEARNERS

Photograph Vocabulary Guide students at the **Beginning** level in understanding and using appropriate vocabulary to discuss and write about the photographs in the lesson. Explain that *terra-cotta* is baked clay, another word for *warriors* is *soldiers*, and that a *photograph* is a picture taken with a camera. Point to and name any features of the warriors that students are unsure of and ask students to repeat each word. Then guide them to use the word in a simple sentence. Provide **Intermediate** level students with sentence frames to help them describe the photographs, such as: Each terra-cotta warrior is _____. Each face has different _____. One warrior is looking _____. Their armor looks like _____.

PRE-AP

Write a Profile Tell students to write a profile of photographer O. Louis Mazzatenta and his travels around the world to photograph for *National Geographic*. Ask them to conduct online research and draw on primary and secondary sources to supplement information from the text. Invite students to post their completed profiles on a class blog or school website or read them to the class.

See the Chapter Planner for more strategies for differentiation.

ANSWER

Possible response: The terra-cotta warriors are life-size and they are very realistic. Their eyes appear to be looking right at the viewer.

VOCABULARY

Write one or more sentences that explain the connection between the two concepts.

1. Sanskrit; Vedic
2. reincarnation; karma
3. varna; caste system
4. enlightenment; nirvana
5. oracle bone; ancestor worship
6. Mandate of Heaven; dynastic cycle
7. meritocracy; bureaucracy

READING STRATEGY
DETERMINE CHRONOLOGY

Use a time line like the one below to organize the major events of the 1,500 years of history in this chapter. Place the following events in their correct order along with their dates: birth of Confucius, death of the Buddha, beginning of Shang dynasty, beginning of Zhou dynasty, beginning of Qin dynasty.

8. Of the Chinese dynasties shown on your time line, which two Chinese dynasties began before the Maurya Empire arose in India?

MAIN IDEAS

Answer the following questions. Support your answers with evidence from the chapter.

9. How do the excavations of Harappan cities show that the people of the Indus Valley had developed a sophisticated civilization? LESSON 1.1
10. What does the Rig Veda reveal about the lives and beliefs of the Indo-Aryans? LESSON 1.2
11. What are some of the actions that Siddhartha Gautama took in his search for an end to suffering? LESSON 2.1
12. What effect did the conquest of Kalinga have on Ashoka and his reign? LESSON 2.3
13. What are some of the ideas that spread because of early trade across the Indian Ocean? LESSON 2.4
14. How did the loess of the Huang He contribute to the development of civilization along the North China Plain? LESSON 3.1
15. What difficulties did the Zhou face during the Warring States Period? LESSON 3.2
16. What did Confucius teach about the roles of parents and children? LESSON 3.3
17. Did the practice of legalism benefit the Qin dynasty? Explain. LESSON 4.1

HISTORICAL THINKING

Answer the following questions. Support your answers with evidence from the chapter.

18. MAKE INFERENCES What do the Harappan stone seals and the *Periplus* reveal about trade in ancient India?
19. DESCRIBE How did rulers in India and China seek to justify their methods of governing? Provide one example from each area.
20. DRAW CONCLUSIONS How has the discovery of ancient texts aided scholars in understanding early societies in India and China?
21. COMPARE AND CONTRAST Compare and contrast the governing strategies employed by Ashoka in India and Shi Huangdi in China.
22. FORM AND SUPPORT OPINIONS Would Confucius support Ashoka's practice of governing by example? Explain your reasoning.

INTERPRET MAPS

Study the map of the Shang, Zhou, and Qin dynasties. Then answer the questions below.

23. How did the Qin emperor define his northern border? How did this benefit his empire?
24. What physical features influenced the choice of location for the capitals of these first dynasties?

Shang, Zhou, and Qin Dynasties

ANALYZE SOURCES

One of the main tenets of Confucianism is the practice of filial piety. The following excerpt from *The Analects* describes the importance of this concept. Read the excerpt below and answer the question that follows.

> Master You said: "A man who respects his parents and his elders would hardly be inclined to defy his superiors. A man who is not inclined to defy his superiors will never foment a rebellion. A gentleman works at the root. Once the root is secured, the Way unfolds. To respect parents and elders is the root of humanity."

25. According to the excerpt, how does one's individual roots, or practices from an early age, lead to an orderly and humane society?

CONNECT TO YOUR LIFE

26. EXPLANATORY Qin emperor Shi Huangdi undertook a number of large public works projects. Research a large public works project that affects the United States today. Why was this project undertaken? Did it achieve its purpose? Write a paragraph to compare your recent project with a public works project undertaken by Shi Huangdi. Conclude with a statement that evaluates the value of public works projects in your community or state.

TIPS

- Review the discussions of Shi Huangdi's large public works projects in the chapter.
- Conduct research into large public works projects in the United States. Choose one of these projects that interests you.
- Compare one of Shi Huangdi's projects with the U.S. public works project.
- State your main idea about the two projects clearly at the beginning of the paragraph.
- Provide a concluding sentence that evaluates the value of public works projects today.

VOCABULARY ANSWERS

1. During the Vedic period, the earliest known sacred texts were written in Sanskrit.
2. If you live your life with virtue, you will gain karma, which will enable you to advance in your next life through reincarnation.
3. Because of varna, ancient Indians were born into a strict hierarchy, or caste system, that they could not escape.
4. The Buddha meditated under a tree and finally understood how to be free from suffering, thus he achieved enlightenment and nirvana, or the end of suffering.
5. The Shang practiced ancestor worship and used oracle bones to communicate with their deceased ancestors.
6. The Zhou developed a concept known as the Mandate of Heaven, which led to a pattern in the rise and fall of dynasties in China called the dynastic cycle.
7. The Qin introduced a type of bureaucracy known as meritocracy that allowed people to be promoted based on their personal merit and achievement.

READING STRATEGY ANSWER

Shang dynasty begins: 1600 B.C.E.	Confucius born: 551 B.C.E.	Maurya Empire begins: 320 B.C.E.

Zhou dynasty begins: 1045 B.C.E.	Buddha dies: 550s B.C.E.	Qin dynasty begins: 221 B.C.E.

8. The Shang and Zhou dynasties began in China before the Maurya Empire arose in India.

MAIN IDEAS ANSWERS

9. Excavations of Harappan cities show the sophisticated use of standardized measurements and a planning grid. Also, these cities had advanced plumbing and sewer systems.
10. The Rig Veda revealed changes in women's roles, the worship of numerous gods, and the way people of a variety of different occupations worked at that time.
11. Siddhartha left his family, gave up all his possessions, and searched for an understanding of how to be free from suffering.

12. Ashoka felt great remorse for having conquered Kalinga so brutally. Therefore, he adopted Buddhism and began a humanitarian rule.

13. Buddhism was the most important idea that spread due to early Indian Ocean trade. However, knowledge of new ideas about medicine, agriculture, and technology were also spread through trade.

14. The loess deposited along the river valley created fertile soil that enabled the development and growth of agriculture.

15. The Zhou king lost control as local lords gained power and fought against each other during the Warring States Period.

16. Confucius taught that children should respect and obey their parents.

17. Yes, legalism helped the Qin develop a strong government with strictly enforced laws.

HISTORICAL THINKING ANSWERS

18. The discovery of stone seals far from the Indus River Valley and documentation in the *Periplus* reveal that ancient Indians were heavily involved in trade.

19. Ashoka used inscriptions on stone pillars to portray himself as virtuous and humane in hopes that people would view his reign as worthy of support. The Zhou claimed that the dynasty had gained the Mandate of Heaven, which was a guiding force for rulers.

20. Texts written in Sanskrit revealed many aspects of Indo-Aryan society, including family dynamics, religion, and lifestyles. Texts written on oracle bones reveal the Shang belief in ancestor worships. These texts also describe events, such as battles.

21. Possible response: Ashoka ruled by example, which was effective because people believed he was virtuous and supported him. In contrast, Shi Huangdi used detailed laws, forced labor, and a meritocracy, or merit-based system.

22. Possible response: I believe Confucius would support Ashoka's practice of governing by example because Confucius taught that leaders who presented an inspiring example would lead people to goodness. Ashoka and Confucius both promoted benevolence, goodness, and virtue.

INTERPRET MAPS ANSWERS

23. He marked his northern border by constructing the Great Wall. The Great Wall distinguished the border as well as his power. It also blocked invaders from the north.

24. The Huang He influenced the choice of locations because all of these first dynasties established their capitals along the Huang He, which provided water, loess, and fertile soil.

ANALYZE SOURCES ANSWER

25. Possible response: If an individual learns from an early age to respect and obey his/her parents, then respect for others will come naturally throughout life, creating an orderly and humane society. Rebellion would be unnecessary in a society in which people respect one another and respect authority.

CONNECT TO YOUR LIFE ANSWER

26. Students' explanatory paragraphs will vary but should contain a thesis; develop the thesis with relevant, supporting details; and provide a summarizing statement that evaluates the value of public works projects in their community or state.

NATIONAL GEOGRAPHIC | CONNECTION

Cities of Silence
(Thoughts on the Harappan Culture)

BY PAUL SALOPEK   Adapted from "Cities of Silence," Out of Eden Walk dispatch
from Kalibangan, Rajasthan, India, August 30, 2018

When it's all said and done, what essence of our days will survive? What shard of human experience endures past the shallows of memory—beyond one generation? Or at most, two? Walking through the world it is impossible not to ask such questions.

The Indus Valley civilization, also called the Harappan culture, was both extraordinarily old and fantastically advanced. The biggest Harappan metropolis ever found is located at Mohenjo-Daro, in Pakistan. In India I visited a smaller and less known site in the desert called Kalibangan. Walking across it today, Kalibangan doesn't look like much. Flat-topped mounds of cobbles and broken bricks rise where the city walls once stood. The sand is littered with millions of 4,000-year-old pottery shards. It is impossible not to step on them. Local shepherds push their cows through the ruin.

Kalibangan has architectural features typical of most Harappan cities. A citadel ringed by 20-foot-thick walls protects a complex of fire altars. Most of the population lived, organized in neighborhoods of artisans, on a nearby grid of streets where wooden bumpers once were installed at the corners, presumably to shield buildings from clumsy cart traffic. Kalibangan's most famous relic is an anonymous-looking patch of earth: the oldest plowed field in the world, believed to date back 4,800 years. Even here the technology is elegant: The furrows are crossed-plowed at 90-degree angles, presumably allowing intercropping with different seeds, most likely cereals and mustard.

Swaying dizzily under the white desert sun, I dripped sweat from each fingertip and marveled at humankind's capacity for forgetting.

Why is the Indus Valley civilization—by any measure, one of the most accomplished ancient societies in the world—so little known?

Was it because a world-class culture vanished so utterly and mysteriously? By 1800 B.C.E., Harappan cities were

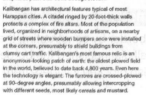

National Geographic Explorer Paul Salopek walks across broken 4,000-year-old pottery at the ancient Harappan city of Kalibangan, one of the earliest urban centers in the world.

being abandoned. Theories explaining their demise range from climate changes that unleashed flooding on the Indus to invasions from Central Asian tribes to an earthquake that may have shifted the course of vital rivers, such as the Saraswati, which exists today only as a ghostly channel of cobblestones in the waterless Thar desert.

Or maybe Harappan culture was simply too peaceful.

The Harappans did not appear to have left us any horror stories, the way violent colonizers like Alexander and the pharaohs did. Instead, the pioneers of urban living bequeathed to us the most efficient brick size, whose dimensional ratio of 1:2:4 is still favored in construction today. Harappa was an antique Switzerland.

"This is not a 'spectacular' civilization," writes Michel Danino in *The Lost River*, a book on the vanished Saraswati River. "[A]s a matter of fact, early archaeologists, especially European ones, complained at times of its 'monotony': no great pyramid, no glorious tomb, no awe-inspiring palace or temple, no breathtaking fresco or monumental sculpture."

I walked on.

94 UNIT 1

UNIT INQUIRY
UNIT 1 Design a Civilization-Building Game

Staging the Question

In this unit, you learned about how and why humans stopped roaming as nomads, settled into the first villages, and formed the earliest civilizations. Each society in the ancient Middle East, the Mediterranean, Africa, and Asia followed its own unique path toward increasingly complex civilizations. At the same time, however, they were all influenced by similar unifying forces, such as religion, and faced similar challenges, such as war. Which factors were the most important to the building—and decline—of the first civilizations?

ASSIGNMENT

List at least five factors that helped early civilizations develop and four challenges the civilizations faced. You might include people, new ideas, and geographic advantages or disadvantages.

Analyze the factors you listed and decide how they contributed to the formation or destruction of a civilization.

Rank the factors in terms of how strongly they influenced the civilizations. You could assign each factor a point value.

Based on your analysis of how early civilizations developed, design a civilization-building game that realistically shows how and why civilizations grow or fail.

Supporting Questions: Begin by developing supporting questions to guide your thinking. For example: How does having a strong ruler affect a developing society? Research the answers in this unit and in other sources, both print and online.

Cause		Effect
	→	

Summative Performance Task: Use the answers to your questions to help you determine which positive and negative factors you want to include in your game and how these forces will affect game play. You may format your game in a number of ways, such as a card game, a board game, a role-playing game, or even an online game. Consider researching existing online and board-based civilization-building games for inspiration. You might want to use a graphic organizer like this one to help you plan the steps in your game.

Present: Share your game with the class. You might consider one of these options:

PLAY THE GAME
Gather a group of classmates to play your game. Explain the rules and why certain elements of the game allow players to advance more quickly toward civilization—or set them back further.

PITCH THE GAME
Hold a "pitch session" in which game developers present their games to the class, which acts as the board of directors of a game company. The game developers must explain why their game is realistic and why the company should buy it.

Take Informed Action:

UNDERSTAND Examine current events and identify factors from your game that seem to be at work in societies today.

ASSESS Draw conclusions about why it is important to understand the forces that have contributed to the rise and fall of civilizations.

ACT Make a presentation to share with other classes or in your community about what we gain by studying the forces that shape civilizations.

Ancient Worlds 95

NATIONAL GEOGRAPHIC CONNECTION

GUIDED DISCUSSION FOR "CITIES OF SILENCE (THOUGHTS ON THE HARAPPAN CULTURE)"

1. **Form and Support Opinions** Which presented theory best supports the reason that Harappan cities were abandoned? Explain your response. *(Answers will vary. Possible responses: I think the theory that climate changes unleashed flooding supports why Harappan cities were abandoned because history shows that melting ice from the Ice Age caused water levels to rise. I think the theory that an invasion from Central Asian tribes supports why Harappan cities were abandoned because as the tribes conquered territory, they often brutally murdered people and then marched on to the next territory. I think the theory that a great earthquake affected the habitat and shifted the course of rivers supports why Harappan cities were abandoned because the quake altered the landscape, and people had to find a new place to settle.)*

2. **Make Connections** What makes the Harappans unique, and why is it important to learn about their culture? *(Possible response: The Harappans may be the most accomplished ancient society in the world, so it is important to understand their architecture, agriculture practices, city structure, and religious beliefs so that we may grow as a society and learn from others' successes and mistakes.)*

History Notebook

Encourage students to complete the Unit Wrap-Up page for Unit 1 in their History Notebooks.

UNIT INQUIRY PROJECT RUBRIC

ASSESS

Use the rubric to assess each student's participation and performance.

SCORE	ASSIGNMENT	PRODUCT	PRESENTATION
3 GREAT	• Student thoroughly understands the assignment. • Student develops thoughtful supporting questions to guide research.	• The game is well thought out, shows creativity, and has a variety of questions. • The game reflects all of the key elements listed in the assignment.	• The game pitch or game directions are clear, concise, and logical. • The game is factual but also creative and engaging.
2 GOOD	• Student mostly understands the assignment. • Student develops somewhat thoughtful supporting questions to guide research.	• The game is fairly well thought out and shows some creativity and variety. • The game reflects most of the key elements listed in the assignment.	• The game pitch or game directions are fairly clear, concise, and logical. • The game is somewhat creative and engaging.
1 NEEDS WORK	• Student does not understand the assignment. • Student does not develop thoughtful questions to guide research.	• The game is not well thought out and shows no creativity. • The game reflects few or none of the key elements listed in the assignment.	• The game pitch or game directions are not clear, concise, or logical. • The game is not creative or engaging.

PHILIPPI AND THE END OF THE ROMAN REPUBLIC

Along with its importance in the history of Christianity, the city of Philippi was also the site of an important battle. In October 42 B.C.E., two armies clashed on the plains just west of the city. One army was headed by Brutus and Cassius, the assassins of Julius Caesar and defenders of the republican form of government in Rome; the other was headed by Mark Antony and Octavian, who wished to avenge the murder of Caesar and continue his legacy. The battle began when Antony and Octavian launched an assault on Brutus and Cassius. Antony captured Cassius's camp but then had to go to the aid of Octavian, whose troops were captured by Brutus. Not knowing that his counterpart had been successful, the defeated Cassius committed suicide. Antony then began building a fortified causeway across a marsh to move around Brutus's troops. On October 23, Brutus launched an attack on the causeway but ended up surrounded by Antony's cavalry. Brutus committed suicide and his troops surrendered. The battle marked the effective death of the Roman Republic. Eleven years later, Octavian defeated Mark Antony at Actium and became the sole ruler of the Roman Empire.

Direct students' attention to the photograph. **ASK:** What features of Roman architecture are evident in the photographed remains? *(Possible response: the theater, arch entrance, stonework)*

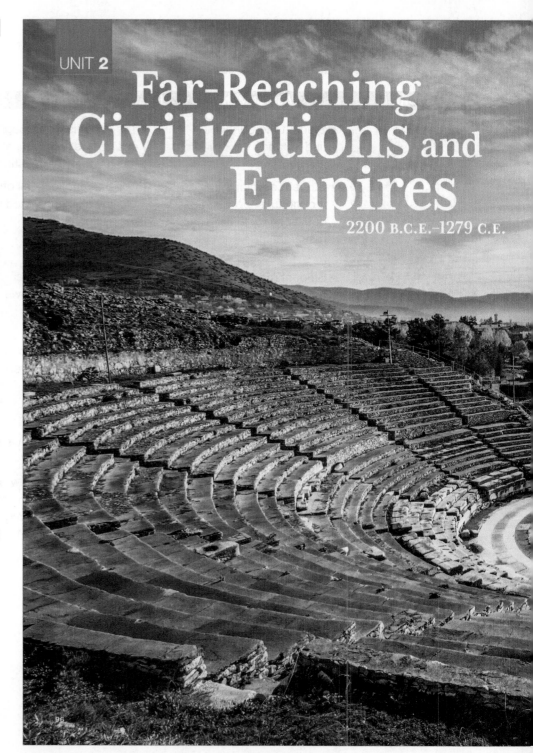

Far-Reaching Civilizations and Empires

2200 B.C.E.–1279 C.E.

CRITICAL VIEWING Possible response: The fact that the site provides clues to ancient Greek, Roman, and Christian cultures is why the site is culturally significant and important to preserve today.

INTRODUCE TIME LINE EVENTS

IDENTIFY PATTERNS AND THEMES

Have volunteers read aloud each of the world events in the time line. **ASK:** What are some common themes or patterns that you notice with regard to these events? *(Possible responses: Some common themes or patterns include powerful empires, conquest, and cultural developments.)* Sort the themes and patterns into categories and put them in Concept Clusters like the ones shown here.

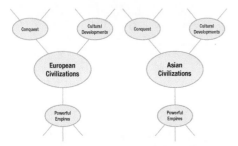

As students read the lessons for each chapter in the unit, have them add the lesson titles to the appropriate cluster. Advise students that they may also add or revise categories as necessary. At the end of the unit, revisit students' clusters and create a final list of categories to summarize the historical themes students encountered as they read each chapter.

UNIT 2 Far-Reaching Civilizations and Empires

WORLD EVENTS
2200 B.C.E.–1200 C.E.

c. 760 B.C.E. EUROPE The first important work of Western literature, *The Iliad*, is written. *(Greek amphora depicting the Trojan horse)*

522 B.C.E. ASIA King Darius I ascends the throne of the Persian Empire and ushers in the empire's golden age. *(Persian coin depicting Darius I)*

490 B.C.E. EUROPE Greatly outnumbered Greek forces defeat Persian aggressors in the Battle of Marathon, a major battle of the Greco-Persian Wars.

2200 B.C.E. // 1000 B.C.E. 500 B.C.E.

509 B.C.E. EUROPE Romans overthrow Etruscan King Tarquin and establish the first republic.

2000 B.C.E. EUROPE The first major Phoenician city-states—Tyre and Sidon— arise on the shores of the Mediterranean. *(figurines from the ancient Phoenician city of Byblos)*

508 B.C.E. EUROPE Cleisthenes establishes the world's first democracy in ancient Greece.

330 B.C.E. ASIA Alexander the Great overthrows the Persian Empire. *(17th-century French painting of Alexander the Great)*

98

206 B.C.E. ASIA
In China, the peasant leader Liu Bang conquers the Qin to found the Han dynasty. *(Han-era painted warrior with spear)*

HISTORICAL THINKING

ANALYZE CAUSE AND EFFECT How might the failure of the Jewish uprising against the Romans in 70 B.C.E. have contributed to Christianity becoming the official religion of the Roman Empire?

70 C.E. ASIA In Jerusalem, Roman general Titus crushes a Jewish uprising and destroys the city, causing the Jewish people to disperse throughout the empire.

380 C.E. EUROPE Emperor Theodosius declares Christianity the official religion of the Roman Empire. *(mosaic of Jesus Christ)*

649 C.E. ASIA Empress Wu becomes China's first and only female emperor. *(portrait of Empress Wu)*

105 C.E. ASIA
The Chinese invent paper.

500 C.E. — **1200 C.E.**

476 C.E. EUROPE Germanic leader Odoacer leads his army into Rome and conquers the city without a fight, ending the Roman Empire.

320 C.E. ASIA
The Gupta dynasty takes control of northern India and ushers in a golden age. *(Gupta-era statue of the Hindu deity Vishnu)*

C. 1000 C.E. ASIA Lady Murasaki Shikibu of Japan writes *The Tale of Genji*, the world's first novel. *(woodcut portrait of Lady Murasaki Shikibu)*

99

HISTORICAL THINKING

Analyze Cause and Effect

Possible response: After the failure of the uprising, Jewish people spread out across the empire, which made room for Christianity to grow and flourish. This may have increased the religion's popularity in the empire, laying the groundwork for Theodosius's declaration in 380.

Student eEdition online

Additional content, including the unit map and Global Perspective feature, is available online.

UNIT 2 RESOURCES

UNIT INTRODUCTION

UNIT TIME LINE

UNIT MAP online

THE GLOBAL PERSPECTIVE: Astronomy: The Search for Meaning and Survival

- National Geographic Explorers: Kevin Hand, Neil deGrasse Tyson, and Jedidah Isler
- On Your Feet: Roundtable

| **NG Learning Framework**
Research National Geographic Explorers

UNIT WRAP-UP

National Geographic Magazine Adapted Article
- "The Land of the Stars"

Unit 2 Inquiry: Curate a Museum Exhibit

Unit 2 Formal Assessment

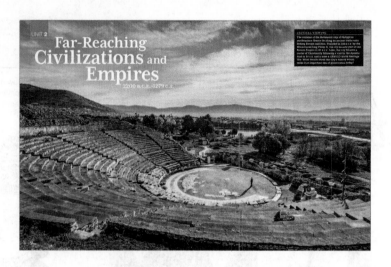

CHAPTER 4 RESOURCES

Available in the Teacher eEdition

TEACHER RESOURCES & ASSESSMENT

Reading and Note-Taking

Vocabulary Practice

Document-Based Question Template

Social Studies Skills Lessons
- Reading: Analyze Cause and Effect
- Writing: Explanatory

Formal Assessment
- Chapter 4 Pretest
- Chapter 4 Tests A & B
- Section Quizzes

Chapter 4 Answer Key

Cognero®

STUDENT DIGITAL RESOURCES

Available in the Student eEdition

- eEdition (English)
- Handbooks
- National Geographic Atlas
- History Notebook
- Biographies
- Literature Analysis

STRATEGY **1**

Focus on Main Ideas

Tell students to locate the Main Idea statement at the beginning of each lesson. Explain that these statements summarize the important ideas of the lesson and help students focus on key facts and ideas. Ask students to copy each Main Idea statement into a graphic organizer and then list details from the lesson that support it.

Use with All Lessons *For example, key details from Lesson 1.2 may include the following: when the Persians overthrew the Medes, where the Persian Empire was, why Cyrus was called "Cyrus the Great," and what he did that made him "a good and tolerant ruler."*

STRATEGY **2**

Pose and Answer Questions

Arrange students in pairs and ask them to reread a lesson from the chapter together. Instruct them to pause after each paragraph from a lesson and ask each other *who, what, when, where,* and *why* questions about what they have just read. Suggest that students use a 5Ws Chart to help organize their questions and answers. Encourage partners to assist each other as needed.

Use with All Lessons

STRATEGY **3**

Summarize a Lesson

Instruct pairs of students to read each paragraph from a lesson silently and write a sentence to summarize what they read. Tell partners to trade sentences and then work together to clarify the meaning of each paragraph. Point out to students that, taken together, the sentences represent a summary of the whole lesson.

Use with All Lessons *Throughout the chapter, encourage students to get in the habit of summarizing paragraphs and sections as they read.*

STRATEGY **1**

Use Supported Reading

Pair proficient readers with students who have reading or perception issues. Assign partners paragraphs from one of the lessons to read aloud together. At the end of each paragraph, have students use the following sentence frames to monitor their comprehension:

- This paragraph is about _____ .
- One fact that stood out to me was _____ .
- I don't think I understand _____ .

Review ideas that confuse students and be sure all students understand the content before moving on to the next paragraph.

Use with All Lessons

STRATEGY **2**

Modify Vocabulary Lists

You can modify the number of Key Vocabulary words that students will be required to master. As they read, instruct students to create a vocabulary card, such as the one shown, for each word in the modified list. Encourage them to write definitions, synonyms, antonyms, or examples on each word card. Direct students to refer to their vocabulary cards often as they read.

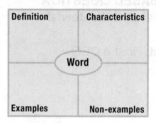

Use with All Lessons

STRATEGY **1**

Create a Word Wall

Work with students at the **Beginning** and **Intermediate** levels to select five terms from each lesson to display on a Word Wall. Choose terms students are likely to encounter in other lessons in the unit, such as *diverse, tribute, conquests, repressive,* and *regime.* Keep the words displayed throughout the chapter, adding terms for each new lesson. Discuss each term as it comes up during reading.

Use with All Lessons

STRATEGY ②

Teach and Learn

Pair students at the **Beginning** or **Intermediate** level with students at the **Advanced** level. Have the more English-proficient students teach words that appear in various forms, such as an adjective and a noun. Direct pairs to compose a sentence for each word and invite them to share their sentences with other pairs. Suggest the following words:

culture/cultural
provinces/provincial
administer/administrative/administrator
tolerance/tolerant

Use with Lesson 1.2 *You may use a similar strategy for other lessons. For example, in Lesson 2.3, you could instruct students to write sentences for related words such as* rebels/rebelled/rebellion *and* invaders/invaded.

STRATEGY ③

Create Word Charts

Help students understand unfamiliar words by completing charts like the one shown. Pair students at the **Beginning** level with students at either the **Intermediate** or **Advanced** level. Ask pairs to copy the chart and then work together to complete it as they encounter unfamiliar words.

Definition of _____.	Draw a visual of the word.
Tell how the word relates to the Persian Empire.	Use the word in a sentence.

Use with All Lessons

STRATEGY ①

Conduct an Interview

Tell students to work in pairs to gather information from the lessons on Cyrus or Darius. Prompt students to write questions a journalist might have used to interview either ruler, focusing on his experiences, motivations, challenges, and achievements/defeats. Then tell students to work together to write the answers the ruler might have given to those questions. Have pairs conduct their interview before the class.

Use with Lessons 1.2, 1.3, and 2.1

STRATEGY ②

Report on a Battle

Prompt students to choose one of the battles detailed in Lesson 2.3 "The Greco-Persian Wars" and write a news report describing it. Have them conduct additional research as needed on the strategies employed by both sides in the battle. Instruct students to describe motivations and forces for both sides, how one side took advantage of the other, and who won. Encourage them to include an eye-catching headline and an attention-grabbing introduction in their news reports.

Use with Lesson 2.3

STRATEGY ①

Study Historic Documents

Direct students to conduct online research on the historian Herodotus and his work, *The Histories*. Encourage them to read sections of *The Histories* that refer to topics in the chapter and write an essay analyzing how Herodotus brings the topic to life.

Use with All Lessons

STRATEGY ②

Evaluate Persian Influence

Ask students to choose one legacy of the Persian Empire and research to learn more about the way in which it influences governments and people today. Students may also wish to discuss the impact of Persia's legacy on their own lives.

Use with Lesson 2.4

HISTORICAL THINKING How did the Persians create a
well-ordered empire that lasted for 200 years?

SECTION 1 Ancient Iran

SECTION 2 The Reign of Darius

CRITICAL VIEWING
Columns and sculpted carvings recall the grandeur
of the ancient Persian capital of Persepolis, built
around 500 B.C.E. What do the ruins of the city
suggest about the Persian Empire at that time?

INTRODUCE THE PHOTOGRAPH

PERSIAN RUINS

Have students study the ruins at Persepolis in the photo.
ASK: What events are depicted in the sculpted carvings
in the wall? *(Possible response: A procession of people,
possibly soldiers carrying shields and spears, appears
on the left. On the right, a lion attacks a horse.)* Explain
that these carvings are called the Parade of Nations and
show people of the empire bringing gifts to the king. Tell
students that in this chapter they will learn about the rise
of the Achaemenid Empire in Persia and its powerful
leaders.

SHARE BACKGROUND

Achaemenid emperor Darius constructed a magnificent
terrace at Persepolis. It featured a double staircase,
slender columns, intricate friezes, and massive winged
bulls.

Darius began construction of the monument in 515 B.C.E.
when he came to power, and the complex reflects the
diversity of the Persian Empire's population. Xerxes
completed the monument in 480 B.C.E.

CRITICAL VIEWING Answers will vary. Possible
response: They suggest the power of the empire and
the skill of its architects and artists.

How did the Persians create a well-ordered empire that lasted for 200 years?

Team Word Webbing Activity: The Well-Ordered Persian Empire This activity will help students consider what social, economic, and political factors enabled the Persians to create a strong and orderly empire. Organize students into teams and provide each with a large sheet of paper. Assign each team one of the following questions:

- What political factors helped create a well-ordered empire?
- What economic factors helped create a well-ordered empire?
- What socio-cultural factors helped create a well-ordered empire?

Tell teams to draw a concept web on their paper and write their question in the central oval. Have team members brainstorm answers and then take turns writing them in the web. Each student adds to the part of the web nearest to him or her. Once one team member has finished, students should rotate the paper until all students have written an answer. Then call on volunteers from each team to read from their webs.

KEY DATES FOR CHAPTER 4

550 B.C.E.	Persian leader Cyrus II overthrows the Medes and incorporates their land into the Persian Empire.
539 B.C.E.	Cyrus frees the Jews.
522 B.C.E.	Darius overthrows the Persian government and later moves the capital of the empire to Persepolis.
499–479 B.C.E.	The most intense fighting occurs in the Greco-Persian Wars, which lasted from 492 to 449 B.C.E.
449 B.C.E.	The Peace of Callias is signed and brings the Greco-Persian Wars to an end.
440 B.C.E.	Herodotus publishes *The Histories*.
331 B.C.E.	The Macedonians under Alexander the Great defeat the Persian Empire.
224 B.C.E.	The Sasanians overthrow the Parthians.
651 C.E.	The Sasanian Empire ends.

ANALYZE CAUSE AND EFFECT

Explain that analyzing cause and effect can help students understand the complexity of historical events and their multiple causes and effects. Turn to the Chapter Review and preview the graphic organizer with students. As they read the chapter, tell students to analyze and record the causes and effects of the rise of the Persian Empire, Persia's golden age, and the Greco-Persian Wars.

KEY VOCABULARY

SECTION 1

satrap

SECTION 2

coup	phalanx	trireme

DEFINITION CHART

As they read the chapter, encourage students to complete a Definition Chart for Key Vocabulary terms. Instruct students to list the Key Vocabulary terms in the first column of the chart. They should add each term's definition in the center column as they encounter the term in the chapter and then restate the definition in their own words in the third column. Model an example on the board, using the graphic organizer shown.

Word	Definition	In My Own Words
satrap	a provincial governor	the person who leads the government of a province

Traveler: Herodotus
The World's First Historian

c. 145–87 B.C.E.

A good travel writer uses vivid description and gripping stories to make the history and culture of a place come alive. The historian Herodotus first used these techniques about 2,500 years ago when he wrote about the Persians, Greeks, and other ancient societies.

LIFE AND TRAVELS

Like travelers who write about their experiences today, those of the past introduced their readers to people and places in distant lands. Because the writings of Herodotus survived, they have reached across time to enhance our understanding and knowledge of the ancient world. Modern historians still consider Herodotus's book an important source for information about ancient Greece and the Persian Empire. Many scholars have called him the world's first historian.

Little is known about Herodotus's life, including the exact years of his birth and death. Most historians today believe he was born around 484 B.C.E. in Halicarnassus—present-day Bodrum, Turkey—a mostly Greek city within the Persian Empire. At that time, the empire was ruled by a dynasty of kings called the **Achaemenids** (ah-KEE-muh-nihdz). The lands of the Persian Empire, centered in Iran, stretched from Anatolia (the Asian part of modern Turkey) and Egypt across western Asia to northern India and central Asia.

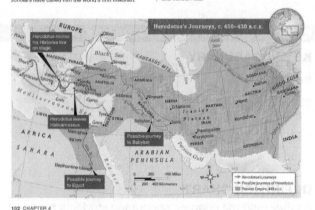

Herodotus's Journeys, c. 450–430 B.C.E.

Herodotus probably lived for a time in Athens, Greece, but he is best known for his extensive travels. Over the course of many years, he journeyed through parts of the Persian Empire, including Anatolia, Lydia, Egypt, Syria, and Babylonia. He also traveled throughout Greece and Italy. His interest in other cultures and keen observational skills made him a savvy traveler. These qualities served him well as a historian.

"GREAT AND MARVELOUS DEEDS"

Herodotus wrote and published his masterpiece, *The Histories*, in Greek around 440 B.C.E. The book is the only one Herodotus produced, and he spent most of his life working on it. From the beginning, *The Histories* was a great success, and Herodotus recited the work before appreciative audiences in Athens. After his death, *The Histories* was divided into nine books. The first five books focus on the rise of the Persian Empire and describe its geography, people, and customs. These books set the stage for Herodotus's history of the **Greco-Persian Wars**, which is the subject of the last four books.

During the wars, the most intense fighting between various Greek city-states and the mighty Persian Empire took place between about 499–479 B.C.E. While Persia was a great empire, the Greeks were largely organized in much smaller city-states, where male citizens actively participated in civic life. Herodotus discusses important battles and provides insight into the leaders of both armies. Although the imperial army of the Achaemenids was far more powerful than those of the much smaller Greek cities, Greek forces were able to repel the imperial invaders twice and, eventually, defeat Persia. In part, Herodotus wrote *The Histories* to understand the Greeks' improbable victory. You will learn more about the Greco-Persian Wars later in this chapter.

Herodotus used methodical research and multiple sources to explain how and why past events occurred. In fact, in ancient Greek, the title of his book means "inquiries" or "research" and is the basis of the English word *history*. Herodotus also distinguished his work by filling his narrative with entertaining stories, dialogue, and speeches by historical figures. He structured the material by weaving themes and morals throughout. For example, to illustrate the moral "pride comes before a fall," Herodotus points out the arrogance and

PRIMARY SOURCE

Herodotus of Halicarnassus here displays his inquiry, so that human achievements may not become forgotten in time, and great and marvelous deeds—some displayed by Greeks, some by barbarians [non-Greeks]—may not be without their glory; and especially to show why the two peoples fought with each other. . . .

If, like ours [the Greeks'], their troops were subject to the control of a single man, then possibly for fear of him, in spite of the disparity in numbers, they might show some sort of factitious [false] courage, or let themselves be whipped into battle; but, as every man is free to follow his fancy, it is not conceivable that they should do either.

cruelty of the Persian king **Xerxes I** (ZURK-seez) and then describes the king's failure to conquer Greece in 480 B.C.E. Herodotus emphasized the impact of humans on historical events.

On the other hand, he also sometimes stretched the facts to tell a good story. Throughout his book, Herodotus exaggerated the truth, relied on hearsay, invented stories, and made outright mistakes. Many historians who came after Herodotus criticized his work and tried to discredit it. But most scholars today agree that the inaccuracies in *The Histories* do not detract from the book or diminish its significance.

Before Herodotus, travelers wrote disjointed chronicles about people and places that didn't form a unified whole. *The Histories* led to the development of historiography, which as you learned earlier is based on examining sources, selecting details from the sources, and synthesizing those details into a coherent story. As a result of his questions and explorations, Herodotus wrote a narrative that provides a window on the past.

HISTORICAL THINKING

1. **READING CHECK** What techniques did Herodotus use to hold his readers' attention?

2. **ANALYZE SOURCES** According to Xerxes, what would have happened if the Greek troops had been under the control of one man?

3. **INTERPRET MAPS** How might Herodotus have traveled from Halicarnassus to Athens?

PLAN: 2-PAGE LESSON

OBJECTIVE

Explain how Herodotus produced a work that came to define how history should be written.

CRITICAL THINKING SKILLS FOR LESSON 1.1

- Analyze Sources
- Interpret Maps
- Compare and Contrast
- Form and Support Opinions
- Analyze Primary Sources

HISTORICAL THINKING FOR CHAPTER 4

How did the Persians create a well-ordered empire that lasted for 200 years?

Lesson 1.1 discusses the contribution of Herodotus's *The Histories* as a significant resource in our understanding of the Persian Empire.

BACKGROUND FOR THE TEACHER

Technique and Topics in *The Histories* Herodotus makes it clear when he uses a hearsay account rather than his own observations and openly expresses doubt about some of the taller tales he presents. *The Histories* is also more than a first-person travel account. It presents the history, folklore, geography, plants, and customs of the known world at the time. Because of his extensive travels, Herodotus had many experiences that shaped his view. Yet he was also Greek and favored Greek ideas, both culturally and politically.

History Notebook

Encourage students to complete the Traveler page for Chapter 4 in their History Notebooks as they read.

INTRODUCE & ENGAGE

DISCUSS ANCIENT TRAVEL

Direct students to look at the map of Herodotus's journeys in the lesson. Explain that travel at this time was long, tedious, and often dangerous. Ask volunteers to suggest how Herodotus traveled to the different places shown on the map and what travel challenges and delays he might have experienced. *(Possible response: Travel by ship across the Black and Mediterranean seas might have been difficult and long and his journey across Anatolia might have been done by foot or on a horse.)* Tell students that in this lesson they will learn about Herodotus and his book, *The Histories*, which describes his experiences and travels.

TEACH

GUIDED DISCUSSION

1. **Compare and Contrast** In what way was Herodotus's *The Histories* different from earlier works by other writers? *(Herodotus carefully researched different sources and then synthesized the details to create a unified work.)*

2. **Form and Support Opinions** Do you think Herodotus's account of the Greco-Persian Wars can be trusted? Why or why not? *(Possible response: Yes, but the reader must be careful and check other sources to verify facts and opinions expressed by Herodotus.)*

ANALYZE PRIMARY SOURCES

Tell students to read and analyze the two primary source excerpts from *The Histories* in the lesson. **ASK:** Why does Xerxes say that the Greeks have more freedom than his people? *(Possible response: because the Greeks practice democracy and the Persians do not)* Prompt pairs to ask each other questions about the excerpts. Have them discuss possible answers and then pose the same questions with another pair.

ACTIVE OPTIONS

On Your Feet: Create a Quiz Arrange students in teams and direct them to create a quiz about information in the lesson. Allow time for teams to write a variety of true-false, short answer, or complete-the-sentence questions. Then have teams alternate posing a question to which the other team responds. Clarify incorrect answers and keep track of the number of correct answers for each team.

| **NG Learning Framework: Create a Composite Illustration**
| **ATTITUDE** Curiosity
| **SKILLS** Communication, Collaboration

Have small groups create a composite illustration that shows a scene from *The Histories*. Some students in each group could research artwork of the scene; others may make a digital composite or collage using prints of the artwork. If necessary, direct students to online instructions for photographing artwork and creating digital composite photos. Invite groups to present their completed work to the class and explain the concept behind it, including why they chose this detail to feature.

DIFFERENTIATE

STRIVING READERS

Paraphrase Primary Sources Some students may find the primary source difficult to understand because of its vocabulary and challenging sentence structure. Pair students who are struggling with students who are not. Have them discuss unfamiliar words and phrases. Then direct partners to work together to paraphrase each excerpt.

GIFTED & TALENTED

Create a Web Page Prompt students to conduct online research to find other passages from *The Histories* or information about Herodotus's travels. Challenge them to design a web page about his writings, his perspective, and related information. Suggest that they include information about his methodology for writing *The Histories* and details about his travels. Encourage students to post their web page on a school or class website.

See the Chapter Planner for more strategies for differentiation.

HISTORICAL THINKING

ANSWERS

1. He included entertaining stories, dialogue, and speeches by historical figures, and he structured his material by weaving themes and morals throughout it.

2. They would fight out of fear of their commander or be forced into battle.

3. by ship

Early Persia

The desire to acquire land and exercise power over many people was as great a drive in the ancient world as it has been in modern times. Around the 600s and 500s B.C.E., two groups fought for domination over Iran, an important region in Southwest Asia. History suggests that the best man won.

THE RISE OF THE PERSIANS

Humans had lived on the Iranian Plateau, the region of Southwest Asia that roughly includes the boundaries of present-day Iran, for thousands of years. Some may have been drawn by the abundant pearl oyster beds in the Persian Gulf, the center of pearl trade in the ancient world. Many different cultures arose in the region and developed in relative isolation. Around 1300 B.C.E., however, nomadic groups of Indo-Europeans began migrating there. Two ancient Iranian groups, the Medes (meedz) and the Parsa, grew especially powerful. The Medes settled in an area of northwestern Iran called Media and spoke the Median language. The Parsa—or the Persians, as they came to be known—lived in an area called Persis in southwestern Iran and spoke Persian.

Little is known about Median culture and religion. But historians know that many Persians practiced **Zoroastrianism**, a religion founded by the prophet Zoroaster (also known as Zarathustra) about 3,500 years ago. Zoroastrianism is one of the world's oldest monotheistic religions. Its core teachings are contained in the Avesta, the religion's sacred book. The Avesta describes a supreme god, Ahura Mazda, who created twin spirits of good and evil. The struggle between the two spirits reflects the constant battle humans face in their daily lives.

Both the Medes and the Persians established kingdoms in Iran. In 550 B.C.E., however, the Persian leader **Cyrus II** overthrew the Medes, and the Median Empire came under his control. The Median lands, which included Assyria and its capital of Nineveh, became the first part of the Persian Empire. Cyrus then conquered lands north and west of Persia, including the regions of Lydia, Babylonia, Syria, Palestine, and the Greek city-states on the eastern Aegean Sea. Lydia was an enormously wealthy region. People there had been minting coins from an alloy of gold and silver since around 600 B.C.E.. These Lydian coins were the first metal coins used anywhere in the world.

Remember reading about the Achaemenids? Cyrus was part of that dynasty, which was named for a legendary king. The Persian Empire that Cyrus established is sometimes referred to as the Achaemenid Empire. Cyrus took the title King of Kings, as did all the Achaemenid rulers who came after him. Between 550 and 330 B.C.E., the Achaemenids would rule over about 30 to 35 million people. It was the most diverse empire the world had ever seen. Its subjects came from a mix of cultures, spoke many different languages, and practiced a wide variety of religions. The Persian Empire also contained some of the world's most advanced cities, including Babylon and Susa in southwestern Iran.

THE REIGN OF CYRUS THE GREAT

Cyrus controlled his empire by maintaining a huge army manned not only by Persians but also by peoples of conquered lands, including the Medes. He recruited soldiers from different groups within the empire, so all would share in the wealth that came from further conquests. The new emperor believed doing so would help inspire allegiance, or loyalty, toward his dynasty and his officials. And he was willing to learn from those he conquered. Historians believe Cyrus made a Mede one of his closest advisors.

The Persian leader also adapted cultural traditions from other peoples and borrowed aspects of the governmental systems of other rulers to guide his empire. To administer his lands, Cyrus divided the empire into provinces. Other empires had used this system, but unlike other rulers, Cyrus appointed local people as provincial governors, or **satraps**

(SAY-traps). A satrap collected taxes, maintained order within the province, and defended against external threats. The administrative structures Cyrus put into place were so effective that they continued for about two centuries.

While an excellent administrator, Cyrus is most renowned for his tolerance of others' beliefs and practices. He allowed conquered kings to maintain their thrones, and he let his subjects keep their religions, languages, and customs. Cyrus demanded only tribute that defeated people could afford, thus sparing them great hardship. The most famous example of his religious tolerance involved the Jews in Babylonia who, as you have learned, had been held captive there since the conquest of Judah. After Babylonia became part of the Persian Empire, Cyrus freed the Jews. In 539 B.C.E. he allowed them to return to their homeland to rebuild the Jerusalem Temple, which had been destroyed by the Babylonian king Nebuchadnezzar.

Cyrus laid the foundation for Persian civilization. His policy of extending generosity rather than reigning over a repressive regime probably made him a popular leader. In fact, the Persians are said to have called Cyrus their father. As a brave and skilled conqueror and a wise and tolerant ruler, it's no wonder he came to be known as Cyrus the Great.

CRITICAL VIEWING People in this photo are visiting the Tomb of Cyrus, which stands in Pasargadae, the king's ancient capital. The tomb chamber sits atop a massive base. In what way might the design of this tomb, made to contain the remains of a king, be surprising?

HISTORICAL THINKING

1. **READING CHECK** Which two groups founded kingdoms in ancient Iran?

2. **DRAW CONCLUSIONS** How did the policies of Cyrus II help unite and keep peace in his diverse empire?

3. **MAKE INFERENCES** What were the benefits of appointing locals to serve as satraps?

PLAN: 2-PAGE LESSON

OBJECTIVE
Describe how the Persian Empire rose and became unified under Cyrus the Great.

CRITICAL THINKING SKILLS FOR LESSON 1.2
- Draw Conclusions
- Make Inferences
- Identify Main Ideas and Details
- Make Predictions
- Analyze Cause and Effect

HISTORICAL THINKING FOR CHAPTER 4
How did the Persians create a well-ordered empire that lasted for 200 years?

After the Persians overthrew the Medes, a great empire developed under Cyrus II, a good and tolerant leader. Lesson 1.2 discusses how Cyrus II made the Persian Empire great by unifying the many different peoples who made up the empire, and by developing a strong army, economy, and government.

Student eEdition online
Additional content for this lesson, including a Global Commodity feature, is available online.

BACKGROUND FOR THE TEACHER
Unifying the Empire The Persians unified their empire through the use of an extensive transportation network. Some of the roads were simple caravan tracks through the desert, while others, usually serving main cities like Babylon, were paved with bricks or rock. The government took advantage of this road network, sending government couriers to maintain communication amongst military generals. Sometimes couriers traveled 90 miles in a day or 1,600 miles in about 20 days, while regular travelers took about 3 months to cover the same distance.

History Notebook
Encourage students to complete the Global Commodity page for Chapter 4 in their History Notebooks as they read.

INTRODUCE & ENGAGE

DISCUSS THE SIZE OF THE PERSIAN EMPIRE

Remind students that Cyrus II founded the Achaemenid dynasty and that this dynasty ruled about 30 to 35 million people between 550 and 330 B.C.E. Point out that, around this same time, ancient Egypt's Late New Kingdom had an estimated population of only about 5 or 6 million people. **ASK:** Why do you think the population of the Persian Empire was so much larger than that of the Egyptian Empire? *(Possible response: The Persian Empire contained many people from lands beyond Iran.)* Tell students that in this lesson they will learn about how the Persian Empire rose and expanded to become the most diverse empire the world had ever seen.

TEACH

GUIDED DISCUSSION

1. **Identify Main Ideas and Details** How did Cyrus's treatment of the Jews in Babylonia reflect his policy of tolerance? *(Cyrus freed the Jews and allowed them to rebuild their temple.)*

2. **Make Predictions** Do you think that the Persian Empire continued to expand after Cyrus's death? Why or why not? *(Possible response: Yes, Cyrus set an excellent precedent and put systems in place that would benefit the empire for a long time.)*

ANALYZE CAUSE AND EFFECT

Remind students that a cause tells why something happened and an effect tells what happened. Then refer students to the Global Commodity feature on pearls (available in the Student eEdition) and discuss causes and effects that changed the value of pearls over history. **ASK:** Why were natural pearls reserved for the wealthy for thousands of years? *(Possible response: because they were rare, hard to obtain, and very expensive)* What effect did Mikimoto's cultured pearls have on the value of pearls? *(Possible response: The process that Mikimoto developed not only made pearls more affordable but also made them less unique and people of lower social status could buy them.)*

ACTIVE OPTIONS

On Your Feet: Compete in a True-False Quiz Divide the class into two teams and have each write a series of True-False questions about the lesson for a quiz competition. Choose one team to begin the competition and then have teams take turns reading questions. The team with the most correct answers is the winner.

> **NG Learning Framework: Design a Policy**
> ATTITUDE Responsibility
> SKILL Problem-Solving

Guide students to think more deeply about the precedent that Cyrus set by tolerating the religions and cultures of people within his empire. Instruct them to use information from the chapter and additional print or online sources to design a policy today that incorporates those same principles. Invite students to share their finished policy with the class, explaining how it fits with Cyrus's policy.

DIFFERENTIATE

INCLUSION

Analyze Photographs Pair students who are sight impaired with students who are not. Have the pairs study the photograph of Cyrus's tomb. Ask them to consider the size, material, and structure of the tomb. Then have the pairs of students work together to answer the Critical Viewing question regarding the Tomb of Cyrus.

PRE-AP

Write an Essay Instruct students to review the lesson and decide which events were most important to the development of the Persian Empire under Cyrus. Students should conduct research to find additional details, images, or maps. Then have students use the information they've gathered to write an essay in which they explain why the events they chose were important.

See the Chapter Planner for more strategies for differentiation.

HISTORICAL THINKING

ANSWERS

1. the Medes and the Persians

2. Cyrus's use of satraps helped him learn what was happening in all parts of his empire. His tolerance inspired loyalty and helped prevent rebellions.

3. Answers will vary. Possible response: Locals knew their territory and the culture and customs of the people there. In addition, the people in the territory would have felt that they were being more fairly represented.

CRITICAL VIEWING Answers will vary. Possible response: The design seems too modest and plain for a king.

1.3 Cyrus the Great and the Jewish Exiles

People often say that history is written by the victors. Cyrus the Great was no exception. He had his bravery and deeds memorialized on a clay cylinder. The Jewish people benefited from Cyrus's victory, but they told the story in their own way.

As you know, Cyrus showed tolerance for the customs and religions of those he conquered. But he wasn't above "blowing his own horn" and taking credit for this policy. He issued the Cyrus Cylinder around 539 B.C.E., after he defeated the Babylonian Empire.

The first part of the cylinder is written in the third person and describes Cyrus's deeds and criticizes the rule of Nabonidus, the Babylonian king. The script claims that the people of Babylon were happy to have Cyrus as their new king. In the second part, Cyrus speaks in the first person and discusses his treatment of the deported people in Babylon.

During Cyrus's rule, royal inscriptions were typically presented in a cylindrical form. And those inscriptions usually praised the bravery and wisdom of the victor and denounced those who were defeated. Many historians believe the portrayal of Nabonidus is exaggerated and unfair. But Cyrus did earn a high reputation for his deeds, and he became a hero to the Jewish people. The Hebrew Bible mentions Cyrus 23 times by name.

CRITICAL VIEWING Dutch artist Jacob van Loo painted *Zerubbabel Showing a Plan of Jerusalem to Cyrus* around 1655. Zerubbabel served as the satrap of the Persian province of Judah under Cyrus and led the first group of Jews from Babylonian captivity to Jerusalem. How would you describe Cyrus's attitude toward Zerubbabel as the satrap points to the plan?

DOCUMENT ONE

Primary Source: Artifact
The Cyrus Cylinder, c. 539 B.C.E.

This clay cylinder was created on Cyrus's orders after he conquered Babylon. The Cyrus Cylinder measures about nine by four inches and is covered in Babylonian script. It provides an account of Cyrus's victory, praises Cyrus, and refers to his repatriation of exiled peoples. The cylinder was buried in Babylon's city wall.

CONSTRUCTED RESPONSE
Why do you think Cyrus wanted the cylinder made?

DOCUMENT TWO

Primary Source: Inscription
from the Cyrus Cylinder, c. 539 B.C.E.

The Babylonian rulers sacked temples and forced conquered peoples to resettle in their empire. After his conquest of Babylon, Cyrus allowed these people to return to their homelands. In this excerpt from the Cyrus Cylinder, the script is written as if Cyrus himself were speaking.

CONSTRUCTED RESPONSE How is Cyrus portrayed in this excerpt?

I am Cyrus, king of the world, great king, mighty king, king of Babylon, king of Sumer and Akkad, king of the four quarters. . . . My vast army marched into Babylon in peace; I did not permit anyone to frighten the people of Sumer and Akkad. . . . As for the citizens of Babylon, . . . I relieved their weariness and freed them. . . . I returned the images of the gods, who had resided there [in Babylon] to their places and I let them dwell in eternal abodes [temples].

DOCUMENT THREE

Primary Source: Sacred Text
from the Book of Ezra

In the Hebrew Bible, the Book of Ezra, chapter 1, verses 1–3, discusses Cyrus and his proclamation regarding the exiled Jews in Babylonia. In this selection from the verses, Cyrus speaks directly to the exiles.

CONSTRUCTED RESPONSE What does Cyrus tell the Jewish exiles to do?

[T]he Lord stirred up the spirit of Cyrus king of Persia so that he made a proclamation throughout all his kingdom and also put it in writing: "Thus says Cyrus king of Persia: The Lord, the God of heaven, has given me all the kingdoms of the earth, and he has charged me to build him a house in Jerusalem, which is in Judah. Whoever is among you of all his people, may his God be with him, and let him go up to Jerusalem, which is in Judah, and rebuild the house of the Lord, the God of Israel."

SYNTHESIZE & WRITE

1. **REVIEW** Review what you have learned about Cyrus II, his conquest of the Babylonian Empire, and his treatment of the Jewish exiles.

2. **RECALL** On your own paper, write down what the three documents tell you about Cyrus and the Babylonian exiles.

3. **CONSTRUCT** Construct a topic sentence that answers this question: How does the account of Cyrus in the Hebrew Bible compare with the inscriptions on the Cyrus Cylinder?

4. **WRITE** Using evidence from this chapter and the documents, write an informative paragraph that supports your topic sentence in Step 3.

PLAN: 2-PAGE LESSON

OBJECTIVE
Analyze ancient sources that recount the deeds of Cyrus the Great.

CRITICAL THINKING SKILLS FOR LESSON 1.3
- Synthesize
- Identify Main Ideas and Details
- Form and Support Opinions
- Evaluate

HISTORICAL THINKING FOR CHAPTER 4
How did the Persians create a well-ordered empire that lasted for 200 years?

Lesson 1.3 introduces documents that detail Cyrus's victories and wise treatment of those he conquered, which contributed to the success and unity of the Persian Empire.

BACKGROUND FOR THE TEACHER

Jews in Babylonia After Babylonia defeated Judah, deportations of Jews from the conquered land began. Many Jews were held captive in Babylonia for about 50 to 70 years. During that time, the Jews kept their traditions alive by observing the Sabbath and religious holidays. When Cyrus freed the Jews, they looked upon him as their benefactor.

INTRODUCE & ENGAGE

PREPARE FOR THE DOCUMENT-BASED QUESTION

Before students start on the activity, briefly preview the three documents. Remind students that a constructed response requires full explanations in complete sentences. Emphasize that students should use what they have learned about Cyrus the Great in addition to the information in the documents.

TEACH

GUIDED DISCUSSION

1. **Identify Main Ideas and Details** According to Document Two, what did Cyrus and his army do? *(When Cyrus marched into Babylon, he did not allow his army to frighten the people of Sumer and Akkad. He freed the people of Babylon, returned religious objects to their places, and let the people return to their temples.)*

2. **Form and Support Opinions** Why do you think the Bible passage in Document Three stresses that "the Lord stirred up the spirit of Cyrus" to deliver his proclamation to the Jews? *(Possible response: The writer wanted to suggest that God was actually responsible for Cyrus's actions.)*

EVALUATE

After students have completed the Synthesize & Write activity, allow time for them to exchange paragraphs and read and comment on the work of their peers. Establish guidelines for comments prior to the activity so that feedback is constructive and encouraging. Comments should focus on the most significant parts that address the purpose of the activity and the audience.

ACTIVE OPTION

On Your Feet: Host a DBQ Roundtable Direct students to gather into groups of four. Pose the following question: Why is it important to study the literature, philosophy, and history of the past? Instruct the first student in each group to write an answer, read it aloud, and pass the paper clockwise to the next student. The paper may circulate around the table several times. Then reconvene the class and discuss the groups' responses.

DIFFERENTIATE

STRIVING READERS

Use Reciprocal Teaching Have partners take turns reading the two written documents aloud. The reading student should then ask the listening student questions about the document. Students may ask their partners to state the main idea and details or summarize the document in their own words. Then have them work together to answer the Constructed Response questions.

PRE-AP

Research Cyrus the Great Tell students that while Cyrus the Great is generally regarded as a brave and generous ruler, there are some scholars that feel his contributions to the Persian Empire are overstated. Invite students to research Cyrus in greater depth and make an argument regarding his political attitudes and character.

See the Chapter Planner for more strategies for differentiation.

SYNTHESIZE & WRITE

ANSWERS

1. Answers will vary.

2. Answers will vary. Possible response: Document One: The cylinder suggests that Cyrus was proud of his conquests, desired praise, and wanted his deeds to be documented and preserved. Document Two: The excerpt also extols his deeds but does not specifically mention the Jewish people. Document Three: The Bible excerpt credits God with inspiring Cyrus to free the Jews and charges them with rebuilding the temple in Jerusalem.

3. Answers will vary. Possible response: The inscriptions on the cylinder praise the conqueror, but the Hebrew Bible has a slightly different take.

4. Answers will vary. Students' paragraphs should include their topic sentence from Step 3 and provide several details from the documents to support it.

CONSTRUCTED RESPONSE

Document One: It preserved his deeds for posterity.

Document Two: He is portrayed as powerful and caring.

Document Three: He tells them to go to Jerusalem and build their temple.

CRITICAL VIEWING Answers will vary. Possible response: Cyrus appears respectful and attentive.

What a Cooking Pot
Can Tell Us

"Studying history lets us look back on all that we have accomplished and to consider where we are going now!" –Chris Thornton

Chris Thornton takes a break from working at the archaeological site of Bat in Oman.

Speaking to an audience of fellow archaeologists at Brown University, Chris Thornton posed the question that has motivated generations of researchers: "How do we understand ancient peoples from the materials they left behind?" By examining items such as a humble cooking pot, Thornton seeks to understand what daily life was like in early societies. Although materials such as copper and pottery were essential to everyday life in the past and are frequently found on archaeological digs, they are "frustratingly silent" about the people who used them. Thornton's job is to make these items talk.

MAIN IDEA Working in the field and at National Geographic headquarters, Christopher Thornton helps expand our understanding of the world—both past and present.

IN THE OFFICE AND IN THE FIELD

As the saying goes, Thornton wears many hats. When he's in his office hat, he works in Washington, D.C., as the National Geographic Society's Lead Program Officer for the Committee for Research and Exploration. In this capacity, he manages the process of granting funds to researchers and explorers. "I act as NatGeo's resident 'expert' in six disciplines [anthropology, archaeology, astronomy, geography, geology, and paleontology]," he says, "and serve these six disciplines by helping scholars to get research grants and media attention from NatGeo." On a normal workday, he might be meeting with film producers and explorers in the morning and analyzing the proportion of grants awarded to male and female applicants in the afternoon.

Out in the field, Thornton is the Director of Excavations at the UNESCO World Heritage Site of Bat in the Sultanate of Oman, on the Arabian Peninsula. Bat was a Bronze Age settlement in the region, referred to by ancient Mesopotamian texts as *Magan*. Part of Magan came under Persian control during Cyrus's rule. Archaeologists studied some Magan sites during the 1970s, but very little information was published. When Thornton began working at Bat in 2007, he used up-to-date methodologies, including radiocarbon dating. "Because this region had very limited literacy during the late prehistoric and early historic periods, it needs an archaeologist's eye to investigate and figure out what was going on then," he explains.

RECONSTRUCTING HISTORY

Bat is located at the intersection of several wadis, or dry riverbeds that occasionally fill with water. In the Bronze Age, people settled within wadi systems, which allowed them to survive and farm in the region's dry climate. The same holds true for farmers in present-day Oman.

"One of the key questions I'm trying to answer is how and why people living in arid regions like present-day Oman managed to create relatively large settlements 4,000 years ago," Thornton explains. He believes one clue to the answer lies with copper. He and his team have discovered evidence of copper production and indications of the local use of copper in tools, weapons, and jewelry. According to Thornton, "This suggests that despite the harsh geography of the region, the people of Magan were a very important part of the Bronze Age economic trade networks that led to the rise of cities." In fact, Magan was a major producer of copper for the entire Southwest Asian region for at least 500 years.

Recently, Thornton has been looking to another basic material for clues about life in Bronze Age Bat—pottery. His team has found prehistoric fragments of pottery, or sherds, of cooking pots made in a style that was once thought to exist only in South Asia's Indus Valley. These fragments raise intriguing questions. Are they evidence of a migration of people from the Indus Valley into Magan thousands of years ago? Or do they indicate that the people of Magan admired elements of Indus Valley civilization and imported some of their styles—in the same way that people do today? The pots may also reflect the cultural and technological mixing that took place when Indus Valley people married into Magan families, bringing their cooking techniques with them. At this point, there are many more questions than answers.

Thornton is excited about using contemporary archaeological techniques to study the everyday materials of Bat. By breaking the silence of copper and cooking pots, as well as other items the people of Magan left behind, he hopes to learn how farmers became settlers, and how settlements grew into cities. Ultimately, perhaps, he will help the world understand Magan and the cultural bonds that link it with Oman.

HISTORICAL THINKING

1. **READING CHECK** What does Christopher Thornton do in his two jobs?

2. **ANALYZE CAUSE AND EFFECT** What may have led to the rise of cities in Magan?

PLAN: 2-PAGE LESSON

OBJECTIVE
Explain how Christopher Thornton's work has helped expand our understanding of the world, both past and present.

CRITICAL THINKING SKILLS FOR LESSON 1.4
- Analyze Cause and Effect
- Synthesize
- Draw Conclusions
- Analyze Visuals

HISTORICAL THINKING FOR CHAPTER 4
How did the Persians create a well-ordered empire that lasted for 200 years?

The Persians had to adapt to their dry environment and develop technology in order to survive. Lesson 1.4 discusses Christopher Thornton's findings on Magan, which may have come under Achaemenid control during Cyrus's rule. Thornton reveals how the people of Magan adapted to the region's dry climate and built a large settlement.

BACKGROUND FOR THE TEACHER

Christopher Thornton Chris Thornton has not only worked extensively to better understand how ancient peoples lived in Oman, but he has also helped encourage tourism there. In 2015, he worked with National Geographic to set up an overland tour in the country. The trip, called Traveling the Sands of Time, started in Muscat, Oman, and ended in Dubai, in the United Arab Emirates. Travelers perused items at bazaars, toured a mud-brick village, and learned about the traditions of falconry, among other interesting activities. In addition, experts accompanied the tourists to provide further information, which was especially useful when they arrived at the UNESCO World Heritage Site of Bat.

History Notebook
Encourage students to complete the National Geographic Explorer page for Chapter 4 in their History Notebooks as they read.

Student eEdition online
Additional content for this lesson, including a video and a photo, is available online.

INTRODUCE & ENGAGE

ACTIVATE PRIOR KNOWLEDGE

Engage students in a discussion of the importance of modern trade. **ASK:** What are some examples of popular trade goods today, and how do countries benefit from trading them? *(Possible response: electronics, oil, gas; countries can become rich and powerful from trading these commodities.)* Tell students that in this lesson they will learn about people who lived long ago in a region of present-day Oman and used their copper production to become an important part of the Bronze Age economic trade networks.

TEACH

GUIDED DISCUSSION

1. **Synthesize** What has Thornton been able to deduce from his examination of copper and the style of the pottery he has uncovered? *(Possible response: that people either migrated to the area from the Indus Valley and brought new technology and styles with them, or they admired elements of the Indus Valley civilizations and copied them)*

2. **Draw Conclusions** Why have everyday objects from the past been frustrating to Thornton but also valuable evidence to support his inferences? *(Possible response: They can't reveal the past, but he can use them as clues to help him in his analysis of how early people lived.)*

ANALYZE VISUALS

Have students reread the information about cooking pots in the lesson and then examine the photograph of the pottery sherd (available in the Student eEdition). **ASK:** What can Thornton learn from studying pottery sherds? *(Possible response: He can learn what kind of technologies people employed to make their pottery.)*

ACTIVE OPTIONS

On Your Feet: Numbered Heads Have students number off within small groups and review the text and the video (available in the Student eEdition) as they consider the following topic sentence: Thornton's work has helped us to better understand how people in Bat lived and thrived. Tell students to think about the topic and then discuss it as a group. Ask them to work together to build a paragraph on the topic by having each group member contribute one sentence. Then call a number and have students with that number read their group's paragraph to the class.

> **NG Learning Framework: Create a Presentation About Thornton's Finds**
> **ATTITUDE** Curiosity
> **KNOWLEDGE** Our Human Story

Have students use online sources to prepare a short presentation on Thornton's discoveries, including details about his work at Bat and his research on the daily lives of the people of Magan. Invite students to work in pairs or small groups and to share their presentations with the class or record them on video and post them on a class blog.

DIFFERENTIATE

ENGLISH LANGUAGE LEARNERS

Summarize Pair students at the **Beginning** level with students from a higher proficiency level. Assign each pair one of the six disciplines in which Thornton serves as an expert: anthropology, archaeology, astronomy, geography, geology, and paleontology. Tell partners to read the lesson from the perspective of their assigned discipline and then work together to write a summary connecting that discipline to Thornton's work and findings. Provide the following sentence frames to help pairs create their summaries.

- Intermediate: This discipline relates to _____. Thornton uses it by _____.
- Advanced: Thornton uses this discipline by _____. He has discovered that _____.

GIFTED & TALENTED

Write an Interview Have pairs write interview questions to pose to Thornton. Tell students to create a list of questions covering every aspect of the "hats" that he wears. Then instruct students to conduct online research, if needed, to answer their questions. Tell students to write their answers in Thornton's voice. When students have completed writing and rehearsing their interview, invite pairs to perform it for the class.

See the Chapter Planner for more strategies for differentiation.

HISTORICAL THINKING

ANSWERS

1. Thornton works in Washington, D.C., as the National Geographic Society's Lead Program Officer for the Committee on Research, Conservation, and Exploration and as the Director of Excavations at the UNESCO World Heritage Site of Bat in the Sultanate of Oman.

2. trade in copper and copper tools, weapons, and jewelry

Darius and Persia's Golden Age

In the ancient world, rulers often used violence to gain power. The Persian Empire was no different—one man used murder, lies, and intrigue to become its leader. In spite of his ruthlessness, however, that leader turned out to be a great one.

SEIZING POWER

After Cyrus's death around 529 B.C.E., his son Cambyses (kam-BY-seez) succeeded him. Cambyses continued his father's conquests and added Egypt and Libya to the Persian Empire. But he only ruled for about seven years. After Cambyses's death in 522 B.C.E., one of his royal bodyguards, a man named **Darius** (duh-RY-uhs), staged a **coup**, or a sudden overthrow of government. He traveled to Media and, with the help of six Persian noblemen, murdered Bardiya, another son of Cyrus who had assumed the throne several months before. Darius claimed that he had actually killed a priest named Gaumata (GOW-mah-tah), who was impersonating Bardiya.

After the murder, the conspirators discussed what political system they would implement to rule the empire. Some believed the government should be led by a representative form of government or by a group of noblemen. But Darius called for a monarchy, the form of government that had been in place under Cyrus. Although the discussion between Darius and the conspirators took place long before Herodotus was born, the historian presented a lively version in *The Histories* of what they might have said. According to Herodotus, Darius defended his choice by declaring, "One ruler: it is impossible to improve upon that—provided he is the best. His judgment will be in keeping with his character; his control of the people will

be beyond reproach; his measures against enemies and traitors will be kept secret more easily than under other forms of government."

Darius got his way. Herodotus tells us that the conspirators agreed to select the monarch by seeing whose horse neighed first after the sun came up. Darius won the contest (he cheated) and reigned as King Darius I. And because he was an Achaemenid—Darius was a distant cousin of Cyrus—he continued the Achaemenid Empire.

RULING THE EMPIRE

In spite of the means he used to gain power, Darius was an effectiveruler. He expanded the empire until it extended from India in the east to southeastern Europe in the west. The Persian Empire reached its height under Darius and became the largest empire the world had yet seen. Darius followed Cyrus's example by respecting the religious beliefs of others. He also helped carry out Cyrus's decree, which called for the Jews to rebuild the Temple at Jerusalem. And Darius protected his people by introducing a uniform law code for his subjects and appointing judges to administer those laws. Darius also imposed taxes on his subjects, efficiently collecting them through local officials recruited as satraps.

Darius expanded Cyrus's administrative system to maintain control of his huge empire. He divided his lands into 20 satrapies, or provinces, each one run by a centrally appointed satrap. To prevent the satraps from becoming too powerful, Darius appointed inspectors, known as the "eyes and ears of the king," to report problems directly to him.

He also regularized the tax system by requiring each province to pay a fixed amount of revenue based on what its people could afford to pay. Most provinces paid taxes in silver, but Darius allowed some to pay using other commodities. For instance, Egyptians sometimes paid with grain, Indians with gold dust, and Ethiopians with gold, ebony, and elephant tusks. In addition, Darius introduced a single currency and a standardized system of weights and measures.

Understanding that a good government depended on good communication, Darius built the 1,500-mile-long Royal Road, which ran from Susa in Persia to Sardis in Anatolia. Additional roads connected the 20 satrapies. These roads unified the diverse cultures of the empire.

During Darius's reign, the Persian Empire reached its golden age—a period of great cultural achievement. The king carried out ambitious building projects. As a result, Persian architecture flourished. Darius also built a new capital called **Persepolis**. Located in a remote mountainous region in southwestern Iran, Persepolis was mainly used for ceremonial purposes. Darius decorated the capital with palaces and jeweled statues, and Persepolis came to symbolize the magnificence of the Persian Empire. With all his accomplishments, it's no wonder that, like Cyrus, Darius earned the title "the Great."

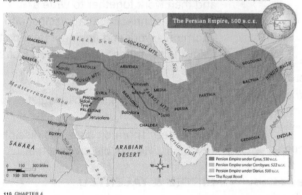

The Persian Empire, 500 B.C.E.

This relief of a lion attacking a bull decorates what was the eastern stairway of the Apadana, the largest building at Persepolis.

HISTORICAL THINKING

1. **READING CHECK** How did Darius become king of Persia?

2. **MAKE INFERENCES** How do you think a single form of currency and a standardized system of weights and measures benefited the people of the Persian Empire?

3. **INTERPRET MAPS** What parts of the ancient world did both Cambyses and Darius add to the Persian Empire?

PLAN: 2-PAGE LESSON

OBJECTIVE

Examine how Darius I expanded the Persian Empire to its greatest extent and put measures in place to govern and unite its many different peoples.

CRITICAL THINKING SKILLS FOR LESSON 2.1

- Make Inferences
- Interpret Maps
- Draw Conclusions
- Evaluate
- Analyze Visuals

HISTORICAL THINKING FOR CHAPTER 4

How did the Persians create a well-ordered empire that lasted for 200 years?

Lesson 2.1 discusses Darius I, who took power and expanded the Persian Empire further. Darius also continued Cyrus's policies, strengthened the administrative system, and helped unite the empire by building the Royal Road.

Student eEdition online

Additional content for this lesson, including a video and a photo, is available online.

BACKGROUND FOR THE TEACHER

Darius and Darics Darius's standardized system of weights and measures was important to the growth of trade in the region, as was establishing a single currency. Coins had already been in circulation thanks to the Lydians. Darius ordered the use of shekels and introduced the gold Daric (which was most likely named for Darius). Heavier than the Lydian coins, the gold Daric also had a silver equivalent. Many of Darius's coins were uncovered in Persepolis. Some of the coins show Darius charging into battle. Having a common currency helped Darius further unify the empire. Rulers who succeeded Darius adopted the coins and simply replaced his image with theirs. Daric coins were minted until the empire declined and were later replaced with Macedonian coins.

INTRODUCE & ENGAGE

DISCUSS CHOOSING A GOVERNMENT

Ask students the following question: How do people select a form of government? Prompt students to consider how the Founders of the United States decided which kind of government to create for their new country. Access their prior knowledge of America's 13 colonies and the circumstances that led to the American Revolution. Explain to students that in this lesson they will learn that Darius continued the form of government that Cyrus the Great had established, a monarchy.

TEACH

GUIDED DISCUSSION

1. **Draw Conclusions** Why do you think the Persian Empire experienced a golden age under Darius? *(Darius encouraged achievement, particularly in architecture. He wanted to display the grandeur of the Persian Empire.)*

2. **Evaluate** How did Darius's policy of respecting the customs and beliefs of the people he conquered help unite the empire? *(Possible response: The policy increased the people's loyalty to the empire and willingness to be part of it.)*

ANALYZE VISUALS

Show the video of Persepolis (available in the Student eEdition) to students and have them discuss the video and the photo of the Hall of 100 Columns (available in the Student eEdition). **ASK:** How do both the video and photograph illustrate the grandeur of the Persian Empire? *(Possible response: They both show large buildings and columns, carvings, and elaborate décor.)* Invite students to share details from the visuals that struck them as interesting or particularly engaging.

ACTIVE OPTIONS

On Your Feet: Think, Pair, Share Ask students to study the map and then discuss the expanse of the Persian Empire. Have students compare this map to the one in Lesson 1.1, which shows the extent of the empire about 70 years earlier. Ask them to think about where the growth of the empire occurred, why the empire expanded in those directions, and how such expansion benefited the empire. Then instruct students to form pairs and discuss the two maps. Have a student from each pair share their ideas with the rest of the class.

> **NG Learning Framework: Create a Monument or Mural**
> SKILL Communication
> KNOWLEDGE Our Human Story

Tell students to create a monument or digital mural that depicts an aspect of Darius's rule or one of his achievements. For example, students might create a mural of travelers on the Royal Road or draw a monument to Persepolis. Invite volunteers to present their creations to the class, explaining the concept behind it and describing its features.

DIFFERENTIATE

STRIVING READERS

Create a Concept Cluster On the board, write *Darius's Rule* in the center oval of a Concept Cluster. Write *economy, government,* and *culture* in the other three ovals. Instruct students to review the lesson and then call out specific examples of each topic, which you can add to the cluster.

PRE-AP

Research the Royal Road Instruct students to learn more about the Royal Road. They should research what towns developed along it and describe interesting stops or locations along the road. Ask volunteers to share the information with the class.

See the Chapter Planner for more strategies for differentiation.

HISTORICAL THINKING

ANSWERS

1. He murdered the son of Cyrus who had assumed the throne after Cambyses and made himself sole ruler of the Persian Empire.

2. Answers will vary. Possible response: A single form of currency allowed people to compare prices and made it easier for them to buy and trade goods. A standardized system of weights and measures helped prevent people from being cheated when they bought goods.

3. Egypt, part of northeastern Africa

2.2 Material Culture

PERSIAN MONUMENTS AND SCYTHIAN GOLD

Before the Persians rose to power in Iran, a nomadic people called the Scythians inhabited the region around the ninth century B.C.E. Over the next 200 years or so, however, the nomads migrated to what is now southern Russia and Ukraine, where they founded a powerful empire. The Scythians were great warriors and horsemen. In fact, they were among the first people to harness and ride horses. Unlike the Persians, the Scythians did not leave behind any monuments or written records—they didn't have a writing system. Most of what we know about the Scythians has been gleaned from the artifacts they left behind and from Herodotus. But those items, like the monuments and artifacts of the Persians, have provided great insight into their culture and everyday life.

The Tolstaya Mogila Pectoral
In 1971, a Russian archaeologist excavated a royal Scythian burial mound known as Tolstaya Mogila in present-day southern Ukraine. Dating from the fourth century B.C.E., the mound contained burials of rulers, their families, and their possessions. The greatest find was this beautiful piece of gold jewelry called a pectoral, which would have been worn around the neck. Historians believe Greek artisans made the pectoral for a Scythian ruler.

The pectoral contains three sections that are decorated with a host of animals and scenes from Scythian daily life. This detail from the top section shows two men—possibly chieftains—sewing a sheepskin shirt. A pair of quivers containing the warriors' bows and arrows lies close at hand.

Faravahar This winged symbol of Zoroastrianism was carved over a doorway at Persepolis. All parts of the symbol represent different aspects of Zoroastrian philosophy. The circle in the center represents the eternity of the universe and the soul, while the man atop it represents wisdom. The rows of feathers on the wings stand for the three pillars of the faith.

Gold Griffin This Persian gold plaque from the Achaemenid Period features a pair of griffins with a twist: instead of lions' ears, they have those of a bull. Identical feathered wings further balance the design. Rings attached to the back of the plaque suggest that the ornament might have been worn on a belt.

The Oxus Treasure Around 1880, a hoard of Persian artifacts was discovered along the Oxus River in present-day Tajikistan. The Oxus Treasure consists of about 180 pieces of metalwork that have survived from the Achaemenid Empire. The lion heads on the knob of the staff shown here are made from lapis lazuli, a rock prized for its deep blue color.

HISTORICAL THINKING

1. **READING CHECK** What sources have historians used to gather information about the Scythians?

2. **COMPARE AND CONTRAST** How is the artistry of the Persians and the Scythians similar?

3. **DRAW CONCLUSIONS** Based on the artifacts in this lesson, what was important to the Persians and to the Scythians?

PLAN: 2-PAGE LESSON

OBJECTIVE
Examine artifacts and monuments to learn about the culture and everyday life of the Persians and Scythians.

CRITICAL THINKING SKILLS FOR LESSON 2.2
- Analyze Visuals
- Make Connections
- Compare and Contrast
- Draw Conclusions
- Make Inferences

HISTORICAL THINKING FOR CHAPTER 4
How did the Persians create a well-ordered empire that lasted for 200 years?

Lesson 2.2 takes a closer look at the monuments the Persians left behind and also explores the culture of the Scythians, who inhabited the region that would later become home to the Persian Empire.

Student eEdition online
Additional content for this lesson, including photos, is available online.

BACKGROUND FOR THE TEACHER
Scythian Style Archaeologists have been able to identify Scythians in Persian artwork because of certain identifiable traits. A frieze from the left side of the staircase at Darius's Palace at Persepolis shows Scythians wearing pointed hoods or headdresses and leading fine horses. Most hoods were likely made of leather or plant reeds and represented a person's rank. This style of hood was commonly worn in western Asia. Even nomads from this region wore these headdresses, but the nomads' styles were simpler. Some Scythian hoods were quite decorative and sported gold plaques. These could have symbolized a higher social rank, royalty, or even god-like status.

History Notebook
Encourage students to complete the Material Culture page for Chapter 4 in their History Notebooks as they read.

INTRODUCE & ENGAGE

EXPLORE HISTORY USING PHOTOGRAPHS

Tell students that the photographs in this lesson represent only a few examples of the many magnificent monuments and artwork left behind by the Persians and Scythians. **ASK:** What types of art are represented in these photos? *(Possible response: stone reliefs, gold and wooden artifacts)* What common details do you see in these photographs? *(Possible response: many animals and people or some combination of both)*

TEACH

GUIDED DISCUSSION

1. **Compare and Contrast** How are the photos of the gold armlet (available in the Student eEdition) and staff from the Oxus Treasure similar and different? *(Possible response: They both show two heads of an animal. The gold armlet shows the animals facing one another, while the staff shows the lion heads facing away from one another.)*

2. **Make Inferences** Why might the Persians and Scythians have placed such importance on showing animals in their artwork? *(Possible response: Animals might have been part of their spiritual beliefs and were depicted to symbolize strength and power. The Persians and Scythians also may have relied on animals to do work and depended on them for food and protection.)*

MATERIAL CULTURE

Provide time for students to study the monuments and artifacts shown in the lesson. Point out that many of the items fall into the following categories: commemorations of people or events, religious artifacts, and decorative art. Encourage students to think of modern works they've seen that fall into these categories. Then initiate a class discussion of the similarities and differences between those modern works and Persian and Scythian artifacts.

ACTIVE OPTION

On Your Feet: Research Cultural Contributions Instruct students to form two teams. Have one team research to learn more about Persian culture and have the other research Scythian culture. Provide guiding questions, such as "What aspects of culture are revealed through their artwork?" and "How did their contributions shape or influence culture in the region?" Reconvene as a class and ask a volunteer from each group to share the group's findings.

DIFFERENTIATE

INCLUSION

Describe Details in Photos Pair students who are visually impaired with students who are not. Ask the latter to describe each photo in the lesson and answer any questions their partners might have. Then have the students work together to answer the Historical Thinking questions.

GIFTED & TALENTED

Copy a Pattern Direct students to choose a piece of artwork from the photographs and copy it using a pencil or pen and paper. Invite them to discuss what they learned from the process of copying the details. What challenges did they face? What new appreciation of the original craftsmanship did they gain through the process of making the copy?

See the Chapter Planner for more strategies for differentiation.

HISTORICAL THINKING

ANSWERS

1. the writings of Herodotus and Scythian artifacts from burial mounds

2. Answers will vary. Possible response: Both reveal great skill and workmanship, aspects of their culture, and daily life.

3. Answers will vary. Possible response: for the Persians: their empire, power, and religion; for the Scythians: their warrior culture, horses, and nomadic lifestyle

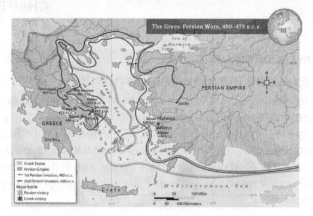
The Greco-Persian Wars, 490–479 B.C.E.

The Greco-Persian Wars

We often root for the underdogs in a contest because their chance of beating their stronger opponents is so small. Most of the time they lose, but sometimes, miraculously, they win. Such a miracle occurred during the Greco-Persian Wars.

THE BATTLE OF MARATHON

At the beginning of *The Histories*, Herodotus declared that he wished to record the "great and marvelous deeds" displayed during the Greco-Persian Wars. The wars lasted for nearly 50 years, from about 492 to 449 B.C.E., and were triggered by Persian expansion into Greece. In 546 B.C.E., Cyrus II conquered Ionia, an area of Greek city-states along the west Anatolian coast, and made it part of the Persian Empire. The city-states rebelled against Persia in 500 B.C.E., during Darius's reign, and fought for about six years. Although the rebellion, known as the Ionian Revolt, failed, it set the stage for the Greco-Persian Wars.

Marathon Race According to legend, a messenger was charged with running the 25 miles or so from Marathon to Athens to deliver the news of the Persian defeat there. Immediately after he reached Athens, he died of exhaustion. The modern marathon race, which today covers a distance of just over 26 miles, commemorates this story. We have no way of knowing if the story is true, but, as this detail from a Greek vase from the 500s B.C.E. suggests, running as a sport was taken seriously in ancient Greece and was part of a soldier's training.

During the revolt, city-states on the Greek mainland, including Athens, sent a few ships to support the rebels. In revenge, Darius invaded—and tried to conquer—the mainland. The first fleet he sent to Greece in 492 B.C.E. was destroyed in a storm. In 490 B.C.E., however, 25,000 Persian soldiers reached the Greek mainland and marched to the Plain of Marathon, about 25 miles outside of Athens. But the **Battle of Marathon** didn't go as the Persians planned.

With only about 11,000 men, the Greek forces seemed hopelessly outnumbered, yet fortune was on their side. After they learned that the Persian cavalry—soldiers on horseback—had withdrawn temporarily from the battlefield, they decided to seize their opportunity to attack the Persian infantry, which had stayed behind. The Athenian general Miltiades devised a maneuver that allowed his men to surround many of the Persian troops. It resulted in a rout. The Persians fled to their ships but not before suffering thousands of casualties. According to Herodotus, the Athenians lost 192 men while the Persians lost 6,400.

Several factors contributed to the victory of the Ionian rebels and their Athenian allies. For one thing, the rebel soldiers were fighting for their homeland. Greek soldiers also had better weapons than the Persians, with stronger armor and superior swords and spears. Even the military formations used by the Greeks gave them an advantage. Heavily armed soldiers advanced together in **phalanxes**, tight rows of eight men each. If the first row of soldiers fell, the row behind them pressed forward to meet the attack.

The Greek victory at the Battle of Marathon meant that the representative form of government developing in Athens would survive and be a legacy for future civilizations. In the short run, though, the victory would inspire other Greeks to resist the Persian Empire.

THERMOPYLAE AND SALAMIS

They got their chance 10 years after the Battle of Marathon when Persian armies once again invaded. By that time, Xerxes I, Darius's son and successor, was Persia's king. In 480 B.C.E., Xerxes sent hundreds of ships and more than 150,000 soldiers to Athens. But the size of these forces made progress slow, which gave Athens time to organize alliances with other Greek city-states, including Sparta. Athens took charge of the navy, and Sparta commanded the army.

The first battle was fought at **Thermopylae** (thur-MAHP-uh-lee), an important mountain pass north of Athens. The Spartan king Leonidas led 6,000 Greeks in a fight against more than 100,000 Persian soldiers. The Greeks battled bravely, but Leonidas knew it was hopeless and ordered most of the soldiers to withdraw. However, the king and 300 of his finest Spartan warriors stayed at Thermopylae to protect the retreating army. According to Herodotus, they battled fiercely—using their bare hands when their swords broke. All of them died.

While the Spartans battled at Thermopylae, the Athenians fought in the strait at Salamis. A Greek fleet of about 370 **triremes**, warships with three levels of oars on each side, faced off against about 800 ships of the Persian navy. The Greeks lured the Persians into the narrow strait and sank more than a third of their vessels.

One of the Persian commanders at the Battle of Salamis was Artemisia, queen of Halicarnassus. Although Artemisia was Greek, she was loyal to Xerxes. But during the chaos of battle, she betrayed the Persians after her ship became trapped between the Greek and Persian ships. Thinking quickly, she rammed her ship into a Persian vessel and made her escape. The Greeks believed she was on their side and let her go.

The Persian invaders finally left Greece in 479 B.C.E. after an alliance of Greek armies defeated them at the Battle of Platea. Persia never invaded Greece again, though the war continued off and on for another 30 years. Finally, however, the Greeks and Persians signed the Peace of Callias around 449 B.C.E., bringing the Greco-Persian Wars to an end.

HISTORICAL THINKING

1. **READING CHECK** Why didn't the Battle of Marathon go as the Persians had imagined?

2. **ANALYZE CAUSE AND EFFECT** What led to the Greco-Persian Wars?

3. **INTERPRET MAPS** Near which Greek city-state were most of the major battles fought?

PLAN: 2-PAGE LESSON

OBJECTIVE
Explain how the Greek city-states united twice to defeat the invading forces of the Persian Empire.

CRITICAL THINKING SKILLS FOR LESSON 2.3
- Analyze Cause and Effect
- Interpret Maps
- Draw Conclusions
- Explain
- Interpret Models

HISTORICAL THINKING FOR CHAPTER 4
How did the Persians create a well-ordered empire that lasted for 200 years?

Lesson 2.3 discusses how the Persians tried unsuccessfully to extend their empire and conquer and defeat the Greeks in the Greco-Persian Wars.

Student eEdition online
Additional content for this lesson, including a diagram, is available online.

BACKGROUND FOR THE TEACHER
The Mighty Persian Army The Persian army was made up of highly trained soldiers, called Immortals, a regiment that Cyrus II first established as his personal guards. Some Immortals served as the cavalry archers. The regular cavalry and infantry supported the cavalry archers. Other Immortals rode to battle in chariots, but these were so heavy that they required four horses to pull them. Because the Persian army was so immense, it was not easy to move and supply. It also required massive encampments, which were difficult and time-consuming to set up.

INTRODUCE & ENGAGE

DISCUSS COMPETITION

Ask students to recall a time when they were engaged in a competition in which the sides were not quite evenly matched. Invite them to share examples and experiences, including which side won and what made the competition uneven. Then explain that in this lesson they will learn about an uneven match in which the smaller side won.

TEACH

GUIDED DISCUSSION

1. **Draw Conclusions** Why did the Greco-Persian Wars drag on for so many years? *(Possible response: Persian kings did not want to give up. They wanted to expand the empire onto the Greek mainland, but the Greeks were fierce fighters and would not back down.)*

2. **Explain** What was significant about Artemisia during the Greco-Persian Wars? *(Possible response: She commanded a fleet of Persian ships at the Battle of Salamis, which was unusual because she was a woman.)*

INTERPRET MODELS

Direct students' attention to the diagram of the trireme (available in the Student eEdition) and have them study its details. **ASK:** How do you think this Greek ship got its name? *(Possible response:* Tri *means "three," and the ship had three levels of oars.)* What features of the ship gave the Greeks an advantage in fighting? *(Possible responses: the spearmen at the front of the ship, the ram at the front of the ship)* What advantage did the triremes have over Persian ships in narrow straits? *(The triremes were narrow and could maneuver easily through the straits while the Persian ships could not.)*

ACTIVE OPTIONS

On Your Feet: Inside-Outside Circle Have students form concentric circles facing each other. Allow students time to write questions about the events of the Greco-Persian Wars. Then have students in the inside circle pose questions to students in the outside circle. Have students switch roles. Students may ask for help from other students in their circle if they are unable to answer a question.

> **NG Learning Framework: Learn More About Triremes** STEM
> **ATTITUDE** Curiosity
> **SKILL** Problem-Solving

Invite students to review the text and diagram (available in the Student eEdition) in the lesson. Encourage them to share their observations about how the triremes were constructed, how rowers had to work together, and how wind and water conditions might have affected a battle. **ASK:** What might be one of the problems a rower on a trireme would have had to solve?

DIFFERENTIATE

STRIVING READERS

Set a Purpose for Reading Before reading, have students use the lesson headings and features to create purpose-setting questions:

- Who were the Ionians? Why did they revolt?
- Who defeated the Persian Empire? How did they do it?
- What is a trireme?

PRE-AP

Annotate a Time Line Have students annotate a time line of the Persian Wars. They should conduct independent research to support the reading in the lesson and to include more details and dates. Their time lines should extend from 546 B.C.E. to 479 B.C.E. Encourage students to include visuals on their time lines that might illustrate events. Have students post their time lines on the wall in the classroom.

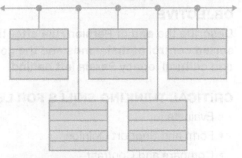

The Greco-Persian Wars

See the Chapter Planner for more strategies for differentiation.

HISTORICAL THINKING

ANSWERS

1. The Greeks staged a surprise attack and out-maneuvered the Persians.

2. the conquest of the Ionian Greek city-states and the Ionian Revolt

3. Athens

The Legacy of Ancient Iran

Nothing lasts forever. The greatest kings die and their monuments crumble to dust. But if those kings and their deeds are great enough, their impact may be felt years—and even centuries—later.

DECLINE OF THE PERSIAN EMPIRE

After his defeat at the hands of the Greeks during the Greco-Persian Wars, Xerxes I withdrew from political life and became an ineffective ruler. In 465 b.c.e., the king and his elder son were assassinated. A series of mostly weak rulers followed, and the Achaemenid Empire began to decline. The next 100 years or so were characterized by rebellions, assassinations, and corruption. It is due to the strong foundation laid by Cyrus, Cambyses, and Darius that the empire endured for so many years. At last, however, a ruler from Macedonia, an ancient kingdom located just to the north of Greece, overthrew the Persian Empire in 331 b.c.e. The young conqueror was called Alexander the Great, and he would adopt many aspects of Persian culture and spread its influences to the west. You will learn much more about Alexander in the next chapter.

Eventually, a group called the Parthians established an empire in Iran and ruled there until 224 c.e., when they were overthrown by the Sasanians. Like the Achaemenids, the Sasanians hailed from Persis. Often called the Second Persian Empire, the Sasanian Empire promoted Iranian art and culture, and Zoroastrianism became the state religion. But unlike the Achaemenids, the Sasanians did not always tolerate those who practiced other religions. Government structures were similar to those of the Achaemenids, however. Provincial officials reported to the Sasanian kings, and the government invested in roads and building projects. The Sasanian Empire ended in 651 after it came under Arab control. Later, many Arabic empires would reflect a strong Persian influence in art, architecture, and poetry.

A LASTING INFLUENCE

In fact, the Persians continued to influence other civilizations for centuries. One of the Persians' greatest legacies was the policy of cultural and religious tolerance that Cyrus II first established in the empire.

CRITICAL VIEWING This gold model chariot is part of the Oxus Treasure. The figures are thought to represent a driver and a satrap as they traveled the Royal Road. What details in this piece convey the skill of the artist?

The policy would serve as a model for other rulers. In addition, because Persian kings respected the many cultures in their empire and allowed them to flourish, the cultures were preserved for the future.

The Persians also brought political order to Southwest Asia. Their well-organized central government was more efficient and humane than any that had been seen before in the region. And the imperial roads helped unite the empire. One of the world's first postal systems even developed on the Royal Road. Similar to the Pony Express, a mail service that arose in the American West in the 1860s, horseback-riding couriers carried letters for the king and other leaders along the road.

As you've learned, many Persians were Zoroastrians. Their devotion to the religion helped keep Zoroaster's teachings alive. And traces of the religion—including the belief in Satan and angels—can be found in later religions, including Christianity and Islam. Zoroastrianism declined in Southwest Asia after the

Arab conquest, but it spread to India and other parts of the world. Today, the followers of Zoroastrianism in India are called *Parsis*, which means "Persians."

The Persians also left behind a legacy in art and architecture. They created beautiful gold and silver coins, jewelry, and decorative objects. Achaemenid artists also excelled at relief sculpture, a work, as you may recall, in which three-dimensional elements project from a flat base. The artists combined Greek and Iranian traditions to carve detailed human and animal figures. Persians also adopted techniques, designs, and materials from across the empire to create a new architectural style. Architects built magnificent cities, temples, palaces, and gardens. The largest building among the royal residences at Persepolis was the Apadana. It was used for receptions and could hold 10,000 people. Much of Persepolis and other ancient Persian cities has been reduced to ruins, but many archaeologists are working today to preserve Iran's cultural heritage. After all—as some historians say—the Persians defined the meaning of empire.

The Persians may have influenced our modern postal service. In the following excerpt from *The Histories*, Herodotus describes the couriers who carried messages on the Royal Road from station to station. The last sentence in the excerpt was adapted by the U.S. Postal Service and became its unofficial motto: "Neither snow nor rain nor heat nor gloom of night stays these couriers from the swift completion of their appointed rounds."

PRIMARY SOURCE

No mortal thing travels faster than these Persian couriers. The whole idea is a Persian invention, and works like this: riders are stationed along the road, equal in number to the number of days the journey takes—a man and a horse for each day. Nothing stops these couriers from covering their allotted stage in the quickest possible time—neither snow, rain, heat, nor darkness.

—from *Herodotus: The Histories* translated by Aubrey de Sélincourt

Fire represents the light and purity of the god worshiped by followers of Zoroastrianism, a religion that developed in ancient Iran. In Zoroastrian temples, like this one in the southwest Asian country of Azerbaijan, the fire is never extinguished.

HISTORICAL THINKING

1. **READING CHECK** Which Persian groups established empires in Iran after the Achaemenids?

2. **EVALUATE** In what ways might the Persians have defined the meaning of empire?

3. **FORM AND SUPPORT OPINIONS** What do you think is Persia's greatest legacy? Explain your answer.

PLAN: 2-PAGE LESSON

OBJECTIVE
Describe the end of Persian rule after the Arabs seized control of their lands and the governmental and cultural legacy Persia left behind.

CRITICAL THINKING SKILLS FOR LESSON 2.4
- Evaluate
- Form and Support Opinions
- Compare and Contrast
- Make Generalizations
- Analyze Primary Sources

HISTORICAL THINKING FOR CHAPTER 4
How did the Persians create a well-ordered empire that lasted for 200 years?

Lesson 2.4 discusses what led to the decline and eventual fall of the Persian Empire but also discusses Persia's lasting legacy.

BACKGROUND FOR THE TEACHER
The Rise of the Parthian Empire After Alexander the Great's death, the Seleucids established a Persian kingdom in the lands that had belonged to the Achaemenids. In 247 b.c.e., the Parthians broke away from the kingdom and established their own empire. Parthia, a territory in northeastern Iran, had been part of a satrapy under the Achaemenids. The Parthians were probably nomads who migrated to Iran from Central Asia. They ruled Iran until the Sasanians rose to power.

INTRODUCE & ENGAGE

ACTIVATE PRIOR KNOWLEDGE

Tell students that in this lesson they will learn about the enduring legacy of ancient Iran. Review with students the Persian Empire under Cyrus and Darius. Ask students to predict what might be part of ancient Iran's legacy in government and culture based on the rule of these two kings.

TEACH

GUIDED DISCUSSION

1. **Compare and Contrast** How did the rule of the Sasanians differ from that of the Achaemenids? *(Possible response: The Sasanians were not as tolerant of other religions.)*

2. **Make Generalizations** Which was the greatest cultural contribution of the Persians? Explain your response. *(Possible response: Architecture was the Persians' greatest cultural contribution, because the architecture and carvings at Persepolis are impressive and have influenced other cultures.)*

ANALYZE PRIMARY SOURCES

Read aloud the primary source from *The Histories*. **ASK:** What qualities were probably necessary to be a Persian courier on the Royal Road? *(Possible response: A courier had to be reliable, intrepid, and brave.)* Then have the class consider why the U.S. Postal Service adapted the last line of the primary source and began using it as its motto.

ACTIVE OPTIONS

On Your Feet: Discuss the Decline of the Persian Empire Organize the class into groups of four. Ask each group to discuss the following question: Was the decline of the Persian Empire inevitable? After students have finished their discussions, have representatives from each group summarize their answer.

> **NG Learning Framework: Develop Guidelines for Governance**
> **ATTITUDE** Empowerment
> **SKILL** Communication

Using the Persian Empire as an example, have students form small groups to develop guidelines on governance for ancient civilizations. Encourage students to consider what aspects of the Persian Empire subsequent civilizations might adopt. Encourage students to also come up with their own ideas for governments in ancient civilizations. Invite groups to share their work with the class.

DIFFERENTIATE

ENGLISH LANGUAGE LEARNERS

Use Sentence Strips Choose a paragraph from the lesson and make sentence strips out of it. Read the paragraph aloud, having students follow along. Without using the text, have students put the sentence strips in order. Then ask them to read the paragraph aloud. Have students at the **Beginning** and **Intermediate** levels work in pairs and students at the **Advanced** level work independently.

PRE-AP

Form and Support a Thesis Have students review what they learned about the rise and fall of the Persian Empire. Then instruct them to develop a thesis regarding what economic, political, and social factors led to the empire's rise and expansion and to its decline. Tell students to conduct research using a variety of print and online sources and write an essay supporting their thesis with evidence. Encourage students to share their essays on a class or school blog.

See the Chapter Planner for more strategies for differentiation.

HISTORICAL THINKING

ANSWERS

1. the Parthians and the Sasanians

2. Possible response: by demonstrating that a ruler should treat his or her multicultural citizens with respect, people should be governed fairly, and communications and infrastructure should unite the land

3. Answers will vary. Possible response: religious and cultural tolerance because it set a standard for other leaders of multicultural nations

CRITICAL VIEWING Answers will vary. Possible response: figures' faces and clothes; the knobs and spokes on the wheels; the horses' features

VOCABULARY

Use each of the following vocabulary words in a sentence that shows an understanding of the term's meaning.

1. satrap
2. coup
3. Zoroastrianism
4. phalanx
5. trireme
6. Greco-Persian Wars

READING STRATEGY
ANALYZE CAUSE AND EFFECT

Use a graphic organizer like the one below to list the causes and effects of the Greco-Persian Wars. Then answer the questions that follow.

Greco-Persian Wars

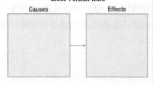

Causes

Effects

7. What happened when Athens sent a few ships to support the rebels in the Ionian Revolt?
8. How did the size of the forces Xerxes sent to Greece impact the Persians' second invasion?

MAIN IDEAS

Answer the following questions. Support your answers with evidence from the chapter.

9. What subjects does Herodotus write about in *The Histories*? LESSON 1.1
10. How did Cyrus II administer his lands? LESSON 1.2
11. In what way did Cyrus demonstrate his religious tolerance after he conquered Babylonia? LESSON 1.2
12. What was the Royal Road? LESSON 2.1
13. Why was the phalanx formation an effective strategy in battle? LESSON 2.3
14. What happened at the Battle of Thermopylae? LESSON 2.3
15. Why is the Sasanian Empire sometimes called the Second Persian Empire? LESSON 2.4

HISTORICAL THINKING

Answer the following questions. Support your answers with evidence from the chapter.

16. **MAKE INFERENCES** Why do you think Herodotus's book was an instant success?
17. **EVALUATE** In what way did Cyrus's appointment of a Mede as one of his closest advisors demonstrate great wisdom?
18. **DRAW CONCLUSIONS** How might the inspectors Darius appointed to oversee the satraps have functioned as spies?
19. **SYNTHESIZE** Why were the Greco-Persian Wars significant for both the ancient Greeks and the Persians?
20. **ANALYZE CAUSE AND EFFECT** What happened because weak rulers came to power after Xerxes?
21. **FORM AND SUPPORT OPINIONS** Who do you think was the better leader, Cyrus or Darius? Explain your answer.

INTERPRET VISUALS

After Darius took the throne he had this relief carved into rock on the Zagros Mountains in Behistun, Iran. Darius, the third figure from the left, stands with his foot on Gaumata, who is lying on the ground. Those who opposed Darius's ascension to the throne have been captured and appear before him. Study the relief below. Then answer the questions that follow.

22. How does Darius appear in the sculpture as compared with the rebels standing before him?
23. What message was Darius trying to send to his enemies with this monument?

ANALYZE SOURCES

In *The Histories*, Herodotus presents Artemisia as an advisor and ally of Xerxes during the invasion of Greece. In this excerpt from his work, Herodotus describes Xerxes' reaction after Artemisia sank a Persian ship—the Calyndian—to escape from the Greek triremes at the Battle of Salamis. The "bystander" mistakenly believes Artemisia has sunk a Greek ship. Read the excerpt and then answer the following question.

> For the story goes that Xerxes, who was watching the battle, observed the incident, and that one of the bystanders remarked: "Do you see, my lord, how well Artemisia is fighting? She has sunk an enemy ship." Xerxes asked if they were sure it was really Artemisia, and was told there was no doubt whatever. . . . She was, indeed, lucky in every way—not least in the fact that there were no survivors from the Calyndian ship to accuse her. Xerxes' comment on what was told him is said to have been: "My men have turned into women, my women into men."

24. How did the incident affect Xerxes' opinion of Artemisia?

CONNECT TO YOUR LIFE

25. **EXPLANATORY** Think about the Persian Empire's policy of inclusion and tolerance and how the Persian legacy is relevant to American society. How does the U.S. government reflect inclusion? How does American culture demonstrate tolerance? Do you think our nation could be more inclusive and tolerant? Write an essay explaining how well the Persian example of tolerance is also found in the United States today.

TIPS

* Review what you've learned about tolerance in the Persian Empire and then consider how this policy is also found in the United States. You may wish to jot down your ideas in a graphic organizer.
* State your main ideas clearly and support them with relevant facts, details, and examples.
* Use two or three vocabulary words from the chapter in your essay.
* Provide a concluding statement about the continuation of the Persian legacy.

VOCABULARY ANSWERS

1. Possible response: Cyrus II appointed **satraps**, or provincial governors, to collect taxes and maintain order within their province.
2. Possible response: The military staged a **coup** and took over the government.
3. Possible response: Many Persians practiced **Zoroastrianism**, a monotheistic religion founded by Zoroaster.
4. Possible response: The soldiers formed a **phalanx** of several lines and stood in tight formation.
5. Possible response: Grasping the three sets of oars, the Greeks steered the **trireme** swiftly and effortlessly into battle.
6. Possible response: The Greeks fought off two invasions by the Persians during the **Greco-Persian Wars**.

READING STRATEGY ANSWERS

Greco-Persian Wars

Causes	Effects
Cyrus II conquered Ionia and made it part of the Persian Empire.	The Ionian city-states rebelled against Persia.
Athens and other Greek city-states supported the rebels.	Darius invaded mainland Greece, but the Persians were defeated at Marathon.
Xerxes I sent hundreds of ships and more than 150,000 soldiers to Athens.	Athens organized alliances with other Greek city-states and defeated the Persians at Thermopylae and Salamis.

7. Darius decided to invade mainland Greece.
8. Because the size of the Persian forces made progress slow, the Greeks had time to form alliances and prepare for battle.

MAIN IDEAS ANSWERS

9. The first five books focus on the rise of the Persian Empire and describe its geography, people, and customs; the Greco-Persian Wars are the subject of the last four books.

10. He divided his empire into provinces and appointed satraps as provincial governors.

11. He freed the Jews who had been held captive in Babylonia and allowed them to return to their homeland to rebuild the Jerusalem Temple.

12. The Royal Road, built by Darius, was 1,500 miles long and ran from Susa in Persia to Sardis in Anatolia.

13. If one row of soldiers fell, the row behind would advance to fight the enemy.

14. Hopelessly outnumbered by the Persians, many of the Greek soldiers were ordered to retreat. Three hundred Spartan soldiers stayed behind to protect the retreating forces and fought to the death.

15. Like the Achaemenids, the Sasanians hailed from Persis; they promoted Iranian art and culture; provincial officials reported to the Sasanian kings; and the government invested in roads and building projects.

HISTORICAL THINKING ANSWERS

16. Answers will vary. Possible response: Herodotus's book was immediately successful because his narrative was entertaining, exciting, and filled with speeches and dialogue.

17. Answers will vary. Possible response: He gained people's trust by showing that he was willing to listen to and learn from those he had conquered and who had once been his enemies.

18. Answers will vary. Possible response: The inspectors, the "eyes and ears of the king," could scrutinize the activities and behavior of a satrap, investigate any wrong-doing, and then report it to Darius.

19. Answers will vary. Possible response: Greece's victory in the Greco-Persian Wars allowed the Athenian form of government and culture to survive. Persia's defeat would spell the end of the Persian Empire.

20. The Persian Empire declined.

21. Answers will vary. Possible response: Cyrus was a better leader because he founded the empire and instituted the policies and government systems that Darius would follow and build on.

INTERPRET VISUALS ANSWERS

22. He is much bigger and, with his robe, raised hand, and beard, appears authoritative and powerful.

23. Answers will vary. Possible response: Darius was letting his enemies know that he was strong and ruthless.

ANALYZE SOURCES ANSWER

24. It raised her in his esteem because he thought, erroneously, that she had fought like a man in the battle and sunk an enemy ship.

CONNECT TO YOUR LIFE ANSWER

25. Essays will vary but should contain main ideas and relevant supporting details to explain how the Persian Empire's policy of inclusion and tolerance is carried on in the United States today.

UNIT 2 RESOURCES

UNIT INTRODUCTION

UNIT TIME LINE

UNIT MAP online

THE GLOBAL PERSPECTIVE: Astronomy: The Search for Meaning and Survival

- National Geographic Explorers: Kevin Hand, Neil deGrasse Tyson, and Jedidah Isler
- On Your Feet: Roundtable

  NG Learning Framework
  Research National Geographic Explorers

UNIT WRAP-UP

National Geographic Magazine Adapted Article
- "The Land of the Stars"

Unit 2 Inquiry: Curate a Museum Exhibit

Unit 2 Formal Assessment

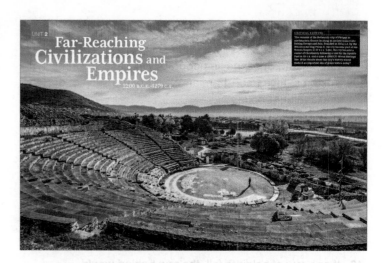

CHAPTER 5 RESOURCES

Available in the Teacher eEdition

TEACHER RESOURCES & ASSESSMENT

Reading and Note-Taking

Vocabulary Practice

Social Studies Skills Lessons
- Reading: Identify Main Ideas and Details
- Writing: Narrative

Formal Assessment
- Chapter 5 Pretest
- Chapter 5 Tests A & B
- Section Quizzes

Chapter 5 Answer Key

Cognero®

STUDENT DIGITAL RESOURCES

Available in the Student eEdition

- eEdition (English)
- Handbooks
- National Geographic Atlas
- History Notebook
- Biographies
- Literature Analysis

STRATEGY ❶
Focus on Main Ideas

Tell students to reread the lesson and review the visuals. Then ask them to close the book and write five facts that they remember from the lesson. Have partners compare lists and consolidate the two lists into one final list.

Use with All Lessons *Help students develop the habit of making lists of facts as they read.*

STRATEGY ❷
Turn Headings into Outlines

Explain to students that headings can provide a good outline for the content of each lesson. Model for students how to use a lesson title and headings to create a basic outline structure. Encourage students to add to their outlines as they read.

Use with All Lessons *You might choose to pair students of mixed proficiency.*

STRATEGY ❸
Use Reciprocal Teaching

Instruct partners to take turns reading each paragraph of the lesson aloud. At the end of the paragraph, the reading student asks the listening student questions about the paragraph. Students may ask their partners to state the main idea, identify important details that support the main idea, or summarize the paragraph. Then have pairs answer the Historical Thinking questions.

Use with All Lessons

STRATEGY ❶
Trace Visuals

Pair a sight-impaired student with a sighted student. Have the sighted student guide the sight-impaired student's hand to trace photographs and other visuals with their fingers. Then encourage the pair to discuss memorable parts of each visual. The tactile tracing and discussion will help the student understand and remember the content contained in each visual.

Use with All Lessons

STRATEGY ❷
Modify Main Idea Statements

To help students anticipate and organize content, provide modified Main Idea statements before reading. Several examples are provided below.

1.1 The archaeologist William Parkinson studies early Greek farming towns and how they eventually became cities.

1.2 Groups that lived on the Mediterranean Sea before the Greeks lived there got rich from trade.

1.3 The Phoenicians sailed and set up outposts around the Mediterranean Sea, created a new way of writing, and made a valuable dye to make purple cloth.

2.1 The people of Athens started a government in which common citizens help make decisions and choose leaders.

2.2 When Pericles led Athens, Greek people wrote and performed plays and built impressive buildings.

3.1 Because the Greek city-states kept fighting with each other, they created a chance for the Macedonians to invade Greece.

3.2 Alexander the Great fought and defeated Persia, which led to the mixing and sharing of ideas across the ancient world.

Use with All Lessons

STRATEGY ❶
Use Terms in a Sentence

Pair students at the **Beginning** level with students at the **Intermediate** or **Advanced** level. Instruct pairs to work together to compose a sentence using selected Key Vocabulary words and terms. Ask the more proficient students to assist their partners in checking the accuracy of the sentences. Invite pairs to share their sentences and discuss different ways to use each word or term.

Use with All Lessons

STRATEGY 2
Pronounce Words

Before reading, preview with students at **All Proficiencies** the terms *papyrus, alphabetic text, hieroglyphics,* and *cuneiform.* Say each word slowly, and have students repeat after you. Suggest students make word cards for the terms, writing definitions and pronunciation hints for themselves. You may wish to preview additional terms from the lesson, such as *exported, cedar, coastlines, consonants, vowels, accessible,* and *script.*

Use with Lesson 1.3 *You may wish to use this strategy with other lessons that contain words students find difficult to pronounce.*

STRATEGY 3
Compose Captions

Review the artwork and photographs in a lesson, as needed. Then pair students at the **Beginning** and **Intermediate** levels with English-proficient students and instruct them to write original captions for the photos—and, if applicable, any artwork—in the chapter. Ask volunteers to share their captions.

Use with All Lessons *For lessons with more than one photograph or piece of art, make sure students write original captions for all photos and artwork.*

GIFTED & TALENTED

STRATEGY 1
Research and Role-Play

Invite students to choose one advocate or opponent of the government in Athens that led to democracy and prepare to role-play the part of that individual. The person might be an aristocrat who was elected one of the nine archons, a male peasant, Solon, Cleisthenes, Pericles, or a woman not allowed to participate in the assembly. Instruct students to conduct research to learn why the individual they chose would have supported or opposed one level of democracy formed in Athens. Pair students who hold opposing views and invite them to role-play their parts with each other.

Use with Lesson 2.1 *If students role-play for the class, discuss how the performances enhance students' understanding of how democracy developed and why it was different from other forms of government at the time.*

STRATEGY 2
Review a Performance

Prompt students to choose one of the playwrights described in the chapter and pretend to be a critic watching a performance of one of his plays. Have them conduct more research as needed on the playwright and his plays. Instruct students to describe how the play was unlike earlier dramas and why it was entertaining. Students may also comment on why they think these plays still survive today.

Use with Lessons 2.2 and 3.4

PRE-AP

STRATEGY 1
Study a Historic Philosopher

Direct students to select Socrates, Plato, or Aristotle and conduct online research on how their chosen famous Athenian philosopher has influenced modern thinking. Encourage students to read some of this philosopher's writings and to write an essay evaluating how he explored ideas and proposed new ways of thinking. Invite them to speculate why these philosophers are still studied in modern classes and how their ideas could affect present-day life.

Use with Lessons 3.2 and 3.4

STRATEGY 2
Extend Knowledge

Invite students to show the relevance of a topic, person, idea, or event introduced in Chapter 5 to current events or issues that are still relevant today. For example, students might research how the epic poems the *Iliad* and the *Odyssey* have influenced modern movies, how the Phoenician alphabet influenced modern languages, how Spartan warriors are used as mascots, how Athens's democracy influenced the democracy of the United States, and how Greek architecture influences modern architecture. Invite students to report their findings to the class.

Use with All Lessons

**Greek
Civilization**

2200 B.C.E–200 B.C.E

HISTORICAL THINKING How did the arts,
sciences, and government of ancient Greece
influence later civilizations?

SECTION 1 **Early Greece**
SECTION 2 **The Golden Age**
SECTION 3 **Hellenism: A Cultural Synthesis**

CRITICAL VIEWING
People bustle through the streets of Plaka, or old town,
of Athens, Greece, with the Parthenon and Acropolis
overlooking the city. Compare and contrast the buildings.
What do they have in common? How are they different?

INTRODUCE THE PHOTOGRAPH

THE ACROPOLIS AT ATHENS

Have students study the photograph of Athens, Greece.
Draw students' attention to the Acropolis at the top of the
photo and the Parthenon, which is the most prominent
structure. **ASK:** What inferences can you draw about the
Acropolis and the Parthenon, based on the photograph?
*(The Parthenon must be very, very old, because it is
greyish and faded, compared to the modern buildings
in the foreground. Also, only part of its structure is still
standing, which suggests time and the natural elements
have worn it away. The Acropolis was built on a raised
area—perhaps a mountain or a hill. That suggests that it
may have been important.)* Explain to students that in this
chapter they will learn about the civilization of Ancient
Greece, the achievements of which form the foundation
of the Western world.

SHARE BACKGROUND

In Ancient Greece, an acropolis was a district that served
as the center of a city-state's municipal, military, and
religious activity. It was typically built atop a high hill
or mountain, which served a dual purpose: to give the
military the ability to see invaders and to give people
closer proximity to the gods. The Acropolis at Athens was
built during the fifth century B.C.E., and on it stood a series
of marble temples, bronze statues, and other monuments
that Athenians could observe from lower ground. The
most magnificent of all the structures on the Athenian
Acropolis was the Parthenon, a huge, marble temple built
to honor Athena, the goddess of war and wisdom. Athena
was believed to be the protector of Athens; indeed, the
city was named for her. The Parthenon, so beautifully
symmetrical and balanced, is one of the most admired
works of architecture in the world.

CRITICAL VIEWING Answers will vary. Possible
response: Several of the new and ancient structures have
columns and square foundations. The Parthenon and
other ancient structures are made from pale stone
and are incomplete. The newer buildings are colorful and
have walls, doors, windows, and roofs.

HISTORICAL THINKING QUESTION

How did the arts, sciences, and government of ancient Greece influence later civilizations?

Brainstorm the Legacy of Ancient Greece Invite students to begin thinking about the legacy and influence of Ancient Greece. Ask students to brainstorm ideas in response to the following questions.

1. Look at the photograph of the Parthenon. Does it remind you of any buildings you've seen in photographs or in person? Explain.

2. Think about your prior knowledge of mathematics. Are there any mathematical concepts—especially in geometry—that have Greek names, use Greek terms, or you know originated in Greece?

3. Can you describe the features of a Greek sculpture without first looking at an example? If you can, what does that tell you about Greek sculpture?

4. When you hear the term *democracy*, what do you think of?

5. Think about your favorite book, movie, or TV show. Does the story have a protagonist and an antagonist? What is the main conflict of the story?

6. Have you ever had a parent or teacher respond to your question with another question? Relate an example.

Write each question on chart paper and add students' ideas. Revisit the questions at the end of each lesson and ask students to suggest additional answers based on what they have learned and to explain how each question relates to influences from ancient Greece.

KEY DATES FOR CHAPTER 5

c. 2000 B.C.E.	The Minoans build Knossos.
c. 1700–1500 B.C.E.	The Phoenicians develop their alphabet.
c. 1600 B.C.E.	The Minoans encounter the Mycenaeans.
c. 800 B.C.E.	The *Iliad* is written.
508 B.C.E.	Cleisthenes reforms Athenian democracy.
490–479 B.C.E.	The Greco-Persian Wars are fought.
447–432 B.C.E.	The Parthenon is built.
431–404 B.C.E.	The Peloponnesian War is fought.
338 B.C.E.	Philip II and the Macedonians defeat the Greeks.
333 B.C.E.	Alexander the Great defeats the Persians.

INTRODUCE THE READING STRATEGY

IDENTIFY MAIN IDEAS AND DETAILS

Explain to students that identifying the main ideas and details of a paragraph, a lesson, or even an entire chapter can help them recognize important concepts. It also enables them to locate supporting evidence for answers or arguments. Go to the Chapter Review and preview the graphic organizer with students. As they read the chapter, have students look for details about Greek democracy.

INTRODUCE CHAPTER VOCABULARY

KEY VOCABULARY

SECTION 1

agora	alphabet	fresco
helot	hoplite	Linear B
oligarchy	oral tradition	polis
redistributive economy	veto	

SECTION 2

archon	aristocrat	commodity
deity	democracy	quorum
satire		

SECTION 3

coalition	Hellenization

WORD MAPS

As students read the chapter, ask them to complete a Word Map for each Key Vocabulary term. Tell them to write the term in the oval and, as they encounter the term in the chapter, complete the Word Map. Model an example using the graphic organizer below.

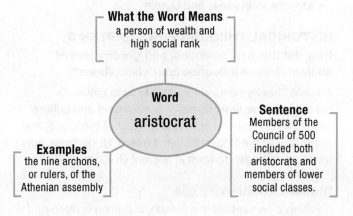

What the Word Means
a person of wealth and high social rank

Word
aristocrat

Sentence
Members of the Council of 500 included both aristocrats and members of lower social classes.

Examples
the nine archons, or rulers, of the Athenian assembly

Embracing Our
Greek Heritage

"To some extent, we're all Greeks." —Bill Parkinson

Parkinson is certain the bodies buried in Alepotrypa Cave were deliberately placed in the position revealed by their skeletons. "Their arms are draped over each other, their legs are intertwined," he says. "It's unmistakable."

122 CHAPTER 5

Sometimes an archaeological find strikes right at the heart—like the pair of skeletons uncovered near Alepotrypa (ah-leh-POH-trih-pah) Cave in Greece in 2015. Archaeologists were stunned to find the 5,800-year-old bones of a man and woman in their twenties locked in an embrace. The remains raised hard-to-answer questions: Were the couple young lovers? husband and wife? brother and sister? How did they die? "Like most things in Greece, it's complicated," says National Geographic Explorer William Parkinson.

MAIN IDEA
Bill Parkinson studies ancient Greek society, focusing on how early farming villages developed and turned into cities.

SOLVING MYSTERIES
The relationship of the embracing couple—and how they died—may always remain unknown. However, examinations of other skeletons at the cave site suggest the couple lived during a violent time. According to the work of Parkinson's colleague, Dr. Anastasia Papathanasiou, a third of the skeletons show evidence of head trauma, probably caused by rocks or clubs. Archaeologists hope to gain a fuller picture of ancient Greek life from ongoing studies of the site.

Parkinson, a curator at the Field Museum and professor at the University of Illinois at Chicago, is one of those archaeologists. He codirects the Diros Project, a shared Greek and American research venture focused on Alepotrypa Cave, which lies along Diros Bay on the Mani Peninsula in southern mainland Greece. More than 8,000 years ago, Neolithic farmers began using the cave for burials and religious ceremonies. About 6,500 years ago, farmers established a village outside the cave. For unknown reasons, people abandoned the settlement about 5,000 years ago.

Parkinson and his team are working to solve some of the mysteries surrounding this important ancient site. They have gained insight into how early farming villages developed in Greece and are working to piece together how these villages transformed into towns and cities.

Parkinson appreciates Western society's strong connection to the ancient Greeks. "So many aspects of our culture and our civilization derive from what happened over 2,000 years ago in the southeastern corner of Europe," he notes, "from our political systems to many of the sports that still hold the American imagination to much of our language, medicine, philosophy."

NEVER GETTING OLD
Growing up outside Joliet, Illinois, Parkinson liked to search for arrowheads in nearby fields and woods. Originally focused on becoming a journalist when he entered college, he instead became attracted to archaeology for a variety of reasons. For one, much of the work is hands-on. In addition to drawing upon a wide range of skills and knowledge, archaeology is also a "team sport"—one requiring collaboration with many kinds of specialists.

Perhaps the greatest thing about shoveling dirt, Parkinson says, is that it never gets old. He claims, "Nothing can describe how exciting it is to put your trowel in the ground and uncover something nobody has seen for several thousand years." Like the bones of an embracing couple, for example.

What has Parkinson discovered from his fieldwork about the growth of cities from small farming villages? An old theory is that people banded together and formed cities to defend themselves against attackers. According to Parkinson, safety wasn't the only reason. His fieldwork indicates that the early Greeks were drawn to populated places because "there were things going on—in the same way it happens today." And over time, those small beginnings led to the magnificent cities of Greek civilization.

HISTORICAL THINKING

1. **READING CHECK** What attracted William Parkinson to the field of archaeology?

2. **ANALYZE CAUSE AND EFFECT** What has Parkinson's research revealed about the reasons ancient Greek farming villages grew into cities?

Greek Civilization 123

PLAN: 2-PAGE LESSON

OBJECTIVE
Understand William Parkinson's studies of ancient Greek society, focusing on how early farm villages developed and turned into cities.

CRITICAL THINKING SKILLS FOR LESSON 1.1
- Analyze Cause and Effect
- Make Inferences
- Make Connections
- Identify Main Ideas and Details

HISTORICAL THINKING FOR CHAPTER 5
How did the arts, sciences, and government of ancient Greece influence later civilizations?

Ancient Greeks banded together to form cities. As cities grew over time, forms of government and culture spread throughout Greece and the rest of the world, and eventually to the United States. Lesson 1.1 explores how these cities began to form in ancient Greece.

Student eEdition online
Additional content for this lesson, including a video and a photo, is available online.

BACKGROUND FOR THE TEACHER
Körös Regional Archaeological Project William Parkinson, along with a team of international specialists, studies the social changes in Körös River Valley during the transition from the Neolithic to the Copper Age—a time when the organization of households and settlements went through many significant changes. The project focuses on the Neolithic site of Szeghalom-Kovácshalom in the Körös River Valley—home to a group called the Tisza from around 5000 B.C.E. to 4500 B.C.E.—where a *tell* protrudes from the landscape. A *tell* is a flat-topped mound composed of debris and cultural materials that developed over time as people rebuilt cities on top of the ruins of previous settlements. The project is exploring potential environmental, ecological, and social changes that may have led people to live on these fortified settlements over their scattered villages. Parkinson and his team hope to reconstruct the cultures of the early Great Hungarian Plain inhabitants and learn more about the influences and aspects of complex societies worldwide.

History Notebook
Encourage students to complete the National Geographic Explorer page for Chapter 5 in their History Notebooks as they read.

INTRODUCE & ENGAGE

DISCUSS COMMUNITIES

Have students provide examples of different communities in which people may live, such as urban, suburban, and rural. Discuss with students the characteristics of each. Encourage them to supply pros and cons for living in each type of community. Tell students that in this lesson they will learn what led people to move closer together and form cities.

TEACH

GUIDED DISCUSSION

1. **Make Inferences** How have Parkinson's methods of studying history likely evolved since he was a child? *(Possible responses: Parkinson now studies ancient civilizations halfway across the world rather than in his own backyard. Parkinson likely uses advanced technology to excavate and study ancient sites.)*

2. **Make Connections** What aspects of our culture and civilization does Parkinson say were influenced by ancient Greece? *(political systems, sports, language, medicine, philosophy)*

IDENTIFY MAIN IDEAS AND DETAILS

Direct students to the video (available in the Student eEdition). **ASK:** What details in the video explain how early farming villages turned into cities? *(Small groups of hunter-gatherers settled down and began domesticating plants and animals and growing their own food. Specialization of crafts such as tool and pottery production led to trade, as materials were needed from outside the original location. The beginning of local trade and the production of bronze led to massive trade networks. As the societies grew and leaders and kings attempted to govern and failed, leaders realized that giving people a voice would make their form of government and their society last. People moved to cities that had what they could not get back at home, whether it was a type of good or a special place such as a ritual center.)*

ACTIVE OPTIONS

On Your Feet: Think, Pair, Share Remind students that the couple in the photo was found in a burial site in which "about one-third of the skeletons show evidence of head trauma" and that it is unknown how the couple died. Tell them to consider this as they think about the following questions: Why is it strange that the skeletons in the grave are embracing? Why might they have been placed together in their grave like this? Have students discuss possible reasons with a partner. Then have them share their thoughts with the class.

> **NG Learning Framework: Investigate Previous Societies**
> **ATTITUDE** Curiosity
> **KNOWLEDGE** Our Human Story

Have students research what they might find in their own "backyards" as Parkinson found in his. Have them find answers to the following questions: Who lived here before? When? What do we know about these people? Who came before them? Invite students to share their findings with the class.

DIFFERENTIATE

ENGLISH LANGUAGE LEARNERS

Ask Yes/No Questions Ask the questions below and have students say or write *yes* or *no* in response. Then reread the questions and ask students to correct the information in any question that has *no* as an answer. *(numbers 1, 3, 4)*

1. Does William Parkinson know how the young embracing couple died?

2. Did the couple live during a violent time?

3. Did Parkinson know he wanted to be an archaeologist when he was a child?

4. Do archaeologists work alone?

PRE-AP STEM

Build a City Ask students to imagine they are rulers of an early Greek civilization and want to build a city to suit their economic, political, and social needs. Encourage them to consider water sources, climate, and natural defenses when choosing a location; the availability of materials and tools needed to erect the structures; the purpose of each structure within the city; and the number of people the city could safely house. Then have them create detailed building plans for their city. Encourage students to use their plans to build their city out of small building blocks or other available materials.

See the Chapter Planner for more strategies for differentiation.

HISTORICAL THINKING

ANSWERS

1. the work is hands-on, draws on a wide range of skills and knowledge, and involves collaboration with many kinds of specialists

2. In addition to safety, the ancient Greeks were also drawn to populated places for the opportunities.

Crete and Trading Centers

You've probably heard people talk about how innovation and productivity are important to a successful economy today. For ancient civilizations, thriving agriculture and trade were the keys to success. One example is a society from about 4,000 years ago on an island in the Mediterranean.

MINOAN SEA TRADE

Geography played an important role in the development of ancient Greek civilization. Greece's mainland consists of a mountainous peninsula extending south into the vast Mediterranean Sea. To its west lies the Ionian Sea and to its east the Aegean Sea. The Aegean, especially, contains many small islands. The much larger island of Crete, the center of the Minoan civilization, sits about 100 miles to the south of the mainland. The **Minoans** are named after King Minos, who according to Greek legend ruled a large empire with many ships. The Minoans did not speak Greek like later peoples who settled in the region did, but the Minoans did engage in long-distance sea trade.

Crete had a limited amount of fertile agricultural land, but it produced enough grain and livestock to feed the population with some left over for trade. The Minoans also crafted textiles, metalwork, pottery, and fine jewelry. By about 2000 B.C.E., they had built large palace complexes with storage areas for farm produce, various raw materials, and craft goods. Their economy was a **redistributive economy**, in which farmers and artisans delivered large amounts of produce and goods to the palace, and palace authorities stored, sorted, and distributed the items to the people as needed.

Many Minoans settled in areas near the palaces, which also served as public meeting places and perhaps religious centers. The palace at **Knossos** became the main center of the Minoan civilization. This structure had indoor plumbing and hundreds of rooms. Colorful **frescoes**, or paintings drawn on wet plaster, covered the walls of the palace and often showed scenes related to seafaring.

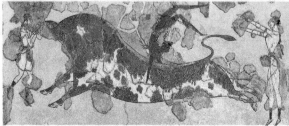

CRITICAL VIEWING The Bull-Leaping Fresco, painted about 1550 B.C.E., originally decorated a wall in the palace at Knossos in Crete, Greece. It shows a man flipping over a bull as two women observe. Why do you think the artist chose this subject?

In addition to redistributing food and craft goods, people in the palaces may have also managed the sea trade. Minoan sailors carried foodstuffs, textiles, wood, olive oil, and luxury goods such as jewelry to the Greek mainland, the lands of the eastern Mediterranean, and Egypt. They brought back mainly raw materials: tin and copper for making bronze, as well as gold, silver, gemstones, and ivory.

To keep track of so much activity, early Minoans kept records on clay tablets using script in which pictures represent objects. Later, the Minoans established a writing system in which characters stood for sounds. Today, this script, called Linear A, is still a mystery—nobody has been able to decipher it.

HOMER'S EPICS The characters in Homer's classic epics chase glory on the battlefield and beyond. The *Iliad* tells of events during a period of the Trojan War, including the story line of the great warrior Achilles. The *Odyssey* chronicles the adventures of Odysseus, the king of Ithaca who fought in the war on the side of the Greeks, as he attempts to sail home. Hindered by some gods and aided by others, Odysseus and his crew face obstacles, including dangerous mythical creatures such as the Cyclops shown here.

MYCENAEAN GREECE

Around 1600 B.C.E., Minoan traders sailing to the mainland encountered a Greek-speaking people that we know as the **Mycenaeans**. Their name comes from Mycenae, a city that appears in the epic poem the *Iliad*. Written around 800 B.C.E., the *Iliad* tells how King Agamemnon of Mycenae led a Greek army against Troy, a city located across the Aegean Sea in present-day Turkey. An archaeologist who excavated a palace site in southern Greece in the 1870s thought he had discovered Mycenae. Thereafter, historians referred to the Greek-speaking people who had settled on the mainland as Mycenaeans.

The war described in the *Iliad* was known as the Trojan War, and the story remains a literary classic. However, such a war may or may not have actually taken place. Additionally, although many scholars attribute the *Iliad* and the *Odyssey*, another epic poem, to a writer named **Homer**, some experts believe that *Homer* is merely the name attached to an **oral tradition**, or a group of stories that are passed down through the generations by people talking with one another.

The *Iliad* did, however, have some basis in fact. Archaeologists have found evidence that the Mycenaeans were, indeed, a warrior people. The graves of wealthy Mycenaean men typically contained bronze weapons and armor. Unlike the palaces of the Minoans, Mycenaean palaces were fortresses surrounded by thick walls. Warriors rode into battle in horse-drawn two-wheeled chariots.

By about 1500 B.C.E., the Minoan civilization was in decline, but historians do not know why. Perhaps the Mycenaeans conquered Crete, or perhaps earthquakes or droughts brought the civilization to an end. Whatever the cause, by 1400 B.C.E. the Mycenaean writing system, known as **Linear B**, was used for palace records on Crete. This system has been deciphered and has been shown to be an early form of the Greek language.

During the time that the two cultures overlapped, the Minoans exerted a great influence on the Mycenaeans, especially their art. Minoan artifacts and artistic styles appeared throughout the Mycenaean world. Like the Minoans, the Mycenaeans had a redistributive economy, and they prospered from a wide-ranging trade network that brought them into contact with other cultures.

Archaeological evidence of the Mycenaeans dates to no later than about 1200 B.C.E. Foreign raiders might have invaded, or infighting among the Mycenaeans might have caused their civilization to collapse.

HISTORICAL THINKING

1. **READING CHECK** How did sea trade affect the Minoan and Mycenaean civilizations?

2. **COMPARE AND CONTRAST** What key characteristics did the Minoan and Mycenaean civilizations share? How did the two cultures differ?

3. **DRAW CONCLUSIONS** How does Homer's *Iliad* reflect the history of ancient Greek civilization?

INTRODUCE & ENGAGE

OUTLINE A PERSONAL EPIC POEM

Inform students that in this lesson they will learn about the epic poems of Homer. Then invite them to outline an epic poem that would tell the story of their own life. Encourage them to select the major events of their lives and how those events might be described. Ask them to think about which events might be sung, rather than spoken. Have them consider what they would want later generations to understand about their life and their times.

TEACH

GUIDED DISCUSSION

1. **Identify Main Ideas and Details** How did geography affect the development of the Minoan civilization? *(The Minoans were centered on the island of Crete. Crete had some farmable land that allowed them to sustain themselves. However, they also had to become traders so that they could obtain needed raw materials. They developed a written language, called Linear A, to keep track of their trading activities.)*

2. **Explain** What aspect of Mycenaean civilization is described in the *Iliad*? Explain your response. *(The* Iliad *describes the Mycenaeans as a warrior people, and archaeologists have unearthed relevant evidence in Mycenaean palaces as well as the graves of Mycenaean men.)*

IDENTIFY MAIN IDEAS AND DETAILS

Have students review the photograph and caption of the first Mycenaean dagger blade in the gallery (available in the Student eEdition). **ASK**: What details about the blade support the main idea that the Mycenaeans were a warrior people? *(Possible answer: The blade depicts a lion hunt in which some Mycenaeans are armed with weapons and shields. The caption says that men were typically buried with multiple blades, which suggests that weapons were highly valued. Also, the blade is ornately decorated with what appears to be gold and perhaps silver; a warrior people would probably decorate weapons this way.)*

ACTIVE OPTIONS

On Your Feet: Roundtable Divide the class into groups of four or five. Hand each group a sheet of paper containing the following question: In what ways can trade and warfare make a civilization more powerful? The first student in each group should write an answer, read it aloud, and pass the paper clockwise to the next student. Have students circulate the paper until they run out of answers or the time is up.

> **NG Learning Framework: Compare and Contrast the Minoans and the Mycenaeans**
> **SKILL** Collaboration
> **KNOWLEDGE** Our Human Story

Ask small groups to create a chart summarizing the similarities and differences between the Minoans and the Mycenaeans in the following categories: economy, geography, society and the role of women, and arts and culture. Have students supplement information in the text with online sources. Display charts on a class website or around the classroom.

DIFFERENTIATE

STRIVING READERS

Summarize Arrange students in pairs and tell them to read and summarize the text by writing at least three notes for each of the lesson's two sections. After they have completed taking notes, guide students to review their notes and create a summary statement for each section. Then have students write a summary statement for the whole lesson.

PRE-AP

Investigate a Minoan Fresco Ask students to select a fresco, other than the Bull-Leaping fresco in the lesson. Have them gather information from a variety of sources and create an oral report detailing the history of the fresco, which characteristics of Minoan art it demonstrates, and what historians have learned about the Minoans by studying the fresco. Invite volunteers to share their findings with the class.

See the Chapter Planner for more strategies for differentiation.

HISTORICAL THINKING

ANSWERS

1. It helped both prosper economically and linked them to other cultures that likely influenced them.

2. Both engaged in sea trade, built palace centers, supported artisans, used a writing system, and collapsed for unknown reasons. The Mycenaeans spoke Greek and were a warrior people whose palace centers were fortresses.

3. It tells a story of how an ancient Greek culture attacked a distant city during the Trojan War. As a warrior people, the Mycenaeans may have engaged in such a war.

CRITICAL VIEWING Possible response: A person flipping over a running bull is both dangerous and exciting, which makes it an interesting event to depict in art.

The Phoenicians and Their Alphabet

Family, friends, and life experiences all help shape your personality and make you who you are. What factors shape a culture? For the ancient Greeks, the list of key influences must include the Phoenicians.

Phoenician script appears on a sarcophagus, or coffin, from the fifth century B.C.E.

PHOENICIAN CITY-STATES

The **Phoenicians** (fih-NEE-shuhnz) occupied a sizable stretch of land along the far-eastern shore of the Mediterranean Sea. This territory included parts of present-day Syria, Lebanon, Israel, and the Palestinian territories. Phoenicia, however, more accurately consisted of a group of independent city-states within that territory. As you have learned, a city-state is a city whose ruler governs both the city and the surrounding countryside. The first major Phoenician city-states—Tyre and Sidon—arose around 2000 B.C.E. Other powerful city-states included Byblos, Aradus, and Berot (modern Beirut). Together, the city-states of Phoenicia dominated the Mediterranean Sea from the ninth to the sixth centuries B.C.E.

The Phoenician city-states prospered mainly from trade. Their trading partners included Egypt, Syria, Mesopotamia, the Greek mainland, and the Aegean islands. People in Phoenicia exported cedarwood, metalwork, fine glass, and cloth colored with a rare reddish-purple dye extracted from snails. They also exported the dye itself, called Tyrian purple after

the city-state of Tyre. (The name *Phoenician* comes from the Greek word for the dye.) Phoenician imports included papyrus, silk, spices, horses, precious metals, and gemstones. Although kings ruled most city-states, they often shared political power with merchant families.

The Phoenicians, master seafarers and shipbuilders, sailed west, establishing settlements on the island of Cyprus and the far reaches of the western Mediterranean Sea. By 814 B.C.E., they had built a thriving trading post at **Carthage** (near present-day Tunis) and set up commercial outposts and other small settlements along the North African and Spanish coastlines. Control of these areas gave the Phoenicians access to valuable natural resources, especially precious metals. Some Phoenician sailors voyaged even farther west, passing through the narrow Strait of Gibraltar to reach coastal lands on the Atlantic Ocean.

DIFFUSION OF PHOENICIAN IDEAS

As you have already learned, the exchange of goods has typically also included an exchange of ideas. Participation in a trade network that stretched from the western Mediterranean to Southwest Asia exposed the Phoenicians to a broad range of concepts and viewpoints. The Phoenicians also spread ideas to their trading partners, including the Greeks.

One of those concepts, a new type of writing system developed between 1700 and 1500 B.C.E., was the **alphabet**. In writing based on an alphabet, a single letter represents a single sound. This simplicity helped the writing system spread to other cultures. The alphabet consisted of 22 letters—all of them consonants. Readers supplied vowels on their own. Peoples in various areas of the eastern Mediterranean, including the Phoenicians, likely contributed to the alphabet's development. Early forms of the alphabet found on written records at Byblos have been dated to the 15th century B.C.E.

The exact origins of the alphabet are unknown. It may have evolved from Egyptian hieroglyphics, which included some syllables based on sounds. However, unlike hieroglyphics—a complex system of pictures representing objects, sounds, or ideas that few people other than highly trained scribes could understand—the alphabet was easy to learn and use, which made it accessible to more people. And, unlike cuneiform, it lent itself to writing on papyrus as well as on pottery or stone. In addition, letters could be used in many different combinations to form words, and they could represent nearly any spoken language. The alphabetic system was more flexible than hieroglyphics, cuneiform, or the Mycenaeans' Linear B.

By around 1100 B.C.E., the Phoenician alphabet had settled into a consistent form. The sequence of the 22 letters was set, and lines of alphabetic text were written from right to left. The Mycenaean Linear B writing system seems to have disappeared from Greece around 1200 B.C.E., along with that civilization. The

Phoenician system, which arrived in the Aegean lands (Greece) between 950 and 750 B.C.E., took its place.

At first, the Greeks accepted the Phoenician alphabet as it was. They included all its letters, even though some did not represent sounds found in their own language. They also wrote text from right to left. By 700 B.C.E., however, the Greeks had adapted the alphabet to better suit their speech by converting some unused letters into vowels and adding more vowels. In time, they also shifted to a left-to-right form of writing.

The Phoenicians passed along to the Greeks—and others—their knowledge of Mediterranean geography as well. They had an extensive understanding of the Mediterranean Sea and coastal lands. Following the example of the Phoenicians and using what they learned from them, the Greeks established their own colonies in the Mediterranean area during the period 750–550 B.C.E.

Phoenician and Greek Settlement in the Mediterranean

HISTORICAL THINKING

1. **READING CHECK** Why was an alphabetic writing system easier to learn and use than existing writing systems?

2. **INTERPRET MAPS** Which outpost did the Phoenicians likely establish first, Citium or Carthage? Use the map scale to support your answer.

3. **DRAW CONCLUSIONS** Why did some merchant families have considerable power in Phoenician city-states?

PLAN: 2-PAGE LESSON

OBJECTIVE

Examine the society and accomplishments of the sea-faring Phoenicians, including the significance of their writing system.

CRITICAL THINKING SKILLS FOR LESSON 1.3

- Interpret Maps
- Draw Conclusions
- Make Connections
- Sequence Events
- Interpret Charts

HISTORICAL THINKING FOR CHAPTER 5

How did the arts, sciences, and government of ancient Greece influence later civilizations?

The Phoenicians were a seafaring people located in Southwest Asia who developed an alphabet that was the precursor to the Roman alphabet, which we still use today. Lesson 1.3 describes the Phoenicians, their achievements, and how they developed their alphabet.

Student eEdition online

Additional content for this lesson, including a chart, is available online.

BACKGROUND FOR THE TEACHER

Travel and Trade The Phoenicians were extraordinary travelers. Driven by trade, the earliest Phoenicians built great "round ships" and set sail on the Mediterranean Sea around 3000 B.C.E. Egypt's and Mesopotamia's climates were not conducive to growing trees, so the Phoenicians' cedar timber (from today's Lebanon) was highly coveted. Trading timber for gold brought the Phoenicians to Nubia, and a desire for copper took them to Cyprus. Between 1200 B.C.E. and 334 B.C.E., Phoenician traders traveled beyond the Mediterranean. In fact, so renowned were Phoenician sailors, other kingdoms chartered them for their own interests. King Solomon of Israel ordered Phoenician trading ships to Ophir, which historians believe was in present-day India. About 600 B.C.E., Egyptian pharaoh Necho II hired Phoenicians to circle around Africa—an incredible accomplishment that remained unequalled for 20 centuries. Later, after their great city-state of Carthage was well-established, Phoenician traders trekked even farther, up the Atlantic coast to the Azores, off the coast of Portugal, and perhaps to the British Isles, where the Phoenicians would have traded for tin.

INTRODUCE & ENGAGE

SHARE TRAVEL EXPERIENCES

Ask students to share personal experiences about trips they have taken or information about places they would like to visit. Have them discuss their motivations for travel. **ASK:** How do the reasons people travel today differ from those of people in the past? *(Answers will vary. Possible response: Modern people travel for leisure, for business, or to aid others. People in previous eras traveled for economic reasons or to share their cultures.)* Tell students that they will learn about the Phoenicians, a trading civilization who traveled within and beyond the Mediterranean Sea.

TEACH

GUIDED DISCUSSION

1. **Make Connections** What was the connection between the reddish-purple dye called Tyrian purple and the spread of Phoenician ideas? *(Tyrian purple was rare; Phoenicians dyed cloth with it. They traded the cloth and the dye itself; Phoenician ideas traveled along with this and other goods.)*

2. **Sequence Events** Sequence the following events: Mycenaean Linear B writing system disappears from Greece; Phoenicians develop a new writing system; Phoenician writing system replaces the Mycenaean Linear B writing system. *(Phoenicians develop a new writing system (1700 B.C.E.–1500 B.C.E.); Mycenaean Linear B writing system disappears from Greece (around 1200 B.C.E.); Phoenician writing system replaces the Mycenaean Linear B writing system (950 B.C.E.–750 B.C.E.)*

INTERPRET CHARTS

Direct students to the chart of Phoenician and English letters (available in the Student eEdition). **ASK:** Which English and Phoenician letters are similar and which are different? Describe one example of each. *(Possible response: The letter A is similar. It's a V-shape with a line through it, but the line of the Phoenician A is longer, and the letter is turned on its side. The letter C is different; the Phoenician C is made with two straight lines.)*

ACTIVE OPTIONS

On Your Feet: Inside-Outside Circle Arrange students in concentric circles facing each other. Direct students in the outer circle to pose the following questions to students in the inner circle: In what ways was the Phoenician alphabet simpler than previous writing systems? What did each letter stand for? How did the Greeks modify it? Ask students to trade inside/outside roles and rotate to create new partnerships.

NG Learning Framework: Research a Phoenician Cultural Legacy
ATTITUDE Curiosity
SKILL Collaboration

Instruct pairs to create a web page about the cultural legacy of the Phoenicians. Have them focus on one aspect of Phoenician civilization, such as the alphabet, the trading network, or a city-state, such as Carthage. Ask them to include visuals, explanations, and hyperlinks.

DIFFERENTIATE

INCLUSION

Connect Letters Pair students who are strong readers with those who have reading or perception difficulties. Instruct partners to study the information presented in the chart comparing Phoenician letters with modern English letters (available in the Student eEdition) as well as the photograph of the tablet. Direct them to look together and use a finger to connect the modern English letter with its Phoenician counterpart. Then have them look for Phoenician letters in the photograph of the tablet.

PRE-AP

Extend a Chart Ask students to research the other letters of the Phoenician alphabet and create a complete chart of the alphabet. They should show all 22 letters of the Phoenician alphabet and their modern English (Latin) counterparts. Then have them research the phoneme for each letter and be prepared to demonstrate the sounds for the class. As a final challenge, have them write a short sentence in English using the Phoenician alphabet.

See the Chapter Planner for more strategies for differentiation.

HISTORICAL THINKING

ANSWERS

1. It was less complex, could be used to write on many different materials, and was more flexible than other writing systems.

2. Citium, on the island of Cypress, is located about 125 miles from Phoenicia, but Carthage is nearly 1,500 miles away. The Phoenicians likely established Citium first.

3. Possible response: The main source of a city-state's prosperity was trade. Merchant families held political power because they controlled trade.

The Rise of Greek City-States

Life can be difficult. An accident or tragic event can leave a person feeling lost. After the collapse of the Mycenaean civilization, the Greeks seemed lost to history. But they bounced back—and became even stronger.

A PERIOD OF RECOVERY

About 1200 B.C.E., after the Mycenaean civilization fell, the entire population of Greece dropped sharply. Survivors abandoned the palace centers, and agriculture declined. Little evidence exists of social or cultural progress for several centuries. By around 900 B.C.E., however, the population had made a comeback, as had agriculture—assisted by the increasing production of iron tools. Iron had taken the place of bronze as the metal of choice for tools and for weapons.

As you already learned, sometime after the eighth century B.C.E. the Phoenicians introduced the Greeks to their alphabet. This transfer or sharing of information not only gave the Greeks a writing system to replace the one that had largely been lost but also made written language more available to people in general. The oral transmission of poetry and songs had preserved Greek culture through these difficult times, and those forms of expression would soon begin to appear in writing. Recall that the epic works by the poet or group of poets known as Homer were written in the 700s B.C.E.

At about this same time, families began to organize into communities on the Greek mainland and islands. They established borders and exerted control over villages and farms within those borders. They built temples dedicated to a god or goddess within a sanctuary, or sacred area. They set aside land

for an **agora**, an open-air marketplace where citizens could gather to discuss politics and other matters of local interest. Later communities often built an outdoor theater and usually surrounded their city center with a wall. These elements came to define the Greek city-state, known to the Greeks as a **polis** (PAW-luhs).

ORGANIZATION AND SPREAD OF CITY-STATES

Recall that mountains cover much of Greece. In ancient times, this terrain made overland travel and communication difficult, so Greeks tended to orient themselves toward the sea. Since mountain ranges divided the landmass, developing city-states were isolated.

Greek City-States, c. 500 B.C.E.

Those city-states tended to be located in fertile valleys or on coastal plains, often with no land route directly linking them to other population centers. Unlike the diverse Persian Empire, all Greeks spoke the same language and worshiped the same gods. But isolation limited cooperation among city-states and also made it highly unlikely that a single ruler could control all of them. As a result, there was no unified nation called Greece. Each city-state ruled itself. Most remained small, with perhaps a few thousand people, but each one had its own food sources, court system, and army.

As early as the 800s B.C.E., Greeks began to migrate eastward across the Aegean Sea, settling in coastal Anatolia and nearby islands. There they established trading posts. Over the next 200 years, Greek emigrants formed their own small city-states, not only in the eastern Aegean but along the Black Sea and in what is today southern Italy, Sicily, France, Spain, and northern Africa. These communities remained linked to the metropolis, or "mother city," through trade.

SPARTA AND ATHENS

The evolution of the polis brought with it some novel political ideas. One was citizenship; all residents of a city-state, except foreigners and slaves, were citizens. Another was freedom of speech; citizens could speak freely about political issues. Yet another was the rule of law; citizens were subject to the laws and, whether rich or poor, enjoyed legal equality. (Women, though citizens, lacked certain rights; they could not participate in politics or own property.) Two dominant city-states, **Sparta** and **Athens**, are credited with promoting these and other groundbreaking political concepts.

Until around 600 B.C.E., a group of wealthy landowners or merchants governed most city-states. The warrior society Sparta took a different path. Two military leaders served as its kings but had limited power, and a council of about 30 elders, joined by the two kings, proposed the laws. This "rule by the few" made Sparta an **oligarchy**. An assembly of all free adult men voted on the laws, although they rarely **vetoed**, or voted against, any of them. This assembly marked Sparta as one of the first city-states to grant substantial political rights to its male citizens.

CRITICAL VIEWING On this vase from the sixth century B.C.E., armed citizen-soldiers cluster closely together. What does this formation suggest about Greek armies?

Men who descended from the original Spartans served full-time as citizen-soldiers, or **hoplites**. Spartan hoplites were not permitted to farm or engage in business, but they could vote in the assembly. Male descendants of the first peoples conquered by Sparta could own land and work as artisans and traders. However, unlike citizens, they could not vote in the assembly. Women could not vote either, but they enjoyed more freedoms than women in some other city-states. For example, they ran their husbands' estates when men were away at war. State-owned slaves known as **helots** did the farming and domestic work.

Athens was not a warrior society, but—like Sparta—it could field a powerful army of citizen-soldiers. Recall that when the Persian army invaded in 490 B.C.E., the Athenians beat them back at the Battle of Marathon. Athenians and Spartans later joined forces to repel a second Persian invasion in 480 B.C.E. In the key battle, the Athenian navy destroyed the Persian fleet.

In both Athens and Sparta, citizens had significant rights and freedoms. However, Athenians outdid Spartans by establishing a more open political system: the world's first democracy.

HISTORICAL THINKING

1. **READING CHECK** How did geography impact ancient Greece's attempt to form a united country?

2. **ANALYZE CAUSE AND EFFECT** What factors helped rebuild the ancient Greek civilization?

3. **COMPARE AND CONTRAST** How do the rights of citizens in the Greek polis compare with the rights citizens enjoy today in similar societies?

PLAN: 2-PAGE LESSON

OBJECTIVE

Explain the causes and effects of the rise of Greek city-states such as Athens and Sparta.

CRITICAL THINKING SKILLS FOR LESSON 1.4

- Analyze Cause and Effect
- Compare and Contrast
- Make Inferences
- Interpret Maps

HISTORICAL THINKING FOR CHAPTER 5

How did the arts, sciences, and government of ancient Greece influence later civilizations?

After a long, fallow period, Greek civilization began to make a comeback in the eighth century B.C.E. As city-states such as Athens and Sparta became organized socially and politically, Greek culture experienced a renewal. Lesson 1.4 describes the rise of Athens and Sparta and the emergence of new and enduring political ideas.

Student eEdition   online

Additional content for this lesson, including a sidebar, is available online.

BACKGROUND FOR THE TEACHER

A Warrior City-State Sparta's reputation as an aggressive, warrior city-state was well-earned. From its earliest days, Sparta used its military might to conquer surrounding towns. For example, Sparta invaded Messenia and forced the Messenians to become helots, enslaved people owned by the state. The more peoples the Spartans conquered, the larger the helot population became. Fearing revolt, Spartan leaders became more militaristic and ruled with an iron fist. By the fifth century B.C.E., Spartan rulers were committed to building a powerful military state dedicated to war. Spartans were reared to be soldiers. Babies deemed weak and fragile were exposed to the elements and rarely survived. Boys were raised to be both mentally and physically tough, and school was a harsh, disciplinary place where boys were taught to be warriors. When they were a little older, boys had to demonstrate survival techniques in remote natural environments. Eventually, around age 30, Spartan men were free to leave the army, go home, and become regular citizens.

INTRODUCE & ENGAGE

COMPARE ATHENS AND SPARTA

Lead students in a brainstorming session about what they already know about Athens and Sparta. Ask them to record their knowledge in a Venn diagram. Remind them that the middle section is where they can record characteristics that both city-states share. Allow time during the lesson for students to add to the diagram as they read.

TEACH

GUIDED DISCUSSION

1. **Make Inferences** How did the features of a polis lead to new political ideas? (*A polis was an organized community of people. It included an agora, where people congregated and debated politics, as well as an outdoor theater, where people gathered to watch performances. Because people were coming together in an organized way, certain social and political norms—and rules—began to emerge. For example, the concept of citizenship emerged. Citizens could speak freely but were also subject to laws.*)

2. **Compare and Contrast** In Sparta, what was the difference between hoplites and helots? (*Hoplites were full-time, male citizen-soldiers. They could vote in the assembly, but they could not farm or engage in commerce. Helots were state-owned slaves who farmed and performed domestic work. Helots could not vote.*)

INTEPRET MAPS

Ask students to study the map of Greek City-States, c. 500 B.C.E. **ASK:** What do you notice about the locations of the city-states shown on the map? (*The city-states shown on the map are located on or close to a coast.*) What aspect of ancient Greek civilization does this fact support? (*Ancient Greece was a seafaring—and sea trading—civilization.*)

ACTIVE OPTIONS

On Your Feet: Think, Pair, Share Ask students to use the Think, Pair, Share strategy as they consider the following question: What were the advantages and disadvantages of the Spartan way of life? Allow a few minutes for students to think, and then tell students to choose partners and discuss their ideas for five minutes. After discussion time, invite students to share their ideas with the class.

> **NG Learning Framework: Compose a Journal Entry**
> SKILL Communication
> KNOWLEDGE Our Human Story

Tell students to conduct online research to explore the lives of women in either Athens or Sparta. Encourage students to take notes and analyze what women's day-to-day experiences might have been like. Then instruct them to compose a journal entry from the perspective of one such woman from either city-state, discussing work, leisure, household tasks, and citizenship. Point out that journals are a forum for self-expression—where writers seek to clarify their own thoughts or work out problems. When students have completed their journal entries, invite volunteers to share their work with the class.

DIFFERENTIATE

ENGLISH LANGUAGE LEARNERS

Understand Greek Words Direct students' attention to the words *agora, polis, hoplite,* and *helot.* Pair students at the **Beginning** or **Intermediate** level with more proficient English speakers and have them make word cards with each word's definition, pronunciation, and a sentence using the word.

PRE-AP

Explore Greek Roots Many words in modern English have Greek roots. Ask students to conduct online research and create a three-column chart that lists common Greek roots, their meanings, and examples of words that use the roots. For example, *geo-* means "earth," *-graph* means "draw" or "write," and *micro-* means "small." Tell students to be careful not to confuse Greek roots with Latin roots.

See the Chapter Planner for more strategies for differentiation.

HISTORICAL THINKING

ANSWERS

1. The geographic isolation of many Greek city-states, a barrier to communication and travel, made it unlikely that a single ruler could unite and govern them all as one country.

2. Factors leading to the rebuilding of the ancient Greek civilization included the use of iron tools in agriculture, the introduction of the Phoenician alphabet, and the organization of communities into city-states.

3. Citizens in the polis could speak out freely on political issues, they were protected by the rule of law, and they enjoyed legal equality. Today, women have the right to vote and can also participate in politics.

CRITICAL VIEWING This tightly packed formation suggests that Greek armies were heavily armed, well trained, and held advantages over their enemies.

Democracy in Athens

In a world of pharaohs, kings, and emperors, how did Athens end up ruled by the people? Democracy did not just suddenly appear. It developed slowly, sparked by popular discontent and brought to life by a few reform-minded politicians.

GOVERNMENT REFORMS

By the 600s B.C.E., the sharp rise in agricultural productivity had boosted the population of Athens's peasant farmers. Some free owners of small farms started to demand a greater say in governing the city-state. At this time, every male citizen, whether poor or prosperous, had the right to take part in the assembly, whose main job was to elect the nine archons, or chief rulers. However, all candidates for the position of archon were aristocrats, people of wealth and high social rank. Athens was not yet a democracy, the form of government in which common citizens have a voice in making decisions and choosing leaders.

ELECTED BY LOTTERY Athenians used this machine, known as a *kleroterion*, to elect officials. Each eligible male placed a token with his name on it in one of the slots. A series of balls were then released from a tube to determine whose tokens would be chosen.

Conflict among the archons, along with a declining economy, led to instability in Athens; peasants suffered greatly during this uncertainty and threatened to rebel. In 594 B.C.E., Athenians gave special powers to a single leader named Solon (SOH-luhn). To restore peace, he enacted reforms aimed at lessening the financial burden on the poor and increasing political participation. He abolished a tax on crops, canceled debts, and freed peasants and others who had been sold into slavery to pay their debts.

Solon also reformed the political process by establishing four categories of Athenians that had varying levels of political power. Male citizens were assigned to each category based on how much income their land produced. As a result, the wealthiest Athenians in the top two categories filled the most important government roles. Hoplites, including some landowning peasants, gained other positions. As members of a lower class, laborers were not eligible for office, but as citizens, they could vote on substantive issues in the assembly. The matters up for a vote were drafted by a Council of 400, which still consisted mainly of aristocrats. Athens was slowly becoming more democratic.

DEMOCRACY IN ACTION

In 508 B.C.E., additional popular reforms were promoted by an archon named Cleisthenes (KLYS-thuh-neez) who established a new form of government. All male citizens over the age of 20—roughly 10 percent of a total population of some 300,000—could join the assembly and had an equal right to speak and to vote on issues of public policy. Democracy was still limited, though, since women and slaves were not allowed to participate.

The City of Athens, c. 400 B.C.E.
ACROPOLIS — Odeon of Pericles
Erechtheion — Parthenon — Theatre of Dionysus Eleuthereus — Propylaea — Temple of Athena Nike
AGORA — Stoa Poikile — Altar of the Twelve Gods — Monument of Eponymous Heroes — South Stoa — Tholos — Temple of Hephaestus — Bouleuterion

The assembly met outdoors about 40 times a year. At least 6,000 citizens had to attend to ensure a quorum, or the minimum number required to conduct the assembly's business. During the assembly, which typically lasted a few hours, citizens voted by a show of hands. A newly formed council prepared the agenda for each assembly. Unlike Solon's council, this Council of 500 represented a cross-section of the Athenian population, not just aristocrats, and its members came from all parts of the city-state. Athens had created the world's first democracy. It is known as a direct democracy because individual citizens participated directly in the making of laws and policies.

In the 450s B.C.E., an Athenian general and politician named Pericles (PEHR-uh-kleez) helped expand that democracy. Based on his proposal, members of the council started to receive a small stipend, or living allowance, and so did jurors—the 6,000 citizens over the age of 30 who, in groups of various sizes, had the right to decide legal cases. Pericles believed that individuals had a duty to take part in their political system. Paying citizens for their service made it much more likely that even poor Athenians would be able to participate.

Athenian citizens were proud of their achievements. They had the liberty to participate in decision making, freedom of speech, and political equality. The opportunity existed for every male citizen, whether rich or poor, to offer opinions in the council, speak his mind at the assembly, or judge cases brought before a court.

Around 431 B.C.E., Pericles spoke publicly to honor soldiers who had died in a recent battle. In his speech, Pericles spoke highly of Athenian democracy. The Greek historian Thucydides (thoo-SIH-duh-deez) wrote an account of the speech.

PRIMARY SOURCE

In our form of government we are not imitators, but set the pattern for others. We are a democracy. Equality is at the basis of our laws, merit at the basis of our public preferment [advancement, as in rank or office]. The poor and the rich have an equal chance to contribute to the public weal [well-being], as well as to enjoy the honors in the gift of the state. The same spirit pervades throughout the private life of our citizens and we render cheerful obedience both to the written laws of the state and to the unwritten laws of society.

—from *The Funeral Oration of Pericles*

HISTORICAL THINKING

1. **READING CHECK** What significant democratic change did Cleisthenes make to the council?

2. **IDENTIFY** How did Solon try to balance political power between the wealthy and less wealthy?

3. **FORM AND SUPPORT OPINIONS** How do you think people living in Athens felt about the Athenian assembly as established under Cleisthenes? Respond from the perspective of one of the following: an aristocrat, a peasant, a laborer, or a woman.

PLAN: 2-PAGE LESSON

OBJECTIVE
Summarize the development of democratic ideals in Athenian government.

CRITICAL THINKING SKILLS FOR LESSON 2.1
- Identify
- Form and Support Opinions
- Identify Problems and Solutions
- Make Inferences
- Analyze Visuals

HISTORICAL THINKING FOR CHAPTER 5
How did the arts, sciences, and government of ancient Greece influence later civilizations?

The democratic reforms that developed in Athens beginning around 500 B.C.E. influenced political systems and their related documents for generations to come, including the Magna Carta, the English Bill of Rights, and the U.S. Constitution. Lesson 2.1 explores how Athens developed the world's first democracy—a system of government in which common citizens have a voice in making decisions and choosing leaders.

BACKGROUND FOR THE TEACHER
Solon Solon's economic and legal reforms were as important as his political reforms. Debt and poverty were overriding problems among the lower and middle classes. Under Solon's reforms, Athenians who had given up their land to pay debts had it returned to them; those indebted to the point of becoming enslaved were set free. Farmers who could not sustain themselves were allowed to learn a new trade and change professions. New coins, standardized in Athens rather than other city-states, were minted and circulated. Limits on exports of grain and produce were also put in place to combat food shortages. Solon's legal reforms replaced the existing code, a set of harsh edicts established by an earlier statesman named Draco. Draconian laws punished most crimes with death; Solon's code eliminated those penalties except in cases involving murder. Solon's other legal reforms included allowing any Athenian—not just crime victims—to sue, and a process by which citizens could appeal a judge's verdict.

Student eEdition online
Additional content for this lesson, including a video, is available online.

INTRODUCE & ENGAGE

BRAINSTORM A LIST

Write the word *democracy* on the board. Invite students to brainstorm words, ideas, and phrases they associate with it. List their responses on the board. Tell students that in this lesson they will learn about the characteristics of Athenian democracy and how it developed over time.

TEACH

GUIDED DISCUSSION

1. **Identify Problems and Solutions** What problem did owners of small farms have that Solon's reforms helped to solve? *(They wanted more say in electing archons, but the candidates were typically aristocrats, so the small farmers were shut out of the process. Solon's reforms established more political participation for lower-ranked citizens.)*

2. **Make Inferences** Why did the Council of 500 prepare an agenda for the assembly? *(A meeting of the assembly would have a minimum of 6,000 people attending; a smaller council was more practical and effective in doing things like setting an agenda.)*

ANALYZE VISUALS

Direct students to watch the video History 101: Ancient Greece (available in the Student eEdition) and examine the diagram The City of Athens, c. 400 B.C.E. **ASK:** What is one artistic contribution ancient Greeks made to the western world? *(They developed three types of columns and used them in their structures. These columns were used in other buildings all over the world for thousands of years.)* Where are these elements visible in the diagram? *(Possible response: in the Temple of Hephaestus in the Agora and in the Parthenon and other Acropolis buildings)* What is the legacy of the Greek language? *(It is the basis of many modern languages. Modern English has thousands of words with Greek roots and word parts.)*

ACTIVE OPTIONS

On Your Feet: Roundtable Arrange students in groups of four, and give each group a large sheet of paper with the question: How is Athenian democracy different from modern American democracy? Tell each student in every group to write an opinion that he or she can support with evidence from the text, including the primary source. After students have written their opinions, allow time for groups to discuss the opinions and supporting evidence. Then call on volunteers to share their group's ideas.

> **NG Learning Framework: Trace a System of Government Across Time**
> **ATTITUDE** Curiosity
> **KNOWLEDGE** Our Human Story

Remind students that Solon, Cleisthenes, and Pericles established different kinds of democracy in ancient Greece. Ask small groups to research the development of Athenian democracy through the periods of the three reformers. Tell students to summarize the pros and cons of each system of government. Then ask groups to choose one of the leaders and prepare a short presentation outlining his democratic viewpoints. As a class, compare and contrast the policies of the three politicians.

DIFFERENTIATE

STRIVING READERS

Use Context Clues Tell students to copy the sentences from the text that contain the Key Vocabulary words *democracy* and *quorum* on a piece of paper. Ask them to underline the context clue that provides the meaning of each word. Have students identify context clues when they encounter unfamiliar words.

GIFTED & TALENTED

Plan a Streaming TV Series Have students plan a four-episode TV series to air on a streaming platform. The series is set in ancient Athens and is about the political machinations within the Athenian assembly. Students should create three or four main characters, one of which must be an antagonist. Have them use what they have learned in the lesson to devise a simple plot that contains a conflict (for example, one character wants a certain kind of reform and the antagonist opposes it). The characters and the conflict should be introduced in Episode 1, developed in Episodes 2 and 3, and resolved in Episode 4. They are not writing actual scenes and dialogue—only the plan for the series that they will then share with each other.

See the Chapter Planner for more strategies for differentiation.

HISTORICAL THINKING

ANSWERS

1. made the Council of 500 a cross-section of people from all parts of Athens, rather than only aristocrats

2. Possible response: The wealthy gained better positions in government. The council determined what would be voted on in the assembly. Some landowning peasants gained positions that might not have been open to them before. Peasants and laborers could vote on substantive issues rather than just voting for archons.

3. Answers will vary.

Pericles and Cultural Advances

From time to time, a society defines what it means to be great. For a period in the fifth century B.C.E., Athens embodied this excellence. This Greek city-state could boast not only a powerful military and a democratic government but also an exceptional culture that left a powerful global legacy.

GOLDEN AGE OF ATHENS

With the Greek victory in the Greco-Persian Wars (490–479 B.C.E.), Athens rose to a position of leadership in an alliance of Greek city-states. Its superiority, however, rested on more than its military and economic strength. In the decades that followed, Athens forged a remarkable culture. The power and prosperity of Athens, along with a flowering of literature and architecture, made this a golden age, a period of great cultural achievement.

In 472 B.C.E., the Athenian playwright **Aeschylus** (EH-skuh-luhs) wrote a play, a tragedy that still survives today. Titled *The Persians*, it explores the story of the Greco-Persian Wars from the point of view of the Persians—and with some sympathy for their fate. Unlike earlier dramas, which had a single character, *The Persians* introduced a second character to the stage. Having two characters onstage allowed the plot to include conflict. Greek dramas also relied on a chorus, a group of players who commented on the action, usually through song.

The Parthenon at the Acropolis, shown here at dawn, is one of the most recognizable buildings in the world.

Hundreds of plays, most of which were tragedies, would appear during this century, including those written by **Sophocles** (SAH-fuh-kleez) and **Euripides** (yoo-RIHP-uh-deez). Sophocles added a third character to his plays and introduced painted scenery. Euripides is known for the strong, heroic women in his dramas. Another literary genre, the Greek comedy, also flourished during this time. Its leading playwright, **Aristophanes** (air-ih-STAH-fuh-neez), poked fun at well-known members of Athenian society through the use of colorful language, nonsense, and **satire**—humor and sarcasm used to expose or ridicule human foolishness or weakness.

THE PARTHENON AND RELIGION

Sophocles may have modeled one of his characters on Pericles; the two men knew each other and may even have been friends. As you have read, Pericles supported democratic government in the 450s B.C.E. He also promoted the arts, including theater and the fine arts of sculpture and vase painting.

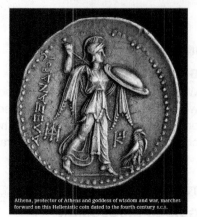

Athena, protector of Athens and goddess of wisdom and war, marches forward on this Hellenistic coin dated to the fourth century B.C.E.

In addition, Pericles used his influence with the assembly to pursue a building campaign in Athens. His goal was to make the city as physically impressive as it was politically powerful. The centerpiece of Athens's reconstruction was the **Parthenon**, built between 447 and 432 B.C.E. This temple honored Athena, goddess of wisdom and war and protector of the city-state, and also served as a memorial to people who had died in the Greco-Persian Wars. A two-room structure surrounded by tall columns, the Parthenon sat atop the Acropolis, a rocky hill jutting up from the center of Athens.

Athena was one of many **deities**—gods and goddesses—worshiped by Athenians, who also built sanctuaries and other structures to honor Zeus (king of the gods), Hephaestus (god of fire), and Dionysus (god of wine and theater). The Greeks believed their gods and goddesses observed people from high upon Mount Olympus, the tallest mountain in mainland Greece. The ancient Greeks showed their devotion to their deities through animal sacrifices, which took place within a sanctuary.

Women played a central role as priestesses in these rituals. Although women were shut out of the political realm, they could still participate in Greek culture in this meaningful way. The worship of Athena and other powerful goddesses, such as Artemis (goddess of the hunt), Aphrodite (goddess of love), and Demeter (goddess of agriculture), also indicates how much ancient Greek society valued women.

As Greeks, the Athenians and Spartans had much in common culturally and historically. They worshiped most of the same gods and goddesses. They had cooperated to defeat the invading Persians. However, in the late fifth century B.C.E., these two city-states competed to dominate the Greek world. This competition led to conflict.

HISTORICAL THINKING

1. **READING CHECK** How did Pericles influence Athenian culture?

2. **DRAW CONCLUSIONS** What other culture, ancient or otherwise, do you think deserves to be described as "great"? Why?

3. **MAKE GENERALIZATIONS** Why do you think people today still enjoy Greek drama and find beauty in Greek art and architecture?

PLAN: 2-PAGE LESSON

OBJECTIVE

Describe the cultural achievements of Athens during its Periclean golden age.

CRITICAL THINKING SKILLS FOR LESSON 2.2

- Draw Conclusions
- Make Generalizations
- Explain
- Analyze Visuals

HISTORICAL THINKING FOR CHAPTER 5

How did the arts, sciences, and government of ancient Greece influence later civilizations?

The cultural achievements of Athens's golden age—and those in literature, drama, and architecture in particular—are the foundation of much of Western arts and humanities. Lesson 2.2 describes some of those achievements.

Student eEdition online

Additional content for this lesson, including an image gallery, is available online.

BACKGROUND FOR THE TEACHER

Greek Mythology The Greek myths are part of the foundation of Western storytelling. Their precise origin, however, remains unknown. Some of the earliest appearances of Greek gods and goddesses are found in the eighth- (or ninth-) century B.C.E. epic poems of Homer, including Apollo, a son of Zeus who is mentioned in the *Iliad*. The writing makes it clear that Greek audiences were already familiar with the sun god. Indeed, pottery from the eighth century B.C.E. appears to depict scenes from the Trojan War as described in the *Iliad*. Post-Homeric writers who developed the Greek myths include Hesiod in his *Theogony*, Pindar and Thebes in their odes, and the playwrights Aeschylus, Sophocles, and Euripides. Greek myths endured through the Hellenistic and Roman periods and went on to inspire Western writers from Dante to Shakespeare, and many 20th-century readers learned Edith Hamilton's versions of the myths in her seminal book *Mythology* (1942). Today, films such as *Clash of the Titans* and *Percy Jackson & the Olympians* bring the Greek myths to life.

INTRODUCE & ENGAGE

ACTIVATE PRIOR KNOWLEDGE

To preview the lesson, engage students' prior knowledge and opinions about the portrayal of Greek heroes, gods, and goddesses they have read about or seen in novels, movies, television shows, comics, electronic games, or other forms of media. Discuss why the dramatic stories of the Greeks continue to fire our imaginations centuries and centuries later.

TEACH

GUIDED DISCUSSION

1. **Explain** What was Aeschylus's lasting contribution to the theatrical arts? *(He was the first to have a second character in his play, making conflict part of the plot. Conflict is an essential element of drama and theater.)*

2. **Make Generalizations** How were women regarded in Athenian society? *(They could not participate in politics, so they did not have any real power. However, female goddesses were worshiped and represented in art and drama. Also, women served as priestesses—a special role—during animal sacrifices to the gods.)*

ANALYZE VISUALS

Draw students' attention to the image gallery of Greek gods and goddesses (available in the Student eEdition). **ASK:** Which gods and goddesses are depicted, and what aspect of life or nature does each govern? *(Aphrodite, love and beauty; Ares, war; Artemis, the hunt and protector of the natural world; Athena, war; Hephaestus, fire and blacksmiths; Hera, marriage and women; Hermes, messenger, trade and wealth; Zeus, king of all the Greek gods; Poseidon, god of the sea)* Why do you think the Greeks worshiped these gods and goddesses? *(The gods and goddesses explained the natural world, historical events, and other phenomena; Greeks believed the gods and goddesses protected them, too.)*

ACTIVE OPTIONS

On Your Feet: Three-Step Interview Have students work in pairs. One student should interview the other using these questions: In what way was the Periclean era of Athens a "golden age"? What was achieved? How did those achievements impact Western culture? Then students should reverse roles. Ask students to share their responses in a class discussion.

> **NG Learning Framework: Design an Infographic**
> SKILL Communication
> KNOWLEDGE Our Human Story

Guide groups of four to conduct online research and create a colorful infographic that displays the 12 major Olympian gods and goddesses: Zeus, Hera, Poseidon, Demeter, Athena, Apollo, Artemis, Ares, Aphrodite, Hephaestus, Hermes, and either Hestia or Dionysus. Ask students to begin with visual depictions of the deities that they find online or create themselves. Tell them to label each god or goddess with his or her own name, area of life or nature he or she governs, and a few other key facts. Invite students to share their infographics on a class or school website or in a classroom gallery.

DIFFERENTIATE

INCLUSION

Use Supported Reading Pair proficient with less proficient readers and have them read the lesson aloud paragraph by paragraph. Have pairs stop at the end of each paragraph and use sentence frames to monitor their comprehension:

- This paragraph is about _____.
- Its main idea is _____.
- Details that support the main idea are _____ and _____.
- One question I have is _____.

GIFTED & TALENTED

Perform a Monologue Ask students to conduct online research and find a monologue (a piece of dramatic text that is delivered by one person) from a Classical Greek drama or comedy. Students may choose either a playwright or a play they learned about in the lesson or a less familiar work. Challenge them to prepare it—or even memorize it— and perform it for the rest of the class. Afterwards, lead a class discussion about the ways the monologues differ from what is seen and heard in contemporary theater, film, and TV.

See the Chapter Planner for more strategies for differentiation.

HISTORICAL THINKING

ANSWERS

1. He supported the arts and promoted construction projects, including the Parthenon.

2. Answers will vary. Possible responses: Sumer, because of its writing system or invention of the wheel; the Roman Empire, because of its law codes

3. Possible response: Greek drama deals with universal themes that apply to present-day society. Greek art and architecture have a wide-ranging, influential appeal.

2.3 A Global Commodity: Gold

People have probably been obsessed with gold ever since early humans first spied the lustrous metal in streams. Since then, gold has been prized by cultures and civilizations all over the globe. Its malleability made it easy to work with and shape, but gold's beauty, weight, and permanence made it a fitting symbol of rulers and gods. During Greece's golden age, gold became more than a desirable commodity, or valuable trade good. Greek traders at this time exchanged their goods for gold but also used coins made of gold and silver as money.

The Greeks founded colonies around the Mediterranean in part to obtain raw materials their homeland couldn't provide, including gold. Laborers toiled deep in the underground gold mines of Thrace, setting fires to break down gold-bearing rocks. The ancient Greek philosopher Aristotle believed that gold formed underground when hardened water was transformed by the sun's rays—a fittingly poetic story for this most precious of metals.

Why did myths and stories arise about gold throughout the ancient world?

WORTH ITS WEIGHT IN GOLD

As good as gold. The streets are paved with gold. These are just a few of the phrases that extol the value of gold. Before it was used as money, gold's fundamental value was accepted by all cultures. In ancient times, when gold's uses were mostly decorative, the Egyptians, Chinese, Indians, and others forced prisoners of war and slaves to mine for the metal. And gold continues to dazzle people today. In this photo, a miner holds aloft a stone extracted from a mine in the Central American country of El Salvador that contains precious gold minerals.

OPEN-CUT GOLD MINE

When gold is close to the surface, miners often use the open-cut, or open-pit, method to extract it. First, the vegetation and soil are cleared away, then the rock layer is blasted, and finally the pit is dug. The walls of the pit are stepped to help prevent rock falls. And engineers build a road along the side of the pit so that trucks can haul the ore and rocks away. The mineral belt in this open-cut mine in Cobar, Australia, is clearly visible.

GOLD AT A GLANCE

USES	Ancient cultures used gold to make jewelry and shrines and images to honor their gods.	For thousands of years, gold in the form of standardized coins was used as money in trade.	Today, gold is used in such fields as medicine, industry, electronics, and dentistry.
VALUE	Gold's rarity and the difficulties involved in finding and extracting it have added to its value and desirability.	The Phoenicians traded to obtain many precious metals but determined that gold was worth four times more than silver.	Gold is measured according to weight and was priced at more than $1,300 per ounce by markets in 2017.
PRODUCTION	Placer mining uses water to separate gold from loose materials such as gravel and sand.	Most gold is mined and extracted from deposits of rocks found deep underground or in open pits.	Copper mines often contain significant amounts of gold in addition to copper.
HISTORY	The first pure gold coins were produced in the 5th century B.C.E. in the ancient kingdom of Lydia under King Croesus, whose wealth was legendary.	Gold discovered in the Sacramento Valley in 1848 sparked a rush of immigrants to the area and spurred statehood for California.	Archaeologists feared that the Bactrian Hoard, a trove of Afghan gold dating from the 1st century C.E., had been stolen, but it was found in 2003.
ECONOMICS	When Mali emperor Mansa Musa traveled to Cairo, Egypt, in the 1300s, he spent so much gold there that its value declined.	Between 1871 and 1914, many nations adopted the gold standard, which linked the value of a country's currency directly to gold.	In 2017, the world's leading producer of gold was China, followed by Australia, Russia, and the United States.

PLAN: 4-PAGE LESSON

OBJECTIVE
Understand the history of gold as a highly desired commodity and how gold was used by early civilizations.

CRITICAL THINKING SKILLS FOR LESSON 2.3
- Analyze Visuals
- Make Connections
- Draw Conclusions
- Identify Supporting Details
- Analyze Cause and Effect
- Sequence Events

HISTORICAL THINKING FOR CHAPTER 5
How did the arts, sciences, and government of ancient Greece influence later civilizations?

Early civilizations, including those around the Mediterranean Sea, valued gold as a commodity, or valuable trade good. Gold was used to make money as well as decorative arts. Today, it is still highly desired. Lesson 2.3 explains how gold was used during Greece's golden age.

BACKGROUND FOR THE TEACHER
Thracian Gold The Thracians were a loosely organized group of Mediterranean tribes who lived in a region to the north and east of Greece in present-day Bulgaria, Romania, Serbia, and other Balkan countries. In the fifth century B.C.E., they came into contact with the Ancient Greeks, and Herodotus described them in his writings. The Thracians were fierce horse-riding warriors and allied themselves with the Trojans during the Trojan War. However, they were also skilled metalworkers, particularly with gold. The Thracians buried their rulers in tombs filled with incredible gold objects, including drinking vessels, decorative plates for harnesses, and masks. Recent archaeological finds include solid gold brooches, necklaces, buttons, and ornaments. Archaeologists in Bulgaria believe they have only excavated a fraction of the ancient Thracian artifacts. The incredible opulence demonstrates Thracian wealth and power that was largely underestimated until the late 20th century.

History Notebook
Encourage students to complete the Global Commodity page for Chapter 5 in their History Notebooks as they read.

INTRODUCE & ENGAGE

CONSIDER MODERN COMMODITIES

Explain to students that a *commodity* is any valuable raw material exchanged in large-scale trading. Work with students to guess the top commodities that the United States imports and exports today. After the discussion, inform students that the top five commodity imports are refined and crude petroleum, lumber, gold, aluminum, and coffee. Then tell them that the top five commodity exports are refined and crude petroleum, soybeans, gold, corn, and wheat. Guide the class to compile a list of businesses that might evolve from these commodities. *(Possible responses: oil refining, automobiles, furniture, farming)*

TEACH

GUIDED DISCUSSION

1. **Draw Conclusions** Why has gold been so highly desired throughout history? *(Gold is a relatively soft metal, which means it is malleable and easy to shape and mold. It is also heavy, durable, and relatively permanent, as proved by the gold artifacts that have stood the tests of time. It is also beautiful; gold is lustrous and can be polished into brilliance.)*

2. **Identify Supporting Details** How did Greek traders use gold? *(They exchanged their goods for gold, which was a raw material for them. They also used gold coins as money.)*

A GLOBAL COMMODITY

One reason gold is considered a precious metal is because of its high economic value. Another reason is because it is quite rare. Just how rare is gold? It is estimated that only about 161,000 tons of gold have been mined in all of human history, and more than half of that has been mined just since the 1950s. Gold is also rare because it is expensive and difficult to extract. Today, gold deposits are almost totally depleted, and the rest exists as mere traces in various places around the world. Based on production, the largest gold mine in the world is in the state of Nevada and it is actually comprised of two mines. In 2017, Barrick, Nevada produced 71.9 tonnes of gold. A tonne is a metric ton, which weighs about 2,220 pounds. As proof that gold is a truly global commodity, the second largest gold mine is in Uzbekistan.

DIFFERENTIATE

STRIVING READERS

Write a Tweet As students read the lesson, direct them to pause after each section and write a tweet summarizing the section's main idea in their own words. For the "Gold at a Glance" chart, have them choose one fact, rephrase it in their own words, and compose a tweet about it. Remind students to keep their tweets within the 280-character limit. Direct students to read their tweets aloud to the class, alternating sections throughout the lesson.

PRE-AP

Research Side Effects of Gold Mining Have students conduct online research on the issue of mercury pollution in gold mining. Mercury, a toxic substance, is used in gold mining to separate the gold from the ore. Instruct students to gather information from a variety of unbiased sources. Then have students write an essay analyzing the impact of the mercury on people who work in and live around gold mines. Ask students to share their analyses and recommendations with the class.

See the Chapter Planner for more strategies for differentiation.

"I HAVE GAZED ON THE FACE OF AGAMEMNON"

Thus wrote Heinrich Schliemann after he uncovered a 3,000-year-old mask in a tomb at the archaeological site of Mycenae. The German archaeologist was sure it was the funerary mask of Agamemnon, the powerful king of Mycenae. Schliemann then found another mask, the one shown here, in the same tomb. However, modern research has dated the masks and determined that they were made about 300 years before the king lived, if he did exist. Both masks were made of a very thin sheet of gold, but the features of the second one were much more defined and portrayed a recognizable face of a man. As a result, this mask is often referred to as the Mask of Agamemnon.

GOLD DIADEM

This woven gold diadem, or crown, was found in the tomb of the Macedonian king Philip II, father of Alexander the Great. It is made of tiny movable parts that would make beautiful sounds when the wind blew through its leaves.

BACKGROUND FOR THE TEACHER

A 21st-Century Gold Rush Today, gold is desired more than ever before. Despite the fact that every nation in the world has abandoned the gold standard (the United States was the last to do so, in 1971), gold continues to fascinate. Why? First of all, gold is considered a safe investment. No matter what happens to the global economy, some people believe that there will always be a market for gold. Indeed, in the spring of 2019, gold was selling for more than $1,270 per ounce, up from $271 an ounce in September 2001. Second, the market for gold jewelry is stronger than ever, particularly in 21st-century China and India. Although gold is also used in electronics and dentistry, the jewelry industry consumes most of the world's gold. The high demand for gold has negative effects, however. Gold mines are becoming depleted, and the process by which gold is mined is damaging the environment. Working conditions are unsafe, too. In poor countries, migrant workers toil in mines only to be violently attacked by local armed groups. These groups sell the stolen gold to raise money to purchase more weapons. Gold mining is also rife with child labor. Large corporations push out small miners to make way for large-scale mines, and the displaced workers suffer as a result.

TEACH

GUIDED DISCUSSION

3. **Analyze Cause and Effect** What is the effect of stepping the walls of a gold pit? *(The stepped walls help prevent rocks from falling and injuring people or damaging equipment.)*

4. **Sequence Events** Put the following events in correct chronological order: nations around the world adopt the gold standard; gold is discovered in California; gold hits $1,300 an ounce; the first gold coins are produced. *(the first gold coins are produced; gold is discovered in California; nations around the world adopt the gold standard; gold hits $1,300 an ounce)*

ANALYZE VISUALS

Have students revisit the photo of and caption for King Philip II's gold diadem. **ASK:** In what way does the diadem show how the Macedonians regarded gold? *(The diadem is extremely intricate and beautiful. The caption says that it was constructed so that it would "make beautiful sounds" when wind blew through it. The diadem was buried with the Macedonian king. The fact that something so exceptional and precious was buried with their king shows that the Macedonians regarded gold as very special.)*

ACTIVE OPTION

NG Learning Framework: Explore Gold Mining Controversies
ATTITUDE Responsibility
SKILLS Problem-Solving, Collaboration

Mining gold today is a dangerous undertaking. The process can be harmful to miners, and it can also damage the environment. Divide the class into four or five groups. Have each group briefly research a controversy around modern gold mining—environmental damage or human suffering. Groups should prepare a short report and present the facts to the class. Encourage students to share any possible solutions to the issues they research.

ANSWERS

- Possible response: Gold's beauty and easy malleability must have made the metal seem almost magical, which would have inspired stories about it.

- Possible response: The photos in this lesson illustrate gold's malleability and its beauty.

The Peloponnesian War

What seems like a minor dispute can sometimes lead to major trouble. Although Greek city-states repeatedly quarreled with one another, daily life often went on as usual. When the two most powerful city-states went to war, however, the severe consequences rippled throughout the area.

A CLASH OF ALLIANCES

After the Greco-Persian Wars ended, Athens formed the **Delian League** in 478 B.C.E. This alliance included the city-states along the northern and eastern Aegean coast and nearly all of the Aegean islands. The stated purpose of the league was to eliminate the continued Persian threat to the region. By the mid-450s B.C.E., Athens controlled the league. It forced other members to pay tribute in the form of dues to support the Athenian navy.

The other dominant Greek city-state, Sparta, led an alliance known as the **Peloponnesian League**. Sparta had long controlled much of the land on the Peloponnese, a large peninsula at the far south of the Greek mainland. The Spartans believed that they, not the Athenians, should lead the Greeks. The rivalry between Athens and Sparta led to the **Peloponnesian War**, fought from 431 to 404 B.C.E.

The Delian League and the Peloponnesian League squared off in a series of battles. Athens had naval superiority and plenty of money, mainly from tribute, but Sparta could field a stronger army. The two powers invaded each other's territory, clashing both at sea and on land. Key leaders were killed in battle or by disease—in 429 B.C.E., Pericles died as a result of a plague that swept through Athens. In 404 B.C.E., the Spartan-led Peloponnesian League, with the help of Persian armies, finally defeated Athens and the Delian League.

During the conflict, Athens was home to the influential philosopher **Socrates** (SAH-kruh-teez). Socrates was

CRITICAL VIEWING A frieze from the Nereid Monument (390–380 B.C.E.) found near present-day Turkey shows soldiers clashing in combat. What do you notice about the battling warriors?

accused of corrupting his students by leading them to question the gods and the authorities. He also became entangled in a political conflict. Just after the war, an oligarchy replaced Athens's democracy. Democratic forces quickly regained control of the government, but some leaders suspected that Socrates had sided with the oligarchy. In 399 B.C.E., after a public trial at which he claimed his innocence, he submitted to execution by drinking a cup of hemlock, a poison.

THE AFTERMATH OF WAR

Nearly all the Greek city-states suffered as a result of the Peloponnesian War. Their armies, including that of Sparta, were severely weakened. The war also drained the Athenian treasury and shattered Athens's navy.

Sparta, Athens, and a third city-state, Thebes, had recovered enough by the 370s B.C.E. to continue to attack one another. By the 350s B.C.E., it was clear that none of them had the strength to dominate the Greek world. Exhausted by warfare, the Greeks would find it difficult to respond to an unexpected challenge.

That challenge came from Macedonia, a kingdom in the far-northern mainland with no cities and few farms, mainly populated by Greek-speaking people. Its ruler, **Philip II**, had created a highly skilled army of paid troops. His infantry, or foot soldiers, fought in closely packed units. From the pack they thrust pikes—long poles with sharp spearheads—at the enemy. Philip dreamed of using that army to conquer the Persian Empire, but he first looked southward.

In the 350s and 340s B.C.E., through force of arms as well as bribery, Philip gained the loyalty of much of northern and central Greece. Then, in 338 B.C.E., the Macedonians and their Greek allies defeated a **coalition**, or temporary alliance, of southern Greek city-states. Philip forced people whom he conquered to join his alliance. Greek city-states would keep a measure of political freedom, but never again would they be fully independent actors on the world stage.

The city-states contributed soldiers and other resources to Philip in support of his mission to defeat the Persian Empire. Philip, however, did not live long enough to lead that quest. In 336 B.C.E., a fellow Macedonian assassinated him. It would be up to Philip's son Alexander to carry out his dream.

This 1787 painting by French artist Jacques-Louis David is called *The Death of Socrates.* It shows the philosopher surrounded by his grief-stricken disciples. Socrates continues teaching even as he reaches for the cup of hemlock, a poison that will kill him.

HISTORICAL THINKING

1. **READING CHECK** What were the consequences of the Peloponnesian War and the later conflicts among the Greek city-states?

2. **MAKE INFERENCES** Why do you think the Spartans might have feared the aggressive expansion of Athens's power in the years before the Peloponnesian War?

3. **FORM AND SUPPORT OPINIONS** Do you think the establishment of military alliances may have incited the Peloponnesian War? Why or why not?

PLAN: 2-PAGE LESSON

OBJECTIVE

Summarize the Peloponnesian War and explain how it left Greece vulnerable to invasion.

CRITICAL THINKING SKILLS FOR LESSON 3.1

- Make Inferences
- Form and Support Opinions
- Analyze Cause and Effect
- Identify
- Analyze Visuals

HISTORICAL THINKING FOR CHAPTER 5

How did the arts, sciences, and government of ancient Greece influence later civilizations?

After the Greco-Persian Wars ended, both Athens and Sparta formed their own alliances of city-states. Modern alliances like NATO, the European Union, and the Arab League are the foundation of present-day international relations and diplomacy. However, they are not without their tensions. Lesson 3.1 shows how the rivalry between Athens's and Sparta's alliances led to war and ruin for Greece.

BACKGROUND FOR THE TEACHER

Socrates and Plato The Athenian philosopher Socrates perfected a style of teaching, now known as the Socratic method, in which the instructor asks the student questions without revealing the instructor's own views. Many of the dialogues stress the Greek concept of *areté* (virtue or excellence), which people can attain by doing right. Socrates believed that wisdom allows an individual to determine the right course of action. Plato continued Socrates's method of teaching by asking questions. He founded the Academy, a gymnasium where he could teach students a broad curriculum emphasizing ethics. Gymnasiums had begun simply as an open ground for soldiers to train, but they had evolved into schools where young boys engaged in exercise and studied texts. Plato taught that people could choose the just course of action by using reason to reconcile the conflicting demands of spirit and desire. Reason alone determined the individual's best interests. Plato admitted boys to the Academy as well as some girls. Some scholars contend that all well-off Greek women could read and write, while others think that only a small minority could.

Student eEdition online

Additional content for this lesson, including photos and a diagram, is available online.

INTRODUCE & ENGAGE

SETTLE A CONFLICT

Lead students in discussing tools that a nation might use to resolve conflicts with another nation, such as military force, diplomacy, economic sanctions, and other ideas. Record students' responses, and then prompt a discussion with the following questions: Under what circumstances might a nation go to war? How and why might a nation avoid going to war? Tell students that they will learn about how conflict between the Delian League and the Peloponnesian League led to war.

TEACH

GUIDED DISCUSSION

1. **Analyze Cause and Effect** What events caused the Peloponnesian War? *(Athens and Sparta each formed its own alliance of city-states: the Delian League and the Peloponnesian League, respectively. The Delian League was powerful enough to force other city-states to pay dues. The Spartans resented the Athenians' power and believed that they should lead the Greeks. As a result, an armed conflict broke out.)*

2. **Identify** Who was Philip II, and what did he achieve? *(He was the ruler of Macedonia. When Greece was weakened after the Peloponnesian War, Philip II gained the loyalty of northern city-states. He then conquered the southern city-states before he was assassinated in 336 B.C.E.)*

ANALYZE VISUALS

Direct students' attention to the painting *The Death of Socrates.* **ASK:** What do the details in the painting tell you about Socrates and his students? *(Possible responses: Socrates, though about to drink the cup that contains hemlock, continues to teach. This shows his defiance and strength. The students around him are distressed. One turns away from him, one grabs his thigh, and one is pressed up against a wall. These responses imply that they valued and respected Socrates. The students are also of varying ages, which suggests that Socrates had wide appeal.)*

ACTIVE OPTIONS

On Your Feet: Fishbowl Direct half the class to sit in a circle facing inward and the other half to sit in a larger circle around them. Ask the inner circle to discuss these questions: Could the Greek city-states have done anything to avoid or prevent the challenge from Macedonia? What lessons can ancient Greece's decline teach us today? Have students in the outer circle listen to the discussion and evaluate the points made. Then have the groups reverse roles and continue the discussion.

NG Learning Framework: Write a Profile of Philip II
SKILL Communication
KNOWLEDGE Our Human Story

Invite students to use their text as a jumping off point for writing a short historical profile of Philip II of Macedonia. Direct them to conduct online and library research to learn how he rose to power, how he restored peace in Macedonia, his military innovations, and how he conquered the Greeks. Encourage students to share their profiles with the class.

DIFFERENTIATE

STRIVING READERS

Understand Main Ideas Confirm students' understanding by asking them to correctly complete statements such as the following:

- The city-state of Sparta led an alliance called the _____. *(Peloponnesian League)*
- With the help of Persian armies, the Peloponnesian War was won by _____. *(Sparta)*
- In 338 B.C.E., the Greeks were defeated by a force led by Philip II, ruler of _____. *(Macedonia)*

GIFTED & TALENTED

Create an Illustrated Time Line Direct students to conduct online research into the many wars and battles fought by the Greeks. Have them list the events in the lesson chronologically and then add at least three more armed conflicts. Their time lines should contain at least four images, and each event should have a brief explanation. Ask volunteers to present their time lines to the class.

See the Chapter Planner for more strategies for differentiation.

HISTORICAL THINKING

ANSWERS

1. The war weakened all participating Greek city-states. Athens was left with an empty treasury and a shattered navy. Later conflicts sapped the strength of the strongest city-states, which made it impossible for them to withstand an invasion by the Macedonians. The city-states would never again be independent.

2. Possible response: They feared Athens might turn against Sparta.

3. Answers will vary.

CRITICAL VIEWING different helmets and uniforms; pressing their shields against each other; their hands are raised to attack their enemy

Alexander the Great

What does it take to persuade thousands of people to leave their homeland and travel to hostile, unknown lands, perhaps never to return? Alexander of Macedonia—later known as Alexander the Great—had both the intelligence and the ambition to seize that chance.

CONQUEST OF PERSIA

Alexander, son of Philip II, set off for Persia in 334 B.C.E. with an army of battle-tested Macedonians and Greeks. They traveled east and then south into Anatolia. The first clash against the Persians at the River Granicus revealed Alexander's leadership style. Wearing armor and a brightly colored cloak, he charged into the fray on horseback at the head of his cavalry. Alexander saw himself as a heroic warrior, and he sought to prove that on the battlefield.

Although Alexander's bravery inspired his troops, his brilliance as a military strategist likely was the key to his success. He led his army through Anatolia and south along the Mediterranean coast to Egypt, where the Egyptians welcomed Alexander after his victory there and treated him as if he were a pharaoh.

Many battles followed as Alexander pursued the Persian king, Darius III. By April of 330 B.C.E., Alexander's army had captured the Persian capitals of Susa and Persepolis. That summer, a Persian official murdered Darius, and Alexander's conquest was complete; the empire was his. Still, Alexander and his soldiers marched on. By the time the military campaign was finished, Alexander had led them on a journey of some 11,000 miles that had taken them as far east as present-day Afghanistan and India. Alexander never returned to Macedonia; in 323 B.C.E., at the age of 32, he developed a fever and died.

GREEK INFLUENCE AND CULTURAL CREATIVITY

The effects of Alexander's conquests lasted far longer than his brief reign. For example, his soldiers had a major impact. Thousands of them stayed in different parts of Southwest and Central Asia, and they often

This Roman marble copy of a Greek bronze original sculpture depicts Alexander as Helios, the god and personification of the sun.

married local women. Over time, these men introduced Greek culture and ideas over a large geographic area, and newly opened trade routes in this region had a similar effect. This process by which Greek culture was diffused throughout the Persian Empire is known as **Hellenization**, which comes from the Greek word for Greece: *Hellas*.

Greek culture, however, did not completely overwhelm Persian culture in the Hellenized areas. Alexander himself had adopted Persian dress and Persian customs. As king of Persia, he modeled his army, administration, and tax system on those of the Persians. He also learned from the experience of earlier Persian kings, including Cyrus the Great. Those kings gained the support of local leaders by preserving their authority and respecting local customs and beliefs.

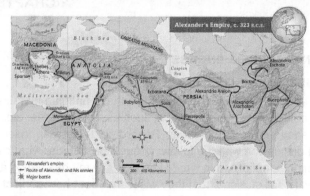

Alexander's Empire, c. 323 B.C.E.

Soldiers who settled in Persia kept many of their Greek ways but not all of them. Archaeologists have unearthed a city in Afghanistan that reflects a creative mix of cultures. Founded in 300 B.C.E., it has all the characteristic buildings of a Greek town. Soil was mounded into an acropolis some 200 feet high, and a semicircular structure served as a theater. The city's palace had rows of Greek columns, but its layout, with huge open spaces, was clearly Persian. Also, temples in the town honored Greek gods as well as those of local civilizations.

Egypt offers an even more striking example, where Greek, Persian, and African cultures intertwined and merged as a result of the Greek conquest. After Alexander died, each of his three generals ruled a main section of the empire. Egypt went to Ptolemy. Like the other generals—and Alexander before them—Ptolemy adopted elements of Persian culture and methods of administration. He established a community of religious worship that merged Greek and Egyptian gods, and he also restored temples that the Persians had destroyed. Ptolemy gave the highest royal posts to Macedonians and Greeks, many of whom had migrated from their

homelands. Even though most government tasks, such as collecting taxes, were carried out by local officials, he opened positions in his army to Egyptians.

Ptolemy moved Egypt's capital from Memphis to **Alexandria**. There, he built what became a renowned library. His successors, during what is called Egypt's Ptolemaic period, further developed this city into a major center of learning.

Scholars from many different fields settled in Alexandria. Inspired by one another, they made a number of important scientific breakthroughs. Around 300 B.C.E., a mathematician named **Euclid** (YOO-kluhd) wrote a book titled *The Elements*, which gave the world its first systematic explanation of geometry. Drawing on Euclid's teachings, **Eratosthenes** (air-uh-TAHS-thuh-neez) devised an ingenious experiment to measure the circumference, or distance around, Earth. Applying his knowledge of parallel lines and angles, Eratosthenes came very close to determining the planet's actual circumference. He surprised everyone by showing that Earth is much larger than they had thought.

HISTORICAL THINKING

1. **READING CHECK** What traits helped Alexander lead his army to victory over the Persians?

2. **INTERPRET MAPS** What labels on the map imply that followers of Alexander settled in those places and likely introduced Greek culture?

3. **SYNTHESIZE** Describe the culture that developed in regions of the Persian Empire conquered by Alexander.

PLAN: 2-PAGE LESSON

OBJECTIVE

Analyze how Greece and parts of Asia and Africa mixed and shared their cultures as a result of Alexander the Great's conquests.

CRITICAL THINKING SKILLS FOR LESSON 1.2

- Interpret Maps
- Synthesize
- Make Generalizations
- Identify Supporting Details
- Analyze Visuals

HISTORICAL THINKING FOR CHAPTER 5

How did the arts, sciences, and government of ancient Greece influence later civilizations?

After Alexander the Great's conquests of parts of Asia and Africa, Greek culture spread and mixed with existing local cultures, which influenced the Greeks in turn. Today, cultural mixing and sharing, especially in diverse nations like the United States, is common. Lesson 3.2 gives information about how Greek culture spread as well as examples of cultural mixing and merging.

BACKGROUND FOR THE TEACHER

The Spread of Greek Culture Modern historians have questioned the depiction of Alexander as primarily distributing Greek culture, noting how much he emulated the Persians. Alexander portrayed himself as a defender of the Persian rulers' tradition and adopted many of their practices, sometimes to the dismay of his Greek followers. Recently discovered leather scrolls show that four years after defeating the Persians, Alexander's government issued orders under his name in the same format and language as their former rulers used. Also, the borders of Alexander's empire overlapped almost entirely with those of the Persian Empire. Some historians also question the one-way concept of Hellenism, a stream of influence in which non-Greek peoples adopted the Greek language, education, sculpture, architecture, and other customs because of the prestige of Greek culture. These scholars argue that Hellenism was one part of a two-way process, with non-Greeks emulating Greeks and Greeks absorbing non-Greek ways.

Student eEdition online

Additional content for this lesson, including a mosaic and an image gallery, is available online.

INTRODUCE & ENGAGE

UNDERSTAND CULTURE

Remind students that a culture region is an area unified by language, religion, or other traits. Discuss how each of the following topics might influence cultures in close contact to change: seeing and learning about other lands, their people, and cultures; creating new styles in art and architecture; adopting and applying ideas to design new inventions; and challenging one's assumptions and being open to new explanations.

TEACH

GUIDED DISCUSSION

1. **Make Generalizations** How would you characterize Alexander's leadership style? *(He was brave but also confident and even flashy, as he wore a brightly colored cloak into battle.)*

2. **Identify Supporting Details** How did Greek culture disseminate throughout the areas conquered by Alexander the Great? *(Many of Alexander's soldiers stayed in the areas he conquered and married local women. New trade routes also opened in these areas, which also spread Greek culture.)*

ANALYZE VISUALS

Draw students' attention to the Alexander the Great image gallery (available in the Student eEdition). **ASK:** What do you notice about the ways Alexander is depicted? *(either as a warrior on horseback or holding a weapon or as a kind of god with a noble, proud look on his face); The images also seem to emphasize Alexander's physical beauty.)* **ASK:** Which object is the most helpful to understanding Alexander's leadership style? Explain. *(The coin showing Alexander attacking enemies on an elephant is very useful because it was made during Alexander's lifetime, so that makes it more likely to be accurate. It also shows him engaged in attack, which shows that he participated in military campaigns himself.)*

ACTIVE OPTIONS

On Your Feet: Numbered Heads Organize the class into groups of four and ask students to count off within each group. Ask students to consider the following questions: Do you think aspects of Greek culture would have spread as far as they did if Alexander the Great had not conquered so many lands? Why or why not? Provide time for groups to discuss the question. Then call a number and have the student with that number from each group summarize the group's discussion for the class.

> **NG Learning Framework: Write a Eulogy**
> SKILL Communication
> KNOWLEDGE Our Human Story

Instruct students to work in pairs to conduct online research to look at examples of eulogies, or speeches crafted to honor someone who has died. Tell them their task is to write a eulogy for Alexander the Great, highlighting his greatest accomplishments. Prompt pairs to collect details for their eulogies from the text and additional online research. Invite them to present their completed eulogies to the class.

DIFFERENTIATE

INCLUSION

Read a Map Have students examine the map of Alexander's empire, c. 323 B.C.E., and ask them questions to ensure they comprehend what the map shows. **ASK:** What region of the world does the map show? *(where Europe, Africa, and Asia meet)* How wide was Alexander's empire at its greatest extent? *(more than 2,400 miles)* Did it extend to the Caucasus Mountains? *(no)*

GIFTED & TALENTED

Create a Podcast Direct students to use information from the text as well as relevant research from other sources to write and record a news podcast about Alexander's military victories and accomplishments. Encourage them to listen to news programs for examples of the tone they should use when reading their scripts aloud. Have volunteers share their podcasts by posting them to the class or school website.

See the Chapter Planner for more strategies for differentiation.

HISTORICAL THINKING

ANSWERS

1. Alexander inspired his troops with his bravery, demonstrated by his willingness to lead them into battle, and he proved to be a brilliant military strategist.

2. Any city labeled Alexandria (such as Alexandria Areion, Alexandria Arachoton, and Alexandria Eschate) was likely settled by followers of Alexander.

3. The culture that developed in the Persian Empire melded elements of Greek culture, such as architecture and religion, with Persian culture as well as other local customs and ways of life.

3.3 Preserving Cultural Heritage

LADY MOON AT THE CROSSROADS

Ai-Khanoum, which means "Lady Moon" in Uzbek, was an ancient Greek city on the Oxus River in present-day Afghanistan that was discovered in 1961. Originally part of the Persian Empire, the area was conquered by Alexander the Great in the fourth century B.C.E. However, the city itself wasn't established until 300 B.C.E., after Alexander's death, by one of his generals, Antiochus I.

Ai-Khanoum was an important crossroads of the ancient world—a vital link between India and the Hellenistic world. As different people passed through the city from Persia, India, and China, they ended up settling in the region and becoming part of the culture. Ai-Khanoum eventually fell to nomad groups but the Greek culture remained.

Archaeological findings from this ancient site illustrate a blend of Greek and Asian traditions, key to understanding the Hellenization of the East. The city had the classic features of a Greek city, such as temples to Greek gods, Corinthian columns, and a gymnasium, but it also reflected cultural influences left behind by different groups. For instance, a main temple built in an early Persian style housed a Greek statue of Zeus, and archaeologists discovered artifacts such as Greek and Indian coins, nomadic jewelry, and an Iranian fire altar.

Years of war and instability along with illegal digs and looting have severely damaged the site. When Russia invaded Afghanistan in 1979, the initial excavation had already stopped. After 10 years of war, Soviet troops finally left, but Afghanistan's troubles were far from over.

Years of instability continued as a civil war progressed, and then in 1996 the Taliban, an extremist Islamic militia, took control. Fighting raged on until 2001.

In 2003, after peace and stability had been re-established, Afghan treasures were revealed, some having been kept safe by the Afghan government who deliberately took them from the National Museum and concealed them. Some of those artifacts came from Ai-Khanoum.

While Ai-Khanoum no longer exists, artifacts remain and efforts are being made to reconstruct the city through computer graphics. In 2005, archaeologists inventoried the Ai-Khanoum collection. It is through these efforts that the cultural legacy of important settlements like Ai-Khanoum can be preserved.

HISTORICAL THINKING

MAKE CONNECTIONS What can preserving an ancient city like Ai-Khanoum tell us about the world?

IVORY STATUETTES, C. FIRST CENTURY C.E.
In the ancient world, ivory was a symbol of luxury. These small sculptures were found in Bagram, a settlement in what is now Afghanistan. Bagram and Ai-Khanoum were both trading outposts on the Silk Roads. The blending of cultural influences in these figures—thought to be furniture ornaments or supports, perhaps for a table—is readily apparent. Each statue features a woman in Hellenistic-style dress standing on the back of a *makara*, a Hindu monster that was half land animal, half sea creature.

This first-century-C.E. goblet is a rare example of an almost complete piece of glassware from the era. Discovered in Bagram, it depicts four people surrounded by palm trees, harvesting dates.

An Afghan worker carefully restores a blue blown-glass vase, also found in Bagram. The carved vessel dates to the first century C.E. and is probably of Greek origin.

On this gilded silver ceremonial plaque from the beginning of the third century B.C.E., Cybele (the Phrygian goddess of nature) and Nike (the Greek goddess of victory) ride together in a lion-drawn chariot. The disk found in Ai-Khanoum includes symbols from both Anatolia and Greece, showing a synthesis of gods from different regions and religions.

PLAN: 2-PAGE LESSON

OBJECTIVE
Examine artifacts from Ai-Khanoum and understand how they demonstrate a blend of cultures from the ancient world.

CRITICAL THINKING SKILLS FOR LESSON 3.3
- Analyze Visuals
- Make Connections
- Identify Supporting Details
- Make Predictions

HISTORICAL THINKING FOR CHAPTER 5
How did the arts, sciences, and government of ancient Greece influence later civilizations?

Ai-Khanoum was an ancient Greek city located in present-day Afghanistan. Its location between India and the Mediterranean caused it to become a cultural crossroads. Lesson 3.3 explains how Ai-Khanoum blended Greek, Persian, Indian, and even Chinese cultures.

Student eEdition online
Additional content for this lesson, including a photo and caption, is available online.

BACKGROUND FOR THE TEACHER
Kabul Museum The National Museum of Afghanistan—also known as the Kabul Museum—houses many artifacts from Ai-Khanoum. It was founded in 1924 and moved to its present location just outside the city of Kabul in 1931. In 1939, an incredible trove of artifacts from India, Rome, Greece, Egypt, and Central Asia was discovered. This collection of 1,800 pieces, called the Bagram Collection, makes up the core of the museum's holdings. In 1993, Kabul was bombed, and the museum was severely damaged. To make matters worse, looters ran off with many of the museum's prized pieces. Then, in early 2001, the Taliban decreed that all pre-Islamic works of art be destroyed. This act devastated the museum's collection, as many irreplaceable works (including the world's tallest statue of a standing Buddha) were destroyed. Today, the Kabul Museum continues to rebuild and restore its collection. A recent addition is a statue of a Buddha in outstanding condition that had been buried since the third century.

History Notebook
Encourage students to complete the Preserving Cultural Heritage page for Chapter 5 in their History Notebooks as they read.

INTRODUCE & ENGAGE

CONNECT TO TODAY

Help students understand the concept of cultural blending by asking them to name contemporary works of art that blend cultures and genres. Encourage students to use examples from pop culture that may be familiar to them. For example, the *Star Wars* film series blends the cinematic genres of space opera and westerns. The musical *Hamilton* blends hip-hop, rap, and musical theater traditions in a Broadway show about one of the founders of the United States. Explain to students that the way cultures and genres blend today is not all that different from the items found at Ai-Khanoum.

TEACH

GUIDED DISCUSSION

1. **Identify Supporting Details** What constitutes the cultural blending in the ivory sculptures shown in the photographs? *(The figures are wearing Hellenistic-style clothing, but they are standing on the back of a creature from Hindu culture.)*

2. **Make Predictions** If archaeologists found more artifacts from Ai-Khanoum, do you think the items would show evidence of cultural blending? Why or why not? *(Possible response: Any newly discovered items would show evidence of cultural blending because Ai-Khanoum was a crossroads culturally; all the artifacts from Ai-Khanoum shown in the lesson demonstrate different cultural traits and influences.)*

PRESERVING CULTURAL HERITAGE

The archaeological site at Tillya Tepe in northern Afghanistan, where the golden crown in the photo (available in the Student eEdition) was found, is well known for producing the Bactrian gold. This collection of tens of thousands of gold pieces was buried by Scythian or Chinese nomads around the time of the birth of Christ. Discovered by a Russian archaeologist in 1978, the Bactrian gold (named for the region where it was found) is notable not only for its volume but for its diversity: the gold pieces originate from all over the world. After the Soviet invasion of Afghanistan in 1979, the Bactrian gold was hidden by Afghans, who later revealed it in the early 2000s. Today it is held and displayed at the National Museum of Afghanistan.

ACTIVE OPTION

NG Learning Framework: Explore Ai-Khanoum Artifacts
SKILL Curiosity
KNOWLEDGE Our Human Story

Ask students to conduct online research into more artifacts from Ai-Khanoum or other archaeological sites in present-day Afghanistan, such as Tillya Tepe. Students should then work in pairs and select two artifacts and research their history and cultural origin. At least one of the artifacts they select should demonstrate cultural blending. After students have completed their research, have them meet with another pair and discuss their findings.

DIFFERENTIATE

INCLUSION

Describe Lesson Visuals Pair sight-impaired students with sighted students to interpret the photographs in this lesson. Ask sighted students to describe each of the visuals in the lesson to the sight-impaired students and read all of the captions. Remind partners to identify details in the photographs and give particular emphasis to the qualities and traits that come from different cultures.

PRE-AP

Research Cultural Influences Have students research one of these ancient cities: Ai-Khanoum, Bagram, or Tillya Tepe. Tell them to include information about their chosen city's main culture as well as other cultures that may have influenced it. Encourage students to present their findings to the class. If there is more than one presentation, determine as a class the similarities and differences among the cultures found in the cities.

See the Chapter Planner for more strategies for differentiation.

HISTORICAL THINKING

ANSWER

Possible response: Preserving an ancient city like Ai-Khanoum can tell us how different cultures may have interacted long ago.

The Legacy of Ancient Greece

When people refer to something today as "classical," it suggests that it meets a traditional standard of excellence. Historians also apply the term *classical* to an era in ancient Greece (from 500 to 323 B.C.E.) that set several standards for later civilizations.

GOVERNMENT AND CITIZENSHIP

Democracy, as a system of government, is practiced in many parts of the world today, and any discussion of the sources of modern democracy must refer to ancient Greece. As you have already learned, the Athenians established a direct democracy, a system in which male citizens (a status that excluded foreigners and slaves) had the right to vote in the assembly. Furthermore, according to leaders such as Pericles, these citizens had the responsibility to participate in civic affairs.

Today, democracy still means the participation of common people in government decision-making, just as it did in ancient Athens. Athenians also believed, as every true democracy does today, that all citizens are subject to the rule of law and all enjoy equality before the law. The rights of citizenship, however, have expanded in most present-day democracies to include women, and, since slavery is illegal throughout the world, each individual in a democracy who meets age and residency requirements has rights and a voice.

ART AND ARCHITECTURE

The Parthenon is one of the best examples of classical Greek architecture. This marble temple, perched high atop the Acropolis in Athens, represented the power and wealth of the Greek city-state. Tall columns similar to the Parthenon's can be found in places such as the Supreme Court Building in Washington, D.C., and the British Museum in London. Modern versions of other types of Greek architecture, such as outdoor theaters and sports stadiums, can be found all over the world.

Within the Parthenon stood a magnificent gold and ivory statue of the goddess Athena. A frieze, or horizontal band of sculpted marble showing a festival procession, adorned an inside wall of the temple. Later Greek sculptors preferred to work in bronze. Their sculptures would influence Roman artists, some of whom crafted marble copies of Greek statues.

Greeks of the classical era are also well known for excellence in several styles of painting. Fresco painters applied pigment directly onto walls covered with freshly wet plaster. Paintings on wooden panels included portraits, still lifes, battle scenes, and legendary figures. Another specialized technique in ancient Greece was vase painting. The subject matter of these various painting styles has given historians insight into ancient Greek society.

Alexander the Great was a great supporter of the arts. Through Hellenization, Greek arts spread throughout the lands of the former Persian Empire. At the same time, Greek colonies in southern Italy transferred artistic styles to local cultures—and eventually to Rome and beyond.

LITERATURE AND PHILOSOPHY

As you have already read, historians credit Homer with writing the *Iliad* and the *Odyssey*—two works key to Western civilization and literature—in the 700s B.C.E. Based on observations of other cultures with an oral tradition, scholars believe these epic poems might well be the product of centuries of storytelling, tales passed from generation to generation until they were written down. Whatever their origin, these classical stories still fascinate readers today. Translations in a variety of languages continue to join the hundreds of previous interpretations of these classics.

What would literature be without letters? Although the Greeks did not invent the alphabet, they refined it. Credit for the invention, however, goes to various peoples of the eastern Mediterranean, including the

CRITICAL VIEWING The Hellenistic masterpiece *Winged Victory of Samothrace* dates from the second century B.C.E. The marble statue depicts Nike, the Greek goddess of victory, and was probably built to celebrate a naval triumph. In what ways does the statue celebrate ancient Greek values?

PLAN: 4-PAGE LESSON

OBJECTIVE

Discuss and explain the lasting influence of classical Greek civilization.

CRITICAL THINKING SKILLS FOR LESSON 3.4

- Form and Support Opinions
- Synthesize
- Make Inferences
- Compare and Contrast
- Make Connections
- Identify Main Ideas and Details
- Analyze Visuals
- Analyze Primary Sources

HISTORICAL THINKING FOR CHAPTER 5

How did the arts, sciences, and government of ancient Greece influence later civilizations?

Classical Greek civilization is in many ways the foundation of the Western world. In government, citizenship, art, architecture, literature, drama, philosophy, mathematics, and science, the roots of the modern world are to be found in ancient Greece. Lesson 3.4 describes the contributions of the Greeks in these areas.

BACKGROUND FOR THE TEACHER

The U.S. Supreme Court Building As the caption of the photo of the U.S. Supreme Court Building (available in the Student eEdition) indicates, the structure includes several Greek architectural elements. The 16 marble columns are of Greek design. The Greeks developed three styles of columns: Doric, Ionic, and Corinthian. The styles feature a variety of elements, but the top section—the capital—helps one identify a column's style. Doric columns have simple capitals; Ionic columns have two (or four) curly-cue scrolls that spill out over the edge; Corinthian columns have ornate, stylish capitals made up of leaves and scrolls. The Greek influence is also seen in the triangular section, called a pediment, over the top of the building's entrance. In the pediment is a relief sculpture of nine figures, six of whom are key figures in the history of U.S. law. The Parthenon in Athens also had a relief sculpture in its pediment. The Greek influence is felt inside the building as well; the main courtroom has four long friezes featuring important individuals in the history of world law and democracy, including the Greek archon Solon and his predecessor Draco.

Student eEdition online

Additional content for this lesson, including a photo, is available online.

INTRODUCE & ENGAGE

K-W-L CHART

Provide students with a K-W-L Chart and ask them to record in the left column what works and ideas from classical Greek civilization they already know. Encourage them to jot down every work of classical Greek literature, philosophy, drama, art, or architecture they can think of. Then ask them to record what they would like to learn about those works in the middle column. Allow time at the end of the lesson for students to complete the chart with information they learned.

TEACH

GUIDED DISCUSSION

1. **Compare and Contrast** What are some key similarities and differences between the democracy practiced by Ancient Greece and the democracy practiced by a modern Western nation, such as the United States? *(Democracy today allows the participation of common people in decision-making and asserts that all citizens are equal in the eyes of the law, just as it did in ancient Athens. The rights of citizenship are different; for example, women can vote in the United States and slavery is illegal in Western democracies.)*

2. **Make Connections** How did Greek art and architecture influence later artists and architects? *(Greek columns were influential; a version of the tall columns of the Parthenon, for example, can be seen at the U.S. Supreme Court Building. Greek sculptors who worked in bronze influenced their Roman successors, who made marble copies of Greek statues.)*

ANALYZE VISUALS

Share the Background for the Teacher information on the Greek elements of the U.S. Supreme Court Building. Then have students discuss the photograph of the U.S. Supreme Court Building (available in the Student eEdition). **ASK:** What details of the columns tell you that they are Corinthian? *(the ornate capitals at the top of each column)* What details about the pediment do you notice? *(a relief sculpture)* What does the prominent inclusion of Greek design elements in the U.S. Supreme Court Building tell you about Greece's legacy? *(Important tenets of Greek democracy, law, and justice were inspirational to the founders of the United States. Including Greek elements in the design of a modern building that houses the top court reflects the importance of Greece's legacy.)*

DIFFERENTIATE

INCLUSION

Work in Pairs Pair students who have visual or learning disabilities with partners who are proficient readers. Encourage the partner without disabilities to also describe the photograph of the *Winged Victory of Samothrace*. Then have students work together to answer the Critical Viewing question.

GIFTED & TALENTED

Locate Greek References Encourage students to explore their everyday worlds and locate references to Greek culture that surround them in our modern world. Offer as an example the Nike brand of athletic gear. Ask students to locate at least three items or ideas that reflect ancient Greek culture. Tell them to bring in examples to share with the class. As students share their examples, list their findings on the board under broad categories, such as *Politics, Sports, Literature, Architecture*, and *Art*.

See the Chapter Planner for more strategies for differentiation.

Phoenicians. Over time, the Greeks transmitted their alphabet to other cultures, and it spread throughout much of the world.

The historian Thucydides lived and wrote in the 400s B.C.E. He based much of his *History of the Peloponnesian War* on personal observation—as an Athenian, he served as a general in the war. He also relied on information provided by eyewitnesses. Thucydides therefore set a standard of objective writing for future historians.

Other Athenian writers of this era focused on drama. The playwrights Aeschylus, Sophocles, and Euripides wrote tragedies, such as the *Orestia, Antigone,* and *Medea,* that are still performed today—and not just in Greece. The comedies of Aristophanes have also enjoyed revivals through the ages. These dramas are classics, and their universal themes such as pride, personal relationships, and justice remain relevant to modern audiences.

Socrates was not the only famous Athenian philosopher. **Plato** (PLAY-toh) and **Aristotle** (AIR-uh-stah-tuhl) were two thinkers who emphasized the power of human reason to describe the world and to guide proper human behavior. Plato was born around 428 B.C.E. He and his pupil Aristotle addressed a question that still provokes debate today: What is reality? Plato proposed the notion that an ideal reality exists beyond the physical world. Within this invisible world are what he called Forms: perfect versions of universal ideas such as Goodness, Beauty, or Justice. Aristotle disagreed, arguing that the earthly forms were all that existed.

PRIMARY SOURCE

Until philosophers are kings, or the kings and princes of this world have the spirit and power of philosophy, and political greatness and wisdom meet in one, and those commoner natures who pursue either to the exclusion of the other are compelled to stand aside, cities will never have rest from their evils—nor the human race, as I believe—and then only will this our State have a possibility of life and behold the light of day.

—from Book V of *The Republic* by Plato, c. 380 B.C.E.

In his best-known work, *The Republic,* Plato examines the concept of justice as it relates to various systems of government. He explores this and other ideas in dialogues in which his teacher, Socrates, and others engage in back-and-forth discussions of often complex philosophical issues. Plato also tried to identify moral and ethical principles, or general rules of proper conduct or behavior, and sought to define a virtuous way of life.

Aristotle, too, wrote about ethics and virtue, which is moral excellence or "right living." For his book *Politics,* he studied Athens and other Greek city-states as a way of determining what an ideal community of virtuous citizens might look like. Aristotle, who lived from 384 to 322 B.C.E., migrated to Athens from Macedonia and lived long enough to witness the conquest of the southern Greek city-states by Philip II.

Another famous Alexandrian was the Jewish philosopher **Philo Judaeus,** who lived during the later Ptolemaic period, many years after Plato's time. Philo was strongly influenced by Plato, and he kept the earlier philosopher and his teachings in mind as Philo attempted to synthesize Greek philosophy and Jewish scripture. His effort emphasizes the impact of cross-cultural influences during the Hellenistic period.

MATHEMATICS AND SCIENCE

Anyone who has taken a course in geometry knows of the Pythagorean theorem. **Pythagoras** was born around 570 B.C.E. on Samos, an island in the eastern Aegean Sea. As an adult, he settled in a Greek colony in southern Italy, where he studied and taught mathematics. Pythagoras promoted the idea that numbers could explain everything about the world, and modern mathematicians and scientists continue to support and expand upon this idea. Pythagoras is also credited with a breakthrough mathematical analysis of musical harmony. His work in geometry led to advancements in astronomy as well.

As you have already learned, in 300 B.C.E. the Greek mathematician Euclid wrote *The Elements,* which is his treatise that developed geometry in a logical way. Translated from Greek into Arabic and then English, it influenced Muslim and European mathematicians for more than 2,000 years. Among his other accomplishments, Euclid devised a proof of the Pythagorean theorem. Later in the same century, Eratosthenes applied his pioneering work in the field of mathematical geography to measure the circumference of Earth. As you learned earlier, his calculation of Earth's circumference was close to Earth's actual circumference of 24,857 miles. Eratosthenes' work

taught the Greeks that the known world occupied only a small section of Earth's northern hemisphere.

Legend has it that in the bath one day, the mathematician **Archimedes** (ahr-kuh-MEE-deez) suddenly shouted "Eureka!" (Greek for "I have found it!") because he had a key insight about the displacement of water as he rose from the tub. Archimedes was born in 287 B.C.E. in the Greek city-state of Syracuse in southern Italy. A genius with numbers, he calculated

the approximate value of pi (π)—the ratio of the circumference of a circle to its diameter. Archimedes also excelled as an inventor; one of his inventions, the Archimedes screw, is still in use today. This simple machine, which is used for raising water, consists of a large screw within a pipe. Its users can dip one end of the device into a pond at an angle and then turn the screw to transport the water up the pipe for irrigation or other purposes.

Greek dramas from thousands of years ago remain relevant today. In 2017, a Japanese director presented his version of Sophocles' *Antigone* at an international theater festival in Avignon, France.

HISTORICAL THINKING

1. **READING CHECK** Which two cities in the Greek world, through their political, artistic, literary, or mathematical advances, had the greatest impact on subsequent civilizations?

2. **FORM AND SUPPORT OPINIONS** Of the writers, philosophers, and mathematicians described in this lesson, whose work do you think had the most practical value? Why?

3. **SYNTHESIZE** Much of the art produced by the ancient Greeks—sculptures and panel paintings, for example—has not survived. The same is true of some literature—for example, no original manuscript exists for the *Iliad.* How do we know about these artistic styles? How do we know the story of the *Iliad?*

4. **MAKE INFERENCES** How did the design of the Parthenon reflect Athenian culture?

BACKGROUND FOR THE TEACHER

Thucydides The historian Thucydides pioneered a more scientific approach to history by focusing exclusively on human, not divine, actors. Thucydides, a general, thought of history as a science. Just as doctors study the health of a human being, historians study people's political behavior. Thucydides's great work, the eight-volume *The History of the Peloponnesian War*, broke ground in its treatment of participants of war. Thucydides did not write about specific individuals; rather, he ascribed human traits to entire city-states. This choice provides realistic portraits of the Athenians (dynamic, inventive, always on the move) and the Spartans (careful, even-keeled, self-confident) that reads more like a play or a novel than a straightforward news report. *The History*'s long narrative abruptly concludes about six-and-a-half years before the actual war ended. Historians believe that Thucydides likely died before he could finish his historical account. It may also mean that the eighth book in the series is less reliable, as Thucydides did not revise it or place it in a larger context of the war. Later historians in the ancient world, including Plutarch, considered Thucydides to be the best ancient Greek historian, particularly compared to Herodotus, an earlier Greek historian who included unbelievable and dubious anecdotes in his reports on the Greco-Persian Wars. In recent years, however, scholars have realized that Thucydides exercised some creativity (unable to know exactly what historical actors said, Thucydides admitted to creating dialogue) and that Herodotus's digressions often turn out to be accurate.

TEACH

GUIDED DISCUSSION

3. **Identify Main Ideas and Details** What is the lasting legacy of the historian Thucydides? *(Thucydides reported on the Peloponnesian War from his own firsthand experience; he set a standard of objective reporting that remains a central tenet of responsible journalism.)*

4. **Make Connections** What was the relationship between the ideas of Pythagoras and Euclid? *(Both were mathematicians; Euclid devised a proof of the Pythagorean theorem.)*

ANALYZE PRIMARY SOURCES

Direct students' attention to the excerpt from Book V of *The Republic* by Plato. Conduct a class discussion about the concept of philosopher kings and queens. **ASK:** Do you agree that the ideal government would be run by highly educated and enlightened philosopher kings and queens? *(Possible response: I think that this is a good idea in theory, but it is problematic. For example, by what criteria are said philosopher kings and queens selected? And who gets to select them?)* Do you think Plato would have a different point of view if he were alive today, living and trying to govern in the modern world? Explain your response. *(Possible response: In today's world, modern conveniences such as airplane travel and the Internet have made it possible for people to see how different cultures work and operate. Plato's Greece was more homogenous and also excluded women and enslaved people from political participation. Therefore, today's governments must contend with the contribution of a greater array of individual voices—something Plato did not have to deal with in his consideration of the ideal government.)*

ACTIVE OPTIONS

On Your Feet: Jigsaw Strategy Organize students into "expert" groups and have students from each group analyze one area of Greek culture: government and citizenship, art and architecture, literature and philosophy, mathematics and science. Ask students in each group to summarize their analysis in their own words. Regroup students so that each new group has at least one member from each expert group. Have students in the new groups take turns sharing their simplified summaries.

| **NG Learning Framework: Explore Greek Pottery**
| **ATTITUDE** Curiosity
| **KNOWLEDGE** Our Human Story

Invite students to conduct online research and study examples of Greek vases and other vessels. Encourage them to look at the different forms (shapes) as well as the two main styles: black figure pottery and red figure pottery. Have students select one piece and analyze it in terms of what they have learned about Ancient Greece—for example, they may want to look at a piece that depicts a military scene and analyze it from that perspective. Have volunteers present their piece of pottery to the class and describe its Greek characteristics.

HISTORICAL THINKING

ANSWERS

1. The two cities that had the greatest impact were Athens and Alexandria.

2. Accept reasonable responses. Students will likely favor the mathematicians over the writers and philosophers, perhaps singling out Archimedes for his invention of the screw.

3. Possible response: Subsequent cultures, such as the Romans, copied sculptures and may have copied or described in writing the panel paintings. Homer's story was carried forward by oral tradition and, probably, other writers.

4. Possible response: The Parthenon's location atop the Acropolis reflected the power and wealth of Athens, while its striking architecture, statue of Athena, and marble frieze reflected the city's status as a cultural center.

CRITICAL VIEWING Possible response: The statue suggests that Nike is on a ship at sea, her drapery rustling as if blown by a strong breeze, with her stance suggesting that the goddess is braced against the wind. These details imply Greece's power and appreciation of beauty.

VOCABULARY

Match each vocabulary word with its definition.

1. alphabet
2. oligarchy
3. agora
4. polis
5. aristocrat
6. democracy
7. quorum
8. coalition
9. Hellenization

a. a temporary alliance

b. a form of government in which common citizens have a voice in making decisions and choosing leaders

c. a Greek city-state

d. the group of letters that form the individual elements of a writing system

e. a minimum number of people who must be present to conduct a group's business

f. the process by which Greek culture was spread throughout the Persian Empire

g. an open-air marketplace in a Greek city-state

h. a form of government ruled by a few powerful citizens

i. a person of wealth and high social rank

READING STRATEGY
IDENTIFY MAIN IDEAS AND DETAILS

Use a graphic organizer like the one below to identify the supporting details about Greek democracy. Then answer the question that follows.

Greek Democracy
Pay citizens for public service

10. Which members of Greek society were excluded from the democratic political process?

MAIN IDEAS

Answer the following questions. Support your answers with evidence from the chapter.

11. To which regions did Minoan sea traders carry their goods? LESSON 1.2

12. What valuable writing system did the Phoenicians introduce to the Greeks? LESSON 1.3

13. Why was Sparta considered a warrior society? LESSON 1.4

14. How did Athenian citizens participate in their democracy? LESSON 2.1

15. Why did Pericles undertake a building campaign in Athens? LESSON 2.2

16. How did the Peloponnesian War weaken the Greek city-states? LESSON 3.1

17. What effect did Alexander the Great's conquest of the Persian Empire have on Greek culture? LESSON 3.2

18. How did Plato's view of reality differ from that of Aristotle? LESSON 3.4

HISTORICAL THINKING

Answer the following questions. Support your answers with evidence from the chapter.

19. MAKE PREDICTIONS How might history have changed if the Persians had invaded Greece immediately after the Peloponnesian War?

20. MAKE INFERENCES Why do you think Pericles is considered one of the greatest Athenians?

21. MAKE CONNECTIONS How could artifacts help experts understand how Greek, Persian, and African cultures influence one another?

22. MAKE GENERALIZATIONS Discuss how the presence of writers, artists, mathematicians, and scientists can affect a civilization.

23. FORM AND SUPPORT OPINIONS Which city-state do you think would have been the more interesting place for a Greek to live, Athens or Alexandria? Explain your answer.

INTERPRET MAPS

Study the map, which shows the Athenian and Spartan alliances during the Peloponnesian War. Then answer the questions that follow.

24. Why do you think Corinth's geographic location made it one of Sparta's most important allies?

25. What information can you gather based on the numbers of Spartan and Athenian victories and their dates? Does this data indicate the winner of the war? Explain.

The Peloponnesian War, 431–404 B.C.E.

ANALYZE SOURCES

In the *Phaedo*, Plato describes the last hours before the death of Socrates. In this excerpt, Plato describes Socrates' attitude upon seeing his friends. Read the excerpt and answer the question that follows.

> Socrates sat up on his couch and bent his leg and rubbed it with his hand, and while he was rubbing it, he said, "What a strange thing, my friends, that seems to be which men call pleasure! How wonderfully it is related to that which seems to be its opposite, pain, in that they will not both come to a man at the same time, and yet if he pursues the one and captures it, he is generally obliged to take the other also, as if the two were joined together in one head. . . . Just so it seems that in my case, after pain was in my leg on account of the fetter [shackle], pleasure appears to have come following after."

26. What does this incident suggest about Socrates' state of mind before his death? Explain your answer.

CONNECT TO YOUR LIFE

27. NARRATIVE Choose one of the figures you read about in this chapter and think of someone alive today who could be regarded as that person's counterpart. Write a few paragraphs to describe the qualities or achievements that earn your respect, and compare and contrast the present-day person with a figure from ancient Greece. Use the tips below to help you plan, organize, and write your essay.

TIPS

* Skim the chapter and choose a figure who intrigues you. Note the characteristics of that person that appeal to you.

* Think of a person in today's world who has some of the same characteristics of the ancient figure you've chosen.

* Describe the two people, noting the qualities or achievements you find worthy of respect.

* Use two or three vocabulary terms from the chapter in your narrative.

* Conclude your narrative with a summary of the ways in which these two individuals are similar and why they are worth our attention.

VOCABULARY ANSWERS

1. d
2. h
3. g
4. c
5. i
6. b
7. e
8. a
9. f

READING STRATEGY ANSWERS

Main Idea: Greek Democracy

Detail: Male citizens over the age of 20 could join the assembly

Detail: Citizens had equal right to speak

Detail: Citizens participated directly in the making of laws and policies

Detail: Citizens could judge court cases

Detail: Pay citizens for public service

10. Women, enslaved people, and men who were foreigners were excluded from the democratic political process.

MAIN IDEAS ANSWERS

11. Minoan traders sailed to the Greek mainland, lands of the eastern Mediterranean, and Egypt.

12. The Phoenicians introduced the alphabet to the Greeks.

13. Sparta was considered a warrior society because two military leaders served as Sparta's kings, and descendants of the original Spartans served as full-time citizen-soldiers.

14. Athenian citizens participated directly in the assembly, where they voted by show of hands, and they also served as jurors.

15. Pericles undertook a building campaign in Athens to make the city as physically impressive as it was politically powerful.

16. The Greek city-states expended so many resources in fighting the Peloponnesian War that they were left much weaker than they had been before the war.

17. Alexander adapted Persian dress and customs, modeled his army, administration, and tax system on those of the Persians, and learned from earlier Persian kings' experiences.

18. Plato believed that an ideal reality existed beyond the physical world, home to what he called Forms, or perfect versions of universal ideas. Aristotle argued that only the earthly forms of those universal ideas existed.

HISTORICAL THINKING ANSWERS

19. Possible response: The Persians might have been able to defeat not only the Greek city-states weakened by the Peloponnesian War but also Macedonia. Accordingly, Alexander the Great might never have been able to conquer the Persian Empire—and the spread of Greek culture might have been much more limited.

20. Possible response: Pericles helped Athenian culture flourish as a patron of the arts and promoter of the building campaign that resulted in the Parthenon. He also strongly supported democracy in Athens.

21. Possible response: By conducting digs at older ancient sites in Persia, archaeologists might discover structures or artifacts that indicate a blend of Greek, Persian, and African cultures or a separation of those cultures, with perhaps one being clearly dominant.

22. Possible response: Writers and artists strengthen a culture by providing its people with intellectual and visual inspiration. Writers' literature and dramas feed people's imagination, and artists' statues and paintings surround people with beauty. Mathematicians and scientists may have more subtle effects on a culture, but they bring people advances in technology, add to people's understanding of the world, and encourage education.

23. Possible responses: Alexandria, because it had a mix of cultures, a renowned library, opportunities for government positions, and mathematicians who were doing fascinating work; Athens, because of its beautiful art and architecture, its writers and philosophers, and its democratic system of government

INTERPRET MAPS ANSWERS

24. Corinth's location likely allowed it to control the narrow land bridge between Sparta and Athens, which made it easier for Spartan armies to cross into Athenian territory.

25. Sparta won all but one of the battles fought on the Greek mainland, and those battles occurred relatively early in the war. The later battles took place east of the Aegean Sea, and Athens won one more battle than Sparta did. However, Sparta won the final battle. The number and dates of the victories on the map do not indicate clearly who won the war.

ANALYZE SOURCES ANSWER

26. Socrates seems calm rather than angry or sad, which suggests that he was aware of his situation.

CONNECT TO YOUR LIFE ANSWER

27. Students' essays should provide the name of a Greek person from the chapter and the name of a person living today, support their choices with qualities or achievements from each person's life that earn their respect, compare the ancient Greek person they chose with that of their present-day choice, support their comparison with examples from the chapter and additional research, and be written in a formal style.

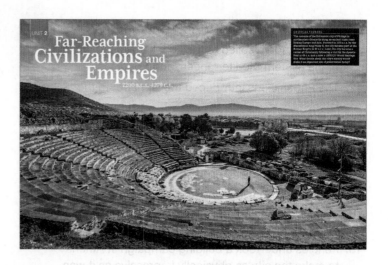

STRATEGY ❶
Preview the Text

Work with students to preview each lesson in the chapter. Guide them to read each lesson's title, captions, and headings. Then tell them to list the information they expect to find in the text. Instruct students to read a lesson and discuss with a partner what they learned and whether or not it matched their expectations.

Use with All Lessons

STRATEGY ❷
Create Idea Webs

Guide students to summarize the chapter by creating an Idea Web for each section. Tell them to write one of the four section titles in the center square of each of the four webs: The Roman Republic; The Roman Empire; The Rise of Christianity; Western Decline, Eastern Renewal. Have students complete each Idea Web with main ideas and relevant information as they read each section's lessons.

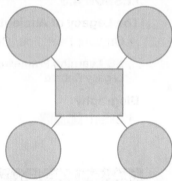

Use with All Lessons *For example, for the lessons in the section titled The Roman Republic, students may add the following information: Early Rome created a new form of government called a republic; laws inscribed in the Twelve Tables protected all Roman citizens; Rome defeated Carthage in the Punic Wars; men dominated both public and family life; Roman gods and goddesses were similar to Greek gods and goddesses.*

STRATEGY ❸
Play the "I am . . ." Game

To reinforce the meanings of key terms and names, assign every student one term or name that appears in the chapter and have them write a one-sentence clue beginning with "I am . . . ." Have students take turns reading clues and calling on other students to guess the answers.

Use with All Lessons

STRATEGY ❶
Provide Terms and Names on Audio

Decide which of the terms and names are important for mastery and have a volunteer record the pronunciations and a short sentence defining each word. Encourage students to listen to the recording as often as necessary.

Use with All Lessons *You might also use the recordings to quiz students on their mastery of the terms. Play one definition at a time from the recording and ask students to identify the term or name described.*

STRATEGY ❷
Preview Content Using a Map

Use the following suggestions to preview content:

- Point to the map key and discuss the ways it helps to explain the content shown on a map. Discuss that the different colors on the map represent different things.
- Remind students that they can identify continents and bodies of water by their labels on the map.
- Call out specific map features, such as rivers, mountain ranges, oceans, and countries, and ask students to point to them.

Use with Lessons 1.2, 2.2, 3.3, 3.4, and 4.2 *Invite volunteers to describe the visuals in detail to help visually-impaired students understand them.*

STRATEGY ❶
Clarify Vocabulary

To help students at **All Proficiencies** clarify vocabulary, tell them to choose an unfamiliar word from the lesson. Guide them to understand the word using frames such as these

I don't know the word _____.

I think it means _____.

A clue I found is _____.

Another clue is _____.

The context and word parts suggest _____.

The most likely meaning of the word is _____.

If necessary, point out context clues and word parts to help guide students to discover the word's meaning.

Use with All Lessons

STRATEGY ❷

Identify Word Parts

Write the following compound words on the board: *outpost, shipwreck, setback, counterattack, stronghold, northeast, outnumbered, homeland.* Instruct students of **All Proficiencies** to copy the words and circle the two smaller words in each compound word. Then place students in mixed-proficiency pairs, and have them work together to define each of the two smaller words and the resulting compound word.

Use with Lesson 1.2 *You may wish to use this strategy with other lessons that contain compound words.*

GIFTED & TALENTED

STRATEGY ❶

Write a Dialogue

Ask students to write a dialogue that might have taken place during events described in the lessons. You might suggest the following imagined dialogues:

- the Carthaginian general Hannibal and one of his officers before they invade Italy
- the slave Spartacus and other slaves as they plan their rebellion against Roman troops
- a group of senators plotting to assassinate Caesar
- Jesus discussing his ideas with one of his disciples

Use with All Lessons

STRATEGY ❷

Present a Museum Exhibit

Have groups of students prepare a museum exhibit featuring the ruins of Pompeii. Have them photocopy or download images of the ruins and write museum-style captions for each one. Once students have compiled their exhibits, have them present the images to the class on a series of posters or in an online format. Encourage students to introduce the exhibit with some background information about Pompeii. Tell them that they should also be prepared to answer any questions as their classmates view the exhibit.

Use with Lesson 2.4

PRE-AP

STRATEGY ❶

Teach a Class

Before beginning the chapter, allow students to choose one of the lessons and prepare to teach the content to the class. Give them a set amount of time in which to present their lesson. Suggest that students think about any visuals or activities they want to use when they teach.

Use with All Lessons

STRATEGY ❷

Consider Multiple Sides

Tell students that historians have different opinions about why the Roman Empire came to an end. Have pairs of students research the issue and make a chart listing the different perspectives about the causes of the fall of the Roman Empire. Have students share and discuss their chart with the class

Use with Lessons 4.1–4.3

HISTORICAL THINKING Why did the Roman Empire
become one of the most influential in history?

CRITICAL VIEWING
The Roman Colosseum opened in 80 C.E., and much
of the open-air theater still stands today. Thousands
of spectators entered through its arches to watch the
brutal games offered as entertainment. In what ways
do many modern stadiums resemble the Colosseum?

INTRODUCE THE PHOTOGRAPH

THE ROMAN COLOSSEUM

Have students study the photograph of the Colosseum in
Rome. Tell students that the Colosseum was a remarkable
feat of engineering that was used for horrifically brutal
entertainment. **ASK:** What do the ruins of the nearly
2,000-year-old structure suggest about the lasting
influence of the Roman Empire? *(Possible response: The
ruins suggest that Roman engineers made monumental
structures designed to endure for centuries.)*

SHARE BACKGROUND

Also known as the Flavian Amphitheater, construction
of the Colosseum was begun by the emperor Vespasian
sometime between 70 and 72 C.E. The site chosen
was on the palace grounds of former emperor Nero's
estate. An extravagant artificial lake was drained and a
theater for the public was built in its place. The choice of
construction was symbolic—paving over the tyrannical
ruler's home. However, the choice was also practical—
nothing to tear down, just drain the lake and prepare
the site for construction. The emperor Titus officially
dedicated the Colosseum in 80 C.E., and Domitian
completed final construction in 82 C.E. Excavations of
the Colosseum in the early 19th century revealed the
Hypogeum, the complex labyrinth of passages and cells
seen at the center of this picture. Gladiators and exotic
animals could be made to appear suddenly on the arena's
wooden stage, from the depths of the hypogeum, via an
ingenious network of trap doors, ramps, and lifts.

CRITICAL VIEWING Answers will vary. Possible
response: Both have tiered seating that encircles a central
stage.

HISTORICAL THINKING QUESTION
Why did the Roman Empire become one of the most influential in history?

Jigsaw Strategy: Preview Content Organize students evenly into "expert" groups and assign each group a topic and question about each section of the chapter to research and discuss in depth. Regroup students and have experts take turns sharing their knowledge with new group members by reporting on their assigned topic.

Group 1 Section 1 is about the birth and growth of the Roman Republic. **ASK:** What obstacles might the rulers and citizens of the republic have faced as it expanded?

Group 2 Section 2 is about the end of the republic and the rise of the Roman Empire. **ASK:** What factors helped the empire grow and prosper?

Group 3 Section 3 is about the spread of Christianity, a religion based on the ideas of an influential teacher named Jesus. **ASK:** What allows religious ideas such as Christianity to spread?

Group 4 Section 4 is about the fall of the Roman Empire and its long-lasting cultural legacy. **ASK:** How has the United States been influenced by Roman culture?

KEY DATES FOR CHAPTER 6

753 B.C.E.	Romulus becomes the first king of Rome and names it after himself.
509 B.C.E.	The Romans overthrow the monarchy of King Tarquin and form a republic.
272 B.C.E.	The Romans take command of the Italian Peninsula.
264 B.C.E.	The First Punic War begins.
201 B.C.E.	The Second Punic War ends, and the entire western Mediterranean comes under Roman control.
146 B.C.E.	Rome takes control of Carthage, invades Macedonia, and conquers Greece.
73 B.C.E.	Spartacus leads 90,000 slaves in rebellion against the Roman army.
March 15, 44 B.C.E. (The Ides of March)	Julius Caesar is assassinated by a group of senators after declaring himself dictator for life.
27 B.C.E.	Augustus overthrows the republic begins a 200-year period of peace and prosperity known as the Pax Romana.
117 C.E.	The Roman Empire spans three continents, reaching its greatest extent.

INTRODUCE THE READING STRATEGY

COMPARE AND CONTRAST
Explain to students that comparing and contrasting two topics or ideas can help them more deeply understand new information. Go to the Chapter Review and preview the Venn diagram with students. As they read the chapter, have students compare and contrast the roles and rights of men and women in Roman society.

INTRODUCE CHAPTER VOCABULARY

KEY VOCABULARY

SECTION 1

dictator	lar	mercenary
pantheon	patriarchy	patrician
plebeian	republic	script
Senate	tribune	

SECTION 2

amphitheater	amphora	aqueduct
edict	gladiator	legionary
principate		

SECTION 3

catacomb	epistle	missionary
pilgrimage		

SECTION 4

oratory	tetrarchy

WORD MAPS
As they read the chapter, encourage students to complete a Word Map for Key Vocabulary terms. Instruct students to write the Key Vocabulary term in the oval and, as they encounter the word in the chapter, complete the Word Map. Model an example on the board, using the graphic organizer shown.

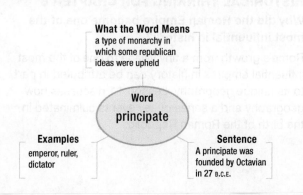

What the Word Means
a type of monarchy in which some republican ideas were upheld

Word
principate

Examples
emperor, ruler, dictator

Sentence
A principate was founded by Octavian in 27 B.C.E.

The Emergence of Rome

It has been said that "mighty oaks from little acorns grow." The "little acorn" that was Rome in its early days grew slowly and steadily until it was mighty enough to control all of Italy. And its growth had just begun.

CRITICAL VIEWING The ruins of the Roman Forum, shown here, represent different periods of Rome's history. During the time of the Roman Republic, the Forum became the center of politics. The Roman Senate met in the Forum, but ordinary Romans gathered there, too. How do these ruins convey the Forum's former glory?

THE FOUNDING OF ROME

Rome lies halfway down the west coast of the boot-shaped peninsula of Italy. The tip of the boot looks as if it's about to kick the island of Sicily toward North Africa. To the north, the soaring Alps form a natural barrier. A chain of smaller mountains, the Apennines (A-puh-nynz), runs down the center of the peninsula. The vast Mediterranean Sea, which the Romans would come to call *Mare Nostrum* (MAHR-ay NOHS-truhm), or "our sea," surrounds the peninsula.

By 1000 B.C.E., many small villages had been settled in the seven hills around the **Tiber** (TY-bur) **River**. The villages merged into one large settlement, early Rome, around 750 B.C.E. However, in ancient times, a legend arose about the founding of Rome. According to this story, the twin brothers Romulus and Remus were abandoned on the Tiber. They were rescued by a wolf and raised by a shepherd. The brothers eventually founded a city, and Romulus became its first king in 753 B.C.E. He named the city Rome after himself.

Rome lay at a point where the shallow Tiber could be crossed easily. And the city became a natural stopping point for the trade routes that ran along the river. Rome's fertile soil, mild climate, and access to water allowed agriculture to flourish. Various peoples were attracted to the area, bringing their technologies and cultures with them and helping the city grow in size and power.

By 700 B.C.E., the Greeks had settled in southern Italy and Sicily, and the **Etruscans** controlled a large area just north of Rome. Both groups influenced Rome. The Etruscans were especially skilled in sewage management, engineering, and city planning, and the Romans learned a great deal from them. They also gained an alphabet from the Etruscans and adapted it around 600 B.C.E. to create their first **script**, or form of writing, in their native language—Latin. The words you are reading now use the Latin alphabet.

Around the late 600s, Etruscan kings came to rule Rome. They laid out the city's streets in a grid pattern and built stone houses, temples, and public buildings. The foundations of Rome as one of the great cities of the ancient world had been laid.

THE EARLY REPUBLIC

The Etruscans ruled Rome until 509 B.C.E., when the Romans overthrew King Tarquin, a cruel tyrant who often had his opponents killed. The Romans replaced the monarchy with a new form of government called a **republic**, in which citizens vote for their leaders and the officials that represent them. This differed from the direct democracy established in Athens. Rome was an indirect democracy, which meant the people did not vote directly on laws and policies.

Two executive leaders called consuls ruled the Roman Republic, and they were elected to serve a one-year term. They were primarily tasked with leading Rome's army. The consuls could veto each other's decisions. They also took advice from the **Senate**, which, in the beginning, was composed entirely of wealthy landowners called **patricians**. Roman society at this time was divided into the patricians and the **plebeians**, who included farmers, artisans, and merchants. Most of Rome's citizens were plebeians.

CINCINNATUS During times of crisis, the Romans appointed a **dictator**, who was granted absolute authority. Once the crisis had passed, the dictator was expected to step down. One such dictator was named Cincinnatus. When the Senate called on him to take charge of Rome in 458 B.C.E., he accepted. After Cincinnatus defeated the enemy, he gave up his power. George Washington followed Cincinnatus's example. When Washington was asked to lead the Continental Army during the American Revolution, he, too, accepted the charge. Once the war was won, he resigned his commission.

The Senate formed Rome's legislative branch along with a much less powerful plebeian assembly. Soon after the formation of the republic, plebeians called for a greater voice in the government. In time, they were allowed to elect their own representatives, called **tribunes**. At first, the Senate's opinions on issues carried greater weight than those of the plebeian assembly. In the 400s B.C.E., however, plebeians demanded and gained political and legal equality. The balance of power between the Senate and the plebeian assembly equalized as well.

Plebeians also called for equal treatment under the law. Laws weren't written down, so patricians often interpreted them in ways that would benefit their friends. The plebeians insisted on having the laws carved into bronze tablets and displayed in public for all to see. They got their wish. The laws became known as the **Twelve Tables**, and they protected all Roman citizens.

After 400 B.C.E., the republic continually fought off invaders from the north. In 390 B.C.E., Rome suffered a defeat at the hands of the Gauls, a people from a region of western Europe that included present-day France.

After the city had recovered, the Romans set out to dominate the region. Once an enemy surrendered, Rome's leaders offered citizenship to any man who spoke Latin. Those who did not had to pay taxes and serve as soldiers but could not participate in politics. This policy greatly increased the size and strength of Rome's army, which conquered more territory. By 272 B.C.E., Rome controlled the entire Italian Peninsula.

HISTORICAL THINKING

1. **READING CHECK** What geographic advantages did Rome possess?

2. **DRAW CONCLUSIONS** What does it say about the Romans that the power of their two elected consuls was primarily limited to military affairs?

3. **MAKE INFERENCES** Why did the plebeians want Roman laws to be displayed in public?

PLAN: 2-PAGE LESSON

OBJECTIVE

Explain how Rome grew from a small settlement to a powerful republic.

CRITICAL THINKING SKILLS FOR LESSON 1.1

- Draw Conclusions
- Make Inferences
- Identify Main Ideas and Details
- Form and Support Opinions
- Analyze Primary Sources

HISTORICAL THINKING FOR CHAPTER 6

Why did the Roman Empire become one of the most influential in history?

Rome's growth from a tiny village to one of the most influential empires in history can be attributed in part to its unique geography. Lesson 1.1 discusses how geography and a series of key events culminated in the birth of the Roman Republic.

BACKGROUND FOR THE TEACHER

The Twelve Tables Although records confirming the precise history of the Twelve Tables have been lost, tradition tells us the code was composed by a commission of 12 men, between 451 and 450 B.C.E. After it was ratified by an assembly of wealthy Roman citizens known as the Centuriate Assembly in 449 B.C.E., the laws were engraved on tablets. The Twelve Tables were then attached to a large platform known as the Rostra at the center of the Roman Forum and witnessed by an assembly of citizen groups called *curiae*. The tables allowed the plebeians to become acquainted with the law and protect themselves against abuses of power at the hands of the patricians.

Student eEdition online

Additional content for this lesson, including a map, primary source excerpt, diagram, and painting, is available online.

INTRODUCE & ENGAGE

BRAINSTORM STRONG, SUCCESSFUL CITIES

Ask students to identify examples of strong, successful U.S. cities, such as New York, Chicago, or San Francisco. Have students record the names of these cities on sticky notes and post them on the wall. Then work together to brainstorm characteristics that make a city strong and successful. Again, record these characteristics on sticky notes and post so students can refer to them while they read the lesson. Tell students they will learn about geographic features that helped the city of Rome grow powerful and strong.

TEACH

GUIDED DISCUSSION

1. **Identify Main Ideas and Details** How did the Etruscans influence Rome? *(Romans learned engineering, city planning, and sewage management techniques from the Etruscans. They also used the Etruscan alphabet to create their first script.)*

2. **Form and Support Opinions** Do you think the Twelve Tables were helpful to most plebeians living in Rome? Why or why not? *(Possible responses: Yes, because they could refer to the laws when defending themselves against patrician abuses of power; no, because most were probably unable to read the laws or vote.)*

ANALYZE PRIMARY SOURCES

Have students read the primary source excerpt (available in the Student eEdition) from Table VII of the Twelve Tables. **ASK:** What right do the last two laws address? *(Possible response: the rights of neighbors)*

ACTIVE OPTIONS

On Your Feet: Fishbowl Review the definitions of direct and indirect democracy with the class. Then organize students into two groups. Have one group sit in a small, inner circle. Have the other group sit in a large, outer circle. Tell students in the inner circle that they are ancient Romans and task them with presenting arguments in favor of Rome's indirect democracy. Have students in the outer circle evaluate their arguments. Then have students switch positions. Tell students sitting in the inner circle that they are ancient Greeks and task them with presenting arguments in favor of direct democracy. Instruct the students in the outer circle to evaluate these arguments. Invite students to ask questions of the presenters.

> **NG Learning Framework: Write a Biography**
> **ATTITUDE** Curiosity
> **SKILL** Communication

Have students write a short biography or profile of the leader Cincinnatus using information from the chapter and additional source material. Suggest students focus on uncovering new details about the life and contributions of this one-time Roman dictator. Invite students to read their biographies aloud to the class.

DIFFERENTIATE

STRIVING READERS

Complete a Venn Diagram Tell students to use a Venn diagram to take notes while they read about the similarities and differences between patricians and plebeians in ancient Roman society. Invite them to compare their completed diagrams with a partner's and discuss any differences. Encourage students to make inferences about the types of challenges and frustrations faced by plebeians based on what they have learned about these two social classes from the text.

PRE-AP

Analyze the Twelve Tables Have students conduct research to find a full copy of the Twelve Tables and analyze each table separately. Then have them write a summary for each of the tables, explaining what laws each table outlined. Ask students to evaluate whether the tables would be sufficient in modern society, and, if not, what changes should be made to each.

See the Chapter Planner for more strategies for differentiation.

HISTORICAL THINKING

ANSWERS

1. mild climate, fertile soil, access to water, location along trade routes

2. Answers will vary. Possible response: The Romans were often at war and valued military leaders.

3. Answers will vary. Possible response: They wanted all people to know the laws so that they could defend themselves against injustice.

CRITICAL VIEWING Answers will vary. Possible response: The tall columns and monument that remain are huge, beautiful, and imposing and convey the Forum's majestic past.

The Republic Expands

Every road has its bumps. For Rome, the city-state of Carthage was a particularly difficult bump on the road to taking control of the Mediterranean Sea and its surrounding region.

THE PUNIC WARS

You may remember that Carthage began as a trading station for the Phoenicians. By the 400s B.C.E., the North African outpost had developed into an independent city-state. No longer a Phoenician colony, Carthage used its wealth and maritime skills to establish its own empire in the western Mediterranean. By the time the Romans took command of the Italian Peninsula in 272 B.C.E., Carthage controlled much of coastal North Africa and Spain, the islands of Corsica and Sardinia, and the western half of Sicily. The Romans and the Carthaginians fought the first of three **Punic Wars** over this chunk of Sicily. (*Punic* is derived from the Latin word for "Phoenician.")

The First Punic War lasted from 264 to 241 B.C.E. Rome's army consisted mainly of farmers. The Carthaginians hired **mercenaries**, or troops who were paid to fight. However, more clashes took place at sea than on land. Carthage was a major sea power, and so Rome was forced to build its first navy. Roman ships, powered by oarsmen, did well in battle. But stormy seas and inexperienced crews led to shipwrecks costing hundreds of vessels and thousands of sailors' lives.

In spite of these setbacks, the Romans managed to rebuild their navy in time to score a major victory against the Carthaginian fleet off the coast of Sicily. By then, the Carthaginians had had enough. They surrendered

Roman Expansion, 264–146 B.C.E.

Controlled by Carthage, 264 B.C.E.
Controlled by Rome, 264 B.C.E.
Added to Rome, 146 B.C.E.
Carthaginian land added to Rome, 146 B.C.E.
Hannibal's route

in 241 B.C.E. and gave up Sicily, Corsica, and Sardinia. The peace was short-lived, though. In 218 B.C.E., a Carthaginian general named **Hannibal** sought to avenge Carthage's earlier defeat and attacked a Roman ally in southern Spain. The Second Punic War had begun.

Hannibal's next move was audacious. While the Romans planned a counterattack in Spain, the Carthaginian general decided to invade Italy itself. Starting from his stronghold on the Iberian Peninsula, he headed northeast, leading a force of more than 50,000 soldiers and 37 war elephants on a grueling five-month march. Their route took them through Gaul to the Alps. Crossing the Alps, which are among the world's tallest mountains, was a daring feat—and perhaps foolhardy. Nearly half of Hannibal's men died from starvation or the bitter cold. In spite of these losses, Hannibal's maneuver worked. He took the Romans by surprise and achieved a string of victories as he and his men marched south toward Rome. Even when his outnumbered forces faced the Roman army at Cannae in southeast Italy, Hannibal defeated his foes.

The Romans, however, did not give up. The Roman general Scipio devised a tactic of his own. He invaded North Africa in an attempt to lure Hannibal out of Italy, and it worked. Hannibal returned to defend his homeland. In 202 B.C.E., at the Battle of Zama on the North African coast, Hannibal and Scipio faced off in a brutal fight. Rome defeated Carthage, and the Second Punic War ended in 201 B.C.E. The entire western Mediterranean was now under Roman control.

FURTHER CONQUESTS

Although the Romans had decisively defeated Carthage, they still considered their old enemy a threat. After the Second Punic War was over, Carthage turned its focus to trade and began accumulating great wealth. Some Romans called for the city-state's total destruction. As a result, Rome provoked Carthage into launching the Third Punic War in 149 B.C.E., but it was short-lived. Rome took control of Carthage in 146 B.C.E. The Roman commander sent the survivors to Rome, where they were sold as slaves, and ordered the utter annihilation of Carthage. The city-state ceased to exist. Carthage and its surrounding lands became the Roman province of Africa.

NATIONAL GEOGRAPHIC EXPLORER
PATRICK HUNT

Tracing Hannibal's Route

Hannibal managed to lead his army through the snow-covered Alps. But where did he cross the mountain range? This question has fascinated National Geographic Explorer Patrick Hunt for years. And he might have found the answer. Hunt reconstructed the past by combining an analysis of documents with archaeology. He followed clues provided in the works of the Greek historian Polybius and Roman historian Livy, who wrote accounts of Hannibal's campaign and described the geographic features Hannibal saw and the distances he traveled. Hunt also studied the ways in which the geology of the Alps may have changed in 2,000 years due to erosion and climate change. His research has led him to believe that Hannibal used the Col du Clapier-Savine Coche mountain pass. According to the archaeologist, landmarks on the route and the view from the summit fit perfectly with the descriptions in the ancient texts. Hunt and his team are still looking for physical evidence, including stones that may mark graves. As Hunt says, "An elephant burial would be fantastic!"

Rome was also dealing with another aggressor. During the Second Punic War, Rome was attacked by the army of Macedonia—the homeland of Alexander the Great. Since the Romans had their hands full with Hannibal, they negotiated a peace deal to end the First Macedonian War. After Hannibal's defeat, Rome invaded Macedonia, starting the Second Macedonian War. The Roman army emerged victorious in 197 B.C.E. and later made Macedonia a province. In 148 B.C.E., Rome conquered Greece and made it a colony as well. With its authority extending over much of the Mediterranean, Rome had become a major power in the ancient world.

HISTORICAL THINKING

1. **READING CHECK** What led to the First Punic War?

2. **COMPARE AND CONTRAST** At the beginning of the Punic Wars, how did the Carthaginian and Roman armies differ?

3. **INTERPRET MAPS** How did the Macedonian wars help Rome dominate the Mediterranean?

PLAN: 2-PAGE LESSON

OBJECTIVE

Explain how the wars between Rome and Carthage launched Rome's conquest of the Mediterranean region.

CRITICAL THINKING SKILLS FOR LESSON 1.2

- Compare and Contrast
- Interpret Maps
- Evaluate
- Summarize
- Analyze Visuals

HISTORICAL THINKING FOR CHAPTER 6

Why did the Roman Empire become one of the most influential in history?

In its journey to becoming one of the most influential empires, the Roman Empire faced the might of the flourishing city-state of Carthage in the Punic Wars. Lesson 1.2 lays out the details of these important conflicts, which paved the way to Rome's dominance of the Mediterranean.

BACKGROUND FOR THE TEACHER

Hannibal's Father Hamilcar Hamilcar Barca was a military commander whose fame would only be eclipsed by that of his son. Hamilcar led Carthaginian forces during the First Punic War, before his son rose to power. In his campaign, Hamilcar hoped to take Sicily back from Roman troops and held his ground until the Romans forced Carthage to sign a treaty ending the war. The treaty required Carthage not only to surrender Sicily but also to pay an enormous sum to Rome as a penalty for its defiance. This demand drove the father to make his son swear to take revenge against the Romans.

Student eEdition online

Additional content for this lesson, including a painting and a photograph, is available online.

INTRODUCE & ENGAGE

PREVIEW USING VISUALS

Direct students' attention to the visuals in this lesson. Draw a two-column chart on the board and label the first column Questions and the second column Answers. Ask students what questions these visuals bring to mind and then discuss and record their questions in the chart. After students have finished reading the lesson, have them revisit the chart and see whether they would change any of their answers.

TEACH

GUIDED DISCUSSION

1. **Evaluate** Rather than counter Rome's attack of Spain, Hannibal invaded Italy. **ASK:** Why was this strategy an effective counterattack? *(Possible response: The attack caught Romans—who were too far from Italy to respond to the invasion of their capital city quickly—by surprise.)*

2. **Summarize** After the Romans defeated Carthage, what events led to the beginning of the Third Punic War? *(Carthage began to accumulate wealth and power through trade, making it a threat to Rome. In response, some Romans called for the city-state's destruction. This provoked Carthage to declare war on Rome again, thus beginning the Third Punic War.)*

ANALYZE VISUALS

Instruct students to study the photograph in this lesson of National Geographic Explorer Patrick Hunt in the Alps (available in the Student eEdition) and describe the landscape. **ASK:** Based on this photograph, what particular challenges do you think the terrain presented to Hannibal's army? *(Possible response: The army probably found the uneven and rocky ground difficult to traverse. The climate was probably too cold for elephants to survive, and food was likely difficult to find.)*

ACTIVE OPTIONS

On Your Feet: Four Corners Organize students into four groups and direct them to the four corners of the room to discuss the following questions about the Punic Wars: Why was Rome outmatched by Carthage in the First Punic War? How did the resources and strategy of the Roman army change in the Second Punic War? How did events during the Second Punic War impact the outcome of the First Macedonian War? Why was the Third Punic War so short? Assign one question to each group. Then hold a class discussion to share the groups' ideas.

| **NG Learning Framework: Create a Web Page**
| **ATTITUDE** Empowerment
| **SKILL** Collaboration

Direct students to work in small groups to design a Web page that describes the key figures and events in the Punic Wars and explains their significance. Have them include special features such as an annotated map, a time line, and biographies to help engage viewers.

DIFFERENTIATE

INCLUSION

Facilitate Comprehension Pair special needs students with proficient readers who can help them understand important details about the Punic Wars and make connections. Have the special needs students jot down the words and ideas that confuse them. Encourage their partners to help define words, explain ideas, and answer questions using information from the text.

STRIVING READERS

Write About It Tell students to imagine they are Roman soldiers battling against Hannibal's army and seeing elephants for the first time in their lives. Have them write short narrative paragraphs explaining this experience and describing their feelings. Then invite volunteers to share their paragraphs with the class.

See the Chapter Planner for more strategies for differentiation.

HISTORICAL THINKING

ANSWERS

1. Carthage had gained control of part of Sicily.

2. The Carthaginian army was made up of professional soldiers and boasted a powerful navy. The Roman army had to conscript farmers and did not have a navy at all.

3. The wars resulted in the conquest of Greece, which provided a strategic foothold in the Mediterranean.

CRITICAL VIEWING (available in the Student eEdition) Answers will vary. Possible response: They were probably terrified and fled from the elephants.

Roman Society

Families around the world have rules. Rules for the children may be intended to keep them safe, teach them how to behave, or clarify what is expected of them. You might find some of the rules governing ancient Roman families a bit harsh.

FAMILY LIFE

Men dominated life in the Roman Republic. Only men could vote, hold public office, join the army, or perform important ceremonies. Rome was a **patriarchy**, or a society in which men have all the power. They were in charge of the family as well. In Roman households, the *paterfamilias* (pah-tur-fuh-MIH-lee-uhs), or male head of the family, made all the decisions. He ruled with complete authority over his wife, children, and extended family members. Laws gave him the power to punish them, sell them into slavery, or even have them killed for serious crimes. Women often did have considerable influence behind the scenes, however, and had the right to divorce and remarry.

Roman women were subject to the men in their families—their

CRITICAL VIEWING This fresco from the first century C.E. shows a Roman woman and man holding writing tools and materials. What conclusions can you draw about the couple based on these items?

husbands, fathers, or brothers. Women were considered citizens but had few rights. During the time of the republic, they could not own property or run a business. Most wives and mothers who performed all of the daily domestic chores. They instructed their daughters in these household skills to prepare the girls for marriage. Most marriages were arranged, and girls could marry as early as 12 years old. The boys in the family often left home at a young age to work or learn a trade.

SOCIAL ORDER

Like the family, Roman society was strictly ordered. Patricians stood at the top of the social ladder. These aristocrats owned most of the land and lived in luxurious country estates, or villas. Unlike the poor, patricians

sent their sons to school. Those boys destined for government jobs were later taught by private tutors. Between the ages of 14 and 17, all free boys became citizens.

The plebeians came next in society, and, as you know, made up the majority of Rome's citizens. Some plebeians were well-off and lived comfortably, but many were very poor. Most of the poor plebeians lived and worked on small farms. You've read that Rome's plebeians achieved greater legal and political equality with patricians in the 400s B.C.E. In time, some plebeian families gained significant wealth and political power. But while the social structure of Rome had changed, the gap between rich and poor remained huge.

Slaves were in the lowest class of Roman society. Some prisoners captured in Rome's conquests were enslaved and sent to Rome, but most slaves were bought from foreign traders. Some became household servants. Others toiled in gold and silver mines. But a large proportion of slaves ended up working on farms.

Military campaigns swelled the numbers of slaves in and around Rome. But, as a result of ongoing Roman conquests, foreigners and migrants from the countryside poured into the city as well. Estimates of Rome's population in the second century B.C.E. vary from around 450,000 to as high as 1 million.

Wars and the ever-increasing need for soldiers also had a major effect on Roman agriculture. In the early years of the republic, most Roman soldiers lived and worked on their family farm. They were farmer-soldiers who left their fields when called to defend their city. As the Roman army fought in more distant places, such as Carthage, soldiers had to be away from home for long periods of time. Many of them sold their fields to rich landowners.

These landowners combined their land purchases into large-scale agricultural enterprises where they grew fruits and vegetables, pressed olives into oil, and produced wine. Instead of working the land themselves, they relied on slaves. The rural population shrank, as landless farmers and former farm laborers migrated to the city. There they lived in overcrowded buildings and worked for very low wages—if they were fortunate enough to find employment.

BELIEFS AND VALUES

As Rome expanded, its culture and the Latin language diffused among the peoples it conquered. But the Romans also absorbed the customs and practices of others and adapted them to their own use. Religion is a prime example. Roman gods had a mix of traits drawn mainly from Greek gods. The Roman **pantheon**, or group of many gods and goddesses, included Jupiter, the king of the gods, who was modeled after the Greek god Zeus. Mars, the god of war, had much in common with the Greek god Ares. And Venus, the goddess of love, was as beautiful as the Greek goddess Aphrodite. The pantheon grew as the Romans adopted some of the gods of the people they conquered.

This sculpted head of Mars, the god of war, is from the second century C.E.

Worship of the gods could take place anywhere—even the home. Most Roman houses contained a shrine to a household god, or **lar**. The paterfamilias made daily offerings to the god, who was considered a guardian of the house and family. Priests conducted rituals for more important gods in temples. In addition, Romans celebrated religious festivals throughout the year in hopes that the deities would grant Rome good harvests and success in war. Like the festivals of ancient Greece, those of Rome featured processions, feasts, music, dance, theater, and sports.

But the Romans didn't always share the same values as the Greeks. While the Greeks valued beauty, grace, and elegance, Romans were a more practical people. They preferred such qualities as discipline, strength, and loyalty. These qualities, Romans believed, would help them achieve success. The qualities also reveal an important aspect of the Roman personality known as *gravitas*, or a serious and solemn approach to life. Their values helped the Romans accomplish great things in politics, engineering, and commerce and came to be known as "the Roman Way."

HISTORICAL THINKING

1. **READING CHECK** What powers did the paterfamilias have in Roman families?

2. **COMPARE AND CONTRAST** How did life for rich and poor citizens in Roman society differ?

3. **MAKE INFERENCES** Why do you think discipline, strength, and loyalty were so important to the Romans?

OBJECTIVE

Determine how Roman society was shaped by its patriarchy, classes, religious beliefs, and practical values.

CRITICAL THINKING SKILLS FOR LESSON 1.3

- Compare and Contrast
- Make Inferences
- Analyze Cause and Effect
- Form and Support Opinions
- Integrate Visuals

HISTORICAL THINKING FOR CHAPTER 6

Why did the Roman Empire become one of the most influential in history?

Many Roman social practices, religious customs, and practical values have influenced the modern world. Lesson 1.3 discusses the values and beliefs that shaped life in Roman society.

Student eEdition online

Additional content for this lesson, including a diagram and an image gallery, is available online.

BACKGROUND FOR THE TEACHER

Roman Men and Women Roman *paterfamilias* were the only people who could own property. Even successful married adult sons could not own property until their fathers died. However, sons were highly valued because they continued the family's name. Roman fathers without sons sometimes adopted a son to ensure the family's name and legacy would carry on after their death.

Roman women did not have many rights and were not given the educational opportunities that men were given. But they were rewarded for bearing many children. Many babies and children died at a young age during the first century C.E., so if a woman gave birth to three or four children who survived, she was given legal freedom. This allowed her to become independent from men if she so chose.

INTRODUCE & ENGAGE

MAKE CONNECTIONS

Post descriptions of two different people for students to read. Describe Person A as practical, strong, disciplined, and loyal. Describe Person B as beautiful or handsome, graceful, and elegant. Ask students to predict which individual would be more valued by the Romans and which would be more valued by the Greeks. Tally students' predictions. Then have students brainstorm people from today's society who might fit each description. Record their names on sticky notes and place them under the appropriate descriptions.

TEACH

GUIDED DISCUSSION

1. **Analyze Cause and Effect** How did military campaigns impact farming in the Roman Empire? *(The ever-increasing need for soldiers led many farmers to join the Roman army and sell their farms to wealthy landowners. The landowners combined the properties to form larger-scale farming operations reliant on slave labor, driving paid laborers into the city in search of work.)*

2. **Form and Support Opinions** In your opinion, did women or men have a harder life in the culture of ancient Rome? *(Possible responses: Men had a harder life because they had to fight in wars and lead their families. Women had a harder life because they had fewer options and had to stay home, do household chores, and take care of the children.)*

INTEGRATE VISUALS

Have students look at the diagram of a wealthy Roman family's home (available in the Student eEdition). **ASK:** What information in the text does this diagram support? *(Possible response: that patrician men were wealthy landowners and had a great deal of power)*

ACTIVE OPTIONS

On Your Feet: Roundtable Arrange students in groups of four or five. Provide a sheet of paper with the following questions to each group: How were Roman and Greek religious beliefs and values alike? How were they different? Instruct a group leader to draw a Venn diagram on the sheet of paper with the heading *Values and Religious Beliefs.* Instruct the student to label one circle *Greeks* and the other circle *Romans.* Ask each student in every group to add an answer to the diagram and read it aloud before passing the paper clockwise to the next student. When the groups have run out of answers, ask the group leaders to share their group's ideas.

| **NG Learning Framework: Compare Ancient Roman and Chinese Ideals**
SKILL Collaboration
KNOWLEDGE Our Human Story

Have small groups of students review the principles of Confucianism and the ways in which the philosophy influenced Chinese government in the early dynasties. Then have groups make comparisons between Confucian principles and the Roman Way. Ask students to consider how each set of ideals strengthened the government and society of the civilization.

DIFFERENTIATE

STRIVING READERS

Make a Chart Instruct students to draw a four-column chart and label the columns with the topics *Women's Rights, Class, Religion,* and *Values.* As they read, tell students to fill in the chart with information from the text about each topic. After reading, encourage students to compare their charts with a partner.

GIFTED & TALENTED

Direct students to find out more about one of the Roman gods or goddesses in the image gallery (available in the Student eEdition) by conducting research. Students should learn how people worshiped the god or goddess and what benefits they hoped to receive. Encourage students to create a presentation that includes photographs of artwork or original drawings. Invite students to present their findings to the class and be prepared to answer questions.

See the Chapter Planner for more strategies for differentiation.

HISTORICAL THINKING

ANSWERS

1. The paterfamilias made all the decisions in the family and ruled with complete authority over his wife, his children, and anyone else in the extended family.

2. The rich lived in villas, owned large tracts of land, sent their sons to school, and had slaves do the hard work on their farms. The poor lived on small farms or in overcrowded buildings. Those in rural areas performed all work on their farms themselves. Those in the city who found employment worked for low wages.

3. Answers will vary. Possible response: These qualities helped them endure hardship and win wars.

CRITICAL VIEWING Answers will vary. Possible response: They are educated, literate, and relatively wealthy.

The End of the Republic

Have you ever heard people talk about the "one percent"? They're referring to the very few Americans who own about 40 percent of the country's wealth. The Roman patricians were the one percenters of their day. Their greed helped bring about the end of the republic.

CHAOS IN THE REPUBLIC

You've read that soldiers leaving for far-flung wars sometimes sold their land to the rich. These patricians soon found other ways to acquire land. When the Roman Republic gained territory through military conquests, the government set it aside as public land. However, wealthy landowning families came to control it, using slaves to grow crops for sale.

As more and more small farmers were driven out of business—unable to compete with the large-scale farms—unemployment and poverty became common in the republic. Yet the rich ignored the problems of the poor. Between 133 B.C.E. and 123 B.C.E., two political reformers put forward bills that would take some of the public land from the rich and give it to the poor, but their actions infuriated the Senate. Members of the legislative body had the reformers assassinated.

Julius Caesar's assassination on March 15, 44 B.C.E.—known as the Ides, or middle, of March—captured the imagination of many historians and writers. As a result, that date has come to represent an unlucky or ill-fated day. In the dramatic painting shown here, Caesar reaches out for help just before the senators attack him.

Political turmoil in Rome increased with conflict at home. The army general Marius had been elected consul in 107 B.C.E. He had allowed landless citizens to join the army and paid them for their service. Other generals began instituting the same policy. As a result, soldiers started to switch their loyalty from the state to their generals. Soon, politically ambitious generals marched their armies to do battle against other Roman generals. A series of civil wars broke out as the generals fought for control of Rome. Other crises arose, including a slave rebellion in 73 B.C.E. A slave named **Spartacus** led about 90,000 other slaves against Roman troops in an effort to flee Italy and return to their homelands. Spartacus was killed and his followers defeated.

Finally, a popular general, **Julius Caesar**, won the civil wars in 45 B.C.E., and the Senate agreed to declare him dictator for a six-month period. Many Romans expected Caesar to restore the republic, but instead, he declared himself dictator for life. This act prompted a group of senators to assassinate him in 44 B.C.E.

After 14 more years of civil war, Caesar's great-nephew Octavian became Rome's sole ruler. In 27 B.C.E., Octavian founded a government known as the **principate**, a type of monarchy in which some republican ideals were upheld. Octavian ruled as an emperor and held the position for life. The Senate gave him the name **Augustus**, which means "exalted one."

Augustus brought an end to the republic, weakening the Senate and undermining Roman democracy. But he did bring peace to the empire. His reign began a period of calm and prosperity that lasted for about 200 years. Historians call this period the **Pax Romana**.

PEACE IN THE EMPIRE

Romans were somewhat uneasy about a ruler granted powers for life. It reminded them of the rule of kings. But the people, tired of political chaos, accepted Augustus because he had been legally approved by the Senate, moved slowly and carefully, dressed simply, and lived in a modest palace. The price for Roman citizens was, as you know, a decline in their long tradition of democracy.

During his rule, Augustus initiated many political and social changes. The Senate continued, but the emperor controlled its decisions. Augustus appointed all military leaders and the governors of the important provinces. He also cut the size of the army in half. However, he gave released soldiers grants of land and offered Roman citizenship to many of them. Augustus created a permanent navy and stationed an elite group of soldiers in Rome, called the Praetorian Guard, to provide security in the city. To help ease poverty, Augustus had free handouts of grain distributed to the poor. In addition, he actively encouraged art, literature, and education. And he transformed Rome into an impressive capital by building magnificent monuments. According to his legend, Augustus said, "I found Rome a city of bricks and left it a city of marble."

Roman law changed throughout the principate period. By the mid-100s C.E., the remaining legal distinctions between patricians and plebeians had faded. Nevertheless, Roman courts favored the wealthy and tended to subject the poor to harsher punishments

Experts believe this colossal marble head of Augustus once formed part of a huge statue that included arms, legs, and a torso.

for the same crime. A woman's legal position also changed. Married daughters were entitled to a share of their father's property, which gave them some financial independence. A Roman wife still remained subject to the authority of her husband. However, if her husband died, she was allowed to manage her business.

During the time of the republic, as you know, Roman law was set down in the Twelve Tables. In addition, officials developed a set of civil laws for Roman citizens and the law of nations for both foreigners and Romans. Another type of written law consisted of **edicts**. These were the official proclamations of the principles an elected magistrate, or judge, would follow during his tenure. Around 131 C.E., Rome standardized and consolidated the edicts. These proclamations could not be changed by anyone but the emperor. The body of Roman law would later influence the development of law codes in many different parts of the world.

HISTORICAL THINKING

1. **READING CHECK** Why did civil war erupt in the Roman Republic?

2. **MAKE INFERENCES** Why do you think Romans didn't want to return to the rule of kings?

3. **IDENTIFY PROBLEMS AND SOLUTIONS** How did Augustus tackle the problems that had plagued the republic?

PLAN: 2-PAGE LESSON

OBJECTIVE

Explain how political chaos and division put an end to the republic and led to imperial rule and a period of peace and prosperity.

CRITICAL THINKING SKILLS FOR LESSON 2.1

- Make Inferences
- Identify Problems and Solutions
- Analyze Cause and Effect
- Compare and Contrast
- Analyze Visuals

HISTORICAL THINKING FOR CHAPTER 6

Why did the Roman Empire become one of the most influential in history?

After the Roman Republic ended, Augustus eventually took power and established the Roman Empire. Lesson 2.1 discusses how Augustus laid the groundwork for an empire that would encompass three continents and leave a lasting influence on the world.

Student eEdition online

Additional content for this lesson, including a photo and a sidebar, is available online.

BACKGROUND FOR THE TEACHER

Julius Caesar Caesar's military victories and legislative reforms gained him admiration from his soldiers and appreciation from the Roman people, but he was not necessarily a beloved ruler. In spite of the surprising generosity Caesar showed toward the opponents he defeated in war, they still disliked him. In fact, his own Senate may have killed him in part because of his generosity toward the people he conquered. Caesar instituted many reforms to benefit his people, at the risk of angering the Senate. He often made decisions without consulting the senators or asking for their support. During his rule, he made it easier for veterans and the poor to gain land, developed a police force, revised the calendar, eliminated the tax system, and demanded that the city of Carthage be rebuilt.

INTRODUCE & ENGAGE

CONDUCT A THREE-STEP INTERVIEW

Ask the class to think about how living in peacetime conditions for 200 years might affect the government. What are possible advantages? Are there any disadvantages? Have pairs of students take turns asking each other those questions. Then ask pairs to share their interview results with the class.

TEACH

GUIDED DISCUSSION

1. **Analyze Cause and Effect** What were the effects of Caesar's conquest of Gaul? *(Rome's territory was extended north, Caesar gained fame, and the Senate agreed to declare him dictator for a six-month period.)*

2. **Compare and Contrast** Compare the leadership of Julius Caesar versus that of Augustus. How were they alike? How did they differ? *(Possible response: Both were popular and successful generals who commanded the loyalty of the military. However, Augustus was better able to work with and appease the Senate and moved slowly and carefully.)*

ANALYZE VISUALS

Study the painting that accompanies the Ides of March sidebar (available in the Student eEdition). Point out that Julius Caesar appears unable to believe that his own countrymen, most of whom he had handpicked to be senators, would assassinate him. **ASK:** What other details in the painting does the artist include to illustrate the intensity of the moment? *(Possible response: The looks of horror on the faces of some of the onlookers as well as their body language illustrate the intensity of the moment.)*

ACTIVE OPTIONS

On Your Feet: Fishbowl Arrange students in two concentric circles. Ask students in the inner circle to discuss this question: How did the growing economic disparity between patricians and plebeians contribute to Rome's political turmoil? Direct students to cite examples from the text to support their ideas. Tell students in the outer circle to listen carefully to the discussion. After a time, direct the two circles to trade places. Then tell the new inner circle students to discuss this question: How did Rome's government change under the rule of an emperor? Tell students in the new outer circle to listen carefully to the discussion. Once students have finished, have them provide a brief oral summary of the discussions.

NG Learning Framework: Write a Biography
ATTITUDE Curiosity
SKILL Collaboration

Have student pairs conduct additional research to learn more about the leader of Rome's slave rebellion, Spartacus, and use the information to write a short biography. Suggest that students focus their research on the outcome of his stand. Have students read their biographies to the class.

DIFFERENTIATE

INCLUSION

Match Key Dates and Events Write the key dates and events presented in this lesson on separate note cards. Pair special needs students with students of a higher proficiency level or with a teacher's aide to reread each note card aloud. Then have students match dates and events and arrange the note cards in chronological order.

PRE-AP

Form a Thesis Have students develop a thesis statement on the end of the Roman Republic. Tell them to be sure the statement makes a claim that is supportable with evidence from the lesson or through further research. Then have pairs compare their statements and determine which makes the stronger or more supportable claim.

See the Chapter Planner for more strategies for differentiation.

HISTORICAL THINKING

ANSWERS

1. The republic had fallen into political chaos, so Roman generals began fighting each other to gain the control of Rome.

2. Answers will vary. Possible response: They had become accustomed to a more democratic form of government.

3. Answers will vary. Possible response: To address poverty, he had free grain distributed to the poor. To quell the political chaos, he took charge of the Senate, appointed military leaders and governors, cut the size of the army, and created the Pretorian Guard. To gain the loyalty of the soldiers, he gave those he retired land grants.

CRITICAL VIEWING (available in the Student eEdition) Answers will vary. Possible response: the body armor; his strong, muscular body; his sense of power

Expanding the Empire's Frontiers

When you hear the word *frontier*, you may think of American pioneers in the mid-1800s pushing west in search of gold and a new life. But most pioneers endured only hardship and often faced strong resistance from local peoples. The Romans could probably relate.

NORTH AFRICA

Augustus and many of the rulers who followed him continued to expand the Roman Empire. Rome's army conquered lands and spread the empire's cultural influence farther than ever before. By around 117 c.e., the empire had reached its greatest extent, with territory on three continents—Europe, Asia, and Africa.

As you may remember, Rome established the province of Africa in 146 b.c.e. after defeating Carthage in the Punic Wars. In the century that followed the conquest, large numbers of traders and farmers migrated to the province, and Julius Caesar settled many discharged veterans there. Together, Julius Caesar and Augustus founded 19 Roman colonies in Africa. One of these colonies, the "new" Carthage, grew to become the second largest city in the western part of the empire.

Augustus—then called Octavian—had conquered Egypt in 31 b.c.e. Rome continued to increase its African territory. By the middle of the first century c.e., the empire controlled the entire North African coast. Wealthy Romans recognized the value of the lands there. During and after the reign of Augustus, they established huge and profitable private estates in the provinces. The estates used slave labor to produce wheat, figs, nuts, beans, olives, and wine. Farmers also raised horses, cattle, sheep, and pigs.

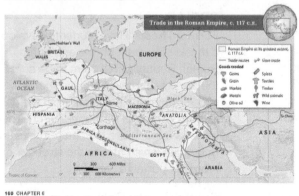

Trade in the Roman Empire, c. 117 c.e.

As the empire expanded, roads were built to connect it, and trade flourished. North Africa provided items such as grain and olive oil. European goods included wine and metals. Wild animals came from Africa and Asia. Most of these goods flowed directly into Rome. The city especially needed food to feed its huge population.

A standardized currency in the empire made it easier to conduct trade, and these coins were even accepted outside the empire. Some traders carried currency and goods well beyond Roman borders, sailing to India or traveling the Silk Roads to China. Traders on these journeys often transported their goods in **amphorae**— large two-handled ceramic jars with narrow necks.

BRITAIN

North Africa marked the southernmost edge of the empire, but in time, Rome would set its sights on what would become its northernmost frontier: Britain. In 55 b.c.e., Julius Caesar crossed the English Channel after defeating Gaul and became the first Roman to invade the island. He formed a relationship with several British tribes, but many Romans at that time didn't think the region had any value. Romans also considered the Britons, the indigenous, or native, tribes of Britain, to be barbarians. (Both the ancient Greeks and Romans viewed anyone outside their culture as barbarians.) Augustus maintained the loose alliances established by Caesar, but another emperor had greater ambitions.

In 43 c.e., the emperor Claudius sent four large army units across the channel to conquer Britain. Then around 60 c.e., the Iceni in the southeastern part of Britain revolted against Roman oppression. Queen Boudicca, who ruled the tribe, led the rebellion. Her forces killed about 70,000 Romans and their Briton allies before the Roman army regained control.

Still, some Britons refused to give up. The people of Wales, in the southwest, fought the Romans for decades until they were finally conquered in 78 c.e. The people of the land known today as Scotland, in the north, had greater success. They repeatedly defeated Roman attempts at conquest.

In the 120s c.e., the emperor Hadrian ordered his army to build a wall at Britain's northwestern frontier to keep out invaders. Hadrian's Wall stood about 13 feet high and ran for about 70 miles from coast to coast.

Meanwhile, a measure of peace had been secured in southern Britain. And Roman culture spread through this region as forums, temples, and theaters were built in the towns. The Romans made the wealthier Britons, many of whom received Roman citizenship, responsible for maintaining order in and around the towns. These Britons collected taxes levied by the Romans—largely in the form of grain needed to feed the army.

Roman influence didn't take hold quite as well in Wales and northern Britain. As a result, a strong army presence remained in these regions to maintain Roman authority and squelch uprisings. Of course, the fighting force of the Roman army was enough to deter almost anyone from causing trouble.

CRITICAL VIEWING During the revolt against Britain, Queen Boudicca's troops sacked several cities, including present-day London. In this 18th-century painting, a British artist imagines what Boudicca might have looked like. With what emotions do Boudicca's people seem to regard her?

HISTORICAL THINKING

1. **READING CHECK** What city became the second largest in the western part of the empire?

2. **INTERPRET MAPS** What goods from the Roman Empire were traded in India?

3. **COMPARE AND CONTRAST** How did the conquest of southern Britain compare with that of Wales and the north?

PLAN: 2-PAGE LESSON

OBJECTIVE

Explain how Rome extended its imperial frontiers to North Africa and Britain.

CRITICAL THINKING SKILLS FOR LESSON 2.2

- Interpret Maps
- Compare and Contrast
- Identify
- Analyze Cause and Effect

HISTORICAL THINKING FOR CHAPTER 6

Why did the Roman Empire become one of the most influential in history?

The Roman Empire was able to conquer territory and expand its influence because of its powerful army. Lesson 2.2 discusses Rome's expansion into North Africa and Britain.

Student eEdition online

Additional content for this lesson, including images, is available online.

BACKGROUND FOR THE TEACHER

Trade in the Empire Trade was a very significant unifying influence in the early Roman Empire. While military campaigns brought new territories under Roman control, trade brought new goods into the empire. Equally as important, military expansion increased the cultural exchange between Rome proper and the frontiers. This financial and cultural interchange contributed to the empire's prosperity and stability over a huge geographic area. Stability allowed various communities and regions to begin specializing in the production of particular goods. Specialization, in turn, allowed for improved processes and products and the development of new products altogether. Glass-blowing, for example, developed during this period.

INTRODUCE & ENGAGE

CONNECT TO MODERN LIFE

Ask students to consider what they know about trade in today's world, especially how goods get to their home. Explain that modern transportation methods (planes, oceangoing ships, etc.) are the bedrock of international trade. Explain that in the Roman Empire, goods arrived along its network of roads or on ships.

TEACH

GUIDED DISCUSSION

1. **Identify** How did a standardized currency increase trade? *(Possible responses: A standardized form of currency made it easier to trade within the empire because the value was consistent. The fact that the standardized Roman currency was also accepted beyond the empire allowed traders to travel farther, to places such as India and China.)*

2. **Analyze Cause and Effect** What happened after the emperor Claudius conquered Britain? *(The Iceni revolted against Roman oppression, and 70,000 Romans and their allies were killed.)*

INTERPRET MAPS

Help students interpret the Trade in the Roman Empire, c. 117 C.E., map. Using the map scale, point out that the empire at this time covered tens of thousands of square miles. The ability to move quickly across such a large area was critical to the success of trade as well as the success of the empire itself. Also point out that the importance of trade by water is shown clearly on the map.

ACTIVE OPTIONS

On Your Feet: Think, Pair, Share Direct students to use the Think, Pair, Share strategy as they consider the following question: What was the relationship between the Roman army and trade? Allow a few minutes for students to think, and then tell students to discuss their ideas for five minutes with a partner. Then invite pairs to share their ideas with the class.

> **NG Learning Framework: Compose a Journal Entry**
> ATTITUDE Curiosity
> KNOWLEDGE Our Human Story

Tell students to use online and library resources to learn more about the construction of Hadrian's Wall. Then ask them to imagine they are engineers engaged in building the wall. Have them write a journal entry about their experiences. Encourage students to describe the challenges and demands of the construction as well as their impressions of the unknown territory. They might also detail an experience fighting off invaders.

DIFFERENTIATE

INCLUSION

Understand Main Ideas Check students' understanding of the main ideas in the lesson by asking them to answer questions such as the following:

- Who was the first Roman to invade the island of Britain—Julius Caesar or Claudius? *(Julius Caesar)*
- What type of trade goods did the city of Rome most need from their European and African settlements—precious metals or food? *(food)*
- What did Rome establish to make trade inside and outside the Roman Empire easier—a standardized currency or relationships with India and China? *(standardized currency)*

GIFTED & TALENTED

Create a Work of Historical Fiction Instruct students to create a story map for a work of historical fiction based on the life of Queen Boudicca. Remind them that an essential element of historical fiction is the depiction of the customs, values, and social conditions of the time. Instruct students to conduct online research to learn more about Boudicca and share their story maps on a class blog or website.

See the Chapter Planner for more strategies for differentiation.

HISTORICAL THINKING

ANSWERS

1. the "new" Carthage

2. grain, textiles, gems, and spices

3. The Roman conquest of the southern region of Britain was relatively easy, and the Britons absorbed Roman culture. In Wales and the northern region of Britain, the people strongly resisted conquest and Roman influence.

CRITICAL VIEWING Answers will vary. Possible response: with awe, fear, love, meekness

Roman Armies and Engineering

How did the Romans do it? They conquered a vast area, with a diverse and often rebellious population, and managed to defend their empire and build marvelous structures throughout it for centuries. The answer lies with Rome's armies and engineers.

MILITARY MIGHT

Wars in places like Britain were physically demanding, but the Roman army was equal to the challenge. During the republic, the army developed a fighting unit called the legion, which consisted of around 4,200 men. It was the ultimate weapon of ancient warfare.

As you know, the army in the republic was peopled by farmer-soldiers, who fought the republic's battles and then went home. However, soldiers in the Roman Empire were no longer farmers. They were paid professionals known as **legionaries**. At first, many of these soldiers came from Italy, but as the empire grew, army leaders recruited more and more men from the provinces. Legionaries joined young and served for a maximum of 16 years. The soldiers were highly disciplined, and they trained, marched, and fought together. They also took part in intensive fighting drills, which a first century c.e. historian called "battles without bloodshed." All were expected to form a strong sense of duty to their fellow soldiers, to the commanders, and to Rome itself. If a soldier disobeyed an order or retreated during battle, his commander could have him executed for putting his comrades in danger.

The army of the Roman Empire was strictly organized. Legionaries were grouped into 80-man centuries, or units. Six centuries formed a cohort, or division. Ten cohorts, comprising a total of 4,800 soldiers, made up a typical legion. From the time of Augustus through the height of the empire some 200 years later, the Roman army commanded anywhere from 25 to 33 legions. Each soldier was a cog in a vast fighting machine. The Roman battlefield formation resembled the Greek phalanx, with legionaries fighting in tight lines, shields held before them.

A legionary carried a staggering amount of equipment. His helmet, armor, shield, and weapons weighed

A legion's unique emblem was painted on the front of a legionary's leather-covered wooden shield. The shield's iron boss and rim (in the center) were used as weapons to punch the enemy during battle.

in at about 50 pounds. And the food, tools, and personal belongings he had to bring as well probably doubled that weight. Many legionaries carried a javelin and wielded a sword and dagger for close fighting. In battle, the Romans sometimes also used a device called a siege engine, a wheeled tower with platforms for weapons and soldiers. Legionaries rolled a tower toward city walls and used its battering rams to knock the fortifications down. Just the sight of a siege engine bearing down on them was sometimes enough to make enemies surrender.

ROADS AND ARCHITECTURE

When the Roman army wasn't fighting, it was often busy building the vast network of roads that connected the empire. The roads not only allowed the army to travel to distant battlefields quickly but also provided messengers, traders, and everyone else in the empire with a faster, safer way to reach their destination.

The first of these extensive roads was the Via Appia, or Appian Way. Built in 312 b.c.e., it ran from Rome to southern Italy. Over time, the army constructed many

CRITICAL VIEWING The towering structure in the center of this photo is an aqueduct, which was built by engineers during the Roman Empire. Aqueducts carried water to citizens throughout the empire, including Spain, where this aqueduct still stands. What does the structure reveal about the skill of Roman engineers?

other major roads that people all over the empire could use to travel to the capital. The web of roadways gave rise to the saying, "All roads lead to Rome." To overcome obstacles along the way, engineers figured out how to build bridges over rivers and tunnels through hills and mountains. At regular intervals, they placed milestones on the roads to mark the distance to major cities. By 300 c.e., about 53,000 miles of roads connected the empire.

Among other materials, engineers used concrete to make bridges and tunnels. An early form of concrete had been in use for centuries. But around the time of Augustus, the Romans developed a more durable type using a secret ingredient—volcanic ash. With this strong new concrete, engineers could build huge, freestanding structures. One of the most famous of these buildings is the Colosseum in Rome. Opened in 80 c.e., the **amphitheater**, or open-air theater with tiers of seats around a central stage, could hold up to 50,000 spectators. The people came to see **gladiators**, usually slaves or criminals, battle wild animals or each other. Other buildings, like the Circus Maximus in Rome, were huge arenas where as many as 250,000 sports fans might gather to watch chariot races. And Rome's Pantheon—the "temple of all the gods"—was completed

around 128 c.e. Its unreinforced concrete dome is the largest in the world.

Roman architects drew on Greek architecture for inspiration. But the addition of domes, arches, and vaults—or lengthened arches—resulted in a distinctive Roman style. Arches are featured in the Colosseum and in some of the long stone channels called **aqueducts**. Roman engineers designed aqueducts to carry a steady flow of clean water from hilltops into cities. Most of the water ran through large underground conduits. But Romans also constructed huge arched bridges to carry the water across valleys. It is a testament to the skill of Roman engineers that many of these structures are still standing today.

HISTORICAL THINKING

1. **READING CHECK** Why was the Roman army so successful?

2. **MAKE INFERENCES** Why do you think so many of the structures in Rome were built on such a large scale?

3. **DRAW CONCLUSIONS** What principle did Roman engineers use to deliver water by means of the aqueducts?

162 CHAPTER 6

The Roman Empire and the Rise of Christianity 163

PLAN: 2-PAGE LESSON

OBJECTIVE

Examine how Rome's armies secured the empire and its engineers built the infrastructure that held it together.

CRITICAL THINKING SKILLS FOR LESSON 2.3

- Make Inferences
- Draw Conclusions
- Form and Support Opinions
- Identify Supporting Details
- Analyze Visuals

HISTORICAL THINKING FOR CHAPTER 6

Why did the Roman Empire become one of the most influential in history?

Rome's armies conquered vast areas, and its engineers built marvelous structures. Lesson 2.3 discusses how Rome's military and engineers contributed to the empire's success.

Student eEdition online

Additional content for this lesson, including an image gallery and a diagram, is available online.

BACKGROUND FOR THE TEACHER

Roman Soldiers Legionaries supplied the Roman armies with the strength they needed in battle to defend and expand the republic. However, legionaries were not the only type of soldiers in the armies, and fighting was not the only thing that Roman soldiers did. Roman auxiliaries were soldiers who weren't Roman citizens but who were paid a small wage to guard forts and sometimes fight in battles. Artillery soldiers used weapons such as catapults and crossbows against enemies, and cavalry battled on horseback. Other soldiers gathered supplies, constructed buildings and roads, made and repaired weapons and shields, and cared for the wounded.

INTRODUCE & ENGAGE

LIFE IN THE MILITARY

Ask students to reflect about and share how they might feel about serving their country as a member of the military. **ASK:** What would you like about it? *(Possible responses: travel, education, room and board, pride in serving my country)* What would you dislike? *(Possible responses: being away from family and friends, danger, difficult living conditions, having to take orders)* Then tell students that they are going to learn what life was like for soldiers in the Roman army.

TEACH

GUIDED DISCUSSION

1. **Form and Support Opinions** How do you think the Roman army appeared to its enemies? *(Possible response: With its fearsome weapons and fighting formations, the Roman army appeared intimidating to its enemies.)*

2. **Identify Supporting Details** What advances did Roman engineering bring to the construction of buildings and roads? *(Engineers designed free-standing structures such as the Colosseum, bridges, and tunnels from concrete. They invented a more durable concrete made from volcanic ash, which made their buildings and roads stronger.)*

ANALYZE VISUALS

Have students study the images in the Roman Armor gallery (available in the Student eEdition) and then use a three-column chart to classify the artifacts into the categories, based on function: Staying Warm, Staying Safe, and Daily Life. Or have the class brainstorm different headings that could be used to categorize the items. Then have students sort the artifacts into the categories, writing each item in the appropriate column. End the activity by inviting volunteers to share their categories and discuss/debate alternative categorizing.

ACTIVE OPTIONS

On Your Feet: Three Corners Have students examine the diagram of the Colosseum (available in the Student eEdition) and read about the events that occurred in the amphitheater. Invite volunteers to discuss examples of other famous Roman architecture. After a brief class discussion, post the following signs in different parts of the room: Arch, Vault, Dome. Show students different examples of these architectural features and ask them to go to the sign matching the photograph.

> **NG Learning Framework: Write a Report**
> SKILL Collaboration
> KNOWLEDGE New Frontiers

Arrange students in small groups and have them conduct research on how Roman aqueducts were built. Instruct them to find out how the systems worked, what materials were used to build them, and how engineers and builders met the challenges of different terrains. Direct students to summarize their findings in a written report that includes visuals. Invite groups to share their work with the class.

DIFFERENTIATE

ENGLISH LANGUAGE LEARNERS

Use Definition Maps Pair students at the **Intermediate** and **Advanced** levels. Have them create a Definition Map for three words they are struggling with in this lesson. Then have students discuss how the words help them understand the main ideas in the lesson.

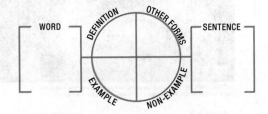

PRE-AP

Extend Knowledge Remind students that Roman architecture was heavily influenced by the Greeks, but it had its own distinctive style. Challenge students to conduct research and write a report on Roman architecture that explains its Greek influences and characteristics that made it distinctly different from Greek architecture. Remind them to evaluate the credibility and accuracy of each of their sources. Invite students to share their reports with the class.

See the Chapter Planner for more strategies for differentiation.

HISTORICAL THINKING

ANSWERS

1. because of its stress on discipline, training of soldiers, organization into legions, and weaponry

2. Answers will vary. Possible response: to accommodate many of the citizens who lived in the capital; to impress people—especially foreigners—with the power and grandeur of Rome

3. gravity

CRITICAL VIEWING Answers will vary. Possible response: They could build very tall structures with precision and with materials that stood the test of time.

Pompeii

"Darkness fell, not the dark of a moonless or cloudy night, but as if the lamp had been put out in a dark room." So wrote the Roman historian Pliny the Younger who, on a sunny summer day, watched darkness descend on Pompeii and bury it alive.

CRITICAL VIEWING This plaster cast preserves a Roman citizen who died at Pompeii nearly 2,000 years ago. What does the man's pose suggest about his death?

CATASTROPHE

In the Roman city of **Pompeii**, August 24, 79 c.e., began much like any other day. Men and women headed to work or went to buy a loaf of bread at the local bakery. Mothers walked with their children, and dogs ran through the streets. About 20,000 people lived within the city walls of Pompeii, located by the Bay of Naples in southwest Italy. Like many Roman towns, Pompeii's streets were laid out in an orderly grid pattern, and its citizens enjoyed all the civic comforts the empire provided. Pompeii was an average city resting in the shadow of Mount Vesuvius about a half-mile away. And then something extraordinary—and terrible—happened.

The historian Pliny the Younger was across the Bay of Naples at the home of his uncle when Vesuvius erupted. He looked on in horror as gas mixed with rock and ash shot high into the sky and then rained down on Pompeii. A thick black cloud of smoke and ash blocked out the sun. Terrified citizens ran through the streets.

Fires in the city added to the terror. Lava pouring from the volcano set buildings ablaze. Many Pompeians were killed by the falling structures and tumbling rocks. Others succumbed to the poisonous gas that filled the air or were suffocated by the smoke and ash. Some people tied pillows on their heads to protect themselves from the rocks or wrapped their tunics over their mouths to keep out the smoke. Recent findings suggest that people also died from the extreme heat created by waves of hot gas and ash.

Lightning, earthquakes, and tidal waves struck Pompeii over the next three days, and many people were buried alive as a blanket of ash nearly 25 feet deep settled over the city. An estimated 2,000 people died, and most of the survivors abandoned the city. Pompeii, with its people and their possessions, remained buried for more than 1,500 years.

FROZEN IN TIME

The city's ruins were first discovered in the late 1500s, but excavation of the site didn't begin until 1748. By the 1800s, archaeologists had discovered that the ash had preserved Pompeii. Household goods, artwork, and jewelry revealed a slice of Roman life. Over the centuries, scientists have uncovered houses containing mosaics and frescoes and graffiti (in Latin!) scrawled on public buildings. They even found an oven with loaves of bread inside. Food scraps retrieved from Pompeii's drainage system indicated that the diet of wealthy Pompeians included such delicacies as sea urchin and flamingos.

The ash also preserved some of its victims by hardening around the bodies and forming a shell. In time, the bodies decayed and left the shells hollow. A 19th-century archaeologist developed the technique of pouring plaster into these spaces to create exact casts of people and animals captured at their moment of death. The lifelike poses of the victims include a man with his face in his hands, a mother trying to protect a child, and a dog on its back with its paws in the air. Recent researchers have studied the plaster casts using sophisticated CT scanning and made digital 3D reconstructions of the victims' skeletons. The images reveal that the Pompeians had perfect teeth—probably the result of a healthy diet.

Archaeologists today still investigate the remains of Pompeii. In fact, it is the longest continually excavated site in the world. Nevertheless, about a third of Pompeii still remains buried. But researchers want to take their time uncovering whatever's still hidden under the ash. Their goal is to preserve and conserve the moving artifacts and victims of the city that were frozen in time.

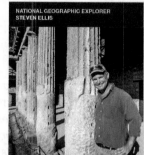

NATIONAL GEOGRAPHIC EXPLORER
STEVEN ELLIS

Excavating the Stories of Ordinary People

In 2005, National Geographic Explorer Steven Ellis became the youngest archaeological director at Pompeii. He wants to use archaeology "to tell the story of ordinary people, the other 98 percent of the population." So Ellis has focused much of his work on a forgotten neighborhood of Pompeii where the working-class people lived. Some of his discoveries, Ellis says, "are changing the way we understand the lives of the sub-elite—for example, the types of food they ate, which were of better quality and variety than is normally supposed." And he's found that, like urban dwellers today, they lived in multicultural neighborhoods, spoke many different languages, and ate at fast-food restaurants. Ellis enjoys digging and discovering artifacts in a part of Pompeii that had been ignored. As he points out, "We're digging in an area where a lot of Pompeians died during the eruption. They don't have fine art, but they do have bones, seeds, and pieces of pottery that tell us a story."

HISTORICAL THINKING

1. **READING CHECK** What happened to Pompeii on August 24, 79 c.e.?

2. **ANALYZE CAUSE AND EFFECT** What multiple effects occurred as a result of the ash that blanketed Pompeii?

3. **DRAW CONCLUSIONS** Why is it important to uncover the stories of ordinary people who lived long ago?

PLAN: 2-PAGE LESSON

OBJECTIVE

Describe the volcanic eruption that destroyed Pompeii in 79 c.e. and the well-preserved site it left behind.

CRITICAL THINKING SKILLS FOR LESSON 2.4

- Analyze Cause and Effect
- Draw Conclusions
- Explain
- Make Inferences
- Integrate Visuals

HISTORICAL THINKING FOR CHAPTER 6

Why did the Roman Empire become one of the most influential in history?

Pompeii is one of the most compelling stories of the ancient world: a city destroyed in a matter of days and hidden away for hundreds of years. Lesson 2.4 examines the end of Pompeii and the excavation and study of the city that continues today.

Student eEdition online

Additional content for this lesson, including an image and a video, is available online.

BACKGROUND FOR THE TEACHER

Early Pompeii Pompeii was a town long before the Romans gained control. Descendants of Neolithic peoples formed the first settlements in the region. Soon after, these settlements came under the influence of Greeks who had settled across the Bay of Naples. Influence in the region shifted to the Etruscans and back to the Greeks, and then the Samnite people conquered the region toward the end of the fifth century B.C.E. After this, a growing Roman presence increasingly came into conflict with the Samnites. Soon after 89 B.C.E., Rome conquered the Samnites, took control of the region, and established a colony of Roman veterans. The town was quickly Romanized but was under Roman control fewer than 100 years before it was destroyed.

INTRODUCE & ENGAGE

ACTIVATE PRIOR KNOWLEDGE

Ask students what they already know about Pompeii. Ask questions such as: What type of natural disaster destroyed the city? What types of photos of Pompeii have you seen? Tell students that in this lesson they will learn about the volcanic eruption, its consequences, and the clues about Roman life it left behind.

TEACH

GUIDED DISCUSSION

1. **Explain** How was an archaeologist in the 19th century able to create casts of the remains of some of Pompeii's people and animals? (*The ash that buried the remains hardened and the bodies decomposed, leaving hollow shells. By filling these hollow shells with plaster, the archaeologist could create casts of the remains themselves.*)

2. **Make Inferences** Why is discovering a well-preserved city that is hundreds of years old so important to archaeologists and historians? (*Possible response: to examine the details of daily life and the daily life of people across a wide range of the socioeconomic spectrum*)

INTEGRATE VISUALS

Have students explore the ruins of Pompeii by watching the video in the lesson (available in the Student eEdition). Tell them to pause the video so they can study the ruins and look for identifiable features, including streets, buildings, fountains, and temples. In addition, present students with selected images of Pompeii's inscriptions and graffiti (with provided translations). Discuss how the inscriptions and graffiti provide evidence of Roman civic contributions and how they are similar to inscriptions and graffiti in the present day.

ACTIVE OPTIONS

On Your Feet: Fishbowl Direct half of the class to sit in a circle facing inward and the other half to sit in a larger circle surrounding them. Ask the inner circle to discuss these questions: What kind of information can archaeologists learn from the graffiti discovered in Pompeii? What can evidence about the diets of Pompeii's citizens help researchers understand about them? What kind of evidence might a researcher study to learn about trade in Pompeii? Students in the outer circle should listen to the discussion and evaluate the points made. Then have the groups reverse roles and continue the discussion.

> **NG Learning Framework: Ask and Answer**
> ATTITUDE Curiosity
> KNOWLEDGE Our Human Story

After reading the sidebar on the work of National Geographic Explorer Steven Ellis, have students write down three questions they would like to have answered about his work. Tell students to research their questions and see if they can find the answers. Then encourage students to get into small groups and share their questions and answers.

DIFFERENTIATE

ENGLISH LANGUAGE LEARNERS

Sequence Events Remind students that they can look at dates and other signal words in a lesson to help them determine the order of events. Have students of **All Proficiencies** form groups after reading the lesson to discuss the organization of events in Pompeii's story. Provide the following sentence frames to help all students participate in the discussion.

First _____ happened. Then/Next _____ happened. Last _____ happened.

GIFTED & TALENTED

Craft a Fictional Account Have students write a fictional account of Pompeii's final days as told from the point of view of one of Pompeii's citizens. Instruct students to use details from the text and outside research to broaden their understanding of the city, its culture, and the eruption of Mount Vesuvius. Invite students to post their accounts on a class website or read them aloud to the class.

See the Chapter Planner for more strategies for differentiation.

HISTORICAL THINKING

ANSWERS

1. A volcanic eruption destroyed the city.

2. The ash suffocated some of Pompeii's victims, preserved its people and their possessions, and hardened to form a shell around bodies of the victims.

3. Answers will vary. Possible response: to gain greater insight into everyday life.

CRITICAL VIEWING (image of Pompeii available in the Student eEdition) Answers will vary. Possible response: It followed a grid pattern. It looks like it had a temple. The architecture is typical of Roman cities.

(plaster cast victim) Answers will vary. Possible response: The man looks as if he's asleep, so his death may have been relatively quick and painless.

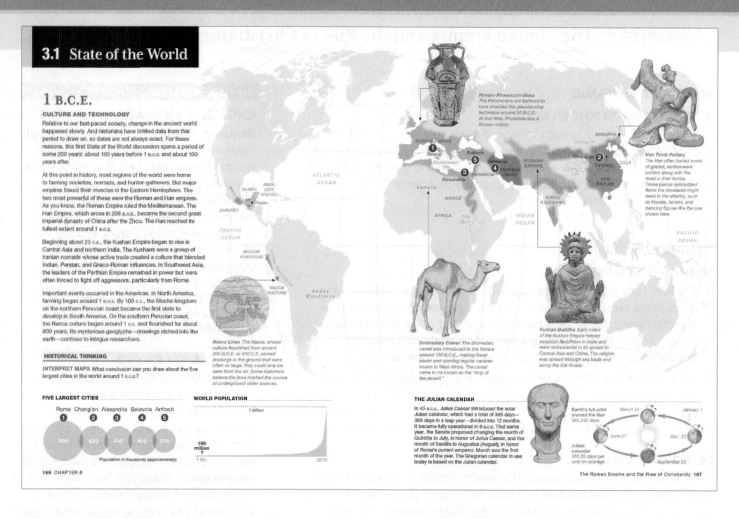

3.1 State of the World

1 B.C.E.

CULTURE AND TECHNOLOGY

Relative to our fast-paced society, change in the ancient world happened slowly. And historians have limited data from this period to draw on, so dates are not always exact. For these reasons, this first State of the World discussion spans a period of some 200 years: about 100 years before 1 B.C.E. and about 100 years after.

At this point in history, most regions of the world were home to farming societies, nomads, and hunter-gatherers. But major empires flexed their muscles in the Eastern Hemisphere. The two most powerful of these were the Roman and Han empires. As you know, the Roman Empire ruled the Mediterranean. The Han Empire, which arose in 206 B.C.E., became the second great imperial dynasty of China after the Zhou. The Han reached its fullest extent around 1 B.C.E.

Beginning about 25 C.E., the Kushan Empire began to rise in Central Asia and northern India. The Kushans were a group of Iranian nomads whose active trade created a culture that blended Indian, Persian, and Greco-Roman influences. In Southwest Asia, the leaders of the Parthian Empire remained in power but were often forced to fight off aggressors, particularly from Rome.

Important events occurred in the Americas. In North America, farming began around 1 B.C.E. By 100 C.E., the Moche kingdom on the northern Peruvian coast became the first state to develop in South America. On the southern Peruvian coast, the Nazca culture began around 1 C.E. and flourished for about 800 years. Its mysterious geoglyphs—drawings etched into the earth—continue to intrigue researchers.

HISTORICAL THINKING

INTERPRET MAPS What conclusion can you draw about the five largest cities in the world around 1 B.C.E.?

Nazca Lines The Nazca, whose culture flourished from around 200 B.C.E. to 600 C.E.,etched drawings in the ground that were often so large, they could only be seen from the air. Some historians believe the lines marked the course of underground water sources.

Roman-Phoenician Glass The Phoenicians are believed to have invented the glassblowing technique around 50 B.C.E. At that time, Phoenicia was a Roman colony.

Han Tomb Pottery The Han often buried works of glazed, earthenware pottery along with the dead in their tombs. These pieces symbolized items the deceased might need in the afterlife, such as houses, horses, and dancing figures like the one shown here.

Dromedary Camel The dromedary camel was introduced to the Sahara around 100 B.C.E., making travel easier and opening regular caravan routes to West Africa. The camel came to be known as the "ship of the desert."

Kushan Buddha Early rulers of the Kushan Empire helped establish Buddhism in India and were instrumental in its spread to Central Asia and China. The religion was spread through sea trade and along the Silk Roads.

FIVE LARGEST CITIES

Rome	Chang'an	Alexandria	Seleucia	Antioch
①	②	③	④	⑤
800	420	400	400	270

*Population in thousands (approximately)

WORLD POPULATION

7 billion

188 million

1 BC — 2010

THE JULIAN CALENDAR

In 45 B.C.E., Julius Caesar introduced the solar Julian calendar, which had a total of 365 days—366 days in a leap year—divided into 12 months. It became fully operational in 8 B.C.E. That same year, the Senate proposed changing the month of Quintilis to July, in honor of Julius Caesar, and the month of Sextilis to Augustus (August), in honor of Rome's current emperor. March was the first month of the year. The Gregorian calendar in use today is based on the Julian calendar.

Earth's full orbit around the Sun 365.242 days

March 21 · January 1 · June 21 · Dec 22 · September 23

Julian calendar 365.25 days per year on average

PLAN: 2-PAGE LESSON

OBJECTIVE
Learn about the cultural and technological innovations throughout the world in and around the first century B.C.E.

CRITICAL THINKING SKILLS FOR LESSON 3.1
- Analyze Visuals
- Make Connections
- Interpret Maps
- Compare and Contrast
- Analyze Cause and Effect

HISTORICAL THINKING FOR CHAPTER 6
Why did the Roman Empire become one of the most influential in history?

The Roman and Han empires were the two most powerful kingdoms in the world at this time. Lesson 3.1 explores the culture and technology that were present around the world during the first century B.C.E.

Student eEdition online
Additional content for this lesson, including a video, is available online.

BACKGROUND FOR THE TEACHER
Julian vs. Gregorian Calendars The Julian calendar was in use from 45 B.C.E. until October 15, 1582 when the Gregorian calendar was adopted. The Julian calendar erred by just 11.14 minutes a year, but after many centuries this time difference made the Julian calendar inaccurate. It was essential that farmers could accurately calculate the seasons, and it was imperative that Christians could accurately calculate the exact date for Easter, making the new calendar essential for westerners. There were four crucial differences between the Julian and the Gregorian calendars: the omission of 10 days from the Julian calendar; the change to a leap year that is divisible by 400 in the Gregorian, not four as in the Julian; the addition of an extra day in a leap year as the day after February 28, rather than the day after February 25; and the introduction of new laws to determine the date of Easter. Although Pope Gregory XIII officially adopted the Gregorian calendar (named after him), it was Pope Paul III, under the suggestion of the astronomer Clavius, who first started the calendar reformation.

History Notebook
Encourage students to complete the State of the World page for Chapter 6 in their History Notebooks as they read.

INTRODUCE & ENGAGE

EXPLORE HISTORY USING VISUALS

Tell students that the photographs, map, and diagrams in this lesson represent important developments that were taking place in the world around 1 B.C.E. **ASK:** What visuals on these pages intrigue you? What questions do you have? *(Answers will vary. Possible responses may include questions about the location of civilizations around the world, the Julian calendar, or the Nasca Lines)* Write down students' questions and have students supply the answers as they read the lesson.

TEACH

GUIDED DISCUSSION

1. **Compare and Contrast** What was the first month of the year in the Julian calendar and how does this differ from the calendar we use today? *(March was the first month of the year in the Julian calendar, but our yearly calendar starts with the month of January.)*

2. **Analyze Cause and Effect** What effect did trade have on the Kushans? *(The Kushans created a blended culture that included Indian, Persian, and Greco-Roman influences.)*

STATE OF THE WORLD

Direct students to watch the video State of the World: Technology and Culture in the First Century B.C.E. (available in the Student eEdition). Remind students of the essential question for this chapter: How did the Roman Empire become one of the most influential in history? **ASK:** Based on the information presented in this lesson and in the video, how would you answer this question? *(Possible response: The location, size, and population of the Roman Empire along with the Romans' quest to conquer other empires and to trade with other kingdoms allowed them to influence empires in other regions of the world for many years.)*

ACTIVE OPTION

On Your Feet: Research Innovations Instruct students to form five teams and assign each team one of the following cultural and technological innovations that are showcased in the lesson: Nasca Lines, Dromedary Camel, Roman-Phoenician Glass, Kushan Buddha, or Han Tomb Pottery. Instruct groups to gather in separate areas of the room to conduct research, including finding additional images, and then to discuss the cultural or technological innovation. Reconvene as a class and ask a volunteer from each group to share two or three additional points that were not covered in the lesson.

DIFFERENTIATE

STRIVING READERS

Create a Chart Group students in pairs and tell them to read and take notes about the cultural and technological innovations found in this lesson. Have partners compare notes and sort their details about cultural and technological innovations into a chart. If time allows, encourage students to research visuals of the innovations to accompany their charts.

PRE-AP

Research Cultural Influences Have students conduct research into one of these ancient cities: Rome, Chang'an, Alexandria, Seleucia, or Antioch. Tell them to include information about their chosen city's main culture as well as other cultures that may have influenced it. Encourage students to present their findings to the class. After the presentations, determine as a class the similarities and differences among the cultures found in the cities.

See the Chapter Planner for more strategies for differentiation.

HISTORICAL THINKING

ANSWER

Possible response: All of the cities were located in the most prominent empires of the time and were likely located on major trade routes.

3.2 Preserving Cultural Heritage

RESTORING THE EDICULE
This view of the Holy Edicule captures light from the candles of the hundreds of pilgrims who visit the Church of the Holy Sepulchre every day. The 2016 conservation project has ensured that this testament to time will endure for many thousands of pilgrims still to make the journey.

Jerusalem: From History to VR

Dr. Fredrik Hiebert is the in-house archaeologist for the National Geographic Society. He's visited many monuments to human achievement, but none has had a greater impact on him than the Church of the Holy Sepulchre in the Old City of Jerusalem, the epicenter of many world religions and events. Below, Dr. Hiebert shares his unique experience in the church.

THE CHURCH OF THE HOLY SEPULCHRE
The church originally dates to 325 c.e., established by the first Christian emperor of Rome, Constantine. Today it is located in the old Christian quarter, where visitors and pilgrims walk through a mazelike covered bazaar that gives way to the brilliant sunlight of the courtyard in front of the church.

At the core of the church is a large shrine, the Edicule or "little house." Over the centuries, the church and the shrine have been subject to damage from earthquakes and invasions and are under threat of fire from pilgrims' candles. In October 2016, National Geographic was invited to document the restoration of the Holy Edicule, where, according to Christian tradition, Jesus' body was laid following his crucifixion.

THE CONSERVATION PROJECT
To restore the Edicule, the church turned to a conservator from the National Technical University of Athens, Professor Antonia Moropoulou, famous for conserving the Hagia Sophia in Istanbul, Turkey. The conservation team used high-tech, noninvasive techniques to peer inside the walls of the Edicule and injected its walls with liquid mortar to reinforce the structure. The upper floors of the church were transformed into a masonry lab where stone slabs were cleaned and repaired—sometimes to reveal painted frescoes under layers of black candle soot. An iron support structure built in 1947 to support the walls of the Edicule was also removed, setting the monument free for the first time in 70 years.

Throughout the night of October 26, 2016, a team of conservators worked to slide off the white slab of marble that covered the top of the inner shrine of the Edicule—something that had not happened for centuries. Peering down into that unseen chamber was a remarkable experience, a chance to look through history. Aside from the dust that had accumulated over the centuries, under the top slab was another partially preserved marble slab engraved with a simple cross. Beneath that was hewn limestone, likely the original bedrock, venerated for generations as the Holy Rock that all of Jerusalem was built on.

The conservation of this shrine is a reminder of the fragile nature of our treasured monuments. Sites that have withstood earthquakes, war, and fire need the stewardship of the world to survive for future generations. National Geographic is one of many organizations committed to preserving the stories and places that are essential parts of understanding our shared past.

PLAN: 6-PAGE LESSON

OBJECTIVE
Explain the historical significance of the Church of the Holy Sepulchre and the Edicule and describe the efforts to restore them.

CRITICAL THINKING SKILLS FOR LESSON 3.2
- Analyze Visuals
- Make Connections
- Form and Support Opinions
- Explain
- Identify Supporting Details
- Identify Problems and Solutions
- Analyze Points of View
- Evaluate

HISTORICAL THINKING FOR CHAPTER 6
Why did the Roman Empire become one of the most influential in history?

Around 325 c.e., Constantine, the first Christian emperor of Rome, had a church built on the traditional site of Jesus' crucifixion and burial. Lesson 3.2 explains how archaeologists have worked to restore the church and the Edicule inside it, which is believed to be Jesus' tomb.

BACKGROUND FOR THE TEACHER

Restoration and Archaeology The restoration of the Holy Edicule raised a quandary: when should restoration give way to archaeological interests? In question was the ground beneath the Edicule itself. Conservators felt the priority was to stabilize the Edicule so that it would not collapse under its own weight or the weight of the 4 million visitors it receives each year. Ground-penetrating radar, robotic cameras, and other tools revealed that the Edicule's foundation was very unstable, the underlying rock was crumbling, and underground tunnels and channels were providing no support. However, scholars like the British archaeologist Martin Biddle believed that if the Edicule's foundation was going to be exposed, then it would be an "intellectual scandal" not to also do a proper archaeological excavation. In the end, both sides were satisfied: the Edicule's complete restoration was finished in 2017, and scientific tests of a mortar sample dated the tomb to around 345 c.e., firmly placing it in the time of Constantine and bolstering the argument that the Edicule sits on the original site of Jesus' burial.

History Notebook
Encourage students to complete the Preserving Cultural Heritage page for Chapter 6 in their History Notebooks as they read.

INTRODUCE & ENGAGE

PREVIEW USING VISUALS

Direct students' attention to the visuals in this lesson. Draw a two-column chart on the board, labeling the first column Questions and the second column Answers. Ask students what questions these visuals bring to mind. Record their questions in the chart. Later, after students have read and discussed the lesson, prompt them to answer as many of the listed questions as they can.

Questions   Answers

TEACH

GUIDED DISCUSSION

1. **Explain** What does the word *edicule* mean, and what is the Edicule in the context of this lesson? *(An edicule is a shrine, and the word means "little house." The Edicule in this lesson is the shrine in the Church of the Holy Sepulchre where Christian tradition says Jesus' body was laid down after he was crucified.)*

2. **Identify Supporting Details** How did Antonia Moropoulou and her team reinforce the structure of the Edicule? *(They injected liquid mortar into its walls.)*

ANALYZE VISUALS

Tell students to re-examine the photograph of the Edicule. **ASK:** If you knew nothing about the Edicule except what you could see in the photograph, what details would tell you that the Edicule is a highly revered place? *(Possible response: There are many hundreds of people with candles surrounding the Edicule. Candles are often used in ceremonies, especially religious ceremonies. Those are clues that the Edicule is a special, perhaps religious, place.)* How does the bird's-eye perspective of the photo enhance the impact of the subject matter? *(Possible response: The bird's-eye view allows the photo to show that large groups of people are visiting the Edicule, which supports the idea that the Edicule is an important place to many people.)*

DIFFERENTIATE

STRIVING READERS

Write a Tweet As students read the lesson, direct them to write a short tweet to summarize each paragraph's main idea in their own words. Encourage students to read their tweets aloud to a partner, alternating so that the first student reads his or her tweet about the first paragraph and the second student reads a tweet about the second paragraph. Partners continue until they reach the end of the lesson. Remind students that tweets can only be 280 characters.

See the Chapter Planner for more strategies for differentiation.

Telling the Story
by Kristin Romey

Kristin Romey is an editor and writer covering archaeology and culture for National Geographic. She documented the historic restoration of the Edicule for the magazine. Here, she describes the experience.

Getting assigned the Church of the Holy Sepulchre story for National Geographic was a pretty good stroke of luck, but being able to share it with our readers took a lot of hard work. In 2016, Dr. Fredrik Hiebert heard about an upcoming project to restore the Edicule at the Church of the Holy Sepulchre in Jerusalem. We decided it would make a great story for National Geographic and ended up spending almost a year traveling back and forth between Washington, D.C., and Jerusalem to report on the conservation work. The project resulted in four National Geographic digital exclusives, a television segment, and the cover story for our December 2017 magazine issue.

For me, the work of reporting begins long before I talk to the people involved in a story. With this assignment, I started by reading up on the history of the Church of the Holy Sepulchre and the tomb that's purported to be the final resting place of Jesus. I learned that the church was built around the tomb in the fourth century and that the

church had been destroyed and rebuilt several times throughout the centuries. This made me wonder: Is the tomb, which is a site of worship for millions of people today, the same one that was first identified in the 330s?

Then I had to delve into the complicated history of the six Christian denominations that claim ownership of a part of the Church of the Holy Sepulchre: the Greek Orthodox Church of Jerusalem, the Roman Catholic Church, the Armenian Orthodox Church, the Syriac Orthodox Church, the Ethiopian Orthodox Church, and the Coptic Christians. There's a ladder on an outside ledge of the church that allegedly hasn't been moved since the 18th century, just because two of the Christian denominations can't agree on whom the ladder belongs to. The family that holds the only key to the church doors is Muslim because the Christian denominations don't trust one another to be the keyholder. So I knew I had to be ready to deal with some unusual situations when I first traveled to Jerusalem.

Like any reporting assignment, this one had its high and low points. The best parts where when I was interviewing the various stakeholders in the church and learning about the different Christian traditions. The Armenians claim theirs is the oldest official Christian country, for instance, while the Franciscan Catholics pride themselves on being the archaeologists of the Holy Land. Many Palestinian Christians worship in the Greek Orthodox Church, which has had a presence in the region as a patriarchate since the fifth century.

Since the Church of the Holy Sepulchre is open every day of the week, the conservators had to do most of their work on the Edicule after the church was closed to visitors for the night, often working until the church reopened at 5 a.m. the next morning. We had this enormous, ancient church complex—absolutely bustling during the daytime—all to ourselves at night, save for a few dozen monks who actually lived inside the church. At first it was magical to explore the nooks and crannies, inspect other 2,000-year-old tombs tucked into side chapels, and marvel at Crusader-era graffiti carved into the walls. After the eighth or ninth night, however, things could get a bit repetitive (there was only so much sandblasting I could watch the conservators do). The church could get quite cold, and we were stuck in there until the Muslim family came with the key in the morning and opened the door to let us out. So it wasn't always a glamorous assignment.

The biggest highlight was the night they opened the tomb. We were given exclusive media access to the opening, but the church authorities wouldn't tell us exactly when it would occur. They just said to be in

Jerusalem during a specific week in October 2016 and be prepared to get to the church at a moment's notice. Only the conservation team, me, our National Geographic film team and photographer, and a small group of high-ranking church representatives were to be present. No news about the tomb was to be made public until it was opened, examined, and resealed, a project that could take up to 60 hours.

I remember I was eating dinner when I got a call to hurry, that it was happening, and that the church doors would remain unlocked for only five minutes. I raced through the streets of Jerusalem's Old City, excitedly thinking about my exclusive story, and got inside the Church of the Holy Sepulchre just in the nick of time. The first thing I saw inside the church were several dozen priests of different denominations, all with their cell phones raised toward the tomb. I quickly realized that while many were taking photos, others were live-streaming the tomb-opening on social media! I knew I had to work fast to make sure that National Geographic could keep its exclusive and be the first media outlet to cover the story.

Fortunately, I had already written most of the background information on the history of the church and the tomb, so I pulled up the text on my cell phone and quickly fleshed out the story of the tomb-opening and the atmosphere inside the church as it happened. Then I went to the top authorities inside the church to plead my case and ask to be allowed to publish the story as soon as possible—and not have to wait until the tomb was resealed. "It's already all over Facebook!" I exclaimed, waving at the crowd of priests holding up their cell phone cameras at the tomb. Finally, the authorities relented, I emailed the text to my editor back in Washington D.C., and within a day the headlines had gone around the world.

Being a journalist comes with a lot of responsibility: It's your job to get your facts right and tell your story in a way that's not only entertaining and interesting but also completely accurate. And if you do good journalism, the karma comes back to you. Not only did millions of people learn about the legacy of the Church of the Holy Sepulchre and the importance of the Edicule, but also the conservation team was pleased with how National Geographic explained their complicated scientific studies to the public. As a result, they gave us the final exclusive discovery from their work: the latest dating results on mortar that bound the earliest parts of the Edicule. It turns out that the building constructed in the fourth century is the same Edicule that pilgrims and tourists flock to today. That's a pretty much unbroken 1,700-year-old history for one of Christianity's most important monuments, and that's pretty cool.

A picture taken on November 4, 2016, shows the Edicule being strengthened as part of the conservation work done by Moropoulou and her team.

BACKGROUND FOR THE TEACHER

The Church Throughout History The history of the Church of the Holy Sepulchre begins with the event of Jesus' crucifixion and burial. In about 30 C.E., an individual named Jesus of Nazareth was crucified on a hill called Golgotha (also called Calvary) and then buried in a tomb about 140 feet away. Surrounding the tomb was a large quarry that archaeologists believe had been used as a Jewish cemetery. About 100 years later, the Roman emperor Hadrian ordered a pagan temple built on the site. The quarry was filled in and paved stone was laid down. A statue of Venus, the Roman goddess of victory and fertility, may have stood on the site of Golgotha.

The next major event in the history of the site took place around 330 C.E., when the emperor Constantine, recently converted to Christianity, ordered Hadrian's temple destroyed. The raising of that structure revealed the original tomb, which was in good condition. As a result of this discovery, Constantine had an edicule built to enclose the remains of the cave where Jesus' body was laid. Rising above it was a large church structure, including a magnificent rotunda. A hall of worship was built and connected to the church, completing a large complex that enshrined all the holy sites.

In 614, the church was burned down by the Persians, then later restored by an abbot named Modestus, only to be totally destroyed by the Muslim caliph al-Hakim Bi-Amr Allah in 1009. In the 11th and 12th centuries, Byzantine Christians and Crusaders rebuilt and restored the site, this time placing the Edicule and the site of Golgotha inside one large church that was dedicated in 1149. The ensuing years required frequent restoration and repair; the current church and Edicule date from around 1810.

TEACH

GUIDED DISCUSSION

3. **Identify Problems and Solutions** What problem did Kristin Romey run into when it came time to publicize the opening of the tomb, and what was her solution? *(National Geographic had exclusive rights to the story of the tomb, but the priests of different denominations who were present at the tomb's opening were recording live video of the event and broadcasting it on social media. Romey went to the church authorities and asked that her story—most of which she had already written—be published immediately. They agreed.)*

4. **Identify Problems and Solutions** What aspect of the church's history became problematic when deciding to go forward with the renovation? *(There are six Christian denominations that claim ownership of the church. These groups all had to be in agreement to go forward with the renovation.)*

ANALYZE VISUALS

Ask students to study the photograph of the Edicule being restored. **ASK:** What details in the photograph tell you that the restoration of the Edicule was an enormous undertaking? *(Possible response: There is a lot of equipment around the Edicule that probably required the presence of a number of well-trained professional archaeologists and other experts. Also, the Edicule itself is covered in scaffolding and other support structures, which shows that the restoration was not a quick and easy job.)* What questions do you have about the restoration of the Edicule, based on the photo? *(Possible responses: How much of the surrounding church had to be restored? Was the Edicule at all damaged during the restoration? What new archaeological discoveries were made during the restoration?)*

GIFTED & TALENTED

Create an Annotated Time Line Share the second Background for the Teacher Information with students. Ask small groups to use that information plus their own online research to develop a list of events in the history of the Church of the Holy Sepulchre. Then provide a large sheet of paper to each group and tell members to work together to create a time line of events that are labeled and annotated. They may add illustrations to some of the events if they wish. Tell students that their time lines should go all the way up to recent years when the church was renovated. Direct groups to present their time lines to the class.

See the Chapter Planner for more strategies for differentiation.

Visitors take part in National Geographic's immersive exhibition *Tomb of Christ: The Church of the Holy Sepulchre Experience*, which virtually transports visitors to the Church of the Holy Sepulchre.

This fly-in view of the Edicule shows what visitors see as part of the VR experience.

Building a Virtual World

When the National Geographic museum team prepares a new exhibition, Creative Director Alan Parente is usually on the front lines. Parente has headed up the design work for some of the museum's most popular shows, including *Peruvian Gold* (2015) and *The Greeks: Agamemnon to Alexander* (2016). But the *Tomb of Christ* exhibition in 2017 offered new opportunities—and new challenges. Parente shared his experience with National Geographic Learning.

NGL: What was the team's primary goal in developing the *Tomb of Christ* exhibition?

ALAN: This exhibition raised exciting new questions about museum exhibitions in general. With so much change in design technology, as a team we stepped back to ask, "How do we best study a place?" And we knew we wanted to make as much information as possible accessible to as many people as possible—to let people study a place, to really experience it, without having to travel there. So the chance to let visitors experience the Church of the Holy Sepulchre through VR and 3-D technology was a great opportunity for us. We wanted both to teach and to thrill.

NGL: How did you go about creating this virtual experience?

ALAN: It can be a complex process, but ultimately it is only as good as the data and imagery you have available to create it—the difference between something that looks real or animated. Our team used advanced tools like LiDAR to gather extensive data and high resolution cameras to film the location. LiDAR is remote sensing technology that can be used to create 3-D models and maps that are accurate to the millimeter. In theory, we could 3-D print these places at full size if we wanted to. These tools not only provide incredibly accurate data, they guarantee a beautiful user experience—as close to real as you can get without being there.

NGL: What special challenges did the Church of the Holy Sepulcre offer?

ALAN: We had to consider the historical and religious significance of the church. This is a cultural site that draws hundreds of thousands of pilgrims and tourists each year, and we were mandated to conduct our work without interrupting visitors' experiences. This meant deploying a very small team working simultaneously in relatively short periods of time—even in the middle of the night. And the structure of the Edicule itself was a challenge.

NGL: In what way?

ALAN: The Edicule was somewhat fragile after centuries of pilgrims' attention. There's an expression that we can "love a place to death." These historical monuments aren't built to withstand that much traffic. And that's what's so great about the possibilities of VR—we can make the site accessible to so many more people without risking more damage to the site itself. And it allows us to tell stories in brand new ways, like changing lighting, getting camera angles and close-ups that would be impossible for a real-life visitor, even taking you back and forth in time.

NGL: How has the *Tomb of Christ* exhibition been received by the public?

ALAN: It was our second-most popular show! But best, I think it surprised our visitors. People came in expecting one type of exhibition—maybe one with artifacts, for example—and instead found something very different. Many people came in specifically because it was the Church of the Holy Sepulchre, but these new technologies and methods of storytelling are usable for all kinds of locations. Our explorers are out there capturing data all over the globe that will let us take visitors along with them. The bottom line is VR is an exciting new way to help visitors explore aspects of human history in a new way. ■

HISTORICAL THINKING

FORM AND SUPPORT OPINIONS Do you think it is a good idea to use VR to help people explore historic sites? What are some of the benefits? What are some of the drawbacks?

BACKGROUND FOR THE TEACHER

St. Helena The emperor Constantine credited his Christian faith with aiding his rise to power, and he converted many people around him, including his mother, Helena. Helena was charged with a series of pilgrimages to places of Christian significance. Upon her visits to certain holy sites, she ordered that churches be built there. For example, in Bethlehem, the Church of the Nativity was built on the site where Jesus was born, and the Church of Eleona was built on the Mount of Olives where Jesus ascended to heaven. Tradition holds that during the building of Constantine's church and the Edicule, Helena discovered the original three crosses used in Jesus' crucifixion. Today, adjacent to the chamber where the crosses were believed to have been found, there stands a chapel named in Helena's honor. Helena died around 328 C.E. and was revered as a saint by the ninth century.

TEACH

GUIDED DISCUSSION

5. **Analyze Points of View** What is Alan Parente's opinion of VR, and what details does he give to support his point of view? *(Parente likes VR and believes it is a useful tool when designing an exhibition about an archaeological site. He says that VR allows people who cannot afford to travel to the exhibition or the site to experience both. He also says that VR allows people to experience a fragile historical site without causing further damage to it.)*

6. **Evaluate** Do you think the restoration of the Church of the Holy Sepulchre was a worthwhile endeavor? Explain your answer. *(Answers will vary. Possible response: The restoration was worthwhile because the church and the Edicule are significant in many ways. Historically, they are a key place in the history of Christianity. For Christians, they are sacred holy sites. For archaeologists, they are a chance to try new techniques like VR that can be applied to other archaeological projects.)*

PRESERVING CULTURAL HERITAGE

Virtual Reality (VR) is being used in archaeological work all over the world and for many reasons. As in the case of the Church of the Holy Sepulchre, VR is allowing people to experience fragile sites without damaging them. VR is also being employed in places that are physically difficult to get to. For example, in Southern California, Pleito and Cache Cave are two remote archaeological sites associated with the Tejon Indians. The sites are very narrow and difficult to navigate. Using VR, a team of researchers has enabled people to experience the incredible Tejon cave paintings and rock art located there without having to visit the site. Some of the people experiencing the Tejon culture are themselves Tejon. The caves are too rugged for older members of the tribe to navigate, and younger Tejon are using the VR to do a kind of gaming with the ancestral places of their culture. VR is being hailed as an innovative new way of preserving and restoring Native American culture.

ACTIVE OPTION

NG Learning Framework: Explore the Church of the Holy Sepulchre
ATTITUDE Curiosity
KNOWLEDGE Our Human Story

Ask students to conduct online research into other aspects of the Church of the Holy Sepulchre, such as the uncovered frescoes that decorate the entryway, the Chapel of the Angel, the Chapel of Saint Helena, the Chapel of the Finding of the True Cross, or some other part. Students should work in pairs as they research, and when they are finished, have them meet with another pair and discuss their findings. You may wish to ask pairs to volunteer to share their research with the entire class.

HISTORICAL THINKING

ANSWER

Possible response: It is a good idea to use VR to help people explore historic sites. Many people would not be able to afford to travel around the world to see these sites, so VR brings the experience to them, which is a benefit. A drawback might be that the VR experience wouldn't seem as special as experiencing the real thing.

The Spread of Christianity

A great teacher can change lives. Jesus had this power. His message of love and everlasting life brought hope and joy to his followers and laid the foundation of a religion that continues to influence the world today.

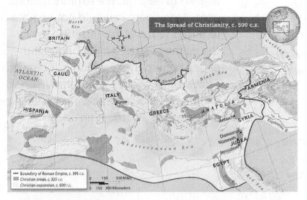

The Spread of Christianity, c. 500 C.E.

Boundary of Roman Empire, c. 395 C.E.
Christian areas, c. 325 C.E.
Christian expansion, c. 500 C.E.

TEACHINGS OF JESUS

The Romans captured Jerusalem in 63 B.C.E. and brought the Jewish people under their control. For many years, Roman emperors allowed the Jews to worship their God, just as they tolerated the practices of many other religions in the empire. But when the Roman rulers began to enforce emperor worship, the Jews resisted and rose up against Rome. The Jews were defeated in 70 C.E., and the future emperor Titus destroyed Jerusalem and the temple. Many of the Jewish people left the city and scattered throughout the empire. Their dispersion helped spread a new religion that was gaining ground in the Jewish community. The religion was **Christianity**, and it was based on the teachings of a Jew from Nazareth named **Jesus**.

Most of what we know about Jesus and his teachings comes from the four Gospels, which were written after his death by four of his disciples, or followers: Matthew, Mark, Luke, and John. The books are part of the Christian Bible's New Testament. Through these sources, we know that Jesus worked as a carpenter and began to speak openly about his new ideas when he was about 30 years old, around 28 C.E. The Gospels also claim that Jesus could perform such miracles as healing the sick and bringing the dead back to life.

Jesus taught that obedience to God's laws was more important than following the laws of men. This Judeo-Christian view of law differed from the Greco-Roman view, which insisted that laws were made by citizens.

Both cultures asserted that everyone should follow laws, but the Judeo-Christian tradition influenced democratic law with its principles of equality and ethical behavior. In Greco-Roman culture, philosophers upheld the power of reason and logic, while Judeo-Christian adherents put their faith in God. And while the Judeo-Christian tradition taught that it is the duty of every individual to live a moral life and practice charity and love toward all, the Greco-Roman world emphasized the civic duty of the individual citizen to vote and contribute to public life.

Jesus' teachings appealed to ordinary people. He declared that God loved everyone equally—not just the wealthy and powerful. Jesus also promised that those who loved God and sought his forgiveness for their sins would go to heaven after death. To his disciples, Jesus was Christ, "the anointed one." That is, they believed Jesus was the Messiah, the one who would free them.

SPREADING THE MESSAGE

As Jesus traveled through the Roman province of Judea preaching his message, he chose his closest disciples, known as the **Twelve Apostles**, to help him spread it. Like Jesus, the apostles stressed the importance of living a simple life and helping the less fortunate. After Jesus was denounced, or condemned, by some conservative Jewish authorities for his new ideas, he was arrested by the Romans as a dangerous popular leader. Jesus was executed by crucifixion.

After Jesus' death, his apostles and other followers continued to spread his teachings. Traveling on the Roman road network, they carried Christianity to Jewish communities throughout the empire. They also began encouraging Gentiles, or non-Jews, to worship with them. Soon, Christianity split from Judaism, developed its own identity, and grew rapidly. But Roman authorities still didn't realize that Christianity was separate from Judaism, which allowed Christians to operate without attracting much attention from the Romans.

Nevertheless, the Romans sometimes persecuted, or punished, Christians for their beliefs. One of the fiercest of these persecutors was **Paul**, a Greek-speaking Jew from Anatolia born around the same time as Jesus. But Paul became Christianity's greatest champion. According to the New Testament, Jesus appeared as the Son of God to Paul in a vision. Soon after, Paul converted to Christianity and began spreading Jesus'

CRITICAL VIEWING *The Last Supper*, painted by Italian artist Leonardo da Vinci in 1498, depicts the moment when Jesus announces to his 12 closest followers that one of them will betray him. Jesus is seated in the middle of the table. Judas, his betrayer, is the second man to Jesus' right. What emotions are vividly expressed by the followers in this moment?

teachings himself. In fact, he became a **missionary**, a person who travels to another country to do religious work.

Paul traveled throughout the eastern Mediterranean, Greece, and Italy and established several churches in these regions. He also reached out to Christian communities through his **epistles**, or letters, in which he answered questions, resolved issues, and generally kept up the spirits of persecuted Christians. Paul was often arrested for his activities, but he always escaped to preach again.

In 64 C.E., the Roman emperor Nero blamed Christians for a devastating fire that swept through Rome. By then, the Romans had realized that Christianity was a separate religion and that it was becoming increasingly popular. Fearing that it might destabilize the empire, Nero made the practice of Christianity illegal. He had thousands of Christians massacred, including Paul, according to traditional belief. Because anyone could be put to death for simply being a Christian, worshipers met in secret and buried their dead in underground chambers called **catacombs**. The suffering of Christians would continue for more than 250 years, but their courage and determination ensured Christianity's survival and later growth as the world's largest religion.

HISTORICAL THINKING

1. **READING CHECK** Who was Jesus?

2. **INTERPRET MAPS** Where did Christianity spread outside of the Roman Empire?

3. **DESCRIBE** What are key beliefs of the Judeo-Christian culture?

PLAN: 2-PAGE LESSON

OBJECTIVE

Understand that Christianity was based on the teachings of Jesus and spread by his followers.

CRITICAL THINKING SKILLS FOR LESSON 3.3

- Interpret Maps
- Analyze Sources
- Identify Main Ideas and Details
- Summarize
- Analyze Primary Sources

HISTORICAL THINKING FOR CHAPTER 6

Why did the Roman Empire become one of the most influential in history?

Christianity developed out of the Jewish community during the time of the Roman Empire. Lesson 3.3 discusses the origins of Christianity, the role of Jesus, and the spread of the religion throughout the Roman Empire and beyond.

Student eEdition online

Additional content for this lesson, including a primary source and a photo, is available online.

BACKGROUND FOR THE TEACHER

The Twelve Apostles *Apostle* comes from the Greek word *apostolos*, which means "person sent" and refers to Jesus' 12 closest disciples who spread his ideas. The names of these men were Peter, James, John, Andrew, Phillip, Bartholomew, Matthew, Thomas, James, Thaddeus, Simon, and Judas Iscariot. Many scholars believe it was important to Christians at the time that there were exactly 12 of these apostles. The number may recall the 12 tribes of Israel, who the Jews believe were the direct descendants of Jacob. According to Jewish belief, Jacob is the father from whom all Israelites descended and God promised to protect.

INTRODUCE & ENGAGE

QUICKWRITE ABOUT CHRISTIANITY

Ask students to write what they already know about Christianity. Questions for students to consider might include the following: What do Christians believe? Where did the first Christians come from? Who is Jesus and why is he important to Christians? What did Jesus teach? Invite volunteers to share their answers with the class. Explain that in this lesson students will learn about the rise of Christianity in the Roman Empire.

TEACH

GUIDED DISCUSSION

1. **Identify Main Ideas and Details** Where does most of the information we have about Jesus and his teachings come from? *(the Four Gospels of the Bible)*

2. **Summarize** Why did Jesus' teachings appeal to ordinary people? *(In a highly stratified society, Jesus taught that God loved everyone, not just the wealthy and powerful; he promised his followers life after death during a time when people died at a young age.)*

ANALYZE PRIMARY SOURCES

As a class, examine the primary source feature (available in the Student eEdition). **ASK:** Why do you think Jesus often used parables to teach moral lessons? *(Possible response: because stories can make information easier to understand and more interesting)*

ACTIVE OPTIONS

On Your Feet: Jigsaw Strategy Organize students into four expert groups. Assign each group one of the following topics: Jesus' life, the conversion of Paul, Leonardo da Vinci's *The Last Supper*, and the catacombs. Ask the groups to discuss their topic. Have them create a summary of what they learned. Then regroup students so that each has at least one member from each expert group. Have students in the new group take turns sharing the summary they created in their expert groups.

NG Learning Framework: Write a Feature Article
ATTITUDE Curiosity
SKILL Collaboration

Encourage students to learn more about the people and places mentioned in this lesson. Instruct them to work in pairs to conduct further research on a person or place that interests them, then prepare a short, informative feature article on the topic. Suggest that students include maps and other visuals in their features. Invite students to publish their features electronically, on a class blog or website, or in a class magazine.

DIFFERENTIATE

STRIVING READERS

Complete a Venn Diagram Tell students to use a Venn diagram to take notes while they read about the similarities and differences between Judeo-Christian and Greco-Roman cultures. Invite them to compare their completed diagrams with a partner's and discuss any differences.

ENGLISH LANGUAGE LEARNERS

Make Vocabulary Cards Have students use flash cards to learn and practice unfamiliar words they encounter in this lesson. They should write the target word on one side of each card. On the other side, they should write related words they are familiar with, draw or paste images that will help them recall the meaning of the target word, or use other mnemonic devices. Encourage students to use their flash cards for review. Have students at the **Beginning** and **Intermediate** levels work in pairs. Have those at the **Advanced** level work independently.

See the Chapter Planner for more strategies for differentiation.

HISTORICAL THINKING

ANSWERS

1. a Jew from Nazareth on whose teachings Christianity is based

2. to Armenia and places along the Tigris and Euphrates rivers

3. Key beliefs include obeying God's laws over the laws of men and living a moral life.

CRITICAL VIEWING (Last Supper) Answers will vary. Possible response: shock, horror, disbelief, sadness, fear

(catacomb, available in the Student eEdition) Answers will vary. Possible response: It's dark, cramped, and probably very quiet.

Traveler: Egeria
An Early Christian Pilgrim

C. LATER 4TH CENTURY–EARLY 5TH CENTURY C.E.

Egeria is a woman of mystery. We don't know when she was born or when she died. We're not even entirely sure that Egeria was her name. What we do know is that around 379 C.E. she set off for Jerusalem for the trip of a lifetime.

PILGRIMAGE

Most historians believe Egeria was born in the second half of the fourth century to a well-to-do family in the Galicia region of Roman Spain. Although she bore a pagan name—Egeria is the name of a water spirit in the polytheistic religion of ancient Rome—she had a strong Christian faith. As a young woman, Egeria decided to leave home and take a **pilgrimage**, a journey to a holy place.

Like Paul a few hundred years before, Egeria took to the Roman roads on a religious journey. Unlike Paul, she didn't set out to spread Jesus' teachings, and she didn't have to worry about being arrested. In 312, Rome put an end to the persecution of Christians. And in 380, Christianity became the official religion of the Roman Empire. (You'll learn more about this surprising turn of events later in the chapter.) Traveling mostly by foot, Egeria went to visit sites in the Holy Land and beyond. Egeria had studied the Bible thoroughly. She wanted to visit biblical sites and talk about biblical events with the local Christians she would meet along the way.

Egeria's primary destination was Jerusalem, at the time a center of Christian thought and a holy city for both Christians and Jews. She remained there for three years, likely from 381 to 384. During her stay in Jerusalem, she took trips to other biblical sites in the region, including a lengthy expedition south to Mount Sinai on Egypt's Sinai Peninsula. In Egypt, Egeria also visited Alexandria and sailed south on the Nile River as far as Thebes. Her homeward trip took her north along the coast of Syria to present-day Turkey and the city of Constantinople, now Istanbul.

A LETTER HOME

Near the end of her pilgrimage, Egeria wrote a long letter to a circle of women in her hometown, based on notes she had kept during her travels. She addressed the letter to her *sorores*, Latin for "sisters." This term could mean that she herself was a sister, or nun, in a religious society. But it might just have been the way she addressed her female Christian friends. Egeria wrote expressively, mainly in Latin but with occasional Greek phrases. She offered detailed descriptions of what she saw, perhaps to help her friends imagine what she was experiencing.

> **PRIMARY SOURCE**
>
> The fragment of Egeria's letter that has survived begins with her trip to Mount Sinai. In the following excerpt from her letter, Egeria describes the view from Sinai's summit. Note that she refers to the eastern Mediterranean as the Parthenian Sea and uses the term Saracens to indicate the Arabs of the Sinai Peninsula.
>
> I want you to be quite clear about these mountains, reverend ladies my sisters, which surrounded us as we stood beside the church looking down from the summit of the mountain in the middle. They had been almost too much for us to climb, and I really do not think I have ever seen any that were higher (apart from the central one which is higher still) even though they only looked like little hillocks to us as we stood on the central mountain. From there we were able to see Egypt and Palestine, the Red Sea and the Parthenian Sea (the part that takes you to Alexandria), as well as the vast lands of the Saracens—all unbelievably far below us.
>
> —from *Egeria's Travels* by John Wilkinson, 1999

Egeria also discussed her encounters with monks and clergy. She visited several of the Christian churches in Jerusalem. Egeria described the daily services in one by writing that all the doors of the church "are opened before cockcrow [very early morning] each day." And after the monks and men and women "who are willing to wake at such an hour" arrive, "they start the morning hymns and the bishop with his clergy comes and joins them."

Only the middle part of her letter, which includes descriptions of her trips to Palestine and Egypt, survived. In the 11th century, this fragment of the letter was copied in a manuscript and preserved in an Italian monastery. The manuscript lay forgotten in the monastery for about 700 years until it was rediscovered in the late 1800s.

Egeria's account of her travels is among the earliest written by a Christian on a pilgrimage to the Holy Land. Her letter has been a treasure trove for scholars, who have studied it to learn about the evolution of the Latin language in the later period of the ancient world. Religious scholars have also gleaned information about the development of Christian church services in the fourth century. But most of all, Egeria's observations during her travels and her religious passion strike a common chord with the many pilgrims who have since followed in her footsteps.

HISTORICAL THINKING

1. **READING CHECK** Why did Egeria undertake her pilgrimage?

2. **COMPARE AND CONTRAST** How do Egeria's travels in the Roman Empire compare with those of Paul?

3. **INTERPRET MAPS** According to the maps, what possible route did Egeria take to Jerusalem?

PLAN: 2-PAGE LESSON

OBJECTIVE

Describe the travels of Egeria who made a pilgrimage to the eastern Mediterranean and wrote a descriptive account about her journey.

CRITICAL THINKING SKILLS FOR LESSON 3.4

- Compare and Contrast
- Interpret Maps
- Describe
- Identify Main Ideas and Details
- Analyze Primary Sources

HISTORICAL THINKING FOR CHAPTER 6

Why did the Roman Empire become one of the most influential in history?

Christian missionaries walked the Roman roads, spreading their faith. Lesson 3.4 describes the pilgrimage of a Christian woman known as Egeria on these roads.

Student eEdition online

Additional content for this lesson, including a photo, is available online.

BACKGROUND FOR THE TEACHER

In 312, Constantine became emperor of Rome and converted to Christianity. Sometime during the fourth century, Constantine asked his mother Helena to visit holy places in Jerusalem, Bethlehem, and Sinai and to establish churches on the holiest sites. When Helena visited Mount Sinai, she found small monastic communities living there. A monk described the area as "the edge of the inhabitable world. . . . People came here for the silence and because this had been the place sanctified by the revelations of God." Working with the monks, Helena had a church built on Mount Sinai that is the oldest structure at the site. Most likely, this is the church Egeria refers to in her letter.

History Notebook

Encourage students to complete the Traveler page for Chapter 6 in their History Notebooks as they read.

INTRODUCE & ENGAGE

DISCUSS FAVORITE PLACES

Invite students to discuss places that are meaningful to them. They might like to go to a favorite park where they can relax and enjoy nature, or they might have a favorite hangout where they can be with their friends. Encourage students to explain why their spot is meaningful. Then tell them that in this lesson, they will read about a woman called Egeria who took a pilgrimage to biblical sites to talk about biblical events with local Christians.

TEACH

GUIDED DISCUSSION

1. **Describe** Where did Egeria go on her pilgrimage? *(She went to the Holy Land and spent much of her time in Jerusalem and biblical sites in the region. She also visited places in Africa and Southwest Asia.)*

2. **Identify Main Ideas and Details** Why is her letter considered a "treasure trove"? *(Possible response: The letter is among the earliest written by a Christian on a pilgrimage to the Holy Land. It describes fourth century church services, and scholars have studied it to learn about the evolution of the Latin language.)*

ANALYZE PRIMARY SOURCES

Discuss the primary source in class. **ASK:** How have the names of some geographic features and groups of people changed? *(Parthenian Sea is now called Mediterranean Sea, and the Saracens are now the Arabs.)* What do you think Egeria means when she writes in her letter that she wants her readers "to be quite clear about these mountains"? *(Possible response: She wants her "reverend ladies my sisters" to understand the majesty and religious importance of Mount Sinai.)*

ACTIVE OPTIONS

On Your Feet: Three-Step Interview Have students form pairs. Then ask Student A to interview Student B about what he or she has learned about Egeria's travels. Then have partners reverse roles. When the interviews are complete, Student A should share with the class information from Student B, and then Student B should share information from Student A.

> **NG Learning Framework: Write a Letter**
> SKILL Observation
> KNOWLEDGE Our Human Story

Invite students to think of a place they have visited that made a strong impression on them. Tell them to write a description of the place in a letter to someone who has never seen the place, including details that help the person visualize it.

DIFFERENTIATE

STRIVING READERS

Understand Main Ideas Check students' understanding of the main ideas in the lesson by asking them to choose the word or phrase that correctly completes the following statements:

- Egeria was a young woman with a strong polytheistic or Christian faith. *(Christian)*
- Egeria went on a pilgrimage to visit biblical or Roman sites. *(biblical)*
- Egeria's primary destination was Constantinople or Jerusalem, where she stayed for three years. *(Jerusalem)*
- Egeria wrote a long letter to her "sisters" or an Italian monastery, giving detailed descriptions of what she saw. *(her "sisters")*

GIFTED & TALENTED

Fill in Missing Details Tell students to consider the facts about Egeria and her letter provided in the lesson and to fill in some of the missing details. Was Egeria a nun? Who received her letter? What did they do with it? How did an Italian monastery come to have the letter about 700 years later? Invite students to write their version of the mystery and share it with the class.

See the Chapter Planner for more strategies for differentiation.

HISTORICAL THINKING

ANSWERS

1. She wanted to see the many places that she had read about in the Bible and talk with other Christians about biblical events.

2. Answers will vary. Possible response: Unlike Paul, Egeria could be more open about her religious beliefs without fear of arrest. Like Paul, Egeria's journey was driven by her devotion to Christianity.

3. She sailed along the Mediterranean, passing through Italy and along the Egyptian coast before arriving in Jerusalem.

3.5 The Romans and the Christians

You probably take freedom of religion for granted. It's a basic right in the United States. The Roman Empire didn't go quite that far. It did tolerate many gods, including those worshiped by conquered peoples. But in time, the Romans came to require that people worship the emperor. Both Jews and Christians believed in one single almighty God, and many were willing to die rather than worship another.

The Temple of Saturn, shown here, has stood in the Roman Forum since around 497 B.C.E. It was dedicated to the Roman god of agriculture. The temple was restored in 42 B.C.E. and then again before 380 C.E. The second restoration was designed to demonstrate Rome's continuing resistance to Christianity.

Emperor worship began with the death of Julius Caesar, when he was officially recognized as a god. Once Augustus became emperor, he allowed people in some parts of the empire to build temples to him. However, in Rome and throughout Italy, an emperor was traditionally only worshiped—often with sacrificial offerings—after his death. Members of an emperor's family were also worshiped.

Roman rulers believed emperor worship helped unify the empire and center the people's loyalty on the ruler. When Christianity became too big to ignore, the Christian refusal to honor the emperor with sacrifices at public festivals was seen as endangering the empire. As you

know, Nero blamed the Christians after fire destroyed much of Rome in 64 C.E. Nero may have made them his scapegoat because he was responsible for the fire.

Following Nero's persecution of the Christians, the emperor Trajan, who ruled from 98 to 117, determined that a person could be punished if proven guilty of being Christian. Many Romans also objected to Christianity's ceremonies. The Roman historian Tacitus suggested that Christians were "hated because of their outrageous practices." One such practice, Holy Communion—the consumption of bread and wine believed by Christians to be the body and blood of Jesus—led to charges of cannibalism.

DOCUMENT ONE

Primary Source: Book
from *The Annals* by Tacitus, 109 C.E.

The Annals is a history of the Roman Empire from the reign of Tiberius to that of Nero. In this work, Tacitus refers to Jesus and Christians only once—and by so doing, provided convincing evidence for most scholars that Jesus really did exist. In the following excerpt, Tacitus discusses the execution of Jesus ("Christus") and then refers to the fire in Rome for which Christians were held responsible.

CONSTRUCTED RESPONSE How does Tacitus characterize Christianity?

Christus, from whom the name [Christian] had its origin, suffered the extreme penalty during the reign of Tiberius at the hands of one of our procurators, Pontius Pilate, and a most mischievous superstition, thus checked for the moment, again broke out not only in Judea, the first source of the evil, but even in Rome. . . . Accordingly, an arrest was first made of all who pleaded guilty; then, upon their information, an immense multitude was convicted, not so much of the crime of firing the city, as of hatred against mankind.

DOCUMENT TWO

Primary Source: Letter
from *Letters of Pliny* by Gaius Plinius Caecilius Secundus, c.E. 112

From 111 to 113, Pliny the Younger, then a respected Roman politician, served as the governor of a province in Anatolia. A number of Christians had appeared in his court, and Pliny wrote to Emperor Trajan to explain his method for punishing them.

CONSTRUCTED RESPONSE What method did Pliny use to determine whether Christians should be punished?

[T]he method I have observed towards those who have been brought before me as Christians is this: I asked them whether they were Christians; if they admitted it, I repeated the question twice, and threatened them with punishment; if they persisted, I ordered them to be at once punished: for I was persuaded, whatever the nature of their opinions might be, a contumacious [rebellious] and inflexible obstinacy [stubbornness] certainly deserved correction.

DOCUMENT THREE

Primary Source: Official Proclamation
from the Edict of Toleration issued by Emperor Galerius, c.E. 311

Gaius Galerius Valerius Maximianus was a Roman emperor from 305 to 311. Galerius persecuted Christians mercilessly—until 311 when he came down with a painful disease. Some historians speculate that Galerius issued his Edict of Toleration because he feared the Christian God was punishing him for his persecutions.

CONSTRUCTED RESPONSE How does Galerius characterize Christians and himself?

After the publication, on our part, of an order commanding Christians to return to the observance of the ancient [Roman] customs, many of them, it is true, submitted in view of the danger, while many others suffered death. Nevertheless, since many of them have continued to persist in their opinions and we see that in the present situation they neither duly [properly] adore and venerate [honor] the gods nor yet worship the god of the Christians, we, with our wonted clemency [customary mercy], have judged it is wise to extend a pardon even to these men and permit them once more to become Christians and re-establish their places of meetings.

SYNTHESIZE & WRITE

1. **REVIEW** Review what you have learned about the Roman Empire, Roman religion, and Christianity.

2. **RECALL** On your own paper, write down the main idea expressed in each document.

3. **CONSTRUCT** Construct a topic sentence that answers this question: How did Roman authorities and writers view Christianity?

4. **WRITE** Using evidence from this chapter and the documents, write an informative paragraph that supports your topic sentence in Step 3.

PLAN: 2-PAGE LESSON

OBJECTIVE
Explain how Roman authorities and writers viewed Christianity.

CRITICAL THINKING SKILLS FOR LESSON 3.5
- Synthesize
- Make Inferences
- Draw Conclusions
- Evaluate

HISTORICAL THINKING FOR CHAPTER 6
Why did the Roman Empire become one of the most influential in history?

Lesson 3.5 provides documents showing that many Roman authorities and writers viewed Christianity as an evil and a threat to the empire. However, in time, Rome allowed Christians to practice their religion, and Christianity's influence spread throughout the world.

BACKGROUND FOR THE TEACHER
Secret Symbol During the time of the Christian persecutions, believers used a secret fish symbol to distinguish friends from foes or indicate a meeting place. The symbol consisted of two arched, intersecting lines to form the profile of a fish. Unlike the Christian symbol of the cross, the fish wasn't recognized by the Romans and didn't arouse their suspicion. Early Christians based the symbol on the Greek word for fish: *ichthys*. They used the initials of the Greek word to form an acronym that, in English, stands for "Jesus Christ God's Son Saviour." The symbol had further relevance to Christians because Jesus had called his disciples—most of whom worked as fishermen—"fishers of men."

INTRODUCE & ENGAGE

PREPARE FOR THE DOCUMENT-BASED QUESTION

Before students start on the activity, briefly preview the three documents. Remind students that a constructed response requires full explanations in complete sentences. Emphasize that students should use what they have learned about the Roman Empire and Christianity in addition to the information in the documents.

TEACH

GUIDED DISCUSSION

1. **Make Inferences** In the excerpt by Tacitus, what is the "extreme penalty" suffered by Christus? *(The extreme penalty is death.)*

2. **Draw Conclusions** How does Pliny view the Christians who refused to renounce their faith? *(as rebellious and stubborn)*

EVALUATE

After students have completed the Synthesize & Write activity, allow time for them to exchange paragraphs and read and comment on the work of their peers. Establish guidelines for comments prior to the activity so that feedback is constructive and encouraging. Comments should focus on the most significant parts that address the purpose of the activity and the audience.

ACTIVE OPTION

On Your Feet: Jigsaw Strategy Organize students into "expert" groups and assign each group one of the documents to analyze and summarize its main ideas into their own words. Then regroup students into new groups so that each group has at least one member from each expert group. Students in the new groups take turns sharing the summaries from their expert groups.

DIFFERENTIATE

STRIVING READERS

Summarize Have two students work together to summarize the documents. One student should read a document aloud, and then the other should summarize its content. After each document has been summarized, ask students to answer the constructed response question.

INCLUSION

Synthesize Help students minimize distractions by typing the three excerpts on one sheet of paper. Give photocopies of these to students along with highlighters. Tell students to highlight important words that appear in all of the documents. Then have them write a summary using several of the words.

SYNTHESIZE & WRITE

ANSWERS

1. Students should record notes on what they have learned about the Roman Empire, Roman religion, and Christianity.

2. Answers will vary. Possible response: Document 1: Christianity is an evil that threatens Rome and mankind. Document 2: Christians who persist in their faith should be punished. Document 3: Christians continue to be obstinate, but Rome will be merciful and let them practice their faith.

3. Answers will vary. Possible response: The Romans viewed Christians as rebels and Christianity as an evil that should be punished.

4. Answers will vary. Students' paragraphs should include their topic sentence from Step 3 and provide several details from the documents to support it.

CONSTRUCTED RESPONSE

Document One: as a "most mischievous superstition" and promoting "hatred against mankind"

Document Two: If they persisted in maintaining they were Christians, Pliny had them punished at once for their rebelliousness and obstinacy.

Document Three: He characterizes the Christians as doggedly persistent and himself as merciful and wise.

Decline of the Roman Empire

When you hear today that a company is too big to fail, that means it's too important to the economy to be allowed to fail. That concept didn't exist in ancient Rome. The empire was becoming too big to manage from Rome, and things began to fall apart.

ROMAN WORLD IN CRISIS

For about 200 years, the Roman Empire ran relatively smoothly, largely under the rule of the so-called "Five Good Emperors." The five were Nerva, Trajan, Hadrian, Antoninus Pius, and Marcus Aurelius, whose reigns spanned the years from 96 to 180 c.e. They were strong rulers who had managed to maintain order in the empire. But with its diverse geography and cultures, the vast empire was becoming increasingly difficult for an emperor to govern.

Defending it was challenging, too. During the last years of Marcus Aurelius's rule, wars broke out on Rome's northern and eastern borders. In the north, Germanic tribes launched raids along the Danube River. In the east, Rome fought the powerful Parthian Empire from Persia. Conflicts on these two fronts strained the empire's money and resources.

After the death of Marcus Aurelius, the empire descended into civil war, as warring groups fought over who would be emperor. While Roman soldiers battled both at home and abroad, invaders plundered riches from unguarded Roman provinces. As the empire became increasingly unsafe, people blamed their leaders. Between 235 and 285, more than 25 different emperors ruled, many of whom were either replaced or murdered. In the Iberian Peninsula, France, and Britain, the people broke from Rome to form a separate Gallic Empire. They preferred the rule of local leaders.

A DIVIDED EMPIRE

At last, in 284, the throne was seized by **Diocletian** (dy-uh-KLEE-shun), who came up with a plan for keeping the empire alive. The new emperor put an end to the principate and, in 285, divided the empire in two: the Western Roman Empire and the Eastern Roman Empire. Diocletian set up a rule by four emperors called a **tetrarchy**. Diocletian ruled the Eastern Roman Empire, and his trusted friend Maximian ruled the Western Roman Empire. Diocletian named the two junior emperors.

Diocletian and Maximian began to institute reforms. They strengthened the army by increasing the number of soldiers to 400,000 men and creating new forces that could be sent to put down trouble wherever it broke out. They also divided the provinces into smaller, more manageable units. In an effort to promote unity, Diocletian and Maximian enforced emperor worship and the use of the Latin language, although Greek was commonly used in the eastern empire. To increase revenue, the emperors regulated the tax system and stabilized the currency. After 20 years, and with the empires recovering, Diocletian and Maximian stepped down and let the junior emperors take over.

The tetrarchy did not last long after that, however. **Constantine**, the son of a former senior emperor of the Western Roman Empire, began a quest for power and sparked a civil war. Constantine became the emperor of the Western Roman Empire in 312 and emperor of both empires in 324. However, he was more interested in the Eastern Roman Empire.

By that time, Rome and the west had weakened considerably. The east had a larger population and produced more food, taxes, and soldiers than the west. So Constantine decided to move the imperial capital from Rome to the ancient Greek city of Byzantium in the Eastern Roman Empire. He renamed the city Constantinople, which means "city of Constantine." The capital was located on the strategically important Bosporus, a narrow stretch of water between Europe and Asia. Constantine rebuilt the city on a monumental scale similar to that of Rome, and so it was sometimes known as "New Rome." He also continued the reforms begun by Diocletian and Maximian, thereby earning the title "Constantine the Great."

CHRISTIANITY RISES

As you know, after Christianity continued to grow in the Roman Empire, emperors began to perceive the religion as a threat. Christians suffered persecution for hundreds of years. In 303, Diocletian's junior emperor, Galerius, launched a particularly violent persecution of Christians. He imprisoned church leaders, destroyed churches, and executed those who would not sacrifice to Roman gods. You may remember that Galerius ended Christian persecution with the Edict of Toleration in 311.

In 312, on the eve of a battle for control of the empire, the fate of Christianity changed even more dramatically. According to legend, Constantine had a vision of the Christian cross in the sky before battle. As a result, he had the cross painted on his soldiers' shields, and they marched into battle as "Christian soldiers." Constantine won the battle, became emperor, and converted to Christianity. In 313, he issued the Edict of Milan, legalizing Christianity.

In 325, Constantine summoned a group of Christian leaders to meet in the city of Nicaea (nye-SEE-uh), in Anatolia, not far from the new capital. The leaders drew up a basic statement of faith, known as the Nicene Creed. The creed defined God as a Holy Trinity: the union of Father, Son (Jesus), and Holy Spirit. It also established common Christian sacraments, or religious ceremonies, including Baptism.

This meeting began the practice of gathering Christian leaders together to discuss beliefs and practices, which were then communicated to churches throughout the empire and beyond. Each church was led by a priest, and groups of churches were overseen by a bishop. According to biblical tradition, the first bishop was the apostle Peter, who was killed during the persecutions in 64 c.e. Another bishop named Augustine, who served in the port city of Hippo in northern Africa from 396 to his death in 430, continues to influence Christian thought today. In time, the bishop of Rome became the most important bishop, or pope, and led the unified Roman Catholic Church.

In 380, the emperor Theodosius declared Christianity the official religion of the Roman Empire. Christianity eventually replaced the polytheistic Roman traditions and became a powerful, organized religion.

The *Colossus of Constantine*, carved around 315, was originally placed near the Roman Forum and showed the emperor seated on a throne. The statue was about 40 feet high. Today, only these marble fragments remain, including Constantine's huge head and hand, and are exhibited in the courtyard of a museum in Rome.

HISTORICAL THINKING

1. **READING CHECK** Why was the Roman Empire in crisis?

2. **COMPARE AND CONTRAST** In what ways were the Western and Eastern Roman empires similar and different?

3. **MAKE INFERENCES** Why do you think Constantinople was a strategic location for Roman trade?

PLAN: 2-PAGE LESSON

OBJECTIVE

Explain how the decline of the Roman Empire in the third and fourth centuries led to far-reaching political and religious changes.

CRITICAL THINKING SKILLS FOR LESSON 4.1

- Compare and Contrast
- Interpret Maps
- Analyze Cause and Effect
- Summarize

HISTORICAL THINKING FOR CHAPTER 6

Why did the Roman Empire become one of the most influential in history?

As the Roman Empire declined, Christianity's influence grew, and the religion was eventually legalized. Lesson 4.1 discusses the political and religious changes that took place as the empire began to crumble.

Student eEdition online

Additional content for this lesson, including photos and a map, is available online.

BACKGROUND FOR THE TEACHER

Constantine Constantine was declared emperor of Rome in 306 c.e. after the death of his father Constantius. Shortly after, he began to battle Rome's remaining rulers for power. Some scholars believe Constantine's conversion to Christianity was a stunt to win the hearts of Romans. Regardless, his most important contribution, the Edict of Milan, granted Romans the right to observe whichever religion they chose and began the process of making Christianity the official religion of the empire.

INTRODUCE & ENGAGE

REVIEW

Review with students the amount of area covered by the Roman Empire. Then discuss the challenges Roman emperors might have faced as they ruled such a large area. Ask students if they think ruling the empire might have been easier with some help. Tell them that in this lesson they will learn about a Roman emperor who decided to take that course.

TEACH

GUIDED DISCUSSION

1. **Analyze Cause and Effect** What happened as a result of Rome's loss of effective leadership? *(Wars broke out, including civil war; invaders attacked provinces; the empire became increasingly unsafe; and people blamed their leaders.)*

2. **Summarize** Summarize the events of Constantine's conversion and his actions afterwards. *(Constantine had a vision of the Christian cross before going into battle, and he painted the symbol on his soldiers' shields. Constantine won the battle, became emperor, and converted to Christianity. In 313, he issued the Edict of Milan, legalizing Christianity.)*

INTERPRET MAPS

Have students review the map (available in the Student eEdition). Tell students that Diocletian's decision to rule the Eastern Roman Empire made it clear that Rome was no longer the center of political power. Point out that the Rhine and Danube rivers on the northern border of the Western Roman Empire were difficult to cross, which made it easier for the Roman army to defend that border. **ASK:** In what ways was Rome's location similar to that of Constantinople? *(Possible response: They were both near water, and they were both near the center of the respective spheres of influence when they were established.)*

ACTIVE OPTIONS

On Your Feet: Roundtable on Diocletian Arrange students in groups of four to answer the following question: What steps did Diocletian take to halt the Roman Empire's decline? Provide each group with a sheet of paper. The first student in the group writes one step of Diocletian's plan, reads it aloud, and passes the paper clockwise to the next student. Each student adds at least one answer. Students circulate the paper around the table until they run out of answers. Call on volunteers from each group to share their answers.

| **NG Learning Framework: Create a Time Line**
ATTITUDE Empowerment
SKILL Communication

Have students work in pairs to create an annotated time line of the events discussed in this lesson. Encourage them to discuss how each of these events affected the Roman Empire. Invite volunteers to share their completed time lines with the class.

DIFFERENTIATE

STRIVING READERS

Pose and Answer Questions Have students work in pairs to read the lesson. Instruct them to pause after each paragraph and ask one another *who, what, when, where*, and *how* questions about what they have just read. Advise students to read more slowly and focus on specific details if they have difficulty answering the questions or to reread a paragraph to find the answers.

GIFTED & TALENTED

Teach a Mini-Lesson Allow students to select a topic of interest from the lesson and conduct further research on it. Then have students prepare to teach a mini-lesson on the topic to the class. Suggest that students think about the visuals and activities they want to use to capture their audience's attention. Give presenters a specified length of time in which to teach their topics.

See the Chapter Planner for more strategies for differentiation.

HISTORICAL THINKING

ANSWERS

1. The empire had grown too large to be governed effectively by a single emperor.

2. Both were ruled by a senior and a junior emperor, but the eastern empire had more people, food, taxes, and soldiers than the western empire.

3. Answers will vary. Possible response: Constantinople was located on the Bosporus, which allowed the empire to control and facilitate trade among Europe, Asia, and Africa.

CRITICAL VIEWING (available in the Student eEdition) Answers will vary. Possible response: By then, Christianity was powerful, wealthy, and influential.

Fall of the Western Roman Empire

In spite of the problems that plagued the Western Roman Empire, most people probably couldn't imagine the world without it. But danger stood just outside the empire's frontiers. It was the beginning of the end.

INVADING TRIBES

After Constantine's death in 337, his sons came to power, but they soon plunged the empire into another civil war. Theodosius, who, as you know, made Christianity the official religion of Rome, reunited the empire. But after his death in 395, the division of the eastern and western empires became permanent.

Meanwhile, Germanic tribes from northern Europe—the Goths (comprising two branches, the Ostrogoths and the Visigoths) and the Vandals—continued to try to cross into the western empire along the Danube-Rhine border. They came in search of better farmland and so migrated south toward the Roman frontier. However, the Romans considered the tribes barbarians and resisted their request to settle on Roman soil.

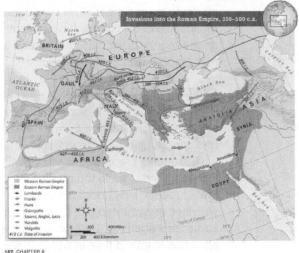

Invasions into the Roman Empire, 350–500 C.E.

The Goths' request became more urgent in the 370s when the Huns, a nomadic group from Central Asia, threatened the tribe's homeland. The Huns' skill with horses and bows made them a ferocious fighting force. After the Goths were forced to cross the Danube into the Western Roman Empire, a Roman commander attacked them, inciting war. In the early 400s, the Vandals, with as many as 80,000 soldiers, invaded Gaul and then Spain. With few Roman soldiers at their command, the Roman emperors had to enlist "barbarian" fighters to defend the empire.

And then the unthinkable happened. On August 24, 410, Alaric, the chief of the Visigoths, led his army into Rome. Alaric had been trained in the Roman army. Over three days, he and his soldiers completely sacked Rome. About 6,000 Roman soldiers came to defend the city, but they were quickly defeated. This was the first time since the fourth century B.C.E. that a foreign army had entered the city. It would not be the last time.

New invaders appeared again and again, as other Germanic tribes, including the Lombards, Franks, Angles, Saxons, and Jutes, went on the attack against the western empire. Roman armies fought back but to no avail. Province after province fell to the invaders. The Vandals crossed the Mediterranean to North Africa, where they captured Carthage in 439. Angles, Saxons, and Jutes crossed the sea into Britain. Ostrogoths and Lombards streamed into northern Italy and Gaul, where they settled. Led by their ruler, **Attila**, the Huns attacked Gaul in 451 but were defeated by the Romans and the Visigoths. A year later, Attila invaded Italy and sacked several cities. In 455, Vandal forces sailed to Italy. They occupied Rome for two weeks.

END OF THE WESTERN EMPIRE

For the next 20 years or so, different Germanic groups gained control of Rome. Finally, in 476, the Germanic leader Odoacer entered the city with his army. Unopposed, he removed the final Roman ruler of the western empire, a 16-year-old named Romulus, and became the first king of Italy. The Roman Empire was over. The Western Roman Empire was broken up into many Germanic kingdoms. The Eastern Roman Empire, with its capital at Constantinople, remained powerful and united. Later known as the Byzantine Empire, it would continue imperial traditions for nearly 1,000 years.

So what led to the fall of the Western Roman Empire? Historians have been debating the question for centuries. Most agree that the internal problems that weakened Rome had existed for many years and rendered the empire vulnerable to the invaders.

Perhaps the main reason for Rome's fall was its financial woes. Constant warfare ruined Rome's economy and disrupted its trade. The Vandals struck a major blow when they claimed North Africa and seized control of the Mediterranean. Because of the empire's inadequate agricultural production, people suffered food shortages. They also faced higher taxes. The empire expected its citizens to pay for all the expensive wars being fought. Both the rich and the poor suffered as a result of the failing economy, but the poor suffered more. Unrest arose as the gap between the two classes widened.

Rome's declining economy also undermined defense. In the early 400s, the Roman army consisted of an estimated 350,000 troops stationed at frontier outposts and 150,000 mobile troops. To maintain the army's strength, soldiers had to be paid. But decreasing revenues sometimes meant no recompense for soldiers. When they weren't paid, they didn't fight.

The army suffered from a lack of manpower for another reason. After expansion ended in the second century, the influx of conquered people and slaves to the empire began to come to a halt. The economy, in part, depended on slave labor, and the army relied on those taken in war to fill its ranks. In time, the army had to hire Germanic peoples to fight Rome's battles. And those soldiers felt little, if any, loyalty toward the empire.

After the division of the empire, the west began to suffer politically as well. Ineffective and corrupt leaders created instability in the western empire. No longer able to trust the leadership of their government, ordinary citizens began to look out for themselves rather than the empire. The Roman virtue of civic responsibility no longer seemed very important.

The Roman Empire lasted about 500 years and, for much of that time, dominated the Mediterranean. Rome fell, but it left a legacy in such areas as law and government, culture and language, and architecture and engineering. This legacy continues to influence much of the world today.

HISTORICAL THINKING

1. **READING CHECK** What happened on August 24, 410?

2. **INTERPRET MAPS** Which groups invaded the Eastern Roman Empire?

3. **DRAW CONCLUSIONS** How did bringing Germanic peoples into the Roman army sometimes backfire on Rome?

The Roman Empire and the Rise of Christianity 183

PLAN: 2-PAGE LESSON

OBJECTIVE

Identify the external and internal factors that brought the Western Roman Empire to an end.

CRITICAL THINKING SKILLS FOR LESSON 4.2

- Interpret Maps
- Draw Conclusions
- Explain
- Analyze Visuals

HISTORICAL THINKING FOR CHAPTER 6

Why did the Roman Empire become one of the most influential in history?

The Roman Empire eventually fell after dominating the Mediterranean for about 500 years. Lesson 4.2 discusses the fall of the Western Roman Empire.

Student eEdition online

Additional content for this lesson, including a painting, is available online.

BACKGROUND FOR THE TEACHER

The Goths According to legend, the Goths came from Scandinavia and crossed the Baltic Sea in the second century C.E. They defeated the Vandals and settled on the sea's southern shore. From there they migrated south, eventually making their way to the Black Sea. The Goths were ambitious in their conquests. Historians hypothesize that pressure from the Goths was what drove other Germanic tribes, such as the Lombards, Franks, Saxons, and Jutes, to the Roman Empire's western border. The Goths living between the Danube and Dniester rivers became known as the Visigoths, while those settled in modern-day Ukraine became known as the Ostrogoths.

INTRODUCE & ENGAGE

END OF EMPIRE

Ask students to recall what they have learned about the downfall of other ancient empires. Then ask them what they know about the collapse of the Soviet Union in modern times. **ASK:** What factors contribute to the fall of a powerful country or empire? *(Possible responses: The country or empire might have become too large to govern. The different ethnic groups in the region might demand their freedom and overthrow the government.)* Tell students that in this lesson they will learn about the fall of the Western Roman Empire.

TEACH

GUIDED DISCUSSION

1. **Explain** Why would multiple groups attacking the Western Roman Empire at the same time be challenging to defend against? *(The Roman army would have been spread thin in an effort to cover the places under attack. Additionally, the various groups had different motivations for attacking, so it would have been hard to predict where their forces were headed.)*

2. **Draw Conclusions** Why was the Visigoths' invasion of Rome a pivotal event in the fall of the Western Roman Empire? *(The Visigoths were the first to invade the city of Rome in more than 700 years. The attack revealed the city's vulnerability and led to multiple attacks from other German tribes.)*

ANALYZE VISUALS

Have students study the painting *The Course of Empire: Destruction* (available in the Student eEdition) and discuss what they see. Point out that many people think the painting depicts the sack of Rome by the Vandals. **ASK:** How do the buildings shown in the painting support that claim? *(The architectural style of the buildings, with their columns, arches, and monumental appearance support the claim.)* Then pose the Critical Viewing question and encourage students to share their ideas with the class.

ACTIVE OPTIONS

On Your Feet: Prevent the Fall of the Western Roman Empire
Organize the class into groups of four and instruct members to number off from one to four. Ask each student to think about and discuss as a group the following question: What, if anything, could the Romans have done to prevent the fall of the Western Roman Empire? After a time, call out a number and ask students with that number to report for the group.

| **NG Learning Framework: Support an Argument**
| **SKILL** Collaboration
| **KNOWLEDGE** Our Human Story

Invite students to pair up and choose one of the four reasons they believe was most responsible for Western Rome's decline: military, political, economic, or social. Have each pair research support for their choice. Ask all the pairs for each topic to get together to share their findings and then present the material to the class.

DIFFERENTIATE

STRIVING READERS

Create Sequence Chains Have students work in pairs to create a Sequence Chain that shows the events leading to the fall of the Western Roman Empire. Remind students to refer to the text to help them. Ask the pairs to discuss their Sequence Chains in a group so you can assess their comprehension.

PRE-AP

Create a Multimedia Presentation
Ask students to create multimedia presentations about the fall of Rome using photos, text, and audio. Point out that their presentations should describe the events that led to the last emperor of Rome leaving the throne. Invite volunteers to share their presentations with the class.

See the Chapter Planner for more strategies for differentiation.

HISTORICAL THINKING

ANSWERS

1. Alaric, the chief of the Visigoths, led his army into Rome, and he and his soldiers completely sacked Rome over a period of three days.

2. the Huns and the Visigoths

3. Answers will vary. Possible response: Some of the Germanic fighters turned against Rome and supported the invaders.

CRITICAL VIEWING (available in the Student eEdition) Answers will vary. Possible responses: the dark, ominous clouds; the fires; the collapsing bridge; the barbarians overrunning the city and its inhabitants; the headless classical statue

The Legacy of Ancient Rome

How, you may wonder, can an ancient civilization influence our lives today? Let us count the ways. From the words we speak to the laws that govern us, Rome's legacy is everywhere.

LANGUAGE AND LITERATURE

You may remember that the early Romans adapted the Etruscan alphabet to develop a Latin one. As the Roman Empire grew, Latin writing spread to northern Europe. Over time, five Romance languages—French, Spanish, Italian, Portuguese, and Romanian—developed from Latin. The English language uses the Latin alphabet, and many English words have Latin roots, including *subway* (*sub-* is a Latin prefix meaning "under") and *statement* (the suffix *-ment* is used to form a noun from a verb). Furthermore, the English language adopted Latin words such as *campus*, *census*, and *stadium*. Legal documents are rich with Latin text, including common expressions such as *ex post facto*, *per se*, and *quid pro quo*, and the language also makes appearances in science papers and memorial inscriptions.

The Romans also left a legacy in poetry. For the Romans, the ultimate poem was the epic. This long poetic form, based on Greek traditions, recounts a hero's adventures. The most celebrated Roman epic is the *Aeneid* by the poet **Virgil**. Written between 30 and 19 B.C.E.—during the early years of the Roman Empire—the work tells the story of Aeneas, a mythical Roman hero said to have fled to Italy from his Trojan homeland to become the legendary father of the Romans.

Public speaking, or **oratory**, was highly prized in ancient Rome as well. A young male patrician's education typically included training in the art of argument and persuasion. The Roman statesman **Cicero**, who served as a consul in 63 B.C.E., was one of Rome's greatest orators. Serious students of debate and public speaking still study his speeches today.

CRITICAL VIEWING The exterior of the Pantheon is relatively plain, but the interior, shown here, is lined with colored marble and is dominated by its great concrete dome. No one knows what method Roman engineers used to support the Pantheon's dome. The oculus, or "eye"—the opening you see here in the center of the dome—provides the structure's sole source of light. How would you describe the dome?

CRITICAL VIEWING When he served as a consul of the Roman Republic in 63 B.C.E., Cicero stood before the Senate and denounced Catiline, a senator who had plotted to overthrow the republic. The event is depicted in this 19th-century painting by Italian artist Cesare Maccari and shows Catiline sitting alone while Cicero attacks him. What details in the painting convey Cicero's skill as a public speaker?

MATHEMATICS AND PHILOSOPHY

Math may not come to mind when you think about ancient Rome, but the Roman numeral system was superior to any other that had been known in Europe up to that time. Roman numerals used the symbols I (1), V (5), X (10), L (50), C (100), and D (500). The symbol M, for 1,000, emerged after the fall of Rome. These numerals made simple math problems easier to solve. The Romans probably adopted the numerical system from the Etruscans. But while the Etruscans read their numbers from right to left, the Romans read theirs from left to right. Roman numerals are no longer used in mathematics—they were replaced by Arabic numerals around the 10th century—but are sometimes seen on public buildings, among many other uses.

Greek ideas inspired much of Roman philosophy. As you know, the Romans were practical people, so ethical and scientific arguments interested them more than theory and speculation. They were especially influenced by the Greek Stoic philosophy, which stressed civic duty and an acceptance of one's circumstances. Both ancient Greek and Roman philosophy taught moral and ethical principles—in particular, living a good and virtuous life. Similar values formed the basis of Judaism and Christianity and were central to the development of Western political thought. Their example had a deep influence on Thomas Jefferson, George Washington, and other founders of the United States.

ART, SCIENCE, AND TECHNOLOGY

The Romans took a realistic approach to art as well. Their statues and paintings portrayed subjects realistically. Like people today, many Romans decorated their homes with these works of art—although we usually display photos and paintings rather than heavy statues. In wealthier homes, mosaics and frescoes might have ornamented the floors and walls. Frescoes can be compared to modern murals and even some street art.

PLAN: 4-PAGE LESSON

OBJECTIVE

Describe ancient Rome's lasting legacy in the arts, sciences, religion, and government.

CRITICAL THINKING SKILLS FOR LESSON 4.3

- Draw Conclusions
- Make Inferences
- Evaluate
- Identify Main Ideas and Details
- Synthesize
- Analyze Cause and Effect
- Analyze Visuals

HISTORICAL THINKING FOR CHAPTER 6

Why did the Roman Empire become one of the most influential in history?

Roman language, literature, art, science, technology, religion, and law profoundly influenced the development of Western society. Lesson 4.3 discusses the lasting legacy of the Roman Empire.

BACKGROUND FOR THE TEACHER

Aqueducts Aqueducts are systems for providing water. Although the Roman aqueducts are the most famous water delivery system of the ancient world, they were not the first. Persia, India, and Egypt all had water supply systems in place hundreds of years before Rome. Still, the engineering mastery shown in the system of aqueducts that supplied the city of Rome with water was unmatched in the ancient world and would remain so until modern times.

INTRODUCE & ENGAGE

BRAINSTORM ROMAN LEGACIES

Tell students that there are legacies of Roman culture that are clearly visible to us every day. As a class, brainstorm objects, artwork, and ideas that derive, in part, from Rome. *(Possible responses: language, government, buildings, sculpture)*

TEACH

GUIDED DISCUSSION

1. **Make Inferences** Why is language one of the most influential legacies a culture or civilization can leave behind? *(Possible response: Language is the means by which ideas are passed from one person to another, from one culture to another. A language reflects a world view, and if that language survives, it carries a significant aspect of the culture into the future.)*

2. **Identify Main Ideas and Details** Which Roman values have become central to Western thought today? *(the Roman values of morality, virtue, and ethical behavior)*

ANALYZE VISUALS

Have students study the photo of the Pantheon. **ASK:** Why do you think the builders decided to make the oculus the sole source of light? *(Possible response: The light pouring down would inspire religious awe.)*

DIFFERENTIATE

ENGLISH LANGUAGE LEARNERS

Strengthen Vocabulary Ask students to write the word *oratory* in a Word Map and then write its definition and characteristics. Have students provide examples and non-examples of the word. After students complete the Word Map, ask them to create additional Word Maps for other words in the lesson they may be struggling with.

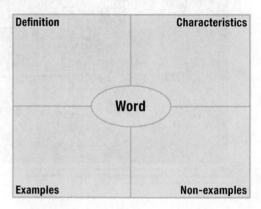

PRE-AP

Research the *Aeneid* Have students find an English translation of Virgil's *Aeneid*. Point out that the epic poem was written in hexameters, which is not a very widely used style in English because the language does not easily lend itself to the format. Ask them to scan the text and find a passage they like. Have them copy the passage and explain it to the class.

See the Chapter Planner for more strategies for differentiation.

Roman artists frequently carved a relief, a sculpture with figures raised against a flat background, on monuments, tombs, and important public buildings. The sculptures often featured soldiers in battle, heroes and heroic deeds, and symbols of patriotism—universal themes that modern reliefs convey, including those at the National World War II Memorial in Washington, D.C.

With their improved form of concrete, Romans constructed all-weather roads, bridges, and buildings that can still be seen today. European roads still follow Roman routes and sometimes cross original Roman bridges. When building streets for a new town, Roman city planners took its geography and climate into account. They usually designed cities in a grid pattern, creating a network of intersecting horizontal and vertical lines. Many modern towns and cities use this pattern.

Roman architects used their durable concrete to create monuments and aqueducts throughout the empire. The columns, arches, and domes they included in these structures are also seen in the U.S. Capitol and other buildings. And many of today's stadiums are modeled on the design for Rome's Colosseum. Even some of the sports played in today's arenas resemble Roman gladiator games, in which opponents were pitted against each other. Of course, while modern athletes sometimes get hurt during a game, they no longer fight to the death.

RELIGION AND GOVERNMENT

One of Rome's most enduring legacies is its impact on religion. You probably remember that Constantine the Great had legitimized Christianity in 313, and Theodosius made it the official religion of the Roman Empire in 380. With the legalization of their religion, Christians quickly organized and spread their faith throughout the empire. The city of Rome soon became the home of the Roman Catholic Church. The church would go on to exert an enormous influence on European and global history. Today Christianity is the largest religion in the world.

In the Judeo-Christian legal tradition, all people are equal before God and before the law. And both the Hebrew Bible and the New Testament state that, when

PRIMARY SOURCE

Table I. Proceedings Preliminary to Trial

1. If the plaintiff summons the defendant to court, the defendant shall go. If the defendant does not go, the plaintiff shall call a witness thereto. Only then the plaintiff shall seize the defendant.

7. If they agree not on terms, the parties shall state their case before the assembly in the meeting place or before the magistrate in the marketplace before noon. Both parties being present shall plead the case throughout together.

Table IX. Public Law

1–2. Laws of personal exception shall not be proposed. Laws concerning capital punishment of a citizen shall not be passed . . . except by the Greatest Assembly . . .

6. For anyone whomsoever to be put to death without a trial and unconvicted . . . is forbidden.

someone is accused of a crime, several witnesses must be brought forward to testify. A single witness is not enough to convict the person charged. The Romans had similar ideas, and these political concepts still influence the justice systems of many countries today, including that of the United States. The U.S. Constitution enforces equality before the law and declares that a person accused of a crime is innocent until proven guilty and has a right to a trial by a jury of peers, or fellow citizens.

The structure of the U.S. government also reflects elements of the Roman Republic's government, including representative assemblies and the system of checks and balances. And the Roman ideal of civic duty is encouraged in the United States and elsewhere. By the way, civic comes from the Latin word civis, meaning "relating to a citizen." It turns out that the Romans and their Latin language still influence the way we live today.

HISTORICAL THINKING

1. **READING CHECK** How has Latin influenced the English language?

2. **DRAW CONCLUSIONS** How might a philosophy that includes the idea of accepting one's circumstances help maintain the social order?

3. **MAKE INFERENCES** Why do you think many modern stadiums have been modeled on the Colosseum?

4. **EVALUTE** Why is it important to have several witnesses testify when someone is charged with a crime rather than rely on the testimony of a single witness?

Erected in Rome in 315 c.e., the Arch of Constantine celebrates the emperor's victory in 312 when he fought for control of the empire. At about 70 feet high, the monument is Rome's largest surviving triumphal arch.

BACKGROUND FOR THE TEACHER

City Planning City planning was a deliberate and thoughtful process in the Roman Empire. The preferred shape was a square. Wide avenues would run from the mid-point of each side directly across to the opposite side. Side streets were based off that grid. The forum was located near the center of Roman towns. Forums were open spaces where commerce was conducted and the business of politics took place. Structures such as shops and temples often appeared on the perimeter of the forum. Large cities might have multiple forums dedicated to specific activities such as finance or administration.

TEACH

GUIDED DISCUSSION

3. **Synthesize** Why are legal concepts such as a fair judge, a presumption of innocence, and equality under the law important? *(Possible response: All of these concepts are designed to protect the innocent and help ensure that the law is applied the same way for all people.)*

4. **Analyze Cause and Effect** Why is religion one of Rome's most enduring legacies? *(After Rome made Christianity the empire's official religion, it spread and eventually became the world's largest religion.)*

ANALYZE VISUALS

Discuss the photograph of the Arch of Constantine with students. **ASK:** What details of the arch are characteristic of Roman art and architecture? *(Possible responses: its size, columns, arches, and carved reliefs)*

ACTIVE OPTIONS

On Your Feet: Four Corners Post the headings in this lesson in the four corners of the classroom: Language and Literature; Mathematics and Philosophy; Art, Science, and Technology; Religion and Government. Have students choose the topic that interests them, go to the corner of their choice, and discuss the topic. Then have volunteers from each corner share their discussion with the class.

> **NG Learning Framework: Legacy Debate**
> **SKILLS** Communication, Collaboration
> **KNOWLEDGE** Our Human Story

Divide the class into four teams: Art and Language, Architecture and Technology, Law, and Religion. Give the teams some time to develop their reasons for why their Roman legacy is the most enduring aspect of Roman culture today. Then have the teams debate their ideas.

HISTORICAL THINKING

ANSWERS

1. English uses the Latin alphabet, many English words have Latin roots, and English adopted many Latin words.

2. Answers will vary. Possible response: The philosophy would encourage people to accept their status in society—no matter how lowly—and make them less likely to rebel or call for change.

3. Answers will vary. Possible response: With its many arched entrances, the Colosseum allowed crowds of people to enter and exit quickly, and the arrangement of seats around a central stage gave all spectators a good view of the action.

4. Answers will vary. Possible response: The witness may have a grudge against the person charged, and so his or her testimony would need to be corroborated.

CRITICAL VIEWING (Cicero painting) Answers will vary. Possible responses: Cicero's stance and gestures, the rapt attention of the senators

(Pantheon) Answers will vary. Possible responses: beautiful, awe-inspiring, a great achievement, perfect

VOCABULARY

Write a sentence to explain the connection between each of the following pairs of vocabulary words.

1. republic; dictator
2. patrician; plebeian
3. legionary; mercenary
4. gladiator; amphitheater
5. missionary; pilgrimage

READING STRATEGY
COMPARE AND CONTRAST

Use a comparison chart like the one below to compare and contrast the role and rights of men and women in Roman society. Then answer the questions.

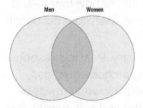

Men   Women

6. How did the roles of men and women differ?
7. What rights did men and women share?

MAIN IDEAS

Answer the following questions. Support your answers with evidence from the chapter.

8. How did the government of the Roman Republic differ from that of ancient Greece? LESSON 1.1
9. What surprise tactic did Hannibal use against the Romans during the Second Punic War? LESSON 1.2
10. What three classes made up the social order in the Roman Republic? LESSON 1.3

188 CHAPTER 6

11. What did Julius Caesar do soon after he gained control of Rome? LESSON 2.1
12. Why did the emperor Hadrian build a wall in Britain? LESSON 2.2
13. How did the Roman Empire connect its far-flung lands? LESSON 2.3
14. How did the apostle Paul spread the story and teachings of Jesus? LESSON 3.3
15. What new type of government did Diocletian put in place? LESSON 4.1
16. How did the declining economy undermine the defense of the Western Roman Empire in the 300s and 400s? LESSON 4.2

HISTORICAL THINKING

Answer the following questions. Support your answers with evidence from the chapter.

17. EVALUATE How did Cincinnatus demonstrate the Roman virtue of civic duty?
18. MAKE PREDICTIONS What do you think might have happened if Julius Caesar had restored the republic?
19. SYNTHESIZE Why was concrete a critical material in the Roman Empire?
20. COMPARE AND CONTRAST How did the lives of slaves differ from those of patricians and plebeians in Roman society?
21. DRAW CONCLUSIONS What did Jesus' teachings have in common with democratic values?
22. ANALYZE CAUSE AND EFFECT What happened as a result of the division of the empire and the political and cultural shift toward the east?
23. MAKE INFERENCES Why do you think the Romans embraced the Greek epic poem?
24. FORM AND SUPPORT OPINIONS Do you think the Roman people were better off during the time of the republic or the empire, or were their lives similar during both periods? Explain your answer.

INTERPRET CHARTS

Study the chart below, which compares the government of the Roman Republic with that of the United States. Then answer the questions that follow.

Roman Republic vs. United States

Government	Roman Republic	United States
EXECUTIVE BRANCH	Led by two consuls elected for a one-year term; led government and army; could veto each other's decisions; took advice from the Senate	Led by a president elected for a four-year term; heads government and military; has veto power over legislation; takes advice from Cabinet members
LEGISLATIVE BRANCH	• Senate of 300 members • Senate advised consuls and set policies • Plebeian assembly made laws and elected representatives	• Congress made up of Senate and House of Representatives • Senate of 100 members • House of Representatives of 435 members	• Laws approved by both groups • Congress with power to override a presidential veto
JUDICIAL BRANCH	• Eight judges oversaw courts and governed provinces	• Supreme Court of nine justices	• Supreme Court interprets the Constitution and federal law
LEGAL CODE	Twelve Tables basis of Roman law • Twelve Tables established laws protecting citizens' rights • Edicts made by magistrates	U.S. Constitution basis of U.S. law • Constitution established individual rights of citizens and powers of government	• Congress has the power to propose and pass amendments to the Constitution

25. What legislative check on the executive branch is part of the U.S. government but was not part of the Roman Republic's government?
26. How is the Constitution similar to the Twelve Tables?

ANALYZE SOURCES

According to the Gospel of Matthew, Jesus gathered his disciples on a mountain, where he "opened his mouth and taught them." In this excerpt from the Sermon on the Mount, as the teachings came to be known, Jesus addresses persecuted Christians. Read the excerpt and answer the question that follows.

> Blessed are those who are persecuted for righteousness' sake, for theirs is the kingdom of heaven. Blessed are you when men revile [insult] you and persecute you and utter all kinds of evil against you falsely on my account. Rejoice and be glad, for your reward is great in heaven, for so men persecuted the prophets who were before you.
>
> —Matthew 5:10–11

27. What impact do you think these teachings had on those who suffered persecution?

CONNECT TO YOUR LIFE

28. EXPLANATORY Just as many diverse people searching for security and opportunity in ancient times became Roman citizens, many people today want to leave their homeland for a chance at a better life in other countries. Do you think today's immigrants to the United States should be allowed to settle here? Or should they be kept from entering the country? Write a brief essay explaining your views on immigration today.

TIPS

• Review how foreigners were regarded by Romans at various times during the republic and the empire. What did the Romans gain and suffer in their dealings with foreigners?
• Conduct research on our country's policy toward immigration today, and consider the advantages and disadvantages of admitting immigrants.
• Use two or three vocabulary terms from the chapter in your explanation.
• Provide a concluding statement that summarizes your views on immigration.

The Roman Empire and the Rise of Christianity 189

VOCABULARY ANSWERS

Answers will vary.

1. Possible response: Roman citizens voted for the leaders in their republic, but during a crisis, they appointed a dictator who was granted complete authority for a time.
2. Possible response: In the Roman Republic, a patrician was a member of a higher social class than a plebeian.
3. Possible response: The Roman army was manned by professional soldiers known as legionaries and also sometimes by paid soldiers, or mercenaries.
4. Possible response: Gladiators in ancient Rome used to fight animals and other men in an amphitheater.
5. Possible response: During Roman times, early missionaries traveled to other countries to do religious work, while, later in the empire, others took pilgrimages to visit important Christian sites.

READING STRATEGY ANSWERS

Men   **Women**

total authority

could vote, hold public office, and perform important ceremonies

considered to be citizens

could divorce and remarry

could not own property or run a business

performed daily domestic chores

6. Men had total authority in the family and could vote, hold public office, and perform important ceremonies. The women performed all household duties and instructed their daughters in the domestic chores to prepare them for marriage.
7. Both were citizens and could divorce and remarry.

MAIN IDEAS ANSWERS

8. Rome had an indirect democracy, while ancient Greece had a direct democracy.

9. He crossed the Alps when he invaded Italy and took the Romans by surprise.

10. the patricians, the plebeians, and slaves

11. Caesar declared himself dictator for life.

12. to keep out invaders

13. by building a vast network of roads

14. Paul traveled through much of the Roman Empire, personally presenting Jesus' message, and wrote letters to new Christian communities.

15. Diocletian set up a rule by four emperors called a tetrarchy.

16. Government revenues could not keep up with the cost of defending the imperial frontiers, which meant that money was not always available to pay Roman troops. The soldiers didn't fight if they weren't paid.

HISTORICAL THINKING ANSWERS

17. Possible response: When called upon by his government to serve as dictator, Cincinnatus answered the call. After his job was done, he relinquished his power.

18. Possible response: There might never have been a Roman Empire, and its roads and structures would not have been built. The Roman influence might not have spread as far as it did, and so its legacy might have been less enduring.

19. Possible response: Roman engineers developed a more durable form of concrete, and it was used to build the empire's roads, aqueducts, and monuments. All of these structures united the empire and instilled pride in Romans and awe in outsiders.

20. Possible response: Slaves were not citizens and had no rights. They were forced to perform whatever work their masters chose.

21. Possible response: Jesus maintained that all people were equal before God.

22. Possible response: The western empire weakened and eventually fell.

23. Possible response: The Romans wanted their civilization to be compared with that of the Greeks and to have heroes associated with their founding and empire.

24. Possible response: Their lives were similar under both the republic and the empire because, even though the republic had a more democratic form of government, the patricians were still largely in charge.

INTERPRET CHARTS ANSWERS

25. The U.S. Congress has the power to override the presidential veto.

26. Both protect the individual rights of citizens.

ANALYZE SOURCES ANSWER

27. Answers will vary. Possible response: The teachings probably gave hope to and inspired courage in those who faced persecution.

CONNECT TO YOUR LIFE ANSWER

28. Essays will vary but should contain main ideas and relevant supporting details to explain the students' views on immigration.

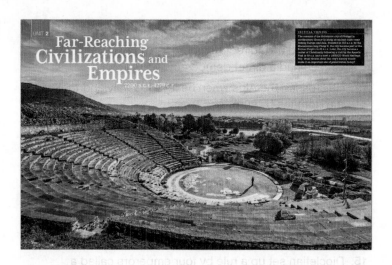

STRATEGY 1

Set a Purpose for Reading

Before beginning a lesson, help students set a purpose for reading by prompting them to read the title, main idea statement, and headings. Encourage them also to look at the visuals and read the captions. Tell students to write a question they expect the lesson to answer. If needed, show them how to turn the main idea statement into a question. After they have read the lesson, instruct students to answer the question in writing.

Use with All Lessons *For example, a question for Lesson 1.1 might be: How did Hinduism spread throughout India and the world?*

STRATEGY 2

Connect Main Ideas and Details

As they read each lesson, encourage students to work in pairs to complete a Main Ideas and Details Chart. Point out the kinds of details (facts, dates, events, reasons) that support main ideas. Then ask each pair to alternate reading paragraphs aloud and writing down main ideas and details. Tell them this process will help them identify and remember the most important information in the lesson. Ask volunteers to share their completed chart with other student pairs and discuss the similarities and differences in their charts.

Use with All Lessons

STRATEGY 3

Use Text Evidence to Draw Conclusions

Tell students that when they read they will often need to analyze the evidence in the text and use their own judgment to form an idea or draw a conclusion. When they draw a conclusion, they are developing an idea as the next logical step using the information they have been given. Practice drawing simple conclusions that are familiar to students, such as Evidence: the guest room has been cleaned, fresh towels are laid out, your grandma's favorite pillow is lying on the bed, and Conclusion: your grandma is coming to visit. After students read each lesson, pair them and have them write three examples of evidence from the text and a conclusion they draw based on the evidence.

Use with All Lessons

STRATEGY 1

Assign Writing Partners

If a student with a disability struggles to produce an assigned piece of writing, have another student or a teacher's aide work with the student to create the assignment. The student with the disability can dictate his or her thoughts to the other student or teacher's aide. The pair can then work together to revise the student's writing and ensure it states the student's ideas clearly.

Use with All Lessons

STRATEGY 2

Use Echo Reading

Point out that the Main Idea statements all relate to important ideas and events that impacted societies in India, China, Korea, Vietnam, and Japan from about 1200 B.C.E. to 200 B.C.E. Pair students with proficient readers who can read aloud the Main Idea statement at the beginning of each lesson. Tell the partner to "echo" the statement and then restate it in his or her own words to check comprehension.

Use with All Lessons *Pairs might continue to echo read selected paragraphs or entire sections of each lesson.*

STRATEGY 1

Build Vocabulary

Help students at **All Proficiencies** learn unfamiliar words by introducing synonyms. Display difficult words paired with more familiar words, as with these from Lesson 1.1:

> evolved into / turned into
> coined / created
> depict / show
> depiction / portrayal
> purifying / cleaning

Tell students that when they encounter a confusing or difficult word, such as *coined*, they should try to replace it with a word they are familiar with, such as *created*. Guide students to use a thesaurus to practice looking up and substituting words to find a synonym that makes sense in the context of the sentence.

Use with All Lessons *Students at the **Advanced** level could help students at the **Beginning** or **Intermediate** level find appropriate synonyms. Look for opportunities to use synonyms and a thesaurus to aid comprehension.*

STRATEGY ②
Review Transitional Words

To help students put events in chronological order and summarize what they read, write these transitional words on the board: *first, next, then, also, while, later, earlier, meanwhile, whenever, simultaneously, during, following, before, afterward,* and *finally.* Direct students at the **Beginning** and **Intermediate** levels to work together to write a series of sentences that tell what happens in each lesson. Encourage them to add transitional words to their sentences to tell about the time order of events. Prompt students at the **Advanced** level to construct a paragraph that summarizes the lesson. Encourage them to use a variety of transitional words and sentence structures.

Use with All Lessons

STRATEGY ③
Use Paired Reading

Pair students at the **Intermediate** and **Advanced** levels and have them read passages from the text aloud.

1. Partner 1 reads a passage. Partner 2 retells the passage in his or her own words.
2. Partner 2 reads a different passage. Partner 1 retells it.
3. Pairs repeat the process, switching roles.

Use with All Lessons

GIFTED & TALENTED

STRATEGY ①
Write a News Report

Instruct students to choose one of the societies presented in the chapter and conduct online research to learn more about one of the achievements made by this society, such as Aryabhata's discovery that Earth is round and orbits the sun (Lesson 1.2) or the invention of paper (Lesson 2.3). Tell students to write a news report about this achievement as if they are journalists writing a feature for a magazine or newspaper. Remind students that news reports have a catchy headline, begin with the most important information, and usually answer the questions *who, what, where, when, why,* and *how.* Invite students to make a class newspaper from their reports.

Use with All Lessons

STRATEGY ②
Compare and Contrast Two Societies

Direct students to choose two of the societies presented in the chapter and create a comparison chart or a Venn diagram listing the similarities and differences. Encourage them to conduct online research and use the facts in the text to compare and contrast the two societies. Have them present their graphic organizers to the class to help other students understand the two societies.

Use with All Lessons

PRE-AP

STRATEGY ①
Explore Short- and Long-Term Impacts

Point out that the text in Lesson 1.3 says that historians "hardly remember the Chola kingdom at all." Encourage students to consider what ancient societies left behind that impacts their place in history. For example, does a written history exist, such as the grand historian Siam Qian created for Chinese history? Invite them to explain how a society can leave a lasting impact without a written history. Tell students to choose one of the societies presented in the chapter and write a report explaining its short- or long-term impact on history.

Use with All Lessons

STRATEGY ②
Report on the Silk Roads

Direct students to gather information from library or online sources to write a report about the different caravans of traders that traveled the ancient trade routes of the Silk Roads. Suggest that they focus on specific details, such as the dangers the traders faced and why they were willing to face them, the distance they traveled and how long it took to travel that distance, how they communicated with traders who spoke different languages, and how they brought back ideas as well as goods. Invite students to share their reports with the class.

Use with Lesson 2.2

HISTORICAL THINKING How did societies in East and South Asia influence one another's cultures over time?

SECTION 1 **Indian Cultures and Dynasties**
SECTION 2 **China's Han and Tang Empires**
SECTION 3 **East and Southeast Asian Kingdoms**

CRITICAL VIEWING
Mount Fuji, the highest mountain in Japan, is located on the island of Honshu. Based on details in the photo, why do you think many Japanese people consider Mount Fuji to be sacred?

196 CHAPTER 7

INTRODUCE THE PHOTOGRAPH

MOUNT FUJI

Have students study the photograph of Mount Fuji and the small city in the valley below it. **ASK:** What do you think living in the shadow of an active volcano might be like? (*Possible response: I might live in fear that the volcano will one day erupt.*) Explain that while Mount Fuji is still considered active by geologists, it has not erupted since 1707. Today, it is part of a national park and also has been named a World Heritage site by the United Nations Educational, Scientific, and Cultural Organization (UNESCO). World Heritage sites are those that have "outstanding universal value," according to UNESCO. Tell students that in this chapter they will learn more about how geography and other aspects of this region impacted the development of Japan and other societies in East and South Asia.

SHARE BACKGROUND

Mount Fuji is known by a handful of other names, including Fuji-san and Fujiyama. No one knows for certain how the mountain got its name, but some believe that it comes from a combination of an Ainu term for fire and the Japanese word *san*, which means mountain. Tradition also holds that the mountain was created by an earthquake in 286 B.C.E. However, geologists say that it is more likely that the mountain top is around 2.6 million years old, while its base is much older. Mount Fuji is made up of more than one volcano, each of which topped the others over the course of its history. The newest volcano is named as such—Shin Fuji, which means "New Fuji." As the photo caption states, the Japanese consider the mountain to be sacred. At its peak is a shrine to which thousands of Japanese hike every year.

CRITICAL VIEWING Answers will vary. Possible responses might mention the height of the mountain in comparison to the land around it or the cloud cover, or the fact that ancient people likely did not have an explanation for its eruptions.

HISTORICAL THINKING QUESTION

How did societies in East and South Asia influence one another's cultures over time?

On Your Feet: Team Word Webbing Arrange students in groups of four or five. Hand each group a sheet of paper containing the following question: What cultural elements of a society might influence the development of another society? Have the first students in each group write an idea with a short explanation and pass the paper clockwise to the next student. Each student in the group then adds at least one answer. Students circulate the paper until they run out of answers. Then direct each group to choose what they think are the best ideas. Call on volunteers from each group to share their list with the class.

KEY DATES FOR CHAPTER 7

206 B.C.E.	Liu Bang establishes the Han dynasty.
139 B.C.E.	Zhang Qian is sent as an envoy by Emperor Wu on what becomes the Silk Roads.
90 B.C.E.	Sima Qian completes *Records of the Grand Historian*, or *Shiji*.
1 C.E.	Hinduism reaches Nepal, Bhutan, and Sri Lanka.
200 C.E.	Paper is commonly used for books.
320 C.E.	The Gupta dynasty begins.
c. 400 C.E.	The Iron Pillar of Delhi is built.
622 C.E.	Prince Shotoku of Japan dies.
668 C.E.	Korea is unified by the Silla and the Tang.

INTRODUCE THE READING STRATEGY

DRAW CONCLUSIONS

Explain to students that drawing conclusions about an event or a series of events involves using evidence in order to make a judgment. Go to the Chapter Review and preview the chart with students. As they read the chapter, have students use the chart to record evidence from the text that reflects the effects of Han and Tang China on Korea, Vietnam, and Japan.

INTRODUCE CHAPTER VOCABULARY

KEY VOCABULARY

SECTION 1

Hindu-Arabic numerals	metallurgy	omnipotence
tribute		

SECTION 2

abdicate	bioarchaeologist	celibate
census	chronicle	cosmopolitan
delegation	garrison town	maritime
treason		

SECTION 3

archipelago	clan	depose
regent		

WORD MAPS

As students read the chapter, ask them to complete a Word Map for each Key Vocabulary word. Tell them to write the word in the oval and, as they encounter the word in the chapter, complete the Word Map. Model an example using the graphic organizer below.

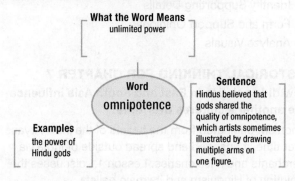

What the Word Means
unlimited power

Word
omnipotence

Examples
the power of Hindu gods

Sentence
Hindus believed that gods shared the quality of omnipotence, which artists sometimes illustrated by drawing multiple arms on one figure.

Developments in Hinduism

Have your beliefs changed as you've grown older? What influenced those changes? The religious beliefs brought by the Indo-Aryans changed over time and these changes evolved into the religion we know as Hinduism.

Hindus make pilgrimages to Varanasi, an ancient city on the Ganges River, where they bathe in the river's water, which is believed to have purifying powers.

CRITICAL VIEWING Most Hindu temples in India are dedicated to one deity. In southern India, the towers of a temple have a pyramid shape and are decorated with sculptures of mythological figures. The Meenakshi Temple (far left) in the city of Madurai is one of the oldest Hindu temples in India. Temples in the United States are often dedicated to multiple deities. They serve as both places of worship and community centers. Today, there are more than 450 Hindu temples in the United States. The BAPS Shri Swaminarayan Mandir (left), located in Atlanta, Georgia, is the largest Hindu temple in the United States. How are the the two temples alike? How are they different?

DEVELOPMENTS AND CENTRAL IDEAS

As you've read previously, the Rig Veda told stories of Indo-Aryan gods and goddesses. Hinduism grew out of these Indo-Aryan beliefs and developed slowly over many centuries. However, the term *Hinduism* wasn't used until the 19th century when the British of colonial India coined the term to refer to traditions and practices not associated with Islam, Jainism, or Christianity. Unlike Buddhism, Hinduism has no single founder, and it doesn't have an agreed upon set of beliefs. Because Hindus worship different Hindu deities, many people didn't consider themselves to be members of a single religious community until the 1800s.

The Upanishads, which you read about in an earlier chapter, introduced the concept of **Brahman** as a universal spirit. Hindus believe Brahman created the universe and exists in everything—a belief that became central to Hinduism. As new scriptures such as the Sanskrit epics the *Mahabharata* and the *Ramayana* appeared, Hindus began to see all Hindu deities as expressions of Brahman. Vishnu and Shiva became two of the most venerated, or revered, deities. These deities take many avatars, or forms with various names. In some cases, artists depict them as having four or more arms. This depiction represents **omnipotence**, or unlimited power, and the ability to overcome evil by performing multiple feats at once.

Hindus believe the human soul is eternal and that after death people undergo reincarnation, in which their souls are reborn in different bodies over different life cycles. The things people do during their lifetimes affect their karma (the sum of their good and bad actions) and determine the kind of life into which each person will be reborn. The ultimate goal of a Hindu is to end this cycle of birth and rebirth by living selflessly and overcoming material desires.

RELIGIOUS PRACTICES

Hindu worship has both public and private aspects. Temples are the center of public worship. Hindus carry out private worship in their homes, where they express devotion to a personal deity.

Hindu rites are further classified into daily worship in the home, worship during religious holidays, and pilgrimages. Each year many Hindus travel to the Ganges River to bathe in its holy waters. They believe the river has purifying powers that will wash away sins. They also scatter the cremated remains of their loved ones there, believing the waters will elevate the loved ones' karma and assist the dead in reincarnation.

Pilgrims from around the world visit temples, shrines, and palaces in Varanasi, one of the oldest cities in the world. Located on the banks of the Ganges, it is revered as the home of Shiva. Varanasi is also an important city for India's Muslims and has ancient Buddhist ruins as well. The city is also a center of learning for those who study ancient Sanskrit texts.

THE SPREAD OF HINDUISM

The beliefs and rituals that would later be called Hinduism were primarily practiced in India. By 1 c.e., merchants and missionaries had carried the religion into present-day Nepal, Bhutan, and Sri Lanka. From there, they continued to spread Hinduism east throughout Southeast Asia.

Today Hinduism is growing in Britain, the United States, and Canada as immigrants from India move to these areas. There are approximately one million Hindus living in Britain and two million living in the United States. As the third largest religion in the world, after Christianity and Islam, Hinduism has nearly one billion practitioners worldwide.

HISTORICAL THINKING

1. **READING CHECK** What new religious concept about Brahman changed Hindus' beliefs about Hindu deities?

2. **DESCRIBE** Describe private and public worship in the Hindu religion and explain the role of pilgrimages.

3. **COMPARE AND CONTRAST** What are some of the similarities and differences between Hindu temples in India and the United States? Why are they different?

PLAN: 2-PAGE LESSON

OBJECTIVE

Learn how the texts, practices, and beliefs of Hinduism evolved and how Hinduism spread in India and around the world.

CRITICAL THINKING SKILLS FOR LESSON 1.1

- Describe
- Compare and Contrast
- Identify Supporting Details
- Form and Support Opinions
- Analyze Visuals

HISTORICAL THINKING FOR CHAPTER 7

How did societies in East and South Asia influence one another's cultures over time?

Hinduism originated from the beliefs of the Indo-Aryans. Over time, it changed and spread outside of India via merchants and missionaries. Lesson 1.1 discusses the evolution of Hinduism and its main beliefs.

BACKGROUND FOR THE TEACHER

The Ganges The Ganges River begins in the Himalaya Mountains at the border of Tibet and empties into the Bay of Bengal. Even though the Ganges is somewhat short and, at points, slow moving and shallow, the area around it supports hundreds of millions of Indians and Bangladeshis. During the snow melt and monsoon seasons, there is great danger of flooding, particularly in the delta region. Cyclones in this region during monsoon season have killed hundreds of thousands of people. At one time, the basin area of the Ganges was heavily forested and home to many animals, including rhinoceroses and lions. Today, these areas are farmland, and there are few large animals. The river supports many types of fish and birds and is even home to the mostly sightless Ganges river dolphin, which is endangered due to human activities.

INTRODUCE & ENGAGE

DISCUSS INFLUENCES ON BELIEFS AND VIEWPOINTS

Direct students to the lesson introduction, where the text asks about how their beliefs have changed as they've gotten older. **ASK:** What typically drives changes in beliefs? Is it things you've read? Is it things you've seen or heard? *(Possible responses: online news; printed media, such as newspapers or magazines; televised debates; school lectures; or beliefs of family or friends)* Explain that Hinduism originated out of the stories of the Rig Veda but gradually grew and changed as new scriptures were written. Tell students that in this lesson they will learn more about these changes and how they contributed to the development of a world religion.

TEACH

GUIDED DISCUSSION

1. **Identify Supporting Details** Why did the British begin to refer to the beliefs and practices of some Indians as Hinduism? *(They were distinguishing them from the beliefs and practices of Islam, Jainism, and Christianity.)*

2. **Form and Support Opinions** Why do you think merchants and missionaries spread the Hindu religion to other places? *(Possible response: They wanted to gain more followers through conversion.)*

ANALYZE VISUALS

Have students examine the photographs of the Hindu temples in India and the United States. **ASK:** Based on what you see, how do you think these elaborate buildings were constructed? *(Possible response: They must have a strong framework of wood, metal, or stone underneath the carvings and multiple layers for support.)*

ACTIVE OPTIONS

On Your Feet: Roundtable Discussion Ask students to reread the information about Hindu religious practices. Then arrange the class into groups of four and ask them to discuss the following question: What are the principle differences between public and private worship? Have each group discuss what is involved in each type of practice and which aspects of public worship unite all Hindus. At the end, ask a volunteer from each group to summarize the main points of their discussion.

> **NG Learning Framework: Hindu Pilgrimages Encyclopedia Entry**
> SKILL Communication
> KNOWLEDGE Our Human Story

Have students research and write an encyclopedia entry about the religious pilgrims who visit revered Hindu sites such as Varanasi. Ask students to find out why people make the pilgrimage and what they take with them when they go. Invite students to read their entries aloud to the class.

DIFFERENTIATE

STRIVING READERS

Summarize Using a Concept Cluster Help pairs summarize the lesson by creating a Concept Cluster with the lesson title in the center oval and the section headings in the smaller ones. As students read each section, tell them to record key facts and ideas on the spokes.

PRE-AP

Explore the Spread of Hinduism Instruct students to conduct research to write a short essay that examines the spread of Hinduism to other parts of the world from India. Ask them to include a world outline map to show the spread.

See the Chapter Planner for more strategies for differentiation.

HISTORICAL THINKING

ANSWERS

1. Brahman as a universal spirit; changed beliefs as they saw all Hindu deities as expressions of Brahman

2. Public worship: at a temple; Private worship: at home with a shrine to a personal god; Pilgrimages: one of three different categories of rites, Hindus travel to the Ganges or to Varanasi

3. India: dedicated to a single god; United States: dedicated to multiple, unrelated gods. The Hindu community in the United States is diverse and one temple must support the worship of different gods. Hindu immigrants use temples as community centers. Reasons: U.S. temples are not as old; immigrants may not have had the finances to build elaborate structures.

CRITICAL VIEWING Both: elaborate carvings and a pyramidal shape; temple in India: colorful; temple in the United States: all white, separate spires and domes

The Gupta Dynasty

Who first discovered that the planet Earth is round and orbits around the sun? Where did the numbers you use in math come from? You might be surprised to learn that these ideas first came from India during the Gupta dynasty.

RISE OF THE GUPTAS

After the fall of the Maurya Empire, India experienced a period of upheaval that lasted for approximately 500 years. During this time, various dynasties arose in different regions of South Asia. One of the most powerful was the Gupta dynasty, which controlled much of northern India between 320 and 600 C.E.

An admirer of the earlier Maurya Empire, the founder of the Gupta dynasty, **Chandragupta I**, took the name Chandragupta from the Maurya founder and governed from the former capital at Pataliputra. Unlike the Maurya rulers, Gupta rulers followed Hindu practices and sponsored the building of temples at which Brahmin priests led public worship. However, they tolerated other religions and included Buddhists among their court advisors.

Chandragupta I ruled the Gupta dynasty from 320 to 330. Both he and his son Samudragupta conquered neighboring kingdoms to expand the northern territory. However, they allowed the defeated kings to continue ruling their kingdoms as long as they provided military assistance or paid **tribute**, a tax required of conquered people.

This large-scale sculpture in the Udayagiri Caves dates to the early fifth century. It depicts the myth of Vishnu in the form of an avatar, rescuing goddess Earth from the cosmic ocean.

Gupta rulers divided the land into provinces governed by high imperial officers. This decentralized power gave more autonomy to the provinces, but they eventually began to seek independence. These internal struggles were compounded by foreign invasions. By approximately 600, invasions and independence movements had so weakened the dynasty that the Gupta were unable to retain control, and the dynasty fell apart after 300 years of rule.

RELIGION REFLECTED IN ART, LITERATURE, AND ARCHITECTURE

The classical Gupta dynasty is widely considered to have been the golden age in India when architecture and art flourished. Before the Gupta, temples were built of wood or brick, but Gupta dynasty builders constructed freestanding temples out of stone. Cave temples embellished with Hindu paintings and sculptures were also carved into sandstone hills at Udayagiri.

The Gupta rulers supported writers as well. The work of poet and playwright **Kalidasa**, considered the greatest of India's Sanskrit authors, reflects the sophisticated values of the Gupta dynasty and makes use of the literary possibilities of the Sanskrit language. In one of his poems, he wrote: "Yesterday is but a dream, Tomorrow is only a vision. But today well lived makes every yesterday a dream of happiness, and every tomorrow a vision of hope." Little is known about Kalidasa's life, and yet he had a significant impact on the work of writers who followed him.

ADVANCES IN MATHEMATICS, ASTRONOMY, AND METALLURGY

The oldest representation of the zero as a symbol was found on an ancient manuscript from the Gupta period, and a Gupta-era mathematician developed rules in rhymed verse for multiplying and dividing by zero. Independently, on the other side of the globe, the Maya of present-day southern Mexico and Central America started using the zero at roughly the same time.

The great mathematician and astronomer Aryabhata wrote books in which he furthered development of the decimal system, calculated pi to 3.1416, and calculated area and volume. One of his books explained that Earth is round and rotates around the sun. **Hindu-Arabic numerals** (1, 2, 3, . . . etc.) also came from Sanskrit of this period. These numerals are often called *Arabic* because Arab traders brought them to the west where they eventually replaced Roman numerals.

Gupta **metallurgy**, metal technology, also improved during this period. The Gupta imported gold to create beautifully crafted coins and used iron to construct tall pillars, such as the Iron Pillar of Delhi. This 23-foot tall pillar, erected around 400 C.E., is made of iron so pure that it has never rusted. It would be more than 1,000 years before metalworkers in other parts of the world would have the skill to create such a large object out of iron.

Roman, Sanskrit, and Western Numerals		
Roman first used c. 900-800 B.C.E.	Sanskrit first used c. 460 B.C.E.	Western Arabic today
	•	0
I	~	1
II	ℛ	2
III	३	3
IV	४	4
V	५	5
VI	६	6
VII	ℓ	7
VIII	८	8
IX	९	9

HISTORICAL THINKING

1. **READING CHECK** Describe two advancements in literature and two advancements in mathematics during the Gupta dynasty.

2. **ANALYZE CAUSE AND EFFECT** What factors caused the decline and fall of the Gupta dynasty?

3. **INTERPRET CHARTS** How do the numerals in Sanskrit compare to our numerals today? Why did the Hindu-Arabic numerals replace the Roman numerals in the west?

PLAN: 2-PAGE LESSON

OBJECTIVE

Identify how literature, art, mathematics, and science flourished during India's Gupta dynasty.

CRITICAL THINKING SKILLS FOR LESSON 1.2

- Analyze Cause and Effect
- Interpret Charts
- Compare and Contrast
- Draw Conclusions

HISTORICAL THINKING FOR CHAPTER 7

How did societies in East and South Asia influence one another's cultures over time?

The founder of the Gupta dynasty, Chandragupta I, admired the earlier Maurya dynasty. Lesson 1.2 tells how he took the name of this dynasty and then built his own great empire.

Student eEdition online

Additional content for this lesson, including a primary source, is available online.

BACKGROUND FOR THE TEACHER

Samudragupta The son of Chandragupta I, Samudragupta ruled the Gupta dynasty beginning in 330 C.E. He was selected by his father over many other choices for the throne. Writers and artists of the period portrayed Samudragupta as a hero and an ideal king who was muscular and had many battle wounds. He was well known for his heroic conquests and, at his most powerful, ruled all of the Ganges valley. Samudragupta was also said to be a poet and a musician who played the harp. Toward the end of his rule, he brought back the Vedic ritual of horse sacrifice, in which a fine horse was selected to roam free across the land while being protected by a royal guard. If the horse entered another country's territory, its ruler had to fight to defend the territory. If the horse avoided capture, it was returned to the capital, where it was sacrificed with a great deal of ceremony. The purpose of the ritual was to celebrate the king but also to bring prosperity and fertility to the people.

INTRODUCE & ENGAGE

DISCUSS THE DAWNING OF THE GUPTA EMPIRE

Ask students to recall what they learned previously about the Maurya Empire. *(Students may recall that it was an Indian empire that controlled the Ganges region and was ruled by a strong government. It was well known for its art and for the last emperor, Ashoka.)* As a class, discuss how a new Indian dynasty, the Gupta, arose in 320 C.E., 500 years after the fall of the Maurya Empire. Then explain that even though the Maurya had fallen 500 years earlier, the first Gupta ruler, Chandragupta I, took the name of their founder. In this lesson, students will learn about the Gupta dynasty and its achievements in the arts and sciences.

TEACH

GUIDED DISCUSSION

1. **Compare and Contrast** How did the religious practices of the Gupta differ from those of the Maurya? *(The Gupta were Hindu; the Maurya were Buddhist.)*

2. **Draw Conclusions** What led to the Gupta's downfall? *(Possible response: They allowed the provinces too much power, which led to independence movements.)*

INTERPRET CHARTS

Have students look at the chart in the lesson. **ASK:** Which numerals are the most concrete? Why? *(Possible response: Modern numerals in the West are the most concrete because they cannot be mistaken for letters, such as Roman numeral one for the letter I or Sanskrit numeral four for the letter y.)*

ACTIVE OPTIONS

On Your Feet: Jigsaw Strategy Organize students into four groups and have students from each group research four areas of Gupta achievements: architecture, literature, mathematics, and science. Have each group create a simplified summary of its research. Regroup students into four new groups so each group has at least one person from each of the four original groups. Have students in the new group take turns sharing the simplified summary they created in their original groups.

| **NG Learning Framework: Design an Infographic**
| **ATTITUDE** Curiosity
| **SKILL** Problem-Solving

Have students read the primary source from the *Ramayana* (available in the Student eEdition). **ASK:** What traits does Rama demonstrate in this excerpt? *(Possible responses: compassion, empathy)* Remind them that this epic poem tells the story of the god Rama. Have them research more about this Hindu god, such as his character traits and how he is portrayed visually and in text. Then have them research more quotations from the *Ramayana* that demonstrate his character traits. Have students create an infographic in which they display their research about Rama and the quotes that they found. Tell students to explain how each of the quotes demonstrates the character traits they have described.

DIFFERENTIATE

STRIVING READERS

Understand Main Ideas Check students' understanding of the main ideas in the lesson by asking them to complete the following statements:

- Unlike the Maurya, the Gupta practiced Hinduism or Buddhism. *(Hinduism)*
- The founder of the Gupta dynasty was Chandragupta I or Samudragupta. *(Chandragupta I)*
- Gupta rulers built temples out of wood or stone. *(stone)*
- A mathematician in the Gupta era calculated the decimal value of pi or zero. *(pi)*

PRE-AP

Research and Write a Report Ask students to write three questions about the temple architecture of the Gupta dynasty and to think of how forms of architecture and building materials can characterize a culture. Tell them to use a variety of sources to help them answer their questions and to write a report of their findings, including how building during this period differed from earlier techniques and materials. Invite them to read their reports to the class.

See the Chapter Planner for more strategies for differentiation.

HISTORICAL THINKING

ANSWERS

1. Literature: The *Mahabharata* and *Ramayana* were written down; Kalidasa wrote his poems and plays. Mathematics: The numerals we use today were developed, including the concept of zero; Aryabhata learned that Earth rotates around the sun.

2. local provinces seeking independence and outside invasions

3. The zero, two, three, four, seven, and nine look similar to our numerals today; because they include the zero

The Chola Kingdom

If you could build a structure that both honors your heroes and represents you, what would it look like? The rulers of the Chola kingdom are remembered for huge temples that not only convey a deep devotion to their gods, but also promote their own power.

LIFE UNDER THE CHOLA KINGDOM

While historians remember the Gupta period as the golden age in India, they hardly remember the Chola kingdom at all. Yet, the Chola kingdom of southern India, established in 907, rivals the Gupta Empire in its contributions to architecture, education, religion, and governance. The kingdom promoted dance and music at services in the temples. The Chola spoke Tamil, a Dravidian language that is unrelated to Sanskrit and other Indo-Aryan languages, and children learned to read and write Tamil. The Chola built colleges, and students were well educated in mathematics, astronomy, and literacy, as well as religion. In fact, the literacy rate was 20 percent, the highest in the world at the time.

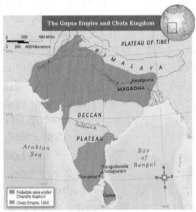

The Gupta Empire and Chola Kingdom

Large irrigation projects also improved the Chola economy. The Chola built a 1,079-foot-long dam to divert water to six canals to irrigate thousands of acres. This dam, known at the Kallanai dam, is one of the oldest irrigation systems in the world that is still in use.

Despite the achievements of the Chola, not everyone was satisfied. By this time, the caste system had become much more rigid. The poor and the outcast had no chance of escape. One Hindu sect called the Lingayats questioned the ideas of reincarnation, rejected the caste system, cautioned against child marriage, and encouraged widows to remarry, a practice that was not allowed in the Chola world. People who expressed these ideas were forced to flee the kingdom. The Lingayats' ideas predated the social reform movements of the 19th century, and centuries later, their movement for greater social equality has lived on in southern India today. These reformers continue to challenge ancient beliefs and practices in southern India today.

TEMPLES MIX RELIGION AND POLITICS

The Chola kingdom is renowned for its many elaborate temples, which displayed the kings' devotion to Hindu rituals. These architectural masterpieces lined the rivers

The Chola temples in Tamil Nadu, including the Brihadisvara Temple at Thanjavur shown here, are UNESCO World Heritage Sites. The Brihadisvara Temple is decorated with sculptures depicting Hindu deities.

and filled Chola cities. Today, a visitor to Tamil Nadu will find nearly a hundred temples in the Chola capital of Thanjavur alone.

The most famous of these Chola temples still stands over 200 feet tall, the tallest building of its time. The Chola king Rajaraja commissioned the temple and dedicated it to the deity Shiva in 1010. Frescos depicting the king and the deity line the interior walls of the temple, and inscriptions provide details about Rajaraja's victories and accomplishments. The temple reveals the king's dedication to Shiva, as well as his belief that, as king, he was Shiva's representative on Earth.

After Rajaraja died, his son Rajendra moved the capital east and built his own temple. While Rajendra's structure is smaller than his father's, its graceful, curved tower and exceptional cast bronze and stone sculptures show a very high level of craftsmanship.

SUCCESS IN GOVERNMENT

The Chola ruled from 907 to 1279, longer than any other Indian kingdom. Chola leaders controlled the immediate vicinity of the capital and possibly the other large cities in the district. Elected district councils governed villages surrounding the cities and those in more distant areas. Every household was given one vote in elections, and subcommittees oversaw local matters. The Chola expanded south onto the island of Sri Lanka and out into the Indian Ocean. There they allowed local leaders to continue to rule, but they encouraged local rulers to build Hindu temples and to adopt Chola principles of government. The kingdom's stability may be attributed to this practice of self-government.

In 1257, the Chola were defeated by their neighbors, the Pandyas, in the southwest, and the kingdom finally fell in 1279.

HISTORICAL THINKING

1. **READING CHECK** What do the Chola temples reveal about their kings?

2. **ANALYZE CAUSE AND EFFECT** How did Chola government principles impact the success of the kingdom?

3. **EVALUATE** Why might historians question the inscriptions on temple walls describing Rajaraja's victories and accomplishments?

PLAN: 2-PAGE LESSON

OBJECTIVE

Understand how religion and politics merged and produced a better quality of life in the nearly forgotten Chola kingdom.

CRITICAL THINKING SKILLS FOR LESSON 1.3

- Analyze Cause and Effect
- Evaluate
- Make Inferences
- Draw Conclusions

HISTORICAL THINKING FOR CHAPTER 7

How did societies in East and South Asia influence one another's cultures over time?

The Chola kingdom of southern India shared many traits with other Indian dynasties, including its Hindu religion. Lesson 1.3 discusses both the similarities and differences between the Chola and other early Indian kingdoms.

BACKGROUND FOR THE TEACHER

Tamil Nadu The modern-day state of Tamil Nadu occupies part of the southern tip of India. It and the surrounding states once made up the domain of the Chola kingdom. The Tamil still speak the Tamil language today, in spite of the fact that the Indian government wants to make Hindi the official language. Unlike Hindi, which is an Indo-Aryan language, the Tamil language is a part of the Dravidian language group. These languages are spoken primarily in South Asia. Tamil is also an official language in Sri Lanka and Singapore, and it is commonly spoken in South Africa, Fiji, Malaysia, and Mauritius. Tamil has been named an official "classical language" of India, which means, among other things, that it has an ancient heritage and body of literature.

INTRODUCE & ENGAGE

DISCUSS MONUMENTAL ARCHITECTURE

Direct students to the text introducing the lesson, in which they are asked to think about what kind of structure they would build to honor their heroes. Then have them examine the photograph of the Chola temple in Tamil Nadu. **ASK:** What do you think the builders of this temple wanted their work to show? *(Possible response: The height of the temple and the elaborate carvings are grand and probably required a lot of work. The builders wanted to honor their gods.)* Tell students that in this lesson they will learn more about the Chola kingdom's architecture as well as their other achievements.

TEACH

GUIDED DISCUSSION

1. **Make Inferences** Based on the text, how important do you think education was to the Chola? *(Possible response: Education was very important. The Chola built colleges and had the highest literacy rate in the world at the time.)*

2. **Draw Conclusions** Why didn't everyone in Chola society benefit from Chola achievements? *(Possible response: The caste system was very rigid and the poor and others were outcasts who did not receive education or economic improvements.)*

DRAW CONCLUSIONS

Have students review the lesson text and examine the map of the Chola kingdom. **ASK:** Based on the map and the text, how important do you think the sea was to the Chola kingdom? *(Possible response: It was likely very important; the major cities are located close to it, and Chola leaders expanded to Ceylon, which is across the sea from the mainland.)*

ACTIVE OPTIONS

On Your Feet: Four Corners Organize the classroom into four corners, with each corner focused on an area of Chola kingdom contributions: education, architecture, religion, and government. Have students first spend time on their own, thinking and writing about one of these topics. Then have students group into the corner of their choice and discuss their chosen topic. Finally, have at least one student from each corner share the corner discussion.

> **NG Learning Framework: Create a Composite Photograph**
> ATTITUDE Curiosity
> SKILL Communication

Tell students to create a composite photograph that shows features of the Tamil culture. They may focus on the Tamil Nadu state or one of its cities, such as Thanjavur. They may make a digital composite or make a collage using printed photographs. If necessary, direct students to online instructions for photographing or taking a screen shot and then creating a digital composite photo. Invite volunteers to present their completed work to the class, explaining the concept behind it, including why they chose the subject matter, and how they constructed it.

DIFFERENTIATE

ENGLISH LANGUAGE LEARNERS

Pronounce Words Remind students of the three pronunciations of *ch* in English: /ch/ as in child, /k/ as in school, and /sh/ as in machine. Point out that two of these pronunciations appear in the lesson: /ch/ in Chola, children, and achievements, and /k/ in architecture and architectural. Model pronunciations and have students repeat. Suggest that they make word cards, noting definitions and pronunciation hints.

GIFTED & TALENTED

Create a Web Page Prompt students to research the Tamil caste system. Have them design an informative web page about the subject, including links to related information. Suggest that they include information about the differing levels, including a graphic depiction of the system, and how people have worked to eliminate the caste system and ensure social justice for all. Ask students to post their web page on a school or class website.

See the Chapter Planner for more strategies for differentiation.

HISTORICAL THINKING

ANSWERS

1. a deep commitment to Hinduism; the temples built for Rajaraja convey his devotion to Shiva and his desire to boast of his own accomplishments.

2. They allowed a great degree of self-government. This allowed people more control over their own lives, so they didn't need to rebel.

3. The inscriptions are probably biased in favor of Rajaraja's rule. However, these sources provide historical information that historians can analyze in terms of historical context, frame of reference, and point of view of the original writers.

Traveler: Sima Qian
The Grand Historian c. 145–87 B.C.E.

If there had been a Lifetime Achievement Award in ancient China, Grand Historian Sima Qian would have been the ideal nominee. He took on a lifelong mission: writing the whole of Chinese history.

FINDING PATTERNS

Around 90 B.C.E., Sima Qian (SUH-mah CHEE-en) completed a history of China called *Records of the Grand Historian*, or *Shiji*. He described thousands of years of Chinese history in an account of more than 500,000 words, the equivalent of 50 thick books in English. Later historians valued his records and point of view. He presented events through the eyes of the people who lived through them and produced a gripping story that is still popular in China.

Sima Qian searched for patterns in the ways in which important rulers and generals of past political eras made decisions. Which decisions led to success and prosperity? Which led to defeat and decay? He included lively descriptions of assassins, merchants, court actors, and bandits. His history brought all these people to life through his empathy, or ability to understand the feelings and actions of others.

PRIMARY SOURCE

I have traveled to the northern border and returned by the Direct Road. As I went along I saw the towers of the Great Wall, which Meng Tian had constructed for the Qin. He cut through the mountains and filled up the valleys . . . Truly he made free with the strength of the common people! Qin had only recently destroyed the feudal states; the hearts of the people of the world were not yet at rest and the wounded were not yet healed. Tian was a renowned general, yet he did not take this opportunity to urge that the ills of the common people be attended to.

—from *Ssu-ma Ch'ien, Grand Historian of China* by Burton Watson, 1958

TRAVELS AND WRITINGS

As a young man, Sima Qian traveled throughout China. He saw the Great Wall, and he ends his biography of the general Meng Tian, who oversaw the building of the Great Wall, by noting that the general "made free with," or explicited, "the strength of the common people" and did not worry about their "ills," or problems. In other words, they were not treated well.

The Great Wall Sima Qian saw was not the massive structure of today. It was made of pounded dirt that stretched for miles and was dotted with watchtowers. Centuries later, workers built a wall of brick and stone over the dirt foundations.

Sima Qian lived during the reign of Emperor Wu of the Han dynasty. The emperor sent **delegations**, groups to represent him, to gather information on people and territories outside his empire. One delegation traveled for years into unknown lands, even through the Taklamakan Desert, whose name means "those who enter do not return." These explorations found the early routes of the Silk Roads that allowed trade between China and Central Asia.

Emperor Wu heard tales of horses with celestial, or heavenly, powers and thought such beasts would be useful for his military goals. They might also reveal secrets of immortality, or living forever. He sent soldiers on long-distance treks to find and capture these horses.

Sima Qian did not write about Emperor Wu. That would have been dangerous. *Shiji* was a personal project that covered China's history only to the Qin period, the first Chinese dynasty. In judging the strengths and weaknesses of its rulers, Sima Qian wrote: "Evil destroys the doer, but good endures, through the sons of the father, the subjects of the ruler, the disciple of the

teacher. It is the function of the historian to prolong the memory of goodness by preserving its record for all ages to see."

Sima Qian was Grand Historian for 20 years. In his court post, he kept a **chronicle**, or factual daily record, of events and ceremonies. He fell from royal favor when he spoke in defense of a general who had angered the emperor. This was **treason**, the crime of betraying the government. Sima Qian had to leave the court, but he continued writing *Shiji*. The story goes that after he died, his daughter hid his writing to protect it. When *Shiji* was brought into the open years later, it changed the way Chinese writers recorded their history and brought belated fame and honor to Sima Qian.

Sima Qian, like Herodotus and other travelers who came before him and those who have continued to journey, extended human understanding across regions with limited contact with each other. Their questions and explorations help us develop a fuller picture of the past as well as the present state of humanity.

Sima Qian's Journeys

CRITICAL VIEWING
Sima Qian wrote his manuscript on individual bamboo slips, which were then assembled into bundles. How does the writing process of his time contrast with today's?

HISTORICAL THINKING

1. **READING CHECK** How was Sima Qian's *Shiji* different from the writing he did as Grand Historian?

2. **IDENTIFY MAIN IDEAS AND DETAILS** What words in the primary source excerpt support the idea that Sima Qian showed empathy?

3. **ANALYZE** What was one result of sending delegations outside the empire's boundaries?

4. **FORM AND SUPPORT OPINIONS** What impact might Sima Qian's travels have had on his approach to writing history?

PLAN: 2-PAGE LESSON

OBJECTIVE

Describe the travels and writings of Sima Qian who devoted his life to recording the entire history of China.

CRITICAL THINKING SKILLS FOR LESSON 2.1

- Identify Main Ideas and Details
- Analyze
- Form and Support Opinions
- Make Connections
- Analyze Cause and Effect
- Analyze Primary Sources

HISTORICAL THINKING FOR CHAPTER 7

How did societies in East and South Asia influence one another's cultures over time?

Emperor Wu sent delegations outside his empire to learn about other lands. One such delegation found the early routes of the Silk Roads. Lesson 2.1 describes the Chinese historian Sima Qian who recorded such events and influenced others with his writings.

BACKGROUND FOR THE TEACHER

Sima Qian was the son of Sima Tan, who was the Grand Astrologer at the imperial court. The responsibilities of the Grand Astrologer included observing natural occurrences, keeping records, and making calendars. In the *Shiji*, Sima Qian writes that his father had started organizing historical records of the feudal lords of China and, before he died, asked his son to set all the historical records in order. Sima Qian agreed to take on this work and made it his life mission. He succeeded his father in the position at the imperial court where he had access to many historical records. However, Sima Qian took the additional step of traveling throughout the country so that he could see places for himself and interview specialists on different topics. These first-hand experiences gave him a better understanding of the people and locations he recorded. He then organized his history in a new way, using a five-part plan that included Basic Annals, Chronological Tables, Treatises, Histories of Hereditary Houses, and a collection of Biographies of famous individuals.

History Notebook

Encourage students to complete the Traveler page for Chapter 7 in their History Notebooks as they read.

INTRODUCE & ENGAGE

DISCUSS WHO BELONGS IN HISTORY BOOKS

Tell students that they are going to read about a historian who "included lively descriptions of assassins, merchants, court actors, and bandits." Then ask: Do you think such descriptions belong in a history book? Why or why not? How does including such lively descriptions help history come alive for readers who lived hundreds or thousands of years later? Ask students to name two people they think should be included in a history book and to explain why.

TEACH

GUIDED DISCUSSION

1. **Make Connections** What kinds of patterns did Sima Qian include in his history, and why do you think he included these? *(He included ways past political leaders made decisions, which led to success and which led to defeat. He most likely included these for later leaders to learn from and use.)*

2. **Analyze Cause and Effect** Why did Sima Qian's daughter hide his writing for years, and what effect did her actions have? *(Possible response: Sima Qian had been accused of treason, so the government may have destroyed his writings; they were preserved and respected when they were brought into the open.)*

ANALYZE PRIMARY SOURCES

Direct students to the primary source. **ASK:** What does Sima Qian describe that would have required "the strength of the common people"? *(the building of the Great Wall, which would have required great strength to cut through mountains by hand)* Why was it important for Sima Qian to travel to the northern border to see the Great Wall? *(Possible response: to see the great amount of work required to build the wall; he possibly saw graves of workers and spoke to people living nearby who witnessed or whose ancestors witnessed the building of the wall.)*

ACTIVE OPTIONS

On Your Feet: Jigsaw Strategy Share the Background for the Teacher. Organize students into groups and assign each group one part of Sima Qian's history to research: Basic Annals, Chronological Tables, Treatises, Histories of Hereditary Houses, and a collection of Biographies. Regroup students so that each new group has at least one member from each expert group. Experts should report on their part of Sima Qian's history.

NG Learning Framework: Write a Historical Record
ATTITUDE Responsibility
SKILLS Observation, Communication

Discuss how Sima Qian felt a personal responsibility to communicate "the memory of goodness by preserving its record." Discuss why memories of "goodness" are important to preserve. Invite students to record a "memory of goodness" that they have observed and that others could learn from. Encourage students to share their historical records with the class.

DIFFERENTIATE

INCLUSION

Adapt Assignments If students with disabilities have difficulty producing a piece of writing, have them create a visual essay with photos or drawings of their historical "memory of goodness" that they have observed and present it to the class.

PRE-AP

Analyze a Legend Invite students to research the "tales of horses with celestial, or heavenly, powers" that Emperor Wu wanted his soldiers to find and capture. Encourage students to compare and contrast the horses in the lands north of China to the smaller horses that the Chinese had. Then ask students to analyze why such horses may have become the subject of legends.

See the Chapter Planner for more strategies for differentiation.

HISTORICAL THINKING

ANSWERS

1. *Shiji*: a personal project that covered China's history only to the Qin dynasty; narrated events through the eyes of people who lived them; included lively descriptions of people; Grand Historian: daily record of events and ceremonies

2. Possible response: "… he made free with the strength of the common people"; "the wounded were not yet healed."

3. Possible response: the discovery of the early routes of the Silk Roads

4. Possible response: Different people, places, and events had an impact on how he viewed the relationship between humanity and history, which probably deepened his sense of empathy for people.

CRITICAL VIEWING Possible response: Today, writing is done on a computer, printed on paper, and then bound into a book, or it is read electronically.

Early History of the Silk Roads

The desert sand swirls in your face and the scorching sun leaves you parched and exhausted. But your caravan of traders trudges onward despite the difficult journey because of what awaits you at the market—silk, spices, gold, and jewels, glittering in the sunlight.

EARLY TRADE ROUTES ACROSS ASIA

The overland routes through Central Asia are known today as the **Silk Roads**. National Geographic Archaeologist-in-Residence, Fredrik Hiebert, describes the Silk Roads as "a metaphor for ancient trade that went east and west." Based on his discoveries, Hiebert has concluded that ancient cultures were always connected and that traders began traveling along the Silk Roads about 4,000 or 5,000 years ago—much earlier than historians had once thought.

The 4,000-mile routes began in the ancient city of Chang'an and followed the Great Wall of China. Originally a network of local overland routes, the Silk Roads eventually joined to form a vast network that connected China with the rest of Asia, Europe, and Africa. The Silk Roads also included **maritime**, or sea, routes that allowed traders to sail to the Mediterranean Sea and Europe. Other maritime routes led across the Indian Ocean to Arabia and East Africa and across the Pacific Ocean to Korea, Japan, and Southeast Asia.

Chinese goods may have traveled thousands of miles along the Silk Roads, but few traders made the entire journey from one end of the route to the other. The trip over the rugged terrain would have taken at least six months. Chinese traders, traveling in caravans of camels, traded their goods somewhere around Kashgar, near the Han Empire's western border, passing their goods along to Central Asian nomads. The nomads, in turn, may have gone on to trade the goods with other merchants from Asia, Africa, and Europe.

The Silk Roads depended on strong governments to protect travelers and allow trade to flourish. Beyond China, empires in Persia and Rome protected the routes. When the Han dynasty declined after 204, trade fell off until the time of the Tang dynasty in the 600s.

CRITICAL VIEWING The Mogao Caves are located near an ancient Silk Roads oasis town in China. Hundreds of Buddhist paintings such as this one adorn the walls of the caves. How might these paintings have influenced traders and travelers and helped spread Buddhism?

THE SPREAD OF GOODS

In addition to silk, Chinese merchants also traded paper, decorative lacquerware, and objects made of iron or bronze. In exchange for these goods, Chinese merchants often sought gold, silver, olive oil, and especially Central Asian horses.

All along the Silk Roads in China, market towns sprang up. Some of these Central Asian markets, in turn, grew into great cities. In these market towns, a dazzling variety of goods filled the stalls: Central Asian rugs and blankets; Indian spices, such as cinnamon and pepper; Korean celadon; and European wool and honey.

Traders from these and many other places used different currencies, and many had no money at all. As a result, the traders often bartered for other goods. In fact, at the high point of the Silk Roads trade, Chinese armies stationed in Central Asia bought goods from the local people using their pay, which they often received in bolts of silk because of coin shortages.

THE SPREAD OF IDEAS AND INVENTIONS

The Silk Roads were conduits not just for traders, but also for religious pilgrims, soldiers, and refugees fleeing dangerous areas. These travelers exchanged ideas, technologies, languages, and religions, and ideas spread from one culture to another, a process called cultural diffusion. In this way, for example, Chinese ideas about papermaking, metalwork, and farming techniques began to spread beyond China's borders, even reaching, in time, as far as western Europe.

Chief among the new ideas brought to and absorbed by China was Buddhism. Indian merchants introduced Buddhist ideas to Chinese traders and even established Buddhist shrines along the Silk Roads. Sea trade routes also helped spread religious ideas. The routes connected Southeast Asia with both India and China, facilitating travel by missionaries and followers. The regions closest to China, particularly Vietnam, became predominantly Buddhist, like China. Rulers of other regions, including Cambodia, patronized both Buddhism and Hinduism, as did most rulers in India.

By the year 600, Buddhism was firmly implanted in the Chinese countryside. Eventually, it became an important part of Chinese life with many Chinese blending Buddhist practices with Confucian beliefs. Thanks to the Silk Roads and maritime trade, other ideas also reached China, including Greek and Indian styles in sculpture, painting, and temple building—all of which enriched Chinese culture and civilization.

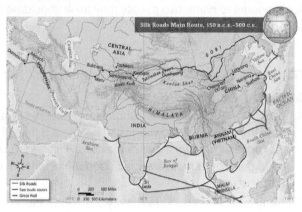

Silk Roads Main Route, 150 B.C.E.–500 C.E.

HISTORICAL THINKING

1. **READING CHECK** What were some of the goods and ideas exchanged on the Silk Roads?

2. **INTERPRET MAPS** What geographic features made traveling along the Silk Roads difficult and even dangerous?

3. **MAKE INFERENCES** What role do you think the early Silk Roads played in China's prosperity?

PLAN: 2-PAGE LESSON

OBJECTIVE

Identify how the Silk Roads, a series of ancient trade routes, facilitated the spread of goods and ideas throughout the Asian continent and beyond.

CRITICAL THINKING SKILLS FOR LESSON 2.2

- Interpret Maps
- Make Inferences
- Identify Main Ideas and Details
- Identify Supporting Details
- Draw Conclusions

HISTORICAL THINKING FOR CHAPTER 7

How did societies in East and South Asia influence one another's cultures over time?

The trade routes known as the Silk Roads were actually several caravan trails that connected China to the rest of Asia, Europe, and Africa. They also followed maritime routes to the Mediterranean and Europe. Lesson 2.2 describes the locations of these routes, what goods were traded on them, and how cultural elements, such as Buddhism, were diffused along these routes.

BACKGROUND FOR THE TEACHER

The Silk Roads One of the routes of the Silk Roads involved bypassing a desert and crossing over the Pamirs, which are mountains and highlands found mostly in Tajikistan but also in parts of China, Afghanistan, and Kyrgyzstan. The route was well traveled between China and the Mediterranean until the Roman Empire lost some of its territory in Asia and travel became unsafe. During the 1200s and 1300s, the Mongols once again began using the routes for trade. It was during this period that Marco Polo traveled on them. Today, a section of the Silk Roads between Pakistan and China remains intact. It is now a paved highway, and the United Nations wants to make it into a trans-Asian highway and/or a railway that spans Asia.

History Notebook

Encourage students to complete the Global Commodity page for Chapter 7 in their History Notebooks as they read.

Student eEdition online

Additional content for this lesson, including an image gallery and a Global Commodity feature, is available online.

INTRODUCE & ENGAGE

DISCUSS TRAVEL ROUTES

Direct students to examine the Silk Roads Main Route map that appears in the lesson. Direct them to note the relief on the map. Point out that travelers did not have the modern transportation methods that we have today. **ASK:** Which features on the map does it look like travelers avoided? Why? *(Possible responses: the Gobi, the Talimakan Desert, the Kunlun Shan, and high-altitude areas of the Hindu Kush. Traders were traveling by camel or on foot, which would take a long time. They would not have risked spending too much time in the desert or in the mountains.)* Tell students that in this lesson they will learn more about how goods were transported along these routes.

TEACH

GUIDED DISCUSSION

1. **Identify Main Ideas and Details** Were the Silk Roads only land based? Explain. *(No, the Silk Roads also included maritime routes that allowed traders to reach the Mediterranean and Europe.)*

2. **Identify Supporting Details** How did the arrival of Buddhism in China affect Chinese society? *(Possible responses: Buddhism eventually became an important part of Chinese life.)*

DRAW CONCLUSIONS

Have students read the feature A Global Commodity: Lapis Lazuli (available in the Student eEdition). **ASK:** What were some of the uses of lapis lazuli? *(Possible response: It was used for jewelry, decorative and sacred objects, carvings, vases, and makeup. It was also used as pigment for painting.)*

ACTIVE OPTIONS

On Your Feet: Numbered Heads Organize students in groups of four and have the members number off. Direct groups to discuss the cultural ideas and practices that were passed along on the Silk Roads. Have them discuss the lesson text and then conduct research to find out more about the ideas and practices. For example, groups might explore which ideas and technologies made their way to new areas as a result of cultural diffusion, such as papermaking and metal/bronze work or the spread of religious beliefs or languages. Then call out a number and have students with that number report on their group's findings.

NG Learning Framework: Write a Journal Entry
ATTITUDE Curiosity
SKILL Communication

Instruct students to imagine they are traveling the main route of the Silk Roads in 250 B.C.E. and are keeping a travel journal about what they see and experience along the way. Ask them to combine information from the text and the image gallery (available in the Student eEdition), with other sources they find online to provide further background for their journal entries. Encourage students to focus on trade goods, routes, and fellow travelers. Invite students to read their completed entries to the class.

DIFFERENTIATE

INCLUSION

Support Critical Viewing Pair sight-impaired students with a partner who can describe the elements of the map in detail, including the key items, the relief, and the locator map. Instruct pairs to ask and answer questions about the map.

GIFTED & TALENTED

Create a Poster Direct students to conduct online research to find more information about the Silk Roads, including the goods that were traded and which types of products were popular in certain areas. Have students write captions for visuals that they have found to illustrate Silk Roads trade and then create their own poster that includes both the visuals and the captions. Encourage students to display their posters and discuss the items they included.

See the Chapter Planner for more strategies for differentiation.

HISTORICAL THINKING

ANSWERS

1. Goods: silk, paper, lacquerware, iron and bronze objects, gold, silver, spices, rugs, honey, wool, and horses. Ideas: papermaking techniques, metalwork, farming techniques, and religions, particularly Buddhism.

2. hot deserts and rugged mountain terrain; the maps show the route of the Silk Roads divides between Dunhuang and Kashgar to bypass the Taklimakan Desert.

3. They facilitated the trade of goods—especially China's highly valued silk—which must have resulted in wealth and bolstered China's economy.

CRITICAL VIEWING Possible response: They may have been attracted to the beautiful colors and decorative nature of the paintings and intrigued by the ideas that inspired such works of art.

Han Expansion and Collapse

Imagine if your teachers told you to memorize everything they said and then recite it back to them. That was what education was like before the Han Chinese invented paper.

QIN FALL AND HAN RISE

After the death of Qin emperor Shi Huangdi in 210 B.C.E., some regions rebelled against the weak, unpopular second Qin emperor. An ambitious peasant by the name of Liu Bang (lee-oo bahng), who had served as a low-ranking official under the Qin, sided with the rebels. Liu Bang was charismatic, and the peasants elevated him to leader of one of the competing rebel groups. After defeating a rival rebel leader, Liu Bang successfully overcame the Qin to found the Han dynasty in 206 B.C.E. Liu Bang, one of only two emperors born as a peasant, ruled until 195 B.C.E.

When Han forces took power, they faced the immediate problem of staffing a government large enough to govern the empire. They continued the Qin Legalist structure of a central government with the emperor at the head and a prime minister as the top official. Underneath the prime minister were three main divisions: tax collection, military supervision, and personnel recruitment. As the Chinese empire expanded to include diverse peoples, the Han Chinese majority was named after this early dynasty.

In 140 B.C.E., Emperor **Wudi** came to the throne. He became one of the most powerful Han emperors. In 124 B.C.E., he established the Imperial Academy to encourage the study of Confucian texts. Like others before him, Emperor Wudi believed that knowledge of Confucian ritual, history, poetry, and the *Analects* would produce more virtuous, and thus better, officials. Before promoting officers, the central government tested the officers' knowledge of the Confucian classics.

The Han Dynasty, 206 B.C.E.–220 C.E.

PAPER AND MATHEMATICS

Paper was first discovered by simple ragpickers who washed and recycled old fabric, left fibers on a screen, and accidentally discovered how to make paper. Initially, the Chinese used paper to wrap fragile items, but they quickly saw that paper was a good surface for writing that was cheap to make. By 200 C.E., it was commonly used for books and letters instead of the silk or bamboo slips used earlier.

With the adoption of paper as the primary writing material, the culture of learning in China shifted from an oral one to a written one. Before the invention of paper, students and poets memorized texts and recited them orally, but by the end of the Han dynasty students read books and poets composed poems on paper. Buddhist monks also benefited from the new invention. They wrote prayers on slips of paper and distributed them to large numbers of devoted followers.

Paper became one of China's most important inventions because it was cheap to produce, durable, and lightweight. Around the world, societies that had previously written on other materials shifted to paper almost as soon as they encountered it.

China's mathematics were also influential. One work called *Jiuzhang Suanshu (Nine Chapters on the Mathematical Art)* was written during the Han dynasty. The text provided arithmetic, algebraic, and geometric algorithms for everyday problems such as land surveying, tax collection, civil engineering, and wage distribution. Historians disagree on the origin of the text, but many believe it was written around 200 B.C.E. Used as a textbook in China and neighboring countries for 2,000 years, it is often compared with *The Elements*, which was written by the Greek mathematician Euclid.

EXPANSION OF THE HAN DYNASTY

During the long reign of Emperor Wudi, the Han dynasty expanded its empire west into the Taklimakan Desert, east into present-day Korea, and south into present-day Vietnam. However, officials living in the **garrison towns**, where soldiers of the empire were based, had little control over the people native to the region.

The Han dynasty gained much of its northwestern territory between 201 and 60 B.C.E. in wars against the Xiongnu, a nomadic people who moved across present-day Mongolia in search of grass to feed their sheep and horses. The Xiongnu had a strong army with brilliant horsemanship. In battle after battle, the Xiongnu used their military strength to threaten and weaken the Han.

In 139 B.C.E., Emperor Wu dispatched the envoy Zhang Qian to Central Asia to create an alliance against the Xiongnu. Although Zhang Qian failed in his mission, he visited local markets and learned about trade with outside societies. The information

he brought back to Emperor Wudi opened the Silk Roads as trade routes through which China could trade silk for animal hides and semiprecious gems, such as lapis lazuli and jade.

FACTORS LEADING TO COLLAPSE

The Han dynasty ruled for 400 years, with only one interruption when a usurper founded his own short-lived dynasty. Natural disasters such as earthquakes, floods, and locust plagues were worrisome, but corruption and internal conflicts strained the dynasty even further. Confucian officials and military leaders vied for power. Exhausted by taxes, reduced plots of land to farm, and new policies of strict control, peasants rebelled. In 184 C.E., a large group of peasants attempted to overtake the capital.

External forces also threatened the Han. Continued invasions from the Xiongnu and other neighbors weakened the dynasty and drained military funds. Strained relations with neighbors also disrupted trade along the Silk Roads, causing further economic shortfalls. Continuous internal and external conflicts further weakened the dynasty until the last emperor **abdicated**, or gave up, his throne in 220 C.E.

Factors Contributing to the Collapse of the Han Dynasty and the Roman Empire

	Han Dynasty	Roman Empire
INTERNAL FACTORS	• Corruption • Economic decline • Peasant rebellions • Power plays as officials and military leaders vied for power	• Corruption • Economic decline • Religious divisions and intolerance • Power plays as military leaders vied for power • Civil war and division • Iron contamination of water pipes
EXTERNAL FACTORS	• Locust plagues • Earthquakes and floods • Trade disruption along the Silk Roads • Invasions from Xiongnu and other neighbors	• Mosquito infestations and malaria • Trade disruption due to war • Invasions from Huns, Vandals, and Goths

HISTORICAL THINKING

1. **READING CHECK** How did the Han expand Chinese territories? How much influence did they have on those new lands?

2. **INTERPRET MAPS** How does the size of the Han dynasty compare to that of the former Qin dynasty?

3. **COMPARE AND CONTRAST** How was the decline and collapse of the Han dynasty similar to and different from that of the Roman Empire?

PLAN: 2-PAGE LESSON

OBJECTIVE

Explain how the Han dynasty expanded Chinese territory, the economy, and education, but then declined due to rebellions and invasions.

CRITICAL THINKING SKILLS FOR LESSON 2.3

- Interpret Maps
- Compare and Contrast
- Draw Conclusions
- Identify Supporting Details
- Interpret Charts

HISTORICAL THINKING FOR CHAPTER 7

How did societies in East and South Asia influence one another's cultures over time?

The Han continued the Qin Legalist government structure and encouraged the study of Confucian texts. Lesson 2.3 discusses how they built on these past traditions to make new advances in learning and technology.

Student eEdition online

Additional content for this lesson, including images, is available online.

BACKGROUND FOR THE TEACHER

Empires in Western Europe and China Historians have compared the history of empires in Western Europe and China and have noticed a big difference. After the fall of the Han dynasty, it was not long before other Chinese rulers reunited and expanded the empire. In Western Europe, by contrast, the fall of Rome resulted in the fragmentation of the once mighty empire into smaller states. Before their collapse, the empires experienced similar problems. Both faced corruption in government and financial problems as a result of warfare and high taxation. Both experienced invasions by outsiders. In Han China, local provinces controlled by warlords gradually gained more power than the central government. In Rome, civil war broke out. Both empires also split into parts—the Han split into the Three Kingdoms for a period of more than 350 years. Rome split into East and West. The West eventually completely crumbled, while the East lasted until the 1400s, when it was overtaken by the Ottoman Empire. In China, the Sui dynasty reunited the empire in 589. The great Roman Empire never reunited.

INTRODUCE & ENGAGE

DISCUSS PAPERMAKING

Tell students that the first person to make a sheet of paper was an official of the Chinese court named Ts'ai Lun. He combined ground-up fishing nets, plant fibers, old rags, tree bark, and waste from the hemp plant to make a pulp. Direct students to pull out a sheet of paper, hold it up to the light, and look at it closely. **ASK:** Can you see the variations in the material that makes up the paper? *(Students may say that the paper isn't uniformly one shade—they can see some variation once they hold it up to the light.)* What do you think a sheet of the early Chinese paper would look like if you held it up to the light? *(Students might say the variations would be much more pronounced, and the texture would probably be rough.)* Tell students that in this lesson they will learn about the invention of paper in China and other achievements of the Han.

TEACH

GUIDED DISCUSSION

1. **Draw Conclusions** Why do you think Liu Bang was able to become an emperor, even though he was a peasant? *(He was charismatic and powerful.)*

2. **Identify Supporting Details** Why did Emperor Wudi establish the Imperial Academy? *(Possible responses: He wanted to ensure the study of Confucian texts by government officials. He believed education created better leaders.)*

INTERPRET CHARTS

Have students examine the diagram comparing the falls of the Han dynasty and the Roman Empire. **ASK:** What internal factors were shared by the two? *(The shared factors are corruption, economic decline, and power plays as military leaders vied for power.)*

ACTIVE OPTIONS

On Your Feet: Fishbowl Arrange students in two concentric circles and tell the inner circle to discuss the following question: What was the Han's greatest contribution to future civilizations? The outer circle listens to the discussion, and then, at a signal, the inner and outer circles reverse positions. The new inner circle continues the discussion by focusing on this question: How does this contribution affect the world today? At the end of the activity, have students summarize their discussions.

NG Learning Framework: Write an Editorial
ATTITUDE Empowerment
KNOWLEDGE Our Human Story

Direct students to work in small groups to write an editorial about one of the events or people discussed in the lesson. Tell them to conduct additional research about the topic they select, including how the person or event influenced ancient China. Inform students that their editorials should express an opinion about their topic and include evidence from their research to support their viewpoints. Ask students to read their editorials to the class or post them on a class blog or website.

DIFFERENTIATE

STRIVING READERS

Summarize Using a Concept Cluster
Instruct pairs to summarize the lesson by creating a Concept Cluster. Tell students to write the lesson title in the center oval and the section headings in the outer ovals. As pairs read each section, have them enter key events and ideas on the spokes, adding spokes as needed. After students complete their Concept Clusters, invite volunteers to summarize the lesson.

PRE-AP

Create a Time Line Ask students to review the events and dates found in this lesson, conduct online and print research to learn more about four of them, and use their findings to construct an annotated time line. Direct students to access reliable sources as they locate maps, visuals, and in-depth descriptions of the events they selected. Invite them to post their completed time lines around the classroom.

See the Chapter Planner for more strategies for differentiation.

HISTORICAL THINKING

ANSWERS

1. The Han expanded into the Taklimakan Desert, Korea, and Vietnam by conquering these lands, but they failed to exert control over these areas.

2. The Han dynasty more than doubled in size compared to that of the former Qin dynasty.

3. They shared certain negatives, such as corruption, invasions, power struggles, environmental problems, and economic decline, but Rome was also plagued by religious divisions and iron contamination of water pipes.

The Tang Empire

Today in our global economy, millions of products are imported and exported through a complex system of trade with other countries. Centuries ago, the people of Tang China benefited from trade along the Silk Roads and the Grand Canal.

A Tang artisan portrayed a whimsical camel and its sleepy driver in this porcelain sculpture created c. 7th–9th century c.e.

CHINA REUNITES

The Han dynasty ended in 220, and China experienced more than 300 years of disunity before the founder of the Sui (sway) dynasty reunified China in 589. The Sui dynasty lasted only until 618, barely 30 years. But a Sui general, Li Yuan, wrested power from rivals to found the Tang dynasty, which lasted nearly 300 years. **Taizong** (ty-johng), who was the second Tang emperor, is probably the dynasty's most famous. He ruled from 626 to 649 and extended the borders of the Tang empire far into Central Asia and south into Vietnam, an expansion that protected China's trade along the Silk Roads. It also protected the dynasty from invasions by nomadic Turkish-speaking people.

One of Taizong's greatest accomplishments was a comprehensive law code, the Tang code, that was designed to help local magistrates govern and solve disputes. The Tang code also described the equal-field system, which was the basis of the Tang dynasty tax system. Based on a **census**, or an official count of the population, the equal-field system divided land according to rank and determined how much each individual would pay in taxes. This system gave Tang officials an unprecedented degree of control over their 50 million subjects. The first half of the Tang dynasty was one of the most prosperous and peaceful eras in Chinese history.

After Taizong's death, a woman who called herself **Emperor Wu** held power for a short time. She was the only woman to rule China as emperor in her own right. Emperor Wu promoted *The Great Cloud Sutra*, a Buddhist text that prophesied a kingdom ruled by a woman would be transformed into a Buddhist paradise.

Although few women were literate at the time, a small number of women were educated in the palace school, and Emperor Wu hired them as scribes. After serving five years as a Tang emperor, Emperor Wu proclaimed a new dynasty named the Zhou (jow). However, in 705, she was overthrown in a palace coup and the Tang dynasty was restored.

After a period of relative stability, a general led the army in a mutiny against the Tang emperor in 755. The Tang suppressed the rebellion, but they never regained full control of the provinces. Court officials began to take control, and regional leaders gained power. After a long period of decline, the Tang dynasty fell in 907. It would not be long, however, before the new Song dynasty re-established imperial control in 960.

THE SPREAD OF BUDDHISM

Beginning in the Han dynasty, Buddhism began to spread to China via the Silk Roads. Initially Buddhism was slow to take hold because it encouraged followers to leave their families and remain **celibate**, or unmarried. This was in conflict with Confucian respect for parents and family. However, in 310 a local ruler converted to Buddhism and granted Buddhists land to build monasteries. By the year 600, Buddhism had become established in China.

Buddhist art and architecture flourished as Tang leaders embraced Buddhism and donated money and land to Buddhist monasteries. Emperor Taizong combined Buddhist ideals with Confucian policies to create a new model of governance. The Tang support of Buddhism continued until late in the dynasty when weakened leaders began to criticize Buddhism and other "foreign" religions. During the reign of Emperor Wuzong from 841 to 846, imperial hostilities toward Buddhism led to the destruction of some 5,000 monasteries. But this was only a temporary setback. Buddhism was now so strong in China that it survived far into the future.

TANG INFLUENCES

International trade boomed in Tang China, and the capital of Chang'an became a **cosmopolitan** city, a diverse place with people, goods, and ideas from around the world. Traders brought music and dance from the west. Equestrian sports, or those performed on horseback, came from the north.

During the Tang dynasty, the wood buildings characteristic of Chinese architecture became more elaborate. Tang builders added curved tile roofs, towers, raised walkways, and bright tiles on floors. Gardens featured ponds and bridges. Many Buddhist temples and monasteries were also built during this time, and many survived the anti-Buddhist backlash.

The Tang were known for their visual arts, which were imported and copied by Korean and Japanese Buddhists and artisans. Tang poetry was also highly valued in Korea and Japan, where it was studied by men of the higher classes.

Perhaps the Tang advancement with the widest influence was woodblock printing. Artisans carved Chinese characters into woodblocks, which were then coated with ink and pressed onto sheets of paper. Woodblock printing led to a communications revolution. People turned to books to learn about everything from cooking to mathematics, agriculture, warfare, and medicine. Buddhists promoted the art of printing, and Buddhist texts spread the religion. Woodblock printing spread the Chinese writing system to Korea, Vietnam, and Japan, and Chinese writing carried the influence of Tang ideas and arts throughout these societies.

NATIONAL GEOGRAPHIC EXPLORER
CHRISTINE LEE

Reconstructing Lives

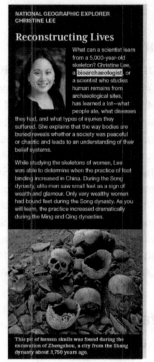

What can a scientist learn from a 5,000-year-old skeleton? Christine Lee, a **bioarchaeologist**, or a scientist who studies human remains from archaeological sites, has learned a lot—what people ate, what diseases they had, and what types of injuries they suffered. She explains that the way bodies are buried reveals whether a society was peaceful or chaotic and leads to an understanding of their belief systems.

While studying the skeletons of women, Lee was able to determine when the practice of foot binding increased in China. During the Song dynasty, elite men saw small feet as a sign of wealth and glamour. Only very wealthy women had bound feet during the Song dynasty. As you will learn, the practice increased dramatically during the Ming and Qing dynasties.

This pit of human skulls was found during the excavation of Zhengzhou, a city from the Shang dynasty about 3,750 years ago.

HISTORICAL THINKING

1. **READING CHECK** What are some of the ideas that the Tang imported and exported through trade with neighboring countries?

2. **DESCRIBE** What does the bioarchaeological study of human skeletons reveal about life in China's past?

3. **DETERMINE CHRONOLOGY** Create a flowchart showing how Buddhism spread to China, how it grew in China, and how it expanded outside of China.

PLAN: 2-PAGE LESSON

OBJECTIVE
Learn how expansion and trade led to prosperity and advancement under the Tang dynasty.

CRITICAL THINKING SKILLS FOR LESSON 2.4
- Describe
- Determine Chronology
- Explain
- Analyze Visuals

HISTORICAL THINKING FOR CHAPTER 7
How did societies in East and South Asia influence one another's cultures over time?

The Tang established an empire influenced by Buddhist and Confucian beliefs. Lesson 2.4 discusses the achievements of the Tang, whose large empire was built on trade.

Student eEdition online
Additional content for this lesson, including an image gallery, is available online.

BACKGROUND FOR THE TEACHER

Empress Wu After Taizong's death, his heir, Gaozong, became emperor. Gaozong was married to Lady Wang but was actually in love with a concubine, Wu Zetian. Lady Wang had no children. Wu had two sons and a daughter with Gaozong. One night, Wu's daughter was strangled in her crib, and Lady Wang was accused of the crime. The emperor banished her from the court and made Wu his wife and empress. The high officials in the government objected to her position because she was not a member of a noble family. Gaozong was weak and sickly, and Wu ruled in his place. She ensured that all who opposed her power were dismissed, exiled, or executed. Upon Gaozong's death, Wu's first son became emperor, but she removed him from power to protect her own power as empress. She made her second son emperor instead, but in reality, she controlled the government. Eventually, Wu assumed total power for herself and ruled until she was overthrown. Many historians believe that it was actually Wu who strangled her own daughter, in an effort to frame Lady Wang.

INTRODUCE & ENGAGE

DISCUSS GENDER ROLES

Prompt students to recall the Chinese leaders they have read about so far. **ASK:** Were any of these leaders women? *(Students should agree that no women had been leaders in China up to that point.)* Explain to students that most Chinese women during this period were typically illiterate and uneducated. Men assumed all power roles in ancient Chinese society. Then tell them that in this lesson they will learn about leaders of the Tang dynasty, including the only Chinese woman to rule as emperor in her own right.

TEACH

GUIDED DISCUSSION

1. **Explain** What was the purpose of the Tang code? *(The purpose of the Tang code was to help magistrates govern and to provide the basis for the tax system.)*

2. **Describe** How did Buddhism come to China? *(Buddhism came to China via the Silk Roads.)*

ANALYZE VISUALS

Tell students to examine the Tang Artifacts and Inventions image gallery (available in the Student eEdition). Direct their attention to the Chinese star chart. **ASK:** What do you think might be the purpose of the connected lines and circles? *(Possible responses: They might be mappings of constellations. They appear to have character labels, which might be names given to the constellations.)*

ACTIVE OPTIONS

On Your Feet: Roundtable Arrange students in groups of four for a Roundtable discussion. Ask them the following question: Why might Tang leaders have blamed Buddhism and other "foreign" religions for the dynasty's decline? Instruct groups to have each member contribute to the answer and then come to a consensus about the answer. Invite groups to share their ideas with the class.

> **NG Learning Framework: Create an Exhibit on the Tang**
> SKILL Collaboration
> KNOWLEDGE Our Human Story

Arrange students in groups. Ask each group to choose an area in which the Tang were influential: architecture, visual arts, poetry, or printing. Instruct groups to use photographs, time lines, or other visuals to create an appropriate visual display about the chosen area. Then direct students to write a brief summary describing their chosen influence. When groups have finished, invite them to share their exhibit with the class.

DIFFERENTIATE

STRIVING READERS

Make a Chart Before they read the lesson, instruct pairs of students to make a chart titled Tang Achievements, and have them label four columns: Law, Architecture, Visual Arts, and Literature. When pairs have finished reading, prompt them to list as many details as they can about Tang achievements for each category. One student can reread paragraphs aloud while the other adds details to the lists. Invite pairs to share their lists with the class.

PRE-AP

Research and Write an Essay Tell students to research music and dance during the Tang period. Describe some of the instruments played by musicians during this period, such as stone chimes and zithers, and point out that western music and dance became more popular and influential in China during this time. Direct students to use their notes to write an essay about the music and dance that were popular under the Tang. Ask volunteers to read their essays to the class.

See the Chapter Planner for more strategies for differentiation.

HISTORICAL THINKING

ANSWERS

1. Imports: new music, dance, and sports; Exports: Chinese characters, woodblock printing, Buddhism, and the arts

2. The study of skeletons reveals how people lived, what they ate, their diseases, as well as information about their society and belief systems.

3. Flowcharts should show the introduction of Buddhism during the Han dynasty. The growth of Buddhism might show missionaries traveling the Silk Roads, the building of Buddhist temples within China, and the expansion of Buddhism into Korea, Japan, and Vietnam through printed books. Flowcharts may also mention the Tang suppression of Buddhism in 845.

Kingdoms in Korea and Vietnam

How long would you tolerate someone telling you what to do? The Koreans and Vietnamese struggled against Chinese political control for hundreds of years. While they borrowed freely from China, they still hung on to aspects of their culture that made them unique.

THE THREE KINGDOMS

From approximately 57 B.C.E. through 668 C.E., the Korean Peninsula was divided into small chiefdoms. The greatest of these chiefdoms were the Koguryo (koh-gur-YOO) in the north, the Paekche (pahk-chay) in the southwest, and the Silla (SIHL-uh) in the southeast. These three kingdoms vied for territory and influence from 313 to 668 C.E., an era known as the Three Kingdoms period.

The Han of China conquered the Koguryo in northern Korea and sent officials and merchants to live in four commanderies, or military cities. The largest of these, Lelang, was near present-day Pyongyang. The Koguryo regained control of the four cities one by one, expelling the last Chinese from Lelang in 313.

As the Sui and Tang dynasties took power in China, the Korean rulers sent officials to China to learn about Chinese culture and governance. The kings of Koguryo and Paekche adopted Buddhism in the 370s and 380s, believing that combining Confucian education with Buddhism would strengthen their kingdoms. However, Buddhism was a contentious issue among the Silla. Many in the Silla kingdom opposed the religion, but King Pophung was determined to build a shrine to the Buddha. In 527, according to legend, a miracle silenced the opposition, when a Buddhist official survived execution, bleeding milk rather than blood.

The Sui and Tang dynasties attempted to take over Korea but failed in several attacks on the peninsula. Then in 660, the Silla joined forces with the Tang to defeat the Paekche and Koguryo. They succeeded and unified Korea in 668. However, the Tang saw the unification as an opportunity to **depose**, or remove from power, the Silla and take control of the entire peninsula. The Silla held out against the Chinese army and navy and defeated Chinese forces to unify Korea again in 676.

For the most part, the Silla followed Tang government principles. However, they rejected the equal-field system, which distributed lands to every household. Instead, the Silla granted entire villages to aristocratic families who appointed officials and paid their salaries. Like the Tang, the Silla used civil service exams, but only members of the highest-ranking families were allowed to take them. The Silla entered a period of decline after 780, when different branches of the royal family fought for control of the throne, and no one ruled for long.

THE PEOPLE OF VIETNAM

While Korea marked the northern extent of Chinese influence, Vietnam marked the southern. Under different dynasties, the Chinese ruled Vietnam from 111 B.C.E. to 938 C.E. During this time, the Vietnamese embraced Buddhism, Confucianism, and Daoism, calling this combination of beliefs the Three Teachings. But they never gave up their traditional practice of ancestor reverence and spirit worship. Throughout their history, they repeatedly rebelled against Chinese control and refused to identify as Chinese. In fact, they built temples in honor of heroes who fought the Chinese, such as **Trung Trac** and **Trung Nhi**, two sisters who organized an army that pushed the Han back and formed an independent state near the Red River in northern Vietnam in 40 C.E. Three years later, the Chinese regained control, but today these sisters are two of Vietnam's greatest heroes.

A DIFFERENT CULTURE IN THE SOUTH

In the southern part of Vietnam, people lived quite differently from their neighbors in the north. The Champa kingdom formed in 192 C.E. Its people, known as the Cham, practiced Hinduism and adopted cultural traditions from India.

Skilled sailors, the Cham traded widely, and goods from their kingdom have been found in Taiwan, the Philippines, and Malaysia. Within southern Vietnam, excavations have uncovered rare gold, agate, and glass beads from India, Iran, and the Mediterranean.

Like their neighbors in the north, the Cham continuously fought off invasions from the Chinese as well as attacks from other countries in Southeast Asia.

Sunrise breaks over the mountains in Bukhansan National Park, Seoul, South Korea.

Statues of the heroic Trung sisters hold a place of honor in the Hai Ba Trung Temple in Hanoi.

HISTORICAL THINKING

1. **READING CHECK** Which aspects of Chinese culture and governance did the Koreans adopt? Which did they reject? Why?

2. **SEQUENCE EVENTS** Create a timeline of events in Korea from 313 to 676 C.E.

3. **DRAW CONCLUSIONS** What do the temples dedicated to heroes reveal about Vietnamese culture and beliefs?

PLAN: 2-PAGE LESSON

OBJECTIVE

Understand that though they were heavily influenced by the Chinese, the people of Korea and Vietnam fought to maintain their own identity.

CRITICAL THINKING SKILLS FOR LESSON 3.1

- Sequence Events
- Draw Conclusions
- Analyze Cause and Effect
- Identify Supporting Details
- Synthesize

HISTORICAL THINKING FOR CHAPTER 7

How did societies in East and South Asia influence one another's cultures over time?

The development of Korea and Vietnam was heavily influenced by China. Lesson 3.1 discusses how each kingdom continued to maintain its own identity in spite of repeated invasions.

BACKGROUND FOR THE TEACHER

Trung Sisters The Vietnamese revolutionaries known as the Trung sisters were upper-class women who organized a full-scale rebellion against the Han Chinese. One of the sisters, Trung Trac, had been married to another revolutionary who was assassinated by a Chinese general because of his attempt to overthrow the ruling Chinese. Trung Trac took up the fight, and her sister, Trung Nhi, joined her. At first, the two were successful. They drove the Chinese out of many areas of Vietnam. The Trung sisters then named themselves joint queens of their own independent state. But when the Chinese army returned, they could not put up a strong enough fight. Soon their supplies ran short and they did not have enough soldiers. Instead of being captured, the two sisters drowned themselves in a river. Today, an avenue in downtown Hanoi is named for them in honor of their efforts.

INTRODUCE & ENGAGE

DISCUSS THE IMPACT OF CONQUEST

Guide students to recall the reason for the downfall of most of the ancient kingdoms and civilizations they have previously studied. **ASK:** What is one common reason for a society's downfall? *(Possible response: Invasions and conquests are one of the most common reasons.)* Then ask them to think about what the people in a conquered civilization might want to preserve from their way of life. Elicit and display volunteers' responses on the board. Tell students that Lesson 3.1 explains how China impacted the kingdoms of Korea and Vietnam. After students have read the lesson, revisit the notes on the board for comparison to the text.

TEACH

GUIDED DISCUSSION

1. **Analyze Cause and Effect** How did the Silla manage to gain control over Paekche and Koguryo? *(They united with the Tang.)*

2. **Identify Supporting Details** What were the Three Teachings? *(The Three Teachings were the combination of Buddhism, Confucianism, and Daoism that was practiced by the Vietnamese.)*

SYNTHESIZE

Have students read A Global Commodity: Celadon (available in the Student eEdition). **ASK:** What properties made celadon valuable? *(Possible response: its greenish color, beauty, and potentially magical properties—it supposedly could detect poison in food)*

ACTIVE OPTIONS

On Your Feet: Numbered Heads Organize students into groups of four and have them number off. Ask the following question: How did Vietnam resist Chinese control both culturally and militarily? Give the group members time to think about the question individually. Then tell groups to discuss the topic so that any member can report for the group. After sufficient time, call a number and ask students with that number to report for their group.

NG Learning Framework: Write a Letter
ATTITUDE Responsibility
SKILLS Communication, Collaboration

Ask students to work in groups to write a letter to the Chinese government from the perspective of the Trung sisters. The letter should express the sisters' concerns and why they are fighting the Chinese takeover of Vietnam. Direct students to conduct research about the perspective they are assuming. When groups finish writing their letters, invite representatives from each to read their letters to the class.

DIFFERENTIATE

ENGLISH LANGUAGE LEARNERS

PREP Before Reading Encourage students to use the PREP strategy to prepare for reading. Write this acrostic on the board:
PREP
Preview the title.
Read the Main Idea statement.
Examine the visuals.
Predict what you will learn.

GIFTED & TALENTED

Write a Dramatic Skit Invite students to use a variety of documents to deepen their understanding of the Korean Three Kingdoms and the takeover of Korea by the Tang. Instruct them to choose one event illustrating the events of this period and use it as the basis of a short skit. Allow time for students to prepare and practice their skits. After they have practiced, invite them to perform their skits for the class.

See the Chapter Planner for more strategies for differentiation.

HISTORICAL THINKING

ANSWERS

1. Koreans adopted the writing system, Buddhism, Tang laws, and civil service exams. However, they rejected the equal-field system and instead allowed aristocratic families to control.

2. Time lines should show the following dates and events: 313—Koguryo expel the Chinese; 313–668—Three Kingdoms Period in which Koguryo, Paekche, and Silla all vie for control; 660—The Silla join forces with the Tang; 668—Silla unify Korea; 668–676—Silla and Tang vie for control; 676—The Silla reunify Korea.

3. Possible response: There was a strong desire to maintain cultural and political independence, and those who acted on that desire had divine support.

The Emergence of Japan

You may learn a lot from textbooks, but what can you learn from a novel? Quite a bit. The world's first novel was written by a Japanese woman around 1000, and it reveals much about Japanese culture at that time.

CRITICAL VIEWING An 1853 woodblock print triptych, a three-paneled artwork, by Japanese artists Utagawa Toyokuni and Utagawa Hiroshige illustrates a snowy winter scene from *The Tale of Genji*. Prince Genji, depicted on the right, is the central character in the novel. How do the artists use images of nature to express Genji's feelings and the action taking place?

EARLY JAPAN

Japan is an island chain, or **archipelago**, made up of four large islands and many smaller ones. Its closest neighbor, South Korea, is only 120 miles away, and that proximity explains the mainland's influences on Japan. For example, Japan adopted Korea's practices in growing rice. As an archipelago, however, Japan long escaped invasions and migrations, forming a unique culture that developed largely from one ethnic group.

Japan has no indigenous writing system, so archaeologists have pieced together its early history from archaeological materials and later sources. One of those sources explains that the Yamato clan was directly descended from the sun-goddess Amaterasu.

A **clan** is a group of people with a common ancestor. The earliest known religion of Japan, **Shinto**, included the worship of the spirits of trees, streams, and mountains, as well as of deceased rulers.

During the 300s and 400s, the Yamato was one of many clans that ruled different regions of Japan. However, by the sixth century, these clans had united under the leadership of a Yamato emperor. According to legend, the Yamato line has run unbroken from 660 B.C.E. until today, the oldest line of monarchs in the world.

As the Koguryo, Paekche, and Silla kingdoms fought for dominance on the Korean peninsula, many Koreans fled instability by migrating to Japan. These refugees introduced Korean military practices, methods of government, and a writing system that used Chinese characters. The Yamato modeled their government on the Korean form and adopted Chinese characters and Korean military practices. They also allied with the Paekche kingdom against the Silla.

For nearly 50 years, Paekche rulers pressured the Yamato to adopt Buddhism, but the Japanese hesitated to adopt the new religion. One clan related to the Yamato, the Soga, supported Buddhism, though. In 587, an armed conflict broke out between the Soga and clans opposed to Buddhism. After the victory of the Soga, the Japanese court converted to Buddhism. The Soga appointed **Prince Shotoku as regent**, which meant that Prince Shotoku would rule in the place of the Soga family.

Along with Buddhism, Prince Shotoku studied the teachings of Confucius and, beginning in 600, sent several delegations to China to learn from the newly formed Sui dynasty. The delegations, which included officials, Buddhist monks, students, and translators, brought back political, artistic, economic, and religious ideas that would influence Japan for centuries.

Prince Shotoku died in 622, but Chinese influence continued. Successive Japanese rulers sought to implement the Tang blueprint for rule, including a written law code. In doing so, they sought to strengthen their country and enhance their own rule, because a Chinese-style emperor had much more power than a Japanese chieftain.

In 710, the Japanese moved their capital to Nara, their first Chinese-style city with gridded streets, walls, and gates. After 710, the Japanese adopted Chinese building practices, using tiled roofs and stone bases for timber columns so that they did not rot.

Korea and Japan, c. 550

THE WORLD'S FIRST NOVEL

During the fifth century, Japan adopted the Chinese writing system. However, Japanese was from a different language family than Chinese. Chinese characters, called *kanji*, did not capture the full meaning of the Japanese language. In the ninth century, the Japanese developed a syllabic alphabet, called *kana*. Each kana character represented a syllable, so Japanese words could be written as they were pronounced.

Aristocratic men continued to use kanji, but aristocratic women were forbidden from using these characters, so they used kana instead. One woman named **Murasaki Shikibu** used kana to write *The Tale of Genji*, the world's first novel. The book describes the life of Prince Genji and his descendants. Shikibu's book describes fashion, entertainment, and romance in a world that valued skill in poetry, music, and calligraphy. The novel provides a wealth of insight into daily lives, such as the courtship of young men and women of the aristocracy and life at the emperor's court around 1000.

HISTORICAL THINKING

1. **READING CHECK** How did China and Korea influence the culture and politics of Japan?

2. **MAKE INFERENCES** What do Japanese kana and *The Tale of Genji* reveal about the lives of Japanese people around 1000?

3. **INTERPRET MAPS** Which Japanese island provided a convenient port of entry from the Korean peninsula to the Japanese archipelago?

208 CHAPTER 7

Societies in East and South Asia 209

PLAN: 2-PAGE LESSON

OBJECTIVE

Describe how Korea and China influenced the culture and government of Japan.

CRITICAL THINKING SKILLS FOR LESSON 3.2
• Make Inferences
• Interpret Maps
• Explain
• Compare and Contrast
• Analyze Primary Sources

HISTORICAL THINKING FOR CHAPTER 7

How did societies in East and South Asia influence one another's cultures over time?

Japan's geography kept it from being easily overrun by invaders and limited the effects of outside influences on the development of its culture. Lesson 3.2 discusses the ways in which China and Korea were able to impact Japanese cultural development.

Student eEdition online

Additional content for this lesson, including a sidebar and a primary source, is available online.

BACKGROUND FOR THE TEACHER

Shinto The word *Shinto* means "the way of kami." Kami are divine powers. These powers are found not just in objects like trees or mountains but also in people, such as deceased rulers, and in ideas, such as growth or judgment. The beliefs that make up Shinto are reflected in the everyday actions and value systems of those who practice it. The Shinto religion has no official text or prescribed way of worshiping. It also has no official founder, unlike the monotheistic religions of Islam, Judaism, or Christianity. The name *Shinto* was created only as a way of distinguishing the old beliefs of native Japanese people from Buddhism once it arrived in Japan. After Buddhism was introduced in Japan, many of the ideas and beliefs of Shinto and those of Buddhism were merged by Japanese followers.

INTRODUCE & ENGAGE

DISCUSS JAPANESE ARTWORK

Direct students to look at the woodblock print triptych in the lesson. Ask volunteers to speculate what early Japan must have been like, based on the artwork. *(Possible responses: beautiful, tree covered, advanced, formal culture)* Tell students that in this lesson they will learn about the development of Japanese society after the Yamato clan assumed power.

TEACH

GUIDED DISCUSSION

1. **Explain** What cultural influences did the Koreans have on the Yamato? *(The Yamato adopted the Korean form of government and military practices and the use of Chinese characters.)*

2. **Compare and Contrast** How were Chinese characters and kana different? *(Possible response: Kana represented symbols only, so words could be written as they were pronounced.)*

ANALYZE PRIMARY SOURCES

Direct students to the primary source excerpt (available in the Student eEdition). **ASK:** What is the excerpt describing? *(the process of making up stories and writing them down so they can be read)*

ACTIVE OPTIONS

On Your Feet: Jigsaw Strategy Organize students into four expert groups and have students from each group research one of the following different ways Korea and China influenced Japan: writing system, religion, government, and architecture. Have each group create a simplified summary of what they learned about the topic they researched. Regroup students into four new groups so each group has at least one person from each of the four expert groups. Have students in the new group take turns sharing the simplified summary they created in their expert groups.

NG Learning Framework: Write a Historical Profile
ATTITUDE Curiosity
KNOWLEDGE Our Human Story

Ask students to create a historical profile of the Japanese city of Nara, where the capital was moved in 710. Direct them to conduct online and library research to learn how the city has changed over the centuries. Prompt them to consider areas such as population, trade, quality of life, and other social, political, and economic factors. Also point out that many ancient Japanese buildings remain standing in Nara and ask them to include some information and visuals about them in their profiles. Have volunteers share their profiles with the class.

DIFFERENTIATE

STRIVING READERS

Make Word Cards As they read the lesson, prompt students at the **Intermediate** and **Advanced** levels to keep a list of unfamiliar words, such as *proximity, migrations, ethnic, unique, descended, hesitated, delegations,* and *implement.* Have students look up each word in a dictionary and make a word card to help them understand and pronounce the word. Tell them to write the word on one side of a card and define the word and spell it phonetically on the other side.

PRE-AP

Extend Knowledge Have students use a variety of sources to learn more about Prince Shotoku, the events of his rule, and his incorporation of Chinese elements into Japanese culture. Ask them to quote or paraphrase and cite secondary sources as appropriate. Invite volunteers to share their findings in an oral or written report.

See the Chapter Planner for more strategies for differentiation.

HISTORICAL THINKING

ANSWERS

1. The Yamato adopted military techniques, strategies for governing, and Buddhism from the Koreans. They adopted the Chinese writing system (by way of Korea), Confucianism, architecture, laws, and city layout from the Chinese.

2. Japanese women used kana because they were forbidden to learn Chinese characters. This shows that women were not expected to be educated in the same way as men. *The Tale of Genji* reveals details about how people of the aristocracy lived.

3. Kyushu

Possible response: The landscape shows the distance between the characters and reflects their hesitance at bridging the space between them.

3.3 Preserving Cultural Heritage

Temple Spires Against the Elements

The Khmer Empire, one of the most successful and sophisticated kingdoms in Southeast Asia's history, made the city of Angkor in present-day Cambodia its capital. It was in that city that Angkor Wat, a massive temple complex, was built in the 12th century by King Suryavarman II.

One of the greatest works of Khmer architecture, Angkor Wat is an important part of Cambodian culture and history. Originally dedicated to the Hindu god Vishnu, Angkor Wat features sculptural reliefs with Hindu motifs and ancient Khmer scenes along the temple walls. Later, during the reign of King Jayavarman VII (1181–1220), a new capital was built, Angkor Thom, dedicated to Buddhism. Angkor Wat then also became a Buddhist temple and much of the Hindu art was replaced with Buddhist art. Today, both styles can be seen throughout the temple.

ANGKOR WAT
Built to honor the Hindu god Vishnu, the central temple at Angkor Wat is a five-towered pyramid. Each tower is shaped like a lotus bud, which in Hinduism represents beauty and purity. Today, the temple complex is threatened by sinking ground due to increased tourism and depleted water levels.

PLAN: 4-PAGE LESSON

OBJECTIVE
Describe the history of the temple complex Angkor Wat and the environmental elements it has survived.

CRITICAL THINKING SKILLS FOR LESSON 3.3
- Analyze Visuals
- Make Connections
- Analyze Cause and Effect
- Explain
- Make Inferences
- Identify Problems and Solutions

HISTORICAL THINKING FOR CHAPTER 7
How did societies in East and South Asia influence one another's cultures over time?

The temple complex Angkor Wat is an example of how societies in South Asia influenced religion. It was built as a Hindu temple but was converted into a Buddhist temple. Lesson 3.3 discusses how Angkor Wat has survived 900 years and the efforts being made to preserve it.

BACKGROUND FOR THE TEACHER
Angkor Archaeological Park Angkor Archaeological Park stretches over 240 square miles and is one of the largest archaeological sites in the world. The park contains magnificent architectural remains and hydrological engineering systems (reservoirs and canals) from the Khmer period. These numerous ancient features provide evidence that an exceptional civilization lived here long ago. Although Khmer architecture was influenced by cultures from the Indian sub-continent, it developed clearly distinct features that made it unique. The Angkor Archaeological Park represents the Khmer art and architecture that influenced much of Southeast Asia. The park is a living heritage site that has many villages scattered throughout, inhabited by people whose ancestors date back to the Khmer Empire.

History Notebook
Encourage students to complete the Preserving Cultural Heritage page for Chapter 7 in their History Notebooks as they read.

INTRODUCE & ENGAGE

PREVIEW WITH VISUALS

Direct students' attention to the photographs presented in the lesson. Write "Environmental Threats" at the center of a Concept Cluster and ask volunteers to list threats to the temples shown based on their observation of the photographs. Arrange the noted threats into groups on the cluster. At the end of the lesson, revisit the Concept Cluster and add or remove traits based on what students learned.

TEACH

GUIDED DISCUSSION

1. **Explain** How was Angkor Wat changed during the reign of King Jayavarman VII? *(Angkor Wat was originally dedicated to the Hindu god Vishnu, but was changed into a Buddhist temple. Much of the Hindu art was replaced with Buddhist art.)*

2. **Analyze Cause and Effect** What caused the demise of the city of Angkor? *(Long droughts followed by heavy monsoon rains destroyed the city's infrastructure.)*

PRESERVING CULTURAL HERITAGE

Angkor Wat is one of the largest religious monuments ever built. The name *Angkor Wat* means "temple city." It is a temple complex spread over more than 200 acres. When Angkor Wat was built in the 12th century, a 15-foot-tall wall surrounded the city of Angkor to protect the temple and the people from invasion. The wall and temple were made from blocks of sandstone which have mostly survived the ages, but the structures around the temple were built from wood and other materials that did not survive. The temple's design is supposed to look like Mount Meru, the home of the gods, according to both Hindu and Buddhist faiths, which lies somewhere beyond the Himalaya. The five towers represent the five peaks of Mount Meru. The tower above the main shrine is nearly 70 feet tall. The many groups of people working to preserve Angkor Wat have been extremely careful not to impact its overall authenticity.

DIFFERENTIATE

ENGLISH LANGUAGE LEARNERS

Dictate Sentence Summaries Pair students at the **Beginning** level with those at the **Advanced** level. After students read the lesson, direct them to identify three sentences that contain an important idea. Then tell each student to write that idea in a summary sentence using his or her own words. Partners then take turns dictating their sentences to each other. Encourage them to work together to check each other's work for accuracy and spelling.

PRE-AP

Explore More Direct students to conduct online research on a topic related to Angkor Wat, such as the French explorer Henri Mouhot who discovered the temple city in the mid-1800s, the hidden paintings archaeologists have found inside some temples, or the new discoveries made around the temple complex using Lidar. Invite them to share their research in an oral presentation to the class.

See the Chapter Planner for more strategies for differentiation.

Strangler fig trees and creeping lichens devour ruins at Ta Prohm—another temple located northeast of Angkor Wat.

By the early 15th century, the once grand Angkor kingdom fell. Researchers found that Angkor's demise wasn't due to enemy invaders but to the changing climate. Long droughts followed by heavy monsoon rains destroyed the city's infrastructure and the empire collapsed.

Once the Khmer Empire fell, Angkor was abandoned and eventually covered up by the jungle—not to be discovered again until the mid-19th century. Restoration efforts began in the early 20th century but were halted in the 1970s and 1980s because of political instability and wars in Cambodia.

After withstanding the tests of time and war, the Angkor complex—and Angkor Wat—was designated a UNESCO World Heritage Site in 1992. Yet once again, environmental issues plague the Angkor region and endanger the stability and structure of Angkor Wat.

Once Cambodia became safe to visit, tourists flocked to Siem Reap, the resort city near the Angkor region.

The increasing number of people has taxed the city's systems and resources—especially water. As water levels have dropped, archaeologists have noticed some sinking and movement in some of the structures in Angkor.

These environmental issues combined with previously poor preservation efforts are threatening the future of Angkor Wat. While the structure is somewhat stable now, archaeologists, architects, restoration specialists, museum curators, and conservationists are working to prevent even greater damage from occurring. Preserving Angkor Wat's cultural heritage is truly a global effort. The World Monuments Fund, a U.S. conservation group, is working with Cambodian professionals and other conservation groups from around the world to protect the historic site from the elements.

HISTORICAL THINKING

ANALYZE CAUSE AND EFFECT In what ways can the environment affect cultural heritage?

BACKGROUND FOR THE TEACHER

National Geographic Photographer Robert Clark All of the photographs in the lesson were taken by photographer Robert Clark, who is known for his innovation. He has photographed more than 40 stories for *National Geographic* over a 20-year association with the magazine. His photographs for the cover article "Was Darwin Wrong?" helped the magazine earn a National Magazine award in 2005. Clark was also recognized at the World Press Photo awards in Amsterdam for his photographs of the attack on the World Trade Center, which he witnessed from his rooftop, approximately three miles away. He has done numerous other independent projects and authored four books, including *Image America*, in which he traveled the country taking photos only with his cell phone camera. Some of his earlier work included documenting a high school football team in Odessa, Texas, for H.G. "Buzz" Bissenger's best-selling book *Friday Night Lights*, which was turned into a movie as well as a television series. In 2003, another project brought Clark back to photographing football players in Texas. This time, it was a new NFL team, the Houston Texans, the publication of a black-and-white photo book, and a popular exhibit at Houston's Museum of Fine Arts. Clark's photographs have been featured in magazines such as *Time, Sports Illustrated,* and *Vanity Fair,* among others. A recent project of Clark's is a book documenting the birth of the science of evolution with *National Geographic.*

TEACH

GUIDED DISCUSSION

3. **Make Inferences** How long was Angkor abandoned, and how could this length of time have affected restoration efforts? *(Angkor was abandoned for more than 400 years, during which the jungle grew over it. The jungle probably grew very thick during 400 years and greatly hampered restoration efforts.)*

4. **Identify Problems and Solutions** How have tourists endangered some of the structures in Angkor and areas nearby, and what has been done to help? *(Tourists have flocked to a resort city near the Angkor region and used so much water that water levels have dropped, causing some structures in Angkor to sink and shift. Tourism has been somewhat regulated.)*

ANALYZE VISUALS

Share the Background for the Teacher information on the Angkor Archaeological Park and the Preserving Cultural Heritage information. Then have students examine the photographs of the temples in the lesson, explaining that all temples are now protected in the park. **ASK:** How are the temples similar and different? *(Possible responses: They all look to be made of sandstone but are very different shapes. Angkor Wat has tall spires, but the temple of Phonom Bakheng is square-shaped. Some have trees growing on them or nearby, while others appear to be free of vegetation.)* Why is it important to limit the number of tourists visiting the temples? *(Possible response: Too many tourists have depleted water levels and threatened the stability of the temples.)*

ACTIVE OPTION

NG Learning Framework: Explore Angkor Temples
ATTITUDE Curiosity
KNOWLEDGE Our Human Story

Invite students to conduct online research on one of the temples mentioned in the lesson. Encourage them to learn about the art and architecture of the temple as well as past and current efforts to restore and preserve the temple. Have volunteers present a visual of their temple to the class and describe its characteristics.

HISTORICAL THINKING

ANSWERS

Possible response: The environment can have a negative effect on cultural heritage, as seen at Angkor Wat. The overgrown trees and roots threaten the temples along with reduced water levels, which are causing some of the existing structures to sink.

7 REVIEW

VOCABULARY

Complete each of the following sentences using one of the vocabulary words from the chapter.

1. Believers of Christianity, Islam, and Hinduism often believe in their God's _____, or unlimited power.

2. The fact that the Iron Pillar of Delhi has never rusted is evidence of Gupta expertise in _____.

3. Conquered people often have to pay _____ to their conquerors.

4. The Tang dynasty tax system was based on a _____, or an official count of the population.

5. Filled with people from around the world, the Chinese capital of Chang'an was very _____.

6. A _____ is more interested in human skeletons and teeth than in pieces of pottery or bronze.

7. The ruling Soga family appointed a _____ to run the government in their place.

8. Four large islands and many small islands make up Japan's _____.

READING STRATEGY
DRAW CONCLUSIONS

When you draw conclusions, you make a judgment based on what you have read. Use a chart like this one to draw a conclusion about the influence of Han and Tang China on Korea, Vietnam, and Japan. Then answer the question.

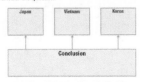

9. Why do you think Korea, Vietnam, and Japan resisted China's control while embracing some elements of its influence?

MAIN IDEAS

Answer the following questions. Support your answers with evidence from the chapter.

10. What are two dimensions of Hindu religious practice? LESSON 1.1

11. Why is the Gupta dynasty considered to be India's golden age? LESSON 1.2

12. In what ways did the Chola kings merge religious devotion and political advancement? LESSON 1.3

13. Why was Zhang Qian's travel through Central Asia important to China's economy? LESSON 2.3

14. What events contributed to the prosperity of the Tang dynasty? LESSON 2.4

15. Which traditions did the Koreans and Vietnamese keep even after adopting many Chinese ways? LESSON 3.1

16. What geographic factor influenced Japan's acceptance of Korean and Chinese cultural and political ideas? LESSON 3.2

HISTORICAL THINKING

Answer the following questions. Support your answers with evidence from the chapter.

17. EXPLAIN Why did the Hindus depict deities as having more than two arms? How did this depiction help followers understand the deities?

18. COMPARE AND CONTRAST How were the Gupta dynasty and the Chola kingdom similar? How were they different?

19. IDENTIFY PROBLEMS AND SOLUTIONS What problems did the Tang emperors face? How did they solve them? Which were they unable to solve?

20. ANALYZE CAUSE AND EFFECT How did alliances with the Tang influence the outcome of the Three Kingdoms period in Korea?

21. FORM AND SUPPORT OPINIONS Do you think *The Tale of Genji* is a reliable resource for researching Japanese history? Why or why not?

INTERPRET TIME LINES

Study the time line of events in Buddhism and Hinduism. Then answer the questions that follow.

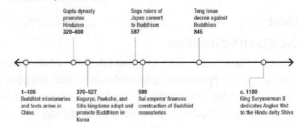

22. How long did Buddhism prosper in China before the Tang backlash?

23. Which event shown on the time line do you think most contributed to the spread of Buddhism and Hinduism?

ANALYZE SOURCES

The daughter of a Han poet and historian, Ban Zhao wrote a book that taught young Chinese women how to be worthy wives. She also delivered strong messages to men. Read the two excerpts below and answer the question that follows.

> If a husband does not control his wife, then the rules of conduct manifesting his authority are abandoned and broken. If a wife does not serve her husband, then the proper relationship between men and women and the natural order of things are neglected and destroyed. . . .
>
> Yet only to teach men and not to teach women—is that not ignoring the essential relation between them? . . . It is the rule to begin to teach children to read at the age of eight. . . . Only why should it not be that girls' education as well as boys' be according to this principle?
>
> —from *Lessons for Women* by Ban Zhao

24. How did the teachings of Ban Zhao both limit women and promote their advancement?

CONNECT TO YOUR LIFE

25. INFORMATIVE Chinese influence did not end with East Asia. Research China's influence on your life, either through ancient inventions used around the world today, current systems of trade and economy, or cultural influences in food and medicine. Then write a short essay describing this influence.

TIPS

• Review Chinese advances in government, technology, and other fields described in this chapter or earlier lessons.

• Investigate the present-day influence of China on global trade and the economy.

• Decide whether you want to write about past or present influences and do further research based on your decision.

• Use two or three vocabulary terms from this chapter in your essay.

• Conclude your essay with a statement that summarizes the influence of China on your life today.

VOCABULARY ANSWERS

1. omnipotence
2. metallurgy
3. tribute
4. census
5. cosmopolitan
6. bioarchaeologist
7. regent
8. archipelago

READING STRATEGY ANSWER

Japan	Vietnam	Korea
Buddhism; sculptures; paintings; porcelain-making techniques; Chinese writing system and woodblock printing; political, artistic, economic, and religious ideas; a written law code; Chinese-style city with gridded streets, walls, and gates; tiled roofs and stone bases for timber columns	Buddhism; Chinese writing system and woodblock printing	Buddhism; sculptures; paintings; porcelain-making techniques; Chinese writing system and woodblock printing; Chinese culture and governance

Conclusion
Japan, Vietnam, and Korea all allowed some Chinese influence into their societies, particularly Buddhism and a writing system. However, Vietnam was most resistant to Chinese influence in the arts, politics, economy, and culture.

9. Possible answer: These cultures recognized the value of some Chinese innovations and practices but wanted to preserve their own traditions, and they feared that Chinese control would not allow that.

MAIN IDEAS ANSWERS

10. Public and private worship are two dimensions of Hindu religious practice. Hindus practice their religion publicly through worship in temples, as well as privately through devotion to a personal deity.

11. During the Gupta dynasty, art, literature, and architecture flourished in India, as did math, science, and technology.

12. The Chola kings built many temples and promoted Hinduism. Their temples showed great devotion to their Hindu deities, but the temples were also places where the kings promoted their own political and military achievements.

13. The information about markets and trade that Zhang Qian brought back to China opened the Silk Roads as a route through which China could trade with the outside world.

14. Trade with other countries contributed greatly to Tang prosperity, as did the Tang practices of developing a census, distributing land, and taxing citizens.

15. The Koreans retained a hierarchical system. The Vietnamese held on to their religious traditions while also adopting Chinese religions and beliefs.

16. Japan's proximity to Korea and China increased communication and allowed for cultural diffusion.

HISTORICAL THINKING ANSWERS

17. The multiple arms represented the deities' power to overcome evil.

18. Both the Gupta and the Chola were accomplished and prosperous. Both dynasties were Hindu and built great temples. Both achieved high levels of education. The Gupta made great advancements in math and astronomy. The Chola had the highest literacy rate of their time. The Gupta were masters of metallurgy while the Chola built a huge irrigation system to master agricultural development. Both allowed a large degree of autonomy in their governance.

19. The Tang created law codes to resolve disputes and to divide up land and collect taxes. At one point in their history, Emperor Wu took over. However, she was deposed in a coup, and the Tang continued their rule. Later, a general rebelled. The Tang suppressed the rebellion, but the dynasty never fully recovered.

20. The Silla formed an alliance with the Tang to take control of the Korean peninsula. This alliance succeeded except that the Tang attempted to overthrow the Silla once Korea was unified. However, the Silla held out against the Chinese. The Paekche alliance with the Japanese didn't result in defeat of the Silla, but it allowed the Paekche and the Buddhists to gain influence in Japan.

21. *The Tale of Genji* is a novel, or work of fiction, so it cannot be trusted to provide accurate historical events. However, descriptions of life and beliefs at the time of its writing reveal what life was like in the imperial court when Murasaki Shikibu lived and wrote.

INTERPRET TIME LINES ANSWERS

22. Buddhism prospered for 744 to 844 years before the Tang dynasty issued decrees against it.

23. The adoption by and support of each country's leaders were important to the spread of both religions.

ANALYZE SOURCES ANSWER

24. Her writings taught women to obey their husbands and taught men to control their wives. These teachings limited women because they were not allowed to be equal to men. However, she also argued for the education of women. In this way, she promoted their advancement.

CONNECT TO YOUR LIFE ANSWER

25. Students' informative essays will vary but should contain a thesis; develop the thesis with relevant, supporting details; include two or three vocabulary terms from the chapter; and provide a concluding statement that describes the influence of China on their life today.

The Land of the Stars

BY NADIA DRAKE Adapted from "How 'The Land of the Stars' Shaped Astronomy (and Me)" by Nadia Drake, news.nationalgeographic.com, August 2, 2016

My father may have dedicated a lifetime to studying the heavens, but my mother comes from the land of the stars. In the Middle East, the night sky's stories have been known for millennia, told by those who named its lights, aligned their tombs and temples with its shifting shapes, and divined the movements of the worlds wandering our solar system.

I came to the Middle East for the first time not knowing what to expect yet anticipating the awakening of a sleepy part of myself. I'd grown up hearing Arabic and knowing the recipe for proper tabbouleh, but Lebanon was a place I'd only seen in my dreams.

As the mountains and buildings of Beirut emerged from the haze, I felt like I was coming home. I was that youth whose universe was right there among the salt and the cedars and the centuries of richness and strife, staring wide-eyed at a realm where the first twinklings of the stars were recorded.

I've always felt like a bit of an impostor Arab. My blondish hair and bluish eyes don't fit the stereotypical image of my darker-eyed kin—but walking the streets of Beirut meant seeing that so many Lebanese women look just like me. It was an observation that offered solace, and I felt like I belonged—a nearly impossible privilege in a part of the world where wars are fought to make "belonging" even a smidge more possible. But there I was.

One evening, we camped in the Wadi Rum desert near Jordan's southern border. Also known as the Valley of the Moon, the Wadi Rum is moody and otherworldly in a harsh and commanding way. There, lumpy sandstone walls erupt from scorched, reddish sands crisscrossed by herds of camels and Bedouin shepherding tourists around in rickety Jeeps.

Too hot to sleep, I wandered outside and found myself completely distracted by one of the most dazzling skies I'd ever seen. A half moon bright enough to cast shadows obliterated the stars until it sank behind a ridge—and then, in the Valley of the Moon, those stars started screaming for attention.

Stars sprinkle the night sky over the Wadi Rum desert in Jordan.

I settled into the sand and lay there silently for hours, transfixed by the lights tracing paths across the sky. Antares, the red supergiant beating at the heart of Scorpius, soon emerged, and then the entire scorpion's tail curled across the sky and dipped into the stream of stars that is the Milky Way. Cygnus glittered overhead, next to the starfield where NASA's Kepler telescope has made such monumental planet discoveries. In the north, Cassiopeia clung to her throne, while in the south, the Sagittarius teapot pointed to the spot where a supermassive black hole churns away in the core of our galaxy.

I can only imagine how captivating this evening light show must have been during the ages when Earth's skies were uncontaminated by artificial lights. It's no wonder cultures all over the planet have their own version of its stories, their own solutions to its mysteries. What did the ancient Arabs think these shapes in the sky represented?

The Middle East is far from perfect, as is every place on Earth. Conflict disfigures the region in profoundly troubling ways. Yet if you ever doubt that we are all connected, just look up: Twinkling overhead are the same exact stars humans all over the world have gazed at forever, beckoning to us and inviting us to solve their riddles. ■

Staging the Question

In this unit, you examined three civilizations that had a tremendous influence on later cultures. One theme that unites the Persians, Greeks, Romans, and Han dynasty is the drive to further human knowledge in numerous realms. All four cultures made remarkable advances in astronomy and other sciences, writing, visual and performing arts, economics, engineering, and various other fields. By scrutinizing Persian, Greek, Roman, and Chinese artifacts and writings, researchers have learned a great deal about each civilization's attainments in learning. What can we learn about a culture from studying its advancements?

Supporting Questions: Begin by developing supporting questions to guide your research. For example: How does this object help me understand the importance of writing to the Persian empire? Research the answers in this unit and in other sources, both print and online. You might want to use a web like this one to record the answers to your questions about each artifact.

Summative Performance Task: Write an explanatory label for each object or image you chose. Your labels will tell museum visitors how each item represents the civilization's advancements in at least one field of learning. Write two or three paragraphs for the exhibit introduction explaining why you chose these particular artifacts and sharing your ideas about how the civilization was changed by its advancements in knowledge.

Present: Share your exhibit with the class. You might consider one of these options:

ASSIGNMENT

Select five artifacts or images from either the Persian, Greek, Roman, or Han empire. You may choose images from this unit or from your own research.

Identify the fields of knowledge—such as science, art, economics, or engineering—that each object or image represents.

Explain how each object or image illustrates the civilization's understanding of the fields it represents.

Use the objects and the information you learned about them to create a museum exhibit about the Persians, Greeks, Romans, or Han dynasty.

MAKE A GALLERY
Combine your exhibit with those of other students who focused on the same civilization. Curate your gallery by choosing artifacts that fit together logically to illustrate the civilization's advancements in at least three fields. Display your exhibit in the classroom or create an online gallery.

GIVE AN EXPLORER LECTURE
Watch lectures by National Geographic Explorers online, then follow their model to write your own Explorer lecture. Create an online slideshow of the artifacts you selected and give your lecture to the class. Use gestures and expressions to convey an Explorer's enthusiasm for the topic.

Take Informed Action:

UNDERSTAND Conduct research online or on social media to learn about artifacts from ancient civilizations that are in danger of destruction.

ASSESS Choose an artifact and think about how it illustrates the culture's understanding of certain fields of knowledge.

ACT Comment on the posts or articles you found about the artifact, sharing your arguments about why it should be preserved.

NATIONAL GEOGRAPHIC CONNECTION

GUIDED DISCUSSION FOR "THE LAND OF THE STARS"

1. **Make Connections** How have cultures other than those near the Valley of the Moon used astronomy? *(Answers will vary. Encourage students to use information from the unit. Possible responses: Egyptians used the star Sirius to determine when the Nile River would flood each year; the Aztec used the movement of objects in space to create a complex calendar; today, astronomers are searching for habitable environments in space.)*

2. **Evaluate** How have sciences such as astronomy prevailed throughout millennia despite conflicts? *(Answers will vary. Possible responses: People likely used the stars to guide them on their explorations and across trade routes, regardless of who or what they might encounter; people used the stars and the universe to explain phenomena on Earth by attributing them to gods, which became the basis for some religious practices; despite different interpretations of the heavens and conflicting ideas about society and religion, people across the world have similarly turned to astronomy to guide them.)*

History Notebook

Encourage students to complete the Unit Wrap-Up page for Unit 2 in their History Notebooks.

UNIT INQUIRY PROJECT RUBRIC

ASSESS

Use the rubric to assess each student's participation and performance.

SCORE	ASSIGNMENT	PRODUCT	PRESENTATION
3 GREAT	• Student thoroughly understands the assignment. • Student develops thoughtful supporting questions to guide research.	• Exhibit is well thought out with a variety of objects and images. • Exhibit reflects all of the key elements listed in the assignment.	• Presentation is clear, concise, and logical. • Presentation is creative and engaging.
2 GOOD	• Student mostly understands the assignment. • Student develops somewhat thoughtful supporting questions to guide research.	• Exhibit is fairly well thought out with some objects and images. • Exhibit reflects most of the key elements listed in the assignment.	• Presentation is fairly clear, concise, and logical. • Presentation is somewhat creative and engaging.
1 NEEDS WORK	• Student does not understand the assignment. • Student does not develop thoughtful questions to guide research.	• Exhibit is not well thought out and contains few objects and images. • Exhibit reflects few or none of the key elements listed in the assignment.	• Presentation is not clear, concise, or logical. • Presentation is not creative or engaging.

INTRODUCE THE PHOTOGRAPH

SHEIKH LOTFOLLAH MOSQUE

The Masjed-e Shaykh Lutf Allah, or the Sheikh Lotfollah Mosque, was constructed in the center of Isfahan, Iran, during the Safavid period. Mosques, generally the most important feature of a town, were more than places of worship for believers in Islam; they were symbols of wealth and power. The Sheikh Lotfollah Mosque is on the eastern side of Naqsh-e Jahan ("Image of the World") Square, which is one of the largest public urban squares in the world and is also registered as a UNESCO World Heritage Site.

The Sheikh Lotfollah Mosque stands about 105 feet tall and was built for the private worship of the royal court. It consists of a single domed chamber, which is unusual for this type of holy structure. This mosque does not include a courtyard or minarets. However, the mosque is decorated with intricate, repetitious patterns on both its interior and exterior, continuing earlier styles of Islamic art. Tiny tiles shift from cream to pink throughout the day, with some people saying the best time to see this transformation is at sunset. In July 2019, restorers began installing 48,000 cream colored tiles on the dome, about one-quarter of the total.

Direct students' attention to the photograph. **ASK:** Is it possible for a building to be a work of art? Explain your response and provide an example. *(Possible response: Yes. Throughout history, artists have been commissioned to construct and paint architectural marvels, such as the Egyptian pyramids, the Colosseum in Rome, or the Sistine Chapel.)*

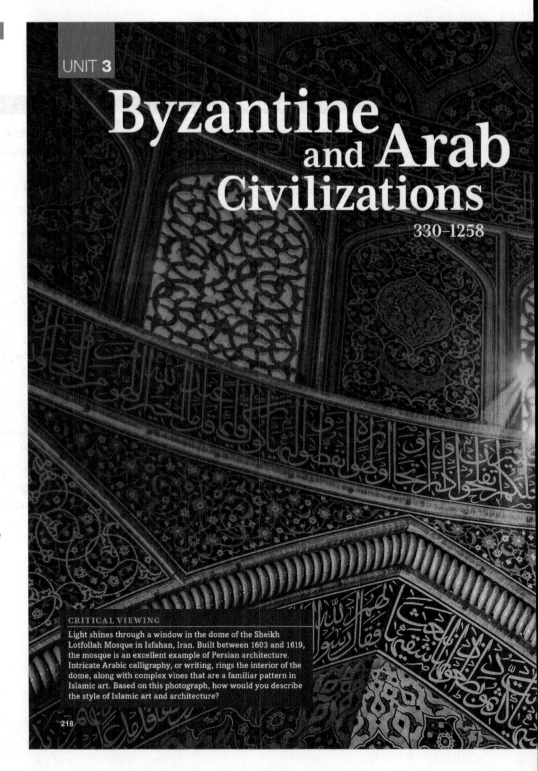

UNIT 3

Byzantine and Arab Civilizations

330–1258

CRITICAL VIEWING

Light shines through a window in the dome of the Sheikh Lotfollah Mosque in Isfahan, Iran. Built between 1603 and 1619, the mosque is an excellent example of Persian architecture. Intricate Arabic calligraphy, or writing, rings the interior of the dome, along with complex vines that are a familiar pattern in Islamic art. Based on this photograph, how would you describe the style of Islamic art and architecture?

218

IDENTIFY PATTERNS AND THEMES

Have volunteers read aloud each of the world events in the time line. **ASK:** What are some common themes or patterns that you notice with regard to these events? *(Possible responses: Some common themes or patterns include exploration, conquest, expansion, powerful empires, religious reform, and technological innovation.)* Sort the themes and patterns into categories and put them into charts as shown here.

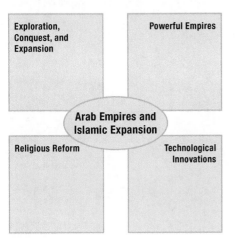

As students read the lessons for each chapter in the unit, have them add the information to the appropriate section in the chart. Advise students that they may also add or revise categories as necessary. At the end of the unit, revisit students' charts and create a final list of categories to summarize the historical themes students encountered as they read each chapter.

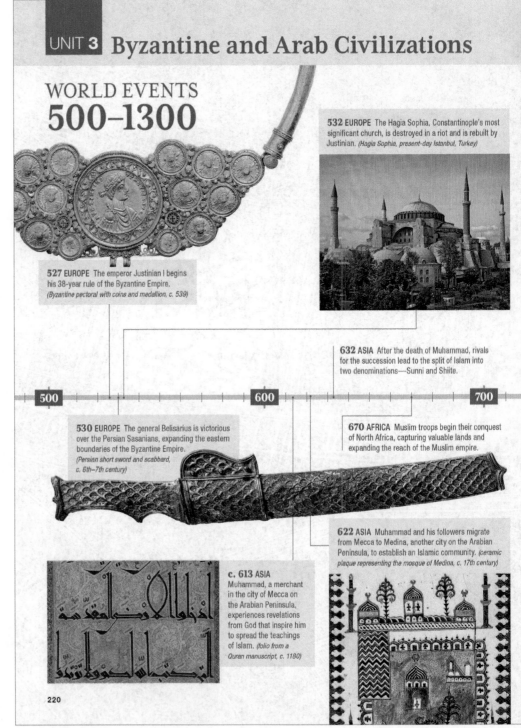

UNIT 3 **Byzantine and Arab Civilizations**

WORLD EVENTS
500–1300

527 EUROPE The emperor Justinian I begins his 38-year rule of the Byzantine Empire. *(Byzantine pectoral with coins and medallion, c. 539)*

532 EUROPE The Hagia Sophia, Constantinople's most significant church, is destroyed in a riot and is rebuilt by Justinian. *(Hagia Sophia, present-day Istanbul, Turkey)*

632 ASIA After the death of Muhammad, rivals for the succession lead to the split of Islam into two denominations—Sunni and Shiite.

500   **600**   **700**

530 EUROPE The general Belisarius is victorious over the Persian Sasanians, expanding the eastern boundaries of the Byzantine Empire. *(Persian short sword and scabbard, c. 6th–7th century)*

670 AFRICA Muslim troops begin their conquest of North Africa, capturing valuable lands and expanding the reach of the Muslim empire.

622 ASIA Muhammad and his followers migrate from Mecca to Medina, another city on the Arabian Peninsula, to establish an Islamic community. *(ceramic plaque representing the mosque of Medina, c. 17th century)*

c. 613 ASIA Muhammad, a merchant in the city of Mecca on the Arabian Peninsula, experiences revelations from God that inspire him to spread the teachings of Islam. *(folio from a Quran manuscript, c. 1180)*

220

HISTORICAL THINKING

COMPARE AND CONTRAST How do the religions of Christianity and Islam compare in terms of growth during this period?

744 ASIA The Abbasids, a family claiming to be direct descendants of Muhammad's uncle Abbas, gain control of the Muslim empire after the assassination of the caliph. *(piece of column from a building in the former Abbasid capital of Raqqa, Syria, c. mid-700s)*

c. early 800s ASIA The caliph Al-Mamun rules the Muslim empire and champions scientific advances, inviting scientists to study in Baghdad at a center known as the House of Wisdom. *(Indian miniature of Caliph Al-Mamun, c. 1593)*

762 ASIA The Abbasid caliph Mansur establishes a new capital at Baghdad, which becomes an important center for learning and trade.

867 EUROPE The Macedonian dynasty ushers in the golden age of the Byzantine Empire, during which the arts and literature flourish and knowledge of mathematics expands.

1258 ASIA Muslim leaders no longer control the territories that were once united under the Abbasid empire.

800 // // **1000** // **1300**

1071 EUROPE The decline of the Byzantine Empire is hastened after Byzantines are first driven out of southern Italy and later defeated at a battle in present-day Turkey.

1054 EUROPE The Christian Church formally splits into the Orthodox Church in the east and the Roman Catholic Church in the west, an event known as the East-West Schism. *(Byzantine icon of the Virgin Mary, c. 1100)*

c. 860 EUROPE Construction of the Alhambra, a building that is considered a remarkable architectural achievement in Islamic Spain, begins in the city of Granada. *(view of the Alhambra, Granada, Spain)*

221

HISTORICAL THINKING

Compare and Contrast

Possible response: The religions of Christianity and Islam follow similar but opposite paths. Islam splits into two denominations after the death of Muhammad, but it grows as it spreads across Africa, Asia, and into Europe. Christianity splits into two distinct branches and is overtaken by Islam after the defeat of the Byzantine Empire.

Student eEdition online

Additional content, including the unit map and Global Perspective feature, is available online.

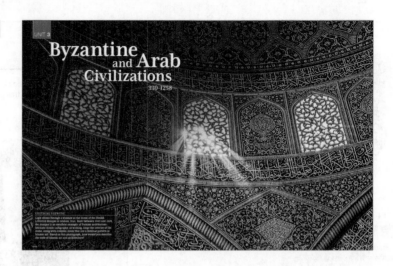

STRATEGY ❶

Use K-W-L Charts

Provide pairs with a K-W-L Chart. Have them brainstorm what they know about the lesson topic and add their ideas to the first column of the chart. Have them preview headings, photographs, and maps and write at least three questions they have in the second column. After they have read the lesson, remind pairs to write the answers to their questions and other information they learned in the third column. Ask them to keep their charts for each lesson to help them review the entire chapter.

Use with All Lessons

STRATEGY ❷

Clarify Information

Students may have trouble understanding different topics in the lessons, such as the devastation of the plague, because they do not realize that people in the past knew nothing about germs or how diseases spread. To help students organize their reading and clarify information, encourage them to use a 5Ws Chart to take notes on the information under each heading in the lessons.

Use with All Lessons

STRATEGY ❸

Read and Recall

Tell students to read the lesson independently. Then pair students and have them take notes as they share the content that they recall. Direct them to review the lesson and decide what to add or change in their notes.

Use with All Lessons

STRATEGY ❶

Describe Artwork

Pair sight-impaired students with a teacher aide or another student to examine the artwork in the chapter. Ask the student to describe what he or she can see, if anything, in the artwork. Instruct the sighted partner to describe details that can be difficult to see, such as the small pieces in the mosaics or the pale circles around the heads of the Virgin Mary and the Christ-child. Have pairs discuss why the artwork has been included in the text.

Use with All Lessons

STRATEGY ❷

Use a Graphic Organizer

Point out that readers often have to put together ideas in a text with what they already know about the ideas to make an inference, or an educated guess or conclusion about what happened or why it happened. Encourage students to use a graphic organizer to help them make inferences. Students can write the evidence or facts that the text provides in the first column, write what they know about the ideas or how their experiences help them understand in the second column, and their inference or educated guess in the third column. Tell students to compare their inference charts with a partner and discuss how the charts are the same and different.

Use with All Lessons

STRATEGY ❶

Activate Prior Knowledge

Display the terms below in a random "splash" arrangement. Tell students that all terms relate to the growth and decline of the early Byzantine Empire. Ask them to discuss ideas that the terms bring to mind, and which terms still relate to important issues today. Then instruct them to work in pairs to write sentences using one or two of the terms. You may wish to pair students at the **Beginning** level with students at the **Intermediate** or **Advanced** level.

outbreak strait plague women's rights geographic barriers immigrants books of law devout mosaic controversy iconoclasts icons legal codes cultural diversity

Use with All Lessons

STRATEGY 2
PREP Before Reading

Encourage students at **All Proficiencies** to use the PREP strategy to prepare for reading. Write this acrostic on the board:

Preview the title.
Read the Main Idea statement.
Examine the visuals.
Predict what you will learn.

Use with All Lessons *Encourage students at the* ***Beginning*** *level to ask questions if they have trouble writing a prediction. Students at the* ***Advanced*** *level may be able to help.*

STRATEGY 3
Use Sentence Strips

Choose a paragraph from the lesson and make sentence strips from it. Read the paragraph aloud while students follow along with the text. Pair students at the **Beginning** and **Intermediate** levels. Then give pairs the set of sentence strips and instruct them to put the strips in order, without using the text. Invite students to take turns reading the resulting paragraph aloud.

Use with All Lessons *You may ask students at the* ***Beginning*** *level to read the sentences aloud and ask their partners to explain unfamiliar words before working together to arrange the sentences in the correct order.*

GIFTED & TALENTED

STRATEGY 1
Create an Invasion Plan

Remind students that many parts of the Byzantine Empire were vulnerable to attack by its enemies. Ask students to use the map of the Byzantine Empire in Lesson 1.1 and to research geographic features of the area that would have helped protect the empire and that would have helped the enemies of the empire. Encourage them to choose one or more of the empire's enemies and to create a plan for invasion of the Byzantine Empire. Have them draw up a diagram of their plan and present it to the class.

Use with Lessons 1.1 and 2.2

STRATEGY 2
Present a Debate

Direct students to further research the icons of the Byzantine Empire and why they were believed to have special powers. Then have one or more students choose the side of the iconophiles, who venerated the icons, and one or more students choose the side of the iconoclasts, who believed the icons violated the Second Commandment of the Hebrew Bible. Encourage them to list reasons that support their side of the controversy and to consider ways to counterattack the other side's reasons. Invite students to debate the issue in front of the class.

Use with Lesson 2.1

PRE-AP

STRATEGY 1
Form a Thesis

Ask students to develop a thesis statement for a specific topic related to one of the lessons in the chapter. The statement must make a claim that is supportable with evidence either from the chapter or through further research. Ask students to present their thesis statements and the supporting evidence to the class.

Use with All Lessons

STRATEGY 2
Write a Biographical Profile

Instruct students to locate a historical biography on Justinian or Theodora. Tell students to read the biography independently and then develop a profile for the emperor or empress that explains his or her influence on the Byzantine Empire, how his or her actions relate to people of today, and why he or she is a good historical figure to know. Encourage students to post their completed profile on a class blog or school website.

Use with Lesson 1.2

The Early Byzantine Empire
330–1081

HISTORICAL THINKING How can a strong leader impact an empire?

SECTION 1 **Constantinople**
SECTION 2 **Christianity in the East**

CRITICAL VIEWING
The Basilica of Sant'Apollinare in Classe in Ravenna, Italy, was built in the sixth century. The area around its altar is covered with an elaborate mosaic scene showing Saint Apollinaris outdoors, surrounded by lambs. What other religious symbols do you see in the scene?

222 CHAPTER 8   The Early Byzantine Empire 223

INTRODUCE THE PHOTOGRAPH

BASILICA OF SANT'APOLLINARE IN CLASSE

Direct students to examine the photograph of the basilica, which is known as one of the most magnificent basilicas of the early Christian Church. Explain to students that Saint Apollinaris led a group of believers, or his flock, in the teachings of Christianity. He was arrested and tortured to death by the Roman Empire. **ASK:** Why do you think Saint Apollinaris is shown standing among lambs? *(Possible response: A group of lambs is known as a flock, and Saint Apollinaris led a flock of believers.)* Tell students that in this chapter they will learn about a devout Christian emperor who ruled what became known as the "New Rome." The empire covered nearly all of the land that Rome had once ruled.

SHARE BACKGROUND

Church building was a passion of Emperor Justinian. It was a key aspect of the vast building projects that he undertook during his reign. Justinian conquered Ravenna in northern Italy, the place where the Basilica of Sant'Apollinare in Classe stands. His masterful rebuilding of the Hagia Sophia is probably his best-known project and it served as a key symbol of the Christian world during this time. The Hagia Sophia has mosaics that feature Jesus and the disciples. Most Byzantine art was inspired by the Christian Church.

The Byzantine Empire celebrated Greco-Roman culture and also preserved it. It built upon Roman mosaic techniques to craft Byzantine mosaics. They used stone and marble pieces in different colors, jewels, colored or clear glass, and brick or terra-cotta. Other architectural styles were adopted or modified. For example, the large dome of the Hagia Sophia may have been inspired by Roman dome architecture as seen in the Pantheon but used a square instead of a round base.

CRITICAL VIEWING Answers will vary. Possible response: There is a cross, a hand coming from above which could be God's hand, and what appear to be two angels in the heavens.

HISTORICAL THINKING QUESTION
How can a strong leader impact an empire?

Numbered Heads Activity: Leadership Role of Emperors Divide the class into groups of four, asking students to count off within each group. Pose the following question: Based on what you've already learned, how has the leadership role of emperors affected their empires? Instruct group members to think about the question individually and then discuss their answers. Tell students that many emperors who expanded the borders of their empires had to figure out how to handle groups of people who held different beliefs. Ask group members to discuss and predict the impact religious tolerance versus lack of tolerance might have on the unity and strength of the empire. Call out a number and invite the person with that number in each group to summarize the group's discussion for the class.

KEY DATES FOR CHAPTER 8

330	Emperor Constantine names the capital of Byzantium Constantinople.
527	Justinian becomes emperor of the Byzantine Empire.
532	Residents of Constantinople burn the city, including the Hagia Sophia.
534	The Code of Justinian is completed.
541	The first outbreak of the plague is recorded in the Byzantine Empire.
548	Theodora dies.
550	The Eastern Roman Empire gives way to the medieval Byzantine Empire.
565	Justinian dies.
726	The first iconoclast period begins; a new code of laws, *Ecloga*, is written by Leo III.
867	The Iconoclastic Controversy ends; the Macedonian dynasty begins.
1071	The Normans and the Turks invade the Byzantine Empire, greatly reducing the size of the empire.

INTRODUCE THE READING STRATEGY

MAKE INFERENCES
Explain that making inferences can help students understand the complexity of historical events by using what they already know to make a reasoned judgment about something. Turn to the Chapter Review and preview the graphic organizer with students. As they read the chapter, tell students to analyze and record their inferences about the Byzantine Empire and its success.

INTRODUCE CHAPTER VOCABULARY

KEY VOCABULARY

SECTION 1

medieval	plague	stagnation

SECTION 2

icon	iconoclast	mosaic
venerate		

DEFINITION CHART
As they read the chapter, encourage students to complete a Definition Chart for Key Vocabulary terms. Instruct students to list the Key Vocabulary terms in the first column of the chart. They should add each term's definition in the center column as they encounter the term in the chapter and then restate the definition in their own words in the third column. Model an example on the board, using the graphic organizer shown.

Word	Definition	In My Own Words
iconoclast	a member of Byzantine society who opposed the use of icons; literally means "image breaker"	someone who was against using sacred or religious pictures

Byzantium's New Rome

Empires don't last forever. But some reorganize and reinvent themselves, becoming something new. This is what happened with the Roman Empire. After the fall of Rome and the western empire, the eastern empire continued on for another thousand years as the Byzantine Empire.

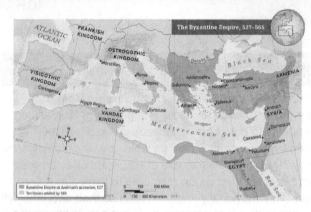

The Byzantine Empire, 527–565

CONSTANTINOPLE CONNECTS EAST AND WEST

As you have read, the emperor Diocletian divided the Roman Empire in 285 and appointed separate rulers to the eastern and western halves. The Eastern Roman Empire became known as the Byzantine Empire because its capital was built on the old Greek town of Byzantium. By 330, the emperor Constantine had transformed Byzantium into a grand "New Rome." He named the city Constantinople, which means "city of Constantine" in Greek. Today it is called Istanbul.

While the Western Roman Empire was torn apart by invading Germanic tribes, the Byzantine Empire managed to survive similar attacks. A series of strong emperors fought off enemies and strengthened the empire, which allowed it to continue the traditions of Roman civilization for another thousand years after the collapse of the Western Roman Empire. The people that historians call Byzantines, most of whom spoke Greek, proudly called themselves Romans.

Constantinople occupied one of the ancient world's most important geographic locations. At the heart of the empire was the small but important land link between Asia and Europe that permitted trade between east and west. The empire itself reached into both continents, with its center in present-day Greece and Turkey.

The Bosporus, a strait that runs through Istanbul, Turkey, still serves as a link between Europe and Asia—much as it did during the Byzantine Empire, when the city was known as Constantinople.

Constantinople was also located on the Bosporus, a strait that links the Black and Mediterranean seas. The city served as a major trade center for goods traveling by land and sea from Europe, Asia, and Africa. It also attracted people from Europe, Asia, and Africa, who came to trade goods from their homelands and ended up living in the thriving city. These immigrants gave Constantinople the cultural diversity for which it was famous.

THE EMPIRE EXPANDS

The Byzantine Empire's location brought problems as well as advantages. Although Constantinople was well protected, the rest of the empire was surrounded by enemies. To the north and west were Germanic kingdoms forcefully pressing on the empire's borders. To the east was an age-old enemy, the powerful and hostile Persian Empire.

The rich resources and great wealth of the Byzantine Empire made it a tempting target for raids and invasions. With no strong geographic barriers to prevent invasion by enemies, the empire was dangerously exposed, and its borders were constantly under attack by invading neighbors.

The Byzantine Empire needed strong leadership to hold it together in the face of so many threats. Over a thousand years, its borders grew and shrank depending on the ability of its rulers and the eagerness of its enemies to wage war. At its greatest extent, the empire completely encircled the Mediterranean Sea.

The greatest Byzantine ruler was one of its earliest—Justinian, who reigned from 527 until his death in 565. He not only recaptured lost Byzantine lands but also reconquered large areas of the old Western Roman Empire. His armies defeated the Persians and reconquered North Africa, the Italian Peninsula, and parts of present-day Spain. For a brief time, Justinian reunited the Eastern and Western Roman empires. He built up the strength of the Byzantine Empire, even while Rome was being overrun by invaders. Justinian's legacy of leadership remained influential throughout the time of the Byzantine Empire and beyond.

HISTORICAL THINKING

1. **READING CHECK** Why was Constantinople's geographic location an advantage for trade?

2. **DRAW CONCLUSIONS** Why was the Byzantine Empire a prime target for invasions?

3. **INTERPRET MAPS** How did the Byzantine Empire expand during Justinian's lifetime?

PLAN: 2-PAGE LESSON

OBJECTIVE
Explain how the Byzantine Empire's location was ideal for trade but also made it vulnerable to attack.

CRITICAL THINKING SKILLS FOR LESSON 1.1
- Draw Conclusions
- Interpret Maps
- Make Generalizations
- Analyze Cause and Effect

HISTORICAL THINKING FOR CHAPTER 8
How can a strong leader impact an empire?

Justinian was an ambitious emperor who wanted to restore the ancient Roman Empire by regaining territory it had lost. He was also a devout Christian but tolerant of other religions. Lesson 1.1 discusses the beginnings of the Byzantine Empire and introduces Emperor Justinian, one of the empire's greatest leaders.

BACKGROUND FOR THE TEACHER
The Plague vs. the Black Death The outbreak of the plague that swept through the Byzantine Empire during the reign of Justinian was the first of several plagues that Europe and Asia suffered through. Rodents traveling on grain ships and carts transmitted the disease to humans. As it was transferred from human to human, it became more deadly. There are three different kinds of plagues: bubonic, pneumonic, and septicemic. The most common form is bubonic. The first major outbreak of the bubonic plague was Justinian's plague. The Black Death that occurred in the 1300s was the next major plague in Europe.

The plague bacillus that struck the Byzantines in 541 is one of 155 known strands. Scientists managed to extract the genome from two teeth of a victim buried in a southern German graveyard. After analyzing the genome carefully, they have concluded that this particular strand, which originated in Asia, no longer survives. Yet other strands, like the one from the Black Death, continue to evolve.

INTRODUCE & ENGAGE

DISCUSS THE IMPORTANCE OF LOCATION

Direct students to examine the map of the Byzantine Empire in the lesson, emphasizing where Constantinople is situated. Explain the advantages and disadvantages of being located on a body of water such as the Bosporus as well as a land link between two continents. Ask students to weigh the advantages and disadvantages and do a cost-benefit analysis. Tell students that in this lesson they will learn about how the great resources and riches of the Byzantine Empire drew invaders, but a strong leader emerged who was able to meet this challenge.

TEACH

GUIDED DISCUSSION

1. **Make Generalizations** Why did the Byzantines consider themselves Romans? *(The Byzantine Empire was a continuation of the Eastern Roman Empire that persisted another 1,000 years after the collapse of the Western Roman Empire. They considered themselves Romans even though they spoke Greek.)*

2. **Analyze Cause and Effect** How did stronger and weaker leaders of the Byzantine Empire affect its growth? *(Possible response: The empire expanded under stronger leaders and shrank due to loss of land under weaker leaders.)*

INTERPRET MAPS

Ask students to make connections between the text and the details on the map. **ASK:** What conclusion can you draw about trade routes and how they affected the economy of the Byzantine Empire? *(Possible response: Trade routes linked the Byzantine Empire with three continents, giving the empire economic security.)* Prompt pairs to draw another conclusion or identify an example of how the map supports the text.

ACTIVE OPTIONS

On Your Feet: Jigsaw Strategy Organize students into expert groups and have each group analyze one of the following topics in the lesson: trade, location, expansion, cultural diversity. Ask groups to summarize their analysis in their own words. Regroup students so that each new group has at least one member from each expert group. Have students in the new groups take turns sharing their simplified summaries.

> **NG Learning Framework: Compare the "Old" Rome and the "New" Rome**
> ATTITUDE Curiosity
> SKILL Communication

Instruct teams to create a list of what they already know and have learned about the "Old" Rome of the ancient Roman Empire and a list about the "New" Rome of the Byzantine Empire. Once they have completed their lists, have teams exchange lists. Ask teams to note similarities and differences between the lists in regard to both conclusions and categories. As a class, review the lists, discussing differences and the causes of those differences.

HISTORICAL THINKING

ANSWERS

1. It was located on a strip of land between Europe and Asia. The city served as a major trade center for goods traveling by land and sea from all over the world.

2. Possible response: It was a rich empire with good resources and was located near trade routes.

3. The Byzantine Empire expanded to the west around the Mediterranean Sea in Africa and Europe to take over parts of the Ostrogothic, Vandal, and Visigothic kingdoms.

Justinian and Theodora

Antony and Cleopatra, Henry VIII and Anne Boleyn, John and Jackie Kennedy—power couples don't always have it easy, but they always have influence. Justinian and Theodora were one of the world's first power couples.

RISE OF JUSTINIAN AND THEODORA

The emperor Justinian I rose to power in 527 and ruled for 38 years. A native of Thrace, a region north of Greece, Justinian was the child of peasants and grew up speaking the local language and Latin. He was adopted by his predecessor, his uncle Justin I, and raised in Byzantium, where he studied law, theology, and Roman history. Even before he was named emperor, he served by his uncle's side as virtual co-emperor.

In 520, Justinian met his future wife, **Theodora**. Not much is known about her early life except that she was an actress and her father was a bear keeper at the Hippodrome, or circus. A Roman law from Constantine's time almost stood in the way of their marriage because of the difference in their social ranks. There are benefits to supreme power, though. Justinian simply had the law changed and married the woman he loved. When Justinian gained the throne, Theodora was proclaimed empress. They ruled together for more than 20 years.

Theodora was Justinian's most trusted and influential advisor. She was intelligent and politically skilled and used her considerable influence to recognize the rights of women, a controversial idea in male-dominated Byzantine society. She was responsible for passing strict laws that protected women and gave them more benefits when seeking a divorce. When Justinian became severely ill during the **plague**, a deadly epidemic disease, and was unable to govern, Theodora served as the sole ruler of the empire. Historians have also noted that Justinian passed only a few important laws after Theodora's death, indicating that she may have been the major strategist of the pair.

BYZANTIUM UNDER JUSTINIAN

Justinian believed it was his duty to restore the Roman Empire to its historical boundaries. He achieved his goal with the help of a brilliant general named **Belisarius**. After expanding the eastern boundaries of the empire with a victory over the Persian Sasanians in 530, Belisarius reconquered the Vandal kingdom in North Africa and parts of Spain and retook most of Italy from the Goths, reaching Rome in 540. Justinian and Belisarius were successful in large part because, like the Persians and Western Romans before them, they recruited soldiers from diverse groups, including Goths, Armenians, Arabs, and Persians.

In this mosaic, the empress Theodora is surrounded by her attendants. Theodora is depicted wearing jewels, a crown, and a royal purple robe.

This sixth-century mosaic shows Justinian in the center with religious leaders on the right and government officials on the left.

Even as he expanded his empire, Justinian faced internal threats. In January 532, residents of Constantinople rioted against his policies. The riot lasted a week and burned or destroyed half the city, including the Hagia Sophia, the city's most important church. The military killed as many as 30,000 people in its efforts to put down the uprising. Justinian rebuilt the Hagia Sophia, which is regarded today as the most important structure of the Byzantine Empire.

Justinian was a devout Christian who provided funding for many churches and monasteries. He also developed the empire's infrastructure with new bridges and forts. Justinian's building projects were so numerous that his biographer wrote an entire volume just on that subject.

THE CODE OF JUSTINIAN

Justinian's *Corpus of Civil Law*, familiarly known as the **Code of Justinian**, eclipsed all his other achievements. When Justinian became emperor, he undertook an ambitious project to create a unified set of clear and consistent laws across the empire. Like Hammurabi long before him, Justinian created a legal system to bring peace and stability to his domain.

He appointed a commission of legal experts to review all known laws. From 529 to 534, this commission gathered all the laws of the Roman Empire, which numbered around three million. They edited, adapted, and revised those laws to create a manageable law code. Obsolete or confusing laws were eliminated and new laws concerning slavery and women's rights were added. (The code is 1,500 pages long in its modern edition.)

Justinian ended up with four books of law: one of laws borrowed from the older Roman Empire, one a collection of opinions by legal experts, one textbook for law students, and finally a collection of new laws devised by Justinian himself. The Code of Justinian includes laws on subjects ranging from religion, trade, and property to marriage and adoption. One of the most important principles of Justinian's code is one still used in our courts today—"No one suffers penalty for merely thinking." Justinian's *Corpus* preserved the core of Roman law not simply for sixth-century judges and lawyers, but for all time.

PLAGUE AND THE END OF AN ERA

In spite of Justinian's many achievements, the heights of his reign were followed by years of **stagnation**, or lack of growth and development, due in part to the ravages of the plague. The first recorded outbreak of what came to be known as Justinian's plague occurred in 541 in the Egyptian port of Pelusium at the mouth of the Nile. Rats in shipments of grain sent as tribute to Constantinople

carried the disease across the Mediterranean the next year. The death toll from the plague may have been as high as one-quarter of the empire's population during Justinian's reign. Over the next 200 years, at least 15 outbreaks devastated the empire and millions died throughout the region.

The final outbreak of plague hit Constantinople in 747 and ended in 767. In the following years, a slow revival began. However, society had changed. Before the plague, the Byzantine Empire had been an urban society in which people met at the marketplace to discuss their affairs or enjoy theater and circus performances. By 600, urban life had faded. In Constantinople alone, 230,000 out of 375,000 people had died. On a positive note, the empire's scholars never stopped preserving Greek learning, systematizing Roman law, and writing new Christian texts.

Theodora died in 548, and historians mark the last period of Justinian's rule from 550 onward as the point where the Eastern Roman Empire gave way to the **medieval** Byzantine Empire, which lasted from about 500 to 1500. This new phase was marked by struggle and loss of territory.

HISTORICAL THINKING

1. **READING CHECK** What was Justinian's main military goal?

2. **IDENTIFY PROBLEMS AND SOLUTIONS** How did Justinian address the problem of a disorganized and oversized legal code?

3. **EVALUATE** Why is Theodora considered a major figure in the Byzantine Empire?

PLAN: 2-PAGE LESSON

OBJECTIVE

Explain how the Byzantine Empire reached new heights under the rule of Justinian and Theodora.

CRITICAL THINKING SKILLS FOR LESSON 1.2
- Identify Problems and Solutions
- Evaluate
- Identify Main Ideas and Details
- Analyze Cause and Effect
- Make Inferences

HISTORICAL THINKING FOR CHAPTER 8
How can a strong leader impact an empire?

Emperor Justinian made great contributions to the Byzantine Empire. Through Justinian's and his wife Theodora's leadership, the Byzantine Empire expanded and Constantinople became a thriving economic center. Lesson 1.2 explores Justinian's background and reign and how he left a lasting legacy for the Byzantine Empire.

Student eEdition online

Additional content for this lesson, including a diagram, is available online.

BACKGROUND FOR THE TEACHER

Sports Fans and the Nika Riots Sports fans date back to ancient times, which can be documented with the excitement of enthusiasts who gathered to watch chariot racing. Many commoners enjoyed chariot races at the Hippodrome, just as the Romans had enjoyed such races in the Colosseum. During the Byzantine Empire, the masses were passionate about two teams, the Blues and the Greens. Riots were not uncommon at chariot races. One in particular broke out in 532, after which Theodora was able to use it to teach Justinian a valuable lesson about standing one's ground. When an earlier riot had broken out, Justinian ordered the execution of some of the rioters. Upset by this decision and rising taxes, fans retaliated and rioted. The rioters shouted, "Nika, Nika!" (which means "win" or "conquer"). Rioting led to looting. Justinian fired his tax minister to try to appease the rioters, but his plan did not work. Then he thought about running away, but Theodora insisted they stay and show their power. Justinian followed her advice and sent in soldiers to crush the dissent. Thousands of rioters were killed.

INTRODUCE & ENGAGE

ACTIVATE PRIOR KNOWLEDGE

Invite students to recall what they learned in the previous lesson about the rise of the Byzantine Empire. Tell students to identify some issues the Byzantine Empire faced before Justinian became emperor. Discuss how a strong power couple such as Justinian and Theodora might handle those issues. Ask students to look in this lesson for new issues that the emperor and his wife had to face.

TEACH

GUIDED DISCUSSION

1. **Identify Main Ideas and Details** What Roman traditions were adopted and/or adapted by the Byzantine Empire? *(Possible responses: chariot racing, military composition, religion, law code, building projects)*

2. **Analyze Cause and Effect** How did the plague affect the fortitude of the Byzantine Empire? *(Possible response: The large population loss weakened the empire so much that it also lost territory.)*

MAKE INFERENCES

Prompt students to read the excerpt from the *Institutiones*. Explain that this first-year law book was published in 533. **ASK:** What basic distinction does this excerpt make? *(Possible response: the difference between civil law and the laws of nations)* How are the laws that he describes different? *(Possible response: They are based on two types of laws. Civil laws are specific to a state, while the laws of nations are for all mankind.)* Why would this information be included in a book for first-year students but not for later students? *(Possible response: The information is very basic knowledge that a law student would learn early on. All of the legal knowledge a student learned from that point forward would build on this concept.)*

ACTIVE OPTIONS

On Your Feet: Compare Constantinople and Istanbul Direct students in small groups to the diagram of Constantinople (available in the Student eEdition). Prompt groups to find photographs of the city today and compare its design and buildings with the diagram in the lesson. Lead students in a discussion about which early influences and contributions lasted, which were replaced, and the reasons for both.

> **NG Learning Framework: Write an Evaluation**
> ATTITUDE Responsibility
> SKILL Problem-Solving

Ask students to evaluate how Justinian and Theodora handled the riot that led to the burning of the Hagia Sophia. Instruct them to use information from the lesson and additional sources to evaluate their decision, taking into careful consideration the causes of the riot and Justinian's actions and policies before the riot broke out. Invite students to share their evaluations with the class, and then use them as a discussion starter about how leaders problem-solve in the past and in the modern world.

DIFFERENTIATE

INCLUSION

Analyze a Diagram Pair students who are sight-impaired with students who are not. Together, they can discuss the diagram "Constantinople: The Heart of the Empire" (available in the Student eEdition). As they read the call-outs, the student with visual impairments can ask questions about where the site is located and what modern structures the visuals resemble. As the other student describes the locations, the partner can discuss why certain structures are located closer to the water and away from the wall.

PRE-AP

Create a Time Line and Essay Instruct students to review the lesson and decide which events were most important during Justinian's reign. Then instruct students to create an annotated time line. Each event should include the date and at least two details. Students should conduct research to supplement their time line with additional details, images, or maps. Prompt students to use their time lines as the basis for an essay arguing why the events they chose were important.

See the Chapter Planner for more strategies for differentiation.

HISTORICAL THINKING

ANSWERS

1. to restore the Roman Empire to its historic boundaries

2. He organized a commission to gather all the laws and to review, revise, and consolidate them into a new code.

3. Possible response: She was a powerful and influential advisor to the emperor who changed laws relating to women and even ruled when the emperor was too ill to govern.

1.3 Preserving Cultural Heritage

"Suspended From Heaven"

Istanbul, Turkey, strategically located between the Black Sea and the Sea of Marmara and straddling Europe and Asia, has been home to significant political, religious, and artistic history. A bridge between the East and the West, it's no wonder that the Byzantines chose what was then called Constantinople as the capital of their empire.

It was in Constantinople in 532 that the Byzantine emperor Justinian I commissioned the Hagia Sophia, a Christian church and one of the finest examples of Byzantine architecture. Hagia Sophia, which means "Divine, or Holy, Wisdom" in Greek, was built in a short time—about 6 years—and completed in 537.

An engineering marvel, the main structure of the Hagia Sophia consists of a central dome that rests on top of four huge arches supported by four giant columns and two semi-domes. Forty arched windows encircle the center dome, which gives it the appearance of floating over the church as if it is, in the words of the writer Procopius, "suspended from heaven."

The complicated construction of the main structure made it prone to problems. In 558, an earthquake destroyed the first dome, which was then rebuilt in 562. The surviving main structure is the original that was first constructed between 532 and 537.

PLAN: 4-PAGE LESSON

OBJECTIVE
Describe the history, construction, and interior details of the Hagia Sophia and how it is susceptible to earthquake damage.

CRITICAL THINKING SKILLS FOR LESSON 1.3
- Analyze Visuals
- Make Connections
- Form and Support Opinions
- Explain
- Make Inferences
- Identify Problems and Solutions
- Identify Supporting Details

HISTORICAL THINKING FOR CHAPTER 8
How can a strong leader impact an empire?

Among the accomplishments of the Byzantine emperor Justinian I was the commissioning of the Great Church, later called the Hagia Sophia. Lesson 1.3 describes the history of the church, its magnificent interior details, and its vulnerability to earthquakes.

BACKGROUND FOR THE TEACHER

A Historic Place of Worship The site of the Hagia Sophia, historians believe, has long been home to places of worship. First, a pagan temple was likely located there. Then, in the year 325, a Christian church was ordered built by the Roman emperor Constantine I. That church endured a series of disasters in its early history; it had to be rebuilt after a fire in 404 and then again after the Nika Riots in 532. During the riots, the church was set on fire and destroyed, leading to the construction of the structure that (largely) stands there today. When it was finished, the Hagia Sophia was not only a triumph for Christianity, but also for Justinian.

History Notebook
Encourage students to complete the Preserving Cultural Heritage page for Chapter 8 in their History Notebooks as they read.

INTRODUCE & ENGAGE

SHARE MEMORIES OF GREAT BUILDINGS

Encourage students to share personal experiences of great buildings they have visited. They may choose examples of places of worship, but the discussion need not be limited to them. They may mention a famous museum, monument, or concert hall. Ask them to describe what was memorable about the place they went to, with a particular emphasis on the building's architecture and symbolic meaning, if any. **ASK:** What was architecturally interesting about the building you visited? *(Answers will vary. Students' responses may focus on the building's exterior; others will mention something about the interior.)* Why do you think people visit that building? *(Answers will vary. Students' responses should acknowledge the building's social, political, cultural, religious, or symbolic meaning.)*

TEACH

GUIDED DISCUSSION

1. **Explain** Why is the Hagia Sophia said to be "suspended from heaven"? *(Numerous arched windows surround the central dome, and when light flows in through the windows, it makes the central dome appear to float over the entire church.)*

2. **Make Inferences** What may have been some of the reasons why the Turkish government turned the Hagia Sophia into a museum in 1934? *(Possible responses: Making it into a museum was the best way to ensure that it would be preserved and protected for years to come; as a museum, many people can visit it and admire its magnificence; a museum attracts paying tourists and those funds can be used to support the Hagia Sophia's preservation.)*

PRESERVING CULTURAL HERITAGE

The Hagia Sophia has been a museum since 1934, when Kemal Atatürk, the founder and first president of the Republic of Turkey, secularized the building. However, in recent years, there has been a movement inside Turkey to turn the Hagia Sophia back into a mosque. A key moment came in 2016, when Pope Francis officially acknowledged the Armenian genocide, the World War I-era mass killing of 1.5 million Armenians by Ottoman-era Turks. Though widely accepted as truth, some nations, including Turkey, refuse to label the event as an actual genocide. The pontiff's remark enraged Recep Tayyip Erdogan, the president of Turkey, and stirred religious passion among many Muslims there. In 2018, President Erdogan recited a portion of the Quran in the Hagia Sophia, and in 2019 declared his firm intention to convert the building. Time will tell if his efforts are successful; the Hagia Sophia's history as a place of worship for both Christians and Muslims has caused objections from Christian leaders, especially in neighboring Greece. Additionally, the Hagia Sophia is a UNESCO World Heritage Site and, as such, would need the approval of UNESCO's World Heritage Committee before the building's status could change.

DIFFERENTIATE

INCLUSION

Visual Partners Pair sight-impaired students with sighted students to interpret the photographs in this lesson. Ask sighted students to describe each of the photographs of the Hagia Sophia to the sight-impaired students. Remind partners to identify details in the photographs and give particular emphasis to the Hagia Sophia's architectural traits.

GIFTED & TALENTED

Research Architectural Details Tell students to conduct online research about the stylistic blending expressed in the architecture of the Hagia Sophia. Ask students to investigate its classical Greek roots (as seen, for example, in its column capitals), its Byzantine details (its dome and pendentives), and its Islamic features (its minarets, mihrabs, and minbars). Ask students to present their research to the entire class in the form of a short oral report. Use student reports as a starting point for a larger class discussion about stylistic and cultural blending in the arts. Ask students to think of other examples of buildings that blend certain styles, especially those borrowed from other cultures.

See the Chapter Planner for more strategies for differentiation.

The Hagia Sophia's central dome is 182 feet from ground level and 102 feet in diameter.

The interior of the Hagia Sophia, which has served as a church, a mosque, and a museum, contains both Byzantine mosaics and Arabic calligraphy, illustrating a blend of two different cultures.

The original interior of the Hagia Sophia was minimally decorated, but as new Byzantine rulers came into power, they filled the walls with mosaics and frescoes depicting art and religious life in the Eastern Roman Empire. For almost a thousand years, the church served as the center of Eastern Christianity.

Then in 1453, the Ottomans conquered Constantinople and converted the Hagia Sophia into a mosque. Minarets were added around the perimeter of the building and the mosaics and frescoes were plastered over. It remained a mosque until the fall of the Ottoman Empire. In 1934, the Turkish government secularized the building, made it into a museum, and began to restore the original mosaics.

The Hagia Sophia represents the interconnected histories of Rome, Byzantium, and the Ottomans, with both Christian and Islamic art decorating the walls. Over the centuries, successive earthquakes have damaged the Hagia Sophia—and continue to threaten the integrity of the building.

While Istanbul's strategic location made it an ideal place for an empire's capital, it also makes it vulnerable to earthquakes. Istanbul lies on the North Anatolian Fault, a crack in Earth's crust that spreads in a line from east to west across the northern part of Turkey. Typically when an earthquake occurs along this fault line, the stress migrates west. Based on this pattern, scientists have determined that Istanbul, home to the Hagia Sophia, is also at risk. Unfortunately, they can't predict when the next earthquake may hit or how large it may be.

After one of the largest earthquakes struck the town of Izmit in 1999, the Turkish government made earthquake safety a priority on their agenda. Today, scientists monitor the structural integrity of the Hagia Sophia and test potential earthquake damage to assess the risks.

HISTORICAL THINKING

FORM AND SUPPORT OPINIONS Do you believe ancient buildings like the Hagia Sophia are important to preserve? Why or why not?

BACKGROUND FOR THE TEACHER

The Architecture The Hagia Sophia's two architects, Anthemios of Tralles and Isidore of Miletus, faced numerous architectural problems that needed solving. First, the area was prone to earthquakes. That meant the building material for the top dome needed to be very strong. The material also had to be sufficiently lightweight, however, because the dome was going to rise some 180 feet above a square base—a great height in that era. The architects solved the weight issue by resting the dome on top of four huge arches, with the resulting triangular-shaped, concave curves (called pendentives) providing the needed support. The pendentives had the effect of directing the weight of the dome into the four upright supports, called piers, that sat on the ground.

Another issue arose from the fact that Justinian wanted the church to be the largest basilica in the Roman Empire. Enlarging the nave (the central part of the church) caused concerns that the main dome could collapse, so Anthemios and Isidore designed a series of supporting semi-domes that extended out from the arches that formed the pendentives. These smaller domes created a longer nave, thereby eliminating the need for the main dome to become larger (and heavier).

Despite Anthemios and Isidore's historic accomplishment, in 557 the original main dome did partially collapse. It was left to Isidore's nephew, Isidore the Younger, to design a second dome with structural ribs to prevent it from also collapsing. The newer dome also had a larger arc; the original dome's arc was too shallow, which caused it to push out and force its weight into the supporting piers. Isidore the Younger also had to rebuild many of the supporting walls and semi-domes in order to support the new dome.

TEACH

GUIDED DISCUSSION

3. **Identify Problems and Solutions** Why is the Hagia Sophia vulnerable to earthquakes? *(It lies on the North Anatolian Fault. When an earthquake occurs, the tremors move west, impacting Istanbul and the Hagia Sophia.)*

4. **Identify Supporting Details** How is the continued safety of the Hagia Sophia being prioritized? *(Scientists are working to anticipate the danger that the Hagia Sophia could be in from future earthquakes. They study the structure's integrity for any changes, and they also test to see what the potential damage would be from a future earthquake.)*

ANALYZE VISUALS

Prompt students to study the photographs of the Hagia Sophia. **ASK:** What surrounds the Hagia Sophia's central dome? *(four other arches)* What details in the photograph remind you of other places of worship you have seen or been to, and what details seem unique? *(Answers will vary. Students who compare the Hagia Sophia to a Christian church may mention that the Hagia Sophia has an altar in the rear of the church, which is common in Christian churches. Unique elements they may mention are the large, circular calligraphic panes that hang high on the walls.)*

ACTIVE OPTION

NG Learning Framework: Create an Online Presentation
SKILLS Observation, Collaboration
KNOWLEDGE Our Human Story

Organize students into four groups and ask each group to investigate two of the eight major mosaics found in the Hagia Sophia: the Imperial Door Mosaic, the Southwestern Vestibule mosaic, the North Tympanum mosaic, the Apse Mosaic, the Emperor Alexander mosaic, the Empress Zoe mosaic, the Comnenus, or the Deesis. Have them conduct online research on the content and symbolism of the scene or person(s) depicted in the mosaics. Tell groups to use an online presentation tool to create a short presentation of their findings. Then have groups share their presentations with the rest of the class.

HISTORICAL THINKING

ANSWER

Possible response: Yes, buildings like the Hagia Sophia are important to preserve because they are a part of our cultural heritage and identity.

Traveler: Procopius
Plague Witness c. 500–554

Today every major political leader is followed by photographers, video crews, and reporters who record their every move. But what about the leaders of the distant past? How do we know about their lives?

EMBEDDED WITH THE BYZANTINE ARMY

Just as Herodotus created a record of the Greco-Persian Wars, the traveler and writer Procopius (pruh-KOH-pee-uhs) recorded Justinian's expansion of the Byzantine Empire. Not much is known about the early life of Procopius except that he was born in Palestine in about 500 and that he learned Greek and studied law. As a young man, he traveled to Constantinople and went to work as a legal advisor and secretary to General Belisarius. During his 13 years with Belisarius and the Byzantine army, Procopius traveled throughout the empire, witnessed its expansion, and learned about its inhabitants. He was with the general during campaigns against the Sasanians in Persia, the Vandals in North Africa, and the Goths in Italy.

Over the course of his life, Procopius wrote three books. *The Wars of Justinian* is about the wars to defend and expand the empire. *Buildings* is about Justinian's public works and was probably commissioned by the emperor. Procopius's final book was called *The Secret History* and was in fact kept a secret and published only after his death. Here, Procopius describes Justinian, Theodora, and Belisarius as corrupt and untrustworthy people with low morals. Today, many historians do not take it very seriously as a historical source. Some speculate that it was a way for the author to "let off some steam" and no one knows for certain why Procopius wrote the book.

In all his work, Procopius wrote for his contemporaries, not for historians of the future. Some of what he recorded came from his own observations. Other information came from the people he met. He followed the style of other classical historians such as Herodotus and Thucydides. Like Herodotus, Procopius must be read critically, but he is the source of the most extensive information about Justinian's world. Like Thucydides, Procopius is most accurate when he is relaying his personal observations, rather than in his historical writing.

CRITICAL VIEWING This Iranian miniature shows Sasanian soldiers laying siege to a Byzantine fortress during the second war between the two empires. Based on this image, what weapons did the Sasanian army use?

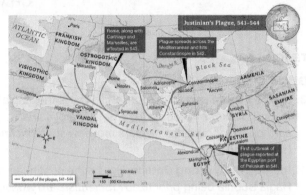

Justinian's Plague, 541–544

Rome, along with Carthage and Marseilles, are affected in 543.

Plague spreads across the Mediterranean and hits Constantinople in 542.

First outbreak of plague reported at the Egyptian port of Pelusium in 541.

Spread of the plague, 541–544

WITNESS TO JUSTINIAN'S PLAGUE

Much of what historians know about the plague during Justinian's reign comes from Procopius. Procopius returned to Constantinople around 541, just before the plague's outbreak. He observed that the disease first appeared in towns along the coast and then moved inland, but he did not know why. Only in the late 19th century did scientists realize that black rats living on ships were the main agents responsible for spreading the disease.

In *The Wars of Justinian*, Procopius describes scenes where there are so many bodies needing to be buried that all rites and rituals are ignored. Rival clans and factions put aside their differences to carry each other's dead. Justinian's government paid men to remove bodies. First, the people placed the bodies in tombs. Then all the tombs filled up. Trenches were dug for the bodies, and soon there was no more space for trenches. Finally, bodies were taken to the towers of a citadel in the outskirts of Constantinople and placed there. According to Procopius, more than half the city died of plague.

In the absence of accurate population statistics, historians have to estimate the deaths resulting from the plague. As you have read, the deaths in the empire's large cities were massive. High estimates put the death toll from the plague at one-fourth of the empire's population—of 26 million subjects, only 19 million survived.

PRIMARY SOURCE

During these times there was a pestilence [epidemic], by which the whole human race came near to being annihilated [utterly destroyed]. Now in the case of all other scourges [afflictions] sent from heaven some explanation of a cause might be given by daring men. . . . But for this calamity it is quite impossible either to express in words or to conceive in thought any explanation, except indeed to refer it to God. For it did not come in a part of the world nor upon certain men, nor did it confine itself to any season of the year, so that from such circumstances it might be possible to find subtle explanations of a cause, but it embraced the entire world, and blighted [destroyed] the lives of all men . . . respecting neither sex nor age.

—*The Wars of Justinian* by Procopius

HISTORICAL THINKING

1. **READING CHECK** How do we know so much about the Byzantine Empire during Justinian's reign?

2. **DRAW CONCLUSIONS** Why did Procopius believe the reason for the plague must be "referred to God"?

3. **IDENTIFY DETAILS** How did Procopius convey the number of people who died during the plague?

PLAN: 2-PAGE LESSON

OBJECTIVE
Explain how Procopius created an historical record of the Byzantine Empire during Justinian's reign.

CRITICAL THINKING SKILLS FOR LESSON 1.4
- Draw Conclusions
- Identify Details
- Determine Chronology
- Synthesize
- Analyze Primary Sources

HISTORICAL THINKING FOR CHAPTER 8
How can a strong leader impact an empire?

Emperor Justinian's reign and the strength of the empire were significantly affected by the plague. Through the eyewitness account of the famous historian Procopius, we have a record of the devastation that it caused. Lesson 1.4 explores the impact of the plague on the Byzantine Empire.

BACKGROUND FOR THE TEACHER

The Plague Today The plague is not a disease of the past. Outbreaks still occur, as in 2014, when a dog, apparently infected by fleas, transmitted the plague to four people in Denver. No one died there, but the death toll can be high if proper medical care is unavailable. One recent occurrence killed 20 people in a Madagascar village in a single week.

In 1994, the largest recent instance of the plague, the Indian city of Surat experienced an outbreak that caused more than 100,000 of the city's residents to flee. Although neighboring cities dreaded a massive epidemic, that particular strain responded to an antibiotic. The final death toll was 56, far lower than most had feared.

Most of the time, the strains that are descendants of the Black Death plague that struck Europe in 1348 lie dormant in rodents, usually rats, but when a new variant appears, it can transmit to humans, causing an outbreak. The strain that caused the 1994 outbreak in Surat was related to the Black Death.

History Notebook
Encourage students to complete the Traveler page for Chapter 8 in their History Notebooks as they read.

INTRODUCE & ENGAGE

DISCUSS *HISTORIOGRAPHY*

Invite a volunteer to share the definition of the word *historiography*. Then invite others to share why they think historiography is important to our understanding of the past. Explain that even though Procopius did not conduct a careful examination of sources in his record of the plague, he contributes substantially to our understanding of a key event that affected the political, economic, and social life of the Byzantine Empire.

TEACH

GUIDED DISCUSSION

1. **Determine Chronology** Why is the timing of when Procopius wrote *The Wars of Justinian* significant? *(He wrote the book, which is about the expansion of the empire, after he served under Belisarius and had traveled widely with the army.)*

2. **Synthesize** Based on what you have learned from reading excerpts from both Herodotus and Procopius, are these two historians credible sources? Take into account how they gathered and presented the information in their books. *(Possible response: Yes, even though sometimes they are biased. Both considered other eyewitness accounts and traveled widely, giving them a more worldly perspective.)*

ANALYZE PRIMARY SOURCES

Tell students to read and analyze the primary source excerpt. **ASK:** Why does Procopius say, "For it did not come in a part of the world nor upon certain men, nor did it confine itself to any season of the year"? *(Possible response: because the plague has not singled out one group of people or appeared at one particular time, it is random)* Pair students and prompt them to pose a question in which one must draw conclusions based on what is known but not explicitly stated in the primary source. Have them discuss possible answers before posing the question to another pair.

ACTIVE OPTIONS

On Your Feet: Descriptive Words Distribute five sticky notes to each student and ask them to reread the lesson. Direct students to write one word or short phrase describing Procopius or his works on each sticky note. Tell students to place their notes on the board or a wall. As a class, discuss the posted descriptions.

NG Learning Framework: Evaluate Procopius's Job Performance
SKILL Communication
KNOWLEDGE Our Human Story

Have small groups gather information from the lesson and from their own research about Procopius. Tell them to use the information to write an evaluation of his job performance, appearance, oratory skills, and arguments. Ask students to include direct quotations from his books in their evaluation. Invite groups to share their evaluations with the class.

DIFFERENTIATE

STRIVING READERS

List Facts Post this heading: Five Facts About the Plague. After students read the lesson, ask them to copy the heading onto a piece of paper and write five sentences that each contain one fact about the plague, as witnessed by Procopius. Invite volunteers to share their sentences with the class.

PRE-AP

Investigate Primary Sources Prompt students to research text excerpts from *The Secret History*. Challenge them to find information that clearly contrasts the tone of his other two books. Tell students to analyze the evidence and compare and contrast the tone in both. Invite students to present their findings in an oral or written report.

See the Chapter Planner for more strategies for differentiation.

HISTORICAL THINKING

ANSWERS

1. Procopius recorded and published books about it.

2. Possible response: because there was no known cause for the plague; It was universal and attacked all people, at all times of the year, in all areas.

3. Possible response: He says the whole human race came near to being annihilated.

CRITICAL VIEWING Answers will vary. Possible response: They used shields, maces, swords, and bows and arrows.

The Iconoclasts

A typical smartphone or tablet screen has many colored squares with graphic symbols and letters. We call them icons, and chances are that you know immediately what a lot of them mean. People of the ancient Byzantine Empire had icons, too, but their meanings were very different.

CHRISTIAN ICONS

As Christianity grew and spread in the sixth and seventh centuries, a Christian culture grew with it. Art, in the form of **icons**, or sacred or religious images, was an important part of that culture. The word *icon* comes from the Greek word *eikon*, which means "image, figure, or likeness." An icon is historically an image of Christ, the saints, the Virgin Mary, or an angel—all important people to Christians.

Icons were not produced as art, but rather as sacred objects; the artists were generally unknown, the works unsigned. Many icons were thought to have appeared miraculously, not created by an artist. These icons in particular were believed to have special powers, such as answering prayers, healing the sick, and offering protection.

A woman lights candles in front of a religious icon at a Greek Orthodox church in Istanbul, Turkey. At one time, these icons were banned in the eastern branch of the Christian Church.

Icons were important and adored, in homes and churches and carried through the streets in religious processions.

Icons were important in the Christian Church during a time of instability and economic and societal change for the empire. Starting in 541 as a result of the plague, the population declined, cities shrank, the economy contracted, and tax revenues plummeted.

In the early seventh century, the structure of the empire began to change. Because the government could no longer afford to pay soldiers, local militias consisted of part-time soldiers who farmed the land during peacetime. Conquered people were moved into less populated rural areas. The tradition of separate civil and military powers that had existed since Constantine's time was replaced by a combined military and civil power structure. The empire was divided into military districts, each headed by a governor who heard legal disputes, collected taxes, and commanded the militia.

In the middle of the seventh century, Arabs conquered lands that had previously been held by the Byzantine Empire, including Syria, Palestine, Egypt, and much of North Africa. Most of Italy was lost, while the Balkans north of Greece fell to the Avars and the Slavs, who lived north of Constantinople.

During this period, the upper and lower classes began to lead almost identical lives. Fewer people knew Latin, so the most common language, Greek, was more widely used. Some people owned more land than others, but they now worked the land alongside their poorer dependents. Slavery declined as well because no one could afford to feed slaves. Most farmers were peasants who worked the land themselves with two oxen and a plow and grew only enough food for their own families.

Icons served as a powerful source of solace to the Byzantine people during this time of change. Some scholars believe icons held the Byzantine identity and empire together. In 626, an icon of the Virgin Mary was credited with saving Constantinople from a Persian attack. But attitudes began to change and by the beginning of the eighth century, the veneration of icons had become controversial.

THE ICONOCLASTIC CONTROVERSY

The Second Commandment of the Hebrew Bible forbids the creation of graven, or engraved, images. In Judaism and Islam, this commandment is interpreted to forbid portrayals of religious figures. Christians have had a variety of interpretations. In the eighth century, some Eastern Christians began to believe that icons violated the Second Commandment. They may have been influenced by neighboring Muslims, or they may have been reacting to the growing power and wealth of the Christian Church. The people opposed to these images were known as **iconoclasts**, or "image breakers." They supported iconoclasm, which is the rejection or destruction of religious images. The people who venerated icons were known as iconophiles.

The split sharply divided the empire for over a century and caused rifts within the Christian Church. The first period of iconoclasm was from 726 to 787. It was started by the emperor Leo III, who banned the worship of icons. In 730, he ordered the destruction of all icons, including the largest icon in Constantinople, the golden Christ, which hung above his own palace gates. This action angered people so much that—according to one version of events—a mob of women killed the man who removed it. One of the most vocal religious leaders who defended icons against Leo's attacks was John of Damascus, a scholar and monk. He argued that there was a difference between veneration and worship.

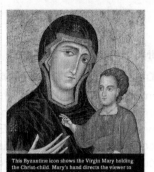

This Byzantine icon shows the Virgin Mary holding the Christ-child. Mary's hand directs the viewer to the child, who holds out his hand in a blessing.

After the emperor Leo III, the Byzantine rulers went back and forth. Constantine V, Leo's successor and son, was also an iconoclast. He went even further, burning down a monastery on Mount Olympus and actively persecuting iconophiles. After Constantine, the iconophiles experienced a brief period of relief under the reign of Empress Irene in the late 700s. Emperor Leo V reinstated iconoclasm in 815. Similar to prior iconoclastic emperors, Leo V attacked the monks who produced icons. Many icon painters had their foreheads branded as a warning to others. The prohibition against the veneration of icons remained in place until 843, when the mother of Michael III, an iconophile serving as regent for her son, ended the controversy. Icons became an integral part of Byzantine Christianity.

The years when icons were banned in the Byzantine Empire increased an existing rift between the Christian Church in the east and west, which was never healed. At the same time, the controversy helped define Byzantine identity and the eastern branch of the Christian Church. The church came out of the controversy newly unified, and the patriarch, or bishop of Constantinople, became even more independent of papal authority in Rome.

HISTORICAL THINKING

1. **READING CHECK** How did attitudes toward icons start to change in the eighth century?

2. **MAKE INFERENCES** Why do you think icons became important to the Byzantine people during a time of economic and societal change?

3. **ANALYZE POINTS OF VIEW** Why does John of Damascus make a distinction between *worship* and *venerate*?

PLAN: 2-PAGE LESSON

OBJECTIVE

Identify how the Byzantine Empire and Christian Church faced more than a century of discord over the use of icons.

CRITICAL THINKING SKILLS FOR LESSON 2.1

- Make Inferences
- Analyze Points of View
- Compare and Contrast
- Make Predictions
- Analyze Visuals

HISTORICAL THINKING FOR CHAPTER 8

How can a strong leader impact an empire?

Different beliefs started to create a division between Eastern and Western Christians. Emperor Leo III banned the worship of icons, which many people venerated. Lesson 2.1 explores the causes of this division and how it affected Christianity in the empire.

BACKGROUND FOR THE TEACHER

Sources of the Iconoclastic Controversy Some historians believe that the growing division within the Christian Church over the use or non-use of icons was a result of Jewish and Muslim influences, as those faiths did not use images in worship. Others believe that it came from the difference in opinion with regard to the nature of the Trinity (God in three persons: Father, Son, and Holy Spirit) and the two natures of Jesus. Whatever the specific cause, there were many questions that were debated by Christians in the Byzantine Empire, such as:

- What is the role of art in worship?
- Should religious images be used to represent Jesus?
- What role does the human aspect of Jesus play in salvation?
- Does the resurrection of Jesus' body have a form that can be reproduced in art?
- Can Christ (or any of his natures) be shown in art form?
- Can the Incarnation be something that is observed?

These and other questions would eventually lead to the Great Schism in 1054, causing the Christian Church to split between the Roman Catholic Church and Eastern Orthodox Church.

INTRODUCE & ENGAGE

CREATE A WORD WEB

Make a Word Web with *icon* written in the center. Ask students what the word means and then add their ideas to the web. Encourage students to suggest words or phrases they associate with icons such as famous singers, athletes, or political figures. Tell students that this lesson examines how an icon in the Christian Church caused the iconoclastic controversy and the controversy's effects on the Byzantine Empire.

TEACH

GUIDED DISCUSSION

1. **Compare and Contrast** How did the Byzantine views of icons differ during the Iconoclastic Controversy? *(One view of icons was that they were graven images and should not be worshiped. The other view of icons was that they were holy images and held special powers.)*

2. **Make Predictions** Why would the worship of icons help strengthen Byzantine Christianity? *(Possible response: It would give Byzantine Christianity its own identity that was separate from the Western Christian Church.)*

ANALYZE VISUALS

Tell students to examine the photograph of a woman lighting candles in front of an icon. Encourage them to find other icons in the photograph. **ASK:** How are the icons similar, and how are they being used in the church? *(Possible response: The icons appear to be in the same style, and the people are looking at the icons admirably, as if they are honoring them.)* Invite students to share details in the photograph that struck them as interesting or particularly engaging.

ACTIVE OPTIONS

On Your Feet: Turn and Talk on Topic Arrange students into three groups. Give each group this topic sentence: The Iconoclastic Controversy divided the Byzantine Empire. Tell students to build a paragraph on the topic by having each student contribute one sentence. Suggest that the groups first discuss why icon veneration divided the Christian Church. Ask a volunteer from each group to present the group's paragraph to the class.

> **NG Learning Framework: Evaluate Points of View**
> **ATTITUDE** Responsibility
> **SKILLS** Observation, Communication

Place students in groups or pairs to further research the causes and effects of the Iconoclastic Controversy. Have students evaluate different primary and secondary sources and different points of view. Then have them use evidence and claims to construct a hypothesis about how the different sides of the controversy clashed, including what they said about each other. Have groups prepare reports that explore what made the situation so controversial and how individuals might have made the controversy worse. Ask groups to present their reports to the class as a panel, with individuals each reading a section to the class.

DIFFERENTIATE

INCLUSION

Use Clarifying Questions Pair inclusion students with students who can read the lesson aloud to them. Ask the inclusion students' partners to summarize the main idea of each paragraph in the lesson. Encourage inclusion students to ask clarifying questions as needed.

GIFTED & TALENTED

Host a Talk Show Arrange students in pairs and direct them to reread the paragraph about the first period of iconoclasm when Leo III banned the veneration of icons. Tell students to assume the roles of a talk show host and Leo III and to plan, write, and perform an interview focusing on the views and reasoning of iconoclasts. Invite pairs to present their talk show to the class.

See the Chapter Planner for more strategies for differentiation.

HISTORICAL THINKING

ANSWERS

1. Some people believed that icons broke the Second Commandment of the Hebrew Bible.

2. Life was uncertain during this time of economic and societal change, so the veneration of icons, which were believed to have special powers, must have been comforting.

3. He is trying to express that he does not believe that the icon is actually God but that through respecting the icon, it brings him closer to God.

Byzantine Growth and Decline

What makes an empire great? Is it the breadth of its territory? The power of its rulers? Or the beauty and innovation of its arts and sciences? As you have read, the Byzantine Empire experienced great heights, but another glorious period was still to come. Yet the empire eventually weakened and faced a long, slow decline.

REVITALIZING THE EMPIRE

After the Iconoclastic Controversy ended in 867, a new dynasty arose that changed the fortunes of the empire and led it into a golden age. The Macedonian dynasty was founded by Basil I who, like Justinian, came from humble peasant beginnings. His successors began reconquering territory that had once made up the extended Byzantine Empire.

More than 100 years after Basil I gained the throne, a descendant, **Basil II**, conquered the Bulgarian Empire and added parts of Syria, Mesopotamia, and Armenia, among others, to his territory. The Byzantine Empire was again a major power in the region. On the home front, Basil II worked to control the growing power of the regional governors and their families who had become a landed aristocracy. He required that land taken from peasants be returned, and he changed the system of taxation so the responsibility for paying more in taxes fell to the large landowners.

The Macedonian dynasty in general and Basil II's rule in particular are considered the golden age of the Byzantine Empire. Some scholars even call it the Byzantine or Macedonian Renaissance. Arts of all kinds were funded and promoted, literature flourished, and scholars, such as Leo the Mathematician, expanded on Greco-Roman knowledge.

The Byzantine Empire, c. 1071

EXTENDING THE FAITH

The period following the Iconoclastic Controversy was an important period for the eastern branch of the Christian Church as it expanded into new regions. This extension of the faith was to have revolutionary consequences that still shape our world today.

In 863, at the request of the ruler of Moravia (present-day Czech Republic), two Byzantine Greek brothers, Cyril and Methodius, became missionaries to the Slavic people of eastern Europe. Chosen because they spoke a Slavic dialect, Cyril and Methodius

proved to be enormously successful. The brothers and their missionary successors ultimately reached out and converted the Bulgarians, Serbs, and Rus peoples (Russians).

But Cyril and Methodius's importance reaches far beyond the spread of religion. To reach the people he wanted to convert, Cyril translated the Bible into local languages, inventing an alphabet made up of a combination of Greek and local letters. This became the precursor of the modern Cyrillic alphabet. Today, over 50 languages, including Russian, use an alphabet derived from the Cyrillic. Byzantine trade and culture traveled the same paths as the missionaries, adding to the wealth of the Byzantine Empire and influencing Russian and eastern European art and architecture.

Cyril and Methodius's work of translating the Bible further increased tensions between the western and eastern branches of the Christian Church, as many leaders in the western branch believed the Bible should only be written in Latin. This and other tensions would eventually lead to a formal division of the church into the

Orthodox Church in the east and the Roman Catholic Church in the west. You will learn more about this split in a later chapter.

THE DECLINE

After the rule of Basil II ended, the Byzantine Empire went into steep decline. Large landowners took back control and regained power. More than ten emperors ruled in the 56 years between 1025 and 1081. Then, shortly after the split of the Christian Church, the Byzantine Empire faced a new enemy, the Latin Christians of western Europe.

In 1071, the Byzantines experienced what is known as the "Double Disasters." First, the Normans, Viking descendants who had settled in northern France, drove the Byzantines out of southern Italy. Then, in August, the Seljuk Turks, skilled horsemen from Central Asia, captured the emperor in a massive defeat for the Byzantines at the battle of Manzikert. After 1071, Byzantine emperors ruled a much smaller empire with a much-weakened army.

This fresco of Saint Basil performing a religious ceremony is located in the Church of St. Sophia in Macedonia. Initially part of the First Bulgarian Empire, the church was built after the region's official conversion to Christianity.

HISTORICAL THINKING

1. **READING CHECK** Why was the period of the Macedonian dynasty called the Byzantine Empire's golden age?

2. **IDENTIFY PROBLEMS AND SOLUTIONS** How did Cyril address the problem of converting the Slavs?

3. **INTERPRET MAPS** What area was still part of the Byzantine Empire after 1071?

PLAN: 2-PAGE LESSON

OBJECTIVE

Explain how the Byzantine Empire reached its golden age and spread Christianity into Eastern Europe and Russia before its decline.

CRITICAL THINKING SKILLS FOR LESSON 2.2

- Identify Problems and Solutions
- Interpret Maps
- Compare and Contrast
- Analyze Cause and Effect

HISTORICAL THINKING FOR CHAPTER 8

How can a strong leader impact an empire?

Strong leaders Basil I and Basil II reconquered territory that the Byzantine Empire had lost and brought about a golden age for the empire. Lesson 2.2 explores how the Byzantine Empire transitioned from a golden age to an empire in steep decline.

BACKGROUND FOR THE TEACHER

The Rise of a Multi-Centered Europe In 500, Constantinople had dominated Christian Europe much as Baghdad shaped the Islamic world before the Abbasid Empire broke apart. Just as Cordoba and Cairo became important Islamic centers, so too did new centers challenge the Byzantines' supremacy. Other regions in Europe converted to Christianity and became new centers. The Anglo-Saxons adopted Christianity in the 500s and 600s. Farther to the north, the Scandinavians converted around 1000. The decision of these individual rulers to adopt Christianity, whether the Roman Catholicism of Rome or the Orthodoxy of Constantinople, had long-term consequences that forever altered culture throughout Europe.

INTRODUCE & ENGAGE

DEFINE *GOLDEN AGE*

Guide students to discuss the meaning of the term *golden age*. Place the term in the center of a Word Web. **ASK:** What are some concepts or events that you associate with the term? *(Answers will vary. Possible responses: a flourishing culture, accomplishments, advancements, technology, rise in the arts)* Have students consider whether a golden age must always come at the height of an empire. Tell students they will read about the golden age that the Byzantine Empire experienced under the Macedonian dynasty.

TEACH

GUIDED DISCUSSION

1. **Compare and Contrast** How were the reigns of the emperors Justinian and Basil II similar? *(Possible response: Justinian wanted to restore lost lands that were once part of the ancient Roman Empire. Basil II wanted to restore lands that were lost under the Byzantine Empire.)*

2. **Analyze Cause and Effect** How did the end of Basil II's rule affect the Byzantine Empire? *(Possible response: It led to the decline of the empire and the end of the golden age.)*

INTERPRET MAPS

Direct students' attention to the map, The Byzantine Empire, c. 1071. **ASK:** Based on map details, where was much of the land in the Byzantine Empire located? *(Possible response: in Europe and the coast of Eurasia)* How does the map support the text with regard to the Byzantine Empire's loss of land? *(By 1071, the Byzantines had been driven out of southern Italy. They lost much of their lands to the east due to invasion by the Turks.)*

ACTIVE OPTIONS

On Your Feet: Three-Step Interview Have students work in pairs. One student interviews the other student using questions such as: How did the new alphabet that Cyril and Methodius created affect local peoples? Do you think that the existence of a new alphabet caused more people to convert to Christianity? Why or why not? Then direct students to reverse roles.

NG Learning Framework: Write a Dual Biography
ATTITUDE Curiosity
KNOWLEDGE Our Human Story

Instruct students to write profiles about Cyril and Methodius, using information from the lesson and additional source materials. Encourage students to connect the two monks' religious contribution of the Cyrillic alphabet to the alphabet's political, economic, and cultural effects. Students should include the rise in tensions between the western and eastern branches of the Christian Church in their profiles.

DIFFERENTIATE

STRIVING READERS

Connect Details to a Main Idea Have student pairs complete a Main-Idea Diagram. Tell students to take turns reading the lesson, pausing after each paragraph to record relevant details, adding more boxes if necessary. Then have pairs work together to write a main-idea statement supported by details for each paragraph.

PRE-AP

The Fall of Empires Point out that empires have risen and fallen throughout history for various reasons, but some factors have been consistent in all of their declines. Have students conduct online research to compare the fall of the Byzantine Empire with the fall of the Roman Empire. Encourage students to consider both social and political causes and effects, such as leaders' decisions and the ethnic composition of the empires. Students can list factors that the declines had in common. Invite students to share their findings with the class.

See the Chapter Planner for more strategies for differentiation.

HISTORICAL THINKING

ANSWERS

1. The empire expanded its territory and had great achievements in the arts and sciences.

2. He created an alphabet and translated the Bible into the local languages so the people could understand the message of Christianity.

3. After 1071, the Byzantine Empire controlled the land on the eastern shores of the Mediterranean Sea and the southern shores of the Black Sea. This included the land around Constantinople.

Imprint of an Early Empire

For many years, a famous historian named Edward Gibbon was the leading authority on the ancient Roman world. He wrote that the Byzantine Empire was corrupt, decadent, immoral, and overly bureaucratic. Essentially, he portrayed it as being the opposite of the enlightened and efficient western Europe. He was wrong.

INFLUENCING EAST AND WEST

Historians now realize the important role played by the Byzantine Empire in preserving the traditions of the classical age. The empire was an essential link that passed Greco-Roman knowledge and culture to the medieval west and also to the Islamic east, for example to Arabia and Persia. The people of the Byzantine Empire protected Greco-Roman knowledge and culture for future generations, developed artistic and architectural styles that influenced artists and builders of the Muslim Golden Age and the European Renaissance (about which you'll learn more later), and gave birth to a branch of Christianity that developed into the Russian, Serbian, and Greek Orthodox Churches.

The empire began as a literal "New Rome," an extension of the Roman Empire, under Constantine, but as the centuries passed the main language shifted from Latin to Greek and a unique tradition and culture developed.

LASTING LEGACIES

Although at times the Byzantine Empire ruled over most of the Mediterranean world, one of its most lasting legacies is not armed conquest but diplomacy. Many Byzantine leaders were adept treaty makers and developed a tradition of negotiating and making deals with their neighbors, often playing one against another.

One reason the empire maintained its power during periods of both decline and ascent was that

its economic and financial system remained strong throughout. Some historians believe that the reliability of its gold currency was possible because it was introduced at the same time that trade increased with West Africa, which made gold more available. The empire also traded with China and developed one of the only silk industries outside China after smuggling out some silkworms around 560.

Most famously, the Byzantine Empire preserved and improved upon the legal codes of the Romans. The Code of Justinian formed the foundation for much of European law and still influences international law today. The emperor Leo III created a new law code in 726, the *Ecloga*. The *Ecloga* revised Roman law to incorporate Christian principles and it was written in Greek, so it could be read by more people. The *Ecloga* became part of the legal institutions of the Slavic world, for example in Russia.

The Byzantine Empire developed an influential artistic culture. Its distinctive style is well represented by the remarkable **mosaics**—groups of tiny colored stone cubes set in mortar to create a picture or design—found in churches such as the Hagia Sophia. Byzantine mosaics were known for their exceptional quality and craftsmanship. Large expanses of gold-backed glass created a rich glow, and natural stone cubes helped create vibrant, detailed scenes. Byzantine artists used techniques from Greece and Rome in painting and mosaic and mixed them with Christian themes, developments that would capture the attention of Renaissance painters a few centuries later. Furthermore, Byzantine art and culture traveled with missionaries and traders to the Slavic world where it had an enormous influence.

WOMEN IN BYZANTIUM

As you have seen, powerful women like Theodora had a strong impact on Byzantine history even if they were still legally inferior to men. In fact, women in the empire had more rights than in many other societies both before and after the Byzantine era.

Under Byzantine law, a woman could be the guardian of an emperor who was still a child and serve as a de facto ruler or regent. Because of this law, Theodora possessed a leadership role in the running of Justinian's empire, and the empress Irene restored the use of icons and plotted against her own son to hold onto her position as emperor.

Throughout the empire, a woman could become the legal head of her household and gain control of her family's resources when her husband died. All Byzantine women, even married women, could sign contracts and make their own wills. The United States did not grant women these kinds of property rights until the 19th century.

CRITICAL VIEWING This mosaic adorns a huge arch in the Basilica of San Vitale in Ravenna, Italy. The arch shows Jesus and the apostles. Why do you think Jesus is shown at the top of the arch with a different orientation than the images of the apostles?

HISTORICAL THINKING

1. **READING CHECK** Why is the Byzantine Empire considered important to the later development of western Europe?

2. **COMPARE AND CONTRAST** What are the similarities and differences between the Code of Justinian and the *Ecloga*?

3. **DRAW CONCLUSIONS** How do you think the rights granted to women in the Byzantine Empire affected women's quality of life? Explain your reasoning.

Byzantine Mosaics

REALISTIC ANIMALS Mosaics often contained realistic animals, such as the sheep shown here.

DAZZLING GOLD Many mosaics contained shiny pieces of gold leaf to create a sparkling effect.

INTRICATE PATTERNS The mosaic floor of the Basilica San Vitale contains intricate patterns.

PLAN: 2-PAGE LESSON

OBJECTIVE

Describe how the Byzantine Empire had an impact on the development of western European, Islamic, and Slavic civilizations.

CRITICAL THINKING SKILLS FOR LESSON 2.3

- Compare and Contrast
- Draw Conclusions
- Make Inferences
- Analyze Visuals

HISTORICAL THINKING FOR CHAPTER 8

How can a strong leader impact an empire?

Despite the fact that the Byzantine Empire came to an end, it had some great leaders who improved its economy and legal system and encouraged culture to flourish. Lesson 2.3 explores some of the accomplishments of these emperors and the impact of their contributions not just on the Byzantine Empire but on future generations.

BACKGROUND FOR THE TEACHER

Women Leaders Women were influential leaders in Byzantium, which was unusual, and they had a lasting impact on the empire and beyond. Along with Theodora, Irene also had a prominent role in the empire. She was the widow of emperor Leo IV, assuming power after his death because their son was only nine years old at the time. Irene tried to devise a solution to the iconoclast controversy. She wanted there to be a compromise, so she organized a church council meeting in Constantinople. In 787, the Second Council of Nicaea met and condemned iconoclasm. As a result, icons that had been removed from different churches were returned.

During her reign, Irene made many payments to keep the Abbasid armies from taking the city of Constantinople. Still, the powerful Islamic army chomped away at the Byzantine Empire's territory, bit by bit. To stay in power, she even overthrew her son, who had taken the throne when he came of age. Finally, her courtiers deposed her and installed a general as her successor in 802. Even though the Byzantine Empire had lost one-third of its land by this time, it likely would have also lost its capital city had Irene not given money to the Abbasid Empire.

INTRODUCE & ENGAGE

CONNECT THE PRESENT WITH THE PAST

Ask students to identify the problem the lesson introduction describes. *(historian Edward Gibbon's biased opinion of the Byzantine Empire)* Have them brainstorm a list of examples of when their thinking about an historic topic or event was inaccurate or contained omissions that distorted the truth or facts. Ask students why they think it is important to read widely about a topic and to consult both primary and secondary sources before writing or speaking about it.

TEACH

GUIDED DISCUSSION

1. **Draw Conclusions** Why do you think many Byzantine leaders were good treaty makers? *(Possible response: Because of the empire's location, it was vulnerable to attack, so the leaders needed to have allies on both continents in hopes of securing the empire.)*

2. **Make Inferences** Why do you think women had more rights and held more positions of power in the Byzantine Empire? *(Possible response: Byzantine law, which was largely impacted by the Code of Justinian, enabled women to have more rights and influence in powerful positions.)*

ANALYZE VISUALS

Direct students' attention to the mosaics in the lesson. **ASK:** What similarities can you draw between the mosaics in the Basilica of San Vitale in Ravenna? *(the patterns of the mosaics are extremely intricate)* What is different about the floor mosaic than the rest of the mosaics? *(The floor mosaic only features patterns, whereas the other mosaics show realistic images of people, animals, and landscapes.)*

ACTIVE OPTIONS

On Your Feet: Create a Team Word Web Ask teams of four to gather around a large sheet of paper. Each student should write a word or phrase related to the legacy of the law codes of the Byzantine Empire on the part of the web nearest him or her. At your signal, students should rotate the paper and continue to add words or phrases. Tell teams to use their completed web to summarize a main idea about how the Byzantine Empire left a legal legacy that was adopted by other legal institutions.

> **NG Learning Framework: Explore Byzantine Influence Abroad**
> SKILLS Observation, Collaboration
> KNOWLEDGE Our Human Story

Ask students to work in small groups to research examples of Byzantine influence in art, architecture, or culture in Europe or Asia. Invite students to present their findings, including visuals, and to point out the connection to Byzantine art and culture.

DIFFERENTIATE

STRIVING READERS

Read and Recall Have each student read the lesson independently. After reading, student pairs should meet without the text and take notes as they share ideas they recall. Then tell them to review the lesson together and decide what to add or change in their notes.

GIFTED & TALENTED

Investigate a Byzantine Emperor Ask students to research information about a Byzantine leader they did not learn about in the chapter. Encourage them to select a leader that made a contribution or is significant to understanding this time period. Invite them to share their findings with the class.

See the Chapter Planner for more strategies for differentiation.

HISTORICAL THINKING

ANSWERS

1. Possible response: It preserved Greco-Roman knowledge and culture and developed artistic and architectural techniques that influenced Renaissance artists.

2. Both were based on Roman law. The Justinian Code was written mainly in Latin and was influential in the West. The *Ecloga* was written in Greek, incorporated Christian principles, and was influential in the Slavic world.

3. Possible response: It allowed them to live an improved lifestyle over women in other ancient civilizations because they could do things like retain inheritances and sign contracts.

CRITICAL VIEWING Possible response: Jesus was the focus of Christianity and the most important person to Christians. The apostles carried on Jesus' teachings after his death, so they were important but more in a supportive role.

VOCABULARY

Choose the vocabulary word that best completes each of the following sentences.

1. An outbreak of a deadly _____ resulted in loss of life and a struggling economy.

2. The Byzantine economy experienced _____ after the reign of Justinian.

3. The _____ period in European history lasted from about 500 to 1500.

4. The _____ of the Virgin Mary glowed beautifully in the candlelight.

5. People would adore and _____ pictures of religious figures.

6. An _____ believed that images of religious figures went against the Second Commandment.

7. Byzantine _____ were part of the empire's artistic legacy.

READING STRATEGY
MAKE INFERENCES

Complete a graphic organizer like the one below to make an inference about the Byzantine Empire and its success. Tell what you know about the subject in the "I Know" section. Write your inference in the "And So" section. Then answer the question that follows.

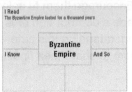

I Read
The Byzantine Empire lasted for a thousand years

Byzantine Empire

I Know

And So

8. What caused the downfall of the Western Roman Empire, and what can you infer about the Eastern Roman Empire in contrast?

MAIN IDEAS

Answer the following questions. Support your answers with evidence from the chapter.

9. What was important about Constantinople's location? LESSON 1.1

10. Why was the Justinian Code an important legacy of Justinian's reign? LESSON 1.2

11. What did iconophiles want? LESSON 2.1

12. What qualities marked the golden age of the Macedonian dynasty? LESSON 2.2

13. How did the Byzantine Empire impact the Slavic world? LESSON 2.3

HISTORICAL THINKING

Answer the following questions. Support your answers with evidence from the chapter.

14. EXPLAIN How did trade with West Africa influence the Byzantine economy?

15. DRAW CONCLUSIONS Why are Procopius's writings important to modern historians?

16. MAKE GENERALIZATIONS How did Byzantine laws of inheritance influence women's lives? Did that make any significant difference to the historic course of the empire? Provide support from the text in your answer.

17. EVALUATE Write a few sentences arguing for or against use of the term *golden age* to describe the Macedonian dynasty.

18. ANALYZE CAUSE AND EFFECT What is the connection between Egyptian grain and the spread of the plague?

19. FORM OR SUPPORT OPINIONS Was the translation of the Bible into the Slavic languages truly important in the conversion of the Slavs to Christianity? Why or why not?

20. DRAW CONCLUSIONS How did Christianity both unify the Byzantine Empire and help form the Byzantine identity?

INTERPRET VISUALS

Study the icon. Then answer the questions that follow.

21. How does the use of gold leaf affect the painting?

22. Why might gold leaf have been such an essential part of the style of icons?

Saint Michael, c. 14th century

ANALYZE SOURCES

Basil II ruled Byzantium during its golden age, and unlike most emperors, he was buried outside the city of Constantinople at the Hebdomon Palace complex. The epitaph below was found in later manuscripts, not on or near his tomb. Read it and answer the questions that follow.

> Other past emperors
> previously designated for themselves other burial places
> But I Basil, born in the purple chamber,
> place my tomb on the site of the Hebdomon [Palace]
> and take sabbath's rest from the endless toils
> which I satisfied in wars and which I endured.
> For nobody saw my spear at rest,
> from when the Emperor of Heaven called me
> to the rulership of this great empire on earth,
> but I kept vigilant through the whole span of my life
> guarding the children of New Rome
> marching bravely to the West,
> and as far as the very frontiers of the East.
> The Persians and Scythians bear witness to this
> and along with them Abasgos, Ismael, Araps, Iber.
> And now, good man, looking upon this tomb
> reward it with prayers in return for my campaigns.
>
> —Epitaph of Basil II

23. According to the epitaph, what did Basil think was the most important achievement of his reign?

24. What does the use of the term "New Rome" tell us about Byzantine identity in the 11th century?

CONNECT TO YOUR LIFE

25. NARRATIVE The plague in Constantinople lasted 20 years and changed the city in profound ways. Write a story in which you are a traveler who has left the city before the outbreak of the plague and then returned after it is over, 20 years later.

TIPS

* Review the lesson that describes the plague and then imagine yourself being one of the people who witnessed this event.

* Use sensory details to describe the city before and after the plague: think of sounds, smells, tastes, and feelings as well as what you would see.

* Use vivid language to help readers visualize the scene.

* Include two or three vocabulary terms from the chapter in your narrative.

* Conclude your narrative by expressing an emotional response to the changes.

VOCABULARY ANSWERS

1. plague
2. stagnation
3. medieval
4. icon
5. venerate
6. iconoclast
7. mosaics

READING STRATEGY ANSWERS

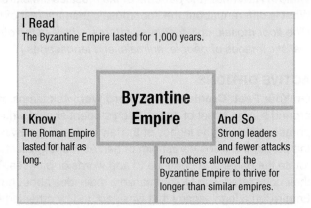

I Read
The Byzantine Empire lasted for 1,000 years.

Byzantine Empire

I Know
The Roman Empire lasted for half as long.

And So
Strong leaders and fewer attacks from others allowed the Byzantine Empire to thrive for longer than similar empires.

8. Possible answers include that poor leadership and social and economic inequality as well as attacks from border peoples led to the downfall of the Western Empire. We can infer that the Eastern Empire did not have these kinds of problems, or at least, they were not so severe as to cause the downfall as in the west.

MAIN IDEAS ANSWERS

9. It was located on a strip of land between Europe and Asia. The city served as a major trade center for goods traveling by land and sea from all over the world.

10. The Justinian Code revised and clarified all previous Roman law, saved it for posterity, and is still influential today.

11. Iconophiles wanted to be able to keep icons as objects of veneration.

12. During the Macedonian dynasty, the literature, arts, and sciences of the Byzantine Empire reached their greatest forms of expression.

13. The Slavic world adopted the religion and many cultural elements of the Byzantine Empire.

HISTORICAL THINKING ANSWERS

14. Trade across the Sahara became easier and more consistent after camels began to be used to cross the desert. This meant that access to West African gold was consistently and readily available in the empire, which stabilized Byzantine currency.

15. Procopius provides firsthand evidence of the Justinian period, including its wars and Justinian's building programs.

16. Possible response: Because of laws allowing women to inherit, women had more freedom and power in the Byzantine Empire than in many other societies at the time. This led to women being more actively engaged in Byzantine society and religion and may have influenced the fervor of the Iconoclast Controversy.

17. Students will have a variety of responses. A student arguing for the term *golden age* might point to the heights reached in the arts during the Macedonian dynasty. A student arguing against the phrase might point out that the Macedonian dynasty did not reach the heights of Justinian's reign.

18. Egyptian grain supplied food to the entire empire. The grain contained rats, which carried the plague. The plague transmitted from the rats to humans.

19. Student responses will vary. A student arguing for the importance of translating the Bible in converting the Slavs might write that having sacred texts available to the common people made Christianity more relatable and attractive. A student arguing the opposite might write that with effective missionaries spreading the message, the Slavs would have converted anyway.

20. Possible response: Even though there were many ethnicities under Byzantine rule, the practice of Christianity gave them all something in common. By making Christianity the state religion and by not allowing people of other religions to become citizens, the Byzantines made Christianity central to their identity.

INTERPRET VISUALS ANSWERS

21. Possible response: The gold leaf makes the painting seem rich and warm.

22. Possible response: The gold leaf made the icon literally rich. It was an expensive component of the paintings. It also reflected candlelight, making the image seem warmer and more alive.

ANALYZE SOURCES ANSWERS

23. Possible response: The epitaph shows that Basil considered wars and conquest his most important achievement.

24. Possible response: The use of the term "New Rome" shows that Byzantines of the 11th century still believed that they were part of the ancient Roman Empire.

CONNECT TO YOUR LIFE ANSWER

25. Narratives will vary but should contain sensory details and vivid language to help convey the narrator's impressions of Constantinople after the plague.

UNIT 3 RESOURCES

UNIT INTRODUCTION

UNIT TIME LINE

UNIT MAP online

THE GLOBAL PERSPECTIVE: Many Paths to God online

| **NG Learning Framework**
Compare and Contrast Religions

UNIT WRAP-UP

National Geographic **Magazine Adapted Article**
• "The World's Newest Major Religion: No Religion"

Unit 3 Inquiry: Argue Before the Emperor

Unit 3 Formal Assessment

CHAPTER 9 RESOURCES

Available in the Teacher eEdition

TEACHER RESOURCES & ASSESSMENT

Reading and Note-Taking

Vocabulary Practice

Document-Based Question Template

Social Studies Skills Lessons
• Reading: Determine Chronology
• Writing: Argument

Formal Assessment
• Chapter 9 Pretest
• Chapter 9 Tests A & B
• Section Quizzes

Chapter 9 Answer Key

Cognero®

STUDENT DIGITAL RESOURCES

Available in the Student eEdition

• **eEdition** (English)	• **National Geographic Atlas**	• **Biographies**
• **Handbooks**	• **History Notebook**	• **Literature Analysis**

SECTION 1 RESOURCES

ORIGINS OF ISLAM

LESSON 1.1   p. 244

The Prophet Muhammad

- On Your Feet: Think, Pair, Share

| **NG Learning Framework**
Discuss the Umma's Influence

Biography

- Khadijah online

LESSON 1.2   p. 246

The Early Caliphs

- On Your Feet: Three-Step Interview

| **NG Learning Framework**
Write a News Story

LESSON 1.3   p. 248

DOCUMENT-BASED QUESTION
Comparing Calendars

- On Your Feet: Roundtable

SECTION 2 RESOURCES

ISLAMIC EXPANSION

LESSON 2.1   p. 250

Conquering the Arabian Peninsula

- On Your Feet: Numbered Heads

| **NG Learning Framework**
Write an Essay

LESSON 2.2   p. 252

The Umayyad Caliphate and North Africa

- On Your Feet: Think, Pair, Share

| **NG Learning Framework**
Create a Presentation About Islamic Architecture

LESSON 2.3   p. 254

STATE OF THE WORLD 800 C.E.

- On Your Feet: Research Religious Structures

SECTION 3 RESOURCES

THE ABBASID EMPIRE

LESSON 3.1   p. 256

Baghdad, City of Learning

- On Your Feet: Jigsaw Strategy

| **NG Learning Framework**
Research Abbasid Control

LESSON 3.2   p. 258

The Islamic Golden Age

- On Your Feet: Roundtable

| **NG Learning Framework**
Explore Islamic Achievements

Biography

- Al-Zahrawi online

CHAPTER 9 REVIEW

STRATEGY ❶
Turn Headings into Outlines

To help Striving Readers organize and understand lesson content, explain that headings can provide a high-level outline of the lesson. Model how to use the lesson title and headings to create a basic outline structure. Have them take notes and flesh out their outlines as they read.

Use with All Lessons

STRATEGY ❷
Sequence Events

Encourage students to use a Sequence Chain to build understanding of the critical events in a section and their relationship to one another in time. Have them use the Sequence Chain to trace the sequence of events related to the prophet Muhammad and the spread of Islam.

Use with All Lessons

STRATEGY ❸
Create Idea Webs

Prompt students to summarize the chapter by creating three Idea Webs, one for each section. Instruct students to complete each web with relevant information as they read the corresponding set of lessons.

Use with All Lessons

INCLUSION

STRATEGY ❶
Preview and Predict

Pair students who have reading or perception challenges with proficient readers and direct them to read the lesson title and headings together. Ask proficient students to guide their partners in describing details in visuals and reading the captions, working together to write notes predicting what the lesson will be about. After reading, ask pairs to review their notes to confirm their predictions and correct inaccuracies.

Use with All Lessons *For example, in Lesson 1.2, after proficient students preview the title, headings, visuals, and captions, have students write predictions, such as the following: This lesson will be about the basic beliefs of Islam and the split that formed between its followers.*

STRATEGY ❷
Use Modified Main Idea Statements

To help students anticipate and organize content, provide modified Main Idea statements before reading:

1.1 Muhammad taught Islam to the people living in the deserts of the Arabian Peninsula, who joined together in the Muslim faith.

1.2 After Muhammad died, Islam experienced growth but also divided into two groups, the Shiite and the Sunni, who had different ideas about the faith.

2.1 The leaders of Islam who came after Muhammad led a powerful army that conquered non-Muslim lands.

2.2 The leaders of the Sunni part of Islam, the Umayyads, made changes and expanded the Muslim empire.

3.1 The next dynasty of the Muslim empire, the Abbasid dynasty, built the capital city of Baghdad and made the empire strong through trade and unity.

3.2 The Muslim people achieved great things during the Islamic Golden Age.

Use with All Lessons

ENGLISH LANGUAGE LEARNERS

STRATEGY ❶
Create Word Charts

Help students understand unfamiliar words by completing word charts such as the one below. Pair students at the **Beginning** level with those at the **Intermediate** or **Advanced** level. Ask students to copy the chart and then work together to complete the four parts for unfamiliar words they encounter.

Definition of _____ .	Draw a visual.
Tell how the word relates to the Arab empires and Islamic expansion.	Use it in a sentence.

Use with All Lessons

STRATEGY ②
Use Paired Reading

Pair students at the **Intermediate** and **Advanced** levels to read passages from the text aloud.

1. Partner 1 reads a passage; partner 2 retells the passage in his or her own words.
2. Partner 2 reads a different passage; partner 1 retells it.
3. Pairs repeat the process, switching roles.

Use with All Lessons

STRATEGY ③
Look for Cognates

Suggest to students that, as they read, they should look for words that are similar in spelling and meaning to words in their home language. For each word they identify, have students of All Proficiencies make a vocabulary card with the English word and definition on one side and the word and definition in their home language on the other side. Encourage them to note any differences in the meanings of the two words.

Use with All Lessons *For example, in Lesson 1.1, the words* desert, rock, religion, *and* prophet *have cognates in Spanish:* desierto, roca, religión, profeta.

GIFTED & TALENTED

STRATEGY ①
Write a Letter

Tell students to put themselves in the place of people who experienced one of the following events: they heard the message of Muhammad; they made the hajj to the holy city of Mecca; they visited the Alhambra in Granada, Spain; or another event from one of the lessons. Tell them to conduct online research to learn more about their chosen event. Instruct them to write a letter to a friend or family member about the experience, describing in detail what happened and how they felt about it. Have students post their letters on a class blog or read them to the class.

Use with All Lessons

STRATEGY ②
Design an Infographic

Direct students to create an infographic that presents information about a specific achievement of the Muslim empire, such as Islamic art, literature, or improvements made in science or mathematics. Guide them to conduct research to learn more about the achievement and collect interesting details and visual information before designing their infographic. Invite students to share their infographic with the class.

Use with Lesson 3.2

PRE-AP

STRATEGY ①
Research Muslim Architecture

Ask students to choose one of the mosques included in the chapter and conduct print and online research about the building. Tell them to write an essay describing the construction, the layout, and the location of the building. Encourage them to include a time line and visuals of the mosque. Ask students to read their essays to the class.

Use with All Lessons

STRATEGY ②
Create an Oral Presentation

Invite students to choose one of the terms below to investigate or to choose another term from one of the lessons. Students will then design and deliver an oral presentation that explains the significance of the term to the history of the Muslim empire.

bureaucracy
mosque
caliph
prayer
conquests
religious revelation
hajj
religious tolerance
monotheistic
sharia

Use with All Lessons

CHAPTER
9
Arab Empires and
Islamic Expansion
550–1258

HISTORICAL THINKING How does religion affect
world civilizations?

SECTION 1 Origins of Islam
SECTION 2 Islamic Expansion
SECTION 3 The Abbasid Empire

CRITICAL VIEWING
The Great Mosque of Córdoba in what is now
Spain is one of the best-known examples of
Muslim architecture. What generalizations
can you make about the art and architecture
of Islam based on this photo of a prayer hall?

242 CHAPTER 9

INTRODUCE THE PHOTOGRAPH

ISLAMIC ART AND ARCHITECTURE

Have students study the photograph of the prayer
hall, part of the Great Mosque of Córdoba, that opens
the chapter. Direct students to look closely at the
architectural features and decorative designs. **ASK:** What
inference can you make about the skill of the Muslims
who designed the prayer hall? *(Possible response: The
Muslims were highly skilled at constructing elaborate
arches and columns. They created intricate designs on
the walls.)* Explain that the Great Mosque is located in the
Historic Center of Córdoba, Spain. It is regarded as one
of the best examples of Western Islamic architecture. Tell
students that in this chapter they will learn about the ways
in which the religion of Islam interacted with the diverse
civilizations that came under its control.

SHARE BACKGROUND

The Great Mosque of Córdoba was named a UNESCO
World Heritage Site in 1984, partly because of its value
representing different cultural civilizations. Historians
believe that a temple to a Roman god first existed on the
site of the mosque. In about 500 C.E., invading Visigoths
converted the temple into the Christian church of San
Vicente. Then, in about 785, the first ruler of the Umayyad
dynasty in Spain developed the church into a mosque.
Umayyad builders blended regional and innovative
Islamic styles. They used stone and brick in the prayer
hall, recycling the materials and techniques of the
Romans and Visigoths. The builders also incorporated
horseshoe arches, which were common in Visigoth
architecture. The decorative art on the walls integrates
the geometric designs typical of Islamic art and the style
of the Moors, Muslim people of North Africa, who used
repeated patterns.

CRITICAL VIEWING Answers will vary. Possible
response: The prayer hall's patterns, double arches, and
tall columns reflect the importance of symmetry. The
repeated designs might signal the importance of order.

HISTORICAL THINKING QUESTION
How does religion affect world civilizations?

Fishbowl Activity: Preview Content This activity will help students preview the topics covered in the chapter by exploring how religion spreads and affects different cultures. Encourage students to use prior knowledge about the effect of religious beliefs on laws and ways of life in the following discussions.

Tell one half of the class to sit or stand in a close circle, facing inward, and the other half of the class to sit or stand in a larger circle around them. Ask students to consider the following question: In what ways do religious convictions shape government and the development of laws? Students in the inner circle should discuss the question for five minutes while those in the outer circle listen and take notes. Then have the groups reverse and consider the following question: How do religious beliefs affect the artistic creations and scientific goals of a society? Like before, students in the inner circle discuss the question for five minutes while those in the outer circle listen and take notes. Reconvene as a class and discuss the common themes each circle touched upon in their discussions. Tell students that in this chapter they will learn how the religion of Islam spread, shaped governments, and affected diverse cultures as the Muslim empire formed.

KEY DATES FOR CHAPTER 9

c. 613	Muhammad has religious visions in Mecca.
c. 622	Hijrah begins the Muslim era.
656	Islam is split into two groups—Shiite and Sunni—over the line of succession.
661	Umayyads seize power and initiate expansion.
744	The Abbasid dynasty begins to rule and expand its empire.
750	Ummayyad Abd al-Rahman founds al-Andalus in Spain.
762	Al-Mansur founds Baghdad at a trading crossroads.
786	Haran al-Rashid takes power and encourages arts and learning.
early 800s	Al-Ma'mun rules the empire and promotes the House of Wisdom.
945	Buyids take over government and reduce caliphs to figureheads.

INTRODUCE THE READING STRATEGY

DETERMINE CHRONOLOGY
Explain to students that creating a time line can help them organize main events to gain a deeper understanding of how they are related and how they develop. Go to the Chapter Review and preview the time line with students. As they read the chapter, have students record the main events and dates pertaining to the origins and spread of Islam.

INTRODUCE CHAPTER VOCABULARY

KEY VOCABULARY

SECTION 1

caliph	hajj	mosque
oasis	sharia	sheikh

SECTION 2

dhimmitude	minaret	religious tolerance

SECTION 3

arabesque	astrolabe	calligraphy
figurehead	qadi	

DEFINITION CHART
As they read the chapter, have students complete a Definition Chart for Key Vocabulary terms. Instruct students to list the Key Vocabulary terms in the left column of the chart. They should add each term's definition in the center column as they encounter the term in the chapter and then restate the definition in their own words in the right column. Model an example on the board, using the graphic organizer shown.

Word	Definition	In My Own Words
mosque	a Muslim place of worship	a place like a church or synagogue where Muslims gather in groups to pray

Muslims from all over the world journey to pray at the Kaaba in Mecca, Saudi Arabia. (The word *Kaaba* means "cube" in Arabic.) The shrine contains a holy rock called the Black Stone.

The Prophet Muhammad

Think about leaders who have affected your life or the lives of others. Leaders can cause political change, social change, or spiritual change. Long ago, the actions of Muhammad led to all of these changes at the same time.

ORIGINS OF ISLAM

Imagine living in the dry, scorching desert of the Arabian Peninsula. The land was so parched that it was difficult to farm there. Instead, many people who lived in the region herded animals such as sheep, cattle, camels, and goats. These people were known as the **Bedouin** (BEH-duh-wuhn), an Arabic word meaning "desert dweller." Living a nomadic life, they moved with their herds to find locations where water and grazing land were available at different times of the year. Luckily, **oases**, isolated places with water where plants can grow, dotted the land, and the Bedouin could find not only water but also areas of grasses for their animals.

The Bedouin traveled together in clans, or groups of people with a common ancestor. Each clan elected its own **sheikh** (SHAYK) to lead them as they conducted their day-to-day affairs. Like most of the people on the peninsula, the clan members communicated with one another in Arabic.

By the time of the Roman Empire, cities such as **Mecca** rose up around the oases and became trade centers where people from Persia, Egypt, the Byzantine Empire, and elsewhere exchanged goods. Arabs, Jews, and Christians lived together and interacted with and influenced one another. The Arab people, who practiced polytheism, believed that their deities lived in objects found in nature, such as trees or rocks. One of the most revered objects was a large black rock in a cube-shaped shrine called the Kaaba (KAH-buh), which was—and still is—located in Mecca.

Many Arabs traveled to Mecca to pray to one of the gods represented in the Kaaba. This steady stream of visitors brought wealth to the merchants and leaders of this prosperous city, which provided the setting for the introduction of the religion of **Islam**. The word *Islam* translates from Arabic to English as "submission to the will of God." In fact, the central idea of Islam is that entry to heaven and an afterlife is attainable only through full surrender to God. Today, Islam is one of the world's major religions, with more than 1.5 billion followers called **Muslims**.

Like Jews and Christians, Muslims are monotheistic. You learned that monotheism is the belief in one God, and the concept of God's forgiveness of sin. Because all three religions honor Abraham as the first religious prophet, they are known as Abrahamic religions. All three religions accept Moses as a prophet as well, but they disagree about other prophets. Only Muslims accept Muhammad as a prophet, and Muslims see Jesus as a prophet rather than as the Son of God as Christians do. Also, while Judaism, Christianity, and Islam all include rituals as part of worshiping God, the rituals vary from religion to religion. For example, both Muslims and Jews follow a set of dietary restrictions. Although these rules differ between each religion, Islam and Judaism share at least one common ban in their diets: followers are forbidden from eating pork.

LIFE AND LEADERSHIP OF MUHAMMAD

Considered a prophet by Muslims, **Muhammad** is credited with introducing Islam to the Arab people. Muslims do not call Muhammad the founder of Islam because they believe God's teachings are timeless, and therefore Islam has no definite origin. Instead, Muslims believe that Muhammad, who was born around 570, was the last messenger of Allah, the Arabic word for God. Historians have learned most of what they know about Muhammad from the writings of others in the centuries following his death. The religious texts of Islam provide few details about his life.

Muhammad was a successful merchant in Mecca and about 40 years old when he began visiting a secluded cave to pray. He was concerned that people focused too much on wealth rather than on the welfare of others.

Around 613, he had a series of visions that included a figure. Muslims believe that Allah spoke to Muhammad through the angel Gabriel, who called on Muhammad to spread the message of submission to God. Followers see Muhammad's teachings as the direct result of his hearing the word of God.

After his religious revelations, Muhammad began spreading the word of Islam, and his wife Khadijah (ka-DEE-juh) and cousin Ali were among his early followers. Khadijah met and hired Muhammad to work as an agent for her successful trading business and soon asked him to marry her. She had a reputation for being generous, sharing her wealth, and caring for the poor. Khadijah believed in Muhammad's revelations immediately and supported him as he preached his ideas.

Muhammad's message was not well-received in much of Mecca at first; leaders feared the growing belief in Islam might have a negative effect on religious pilgrimages to their city and cause losses of income. At the same time, some people in **Medina** (muh-DEE-nuh)—another oasis city that was 210 miles away—grew enthusiastic about Islam and hoped its message might bring an end to feuding among various Arab clans. Feeling unsafe in Mecca, Muhammad and his supporters moved to Medina in 622. This migration of Muhammad and his followers from Mecca to Medina, called the **Hijrah** (HIHJ-ruh), marked a turning point in Islam. All dates in the Islamic calendar are calculated from the year of the Hijrah.

In Medina, Muhammed and other Muslims established an Islamic community called the umma (OO-muh).

Muhammad encouraged Arabs to submit to God, accept Muhammad as God's messenger, pledge loyalty to the umma, and give up their old clan rivalries. In these ways, Islam unified the people of Medina and later the entire Arabian Peninsula. The community was open to everyone who chose to believe. Women gained more status under Islam, with the right to own and inherit property. Strict rules regulated the treatment of slaves.

Meccan leaders worried about the growing strength of Islam. They prepared to attack Medina, but they did not realize that Muhammad had his own military force. He believed that Allah had given him instructions to fight if necessary to expand Islam. Muslim troops swept into Mecca, conquering the city and dedicating the Kaaba to the worship of Allah alone. This conquest's long-term effects included the rapid spread of Islam from Mecca and Medina through the rest of Arabia. By the time of Muhammad's death in 632, most Arabs had converted to Islam. Today, all Muslims are expected to make the **hajj**, or pilgrimage to the holy city of Mecca, if possible.

HISTORICAL THINKING

1. **READING CHECK** How did Muhammad unite the Arab people?

2. **ANALYZE CAUSE AND EFFECT** What were the effects of geography on the settlement and interaction of people who lived on the Arabian Peninsula during Muhammad's time?

3. **DRAW CONCLUSIONS** Why do you think Muhammad opened the doors of his umma to everyone?

PLAN: 2-PAGE LESSON

OBJECTIVE

Explain how Muhammad introduced Islam and united the people of the Arabian Peninsula.

CRITICAL THINKING SKILLS FOR LESSON 1.1

- Analyze Cause and Effect
- Draw Conclusions
- Form and Support Opinions
- Make Inferences
- Analyze Visuals

HISTORICAL THINKING FOR CHAPTER 9

How does religion affect world civilizations?

Lesson 1.1 discusses the geographic and spiritual interactions of people on the Arabian Peninsula with a focus on the introduction of Islam by Muhammad and his leadership in its diffusion.

Student eEdition online

Additional content for this lesson, including a photo, video, and map, is available online.

BACKGROUND FOR THE TEACHER

The Kaaba Millions of Muslims make a pilgrimage each year to the Kaaba in the city of Mecca, Saudi Arabia. The Kaaba is a cube-shaped structure, roughly 50 feet high, located in the center of the Great Mosque. Muslims circle the Kaaba seven times as part of the pilgrimage. The pilgrims try to get close enough to the Black Stone set in the eastern corner and kiss it as Muhammad is believed to have done. According to Islamic tradition, the prophet Abraham and his son Ishmael raised the foundations of the Kaaba on a site linked to the biblical Adam and Eve. Centuries later, polytheistic Arabs used the structure to store idols, but Muhammad restored the Kaaba to monotheistic worship. The Kaaba is cleansed customarily and covered otherwise with an enormous black covering called the *kiswah*.

INTRODUCE & ENGAGE

ACTIVATE PRIOR KNOWLEDGE

Have students work in small groups to create a list of ways in which a person's religion can influence his or her life in terms of religious ceremonies, practices, and holidays as well as other aspects of daily life. Tell students they will learn more about the teachings of Muhammad and how the religion of Islam affected people's lives.

TEACH

GUIDED DISCUSSION

1. **Form and Support Opinions** Why do you think the people of Medina believed the religion of Islam would appeal to and unify Arab clans more than the Jewish and Christian religions? *(Possible response: Arab clans had been exposed to the Jewish and Christian religions for centuries at the trading center of Mecca, but feuding continued. The Islamic faith was new and more likely to take hold at Medina, where trade and pilgrimages were not as common.)*

2. **Make Inferences** What was the major factor in the spread of Islam across Arabia: force of conquest or genuine faith in the new religion? *(Possible responses: Conquest, because Muslim troops had all the power; Religious faith, because invading Muslims likely explained Islam with enthusiasm and conquered peoples found the faith attractive)*

ANALYZE VISUALS

Have students watch the video of people circling the Kaaba (available in the Student eEdition). **ASK:** What types of feelings does the group circling and praying evoke? *(Possible response: Circling the Kaaba and praying in a group evoke a feeling of oneness with others who practice Islam.)* How are the sizes of the space and the cube put into perspective? *(Possible response: The massive size of the space and the cube are put into perspective in the video through the people and through the multistory surrounding building.)*

ACTIVE OPTIONS

On Your Feet: Think, Pair, Share Have students work in pairs. Ask each student to think of three questions about how the actions of Muhammad caused political, social, and spiritual changes. One student in each pair poses questions to his or her partner and the partner answers. Then have students switch roles. Discuss pairs' questions and answers as a class.

> **NG Learning Framework: Discuss the Umma's Influence**
> **SKILL** Communication
> **KNOWLEDGE** Our Human Story

Instruct groups to research the relationships early Muslims had with the umma. Ask students to compare those relationships with connections that other Arabs had with clans and among themselves. Students should also investigate how loyalty to the umma empowered Muhammad, changed society in Arabia, and contributed to the rise of Islam in the Arabian Peninsula. Have groups report back to the class what they learned.

DIFFERENTIATE

STRIVING READERS

Pose and Answer Questions Have students work in pairs to read the lesson. Have one partner ask the other a *what, who, where, when,* or *why* question about what they have just read. Then have partners switch roles and have the other partner ask the questions. Suggest that students use a 5Ws Chart to help organize their questions and answers.

PRE-AP

Create a Group Presentation Have students work in small groups to conduct research about the Bedouin, both as they lived in Arabia in the 600s and as they live in the Arabian Peninsula today. Then ask students to discuss the impact of modern society on the lifestyle of nomadic Bedouins. Students should focus on similarities and differences such as daily activities, housing, food, customs, and livelihoods. Have each group create a report to present to the class.

See the Chapter Planner for more strategies for differentiation.

HISTORICAL THINKING

ANSWERS

1. Muhammad united the Arab people by introducing them to the religion of Islam and by encouraging them to connect to all Arabs, not just members of their clan. He used both peaceful and military means to bring the Arab people together.

2. A dry environment caused people to settle near oases, and settlements grew into cities where people of different backgrounds traded.

3. Possible response: Muhammad opened his umma to everyone because he wanted as many people as possible to surrender to God and become Muslims. He also wanted to unite the Arab people.

The Early Caliphs

Sometimes when people lose a leader, they fear that their lives will change. Although Muhammad's death brought uncertainty about the future of Islam, strong leaders followed in Muhammad's footsteps and spread his ideas.

CRITICAL VIEWING A group of people in Kolkata, India, pray on a city roof and in the streets. According to the Five Pillars of Islam, in what direction should these Muslims face during prayer?

BASIC BELIEFS OF ISLAM

During Muhammad's lifetime, a group of followers committed his teachings to memory. Soon after his death, they compiled his ideas and principles to form the Quran (kuh-RAN), the holy book of Islam. Muslims believe the Quran is the direct word of God as revealed to Muhammad.

Other written texts important to Muslims are hadith (huh-DEETH), accounts of Muhammad's words and actions from those who knew him. A collection of customs called the Sunna (SOO-nuh) describes Islamic practices in detail. These three sacred sources—the Quran, hadith, and the Sunna—form the basis of Islamic law, or sharia (shuh-REE-uh). Sharia focuses on a wide variety of topics ranging from family life to prayer to business. It controls not only the religious parts of life but political and social aspects as well. For example, sharia expressly prohibits consuming alcohol and gambling.

The Five Pillars of Islam

Faith To believe "There is no God but God, and Muhammad is his messenger."

Prayer To pray five times a day in the direction of Mecca

Alms To pay a fixed share of one's income to support the poor

Fasting To refrain from eating and drinking during the daytime hours of the month of Ramadan

Pilgrimage To make the hajj to Mecca at least once in your lifetime, if possible

The Prophet's Mosque in Medina in present-day Saudi Arabia contains the tomb of Muhammad and is a holy site for Muslims.

In addition, the Quran and hadith outline the basic requirements of Islamic faith, which have become known as the Five Pillars of Islam. Following the Five Pillars of Islam shows that a Muslim is willing to make Islam an integral part of his or her life.

Early Muslims felt a connection to Jews and Christians, who also practiced monotheism and had holy texts that contained similar teachings to those found in the Quran. These "people of the book" who lived in Muslim regions sometimes benefited from special privileges, such as lower taxes. Those who believed in multiple gods did not receive these advantages.

In the early days of Islam on the Arabian Peninsula, Muslim traditions began to take shape. Like Muslims today, early believers prayed in a **mosque**, or Muslim place of worship, under the direction of a religious teacher known as an imam (ih-MAHM). Muslims are expected to face Mecca, kneel, and pray five times a day.

Muhammad's death caused the young Muslim community to think carefully about how Islam would continue—and who would lead it. The umma decided that the prophet's father-in-law Abu Bakr (uh-boo BA-kuhr) would serve as the first **caliph** (KAY-luhf), or successor to Muhammad. Under Abu Bakr's leadership, Muslim troops conquered all the Arabian Peninsula and moved into Egypt, Iraq, and Syria.

Abu Bakr was followed as caliph by another "companion of the Prophet" who had known Muhammad. Later, the transition from one caliph to the next was not always smooth, but the decision to install a caliph as the successor of Muhammad had the effect of ensuring the growth and longevity of Islam.

SUNNI AND SHIITE SPLIT

Disagreements about leadership of the umma emerged soon after Muhammad's death. Both the third caliph, Uthman, and the fourth caliph, Ali, were assassinated. Ali and his wife Fatima were both related to Muhammad and considered by many—but not all—to be the rightful heirs to the Muslim empire. Following Ali's death, a family known as the **Umayyads** (oo-MY-uhdz) seized power, and it began a dynasty in which a member of the family would always be caliph. Some Muslims strongly opposed these actions, and conflicting opinions led to a rift in Islam.

One group, called the **Shiite** (SHEE-yt), believed that all caliphs must be direct descendants of Muhammad through Ali, and still grieved the death of Ali's son Hussein at the Battle of Karbala in 680. In contrast, the majority of Muslims, called the **Sunni** (SOO-nee), thought that any devout Muslim could rise to become caliph. Because of this belief, the Sunni supported the Umayyads and acknowledged Umayyad caliphs as legitimate rulers. These two branches of Islam—Sunni and Shiite—still exist to this day.

HISTORICAL THINKING

1. **READING CHECK** How did the rule of the first caliphs bring about both growth and division?

2. **FORM AND SUPPORT OPINIONS** Which of the Five Pillars of Islam is the hardest to comply with, and why?

3. **IDENTIFY MAIN IDEAS AND DETAILS** Why did Jews and Christians living under the rule of the Muslim empire sometimes receive special benefits?

Arab Empires and Islamic Expansion **247**

PLAN: 2-PAGE LESSON

OBJECTIVE

Analyze how after Muhammad's death, Muslim leaders established basic requirements of Islam and formed a powerful empire through expansion.

CRITICAL THINKING SKILLS FOR LESSON 1.2

- Form and Support Opinions
- Identify Main Ideas and Details
- Identify Problems and Solutions
- Make Inferences
- Interpret Charts

HISTORICAL THINKING FOR CHAPTER 9

How does religion affect world civilizations?

The death of Muhammad caused Muslims to determine the basic requirements of the Islamic faith. Lesson 1.2 discusses the future of Islam with a special focus on the Shiite and Sunni split over the line of succession.

BACKGROUND FOR THE TEACHER

The Quran Muslims recite passages from the Quran at daily prayers and at all important events. Muslims who know the entire Quran by heart are given the title *hafiz*, which means "one who has memorized the sacred text." Verses from the Quran are inscribed on mosques and other public buildings. These inscriptions show how important it is to Muslims to connect with God in their daily lives. Everything related to the Quran is considered sacred to Muslims, and the first four caliphs were guided by the principles of the Quran. The Quran is always treated with respect, kept clean, and kept in a place of honor. Muslims make sure that it is never put on the ground.

INTRODUCE & ENGAGE

CONSIDER GROUP DIVISIONS

Ask students to consider what might happen when a group with common beliefs loses its leader and splits into factions. Invite students to share personal experiences or suggest a group whose members became divided, such as a political party or an organization. Have students describe the differences that arose and how the group changed as a result. Tell students that they will learn how Muslims defined their common beliefs and then split into factions after the death of Muhammad.

TEACH

GUIDED DISCUSSION

1. **Identify Problems and Solutions** What problem did Muslims confront after Muhammad died without leaving a complete document that recorded Islam's basic principles? *(piecing together the thoughts of Muhammad and developing basic requirements of the Islamic faith)*

2. **Make Inferences** Why was Abu Bakr important to the survival of the Muslim empire? *(He followed the practices of Islam, was a strong leader who led the Muslim empire in areas of religion, politics, and military power, crushed rebellions, and kept Arabia united under Islam.)*

INTERPRET CHARTS

Draw students' attention to "The Five Pillars of Islam" chart. **ASK:** Which of the Five Pillars of Islam most indicates that followers of Muhammad are expected to show concern for others? *(the third pillar, Alms, which requires paying a share of one's income to support the poor)*

ACTIVE OPTIONS

On Your Feet: Three-Step Interview Have partners interview each other regarding the problems of faith and leadership faced by Muslims immediately after the death of Muhammad. One student poses this question: What spiritual challenge did Muhammad's followers face to preserve the future of Islam? Urge the interviewer to ask follow-up questions based on the answers provided. Then tell students to reverse roles, with the second student asking this question: What leadership issue did Muhammad's followers face to preserve the future of Islam? Finally, ask students to share information from the interviews with the class.

> **NG Learning Framework: Write a News Story**
> **SKILLS** Communication, Collaboration
> **KNOWLEDGE** Our Human Story

Instruct small groups to discuss the role the caliphs played in the growing Muslim empire. Tell them to conduct online research, using credible primary and secondary sources, to learn about the ways the caliphs followed the example set by Muhammad and how they were guided by the principles of the Quran. Have students use their findings to collaborate on writing a news story about how caliphs considered the victories of their armies and the expansion of the empire to be signs that Allah supported them. Encourage groups to present their stories to the class.

DIFFERENTIATE

ENGLISH LANGUAGE LEARNERS

Review Vocabulary After students read the lesson, write the following words on the board: *Quran, sharia, mosque, caliph, Umayyad, Shiite, Sunni.* Invite students to suggest related words from the text. Pair **Beginning** and **Intermediate** level students with those at the **Advanced** level to reread the text, discussing the words as they encounter them. Ask pairs to share their ideas in complete sentences.

GIFTED & TALENTED

Write a Report Instruct small groups to research the rift between the Shiite and Sunni. Have them explore the early history before they investigate more recent events. Then have them write a report in which they provide historical background and explain how the centuries-old division between the Shiite and Sunni still affects the world today. Each group member should contribute to the report. Invite students to share their reports on a class blog or website.

See the Chapter Planner for more strategies for differentiation.

HISTORICAL THINKING

ANSWERS

1. They continued Muhammad's ideas of an Islamic community and placed more people under Muslim control. However, disagreements over who had the right to be caliph caused division among Muslims.

2. Possible response: The fifth pillar could be a hardship or an impossibility for family, financial, or other reasons.

3. They believed in monotheism, like Muslims did, and also had holy texts similar to the Quran. "People of the book" were considered worthier than people who believed in polytheism.

CRITICAL VIEWING toward Mecca; In India, they would face west.

Comparing Calendars

How do you know whether you are busy or free next Wednesday? You may have written a note in a paper calendar or planner. Or you might check a calendar app online or on your phone. People have been consulting calendars for more than 4,000 years. The earliest calendars helped farmers know when to plant and harvest crops.

The Egyptians were among the earliest people to develop a calendar, which they used to keep track of their three seasons. Consulting their calendar let them know when the Nile River would flood and when they could plant and harvest wheat. People today owe a debt to the ancient Egyptians for developing an early solar calendar, which was based on where the sun appeared in the sky at different times.

As the Egyptian civilization declined, the Romans also developed a calendar based on the way the sun seemed to move. Remember that at the time, people believed that the sun revolved around Earth. This calendar, known as the Julian calendar, would be the basis of the Gregorian calendar that is commonly used today. This calendar is remarkable because it addresses not only the relationship between Earth and the moon but also between Earth and the sun.

Another example of a civilization that made many advances in astronomy is the Maya civilization, which flourished in what is now Mexico at about the same time as the Muslim empire. Careful observations of the sun's place in the sky allowed Maya astronomers to create an extremely accurate 365-day calendar. They kept track of the seasons with this calendar, but they used a 260-day calendar for religious purposes. You will learn more about the Maya in a later chapter.

In contrast, the earliest calendars of Southwest Asia used the phases of the moon to create a lunar calendar. (The word *lunar* comes from the Latin word for *moon*.) The Sumerians, the Hebrews, and astronomers in the Muslim empire all devised lunar calendars. Present-day Jewish and Muslim calendars are still based on the movement of the moon, which is why Jewish and Islamic holidays occur on different days from year to year.

In this image from a 16th-century Ottoman manuscript, an astronomer uses a compass and an armillary sphere to study the movements of the sun. An armillary sphere is an astronomical device used to to show the position of the stars and planets.

ARTIFACT ONE

Primary Source: Islamic Calendar Detail
from a calendar almanac, signed and dated by Katib Muhammad Ma'ruf Na'ili, 1224 A.H./1810 C.E.

In the Islamic calendar, like this one from Turkey, each of the 12 lunar months includes 29.5 days, which totals 354 days. Astronomers today use a solar year of 365.25 days. Because the Islamic calendar does not account for the extra days, each day falls at a slightly different time each year. For example, the first day of Ramadan, the holy month of fasting, falls 10 or 11 days earlier than it did the previous year.

CONSTRUCTED RESPONSE Why do you think this Islamic calendar appears to be so complex?

ARTIFACT TWO

Primary Source: Gregorian Calendar Detail
from the Prague Orloj (Prague astronomical clock), 15th century

Many nations around the world use the Gregorian calendar, in which one revolution of Earth around the sun marks a year (365 days) and one revolution of the moon around Earth is a month (29.5 days). This calendar dial from the astronomical clock in Prague displays the 12 months with zodiac signs and symbols in its inner circle. The rotating outer circle includes every day of the year, with the current day appearing at the top.

CONSTRUCTED RESPONSE How does this calendar differ from most calendars used in the United States today?

ARTIFACT THREE

Primary Source: Chinese Calendar Detail
from Song dynasty calendar, 960–1279

The Chinese calendar was based on cycles of 12 for months and also for years. Each period was associated with a different animal: rat, ox, tiger, rabbit, dragon, snake, horse, sheep, monkey, rooster, dog, and pig. In this calendar, the 12 cycles can be seen around the yin and yang symbol. Today, the Chinese still use their traditional calendar for religious festivals but generally use the Gregorian calendar on a day-to-day basis.

CONSTRUCTED RESPONSE What does the shape of the calendar reveal about how the ancient Chinese perceived the passage of time?

SYNTHESIZE & WRITE

1. **REVIEW** Review what you have read and observed about the calendars of various cultures.

2. **RECALL** On your own paper, list two details you learned by reading about one of the calendars described and two details you observed by looking at that calendar.

3. **CONSTRUCT** Construct a topic sentence that answers this question: How are the three calendars similar to and different from one another?

4. **WRITE** Using evidence from this chapter and the documents, write an informative paragraph that supports your topic sentence in Step 3.

PLAN: 2-PAGE LESSON

OBJECTIVE

Synthesize information about calendars from primary source photographs.

CRITICAL THINKING SKILLS FOR LESSON 1.3

- Synthesize
- Compare and Contrast
- Describe
- Evaluate

HISTORICAL THINKING FOR CHAPTER 9

How does religion affect world civilizations?

Lesson 1.3 focuses on photographs of Islamic, Gregorian, and Chinese calendars. Each calendar reflects the religious and cultural beliefs of the civilization in which the calendar was created.

BACKGROUND FOR THE TEACHER

The Beginning of Time According to the Hebrew Bible, the first year of the Jewish calendar, 1 C.E., coincides with God's creation of the world. In Christianity, the birth of Jesus—who Christians believe is the Son of God—starts the Christian calendar. All dates in the Islamic calendar are calculated from the year of the Hijrah, which students learned was the migration of early Muslims from Mecca to Medina. So, to compare, the year 5781 in the Jewish calendar is 2020 C.E. in the Christian calendar and 1440 A.H. in the Muslim calendar.

INTRODUCE & ENGAGE

PREPARE FOR THE DOCUMENT-BASED QUESTION

Before students start on the activity, briefly preview the artifacts. Remind students that a constructed response requires full explanations in complete sentences. Emphasize that students should use what they have learned about early calendars in addition to the information in the artifacts.

TEACH

GUIDED DISCUSSION

1. **Compare and Contrast** How were Egyptian and Maya calendars different from calendars developed by the Sumerians, the Hebrews, and Muslim astronomers? *(Egyptian and Maya calendars were based on the movement of the sun. The Sumerians, the Hebrews, and Muslim astronomers devised lunar calendars.)*

2. **Describe** Explain the design of the Prague Orloj. *(The circular calendar of this astronomical clock shows the 12 zodiac signs. There are also 12 circular scenes that depict groups of people doing various activities. The calendar has painted figures on the sides, including an angel, and carved figures underneath. The outer circle has 365 individual dates, with the current day appearing at the top of the dial.)*

EVALUATE

After students have completed the Synthesize & Write activity, allow time for them to exchange paragraphs and read and comment on the work of their peers. Establish guidelines for comments prior to the activity so that feedback is constructive and encouraging in nature. Comments should focus on the most significant parts that address the purpose of the activity and the audience.

ACTIVE OPTION

On Your Feet: Roundtable Divide the class into groups of four. Hand each group a sheet of paper with the following question: How did different civilizations develop calendars? Instruct the first student in each group to write an answer, read it aloud, and pass the paper clockwise to the next student. The paper may circulate around the table several times. Then reconvene the class and discuss the groups' responses.

DIFFERENTIATE

INCLUSION

Trace Visuals Pair a sight-impaired student with a sighted student. Have the sighted student guide the sight-impared student's hand to trace photographs of the artifacts with their fingers. Then encourage the pair to discuss memorable parts of each visual. The tactile tracing and discussion will help the student understand and remember the content contained in each visual.

PRE-AP

Research Ancient Calendars Ask students to review information they learned about Egyptian and Maya calendars. Tell them to use print and online resources to dig deeper and find two or three additional facts. Ask students to prepare a short oral report about their findings and present it to the whole class.

See the Chapter Planner for more strategies for differentiation.

SYNTHESIZE & WRITE

ANSWERS

1. Answers will vary.
2. Answers will vary. Students' responses should include two details they learned from the descriptions and two details they observed by looking at the calendar.
3. Answers will vary. Students' topic sentences should address the similarities and differences between the calendars.
4. Answers will vary. Students' paragraphs should include their topic sentence from Step 3 and provide several details from the documents to support it.

CONSTRUCTED RESPONSE

Artifact One: The lunar calculations of Muslim astronomers did not take into account the solar cycle, which has 11 more days than a lunar year.

Artifact Two: Most calendars used in the United States today are in a grid that shows days, weeks, months, and years. This calendar plate uses circles to indicate months, and each day is one line; it does not include weeks or years.

Artifact Three: The ancient Chinese saw time as a cycle, symbolized by the circular shape of the yin and yang symbol.

Conquering the Arabian Peninsula

Conquered people do not simply fade away. They must find ways to adapt to life under their new leaders. Groups who fell under the control of the Muslims felt not only political impacts but social and economic effects as well.

In this 11th-century illustration, Arab foot soldiers—wearing blue head coverings and carrying round shields—attack a Byzantine general and his deserting troops.

EARLY CONQUESTS

Earlier, you learned that Abu Bakr and the caliphs who immediately followed him formed a powerful army that set out to conquer non-Muslim lands. The main goals of the invasions were to expand the umma, spread the message of Islam, increase Islamic influence in regional affairs, and gain wealth. The Muslims were helped in their efforts by the fact that other ruling powers in the area had weakened and had little will to resist. In some cases, the people were eager to escape their current oppressors and imagined a better life under Muslim rule.

The Muslim army was divided into units of 100 and subunits of 10. The Muslims developed a successful strategy for defeating their enemies. First, their infantry, or foot soldiers, advanced with bows and arrows and crossbows. Next, their cavalry galloped in on horseback to overpower their opponents. The troops were led into battle by the caliph, who headed the army.

Overpowering city after city, the Muslims soon ruled the entire Arabian Peninsula. The army then headed south and gained control of Egypt by 642. By 650, the Muslims controlled an even larger swath of territory from Libya to Central Asia. Soon, they were ruling over more non-Arab people than Arabs. Everywhere they claimed land, they erected mosques for the worship of God.

Writings left behind by defeated peoples tell tales of great destruction at the hands of Arab armies. However, archaeologists have yet to uncover proof of this supposed devastation, so some

experts believe that the Muslim invaders attempted to preserve as much of the conquered cultures as they could so that their own empire would flourish.

UNITING DIVERSE PEOPLES

Early Arab leaders knew conquest alone would not create a stable empire. Whenever they seized a new region, they immediately began the sometimes lengthy process of making the vanquished people feel included in the new regime. Occasionally, this process of pacifying the people took several generations.

The Arabs levied, or charged and collected, the same tax rates on conquering and conquered people alike. The only catch was that the conquered people had to convert to Islam to receive this tax break. Once they became Muslims, they received similar

Growth of the Muslim Empire, 661

rights to those born into the religion. After all, Islam stressed the equality of all believers before God. All Muslims, whether converts or born to Muslim parents, paid two types of taxes. A tax on land required that Muslims pay the government one-tenth of their yearly harvest. As specified in the Five Pillars of Islam, Muslims paid alms through a *zakat* (zuh-KAHT) tax to help the needy or serve God. Non-Muslims paid a fixed *jizya* (JIHZ-yuh) tax, which was higher than taxes paid by Muslims.

The empire's armies divided conquered people into three groups. As you have read, those who converted became Muslims. Those who continued to practice Judaism or Christianity were granted the status of "protected subjects." The Arabic word for a protected person is *dhimmi* (DIH-mee); through **dhimmitude**, protected status was awarded to certain non-Muslims. Later, Zoroastrians also received *dhimmi* status, joining Jews and Christians. Polytheists formed the lowest group and received less protection than the other two groups. The granting of *dhimmi* status to certain non-Muslims is a special characteristic of Islam.

Almost all religions distinguish between believers and those outside their religions. However, very few award privileges to some nonbelievers but not to others.

Conquered people under Muslim rule had more freedoms than most defeated people of the time. Jews and Christians were allowed to continue practicing their religion even though they sometimes suffered for their beliefs. In fact, the Muslims who controlled the conquered regions did not press them to convert. Later, however, Jews and Christians faced many restrictions, such as not being able to ride on horseback or build new houses of worship.

For many vanquished people, conversion to Islam seemed the best choice. Becoming a Muslim would definitely impact one's political, social, and economic future in positive ways. Some converted to avoid paying the *jizya* tax, and others converted to Islam because they came to believe in the main principles of the religion. Other incentives to conversion to Islam included stronger trade connections and access to literacy and education in Arabic.

HISTORICAL THINKING

1. **READING CHECK** Why did the Muslim caliphs set out to conquer the Arabian Peninsula?

2. **INTERPRET MAPS** How might the conquest of Egypt have benefited the Muslim caliphs?

3. **DRAW CONCLUSIONS** What might have happened if strong caliphs had not begun a path of conquest?

PLAN: 2-PAGE LESSON

OBJECTIVE

Explain how Muslim caliphs formed an empire and united the Arabian Peninsula.

CRITICAL THINKING SKILLS FOR LESSON 2.1

- Interpret Maps
- Draw Conclusions
- Analyze Cause and Effect
- Identify Main Ideas and Details
- Determine Chronology

HISTORICAL THINKING FOR CHAPTER 9

How does religion affect world civilizations?

The spread of Islam had political, social, and economic effects across a vast area. Lesson 2.1 discusses the Muslim conquest of the Arabian Peninsula with a focus on pacifying and ruling diverse populations.

BACKGROUND FOR THE TEACHER

Muslim Expansion Students learned in the previous chapter that Muslims from the Islamic empire conquered lands that had previously been held by the Byzantine Empire, including Syria. In 635, three years after the death of Muhammad, the people of Damascus surrendered. The following year, Muslim and Byzantine forces clashed in the decisive Battle of Yarmuk at the Yarmuk (also Yarmouk) River. Khalid ibn al-Walid—a highly successful general known as the "Sword of Islam"—led his troops against the armies of Byzantine emperor Heraclius. Although the Muslims were outnumbered, they destroyed the Byzantine forces. Estimates vary, but as many as 40,000 Byzantines might have been killed, with Muslims suffering a much smaller loss. Early accounts suggest that some Muslim women accompanied the soldiers on their campaigns. And early historians recorded the preference of Jews and Christians under Muslim rule; the "people of the book" claimed that they endured tyranny under Heraclius.

INTRODUCE & ENGAGE

CONSIDER IMPACTS OF CONQUEST

Direct students' attention to the map of the growth of the Muslim empire. As a class, note the many cultures under Muslim control at that time. **ASK:** How might you feel if another government took over the United States? *(Answers will vary. Possible responses: scared, frustrated, angry, helpless)* Tell students that in this lesson they will learn about Muslim conquests and efforts to rule and convert conquered peoples.

TEACH

GUIDED DISCUSSION

1. **Analyze Cause and Effect** How might the Muslim policy of categorizing conquered peoples into three groups have encouraged the growth of monotheism? *(Two groups consisted of monotheists: people who converted to Islam and people who practiced Judaism or Christianity. Jews and Christians were granted protected status because they believed in one god. Polytheistic nonbelievers had the lowest status and less protection, which would have encouraged some of them to convert to one of the monotheistic religions.)*

2. **Identify Main Ideas and Details** What factors enabled the Muslim armies to gain control over diverse cultures? *(Possible response: The army was well organized; local ruling powers had weakened; Muslims developed a policy of inclusion to pacify conquered peoples; conversion to Islam brought benefits.)*

DETERMINE CHRONOLOGY

Direct students' attention to the dates of events recorded in the chapter. **ASK:** In what year did the Muslim army first control a country beyond the Arabian Peninsula? *(The army gained control of Egypt by 642.)* How many years later did the empire extend into Central Asia? *(The empire extended into Central Asia eight years later, by 650.)*

ACTIVE OPTIONS

On Your Feet: Numbered Heads Organize students into groups of four, giving each student in the group a number from one to four. **ASK:** How was Muslim control an advantage and a disadvantage for conquered peoples? Tell students to think about the social, economic, and religious impacts. Then direct groups to discuss the topics for several minutes. Finally, call a number from one to four and have the student in each group with that number summarize the group's discussion.

| NG Learning Framework: Write an Essay
ATTITUDE Responsibility
SKILL Communication

Have students write a short essay to further explain the concept of dhimmitude. Ask them to focus on the seventh century and how early Muslim conquests affected Jewish and Christian communities on the Arabian Peninsula. Have students use information from the chapter and additional source material. Invite them to read their essays aloud to the class.

DIFFERENTIATE

STRIVING READERS

Summarize Arrange students in pairs and tell them to read and summarize the text by writing at least three notes for each of the lesson's two sections. After they have completed taking notes, guide students to review their notes and create a summary statement for a section. Then have students write a summary statement for the whole lesson.

GIFTED AND TALENTED

Create an Annotated Time Line Instruct students to create and annotate a time line of Muslim conquests through 661, the year shown on the map. Remind students to include dates and a brief statement of the places and caliphs associated with each event. Tell them to conduct online research and use maps or illustrations to enhance the information. Encourage them to use a graphics program if available. Invite students to present their finished time lines to the class and to answer classmates' questions.

See the Chapter Planner for more strategies for differentiation.

HISTORICAL THINKING

ANSWERS

1. They wanted to conquer the Arabian Peninsula to expand the umma, spread the message of Islam, increase Islamic influence in regional affairs, and gain more wealth.

2. The Muslim caliphs would have gained fertile territory for raising crops, the resources found in Egypt, access to trade routes that exchanged sub-Saharan products, more coastal land, and a new transportation route.

3. Possible response: The umma might have fallen apart, other people might have gained control over the Muslims, and the religion of Islam might not have spread.

The Umayyad Caliphate and North Africa

Religion can bring people together—but it can also divide them. In the case of the early Muslims, a division led to changes within the empire. However, strong leadership allowed the empire to strengthen and expand rather than wither away, and Islam became part of daily life in many areas of Asia, Africa, and Europe.

BUILDING, EXPANSION, AND SOUND GOVERNMENT

Muhammad had left no directive about who should succeed him as the leader of the Islamic community. A civil war, now known as the first *fitnah*, broke out between the Shiite and Sunni factions in 656. The *fitnah* ended in 661 with a victory for the Umayyads, who ruled until 750. Muawiya (moo-AH-wee-ya), the fifth caliph, was the first leader of the Umayyad dynasty.

The Umayyads moved their capital from Medina to **Damascus**, Syria. Although this action outraged many Muslims, the Umayyad leaders believed they could rule their growing empire more capably from this location. They also made Arabic the official language even though they were no longer headquartered on the Arabian Peninsula. As people who spoke languages like Persian and Greek converted to Islam, these new Muslims needed to learn the Arabic language. In Islam, daily prayers must be said in Arabic, and the Quran can only properly be read in that language.

The Umayyads fashioned the Great Mosque of Damascus from a former Christian church. Architects created a large space where Muslim worshipers could pray toward Mecca. The Great Mosque contained a number of firsts for an Islamic building—a place to wash hands and feet, a large courtyard, and a tall, slender tower called a **minaret** from which specially trained Muslims issued the call to prayer. No artwork showing human figures or living animals appeared in the building, reflecting Islamic beliefs. The Muslims honored and followed the Ten Commandments, including the Second Commandment: "You shall not make for yourself a graven image."

While some Muslims believed Muawiya was more interested in wealth than in advancing Islam, he did succeed in reuniting Muslims and expanding the empire. He and his successors influenced Asia, Africa, and Europe politically, economically, and socially through their conquests. They pushed into North Africa in the years between 670 and 711 and captured the land called Maghreb, meaning *west* in Arabic, the location of the present-day countries Morocco, Algeria, and Tunisia. Farms in the Maghreb provided the entire Mediterranean region with grain, olive oil, and fruit. The area was also a center for the transport of gold and other trade goods from sub-Saharan Africa across the Mediterranean Sea.

The Muslim conquest of North Africa changed the ways of life and beliefs of the people who lived there. Formerly under the control of the Romans, North Africa had become primarily Christian. Over time, Arabic culture, the Arabic language, and the religion of Islam took root and dominated the region.

From Africa, Umayyad forces crossed the Strait of Gibraltar to take control of parts of the Iberian Peninsula. Additional regions of Southwest and Central Asia fell to the invaders as well. Muslim troops also headed southeast into the Indian subcontinent. Local armies prevented the Umayyads from advancing farther, but the Muslim empire had grown to cover more than four million square miles.

Muawiya and later caliphs realized they needed a strong government to maintain their large domain. They ruled with a firm hand and organized a bureaucracy, which you learned is a group of administrative government officials. The appointed officials ran different bureaus, or

The Dome of the Rock on the Temple Mount in Jerusalem was completed in 691. This gold-domed Islamic mosque, one of the earliest surviving Islamic monuments, stands where Judaism's First Temple was destroyed in 587 B.C.E. Important Christian sites are also nearby.

departments. The caliphs also selected loyal governors to oversee distant provinces. The Umayyads made it clear they intended to leave a lasting mark. They issued their own coined money and built the monumental Dome of the Rock in Jerusalem, alongside Jewish and Christian buildings.

ESCAPE TO THE IBERIAN PENINSULA

After losing control of the empire to rival Muslims in 750, some Umayyads fled to the Iberian Peninsula. There, an Umayyad prince named Abd al-Rahman set up the independent Islamic state of al-Andalus (al-an-duh-LUS). The new Umayyad capital of **Córdoba** had gardens, fountains, paved streets, and running water. Gold and other raw materials flowed into the city, where they were transformed into finished products.

By the year 1000, Córdoba had become a leading center of Islamic learning where many people, including Jews and Christians, could interact in relative harmony. Although the Muslim government practiced **religious**

tolerance, or the acceptance of the beliefs and practices of others, non-Muslims faced a number of restrictions. They were required to wear a badge and were prohibited from owning weapons. But scientists, doctors, mathematicians, architects, writers, and artists of various religions came to Córdoba to study and work. The prominent Jewish philosopher and physician Maimonides—who was born in Córdoba—was widely respected by Muslim and Christian scholars as well as by Jews living throughout the Mediterranean.

HISTORICAL THINKING

1. **READING CHECK** What lands did the Umayyads add to the Muslim empire?

2. **IDENTIFY MAIN IDEAS AND DETAILS** How did the Muslim conquest of North Africa affect Jews, Christians, and others in the region who did not practice Islam?

3. **CATEGORIZE** How did Muslim expansion affect North Africa politically, socially, and economically?

PLAN: 2-PAGE LESSON

OBJECTIVE

Describe the changes initiated by Umayyad caliphs of the Muslim empire.

CRITICAL THINKING SKILLS FOR LESSON 2.2

- Identify Main Ideas and Details
- Categorize
- Draw Conclusions
- Analyze Visuals

HISTORICAL THINKING FOR CHAPTER 9

How does religion affect world civilizations?

The death of Muhammad left his followers with the issue of choosing a suitable successor. Lesson 2.2 discusses the accession to power of the Umayyads with a focus on governance and expansion.

Student eEdition online

Additional content for this lesson, including a photo, is available online.

BACKGROUND FOR THE TEACHER

The City of Damascus One popular story recounts a journey to Damascus in which Muhammad was so impressed by its lush beauty that he refused to enter the city, as a man should enter paradise only once. Damascus was founded in the third millennium B.C.E., and historians believe it might be the oldest continuously inhabited city in the world. Experts have found evidence supporting that Greek, Roman, Byzantine, and Islamic civilizations flourished at Damascus. The Umayyad Mosque at Damascus (pictured in Lesson 3.2) is the earliest Islamic great mosque, ranked in holiness below only the mosques of Mecca and Medina. The site once held an ancient Aramean temple, a Roman temple to the god Jupiter, and a Christian church during the time of Roman emperor Constantine. The UNESCO World Heritage Centre cites Damascus, as capital of the Islamic caliphate, of key importance in the development of later Arab cities. The city, its city walls, its gates, and 125 protected monuments—including the Umayyad Mosque—are all included in this present-day UNESCO World Heritage Site.

INTRODUCE & ENGAGE

BRAINSTORM NEXT STEPS

Ask students to recall what they have learned about the ways in which leaders act after they have conquered new lands. Point out that some new rulers attempted tolerance and mixing different cultures, while others used authoritarianism. Have students brainstorm several different options of steps leaders could take, discussing the probability of each and how the new rulers might accomplish them. Tell students that in this lesson they will learn the steps taken by a new Muslim dynasty to acquire wealth and land and to strengthen control over the peoples they conquered.

TEACH

GUIDED DISCUSSION

1. **Identify Main Ideas and Details** What factors enabled the Umayyads to strengthen their rule of the expanding empire? *(The Umayyads organized a bureaucracy. They appointed officials to run government departments and governors to oversee distant provinces.)*

2. **Draw Conclusions** Why did Córdoba become an international center of learning by the year 1000? *(The government practiced religious tolerance, creating an intellectual environment in which Muslims, Jews, and Christians could work together. The city developed a reputation as a center of learning. Thus, the city attracted scholars and students.)*

ANALYZE VISUALS

Have students look at the photograph of the Dome of the Rock and the photograph of the interior of the Alhambra (available in the Student eEdition). **ASK:** How do the arches on the Dome of the Rock compare to those on the Alhambra? *(Possible response: Alhambra arches are much fancier than Dome of the Rock arches. Alhambra arches have intricate designs in repeated patterns, symbolic of Islamic architecture.)*

ACTIVE OPTIONS

On Your Feet: Think, Pair, Share Give students a few minutes to think about the following question: Was Muawiya more interested in wealth than in advancing Islam? Then have students choose partners and discuss the question for five minutes. Finally, allow individual students to share their ideas with the class.

> **NG Learning Framework: Create a Presentation About Islamic Architecture**
> **ATTITUDE** Curiosity
> **KNOWLEDGE** Our Human Story

Explain that architectural historians interpret architecture by studying its features, purposes, and evolution. Instruct individual students, pairs, or small groups to use online source material to prepare a short presentation on an example of Islamic architecture not represented in this chapter. Presentations should include design details about the structure and information about how the building represents Islam, as well as drawings, paintings, and photographs. Invite students to share their presentations with the class or record them on video and post them to a class blog.

DIFFERENTIATE

ENGLISH LANGUAGE LEARNERS

Create a Word Web Pair students at the **Beginning** and **Intermediate** levels with students at the **Advanced** level. Display a Word Web with the topic *Umayyads* in the center. Tell students to reread the text, noting and adding important words and phrases to the organizer. Then ask pairs to share and discuss their Word Webs, stating their ideas in complete sentences.

PRE-AP

Research and Report Ask students to review information they learned about Abd al-Rahman and how he established al-Andalus. Tell them to use reliable print and online resources to dig deeper and find two or three additional facts. Invite students to present their findings to the class in a short written report that can also be posted on a class or school website.

See the Chapter Planner for more strategies for differentiation.

HISTORICAL THINKING

ANSWERS

1. The Umayyads added North Africa, parts of the Iberian Peninsula, northwestern India, and additional sections of Southwest Asia and Central Asia to the Muslim empire.

2. Possible response: Although non-Muslims were free to practice their own religions, they had to wear a badge and were not allowed to own weapons.

3. Possible response: Politically, North Africa became part of the Muslim empire and its government. Socially, many North Africans became Muslim and learned to speak Arabic. Economically, trade increased between North Africa and other parts of the empire, and all the people of the empire grew to depend on crops from Maghreb.

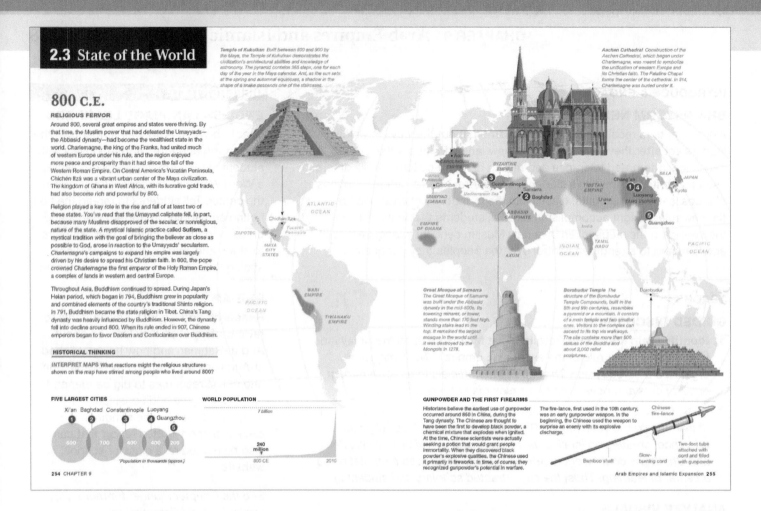

2.3 State of the World

Temple of Kukulkan Built between 800 and 900 by the Maya, the Temple of Kukulkan demonstrates the civilization's architectural abilities and knowledge of astronomy. The pyramid contains 365 steps, one for each day of the year in the Maya calendar. And, as the sun sets at the spring and autumnal equinoxes, a shadow in the shape of a snake descends one of the staircases.

Aachen Cathedral Construction of the Aachen Cathedral, which began under Charlemagne, was meant to symbolize the unification of western Europe and its Christian faith. The Palatine Chapel forms the center of the cathedral. In 814, Charlemagne was buried under it.

800 C.E.

RELIGIOUS FERVOR

Around 800, several great empires and states were thriving. By that time, the Muslim power that had defeated the Umayyads—the Abbasid dynasty—had become the wealthiest state in the world. Charlemagne, the king of the Franks, had united much of western Europe under his rule, and the region enjoyed more peace and prosperity than it had since the fall of the Western Roman Empire. On Central America's Yucatán Peninsula, Chichén Itzá was a vibrant urban center of the Maya civilization. The kingdom of Ghana in West Africa, with its lucrative gold trade, had also become rich and powerful by 800.

Religion played a key role in the rise and fall of at least two of these states. You've read that the Umayyad caliphate fell, in part, because many Muslims disapproved of the secular, or nonreligious, nature of the state. A mystical Islamic practice called **Sufism**, a mystical tradition with the goal of bringing the believer as close as possible to God, arose in reaction to the Umayyads' secularism. Charlemagne's campaigns to expand his empire was largely driven by his desire to spread his Christian faith. In 800, the pope crowned Charlemagne the first emperor of the Holy Roman Empire, a complex of lands in western and central Europe.

Throughout Asia, Buddhism continued to spread. During Japan's Heian period, which began in 794, Buddhism grew in popularity and combined elements of the country's traditional Shinto religion. In 791, Buddhism became the state religion in Tibet. China's Tang dynasty was heavily influenced by Buddhism. However, the dynasty fell into decline around 800. When its rule ended in 907, Chinese emperors began to favor Daoism and Confucianism over Buddhism.

HISTORICAL THINKING

INTERPRET MAPS What reactions might the religious structures shown on the map have stirred among people who lived around 800?

FIVE LARGEST CITIES

Xi'an Baghdad Constantinople Luoyang
① ② ③ ④ Guangzhou
⑤

600 700 400 400 200

Population in thousands (approx.)

WORLD POPULATION

7 billion

240 million

800 CE   2010

Great Mosque of Samarra The Great Mosque of Samarra was built under the Abbasid dynasty in the mid-800s. Its towering minaret, or tower, stands more than 170 feet high. Winding stairs lead to the top. It remained the largest mosque in the world until it was destroyed by the Mongols in 1278.

Borobudur Temple The structure of the Borobudur Temple Compounds, built in the 8th and 9th centuries, resembles a pyramid or a mountain. It consists of a main temple and two smaller ones. Visitors to the complex can ascend to its top via walkways. The site contains more than 500 statues of the Buddha and about 3,000 relief sculptures.

GUNPOWDER AND THE FIRST FIREARMS

Historians believe the earliest use of gunpowder occurred around 850 in China, during the Tang dynasty. The Chinese are thought to have been the first to develop black powder, a chemical mixture that explodes when ignited. At the time, Chinese scientists were actually seeking a potion that would grant people immortality. When they discovered black powder's explosive qualities, the Chinese used it primarily in fireworks. In time, of course, they recognized gunpowder's potential in warfare.

The fire-lance, first used in the 10th century, was an early gunpowder weapon. In the beginning, the Chinese used the weapon to surprise an enemy with its explosive discharge.

Chinese fire-lance

Two-foot tube attached with cord and filled with gunpowder

Slow-burning cord

Bamboo shaft

PLAN: 2-PAGE LESSON

OBJECTIVE

Learn about the religious fervor that took place all over the world around 800 C.E.

CRITICAL THINKING SKILLS FOR LESSON 2.3

- Analyze Visuals
- Make Connections
- Interpret Visuals
- Identify Supporting Details
- Draw Conclusions

HISTORICAL THINKING FOR CHAPTER 9

How does religion affect world civilizations?

Religion played a major role in the expansion and decline of several prominent empires and states throughout history. Lesson 2.3 explores the religious fervor that took place in the world around 800 C.E.

Student eEdition online

Additional content for this lesson, including a video, is available online.

BACKGROUND FOR THE TEACHER

Nature Worship Natural phenomena—celestial objects such as the sun, moon, and stars, or terrestrial objects such as water, fire, and mountains—are part of a system of religion known as *nature worship*. Ancient civilizations needed a way to understand the natural phenomena that surrounded them. Water is viewed as the foundation of all things and represents survival. Its positive qualities symbolize purification of the soul and refreshment and life to plants, animals, and humans. Its negative qualities represent destructive flooding, tidal waves, and storms. Although the sun is sometimes an attribute of the highest being, it is the moon and its phases that are most often personified and worshiped with ritual customs. Many ancient civilizations viewed the moon's phases as childhood (waxing, first quarter), maturity (full moon), dying (waning, last quarter or no moon), and rebirth (new moon). Cultures around the world interpret eclipses of the sun and the moon as illness or death of a heavenly body. Some civilizations have comprehended nature worship as natural objects in need of veneration and placation.

History Notebook

Encourage students to complete the State of the World page for Chapter 9 in their History Notebooks as they read.

INTRODUCE & ENGAGE

EXPLORE HISTORY USING VISUALS

Tell students that the photographs, map, and diagrams in this lesson represent the important developments that were taking place in the world around 800 C.E. **ASK:** What visuals in the lesson intrigue you? What questions do you have about these visuals? (Answers will vary. Possible responses may include questions about the location of the largest cities in the world, the Chinese fire-lance, or the Temple of Kukulkan.) Write down students' questions and have them supply the answers as they read the lesson.

TEACH

GUIDED DISCUSSION

1. **Identify Supporting Details** Where did Buddhism spread, and what changes took place from 794–907 that slowed the spread of Buddhism? (Buddhism spread throughout Asia, including to Japan and Tibet, and was the major religious influence in Tang China until 907, when the new Chinese emperors started favoring Daoism and Confucianism.)

2. **Draw Conclusions** Why do you think a slow-burning cord was included on the Chinese fire-lance? (Possible response: The cord allowed the Chinese to light the fire-lance and then move away from the weapon before it exploded or to know the approximate time that the weapon would release the explosive.)

STATE OF THE WORLD

Direct students to watch the State of the World: Religion in the 800s video (available in the Student eEdition). Remind students of the essential question for this chapter: How does religion affect world civilizations? **ASK:** Based on the information presented in this lesson and in the video, how would you answer this question? (Possible response: Religion becomes the focus of many civilizations during this time period. People build shrines, churches, temples, and statues for worship.) Discuss specific examples from the video of the ways in which religion affected various civilizations.

ACTIVE OPTION

On Your Feet: Research Religious Structures Instruct students to form four teams, and assign each team one of the following religious structures that are shown in the lesson: Temple of Kukulkan, Aachen Cathedral, Great Mosque of Samarra, or Borobudur Temple. Instruct groups to gather in separate areas of the room to conduct research, including finding additional images of the structures, and then to discuss the information about the religious structure. Reconvene as a class and ask a volunteer from each group to share two or three additional points that were not covered in the lesson.

DIFFERENTIATE

STRIVING READERS

Create a Chart Group students in pairs and tell them to read and take notes about the religions and religious practices found in this lesson. Have partners compare notes and sort their details about each religion and where it is practiced into a chart.

PRE-AP

Research Religious Influences Have students conduct research on one of these religious practices: Tibet's traditional religion Bon, Hindu deities, Shintoism's worship of spirits that personify the natural world, the kingdom of Ghana's worship of nature gods, or Mesoamerican temples built to worship various gods and beliefs. Tell students to include information about their chosen religious practice, as well as other religions that may have influenced it. Encourage students to present their findings to the class. After the presentations, determine as a class the similarities and differences between the religions that are presented.

See the Chapter Planner for more strategies for differentiation.

HISTORICAL THINKING

ANSWER

Possible response: The religious structures might have inspired a feeling of awe, which would have strengthened people's religious beliefs.

Baghdad, City of Learning

Islamic law divided the world into two distinct parts. The areas that had accepted the religion of Islam were known as Dar-al-Islam, or the "abode of Islam." Bordering areas that had not accepted Islam were referred to as Dar-al-Harb, or "abode of war." The Umayyads had increased the size of Dar-al-Islam, but a new dynasty would lead this Muslim world to a time of greatness.

The Abbasid Empire, c. 850

A NEW CAPITAL FOR A NEW DYNASTY

When Syrian soldiers assassinated the Umayyad caliph in 744, the **Abbasids**, a family claiming descent from Muhammad's uncle Abbas, seized power. In 762, an Abbasid caliph named Mansur ordered that a new capital be built along the Tigris River in Mesopotamia. Mansur specified that the city of **Baghdad** be built in the shape of a circle.

The city's location at the crossroads of Africa, Europe, and Asia dramatically increased trade. Ships sailed to India and China loaded with Arabian horses and locally produced goods such as cloth and carpets. The ships also carried foreign goods, including African ivory and Southeast Asian pearls, and returned with spices, medicines, silk, and other fine cloth. The trade conducted by the Baghdad merchants impacted all three continents by introducing an array of new products to those regions.

Under the Abbasids, non-Arab Muslims, such as Persians, rose in status and gained the same rights as Arab Muslims. Muslims, Christians, Jews, and Zoroastrians lived side by side and interacted with one another daily. The Abbasids lifted some of the restrictions on non-Muslims and created a more equal society. Some people in the new capital became used to the finer things in life, such as large houses, perfectly tailored clothing, and other luxuries. Other peoples from the far reaches of the empire—Africans, Turks, and Persians—also moved to Baghdad, and a variety of languages, including Arabic, Persian, Greek, and Hebrew, could be heard throughout the city. However, there was not full equality for everyone. Baghdad was also a center for the slave trade and had a slave market where captured people were bought and sold.

The Abbasid caliphs developed a strong interest in past knowledge and encouraged the translation of books from other cultures, especially Greek, into Arabic. The libraries that stored these translations attracted many scholars, and Baghdad soon became known as a center of learning. Translating early texts into Arabic proved to be instrumental to the survival of this early information. Often, the original texts did not survive, and the Arabic translations provided an interpretation of the initial material. Baghdad scholars carefully studied astronomy, medicine, mathematics, geography, and other subjects described in the books. They used the past knowledge they researched to make discoveries of their own.

ABBASID GOVERNMENT

The Abbasid caliph portrayed himself as hand-selected by God. He oversaw the military, the bureaucracy, and the courts. An executive officer known as a vizier managed the government so that the caliph could concentrate on the royal court and its ceremonies. Regional governors supervised distant lands, and mercenaries and enslaved Turks formed the army. The Abbasids continued the bureaucracy of the Umayyads but also introduced ideas about governing from other areas, particularly Persia. Many Persians were appointed as administrators within the bureaucracy, and as a result a number of Persian ideas and customs became a part of general Muslim culture.

The Abbasids created a judicial system based on Islamic law. The caliph appointed a **qadi** (KAH-dee), or judge, for Baghdad and each of the empire's provinces. The judges were selected from a group of well-educated men who knew Islamic law and who usually had the final say in legal matters. The judges' enforcement of sharia shows the continuing close connection between religion and government.

ABBASID SOCIETY

Most people in the Abbasid empire could change their status. For example, non-Muslims could convert to Islam, and slaves could gain freedom. Islam guaranteed specific rights to women, such as the right to divorce. However, these rights were inferior to those of men. Under sharia, women inherited property from their fathers but only one-fourth their brother's share. In general, the higher the status of their husbands, the more women were restricted.

Anyone related to Muhammad, including the Abbasids, had the most prestige. The highest-status person was the caliph. Visitors had to kiss the ground in front of his throne, and an executioner stayed close, ready to kill anyone who displeased the Muslim leader.

The bulk of Muslim society consisted of workers in the city and farmers in the countryside. Young boys studied at a mosque, while many girls learned at home. Boys of promise trained to become members of a well-educated elite or merchants. Merchants were highly respected in Baghdad because trade was so important to the city's economic success. Also, merchants often donated money for the upkeep of mosques and to assist the needy.

Some slaves in the Abbasid empire came from eastern Africa and central Asia, but the largest number came from the Slavic areas of central and eastern Europe. In fact, the English word *slave* comes from the Latin word for *slav* because so many enslaved people were Slavic.

Building on the Indian Ocean trading networks you read about, Muslim merchants traveled to coastal East Africa and Southeast Asia. Trade exchanges, rather than conquest, introduced people of these regions to Islam and had an enormous impact for centuries to come.

In time, Abbasid caliphs found it increasingly difficult to control their sprawling empire. Regional governors often kept the taxes they collected for themselves. As a result, the central government did not have enough money to maintain itself. A group from Persia known as the Buyids took over the government in 945. They allowed the caliph to remain as a **figurehead**, or leader in name only. The once-strong Abbasid empire broke apart into different regions, but the Islamic culture and religion remained. Though no longer part of a single empire, the territory would remain under Muslim control until 1258.

HISTORICAL THINKING

1. **READING CHECK** What major impacts did the Abbasid caliphs have on the people who lived in their empire?

2. **INTERPRET MAPS** What were the geographic advantages and disadvantages of Damascus and Baghdad as centers of trade?

3. **EVALUATE** Why did the Abbasid caliphs hold the point of view that merchants were an important part of Muslim society?

PLAN: 2-PAGE LESSON

OBJECTIVE

Explain how the Abbasid dynasty—ruling from Baghdad—increased trade, strengthened government, and united a vast empire.

CRITICAL THINKING SKILLS FOR LESSON 3.1

- Interpret Maps
- Evaluate
- Analyze Cause and Effect
- Form and Support Opinions

HISTORICAL THINKING FOR CHAPTER 9

How does religion affect world civilizations?

The Abbasid seizure of power initiated a time of greatness for the empire. Lesson 3.1 discusses the Islamic empire under Abbasid rule and the rise of Baghdad as a center of learning.

Student eEdition online

Additional content for this lesson, including illustrations, is available online.

BACKGROUND FOR THE TEACHER

The Abbasid City of Baghdad Historians generally agree that the Muslim empire flourished after the Abbasids relocated the capital city from Damascus to Baghdad. The second Abbasid caliph, al-Mansur, is credited with choosing the site in 762. Baghdad is situated along the Tigris River, some 30 miles from the Euphrates River. In its height in the eighth and ninth centuries, the city became known for great prosperity and sumptuous entertainment, especially during the rule of the fifth Abbasid caliph, Harun al-Rashid (786–809). Al-Rashid and his son al-Ma'mun developed the House of Wisdom, which made Baghdad a famous center of studies in the arts and sciences. A writer of the period described Baghdad as a city of fine mosques, parks, gardens, bazaars, and clean-swept streets. Overseers controlled the city sections and ensured cleanliness and the comfort of inhabitants. Every household had a water supply.

INTRODUCE & ENGAGE

USE VISUALS AS A SPRINGBOARD

Direct students' attention to the illustrations (available in the Student eEdition) and the map in the lesson. Draw a T-Chart on the board, labeling the first column *Visuals* and the second column *Questions*. Ask students what questions these visuals bring to mind. Record their questions in the T-Chart. After students have read and discussed the lesson, prompt them to answer as many of the listed questions as they can.

TEACH

GUIDED DISCUSSION

1. **Analyze Cause and Effect** What were the economic and cultural effects of relocating the empire's capital to Baghdad? *(Baghdad was located at a crossroads of Africa, Europe, and Asia, increasing trade. Ships carrying foreign goods reached the city. People of different religions and cultures interacted at Baghdad, helping Islam to spread.)*

2. **Form and Support Opinions** Why do you think women married to men of higher status faced more restrictions? *(Possible response: Men of higher status would possess some measure of wealth, perhaps from professional work or inheritance. Their wives would have no need to contribute to the household income. These wives would be expected to remain in the home instead of working, limiting their freedom. They would be required to display behavior that was socially acceptable for that time.)*

INTERPRET MAPS

Instruct students to study the map in the lesson. **ASK:** How would you describe the extent of the Abbasid empire? *(The empire includes all of the Arabian Peninsula and extends well into Asia. It includes parts of North Africa, including the Maghreb region, and spreads across the sea into Spain.)* Why does the map include an inset globe and a rectangular space marked in red? *(The globe emphasizes the extent of the empire on a world scale and shows that the Abbasids also had control of sea routes.)*

ACTIVE OPTIONS

On Your Feet: Jigsaw Strategy Organize students into five "expert" groups. Assign each group one of the following topics related to the Abbasid empire: trade, government, religion, society, learning. After groups have studied their topic in depth, regroup students so each new group has at least one member from each expert group. Then ask experts to share the results of their study.

NG Learning Framework: Research Abbasid Control
ATTITUDE Empowerment
SKILL Problem-Solving

Direct students to use information from this chapter and print and online sources to better understand the Abbasids. Suggest students focus on the Abbasid approach to effectively controlling an expanding empire. Invite students to present their information to the class.

INCLUSION

Identify Details in Visuals Pair students who have disabilities with students who can read the lesson aloud to them. Encourage the partner without disabilities to describe in detail the illustrations (available in the Student eEdition) and the map. When pairs have finished reading the lesson, invite them to work together to answer the Historical Thinking questions.

GIFTED & TALENTED

Interview a Caliph Have pairs plan, write, and perform a simulated interview with an Abbasid caliph, focusing on his reign and his accomplishments. Ask pairs to include questions and answers about how the caliph applied Muslim ideals and spread Islam throughout the empire.

See the Chapter Planner for more strategies for differentiation.

HISTORICAL THINKING

ANSWERS

1. They granted more rights, encouraged trade and learning, and maintained peace and unity.

2. Possible response: Damascus was closer to the Mediterranean Sea; Baghdad was next to the Tigris and Euphrates rivers, allowing access to the Persian Gulf, Europe, and northern Asia.

3. Possible response: Trade was vital to supplying the empire with wealth. Merchants donated money for the upkeep of mosques and to assist the needy.

CRITICAL VIEWING (illustration of Baghdad available in the Student eEdition) its circular shape; a moat and a mud-brick wall with four gates, a grand palace, government buildings, and the homes of the elite (illustration from manuscript available in the Student eEdition) The well-dressed scholars' garments and formal head coverings suggest that they held a higher status and had more wealth than farmers.

The Islamic Golden Age

Some civilizations—including the Muslim empire—are known for their impressive achievements in learning and innovation, which ushered in an era of celebrated accomplishments. This period of great advancement in the arts and sciences during Abbasid rule has been dubbed the Islamic Golden Age.

ARCHITECTURE AND ART

One achievement of the Muslim empire was the construction of elaborate mosques and their minarets and gigantic domes. The mosques provided central places for Muslims to pray, but they were also beautiful and perfectly embodied the artistic ideals of Muslim artists and worshipers. In addition, their imposing size showcased the empire's tremendous power.

These early Muslim mosques were richly decorated but void of the human figures prohibited by Islam. Instead, the walls and archways contained abstract designs in repeating patterns, including geometric shapes and floral images, in the art style called **arabesque**. Muslim artists purposefully duplicated designs to show the universal theme of the infinity of God's creation. In addition to geometry, mathematical patterns such as symmetry and algorithms influenced the style. **Calligraphy**, or a form of elegant handwriting, transformed quotations from the Quran into elaborate art.

The mosaics on the exterior of the Umayyad Mosque in Damascus, Syria, include trees growing naturally from the columns. This composition portrays part of the paradise that Muhammad promised his followers would enter after their deaths.

LITERATURE

Early Muslim people immensely enjoyed poetry, admiring it more than other forms of literature. Many poets wrote about love. The Persian mathematician and poet **Omar Khayyam** is credited with popularizing quatrains, or four-line rhyming poems. His works centered on love and other topics, including the meaning of life and the relationship between Allah and humans. The *Rubaiyat of Omar Khayyam* has been translated into every major language.

Rumi was another influential poet from the Muslim world. He was Persian, practiced Sufism, and was famous for his "spiritual couplets." Rumi largely wrote in the Iranian language of Farsi, but he sometimes wrote in Arabic and Turkish as well.

Khayyam also composed an important book about mathematics. Other Muslims wrote about mathematics, geography, history, medicine, and astronomy as well as fiction. A series of popular stories was compiled under the title *The Thousand and One Nights*. This well-known collection centers around a princess, Scheherazade, who must entertain a ruthless king with a different fascinating story each night to keep herself alive.

Although early Muslims loved the adventures of *The Thousand and One Nights*, the most important Islamic book remained the Quran. Muslims began to study the Quran at an early age, learning Arabic to do so if that was not their native language. All Muslims marveled at the beauty of what they considered the word of God.

SCIENCE AND MATHEMATICS

Islamic scholars used sophisticated devices to determine the direction of Mecca for prayer. Muslims improved a Greek instrument known as the **astrolabe** that allowed users to calculate their location on Earth using the date, time of day, and angle of the sun. Later, sailors from many different cultures would use the Muslim astrolabe to find their way around the world.

Early Muslim astronomers used observatories to study the position of the stars at different times. The information they gathered helped set the dates for religious ceremonies. This knowledge also allowed the development of an accurate world map and gave geographers the information they needed to calculate the circumference of Earth.

Al-Mamun, a caliph who ruled during the early 800s, strongly encouraged innovation in astronomy and other fields of science. He invited scientists to Baghdad, where they studied in a large library. In the House of Wisdom, as the building in which they worked was known, scribes also translated books into Arabic. Under Abbasid rule, different schools, or groups of scholars, discussed and debated proper application of sharia.

Islam's emphasis on caring for those less fortunate, including the sick, led to many advances in medicine. Muslim, Christian, and Jewish doctors developed new medical procedures and wrote books that served as guides for other physicians in newly built hospitals across the empire.

In the 1000s, al-Zahrawi of al-Andalus wrote a medical encyclopedia that was the leading medical textbook in Europe for nearly 500 years. Physician and philosopher **al-Razi** is considered the greatest physician of this era. In *The Comprehensive Book on Medicine*, he carefully describes a variety of diseases and their treatments.

A renowned thinker as well as physician, Ibn Sina used Greek, Persian, and Indian texts to write an

In this 14th-century Persian copy of the *Maqamat*, a series of short stories, a doctor visits a patient.

encyclopedia in the early 1000s that included many medical facts. He also explained how and why God created an imperfect world and how science and religion support each other. Another philosopher, **Ibn Rushd**, studied Greek philosophy. Writing in Córdoba in the 1100s, he attempted to show how the logic of the Greek philosophers Plato and Aristotle could relate to religious teachings. Ibn Rushd's ideas later influenced Christian and Jewish philosophers.

You have read that Muslim scholars carefully examined ancient Greek mathematics texts and also made new scientific advances. These scholars looked at the innovations of other cultures as well. From the people of India, they borrowed the numbering system in use throughout much of the world today, now known as the Hindu-Arabic number system. Adopting the use of the numerals 1, 2, 3, 4, 5, 6, 7, 8, 9, and 0 allowed Muslim mathematicians to make amazing strides in their field. The mathematician al-Khwarizmi not only popularized the decimal system among Muslims but also built on Greek ideas to create *al-jabr*, or algebra. His mathematical texts made their way to Europe, allowing Europeans to learn about the number system developed in India.

HISTORICAL THINKING

1. **READING CHECK** In which fields of study did the Muslims excel during the Islamic Golden Age?

2. **ANALYZE CAUSE AND EFFECT** What were the effects of religion on Muslim achievement during the Islamic Golden Age?

3. **FORM AND SUPPORT OPINIONS** Which Muslim accomplishment do you think had the greatest effect on the larger world? Explain.

PLAN: 2-PAGE LESSON

OBJECTIVE

Identify the significant achievements of Muslim people during the Islamic Golden Age.

CRITICAL THINKING SKILLS FOR LESSON 3.2

- Analyze Cause and Effect
- Form and Support Opinions
- Draw Conclusions
- Make Connections
- Evaluate

HISTORICAL THINKING FOR CHAPTER 9

How does religion affect world civilizations?

Muslim scholars rediscovered—and further developed—classical Greek and Roman ideas. Lesson 3.2 discusses key figures and developments in the arts, literature, science, medicine, and mathematics.

Student eEdition online

Additional content for this lesson, including images, is available online.

BACKGROUND FOR THE TEACHER

The Thousand and One Nights Also known as the *Arabian Nights,* this work contains Middle Eastern and Indian tales of uncertain authorship. The tales are tied together by a frame story about King Shahryar, who marries and kills a new wife every day. When the clever Scheherazade marries him, she postpones her death by telling him a fascinating tale every night for 1,001 nights. The king falls in love with her, and he spares Scheherazade's life. The stories were passed down through many generations in Arabia, India, and Persia. In many cases, the tales were changed as they were translated into Arabic to appeal to a Muslim audience; caliphs, Islamic religious practices, and Arab heroes became integrated into the action. The stories reached Europe in the early 18th century, when the collection was published in French. Many translations in various European languages followed, and some of the stories from the collection have become part of Western folklore.

INTRODUCE & ENGAGE

COMPOSE A POEM

Tell students that a quatrain is a four-line stanza. Organize students into groups of four to write a quatrain with an *aaba* rhyme scheme about their school. Each member of the group should contribute a line to the quatrain. Ask groups to share their quatrains with the class. Tell students that they will learn about Muslim contributions in architecture, art, and writing. Explain that they will read about a poem by Omar Khayyam that was composed of quatrains with an *aaba* rhyme scheme.

TEACH

GUIDED DISCUSSION

1. **Draw Conclusions** Would you expect to find statues in a mosque? Why or why not? (*Statues would not be found in a mosque because Muslim artists do not portray people or animals. According to an interpretation of the Quran, doing so would imitate God's act of creation and might encourage the worship of images.*)

2. **Make Connections** How did different cultures influence the development of mathematics during the Islamic Golden Age? (*Muslim mathematicians borrowed the numbering system from the people of India. Al-Khwarizmi used Indian and Greek ideas to create algebra.*)

EVALUATE

Have students study photographs of the mosques in this chapter as well as the Islamic Art gallery in this lesson (available in the Student eEdition). **ASK:** What qualities of Muslim architecture and art do you find most appealing? (*Answers will vary. Possible response: I like the calligraphy and the arabesques. I find it interesting that Muslims initially created calligraphy to make the Quran, their holiest book, look like art.*)

ACTIVE OPTIONS

On Your Feet: Roundtable Arrange students in groups of four. Provide a sheet of paper for each group with the following question: In what ways did the teachings of Islam impact art, literature, science, medicine, and mathematics? The first student in each group should write an answer, read it aloud, and pass the paper clockwise to the next student, who should do the same. The paper should circulate around the table several times. Reconvene as a class and discuss the groups' responses.

| **NG Learning Framework: Explore Islamic Achievements**
| ATTITUDE Empowerment
| KNOWLEDGE New Frontiers

Invite students to search online for additional information about Islamic scholars and their groundbreaking discoveries in science, medicine, and mathematics. Instruct students to focus on one development, such as the astrolabe, or one scholar, such as al-Razi, discussed in the text. Ask students to find additional facts about the impact of their chosen achievement or individual in later centuries. Have students report what they have learned to the class.

DIFFERENTIATE

INCLUSION

Highlight and Paraphrase Help minimize distractions for students with learning or perception issues by giving each student a handout that includes a section of text. Pair these students with strong readers and instruct partners to work together to highlight important words and ideas. Then ask pairs to write a sentence in their own words that summarizes the main ideas in the text section.

GIFTED & TALENTED

Write a Modern Tale Have students find a copy of *The Thousand and One Nights* at the library or online. Tell each student to choose one tale and rewrite it so that it takes place in the present day. Have students read their tales aloud to the class.

See the Chapter Planner for more strategies for differentiation.

HISTORICAL THINKING

ANSWERS

1. During the Islamic Golden Age, Muslims made many advances in architecture, art, literature, astronomy, medicine, philosophy, and mathematics.

2. Islamic beliefs led to construction of mosques throughout Muslim lands and to the type of art included in these structures. The religion of Islam also impacted the development of technology such as the astrolabe, the building of observatories, and the advancement of medicine.

3. Answers will vary. Some students may say the creation of algebra because people around the world study it. Others may say surgical techniques because they led the way to modern surgery. Still others may say the translation of ancient texts because it allowed the information to survive through time.

VOCABULARY

Complete each of the following sentences using one of the vocabulary words from the chapter.

1. Muslims are required to make a _____ to Mecca.

2. Following Muhammad's death, Abu Bakr became the first _____ to lead the Muslim people.

3. Both the Quran and hadith serve as the basis for Islamic law, or _____.

4. The traditional act of awarding protected status to some non-Muslims is known as _____.

5. During the Abbasid dynasty, each province had a _____ who enforced Islamic law.

6. After the Abbasids lost control of their empire, the caliph became a mere _____ with no power.

7. Geometric shapes and floral images are examples of the Muslim art style called _____.

8. Quotations in elaborate handwriting known as _____ often decorate mosque walls.

9. Sailors around the world used the Muslim _____ to calculate their location on Earth.

READING STRATEGY
DETERMINE CHRONOLOGY

Use a time line like the one below to organize major events in the origins and spread of Islam. Then answer the question below.

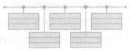

10. In what year did the Hijrah occur?

MAIN IDEAS

Answer the following questions. Support your answers with evidence from the chapter.

11. How did the religion of Islam gain its first followers in the Arabian Peninsula? LESSON 1.1

12. What caused Muslims to split into two groups, Shiites and Sunnis? LESSON 1.2

13. What impact did the expanding Muslim empire have on Asia, Africa, and Europe? LESSON 2.1

14. How did the Umayyad conquest of North Africa change the Muslim empire? LESSON 2.2

15. How did Islam influence law and government in the Abbasid empire? LESSON 3.1

16. How did each of these people contribute to the Islamic Golden Age: Ibn Sina, Ibn Rushd, al-Razi? LESSON 3.2

HISTORICAL THINKING

Answer the following questions. Support your answers with evidence from the chapter.

17. COMPARE AND CONTRAST Why do you think some Arab people readily accepted Islam and others were resistant to it?

18. IDENTIFY MAIN IDEAS AND DETAILS How do Muslims, Christians, and Jews differ in their beliefs about prophets?

19. ANALYZE CAUSE AND EFFECT What effects did the introduction of the position of caliph have on the Muslim people?

20. DISTINGUISH FACT AND OPINION What is one fact and one opinion about the life of Christians and Jews under Muslim rule?

21. MAKE INFERENCES Why and how did Muslim architects change the design of the church they converted into the Great Mosque of Damascus?

22. IDENTIFY PROBLEMS AND SOLUTIONS What problems do you think the Abbasid caliphs' way of governing may have caused, and how do you think this affected their empire?

23. DRAW CONCLUSIONS How did lifting restrictions on Christians and Jews likely affect the Abbasid empire?

24. EVALUATE How important was the Islamic Golden Age to the world? Explain.

INTERPRET CHARTS

Study the chart below, which compares the three Abrahamic religions. Then answer the questions that follow.

Comparison of the Three Abrahamic Religions

CATEGORY	JUDAISM	CHRISTIANITY	ISLAM
Name of God	Hebrew: Yahweh	Various languages: God, Gott, Dieu, Dios, Deus, Mungu, Alaha	Arabic: Allah
Founder	Abraham	Jesus	No founder, but spread by Muhammad
Sacred Texts	Hebrew Bible (including the Torah), Talmud	Christian Bible (Old Testament—similar to Hebrew Bible—and New Testament)	Quran, Hadith, Sunna
Origination	Southern Levant (Israel, Palestinian territories, Jordan)	Southern Levant	Arabian Peninsula
Great Prophets	Noah, Abraham, Moses, Joshua	Noah, Abraham, Moses, Joshua	Noah, Abraham, Moses, Joshua, Jesus
Major Branches	Orthodox, Conservative, Reform	Catholic, Orthodox, Protestant	Shia, Sunni

25. In addition to Abraham, what other important figures do all three religions have in common?

26. Which religions share a sacred text?

ANALYZE SOURCES

Al-Jahiz (776–868) was a scholar during the Muslim empire. This excerpt from *The Uthmanis* describes his thoughts about Muslim succession following the death of Muhammad. Read the excerpt and answer the question that follows.

> Which is better for the community, to choose its own leader or guide, or for the Prophet to have chosen him for us? Had the Prophet chosen him, that would of course have been preferable to the community's own choice, but since he did not, it is well for it that he left the choice in its own hands. . . . Had God laid down the procedure for the nomination of the Imam [Caliph] in a detailed formula with his own precise directions and clear signs, that would indeed have been a blessing. But since He did not make specific provision [for the office of Caliph], it is preferable for us to have been left in our present situation. How can anyone oblige or constrain God to establish an Imam according to a formula simply because in your view such a solution would be more advantageous and less troublesome, and better calculated to avoid error and problems.

27. Does al-Jahiz's argument support the Sunni or Shiite view of how a caliph should be chosen?

CONNECT TO YOUR LIFE

28. ARGUMENT Often, people complain about government bureaucracy. However, you have read how the Umayyad dynasty used a bureaucracy to successfully govern its large empire. Many other governments, ancient and modern, have employed bureaucracies. Write an essay in which you make an argument for or against government bureaucracy, citing examples from the chapter and your own research. Use the tips below to help you plan, organize, and write your essay.

TIPS

* List pros and cons of a bureaucracy.

* State your position for or against government bureaucracy.

* Use information from the chapter as well as examples of bureaucracy to support your ideas.

* Address counterarguments.

* Use two or three vocabulary terms from the chapter in your essay.

* Conclude your argument with a sentence summarizing your position.

VOCABULARY ANSWERS

1. hajj

2. caliph

3. sharia

4. dhimmitude

5. qadi

6. figurehead

7. arabesque

8. calligraphy

9. astrolabe

READING STRATEGY ANSWER

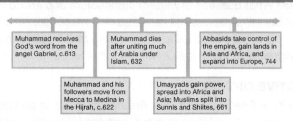

Muhammad receives God's word from the angel Gabriel, c.613	Muhammad dies after uniting much of Arabia under Islam, 632	Abbasids take control of the empire, gain lands in Asia and Africa, and expand into Europe, 744
Muhammad and his followers move from Mecca to Medina in the Hijrah, c.622	Umayyads gain power, spread into Africa and Asia; Muslims split into Sunnis and Shiites, 661	

10. The Hijrah occurred in 622.

MAIN IDEAS ANSWERS

11. After claiming to have heard the message of submission to God through the angel Gabriel, Muhammad began teaching it to friends and family.

12. Muslims split into Shiites and Sunnis because they disagreed about who should be the next caliph.

13. The conquests of the Islamic caliphates placed lands in parts of Asia, Africa, and Europe under Muslim control, introduced Islam to the lands, gave the people who lived there a united identity, and often allowed those people more freedoms.

14. The Umayyads moved the empire's capital to Damascus and made Arabic the official language throughout the empire. They also instituted an age of building and set up a strong government that could rule distant peoples. In addition, they extended the empire into Africa and India.

15. A strong belief in Islam by the people of the Abbasid empire led its caliph to closely associate himself with God as a way to retain authority. The government's support of Islam caused many people within the empire to convert to the religion. Islamic beliefs caused the government's laws to be based on sharia and judges to make many legal decisions based on this Islamic law.

16. Ibn Sina wrote about medicine and the connection between science and religion. Ibn Rushd described how the logical thought of Plato and Aristotle related to religion. Al-Razi made medical advancements in the treatment of diseases.

HISTORICAL THINKING ANSWERS

17. Possible response: Some Arabs were attracted to the message of Islam and thought the religion might affect their lives in positive ways. Others were likely attached to their own beliefs or thought that Islam would negatively affect them economically.

18. Members of all three groups agree that Abraham and Moses were prophets. Muslims see Jesus as a prophet rather than as the Son of God. Only Muslims regard Muhammad as a prophet.

19. Possible response: The establishment of the position of caliph led to the growth and flourishing of the Muslim empire, to Muslim conquests, and to divisions of the Muslims into two main groups.

20. Possible response: Fact: Under Muslim rule, Jews and Christians were allowed to practice their religions. Opinion: Jews and Christians were better off under Muslim rule than the rule of other groups.

21. Possible response: Muslim architects redesigned the building that became the Great Mosque of Damascus to meet the requirements of Islamic worship. They included a large courtyard for prayer, a place for washing hands and feet, minarets for the call to prayer, and appropriate Islamic artwork.

22. Possible response: The caliphs concentrated on their court rather than the day-to-day business of government. This might have caused subjects to lose respect for the caliphs and for regional leaders to gain power, both of which might have led to the weakening of the Abbasid empire.

23. Possible response: Christians and Jews were able to contribute economically and intellectually to the Abbasids. Also, the lifting of the restrictions made it more likely that the time of Abbasid rule would be peaceful. In addition, a variety of ideas from various cultures likely advanced the Abbasid empire.

24. Possible response: The Islamic Golden Age was extremely important to the world because of the advancements made in science and math, the preservation of ancient Greek manuscripts, the contributions to philosophical thought, and the diffusion of knowledge to Europe.

INTERPRET CHARTS ANSWERS

25. Moses

26. Judaism and Christianity share the Hebrew Bible, though it is known as the Old Testament in the Christian Bible.

ANALYZE SOURCES ANSWER

27. Al-Jahiz's argument supports the Sunni view of how a caliph should be chosen because he argues for "the community's own choice."

CONNECT TO YOUR LIFE ANSWER

28. Students' essays should provide a list of bureaucracy pros and cons, include a strong, well-written argument for or against bureaucracy, support their argument with details from the chapter and from examples that each person knows, address the opposing viewpoint, conclude with a summary sentence, and be written in a formal style.

The World's Newest Major Religion:
No Religion

BY GABE BULLARD Adapted from "The World's Newest Major Religion: No Religion," by Gabe Bullard, news.nationalgeographic.com, April 22, 2016.

Around the world, when asked about their feelings on religion, more and more people are responding with a *meh*. The religiously unaffiliated, called "nones," are growing significantly. They're the second largest religious group in North America and most of Europe. In the United States, nones make up almost a quarter of the population. In the past decade, U.S. nones have overtaken Catholics, mainline Protestants, and all followers of non-Christian faiths.

There have long been predictions that religion would fade from relevancy as the world modernizes, but all the recent surveys are finding that it's happening startlingly fast. France will have a majority secular—or nonreligious—population soon. So will the Netherlands and New Zealand. The United Kingdom and Australia will soon lose Christian majorities. Religion is rapidly becoming less important than it's ever been; even to people who live in countries where faith has affected everything from rulers to borders to architecture.

But nones aren't inheriting the Earth just yet. In many parts of the world—sub-Saharan Africa in particular—religion is growing so fast that nones' share of the global population will actually shrink in 25 years as the world turns into what one researcher has described as "the secularizing West and the rapidly growing rest." (The other highly secular part of the world is China, where the Cultural Revolution tamped down religion for decades, while in some former Communist countries, religion is on the increase.)

Within the ranks of the unaffiliated, divisions run deep. Some are avowed atheists. Others are agnostic, which means they do not claim to have faith or disbelief in God. And many more simply don't care to state a preference. Organized around skepticism toward organizations and united by a common belief that they do not believe, nones as a group are just as internally complex as many religions. And as with religions, these internal contradictions could keep new followers away.

A billboard created by a coalition of atheist and agnostic groups appears in Sacramento, California, in 2010.

If the world is at a religious precipice, then we've been moving slowly toward it for decades. Fifty years ago, *Time* asked in a famous headline, "Is God Dead?" The magazine wondered whether religion was relevant to modern life in the post-atomic age when communism was spreading and science was explaining more about our natural world than ever before.

We're still asking the same question. But the response isn't limited to yes or no. A chunk of the population born after the article was printed may respond to the provocative question with, "God who?" In Europe and North America, the unaffiliated tend to be several years younger than the population average. And 11 percent of Americans born after 1970 were raised in secular homes.

Scientific advancement isn't just making people question God, it's also connecting those who question. It's easy to find atheist and agnostic discussion groups online, even if you come from a religious family or community. And anyone who wants the companionship that might otherwise come from church can attend a secular Sunday Assembly or one of a plethora of Meetups for humanists, atheists, agnostics, or skeptics.

The groups behind the web forums and meetings do more than give skeptics witty rejoinders for religious relatives who pressure them to go to church—they let budding agnostics know they aren't alone. ∎

262 UNIT 3

Staging the Question

In this unit, you learned that religion permeated most aspects of both public and private life in the Byzantine and Muslim empires. Government and laws were dictated by religious beliefs, and people could be penalized for not professing Christianity or Islam. You have also read that the Byzantine and Muslim emperors practiced different levels of religious tolerance—willingness to allow people under their rule to follow different religions. Perhaps the emperors made these choices for reasons of faith, or perhaps they had practical purposes. How can religious tolerance help or hinder a ruler trying to effectively govern an empire?

ASSIGNMENT

Research the policies on religious tolerance in the Byzantine and Muslim empires.

Analyze how these policies affected people and institutions within the empires.

Draw conclusions about how religious tolerance helped rulers expand their empires and govern effectively—or how it held them back from those goals.

Develop a claim about the value of religious tolerance to an empire, and construct an argument supporting your claim.

Supporting Questions: Begin by developing supporting questions to guide your research. For example: What was the level of religious tolerance under Emperor Justinian? Who was helped or harmed by Justinian's policy? Research the answers in this unit and in other sources, both print and online.

Summative Performance Task: In this unit, you learned that both the Byzantines and the Muslims valued oration and debate. Make a case for or against religious tolerance to present before a Byzantine or Muslim emperor. Write your claim, and then list your reasons and the supporting examples you found in your research. You might want to use an organizer like this one to help you organize your argument.

| TOPIC |
| SUBTOPIC |
| DETAILS |

Present: Share your argument with the class. You might consider one of these options:

HOLD A DEBATE

Form a team with other students whose claims are similar to yours. Debate your ideas against a team that has an opposing view. Have the teacher or another student act as the emperor who listens and judges the debate.

HOLD AN ORATORS' FORUM

Take turns with your classmates giving an oration, or persuasive speech, as if you are speaking in an open forum before the emperor. Use your organizer to give your speech; do not write it out word for word. Practice beforehand so that you can speak expressively and with confidence.

Take Informed Action:

UNDERSTAND Identify and describe an example of religious intolerance by a government in current or recent news.

ASSESS Determine whether this behavior is doing harm to individuals or to the country in general.

ACT Draft a letter to your government representatives encouraging them to speak out against the instance of religious intolerance that you identified.

Byzantine and Arab Civilizations 263

NATIONAL GEOGRAPHIC CONNECTION

GUIDED DISCUSSION FOR "THE WORLD'S NEWEST MAJOR RELIGION: NO RELIGION"

1. **Compare and Contrast** How do different parts of the world feel about religion? *(In France, the Netherlands, and New Zealand, the majority of people will soon be nonreligious. In the United States and most of Europe, almost one-quarter of the population is nonreligious. However, in China and many former communist countries, and in sub-Saharan Africa, many more people are embracing religion.)*

2. **Make Connections** Think about what you have learned in this unit. How did religion influence the Byzantine and early Muslim empires? *(Possible response: Both the Byzantine and the early Muslim empires built their culture, government, and society around religious beliefs. The Byzantines followed Christianity, and the Muslims followed Islam.)*

History Notebook

Encourage students to complete the Unit Wrap-Up page for Unit 3 in their History Notebooks.

ASSESS

Use the rubric to assess each student's participation and performance.

SCORE	ASSIGNMENT	PRODUCT	PRESENTATION
3 GREAT	• Student thoroughly understands the assignment. • Student develops thoughtful supporting questions to guide research.	• Argument is well thought out with a variety of reasons and supporting examples. • Argument reflects all of the key elements listed in the assignment.	• Presentation is clear, concise, and logical. • Presentation is persuasive and engaging.
2 GOOD	• Student mostly understands the assignment. • Student develops somewhat thoughtful supporting questions to guide research.	• Argument is fairly well thought out with some reasons and supporting examples. • Argument reflects most of the key elements listed in the assignment.	• Presentation is fairly clear, concise, and logical. • Presentation is somewhat persuasive and engaging.
1 NEEDS WORK	• Student does not understand the assignment. • Student does not develop thoughtful questions to guide research.	• Argument is not well thought out and contains few reasons and supporting examples. • Argument reflects few or none of the key elements listed in the assignment.	• Presentation is not clear, concise, or logical. • Presentation is not persuasive or engaging.

EPIC COMPARISON

The epic tales of the Greek poem the *Iliad* (8th century B.C.E.) and the Japanese story *The Tale of the Heike* (13th century C.E.) have often been compared. Both involve tales written about war and the love for a beautiful woman. *The Tale of the Heike* provides an account of the Genpei War, which was a power struggle for the throne between two rival clans, the Minamoto and the Taira. However, the tale also involves an emperor and his love for a beautiful woman of lowly rank. The Minamoto were victorious and, factually, this led to the Kamakura Period. The *Iliad* conveys the mythical Trojan War fought between the defenders of the city of Troy and the Mycenaean Greeks, led by the king of Sparta, Menelaus, after his beautiful wife, Helen, was kidnapped. The Greeks were eventually victorious through the strategic use of the fabled wooden horse.

Both tales depict the fall of a dynasty and the loss of fortunes. Both tales also depict the tragic consequences of war, which focus on loss for both the victors and the defeated. The warriors in both tales fight bravely and fear disgrace more than death.

However, there are differences in the two epic tales, especially between the ethics of the warriors. In *The Tale of the Heike,* warriors and characters in the epic preserve their honor by killing themselves rather than living in shame; and the suicides are often portrayed as idealized. In the *Iliad,* the shamed warriors have suicidal thoughts but never commit suicide.

CRITICAL VIEWING

This detail from a 17th-century Japanese screen depicts a clash between samurai from Japan's Taira and Minamoto clans during the 12th-century Genpei War in which the Minamoto eventually defeated the Taira for control of Japan. The struggle between the two clans was recorded in an epic called *The Tale of the Heike* sometime before 1330. This work is often likened to a Japanese *Iliad*. What does the existence of both the screen and the epic suggest about the role of the Genpei War in feudal Japan?

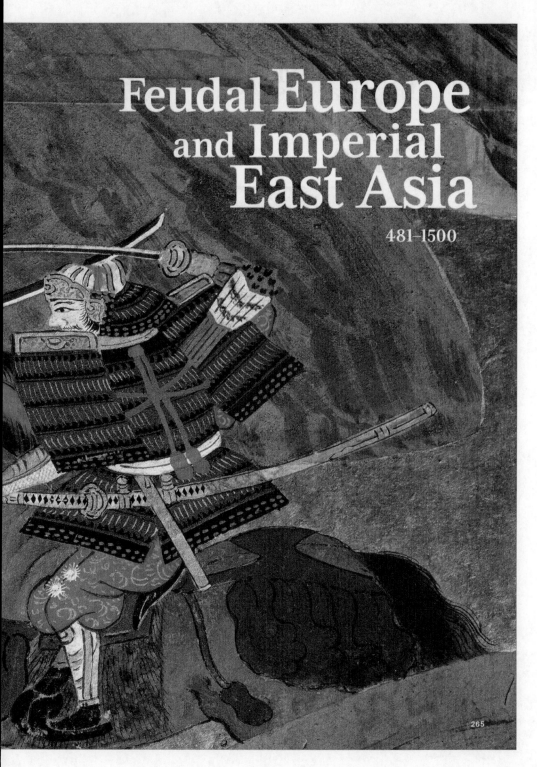

Feudal Europe and Imperial East Asia

481–1500

265

Read the information about the two epic tales as a class. Then direct students' attention to the photograph of the screen. **ASK:** What can you learn about the Genpei War from the screen? *(Possible responses: The warriors used swords and fought on horseback; they appear to also have arrows; they wore extravagant armor.)* Lead a class discussion asking students to share their thoughts about the Genpei War and the two epic tales.

CRITICAL VIEWING Possible responses: The screen and the epic tell us that the Genpei War was a center of focus in feudal Japan.

INTRODUCE TIME LINE EVENTS

IDENTIFY PATTERNS AND THEMES

Have volunteers read aloud each of the world events in the time line. **ASK:** What are some common themes or patterns that you notice with regard to these events? *(Possible responses: Some common themes or patterns include conquest, religious strife, and power struggles.)* Ask students to categorize events in a chart like the one below.

Who	Conquest	Religious Strife	Power Struggles

As students read the lessons for each chapter in the unit, have them add the information to the appropriate column in the chart. Advise students that they may also add or revise categories as necessary. At the end of the unit, revisit students' charts and create a final list of categories to summarize the historical themes students encountered as they read each chapter.

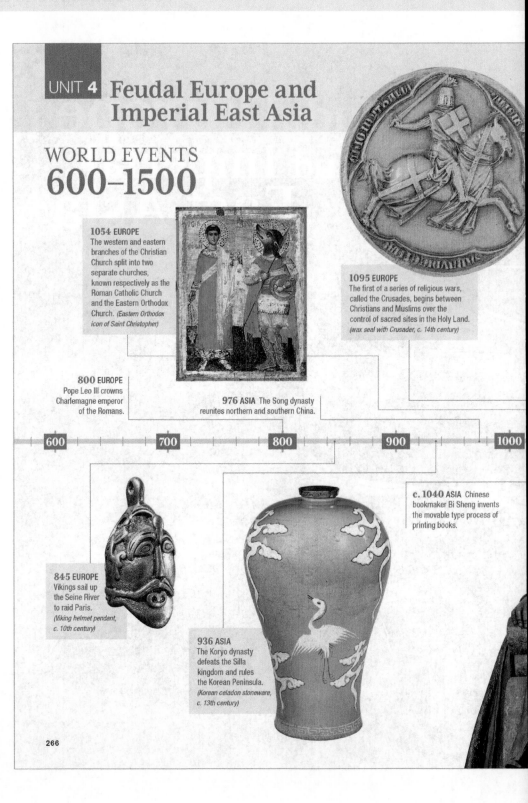

UNIT **4** Feudal Europe and Imperial East Asia

WORLD EVENTS 600–1500

1054 EUROPE The western and eastern branches of the Christian Church split into two separate churches, known respectively as the Roman Catholic Church and the Eastern Orthodox Church. *(Eastern Orthodox icon of Saint Christopher)*

1095 EUROPE The first of a series of religious wars, called the Crusades, begins between Christians and Muslims over the control of sacred sites in the Holy Land. *(wax seal with Crusader, c. 14th century)*

800 EUROPE Pope Leo III crowns Charlemagne emperor of the Romans.

976 ASIA The Song dynasty reunites northern and southern China.

600   700   800   900   1000

c. 1040 ASIA Chinese bookmaker Bi Sheng invents the movable type process of printing books.

845 EUROPE Vikings sail up the Seine River to raid Paris. *(Viking helmet pendant, c. 10th century)*

936 ASIA The Koryo dynasty defeats the Silla kingdom and rules the Korean Peninsula. *(Korean celadon stoneware, c. 13th century)*

266

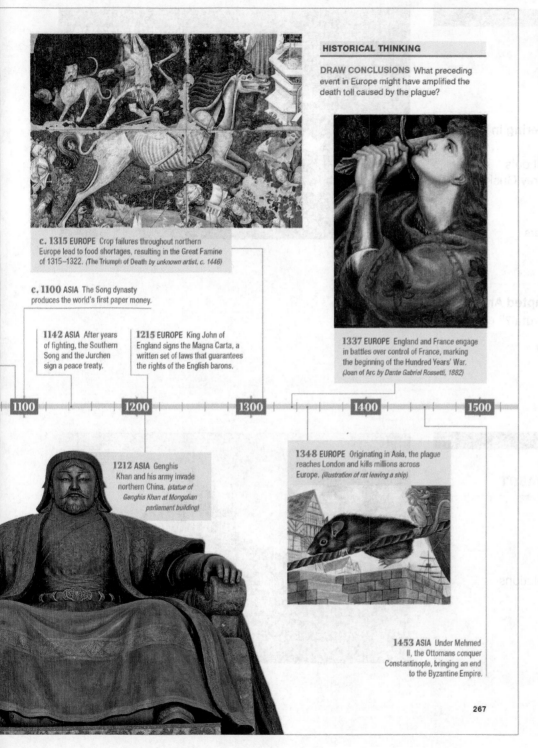

DRAW CONCLUSIONS What preceding event in Europe might have amplified the death toll caused by the plague?

c. 1315 EUROPE Crop failures throughout northern Europe lead to food shortages, resulting in the Great Famine of 1315–1322. *(The Triumph of Death by unknown artist, c. 1446)*

c. 1100 ASIA The Song dynasty produces the world's first paper money.

1142 ASIA After years of fighting, the Southern Song and the Jurchen sign a peace treaty.

1215 EUROPE King John of England signs the Magna Carta, a written set of laws that guarantees the rights of the English barons.

1337 EUROPE England and France engage in battles over control of France, marking the beginning of the Hundred Years' War. *(Joan of Arc by Dante Gabriel Rossetti, 1882)*

1100 1200 1300 1400 1500

1212 ASIA Genghis Khan and his army invade northern China. *(statue of Genghis Khan at Mongolian parliament building)*

1348 EUROPE Originating in Asia, the plague reaches London and kills millions across Europe. *(illustration of rat leaving a ship)*

1453 ASIA Under Mehmed II, the Ottomans conquer Constantinople, bringing an end to the Byzantine Empire.

267

HISTORICAL THINKING

Draw Conclusions

Possible response: The Great Famine may have contributed to such a high death toll as a result of the Black Death. People who were weakened from hunger wouldn't have been able to fight disease very well.

Student eEdition online

Additional content, including the unit map and Global Perspective feature, is available online.

UNIT 4 RESOURCES

UNIT INTRODUCTION

UNIT TIME LINE

UNIT MAP `online`

THE GLOBAL PERSPECTIVE: Soldiering in History `online`

- National Geographic Explorers: O. Louis Mazzatenta, Patrick Hunt, and Jeffrey Gusky
- On Your Feet: Jigsaw Strategy

  NG Learning Framework
  Research National Geographic Explorers

UNIT WRAP-UP

National Geographic Magazine Adapted Article
- "Were Viking Warriors Especially Brutal?"

Unit 4 Inquiry: Broker a Peace Treaty

Unit 4 Formal Assessment

CHAPTER 10 RESOURCES

Available in the Teacher eEdition

TEACHER RESOURCES & ASSESSMENT

Reading and Note-Taking

Vocabulary Practice

Social Studies Skills Lessons
- Reading: Identify Problems and Solutions
- Writing: Informative

Formal Assessment
- Chapter 10 Pretest
- Chapter 10 Tests A & B
- Section Quizzes

Chapter 10 Answer Key

Cognero®

STUDENT DIGITAL RESOURCES

Available in the Student eEdition

- **eEdition** (English)
- **Handbooks**
- **National Geographic Atlas**
- **History Notebook**
- **Biographies**
- **Literature Analysis**

STRATEGY ❶
Outline and Take Notes

Help students develop their reading and comprehension skills by asking them to work in pairs to write an outline for each lesson. Model using an outline format. Tell them to identify main ideas and then look for the most important details that support each one.

Use with All Lessons *You might want to suggest using lesson headings to construct a main idea. Students may find it useful to use the phrases in sentences to state the main ideas.*

STRATEGY ❷
Make a Chart

Instruct students to make a chart to help them understand the problems and solutions discussed in the chapter. Tell them to note in the chart the problems faced by the people of Europe's medieval era, details related to those problems, and the eventual solutions to the problems. Tell students to read independently first and then to work in pairs to identify one of the problems and write it in the first column. Then tell them to take turns, with one partner rereading paragraphs related to the problem aloud, while the other listens and identifies details to list in the second column and a solution to list in the third column.

Problem	Important Details	Solution

Use with All Lessons

STRATEGY ❸
Make "Top Five Facts" Lists

After students finish a lesson, direct them to write in their own words five important facts they have learned. Ask them to compare lists with a partner and consolidate their two lists into one. If time permits, have each pair turn their facts into questions and work with another pair, taking turns asking and answering their "Top Five" questions.

Use with All Lessons

STRATEGY ❶
Preview Using Maps

Preview maps to orient students to the lesson topic and to help them comprehend lesson text. Tell students to read the map title and legend and then place a finger on relevant information and trace arrows if present. For example, for the map of the Crusades in Lesson 3.2, point out the color in the legend that represents each Crusade and tell students to use a finger to trace the journey Crusaders made to the Holy Land.

Use with Lessons 1.3, 3.2, and 4.1

STRATEGY ❷
Use a Time Line

To increase understanding of societal changes during Europe's medieval period, instruct students to identify and list key events in a time line. Each entry should include the date and a brief summary of the event and its significance. Encourage students to add graphics or photographs to the time line.

Use with All Lessons *For example, key events from Lesson 1.2 might include: Viking warriors terrorized Europe (late 700s); Paris paid off Vikings with 7,000 pounds of silver (845); Vikings settled in Iceland (870s); a Viking may have founded Kievan Rus, giving Russia its name (late 800s); Erik the Red led Vikings to Greenland (late 900s); Lief Eriksson, son of Erik the Red, sailed from Greenland to Newfoundland (around 1000).*

STRATEGY ❶
Create a Word Wall

Work with students at the **Beginning** and **Intermediate** levels to select three words from each lesson to display in a grouping on a Word Wall. Choose words students are likely to encounter in other lessons, such as *convert, raid,* and *reign* from Lesson 1.1. Keep the words displayed throughout the chapter and discuss each one as it comes up during reading. Suggest that students at the **Advanced** level contribute by adding phrases or examples to each word to develop understanding.

Use with All Lessons

STRATEGY 2
Use Pronunciation Keys
Preteach the meaning and pronunciation of Key Vocabulary terms for students at **All Proficiencies**. Model pronunciation and help students create a pronunciation key on note cards. Ask students to use the words to write sentences about the lesson and read them aloud. Encourage students at the **Advanced** level to develop more complex sentences for each word and to share their sentences with the group.

Use with All Lessons

STRATEGY 3
Use Context Clues
Pair students at the **Beginning** level with those at the **Intermediate** or **Advanced** level. Instruct pairs to underline the context clues or textual definitions that provide the meaning of Key Vocabulary words. Then have students write original sentences using the words. Have the more proficient students assist others in checking the accuracy of the sentences. Invite pairs to share their sentences and discuss different ways to use each term.

Use with All Lessons *For example, in Lesson 2.1, have pairs underline context clues that help them determine the meaning of the following words:* serfs *(agricultural workers, bound to the land),* knights *(horse-riding warriors),* capital *(money for use in starting a business).*

GIFTED & TALENTED

STRATEGY 1
Create a Podcast
Direct students to choose one of the lessons or part of a lesson as the basis for an episode of a history podcast. Tell students that their podcast should express a point of view so that it is both informative and entertaining. Suggest they write a script for their podcast and include sound effects and music. Then have students either present their episode to the class or record it on a phone or other device.

Use with All Lessons

STRATEGY 2
Write an Online Profile
Direct students to choose one of the following influential religious leaders: Anselm of Canterbury, Bernard of Clairvaux, Hildegaard of Bingen, or Thomas Aquinas. Instruct students to use multiple print and digital sources to research his or her beliefs and influence on the Christian Church from the late 1070s to the 1200s. Ask students to create an online profile with both text and visuals to describe and evaluate his or her beliefs and influence and how they may relate to religion of today. Invite volunteers to share their profiles with the class.

Use with Lesson 2.2

PRE-AP

STRATEGY 1
Review Medieval Literature
Challenge students to read and review parts of one of the great works of world literature from the Middle Ages, such as *Beowulf, The Divine Comedy,* or *The Canterbury Tales.* Remind them that a review briefly summarizes the main topic and then provides a critical assessment of the work's strengths and weaknesses. Students may conclude their reviews by suggesting reasons that their classmates should or should not read the work. Encourage them to post their reviews on a class blog or read them aloud in class.

Use with Lesson 2.3

STRATEGY 2
Extend Knowledge
Invite students to conduct online research to learn more about a topic, person, or event introduced in this chapter. For example, students might choose to research Charlemagne, Otto the Great, Viking longboats, Kievan Rus, Leif Eriksson, William the Conqueror, the rise of banking, Anselm of Canterbury, Bernard of Clairvaux, Hildegaard of Bingen, Thomas Aquinas, the Magna Carta, Francis of Assisi, the legacy of the Crusades, or the bubonic versus the pneumonic plague. Students should construct a thesis regarding the topic's, person's, or event's significance on the era and then gather evidence to support the thesis. Invite students to present their findings in an oral report to the class or in a digital report posted on a class website or blog.

Use with All Lessons

HISTORICAL THINKING What should be the relationship between church and state?

CRITICAL VIEWING
The island of Mont-Saint-Michel, which lies off the coast of Normandy, France, served as the site of a medieval monastery and town. Based on the structure of the town, what might you conclude were important concerns in medieval society?

INTRODUCE THE PHOTOGRAPH

MONT-SAINT-MICHEL

Have students examine the photograph of the island of Mont-Saint-Michel. Explain to students that in its history, Mont-Saint-Michel has been home to an oratory, an abbey, and, since the 1200s, a monastery. Also in the 1200s, Mont-Saint-Michel was fortified in order to withstand English attacks during the Hundred Years' War. **ASK:** In what way is Mont-Saint-Michel a synthesis of religion and politics? *(It has played a dual role since the 1200s as a religious center and a military fortress.)* Explain to students that in this chapter they will learn about Europe's medieval era, a time of deepening relations between the Catholic Church and Europe's political leaders.

SHARE BACKGROUND

The 1,000 years that encompass Europe's medieval era, also known as the Middle Ages, was a period of enormous change. Politically, the Middle Ages began in the year 481. At the time, the Byzantine Empire, with its capital of Constantinople, dominated much of Europe. Five hundred years later, Europe was home to multiple dominant regions—France, Germany, Scandinavia, and Russia—that are still important European centers of power today.

Economically, Europe underwent a dramatic commercial revolution beginning in 1000, especially in agriculture. Most of the land in Europe was brought under cultivation, which resulted in an increase in production. This economic surplus financed the first universities of Europe, new religious institutions, the Crusades, and trade with East Asia, all of which made the Europeans in 1400 richer and more knowledgeable about distant places than they had been in 1000.

CRITICAL VIEWING Answers will vary. Possible response: Since the church is at the top of the mount, you might conclude religion was an important concern in medieval society. The walls around much of the town indicate that safety from attack was another major concern.

What should be the relationship between church and state?

Roundtable: Church and State Arrange students into an even number of small groups and number each group. Assign odd-numbered groups these two questions: How can religion unify a large group of people? What kinds of conflicts can occur between people of different religions? Assign even-numbered groups these two questions: What responsibilities do political leaders have to their people? What happens when political leaders try to attain too much power? Have the first student in each group write an answer to each question on a sheet of paper and pass the paper clockwise to the next student, who adds an answer, continuing until students are out of ideas. As a class, compile a master list of answers for each question. Then tell students that in Chapter 10 they will learn about the complex relationship between the Catholic Church and European leaders during the medieval era.

KEY DATES FOR CHAPTER 10

800	Charlemagne is crowned Holy Roman Emperor.
1054	Schism of 1054 occurs.
1066	William the Conqueror becomes king of England.
1096	The First Crusade begins.
1215	The Magna Carta is signed by King John.
1231	The Inquisitions begin.
c. 1265–1322	Thomas Aquinas writes *Summa Theologica*.
1315–1322	The Great Famine devastates Europe.
1347–1351	The Black Death kills about 20 million people.
1453	The Hundred Years' War ends.

INTRODUCE THE READING STRATEGY

IDENTIFY PROBLEMS AND SOLUTIONS

Explain to students that identifying the problems and solutions of people in the past can help them understand how the events of history unfolded. Go to the Chapter Review and preview the graphic organizer with students. As they read the chapter, have students look for problems of key individuals or groups, how they solved them, and how their solutions impacted others.

INTRODUCE CHAPTER VOCABULARY

KEY VOCABULARY

SECTION 1

assimilate	duchy	excommunication
monastery		

SECTION 2

capital	cathedral	clergy
commerce	feudalism	guild
habeas corpus	knight	manorialism
mystic	Parliament	serf
vassal	vernacular	

SECTION 3

anti-Semitism	Crusade	doctrine
ghetto	heretic	holy war
Inquisition	laity	pogrom
secular	tithe	truce

SECTION 4

consolidate	famine

DEFINITION CHART

As they read the chapter, encourage students to complete a Definition Chart. Ask them to list the Key Vocabulary terms in the left column of their charts. As students encounter each Key Vocabulary term in the chapter, they should write its definition in the center column and explain what it means, using their own words, in the right column. Model an example on the board, using the graphic organizer below.

Word	Definition	In My Own Words
holy war	warfare in defense of a religious faith	a war that's fought because of strong religious ideas

Christian Rulers in Europe

Americans have always maintained, in the words of Thomas Jefferson, "a wall of separation between Church & State." No such wall existed in Europe during the period following the fall of Rome. In fact, European kings formed close alliances with popes and became leaders in the Christian Church as well.

EMERGENCE OF CHARLEMAGNE

Europe's medieval period, also known as the **Middle Ages**, lasted from about 500 to 1500. The Latin roots of the word *medieval* literally mean "middle age." During this time, Europe underwent many political and cultural changes and emerged as a distinct cultural region.

You may recall that after the fall of the Western Roman Empire in 476, various Germanic tribes spread into the former Roman lands of Europe. For the most part, these settlers kept their own traditions, though they eventually adopted the Roman religion, Christianity.

One of these Germanic tribes was the Franks, who occupied what is today northern France, Belgium, and western Germany. Early in the medieval era, the Franks and other tribes engaged in almost continual warfare. As they had against the Romans, Germanic warriors banded together behind a leader to conduct raids into enemy territory. Ambitious leaders gained the loyalty of many warriors. One Frankish leader, Clovis, established a kingdom in northeastern Gaul, which is now France, in 481. A few years before his death, Clovis became the first Frankish leader to convert to Christianity, after which many of his people converted, too.

Descendants of Clovis ruled the Frankish kingdom until the mid-700s. But by 725, Charles Martel, a palace official from another powerful family, had gathered an army and gained control of the kingdom, though he never called himself king. The Carolingian dynasty, named after Martel, overthrew the former dynasty in 751. The Carolingian dynasty's territory would expand greatly under Martel's grandson, who became known as **Charlemagne**, or "Charles the Great."

Charlemagne emerged as king of the Franks in 768 and soon launched a series of military campaigns against neighboring Germanic tribes, including the

This painting shows Charlemagne being crowned king of the Lombards by the pope in 774.

Lombards and the Saxons. The pope in Rome, Pope Leo III, supported Charlemagne's aggression against the Lombards, who occupied northern and central Italy and posed a threat to papal lands around Rome. Charlemagne eventually conquered not only the Lombard kingdom in Italy but also parts of Spain and much of Germany. Under Charlemagne, the Franks came to dominate much of Europe. In 800, the pope crowned Charlemagne emperor of the Romans, a title that would later be known as Holy Roman Emperor.

The alliance between Pope Leo III and the Carolingians benefited both sides. In Charlemagne, the pope gained a protector and a strong promoter of Christianity. From the pope, Charlemagne gained religious authority that solidified his role as king. As a religious leader, Charlemagne sponsored a series of councils aimed at improving and unifying the Roman Catholic Church.

Medieval Europe, c. 500

Reforms enacted in these councils had the force of law throughout the lands Charlemagne controlled. He also encouraged learning by establishing schools in his royal court and in **monasteries**, which were Christian communities of men living under religious vows.

Charlemagne's conquests and the pope's support marked the kingdom of the Franks as a true European empire—a potential heir to the fallen Roman Empire. After Charlemagne died in 814, however, the empire he had formed soon fell apart.

OTTO THE GREAT

In 843, Charlemagne's empire was split into three kingdoms—West Francia, Middle Francia, and East Francia. The kingdom of East Francia, which included much of modern-day Germany, consisted of several **duchies**. A duchy is a territory ruled by a duke or duchess. In 936, the various dukes elected the duke of Saxony as king of the Germans. Named Otto I, he would earn the title **Otto the Great**.

In the first years of his rule, Otto attempted to exert strict control over the other German dukes, which

provoked rebellions. But he was able to quash the rebellions and restore order in the kingdom. In addition to overcoming internal threats to his power, Otto also had to deal with enemy invasions. The biggest external threat came from the Magyars, a people from the Hungarian plains. Since the early 900s, the Magyars had made several incursions into German lands. In 955, during one of their raids, Otto won a decisive victory that ended the Magyars' attacks.

Like Charlemagne, Otto extended the frontiers of his kingdom. In 951, he marched south into Italy and claimed the title of king of the Lombards. A decade later, in 962, Otto marched into Italy again, this time to help the pope fend off an attacker. Shortly after Otto reached Rome, the pope crowned him Holy Roman Emperor.

Through a treaty, Otto gained the power to ratify papal elections. In 963, he took that power a step further. Feeling betrayed when the pope made a treaty with one of his enemies, Otto replaced the pope with a candidate he chose himself. Similar power struggles between popes and emperors would be a regular feature of European politics for centuries to come.

HISTORICAL THINKING

1. **READING CHECK** When did Charlemagne rise to power, and what were his major achievements?

2. **COMPARE AND CONTRAST** How was the reign of Otto the Great similar to that of Charlemagne?

3. **INTERPRET MAPS** How did the kingdom of the Franks compare in size with other European kingdoms around 500?

PLAN: 2-PAGE LESSON

OBJECTIVE

Explore how medieval European rulers developed powerful empires and promoted Christianity.

CRITICAL THINKING SKILLS FOR LESSON 1.1

- Compare and Contrast
- Interpret Maps
- Identify Main Ideas and Details
- Analyze Cause and Effect
- Analyze Visuals

HISTORICAL THINKING FOR CHAPTER 10

What should be the relationship between church and state?

The leaders who amassed power in Europe after the fall of the Western Roman Empire aligned themselves with popes as a way of consolidating—and expanding—their power. Lesson 1.1 explains how some of these relationships developed.

Student eEdition online

Additional content for this lesson, including an image, is available online.

BACKGROUND FOR THE TEACHER

Charlemagne and Carolingian Society Charlemagne, or Charles "the Great" (*le Magne* in old French), was the most powerful of the Carolingian rulers. Carolingian society was divided into two groups: the powerful (*potentes* in Latin) and the powerless (*paupers*, literally "the poor"). The powerful owned their own land and could command others to obey them. Although some paupers owned land, they had no one to command. Among the powerless were slaves, a minority of the laborers in the countryside. During Charlemagne's many conquests, his armies took vast numbers of prisoners from enemy forces whom they sold as slaves to buyers, sometimes in distant lands. Writers in the eighth and ninth centuries used the word *captive*, not *slave*, for these prisoners of war. Charlemagne's Christian advisors urged him to stop the sale of Christian slaves to non-Christians, but he continued the practice.

INTRODUCE & ENGAGE

PREVIEW USING VISUALS

Direct students' attention to the visuals in this lesson. Draw a two-column chart on the board, labeling the first column *Questions* and the second column *Answers*. Ask students what questions these visuals bring to mind. Record their questions in the chart. After students have read and discussed the lesson, prompt them to answer as many of the listed questions as they can.

TEACH

GUIDED DISCUSSION

1. **Identify Main Ideas and Details** Who was Clovis and what is he remembered for? *(king of the Franks who converted to Christianity; many of his followers converted and Christianity spread)*

2. **Analyze Cause and Effect** How did Otto the Great first gain power, and how did he hold on to it? *(elected king by various German dukes; held on to power by suppressing rebellions among the other dukes; His power was also solidified when he defeated the Magyar invasion.)*

ANALYZE VISUALS

Have students compare the painting of Charlemagne being crowned king with the painting of Otto the Great as king (available in the Student eEdition). **ASK:** What unique details do you notice in the painting of Otto the Great that do not appear in the painting of Charlemagne? Explain. *(In the painting of Otto the Great, his shield and cloak have crosses on them. In the painting of Charlemagne, there are no crosses. Also, Otto the Great is standing and wearing his crown; Charlemagne is kneeling before the pope and is about to receive his crown.)*

ACTIVE OPTIONS

On Your Feet: Three-Step Interview Direct pairs to interview each other about Charlemagne and his acquisition of power. First, one student asks the other the following questions: How did Charlemagne use the military to gain power? How did he use his alliance with the pope to gain even more power? Then have students reverse roles and use the following question: How did both Charlemagne and the pope benefit from their alliance? Invite students to share the results of their interviews.

| **NG Learning Framework: Analyze a Historical Figure**
| **SKILL** Observation
| **KNOWLEDGE** Our Human Story

Have students find Einhard's biography of Charlemagne called *The Life of Charlemagne*. Translations of the book, such as one by A. J. Grant, are available for free online or in the public library. As a class, read sections 18–19 about the character and private life of Charlemagne. Then have groups discuss what the text tells them about the kind of person Charlemagne was. Groups should come up with a statement that tells how they think Charlemagne's time period shaped his character and what surprised them about his character.

DIFFERENTIATE

STRIVING READERS

Summarize Using Sentence Frames Assign partners to read each section of the lesson together and then write a summary. When pairs are finished, call on them to read their summaries aloud in the order in which the material appears in the text. Provide the following sentence frames to help students write effective summaries.

- This section is about _____.
- In summary, this section states _____.
- This section makes the following points: _____.

GIFTED & TALENTED

Create a Map Challenge students to design a map of Europe around the year 800 showing the height of Charlemagne's power. They should identify three areas on the map: the Carolingian realm, the areas conquered by Charlemagne during his rule, and Byzantine territory. They should also label the following kingdoms: Lombardy, Flanders, Burgundy, Austrasia, Saxony, Bavaria, Neustria, Gascony, Aquitaine, Venetia, and the Papal States. Invite them to display their maps on a class bulletin board, website, or blog.

See the Chapter Planner for more strategies for differentiation.

HISTORICAL THINKING

ANSWERS

1. 768; He established a European empire aligned with the Christian Church and became the first Holy Roman Emperor.

2. Both rulers established prosperous European empires strongly linked to the Christian Church.

3. among the three largest kingdoms, along with the kingdoms of the Ostrogoths and Visigoths; larger than the Burgundian kingdom, the kingdom of the Sueves, and the kingdom of the Vandals

The Age of Vikings

You may have heard of the Vikings but not know who they really were. The Vikings were skilled farmers and traders who lived in Scandinavia, or present-day Norway, Sweden, and Denmark, in the Middle Ages. But the Vikings are best known as brutal raiders, skilled at looting, burning, and killing.

CRITICAL VIEWING The annual Viking festival in Wolin, Poland, is one of the largest events in which Europeans dress as Viking and Slav warriors to reenact medieval battles between the two groups. Based on this reenactment, how would you describe medieval battle conditions?

VIKING RAIDS

While the German king Otto I was fighting off an invading Magyar force in the mid-900s, a group of invaders from the north, the Vikings, plagued much of the rest of Europe. These fearsome warriors sailed their longboats out of Scandinavia in search of valuable goods they could steal. For more than two centuries, starting in the late 700s, they terrorized the European continent.

Small Viking fleets sailed west across the North Sea to present-day Scotland, Ireland, and England. There they targeted monasteries because these communities often contained large amounts of silver and other treasures.

Larger bands of Vikings also plundered and burned towns along the coasts of Germany, France, Spain, and islands in the western Mediterranean Sea. They often made quick strikes, staying just long enough to steal much of a town's wealth—and killing anyone who tried to stop them.

The Vikings were not restricted to coastal routes. Their longboats were constructed not only to withstand sea travel but also to navigate shallower rivers. As a result, the Vikings could raid wealthy inland towns. In 845, they used their longboats to sail up the Seine River to Paris. The citizens of Paris avoided being plundered only by paying off the Vikings with 7,000 pounds of silver.

Across the Baltic Sea from Scandinavia lay a region inhabited mainly by Slavs—present-day Russia. In the early 800s, Vikings from Sweden crossed the sea and followed rivers into this region. These Vikings engaged in trading as well as raiding. Later, some Vikings followed rivers south all the way to the Black Sea and Constantinople, where they traded furs and slaves for spices and silks from as far east as China.

A traditional Russian chronicle says that in the late 800s a Viking founded Kievan Rus (KEE-ehf-uhn ROOS), a state centered on the trading town of Kiev in present-day Ukraine. Historians still debate whether the Vikings had any role in this event. They also disagree about whether the people known as the Rus were Slavs or Vikings or a mix of peoples. But whoever they were, the Rus gave Russia its name.

VIKING SETTLEMENTS

Some Vikings chose to settle down and farm the lands they had previously raided. Danish Vikings settled in northern and eastern England in the late 800s, while Norwegian Vikings settled in Scotland and Ireland. In the tenth century, another Viking group from Denmark settled in Normandy, in present-day France.

Over time, British and French kings built fortresses and enlarged their armies to resist Viking incursions. In other places, Viking settlers **assimilated**, or integrated, into local populations. The Slavic lands of Russia fairly quickly absorbed the Vikings from Sweden. Viking settlers in Normandy eventually merged into the culture of Western Francia, the westernmost Frankish kingdom.

At a time when most sailors stayed within sight of a coastline, the seafaring Vikings set out across the open Atlantic Ocean. By the 870s, Scandinavians had settled in Iceland, a large island more than 800 miles west of Norway. In the late 900s, a Viking leader named Erik the Red led approximately 400 to 500 followers an additional 200 miles west to Greenland in search of fertile land.

Tales of the adventures of Erik the Red appear in *The Vinland Sagas*, orally transmitted stories written down sometime after 1200. The Scandinavians called the land of North America *Vinland*, which means "land of wild grapes." Erik the Red's son, **Leif Eriksson**, headed toward Vinland around 1000. He and 40 companions sailed from Greenland to Newfoundland, becoming the first Europeans to visit what is today Canada.

The remains of a Viking settlement have been unearthed at L'Anse aux Meadows in southern Newfoundland. Some archaeologists believe that more Viking settlements will be uncovered in the years to come, some perhaps as far south as New England.

NATIONAL GEOGRAPHIC EXPLORER
SARAH PARCAK

Sarah Parcak searches for Viking artifacts at Point Rosee in Newfoundland.

Citizen-Science Technology

The search for Viking settlements in North America has benefited from the expertise of Sarah Parcak, a National Geographic Explorer. Known as a space archaeologist, Parcak examines high-resolution satellite images for possible historic sites hidden just below Earth's surface. "We're using satellites to help map and model cultural features that could never be seen on the ground because they're obscured by modernization, forest, or soil," Parcak explains.

This technology led her to a spot in Newfoundland known as Point Rosee. An archaeological dig at the spot has turned up Viking-style turf walls and signs of ironworking.

Parcak also uses satellite technology to protect ancient sites, and she wants to create a global network of citizen-scientists to help her. Using an online satellite imagery program, volunteers can help stop looters from stealing valuable artifacts. They can also join the hunt for as-yet-undiscovered sites.

HISTORICAL THINKING

1. **READING CHECK** Why did early Viking raiders target monasteries?

2. **IDENTIFY MAIN IDEAS AND DETAILS** What methods have archaeologists used to learn about the Vikings?

3. **ASK AND ANSWER QUESTIONS** What questions do you have about the Vikings, and where might you find answers to your questions?

PLAN: 2-PAGE LESSON

OBJECTIVE
Describe the Vikings and their excursions into Europe and North America.

CRITICAL THINKING SKILLS FOR LESSON 1.2
- Identify Main Ideas and Details
- Ask and Answer Questions
- Make Connections
- Identify
- Integrate Visuals

HISTORICAL THINKING FOR CHAPTER 10
What should be the relationship between church and state?

The leaders of medieval Europe expanded their kingdoms with support from the western church. By contrast, the Vikings had no such relationship with a religious entity. They advanced by pure brute force. Lesson 1.2 describes the Vikings and the areas of Europe they targeted.

Student eEdition online
Additional content for this lesson, including an illustration and an image gallery, is available online.

BACKGROUND FOR THE TEACHER
Viking Longboats The greatest difference between the seafaring Vikings and the land-based Frankish armies was the large wooden Viking longboat held together by iron rivets and washers. These craft ranged between 50 and 100 feet (15 and 30 meters) long. The combination of oars and sails made these boats (along with Polynesian canoes in the east-central Pacific Ocean) the fastest mode of transport in the world before 1000. Longboats had a shallow draft, which made them ideal for inland raids. Like the ancient Polynesians, the Scandinavian navigators did not use navigational instruments. Instead, they used the shapes of different landmasses for orientation. Unlike the Polynesians, however, the Vikings did not designate certain individuals as navigators or transmit geographical knowledge secretly; all men knew how to steer the longboats, and they announced their discoveries to everyone in their army.

INTRODUCE & ENGAGE

K-W-L CHART

Ask students to record what they already know about the Vikings and their incursions into Europe and North America in the first row of a K-W-L Chart. Then ask students to write questions they would like to have answered as they study Lesson 1.2. Allow time at the end of the lesson for students to complete the K-W-L Chart with what they have learned. They will have a chance to add additional questions to the chart as they work on the Historical Thinking section.

TEACH

GUIDED DISCUSSION

1. **Make Connections** How did the Vikings impact modern-day Russia? *(In the early 800s, Vikings from Sweden crossed the Baltic Sea and followed rivers into what is today Russia. They raided towns there and traded with local people. Some Vikings continued down rivers to as far south as Constantinople, where they traded for goods from as far away as China. There is also a theory that the Vikings founded the city of Kiev in present-day Ukraine.)*

2. **Identify** What were some of the many uses for Viking ships? *(exploration, trade, warfare, burial)*

INTEGRATE VISUALS

Draw students' attention to the image gallery (available in the Student eEdition). **ASK:** What trait of the Vikings is represented by the artifacts? *(Possible response: The Vikings were warriors. All the artifacts shown are related to war. There are shields, weapons, and a helmet.)* Which artifacts have representations of animals? *(The shield shows a lizard-like animal; the helmets are horned like an elk.)* What can you infer about the Vikings from the representations of animals on the artifacts? *(Possible response: The Vikings may have regarded animals as strong and perhaps protective, since they depicted them on their weapons.)*

ACTIVE OPTIONS

On Your Feet: Think, Pair, Share Direct students to consider the following question: Why must an examination of medieval Europe include the Vikings? Allow a few minutes for students to think, and then tell students to choose partners and discuss their ideas for five minutes. After discussion time, invite students to share their ideas with the class.

> **NG Learning Framework: Craft an Oral Report**
> SKILL Collaboration
> KNOWLEDGE Our Human Story

Ask pairs to read the National Geographic Explorer sidebar information about Sarah Parcak and find out more about Viking settlements that developed in places where the Vikings conducted invasions. Tell them to develop an oral report that discusses the way Viking culture blended with local culture in these places. Partners can investigate separate cultural traits, such as trade and religion. Invite pairs to share their findings with the class.

DIFFERENTIATE

INCLUSION

Visual Partners Pair sight-impaired students with sighted students to interpret the photographs in this lesson, especially the "Fearsome Fleet" infographic and the Viking Artifacts image gallery (available in the Student eEdition). Ask sighted students to describe each of the visuals to the sight-impaired students, including details that they notice. Partners can then discuss how the details in the image relate to the information in the text.

PRE-AP

Vikings in Popular Culture Have students research how Vikings used to be represented in popular culture, such as in movies and cartoons from several decades ago. Using the original media or still images and synopses they find online, students should compare the depiction to factual information they unearth about the Vikings. Students can explain to the class the accuracy of the media and what would need to be altered for a more truthful depiction.

See the Chapter Planner for more strategies for differentiation.

HISTORICAL THINKING

ANSWERS

1. Viking raiders sought items of value, and monasteries tended to have large amounts of silver and other treasures.

2. They have unearthed and examined archaeological sites, one of which was discovered through the use of high-resolution satellite images. They have also studied oral stories that were written down in later centuries.

3. Answers will vary.

CRITICAL VIEWING The warriors fought in very close quarters. Their armor protected only their heads and their chests. The battle scene appears chaotic.

Conquest and Division

Ruling a large group of people with differing interests is never an easy task.
But a strong leader managed to do just that in medieval England. The Christian
Church, however, moved in the opposite direction—and became divided.

WILLIAM THE CONQUEROR

The Danish Vikings who invaded England in 866 and
settled in the north and east did not dominate England.
They continually vied with the Anglo-Saxons, a mix
of Germanic peoples from present-day Denmark and
northern Germany, for control of the island. The Anglo-
Saxons had invaded England in the 400s and pushed
out the Romans. More than four centuries later, in
the 900s, the tables had turned.
The Anglo-Saxons were the ones
battling "barbarian" invaders.

Meanwhile, the Viking settlers
across the English Channel thrived.
A steady stream of Scandinavians
migrated to the Viking colony in
Normandy. In the 900s, after people
from Normandy, called Normans,
conducted a series of destructive
raids inland, the French king
accepted the colony as a legal—
and largely independent—duchy.
The Normans, in turn, adopted the
French language and the Christian
religion. Normandy had stabilized,
but England was still in a state
of upheaval.

By 954, an Anglo-Saxon king
had conquered the Danes and
established his rule over all of
England. But in the early 1000s,
a new group of Viking invaders
overpowered the Anglo-Saxons.
Several Scandinavians ruled as
kings of England until 1042, when
an Anglo-Saxon noble with family
ties to Normandy gained the throne.
This king promised that, upon his
death, the English throne would go

to William, Duke of Normandy. But the English nobility
chose instead to elect an Anglo-Saxon, Harold, as king.

This decision did not please William, who believed he
was the rightful heir to the throne. In September 1066,
he sailed for England with an army to claim the crown.
Harold, the new king of England, already had his hands
full with yet another Viking invasion. On September 25,
Harold met and defeated a large force of Viking warriors

CRITICAL VIEWING The Bayeux Tapestry, a work of embroidery produced
around 1092, depicts more than 70 scenes leading up to the Norman conquest
of England. In this scene, the Norman cavalry rides toward the site of the
Battle of Hastings. How are these Norman soldiers equipped?

in northern England. Just three
days later, William and his Norman
army landed on the southeast coast
of England.

Harold rushed his forces southward
to meet this new threat. The two
armies clashed near the town of
Hastings. In the Battle of Hastings,
the Normans defeated the Anglo-
Saxons, and Harold died on the
battlefield. Thus, William gained the
English throne and the title **William
the Conqueror.**

William the Conqueror now
reigned over all of England as
well as Normandy. In his first
few years in power, he put down
several rebellions, often brutally.
He brought in loyal friends to
serve as his closest officials and
redistributed Anglo-Saxon lands
to Normans. French became the
official language of the court.

A Christian, William strongly
supported the church and the
pope. He insisted, however, on
filling high church positions in England with Normans.
Later Norman kings, who ruled for another 70 years,
also demanded a role in church matters.

THE SCHISM OF 1054

As you have learned, relations between the western, or
Roman, church and the eastern, or Byzantine, church
began to deteriorate in the fifth century. The churches
used different languages in their services—Latin in the
Roman church and Greek in the Byzantine. With the rise
of the Carolingian dynasty in the mid-700s, the pope in
Rome allied politically with the Frankish rulers, not the
Byzantine emperors.

By 1000, the Roman and Byzantine churches had
begun to diverge further. Members of the Roman
church recognized the pope in Rome as their leader,
while members of the Byzantine church recognized the
patriarch of Constantinople. Doctrines and practices

varied as well. For example, Byzantine priests were
required to have beards, but Roman priests were not.

In 1054, a bishop in a Byzantine province wrote to an
Italian bishop criticizing certain practices of the western
church. These practices included using unleavened
bread, or bread without yeast, during a service called
communion and failing to fast on Saturdays. In two
lengthy letters to the patriarch in Constantinople, the
pope in Rome defended these practices. But the pope
made the inflammatory assertion that he had the right to
rule over all bishops, even those of the eastern church.

The pope and the patriarch argued until they finally
expelled each other from membership in the Christian
Church, a punishment called **excommunication.** As
a result, the western and eastern churches split into
two separate religions, which are now called Roman
Catholicism and Eastern Orthodoxy. Historians refer to
this event as the **Schism of 1054.**

HISTORICAL THINKING

1. **READING CHECK** How did
William the Conqueror rise to the
throne of England?

2. **COMPARE AND CONTRAST**
How did the western Christian
Church differ from the eastern
Christian Church?

3. **INTERPRET MAPS** What lands
were under the authority of the
Eastern Orthodox Church after the
Schism of 1054?

PLAN: 2-PAGE LESSON

OBJECTIVE
**Understand how William the Conqueror became king
of England and how the Christian Church suffered a
permanent split.**

CRITICAL THINKING SKILLS FOR LESSON 1.3
- Compare and Contrast
- Interpret Maps
- Make Connections
- Analyze Cause and Effect
- Identify Problems and Solutions

HISTORICAL THINKING FOR CHAPTER 10
**What should be the relationship between church and
state?**

The western Christian Church and the eastern Christian
Church had been drifting apart for centuries—in practice,
in language, and in politics. Lesson 1.3 describes how
they permanently split into two different religions in 1054.

BACKGROUND FOR THE TEACHER
The Legend of King Arthur One of the most enduring
written works from the medieval era is the legend of King
Arthur. It is not certain whether Arthur was a real king,
but researchers agree that the story probably originated
either in Wales or among Celts in northern Britain. Among
the earliest written works to mention Arthur are two
Welsh texts, the ninth-century *Historia Brittonum* and the
tenth-century *Annales Cambriae*, both of which place
Arthur's exploits in the sixth century, in the years between
the withdrawal of Roman rule and the Norman conquest.
During these "Dark Ages," a number of rulers led small
kingdoms of Anglo-Saxon peoples throughout the British
Isles. Some of these kings were entered in the historical
record. King Arthur was not, but his legend prevails.

INTRODUCE & ENGAGE

CHARACTERISTICS OF INVADING FORCES

Ask students to recall novels, films, or television series in which an invading force overruns a land or a people. Discuss how and why an invading force might conquer a people. **ASK:** Who is their leader? How does the other side resist? What political changes occur as a result? Tell students that Lesson 1.3 describes conflicts between various medieval peoples including the Vikings, the Anglo-Saxons, and the Normans.

TEACH

GUIDED DISCUSSION

1. **Make Connections** Who were the Normans, and how do they connect to William the Conqueror? *(lived in Normandy, an area north of present-day France; recognized as an independent duchy by the French king in the 900s; adopted Christianity, the French language; William was Duke of Normandy before he conquered England.)*

2. **Analyze Cause and Effect** What was the immediate cause of the Schism of 1054? *(The pope asserted his authority over all bishops, including in the eastern church. This led to an argument between the Byzantine patriarch and the pope and the split between the churches.)*

IDENTIFY PROBLEMS AND SOLUTIONS

Ask students to study the map of the Schism of 1054. **ASK:** In what way does the map illustrate the problem that the western Christian Church and the eastern Christian Church were having beginning in the fifth century? *(The churches were diverging, and the map shows that they covered a very large area of land, making it difficult to remain unified.)* In what way does the map also show a solution to the problem? *(Ultimately, the two churches split, overseeing western and eastern lands.)*

ACTIVE OPTIONS

On Your Feet: Inside-Outside Circle Use the Inside-Outside Circle strategy to check students' understanding of the events that led to William the Conqueror becoming king of England. Direct students in the outer circle to pose these questions: Who gained the throne of England in 1042? To whom did he promise the throne upon his death? Why didn't that happen? What happened in 1066? Tell students in the inner circle to answer the questions. Then ask students to trade inside-outside roles.

| **NG Learning Framework: Create an Infographic**
| **SKILLS** Collaboration, Communication
| **KNOWLEDGE** Our Human Story

Organize students into two groups and assign the topics of the western Christian Church and the eastern Christian Church. Tell groups to conduct online research about the following areas: leadership structure, language, beliefs about original sin, approach to the sacraments, lands under their authority, and one other area. Have groups create an infographic with visuals based on their findings. Ask students to use their infographics as visual support as they explain why the Schism of 1054 occurred.

DIFFERENTIATE

ENGLISH LANGUAGE LEARNERS

Make Fact Cards Tell students to make cards that give facts about Danish Vikings, Anglo-Saxons, Normans, King Harold, and William the Conqueror. Have them write the name on one side and a key fact on the other. Then pair students at **All Proficiencies** and have them take turns. Partner 1 holds up the card with the name facing out towards Partner 2. Partner 1 silently reads the fact and offers question clues to Partner 2, such as, "Where were we located?" "Who did we invade?" or "How did I become king?" The goal is for Partner 2 to identify the key fact by answering the question(s).

GIFTED & TALENTED

Investigate the Bayeux Tapestry Invite students to access the full Bayeux Tapestry online and choose one of its 70 scenes. They should learn what the scene shows and how it is shown by its craftsmanship and rendering. They may write a short report or prepare an oral summary. Invite students to share their investigations with the class.

See the Chapter Planner for more strategies for differentiation.

HISTORICAL THINKING

ANSWERS

1. William the Conqueror gathered an army and invaded England, defeated King Harold at the Battle of Hastings, and claimed the throne, which had been promised to him by a former English king.

2. used different languages in their services; different leaders, political allegiances, doctrines, and practices

3. the Byzantine Empire and the Eastern Slavic Principalities

CRITICAL VIEWING wearing helmets and full-body armor; carrying long spears

Manors, Guilds, and the Growth of Towns

Not all revolutions involve armies. Some result from many ordinary people changing the way they do things, often as a result of new technology. That's how one revolution got its start in the medieval era.

Rothenburg ob der Tauber, which lies along the Tauber River, is one of the best-preserved medieval towns in Germany.

LAND AND LABOR

In early medieval times, European economies relied on agriculture, and so fertile land had great value. Large landowners, who were typically nobles or church leaders, established a system called **manorialism** to organize their land and the peasants who worked it.

Manorialism was an economic, social, and political system. The landowner's estate, or manor, produced grains, meats, and crafted goods that supported the peasants, the landowner, and others. Occupants of the manor lived together in a community, where they interacted socially. The landowner, or lord, had legal authority over the manor, essentially serving as its ruler.

Among its cultivated fields, orchards, and pastures, the typical European manor included a variety of buildings. The lord and his family lived in the manor house, usually a fortified stone structure, or castle. Peasants lived in one-room huts. Most manors also had barns, a church, a mill for grinding grain, and a workshop. Thus, the manor was a nearly self-sufficient farming village.

Some peasants farmed small tracts of land of their own. But by the year 1000, most peasants were **serfs**, agricultural workers who were bound to the land of their lord. Serfs were not free to leave the lord's land without his permission. If lords sold their land, they did not take their serfs with them. The serfs stayed with the land.

Each year, the serfs had to turn over a large share of the crops they raised to their lord. They were also required to work the lord's personal fields and do other tasks. In return for their service, the lord promised to protect them against raiders, robbers, and other dangers.

To protect their manors, powerful landowning nobles often commanded the service of horse-riding warriors called **knights**, who were skilled in the use of swords,

crossbows, and other weapons. A knight became a lord's **vassal**. A vassal gave military service and pledged loyalty to a lord in exchange for land to live on. This system of defense emerged after the Frankish and other European kingdoms broke down, leaving it up to powerful local lords to provide people with protection and security.

Traditionally, this legal system has been described as **feudalism**. Yet historians today often avoid the term because no one alive between 1000 and 1350 used the word. The term came into use only after 1600.

Around 1200, manorialism began to fade away. Landowning nobles in western Europe came to rely on free, rent-paying peasants to work their lands. By then, agricultural innovations were increasing productivity. In eastern Europe, however, serfdom continued. Russian peasants remained serfs for centuries to come.

Farmers before 1000 had learned that leaving a third or more of their fields unplanted each year increased soil fertility, as did manure from cattle. Greater fertility meant larger harvests. Farmers later found that rotating crops from year to year—planting different crops that absorbed different nutrients from the soil—allowed them to keep their fields under continuous cultivation.

New technology also expanded yields. A heavier plow, with wheels, allowed peasants to till even the tough clay soils of northern Europe. Attaching iron to a wooden plow blade improved soil cultivation. A newly designed collar helped horses pull the plows more efficiently, while iron horseshoes protected the animals' hooves.

The application of these new methods and technologies resulted in a substantial increase in grain production. This expansion of the food supply led to a population boom in Europe. Between 1000 and 1340, Europe's population nearly doubled, to around 75 million.

THE COMMERCIAL REVOLUTION

As populations grew, so did towns. European towns rose up around local markets that displayed such goods as butter and cheese, textiles, and soap produced by individual households. At first, shoppers traded for the goods they needed. After 1000, with the renewed minting of coins, they began making purchases with money.

As the availability of money increased, so did **commerce**, or the buying and selling of goods on a large scale. Farmers could now sell their food surpluses for money in the growing towns and cities. Artisans and merchants, too, earned money for the goods they sold.

New institutions arose to accommodate these changes. One was the **guild**, an association of artisans or merchants formed to set quality standards, establish prices for goods, and help businesses flourish. Guilds often amassed enough wealth and power to take control of a town's government.

Another new institution was banking. Banks began appearing in northern Italy around 1200, after African discoveries increased the gold supply in the Mediterranean. Business people needed a safe place to keep the money they accumulated and used to run their businesses. Besides protecting deposited money, banks made loans and invested in business ventures. Banking spread from Italy across the Mediterranean and into northern Europe. By 1300, banking networks

served international traders, encouraging further commercial expansion.

In search of larger infusions of **capital**, or money for use in starting a business, merchants began to form partnerships with investors. A merchant would open and manage a business, and the investor would supply the capital and share in the profits. Larger associations of merchants attracted multiple investors. As international trade expanded, a wealthy merchant class arose.

This shift from an economy based on self-sufficient agriculture to one based on international trade is referred to as the **Commercial Revolution**. This revolution advanced the right of individuals to own and manage private property, encouraged competition, and supported the quest for profit.

The Commercial Revolution was just getting started in the late Middle Ages. Its impact would be felt well into the 18th century.

HISTORICAL THINKING

1. **READING CHECK** What factors contributed to the growth of the Commercial Revolution?

2. **DESCRIBE** What were the main characteristics of the economic system of manorialism?

3. **DRAW CONCLUSIONS** How did individuals benefit from the Commercial Revolution?

Europe's Medieval Era 277

PLAN: 2-PAGE LESSON

OBJECTIVE

Explain manorialism and describe how advances in agriculture led to the Commercial Revolution.

CRITICAL THINKING SKILLS FOR LESSON 2.1

- Describe
- Draw Conclusions
- Make Inferences
- Synthesize
- Analyze Visuals

HISTORICAL THINKING FOR CHAPTER 10

What should be the relationship between church and state?

In manorialism, which students will learn about in Lesson 2.1, a large piece of land was owned either by a noble or a church leader. The landowner had legal authority over the manor and its inhabitants. Landholdings by the Christian Church helped to integrate religion into daily life.

Student eEdition online

Additional content for this lesson, including an illustration and diagrams, is available online.

BACKGROUND FOR THE TEACHER

Agricultural Innovations and Farming Families

Agricultural innovations that developed from 1000 to 1300 led to a broad transformation that profoundly affected the structure of society. In addition to the innovations of crop rotation and iron implements, European farmers also began to farm sheep for their wool, while using both horses and oxen for transport. By 1200, horses had gradually replaced oxen on most European farms due to a newly designed horse collar that let the horses pull heavier loads and increased agricultural output, which made feeding and caring for horses a more reasonable prospect than in the past. Members of a farming family performed a wide variety of tasks. Women tended to do the jobs closer to the home, like raising children, cooking, tending the garden, milking cows, and caring for livestock. Men did the plowing and seed sowing, but both sexes helped to bring in the harvest. Many households hired temporary help, both male and female, at busy times of the year to assist with tasks like shearing sheep, picking hops for beer, and mowing hay.

INTRODUCE & ENGAGE

ACTIVATE PRIOR KNOWLEDGE

Invite students to share what they already know about commerce. **ASK:** "What is capital?" "What do banks do?" "How does trade impact the two parties who are trading?" Record and display students' responses in a Concept Cluster. Ask students to use ideas from the Concept Cluster to discuss how commerce can lead to competition and individual economic advancement. Tell students that they will learn how commerce transformed life for individuals in medieval Europe.

TEACH

GUIDED DISCUSSION

1. **Make Inferences** How do you think landowning nobles felt about the Commercial Revolution? *(Possible response: Some landowning nobles may have felt threatened by the changes brought about by the Commercial Revolution. Nobles' power rested in their land ownership but also in their authority over their peasants. As agriculture improved, peasants had surplus crops they could sell at markets. With this money came greater independence from the manor and reduced power for the nobles.)*

2. **Synthesize** How might a peasant take advantage of the changes brought about by the Commercial Revolution? *(Peasants were farmers. They could sell surplus crops at markets and earn money. With this money, they could engage in commerce, such as investing in a business.)*

ANALYZE VISUALS

Have students study the diagram of a manor in the Middle Ages (available in the Student eEdition). **ASK:** What do you think was the effect of peasants and serfs attending church with the lord and his family? *(Possible response: There may have been an increased sense of community among the people living in the manor.)* In what way do the homes of the peasants support the idea that manorialism was a social system as much as an economic one? *(The homes of the peasants are much smaller than the home, or castle, of the lord. This confirms that peasants were in a lower social class than the lord, and that the lord had authority over them.)*

ACTIVE OPTIONS

On Your Feet: Roundtable Divide the class into groups of four. Tell each group to answer the following question: What important long- and short-term consequences arose from the Commercial Revolution? Direct groups to have each member answer the question with a different response. Then reconvene the class and discuss the groups' responses.

NG Learning Framework: Life on a Manor
SKILL Collaboration
KNOWLEDGE Our Human Story

Organize students in small groups to conduct online research on what life on a manor was like for serfs, knights, and vassals. Ask them to compare the responsibilities and way of life of each group. When groups have completed their research, conduct a whole-class discussion in which students share their findings.

DIFFERENTIATE

ENGLISH LANGUAGE LEARNERS

Use New Words in Sentences Pair students at the **Beginning** or **Intermediate** level with students at the **Advanced** level. Direct the latter to pronounce the following words and clarify meanings as necessary: *serfs, knights,* and *vassals.* Instruct pairs to compose an original sentence for each word. Suggest that students compile their own word lists as the basis for additional sentences.

GIFTED & TALENTED

Write and Present a Skit Challenge students to write and present a skit that dramatizes a market during the Commercial Revolution. Prompt them to conduct research to learn more about what markets looked like and who frequented them. Their skits should include roles for peasants, merchants, shoppers, bankers, traders, investors, and/or members of a guild. The plot can be simple; for example, a merchant is looking for investors in his new business. Invite students to present their skits.

See the Chapter Planner for more strategies for differentiation.

HISTORICAL THINKING

ANSWERS

1. Agricultural innovation led to increased production of food, which resulted in a boom in population and sparked the growth of market towns, which stimulated trade, which necessitated banking, which supported the expansion of international trade and commerce.

2. Manor owners ruled over peasants, who produced the food that supported the manors. Manors were self-sufficient farming villages.

3. The Commercial Revolution promoted the right of individuals to own and manage private property and to work for their own profit.

Centers of Learning

Have you read any good books lately—written in Latin? Teenagers who attended school in the Middle Ages were expected to read and write Latin. The language of the Romans remained a key element in a classical education for a long time—until the late 1800s in the United States.

EDUCATION AND THE CHURCH

Large medieval manors generated wealth and provided stability and security for their residents. A traditional practice, aimed at preventing these large estates from being split up, allowed that only the eldest son could inherit a father's property. The other sons in the family often left the manor to get an education and pursue careers. Daughters either married and moved to their husband's property or continued to live with their family.

Three social classes existed in medieval Europe. Known as the three orders of society, they were the nobles, the peasants, and the **clergy**, or religious leaders

appointed by the church to perform ceremonies and explain church teachings. Led by the pope, the clergy included priests, who headed individual churches, and bishops, who oversaw groups of churches.

In the Middle Ages, the church took the main responsibility for educating European youth. Some students attended schools located within monasteries, where monks served as teachers. A monk was a member of a religious order who lived and worked in a monastery, typically following a simple life devoted mainly to prayer and spiritual contemplation. Women who joined similar religious orders were called nuns.

The University of Oxford in England, one of the world's great universities, was established in the 1100s. Many European universities were founded during the Middle Ages, including the University of Bologna in Italy and the University of Paris in France.

They lived and were educated in convents. Like monks, nuns spent much of their time praying and reading, writing, and illustrating religious books. In monastery and convent schools, called monastic schools, the teaching focused on the Christian Bible and its moral lessons.

In addition to being centers of education, Christian monasteries and convents had social, economic, and political importance. They provided charitable support for the poor, sick, and aged. Many monasteries owned large tracts of land, often donated by wealthy landowners. Monasteries contributed to the economy by marketing their surplus agricultural and craft goods. They ruled themselves, and their political independence and power was sometimes threatening to kings.

In addition to monasteries and convents, other centers of learning emerged in towns and cities. Run by priests, these schools were located in a **cathedral**, the principal church of a district administered by a bishop. Cathedral schools originally prepared students to become priests and church administrators, but they later taught those who wanted other careers as well. The schools accepted only males, mostly the sons of nobles.

The curriculum of the cathedral schools was much broader than that of the monastic schools. Cathedral schools focused on classical learning, which was based on the Greek and Roman educational system. All students studied three subjects: grammar, rhetoric, and logic. Cathedral schools also offered courses in arithmetic, geometry, astronomy, and music.

Some cathedral schools expanded and became universities. In the early 1100s, the university at Bologna in Italy became a center for the study of law. Founded around 1200, the University of Paris in France drew students eager to study a variety of disciplines, including religion. As commerce expanded, European towns and cities needed lawyers, accountants, and others with business skills, while the church needed religious scholars. Universities filled both sets of needs.

SCHOLASTICISM

European universities maintained a strong focus on Christianity, with its fixed beliefs and reliance on faith. But they also fostered interest in the natural sciences, which called for the application of logic and reasoning. The two areas of study often presented conflicting ideas.

Some Roman Catholic scholars began looking for a way to unify the study of religion and the study of worldly subjects. They found a way in a philosophy that came to be known as **Scholasticism**. Proponents of Scholasticism sought knowledge, whether religious or otherwise, by applying human reason and logic.

The Italian scholar **Anselm of Canterbury**, considered the founder of Scholasticism, attended a monastic school in Normandy in the 1050s and later became a monk. In the late 1070s, Anselm wrote two lengthy works that presented his ideas about faith and reason. He concluded that the existence of God can be determined through reason alone. In 1093, the Norman king of England appointed Anselm to the top religious post in England—archbishop of Canterbury.

Bernard of Clairvaux, an influential French monk, opposed the application of logic to religious matters. Bernard was a **mystic**, a person who seeks knowledge of God through devotion or meditation. He criticized Scholastics like Anselm for their reliance on logic.

A German nun named **Hildegard of Bingen** was also a mystic. However, she applied reason and logic to the study of the natural sciences, focusing on identifying plants that had medicinal powers. A multitalented woman, she composed poetry and music and wrote persuasively about the equality of men and women. She founded a convent and traveled throughout Germany, preaching to large groups.

One of the greatest Scholastics, the Italian priest **Thomas Aquinas** taught at the University of Paris. He based his philosophy partly on the works of the Greek philosopher Aristotle. Aquinas tried to bridge the gap between faith and reason in Summa Theologica, in which he explains the reasoning for all the church's main teachings. One of the key arguments addresses the question, "Is there a God?" Aquinas states that somebody had to be the first to set events in motion, "and this is what everyone takes to be a God."

In Summa Theologica, Aquinas also presents his philosophy of natural law, a set of moral principles derived from nature. Human beings, he argues, are creatures guided by reason, and so laws or rules of morality should reflect their rational nature. Natural law comes into play, he states, whenever a person uses reason to do what is good and avoid what is evil.

HISTORICAL THINKING

1. **READING CHECK** What social, economic, and political roles did Christian monasteries and convents have in the medieval era?

2. **COMPARE AND CONTRAST** What were the main differences between monastic schools and cathedral schools?

3. **MAKE INFERENCES** How does Thomas Aquinas use reason to explain the existence of God?

PLAN: 2-PAGE LESSON

OBJECTIVE

Describe medieval centers of learning, including universities, and explore how religious scholars addressed the gap between faith and reason.

CRITICAL THINKING SKILLS FOR LESSON 2.2

- Compare and Contrast
- Make Inferences
- Draw Conclusions
- Analyze Primary Sources

HISTORICAL THINKING FOR CHAPTER 10

What should be the relationship between church and state?

The church played a significant role in education in medieval society. Lesson 2.2 explains how the church sponsored schools and thereby maintained its social, political, and economic influence.

Student eEdition online

Additional content for this lesson, including a primary source and images, is available online.

BACKGROUND FOR THE TEACHER

Universities Come of Age The universities at Paris and Bologna gained significant independence in the 1140s. Just as guilds of artisans or merchants (see Lesson 2.1) regulated their own membership, so too did students and instructors decide who could join the university. Modern college degrees have their origins in the different steps needed to reach full membership in the guild for university teachers. Starting students, like apprentices, paid fees, while more advanced bachelors, like journeymen, helped to instruct the starting students. Those who attained the level of masters were the equivalent of full members of the guild. In the 1170s, the masters of Paris gained the right to determine the composition of the assigned reading, the content of examinations, and the recipients for each degree, creating a formalized structure. Most students did not study long enough to get their first degree, which was the equivalent of a modern master's degree. Instead, many concentrated on improving their command of Latin, which remained the language of educated people and the church throughout Europe before 1500.

INTRODUCE & ENGAGE

DISCUSS MEDIEVAL SUBJECTS

Explain to students that they are going to learn about cathedral schools in this lesson. Tell them that the three main subjects taught in cathedral schools were grammar, rhetoric, and logic. Stimulate thinking about these subjects by having students fill out a chart about what each subject is, why it is important to learn it, and how it is used today.

TEACH

GUIDED DISCUSSION

1. **Draw Conclusions** Why do you think universities developed out of cathedral schools, rather than monastic schools? *(The curriculum at cathedral schools was much broader. They taught subjects that could be applied to careers in the newly developing towns and cities.)*

2. **Compare and Contrast** How were the beliefs of Anselm of Canterbury and Bernard of Clairvaux different? *(Anselm of Canterbury believed that one could use reason to prove that God existed. Bernard of Clairvaux felt the opposite; as a mystic, he found God through meditation and devotion.)*

ANALYZE PRIMARY SOURCES

Have students review the excerpt from Aquinas's *Summa Theologica* (available in the Student eEdition). **ASK:** How does Aquinas's argument show that he was influenced by Aristotle? *(Aristotle wrote several books on logic, and Aquinas's argument is very logical.)* What part of Aquinas's argument might be challenged by a skeptic? Explain. *(Possible response: A skeptic might challenge the assertion that the "first mover" would be God. God, likely believing in a physics principle to explain movement.)*

ACTIVE OPTIONS

On Your Feet: Think, Pair, Share Direct students to consider the following question: How does Thomas Aquinas's reasoning in the excerpt from *Summa Theologica* (available in the Student eEdition) reflect the culture that Aquinas lived in? Allow a few minutes for students to think, and then tell students to choose partners and discuss their ideas for five minutes. After discussion time, invite students to share their ideas with the class.

> **NG Learning Framework: Compare Religious Schools Then and Now**
> **ATTITUDE** Curiosity
> **SKILL** Observation

Tell small groups to compare the curriculums of medieval cathedral schools with religion-affiliated schools of today. Ask students to consider both similarities and differences as well as how the contemporary versions educate students for the modern world. Invite students to summarize their findings in a written report, chart, or infographic. Have groups share their work with the class.

DIFFERENTIATE

STRIVING READERS

Dictate Sentence Summaries After students read the lesson, direct them to identify three sentences in the text that contain an important idea. Tell students to write that idea in a summary sentence using their own words. Then have pairs take turns dictating their sentences to each other and check each other's work for accuracy and spelling.

PRE-AP

Explore Christian Mysticism Instruct students to conduct research to write an essay that explores Christian mysticism in the medieval era. Remind students that Bernard of Clairvaux was a mystic. Inform them that the practice of mysticism varied widely and that women could be mystics. Invite volunteers to share their essays with the class and answer any questions.

See the Chapter Planner for more strategies for differentiation.

HISTORICAL THINKING

ANSWERS

1. centers of education; provided charitable support for the poor, sick, and aged; Many monasteries owned large tracts of land and marketed their surplus agricultural and craft goods; ruled themselves and had political independence and power

2. Monastic schools were located in monasteries or convents and prepared students to become monks or nuns. Cathedral schools were associated with cathedrals, originally prepared students to become priests and church administrators but later prepared students for other careers as well, and had a broader curriculum than monastic schools.

3. He explains that everything that is in motion needs to be put in motion by something else, but there has to be something that caused the first action. Aquinas reasons that cause was God.

Medieval Achievements

For many years, historians used the term *Dark Ages* to describe the period immediately after the fall of the Roman Empire. Citing the frequent warfare and disappearance of urban life, they viewed it as a bleak period, a time of ignorance and barbarity. Today, historians rarely use the term and instead tout the achievements that occurred as the Middle Ages progressed.

WRITING

In medieval Europe, Christianity served to unify people socially and politically, with the clergy, the nobles, and the peasants all following the same religion. Not surprisingly, most writers of the time focused on Christian topics and themes, producing works that ranged from scholarly essays to romantic poetry. Until fairly late in the Middle Ages, they wrote in Latin, the language of the Roman Catholic Church.

Before the mid-1100s, few people outside the church could read or write Latin. Monks and nuns learned Latin in the monastic schools and were expected to study the Bible and other religious writings. Because they were literate, many of them played a key role in the spread of literature by serving as scribes. Working alone or together in a scriptorium, a room in a monastery set aside for writing and copying manuscripts, scribes copied biblical and other texts onto sheets of parchment. They often included beautiful illuminations, or decorations produced with brightly colored inks, and bound the manuscripts into books. An illuminated manuscript often contained large, ornamental capital letters as well as detailed illustrations and designs.

This detail from the *Peterborough Psalter* shows David, a king of the Israelites in the Bible, playing the harp. The psalter, or book of psalms, was made in England in the early 1300s.

Nearly all monasteries and convents had a library for storing manuscripts, as did universities. Some manuscripts were available for lending to scholars, and a few libraries even arranged for interlibrary loans. Religious and scholarly works filled a large portion of a library's shelves. These works included histories and biographies, collections of letters and sermons, and books of philosophy and science.

A shift away from Latin toward the **vernacular**, or the language spoken by ordinary people, led to an increase in fictional works in the form of heroic and romantic poetry. The first epic in English, *Beowulf*, appeared as a manuscript around 985. The story had been part of the Germanic oral tradition for about two centuries. Set in Denmark, *Beowulf* tells the tale of a heroic prince who slays an evil monster.

Two medieval writers of vernacular poetry were **Dante Alighieri** and **Geoffrey Chaucer**. Dante, an Italian who was inspired by his love for a woman, completed *The Divine Comedy* around 1321. Written in Italian, the long narrative poem tells of the author's travels through hell, purgatory, and heaven. Chaucer, an English writer, finished *The Canterbury Tales* around 1400. This poetic work offers amusing and colorful descriptions of a group of pilgrims, including a monk, a merchant, and a knight, who journey to a shrine in Canterbury, England, and tell tales along the way.

ART AND ARCHITECTURE

The medieval period saw a return to Roman-influenced styles of art and architecture in Europe. By around 950, the turmoil caused by the barbarian invasions had subsided, and the Roman Catholic Church had regained its influence. About 1000, the Romanesque style in art and architecture emerged, fusing Roman, Byzantine, and Germanic traditions. New cathedrals—featuring massive stone walls, rounded arches, and small windows and decorated with religious sculptures and paintings—arose in France, Germany, Italy, England, and Spain.

By the mid-1100s, the architectural style of cathedrals began to shift from Romanesque to Gothic. The Gothic cathedrals featured pointed arches, tall and thin walls, and large windows that let in great amounts of light. This style emerged in the monastery church at Saint-Denis in France, which was rebuilt starting in 1140. Throughout Europe, the construction of Gothic cathedrals was financed not only by the church but also by guilds flush with profits from the Commercial Revolution.

Art historians often point to the Cathedral of Notre-Dame at Chartres, near Paris, as one of the best examples of a Gothic cathedral. Reconstructed after a fire in 1194, its structural changes included the use of flying buttresses, which are exterior, arched supports for walls. This innovation permitted artisans to construct the high, arched ceilings found in Gothic cathedrals. It also allowed walls to be thinner and much taller—so tall that a viewer at street level would see a structure soaring as if to the heavens. The cathedral's many stained-glass windows filtered all the light that entered, creating a warm glow inside.

ADVANCES IN TECHNOLOGY AND SCIENCE

The construction of soaring cathedrals in the medieval era called for advanced engineering skills. Europeans applied new skills and technologies not only in architecture but also in agriculture and industry.

To produce more food, Europeans opened new land to cultivation and farmed land more intensely than they had before. Earlier in this chapter, you read about some of the agricultural innovations that increased productivity, such as the use of manure as a soil fertilizer and the practice of crop rotation. One popular rotation of turnips, clover, and grain took advantage of different nutrients in the soil each year.

Once grain was harvested, it had to be ground into meal or flour. As early as 500, but particularly after 1000, farmers began to harness the power of water in flowing

Geoffrey Chaucer wrote *The Canterbury Tales* in Middle English, which is the form of English spoken between about 1100 and 1400. In this excerpt, the author describes a nun who tries to impress others with her courtly manners.

PRIMARY SOURCE

Original	Translation
At mete wel y-taught was she with-alle;	At meals she was well taught indeed;
She leet no morsel from hir lippes falle,	She let no morsel fall from her lips,
Ne wette hir fingres in hir sauce depe;	Nor wet her fingers deep in her sauce;
Wel coude she carie a morsel, wel kepe,	She well knew how to carry a morsel and take good care
That no drope ne fille up-on hir brest.	That no drop fell upon her breast.

—from the Prologue to *The Canterbury Tales* by Geoffrey Chaucer, c. 1400, translated by Larry D. Benson

---

PLAN: 4-PAGE LESSON

OBJECTIVE

Explore the achievements in the arts, technology, science, agriculture, and political thought that occurred during the Middle Ages.

CRITICAL THINKING SKILLS FOR LESSON 2.3

- Make Inferences
- Identify Main Ideas and Details
- Draw Conclusions
- Compare and Contrast
- Explain
- Analyze Visuals
- Analyze Primary Sources

HISTORICAL THINKING FOR CHAPTER 10

What should be the relationship between church and state?

The Catholic Church played an important role in fostering intellectual progress during medieval times. Lesson 2.3 describes how monks and nuns copied texts so that they could be distributed and shared, and how libraries in monasteries and convents lent manuscripts to scholars.

BACKGROUND FOR THE TEACHER

Gothic Architecture Medieval builders engineered the walls of Gothic cathedrals in such a way that they did not have to bear the weight of the ceiling. As a result, walls could be cut away to hold glass windows. The cathedral's dark, shadowy corridors suddenly opened up into illuminated areas where beams of light poured through the stained glass, symbolizing the power of God to illuminate the imperfect world. The Cathedral of Notre-Dame in Paris preserves much of its original stained glass, which was made in multiple steps using state-of-the-art technology. The first step was to make a drawing with different colors marked. Using minerals to color the glass, glassmakers produced flat panes that could be cut to fit the outline of the original drawing. An artist painted metallic oxide onto the cut glass and then heated it in an annealing oven to fix the design. Then a metalworker used a soldering iron to melt lead strips that held together the different pieces of glass to form the window, which was then raised and inserted into the wall.

Student eEdition online

Additional content for this lesson, including images, is available online.

INTRODUCE & ENGAGE

ACTIVATE PRIOR KNOWLEDGE

Discuss with students what they already know about the democratic system of government in Great Britain. Write the term *parliament* on the board and discuss what students know about Britain's Parliament. Explain that in this lesson they will learn about how a document called the Magna Carta led to the establishment of Parliament.

TEACH

GUIDED DISCUSSION

1. **Make Inferences** Why do you think the shift from Latin to the vernacular caused an increase in fiction writing? *(Fiction writing, such as romantic poetry, lends itself to common, everyday speech. One can write characters who speak in a contemporary way. Also, writing in vernacular distinguished fictional works from religious writings and scholarly essays.)*

2. **Compare and Contrast** How were Romanesque and Gothic architecture different? *(Romanesque architecture featured rounded arches, thick stone walls, and small windows. Gothic architecture featured pointed arches; tall, thin walls; and large windows.)*

ANALYZE VISUALS

Guide students to review the image gallery of medieval illuminated manuscripts (available in the Student eEdition). **ASK:** Why are the manuscripts so elaborately illustrated? *(Possible response: The illustrations help tell the story of the text and also capture the interest of the reader.)* How might common people of that time period have reacted to the illustration of the elephant? Explain your reasoning. *(The illustration of the elephant must have astonished most common people. Travel was much more difficult back then, and many people had probably never seen an elephant.)*

DIFFERENTIATE

ENGLISH LANGUAGE LEARNERS

Write an Original Sentence Pair students at the **Beginning** level with students at the **Intermediate** or **Advanced** levels. Instruct pairs to work together to write an original sentence using selected words and terms. Have the more English-proficient partner assist in checking the accuracy of the sentences. Invite pairs to share their sentences and discuss ways to use each word or term. Suggest the following terms:

vernacular
habeas corpus
Parliament

GIFTED & TALENTED STEM

Create an Illustrated Cutaway Diagram Tell students to research the Gothic elements of the cathedral at Notre-Dame and create a cutaway diagram that identifies each characteristic element. Have them include a brief explanation of each element. Encourage the use of an online tool, such as one that creates 3-D drawings and models. Invite students to share their completed diagrams with the class.

See the Chapter Planner for more strategies for differentiation.

This stained glass window in the Mansion House, the official residence of the mayor of London, depicts King John signing the Magna Carta in 1215.

rivers to operate mills. Water mills were first used to grind grain and then were adapted to other uses, such as sawing wood and sharpening or polishing iron. By 1100, at least 5,000 water mills existed throughout England, or one mill for every 35 families. Europeans also developed their own version of a Persian invention, the windmill, for use in places that lacked flowing water.

Science also advanced during the Middle Ages. The English philosopher Roger Bacon was an early proponent of experimental science. In the mid-1200s, Bacon undertook experimental research in areas ranging from astronomy to optics, the science of light. From his studies of light and the eye, Bacon predicted the invention of glasses and developed a pinhole camera for observing an eclipse of the sun. He was far ahead of his time in proposing motorized ships and carriages and flying machines.

MAGNA CARTA AND PARLIAMENT

Political changes also occurred during the Middle Ages. Although William the Conqueror established a strong monarchy in England after his invasion in 1066, the dominance of English kings did not mean all was quiet throughout the land. Disputes frequently occurred between the king and the church, lords and their vassals, and merchants and their customers.

During the 1100s, not just in England but throughout Europe, people increasingly used the law to resolve disputes. The University of Bologna, in Italy, offered courses in law, based in part on Byzantine and Roman legal texts. Working in monasteries, guilds, and universities, Europeans began to write down previously unwritten laws.

In 1215, a dispute arose between England's King John and his barons, or landholding nobles. The rebellious barons complained of high taxes and claimed that the king, as their lord, had failed to preserve their rights and privileges as vassals in England's feudal system. The dispute ended only after the barons forced the king to put his seal on a written set of laws.

The main purpose of this set of laws, called the **Magna Carta**, or "Great Charter," was to define the obligations

of the king to his barons. But the document's 63 clauses also established fundamental principles that would become the basis for English constitutional law. Those principles, later incorporated into the legal systems of other countries, supported the rise of modern constitutional government.

The Magna Carta limited the king's authority and established that the law applied to everyone, including the king. It guaranteed a free man's right to a trial by his peers—and within a reasonable amount of time. The legal procedure that prevents the government from holding a person indefinitely, without appearing before a judge, is known today as **habeas corpus**.

Another clause established that the king could not impose new taxes without getting the approval of the barons and high church officials. Thus, the Magna Carta signaled the beginning of a transfer of power from the king to a lawmaking body, called **Parliament** in England. Later events during the Middle Ages advanced the development of Parliament and solidified the role of aristocratic landowners in governing England.

CRITICAL VIEWING Begun in 1063, the Cathedral of Santa Maria Assunta in Pisa, Italy (top), is a prime example of Romanesque architecture. Westminster Abbey, one of the most important Gothic buildings in England, was begun in 1245. How does Westminster Abbey differ in style from the Cathedral of Santa Maria Assunta?

HISTORICAL THINKING

1. **READING CHECK** What technological advances in agriculture occurred during the Middle Ages in Europe?

2. **MAKE INFERENCES** How do the works of Dante Alighieri and Geoffrey Chaucer reflect the importance of religion in medieval society?

3. **IDENTIFY MAIN IDEAS AND DETAILS** How did the Magna Carta contribute to the rise of modern democratic institutions and procedures?

4. **DRAW CONCLUSIONS** An important principle of the American legal system is that "justice delayed is justice denied." How is this idea reflected in the Magna Carta?

BACKGROUND FOR THE TEACHER

The Magna Carta The Magna Carta is a major milestone in the history of world democracy. Democracy was born in Greece and adopted by the Romans, but modern democracy has its roots in medieval England and the Magna Carta. Before the Magna Carta, England was governed by common law: rules that remedied crimes and local disputes. Importantly, this early common law was crafted by judges, not legislatures or lawmakers. As medieval society progressed and became more complex, there was a need for laws to be defined, written down, administered, and applied equally. That need was coupled with a strong desire by many to limit the power of the monarch. Indeed, King John signed the Magna Carta not only to meet the demands of his barons but to avoid a civil war. The document was reissued several times, and on each occasion it was slightly revised, but it remained unchanged after 1225.

There is no better demonstration of the document's endurance than its influence on the American colonists and their fight for independence in the 1770s. In fact, so precious were the protections granted by the Magna Carta that many colonial charters included language tying themselves to England. For example, the Virginia Charter stated that its people "shall have and enjoy Liberties, Franchises, Immunities, within any of our other Dominions . . . as if they had been abiding and born, within this our Realm of England."

After the colonies broke away from England and formed their own government, the ideals of the Magna Carta made their way into America's founding documents. The right to a trial by jury and the writ of habeas corpus have their origins in the Magna Carta. So does the concept of due process, which figures prominently in the United States Constitution and the Bill of Rights.

TEACH

GUIDED DISCUSSION

3. **Make Inferences** How do you think the invention of the mill impacted medieval life? *(Mills were used for grinding grain into flour, sawing wood, and sharpening tools. Each of these processes became faster and more efficient. That would lead to increased production. Surpluses could be sold at market, resulting in increased wealth for farmers and merchants.)*

4. **Explain** What is habeas corpus? *(the right of the accused to appear before a judge and not be held indefinitely)*

ANALYZE PRIMARY SOURCES

Ask students to reread the excerpt from *The Canterbury Tales*. **ASK:** How is the nun described in the excerpt? *(The nun has good manners. She is very neat when she eats.)* What questions do you have about the excerpt? *(Possible questions: Who is the nun? Is she a fellow pilgrim or someone the pilgrims meet along the way? Is Chaucer making a statement about the church by pointing out the nun's manners?)*

ACTIVE OPTIONS

On Your Feet: Four Corners Post the following signs in four corners of the classroom: Writing, Art and Architecture, Technology and Science, Magna Carta. Organize students into groups around each sign and prompt them to discuss achievements in each area during the medieval era. Then have at least one student from each corner summarize the group's discussion for the other three groups.

| **NG Learning Framework: Devise an Innovation**
SKILL Problem-Solving
KNOWLEDGE New Frontiers

Remind students that the medieval era saw agricultural technology like water-powered mills come into wider use. Ask students to work with a partner and come up with an innovation related to water that could help people today. For example, they might think of better ways of delivering water to isolated populations or ways of purifying contaminated water. Encourage them to research the issue they choose and then give a short report about their proposed innovation.

HISTORICAL THINKING

ANSWERS

1. Technological advances affecting agriculture during the Middle Ages included the use of manure as fertilizer, crop rotation, water mills, and windmills.

2. Dante's *The Divine Comedy* describes a trip through hell, purgatory, and heaven. Chaucer's *The Canterbury Tales* describes a pilgrimage in which at least two of the characters had ties to the church—a monk and a nun.

3. The Magna Carta began the transfer of power from the king to a lawmaking body, and it outlined some rights of citizens.

4. The idea that justice should not be delayed is reflected in the Magna Carta, which says that a free man has a right to a trial by his peers within a reasonable period of time.

CRITICAL VIEWING Sample response: The Cathedral of Santa Maria Assunta has rounded arches, small windows, and no towers. Westminster Abbey has pointed arches, large windows, towers, and flying buttresses.

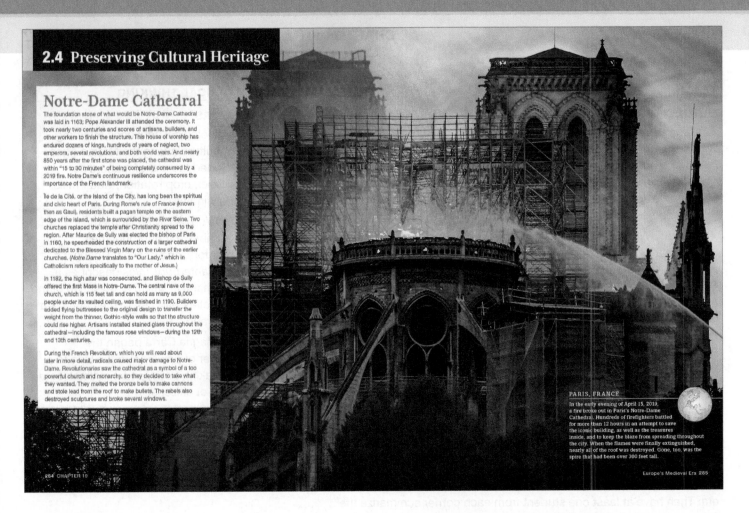

2.4 Preserving Cultural Heritage

Notre-Dame Cathedral

The foundation stone of what would be Notre-Dame Cathedral was laid in 1163; Pope Alexander III attended the ceremony. It took nearly two centuries and scores of artisans, builders, and other workers to finish the structure. This house of worship has endured dozens of kings, hundreds of years of neglect, two emperors, several revolutions, and both world wars. And nearly 850 years after the first stone was placed, the cathedral was within "15 to 30 minutes" of being completely consumed by a 2019 fire. Notre-Dame's continuous resilience underscores the importance of the French landmark.

Île de la Cité, or the Island of the City, has long been the spiritual and civic heart of Paris. During Rome's rule of France (known then as Gaul), residents built a pagan temple on the eastern edge of the island, which is surrounded by the River Seine. Two churches replaced the temple after Christianity spread to the region. After Maurice de Sully was elected the bishop of Paris in 1160, he spearheaded the construction of a larger cathedral dedicated to the Blessed Virgin Mary on the ruins of the earlier churches. (*Notre Dame* translates to "Our Lady," which in Catholicism refers specifically to the mother of Jesus.)

In 1182, the high altar was consecrated, and Bishop de Sully offered the first Mass in Notre-Dame. The central nave of the church, which is 115 feet tall and can hold as many as 9,000 people under its vaulted ceiling, was finished in 1190. Builders added flying buttresses to the original design to transfer the weight from the thinner, Gothic-style walls so that the structure could rise higher. Artisans installed stained glass throughout the cathedral—including the famous rose windows—during the 12th and 13th centuries.

During the French Revolution, which you will read about later in more detail, radicals caused major damage to Notre-Dame. Revolutionaries saw the cathedral as a symbol of a too powerful church and monarchy, so they decided to take what they wanted. They melted the bronze bells to make cannons and stole lead from the roof to make bullets. The rebels also destroyed sculptures and broke several windows.

PARIS, FRANCE

In the early evening of April 15, 2019, a fire broke out in Paris's Notre-Dame Cathedral. Hundreds of firefighters battled for more than 12 hours in an attempt to save the iconic building, as well as the treasures inside, and to keep the blaze from spreading throughout the city. When the flames were finally extinguished, nearly all of the roof was destroyed. Gone, too, was the spire that had been over 300 feet tall.

PLAN: 4-PAGE LESSON

OBJECTIVE
Summarize the history of Notre-Dame Cathedral and describe the fire that blazed through it in 2019.

CRITICAL THINKING SKILLS FOR LESSON 2.4
- Analyze Visuals
- Make Connections
- Integrate Visuals
- Synthesize
- Analyze Cause and Effect
- Analyze Points of View
- Explain

HISTORICAL THINKING FOR CHAPTER 10
What should be the relationship between church and state?

Notre-Dame Cathedral in Paris has seen numerous popes, monarchs, emperors, and other French leaders walk through its doors throughout its 850-year history. Lesson 2.4 describes the history of Notre-Dame and the terrible fire that almost destroyed the structure in 2019.

BACKGROUND FOR THE TEACHER
Fighting the Fire The fire that destroyed the roof and the wooden spire of Notre-Dame could have been much more destructive and could perhaps have been prevented. Notre-Dame was equipped with a fire-warning system, and at 6:18 p.m. local time, a member of the church's security force was alerted to the fire by a flashing red light on a smoke alarm panel. Unfortunately, the guard went to the wrong building; he went to the sacristy, which is the room where priests prepare for service, rather than the cathedral's attic where the fire was ablaze. It took 30 minutes for security personnel to figure out the error, costing valuable time for the firefighters who arrived to face a fire that was already burning out of control. It was hours later when a small group of firefighters bravely marched into the center of the fire and managed to extinguish it, preventing a much more enormous calamity.

History Notebook
Encourage students to complete the Preserving Cultural Heritage page for Chapter 10 in their History Notebooks as they read.

Student eEdition online
Additional content for this lesson, including photos, is available online.

INTRODUCE & ENGAGE

ACTIVATE PRIOR KNOWLEDGE

Draw a Word Web on the board and write *Notre-Dame* in the center. Ask students to come up with words and phrases they associate with Notre-Dame, drawing on their knowledge of France, world history, and artistic works, such as *The Hunchback of Notre Dame.* Then explain that this lesson details Notre-Dame's history and the damage it suffered during a 2019 fire.

TEACH

GUIDED DISCUSSION

1. **Synthesize** Why is Notre-Dame Cathedral such an important French landmark? *(Possible response: The cathedral sits in the center of the city. It is very old and has endured through many eras of French history and survived other destructive events.)*

2. **Analyze Cause and Effect** Why had the original design of the cathedral been altered by the time it was completed in 1190? *(Flying buttresses were added to the design in order to more properly distribute the building's weight, which allowed the ceiling to be made higher.)*

PRESERVING CULTURAL HERITAGE

If the restoration of Notre-Dame is a success, the world may have an American historian and technology enthusiast to thank. Before he died from brain cancer in 2018 at the age of 49, Andrew Tallon, a professor of art at Vassar College and a passionate scholar of Gothic architecture, constructed a complete three-dimensional image of Notre-Dame using laser scanners. Mounted on tripods, the laser scanners rotate and measure every point of a space. Those points are then assembled into a three-dimensional image. At the same time, photographs are taken that are then mapped on to the image, creating a 3-D model that is said to be accurate within five millimeters. In the case of Notre-Dame, it took Tallon five days and 50 different camera set-ups, both inside and outside, to fully capture the 1 billion data points that represent the cathedral. Tallon's high-resolution digital model is currently being used by restorers, architects, and historians in the reconstruction of Notre-Dame.

ENGLISH LANGUAGE LEARNERS

Read in Pairs Pair English language learners at the **Beginning** or **Intermediate** level with English-proficient speakers and have them read the lesson together. Instruct English language learners to ask their partners to pause whenever they hear a word or sentence construction that is confusing. Provide the following sentence frames to help students at different proficiency levels clarify information.

- **Beginning:** Please help me understand this (word, sentence, paragraph).
- **Intermediate:** I need some help understanding this (word, sentence, paragraph).

Suggest that English-proficient speakers point out context clues to help their partners understand the meanings of unfamiliar terms or constructions. Encourage English language learners to restate sentences in their own words.

GIFTED & TALENTED

Create a Photo or Multimedia Essay Ask students to use online and print sources to locate photos of the fire at Notre-Dame Cathedral. Then have students create a photo essay. Their photos should be arranged chronologically, showing the cathedral before, during, and after the fire. Students who want to create a multimedia essay should be encouraged to do so. Ask these students to research a selection of videos from the event, including live, eyewitness footage as well as news reports that followed. Remind students to cite the sources of their photos and videos and prepare brief explanations of how each photo or video illustrates the sequence of events. Invite students to present their essays to the class.

See the Chapter Planner for more strategies for differentiation.

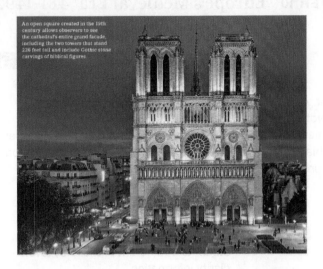

An open square created in the 19th century allows observers to see the cathedral's entire grand facade, including the two towers that stand 226 feet tall and include Gothic stone carvings of biblical figures.

Flames from the fire did not reach Notre-Dame's famous 18th-century Great Organ. However, each of the 8,000 pipes—a few of which date back to the 13th century—and the instrument's wind chest and electrical system needed to be cleaned of dust. The western rose window also survived. The first and smallest of the cathedral's three rose windows was completed about 1225 and restored between 1844 and 1867.

The Catholic Church regained control of the cathedral after the revolution, and French author Victor Hugo's 1831 novel *The Hunchback of Notre-Dame* renewed the public's interest in the building. In 1844, French Gothic architect Eugène-Emmanuel Viollet-le-Duc was chosen to lead the effort to restore the structure to its former glory; it took him nearly 25 years to complete the project. Viollet-le-Duc also added several new elements—the soaring spire, statues of the Twelve Apostles, and Notre-Dame's famous and fearsome stone gargoyles.

In 1914, Notre-Dame was slightly damaged when 50 bombs were dropped on Paris during World War I. And when Charles de Gaulle made his way to the French capital in 1944 to liberate France from Germany in World War II, several bullets struck the cathedral. But the blaze of April 2019 outpaced any other previous threats to the Gothic structure. At the time, Notre-Dame was undergoing a $6.8 million renovation to repair cracks in the stone, and workers had removed copper statues of evangelists and apostles from the roof a week before the tragedy. Other items that remained when the smoke cleared were all three rose windows, the Grand Organ, St. Louis's tunic, and the Holy Crown of Thorns, believed to be worn by Jesus at his crucifixion.

Unfortunately, other treasures and relics were forever lost to the flames. But the people of France—and the world—will not be defeated by this setback. Soon after the blaze, architects and other designers offered sketches of possible options to replace the cathedral's roof and other missing parts. And French president Emmanuel Macron said, "The fire at Notre-Dame reminds us that our history never stops and we will always have challenges to overcome." He also vowed, "We will rebuild it together. It will undoubtedly be part of French destiny and our project for the years to come."

HISTORICAL THINKING

INTEGRATE VISUALS How do the photos and history of Notre-Dame Cathedral reflect France's history?

BACKGROUND FOR THE TEACHER

Gothic Architecture Notre-Dame is a significant and outstanding example of French Gothic architecture. More broadly, Gothic architecture lasted in Europe from the mid-1100s to the 1500s. Some of the characteristics of the Gothic style include arches, rib vaulting, flying buttresses, transepts, large stained-glass windows, and gargoyles. Many of these features were borne out of necessity as Gothic builders sought to build very large structures.

A Gothic arch is recognizable by its pointed apex. Gothic arches helped large-scale structures maintain their integrity while allowing for more natural light to enter. A vault is a series of arches that provide structure, usually to a building's roof. Earlier vaults had rounded tops; the rib vault introduced a pointed top along which a line of ribbing ran. Stone could be laid on this ribbing, and the pointed tops allowed for greater height.

A flying buttress is a supporting bar that rests on an arch and connects a wall to a vertical post or column by "flying" between them. Before the Gothic era, buttresses were usually hidden, but flying buttresses were built out in the open and became important visual elements of the Gothic style. A transept is the space in a church that crosses the nave. Churches of that era were cruciform (shaped like a cross); the nave is the long vertical space of the church, and the transept is the shorter, horizontal space. The large stained-glass windows of the Gothic style allowed for a depiction of religious scenes through which natural light cascaded into the church interior. Notre-Dame's gargoyles appear to be decorative; however, they are actually waterspouts that carry rainwater collected in gutters away from the church's exterior. The other, non-functional grotesque beasts sitting atop the cathedral are called *chimeras*.

TEACH

GUIDED DISCUSSION

3. **Analyze Points of View** How might radicals from the French Revolution have defended their treatment of Notre-Dame? *(Possible response: The radicals viewed the cathedral as a symbol of the monarchy and the Catholic Church, so they had no reason to respect it. Also, they needed metal to make cannons and bullets to fight their side of the revolution, so they melted bronze bells and stole lead from the roof.)*

4. **Explain** Why was the Tunic of St. Louis (shown in the Student eEdition) such an important relic to save from the fire? *(It is believed to have belonged to King Louis IX, whose funeral was held at Notre-Dame.)*

ANALYZE VISUALS

Ask students to study the photographs of Notre-Dame. **ASK:** What are some of the objects shown in the photos that were particularly important to attempt to save? *(Possible response: The first photo shows the two towers; the second photo also shows the wooden spire; the third photo shows the rose window and the Great Organ.)* In the photo of the charred debris (available in the Student eEdition), what objects appear to have survived the fire? *(In that photo, the giant cross is visible, as are some statues around the altar. The wooden pews in the foreground appear to be intact, as well.)*

ACTIVE OPTION

NG Learning Framework: Create a Virtual Museum Exhibit
SKILLS Collaboration, Communication
KNOWLEDGE New Frontiers

Arrange students in groups and explain that each group will create a multimedia presentation about the architectural and artistic features of Notre-Dame Cathedral. Guide each group to choose one of the following topics: the Great Organ and the bells and drones; the paintings; the statuary; the stained glass; the portals; the wooden spire called "the arrow"; the wooden frame called "the forest"; or another of their own choosing. Encourage students to include photographs and other visuals to enhance their presentation. Allow time for groups to share their presentations and answer questions.

HISTORICAL THINKING

ANSWER

Possible response: The fact that the cathedral has gone through turbulent times reflects France's history. Notre-Dame has withstood revolutions, wars, and fire. It has also been immortalized in French literature and as an important Christian site.

Changing Roles of the Church

There's an old saying that money opens doors. In medieval Europe, money could buy a person a position in the church, like that of a bishop or even pope.

STRUCTURE OF THE CHURCH

By 1000, the European countryside was blanketed with churches, each one the center of a parish in which the clergy lived alongside the **laity**, or members of the church who are not clergy. Many churches, especially the cathedrals, owned valuable lands that brought them wealth, but others had little land of their own. The laity were expected to pay a **tithe**, or 10 percent of their income, to their local parish priest. He, in turn, performed the sacraments, or holy rituals, for them, including baptism and marriage. The priest also celebrated Mass, in which he administered the sacrament of the Eucharist, or Holy Communion. In this sacrament, Roman Catholics eat bread and drink wine that they believe become the body and blood of Jesus.

The clergy fell into two categories: the secular clergy and the regular clergy. The **secular** clergy did not belong to a monastic order or live in a monastery. They lived out in the community and worked with the laity as local priests or as teachers in cathedral schools. Regular clergy lived in monasteries and followed the rules of their monastic order, most of which were modeled on the Benedictine Rule, a guide for monastic life written by an Italian monk named Benedict around 530 c.e. The Benedictine Rule called for strict obedience to the abbot, or head of the monastery, and required that monks remain unmarried, have few possessions, wear simple clothing, and follow a daily schedule of prayer and work.

Sacra di San Michele, an abbey built between 983 and 987, sits on top of Mount Pirchiriano in Italy. Like other churches devoted to St. Michael, including Mont-Saint-Michel in France (shown at the beginning of this chapter), Sacra di San Michele was constructed on a hard-to-reach site.

288 CHAPTER 10

MONASTIC REFORMS

The Roman Catholic Church had started out as many individual churches that developed their own **doctrines**, or official beliefs, and practices. As time passed, official church councils sought to standardize doctrines and practices. Although the pope in Rome was the supreme authority in church matters, the monastery system allowed a variety of practices to flourish.

One monastery at Cluny, in eastern France, was the largest in Europe, with holdings in land and money greater than those of the church in Rome. Cluny's abbot was more powerful than anyone in the church except the pope. By the late 1000s, some 300 monks lived at Cluny. In addition, about 1,000 monasteries, home to 20,000 monks, were associated with Cluny. But Cluny's growth meant the abbot was too busy to visit most of these monasteries, and monastic discipline suffered.

In 1098, several monks broke away from Cluny and began a new order, the Cistercians, and called for a return to enforcement of the Benedictine Rule. Unlike the Cluny monasteries, each Cistercian monastery had its own abbot. All abbots met at regular intervals to ensure that everyone followed the same regulations. Cistercian monks lived more simply than those at Cluny. They wore clothes of undyed wool, ate only vegetarian foods, and built undecorated churches.

Some reformers urged monks to live exactly as Jesus and his followers had, not in monasteries with their own incomes but on the streets as beggars dependent on ordinary people for contributions. Between 1100 and 1200, these reformers established at least nine begging orders. Their members were known as friars. The new begging orders explicitly rejected what they saw as lavish spending by the church.

An Italian Catholic named **Francis of Assisi** founded the most important begging order, the Franciscans, which had some 28,000 members by 1326. Franciscans were not allowed to live in a permanent dwelling or to keep any money, books, or extra clothes. Another begging order, the Dominicans, arose in Spain in the early 1200s. Its founder stressed education and sent some of his followers to attend universities.

St. Francis of Assisi, shown on the right, is the patron saint of animals and ecology. He felt a connection and brotherhood with all living creatures.

PAPAL AND SECULAR STRUGGLES

By the early 1000s, the practice of buying and selling church offices had become widespread in Europe. In 1046, three men competed to become pope. One of them had bought the position from an earlier pope. The ruler of Germany, Henry III, intervened in the dispute and paved the way for a German bishop to assume the papacy. The new pope, Clement II, then crowned Henry as the new Holy Roman Emperor. Henry had effectively taken control of the papacy, which allowed him to arrange for the appointment of three later popes.

In 1075, however, Pope Gregory VII renewed that struggle. He declared that only popes could invest bishops, or formally install them in office, and the penalty for breaking this rule would be excommunication. The pope and the next Holy Roman Emperor, Henry IV, soon clashed when they put forward rival candidates for bishop of Milan, Italy.

Pope Gregory excommunicated Henry, who later sought and received the pope's forgiveness. In 1075, the pope drafted 27 declarations asserting the independence of the church from secular rulers. Pope Gregory had regained control of his office.

HISTORICAL THINKING

1. **READING CHECK** What reforms in monastic life did the Cistercians make?

2. **DRAW CONCLUSIONS** Why was the buying and selling of church offices a serious problem?

3. **MAKE PREDICTIONS** Do you think the "victory" of Pope Gregory VII ended the struggle for power between popes and kings? Why or why not?

Europe's Medieval Era 289

PLAN: 2-PAGE LESSON

OBJECTIVE
Understand the attempted reforms to the Roman Catholic Church in the 1000s.

CRITICAL THINKING SKILLS FOR LESSON 3.1
- Draw Conclusions
- Make Predictions
- Identify Problems and Solutions
- Identify Supporting Details
- Analyze Visuals

HISTORICAL THINKING FOR CHAPTER 10
What should be the relationship between church and state?

In the 1000s, the bond between popes and European leaders remained strong. Lesson 3.1 describes the struggles that occurred between them in the midst of monastic reforms.

Student eEdition online
Additional content for this lesson, including an image, is available online.

BACKGROUND FOR THE TEACHER
The Cistercians Although the Cistercians thought of themselves as reformers, they still accepted the need for groups of men or women to live in landed monasteries or nunneries. About half of the Cistercian monasteries were nunneries for women. After 1000, as Europe's population surged, many more women joined nunneries. But because their contemporaries did not think it appropriate for them to do the work monks did, a nunnery needed male staff to run its estates, farm the land, and perform religious services. Despite their strictness, the Cistercians experienced a decline in the discipline of their members by the 15th century. Some abbeys began collecting tithes, which had been forbidden. Others sold wool and grain for profit. Even the election of independent abbots, which was a cornerstone belief, was corrupted as secular rulers put greedy abbots in charge. Often, these abbots were not even members of the local order. In many ways, the Cistercians were victims of their own success; the order had become so large, it was impossible to enforce their own reforms.

INTRODUCE & ENGAGE

DISCUSS REFORM

Write *reform* on the board and ask students to call out words they associate with this term. Invite the class to collaborate on a formal definition of the term (as a noun). *(the improvement of something that is corrupt)* **ASK:** What are some areas of law and politics today that you feel need reform? *(Answers will vary. Possible responses: money in politics, environmental policies, laws having to do with race, laws that protect children, laws that protect women, gun laws)* Tell students that in this lesson they will learn about the reforms that the Catholic Church underwent in the 1000s.

TEACH

GUIDED DISCUSSION

1. **Identify Problems and Solutions** In what ways did reformers cause problems for the Catholic Church? *(Reformers believed that the clergy should not earn incomes. They also opposed the lavish spending of the church, which caused a problem because church offices could be bought and sold, undermining church authority. Also, local parishes required the laity to pay a tithe in exchange for performing sacraments, which meant that church laity members were collecting the tithe payments, thus earning money.)*

2. **Identify Supporting Details** What "victory" did Henry III claim? *(Henry III became Holy Roman Emperor and used his power to take over the papacy and control the appointments of three popes. In this sense, he had a victory over the church.)*

ANALYZE VISUALS

Ask students to look at the photograph of the monastery Sacra di San Michele. **ASK:** Why do you think the monastery was built on top of a mountain? *(Putting the monastery in a hard-to-reach place symbolized the strict, ascetic lifestyle of the monks who lived there. They could not marry or own many personal possessions. They followed a rigorous daily schedule of prayer and work.)*

ACTIVE OPTIONS

On Your Feet: Roundtable Arrange students in groups of four and give each group a large sheet of paper with the following question: What is the value of living a very simple, even strict, life? Tell each student in every group to write an opinion that they can support with examples from the text. After all students have written their opinions, allow time for each group to discuss the opinions and supporting text evidence. Then call on volunteers to share their group's ideas.

NG Learning Framework: Investigate the Franciscans
SKILL Collaboration
KNOWLEDGE Our Human Story

Instruct groups to conduct online research about the Franciscans and St. Francis of Assisi. Tell groups to discuss St. Francis's life and what caused him to form the Franciscans. Then discuss the Franciscans as a class.

DIFFERENTIATE

ENGLISH LANGUAGE LEARNERS

Practice Pronunciation Write the following words on the board: *laity, tithe, secular, doctrine.* Pronounce each word and have students repeat. Pair students at the **Advanced** level with those at the **Beginning** or **Intermediate** level and instruct them to take turns finding passages in the lesson that contain any of the four words and reading the passages aloud.

GIFTED & TALENTED

Interview a Reformer Have pairs plan, write, and perform an in-depth news interview with a church reformer from the 1000s. Tell pairs to review the lesson and then conduct online research to gather details about the reforms that took place during that period. Encourage them to formulate questions that will elicit in-depth answers from their interviewee. Allow pairs time to practice their interview and then record it for playback or perform it live for the class.

See the Chapter Planner for more strategies for differentiation.

HISTORICAL THINKING

ANSWERS

1. Each monastery had its own abbot, who enforced the Benedictine Rule. The Cistercian monks lived more simply than those at Cluny. They wore clothes of undyed wool, ate only vegetarian foods, and built undecorated churches.

2. The buying and selling of church offices was a serious offense because it undermined the moral authority of the church and resulted in unethical people assuming positions of authority.

3. Possible response: The struggle for power between popes and kings probably continued because church and state matters were so closely intertwined.

Waves of Crusades

You've probably heard the saying "The ends justify the means." Christians of the Middle Ages relied on similar reasoning when they launched violent attacks against non-Christians in the name of Jesus, the "Prince of Peace."

BYZANTINE EMPIRE UNDER ATTACK

In 1095, **Pope Urban II** addressed a large meeting of church leaders, telling them that the Byzantine emperor had requested help against the Seljuk Turks, a nomadic tribe from Central Asia. At the time, the Byzantine Empire was shrinking, much of its territory having been captured by Arab Muslims. The Seljuks had begun to carve out a Seljuk empire in central Anatolia that would extend south into Syria and Palestine. They also initiated a quest to topple Constantinople, the heavily fortified Byzantine capital. Meanwhile, the Normans of France had attacked the Byzantine Empire and aimed to conquer Constantinople, too.

The Byzantine Empire, in spite of its wealth and well-trained military, seemed unable to adequately defend itself. Part of the problem was a lack of consistent and competent leadership. Over a span of 50 years before 1081, the empire had gone through 13 rulers, many of them inept. The year 1081, however, brought the Byzantine leader **Alexius Comnenus** to the throne.

Alexius stopped the advance of the Normans in western Greece in 1085. He also achieved a **truce**, or a temporary halt of warfare, with the Seljuks and other Muslim Turks on the empire's eastern border. But the Seljuks remained within striking distance of Constantinople—and they had control of Palestine, called the Holy Land by Christians. The Holy Land included the city of Jerusalem and the area around it, where Jesus had preached and died and was buried. Christians, Jews, and Muslims all believed the land rightfully belonged to them.

FIRST CRUSADE: A CALL AND A RESPONSE

The Holy Land, and especially Jerusalem, had long attracted Christian pilgrims who wanted to visit the sites where Jesus had lived and died and was buried. Muslims, too, considered several sites in Jerusalem sacred, including the Dome of the Rock, from which the prophet Muhammad reportedly ascended into heaven. After taking control of the region, the Seljuk Turks blocked Christian pilgrimage routes to the Holy Land.

Pope Urban II was concerned about the threat Muslims posed to the Holy Land and to the Byzantine Empire. He had heard stories of pilgrims being harassed and holy places being damaged or destroyed. In his speech to the meeting of church leaders, he called for what historians refer to as the First **Crusade**, a Christian military expedition to invade and conquer Palestine. He asked Europe's nobles, the warrior class, to march against the Muslim "infidels," or unfaithful ones. The word Crusader referred to anyone belonging to a large, volunteer force fighting against Muslims. The Crusaders wore a cross on their clothing.

Pope Urban II had determined that warfare designed to defend Christians and sacred Christian sites served a holy purpose. Such a **holy war**, he believed, was morally justified. In his speech, the pope declared that all Crusaders who died en route to the Holy Land could be certain that God would forgive their sins. The Crusaders, he said, were pilgrims, and God forgave all pilgrims' sins.

Some 50,000 combatants responded to the pope's plea. Out of these, several armies of volunteer fighters were organized. The first force set out in August 1096 under the leadership of **Godfrey of Bouillon**, a German duke. A Norman leader known as Bohemond led another group. Both armies marched overland to Constantinople. The Byzantines had not forgotten the earlier Norman attacks on their empire. **Anna Comnena**, the emperor's daughter, later wrote a history of the period, in which she praised the Norman leaders for their courage in battle but criticized them as cunning, or devious, schemers. Emperor Alexius, fearing trouble from the Normans, hurried the Crusaders away from his capital and on their way to Jerusalem.

CRITICAL VIEWING In this detail from an illuminated manuscript, Christian soldiers amass for the siege of Antioch in 1098 during the First Crusade. How would you characterize these volunteer troops?

PLAN: 4-PAGE LESSON

OBJECTIVE

Recount the series of Christian Crusades that were first launched in 1096.

CRITICAL THINKING SKILLS FOR LESSON 3.2

- Evaluate
- Draw Conclusions
- Interpret Maps
- Analyze Cause and Effect
- Explain
- Make Generalizations
- Analyze Primary Sources
- Analyze Maps

HISTORICAL THINKING FOR CHAPTER 10

What should be the relationship between church and state?

The Catholic Church was always mindful of outside threats to its power, influence, territory, and holy sites. Lesson 3.2 describes the four Crusades against non-Christians that began in 1096.

BACKGROUND FOR THE TEACHER

Saladin's Army In 1176, Saladin, the Muslim ruler of the Ayyubid dynasty, married the widow of the Seljuk ruler of Central Asia, effectively allying the two great powers of the Islamic world. With this combined power, he devoted himself to raising an army strong enough to guard against the Crusaders. By 1187, Saladin had gathered an army of 30,000 men on horseback carrying lances and swords like knights but without chain-mail armor. Half of his army consisted of light cavalry who could maneuver much more quickly than the 20,000 Crusaders they faced. Saladin laid a trap for the Crusaders in an extinct Syrian volcano called the Horns of Hattin. The Crusader forces had no way to replenish their water supply, but the Muslim armies made sure that each of their camps had storage tanks supplied by camels carrying goat skins filled with water. On the day of the battle, Saladin's well-rested forces easily defeated the parched and exhausted Crusaders, baiting them by pouring fresh water out on the ground instead of giving it to them to drink.

INTRODUCE & ENGAGE

PREVIEW USING MAPS

Direct students' attention to the Crusades map. **ASK:** What information in the map tells you that the Crusades were an important venture for Christians? *(Possible response: The map shows that the Crusades went on for hundreds of years in four phases and went all over Europe and the Mediterranean via a variety of sea and overland routes.)*

TEACH

GUIDED DISCUSSION

1. **Analyze Cause and Effect** Why was the Byzantine Empire susceptible to attack from the Seljuk Turks? *(The Byzantine Empire had not had consistent or competent leadership. As a result, it seemed unable to defend itself.)*

2. **Explain** Why did both Christians and Muslims believe the Holy Land belonged to them? *(For Christians, the Holy Land was where Jesus had preached and died. For Muslims, several sites in Jerusalem were sacred, including the Dome of the Rock, which was where the prophet Muhammad was believed to have ascended into heaven.)*

ANALYZE PRIMARY SOURCES

Ask students to reread the excerpt from *Alexiad*. **ASK:** How does Anna Comnena describe Bohemond? *(She says he is strong and brave, but violent and hot-tempered.)* What does she mean when she says Bohemond and his father were like "the caterpillar and the locust"? *(Bohemond was like a locust in that whatever his father (the caterpillar) didn't destroy ("devour"), he (Bohemond) would. Between the two of them, they destroyed everything in their paths.)*

DIFFERENTIATE

ENGLISH LANGUAGE LEARNERS

Practice Pronunciation Write the following names on the board: Urban, Alexius Comnenus, Godfrey of Bouillon, Anna Comnena, and Saladin. Pronounce each name and have students repeat. Pair students at the **Advanced** level with those at the **Beginning** or **Intermediate** level and instruct them to take turns finding passages in the lesson that contain any of the four names and reading the passages aloud.

PRE-AP

Write a News Report Direct students to select one of the four Crusades' locations to write a news report about. Guide them to conduct online research to find more information to write an article that includes an interview with an innocent civilian or a community leader whose city was sacked by a group of Crusaders. Have students share their news reports with the class. Then conduct a roundtable discussion in which students explore elements of bias in the news report and how it would have fit or fought against different groups' agendas at the time.

See the Chapter Planner for more strategies for differentiation.

The Crusades, 1096–1270

Map legend:
- Eastern Orthodox Church lands
- Roman Catholic Church lands
- Crusader kingdoms, 1140
- Muslim lands
- First Crusade, 1096–1099
- Second Crusade, 1147–1149
- Third Crusade, 1189–1192
- Fourth Crusade, 1202–1204
- Crusades of Louis IX, 1248–1254 and 1270
- Boundaries, 1097
- Battle

The Crusaders marched from Constantinople southwest across Anatolia toward the historically Christian center of Antioch in Syria. They conquered Antioch in 1098 after an eight-month siege. The following year, they accomplished their main goal by capturing Jerusalem, and Godfrey of Bouillon became the ruler of Palestine. After this victory, the Crusaders massacred thousands of the city's Jewish and Arab residents. Although the Crusaders succeeded in conquering Jerusalem, they would hold it for only 88 years.

DEFEAT AND MORE CRUSADES

By 1140, the Crusaders had set up four small states in the Holy Land: the Kingdom of Jerusalem, the County of Tripoli, the Principality of Antioch, and the County of Edessa. Together, these states became known as the Latin East, because the Crusaders spoke Latin. Of all the Crusader states, Edessa, bordering Seljuk lands,

was the most vulnerable to Muslim attack. In 1144, the Seljuk Turks conquered Edessa.

The loss of Edessa alarmed Christians and moved a new pope to call for a Second Crusade. Bernard of Clairvaux, a monk you read about earlier, depicted the Crusade as a road to salvation in his preaching, which stimulated widespread support. His eloquent sermons prompted the kings of both France and Germany to lead large armies to Edessa in 1147.

The Second Crusade failed completely. After discovering that the Turks had killed the Christian inhabitants of Edessa, the Crusaders gave up on trying to recapture the state. They decided instead to lay siege to Damascus, a fortified Muslim city in Syria. They retreated after four days, however, when it became clear they could not conquer the city. The failure of the Second Crusade dismayed Christians and greatly encouraged Muslims.

The Muslim ruler **Saladin**, founder of a new dynasty in Egypt, joined with the Seljuks to dislodge the Crusaders. In 1187, Saladin's army retook Jerusalem. The Crusaders in Jerusalem who weren't killed were held for ransom or sold into slavery. Saladin's troops restored the mosques as houses of worship and removed the crosses from all Christian churches, though Muslims later allowed Christian pilgrims to visit the city.

Subsequent major Crusades failed to recapture Jerusalem. In the Third Crusade launched in 1189, England's King **Richard the Lionheart** sailed to the Holy Land with his army, landing at Acre, just north of Jerusalem. Richard exemplified the Code of Chivalry, a code of honorable conduct that called for knights to be skilled at combat, brave, fair, and courteous. Richard demonstrated this code in the courtesy he showed his Muslim opponent Saladin, and it may have been mutual respect that allowed these powerful men to negotiate a peace treaty in 1192. Acre fell to the Crusaders, as did several other seaports to the north and the island of Cyprus. The Third Crusade was generally a success, though Jerusalem remained in Muslim hands.

Europeans decided to make a further attempt to retake Jerusalem and launched the Fourth Crusade

PRIMARY SOURCE

In *Alexiad*, her work about her father's reign as Byzantine emperor, Anna Comnena described the Norman leader Bohemond and his father, Robert Guiscard. She characterized these two Norman nobles as equally tough, warlike, and despicable.

Now, Bohemond took after his father in all things, in audacity, bodily strength, bravery, and untamable temper; for he was of exactly the same stamp as his father, and a living model of the latter's character. Immediately on arrival, he fell like a thunderbolt, with threats and irresistible dash upon Canina, Hiericho, and Valona [three Byzantine sites], and seized them, and as he fought his way on, he would ever devastate and set fire to the surrounding districts. He was, in very truth, like the pungent smoke which precedes a fire, and a prelude of attack before the actual attack. These two, father and son, might rightly be termed "the caterpillar and the locust"; for whatever escaped Robert, that his son Bohemond took to him and devoured.

—from *Alexiad* by Anna Comnena, c. 1148, translated by Elizabeth A. Dawes

Saladin developed a reputation among Muslims as a firm but generous ruler. He demonstrated his great military leadership in the struggle against the Christian Crusaders.

in 1202. However, the Crusade leaders agreed to first take part in a plot to unseat the Byzantine emperor in Constantinople, for which they would be paid by a Byzantine prince who sought the throne. Although they were successful, the expected payment for their deed did not materialize, and so the Crusaders sacked the magnificent city in 1204, killing all who opposed them. They took everything that could be taken, including not only valuable works of religious art, rare books, and precious manuscripts, but even doors and tiles from roofs. Many of the stolen objects were destroyed or lost, though some can still be found in cities in Italy, France, and Germany. As a result of the Fourth Crusade, Constantinople and its population declined dramatically.

During this period, many minor Crusades also took place, but most of them were short-lived and never reached the Holy Land. In 1248 and again in 1270, Louis IX of France led two Crusades. The first, aimed at conquering Muslim Egypt, ran afoul of Baybars, a Turkish slave who was then commander of Egypt's army and later ruler of Egypt and Syria. The conflict ended in many Crusader deaths and the capture and ransom of Louis. The next Crusade ended in North Africa, where Louis and many of his troops died of disease.

HISTORICAL THINKING

1. **READING CHECK** What factors led Pope Urban II to call for the First Crusade?

2. **EVALUATE** Did the Crusades align with the teachings of Jesus? Explain your answer.

3. **DRAW CONCLUSIONS** How did the plight of the Byzantine Empire change from the First through the Fourth Crusade?

4. **INTERPRET MAPS** On which Crusade did the armies travel entirely by land?

BACKGROUND FOR THE TEACHER

T-O Maps Reflecting Jerusalem's profound significance for Christians, European mapmakers often placed it in the exact center of world maps that we now call T-O maps because they located Afro-Eurasia inside a circle (the "O") divided by a T that symbolized rivers and the Mediterranean Sea. Most often, Asia occupied the top half of the circle, with Africa on the lower right and Europe on the lower left. T-O maps were stylized; European geographers realized that Jerusalem did not lie at the midpoint of the world. They knew, too, that Earth was sphere-shaped. The two-dimensional T-O maps depicted only the Northern Hemisphere because geographers believed a torrid zone, too hot for human habitation, separated the Northern and Southern Hemispheres. As the Crusaders reported what they saw of the Islamic world and what they learned from Islamic geographers about the world beyond (including Africa), T-O maps showed more and more places.

The Ebstorf Map is a good example of a T-O map. It was made in the 1200s and it shows the world known to the cartographer, who combines knowledge of Afro-Eurasian geography with religious symbolism. Because the world is the body of Jesus, his head appears at the top of the map (the east, where Paradise is located), his feet at the bottom, and his hands on both sides. The walled city of Jerusalem, thought by Christians to be the center of the world, appears at his navel with several large buildings inside it. The map follows the standard T-O format of Asia at the top, Europe at the lower left, and Africa to the lower right.

TEACH

GUIDED DISCUSSION

3. **Evaluate** From the point of view of the Christians, what was the low point of the Crusades? *(Christians would likely say the Second Crusade was their lowest point. They were unable to recapture the state of Edessa and they failed to conquer the city of Damascus.)*

4. **Make Generalizations** What was unique about the Third Crusade? *(In the Third Crusade, King Richard the Lionheart negotiated a peace treaty with Saladin, the Muslim ruler. Crusaders considered the Third Crusade a success, though they did not recapture Jerusalem from the Muslims.)*

ANALYZE MAPS

Tell students to review the map of the Crusades. **ASK:** Do any of the Crusades follow similar paths? Explain. *(The First, Second, and Third Crusades all follow—in part—a southeasterly route from Vienna through the northern part of the Byzantine Empire.)* From the map, what is unique about the Third Crusade? *(It was made mostly by sea, and it started in western France and went around the coast of what are today Spain and Portugal.)*

ACTIVE OPTIONS

On Your Feet: Jigsaw Strategy Organize students into "expert" groups. Assign each group one of the four Crusades. Tell groups to research and discuss the major players and events of their assigned Crusade and summarize their findings. Then regroup students so that each new group has at least one member from each expert group. Students in the new groups take turns sharing the summaries from their expert groups.

> **NG Learning Framework: Investigate T-O Maps**
> **SKILL** Communication
> **KNOWLEDGE** New Frontiers

Direct students to work in small groups to investigate T-O maps and how cartographers depicted the world in the medieval era. Encourage students to find an example of a T-O map, such as the Ebstorf Map, and learn about its details, focusing on what parts of the world are represented on the map. They may consider how a T-O map differs from modern map formats. Invite groups to share their findings with the rest of the class.

HISTORICAL THINKING

ANSWERS

1. The Byzantine emperor had asked for help against the invading Seljuk Turks. Pope Urban II was concerned about the threat Muslims posed to the Holy Land and to the Byzantine Empire. Muslims had harassed pilgrims in the Holy Land and had damaged or destroyed holy places.

2. Most students will likely respond that the Crusades did not align with the teachings of Jesus, who promoted peace and showing love to all people.

3. One aim of the First Crusade was to defend the Byzantine Empire against Muslims, but in the Fourth Crusade, the Crusaders took part in overthrowing the Byzantine emperor and sacked Constantinople, the capital city of the Byzantine Empire.

4. The armies traveled entirely by land on the First Crusade.

CRITICAL VIEWING The soldiers are uniformly dressed and equipped and look like a professional army.

Crusades Within Europe

History is full of examples of groups whose members believed they were superior to others and committed brutal acts against those outside their group. The Crusaders were one example. You won't have to look hard to find many others.

ATTACKS ON NON-CHRISTIANS

The main goal of the major Crusades was to free Palestine from the Muslims, who had "invaded the land of the Christians," according to Pope Urban II. The restoration of Muslim power in Palestine and the threat of Turkish armies to the Byzantine Empire led the pope to feel justified in waging a holy war. However, that war led to attacks on people who had nothing to do with Palestine or the Byzantine Empire.

Many European Christians believed that Christianity was superior to other religions and, in fact, was the one true religion. Infused with the spirit of holy war, they sometimes attacked perceived enemies of Christianity in Europe. At times they acted on their own, and at other times in direct response to a pope's command.

Anti-Semitism, hostility toward and discrimination against Jews, was widespread in Europe during the Middle Ages. Many European Christians looked down on Jews, who were banned from certain occupations, denied citizenship, and prevented from marrying Christians. Jews often resided in **ghettos**, separate areas of cities in which they were required to live. Christians resented Jews who made their living as moneylenders, even though Jews were pushed into moneylending because they were restricted from working in many other occupations.

Before 1096, however, European Christians had largely tolerated Jews and respected their right to practice their own religion. That year, as preparations began for the First Crusade, a French preacher named Peter the Hermit started gathering an army of eager Christian soldiers. Consisting mainly of peasants and urban poor led by knights, this army, called the People's Crusade, set off for the Holy Land. While marching through the Rhine River region of Germany, the Crusaders attacked a number of towns with large Jewish communities. They carried out **pogroms**, or organized massacres, in which

they slaughtered several thousand Jews—men, women, and children. They threatened to kill others unless they converted to Christianity. Later Crusader armies carried out similar pogroms as they traveled through Europe.

In 1212, Pope Innocent III approved a Crusade against non-Christians in Spain. Historians refer to this Crusade and other military campaigns against the Muslims of Spain and Portugal as the **Reconquista** (ray-kohn-KEE-stah), a Spanish word meaning "reconquest." In 711, Arabs had invaded Spain from North Africa and established Muslim states there. Before 1200, Christian rulers had recovered isolated cities in the region, such as Toledo in Spain and Lisbon in Portugal. A decisive Crusader victory in 1212 began a string of conquests until only a single state, Granada, remained under Muslim control by 1249. Two centuries later, the Christian monarchs **Isabella and Ferdinand** of Spain completed the Reconquista. In 1492, after a 10-year, state-sponsored Crusade, they conquered Granada.

In the same year, the Spanish monarchs completed what they called the "purification" of Spain. They gave Jews the option of converting to Christianity. Jews who refused to convert were expelled. Likewise, numerous Muslims living in Spain were exiled, and many moved to North Africa. The anti-Semitism of the Spanish leaders was not unique in Europe. The English and French monarchies, for example, had earlier given in to religious prejudice and banished their Jewish populations.

PURIFYING THE CHURCH

During the time of the Crusades, various popes launched campaigns against enemies *within* the church as well as those outside. These campaigns aimed to rid the church of **heretics**, or church members who hold religious views contrary to official doctrine.

One way that popes chose to eliminate heretics was through an **Inquisition**, a judicial procedure that evolved into a special court for hearing charges against accused heretics. Unlike other church courts, which operated according to established legal norms, an Inquisition used anonymous informants, forced interrogations, and torture to identify heretics. Offenders who refused to renounce their beliefs could be sentenced to life imprisonment or death. The church established a series of Inquisitions beginning in 1231.

Both a Crusade and an Inquisition were used to extinguish the heretical Christian sect known as the Cathars, which arose in southern France in the 11th century. The Cathars considered the spiritual world good and the material world evil. They accused the Roman Catholic Church of becoming too materialistic and losing sight of its spiritual mission. The Cathars also questioned some of the sacraments and viewed Jesus as an angel and not as the Son of God, which the church taught. The Cathars flourished over the next century, attracting followers in France, Germany, and Italy and gaining the support of many nobles and clergy. One French subgroup of Cathars, the Albigensians, grew especially influential. They criticized the church as corrupt, arguing that its priests shirked their religious duties to pursue wealth and political power.

In 1209, Pope Innocent III called for a Crusade against the Cathars, and nobles from northern France undertook what became known as the Albigensian Crusade. Over the next 20 years, the Crusaders slaughtered large numbers of Cathars, including bishops and other clergy. In 1231, Pope Gregory IX directed an Inquisition against the Cathars. Many of those who would not renounce their beliefs were imprisoned, tortured, or burned to death. The church succeeded in putting an end to Catharism by the late 1300s.

LEGACY OF THE CRUSADES

The quest to conquer Palestine, the original goal of the Crusades, ended in failure in 1291, when Muslim forces captured the last of the coastal towns in the region held by Crusaders. Palestine, including Jerusalem, remained firmly in the hands of those the church considered infidels. Moreover, the Crusades had further weakened the Byzantine Empire and made it more vulnerable to aggressors.

CRITICAL VIEWING Ferdinand and Isabella of Spain completed the Reconquista by retaking Granada, the last territory held by Muslims in Spain. What details stand out in this wedding portrait of the Catholic monarchs?

The Fourth Crusade's assault on Constantinople, in which the Crusaders treated Eastern Orthodox Christians as if they were Muslim enemies, created a genuine and lasting schism between Roman Catholics and Eastern Orthodox adherents. Byzantines regained control of Constantinople in 1261, but it was no longer the beautiful and prosperous capital of a powerful Eastern empire.

The Crusades also solidified the hostility between Christians and Muslims. The brutally violent behavior of Roman Christians toward Muslims and Orthodox Christians would not quickly be forgotten, and neither would their behavior toward Jews.

The Crusades did give Europeans a closer connection with the eastern Mediterranean region. Some Crusaders found much to admire and copy in the Islamic world. Even the Europeans who stayed home were affected by imports from Muslim regions, such as eyeglasses, new medical ideas, and a more flexible number system. Other imports that originated in China, such as paper, also came to Europe via the Islamic world. The increased trade with the eastern Mediterranean region contributed to the growth of the merchant class in Europe.

HISTORICAL THINKING

1. **READING CHECK** What were the main effects of the Crusades?

2. **COMPARE AND CONTRAST** How were the Crusades and the Inquisitions similar? How were they different?

3. **SEQUENCE EVENTS** List the main events of the Reconquista in chronological order.

PLAN: 2-PAGE LESSON

OBJECTIVE

Understand the ways in which European Christians persecuted non-believers in the Middle Ages.

CRITICAL THINKING SKILLS FOR LESSON 3.3

- Compare and Contrast
- Sequence Events
- Analyze Cause and Effect
- Explain
- Analyze Visuals

HISTORICAL THINKING FOR CHAPTER 10

What should be the relationship between church and state?

The fervent belief of European Christians that their religion was superior to others led to hostile acts against non-believers. Lesson 3.3 identifies groups targeted by the Catholic Church during the Middle Ages.

Student eEdition online

Additional content for this lesson, including an image, is available online.

BACKGROUND FOR THE TEACHER

The Inquisition The Inquisition process typically began with an inquisitor arriving in a place and asking heretics to come forward and admit their guilt. Those who volunteered in this way were then ordered to stand trial at a tribunal. Tribunals were unfair to the accused in numerous ways: no lawyer was assigned to aid in the accused's defense, and the accused often had no idea what the charge was or who had charged them. Also, filing an appeal to the pope was prohibitively expensive. The guilty were exposed in public, and their punishment depended on whether or not they recanted. If they did not recant, they were burned at the stake. If they did recant, they were forced to make a pilgrimage, wear a yellow cross on their garments, and serve a prison sentence. There were two types of prisons. One had cells surrounding an open courtyard. The other was much stricter—heretics were chained up and kept in solitary confinement.

INTRODUCE & ENGAGE

CONNECT TO TODAY

On the board, write the term *anti-Semitism* in the center of a Word Web. Ask students to supply words and phrases that come to mind when they hear this word. As students offer their ideas, add them to the web. Explain that in this lesson they will learn how European Christians persecuted Jews beginning in 1096.

TEACH

GUIDED DISCUSSION

1. **Analyze Cause and Effect** How did the "purification" of Spain by Spanish monarchs impact Jews and Muslims living there? *(Jews were given a chance to convert to Christianity. If they did not, they were expelled from the country. Similarly, Muslims were exiled and forced to leave.)*

2. **Explain** Who were the Cathars and what brought about their demise? *(The Cathars were an 11th-century Christian sect that was deemed heretical due to their unorthodox beliefs. After a century or so of influence, a Crusade and an Inquisition brought them to a violent end in the late 1300s.)*

ANALYZE VISUALS

Ask students to study the photograph of the Alhambra (available in the Student eEdition). **ASK:** What details of the Alhambra appear to make it a good place for Muslims to take refuge from Christians? *(The Alhambra was a fortress, and it has many high, stone walls with few windows for withstanding attacks from outside forces. Its location appears to be ideal; it is nestled in a forested area and it is surrounded by mountains.)*

ACTIVE OPTIONS

On Your Feet: Roundtable Divide the class into groups of four. Tell each group to move desks together to form a table where they can all sit. Hand each group a sheet of paper containing the following question: What were ways that non-Christians were persecuted? The first student in each group should write an answer, read it aloud, and pass the paper clockwise to the next student. The paper should circulate around the table until students run out of answers.

NG Learning Framework: Examine Islamic Influence
ATTITUDE Curiosity
KNOWLEDGE Our Human Story

Organize students into small groups. Direct them to research one aspect of the Islamic world that was encountered and then adopted by Europeans as a result of the Crusades, such as medicine, paper, or a new numbering system. They should write a short analysis of the impact, including details to support their analysis. Have one member from each group share their findings with the class.

DIFFERENTIATE

ENGLISH LANGUAGE LEARNERS

Use Terms in Sentences Pair students at the **Beginning** level with those at the **Intermediate** or **Advanced** level. Direct partners to take turns creating sentences for the terms *ghetto* and *pogrom*. You may want to expand the exercise to other words from the lesson, such as *anti-Semitism*, *heretic*, and *Inquisition*. Invite pairs to share their sentences and discuss different ways to use each word.

PRE-AP

Analyze Historical Developments Tell students to gather information about anti-Semitism as a driving force throughout history. Ask them to choose one example and write a brief report on the ways Jews were targeted. Have them include quotes from persecuted Jews. Invite volunteers to read their reports to the class.

See the Chapter Planner for more strategies for differentiation.

HISTORICAL THINKING

ANSWERS

1. the deaths of many Christians, Jews, and Muslims; further weakened the Byzantine Empire; division between Roman Catholics and Eastern Orthodox adherents; broadened the worldview of Europeans, introduced them to Islamic ideas, and opened them up to international trade

2. All: directed against enemies of the Catholic Church; Crusades: warfare against Jews and Muslims; Inquisitions: trials and punishments against heretics within the church

3. The Reconquista begins (1212); one Muslim state, Granada, remains in Spain (1249); Granada falls to Isabella and Ferdinand (1492).

CRITICAL VIEWING Possible response: the king's unshaven face, the queen's casual hairstyle, the simple style of dress

Trade, Famine, and Plague

In the 1300s, Europeans did not know the cause of a deadly disease that was wiping out almost the entire population of some towns. Many people thought it was God's punishment for their sins. Doctors blamed it on bad air. The real cause wouldn't be discovered for hundreds of years.

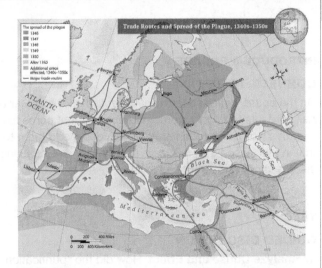

Trade Routes and Spread of the Plague, 1340s–1350s

The spread of the plague
- 1346
- 1347
- 1348
- 1349
- 1350
- After 1350
- Additional areas affected, 1340s–1350s
- Major trade routes

THE SPICE TRADE

By 1300, Europe was prosperous and peaceful. Nearly all the Crusaders had come home from the Holy Land, bringing back new information about the world beyond Europe. They also brought back a taste for spices.

Merchants from Italian city-states sailed to such ports as Acre in Palestine, Alexandria in Egypt, and Constantinople. There they loaded their ships with silks, gems, and other goods. But spices dominated their cargoes. Europeans were consuming more and more of such spices as pepper, cinnamon, and nutmeg. They used the spices to enhance the flavor of foods and to treat illnesses. The growth in trade would have an unexpected downside, however, as Christian and Muslim societies became exposed to a deadly disease.

THE GREAT FAMINE

Until the early 1300s, Europeans generally had sufficient food to eat. Improved agricultural techniques had steadily increased crop yields enough to feed the ever-growing population. Local shortages sometimes occurred, but they did not last long. But then disaster struck. Crop failures throughout northern Europe led to food shortages, resulting in the **Great Famine of 1315–1322.** A famine is an extreme shortage of food in a country or large geographic region.

In the period leading up to the famine, a small shift in climate brought cooler temperatures and more rain to Europe, especially in the north. In 1315 and 1316, spring rains kept peasants from plowing all of their fields. Much of the seed they planted rotted in the ground, and further heavy rains ruined the crops that did sprout.

A poor harvest two years in a row forced peasants to take drastic measures. They killed and ate their draft animals—the horses and oxen they used to pull their plows—and gobbled the seed they had saved for

planting in the spring. Still, many of them starved, and even nobles and clergy began dying from lack of food.

The weather improved in 1317, but the lack of seed grain and draft animals, along with the physical weakness of the malnourished peasants, meant that food stocks could not be restored quickly. Many people continued to die of starvation, and thousands of peasants fled their fields to beg in the cities. This and other changes accelerated the decline of the manorial system.

The Great Famine lasted seven years, during which more than 10 percent of the population of northern Europe died. The supply of food did not return to normal until around 1325.

CRITICAL VIEWING In this 16th-century painting *The Triumph of Death*, Flemish painter Pieter Bruegel portrays death as an army of skeletons. What aspects of life in the Middle Ages does this painting bring to mind?

THE BLACK DEATH

The Great Famine was followed by an even worse disaster. In 1347, a merchant ship sailed out of a Black Sea port carrying rats infected with plague, a highly contagious disease that had spread along the trade routes crossing central Asia. The ship transported its deadly cargo back to several Mediterranean ports, from which the disease spread inland to Arabia, North Africa, and Western Europe over the next four years.

The plague was carried not only by rats but also by the fleas that bit them. It came in two main forms, bubonic and pneumonic. A person bitten by an infected flea contracted the bubonic form, marked by egg-sized, painful boils that turned black. Droplets from that person's cough or sneeze could infect people who inhaled them. Those people got the pneumonic form.

The plague was called the **Black Death,** after the black boils. But it was mainly the pneumonic form that spread death throughout Europe from 1347 to 1351, reducing the population from around 75 million to 55 million.

Some scholars link the high death rate from the plague with the Great Famine, arguing that European peasants had not fully recovered physically from the famine when the plague hit. Thus, they were less able to combat the disease. A related theory holds that peasants had been weakened by their diet on the manor—mainly grains and such legumes as beans and peas. Large swaths of woodland, once habitat for game animals, had been turned into farmland. The loss of hunting land meant peasants no longer consumed enough protein from meat to keep them healthy.

HISTORICAL THINKING

1. **READING CHECK** What caused a large drop in the population of Europe in the first half of the 1300s?

2. **ANALYZE CAUSE AND EFFECT** What were the causes and effects of the Great Famine of 1315–1322?

3. **INTERPRET MAPS** What does the map in this lesson indicate about the relationship between trade routes and the spread of the plague across Western Europe?

PLAN: 2-PAGE LESSON

OBJECTIVE
Understand the causes and effects of the Great Famine and the Black Death.

CRITICAL THINKING SKILLS FOR LESSON 4.1
- Analyze Cause and Effect
- Interpret Maps
- Make Inferences
- Evaluate

HISTORICAL THINKING FOR CHAPTER 10
What should be the relationship between church and state?

Lesson 4.1 describes how Europe in the 1300s was struck with a terrible famine and a horrible plague. While some believed it was a punishment from God, historians claim the actual cause was much different.

Student eEdition online
Additional content for this lesson, including a video, is available online.

BACKGROUND FOR THE TEACHER
Use of Spices In the 12th and 13th centuries, Europeans used the new spices that came back from India and Southeast Asia to enhance flavor, not to preserve meat, as is often said. (Unpreserved meat spoiled and could not be salvaged; the wealthy ate freshly killed meat.) Surprisingly large quantities of spices went into a single meal; in 1319, the pope presided at a dinner for six guests in which he served lamb, pork, chicken, and partridges seasoned with one pound each of ginger and cloves. Spices were also used as medicine. The belief that spices had medicinal use depended on the medieval theory that the human body was composed of four humors: blood, yellow bile, black bile, and phlegm. Each humor was characterized with a quality of cold, hot, wet, or dry. If the humors became imbalanced, it was thought, a person would become sick. Therefore, administering a "hot" and "dry" spice like pepper could help remedy an imbalance of a cold humor.

INTRODUCE & ENGAGE

CONSIDER MODERN RESPONSE TO DISEASE

Discuss what happens today when there is a large-scale outbreak of a disease, like COVID-19. What governmental structures are in place to help manage such an event? How might the seriousness of the event depend on where in the world it occurs? What role does modern medicine play? Encourage students to consider how these questions might have been answered—or not answered—during the Middle Ages. Tell them that they will learn about the Black Death, a medieval plague that killed millions.

TEACH

GUIDED DISCUSSION

1. **Make Inferences** Why did the Great Famine kill more peasants than nobles and clergy? *(Nobles and clergy were a wealthier class and likely had more access to stored food. Also, peasants labored physically, which strained the body and lowered the immune system.)*

2. **Analyze Cause and Effect** What caused the Black Death, and what were its effects? *(A merchant ship from Genoa carried rats infected with plague. The rats—and fleas that bit them—spread a bubonic and pneumonic plague. Millions of Europeans died as a result.)*

EVALUATE

Direct students to watch the video (available in the Student eEdition). **ASK:** What do the three historical plagues all have in common? *(They shared similar causes.)* What is one positive effect of past plagues? *(Studying past plagues has helped medical researchers and microbiologists learn more about treating and managing infectious diseases. It has also caused public officials to make changes in urban planning and sanitation.)*

ACTIVE OPTIONS

On Your Feet: Just the Facts Organize students into two teams, one to focus on the Great Famine and the other on the Black Death. Direct teams to write a list of facts about their topic and to include three believable but false statements. Explain that teams will take turns stating their facts and false statements to each other. When a team member presents a false statement, members of the other team should call out, "Just the facts!" Teams get a point when they correctly identify a false statement, when the opposing team fails to identify one of their false statements, or when the opposing team incorrectly identifies a fact as false. Continue until teams run out of statements. The team with the most points wins.

NG Learning Framework: Develop a Multimedia Presentation
ATTITUDE Curiosity
SKILL Communication

Ask groups to research the Black Death. Have them research at least three different places that were affected and learn how each locality varied in terms of who was affected, how they were affected, and how the plague was treated. Instruct groups to develop and present a multimedia presentation that includes historical statistics, background information, first-person accounts, photos, and video segments.

DIFFERENTIATE

STRIVING READERS

Complete a T-Chart Assign two groups the topics of the Great Famine and the Black Death. Instruct each group to create a T-Chart listing the causes and effects of their event. As students read, tell them to complete the T-Chart with details. Encourage students to compare their completed T-Charts and revise them as necessary.

GIFTED & TALENTED

Write Diary Entries Instruct students to research either the Great Famine or the Black Death. Ask students to imagine that they are living through either event and write three or four diary entries describing their thoughts and feelings. They should include facts about how the event is being remedied, such as by describing the medical treatment for people suffering from the plague, and any actions being taken by their leaders. Invite students to share their diary entries.

See the Chapter Planner for more strategies for differentiation.

HISTORICAL THINKING

ANSWERS

1. the Great Famine and the spread of the plague

2. A small shift in climate resulted in poor harvests for two years, during which hungry peasants ate their seed grain and draft animals. When the weather improved, they were unable to plant and replenish their food stocks quickly. The famine also caused financial strains and led to the decline of the manorial system.

3. The plague spread along trade routes from central Asia to ports in the Mediterranean Sea and then inland across the continent in just a few years.

CRITICAL VIEWING the constant wars, the food shortages, the plague

War and Division

The Spanish-American philosopher George Santayana wrote, "Those who cannot remember the past are condemned to repeat it." In 1066, the nobles of England denied the English throne to William of Normandy. William crossed the English Channel and started a war. Nearly three centuries later, the nobles of France denied the French throne to Edward III of England. How do you think he reacted?

THE HUNDRED YEARS' WAR

The Great Famine and the plague created turmoil throughout Europe for much of the 14th century. Adding to the widespread hopelessness and fear, the continent was also plunged into a bloody conflict. The rulers of England and France engaged in a long series of battles between 1337 and 1453 that came to be known as the **Hundred Years' War.**

The immediate cause of the war was a political dispute. In 1328, the king of France died, and Edward III of England considered himself next in line to the French throne. But the nobles of France selected his cousin as king instead. In 1337, reasserting his claim, Edward sent an army across the English Channel to France, sparking a war that would continue for more than a century.

The roots of the war went far beyond a straightforward dispute over who should rule France, however. England and France had long been bitter rivals. By the 1330s, the two countries were engaged in many complicated territorial disputes. English kings had large landholdings in France but had trouble controlling them. French kings sought to extend their rule over all of France, but they faced challenges from French princes. France backed Scotland in its quest to gain independence from England. England aligned itself with Flanders, a province of France whose prosperous commercial centers sought the status of independent city-states.

France, with a population of some 15 million, was far richer than England, which had only about 4 million people. France's larger population and wealth allowed it to field bigger armies and hire foreign soldiers. The war took place entirely on French soil. Between battles,

English troops launched raids across the French countryside, capturing and plundering towns and burning crops.

The Hundred Years' War marked a shift in the technology of warfare. The era of heavily armored knights on horseback fighting with spears and swords was coming to an end. Knights had donned heavier armor to protect themselves, but they could not protect their horses. Moreover, the armor was so heavy that a knight who fell off his horse could not get up to fight an assailant on foot. Early in the war, the English won significant victories because they used a new type of longbow, 6 feet tall, that shot metal-tipped arrows farther and more accurately than the crossbows then in use.

By the final years of the war, both sides had turned to gunpowder, a Chinese invention that had spread to Europe in the 1200s. In the 1400s, it powered primitive cannons that shot stones, bolts, or lead bullets. Although difficult to aim accurately, these new weapons could destroy the walls surrounding a castle or town under siege and make it possible to overtake the site. The French army used gunpowder weapons in conjunction with crossbows to finally defeat the English in 1453. They expelled English forces from all of France except the northern port of Calais, located just across the English Channel.

The Hundred Years' War significantly changed the political structure of France and England. At the beginning of the war, the two kingdoms consisted of patchworks of territory ruled by a king who shared power with his nobles. By the end of the war, the two

countries had become centralized monarchies governed by kings with considerably more power.

While the English and French kings **consolidated**, or unified and strengthened, their power, they also consulted with advisory groups in their countries, particularly on the subject of taxes. As you have read, this advisory group was called Parliament in England and included nobles, clergy, and later other subjects of the king. The French equivalent was called the Estates-General. The newly centralized monarchies in France and England proved effective at governing, and the existence of representative assemblies helped kings gain the allegiance of their subjects. Those ruled by these monarchies began to feel a sense of national identity.

THE GREAT SCHISM OF 1378

As the Hundred Years' War wore on, a crisis of authority erupted in the Roman Catholic Church. In 1378, a political rivalry resulted in the election of more than one pope, causing a split within the church.

The rivalry occurred between French and Italian leaders in the church. The French bishop who became Pope Clement V in 1305 decided not to reside in Rome, a city beset by political turmoil. In 1309, at the urging of the French king, he moved the papacy to Avignon, a city within a region of southern France controlled by the papacy. The Avignon papacy continued, through six additional French popes, until 1377. During this time, the papacy functioned fairly normally. The popes promoted missionary work and sought an end to the Hundred Years' War. But many Catholics believed the French kings controlled the Avignon popes and that greed had corrupted the papacy.

In 1377, a newly elected French pope returned the papacy to Rome, but he died the next year. Pressured by the people of Rome, the College of Cardinals—the senior clergy who elect the pope—chose an Italian as his replacement. But some of the French cardinals, opposed to the new pope, elected their own pope. This French "antipope" took up residence in Avignon. This period of two popes in the Roman Catholic Church became known as the **Great Schism of 1378.**

CRITICAL VIEWING The Battle of Poitiers, which took place in France in 1356, was an early victory for the English in the Hundred Years' War. In this painting of the battle, John II of France surrenders to Edward, Prince of Wales, who was called the Black Prince. What symbol, long associated with the French crown, appears on the cloak of the French king?

In the years that followed, popes and antipopes declared each other—and all opposing cardinals, bishops, and priests—to be heretics. The Great Schism not only divided the church leadership in two, it also split the population and countries of Europe nearly evenly as well.

In 1409, realizing that the schism was a disaster for the church, the opposing groups of cardinals met to find a solution. But they only made matters worse by electing yet another pope. Finally, in 1417, at the Council of Constance, all the cardinals agreed on a way to solve the problem they had created. They pushed aside all three popes and elected a new one, an Italian acceptable to all, who would reside in Rome.

HISTORICAL THINKING

1. **READING CHECK** What event started the Hundred Years' War?

2. **ANALYZE CAUSE AND EFFECT** What were some political effects of the Hundred Years' War?

3. **SEQUENCE EVENTS** How did the Great Schism of 1378 start, and how did it end?

Europe's Medieval Era **299**

PLAN: 2-PAGE LESSON

OBJECTIVE

Understand the causes and effects of the Hundred Years' War and the Great Schism of 1378.

CRITICAL THINKING SKILLS FOR LESSON 4.2

- Analyze Cause and Effect
- Sequence
- Make Connections
- Identify Supporting Details
- Integrate Visuals

HISTORICAL THINKING FOR CHAPTER 10

What should be the relationship between church and state?

The Roman Catholic Church experienced internal political tensions in the late 1300s as French and Italian leaders vied for power. Lesson 4.2 explains this division and its effects on Catholics in Europe.

Student eEdition online

Additional content for this lesson, including an image, is available online.

BACKGROUND FOR THE TEACHER

Gunpowder Before gunpowder was invented, the effectiveness of most weapons was dependent on the physical strength of whomever wielded them. Gunpowder changed that. Gunpowder was invented by the Chinese in the ninth century. Their black powder was an alchemical mixture of potassium nitrate (also called saltpeter), charcoal, and sulfur. The gas that was produced by igniting it could be harnessed to launch a projectile, such as an arrow or a bullet, at great speed and force. The Chinese used gunpowder in rockets, cannons, and perhaps bombs, but historians are not certain of the latter. Europeans readily applied gunpowder to their weaponry, having attained it either in the 13th century from Mongols or via the Islamic world around 1300. The earliest guns powered by gunpowder appeared around this time, too. Chinese guns were made of metal, and Arabic guns were made of tubes of metal-reinforced bamboo. European guns appeared in the 1300s as well and were used during the Hundred Years' War.

INTRODUCE & ENGAGE

REVIEW AND PREVIEW

Tell students to review with a classmate the section of Lesson 1.3 about the Schism of 1054. Explain to students that in this lesson they will learn about another schism, or split, in the Catholic Church that took place in 1378, this time between French and Italian leaders. Students should think about the ways in which this lesson's schism might be similar to and different from the Schism of 1054. Prompt them to write down three things they would like to know about the Great Schism of 1378. If the lesson does not answer their questions, urge them to conduct online research.

TEACH

GUIDED DISCUSSION

1. **Make Connections** How did warfare change during the Hundred Years' War? *(the introduction of gunpowder; a new type of longbow that was more accurate and could go farther than crossbows; an end to the era of heavily armored knights on horseback)*

2. **Identify Supporting Details** How did the city of Avignon figure in the Great Schism of 1378? *(Pope Clement V moved the papacy to Avignon in 1309. A subsequent French pope moved the papacy back to Rome; French bishops elected and installed their own antipope at Avignon.)*

INTEGRATE VISUALS

Ask students to study the painting of the Battle of Poitiers and think about what they learned in the lesson. **ASK:** What details in the painting give clues that the battle it depicts must have occurred early in the war? *(There are knights holding spears mounted on horseback. Armored knights disappeared from warfare by the end of the Hundred Years' War. Also, one solider appears to be using a 6-foot longbow, which the English used early in the war.)*

ACTIVE OPTIONS

On Your Feet: Fishbowl Divide the class in half, with one half sitting in a circle facing inward and the other half sitting in a larger circle around them. Tell students in the inside circle to discuss the following question: Why did the French and the English develop a sense of national identity as a result of the Hundred Years' War? Ask students in the outside circle to listen for new information. Then tell students to reverse positions. Call on volunteers to name key points from their discussion.

| NG Learning Framework: Create a Storyboard
| SKILL Communication
| KNOWLEDGE Our Human Story

Direct students to conduct online research to learn more about the Hundred Years' War in order to create a storyboard that illustrates the war's main events. Each illustration should include a caption or short paragraph explaining what the scene depicts. Invite students to display the storyboards in the classroom and to narrate their work.

DIFFERENTIATE

STRIVING READERS

Use a Main Idea Cluster Direct pairs to use a Main Idea Cluster to check their understanding of each section in the lesson. First tell students to take turns reading the paragraphs in a section of the lesson. Then have them record the main idea of the section and four details that support the main idea. Instruct pairs to trade and compare clusters.

PRE-AP

Write a Biographical Sketch Instruct students to choose one of the French popes who held office in the 1300s (or the French antipope installed at Avignon in 1377) as the subject of a biographical sketch. Have them conduct research to find details about the pope, focusing on their pope's position in the midst of the tensions between French and Italian Catholics that were felt during that time. Tell students to look for primary sources, like writings by their pope or his contemporaries, that could be quoted. Invite students to read their sketches to the class.

See the Chapter Planner for more strategies for differentiation.

HISTORICAL THINKING

ANSWERS

1. The nobles of France denied the French throne to Edward III of England; he invaded France to claim the throne.

2. France and England became centralized monarchies with representative assemblies; people in the two countries developed a sense of national identity.

3. started in 1378 when the College of Cardinals elected an Italian as pope and a group of French cardinals decided to elect a French pope, who moved to Avignon; ended in 1417 when the cardinals elected an Italian pope who was acceptable to all

CRITICAL VIEWING the fleur-de-lis

4.3 Material Culture

PICTURING JOAN

Far into the Hundred Years' War, a teenage peasant named Joan of Arc claimed to hear divine voices calling upon her to save France from being taken over by the English. She marshalled French troops to an important victory against the English at the city of Orléans in 1429 and boosted the morale of the French. Captured a year later, she was imprisoned by the English, tried for heresy, and then burned alive in 1431. While Joan of Arc—or Jeanne d'Arc in French— was a real person, the portrayals of her life approach mythic proportions. No portrait of Joan of Arc from her lifetime has survived. But her image has been represented in myriad ways over the centuries to serve a variety of political, religious, and commercial purposes.

Symbol of France After her death, Joan of Arc became a patriotic symbol of France and the subject of many public sculptures over the following centuries. In the late 1800s, the French sculptor Paul Dubois created this equestrian statue of Joan of Arc, portraying her as a triumphant warrior. The statue stands in front of the Church of St. Augustine in Paris, and copies of it appear in other cities in France as well as in Washington, D.C.

Jeanne D'Arc During Her Lifetime This sketch is the only existing image of Joan of Arc made during her lifetime. A clerk drew it in the margins of the Paris Parliament's register after receiving news of the French victory at Orléans. The clerk depicted Joan with flowing hair and dressed in a long skirt. In fact, Joan wore men's clothing and cut her hair short for battle.

The Struggle Over Gender This miniature from the 15th century depicting Joan in a soldier's armor contrasts with images of her in women's clothing with long, flowing hair. Artists had to decide: should Joan be portrayed as a woman or as a warrior? In the 1400s, it was considered not only shocking but also heresy for a woman to wear men's clothing.

Political Symbol French political parties on both the right and the left have used Joan of Arc as a symbol to espouse their views.

This 19th-century statue of Joan of Arc by the French sculptor Prosper d'Épinay stands in the Notre-Dame de Reims Cathedral in France. After the French victory at Orléans in 1429, Joan attended the coronation of Charles VII in the Reims Cathedral. The sculpture depicts Joan wearing a smock covered with fleurs-de-lis, an emblem of the French monarchy, over her armor. A replica of her banner appears behind her.

This 1926 statue of Joan stands in Rouen, France, where Joan was burned at the stake. The statue was created by the French sculptor Maxime Réal del Sarte, who was active in Action Française, a right-wing nationalist organization that promoted the restoration of the monarchy and Roman Catholicism as the state religion in France in the early 1900s. The organization used Joan as its symbol.

PLAN: 4-PAGE LESSON

OBJECTIVE

Describe the many different ways Joan of Arc has been portrayed over the centuries.

CRITICAL THINKING SKILLS FOR LESSON 4.3

- Analyze Visuals
- Make Connections
- Compare and Contrast
- Make Inferences
- Explain
- Identify Problems and Solutions
- Analyze Points of View
- Form and Support Opinions

HISTORICAL THINKING FOR CHAPTER 10

What should be the relationship between church and state?

Joan of Arc claimed to hear divine voices calling her to help save France. She saw the relationship between church and state as intertwined. Lesson 4.3 discusses the variety of ways Joan of Arc has been portrayed since 1429, when she led French troops to victory.

BACKGROUND FOR THE TEACHER

Early History of Joan of Arc Joan of Arc was born around 1412 in the village of Domrémy in northeastern France. She was the daughter of a tenant farmer and was raised to be a pious Christian. Her village was not far from the border of the lands controlled by the English. France and England were at war her entire life. She was only 13 when she claimed to begin hearing divine voices and seeing visions directing her to help Charles of Valois, the son of Charles VI, become the rightful king of France. She finally met with Charles when she was 17. Charles had her examined thoroughly by theologians to verify her claims. Only after their approval did he agree to let her join the French forces despite the fact that she was a woman. After several French victories, Joan attended the coronation of Charles VII in the cathedral of Reims in July 1429.

History Notebook

Encourage students to complete the Material Culture page for Chapter 10 in their History Notebooks as they read.

INTRODUCE & ENGAGE

PREVIEW WITH VISUALS

Direct students' attention to the paintings and statues presented in the lesson. Write *Joan of Arc* at the center of a Concept Cluster and ask volunteers to list Joan's characteristics based on their observation of the paintings and statues. Arrange the characteristics into groups on the cluster. At the end of the lesson, revisit the Concept Cluster and add or remove characteristics based on what students learned.

TEACH

GUIDED DISCUSSION

1. **Explain** Why should the only sketch of Joan of Arc made during her lifetime be considered unreliable? *(A clerk who had never seen Joan drew the sketch as he imagined her.)*

2. **Identify Problems and Solutions** What problem did artists face as they portrayed Joan of Arc? *(It was heresy for a woman to wear men's clothing in the 1400s; therefore, artists had to decide whether to portray Joan in the men's armor that she actually wore or to portray her as a woman, which would be more acceptable to the public.)*

MATERIAL CULTURE

Have students consider the following statement: Joan of Arc is a national hero and symbol of France. **ASK:** How do the information and visuals presented in this lesson support this statement? *(Possible response: These visuals show a young woman devoted to her country and her faith who was willing to die an agonizing death for her beliefs. Though conflicts are different, and the role of religion in society is constantly changing, the themes of bravery and sacrifice apply to all eras.)*

DIFFERENTIATE

ENGLISH LANGUAGE LEARNERS

Build Vocabulary Help students at **All Proficiencies** learn unfamiliar words by introducing synonyms they might know. Display difficult words paired with more familiar words, as with these examples from the lesson:

divine / saintly
marshalled / organized
morale / confidence
imprisoned / jailed
mythic / exaggerated
myriad / countless

Tell students that when they encounter a difficult word, they should try to replace it with a word they may be familiar with. Guide students to use a thesaurus to practice looking up and substituting words, encouraging them to look among the synonyms to find one that makes sense in context.

PRE-AP

Explore Pop Culture Depictions Have students find examples of film depictions of Joan of Arc. They can read about the production of each film and its synopsis and find still images or video clips online. Students can prepare for a panel discussion, telling what messages the films have about the historical figure as well as how they reflect the periods in which they were filmed.

See the Chapter Planner for more strategies for differentiation.

BACKGROUND FOR THE TEACHER

Witch or Saint? During a battle on May 23, 1430, Joan was thrown from her horse and captured by her enemies. People started questioning her claims, wondering how someone truly sent by God could have been captured so soon. The English wanted to discredit her and the coronation of Charles VII. They claimed the voices she heard came not from God, but from the devil. Although the charges against her were religious, she was kept in a military prison surrounded by men rather than a church prison where she would have been guarded by nuns. Transcripts of her interrogations by church officials still exist. Threatened with death, she briefly recanted the voices, but within four days claimed, "God was telling me, through them, that I had endangered my soul by recanting, and that I had condemned myself for having tried to save my life. . . . Everything I have recanted, I have done so only because of the fear of the fire. If it does not please God to recant, then I will not do so." Two days later she was burned at the stake.

TEACH

GUIDED DISCUSSION

3. **Analyze Points of View** How was the message of the two posters made in the early 1900s different from the other portrayals of Joan of Arc? *(The two posters were directed at American and British women to inspire them to support war efforts and to fight for the right to vote, unlike the other portrayals that were directed to the French people to remember their history.)*

4. **Form and Support Opinions** Choose one of the portrayals and describe how in your opinion it could be used to inspire people today. *(Answers will vary. Possible response: The painting of* The Maid *could be used to discuss the emotions people feel when faced with a difficult decision.)*

ANALYZE VISUALS

Share the Background for the Teacher information on Joan of Arc with students, pointing out that she was just about their age when these historical events happened to her. Then have students examine the paintings and statues in the lesson. **ASK:** Which is the only portrayal of Joan before she started fighting for France? *(The Maid)* How is this painting different from the other portrayals? *(Possible responses: This is the only one that depicts the divine voices, her home, her emotions before she was committed to her task.)* Why might the painter have wanted to show this side of Joan of Arc? *(Possible response: To show she had feelings like most people.)*

ACTIVE OPTION

On Your Feet: Jigsaw Strategy Group students evenly into five expert groups. Then assign each of the groups one of the following views of Joan of Arc to research in depth: historical figure, patriotic symbol of France, martyred saint, witch/heretic, and role model for women. When they finish their research, regroup the students so that each new group has at least one member from each expert group. The experts should then report on their view of Joan of Arc, so that every student learns more about each view.

HISTORICAL THINKING

ANSWERS

1. Joan of Arc stands out as a young woman who defied gender and age expectations and showed tremendous courage in an attempt to maintain France's independence as a nation during the Hundred Years' War. Though at a disadvantage due to her young age and her gender, she was able to convince the future French king to allow her to lead an army in battle, and she emerged victorious. Her unusual actions earned her widespread respect and made her an enduring national hero and symbol.

2. Possible response: In the painting of Joan of Arc being interrogated in prison, Joan appears as a common young peasant girl who is calm and focused on her faith. She's looking up to heaven and her hands are folded. In the World War I poster, Joan appears as an attractive, modern young woman. She is wearing makeup and her hair is styled. However, she's dressed in armor and carrying a sword and looking straight forward, which makes her appear focused on carrying out her task. Both the painting and the poster portray Joan as an attractive young woman, but the poster modernizes her and focuses on her warrior status rather than her holiness.

3. The English might have felt particularly threatened by Joan of Arc because she claimed to be guided by God, and she was building up the morale of the French and encouraging them to fight with the belief that God was on their side.

VOCABULARY

Use each of the following vocabulary words in a sentence that shows an understanding of the term's meaning.

1. serf
2. vassal
3. commerce
4. capital
5. clergy
6. vernacular
7. holy war
8. pogrom

READING STRATEGY
IDENTIFY PROBLEMS AND SOLUTIONS

Identifying problems faced by people of the past and noting their solutions can help you understand the way history unfolded. Complete the Problem-and-Solution Chart to analyze the way European peasants solved the problem of producing more food on agricultural land during the Middle Ages.

Problem: How to increase agricultural yield

Solution 1   Solution 2   Solution 3

Result

9. How did solutions to the problem of increasing agricultural yield impact Europe's population in the years between 1000 and 1340?

MAIN IDEAS

Answer the following questions. Support your answers with evidence from the chapter.

10. How did Christianity spread through Europe? LESSON 1.1

11. How did William of Normandy gain the title "Conqueror"? LESSON 1.3

12. What economic changes did the Commercial Revolution bring to Europe? LESSON 2.1

13. Why were Scholastics considered unifiers? LESSON 2.2

14. How did reformers try to change the Roman Catholic Church in the 1000s? LESSON 3.1

15. What was the main goal of the First Crusade? LESSON 3.2

16. How did the Great Famine of 1315–1322 accelerate the decline of the manorial system? LESSON 4.1

17. How was the government of England similar to that of France after the Hundred Years' War? LESSON 4.2

HISTORICAL THINKING

Answer the following questions. Support your answers with evidence from the chapter.

18. MAKE INFERENCES Why was Hildegaard of Bingen an unusual woman for her time?

19. ANALYZE CAUSE AND EFFECT What were the results of increased participation in government by the nobles of England during the medieval era?

20. MAKE GENERALIZATIONS How did monasteries and convents contribute to European culture and society during the Middle Ages?

21. DRAW CONCLUSIONS How did the Roman Catholic Church both unify and divide people during the Middle Ages?

22. SEQUENCE EVENTS Write the following events in chronological order, from earliest to latest: the First Crusade; the writing of the Magna Carta; Charlemagne's alliance with the pope; the end of the Hundred Years' War; the Great Famine.

23. FORM AND SUPPORT OPINIONS What do you consider the best and worst aspects of the life of a serf during the Middle Ages?

INTERPRET VISUALS

Study the graph of Europe's population between 1000 and 1450. Then answer the questions that follow.

24. Describe the population trends that occurred in Europe between 1000 and 1450.

25. What events contributed to the population decline that occurred in Europe after 1340?

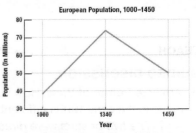

European Population, 1000–1450

Source: Josiah C. Russell, "Population in Europe" in Carlo M. Cipolla, ed., The Fontana Economic History of Europe, Vol. I: The Middle Ages (Glasgow: Collins/Fontana, 1972) 25–71

ANALYZE SOURCES

During the time of the Black Death, many Europeans blamed Jews for causing the plague. In 1349, a German member of the clergy wrote an account of pogroms against Jews throughout Germany. This excerpt from his account focuses on one German town. Read the excerpt and answer the questions that follow.

The persecution of the Jews began in November 1348, and the first outbreak in Germany was at Sölden, where all the Jews were burnt on the strength of a rumor that they had poisoned wells and rivers, as was afterwards confirmed by their own confessions and also by the confessions of Christians whom they had corrupted and who had been induced by the Jews to carry out the deed. And some of the Jews who were newly baptized said the same. Some of these remained in the faith but some others relapsed, and when these were placed upon the wheel [a type of torture] they confessed that they themselves sprinkled poison or poisoned rivers.

—from "The Persecution of the Jews," in The Black Death, translated and edited by Rosemary Horrox, 1994

26. According to this excerpt, what did the people of Sölden believe was causing people to die from the plague, or the Black Death?

27. On what evidence was the guilt of the Jews based? How do you think this evidence was obtained?

CONNECT TO YOUR LIFE

28. INFORMATIVE This chapter describes the gradual transfer of law-making power from the king to a representative body in England between the 1200s and the 1400s. Review this information and identify two principles established during the period that are reflected in current laws in the United States. Write a short essay explaining how these principles continue to protect the rights of people today.

TIPS

• Reread the section on the Magna Carta and Parliament and note the changes to English law that occurred between 1215 and 1430.

• Select two changes or principles that you consider important and locate a section of your state constitution or the U.S. Constitution that expresses the same idea or furthers the idea.

• Write a topic sentence describing the connection between English law of hundreds of years ago and certain legal protections you enjoy today.

• Using evidence from the text or your research, support your topic sentence with relevant facts or examples.

VOCABULARY ANSWERS

Answers will vary. Possible sentences are below.

1. The **serfs** who labored on the manor did not own the land they farmed, but they were bound to it.

2. A **vassal**, if called upon, was expected to support his lord militarily.

3. **Commerce** increased during the Middle Ages as more and more people were able to use money to buy goods.

4. Medieval merchants formed business relationships with investors to gain **capital** for their businesses.

5. Christian priests, monks, and other members of the **clergy** promoted education during the Middle Ages.

6. Some medieval writers, such as Chaucer, wrote in the **vernacular** instead of Latin, which allowed more people to read their work.

7. The pope declared a **holy war** aimed at defending Christian sites in the Holy Land.

8. The violent attack on Jews in a German town was the first of several **pogroms** carried out by Crusaders.

READING STRATEGY ANSWERS

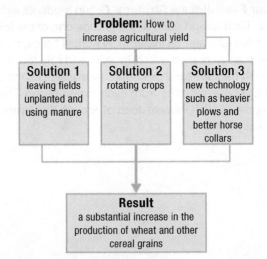

Problem: How to increase agricultural yield

Solution 1 leaving fields unplanted and using manure

Solution 2 rotating crops

Solution 3 new technology such as heavier plows and better horse collars

Result a substantial increase in the production of wheat and other cereal grains

9. In the years between 1000 and 1340, Europe's population nearly doubled, to 75 million.

MAIN IDEAS ANSWERS

10. European rulers, beginning with Clovis, converted to Christianity, and many of their people did too.

11. William sailed with an army from Normandy to England, and he defeated King Harold and became king of England, thus earning the title "Conqueror."

12. The Commercial Revolution resulted in the use of money to buy goods; the growth of commerce; profits for farmers, artisans, and merchants; the rise of guilds and banks; partnerships between merchants and investors; and expansion of international trade.

13. Scholastics searched for a way to unify the study of religion with the study of more worldly subjects, such as science.

14. Reformers tried to make the doctrines and practices of the church more uniform, get monks to follow the example of Jesus in the way they lived, and end the buying and selling of church offices.

15. The main goal of the First Crusade was to gain control of the Holy Land from Muslims.

16. The Great Famine of 1315–1322 caused many peasants to leave the manors to beg in the cities, and it caused financial strains that led lords to free the serfs from the land.

17. Both England and France had centralized monarchies governed by powerful kings who consulted with advisory groups in their countries.

HISTORICAL THINKING ANSWERS

18. Hildegaard of Bingen was an unusual woman for her time because she wrote about the equality of men and women, and she traveled to preach to large groups.

19. English nobles forced King John to put his seal on the Magna Carta, which defined the king's obligations to them and outlined their rights. It limited the king's authority and established that the law applied to everyone. It also gave the nobles some control over taxes.

20. Monasteries and convents served as centers of education. Monks and nuns cared for the poor and the sick and sent out missionaries to spread Christianity. Some of them marketed their surplus crops and craft goods.

21. It unified most of the people under one religion, but it fostered hostility toward those who held differing beliefs.

22. Sequence of medieval events, from earliest to latest: Charlemagne's alliance with the pope; the First Crusade; the writing of the Magna Carta; the Great Famine; the end of the Hundred Years' War

23. Sample response: I think the best aspect of the life of a serf in the Middle Ages was that it was simple: you lived on a small manor and knew everyone there, and you raised or made most things you needed. I think the worst aspect of life was the lack of choice. You were bound to the land and could not move or do something different with your life.

INTERPRET VISUALS ANSWERS

24. The population rose until about 1340 and then dropped.

25. The Great Famine, the Black Death, and the Hundred Years' War contributed to the population decline in Europe after 1340.

ANALYZE SOURCES ANSWERS

26. The people of Sölden believed that people were dying from the Black Death because Jews had poisoned their drinking water.

27. The evidence consisted of a rumor backed up by confessions. The confessions were probably obtained by torturing people.

CONNECT TO YOUR LIFE ANSWER

28. Essays will vary but should include a clear topic sentence supported with relevant facts and examples.

UNIT 4

STRATEGY ❶

Set a Purpose for Reading

Before beginning a lesson, help students set a purpose for reading by turning the Main Idea statement into a question. Tell students to answer the question in writing after they read.

Below are sample questions for Lessons 1.1 and 1.2.

1.1 What led China to a time of prosperity and growth during the Song dynasty?

1.2 What were the great achievements in publishing, agriculture, education, and metalworking in Song China?

Use with All Lessons

STRATEGY ❷

Clarify Multiple Meaning Words

To help improve striving readers' text comprehension, point out words that likely have more familiar meanings. List these words and definitions on the board:

- *commercial:* an advertisement broadcast on TV; relating to commerce, or business
- *staple:* to attach papers with a metal loop; the sustaining or principal element
- *boom:* loud noise; a rapid expansion
- *characters:* people in a story; letters or graphic symbols used in writing

Tell students to identify which meaning fits the context of the sentence in which the word is used.

Use with All Lessons

STRATEGY ❸

Pose and Answer Questions

Arrange students in pairs and ask them to reread the lesson together. Instruct them to pause after each paragraph and ask each other *who, what, where, when,* and *why* questions about what they have just read. Suggest students use a 5Ws Chart to help organize their questions and answers. Encourage partners to assist each other as needed.

Use with All Lessons

STRATEGY ❶

Echo Main Ideas

Point out that the Main Idea statements all relate to important aspects of the East Asia cultures of China, Korea, Vietnam, and Japan. Pair students with a proficient reader. Ask the proficient reader to read the Main Idea statement at the beginning of a lesson aloud. Tell the less proficient partner to "echo" the statement and then restate it in his or her own words. Encourage partners to agree on what they anticipate the lesson to be about. Have them continue to read together and verify the main ideas as they read.

Use with All Lessons

STRATEGY ❷

Use Supported Reading

Ask students to read the chapter aloud lesson by lesson. Instruct them to stop at the end of each lesson and use these sentence frames to monitor their comprehension of the text:

- This lesson is mostly about _____.
- Other topics in this lesson are _____ and _____.
- One question I have is _____.
- One of the vocabulary words is _____, and it means _____.
- One word I don't recognize is _____.

Use with All Lessons

ENGLISH LANGUAGE LEARNERS

STRATEGY 1
Modify Vocabulary Lists

Limit the number of vocabulary words, terms, and names **Beginning** level students will be required to master. Direct students to write each word from your modified list on a colored sticky note and put it on the page next to where the word appears in context.

Use with All Lessons

STRATEGY 2
Create a Definition Chart

Place students in mixed pairs, such as students at the **Beginning** level with those at the **Advanced** level. Tell pairs to work together to identify at least three words from the lesson that they have had difficulty understanding. Instruct students to create a Definition Chart for those words. Then tell pairs to trade their chart with another pair and ask and answer questions about the information.

Use with All Lessons

STRATEGY 3
Summarize Main Ideas

After reading a lesson, ask students at **All Proficiencies** to write a sentence summarizing its main idea. Arrange students in pairs and ask them to dictate their sentences to each other. Then tell partners to work together to check the sentences for spelling and accuracy.

Use with All Lessons *You may wish to pair students at the **Beginning** level with those at the **Advanced** level and students at the **Intermediate** level with one another.*

GIFTED & TALENTED

STRATEGY 1
Design an Infographic

Direct students to create an infographic that presents information about a specific achievement or influence from one of the East Asia cultures in the chapter, such as Bi Sheng's printing process, iron production, paper currency, or Japanese gardens. Guide them to conduct research about their chosen topic and collect visual information before designing their infographic. Invite students to share their infographics with the class.

Use with All Lessons

STRATEGY 2
Debate Historical Views

Direct students to choose either Bi Sheng or Johannes Gutenberg to research and develop an argument about who deserves more credit for inventing movable type and the printing process that greatly increased the amount of printed materials and improved education. Invite students to present their debate in front of the class.

Use with Lesson 1.2

PRE-AP

STRATEGY 1
Explore East Asia Religious Influences

Challenge students to research the teachings of Neo-Confucianism or the form of Buddhism known as Zen Buddhism practiced by the samurai of Japan. Have them write a report on how this form of religion helped people in East Asia during the time period profiled in the chapter, but also how it can help people today through its emphasis on self-improvement. Encourage students to read their reports aloud in class.

Use with Lessons 1.2 and 2.2

STRATEGY 2
Extend Knowledge

Invite students to conduct online research to learn more about the influence of tea on the East Asia cultures profiled in the chapter, but also eventually on European countries, such as Britain. Prompt them to describe one of the tea ceremonies in detail or to research how boiling water for tea saved the lives of people in areas where the water was unsafe to drink. Invite students to present their findings in an oral report to the class or in a digital report posted on a class website or blog.

Use with Lessons 1.1 and 2.3

CHAPTER
11 East Asia and
Chinese Influences
938–1392

HISTORICAL THINKING How does one culture adopt
influences from other cultures and adapt them to its own?

SECTION 1 The Song Dynasty
SECTION 2 Korea, Vietnam, and Japan

The Matsumoto Castle in Nagano is the oldest existing castle in
Japan. Built in the late 1500s of wood and stone and set against
the Japanese Alps, the feudal castle is noted for its many unique
architectural elements, including a pavilion for viewing the
moon. What are some other distinctive features of the castle?

306 CHAPTER 11

East Asia and Chinese Influences 307

INTRODUCE THE PHOTOGRAPH

MATSUMOTO CASTLE

Have students study the photograph of Matsumoto
Castle that appears at the beginning of the chapter. Direct
them to focus on the dark walls, and point out the small
openings. **ASK:** For what do you think these openings
were used? *(Possible response: The openings might
have been used for ventilation or defense.)* Explain that
the openings in the walls were once used by archers
and gunmen for defense of the castle. They also allowed
defenders to drop stones on those who approached.
Next, point out the dark wainscoting below the roof line.
Tell students that the dark walls earned the castle the
nickname "Crow Castle," because crows are also dark in
color.

SHARE BACKGROUND

The current structure of Matsumoto Castle was built
beginning in 1592, during an era in Japan known as the
Warring States period. Defense was particularly important
during this period, because warfare was frequent. Many
of the original elements of the castle remain today,
including its steep wooden stairs and low ceilings. From
the windows, one can see the castle's moat below, the
Japanese Alps in the distance, and the city of Matsumoto.

The city of Matsumoto is still known for its silk industry,
which began during the Japanese feudal period. Today,
it draws tourists for skiing and to bathe in its hot springs.
Matsumoto Castle is one of two castles in the area, both
of which were originally built for provincial governors but
were then passed on to daimyo during the feudal period.

CRITICAL VIEWING Answers will vary. Possible
response: Distinctive features include the curving
rooflines, the dark walls, and the bright modern lighting
that accentuates the roof lines.

HISTORICAL THINKING QUESTION
How does one culture adopt influences from other cultures and adapt them to its own?

On Your Feet: Team Word Webbing Arrange the class into teams of four and provide each with a large sheet of paper. Give each team member a different colored marker and ask them to record ideas of cultural elements that might pass from one culture to another. Encourage students to build on their teammates' entries as they rotate the paper from one member to the next. Then call on volunteers from each group to make statements about what kinds of influences one culture might have on another, and how those elements might be adapted by the new culture.

KEY DATES FOR CHAPTER 11

936	The Koryo kingdom defeats the Silla.
976	The Song dynasty unites north and south China.
c. 1000	The Song introduce the world's first paper money.
1040	Bi Sheng invents a process for book printing.
1125	The Song defeat the Kitan.
1127	Kaifeng surrenders to the Jurchen.
1142	The Southern Song and Jurchen sign a peace treaty.
1185	Rule by the Minamoto clan begins in Japan.
1225	Zhao publishes *The Description of Foreign Peoples*.
1377	The world's earliest surviving book is printed with movable type in Korea.

INTRODUCE THE READING STRATEGY

COMPARE AND CONTRAST
Explain to students that comparing and contrasting can help them more deeply understand the differences and similarities among several cultures in a region. Go to the Chapter Review and preview the Venn Diagram with students. As students read the chapter, have them compare and contrast the effects of Chinese culture on Korea and Japan.

INTRODUCE CHAPTER VOCABULARY

KEY VOCABULARY

SECTION 1

currency	demographics	dialect
movable type		

SECTION 2

daimyo	infrastructure	physiography
shogun		

WORD WEBS
Tell students to complete a Word Web for Key Vocabulary words as they read the chapter. Direct them to write each word in the center of an oval and then look through the chapter to find examples, characteristics, and descriptive words that may be associated with the vocabulary word. After reading the chapter, ask students to share what they learned about each word. Model an example using the following graphic organizer.

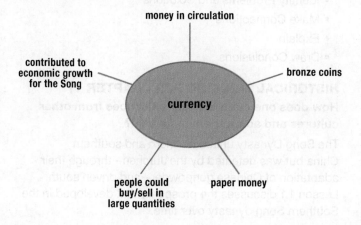

The Rise of Song China

People often say that adversity makes a person stronger. For the Song, the humiliation of admitting weaknesses and paying tribute to their conquerors eventually led to a time of great prosperity and commercial success.

THE SONG DYNASTY RISES

As you've read, after the Tang dynasty came to an end, China fell into chaos until 960, when the Song dynasty was founded and restored order. By 976, the Song had united both north and south China and established its capital at Kaifeng in the Huang He Valley.

The Song founder kept in place the Tang political structure, with the emperor at the top of a central bureaucracy that oversaw local government. However,

the Song believed that generals had exercised too much power in the Tang dynasty. So the Song initiated a period of greater civilian rule with power residing in the hands of bureaucrats rather than with generals.

The Song dynasty faced a problem common to earlier dynasties: keeping peace with the nomads to the north, in this case the Kitan. To counter this threat, the Song formed an alliance with the Jurchen who had formed the Jin dynasty. With their help, the Song defeated the

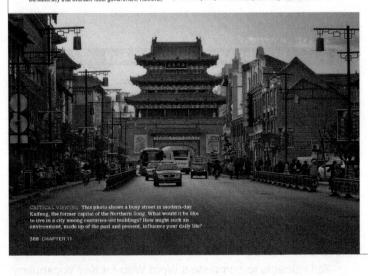

CRITICAL VIEWING This photo shows a busy street in modern-day Kaifeng, the former capital of the Northern Song. What would it be like to live in a city among centuries-old buildings? How might such an environment, made up of the past and present, influence your daily life?

Kitan in 1125. However, the Jurchen immediately turned and attacked the Song. They built siege towers that rose over the walls of Kaifeng, the Song capital. Then the Jurchen used the Chinese invention of gunpowder to fight the Chinese. They also employed a more technologically complex use of gunpowder. Rather than tying gunpowder to arrows to shoot at the enemy as the Chinese had, the Jurchen shot bombs made of bamboo shells containing gunpowder and porcelain shards. Unable to devise an effective defense, the residents of Kaifeng surrendered in January 1127.

THE SONG DYNASTY IS FORCED SOUTH

Taking control of northern China, the Jurchen modeled their government after the Song and ruled 40 million Chinese. Refusing to live under the Jurchen, 500,000 Song Chinese fled south in one of the largest migrations in human history. The Jurchen captured the former Song emperor, but one of the emperor's sons joined the migration south, became the new emperor, and formed a new capital at Hangzhou. Historians now refer to the period when the Song capital was in Kaifeng as the Northern Song and the period when the Song capital was in Hangzhou as the Southern Song.

At first, life in the south was extremely difficult for those who fled as well as for those who were already there. The north and south were distinct cultural regions with many differences. Northerners were accustomed to eating noodles and bread, whereas rice was the main staple in the south. Also, the northern and southern **dialects**, or regional variations in language, were different, so northerners and southerners couldn't understand each other. The huge influx of new residents into southern cities changed the **demographics**, or the characteristics of the population. Hangzhou had been a small, regional city, but within a few years it is one million residents had built it into a worthy successor of the former capital at Kaifeng. By the end of the 12th century, Hangzhou had become the largest city in the world.

For the next 14 years, the Southern Song fought to regain control of the north and to keep the Jurchen from invading the south. Finally, in 1142 the Southern Song and the Jurchen signed a peace treaty. But the terms of the treaty were humiliating to the Song. They were forced to pay a tribute of 250,000 ounces of silver and 250,000 bolts of silk each year to the Jurchen. They also became the first Chinese dynasty to formally accept another dynasty as a "superior state."

The payments, however, stimulated trade and economic growth in the Song dynasty because the Jurchen used the tribute money to buy large quantities of Chinese goods. The Southern Song rebuilt their economy

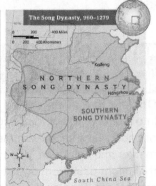

The Song Dynasty, 960–1279

NORTHERN SONG DYNASTY

SOUTHERN SONG DYNASTY

Kaifeng

Hangzhou

South China Sea

and became one of the richest societies in the world. China's farmers realized that they could grow more food in southern China than they had in the north, so they began to grow cash crops to sell at markets. Peasants turned into part-time or full-time artisans and sold pottery, baskets, and textiles. Commercial growth through markets, as well as advances in technology, book publishing, currency, and education, all led to an improved quality of life for many Chinese.

Life was better, and so was travel. Improvements in mapmaking, boat building, and navigational instruments allowed Song ships to sail on deepwater routes to Vietnam and Cambodia for the first time. Through increased trade, the Song learned much more about the peoples and products of the outside world. China's economic transformation affected the whole region, and Song coins circulated widely throughout Korea, Japan, and Vietnam.

HISTORICAL THINKING

1. **READING CHECK** In what ways did China prosper under the Song dynasty?

2. **IDENTIFY PROBLEMS AND SOLUTIONS** What problems did war with the Jurchen pose to the Song? What solutions did the Song develop as a result?

3. **MAKE CONNECTIONS** How do the challenges that the Southern Song faced with large migrations compare with immigration issues the world faces today?

PLAN: 2-PAGE LESSON

OBJECTIVE

Explore the Song dynasty period of prosperity and growth in China.

CRITICAL THINKING SKILLS FOR LESSON 1.1

- Identify Problems and Solutions
- Make Connections
- Explain
- Draw Conclusions

HISTORICAL THINKING FOR CHAPTER 11

How does one culture adopt influences from other cultures and adapt them to its own?

The Song Dynasty united northern and southern China but was defeated by the Jurchen—through their adaptation of Chinese gunpowder—and driven south. Lesson 1.1 discusses the prosperity that developed in the Southern Song dynasty over time.

Student eEdition online

Additional content for this lesson, including a Global Commodity feature, is available online.

BACKGROUND FOR THE TEACHER

The Jurchen After defeating the Song, the Jurchen established their northern Chinese empire in the capital city at Huining. Later, they moved the capital to what today is Beijing, and then to modern-day Kaifeng. The Jurchen wanted to keep their cultural identity—they were a Manchurian tribe—and they kept their own speech and alphabet. They banned their soldiers from taking Chinese names, wearing Chinese clothing styles, and incorporating Chinese cultural customs into their daily lives. However, the Jurchen did establish a Chinese-style bureaucratic government over part of their territory.

History Notebook

Encourage students to complete the Global Commodity page for Chapter 11 in their History Notebooks as they read.

INTRODUCE & ENGAGE

DISCUSS GEOGRAPHIC LOCATION

Direct students to look at the map of the Song dynasty. Point out the eastern edge of the Southern Song dynasty. **ASK:** What makes up the eastern border and what are some advantages to this type of border? *(Possible response: A sea that provides separation and isolation and a definite border that is better protected.)* Discuss with students how a large seacoast might impact cultural development in the region. **ASK:** How might improvements in seafaring technology affect the people who live here? *(Possible response: Better technology allows sailors and traders to go farther and learn about cultures in new lands.)* Tell students that in this lesson they will learn about the development of the Southern Song and how its location and technological improvements affected the dynasty and culture.

TEACH

GUIDED DISCUSSION

1. **Explain** Why did the Song form an alliance with the Jurchen? *(The Song needed help defeating the Kitan, so they formed an alliance with the Jurchen to fight the Kitan.)*

2. **Draw Conclusions** How did the Jurchen's adoption of Chinese technology impact the Song? *(Possible responses: The Jurchen were able to adopt the Chinese technology of gunpowder, adapt and improve it, and then use it to defeat the Song.)*

A GLOBAL COMMODITY

Direct students to read the Global Commodity feature on tea. **ASK:** Why was tea originally consumed only by the upper classes, and why was it possible for all classes to enjoy tea by the 1900s? *(Possible response: Tea was initially very expensive and only the wealthy could afford it. Eventually, the prices dropped and more people could buy it.)*

ACTIVE OPTIONS

On Your Feet: Numbered Heads Organize the class into groups of four, instructing group members to number off from one to four. Point students to the text about Li Qingzhao. Ask groups to discuss questions they might pose if given the opportunity to interview Li Qingzhao and how she might answer the questions. Call a number and invite students with that number to present the questions and answers for their groups.

NG Learning Framework: Craft an Informative Report
SKILL Communication
KNOWLEDGE Our Human Story

Have students review the cultural differences between the northern and southern regions of China during the Song period. Invite students to work in pairs to research foods and languages. Tell partners to collaborate on an oral report and to include a map that shows where different languages and food types predominate. If partners discover conflicting information, prompt them to work together to resolve the issue if they can. Have pairs communicate their findings to the class.

DIFFERENTIATE

INCLUSION

Use Clarifying Questions Pair students with disabilities with students who can read the lesson aloud to them. Encourage students to ask and answer clarifying questions. Have the partner without disabilities describe the map of the Song dynasty and read the labels and describe the migration of the Song to the south.

See the Chapter Planner for more strategies for differentiation.

HISTORICAL THINKING

ANSWERS

1. Mapmaking, boat building, and advances in navigation led to increased trade. People sold goods in markets. Farmers and artisans produced for more than self-sufficiency. Education also improved.

2. The Song were defeated by the Jurchen and forced south in a large migration. They also had to pay tribute and admit to being inferior to the Jurchen. However, paying tribute stimulated the need for increased production of goods that they could sell.

3. Cities in southern China grew rapidly and probably didn't have the infrastructure to handle so many new residents. They had to deal with different cultural issues. The world is experiencing many similar issues today as refugees from around the world migrate to cities in different countries. In China, people at least shared much of the same culture, so accommodating the northerners may not have been as difficult as it is today, as the refugees come from many different countries and cultures.

CRITICAL VIEWING Possible response: Living in a city with many old buildings provides a good sense of your country's history and your place within that history.

Books, Steel, and Currency

Sometimes the person who invents something doesn't get the credit for it because how and when an invention is used makes a big difference. In 1040, a Chinese man named Bi Sheng invented a process for printing books. More than 400 years later, a German printer, Johannes Gutenberg, invented a similar process. Today, Gutenberg gets most of the credit for developing the printing press.

BOOK PUBLISHING AND EDUCATION

The boom in the Chinese commercial economy brought about an information revolution. You've read that woodblock printing began in the Tang dynasty. During the Song dynasty, the production of books increased dramatically. Shortly after 1040, the Chinese bookmaker Bi Sheng invented a printing process that involved arranging **movable type**—individual clay characters—into a frame to form a page. This process was tedious since the Chinese language has thousands of different characters, but for large print runs of more than 100,000 copies, the innovation of movable type made sense.

The low cost of books and economic growth produced a boom in education. Parents who could afford it hired tutors for their sons in hopes that their sons would pass civil service exams and get prestigious government jobs. Although women were not allowed to take civil service exams, many women did learn to read and write, and women took pride in educating their children and managing household finances.

During the Song dynasty, civil service examinations were held every three years. To assure that no preference was given to known students, the candidates' names were removed from the exams and the answers were recopied so that a candidate's handwriting could not be recognized. Those students with the highest scores would move on to the next level of exams. The best students advanced as far as the palace examinations, where the emperor gave orally.

At the time of the Song dynasty's founding, civil service exams had already been in use for more than a thousand years. But it was only in the Southern Song era that the literacy rate increased such that 1 in 250 people took the exams, and government appointments

became almost fully merit-based, or awarded by test scores. As a result, the Song era saw a major shift from government by aristocracy to government by merit-based bureaucracy.

COMMERCIAL REVOLUTION

In northern China, farmers grew wheat and millet, but rice was the most plentiful crop in the south where there was much more rain. Farmers planted rice seeds in small gardens, and then they transported the rice plants to the fields. The farmers used pumps and water wheels to regulate the flow of water into rice fields. Once the plants took root, farmers flooded the fields with water until the crop ripened. In the late 10th century, southern farmers imported a strain of rice from Vietnam that had a shorter growing season and produced two crops a year. With this type of rice, farmers doubled their yields, which helped feed the rapidly growing population.

During the Song dynasty, there was an increase in all goods, not just rice. Iron production surged as well, and metalworkers made both wrought iron, softer iron formed into shapes with tools, and cast iron, which was melted and poured into molds. Cast iron was so hard it could not be worked with a hammer. Song-era blacksmiths also learned to produce steel, one of the strongest metals known, by heating sheets of iron together in a superhot furnace.

Demand for iron goods increased so much that individual workshops could not meet it. Metalworkers worked full time in factory-like spaces where they cast iron armor, weapons, tools, and fittings such as nails and locks that were used for buildings and bridges.

These large-scale foundries housed hundreds of workers who produced identical items in large quantities

In this painting from the Song dynasty, students take the civil service examination at the imperial palace in Kaifeng.

and at low prices. By 1078, China was producing 125,000 tons of iron, or 3.1 pounds per person. It wasn't until 1700, just before the Industrial Revolution, that Europe matched this level of production.

Farmers and foundries sold their goods at markets, and people needed a way to pay for their purchases. In response, Song authorities increased the money supply. During the previous Tang dynasty, **currency**, money in circulation, consisted of round bronze coins with square holes. Carrying strings of heavy bronze coins became cumbersome for merchants and buyers alike, especially for large transactions. Sometime around 1000, the Song government introduced the world's first paper money. Over time, the use of bank seals and increasingly complex designs helped discourage counterfeiting. Paper money allowed people to buy and sell in larger quantities, further contributing to economic growth.

During the Northern Song dynasty, Kaifeng was one of the three largest cities in the world, and Kaifeng's residents lived at a density of 32,000 people per square mile. Along with its many markets, Kaifeng had 72 major restaurants, each standing three floors high and licensed by the government. Just as in ancient Rome, residents of Kaifeng and other Song cities could enjoy public restaurants and stopping for meals, noodles, or snacks at small stands and major restaurants.

RELIGIOUS LIFE

Prosperity also allowed the Chinese to give money to many different religious institutions. Many educated Chinese were drawn to the teachings of Neo-Confucianism. Traditional Confucianism had focused on society, ritual, and morality. But Neo-Confucians sought self-development through the study of four Confucian classics known as The Four Books. Followers learned to examine everything in the world around them to discover an underlying pattern and understand the all-inclusive life force called qi. The ultimate goal of Neo-Confucian education was to attain sagehood, which was a state of ultimate wisdom. By the 17th century, Neo-Confucianism had gained a wide following in Japan, Korea, and Vietnam as well as in China.

HISTORICAL THINKING

1. READING CHECK How did the expansion of markets lead to advances in education, agriculture, and the production of iron and steel?

2. SYNTHESIZE Why was it necessary to double crop yields in southern China after 1126? How did the Chinese accomplish this?

3. ANALYZE CAUSE AND EFFECT What events in the Tang dynasty led to the use of paper currency during the Song dynasty?

PLAN: 2-PAGE LESSON

OBJECTIVE

Explain how rapid growth in commerce led to great achievements in publishing, agriculture, education, and metalworking in Song China.

CRITICAL THINKING SKILLS FOR LESSON 1.2

- Synthesize
- Analyze Cause and Effect
- Explain
- Describe
- Analyze Visuals

HISTORICAL THINKING FOR CHAPTER 11

How does one culture adopt influences from other cultures and adapt them to its own?

The Song dynasty prospered due to advances in publishing, education, and commerce. Lesson 1.2 discusses the reasons for Song prosperity and how it affected Chinese culture.

BACKGROUND FOR THE TEACHER

Education Under the Song Dynasty The importance of education grew during the Song period. In addition to the lower and higher level schools and technical schools offered to many Chinese students, a mostly private academy system developed. These academies were called *shuyuan*, and they were paid for partly by the state and partly by wealthy donors. They were located in the mountains or in the woods, and in addition to teaching classical subjects, they emphasized quiet study away from the bureaucracy of everyday life. Classes were taught by important scholars who frequently focused on the principles of Buddhism and Daoism. One important shuyuan in the Wuyi Mountains was Ziyang Shuyuan, which was founded in 1183 by Zhu Xi, a Neo-Confucian scholar. The academy system served as a base for the Neo-Confucian thought that spread during this time period.

Student eEdition online

Additional content for this lesson, including a painting, a photograph, and a Primary Source feature, is available online.

INTRODUCE & ENGAGE

PREVIEW WITH VISUALS

Direct students' attention to the photograph of the rice harvester. Write *Southern China* at the center of a Concept Cluster and ask volunteers to list geographical features that they notice in the photograph. At the end of the lesson, revisit the Concept Cluster and reflect on how the geography of southern China differed from that of northern China, and how this affected the Southern Song dynasty.

TEACH

GUIDED DISCUSSION

1. **Explain** Why did book printing increase under the Song? *(Bi Sheng invented a process using movable type that enabled multiple copies of books to be printed more easily.)*

2. **Describe** How did rice and iron affect China under the Song? *(Possible response: The products helped launch a commercial revolution—a new strain of rice from Vietnam grew much more quickly and thus could be used to feed the rapidly growing population. Improvements in iron working, including the development of steel, led to a surge in demand for iron goods.)*

ANALYZE VISUALS

Discuss the painting of the students taking the civil service examination. Have students read the caption, and explain that the last stage of the examinations took place in the imperial palace, where the emperor judged the results. **ASK:** What do you notice about the figures in this painting? *(Possible responses may include that they are all men, that they are all wearing similar clothing, have similar hair, and most have facial hair.)* How does this painting illustrate the gender roles in China during this period? *(Possible response: Women were not allowed to take the exams.)*

ACTIVE OPTIONS

On Your Feet: Turn and Talk on Topic Arrange students in small groups. Give the groups the following topic question: Which Song advancement had the greatest impact on the future of China and the world? Tell the groups to write a paragraph on this topic with each student contributing at least one unique sentence. Suggest that each group first discuss the wide-ranging implications of their chosen advancement. Ask the groups to read their paragraphs to the class.

| **NG Learning Framework: Create an Infographic on Neo-Confucianism**
ATTITUDE Curiosity
KNOWLEDGE Our Human Story

Organize students into four groups and assign each group one of *The Four Books* of Confucianism. Tell students to conduct online research about their assigned book and create an infographic based on their findings. Encourage groups to include graphs or other visuals in their infographics and to display them in the classroom. Use the completed infographics to discuss how Confucianism impacted the development of Chinese culture during this period.

DIFFERENTIATE

ENGLISH LANGUAGE LEARNERS

Make Word Cards Tell students to use sticky notes to make word cards defining *movable type, currency,* and *Neo-Confucianism,* writing the term on one side and the definition on the other.

PRE-AP

Analyze a Primary Source Invite students to access a primary source of the Song period that describes a student's difficulty in understanding why people act a certain way, even when they know they should not. Ask students to write one or two sentences explaining the issue addressed in the primary source.

See the Chapter Planner for more strategies for differentiation.

HISTORICAL THINKING

ANSWERS

1. Because people were selling their goods at market, they had more money to spend on books and education, on seeds for farming, and on steel for tools and weapons. In turn, increases in book sales and higher levels of education led to higher paying jobs and better skills.

2. The population of Southern China grew by 500,000 from 1126 to 1127 as the Northern Song moved south. Farmers imported a new strain of rice from Vietnam to feed the large influx of people.

3. In the Tang dynasty, people began to use coins, but the coins were heavy. The use of paper currency led to increased commerce in the Song dynasty.

CRITICAL VIEWING Possible responses: Silk producers may have believed that women would be better caretakers for the silkworms, or that they had greater dexterity for handling tasks that involved fine-motor skills.

1.3 Knowledge of the World's Islands

How much can you really learn about the world from reading books and talking with others? Is it necessary to travel to other countries to learn about them? Without ever setting foot on another country's soil, Song official Zhao Rugua (JOW ROO-gwah) wrote a two-volume book all about the lands and cultures of the world.

Zhao Rugua was the director of overseas trade in China's largest international trade port, Quanzhou (chwahn-joh). In this position, he met many foreign and domestic traders and talked to them about the places they visited, the people they met, and the goods they traded. Zhao never traveled outside of China, but he learned from others and from written records, including Muslim geographers' accounts that he probably heard about from Muslim travelers.

Around 1225, Zhao combined the information he obtained into a two-volume book he titled *The Description of Foreign Peoples*. The first volume tells about the location of each country, its people, and its products. The second volume is a catalogue of products from each country.

CRITICAL VIEWING Mount Etna is located on the east coast of Sicily and is the most active volcano in Europe. What words and phrases did Zhao Rugua use to describe the volcano's activity?

DOCUMENT ONE

Primary Source: Book
from *Zhu Fan Zhi* by Zhao Rugua, c. 1225

In this excerpt, Zhao describes his impressions of the African islands of Pemba and Madagascar.

CONSTRUCTED RESPONSE
Which parts of this description seem credible? Which do not? Why?

This country is in the sea to the southwest. It is adjacent to a large island. There are usually on the great island great peng birds that are so large that they cover the sun when they fly by and the sun's shadow shifts so much that it gives a different reading on the sundial. If the great peng bird finds a wild camel, it swallows it. If one should happen to find a peng feather, after cutting off the hollow quill, you can use it to make a water pail.

The products of the country are big elephants' tusks and rhinoceros horns.

. . . Enticed by offers of food, [the people of this country] are caught and then carried off to be sold as slaves in the Arab countries where they command a high price. They work as gatekeepers. People say that they do not miss their families.

DOCUMENT TWO

In this excerpt, Zhao describes the kingdom of northern Taiwan.

CONSTRUCTED RESPONSE
Taiwan is a mere 150 miles from Quanzhou, yet Zhao's description was actually recycled from earlier documentation written in the 600s. What information in the excerpt explains why the Chinese had little contact with Taiwan?

The country of northern Taiwan is some five or six days' sail east of Quanzhou. . . . The king's residence is called Poluotan Cave; around it [are] three separate wooden palisades surrounded by running water and protected by thorn hedges, and the palace roof has many carvings of birds and animals. . . .

Their soldiers are armed with weapons of every kind, such as knives, pikes, bows and arrows, and swords; they use drums, and make armor from bear and leopard skins. . . .

They have no unusual goods; the locals tend to be robbers, which is why traders do not go there. Still, the locals . . . collect yellow wax, locally mined gold, buffalo tails and jerked leopard meat and take it to the Philippines to sell it.

DOCUMENT THREE

In this excerpt, Zhao describes the island of Sicily off the coast of the Italian Peninsula. The mountain he refers to is Mount Etna, which still erupts today.

CONSTRUCTED RESPONSE
What information has Zhao included about Madagascar and Taiwan but omitted from his information about Sicily?

The country of Sicily is near the border with Rome. It is a sea island one thousand li [roughly 0.33 miles] in breadth. The clothing, customs, and language of the people are the same as those of Rome. This country has a mountain with a very deep cavern in it that emits fire the four seasons of the year. When seen from afar it looks like smoke in the morning and fire in the evening; when seen up close it is a wildly roaring fire. . . .

Once every five years fire and stones break out and flow down to the sea-coast and then flow back again. The trees in the woods through which this stream of fire flows are not burned, but the stones it meets in its course turn to ashes.

SYNTHESIZE & WRITE

1. **REVIEW** Review what you have learned about Chinese trade with the "outside world" during the Song dynasty.

2. **RECALL** On your own paper, list details about each country's land, people, and products.

3. **CONSTRUCT** Construct a topic sentence that answers this question: Was Zhao Rugua's book a valuable resource for Chinese merchants who were traveling abroad during the late Song dynasty?

4. **WRITE** Using evidence from this chapter, information about the author, and the excerpts, write an argumentative paragraph that supports your topic sentence in Step 3.

PLAN: 2-PAGE LESSON

OBJECTIVE
Synthesize knowledge the Chinese had about foreign traders and the lands in which they resided during the Song dynasty.

CRITICAL THINKING SKILLS FOR LESSON 1.3
- Synthesize
- Monitor Comprehension
- Form and Support Opinions
- Evaluate

HISTORICAL THINKING FOR CHAPTER 11
How does one culture adopt influences from other cultures and adapt them to its own?

Lesson 1.3 focuses on excerpts from *The Descriptions of Foreign Peoples (Zhufan Zhi)*, a two-volume text written by Zhao Rugua. These excerpts help us to understand how trade quickly spread cultural ideas around the world.

BACKGROUND FOR THE TEACHER

Zhao Rugua Zhao was born in 1170 in the Zhejiang province in China. He was part of the Song imperial family. After passing the civil service examination and obtaining a degree, he became the superintendent of customs at the port of Quanzhou, Fujian along the southeast coast of China. As superintendent and inspector of foreign trade at one of the largest ports in China, Zhao Rugua met many foreign traders from Africa, Arabia, Europe, India, Japan, Korea, Persia, and the Philippines wanting to trade and buy Chinese goods. In order to write his book, he studied maps and took information from an older work titled *Lingwai Diada*, written by geographer Zhou Qufei in 1178. In the preface of his book, Zhao Rugua states that his motivation for writing was to advance Chinese knowledge about the world. His curiosity led him to record information about the geography, legends, fauna, and flora found in the lands where the merchants resided. In his writing, Zhao Rugua depicts others, using China as his basis for scholarly culture. As an example, he thought people who did not wear shoes were far beneath him. Some of his exotic accounts are embellishments, which is typical of many stories that have been passed along from person to person. Zhao Rugua died in 1231.

PREPARE FOR THE DOCUMENT-BASED QUESTION

Before students start on the activity, briefly preview the three documents. Remind students that a constructed response requires full explanations in complete sentences. Emphasize that students should use what they have learned about trade in China during the Song dynasty in addition to the information in the documents.

GUIDED DISCUSSION

1. **Monitor Comprehension** Based on the excerpts, what were Zhao Rugua's primary interests? *(He was interested in the geography, animals, plants, and the people found in the lands where the merchants resided.)*

2. **Form and Support Opinions** What was Zhao Rugua's attitude toward merchants and people from other places, and how might his job have influenced his opinion about merchants? *(Possible response: In some excerpts he has a negative opinion of people. For instance, he feels the merchants in Pemba and Madagascar trick people with food and then sell them as slaves, and the people of Taiwan are all "robbers." Because he is a trade inspector, he has likely seen many negative things, so his job greatly influences his opinions of others.)*

EVALUATE

After students have completed the Synthesize & Write activity, allow time for them to exchange paragraphs and read and comment on the work of their peers. Establish guidelines for comments prior to the activity so feedback is constructive and encouraging. Comments should focus on the most significant parts that address the purpose of the activity and the audience.

ACTIVE OPTION

On Your Feet: Host a DBQ Roundtable Divide the class into groups of four. Hand each group a sheet of paper with the following question: What cultural ideas spread because of trade? Instruct the first student in each group to write an answer, read it aloud, and pass the paper clockwise to the next student. The paper may circulate around the table several times. Then reconvene the class and discuss the groups' responses.

STRIVING READERS

Summarize Read each document aloud, asking students to summarize. Then read the constructed response question and have volunteers suggest responses.

PRE-AP

Research Excerpts Invite students to research other excerpts from Zhao Rugua's *The Description of Foreign Peoples.* Have them identify the country the excerpt is about and research whether the information is factual.

ANSWERS

1. Answers will vary.

2. Possible response: Pemba and Madagascar are both islands in the southwest. They trade elephant tusks and rhinoceros horns. The people were carried off as slaves. Taiwan is east of Quanzhou. Taiwan trades wax, gold, and jerky with the Philippines. Sicily is a small island near Rome. There are active volcanoes. Trade products are not mentioned.

3. Possible response: Zhao Rugua's descriptions contain a wealth of knowledge about other places that would be very valuable to merchants. OR: He provides some accurate information about other places, but there are too many inaccuracies and biases for his accounts to be useful to merchants.

4. Answers will vary. Students' argumentative paragraphs should include their topic sentence from Step 3 and provide several details.

CONSTRUCTED RESPONSE

Document One: The location of the islands, the products they traded, and the fact that the people were enslaved all seem credible. However, the information about the huge bird that swallowed camels is unbelievable.

Document Two: The excerpt describes a dangerous place fortified with a strong military and high crime. It also states that few went there for trade. If merchants didn't feel safe in Taiwan, the Chinese probably didn't have much contact with or information about Taiwan.

Document Three: Zhao mentions the location of Sicily and the people. However, the description focuses on volcanoes rather than trade.

CRITICAL VIEWING Possible response: He describes it as a mountain with a deep cavern that emits fire.

Koryo Korea and Vietnam's Ly Dynasty

Have you ever admired someone you also disliked? Korea and Vietnam both admired China and adapted many Chinese ideas and practices to meet their own needs. But they also maintained a strong aversion to Chinese control.

KOREA UNDER THE KORYO DYNASTY

Although the Chinese considered Korea to be part of China, the Koreans did not. After the defeat and withdrawal of the Chinese in 676, the Korean Silla kingdom ruled. But in 936, the Koryo kingdom defeated the Silla and founded the dynasty from which Korea takes its name. Starting with King Taejo, whose title means "Great Founder," the Koryo dynasty modeled the structure of its central government on China's Tang dynasty and divided the region into administrative districts as China had. It also followed Chinese practice in sponsoring Buddhism while adopting Confucianism. Taejo applied a traditional Korean emphasis on nature by assessing the life forces of trees and streams in selecting sites for his cities and palaces.

The Koryo king also used a Chinese-style exam to recruit officials by merit and to reduce the influence of powerful families who formed a hereditary local aristocracy. This policy succeeded for over 200 years, but in 1170, aristocratic families and their military supporters overthrew the Chinese-style administration and implemented their own. As a result, Koryo kings continued to rule as figureheads, but Koryo's professional bureaucracy came almost entirely from its hereditary nobility.

Trade continued between Korea and China even during politically unstable times. Korea exported precious metals and edible goods in exchange for Chinese silks, books, and ceramics. Koryo potters also imported advanced Chinese techniques, but they introduced an important innovation to Chinese ceramic wares. Improving on the porcelain-making process used in China, Korean potters built high-firing kilns, ovens for pottery, to make their pale green, inlaid celadon pots. Many people considered Korean celadon to be the finest porcelain in the world.

Similarly, woodblock printing reached new levels of sophistication in the hands of Korean printers. Between 1237 and 1248, Korean monks carved Buddhist teachings onto approximately 80,000 woodblocks known collectively as the Tripitaka Koreana. Koreans also adopted the technology of printing with movable type. However, rather than carving characters into separate clay blocks, the Koreans improved the process and used metal type. The world's earliest book printed with movable metal type was made in Korea in 1377.

Some religious texts had been brought back from China by Korean monks. For example, a monk named Uichon went to China to study in 1085, and he later donated some of his 5,000 books to the Tripitaka Koreana. Uichon was hoping to find a way to bridge two schools of Buddhist thought, one which believed that the study of texts was most important, the other placing emphasis on meditation.

In 1402, shortly after the end of the Koryo dynasty, royal astronomers, or scientists who study stars and planets, designed Korea's earliest surviving map of East Asia. The map shows China as the largest country in the world. But it distorts the size of Korea, making it look much larger than its actual size. This may have been the first time a map showed north at the top, a common practice today. Yet this map, like all maps that try to translate the shape of Earth to a flat piece of paper, reflects the culture of those who made it.

THE LY DYNASTY RISES IN VIETNAM

As the Tang dynasty weakened in China, resistance to Chinese control grew in Vietnam. Vietnamese general Ngo Quyen (noh kwehn) revolted in 939, defeating the Chinese by planting iron-tipped stakes in a riverbed to sink China's warships. He claimed independence for Vietnam and named himself king. China acknowledged

A monk holds one of the 80,000 woodblocks from the Tripitaka Koreana collection, which is kept at the Haiensa Temple in present-day South Korea. These are a replication of the original blocks, commissioned in 1237. The originals were destroyed by the Mongols in 1232.

the independence of the new **Dai Vet** state in exchange for tribute payments. This began 1,000 years of independence for Vietnam.

Ngo's rule lasted for 30 years, and the rulers who followed him built up the military to defend Vietnam against China's Song dynasty. To assure that the Chinese would not attempt a takeover, the Vietnamese sent a delegation to China. However, the Song rulers refused to recognize Vietnam's independence until 1009 when the Ly (lee) dynasty came to power.

Even as an independent state, the Ly dynasty acknowledged the superiority of the Chinese emperor, and periodically sent delegations to present the emperor with gifts. The Chinese emperor bestowed gifts on the emissaries in return. Trade between the Chinese and Vietnamese continued as it had for the previous 1,000 years. The Vietnamese exported medicines and resources such as timber and elephant tusks, which the Chinese used to carve ornaments and jewelry.

Chinese-educated scholars of the Ly dynasty argued that the Vietnamese king ruled Vietnam because he, like the Chinese emperor, held the Mandate of Heaven. Vietnamese kings credited local spirits with protecting the royal house, but at the same time, they reinforced Buddhism as the state religion.

The Ly dynasty's rulers moved the Vietnamese capital to what is now Hanoi, established a strong central government based on Chinese law and Confucian values, and recruited a professional army.

Dedicated to the study of Confucian texts, the Ly dynasty king founded a temple of literature in 1070, and by 1076, the government had set up an imperial academy. Following a centralized curriculum, students studied for civil service exams similar to those used in China.

Along with establishing the government, army, and education, the Ly dynasty worked on its **infrastructure**, or transportation networks. Ly dynasty builders built a successful road system and a system of canals that improved year-round rice farming. The Ly dynasty remained in power until 1225.

HISTORICAL THINKING

1. **READING CHECK** How did the Koreans improve upon some of the technology they adopted from China?

2. **ANALYZE CAUSE AND EFFECT** What events in China may have caused Ngo Quyen to seek independence for Vietnam?

3. **IDENTIFY** What are some of the major accomplishments of the Ly dynasty?

PLAN: 2-PAGE LESSON

OBJECTIVE
Identify how Korea and Vietnam continued to adopt and adapt Chinese ways while prospering as somewhat independent countries.

CRITICAL THINKING SKILLS FOR LESSON 2.1
- Analyze Cause and Effect
- Identify
- Compare and Contrast
- Explain
- Analyze Visuals

HISTORICAL THINKING FOR CHAPTER 11
How does one culture adopt influences from other cultures and adapt them to its own?

Korea and Vietnam adapted Chinese practices and technologies for their own use. Lesson 2.1 discusses the formation of their unique cultural practices in government, printing, the arts, and other areas.

Student eEdition online
Additional content for this lesson, including a map and photographs, is available online.

BACKGROUND FOR THE TEACHER
Celadon Celadon is a form of stoneware, which is a term for pottery that has been fired at a very high heat so that it is more like glass and no longer porous. Stoneware was first made in China during the Shang Dynasty. Stoneware does not require a glaze, but artisans often add one for decoration. In order to obtain the greenish color in celadon, artists coat the stoneware with a liquefied clay that is very high in iron before firing. The iron reacts with the heat and turns green. To create a design, the maker may carve the clay off the object to show different shades of color. Korean artists also often carved decorations under the glaze or used a stamp to produce them. The decorations were frequently black and white and featured birds, flowers, or clouds. These features and the colors of Korean celadon differentiated it from Chinese celadon.

INTRODUCE & ENGAGE

DISCUSS THE IMPORTANCE OF CULTURAL TIES

Direct students to look at the photograph of the monk with the Tripitaka Koreana that appears in the lesson, and have them read the caption. Explain that these woodblocks are one of the most complete bodies of Buddhist texts in the world. **ASK:** Why do you think the Mongols destroyed the blocks? *(Possible responses might include the Mongols' desire to destroy religious and other cultural elements of their subjects.)* Why do you think the woodblocks were remade after the Mongol conquest? *(Possible response: The woodblocks were extremely important to Korean culture and religion.)*

TEACH

GUIDED DISCUSSION

1. **Compare and Contrast** What was similar about Chinese and Korean government? *(Both the Chinese and the Koreans divided the region into administrative districts and implemented a civil service exam.)*

2. **Explain** What condition did the Chinese place on acknowledging Vietnamese independence? *(The Vietnamese had to make tribute payments.)*

ANALYZE VISUALS

Have students look at the photo of the Thang Long Imperial Citadel in Hanoi. **ASK:** What similarities do you notice between this Vietnamese building and the Chinese buildings under the Song you read about earlier? *(Possible response: Both are often made of stone and have curved roof corners.)*

ACTIVE OPTIONS

On Your Feet: True or False? Tell half the class to write True-False statements based on the information about government in Korea and Vietnam. Tell the other half to create answer cards, with "True" written on one side and "False" on the other. Then ask students who wrote statements to read them aloud. Direct students in the second group to respond by holding up either "True" or "False." When discrepancies occur, review the statement and the text and discuss which answer is correct. After all statements are answered, if time permits, have groups reverse roles.

| **NG Learning Framework: Compare and Contrast Korea and Vietnam**
SKILLS Communication, Collaboration
KNOWLEDGE Our Human Story

Arrange students in small groups and ask them to create a chart summarizing the similarities and differences between Korea and Vietnam in the following categories: relationship with the Chinese, religion, and government structure. Encourage students to conduct online research as needed to supplement information in the text. Invite students to display their charts on a class website or around the classroom.

DIFFERENTIATE

INCLUSION

Describe a Map Pair students who are sight impaired with students who are not. Ask the latter to describe in detail the map of China's Trade Relations with Korea and Vietnam, 1225. Have the students read the labels, point out the trade route lines, read the trade goods lists, and answer any questions their partners may have.

PRE-AP

Analyze Cross-Cultural Relationships Ask students to reflect on the relationship between the Chinese and the Koreans or Vietnamese. Then have them choose either Korea or Vietnam to conduct online research about present-day relationships between their chosen culture and China. Assign a moderator and have a panel discussion in which they discuss the similarities between present-day and early relationships and their impact on cross-cultural interactions.

See the Chapter Planner for more strategies for differentiation.

HISTORICAL THINKING

ANSWERS

1. The Koreans made high-firing kilns to produce celadon. They also used Chinese woodblock technology to create a huge library of Buddhist texts. They improved on the invention of movable type to metal type.

2. China's Tang dynasty had collapsed, and China was in a state of disunity, so Ngo Quyen probably assumed that China lacked the strength to fight the Vietnamese.

3. They established a strong central government and army. They set up a centralized education system, an academy, and civil service exams. They also built a road system and canals to regulate the irrigation of rice.

Shoguns of Japan

Just how loyal should you be to your teacher, your parents, or a boss?
In feudal Japan, a warrior would give his life for his lord. This dedication to the lord was even stronger than the warrior's loyalty to a family member or the emperor himself.

JAPAN'S GEOGRAPHY

The physical geography, or **physiography**, of Japan affected many aspects of life in this nation and still does today. As you may recall, Japan is an archipelago made up of four large islands and many smaller ones. The islands are actually the peaks of mostly submerged mountains. Japan's mountains are part of a vast network of volcanoes and intense earthquakes that line both sides of the Pacific in what is known as the Ring of

Fire. Thick forests comprise another large portion of the Japanese islands' geography. Japan's terrain of rugged mountains and dense forests may have inspired Japan's ancient religion, **Shinto**, which means "way of the gods." Followers of Shinto believe that spiritual powers called *kami* reside in anything in nature that inspires a sense of religious wonder. Followers of Shinto regard mountains as especially important, particularly Mount Fuji, near Tokyo, which has long been considered sacred.

CRITICAL VIEWING The mountainous Shakotan Peninsula on the west coast of Hokkaido, Japan, projects into the Sea of Japan. From details in this aerial photo, what impact do you think Japan's physical geography has on where and how people live?

316 CHAPTER 11

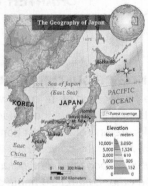

The Geography of Japan

Elevation

feet	meters
10,000+	3,050+
5,000	1,524
2,000	610
1,000	305
500	152
0	0

Japan's landscapes are breathtaking, but the space available for agriculture and construction is very limited. Only about 12 percent of Japan's total land is available for farming, and Japan's population is crowded onto a few coastal plains. However, Japan's temperate climate is ideal for growing rice, a major staple of the Japanese diet. Fish and other seafood are also central to Japanese cuisine since most people live near the ocean.

During the 9th and 10th centuries, Japan continued to trade with China and Korea. Japan's main export was lumber from its vast forests. Because Japan did not mint its own coins at the time, Chinese Song dynasty coins became the unofficial currency.

FEUDALISM IN JAPAN

Partially due to the scarcity of land, the **daimyo** (DY-mee-oh), or wealthy landowners, gained power and built up strong alliances to protect their property. As their power increased, the central government and the emperor's power faded. Around the time that the Song dynasty came to rule in China, Japanese warrior clans under daimyo were gaining power. They forced the Japanese emperor to retire to the capital, which had

moved from Nara to Kyoto in 794. He remained in Kyoto as a figurehead, and his responsibilities were limited to religious and ritual functions.

Each daimyo retained an army of warriors called samurai. In Japan at this time, real power lay with the daimyo in the countryside, loyally served by their samurai. Meanwhile, the emperor was only a shadowy figure, while the **shogun**, or general, had little real authority. The situation was similar to the feudalism of medieval Europe, where knights were bound as vassals to their lords, who dominated rural society. Powerful daimyo commanded the allegiance of lesser lords, armies, and peasants, creating rival clans that battled for control of Japan.

The Minamoto clan ruled during what is known as the Kamakura period (1185–1333), named for its capital of Kamakura, a city just outside present-day Tokyo. Political power rested in the hands of the Minamoto leader, Yoritomo. He became shogun, who claimed to govern on behalf of the emperor while struggling to command the daimyo. The shogun discontinued the use of Chinese-style civil service examinations, opting instead to appoint members of powerful clans to office. Still, scholars continued to study both Buddhist and Confucian texts, many of which were imported from China.

In 1333, the Ashikaga clan toppled the Minamoto and moved the capital back to Kyoto. However, political power was decentralized and the Ashikaga shoguns had little control over the daimyo who ruled their own rural domains. Since each daimyo had a separate army of samurai, incessant warfare spread chaos throughout the islands. The introduction of gunpowder weapons in this period, as in Europe and western Asia, was making warfare even more deadly. Still, the Ashikaga remained in power for more than 200 years until 1573.

The samurai warriors followed a strict code of behavior called *bushido* (BUSH-ih-doh), or "way of the warrior." Like the knight's code of chivalry in Europe, bushido promoted loyalty, bravery, and honor. Most samurai practiced a form of Buddhism known as **Zen Buddhism** because of its emphasis on self-discipline, inward contemplation, and fearlessness. The Shinto value of devotion to family and ruler and the Confucian emphasis on service to state and country also influenced the code.

HISTORICAL THINKING

1. **READING CHECK** What were the official roles of the shogun and the emperor? What were their roles in reality?

2. **ANALYZE CAUSE AND EFFECT** How did Japanese physiography influence the country's religion, economy, and rise of the daimyo?

3. **COMPARE AND CONTRAST** In what ways were Japanese samurai similar to European knights? In what ways were they different?

East Asia and Chinese Influences 317

PLAN: 2-PAGE LESSON

OBJECTIVE

Understand how power shifted from the hands of the emperor to those of landowners and warriors during Japan's feudal period.

CRITICAL THINKING SKILLS FOR LESSON 2.2

- Analyze Cause and Effect
- Compare and Contrast
- Categorize
- Explain
- Interpret Charts

HISTORICAL THINKING FOR CHAPTER 11

How does one culture adopt influences from other cultures and adapt them to its own?

During Japan's feudal period, power shifted from a single emperor to multiple shoguns. Lesson 2.2 discusses this period of Japanese history and how under this new hierarchy of allegiance Japan retained some cultural elements that originated in China but rejected other elements.

BACKGROUND FOR THE TEACHER

Shoguns The Japanese word *shogun* literally translates to "barbarian-quelling generalissimo," an apt description for these warrior rulers. Though the emperor was still technically the head of Japan, the shoguns, or warrior class, held all the real power in its feudal government. Whichever shogun controlled the Japanese military was, in effect, the leader of Japan. A period of rule by a Japanese shogun is called a shogunate, and there were several shogunates during Japan's feudal period. The first shogunate was established by samurai Minamoto Yoritomo. The samurai were the military caste of Japanese society, an aristocratic social class known for its military skills and rigid discipline.

Student eEdition online

Additional content for this lesson, including a diagram, is available online.

INTRODUCE & ENGAGE

DISCUSS THE RING OF FIRE

Tell students that they will soon learn that Japan is located within the Ring of Fire, a network of volcanoes and earthquakes that line both sides of the Pacific. Hold a class discussion on how living in this region might impact a culture. Ask volunteers to list cultural elements that they think might be impacted by living in close proximity to active volcanoes. *(Possible responses might include cultural elements such as architecture, art, or religion.)* Tell students that in this lesson they will learn about how the Ring of Fire and other geographical features impacted the development of Japanese society and culture.

TEACH

GUIDED DISCUSSION

1. **Categorize** Name three key features of Japan's geography. *(Possible responses include location in the Ring of Fire, archipelago, thick forests, and rugged mountains.)*

2. **Explain** What characterized the period of rule by the Ashikaga clan? *(Possible response: constant warfare and chaos)*

INTERPRET CHARTS

Have students examine the Hierarchical Society in Feudal Japan diagram. **ASK:** Who was at the bottom of the Japanese social hierarchy? *(Peasants and artisans were at the bottom.)* Why do you think artisans were at the bottom of the social hierarchy? *(Answers will vary, but students may say that the other layers require you to be born into a particular social class, or that perhaps the Japanese considered making things with your hands to be lower class activities.)*

ACTIVE OPTIONS

On Your Feet: Discuss Feudal Japan Arrange students in an Inside-Outside Circle configuration. Allow students time to write questions about Japan during the feudal period. Ask them to focus their questions on the reasons for the development of the feudal system, the power of the daimyo, the role of the samurai, and what life was like during this time in Japanese history. Then tell students in the inside circle to pose questions to students in the outside circle. Have students switch roles. Students may ask for help from other students in their circle if they are unable to answer a question.

NG Learning Framework: Write a Biography
ATTITUDE Curiosity
SKILL Communication

Have students write a short biography or profile of the Minamoto leader Yoritomo using information from the chapter and additional source material. Suggest students focus on Yoritomo's approach to maintaining control over the daimyo. Invite students to read their biographies aloud to the class.

DIFFERENTIATE

STRIVING READERS

Rewrite a Passage Instruct pairs to read the text under the heading Feudalism in Japan and define the following words: *scarcity* (short supply), *figurehead* (leader without real power), *allegiance* (loyalty), and *incessant* (nonstop). Tell pairs to work together to choose one paragraph from this excerpt of the lesson and write it in conversational, or informal, English.

PRE-AP

Research Religion and Philosophy in Feudal Japan Ask students to generate a research question based on information in the text about the role of Confucianism and Buddhism in feudal Japan. Ask students to conduct online research and share their findings with the class.

See the Chapter Planner for more strategies for differentiation.

HISTORICAL THINKING

ANSWERS

1. The emperor remained the head of the country; the shogun acted on behalf of the emperor and held the greatest power.

2. Japan's natural beauty may have influenced the Shinto religion, which focused on nature. Japan has many mountains and forests, so there is little land to build cities. However, the climate is ideal for rice farming, fishing, and timber industries. The lack of land caused daimyo to protect their land.

3. Both lived by a strict code of bravery and honor. However, the European knight was Christian while the samurai practiced a combination of Zen Buddhism, Shinto, and Confucianism.

CRITICAL VIEWING Possible response: Based on this photo, most people live on the coasts and in the valleys, because the rest of the land is mountainous and forested.

2.3 Material Culture

SHARING CULTURES, KEEPING TRADITIONS

You've learned about Chinese influences in East Asia during the 10th–14th centuries. As Chinese influence grew in East Asia, the people of Japan, Korea, and Vietnam adopted and adapted many aspects of Chinese culture, including new ideas and technology. However, as they adapted Chinese ideas to suit their own needs and cultures, they often made significant improvements that led to new discoveries and traditions.

Japanese Gardens In the ancient Shinto tradition of worshiping kami and seeking harmony with nature, the earliest Japanese gardens were considered sacred places. The Japanese developed many varieties of gardens, but they can be categorized into two distinct types: strolling gardens and viewing gardens. Strolling gardens feature carefully designed landscapes along a walking path. The garden shown here is a moss garden, one of the many viewing gardens at Kennin-ji, a Zen Buddhist temple built in Kyoto in 1202. Zen Buddhism greatly influenced

Japanese garden traditions. The main purpose of Zen viewing gardens is to create a calm state of mind for meditation. Zen Buddhism inspired Japanese gardeners to create landscapes that represent the world in miniature, using simple elements, such as stone and gravel, to stand for something larger. In a dry landscape garden, for instance, gravel raked in various ways might represent the ocean and larger stones might symbolize hills and mountains, while arrangements of smaller stones might portray a waterfall or a stream.

Japanese Tea Ceremony The photograph above shows a chawan of matcha tea. A chawan—a bowl used for preparing and drinking tea—is one of the traditional utensils used in the Japanese tea ceremony, as is the chasen, or bamboo tea whisk, shown beside the chawan. Introduced by a Japanese Zen Buddhist priest, the tea ceremony is a ritual rooted in the principles of Zen Buddhism, focusing attention on the beauty of simple, everyday activity. It wasn't until the 17th century that tea from China and Japan arrived in Europe, eventually becoming a traditional beverage in Britain and Russia, too.

Japanese Writing System In this 1897 Japanese woodblock print by Toyohara Chikanobu, a young woman practices kanji, the Japanese word for Chinese characters. As you'll recall from an earlier chapter, the Japanese adopted the Chinese writing system in the fifth century. Four centuries later, they developed a syllabic alphabet called kana that better captured the full meaning and inflection of the Japanese language.

Korean Celadon Pottery Korea imported a porcelain-making process first developed during the Song dynasty in China. Sometime after 1150, Korean potters improved the Chinese process by using iron pigments and high-firing kilns to create the unique and coveted pale blue-green color of celadon. Popular items of Koryo celadon pottery included vases, bowls, and jugs, as well as ceramic pillows with cut-out designs, such as the one shown here.

PLAN: 4-PAGE LESSON

OBJECTIVE

Learn how the people of Japan, Korea, and Vietnam adopted many aspects of Chinese culture and adapted them to suit their own needs and cultures.

CRITICAL THINKING SKILLS FOR LESSON 2.3

- Analyze Visuals
- Make Connections
- Compare and Contrast
- Make Inferences
- Draw Conclusions

HISTORICAL THINKING FOR CHAPTER 11

How does one culture adopt influences from other cultures and adapt them to its own?

Japan, Korea, and Vietnam incorporated elements of Chinese culture into their own cultures and created unique traditions. Lesson 2.3 explores how Chinese religion and philosophy, written language, the arts, and other cultural elements were adopted, practiced, and adapted in East Asia and beyond.

BACKGROUND FOR THE TEACHER

Bonsai Another Japanese gardening tradition influenced by the Chinese is the art of bonsai—the cultivation of living trees in small containers. Bonsai trees are dwarfed through careful pruning and are meant to look like full-size trees. Bonsai cultivation is inspired by how nature impacts the growth of full-size trees when trees grow in places that limit their expansion. Full-size, natural trees in these locations become dwarfed and twisted. It is believed that the Chinese began the practice of cultivating dwarf trees more than 1,000 years ago, but the Japanese adapted the practice. Japanese cultivated bonsai should reflect the ways in which the natural world can change the form of a living thing. Bonsai have specific desirable qualities, including the amount of space between branches, proportion, the amount of bare trunk showing, and the visual relationship between the type of specimen chosen and the container in which it is grown. Some bonsai may be as small as two inches tall, while larger varieties can be as tall as 47 inches.

History Notebook

Encourage students to complete the Material Culture page for Chapter 11 in their History Notebooks as they read.

INTRODUCE & ENGAGE

EXPLORE HISTORY USING A PHOTOGRAPH

Have students view the photograph of the Temple of Literature in Vietnam. **ASK:** What architectural details do you notice in this building? *(Possible response: The building has a symmetrical nature, intricate carvings, and the building elements are common to Chinese architecture, such as the curved roof corners.)* Explain to students that one important element in Confucianism is the concept of order in the world. **ASK:** How does this building reflect Confucianism's focus on order? *(Possible response: Confucianism is reflected in the building's symmetry and high level of detail.)*

TEACH

GUIDED DISCUSSION

1. **Make Connections** What role do gardens play in the practice of Zen Buddhism? *(They provide a calm and sacred space for meditation.)*

2. **Compare and Contrast** How are the elements of the Japanese tea ceremony similar to those for Japanese gardens? *(Both involve Zen Buddhist ritual, and gardens are often used as a space for tea ceremonies.)*

MATERIAL CULTURE

Remind students of the Historical Thinking question for this chapter: How does one culture adopt influences from other cultures and adapt them to its own? **ASK:** Based on the information and photographs presented in this lesson, how would you answer this question? *(Possible response: Chinese culture was and is highly influential throughout world, especially in nearby Korea, Japan, and Vietnam. Each of these kingdoms adopted multiple aspects of Chinese society. However, they made changes to them to suit their own needs and cultures. For example, tea made its way from China to Japan, and the Japanese took the Chinese tea-drinking tradition and created an elaborate ritual around this popular drink.)*

DIFFERENTIATE

ENGLISH LANGUAGE LEARNERS

Identify Word Parts to Clarify Meaning Explain to students that when they encounter a new word, they can look for familiar word parts to help understand its meaning. Pair students at the **Beginning** level with students at the **Intermediate** or **Advanced** level. Have pairs identify the three parts of the word *inflection* (in-, -flect-, and -ion) and discuss the meaning of each word part. *(in: toward; flect: bend; ion: act or process)* Partners then review the definition of *inflection*—the changing (or "bending") in pitch of the voice. Have them use their understanding of this word to review the text about the Japanese writing system.

GIFTED & TALENTED

Create a Celadon Piece Direct students to choose an example of celadon from the text or from another source and attempt to copy it and its pattern using pencil or pen and paper, or to create an object of their own design. Invite them to discuss what they learned from the process of copying the piece and its pattern. What difficulties did they face? What role do symmetry, repetition, and intricate detail play in their copied piece?

See the Chapter Planner for more strategies for differentiation.

European Chinoiserie The term *chinoiserie* (SHEEN-wahz-ree) refers to a style in European arts and crafts that became popular in the 17th and 18th centuries. *Chinoiserie* is borrowed from the French word *chinois*, meaning "Chinese." Reflecting an increased interest in China and East Asia, European craftsmen created works that were fanciful interpretations of Chinese styles and motifs rather than authentic adaptations of Chinese art.

Confucianism in Vietnam Built in 1070 during the Ly dynasty, the Temple of Literature, shown here, is located in Hanoi, Vietnam. Dedicated to the Chinese philosopher Confucius, the temple features statues and altars dedicated to Confucius and his disciples. In 1076, the Imperial Academy—Vietnam's first university—was established inside the temple.

Students studied Chinese literature, history, and philosophy. The government also held civil service examinations here, and the emperor himself asked the questions. The temple is an example of how Ly dynasty rulers and their Chinese-educated scholars adopted and promoted Confucian values and principles in education, government, and society.

▲ In keeping with the chinoiserie decorative style, Chinese landscape scenes adorn the walls of the Troja Palace in Prague, the capital of the Czech Republic.

◄ This secretary, or writing desk, is an excellent example of French chinoiserie with its pagoda-shaped top, front panels in imitation lacquer, and charming tea-drinking scenes.

Japanese Buddhism This four-panel Japanese folding screen (c. 1700) by Ogata Korin depicts Raijin, the thunder god (above), and his brother Fujin, the wind god (right). Often portrayed together, Raijin and Fujin are Shinto gods, or kami. In Japan's Shinto religion, the brothers are viewed as protectors of Japan. As Buddhism spread from China to Japan, Shinto kami came to be seen as protectors of Buddhism, too. In time, certain Buddhist and Shinto rituals integrated, and Shinto gods were incorporated into Japanese Buddhist traditions.

HISTORICAL THINKING

1. **READING CHECK** What is one example of a culture adapting and improving upon an idea or technology from China?

2. **COMPARE AND CONTRAST** In what way is the chinoiserie style different from other adaptations of Chinese culture?

3. **MAKE CONNECTIONS** Which example of cultural adaptation included in this lesson do you find most interesting? Why?

BACKGROUND FOR THE TEACHER

Chinoiserie The first appearance of a chinoiserie design scheme was incorporated into a room at Versailles for Louis XIV's mistress. The trend became so popular as a result that most European palaces had a "Chinese room" during this period, typically used for the royal ruler's mistress.

Chinoiserie was also popular in European fine arts during this period. Chinoiserie is characterized by asymmetrical design and the use of Chinese figures and scenes, gold overlay, and heavy lacquer. In porcelain, the colors blue and white are often used for the motifs.

Europeans also adopted Asian garden designs during this period. Gazebos, tea houses, and pagodas were commonly seen in European parks during the 1700s. However, Europeans lost interest in incorporating Chinese, Japanese, and Korean influences into art and design during the 1800s, when they became more interested in Southwest Asian and Greek influences.

TEACH

GUIDED DISCUSSION

3. **Make Inferences** What is one reason celadon's green color was desirable? *(Possible response: It resembled the valuable stone jade.)*

4. **Draw Conclusions** Why do you think Europeans were drawn to chinoiserie? *(The Asian world probably seemed very exotic and distant to them.)*

ANALYZE VISUALS

Have students examine the painting of the Japanese woman practicing writing Chinese characters. **ASK:** How does this painting and its accompanying text reflect a different pattern of adoption and adaptation of Chinese influences in Japan? *(Possible response: The Japanese initially adopted Chinese writing but then later created their own writing system because the Chinese system did not fully address all nuances of their language.)*

ACTIVE OPTION

On Your Feet: Chinese Influences on the Arts Word Web Arrange students into teams of four for a Team Word Webbing activity. Provide each team with a large sheet of paper, and give each student a different colored marker. Invite students to create a Word Web for the topic: Chinese Influences on the Arts. Ask each team member to contribute a word to the part of the web nearest to him or her. Then have students rotate the paper and add words to the nearest part of the web again. Encourage teams to share, discuss, and display their completed Word Webs around the classroom.

HISTORICAL THINKING

ANSWERS

1. Answers will vary. Possible response: One example is Korean potters adapting the porcelain-making process from China and improving on the technique by using iron pigments and high-firing wood kilns. These improvements by Korean potters led to the creation of greatly admired celadon.

2. Possible response: Chinoiserie is a more stylized and fanciful view of Chinese culture, rather than an authentic adaptation of cultural elements.

3. Responses will vary. Students should support their answer with details explaining why.

VOCABULARY

Match each vocabulary word with its definition.

1. dialect
2. demographics
3. movable type
4. currency
5. infrastructure
6. physiography
7. daimyo
8. shogun

a. the general and military ruler of Japan
b. individual tablets arranged in a frame for printing
c. money in circulation
d. the characteristics of a particular population
e. a wealthy landowner
f. networks for transportation
g. a regional variation in language
h. the physical geography of a place

READING STRATEGY
COMPARE AND CONTRAST

Comparing and contrasting characteristics of different societies can help you better understand the similarities and differences between them. In a Venn diagram like the one below, list ways in which the effect of Chinese culture on Korea and Japan were similar and different. Then answer the question below.

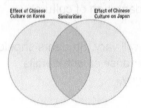

Effect of Chinese Culture on Korea   Similarities   Effect of Chinese Culture on Japan

9. Compare and contrast the effect of Chinese culture on Korea and Japan. How was the effect similar? How was it different?

MAIN IDEAS

Answer the following questions. Support your answers with evidence from the chapter.

10. How did tribute payments to the Jurchen eventually help the Southern Song prosper? LESSON 1.1
11. How did farming practices change over the course of the Song dynasty? LESSON 1.2
12. What effect did woodblock printing have on education in Song China? LESSON 1.2
13. What changes did women and children, particularly young boys, experience during the Song dynasty? LESSON 1.2
14. How was China able to produce extremely large quantities of iron? LESSON 1.2
15. How do Korea's accomplishments during the Koryo dynasty reflect Chinese influence? LESSON 2.1
16. How did Vietnam avoid a Chinese takeover during the Ly dynasty? LESSON 2.1
17. What was the role of the samurai in feudal Japan? LESSON 2.2

HISTORICAL THINKING

Answer the following questions. Support your answers with evidence from the chapter.

18. SYNTHESIZE How did Song inventions help Zhao Rugua write books that facilitated trade between China and other countries?
19. FORM AND SUPPORT OPINIONS What qualities and advances were women admired for in the Song dynasty? Does this show that women were held in high esteem or that they were subservient? Support your opinion.
20. DRAW CONCLUSIONS Why did common people give more money to religious institutions during the Song dynasty?

21. COMPARE AND CONTRAST How was life for the Koryo king in 1170 similar to the life of emperors in feudal Japan?
22. SEQUENCE EVENTS Create a flow chart to show how power shifted from the Japanese emperor to the shogun.

INTERPRET CHARTS

The following chart shows the structure of society in feudal Japan and feudal Europe. Study the chart and then answer the questions that follow.

Hierarchical Society in Feudal Japan

Emperor	Figurehead with a religious role
Shogun	General with absolute power
Daimyo	Landowners
Samurai	Noble warriors (vassals)
Peasants, artisans, and merchants	Lowest class

Hierarchical Society in Feudal Europe

The Pope	Religious ruler
King	Ruler of a regional country
Nobility	Landowners
Knights	Noble warriors (vassals)
Peasants and Serfs	Lowest class

23. How were the roles of the Japanese emperor and the Pope similar? How were they different?
24. Who held more power, a shogun or a king?

ANALYZE SOURCES

Ono no Komachi is known as one of Japan's greatest poets. Read the poem below and answer the questions that follow.

Watching the wan moonlight
illuminate tree limbs,
my heart also brims,
overflowing with autumn.

—Ono no Komachi (c. 833–857)

25. What emotions does this poem convey?
26. How does this poem reflect Shinto ideas as well as universal themes?

CONNECT TO YOUR LIFE

27. EXPLANATORY Two of the great innovations of the Song dynasty were the book and paper currency. Write a short paragraph describing how your life and society at large would be different if these innovations had not been introduced.

TIPS

• List ways paper currency and books affect your life today. Review the lesson on Song contributions to better understand how they changed life for people of the time.

• Draft a main idea statement that expresses your view of the importance of these innovations.

• Use evidence from the text and your own experience to support your main idea.

• Use two or three vocabulary terms in your paragraph.

VOCABULARY ANSWERS

1. g
2. d
3. b
4. c
5. f
6. h
7. e
8. a

READING STRATEGY ANSWER

9. Answers will vary. Sample answer: Chinese culture greatly influenced both Korea and Japan, but in different ways. The effect of Chinese influence in Korea, for example, included the structure of central government, sponsorship of Buddhism, adoption of Confucianism, and the adoption of porcelain-making techniques. However, the Koreans made many improvements and innovations on elements adopted from Chinese culture. For example, the Koreans made an important innovation to Chinese celadon ware, which led to the Koreans creating the finest porcelain in the world. The Japanese carefully selected what elements of Chinese culture suited them and then adapted those elements. The Japanese, for example, embraced the use of tea, which spread from China, but refined tea ceremonies to reflect their own culture. Zen Buddhism had a tremendous effect on Japanese culture, influencing not only religious practices, but tea ceremonies and gardening as well. Zen Buddhism, Confucianism, and the Japanese Shinto religion all influenced the samurai code of behavior.

MAIN IDEAS ANSWERS

10. The Jurchen imported large quantities of Southern Song goods as tribute, so the south was forced to improve production to meet the demand. The Song learned ways to become more efficient.

11. Farmers who had previously grown food to be self-sufficient began to grow surplus food to sell in markets. Northerners also realized that they could grow larger harvests of rice in the south than the crops of wheat and millet that they had grown in the north.

12. An increase in printed books gave students more access to books to study and learn.

13. Women were no longer admired only for their physical beauty and ancestry. Instead, they learned to read and write and were admired for educating their children and managing family finances. More children, particularly young boys, were educated during this time because of increased access to books, so they had more opportunities to take the civil service exams and advance, even if they weren't from the highest class.

14. They developed factories that employed hundreds of workers.

15. Koreans built upon Chinese inventions. They improved upon the Chinese art of porcelain, developing their own process for making celadon in high-firing kilns. They also improved upon the process of printing with movable type by creating movable type with metal rather than with clay.

16. The Ly dynasty paid tribute to China, sent gifts to the Chinese emperor, and sent delegations to meet with the new Song dynasty. They also continued to trade with China. These actions probably helped to stabilize relationships so that China would not take over.

17. The samurai was a vassal. He swore allegiance to the daimyo and fought battles for the daimyo in exchange for land and money.

HISTORICAL THINKING ANSWERS

18. Advances in mapmaking, boat building, and navigational instruments allowed for easier trade on deep-water routes. More trade meant more sharing of goods and information between different countries and cultures, all of which gave Zhao Rugua information about the world outside China.

19. Answers will vary. Students may say that the fact that women could read and write was an advancement that allowed them to prosper. They may also explain that women did divorce their husbands and remarry even though these practices were looked down upon. Other students may argue that women were only valued for serving others, not for their individuality.

20. People were more prosperous, so they had more money to give to religious institutions.

21. The Koryo king lost power and became a figurehead, as did the Japanese emperor.

22. Students' flowcharts should show the following sequence:
The daimyo gained power by forming clans of samurai.
The emperor lost power and became a figurehead.
Daimyo clans fought each other for power.
The most powerful daimyo clan took control, and its leader became the shogun.

INTERPRET CHARTS ANSWERS

23. They both held a religious function. The emperor had a religious role, but he was only a figurehead. The Pope, however, was the religious ruler over all.

24. A shogun held more power because the shogun ruled over all of Japan with absolute power, while European kings were regional rulers.

ANALYZE SOURCES ANSWERS

25. The phrases "wan moonlight" and "overflowing with autumn" express a feeling of sadness or melancholy. The phrase "my heart also brims" suggests that the narrator's heart is full of emotion.

26. By focusing on natural elements and the emotions they evoke, the poem reflects Shinto ideas about nature and the sense of wonder that it arouses. Nature and its sense of wonder and the emotions or feelings people have about nature are also universal, or common to everyone.

CONNECT TO YOUR LIFE ANSWER

27. Students' paragraphs will vary but should contain a thesis; develop the thesis with relevant, supporting details; include vocabulary terms and provide a concluding statement that describes the influence of the Song dynasty.

UNIT 4

Feudal **Europe** and Imperial **East Asia** 481–1500

12 The Mongol Empire, Ming Dynasty, and Ottoman Rise 1150–1500

HISTORICAL THINKING How did nomads from Central Asia build (and unpush) empires?

SECTION 1 The Mongols
SECTION 2 China and the Ming Dynasty
SECTION 3 Rise of the Ottoman Empire

CHAPTER 12 REVIEW

STRATEGY ❶
Analyze Main Ideas
Direct students to read the Main Idea statements aloud for each lesson. Explain that these statements identify and summarize the key idea for each lesson. As students read the lessons, encourage them to make notes about details they find in the text that connect to the Main Idea statements. Tell them this process will help them identify and remember the most important information.

Use with All Lessons

STRATEGY ❷
Analyze Maps Using a TASKS Approach
Help students analyze maps to obtain information by using the following TASKS strategy.

T   Look for a **title** that may give the main idea.
A   **Ask** yourself what the map is trying to show.
S   Determine how any **symbols** are used.
K   Look for a **key** or legend.
S   **Summarize** what you learned.

Use with Lessons 1.1, 1.3, 2.2, and 3.1

STRATEGY ❸
Summarize with Idea Webs
Prompt students to summarize the chapter by creating three Idea Webs, one for each section, and label the center sections as follows: The Mongol Empire, The Ming Dynasty, The Ottoman Empire. Instruct students to complete each web with relevant information as they read the corresponding set of lessons. Encourage students to share their Idea Webs.

The Mongol Empire

Use with All Lessons

STRATEGY ❶
Preview Visuals to Predict
Ask students to preview the title and visuals in each lesson. Then have students tell what they think the lesson will be about. After reading, ask them to repeat the activity to see whether their predictions were confirmed.

Use with All Lessons *Invite volunteers to describe the visuals in detail to help visually impaired students see them.*

STRATEGY ❷
Sequence Events
Write the main events of a lesson on index cards. There should be one event on each index card. Then have pairs of students work together to place the events in the order they occurred. Use the following main events for Lesson 1.1:

- The Mongols were a group of independent tribes who wandered the grassy plains with their herds of sheep, goats, and horses.
- Temujin formed alliances with other Mongol tribes and defeated his rivals to unite all the tribes.
- The Mongol chieftains gave Temujin the title Genghis Khan, which means "universal ruler."
- Genghis Khan and his army invaded northern China and took the Jin capital.
- Genghis Khan and his army seized lands throughout Central Asia.
- Genghis Khan divided his empire into four sections, one for each of his sons.
- Genghis Khan died in 1227.
- Genghis Khan's son Ogodei and his army expanded the empire into Russia and Europe.

Use with All Lessons

STRATEGY ❶
Pronounce Words
Before reading, preview with students at **All Proficiencies** vocabulary terms such as *steppe, ger, khanate, envoy, despotic, omnipotence, ghazi,* and *sultan.* Say each word slowly and have students repeat, noting the pronunciation and syllable stress. Suggest students make a card for each word and write its definition and pronunciation for themselves.

Use with All Lessons

STRATEGY ❷
Develop Vocabulary

Work with students at each proficiency level to develop understanding of the vocabulary words. Post the words in class and keep them displayed throughout the chapter, adding terms for each new lesson. Discuss each term as it comes up during reading. Then use the following sentence frames to assess their understanding of the terms.

- **Beginning** Use vocabulary words in either/or questions, such as: Are **steppes** grassy hills or plains? *(plains)* Do people who live in **gers** live in tents or cabins? *(tents)*
- **Intermediate** Use sentence frames with one blank, such as: **Khanates** are ruled by _____. *(khans)* A **despotic** ruler is a _____. *(tyrant)* Dragons were a symbol of an emperor's **omnipotence**, or _____. *(power)*
- **Advanced** Use sentence frames with two blanks, such as: _____ live in **gers** and _____ from place to place. *(Nomads/travel)* **Ghazis** are _____ for Islam who were bound by a strict code of _____. *(warriors/conduct)*

Use with All Lessons

STRATEGY ❸
Review Sequence Words

To help students put events from the lessons in chronological order, write these sequence words on the board: *first, second, next, then, finally, before, after, earlier, later.* Direct students at the **Beginning** and **Intermediate** levels to work together to write a series of sentences that explain what happens in each lesson. Encourage them to use a variety of sequence words and to vary sentence structure.

Use with All Lessons

GIFTED & TALENTED

STRATEGY ❶
Report on a Conquest

Prompt students to choose one of the leaders described in the chapter and write a news report giving the details of one of his conquests. Have students conduct more research as needed on the strategies employed by the leader to overpower the area that his armies invaded. Instruct students to describe the weapons and methods used to conquer and control people. Encourage them to write an eye-catching headline and an attention-grabbing introduction.

Use with All Lessons

STRATEGY ❷
Write Journal Entries

Tell students to access primary and secondary source materials to learn more about the experiences of the traveler Zheng He or Marco Polo. Then ask them to choose one of the travelers and write journal entries from his perspective. Encourage students to write what the traveler might have experienced, thought, felt, and hoped. Invite students to read their journal entries to the class.

Use with Lessons 2.1 and 2.2

PRE-AP

STRATEGY ❶
Consider Both Sides of an Issue

Suggest that students make a list of both positives and negatives for the rule of one of the leaders discussed in this chapter, such as Genghis Khan or Yongle. Then have them analyze their list and write a paragraph stating their own judgment about this emperor. They should present both positive and negative sides of the emperor's rule, tell their conclusion, and provide other evidence supporting their conclusion. Then have pairs compare their paragraphs and determine which judgment is the most convincing based on the evidence.

Use with All Lessons

STRATEGY ❷
Present a Biography

Invite students to choose a historical figure from the chapter and conduct online research to learn more about this person. Encourage them to write a biography of the person, describing in detail how this person is remembered in history. Invite students to present their biographies orally to the class.

Use with All Lessons

HISTORICAL THINKING How did nomads from Central Asia build great empires?

SECTION 1 The Mongols
SECTION 2 China and the Ming Dynasty
SECTION 3 Rise of the Ottoman Empire

CRITICAL VIEWING
The Hall of Supreme Harmony dominates Beijing's Forbidden City, a huge complex of buildings that once served as the center of Chinese imperial power and government. What details in the photo help indicate the size of the hall?

INTRODUCE THE PHOTOGRAPH

THE HALL OF SUPREME HARMONY

Tell students to examine the photograph of the Hall of Supreme Harmony in Beijing's Forbidden City. Encourage students to compare the Hall of Supreme Harmony to the other structures in the photograph and to think about its relationship to its surroundings. **ASK:** What can you infer about the Hall of Supreme Harmony based on its position relative to the other buildings? *(Possible response: Important events must have taken place in the Hall of Supreme Harmony, since it is much larger than the other buildings.)* **ASK:** What impression was the Hall of Supreme Harmony probably meant to convey? *(Possible response: a sense of power and prestige or the strength of an empire)*

SHARE BACKGROUND

The Forbidden City was designed along a straight north-south axis. The axis symbolizes power and reverence for the government, so many government buildings and public works are situated along the north-south axis. During the Ming dynasty, 16 city gates were built and arranged in relation to the north-south axis with 7 on each side and 2 directly on top of the axis. Today the Forbidden City operates as a museum that draws visitors from around the world.

CRITICAL VIEWING Answers will vary. Possible responses: the tiny-looking people standing near the large buildings; the relative sizes of the other buildings seen in the Forbidden City

HISTORICAL THINKING QUESTION
How did nomads from Central Asia build great empires?

Roundtable: Preview Content Seat students around a table in groups of four. Ask them to consider the following question: What qualities make an empire great? Encourage them to think about why some societies were motivated to expand their control over vast regions and how different leadership styles can affect the people within an empire. Each student around the table should name a different characteristic of a successful empire. One student in each group should record the answers. After groups finish, collect the papers and save them until students have read the chapter. Then have groups add or correct information.

KEY DATES FOR CHAPTER 12

1206	Temujin unites nomadic Mongolian tribes and becomes Genghis Khan.
1212	Genghis Khan invades China.
1218	Genghis Khan begins his conquest of Central Asia.
1227	Genghis Khan dies.
1229	Ogodei, the son of Genghis Khan, becomes the Great Khan.
1241	Ogodei dies, and the Mongols retreat from Europe.
1279	Kublai Khan becomes the first emperor of the Yuan dynasty.
1300	Osmon begins establishing a Turkish state.
1403	Yongle becomes the ruler of the Ming dynasty.
1405	Zheng He embarks on his first naval voyage.
1451	Mehmed II comes to power in the Ottoman Empire.
1453	Mehmed II seizes Constantinople for the Turks.

INTRODUCE THE READING STRATEGY

ANALYZE CAUSE AND EFFECT
Explain to students that analyzing causes and effects can help them understand why actions and events happened, what led up to the actions and events, and what happened afterwards. Go to the Chapter Review and preview the cause-and-effect chart with students. As they read the chapter, have students fill in their own charts with causes and effects of the expansion of the Mongol, Ming, and Ottoman empires.

INTRODUCE CHAPTER VOCABULARY

KEY VOCABULARY

SECTION 1
ger	khanate	steppe

SECTION 2
despotic	envoy	omnipotence

SECTION 3
ghazi	sultan

DEFINITION CHART
As they read the chapter, encourage students to complete a Definition Chart for Key Vocabulary terms. Instruct students to list the Key Vocabulary terms in the first column of the chart. They should add each term's definition in the center column as they encounter the term in the chapter and then restate the definition in their own words in the third column. Model an example on the board, using the graphic organizer shown.

Word	Definition	In My Own Words
omnipotence	unlimited power	having total power over everyone

From Nomads to Conquerors

You've read about the Persian Empire and the Roman Empire, but there was another one that topped them both in size and might: the Mongol Empire. The Mongols swept across Asia in one of history's most impressive conquests.

NOMADIC LIFE

Before the 13th century, the Mongols were a loose collection of independent nomadic tribes from the **steppes**—or vast, grassy plains—beyond the Great Wall, northwest of China. These grasslands were perfect for raising sheep, goats, yaks, and horses. The Mongols' lives were centered on these herds and the products they obtained from them. They made their clothes out of sheep, goat, and yak wool. They ate the animals' meat and made cheese from their milk. The nomads traded these animal products for grain, wood, silk and cotton textiles, and metal products such as knives, daggers, and spears. Mongol tribes traveled with their herds, roaming the steppes and living in portable felt tents called **gers**.

Horses were essential to the Mongols' culture and identity. Children quickly became skilled riders who could shoot a bow and arrow while riding on horseback. Mongol horses were small and stocky and had incredible stamina. They could run for six miles without stopping and pull carts loaded with goods. Most important, the fast, agile horses were the Mongols' best weapon in warfare.

Traditionally, the men looked after the horses, built the gers and carts, and led their herds to new grazing areas. Mongol women had more freedom than women in most sedentary societies. For example, they ran the households when the men were away. Women also set up and took down the gers, milked the animals, and prepared the food. Mongol women often sat beside their husbands during meetings, participating in decision-making. As a result, women had the power to influence decisions at all levels of society.

Mongols belonged to clans, groups of people recognizing a common ancestor. Men served as both herders and soldiers. Different clans were united by chiefs and often fought in battles against rival clans. They also conducted raids to steal cattle or capture prisoners. Although differences in wealth existed among the families, there was no strict social order. And they were treated fairly by their chief, who periodically collected taxes by claiming one of every hundred animals in a herd.

GENGHIS KHAN

A man named Temujin (TEE-moo-juhn) would become a political leader in the early 1200s. He was born around 1162 as the son of a chieftain of a small Mongol tribe. When Temujin was nine, his father was poisoned by someone from another nomadic group. Temujin sought to claim his position as the new leader, but his people refused to acknowledge him. He and his mother and siblings were ostracized, or banished, from the tribe and survived for a time by eating fish and wild plants rather than the traditional nomad diet of meat and milk.

When he grew older, Temujin began forming alliances with other clans and building an army. Temujin trained his soldiers and used strict discipline to create a powerful military machine. As he gathered more followers, he weakened their loyalty to a particular clan by dividing the soldiers into units composed of men from various clans. Temujin wanted his soldiers to be loyal only to him.

Many Mongolians in rural areas still live in gers, and urban dwellers also head to the countryside to spend time in the felt tents. Gers, like the ones shown here on the Mongolian steppes, are often set up in valleys for protection from the wind.

CRITICAL VIEWING Standing more than 130 feet high, this stainless-steel statue of Genghis Khan is the tallest equestrian statue in the world. Visitors can walk through the horse's neck and chest and stand on the animal's head. How does the statue convey Genghis Khan's power?

By 1206, Temujin had defeated his rivals and united the nomadic tribes under his leadership. That same year, the Mongol chieftains gave him the title **Genghis Khan** (JEHNG-gihs KAHN), which means "universal ruler." The title conferred upon him divine status. And that may have been what compelled Genghis Khan to set out to conquer the world. He and the Mongols believed it was his destiny.

Actually, we don't really know very much about Genghis Khan and his motives. The main source for information on the ruler is a book called *The Secret History of the Mongols*, an oral history dating from around 1228 and written down about 100 years later. Historians have theorized about Genghis Khan's life and why he set off on his conquests. Some scholars believe that, with a growing population, the Mongols needed more food and grazing land. Others claim that trade disputes with China meant that the Mongols had to expand to obtain the goods they couldn't produce.

Whatever the reason, Genghis Khan and his army invaded northern China in 1212. Their approach must have been a terrifying sight. As drums sounded the charge, thousands of soldiers galloped toward the enemy. The Mongols designed improved stirrups of leather and metal that allowed them to control their

The Mongol Empire, Ming Dynasty, and Ottoman Rise 327

PLAN: 4-PAGE LESSON

OBJECTIVE
Explain how Genghis Khan led the Mongols to conquer much of Asia and eastern Europe and ruled the largest land empire in history.

CRITICAL THINKING SKILLS FOR LESSON 1.1
- Interpret Maps
- Make Predictions
- Draw Conclusions
- Evaluate
- Explain
- Identify Main Ideas and Details
- Make Inferences
- Analyze Cause and Effect

HISTORICAL THINKING FOR CHAPTER 12
How did nomads from Central Asia build great empires?

For centuries, the Mongols were disjointed groups of nomadic tribes. Lesson 1.1 discusses how Genghis Khan defeated his rivals and united the Mongols in a quest to build an empire.

BACKGROUND FOR THE TEACHER
Mongolian Gers The design of a ger made the structure easy to take down, move, and reassemble—ideal for a nomad's life. A ger is constructed of light wooden poles tied together with ropes made of leather or animal hair. After erecting the pole structure, it is covered in felt made from the wool of sheep, goats, or yaks. Gers are about six feet high at the edge and, because the roof slopes up towards the middle, about nine feet high in the center. A stove or other heat source is located in the center, and a chimney carries smoke up through a hole in the center of the roof. The ger's round design is ideal for windy weather on the Mongolian steppes. Today, about 61 percent of the urban population and 90 percent of the rural population call a ger home. Typically, between 5–15 people live in one ger.

INTRODUCE & ENGAGE

DISCUSS LEADERSHIP STRATEGIES

Invite students to imagine they are leaders bent on conquest and establishing an empire. Ask students to consider several alternatives for how they might deal with newly conquered peoples, such as allowing existing governments to maintain decision-making abilities or imposing their own decisions and customs. Ask volunteers to list the potential benefits and drawbacks of each strategy. Then tell students that in this lesson they will learn about Genghis Khan and the strategies he used with newly conquered peoples.

TEACH

GUIDED DISCUSSION

1. **Evaluate** What personality traits and abilities did Genghis Khan have that enabled him to become the "universal ruler"? *(Possible response: great military ability, strength, ruthlessness, organization, leadership, ambition, intelligence, cruelty)*

2. **Explain** Why did Mongol soldiers control their horses with their legs? *(They controlled their horses with their legs so that their hands would be free to fire weapons.)*

ANALYZE CAUSE AND EFFECT

Discuss the National Geographic Explorer feature on Albert Lin's search for Genghis Khan's tomb. **ASK:** Why did Lin use technology to search for Genghis Khan's tomb? *(Mongol legend warns against disturbing Genghis Khan's grave, so Lin used technology to search for the tomb in a noninvasive manner.)* What might result from using crowdsourcing to enlist help from others? *(Possible response: Lin could generate more interest across the world in locating the tomb.)* What do you think would happen if someone were to find Genghis Khan's tomb? *(Possible responses: People might learn details about Mongolian culture that were previously unknown; Mongolians might be upset that his grave had been disturbed.)*

DIFFERENTIATE

ENGLISH LANGUAGE LEARNERS

Read in Pairs Pair students at the **Beginning** or **Intermediate** level with an English-proficient partner and have them read the lesson together. Instruct the English learners to ask their partners for clarification whenever they encounter a word or sentence construction that is confusing. Suggest that partners point out context clues to help students understand the meanings of unfamiliar terms or constructions. Encourage them to restate sentences in their own words.

GIFTED & TALENTED

Research the Mongolian Army The Mongolian army accomplished incredible feats and conquered a vast amount of the world. Have students conduct online research to find out how the army worked and why it was so successful. Suggest that students divide up the following topics: training, weapons, mobility, organization, strategy, and ground tactics. They should organize their findings into a presentation for the class.

See the Chapter Planner for more strategies for differentiation.

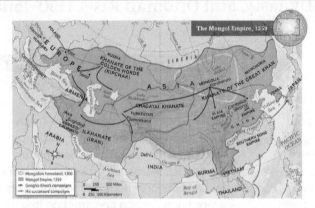

The Mongol Empire, 1259

Key:
- Mongolian homeland, 1300
- Mongol Empire, 1259
- Genghis Khan's campaigns
- His successors' campaigns

Albert Lin teamed up with other National Geographic Explorers as part of his Valley of the Khans Project. Here, he lays out a grid at an archaeological site in the forests of Mongolia.

horses with their legs, leaving their arms free to fire wave after wave of arrows at their foes. Genghis Khan also devised brilliant tactics to outwit the opposition. One of his favorites was to pretend to withdraw his troops. When the opposing army pursued them, other Mongol units would suddenly appear and overwhelm the army. And, of course, the Mongols depended on their horses. A Mongol soldier traveled with three or four horses so that each animal could get a break from carrying the rider—and the warrior could keep moving.

The Jin dynasty in China had fortified the Great Wall against Mongol attack, but it made no difference. After taking the Jin capital in 1215, Genghis Khan turned west. In 1218, he began his conquest of Central Asia and seized lands as far west as the Caspian Sea. Meanwhile, he sent other warriors into southern Russia where they defeated the Kipchaks, a group of nomadic people. Soon after, Genghis Khan returned to invade northwestern China. While on campaign there, Genghis Khan died in 1227. The exact cause of his death is a mystery.

THE GREAT KHAN

Before his death, Genghis Khan divided his empire into four **khanates**, or areas ruled by khans—one for each of his sons. But he intended the empire to remain a single entity with a single leader. In 1229, Genghis Khan's third son, **Ogodei** (AH-gah-day), took the title Great Khan and became the ruler of the Mongol Empire.

Ogodei, along with his brothers, had joined his father in battle and commanded troops during the invasions across Central Asia.

Following in his father's footsteps, Ogodei began to expand the empire. He launched a series of simultaneous campaigns in Asia and Europe. In 1234, the Mongol armies consolidated Genghis Khan's victories in China and overthrew the Jin dynasty. That same year, the Mongols occupied the northern part of Korea. Ogodei also sent soldiers to Iran, Iraq, and Russia where they sacked Kiev, the Russian capital. In 1240. Then in 1241, they marched through Hungary, defeated mounted European knights in battle in Poland, and crossed the Danube River heading for the city of Vienna. It seemed that western Europe would fall to the Mongols as well, but suddenly the Mongol armies retreated. The Europeans did not know why, but it was because of the death of Ogodei. Mongol custom dictated that they return to Karakorum, their capital, to choose a new leader. They never returned.

After the overthrow of the Jin dynasty, Ogodei decided to spare the people and lands of the northern Chinese region from destruction. As a result, Ogodei preserved Chinese culture in north China and benefited from the technologies that had developed there. The Mongols also learned new governmental techniques from the Chinese. In fact, they often profited from the knowledge and skills of those they defeated by bringing

astronomers, engineers, metallurgists, artisans, and merchants to Karakorum. In addition, the Mongols left many local governments intact and allowed conquered peoples to practice their own religions and customs. Some of the people who demonstrated great loyalty to the empire were even permitted to join the Mongol armies.

Under Ogodei's rule, the Mongol Empire expanded to its greatest extent. After his death, however, the rulers of the khanates struggled for power, and the empire began to fall apart.

NATIONAL GEOGRAPHIC EXPLORER **ALBERT LIN**

Searching For Genghis Khan's Tomb

Genghis Khan wanted his burial site to remain a secret, and he got his wish. That didn't stop National Geographic Explorer Albert Lin from trying to find it, though. He began his search for Genghis's tomb in 2009. But since, as Lin says, "Mongolian custom warns that disturbing Genghis Khan's burial site will unleash a curse that could end the world," he figured out how to look for the tomb without using a shovel. Instead, Lin used noninvasive computer-based technologies,

such as satellite imagery, ground-penetrating radar, and remote sensors. He also tried crowdsourcing, inviting volunteers to examine satellite images online and tag anything that warranted further investigation. Lin didn't find Genghis Khan's tomb, but the explorer remains undaunted and continues to apply similar approaches in his other undertakings. As he says, "The most exciting thing about science is the unknown—anything is possible."

HISTORICAL THINKING

1. **READING CHECK** Who were the Mongols?

2. **INTERPRET MAPS** Why do you think the Mongols made Karakorum the capital of their empire?

3. **MAKE PREDICTIONS** What might have happened if Ogodei hadn't died during the Mongol army's invasion of Europe?

4. **DRAW CONCLUSIONS** Why was it wise to allow conquered peoples to keep their local government and practice their religions?

BACKGROUND FOR THE TEACHER

Ogodei's Personality and Accomplishments Although Ogodei was the third son of Genghis Khan, historians credit him as his father's favorite. This was due primarily to his humility, pragmatism, and charisma. Ogodei did not perceive himself as morally or intellectually superior to others and led the Mongol armies by soliciting the opinions of generals he respected. He was also a skilled debater, another trait that served him well as he expanded the Mongol Empire. By expanding the empire throughout Asia, Ogodei brought previously disparate regions together. Supporting the Silk Roads increased trade throughout Asia, and communities that became part of the Mongol Empire gained exposure to one another's technologies and cultures.

TEACH

GUIDED DISCUSSION

3. **Identify Main Ideas and Details** How did the Mongols benefit from preserving Chinese culture in northern China? *(The Mongols benefited by learning from Chinese technologies and methods of government.)*

4. **Make Inferences** Why would being allowed to join the Mongol army be perceived as a reward for people conquered by the Mongols? *(Possible response: Because the Mongol army was incredibly strong, being associated with such a force could convey power and prestige.)*

INTERPRET MAPS

Direct students to the map of the Mongol Empire in 1259. **ASK:** What obstacles might the Mongolian army have faced as they retreated from western Europe and returned to Karakorum after learning about Ogodei's death? *(Possible response: They would have faced physical obstacles, such as rivers and deserts.)* Why might the life of a person living in Armenia have been affected by the Mongol Empire? *(Possible response: Even though Armenia was not part of the Mongol Empire, it was surrounded by the Mongol Empire and would have likely been influenced by its culture and governmental decisions.)*

ACTIVE OPTIONS

On Your Feet: Inside-Outside Circle Have students stand in concentric circles facing each other. Ask students in the outside circle to pose questions about the rule of Genghis Khan and Ogodei to those in the inside circle. On your signal, students should rotate to create new partnerships. Then on another signal, have students trade their inside/outside roles.

> **NG Learning Framework: Theorize About Mongol Motivation**
> **ATTITUDE** Curiosity
> **KNOWLEDGE** Our Human Story

Invite students to read passages from *The Secret History of the Mongols* or conduct online research about the book and its content to further understand historians' theories about Genghis Khan's motivation for setting out to conquer the world. Then have students draw their own conclusions about the leader's motivation and write a paragraph explaining their ideas. Ask volunteers to share their theories with the class.

HISTORICAL THINKING

ANSWERS

1. a loose collection of independent nomadic tribes from the steppes of northwest China

2. Answers will vary. Possible response: because Karakorum was part of their original homeland

3. Answers will vary. Possible response: The Mongols might have conquered all of Europe and put an end to western civilization.

4. Answers will vary. Possible response: The conquered peoples might be less likely to rebel.

CRITICAL VIEWING Answers will vary. Possible response: his size, his posture on the horse, his direct gaze, the crop in his hand all convey the power of Genghis Khan

1.2 Early Accounts of the Mongols

Barbarians. Plunderers. Ferocious Mongol hordes. These are just some of the terms used to describe the invading Mongol armies. But most of these descriptions were penned by early Arab, Persian, and central Asian historians. Recent scholars have challenged this view. While it's certainly true that the Mongols were often brutal during their conquests—by some accounts, the Mongols killed more than 40 million people—studies now suggest that this violence may have been exaggerated. Perhaps there's another side to their story.

It seems there was some method to the Mongols' madness. When they galloped onto the battlefield, they were ready for action. If the opposing army and local people put up a fight, the Mongols were merciless. They slaughtered everyone in their path and leveled the town. However, if the Mongols were offered no resistance, the people were allowed to live.

Genghis Khan may have encouraged foreigners to fear him. He called himself "the punishment of God" and was said to be pleased when others perceived him as such. Sometimes, when he and his army appeared, the frightened townspeople surrendered immediately. The terror his words and presence inspired saved their lives. The Mongols were a pragmatic, or practical, people. If they laid waste to a town, they'd have to rebuild it. And the destruction would interrupt commerce and trade, which the Mongols valued and depended on.

The Mongols were pragmatic about governing as well. Genghis Khan tried to unite the people in his empire both politically and culturally. He established a set of laws that he enforced equally for all his subjects. And as you've read, the Mongols believed in religious freedom. They usually spared the lives of the religious leaders in the lands they invaded. Artisans often enjoyed favored status as well. Genghis also advocated literacy. The leader had the first Mongol writing system created and had it taught to his people.

In this 14th-century Persian miniature depicting the Battle of Ain Jalut, the Mongols—in black caps—battle the Egyptian army in Palestine. The Mongols lost the 1260 battle, which put an end to their effort to conquer Southwest Asia.

DOCUMENT ONE

Primary Source: Book
from *The Complete History* by Ibn al-Athir, c. 1231

The Arab historian Ibn al-Athir spent much of his life in Mosul, a city in present-day Iraq. His chief work, *The Complete History*, is a history of the world. One of the sections in the work deals with the Mongols. In this excerpt from the book, the historian describes what he calls "the announcement of the death-blow of Islam and the Muslims" delivered by the Mongol army.

CONSTRUCTED RESPONSE What words does Ibn al-Athir use to convey the brutality of the Mongols?

For some years I continued averse [unwilling] from mentioning this event, deeming it so horrible that I shrank from recording it. . . . [T]his thing involves the description of the greatest catastrophe and the most dire calamity . . . which befell all men generally and the Muslims in particular. . . . For truly those whom they [the Mongols] massacred in a single city exceeded all the children of Israel. Nay, it is unlikely that all mankind will see the like of this calamity, until the world comes to an end and perishes. . . . These Mongols spared none, slaying women and men and children. . . . The hurt was universal; and which passed over the land like clouds driven by the wind.

DOCUMENT TWO

Primary Source: Book
from *The History of the World Conqueror* by Ala-ad-Din Ata-Malik Juvaini, 1258

Persian historian and official Ala-ad-Din Ata-Malik Juvaini served at the Mongol court in Persia. His book, *The History of the World Conqueror*, is considered one of the most complete histories of Genghis Khan and his successors. In the following, Juvaini discusses the empire-wide postal system established by Genghis. Note that a yam is a relay station that appeared every 20 or 30 miles along the system's route where a rider could eat, sleep, or get a fresh horse.

CONSTRUCTED RESPONSE What conclusions can you draw about the Mongol postal system?

When the extent of their [Mongol] territories became broad and vast, . . . it became essential to ascertain [determine] the activities of their enemies, and it was also necessary to transport goods from the West to the East. . . . Therefore throughout the length and breadth of the land they established yams and made arrangements for the upkeep and expenses of each yam. . . . [M]essengers need make no long detour in order to obtain fresh mounts while at the same time the peasantry and the army are not placed in constant inconvenience. . . . Every year the yams are inspected, and whatever is missing or lost has to be replaced by the peasantry.

DOCUMENT THREE

Primary Source: Book
from *Compendium of Chronicles* by Rashid al-Din, c. 1314

Rashid al-Din was a doctor, historian, and chief minister for the Mongol ruler of Iran. His *Compendium of Chronicles* includes the history of the Mongol Empire. In the excerpt below, Rashid al-Din provides his observations of Ogodei, the Great Khan, while the author was a government official.

CONSTRUCTED RESPONSE How does the historian portray Ogodei?

During the seven years [1235–1241] Ogodei enjoyed life and amused himself. He moved from summer camp to winter camp and vice versa, serene and happy. . . . At every opportunity, he allowed his sublime [inspiring] thoughts to overflow lavishly into the most just and charitable of good deeds, into the eradication [elimination] of injustice and enmity [hatred], into the development of cities and districts, as well as into the construction of various buildings. He never neglected any measure designed to strengthen the framework of peace, and to lay the foundation of prosperity.

SYNTHESIZE & WRITE

1. REVIEW Review what you have learned about the Mongols and their conquests.

2. RECALL On your own paper, write down the main idea expressed in each document.

3. CONSTRUCT Construct a topic sentence that answers this question: How did early historians represent the Mongols?

4. WRITE Using evidence from this chapter and the documents, write an informative paragraph that supports your topic sentence in Step 3.

PLAN: 2-PAGE LESSON

OBJECTIVE
Synthesize information from three primary source documents containing early views of the Mongols.

CRITICAL THINKING SKILLS FOR LESSON 1.2
- Synthesize
- Identify
- Identify Supporting Details
- Analyze Cause and Effect
- Evaluate

HISTORICAL THINKING FOR CHAPTER 12
How did nomads from Central Asia build great empires?

Mongol rulers used cruel methods to conquer new lands, but they often demonstrated good leadership. Lesson 1.2 focuses on how the Mongols were perceived by early historians.

BACKGROUND FOR THE TEACHER
Genghis Khan Genghis Khan was a ruthless military conqueror who caused the deaths of millions of people, especially in Iran and China. However, as a ruler he did some good things. He granted freedom of religion to his diverse subjects; he created an international postal system; he adopted a system of writing; he held regular censuses; he abolished torture; and he encouraged trade. He also fathered hundreds of children, leading modern genealogists to believe that over 16 million men in the world are direct descendants of Genghis Khan. He never allowed images of himself to be made; visual depictions were only created after his death.

INTRODUCE & ENGAGE

PREPARE FOR THE DOCUMENT-BASED QUESTION

Before students start on the activity, briefly preview the three documents. Remind students that a constructed response requires full explanations in complete sentences. Emphasize that students should use what they have learned about the Mongol Empire in addition to the information in the documents.

TEACH

GUIDED DISCUSSION

1. **Identify** In Document One, what does the writer compare the Mongol invasion to? *(The writer compares the Mongol invasion to a storm that he states, "passed over the land like clouds driven by the wind.")*

2. **Identify Supporting Details** Based on the documents and the information about them, what accomplishments did the Mongols achieve? *(Possible responses: created a writing system and taught it to the people, established a set of laws, constructed a postal system, developed and rebuilt cities and districts, constructed new buildings, laid a foundation of prosperity)*

3. **Analyze Cause and Effect** According to the author of Document Three, what happened as a result of Ogodei's "sublime" thoughts? *(Ogodei's sublime thoughts led to good deeds, the end of injustice and hatred, and brought about the construction of cities, districts, and buildings.)*

EVALUATE

After students have completed the Synthesize & Write activity, allow time for them to exchange paragraphs and read and comment on the work of their peers. Establish guidelines for comments prior to the activity so feedback is constructive and encouraging in nature. Comments should focus on the most significant parts that address the purpose of the activity and the audience.

ACTIVE OPTION

On Your Feet: Jigsaw Strategy Organize students into "expert" groups and assign each group one of the documents to analyze and summarize its main ideas into their own words. Then regroup students into new groups so that each group has at least one member from each expert group. Students in the new groups take turns sharing the summaries from their expert groups.

DIFFERENTIATE

ENGLISH LANGUAGE LEARNERS

Summarize Pair **Beginning** and **Intermediate** proficiency students. Assign each pair a document to read and summarize. Provide the following to help students effectively summarize each document.

- **Document One:** This document is about _____. The writer is _____ from _____. He says the Mongols _____. Then the Mongols _____.
- **Document Two:** This document is about _____. The writer is _____ from _____. He says the Mongols _____, which is _____. Every year the Mongols _____.
- **Document Three:** This document is about _____. The writer is _____ from _____. He says Ogodei _____. Then Ogodei _____.

PRE-AP

Research a Battle Have students conduct research to learn about the Battle of Ain Jalut to find out who fought the battle, what tactics were used, and how its outcome affected the people involved and their history.

SYNTHESIZE & WRITE

ANSWERS

1. Answers will vary.

2. Answers will vary. Possible response: Document 1: The Mongols were bloodthirsty murderers who showed no mercy to their victims. Document 2: The Mongol postal system spanned the empire and was well-run and efficient. Document 3: Ogodei was a great leader who constantly considered new measures to improve the lives of his subjects.

3. Answers will vary. Possible response: While some early historians reviled the Mongols, others praised their institutions and leadership.

4. Answers will vary. Students' paragraphs should include their topic sentence from Step 3 and provide several details from the documents to support it.

CONSTRUCTED RESPONSE

Document One: He uses words such as "horrible," "catastrophe," "dire calamity," and "massacred."

Document Two: Possible response: It was efficient and well maintained.

Document Three: Possible response: happy, wise, serene, caring, charitable, just, a great leader and administrator

A Fragmenting Empire

Family feuds rarely end well. When Genghis Khan's descendants squabbled over who would be sole ruler of the Mongol Empire, it broke into four dominions. The ruler of one of them would be the greatest khan since Genghis.

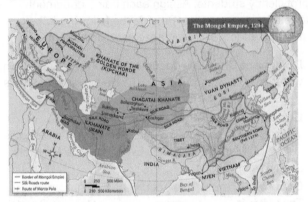

The Mongol Empire, 1294

DIVISION OF THE EMPIRE

As you've read, a struggle for power erupted after Ogodei's death in 1241. At last, 10 years later, Mongke, one of Genghis Khan's grandsons, asserted himself as Great Khan. Mongke continued to expand the empire. His armies marched through Southwest Asia where they conquered Iran, Iraq, and Syria. In 1258, the Mongols killed the last Abbasid caliph in Baghdad, bringing an end to the Abbasid Empire. Mongol soldiers also headed east and advanced against China. In 1257, Mongke himself took charge of the army in China. Two years later, however, he died.

Mongke had been a relatively kind and popular ruler. He brought economic stability to the empire and instituted

measures that protected ordinary civilians. He was also the last of the Great Khans to hold the enormous empire together. Mongke's brothers fought for control, and **Kublai Khan** (KOO-bluh KAHN) emerged the victor. In 1260, he declared himself the Great Khan. By that time, the Mongol Empire had fractured into four khanates: the Golden Horde, or Kipchak Khanate; the Chagatai Khanate; the Ilkhanate; and the Khanate of the Great Khan.

The Golden Horde stretched from Hungary to the steppes of Siberia and included the Russian principalities of Kiev and Moscow. Chagatai Khan, a son of Genghis Khan, ruled the central Asian khanate that bore his name and was succeeded by his grandson.

332 CHAPTER 12

The Ilkhanate, centered in Iran and including the former Abbasid capital of Baghdad, was less successful. Its economy was impoverished by the high taxes imposed by its Mongol rulers.

KUBLAI KHAN

Kublai Khan seized control of the Khanate of the Great Khan, which included Mongolia, Korea, Tibet, and northern China. But he was determined to add to his empire by conquering all of southern China. Remember reading about China's Song dynasty? The leaders of the dynasty fought off Kublai's forces during much of the 1270s but finally surrendered in 1279. As a result, Kublai Khan became ruler of all China, the first to unite the lands in more than 300 years. He was also the first foreigner to rule the entire country. As China's new emperor, Kublai moved his capital to the site of modern Beijing and founded a new dynasty called Yuan (YOO-AHN). He would try to further extend his empire to Japan and, later, into Southeast Asia, but these attempts failed.

Under the Yuan dynasty, the Chinese government continued much as before, with a strong central state built around a bureaucracy. But each Chinese official had to report to a Mongol or other Central Asian superior. Because the number of Chinese in the empire far exceeded the number of Mongols, Kublai feared putting too much power in their hands. For the most part, the Mongols lived apart from the Chinese.

Many Chinese hated Mongol rule and resented being subjects of a "barbarian" king from Central Asia. Kublai forced Chinese peasant farmers to work on his extravagant building projects, particularly in his capital. Beijing became a wealthy city filled with magnificent palaces and gardens—all for the enjoyment of rich foreigners. And many of the farmers were forced off their land when they couldn't pay their taxes. Aware of Chinese unrest and fearful of rebellion, the Yuan

This painting from a French illustrated manuscript from around 1400 shows the departure of Marco Polo and his father and uncle from Venice in 1271. In the painting, Polo, dressed in a light pink robe and portrayed as an older man, speaks to a group of dignitaries before he boards the boat that will take him to the court of Kublai Khan.

dynasty enforced laws that restricted the activities of the local people.

Still, Kublai Khan was an effective leader. He extended the Grand Canal initially built during the Qin dynasty to Beijing and built roads along its banks. Grains and other goods moved from the south of China to the north on these land and water routes. Above all, Kublai encouraged foreign trade. Caravan routes across Central Asia—including the Silk Roads—were largely safe, thanks to the **Pax Mongolica**, or Mongol peace. This period of peace, which continued from the mid-1200s to the mid-1300s, was due to the law and order imposed by the Mongols across Eurasia.

Kublai also invited foreign merchants to visit China. The most famous of these was the Venetian trader **Marco Polo**, who traveled as a teenager with his father and uncle along the Silk Roads and arrived at Kublai Khan's court around 1275. Polo came to be employed by Kublai Khan and was sent on government missions throughout China and beyond. After serving the emperor for nearly 20 years, Polo returned home greatly impressed with Kublai Khan's wealth and power.

HISTORICAL THINKING

1. **READING CHECK** What happened after Mongke's death?

2. **ANALYZE CAUSE AND EFFECT** Why did the Chinese feel like second-class citizens under Kublai Khan's rule?

3. **INTERPRET MAPS** Why was it important to the Mongols to make sure the routes of the Silk Roads were safe?

The Mongol Empire, Ming Dynasty, and Ottoman Rise 333

PLAN: 2-PAGE LESSON

OBJECTIVE

Explain how Kublai Khan brought all of China under his control after the Mongol Empire split into the four khanates.

CRITICAL THINKING SKILLS FOR LESSON 1.3

- Analyze Cause and Effect
- Interpret Maps
- Compare and Contrast
- Analyze Visuals

HISTORICAL THINKING FOR CHAPTER 12

How did nomads from Central Asia build great empires?

After a period of expansion, the Mongol Empire fractured into four khanates. Lesson 1.3 discusses how Kublai Khan expanded his khanate and became ruler of all of China.

BACKGROUND FOR THE TEACHER

The Travels of Marco Polo When Marco Polo returned to Europe, he was briefly imprisoned by the Genoese, a group hostile to the Venetians. He met another prisoner named Rustichello, who was a writer. Polo recounted stories of his travels in Asia to Rustichello, who wrote them down. The stories were published in a book known in English as *The Travels of Marco Polo*. Many historians today question the book's historical accuracy. Some scholars believe that parts of the text do not depict Polo's travels exactly as they happened, but rather contain information he heard from other travelers. A lack of concrete detail led some to believe that portions of the book had been fabricated. Furthermore, the original manuscript is not available, and Rustichello wrote it in his own style rather than recording the exact words of Marco Polo. In addition, *The Travels of Marco Polo* had been copied many times before the invention of the printing press. These copiers likely took liberties with which aspects of the manuscript were included or left out.

INTRODUCE & ENGAGE

WALK IN THEIR SHOES

Present a "what-if" scenario to students: Suppose another country defeated the United States and took over the government. What if the foreign country's people were in charge, and Americans had to obey their wishes? How would you feel? How would your life change? After students discuss the changes and their feelings, tell them that when Kublai Khan took control of China, that's what happened to the Chinese.

TEACH

GUIDED DISCUSSION

1. **Analyze Cause and Effect** Which of the four khanates was less successful, and why? *(The Ilkhanate was impoverished because its Mongol rulers imposed high taxes that prevented citizens from spending more money on goods and services.)*

2. **Compare and Contrast** How did the leadership styles of Mongke and Kublai Khan differ? *(Possible response: Mongke held the enormous empire together through kindness and respect for local customs. Kublai Khan was more authoritative, kept the Chinese people subjugated, and imposed strict rules.)*

ANALYZE VISUALS

Encourage students to examine the painting of Marco Polo preparing to leave Venice. **ASK:** Why do you think Marco Polo is portrayed as much older than he actually was when he embarked on his travels? *(Possible response: He was portrayed as older to convey the greater wisdom of an older man.)*

ACTIVE OPTIONS

On Your Feet: Jigsaw Strategy Group students into four "expert" groups, and have each one conduct research to learn more about one of the khanates: the Golden Horde, the Chagatai Khanate, the Ilkhanate, and the Khanate of the Great Khan. After the groups have concluded their study, regroup students so that each new group has at least one member from each expert group. Then have experts report on their study to the new group.

NG Learning Framework: Discuss Systems of Oppression
SKILL Communication
KNOWLEDGE Our Human Story

Tell students to conduct online research to learn more about the experiences of Chinese people living under Mongol rule during the Yuan dynasty. Instruct them to write notes summarizing their findings, and then lead a discussion comparing the Mongol oppression of the Chinese to the experiences of other groups of oppressed people that students have studied.

DIFFERENTIATE

STRIVING READERS

Preview Text Help students preview Lesson 1.3. Point out the text features, such as the lesson title, Main Idea statement, and headings. Ask students what they expect the lesson to be about based on the headings. As students begin reading, help them confirm their understanding of each paragraph before they move on to the next one.

ENGLISH LANGUAGE LEARNERS

Make Word Cards As they read the lesson, prompt students at the **Intermediate** level to keep a list of the unfamiliar words they encounter, such as *descendants, dominions, succeeded,* and *imposed*. Direct students to look up each word in a dictionary and make a word card to help them understand and pronounce the word. Tell them to write the word on one side of a card and its definition and phonetic spelling, if needed, on the other side.

See the Chapter Planner for more strategies for differentiation.

HISTORICAL THINKING

ANSWERS

1. The Mongol Empire split into four khanates with four different rulers.

2. because he excluded them from high positions in the government and imposed strict laws on their behavior

3. because the routes ran through the entire Mongol Empire

Out of Eden:
Ten Million Steps

"We walk on. At dawn we inch steadily toward our own blue shadows that stretch, bending, far behind us: shades that slip backwards over the desert horizon. We will meet them one day." –Paul Salopek

The stone ruins of the Beleuli caravanserai Salopek mentions in his journal stand on an Uzbek steppe that was once the scene of a busy marketplace.

In Chapter 1, you read about Paul Salopek's long walk to retrace the path of human migration from Ethiopia to the southernmost tip of South America. He began his trek in January 2013. Three and a half years later, Salopek had traveled 3,600 of the planned 21,000 miles. He found himself on the Ustyurt Plateau of Uzbekistan, following the path of the Silk Roads, the historic trade routes between East Asia and the Mediterranean. There, in land once conquered by Genghis Khan, Salopek visited the ruins of one of many ancient travelers' inns that dotted the landscape and noted the irony of the fact that the ruthless Mongols had built such peaceful, practical rest stops.

> PRIMARY SOURCE

JULY 2016—UZBEKISTAN:
DISCOVERING A MEDIEVAL MOON BASE IN THE HEART OF CENTRAL ASIA

We are moving slowly through the world.

The sun melts a hole in the sky: white-hot as the focused beam of a magnifying glass. The steppe is sweltering. Cloudless. Windless. We create our own paltry wind by walking.

There are three of us. Aziz Khalmuradov, my Uzbek guide, limps behind on blister-broke feet. The donkey wrangler, Jaikhan Bekniyazov, is dizzy with some mysterious ailment—sunstroke, or perhaps extreme homesickness. We slog eastward 15 or 20 miles a day across the burning steppe. . . . The planet creaks underfoot, carrying us forever toward sunrise. Toward Khiva—the old mud-walled khanate. Toward the unimaginable cold of Siberia. Toward Beleuli.

Beleuli: a stone ruin. A Silk Road caravanserai [inn for travelers] lost on the grasslands of Karakalpakstan. Built in late 13th century. A pioneering artifact of globalization. A work of art. A cautionary tale.

"The construction was clever," Shamil Amirov, an archaeologist with the Karakalpak branch of the Academy of Sciences of Uzbekistan, tells me. "Beleuli was extremely remote. So they built it for self-sufficiency."

The outpost's defensive walls were turreted to protect treasure-laden caravans against local nomad attacks. To catch the stray breezes, passing merchants occupied second-floor apartments above a grand central square. (The ground-level rooms served as stables for camels, horses, donkeys—the cargo animals.) There were market stalls, craftsmen's workshops, baths, soldiers' barracks. Shipments of gold, spices, silks, medicines, carpets, porcelain, and other luxury goods packed the warehouses. At the center of Beleuli's courtyard: a public drinking reservoir the size of a hotel swimming pool.

Beleuli was a medieval moon base.

Wheat was sown nearby on the banks of seasonal ponds. These crops supplied the caravanserai's bakery and fed its cattle herd. Most impressive of all, a system of stone-domed cisterns, called sardobas, stored scarce rainwater. This water was collected—via a complex network of underground brick gutters—from erratic steppe thunderstorms. While Beleuli's traders sipped clean water from faucets, London's 40,000 unwashed citizens waded through ankle-deep slops.

Who conceived Beleuli?

The answer is improbable: the Mongols. Warrior-nomads. The supposed destroyers of civilizations, the horsemen of apocalypse, the urbanite's nightmare, the human locusts.

Having destroyed the powerful Central Asian trading empire of Khorezm in 1221, Genghis Khan's hordes began to impose their own taxes on the commerce bumping through the region by camelback from India, China, and Europe. Pillage and mass slaughter were dandy. But business was business. To promote this lucrative traffic, the Mongol overlords ordered a string of travelers' inns, spaced a day's camel ride apart, to be built across the Ustyurt Plateau, an immense wilderness of salt flats and prickly grasses that isolated the rich Central Asian cities of the Oxus River from the mercantile hub of the Caspian Sea. (Today the Ustyurt Plateau, straddling Uzbekistan and Kazakhstan, is more desolate than ever.) In effect, the Mongols bankrolled a primordial interstate highway system, complete with fortified truck stops.

HISTORICAL THINKING

READING CHECK Why does Salopek express surprise that the caravanserai was conceived and built by the Mongols?

PLAN: 4-PAGE LESSON

OBJECTIVE

Describe what Paul Salopek has discovered and learned during his walk through Central Asia.

CRITICAL THINKING SKILLS FOR LESSON 1.4

- Identify Main Ideas and Details
- Make Inferences
- Draw Conclusions
- Form and Support Opinions
- Analyze Primary Sources

HISTORICAL THINKING FOR CHAPTER 12

How did nomads from Central Asia build great empires?

Mongols developed rest stops along trade routes that kept traders safe and nourished as they trekked through the desert. Lesson 1.4 describes these rest stops as well as the encounters Paul Salopek has had while on his journey through Central Asia.

BACKGROUND FOR THE TEACHER

Ten Million Steps Jeff Blossom, Chief Cartographer for the Out of Eden Walk, is responsible for the maps and calculations of Salopek's journey. In his story "Mapping Ten Million Footsteps," Blossom explains how he used Salopek's 32-inch stride and the miles tracked on Salopek's GPS to calculate the explorer's first 10 million steps. Blossom uses a variety of maps to illustrate both the steps Salopek has taken and the steps he has been unable to take while crossing bodies of water. His maps also detail the terrain Salopek is forced to traverse, such as the Caucasus Mountains through Azerbaijan. Salopek's GPS determines his location every 15 seconds, allowing for accurate calculations and maps. The GPS, carried in Salopek's backpack, provides Blossom—and the rest of the world—with a view of each of Salopek's steps.

History Notebook

Encourage students to complete the National Geographic Explorer and Traveler page for Chapter 12 in their History Notebooks as they read.

INTRODUCE & ENGAGE

ACTIVATE PRIOR KNOWLEDGE

Remind students that in Chapter 1 they learned about National Geographic Explorer and Traveler Paul Salopek and his Out of Eden Walk: the 21,000-mile trek to retrace the path of human migration from Ethiopia to the southern tip of South America. Have students discuss what they remember reading about Salopek and his travels. Ask them why he embarked on the walk and what he hopes to learn. Tell students they will learn more about Salopek's journey in this lesson.

TEACH

GUIDED DISCUSSION

1. **Identify Main Ideas and Details** What structures built by the Mongols does Salopek visit during his journey? *(He visits the ruins of a caravanserai they built on the Silk Roads.)*

2. **Make Inferences** Why do you think Salopek refers to the stone ruin of the caravanserai at Beleuli as "a cautionary tale"? *(Possible response: The ruin is a reminder of the impermanence of empires, cultures, and ways of life.)*

ANALYZE PRIMARY SOURCES

Direct students to the first primary source. **ASK:** How does Salopek describe the road to Beleuli? *(sweltering, cloudless, windless)* **ASK:** What did Beleuli and other caravanserai provide, and why did the Mongols build them? *(Caravanserai provided a safe place for traders to rest, eat, and drink water. The Mongols built these oases so traders could continue to travel through the desolate region and pay the Mongols taxes on the goods they carried.)*

DIFFERENTIATE

STRIVING READERS

Use Sentence Starters Provide these sentence starters for students to complete after reading:

1. Salopek says his journey across the desert was _____.

2. A caravanserai is _____.

3. Beleuli and other caravanserai were conceived by _____.

4. The point of slow journalism is _____.

5. Safina Shohaydarova and Furough Shakarmamadova are _____.

GIFTED AND TALENTED STEM

Design a Caravanserai Have students design a caravanserai based on the information in the lesson. Students may sketch or use a computer to provide a visual representation of what a caravanserai may have looked like in the time of Genghis Khan. Students should label each of the features and prepare to present their design to the class or share it on a class website.

See the Chapter Planner for more strategies for differentiation.

Crossroads Revival

More a network than a single path, the Silk Roads emerged over centuries of interaction and trade. Routes shifted as empires rose and fell; traffic declined after the rise of maritime trade. Regional powers now want to revive these historic commercial lifelines to better connect Asia with Europe and beyond.

AREA ENLARGED

Planned route

Completed

NORTH AMERICA

ASIA

AFRICA

SOUTH AMERICA

Paul Salopek's 21,000-mile journey on foot traces human migrations from East Africa to Patagonia.

Out of Eden Walk: January 2013–October 2017

RUSSIA

— Paul Salopek's route
— Infrastructure projects, 2006–2017*
▲ Ruin
— Ancient Silk Road corridor

KAZAKHSTAN

A New Silk Road
China is leading the Belt and Road Initiative to revitalize and expand trade routes, pledging one trillion dollars in what it calls "the plan of the century."

Astrakhan
Astana
Aral Sea
Caspian Sea
Lake Balkhash
GEORGIA
Day 1 of section
Aktau
USTYURT PLATEAU
Tbilisi
Travel by boat
ARM.
AZER.
Baku
QIZILQUM
Bishkek
KYRGYZSTAN
TIAN SHAN
TURKEY
AZER.
Khiva
Turtkul
UZBEKISTAN
Tashkent
Day 100
Kashgar
CHINA
Bukhara
Samarqand
Tashkurgan
Nisa
Merv
TAJIKISTAN
TURKMENISTAN
Amu Darya
Mosul
IRAQ
Balkh
Mashhad
PAKISTAN
Baghdad
I R A N
Herat
Kabul
Islamabad
AFGHANISTAN
Tehran
Lahore
The Old Silk Road
From silk and spices to livestock and religions, the trade of goods and ideas ebbed and flowed between the second century B.C.E. and the 14th century C.E.
Kandahar
INDIA
Persian Gulf
New Delhi

*Includes belt and road initiative as well as other projects. Lauren C. Tierney and Ryan T. Williams, NGM Staff.
SOURCES: Patrick Wellever, Reconnecting Asia Project, Center for Strategic and International Studies

Salopek's original plan was to complete his 21,000-mile journey in seven years. But three years into the odyssey, it was clear that he would need more time. The weather, the terrain, and the politics of a given region had slowed his pace. Salopek revised his plans, expecting the entire journey to take about a decade. But the delays did not dampen Salopek's spirits. In fact, for this slow journalism project, the deliberate pace is the point.

PRIMARY SOURCE

APRIL 2016—WHAT I'M LEARNING FROM WALKING 21,000 MILES AROUND THE WORLD

Naturally, since setting out from the Horn of Africa in 2013, walking has made my legs and heart stronger. But more important, it's limbered up my mind. Spanning nations, continents, and time zones on foot—day after day, month after month—has altered the way I experience life on the planet.

I've learned quickly, for instance, that the poorest parts of the globe are the most congenial to foot travel. In Ethiopia, where few people own cars, everybody walks. Even the smallest child could guide me through complex landscapes still netted by human trails. In more affluent and motorized countries, by contrast, people lose connection not only with their environment but with the shape of the world itself. Cars annihilate time and distance. Locked inside bubbles of metal and glass, confined to narrow strips of asphalt, we become drugged with speed. . . . On foot in car-crazy Saudi Arabia, I discovered the pointlessness of asking directions. . . .

One step at a time, Paul Salopek is exploring lands that early humans, Silk Road traders, and Central Asian armies once traveled. In this 2016 photo, Salopek walks along the Caspian Sea in Kazakhstan with his traveling companion—a cargo pony named Alex Moen.

Walking across the Earth, I have relearned the old ceremony of departures and arrivals. (Making and striking campsites, packing and unpacking rucksacks, an antique and comforting ritual.) I have absorbed landscapes through my taste buds, by gleaning farmers' harvests. And I have reconnected with fellow human beings in ways I could never conceive as a reporter crisscrossing maps by jet and car. Out walking, I constantly meet people. I cannot ignore them or drive by them. I greet them. I chat with strangers five, ten, twenty times a day. I am engaged in a meandering, three-mile-an-hour conversation that spans two hemispheres. In this way walking builds a home everywhere.

HISTORICAL THINKING

READING CHECK According to Salopek, how has walking enhanced his experience as he travels across the world?

BACKGROUND FOR THE TEACHER

"How Is It Possible for a Girl?" Throughout his journey, Salopek has enlisted the company of local journalists, interpreters, or trekking guides. Fourteen of these successful, capable companions have been women. Expert trekkers Furough Shakarmamadova and Safina Shohaydarova walked for more than 100 miles with Salopek at separate times. Many of Salopek's female companions admitted that they were not sure they could complete their portion of the walk. However, after facing the judgment of villagers and their own fears, they feel like they could go back and do it on their own. The experiences have proven to be empowering to the women. They hope to see young women someday taking on challenges like Salopek's and are determined to make political and social changes to give women a voice. They have also served as an inspiration to young girls who plan to become soldiers, lawyers, or journalists, too.

TEACH

GUIDED DISCUSSION

3. **Draw Conclusions** In what way is a "deliberate pace" the point of Salopek's journey? *(Possible response: Early humans probably traveled at a slow and deliberate pace during their migration, and such a pace allows Salopek to understand their challenges, make his own observations, and talk to people along the way.)*

4. **Form and Support Opinions** Do you agree with Salopek's view that people in motorized countries lose their connection with their environment and with the shape of the world itself? Explain. *(Possible responses: Yes, people do lose their connection because they are focused on operating a vehicle and aren't paying attention to the world around them. They also don't feel every hill and valley in a car as they would if they were walking. No, people don't lose their connection. They get to see even more places if they can travel by car than they could travel by walking.)*

ANALYZE PRIMARY SOURCES

Direct students to the second primary source. Point out that Salopek says everyone walks in Ethiopia because few people own cars. **ASK:** What does Salopek say results when people rely too much on traveling by car? *(They lose connection with their environment and with the shape of the world.)* Then tell students that Salopek's ritual of making and striking campsites mimics what early humans might have done during their migration. **ASK:** What does he mean when he says, "I am engaged in a meandering three-mile-an-hour conversation that spans two hemispheres"? *(Possible response: He is conversing with the people he meets on his long journey, and he is also communicating with the land he's slowly traversing.)*

ACTIVE OPTIONS

On Your Feet: Think, Pair, Share Have students think about the challenges Salopek encounters daily on his journey. Then have pairs get together to discuss the topic. Following this discussion, encourage students to share their thoughts with the class.

> **NG Learning Framework: Map Paul Salopek's Progress**
> **ATTITUDE** Curiosity
> **KNOWLEDGE** Our Human Story

Have groups of students work together to add to the map of Salopek's travels shown in the lesson. Ask them to conduct online research to find where the explorer is now and indicate his progress on their map. Students should also add labels and visuals to the map to describe Salopek's experiences and illustrate what he has seen. Ask groups to post their maps on a class website or display them in the classroom.

HISTORICAL THINKING

ANSWERS

1. Possible response: The Mongols' reputation is that they were ruthless warriors devoted to conquering new lands, so the fact that they devised a practical, safe haven for travelers is unexpected.

2. Possible response: Walking has allowed Salopek to experience connections with people that he wouldn't have experienced traveling by car.

The Impact of the Mongols

All things—both good and bad—must come to an end. This old adage
certainly seems to apply to great empires. The Mongol Empire was ending,
but its impact would resound throughout much of the world.

END OF THE EMPIRE

Kublai Khan's treatment of the Chinese led to hostility
among the people. Some formed secret societies and
plotted rebellion. But Kublai was a strong leader who
knew how to control his kingdom. After his death in
1294, however, the Yuan dynasty gradually declined.
Seven emperors ruled China over the next 40 years, but
none of them possessed Kublai's leadership skills.

During the 1360s, rebellions broke out in China, and
Zhu Yuanzhang (JOO YOO-AHN-JAHNG), the son of
a peasant, became the rebels' leader. In 1368, they
drove the Mongols out of China, bringing the Yuan
dynasty to an end. Zhu declared a new dynasty, the
Ming, or "brilliant," dynasty, and chose for himself the
title **Hongwu** (HUNG-WOO), which roughly translates
as "vastly martial." You'll learn more about the Ming
dynasty in the next lesson.

By the time the Yuan dynasty collapsed, most of the
other khanates had disintegrated as well. In the 1330s,
the government of the Ilkhanate fell apart. The Chagatai
khans ruled Central Asia until the 1370s when the
Turkish conqueror Timur—also known as **Timur the
Lame**—proclaimed himself ruler of the western part
of the khanate. After his conquest, khans with no real
power occupied the throne. The khans who ruled the
Golden Horde in Russia stayed in power the longest.
They ruled Russia for 250 years. Russian leader **Ivan III**
finally led Russia to independence from Mongol rule in
1480. The great Mongol Empire had come to a close.

CRITICAL VIEWING Markets still thrive in some of the
cities and towns along the Silk Roads. The women in
this photo are selling food at a market in Samarkand,
Uzbekistan. What other traditions are evident in the photo?

MONGOLIAN INFLUENCE

The Mongol Empire was gone but not forgotten. Its
influence was felt long after the Mongols retreated to
the steppes of Central Asia. Perhaps the Mongols'
greatest legacy was linking Europe and Asia through
trade. Merchants from Europe, China, Southwest Asia,
and India traveled the Silk Roads and traded ideas
as well as goods. Although many Mongols practiced
shamanism, a worship of nature spirits, they were open
to the religious beliefs of others. Different religions
gained followers along the routes. Islam became the
dominant religion of people along the Silk Roads and
was adopted by Mongols in several of the khanates.
Unfortunately, disease was sometimes carried along
the trade routes. Some scholars believe the terrible
plague that devastated western Asia, North Africa, and
Europe in the 1300s may have arrived in lands along the
Mediterranean Sea, in part, via the Silk Roads.

Contacts between Europe and Asia also spread new
ideas in science. Paper production and gunpowder,
both Chinese innovations, reached Europe during this
period. The Chinese adopted Islamic medical advances
in treating wounds, while Indian scientists learned to
question the idea of a geocentric, or Earth-centered,
universe from Muslim astronomers.

Cross-cultural exchanges took place in the arts. Muslim
artists were influenced by artistic techniques from China
and India. Human figures, featured in both countries'
artistic works but traditionally forbidden in Islamic
art, began to appear in Muslim creations, particularly
Persian miniatures. In addition, influenced by Indian
narrative art, murals in mosques sometimes depicted
stories from sacred Islamic texts. In Europe, artists
began using the Chinese dragon in their works. The
Mongols themselves had a great impact on the arts.
Chinese painting, ceramics, and literature flourished
under the rule of Kublai Khan. And Ogodei brought
artists and architects to build and decorate his capital
at Karakorum. Russian architecture was influenced by
Central Asian styles, though after the rule of the Golden
Horde, Russian leaders remained suspicious of the
nomadic societies to their south and east.

The network of roads built by the Mongols across
Eurasia also brought the East and West into contact.
Craftsmen, scientists, engineers, and merchants from
Europe could travel as far as China for the first time.

This blue-glazed Persian jar was probably bartered
on the Silk Roads around 1280.

And the postal system established by Genghis Khan
functioned as the central nervous system of the huge
empire. The Mongols used the postal relay stations to
provide visiting **envoys**, or diplomatic representatives,
with guides, guards, food, and shelter.

During Mongol rule, European merchants carried Asian
goods to their home markets where demand for these
items, especially silk, quickly rose. But traveling over
land to obtain the products took a lot of time. Eventually,
Europeans would begin to search for a sea route to
China. This search, in part, led to the European Age
of Exploration in the 1400s, which you will read about
later. In their quest for the sea route, Europeans were
aided by the descriptions of places and distances in
Marco Polo's book. Some of the information was used
to create maps of the East. And the Italian explorer
Christopher Columbus is said to have taken Polo's
writings with him when he set off on the voyages that
led him to the Americas.

HISTORICAL THINKING

1. **READING CHECK** How did the
Yuan dynasty fall?

2. **ANALYZE CAUSE AND EFFECT**
How do you think Islam spread
along the Silk Roads?

3. **SYNTHESIZE** In what way are the
Mongols, Marco Polo, and later
European exploration connected?

PLAN: 2-PAGE LESSON

OBJECTIVE

**Explain how the Mongol Empire fell and describe its
lasting impact on Asia and Europe.**

CRITICAL THINKING SKILLS FOR LESSON 2.1

- Analyze Cause and Effect
- Synthesize
- Make Predictions
- Analyze Visuals

HISTORICAL THINKING FOR CHAPTER 12

**How did nomads from Central Asia build great
empires?**

The Yuan dynasty and the other khanates ended, but
the Mongol Empire was highly influential. Lesson 2.1
discusses the legacy of the Mongol Empire.

Student eEdition online

Additional content for this lesson, including an image
gallery and a video, is available online.

BACKGROUND FOR THE TEACHER

The Mongols' Deep Nomadic Roots The tensions
between the Chinese and the Mongols can be traced
back to the latter's nomadic roots. Chinese peasants
depended on crops for their livelihood. While China
was under the rule of the Yuan dynasty, however, the
government kept game animals available for the Mongol
hunters. Peasants were not allowed to harm the animals,
even if the animals ate their crops. This is one of the
primary issues that eventually led the Chinese to rebel.
After the Mongol Empire ended, many Mongolians
returned to living nomadic, tribal lives on the steppes,
just as they had before the empire rose to power. Over
the course of the next several hundred years, Ming China
tried and failed several times to occupy Mongolia and
incorporate it as a part of China.

INTRODUCE & ENGAGE

CREATE A WORD WEB

Create a Word Web with the term *cultural exchange* in the center. Ask students to suggest words or phrases that they associate with cultural exchanges, such as *religion* or *technology* and add these to the Word Web. Tell students that in this lesson they will learn about cultural exchanges that took place along the Silk Roads.

TEACH

GUIDED DISCUSSION

1. **Make Predictions** How might the history of the Yuan dynasty have played out differently if Kublai Khan had treated the Chinese people with more respect? *(Possible response: After Kublai Khan's death, the Chinese people might not have rebelled.)*

2. **Analyze Cause and Effect** How did cross-cultural exchange on the Silk Roads help trigger the European Age of Exploration? *(Demand for the items traded on the Silk Roads grew, but traveling over land took a lot of time. Europeans wanted to find a sea route to China.)*

ANALYZE VISUALS

Review the images in the Cross-Cultural Exchange on the Silk Roads gallery (available in the Student eEdition). **ASK:** What do the images suggest about the artists who created these pieces? *(Possible response: They were highly skilled.)* Then have students form small groups to discuss their favorite pieces. Encourage students to explain why they like a particular piece and what it suggests about the culture of the place where it was made.

ACTIVE OPTIONS

On Your Feet: Numbered Heads Organize students into groups of four, and tell students in each group to number off. Instruct students to think about how the Mongol Empire influenced Europe and Asia and how its influence continues to be felt today. Then have groups discuss the topic so that any member can report for the group. Call a number and have that student report for each group.

NG Learning Framework: Build Best Practices for Exploring
ATTITUDE Empowerment
SKILLS Communication, Collaboration

Have students watch the Albert Lin video, *The Search for Genghis Khan.* Based on the video, have students come up with a list of best practices for conducting an exploration. Then have students use it to carry out an exploration of their own. They might want to work as a group to find out why their school is located where it is, for instance, or explore a local museum's items that are not on public display.

DIFFERENTIATE

STRIVING READERS

Determine Chronology Assign students to work in pairs to determine the chronology of the end of the Mongol Empire. Have them read the lesson, pausing to jot down notes and dates in a Sequence Chain. When they have finished, instruct students to take turns reading the notes in their Sequence Chains aloud, using transitional phrases such as *and then* or *after that* to indicate connections between events.

PRE-AP

Use the "Persia" Approach Have students research to write an essay about the legacy of the Mongol Empire. Copy the following "Persia" mnemonic on the board to guide students' research:
Political
Economic
Religious
Social
Intellectual
Artistic

See the Chapter Planner for more strategies for differentiation.

HISTORICAL THINKING

ANSWERS

1. Chinese rebels drove the Mongols out of China, bringing Mongol rule there to an end.

2. Answers will vary. Possible response: Muslim traders on the routes talked to other merchants about their religion.

3. Answers will vary. Possible response: The Mongols opened up trade with foreigners, allowing Europeans to come to China for the first time. European mapmakers used the information in Polo's book to create their maps.

CRITICAL VIEWING Possible response: The women are wearing traditional clothing, and the food is displayed as it might have been during the Mongol Empire.

The Ming Dynasty

Sometimes, unlikely leaders emerge during times of crisis. Hongwu—a peasant and, for a time, a monk—had led China's rebellion and seized power. Now he was determined to restore Chinese traditions and Chinese government.

RETURN TO CHINESE RULE

Hongwu set out to restore China to greatness, but he proved to be a **despotic**, or tyrannical, ruler. After Hongwu's prime minister plotted to overthrow him, the emperor had the minister executed and abolished the office. Hongwu engaged a number of "grand secretaries" to handle routine administrative matters, but the emperor exercised direct control over his empire.

Because Hongwu had been born a poor peasant himself, he protected the interests of farmers. He rebuilt China's agricultural system and supported the growth of manufacturing. He also cut government spending and punished corruption within his administration. Although Hongwu distrusted scholars, he based his rule on the principles of the Tang and Song dynasties and restored Confucian values. He believed that an efficient government depended on a bureaucracy filled with

Powerful dragons were frequently depicted on works of art made during the reign of the Ming emperor Yongle. This box, made to hold a Buddhist scripture, was created for use at court.

Confucian scholars. The emperor established schools across China to train students to take the civil service examination and prepare for government service. But to prevent the scholar-officials from gaining too much power, Hongwu enforced strict rules and severely punished them for the slightest infraction.

Hongwu expanded his empire to include part of Manchuria, located in present-day northeastern China. He also demanded tribute from states whose foreign affairs he controlled, including Korea. The emperor sent his ambassadors to the city of Samarkand in Central Asia to demand tribute, but they were imprisoned by Timur who, as you may recall, ruled the western part of the Chagatai Khanate at that time. Timur was actually planning to invade China itself, but the great conqueror died in 1405, and the mission was canceled.

After Hongwu's own death in 1398, his son Zhu Di (JOO DEE) became the next ruler of Ming China. Zhu Di came to power in 1403 and took the name **Yongle** (YUNG LOH), meaning "perpetual happiness." Like his father, Yongle was a suspicious, ruthless, and tyrannical ruler. He established a sort of secret service agency to search out and report to him any treasonous activity in the empire. And although Yongle had little interest in high culture, the emperor sponsored the publication of a huge body of Chinese literature that filled more than 11,000 volumes called *The Great Canon of the Yongle Era*.

THE FORBIDDEN CITY

Soon after Yongle became emperor, he authorized the transfer of the imperial capital from Nanjing to Beijing. As the capital during the Yuan dynasty, Beijing was associated with "barbarian" rulers, but it placed Yongle near his supporters. The location also allowed him to keep an eye on the northern defenses. And Beijing was well protected: it was surrounded by 14 miles of 40-foot walls.

In the heart of the new capital, Yongle commissioned the construction of the Imperial Palace, a huge complex of buildings that would be the center of imperial power and government for the next 500 years. The Imperial Palace was also known as the **Forbidden City** because few people were allowed to enter it and then only with the emperor's permission.

An estimated one million workers labored for almost 15 years to complete the complex, which contained hundreds of buildings. Some of the buildings were residences for the imperial family and their more than 100,000 servants. For defense purposes, the Imperial Palace was surrounded by a wall more than 30 feet high and a moat about 170 feet wide.

The rectangular, symmetrical, and compass-aligned design of the Forbidden City was said to be in perfect harmony with the world. Even the colors used in the complex had symbolic meanings. For example, yellow, which the Chinese believed represented the earth, the producer of all life, was used in the glaze for roof tiles. And red, a color the Chinese associated with power, happiness, wealth, and honor, appears throughout the complex. Dragons were a symbol of the emperor's **omnipotence**, or unlimited power. Artists carved a coiled dragon in the ceiling of the Hall of Supreme Harmony, the Forbidden City's tallest building. The building also housed the emperor's golden Dragon Throne.

While the Imperial Palace was being built, Yongle oversaw another construction project. You probably remember that Kublai Khan had extended the Grand Canal. To make the transport of grain to Beijing even more efficient, Yongle extended the Grand Canal even farther and deepened and widened it. In the process, his engineers built a dam to divert water from a river to the Grand Canal and dug reservoirs to control water levels.

THE VOYAGES OF ZHENG HE

Like Hongwu, Yongle sent ambassadors to receive tribute from leaders in Southeast Asia and Central Asia and, for a time, Japan. However, Yongle also wanted to expand his empire. In 1406, his forces occupied the southeast Asian state of Dai Viet, which you read about earlier. The following year, Yongle claimed Dai Viet as a province. Resistance to the Chinese soon erupted and continued for years. The Ming dynasty finally left Dai Viet in 1428 and abandoned its direct rule there.

As you have read, the Indian Ocean had long been a zone of interaction, with people and commodities moving between Africa, Arabia, Iran, India, and Southeast Asia. Now the Yongle emperor decided to follow those routes on a grand tribute-seeking mission. For about 300 years, China's navy had been expanding, and the Ming dynasty had overseen technological advances in shipbuilding. The accuracy of Chinese navigation was also the best in the world. Yongle wanted to display his naval power, so in 1405, he ordered the first in a series of seven voyages to Asia and Africa. He selected a young Chinese Muslim called **Zheng He** (JUNG HUH) to command the expeditions.

China had developed an extensive sea trade to obtain spices and other items, but the expeditions were about more than exploration and trade. Zheng He's main mission was to glorify Yongle by asserting Chinese control over trade routes and weaker countries. On

---

PLAN: 4-PAGE LESSON

OBJECTIVE

Describe how the Ming dynasty restored Chinese rule and initiated a period of political and cultural power and influence.

CRITICAL THINKING SKILLS FOR LESSON 2.2

- Make Inferences
- Interpret Maps
- Make Predictions
- Explain
- Draw Conclusions
- Synthesize
- Analyze Images

HISTORICAL THINKING FOR CHAPTER 12

How did nomads from Central Asia build great empires?

After China rebelled against the Mongols and established the Ming dynasty, China returned to Confucian ideals and a bureaucratic system of government. Lesson 2.2 discusses key accomplishments during the Ming dynasty, including China's period of naval exploration.

BACKGROUND FOR THE TEACHER

Zheng He's Voyages Zheng He's wooden treasure ships were first developed in the 11th century. Some were 440 feet long and 185 feet across with multiple decks and watertight compartments below the decks. The ships were designed with a deep keel, a very large rudder in the stern, and a complex system of rigging in the sails. Most of the official records of Zheng He's voyages were destroyed after his death. New laws made it illegal to build large ships to sail the oceans. The Chinese still exported silk, porcelain, and tea, but they stopped importing European goods and thought Western influence would weaken their culture. As a result, European and Japanese merchants and pirates took control of the seas. More foreign visitors and missionaries began coming to China in the mid-1500s.

Student eEdition online

Additional content for this lesson, including a diagram, is available online.

INTRODUCE & ENGAGE

COMPARE AND CONTRAST

Ask students if they have visited the White House or the U.S. Capitol in Washington, D.C. Encourage those who have to give a brief description of each building. **ASK:** Who lives in a palace? *(kings, queens)* Why doesn't the U.S. president live in a palace? *(Possible response: The United States is a democracy, and the president is elected by the people. A palace suggests more power than a U.S. president is given.)* Tell students that in this lesson they will learn about a great palace built during the Ming dynasty.

TEACH

GUIDED DISCUSSION

1. **Explain** Why did Hongwu prioritize rebuilding China's agricultural system? *(Hongwu was born a peasant farmer, so he was sympathetic to their needs.)*

2. **Make Inferences** Why do you think Yongle had *The Great Canon of the Yongle Era* published? *(Possible response: He knew that publishing this literature would become part of his legacy.)*

ANALYZE IMAGES

Have students examine the image of the dragon box. Point out the elaborate dragon designs etched into the wooden box. Have a volunteer read the caption that describes the art and its use. **ASK:** After examining the art on the box, what values does the wooden box characterize about the Yongle emperor? *(Possible responses: The art shows that dragons and designs were popular during this time period. The artist uses the colors yellow and red, which were important colors also used as the colors of the Forbidden City. The fact that this box was made to hold a Buddhist scripture for use at court explains that the emperor practiced the beliefs of Buddha.)* Tell students that the symbolism found in this dragon box mirrored the symbolism used in the Forbidden City, such as a dragon to represent power, a dragon carved in the ceiling, and even a Dragon Throne. Encourage students to give their opinions about the design of the artwork.

DIFFERENTIATE

INCLUSION

Read the Map Have students study the map of Zheng He's voyages. Help them understand the map and the captions that go with it. Point out that Zheng He traveled west from the point where he started in China. Explain that the callouts are in chronological order, but, like the map, need to be read from right to left. Call on volunteers to read each callout and point to the places referred to on the map.

GIFTED AND TALENTED

Research the Forbidden City Have students choose one part of the Forbidden City and conduct online research to learn about it. Their assignment is to provide more visual detail about that part of the complex. They can focus on a particular building, garden, or structure or on the layout of an area. Students can sketch, diagram, or print out pictures of the structure or area. Have them label and post the visuals around the classroom for viewing.

See the Chapter Planner for more strategies for differentiation.

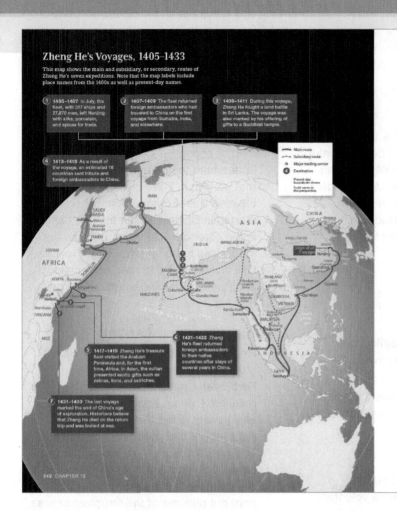

Zheng He's Voyages, 1405–1433

This map shows the main and subsidiary, or secondary, routes of Zheng He's seven expeditions. Note that the map labels include place names from the 1400s as well as present-day names.

1 1405–1407 In July, the fleet, with 317 ships and 27,870 men, left Nanjing with silks, porcelain, and spices for trade.

2 1407–1409 The fleet returned foreign ambassadors who had traveled to China on the first voyage from Sumatra, India, and elsewhere.

3 1409–1411 During this voyage, Zheng He fought a land battle in Sri Lanka. The voyage was also marked by his offering of gifts to a Buddhist temple.

4 1413–1415 As a result of the voyage, an estimated 18 countries sent tribute and foreign ambassadors to China.

5 1417–1419 Zheng He's treasure fleet visited the Arabian Peninsula and, for the first time, Africa. In Aden, the sultan presented exotic gifts such as zebras, lions, and ostriches.

6 1421–1422 Zheng He's fleet returned foreign ambassadors to their native countries after stays of several years in China.

7 1431–1433 The last voyage marked the end of China's age of exploration. Historians believe that Zheng He died on the return trip and was buried at sea.

— Main route
- - - Subsidiary route
⊙ Major trading center
4 Destination
Present-day boundaries shown
Scale varies in this perspective.

his first expedition, Zheng He led a fleet of more than 60 ships manned by more than 27,000 sailors. His expeditions included treasure ships to carry tribute and trade items back to China. At more than 400 feet long and 160 feet wide, the treasure ships were far bigger than any other ships at that time.

For three decades, Zheng He sailed some 40,000 miles around Southeast Asia, India, Southwest Asia, and East Africa. He returned with tribute that included such exotic items as gold, gems, rare spices, giraffes, and zebras. Although the expeditions mainly served to fuel Yongle's vanity, they also helped expand China's connections to other Asian and African societies. On his seventh and final journey, Zheng He left the main fleet for a personal journey. Following the example of his grandfather and his father, he went to Arabia to visit the holy sites of Mecca and Medina. As a Muslim, it was his duty to perform the hajj pilgrimage.

A CONSERVATIVE TURN

Zheng He died during his seventh voyage in 1433. Two years later, a new emperor, Zhengtong (JUNG-TUNG), took power and stopped all future voyages. Zhengtong claimed the expeditions were too expensive. He also believed that the Chinese were the most civilized people on Earth and had nothing to learn from foreigners. After Yongle, conservative Ming emperors tried to restore what they saw as the glories of the imperial Chinese tradition in governance and the arts. As part of that conservative turn, they gave up on the sea voyages, returning to the long imperial tradition of focusing on defense of the interior border with Central Asia.

To prevent another invasion of nomadic horsemen, Ming rulers strengthened the Great Wall. They extended the stone wall to a length of about 5,500 miles and built 25,000 watchtowers along it. Most of the Great Wall that stands today was constructed during the Ming dynasty.

Many Ming artists also took a conservative approach by focusing on the revival of traditional artistic styles. Many Chinese artists carved small decorative items out of wood and jade and produced beautiful porcelain vases. Ming dynasty artists particularly excelled in painting and pottery. The paintings reflected the artists' personal styles, and ceramics combined new developments with old traditions. One new technique involved the use of a blue overglaze, which was applied on top of an already glazed piece and is sometimes called "blue and white." This style was imitated in Vietnam, Japan, and, around the 17th century, in Europe, where all fine porcelain became known as "china."

Yongle had strengthened and stabilized China's economy when he rose to power, and it continued to be robust for many years. Even in the late 1500s, the magnificence, wealth, and power of the Ming impressed foreign visitors. But by 1600, the old cycle of imperial decline had begun. The court became corrupt, pirates raided the coasts, bandits came down from the mountains, and people lived in greater poverty and insecurity. It seemed the Ming dynasty was losing the Mandate of Heaven.

A EUROPEAN IN MING CHINA The Italian missionary Matteo Ricci arrived in China in 1582, having sailed around Africa and stopping for several years in India. His goal was to convert the Chinese to Christianity, and he hoped to do it from the top down by convincing elite scholar-officials that his faith was compatible with Confucianism. Ricci learned Chinese and wrote a book showing how one could convert to Roman Catholicism and remain a good Confucian. He was an accomplished mathematician and cartographer, but what Ming officials most appreciated was Ricci's ability to memorize a long list of information and then flawlessly repeat it—even backwards! That was a very useful talent in a society where officials had to pass difficult examinations to move up the ranks. For his part, Ricci noted with approval that, in Ming China, the highest status went to men of learning (like himself) rather than, as in Europe, to military leaders: "[T]he entire kingdom is administered by . . . Philosophers. The responsibility for orderly management of the entire realm is wholly and completely committed to their charge and care . . ." In the end, Matteo Ricci made only a few converts before he died in China in 1610.

HISTORICAL THINKING

1. **READING CHECK** How did Hongwu establish an efficient government?

2. **MAKE INFERENCES** Why do you think Yongle built the Imperial Palace?

3. **INTERPRET MAPS** What conclusion can you draw from the fact that the final destination of Zheng He's first three expeditions was India?

4. **MAKE PREDICTIONS** What might have happened if China had not ended its maritime expeditions?

BACKGROUND FOR THE TEACHER

Chinese Porcelain While Chinese porcelain gained popularity in Europe during the Ming dynasty, the Chinese had been producing variations of it for hundreds of years prior, dating back to the Shang dynasty. The well-known blue and white porcelain was first made during the Yuan dynasty in Jingdezhen, a city that became known as the "Capital of Porcelain." Not surprisingly, during the Ming dynasty when China was shifting back to a focus on Confucian values, Chinese porcelain makers used traditions and techniques developed during the Song dynasty to produce their wares.

TEACH

GUIDED DISCUSSION

3. **Draw Conclusions** Why were Ming rulers concerned about an invasion from the north? *(Possible response: Since the Mongols invaded from the north and ruled China for many years, Ming leaders wanted to be sure this would not happen again.)*

4. **Synthesize** How might other societies in Asia and Africa have benefited from Zheng He's voyages? *(Possible response: Zheng He's voyages were an opportunity for cultural exchange, and other societies could have learned about Chinese technology and culture.)*

INTERPRET MAPS

Have students study the map of Zheng He's voyages, paying particular attention to his destinations and the solid line that shows his main route. Conduct a class Map Bee to see who can answer these questions accurately and quickly:

- What present-day country did he reach on his first three voyages? *(India)*
- What islands did he visit on the way? *(Java, Sumatra, Malaysia, Sri Lanka)*
- What was the destination of the fourth voyage? *(Iran and the Red Sea)*
- Why would Zheng He take a side trip to Mecca off the Red Sea? *(Mecca is sacred to Muslims.)*
- What continent did he visit for his last three voyages? *(Africa)*

ACTIVE OPTIONS

On Your Feet: Roundtable Seat students around a table in groups of four, and ask them whether they think Hongwu and Yongle were good leaders, bad leaders, or a combination of both. Each student around a table should answer the question in a different way.

> **NG Learning Framework: Learn About Zheng He**
> **ATTITUDE** Curiosity
> **KNOWLEDGE** Our Human Story

Ask students to choose one destination of Zheng He's voyages and find out what he might have seen and experienced in that place at that time. They should research the people and culture of the destination. Then ask students to write their observations as Zheng He might have written them in a journal.

HISTORICAL THINKING

ANSWERS

1. He filled his government bureaucracy with Confucian scholars.

2. Answers will vary. Possible response: to demonstrate his power and wealth

3. Answers will vary. Possible response: The Chinese wanted to obtain many goods from India.

4. Answers will vary. Possible response: Instead of Europe, China might have dominated maritime exploration.

The Rise of the Ottomans

When you hear about nomads from Central Asia seeking to forge an empire, you probably think of the Mongols. But in the 14th century, the nomads were Turks, and they were on a religious mission.

TURKISH ORIGINS

In the 10th century, Turkish peoples from central Eurasia began migrating to Southwest Asia. Many of these nomadic groups had converted to Islam. One of the Islamic groups, the Seljuks, grew in number and power and captured Baghdad from the Persians in 1055. The Seljuks expanded across much of Southwest Asia and, in 1071, marched on the Byzantine Empire. By the early 12th century, the Seljuks occupied most of Anatolia.

By the late 1100s, however, the Seljuk empire had weakened. When the Mongols stormed across Asia in the early 1200s, the invading armies reached Anatolia and defeated the Seljuks. A small Seljuk kingdom continued as a Mongol province for a time, but the dynasty finally died out in 1293. Around that time,

as you may remember, the Mongol Empire was also beginning to decline, and small Muslim-ruled states emerged in northwestern Anatolia.

A large number of Turks inhabited Anatolia. Many of these Anatolian Turks saw themselves as **ghazis** (GAH-zees), or warriors for Islam. The ghazis were led by a commander, or emir, and were bound by a strict Islamic code of conduct. Between 1300 and 1326, a powerful ghazi named Osman developed the small Turkish state that his father had founded along the frontier of the Byzantine Empire. **Osman** became the leader of the Ottoman Turks. *Ottoman* comes from the Arabic form of his name—Uthman—and would be the name of his dynasty and the empire that would eventually arise.

CRITICAL VIEWING After his defeat at the Battle of Ankara, Sultan Bayezid is taken prisoner and brought before Timur in this 16th-century miniature painting from India. What details in the painting convey Bayezid's defeat and Timur's triumph?

OTTOMAN EXPANSION

The Ottomans set out to conquer poorly defended areas along the Byzantine frontier. Osman united nomadic tribes and city-dwelling Muslims who wanted to expand the amount of territory under Islamic rule. After the death of Osman in 1326, his son, Orhan, began hiring Christian mercenaries to join the fight and lessen Ottoman dependence on the nomads. Orhan captured important towns in northwestern Anatolia and declared himself **sultan**, meaning "strength" or "one with power."

Throughout the 1300s, the Ottomans took over territories in western Anatolia and southeastern Europe. In 1361, the Ottomans captured Adrianople (ah-dree-uh-NOH-puhl), the second most important city in the Byzantine Empire after Constantinople, and made it their capital. They also defeated other Turkish states and gained eastern Anatolia. As the Ottomans established their new empire, their wise treatment of those they conquered helped gain peoples' trust. The Ottomans appointed local officials to govern the territories and improved the lives of the peasants. Most Muslims were required to fight in Ottoman armies, but non-Muslims were not. In exchange for this exemption, however, they had to pay a tax.

You have read about Timur, who had earlier taken over the Chagatai khanate from the Mongols. Now he turned west and, in 1402, briefly halted further Ottoman expansion. The Ottomans were preparing to invade

Constantinople when they learned that Timur was advancing on Anatolia. The two armies clashed at the Battle of Ankara in central Anatolia, and the Ottomans were soundly defeated. Timur captured Sultan Bayezid (BAY-uh-zihd), who commanded the Ottoman army. According to legend, Timur kept Bayezid in a golden cage until the sultan's death in 1403. Timur's empire ended after his death in 1405, while the Ottomans continued to expand.

And so, what was the secret to the Ottomans' success? For the most part, the answer is gunpowder, which, as you may recall, was invented by the Chinese. The technology had been passed along to Europe and the Islamic world through trade on the Silk Roads. Instead of sending in the cavalry, with soldiers on horseback shooting bows and arrows as the Mongols had, the Ottomans employed infantry soldiers carrying muskets. Under a powerful sultan, the Ottomans would also use gunpowder to fire cannons that could blast down city walls to achieve one of their greatest victories.

HISTORICAL THINKING

1. **READING CHECK** Who was Osman?

2. **COMPARE AND CONTRAST** How did the motivation behind Mongol and Ottoman expansion differ?

3. **INTERPRET MAPS** Which city was situated in the center of the Ottoman Empire by 1481?

The Ottoman Empire, 1481

AUSTRIA
HUNGARY
CRIMEA
Belgrade
Danube R.
Black Sea
Adriatic Sea
Taranto
Adrianople
Golden Horn
BYZANTINE EMPIRE
Constantinople (Istanbul)
Ankara
GREECE
ANATOLIA
Athens
Turkey
SYRIA

0   100   200 Miles
0   100   200 Kilometers

■ Ottoman Turks, 1300
■ Acquisitions, 1300–1359
■ Acquisitions, 1359–1451
■ Acquisitions, 1451–1481

PLAN: 2-PAGE LESSON

OBJECTIVE
Explain how the Ottoman Turks, a group of central Asian nomads, gave rise to a dynasty and, later, a mighty empire.

CRITICAL THINKING SKILLS FOR LESSON 3.1
- Compare and Contrast
- Interpret Maps
- Identify Main Ideas and Details
- Make Generalizations

HISTORICAL THINKING FOR CHAPTER 12
How did nomads from Central Asia build great empires?

Osman founded a Muslim dynasty and became the leader of the Ottoman Turks. Lesson 3.1 discusses the early rise of the Ottoman Empire and its early leaders.

Student eEdition online
Additional content for this lesson, including a portrait, is available online.

BACKGROUND FOR THE TEACHER
Orhan Osman's son, Orhan, continued to expand the Ottoman Empire after his father's death. Although he initially clashed with the Byzantines, he formed an alliance with Greek statesman John VI Cantacuzenus, who would eventually become the Byzantine emperor. The alliance between Orhan and Cantacuzenus was so strong that Orhan married Cantacuzenus's daughter, Theodora. As a leader, Orhan stimulated the economy by minting the first Ottoman coins. He also formalized the organization of the Ottoman army. His other primary accomplishments include erecting infrastructure such as mosques and medreses—colleges for Islamic instruction—that facilitated the spread of Islam as the empire expanded.

INTRODUCE & ENGAGE

CREATE A 5Ws CHART

Have students use the lesson's introduction, headings, and visuals to preview the lesson. **ASK:** Based on these features, what questions do you expect this lesson to answer? *(Possible response: Who was Osman? When did he rise to power? What motivated the expansion of the Ottoman Empire? What values did the Ottomans have?)* Create and display a 5Ws Chart to list students' questions. Return to the chart at the end of the lesson and ask volunteers to research any unanswered questions.

TEACH

GUIDED DISCUSSION

1. **Identify Main Ideas and Details** How did Osman unite city-dwellers and nomadic tribes? *(He united them over their desire to expand Islamic rule.)*

2. **Make Generalizations** How did the Ottomans benefit from their treatment of those they captured? *(Possible response: By treating those they captured respectfully, the Ottomans gained the people's trust and did not face threats of rebellion.)*

INTERPRET MAPS

Have students study the map of the Ottoman Empire in 1481. **ASK:** By what date had the Ottomans taken over all of Anatolia? *(by 1481)* Point out that the most far-flung region of the empire by 1481 was in Crimea. **ASK:** What might the benefits and drawbacks of controlling that land have been? *(Benefits: control of the Black Sea; Drawbacks: difficult to govern)*

ACTIVE OPTIONS

On Your Feet: Think, Pair, Share Organize students into pairs. Ask them to consider what might have happened if Timur had lived and continued his conquests. Would he have halted Ottoman expansion? Then have pairs discuss the topic. After the one-on-one discussions, invite volunteers to share their ideas with the class.

NG Learning Framework: Compile a Code of Conduct
ATTITUDE Empowerment
SKILL Collaboration

Tell students that the ghazis lived by a code of conduct that valued bravery and honor. Ask groups of students to collaborate and come up with a code of conduct for themselves and their peers at school. Encourage them to think about how students should conduct themselves in class, outside of class, with teachers, and with other students. After groups have compiled their codes, post and discuss them in class.

DIFFERENTIATE

STRIVING READERS

Use a Main-Idea Cluster Direct pairs of students to complete a Main-Idea Cluster for each heading in the lesson. Tell partners to take turns reading paragraphs aloud and then work together to record the main idea and four details before moving on to the next heading.

PRE-AP

Create a TV News Report Invite students to research the Battle of Ankara fought between the Ottomans and Timur to answer the following questions:

1. Why did the two sides engage in battle?
2. Where did they fight?
3. What battle tactics did each side use?
4. How many soldiers died in the battle?
5. What happened as a result of the battle?

Have students present their information to the class in the form of a TV news report.

See the Chapter Planner for more strategies for differentiation.

HISTORICAL THINKING

ANSWERS

1. Osman was a ghazi who became the leader of the Ottoman Turks between 1300 and 1326.
2. While the Mongols probably began empire-building to gain access to more food, goods, and grazing land, the Ottomans wanted to expand the amount of territory under Islamic rule.
3. Constantinople/Istanbul

CRITICAL VIEWING Answers will vary. Possible response: The defeated Bayezid is stooped and does not look Timur in the eyes. The great conqueror looks proud and stares haughtily at his captive.

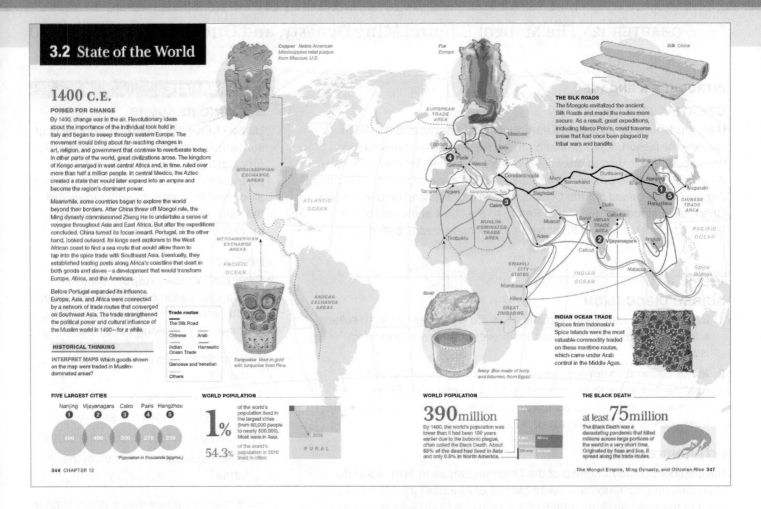

3.2 State of the World

1400 C.E.

POISED FOR CHANGE

By 1400, change was in the air. Revolutionary ideas about the importance of the individual took hold in Italy and began to sweep through western Europe. The movement would bring about far-reaching changes in art, religion, and government that continue to reverberate today. In other parts of the world, great civilizations arose. The kingdom of Kongo emerged in west central Africa and, in time, ruled over more than half a million people. In central Mexico, the Aztec created a state that would later expand into an empire and become the region's dominant power.

Meanwhile, some countries began to explore the world beyond their borders. After China threw off Mongol rule, the Ming dynasty commissioned Zheng He to undertake a series of voyages throughout Asia and East Africa. But after the expeditions concluded, China turned its focus inward. Portugal, on the other hand, looked outward. Its kings sent explorers to the West African coast to find a sea route that would allow them to tap into the spice trade with Southeast Asia. Eventually, they established trading posts along Africa's coastline that dealt in both goods and slaves—a development that would transform Europe, Africa, and the Americas.

Before Portugal expanded its influence, Europe, Asia, and Africa were connected by a network of trade routes that converged on Southwest Asia. The trade strengthened the political power and cultural influence of the Muslim world in 1400—for a while.

HISTORICAL THINKING

INTERPRET MAPS Which goods shown on the map were traded in Muslim-dominated areas?

Trade routes
The Silk Road
Chinese — Arab
Indian Ocean Trade — Hanseatic
Genoese and Venetian
Others

Copper *Native American Mississippian relief plaque from Missouri, U.S.*

Fur *Europe*

Silk *China*

THE SILK ROADS
The Mongols revitalized the ancient Silk Roads and made the routes more secure. As a result, great expeditions, including Marco Polo's, could traverse areas that had once been plagued by tribal wars and bandits.

Turquoise Vase in gold with turquoise from Peru

Ivory Box made of ivory and bitumen, from Egypt

INDIAN OCEAN TRADE
Spices from Indonesia's Spice Islands were the most valuable commodity traded on these maritime routes, which came under Arab control in the Middle Ages.

FIVE LARGEST CITIES

Nanjing ❶ 490 Vijayanagara ❷ 400 Cairo ❸ 300 Paris ❹ 275 Hangzhou ❺ 235

Population in thousands (approx.)

WORLD POPULATION

1% of the world's population lived in the largest cities (from 80,000 people to nearly 500,000). Most were in Asia.

54.3% of the world's population in 2016 lived in cities.

WORLD POPULATION

390 million By 1400, the world's population was lower than it had been 100 years earlier due to the bubonic plague, often called the Black Death. About 55% of the dead had lived in Asia and only 0.5% in North America.

THE BLACK DEATH

at least **75 million** The Black Death was a devastating pandemic that killed millions across large portions of the world in a very short time. Originated by fleas and lice, it spread along the trade routes.

PLAN: 2-PAGE LESSON

OBJECTIVE
Learn how exploration brought about the changes that took place throughout the world in and around 1400 C.E.

CRITICAL THINKING SKILLS FOR LESSON 3.2
- Analyze Visuals
- Make Connections
- Identify Supporting Details

HISTORICAL THINKING FOR CHAPTER 12
How did nomads from Central Asia build great empires?

Lesson 3.2 explores how revolutionary ideas brought about change, how exploration brought about new empires, and how trade networks brought about political power and cultural influences.

Student eEdition online
Additional content for this lesson, including a video, is available online.

BACKGROUND FOR THE TEACHER
Portuguese Expansion The Portuguese were seen as the pioneers of the European sea trade and as the developers of oceanic trade routes to Africa and Asia in the 15th century. Their main goal was to establish better trade routes to Asia, but they needed to circumnavigate Africa to reach Asia. They colonized the Cape Verde Islands in 1460, which provided a trade base with the Mali Empire. Then in 1471, a Portuguese captain reached the coast of Guinea and discovered that the Akan peoples were willing to trade gold for base metals, cloth, and other manufactures; the captain soon realized the importance of this discovery, thus altering Portugal's focus. By this time, the Portuguese had already established settlements on the Canary and Madeira islands. They moved on to establish the island of São Tomé, where they planted sugarcane and built sugar mills. The need to find workers brought about the need for slaves, making this Portuguese-controlled island the first stepping-stone in the Atlantic slave trade.

History Notebook
Encourage students to complete the State of the World page for Chapter 12 in their History Notebooks as they read.

INTRODUCE & ENGAGE

EXPLORE HISTORY USING VISUALS

Tell students that the photographs, map, and diagrams in this lesson represent the important developments that were taking place in the world around 1400 C.E. **ASK:** What visuals in this lesson intrigue you? What questions do you have? *(Answers will vary. Possible responses may include questions about the trade routes or trade goods or about the Black Death.)* Write down students' questions and have students supply the answers as they read the lesson and watch the video.

TEACH

GUIDED DISCUSSION

1. **Identify Supporting Details** How did the Black Death spread? *(Traders carried the fleas and lice that carried the disease with them along the trade routes, spreading the disease and killing millions of people in a short time.)*

2. **Make Connections** What trade goods from the 15th century are still valued today? *(Possible responses: gold, silk, spices, precious gems, and metals)*

STATE OF THE WORLD

Direct students to watch the video "State of the World: Time-Travel the Trade Routes in 1400" (available in the Student eEdition). Remind students of the essential question for this chapter: How did nomads from Central Asia build great empires? **ASK:** Based on the information presented in this lesson and in the video, how would you answer this question? *(Possible response: Trade routes and the wealth they brought allowed many Asian nomads to settle into cities.)*

ANALYZE VISUALS

Have students examine the Five Largest Cities diagram and the World Population map. **ASK:** Where did most of the world's population live in 1400 C.E.? *(Asia)* After viewing the Silk Roads route, why do you think Nanjing may have become the largest city during this time period? *(The Silk Roads began in Nanjing. Many people traveled to and from this city and may have eventually settled in Nanjing.)* Based on the routes of the Silk Roads, which trade route do you think was the most difficult to travel? *(Answers will vary. Possible responses: The Indian Ocean route because sea travel was unpredictable. OR The Arab route because they had to cross the Sahara.)*

ACTIVE OPTION

On Your Feet: Research Innovations Instruct students to form six teams and assign each team one of the following trade goods that are showcased in the image gallery: copper, turquoise, fur, silk, cotton cloth, or gold and ivory. Instruct groups to conduct research to find additional information about the trade good, where each was traded, and aspects about the goods that are surprising or interesting. Allow time for teams to discuss and then ask groups to share their information.

DIFFERENTIATE

STRIVING READERS

Use Reciprocal Teaching Have students read this lesson with a partner. Instruct students to take turns reading each paragraph aloud. At the end of each paragraph, the reading student should ask the listening student a question or two about what the listening student just heard. After reading the lesson, encourage students to discuss the visuals in this lesson and to ask and answer questions with each other about the information found in the visuals.

PRE-AP

Research Cultural Influences Have students conduct research into one of these cities: Nanjing, Vijayanagara, Cairo, Paris, or Hangzhou. Tell them to include information about the changes and influences that trade routes brought to the city and the lasting effect of trade on the city. Encourage students to present their findings as an oral report to the class.

See the Chapter Planner for more strategies for differentiation.

HISTORICAL THINKING

ANSWER

Gold and ivory were traded in Muslim-dominated areas.

The Conquest of Constantinople

By the mid-15th century, Constantinople had been reduced to a shadow of its former glory. And it was surrounded by Ottoman territory. The Ottomans wanted to take advantage of its isolation and vulnerability.

CRITICAL VIEWING The Ottomans battle the Byzantines at Constantinople in this painting called *First Turkish Attack on Constantinople in 1453* by Italian artist Palma il Giovane. How would you describe the battle as depicted in this painting?

348 CHAPTER 12

MEHMED THE CONQUEROR

By 1450, all that remained of the Byzantine Empire was the city of Constantinople, but its fortified walls presented a seemingly impregnable, or indestructible, barrier. Still, it was a tantalizing target. The city's population had fallen from about a million people in ancient times to only around 50,000 in the 1400s. And through Constantinople, the Byzantines controlled the Bosporus and the trade and traffic on the waterway. In religious terms, the city was still the center of the Orthodox Christian faith.

The Ottomans had tried to seize Constantinople in 1422, but their bid was unsuccessful. Then in 1451, a young sultan rose to power who was determined to accomplish the feat. His name was **Mehmed II**, and he came to be known as Mehmed the Conqueror. "Give me Constantinople," he declared early in his reign.

Mehmed carefully prepared his attack. He constructed a castle on the Bosporus and placed armed guards inside it ready to shoot at ships attempting to bring provisions to Constantinople. He also had a powerful cannon built that could bring down the city's walls. The cannon was 26 feet long and could shoot 1,200-pound boulders.

In 1453, at the age of 21, Mehmed launched his assault. The Ottomans began by firing their cannons at Constantinople's walls. At the same time, their fleet attempted to enter the city's harbor. But the Byzantines had blocked access to the Golden Horn, the inlet to the Bosporus, with a chain. Mehmed devised a plan to circumvent the problem. At night, he had his army pull 70 ships out of the Bosporus, haul them over a hill on greased logs, and then refloat them in the waters of the Golden Horn.

While Mehmed commanded a force of as many as 100,000 soldiers and a large fleet of ships, the opposition army numbered only about 8,000. Nevertheless, the Byzantines held off the Ottomans for over seven weeks. At last, however, the Turks broke through the city's walls. Many civilians as well as soldiers died on both sides during street-to-street fighting. Constantinople had not seen such bloodshed since the horrible violence of the Fourth Crusade in 1402. But Mehmet was now in control. After permitting several days of looting, he ordered his soldiers to allow the remaining inhabitants to return to their homes in peace. The Byzantine Empire had finally come to an end.

REBUILDING ISTANBUL

After Constantinople fell, Mehmed rode on a white horse to the Hagia Sophia, the city's cathedral, to deliver prayers of thanks for his victory. He soon converted the church to a mosque, underscoring the Muslim takeover of the city. Mehmed also set about rebuilding Constantinople, which he renamed Istanbul and made the new Ottoman capital. He constructed a great mosque and eight colleges around it. For nearly 100 years, the schools were renowned for their excellence in teaching the sciences. Borrowing from and building on the long tradition of Arab scholarship, learning in mathematics and astronomy reached an even higher level during the Ottoman Empire under Mehmed.

The great conqueror opened Istanbul to everyone: Muslims, Jews, Christians, Turks, and non-Turks. An envoy from Venice arrived in the city within months of the conquest to renew trade with the new ruler. A well-read man himself, Mehmed drew Italian and Greek scholars to his court and collected works in Greek and Latin for his palace library. He also hired Italian architects to help rebuild Istanbul.

The Ottoman conquest of Constantinople—the last remnant of the Eastern Roman Empire—shifted the military balance in western Eurasia away from Christian rulers and toward Muslim rulers. But Mehmed saw himself as the successor of the Roman emperors as well as a champion of Islam. His victory helped pave the way to the growth of one of the greatest empires in history.

The Greek historian Kritovoulos served as an official under Mehmed and wrote a history of the conquest of Constantinople. Although the historian wasn't present at the siege, he describes here how Mehmed may have felt upon seeing the sacked city.

PRIMARY SOURCE

When he saw what a large number had been killed, and the ruin of the buildings, and the wholesale [total] ruin and destruction of the City, he was filled with compassion and repented not a little at the destruction and plundering. Tears fell from his eyes as he groaned deeply and passionately: "What a city we have given over to plunder and destruction."

—from *History of Mehmed the Conqueror* by Kritovoulos

HISTORICAL THINKING

1. **READING CHECK** How did Mehmed prepare for his attack on Constantinople?

2. **ANALYZE CAUSE AND EFFECT** What happened as a result of Mehmed's victory?

3. **ANALYZE SOURCES** How does Kritovoulos's description of Mehmed contrast with what you've read about the conqueror's actions in Constantinople?

PLAN: 2-PAGE LESSON

OBJECTIVE

Explain how the Ottoman conquest of Constantinople marked the end of the Byzantine Empire and the start of a major Muslim empire.

CRITICAL THINKING SKILLS FOR LESSON 3.3

- Analyze Cause and Effect
- Analyze Sources
- Identify Supporting Details
- Make Inferences
- Analyze Primary Sources

HISTORICAL THINKING FOR CHAPTER 12

How did nomads from Central Asia build great empires?

The Ottomans wanted to seize Constantinople, the last remnant of the Byzantine Empire. Lesson 3.3 discusses how Ottoman sultan Mehmed the Conqueror took control of Constantinople and expanded the Ottoman Empire.

Student eEdition online

Additional content for this lesson, including an image, is available online.

BACKGROUND FOR THE TEACHER

Greek Fire Constantinople may have been able to withstand the Ottomans as long as it did because of the Byzantine army's secret weapon: Greek fire. This was a liquid fire soldiers could propel at enemy troops. It burned with an incredible intensity, and not even water could extinguish it. The formula for making Greek fire was a closely guarded secret that died with the Byzantine Empire.

INTRODUCE & ENGAGE

ANALYZE VISUALS

Show and discuss the painting of the invasion of Constantinople. Have students study the painting and its caption and then answer the following questions:

- What does the painting show?
- What details do you see?
- Which two groups are represented in the painting?
- Which group appears to have the upper hand? What details in the painting lead you to think so?

Tell students that in this lesson they will learn about the fall of Constantinople and the Byzantine Empire.

TEACH

GUIDED DISCUSSION

1. **Identify Supporting Details** How did the Byzantines try to defend against Mehmed's attack on Constantinople? *(They blocked access to the Bosporus with a chain.)*

2. **Make Inferences** Why do you think Mehmed converted the Hagia Sophia to a mosque soon after he seized Constantinople? *(Possible response: He wanted to declare that the former Christian Byzantine Empire was now under Muslim rule.)*

ANALYZE PRIMARY SOURCES

Have students read the primary source. **ASK:** How might Kritovoulos's relationship with Mehmed have influenced his opinion of the Turkish sultan? *(Possible response: Because Kritovoulos was a government official who worked for Mehmed, he wanted to show Mehmed in a positive light rather than as a ruthless conqueror.)*

ACTIVE OPTIONS

On Your Feet: Three-Step Interview Tell pairs to interview one another on their opinions of Mehmed's leadership style and strategies. First have Student A interview Student B, and then instruct partners to reverse roles. Have Student A share with the class information from Student B, and have Student B share information from Student A. Finally, as a class, discuss Mehmed's leadership.

> **NG Learning Framework: Debate Ecological Consequences**
> ATTITUDE Responsibility
> KNOWLEDGE Our Living Planet

Tell students that Turkey has proposed building a canal to decrease the traffic on the very busy Bosporus Strait. However, some experts have warned that the project will result in serious ecological consequences. Have students research to learn more about the proposed canal and its impact, both positive and negative. Ask them to form groups to debate the scheme before the class.

DIFFERENTIATE

STRIVING READERS

List Details After students read the lesson, have pairs create a two-column chart using the headings in the lesson: *Mehmed the Conqueror* and *Rebuilding Istanbul*. Encourage pairs to take turns rereading paragraphs aloud, while their partner listens and adds details.

ENGLISH LANGUAGE LEARNERS

Summarize Lesson 3.3 has eight paragraphs. Have students work in pairs assigning each one paragraph to read. Then each pair or group should write a brief summary of their paragraph. Provide the following sentence frames to help students write an effective summary.

- **Beginning and Intermediate**
  This paragraph is about _____.
  First, _____. Then _____.
  At the end, _____.

- **Advanced**
  The paragraph begins by _____.
  It then _____ and concludes by _____.

  To summarize, the paragraph provides information about _____.

See the Chapter Planner for more strategies for differentiation.

HISTORICAL THINKING

ANSWERS

1. He constructed a castle and placed armed guards ready to fire at ships attempting to bring provisions to Constantinople and had a powerful cannon built that could bring down the city's walls.

2. Possible response: The Byzantine Empire ended, many people were killed, and the city was destroyed.

3. Possible response: He describes Mehmed as repentant and compassionate; the text describes his brutality.

CRITICAL VIEWING Answers will vary. Possible response: violent, intense

REVIEW

VOCABULARY

Match each vocabulary word below with its definition.

1. steppe
2. ger
3. khanate
4. envoy
5. omnipotence
6. despotic
7. ghazi
8. sultan

a. a Muslim ruler
b. an area of the Mongol Empire
c. a vast, grassy plain
d. a warrior for Islam
e. a diplomatic representative
f. unlimited power
g. nomadic tent
h. tyrannical

READING STRATEGY
ANALYZE CAUSE AND EFFECT

Use a cause-and-effect chart like the one below to describe the impact of the Mongol invasions. Then answer the questions.

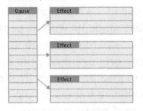

9. What happened in 1241 as a result of Ogodei's death?

10. How did Ogodei's decision to spare the people and lands of northern China from destruction affect the region culturally?

MAIN IDEAS

Answer the following questions. Support your answers with evidence from the chapter.

11. Who was Genghis Khan? LESSON 1.1
12. How did Kublai Khan treat the Chinese after he founded the Yuan dynasty? LESSON 1.3
13. How did the Mongol Empire link Europe and Asia through trade? LESSON 2.1
14. Why did later Ming emperors put an end to the voyages of exploration? LESSON 2.2
15. What defeat briefly interrupted Ottoman expansion? LESSON 3.1
16. What surprise tactic did Mehmed II use to enter Constantinople's harbor? LESSON 3.3

HISTORICAL THINKING

Answer the following questions. Support your answers with evidence from the chapter.

17. MAKE INFERENCES Why do you think Genghis Khan wanted his burial site to remain a secret?
18. ANALYZE CAUSE AND EFFECT What impact did the Mongol invasion of Southwest Asia have on the Abbasid Empire?
19. DRAW CONCLUSIONS Why was Kublai Khan's decision to move his capital to Beijing significant?
20. FORM AND SUPPORT OPINIONS What do you think is the Mongol Empire's greatest legacy? Explain your answer.
21. EVALUATE How did Zheng He's expeditions help expand China's dominance over maritime global trade in Asia?
22. SYNTHESIZE How did China indirectly help the Ottoman Turks establish an empire?
23. MAKE CONNECTIONS Why did Mehmed II want to be seen as the heir to the Roman emperors?

INTERPRET VISUALS

This full-size replica of one of Zheng He's treasure ships stands in Nanjing, China. The people in the foreground of the photo help convey the ship's immensity. Study the photo. Then answer the questions that follow.

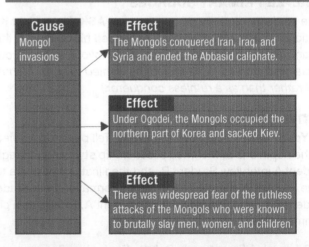

24. How did local people probably react when they saw Zheng He's treasure ships pulling into their port?

25. What does the size of the treasure ship suggest about what Ming emperor Yongle expected from the expeditions?

ANALYZE SOURCES

Marco Polo's stories about his travels and adventures were gathered into a book around 1300, and it was an instant success. In this excerpt from the book, Polo describes the trade that flowed through Beijing during the Yuan dynasty. Read the excerpt and then answer the following question.

> You may take it for a fact that more precious and costly wares are imported into Khan-balik [Beijing] than into any other city in the world. Let me give you particulars. All the treasures that come from India—precious stones, pearls, and other rarities—are brought here. So too are the choicest and costliest products of Cathay [China] itself. . . . This is on account of the Great Khan [Kublai] himself, who lives here, and of the lords and ladies and the enormous multitude of hotel-keepers and other residents and of visitors who attend the courts held here by the Khan.

26. What impression of Beijing and Kublai Khan does Polo convey?

CONNECT TO YOUR LIFE

27. EXPLANATORY Mehmed II rebuilt Constantinople to make it an important center of art, education, and business. Review the measures he took to accomplish this, and then think about a city or region today that has suffered from war or a natural disaster. What did people do to rebuild that area? What do you think they might have learned from Mehmed's actions in Constantinople? Write a short essay explaining what local people and the government have done to rebuild a ravaged area and what actions or policies of Mehmed they might have adopted.

TIPS

* Review Mehmed's actions and policies when he rebuilt Constantinople.
* Do research to learn what was done recently to rebuild an area that was damaged or destroyed by war or a natural disaster.
* Consider which of Mehmed's actions and policies might have helped in the modern-day rebuilding.
* Use two or three vocabulary terms from the chapter in your essay.
* Provide a concluding statement that summarizes your ideas on how adopting Mehmed's actions and policies might have helped.

VOCABULARY ANSWERS

1. c
2. g
3. b
4. e
5. f
6. h
7. d
8. a

READING STRATEGY ANSWERS

Cause	Effect
Mongol invasions	The Mongols conquered Iran, Iraq, and Syria and ended the Abbasid caliphate.
	Under Ogodei, the Mongols occupied the northern part of Korea and sacked Kiev.
	There was widespread fear of the ruthless attacks of the Mongols who were known to brutally slay men, women, and children.

9. His soldiers ended their invasion of Europe and returned to Mongolia.

10. His decision helped preserve Chinese culture in north China, and the Mongols benefited from the technologies that had developed there and learned new governmental techniques.

MAIN IDEAS ANSWERS

11. the Mongol warrior who conquered lands in Central Asia, China, and Russia and founded the Mongol Empire

12. He treated them like second-class citizens, forcing Chinese peasants to work on his building projects and not allowing Chinese scholars to occupy the top government jobs.

13. Merchants from Europe, China, Southwest Asia, and India traveled the Silk Roads and traded goods as well as ideas.

14. They wanted to restore what they saw as the glories of the imperial Chinese tradition in governance and the arts.

15. the defeat at the Battle of Ankara when the Ottomans fought Timur and his army

16. He had his army pull 70 ships out of the Bosporus, haul them over a hill on greased logs, and then refloat them in the waters of the Golden Horn.

HISTORICAL THINKING ANSWERS

17. Answers will vary. Possible response: He feared that his enemies might desecrate and rob his grave.

18. The Mongols killed the last Abbasid caliph in Baghdad and brought an end to the Abbasid caliphate.

19. Answers will vary. Possible response: He chose to establish his capital in China rather than in a Mongol city.

20. Answers will vary. Possible response: making the Silk Roads safe to travel and linking Europe and Asia through trade along the routes

21. Answers will vary. Possible response: The expeditions demonstrated China's naval and political power, its variety of trade goods, and its control over trade routes and weaker countries.

22. The Chinese invention of gunpowder helped the Ottomans in their quest to expand their territory.

23. Answers will vary. Possible response: He wanted to be associated with their power, greatness, and huge empire.

INTERPRET VISUALS ANSWERS

24. Answers will vary. Possible response: with fear and awe

25. Answers will vary. Possible response: The emperor expected Zheng He to return with a lot of tribute and trade goods—enough to fill the huge treasure ships.

ANALYZE SOURCES ANSWER

26. Answers will vary. Possible response: He conveys Beijing's wealth and opulence and Kublai Khan's great leadership and power.

CONNECT TO YOUR LIFE ANSWER

27. Essays will vary but should contain main ideas and relevant supporting details to explain how adopting Mehmed's actions and policies might have helped people today rebuild a city.

Were Viking Warriors
Especially Brutal?

BY CHRISTOPHER SHEA Adapted from "Did the Vikings Get a Bum Rap?" by
Christopher Shea, news.nationalgeographic.com, September 28, 2014

You've read about the motivations and characteristics of soldiers throughout history. Many accounts of warriors in medieval times focus on their brutality. The Vikings of Scandinavia have especially been portrayed as monstrous warriors who launched raids throughout Europe, supposedly decimating towns and needlessly slaughtering priests.

But according to Anders Winroth, a Yale history professor and author of the book *The Age of the Vikings*, the Vikings were no more bloodthirsty than other warriors of the period. They suffered from bad public relations, however, partly because they attacked a society more literate than their own. Therefore, most accounts of them come from their victims. Moreover, because the Vikings were pagan, Christian writers cast them as a devilish outside force.

To be sure, scholars have for decades been stressing aspects of Viking life beyond the warlike. They point to the craftsmanship of the Norse (a term that refers more generally to Scandinavians) and the ingenuity of their ships. They also highlight their trade with the Arab world, their settlements in Greenland and Newfoundland, and the fact that the majority of them stayed behind during raids. But Winroth wants to put the final nail in the coffin on the notion that the Vikings were the "Nazis of the North," as British journalist Patrick Cockburn has argued.

It used to be routine for scholars to claim that the Vikings killed some of their victims by means of the so-called blood eagle. The form of an eagle reportedly was carved onto a victim's back, the rib cage severed, and the lungs pulled out the back. But Winroth holds strongly to the view that this story comes from a misreading of Norse verse. Norse poetry is full of birds, including eagles, that feast on the bodies of one's enemies. Authors of Scandinavian sagas, writing centuries after the Viking raids, turned an eagle cutting into a man's back into an eagle being carved on the back.

This illustration shows the stereotype of Viking marauders wreaking mayhem, even on clergy. The scene depicts the monastery at Clonmacnoise, Ireland.

Winroth also wants us to rethink the berserkers, the supposedly near-psychopathic warriors in the front line of Viking attacks. The berserkers were said to be immune to pain. More colorful accounts add that they chewed on their shields and ate burning coals. Winroth argues that references to berserkers first appear in the poetry of 13th- and 14th-century Iceland. In the poetry, the berserkers are plainly described as people who lived "once upon a time."

Winroth proposes that "the Vikings were sort of free-market entrepreneurs." Rather than being primed for battle by an irrational love of mayhem, the Vikings went raiding mainly for pragmatic reasons. They sought to build personal fortunes and enhance the power of their chieftains. As evidence, Winroth enumerates cases in which Viking leaders negotiated for payment, or tried to, rather than immediately attack.

Winroth believes the Vikings need to be seen in context. For a historian, he says, putting people in the context of their times humanizes them. And that's good, even when we're talking about people best known as warriors who plundered villages and slaughtered monks. ∎

Staging the Question

In this unit, you followed the rise of several combative dynasties. The kings and nations you have read about went to war for varying reasons. According to one chronicler, Genghis Khan fought for the sheer joy of it, saying, "Man's greatest good fortune is to chase and defeat his enemy, seize his total possessions, leave his married women weeping and wailing." Like Charlemagne, Osman, and others, however, Genghis Khan was an astute ruler as well as a warlord and most likely had more complex motivations. But was war the only choice? By examining the causes of war, how can cultures in conflict make peace?

ASSIGNMENT

Identify the root causes for the wars and conquests described in this unit. Choose one of the conflicts to explore in greater depth.

Research the causes of the war, as well as the resources each side in the war controlled.

Synthesize ideas for how the warring nations could exchange resources or find other ways to make peace.

Develop a peace plan for two warring empires or nations from this unit, laying out terms that would allow each side to gain what it had sought through conflict.

Supporting Questions: Begin by developing supporting questions to guide your research. For example: What did the Song have that the Jurchen needed? Were there other reasons for the Song and Jurchen to fight? Research the answers in this unit and in other sources, both print and online. You might want to use a graphic organizer like this one to record your answers.

Summative Performance Task: Develop a peace plan that you will present to both powers in the war. Include specific details about the conditions each side will have to accept and explain the advantages each side will gain by agreeing to them. Use what you know about the causes of the war to help you create peace terms that will appeal to the combatants.

Present: Share your plan with the class. You might consider one of these options:

MAKE A PRESENTATION

Create a slideshow or video to present before an international body such as the United Nations, laying out the peace terms and their advantages. Include graphics, photos, or other visuals to support your points.

BROKER A TREATY

Meet with classmates who are acting as representatives for the warring powers. Explain the points of your plan, and negotiate the final terms of the peace.

Take Informed Action:

UNDERSTAND Understanding the causes of a disagreement can lead to a peaceful solution, even when there is no war involved. Identify a disagreement in your school or community.

ASSESS Determine the causes of the disagreement and think of solutions that address these causes.

ACT Create a "peace plan" to solve the disagreement and present it to the two sides. You may meet with representatives of both sides, write a letter, or communicate your plan in some other way.

NATIONAL GEOGRAPHIC CONNECTION

GUIDED DISCUSSION FOR "WERE VIKING WARRIORS ESPECIALLY BRUTAL?"

1. **Form and Support Opinions** Do you think the Vikings were more brutal than other warriors? Use the text to explain your reasoning. *(Answers will vary. Possible responses: No, it seems as though the Vikings were more or less the same as other warriors in empires and kingdoms throughout history. The Vikings attacked Christians, who thought the Vikings were barbarians without religion. They also attacked many places where people were literate, so the victims could write about the Vikings' attacks.)*

2. **Make Connections** What makes the Vikings of Scandinavia unique and why is it important to learn about them as more than just warriors? *(Answers will vary. Possible responses: It is important to learn about them because the Vikings were a dominant clan with settlements in Greenland and Newfoundland. Vikings had advanced navigation skills and knowledge of the seas. The Vikings were known for their craftsmanship and ingenuity of their shipbuilding. It is important to learn about all aspects of people and about all civilizations.)*

History Notebook

Encourage students to complete the Unit Wrap-Up page for Unit 4 in their History Notebooks.

UNIT INQUIRY PROJECT RUBRIC

ASSESS

Use the rubric to assess each student's participation and performance.

SCORE	ASSIGNMENT	PRODUCT	PRESENTATION
3 GREAT	• Student thoroughly understands the assignment. • Student develops thoughtful supporting questions to guide research.	• Peace treaty is well thought out and includes many specific details and advantages for each side. • Peace treaty reflects all of the key elements listed in the assignment.	• Presentation clearly lays out the peace terms and the advantages to both sides. • Presentation is concise, logical, and engaging.
2 GOOD	• Student mostly understands the assignment. • Student develops somewhat thoughtful supporting questions to guide research.	• Peace treaty is fairly well thought out and includes some specific details and advantages for each side. • Peace treaty reflects most of the key elements listed in the assignment.	• Presentation is fairly clear as it lays out the peace terms and the advantages. • Presentation is fairly concise, logical, and engaging.
1 NEEDS WORK	• Student does not understand the assignment. • Student does not develop thoughtful questions to guide research.	• Peace treaty is not well thought out and includes few specific details and advantages for each side. • Peace treaty reflects few or none of the key elements listed in the assignment.	• Presentation is not clear as it lays out the peace terms and the advantages. • Presentation is not logical or engaging.

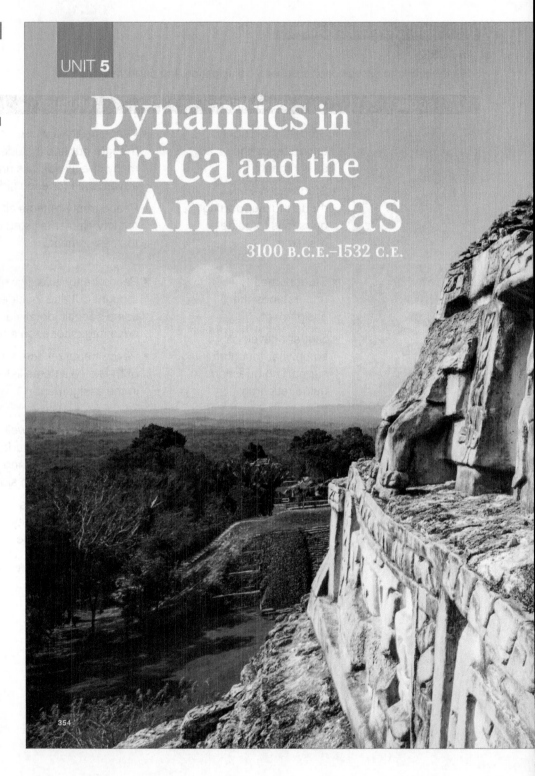

Dynamics in Africa and the Americas

3100 B.C.E.–1532 C.E.

THE MAYA CITY OF XUNANTUNICH

Xunantunich, a lesser known Maya settlement, was named for the "stone woman" who appeared in a local legend at the end of the 1800s. According to the legend, a local villager was hunting near the site and was captivated by a beautiful woman dressed in traditional Maya clothing standing at the opening of a cave at the base of El Castillo. The stone woman appeared to other locals later, but none were able to find her in the cave.

The city of Xunantunich, surrounded by fertile farmland, lies roughly 600 feet above sea level on an artificially leveled limestone ridge above the Mopan River. The city's core is about one square mile and consists of four architectural groups that include palaces, temples, ball courts, and hundreds of unearthed mounds. The most prominent group is dominated by El Castillo, a large complex that was used by the Maya as a dwelling, shrine, and administrative hub for elite rulers. The structure's exterior features detailed carvings that represent astronomical symbols and Maya gods of creation, among others.

It is believed that early Maya settled a small village at the site during the Middle Preclassic period and rose rapidly between 800 and 900 C.E., when most other cities in the region were declining. An excavation that began in 1959 revealed that the layout of Xunantunich was similar to the Maya city Naranjo, located in what is now Guatemala. This and other evidence suggests that the Maya traded and communicated with one another. As Naranjo authority declined, local Maya likely gained control of Xunantunich and began to develop it, as evidenced by the construction of El Castillo and other buildings. The last recorded Mayan

CRITICAL VIEWING

In western Belize, stone carvings adorn the Maya temple El Castillo ("The Castle") at the Xunantunich archaeological site. This structure at Xunantunich, which is ancient Mayan for "stone woman," stretches to 130 feet above the main plaza. Based on the details in this photograph, what can you infer about the Maya people and their religion?

date, found on a stela at the site, is 830 C.E. The activity that followed likely came from other groups who attempted to occupy the abandoned settlement. Structural damage indicates that the city was hit with an earthquake or other sudden disaster around 900 C.E.

Direct students' attention to the photograph. **ASK:** From what location is the photograph taken? *(along the side of El Castillo)* What is the photographer able to accomplish from this vantage point? *(The photographer is able to capture both the intricate details of the stone carvings and provide perspective of the height and size of the temple as compared with the surrounding land.)*

CRITICAL VIEWING Possible response: Religion was probably important to the Maya people, based on the ornate carvings on the temple. The Maya also appear to have been skilled architects who were able to construct such a tall structure.

INTRODUCE TIME LINE EVENTS

IDENTIFY PATTERNS AND THEMES

Have volunteers read aloud each of the world events in the time line. **ASK:** What are some common themes or patterns that you notice with regard to these events? *(Possible responses: Some common themes or patterns include migration, trade, and the emergence of powerful empires.)* Sort the themes and patterns into categories and put them in graphic organizers like the ones shown here.

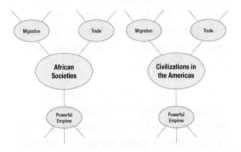

As students read the lessons for each chapter in the unit, have them add the lesson titles to the appropriate line on the related graphic organizer. Advise students that they may also add or revise categories as necessary. At the end of the unit, revisit students' graphic organizers and create a final list of categories to summarize the historical themes students encountered as they read each chapter.

UNIT 5 **Dynamics in Africa and the Americas**

WORLD EVENTS
1500 B.C.E.–1600 C.E.

c. 1000 C.E. AMERICAS The Mississippian culture builds the prehistoric city of Cahokia in present-day Illinois. *(flint clay artifact called the Rattler Frog Pipe, c. 1000–1250)*

c. 1200 B.C.E. AMERICAS The Olmec develop their civilization in Mesoamerica. *(Olmec colossal stone head, c. 1200 B.C.E.)*

c. 500 C.E. AFRICA Ghana becomes the first great trading state in West Africa.

| 1500 B.C.E. | // | 1200 B.C.E. | // | 1 C.E. | | 200 C.E. | | 400 C.E. | | 600 C |

400s C.E. AFRICA Bantu speakers from West Africa migrate to sub-Saharan Africa.

700 C.E. AMERICAS The Anasazi expand their territory and begin to live in small villages in what is now the southwestern United States. *(ancestral Pueblo earthenware jar, c. 1300)*

250 C.E. AMERICAS The Maya Classic Period begins. *(earthenware head of Oaxaca, Maya corn god, c. 500)*

Dynamics in Africa and the Americas 3100 B.C.E.–1532 C.E.

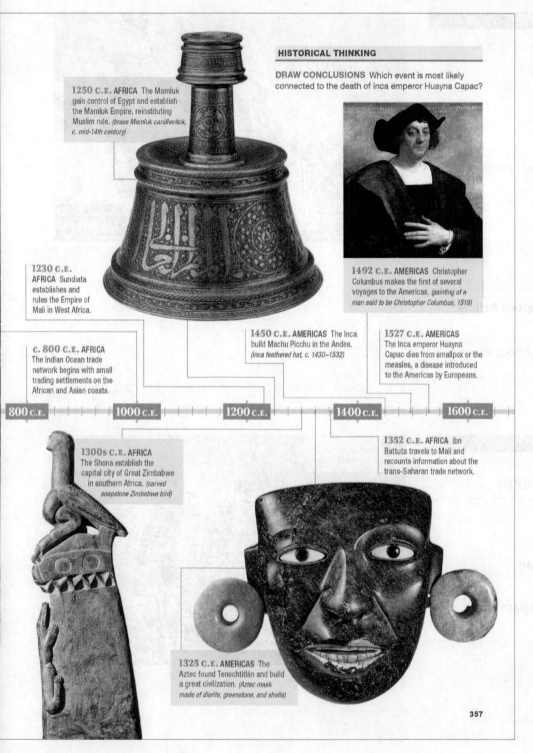

1250 C.E. AFRICA The Mamluk gain control of Egypt and establish the Mamluk Empire, reinstituting Muslim rule. *(brass Mamluk candlestick, c. mid-14th century)*

HISTORICAL THINKING

DRAW CONCLUSIONS Which event is most likely connected to the death of Inca emperor Huayna Capac?

1230 C.E. AFRICA Sundiata establishes and rules the Empire of Mali in West Africa.

1492 C.E. AMERICAS Christopher Columbus makes the first of several voyages to the Americas. *(painting of a man said to be Christopher Columbus, 1519)*

c. 800 C.E. AFRICA The Indian Ocean trade network begins with small trading settlements on the African and Asian coasts.

1450 C.E. AMERICAS The Inca build Machu Picchu in the Andes. *(Inca feathered hat, c. 1430–1532)*

1527 C.E. AMERICAS The Inca emperor Huayna Capac dies from smallpox or the measles, a disease introduced to the Americas by Europeans.

| 800 C.E. | 1000 C.E. | 1200 C.E. | 1400 C.E. | 1600 C.E. |

1300s C.E. AFRICA The Shona establish the capital city of Great Zimbabwe in southern Africa. *(carved soapstone Zimbabwe bird)*

1352 C.E. AFRICA Ibn Battuta travels to Mali and recounts information about the trans-Saharan trade network.

1325 C.E. AMERICAS The Aztec found Tenochtitlán and build a great civilization. *(Aztec mask made of diorite, greenstone, and shells)*

357

HISTORICAL THINKING

Draw Conclusions

Possible response: Columbus's 1492 voyage brought Europeans and their diseases, including smallpox and measles, to the Americas.

Student eEdition online

Additional content, including the unit map and Global Perspective feature, is available online.

UNIT 5 Dynamics in Africa and the Americas

UNIT 5 RESOURCES

UNIT INTRODUCTION

UNIT TIME LINE

UNIT MAP online

THE GLOBAL PERSPECTIVE:
Power Objects online

- National Geographic Explorers: Fred Hiebert and Ken Garrett
- On Your Feet: Corners

| **NG Learning Framework**
Research Museum Exhibitions

UNIT WRAP-UP

National Geographic Magazine Adapted Article
- "The Real Price of Gold"

Unit 5 Inquiry: Make a Documentary About Power Objects

Unit 5 Formal Assessment

CHAPTER 13 RESOURCES

Available in the Teacher eEdition

TEACHER RESOURCES & ASSESSMENT

Reading and Note-Taking

Vocabulary Practice

Document-Based Question Template

Social Studies Skills Lessons
- Reading: Identify Main Ideas and Details
- Writing: Argument

Formal Assessment
- Chapter 13 Pretest
- Chapter 13 Tests A & B
- Section Quizzes

Chapter 13 Answer Key

Cognero®

STUDENT DIGITAL RESOURCES

Available in the Student eEdition

- eEdition (English)
- National Geographic Atlas
- Biographies
- Handbooks
- History Notebook
- Literature Analysis

STRATEGY ❶
Focus on Main Ideas

Tell students to locate the Main Idea statement for each lesson. Explain that these statements summarize the important ideas of the lesson and help students focus on key facts and ideas. Ask students to copy the Main Idea statement into a Main Idea and Details List and list details that support the Main Idea as they read the lesson.

Use with All Lessons *For example, key details from Lesson 1.1 may include where sub-Saharan societies lived in Africa, who speakers of the Bantu language family were and how they lived, and how the oral historians called* griots *have preserved the African past.*

STRATEGY ❷
Turn Headings into Outlines

Explain that headings can provide a high-level outline of the lesson. Model for students how to use the lesson title and headings to create a basic outline, leaving space after each heading to take notes. Encourage students to add information to the outline after reading each section.

Use with All Lessons

STRATEGY ❸
Ask Either/Or Questions

Monitor students' comprehension of the lesson by asking them to answer either/or questions. Ask partners to check one another's answers.

Use with All Lessons *For example, you may ask questions such as these for Lesson 2.1: Did Mansa Musa gain his wealth through taxes on trade or gold mining? (taxes on trade); Was the cultural center of the Mamluk Empire the city of Baghdad or Cairo? (Cairo)*

STRATEGY ❶
Provide Terms and Names on Audio

Decide which of the terms and names are important for mastery and ask a volunteer to record the pronunciations and a short sentence defining each. Tell students to listen to the recording until they can use the terms in discussion.

Use with All Lessons *To quiz students on their mastery of the terms, play one definition at a time and ask students to identify the term or name described.*

STRATEGY ❷
Use Supported Reading

Pair proficient readers with students who have reading or perception issues and assign partners paragraphs to read aloud together. At the end of each paragraph, have students use the following sentence frames to monitor their comprehension:

- This paragraph is about _____.
- One fact that stood out to me was _____.
- One question I have is _____.
- One word I don't recognize is _____.

Review ideas that confuse students and be sure all students understand the content before moving on to the next paragraph.

Use with All Lessons

STRATEGY ❶
Create Meaning Maps

Pair students at the **Beginning** level with those at the **Intermediate** or **Advanced** level. Demonstrate how to use a Meaning Map for any of the Key Vocabulary or other important terms in the lesson. Encourage pairs to discuss the words and clear up any misunderstandings.

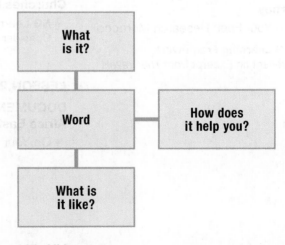

Use with All Lessons

STRATEGY 2
Develop Word Knowledge
Help students develop understanding and usage of unknown words and vocabulary words by using the words in context.

For **Beginning** level students, display sentences with choices: Griots passed historical information on by telling stories/writing books. *(telling stories)*

For **Intermediate** level students, display individual sentence frames with only one blank: People of an African village belonged to a lineage and had a _____ ancestor. *(common)*

For **Advanced** level students, display sentences with more than one blank: A mansa was a _____ who oversaw the religious, political, and _____ aspects of an empire. *(ruler, economic)*

Use with All Lessons

STRATEGY 3
Connect Visuals to Lesson Content
Direct students at the **Beginning** and **Intermediate** levels to read each lesson and study the visuals. Then ask them to explain how the visuals are related to the lesson.

Use with All Lessons *Encourage students at the **Beginning** level to ask questions if they have trouble connecting a visual with its lesson. Suggest students at the **Advanced** level help students at the **Beginning** and **Intermediate** levels.*

STRATEGY 1
Develop a Nature Program
Prompt students to choose one of the African societies described in the chapter and develop a nature program about the group of people. Have them conduct more research as needed on the climate and natural resources of the area and how these impacted the lives of the people. Instruct students to describe the impact on the common people as well as the wealthy people of the society. Encourage them to find interesting visuals to display as they present their nature facts to the class.

Use with All Lessons

STRATEGY 2
Analyze Historical Records
Tell students to conduct more research into one of the ways historians have learned about an early African society, such as through the oral tradition of griots, through the buildings they left behind, through the discovery of a hoard, or through written records. Invite them to analyze the positive and negative aspects of this kind of historical record and what it does and does not tell us. Have them write their analysis and post it on a class website.

Use with All Lessons

STRATEGY 1
Write a Cause-and-Effect Essay
Remind students that most historical events have many causal factors and bring about many consequences. Challenge students to choose one of the African societies described in the chapter and find out more about what caused their success and decline. Encourage them to use a graphic organizer to map out cause-and-effect relationships before they write their essay about both the causes and effects. Invite them to share their essays with the class.

Use with All Lessons

STRATEGY 2
Form and Support a Thesis
Direct students to construct a hypothesis and use it to develop a thesis statement for a historical event from the chapter. Tell students to support their thesis statement with evidence from the lessons and from multiple primary and secondary sources. Invite students to present their thesis statement and supporting evidence to the class. Discuss the process with the entire class, asking students to point out evidence used and how it relates to the original hypothesis.

Use with All Lessons

CHAPTER
13 Achievements of African Societies
300–1525

HISTORICAL THINKING How did African societies influence other cultures?

SECTION 1 Diverse Societies, Powerful Kingdoms
SECTION 2 Trade and Cultural Interactions

CRITICAL VIEWING
The Great Mosque of Djenné is an important religious site in Mali. What materials were used to construct the mosque?

INTRODUCE THE PHOTOGRAPH

ISLAMIC ARCHITECTURE

Have students study the Great Mosque of Djenné that appears at the beginning of the chapter. Direct students to focus on the materials used to build it, as well as its design. Have students discuss and answer the Critical Viewing question. **ASK:** How do the materials used to build this mosque compare to the materials used for other mosques you may have seen? *(Possible response: Photographs of other mosques show that some mosques are made of stone, wood, and glass.)* Besides the materials used, does this mosque look the same as or different from other mosques? Explain. *(Possible response: It looks different. Some mosques have domes, towers, or geometric shapes and this mosque does not have these features.)* Explain that the resources an environment offers differ and that often people will use resources that are plentiful in their environment to meet their needs. Tell students that in this chapter they will learn about African achievements over many centuries, including adaptations societies made due to environmental challenges.

SHARE BACKGROUND

Islam arrived in Africa centuries before the Great Mosque was built in the 1200s or 1300s. As it took hold, the people of Africa who adopted the religion influenced Islamic culture just as much as Islamic culture influenced them. Yet the Great Mosque may have had yet another influence—the French.

Some archaeologists and historians argue whether the French rebuilt the Great Mosque in 1907, because it is in a style that the French preferred for all of its West African colonies. That means the style may be different and less "West African" than the original mosque. One detail that supports this argument is that dried mud-brick does not hold up well when there are heavy rains, which West Africa experiences at certain times of the year. Because of this issue, the exterior of the mosque has to be brushed with more mud to fill any cracks, holes, and uneven surfaces.

CRITICAL VIEWING Possible responses include that the mosque is made of dirt, mud, or clay, and wood.

HISTORICAL THINKING QUESTION
How did African societies influence other cultures?

Four Corners: Preview Content This activity will help students preview and discuss the topics covered in the chapter. Provide a brief description and question for each region discussed in the chapter, such as the ones shown below, and designate each of the four corners as being "home" to one of the regions of Africa. Divide the class into four groups and direct each group to go to one of the corners and discuss an African region's influence on other cultures for a short time.

Group 1 Northern Africa. **ASK:** How have France and Italy been influenced by this region?

Group 2 Western Africa. **ASK:** How has U.S. culture been influenced by this region?

Group 3 Eastern Africa. **ASK:** How has the culture of southwest Asia been influenced by this region?

Group 4 Southern Africa. **ASK:** How have British and Dutch cultures been influenced by this region?

KEY DATES FOR CHAPTER 13

1000 B.C.E.	Bantu speakers begin moving east and south through sub-Saharan Africa.
400s C.E.	Bantu speakers reach southern Africa.
800	Ghana becomes a wealthy empire through trade.
1200s	An Ethiopian king begins building the rock churches at Lalibela.
1230s	The Mali Empire begins.
1250	The Mamluks gain control of Egypt.
early 1300s	The Shona people establish Great Zimbabwe.
1307	Mansa Musa becomes ruler of the Mali Empire.
1325	Ibn Battuta begins his pilgrimage to Mecca.
1354	Ibn Battuta returns from his travels and dictates a book called *The Travels*.
1450	The Songhai conquer the Mali Empire.

INTRODUCE THE READING STRATEGY

IDENTIFY MAIN IDEAS AND DETAILS

Explain to students that identifying main ideas and details can help them gain an understanding of the central idea of a text and the details that support it. Go to the Chapter Review and preview the Main Ideas and Details chart with students. As they read the chapter, have students take notes about the main ideas about African achievements and the details that support these ideas.

INTRODUCE CHAPTER VOCABULARY

KEY VOCABULARY

SECTION 1

caravan	griot	intermediary
lineage	mansa	monopoly
Sahel	savanna	

SECTION 2

dhow	trans-Saharan trade network

WORD MAPS

As students read the chapter, ask them to complete a Word Map for each Key Vocabulary word. Tell them to write the word in the oval and, as they encounter the word in the chapter, complete the Word Map. Model an example using the graphic organizer below.

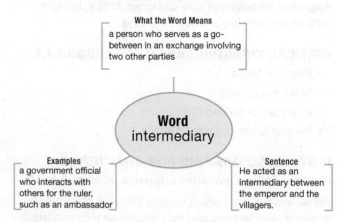

What the Word Means
a person who serves as a go-between in an exchange involving two other parties

Word
intermediary

Examples
a government official who interacts with others for the ruler, such as an ambassador

Sentence
He acted as an intermediary between the emperor and the villagers.

Sub-Saharan African Societies

When you think of Africa, do you think of the Sahara? This vast desert divides the enormous continent into two parts: North and East Africa and sub-Saharan Africa. More than 2,000 years ago, a group of people in western Africa started migrating throughout sub-Saharan Africa, spreading their language and culture.

SUB-SAHARAN AFRICA AND BANTU MIGRATIONS

Africa is a large continent with an area greater than that of the United States, Europe, and China combined. It is also a land of varying climate zones. The northern coast of Africa borders the Mediterranean Sea and is separated from southern regions by the mighty Sahara. Immediately to the south of the Sahara is a semidesert region called the **Sahel**. South of the Sahel is the **savanna**, an area of fertile grasslands, followed by rain forest, more savanna, and the Kalahari Desert near the southern tip of Africa.

You have already learned about Africa's earliest civilizations in Egypt and Nubia, and you have heard about African participation in Indian Ocean trade. You have also read about the spread of Islam in North Africa. In fact, much of what we know about early North and East Africa comes from accounts by Arab travelers.

Historians know less about early sub-Saharan Africa since few Arab travelers entered the region before the year 1000. Instead, they must look at evidence from archaeological excavations, oral traditions, and the distribution of languages. Africans today speak nearly 2,000 languages, or about one-third of all the world's languages. They fall into a few main language categories. Speakers of Arabic in North Africa and of Amharic in East Africa, for example, speak languages that are part of the wider Afrasian family. Many West Africans

speak languages of the Niger-Congo family. The Bantu languages are part of that family, and Bantu speakers would have a huge impact on sub-Saharan Africa.

Bantu means "people" and is a general name for many different peoples of Africa who speak more than 500 different languages yet share a common ancestry. By studying the different Bantu languages, linguists, people who study human speech, know that the Bantu originated in western Africa around present-day Nigeria and Cameroon. Research suggests that speakers of Bantu languages began moving east and south from their original homes as early as 1000 B.C.E. Over generations, these Bantu societies developed differences

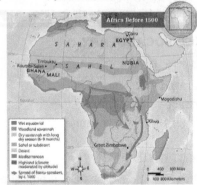

in their speech, culture, and mode of living. For example, those groups who moved south into the rain forest focused on crops that were successful in a warm and humid atmosphere. Those who moved east encountered cattle-herding peoples in the Nile River Valley from whom they borrowed a focus on cattle-herding. In western and southern Africa, farming and cattle-herding went together.

Bantu societies were skilled in agriculture and ironworking and brought these technologies with them as they migrated. As you have learned, farming supports much denser populations than hunting and gathering. That is why the Bantu moving both south into the rain forest and east across savanna lands either absorbed the ancient hunting and gathering societies they found in those places or forced such foragers to move to more remote areas. By the 400s, Bantu societies had come to southern Africa, a frontier of settlement almost 4,000 miles in distance.

EARLY AFRICAN WAYS OF LIFE

All African societies, including those of Bantu speakers, used oral traditions to remember the past as a guide to the present. In some West African societies, there was even a special class of oral historians known as **griots** who passed historical knowledge from father to son across the centuries. When historians began studying the stories of the griots in the 20th century, they found that they could learn a great deal about the African past that had previously not been known.

The core of African life lay in the village. Usually, residents of a village belonged to a **lineage**, descendants from a common ancestor. The residents' lineage defined their rights and responsibilities. It was the elders of the lineage who made the most important decisions. Over time, groups of lineages might come together to form clans, larger networks that might include thousands of people. Similarly, related clans might sometimes band together and accept a chief or king as their common leader. However powerful African kings might become, for many people the most important thing was still their lineage and clan.

Like most farming societies, African villages were patriarchal. Men had more power and authority than

CRITICAL VIEWING The Sahel has a dry season (left) and a wet season (right). How is the land different during the two seasons?

women. Men usually did jobs that were considered more prestigious, such as hunting, working with metals, going on military conquests, looking after cattle, and trading. Women more often did the tough day-to-day work of farming, gathering wild fruits and vegetables, carrying water, gathering wood, and preparing meals. But it was also true that in many village societies, older women, as elders, had a voice in decision-making. Women often had their own councils where they made decisions to protect women's interests. In some African kingdoms, there was even an official role for the Queen Mother, a person nearly equal in power to the king.

A man with many children and great wealth was a "great man." Great men often became leaders of clans or groups of clans that formed chiefdoms or kingdoms. Further conquest might expand the kingdom even further. In the next lesson, you will learn about two powerful kingdoms that grew out of this practice—Ghana and Mali.

HISTORICAL THINKING

1. **READING CHECK** How did farming techniques and ironworking skills spread throughout sub-Saharan Africa?

2. **INTERPRET MAPS** Look at the map in this lesson. In what ways did the sub-Saharan lands on which Bantu-speaking peoples settled vary?

3. **MAKE INFERENCES** Why did men take on the more prestigious tasks in sub-Saharan African society?

PLAN: 2-PAGE LESSON

OBJECTIVE
Describe how speakers of the Bantu languages migrated throughout sub-Saharan Africa, bringing with them farming and ironworking.

CRITICAL THINKING SKILLS FOR LESSON 1.1
- Interpret Maps
- Make Inferences
- Analyze Cause and Effect
- Identify Main Ideas and Details

HISTORICAL THINKING FOR CHAPTER 13
How did African societies influence other cultures?

Bantu-language speakers spread their rich culture and knowledge of farming and ironworking as they migrated from western Africa to sub-Saharan Africa. Lesson 1.1 discusses the influence of Bantu speakers and their culture as they migrated throughout sub-Saharan Africa.

BACKGROUND FOR THE TEACHER

Glottochronology African historians pioneered the use of a linguistic method called *glottochronology* to analyze the history of languages. By comparing vocabulary lists, linguists can count how many words in two languages are the same and how many have changed. The greater the number of shared words, the closer two languages are; the fewer the number, the more distant. Glottochronology can indicate which languages broke off from others and in what order but not always exactly when. Close analysis of the linguistic variation among modern Bantu languages suggests that multiple waves of change occurred. Accordingly, scholars today have discarded the theory of a single wave of Bantu migration. A persuasive model for the spread of Bantu languages sees three different, and often overlapping, processes taking place over an extended period: the planting of the first crops, the development of metallurgy, and the spread of the Bantu languages. Habitat influenced where the Bantu settled. Savannas were more populated than more unfamiliar environments, such as rainforests, because the Bantu better understood the habitat, and it better supported their farming practices.

INTRODUCE & ENGAGE

DISCUSS CULTURAL INFLUENCES

Invite students to discuss any cultural influences that they think may have come from Africa, such as music, an artistic style, food, clothing, or dance that they have observed in the United States. *(Possible responses: dances, sweet potatoes, stews, brightly colored textiles)* Tell students that they will learn about the achievements of African societies, including the influence of African culture on other cultures around the world.

TEACH

GUIDED DISCUSSION

1. **Analyze Cause and Effect** What other cultures may have been influenced by griots and storytelling, and what cultures may have used or developed storytelling independently? *(Possible responses: African-American culture; Native American cultures)*

2. **Identify Main Ideas and Details** Which detail in the text supports the main idea that African villages were patriarchal? *(Possible response: Jobs done by men were considered more prestigious.)*

IDENTIFY MAIN IDEAS AND DETAILS

Discuss the sentence, "Instead, they must look at evidence from archaeological excavations, oral traditions, and the distribution of languages." Point out that this states an important main idea in this section of the text: historians use the above techniques to learn about early sub-Saharan Africa. Have students read the rest of the paragraph and the one following it. **ASK:** What historical technique mentioned in the main idea statement for this section of text is supported by the text? *(Possible response: the technique of looking at the distribution of languages)* Have students identify details about this historical technique that support the main idea statement.

ACTIVE OPTIONS

On Your Feet: Ready, Set, Recall Have small, numbered groups write down all the details they recall from the lesson. Then have them take turns sharing one fact at a time from their lists with the class. Write all contributions on the board under the group's number. When a group runs out of items, the members must drop out of the game, but they can rejoin if they recall a fact that has not yet been shared. Continue until time runs out. The group with the most facts listed is the winner.

> **NG Learning Framework: Research Homes and Clothing in Early Sub-Saharan Africa**
> **ATTITUDE** Curiosity
> **SKILLS** Collaboration, Communication

Assign groups to learn more about the styles of homes and clothing that were prevalent in early sub-Saharan Africa. Have them compare and contrast their findings and consider how the environment and climate affected the materials used for both homes and clothing. Groups should create a chart or profile of the information they have gathered, including photos or illustrations. Invite groups to share their work with the class.

DIFFERENTIATE

ENGLISH LANGUAGE LEARNERS

Explore the 5Ws Remind students of the 5Ws: *Who? What? Where? When?* and *Why?* Pair students with English-proficient students to take turns asking and answering questions about the lesson visuals using these question words. Tell English-proficient students to help their partners understand any new terms.

PRE-AP

Compare the Sahel Then and Now Have students research and analyze how the climate of the Sahel has changed from the time of the Bantu migrations. Students should create or use visuals such as diagrams, charts, animation, or videos to illustrate the changes that the Sahel has undergone over centuries and how it has affected the people who live there. They may explain their findings in an essay or a multimedia presentation.

See the Chapter Planner for more strategies for differentiation.

HISTORICAL THINKING

ANSWERS

1. Bantu-speaking people introduced them as they migrated south.

2. Possible response: They spread into wet equatorial, woodland savanna, dry savanna, and the Sahel. Some land was near water and flat; other land was far from water and possibly hilly or mountainous. Some land was farther from the Equator.

3. Possible response: Society was dominated by males; males served as leaders. Men chose the jobs that were most important and satisfying to them. They may have assumed that jobs requiring physical strength would be better handled by men.

CRITICAL VIEWING dry: very dry, lacks lush vegetation; wet: lush and green

Ghana and Mali

Location! Location! Location! is often said to be the key to economic success. The early history of West Africa supports the idea that people can profit from their location. West African kingdoms and empires flourished based on their ideal trade positions.

THE RISE OF THE KINGDOM OF GHANA

Around 300, a people called the Soninke (sah-NEENG-kay) lived in small agricultural villages in West Africa. Their location was ideal for economic growth. To the north lay mines filled with salt, important for flavoring food and maintaining health. Directly south were mines filled with gold. Both gold and salt proved to be valuable commodities and brought wealth to the Soninke.

Over time, Soninke clans joined together under a strong leader to form the kingdom of Ghana. By the 500s, the kingdom's location on the Niger River allowed its people to become **intermediaries**, or go-betweens, in the salt–gold trade. The king of Ghana established a taxation system for collecting fees for all goods going in and out of the lands he ruled. He carefully monitored the amount of gold that flowed through his lands. All gold nuggets were possessions of the king, and only gold dust could be traded. In this way, Ghana gained a **monopoly**, or sole control, over gold and its trade and became a wealthy empire by 800.

In the mid-1000s, the Muslim historian al-Bakri reported that the capital of Ghana, Koumbi-Saleh (KUHM-bee SAHL-uh), was actually two towns in one. One part was Islamic, filled with mosques as well as Muslim traders and scholars. The other part was where the king, nobles, and the common people practiced a polytheistic religion, involving a belief in many gods. The common people made their living mainly through farming, fishing, herding, and craftmaking. Though often rich, traders in Ghana received little respect because they did not produce a product.

In the 11th century, the Almoravid dynasty in the north was on the rise. From their base in Morocco, the Almoravids competed with Ghana for control of valuable resources like salt. The kings of Ghana resisted Almoravid attacks, but by 1075 they lost control of Koumbi-Saleh and the kingdom went into sharp decline.

SUNDIATA AND THE MALI EMPIRE

The people under the control of Ghana had begun to rebel as the kingdom weakened. Among them were the Malinke (meh-LING-kay), whose rulers would later establish an even more powerful kingdom. It was the griots, custodians of Malinke oral traditions, who kept alive the story of **Sundiata** (sun-JAHT-ah), a sickly prince who gained the strength to lead his people to victory.

The story begins with Sundiata's mother, Sogolon. Sogolon had married the Malinke king, but she delivered a disabled son who could not even raise himself from the ground. She and Sundiata suffered humiliating insults and were finally driven away. Then one day, according to the griots, a blacksmith with magical powers gave young Sundiata an iron rod that he used to raise himself and stand. Sundiata returned and took his father's kingdom, Sogolon was showered with wealth, and the Mali Empire rose to power.

Starting from these beginnings in about the 1230s, the Mali Empire grew until it stretched from West Africa's Atlantic coast to the rich lands of the upper Niger River, where the city of **Timbuktu** became a center of trade and learning. After Sundiata, a ruler, or **mansa**, converted to Islam, and the later emperors of Mali oversaw the religious, political, and economic aspects of the large empire. While the mansas practiced Islam, they did not force their subjects to convert to Islam and many subjects retained their traditional religion. To keep political order, the mansas hired well-educated Muslims as administrators. Local rulers who sent tribute were allowed to retain much of their authority. Yet the

The village of Goumins sits on an island in the middle of the Niger River in Mali. Like their ancestors, people here still rely on the river to flood every summer to irrigate their rice crop and to supply them with transportation to trading centers along the river.

mansa's standing army made sure no one overstepped the central government's power.

Both the farming of crops such as millet, rice, and sorghum and the herding of sheep, goats, and camels were important economic activities in Mali. However, trade brought riches to the mansas and allowed them to maintain the government. All trade items that passed through the empire were heavily taxed, including the goods that crossed the Sahara, as you will learn later in this chapter.

HISTORICAL THINKING

1. **READING CHECK** What led the people of Ghana and Mali to gain profits through trade?

2. **COMPARE AND CONTRAST** How were the empires of Ghana and Mali similar and different?

3. **DRAW CONCLUSIONS** Why did Muslim mansas allow the people of Mali to keep their traditional religions rather than force the people to convert to Islam?

PLAN: 2-PAGE LESSON

OBJECTIVE
Explain how trade allowed the kingdoms of Ghana and Mali to thrive in West Africa.

CRITICAL THINKING SKILLS FOR LESSON 1.2
- Compare and Contrast
- Draw Conclusions
- Analyze Cause and Effect
- Make Inferences
- Integrate Visuals

HISTORICAL THINKING FOR CHAPTER 13
How did African societies influence other cultures?

The West African kingdoms of Ghana and Mali gained so much wealth through trade that other kingdoms looked to them as inspiration. Lesson 1.2 discusses how Ghana's and Mali's location in the trade network helped them to flourish.

Student eEdition online
Additional content for this lesson, including a diagram, is available online.

BACKGROUND FOR THE TEACHER

Griots With no indigenous written sources before 1800, historians of Africa have exercised great ingenuity in reconstructing the past by drawing on oral histories, some of which were transmitted over the centuries by griots. Some griots have celebrity status, appearing on television, radio, and other media as they perform and reinterpret traditional African songs. Many griots lead ceremonies and take part in performances that feature storytelling. Even today, griots still recite stories, sometimes on the radio, and receive high payments for doing so. Exciting breakthroughs in African history have come when historians have linked events from oral histories with archaeological finds or Arabic-language sources. Many of today's griots are musicians who tell Africa's stories. They are both men and women, but women tend to use singing rather than traditional storytelling. Key instruments that griots use in storytelling are the kora, lute, and balafon.

INTRODUCE & ENGAGE

DISCUSS GEOGRAPHIC INFLUENCE

Invite students to discuss how and what geographic factors influence where people live, how places develop, and the economic activities that are supported. Ask them to provide specific examples either based on your community or a place they have read about or visited. Tell students that they will learn about the geographic setting of the African kingdoms of Ghana and Mali and how it influenced their growth and development.

TEACH

GUIDED DISCUSSION

1. **Analyze Cause and Effect** How did Ghana respond to the influence of Islam? *(Ghana's capital was tolerant of both Islam and the local polytheistic religion.)*

2. **Make Inferences** Why do you think the mansas of Mali consolidated their power? *(Possible response: because the empire was very wealthy from trade and the mansas knew that to maintain power they needed a strong administration and army to help them)*

INTEGRATE VISUALS

Have students look at the diagram of Timbuktu (available in the Student eEdition). **ASK:** How does this diagram support what you read in the text about Timbuktu? *(Possible response: The text says that Timbuktu was a center for trade and learning. In the diagram, there are tents where goods were probably sold and camels that probably transported the goods.)* What cultural influences do you see throughout the city? *(Possible response: Greek and Roman classical architecture in the columns on the building in the far back left; a more unique African style in the mosque with the conical columns and support timbers jutting out)*

ACTIVE OPTIONS

On Your Feet: Roundtable Assign groups of four to Ghana or to Mali. Assign one student in each group the role of griot or storyteller, a teen villager, a government official, and a merchant. Instruct students to think about what a person in their assigned role might have experienced living in either Ghana or Mali when the empire was at its height. Ask students to answer the following question from their assigned perspective: What is it like living in this kingdom? Encourage students to conduct research and draw on information from the lesson to help them to answer the question.

> **NG Learning Framework: Investigate Timbuktu and Koumbi-Saleh Today**
> **SKILL** Communication
> **KNOWLEDGE** Our Human Story

Tell pairs or small groups to research Timbuktu and Koumbi-Saleh today and describe how they have changed or stayed the same over time. Have them investigate their names today as well as their cultures. Other details that students should consider examining are imported and exported trade items, the strength of their economy, as well as their ethnic composition. Ask students to share their research with the class.

DIFFERENTIATE

STRIVING READERS

Summarize Instruct students to work in pairs to read and summarize the text and captions. Tell students to write at least three notes for each of the two sections of the lesson. Guide students to first create a summary statement for each section and then a summary statement for the entire lesson. Invite pairs to compare their summary statements and note any similarities and differences.

GIFTED & TALENTED

Write a Travel Log Have students write a travel log from the perspective of a merchant traveling through the Mali Empire at its height. Students should use the lesson content and conduct additional research as necessary. Travel logs should include observations about the people who live there, cultural aspects, trade item transactions, and overall thoughts about the empire as compared to other trading kingdoms in the region. Invite students to share their travel logs with the class or post on a class blog.

See the Chapter Planner for more strategies for differentiation.

HISTORICAL THINKING

ANSWERS

1. Their location between gold mines to the south and salt mines to the north made it ideal for the people who lived there to become middlemen in the trade of both salt and gold.

2. Both: located in West Africa near the Niger River; gained wealth through trade and taxation; Mali: empire formed later; was larger; gold mines of West Africa lay within territory; founded by Malinke; influenced by Islam; Ghana: founded by Soninke

3. Possible response: The people of Mali had a strong attachment to their traditional religion, and the mansas did not want to lose their loyalty by questioning their beliefs.

Great Zimbabwe

Consider how various peoples of the past have demonstrated their authority and strength. Some formed fierce armies, while others built ornate palaces. Some spread news of great feats through messages on stelae. The early rulers of southeastern Africa announced the power of their kingdoms through massive stone structures.

These ruins are the remains of the Great Enclosure from the ancient capital city of Great Zimbabwe.

GREAT STONE HOUSES

As you have already read, groups of Bantu speakers migrated throughout sub-Saharan Africa. One group settled as far south as the high plateau beyond the Zambezi River. There, the **Shona** people established the state that reached its greatest extent in the early 1300s. Its center was the imposing capital city known as Great Zimbabwe. That spot was likely chosen as the location of the capital because of its mild climate and fertile soil as well as its strategic position. Great Zimbabwe was situated along a much-traveled trade route that carried gold and other items. Taxes collected on goods that passed through Great Zimbabwe brought enormous wealth to its leaders.

Like many other Bantu settlers in sub-Saharan Africa, the Shona lived as cattle herders and farmers. They made efficient use of iron tools in their day-to-day life. Before 1000, most people lived in small villages of houses made from wood beams. Then some villagers became rich enough to build their own stone structures. By the 13th and 14th centuries, the population of the region had reached 10,000. The villages built some 300 stone enclosures, or areas surrounded by walls, across the plateau. The word for these enclosures in the Shona language is *Zimbabwe*, or "place of stone houses." This word is the source of the name of the present-day nation of Zimbabwe where the structures are located. The largest of these enclosures, Great Zimbabwe, prospered for about 250 years.

After 1450, the inhabitants of Great Zimbabwe deserted their walled complex. Perhaps they had depleted natural resources by cutting down forests for fuel to make iron. Perhaps their population grew too large for the area. The shifting of trade routes also contributed to the demise of Great Zimbabwe.

STUDYING THE RUINS

The ruins of Great Zimbabwe cover almost 1,800 acres near the present-day city of Masvingo. One point of interest at the site is the Great Enclosure, a large circular wall that is 15 feet thick and more than 30 feet in height. It is the largest single stone structure in sub-Saharan Africa built before 1500. One estimate holds that it might have taken 400 workers four years to complete the project. In any case, the remains of the wall show the skill of those who built it. It is made of evenly cut granite blocks placed so closely together that mortar was not necessary. The Great Enclosure was reserved for the ruler and other elites, keeping them separate from the common people.

Since the people of Great Zimbabwe did not keep written records, oral traditions and archaeological finds provide the only sources of information about their way of life. Of special interest to scholars is the discovery of a hoard, or a hidden supply of stored items, unearthed at one of the smaller enclosures. The hoard included Chinese ceramics, beads from India, and colorful Persian plates. Other artifacts at the site indicate that skilled Shona craftworkers created fine gold jewelry. All these findings provide evidence of participation in trade networks. In fact, East African traders were exporting the gold of Great Zimbabwe to Indian Ocean markets and bringing valuable goods back in return. Archaeologists have found fine porcelain from Ming China at the site of Great Zimbabwe, reminding us of the voyages of Zheng He.

Africans are proud of the architectural achievement of Great Zimbabwe, so much so that when they gained their independence and had a chance to pick a new name, the people of this region chose *Zimbabwe*.

SHONA SCULPTURE
The only surviving sculptures from Great Zimbabwe are stylized birds carved out of soapstone. The birds resemble fish eagles, a common species in the region. Today the people of Zimbabwe are entranced by the birds made long ago, and an image of a bird even appears on Zimbabwe's national flag.

HISTORICAL THINKING

1. **READING CHECK** For what reason are the people of Great Zimbabwe most remembered today?

2. **MAKE INFERENCES** Why did the Great Enclosure require so many workers and take four years to complete?

3. **ASK AND ANSWER QUESTIONS** What are three questions about Great Zimbabwe that you might like to research?

PLAN: 2-PAGE LESSON

OBJECTIVE
Explain how powerful trading empire Great Zimbabwe demonstrated its strength and power through massive stone structures.

CRITICAL THINKING SKILLS FOR LESSON 1.3
- Make Inferences
- Ask and Answer Questions
- Compare and Contrast
- Form and Support Opinions
- Analyze Visuals

HISTORICAL THINKING FOR CHAPTER 13
How did African societies influence other cultures?

In southern Africa, Great Zimbabwe developed into a strong trading empire. Lesson 1.3 discusses the rise of this great civilization, how it was influenced by other societies, and how it left behind amazing rock structures to show its power.

BACKGROUND FOR THE TEACHER

Hill Complex and Valley Complex The ruins of Great Zimbabwe fall into three groups: the Hill Complex, the Valley Complex, and the Great Enclosure. The Hill Complex included a group of stone buildings forming a ritual space. It stood above a granite cliff 330 feet long and 100 feet high on the northern edge of the site. In the Valley Complex, Enclosure 12 contained the largest hoard found on the site: over 220 pounds of iron hoes, 44 pounds of iron for wire, warthog and elephant tusks, thousands of Indian beads, and broken ceramic vessels from China and Iran. With three entrances, the Great Enclosure contains the Elliptical Building, the Conical Tower, and mud and thatch huts where individual families lived. The Elliptical Building has an outer wall that runs 800 feet long and contains 182,000 cubic feet of stone. Eight bird statues averaging 16 inches tall were found at the site; each was placed on a pillar three feet tall. The birds are so striking that a stylized representation has appeared on every version of Zimbabwe's national flag since 1968.

INTRODUCE & ENGAGE

DISCUSS LOCATION AND SETTLEMENT

Invite students to discuss what they know about ideal factors for a settlement to thrive, including climate, natural resources, and proximity to bodies of water. Make a list on the board as students share their ideas. Discuss the factors that influence settlement location. As students read the lesson, have them look back at the class list to see which ones were present at Great Zimbabwe. Tell students that they will learn about the ruins of Great Zimbabwe and what they have taught us.

TEACH

GUIDED DISCUSSION

1. **Compare and Contrast** How was Great Zimbabwe similar to and different from the West African kingdoms? *(Possible response: Similar: all became wealthy from trade; Different: There is no evidence that the West African kingdoms built a great wall or enclosure like the Shona did; Great Zimbabwe might have been prone to invaders and attacks.)*

2. **Form and Support Opinions** What do you think were the major factors in Great Zimbabwe's decline? Use evidence from the text to support your opinion. *(Possible response: dwindling resources and possibly deforestation; If the Shona could no longer produce enough iron to trade, trade probably decreased. If the cattle ate the grass and deforestation hurt the fields, then the soil would not be productive enough to feed a growing population.)*

ANALYZE VISUALS

Have students look at the photos of the bird sculpture and the Great Enclosure. **ASK:** How do you think the environment shown around the Great Enclosure would have been ideal for birds such as the fish eagle? *(Possible response: trees for birds to perch on and rest, a lot of open land where the birds could easily find prey from trees above)* Why do you think the Shona people carved figures out of soapstone? *(Possible response: It was likely found in the environment and was easy to work with.)*

ACTIVE OPTIONS

On Your Feet: Create an Acrostic Write the words *Great Zimbabwe* vertically on the board or on a large sheet of paper. Assign each letter to pairs or individual students. Have them come up with a word, phrase, or sentence beginning with their assigned letter that relates Great Zimbabwe to the people who built it, its structures, and its surroundings. Invite students to write their responses next to their assigned letter.

NG Learning Framework: Investigate Construction Methods STEM
ATTITUDE Curiosity
SKILL Problem-Solving

Pose the following question: How did the Shona successfully build the rock structures of Great Zimbabwe without using mortar? Instruct pairs or small groups to construct and test their hypotheses and then collect information to find out how the stones had to be laid to fit tightly without mortar. Have them use drawings or models to illustrate the process.

DIFFERENTIATE

INCLUSION

Support Visual Understanding Pair students to work with a partner who can describe the ruins of Great Zimbabwe and read the caption to them. Ask their partner to describe the elements in detail, including the stone enclosures, environment, and resources. Instruct pairs to ask and answer questions about the photograph.

PRE-AP STEM

Create a Website Prompt students to conduct online research to identify more details about the discovery of the ruins of Great Zimbabwe and the debate that followed about who actually built the structures. Instruct them to design a home page and then create a site map for the supporting pages. The website should include information about the find itself, the people who discussed the origin of the structures, and the most recent evidence to support current assertions. Encourage students to share their website designs with the class. Some students may wish to use website templates or design software to create and publish their websites.

See the Chapter Planner for more strategies for differentiation.

HISTORICAL THINKING

ANSWERS

1. Their architectural achievements; The construction skills evidenced by the ruins of their stone enclosures are still admired today.

2. Possible response: The project was a massive one, and the fine craftwork took a lot of time.

3. Possible response: How did the stonemasons cut the granite blocks? In what type of structures did the working people live? What other artifacts did archaeologists find in the hoard in Great Zimbabwe?

Traveler: Ibn Battuta
The Longest-Known Journey 1304–1368

No two places are alike, even if they share many characteristics and are united under a single ruler. Sometimes, it is only possible to discern the differences and similarities through first-hand observation. World travelers do just that. They make extended trips to discover what makes each place on Earth unique and what ties various places together.

WHERE HE WENT

Ibn Battuta (IB-uhn bah-TOO-tuh) is remembered today for his invaluable descriptions of the Muslim world. As a 20-year-old legal scholar, the young Muslim had no idea that he would become a world traveler. At first, he embarked from his home in Tangier, Morocco, to make the hajj pilgrimage to Mecca, fulfilling one of the five pillars of Islam. It was only after this pilgrimage that he decided to continue traveling with no fixed destination and no set time of return. He spent the next 29 years following the trade routes that knit the Islamic world together. After his journey, Ibn Battuta dictated his adventures to another writer to create a book called *The Travels*.

In all, Ibn Battuta traveled about 75,000 miles throughout the *dar-al Islam*, Arabic for "abode of Islam." His journey led him to Egypt, Muslim-ruled areas of Spain, Arabia, Persia, and south into India. He traveled along China's Pacific coast with Muslim sea merchants, and he toured the northern and eastern coasts of Africa. He explored deep into West Africa. He traveled on foot, rode camels and donkeys, and sailed by boat.

To finance his journey, Ibn Battuta relied on donations from other Muslims. The Five Pillars encouraged donations not only to the poor but also to travelers. Ibn Battuta's dependence on Muslim support kept him from venturing beyond the realm of Islam. For example, he never visited the majestic Great Zimbabwe, which you

In this excerpt from *The Travels*, Ibn Battuta describes his first stop in Mali at Taghaza, an important center of the salt trade.

PRIMARY SOURCE

After 25 days we arrived at Taghaza. This is a village with nothing good about it. One of its marvels is that its houses and mosque are of rock salt and its roofs of camel skins. It has no trees, but is nothing but sand with a salt mine. They dig in the earth for the salt, which is found in great slabs lying one upon the other as though they have been shaped and placed underground. A camel carries two slabs of it. Nobody lives there except the slaves ... who dig for the salt. They live on the dates imported to them, ... on camel-meat, and on anili [a type of grain]. ...

read about in the last lesson. But he did visit the African Muslim cities on the Indian Ocean coast. You will read more about them later.

WHAT HE SAW

During his long journey, Ibn Battuta frequently accompanied Muslim merchants on established land and sea routes. His reports include descriptions of trade items, trade processes, and the people he met along the way. It appears that he mainly encountered rulers, high-ranking judges, and religious leaders. His account includes many details about political events, ways of governing, and social interactions with male Muslims. Little is mentioned of local economies or the ways of life of women and non-Muslims.

Ibn Battuta was the first traveler to record an eyewitness description of sub-Saharan Africa. Some of the details you read earlier about the Mali Empire are known only because of Ibn Battuta's eyewitness

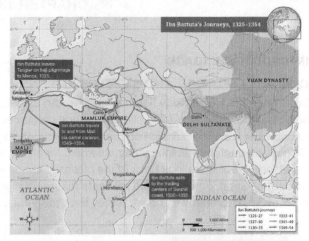

account. For example, Ibn Battuta describes a grueling 25-day trip to get to Mali with a caravan, or group of people who travel together. He also describes the city of Timbuktu.

A devout Muslim, Ibn Battuta was shocked at the way in which the people of Mali practiced Islam. For example, he disapproved of the fact that women were not secluded. Yet he was pleased that many people worshiped at mosques and memorized the Quran. He did approve when he saw that children who failed at their Quranic lessons were sternly punished.

You read in a previous chapter that the people of Arabia were the first people to practice Islam. Ibn Battuta believed this region was a model for how Islam should be practiced.

Many legs of Ibn Battuta's journey would not have been possible 300 years earlier. By 1450, however, West and East Africa were important stops along trade routes within the broader Islamic world. You will learn more about these early trade routes as you read the next lesson.

Ibn Battuta's account of a 1348 visit to Damascus, Syria, portrays the suffering caused by the Black Death, or plague. As you know, the plague caused many deaths in Europe as well.

PRIMARY SOURCE

The entire population of the city joined in the exodus, male and female, small and large; the Jews went out with their book of the Law and the Christians with their Gospel, their women and children with them; ... in tears and humble supplications, imploring the favor of God through His Books and his Prophets.

HISTORICAL THINKING

1. **READING CHECK** Why has Ibn Battuta gained a place in history?

2. **INTERPRET MAPS** Did Ibn Battuta visit West Africa before or after he visited China?

3. **MAKE GENERALIZATIONS** In what ways are the reports of Ibn Battuta biased?

4. **EVALUATE** How trustworthy do you think *The Travels* is as a historical source?

PLAN: 2-PAGE LESSON

OBJECTIVE

Explain how Ibn Battuta traveled the Muslim world and learned fascinating details about the people and places he encountered.

CRITICAL THINKING SKILLS FOR LESSON 1.4

- Interpret Maps
- Make Generalizations
- Evaluate
- Analyze Points of View
- Form and Support Opinions
- Analyze Primary Sources

HISTORICAL THINKING FOR CHAPTER 13

How did African societies influence other cultures?

Ibn Battuta thought he was just making a pilgrimage to Mecca, but he encountered so many interesting places and people along the way that it became a journey of a lifetime. Lesson 1.4 discusses Ibn Battuta's travels and his reflections about the societies and cultural practices of the places he visited.

BACKGROUND FOR THE TEACHER

His Journeys by the Numbers Ibn Battuta traveled from North Africa to Cairo for the first leg of his trip. On his way, he met up with a caravan, which was on its way to Mecca. They arrived in Algiers and camped overnight before continuing on their pilgrimage. It wasn't long before Ibn Battuta became ill in the city of Bijaya. He persevered on to Cairo, arriving in 1326. During 1326, he traveled to Jerusalem, Damascus, Medina, and Mecca and then on to Iraq and Persia into 1327. From 1328–1330, he rode on a dhow across the Red Sea to East Africa and then on to the Arabian Sea. Then he traveled to Anatolia (the Asian part of modern-day Turkey) in 1330–1331, the Lands of the Golden Horde and the Chagatai from 1332–1333, Delhi in 1334, the Maldive Islands and Sri Lanka from 1341–1344, through the Strait of Malacca to China in 1345–1346, and back home from 1346–1349. He continued by traveling to al-Andalus and Morocco that same year and Mali in 1350–1351.

History Notebook

Encourage students to complete the Traveler page for Chapter 13 in their History Notebooks as they read.

INTRODUCE & ENGAGE

DISCUSS BOOK TITLES

When Ibn Battuta first dictated his story to a scholar, the name of the book was *Gift to Those Who Contemplate the Wonders of Cities and the Marvels of Traveling* instead of *The Travels*, the name by which we know the book today. Discuss with students if they would be drawn to a book by this title if they were living in the 1300s. Invite students to discuss why this original title may have been chosen. Then ask students to consider the significance of travels such as those of Ibn Battuta then and also today. Tell students that they will learn about Ibn Battuta and how his travels and the book that followed became an important record in our understanding of the Muslim world during this time period.

TEACH

GUIDED DISCUSSION

1. **Analyze Points of View** Why do you think Ibn Battuta showed bias about different Muslim customs? *(Possible response: He had never traveled outside his homeland; was not used to different customs)*

2. **Form and Support Opinions** Do you think that Ibn Battuta's attitude regarding his faith changed from the beginning of his trip to the end? Explain. *(Possible response: probably remained just as strict; relied on alms from Muslims to finance his travels; thought his homeland should be a model for other Muslims; probably stayed true to his faith)*

ANALYZE PRIMARY SOURCES

Tell students to read and analyze the second primary source. **ASK:** What is Ibn Battuta describing in this excerpt? Explain your response. *(Possible response: People are fleeing the city possibly to escape the plague. They are asking for God's help because what they are fleeing must be something terrible and only God can help them.)* Encourage students to compare this excerpt with that of Procopius, who also gave an eyewitness account of the plague.

ACTIVE OPTIONS

On Your Feet: Research Morocco Ask groups of four or five students to conduct online research on the history of Morocco in the 1300s. Tell students to investigate the country's economy, social structure, and customs. After groups have conducted their research, lead a class discussion about why Ibn Battuta might have held his attitudes and beliefs based on where he lived.

> **NG Learning Framework: Present an Excerpt from *The Travels***
> **SKILL** Communication
> **KNOWLEDGE** Our Human Story

Invite students to present an excerpt from Ibn Battuta's *The Travels* that reflects a vivid opinion about his observations of how Islam is practiced in the lands he visited. Tell them to make their delivery interesting and engaging, using inflection and pausing as appropriate. The audience should take notes during and ask questions after each presentation.

DIFFERENTIATE

STRIVING READERS

List Biographical Facts Post this heading: Five Facts About Ibn Battuta. After reading the lesson, ask students to copy the heading onto a piece of paper and write five sentences that each contain one fact about Ibn Battuta's life. Invite volunteers to share their sentences.

PRE-AP

Investigate Primary Sources Prompt students to research excerpts from *The Travels*. Have them find passages that describe the diversity in the towns and cities Ibn Battuta visits or passes through. Ask students to write a short essay that explains the diversity of the people and places Ibn Battuta sees. Invite students to present their essays to the class.

See the Chapter Planner for more strategies for differentiation.

HISTORICAL THINKING

ANSWERS

1. because of his detailed reports on a variety of places along trade routes that lay within the Muslim world

2. He visited China before Mali. The map shows that Ibn Battuta visited China between the years 1341–1349 but did not visit Mali until 1349–1354.

3. Possible response: Ibn Battuta may have been biased toward Muslims and particularly toward Muslims who practiced Islam as he did; toward the wealthy who provided him with support; biased against women who did not accept their place in Islamic society

4. Possible response: *The Travels* ranks high as a historical source; Ibn Battuta presented a comprehensive first-person account of the early Muslim world. His extensive travels ensured that he addressed all parts of the empire and could reasonably compare and contrast regions.

Trans-Saharan Trade

Throughout history, people have taken risks in hopes of receiving rewards for their efforts. Traders in Africa trekked through the harsh Sahara for weeks at a time to gain wealth from the trade of West African resources.

THE SALT, GOLD, AND SLAVE TRADE

You read about how Sundiata founded the Mali Empire. His wealthiest successor was **Mansa Musa** (MAHN-sa MOO-sa), who ruled from 1307 to 1332. On a trip to Cairo during a hajj, Mansa Musa made a grand display of his riches. Early sources say that 500 slaves marched in front of him, each carrying a gold walking stick. One hundred camels transported the leader's travel money—700 pounds of gold—which he spent freely. In Cairo, legend says, he spent so much that he flooded the market with gold and seriously reduced the value of the Egyptian currency.

Mansa Musa had gained his wealth through taxes on trade that passed through the empire along the **trans-Saharan trade network**, a set of well-established trade routes across the Sahara. Crossing the Sahara to reach Mali required weeks of travel over scorching sand. Travelers from the north risked this trip because of the salt and gold they could acquire in Mali. Some towns in Mali seemed to overflow with salt, which was highly valued in places where it was scarce. In other locations, gold was a prized commodity. Mining gold was profitable but dangerous as mines often collapsed. However, farmers were willing to do it to add to their income.

In addition to exchanging salt and gold, the people of Mali also participated in the slave trade. An estimated 5,500 slaves crossed the desert yearly. The slave

The *Catalan Atlas* shows trade routes of various places in Africa. Mansa Musa (right) is shown as a prominent figure on the atlas.

traders of Mali did not enslave people from their own country. Instead, they captured people in the forest belt to the south and sold them across the desert to Arab traders.

Other people of West Africa envied Mali's wealth. Armored soldiers on horseback captured major cities, including Timbuktu. By 1450, the neighboring Songhai (SAHNG-gy) people, who had also gained riches through trade, had conquered Mali and claimed rulership over many West African societies. You will learn more about the Songhai people in a later chapter.

MAMLUK TRADE NETWORKS

You learned about the ruler Saladin who had founded a new dynasty in Egypt in the 12th century and retook Jerusalem from the Crusaders. His dynasty was replaced by the Mamluks (MAM-looks). They started as enslaved Turkish soldiers. Once the Mamluks converted to Islam, they were granted freedom, and some gained high positions in the military and in government. In 1250, they gained control of Egypt and established their own dynasty. Soon after, the Mamluk Empire extended to include Syria. The Mamluks would retain control of these lands until 1517.

As converts to the faith, the Mamluks took the defense of Islam very seriously, reviving the faith after the Mongol sack of Baghdad in 1258. The new government of the Mamluks was based in Cairo and led by a sultan. Many Muslims, especially Muslim scholars, poured into the city. With its many colleges, called *madrasas*, Cairo replaced Baghdad as the cultural center for Islam. It grew to become one of the largest cities of the day with a population of more than 400,000 people. It was this impressive city that was visited by both Mansa Musa and Ibn Battuta.

During this time, North Africa continued to be the end African destination for salt, gold, and slaves from West Africa. From there, other traders transported the trade items and enslaved people to markets in Europe and Asia across the Mediterranean. Traders also transported goods to locations on the Indian Ocean by way of the Red Sea. In return, products such as Chinese silk and spices from India reached North Africa.

Eventually, such problems as drought, government corruption, and the bubonic plague caused severe economic distress. To keep his government going, the Mamluk sultan increased taxes on trade. Traders looked elsewhere for the items they desired. By the early 1500s, the Mamluks had lost control of their lands.

HISTORICAL THINKING

1. **READING CHECK** Why was salt important to the people of Mali?

2. **IDENTIFY** Which historical figure is most often used as an example of Mali's wealth? Why?

3. **MAKE INFERENCES** What might have led the people of Mali to take part in the African slave trade?

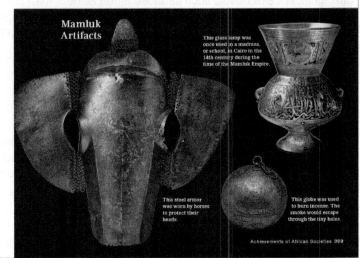

Mamluk Artifacts

This glass lamp was once used in a madrasa, or school, in Cairo in the 14th century during the time of the Mamluk Empire.

This steel armor was worn by horses to protect their heads.

This globe was used to burn incense. The smoke would escape through the tiny holes.

PLAN: 2-PAGE LESSON

OBJECTIVE

Analyze how the robust trade in salt, gold, and slaves over Saharan trade routes brought wealth to West and North Africa.

CRITICAL THINKING SKILLS FOR LESSON 2.1

- Identify
- Make Inferences
- Draw Conclusions
- Identify Problems and Solutions
- Analyze Visuals

HISTORICAL THINKING FOR CHAPTER 13

How did African societies influence other cultures?

Salt, gold, slaves, and Islam traveled from West and North Africa to Europe and Asia. Lesson 2.1 discusses how the trans-Saharan trade network linked traders who were willing to make the long, difficult journey to West Africa.

Student eEdition online

Additional content for this lesson, including images, is available online.

BACKGROUND FOR THE TEACHER

The Catalan Atlas In 1375, a European cartographer named Abraham Cresques created a map that was highly accurate for the time. Mapmaking was in its infancy because the Age of Exploration had not yet begun; therefore, many maps were inaccurate, unreliable sources. Cresques worked for the king of Aragon, who asked that the map be created. Cresques wrote notes on the map that identify the figure on the lower right corner as Mansa Musa, the king of the Mali Empire in West Africa. At the time, Mansa Musa was the richest king in the region because of the vast amounts of gold he had acquired through trade.

The name *Catalan* comes from the historic region called Catalonia. It is comprised of four provinces, including Barcelona, in Spain. Aragon, which lies to the west, began as a community around 1035. In the 1100s, Aragon and Catalonia were joined together, a union that lasted until the early 1400s. During this time, Catalonia focused on the development of commerce and sea expansion, while Aragon supported these endeavors financially and militarily.

INTRODUCE & ENGAGE

DISCUSS TRADE

Ask students what they know about why civilizations have relied on trade to meet their needs. Discuss factors such as location, natural and mineral resources, and supply and demand in relation to economic development and strength. Tell students that they will learn about how the Mali Empire and other civilizations in West Africa and North Africa gained wealth from a trade network that stretched across the Sahara.

TEACH

GUIDED DISCUSSION

1. **Draw Conclusions** Why do you think Mansa Musa gave away his gold? *(Possible response: showing off; other empires and kingdoms would see how wealthy and powerful the Mali Empire was under him)*

2. **Identify Problems and Solutions** What problem led to the downfall of Mamluk power, and why was the Mamluk sultan's solution ineffective? *(Possible response: Government corruption, drought, and the plague hurt the economy, so the sultan increased taxes on trade. Traders who did not want to pay the taxes took other routes where they sold their trade items for a larger profit. The sultan's solution didn't work. Merchants and traders didn't want to lose profits from paying higher taxes.)*

ANALYZE VISUALS

Have students look at the gallery of the Mamluk artifacts (available in the Student eEdition). **ASK:** How does the first artifact illustrate the ways in which the Mamluk used the resources in their environment and traded to meet their needs? *(Possible response: The helmet is made of different metals that were either found in North Africa or acquired through trade.)* Why would this helmet have been particularly important to the Mamluks? *(Possible response: Because they were fierce defenders of Islam, they needed strong materials such as steel to produce such helmets.)*

ACTIVE OPTIONS

On Your Feet: Become an Expert Four "expert" groups research the following: West African slave trade, West African gold and salt trade, kingdoms and empires of West Africa, influence of Islam in West Africa. Students regroup so that each new group has at least one member from each expert group. Experts report on their study. As a class, discuss the factors that led to the development of West Africa before 1500.

> **NG Learning Framework: Trace the Trans-Saharan Trade Network Across Time**
> **ATTITUDE** Curiosity
> **KNOWLEDGE** Our Human Story

Explain that the trans-Saharan trade network led to much economic growth and wealth but that it came to an end by the 19th century. Ask small groups to research what factors led to its decline. Tell them to find statistics about the value of goods traded on this network over time and key events that caused the network to weaken. Have groups present their findings in a large-group discussion format.

DIFFERENTIATE

ENGLISH LANGUAGE LEARNERS

Look for Cognates Suggest that as students read, they look for words that are similar in spelling and meaning to words in their home language. For example, the words *found, conquer, pass,* and *transport* have cognates in Spanish. For each word they identify, have students make a vocabulary card with the English word and definition on one side and the cognate on the other side.

GIFTED & TALENTED

Create an Annotated Time Line Instruct students to research events that were going on in Europe and Asia during the time of Mansa Musa's pilgrimage to Mecca and create an annotated time line of key events. Remind students to include dates and brief descriptions of people, places, and actions associated with the events. Students may use maps and other visuals to add further information. Encourage students to compare their finished time lines and discuss items they chose to include or omit and why.

See the Chapter Planner for more strategies for differentiation.

HISTORICAL THINKING

ANSWERS

1. Salt was important to the people of Mali because it was an abundant resource in their region and was highly desired by other people who faced a scarcity of it.

2. Mansa Musa is most often associated with Mali's wealth because of the riches he displayed while on a hajj.

3. Possible response: There was a high demand for slaves in Europe and Asia and the people of Mali realized they could gain profits by supplying slaves from elsewhere in Africa.

2.2 A Global Commodity: Salt

For centuries, salt was a scarce and precious commodity. Traded across continents, it established the wealth of empires for much of human history. You've already read that in the 12th century, merchants traveled to Timbuktu on the trans-Saharan caravan route to trade a measure of gold for an equal weight of salt. (Imagine such an exchange today!) Mighty African empires even went to war to control sources of salt.

Although salt is no longer scarce, in present-day Africa, traditional camel caravans still make the 500-mile trek between Timbuktu and the continent's salt mines to move this simple but vital substance. Today, there are an estimated 14,000 uses for salt, the most important of which is keeping us alive. No wonder it's a treasured commodity—and one that has profoundly shaped and influenced history.

What factors might influence the changing value of a commodity like salt throughout history?

BACK TO THE SALT MINES
A salt miner in Uganda displays a handful of salt harvested from Lake Katwe. Work in salt mines can be dangerous and physically demanding, as evidenced by the film of salt covering this worker's skin. The modern expression "back to the salt mines," a reference to reluctantly returning to one's job after time away, acknowledges the unpleasantness of salt mining and possibly the fact that some countries forced prisoners to toil in salt mines as a punishment.

SALT AT A GLANCE

LIFE	Life-sustaining salt consists of two important elements: sodium and chloride.	Sodium aids communication between cells and allows muscle and nerve function.	Chloride regulates blood pressure and acidity and is used to make stomach acid.
VALUE	Salt exists only in small amounts on Earth's surface, but is no longer scarce because it is inexpensive and easy to produce.	Salt is used to preserve food and in medication, although too much salt can be unhealthy. It's also a key ingredient in PVC plastic.	Production of salt has increased to meet worldwide demands. China and the United States produce the most salt.
PRODUCTION	Salt can be mined from underground deposits left behind by ancient seas and harvested from the ocean through evaporation.	Solution mining injects water into salt deposits, removes the solution, and evaporates the water to yield salt.	Solar recovery methods use energy from the sun to produce salt. The sun and wind provide energy to evaporate water from salt.
HISTORY	The camel was introduced to Saharan trade around 200 c.e., marking the start of the salt trade.	Ancient Rome's Via Salaria, or "salt road," was one of the oldest salt trade routes.	Wagons of "white gold" made the 62-mile journey along the Old Salt Road across Europe during the Middle Ages.
ECONOMICS	The salt trade built the wealth of countries and empires and financed the construction of the Great Wall of China.	Salt was used to pay Roman soldiers and traded for slaves in ancient Greece—a lazy slave was "not worth his salt."	Today, China leads the world in salt production, and international trade of this commodity is minimal due to global availability.

370 CHAPTER 13

Achievements of African Societies 371

PLAN: 4-PAGE LESSON

OBJECTIVE
Describe the value of salt and how its importance and availability has changed over time.

CRITICAL THINKING SKILLS FOR LESSON 2.2
- Analyze Visuals
- Make Connections
- Interpret Charts
- Make Inferences

HISTORICAL THINKING FOR CHAPTER 13
How did African societies influence other cultures?

Salt is an element that humans have always needed for survival. Long ago, it was not easy to find. Its widespread demand made some African societies very rich from the salt trade. Lesson 2.2 discusses the history of salt and its value and importance over time.

BACKGROUND FOR THE TEACHER
The Salt Chain The earliest camel caravans departed across the western Sahara and were led by cameleers (nomadic Berbers) hired by Ibadi merchants. They usually left in the winter when the days were cooler to avoid scorching hot sunny days. Desert wells provided much needed water for both the travelers and camels, and routes often ran between them. Along the way, caravans stopped at salt mines to load blocks of salt onto the camels. Each camel carried about four large blocks of salt, each weighing about 308 pounds (140 kg). Gold-seeking caravans went to Wagadu, where Wangara merchants engaged in the trade of gold for salt. Here, salt blocks were transferred from camels to donkeys. Donkeys then carried the salt as far as the area near where tsetse flies were rampant. Unable to penetrate this area, donkeys would be forced to stop and humans would take the salt from here, carrying it to its final destination in the rain forest. As the salt traveled from camel to donkey to human, it was taxed, and its price could increase greatly.

History Notebook
Encourage students to complete the Global Commodity page for Chapter 13 in their History Notebooks as they read.

INTRODUCE & ENGAGE

PREVIEW WITH VISUALS

Direct students' attention to the photograph of a salt miner's hand in the lesson. Write "salt" at the center of a Concept Cluster and ask volunteers to list characteristics of salt and its influence throughout history based on their observation of the photographs. At the end of the lesson, revisit the Concept Cluster and add or remove characteristics and influences based on what students learned.

TEACH

GUIDED DISCUSSION

1. **Analyze Visuals** What does the photograph of the salt miner's hand reveal about the qualities and characteristics of salt? *(It is chalky and can cause dryness and cracking.)*

2. **Make Connections** Why does it seem difficult for people today to understand how salt made traders rich and how it also drove people to war? *(Possible response: Today, salt is no longer a scarce commodity.)*

A GLOBAL COMMODITY

Salt is critical to human life, but it is also important for animals. Humans can naturally get the salt that they need by consuming foods. Farmers provide salt blocks for animals such as cattle and horses to make sure they are getting enough salt in their diets. Birds and wild mammals may seek out mineral deposits known as salt licks in the natural environment. Saltwater fish can get the salt that they need by ingesting salt water. Animals who consume large amounts of salt water have adapted to eliminate the excess salt. Some saltwater fish are able to dispose of extra salt through their kidneys or gills. Some ocean birds who drink salt water can secrete excess salt through evolutionary traits called salt glands, which excrete salt through their beaks.

ENGLISH LANGUAGE LEARNERS

Content Word Search Pair students together to reread the lesson to identify key content words to understanding the material. Ask pairs to make a list of these words and then to use context clues or word parts to determine the meaning of the words. They may also use a dictionary to help them. On their lists, students should write the content word, its meaning, and an example.

PRE-AP

Analyze Primary Sources Direct students to conduct online research to locate primary sources about working in the salt mines in Africa. Encourage students to find African perspectives, if possible. Ask students to identify key excerpts from these sources to deliver orally to the class. Then invite students to provide a brief analysis of the primary source during their presentation.

See the Chapter Planner for more strategies for differentiation.

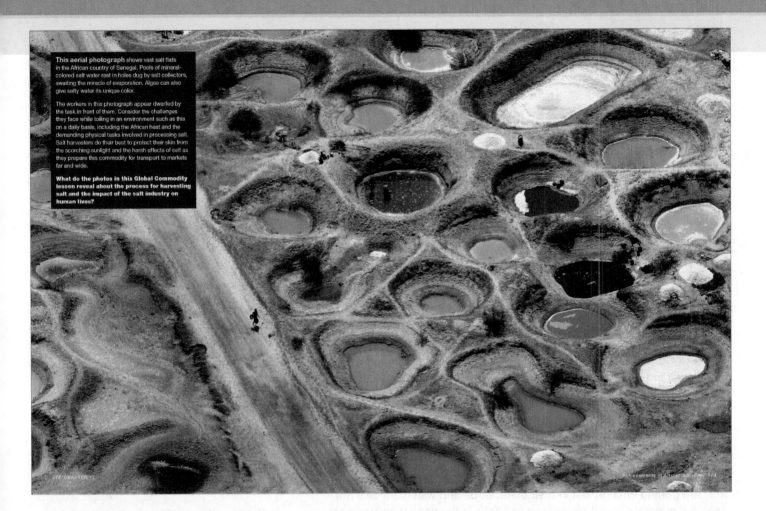

BACKGROUND FOR THE TEACHER

Senegal Salt The largest producer of salt in West Africa, Senegal is also making strides in another area: female salt entrepreneurs. Marie Diouf is a major salt producer in the country; about one-third of the country's salt comes from her salt flats. She lives in a village called Ndiemou, has become a role model for women, and is paving the way for the future of Senegal. In the local language, the town's name means "salt," which clearly illustrates the importance of it to the economy. Diouf made the investment in her salt mines in 2000 after Senegal privatized the area. She provides jobs to both women and men. Her husband is one of her employees. She has also taken the initiative to educate people in her local area to learn about the importance of consuming iodized salt, because the government asserted that by iodizing salt, the country should be able to reduce iodine deficiency, especially for pregnant women, as iodine deficiencies can lead to miscarriages. After learning about government initiatives to reduce iodine deficiency in Senegal, Diouf has been working to add potassium iodate into the salt that her flats produce before it is distributed. Through the work of Diouf and Nutrition International, the early results of their efforts have been positive.

TEACH

GUIDED DISCUSSION

3. **Interpret Charts** What facts in the chart reveal the importance and value of salt long ago? *(Possible response: Rome's Via Salaria; paying Roman soldiers in salt instead of money; used interchangeably with money as it was traded for slaves)*

4. **Make Inferences** Why do you think people risk working as salt harvesters in present-day Africa when the conditions on the human body are harsh? *(Possible responses: There are probably few other industries in the area in which they can work; there are not a lot of job opportunities; the jobs may pay better because of the risks workers must take.)*

INTERPRET CHARTS

Discuss the chart that appears in the lesson. Have students read each section horizontally and think about how it relates to the head for that row. **ASK:** Why are sodium and chloride important to sustaining life? *(Possible responses may include that they help in cell function, with the regulation of blood pressure, and in making stomach acid.)* Why do you think salt has been used to make PVC plastic? *(Possible response: PVC plastic is used in many products, and since salt is plentiful, people have tried to figure out what other uses it has.)* Why do you think there are so many different ways to produce salt today? *(Possible responses: because we need it to live, people probably want to have many methods available to produce it in case one method no longer works)*

ACTIVE OPTION

NG Learning Framework: Explore Camel Caravans
SKILLS Collaboration, Communication
KNOWLEDGE Our Human Story

Invite students to search online for information about camel caravans that still make the 500-mile trek between Timbuktu and Africa's salt mines. Encourage them to find out how much salt is transported, how long the journey takes, and any primary sources about the experience of workers on these caravans. Students may sketch a map and annotate it with the information that they find or present a multimedia presentation.

ANSWERS

- Factors such as availability and need might influence the value of a commodity like salt.

- The photos in this lesson reveal that the process of harvesting salt is hard, dirty work, which might have a negative impact on people who do this work.

Africa's Eastern Networks

While African resources flowed through North Africa to Europe across the Mediterranean, another trade network bustled to the east. This set of trade routes spanned the Indian Ocean and was driven primarily by Muslim traders and sultans.

The fort at Kilwa, shown here, was built by the Portuguese after they arrived in East Africa in 1498 and took control of the region's trade.

374 CHAPTER 13

INDIAN OCEAN TRADE

Varied lands and people surrounded the Indian Ocean long ago. The East African coast, the southern edge of the Arabian Peninsula, the Persian Gulf, and the west coast of India had various languages, cultures, and political units. Yet all the city-states and larger political units surrounding the large body of water joined together as part of the Indian Ocean trade network. Just as rulers of North and West Africa taxed overland trade, so too did the sultans of these coastal regions tax Indian Ocean sea trade. Sultanates, the territories governed by the sultans, could be as small as a single city-state or a large kingdom. For example, small Muslim sultanates dotted East Africa's coast while an enormous Muslim kingdom prospered in northern India.

The people of these three regions traveled the Indian Ocean on ships called **dhows** (dows), boats with triangular sails that were common in the Arab world. These early vessels carried goods between ports, much like camels of the desert. Dhows had no deck, so passengers sat and slept next to the ships' cargo. Indian ocean winds powered the boats as they beat against their large sails. Little human labor was required on these voyages, so traders and their families staffed their own boats. As people of three regions traveled to other lands, they often intermarried, bringing about a mixing of cultures.

One such culture was that of the **Swahili** (swah-HEE-lee) people. The ancestors of the Swahili were Bantu-speaking migrants who settled on the coast. As they interacted with traders from other lands, they borrowed words from Arabic, Farsi, and the Indian language Gujarati. The Swahili converted to Islam and began to focus more on trade than farming.

One of their important trading cities was Kilwa, located on a small island off the coast of present-day Tanzania. Among Kilwa's main exports were gold from interior regions like Great Zimbabwe, elephant tusks, and slaves. Many goods from Africa's interior traveled to ocean ports, then to Kilwa, and on to their final destination. Kilwa was just one of about 40 East African trading settlements where African resources were traded for goods such as spices, beads, silk and cotton cloth, and porcelain from other locations. Those who participated in trade were highly regarded in society.

This Ethiopian miniature illustrates the legendary meeting of King Solomon and the Queen of Sheba.

THE KINGDOM OF ETHIOPIA

Another East African society with wider connections was the kingdom of Ethiopia. In this mountainous region, the rulers had long been Christians. Though later encircled by Muslim-dominated societies, they held fast to their ancient Coptic form of the Christian faith, which was connected to the Eastern Orthodox Church. Ethiopian priests, monks, and nuns still use their own sacred script, called Ge'ez (gee-EHZ), for religious purposes. When Christian pilgrims arrived in Jerusalem during the Middle Ages, they found Ethiopian visitors there as well.

One of the most famous churches in all of Africa is St. George's Church at Lalibela, built by an Ethiopian king in the 1200s. Instead of building the church upward, the king had his architects design the Lalibela church to be dug out of the living rock, below ground. You will learn more about this church and others like it in the next lesson.

The Christian kings of Ethiopia even traced their ancestry back to the Hebrew Bible. The Queen of Sheba, they claimed, was Ethiopian, and when she returned home after visiting Jerusalem, she delivered a child, the son of King Solomon, and called him **Menelik** (MEH-nuh-lihk). Menelik was the legendary founder of a line of emperors who ruled Ethiopia until the 1970s.

HISTORICAL THINKING

1. **READING CHECK** How did trade affect the people living in areas that bordered the Indian Ocean?

2. **DRAW CONCLUSIONS** Why were East Africans who participated in trade highly regarded in society?

3. **MAKE INFERENCES** Why was it important for the kings of Ethiopia to trace their lineage to the Hebrew Bible?

Achievements of African Societies 375

PLAN: 2-PAGE LESSON

OBJECTIVE
Explain how the Muslim kingdoms and city-states in East Africa primarily dominated Indian Ocean trade in the 1200s through the 1500s.

CRITICAL THINKING SKILLS FOR LESSON 2.3
- Draw Conclusions
- Make Inferences
- Identify Main Ideas and Details
- Make Connections
- Analyze Visuals

HISTORICAL THINKING FOR CHAPTER 13
How did African societies influence other cultures?

Like kingdoms in West and North Africa, East African kingdoms also became wealthy through trade. Lesson 2.3 discusses how the Indian Ocean trade network connected the region to Muslim kingdoms in India, the Persian Gulf, and the Arabian Peninsula.

BACKGROUND FOR THE TEACHER
East African City-States and Dhows More than two dozen city-states sat along the coast of East Africa. Mogadishu was the northernmost city and Sofala was the farthest south. They all had specialty trade products. Asian manufactured goods were imported, and trade goods from Africa such as ivory, tortoise shells, gold, leopard skins, and rhinoceros horns were exported to the Arabian Peninsula. Some East African cities also made cloth or iron for export.

For sea routes, dhows were primarily used because they could make good use of the monsoon winds in the western Indian Ocean. The dhows in this region were unlike most other boats because they were sewn together rather than nailed together. This method made the ship more flexible. Boatmakers sewed planks of teak (from India) or coconut trees together with a cord and added a single sail. This boat design was so practical that it is still in use today, yet many modern dhows make use of auxiliary engines.

INTRODUCE & ENGAGE

DISCUSS CULTURAL DIVERSITY

Discuss how new peoples and ideas affect the culture that is already present in an area. Sometimes these cultures blend or become dominant as other cultures migrate. Other times, they may take on a more minor role in a society but are still rich and contribute to the diversity. Have students discuss how places are affected by new languages, political and economic ideas, religions, and other aspects of culture.

TEACH

GUIDED DISCUSSION

1. **Identify Main Ideas and Details** How do details about dhows relate to the lesson's Main Idea statement? *(Dhows made Indian Ocean travel without large boat crews possible, allowing Muslim kingdoms and city-states in Africa to dominate Indian Ocean trade.)*

2. **Make Connections** Why do you think that a Christian community was able to exist in the kingdom of Ethiopia when it was surrounded by Muslim societies? *(Possible response: The Christian community was protected by the mountains. The Christians probably lived separately and independently of the Muslim societies, and they did not interact because of the physical geography.)*

ANALYZE VISUALS

Have students look at the photograph of the old fort at Kilwa. **ASK:** How do you think geographic setting influenced the location of this fort? *(Possible response: The fort was made to protect the port where traders would arrive.)* Why was this fort built? *(Possible response: With so many valuable trade goods such as gold and ivory being exchanged at the port, the fort was needed to make sure the goods weren't stolen.)*

ACTIVE OPTIONS

On Your Feet: Fishbowl Arrange students in two concentric circles facing inward. Pose the following questions: How did Ethiopia's religious diversity affect its development? How was it different from other societies in East Africa? As students in the inner circle discuss the questions, students in the outer circle listen and evaluate the ideas they hear. Then students reverse roles and the new inner circle continues the discussion by supporting or refuting the ideas they just heard. Provide time for both groups to exchange ideas and summarize the results of the discussions.

NG Learning Framework: Compare the Trans-Saharan and Indian Ocean Trade Networks
ATTITUDE Curiosity
SKILL Our Human Story

Explain that the trans-Saharan and Indian Ocean trade networks were connected through other trade routes such as those that linked the Arabian Peninsula. Ask small groups to research their similarities and differences besides the trade goods that were exchanged on them. Students may create guiding questions that relate to travel, taxes, trading partners or relations, and volume of trade goods. Have them present their findings.

DIFFERENTIATE

INCLUSION

Work in Pairs Allow students with disabilities to work with students who can read the lesson aloud to them. Encourage the partner without disabilities to describe the photographs and explain how they support the lesson content about East African trade networks. When pairs have finished the lesson, direct them to work together to answer the Historical Thinking questions.

PRE-AP

Research and Write a Trader Narrative Instruct students to write a narrative from the perspective of an East African trader who describes what life is like traveling and trading on the Indian Ocean trade network. Students should provide sources for the information in their narrative, and details should be accurate. Encourage students to include cities visited, travel durations, challenges, successes, specifics about trade goods, and new ideas and peoples. Invite students to read their narratives to the class or post on a class blog.

See the Chapter Planner for more strategies for differentiation.

HISTORICAL THINKING

ANSWERS

1. Trade provided the people living near the Indian Ocean with a wide variety of products and led to interactions of the various people and the mixing of cultures.

2. Possible response: Merchants were likely most highly regarded in society because they held the most wealth, had access to luxury items, and probably gained knowledge from their interactions.

3. Possible response: The Ethiopians had long been Christians and held fast to their ancient Coptic form of the Christian faith.

2.4 Preserving Cultural Heritage

CHURCHES CARVED INTO ROCK

Lalibela, a town north of Addis Ababa in Ethiopia, is home to 11 monolithic churches, each formed from a single large block of stone. These Christian churches are a vital part of Ethiopian history and culture, yet they are under threat. Without immediate attention, the churches—and their history—may deteriorate.

The town, which was named for King Lalibela, became the center of Ethiopian Christianity during the 12th century. After the capture of Jerusalem by Muslim forces in 1187, King Lalibela commissioned the churches and declared the town to be a new Jerusalem.

The churches were carved from volcanic rock below Earth's surface. Trenches were carved in a rectangle isolating a single stone block. The block was then carved inside and out, creating the churches from the top down rather than from the ground up. The roofs of each of the churches are level with the ground. Long underground tunnels provide passageways from one church to another.

These churches are still in use today, and the town is visited every year by hundreds of thousands of religious pilgrims. Preservation efforts for the site started as early

as the 1960s, with the World Monuments Fund (WMF) working with conservators to document information, stabilize construction, and raise international attention for the protection of the site. In 1978, UNESCO designated the churches as a World Heritage Site.

As transportation conditions to Ethiopia improved, the number of visitors to Lalibela increased. This growth in tourism along with water filtration problems has caused damage and structural problems.

In 2007, temporary shelters were built over four churches to address water problems caused by rain. However, it was later discovered that the shelters caused additional damage to the churches. In 2018, a group was commissioned to study the current state of conservation and make recommendations for further actions to ensure that the Lalibela churches—and Ethiopia's cultural heritage—are preserved now and for the future.

HISTORICAL THINKING

DRAW CONCLUSIONS How do human interaction and the environment affect cultural sites like the churches of Lalibela?

A priest stands at the entrance to the Church of Gabriel-Raphael. The entrance to this church is up at the top of the structure instead of down at the bottom.

376 CHAPTER 13

LALIBELA, ETHIOPIA
The Church of Saint George is one of 11 rock-hewn monolithic—or carved from a single stone—churches in this Ethiopian town. The church is formed in the shape of a cross and extends 40 feet down below the surface.

Achievements of African Societies

PLAN: 2-PAGE LESSON

OBJECTIVE

Describe the monolithic churches of Lalibela, Ethiopia; the problems that threaten them; and the efforts being made to preserve them.

CRITICAL THINKING SKILLS FOR LESSON 2.4

- Analyze Visuals
- Make Connections
- Draw Conclusions
- Sequence
- Analyze Cause and Effect

HISTORICAL THINKING FOR CHAPTER 13

How did African societies influence other cultures?

Lalibela became the center of Ethiopian Christianity during the 12th century. Lesson 2.4 discusses the 11 monolithic churches of Lalibela that hundreds of thousands of religious pilgrims visit every year and the international efforts being made to preserve the churches.

BACKGROUND FOR THE TEACHER

A Symbol of the Holy Land There are two main groups of the monolithic churches of Lalibela. Five of the churches were carved from rock north of the river Jordan, and five were carved from rock south of the river. The Church of Saint George is separate from the other 10 but connected by a system of trenches. The churches contain replicas of the tomb of Christ and the crib of the Nativity so that religious pilgrims could visit these holy symbols of Jerusalem and Bethlehem when those cities were not safe to visit. The holy site of Lalibela is home to a large community of priests and monks that serve the residents of Lalibela and the pilgrims who travel there. The priests and monks at the Church of Saint George have maintained the original purpose of the site over the centuries.

History Notebook

Encourage students to complete the Preserving Cultural Heritage page for Chapter 13 in their History Notebooks as they read.

Student eEdition online

Additional content for this lesson, including a video and a photo, is available online.

INTRODUCE & ENGAGE

PREVIEW WITH VISUALS

Direct students' attention to the photograph of the Church of Saint George in the lesson. Invite students to predict how the church shown was built based on the caption and their observation of the photograph. Make a list of their ideas. At the end of the lesson, revisit the list to confirm or revise predictions based on what students learned.

TEACH

GUIDED DISCUSSION

1. **Sequence** What steps were followed to create each of the churches? *(Trenches were carved in a rectangle. A single stone block was isolated. The block was carved inside and out from the top down.)*

2. **Analyze Cause and Effect** Why did the king declare the town of Lalibela to be a new Jerusalem? *(Because Muslim forces had captured Jerusalem in 1187, King Lalibela had 11 churches built in the town for Christian pilgrims to visit as a new Jerusalem.)*

PRESERVING CULTURAL HERITAGE

An extensive system of drainage ditches was built when the Lalibela churches were created to drain rainwater away from the churches. However, over the centuries, dirt collected in the ditches and blocked many of them. The ditches were not cleared until the 20th century. Seismic activity in the region has also damaged some of these drainage ditches. Unfortunately, these problems have caused severe degradation of the churches from water damage. Erosion to the rock has also caused structural problems that are being addressed or need to be. New public and private construction in the area, partly to house tourists and religious pilgrims, has also threatened the stability of the churches. International efforts are being made to address all these problems in the hopes of preserving these unique and exceptional churches of Ethiopia.

ACTIVE OPTION

NG Learning Framework: Consider Complexity of Construction STEM
ATTITUDE Curiosity
SKILL Observation

Invite students to watch the video clip (available in the Student eEdition) and consider how complex the construction of the Lalibela churches was, especially in the 12th and 13th centuries, without the use of computers and modern machinery. Encourage them to conduct online research to learn about the construction theories archaeologists have made based on their observations and the mysteries still unresolved, such as what happened to the enormous amount of rock excavated inside and out from the 11 churches. Have students write a summary paragraph of their research and observations. Then lead a class discussion about their findings.

DIFFERENTIATE

INCLUSION

Visual Perspective Pair proficient readers with students who have perception issues to examine the photographs together. Encourage the proficient students to point out the people at the base of the trenches that surround two of the churches and the priest inside the church in the third photo. Invite them to use rulers or other ways to compare the size of the people to the size of the structures to help them comprehend the immensity of the churches and complexity of their construction.

GIFTED & TALENTED

Portrait of an Individual Church Direct students to conduct online research on one of the 11 monolithic churches of Lalibela. For example, they might choose the Church of the Saviour of the World, which has five aisles and is believed to be the largest monolithic church in the world, or they might choose the Church of Gabriel Raphael, which may have been a royal residence prior to being a church. Encourage them to collect photos of the church as well as facts about it and to use these to create a portrait to share. Invite them to share their portrait in an oral presentation to the class.

See the Chapter Planner for more strategies for differentiation.

HISTORICAL THINKING

ANSWER

Possible response: They can cause deterioration of the structures, which can inadvertently lead to the destruction of the culture site.

2.5 Africa East and West

A variety of factors affected life in West Africa and along the Swahili Coast between 1000 and 1500, including climate, available resources, basic beliefs, and cultural diffusion. The term *Swahili Coast* refers to the East African lands along the Indian Ocean where people developed the Swahili language and built Muslim trading cities.

Political, social, and religious aspects of life in various parts of Africa influenced building styles in particular. Places where Islam was well established, such as North Africa, the cities of the Sahel, and the Swahili Coast, became home to many mosques, some of which were large and impressive. African rulers also became used to sturdy and elaborate palaces. In addition, the multiroom houses of traders and other wealthy individuals provided visual confirmation of their high status in society. Stone proved to be the ideal resource for such imposing structures, though Swahili structures were also built of coral cut from Indian Ocean reefs.

Less-wealthy people made do with whichever resources were available in their area. Traditional building materials such as mud, wattle, grasses, tree branches, and even salt formed many one-room homes in much of West and East Africa. Wattle is formed by interweaving poles, branches, and reeds. Originally, many people in sub-Saharan Africa resided in circular homes with dome-shaped roofs. Later, Africans began building rectangular homes with flat roofs, an idea they borrowed from Arab visitors.

Wood was abundant in some parts of Africa and therefore was the main resource for doors used not only in African homes but also sold as export items. Swahili craftsmen were experts at carving intricate designs for these doors. The most ornate doors featured ebony wood with inlays of ivory. East African merchants also found a good market for the mangroves they harvested from coastal wetlands. These were in high demand in Arabia, where there is very little local wood for use in construction.

CRITICAL VIEWING The Sankore (sayn-KOHR) Mosque still stands in Timbuktu. It has features you will find in mosques anywhere. But the architects of Mali also brought their own culture and building knowledge to the task, for example including beams within its thick mud walls. These beams can be seen protruding through the walls of the mosque. What do you think the inside of the mosque looks like based on its appearance from the outside?

DOCUMENT ONE

Primary Source: Book
from *Book of Highways and of Kingdoms*
by Abu U'bayd al-Bakri, 1068

Al-Bakri provided early descriptions of Ghana in his *Book of Highways and of Kingdoms*. He did not actually travel to West Africa, so his account is based on observations of others. Geographers and historians today rely on the descriptions of al-Bakri to gain much of their knowledge of Ghana long ago.

CONSTRUCTED RESPONSE What can you infer about the king's attitude toward Muslim merchants based on the architecture of the town?

The city of Ghana consists of two towns situated on a plain. One of these towns, which is inhabited by Muslims, is large and possesses 12 mosques, in one of which they assemble for the Friday prayer. . . . In the environs are wells with sweet water, from which they drink and with which they grow vegetables. The king's town is six miles distant from this one and bears the name of Al-Ghaba. Between these two towns there are continuous habitations. The houses of the inhabitants are of stone and acacia wood. The king has a palace and a number of domed dwellings all surrounded with an enclosure like a city wall. In the king's town, and not far from his court of justice, is a mosque where the Muslims who arrive at his court pray.

DOCUMENT TWO

Primary Source: Book
from *The Book of Duarte Barbosa* by Duarte Barbosa, 1518

Searching for new sea-trade routes to southern India, the Portuguese came into contact with booming East African trading cities such as Kilwa. They were shocked to find such well-developed communities. Duarte Barbosa, a Portuguese government official, traveled throughout the Indian Ocean region to see for himself the richness of that trade.

CONSTRUCTED RESPONSE Why is Duarte Barbosa so impressed with Kilwa?

Going along the coast from the town of Mozambique, there is an island which is called Kilwa, in which is a Muslim town with many fair houses of stone and mortar, with many windows after our fashion, very well arranged in streets, with many flat roofs. The doors are of wood, well carved with excellent joinery. Around it are streams and orchards and fruit-gardens with many channels of sweet water. It has a Muslim king over it. From this place they trade with Sofala, whence they bring back gold. Before the King our Lord sent out his expedition to discover India, the Muslims of Sofala, Cuama, Angoya and Mozambique were all subject to the King of Kilwa.

DOCUMENT THREE

Primary Source: Book
from *A Geographical Historie of Africa* by Leo Africanus, 1526

Leo Africanus grew up in Muslim-ruled Grenada in Spain and went with his father on a diplomatic mission to the Songhai Empire. Determined to learn more about the world, he traveled throughout North Africa and into West Africa. In his book, he describes in detail the trading city of Timbuktu, which, at the time of his writings, featured majestic mosques and was a center of learning where books were highly valued.

CONSTRUCTED RESPONSE Why do you think the houses of Timbuktu were made of clay-covered wattles with thatched roofs rather than stone?

The houses of Timbuktu are huts made of clay-covered wattles with thatched roofs. In the center of the city is a temple built of stone and mortar, and in addition there is a large palace where the king lives. The shops of the artisans, the merchants and especially weavers of cotton cloth are very numerous. Fabrics are also imported from Europe to Timbuktu, borne by Berber merchants.

The women of the city maintain the custom of veiling their faces, except for the slaves who sell all the foodstuffs. The inhabitants are very rich, especially the strangers who have settled in the country.

SYNTHESIZE & WRITE

1. REVIEW Review what you have read and observed about the construction of houses in early East Africa and West Africa.

2. RECALL On your own paper, list key details about the architecture at each of the three locations described.

3. CONSTRUCT Construct a topic sentence that answers this question: How are the three types of houses described in the primary sources similar to and different from one another?

4. WRITE Using evidence from this chapter and the documents, write an informative paragraph that supports your topic sentence in Step 3.

PLAN: 2-PAGE LESSON

OBJECTIVE
Synthesize information about societies in East and West Africa.

CRITICAL THINKING SKILLS FOR LESSON 2.5
- Synthesize
- Form and Support Opinions
- Generalize
- Evaluate

HISTORICAL THINKING FOR CHAPTER 13
How did African societies influence other cultures?

Political, social, and religious aspects of life are evident in eastern and western African architecture. Lesson 2.5 focuses on three documents about early descriptions of the cities of Ghana and Timbuktu in West Africa and the East African city of Kilwa.

BACKGROUND FOR THE TEACHER

Mosque Construction The Mosque of Sankore is considered an architectural marvel at the center of Timbuktu and is part of a UNESCO World Heritage Site. Sankore is one of western Africa's oldest mosques, designed by architect Ishaq al-Shahili. He incorporated a wooden framework that helped to support the mud walls. After the rainy season, the mud walls require repairs, so a celebration is held each year in which residents re-plaster the walls of the mosque. People climb up and sit on the timber while applying new mud to the wall by hand, which creates the rounded edges.

The Great Mosque of Kilwa stands on the island of Kisiwani in Tanzania and is also a UNESCO World Heritage Site. The stone coral roof, with its symmetrical domes and vault ceilings, reflects the architecture of a cosmopolitan city that was a favorite trading and meeting spot for Europeans during the 10th century. The strong coral walls, filled with thick mortar, display the impressive design of what is probably one of the oldest mosques in East Africa. In the 15th century, under the reign of Süleyman, the mosque was repaired, and a large vaulted dome was built over a southern extension, making the Great Mosque at Kilwa the largest covered mosque in East Africa to date.

INTRODUCE & ENGAGE

PREPARE FOR THE DOCUMENT-BASED QUESTION

Before students start the activity, briefly preview the three documents. Remind students that a constructed response requires full explanations in complete sentences. Emphasize that students should use what they have learned about East and West Africa in addition to the information in the documents.

TEACH

GUIDED DISCUSSION

1. **Form and Support Opinions** After reading the documents, which city do you think is the largest and most established? Explain why. *(Possible response: The city of Ghana seems to be the largest because there are 2 towns and 12 mosques; it also seems to be the most established because the dwellings and buildings are constructed with stone. Building with stone takes a long time to do and is very permanent, which means that its setting was an established city.)*

2. **Generalize** What can archaeologists learn about civilizations by studying their architecture? *(Possible response: They can learn about the materials they used, the types of structures that were important to the people, and the political, social, and religious aspects of life.)*

EVALUATE

After students have completed the Synthesize & Write activity, allow time for them to exchange paragraphs and read and comment on the work of their peers. Establish guidelines for comments prior to the activity so that feedback is constructive and encouraging in nature. Comments should focus on the most significant parts that address the purpose of the activity and the audience.

ACTIVE OPTION

On Your Feet: Think, Pair, Share Ask the following question and then allow a few minutes for students to think about it: What details from the documents do you find interesting? Then tell students to choose partners and talk about the question for five minutes. After discussion time, invite students to share their ideas with the class.

DIFFERENTIATE

STRIVING READERS

Summarize Main Ideas Ask pairs to read information about each document presented in the lesson. Instruct them to pause after reading about a document and ask each other *Who? What? Where? When?* and *Why?* questions. Students may use a 5Ws chart to organize their questions and answers. Have them summarize the main ideas about each document, using their responses.

GIFTED & TALENTED

Create a Map Ask students to research architecture in eastern and western Africa. Instruct them to create an "Interesting African Architecture" map showing the location and a visual of 5 to 10 of the most interesting buildings that they discovered in their research. Have them list a few details about the architecture of each building. Encourage students to be creative in their designs. Ask them to present their maps to the class.

SYNTHESIZE & WRITE

ANSWERS

1. Answers will vary.

2. Possible response: Excerpt 1: stone and acacia wood, palace, domed dwellings, city wall, mosque; Excerpt 2: fair houses, stone and mortar, windows, well arranged, flat roofs, wooden doors, excellent joinery; Excerpt 3: huts, clay-covered wattles, thatched roofs, temple, stone and mortar, palace

3. Possible response: Available resources and beliefs of various African cultures affected their architecture.

4. Answers will vary. Students' paragraphs should include their topic sentence from Step 3 and several details from the documents to support the sentence.

CONSTRUCTED RESPONSE

Document One: Possible response: The king values Muslim merchants and wants them to feel welcome.

Document Two: Possible response: The houses are somewhat like those he is used to seeing, are arranged in an orderly fashion, and appear to be well-crafted.

Document Three: Possible responses: Clay, wattle, and thatch might be more readily available than stone and were traditional materials used to build houses; stone might be reserved for other uses; building with stone is more labor-intensive and time-consuming.

CRITICAL VIEWING Possible response: the walls and ceilings are lined with timber; the inside is probably dark

REVIEW

VOCABULARY

Use each of the following vocabulary words in a sentence that shows an understanding of the term's meaning.

1. griot
2. lineage
3. intermediary
4. monopoly
5. mansa
6. caravan
7. trans-Saharan trade network
8. dhow

READING STRATEGY
IDENTIFY MAIN IDEAS AND DETAILS

Use a graphic organizer like the one below to list a main idea and details about each of the following: Mansa Musa, Ibn Battuta, and Sundiata. Then answer the question that follows.

Main Ideas	Details

9. Use the details you listed to describe how one of the people mentioned above contributed to the growth of a kingdom or an empire of sub-Saharan Africa.

MAIN IDEAS

Answer the following questions. Support your answers with evidence from the chapter.

10. In what different ways were African societies governed? LESSON 1.1

11. How did Ghana and Mali profit from trade? LESSON 1.2

12. What have archaeological finds revealed about Great Zimbabwe? LESSON 1.3

13. How did Ibn Battuta's Islamic faith affect his travel? LESSON 2.1

14. What was the purpose of the trans-Saharan trade network? LESSON 2.2

15. Why was the Indian Ocean trade network significant in history? LESSON 2.4

HISTORICAL THINKING

Answer the following questions. Support your answers with evidence from the chapter.

16. EXPLAIN How did the different climates of sub-Saharan Africa affect the economy of the region?

17. MAKE INFERENCES Why might historians want to verify the information found in the stories of griots through architectural findings?

18. ANALYZE CAUSE AND EFFECT What was the effect of the Bantu migrations on hunter-gatherer societies in southern and eastern Africa?

19. CATEGORIZE How did both internal and external factors lead to the break-up of the Ghana empire?

20. FORM AND SUPPORT OPINIONS Did Sundiata or Mansa Musa have a greater effect on Mali? Explain your answer.

21. EVALUATE How closely can a modern-day traveler follow in Ibn Battuta's footsteps? Explain.

22. DRAW CONCLUSIONS Why did the Mamluks convert to Islam and support its expansion?

23. MAKE INFERENCES Why did Ethiopian kings connect their dynasty to the Hebrew Bible?

INTERPRET VISUALS

Study the map at right, which shows the trans-Saharan trade network. Then answer the questions below.

24. Was the Sahara a barrier to trade in North and West Africa? Why or why not?

25. Based on the map, which resource appears to be available in the largest amount?

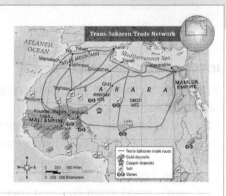
Trans-Saharan Trade Network

ANALYZE SOURCES

In this excerpt, Ibn Battuta describes a visit to the royal court of Mali, where he observes griots orally relaying history to the king. He uses the word *sultan* for the Mali king since earlier rulers of the empire had converted to Islam. Read the excerpt and then answer the questions that follow.

> Each of them is inside a costume made of feathers resembling the green woodpecker on which is a wooden head with a red beak. . . . They stand before the Sultan in this laughable get-up and recite their poems. . . . They say to the Sultan: "This platform, formerly such and such a king sat on it and performed noble actions, and so and so did such and such; do you do noble acts which will be recounted after you?"
>
> —from *The Travels of Ibn Battuta*, 1350–1351

26. What attitude does Ibn Battuta hold toward the griots?

27. Why might he have formed this attitude?

CONNECT TO YOUR LIFE

28. ARGUMENT In 2012, Islamist rebels, who believe that the government should impose a strict form of religious law, pushed back the army of the government of Mali and temporarily took over the city of Timbuktu. To impose their extreme version of the faith, they attacked holy sites they saw as lacking in purity. Research to find out more about these rebels and then think about the following: Can you think of other times when wars have been fought to force people to believe and behave in a certain way? Is it ever justified for religious leaders to use violence to impose their own version of religion on other people? Write a short argument stating your position, using present-day or past examples.

TIPS

• List possible examples and choose one or two to use in making your argument.

• Summarize your viewpoint clearly before you present your points in more depth.

• Include reasons and specific details to support your position.

• Counter the strengths of an opposing viewpoint with your own position.

VOCABULARY ANSWERS

1. Possible response: A griot in the royal court of West Africa orally recounted the actions of past kings.

2. Possible response: The distant cousins were able to trace their lineage back to a common ancestor, their great-grandfather.

3. Possible response: Their location between gold mines to the south and salt mines to the north allowed West Africans to profit as intermediaries in the trade of these resources.

4. Possible response: Anyone with sole control of the manufacture and sale of a product has a monopoly on that product.

5. Possible response: The leader of the Mali Empire held the title of mansa.

6. Possible response: The members of the desert caravan consisted of Muslim traders on camelback.

7. Possible response: The trans-Saharan trade network allowed resources such as gold and salt from West Africa to be transported to port cities on North Africa's coast.

8. Possible response: The wind blew fiercely on the sail of the dhow, allowing the ship to move quickly over the Indian Ocean with its cargo.

READING STRATEGY ANSWER

Possible responses shown.

Main Ideas	Details
Mansa Musa was a wealthy ruler of the Mali Empire.	• displayed his riches during a hajj
Ibn Battuta was a traveler in the Muslim world.	• spent 29 years traveling • wrote *The Travels*
Sundiata was a ruler of Mali.	• became ruler as the Mali Empire rose to power

9. Sample answer: Sundiata defeated the empire of Ghana and established the Mali Empire.

MAIN IDEAS ANSWERS

10. Some villages were ruled by elders of the lineage. The elders made the most important decisions. Sometimes groups of lineages came together to form clans. Sometimes the clans formed kingdoms.

11. Traders of both Ghana and Mali served as middlemen in the gold–salt trade. Their leaders collected taxes on all goods that passed through the empire.

12. Archaeological finds have revealed that the people were highly skilled builders and craft-workers, had social distinctions, had not adopted Islam, and traded with places as far away as China and India.

13. Possible response: Ibn Battuta began his travels because of his experience on a hajj. He traveled mainly in Muslim lands or to areas frequented by Muslim traders and used the beliefs of Islam as a way of evaluating the cultures he encountered. Also, the Islamic belief in alms supported his journey.

14. It provided a way to transport goods over land between West Africa and North Africa using established trade routes.

15. It connected the East African coast, the southern edge of the Arabian Peninsula, and the west coast of India in trade and led to the mixing of the different cultures there. It operated free of European influence, showing that many different peoples participated in trade.

HISTORICAL THINKING ANSWERS

16. The different climates led people to do different things in order to survive. For example, people who lived in the desert traded or worked in the salt mines, while people who lived on the savanna farmed or herded.

17. Possible responses: The stories of griots may not be completely based on facts, and they may have been embellished or altered as they passed through the centuries by word of mouth. Historians can only confirm the accuracy of griots' stories through hard evidence found at archaeological sites.

18. Possible response: Bantu speakers brought their farming techniques to areas where farming had not yet been established.

19. Possible response: Internal factors leading to the break-up of the Ghana Empire included the degradation of its soil and the overuse of resources. External factors included invasions of its land, causing disruptions in trade.

20. Answers will vary. Some students might say Sundiata had the greatest effect because he founded the Mali Empire and set it on a path of growth and wealth. Others might mention Mansa Musa because his hajj made Mali known in other parts of the world, expanded the empire, and encouraged the growth of the arts, learning, and Islam.

21. Answers will vary. Some students may say that a modern-day traveler can closely follow in Ibn Battuta's footsteps by conducting historical research, mimicking the routes the early traveler took, and using the same types of transportation. Other students may say that the people, places, modes of transportation, and forms of communication are too different today to authentically duplicate Ibn Battuta's voyage.

22. Possible response: The Mamluks converted to Islam because it helped them gain their freedom, and it helped them gain higher positions in military and government.

23. Possible response: The Ethiopians had long been Christians and held fast to their ancient Coptic form of the Christian faith.

INTERPRET VISUALS ANSWERS

24. No. While the Sahara was an obstacle, people created a trans-Saharan trade network that connected the gold, salt, and copper deposits in West Africa and the port cities of North Africa.

25. Both gold and salt appear to be the most available resources.

ANALYZE SOURCES ANSWERS

26. His mention of "laughable get-up" indicates that he does not respect the griots or their activities.

27. Possible response: He is from a literate culture and might find a culture that relies on oral culture to be inferior. He may be used to more formal and refined court ceremony.

CONNECT TO YOUR LIFE ANSWER

28. Answers will vary. Students' arguments should include evidence supporting their position as well as a response to a perceived counterargument.

UNIT 5

Dynamics in Africa and the Americas
3100 B.C.E.–1592 C.E.

CRITICAL VIEWING
In western Belize, stone carvings adorn the Maya temple El Castillo ("The Castle") at the Xunantunich archaeological site. This structure at Xunantunich, which is sacred Mayan for "stone woman," stretches to 130 feet above the main plaza. Based on the details in this photograph, what can you infer about the Maya people and their religion?

14 **Civilizations in the Americas**
3100 B.C.E.–1532 C.E.

HISTORICAL THINKING How did early American societies emerge and interact before European contact?

SECTION 1 Fishing, Hunting, and Farming
SECTION 2 Mesoamerican and Andean Societies

CRITICAL VIEWING
This view from the Pyramid of the Moon in Teotihuacan in modern Mexico shows a terrace descending steps to the Avenue of the Dead. The Pyramid of the Sun exists in the background. What generalization can you make about the people who lived here more than 2,000 years ago?

STRATEGY ❶
Turn Titles into Questions
To help students set a purpose for reading, tell them to read the title of each lesson in a section and then turn that title into a question they believe will be answered in the lesson. Students can record their questions and write their own answers, or they can ask each other questions.

Use with All Lessons *For example, Section 1 questions could be: How (or When) were the Americas settled? What were the early complex societies of the Americas? What characterized the Classic and Post-Classic Maya civilization? What Maya secrets have been discovered underwater? What were the northern cultures like?*

STRATEGY ❷
Sequence Events
To build understanding of a lesson, direct students to note critical events in a Sequence Chain, such as the one shown, including the date and a brief summary of each event. Encourage students to add circles and arrows as necessary to show the number and complexity of the causes and effects of historical events and their relationship to each other.

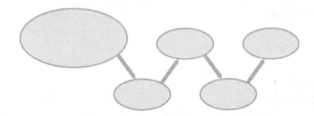

Use with All Lessons

STRATEGY ❸
Identify Facts
Arrange students in mixed-proficiency pairs and guide them to conduct a Round Robin activity to review what they have learned. Ask pairs to generate facts for about three to five minutes and then invite one student from each pair to share their facts. Display all facts on the board and invite comments from the rest of the group.

Use with All Lessons

STRATEGY ❶
Sequence Events
Write the main events of a lesson on index cards. There should be one event on each index card. Have each student work with another student or a teacher aide to read the section. Then have the student place the cards listing the events in the order they occurred. Use the following main events for Lesson 2.1:

- Around the 10th century, the Toltec emerged in what is now the Valley of Mexico.
- The Toltec conquered the city of Teotihuacán around 900.
- The Toltec civilization ended around 1100.
- Around 1325, the Mexica, who would become the Aztec, traveled to the Valley of Mexico.
- By 1500, the Aztec ruled over a population between 6 and 11 million.

Use with All Lessons

STRATEGY ❷
Provide Alternative Ways of Assessing Knowledge
Adapt tests or quizzes for students with disabilities by having teacher aides or other students read tests and quizzes aloud to students with disabilities. Break multi-step questions into parts, so that each part is more manageable for students with disabilities to answer by writing or speaking. Accept oral responses rather than written responses when appropriate.

Use with All Lessons

STRATEGY ❶
Build Vocabulary
Help students at **All Proficiencies** learn unfamiliar words by introducing synonyms they might know. Display difficult words paired with more familiar words, as with these examples from Lesson 1.1:

evolving / changing
vessels / boats
organic / living
foraged / searched

hospitable / friendly
ample / enough

Tell students that when they encounter a difficult word, such as *evolving*, they should try to replace it with a word they may be familiar with, such as *changing*. Guide students to use a thesaurus to practice looking up and substituting words, encouraging them to look among the synonyms to find one that makes sense in context.

Use with All Lessons *Students at the Advanced level could help students at the Beginning and Intermediate levels find appropriate synonyms. Look for opportunities in all lessons to use synonyms and a thesaurus to aid comprehension.*

STRATEGY ❷
Create a Word Wall

Work with students at the **Beginning** and **Intermediate** levels to select five terms from each lesson to display on a Word Wall. Choose terms students are likely to encounter in other lessons in the text, such as *barrier, extinct, dispersed, aquatic,* and *mode*. Keep the words displayed throughout the chapter, adding terms for each new lesson. Discuss each term as it comes up during reading.

Use with All Lessons

STRATEGY ❸
Use Paired Reading

Pair students at the **Intermediate** or **Advanced** levels and have them read passages from the text aloud.

1. Partner 1 reads a passage. Partner 2 retells the passage in his or her own words.
2. Partner 2 reads a different passage. Partner 1 retells it.
3. Pairs repeat the process, switching roles.

Use with All Lessons

GIFTED & TALENTED

STRATEGY ❶
Present an Artistic History

Prompt students to choose one of the American civilizations described in the chapter and develop a visual display of its artistic achievements. Have them conduct

more research to collect visuals of pyramids, statues, building decorations, carvings, pottery, weavings, jewelry, and paintings. Instruct students to describe each visual and what it reveals about the people. Encourage them to display the visuals as they present their artistic history to the class.

Use with All Lessons

STRATEGY ❷
Research Ball Courts

Tell students to conduct research into one of the ball courts used by one of the American civilizations presented in the chapter. Encourage them to describe the court and how it was used. Invite them to hypothesize why the court was significant and how some of them have survived hundreds of years. Tell them to create a poster of their findings that they can display in the classroom.

Use with Lessons 1.2, 1.3, 1.5, and 2.1

PRE-AP

STRATEGY ❶
Teach a Class

Before beginning the chapter, allow students to choose one of the lessons and prepare to teach the content to the class. Give them a set amount of time in which to present their lesson. Suggest that students think about any visuals or activities they want to use when they teach.

Use with All Lessons

STRATEGY ❷
Compare and Contrast Calendars

Direct students to conduct research into the calendars of the Maya and the Aztec. Encourage them to use a Venn diagram or other graphic organizer to list similarities and differences between the two calendars. Have them use their research to analyze and evaluate which calendar was more accurate and useful for its people. Invite students to make an oral presentation of their research and evaluation to the class.

Use with Lessons 1.3 and 2.1

HISTORICAL THINKING How did early American
societies emerge and interact before European contact?

SECTION 1 Fishing, Hunting, and Farming
SECTION 2 Mesoamerican and Andean Societies

CRITICAL VIEWING
This view from the Pyramid of the Moon in
Teotihuacán in modern Mexico shows tourists
descending steps to the Avenue of the Dead. The
Pyramid of the Sun looms in the background.
What generalization can you make about the
people who lived here more than 2,000 years ago?

INTRODUCE THE PHOTOGRAPH

TEOTIHUACÁN

Have students study the photograph of pyramids in
the ancient city of Teotihuacán. Direct them to read the
caption and find the Pyramid of the Sun in the photo.
Explain that this pyramid is the largest of its kind in North
America and was built around 200 B.C.E. **ASK:** Based on
your background knowledge of pyramids, what purpose
do you think the Pyramid of the Sun and the Pyramid of
the Moon served? (Possible responses: Like the pyramids
in Egypt, the pyramids may be tombs for their rulers. They
may be places for religious rituals or worship.) What do
you think was the purpose of the platforms at the tops of
the other pyramids? (Possible response: Each platform
was probably a foundation for a building or a stage for an
event.) Tell students that the information they learn about
early civilizations in the Americas will help them make
inferences about the people who lived there.

SHARE BACKGROUND

Teotihuacán, which means "place where the gods were
created," was one of the most powerful cultural centers in
Mesoamerica and is located about 30 miles from Mexico
City. Its ceremonial center covered more than 22 square
miles at its peak. The compound had 2,000 apartments,
great plazas, temples, and palaces where the nobles
and priests lived. In ancient times, the terraced levels of
the Pyramid of the Sun would have been decorated with
bright, multicolored murals.

CRITICAL VIEWING Answers will vary. Possible
response: People lived in large, monumental cities. The
civilization's builders were highly skilled architects.

HISTORICAL THINKING QUESTION

How did early American societies emerge and interact before European contact?

Roundtable: Emergence and Interaction of Early American Societies Arrange students in groups of four. Assign half of the groups this question: What events and characteristics have contributed to the growth of the civilizations we have studied so far? Assign the remaining groups this question: What are some of the ways societies today interact? Have one student in each group write an answer to the question on a sheet of paper and pass the paper clockwise to the next student, who adds an answer, continuing until students are out of ideas. As a class, compile a master list of answers for each question. Then tell students that in Chapter 14, they will learn how early American societies emerged and interacted with one another before the arrival of Europeans.

KEY DATES FOR CHAPTER 14

3100 B.C.E.	The Americas' first large urban community, Caral, develops in Peru.
1000 B.C.E.	The Maya develop an advanced civilization.
500 B.C.E.	The Adena settle along the Ohio and Illinois river valleys.
200 B.C.E.	The Hopewell settle along the Ohio, Illinois, and Mississippi rivers.
650 C.E.	The Toltec emerge in the Valley of Mexico.
800 C.E.	The Maya era begins to decline.
900 C.E.	The Toltec conquer the city of Teotihuacán.
1150 C.E.	The Anasazi build cliff dwellings in Arizona and Colorado.
c. 1400 C.E.	The Inca civilization develops in the Andes.
1500 C.E.	The Aztec conquer more than 450 city-states.

INTRODUCE THE READING STRATEGY

MAKE INFERENCES

Explain to students that making inferences will help them build understanding and gain additional insight into the concepts and events in this chapter. Go to the Chapter Review and preview the graphic organizer there with students. As they read the chapter, remind students to support their understanding of new ideas by making connections to what they already know.

INTRODUCE CHAPTER VOCABULARY

KEY VOCABULARY

SECTION 1

cenote	Clovis point	codex
earthwork	maize	mother culture
slash-and-burn agriculture	terrace	

SECTION 2

chinampa	compulsory education
geoglyph	quipu

WORD MAPS

As students read the chapter, ask them to complete a Word Map for each Key Vocabulary word. Tell them to write the word in the oval and, as they encounter the word in the chapter, complete the Word Map. Model an example using the graphic organizer below.

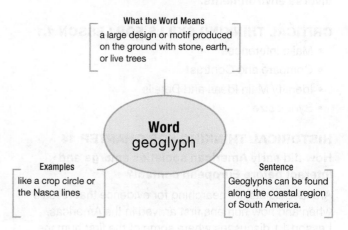

What the Word Means
a large design or motif produced on the ground with stone, earth, or live trees

Word
geoglyph

Examples
like a crop circle or the Nasca lines

Sentence
Geoglyphs can be found along the coastal region of South America.

The Settling of the Americas

Imagine finding lands and waters untouched by human beings. How would you and the people with you survive in these new places? The first people to set foot in North and South America, the last continents to be settled by humankind, accepted that challenge and developed a myriad of distinct cultures.

HOW THE FIRST AMERICANS LIVED

As you have read, the story of how and when humans came to the Americas is ever evolving. New discoveries constantly challenge what experts think they know. The best evidence for the first wave of migration comes from far down the west coast of the Americas at a settlement called **Monte Verde**, in what is now Chile. The Rocky Mountains and the Andes Mountains form a bony spine running along the western edge of the Americas. This barrier kept the first settlers in the coastal zones west of the mountain chain. Early humans probably traveled down the west coast of North and South America in small boats. These vessels were likely not that different from those used by early humans to sail to Australia.

Although no human remains have been found at Monte Verde so far, experts have discovered the 14,000-year-old footprints of a child. The site is under a layer of peat, which preserved organic materials such as wood, skin, and plants that almost never survive. This unusual preservation means that scholars know exactly which tools the first Americans used. When hunting, Monte Verde's residents used stone flakes on wooden sticks, spear points, and bolas—long strings with stones tied at both ends. The main weapon used to kill large game was the *atlatl*. The atlatl was a powerful two-part spear-thrower that people used over thousands of years.

The people who lived in Monte Verde hunted mastodon, a relative of the modern elephant that became extinct about 9000 B.C.E. They also foraged along the coast for shellfish, which could be eaten raw, and many other types of food. In the initial stages of migration, the settlers found a coastal environment much more hospitable than an inland one. Hunting parties could leave for long periods, knowing that people left behind had ample food supplies.

By 11,000 B.C.E., small bands of people had settled all of the Americas. For weapons, they used atlatls as well as wooden sticks with sharp slivers of rock, called microblades, attached to the shafts. Studies of different sites have determined that while the people in these regions shared many common traits, different technological traditions also existed in different North American regions. Each group left behind distinct artifacts, usually a spear point of a certain type.

Like the residents of Monte Verde, these later peoples combined hunting with the gathering of wild fruits and seeds. They lived in an area stretching from present-day Oregon to Texas, with heavy concentration in the Great Plains. They hunted a wide variety of game using atlatls tipped with stone spear points called **Clovis points**. Archaeologists call these characteristic artifacts Clovis points because the first such spear points were found in Clovis, New Mexico.

DIVERSE ENVIRONMENTAL ADAPTATIONS

The migrations to the Americas ended when the world's climate warmed quickly at the end of the last Ice Age. After 8300 B.C.E., the sea level rose. By 7000 B.C.E., most of Beringia was underwater once again. After 7000 B.C.E., the ancestors of modern American Indians dispersed over North and South America and began settling in diverse environments. Hunting, farming, gathering, and fishing were the principle activities that sustained these communities.

Hunting was common across the Americas. In fact, in some environments, it was the primary source of food. In the polar north, the ancestors of people like the Inuit developed great skills in hunting sea mammals such as whales and walruses. American Indians in the Clovis tradition hunted huge megafauna like wooly mammoths across the Great Plains. They were so successful that scientists believe that prehistoric people hunted these giant creatures into extinction, a reminder that humans not only adapt to environments but change them as well.

In other areas, farming became a common way of life after several separate Neolithic revolutions. As you will learn, farming sustained large populations and powerful empires in Mesoamerica—the region that stretches from today's Mexico into Central America—and in the Andes of South America. Woodland communities along the eastern seaboard also included skilled farmers and hunters. In the Mississippi River Valley and the Great Lakes region of North America, indigenous communities combined farming, hunting, fishing, and the gathering of foods such as honey, wild rice, and berries.

In some environments, aquatic resources were key to sustaining the population. Fishing and the gathering of seafood played a central role in the livelihoods of people in places such as the Amazon River basin, the swamps and bayous of what are now the states of Louisiana and Florida, and along the Pacific coast.

While adapting to varying environments, First Nations communities (as they are called in Canada) also developed hundreds of distinctive cultures, languages, and modes of living. Long separated from the peoples of the Eastern Hemisphere, the earliest Americans undertook their historical journeys in a unique geographic laboratory.

HISTORICAL THINKING

1. **READING CHECK** How and when did the first humans settle in the Americas?

2. **MAKE INFERENCES** What makes Monte Verde an important archaeological site?

3. **COMPARE AND CONTRAST** What were the similarities and differences between the ways in which the first Americans adapted to their various environments?

Clovis Point Discoveries

Coastline at 75m below current sea level
Glacial ice 12,000 years before present
Glacial ice 13,000 years before present

CLOVIS POINT DISTRIBUTION
1–4 5–12 13–34 35–54 88–142
No sites reported finding 55–87 Clovis points.

Makers of Clovis spear points chose glassy rocks of striking colors to craft finely worked stone points.

0 250 500 Miles
0 250 500 Kilometers

PLAN: 2-PAGE LESSON

OBJECTIVE

Explain how descendants of early humans fanned out across North and South America and adapted to diverse environments.

CRITICAL THINKING SKILLS FOR LESSON 1.1

- Make Inferences
- Compare and Contrast
- Identify Main Ideas and Details
- Synthesize

HISTORICAL THINKING FOR CHAPTER 14

How did early American societies emerge and interact before European contact?

Archaeologists are searching for evidence that reveals when and how humans first arrived in the Americas. Lesson 1.1 discusses where some of the first humans settled and describes how they adapted to their new environments in the Americas.

Student eEdition online

Additional content for this lesson, including an illustration, is available online.

BACKGROUND FOR THE TEACHER

The Americas' First Inhabitants Monte Verde is located near the southern tip of Chile, where Chilean lumbermen once stumbled across the ancient bones of a mastodon. Excavation of the site has since revealed the wooden posts of a 60-foot-long structure, the remains of two hearths, fragments of preserved meat, firewood, wooden slabs for grinding, and the broken pieces of rudimentary stone tools, all dating back between 17,000 and 19,000 years ago. The discovery at this and other coastal settlements has challenged an important earlier hypothesis that the Americas' first human inhabitants were large game hunters who had arrived on foot in North America about 13,000 years ago. Distinctive Clovis spearpoints uncovered across the lower 48 states seemed to support this theory, and radiocarbon dating of the spears determined the age of most to be around 13,000 years old. In another coastal settlement, the Paisley Caves in present-day Oregon, archaeologists have found evidence of baskets and ropes older than 14,000 years.

INTRODUCE & ENGAGE

DISCUSS ARCHAEOLOGICAL EVIDENCE

Direct students to the illustration of the hunter (available in the Student eEdition) and point out that archaeologists in North and South America have discovered fragments of weapons such as the bolo. **ASK:** What other types of evidence do you think archaeologists have found, and what can these artifacts tell us about the first inhabitants of the Americas? *(Possible response: Archaeologists have probably found fragments of pots and tools that can tell us what the people ate and how they hunted.)* Tell students that they will learn how the first Americans lived and adapted to diverse environments.

TEACH

GUIDED DISCUSSION

1. **Identify Main Ideas and Details** What differences did early Americans begin to develop as they adapted to various environments across North and South America? *(Early Americans began to develop differences in language, culture, and modes of living.)*

2. **Synthesize** What do the tools found at Monte Verde suggest about the ability of early Americans to adapt to various environments? *(Possible response: that early Americans were resourceful, inventive, and devised tools to hunt different kinds of prey)*

MAKE INFERENCES

Have students examine the photograph of the Clovis spear points. **ASK:** Why do you think spear points are a common archaeological discovery in the Americas? *(Possible response: They don't break down like other artifacts and are numerous because hunting was a regular necessity.)* What can you infer about the Americas' first inhabitants based on these artifacts? *(Possible response: I can infer that they were skilled hunters, and wild game was an important food source.)*

ACTIVE OPTIONS

On Your Feet: Jigsaw Strategy Organize students into four "expert" groups and assign each group one of the following lesson topics: migration, hunting and gathering, farming, and adaptation. Instruct groups to review important ideas and details related to their assigned topics. Then regroup students into new groups so that each new group has at least one member from each expert group. Students in the new groups take turns sharing information from their expert groups.

| **NG Learning Framework: Create a Multimedia Presentation**
| **SKILL** Communication
| **KNOWLEDGE** Our Human Story

Arrange students in small groups and ask them to develop a multimedia presentation on some of the settlements and communities that arose in the Americas. Tell students that their presentations should cover the topics of migration and adaption. Encourage them to present information in a way that is clear and engaging, using visuals to enhance the information they share with the class.

DIFFERENTIATE

ENGLISH LANGUAGE LEARNERS

Use Word Parts Pair students at the **Beginning** or **Intermediate** level with students at the **Advanced** level. Direct pairs to identify the parts of the word *megafauna* and use a dictionary to investigate the meanings. Instruct students to write one sentence using the word and another using the root (*fauna*). Suggest that as students encounter unfamiliar compound words like this, they use word parts to determine meaning.

PRE-AP

Form and Support a Thesis Have students conduct research to learn more about the Wisconsin Ice Age. Then instruct them to develop a thesis regarding how the climate change impacted human migration and the societies settling in affected regions. Tell students to write an essay supporting their thesis with primary and secondary sources. Encourage students to share their essays on a class website or blog.

See the Chapter Planner for more strategies for differentiation.

HISTORICAL THINKING

ANSWERS

1. The first Americans arrived by traveling down the west coast of North and South America in small boats more than 14,000 years ago.

2. Monte Verde contains the earliest proof of humans in the Americas. The peat there preserved organic materials like wood, skin, and plants that can be studied by archaeologists.

3. Residents of South and North America both hunted wild game and gathered wild fruits and seeds. But the two groups used different types of weapons to kill animals for food. South American people also foraged along the coast.

Early Complex Societies

Indigenous peoples from the Arctic to Patagonia successfully adapted to varied surroundings and habitats. It was only in places where agricultural surpluses led to significant population density, however, that we find the transition to complex societies.

FOUNDATIONS OF COMPLEX SOCIETIES

The history of farming in the Americas began independently from the Neolithic revolution in Eurasia, and it is nearly as old. Squash was first domesticated in the Americas about 10,000 years ago. Soon, the people of Mesoamerica began to grow maize—which is similar to corn—squash, and beans. These foods offer excellent nutritional benefits when eaten together. Because of this advanced nutrition, by 2500 B.C.E., the population of Mesoamerica had increased by about 25 times. Mesoamericans did not start to domesticate animals, such as turkeys, until much later, around 800 B.C.E.

In the Andes Mountains in South America, agriculture developed differently. While Andean people also ate squash, beans, and maize, the main diet staple was potatoes. Over time, they developed many types of potatoes to improve their diets. Also, by planting different crops at different altitudes, Andean farmers increased their food security: if one crop failed, others might still grow well.

Around 4000 B.C.E., the Andeans domesticated the llama, the alpaca, and the capybara, a mammal that resembles a modern guinea pig but weighs 145 pounds or more in adulthood. Llamas and alpacas were used for their wool and as pack animals. Capybaras were raised for their meat. Unlike people in other parts of the world, early Americans never used the wheel or the plow to help them farm.

The earliest complex societies in the Americas developed in present-day Peru in the Andean region of South America, which extends from the Amazon rain forest in the east to the Pacific coast in the west. The earliest large urban community, Caral, arose in about 3100 B.C.E., around the same time cities first appeared in Mesopotamia. Caral's social classes were revealed in its architecture. Wealthy people lived in large dwellings on top of pyramids, artisans resided in smaller houses at the base of pyramids, and unskilled laborers had much simpler homes at the edge of the city. About 20 smaller towns have been found near Caral.

Early Complex Societies in the Americas

Several hundred years after the decline of Caral in 1800 B.C.E., the Chavín civilization developed. The Chavín people built cities with large temples and stone sculptures and developed a religion that would influence later Andean civilizations. The most famous Chavín site is Chavín de Huantar, which had a population of 2,000–3,000 people and stretched out over 100 acres. No one is certain why the Chavín civilization declined, but earthquakes or drought may have played a part.

LEGACIES OF THE OLMEC, ZAPOTEC, AND TEOTIHUACÁN

The Olmec civilization developed in Mesoamerica at about the same time as the Chavín. The Olmec are considered the first advanced technological culture in the Americas. Their civilization consisted of at least five cities in the coastal region of what are now the Mexican states of Veracruz and Tabasco. Scholars are still learning about the Olmec, but they consider the Olmec the **mother culture** of the Mesoamerican societies that followed.

Scholars do know that the Olmec had social classes, a basic writing system, and an organized religion. The Olmec traded extensively and as far south as present-day Nicaragua. They drank chocolate, built pyramids, played ball games, and created incredible works of art, including small sculptures and colossal stone heads.

Several cultures that traded with the Olmec developed their own complex civilizations, including the Zapotec. The Zapotec lived in the southern highlands in the Oaxaca Valley and built the cities of San José Mogote and Monte Albán. Like other Mesoamerican civilizations, Zapotec cities had plazas, pyramids, palaces, and an astronomical observatory. Like other mountain peoples, the Zapotec built **terraces**, or stepped platforms, in the hills to create more room for their crops.

Another important Mesoamerican culture was centered in the city of Teotihuacán, which lasted from 200 B.C.E. to 650 C.E., and is the earliest known civilization in the Valley of Mexico. This area would later become home to the Toltec and Aztec cultures, both of which were heavily influenced by Teotihuacán. The largest city in the Americas before 1500, Teotihuacán covered 8 square

NATIONAL GEOGRAPHIC EXPLORER MATTHEW PISCITELLI

Exploring Peru's Ancient Past

About 5,000 years ago, the first complex societies in the Americas developed in a region along the north central coast of modern-day Peru called Norte Chico, or "Little North." In four river valleys in the region, people established permanent farming villages and built monumental structures for conducting religious ceremonies. Archaeologist and National Geographic Explorer Matthew Piscitelli works to investigate and preserve what remains of these settlements. In his research, he incorporates scientific tools such as drones and radar to map sites and identify buried structures.

Archaeologists have discovered about 30 large settlements with stepped platform mounds and sunken circular plazas in Norte Chico. According to Piscitelli, these large-scale structures served as religious centers that attracted visitors from outlying areas. He regards the Norte Chico settlements as a mother culture that greatly influenced cultures that followed. The Norte Chico culture set the stage for later Andean cultures, including the mighty Inca Empire.

miles and had a population of 200,000. Most people lived in one-story apartment compounds that were divided among several families. The outsides of the compounds had no windows and were painted white, while the interiors were covered with colorful frescoes. The city had a plumbing system that drained wastewater into underground channels that drained into canals.

Sometime around 600 C.E., major buildings in Teotihuacán were set on fire and artworks destroyed. The damage may have been the work of invaders, as it seems the city had no military fortifications. Many scholars, however, believe that the violence shows a revolt by the poor against the wealthy elite. In any case, Teotihuacán's population began to decline. By 750, the city was abandoned.

HISTORICAL THINKING

1. **READING CHECK** What major crops did the earliest societies in the Americas develop, and why were they so important to the development of complex civilizations?

2. **INTERPRET MAPS** Why do you think ancient American civilizations developed along coastal areas?

3. **DRAW CONCLUSIONS** Why would the existence of large buildings or extensive irrigation projects be a sign of a complex society?

PLAN: 2-PAGE LESSON

OBJECTIVE

Explain how early inhabitants of the Americas developed agriculture and complex societies similar to others around the world.

CRITICAL THINKING SKILLS FOR LESSON 1.2

- Interpret Maps
- Draw Conclusions
- Analyze Cause and Effect
- Identify
- Make Connections

HISTORICAL THINKING FOR CHAPTER 14

How did early American societies emerge and interact before European contact?

Lesson 1.2 discusses the importance of agriculture and animal domestication in the emergence of Mesoamerica's and South America's first complex societies.

BACKGROUND FOR THE TEACHER

Olmec Heads Only 17 stone Olmec heads have been uncovered, 10 of which have been found in San Lorenzo and La Venta. Archaeologists have determined that each head was carved from a single basalt boulder. Experts theorize that sculptors only depicted the head because, according to Mesoamerican culture, the head was believed to be where the soul resided. Artists carved the heads using hard stones. They used reeds and wet sand to form the eyes, nose, mouth, and ears. Originally, the heads were probably painted in bright colors, but these have long since worn off.

Student eEdition online

Additional content for this lesson, including images, is available online.

INTRODUCE & ENGAGE

DISCUSS CLIMATE AND GEOGRAPHY

Direct students to the map of early complex societies in the Americas. Invite volunteers to point out geographical features near each settlement and share what they know about the climates of these regions. Discuss the ways climate and geography may have influenced how these societies adapted to life in the Americas, based on what they have learned about other emerging societies. Then tell students that in Lesson 1.2 they will learn that these societies embraced new agricultural practices and technologies to thrive.

TEACH

GUIDED DISCUSSION

1. **Analyze Cause and Effect** What key resources led to the development of complex societies in Mesoamerica and why? *(The ability to farm and produce agricultural surpluses allowed people to stay in one place and led to an increase in population and the development of more complex societies.)*

2. **Identify** What technologies did the Olmec develop? *(a writing system, pyramids, colossal works of art)*

DRAW CONCLUSIONS

Discuss the work of National Geographic Explorer Matthew Piscitelli with the class. Point out that the archaeologist focuses on preserving the remains of sites in the Norte Chico region of Peru. **ASK:** What purpose did the platform mounds and sunken plazas in the Norte Chico settlements serve? *(They were used as religious centers.)* Why does Piscitelli regard Norte Chico as a mother culture? *(It influenced many Andean cultures that followed.)* Then have students study the photo of Piscitelli. **ASK:** Based on the photo, what challenges do you think the archaeologist faces in his work? *(Possible response: hard physical work; uncertainties about where to dig; having to deal with weather, mud, and bugs)*

ACTIVE OPTIONS

On Your Feet: Four Corners Arrange students into four teams and have each team go to a different corner of the room. Assign each group one of the civilizations discussed in this lesson—Chavín, Olmec, Zapotec, or Teotihuacán—and instruct students to discuss what they've learned about the civilization. Then have at least one student from each corner summarize the group's discussion for the other three groups.

| NG Learning Framework: Research Mesoamerican Achievements
| ATTITUDE Observation
| KNOWLEDGE Our Human Story

Encourage groups of students to research Mesoamerican achievements in astronomy, mathematics, and the development of the calendar. Have each group select one topic and find three facts about it to share with the class. Then have groups take turns presenting their sets of facts to the class.

DIFFERENTIATE

STRIVING READERS

Understand Main Ideas Check students' understanding of the main ideas by asking the following questions:

- What was one of the first animals domesticated by Mesoamericans—the turkey or the capybara? *(turkey)*
- Where did the earliest complex societies develop in the Americas— present-day Mexico or present-day Peru? *(present-day Peru)*
- What common farming technology was never used by early Americans— animal domestication or the wheel and plow? *(the wheel and plow)*
- What archaeological findings reveal Caral's social class system— tablet inscriptions or architecture? *(architecture)*

GIFTED & TALENTED

Create a 3-D Model Have students research and create a 3-D model of one of the archaeological sites referenced in the lesson. Invite volunteers to present their models to the class.

See the Chapter Planner for more strategies for differentiation.

HISTORICAL THINKING

ANSWERS

1. Early Americans grew maize, squash, beans, and potatoes, which are extremely nutritious, which led to population growth. Larger populations allowed complex societies to form.

2. They built their communities along the coast to be close to water sources.

3. Because these types of projects require specialized skills and the coordinated activity of a large group of people with enough free time to engage in an activity not related to day-to-day survival.

CRITICAL VIEWING Possible response: Olmec leaders were powerful and respected.

Classic and Post-Classic Maya Civilization

In 2018, scientists scanned a section of the Guatemalan lowlands and digitally removed the forest cover. They discovered something that amazed the world: huge numbers of previously unknown buildings, raised roads, quarries, irrigation systems, and terraced fields. All these features were created by the Maya, an ancient American culture that flourished for thousands of years.

ECONOMY AND POLITICS

For many years, experts understood that the Maya developed an advanced civilization that, starting in 1500 B.C.E., thrived for more than three millennia on the Yucatán Peninsula between the Gulf of Mexico and the Caribbean Sea. The Maya built a series of independent city-states, developed an accurate calendar, and were constantly at war with one another—or so archaeologists thought. The structures revealed by the land scans in 2018 showed that Maya city-states did not only interact through war. In fact, scientists now believe that Maya society was more interconnected and densely populated than anyone had realized.

The understanding of Maya society is still defined by its cities and architecture, however. Some Maya cities from the Classic Period (250–900 C.E.) include Copán, Tikal, Chichén Itzá (chee-CHEHN eet-SAH), and Palenque (pah-LEHNG-kay). Each city had a large central plaza that was used both as a market and for religious ceremonies, a palace, government buildings, temples, pyramids, and at least one ball court. The Maya ball game dated back to the Olmec and was a central part of Maya life. The ball game was not only an entertainment; it also had significant religious meaning.

To feed people in these cities, the Maya conquered the landscape, learning to control water to their advantage; they built canals, reservoirs, and dykes—or dams—even in swampy areas that modern scientists thought were uninhabitable. Their raised roadways were passable even during floods. Like the Zapotec, they terraced fields. And like earlier Mesoamerican peoples, the Maya practiced **slash-and-burn agriculture**, a method of clearing fields for planting in which people cut down trees, burned them, and used the ash as fertilizer.

This colorful fresco in a Maya temple in Bonampak, Mexico, shows a procession of musicians. The temples that contain these murals were suddenly abandoned around 800, a time when work on many other monuments stopped abruptly, marking the end of the Classic Period.

Maya city-states were ruled by kings who believed that they were descended from the gods. However, these rulers were not always completely independent of one another. In some cases, a ruler could be a vassal to a more powerful king. And queens were religiously important and could hold power in their own right. Recent analysis reveals a tradition of warrior queens, shown on carvings as armed for battle. On one, a queen known as Ix Naah Ek' wears the helmet of the Maya god of war. On other carvings, women are depicted standing on the heads of conquered enemies.

Pacal the Great was one of the most impressive Maya kings. He ruled the city of Palenque in present-day southeastern Mexico, near the Guatemalan border. Before Pacal ascended the throne at age 12, Lady Sak K'uk, his mother, served as regent. Pacal ruled his city for almost 70 years and took Palenque from a small, relatively unimportant place to one of the greatest cities in Mesoamerican history. Today, only a small part of the city has been studied.

Maya society was strictly divided into classes. The nobility included priests, warriors, and scribes. Below the nobility came merchants, artisans, and architects. Next were the farmers, who made up the majority of the population. The lowest class was made up of enslaved people. They were usually acquired through war, did much of the agricultural work, and sometimes served as sacrifices to the gods.

PEOPLE, CULTURE, AND TECHNOLOGY

Maya civilization seems to have been defined by warfare. Leaders of individual city-states battled one another to extend their territory, power, and influence. The Maya also needed captives to use in the frequent blood sacrifices demanded by their religion. Sometimes the people of a city, especially the king and queen, provided the blood themselves, but most often the blood was provided by sacrificing warriors who had been captured in battle.

The Maya were skilled artists who created beautiful works of pottery, sculpture, weaving, and painting. They worked with gold and copper but no other metals. They were the only ancient American civilization to develop a complex system of writing, which they used on stelae, in tomb art, and in folded books made of tree-bark paper called **codices**. (The singular term is *codex*.) Their

THE POPOL VUH Much of the Maya belief system is recorded in the oral epic *Popul Vuh* (POHP-uhl voo), or "The Council Book," which is the most complete surviving pre-Columbian text in the Americas and tells the story of the origins of the gods, humanity, and the Maya people. It was written down after the Spanish conquest, using Roman script but the Mayan language. Recently, archaeologists discovered sections of the story inscribed on stelae, proving that at least parts of the epic were written down before the Spanish arrived.

writing also recorded their sophisticated mathematical and scientific calculations.

At the time, the Maya numerical system was more advanced than any in the world. The Maya understood the concept of zero and were able to calculate sums into the hundreds of millions. Astronomers built observatories and used their mathematical skills to track the movements of the sun, moon, and stars. They observed the stars and planets so closely that they could predict eclipses. The Maya also created a complex ritual calendar as well as a 365-day solar calendar that is nearly as accurate as the one used today.

The Maya were great writers. Though many of their works included mathematical and scientific calculations, the Maya also wrote about their gods and their history. They left inscriptions on temples, in pyramids, on pottery, and in codices. It took hundreds of years of study for experts to discover how to read the Mayan script, which is made up of about 800 glyphs.

After about 800 C.E., the Maya entered an era of decline, which could have been the result of their unending wars. Another cause may have been environmental. The tropical environment around the main cities is highly sensitive and can easily be overfarmed. Competition for scarce land and food may have fed into the vicious cycle of warfare. A long drought between 800 and 1050 may have played a role as well. The urban-temple complex revived between 910 and 1500 but never achieved its former glory. Today, about 10 million Mayan speakers live in Guatemala, Honduras, Belize, El Salvador, Mexico, and the United States.

HISTORICAL THINKING

1. **READING CHECK** Why are the Maya considered one of the world's great civilizations?

2. **EVALUATE** How did the carvings of queens reveal their role in Maya society?

3. **ANALYZE CAUSE AND EFFECT** How might overfarming have contributed to the decline of the Maya civilization?

PLAN: 2-PAGE LESSON

OBJECTIVE

Examine the Maya, a complex and sophisticated urban society that flourished for thousands of years.

CRITICAL THINKING SKILLS FOR LESSON 1.3

- Evaluate
- Analyze Cause and Effect
- Make Inferences
- Analyze Visuals

HISTORICAL THINKING FOR CHAPTER 14

How did early American societies emerge and interact before European contact?

Lesson 1.3 discusses the emergence and growth of the Maya, a sophisticated civilization that in its Classic and Post-Classic periods rivaled the civilizations of Greece and China.

Student eEdition online

Additional content for this lesson, including a sidebar, an image, an illustration, a map, a video, and a Global Commodity feature, is available online.

BACKGROUND FOR THE TEACHER

Maya Warrior Queens The theory that Maya women participated in battles, captured enemies, and ruled independently is a relatively new one and was the result of a painstaking re-examination of existing Maya artifacts and studies. Archaeologists were able to glean new information and insight into the lives of royal women from frescoes, hieroglyphic inscriptions, and carved stelae. For instance, based on a closer study of the styles of dress ornamentation depicted in carvings, archaeologists were able to identify female figures who had been mistaken as male figures. Similarly, through closer study of Maya writing found in inscriptions on key artifacts, researchers were able to develop a better understanding of Maya family dynasties. This allowed them to form new hypotheses about the cultural and political shifts that put women into positions of power. Their research shows that women during the seventh and eighth centuries C.E. frequently ruled during times of war.

History Notebook

Encourage students to complete the "Chocolate" Global Commodity page for Chapter 14 in their History Notebooks as they read.

INTRODUCE & ENGAGE

PREVIEW USING VISUALS

Draw students' attention to the visuals in this lesson—the photographs of the Maya tomb and the stone ring, the illustration of the Mesoamerican ball game, and the map (available in the Student eEdition). Draw a two-column chart on the board, labeling the left column *Questions* and the right column *Answers*. Ask students what questions these visuals bring to mind. Record their questions in the chart. Later, after students have read and discussed the lesson, prompt them to answer as many of the listed questions as they can.

TEACH

GUIDED DISCUSSION

1. **Make Inferences** Why were farmers and enslaved people critical to the emergence and growth of Maya society? *(They did most of the agricultural work necessary, which allowed others to develop and perform the specialized jobs that help a society grow.)*

2. **Analyze Visuals** Which modern sports today most resemble the Mesoamerican ball game? *(basketball, soccer)*

ANALYZE VISUALS

Discuss the Global Commodity feature on chocolate (available in the Student eEdition) with the class. **ASK:** Why was chocolate reserved for the upper classes in Maya and Aztec society? *(The Maya and Aztec believed chocolate had divine properties, so they probably thought the lower classes weren't worthy of it. In addition, cacao beans were valuable, so the lower classes almost certainly couldn't afford to buy them.)* Have students look at the images of chocolate in the feature and read the captions. Ask students what they find interesting or surprising about the images.

ACTIVE OPTIONS

On Your Feet: Roundtable Arrange students in groups of four to take part in a Roundtable discussion about the various ways Maya society adapted to their natural environment and flourished as a culture. Ask each member of the group to name one fact they learned about Maya practices and inventions, such as slash-and-burn agriculture, a complex writing system, a numerical system, observatories, and a calendar. Then instruct each group to discuss and decide which of these developments is most important and why.

> **NG Learning Framework: Research Maya Cities**
> **ATTITUDE** Curiosity
> **SKILL** Communication

Organize students in groups of two or three and instruct them to research a Maya city from the Classic period discussed in this lesson—Copán, Tikal, Chichén Itzá, or Palenque—and the people who lived there. Instruct students to organize their findings in a list of key details. Once they have completed their lists, prompt each group to exchange lists with another group. Ask groups to note similarities and differences between the lists. Finally, have the class review the lists and discuss the students' findings.

DIFFERENTIATE

STRIVING READERS

Create an Annotated Chart To help students learn about the social structure of Maya society, provide pairs with a pyramid-shaped chart divided into four rows. Then have pairs review the text about Maya social structure and add facts to the chart. Invite pairs to compare and discuss their completed charts, making changes or additions.

ENGLISH LANGUAGE LEARNERS

Read in Pairs Pair students at the **Beginning** and **Advanced** levels with English-proficient students and have them read the lesson together. Instruct the native speakers to pause whenever they encounter a word or sentence that is confusing. Suggest that the native speakers point out context clues to help their partners understand the meanings of unfamiliar terms. Encourage English language learners to restate sentences in their own words.

See the Chapter Planner for more strategies for differentiation.

HISTORICAL THINKING

ANSWERS

1. The Maya built large cities, which required sophisticated technology. They had advanced mathematical and astronomical understanding, an accurate solar calendar, and a complex writing system.

2. The carvings depict queens armed for battle standing on the heads of conquered enemies, which shows that the queens were powerful in Maya society.

3. Land that is overfarmed is less productive and not able to support as many people. Fewer people and less food production probably drove people from the Maya civilization.

Discovering Maya Secrets
Underwater

"The sacred geography of the Maya is important because it's exactly why we are doing our work." –Guillermo de Anda

Archaeologist Guillermo de Anda descends into the Holtún cenote in Chichén Itzá, Mexico.

Guillermo de Anda is not a typical archaeologist. He doesn't excavate remains covered by dirt at a dry and dusty site. Instead, he puts on a wetsuit and rappels several stories into caves full of water. De Anda then straps on his underwater gear, organizes any necessary scientific equipment, and swims back to the time of the Maya. It's dangerous and precise work. "We have a saying that it's easier to train someone to be an archaeologist than to be a cave diver," he says.

MAIN IDEA National Geographic Explorer Guillermo de Anda's explorations of underwater caves in Mexico have revealed new information about the Maya and their way of life.

PRAYING FOR RAIN

Scientists such as de Anda use the latest technology to investigate new environments and provide new information about the first peoples of the Americas. One such environment is the *cenote*, a large natural pool or open cave. The Maya believed caves served as portals between the world of the living and the underworld. There, they practiced sacred ceremonies, including human sacrifices and communication with the dead.

De Anda specializes in mapping and exploring cenotes and underwater caves to research the Maya. In 2010, he explored the Holtún cenote. This cenote is located 1.6 miles northwest of El Castillo, the large Maya pyramid at Chichén Itzá. He found carefully arranged human skeletons and items such as pottery, fragments of carved figures, a flint knife, and the remains of birds, dogs, and stingrays. Some experts believe that the Maya sacrifices and gifts were an appeal to the rain god Chaak to provide needed rainfall for their crops.

According to the *Popul Vuh*, the Maya cosmos had four sides and four corners. El Castillo stands in the middle of four cenotes: Holtún, Xtoloc, Kanjuyum, and the Sacred Cenote. In February 2018, de Anda and his team began an attempt to reach a hidden, blocked cenote under the pyramid itself. He believes a successful excavation could lead to evidence of a "fifth direction" or other clues to Maya beliefs and rituals.

PLUNGING INTO THE PAST

Accessing and studying cenotes requires a lot of experience and a lot of preparation in challenging conditions. "You also have to stay a long time under the water," de Anda explains. "Sometimes we will spend six or seven hours in the water. That's the most demanding part because you still have to go back, you're tired, cold, hungry."

In addition to their scuba gear, underwater archaeologists also have to contend with bulky technology that helps them gather information. One such tool is ground-penetrating radar, or GPR. GPR can be used to find and map hidden tunnels or caves, including cenotes. Thermal imaging and LiDAR can detect some of the estimated 3,000 cenotes in southern Mexico that are concealed by dense forests. Researchers also mount sonar equipment on kayaks and use laser-scanning and photogrammetry to generate 3-D versions of the caves.

In January 2018, de Anda and a team of archaeologists discovered a passage that links the flooded cavern systems of Sac Actun and Dos Ojos. This flooded freshwater cave in the Yucatán Peninsula is now the world's largest and measures 215 miles long. It contains important evidence of the Maya as well as the very first Americans.

In March 2019, de Anda and other specialists announced the discovery of a cave system under Chichén Itzá that contains well-preserved ritual items dating back more than a thousand years. To reach the cave known to locals as Balamkú, or Jaguar God, de Anda had to crawl on his stomach for hours through incredibly narrow tunnels. "When I get to the first offering," he notes, "I realized I was in a very very very sacred place." He adds, "You almost feel the presence of the Maya who deposited these things in there." Continuing studies may provide additional clues to the rise and fall of this mighty civilization. "Balamkú will help rewrite the story of Chichen Itzá," de Anda claims.

HISTORICAL THINKING

1. **READING CHECK** Why are the discoveries of Guillermo de Anda and his team important?

2. **ANALYZE CAUSE AND EFFECT** What is the effect of technology on the work of de Anda and other archaeologists?

Civilizations in the Americas 391

PLAN: 2-PAGE LESSON

OBJECTIVE
Identify what new information Guillermo de Anda's explorations of underwater caves in Mexico have revealed about the Maya and their way of life.

CRITICAL THINKING SKILLS FOR LESSON 1.4
- Analyze Cause and Effect
- Identify
- Explain
- Analyze Visuals

HISTORICAL THINKING FOR CHAPTER 14
How did early American societies emerge and interact before European contact?

Lesson 1.4 explores the information gained from underwater archaeological investigations of flooded caves where the Maya performed sacred rituals and buried their dead.

Student eEdition online
Additional content for this lesson, including a diagram, is available online.

BACKGROUND FOR THE TEACHER

Guillermo de Anda Authorities had known about the cave system at Balamkú for more than 50 years, but the entrance to it had remained sealed to protect the cave's contents. Guillermo de Anda was among the first archaeologists to explore the site. He found at least 200 artifacts there, which dated to around 700 to 1000 C.E. The items he found included ceramic incense holders and containers, which probably held offerings for the gods. The likeness of Tlaloc, the rain god of Central Mexico, appears on some of the incense holders, suggesting that the Maya closely interacted with other civilizations. Because he found so many artifacts—and they were in such hard-to-reach places in the cave—de Anda believes the site was highly important in Chichén Itzá.

History Notebook
Encourage students to complete the National Geographic Explorer page for Chapter 14 in their History Notebooks as they read.

INTRODUCE & ENGAGE

PREVIEW VOCABULARY

Ask students to name land formations with which they are familiar. Then ask them if they are familiar with the word *cenote*. Explain that a cenote is an underground cave formation created by the collapse of a limestone surface, revealing a store of freshwater beneath. Cenotes can be found in other parts of the world, where they are more often called sinkholes, but are especially prevalent in the Yucatán Peninsula in Mexico. Tell students that in this lesson they will learn about the cenotes that National Geographic Explorer Guillermo de Anda has investigated.

TEACH

GUIDED DISCUSSION

1. **Identify** What were cenotes used for by the Maya? *(Cenotes were used for practicing sacred ceremonies, such as human sacrifices and rituals related to communicating with the dead, and as a primary water source.)*

2. **Explain** What is Balamkú, and why is it significant? *(It is a cave system under Chichén Itzá, which de Anda reached by crawling through narrow tunnels for hours. The site may provide clues to the rise and fall of the Maya.)*

ANALYZE VISUALS

Direct students to view the features of the Holtún cenote diagram (available in the Student eEdition). Explain that the Maya used the cenotes as sacred sundials, using the sun's zenith to calibrate their agricultural calendar. **ASK:** How did the Maya adapt the naturally occurring cenote to aid their solar observations? *(They carved the jagged mouth into a rectangle to allow the sunlight to flow straight in.)* How does the diagram put the size of the cenote into perspective? *(Possible response: The diagram includes trees on the land above the cenote, figures of people at the top and on the shelf, and a scale showing the depth from the top to the bottom.)*

ACTIVE OPTIONS

On Your Feet: Numbered Heads Organize students into groups of four. Tell students to think about and discuss a response to this question: What has Guillermo de Anda discovered in his explorations of Maya cenotes? Then call a number and have the student from each group with that number report for the group.

> **NG Learning Framework: Create a Travel Brochure**
> **ATTITUDE** Curiosity
> **SKILL** Communication

Tell students that many cenotes are popular tourist attractions. Have them conduct research to create a travel brochure for a chosen cenote in the Yucatán with photos and information for prospective travelers that answer the following questions: What is a cenote? Where is this cenote? Why should I visit it? What are its features? What flora and fauna may I encounter? What else do I need to know (temperature, items to bring, and so on)? Encourage students to choose different cenotes to provide variety. Have students share their completed brochures with the class.

DIFFERENTIATE

STRIVING READERS

Understand Unfamiliar Terms Point out terms used in the lesson that students might not be familiar with, such as *portal*, *anemic*, *contend*, and *photogrammetry*. Tell pairs to use the text and a dictionary, if needed, to clarify the meanings of these terms and any other unfamiliar words they encounter and then to create sentences using the terms.

GIFTED & TALENTED

Write Journal Entries Ask students to imagine that they are archaeologists searching for Maya artifacts in a cenote for the first time. Have them write several journal entries describing their work, the moment of discovery, and their emotions. Then have volunteers share their journal entries with the class.

See the Chapter Planner for more strategies for differentiation.

HISTORICAL THINKING

ANSWERS

1. Discoveries made by Guillermo de Anda and his team are important because the finds provide more clues about the Maya people and their culture.

2. Technology has enabled de Anda and other archaeologists to make new discoveries, which has expanded people's understanding of early cultures.

Northern Cultures

What was North America like when Europeans arrived? For generations, students were taught it was an empty, wild land sparsely populated with small bands of Native Americans hunting and fighting one another. The truth is quite different— and far more interesting.

EARLY NORTH AMERICANS

Millions of Native American people lived across vast territories in what are now the United States and Canada. They were organized into hundreds of different societies.

Many early North American archaeological sites are located along the rivers of the midwestern United States. The Adena culture, the oldest known complex society, built large **earthworks**, or constructions of soil and rocks, along the Ohio River Valley in Ohio and Illinois between 500 B.C.E. and 100 C.E. No evidence demonstrates that the Adena raised crops, but they did trade with other groups and engaged in mound-building.

The Hopewell people, who established themselves between 200 B.C.E. and 500 C.E., were both farmers and mound-builders. They grew crops and built large earthworks in the valleys of the Ohio, Illinois, and Mississippi rivers. The Hopewell had a larger trade network than the Adena, and archaeologists believe that the Hopewell mounds were also well-known religious sites that attracted Native American pilgrims.

Between 800 and 1450, the Mississippian culture developed one of the first urban societies in North America. This society was centered around the Mississippi River Valley, but it reached as far east as present-day Georgia and as far south as New Orleans. The Mississippian people built large urban centers and were the first known group in the Americas to use bows and arrows.

North American Civilizations, 1000 B.C.E.–1500 C.E.

More than 100 different Mississippian sites have been discovered. These towns and cities followed a plan similar to that used by the Maya, with temples and mounds around a central plaza. Recent investigations have focused on evidence of cultural and archaeological influences flowing from the Yucatán Peninsula to places such as Cahokia, the largest of the Mississippian cities.

Located in present-day Illinois, experts claim that Cahokia sprang up between 1000 and 1100, its population swelling from about 7,000 to 15,000. The Cahokians built houses, an expansive plaza as large as 45 football fields, and more than 100 mounds. The largest mound—Mound 38—stands nearly 100 feet high and has a base larger than that of the Great Pyramid of Giza in Egypt.

Recent studies have shown that Cahokia was a place of pilgrimage and an astronomical site. It may have been used for complex calculations, showing that the people of Cahokia—perhaps learning from the Maya—may have had the advanced knowledge to predict eclipses.

Archaeologists recently found evidence of another ancient city in the Midwest. Etzanoa is located between the Arkansas and Walnut rivers near Wichita, Kansas. It is thought to have flourished between 1450 and 1700 and been home to at least 20,000 people. Ancestors of the Wichita people, the people of Etzanoa were farmers and buffalo hunters from today's Oklahoma and Texas who traded meat and hides to the Pueblo people in return for cotton, obsidian, and turquoise.

THE ANASAZI

The Pueblo peoples—Hopi, Zuni, Acoma, and Laguna—located in what is now the southwestern United States have a long and intriguing history. Their predecessors were the ancestral Pueblo, or Anasazi, who flourished between 100 and 1600. One of the most famous civilizations in North America, the Anasazi originated in present-day Colorado, Arizona, Utah, and New Mexico. At their height, they may have lived in thousands of different communities connected by a 400-mile network of roads and spread over almost 30,000 square miles.

Anasazi villages and towns show signs of contact with the Mesoamerican cultures, particularly in the design of their ball courts. The Anasazi used irrigation to farm, and their craftspeople made distinctive pottery, cotton and feather clothing, and turquoise jewelry. Early Anasazi lived in caves or pit houses carved out of the ground. Starting in about 700, they expanded their territory and began to live in small villages. Their buildings were made with bricks and mortar and had log roofs. Some of these buildings had as many as 100 connected rooms.

The Chaco culture thrived between 850 and 1250 during a particularly mysterious period of Anasazi history centered around Chaco Canyon, New Mexico. The Chacoans were skilled astronomers and used advanced water control and collection techniques. They erected huge stone buildings called "great houses." The great houses were often oriented to the sun and moon and were within direct view of one another, which enabled quick communication over long distances. It is possible

CRITICAL VIEWING The ancient Pueblo built individual dwellings connected to one another, as shown here in Mesa Verde. Based on details from the photograph, why do you think the people chose to build Mesa Verde where they did?

that these great houses were not villages but political, religious, or trading centers that were populated only at particular times or for specific events. No one is certain.

After 1150, the Anasazi abandoned the towns and great houses and started to live in large communities built into the sides of cliffs. The most famous Anasazi cliff city is **Mesa Verde**, in Colorado. After only about 50 years, the Anasazi began to vacate their cliff homes. No one is sure why the Anasazi moved to the cliffs or why they left them. One recent theory is that the Anasazi were driven out by internal strife. Whatever the reason, the Anasazi deserted their cliff dwellings and moved to other parts of the Southwest, including the White Mountains of Arizona and the Rio Grande Valley

HISTORICAL THINKING

1. **READING CHECK** In what types of environments did the oldest complex societies develop in North America?

2. **COMPARE AND CONTRAST** How were many North American civilizations similar to and different from Mesoamerican cultures?

3. **INTERPRET MAPS** Where were most of the mound builders' sites located, and why?

PLAN: 2-PAGE LESSON

OBJECTIVE

Explain how early modern humans who migrated and settled in present-day Canada and the United States developed complex societies.

CRITICAL THINKING SKILLS FOR LESSON 1.5

- Compare and Contrast
- Interpret Maps
- Draw Conclusions
- Make Inferences

HISTORICAL THINKING FOR CHAPTER 14

How did early American societies emerge and interact before European contact?

Lesson 1.5 discusses the emergence and growth of complex societies across North America and examines the ways they interacted with one another as farmers and traders.

Student eEdition online

Additional content for this lesson, including images and a Global Commodity feature, is available online.

BACKGROUND FOR THE TEACHER

Cahokia Mounds Cahokia Mounds, a UNESCO World Heritage Site, is the largest and most complex archaeological site in North America that is located north of Mexico. Based on the artifacts found there, it was also one of the most sophisticated societies in the region. Cahokia's size and layout suggest it was a pre-urban society with a powerful political and economic hierarchy built on wealth derived from communal agriculture, trade, and highly organized divisions of labor. Archaeologists estimate that at its height, Cahokia covered almost six square miles and contained about 120 earthen mounds.

History Notebook

Encourage students to complete the "Turquoise" Global Commodity page for Chapter 14 in their History Notebooks as they read.

INTRODUCE & ENGAGE

PREVIEW VISUALS

Direct students to the photograph of the Pueblo dwellings and the map of the North American Civilizations. Explain that many earthworks, made of soil and rocks, can be found in the West and across the Midwest and are remnants of societies that flourished throughout North America. Ask students to recall the Mesoamerican civilizations they've studied so far and discuss the importance of location to archaeological sites such as Monte Albán and Chichén Itzá. *(Possible response: The locations are often located near water sources.)* Tell students that in this lesson, they will learn about complex societies in North America.

TEACH

GUIDED DISCUSSION

1. **Compare and Contrast** In what ways were the Adena, Hopewell, and Mississippians similar and different? *(Possible response: They all built mounds and engaged in trade. While the Hopewell and the Mississippians farmed, the Adena likely did not.)*

2. **Draw Conclusions** How did the Anasazi show their skill as architects and engineers? *(Possible response: They built huge buildings and learned to carve cliff dwellings. They also used advanced water control and collection techniques.)*

MAKE INFERENCES

Have students review the information about turquoise found in the Global Commodity feature (available in the Student eEdition). **ASK:** Based on this information and your own background knowledge, how did the close control of turquoise mines by Chacoan leaders influence the stone's value? *(Possible response: Controlling the supply of turquoise probably helped the stone increase in value.)*

ACTIVE OPTIONS

On Your Feet: True or False? Have students write True-False statements based on the information about early North American civilizations in the lesson. Then distribute one index card to each student and instruct them to write "True" on one side and "False" on the other. Invite volunteers to read their statements aloud to the class. Ask the rest of the class to respond to the statements by holding up either "True" or "False." When discrepancies occur, review the statement and the text and discuss which answer is correct. Continue this cycle until students run out of statements.

NG Learning Framework: Explore Native American Cultures
SKILL Collaboration
KNOWLEDGE Our Human Story

Have students select something about one of the societies that they would like to know about in depth. For example, students might be interested in learning more about the cliff dwellings in Mesa Verde or what archaeologists have uncovered in Cahokia. Have students work in pairs to research their topic, making sure they share the work equally. Ask pairs to prepare an oral report that gives details about their topic. Encourage students to share their reports with the class.

DIFFERENTIATE

INCLUSION

Identify Image and Map Details Pair students who can read the lesson aloud with students who are visually impaired. Encourage the reader to describe the images and maps in detail and explain their significance. When pairs have finished reading the lesson, invite them to work together to answer the Historical Thinking questions.

PRE-AP

Compare Across Regions Encourage students to compare Native American groups across regions. Have students make a chart with categories such as physical geography, food sources, and shelter. Tell them to conduct research to supplement the information in the text. Then have students present their findings to the class.

See the Chapter Planner for more strategies for differentiation.

HISTORICAL THINKING

ANSWERS

1. Complex societies developed along rivers in the Midwest and in the dry canyon lands of the Southwest.

2. Answers will vary. Possible response: The Anasazi grew maize and had ball courts. The Hopewell grew maize, beans, and squash. The Mississippians laid out their cities in a similar way to the Maya. The Adena, Hopewell, and Mississippians created earthworks rather than build with stone.

3. Most of the mound builders' sites were located next to rivers, which the people probably used as water sources and for trade and travel.

CRITICAL VIEWING Answers will vary. Possible response: Putting the buildings close together on a cliff probably protected the Pueblo from invaders.

Toltec and Aztec Civilizations

Kingdoms come and go, but beliefs and traditions continue. The feathered serpent god traveled through the centuries taking bits of knowledge and culture with him. Born among the Olmec, he visited San José Mogote and Teotihuacán before he settled among the Toltec and then the Aztec, where he was called Quetzalcoatl (kweht-suhl-kuh-WAH-tuhl).

CHARACTERISTICS OF THE TOLTEC

A new Mesoamerican society, the Toltec, began to rise about the 10th century c.e. The Toltec conquered the city of Teotihuacán around 900, which began a period of wealth and local influence that lasted until about 1100. Some archaeologists believe the Toltec were descendants of the Teotihuacán people, and others think they migrated to central Mexico from the north.

The Toltec were excellent potters, metalworkers, and warriors. Once they were established in the area, they built a capital called Tollan. Ultimately, the city covered around five square miles and was home to 30,000–40,000 people. The remains of the city reveal at least two large pyramids, a palace, and a ball court. Dwellings were organized into groups of homes around a central courtyard surrounded by a wall. Each courtyard contained an altar in the center.

No one is certain why the Toltec civilization weakened and ended around 1100. Reasons for the decline may have been environmental or political. The city of Tollan was certainly lost through violent overthrow: it was burned, buried, and later looted by the next dominant group in the Valley of Mexico, the Aztec. These people adopted much of Toltec culture and technology, and even though they migrated from the north, they claimed to be the Toltec's descendants.

THE AZTEC EMPIRE

Around 1325, a people known as the Mexica traveled to the Valley of Mexico from what is now western Mexico. When they arrived, they found some 50 established city-states. Because the area was already occupied, the Mexica were forced to settle in the surrounding swampland and on an island in the middle of Lake Texcoco. They called their city **Tenochtitlán**.

After they had been in the region for about 100 years, the Mexica formed an alliance with the Texcoco and Tlacopan city-states. This Triple Alliance became what historians call the Aztec. Under the rule of **Moctezuma**, the Mexica became the dominant group in the Triple Alliance, and Tenochtitlán became the center of the Aztec Empire.

Toltec and Aztec Civilizations, 900–1500 c.e.

At its height, Tenochtitlán contained 60,000 homes, covered an area of five square miles, and had a population of around 200,000 people. Residents traveled large canals by canoe, and **chinampas**—artificial islands created to raise crops—supplied ample food. Reservoirs held fresh water, and flower gardens were everywhere. The central marketplace offered cooked and uncooked food, enslaved people, and luxury goods made from gold, silver, and feathers.

By 1500, the Aztec had conquered 450 city-states and ruled over a population of between 6 and 11 million. They maintained their military by drafting all adult men from among their own as well as conquered people. Once the Aztec defeated a people, they demanded tribute and chose sacrificial victims from the conquered. Not surprisingly, the Aztec faced frequent rebellions.

Like many other societies in the Americas, the Aztec engaged in human sacrifice, but they have become known for killing unusually high numbers of people at one time. The term for human blood in the Aztec language was "precious water," and the Aztec believed that their gods needed that precious water to keep the soil fertile, the harvest plentiful, and the seasons regular.

Aztec society was strictly organized. The Aztec leader was considered a god. Next in the hierarchy were local rulers, then nobles and priests, and finally commoners, serfs, and slaves. The position of emperor was not strictly hereditary, though it often stayed within the same family. A group of nobles, priests, and successful warriors chose each new leader and could depose him if they did not approve of his rule. While there was some flexibility, everyday life was generally extremely structured and rule-oriented. Crafts were specialized, and sons were trained in the professions of their fathers.

Although the Aztec were fierce warriors, they were skilled farmers, successful traders, expert architects, and accomplished artists as well. Aztec priests were also the scientists and in many cases the scribes of society. Both boys and girls went to school, and some scholars believe that the Aztec were the first society with **compulsory education**, or education required by law, for all boys under the age of 16.

CRITICAL VIEWING Quetzalcoatl (at right in the main panel) devours a person in this image from the Codex Borgia, which scholars think the Aztec wrote before the arrival of European explorers. Which details in the illustration help you identify Quetzalcoatl?

Gender relations in Aztec society were complex. On a public level, this was a decidedly male-dominated culture with war, politics, and blood rituals as the special domain of men. But modern scholars acknowledge the parallel institutions in which women had significant power as doctors, priestesses, teachers, merchants, and skilled artisans. In Tenochtitlán, it seems that a shared system of childcare freed mothers to take on specialized roles.

The Aztec Empire had many characteristics found in other empires both nearby and on the other side of the world. Like the Maya, the Aztec had complex ritual and solar calendars, worshiped a feathered serpent god, built large stone monuments, and played a ritual ball game. Like many societies in Africa and Eurasia, ordinary Aztec people were required to pay tribute to their leaders by contributing a share of their crops, performing labor, or providing other goods. The Aztec also shared similarities with another American empire that ruled farther south at the same time: the Inca.

HISTORICAL THINKING

1. **READING CHECK** What influence did the Toltec have on the Aztec?

2. **MAKE CONNECTIONS** How did the Aztec manipulate their environment to help increase their power?

3. **DRAW CONCLUSIONS** Why did the Aztec face many rebellions from the people they conquered?

PLAN: 2-PAGE LESSON

OBJECTIVE

Explain how two cultures—first the Toltec and then the Aztec—emerged and developed complex social structures in what is now the Valley of Mexico in the 10th and 12th centuries.

CRITICAL THINKING SKILLS FOR LESSON 2.1

- Make Connections
- Draw Conclusions
- Identify Main Ideas and Details
- Make Inferences
- Interpret Maps

HISTORICAL THINKING FOR CHAPTER 14

How did early American societies emerge and interact before European contact?

Lesson 2.1 discusses the emergence and growth of the Toltec and the Aztec. The Aztec grew to become a powerful and wealthy empire.

Student eEdition online

Additional content for this lesson, including an image, is available online.

BACKGROUND FOR THE TEACHER

Tenochtitlán Tenochtitlán was located in modern-day Mexico City. It consisted of a network of streets and canals built on wooden piles that had been driven deep into Lake Texcoco's marshy soil. The city was linked to the shore by three raised causeways. The Templo Mayor, or Great Temple, was Tenochtitlán's main religious building and dominated the city's sacred precinct. The pyramid had two temples on the top. One of the temples was dedicated to the Aztec god of the sun and war. The other temple was dedicated to the god of rain. Both gods, experts believe, required many human sacrifices.

INTRODUCE & ENGAGE

ANALYZE VISUALS

Direct students' attention to the illustration of Quetzalcoatl in this lesson. Explain that it shows a panel from the Codex Borgia, an important Aztec manuscript. **ASK:** What do the details in the panel suggest about the culture and values of the Aztec people? *(Possible response: The bright shades of red and green suggest the Aztec belonged to a vibrant and creative culture. The battle shield and serpent suggest the culture may also have been consumed with war and violence.)* Tell students that in this lesson they will learn about the Aztec as well as another Mesoamerican people known as the Toltec.

TEACH

GUIDED DISCUSSION

1. **Identify Main Ideas and Details** What key event led to the establishment and growth of the Toltec civilization, and why? *(The Toltec conquered Teotihuacán around 900, which led to a period of wealth and influence that lasted about 200 years.)*

2. **Make Inferences** Why do you think priests in Aztec society also filled the role of scientist and scribe? *(Possible response: As in other complex societies, Aztec priests were probably among the most highly educated; their occupation allowed them the time, freedom, and resources necessary for a lifetime of study.)*

INTERPRET MAPS

Have students study the map of the Toltec and Aztec empires. Discuss the relative size of the two empires. **ASK:** Which regions were completely surrounded by the Aztec? *(Tlaxcala, Teotitlán, and Yopitzinco)* What kind of pressure might the Aztec have exerted on these regions? *(Possible response: to engage in trade, to join the empire)*

ACTIVE OPTIONS

On Your Feet: Fishbowl Arrange students in two concentric circles. Ask the inner circle to discuss the following question: How did cultural exchange shape the Mesoamerican civilizations of the Toltec and Aztec? Students on the inside circle should discuss the question, while those on the outside circle should listen for new information. Then direct the students in the two circles to switch places. Encourage volunteers to summarize the conclusions discussed in their circle.

> **NG Learning Framework: Write a Narrative**
> **ATTITUDE** Curiosity
> **KNOWLEDGE** Our Human Story

Based on what they've learned about the social structure of Aztec society, have students write a short narrative describing a day in the life of an artisan's 15-year-old son. Suggest that students conduct online research to enrich their narratives with additional facts and details. Invite students to share their narratives on a class website or blog.

DIFFERENTIATE

STRIVING READERS

Complete Sentence Starters Provide these sentence starters for students to complete after reading.

- The Aztec founded a city called _____.

- To grow their crops, Aztec farmers made _____.

- The Aztec built a great empire in _____.

- The Aztec leader was considered a _____.

GIFTED & TALENTED STEM

Create Models Invite groups of students to conduct research to learn more about a chinampa and then make a model of the artificial island. Students may draw a detailed model or make the model out of clay or cardboard. Once students have completed their model, have them present it to the class. Ask them to use the model to explain how a chinampa was made and be prepared to answer their classmates' questions.

See the Chapter Planner for more strategies for differentiation.

HISTORICAL THINKING

ANSWERS

1. The Aztec adopted Toltec technologies and cultural aspects, claiming to be the Toltec's descendants.

2. The Aztec built artificial islands and developed systems for water management and agriculture, which helped the Aztec gain power and flourish.

3. The Aztec faced rebellions because they demanded tribute and human sacrifice from conquered people.

CRITICAL VIEWING Quetzalcoatl is a feathered serpent god. In the illustration, Quetzalcoatl is limbless like a serpent and has feathers on its head and back.

Andean Cultures and the Inca

For a long time, historians and other scholars claimed that a writing system was essential to a complex culture. Yet one great empire—the Inca—managed a population of millions over far-reaching, difficult terrain without having a conventional written script.

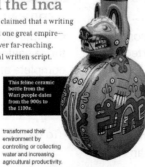

This feline ceramic bottle from the Wari people dates from the 900s to the 1100s.

EARLY SOUTH AMERICAN SOCIETIES

In what is now northern Bolivia, archaeology shows an ancient tradition of intensive agriculture supporting the earthworks, canals, raised fields, and causeways that indicate the beginnings of complex societies. The Andean region contains extreme climates—including oxygen-poor high altitudes, steamy jungles, and dry coastal deserts—and many different societies developed in the vicinity.

The Paracas and the Topará peoples created **geoglyphs**. Geoglyphs are large geometric designs and shapes drawn on the ground, created by scraping away dark surface dirt and rocks to reveal lighter-colored soil. The geoglyphs made by the Paracas and the Topará date from 500 B.C.E. to 200 C.E. From 200 to 700 C.E., the Nasca people produced their own glyphs now known as the Nasca Lines. These designs were made in a variety of shapes including spirals, fanciful animals, and humanlike figures. Some archaeologists believe people walked the patterns in spiritual rituals.

Other early Andean societies include the Moche (MOH-chay), who flourished between 100 and 700 C.E. They were best known for the sophisticated pottery and metalworking they left behind. The militaristic Wari may have invaded and brought down—or helped bring down—both the Moche and the Nasca, while the neighboring Tiwanaku (tee-WAH-nuh-koo) culture built their city-state on reclaimed marshland, like the Aztec's Tenochtitlán. The Chimú (chee-MOO) people stabilized their empire by allowing people they defeated to retain some control over local governments. They also made a very early form of the telephone.

These early cultures all developed road systems and established trading networks, some more extensive than others. They built irrigation and canal systems and raised or terraced their fields. These civilizations survived for hundreds of years because they

transformed their environment by controlling or collecting water and increasing agricultural productivity.

All of these societies also had skilled artisans. Expert weavers made exquisite textiles, architects built impressive cities, sculptors carved stone statues, and craftspeople made jewelry from jade and decorations from gold and silver. Sometime around 700 to 800, the peoples of the Andes Mountains combined tin and copper to make bronze and also added copper and silver to gold to make an alloy that was easier to work with than pure gold. They used different quantities of metals to make different colors. Unlike the peoples of Eurasia, the Andeans never used these metals for weapons or tools.

Around 1400, a new culture arose in the Andes. From its capital city high in the mountains, this society created an empire that would eclipse all others.

THE INCA EMPIRE

The Inca civilization, which lasted from 1400 to 1532, started in the same region as the Wari and Tiwanaku, whom the Inca greatly admired. The Inca capital, **Cusco** (KOO-skoh), was located in the Andes at 11,300 feet. With an estimated peak population of up to 150,000, the city had vast plazas, parklands, shrines, fountains, and canals. Later, as the empire expanded, a second capital was established at **Quito** (KEE-toh).

Archaeologists believe the Inca moved to Cusco around 1400. The first great ruler was **Pachacuti** (pah-chah-KOO-tee), who seized the throne from his brother in a coup in 1438 and began to expand the Inca domain at an amazing speed. In only 100 years, Pachacuti and his successors conquered large chunks of present-day Peru, Ecuador, Bolivia, Argentina, and Chile to rule over a population of about 10–12 million.

Compared with other world empires, the Inca were remarkably centralized and authoritarian. Rather than accept tribute but otherwise leave conquered peoples with their own languages and customs, the Inca overpowered them. They held the gods of conquered people hostage by taking images of those deities to Cusco. They built their own temples on sites sacred to the people they defeated. They resettled thousands, forcing people to move to regions far from their original homes. And they encouraged submission by treating those who surrendered more gently than those who resisted.

The Inca integrated people they conquered into their empire. Vanquished people were forced to perform labor and serve in the military. In fact, most of the soldiers in the Inca army were defeated people. The Inca kept local leaders in power but required them to give up their lands and swear loyalty to the emperor. They also allowed these leaders to serve in the central government—though only at lower levels—as long as the leaders learned Quechua (KEH-chuh-wuh), the Inca language.

The Inca did not have an orderly system of succession, and this flaw weakened their empire. Each time an Inca ruler died, all the male relatives who hoped to succeed him launched an all-out war until a single man won.

CHARACTERISTICS OF INCA RELIGION, CULTURE, AND SOCIETY

The Inca believed in many gods, with the most powerful being Inti, the sun god. The Inca were certain that they were chosen people who derived from Inti and that the emperor was a direct descendant of Inti. Below the gods were ancestor spirits and wak'a, spirits who inhabited places such as streams, caves, rocks, and hills. The Inca also believed that their nobles lived after death. Rulers and close family members were mummified. These mummies were removed from their tombs during important ceremonies, given food and drink, and consulted about important issues.

Like the Maya and the Aztec, the Inca developed a complex, organized ritual calendar. The Inca also practiced human sacrifice like other Andean and Mesoamerican societies did. Scholars believe

Early South American Societies, 600–1532 C.E.

AMAZON BASIN

PACIFIC OCEAN

Quito · Farfán · Chan Chan · Moche/Sicán · Cusco · Lake Titicaca · Tiwanaku

ANDES

0 200 400 Miles
0 200 400 Kilometers

- Nasca, c. 600 C.E.
- Moche, c. 700 C.E.
- Wari, c. 1000 C.E.
- Tiwanaku, c. 1000 C.E.
- Chimú, c. 1475 C.E.
- Inca, c. 1532 C.E.
- Inca roads

Inca sacrifices were not as frequent as those in Mesoamerican societies and usually occurred in times of hardship, such as droughts or floods, or during unusual astronomical events, such as eclipses. Occasionally, events demanded a larger number of sacrifices, such as when a ruler died. One source gives the largest number of Inca people killed at a single time as 4,000.

Inca society was strictly organized. The aristocracy was divided into three tiers: the close relatives of the emperor and previous rulers, more distant relatives, and leaders of conquered peoples. During his reign, the emperor lived as a god among his subjects. Even so, he had to maintain support from the nobles, who could overthrow him at any time.

The ordinary people of the Andes lived in family groups. Each group farmed land in several connected ecological

---

PLAN: 4-PAGE LESSON

OBJECTIVE
Examine the Inca Empire and other civilizations found in the Andean region of South America.

CRITICAL THINKING SKILLS FOR LESSON 2.2
- Interpret Maps
- Identify
- Analyze Cause and Effect
- Identify Main Ideas and Details
- Make Generalizations
- Make Inferences
- Describe
- Analyze Visuals

HISTORICAL THINKING FOR CHAPTER 14
How did early American societies emerge and interact before European contact?

Lesson 2.2 discusses the emergence and interaction of the Inca Empire and other complex early Andean societies.

BACKGROUND FOR THE TEACHER
The Nasca Geoglyphs There are more than 1,000 Nasca Lines in Peru, which include figures of animals and plants, geometric shapes, and long lines. (The longest line is 30 miles long.) Broad archaeological study of these lines didn't begin until the 1940s, after the advent of commercial flight, because the shapes are nearly impossible to distinguish from the ground. Since then, many theories about the purpose of the lines have been proposed. Until the 1970s, researchers theorized that they had calendrical purposes. In the 1960s, radical theories involving aliens and astronauts were proposed. Current research by National Geographic Explorer Johan Reinhard suggests the geoglyphs led the way to the location of water and fertility rituals. In his study, he points out that animal symbolism was common in early Peruvian culture, and cultural symbols like spiders (a sign of rain), hummingbirds (symbolic of fertility), and monkeys (associated with the Amazon and an abundance of water) are also found among the Nasca geoglyphs.

Student eEdition online
Additional content for this lesson, including images, a video, and an image gallery, is available online.

ACTIVATE PRIOR KNOWLEDGE

Explain that in this lesson students will learn about the rise and fall of the mighty Inca Empire. Prompt students to recall other empires they have studied in this text. **ASK:** What circumstances are necessary for an empire to grow, and what might cause an empire to fall into decline? *(Possible response: Established trade networks, a strong military, and geography favorable to growth and prosperity are necessary for an empire to grow. Distrust of leadership, political infighting, and a territory too large to rule can lead to an empire's decline.)* List students' responses on the board. At the end of the lesson, revisit the list and add or remove items based on what students have learned.

TEACH

GUIDED DISCUSSION

1. **Identify Main Ideas and Details** What various geographic challenges did early South American societies have to deal with? *(oxygen-poor high altitudes, steamy jungles, dry coastal areas, mountainous regions)*

2. **Make Generalizations** How were Andean civilizations able to survive for hundreds of years? *(They transformed their environments by controlling water sources and increasing agricultural production.)*

ANALYZE VISUALS

Direct students' attention to the image gallery (available in the Student eEdition) of pre-Inca artifacts and have students read the captions. **ASK:** What common themes do you notice represented in the artifacts? *(Possible response: the use of animals and faces; the use of precious metals such as gold and turquoise; evidence of elaborate metalwork)* Which of the artifacts were probably primarily functional or decorative? *(the Wari ceramic bottle and the Chimú vase)* Which of the artifacts might have been used in religious or ritual ceremonies? *(the Nasca bowl, the Moche gold-plated hands, and the Chimú gold funerary mask)*

ENGLISH LANGUAGE LEARNERS

Identify Word Parts to Clarify Meaning Explain to students that when they encounter a new word, they can look for familiar word parts to help them understand its meaning. Pair students at the **Beginning** level with students at the **Intermediate** and **Advanced** levels. Have pairs identify the three parts of the word *relocated (re-, locate,* and *-ed)* and discuss the meaning of each word part. Partners then review the definition of *relocated,* or the act of moving something from its original place.

STRIVING READERS

Create a Culture Chart Help students organize information about the different cultures discussed in the lesson by having them record facts in a chart. Have students work in pairs to write two facts about the pre-Inca culture and five facts for the Inca. Then have student pairs trade charts to check their facts.

See the Chapter Planner for more strategies for differentiation.

Machu Picchu, which stands 8,000 feet above sea level, embodies the Inca talent for engineering. The site's even stone houses on multiple levels are connected by man-made waterways and more than 100 stairways. Built around 1450 as a summer palace for Pachacuti, Machu Picchu was abandoned after the collapse of the Inca Empire.

zones so that everyone could have food even if the crops in one zone failed. All agricultural produce was divided—one-third was given to the priests, one-third went to the ruler, and one-third stayed with the farmer. Family groups were governed by local nobles, including women.

Like the Aztec, the Inca had parallel spheres for men and women. For example, men controlled the cult of the sun god, associated with war, while women led the lunar cult, responsible for fertility. "Chosen women" were sent from the provinces to special schools in Cusco where they learned leadership skills in the women's sphere, as well as legends of the Inca gods.

INCA ACHIEVEMENTS

Like other Andean societies, the Inca adapted to prosper in extreme landscapes. They terraced the land for agriculture, transported water over long distances, built underground water systems, and adorned their cities with impressive fountains. The Inca Empire stretched across multiple environments, from the Pacific Ocean, through a coastal plain fertile for agriculture, to the steepest mountains, and to the tropical rain forest on the other side. Trade across such diverse terrains with different crops and natural resources made the Inca rich.

The Inca are particularly famous for their incredible architecture. Like the master stonemasons of Great Zimbabwe in Africa, Inca builders created huge structures with blocks of stone fitted together so well that mortar, a mixture used to keep larger materials together, was not necessary. One of the most famous examples of Inca architecture is the mountain-top city of **Machu Picchu** (mah-choo PEE-choo).

Another major legacy of the Inca Empire was its impressive road system. While some roads in the region were built as early as 1000 B.C.E., it was the Inca who linked existing roads with new roads to create one huge highway network. While other empires—the Persians, the Romans, and the Chinese—had impressive engineering systems, none but the Inca had the skill to build at such high altitudes. With no wheel, the Inca constructed roads across deserts, deep chasms, and mountains taller than 16,000 feet.

Most of the traffic on these roads was by foot, with llamas carrying small loads. These routes included rest stations and a messenger system. Inca messengers most likely switched off often to travel so quickly. These roads allowed not only the rapid deployment of the Inca

army but also allowed efficient delivery of messages between the capital and provinces, reinforcing the centralization of Inca power in spite of enormous spaces and difficult terrain.

The Inca mathematical system was quite advanced and almost identical to the one used today. The Inca developed an agricultural calendar and calculated the correct days to plant and harvest, as well as when to celebrate important festival days. They also produced beautiful textiles, pottery, and metal sculpture. They were influenced by the Chimú as well as other Andean cultures, but their work was more technically advanced than the art of previous societies.

Much about the Inca remains a mystery because they did not have a writing system. However, they did develop the **quipu** (KEY-poo), a series of knotted strings that the Inca used to keep records, including business accounts, population censuses, and calendars. Interestingly, recent theories claim that some quipu also include historical and religious stories and songs.

Despite its accomplishments, the Inca Empire was not as strong or stable as it appeared. Conquered people resented their heavy labor obligations, but if they failed to cooperate, the Inca sent loyal subjects as colonists to take their land. If they still rose up, Inca officials would move troublemakers to distant regions. Succession disputes also destabilized the empire. It is possible that the Inca might have withstood or even overcome these failings, but by 1500, they faced a new and unexpected enemy: diseases brought by Europeans to the Americas.

HISTORICAL THINKING

1. **READING CHECK** Why is the Inca Empire considered a major world empire?
2. **INTERPRET MAPS** What physical features limited the expansion of early South American civilizations?
3. **IDENTIFY** How did earlier Andean civilizations influence the Inca?
4. **ANALYZE CAUSE AND EFFECT** What effect did the road system have on the Inca Empire?

BACKGROUND FOR THE TEACHER

Machu Picchu American archaeologist Hiram Bingham located Machu Picchu in 1911 and initiated its scientific study. The stones of Machu Picchu's structures—its palaces, temples, dwellings, and storehouses—are fitted so tightly together that even a knife cannot be wedged between them. Although it is unlikely that researchers will be able to determine the exact purpose of this citadel, they continue to excavate the site, adding to existing theories about its origin and proposing new ones. Bingham theorized that it was a convent where Inca women trained to serve the Inca leader. Modern researchers have since disproved this theory. Some hypothesize that it was built as a summer residence for Pachacuti, while others believe it was built as a retreat for Peru's political elite. All agree on its significance as a gathering place of spiritual significance for early South American societies.

TEACH

GUIDED DISCUSSION

3. **Make Inferences** Why do you think the Inca built their own temples on sites that were sacred to those they conquered? *(Possible response: The Inca wanted not only to subdue the people they defeated but also to annihilate their culture.)*

4. **Describe** What are the major legacies of the Inca? *(Possible responses: architectural achievements, including Machu Picchu; an impressive road system; an advanced mathematical system; a calendar; beautiful textiles, pottery, and metal sculptures)*

ANALYZE VISUALS

Have students watch the video (available in the Student eEdition) on Machu Picchu and then answer the following questions:

- Why does Machu Picchu look undamaged? *(Its buildings are made of stone and were constructed to withstand earthquakes.)*

- Why would it have been hard for an enemy to invade Machu Picchu? *(It's located on top of a mountain and hidden from view.)*

- Why is the construction of the structures on Machu Picchu particularly notable? *(They were built without the help of wheels, iron or steel tools, and mortar.)*

ACTIVE OPTIONS

On Your Feet: Team Word Webbing Arrange students in groups of four and give each group a large sheet of paper and each student on the team a different colored marker. Assign teams the following topic: What are the characteristics of Inca religion, culture, and society? Each student should write an answer to the question on the part of the web nearest to him or her. Then, on your signal, students should rotate the paper, and each student should add to the nearest part. When teams are done, initiate a class discussion on the topic.

> **NG Learning Framework: Investigate an Andean Archaeological Site**
> **ATTITUDE** Curiosity
> **SKILL** Collaboration

Assign students to work with a partner to create a web page or blog about an Andean archaeological site discussed in this lesson such as the Nasca geoglyphs, Cusco, or Machu Picchu. Encourage students to include visuals, text explanations, and hyperlinks in their web pages. Invite volunteers to share their website designs with the class.

HISTORICAL THINKING

ANSWERS

1. The Inca Empire had advanced technology and science, excelled in the arts and in architecture, and manipulated a variety of environments to advance and grow.

2. The Pacific Ocean prevented expansion to the west, and the Andes Mountains restricted expansion to the east.

3. The Inca adopted methods of adaptation and survival in extreme landscapes from early Andean civilizations.

4. The Inca road system made communication, trade, and military control easier.

Pacific and Caribbean Island Societies

Imagine being at sea in a simple canoe with everything you need to survive onboard. You are surrounded by the sea. There is no land in sight—and you have no idea when you might see any. This is what great Polynesian explorers and settlers experienced.

POLYNESIAN SOCIETIES

Sometime before 300 c.e., the first settlers reached present-day Hawaii, traveling the great distance from the Marquesas Islands without a clear idea of what might lay ahead. By this time, Polynesian sailors had developed a strong double canoe, two wooden frames lashed together with rope. These sail-driven vessels could carry tons of cargo and travel over a hundred miles a day. The Polynesians carried with them not just food and water but breadfruit and taro

seedlings for planting and the pigs they relied on for meat. With deep knowledge of the ocean environment, Tahitian navigators headed into the unknown, eventually establishing communities on the Hawaiian Islands.

Sometime after 400, the first settlers reached Rapa Nui (RAH-puh NOO-ee), also known as Easter Island. Their final migration, in 1350, was to New Zealand, where they became the Maori (MAW-ree). Experts believe the Polynesians also reached the coast of South America

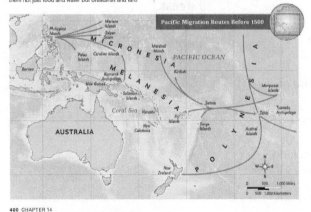

Pacific Migration Routes Before 1500

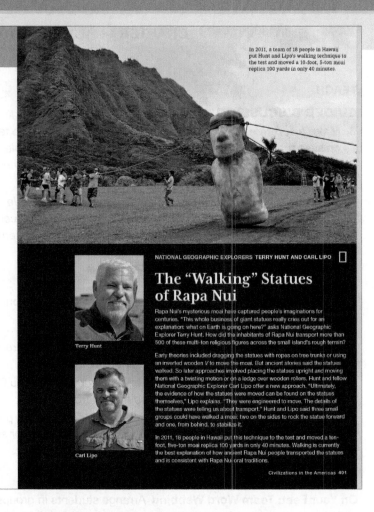

In 2011, a team of 18 people in Hawaii put Hunt and Lipo's walking technique to the test and moved a 10-foot, 5-ton moai replica 100 yards in only 40 minutes.

NATIONAL GEOGRAPHIC EXPLORERS TERRY HUNT AND CARL LIPO

Terry Hunt

Carl Lipo

The "Walking" Statues of Rapa Nui

Rapa Nui's mysterious moai have captured people's imaginations for centuries. "This whole business of giant statues really cries out for an explanation: what on Earth is going on here?" asks National Geographic Explorer Terry Hunt. How did the inhabitants of Rapa Nui transport more than 500 of these multi-ton religious figures across the small island's rough terrain?

Early theories included dragging the statues with ropes on tree trunks or using an inverted wooden V to move the moai. But ancient stories said the statues walked. So later approaches involved placing the statues upright and moving them with a twisting motion or on a ledge over wooden rollers. Hunt and fellow National Geographic Explorer Carl Lipo offer a new approach. "Ultimately, the evidence of how the statues were moved can be found on the statues themselves," Lipo explains. "They were engineered to move. The details of the statues were telling us about transport." Hunt and Lipo said three small groups could have walked a moai: two on the sides to rock the statue forward and one, from behind, to stabilize it.

In 2011, 18 people in Hawaii put this technique to the test and moved a ten-foot, five-ton moai replica 100 yards in only 40 minutes. Walking is currently the best explanation of how ancient Rapa Nui people transported the statues and is consistent with Rapa Nui oral traditions.

PLAN: 4-PAGE LESSON

OBJECTIVE

Discuss how people of the Pacific and Atlantic traveled great distances, bringing complex societies to ocean islands.

CRITICAL THINKING SKILLS FOR LESSON 2.3

- Interpret Maps
- Synthesize
- Identify Main Ideas and Details
- Draw Conclusions
- Compare and Contrast
- Make Inferences
- Evaluate

HISTORICAL THINKING FOR CHAPTER 14

How did early American societies emerge and interact before European contact?

The first inhabitants of the Pacific and Atlantic islands came by boat, thanks to their advanced navigation and sailing skills. Lesson 2.3 introduces the Polynesians and examines the emergence of island societies in the Pacific and the Caribbean.

BACKGROUND FOR THE TEACHER

Rewriting the Story of Rapa Nui When archaeologists Terry Hunt and Carl Lipo arrived in 2001, most experts agreed that the 600-square-mile island had been settled by Polynesians between 400 and 800 c.e. and had become quickly overpopulated. These experts believed the overpopulation led to a fight for dwindling resources that resulted in warfare, cannibalism, and eventually societal collapse. But Hunt and Lipo could find no evidence to support this theory. Nor could they find evidence of a pre-European collapse. Based on their findings, Polynesians arrived on Rapa Nui as late as 1200. When the Polynesians established a method for growing taro and sweet potatoes in the island's poor soil, the population stabilized enough to last for the next 500 years, until European invaders conquered the island in the 18th century.

Student eEdition online

Additional content for this lesson, including video clips, is available online.

INTRODUCE & ENGAGE

TRACK PACIFIC ISLAND MIGRATIONS

Help students locate Tahiti, the Hawaiian Islands, and Rapa Nui on a world map or globe and then trace the distance between them. Explain that in this lesson students will learn how Polynesians from Tahiti arrived at the Hawaiian Islands and Rapa Nui beginning around 300 C.E. to establish complex and long-lasting societies. **ASK:** What skills and technologies do you think the Polynesians had that allowed them to travel these great distances? *(Possible responses: accurate and reliable navigation tools, efficient boats or ships able to travel long distances across the ocean.)*

TEACH

GUIDED DISCUSSION

1. **Identify Main Ideas and Details** What distinguished far-flung Polynesian societies from other societies similarly spread out over long distances? *(The Polynesians had a uniquely unified culture and similar tools and artistic styles.)*

2. **Draw Conclusions** Why might it have appeared as if the moai of Rapa Nui could walk? *(Possible response: If the statues were moved by rocking them back and forth, it would have looked as though they were walking.)*

INTERPRET MAPS

Instruct students to study the map of Pacific migration routes found in this lesson. **ASK:** How are the migration routes indicated on the map? *(green arrows pointed in the direction of the migration)* According to this map, from where did most of the Pacific islands' settlers come? *(the Philippine Islands)* From where did settlers in the Marshall Islands probably originate? *(the Fiji Islands)* Based on this map, what conclusion can you draw about Pacific migration routes before 1500? *(Possible response: Settlers hopped from one island to the next in their quest to find a favorable place to settle.)*

DIFFERENTIATE

STRIVING READERS

Complete a Venn Diagram Tell students to use a Venn diagram to take notes as they read about the similarities and differences between Polynesian and Caribbean societies. Invite them to compare their completed diagrams with a partner's and discuss any differences. Encourage students to think about the aspects of each culture that allowed their societies to flourish and how they may have influenced other cultures through trade or cultural exchange.

PRE-AP

Learn About Hunt and Lipo's Work Have students research to learn more about Terry Hunt and Carl Lipo's study of Rapa Nui. Ask students to find out about the explorers' archaeological work on the island and their theories about the time line of the Polynesians' arrival and island life. Invite students to present their summaries to the class in a written or oral report.

See the Chapter Planner for more strategies for differentiation.

These giant stone figures on Rapa Nui, or Easter Island, portray ancestral leaders. When alive, a ruler would commission a statue of himself that remained horizontal. After leaders died, the statues were placed in an upright position.

at some point because sweet potatoes, a South American plant, have been found on Polynesian islands as well. And chickens, which were domesticated by the Polynesians, were also in South America before the Spanish arrived.

That Rapa Nui was settled at all is as amazing as it is unlikely; it is truly a speck in a wide sea. It lies 1,300 miles southeast of its nearest neighbor, Pitcairn Island, and is only 14 miles across at its widest point. It was probably settled by a small party of Polynesians blown extremely far off their original course. Rapa Nui is well known around the world because of its ancient *moai* (MOW-eye) statues that resemble humans with large heads.

The Polynesians were master shipbuilders, navigators, sailors, and fishermen. They had no navigational instruments, so they relied on their expert knowledge of astronomy. They used observation not only of the stars but also of clouds, waves, and bird flight patterns to navigate across vast distances in all types of weather. The Polynesians established trading networks but also warred with one another, depending on island proximity.

Polynesian communities ranged from a few houses around a lagoon to large protected villages on the larger islands. The more people lived in one area, the stronger the chiefs became, and the more elaborate their religious rituals. Polynesian law was based on what the Hawaiians called *kapu*. Kapu was a long list of taboos that regulated each person's behavior. If a person of low rank ate food prepared for a chief, for example, or if a woman entered a warrior's canoe, he or she could face severe punishment.

Considering the extensive distances between some of the islands, the culture of Polynesia is exceptionally unified. Polynesians separated by thousands of miles share many of the same words. Tools and artistic styles are also remarkably similar across the many islands.

CARIBBEAN ISLAND SOCIETIES

Like the Polynesians, the people of the Caribbean islands in the western Atlantic had to migrate by sea to find new homes. However, they did not have to travel nearly as far. Central and South America are separated from their closest island neighbors by only 200–500 miles, compared with the thousands of miles that separate the islands of Polynesia.

Today, the Caribbean islands are usually divided into three groups: the Greater Antilles (including Cuba, Hispaniola, Jamaica, and Puerto Rico), the Lesser Antilles (including Grenada in the south to the Virgin Islands in the north); and the Bahamian Archipelago. There were three main waves of migration to the Caribbean islands. The first wave came from Central America to Cuba and Hispaniola in about 5000 B.C.E. The people who settled there used stone tools, hunted, and foraged. In about 1000 B.C.E., a different group came from South America. They settled these same islands and later expanded into the Bahamian Archipelago. These people were farmers and fishers, and they also made pottery. Many historians believe these are the ancestors of the Taíno people first encountered by Christopher Columbus. Finally, from about 250 B.C.E. to 1450 C.E., groups began to migrate to the Lesser Antilles from the Orinoco river delta in present-day Venezuela.

Ultimately, the peoples of the Caribbean became two closely related groups who both spoke a language called Arawak (A-ruh-wahk). The Island Caribs lived in the Lesser Antilles, while the Taíno lived in the Greater Antilles and the Bahamas. Like the Polynesians, Caribbean peoples were expert navigators and seafarers. They, too, fought with one another but also developed complex trade networks. They had expert astronomical knowledge, built thatched buildings, grew crops, and developed skills such as weaving and making pottery and baskets.

While they shared many characteristics, civilizations in the Caribbean islands were culturally diverse. In general, Island Caribs lived in smaller, less permanent villages, had more communal societies, and were influenced culturally by South American peoples. The Greater Antilles islands, on the other hand, were more densely populated. The Taíno had bigger, more permanent towns and more hierarchical societies, and their villages were led by chiefs. There is evidence they traded with and were influenced culturally by Mesoamerican societies.

HISTORICAL THINKING

1. **READING CHECK** What skill made both Polynesian and Caribbean migrations possible?

2. **INTERPRET MAPS** Which Pacific island served as a base for possible migrations to present-day North America, South America, and New Zealand?

3. **SYNTHESIZE** How do the locations of the Caribbean island groups relate to which mainland cultures influenced them?

Art in the Heart of the Caribbean

On the tiny island of Mona, 41 miles west of Puerto Rico, anthropologist and National Geographic Explorer Jago Cooper researches cave art created by indigenous peoples as early as the 12th century. The images are painted or carved (like the one shown above). They include people, animals, and patterns that twist across the rock surfaces. Cooper, the British Museum's curator of the Americas, says, "These finger-fluted designs reflect the spiritual beliefs of the indigenous people."

He explains, "For the millions of indigenous peoples living in the Caribbean before European arrival, caves represented portals into a spiritual realm, and therefore these new discoveries of the artists at work within them captures the essence of their belief systems and the building blocks of their cultural identity."

Mona is one of the most cavernous areas in the world. Cooper points out that the Caribbean people "deliberately explored caves that were difficult to access." As of 2016, Cooper and his team found extensive evidence of pre-Columbian iconography on the walls and ceilings in more than 25 caves on the island. Cooper is also investigating similar art in Cuba and the Dominican Republic.

BACKGROUND FOR THE TEACHER

Mona Island's Indigenous People Jago Cooper's findings are changing our understanding of an indigenous island people. His research of the Mona Island cave drawings suggests a relationship between islanders and European explorers that is very different from what has been commonly believed. Some of the cave art he has encountered was left by Europeans, and neither the markings of Mona's indigenous people nor those of its European visitors include images that suggest conflict. Instead they show a dialogue between the two groups. The art seems to be evidence of a time in which two groups of strangers were simply getting to know one another. As Cooper has pointed out, it is unlikely Europeans would have found these caves without the help of local guides.

TEACH

GUIDED DISCUSSION

3. **Compare and Contrast** In what ways were Polynesian and Caribbean societies similar? *(The people of both societies were expert navigators and seafarers, established trade networks, had advanced astronomical knowledge, built thatch buildings, grew crops, and developed skills such as weaving and making pottery and baskets.)*

4. **Make Inferences** What details about the people of the Great Antilles Islands suggest that they were influenced culturally by Mesoamerican societies? *(Possible response: the fact that they had hierarchical societies, built more permanent towns, and were led by chiefs)*

EVALUATE

Instruct students to review the National Geographic Explorer feature on Jago Cooper. **ASK:** Why do you think Caribbean people might have "deliberately explored caves that were difficult to access"? *(Possible response: They may have been seeking difficult-to-reach places to conduct sacred rituals and store valuable objects.)*

ACTIVE OPTIONS

On Your Feet: Inside-Outside Circle Have students stand in concentric circles facing each other. Direct students in the outside circle to pose questions such as the following: Where did the first human settlers in the Caribbean Islands come from? When and how did they arrive? What evidence suggests settlers in the Caribbean had interacted with Mesoamerican societies? Tell students in the inside circle to answer the questions. On your signal, have students rotate to create new partnerships. Then on another signal, have students trade inside/outside roles.

> **NG Learning Framework: Research Pacific and Caribbean Societies**
> **ATTITUDE** Curiosity
> **KNOWLEDGE** Our Human Story

Organize students into small groups. Instruct groups to select a specific topic of interest from the lesson, such as the walking moai in Rapa Nui, Polynesian laws and the Kapu, or the Taíno people. Have students conduct research and organize their findings in a brief presentation. Invite volunteers to present their findings to the class.

HISTORICAL THINKING

ANSWERS

1. Both societies had excellent navigation and seafaring skills.

2. Tahiti

3. Answers will vary. Possible response: The Island Caribs in the Lesser Antilles were closer to South America and influenced more by South American cultures, while the Taíno in the Greater Antilles were closer to Mesoamerica and influenced more by cultures in that region.

VOCABULARY

Use each of the following vocabulary words in a sentence that shows an understanding of the term's meaning.

1. terrace
2. slash-and-burn agriculture
3. geoglyph
4. cenote
5. earthworks
6. codex
7. chinampa
8. maize

READING STRATEGY
MAKE INFERENCES

Complete a graphic organizer like the one shown to make an inference about why it is important to scholars to decipher Inca quipu. Summarize what you've read in the "I Read" section. Tell what you know in the "I Know" section. Then write your inference in the "And So" section.

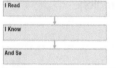

I Read

I Know

And So

9. Why is it so difficult for researchers to decode Inca quipu?

MAIN IDEAS

Answer the following questions. Support your answers with evidence from the chapter.

10. What did the Caral, Chavín, Olmec, Zapotec, and Teotihuacán have in common? LESSON 1.1
11. How did the Maya use advanced mathematics? LESSON 1.2
12. What links the Anasazi culture to Mesoamerica? LESSON 1.5
13. Why are the Aztec considered a complex civilization? LESSON 2.1
14. How did early Andean civilizations express themselves through art? LESSON 2.2
15. What are the three main groups of the Caribbean islands? LESSON 2.3

HISTORICAL THINKING

Answer the following questions. Support your answers with evidence from the chapter.

16. IDENTIFY How did the closing of the Beringia land bridge affect the civilizations of the Americas?
17. MAKE PREDICTIONS How do you think the practice of human sacrifice will influence how Europeans interpret American civilizations?
18. IDENTIFY PROBLEMS AND SOLUTIONS In what ways did American civilizations modify their environments, and how do those modifications help people understand those civilizations?
19. SYNTHESIZE How did different physical environments affect the lack of knowledge about ancient American civilizations when compared with Eurasian civilizations from the same era?
20. MAKE CONNECTIONS What were the legacies of the Olmec, Zapotec, and Teotihuacán societies? Support your answer with specific examples.
21. FORM AND SUPPORT OPINIONS In your opinion, which civilization—Maya, Aztec, or Inca—was greater than the others, and why?
22. COMPARE AND CONTRAST What are three similarities between American and Eurasian civilizations?
23. DRAW CONCLUSIONS What were two main reasons that civilizations in the Americas declined? Use examples from the chapter.

INTERPRET VISUALS

Study the images of a Maya pyramid (top) and an ancient Egyptian pyramid (bottom). Then answer the questions that follow.

24. How are the pyramids similar, and how are they different?
25. What difficulties did people face when building these pyramids?

ANALYZE SOURCES

In this excerpt from the *Popol Vuh*, the hero twins—who often represent pairs such as life and death, sky and earth, day and night, or sun and moon—do some work for their grandmother. Read the excerpt and answer the question that follows.

> Then they [Hunahpu and Xbalanque] began to work, in order to be well thought of by their grandmother and their mother. The first thing they made was the cornfield. "We are going to plant the cornfield, grandmother and mother," they said. "Do not grieve; here we are, your grandchildren, we who shall take the place of our brothers," said Hunahpu and Xbalanque.
>
> At once they took their axes, their picks, and their wooden hoes and went, each carrying his blowgun on his shoulder. As they left the house they asked their grandmother to bring them their midday meal.

26. What conclusions can you draw about corn and how it was farmed in ancient Maya society?

CONNECT TO YOUR LIFE

27. NARRATIVE You have read that the Inca were weakened by unknown European diseases. Put yourself in the place of someone from the empire, such as a member of the royal family, a conquered subject who has taken part in a rebellion, a priest, or a local leader. Write a story in which you are a main character and explore what you may have thought or done when an unknown illness affected your community. Use the tips below to help you plan, organize, and write your story.

TIPS

- Choose your role carefully, considering the different interests of various people at that time.
- Identify your character's thoughts and feelings about the illness and what may happen next.
- Use vivid language to describe the location, events, and the other characters in the story.
- Include realistic dialogue in your narrative.
- Use two or three vocabulary terms from the chapter.
- End the narrative with a prediction of future events on the part of your character.

VOCABULARY ANSWERS

1. Possible response: Early Americans built **terraces** on hillsides to have more room to grow crops.
2. Possible response: The Maya cleared their fields by using **slash-and-burn agriculture**.
3. Possible response: The **geoglyphs** carved in the ground were only visible from the air.
4. Possible response: Archaeologists explore **cenotes** to find underwater Maya artifacts.
5. Possible response: Unlike the Mesoamericans who built stone monuments, early North Americans built **earthworks**, or constructions of soil and rock.
6. Possible response: The **codex** contained the history and origin stories of the newly discovered culture.
7. Possible response: **Chinampas**, or artificial islands, were created to raise crops.
8. Possible response: Both South Americans and Mesoamericans grew **maize**, or corn.

READING STRATEGY ANSWERS

I Read
Glyphs are symbolic pictures that represent words, symbols, and sounds. Quipu is a series of knotted strings the Inca used to keep records.

I Know
The Maya and the Inca did not use letters to record their information and histories.

And So
Deciphering Maya glyphs and Inca quipu can help experts better understand these early American peoples and their cultures.

9. Possible response: The quipus are unique, so they cannot be cracked by using known systems.

MAIN IDEAS ANSWERS

10. They were all early American complex societies that built cities.
11. The Maya used advanced mathematics to calculate the movement of the sun, moon, and stars.

12. Like many Mesoamerican cultures, the Anasazi used irrigation to farm, made pottery, wove cloth, and used feathers and turquoise. They played a ball game like the Maya and were astronomers.

13. The Aztec controlled a large empire, extensively traded, had a strict social structure, used advanced mathematics and astronomy, and were expert artists and architects.

14. Andean societies created large geoglyphs, made pottery, wove textiles, carved statues from stone, created jewelry, and combined metals.

15. the Greater Antilles, the Lesser Antilles, and the Bahamian Archipelago

HISTORICAL THINKING ANSWERS

16. The closing of the Beringian land bridge meant that American societies developed isolated from Eurasian societies.

17. Possible response: The practice of human sacrifice probably made Europeans think that American civilizations were cruel and lacked moral or ethical principles. This interpretation might have made the Europeans underestimate the Americans.

18. Possible response: The civilizations of the Americas controlled and manipulated water, slashed and burned to clear land, and created terraced fields to extend growing areas. This showed the level of technology it reached, other cultures that influenced it, and the degree to which large-scale labor-intensive projects could be organized.

19. Possible response: Many ancient American civilizations developed in environments where buildings and relics could easily decay and disappear, or where structures and objects have been hidden by jungle growth.

20. Possible response: The Olmec, Zapotec, and Teotihuacán civilizations all influenced the later Maya, Aztec, and Toltec civilizations in the technology they used, in their artistic and architectural styles, and in their religious beliefs. Examples include the feathered serpent god in Mesoamerican religion and the ball game played by the Olmec, Maya, and Aztec.

21. Possible response: I think the Inca was the greatest American empire. At one time, it had the best road system and used the complex quipu to track information ranging from math to history.

22. Possible response: Like many Eurasian societies, Aztec emperors demanded tribute from the people they defeated, and serfs had to give the ruler a portion of their crop. Like the early Persians, the Inca integrated people into their empire. The Inca, like the Mongols, resettled thousands of people. Like the Chinese, Mongols, and Persians, the Inca had an advanced and extended road and messenger system.

23. Possible response: Two main reasons civilizations declined were environmental problems and political problems. Many societies faced extreme environmental conditions such as drought that led to widespread hunger and the decline of populations either through death or migration. This, in turn, caused the structures of the culture to fall apart. Political problems were caused by invasion and conquest by a more powerful group, or by internal rebellions.

INTERPRET VISUALS ANSWERS

24. Possible response: Both pyramids have a triangular shape and are built from stone. The Maya pyramid has steps on each of its sides and has a flat top. The Egyptian pyramid has a smoother surface and ends with a point at the top.

25. Possible response: The people who designed the buildings needed to make exact calculations for each pyramid to make sure the proportions were right and enough building materials were gathered. A large labor force was needed to build the pyramids.

ANALYZE SOURCES ANSWER

26. Possible response: Corn was part of the diet and maybe the essential crop. The people did not rely on animals or plows to farm but rather used axes, picks, and hoes. The fields must have been dangerous because they carried blowguns.

CONNECT TO YOUR LIFE ANSWER

27. Students' narratives should include their role as a person who lived in the Inca Empire after Huayna Capac's death; reveal their thoughts and feelings about the emperor's health as well as what may happen next; describe the location, events, and other characters in vivid language; use realistic dialogue and two or three chapter vocabulary terms; predict what will happen to their character.

The Real Price of Gold

BY BROOK LARMER Adapted from "The Real Price of Gold" by Brook Larmer, *National Geographic*, January 2009

No single element has excited and tormented the human imagination more than the shimmering metal known by the chemical symbol Au. For thousands of years, the desire to possess gold has driven people to extremes, fueling wars and conquests, girding empires and currencies, leveling mountains and forests. Gold is not vital to human existence; it has, in fact, relatively few practical uses. Yet its chief virtues—its unusual density and malleability along with its imperishable shine—have made it one of the world's most coveted commodities. It has long been a symbol of beauty, wealth, and immortality. Nearly every society through the ages has invested gold with an almost mythological power.

At this improvised mine in Ghana, a 13-year-old boy sluices for gold.

For all of its allure, gold's human and environmental toll has never been so steep. Part of the challenge, as well as the fascination, is that there is so little of it. In all of history, only 161,000 tons of gold have been mined, barely enough to fill two Olympic-size swimming pools. More than half of that has been extracted in the past 60 years. Now the world's richest deposits are fast being depleted, and new discoveries are rare. Most of the gold left to mine exists as traces buried in remote and fragile corners of the globe. It's an invitation to destruction. But there is no shortage of miners, big and small, who are willing to accept.

At one end of the spectrum are the armies of poor migrant workers converging on small-scale mines. According to the United Nations Industrial Development Organization (UNIDO), there are between 10 million and 15 million so-called artisanal miners around the world, from Mongolia to Brazil. Employing crude methods that have hardly changed in centuries, they produce about 25 percent of the world's gold and support a total of 100 million people. It's a vital activity for these people—and deadly too.

In the Democratic Republic of the Congo in the past decade, local armed groups fighting for control of gold mines and trading routes have routinely terrorized and tortured miners. They have used profits from gold to buy weapons and fund their activities. In the Indonesian province of East Kalimantan, the military, along with

security forces of an Anglo-Australian gold company, forcibly evicted small-scale miners and burned their villages to make way for a large-scale mine. Thousands of protestors against expansion of a mine in Cajamarca, Peru, faced tear gas and police violence.

The deadly effects of mercury are equally hazardous to small-scale miners. Most of them use mercury to separate gold from rock, spreading poison in both gas and liquid forms. UNIDO estimates that one-third of all mercury released by humans into the environment comes from artisanal gold mining.

At the other end of the spectrum are vast, open-pit mines run by the world's largest mining companies. Using armadas of supersize machines, these big-footprint mines produce three-quarters of the world's gold. They can also bring jobs, technologies, and development to forgotten frontiers. Gold mining, however, generates more waste per ounce than any other metal, and the mines' mind-bending disparities of scale show why. The mining gashes in the earth are so massive they can be seen from space. But the particles being mined are so microscopic that, in many cases, more than 200 could fit on the head of a pin. At a mining operation in eastern Indonesia, extracting a single ounce of gold—the amount in a typical wedding ring—requires the removal of more than 250 tons of rock and ore.

And so the real cost of gold keeps rising. ∎

Make a Documentary About Power Objects

Staging the Question

In this unit, you learned about some objects and commodities—such as masks, gold, and enigmatic stone carvings—that possessed power or significance in Africa and the Americas. The Global Perspective further explored the nature of power objects and why they matter so deeply to the people who create them. As you have discovered, these items can explain much about an early society, including what qualities it valued, what the people's religion taught them about the world, and what they viewed as wealth. What do our own society's power objects say about us?

ASSIGNMENT

Research the power objects treasured by at least three of the civilizations discussed in this unit.

Identify at least three items that you believe are power objects of your own culture.

Compare these modern-day power objects with those of the earlier civilizations. Consider what each society's power objects say about its culture's priorities and beliefs.

Make a documentary film about some modern-day power objects and their significance. Use the insights you gained from analyzing historical artifacts.

Supporting Questions: Begin by developing supporting questions to guide your research. For example: Does this object exemplify religious or secular beliefs? Research the answers in this unit and in other sources, both print and online. You might want to use a matrix like this one to record your answers.

	Object 1	Object 2	Object 3
Religious Meaning			
Monetary Value			
Other Significance			

Summative Performance Task: Make a documentary about the modern-day power objects you chose. In the script, explain what the objects say about the culture they embody, and discuss their similarities with historical power objects. You may include video clips or images of the present-day and historical objects, interviews with people discussing present-day objects, and any other footage that supports your ideas.

Present: Share your documentary with the class. You might consider one of these options:

POST IT ONLINE
Post the documentary on a class website and invite your classmates and friends to view it. Invite viewers to share their feedback and questions with you. Respond to the feedback and questions you receive.

VIEW IT IN CLASS
Work with your teacher to schedule a class viewing of the documentary. After the viewing, ask classmates for their reactions and lead a class discussion about modern-day power objects.

Take Informed Action:

UNDERSTAND Think about the value of understanding your own culture's power objects. Identify the ideas you learned from the present-day power objects that you believe are important to share.

ASSESS Choose the power object that most clearly stands for your culture. Think about the best place to share information about the object.

ACT Create an informational poster about the power object to display in your school, the public library, or another place in your community. You may also look for opportunities to screen your documentary.

NATIONAL GEOGRAPHIC CONNECTION

GUIDED DISCUSSION FOR "THE REAL PRICE OF GOLD"

1. **Identify Cause and Effect** What are the effects of gold mining? *(Answers will vary. Possible responses: Groups fighting for control of gold mines terrorize and torture miners; small-scale miners are evicted by larger-scale mines; poison gas and liquid mercury are released into the environment; gold mining produces more waste per ounce than any other metal.)*

2. **Form and Support Opinions** Do you think mining gold is worth the challenges? Explain your reasoning. *(Answers will vary. Possible responses: Yes, gold is an extremely sought-after commodity and its production can lead to jobs. OR No, the negative impacts on humans and the environment are not worth the trouble, especially with such low yields.)*

History Notebook
Encourage students to complete the Unit Wrap-Up page for Unit 5 in their History Notebooks.

ASSESS

Use the rubric to assess each student's participation and performance.

SCORE	ASSIGNMENT	PRODUCT	PRESENTATION
3 GREAT	• Student thoroughly understands the assignment. • Student develops thoughtful supporting questions to guide research.	• Documentary is well thought out with a variety of power objects. • Documentary reflects all of the key elements listed in the assignment.	• Presentation is clear, concise, and logical. • Presentation is creative and engaging.
2 GOOD	• Student mostly understands the assignment. • Student develops somewhat thoughtful supporting questions to guide research.	• Documentary is fairly well thought out with some power objects. • Documentary reflects most of the key elements listed in the assignment.	• Presentation is fairly clear, concise, and logical. • Presentation is somewhat creative and engaging.
1 NEEDS WORK	• Student does not understand the assignment. • Student does not develop thoughtful questions to guide research.	• Documentary is not well thought out and contains few power objects. • Documentary reflects few or none of the key elements listed in the assignment.	• Presentation is not clear, concise, or logical. • Presentation is not creative or engaging.

INTRODUCE THE PAINTING

VIEW OF NAPLES (DETAIL)

This painting by the Dutch painter Gaspar van Wittel shows the bustling port city of Naples as it looked during the early 18th century. Founded by the Greeks in the seventh century B.C.E., Naples is one of the oldest cities in Italy. Its long history also includes periods of rule by the Romans, the Byzantines, the French, and the Spanish. During the early Renaissance, the city was a gateway through which Greek and Arab learning entered western Europe. At the time of the painting, Naples was governed by the Spanish branch of the powerful Habsburg family.

Direct students' attention to the painting. **ASK:** From what location is the artist viewing the city? *(from the Tyrrhenian Sea)* How does the artist's vantage point affect his portrayal of the city? *(The artist is able to view the city from a distance, which gives him a broad view of both the buildings near the water and the buildings higher up in the hills.)*

Gaspar Van Wittel was a Dutch painter who immigrated to Italy in the late 17th century. He is known as one of the founders of the Italian *veduta*, a highly-detailed large-scale painting of a city or some other landscape. Van Wittel spent most of his time in Rome, but in 1699 he moved to Naples and stayed for two years in the service of the viceroy, or governor. He painted several views of Naples during this time.

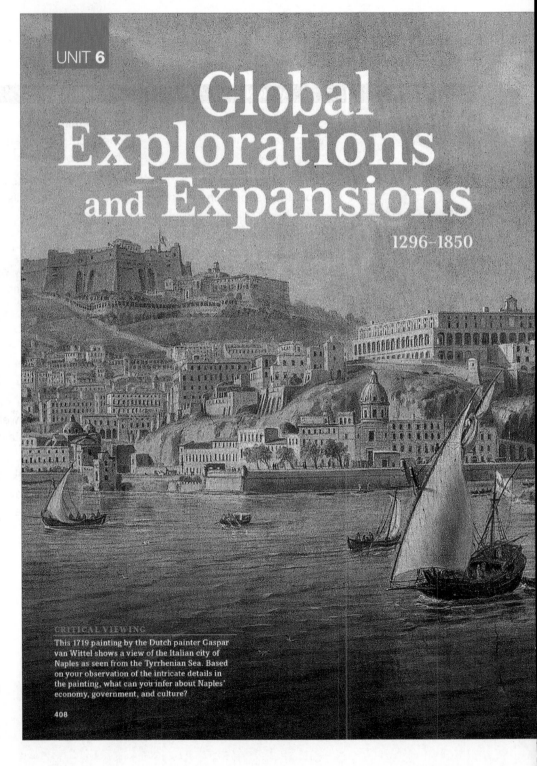

UNIT 6

Global Explorations and Expansions

1296–1850

CRITICAL VIEWING

This 1719 painting by the Dutch painter Gaspar van Wittel shows a view of the Italian city of Naples as seen from the Tyrrhenian Sea. Based on your observation of the intricate details in the painting, what can you infer about Naples' economy, government, and culture?

408

CRITICAL VIEWING Based on the city's location on the water and the number of boats sailing there, the economy is probably based on either trade or fishing. The many castle-like buildings that dot the landscape suggest that there is some type of royal government, and the domed building that looks like a church suggests that religion is important to the culture.

INTRODUCE TIME LINE EVENTS

IDENTIFY PATTERNS AND THEMES

Have volunteers read aloud each of the world events in the time line.

ASK: What are some common themes or patterns that you notice with regard to these events? *(Possible responses: Some common themes or patterns include exploration, expansion, powerful empires, conquest, religious reform, and technological innovation.)* Sort the themes and patterns into categories and put them in a chart like the one shown here.

Exploration and Conquest	Innovation and Reform	Growth of Empires

As students read the lessons for each chapter in the unit, have them add the lesson titles to the appropriate column in the chart. Advise students that they may also add or revise categories as necessary. At the end of the unit, revisit students' charts and create a final list of categories to summarize the historical themes students encountered as they read each chapter.

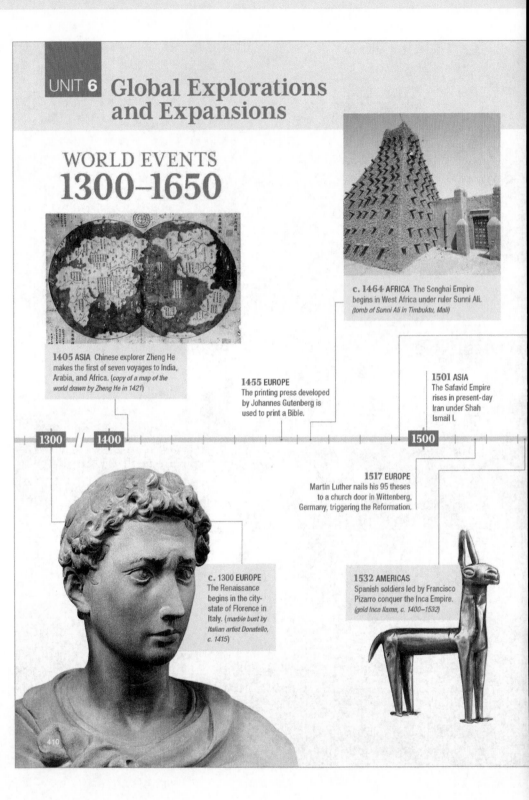

UNIT 6 Global Explorations and Expansions

WORLD EVENTS
1300–1650

1405 ASIA Chinese explorer Zheng He makes the first of seven voyages to India, Arabia, and Africa. *(copy of a map of the world drawn by Zheng He in 1421)*

c. 1464 AFRICA The Songhai Empire begins in West Africa under ruler Sunni Ali. *(tomb of Sunni Ali in Timbuktu, Mali)*

1455 EUROPE The printing press developed by Johannes Gutenberg is used to print a Bible.

1501 ASIA The Safavid Empire rises in present-day Iran under Shah Ismail I.

1300 // **1400**   **1500**

1517 EUROPE Martin Luther nails his 95 theses to a church door in Wittenberg, Germany, triggering the Reformation.

c. 1300 EUROPE The Renaissance begins in the city-state of Florence in Italy. *(marble bust by Italian artist Donatello, c. 1415)*

1532 AMERICAS Spanish soldiers led by Francisco Pizarro conquer the Inca Empire. *(gold Inca llama, c. 1400–1532)*

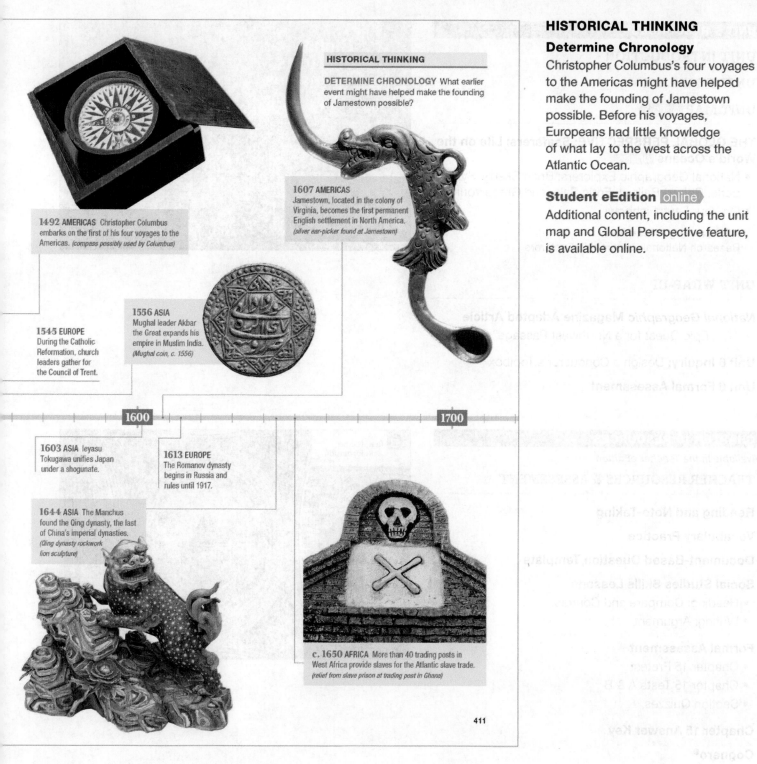

HISTORICAL THINKING

DETERMINE CHRONOLOGY What earlier event might have helped make the founding of Jamestown possible?

1607 AMERICAS
Jamestown, located in the colony of Virginia, becomes the first permanent English settlement in North America. *(silver ear-picker found at Jamestown)*

1492 AMERICAS Christopher Columbus embarks on the first of his four voyages to the Americas. *(compass possibly used by Columbus)*

1556 ASIA
Mughal leader Akbar the Great expands his empire in Muslim India. *(Mughal coin, c. 1556)*

1545 EUROPE
During the Catholic Reformation, church leaders gather for the Council of Trent.

1600

1700

1603 ASIA Ieyasu Tokugawa unifies Japan under a shogunate.

1613 EUROPE
The Romanov dynasty begins in Russia and rules until 1917.

1644 ASIA The Manchus found the Qing dynasty, the last of China's imperial dynasties. *(Qing dynasty rockwork lion sculpture)*

c. 1650 AFRICA More than 40 trading posts in West Africa provide slaves for the Atlantic slave trade. *(relief from slave prison at trading post in Ghana)*

HISTORICAL THINKING

Determine Chronology

Christopher Columbus's four voyages to the Americas might have helped make the founding of Jamestown possible. Before his voyages, Europeans had little knowledge of what lay to the west across the Atlantic Ocean.

Student eEdition online

Additional content, including the unit map and Global Perspective feature, is available online.

411

UNIT 6

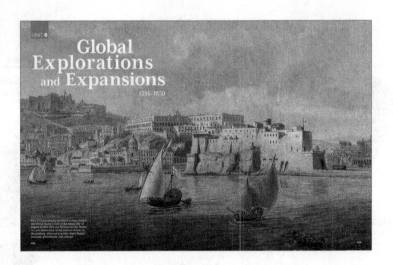

STRIVING READERS

STRATEGY ❶
Read and Recall
Arrange students in pairs. First have each student read the lesson independently. After reading, direct students to meet without the text, share ideas they recall, and take notes. Then tell students to use the text to review the lesson and decide what to add or change in their notes.

Use with All Lessons

STRATEGY ❷
Use a Sorting Activity
Write the following terms on the board and tell students to sort them into four groups of three related terms. Then instruct students to write a paragraph that shows how the terms in each set are related.

piety	anatomy	satire
indulgence	naturalism	Protestant
dissident	canonize	patron
liturgy	humanism	linear perspective

Use with All Lessons *You may use this activity at the beginning of the chapter and again after students study the lessons.*

STRATEGY ❸
Create Idea Webs
Have students summarize the chapter by creating two Idea Webs, one for the Renaissance and one for the Reformations (Protestant and Catholic). Tell students to complete each web with relevant information as they read the lessons.

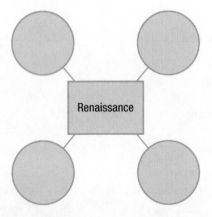

Use with All Lessons

INCLUSION

STRATEGY ❶
Use Supported Reading
Tell students to work in pairs and read the chapter aloud lesson by lesson. Instruct them to stop at the end of each lesson and use these sentence frames to monitor their comprehension of the text:

- This lesson is mostly about _____.
- Other topics in this lesson are _____.
- One question I have about the lesson is _____.
- One of the vocabulary words is _____. It means _____.
- One word I do not recognize is _____.
- I don't think I understand _____.

Use with All Lessons

STRATEGY ❷
Use Echo Reading
Point out that the Main Idea statements all relate to important aspects of the Renaissance or Reformation. Pair each student with a proficient reader. Ask the proficient reader to read aloud the Main Idea statement at the beginning of a lesson. The less proficient partner will "echo" by reading the same statement.

Use with All Lessons

ENGLISH LANGUAGE LEARNERS

STRATEGY ❶
Use Visuals to Predict Content
Direct students at the **Beginning** and **Intermediate** levels to read the lesson title and look at the visuals. Then ask them to write a sentence predicting how the visuals will relate to the lesson. After reading, you may wish to have students verify their predictions and reword sentences if necessary.

Use with All Lessons *Encourage students at the **Beginning** level to ask questions if they have trouble writing a prediction. Students at the **Advanced** level could help students at the **Beginning** and **Intermediate** levels write their predictions.*

STRATEGY 2

Pair Partners for Dictation

After reading a lesson, direct students at **All Proficiencies** to write in their own words a sentence expressing an important idea from the lesson. Pair students and let them take turns dictating their sentence to each other. Then encourage them to work together to check spelling and accuracy.

Use with All Lessons

GIFTED & TALENTED

STRATEGY 1

Create a Graphic Biography

Tell students to conduct online research about one of the important artists, writers, or reformers in this chapter. Examples include Leonardo da Vinci, Michelangelo, Petrarch, Desiderius Erasmus, Martin Luther, John Calvin, Ignatius of Loyola, or Teresa of Ávila. Ask students to then create a graphic biography, encouraging them to interpret the person's thoughts and actions based on their research. Invite students to share their completed work and answer any questions.

Use with All Lessons

STRATEGY 2

Write a Historical Dialogue

Tell students to write a fictional dialogue between pairs of figures in this chapter, such as Leonardo da Vinci and Michelangelo, Martin Luther and the pope, or John Calvin and Erasmus. Dialogues should convey each character's philosophy and views on art or religion as appropriate. Students should conduct online research to flesh out their dialogues. Encourage students to perform their completed dialogues for the class and answer questions.

Use with All Lessons

PRE-AP

STRATEGY 1

Create an Annotated Time Line

Instruct students to create and annotate a time line of events of the Renaissance and Reformation. Encourage students to illustrate their time line with thumbnail portraits of people or of buildings or details of art. Ask students to share their completed time lines with the class and to explain in depth the connection—causal and otherwise—between one event and a larger artistic or religious development that came later.

Use with All Lessons

STRATEGY 2

Extend Knowledge

Ask students to conduct online research to find out more about a topic, a person, or an event introduced in the chapter. For example, students might choose to research the Medici, the northern Renaissance, early critics of the Catholic Church, Henry VIII, the Holy Roman Empire, the Ottoman Empire, the Inquisition, or the Jesuits. Have students present their findings in an oral report to the class or in a digital report posted on a class blog.

Use with All Lessons

CHAPTER
15 Renaissance and **Reformation**
1296–1622

HISTORICAL THINKING Can tradition coexist with transformation?

SECTION 1 **The European Renaissance**
SECTION 2 **The Renaissance Impact**
SECTION 3 **The Protestant Reformation**
SECTION 4 **Global Impact of Religious Reforms**

CRITICAL VIEWING
This fresco of the Virgin Mary surrounded by saints adorns the ceiling of a chapel in the Church of the Gesù in Rome. Completed in 1564, the church is the primary church of the Jesuits, a religious order that emerged during the Catholic Reformation. What are characteristics of the artistic style of the painting?

INTRODUCE THE PAINTING

BAROQUE ART

Have students study the fresco of the Virgin Mary that appears at the beginning of the chapter. Direct students to focus on the central image and the details around it. **ASK:** What is happening in this painting? *(Possible response: The Virgin Mary, surrounded by angels, is rising up into heaven while a variety of people look on in awe.)* Explain that this style of painting is known as Baroque and that Baroque artists tried to create a sense of drama, exuberance, and grandeur through the use of ornate details and sensuous richness. Tell students that in this chapter they will learn about developments in European art that eventually evolved into the Baroque style.

SHARE BACKGROUND

Baroque art served as a tool of outreach for the Roman Catholic Church after the Protestant Reformation. The Baroque appeal to emotions and senses was meant to evoke a spiritual or mystical experience. Naturalistic techniques allowed viewers to identify with and feel a connection to religious figures, while drama and illusion were used to evoke a heavenly or divine splendor. As in the fresco of the Virgin Mary, paintings often depicted holy figures against a backdrop of heavenly glory.

Appropriately, the Baroque style began in Rome. Baroque sculptors and architects such as Gian Lorenzo Bernini created dramatic spaces and lighting using contrasting textures, vivid colors, and precious materials to thrill and delight viewers. The Baroque style traveled to other parts of Catholic Europe—especially to Spain and Spain's colonies in Latin America.

CRITICAL VIEWING Answers will vary. Possible responses include words such as *grand, fancy, ornate, elaborate,* or *dramatic.*

Four Corners: Preview Content This activity will help students preview and discuss the topics covered in the chapter. Provide a brief description and question for each section of the chapter, such as the ones shown below, and designate each of four corners as being "home" to one of the sections. Divide the class into four groups and direct each group to go to one of the corners and discuss the topic of the section for a short time.

Group 1 **Section 1** is about the European Renaissance. **ASK:** How do artistic styles reflect the concerns of a culture or society?

Group 2 **Section 2** is about the impact of the European Renaissance and the intellectual movement known as humanism. **ASK:** What goals and expectations do we have for education and educated people today?

Group 3 **Section 3** is about the Protestant Reformation. **ASK:** How do people express disagreement with mainstream views and what happens when they do so?

Group 4 **Section 4** is about the global impact of religious reforms. **ASK:** What causes religious ideas to spread to new areas?

KEY DATES FOR CHAPTER 15

1436	Brunelleschi's dome is completed in Florence.
c. 1450	Gutenberg invents the printing press.
1508	Michelangelo begins work on the Sistine Chapel ceiling.
1511	*The Praise of Folly* is published by Desiderius Erasmus.
1511	Raphael paints *School of Athens*.
1517	Martin Luther publicizes his 95 theses.
1520	Charles V is crowned Holy Roman Emperor.
1536	John Calvin flees to Geneva.
1545	The first meeting of the Council of Trent takes place.
1582	Matteo Ricci travels to China.

INTRODUCE THE READING STRATEGY

COMPARE AND CONTRAST

Explain to students that comparing and contrasting can help them more deeply understand concepts and events. Go to the Chapter Review and preview the Venn diagram with students. As they read the chapter, have students compare and contrast aspects of events pertaining to the European Renaissance and religious reformations.

INTRODUCE CHAPTER VOCABULARY

KEY VOCABULARY

SECTION 1

anatomy	commission	naturalism
patron		

SECTION 2

humanism	linear perspective	satire

SECTION 3

indulgence	liturgy	Protestant

SECTION 4

canonize	dissident	piety
religious syncretism		

DEFINITION CHART

As they read the chapter, encourage students to complete a Definition Chart for Key Vocabulary terms. Instruct students to list the Key Vocabulary terms in the first column of the chart. They should add each term's definition in the center column as they encounter the term in the chapter and then restate the definition in their own words in the third column. Model an example on the board, using the graphic organizer shown.

Word	Definition	In My Own Words
satire	a style of writing that makes humorous but critical observations	like *The Onion* or *Saturday Night Live*

The Rise of Italian City-States

Imagine a time when political power seemed up for grabs. In the 1300s,
Italy was divided into smaller kingdoms, city-states, and papal territories.
Regions battled for land and resources or to control trade. Wealthy families
battled for control as well.

EXPANDING CITY-STATES

Though growing in wealth, Italy in the 1300s could be violent and unstable. Farmland for growing olives, grapes, or wheat surrounded walled towns and cities. Some cities had to raise armies to defend themselves against attack from other cities. They fought to take over successful industries or a region's natural resources. Over time, stronger cities controlled larger areas.

In times of turmoil and in times of peace, Italian merchants carried on their centuries-old trade with northern Europe, northern Africa, and societies across Asia. As city-states grew wealthier into the 1400s, traders imported luxury goods for the rich. Carpets, gems, tulips, horses, and expensive dyes for brilliant colors in fabrics and paint came from bazaars, or large outdoor markets, in Muslim cities along the Mediterranean.

Controlling trade connections was essential to Italy's city-state economies. The city-states of Venice, Milan, Rome, and Florence were among the most powerful. Venice, a major port city, built a coastal trading empire that included many islands and trading stations along the Mediterranean as well as a colony in Constantinople. Milan, ruled by aggressive dukes, allied itself with France to take over northern and central Italy. Popes had been forced out of Rome by those who wanted a government that was independent of the church. The effort failed. When popes returned to govern, they used new ideas in mathematics and learning, along with growing wealth in trade, to rebuild the city.

Florence prospered through banking and wool and silk manufacturing. A republic, Florence was governed by members of guilds, organizations of people in the same field of work. The guilds for lawyers, bankers, or silk weavers had more power than guilds for stone masons, blacksmiths, or saddle makers. Workshops and offices

hired apprentices, who were workers training to learn a craft or discipline. Those who achieved mastery could join a guild and open their own workshops. Without a king, duke, or ruling dynasty, Florence relied on the active participation of its citizens to achieve stability.

FLORENCE'S DOME

City leaders of Florence turned to art and architecture to display the city's growing success. The city's centerpiece, its cathedral, had been under construction since 1296. Work slowed when plague spread in the mid-1300s, devastating Italy, western Asia, and North Africa. The disease reduced Florence's population from 120,000 to 50,000. But by 1418, all but the cathedral's dome had been completed. The dome would have to be huge—138 feet across at its base, which was more than 170 feet off the ground. How could workers haul up materials to begin construction? What would keep the dome from collapsing? The master builders of Florence had no solutions, so city leaders announced a public competition. Competitors had to build a model and describe how the dome could be accomplished.

Filippo Brunelleschi (broo-nuhl-LEHS-kee) had apprenticed as a goldsmith but pursued architecture instead. He studied mathematics and lived in Rome briefly to examine classical Roman buildings and ruins. For the dome competition, he described his ideas for a crane and a giant hoist, or lift, for safely moving workers and materials. These inventions and his model, with its Roman influences, were brilliant. He was given the job. Even before the dome was completed in 1436, Brunelleschi became the most sought-after architect in Florence.

Structures symbolizing a city's identity were meant to be seen from miles around. They were a source of pride for the people in the street and farmers in the valleys. Florence's cathedral is called Il Duomo in Italian.

(Duomo is Italian for "cathedral.") The cathedral had been planned to show off one of Europe's most powerful cities. Now with its magnificent dome, Florence could claim an architectural wonder.

THE MEDICI FAMILY

Florence's greatest family, the Medici (MEHD-ih-chee), controlled Europe's wool manufacturing and banking. Bankers who spoke multiple languages, knew the values of coins in different societies, and could negotiate and calculate exchange rates were essential to growth in trade. The Medici established banks in Venice, Rome, London, and other cities.

The economy of Florence weakened after the plague, and guilds became less powerful. In 1434, Cosimo de Medici took over the government. He was a **patron** of artists, which meant he gave artists financial support. He promoted the Medici reputation with art, building projects, and pageantry, or grand public displays. Cosimo admired Plato and learning from ancient Greece. He founded a public library in Florence, the first in western Europe since ancient times.

By the time control of Florence passed to Cosimo's grandson, **Lorenzo de Medici**, the former republic was, in effect, ruled by a Medici prince. Lorenzo became known as "the Magnificent" for his learning and his support of scholars and artists, but some citizens of Florence were upset that the Medici had undermined their republic by establishing a ruling dynasty. By the end of the 1500s, the absolute rule of the Medici would bring an end to the cultural and political conditions that once made Florence a center of artistic achievement.

The Dome

When the dome was completed in 1436, it soared to a height of about 374 feet. Engineers today still do not fully understand how Brunelleschi constructed his masterpiece.

Because the base of the dome was not built with precision, opposite pairs of diagonal lines cross at four different points, not the center.

HISTORICAL THINKING

1. **READING CHECK** How did Florence stand out from the other major city-states?

2. **IDENTIFY PROBLEMS AND SOLUTIONS** How was engineering important to the solution of the dome's design?

3. **DRAW CONCLUSIONS** Why do you think banking was essential to trade at this time?

PLAN: 2-PAGE LESSON

OBJECTIVE

Identify the causes and effects of Florence's influence in the 15th and 16th centuries.

CRITICAL THINKING SKILLS FOR LESSON 1.1

- Identify Problems and Solutions
- Draw Conclusions
- Categorize
- Form and Support Opinions
- Analyze Visuals

HISTORICAL THINKING FOR CHAPTER 15

Can tradition coexist with transformation?

The growth of Italian city-states preceded the events now known as the European Renaissance. Lesson 1.1 discusses the city-states' rise to power with a special focus on Florence and the ruling Medici family.

Student eEdition online

Additional content for this lesson, including a video, is available online.

BACKGROUND FOR THE TEACHER

Florence's *Signoria* In 1293, Florence adopted the Ordinances of Justice, a city constitution that required eight of Florence's nine city council (*Signoria*) members to be elected from members of the guilds. It barred non-guild members, including nobles, from political power. Candidates were chosen at random from names written on slips of paper and placed in a leather bag. The only requirements were that they had to be male, at least 30 years old, free of debt, and have no relative already serving on the *Signoria*. Terms lasted for only two months. The job of the nine-member council was to introduce legislation. Laws introduced by the *Signoria* had to be passed by the Council of the People and the Council of the Commune, each of which had about 300 members. Because such a high proportion of the male population was likely to hold political office at some time, Florentines saw themselves as a community of civil servants who were interested in and informed about current affairs.

INTRODUCE & ENGAGE

DISCUSS MONUMENTAL ARCHITECTURE

Direct students to look at the diagram and photographs of *il Duomo* that appear in the lesson. Explain that structures such as this cathedral often come to symbolize a city's identity. Ask volunteers to name other cities and the key architectural features that define them—including the local community. *(Possible responses might include the Empire State Building for New York City, the Willis Tower for Chicago, or the Space Needle for Seattle.)* Tell students that in this lesson they will learn about the Italian city of Florence and how it became a center of artistic achievement.

TEACH

GUIDED DISCUSSION

1. **Categorize** Why do you think the bankers' and silk weavers' guilds had more power than the stone masons' or saddle makers' guilds? *(The fields of banking and silk weaving probably involved more money than stone masonry or saddle making, and money is often linked to power.)*

2. **Form and Support Opinions** Do you think Lorenzo de Medici deserved the title "the Magnificent"? Why or why not? *(Possible responses: Yes, because of his support for art and learning; no, because he and his family brought an end to the republican government and the conditions that made Florence a center of achievement.)*

ANALYZE VISUALS STEM

Have students look at the images and video of *il Duomo* (available in the Student eEdition). **ASK:** Based on what you saw, how did Brunelleschi keep the heavy structure from collapsing in on itself? *(Possible response: He created an inner shell and an outer shell with a wooden skeleton between them.)*

ACTIVE OPTIONS

On Your Feet: Jigsaw Strategy Organize students into four "expert" groups and have students from each group research the Italian cities Venice, Milan, Rome, and Naples during the 15th and 16th centuries. Have each group work to create a simplified summary of what they learned about the city they researched. Then have students in each group count off using A, B, C, and D. Regroup students into four new groups so each group has at least one person from each of the four expert groups. Have students in the new group take turns sharing the simplified summary they created in their "expert" groups.

> **NG Learning Framework: Write a Biography**
> **ATTITUDE** Empowerment
> **SKILL** Problem-Solving

Have students write a short biography or profile of Filippo Brunelleschi using information from the chapter and additional source material. Suggest students focus on Brunelleschi's approach to problem-solving. Invite students to read their biographies aloud to the class.

DIFFERENTIATE

STRIVING READERS

Understand Main Ideas Check students' understanding of the main ideas in the lesson by asking them to correctly complete statements such as the following:

- Italian city-states built empires based on (technology or trade). *(trade)*
- Florence was governed by (guilds or nobles). *(guilds)*
- Leaders of Florence wanted to display their (engineering skill or financial success) by building a huge dome. *(financial success)*
- To succeed, bankers (did business only with the rich or spoke many languages). *(spoke many languages)*

PRE-AP

Analyze a Paradox Have students analyze the paradoxical effect of the Medici family on Florence: The Medici supported the arts, founded a library, and promoted the city with building projects; however, they also seized power and brought an end to the conditions that once made Florence a center of artistic achievement. Direct students to conduct online research to analyze the paradox and write an essay. Ask them to share their essays on a class blog or website.

See the Chapter Planner for more strategies for differentiation.

HISTORICAL THINKING

ANSWERS

1. It was a republic ruled by members of guilds.

2. A crane and a giant hoist, as well as a structure that would not collapse, were required for its success.

3. Possible response: because trade was carried out over wide areas involving different languages and currencies; Also, large amounts of money were exchanged as valuable goods were bought and sold.

A Cultural Rebirth

As is sometimes the case, historians look back on the past and give a name or label to a group of events. This was true in the 1800s, when historians applied the term *renaissance*, meaning "rebirth," to Italy's renewed interest in ancient ideas during the 14th and 15th centuries.

Many of the Renaissance artist Giotto's paintings portray the life of St. Francis, an Italian monk known for his care of the poor and animals. In this fresco, St. Francis (with a halo at right), addresses the throned sultan Al-Kamil, ruler of Egypt, Palestine, and Syria.

TRADE AND CULTURE

The European Renaissance, which lasted from the 1300s into the 1600s, had international roots. As you have already read, scholars in cities such as Córdoba, Baghdad, and Timbuktu had been translating classical Greek writings for hundreds of years. While Arab and Jewish scholars studied these texts to make advances in science and mathematics, European Christian scholars focused on religion.

Through trade with Asian and African societies, Italians became aware of these translated works. They learned, too, about texts that described Chinese inventions and Muslim medicine and astronomy. Italian scholars traveled to Christian monasteries and to libraries in Muslim cities in search of classical writings, even if only in fragments. Works by the philosophers Aristotle and Plato, the mathematicians Euclid and Ptolemy, and the great Roman orator Cicero generated excitement and

were in demand. Italians founded academies, or Greek-style schools, and read classical writings that explored how to be ethical in society and what was harmonious or ideal in art and architecture.

Asian goods were also valued. Intricately painted ceramics and silks woven with gold threads came into Venice from Mongol and Ottoman trading sources. Wealthy Italians also prized thick, hand-knotted carpets in geometric designs. Some commissioned painters to include luxury goods in their portraits. A **commission** was a request for a specific art or design project, usually from a rich patron. A painting showing an expensive carpet, whether spread on a table or hung from a window during a festival, signaled the patron's high status or prestige.

Trading cities were sources of fascination. However, most Italian painters never saw Ottoman cities and their busy bazaars. Painters may have based their images of these places on stories from travelers, traders, and soldiers. One artist who drew on such stories was **Giotto**, who lived in the 1300s.

Giotto was one of the earliest and most influential of the Italian Renaissance painters. Although his work had Byzantine influences, Giotto portrayed people with expressive faces and natural postures in realistic backgrounds and settings. Painters who followed him admired him for "painting from life." This opened the way for the three-dimensional characteristics of Renaissance painting.

THE PRINTED WORD

As you have already learned, China and Korea had used woodblock printing and movable type since the 11th century. Printers coated the blocks with ink and pressed them into paper. In the 1200s, Spanish Muslims were the first Europeans to follow the ancient Chinese technique for making paper. They shredded and soaked cloth rags, pressed the fibers into single sheets, and then let them dry. Scribes wrote on this paper, and bookbinders sewed pages together to form books.

This labor-intensive method of bookmaking changed in the mid-1400s. A German printer, **Johannes Gutenberg**, made metal castings of individual letters of the German alphabet. This metal type could be

GUTENBERG'S BIBLE The first book Gutenberg printed on his new press was a Latin Bible. The Gutenberg Bible, as it came to be called, contained 1,286 pages with about 42 lines on each page. It was remarkable for its neat, even letters and hand-painted illustrations of nature. Gutenberg printed 180 copies of his Bible, of which about 50 survive today.

rearranged, inked, pressed, and reused. The metal letters could print multiple copies without breaking or wearing out. Gutenberg's method was soon used to print thousands of books far more cheaply and quickly than copying books by hand.

The printing press came to Italy in 1465. By 1500, Italy had 73 workshops for printing and selling books, and throughout Europe several million books had been produced. Many were printed in the vernacular European languages—such as German, Italian, Spanish, French, and English—rather than in Latin. Before that, most writings had been documents of the church, written in Latin. As people read or heard works read in their native language, they began to think of themselves as German, French, Italian, or Spanish.

Printing presses provided greater access to printed materials. As a result, more people learned to read, even in rural areas, and they shared books, and the stories and information within them, at social gatherings. The technological advance of the printing press allowed ancient and global ideas and creative expression to reach new readers. The revolution in print materials transformed learning and communication in Europe.

HISTORICAL THINKING

1. **READING CHECK** Why did many painters include carpets in their pictures?

2. **DRAW CONCLUSIONS** How might Giotto's painted figures have affected viewers who had only seen religious stories in earlier art?

3. **ANALYZE CAUSE AND EFFECT** What was one effect of the use of vernacular languages in printed books on those who read them?

PLAN: 2-PAGE LESSON

OBJECTIVE

Explain how trade with Asian and African societies and the development of the printing press transformed learning and communication in Europe.

CRITICAL THINKING SKILLS FOR LESSON 1.2

- Draw Conclusions
- Analyze Cause and Effect
- Make Inferences

HISTORICAL THINKING FOR CHAPTER 15

Can tradition coexist with transformation?

Trade and technology were behind a series of cultural changes in 14th-century Europe. Lesson 1.2 explains how global trade and the invention of the printing press gave Europeans a greater awareness of ancient writings and ideas from different cultures.

BACKGROUND FOR THE TEACHER

Gutenberg and the Printing Press Johannes Gutenberg may have used existing technologies—such as the wine press—to create the printing press, but he also invented his own ink and developed the special metal alloy used to create his movable type. While the press greatly reduced the time and cost of making books, printing was still labor intensive. Each letter had to be placed by hand in the frame used to print a page. Approximately 2,500 pieces of type had to be set for each page of the 1,286 pages of Gutenberg's three-volume Bible. Historians believe it took three to five years to complete that first printing of the Bible.

While Gutenberg's printing press is widely recognized as one of the most important inventions in world history, it did not solve his considerable financial problems. He needed investors to pay for the enterprise. Conflicts led to lawsuits, and Gutenberg never received much money for his invention. Even so, his name lives on in Project Gutenberg, an organization devoted to digitizing public domain books and making them available at no cost to anyone who wants to read them.

INTRODUCE & ENGAGE

DISCUSS CULTURES

Pair students and encourage them to discuss elements of other cultures that have become familiar in the United States. Have pairs share their ideas and write them on the board. **ASK:** How do these cultural elements affect your view of the world? *(Possible response: They make me feel more connected to people from other places; they make me realize that new and different experiences can be enlightening.)* Tell students that in this lesson they will learn how exposure to new ideas and technology led to a period of cultural change in Europe.

TEACH

GUIDED DISCUSSION

1. **Make Inferences** What can you infer about the value of books from the information about Italian scholars? *(The fact that they traveled in search of books and even fragments tells us that books were rare and difficult to find.)*

2. **Draw Conclusions** What do you think motivated most of those who commissioned works of art? *(They wanted to portray themselves as powerful and successful.)*

MORE INFORMATION

The Giotto fresco that appears in this lesson is known as *Trial by Fire*. During the Fifth Crusade in 1219, the Italian monk Francis of Assisi went to Egypt to meet with Sultan Al-Kamil. Francis is said to have offered to walk through fire if the sultan would become a Christian. While neither the sultan nor Francis changed their religious views, the two men spent several days together talking. They were unable to end the fighting between Christians and Muslims, but both are believed to have gained respect for each other. Later, when the sultan's armies surrounded Christian crusaders, he sent the enemy soldiers and their animals food rather than killing them.

ACTIVE OPTIONS

On Your Feet: Card Responses Direct students to work in groups to create a quiz about what they learned in the lesson. Students can write true-false, complete-the-sentence, or short-answer questions. Have groups trade sets of questions and answer them. Encourage groups to check answers against the text and to keep track of group scores.

> **NG Learning Framework: Create a Marketing Plan**
> **SKILL** Problem-Solving
> **KNOWLEDGE** New Frontiers

Have groups create a marketing plan for Gutenberg's printing press. Tell students that Gutenberg's motivation for inventing the press was his need to make money. Ask students to develop a campaign that Gutenberg could have used to explain to people why his idea was important and something they should use. Have students start by creating an ad that Gutenberg might have printed himself on his press. Students may also choose to extend the marketing campaign to include digital and social media.

DIFFERENTIATE

INCLUSION

Describe Images Pair students who are visually impaired with students who are not. Ask the latter to describe the Giotto painting and the photograph of the Gutenberg Bible in detail, responding to questions from their partners.

PRE-AP

Present an Oral Report Ask students to prepare and present oral reports on a painting or series of paintings by Giotto. Instruct students to focus on the ways in which Giotto's work was innovative in his time. Ask students to include visuals in their reports to enhance interest and understanding.

See the Chapter Planner for more strategies for differentiation.

HISTORICAL THINKING

ANSWERS

1. Carpets were expensive, valued possessions. Including them in a commissioned portrait was a way to indicate the patron's wealth and prestige.

2. Paintings of ordinary mortals may have startled viewers and encouraged them to view themselves and other people as newly significant.

3. People who read or heard books read in the vernacular language slowly began to identify with their language group.

Renaissance Arts

Imagine a world in which no one has heard of superstar
artists and musicians. But that's how it was in Europe until
the 15th century, when some Renaissance artists became
the superstars of their day.

"TRUTH TO NATURE"

During the Renaissance, rediscovered classical writings
in math, science, and philosophy fueled a new direction
in the arts, called a "truth to nature," or **naturalism**.
Renaissance artists strove for accuracy in their
depictions of people or of the natural world.

Leonardo da Vinci is famous for being an artist,
a scientist, an inventor, and a keen observer of the
natural world. Maybe you have heard or read about a
"renaissance man" or "renaissance woman." Those
terms refer to someone who has many talents, and they
come from Leonardo's time. To develop oneself as fully
as possible was a Renaissance goal.

In 1465, when he was about 15, Leonardo traveled to
Florence to train to be a painter. Throughout his life,
until his death in 1519, he traveled to escape political
upheavals or to compete for commissions. The Duke of
Milan, whose court rivaled the splendors of the Medici
court in Florence, hired him as a military engineer.
Leonardo also lived in Rome and in France. In 1517, the
royal court in France gave him the title "First Painter,
Engineer, and Architect of the King."

In Florence, artists were trained to draw as the first
stage of making a painting. But Leonardo's drawings
accomplished far more. He drew plant life, the flight
of birds, and images of **anatomy**, or the interior and
exterior structures of living things. His drawings showed
how water moves and how machines work. He sketched
his ideas for a parachute, an adding machine, a giant
crossbow, flying machines, and elaborate theatrical
displays. His many inventions, whether for entertainment
or military use, were not all built but were remarkably far
ahead of their time.

In his paintings, Leonardo based his choices of color
on his observations, such as the effects of light in the

atmosphere. Nearer objects were their true color, he
wrote, but distant objects were bluer, as if in a mist or
haze. His ideas influenced painters throughout Italy.
Leonardo's *Last Supper* and the portrait *Mona Lisa* are
today two of the most famous images of European art.

ART THAT INSPIRES AWE

About 25 years younger than Leonardo, **Michelangelo
Buonarotti** also studied in Florence. He was educated
at the Medici Palace and became a painter, sculptor,
architect, and poet. At 23, he completed his first
sculpted masterpiece in marble, the *Pietà*, or "Pity,"
in which Mary mourns the death of her son Jesus. Six
years later, Michelangelo finished his 13-foot sculpture,
David, the larger-than-life statue of the young man
who killed a giant, according to the biblical account.
This second marble masterpiece was a commission
from the supporters of a renewed republic that had
temporarily expelled the Medici family. *David* became
a symbol of victory over tyranny. Both sculptures made
Michelangelo famous. Proud and competitive, he was
said to care more for his work as an artist than for
money or celebrity.

In 1508, he accepted a commission to paint, in fresco,
the ceiling of the Sistine Chapel in Rome. *Pittura a
fresco* is an Italian term meaning "painting freshly." In
fresco painting, artists ground minerals into powders
to create pigments of different colors. They mixed the
pigments with water and then brushed the mixture onto
a damp, newly plastered surface. When dry, the color
was chemically bound to the surface.

Michelangelo spent about four years working on the
ceiling. Much of that time he spent lying on his back on
a scaffold. He painted Old Testament figures in active
poses. Among them are prophets, whom he painted
holding books or reading. Michelangelo's human forms

418   CHAPTER 15

LYBIAN SIBYL (detail of Sistine Chapel Ceiling)
This sibyl, or female prophet, faces the church altar. The twist
of her body and the placement of her foot make her appear as
though she is about to stand, the kind of realistic "action" in
paint Michelangelo was known for. The sketch is known as
a study. Completed in red chalk, it demonstrates the artist's
approach as he worked out the figure's pose.

Renaissance and Reformation   419

PLAN: 4-PAGE LESSON

OBJECTIVE

**Describe the innovative methods and materials used
by Italian and Northern Renaissance artists.**

CRITICAL THINKING SKILLS FOR LESSON 1.3

- Make Inferences
- Describe
- Identify Main Ideas and Details
- Make Connections
- Synthesize
- Form and Support Opinions
- Analyze Visuals

HISTORICAL THINKING FOR CHAPTER 15

Can tradition coexist with transformation?

Renaissance scholars rediscovered classical Greek
and Roman ideas that inspired new ways to think about
people and the natural world. Lesson 1.3 discusses key
figures and developments in painting, sculpture, and
other arts.

BACKGROUND FOR THE TEACHER

The *Mona Lisa* Leonardo da Vinci's *Mona Lisa* is
probably the most famous and recognizable painting in
the world, and this familiarity makes it hard for modern
viewers to understand its importance. Yet according to
art experts, this painting has inspired Western portraiture
ever since. Prior to *Mona Lisa*, Florentine painters
outlined their subjects. You can see this technique in
Michelangelo's Libyan Sibyl shown in this lesson. For the
Mona Lisa, Leonardo used a technique known as *sfumato*
(smoke) to create the subtlest of transitions between
colors. The edge of the woman's hair and the shadows
around her eyes are created with minute brushstrokes too
fine to be seen. Viewers of Leonardo's time thought the
woman in the picture did not even appear to be painted,
but was "truly of flesh and blood."

INTRODUCE & ENGAGE

PREVIEW WITH VISUALS

Direct students' attention to the art presented in the lesson. Write "Renaissance Arts" at the center of a Concept Cluster and ask volunteers to list traits of Renaissance painting based on their observation of the art and arrange them into groups on the cluster. At the end of the lesson, revisit the Concept Cluster and add or remove traits based on what students learned.

TEACH

GUIDED DISCUSSION

1. **Make Connections** How did Leonardo da Vinci and Michelangelo Buonarroti exemplify the idea of the "Renaissance man"? *(Leonardo was a painter, scientist, and inventor; Michelangelo was a painter, sculptor, architect, and poet. This wide range of accomplishments by both men reflected the ideal of exceptional achievement in many different areas.)*

2. **Synthesize** Review the descriptions of Leonardo da Vinci's most famous works and those of Michelangelo. What common feature do most of them share? Which one is distinctive? *(The Last Supper, the Pietá, David, and the Sistine Chapel share a biblical or religious inspiration. The Mona Lisa is distinctive in that it has no religious connection.)*

ANALYZE VISUALS

Discuss the painting of the sibyl that appears in the lesson. Have students read the caption and explain that sibyls originated in classical Greece but were regarded as similar to prophets by later Christians. According to legend, sibyls wrote out their prophecies of the future and kept them secret. **ASK:** What stands out for you in this depiction of the sibyl? *(Possible responses may include the musculature of her body or the drapery of her clothing.)* How does Michelangelo convey the muscles and drapery? *(He uses shadow and highlights to create the illusion of muscles and drapery.)* Do you think the sibyl is lifting her book up or setting it down? How does your perception of what she is doing with the book affect your interpretation of the painting? *(Possible response: She is setting it down because she has just finished writing down a prophecy, or she is lifting the book because she is about to reveal her prophecy for the first time, or alternatively, about to enter a new prophecy.)*

DIFFERENTIATE

ENGLISH LANGUAGE LEARNERS

Dictate Sentence Summaries Pair students at the **Beginning** level with those at the **Advanced** level. After students read the sections on Leonardo and Michelangelo, direct them to identify three sentences that contain an important idea. Then tell each student to write that idea in a summary sentence using his or her own words. Partners then take turns dictating their sentences to each other. Encourage them to work together to check each other's work for accuracy and spelling.

GIFTED & TALENTED

Evaluate Exhibition Posters Direct students to conduct online research to find posters announcing major museum exhibits for Leonardo and Michelangelo. Have each student choose three to five posters they like and then identify the visual and text elements that make these posters effective. Ask students to prepare a brief presentation to discuss the posters and explain how they present the work of the artist in question.

See the Chapter Planner for more strategies for differentiation.

were unmatched by any other artist in their intensity and power. One dramatic section is as widely recognized as Leonardo's great *Mona Lisa*. Titled *Creation of Adam*, a figure who represents God reaches out toward Adam to convey the spark of life.

NORTHERN PAINTERS

Italian artists influenced artists in the Netherlands, Germany, and other northern European regions. These artists did not abandon their tradition of precision, attention to detail, and mastery of landscapes. Their work, in turn, influenced Italians.

Jan van Eyck (yahn vahn IKE) of the Netherlands was an early northern Renaissance artist. He perfected the technique of mixing pigments with oil. Thin layers or glazes of oil paint caught the light, giving colors a jewel-like quality not possible in fresco painting. Lorenzo de Medici collected van Eyck's paintings. Leonardo, along with many other Italian artists, adopted and experimented with oil painting technique.

In the 1300s and 1400s, artists sometimes included themselves in a group of figures in a painting, but van Eyck may have been the first to simply paint himself. *Portrait of a Man* shows him in a red chaperon, or head covering. His gaze, the roughness of his skin, and the glint in his eyes look real. Van Eyck was proud of his

work. He wrote on the frame of the portrait, "As I can . . . Jan van Eyck made me on 21 October 1433."

Albrecht Dürer (AHL-brekht DYOO-ruh) of Nuremberg, Germany, was the first northern artist to apply the innovations of Italian artists to his own work. Born in 1471, his life overlapped that of many of Italy's famous artists. At 23, he traveled to Venice, painted watercolors of the great works he saw, and later returned to Italy to stay longer and learn more. In his writings, he said, "art was extinct until it came to light again [in Italy]."

Dürer was an accomplished maker of woodblock prints and engravings and is credited with elevating these techniques to a fine art. He noticed that many artists in Italy were literate and well read and had a higher social position than artists in Germany did. He wanted to bring the desire for scientific knowledge to Germany and raise artistic standards. He succeeded for himself and influenced many others.

SPANISH RENAISSANCE

El Greco ("the Greek"), was born in Crete in 1541. As a young man, he moved to Venice to study art. Later, he chose to paint in nearby Toledo, an ancient city with a history of Roman occupation and rule by Arabic-speaking Christians and Muslims.

CRITICAL VIEWING Van Eyck's *Madonna of Chancellor Rolin* (above left, 1435) introduces the illusion of space by including a background scene, while El Greco's *View of Toledo* (above right, c. 1599–1600) introduces emotion through the somber clouds in the sky. What are some differences between the two painting styles?

Self-Portrait Holding a Medallion, c. 1556

PAINTED FROM A MIRROR Michelangelo's monumental works brought him great fame. Another northern Italian artist, Sofonisba Anguissola (ah-gwih-SOH-lah), has been called Europe's first famous woman artist. Because women weren't allowed to study anatomy at this time, female artists tended to paint portraits. Anguissola gained renown for her self-portraits.

Anguissola's father sent her drawings to Michelangelo and her paintings to potential patrons. Her exceptional skill attracted the attention of King Philip II of Spain, and in 1559 at age 27, she moved to the Spanish court in Madrid. For ten years, she painted royal portraits. Such portraits asserted the importance, even majesty, of a ruler. Rulers chose virtuosos, or those of exceptional skill, who could duplicate in paint the look of velvet, brocade, silk, lace, or gems to emphasize their wealth. Anguissola continued painting self-portraits into old age.

The self-portrait shown here is a miniature, an artwork designed to be worn or carried.

Toledo's population was a mix of Jewish and Catholic Spaniards, and the town was full of scholars and poets. El Greco received commissions to paint for churches and monasteries. He had brought the Renaissance to Spain, but his style rejected naturalism. For example, he did not use realistic colors, nor did he apply the ancient Greek and Roman ideals for human proportions. Instead, he elongated, or distorted, his figures, giving them a restless and emotional quality that many critics praise.

OTTOMAN CONNECTIONS

Just as trade connected Italy to the Ottomans, so did the arts. In the late 1400s, the Venetian artist Gentile Bellini went to the Ottoman court. Sultan Mehmed II wanted an artist to use Italian techniques to paint and

cast bronze medals of his image so it could be seen throughout Europe.

Then in the early 1500s, the sultan invited Leonardo to submit drawings for a bridge to cross the Golden Horne, part of the Bosporus that runs through present-day Istanbul. Another drawing was submitted by the military engineer Mimar Sinan, who was to become the greatest architect in Ottoman history. Living at the same time as Michelangelo, Sinan created mosques whose domes seem to float in the air while flooding interior spaces with light. We see the flow of ideas across cultures when Michelangelo used the Byzantine architecture of Istanbul as inspiration for the dome of Saint Peter's Basilica in Rome and when Sinan was then influenced by Michelangelo in his design of the magnificent Süleymaniye Mosque.

HISTORICAL THINKING

1. **READING CHECK** How did observations of the natural world bring change to the arts of Italy?

2. **MAKE INFERENCES** Why do you think artists like Leonardo and Michelangelo had to be competitive?

3. **DESCRIBE** What elements of van Eyck's paintings astonished viewers?

4. **IDENTIFY MAIN IDEAS AND DETAILS** What evidence indicates that artists in Renaissance Italy and the Ottoman Empire influenced one another?

BACKGROUND FOR THE TEACHER

The Development of Oil Painting Jan van Eyck has long been credited with inventing oil painting, but art historians no longer believe this was the case, citing evidence of its use in northern Europe for more than a century before van Eyck was born. No one disputes, however, that it was van Eyck's mastery of the medium in the early 1400s that led to its widespread adoption throughout Europe in the 1500s. Before this time, artists in southern Europe used egg-based tempera paint. Tempera dries quickly and produces bright colors, but it does not have the transparent qualities of oil paint. Because oil dries slowly, it can be blended to create different effects. In the hands of a master such as van Eyck, it can portray smooth polished marble, reflective glittering jewels, sumptuous velvet, or swirling transparent water.

TEACH

GUIDED DISCUSSION

3. **Form and Support Opinions** What do you think Dürer meant by the following comment: "[A]rt was extinct until it came to light again [in Italy]?" *(Possible response: In Italy, Dürer saw artists creating work that showed greater technical skill and vision than he had seen in other areas of Europe.)*

4. **Describe** How would you describe the emotions in El Greco's *View of Toledo*? How does the artist convey these emotions? *(Possible response: He uses grays and blacks to create a sense of threat or foreboding both in the dark clouds in the sky and in the deep hollows of the earth. There is also a feeling of movement, as though things are about to change, created by the clouds that appear to be in motion across the sky.)*

ANALYZE VISUALS

Share the Background for the Teacher information on the development of oil painting with students. Then have students examine van Eyck's *Madonna of Chancellor Rolin*, which appears in the lesson. **ASK:** What effects does van Eyck create with the use of oil paint in this work of art? *(Possible response: He shows the reflection of the boat on the river in the background of the painting, the ornate detail on the columns in the room, and the shine of the gold crown being placed on the Madonna's head.)*

ACTIVE OPTIONS

On Your Feet: Tell Me More Instruct students to form four teams and assign each team one of the following topics: Northern Renaissance Painters; Spanish Renaissance Painters; Women Painters of the Renaissance; Ottoman Connections to the Renaissance. Each group should write down as many facts about their topic as they can. Reconvene the class and have one group stand up. Invite the rest of the class to call out, "Tell me more about [one of the topics]!" The standing group reads aloud one of their facts. The class again calls out, "Tell me more!" until the group runs out of facts to share. Then the other groups stand, one at a time, to present their facts as classmates ask for more information. Monitor which group shares the most facts, but keep in mind that the last two topics will be more difficult to find information about than the first two topics.

NG Learning Framework: Explore Renaissance Art
| **ATTITUDE** Curiosity
| **KNOWLEDGE** Our Human Story

Invite students to search online for the other Renaissance paintings mentioned but not shown in the lesson or another work by one of the artists mentioned in the lesson. Have them select one of the paintings and analyze it in terms of what they have learned about Renaissance art. Have volunteers present their painting to the class and describe its Renaissance characteristics.

HISTORICAL THINKING

ANSWERS

1. Observations of the natural world affected the way artists used color and depicted human anatomy.

2. Possible response: Artists depended on commissions from wealthy people and institutions such as the Roman Catholic Church and they had to compete to get them.

3. Van Eyck's oil painting technique allowed him to create different surfaces and lighting effects that astonished viewers.

4. The domes of notable mosques and cathedrals offer evidence that artists of Renaissance Italy and the Ottoman Empire influenced one another.

CRITICAL VIEWING Possible response: Van Eyck introduces emotion through gesture, posture, and facial expression, while El Greco creates emotion through color and movement. Van Eyck's brushwork is precise and controlled, while El Greco's brushwork is looser and more active.

Finding a
Lost da Vinci

"You simply have to go beyond what your eyesight can do." –Maurizio Seracini

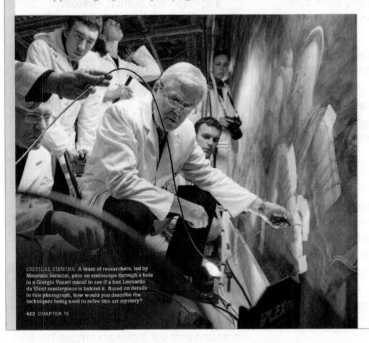

CRITICAL VIEWING A team of researchers, led by Maurizio Seracini, pass an endoscope through a hole in a Giorgio Vasari mural to see if a lost Leonardo da Vinci masterpiece is behind it. Based on details in this photograph, how would you describe the techniques being used to solve this art mystery?

At the Palazzo Vecchio in Florence in 1504, the two greatest artists of the Italian Renaissance faced off—but this was not a duel. It was a battle with pencils and brushes. Leonardo da Vinci, an artist in his early 50s known through all of Europe, had been commissioned to paint a mural on a wall in the enormous Hall of 500 in the Palazzo. The young artist Michelangelo had been commissioned to paint another mural on the same wall. The two men couldn't stand each other. This was a competition to show the world who was the better artist.

> MAIN IDEA National Geographic Explorer Maurizio Seracini uses high-tech methods to analyze art masterpieces.

FINDING THE LOST DA VINCI

Michelangelo drew a detailed, full-size version of his planned scene. But before he started to paint, the pope summoned him to Rome to work on another project. Leonardo's painting, called *The Battle of Anghiari*, was completed, but the paint didn't dry properly and some of it began to drip down the wall. Even so, the painting was much admired, but some 50 years after Leonardo completed his work, artist Giorgio Vasari was hired to paint over it. The artwork was lost forever. Or was it?

Fast-forward hundreds of years. National Geographic Explorer Maurizio Seracini grew up in Florence, then moved to California to attend college, where he received a degree in bioengineering. In the 1970s, Seracini, at the request of his former professor and famed Leonardo historian Carlo Pedretti, applied his understanding of technology to solve the mystery of the lost da Vinci masterpiece. While studying Vasari's mural, Seracini spotted a nearly invisible Italian motto in the upper corner. It read "cerca trova," which translates to "seek and you shall find." Seracini began to suspect that Leonardo's painting was behind Vasari's. Unfortunately, the technology of the 1970s wasn't sophisticated enough to tell.

THE ART DETECTIVES

In 2000, Seracini used 3-D modeling and thermography to reconstruct the Hall of 500 at the time of Leonardo, which allowed him to pinpoint the spot that would have been painted by the artist back in 1504. This spot coincided exactly with the "cerca trova" clue. A radar scan also indicated that there was a small air gap behind this section of the wall. Had Vasari built a wall over Leonardo's masterpiece to protect it before he painted his own mural? The answer seemed impossible to determine without causing harm to Vasari's work.

Turning again to technology, Seracini, with the help of a group of physicists, developed two noninvasive devices that would be able to detect the presence of chemicals in the paint traditionally used by Leonardo. However, getting permission from the city of Florence to use this technology proved difficult because the devices emitted a small amount of radiation. Instead, in 2011 the city decided to send in a team of art restoration experts to drill small holes into parts of the mural that were already damaged. The government then asked Seracini to use an endoscopic camera, a tiny device on a flexible tube, to explore the space behind the wall. Seracini and his team found places behind the mural that looked as if they had been stroked with a brush. The team also retrieved fragments of pigment similar to those used by Leonardo in other paintings. However, Seracini's exploratory work on the mural was stopped in 2012, when local authorities refused to allow the drilling of any new holes.

Today, Seracini lives in Florence and focuses on his company, Editech, which he founded in 1977. It was the first company in Europe to apply engineering sciences to the study of cultural heritage and the authentication of works of art. In addition to the Leonardo mural, he has studied more than 4,000 works of art, including *The Adoration of the Magi*—another Leonardo masterpiece. He determined that the work was completed by another artist who painted over Leonardo's original sketch, changing the layout considerably.

Over the years, Seracini has collaborated with several major museums to solve art mysteries. In many ways, his work could be said to have been inspired by that nearly invisible clue he saw in a corner of Vasari's mural: *cerca trova*—seek and you shall find.

HISTORICAL THINKING

1. **READING CHECK** What evidence did Seracini find that made him think there might be another painting behind the Vasari mural in the Hall of 500?

2. **ANALYZE CAUSE AND EFFECT** What effect does the need to preserve artwork have on the need to study it? Explain how both relate to Seracini's work.

PLAN: 2-PAGE LESSON

OBJECTIVE
Discuss ways in which researchers such as Maurizio Seracini use present-day technology to better understand the techniques of artists of the past.

CRITICAL THINKING SKILLS FOR LESSON 1.4
- Analyze Cause and Effect
- Form and Support Opinions
- Make Predictions
- Evaluate

HISTORICAL THINKING FOR CHAPTER 15
Can tradition coexist with transformation?

Present-day technology deepens our understanding of the ways in which artists and artisans of the past made their creations. Lesson 1.4 introduces National Geographic Explorer Maurizio Seracini and his quest to uncover one of Leonardo da Vinci's lost works.

Student eEdition online
Additional content for this lesson, including a video and a sidebar, is available online.

BACKGROUND FOR THE TEACHER
Artistic Rivalry The rivalry between Leonardo and Michelangelo was not confined to the walls in the Palazzo Vecchio. Earlier, Leonardo, who was more than 20 years older than Michelangelo, had been on a committee of Florentines whose job was to consider the question of where to place Michelangelo's statue *David*, the 16-foot tall "marble giant," as it was known. Leonardo recommended that the statue be placed behind a wall so it would not "interfere" with public events. Most of the others on the committee felt the magnificent work should go in the main plaza of Florence, outside the main entrance of the Palazzo Vecchio, and their opinion carried the day.

Perhaps because of this slight on Leonardo's part, Michelangelo later insulted Leonardo in front of others for being unable to finish a sculpture he had started, and Leonardo in turn criticized pictures of Michelangelo's that depicted bodies as too muscular, warning that such pictures make human beings look like "a sack of walnuts."

History Notebook
Encourage students to complete the Explorer page for Chapter 15 in their History Notebooks as they read.

INTRODUCE & ENGAGE

BRAINSTORM QUESTIONS

Ask students to think about a work of art that inspires them, such as a film or video, book, music, fashion, building, or any type of visual or performance art. If the work of art is recent and the creator is still living, ask them to put themselves in the place of someone viewing or experiencing it 500 years in the future. Ask what questions such a viewer might have about the art or its creator five centuries from now. Note students' questions on a board or screen where the class can see them.

TEACH

GUIDED DISCUSSION

1. **Form and Support Opinions** What might have caused the rivalry between Michelangelo and Leonardo? What effect do you think the rivalry might have had on their work and careers? *(Possible response: They may have seen one another as rivals because both were held in such high regard. Despite the animosity, they may also have recognized one another's talent. Their rivalry might have been like that between two great athletes—they are rivals because they are both so good. The rivalry may have spurred each to greater achievement.)*

2. **Make Predictions** Do you think we will ever know whether there is a painting by Leonardo da Vinci behind the Vasari mural? Explain your answer. *(Possible response: Just as technology in 2012 allowed Seracini to learn things that weren't possible with technology from the 1970s, future technological advances may allow investigators to "see" things behind the Vasari mural without damaging it.)*

EVALUATE

Ask pairs of students to decide whether or not the search for Leonardo's painting should continue. Have them create a list of pros and cons and then share their final decision and reasoning behind it with the class.

ACTIVE OPTIONS

On Your Feet: Think, Pair, Share Give students a few minutes to think about the following question: How did the city government's commissioning of murals by Leonardo and Michelangelo in the Hall of 500 reflect the character of Florence in the early 1500s? Then have students pair off and talk about the question for three to five minutes. Finally, ask volunteers to share their ideas with the class.

> **NG Learning Framework: Research Renaissance Art**
> ATTITUDE Observation
> SKILL Curiosity

Have students work in groups of three or four to research works by Leonardo or Michelangelo. Have each small group choose a painting, sculpture, building, or invention created by one of these artists. Confirm that every group has chosen a different creation and have half the class research creations by Leonardo and half by Michelangelo. After students have found images and conducted research, invite each group to present their findings.

DIFFERENTIATE

ENGLISH LANGUAGE LEARNERS

Sound Out Words Before reading, preview with students at **All Proficiencies** multisyllabic words such as *Renaissance*, *technology*, *thermography*, *endoscopic*, *exploratory*, and *considerably*. Model the pronunciation and have students make word cards for each word, writing definitions and pronunciation hints for themselves. You may also wish to point out words in the lesson that are Italian, such as *Palazzo Vecchio*, *Anghiari*, and *cerca trova*.

GIFTED & TALENTED

Invent a Technology Have students think about what it would be like to be an art detective. What technology that doesn't yet exist would help them in their work? Invite students to draw their imagined invention, list its specs, and explain why it would be valuable.

See the Chapter Planner for more strategies for differentiation.

HISTORICAL THINKING

ANSWERS

1. His radar scan revealed a hollow space behind the Vasari mural and nowhere else in the Hall of 500.

2. The need to preserve artwork prevents certain types of analysis; e.g., scraping away at surfaces to examine materials. At the same time, the study of artwork may allow better preservation. As a researcher who values artistic works and their histories, Seracini must deal with both the need to preserve art and the need to study it.

CRITICAL VIEWING Possible response: The techniques involve drilling a hole into the painting and passing a narrow tube through it. It also looks like something is being shown on a screen that everyone is looking at.

Renaissance Humanism

What qualities do we admire in people today? Many admire those who work to help others, serve in the military, or protect local communities. During the 14th and 15th centuries, the movement known as humanism explored the question of what makes a good person.

PETRARCH AND EARLY HUMANISM

Around 1350, a group of Italian scholars pioneered a new intellectual movement called **humanism**. Humanists studied texts of Greek and Roman thinkers, and these works inspired them to value active participation in public life. They moved the focus away from a life of contemplation and prayer to one that promoted human relationships within society. They admired political and military action as well as devotion to God and the church. Humanists also valued eloquent language and its ability to both persuade and delight.

One of the earliest humanist writers was the Italian historian, poet, and philosopher **Petrarch** (PEH-trahrck), who lived from 1304 to 1374. He came from a well-educated family who introduced him to the classical Latin writers Cicero and Virgil when he was young. Orphaned as a young man, Petrarch at first spent his family's money on clothes, shoes, and hairstyles, but once he ran out of money, he began to think seriously about a profession.

Petrarch wanted work that would allow him to think deeply, and eventually he became a priest. However, his life changed when he saw a woman in church. He called her Laura. No one knows whether that was really her name, whether Petrarch ever spoke to her, or even if she really existed! Nonetheless, Petrarch wrote a series of love poems to Laura in the sonnet form in Italian. A sonnet is a 14-line poem that follows a particular rhyme scheme, or pattern. It was unusual for a serious writer in Italy to write in Italian rather than Latin in the 1300s, and Petrarch had many readers. Sonnets became one of the most popular forms of poetry in Europe.

Apart from his love poems, what drove Petrarch was his effort to answer his questions about how to live a good life. The church at this time was full of conflict and

In 1341, Petrarch was crowned with a wreath of laurels, echoing a traditional Roman ceremony. Today, poets are sometimes recognized for their work with the title *poet laureate*.

corruption, so he did not feel he could rely on church leaders for guidance. Instead, he turned to the Latin writers he had admired as a boy, especially Cicero. He traveled throughout Europe, searching the libraries of old monasteries for forgotten Latin manuscripts. Inspired by these sources, Petrarch wrote letters and imaginary dialogues, or conversations, between himself and Cicero. Like his love poems, these were read throughout Europe. Petrarch's humanist writings inspired the formation of universities in England, Scotland, Ireland, Italy, Germany, and Scandinavia.

ERASMUS AND THE CHURCH

Desiderius Erasmus was born in 1469 in Rotterdam, Holland—nearly 100 years after Petrarch's death. Like Petrarch, Erasmus admired Greek and Latin philosophers, and he wrote one of the first books printed on Europe's printing presses—the Greek New Testament with his Latin translation next to the Greek text. At this time, most educated Europeans could read Latin, so the Latin translation allowed more people to read the New Testament themselves for the first time. Erasmus traveled even more widely than Petrarch, attending university in Paris and then going to England where he became a tutor in the royal court. This position took him to Rome, where he saw what he considered the excessive grandeur of Pope Julius II. He began to write **satire**, humorously critical observations, about Rome and the church. His satirical book *The Praise of Folly*, printed in 1511, was the best-selling book in Europe for several years. Even the pope laughed at the way Erasmus poked fun at human weakness and institutions while ultimately affirming Christian ideals.

Erasmus argued for the importance of education and believed that it should not be controlled by the church. His elegant writing style and ability to see many sides of an issue influenced writers such as the English writer William Shakespeare and the French essayist Michel de Montaigne. Writing some 75 years after Erasmus, Montaigne is credited with having invented the personal essay, a form he used to explore his personal character in order to better understand the human condition.

Portrait of a Young Woman as a Sybil, c. 1620

HUMANISM AND WOMEN Humanist writers looked to classic Latin and Greek authors for inspiration. As you've read, sculptors, architects, and painters turned to the statues and buildings of ancient Greece and Rome for inspiration. Born in 1593, the painter Artimesia Gentileschi was trained by her father. She was the first woman to become an official member of the artistic academy of Florence and received commissions from the Medici family and Charles I of England.

Gentileschi's painting expresses many humanist ideas. For example, her figures seem to express human emotions and appear in realistic settings. Gentileschi worked to overcome the limitations society placed on women in her time, not only in her professional activities but also in her choice of subjects. Of her 60 surviving paintings, 40 portray women.

HISTORICAL THINKING

1. **READING CHECK** What was Petrarch looking for as he visited libraries in different parts of Europe?

2. **IDENTIFY** What poetic form did Petrarch use for his love poems to Laura?

3. **DRAW CONCLUSIONS** Why do you think Erasmus was so popular, even though he criticized many institutions of his time?

PLAN: 2-PAGE LESSON

OBJECTIVE

Discuss ways in which the ideals of Renaissance humanism influenced education, art, and writing.

CRITICAL THINKING SKILLS FOR LESSON 2.1

- Identify
- Draw Conclusions
- Make Inferences
- Evaluate

HISTORICAL THINKING FOR CHAPTER 15

Can tradition coexist with transformation?

Humanists combined Christian and classical traditions to answer old questions and thus sparked changes in education and literature. Lesson 2.1 introduces the concept of Renaissance humanism and its early proponents.

BACKGROUND FOR THE TEACHER

The Spread of Humanism While the ideas of humanism were new, Europe's universities, founded well before the birth of humanism, allowed them to spread. The oldest university, the University of Bologna in Italy, dates from the end of the 11th century. The University of Paris was formed sometime after 1150, followed soon around 1168 by the University of Oxford in England, which was modeled on the University of Paris and may have been formed by students from Paris. By the time of Petrarch's death, universities of Europe, whether in France, Germany, Sweden, Italy, Spain, England, or Denmark, were part of an educational system with shared goals and standards.

The humanist cause was also helped by the conquest of Constantinople in 1453. Scholars fled to Florence and other Italian centers of learning as the Ottomans advanced on and then conquered the Byzantine capital. These scholars, fluent in Greek, made translations of many classical texts accessible to other scholars.

INTRODUCE & ENGAGE

MAKE A LIST

Ask students to list the subjects they think should be studied in high school and college. Then ask them to circle or add any subjects they think that *all* students should study, regardless of their educational or career plans. Explain that this lesson will describe the ideas of a group of writers who still influence the subjects taught in universities and high schools today.

TEACH

GUIDED DISCUSSION

1. **Make Inferences** What can you infer about the fact that Petrarch spent his life writing and revising poems about Laura yet may not have ever spoken to her? *(Possible response: His love for her inspired his poetry, and that was more important to him than having an actual relationship.)*

2. **Evaluate** Based on the description in the text, how do you think *The Praise of Folly* embodies humanist ideals? *(Possible response: It presents more than one side of an issue because it is critical of the Church but it affirms Christian principles.)*

MORE INFORMATION

Many people have questioned whether William Shakespeare wrote the plays credited to him. During the 19th century, some literary critics suggested that it was another English writer, such as Francis Bacon or Christopher Marlowe. An early 20th-century theory, put forth by the Shakespeare Oxford Society, suggests that the English aristocrat Edward de Vere, the 17th Earl of Oxford, was the author of Shakespeare's work. The society cites such evidence as de Vere's knowledge of aristocratic society, his education, and the similarity in structure between his poetry and Shakespeare's. The society believes that Shakespeare did not have the education or literary background needed to create such masterpieces.

ACTIVE OPTIONS

On Your Feet: Create a Team Word Web Ask students in teams of four to gather around a large sheet of paper to write words or phrases related to Renaissance humanism. At your signal, students should rotate the paper and continue to add words or phrases to the web. Tell teams to use their completed web to summarize a main idea about humanism.

> **NG Learning Framework: Research European Universities**
> **ATTITUDE** Curiosity
> **SKILL** Communication
>
> Have students consult a ranking of global universities such as that published by U.S. News and World Report. Ask students to choose three European universities to research. Have them make fact cards for each of their choices, listing information such as year founded, language of instruction, cost of attending, numbers of domestic and international students, special areas of study, and fun facts, along with images of the university campus. Students can post their findings on a wall display.

DIFFERENTIATE

STRIVING READERS

Use a Concept Cluster Guide pairs of students to summarize the lesson by creating a Concept Cluster. Tell them to write the lesson title in the center circle and the lesson headings in the outer circles. Have them draw spokes radiating from each outer circle and, as they read the information under each heading, have them enter key ideas on the spokes. Then invite volunteers to summarize each section using the ideas on the spokes.

GIFTED & TALENTED

Interpret Quotations Ask students to use the Internet or other sources to locate translations of quotations from Petrarch, Erasmus, and Montaigne. Have them choose one quotation from each person and write a short paragraph to explain what they like about the quotation or why they agree or disagree with it.

See the Chapter Planner for more strategies for differentiation.

HISTORICAL THINKING

ANSWERS

1. He was looking for forgotten Latin manuscripts.

2. Petrarch's love poems were written in sonnet form in Italian.

3. Erasmus was probably popular because he used humor to express his criticism.

Raphael's *School of Athens*

Outdoor schools? Not a bad idea in Greece's mild climate. The famous academies of ancient Greece were not buildings but open-air gatherings. But in this painting from 1511, Plato, Aristotle, and other notable philosophers interact in an imaginary scene set in Rome.

HUMANIST LEARNING

In the early 1500s, Italy's cultural center shifted south from Florence and Venice to Rome. The church used its great wealth to become an important patron of the arts. Pope Julius II, who had hired Michelangelo to paint the Sistine Chapel, brought another Florentine artist to Rome, the young and accomplished **Raphael**. The pope commissioned Raphael to paint large frescoes in his papal offices and rooms. The most famous of these works is the *School of Athens* painted in Julius's library. In the painting, philosophers ponder, write, debate, and teach in the pursuit of truth. But instead of an outdoor olive grove, the gathering is set in St. Peter's Basilica. Julius wanted to show the importance of ancient wisdom to Christian beliefs. In his view, a learned individual—one who studied the classics, including poetry and mathematics—could better understand religious ideas.

Raphael's composition leads viewers' eyes to Plato and Aristotle at its center. Plato points up. To him, truth was found in ideals that existed beyond the senses. Aristotle gestures toward the earth; he finds truth in observing the world. Raphael provided no key to the identity of all the ancient figures, nor to their faces, some of which resembled artists he knew. He also included himself in the painting—on the far right. By the time of his death at age 37 in 1520, he was famous for his art and oversaw a large number of apprentices in his workshop.

PERSPECTIVE

School of Athens is painted on a flat wall about 25 feet wide, yet it gives the illusion of depth. Painters made figures, objects, and architectural features appear closer or farther away using mathematical calculations. The architect Brunelleschi, whom you read about earlier in this chapter, had developed the technique a hundred years earlier. Called **linear perspective**, it allowed artists to determine the placement and size of figures on a flat plane, making them appear as if positioned in three dimensions. Today, architects and animators use computer software to create and alter perspective in 3-D.

To create linear perspective, all parallel lines in a painting converge in a single vanishing point on the horizon, creating the illusion of depth.

HISTORICAL THINKING

1. **READING CHECK** Why did Pope Julius II commission the *School of Athens*?

2. **INTERPRET VISUALS** According to Raphael's painting, in what ways did classical thinkers share knowledge?

3. **SYNTHESIZE** How does the architectural structure in the painting show linear perspective?

CRITICAL VIEWING Raphael was only 27 when he completed this fresco, which celebrates the classical period. How does *School of Athens* express the ideals of humanism and Renaissance art?

PYTHAGORAS
This Greek mathematician sits before a slate showing ratios for musical tones. He believed numbers held the key to all aspects of the universe.

IBN RUSHD
Also known as Averroes, this Arab philosopher lived in Spain during the 12th century and sparked interest in Aristotle prior to the Renaissance.

EUCLID
Euclid wrote *Optics and Elements*, books on geometry and mathematics, around 300 B.C.E. He holds a compass over a slate with a geometric drawing on it.

SOCRATES
Socrates talks with figures representing people from different cultures, emphasizing the universal appeal of his philosophy.

ZOROASTER
The ancient Iranian astronomer and philosopher Zoroaster, often viewed as the founder of monotheism, holds a sphere showing the fixed stars.

PTOLEMY
Ptolemy, a Greco-Roman mathematician and astronomer, holds the sphere of Earth. The figure facing the viewer on his right is the painter Raphael.

PLAN: 2-PAGE LESSON

OBJECTIVE
Explain how Renaissance artists used linear perspective to create depth on a two-dimensional surface.

CRITICAL THINKING SKILLS FOR LESSON 2.2
- Interpret Visuals
- Synthesize
- Identify
- Describe
- Make Inferences

HISTORICAL THINKING FOR CHAPTER 15
Can tradition coexist with transformation?

Renaissance artists and leaders sought to show the importance of classical wisdom to Christian beliefs, thus combining ancient traditions with the transformation of a newer religious view. Lesson 2.2 focuses on a painting that embodies this mindset.

BACKGROUND FOR THE TEACHER
Perspective Linear perspective is based on the idea of a single vanishing point, but aerial perspective, also called atmospheric perspective, uses color to create the illusion of depth. A close observer of nature, Leonardo da Vinci first used the term *aerial perspective* and noted that "Colors become weaker in proportion to their distance from the person who is looking at them." Today we know that moisture and tiny particles of dust in the atmosphere scatter light and give distant dark objects such as mountains a bluish tint.

The atmosphere creates other visual effects that landscape painters can use to create a sense of distance. For example, distant objects appear to have softer edges than closer objects. Contrasts between light and dark also diminish as distance increases.

In the 20th century, artists such as Picasso abandoned or redefined perspective, breaking pictures into multiple planes or treating a painting as a two-dimensional object.

INTRODUCE & ENGAGE

PREVIEW USING VISUALS

Have students examine Raphael's *School of Athens*. Invite volunteers to describe what they see. **ASK:** How are the men in the painting dressed? *(They are wearing robes and togas like those of classical Greece or Rome.)* What are most of them doing? *(Most seem to be discussing; a few are looking at books or seem lost in solitary thought.)* Ask a volunteer to read the title of the lesson. Then ask students to recall what they know about Athens from prior lessons. *(It was a center of learning and philosophy.)*

TEACH

GUIDED DISCUSSION

1. **Identify** Where is the vanishing point in the linear perspective of *School of Athens* located? *(In the center of the painting between the figures of Plato and Aristotle.)*

2. **Describe** What is the effect on the viewer of placing the vanishing point in the center of the painting? *(Possible response: draws viewer's eyes to the center; makes viewers feel that these two figures are the most important even though they are among the smallest.)*

MAKE INFERENCES

Explain that Raphael used people he knew as models for the philosophers in the painting, all of whom lived long before he did. Experts believe that the bearded Plato in the center is modeled on Leonardo while the man in the foreground with his head on his hand is modeled on Michelangelo and was added later. **ASK:** What can you infer about Raphael's attitudes toward these other two painters? *(Possible responses: Leonardo may have been at the center of the artistic world as he knew it; Michelangelo might have been viewed as a loner and a latecomer. Michelangelo's place in the foreground may mean that Raphael feels closer to him than to Leonardo.)*

ACTIVE OPTIONS

On Your Feet: Become an Expert Organize students into four groups to become experts on the figures in the painting *School of Athens*: Plato and Aristotle, Pythagoras and Euclid, Ibn Rushd (Averroes) and Socrates, or Zoroaster and Ptolemy. Then regroup students so each new group has at least one member from each expert group. Allow experts to share information with their new groups.

| **NG Learning Framework: Analyze Art Techniques**
| **ATTITUDE** Curiosity
| **SKILL** Communication

Ask pairs to view paintings in library art books, art websites, or a local museum. Have them analyze one painting, asking one another whether the painter has used some of the techniques they have read about such as linear perspective or sfumato. What qualities does the painting share with the Renaissance paintings described in this chapter? How is this painting different from those paintings? Have students prepare a short presentation using a visual of their chosen painting and a bulleted list of similarities and differences to at least one painting in this chapter.

DIFFERENTIATE

INCLUSION

Describe Lesson Visuals Pair visually impaired students with students who are not visually impaired. Ask the latter to describe the lesson visuals in detail and to answer any questions the visually impaired students might have.

GIFTED & TALENTED

Use Art to Study Art Artists often learn their craft by copying paintings that inspire them. Have students experiment with this technique of learning by asking them to choose a detail or section of *School of Athens* to draw, starting with a pencil sketch and adding color and details as they wish. Encourage students to share their sketches and explain why they chose the section they did and what they found challenging or rewarding about copying this section of the painting.

See the Chapter Planner for more strategies for differentiation.

HISTORICAL THINKING

ANSWERS

1. He wanted to show the importance of ancient wisdom to Christian beliefs.

2. The ancients shared knowledge through discussion, lectures, books, drawings, and models such as globes.

3. The archways in the center and back of the painting are smaller than those in the middle distance and front of the painting, indicating that the archways in the back are closer to the central vanishing point.

CRITICAL VIEWING *School of Athens* was painted with linear perspective to make it seem three-dimensional, and the people in the painting are very realistic with detailed features. Both of these characteristics are traits of Renaissance art. The focus on ancient scholars reflects the ideals of humanism.

2.3 Humanist Writings

It's one thing to worry about what people will think of you if you say what's on your mind. It's another thing to fear for your life. Renaissance humanist writers had to be careful not to offend the powerful. They created works that are praised for their elegance and depth and are still read today.

Humanists believed the works of ancient Greece and Rome offered important moral values and fresh perspectives. They may have been right because the ideas of humanism had a broad influence, starting in Italy in the 14th century and affecting all of Europe by the 16th century.

The goals of a humanist education were to teach people to contribute to the common good by taking part in public life. Humanists valued practical careers over contemplation. Eloquence, or the ability to speak and write well, was also important and led to the creation of the field of studies known today as the humanities.

Humanists did not reject religion but rather sought to combine classical and Christian ideas. Northern European humanists, in particular, saw humanist learning as a way to bring about reform within the church.

CRITICAL VIEWING Paintings of the Virgin Mary in classic art usually show her holding the baby Jesus. This 1505 painting by the Italian artist Vittore Carpaccio shows Mary sitting in a garden reading a book. She is dressed in the clothing of a 16th-century Italian noblewoman. How does Carpaccio's painting reflect humanist views of education?

DOCUMENT ONE

Primary Source: Speech
from "An Oration . . . in Praise of Letters" by Cassandra Fedele, c. 1487–1521

Born in 1465 in Venice, Italy, Cassandra Fedele was a prodigy, a young person of unusual talent, who appeared before groups of learned men to display her knowledge while still a teenager. As a woman, she had to find ways to express her extensive learning without threatening powerful men who felt they knew how women should behave.

CONSTRUCTED RESPONSE Based on the excerpt, what qualities would Fedele value in a prince?

The study of literature refines men's minds, forms and makes bright the power of reason, and washes away all stains from the mind, or at any rate, greatly cleanses it. It perfects its gifts and adds much beauty and elegance to the physical and material advantages that one has received by nature. States, however, and their princes who foster and cultivate these studies become much more humane, more gracious, and more noble. For this reason, these studies have won for themselves the sweet appellation, "humanities."

DOCUMENT TWO

Primary Source: Book
from *The Prince*, by Niccolò Machiavelli, completed 1513, published posthumously (after his death) 1532

Machiavelli was a supporter of the republic in Florence and was tortured and expelled from the city when the Medici family retook control. He then tried to regain his place by writing *The Prince*, advising the Medici on how best to rule the city. The book was controversial because it described the reality of politics in harsh terms. Thus, today the term *Machiavellian* means "scheming and unscrupulous."

CONSTRUCTED RESPONSE According to this excerpt, why is it safer for a ruler to be feared than loved?

Upon this a question arises: whether it be better to be loved than feared or feared than loved? It . . . is much safer to be feared than loved. . . . Because [men] are ungrateful, fickle, false, cowardly, covetous, and as long as you succeed they are yours entirely; they will offer you their blood, property, life, and children, as is said above, when the need is far distant; but when it approaches they turn against you. And that prince who, relying entirely on their promises, has neglected other precautions, is ruined; because . . . men have less scruple in offending one who is beloved than one who is feared.

DOCUMENT THREE

Primary Source: Book
from *Utopia* by Thomas More, 1516

Thomas More, born in London in 1478, was an advisor to Henry VIII of England and a friend of Erasmus. But being a humanist did not always mean acting humanely. Henry VIII ordered many executions, and Thomas More had people burned at the stake. In *Utopia*, his most famous book, More describes an imaginary island.

CONSTRUCTED RESPONSE In this excerpt, how does the imaginary Utopia reflect humanist ideals?

It is ordinary to have public lectures every morning before daybreak, at which none are obliged to appear but those who are marked out for literature; yet a great many, both men and women, of all ranks, go to hear lectures of one sort or other, according to their inclinations: but if others that are not made for contemplation choose rather to employ themselves at that time in their trades, as many of them do, they are not hindered, but are rather commended, as men that take care to serve their country. After supper they spend an hour in some diversion, . . . where they entertain each other either with music or discourse.

SYNTHESIZE & WRITE

1. REVIEW Review what you have learned about the values of humanism.

2. RECALL On your own paper, list two details about each of the writers mentioned above and two details about each of the excerpts.

3. CONSTRUCT Construct a topic sentence that answers this question: Does education in the humanities make people more ethical? Why or why not?

4. WRITE Using evidence from this chapter and the documents, write an informative paragraph that supports your topic sentence in Step 3.

PLAN: 2-PAGE LESSON

OBJECTIVE
Synthesize information about humanism from primary source documents.

CRITICAL THINKING SKILLS FOR LESSON 2.3
- Synthesize
- Draw Conclusions
- Form and Support Opinions
- Evaluate

HISTORICAL THINKING FOR CHAPTER 15
Can tradition coexist with transformation?

Humanist writers went back to the writings of ancient philosophers to create a new worldview that ushered in the early modern age in Europe. Lesson 2.3 focuses on important works by Cassandra Fedele, Niccoló Machiavelli, and Thomas More.

BACKGROUND FOR THE TEACHER
The Word *Utopia* Thomas More coined the term *utopia* from the Greek words for "not" (*ou*) and "place" (*topos*)—in other words, "nowhere." More describes a communist and pagan society that contrasted with the greed for power and riches he saw in Christian Europe. Readers are left wondering how seriously to take More's proposals.

Although More coined the word, he was not the first or the last to imagine an ideal utopia. Most were modeled on Plato's *Republic*, but explorations of the Americas stimulated many European writers to describe societies based on religious or economic ideals.

By the 20th century, many writers began to imagine and describe *dystopian* societies, or those in which religious or economic ideals are pursued to their logical conclusions, resulting in authoritarian regimes allowing for little freedom or privacy.

INTRODUCE & ENGAGE

PREPARE FOR THE DOCUMENT-BASED QUESTION

Before students start on the activity, briefly preview the three documents. Remind students that a constructed response requires full explanations in complete sentences. Emphasize that students should use what they have learned about humanism in addition to the information in the documents.

TEACH

GUIDED DISCUSSION

1. **Draw Conclusions** Do humanist ideals guide government and popular choices of leaders today? Should they? *(Possible response: People still value a background in practical careers such as military leadership or business success over contemplative fields, and eloquence, or the ability to persuade through speech or writing, still affects choices of leaders. Some students may argue that eloquence can be deceptive, however.)*

2. **Form and Support Opinions** Based on the documents and the information about them, do you think Cassandra Fedele and Thomas More would agree with Machiavelli that is safer to be feared than loved? Why or why not? *(Possible response: No, they would disagree because Fedele values princes who are gracious and noble rather than feared, while More seems to value a society in which people choose their activities based on their interests and skills.)*

EVALUATE

After students have completed the Synthesize & Write activity, allow time for them to exchange paragraphs and read and comment on the work of their peers. Establish guidelines for comments prior to the activity so feedback is constructive and encouraging. Comments should focus on the most significant parts that address the purpose of the activity and the audience.

ACTIVE OPTION

On Your Feet: Host a DBQ Roundtable Direct students to gather into groups of four. Pose the following question: Why is it important or unimportant for leaders to study the humanities—literature, philosophy, and history—today? Instruct each student in a group to answer the question in a different way. Then ask groups to summarize their answers for the class.

DIFFERENTIATE

ENGLISH LANGUAGE LEARNERS

Summarize Place students at **Beginning** and **Intermediate** proficiencies in pairs and assign each pair a document. Instruct them to read the document together and then write a few sentences to summarize it. When all pairs are finished, call on them to read their summaries aloud in the order in which the material appears to provide an overview of the entire lesson.

PRE-AP

Research Machiavelli Tell students that while Machiavelli is generally regarded as an evil schemer, some of his other writings, not as well-known as *The Prince*, contradict that view. Invite students to research Machiavelli in greater depth and make an argument regarding his political attitudes and character.

SYNTHESIZE & WRITE

ANSWERS

1. Possible response: Humanism valued civic action and the ability to use language effectively.

2. Possible response: Fedele: prodigy who impressed older men with her learning; argues that the study of literature "cleanses" the mind and that princes who study literature become more humane and gracious; Machiavelli: well-educated man who advocated fear and manipulation as tools of government; More: well-educated man who imagined an ideal society; persecuted others for their religion

3. Possible response: Education in the humanities does not make people more ethical.

4. Students' informative paragraphs should support their topic sentences and include evidence from the text and documents.

CONSTRUCTED RESPONSE

Document One: humaneness, grace, and nobility

Document Two: Men are more likely to betray someone they love than they are someone they fear.

Document Three: People are free to pursue an interest in literature; they are free to pursue other interests that are useful to society; this reflects the humanist ideals of both honoring literature and valuing civic participation.

CRITICAL VIEWING those who are gracious and noble, like the Virgin Mary, will pursue study of the humanities, symbolized by the book she holds in the painting

2.4 Material Culture

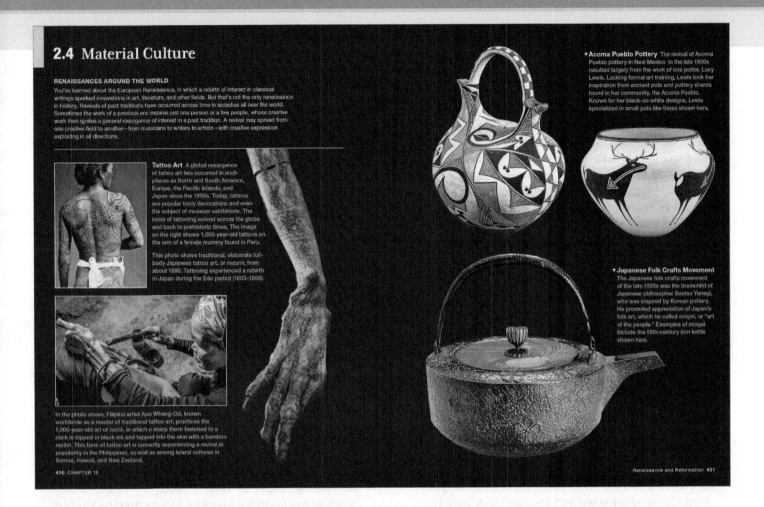

RENAISSANCES AROUND THE WORLD
You've learned about the European Renaissance, in which a rebirth of interest in classical writings sparked innovations in art, literature, and other fields. But that's not the only renaissance in history. Revivals of past traditions have occurred across time in societies all over the world. Sometimes the work of a previous era inspires just one person or a few people, whose creative work then ignites a general resurgence of interest in a past tradition. A revival may spread from one creative field to another—from musicians to writers to artists—with creative expression exploding in all directions.

Tattoo Art A global resurgence of tattoo art has occurred in such places as North and South America, Europe, the Pacific Islands, and Japan since the 1990s. Today, tattoos are popular body decorations and even the subject of museum exhibitions. The roots of tattooing extend across the globe and back to prehistoric times. The image on the right shows 1,600-year-old tattoos on the arm of a female mummy found in Peru.

This photo shows traditional, elaborate full-body Japanese tattoo art, or *irezumi*, from about 1880. Tattooing experienced a rebirth in Japan during the Edo period (1603–1868).

In the photo above, Filipino artist Apo Whang-Od, known worldwide as a master of traditional tattoo art, practices the 1,000-year-old art of *batok*, in which a sharp thorn fastened to a stick is dipped in black ink and tapped into the skin with a bamboo mallet. This form of tattoo art is currently experiencing a revival in popularity in the Philippines, as well as among island cultures in Samoa, Hawaii, and New Zealand.

▼ Acoma Pueblo Pottery The revival of Acoma Pueblo pottery in New Mexico in the late 1900s resulted largely from the work of one potter, Lucy Lewis. Lacking formal art training, Lewis took her inspiration from ancient pots and pottery shards found in her community, the Acoma Pueblo. Known for her black-on-white designs, Lewis specialized in small pots like those shown here.

▼ Japanese Folk Crafts Movement The Japanese folk crafts movement of the late 1920s was the brainchild of Japanese philosopher Soetsu Yanagi, who was inspired by Korean pottery. He promoted appreciation of Japan's folk art, which he called *mingei*, or "art of the people." Examples of *mingei* include the 19th-century iron kettle shown here.

PLAN: 4-PAGE LESSON

OBJECTIVE
Learn how revivals of traditions have brought a resurgence of creativity to many different cultures at different times around the world.

CRITICAL THINKING SKILLS FOR LESSON 2.4
- Analyze Visuals
- Make Connections
- Compare and Contrast
- Categorize
- Make Inferences

HISTORICAL THINKING FOR CHAPTER 15
Can tradition coexist with transformation?

The Italian Renaissance was neither the first nor last time when people turned to older forms of art to transform the culture in which they lived. Lesson 2.4 explores renaissances in other past and present cultures.

BACKGROUND FOR THE TEACHER
Acoma Pueblo Pottery Lucy M. Lewis was born around 1898. She learned to make pottery by watching other women. She never attended art school but lived all her life on the Sky City mesa of the Acoma Pueblo. Like other women of her culture, she did not sign her pots and sold them along the side of highways, and she used local clay from sources known only to the people of the Acoma Pueblo. Over time, however, she began to revive an ancient style of black-and-white pottery, bringing her own interpretations to traditional designs and patterns, and at that point she began signing her work.

By the 1950s, Lewis was winning recognition and awards for her work. Today her pots are owned by a number of leading museums, including the Smithsonian American Art Museum, the National Museum of Women in the Arts, and the Pacific Grove Museum of Natural History. Many of her children and grandchildren have carried on her work and continue making pottery in the Acoma tradition.

History Notebook
Encourage students to complete the Material Culture page for Chapter 15 in their History Notebooks as they read.

INTRODUCE & ENGAGE

EXPLORE HISTORY USING PHOTOGRAPHS

Tell students that the photographs in this lesson represent only a few examples of the many cultural revivals that have occurred as a result of turning to traditional arts. **ASK:** What images on these pages intrigue you? What questions do you have about these images? *(Possible responses may include questions about how painful traditional tattooing was or about the sounds of Hawaiian musical instruments.)* Can you think of places or objects around you that offer insights into traditions that might spark a revival of arts in your own community? *(Possible responses may include murals, buildings, historical museums, or artisans in the local community.)*

TEACH

GUIDED DISCUSSION

1. **Make Connections** Which two forms of material culture shown in the lesson are linked to Japan? *(full-body tattoos from the Edo period and the Japanese folk crafts movement from the late 1920s)*

2. **Categorize** Which of these art forms is practiced most broadly and over the longest period of time? *(Tattooing is practiced in Asia, the Americas, and Europe, and is known to be at least 1,600 years old.)*

MATERIAL CULTURE

Remind students of the essential question for this chapter: Can tradition coexist with transformation? **ASK:** Based on the information and objects presented in this lesson, how would you answer this question? *(Possible response: Yes, tradition can coexist with transformation. In each renaissance mentioned in the lesson, people were turning back to old traditions but expressing them in new ways.)*

DIFFERENTIATE

INCLUSION

Describe Details in Photos Pair students who are visually impaired with students who are not. Ask the latter to describe the details in each photo in the Material Culture lesson and to answer any question their partners might have. Then have the students work together to complete the Analyze Visuals activity.

GIFTED & TALENTED

Copy a Pattern Direct students to choose an example of Acoma pottery from the photograph or from another source and attempt to copy it using pencil or pen and paper or on a pot of their own making. Invite them to discuss what they learned from the process of copying the pattern. What difficulties did they face? What new understanding did they achieve through the process of making the copy?

See the Chapter Planner for more strategies for differentiation.

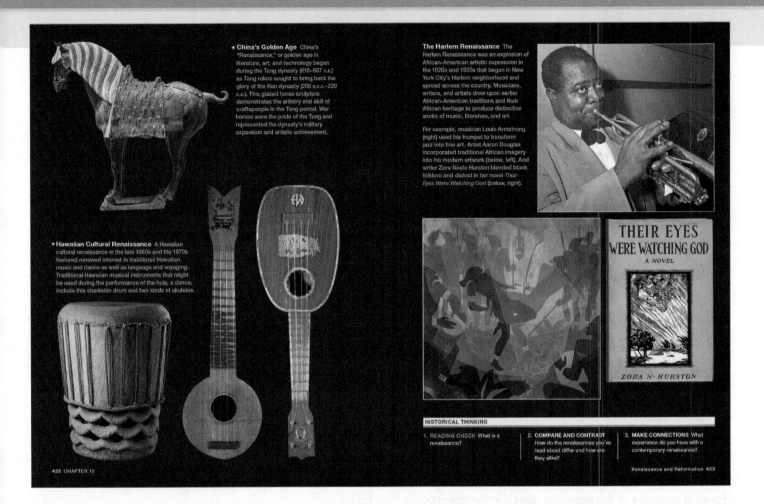

◄ China's Golden Age China's "Renaissance," or golden age in literature, art, and technology began during the Tang dynasty (618–907 c.e.) as Tang rulers sought to bring back the glory of the Han dynasty (206 b.c.e.–220 c.e.). This glazed horse sculpture demonstrates the artistry and skill of craftspeople in the Tang period. War horses were the pride of the Tang and represented the dynasty's military expansion and artistic achievement.

▼ Hawaiian Cultural Renaissance A Hawaiian cultural renaissance in the late 1960s and the 1970s featured renewed interest in traditional Hawaiian music and dance as well as language and voyaging. Traditional Hawaiian musical instruments that might be used during the performance of the hula, a dance, include this sharkskin drum and two kinds of ukuleles.

The Harlem Renaissance The Harlem Renaissance was an explosion of African-American artistic expression in the 1920s and 1930s that began in New York City's Harlem neighborhood and spread across the country. Musicians, writers, and artists drew upon earlier African-American traditions and their African heritage to produce distinctive works of music, literature, and art.

For example, musician Louis Armstrong (right) used his trumpet to transform jazz into fine art. Artist Aaron Douglas incorporated traditional African imagery into his modern artwork (below, left). And writer Zora Neale Hurston blended black folklore and dialect in her novel *Their Eyes Were Watching God* (below, right).

HISTORICAL THINKING

1. **READING CHECK** What is a renaissance?

2. **COMPARE AND CONTRAST** How do the renaissances you've read about differ and how are they alike?

3. **MAKE CONNECTIONS** What experience do you have with a contemporary renaissance?

BACKGROUND FOR THE TEACHER

Hawaiian Cultural Renaissance The creation of the Polynesian Voyaging Society, which revived knowledge and interest in the double-hulled canoes and navigation techniques that brought human beings to Hawaii, also revived interest in linguistic, musical, and artistic traditions. In the 1970s, the Hawaiian language was believed to be dying, but today the language is taught in many schools, and the local newspaper, television station, and public radio regularly offer articles and brief programs in the Hawaiian language.

The Harlem Renaissance Like the Italian Renaissance, the Harlem Renaissance had sources prior to its beginning. For example, late 19th-century writers such as Paul Laurence Dunbar and Henry Tanner influenced early 20th-century writers such as Langston Hughes and Zora Neale Hurston. Just as painters of northern Europe influenced Italian artists, artists from California, Chicago, New Orleans, the Caribbean, and many other places far beyond New York City influenced the Harlem Renaissance. Certain figures, such as W.E.B. Du Bois, Charles Johnson, and Alain Locke, had an outsized influence through their ability to bring the work of artists and writers to the attention of others through publication and patronage in magazines such as *The Crisis* and *Opportunity* and anthologies such as *The New Negro*.

TEACH

GUIDED DISCUSSION

3. **Make Inferences** Why might the Tang rulers have wanted to revive the arts of a dynasty that ruled some 800 years earlier? *(Possible response: The Han dynasty lasted for hundreds of years and was very wealthy. It conquered vast territory through skilled horsemanship.)*

4. **Compare and Contrast** How was China's Tang dynasty golden age different from some of the other artistic revivals in this lesson? *(The Tang golden age was the result of China's rulers seeking to revive the glories of the Han dynasty, while the Hawaiian and Acoma revivals, for example, were the result of ordinary people finding inspiration in the traditions of their culture.)*

ANALYZE VISUALS

Have students examine the painting by Aaron Douglas that appears in the lesson. Explain that this painting is one in a series of four murals Douglas was commissioned to paint for a branch of the New York Public Library in 1934. The title of this particular mural is *Aspects of Negro Life: The Negro in an African Setting.* **ASK:** How does this painting reflect the characteristics of a renaissance? *(Possible response: The painting celebrates traditions from Africa, but it is painted in a modern style— blending old concepts with new ones.)*

ACTIVE OPTION

On Your Feet: Research Artistic Movements Instruct students to form six teams and assign each team one of the following topics: Filipino tattoo traditions, Acoma Pueblo pottery, the Japanese folk crafts movement, China's Golden Age of the Tang dynasty, the Hawaiian cultural renaissance, or the Harlem Renaissance. Instruct groups to gather in separate areas of the room to do additional research, including finding additional images, and then to discuss how their assigned movement brought a renaissance to the culture that created it. Reconvene as a class and have a volunteer from each group share two or three additional points that were not covered in the lesson.

HISTORICAL THINKING

ANSWERS

1. A renaissance is a revival of past traditions that ignites a general resurgence of interest and reinterpretation in one or more fields of creative endeavor.

2. Possible response: Some of the renaissances are sparked by an individual artist, others by a group of artists, and still others by rulers or community leaders.

3. Answers will vary. Some students may be familiar with forms of music or handcrafts sparked by an earlier art form.

Martin Luther and the Protestant Reformation

An impressive building may inspire awe and appreciation in those who see it. Yet others may object to the cost of such a structure. That's how one German monk felt when he visited Rome and saw St. Peter's Basilica under construction.

LUTHER'S 95 THESES

In 1450, the pope ordered that work begin on St. Peter's Basilica in Rome. Drawing on the artistic and architectural advances of the Renaissance, St. Peter's would be a fitting symbol for the Catholic Church. At the time, the church was richer and more powerful than any king or emperor in Europe. The magnificent structure would take 200 years to complete, but in 1517, well before it was completed, the German monk **Martin Luther** would do something that would dramatically alter the religious, political, and social landscape of Europe.

Luther was angry about the way money was being raised to build the great basilica. Catholics were encouraged to buy **indulgences**, or special pardons, from the archbishop to save their own souls as well as those of deceased loved ones. Luther's studies of the Bible led him to believe that faith in God was the only way to save souls. He wrote a list of 95 theses, or ideas, criticizing indulgences and other church practices. In thesis 86, for example, he said, "Why does not the pope, whose wealth is today greater than the riches of the richest, build just his one church of St. Peter with his own money, rather than with the money of poor believers?"

According to legend, Luther nailed his list to the door of Wittenberg's largest church. Then he did something even more courageous: he had copies printed in German and Latin. He mailed a copy to the archbishop, who passed it along to the pope. Church officials dismissed the ideas of the man they thought of as just another small-town monk. But thanks to the printing press, Luther's ideas gained widespread attention, and he became a best-selling author.

This 1529 double portrait by artist Lucas Cranach the Elder commemorates the marriage of Martin Luther to Katharina von Bora.

In addition to criticizing indulgences, Luther believed priests should be allowed to marry and have families. In 1525, he married a former nun, Katharina von Bora, whom he praised for her business sense and managerial abilities. Many historians believe Katharina's abilities helped make Luther successful.

EARLIER INFLUENCES

Luther's ideas led to the changes known today as the Reformation, a political and religious challenge of papal authority. His ideas did not come out of nowhere. Scholars had questioned the power and practices of the church for more than 100 years before Luther printed his 95 theses.

One early critic was the theologian **John Wycliffe**. Wycliffe lived and wrote in Oxford, England, in the late 14th century. As Luther would more than 100 years later, Wycliffe came to believe that the Bible, not the pope, was the source of God's word. He arranged for the Latin Bible to be translated into English so more people could read it. Like Luther, Wycliffe believed priests should be able to marry and that the church should give up its power and wealth.

Soon after Wycliffe published his arguments, his ideas attracted the attention of **Jan Hus**, a priest and philosopher from Prague, in the kingdom of Bohemia (present-day Czech Republic). Hus was impressed by Wycliffe's views toward the reform of Catholic clergy. At that time, the church and its high-ranking officials owned property in Bohemia. Yet many priests were poor, and peasants were forced to pay taxes to the church. Eventually declared a heretic, Hus was burned at the stake in 1415.

Like Hus and Wycliffe, the humanist Desiderius Erasmus, whom you learned about earlier, was critical of the wealth of the Catholic Church. He also disapproved of princes who fought wars over minor insults and priests who supported those wars to advance their own careers. Erasmus agreed with many of Luther's criticisms, but he didn't like Luther's combative tone. As a humanist, Erasmus valued tolerance for diverse opinions, and he did not think it right to punish people for their beliefs.

AN OUTLAW AND A HERO

After his publication of the 95 theses, Luther continued to write extensively. Wittenberg became the publishing center of Germany, with one-third of the books published there written by Luther and another one-fifth by his followers.

In spite of his radical ideas about religion, Martin Luther believed it was a Christian's duty to obey legitimate authority. When the German peasants rebelled in 1524, Luther was appalled by their behavior. He responded by writing a pamphlet to distance himself (and his reform movement) from the peasants' cause and align himself with the nobility.

PRIMARY SOURCE

Since the peasants, then, have brought both God and man down upon them . . . since they submit to no court and wait for no verdict, but only rage on, I must instruct the worldly governors how they are to act in the matter with a clear conscience.

First, I will not oppose a ruler who . . . will smite and punish these peasants without offering to submit the case to judgement. For he is within his rights, since the peasants are not contending any longer for the Gospel, but have become faithless, perjured, disobedient, rebellious murderers, robbers and blasphemers. . . .

—from "Against the Robbing and Murdering Hordes of Peasants," by Martin Luther, 1525

Luther wrote about every aspect of life. He wrote pamphlets offering spiritual inspiration and analysis of the Bible, but he also urged German nobles to take over the lands held by the Catholic Church. In 1520, Luther was given a chance to recant, or take back, his criticisms of the church. Luther refused. He was declared an outlaw, but he also became a hero to many German nobles, shopkeepers, artisans, and students.

German peasants, in particular, were inspired by Luther to question many aspects of their lives. They had been forced to pay high taxes to landowners. They questioned whether babies should be baptized since they were too young to understand the meaning of the ritual. They questioned private property. They wanted to choose their own priests and wanted the right to overthrow princes. In 1524, the peasants rebelled. At first, Luther acknowledged that some demands were valid, but as the uprising spread and mob violence grew, he urged princes to strike down those he described as "murderers and robbers." Armies attacked, and as many as 100,000 died in the uprising known as the Peasants' War. Luther had chosen to support the princes over the common people.

HISTORICAL THINKING

1. **READING CHECK** What new technology helped spread Martin Luther's ideas throughout Europe?

2. **ANALYZE CAUSE AND EFFECT** Why did Wycliffe support the translation of the Bible into English?

3. **MAKE INFERENCES** What are some possible reasons why Martin Luther would side with the nobility against the peasants in the 1525 revolt?

PLAN: 2-PAGE LESSON

OBJECTIVE

Describe Martin Luther's motivations and role in the Protestant Reformation.

CRITICAL THINKING SKILLS FOR LESSON 3.1

- Analyze Cause and Effect
- Make Inferences
- Summarize
- Draw Conclusions
- Analyze Primary Sources

HISTORICAL THINKING FOR CHAPTER 15

Can tradition coexist with transformation?

Martin Luther sought guidance for his spiritual struggles in biblical sources and ended up transforming European Christianity. Lesson 3.1 explores the influences behind and the effects of Luther's 95 theses.

Student eEdition online

Additional content for this lesson, including a video, is available online.

BACKGROUND FOR THE TEACHER

Indulgences and Purgatory At the time of Luther, Christians believed that hell, the home of Satan and a place of eternal torment, was under Earth's core. People who died, including baptized Christians, without repenting of their sins could go straight to hell. Very few people were able to go straight to heaven, the abode of God and the angels, because it was believed that human beings were sinful by nature. Therefore, a merciful God had created purgatory, a place in which Christians could cleanse or purge themselves of their sins and thus be eligible to enter heaven. It was assumed that most people had to spend thousands of years suffering in purgatory before they were ready to enter heaven. Indulgences promised to reduce the amount of time required before souls in purgatory could enter heaven.

INTRODUCE & ENGAGE

ACTIVATE PRIOR KNOWLEDGE

Discuss what students have already learned about the changes brought about after Gutenberg's printing press came into use in the mid-1400s. Remind students that the humanist Desiderius Erasmus translated the New Testament of the Bible from Greek into Latin, a language that most educated people could read at the time, and that Erasmus published *The Praise of Folly* in 1511 and that it became the best-selling book in Europe for several years. **ASK:** Can you recall what Erasmus mocked in this satirical book? *(the church and its seat of power, Rome)* Tell students that they will learn about someone else who wrote and published criticisms of the Roman Catholic Church, but these were not humorous or satirical.

TEACH

GUIDED DISCUSSION

1. **Summarize** Why did Luther object to the selling of indulgences? *(Luther believed that faith in God, not special prayers, was the only way to attain salvation.)*

2. **Draw Conclusions** Why do you think German nobles supported Luther and his ideas? *(Possible response: Luther urged nobles to take over lands held by the Catholic Church, which would have made the nobles richer; Luther said peasants should obey their masters.)*

ANALYZE PRIMARY SOURCES

Direct students' attention to the primary source feature. **ASK:** How does Luther characterize the rebelling peasants? *(as evil human beings whose behavior is condemned by both God and the legal system; He associates them with some of the vilest people at the time—murderers, robbers, and blasphemers.)* How does he characterize the nobility? *("worldly" and concerned with maintaining a "clear conscience")* Why do you think he characterizes both groups in such extreme ways? *(so the nobility feels justified in punishing the peasants; By characterizing them as robbers and murderers, he is implying that they need to be treated as such.)*

ACTIVE OPTIONS

On Your Feet: Inside-Outside Circle Direct students to use the Inside-Outside Circle strategy to discuss questions such as the following: What were Luther's 95 theses about? How did Luther spread his ideas? Why did church officials ignore him at first? Who were John Wycliffe and Jan Hus? What was Luther's role in the Peasants' War?

NG Learning Framework: Explore Perspectives
ATTITUDE Responsibility
SKILL Communication

Have small groups research the Peasants' War to write one paragraph describing the causes of the war from the perspective of the peasants and another to describe it from the perspective of the nobles. Then have students write a one-page flyer that could have been printed and posted supporting or criticizing Luther's position in the war.

DIFFERENTIATE

STRIVING READERS

Create a Biography Square Ask students to complete a Word Square about Martin Luther, as shown below.

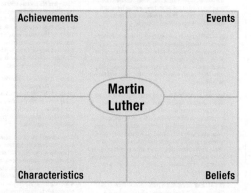

PRE-AP

Examine Evidence for an Event
Historically, people long believed that Luther posted his 95 theses on the door of a church in Wittenberg, Germany. In the 1960s, scholars questioned this view, but later researchers argued that it had indeed occurred. Have students research opinions and evidence on this matter from leading historians and scholars. Ask them to summarize and examine the evidence for each position and state their own opinion, explaining how they came to their position.

See the Chapter Planner for more strategies for differentiation.

HISTORICAL THINKING

ANSWERS

1. the printing press

2. He believed the Bible, not the pope, was the source of God's word; he supported translation so more people could read it.

3. Possible response: Many nobles had supported him in his conflict with Rome, so he may have viewed nobles as his friends and allies who could continue to exercise power on his behalf.

Reforms Across Europe

Reforms can make things better, but not every change is an improvement. Some religious reformers took extreme positions that led to intolerance or violence.

THE REFORMATION SPREADS

Not all the Europeans who left Catholicism became "Lutherans." Other reformers developed a variety of alternative church structures, rituals, and beliefs. Over time, followers of Luther and these other reformers became known as **Protestants** for their protests against the Roman Catholic Church.

Even before Luther published his 95 theses, another reformer, **Ulrich Zwingli**, was preaching directly from the Bible and questioning the teaching and practices of the Catholic Church. Like the Byzantine iconoclasts you read about earlier, Zwingli believed statues and other religious art were idols, or false gods, and should be destroyed.

By 1519, Zwingli had become the priest of the largest church in Zurich, Switzerland, where he preached powerful sermons. By 1524, he had convinced the city council to allow the destruction of all religious art in Zurich's churches. Teams of artisans destroyed religious objects and painted church interiors white to symbolize purity. Zwingli and his followers wanted to create communities that did not allow people to sin. The Swiss reformers created their own institutions—courts, schools, and charities—to carry out their vision of Christian society.

While Luther changed the religious environment of Germany and Zwingli changed Switzerland, **John Calvin** would have the greatest impact on Europe's religious world. Admired as a man of determination and insight, Calvin was also criticized for his coldness and his austere depiction of God. His doctrine that an elect group of believers chosen by God were the only true Christians in England would shape the culture of the English colonies in North America.

After fleeing persecution in France in 1536, Calvin set out to create a Protestant Rome in Geneva, Switzerland. His church had far more power over people's lives than

Zwingli's church. Everyone in Geneva was required to attend religious services. People who arrived late or fell asleep could be punished and even imprisoned.

Calvin and his pastors tried to guide followers toward the "correct" form of Christianity. Church officials regulated clothing and hairstyles, and parents could not give their children names associated with Catholic saints. Innkeepers were expected to report on visitors who played dice or cards, sang indecent songs, stayed up late, or committed blasphemy by speaking disrespectfully about sacred things. Extreme penalties were imposed for offenders.

Geneva became an international city as Protestants who were persecuted in other areas of Europe sought refuge there. They brought wealth and industries which, along with Calvin's planning, transformed Geneva into a modern city with hospitals and educational institutions. Today, many international organizations are headquartered there.

Other reformers took the ideas of Luther, Zwingli, and Calvin and adapted them further. One group, the Anabaptists, rejected the Catholic and Protestant view that churches should answer to state or civil authorities. They also believed that people should be rebaptized as adults, when they could exercise their own free will. A man called John of Leyden carried the Anabaptist perspective to an extreme. He turned Münster, Germany, into an armed encampment of baptized believers in an episode that ended in his execution and continued persecution of moderate Anabaptists.

ENGLAND BREAKS WITH ROME

While theologians and philosophers triggered reformations in Germany and Switzerland, in England the king broke with the Roman Catholic Church for political reasons. **Henry VIII** was a devout Catholic who opposed the changes Luther promoted. But in 1527, Henry asked the pope to annul, or rule invalid, his marriage of 25 years. He and Queen Catherine of

The difference between Catholic and Protestant beliefs and rituals is clearly demonstrated by church architecture. Note the sharp contrast between the Spanish colonial church of Santa Maria Tonantzintla (left) in Mexico and that of the Old Whaling Church in Massachusetts (below). The Spanish church reflects the Catholic preference for ornate interiors associated with elaborate rituals, while the colonial English church reflects the simplicity of Calvinism.

Aragon, the daughter of Spain's Ferdinand and Isabella, had produced only one surviving child, a daughter. The Roman Catholic Church did not allow divorce, and Henry felt he needed a son to inherit the throne.

The pope did not want to offend Catherine's powerful nephew, the Holy Roman Emperor Charles V, and refused to annul Henry's marriage. Henry declared himself head of the new Church of England so he could put Catherine aside and marry Anne Boleyn,

one of Catherine's ladies-in-waiting. This new church kept nearly all the practices and rituals of the Catholic Church but rejected the pope's authority. The Church of England created the Book of Common Prayer, which established a **liturgy**, or form of worship, that has influenced Protestant churches throughout the English-speaking world. Over time, Henry made further changes, such as abolishing monasteries and seizing their land and property. In England, the Reformation led to an increase in the power of the monarchy.

HISTORICAL THINKING

1. **READING CHECK** How did Zwingli feel about Luther's efforts to reform the Catholic Church? Explain.

2. **MAKE INFERENCES** Why did the people of Zurich destroy religious art in their churches?

3. **ANALYZE CAUSE AND EFFECT** What caused Henry VIII to break with the Roman Catholic Church and form the Church of England?

PLAN: 2-PAGE LESSON

OBJECTIVE

Analyze the spread and impact of the Protestant Reformation.

CRITICAL THINKING SKILLS FOR LESSON 3.2

- Make Inferences
- Analyze Cause and Effect
- Compare and Contrast
- Draw Conclusions

HISTORICAL THINKING FOR CHAPTER 15

Can tradition coexist with transformation?

As the Protestant Reformation spread through Europe, many symbols of tradition were destroyed even as new traditions were created. Lesson 3.2 discusses the reformers who came after Luther and the various reasons behind their reforms.

BACKGROUND FOR THE TEACHER

Spread of the Reformation The diversity of the Reformation may have encouraged its spread. Lutheranism spread through German-speaking regions, Scandinavia, Finland, and the Baltic states. It also influenced German-speaking Poles, but Calvinism, which was neither German nor French in flavor, found many adherents in Poland, too. In fact, the nation became a haven not only for Lutherans and Calvinists, but also Socinians (considered the precursors of today's Unitarians) from Italy and pacifist Bohemian Brethren (inspired by Jan Hus). In 1573, Poland granted toleration not only to Roman Catholics, but also to Lutherans, Calvinists, and Bohemian Brethren (but not the Socinians). Hungary was also a region of great religious diversity. Roman Catholics were the majority, but Lutherans, Calvinists, and Socinians were largely tolerated there.

INTRODUCE & ENGAGE

PREVIEW USING VISUALS

Draw students' attention to the photographs of the two churches and the caption. Ask students to identify the locations of the buildings in the pictures. Point out that both places are far from Luther's Germany. Explain that in this lesson and the next one they will learn about how Luther's ideas were transformed by others and carried over great distances.

TEACH

GUIDED DISCUSSION

1. **Compare and Contrast** What qualities did people admire in Calvin? What qualities did they criticize? *(determination, insight, and creation of "the Protestant work ethic"; cold, depicted God as austere)*

2. **Draw Conclusions** Why do you think many people chose to live in Calvin's Geneva even though life there was strictly regulated? *(Possible response: Calvinists felt safe from persecution; people may have valued a community in which standards of behavior were predictable even though deviations from those standards carried punishments.)*

MORE INFORMATION

In 1534, Parliament passed the Act of Supremacy, which proclaimed Henry VIII as the lawful head of the Church of England. Between 1536 and 1540, under the guise of eliminating the monks' excessive wealth and immorality, Henry dissolved 825 monasteries and took their land and wealth. He sold much of the monasteries' lands to the nobility, thereby increasing the royal treasury and ensuring the nobles' loyalty. For years, the common people had looked to the monasteries for charitable assistance and for safe lodging when traveling. After the dissolution, the number of beggars and thieves increased, leading to increased poverty and making travel more dangerous.

ACTIVE OPTIONS

On Your Feet: Jigsaw Strategy Organize students into four "expert" groups. Assign each group one of the following topics: Ulrich Zwingli, John Calvin, Anabaptists, Henry VIII. After groups have studied the topic in depth, regroup students so each new group has at least one member from each expert group. Ask experts to share the results of their study.

> **NG Learning Framework: Research International Organizations**
> ATTITUDE Responsibility
> SKILL Communication

Have small groups research one of the major international organizations in Geneva, such as the World Trade Organization, World Health Organization, International Committee of the Red Cross, International Labor Organization, Doctors Without Borders, or another organization. Direct groups to create fact sheets about the organization they research, including the purpose of the organization, year of founding, size of its budget, and major accomplishments and activities. Give students a chance to present their fact sheets or post them on a bulletin board.

DIFFERENTIATE

ENGLISH LANGUAGE LEARNERS

Dictate Sentence Summaries Pair students at the **Beginning** level with those at the **Advanced** level. After students read the lesson, direct them to identify three sentences that contain an important idea. Then tell each student to write that idea in a summary sentence using his or her own words. Partners should then take turns dictating their sentences to each other. Encourage them to work together to check each other's work for accuracy and spelling.

GIFTED & TALENTED

Create an Architectural Tour Have students locate examples of Protestant and Catholic churches—either churches they can visit and photograph themselves or through online photos. Invite students to put together a virtual tour of the churches, with captions to identify the church and its location and the ways in which the interior or exterior reflects the building's religious tradition.

See the Chapter Planner for more strategies for differentiation.

HISTORICAL THINKING

ANSWERS

1. Zwingli differed from Luther in that he wanted to find ways to communicate with God, while Luther was concerned with how people could be forgiven for their sins.

2. Zwingli was an electrifying speaker who convinced people that statues and religious art were false gods that should be destroyed.

3. The pope's refusal to grant him an annulment caused Henry VIII to break with the Roman Catholic Church and form the Church of England.

Challenges to Habsburg Dominance

Sometimes the winner of a game, an election, or a power struggle seems obvious. But history is full of unexpected outcomes. New factors and unanticipated circumstances can turn everything upside down.

THE HABSBURGS

Originally from central Europe, the Habsburg dynasty extended its rule through a series of strategic marriages between 1492 and 1515. As a result, the Habsburgs held more thrones than any other family in Europe in the 1500s, but religious strife and competition among emperors, kings, and princes challenged the dominance of the Habsburgs.

By 1516, when 16-year-old **Charles I** took the throne, the Habsburgs ruled the Netherlands, southern Italy, and Spain. Very soon, the wealth of silver and gold of the Spanish Empire would make the Habsburgs one of the wealthiest dynasties in the world.

With extensive territory in Europe and the wealth of the Americas at their disposal, it seemed that the Habsburgs might be able to create a Catholic empire and achieve political unity in western Europe. In 1520, the pope crowned Charles as Holy Roman Emperor after he was elected to that position by the archbishops and princes who ruled the German-speaking lands. As Holy Roman Emperor, he was now Charles V and the principal defender of the Catholic faith. But Charles faced challenges to the considerable power of the Habsburgs. France, which was creating a strong centralized government that gave the king sweeping powers, was making efforts to conquer parts of Italy and was a powerful rival in the west.

The Protestant Reformation also created problems. The wave of challenges to the Catholic Church that swept

Europe, c. 1520

through German-speaking Europe led to decades of inconclusive warfare among princes loyal to the pope and those who called themselves Lutherans. Religious division became a fixture of western Europe.

In 1555, Charles finally gave up his attempt to impose Catholicism through military means and agreed to a peace, recognizing the principle that princes could impose either Catholicism or Lutheranism within their own territories. Exhausted, Charles abdicated, or gave up, his throne, retired to a monastery, and split his inheritance between his brother Ferdinand, who took control of the Habsburgs' central European territories, and his son Philip, who became king of Spain. The Habsburgs had failed to hold Europe together.

RELIGIOUS AND POLITICAL CONFLICTS

Charles's son **Philip II** ruled over a magnificent court at Madrid in Spain, the Spanish empire in the Americas, and the new southeast Asian colony of the Philippines. However, even with the vast riches of New Spain, wars severely strained the treasury, and increased taxes led to unrest. Philip's determined efforts to impose Catholicism led to religious conflicts. For example, in 1568, the *moriscos*, Arabic-speaking residents of Spain who had been forced, like the Spanish Jews, to convert to Catholicism in 1492, rebelled when the church imposed stricter rules. It took two years for Philip's forces to crush the uprising; Philip then ordered all the moriscos who had survived to leave Spain.

Religious differences also drove Philip's war on the Calvinists in his Dutch provinces. He tried to seize their property, but they armed themselves and rebelled against him.

Protestant England was another constant source of concern for Philip. Under the rule of Queen Elizabeth I, England harassed the Spanish at every turn. England provided aid to Calvinist rebels in Spain's Dutch provinces, and English pirates raided Spanish treasure ships in the Caribbean. In 1588, Philip sent a great naval armada to invade England. Poor weather, along with clever English strategy, led to the defeat of the Spanish Armada. The English took their victory as a sign that God was indeed on their side.

Religious differences affected one of Spain's chief rivals, France. French Protestants, largely Calvinists known as Huguenots (HYOO-guh-nahtz), were a small but prosperous minority. Catholic persecution of Huguenots reached its extreme in 1572, with the Saint Bartholomew's Day massacre. Huguenot leaders were assassinated, and tens of thousands of Protestants were killed. More than 25 years later, in 1598, the Edict of Nantes gave French Protestants in certain cities limited rights.

Challenges remained, however. The expanding Ottoman Empire threatened the Habsburgs in central Europe and on the Adriatic coast of Italy. Meanwhile, religious tensions increased, not just between the rulers of Spain and England. Competition between Catholic and

Lutheran rulers in German-speaking lands, as well as struggles for power by Europe's major powers, brought about the catastrophic Thirty Years War.

From 1618 to 1648, Catholic and Protestant armies rampaged across central Europe. In some areas, as much as 30 percent of the population was killed as a result of famine and disease, a loss almost as great as that of the Black Death 300 years earlier. Religious intolerance, combined with greed and lust for power, had turned central Europe into a blood bath.

The humanists' emphasis on peaceful contemplation and toleration for diverse views had been largely forgotten. But by 1648, leaders realized that no military solution was possible and agreed to a peace that recognized that the religious divisions of Europe would be permanent.

Philip II (left) of Spain married Mary I of England (right) in 1554. Until her death in 1558, the two kingdoms maintained friendly relations and Catholicism was restored as England's official religion. However, when Mary's sister and heir, Elizabeth I, took the throne, the country returned to Protestantism.

HISTORICAL THINKING

1. **READING CHECK** What was the primary goal of the Habsburg dynasty when Charles I took the throne in 1516?

2. **IDENTIFY MAIN IDEAS AND DETAILS** What three challenges did Charles I face in his efforts to bring about political and religious unity?

3. **IDENTIFY PROBLEMS AND SOLUTIONS** Why did Philip II try to invade England in 1588?

PLAN: 2-PAGE LESSON

OBJECTIVE

Identify military and religious conflicts arising from Habsburg efforts to maintain political and religious control of Europe.

CRITICAL THINKING SKILLS FOR LESSON 4.1

- Identify Main Ideas and Details
- Identify Problems and Solutions
- Identify
- Interpret Maps

HISTORICAL THINKING FOR CHAPTER 15

Can tradition coexist with transformation?

Efforts by powerful rulers to maintain Roman Catholic traditions led to conflicts that created transformation in Europe. Lesson 4.1 discusses the impact of the Reformation on the Habsburg dynasty.

BACKGROUND FOR THE TEACHER

A Dynasty's Downfall While the Habsburgs saw themselves as the defenders of Catholicism in Europe, not all Catholics supported them. In addition to hostility from France (threatened by the extent of Habsburg possessions), the Habsburgs also faced resistance from popes who feared their power. Other European powers tended to sympathize with France in efforts to limit the extent of the Habsburg powers. While the Habsburgs were known for their marriages (a translation of a famous Latin couplet goes: "*Let others wage wars: you, fortunate Austria, marry*") over time they worried that other dynasties would undermine them with a similar strategy. Therefore, they began to intermarry in an effort to protect their holdings. Within a few generations, genetic disorders made it impossible for members of the Habsburg dynasty to reproduce. Ironically, following the death of Charles II, who died in 1700 with no heirs, the French House of Bourbon took the throne of Spain.

INTRODUCE & ENGAGE

BRAINSTORM FORMS OF POWER

Ask students to recall what they have learned about the ways in which different dynasties came to and maintained power. Point out that military conquest, trade, tolerance, and authoritarianism have all been used at different times. Ask if they can think of another way in which a family or government might build an empire, and then tell them that in this lesson they will learn about a dynasty that achieved power in a unique manner.

TEACH

GUIDED DISCUSSION

1. **Identify Main Ideas and Details** What were the challenges that faced the Habsburgs in their efforts to create a unified Catholic empire? *(Protestant Reformation, rivalry from France, rebellions in Spain and the Netherlands, challenges from England, and threats from the Ottomans)*

2. **Identify** Who were the *moriscos*, and what became of them under Philip II? *(The moriscos were Arabic-speaking Spaniards who were forced to convert to Catholicism. After their uprising was defeated, they were ordered to leave Spain.)*

INTERPRET MAPS

Instruct students to look at the Europe, c. 1520 map that appears in the lesson. **ASK:** What geographic and cultural difficulties might the Habsburgs have had in trying to keep their lands unified and in trying to create a Catholic empire? *(The lands were separated by powerful kingdoms such as France, the Germanic kingdoms, and the Italian kingdoms. In addition, the Germanic kingdoms were the center of the Protestant Reformation, which would have made them anti-Catholic.)*

ACTIVE OPTIONS

On Your Feet: Roundtable Have students sit in groups of four around a table to discuss the following question: Why did the Habsburgs, despite their power and wealth, fail to unify Europe as a Catholic empire? Provide each group with a large sheet of paper. Tell group members to take turns jotting down as many answers to the question as possible, urging them to do additional research. Call on a representative from each group to share the group's ideas. You may want to compile a master list of responses.

> **NG Learning Framework: Mapping Habsburg Influence**
> **SKILL** Observation
> **KNOWLEDGE** Our Human Story

Provide or have students create a large outline map of the world. Have small groups review the lesson, marking every place mentioned in the lesson on the map. In addition to places in Europe, they will want to mark locations such as the Philippines, the Americas, the Caribbean, and the Ottoman Empire. Encourage them to review earlier chapters or conduct additional research to determine, for example, the location of the Ottoman Empire or where the *moriscos* went. Invite students to display their maps and provide commentary on the places they have marked.

DIFFERENTIATE

INCLUSION

Trace Maps Direct students to read the caption and legend for the map of Europe in 1520. Have them use a finger to circle the territories held by the Habsburgs, France, England, and the Ottomans. Provide sentence frames for students to complete based on the map.

- The Netherlands was held by _____. *(the Habsburgs)*
- The _____ attacked the Habsburgs from the east. *(Ottoman Empire)*
- _____, also Catholic, was a rival to the west. *(France)*
- _____ defeated Habsburg Spain in a famous sea battle. *(England)*

PRE-AP

Write a Report Direct students to gather relevant information from several library or online sources to write a report on challenges to Habsburg dominance. Suggest students limit their report to one challenge, such as France, the uprising of the *moriscos*, the rebellion in the Netherlands, English privateers, etc.

See the Chapter Planner for more strategies for differentiation.

HISTORICAL THINKING

ANSWERS

1. The primary goal of the Habsburg dynasty when Charles took the throne in 1516 was to create a unified Catholic empire in Europe.

2. The Protestant Reformation, France, England, and the Ottoman Empire were challenges to Charles's efforts.

3. Philip II tried to invade England in 1588 to stop raids on Spanish treasure ships by English privateers.

The Catholic Reformation

Do the ends justify the means? In the 16th and 17th centuries both Protestants and Catholics used cruel methods to convince people of what they each thought was the religion that would save their souls.

THE COUNCIL OF TRENT

Some had pushed for reforms and changes within the Roman Catholic Church before 1517, but once Luther published his 95 theses, the growth of Protestantism became a threat the church could not ignore. This movement to reform and strengthen the Roman Catholic Church from within became known as the Catholic Reformation or the Counter-Reformation. In 1545, the pope called for a meeting in the city of Trent in northern Italy to begin the formal process of reforming the church from within. A group of bishops met 25 times over a period of 18 years in what became known as the **Council of Trent**. These meetings laid out the rituals and structures of the modern Roman Catholic Church. They also clearly defined the differences between Catholics and Protestants.

The Roman Catholic Church published a list, or index, of forbidden books. This list included works by humanist writers such as Erasmus and Machiavelli, as well as translations of the Bible into languages other than Latin. The church also used the Inquisition to enforce conformity. As you may recall, the Inquisition was a group of institutions that investigated people to make sure they were following the teachings of the Catholic Church. The most famous was the Spanish Inquisition, originally created to persecute Jews and Muslims.

After the Protestant Reformation, the Spanish Inquisition was also used to track down Protestants in Spain. After the Council of Trent, it hunted down corrupt priests. The

A prisoner is tortured by the Spanish Inquisition while monks await his confession, c. 1500. Individuals were often punished and even killed by the Inquisition for exercising free thought and speech.

Inquisition was not any crueler than some Protestant-controlled regimes that punished those who did not conform to the religious views of those in power. Europe in the 16th and 17th centuries had little room for freedom of speech, and those who believed they were rooting out people who threatened the religious order, whether Catholic or Protestant, were often cruel.

Through the Council of Trent, the Catholic Church tried to create a truly universal church that would address the spiritual needs of all people, no matter what their language or where they lived. The church conducted all worship in Latin and reduced the number of church holidays and ceremonies. It standardized the rituals used for worship and prayer. The church worked to increase activities that provided charity and expand opportunities for **piety**, or devotion to the church. It also established new rules to reduce corruption among clergy and the monastic orders.

CATHOLIC REFORMERS

Ignatius of Loyola set aside his life as a Spanish noble to live as a beggar. He developed the idea that through simple meditation and prayer, people might come closer to God, and through his book *Spiritual Exercises*, he began to gain disciples, or followers. Convinced of the need for a solid education in order to carry out God's will, he became a university student. Ignatius's perspective was not always welcomed by the Catholic Church; he faced imprisonment and trials, but by 1540, the pope approved of the formation of a new order, or religious community, to be known as the Society of Jesus. Members of the order were called Jesuits.

Jesuit schools became one of the most effective defenses against the Protestant Reformation. Many parts of Europe, including Poland and parts of Germany, returned to Catholicism because of Jesuit schools. Jesuits also emphasized caring for the poor and the sick. They wrote and published widely, providing European readers with reasonable arguments for their religious views. The Jesuits became one of the most active missionary arms of the Catholic Church, spreading the faith to the Americas, Africa, and Asia, and across Europe.

Teresa of Ávila was a Spanish nun and mystic, or person who seeks a direct connection to God. At the age of 13, Teresa was placed in a convent. Although it was founded as an order that emphasized prayer and withdrawal from the world, it had become a retreat that

Gian Lorenzo Bernini sculpted *The Ecstasy of Saint Teresa* in marble and bronze in the mid-1600s. It depicts Teresa of Ávila overwhelmed by a religious vision.

allowed wealthy young women to live in comfort. Teresa began to have religious visions, gave up her worldly goods, and started a new order with women who had been moved by her teaching. Her order required a vow of poverty and gave all the nuns equal status regardless of their prior rank. It also required withdrawal from the world and obedience. Parents of daughters who joined Teresa's convent were suspicious. They feared they would lose contact with their daughters or that their family fortunes would be given away. Teresa and her followers faced persecution, yet her following grew until the church finally recognized her order. Teresa of Ávila and Ignatius of Loyola were **canonized**, or recognized as saints by the Catholic Church, on the same day in 1622.

HISTORICAL THINKING

1. **READING CHECK** Who called the series of meetings known as the Council of Trent, and what was the outcome of those meetings?

2. **DRAW CONCLUSIONS** How did the use of Latin reflect the structure of the Roman Catholic Church?

3. **COMPARE AND CONTRAST** Compare and contrast the efforts of the Inquisition and the Jesuits to strengthen the Catholic Church.

PLAN: 2-PAGE LESSON

OBJECTIVE

Discuss the efforts of the Catholic Church to deal with internal problems and the Protestant Reformation.

CRITICAL THINKING SKILLS FOR LESSON 4.2

- Draw Conclusions
- Compare and Contrast
- Identify Problems and Solutions
- Make Inferences
- Integrate Visuals

HISTORICAL THINKING FOR CHAPTER 15

Can tradition coexist with transformation?

The Roman Catholic Church transformed itself in an effort to maintain its traditions. Lesson 4.2 discusses steps taken by the church to counteract the Protestant Reformation.

BACKGROUND FOR THE TEACHER

The List of Forbidden Books The first *Index Librorum Prohibitorum* was published in 1559, but the Index Congregation, or the consultants whose job it was to consider the suitability of books, continued to meet a few times a year for the next 400 years to discuss books and submit their list for the pope's approval. The index included a list of rules regarding "superstitious" or "heretical" writings and extended the punishment of excommunication to the authors of books, to those who printed or sold them, and to those who read or possessed them. The office that published the index ceased activity in 1966, and the files of the index were opened to researchers in the 1990s.

INTRODUCE & ENGAGE

DISCUSS ETHICAL QUESTIONS

Ask the question in the lesson introduction: Do the ends justify the means? Invite students to weigh in on this issue and explain their reasoning. Tell students to challenge one another in their thinking. Then explain that, in the 1500s, officials of the Roman Catholic Church adopted different measures in their efforts to save souls.

TEACH

GUIDED DISCUSSION

1. **Identify Problems and Solutions** What problems did the Catholic Church face in the early 1500s? What measures did it undertake to solve them? *(the threat of Protestantism as well as internal problems; a group of bishops met over a period of 18 years in the Council of Trent to agree on shared rituals and structures of the church and to clearly define the differences between Catholics and Protestants.)*

2. **Make Inferences** Why did the Catholic Church decide to conduct all worship in Latin after the Council of Trent? *(Catholic leaders wanted to create a universal church that would address the needs of people who spoke different languages; Latin was used throughout Europe.)*

INTEGRATE VISUALS

Have students examine the lithograph of the prisoner being tortured. **ASK:** What is happening in this image? *(A prisoner is attached to a wheel, and the wheel revolves so that the prisoner passes very closely to a fire burning beneath.)* Remind students of the question from the Introduce & Engage activity: Do the ends justify the means? **ASK:** Based on this image and what you read about the Spanish Inquisition, how would you answer this question? *(Possible response: No, the ends did not justify the means. Using cruel methods to strengthen the Roman Catholic Church went against the basic beliefs of Christianity.)*

ACTIVE OPTIONS

On Your Feet: Team Word Webbing Provide teams with a large piece of paper. Give each student a different colored marker. Assign the topic "The Catholic Reformation." Tell each student to add to the part of the web nearest to him or her. On a signal, students should rotate the paper and continue to add to the web. Ask teams to compare their webs.

> **NG Learning Framework: Discuss Ethical Standards**
> **ATTITUDE** Curiosity
> **KNOWLEDGE** Our Human Story

Pose this question: Which of the measures undertaken by the Roman Catholic Church were most effective at achieving the church's goals? Instruct small groups to generate as many responses as they can, referring to as many elements of the Catholic Reformation as they can. Invite groups to share their lists with the class and compile a master list of methods the church used to successfully weather changes.

DIFFERENTIATE

STRIVING READERS

Use a Concept Cluster Guide pairs to summarize the lesson by creating a Concept Cluster. Tell them to write the lesson title in the center circle and the lesson headings in the outer circles: *The Council of Trent* and *Catholic Reformers.* As students read the information under each heading, prompt them to enter key events on the spokes radiating from each section. After students complete their Concept Cluster, invite volunteers to summarize the lesson and explain the effects of the Catholic Reformation.

PRE-AP

Research Catholic Orders Tell students to research major religious orders of Catholicism. Invite them to create infographics to summarize information such as when and where the order was founded and by whom, the order motto, the habit or distinctive clothing, the focus of the spiritual community, and notable saints of the order.

See the Chapter Planner for more strategies for differentiation.

HISTORICAL THINKING

ANSWERS

1. The pope; the rituals and structures of the church were standardized and the differences between Catholics and Protestants were clearly defined.

2. reflected the international structure of the Roman Catholic Church and the clergy and church officials were among the best educated people in Europe of their time

3. Inquisition: strengthen the church by seeking out, investigating, and persecuting those who were believed to hold incorrect religious views; Jesuits: strengthen the church by providing education, care for the poor and the sick, and published arguments in favor of their religious views

Global Christianities

Conflicts over religion occurred at the same time Europeans were expanding trade networks and land claims to areas beyond Europe. This expansion offered new opportunities to spread religious ideas.

DIVERSE CHRISTIAN PRACTICES

Since ancient times, Christian communities have developed diverse rituals and interpretations of the Bible. The Armenian Church and Coptic Christianity in Ethiopia, for example, both have unique sacred languages and rituals inherited from long ago.

The diversity of Christian practices led to conflict in the 11th century when, as you have learned, the Roman Catholic and Eastern Orthodox branches of Christianity finalized a split that had been brewing for centuries by excommunicating one another. Roman Catholics recognized the authority of the pope in Rome and used Latin as the official church language. Orthodox communities, many with Greek as their church language, recognized the patriarch of Constantinople as leader. The Orthodox Church became very influential in Russia, where it deeply affected social and political life. It was not until 1965 that the Roman Catholic

and Orthodox churches recognized one another as valid by lifting their mutual excommunications.

Such splits are part of the evolution of most major religions. Divisions among Buddhists followed the death of the Buddha around 483 B.C.E. In the 600s, following the death of Muhammad, Islam split into Sunni and Shiite groups over disputes about leadership. As in Europe, where political competition was fueled by religious disagreement, differences between Sunnis and Shiites deepened and led to political and military competition in the Islamic world.

Similarly, the deep and bitter divisions that led to religious warfare in Europe at the time of the Protestant and Catholic reformations would also have wider consequences, as missionaries spread their interpretations of the faith using new maritime connections to Africa, Asia, and the Americas.

REFORMATIONS AROUND THE GLOBE

Although the Protestant Reformation started in western Europe, its effects were felt far beyond that region. Some Protestant groups fled the continent to avoid persecution, such as Calvinists fleeing from France and England. Some of these Puritans became known as Pilgrims. The Pilgrims were English **dissidents**, or people who were at odds with the official religion. They left Holland, where they had been living to avoid persecution and sailed to Plymouth, Massachusetts, on the *Mayflower*. Soon after, a much larger group of English settlers arrived to form the Massachusetts Bay Colony farther up the coast. Inspired by Calvin and his followers, who had tried to make Geneva into a city that reflected their beliefs, these Puritans planned to create a haven for what they considered to be a "purified" form of Christianity.

The Catholic Counter-Reformation had an even larger global impact in the 16th century. Roman Catholic

Spread of Protestantism, 1600s

- Anglican
- Calvinist
- Lutheran

CRITICAL VIEWING As Catholic missionaries traveled throughout the world as a result of the Counter-Reformation, they established churches in the Americas, Africa, and Asia, such as this 18th-century Roman Catholic Church in southern China. How would you compare the style of this church to other churches you've seen pictured in this chapter?

missionaries from Spain and Portugal carried their religion into the Americas. In 1524, the first Franciscan friars arrived in Mexico. The Franciscans became the most important missionary order among the Aztec. They searched for parallels between native beliefs and Christian teachings; at the same time, they suppressed practices such as human sacrifice.

Before long, Aztec converts to Catholicism began making the new religion their own. For example, in 1531 a peasant named Juan Diego reported that he had seen a vision of the Virgin Mary, who had appeared to him on the very site of an earlier shrine to the Aztec goddess of fertility. The Catholic Church recognized his vision as authentic, and the cult of the Virgin of Guadalupe was born. Her dark-skinned image became central to the Mexican practice of Catholicism. Historians use the

term **religious syncretism** to describe this merging of indigenous religious rituals and ideas with conversion to a new faith. Another example of religious syncretism is when African converts to Christianity brought their traditions into the new faith, for example, by keeping their old gods but now calling them "saints."

It is true that indigenous peoples sometimes suffered from missionary efforts, as when Jesuits converted people in Brazil to Catholicism and resettled them in villages where they might be killed by disease or sold into slavery. In South Africa and North America, Calvinist settlers deprived indigenous peoples of land and resources. Still, a final outcome of the global expansion of Christianity in the 17th century was a rich and diverse set of faith traditions across the world.

HISTORICAL THINKING

1. **READING CHECK** What were the possible financial benefits to rulers who became Protestants?

2. **INTERPRET MAPS** How did the spread of the Lutheran and Calvinist branches of Protestantism differ from that of the Anglican branch?

3. **ANALYZE CAUSE AND EFFECT** What were the effects of the Reformation and the Counter-Reformation on settlement in the Americas?

PLAN: 2-PAGE LESSON

OBJECTIVE

Explain how expanding European trade and land claims contributed to the spread of religious ideas.

CRITICAL THINKING SKILLS FOR LESSON 4.3

- Interpret Maps
- Analyze Cause and Effect
- Make Connections
- Synthesize
- Create Maps

HISTORICAL THINKING FOR CHAPTER 15

Can tradition coexist with transformation?

Transformation of European conceptions of the world helped spread European religious traditions. Lesson 4.3 discusses the global effects of the Protestant Reformation and Catholic Counter-Reformation.

BACKGROUND FOR THE TEACHER

Students may be curious about who came out ahead in the Reformation efforts. According to the Pew Research Center's Forum on Religion & Public Life, as of 2015 there were about 2.3 billion Christians in the world, making it the world's largest religion. Worldwide, a little over 50 percent of Christians were Catholic in 2010, nearly 38 percent were Protestant, and about 12 percent were Orthodox. As of 2017, most European Christians tended to see Protestantism and Catholicism as more similar than different. But the number of Christians in Europe—Catholic and Protestant—is declining as the population ages and the birth rate falls. Worldwide, Christianity is growing. Christians have the second-highest fertility rate of any religious group, but Muslims have the highest rate. If present trends continue, Muslims are expected to catch up with Christians in absolute numbers as well as in share of the global population.

INTRODUCE & ENGAGE

PREVIEW THE MAP

Direct students' attention to the map of the spread of Protestantism that appears in the lesson. Have students identify the cities that form the epicenter of each strain of Protestantism—Lutheran, Calvinist, and Anglican. Invite students to discuss the direction in which each strain spread and the range. Remind students that both Protestant and Catholic beliefs were eventually carried far beyond Europe.

TEACH

GUIDED DISCUSSION

1. **Make Connections** What are some historical examples of religious division? *(The split between the Roman and Eastern branches of Christianity in the 11th century; the division among Buddhists following the death of the Buddha; the division between Sunni and Shiite Muslims following the death of Muhammad.)*

2. **Synthesize** How did Protestants and Catholics carry their religious views beyond Europe? How were their motivations similar or different? *(Possible response: In general, Protestants sought refuge from persecution and started new settlements and communities; Catholics carried religious ideas to existing cultures via missionaries.)*

CREATE MAPS

Provide students with a blank map of the world (with no country boundaries). Have students reread the final section of the lesson and use the descriptions in the text to create their own map illustrating the spread of both Protestantism and Catholicism around the world as a result of the Protestant and Catholic Reformations.

ACTIVE OPTIONS

On Your Feet: Roundtable Have students gather in groups of four and give each group a large sheet of paper. Ask students to consider the following question: Did conflicts between Protestants and Catholics help or hurt the spread of Christianity? Tell each student in every group to write his or her opinion, supported with evidence from the text. After all students have written their answers, allow time for groups to discuss their responses. Then call on volunteers to share their group's ideas.

> **NG Learning Framework: Chart Religious Pluralism**
> **ATTITUDE** Curiosity
> **SKILL** Communication

Ask small groups to conduct an inventory of religious congregations in their own community. Depending on the size of the school community, this might mean a town or a section or neighborhood of a larger city. Have them use online resources to find and list the name and affiliation of each church, temple, mosque, or other institution. Invite them to find out and include on their chart the country of origin of each religious movement represented in their community. Ask students to share their findings and offer a conclusion about religious activities in their community.

DIFFERENTIATE

ENGLISH LANGUAGE LEARNERS

Make Word Cards Invite students at the **Intermediate** level to make word cards for the terms *excommunicate* and *dissident*. You may also add other words from the lesson. Tell students to write each term on one side of a card and illustrate it on the opposite side. Then have students pair with another student, present each illustration, and ask their partner to determine which term is being illustrated.

GIFTED & TALENTED

Write Journal Entries Instruct students to research the experiences of various people, such as English dissidents who left Holland for Massachusetts, Franciscan missionaries in Mexico, or local people in Asia or the Americas encountering Christian missionaries or settlers. Tell students to use their research to write journal entries, providing specific details of their efforts to spread their religion or their impressions of Christian settlers or missionaries. Have students perform a reading of their journal entries.

See the Chapter Planner for more strategies for differentiation.

HISTORICAL THINKING

ANSWERS

1. They were encouraged to take over the large properties of Catholic monasteries.

2. They spread beyond their kingdoms of origin, while the Anglican branch stayed local to England.

3. encouraged religious dissidents to go to the Americas to build new communities that would allow them to pursue their own forms of worship

CRITICAL VIEWING Possible response: It also has a section that is very high and incorporates elements of the local culture into its design.

15 REVIEW

VOCABULARY

Use each of the following vocabulary words in a sentence that shows an understanding of the term's meaning.

1. patron
2. humanism
3. linear perspective
4. indulgence
5. Protestant
6. liturgy
7. piety
8. dissident

READING STRATEGY
COMPARE AND CONTRAST

Use a Venn diagram like the one below to compare and contrast the Protestant Reformation and the Catholic Reformation. Then answer the questions that follow.

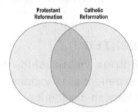

9. Which Reformation movement (Protestant or Catholic) benefited most from the development of the printing press and increased literacy?

10. Which Reformation movement (Protestant or Catholic) employed schools most effectively to further its goals?

MAIN IDEAS

Answer the following questions. Support your answers with evidence from the chapter.

11. What did Italy's city-states hope to gain in their battles with each other in the 1300s? LESSON 1.1

12. Why did Renaissance artists sometimes include carpets in their commissioned paintings? LESSON 1.2

13. What were some ways that Leonardo da Vinci used science and mathematics in his art? LESSON 1.3

14. What sources did Petrarch turn to for moral guidance in the 1300s? LESSON 2.1

15. What technique did artists use to make objects look closer or farther away in their paintings? LESSON 2.2

16. Why did Niccolò Machiavelli write The Prince? LESSON 2.3

17. Why did Zwingli and his followers destroy statues and religious art in Zurich's churches? LESSON 3.2

18. How did Jesuit schools impact the Protestant Reformation? LESSON 4.2

HISTORICAL THINKING

Answer the following questions. Support your answers with evidence from the chapter.

19. ANALYZE CAUSE AND EFFECT How did widespread use of the vernacular in printed books affect Europeans?

20. MAKE GENERALIZATIONS Discuss the ways that three different humanist writers expressed the ideals of humanism in their work.

21. DRAW CONCLUSIONS Why was Martin Luther so successful in spreading his ideas?

22. COMPARE AND CONTRAST Discuss the similarities and differences between the goals and methods of the Protestant Reformation and the Catholic Reformation. In your opinion, was one of these efforts more successful? Why or why not?

23. ANALYZE CAUSE AND EFFECT How were Protestants and Catholics impacted by advances in maritime technology?

INTERPRET VISUALS

Study the graph below, which shows the estimated rates of literacy in Europe between 1475 and 1750. Then answer the questions that follow.

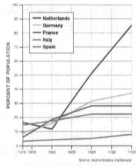

European Literacy Rates, 1475–1750

24. Which two nations had the highest rates of literacy in 1475? Which two had the highest in 1750?

25. How would you describe the change in rates of literacy in Germany between 1550 and 1650? In the Netherlands in this same period?

ANALYZE SOURCES

One of Michelangelo's students, Ascanio Condivi, wrote a biography of his teacher that was published in 1553. In this excerpt, Condivi describes the physical strain of painting the Sistine Chapel ceiling and its effect on Michelangelo. Read the excerpt and answer the question that follows.

> After he had accomplished this work, because he had spent such a long time painting with his eyes looking up at the vault, Michelangelo then could not see much when he looked down; so that, if he had to read a letter or other detailed things, he had to hold them with his arms up over his head. . . . From this we may conceive how great were the attention and diligence with which he did his work.

26. According to his biographer, how did the work of painting the ceiling of the Sistine Chapel affect Michelangelo's vision?

CONNECT TO YOUR LIFE

27. ARGUMENT In a statement that many view as the guiding principal of humanism, the writer Petrarch said, "It is better to will the good than to know the truth." Do you think this statement served as guide for political and religious leaders of the Renaissance and Reformation? Is it a statement that could be used as a guide for moral and ethical living today? Write an essay presenting your answers to both questions, citing examples from the chapter and your own research.

TIPS

• Review the discussions of the Renaissance, humanism, and the Reformations in the chapter.

• Choose two or three figures from the chapter who you think might exemplify or contradict Petrarch's statement. Conduct additional research into these figures if necessary.

• Use two or three vocabulary words from the chapter in your argument.

• Think about your own life and the behavior of leaders you admire today. Does this statement serve as a guide in our present-day world? Why or why not?

VOCABULARY ANSWERS

1. Renaissance artists relied on patrons to give them financial support so they could focus on their work.

2. A new intellectual movement called humanism encouraged the study of classical Greek and Roman texts.

3. The technique of linear perspective allowed Renaissance artists to make a painting seem three-dimensional.

4. The church sold indulgences to people who wished to save their souls.

5. A person who followed a Christian religion that did not recognize the authority of the pope was called a Protestant.

6. One of the major contributions of the Reformation in England was the creation of the Book of Common Prayer, which established a liturgy that is still used today.

7. A person who practiced piety showed extreme devotion to the church.

8. A religious dissident was often forced to seek refuge in a new place to avoid persecution.

READING STRATEGY ANSWERS

Protestant Reformation | Catholic Reformation

Protestant Reformation: Translations of Bible, Printing press, Disagreement over salvation and communication with God

Both: Changes to religious landscape of Europe, Global implications

Catholic Reformation: Council of Trent, Inquisition, Jesuits, Franciscans, other religious orders

9. Protestants benefited most from the development of the printing press and increased literacy because more people were able to read the Bible and make arguments for new ideas.

10. Catholic Jesuits employed schools to spread their religion throughout Europe and other parts of the world, including Asia, the Americas, and Africa.

MAIN IDEAS ANSWERS

11. Italian city-states hoped to gain industries or natural resources.

12. Carpets were prized luxury goods that showed off the wealth of art patrons when shown in paintings.

13. Leonardo's close observations of the effects of light affected his use of color and lines in paintings.

14. Petrarch turned to Latin writers such as Cicero and to the early Christian writer St. Augustine for moral guidance.

15. Use of linear perspective allowed artists to determine the placement and size of figures on a flat plane.

16. Machiavelli wrote *The Prince* to explain how rulers gain and hold onto power.

17. Zwingli and his followers believed statues and other religious art were idols, or false gods.

18. Many parts of Europe, including Poland and parts of Germany, returned to Catholicism because Jesuit schools offered a quality education to children of all faiths.

HISTORICAL THINKING ANSWERS

19. Widespread use of the vernacular in printed books allowed more people to read and access the ideas in books.

20. Cassandra Fedele expressed the ideal that study of the humanities exposed people to important moral values. Machiavelli expressed the view that effective action was more important than contemplation. Thomas More portrayed a society in which both practical skills as well as learning were valued.

21. Martin Luther was successful in spreading his ideas thanks to his abilities as a writer and preacher, the printing press, work by earlier reformers, and the management abilities of his wife Katharina von Bora.

22. Both the Protestant and Catholic Reformations attempted to reach as many people as possible with their views about the correct approach to Christianity. Protestants attempted to reach people with inspiring preachers and translations of the Bible; Catholics sought to create a universal church through the use of Latin and shared rituals. One could argue that both efforts were successful at spreading their form of Christian worship throughout Europe and the world as both have had a significant impact.

23. Advances in maritime technology allowed Protestants and Catholics to spread their faith across the ocean to different parts of the world.

INTERPRET VISUALS ANSWERS

24. The Netherlands and Italy had the highest rates of literacy in 1475 among the countries shown on the graph. The Netherlands and Germany had the highest rates in 1750.

25. Between 1550 and 1650, literacy rates in Germany more than doubled from about 15 percent to more than 30 percent. During the same period after a slight drop, literacy rates in the Netherlands more than quadrupled, from about 12 percent to over 50 percent.

ANALYZE SOURCES ANSWER

26. The strain of the work on the Sistine Chapel ceiling required Michelangelo to hold detailed objects over his head to see them.

CONNECT TO YOUR LIFE ANSWER

27. Answers will vary, but students should include a discussion of two to three people from the chapter. Petrarch may have meant "truth" in the religious sense, and his statement could be taken to mean that he thought having a positive impact on the world was more important than following a strict religious doctrine. Petrarch, Erasmus, and many of the artists covered in this chapter, as well as perhaps Cassandra Fedele and Thomas More, might have agreed with this perspective (though More did not always act on this view). Ignatius of Loyola and Teresa of Ávila might have agreed as well, though generally people of both the Protestant and Catholic Reformations seemed to value religious truth over "the good."

UNIT 6 RESOURCES

UNIT INTRODUCTION

UNIT TIME LINE

UNIT MAP

THE GLOBAL PERSPECTIVE:
Seafarers: Life on the World's Oceans

- National Geographic Explorers: Brian Skerry, Sylvia Earle, Robert Ballard, Enric Sala, and Grace Young
- On Your Feet: Fishbowl

NG Learning Framework
Research National Geographic Explorers

UNIT WRAP-UP

***National Geographic* Magazine Adapted Article**
- "The Epic Quest for a Northwest Passage"

Unit 6 Inquiry: Design a Conqueror's Toolbox

Unit 6 Formal Assessment

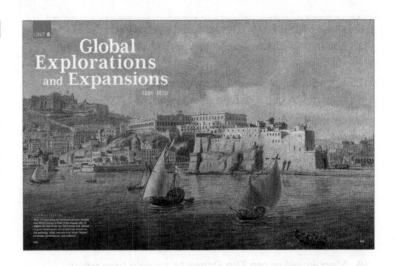

CHAPTER 16 RESOURCES

Available in the Teacher eEdition

TEACHER RESOURCES & ASSESSMENT

Reading and Note-Taking

Vocabulary Practice

Document-Based Question Template

Social Studies Skills Lessons
- Reading: Draw Conclusions
- Writing: Informative

Formal Assessment
- Chapter 16 Pretest
- Chapter 16 Tests A & B
- Section Quizzes

Chapter 16 Answer Key

Cognero®

STUDENT DIGITAL RESOURCES

Available in the Student eEdition

- eEdition (English)
- National Geographic Atlas
- Biographies
- Handbooks
- History Notebook
- Literature Analysis

STRATEGY ❶
Outline and Take Notes

Help students develop their reading and comprehension skills by asking them to work in pairs to write an outline for each lesson. Instruct them in using an outline format such as the one shown. Tell them to identify the main idea and then look for two details that support each main idea.

I. _____
   A. _____
   B. _____
II. _____
   A. _____
   B. _____
III. _____
   A. _____
   B. _____

Use with All Lessons *You might choose to pair students of mixed proficiency. Remind students that section headings in the lesson sometimes serve as the highest level (Roman numerals) of an outline.*

STRATEGY ❷
Make a Top Five Facts List

Assign a lesson to be read. After reading, have students write in their own words five important facts that they have learned. Tell students to meet with a partner to compare lists and consolidate the two lists into one final list. Call on students to offer facts from their lists.

Use with All Lessons

STRATEGY ❸
Clarify Information

Help students clarify information about the Ottomans and Safavids and their struggle for control of the geographic heart of the Islamic world. As they read the lessons in the first section of the chapter, instruct students to create and label a T-Chart. Have them note key facts about each group. Ask students to compare their completed charts, note differences, and make changes as necessary.

Use with Lessons 1.2, 1.3, and 1.4

STRATEGY ❶
Trace Visuals

Pair a sight-impaired student with a teacher aide or another student to trace photographs and other visuals with their fingers. Then encourage the pair to discuss memorable parts of each visual. The tactile tracing and discussion will help the student understand and remember the content contained in each visual.

Use with All Lessons

STRATEGY ❷
Provide a Summary Chart

Tell students that they will be learning about three empires in Asia in Section 2 of this chapter. To help students preview or understand lesson content, provide them with a summary chart of the three empires and their economic prosperity and notable achievements.

Dynasty	Economy	Achievements
Mughal (India)	Trade along the Indian Ocean; exported cotton textiles, sugar, pepper, diamonds	Religious tolerance; Taj Mahal
Qing (China)	Largest industrial economy in the world (18th century); exported silk, porcelain, cotton textiles; controlled European trade with state-approved firms and fixed prices	Territorial expansion; under Qianlong the arts and humanities flourished in China
Tokugawa (Japan)	Internal trade; improved processes increased yields of farmers and fishermen; trade with China and Korea; limited European trade to one Dutch trading mission per year	Established schools; patronized the arts; Haiku poetry; Kabuki drama

Use with Lessons 2.1, 2.3, and 2.5

STRATEGY ❶
Use Terms in a Sentence

Pair students at the **Beginning** level with students at the **Intermediate** or **Advanced** level. Instruct pairs to work together to compose a sentence using the Key Vocabulary words and terms. Ask the more proficient students to assist their partners in checking the accuracy of the sentences. Invite pairs to share their sentences and discuss different ways to use each word or term.

Use with All Lessons

STRATEGY 2
Compose Captions

Review the artwork and photographs in a lesson, as needed. Then pair students at the **Beginning** and **Intermediate** levels with English-proficient students and instruct them to work together to write original captions for the artwork and/or photographs in each lesson of the chapter. After they have finished, ask volunteers to share their captions.

Use with All Lessons *Suggest that students first read the printed caption aloud, then cover it with a piece of paper and write their original caption on the paper. Their caption may paraphrase and expand upon the one in the text. You may then lead a discussion comparing the different captions.*

STRATEGY 3
Create Meaning Maps

Pair students at the **Beginning** level with those at the **Intermediate** or **Advanced** level. Demonstrate how to use a Meaning Map for any of the Key Vocabulary or other important words and terms in the lesson. As students work, encourage them to discuss the words together and clear up any misunderstandings.

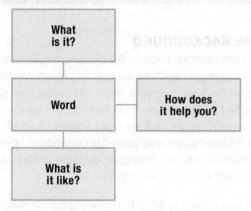

Use with All Lessons

STRATEGY 1
Design an Infographic

Have students conduct additional research about one of the empires discussed in the chapter. Tell them to use the most compelling data and visuals from their research to create an infographic about its leaders, people, economy, and achievements. Invite students to post their infographics on a class website or on the class bulletin board.

Use with All Lessons

STRATEGY 2
Compare Two Leaders

Encourage students to pick two leaders from the lessons in the chapter to compare. Have students conduct additional research about each leader and develop a comparison chart that lists their characteristics, achievements, and faults. Tell them to analyze each leader and then compare the two to decide which in their opinion was the better leader. Invite them to present their chart, analysis, and opinion to the class.

Use with Lessons 1.2, 1.3, 1.4, 2.1, 2.3, 2.5, 3.1, 3.2, and 3.3

STRATEGY 1
Evaluate Voltaire's View of Qianlong

Instruct students to research more of Voltaire's impressions of the Chinese emperor Qianlong. Encourage them to decide if they agree or disagree with his opinion that Qianlong was a great philosopher king who ruled over a model state. Tell them to write a report of their analysis with several details supporting their view.

Use with Lesson 2.4

STRATEGY 2
Analyze Religious Tolerance and Intolerance

Direct students to study examples of religious tolerance and intolerance described in the chapter and to conduct further research as necessary. Invite students to use these examples to write a persuasive speech in support of the First Amendment to the Constitution of the United States allowing freedom of religion and to present their speech to the class.

Use with All Lessons

HISTORICAL THINKING What economic, political,
and cultural impact did the rise of powerful land-based
empires have across Eurasia?

SECTION 1 The Ottoman Empire
SECTION 2 Empires in Asia
SECTION 3 The Russian Empire and
Shifting Powers

INTRODUCE THE PHOTOGRAPH

MUGHAL ARCHITECTURE

Have students study the photograph of the Taj Mahal in Agra, India. Direct students to look closely at the architectural features. **ASK:** What inferences can you make about the architecture? *(Possible response: The architecture displays some features seen in Islamic mosques.)* Explain that the Taj Mahal complex became a UNESCO World Heritage Site in 1983 partly because of the universal significance of its architecture. Mughal architecture, as seen in the Taj Mahal, is a blend of Indian, Persian, and Islamic styles. Tell students that in this chapter they will learn about cultural and other effects of the Mughal Empire as well as information about several land-based empires across Eurasia.

SHARE BACKGROUND

In the 16th century, even as Europeans began to create empires through maritime expansion, which will be discussed in later chapters, most of Eurasia was still dominated by large imperial dynasties. These dynasties relied on agriculture as their main source of wealth. Some of these land-based empires—the Ottoman Empire, Qing dynasty in China, and Romanov dynasty in Russia—would last into the 20th century.

The Mughal dynasty fell into decline after the mid-18th century, but the Taj Mahal remained as evidence of the power and wealth that rulers of such empires could command. More than 20,000 workers built the Taj Mahal tomb complex over a period of some 20 years. Building materials came from regions of India, Central Asia, and beyond. The central dome features acoustics that can cause the single note of a flute to echo five times.

CRITICAL VIEWING Answers will vary. Possible response: The building reflects qualities of grandeur, wealth, timelessness, peace, and/or serenity.

HISTORICAL THINKING QUESTION

What economic, political, and cultural impact did the rise of powerful land-based empires have across Eurasia?

Roundtable: Impact of Empires Arrange students into an even number of small groups and number each group. Assign odd-numbered groups these two questions: What are the advantages and disadvantages of empire expansion? What factors enable an empire to be successfully governed? Assign even-numbered groups these two questions: How might the development of an empire change local economies and cultures? How might different empires interact? Have the first student in each group write an answer to each question on a sheet of paper and pass the paper clockwise to the next student, who adds an answer, continuing until students are out of ideas. As a class, compile a master list of answers for each question. Then tell students that in Chapter 16 they will learn how several land-based empires affected policies, economies, and cultures across Eurasia.

KEY DATES FOR CHAPTER 16

1520	Süleyman I begins his rule and vastly expands the Ottoman Empire.
1526	Turkic prince Babur founds the Mughal dynasty.
1556	Akbar I begins his successful rule of Mughal India.
1597	Abbas I begins his rule that will cause the Safavid Empire to thrive.
1603	The Tokugawa shogunate begins in Japan.
1613	The Romanov dynasty begins in Russia.
1661	Emperor Kangxi begins to mold Qing China into a great empire.
1697	Peter the Great visits Europe and plans to westernize Russia.
1762	Catherine the Great declares herself empress of Russia.
1792	Qing emperor Qianlong rejects British trade negotiations.

INTRODUCE THE READING STRATEGY

DRAW CONCLUSIONS

Explain to students that drawing conclusions means making judgments about what they read. They can draw conclusions by looking for details in the text. Go to the Chapter Review and preview the Reading Strategy chart with students. As they read the chapter, have students draw conclusions about the development and impact of land-based empires across Eurasia.

INTRODUCE CHAPTER VOCABULARY

KEY VOCABULARY

SECTION 1

embellish	inflation	janissary
shah		

SECTION 2

consumption	dowry	entrepreneur
mausoleum	nativism	revenue

SECTION 3

conscription	petition	pull factor
push factor	taiga	tsar
tundra		

WORD MAP

As students read the chapter, ask them to complete a Word Map for each Key Vocabulary word. Tell them to write the word in the oval and, as they encounter the word in the chapter, complete the Word Map. Model an example using the graphic organizer below.

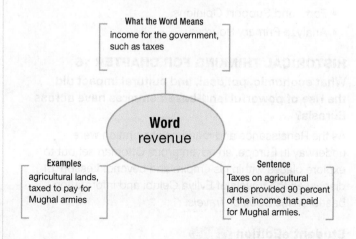

What the Word Means
income for the government, such as taxes

Word
revenue

Examples
agricultural lands, taxed to pay for Mughal armies

Sentence
Taxes on agricultural lands provided 90 percent of the income that paid for Mughal armies.

Traveler: Evliya Çelebi
Tales from Forty Years of Travel 1611–1682

If you could travel anywhere, would you explore your own country, trek to allied lands, or venture into hostile territory? The most famous Ottoman traveler spent most of his time touring the Ottoman Empire, but he also set forth into enemy lands in Iran and Europe.

Evliya Çelebi's Journeys

The Travels of Evliya Çelebi
- Journeys 1640–1670s
- Possible journey, 1663
- The hajj, 1671–1672
- City visited by Çelebi
- Other city
- Boundaries, ca. 1680

BEGINNING A LIFE OF TRAVEL

At the age of 20, Evliya Çelebi (ehv-lee-yuh chuh-LEH-bee) dreamed of a visit from the Prophet Muhammad. Normally, if a person saw the Prophet Muhammad in a dream, he or she would ask for a blessing. Instead, Çelebi asked for the chance to travel. In the dream, the prophet responded, "Thou shalt travel through the whole world and be a marvel among men. Of the countries through which you will pass, of their castles, strongholds, wonderful antiquities, . . . the extent of their provinces and length of the days there, draw up a description which will be a monument worthy of thee."

Çelebi was the son of the chief goldsmith of the powerful sultan of the Ottoman Empire. He had impressed the sultan with his artful recitation of the Quran. Even though Çelebi lived a privileged life in Constantinople, he was passionately curious about the world outside of his home. "I longed," he wrote, "to set out for the Holy Land toward Baghdad and Mecca and Medina and Cairo and Damascus." Çelebi visited those places and many more, which was a great feat in the 17th century. He traveled in luxury, accompanied on each trip by an entourage of men and slaves, cases of fine clothing, libraries of books, and numerous mules and camels. Today Çelebi is recognized as the greatest of all the Ottoman travelers. In 2014, Turkey's Ministry of Culture and Tourism sponsored the country's first 3-D animated movie, *Evliya Çelebi: The Fountain of Youth*. But long before the film was made, the Turkish phrase for a person who feels a constant urge to travel is *Evliya Çelebi gibi*, or "He is like Evliya Çelebi."

RECORDING HIS ADVENTURES

As Çelebi traveled, he recorded his adventures in his *Book of Travels*. After his trips, he returned with both true and fictionalized tales to entertain the sultan and the court.

Early in his travels, Çelebi survived a shipwreck while crossing the Black Sea during a storm. He and his companions retreated to a lifeboat and survived by using their turbans as paddles. However, after this event, Çelebi refused to travel by open sea.

Evliya Çelebi also traveled beyond the Ottoman Empire to Europe and Iran. In Europe he participated in wars between Ottoman forces and the Holy Roman Empire. While in Iran, he described the tense relationships between the Safavid dynasty and the Ottoman rulers.

Çelebi first began to record his adventures after touring his own city of Constantinople. There he watched a parade celebrating an anticipated victory against the Safavid dynasty of Iran.

PRIMARY SOURCE

This procession of the imperial camp begins its march at dawn and continues the whole day until sunset and amounts to the number of 200,000 men all passing like a thundering sea, . . . Nowhere else has such a procession been seen or will be seen. Such is the crown and population of that great capital Constantinople, which may God guard from all celestial and earthly mischief, and let her be inhabited until the end of the world.

—from *The Book of Travels* by Evliya Çelebi

When Çelebi was 60 years old, he made a pilgrimage to the holy cities of Mecca, Medina, and Jerusalem. He described his experience and the proper Muslim ritual for entering Medina.

PRIMARY SOURCE

After one hour of traveling we arrived at the top of a hill. When one reaches this point and turns south one sees the orchards and gardens of Medina and the dome of the Mosque of the Prophet reaching to the sky. From the gleam of the gilded pinnacle on the dome, the plain of Medina becomes light upon light and one's eyes are dazzled. Here the sincere lover gets off his horse or camel or mule and says the following prayer: Peace and blessing be upon you, O Messenger of God; peace and blessing be upon you, O Beloved of God; peace and blessing be upon you, O lord of the first ones and the last ones; and peace be upon the apostles of God. . . . If the pilgrim feels strong enough, he proceeds from here as far as Medina by foot, a five-hour downhill stroll. If he is handicapped or old, he remounts his horse or camel or mule or donkey and continues the journey, repeating again and again the noble blessings on the Prophet.

—from *The Book of Travels* by Evliya Çelebi

HISTORICAL THINKING

1. **READING CHECK** According to Çelebi's own writing, what three cities were his top priority travel destinations? Did he ever visit these places?

2. **ANALYZE POINT OF VIEW** What does Çelebi's description of the royal procession in Constantinople tell readers about his opinion of his own city?

3. **DESCRIBE** What ritual do pilgrims observe as they enter Medina?

4. **ASK AND ANSWER QUESTIONS** Historians claim that Çelebi fabricated many of the details of his travels. What questions might they have asked to lead them to that belief?

PLAN: 2-PAGE LESSON

OBJECTIVE
Describe the 17th-century travels of Ottoman voyager Evliya Çelebi.

CRITICAL THINKING SKILLS FOR LESSON 1.1
- Analyze Points of View
- Describe
- Ask and Answer Questions
- Form and Support Opinions
- Analyze Primary Sources

HISTORICAL THINKING FOR CHAPTER 16
What economic, political, and cultural impact did the rise of powerful land-based empires have across Eurasia?

As the Renaissance and maritime exploration were underway in Europe, an adventurous Ottoman set out to explore places within his empire and beyond. Lesson 1.1 discusses the travels of Evliya Çelebi and information based on his *Book of Travels*.

Student eEdition online
Additional content for this lesson, including images, is available online.

BACKGROUND FOR THE TEACHER
Evliya Çelebi, Traveler Çelebi was the son of a slave woman and the imperial goldsmith. He was born in 1611 and received instruction at an Islamic college. He then attended the palace school of the Ottoman sultan, graduating as a cavalryman. This provided knowledge he later used when he joined military engagements for the empire. Çelebi also served in official and semi-official functions. He accompanied the Ottoman delegation to Vienna for the signing of the 1665 peace treaty with the Habsburgs. His *Book of Travels* comprises 10 volumes of details about his observations and experiences. Although the book mixes fiction and fact, historians find it a useful resource. Çelebi described the towns, geography, social and economic systems, institutions, and culture of the Ottoman Empire and neighboring lands. In 2011, UNESCO held activities in Paris to mark the 400th anniversary of Çelebi's birth. Çelebi died in about 1684.

History Notebook
Encourage students to complete the Traveler page for Chapter 16 in their History Notebooks as they read.

INTRODUCE & ENGAGE

DISCUSS RECORDING TRAVELS

Direct students to recall the times they traveled, such as family vacations or group tours. Ask if a diary of their travels would help future historians understand what life was like today. Have volunteers suggest the kinds of information that a future historian would find useful. *(Possible responses might include events, political issues, recreational activities, or popular music and videos.)* Tell students that in this lesson they will learn about a traveler whose writings help explain what life was like in the 17th-century Ottoman Empire.

TEACH

GUIDED DISCUSSION

1. **Describe** What factors enabled Çelebi to travel extensively? *(Çelebi lived a privileged life close to the court and sultan. He possessed a strong curiosity and the funds to travel in luxury.)*

2. **Form and Support Opinions** Do you think Çelebi deserves recognition as the greatest Ottoman traveler? *(Possible responses: Yes, because he traveled to many places and served the empire in official capacities. No, because he traveled to satisfy his own curiosity and left a record that included fictionalized tales.)*

ANALYZE PRIMARY SOURCES

Direct students to the second primary source. **ASK:** What was Çelebi's main purpose for visiting Medina? *(Çelebi wanted to visit a Muslim holy city.)* Why might Çelebi have used the image of a pinnacle's gleam making the plain "light upon light" that "dazzled" the eyes? *(Possible response: He intended to convey that the power of the mosque and Islam shed spiritual light on the city and visitor.)*

ACTIVE OPTIONS

On Your Feet: Numbered Heads Arrange students in groups of four. Ask group members to number off. Instruct groups to think about and discuss the following question: How important are the traveler's personal qualities and social status in determining the kinds of information captured in a travelogue? Tell groups to use Çelebi as a starting point. Have groups discuss for several minutes. Then call out a number, and have the student with that number in each group summarize the group's discussion.

NG Learning Framework: Write Journal Pages
ATTITUDE Curiosity
SKILL Observation

Have students create one or two journal pages from the point of view of Evliya Çelebi using information and the map from the lesson. They may consult additional source material if needed. Suggest students focus on Çelebi's feelings and thoughts at a particular event. Invite students to share their pages with the class.

DIFFERENTIATE

INCLUSION

Facilitate Interpretation Pair special-needs students with proficient readers who can help them interpret the map and relate it to the text. Encourage special-needs students to ask questions about map features that confuse them. Have proficient readers answer questions and explain how points on the map are related to places and events in the text. Invite pairs to summarize together the travels of Çelebi.

GIFTED & TALENTED

Explore a Book of Travel Invite students to delve further into Çelebi's *Book of Travels*. Have them research the dates, locations, experiences, and fictional accounts recorded by Çelebi. Suggest they include commentaries or reviews of the *Book of Travels* in their research. Ask them to summarize their research in an essay. Invite students to share their essays with the class.

See the Chapter Planner for more strategies for differentiation.

HISTORICAL THINKING

ANSWERS

1. Mecca, Medina, and Jerusalem; yes, when he was around 60 years old

2. proud of his city; believed it to be the greatest in the world; A visitor from the Safavid Empire would probably be offended that such a celebration was made with the assumption that the Ottomans would be victorious over the Safavids.

3. dismount their horses and pray; then hike on foot down to the city; Elderly or unhealthy pilgrims pray and then recite a prayer as they continue to the city on horses or other animals.

4. if he recorded events as others who had been there; if his descriptions matched the actual structures and geographical features of a place; his biases toward cultures compared to historical knowledge of cultures

Süleyman and Ottoman Power

Which would you rather have: political and military power, wealth for a luxurious life, or a virtuous life of religious devotion? The powerful Ottoman sultan Süleyman I managed to have it all: a huge military, too much money to count, and a deep devotion to his religion.

Süleyman I was the 10th sultan of the Ottoman Empire.

OTTOMAN EXPANSION AND MILITARY POWER

Having used gunpowder weapons such as cannons to seize control of Constantinople in 1453, the Ottomans grew in military strength. Over the next 100 years, the Ottoman armies pushed further into Europe and North Africa as well as Arab and Persian lands.

The heart of the Ottomans' power was cavalry warfare, attacks carried out by fighters on horseback. After the conquest of Constantinople, which gave the Ottomans access to both the Black Sea and the Mediterranean, they constructed a navy as well. The Ottomans' greatest force, however, was their elite enslaved soldiers from conquered Christian lands. These soldiers, called **janissaries**, trained year-round and became highly skilled at using gunpowder weapons. While a sultan may not have been able to trust his own brothers or sons because they may well have been vying for his power, the janissaries were completely loyal. They were constantly aware that they had no family to protect them, and if they disobeyed, they would be killed. By the 16th century, the janissaries not only served in the military, they also played a central role in the administration. Even the sultan's chief minister was a slave.

On the Persian frontier, the Ottomans faced pushback from the rising Safavid dynasty. In fact, well before Evliya Çelebi's birth, the Turkish Ottomans and the Iranian Safavids were already struggling for the geographic heart of the Islamic world. Adding to their military competition were religious differences. The Ottomans, who controlled the holy sites of pilgrimage in Arabia, were members of the dominant Sunni branch of Islam. The Safavids, on the other hand, had come to embrace the Shiite tradition.

SÜLEYMAN, THE MAGNIFICENT

The Ottomans' master strategist was the sultan **Süleyman I**, who came to power in 1520. As a strong military leader, Süleyman greatly expanded the empire.

Süleyman's court reflected the ethnic diversity of his empire. Turkish was the language of the government and the military, Arabic was the language of religion and philosophy, and Persian was the language of poetry and the arts. Süleyman and the members of his court led luxurious lives. Visitors from around the world brought so many gifts that at some point they just piled up with no one looking at them. Süleyman seldom wore an item of clothing twice, and observers wrote that four servants

accompanied the sultan at all times in case he desired a drink of water, needed a jacket, or became tired. The sultan also employed his own personal coffeemaker. This lavish lifestyle led the Europeans to call him "Süleyman the Magnificent." However, within the empire he was known as "Süleyman the Lawgiver" because his laws covered such details as the types of clothing that people of different social positions should wear. These laws helped keep stability in the empire and were later used in other parts of the world to form constitutions.

Süleyman was a devoted Muslim who centralized religious authority and sponsored the building of religious schools and mosques. You have read about the sublime works of Sinan, the sultan's favorite architect. Nevertheless, he did not impose religious laws on minority cultural and religious traditions. Instead, he provided legal protections for minorities by allowing them to practice their own religions, govern their own affairs, and maintain their own courts. The only requirement was that they remained loyal and paid their taxes promptly.

Under Süleyman, the Ottomans aggressively expanded into Europe, northern Africa, and western Asia. They dominated Islam's holy pilgrimage sites in Jerusalem, Mecca, and Medina, and they regained control of

Baghdad from the Safavids. The Ottoman navy defeated Christian fleets in the Red Sea, the Persian Gulf, and the Indian Ocean. As you have already read, the Ottomans marched into the German-speaking lands of central Europe, but Austria's Habsburg dynasty pushed Süleyman's forces back when they attempted to lay siege to Vienna in 1529. After Süleyman's death in 1566, a united European fleet defeated the Ottomans in 1571. Still, the Ottomans refused to give up on Europe. Nearly a century later, they again threatened to take Vienna. By that time, the Ottomans held firm control of much of southeastern Europe and were a major player in the European balance of power.

HISTORICAL THINKING

1. **READING CHECK** How did the Ottomans gain power to spread throughout eastern Europe, northern Africa, and Arab lands?

2. **IDENTIFY SUPPORTING DETAILS** What details in the text explain why the Europeans gave Süleyman the title "the Magnificent"? What details explain why the Ottomans called him "Süleyman the Lawgiver"?

3. **INTERPRET MAPS** Along what bodies of water did the Ottoman Empire extend?

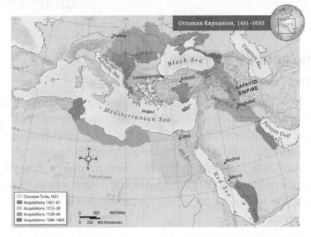

Ottoman Expansion, 1451–1683

Legend:
- Ottoman Turks, 1451
- Acquisitions, 1451–81
- Acquisitions, 1512–20
- Acquisitions, 1520–66
- Acquisitions, 1566–1683

0   200   400 Miles
0   200   400 Kilometers

PLAN: 2-PAGE LESSON

OBJECTIVE

Explain the spread of the Ottoman Empire under Süleyman's leadership.

CRITICAL THINKING SKILLS FOR LESSON 1.2

- Identify Supporting Details
- Interpret Maps
- Make Inferences
- Summarize

HISTORICAL THINKING FOR CHAPTER 16

What economic, political, and cultural impact did the rise of powerful land-based empires have across Eurasia?

As the Renaissance spread across Europe, the Ottoman Empire was increasing in strength and impact. Lesson 1.2 discusses the expansion of the Ottoman Empire with a special focus on the reign and achievements of the 10th sultan, Süleyman I.

Student eEdition online

Additional content for this lesson, including a Global Commodity feature, is available online.

BACKGROUND FOR THE TEACHER

A Portrait of Süleyman I The Ottoman Empire reached great heights under the reign of Süleyman I. Major developments in trade, economic growth, and the arts accompanied significant territorial expansion. Turkish architecture, textiles, ceramics, and calligraphy flourished during Süleyman's reign. Süleyman expressed his own creativity in poetry, mostly writing love poems to his wife Hürrem Sultan, using the pen name Muhibbi. His importance is confirmed by his endurance in books, film, and television, including an award-winning Turkish television series in 2011-2014 and a BBC documentary in 2013. A marble portrait of Süleyman I also appears in the United States Capitol, among 23 marble relief portraits placed above the gallery doors of the House Chamber. According to the Architect of the Capitol website, the portraits depict historical figures noted for their work in establishing the principles that underlie American law. Süleyman is particularly credited with reforming and improving civil and military codes and uniting a group of unstable territories into an empire.

History Notebook

Encourage students to complete the Global Commodity page for Chapter 16 in their History Notebooks as they read.

INTRODUCE & ENGAGE

BRAINSTORM GOOD LEADERSHIP

Invite students to discuss the qualities a person must possess to lead a nation or an empire to greatness. Is it the ability to command a military force? Is it the wisdom to understand different points of view? Is it an attractive personality? Tell students that in this lesson they will learn about a powerful leader who brought the Ottoman Empire to heights of economic, political, and cultural achievement.

TEACH

GUIDED DISCUSSION

1. **Make Inferences** Why might Süleyman's policy of allowing minorities to have their own governments and religious practices help to expand the empire? *(Minorities would be inclined to peacefully accept Ottoman rule because it did not force them to adopt Islam and change their customary ways of life.)*

2. **Summarize** Why did the Ottomans face pushback from the rising Safavid dynasty? *(The two empires were military competitors. In addition, Turkish Ottomans were Sunni Muslims, whereas the Iranian Safavids followed Shiite tradition. The Ottomans controlled the holy sites of pilgrimage in Arabia.)*

A GLOBAL COMMODITY

Have students focus on the Global Commodity feature (available in the Student eEdition). **ASK:** How do you think religious authorities managed to reconcile Islam with Muslim gatherings at coffeehouses? *(Possible response: Religious authorities saw that coffee-drinking Muslims still worshiped at mosques and that coffee caused none of the ill effects produced by alcohol.)*

ACTIVE OPTIONS

On Your Feet: Roundtable Arrange students in groups of four. Provide a sheet of paper with this question for each group: In what ways did Süleyman I promote the economic, political, and cultural impact of the Ottoman Empire? The first student in each group writes an answer and reads it aloud before passing the paper clockwise to the next student. Make sure that every student in the group adds at least one answer. When the groups have run out of answers, invite a volunteer from each to share their ideas.

NG Learning Framework: Write an Article
ATTITUDES Empowerment, Responsibility
SKILLS Communication, Collaboration

Arrange students into small groups. Ask them to write an article about cultural achievements during the reign of Süleyman I. Encourage students to use information from the chapter supplemented by online research as needed. Suggest students focus on architectural achievements and building renovation, painting, and calligraphy. Invite students to share their articles with the class.

DIFFERENTIATE

STRIVING READERS

Understand Main Ideas Ask students to complete statements such as the following:

- The greatest Ottoman force for warfare was (janissaries or cannons). *(janissaries)*
- The Ottoman Empire was governed by (Evliya Çelebi or Süleyman I). *(Süleyman I)*
- The court of Süleyman I reflected (ethnic diversity or Shiite traditions) and led a lavish lifestyle. *(ethnic diversity)*
- Minorities in the Ottoman Empire could govern their own affairs but also (be loyal and pay taxes promptly or learn Islam and the Arabic language). *(be loyal and pay taxes promptly)*

PRE-AP

Prepare a Report Direct students to conduct research about coffee. Have them consider the question of the value of coffee as a commodity today. Suggest they locate statistics about places coffee is grown, its use, and its effects, and information about the benefits or risks of drinking coffee. Ask them to organize their findings in a report with sections indicated by headings and a list of sources. Tell students to include conclusions they draw. Invite them to share their reports and discuss them as a class.

See the Chapter Planner for more strategies for differentiation.

HISTORICAL THINKING

ANSWERS

1. professional cavalry, navy, and enslaved soldiers who were skilled in using gun powder; enslaved janissaries were loyal to the sultan

2. "Magnificent": many gifts bestowed upon him, almost never wore the same item of clothing twice, had servants to address his every desire; "Lawgiver": developed detailed laws that kept stability in the empire, later used to develop constitutions

3. the Black Sea, Adriatic Sea, Aegean Sea, Mediterranean Sea, the Persian Gulf, and the Red Sea

Safavid Rise and Fall

"The enemy of my enemy is my friend" is a saying that has been around for a very long time. But the saying is as true today as it was in the 16th century, when the Safavids of Iran befriended the European Habsburgs to fight together against the Ottomans.

The Safavids built the Shah Mosque in Isfahan, Iran, during the reign of Abbas I. A masterpiece of Persian architecture, engineering, and craftsmanship, the mosque features a magnificent dome decorated with colorful mosaic tiles and calligraphy.

THE SAFAVID EMPIRE OF IRAN

Iran has a long history of influence in Southwest Asia. Because of its location at the center of international trade routes, Iran was constantly under threat from invaders, including Alexander the Great in 330 B.C.E. Much later, other invaders swept down from Azerbaijan, conquered the Persian-speaking lands, and founded the Safavid Empire, which lasted from 1501 until 1722.

The Safavids were members of an Islamic sect that captured the cities of Baghdad and Basra from the Ottomans. As you've read, they adopted Shiite beliefs and imposed them on conquered subjects, including Sunni Muslims and followers of Persia's ancient Zoroastrian faith. The Ottomans retook Baghdad, but the Shiites, who had long been a suppressed minority group, now controlled a large Islamic state.

The greatest Safavid ruler, Abbas I, became **shah**, or king, in 1597 and built the Safavid capital at Isfahan. Under his rule, the economy thrived and the Safavids used their wealth to build palaces, mosques, schools, hospitals, roads, bridges, and new irrigation systems for agriculture. With a population of a half million, Isfahan was a huge city teeming with mosques and public baths. The gardens of Isfahan were legendary, and the city was a showcase for Persian architecture and engineering.

The Safavids also made Iran into a cultural center. Shiite scholars were encouraged to immigrate to the area, and Persian verse influenced poets as far away as East Africa and India. Craftsmen, artists, and traders moved to Iran and sold their work in vast markets. Persians traded silks, carpets, and ceramics by sea, and Europeans eagerly imported these products.

The Safavid Empire, 16th Century

The Safavid Empire was a theocracy in which the ruler was also a religious leader. Under the shah, officials were appointed based on skill rather than heredity, but most were from the nobility. The social structure was organized like a pyramid with the shah and the royal class at the top, followed by the nobility and the clergy, and then rich merchants and urban artists. Commoners were the lowest group. During Abbas's rule, women were treated with respect. A tradition began where the unmarried aunts and daughters of the Shah were admired as patrons of the arts and of religious pilgrims.

The Safavids were constantly at battle with the Ottomans over the lands around Mesopotamia. So although they were antagonistic toward anything Christian or European, the Safavids formed an alliance with the European Habsburgs. Through this alliance, Abbas acquired guns, cannons, and training that his professional soldiers used against the Ottomans.

DECLINE IN LEADERSHIP

Shah Abbas neglected to groom a worthy successor, and after his death in 1629, the quality of leadership declined. The next shah, Süleyman I, was an ineffective ruler who was much more concerned with entertainment and a decadent lifestyle than governance. Corruption spread throughout his court, angering the Shiite clerics who had previously supported the Safavid Empire.

The last Safavid shah attempted to reverse the trend and regain support of the clergy. Like the Puritans in Europe, he imposed harsh conditions on public morality, banning music, coffee, and public entertainment, and he restricted women to their homes. However, people rejected these harsh restrictions, and support for the empire declined even further. The Safavid Empire fell easily to Afghan invaders who descended on Isfahan in 1722, leaving the city in ruins.

HISTORICAL THINKING

1. **READING CHECK** How did the similarities and differences between the Safavids and Ottomans lead to their constant struggle for power?

2. **INTERPRET MAPS** What lands were in dispute between the Safavids and the Ottomans?

3. **ANALYZE CAUSE AND EFFECT** How did the lives of women change after Shah Abbas died? Why did this change occur?

PLAN: 2-PAGE LESSON

OBJECTIVE
Evaluate the Safavid Empire as a Shiite state that rivaled the Sunni Ottomans.

CRITICAL THINKING SKILLS FOR LESSON 1.3
- Interpret Maps
- Analyze Cause and Effect
- Make Connections
- Make Inferences
- Analyze Visuals

HISTORICAL THINKING FOR CHAPTER 16
What economic, political, and cultural impact did the rise of powerful land-based empires have across Eurasia?

The Safavid Empire bordered the 17th-century Ottoman Empire as a hostile rival. Lesson 1.3 discusses the Safavid Empire with a focus on the achievements of Shah Abbas I.

Student eEdition online
Additional content for this lesson, including an image, is available online.

BACKGROUND FOR THE TEACHER
Shah Safi II After the death of Shah Abbas II in 1667, his oldest son, Sām Mirzā, who was raised in the royal harem and known for his arrogance, took the throne at the age of 19 and was given the name Safi II. The first year and a half of his reign was disastrous as Safi II spent a great deal of time being entertained in the harem while court officials handled state affairs. He had also fallen ill, and his empire suffered a drought that led to high food costs, famine, and disease, as well as an earthquake that killed thousands. Because of all of this misfortune, Safi II was given a second chance and re-enthroned under a new name and known as Shah Solaymān, with different spellings such as Sulayman, Sulaiman, and Soleyman. (The Safavid Shah is not to be confused with the Ottoman sultans Süleyman I or Süleyman II.) His second reign proved the shah's faults as he disappeared for weeks at a time into the harem and continued not to participate in state affairs. His 27-year reign was largely unnoteworthy and, with that of his successor, led to the decline of the Safavid Empire.

INTRODUCE & ENGAGE

EVALUATE A TIMEWORN SAYING

Read aloud the saying that opens the lesson: "The enemy of my enemy is my friend." Have volunteers suggest other common sayings. *(Possible responses: "actions speak louder than words," "opposites attract")* Ask students if these sayings are true rules to live by. Tell them that in this lesson they will learn if the Safavids saved their empire by befriending a European enemy to help them defeat the Ottomans.

TEACH

GUIDED DISCUSSION

1. **Make Connections** How might the respect women received during the reign of Abbas I have had an impact on Safavid culture? *(Possible response: His reign began a tradition whereby a shah's unmarried aunts and daughters were honored as patrons of the arts and of religious pilgrims.)*

2. **Make Inferences** Why do you think the Safavid Empire declined in spite of the last shah's efforts to reverse corruption and please the Shiite clergy? *(Possible response: The last shah was probably an unlikable, ineffective leader who could not gain support from either the clergy or the people.)*

ANALYZE VISUALS

Direct students' attention to the painting depicting the court of Shah Süleyman I (available in the Student eEdition). **ASK:** What details in the painting support the text's assertion that the shah led a decadent lifestyle? *(Possible response: The shah is being waited upon and entertained, surrounded by his court in a beautiful setting with lavish carpets and fine foods.)*

ACTIVE OPTIONS

On Your Feet: Three-Step Interview Have students work in pairs to interview each other regarding Safavid leadership. Direct one student to interview the other by asking this question: What made Abbas I the greatest Safavid ruler? Urge the interviewer to ask follow-up questions based on the answers provided. Then tell students to reverse roles with the second student asking this question: Why did the Safavid Empire decline under the leaders who followed Abbas I? Finally, ask students to share information from the interviews with the class.

NG Learning Framework: Write an Interview-Based News Story
ATTITUDE Curiosity
SKILL Communication

Have students write a short news story about Shah Abbas I using information from the chapter and additional research material. Ask students to write the story as though they had conducted an interview with Abbas I. Encourage them to include several quoted statements by Abbas I in the story. Invite students to read their news stories aloud to the class.

DIFFERENTIATE

ENGLISH LANGUAGE LEARNERS

Create a Word Web Pair students at the **Beginning** and **Intermediate** levels with students at the **Advanced** level. Display a Word Web with the topic Abbas I in the center. Tell students to reread the text, noting and adding important words and phrases to the organizer. Then ask pairs to share and discuss their Word Webs, stating their ideas in complete sentences.

GIFTED & TALENTED

Create a Safavid Time Line Direct students to gather additional information about the Safavid Empire beginning with Ismail through the reign of Abbas I. Tell them to create a time line of major events in Safavid history during the period. Ask students to include specific details for each event they cite, either by annotating the time line or in a short explanatory essay. Invite students to share completed time lines with the class.

See the Chapter Planner for more strategies for differentiation.

HISTORICAL THINKING

ANSWERS

1. They were both prosperous Muslim powers and wanted to dominate the lands around Mesopotamia. The Ottomans were Sunni; the Safavids were Shiite. These two Islamic sects had a long history of animosity that must have contributed to their hostilities. Also, the fact that they both wanted control of the same areas made for constant rivalry.

2. between the Black and Caspian seas, the Caspian sea and the Persian Gulf, and northwest from the Persian Gulf to the upper Tigris River

3. Women lost rights and freedoms after Shah Abbas died. This may have been a result of trying to please the clergy who had lost respect for the Safavids when the new shah became corrupt and led a decadent life.

Ottoman Persistence

How much effort do you put into having artistic handwriting or choosing an attractive style of type? During the Ottoman Empire, calligraphy, among other art forms, was highly valued—even as the empire began to show signs of weakness.

While the Safavids were defeated in 1722, the Ottomans persisted as a significant power into the mid-18th century. Their empire continued to include much of southeastern Europe with the same political order.

As a sign of their enduring strength, the Ottomans continued to attack Vienna. More than 100 years after Süleyman's first attack in 1529, Ottoman forces made another attempt in 1638. It wasn't until 1739, though, that the Ottomans finally defeated the Habsburgs, who were forced to cede territory to Constantinople. By that time, however, Ottoman power had waned. Rather than expanding the empire, Ottoman military leaders focused their energies on defending the empire's borders against emerging powers, especially Russia.

Ottoman political strength continued following Süleyman's death. Unlike Safavid Iran, where the quality of the shah's leadership was such a determining factor, Ottoman administrative reforms had created stronger and more reliable institutions for both civilian and military affairs. A clear example occurred in 1648 when both court officials and ordinary citizens of Constantinople grew dissatisfied with a sultan who ignored matters of state, or his official duties, while spending lavishly on a decadent lifestyle. He was assassinated. However, unlike Safavid Iran, where weak leadership led to dynastic decline, Ottoman institutions were strong enough to allow a smooth transition to more effective leadership.

This fresco in Florence, Italy, depicts Süleyman's attack on Vienna in 1529.

454 CHAPTER 16

THE ARTS AND THE ECONOMY

The Ottomans had a long tradition of creating exquisite works of art. During the 16th century, Süleyman hired as many as 120 artists, including painters, textile artists, and architects. Perhaps the most admired artists, however, were the calligraphers, or handwriting artists. Calligraphers trained for many years to create Arabic scripts that symbolized the harmony of God's creation. Quotations from the Quran formed the bulk of the calligraphic text, but artists also used other religious texts, poems, short expressions of wisdom, and words of praise for the Ottoman rulers. Their graceful scripts **embellished**, or decorated, book pages as well as tiles, ceramics, and the walls of buildings.

Painters worked alongside calligraphers in creating illustrated books such as the Quran. Calligraphers used gold or colorful inks as they wrote the text, leaving space for illustrations. You may recall that many Muslims believe the representation of human figures or animals to be forbidden, so artists painted complex floral and geometric patterns known as arabesques to embellish religious texts.

Calligraphers and painters also decorated silk and other textiles. Before the mid-16th century, the Ottomans had imported raw silk from Iran. However, as relations between the two empires deteriorated, the Ottomans were forced to create their own silk. The city of Bursa in present-day Turkey became the silk capital where weavers produced a large variety of silks and velvets. Artists employed by Süleyman wove gold and silver threads into fabrics worn by the sultan and others of the imperial palace. They created large floral designs that could be seen from afar for use in royal processions.

In the 17th century, the Ottoman economy began to weaken. Ottoman agricultural and commercial production was still substantial, but economic expansion no longer kept up with population growth. Also, the flow of silver into Europe from the Americas caused **inflation**, or increased prices, in the Ottoman economy and a weakened balance of trade. It now became difficult to fund further investment in the arts.

These economic difficulties compelled the court to reduce the number of royal artists and royal commissions. Royal workshops continued to produce

This red satin prayer rug, embroidered with gold and silver thread, dates from the 19th-century Ottoman Empire.

calligraphy and books, and the royal architects continued to build mosques. However, textile art was pushed out of the royal palace. Private workshops continued the art, producing the quality of silk fabrics that had been reserved for the royal court. These textiles became available in markets where they were purchased by upper-class Ottomans and European merchants. The textiles were highly valued in Europe where royalty and priests used the fine fabrics for both state and religious ceremonies.

Despite such challenges, however, the Ottomans persisted as a large and stable state, central to the balance of power in western Asia, central Europe, and North Africa.

HISTORICAL THINKING

1. **READING CHECK** Describe signs of weakness in the Ottoman military and economy in the 17th century.

2. **MAKE GENERALIZATIONS** Why did calligraphy and illustrated books remain a priority in Ottoman art?

3. **MAKE INFERENCES** Why were Ottoman textiles popular in Europe?

Land-Based Empires of Eurasia 455

PLAN: 2-PAGE LESSON

OBJECTIVE
Identify signs of weakness and strength in the 17th-century Ottoman Empire.

CRITICAL THINKING SKILLS FOR LESSON 1.4
- Make Generalizations
- Make Inferences
- Identify Main Ideas and Details
- Analyze Visuals

HISTORICAL THINKING FOR CHAPTER 16
What economic, political, and cultural impact did the rise of powerful land-based empires have across Eurasia?

The Ottoman Empire endured long after the Safavid Empire fell. Lesson 1.4 discusses the persistence of the Ottoman Empire with a focus on political strength and the arts in a declining economy.

BACKGROUND FOR THE TEACHER
Bursa and Koza Han The city of Bursa is located about a two-hour drive from Istanbul (Constantinople) in eastern Turkey. Once a Byzantine stronghold, Bursa later became the first great capital of the Ottoman Empire. The son of Osman I, founder of the empire, captured Bursa in 1326. Constantinople became the Ottoman capital in 1458, but Bursa remained under Ottoman rule and flourished. Bursa's Ulu mosque and Green Mosque, built in the late-14th and early-15th centuries, are significant in the history of Ottoman architecture. Bursa is historically important as a major trading center on the Silk Roads. The Koza Han, built in 1491 at Bursa, was a silk market and center of the Ottoman silk industry. Weavers imported silk fabric until, by the 17th century, they acquired cocoons from East Asia and learned to raise silkworms. Koza Han today has tea gardens and 95 rooms of shops. Britain's Queen Elizabeth II purchased silk items at the Koza Han on a state visit to Turkey in 2008.

INTRODUCE & ENGAGE

ACCESS PRIOR KNOWLEDGE WITH VISUALS

Direct students to read the introductory sentences to the lesson and view the photo of the prayer rug. **ASK:** Why was art so valued by the Ottomans? *(Possible response: Art was a form of religious expression for the Ottoman Muslims, so excellent craftsmanship was important.)* Invite volunteers to recall what they have learned about Ottoman art and relate their ideas to the prayer rug. *(The rug displays floral designs in repeated patterns; human figures are forbidden.)* Tell students that in this lesson they will learn about Ottoman arts and royal investments in the arts.

TEACH

GUIDED DISCUSSION

1. **Identify Main Ideas and Details** What factors caused the Ottoman court to curtail investment in the arts? *(Economic expansion failed to keep up with population growth, and the flow of silver from the Americas caused inflation and weakened the balance of trade.)*

2. **Make Inferences** How might the continued production of textile art in private workshops have helped the overall Ottoman economy? *(Possible responses: The ongoing popularity in Europe of Ottoman textiles would have kept money flowing into the empire; the royal court likely benefited from taxes paid by prosperous workshop owners; trade in textiles from private workshops might have encouraged other forms of trade with Europeans.)*

ANALYZE VISUALS

Have students look at the fresco and the prayer rug. **ASK:** Based on the fresco, how did the Ottomans wage war? *(They relied on cavalry warfare.)* How does the prayer rug reflect the Ottoman artistic style? *(The prayer rug primarily displays floral designs in repeated patterns.)*

ACTIVE OPTIONS

On Your Feet: Think, Pair, Share Give students a few minutes to think about the following topic: A declining economy was not a serious problem for the Ottomans because strong leadership was the important factor. Then have students choose partners and talk about the topic for five minutes. Finally, allow individual students to share their ideas with the class.

> **NG Learning Framework: Write a Brief Historical Sketch**
> **SKILL** Collaboration
> **KNOWLEDGE** Our Human Story

Have students write a short historical sketch about the Habsburg-Ottoman conflict using information from the first section of the chapter and additional source material. Suggest students focus on major events and reasons for the conflict. Invite students to share their histories with the class.

DIFFERENTIATE

STRIVING READERS

Summarize Using Sentence Frames Ask pairs to read each section of the lesson together and then write a summary. When all pairs are finished, call on them to read their summaries aloud in the order in which the material appears in the text for an overview of the entire lesson.

PRE-AP

Write a Position Paper Have students analyze the economic impact of government support for the arts. Have students assume that a government committee is discussing the prospect of dropping tax support for the arts. Direct students to conduct online research to determine ways in which the arts might contribute to economic growth. Tell them to think about the situation of the Ottoman court and how cultural forms today, such as art exhibits, concerts, or museums, might pull in tourist dollars and affect local businesses. Ask students to express their ideas and conclusions in a position paper for the committee.

See the Chapter Planner for more strategies for differentiation.

HISTORICAL THINKING

ANSWERS

1. Military: moved from expansion to defense; defending its borders rather than conquering new territories; Economy: beginning to suffer; empire was not expanding and production of agriculture and commerce was not keeping up with population growth

2. sacred arts that expressed ideas of the Islamic religion; Ottomans were devoted to their faith.

3. exquisite in craftsmanship and artistry, making them desirable and popular; gold and silver threads were woven into silks; floral patterns were embroidered into the fabrics; probably difficult to find in Europe

Mughal India

A strong army can conquer a nation, but what does it take to keep people of very different beliefs from revolting? A great Mughal emperor found a solution when he implemented a policy of religious tolerance.

THE DELHI SULTANATE

Islam arrived on the Indian subcontinent via trade with the city-states of East Africa and through invasions by Turks from Central Asia. By the early 1200s, most of northern India was under Muslim rule in the Delhi sultanate, named for its capital city of **Delhi**. The sultanate lasted for three centuries and is credited with preventing the Mongols from invading South Asia.

Five different dynasties ruled the Delhi sultanate between 1210 and 1524. Government officials in Delhi believed the most qualified person in the sultanate, even if not a royal relative, could become sultan. This system of succession led to a free-for-all fight for control whenever a sultan died. One victorious sultan, Muhammad bin Tughluq (TOO-gluhk), conquered most of India. Only parts of southern India remained free of his control. The new sultan staffed his administration solely with foreigners, who he believed would remain loyal if other Muslims tried to overthrow him.

RISE OF THE MUGHAL DYNASTY

Muslim rule in India reached its peak with the Mughal dynasty, which was founded in 1526 by the Turkic prince Babur, who conquered lands in Afghanistan and India, ending the Delhi sultanate. The dynasty reached its height under the emperor **Akbar I**, whose armies controlled most of the Indian subcontinent. Akbar became one of the most powerful men in the world, ruling 100 million subjects from Delhi.

The Mughal state was well positioned to take advantage of expanding trade along the Indian Ocean. The Mughals exported dyed cotton textiles, sugar, pepper, diamonds, and other luxury goods. Imperial mints, factories with government authorization to produce currency, created hundreds of millions of gold, silver, and copper coins.

Akbar invested in roads to help traders move goods to market. The Mughals also granted tax-exempt status to new settlements to encourage people to move into previously underutilized lands. These settlements transformed the eastern half of Bengal (present-day Bangladesh) from tropical forestland into a densely populated rice-producing region.

Agriculture was the ultimate basis of Mughal wealth and power. Taxes on agricultural lands provided 90 percent of the income that paid for

One of Delhi's most recognizable landmarks, Qutb Minar is a high tower with inscriptions from the Quran written on its red and tan sandstone facade. Begun before the founding of the Delhi sultanate, the tower was completed during the reign of the first sultan. As was common practice, the builders used pieces of destroyed Hindu and Jain temples to build both the tower and the nearby mosque.

PLAN: 4-PAGE LESSON

OBJECTIVE

Explain how the Mughal dynasty maintained a stable government in India.

CRITICAL THINKING SKILLS FOR LESSON 2.1

- Analyze Cause and Effect
- Describe
- Make Inferences
- Make Connections
- Compare and Contrast
- Analyze Visuals

HISTORICAL THINKING FOR CHAPTER 16

What economic, political, and cultural impact did the rise of powerful land-based empires have across Eurasia?

The Mughal dynasty rose to power as the Ottomans and Safavids expanded their empires. Lesson 2.1 discusses the establishment of the Mughal dynasty in India with a special focus on the stabilizing policies of the Muslim emperor Akbar I.

BACKGROUND FOR THE TEACHER

Early Mughal Culture Mughal painting developed during the reigns of early Mughal emperors. The Mughal school began with Emperor Humayun, who visited Persia and admired the miniature paintings used to illustrate books. Humayan brought two Persian artists to his court. These artists, Mir Sayyid Ali and Abd-us-Samad, helped to establish the first studios of painting in India. Humayun's son Akbar I developed his love of the arts in a cultured atmosphere. As emperor, Akbar greatly expanded his father's library to some 24,000 volumes. He invited poets, architects, scholars, artists, and religious men to his court for study and discussion. Studios at the royal court included workshops for paper makers, calligraphers, illustrators, and bookbinders. Akbar was also passionate about architecture, and building construction burgeoned during his reign. Artistic and architectural styles evolved in the Mughal period to display Persian/Islamic and Hindu influences. Akbar also was a patron of poets and musicians, including Tansen, the musical genius of the period. Akbar's successor Jahangir, and Jahangir's son Shah Jahan, carried forward the pursuit of the arts and architecture.

INTRODUCE & ENGAGE

BRAINSTORM A LIST

Have students brainstorm ways that a leader might promote a policy of tolerance among different groups of people. **ASK:** What challenges and benefits might such a policy have? *(Possible response: Challenges would include resistance to the idea; benefits could include peace among different groups and shared prosperity.)* Explain that Muslim leaders conquered lands largely populated by Hindus. Tell students that in this lesson they will learn how Muslim emperors developed policies to meet the challenge of ruling people of different religious beliefs that led to a stable social order.

TEACH

GUIDED DISCUSSION

1. **Describe** How did the Mughal state arrive at a favorable position to participate in expanding trade along the Indian Ocean? *(Mughal founder prince Babur conquered lands in Afghanistan and India, and the armies of emperor Akbar I controlled most of the Indian subcontinent.)*

2. **Analyze Cause and Effect** What was the impact of the policy to incorporate existing local Indian rulers into the Mughal government? *(The Mughals were able to retain control from the top and maintain stability.)*

ANALYZE VISUALS

Direct students' attention to the 17th-century miniature. **ASK:** How would you describe the horse and its immediate background? *(Possible response: The miniature depicts a horse against a background of plant and animal life; human figures appear within the horse.)* What words would you use to describe the style of the miniature? *(Possible response: ornate, elaborate, precise, intricate)*

DIFFERENTIATE

ENGLISH LANGUAGE LEARNERS

Ask and Answer Questions Pair students at the **Advanced** level with those at the **Intermediate** level. Tell them to write several short-answer questions such as the following about people and ideas in the lesson. Then have pairs take turns asking and answering questions with another pair.

1. What was the basis of Mughal wealth and power? *(agriculture)*

2. Who was the most powerful Mughal emperor? *(Akbar I)*

3. What was the Mughal policy toward the Hindu majority? *(tolerance and inclusion)*

4. Who ruled the empire with Jahangir? *(his wife Nur Jahan)*

GIFTED & TALENTED

Explore Mughal Architecture Invite students to conduct online research about architecture from the Mughal period. Tell them to omit the Taj Mahal and focus on other structures. Have students prepare a report that includes information about three structures from the Mughal period, such as mosques, tombs, or other types of construction. Encourage students to include information about the architectural features, stylistic influences, and materials used in construction. Invite students to enhance their reports with drawings or photographs. Have students share their reports with the class.

See the Chapter Planner for more strategies for differentiation.

Mughal art was dominated by miniatures—tiny, detailed illustrations that appeared in books or as individual works. This miniature of a horse is from the 17th century.

Nur Jahan was also interested in commerce. She owned a fleet of ships that took religious pilgrims and trade goods to Mecca. Her policies facilitated both domestic and foreign trade even more than Akbar's had. During her time, India had a strong influence on the wider world. Indian merchants, sailors, bankers, and shipbuilders played important roles in Indian Ocean markets. The ports of Mughal India teemed with visitors from Europe, Africa, Arabia, and Southeast Asia.

Jahangir recognized and was grateful for his wife's crucial contributions. While Mughal coins were normally stamped with the name of the emperor, Jahangir had coins minted in Nur Jahan's name.

Jahangir's successor and son Shah Jahan held his wife, Mumtaz Mahal, in great regard as well. Following her death, he had an extensive **mausoleum**, or tomb, built in her honor. The mausoleum, the Taj Mahal, often called a work of "poetry in stone," became one of the most admired and magnificent buildings in the world.

MUGHAL DECLINE

Mughal India was at its height when Aurangzeb (owrang-ZEHB) became emperor in 1649. He called himself *Alamgir*—"world seizer"—to express his goal of extending Mughal power even further. Indeed, when he died many years later in 1707, the empire was at its greatest extent.

The problem was that in order to sustain his rule, Aurangzeb was forced to spend almost all his time away from the capital of Delhi on military campaigns. Regional rulers across India were testing the emperor's authority, for example, by withholding tax revenue and using it to engage in Indian Ocean trade and to purchase gunpowder weapons.

Aurangzeb managed to hold them in check but at a huge cost. His devotion to Islam and his imposition of the special tax on nonbelievers increased tensions with Hindus and other religious minorities. And the costs of his wars emptied the Mughal treasury. After his death, invasions from Iran and Afghanistan weakened Mughal power. As you will see, it was the British who would later benefit from Mughal decline.

In this 16th-century painting from the Mughal dynasty, Akbar I converses with people of different religious beliefs, including Muslim scholars and Jesuits, missionaries from a Catholic religious order.

Mughal armies. The Mughals sent tax clerks out to the provinces to survey the lands and divert **revenue**, or income for the government, to Delhi. The Mughals also continued the practice of allocating 10 percent of tax income to local rulers who had been in place before the Mughal conquest. By recognizing local rulers, the Mughals were able to incorporate existing Indian authorities into their government while maintaining control from the top.

RELIGIOUS TOLERANCE

As Muslims, the Mughals faced a difficult challenge in ruling over the Hindu majority of India. They had conquered by force, but maintaining control of a people with such different beliefs was a more difficult challenge.

Akbar's solution was to develop a policy of tolerance and inclusion. He canceled the special tax that Islamic law allows Muslim rulers to collect from nonbelievers. He also granted Hindu communities the right to follow their own social and legal customs. Hindu princes and rural aristocrats were incorporated into the Mughal administrative system. The Hindus were accustomed to a social system in which people paid little attention to matters outside their group. So Akbar presented the ruling Muslims as simply another caste with their own rituals and beliefs. In this way, the Mughals achieved a stable social order.

Akbar's successor Jahangir and his remarkable wife, **Nur Jahan**, continued Akbar's policy of religious tolerance. Jahangir was a weak ruler, so his wife took charge and kept Mughal power intact. Since women were secluded in separate quarters, Nur Jahan could not appear at court in person. Instead she issued government decrees through trusted family members. Taking a special interest in women's affairs, she donated land and **dowries**, or property that girls could use to start their married lives, to orphans. She was from an Iranian family, and she patronized Persian-influenced art and architecture, building many of the most beautiful mosques and gardens in north India.

HISTORICAL THINKING

1. **READING CHECK** How did Akbar's policy of religious tolerance help the Mughals maintain control of India?

2. **ANALYZE CAUSE AND EFFECT** What was the result of the Mughal policy of granting tax-exempt status to new settlements?

3. **DESCRIBE** How did Nur Jahan's foreign and domestic trade policies support the diffusion of cultures?

4. **MAKE INFERENCES** How did the large size of the Mughal Empire eventually contribute to its decline?

BACKGROUND FOR THE TEACHER

Mughal Women's History Historians in recent years have focused increasing attention on women of Mughal India, notably those whose lives can be traced from knowledge of important rulers to whom they were related. The latest scholarship indicates that many Mughal women were educated and accomplished intellectuals, scholars, and writers. A notable example is Gulbadan Banu Begum. She was the daughter of Babur, founder of the Mughal dynasty; sister of the emperor Humayun, Babur's successor; and aunt of the emperor Akbar I. It was her nephew Akbar who commissioned her to write a biography about her brother Humayun. Although the manuscript was lost for centuries, it was rediscovered with parts missing and can be found under the title *Humayun-Nama*. Recent scholarship on Mughal women has produced a more balanced picture of Nur Jahan, wife of the fourth Mughal emperor Jahangir and thus Akbar's daughter-in-law. Once ignored or portrayed as a scheming female, Nur Jahan is credited with talents for hunting, writing poetry, and building gardens, along with being a patron of the arts and architecture. Her aristocratic father saw that she was well educated in literature, art, and music. She also learned to speak Persian and Arabic. Because of her role as co-ruler with Jahangir, Nur Jahan has inspired works of Indian popular culture. She has been portrayed in books and film, including the 2005 Bollywood movie *Taj Mahal: An Eternal Love Story*. A 2015 television drama was adapted from Indu Sundaresan's *The Twentieth Wife*, a work of historical fiction based on the relationship of Jahangir and Nur Jahan. Jahangir's successor Shah Jahan built the Taj Mahal for Mumtaz Mahal, a daughter of Nur Jahan's brother.

TEACH

GUIDED DISCUSSION

3. **Make Connections** How did the personal background and interests of Nur Jahan affect her policies for Mughal India? *(Through her interest in women's affairs, Nur Jahan donated land and dowries to orphaned girls. As a descendant of an Iranian family, she patronized Persian-influenced art and architecture. Based on her interest in commerce and Muslim faith, she used her fleet of ships to facilitate trade and pilgrimages to Mecca.)*

4. **Compare and Contrast** Why did the policy of Aurangzeb toward nonbelievers in Islam have a different impact from the policy of Akbar? *(Aurangzeb restored the special tax that Islamic law allowed Muslim rulers to impose on nonbelievers, which created tensions among the Hindus and religious minorities; Akbar had canceled the special tax to appease the Hindus and rule by a policy of inclusion, which fostered allegiance and stability.)*

ANALYZE VISUALS

Have students study and read the caption of the 16th-century painting of Akbar I. **ASK:** What conclusions can you draw from the depiction of people conversing with Akbar and the human figures at the bottom of the painting? *(Possible response: The figures are excluded from the court of Akbar by a high wall. They seem to be of the lower class, and three in the left bottom corner might be beggars. The painting implies the separation of classes in Mughal society.)*

ACTIVE OPTIONS

On Your Feet: Roundtable Arrange students in groups of four. Provide each group with a sheet of paper to consider this question: What was the impact of Mughal policies on the economy and government of the empire? Ask the first student in each group to write an answer and read it aloud. Then have the student pass the paper clockwise to the next student. Each student within the group must add an answer. When the groups have no more answers, invite a volunteer from each group to present their ideas. Discuss the ideas as a class.

NG Learning Framework: Write Encyclopedia Entries
SKILL Observation
KNOWLEDGE Our Human Story

Direct students to use information in the chapter and supplement it with online research to write entries for an encyclopedia or reference book. Tell them to take notes from which to compose a paragraph or two about each Mughal ruler discussed in the chapter, from Babur to Aurangzeb. Ask students to list the rulers in order and include the dates of each reign and a few major achievements. Have them include Nur Jahan with the emperor Jahangir. Invite students to post their entries on a class website or blog.

HISTORICAL THINKING

ANSWERS

1. The populace was predominantly Hindu, and Islam was a foreign religion. If Akbar had not been tolerant of Hinduism, people would likely have revolted.

2. Tax exemption was an incentive for people to move to previously underutilized areas. New settlements in these areas promoted rice farming. Because agriculture produced the highest tax revenues, developing land for agriculture would eventually pay off in the revenue.

3. She supported religious pilgrims as they traveled to Mecca in Arabia. By supporting domestic and foreign trade, Indian culture and products spread throughout the world. At the same time, visitors from around the world came to India to sell their products and exchange aspects of their culture.

4. Aurangzeb, the emperor, had to spend much of his time away from the capital on military campaigns, which led lower rulers to test his authority.

2.2 Preserving Cultural Heritage

The Taj Mahal

The Taj Mahal in northern India is considered the greatest work of Mughal architecture, blending Indian, Persian, and Islamic styles. It is also considered one of the most beautiful buildings in the world—one that over three million people come to visit each year.

An enormous mausoleum complex, the Taj Mahal was built in Agra, India, along the banks of the Yamuna River, commissioned in 1632 by Mughal emperor Shah Jahan after the death of his beloved wife Mumtaz Mahal.

In 1631, Mumtaz Mahal died in childbirth. According to legend, Shah Jahan and his wife had been inseparable since their marriage in 1612. Grief-stricken, Shah Jahan ordered the building of the most beautiful tomb in the world as an enduring monument to the love of his wife.

Construction began in 1632 and over 20,000 workers from India, Persia, the Ottoman Empire, and Europe worked to build the magnificent complex. The five main structures of the complex consist of the main gateway, the garden, a mosque, a *jawab*, or guesthouse mirroring the mosque, and the mausoleum.

AGRA, INDIA
Goat shepherds walk with their flocks on the other side of the Yamuna River, across from the Taj Mahal. The heavily polluted river has become a breeding ground for mosquito-like bugs, whose excrement is leaving green stains on the mausoleum's marble.

PLAN: 4-PAGE LESSON

OBJECTIVE
Describe the complex of the Taj Mahal, the problems that threaten it, and the efforts to preserve it.

CRITICAL THINKING SKILLS FOR LESSON 2.2
- Analyze Visuals
- Make Connections
- Evaluate
- Draw Conclusions
- Identify Problems and Solutions

HISTORICAL THINKING FOR CHAPTER 16
What economic, political, and cultural impact did the rise of powerful land-based empires have across Eurasia?

The Taj Mahal is considered the greatest architectural work of the Mughal dynasty. Lesson 2.2 discusses the cultural impact of the mausoleum that was commissioned in 1632 by Mughal emperor Shah Jahan to honor his wife.

Student eEdition online
Additional content for this lesson, including photographs, is available online.

BACKGROUND FOR THE TEACHER
A Vision of Paradise A court poet described Shah Jahan's despair when his wife died at the age of 38, after giving birth to the couple's 14th child: "The color of youth flew away from his cheeks; The flower of his countenance ceased blooming." He wept so often "his tearful eyes sought help from spectacles." Shah Jahan decided to build a magnificent tomb with a mosque and gardens that mirrored the Islamic vision of Paradise. He found a tranquil spot along a sharp bend in the Yamuna River. The bend slowed the movement of the water and reduced the possibility of erosion along the riverbank. Shah Jahan acquired the land. He could have simply seized it, but according to Islamic tradition, a woman who dies in childbirth is a martyr. Since her burial place is holy, it must be acquired justly. He also acquired the land across the river, which is now the Mahtab Bagh (Moonlight Garden), a calm place to gaze at the mausoleum by the light of the moon and stars.

History Notebook
Encourage students to complete the Preserving Cultural Heritage page for Chapter 16 in their History Notebooks as they read.

INTRODUCE & ENGAGE

PREVIEW WITH VISUALS

Direct students' attention to the photographs and captions. Tell students that the emperor Shah Jahan picked the perfect tranquil spot for the Taj Mahal in 1632. Invite students to describe how the site has changed in these modern-day photographs. Ask a volunteer to read the captions aloud. Then discuss how the priorities of the government have also changed since 1632.

TEACH

GUIDED DISCUSSION

1. **Draw Conclusions** How did one of Shah Jahan's sons feel about his father's commitment to building the Taj Mahal, and how did he show these feelings? *(Possible response: One son most likely thought his father was spending too much time and money on the Taj Mahal because he overthrew his father and imprisoned him in a fort.)*

2. **Make Connections** How does the Taj Mahal reflect cultural heritage in India? *(Possible response: It is a prime example of Mughal architecture, and the decorations in the interior reflect India's Islamic cultural heritage.)*

PRESERVING CULTURAL HERITAGE

The city of Agra and the surrounding area are home to about 5 million people. The city also hosts millions of tourists who come to visit the Taj Mahal and other nearby attractions every year. To reduce traffic emissions, battery-charged buses transport tourists from the city to the Taj Mahal, a distance of about five miles. Other steps to reduce pollution include requiring the city's industries to use natural gas instead of coal and planting trees and shrubs in a green buffer zone to help clean the air. The people working to preserve the mausoleum are also applying silicone agents to the marble after cleaning it in the hope that the silicone will help protect it from the corrosive and staining effects of pollution.

DIFFERENTIATE

ENGLISH LANGUAGE LEARNERS

Identify Word Parts Remind students of **All Proficiencies** that two words can be combined to make a new word. Write the following compound words on the board: *childbirth, gateway, guesthouse, overthrown.* Instruct students to copy the words and circle the two smaller words in each compound word. Then place students in mixed-proficiency pairs, and have them work together to define each of the two smaller words and the resulting compound word.

GIFTED & TALENTED

Steps in a Process Direct students to conduct online research on the steps restoration workers are taking to clean the facade of the Taj Mahal and an estimate of the time and money it would take to clean and preserve the entire site. Encourage them to collect photos of the process as well as facts about it and to use these to create an infographic to share in an oral presentation to the class.

See the Chapter Planner for more strategies for differentiation.

The Taj Mahal rises up behind workers from the Archaeological Survey of India, the organization charged with cleaning the mausoleum's facade. India's Supreme Court has called preservation of the structure a "hopeless cause" due to government failures to cut down on pollution.

It took two decades to complete the work. The white-marble mausoleum was completed around 1638 while the remaining buildings and decoration work continued. Shah Jahan intended to build a second mausoleum across the river where his remains would be buried, but before that could be done he was overthrown by one of his sons. He was then imprisoned in the Agra Fort, which had a view of the Taj Mahal.

Notable for its white marble facade, the Taj Mahal's interior is decorated with semiprecious stones and carvings of verses from the Quran. After Mughal rule ended, the iconic white marble mausoleum suffered from neglect and deterioration. Major restoration was carried out in the early 20th century in an effort to preserve India's cultural heritage, and the Taj Mahal was designated a UNESCO World Heritage Site in 1983.

As both industrial development and tourism increased in India, air pollution from neighboring factories and vehicle emissions from increasing traffic threatened the facade of the marble building. Actions have been taken to combat the growing air pollution as well as the vast amounts of visitors. In 1996, the Supreme Court of India ordered environmental protections for the Taj Mahal. As a result, some factories were closed while others installed pollution-control equipment. A buffer zone around the complex and a ban of nearby vehicular traffic has also helped decrease pollution.

Today, the Archaeological Survey of India continues to manage the site and works with the World Monuments Fund to restore and preserve the Taj Mahal, maintaining it as the most magnificent example of Mughal architecture.

HISTORICAL THINKING

EVALUATE Industrialization plays a key role in growing economies in less-developed countries, but it also has consequences for the environment. Should industrial development be strictly regulated to protect cultural sites like the Taj Mahal? Why or why not?

BACKGROUND FOR THE TEACHER

The Mughal Gardens of Agra Another important example of Mughal culture is the gardens that line the banks of the Yamuna River across from the Taj Mahal. From the time of the emperor Babur through the reign of Shah Jahan, the riverfront was covered by walled enclosures, buildings, pavilions, and lush gardens. More than 40 Mughal gardens survive today, providing open green space in the middle of Agra's congestion, but they are facing challenges from urban development. Starting in 2014, the World Monuments Fund (WMF) and the Archaeological Survey of India launched a four-year restoration process for two of the best-known gardens—the Mehtab Bagh ("Moonlight Garden") and the Garden of the Tomb of I'timad-ud-Daulah. One of the most challenging aspects of the restoration was providing water to the gardens. It was believed that the original gardens were irrigated from the Yamuna River, but today the water is too polluted. Engineers had to design a water treatment system that pulls from the site's groundwater. Another challenge was identifying the plant species that once populated the gardens. While it will take some time for the reintroduced trees to fully mature, many of the fragrant plants, such as jasmine, oleander, and hibiscus, are flourishing. The WMF and the Archaeological Survey of India celebrated the completion of the restoration project in January 2019.

TEACH

GUIDED DISCUSSION

3. **Identify Problems and Solutions** What steps did the Supreme Court of India take to try to solve the problems threatening the Taj Mahal? *(The Supreme Court of India ordered environmental protections that closed some factories, installed pollution-control equipment on others, and banned nearby vehicular traffic to help decrease pollution.)*

4. **Evaluate** How do you think the solutions to the environmental threats facing the Taj Mahal will help preserve its cultural heritage? *(Possible response: The solutions will make it easier to preserve the building, which will allow it to remain standing for a longer time. This will allow future generations of people to see and learn about the Taj Mahal.)*

ANALYZE VISUALS

Have students study the photographs of the Taj Mahal that appear in the lesson. Then do an online image search to share other photos of the complex, including the gardens. **ASK:** Do you agree with the assertion that the Taj Mahal is one of the most beautiful buildings in the world? Why or why not? *(Possible responses: Yes, it is one of the most beautiful buildings in the world. There is beauty both in the symmetry of the building and in the intricate designs on the exterior and interior. No, there are many other buildings that surpass the Taj Mahal in beauty depending on your personal taste. Someone who prefers modern architecture might find more beauty in a building that is more streamlined and that blends better with the environment around it.)*

ACTIVE OPTION

NG Learning Framework: Effects of Pollution
ATTITUDE Responsibility
KNOWLEDGE Our Living Planet

Encourage students to consider the effects of pollution not only on the historical site of the Taj Mahal but also on the people and living creatures of the area. Tell them to conduct online research into the effects of air and water pollution on the Agra area, the Yamuna River, and everything living nearby. Then invite them to create innovative posters explaining steps individuals can take to help clean up polluted areas like this to benefit everyone.

HISTORICAL THINKING

ANSWER

Possible responses: Yes, industrial development should be regulated so emerging market countries don't lose culturally important sites. No, development should not be regulated because that will slow down economic growth.

Ming Decline to Qing Power

If you were rich and famous, would you need to try to please others? One Chinese emperor didn't think so. He ruled over a huge and extremely powerful country. He felt no need to pay attention to smaller countries on the other side of the world.

MING FALL AND QING RISE

By the beginning of the 17th century, Ming China, which you read about in an earlier chapter, was starting to show signs of weakness. The Chinese economy relied on silver from Spanish America, but as supplies of silver fell, inflation, or increased prices, triggered a decline in purchasing power. In other words, people were able to buy less with the same amount of money.

This economic crisis occurred at the same time as a government crisis. The aging emperor had lost interest in governing, and without his oversight, corruption increased. While officials vied for power, the country's affairs went unattended. Irrigation works were left unfinished and roads became unsafe as bandits robbed merchants. Peasants began to revolt. These weaknesses made China vulnerable to invasion, and in 1644 armies from neighboring Manchuria overran Beijing, deposed the Ming dynasty, and established the Qing (chihng) dynasty.

The Qing were Manchu (mahn-CHOO), or from Manchuria, and had a different language and identity than the majority Han Chinese. They never fully assimilated into Chinese culture, but they continued many of the policies and philosophies of previous dynasties with the hope that the Chinese people would

Ming and Qing Dynasties, 1405–1783

endorse their rule. They maintained Confucianism as the official ideology and retained the Chinese system of ministries and the examination system.

When the emperor **Kangxi** (KAHNG-shee) ascended the throne in 1661, Ming resistance continued in the south. However, Kangxi, who had been educated by Christian Jesuit tutors, brought knowledge of cannons and the mathematics to use them to successfully

suppress the rebels and to annex the island of Taiwan. He oversaw tremendous economic expansion. Farmers improved agricultural productivity by planting crops such as peanuts, potatoes, and maize from the Americas, and the Chinese population boomed—a sign of prosperity. Over six decades, Kangxi established the Qing as masters of one of the greatest empires the world had known.

QING TRADE AND FOREIGN RELATIONS

The emperor **Qianlong** (CHEE-ahn-lawng) ruled during the empire's greatest prosperity and territorial expansion. China exported luxury goods such as silk and porcelain, and, in return, vast quantities of silver poured into Qing China. Farmers added new crops, and artists and small-scale **entrepreneurs**, people who organize and operate businesses, expanded the glassmaking and coal-mining industries. Cotton textile production also emerged as a major commercial industry at this time, helping 18th-century China retain its position as the largest industrial economy in the world.

Territorial expansion was one of the greatest Qing achievements. Through both diplomacy and force, the Qing dynasty added 600,000 square miles to its empire. However, the Qing were not interested in asserting cultural superiority over the societies they acquired, and Korea and Vietnam remained self-governing through rituals such as annual tribute missions to Beijing in recognition of the Qing as their overlords.

The Russians, who you will read more about later in this chapter, were also expanding territory during this time, and the Qing worried that the Russians might threaten China. After some skirmishes, the Russians and the Chinese agreed to a treaty. The Qing recognized Russian claims west of Mongolia, and the Russians disbanded settlements to the east.

Pearls, silk, and silver and gold thread adorn the pheasant featured in this example of embroidery, or decorative needlework, from the 18th-century Qing dynasty.

Unlike the Russians who came over land, other Europeans came by sea. The Qing restricted European trade to a single port in south China. They also allowed Europeans to trade only with state-approved firms, which gave the Qing exclusive control over the market. They easily fixed prices and amassed huge profits.

The Chinese trade structure frustrated the British, who were the greatest maritime commercial power of the time. With the goal of opening access to the vast Chinese market, King George III sent a mission to China to negotiate formal diplomatic relations in 1792. However, when British representatives refused to recognize Emperor Qianlong as superior to King George, negotiations broke down. The Qing controlled the largest and wealthiest empire in the world. And as Qianlong noted in his response to the British: "We have never valued ingenious articles, nor do we have the slightest need of your country's manufactures." The Qing had no need to look beyond their own imperial borders for resources.

HISTORICAL THINKING

1. **READING CHECK** What were some of the greatest Qing accomplishments?

2. **INTERPRET MAPS** By how much did the Qing Empire expand from the size of the previous Ming dynasty?

3. **MAKE INFERENCES** How did Qing trade practices with Europeans turn the balance of trade in China's favor?

PLAN: 2-PAGE LESSON

OBJECTIVE

Explain how the Manchurians took over China and established a vast and prosperous empire.

CRITICAL THINKING SKILLS FOR LESSON 2.3

- Interpret Maps
- Make Inferences
- Summarize
- Make Connections

HISTORICAL THINKING FOR CHAPTER 16

What economic, political, and cultural impact did the rise of powerful land-based empires have across Eurasia?

Qing China numbered among the strong political and economical land-based empires that arose during this historical period. Lesson 2.3 discusses the rise to power of the Qing with a focus on the emperors Kangxi and Qianlong.

BACKGROUND FOR THE TEACHER

Kangxi as Emperor Kangxi was born in 1654, 10 years after the Qing dynasty began. For his reign, he chose the name of Kangxi, which means "peaceful harmony." Kangxi was a child when his reign began, and four advisors ruled for him. Kangxi involved himself in state affairs as a teenager. As a ruler, he was a strong administrator and military leader. He dealt personally with correspondence and spent time traveling to inspect his lands. He was a patron of the arts and revived the porcelain industry, which resulted in several innovations. European ideas and scientific knowledge fascinated Kangxi. He employed Jesuit missionaries who informed him and supplied scientific equipment. In 1708, Kangxi ordered an accurate atlas of the empire, later published as the *New Atlas of China, of Chinese Tartary, and of Tibet*. It was a standard source for the geography of China into the 19th century. Kangxi died in 1722, after a 61-year reign that laid the foundation for years of stability and prosperity in China.

INTRODUCE & ENGAGE

RULING QING CHINA

Ask students to imagine a child knowing he must rule a territory of people from a different culture. How would they face the challenge? Invite comments. *(Possible responses might include efforts to learn about the people they would rule.)* Explain that the first important emperor of Qing China came to power as a child. Tell students that in this lesson they will learn how that emperor and a famous Qing successor brought political and economic stability and great expansion to the empire.

TEACH

GUIDED DISCUSSION

1. **Summarize** What weaknesses led to Ming China's overthrow by the Qing? *(Inflation brought about an economic crisis. The emperor's lack of interest led to corruption and power struggles. Irrigation works were unfinished and roads were unsafe. Peasants began to revolt.)*

2. **Make Connections** How might the Qing approach to diverse cultures have helped the empire thrive in China and expand? *(The Qing continued the policies and philosophies of previous dynasties. Emperor Qianlong did not assert cultural superiority, which encouraged allegiance from conquered peoples. He allowed self-government for Korea and Vietnam so long as the Qing received annual tribute missions.)*

INTERPRET MAPS

Have students study the map that shows the Ming and Qing dynasties. **ASK:** How might Qing territorial expansion explain the response of Qianlong to King George III? *(The Qing acquired lands that vastly increased agricultural productivity and provided the resources needed for industrial development. Expansion provided Qianlong with all that was needed for prosperity and trade.)*

ACTIVE OPTIONS

On Your Feet: Fishbowl Point out that several factors helped the Qing take control without assimilating existing Chinese culture. Arrange students in a Fishbowl configuration. Assign the inner circle the following topic: Factors in Ming Downfall and Qing Success. Prompt students to discuss the topic. Have students in the outside circle listen and take notes. After a few minutes, have the students change positions and restart the discussion.

NG Learning Framework: Write a Profile
ATTITUDE Curiosity
KNOWLEDGE Our Human Story

Have students write a short profile of the governmental structure of Qing China and compare it to the government of China today. Students may use the text and conduct additional research online. Suggest students focus on a comparison of the Qing Chinese bureaucracy to the system of government in China today. Invite students to share what they have learned with the class.

DIFFERENTIATE

INCLUSION

Understand Information in a Map Pair students who are strong readers with those who have reading and perception difficulties. Instruct pairs to study the Ming and Qing Dynasties map. Direct them to read the legend together and use a finger to trace the perimeter of the territory of each expansion. Have them note relationships to the seas and other empires. Prompt pairs to work together to answer the relevant Historical Thinking question.

PRE-AP

Write an Essay about Trade Direct students to review the section about Qing trade and foreign relations. Instruct them to conduct online research on news websites to identify some of the issues faced by countries trading with China today. Have them take notes about how these issues are similar to or different from trade with China during the Qing period. Ask students to write an essay about their findings, citing all of their sources at the end. Invite students to share and discuss their essays with the class.

See the Chapter Planner for more strategies for differentiation.

HISTORICAL THINKING

ANSWERS

1. The Qing expanded the economy. They developed new farming practices and expanded many other industries. Their greatest accomplishment may have been their land expansion to 4.5 million square miles.

2. During the Qing Empire, China doubled in size from the Ming dynasty.

3. The Qing opened only one port to foreign trade and allowed Europeans to trade only with state-approved firms to have exclusive control of the market.

2.4 Voltaire Writes About Qianlong

Today's technology can help us connect with people in faraway lands pretty quickly. But how much can you really know about someone you have never met? In the 18th century, news of Qianlong's rule of China traveled far, and France's most famous philosopher became a fan of China's emperor.

Well before Qianlong became emperor, his grandfather and father had groomed him for the role. He had a fine education in which he gained skills in writing, art, philosophy, and government. He published more than 44,000 poems and sponsored the compilation of China's greatest works of philosophy. While he held the throne, the arts and humanities flourished in China.

Qianlong's successful rule made an impression on Europe's greatest thinkers. Voltaire was a contemporary of Qianlong and the most outspoken philosopher of his time in France. He used satire, wit, and reason to criticize European corruption and injustice. Although he was in regular contact with the greatest intellectuals of Europe, Voltaire held a man he had never met in the highest regard. In his eyes, Qianlong was a great philosopher king who ruled over a model state. In 1764, Voltaire wrote, "One need not be obsessed with the merits of the Chinese to recognize that their empire is the best that the world has ever seen."

Emperor Qianlong ruled China from 1736 to 1796.

DOCUMENT ONE
Primary Source: Letter
from a letter by Voltaire to Frederick the Great, King of Prussia, 1772

In 1770, Qianlong's 3,000-word poem "Ode to Moukden" was translated into French. As one of the greatest essayists and poets of Europe, Voltaire read and admired the translated poem. The king of Prussia, on the other hand, was not known to be much of a poet. However, when Voltaire wrote this letter, he was seeking financial support from King Frederick the Great.

CONSTRUCTED RESPONSE Why does Voltaire compare Frederick the Great's writing to Qianlong's? Do you think Voltaire really believes that King Frederick's writing is better than Qianlong's? Explain your answer.

I do not know if the emperor of China has some of his discourses recited in his Academy, but I defy him to write better prose, and, with regard to his verses, I am acquainted with a king of the North [Frederick] who can write better ones without too much trouble. . . . Know that the king's poem on the Confederates is infinitely superior to the poem of Moukden [Mukden].

DOCUMENT TWO
Primary Source: Letter
from a letter by Voltaire to the Marquis de Condorcet, 1770

Voltaire was a strong advocate of religious tolerance. He criticized Christians for not being accepting of other faiths. In China, Christian missionaries were sometimes forbidden from preaching and converting Chinese people. However, Qianlong had several Jesuit missionaries as his personal friends. In this letter, Voltaire quotes a dialogue between Qianlong and the Chinese minister of state to argue a point.

CONSTRUCTED RESPONSE How does this anecdote support Qianlong's beliefs about religious tolerance?

[When] a Minister of State accus[ed] a mandarin [Chinese official] of being a Christian, the Emperor Kien-long [Qianlong] asked: "Does his province complain of him?"
"No."
"Does he render justice impartially?"
"Yes."
"Has he failed in his duty towards the state?"
"No."
"Is he a good father to his family?"
"Yes."
"Why then dismiss him for a mere nothing?"

DOCUMENT THREE
Primary Source: Letter
from a letter by Qianlong to King George III of Britain, 1793

Chinese products were in high demand in Europe. However, Europeans found it difficult to convince Qing officials to open up their markets. In an attempt to persuade China to open up to freer trade, King George sent an ambassador to China. This excerpt is from Qianlong's response.

CONSTRUCTED RESPONSE In what way does Qianlong's response to King George further opinions similar to those of Voltaire?

. . . [O]ur Celestial Empire possesses all things in prolific abundance and lacks no product within its own borders. There was therefore no need to import the manufactures of outside barbarians [societies outside China] in exchange for our own produce. But as the tea, silk, and porcelain which the Celestial Empire produces are absolute necessities to European nations and to yourselves, we have permitted, as a signal mark of favor, that foreign hongs [merchant firms] should be established at Canton, so that your wants might be supplied and your country thus participate in our beneficence [generosity].

SYNTHESIZE & WRITE

1. **REVIEW** Review what you have learned about Voltaire and Qianlong.

2. **RECALL** On your own paper, list details about Qianlong from what Voltaire has written and from Qianlong's own words.

3. **CONSTRUCT** Construct a topic sentence that answers the following question: Was Voltaire's belief that Qianlong was a benevolent and wise leader accurate?

4. **WRITE** Using evidence from this chapter and the documents, write an informative paragraph that supports your topic sentence in Step 3.

PLAN: 2-PAGE LESSON

OBJECTIVE
Synthesize information from three primary source documents about Qianlong, the emperor of China during the 18th century.

CRITICAL THINKING SKILLS FOR LESSON 2.4
- Synthesize
- Identify Main Ideas and Details
- Analyze Text
- Evaluate

HISTORICAL THINKING FOR CHAPTER 16
What economic, political, and cultural impact did the rise of powerful land-based empires have across Eurasia?

The three primary source letters display Voltaire's praise for Qianlong and exemplify the economic, political, and cultural impact of the Qing dynasty during the 18th century.

BACKGROUND FOR THE TEACHER
Voltaire François-Marie Arouet was born on November 21, 1694, in Paris, France, into a middle-class family. He lost his mother at the age of seven. He had little to do with his father or brother and preferred to spend time with his godfather, the abbe de Chateauneuf, who was known as a freethinker. His love for literature and the theater came when he attended the Jesuit college of Louis-le-Grand in Paris. After school, a short employment as a secretary at the French embassy, and the death of Louis XIV, he frequented the Temple in Paris, which was the center of freethinking society. It was there that he became "the wit of Parisian society." His famous epigrams landed him in Bastille prison for nearly a year (the first of his two jail terms). In 1718, he became successful for writing *Oedipe*, the first of his tragedies, and adopted the name Voltaire. He became the court poet under King Louis XV, when Queen Marie found favor with him. From here his life at court moved him from country to country, in and out of exile and favor with France. Voltaire went on to become one of the leading historians of the French Enlightenment and one of the most famous writers of the Enlightenment. Voltaire argued for the rights of freedom of religion and speech; he criticized oppression, prejudice, and intolerance. He is still revered today for his letters to European monarchs that helped to pave the way to new reforms and freedoms.

INTRODUCE & ENGAGE

PREPARE FOR THE DOCUMENT-BASED QUESTION

Before students start on the activity, briefly preview the three documents. Remind students that a constructed response requires full explanations in complete sentences. Emphasize that students should use what they have learned about Qianlong and the Qing dynasty in addition to the information in the documents.

TEACH

GUIDED DISCUSSION

1. **Identify Main Ideas and Details** In Document Two, Qianlong asks a series of questions. According to these questions, what traits are valuable? *(Possible responses: Treating provinces/people fairly, upholding justice, doing the state's duty, and being a good father.)*

2. **Analyze Text** What does Qianlong mean when he states "our Celestial Empire"? *(Possible response: Qianlong is referring to China. He is saying that China is the most holy or most splendid of all empires.)*

EVALUATE

After students have completed the Synthesize & Write activity, allow time for them to exchange paragraphs and read and comment on the work of their peers. Establish guidelines for comments prior to the activity so that feedback is constructive and encouraging. Comments should focus on the most significant parts that address the purpose of the activity and the audience.

ACTIVE OPTION

On Your Feet: Host a DBQ Roundtable Direct students to gather into groups of four. Pose the following question: What qualities does Voltaire admire in Qianlong? Instruct the first student in each group to write an answer, read it aloud, and pass the paper clockwise to the next student. The paper may circulate around the table several times. Then reconvene the class and discuss the groups' responses.

DIFFERENTIATE

ENGLISH LANGUAGE LEARNERS

Understand and Pronounce Words Preview the following words: *discourses, recited, infinitely, province, render, impartially, prolific,* and *absolute.* Say each word slowly, and have students at **All Proficiencies** repeat, noting the pronunciation and syllable stress, and make word cards with definitions and pronunciation hints.

PRE-AP

Present a Biography Tell students to research and write a biography about one of the following: Frederick the Great, Marquis de Condorcet, King George III, Qianlong, or Voltaire. Students should describe in detail how this person is remembered in history and decide whether he would have liked to be remembered that way or not. Ask students to display a visual of the person as they present.

SYNTHESIZE & WRITE

ANSWERS

1. Answers will vary.

2. Possible response: a skilled writer of prose and poetry; tolerated Christian officials, if they were also just, impartial, hardworking, and fulfilled their family responsibilities; required people to bow to him and was condescending toward Europeans, which may have been a sign of protectionism for China

3. Possible response: Qianlong was a benevolent and wise leader who stood firm when confronted with others who might try to exploit his country.

4. Answers will vary. Students' paragraphs should include their topic sentence from Step 3 and provide several details from the documents as support.

CONSTRUCTED RESPONSE

Document One: Because Qianlong was held in such high regard, Voltaire hopes that Frederick will be flattered to be compared with him. Voltaire is probably not being honest about Frederick's writing abilities. He uses blatant flattery because he is requesting money from the king and a king would expect to be flattered.

Document Two: It shows he used reason to advocate tolerance toward a person who held different beliefs.

Document Three: Voltaire wrote that the Chinese "empire is the best that the world has ever seen," and Qianlong's condescending letter presents a ruler of the greatest empire, looking down with sympathy on the poor countries that have nothing to offer.

Japan's Tokugawa Shogunate

When things feel chaotic, do you ever feel the need to pull back and take control? This is what the Tokugawa shoguns tried to do when they felt Japanese society was changing too fast.

STABILITY AND PROSPERITY

The 16th century was a time of violence and insecurity in Japan, and as the nation entered the 17th century, the Japanese emperor remained secluded in Kyoto. The Tokugawa (toh-koo-gah-wah) shoguns who ruled from the political capital at Edo, today's Tokyo, had the real political power. These shoguns took control and formed a shogunate—a government ruled by shogun generals—that brought peace and stability to the Japanese islands. Still, the provincial lords, the daimyo, retained substantial authority within their own domains.

Under the Tokugawa, the economy flourished as farmers and fishermen improved their processes and increased their yields. The shoguns and daimyo developed an efficient tax system based on precise appraisals of the land and population. Some of this new tax revenue went toward the improvement of roads and irrigation works, further stimulating economic growth.

Internal trade expanded as Japanese cities and commercial centers grew and peasants geared their production toward urban markets. By 1720, Edo had grown from a small village to a city of more than a million people.

This peacetime economy altered roles for samurai warriors and for women. While samurai remained loyal to their daimyo lords, some positioned themselves as intellectual and cultural leaders. They established schools, wrote Confucian treatises, and patronized the arts. Women's roles began to change, too. Elite women contributed to Japanese literature, including experimenting with a form of poetry called *haiku*. Women from merchant and artisan families claimed some mobility and economic opportunities. Some participated as performers or audience members in theater and dance. Samurai and women enjoyed the new form of drama called *kabuki*.

These artistic trends and societal changes worried the Tokugawa leaders because they wanted to maintain a more traditional society. They demanded that people return to traditional ways of living and ordered them to dress in clothing and live in houses appropriate to their social status.

CHALLENGES, REFORM, AND DECLINE

By the 18th century, the Tokugawa shoguns faced numerous challenges. The population had grown to more than 30 million. While population growth had been a sign of prosperity early in the shogunate, it became a problem in a country with limited farmland. Urban centers grew and encroached on farmland, and constant construction in urban areas depleted Japan's timber resources. Wood became more expensive, and heavy logging led to soil erosion.

The Tokugawa shogun **Yoshimune** (YOH-shih-muhn) supported the use of fertilizer to refresh exhausted soil, but the problem of limited land for agriculture and timber only escalated. The economy took a downturn, and hundreds of thousands perished in a terrible famine in the 1780s.

To curb unnecessary **consumption**, or spending, Yoshimune issued edicts emphasizing frugality. But his edicts did not change people's behavior. He sponsored reforms to curb corruption, reduce imports, and support fishing, and he increased government control over commerce. But these policies undermined new business development, and Japanese business gradually became more regulated and less inventive.

These troubles resulted in a rural uprising. It was becoming clear that the Tokugawa shoguns' policies were inadequate to solve Japan's problems.

JAPAN REJECTS THE EUROPEAN WORLD

The shoguns' conservative policies were most evident in foreign affairs. In the 17th century, Tokugawa leaders outlawed Christianity because the shoguns were alarmed by the early success of Christian missionaries. A series of seclusion edicts strictly limited contact with Europeans. The Tokugawa allowed only one Dutch trading expedition per year. During that expedition, no Bibles or other Christian texts were allowed to enter the country.

The seclusion edicts only applied to Europeans. Trade with Chinese and Korean merchants grew, and overall, Japanese foreign trade increased. Through the Dutch trade expedition, some scientific and philosophical books from Europe reached Japan, and European knowledge became known as "Dutch learning." But for the most part, Japanese thinkers relied on China to learn of advances in science and philosophy.

Some Tokugawa thinkers even downplayed Chinese influence. They rejected Buddhism and Confucianism and elevated Shinto since that was Japan's indigenous religion. The practice of **nativism**, favoring Japanese tradition and ideas rather than those of outsiders, spread. Unlike China, Russia, and Britain, Japan opted out of empire building.

In the early 1790s, Americans and Russians arrived in Japan, hoping to re-establish trade relations. The Japanese responded by attacking their vessels, forcing them to flee. Their commitment to seclusion would later be challenged with an ultimatum from these foreign powers: open your doors to foreign trade, or we will use advanced weapons to destroy them.

This woodblock print by the Japanese artist Utagawa Hiroshige is from his series *One Hundred Famous Views of Edo.* First published in 1856–1859, the series made Hiroshige one of the most popular *ukiyo-e* artists of all time. *Ukiyo-e,* which is Japanese for "pictures of the floating world," was an art style that flourished during the Tokugawa period.

HISTORICAL THINKING

1. **READING CHECK** Why did the Tokugawa shoguns decide to seclude Japan from Europeans?

2. **IDENTIFY PROBLEMS AND SOLUTIONS** Why did population growth become a problem in the 18th century, and how did the Tokugawa government seek to solve the problem?

3. **ANALYZE CAUSE AND EFFECT** What was one effect of the Tokugawa government's attempts to increase control over commerce?

PLAN: 2-PAGE LESSON

OBJECTIVE

Identify the positive and negative impact of Japan's Tokugawa Shogunate in the 17th and 18th centuries.

CRITICAL THINKING SKILLS FOR LESSON 2.5

- Identify Problems and Solutions
- Analyze Cause and Effect
- Summarize
- Form and Support Opinions
- Analyze Visuals

HISTORICAL THINKING FOR CHAPTER 16

What economic, political, and cultural impact did the rise of powerful land-based empires have across Eurasia?

The Tokugawa shogunate was founded in Japan in 1603, a few decades before the Qing took over Ming China. Lesson 2.5 discusses Japan under shogunate rule through successive periods of prosperity, decline, and ultimate isolation.

Student eEdition online

Additional content for this lesson, including images, is available online.

BACKGROUND FOR THE TEACHER

Kabuki and Tokugawa Arts The prosperity of the early Tokugawa period resulted in increasing urbanization and change that favored merchants and common people. The aristocratic daimyo no longer had a monopoly on entertainment. Kabuki theater originated at the start of the Tokugawa period as entertainment for all classes but particularly commoners. According to legend, the founder was a woman who entertained passersby with her dancing. In Japanese, the word *kabuki* means "song-dance-skill." Female song-and-dance troupes began to stage the performances called kabuki theater. The performances were informal and intended to be fun. The somewhat rollicking atmosphere alienated Tokugawa leaders, who saw women performing as a public threat. The leaders banned female dancers and finally allowed performances by adult men only. That rule remains largely true in kabuki today. The art form of woodblock prints that also originated in the Tokugawa period often depicted kabuki. Japan's popular puppet theater, or bunraku, dates from the Tokugawa period as well. Both kabuki and bunraku appear on a UNESCO Intangible Cultural Heritage of Humanity list.

INTRODUCE & ENGAGE

DISCUSS THE VALUE OF TRADITION

Have students think about the place of tradition in society. Invite volunteers to suggest some advantages and disadvantages of adhering to traditional ways. Tell students that in this lesson they will learn about the Tokugawa shoguns who favored Japanese tradition and how Japan became isolated from the world under their rule.

TEACH

GUIDED DISCUSSION

1. **Summarize** What factors caused the economy to flourish during the early Tokugawa period? *(Farmers and fishermen improved their methods and increased yields; the shoguns and daimyo developed an efficient tax system that stimulated economic growth and provided for public works projects; and internal trade expanded as cities grew and urban markets opened up.)*

2. **Form and Support Opinions** Do you think the Tokugawa leaders contributed to economic decline by demanding that people return to traditional ways of living? Why or why not? *(Possible responses: Yes, because the insistence on tradition hindered inventive business practices and the creative thinking needed to solve Japan's numerous challenges. OR No, because problems of urban growth, overpopulation, and limited timber and agricultural lands would have caused economic decline in any case.)*

ANALYZE VISUALS

Have students look at the woodblock print and read the caption. Ask them to note the translation of the Japanese word *ukiyo-e*. **ASK:** What can you infer from the meaning of ukiyo-e? *(Possible response: A floating world means that the world is constantly changing, and the artist is capturing moments of change in pictures.)*

ACTIVE OPTIONS

On Your Feet: Numbered Heads Organize students into groups of four. Ask group members to number off. Instruct groups to discuss the following question: Was the isolation of Japan inevitable, or could the Tokugawa shoguns have found ways to avoid isolation? Tell students to cite evidence from the text to support their responses. Then call out a number and have students with that number summarize their group's discussion.

> **NG Learning Framework: Write a Brief History**
> SKILL Observation
> KNOWLEDGE Our Human Story

Have students write a brief history of Japan's relationship with Europe and foreign powers in the later Tokugawa period. Have students use information from "Japan Rejects the European World" and locate additional source material. Suggest students focus on the shoguns' reasons for isolating Japan. Invite students to share their histories with the class.

DIFFERENTIATE

STRIVING READERS

Dictate Section Summaries After students read each section of the lesson, ask them to write a sentence or two summarizing the main idea. Then pair students to write answers to these questions, checking their answers for accuracy and spelling:

- What is this section about?
- What is the main idea in this section?
- What details support the main idea?

GIFTED & TALENTED

Create a Multimedia Presentation Prompt students to learn more about the arts of the Tokugawa period. Tell students to create a multimedia presentation on the subject of art forms, such as kabuki theater, paintings, and ukiyo-e art. Have students conclude the presentation with comments on Tokugawa influences on Japanese art today.

See the Chapter Planner for more strategies for differentiation.

HISTORICAL THINKING

ANSWERS

1. European missionaries had converted many Japanese people to Christianity. Shoguns wanted a return to tradition and likely feared the loss of a unique Japanese identity.

2. Urban centers encroached on farmland and urban construction depleted timber resources. Heavy logging led to soil erosion. The Tokugawa tried to refresh soil by using fertilizer, but this did not solve the problem of limited land for agriculture and timber.

3. Government reforms failed to change people's behavior. Attempts to control commerce undermined new business development. Japanese business was gradually more regulated and became less inventive.

Control of the Steppes

Have you ever heard the saying "Absolute power corrupts absolutely"? In the case of one Russian monarch, power led not only to corruption but also to a reign of absolute terror.

LIFE ON THE STEPPES

The Eurasian steppes extend approximately 5,000 miles across Europe and Asia from Hungary to Manchuria. The steppe region consists largely of grasslands; few trees grow there, and the soil isn't well suited for farming. These are the lands of nomadic herders like the Mongols, whose great empire you learned about earlier.

Most people lived north of the steppes in the forests, where they raised herds and grew crops on small family farms. Treeless arctic plains called **tundra** and land called **taiga** that was covered with scattered stands of evergreen shrubs lay beyond the forests. People in this region survived by fishing and hunting reindeer, bear, and walrus.

Some of the people living in the region called themselves the Rus, the root of the word *Russia*, which became another name for the area. This multiethnic group spoke many different languages. But starting in around 500, the Slavs, who occupied much of the territory along the southwestern coast of the Black Sea, moved north and east, carrying their language with them. The Slav language is related to Russian, Ukrainian, Polish, and Czech.

Children race horses across the steppes during the summer Naadam Festival, an annual celebration of nomadic culture in Mongolia.

TAKING CONTROL OF THE STEPPES

West of the Slav region were the Magyars, Christian converts known to their neighbors as Hungarians. Two Turkish-speaking communities were also in the area—the Khazars, who lived near **Kiev** and who had converted to Judaism, and the Bulgars, converts to Islam.

Before 930, the Rus paid tribute to rulers like the Khazars and the Bulgars. However, the Rus evolved into early states called principalities. As trade grew, so did the populations of the Rus principalities, with Kiev becoming the largest. After signing a trade treaty with the Byzantine Empire, the Kievan Rus began to eliminate their political rivals, including the Khazars and the Bulgars.

Unlike the other groups, the Rus had not chosen a religion. However, since the middle of the ninth century, Byzantine missionaries had been active among the Rus. Earlier you read about the Byzantine missionary Cyril and how he created the Cyrillic alphabet using a combination of Greek and local languages to provide a written language for the Slavs. The Christian scriptures were then translated using this alphabet, called Old Church Slavonic.

Prince Vladimir of Kiev, who emerged as the leader of the Kievan Rus, converted to Christianity in 987 after he married the sister of a Byzantine emperor. He then ordered all the inhabitants of Kiev to come to the riverbank where he surprised them by performing a mass baptism. Thus, Christianity became the religion of the Rus.

Conquest by the Mongols in the 1230s left the city of Kiev devastated. The principality of Muscovy (Moscow) eventually emerged as Kiev's successor, and Ivan III defeated other Russian families to become the undisputed leader of the region.

By the time **Ivan IV** came to power in 1533, what became known as Russian Orthodox Christianity had taken deep root in Russia. Ivan IV took the title **tsar**, a version of the Latin term *Caesar*, because he considered Russia a continuation of the old Roman Empire. Claiming that God had granted him the divine right to rule, he centralized power and extended Russia's frontiers. He also maintained a large buffer around Russia to protect it from invasion. Ivan's accomplishments came with a price, though. He was known as "Ivan the Terrible" because of his cruelty. For example, when he heard that members of the nobility in the town of Novgorod were plotting against him, he had the entire town destroyed, executing thousands of the town's innocent inhabitants. He also formed an elite force to torture and kill anyone who disobeyed him. In a fit of rage, he even murdered his own son, heir to the throne.

CRITICAL VIEWING This 1897 oil painting by Victor Mikhailovich Vasnetsov portrays Ivan IV. What can you infer about the tsar from details in the painting?

HISTORICAL THINKING

1. **READING CHECK** Describe the religious diversity in the steppes before the 10th century.

2. **DESCRIBE** How did the Slav language come to dominate the vast region of the steppes?

3. **IDENTIFY SUPPORTING DETAILS** Describe some of the events that gave Ivan IV the title "Ivan the Terrible."

PLAN: 2-PAGE LESSON

OBJECTIVE
Explain how Russia formed from diverse peoples living along the Eurasian steppes.

CRITICAL THINKING SKILLS FOR LESSON 3.1
- Describe
- Identify Supporting Details
- Analyze Cause and Effect
- Summarize
- Interpret Maps

HISTORICAL THINKING FOR CHAPTER 16
What economic, political, and cultural impact did the rise of powerful land-based empires have across Eurasia?

Russia emerged as a Eurasian power by the mid-16th century. Lesson 3.1 discusses the evolution of multiethnic Rus populations into states dominated first by Kiev and then by Moscow, with attention to the roots of Russian Orthodox Christianity and the rule of Ivan IV.

Student eEdition online
Additional content for this lesson, including a map, is available online.

BACKGROUND FOR THE TEACHER

The Naadam Festival in Mongolia The Naadam Festival has a rich history rooted in the equestrian culture of nomads from thousands of centuries ago. People relied on horses for travel and conquest, including traders on the ancient Silk Roads. Expert horsemen enabled the Mongolian Genghis Khan to conquer almost the entire steppes in the 13th century. Horseback riding is central to most people of the steppes to this day, and the Naadam Festival celebrates this with horse racing. The races are as long as 18 or 20 miles with horses numbering in the hundreds. The jockeys typically are children as young as five years old, but the prizes are awarded to the horse and its trainer. Naadam is a national holiday celebrated in towns and nomadic camps throughout Mongolia, with the main festival being held in the capital city of Ulaanbaatur. Naadam focuses on two other sports as well, archery and wrestling, all dating back to the days of Genghis Khan. Dancers, singers, and ceremonies are other elements of these mid-summer festivals.

INTRODUCE & ENGAGE

DISCUSS RULE BY FEAR

Ask students to think about a government that relies on terrorizing citizens. Is fear an effective method of control? Have students recall what they have learned and suggest better ways to govern. *(Students' responses will vary.)* Tell students that in this lesson they will learn about the diverse peoples of the Eurasian steppes and how a leader emerged to rule them all through his use of cruelty and terror.

TEACH

GUIDED DISCUSSION

1. **Analyze Cause and Effect** How did the growth of trade affect the Rus principalities? *(The populations of the principalities grew. Kiev became the largest principality and assumed the leading role.)*

2. **Summarize** How did the Cyrillic alphabet pave the way for Christianity to become deeply rooted in Russia? *(The Cyrillic alphabet was created by a Byzantine missionary as a language for Christian Slavs. It was used to translate the Christian scriptures. Prince Vladimir, who led the Kievan Rus, converted to Christianity by marrying a Byzantine woman. He baptized all inhabitants of Kiev so that Christianity became the religion of the Rus.)*

INTERPRET MAPS

Direct students to study the map of the western and eastern steppes (available in the Student eEdition). **ASK:** Where are Kiev and Moscow located in relation to the steppes? *(Kiev is located in the far western end of the steppe region, northeast of Hungary and the Black Sea, and Moscow lies northeast of Kiev and far north of the Black Sea.)*

ACTIVE OPTIONS

On Your Feet: Three-Step Interview Have students work in pairs to interview each other about the living conditions and unification of peoples on the steppes. Direct one student to interview the other by asking this question: What challenges did the steppes present to resident peoples? Encourage the interviewer to ask follow-up questions based on the answers. Then have students reverse roles, with the second student asking the question: How did peoples of the steppes unify under the Kievan Rus but then fall subject to rule by Moscow? After the interviews, ask students to share information with the class.

> **NG Learning Framework: Write a Biography**
> **ATTITUDE** Curiosity
> **KNOWLEDGE** Our Human Story

Have students write a short biography or profile of Ivan IV using information from the lesson and additional material based on online research. Suggest students focus on Ivan IV's approach to leadership. Invite students to read their biographies aloud to the class for discussion and comparison.

DIFFERENTIATE

STRIVING READERS

Understand Main Ideas To help students develop their reading and comprehension skills, pair an English-proficient student with a striving reader. Ask pairs to find two or three main ideas in each section and list the ideas. Then have pairs exchange lists for comparison and discussion.

GIFTED & TALENTED

Write a Travel Brochure Ask students to conduct additional research to learn more about Kiev as it was then and as it is now. Tell students to develop a travel brochure for Kiev. Encourage them to include a time line or brief summary of events that explains how Kiev became a modern city. They might also incorporate illustrations or photographs. Have students post their brochures for the class.

See the Chapter Planner for more strategies for differentiation.

HISTORICAL THINKING

ANSWERS

1. The Magyars in the west were Christians. The Khazars were Jewish, and the Bulgars were Muslim. Byzantine Christian missionaries were also active among the Rus.

2. Around the year 500, the Slavs moved north and east from their home along the southwest coast of the Black Sea. As they moved, they carried their language with them, and it spread.

3. Ivan IV was a brutal leader who killed anyone who disobeyed him. When he heard that some people in one town were plotting against him, he had the entire city destroyed. He also killed his own son.

CRITICAL VIEWING Possible response: The tsar looks cruel, angry, and threatening. His ornate robe and his weapon suggest importance and power.

The Romanov Dynasty

How difficult is it to live up to your values? Most of us have good intentions, but when it comes down to practice, we often fall short. This is what happened to the Russian empress Catherine the Great. She hoped to grant the Russian people more freedoms, but she found that the cost was too high.

RISE OF THE ROMANOVS

It was Russia's fear of disorder and instability that allowed Ivan IV to rule without limitation. But Ivan's death ushered in a "time of troubles" because, as you've read, he killed his own son and failed to leave a clear successor. After 30 years of instability, Russian nobles offered royal power to a noble named Mikhail Romanov. With his ascent in 1613, the Romanov dynasty began, and it endured for a long time. Like the Ottoman Empire and the Qing dynasty, Romanov rule in Russia lasted into the 20th century.

The Romanovs continued Russia's imperial expansion. Animal furs had become fashionable, and profit lured Russian traders to the east, where they traveled across the Ural Mountains into frigid Siberia in search of animal pelts. Although Russians were trading furs on a substantial scale, agricultural surpluses were the main source of revenue for the tsars and the nobility. Peasants worked the fields to provide this revenue stream. While most European countries had given up serfdom, serfs continued to live in oppressive conditions in Russia. Russian peasants were tightly bound to their villages, and the aristocracy increasingly saw these serfs as property to be bought and sold.

Tsar **Peter the Great** visited western Europe as a young monarch in 1697, and he returned to Russia with the realization that it had fallen behind. He was determined to bring Russia up to par with its European counterparts. To bring about rapid transformation, Tsar Peter accumulated greater power for himself by bringing the nobles more tightly under his control. He forced his royal court to dress in the latest European fashions, and he ordered Russian aristocrats to shave off their long beards so they would look more European. Any Russian man who wanted to keep his beard would have to pay a "beard tax" and carry a receipt that read: "the beard is

a superfluous [unnecessary] burden." Tsar Peter's beard policy showed who was in charge and made it clear that change in Russia would flow in one direction: from the top down.

To further Russia's transformation, Peter also brought in the latest military technology from Europe. In a spectacle of military power, he created a regular standing army, larger than any in Europe, as well as a powerful navy fleet. He also sponsored a new educational system to train more efficient civilian and military bureaucrats. Still, the situation of the serfs did not improve. Their heavy taxes paid for the Russian military, and their sons fought in Peter's armies. At the serfs' expense, Peter extended Russian frontiers in wars against Sweden and Poland and laid the groundwork for later conquests of Muslim steppe societies. For all the elegance of Peter's new capital, his insistence on expansion and absolute power left Russia's policies little changed from those of Ivan the Terrible.

EUROPEAN AND ASIAN INFLUENCES

With great expense Peter built the new capital city of St. Petersburg on the Baltic Sea to serve as Russia's "window on the West." He used European architectural styles in St. Petersburg, emulating the elegant baroque buildings of Rome and Vienna. Peter's palace in St. Petersburg was originally planned as the main residence of the Romanov family, but later Romanovs moved the capital back to Moscow. They returned to the "Winter Palace" for winter retreats in the milder climate of St. Petersburg.

A little over a hundred years earlier, in the 1550s, Ivan the Terrible built St. Basil's Cathedral in Moscow to commemorate his conquest of Kazan, a city ruled by Muslims. Some scholars theorize that St. Basil's "onion dome" architecture was inspired by Kazan's central mosque, which was destroyed by Ivan's armies. However,

The Cathedral of Vasily the Blessed, known as St. Basil's Cathedral, is located in Red Square in Moscow. Completed in 1560, the cathedral was ordered by Ivan IV to be built in 1552. In 1860, during restoration, the cathedral was painted with the bright, striking patterns of color for which it is known. Today, the cathedral is a museum and a UNESCO World Heritage Site.

PLAN: 4-PAGE LESSON

OBJECTIVE

Identify efforts by the Romanov dynasty to become European while oppressing the serfs.

CRITICAL THINKING SKILLS FOR LESSON 3.2

- Analyze Language Use
- Compare and Contrast
- Make Predictions
- Summarize
- Form and Support Opinions
- Make Connections
- Make Inferences
- Analyze Visuals

HISTORICAL THINKING FOR CHAPTER 16

What economic, political, and cultural impact did the rise of powerful land-based empires have across Eurasia?

The Romanovs of Russia were similar to other Eurasian emperors in the pursuit of power and expansion. Lesson 3.2 discusses the rise of the Romanovs with a focus on the reigns of Peter the Great and Catherine the Great.

BACKGROUND FOR THE TEACHER

St. Petersburg Peter the Great chose an inhospitable site for his new capital city, but it provided a seaport. The construction of St. Petersburg began in 1703 on islands and marshes where the Neva River flows to the Gulf of Finland and the Baltic Sea. Peter used forced labor. He had tens of thousands of peasants rounded up each year to work at the site. Most died from exhaustion, the weather, or starvation. Peter recruited foreign architects to design the city. He built palaces and government buildings, including a naval academy. St. Petersburg had a police force and lighted streets. Peter's grandson moved the court to Moscow during his reign, but Catherine the Great liked St. Petersburg. She had its embankments covered in granite, but regular flooding still occurred. A disastrous flood in 1824 caused great damage. The flood is depicted in Alexander Pushkin's poem "The Bronze Horseman." Today, St. Petersburg consists of about 40 islands connected by more than 300 bridges. Some 5 million people live there. It is the hometown of Russian president Vladimir Putin.

INTRODUCE & ENGAGE

BRAINSTORM GREAT LEADERSHIP

Invite students to think about leaders whom most people would consider great. Have students share their ideas about the achievements of great leaders. *(Possible examples: The U.S. Founding Fathers established a new nation; George Washington set the tone for the new U.S. presidency; Abraham Lincoln drafted the Emancipation Proclamation and united the nation after the Civil War.)* Tell students that in this lesson they will learn about two leaders considered great for their achievements but whose policies favored some people and oppressed most others.

TEACH

GUIDED DISCUSSION

1. **Summarize** How did Peter the Great use serfs to support his military campaigns? *(The serfs paid heavy taxes to support the army, and the sons of serfs were forced to fight in it. Peter used serfs to extend Russia's frontiers by wars against Sweden and Poland and to lay the groundwork for conquests of Muslim steppe peoples.)*

2. **Form and Support Opinions** Do you think that the reign of Peter the Great brought great advancement in Russia? Why or why not? *(Possible responses: Yes, because Peter worked to modernize Russia, expand its boundaries by upgrading the army, and improve education for military and civilian bureaucrats. OR No, because Peter forced people to dress his way to assert his absolute power, oppressed the serfs, and supported an educational system only for bureaucrats.)*

ANALYZE VISUALS

Direct students' attention to the photograph of St. Basil's Cathedral that appears in the lesson. Have students read the caption. **ASK:** Based on what you have learned about the architecture of different empires, what conclusions can you draw about the style of St. Basil's Cathedral? *(Possible responses may include resemblance to Byzantine architecture because of the domes, arches, and use of color. Responses may also include the mention of unusual features, such as the onion-like twists of the domes or upper floors formed of columns spaced tightly together. Responses overall may conclude that St. Basil's Cathedral is a unique blend of styles.)*

DIFFERENTIATE

INCLUSION

Understand Details in Photographs
Pair students with disabilities with students who can read the lesson aloud to them. Direct the partner without disabilities to describe in detail the photographs in the lesson. Encourage that partner to discuss the photographs in relation to the lesson content. When pairs have finished reading the lesson, you might want to have them work together to answer the Historical Thinking questions.

PRE-AP

Support a Position Ask students to decide whether or not Catherine the Great had no other choice except to impose harsher policies toward the serfs. Have students review the relevant paragraphs in the section. Instruct them to conduct online research to gather evidence about the lives of serfs in Catherine's time and opinions of historians on the subject. Tell students to take notes to construct an argument that supports their position and addresses the opposing viewpoint. Invite students to present their argument as a written or oral report.

See the Chapter Planner for more strategies for differentiation.

dome roofs were characteristic of Byzantine architecture as well, and St. Basil's Cathedral was built with red brick, probably inspired by Italian Renaissance architecture. Russian culture thus absorbed diverse influences, both from Europe to the west and Asia to the east.

REFORM AND REPRESSION UNDER CATHERINE THE GREAT

Catherine the Great was a German princess who married into the Romanov family. Her husband, Peter the Great's grandson, was overthrown in 1762, within a year of taking the throne. However, within hours of the coup, Catherine had herself declared empress. In a short time, she accumulated enough personal power to become one of the dominant figures of 18th-century Eurasian politics.

Catherine continued Russian expansion, adding approximately 200,000 square miles to the country. As Catherine consolidated control over vast new territories, she developed policies that benefited Russia while seeming to be tolerant of the cultures of conquered regions. Rather than encouraging Siberians to convert to the Russian Orthodox Church, she prevented the church from converting them. This policy benefited her regime because converts to Orthodoxy had tax protections, so too many converts meant diminished tax revenues. In Crimea, Catherine protected the rights of Muslims. She understood that the best way to maintain stability was to work with local Muslim leaders.

From the beginning of her rule, Catherine sought to reform Russia. She had studied the ideas of European philosophers, such as Voltaire, and hoped to reorganize the government using liberal ideas. She labored over issues such as the legal code, town planning, and agriculture. She also pushed for the education of both boys and girls, and she supported science and the arts. Although ending serfdom had been part of her plan for reform, Catherine needed the loyalty and service of the landowning nobles to carry out her reforms. In the end, she increased the nobility's power over the serfs, and even expanded serfdom into areas where peasants had previously been free.

Catherine shared Peter the Great's intention to make Russia a European state, and she adopted laws and attitudes that reflected that position. European demand for Russian grain increased, providing a profitable market for Russian landowners. To produce more grain, the Russian nobility made increasingly harsh demands on the serfs. These aristocrats, who lived in elegant townhouses and country estates, saw European luxuries as essential to their lifestyles, and they treated the serfs like slaves.

As the serfs' situation deteriorated, unrest led to rebellion. By the 1770s, rebels who promised an end to serfdom, taxation, and **conscription**—forced enrollment in the military—had gained a following. They looted estates and murdered nobles, but as they neared Moscow, their leader was captured and the rebellion was defeated. After she had crushed the rebels, Catherine tightened her grip on the populace, suppressing those who sought better treatment for the serfs, even though she had originally professed those same ideas.

This bronze statue of Peter the Great stands in Senate Square in St. Petersburg, surrounded by the buildings of the civil and religious governing bodies of pre-revolutionary Russia.

HISTORICAL THINKING

1. **READING CHECK** What did the Romanov tsars Peter the Great and Catherine the Great do to make Russia more European?

2. **ANALYZE LANGUAGE USE** What does the phrase "window on the West" mean with regard to the construction of St. Petersburg?

3. **COMPARE AND CONTRAST** How did Catherine the Great's policies toward newly conquered peoples contrast with her policies toward the serfs?

4. **MAKE PREDICTIONS** What problems do you think the situation with the serfs will create for Russia's future?

BACKGROUND FOR THE TEACHER

Catherine, the Great Collector Catherine the Great promoted Russian culture and avidly collected art. She referred to herself as a "glutton for art" and included the words "I love art" in an epitaph she wrote for herself years before she died. Catherine was determined to show Europeans that Russia was not culturally backward. Her art collection formed the basis of the Hermitage Museum, housed in the Winter Palace in St. Petersburg. Today, it is one of the world's great art museums and contains some 3 million works. Catherine collected thousands of paintings, including portrait paintings and miniatures, along with intaglios and cameos. She commissioned metalwork, porcelain, and glasswork for herself and her court. In imitation of Europe, she favored neoclassicism, or the styles of ancient Greece and Rome. Catherine used portraiture to enhance her royal image, a use of art that was current in Europe. She ordered artists to paint her portraits so that she appeared regal. To strengthen her relationship to Peter the Great's ideas, she commissioned the equestrian statue of Peter that stands in St. Petersburg's Senate Square. The French sculptor Étienne Falconet created the statue, and his assistant Marie-Anne Callot modeled the head. A commissioned sculpted portrait of Voltaire, by Marie-Ann Callot, is evidence of the support Catherine gave to female artists.

TEACH

GUIDED DISCUSSION

3. **Make Connections** How did the European demand for Russian grain affect the lives of Russian serfs? *(Grain was a profitable market for Russian landowners, and they wanted bigger yields. They made harsh demands on the serfs who worked the land like slaves. Bigger yields meant that the landowners could have more income for elegant homes and European luxuries.)*

4. **Make Inferences** How might her foreign birth have influenced Catherine's decision to honor Peter the Great and carry forward his ideas to make Russia like Europe? *(Possible responses: Catherine appreciated Europe because she was born there; she wanted to make herself appear a legitimate successor to the throne by aligning herself with Peter the Great and his ideas.)*

ANALYZE VISUALS

Direct students' attention to the photographs of the Winter Palace and statue of Peter the Great. **ASK:** Based on what you previously learned, what style is suggested by the columns on the Winter Palace and the clothing in which the sculptor depicted Peter the Great? *(Possible response: The columns suggest the influence of Greek and Roman architecture. The figure of Peter resembles the sculptures of important rulers of the Roman Empire.)*

ACTIVE OPTIONS

On Your Feet: Inside-Outside Circle Use the strategy to check students' understanding of Romanov rule. Direct students in the outer circle to pose questions such as the following: How did the Romanovs come to power? What formed the basis of Romanov revenues? Why did Peter the Great impose a European dress code? Why did Catherine the Great adopt different policies toward nobles, Siberians, Tatars, and serfs? Tell students in the inner circle to answer the questions. Then ask students to trade inside-outside roles.

| **NG Learning Framework: Investigate the Bronze Horseman**
ATTITUDE Curiosity
KNOWLEDGE Our Human Story

Direct students to search online for detailed information about the bronze statue of Peter the Great. Tell them that the statue is often referred to as the Bronze Horseman. Invite students to explore its origin, acquisition of the pedestal, meaning of the inscription, and significance of the outstretched arm and rearing horse. Have students report their information for class discussion.

HISTORICAL THINKING

ANSWERS

1. The nobility and court under Peter the Great removed their beards and wore European fashions. Peter's new capital in St. Petersburg was built using European architectural styles. During Catherine the Great's rule, Russia traded with Europe and the Russian aristocracy lived like Europeans in luxurious homes. Catherine hoped to reform Russia with enlightened European ideals, but she could not.

2. The phrase "window on the West" refers to a distinctly "European" city that would rival any of the other great cities in Europe.

3. Catherine allowed the newly conquered people to retain their culture and protected their rights. In contrast, she took away the rights of peasants and allowed the nobility to rule them more harshly. However, her policies toward both the serfs and the conquered people always served her own prosperity. The treatment of the serfs kept the support of the nobility, and by protecting the rights and cultural traditions of the conquered people, she maintained stability and profited from taxes.

4. The serfs might continue to rebel. They could eventually overthrow the tsars and gain control of Russia.

CRITICAL VIEWING Possible response: The styles contrast strongly except that both structures display arches, colorful exteriors, and peaked roofs. The Winter Palace is European in style, punctuated with windows and decorated with columns leading to a roof lined with sculptures. St. Basil's Cathedral above the first floor consists of column-like structures built tightly together and topped with twisted, onion-like domes.

Jewish, Tatar, and Armenian Diasporas

What would it take to convince you to move to a place with a completely different language and culture? Members of the Jewish, Armenian, and Tatar communities left their homes for a variety of reasons, often not by their own choice.

This portrait of Catherine the Great, was painted by Fedor Stepanovich Rokotov, c. 1770.

MEMBERS OF THE JEWISH COMMUNITY PETITION THE TSARINA

One of Catherine the Great's innovations was to invite **petitions**, or formal written requests, from her subjects. People who felt local and provincial officials were misusing their power believed the tsarina would surely correct the injustices if only she knew about them. Catherine encouraged this attitude and invited her subjects (serfs were not included) to submit petitions. One of these was submitted by a group of Jewish leaders in Belarus. You may recall that the Babylonian Exile, which lasted from 586 to 538 B.C.E., marked the beginning of the Jewish Diaspora, in which the Jewish people migrated to different locations around the world. The Jews in Belarus were known as *Ashkenazim* (ahsh-kuh-NAH-zuhm). They spoke Yiddish, a German-derived language mixed with Hebrew and, in the east, with words from Slavic languages. Members of the Ashkenazim were broadly educated. Many lived in peasant villages within the Russian Empire, while those living farther west were more likely to live in cities and engage in commerce. Many Ashkenazim lived apart from other religious groups, partly by their own preference and partly because of exclusion by Christians. They followed their own traditions and married within their own group. The European Jews remained culturally distinctive in their music, cuisine, folktales, and Yiddish language.

They both contributed to and borrowed from the majority communities. However, the Ashkenazim were vulnerable and insecure. In their petition to Catherine the Great, the Ashkenazim explained that after they joined the Russian Empire, they had been allowed to continue to invest in and run certain wholesale and retail businesses. However, a decree by the governor-general of Belarus forbade them from continuing these businesses. The petition explained that many Jews were left completely impoverished.

So many petitions flowed into St. Petersburg that it is unlikely that Catherine had time to read them, and the difficulties the Ashkenazim experienced were not resolved. Loss of business was just one result of the deep prejudices Jews faced. All across Europe, Jewish communities faced terrifying intimidation and abuse. They often suffered theft of property and sometimes even violent attacks from their Christian neighbors. You previously learned how Jews were attacked during the Crusades and how the Jews of Spain were expelled by Christian rulers in 1492.

THE TATARS

The nobility of a group of Muslim, Turkish-speaking people called the Tatars also petitioned Catherine the Great. In the 16th century, the Tatar home, the Kazan region, had been conquered by Ivan the Terrible. Ivan had slaughtered much of the Muslim population and forced many survivors to convert to Orthodox Christianity.

Catherine allowed the Tatars to build new mosques, and she accepted petitions from Tatar nobles. The petition of 1767 described insults Tatars had suffered based on their faith and rank, and they also requested that their region remain Muslim. Catherine initially allowed the Tatars some freedoms and control of their lands, but this didn't continue and Tatar peasants were forced into serfdom.

THE ARMENIAN DIASPORA

The Armenians, who originated in western Asia, are followers of an ancient Orthodox Christian faith. Like the Jews, their diaspora covered a wide area of Eurasia that included Russian and Ottoman lands. Many Armenians also lived in India and Iran. They had distinct Armenian neighborhoods in Constantinople, Jerusalem, Agra, Isfahan, and other cities.

Push and pull factors influenced Armenians to immigrate to places outside their homeland. **Pull factors** entice people to immigrate to new lands. In the late 1500s, the emperor Akbar I invited Armenian merchants to live in Mughal India. He understood that Armenians were skilled at handicrafts and commerce, so he created incentives to attract Armenians to India. He exempted them from paying taxes on the products they imported or exported. He also allowed them to move around India and conduct businesses in areas where other foreigners were not allowed.

Perhaps the biggest **push factor** that caused people to leave Armenia was its location. The Armenian homeland was bordered by the feuding Ottoman and Safavid empires. Partly to secure his border with the Ottomans, the Safavid shah Abbas I forced as many as 150,000 Armenians to move to a separate quarter of Isfahan. By moving Armenian merchants into Isfahan, Shah Abbas was able to advance Iran's silk trade. Although Armenians were forced to live away from their homeland, they were allowed to build churches and look after their own community affairs.

During the Romanov dynasty, many Armenians moved from Isfahan to Russia to take advantage of Russia's growing economy. Armenians were at the center of a commercial network stretching across the Indian Ocean. They had business interests all the way from the Mediterranean to the South China Sea.

HISTORICAL THINKING

1. **READING CHECK** Describe some of the abuses faced by the Jewish, Tatar, and Armenian people.

2. **COMPARE AND CONTRAST** How did the European Jews, Tatars, and Armenians differ from their neighbors?

3. **IDENTIFY** What are some of the push and pull factors that influenced Armenian migration?

OBJECTIVE
Describe the abuses faced by Jews, Tatars, and Armenians in their spread throughout Eurasia.

CRITICAL THINKING SKILLS FOR LESSON 3.3
- Compare and Contrast
- Identify
- Make Inferences
- Analyze Visuals

HISTORICAL THINKING FOR CHAPTER 16
What economic, political, and cultural impact did the rise of powerful land-based empires have across Eurasia?

Conquered peoples in Eurasia represented diverse cultures. Lesson 3.3 describes the different experiences and prejudices faced by the Jewish, Tatar, and Armenian cultural groups.

Student eEdition online
Additional content for this lesson, including a photograph, is available online.

BACKGROUND FOR THE TEACHER
The Armenian Diaspora The Armenians fared better than other groups once they reached Russia. Armenian merchants operated in Russia well before the reign of Peter the Great. They traded from Kazan, a city southeast of Moscow, and from Astrakhan on the Caspian Sea during the time of Ivan IV. Later, Armenians asked Peter the Great for permission to conduct trade from St. Petersburg, and he approved. Armenian merchants were settled in Russia by 1710. They built trade routes that brought European goods to Russia and gave Russians access to the European market. Peter recognized the importance of the Armenian presence in Russia and told his newly formed Senate to welcome Armenians and to encourage more to come. Soon thousands of Armenians came as part of the diaspora from Iran and the Ottoman Empire. The Armenians flourished during the reign of Catherine the Great. Catherine granted the St. Petersburg Armenians the right to construct their own church on Nevsky Prospekt, the main avenue. The Church of St. Catherine stands in St. Petersburg today.

INTRODUCE & ENGAGE

DISCUSS FORCED MIGRATION

Ask students to think about a time they transferred to a new school or moved to a different neighborhood. Did anyone make them feel unwelcome? Invite comments. Then have students consider whole populations forced to relocate and ask them to discuss examples of this that they know of or have heard of recently. Tell students that in this lesson they will learn about the dispersion of Jews, Tatars, and Armenians and their experiences in new locations.

TEACH

GUIDED DISCUSSION

1. **Compare and Contrast** How did the petition of the Jews in Belarus differ from the petition of the Tatars? *(Jewish business owners and investors petitioned to overrule a decree by the Belarus governor-general that forbade the continued operation of their businesses. The Tatar nobles described insults against them and their faith and asked that their region remain Muslim.)*

2. **Make Inferences** Why were the Jews treated worse than the Armenians who similarly operated useful businesses? *(Responses will vary but might include different places of origin. The Jews were from European areas where centuries-long prejudices existed against them, whereas the Armenians originated in western Asia and practiced Christianity in empires that were more tolerant of religious differences.)*

ANALYZE VISUALS

Have students study the portrait of Catherine the Great. **ASK:** What elements suggest that Catherine is a royal figure? *(Possible responses: Catherine is standing instead of sitting, which makes her appear more powerful. She wears an elaborate gown and is surrounded by elegant furnishings. She is painted from the perspective of someone looking up at her, which suggests that she is superior. She holds a scepter or rod in her right hand and points it as though issuing a command.)*

ACTIVE OPTIONS

On Your Feet: Think, Pair, Share Give students about five minutes to think about the following topic: How successful was Catherine the Great's innovation of inviting petitions from her subjects? Then have students form pairs and talk about the topic. After five minutes, invite volunteers from the pairs to share their evaluations with the class.

> **NG Learning Framework: Write a Profile**
> SKILL Collaboration
> KNOWLEDGE Our Human Story

Arrange students into small groups and instruct them to conduct research for a short profile of the Tatars in Russia. Suggest students begin with the reign of Catherine the Great. Have them explore the Tatar experience then and into the present day. Invite student groups to share their profiles.

DIFFERENTIATE

STRIVING READERS

Summarize Details Ask students to work in pairs. Assign a proficient student to each striving reader. Instruct pairs to review sections together and take notes of details about each cultural group. Encourage pairs to discuss their notes and use them to respond to the Historical Thinking questions.

PRE-AP

Analyze the Jewish Experience Have students investigate the decisions made by Catherine the Great for Jewish people. Tell students that many historians believe her decisions had a long-lasting impact. Direct students to conduct research that includes the later impact. Have students create a multimedia presentation with their findings.

See the Chapter Planner for more strategies for differentiation.

HISTORICAL THINKING

ANSWERS

1. Some Christians stole from or attacked Jews. Ivan the Terrible killed many in the Kazan region and forced survivors to become Christians. Under Catherine the Great, Tatar peasants became serfs. Safavid Shah Abbas I forced the Armenians to leave their homeland and move into Isfahan, Iran.

2. The European Jews and the Muslim Tatars were in predominantly Christian areas. The Armenians were Christians living among Muslims or Hindus. All three groups had their own languages and cultures in places with different languages and cultures.

3. The Armenians were pushed out of Armenia by the dangerous location of their homeland and by Shah Abbas I, who forced them to move to Isfahan. They were pulled to both India and Russia for economic benefits, including tax incentives in India and economic growth in Russia.

VOCABULARY

Match each of the following vocabulary words with its definition.

1. janissary
2. shah
3. mausoleum
4. entrepreneur
5. tundra
6. taiga
7. tsar
8. petition
9. push factor
10. pull factor

a. a king in Iran
b. a highly trained soldier and slave in the Ottoman army
c. an incentive that attracts people to a new country
d. land covered with evergreen trees in the far north
e. a formal written request
f. a condition that causes people to leave their country
g. a person who organizes and operates a business
h. a large tomb
i. treeless arctic plains
j. the ruler of imperial Russia

READING STRATEGY
DRAW CONCLUSIONS

When you draw conclusions, you make a judgment based on what you have read. Use a chart like this one to draw a conclusion about the qualities of effective leaders of land-based empires in Eurasia in the 17th and 18th centuries.

Leader	Details
Conclusion	

11. Which of these leaders strengthened their empires through tolerance of religious and cultural groups other than their own?

MAIN IDEAS

Answer the following questions. Support your answers with evidence from the chapter.

12. How did Çelebi fulfill the wishes of the Prophet Muhammad from his dream? LESSON 1.1

478 CHAPTER 16

13. How did Süleyman I treat communities of different religions once they became part of the Ottoman Empire? LESSON 1.2

14. In what ways was the Safavid society prosperous? LESSON 1.3

15. In what ways did the Ottoman Empire persist into the 17th and 18th centuries? LESSON 1.4

16. How were the Mughals different from most of their subjects in India? LESSON 2.1

17. How did the Qing prevent the Russians from expanding into China? LESSON 2.3

18. What was French philosopher Voltaire's opinion of Qianlong? Why did he hold this opinion? LESSON 2.4

19. How did the lives of women and samurai change during the Tokugawa shogunate? How did the Tokugawa respond to these changes? LESSON 2.5

20. How did Ivan IV centralize control of Russia? LESSON 3.1

21. Describe the condition of the serfs under Peter the Great and Catherine the Great. LESSON 3.2

HISTORICAL THINKING

Answer the following questions. Support your answers with evidence from the chapter.

22. **COMPARE AND CONTRAST** How did the Ottomans and the Safavids differ? How were they similar?

23. **ANALYZE CAUSE AND EFFECT** What pull factor did Akbar I use in India to entice immigrants to move into underdeveloped lands?

24. **SYNTHESIZE** What common difficulties did the Mughals in India and the Qing in China have in ruling their countries? How effective were they in dealing with these difficulties?

25. **DESCRIBE** In the Ottoman Empire, Christian children were enslaved to become janissaries. In Russia, the serfs were treated as slaves. Describe how the slaves were treated under each society.

Study the map of the Mughal Empire. Then answer the questions below.

26. What river formed a natural barrier to the north at the extent of the Mughal Empire in 1530?

27. What major bodies of water had the Mughal Empire expanded to by 1605?

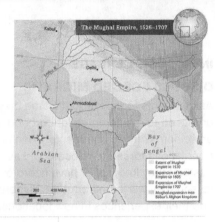

The Mughal Empire, 1526–1707

ANALYZE SOURCES

Matsuo Basho (1644–1694) was probably the most famous of all haiku poets. In this form of poetry, each haiku has 17 syllables in three unrhymed lines of 5, 7, and 5 syllables. In this poem, Basho describes common images from life in 17th-century Japan. Read the poem and answer the question that follows.

An ancient pond,

the frog leaps:

the silver plop and gurgle of water.

—Matsuo Basho, translated by Michael R. Burch

28. What universal, timeless theme is expressed in this haiku?

CONNECT TO YOUR LIFE

29. **INFORMATIVE** You've read about the ways that Ottoman, Safavid, Mughal, and Russian monarchs expressed their power and values through architecture. Research an impressive new building that has been completed in the last 10 years in the United States. Find out who paid for the building and how the building is meant to be used. What values and traditions does the style of the building express? Prepare an informative presentation with text and photos.

TIPS

* Reread the sections on architecture from this chapter.

* Research recent buildings in the United States. Choose a building you can visit, if possible, or choose one you find especially interesting.

* Identify the people or organizations that paid for the building. Find out about the architect and why he or she was chosen to design this building.

* Think about the goals for the building, both practical and symbolic. Do you think the building fulfills those goals? Why or why not?

* Conclude your presentation with a statement that sums up the values and traditions represented by this building.

Land-Based Empires of Eurasia 479

VOCABULARY ANSWERS

1. b
2. a
3. h
4. g
5. i
6. d
7. j
8. e
9. f
10. c

READING STRATEGY ANSWERS

Leader	Details
Süleyman I	strong military leader; supported ethnic diversity; built schools and mosques
Abbas I	built schools, mosques, roads; made Iran a cultural center; valued skill over heredity
Emperor Kangxi	shared knowledge of cannons and mathematics; expanded the empire; promoted farming
Catherine the Great	expanded Russia; practiced tolerance; promoted education
Conclusion Effective leaders must support their people and encourage education and freedom of culture and religion.	

11. Answers will vary. Sample answer: Süleyman the Magnificent, the Muslim Mughals, the Qing dynasty of China, and Catherine the Great of Russia all strengthened their empires through tolerance of the cultures of those they ruled, though the forms and motivations for toleration differed.

MAIN IDEAS ANSWERS

12. The Prophet Muhammed told him Çelebi would "travel through the whole world and become a marvel among men." Çelebi traveled longer distances than most men of his day, and he was invited to share his adventures with the sultan. He became a marvel and remains famous in Turkey.

13. He was tolerant and allowed them to continue their religions, manage their own affairs, and hold their own courts. However, they were required to remain loyal to him and to pay their taxes.

14. The Safavids conquered lands to gain territory and built many mosques, palaces, and public works projects. Their gardens were legendary, and their architecture and engineering were renowned. Their poetry influenced poets around the world. They traded in expensive silk, carpets, and ceramics.

15. They finally defeated the Austrians and were able to defend themselves against outside powers. The government remained stable after an assassination of a sultan. They continued to create beautiful art.

16. The Mughals were Muslim and from Central Asia while the majority of the Indian populous were Hindi.

17. They agreed to a treaty with the Russians that recognized Russian claims west of Mongolia as long as the Russians disbanded settlements to the east.

18. Voltaire held Qianlong in very high regard. He never met him, but stories coming out of China and Qianlong's writing suggested to Voltaire that Qianlong was a talented writer, poet, and philosopher who ruled justly over the most advanced nation on Earth.

19. Women began to write literature, gain economic mobility, and participate in theater. Samurai patronized the arts, established schools, and wrote Confucian treatises. The Tokugawa were uncomfortable with changes to society, so they ordered people to conform to traditional ways.

20. The people were afraid of chaos and insecurity, so they allowed Ivan IV to become an absolute monarch in the hopes that he would maintain order. He extended Russian borders and protected the country from invasion, but he was a brutal leader.

21. They were essentially slaves who were bound to their villages and the nobility. Their taxes paid for Peter's expansions of the borders. Catherine hoped to improve life for the serfs, but instead she sought the support of nobility and the serfs were treated even worse. Many peasants, who were previously free, lost their freedoms under Catherine.

HISTORICAL THINKING ANSWERS

22. They were both Turkic and Muslim. The Safavids were Shiite Muslims and settled in Persia (Iran). The Ottomans were Sunni Muslims and settled in the area around the Mediterranean and Black seas.

23. He gave immigrants tax exemptions for moving into the area and cultivating the land.

24. The Mughals and the Qing had conquered countries with cultures different from their own. The Mughals were Muslims ruling over a population of Hindis. The Qing were Manchus ruling over Chinese. Both were effective in dealing with their differences. The Mughals allowed religious freedom so that the Hindis wouldn't rebel. The Qing supported and continued previous policies and beliefs such as Confucianism and merit-based advancement.

25. In the Ottoman Empire, the janissaries were taken as children and left with no family. They were then highly trained and treated as elite soldiers. Some were even members of the sultan's court. They were completely loyal to the sultan because they knew they had no family to fall back on. The serfs had no rights and were forced to work the land under the Russian nobility. They paid taxes and funded Russia's expansion. Under Catherine the Great, peasants in newly gained territories lost their freedoms and automatically became serfs.

INTERPRET VISUALS ANSWERS

26. the Indus River
27. the Arabian Sea and Bay of Bengal

ANALYZE SOURCES ANSWER

28. The haiku expresses the universal theme of the natural world through its description of the frog leaping into the ancient pond. It is a timeless observance enhanced by the sounds of the "silver plop" and "gurgle of water."

CONNECT TO YOUR LIFE ANSWER

29. Students' informative presentations will vary but should contain a thesis; develop the thesis with relevant, supporting details with both text and photos; and provide a concluding statement that sums up the values and traditions represented in the building they selected for their presentation.

UNIT 6

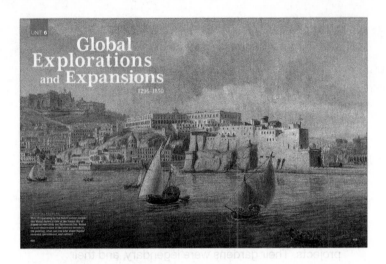

STRATEGY ❶

Use a K-W-L Chart

Arrange students in pairs and provide them with a K-W-L Chart. Have partners brainstorm what they know about the topic of the lesson and add their ideas to the first column of the chart. Then invite students to page through the lesson and preview headings, images, and maps. In the second column, tell students to write at least three questions they have about the topic based on their preview. After they have read the lesson, remind students to write the answers to their questions and other information they learned in the third column. Encourage them to keep their charts for each lesson to help them review the entire chapter.

K What Do I Know	W What Do I Want To Learn?	L What Did I Learn?

Use with All Lessons

STRATEGY ❷

Focus on Main Ideas

Tell students to locate the Main Idea statement at the beginning of each lesson. Explain that these statements summarize the important ideas of the lessons and will be useful for helping them focus on what matters most in the text.

Use with All Lessons *Throughout the chapter, help students get in the habit of using the Main Idea statements to set a purpose for reading.*

STRATEGY ❸

Turn Titles into Questions

Before reading each lesson, display a question based on the lesson title. After reading the lesson, have students work in pairs to answer the question with evidence from the text.

Lesson 1.2 Who made conquests in the Americas?

Lesson 1.4 What was the Columbian Exchange?

Lesson 3.1 Where in the Americas did the Spanish build an empire?

Use with Lessons 1.2, 1.4, and 3.1 *Additional option: Have students choose another lesson from the chapter and rewrite its title as a question. Students can trade questions with a partner and work on answering them after reading the chosen lesson.*

STRATEGY ❶

Preview Maps

Preview maps with students. Remind them that maps show different kinds of information. For example, political maps show regional boundaries and capitals. Physical maps highlight geographic features such as mountain ranges and bodies of water. Point out that the maps in this chapter are thematic maps, which show specialized information. The map in Lesson 1.1, for example, shows the routes of Christopher Columbus's voyages. Tell students that the map's title and key indicate the type of information shown.

Use with Lessons 1.1, 1.4, 2.1, 3.1, and 3.4

STRATEGY ❷

Provide Terms and Names on Audio

Decide which of the terms and names in the chapter are most important for mastery and have a volunteer record the pronunciations and a short sentence defining each word. Encourage students to listen to the recording as often as necessary.

Use with All Lessons *You might also use the recordings to quiz students on their mastery of the terms. Play one definition at a time from the recording and ask students to identify the term or name described.*

ENGLISH LANGUAGE LEARNERS

STRATEGY ❶
Prep Before Reading
Encourage students at **All Proficiencies** to use the PREP strategy to prepare for reading. Write this acrostic on the board:

Preview the title.
Read Main Idea statement.
Examine visuals.
Predict what you will learn.

Use with All Lessons *Encourage students at the* ***Beginning*** *level to ask questions if they have trouble writing a prediction. Students at the* ***Advanced*** *level may be able to help.*

STRATEGY ❷
Look for Cognates
Suggest that as students read they look for words that are similar in spelling and meaning to words in their home language. For each word they identify, have students of **All Proficiencies** make a vocabulary card with the English word and definition on one side and the word and definition in their home language on the other side. Encourage them to note any differences in the meanings of the two words.

Use with All Lessons *For example, in Lesson 1.1, the words* expedition, route, compass, explore, *and* colony *have cognates in Spanish:* expedición, ruta, compás, explorar, colonia.

STRATEGY ❸
Review Transitional Words
To help students put events in chronological order and summarize what they read. Write these transitional words on the board: *first, next, then, also, while, later, earlier, meanwhile, whenever, simultaneously, during, following, before, afterward,* and *finally.* Direct students at the **Beginning** and **Intermediate** levels to work together to write a series of sentences that tell what happens in each lesson. Encourage them to add transitional words to their sentences to tell about the time order of events. Prompt students at the **Advanced** level to construct a paragraph that summarizes the lesson. Encourage them to use a variety of transitional words and to vary their sentence structure.

Use with All Lessons

GIFTED & TALENTED

STRATEGY ❶
Present a Television Documentary
Have students split into small groups to conduct research about Spanish missions in the Americas. Ask them to choose a specific mission and present a short television-style documentary about it. Tell students to include information on the mission's founders, its history, its present-day uses, and its architecture, using images if available. Invite groups to present their documentaries to the class.

Use with Lesson 3.1

STRATEGY ❷
Teach a Class
Have students choose one of the lessons and prepare to teach a class on it. Students should prepare questions to ask the class and be ready to answer classmates' questions as well. Encourage students to use visual or audio materials in their teaching.

Use with All Lessons *Provide students with an appropriate time limit for their teaching presentations.*

PRE-AP

STRATEGY ❶
Form a Thesis
Have students select one of the lessons from the chapter and develop a thesis around one of its related topics. Remind students that the thesis statement must make a claim they can support with evidence from the lesson, chapter, or outside source.

Use with All Lessons

STRATEGY ❷
Create an Annotated Time Line
Have students create and annotate a time line for the explorers and conquerors discussed in the chapter. Time lines may include dates or date ranges for expeditions, conquests, the founding of different settlements, and other political or religious events. Prompt students to illustrate their time lines with images.

Use with All Lessons

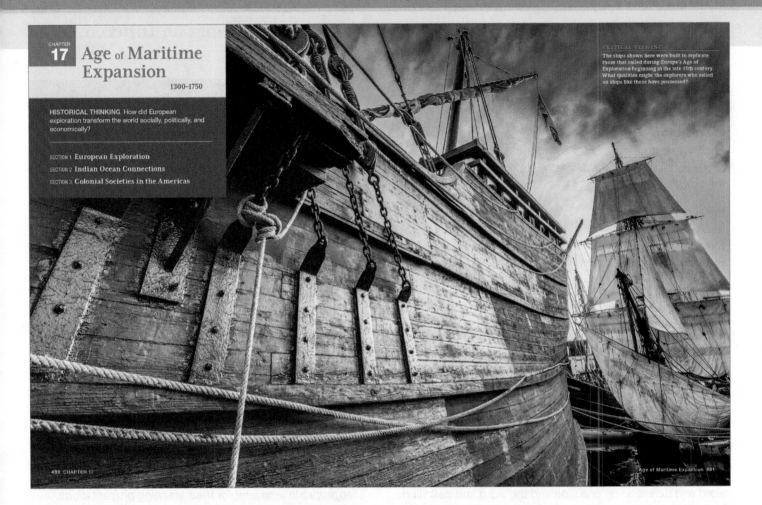

HISTORICAL THINKING How did European exploration transform the world socially, politically, and economically?

SECTION 1 **European Exploration**

SECTION 2 **Indian Ocean Connections**

SECTION 3 **Colonial Societies in the Americas**

CRITICAL VIEWING The ships shown here were built to replicate those that sailed during Europe's Age of Exploration beginning in the late 15th century. What qualities might the explorers who sailed on ships like these have possessed?

INTRODUCE THE PHOTOGRAPH

EUROPEAN SHIPS

Have students examine the photograph of the replicas of 15th-century European ships. **ASK:** What might life have been like during a transatlantic journey on one of these ships? *(Possible response: Life would have been difficult and uncomfortable, living in cramped quarters with limited access to food and clean water.)* If you had lived during this time period, would you have considered sailing on one of these ships? Why or why not? *(Possible response: yes, because of the possibility of adventure and riches in the New World)*

SHARE BACKGROUND

Maritime Life The life of a sailor in the Age of Exploration was grueling. Conditions on a ship were dirty, cramped, and dark below deck, where low ceilings made it difficult to stand. Work on the ship was also tough. Some tasks, such as climbing up to tie the sails, were extremely dangerous. There was barely any safety equipment to prevent a fall, and falling meant certain death. Hierarchies were strictly enforced onboard. While there are few records of crew members receiving punishments, disobeying an officer could result in physical mutilation. Rations were scarce, and if a ship ran out of clean water, its crew would drink ale. Many sailors also had to contend with pirates who preyed on ships traveling to and from South America.

CRITICAL VIEWING Answers will vary. Possible response: daring, reckless, adventurous, brave, strong, foolhardy

HISTORICAL THINKING QUESTION

How did European exploration transform the world socially, politically, and economically?

Brainstorm Activity: Predict Content This activity prompts students to draw on their prior knowledge and make predictions about the ways in which European exploration transformed the world socially, politically, and economically. Divide the class into three groups and assign each one the following questions:

Group 1 How do you think indigenous peoples were affected by the explorers' arrival? Did their lives improve or worsen as a result of the explorations?

Group 2 What do you think happened when explorers claimed a region for their country? Did the explorers allow leaders to remain in power or were the leaders replaced?

Group 3 Who do you think benefited financially from European exploration? Who do you think suffered financially?

Regroup students so each new grouping has at least one member from each original group. Have students share their ideas and predictions.

KEY DATES FOR CHAPTER 17

1419	Prince Harry of Portugal establishes a navigation school.
1492	Christopher Columbus embarks on his first expedition.
1497	Vasco da Gama sails around southern Africa from Portugal to India.
1519	Hernan Cortés invades the Aztec Empire in Mexico.
1532	Francisco Pizzaro invades the Inca Empire in Peru.
1602	The Dutch East India Company is established.
1607	English colonists establish Jamestown in Virginia.
1614	The Dutch establish a trading post that will eventually become New York City.
1754	The French and Indian War begins.

INTRODUCE THE READING STRATEGY

ANALYZE CAUSE AND EFFECT

Explain to students that analyzing cause and effect can help them understand the complexity of historical events. Turn to the Chapter Review and preview the cause-and-effect chain with students. As they read the chapter, have students analyze the causes and effects of European exploration and colonization in the Americas and around the world.

INTRODUCE CHAPTER VOCABULARY

KEY VOCABULARY

SECTION 1

caravel	circumnavigate	Columbian Exchange
mercantilism	conquistador	

SECTION 2

capitalism	joint-stock company	Northwest Passage

SECTION 3

encomienda	hacienda	indentured servant
mestizo	viceroy	viceroyalty

WORD MAP

As students read the chapter, ask them to complete a Word Map for each Key Vocabulary word. Tell them to write the word in the oval and, as they encounter the word in the chapter, complete the Word Map. Model an example using the graphic organizer below.

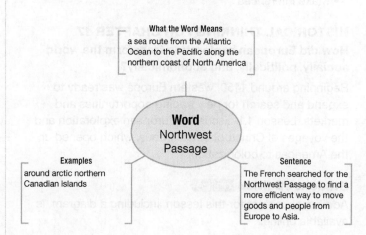

What the Word Means
a sea route from the Atlantic Ocean to the Pacific along the northern coast of North America

Word
Northwest Passage

Examples
around arctic northern Canadian islands

Sentence
The French searched for the Northwest Passage to find a more efficient way to move goods and people from Europe to Asia.

Voyages of Discovery

"Here are dragons." "Land unknown." These warnings sometimes labeled unexplored parts of the world on early European maps and globes. A voyage to these places could be filled with danger. But by the mid-1400s, some navigators were ready to take their chances.

GOLD, GOD, AND GLORY

Around 1450, western Europe was ready to expand. The Renaissance had inspired curiosity about the world, and merchants were eager to find new trading opportunities and markets. But, as you know, the Ottoman Empire controlled the trade routes to Asia where many of the luxury items Europeans desired, including silk and spices, came from. To secure a share of this profitable trade, Europe's leaders and merchants sponsored numerous sailing expeditions to search for an alternative sea route to Asia.

Remember Zheng He, the Chinese admiral who led maritime expeditions to ports in Asia and Africa during the Ming dynasty? His fleets of treasure ships traveled along well-known trade routes across the Indian Ocean. However, between about 1450 and 1750, a period sometimes called the Age of Exploration, European navigators explored largely uncharted waters in the Atlantic. Their explorations were motivated by factors that historians often refer to as "gold, God, and glory." "Gold" represents the profits merchants hoped to gain through the trade of spices, slaves, and precious metals. "God" indicates the European desire to spread Christianity and seize Muslim lands. "Glory" denotes the drive to create an empire and gain political power.

Portugal took the lead in European exploration. In 1419, **Prince Henry the Navigator**, the son of Portugal's king, established a navigation school on the Atlantic coast

The Voyages of Christopher Columbus, 1492–1504

(map showing EUROPE, SPAIN, NORTH AMERICA, ATLANTIC OCEAN, Florida, Bahamas, Hispaniola, Caribbean Sea, PACIFIC OCEAN, SOUTH AMERICA, BRAZIL, AFRICA with routes labeled 1492–1493, 1493–1496, 1498–1500, 1502–1504, Line of Demarcation)

in Sagres, Portugal. There, sailors learned to navigate a course by the stars and by using technological tools such as the magnetic compass and the astrolabe and quadrant, devices for measuring latitude that had been borrowed from Arab prototypes. They also learned shipbuilding and, in particular, how to build a **caravel**. The caravel was a light ship with triangular sails and was also borrowed from Arab mariners. Caravels were quick, easy to maneuver, and could sail into the wind, which earlier European ships could not do.

CHRISTOPHER COLUMBUS

Italian navigator **Christopher Columbus** used caravels during his historic voyage to the Americas. He thought he could find a faster sea route to Asia by sailing west across the Atlantic Ocean. So, in the 1480s, Columbus

OCTOBER 12, 1492

When land was sighted on October 12, Columbus must have been relieved. The voyage had taken longer than expected, and his crew was threatening mutiny. Convinced he had reached Asia, Columbus called the local Carib and Taino people he encountered there "Indians." But Columbus had greatly underestimated Earth's circumference and, as a result, the distance from Europe to Asia. So he unexpectedly found an area unknown to Europeans: the Americas.

CRITICAL VIEWING American artist John Vanderlyn's 1846 painting, *Landing of Columbus*, depicts a romanticized view of the explorer upon his arrival in the West Indies. Members of Columbus's crew express varying emotions and reactions, while local inhabitants watch them warily from behind a tree. How do the figures in the painting convey the motivating factors of gold, God, and glory?

petitioned both the Spanish and the Portuguese monarchs to fund his voyage, but they rejected his proposal. Finally, in 1492, King Ferdinand and Queen Isabella of Spain agreed. You may remember that these monarchs expelled thousands of Jews and Muslims from Spain and Portugal that same year. Spain also conquered the kingdom of Granada in 1492, which helped Ferdinand and Isabella finance Columbus's expeditions.

Columbus departed Spain on August 3, 1492, with three ships, the *Niña*, the *Pinta*, and the *Santa María*. In October, he and his fleet arrived in the Bahamas, off the coast of Florida. From there, Columbus sailed to the islands of the Caribbean—believing the entire time he was exploring islands south of China—and claimed them for Spain. Meanwhile, Ferdinand and Isabella petitioned the pope to allow them to colonize the lands Columbus seized for Spain. Spain's economy was

based on **mercantilism**, a system in which government protects and regulates trade to create wealth at the expense of rival powers. Under this system, the Spanish would maintain the sole right to trade with their colonies.

But Portugal competed with Spain over who would control the lands. In 1494, the two countries agreed to the **Treaty of Tordesillas** (tawr-day-SEE-yahs), which established a boundary, called the **Line of Demarcation**, that passed vertically through the Atlantic Ocean and Brazil. Portugal gained possession of the easterly lands, including Brazil, while Spain would receive any newly encountered lands to the west.

Columbus made three more voyages to the Caribbean islands. Although he didn't find a route to Asia or the riches he dreamed of, he did open up a "new world" to European exploration and colonization. Spain would be the first to capitalize on the opportunities it provided.

HISTORICAL THINKING

1. **READING CHECK** What did sailors learn in Prince Henry's school in Portugal?

2. **ANALYZE CAUSE AND EFFECT** What led Europeans to explore the Atlantic between 1450 and 1750?

3. **INTERPRET MAPS** Why do you think Columbus assumed he had sailed to Asia?

PLAN: 2-PAGE LESSON

OBJECTIVE
Describe the European voyages of exploration that set off to discover a sea route to Asia.

CRITICAL THINKING SKILLS FOR LESSON 1.1
- Analyze Cause and Effect
- Interpret Maps
- Identify Main Ideas and Details
- Make Inferences

HISTORICAL THINKING FOR CHAPTER 17
How did European exploration transform the world socially, politically, and economically?

Beginning around 1450, western Europe was ready to expand and search for new trading opportunities and markets. Lesson 1.1 discusses European exploration and the voyages of Christopher Columbus, which opened up the Americas to colonization.

Student eEdition online
Additional content for this lesson, including a diagram, is available online.

BACKGROUND FOR THE TEACHER

Christopher Columbus's Voyages When Columbus landed on Hispaniola on his first voyage, he established a small settlement of Europeans. When he returned on his second voyage, he learned that the settlement had been destroyed and its people killed by the Taino, indigenous people of the island. Columbus left some of his crew behind to rebuild the settlement, along with hundreds of enslaved Taino. The explorer sailed to Spain with about 500 other Taino to give to Queen Isabella—instead of the gold he hadn't been able to find in the Americas. Isabella was angered by the gesture, however, and had Columbus take them back. He found the Hispaniola settlers in revolt on his third voyage. As a result of his mismanagement, Columbus was arrested and sent back to Spain in chains. His fourth and final voyage also failed to uncover any riches, and he returned home empty-handed. Columbus died in 1506, still believing that he had sailed to Asia.

INTRODUCE & ENGAGE

MAKE CONNECTIONS

Discuss with students the kinds of explorations that are done today. Students might point to the exploration of space or underwater explorations. Ask students why they think such explorations are undertaken and what risks and benefits might result from the expeditions. Write students' responses on the board. Tell students that in this lesson they will learn about European explorations of the world in the 1400s.

TEACH

GUIDED DISCUSSION

1. **Identify Main Ideas and Details** How did the Renaissance spur Europeans' interest in exploration? *(Trade with other parts of the world became more prevalent during the Renaissance, and Europeans were looking for new trade routes and to find greater riches. Exposure to cultures and ideas from around the world also sparked Europeans' curiosity.)*

2. **Make Inferences** How did Christopher Columbus and Spain's rulers seem to view the indigenous people in the Americas? *(Possible response: They believed the indigenous people had no rights and that Columbus and Spain could claim any land that was found.)*

ANALYZE CAUSE AND EFFECT

Ask students to consider the events in Spain that led to Christopher Columbus's voyages. **ASK:** What aspects of the political climate in Spain caused Ferdinand and Isabella to finance Christopher Columbus's voyages? *(Possible responses: Spain's additional wealth from conquering Granada; Spain's mercantile economic system)*

ACTIVE OPTIONS

On Your Feet: Three-Step Interview Instruct pairs to read the sidebar "October 12, 1492" on Columbus's arrival in the Americas and consider the difficulties the crew faced during the voyage. Have Student A interview Student B about the topic, and then have them reverse roles. After the interviews, invite partners to share their thoughts and ideas with the class.

> **NG Learning Framework: Learn About GPS in Navigation**
> ATTITUDE Curiosity
> SKILL Collaboration

Have students review the technological advances that improved navigation in Europe in the 1400s, including the astrolabe, quadrant, and magnetic compass. Then have them work with partners to research the use of the Global Positioning System (GPS) in navigations on land, sea, and in space. Have students collaborate to write a brief description of this modern navigation system and share their reports with the rest of the class.

DIFFERENTIATE

STRIVING READERS

Summarize Arrange students in pairs and have them take notes as they read each of the lesson's two sections. After they have completed taking notes, guide students to review their notes and create a summary for each section. Then have students write a summary for the whole lesson.

PRE-AP

Write an Opinion Piece Ask students to do additional research on the technological advancements that led to European exploration. Then have them use that information and the information in the lesson to write an opinion piece on which technological advancement was the most important to European exploration. Have students share their opinion pieces with the class.

See the Chapter Planner for more strategies for differentiation.

HISTORICAL THINKING

ANSWERS

1. They learned to navigate a course by the stars and by using the astrolabe, quadrant, and magnetic compass. They also learned to build ships, including the caravel.

2. gold, God, and glory

3. Answers will vary. Possible response: He thought the first landmass he would encounter after sailing from Europe would be Asia. He didn't know the Americas existed.

CRITICAL VIEWING Answers will vary. Possible response: Some crew members seem to be searching for gold on the ground; Columbus raises his eyes heavenward, and others hold crosses; Columbus and others carry Spanish flags and banners.

Conquests in the Americas

An uneven fight isn't necessarily determined by numbers. Relatively small Spanish forces—but armed with the latest military technology (and, unknowingly, deadly diseases)—were able to bring the two most powerful empires in the Americas to their knees.

CORTÉS AND THE AZTEC

As Europeans continued their exploration of the Western Hemisphere, they realized that Columbus had not reached Asia but rather lands they would call *America*. After the Treaty of Tordesillas divided these lands, Spanish navigators were quick to explore their new territory. In 1513, **Vasco Núñez Balboa** crossed through Panama with his crew, and they became the first Europeans to see the Pacific Ocean. Balboa claimed everything he saw for Spain. About six years later, **Ferdinand Magellan** led an expedition that would be the first to **circumnavigate**, or travel all around, the world.

By 1549, Spain had conquered lands that extended south to Chile, north to Florida, and west to California. The Spanish soldiers and adventurers who led the conquest of the Americas came to be called **conquistadors** (kahn-KEE-stuh-dawrz). One of the most successful of the conquistadors was **Hernán Cortés**, who launched an invasion of Mexico in 1519 with about 500 men.

After landing on the coast of Mexico, Cortés learned of the gold-rich Aztec Empire and marched inland to conquer it. On the way to the Aztec capital of

CRITICAL VIEWING This mural (painted at a later date) depicts the 1519 meeting of Spanish leader Hernán Cortés and Aztec ruler Moctezuma in Tenochtitlán. Cortés, riding a white horse, appears on the right, while Moctezuma, on the left, is carried by his servants. How does the portrayal of the Spanish soldiers compare with that of the Aztec?

In 1547, Spanish historian Bernardino de Sahagún interviewed people who had witnessed the invasion of Mexico by Cortés and his army. In the following excerpt from one of those interviews, an eyewitness describes Moctezuma's amazement and terror when he saw the conquistadors' weapons.

PRIMARY SOURCE

It especially made him faint when he heard how the guns went off at the Spaniards' command, sounding like thunder. . . . And when it went off, something like a ball came out from inside, and fire went showering and spitting out. . . . And if they shot at a hill, it seemed to crumble and come apart. . . . Their war gear was all iron. They clothed their bodies in iron, they put iron on their heads, their swords were iron. . . . And their deer [horses] that carried them were as tall as the roof.

—from *General History of the Things of New Spain*, by Bernardino de Sahagún, 1569

Tenochtitlán, he recruited allies from some local societies who were unhappy with Aztec rule, as well as the Aztec practice of human sacrifice. A key role in the campaign was played by a young Nahua-speaking woman known as La Malinche, who learned Spanish after joining Cortés's troops and served as his translator.

The Aztec ruler Moctezuma received the Spanish courteously while Aztec officials debated what to do. They were intimidated by the Spanish who, though few in number, were armed with steel weapons, cannons, and horses—all unknown to the Aztec. Also, the bearded and light-skinned Cortés seemed to resemble their feather-serpent god Quetzalcoatl, who, according to legend, had left long ago but promised to return. Cortés used Moctezuma's hesitation against him. He seized the king and forced the Aztec to fight.

Cortés demanded and received gold and other treasure but could not hold onto Tenochtitlán. After a series of bloody battles, Cortés finally laid siege to the magnificent capital city in 1521. The Aztec fought fiercely, but they were weakened by smallpox, a deadly disease brought to the Americas by the Spanish. In the end, Cortés and his army destroyed Tenochtitlán. Spain would eventually build Mexico City on its ruins.

PIZARRO AND THE INCA

Smallpox also played a role in the Spanish conquest of the Inca. In the 1520s, the conquistador **Francisco Pizarro** set off for South America and the gold and silver of the Inca Empire. Like Cortés, Pizarro and his army of about 200 men had the advantage of superior weapons and horses. And the Inca had been weakened by a deadly smallpox epidemic before Pizarro arrived. In addition, a bitter civil war had divided the ruling dynasty. In 1532, the newly appointed Inca emperor, **Atahualpa** (ah-tuh-WAHL-puh), invited Pizarro and his soldiers to a meeting in the northern part of present-day Peru.

Atahualpa, accompanied by about 5,000 of his warriors, received the Spaniards peacefully. He and Pizarro exchanged gifts, and the Inca ruler probably felt safe. But then Pizarro's men opened fire on the mostly unarmed Inca and took Atahualpa prisoner. The Inca ruler offered his captors one room filled with gold and two filled with silver in exchange for his release. Pizarro took the treasure and then executed Atahualpa. The highly centralized Inca Empire began to disintegrate.

The Inca in other parts of the empire continued to resist the Spanish until 1572, when the last Inca ruler was executed. Through military conquest, Spain built one of the richest and most powerful empires in the world in the 1500s.

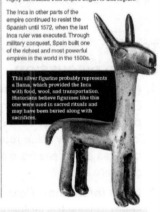

This silver figurine probably represents a llama, which provided the Inca with food, wool, and transportation. Historians believe figurines like this one were used in sacred rituals and may have been buried along with sacrifices.

HISTORICAL THINKING

1. **READING CHECK** Who were the conquistadors?

2. **COMPARE AND CONTRAST** How was Cortés's conquest of the Aztec similar to Pizarro's conquest of the Inca?

3. **ANALYZE SOURCES** What weapons and equipment does the eyewitness describe in the excerpt?

PLAN: 2-PAGE LESSON

OBJECTIVE

Explain how Spain invaded the Americas in the 1500s and conquered the Aztec and Inca empires.

CRITICAL THINKING SKILLS FOR LESSON 1.2

- Compare and Contrast
- Analyze Sources
- Explain
- Analyze Cause and Effect
- Analyze Visuals

HISTORICAL THINKING FOR CHAPTER 17

How did European exploration transform the world socially, politically, and economically?

Christopher Columbus's expeditions to the Americas led to further explorations by Spain. Lesson 1.2 explains how relatively small numbers of Spanish conquerors defeated the powerful Aztec and Inca empires and changed the power structure in much of the Americas.

Student eEdition online

Additional content for this lesson, including an image gallery, is available online.

BACKGROUND FOR THE TEACHER

Tenochtitlán Tenochtitlán, the capital of the Aztec Empire, was located on the site of present-day Mexico City. It was founded in 1325 in the marshes of Lake Texcoco. The city was surrounded by floating gardens called *chinampas*, on which produce for the city's food supply was grown. The city covered about five square miles and was joined to the mainland by several causeways. By 1519, when the Spanish launched their invasion of Mexico, Tenochtitlán's population was estimated to be about 400,000 people. In addition to the hundreds of temples, the palace of the Aztec emperor Moctezuma was also found in Tenochtitlán. The palace was said to have consisted of 300 rooms. The Spanish destroyed the city in 1521.

INTRODUCE & ENGAGE

BRAINSTORM A LIST

Have students brainstorm tactics that leaders might take to protect their people from enemies. Encourage students to consider such factors as population size, military strength, wealth, negotiating ability, and alliances. **ASK:** What might help a smaller fighting force overcome a larger one? *(Possible response: superior weaponry or alliances with other groups)* Explain that in this lesson students will learn what happened when Spanish explorers invaded the Aztec and Inca empires.

TEACH

GUIDED DISCUSSION

1. **Explain** Why did Aztec leaders hesitate to make a decision about how to react to the Spanish? *(The Aztec were intimidated by the explorers' unfamiliar weapons and technology. Cortés also resembled an Aztec god who had left but promised to return.)*

2. **Analyze Cause and Effect** What factors helped bring about the fall of the Inca Empire? *(A civil war had divided the empire, and the people were weakened by a smallpox epidemic.)*

ANALYZE VISUALS

Invite students to look through the Inca Gold and Silver image gallery (available in the Student eEdition) or to observe the silver llama and read the caption. **ASK:** Other than monetary value, why might these pieces have been valuable to the Inca? *(Possible response: The pieces represent aspects of their culture and society.)*

ACTIVE OPTIONS

On Your Feet: Team Word Webbing Organize students into groups of four, and provide each team with a single large piece of paper. Give each student a different colored marker. Tell students that they will be jotting down notes about the Spanish conquest of the Americas on the web. Each student should begin by adding to the part of the web nearest him or her. On a signal, have students rotate the paper and add to the nearest part again.

> **NG Learning Framework: Find Facts on Historical Figures**
> SKILL Communication
> KNOWLEDGE Our Human Story

Have students select one of the historical figures in this lesson. Instruct them to use information from the lesson and additional source material to uncover at least five new facts about their subject. Then have students gather in small groups to share the information they found.

DIFFERENTIATE

INCLUSION

Understand a Primary Source Pair a proficient reader with one who is not and have them read the Primary Source together. Encourage them to pay particular attention to the comparisons in the excerpt and work together to describe them in their own words.

GIFTED & TALENTED

Conduct an Interview Have students imagine they are news broadcasters covering the Spanish conquest of the Americas. Have students work with partners to create an interview with Hernán Cortés, Francisco Pizarro, or Atahualpa. Student partners should develop questions to ask the interviewee. Then have each pair present their interviews to the class.

See the Chapter Planner for more strategies for differentiation.

HISTORICAL THINKING

ANSWERS

1. the Spanish soldiers and adventurers who led the conquest of the Americas

2. Answers will vary. Possible response: Both had small forces and superior weapons and horses; both came looking for riches; both were merciless in dealing with the native peoples.

3. The eyewitness describes the cannon fire, the armor and helmets worn by Cortés and his men, and their huge horses.

CRITICAL VIEWING Answers will vary. Possible response: There are fewer Spanish than Aztec; the Spanish are much more heavily armed; some of the Spanish soldiers are on horseback; both appear a bit wary.

Math Against Malaria

"Science is infectious." –Pardis Sabeti

Pardis Sabeti (above) is a musician, teacher, volleyball player, and research scientist who specializes in the study of infectious diseases. She divides much of her time between working at Harvard University and collecting virus samples in West Africa. Shown here in the genome center at the Broad Institute of MIT and Harvard, Sabeti collaborates with colleagues all over the world to prevent major outbreaks of deadly diseases.

Four of these red blood cells (left) are healthy, but the other two, tinged with yellow, have been infected with malaria. The infection began when a malaria-carrying mosquito bit its victim and the malaria parasite entered the bloodstream. Sabeti believes the microbes that cause malaria and other infectious diseases are continually evolving in a struggle to survive human defenses.

486 CHAPTER 17

It wasn't that long ago that the concept of an epidemic killing a million people seemed like ancient history. However, the 2019 coronavirus outbreak changed everything. Just the mention of a novel, or new, virus can send shivers down the spines of health officials throughout the world. But the difference between today and the past is that modern science can limit and sometimes even prevent the spread of diseases. National Geographic Explorer Pardis Sabeti uses mathematics in her battle against diseases, including malaria.

MAIN IDEA Scientist Pardis Sabeti uses her math skills to understand epidemics.

UNDERSTANDING DISEASE

As you have read, the conquistadors' cannons helped them destroy the powerful Aztec and Inca empires. But the conquistadors had a secret weapon, unknown even to them: smallpox. The ability of European invaders to conquer the Americas had as much to do with deadly diseases as it did with superior weapons. That's because many Europeans had developed an immunity, or a natural resistance, to diseases like smallpox. The indigenous peoples, however, had no such immunity. Smallpox swept through entire regions, decimating a large percentage of the population.

Malaria also played a role in the settlement of the Americas. Brought with the slave trade from Africa, it proved deadly to indigenous peoples and Europeans in the Caribbean. But many Africans had been exposed to the disease in childhood and developed some immunity. As a result, even today, the population of the Caribbean is largely of African descent.

One key to preventing an epidemic is knowing what causes the disease. By 1900, for example, scientists knew that malaria was caused by mosquito bites. Another key is taking steps to eliminate the cause—in the case of malaria, by eliminating standing water where mosquitoes can breed. A third key is vaccination. Today, vaccines provide immunity to a host of diseases such as smallpox and polio. No vaccine, however, has yet proven effective against malaria, which kills more than one million people every year.

Enter Pardis Sabeti. When Sabeti was two years old, she and her family fled from Iran just before the country's 1979 revolution and settled in Florida. While at school, Sabeti fell in love with math. In medical school, she also developed a love of research and data analysis. She would combine these interests to fight malaria and other infectious diseases.

ANALYZING DATA

Sabeti is one of a new breed of scientist, called a computational geneticist, who uses computers to analyze the genetic data of people and diseases. When Sabeti was in graduate school, she developed a groundbreaking algorithm, or a procedure for solving a problem or analyzing data using a computer. She uses her algorithm to analyze a specific gene, the part of a cell that controls growth, appearance, and traits. The information helps her discover how infectious diseases change over time and spread. Sabeti's algorithms can also reveal how people adapt to or resist a disease through changes in their biology. This knowledge can aid scientists in developing strategies for dealing with disease.

While analyzing data gleaned from people who had been exposed to malaria, Sabeti made an important discovery. She explains, "I realized I'd found a trait that had to be the result of natural selection—a trait that likely helped the population I was looking at cope with malaria better than others. It was an amazing feeling because at that moment I knew something about how people evolved that nobody else knew."

Sabeti has done fieldwork in Sierra Leone and other African countries affected by malaria, Lassa fever, and the Ebola virus. Much of the time, however, she can be found in her research lab. There, Sabeti and her colleagues put their math skills to work analyzing data. Their goal is to find better treatments for diseases such as malaria—and eventually, perhaps, a cure.

HISTORICAL THINKING

1. **READING CHECK** Why were the native populations of the Americas vulnerable to diseases like smallpox?

2. **MAKE INFERENCES** Why was Sabeti excited to discover a trait that helped some people cope with and resist malaria?

3. **DRAW CONCLUSIONS** How does fieldwork help Sabeti further understand the infectious diseases she analyzes?

Age of Maritime Expansion 487

PLAN: 2-PAGE LESSON

OBJECTIVE
Learn how Pardis Sabeti uses her math skills to understand epidemics.

CRITICAL THINKING SKILLS FOR LESSON 1.3
- Make Inferences
- Draw Conclusions
- Summarize
- Identify
- Analyze Cause and Effect

HISTORICAL THINKING FOR CHAPTER 17
How did European exploration transform the world socially, politically, and economically?

European explorers brought devastating diseases to the Americas. Lesson 1.3 discusses how Pardis Sabeti is using math to understand diseases and help prevent their spread.

BACKGROUND FOR THE TEACHER
Pardis Sabeti Pardis Sabeti does more than study diseases. She has made a discovery that connects Native Americans to their Asian ancestors. During a study of the genomes of 179 people from around the world, Sabeti discovered a gene that increases the number of sweat glands within people. She found that the gene emerged in China 30,000 years ago and traveled to the Americas as Asian populations migrated there. Sabeti believes the mutation has been passed through the generations because it helps regulate body temperatures during strenuous activity.

History Notebook
Encourage students to complete the National Geographic Explorer page for Chapter 17 in their History Notebooks as they read.

INTRODUCE & ENGAGE

ACTIVATE PRIOR KNOWLEDGE

Write the term *epidemic* on the board. Ask students where they might have heard this term before and what it means. *(Possible responses: news reports about diseases; to describe behavior, such as an epidemic of texting while driving)* Record students' responses on the board. Then explain that *epidemic* refers to something that spreads quickly and affects large numbers of people—especially diseases. Tell students that in this lesson they will be learning about National Geographic Explorer Pardis Sabeti and how her work can help us understand epidemics.

TEACH

GUIDED DISCUSSION

1. **Summarize** Why is the population of the Caribbean today largely of African descent? *(The malaria the Africans brought with them to the Caribbean during the slave trade killed many Europeans and indigenous people who had not developed an immunity to it. The Africans had developed some immunity to the disease.)*

2. **Identify** What discovery did Sabeti make when she used her algorithm to analyze data from people who had been exposed to malaria? *(She found a trait that may have helped the people cope with malaria.)*

ANALYZE CAUSE AND EFFECT

Have students study the visual of the red blood cells. **ASK:** Why are two of the red blood cells tinged with yellow? *(because they are infected with malaria, which attacks red blood cells)* What causes malaria in humans? *(Mosquitoes carrying malaria bite people, and malaria parasites enter the bloodstream.)* Then have students discuss the implication of the last sentence of the image caption.

ACTIVE OPTIONS

On Your Feet: Inside-Outside Circle Organize the class so that students stand in concentric circles facing each other. Then have students in the outside circle ask questions about the lesson and Pardis Sabeti's work, while those inside answer. On a signal, ask students to rotate to create new partnerships. Finally, on another signal, have students trade their inside/outside roles.

> **NG Learning Framework: Research the Researchers**
> **ATTITUDE** Curiosity
> **KNOWLEDGE** New Frontiers

Point out that research science includes a wide variety of topics. Have students work in pairs or small groups to learn more about the different types of research scientists are doing today. They should look for information on where research scientists might work, how much education they need, what fields they work in, and what technologies they use or develop. Have each student create a diagram, such as an idea web, for the type of research scientist he or she finds most interesting, and display the diagrams on the board.

DIFFERENTIATE

STRIVING READERS

Understand Unfamiliar Terms Point out terms introduced in this lesson that students may not be familiar with, such as *immunity*, *decimating*, *computational geneticist*, and *algorithm*. Tell pairs to use the text and a dictionary, if needed, to clarify the meanings of these terms and any other unfamiliar words they encounter and then to create sentences using the terms.

PRE-AP STEM

Map an Epidemic Have students use online and other sources to research a major epidemic from past or recent history, such as COVID-19. Then have them create a map of the epidemic, showing where it began, where it spread and when, and the number of people affected. When students are done, have them present their research to the class. Remind them to briefly introduce the disease they have studied: how it spreads, what its symptoms are, and how it is treated or cured.

See the Chapter Planner for more strategies for differentiation.

HISTORICAL THINKING

ANSWERS

1. They had never been exposed to the diseases, so they had no immunity to them.

2. Answers will vary. Possible response: It was a big step in trying to understand malaria and developing a drug that might cure it.

3. Answers will vary. Possible response: By going to a place where an infectious disease is active, Sabeti can see firsthand how the disease affects its victims and learn details about the disease from the health care workers closely involved with treating patients.

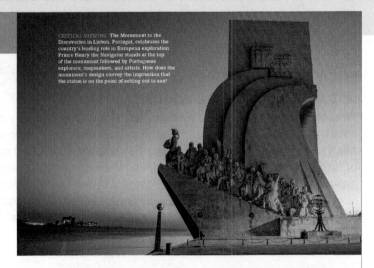

CRITICAL VIEWING The Monument to the Discoveries in Lisbon, Portugal, celebrates the country's leading role in European exploration. Prince Henry the Navigator stands at the top of the monument followed by Portuguese explorers, mapmakers, and artists. How does the monument's design convey the impression that the statue is on the point of setting out to sea?

The Columbian Exchange

Do you like apples, citrus fruit, or grapes? These foods came to our shores through a worldwide movement of goods across the Atlantic that began more than 500 years ago. You might think about that the next time you bite into an apple.

A GLOBAL FOOD EXCHANGE

Columbus's first voyage in 1492 brought the so-called "Old World," the Eastern Hemisphere of Europe, Asia, and Africa, into contact with the "New World," the Western Hemisphere of the Americas. (Of course, the land was only new to the Europeans; diverse indigenous societies had been settled across those lands for thousands of years.) The encounter coincided with improved methods of sea travel and the European desire to explore, settle, and exchange with new lands. The creation of regular interchange between the Eastern and Western hemispheres, and the integration of previously isolated peoples into global networks, is known as the **Columbian Exchange**, named after Columbus. The exchange resulted in a transfer of foods, crops, animals, technology, and medicines between the two hemispheres.

The Europeans who traveled to the Americas intentionally brought food and crops well known to them, such as wheat, barley, grapes, and apples, and livestock including cattle, pigs, chickens, sheep, and horses. All of these plants and animals flourished in the Americas. Wheat became one of the most important crops in North America. And horses brought by the Spanish changed the lives of Native Americans by making buffalo hunting much easier and safer.

Europeans also brought crops from Africa and Asia to the Americas. Sugarcane thrived in the Caribbean islands and Brazil. Later in this book, you will learn more about the slaves brought from Africa who did the harsh work in the cane fields to create huge profits for European plantation owners. By the end of the 1600s, rice had become a staple crop in the Carolinas. Enslaved Africans would also be forced to work the rice fields.

Foods from the Americas traveled to Europe, Africa, and Asia as well. Ships returned to Europe with beans, corn (also called maize), peppers, tomatoes, potatoes, turkeys, and much more. Many of these foods became staples of European diets. West Africans came to rely on American food crops, such as corn, peanuts, squash, and sweet potatoes. And Asian farmers cultivated corn, tomatoes, peppers, peanuts, and sweet potatoes.

Two of the crops from the Americas—corn and potatoes—played an especially important role in Europe, Asia, and Africa. Both produced higher yields than wheat and grew in fields that were hard to cultivate. By the 1700s, corn and potatoes had reached as far as India and China, and populations in both places increased significantly. Today about 30 percent of the foods eaten worldwide originated in the Americas. This early food trade led to our global cuisine. Who could imagine Italian food without tomato sauce, New Zealand without lamb, or Thai food without chili peppers? Kitchens around the world reflect the Columbian Exchange.

NEGATIVE IMPACTS OF THE EXCHANGE

Not everything that traveled in the exchange was beneficial, however. In addition to goods, Europeans introduced deadly new diseases to the Americas for which the Native Americans had no immunity. You have read that the conquistadors spread smallpox when they arrived. Colonizers also brought other diseases, including typhoid, measles, and influenza. As a result, the indigenous population of Central America fell from about 25 million to 2.5 million between 1519 and 1565. And historians estimate that, within about 150 years of Columbus's voyages, epidemics of infectious diseases had killed up to 90 percent of the native population, a pattern that would later be repeated in Australia and Polynesia. With these deaths, the world also lost valuable indigenous knowledge in areas such as agriculture and medicine. For good and bad, the Columbian Exchange transformed the world.

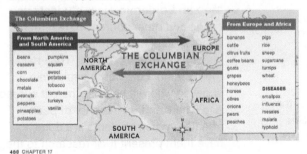

The Columbian Exchange

From North America and South America

beans	pumpkins
cassava	squash
corn	sweet potatoes
chocolate	tobacco
metals	tomatoes
peanuts	turkeys
peppers	vanilla
pineapples	
potatoes	

THE COLUMBIAN EXCHANGE

EUROPE
NORTH AMERICA
AFRICA
SOUTH AMERICA

From Europe and Africa

bananas	pigs
cattle	rice
citrus fruits	sheep
coffee beans	sugarcane
goats	turnips
grapes	wheat
honeybees	
horses	**DISEASES**
olives	smallpox
onions	influenza
pears	measles
peaches	malaria
	typhoid

HISTORICAL THINKING

1. **READING CHECK** What led to the Columbian Exchange?

2. **DRAW CONCLUSIONS** In what way did the Columbian Exchange encourage slavery?

3. **FORM AND SUPPORT OPINIONS** Do you think the positive impact of the Columbian Exchange outweighed the negative impact? Explain your answer.

PLAN: 2-PAGE LESSON

OBJECTIVE

Describe the global exchange of plants, animals, people, and diseases that crossed the Atlantic Ocean after Columbus arrived in the Americas.

CRITICAL THINKING SKILLS FOR LESSON 1.4

- Draw Conclusions
- Form and Support Opinions
- Analyze Cause and Effect
- Make Inferences
- Categorize

HISTORICAL THINKING FOR CHAPTER 17

How did European exploration transform the world socially, politically, and economically?

Regular interchange among Europe, Africa, Asia, and the Americas developed after Columbus's voyages. Lesson 1.4 discusses the Columbian Exchange and the ways in which it impacted cultures around the world.

Student eEdition online

Additional content for this lesson, including a sidebar feature, is available online.

BACKGROUND FOR THE TEACHER

Smallpox While researchers are not exactly sure when smallpox began infecting populations, scholars believe it may go back many thousands of years—as far back as ancient Mesopotamia and the Nile River Valley. Descriptions of diseases with symptoms matching smallpox appear in accounts of terrible plagues from ancient Greece and Rome. Smallpox is thought to have traveled to Europe with soldiers returning from the Crusades. The disease caused fever, aches, vomiting, and a blistering rash that often left permanent, horrible scars. It killed almost a third of its victims. Smallpox is the only infectious disease to be successfully eradicated through vaccination and continual monitoring.

INTRODUCE & ENGAGE

CREATE A CULTURAL EXCHANGE LIST

Have students think of and discuss the foods, music, media, or fashions they enjoy. Write their responses on the board. Ask the class to identify any items that come from another region, country, or culture. Then direct students' attention to the map of the Columbian Exchange. **ASK:** How might the map look different if we were describing cultural exchange today? *(Possible response: The arrows would point to many different areas; the items listed might be clothing, music, art, or technology.)*

TEACH

GUIDED DISCUSSION

1. **Analyze Cause and Effect** How did crops that originated in the Americas affect population trends in the Old World? *(The populations of both India and China grew when these regions gained access to and produced higher yields of food.)*

2. **Make Inferences** Based on what you have read, why might European explorers have brought their own crops and livestock with them? *(Possible response: They may have been unsure about edible food or useful animals in the Americas.)*

CATEGORIZE

Have students examine the Columbian Exchange items listed in the lesson and on the map. Ask them to use a three-column chart to sort the items into one of three categories: Mostly Helpful, Mostly Harmful, Both. *(Possible responses: Mostly Helpful—fruits, vegetables, animals; Mostly Harmful—weapons, diseases; Both—livestock, agriculture/farming)*

ACTIVE OPTIONS

On Your Feet: Think, Pair, Share Have students use the Think, Pair, Share strategy to develop their ideas about the positive and negative effects of the Columbian Exchange. Have pairs decide what they believe to be the greatest benefit of the exchange to Europe, the indigenous populations, and the world, as well as the greatest negative impact on each of the three.

NG Learning Framework: Explore Introduced Species
ATTITUDES Curiosity, Empowerment
KNOWLEDGE Critical Species

Remind students that exchanges of plants, animals, diseases, and other biological elements are continuous. Have them choose a more recent instance of an introduced species in one part of the world and research its features, issues, and contributions. Students should prepare a presentation on their chosen species, explaining how and when it was introduced, the consequences of its introduction, and, in the case of negative impacts, what steps people took to remedy the situation. If students need help choosing a topic, you might suggest the following: rabbits in Australia; zebra mussels in the Great Lakes region; kudzu vines in the southeastern United States; beavers in Argentina.

DIFFERENTIATE

INCLUSION

Describe Visuals Pair students who are visually impaired with those who are not. Have the latter describe the Columbian Exchange map in detail to their partners.

ENGLISH LANGUAGE LEARNERS

Summarize Have students work in pairs or small groups to read and write a one- to two-sentence summary of each paragraph in the lesson. Provide the following sentence frames:

• **Beginning and Intermediate**
This paragraph is about _____.
First, _____. Then _____. At the end, _____.

• **Advanced**
The paragraph begins by _____.
It then _____, and concludes by _____.

To summarize, the paragraph provides information about _____.

See the Chapter Planner for more strategies for differentiation.

HISTORICAL THINKING

ANSWERS

1. The exchange began after Columbus's voyages and coincided with improved methods of sea travel and the European desire to explore and conquer new lands.

2. Some of the crops sent to the Americas became so popular that growers forced slaves to work the crops and produce greater yields.

3. Overall, it was positive because the new foods and crops improved nutrition and increased the world population.

CRITICAL VIEWING Answers will vary. Possible response: The monument is in the shape of a ship; its sails seem to be blown out by the wind; Prince Henry is looking out to sea.

Portugal's Trade Empire

Europeans knew that whoever found a direct sea route to Asia would become fabulously wealthy. The competition was intense, but Portugal would win out and become "Lord of the Seas"—for a time, anyway.

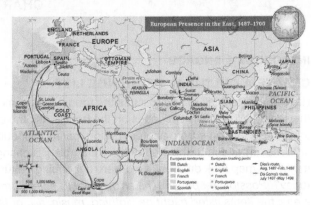

FINDING A ROUTE TO INDIA

The Portuguese had a special incentive to explore the Atlantic Ocean since geography separated them from Mediterranean trade. Remember reading about Prince Henry and his navigation school? Henry also began funding caravel expeditions to explore Africa's western coast. By 1460, Portuguese explorers were trading with Africans from new coastal trading posts, sending spices, gold, and slaves to European markets.

Then, in 1487, Portuguese explorer **Bartholomeu Dias** sailed around the Cape of Good Hope on the Atlantic coast of present-day South Africa. By doing so, he proved that a sea route around Africa to India was

possible. About 10 years later, another Portuguese navigator, **Vasco da Gama**, began exploring the east African coast and crossed the Indian Ocean to India, where he marveled at the merchant ships filled with spices, silks, and precious gems. Da Gama returned to Portugal with Asian spices and knowledge of sea routes and Indian Ocean ports.

Portuguese mariners had a more accurate sense of geography than Columbus, and their success in connecting Europe directly with Asia had a very different outcome. Columbus's connection across the Atlantic was brand new, and the Spanish quickly overwhelmed indigenous societies in the Americas. In the Indian

Ocean, however, the Europeans were entering an established trade network surrounded by powerful land-based empires like the Mughal Empire of India.

The problem for the Portuguese was that they did not have anything of value to offer Asian markets. Their only advantage over Asian competition was their powerful cannons. That is how they defeated a fleet of Muslim ships off the coast of India in 1509 and took control of important trade routes.

BUILDING A TRADE EMPIRE

After the battle, the Portuguese extended their power. In 1510, they captured Goa on India's west coast and made it their chief port. From Goa, they took over important "choke points" of trade, places that Asian and African merchants had to pass through to conduct their business. In 1511, the Portuguese attacked and captured Malacca on the west coast of the Malay Peninsula. The city gave Portugal control of the Strait of Malacca and the Moluccas, islands so rich in spices they were called the Spice Islands.

In 1514, Portugal gained control of the Strait of Hormuz, which provided the only sea passage from the Persian Gulf to the Indian Ocean. Seizing the waterway meant Portugal could charge Muslim traders a fee for passage through the straits between Iran and India. In Africa, the Portuguese diverted the gold trade to their own ships, using their cannons to destroy the old city of Kilwa, and joined forces with Ethiopian Christians to secure trade around the Red Sea. In East Asia, the Portuguese established a strongly fortified trading post on Macao on the eastern coast of China in the 1550s. By the 1570s, they had reached all the way to Japan.

Portuguese merchants profited handsomely from the trade. They purchased luxury items in Asia for about one-fifth the cost the Muslim traders had charged. As a result, prices for these items on the European markets were lower, and more people could afford them. Portugal would remain unrivaled until other, equally aggressive European powers would muscle their way into the Indian Ocean trade.

CRITICAL VIEWING The Cape of Good Hope was once believed to be the southernmost tip of Africa. It marked the spot at which Dias began sailing east rather than south and would have given him hope that he was on course for India. Based on the photo, what challenges did Dias face as he sailed around the cape?

HISTORICAL THINKING

1. **READING CHECK** Why did Portugal want to find a direct sea route to India?

2. **INTERPRET MAPS** By 1700, which European power had taken control of the East Indies from the Portuguese?

3. **ANALYZE CAUSE AND EFFECT** How did Portuguese merchants and European buyers benefit as a result of Portugal's domination of Indian Ocean trade?

PLAN: 2-PAGE LESSON

OBJECTIVE

Explain how Portugal built a powerful trading empire in the Indian Ocean.

CRITICAL THINKING SKILLS FOR LESSON 2.1

- Interpret Maps
- Analyze Cause and Effect
- Compare and Contrast
- Explain

HISTORICAL THINKING FOR CHAPTER 17

How did European exploration transform the world socially, politically, and economically?

Charting a sea route around Africa to Asia helped Portugal establish itself as a maritime powerhouse. Lesson 2.1 discusses how Portugal built a powerful trading empire in the Indian Ocean.

Student eEdition online

Additional content for this lesson, including a primary source, is available online.

BACKGROUND FOR THE TEACHER

Prince Henry's Brothers Although Prince Henry the Navigator receives much of the credit for financing and encouraging Portugal's maritime exploration, he was heavily influenced by his older brothers, Prince Pedro and King Duarte. Prince Pedro traveled throughout Europe, and this travel not only sparked an interest in exploring the world but also alerted him to the extent of Muslim influence in global trade. He came to understand that Portugal would primarily have to compete with Muslim traders for control of ports in the Indian Ocean. Duarte, who would rule Portugal as king for five years, also heavily emphasized exploration. He sponsored many trips to islands off the coast of West Africa, which helped pave the way for the explorations of Bartholomeu Dias and Vasco da Gama.

INTRODUCE & ENGAGE

POSE AND ANSWER QUESTIONS

As a class, complete a K-W-L Chart to explore what students know and what they would like to learn about Portugal's trading empire. Write students' ideas on the board in a chart. Give students the opportunity to return to the chart and review what they have learned after they have read the lesson.

TEACH

GUIDED DISCUSSION

1. **Compare and Contrast** How did Columbus's connection across the Atlantic Ocean differ from that of the Europeans in the Indian Ocean? *(Columbus's connection was brand new, and the Spanish quickly overwhelmed indigenous societies in the Americas. The Europeans entered an established trade network in the Indian Ocean, surrounded by powerful land-based empires.)*

2. **Explain** Why was the port in Goa essential in Portugal's domination of Indian Ocean trade? *(The Portuguese used it to take over "choke points" that merchants had to pass through to conduct business.)*

INTERPRET MAPS

Have students study and discuss the territories held by European powers around 1700. **ASK:** By then, which country controlled the most territory in the Indian Ocean? Which controlled the least? *(the Netherlands; France)* Then have students locate the territory controlled by Portugal. **ASK:** How did controlling land along the east and west coasts of Africa benefit Portugal? *(Possible response: Portugal could control the access of other Europeans who tried to sail around Africa to Asia.)*

ACTIVE OPTIONS

On Your Feet: Roundtable Divide the class into groups of four. Hand each group a sheet of paper with the following question: How did Portugal go about building an empire in the Indian Ocean? The first student in each group should write an answer, read it aloud, and then pass the paper clockwise to the next student. Each student in the group should add at least one answer. The paper should circulate around the table until students run out of answers. At the end of the activity, initiate a class discussion of students' responses.

> **NG Learning Framework: Make a Claim About European and Arab Navigators**
> **SKILL** Collaboration
> **KNOWLEDGE** Our Human Story

Challenge students to conduct online research to learn more about the ideas expressed in Ahmad Ibn Majid's *Book of Useful Information on the Principles and Rules of Navigation.* Then tell students to work in pairs to summarize the relationship between European and Arab maritime navigators in the 15th and 16th centuries.

DIFFERENTIATE

INCLUSION

Use Supported Reading Pair proficient readers with less-proficient readers and have them read the lesson aloud paragraph by paragraph. Instruct pairs to stop at the end of each paragraph and use these sentence frames to monitor their comprehension of the text:

- This paragraph is mostly about _____.
- Its main idea is _____.
- Details that support the main idea are _____ and _____.
- One word I don't recognize is _____.
- One question I have is _____.

GIFTED & TALENTED

Host a Talk Show Instruct students to work in pairs to plan, write, and perform a simulated radio or television talk show in which Bartholomeu Dias and Vasco da Gama are the guests. Encourage students to conduct research to help them come up with questions and answers about the explorers' voyages, including the similarities and differences between their motivations and experiences. Invite pairs to present their talk shows to the class.

See the Chapter Planner for more strategies for differentiation.

HISTORICAL THINKING

ANSWERS

1. The Portuguese wanted to get in on the lucrative trade in the Indian Ocean.

2. the Dutch

3. The merchants paid much less for luxury goods in Asia, and the buyers paid less to buy them in Europe.

CRITICAL VIEWING Answers will vary. Possible response: rocky cliffs, treacherous waters

The Dutch East India Company

In the business world, large companies sometimes "swallow up" smaller companies. In the Indian Ocean, the Dutch made it their business to swallow up their Portuguese competitors.

THE RISE OF THE DUTCH

Portugal tried to keep its sea route to Asia a secret, but it soon attracted the attention of other European countries. Navigators from other countries began to sail to Asia in the early 1600s, and the Netherlands and England became the key challengers to Portugal's pioneering role in developing European trade in the Indian Ocean.

In the mid-1500s, the Netherlands was a collection of provinces governed by the Catholic rulers of Habsburg Spain. In 1568, the provinces began waging a war of independence against the Spanish. Seven of the northern provinces won their independence in 1609 and formed the Dutch Republic. However, fighting continued for many years until Spain finally recognized full Dutch independence in 1648.

The Dutch based their economy on the fishing and shipbuilding industries and soon became a major sea power. Around 1650, they commanded a fleet of about 16,000 ships, the largest in the world. In the 1590s, the first Dutch traders arrived in the Indian Ocean and explored the Spice Islands. They returned to the Netherlands loaded with pepper, cloves, cinnamon, nutmeg, and other spices and made huge profits when they sold the goods.

Soon the Dutch and other Europeans began making the long sea voyage to India. Both England and the Netherlands formed an East India Company to regulate their trade in the region. Established in 1602, the **Dutch East India Company** was richer and more powerful than England's company. It became Europe's largest

Dutch merchants in the 17th century were among the most successful traders in the world. The shipowner and his family in the painting shown here are dressed in the typical Dutch style of the time and are posed before the trading vessels that provided them with great wealth.

commercial enterprise of the 17th century. A charter granted by the government gave the Dutch East India Company exclusive control over Dutch trade with Asia. The company also had the right to build forts, form armies, establish colonies, and make treaties.

The Dutch East India Company operated as a **joint-stock company**, which means that it sold shares of stocks to investors who became partners in the venture. In this new form of business enterprise, investors shared losses as well as profits. Innovations in banking and insurance also gave the Dutch a more stable infrastructure for investment. These institutions would later be valuable in the development of **capitalism**, in which businesses are privately owned and exist to make profits. But the Dutch East India Company was not based on free-market principles. Like other European powers, the Dutch practiced mercantilism and stressed government control over trade monopolies.

Today, the Netherlands is the world's largest producer of tulips with over 70 percent of the market. One of the best places to see Dutch tulips is the Keukenhof, the largest flower park in the world. More than seven million flower bulbs are planted here each year.

DUTCH ENTERPRISE

Over time, the Dutch East India Company eroded Portugal's position in the Indian Ocean by taking over strategic points of trade. In 1619, the company established its headquarters at Batavia (present-day Jakarta) on the island of Java in the East Indies. From there, the Dutch conquered several nearby islands. Dutch warships regularly squared off against Portuguese vessels and won most of the battles. Then in 1641, the Netherlands seized Malacca and the Spice Islands from Portugal. By 1700, the Dutch controlled the spice trade and the Indian Ocean trade routes.

The Dutch ruled some of these areas in Asia directly, such as the Banda Islands where they grew valuable nutmeg. Often the Dutch saw more opportunity in inserting themselves as middlemen into existing markets. For example, India was the world's biggest producer of cotton textiles. Using their faster ships with large cargo capacity, the Dutch profited by transporting such goods around the Indian Ocean as well as by selling the cloth in Europe.

They had also established a colony at Cape Town on the southwestern coast of Africa. This outpost provided fresh water and other services to Dutch ships that rounded the Cape of Good Hope. In time, the colony became part of the slave trade. The Dutch East India Company used slave labor on its settlements, and many of the enslaved people came from South Asia.

In the early 1600s, the Dutch East India Company got involved in the search for the **Northwest Passage**, a sea route from the Atlantic Ocean to the Pacific by way of a series of arctic northern Canadian islands. Such a route would have significantly shortened the voyage between Europe and Asia. In 1609, while under contract with the company, English explorer **Henry Hudson** searched for the passage but failed to find it. He did, however, sail up what is now the Hudson River to present-day Albany, New York. Along the way, he traded for furs with Native Americans. This trade was so lucrative that the Dutch established a post in the area.

With all the goods flowing into and out of the Netherlands—tulips were a hot commodity—Amsterdam, its capital, became a leading center of commerce. Meanwhile, however, other European countries continued to battle for a foothold in the Indian Ocean trade.

HISTORICAL THINKING

1. **READING CHECK** Why were the Dutch in a good position to compete with the Portuguese in the Indian Ocean?

2. **COMPARE AND CONTRAST** In what way was the Dutch East India Company similar to an independent country?

3. **ANALYZE CAUSE AND EFFECT** What was one effect of the Dutch East India Company's search for the Northwest Passage?

PLAN: 2-PAGE LESSON

OBJECTIVE
Explain how the Dutch East India Company gained control of the spice trade in the East Indies.

CRITICAL THINKING SKILLS FOR LESSON 2.2
- Compare and Contrast
- Analyze Cause and Effect
- Analyze Points of View
- Make Connections
- Analyze Visuals

HISTORICAL THINKING FOR CHAPTER 17
How did European exploration transform the world socially, politically, and economically?

In the early 1600s, other European countries competed with Portugal for the Indian Ocean trade. Lesson 2.2 discusses how the Dutch gained control of the spice trade and the Indian Ocean trade routes.

Student eEdition online
Additional content for this lesson, including a map and a Global Commodity feature, is available online.

BACKGROUND FOR THE TEACHER
The End of the Dutch East India Company The Dutch East India Company was a powerful global force for much of the 1600s, but it only lasted for about a century. Its power weakened in the late 1600s, and its responsibilities and priorities shifted to the internal affairs of Java and Indonesian agriculture. By the end of the 1700s, the company was in debt, and its leadership was considered corrupt. In 1799, it was formally disbanded when the Dutch government revoked its charter and assumed its debts and assets.

History Notebook
Encourage students to complete the "Tulips" Global Commodity page for Chapter 17 in their History Notebooks as they read.

INTRODUCE & ENGAGE

CONNECT TO THE PRESENT

Ask students what they know about world trade today. Discuss the leading trade countries as well as the commodities that the United States exports and imports. Then remind students that global exchange networks also existed in the 1600s. Tell them that in this lesson they will read about the competition to control the market in the Indian Ocean, an important trade region at that time.

TEACH

GUIDED DISCUSSION

1. **Analyze Points of View** How did the Dutch tie success in business to their religious beliefs? (The Dutch believed that business success was a sign of God's favor.)

2. **Make Connections** What institutions of the Dutch East India Company influenced the development of capitalism? (joint-stock company, innovations in banking and investment)

ANALYZE VISUALS

Invite students to review the text and photos in the Global Commodity feature on tulips (available in the Student eEdition). Make sure students understand that the story of tulipmania is largely false. Then initiate a discussion about the photographs and painting of tulips. **ASK:** What do the photos of tulips convey about the role of tulips today in the Netherlands? (Possible response: Tulips are still an important commodity in the Netherlands.) How does the painting reflect the story of tulipmania? (Possible response: It shows a buyer who seems ready to purchase some tulip bulbs with a sack of money.)

ACTIVE OPTIONS

On Your Feet: Four Corners Designate each corner of the classroom for a focused discussion on one of four aspects of Dutch economic expansion: its impact on local populations in Asia; its impact on the Dutch economy and standard of living; its effect on relationships with other European powers; and its influence on the development of capitalism. Instruct students to think and write individually about Dutch economic expansion for a short time. Then have them move to a corner of their choice to discuss one aspect of the topic. Finally, invite at least one student from each corner to share about the corner discussion.

> **NG Learning Framework: The Dutch Golden Age**
> **ATTITUDE** Curiosity
> **KNOWLEDGE** Our Human Story

Have students work together in small groups to learn more about the golden age of the Dutch Republic. Suggest that groups research the following topics: Dutch finance, science, military, and art in the 17th century. Students may present their findings in a poster or on a website or class blog. Encourage them to use photographs, graphs, and other visuals in their reports.

DIFFERENTIATE

ENGLISH LANGUAGE LEARNERS

Find Someone Who Knows Have students find classmates who can provide the correct answer to each question below. Encourage students to answer in complete sentences by inverting the questions and turning them into statements.

1. Who ruled the Netherlands in the mid-1500s? (Spain ruled the Netherlands in the mid-1500s.)

2. What was Europe's largest economic enterprise in the 17th century? (The Dutch East India Company was Europe's largest economic enterprise in the 17th century.)

3. Where did the Dutch East India Company establish its headquarters? (The Dutch East India Company established its headquarters in Batavia on the island of Java.)

4. Which English explorer set sail in 1609 to search for the Northwest Passage? (English explorer Henry Hudson set sail in 1609 to search for the Northwest Passage.)

INCLUSION

Sequence Events Write events from the lesson on index cards. Read the events aloud and then have students put the cards in chronological order.

See the Chapter Planner for more strategies for differentiation.

HISTORICAL THINKING

ANSWERS

1. They commanded the largest fleet in the world and had earned a great deal of money through European trade.

2. Like an independent country, the Dutch East India Company could build forts, form armies, establish colonies, and make treaties.

3. The Dutch ended up setting up a trading post on the Hudson River near present-day Albany, New York.

2.3 Trade and Cross-Cultural Encounters

When someone discovers the next great thing, everyone wants to get in on the action. You've learned that the Portuguese and the Dutch established lucrative trade-based empires in the Indian Ocean. Eventually, other European maritime powers followed with their own merchant fleets. As Europeans traveled the Indian Ocean, some of them wrote down their views of the people they encountered. The Muslims and Asians did, too. Impressions on all sides weren't always flattering.

The Dutch established a few substantial settlements along the Indian Ocean, including those on the island of Java in today's Indonesia. For the most part, though, Europeans in the Indian Ocean limited their enterprises to "factories," as they called their trade settlements along the coast. But when they traveled inland to regions such as the Ottoman and Mughal empires or Safavid Iran, they discovered that they had to play by the rules of local leaders.

As Europeans competed for trade and wealth with local competitors in these inland regions, they left records of their cultural encounters. Likewise, Asians recorded accounts of European behavior. These reports frequently revealed the prejudices on both sides. Many Asians referred to Europeans as "Franks" and accused them of being greedy and violent. Europeans tended to view Muslims and other Asians as lazy and deceitful. Their views enforced negative stereotypes that would persist for many years.

Spices displayed in sacks are still sold in traditional open-air markets in India, just as they were when Europeans worked the Indian Ocean trade. Spices shown in this photo include cloves, cardamom, nutmeg, and turmeric.

DOCUMENT ONE
Primary Source: Book
from the *Sejarah Melayu (Malay Annals)* by Tun Sri Lanang, 1612

Tun Sri Lanang was the Chief Minister of the Kingdom of Johor (in present-day Malaysia), which was founded by refugees from Malacca after the Portuguese conquest of 1511. About 100 years later, the sultan commissioned Tun Sri Lanang to rewrite and compile the *Malay Annals*, a history of their leaders before the conquest. In this excerpt from the work, Tun Sri Lanang describes the Portuguese attack on Malacca in 1511, led by Portugal's Viceroy, Alfonso d'Albuquerque.

CONSTRUCTED RESPONSE How does Tun Sri Lanang characterize the Portuguese attack on Malacca?

And the Franks [Portuguese soldiers] engaged the men of Malacca in battle, and they fired their cannon from their ships so that the cannon balls came like rain. . . . The Franks then fiercely engaged the men of Malacca in battle and so vehement [violent] was their onslaught [attack] that the Malacca line was broken, leaving the king on his elephant isolated. And the king fought with the Franks pike to pike, and he was wounded in the palm of the hand. . . . And Malacca fell. The Franks advanced on the King's hall and the men of Malacca fled.

DOCUMENT TWO
Primary Source: Memoir
from *Travels in Persia, 1673–1677* by Jean Chardin, 1686

French jeweler Jean Chardin traveled twice to the Safavid Empire in Iran, where he learned the Persian language and formed strong opinions about the people. While in the capital of Isfahan, Chardin negotiated a deal to create jewelry for the shah. After Chardin returned from his second visit, he detailed his observations of Safavid Iran in *Travels in Persia, 1673–1677*. In this excerpt from the memoir, Chardin relates his impressions of the Persian people.

CONSTRUCTED RESPONSE According to Chardin, what do the Persians expect to receive in exchange for a favor?

As civil as that nation is, they never act out of generosity. . . . And they cannot conceive that there should be such a country where people will do their duty from a motive of virtue only, without any other recompense [reward]. It is quite the contrary with them; they are paid for everything, and beforehand too. One can ask nothing of them, but with a present in one's hand. . . . The poorest and most miserable people never appear before a great man, or one from whom they would ask some favor, but at the same time they offer a present, which is never refused, even by the greatest lords of the kingdom.

DOCUMENT THREE
Primary Source: Memoir
from *The Ship of Sulaiman* by Muhammad Rabi ibn Muhammad Ibrahim, translated by John O'Kane, 1972

In 1685, Muhammad Rabi was the leader of a diplomatic mission to Siam, known today as Thailand. Muhammad Rabi wrote an account of the mission, focusing on the Iranians who resided in Siam at that time and their role in its trade and political affairs. He also discussed the European traders who had joined the Malay, Chinese, and Iranian merchant communities in Siam. In the following excerpt from his book, Muhammad Rabi describes an influential Frenchman at the Siamese court.

CONSTRUCTED RESPONSE How does Muhammad Rabi portray the Frenchman?

[T]he king was not able to find an Iranian to act as prime minister [and] the only candidate who remained was that Frank [the Frenchman] who had originally worked as a sailor. . . . The Frank minister has succeeded in penetrating into the king's affections to such an extent . . . that there is never a moment in public or in private when he is not at the king's side. To the world at large this Christian minister displays a record of service, integrity, thrift and sincerity. . . . However, it is a fact every year he sends huge sums of money from the king's treasury abroad to the Frank kingdoms, supposedly for business purposes. Up until now there have been absolutely no visible returns from that money.

SYNTHESIZE & WRITE

1. **REVIEW** Review what you have learned about the Indian Ocean trade.

2. **RECALL** On your own paper, write down the main idea expressed in each document.

3. **CONSTRUCT** Construct a topic sentence that answers this question: Why do you think Europeans, Asians, and Muslims formed negative impressions of each other during their cross-cultural interactions?

4. **WRITE** Using evidence from this chapter and the documents, write an informative paragraph that supports your topic sentence in Step 3.

PLAN: 2-PAGE LESSON

OBJECTIVE
Analyze how Europeans, Asians, and Muslims viewed each other in the 17th century.

CRITICAL THINKING SKILLS FOR LESSON 2.3
- Synthesize
- Identify Main Ideas and Details
- Form and Support Opinions
- Evaluate

HISTORICAL THINKING FOR CHAPTER 17
How did European exploration transform the world socially, politically, and economically?

New trade networks in the 17th century brought Europeans, Muslims, and Asians in contact. Lesson 2.3 focuses on written historical accounts that show what they thought of each other.

BACKGROUND FOR THE TEACHER
Spice Trade Arab traders were adept at keeping their sources of spices a secret. One way they did this was by making up fanciful stories. For example, they told other traders that the places where cinnamon was grown were infested with poisonous snakes and that cassia, a type of Chinese cinnamon, was grown in lakes guarded by winged animals. For a time, the stories helped discourage competitors, and keep the prices of spices high. At one point, cinnamon was more valuable than gold.

INTRODUCE & ENGAGE

PREPARE FOR THE DOCUMENT-BASED QUESTION

Before students start on the activity, briefly preview the three documents. Remind students that a constructed response requires full explanations in complete sentences. Emphasize that students should use what they have learned about 17th-century Asian, Muslim, and European sea traders in addition to the information in the documents.

TEACH

GUIDED DISCUSSION

1. **Identify Main Ideas and Details** What negative development arose from the cultural encounters among Europeans, Muslims, and Asians? *(Prejudices and stereotypes arose.)*

2. **Form and Support Opinions** What do you think may cause people to form prejudices of others? *(Possible response: fear, ignorance, lack of understanding of other people's cultures)*

EVALUATE

After students have completed the Synthesize & Write activity, allow time for them to exchange paragraphs and read and comment on the work of their peers. Establish guidelines for comments prior to the activity so feedback is constructive and encouraging. Comments should focus on the most significant parts that address the purpose of the activity and the audience.

ACTIVE OPTION

On Your Feet: Jigsaw Strategy Organize students into "expert" groups and assign each group one of the documents to analyze and summarize its main ideas in their own words. Then regroup students into new groups so that each new group has at least one member from each expert group. Students in the new groups take turns sharing the summaries from their expert groups.

DIFFERENTIATE

STRIVING READERS

Summarize Read each document aloud to students. Then ask one small group of students to work together to reread each document and summarize it for the larger group. After each document is summarized, read the Constructed Response question with the larger group and make sure all students understand it. Then have volunteers suggest answers.

INCLUSION

Work in Pairs Allow students with disabilities to work with other students who can read the lesson aloud to them. Encourage the partner without disabilities to read slowly and distinctly, especially when reading the longer words and more formal language of the excerpts. Ask pairs to work together to answer the Constructed Response and Synthesize & Write questions. If possible, give students the option of recording their answers rather than writing them out.

See the Chapter Planner for more strategies for differentiation.

SYNTHESIZE & WRITE

ANSWERS

1. Answers will vary.

2. Answers will vary. Possible response: Document 1: The Portuguese conquered Malacca with overwhelming force. Document 2: The Persians do not perform their duty or help anyone unless they receive recompense. Document 3: A Frenchman at the Siamese court thoroughly deceived the king.

3. Answers will vary. Possible response: Europeans, Asians, and Muslims formed negative impressions of each other during their cross-cultural interactions out of a need to categorize new, confusing social groups—and to feel better about themselves.

4. Answers will vary. Students' paragraphs should include their topic sentence from Step 3 and provide several details from the documents to support it.

CONSTRUCTED RESPONSE

Document One: He characterizes the attack as violent and relentless.

Document Two: The Persians expect to receive a present or money.

Document Three: The Frenchman is portrayed as sly, duplicitous, and a thief.

The Spanish Empire in the Americas

Spanish explorers faced a perilous journey when they sailed for the Americas. But, if successful, they knew Spain would be rewarded with great riches. The same cannot be said for the indigenous peoples they conquered.

NORTHERN EXPANSION

While Cortés and Pizarro were conquering Mexico and Peru, other Spanish conquistadors defeated the Maya in Yucatán and Guatemala. But the Spanish didn't limit their American explorations to Mesoamerica and South America. Soon they began moving north into the present-day United States. In 1513, **Juan Ponce de Léon** (PAWN-say DAY lay-OHN) was the first European to set foot in Florida, and he claimed it for Spain. Over the next 30 years or so, more Spanish explorers pushed deeper into North America in search of new territories and treasures.

One of the largest of these expeditions was led by **Francisco Vásquez de Coronado** from 1540 to 1542. Coronado and his men explored what is now California and parts of the Southwest. They hoped to find the legendary Seven Cities of Cibola (SEE-boh-lah), a kingdom said to be rich in silver and gold. But they found only Native Americans who resisted Spanish rule.

As a result, the Spanish monarchy had Catholic priests explore and colonize some of the new lands. Priests had accompanied explorers during American colonization from the beginning. While the explorers traveled in search of wealth, the priests sought to convert the indigenous peoples to Christianity. To that end, the clergymen established missions, or religious settlements, where they preached Christianity and provided food and shelter. By 1629, more than 25 missions dotted what is now New Mexico.

Some priests brutally punished the Native Americans who would not adopt Christianity. **Bartolomé de Las Casas**, a Spanish priest himself, spoke out against these abuses but to little effect. Some Native Americans converted but didn't entirely abandon their traditions. Instead, they combined their own practices with Christian teachings. As you have learned, this blending of different belief systems is called religious syncretism.

By the mid-1500s, Spain had established an American empire. The king of Spain was the ultimate authority. A group of advisors, called the Council of the Indies, regulated trade, appointed officials, and made laws. The king also divided his territory in the Americas into two **viceroyalties**, or colonies: New Spain, which included portions of Central and North America; and Peru, which covered portions of South America. A **viceroy**, a colonial leader appointed by the king, ruled each viceroyalty. The viceroys governed from their capitals—Mexico City in New Spain and Lima in Peru.

SOCIAL ORDER

A strict hierarchy developed in Spanish colonial society. At the top were Spanish-born settlers called *peninsulares*. They were closely followed by the *criollos* (cree-OH-yohs), Spaniards who were born in the Americas. These two groups were small but held the most power. Next came **mestizos**, people of mixed Spanish and Native American ancestry. Indigenous peoples and African slaves were at the bottom. They made up the largest group but had the least power.

The Spanish government gave the wealthiest colonists large tracts of farmland called **haciendas**. On Caribbean islands, most haciendas were sugarcane plantations. A hacienda included a grant, or **encomienda**, that allowed owners to force Native Americans to labor for them. Under this system, Native Americans farmed, ranched, and mined for the Spanish throughout the Americas. In return for their labor, native peoples received protection from their enemies rather than payment. But Spanish landlords often abused the indigenous people, forcing them to work under harsh conditions, especially in the mines, where many died. In response to criticism of the treatment of Native Americans, the Spanish government put an end to the encomienda system in 1542. But abuse of indigenous workers on farms and in mines continued.

As the Spanish colonies in the Americas developed and thrived, the population of some of its cities steadily increased. Mexico City and Lima grew especially large, and so did some mining towns in South America. By 1580, the population of Potosí, the capital of Bolivia, topped 150,000, making it the largest city in the Americas. Mexico also produced one of the outstanding writers of the Spanish colonial period, a nun and self-taught poet and playwright named Sor Juana Inés de la Cruz. She had served the viceroy's wife and learned Latin. Further studies were not allowed for women, so she joined a convent in Mexico City in the late 1600s, where she was free to write poetry and study philosophy for the rest of her life. Her poems are still popular today.

Spain dominated colonization in the Americas until 1588, when the English defeated the Spanish Armada, a fleet of warships sent by Spain to attack England. After the defeat, other European powers gained momentum and started to take advantage of Spain's vulnerability and establish their own colonies in the Americas.

HISTORICAL THINKING

1. **READING CHECK** How did the king of Spain control his colonial empire in the Americas?

2. **ANALYZE CAUSE AND EFFECT** What happened after Spanish explorers failed to find riches in what is now the southwestern United States?

3. **INTERPRET MAPS** Why might the distance between the two viceroyalties have caused problems for Spain?

CRITICAL VIEWING In *Defeat of the Spanish Armada*, a painting by 18th-century English artist Charles Robinson, the British navy fires on the Spanish fleet. The British victory in 1588 dealt a severe blow to the Spanish Armada and to Spain. How does the artist portray the Spanish sailors of the armada?

PLAN: 2-PAGE LESSON

OBJECTIVE

Describe how Spain pushed deeper into North America and colonized new lands where a hierarchical class system developed.

CRITICAL THINKING SKILLS FOR LESSON 3.1

- Analyze Cause and Effect
- Interpret Maps
- Synthesize
- Evaluate
- Analyze Visuals

HISTORICAL THINKING FOR CHAPTER 17

How did European exploration transform the world socially, politically, and economically?

In the 1500s, Spanish explorers began pushing deeper into the Americas. Lesson 3.1 discusses Spain's colonization of North, South, and Central America and the hierarchical societies they established there.

BACKGROUND FOR THE TEACHER

Francisco Vásquez de Coronado Coronado's soldiers carried a wide variety of armor and equipment. The conquistadors were soldiers, but they were not an army in the way we often think of armies today. They did not wear uniforms, apart from very basic items such as helmets. Soldiers wore and carried whatever they could find. Since they paid for their own equipment, many settled for out-of-date equipment. Wealthier soldiers might wear full suits of metal armor, while poorer soldiers wore partial armor, chain mail, or thick leather to protect themselves against enemy weapons. The leaders of the expedition were best equipped. The equipment list from one of Coronado's expeditions mentions that Coronado brought with him four suits of armor—for his horses.

INTRODUCE & ENGAGE

DISCUSS SOCIAL HIERARCHIES

Ask students to consider social hierarchies they have learned about, such as the caste system in ancient India. **ASK:** What are some causes and effects of social hierarchies? *(Possible response: Some want to maintain power, while others may not have access to vital resources or basic human rights.)* Tell students that in this lesson they will learn about the Spanish colonization of the Americas and the social hierarchies that developed in colonial Spanish society.

TEACH

GUIDED DISCUSSION

1. **Synthesize** Why did Spanish priests try to convert indigenous peoples to Christianity? *(Spreading Christianity was one of the three main goals of European exploration.)*

2. **Evaluate** What role did ancestry play in the social hierarchy of the Spanish colonies? *(It gave most power to those born in Spain or those with Spanish parents, less power to those with partial indigenous ancestry, and the least to full indigenous peoples or Africans.)*

ANALYZE VISUALS

Direct students' attention to the painting, *Defeat of the Spanish Armada.* Invite volunteers to describe the painting. **ASK:** What moods and actions does the painting convey? *(Possible response: chaos, desperation, frenzied activity)* How does the artist use color to show the drama of the battle? *(Possible response: Vivid reds portray the intensity of the battle, grays depict the choking smoke, with a gap of blue sky, perhaps signifying hope.)*

ACTIVE OPTIONS

On Your Feet: Jigsaw Strategy Organize students into four "expert" groups and assign each group one of the following: the expeditions of Juan Ponce de Léon, Cabeza de Vaca, Hernando de Soto, or Francisco Vásquez de Coronado. Encourage students to consider the routes and motivations of the explorers. Each group should create a summary of what they learned. Then regroup students into four new groups so each group has at least one person from each of the four expert groups. Tell students in the new group to take turns sharing the summary they created in their "expert" groups.

> **NG Learning Framework: Write a Persuasive Letter**
> **ATTITUDES** Responsibility, Empowerment
> **SKILL** Communication

Explain to students that Bartolomé de Las Casas wrote letters and books denouncing the abuse of indigenous peoples by the Spanish. Encourage students to follow Las Casas's lead and write a persuasive letter addressed to a person in power, such as a government official. Students should cover an issue they feel strongly about and attempt to convince that person that a change must be made.

DIFFERENTIATE

STRIVING READERS

Write a Tweet As students read the lesson, direct them to write a tweet that summarizes each paragraph's main idea in their own words. Tell students to read their tweets aloud to a partner, alternating paragraphs. Pairs should continue this activity until they reach the end of the lesson.

GIFTED & TALENTED

Research the Spanish Mission System Ask students to research to learn more about the Spanish mission system, which extended from Florida to California. Encourage students to find out what life was like in the missions for the priests and indigenous people. Tell students they can present their research in any way they like. Along with text, they should include a map showing the locations of the missions, photographs of the missions, and other visuals portraying daily life.

See the Chapter Planner for more strategies for differentiation.

HISTORICAL THINKING

ANSWERS

1. He divided the empire into two viceroyalties governed by two viceroys.

2. Spanish priests colonized lands and set up missions to convert Native Americans to Christianity.

3. Answers will vary. Possible response: Communication between the two viceroyalties and with Spain would have been difficult, making it hard to maintain control over the colonies.

CRITICAL VIEWING Answers will vary. Possible response: overwhelmed, desperate, in disarray, defeated

3.2 A Global Commodity: Silver

People in the ancient world discovered silver around 4000 B.C.E.—long after gold and copper—and valued its beauty and ability to reflect light. Silver is the lightest of the precious metals and soft. It can be stretched thinner than a strand of hair. It can also be polished to a brilliant shine that only contact with sulfur can dim. The Inca called silver "tears of the moon" for the metal's milky luster. Silver is rare, and very little of the metal had been mined before 1492. That's the year Spain began its conquest of the Americas and plunder of their resources, including silver.

In the mid-1550s, huge deposits of silver in mines in present-day Mexico, Bolivia, and Peru allowed Spain to begin a lucrative trade with China that lasted 250 years. Once a year, a ship known as the Manila galleon made the long voyage back and forth between Acapulco, Mexico, and Manila, in the Spanish colony of the Philippines, to exchange silver for Chinese goods such as silk and porcelain. During this period, the three mines produced 85 percent of the world's silver.

How do you think silver both connected and divided the world during the age of maritime expansion?

498 CHAPTER 17

A SILVER LINING

Silver often plays second fiddle to gold, but it contains special properties that set it apart from other precious metals. Silver is the best conductor of heat and electricity, and it reflects light better than any other element. As a result, it is used to make mirrors, telescopes, and microscopes. Of course, silver is also beautiful. Silversmiths, like the one at work in Cambodia in this photograph, fashion decorative objects and jewelry from the metal—just as they did in ancient times.

Age of Maritime Expansion 499

PLAN: 4-PAGE LESSON

OBJECTIVE
Explain silver's versatility and the role it has played in ancient and modern economies.

CRITICAL THINKING SKILLS FOR LESSON 3.2
- Identify
- Analyze Cause and Effect
- Synthesize
- Analyze Visuals

HISTORICAL THINKING FOR CHAPTER 17
How did European exploration transform the world socially, politically, and economically?

Europeans explored the Americas to search for riches to boost their economies. Lesson 3.2 explains how the silver found in the Americas in the 1500s affected markets worldwide.

BACKGROUND FOR THE TEACHER
Silver in Nature Silver is found in small concentrations primarily in ores containing lead, copper, and a metalloid element called *antimony*. Often, less than one percent of these ores is pure silver. Silver's lustrous appearance is due to the fact that it reflects all wavelengths of visible light.

History Notebook
Encourage students to complete the "Silver" Global Commodity page for Chapter 17 in their History Notebooks as they read.

INTRODUCE & ENGAGE

SILVER'S USES TODAY

Ask students to name some items that contain silver. They may mention jewelry, tableware, and coins. Then tell them that silver is also used to make batteries, solar panels, and windows and has many medicinal applications. Tell students that in this lesson they will learn about the history of silver and the role it played in European exploration and global trade.

TEACH

GUIDED DISCUSSION

1. **Identify** What are some of silver's unique characteristics? *(It reflects light, is the lightest of the precious metals, and can be polished to a brilliant shine.)*
2. **Analyze Cause and Effect** What happened because the Industrial Revolution released more sulfur into the atmosphere? *(Silver goods lost their luster more quickly.)*

A GLOBAL COMMODITY

Some historians believe the silver mines of Laurium in ancient Greece were worked as early as 1000 B.C.E. Work intensified around 480 B.C.E. during the Greco-Persian Wars. Athenians used the mined silver to finance the building of a large fleet, which was instrumental in defeating the Persians at the Battle of Salamis in 480 B.C.E. As a result of pirate raids and competition from mines in Macedonia, the Laurium mines fell into disuse as ancient Rome became the dominant power in the Mediterranean. Around the time Christianity began to rise, the silver in the mines had been exhausted.

DIFFERENTIATE

STRIVING READERS

Record and Compare Facts After students read the lesson, ask them to write three important facts they learned about silver. Ask pairs of students to compare and check their facts and then combine their facts into one list. Finally, ask one student from each pair to write the most important fact from their list on the board. As a group, decide if the list includes the most important facts about silver, or if something needs to be added or changed.

GIFTED & TALENTED

Create a Multimedia Presentation Instruct students to create a multimedia presentation about silver, using photos, spoken words, and written text. The presentations should describe and illustrate silver mining and processing and explain and show some of silver's many uses. Invite students to share their presentations with the class.

See the Chapter Planner for more strategies for differentiation.

How do the items shown here reflect silver's versatility?

SPANISH COLONIAL COINS

Spain began minting silver coins in 1537, following its conquest of the Americas. The Spanish coins shown here, called reales, were issued in 1723 and are stamped with King Philip V's name. Holes were punched in coins used as currency in Spain's colonies. Spanish reales were used in English colonies as well. Half of the coins in circulation in colonial America were probably reales. In fact, Spanish money would be used as legal tender in the United States until 1857.

SILVER CAULDRON

This silver cauldron, or large pot, was found in 1891 in a bog in the Danish town of Gundestrup. Made around the first century B.C.E., the silver vessel is decorated with people, animals, and unknown gods. Experts believe an ancient people known as the Thracians, who lived in the area of present-day Bulgaria and Romania, made the cauldron. But they have no idea how it got to Denmark.

INCA SILVER

Like the Peruvian societies that came before them, the Inca were known for their beautiful metalwork. Unfortunately, the Spanish melted down almost every artifact of silver or gold. Pieces that survive include this large silver beaker featuring a human face wearing a headdress (far right). Beakers like this one were often used as drinking vessels during Inca rituals.

Standing at just slightly more than four inches tall, this silver female figurine (right) shows a woman with arms and hands held close to the chest. The figure is adorned with inlaid stones.

SILVER AT A GLANCE

USES	• Like gold, silver was used in the ancient world to make jewelry, artwork, and objects for religious rituals.	• Silver became the most used material for coinage in history because it was perfect for smaller denominations.	• Silver is an essential element in modern technology, medicine, and health-care products.
VALUE	• In ancient Egypt, silver was sometimes valued over gold since sources of silver in the region were more rare.	• Silver became so tied to currency that, in some countries, the word for *silver* and *money* is the same.	• The price of silver rose to an average of about $35 an ounce in 2011 but fell to about $19 in 2016.
PRODUCTION	• Silver is rarely found in a pure state and usually combines with ores such as lead and copper.	• Silver-bearing deposits of ores are mined and then smelted or ground to separate the silver.	• In the 1500s, miners in South and Central America crushed and mixed silver-bearing ore by having mules tread over it.
HISTORY	• The Greek silver-lead mine of Laurium, near Athens, was the best-known mine of the ancient world and was worked by slaves from 500 B.C.E. to 100 C.E.	• Silver goods retained their luster longer until the Industrial Revolution of the 18th and 19th centuries, when more sulfur was released into the atmosphere.	• By 1892, $397 million worth of silver had been mined from Nevada's Comstock Lode, which is the equivalent of more than $9 billion today.
ECONOMICS	• In the 16th century, the flow of silver in Spain resulted in inflation in that country and in much of Europe, with sharp increases in the price of food.	• In 1792, the United States based its currency on the value of silver, and silver coins were not removed from circulation until 1967.	• In 2017, the world's four leading producers of silver were Mexico, Peru, China, and Russia.

BACKGROUND FOR THE TEACHER

Silver in Medicine For centuries, silver has been used by doctors because of its antiseptic properties. Sailors placed silver coins into containers of water and wine to keep the beverages from becoming contaminated during weeks or months at sea. During World War I, silver foil was used to wrap wounds before transporting patients to hospitals. In modern medical practice, silver is used to maintain the sterility of bandages, surgical tools, and medical devices that are inserted into the body, including breathing tubes and catheters. It is even used in hospital fixtures, from furniture to linens to doorknobs! Perhaps the most revolutionary use of silver in medicine is targeting bacteria cells with silver ions. These ions can penetrate and kill bacteria cells without damaging healthy cells.

TEACH

GUIDED DISCUSSION

3. **Synthesize** What is suggested by the fact that Mexico and Peru are still major producers of silver? *(It suggests that some of the sources Spain first plundered around the mid-1550s are still rich in silver.)*

4. **Analyze Visuals** What details of the silver cauldron tell you that the person who made it was highly skilled? *(Possible response: the different faces of the gods, the detailed people and animals, the beautiful shape of the vessel)*

ANALYZE VISUALS

Instruct students to examine the photograph of a Thracian silver cauldron and read the caption. **ASK:** What is depicted on the caldron? *(faces, people on horseback, people with weapons)* Based on its decoration, what do you think the cauldron was used for? *(Answers will vary. Possible response: It was used for ceremonies due to the symbolism of its decorations.)*

ACTIVE OPTION

NG Learning Framework: Debate a Silver-Backed Currency
ATTITUDE Responsibility
SKILL Problem-Solving

Organize students into pairs and have them research the decision in 1792 to base the U.S. currency on silver. Students should investigate why this was proposed as well as the positive and negative impact of the decision. Then encourage the two students in each pair to take different positions and debate whether backing currency with silver was the right decision.

ANSWERS

- Possible response: It connected the world because countries involved in the trade of silver, such as Spain and China, came together. It divided the world because some countries exploited the local people who lived where silver was a natural resource.

- Possible response: The items shown illustrate that silver can be used for many different purposes—as money, for creating dishware, or as jewelry and decoration.

CRITICAL VIEWING The upper levels of Elmina Castle, located in present-day Ghana, provided luxurious accommodations for European traders and ship captains. Below, however, filthy cells in the dungeons housed enslaved people before they were shipped across the Atlantic. Why do you think cannons were mounted and pointed toward the sea?

The Portuguese and Dutch in the Americas

Spain was the first to stake a claim on land in the Americas—but it wouldn't be the lone colonizer for long. In the scramble for land in the Americas, Portugal and the Netherlands didn't want to be left out.

THE PORTUGUESE IN BRAZIL

Remember reading about the Treaty of Tordesillas at the beginning of this chapter? According to the terms of the treaty, Portugal received Brazil, one of the areas that remained outside of Spanish control. But the Portuguese didn't explore Brazil until they stumbled across it when they sailed too far west on a trip to India. In 1500, the Portuguese navigator **Pedro Álvares Cabral** landed in Brazil long enough to claim it for Portugal.

At first, the Portuguese had limited interest in Brazil. The only resource the region seemed to provide was brazilwood, a tree that produced a red dye. The tree gave Brazil its name. But after the French began trading with Brazil's native people, Portugal decided to assert its authority over the area and established its first Brazilian colony in 1532. The Portuguese king divided the colony into administrative districts and appointed a governor to rule over each one.

Colonists began arriving and so did priests, who converted many of the indigenous people to Christianity. The Portuguese priests in Brazil tried to protect local people from cruel treatment at the hands of colonial settlers but had little success. The Portuguese government encouraged colonists in Brazil to set up plantations for growing sugarcane. Sugar, as you know, was a luxury in Europe, so Portugal would make great profits by its sale. However, growing and processing sugarcane was labor-intensive and dangerous. So the plantation owners used slave labor to do the work.

In the beginning, the owners enslaved native Brazilians to grow their sugarcane. Some of the indigenous people fled into the heavily forested interior of Brazil, but the Portuguese recaptured many of them. Eventually, the Portuguese imported African slaves to work on the sugarcane plantations. Portugal had already been

using enslaved Africans on its sugar plantations in West Africa and now brought that practice to Brazil. By 1600, about 15,000 enslaved Africans labored on Brazil's sugar plantations. Resistance was widespread among the African slaves. Some even managed to escape to Brazil's interior and form independent farming communities. Most weren't so lucky. Over time, Portugal would import a total of nearly four million slaves. You will learn more about the slave trade later in this book.

Meanwhile, Portuguese colonists pushed further into Brazil. In 1695, gold was discovered in southeastern Brazil, triggering a gold rush. With enslaved Africans providing the labor, Brazilian mines produced enormous amounts of gold. By 1760, gold rivaled sugar as Portugal's main export. And the search for more gold led to the discovery of diamonds. Brazil became Portugal's most important overseas colony.

THE DUTCH IN NORTH AMERICA

As you know, the Dutch were conducting a booming trade in the Indian Ocean and Europe by the early 1600s. They wanted to get in on the equally lucrative opportunities available in the Americas. To that end, the Netherlands formed the Dutch West India Company in 1621. You've read about the Dutch East India Company, which regulated trade in the Indian Ocean. Its counterpart was granted a monopoly on trade with the Americas, the Caribbean islands, and Africa.

The Dutch West India Company was also determined to wage war on the economies of Spain and Portugal. In 1628, Piet Heyn, the company's director and an admiral, captured a Spanish treasure fleet filled with gold and silver from the Americas. He received a hero's welcome when he returned home. The company used some of the treasure to challenge Portugal's hold on Brazil. In 1630, the Dutch seized an area in northeastern Brazil

502 CHAPTER 17

and took over its sugar plantations there. The Dutch company also sponsored a fleet of ships that captured Elmina Castle, a Portuguese fort on the coast of West Africa, and used it to transport slaves to Brazil and the Caribbean. Elmina became a key outpost for the growing slave trade. The Dutch colony in Brazil flourished for nearly 25 years until the Portuguese won it back in 1654.

Meanwhile, the Dutch West India Company established several colonies in the Caribbean, including a group of five islands called the Netherlands Antilles. The islands were captured from Spain in 1634. Like other European colonizers, the Dutch built sugar plantations on these Caribbean islands and forced enslaved Africans to supply the labor.

You've learned that when the Dutch East India Company sent Henry Hudson to find the Northwest Passage, he only got as far as present-day New York state. The fur trade that Hudson had begun in the region gradually expanded, and the Dutch West India Company was authorized to set up a colony there. As a result, in 1624, the company established New Netherland off the tip of what the Native American inhabitants called Manna-hata Island (today's Manhattan) and built **New Amsterdam** (today's New York City) as its capital. Dutch presence on the mainland of North America didn't last long, however. In 1664, the English seized New Netherland without a struggle. By that time, the English and French had come to dominate colonial America.

HISTORICAL THINKING

1. **READING CHECK** What made Brazil Portugal's most important colony?

2. **MAKE INFERENCES** Why did the Dutch West India Company want to undermine the Spanish and Portuguese economies?

3. **ANALYZE CAUSE AND EFFECT** What happened as a result of Henry Hudson's attempt to find the Northwest Passage?

Age of Maritime Expansion 503

PLAN: 2-PAGE LESSON

OBJECTIVE

Explain how Portugal and the Netherlands established profitable colonies in Brazil, the Caribbean, and the mainland of North America.

CRITICAL THINKING SKILLS FOR LESSON 3.3

- Make Inferences
- Analyze Cause and Effect
- Identify Main Ideas and Details
- Compare and Contrast
- Analyze Visuals

HISTORICAL THINKING FOR CHAPTER 17

How did European exploration transform the world socially, politically, and economically?

Following Spain's example, other European countries soon set out to explore the Americas. Lesson 3.3 discusses the impact that Portuguese and Dutch settlements had on the colonization of the Americas.

Student eEdition online

Additional content for this lesson, including an image, is available online.

BACKGROUND FOR THE TEACHER

Pedro Álvares Cabral Pedro Álvares Cabral was educated in Portugal's royal court. In 1500, King Manuel I named him commander of the second Portuguese expedition to India. He was to follow the route taken earlier by Vasco da Gama. Sailing westward, Cabral sighted the coast of Brazil and named it the *True Cross.* Eventually, the country took its present-day name, *Brazil,* from the brazilwood tree found there. Cabral took formal possession of the country and sent a ship back to Portugal to inform the king. Afterward, maps showed Portugal as the ruler of a great area of land. Later voyages used Brazil as a port of call in the journey from Europe to the Cape of Good Hope in Africa and the Indian Ocean.

INTRODUCE & ENGAGE

PREVIEW USING TEXT FEATURES

Guide students in using the lesson's introduction, section headings, and visuals to preview the lesson. **ASK:** Based on these features, what questions do you expect this lesson to answer? (*Possible responses: Why did the Portuguese and Dutch colonize the Americas? What regions in the Americas were colonized by the Portuguese and Dutch?*) Create and display a 5Ws Chart to categorize students' questions. Return to the chart after students have read the lesson and prompt them to provide answers. Urge students to research unanswered questions.

TEACH

GUIDED DISCUSSION

1. **Identify Main Ideas and Details** Why did the Portuguese government encourage Brazilian colonists to set up sugarcane plantations? (*Sugar was a luxury item in Europe, and Portugal expected to make huge profits from its trade.*)

2. **Compare and Contrast** In what ways were the Portuguese and Dutch colonization of the Americas similar? (*Both established sugar plantations in their colonies, engaged in slave trade, used enslaved Africans, and showed little regard for indigenous people.*)

ANALYZE VISUALS

Tell students to examine the photograph of the Dutch silver dish (available in the Student eEdition). **ASK:** Why might nautical themes have been popular during this time? (*Possible response: Because the Dutch were exploring and colonizing the world by sea, Dutch nautical themes represented the spirit of the times.*)

ACTIVE OPTIONS

On Your Feet: Three-Step Interview Organize students into pairs. Tell Student A to interview Student B about the motivations and strategies of the Portuguese in the Americas. Then tell Student B to interview Student A about the motivations and strategies of the Dutch in the Americas. Reconvene as a class, and invite Student A to share information from Student B and Student B to share information from Student A.

NG Learning Framework: The Fur Trade in the 1600s
ATTITUDES Curiosity, Responsibility
KNOWLEDGE Our Living Planet

Encourage students to learn more about the fur trade in North America in the 1600s by conducting research. Have students consider the following questions as they research. Then tell students to prepare a short report to present to the class.

• What kinds of animals were most affected by the fur trade?
• How long was the fur trade in North America active?
• How have attitudes about fur trading changed over time?

DIFFERENTIATE

ENGLISH LANGUAGE LEARNERS

Create Detail Webs Pair students at the **Beginning** and **Intermediate** levels with those at the **Advanced** level to read the first section of the lesson together. To help students keep track of the details, have them complete a Detail Web. Tell students to write "The Portuguese in Brazil" in the center of the web and fill in details from the text that explain what the Portuguese did in Brazil in the outer circles. Then have pairs compare their Detail Webs and add any details they may have missed.

PRE-AP

Research Have students conduct online research to find out more about the Dutch West India Company. Ask them to report to the class about its leaders, activities, successes, and failures. Encourage them to explain how the Dutch West India Company compared to the Dutch East India Company.

See the Chapter Planner for more strategies for differentiation.

HISTORICAL THINKING

ANSWERS

1. Brazil's sugar plantations yielded great profits, as did its gold mines.

2. Answers will vary. Possible response: By weakening their economies, the Dutch hoped to seize some of their colonies and take over much of their trade.

3. The Dutch established a colony called New Netherland on the mainland of North America.

CRITICAL VIEWING Answers will vary. Possible response: to fight off attacks from Europeans and pirates

The English Colonies and New France

The English government established colonies in North America in hopes of finding gold, silver, and a viable sea route to Asia. None of those things turned up, but many of those who settled in the colonies found freedom, work, and a new home.

ENGLISH COLONIES

Due to wars and internal problems during the late 1400s and much of the 1500s, England couldn't compete with other European countries in overseas exploration and colony-building. By the end of the 16th century, however, England had expanding agricultural and mining industries, land shortages, and an increasingly mobile population. These factors set the stage for England to challenge its European rivals.

CRITICAL VIEWING This aerial photo of Jamestown shows the original fort and settlement site. Archaeologists reconstructed the fort and erected fences to mark the dimensions of the original buildings. The colonists built the fort on an island to defend Jamestown against the Spanish. Why might the colonists have feared an attack by Spain?

In 1607, a group of English colonists landed at Chesapeake Bay on the mid-Atlantic coast of North America. There they founded **Jamestown**, England's first permanent settlement in the Americas. They named the surrounding land Virginia, and tobacco became the colony's chief crop. To grow their tobacco, planters began to use **indentured servants**, people who pledged to work for four to seven years in exchange for ocean passage and living costs. Slavery was also introduced to Jamestown. The first slaves, African captives taken from a Portuguese ship by English raiders, arrived in 1619.

Other colonies were soon founded along the Atlantic coast. Slavery would expand throughout the Southern Colonies. As cash crops such as tobacco, cotton, indigo, and rice flourished, a plantation system and distinct social classes arose.

Slavery was not widely practiced in the New England Colonies, which began with the arrival of the Pilgrims and the Puritans, who were seeking religious freedom. More settlers soon arrived for economic reasons. As fishing, whaling, and shipbuilding industries developed, New England became the center of colonial trade.

The Middle Colonies were known for their tolerance. This policy was primarily a legacy of Dutch settlers who had welcomed Jews and Protestants and people from Sweden, Finland, and Norway. The population of these colonies grew as a result of a thriving agricultural industry. And cities, including Philadelphia and New York, became economic and cultural centers.

NEW FRANCE

One year after English colonists arrived in Jamestown, French explorer **Samuel de Champlain** sailed up the St. Lawrence River and founded **Quebec** in present-day Canada. Quebec would be the base of France's colonial empire in North America, known as New France. The colonists began a valuable trade in furs with First Nations communities such as the Algonquin. While the English colonists sought to expand their share of territory and push Native Americans off the land, the French established good relationships with their Algonquin trading partners and even forged alliances with them. French fur traders often traveled into the interior and married local women. Their children often spoke both French and indigenous languages.

Other French explorers pushed deeper into the North American continent. In 1673, Jacques Marquette and Louis Joliet paddled through the Great Lakes and upper Mississippi River. Their account of the extraordinary natural resources they saw there led the French to create a 4,000-mile-long network of trading posts along the bodies of water. Explorer Sieur de La Salle traveled the Illinois and Mississippi rivers and claimed all the land along the rivers for French king Louis XIV in 1682. By the early 1700s, New France covered much of what is today the midwestern United States and eastern Canada.

Despite the size of its territory, however, the population of New France remained sparse. The English wanted to extend their settlements to the west and had their eyes on the lands of New France. In 1754, the **French and Indian War** broke out between France and its Native American allies on one side and England and the American colonists on the other. England would win the war, and New France would lose most of its colonies. But the outcome for the American colonists would not be what they had expected.

New France and English Colonies in North America, 1754 (map)

HISTORICAL THINKING

1. **READING CHECK** Why were indentured servants and enslaved people brought to Jamestown?

2. **INTERPRET MAPS** How would you describe the location of the English colonies in relation to New France?

3. **ANALYZE CAUSE AND EFFECT** What led to the French and Indian War?

PLAN: 2-PAGE LESSON

OBJECTIVE
Explain how England and France established colonies in North America with differing economies and relationships with indigenous peoples.

CRITICAL THINKING SKILLS FOR LESSON 3.4
- Interpret Maps
- Analyze Cause and Effect
- Compare and Contrast
- Analyze Visuals

HISTORICAL THINKING FOR CHAPTER 17
How did European exploration transform the world socially, politically, and economically?

The English settlers of North America came seeking economic opportunities and religious freedom. Lesson 3.4 discusses French and English settlements in North America and their differing treatment of indigenous peoples.

Student eEdition online
Additional content for this lesson, including a Global Commodity feature, is available online.

BACKGROUND FOR THE TEACHER
Jamestown A company called the Virginia Company funded the first settlement of Jamestown. The Virginia Company viewed Jamestown as a business and settlers as company employees. The company instructed the first colonists to search for gold and silver and establish profitable industries and trade. The colonists, many of whom were wealthy adventurers, failed to produce and became aimless. Sir Thomas Dale, who arrived in Jamestown as governor in 1611, quickly established martial law and required reasonable hours of work with harsh punishments for noncompliance. A first offender was tied neck to heels all night. A second offense merited whipping, and punishment for a third offense was death. The harsh laws caused a scandal in England and discouraged settlers from coming to the colony.

History Notebook
Encourage students to complete the "Indigo" Global Commodity page for Chapter 17 in their History Notebooks as they read.

INTRODUCE & ENGAGE

ESTABLISH A COLONY

Tell students that the class will work together to plan a new colony. Guide the planning process by having students consider the following questions: What is the purpose of the colony? Should it be permanent or temporary? What kind of climate and geography would be best for the colony? Why? How will the colony be run? Who is in charge? What rights do the colonists have?

As students offer ideas, write them on the board, editing them as they evolve through discussion.

TEACH

GUIDED DISCUSSION

1. **Analyze Cause and Effect** What factors affected the timing of England's expeditions to the New World? *(England was facing other challenges, so it wasn't until the early 17th century that England began to focus on colonization and world exploration.)*

2. **Compare and Contrast** How did the French and English colonizers in North America differ in their treatment of indigenous peoples? *(The French traded with First Nations communities, and some intermarried. The English practiced segregation and competed with indigenous peoples for resources.)*

ANALYZE VISUALS

Invite students to review the text and photos in the Global Commodity feature on indigo (available in the Student eEdition). Discuss indigo's ties to the North American colonies, the global market, and the slave trade. **ASK:** How would you describe the process for making indigo dye? *(Possible response: labor-intensive, messy)* What does the linen shawl made around 1750 suggest about the dye? *(Possible response: The dye was prized and used to color clothing.)*

ACTIVE OPTIONS

On Your Feet: Fishbowl Have part of the class sit in a close circle facing inward. Direct the other part of the class to sit in a larger circle around the first circle. Ask students on the inside to discuss the different cultures of the Southern Colonies, Middle Colonies, and New England. Those sitting in the outside circle should listen for new information and evaluate the discussion. Then have the groups reverse positions.

> **NG Learning Framework: Write a Biography**
> SKILL Communication
> KNOWLEDGE Our Human Story

When the English settlers arrived in Jamestown, they encountered the Powhatan, a Native American tribe. Then in 1614, Chief Powhatan's daughter, Pocahontas, married colonist John Rolfe. Pocahontas has fascinated people from 17th-century artists to 21st-century filmmakers. Tell students to find out more about her life and the impact of her marriage to Rolfe. Instruct them to create a biographical sketch of Pocahontas and use existing paintings or their own illustrations to share with the class.

DIFFERENTIATE

STRIVING READERS

Record Facts and Details Instruct students to draw a three-column chart and label the columns with the names of the three groups of English colonies: New England, Middle Colonies, and Southern Colonies. As they read, have students jot down important facts and details about each group.

PRE-AP

Design a Poster Have students create a poster for the French government designed to persuade people to move to New France. The poster should feature information about the settlements and the kinds of opportunities available there. Students may also wish to include disclaimers, disclosing the potential drawbacks to settlement.

See the Chapter Planner for more strategies for differentiation.

HISTORICAL THINKING

ANSWERS

1. Demand for tobacco grown in the colony skyrocketed, and farmers needed laborers to grow and harvest it.

2. New England and the Middle and Southern colonies directly bordered New France on the west.

3. the desire to seize the lands of New France from the French

CRITICAL VIEWING Answers will vary. Possible response: Spain had dominated colonization of the Americas and may have wanted to seize Jamestown.

VOCABULARY

Complete each sentence below with the correct vocabulary word.

1. The Portuguese learned how to build a light ship with triangular sails called a _____.

2. Ferdinand Magellan led the first expedition to _____ the world.

3. The _____ of New Spain governed from his capital in Mexico City.

4. After Jamestown was founded, tobacco planters used _____ to supply the labor on their farms.

5. Under the _____ system, Spanish plantation owners forced Native Americans to farm the land.

6. The Spanish explorer Hernán Cortés, also called a _____, conquered the Aztec.

7. Wealthy Spaniards owned large agricultural estates known as _____.

READING STRATEGY
ANALYZE CAUSE AND EFFECT

Use a cause-and-effect chain to identify the multiple causes and effects of the Indian Ocean trade empire established by Portugal. Then answer the questions.

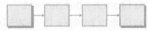

8. How did the legacy of Prince Henry impact the establishment of Portuguese trade in the Indian Ocean?

9. What happened as a result of Portugal's seizure of the Straits of Hormuz?

MAIN IDEAS

Answer the following questions. Support your answers with evidence from the chapter.

10. What did Christopher Columbus hope to achieve on his voyages? LESSON 1.1

11. Who brought about the end of the Aztec and Inca empires? LESSON 1.2

12. What were some of the positive and negative impacts of the Columbian Exchange? LESSON 1.4

13. Why was the 1498 voyage of Vasco da Gama important to Portugal? LESSON 2.1

14. What was the purpose of the Dutch East India Company? LESSON 2.2

15. Which groups made up the social order in Spanish colonial society? LESSON 3.1

16. Why did the Portuguese have limited interest in Brazil when they first colonized it? LESSON 3.3

17. How did raising tobacco help Jamestown succeed? LESSON 3.4

HISTORICAL THINKING

Answer the following questions. Support your answers with evidence from the chapter.

18. ANALYZE CAUSE AND EFFECT What happened as a result of Columbus's voyages?

19. FORM AND SUPPORT OPINIONS Do you think the Spanish would have been able to conquer the Aztec and Inca if the native peoples had not been infected with disease? Why or why not?

20. DRAW CONCLUSIONS Aside from the desire for wealth and power, what else probably encouraged the Portuguese to take away much of the Indian Ocean trade from the Muslims?

21. MAKE INFERENCES Why do you think some of the Native Americans in New Spain combined their spiritual traditions with Christian teachings?

22. SYNTHESIZE In addition to taking over profitable Spanish colonies in the Americas, what might have motivated Dutch attacks on Spain?

23. COMPARE AND CONTRAST How did the Dutch attitude toward settlers in North America compare with their attitude toward those they colonized elsewhere?

INTERPRET MAPS

German cartographer Martin Waldseemüller drew this map of the New World in 1513. The map shows Florida in the top left corner with the Caribbean islands of Cuba (Isabella) and Haiti and the Dominican Republic (Spagnolla) beneath it. Spain and Africa appear on the right, and the area labeled with the Latin words *terra incognita*, meaning "unknown lands" represents Brazil. Study the map, and then answer the questions below.

Waldseemüller Map of the "New World," 1513

24. How does Waldseemüller depict the physical relationship between North America and South America?

25. What does the map suggest about European knowledge of the Western Hemisphere in 1513?

ANALYZE SOURCES

The Spanish missionary Bartolomé de las Casas witnessed the harsh treatment of Native Americans at the hands of Spanish settlers. In 1542, he wrote *A Brief Account of the Destruction of the Indies*, detailing what he had seen. In this excerpt, Las Casas summarizes the Spaniards' brutality toward Native Americans on the Caribbean island of Hispaniola.

> The Spaniards first assaulted the innocent Sheep . . . like most cruel Tygers, Wolves and Lions hunger-starv'd, studying nothing, for the space of Forty Years, after their first landing, but the Massacre of these Wretches, whom they have so inhumanely and barbarously butcher'd and harass'd with several kinds of Torments, never before known, or heard . . . . [O]f Three Millions of Persons, which lived in Hispaniola itself, there is at present but the inconsiderable remnant of scarce Three Hundred.

26. How does Las Casas characterize the Spanish settlers and the Native Americans in Hispaniola?

CONNECT TO YOUR LIFE

27. EXPLANATORY Between 1450 and 1750, Europeans explored lands unknown to them. The expeditions were dangerous and filled with challenges and hardships. What would you like to explore: outer space, the oceans, Antarctica?

Think of where you'd like to go, and then plan your expedition. Consider how you'd get there, what challenges you might face, and what you would want to find or accomplish on your expedition. Write a brief essay explaining where you'd go, how you'd get there, and what the purpose of your expedition would be.

TIPS

* Review what you've read about the experiences of the Spanish, Portuguese, Dutch, French, and English explorers.

* If necessary, do research to learn about the place you've chosen to explore.

* Decide what the goal of your expedition would be. Do you want to study conditions on another planet, discover new life forms, find evidence of climate change? Reflect on the ways in which your goal compares with those of the explorers in this chapter.

* Use two or three vocabulary terms from the chapter in your essay.

* Provide a concluding statement summarizing your trip and comparing your expedition to those conducted by early European explorers.

VOCABULARY ANSWERS

1. caravel
2. circumnavigate
3. viceroy
4. indentured servants
5. encomienda
6. conquistador
7. haciendas

READING STRATEGY ANSWERS

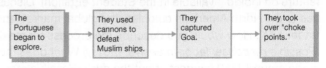

The Portuguese began to explore. → They used cannons to defeat Muslim ships. → They captured Goa. → They took over "choke points."

8. Because of Prince Henry's navigation school, Portuguese navigators explored the coast of Africa, and Vasco da Gama eventually discovered a direct sea route to India.

9. Muslim traders could no longer reach India by sailing through the Persian Gulf to the Indian Ocean.

MAIN IDEAS ANSWERS

10. He hoped to find a faster sea route to Asia by sailing west across the Atlantic Ocean.

11. Cortés ended the Aztec Empire, and Pizarro defeated the Inca.

12. Positive: The availability of such a great variety of foods through the Columbian Exchange improved nutrition around the world. Negative: Europeans introduced deadly new diseases to the Americas for which the local populations had no immunity, and millions of indigenous people were killed.

13. Da Gama found a direct sea route to India, which allowed the Portuguese to take control of the trade there.

14. to have exclusive control over Dutch trade with Asia

15. *Peninsulares* came first, followed by the Creoles and mestizos. Indigenous peoples and African slaves were at the bottom of the social ladder.

16. The only resource the region seemed to provide was brazilwood, a tree that produced a red dye.

17. Demand for tobacco grew in Europe, and the colony benefited from the trade.

HISTORICAL THINKING ANSWERS

18. Answers will vary. Possible response: He opened up the Americas to exploration and colonization.

19. Answers will vary. Possible response: The conquistadors would have conquered the Aztec and Inca even if they hadn't been affected by disease because the Spaniards had much more powerful weapons.

20. Answers will vary. Possible response: the desire to end Muslim influence in the region and spread Christianity among the people

21. Answers will vary. Possible response: The traditions had probably been passed down for hundreds of years and were important parts of the indigenous peoples' lives and culture.

22. Answers will vary. Possible response: The Dutch were engaged in an ongoing war for independence from Spain, so the Dutch wanted to weaken their enemy.

23. Answers will vary. Possible response: While the Dutch tolerated differences among the white settlers in New Netherland, they demonstrated a racist attitude toward the people of color in other parts of the world.

INTERPRET MAPS ANSWERS

24. He connects the two landmasses.

25. It suggests that the knowledge of places and their distances from one another was limited and sketchy.

ANALYZE SOURCES ANSWER

26. Las Casas refers to the native people as innocent sheep and wretches and to the Spaniards as cruel, hunger-starved tigers, wolves, and lions.

CONNECT TO YOUR LIFE ANSWER

27. Essays will vary but should contain main ideas and relevant supporting details to explain the destination and purpose of the expedition.

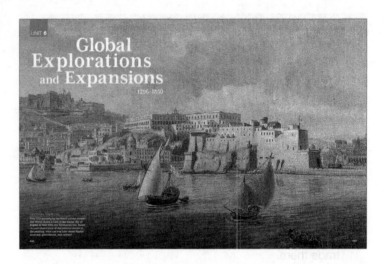

SECTION 1 RESOURCES	SECTION 2 RESOURCES	CHAPTER 18 REVIEW

AFRICA, ASIA, AND EUROPE

THE ATLANTIC SLAVE TRADE

STRATEGY ❶
Use Supported Reading

Have students in small groups read the chapter aloud lesson by lesson. At the end of each lesson, have them stop and use these frames to tell what they comprehended from the text:

- This lesson is about _____.
- One detail or fact that stood out to me is _____.
- A difficult vocabulary word to me is _____. It means _____.
- I don't think I understand _____.

Use with All Lessons

STRATEGY ❷
Use a TASKS Approach

Have students get information from visuals by using the following TASKS strategy:

T Look for a **title** that may give the main idea.
A **Ask** yourself what the visual is trying to show.
S Determine how **symbols** are used.
K Look for a **key** or legend.
S **Summarize** what you learned.

Use with Lessons 1.2, 2.2, and 2.3

STRATEGY ❸
Use Paired Reading

Pair students and assign each pair two passages in the lesson. Tell them that they will each take one passage, read it, take notes, become an expert on it, and share their expertise with their partner. After students have had time to prepare their passages, have them report on their reading to each other. Tell each listener to write two clarifying questions for the other to answer.

Use with All Lessons

STRATEGY ❶
Provide Terms and Names on Audio

Decide which of the terms and names are important for mastery and ask a volunteer to record the pronunciations and a short sentence defining each. Encourage students to listen to the recording as often as needed for them to use the terms comfortably in discussion.

Use with All Lessons *You might also use the recordings to quiz students on their mastery of the terms. Play one definition at a time and ask students to identify the term or name described.*

STRATEGY ❷
Provide Alternative Ways of Reporting

Instead of a written report, allow students to report their knowledge in other ways. For example, students who are comfortable communicating orally can give an oral presentation instead of a written report, or students who struggle with writing and speaking can give a photographic essay on a chapter topic, such as the 2013 attack on Timbuktu or growing, harvesting, and processing sugar today.

Use with All Lessons

STRATEGY ❶
Modify Vocabulary Lists

Limit the number of words, terms, and names students at the **Beginning** level will be required to master. Have students write each word from your modified list on a colored sticky note and put it on the page next to where it appears in context.

Use with Lessons 1.2, 1.3, 2.2, and 2.4

STRATEGY ❷
Use Visuals to Predict

Direct students at the **Beginning** and **Intermediate** levels to read the lesson titles and look at the visuals. Then ask them to write a sentence predicting how the visual is related to the lesson. After reading, you may wish to have students verify their predictions and reword sentences as necessary.

Use with All Lessons

STRATEGY ❸
Build a Concept Cluster

Write the phrase *triangular trade* on the board and ask students for words, phrases, or pictures that come to mind. Have volunteers write the words and draw simple pictures around *triangular trade* to build a Concept Cluster. Call on students to create sentences about the words and pictures. Then tell students to each ask a question they would like answered about the Key Vocabulary term.

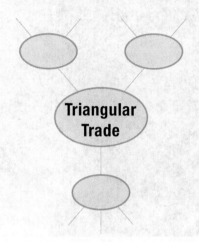

Use with Lessons 2.1 and 2.2 *You might pair students at the **Advanced** level with students at the **Beginning** and **Intermediate** levels and have more proficient students assist less proficient students.*

GIFTED & TALENTED

STRATEGY ❶
Write a Historical Memoir

Tell students to use facts they have learned to write a memoir from someone who was alive during the 1400s as the Songhai rulers took control of West Africa. Students should consider the various rulers, including their strengths and weaknesses, as well as the influence of Muhammad and Islam. Students may want to supplement their memoirs with additional research. Remind them to use academic sources in their research.

Use with Lesson 1.2

STRATEGY ❷
Form a Thesis

Have students develop a thesis statement about an immediate consequence of the Atlantic slave trade. Tell students to make sure the statement makes a claim that is supportable with evidence either from the chapter or through further research. Then have pairs compare their statements and determine which makes the strongest or most supportable claim.

Use with Lessons 2.1, 2.2, 2.3, and 2.4

PRE-AP

STRATEGY ❶
Write a News Story

Instruct students to further research the city of Timbuktu. Have them supplement the information in the text with library or online resources about the history or a current event that relates to the city. Encourage students to include statistics, photos, and first-person accounts in their story, if appropriate. Have students share their news stories with the class.

Use with Lesson 1.1

STRATEGY ❷
Analyze Effects

Tell students to work individually or in pairs to research the long-term effects of the Atlantic slave trade in the United States. Students should consider the following aspects:

- social changes
- economic changes
- political changes

Suggest that students develop a graphic organizer to display the results of their investigation. As an alternative, assign students to research slavery in another country such as England, France, or Spain.

Use with Lessons 2.1, 2.2, 2.3, and 2.4

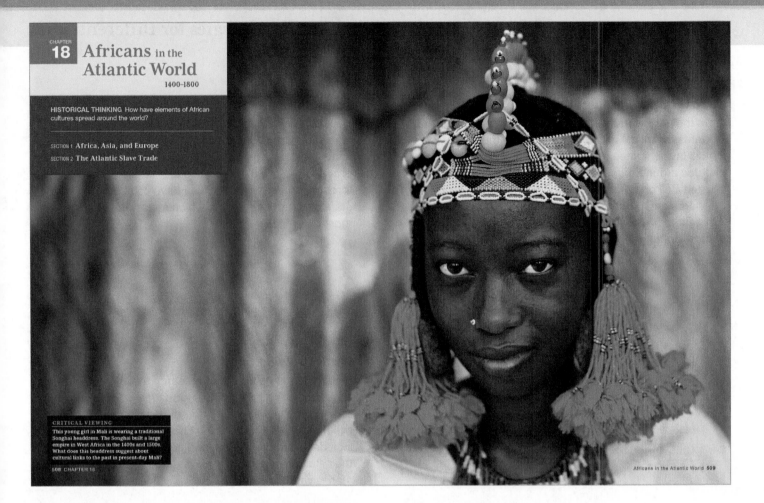

HISTORICAL THINKING How have elements of African cultures spread around the world?

SECTION 1 **Africa, Asia, and Europe**
SECTION 2 **The Atlantic Slave Trade**

CRITICAL VIEWING
This young girl in Mali is wearing a traditional Songhai headdress. The Songhai built a large empire in West Africa in the 1400s and 1500s. What does this headdress suggest about cultural links to the past in present-day Mali?

508 CHAPTER 18

Africans in the Atlantic World 509

INTRODUCE THE PHOTOGRAPH

MALIAN HEADDRESS

Have students examine the photograph of the Malian girl in the traditional Songhai headdress and read the accompanying caption. **ASK:** Based on her expression, how might she feel about wearing the headdress? *(Possible responses: prideful, important, a celebration of her cultural heritage)* Explain that Malian headdresses are traditionally made of beads, gems, fabric, and even fake hair. Tell students that in this chapter they will learn about powerful empires in Africa, how the Atlantic slave trade changed the course of African history, and how enslaved Africans resisted their captivity and formed unique cultures in the New World.

SHARE BACKGROUND

Mali's cultural tradition is a mix of native African and Islamic culture. In 2012–2013, militant Islamist rebels took control of Timbuktu and the surrounding region, trying to repress and destroy any aspects of culture that did not fall in line with sharia law and strict Islamic rules. The rebels destroyed countless historic manuscripts and buildings. Their demands also extended to how people dressed; for example, traditional headdresses were not accepted by the rebels. After the rebels were expelled from Mali through the efforts of Malian and French troops, many Malian people celebrated by donning traditional headdresses, which were traditionally worn by high-ranking people on special occasions.

CRITICAL VIEWING Answers will vary. Possible responses may include that cultural links to the past are strong, since a contemporary person is wearing a style that has been around for hundreds of years.

How have elements of African cultures spread around the world?

Numbered Heads Activity: Reflecting on Africa's Role in the World This activity will help students preview and discuss the topics covered in the chapter. Divide the class into groups of four and have them count off within each group. Pose the following question: How have parts of Africa affected and been affected by other parts of the world? Assign the following topics to each number: religion, the arts, the global economy, and the environment. Students may wish to preview the chapter content while considering the question. Instruct group members to think about the question individually and then discuss the answers within their team, making sure that each team member is knowledgeable enough to report for the group. Then call a number and have that student share the group's thoughts on all four categories with the class.

KEY DATES FOR CHAPTER 18

c. 1460	The Songhai take control of Mali.
1493	Askia Muhammad the Great becomes the leader of the Songhai Empire.
1591	Moroccans conquer the Songhai Empire.
1600s	Rwanda and Buganda flourish in the Great Lakes region.
mid-1600s	Kimpa Vita preaches in the Kongo kingdom.
late 1700s	Europeans realize the abuses of triangular trade.
1789	Olaudah Equiano writes *The Interesting Narrative of the Life of Olaudah Equiano, or Gustavus Vassa, the African, 1789.*
1800s	Harriet Tubman helps enslaved people in the United States escape to freedom.
2013	Islamist rebels seize Timbuktu and destroy priceless artifacts.

INTRODUCE THE READING STRATEGY

IDENTIFY MAIN IDEAS AND DETAILS

Explain to students that identifying a passage's main idea and details can help them more deeply understand concepts and events. Go to the Chapter Review and preview the Main Idea and Details graphic organizer with students. As they read the chapter, have students use graphic organizers like this one to differentiate between main ideas and details pertaining to Africa's interactions with the Atlantic world.

INTRODUCE CHAPTER VOCABULARY

KEY VOCABULARY

SECTION 1

| Islamist | succession |

SECTION 2

abolition	autonomous	manumission
maroon community	Middle Passage	
racism	slave narrative	triangular trade

DEFINITION CHART

As they read the chapter, encourage students to complete a Definition Chart for Key Vocabulary terms. Instruct students to list the Key Vocabulary terms in the first column of the chart. They should add each term's definition in the center column as they encounter the term in the chapter and then restate the definition in their own words in the third column. Model an example on the board, using the graphic organizer shown.

Word	Definition	In My Own Words
abolition	the movement to end slavery	making it illegal to buy, sell, or own another human

African History: 1500s to 1700s

Since ancient times, Africans had formed trade connections with other peoples across the Mediterranean, the Red Sea, and the Indian Ocean. Through the centuries, these trade networks kept expanding, spreading both goods and ideas across the continent and to other parts of the world.

CRITICAL VIEWING People buy and sell goods at a street market in Ibadan, Nigeria. What can you infer about the city's economy based on evidence in the photo?

A DIVERSE CONTINENT

By the 1500s, Africa's geographic diversity—its deserts, grasslands, and rain forests—had been matched by its variety of political systems for a very long time. Some Africans formed small bands of hunter-gatherers, while others lived in kingdoms led by powerful monarchs. In many agricultural communities, ruling dynasties developed along with a complex hierarchy.

In almost all African societies, clan elders played a key role in negotiating consensus, or general agreement, on community decisions. African villages ruled by a distant chief or king retained their own ways of keeping peace and administering justice.

Over time, interaction among various African peoples brought about cultural and economic changes. For example, in the Great Lakes region of east-central

Africa, Bantu-speaking people migrating from the west brought knowledge of grain agriculture and gained access to cattle in exchange. In the societies that resulted from this migration, farming provided most of the food, while cattle were viewed as signs of wealth and social status. Supported by agricultural surpluses and dominated by clans wealthy in cattle, a number of powerful kingdoms, such as Rwanda and Buganda, emerged in the 1600s.

In the Great Lakes region and other parts of Africa, high population density was connected to more centralized politics. That was not true in the Igbo (ee-BWOH)-speaking region of West Africa, however. In this rich agricultural area, with its vibrant markets and trade, powerful kings never emerged. Instead, the people preferred a system in which men and women gained titles and authority based on their achievements rather than on their social rank at birth.

The growth of external markets and the spread of Islam persisted in Africa through the 1500s. Though the Muslim-ruled empire of Mali collapsed in about 1450, trade persisted. West African goods such as gold and leather were transported across the Sahara in return for commodities from its Mediterranean region. From West African cities on the **Niger River**, goods then flowed on this "water highway" into Africa's rain forests. The continual stream of both goods and ideas, as well as religious pilgrims and teachers, reinforced the spread of Islam across much of West Africa.

African trade across the Indian Ocean continued even after the Portuguese disrupted coastal trade with their assault on the East African port of Kilwa in the early 1500s. Muslim Swahili merchants still carried on a lively trade with peoples in India and around the Persian Gulf. In fact, African merchants traded brightly patterned Indian cotton textiles deep into the interior of the continent in the 16th century.

Beginning in 1696, Arab sultans of Oman began to exert control over East African ports. Swahili princes and aristocrats generally accepted the authority of the Arab sultans while continuing to regulate the day-to-day affairs of their own city-states. Traditional Swahili arts and crafts, such as poetry and jewelry, continued to thrive, blending Islamic and African themes.

CHRISTIANITY IN AFRICA

Christianity had been part of North African life since ancient times. As you learned, the Ethiopian Coptic Church, connected to the Eastern Orthodox Church, was already more than 1,000 years old when the Portuguese arrived along Africa's eastern coast in 1498. The many monasteries that had been built in the region were evidence of the strong presence of Christianity.

By this time, Islam was spreading throughout the region. As a result, the Ethiopian and Portuguese Christians formed a military alliance against the expanding Muslim kingdom. The alliance was not a great success. The Portuguese leader was killed in a battle with Muslim forces. In addition, because the Ethiopians had their own Christian beliefs and rituals, they refused to accept the Catholic interpretations of European priests.

A new frontier of Christianity in Africa opened in the Kongo kingdom of Central Africa. King Nzinga, the ruler of the kingdom, converted to Roman Catholicism after the arrival of the Portuguese. Nzinga exchanged ambassadors with the pope and sent his son to school in Lisbon. His alliance with the European Christians became strained, however, when Portuguese slave trading disrupted Kongo society. Nzinga complained to the king of Portugal, but the slave trade continued.

In the mid-1600s, the Kongo kingdom collapsed. A Christian reformer named **Kimpa Vita** quickly stepped in to provide direction to the Kongo people. She declared that she had been visited by Saint Anthony and had spoken with God, who said that the people must unite under a new king. Kimpa Vita taught that Jesus and his apostles were Africans who had lived and died in Kongo, and she mixed Christian beliefs with African religious traditions. Her teachings were popular with many Africans, but Portuguese missionaries regarded her as a heretic. She was captured by rivals, tried for witchcraft, and burned at the stake.

European settlers introduced yet another form of Christianity to the continent. In the 1600s, Dutch Calvinists and French Huguenots brought Protestant Christianity to southern Africa. However, another two centuries passed before significant numbers of southern Africans converted to Christianity.

HISTORICAL THINKING

1. **READING CHECK** How did Muslim traders affect the cultures of North, East, and West Africa?

2. **IDENTIFY MAIN IDEAS** What was one common feature of the political systems in almost all African societies?

3. **COMPARE AND CONTRAST** What were the differences and similarities in Christian beliefs introduced in eastern, central, and southern Africa?

PLAN: 2-PAGE LESSON

OBJECTIVE
Describe how, between the 1500s and 1700s, Africa continued to develop as a politically and culturally diverse continent with expanding international trade networks.

CRITICAL THINKING SKILLS FOR LESSON 1.1
- Identify Main Ideas
- Compare and Contrast
- Explain
- Describe

HISTORICAL THINKING FOR CHAPTER 18
How have elements of African cultures spread around the world?

Countless societies have flourished in Africa, a very geographically and culturally diverse continent. Lesson 1.1 discusses the many political, religious, and cultural characteristics of different people in Africa.

Student eEdition online
Additional content for this lesson, including an image, is available online.

BACKGROUND FOR THE TEACHER
Coptic Christianity in Ethiopia and Egypt Christianity has existed in eastern Africa since the first century C.E. Saint Mark, who wrote the Gospel of Mark in the New Testament, brought Christianity to Egypt, where he eventually was killed and became a martyr for his beliefs. Egyptian Christians became known as *copts*—a term that, over time, was derived from Arabic and Greek words for Egypt.

Ethiopian Christians are also known as copts, and although Ethiopian churches were first established around the same time that Saint Mark was preaching in Alexandria, Christianity's path to Ethiopia did not come through Egypt. The Saints Matthew and Bartholomew began to spread Christianity in Ethiopia, and several centuries later, the religion's adoption by the kings Aksum and Ezana cemented its role in Ethiopian society.

INTRODUCE & ENGAGE

ACTIVATE PRIOR KNOWLEDGE

Discuss with students what they already know about different Christian denominations, such as Catholicism, Protestantism, and Eastern Orthodox Christianity. Have students consider the different traditions, values, and religious beliefs of each of these denominations, as well as any times these differences have caused conflict between various groups. Tell students that in this lesson they will learn about several different kinds of Christianity that developed in Africa and how their belief systems affected their relationships with some Europeans.

TEACH

GUIDED DISCUSSION

1. **Explain** Why was the Niger River considered a "water highway"? *(Goods, people, and ideas were transported along the Niger River from West Africa to the interior of the continent.)*

2. **Describe** How were Jesus and his apostles portrayed in the Kongo tradition? *(They were portrayed as Africans.)*

IDENTIFY MAIN IDEAS AND DETAILS

After reading the first section of the lesson, have students state the main idea and extrapolate supporting details. **ASK:** What is the main idea of this section? *(Many diverse groups of people lived in Africa.)* What details from the text support this idea? *(Possible responses: Some Africans were hunter-gatherers while others lived in large, thriving kingdoms; the Great Lakes region and parts of West Africa had different approaches to government; both Islam and Christianity were prominent in different regions of Africa.)*

ACTIVE OPTIONS

On Your Feet: Jigsaw Strategy Organize students into four "expert" groups and have students from each group research various prominent groups in Africa: the Igbo people of West Africa, the Great Lakes kingdoms of Rwanda and Buganda, the Muslim-ruled empire in Mali, and the Swahili region in East Africa. Have each group create a simplified summary of what they learned about the group they researched. Then have students in each group count off using A, B, C, and D. Regroup students into four new groups so each group has at least one person from each of the four expert groups. Have students in the new group take turns sharing the simplified summary they created in their "expert" groups.

> **NG Learning Framework: Write a Biography**
> SKILL Communication
> KNOWLEDGE Our Human Story

Have students conduct online research to write a short biography or profile of Kimpa Vita. Suggest that students focus on her approach to Christianity, the African traditions that informed her beliefs, and how she was received by the Kongo people and by the Portuguese. Invite students to read their biographies aloud to the class.

DIFFERENTIATE

STRIVING READERS

Create Idea Webs Ask students to summarize the lesson by creating two Idea Webs, one for each section. Instruct them to complete each web with at least four important ideas from the section. Guide students to use their Idea Webs to write a summary statement for each section and then a summary statement for the entire lesson. Invite them to compare their summary statements and note similarities and differences.

GIFTED & TALENTED

Make a Catalog Have students conduct online research to learn more about the goods that were traded between East Africa and India and then create a catalog that shows visuals and descriptions of several items. In their descriptions, students should focus on the desirability and functionality of each item in order to persuade a potential buyer. Invite volunteers to share their catalog with the class.

See the Chapter Planner for more strategies for differentiation.

HISTORICAL THINKING

ANSWERS

1. Muslim traders brought imported goods and the religion of Islam to North, East, and West Africa.

2. In almost all African societies, clan elders played a key role in negotiating agreements on community decisions.

3. Eastern Orthodox Christianity was introduced in east Africa, Roman Catholicism in central Africa, and Protestant Christianity in southern Africa.

CRITICAL VIEWING Possible response: Based on the amount of produce in the market, the city's economy is probably based on agriculture.

The Songhai Empire

What happens when a large, successful company goes out of business? Usually, another company eagerly steps in to fill the void. That's just what happened when the prosperous West African empire of Mali disintegrated. Another group quickly claimed control of regional trade.

EMERGENCE OF SONGHAI

You've read that first Ghana and then Mali grew powerful because of an active trans-Saharan trade network. In the mid-1400s, the once-mighty Mali Empire declined because of weak rulers and struggles over **succession**, or the process by which a new leader is chosen to follow an outgoing leader. Groups of people began breaking away, and the Mali Empire lost control of several major cities, including Timbuktu, in 1433. Then in the 1460s, soldiers on horseback with

iron breastplates beneath their battle tunics attacked Mali from the north and south. They were the elite forces of a group of West African people called the Songhai (SAHNG-gy).

The Songhai ruled from their capital city of Gao, southeast of Timbuktu along the Niger River. The Songhai leader **Sunni Ali**, in power from 1464 to 1492, built a powerful cavalry that quickly won the reputation of being undefeatable as it set out to conquer surrounding lands. On water, his war canoes controlled

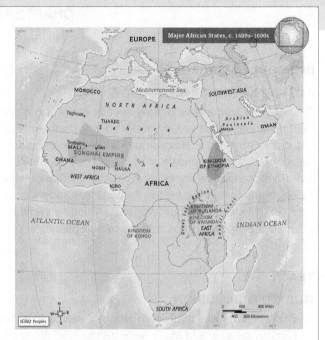

Major African States, c. 1400s–1600s

CRITICAL VIEWING In Gao, Mali, Muslims take part in evening prayer near the tomb of Askia Muhammad the Great, an emperor who championed Islam in the Songhai Empire. What is unusual about the tomb's appearance?

the Niger River. The professional army's many victories allowed Sunni Ali to build the Songhai Empire. In spite of these achievements, Muslim historians portray Sunni Ali as a harsh and unjust ruler because he mistreated the Muslim scholars of Timbuktu during his conquest.

The same was not true of **Askia Muhammad the Great**, who claimed control of Songhai in 1493 after Sunni Ali's death and is remembered as a great supporter of Islam. Askia became the name of the Muslim dynasty that Muhammad established and the title of its rulers. Muhammad followed the example of Mansa Musa by showing off his wealth as he made a pilgrimage to Mecca.

Although Muhammad championed Islam and mandated that the empire's laws be based on Islamic law, the faith spread slowly within the Songhai Empire. Most West Africans lived in small agricultural villages and continued to worship African gods and follow traditional rituals. Eventually, some aspects of Islam blended with traditional West African beliefs, but few villagers became Muslim. Even in cities such as Timbuktu, where many Africans were Muslim, religious syncretism took place. Muslim visitors from other lands often thought Africans did not adhere closely enough to Islamic principles. They particularly criticized the relaxed attitude of Africans toward the veiling of women.

PLAN: 4-PAGE LESSON

OBJECTIVE

Explain how the leaders of the Songhai Empire gained control of interregional and trans-Saharan trade and established an effective system of government in West Africa.

CRITICAL THINKING SKILLS FOR LESSON 1.2

- Explain
- Interpret Maps
- Analyze Cause and Effect
- Evaluate
- Make Inferences
- Make Predictions
- Analyze Visuals

HISTORICAL THINKING FOR CHAPTER 18

How have elements of African cultures spread around the world?

The Songhai Empire was a huge center of west African culture and commerce for several centuries. Lesson 1.2 discusses the rise and fall of the Songhai Empire, along with the values that guided its accomplishments.

BACKGROUND FOR THE TEACHER

Islamic Artistic Styles in Africa Religious syncretism in Africa stretched beyond religious practices themselves and had a profound influence on the arts. Since Islamic artistic traditions discouraged depicting people and animals, these subjects became less prevalent in art from the Islamic regions of Africa. Much of Islamic art and architecture emphasized mathematics and geometric patterns, and these became more prevalent in African architecture, textiles, and other objects as Islam spread throughout the region. Islamic patterns often started with a shape, such as a circle or square. Then the shape would be repeated and interwoven in various permutations to create a complex pattern. African artisans also began to produce talismans, objects inscribed with verses of the Quran that are said to bear protective powers.

Student eEdition online

Additional content for this lesson, including a photograph, is available online.

INTRODUCE & ENGAGE

PREVIEW WITH VISUALS

Direct students' attention to the two photographs in the lesson. Based on the photographs, have students make inferences about the people they will learn about in this lesson. **ASK:** What do these photographs demonstrate about the values of the Songhai people? *(Possible response: The Songhai people were religious and valued learning because in one photograph they appear to be praying and the other photograph shows a scholar reading Islamic manuscripts.)* Tell students that in this lesson they will learn about the emphasis of scholarship in Islamic Africa and Songhai leaders' approach to government.

TEACH

GUIDED DISCUSSION

1. **Explain** How did the use of cowrie shells help the expansion of the Songhai Empire? *(Possible response: Having a fixed currency helped the Songhai Empire gain and manage wealth through trade and taxes.)*

2. **Evaluate** Why was using the borders of conquered lands to designate Songhai provinces a good strategy? *(Possible response: People in each province were part of the same group, so they were more likely to get along with one another rather than fight over power and resources.)*

INTERPRET MAPS

Direct students to the Major African States map. **ASK:** Based on their relative locations on the map, do you think these African societies had much contact with one another? Why or why not? *(Possible response: These societies did not have much contact because they were far from one another geographically, and barriers such as mountains, rivers, and deserts would have made it difficult to travel from one society to another.)* How do you think interactions, or lack thereof, between these societies affected the cultures that developed on the African continent? *(Possible response: Due to the geographic separation of these societies, they developed very different cultures.)*

DIFFERENTIATE

ENGLISH LANGUAGE LEARNERS

Create Word Maps Arrange students at all levels in mixed pairs, and tell them to write the word *succession* in the center oval of a Word Map. Have them consult the text and write the word's definition and characteristics in the appropriate boxes. Then instruct students to write examples and non-examples of *succession* using information from the text, current events, or their own knowledge. Direct pairs to exchange their Word Maps with another pair and ask and answer questions about the information.

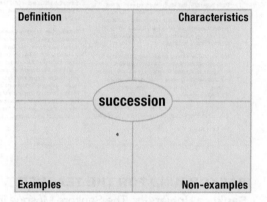

GIFTED & TALENTED

Host a Debate In groups of three, have one student take the role of Sunni Ali, one the role of Askia Muhammad the Great, and one the role of a moderator. Have the moderator craft a list of questions to ask the two leaders about what they believe is the best strategy for ruling the Songhai Empire. Suggest that moderators focus their questions on leadership techniques, motivations, and desired outcomes for the Songhai Empire. Then give the students portraying the leaders time to prepare responses to each of the moderators' questions. Students should conduct online research while crafting their questions and responses. Ask each moderator to initiate a discussion between the two leaders in front of the class, asking each of the questions and listening to each leader's response.

See the Chapter Planner for more strategies for differentiation.

A scholar reads Islamic manuscripts from the 13th century at the Ahmed Baba Institute of Higher Learning and Islamic Research in Timbuktu. About 4,000 ancient manuscripts were burned by radical Islamist militants in Timbuktu before the militants were driven out by French forces in 2013.

TRADE AND GOVERNMENT

Trade both north and south expanded even farther under the Songhai Empire. For example, kola nuts from the forest regions in the south were exchanged for valuable salt from mines in the Sahara region. In turn, gold was traded north for such commodities as ceramics, glass, and Islamic texts.

The Songhai also traded people. At first, the Songhai relied on captured slaves to serve as loyal soldiers and as skilled craftworkers. The supply of enslaved people then increased as Songhai armies conquered new territory, and a larger number of slaves were sold in North African markets.

Within the Songhai Empire, people used cowrie shells as a currency for local trade. Cowrie are a type of snail, and their beautiful shells were highly valued in Africa during the 1400s and 1500s. The Songhai people used fixed amounts of cowrie shells to pay for cloth, food, and other goods.

To strengthen his empire's control of trade, Muhammad shrewdly planned his battles and conquests. He pushed back against the Tuareg people who lived in the desert north of Timbuktu to prevent them from claiming Sahelian trade routes. He conquered Taghaza in northern Africa to gain access to its salt mines and expanded his empire into the Sahara as far as he could. He also defeated the Mossi people of what is now Burkina Faso and the people of present-day Niger and incorporated them into his empire. In addition, he forged new trade connections with the Hausa people who lived to the east of Songhai lands.

Gaining wealth through trade was just one way Muhammad ensured the success of the Songhai Empire. To make sure his government could effectively oversee his growing empire, he established a bureaucracy. Each department within the bureaucracy had a different responsibility, such as handling finances, administering justice, waging war, and regulating agriculture.

Muhammad also controlled his sprawling empire by dividing it into provinces. Generally, each province followed the borders of a particular conquered land. Muhammad installed relatives or close followers as governors of the provinces. These loyalists obeyed his every command. Taxes paid by the conquered territories added to the empire's wealth.

SUPPORT FOR LEARNING

Muhammad and other Songhai rulers used some of the empire's wealth to support Islamic arts and sciences. The Sankore Mosque in Timbuktu, with its impressive library, became a center of intellectual debate, drawing scholars from far and wide. Sankore University was established around the mosque and became a leading center of learning. Timbuktu also became famous for its book market, where Arab and African Muslim scholars could find finely bound editions of books they sought. The opportunity to both trade and gain knowledge drew many Muslims to Timbuktu.

Today, the site of the Sankore Mosque is protected as a UNESCO World Heritage Site. In 2013, however, **Islamists**, who believe in a strict legal interpretation of Islam, destroyed some of Timbuktu's precious manuscripts. They wanted to wipe out all records that demonstrated the blending of African and Islamic cultures. Fortunately, a number of similar manuscripts had already been moved to another location for safekeeping.

END OF AN EMPIRE

The wealth of Songhai's gold and salt mines inspired the envy of the ruler of Morocco in northern Africa. In 1591, he dispatched his army, equipped with firearms from Europe, to conquer Songhai. With the advantage of superior weapons and aided by internal disputes within Songhai, the Moroccans won an easy victory. The invaders forced Timbuktu scholars to flee the city. Later,

the Songhai Empire broke up into smaller kingdoms, chiefdoms, and sultanates.

Never again would a large-scale African state rise to such dominance in the Sahel. Saharan people other than the Moroccans would ultimately gain control of trans-Saharan trade, however.

Even before the demise, or downfall, of Songhai, Europeans were building small settlements along the West African coast. European merchants were looking for ways to control not only the gold trade but also the booming slave trade. The Atlantic Ocean would emerge as an important connection to Europe and the Americas, bringing drastic changes for Africans.

Writing under the name Leo Africanus, a young diplomat who visited Songhai during Askia Muhammad's reign published a description of the empire at its peak. In this excerpt from his writing, he describes the city of Timbuktu. The name Barbarie refers to Berber lands in northern Africa.

PRIMARY SOURCE

Here are many shops of craftsmen and merchants, especially those who weave linen and cotton cloth. To this place Barbarie merchants bring cloth from Europe. All the women of this region except maidservants go with their faces covered and sell all necessary kinds of foods. . . .

The rich king of Timbuktu has many articles of gold, and he keeps a magnificent and well-furnished court. When he travels anywhere he rides upon a camel which is led by some of his noblemen. . . .

Here there are many doctors, judges, priests, and other learned men, that are well maintained at the king's cost. Various manuscripts and written books are brought here out of Barbarie and sold for more money than any other merchandise. . . .

The inhabitants are people of a gentle and cheerful disposition and spend a great part of the night in singing and dancing through all the streets of the city. They keep great store of men and women slaves.

—from *History and Description of Africa* by Leo Africanus, translated by J. Pory and edited by R. Brown, 1896

HISTORICAL THINKING

1. **READING CHECK** What were some major achievements of Askia Muhammad the Great?
2. **EXPLAIN** How did Islam spread in West Africa?
3. **INTERPRET MAPS** What trend do you notice about the locations of the various African civilizations?
4. **ANALYZE CAUSE AND EFFECT** What factors contributed to the fall of the Songhai Empire?

BACKGROUND FOR THE TEACHER

Sankore University The Sankore Mosque in Timbuktu is one of the city's most famous, and its fame derives from the scholarly activity that took place at what came to be known as the University of Sankore. The city of Timbuktu, which was situated along the trans-Saharan trade route, became an important center of Islamic scholarship. The library at Sankore attracted both African and Arab scholars. The organization of scholarly practice here differed widely from European universities of the same era. An imam, or Islamic teacher, would establish a school through the university and work directly with students, teaching classes in courtyards or even in private homes. Students typically worked one-on-one with their specific imam, rather than taking different courses with different instructors, as was the norm in many European schools. Due to this structure, the University of Sankore did not have a formal course registration process nor official programs of study that students followed. Much of the scholarly work that took place at the university was focused on history, Quranic theology, law, logic, and astronomy. In later years, the university trade shops offered coursework in business, carpentry, farming, fishing, and other trades professions. In order to attend the university, students needed to have memorized the Quran and have mastered the Arabic language.

TEACH

GUIDED DISCUSSION

3. **Make Inferences** What attitude did Songhai leaders have toward intellectualism? *(Possible response: They supported intellectual endeavors, which is evident in the establishment of the Sankore University and allowing the book market to flourish in Timbuktu.)*

4. **Make Predictions** How might the history of the Songhai Empire have been different if the Songhai people had had increased access to technology from other parts of the world? *(Possible response: The Songhai people might have been able to stop the attack of the Moroccan army and maintain control of their empire if they had had access to firearms.)*

ANALYZE VISUALS

Direct students to the photograph of the manuscript from the Songhai Empire (available in the Student eEdition). Encourage students to consider how the manuscript is presented, such as the script in which it is written, the way the book is bound, and the visuals that are included on the page. **ASK:** What might the writer have hoped to accomplish based on the way the manuscript is presented? *(Possible responses: The writer might have hoped to convey information concisely, based on the small amount of text on the page, and might have wanted to ensure that the book was durable to protect the information, based on the way the book is bound.)*

ACTIVE OPTIONS

On Your Feet: Fishbowl Organize the class into two groups. Have one group sit in a close circle facing inward and have the other half of the class sit in a larger circle around them. Have the students on the inside discuss Muhammad's leadership of the Songhai Empire, including his bureaucratic system of government, the division of the empire into provinces, his stance toward intellectualism and religion, and his strategies for gaining wealth. The students sitting on the outside of the circle should listen closely to the discussion to take in new information and evaluate the ideas being discussed. Then have groups reverse positions.

| **NG Learning Framework: Diagram Societal Roles**
| **ATTITUDE** Curiosity
| **KNOWLEDGE** Our Human Story

Have students read Leo Africanus's description of the many people he observed in Timbuktu during his visit to the Songhai Empire. Based on Africanus's writing and students' own additional research, have students create a diagram that visually depicts the various societal roles that were an essential part of Songhai society. Encourage students to consider how these different roles overlapped and interacted with each other. Invite volunteers to share their diagrams with the class and to discuss the intersections of each of the societal roles.

HISTORICAL THINKING

ANSWERS

1. Askia Muhammad the Great gained control of the West African gold and salt trade, enlarged the Songhai Empire, established an effective system of government for the empire, and supported Islamic arts and sciences.

2. Islam spread slowly in West Africa after Askia Muhammad championed the religion. He mandated that the empire's laws be based on Islamic law, and he used his Islamic faith to build trade relations with Muslim merchants.

3. The various civilizations are all located near bodies of water.

4. Internal disputes weakened the empire, which was invaded by Moroccans with superior weapons.

CRITICAL VIEWING Possible response: The tomb is held together or built with branches and appears fairly humble for a great leader.

1.3 Preserving Cultural Heritage

TIMBUKTU

Once a prosperous center for trade and learning, Timbuktu is a historically significant city in the West African country of Mali. Its location where the Sahara and the Niger River meet made it an important city along the trans-Saharan trade routes.

In 2012, Tuareg rebels backed by Islamic militants took control of the northern part of Mali. The militants soon replaced the Tuareg and imposed strict sharia, or Islamic, law. They ordered that many of Timbuktu's monuments, tombs, and artifacts be destroyed.

French troops backed by the United States and the European Union drove out the Islamist forces from Timbuktu in 2013. As the rebels fled, they set fire to several buildings, including libraries that housed thousands of ancient texts, with the oldest manuscript dating to around 1204.

Work to repair the resulting damage began immediately. Not all the historic manuscripts were destroyed. A librarian and several others had packed and hidden away many of the manuscripts for safekeeping. To preserve its cultural heritage, Mali's sites were included on the 2014 World Monuments Watch. The French and Malian governments, along with UNESCO, created a plan for the restoration of the sites destroyed by the conflict.

In 2016, The Hague's International Criminal Court (ICC) brought a Malian rebel leader to trial for his alleged crimes. This trial marked the first prosecution of cultural heritage destruction as a war crime. He was found guilty and ordered to pay for the damage.

HISTORICAL THINKING

DESCRIBE What is the historical significance of Timbuktu and what would be lost if the city was not preserved?

A museum guard displays a burnt ancient manuscript in its box at the Ahmed Baba Institute.

TIMBUKTU, MALI
A door and some rubble are all that remain of a mausoleum destroyed by Islamist fighters in a cemetery in Timbuktu, Mali, in 2013. These same fighters set fire to dozens of ancient manuscripts at the Ahmed Baba Institute, the city's biggest and most important library.

PLAN: 2-PAGE LESSON

OBJECTIVE

Explain why Timbuktu is revered around the globe for its cultural significance and why many sites within the city need protection from some groups who wish to destroy their rich history.

CRITICAL THINKING SKILLS FOR LESSON 1.3

- Analyze Visuals
- Make Connections
- Describe
- Form and Support Opinions
- Make Inferences

HISTORICAL THINKING FOR CHAPTER 18

How have elements of African cultures spread around the world?

Timbuktu was a hotbed of intellectual and commercial activity from the rule of Mansa Musa through the Songhai Empire. Lesson 1.3 explores the significance of Timbuktu and the world's effort to preserve its history.

BACKGROUND FOR THE TEACHER

The Ahmed Baba Institute Ahmed Baba was considered a saint of Timbuktu and wrote many of the sacred manuscripts that epitomized African-Islamic culture and beliefs. He strove to bring different ethnic groups together to live harmoniously in Timbuktu during the 16th century. He is admired for his Islamic scholarship and wisdom and for his courage in speaking out against Moroccan slave traders. His writings were controversial because he supported Muslims regardless of their skin color and origin. The Ahmed Baba Institute, named in his honor, is a library in Timbuktu that housed many culturally significant artifacts before it was attacked by Islamist rebels in 2013. The institute was one of the last locations in the city to be sacked, and some journalists postulate that the rebels knew that foreign troops were about to aid the city. Many manuscripts were burned; others may have been stolen. While some content in the manuscripts was of a religious nature, other content consisted of academic accounts of the more popular subjects at Sankore University: astronomy, history, and law.

History Notebook

Encourage students to complete the Preserving Cultural Heritage page for Chapter 18 in their History Notebooks as they read.

INTRODUCE & ENGAGE

CONSIDER CONSEQUENCES

Discuss with students how rules and regulations often come about after something has gone wrong in order to prevent the issue from happening again. **ASK:** What are some examples of government regulations or rules you have encountered that were enacted in response to something that went wrong? *(Answers will vary. Possible responses may include environmental regulations or building codes that were enacted after a tragedy.)* Tell students that in this lesson they will learn about how Islamist rebels tried to destroy centuries-old artifacts in Timbuktu, which prompted the world to take action to preserve the city's heritage going forward.

TEACH

GUIDED DISCUSSION

1. **Form and Support Opinions** How do you think Timbuktu's affluence as a center for trade helped the city become a hub of intellectualism? *(Possible response: As the city grew wealthier from trade, people had more resources to devote to intellectual endeavors.)*

2. **Make Inferences** Why do you think the United States and Europe helped Timbuktu drive out the rebel Islamist forces? *(Answers will vary. Possible responses: The United States and Europe were concerned about human rights in Timbuktu; the United States and Europe had economic interests in Timbuktu; the United States and Europe were concerned that the rebels could eventually pose a larger global threat; the United States and Europe valued preserving the culture and history of Timbuktu.)*

PRESERVING CULTURAL HERITAGE

Direct students to the photograph of the destroyed mausoleum. Explain that a mausoleum is an above-ground tomb, and that mausoleums are often ornate and used as a resting place for prominent people. **ASK:** Why might the Islamist rebels have targeted the mausoleum? *(Possible response: The mausoleum could have been the tomb of people who played an important role in Timbuktu's history and African-Islamic culture, and they wanted to destroy things that celebrated this culture.)*

> **NG Learning Framework: Give a Presentation About Historic Preservation Techniques**
> **SKILL** Problem-Solving
> **KNOWLEDGE** New Frontiers

Invite students to conduct online research about some of the architecture and artifacts that UNESCO is working to preserve in Timbuktu, such as the restoration of medieval shrines or ways to ensure the safety of ancient manuscripts. Encourage students to focus on new technological advances within the field of preservation and how preservationists are using technology to create more accurate restorations and deter the breakdown of original elements. Then have students present their findings to the class.

DIFFERENTIATE

INCLUSION

Analyze Visuals Provide concrete questions to help students describe the photographs in the lesson. Ask students the following questions: What can be seen in the photo of the rubble? What is left of the burned manuscripts? What do the details in the photos tell you? Encourage students to point to details they don't understand and help them frame questions about these details.

PRE-AP

Compare and Evaluate Primary Sources Instruct students to conduct online research to find news articles about the attack on Timbuktu that occurred in 2013. Encourage students to find three or four different articles that are each written from different perspectives. Then have students write an essay comparing and analyzing the sources. Students should make a claim about how trustworthy they perceive each source to be and why. Invite students to share their analyses with the class.

See the Chapter Planner for more strategies for differentiation.

HISTORICAL THINKING

ANSWER

Students' answers will vary. Possible response: Timbuktu is historically significant as a trading hub and as a center of Islamic learning. If the city was not preserved, many old manuscripts would be lost.

Traveler: Olaudah Equiano
An African Voice c. 1745–1797

In the Atlantic slave trade, millions of Africans were forced to sail across the Atlantic to be sold into slavery. Many were destined for the sugar plantations of the West Indies. Much of what we know about their horrific journeys and difficult lives comes from the writings of an enslaved sailor working on a merchant ship that crossed the Atlantic.

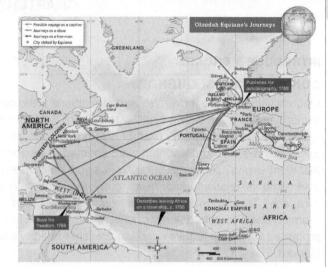

Olaudah Equiano's Journeys

EARLY LIFE AND TRAVELS

In 1789, British antislavery activists were eagerly discussing a new book by a former African slave named Olaudah Equiano (oh–LOW–duh ehk-wee-AHN-oh). In his **slave narrative** called *The Interesting Narrative of the Life of Olaudah Equiano, or Gustavus Vassa, the African*, Equiano vividly described the ordeal of slavery from a first-person point of view.

Equiano was born around 1745, when the Atlantic slave trade was at its height. Hundreds of thousands of captive Africans crossed the Atlantic on sailing ships every year. According to his narrative, Equiano was 11 years old when he was captured and forced onto a slave ship headed to the West Indies. In his narrative, he describes the horrors of the infamous **Middle Passage**, the journey by slave ships across the Atlantic from West Africa to the Americas.

Equiano continues his narrative by describing his sale to a British naval officer. Rather than working on a Caribbean sugar plantation like many African captives, Equiano spent much of his early life aboard ships. Later, he was sold to a Philadelphia merchant who conducted business in the West Indies. Aboard ship, Equiano learned reading, writing, and

mathematics. He tended to his owner's business, which sometimes included trading in slaves. Life as a sailor allowed him more independence than most slaves had, yet he longed for true freedom.

Eventually, Equiano won his freedom through a combination of good fortune and business sense. His final owner was a member of the Society of Friends, or Quakers. The Quakers had strong doubts about whether Christians should own other people. The slaveholder agreed to Equiano's **manumission**, or release from slavery, if Equiano could pay his own purchase price. He allowed Equiano to conduct his own trades in his spare time to earn money.

> In this excerpt from his autobiography, Olaudah Equiano describes his impressions as he was first brought onto a slave ship.
>
> **PRIMARY SOURCE**
>
> The first object which saluted my eyes when I arrived on the coast was the sea, and a slave ship . . . These filled me with astonishment, which was soon converted into terror . . . [T]hey made ready with many fearful noises, and we were all put under deck . . . now that the whole ship's cargo were confined together, [the stench of the hold] became absolutely pestilential [deadly]. The closeness of the place, and the heat of the climate, added to the number in the ship, which was so crowded that each had scarcely room to turn himself, almost suffocated us. . . This wretched situation was again aggravated by the galling of the chains, . . . and the filth of the [latrines], into which the children often fell, and were almost suffocated. The shrieks of the women, and groans of the dying, rendered the whole a scene of horror almost inconceivable.
>
> —from *The Interesting Narrative of the Life of Olaudah Equiano, or Gustavus Vassa, the African*, 1789

518 CHAPTER 18

After paying the man who had enslaved him and gaining his freedom, Equiano moved to London, where he lived as a free man and often set off on new sea adventures. In his later years, he wrote about his experiences and lectured to audiences about the evils of slavery. As an antislavery activist, he hoped his actions would help turn the tide of public opinion against slavery.

IMPORTANCE OF HIS WRITINGS

Historians have confirmed the accuracy of Equiano's account of his adult activities. However, some scholars question the accuracy of his retelling of his earliest life. Some evidence, though inconclusive, suggests

that Equiano was actually born in the Americas and may have used other slaves' stories to create his description of Africa and the voyage across the Atlantic. This possibility serves as an important reminder to be cautious when using memoirs to learn about history.

Still, Equiano's *Interesting Narrative* is important to the study of history because it provides a firsthand account of life under slavery in the 1700s. As one of the first slave narratives, the book aided the cause of **abolition**, the movement to end slavery, as did Equiano's speaking tours. Equiano's earnings from the book made him the wealthiest black man in England at the time.

HISTORICAL THINKING

1. **READING CHECK** What is the significance of *The Interesting Narrative of the Life of Olaudah Equiano, or Gustavus Vassa, the African?*

2. **INTERPRET MAPS** Use the map to describe Equiano's journeys as a slave.

3. **COMPARE AND CONTRAST** How was Equiano's experience different from that of most enslaved Africans in the 1700s?

Africans in the Atlantic World 519

PLAN: 2-PAGE LESSON

OBJECTIVE

Describe how an enslaved African sailor wrote an influential firsthand account of the horrors of slavery, which he witnessed during his sea travels.

CRITICAL THINKING SKILLS FOR LESSON 2.1

- Interpret Maps
- Compare and Contrast
- Make Connections
- Form and Support Opinions
- Analyze Primary Sources

HISTORICAL THINKING FOR CHAPTER 18

How have elements of African cultures spread around the world?

Many atrocities were committed during the slave trade across the Atlantic Ocean. Lesson 2.1 introduces Olaudah Equiano, an enslaved person who eventually gained his freedom and wrote about the horrors of slavery.

Student eEdition online

Additional content for this lesson, including a primary source and an image, is available online.

BACKGROUND FOR THE TEACHER

The Content of Equiano's Writing Equiano's *The Interesting Narrative of the Life of Olaudah Equiano, or Gustavus Vassa, the African, 1789* describes the horrific treatment of enslaved Africans as well as life in western Africa and his collaboration with British abolitionists. His writing idealizes western Africa as a place of social harmony but harshly criticizes Africans who participated in the slave trade by capturing and selling other Africans. While living in England, Equiano describes the kindness of those who helped him settle in a new location and gain access to the resources to publish his book. He even speaks somewhat positively of his former masters, deriding the system of slavery while appreciating some of the individual kindnesses he received. As a whole, his work is strongly rooted in interpersonal interactions, cataloging humanity's capability of both gruesome and empathetic actions. His work had nine editions published in the United Kingdom, one in the United States, and has been translated into Dutch, German, and Russian.

History Notebook

Encourage students to complete the Traveler page for Chapter 18 in their History Notebooks as they read.

INTRODUCE & ENGAGE

PREVIEW VOCABULARY

Write *slave narrative* on the board, and have students consider what this vocabulary term might imply about the lesson. **ASK:** What do you think a slave narrative could be? *(Possible response: Someone who is or had been enslaved telling about his or her experiences in slavery.)* How might a slave narrative influence public opinion about slavery? *(Possible response: A slave narrative could expose some of the evils of slavery to people who were not familiar with its horrors.)* Tell students that in this lesson they will learn about the African writer Olaudah Equiano and how he wrote about his own experiences in order to convince others to put an end to slavery.

TEACH

GUIDED DISCUSSION

1. **Make Connections** How did being enslaved by a naval officer lead to Equiano's opportunity to learn to read and write? *(He learned to read and write while aboard ships with the officer.)*

2. **Form and Support Opinions** Even if some of Equiano's writings were based on information he learned from other Africans, rather than his own life experiences, do you think that takes away from the importance of his work? Why or why not? *(Answers will vary. Possible response: No, because his work still exposed the horrors of the Middle Passage, so it doesn't matter if the information was first-hand or second-hand.)*

ANALYZE PRIMARY SOURCES

Direct students to read the primary source in the text and another in the Student eEdition. **ASK:** Why do you think Equiano chose to describe the sounds and smells of a slave ship? *(Possible response: so that readers would be able to viscerally understand the awful conditions on board; This would appeal to people's emotions when it came to abolishing slavery.)* How do these two passages work together to cover a common theme? *(Possible response: They focus on how enslaved people were mistreated.)*

ACTIVE OPTION

On Your Feet: Think, Pair, Share Instruct students to consider Olaudah Equiano's writing style and how it was influenced by his motivation to write and publish his narrative. First, have them discuss their ideas in pairs and then share with the class. Encourage students to reference the primary source passages when analyzing Equiano's writing style.

| **NG Learning Framework: Create a Chart to Show Conflicting Beliefs About Slavery** |
| **ATTITUDE** Curiosity |
| **KNOWLEDGE** Our Human Story |

Have students conduct online research to understand the Quakers' beliefs about slavery and how those beliefs may have evolved over time. Students should create a chart that compares and contrasts the Quakers' beliefs about and approach to slavery with Olaudah Equiano's descriptions of enslaved people's experiences.

DIFFERENTIATE

STRIVING READERS

Write a Tweet As students read the lesson, direct them to pause after each paragraph and write a tweet summarizing the paragraph's main idea in their own words. Remind students to keep their tweets within the 140-character limit. Allow students to compare their tweets with a partner and make note of any differences in the content of their summaries.

PRE-AP

Write a Book Review Instruct students to conduct online research or use the library to read additional passages from Olaudah Equiano's narrative. Then have them write a book review discussing the importance of his work in the context of the late 18th century. Encourage students to read contemporary book reviews as examples for how to craft their work. Invite volunteers to share their book reviews with the class.

See the Chapter Planner for more strategies for differentiation.

HISTORICAL THINKING

ANSWERS

1. The book was one of the first slave narratives, and its description of the horrors of slavery aided the cause of abolition in England.

2. Olaudah Equiano traveled all over the Atlantic Ocean, reaching such locations as England, the West Indies, the eastern coast of North America, and the Canary Islands. The route of his travels took a triangular shape.

3. Possible response: Olaudah Equiano did not have to work as a field slave, had more independence, learned to read and write, and was allowed to buy his own freedom.

The Middle Passage

As Europeans expanded into the Americas, they created large plantations that depended on cheap labor for economic success. At first, they turned to the indigenous people of the Americas to work on the plantations, but large numbers died of European diseases. Europeans then looked to Africa for people to enslave.

TRIANGULAR TRADE

Enslaved people from West Africa were expensive, but sugar planters believed they were worth the cost. West Africans had long been exposed to smallpox and other European diseases and had built up a resistance to them. Having grown up in the tropics, they also had exposure to tropical diseases such as malaria and yellow fever. Their ability to survive these diseases, along with their experience in agriculture, made them valuable in the fields.

While slavery was common in many places, it had never before been such an integral part of society as it was in the Americas in the 1600s and 1700s. Slavery became central to every aspect of social and economic life in the Americas. In West Africa, many groups had traditionally enslaved their captured enemies, but now they gained wealth by selling slaves to Europeans. Unlike earlier enslaved people, who were often incorporated into their captor's society through marriage, these Africans were stripped of all rights and had little hope of escaping bondage.

The Atlantic slave trade was part of a network often called the **triangular trade**, which connected Europe, Africa, and the Americas from the 1500s through the 1800s. The network is named for the shape the trade route formed. On the first leg of the route, European ships loaded with manufactured goods such as guns and cloth sailed into West African ports. After exchanging these goods for enslaved Africans, European traders then set off on the second leg of the journey, the Middle Passage. This part of the route took enslaved West Africans to the Americas, where they were traded for products such as sugar, tobacco, rum, and timber. On the third leg of the trade network, ships loaded with these products returned to Europe, where

The Triangular Trade, c. 1500–1800

the products were sold or exchanged for cloth or guns, and the cycle began again.

The Europeans who controlled the triangular trade made huge profits. Indian Ocean trade was also connected to this Atlantic trade network because Europeans often included such commodities as Asian textiles as trade items. The largest profits in this slave-based system of sugar production and trade went to Europeans who owned the ships and plantations. But African merchants and kings also profited and increased their local power.

HORRORS ABOARD SLAVE SHIPS

The most horrific part of the triangular trade was the Middle Passage, in which humans were transported as if they were inanimate trade items. European slave traders often rationalized, or attempted to justify, their inhumane treatment of Africans by claiming that, as Christians, they were rescuing Africans from "paganism." As more Africans converted to Christianity, those profiting from

PLAN OF LOWER DECK WITH THE STOWAGE OF 292 SLAVES

130 OF THESE BEING STOWED <u>UNDER</u> THE SHELVES AS SHEWN IN FIGURE 2 & FIGURE 3.

The Slave Ship *Brooks*

Abolitionists used these diagrams of the British slave ship *Brooks* in their campaign against slavery. The diagram above illustrates how captive Africans were tightly packed into the cargo hold while the cross-section at right shows how little headroom captives had, just 2 feet, 7 inches or less. The diagram at the far right provides a closer view of captives crammed into the ship.

slavery turned to **racism**, the belief that the color of a person's skin makes them superior or inferior, to justify their motives.

Enslaved Africans experienced brutal conditions aboard a ship during the Middle Passage. Below the ship's deck, African men lay shackled in a hunched position, so close together they could hardly move. Women and children were allowed more movement because captors believed they were less likely to rise up in rebellion. Small groups of slaves were regularly taken above deck and forced to move their arms and legs wildly to prevent loss of muscle.

On a typical ship, about 400 to 600 slaves were squeezed into the slave quarters, which grew unbearably hot and filled with noxious air. Any slave who showed the slightest hint of rebelling was beaten severely. Many enslaved Africans died of diseases such as dysentery, scurvy, and smallpox. A typical trip took from about 3 to 12 weeks, and as many as 20 percent of the captives did not survive. Slave traders simply regarded such loss as part of the cost of running a business.

In all, more than 12 million Africans endured the long and harrowing voyage across the Atlantic. An unknown number died while held in captivity at the European

slave forts or on the journey from their homes to the coast. The slaves transported over the Middle Passage had little idea of what to expect when they reached their destination. Most would face harsh conditions as enslaved workers on plantations.

Great Britain, France, Holland, and other European nations gained great wealth through the triangular trade, but by the late 1700s, many people began to speak up against the evils of African enslavement. Some were motivated by their belief in the value of all human life, others by Christian religious conviction. Many Christians could not reconcile slavery with their belief that all people should be treated with love and charity. Eventually, Parliament would ban British participation in the slave trade, as you will read about later.

HISTORICAL THINKING

1. **READING CHECK** What was the Middle Passage?
2. **MAKE INFERENCES** Why did slave traders pack so many enslaved Africans on the ships that traveled to the Americas?
3. **INTERPRET MAPS** How did the triangular trade reflect the structure of the colonial economy?

PLAN: 2-PAGE LESSON

OBJECTIVE

Identify that the Middle Passage was the greatest forced migration in human history and one of the most brutal.

CRITICAL THINKING SKILLS FOR LESSON 2.2

- Make Inferences
- Interpret Maps
- Describe
- Compare and Contrast
- Analyze Visuals

HISTORICAL THINKING FOR CHAPTER 18

How have elements of African cultures spread around the world?

Crimes against humanity increased as the slave trade became a more and more lucrative option for Europeans. Lesson 2.2 discusses the awful and abusive conditions endured by enslaved Africans during the Middle Passage across the Atlantic Ocean.

Student eEdition online

Additional content for this lesson, including a Global Commodity feature, is available online.

BACKGROUND FOR THE TEACHER

Africans' Experiences on Slave Ships The abuse of Africans began on the West African coast when they were first sold into slavery and continued throughout the journey across the Atlantic and arrival in the Americas. Before embarking on a slave ship, Africans were forced to forfeit their clothing and personal items and were examined by a surgeon, not out of concern for their health but out of concern for the financial investment of the slave traders. While the men were chained in extremely tight conditions below deck, occasionally women and children were kept above deck. However, this was a mixed blessing as it did allow for some physical movement but also exposed women and children to sexual abuse and violence at the hands of the crew. Enslaved people were usually fed twice daily during the Middle Passage. Some attempted a hunger strike, and were force-fed by their captors. Disease and infection ran rampant on board the ship, as conditions were extremely unsanitary. When enslaved people died, their bodies were tossed into the ocean.

History Notebook

Encourage students to complete the "Humans" Global Commodity page for Chapter 18 in their History Notebooks as they read.

INTRODUCE & ENGAGE

ACTIVATE PRIOR KNOWLEDGE

As students share what they have already learned about slavery and the Middle Passage from Olaudah Equiano's work or other sources, record and display their responses in two Word Webs: one with *slavery* in the center and the other with *Middle Passage* in the center. Ask students to use ideas from the Word Webs to discuss why people eventually became opposed to slavery. Tell students that in this lesson they will learn more about the horrible abuse Africans suffered during the Middle Passage and the difficulties they would face after arrival in the Americas.

TEACH

GUIDED DISCUSSION

1. **Describe** Why did Europeans think that enslaving Africans would be more economical than enslaving native peoples in the Americas? *(Africans had been exposed to both European and tropical diseases; there was less of a risk of them being killed due to disease exposure.)*

2. **Compare and Contrast** How did those in favor of and against slavery use Christianity to justify their opinions? *(People in favor claimed that they were saving Africans by converting them to Christianity; people opposed to slavery said that brutalizing Africans went against Christian values such as treating others with love and compassion.)*

ANALYZE VISUALS

Direct students to the diagrams of the slave ship *Brooks*. **ASK:** How did abolitionists use these diagrams to advance their cause? *(Possible response: The diagrams showed the awful conditions that Africans were subjected to on board slave ships, such as being chained in cramped quarters.)* Why do you think men and women were separated during the Middle Passage? *(Possible response: Captors feared that men were more likely to revolt than women, so the men were treated more harshly and were likely separated so that they could be watched over carefully.)*

ACTIVE OPTIONS

On Your Feet: Roundtable Ask students sitting around a table in groups of four to consider alternative ways that trade between Europe, Africa, the Americas, and Asia could have flourished without relying heavily on the enslavement of Africans. Have each student answer the question in a different way. Invite groups to share their responses with the class.

> **NG Learning Framework: Give a Presentation on Instances of Slavery Around the World**
> **ATTITUDE** Responsibility
> **SKILL** Collaboration

Direct students to the Global Commodity: Humans feature (available in the Student eEdition) and have them read the passage. Then have pairs choose another instance of slavery in human history to further research. Encourage students to focus on how enslaved people were treated, what types of work they were forced to perform, and what their relationship with their captors was like. Have pairs create presentations for the class.

DIFFERENTIATE

INCLUSION

Identify Diagram and Map Details Pair students with disabilities with students who can read the lesson aloud to them. Ask the partner without disabilities to describe the diagram of the slave ship *Brooks* and the map of the triangular trade in detail. Then have pairs answer the Historical Thinking questions.

GIFTED & TALENTED

Prepare and Present an Oral History Tell students that of the millions of enslaved people who endured the Middle Passage, only a few left narratives of their experiences. Instruct students to conduct research using a variety of sources to discover details about the experiences of people who survived the Middle Passage. Then have students select, prepare, and present a partial oral history or narrative to read to the class, prefacing their reading with information about the subject of the oral history.

See the Chapter Planner for more strategies for differentiation.

HISTORICAL THINKING

ANSWERS

1. The Middle Passage was the second leg of the triangular trade and the greatest forced migration in history. During the Middle Passage, enslaved Africans were taken from West Africa to the Americas for sale.

2. Slave traders crammed together so many enslaved Africans on the ships to the Americas to gain greater profits.

3. The mother countries obtained natural resources from their colonies, which they then turned into manufactured goods that were sold to African slavers in return for slaves, who were then transported to the colonies to help procure more natural resources for the mother country.

2.3 A Global Commodity: Sugar

For many people, their first taste of sugar marks the beginning of a lifelong love affair with it. Early in the ancient world, sugarcane only grew in New Guinea, an island in the South Pacific Ocean, but it eventually spread to India and Southwest Asia. After the Arabs turned sugar production and processing into an industry during the Middle Ages, demand for sugar increased. The problem was, the supply of sugarcane was limited because it grew best in a hot, tropical climate.

In part, European explorers sailed to the Americas in search of places to cultivate sugarcane. They discovered that Brazil and the Caribbean islands were perfect for that purpose. But the work involved in growing, harvesting, and processing the cane was brutal. As a result, millions of enslaved Africans were forced to endure the Middle Passage and labor on sugarcane plantations. By the 1700s, sugar—the oil of its day—was a hot commodity on the triangular trade.

In what ways can a commodity such as sugar impact the lives of people all over the world?

A SPOONFUL OF SUGAR
The man shown here is ready to harvest sugarcane on a plantation in present-day Brazil. It's no easy task to farm sugarcane by hand—the tall stalks often grow more than 10 feet high, and farmers can't relax after the stalks are gathered. Sugarcane has to be processed within hours after it's cut. Otherwise, bacteria in the soil can feed on the stalk's sucrose, or natural sugar, and cause significant production loss. Harvesting and processing sugarcane can go on for months. All to satisfy the world's sweet tooth.

PLAN: 4-PAGE LESSON

OBJECTIVE
Describe the value of sugar and its global impact, particularly on millions of enslaved Africans.

CRITICAL THINKING SKILLS FOR LESSON 2.3
- Analyze Visuals
- Make Connections
- Make Inferences
- Identify
- Interpret Charts

HISTORICAL THINKING FOR CHAPTER 18
How have elements of African cultures spread around the world?

Europeans developed sugarcane plantations in the Americas and used enslaved Africans to work on them. Lesson 2.3 discusses the history of sugar and how it was a major factor in the forced migration of Africans.

Student eEdition online
Additional content for this lesson, including photos and captions, is available online.

BACKGROUND FOR THE TEACHER
The Annaberg Plantation (shown in the Student eEdition) The plantation, originally established in 1722, was consolidated with other plantations into a larger, more modern plantation in 1796 with a 40-foot-tall windmill, which crushed double the amount of sugar cane on windy days, and a sugar factory. Slaves were responsible for all aspects of growing, harvesting, and processing sugar. The fieldworkers would cut the cane, cart it to the windmill, and feed it through rollers to extract the sugar juice. Sugar cookers would then heat the juice until it was ready to crystallize, cool the syrup, rake the forming crystals, and load the sugar into barrels where it would cure. After their 18-to-20-hour days in the tropical heat, the slaves had to tend to their own food plots, producing barely (and sometime not) enough to sustain them. They farmed 1,300 acres and produced 100,000 tons of sugar per year. The ruins of the plantation, preserved by the Virgin Islands National Park, depict the village and factory where the slaves lived and worked, including a dungeon that was used to deter slaves from rebelling.

History Notebook
Encourage students to complete the "Sugar" Global Commodity page for Chapter 18 in their History Notebooks as they read.

INTRODUCE & ENGAGE

PREVIEW WITH VISUALS

Direct students' attention to the photographs in the lesson. Write *sugar* at the center of a Concept Cluster and ask volunteers to list characteristics of sugar and its influence throughout history based on their observation of the photographs. At the end of the lesson, revisit the Concept Cluster and add or remove characteristics and influences based on what students learned.

TEACH

GUIDED DISCUSSION

1. **Analyze Visuals** What do the photographs of the burnt sugarcane stalks and the Annaberg Plantation and their captions (available in the Student eEdition) reveal about sugarcane? *(Possible responses: It can grow taller than 10 feet; fields are often burned to remove the leaves and make the stalks easier to cut; stalks are crushed in windmills to extract the liquid; in the 18th and 19th centuries, slaves were forced to work sugarcane plantations.)*

2. **Make Inferences** Why does the text refer to sugar as "the oil of its day"? *(Possible response: Oil is currently a highly sought commodity across the world. Although sugar is widely available today, it was more difficult to attain and thus more valued in the 1700s.)*

A GLOBAL COMMODITY

While processed sugar may not have the health benefits of its liquid form, there are medicinal uses for the granulated product. Sugar is used in medications as a coating or preservative or to add volume, texture, or flavoring. A spoonful of sugar can cure hiccups and relieve pain from eating foods that are too hot or too spicy. It can also be applied to open wounds to help absorb moisture and prevent bacteria growth and to bee stings and bug bites to soothe the pain.

DIFFERENTIATE

ENGLISH LANGUAGE LEARNERS

Use Sentence Stems Before reading, provide students with the sentence stems listed below. Call on volunteers to read the stems aloud and explain any unfamiliar vocabulary. After reading, have students complete the stems in writing and then compare completed sentences with a partner.

1. After the sugarcane stalks are cut, they must be _____.

2. In search of places to grow sugarcane, the Europeans sailed to the _____.

3. Health benefits such as boosting the immune system and fighting infection come from consuming _____.

4. Sugar was as expensive as nutmeg and other luxury spices during the _____.

5. Americans consume far too much sugar per day, averaging about _____.

GIFTED & TALENTED

Market a Product Ask students to consider all of the possible uses for sugar besides in food and create a product using sugar that people might buy. For example, they may choose to develop a product made from sugar that soothes bug bites and stings. Students should come up with a creative name for the product and develop a plan for how they would market it. Their plan should outline who their market would be, how much the product would be worth, where consumers could purchase it, and where and how they would advertise their product. Students should create a sample advertisement for their product and share it with the class.

See the Chapter Planner for more strategies for differentiation.

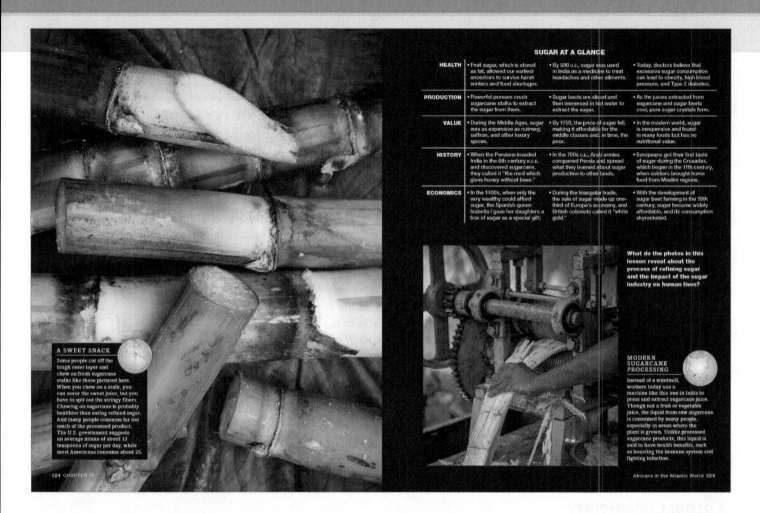

SUGAR AT A GLANCE

HEALTH	• Fruit sugar, which is stored as fat, allowed our earliest ancestors to survive harsh winters and food shortages.	• By 500 c.e., sugar was used in India as a medicine to treat headaches and other ailments.	• Today, doctors believe that excessive sugar consumption can lead to obesity, high blood pressure, and Type 2 diabetes.
PRODUCTION	• Powerful presses crush sugarcane stalks to extract the sugar from them.	• Sugar beets are sliced and then immersed in hot water to extract the sugar.	• As the juices extracted from sugarcane and sugar beets cool, pure sugar crystals form.
VALUE	• During the Middle Ages, sugar was as expensive as nutmeg, saffron, and other luxury spices.	• By 1750, the price of sugar fell, making it affordable for the middle classes and, in time, the poor.	• In the modern world, sugar is inexpensive and found in many foods but has no nutritional value.
HISTORY	• When the Persians invaded India in the 6th century b.c.e. and discovered sugarcane, they called it "the reed which gives honey without bees."	• In the 700s c.e., Arab armies conquered Persia and spread what they learned about sugar production to other lands.	• Europeans got their first taste of sugar during the Crusades, which began in the 11th century, when soldiers brought home food from Muslim regions.
ECONOMICS	• In the 1400s, when only the very wealthy could afford sugar, the Spanish queen Isabella I gave her daughters a box of sugar as a special gift.	• During the triangular trade, the sale of sugar made up one-third of Europe's economy, and British colonists called it "white gold."	• With the development of sugar beet farming in the 19th century, sugar became widely affordable, and its consumption skyrocketed.

What do the photos in this lesson reveal about the process of refining sugar and the impact of the sugar industry on human lives?

A SWEET SNACK
Some people cut off the tough outer layer and chew on fresh sugarcane stalks like those pictured here. When you chew on a stalk, you can savor the sweet juice, but you have to spit out the stringy fibers. Chewing on sugarcane is probably healthier than eating refined sugar. And many people consume far too much of the processed product. The U.S. government suggests an average intake of about 13 teaspoons of sugar per day, while most Americans consume about 25.

MODERN SUGARCANE PROCESSING
Instead of a windmill, workers today use a machine like this one in India to press and extract sugarcane juice. Though not a fruit or vegetable juice, the liquid from raw sugarcane is consumed by many people, especially in areas where the plant is grown. Unlike processed sugarcane products, this liquid is said to have health benefits, such as boosting the immune system and fighting infection.

524 CHAPTER 18

Africans in the Atlantic World 525

BACKGROUND FOR THE TEACHER

White Gold In the mid-1500s, approximately 5,000 sugarcane mills were built in the Caribbean and South America. At one time, sugar was so valuable, people locked it up in sugar safes. By 1830, Louisiana had the largest sugar refinery in the world. By 1897, the candy industry had grown so rapidly that Americans had consumed 26 million pounds of milk chocolate. During Prohibition, soda (made of large amounts of sugar) was added to vending machines. This once rare commodity quickly grew into a staple of the American diet and has been overly consumed. Today, food manufacturers add sugar to many food products to enhance flavor, balance acidity, add texture, increase shelf life and microbial stability, retain moisture, depress freezing points, and aid in fermentation. Some of these foods are fairly obvious, such as soft drinks, sports drinks/energy drinks, cookies, cake, and candy, but other foods are not so obvious, such as yogurt, soup, bread, cured meats, and ketchup. Consuming an excess of sugar, like any other type of calorie, can lead to weight gain. Excessive weight gain, along with other factors, can increase the risk of health problems such as diabetes and heart disease. The Dietary Guidelines for Americans recommend limiting sugar intake to less than 10 percent of total calorie intake per day.

TEACH

GUIDED DISCUSSION

3. **Identify** How has sugarcane processing changed since the 18th and 19th centuries, and are these changes an improvement? *(Possible response: Workers use smaller machines to press the liquid from the stalks, which are likely easier to use and more efficient.)*

4. **Analyze Visuals** What do the close-up photograph of the sugarcane and its caption reveal? *(Possible responses: Sugarcane appears to be very dense. The caption says the stalks have stringy fibers.)*

INTERPRET CHARTS

Direct students to the chart that appears in the lesson. **ASK:** Where did sugarcane originate? *(India)* How did the knowledge of sugar production spread? *(Persians invaded India, and then Arab armies invaded Persia. After that, the Europeans tasted sugar during the Crusades.)* What made sugar more affordable? *(the development of sugar beet farming)* How are sugarcane and sugar beets processed differently? *(Sugarcane stalks are crushed to extract the sugar liquid from them. Sugar beets are sliced and immersed in hot water to extract their sugar.)*

ACTIVE OPTION

NG Learning Framework: Explore the Uses of Bagasse
SKILLS Problem-Solving, Collaboration
KNOWLEDGE New Frontiers

Explain to students that after the sugar liquid is extracted, the fibrous remains of the sugarcane stalk are not wasted. These remains, called *bagasse,* can be used to produce a multitude of products. Have small groups conduct online research into products made with bagasse. Tell them to research how bagasse is turned into these products and how the products are used. Have them choose one of the products and create a visual that details the process of creating the product, any benefits the product may have, and how it is used. Encourage students to share their visuals with the class.

ANSWERS

- Possible response: A commodity such as sugar can impact the lives of the people who use it, harvest it, and transport it—especially if it is a desired commodity that will generate profit for those who control it.

- The photos reveal that the process of refining sugar is hard work that must impact the physical well-being of those who do the work and that most people in the United States consume too much sugar.

Resistance to Slavery

It's almost impossible to imagine what it would be like to be captured suddenly and then face a lifetime of slavery. Undoubtedly, a person would have to draw upon every possible resource to carry on. Among the resources Africans called upon were music, religion, and their sense of community.

SLAVE LABOR ON PLANTATIONS

As you have learned, from the 1500s to the late 1700s, Europeans developed a large-scale form of agriculture in the Americas: the plantation system. Africans became unwilling participants in an enterprise that depended on slave labor to produce agricultural products.

Over time, many successful sugar planters in the Caribbean became absentee owners who used their profits to build impressive country houses, including some of the finest estates in France and Britain. The work of overseeing slave labor usually went to lower-status European immigrants, who were often harsh supervisors. The life of a slave on a sugar plantation was grueling. Enslaved Africans performed all the

backbreaking work of planting, weeding, harvesting, and processing sugarcane. They were treated more like machines than human beings, and many were literally worked to death. Sunday was their only day of rest.

Later, other types of plantations, such as tobacco plantations in Virginia and rice and indigo plantations in the Carolinas, would grow prosperous through the labor of enslaved Africans. As you will learn, a big change came in the late 1700s with the beginning of the Industrial Revolution. British factories needed more and more raw cotton to make clothing and other products, and by the early 1800s, Native Americans were being driven off the land to make way for cotton plantations, which relied on slave labor.

This illustration from 1667 depicts the manufacturing of sugar by enslaved Africans on a Caribbean plantation.

WAYS OF RESISTING BONDAGE

Everywhere in the Americas, enslaved Africans looked for ways to resist their captivity and escape bondage. Slaveholders and overseers were always on the lookout for any resistance—and they reacted to it brutally. In his autobiography, Olaudah Equiano tells of a slave trader who cut off the leg of a slave for running away.

Usually, enslaved Africans found more subtle ways to express their defiance. Although these smaller acts did not lead to freedom, they helped enslaved men and women cope with their situation. Slaves sang songs and told stories based on African cultural traditions. Often, the songs and stories ridiculed plantation owners, using coded language the slaveholders could not understand. Slaveholders knew that Africans frequently used drums to communicate, so they banned the musical instruments from their quarters. Despite this, enslaved people were still able to relay messages through rhythm. Slaves also purposely slowed down their work, broke farm tools, and feigned illness as ways to impede, or hinder, the plantation owners' financial success. However, such resistance often resulted in a beating.

Religion also served as a survival aid. Praying alone or with others helped restore dignity and provide hope for a better life. In areas with large African populations, enslaved people merged their existing beliefs with Christianity. For example, in Brazil and Cuba, Yoruba gods called orishas were transformed into Catholic saints. In British North America, enslaved people focused on aspects of Christianity most closely connected to their plight. They sang hymns of liberation and were inspired by biblical stories, such as that of Moses leading the enslaved Israelites to freedom.

ESCAPING TO FREEDOM

Enslaved people who managed to escape to freedom needed help to survive and to avoid recapture. Options for escaped slaves included joining pirate groups in the Caribbean, settling among Native American populations, or forming their own **autonomous**, or self-governing, communities.

As early as the 16th century, escaped slaves banded together to form their own communities. Called **maroon communities**, these self-governing groups of escaped slaves were common in the Caribbean and in coastal areas of Central and South America. The word *maroon* comes from a Spanish word meaning "wild or untamed," but it came to be used as a name for an escaped slave.

The largest and most powerful maroon community was Palmares in Brazil. Founded in the early 17th century; it had tens of thousands of residents who

Harriet Tubman was a former slave who helped hundreds of enslaved Africans in North America escape to freedom in the 1800s. She often used coded songs to communicate with freedom seekers. On one trip, she used the following song to announce her return to a group she had left in hiding and to tell them it was safe to approach her.

PRIMARY SOURCE

Oh go down, Moses,
Way down into Egypt's land,
Tell old Pharaoh,
Let my people go.

Oh Pharaoh said he would go cross,
Let my people go,
And don't get lost in the wilderness,
Let my people go.

You may hinder me here, but you can't up there,
Let my people go,
He sits in the Heaven and answers prayer,
Let my people go!

—from *Harriet: The Moses of Her People* by Sarah H. Bradford, 1886

PLAN: 4-PAGE LESSON

OBJECTIVE

Describe how, during the years of the Atlantic slave trade, captured Africans relied on a variety of strategies and resources to resist, cope with, and escape from slavery in the Americas.

CRITICAL THINKING SKILLS FOR LESSON 2.4

- Draw Conclusions
- Compare and Contrast
- Analyze Cause and Effect
- Explain
- Evaluate
- Analyze Primary Sources
- Analyze Visuals

HISTORICAL THINKING FOR CHAPTER 18

How have elements of African cultures spread around the world?

Enslaved Africans who were taken to the Americas brought many aspects of their cultures with them. Lesson 2.4 discusses the ways in which enslaved Africans resisted their oppression and the cultural contributions that they made.

BACKGROUND FOR THE TEACHER

South Carolina and the Cowboys South Carolina included early examples of an iconic American figure—the cowboy. Many Africans had experience with herding cattle and were forced to use this skill while enslaved in colonial South Carolina, which was ideal for raising cattle and hogs on its open grasslands. When the cattle were ready for sale, the enslaved cowboys rounded them up, branded them, and drove them to market—practices that predated the American West by nearly 150 years. These African cowboys experienced more freedom than most enslaved Africans in the Carolina colony until the rice plantation system began to take root. The colonists then adopted the Barbados slave codes, the harshest codes in all the colonies, which curtailed the freer life of the early cowboys.

Student eEdition online

Additional content for this lesson, including an image, is available online.

INTRODUCE & ENGAGE

TAKE A POSITION

Have students imagine that they are 17th-century opponents of slavery who have been asked by a local plantation owner why they believe that the practice is wrong. Encourage students to think about the ethical, religious, and economic issues they might consider in their response and then explain and justify their position. Then tell students that in this lesson they will learn about the treatment of enslaved Africans, ways that enslaved Africans resisted their oppression, and the greater effects of slavery on communities in North America, South America, the Caribbean, and Africa.

TEACH

GUIDED DISCUSSION

1. **Analyze Cause and Effect** How did the Industrial Revolution affect Native Americans living in the South? *(The Industrial Revolution increased the demand for products like cotton and indigo in Europe. This caused more land in the American South to be converted to plantations, and Native Americans were forcibly removed from this land.)*

2. **Explain** How did enslaved people use music to communicate? *(They would clap rhythms and sing hymns with coded language.)*

ANALYZE PRIMARY SOURCES

Direct students to the lyrics of the coded song that Harriet Tubman would use to communicate with enslaved people she was helping to escape. **ASK:** Why do you think Harriet Tubman went by the nickname "Moses"? *(Possible response: Moses freed slaves in ancient Egypt, and she was freeing slaves in the United States.)* Why did Tubman communicate by song? *(Possible response: If a hostile people overheard the lyrics, they wouldn't understand the hidden meaning.)*

DIFFERENTIATE

ENGLISH LANGUAGE LEARNERS

Ask and Answer Questions Pair students at the **Beginning** level with those at the **Advanced** level. Tell students to write several short-answer questions about the lesson content, including notable people and groups, the experience of enslaved people, how enslaved people resisted their oppression, and how enslaved people have contributed to the economy and culture of the Americas. Then have each pair take turns asking and answering questions with another pair.

PRE-AP

Create a Flow Chart Direct students to conduct online research and create a flow chart illustrating the long-term impact of the transatlantic slave trade. Tell them to explore connections to later injustices toward African Americans such as Jim Crow laws, institutionalized racism, and mass incarceration, as well as the economic and social difficulties that the slave trade inflicted upon Africa. Invite students to share their flow charts with the class.

See the Chapter Planner for more strategies for differentiation.

Maroon communities still exist in the Caribbean and in parts of South and North America. At the annual Accompong Maroon Festival in Jamaica (shown above) community members commemorate the signing of a peace treaty between the maroons and the British in 1739, which recognized the maroons' freedom.

defended themselves against the Portuguese until the Portuguese defeated them in 1694. Significant maroon communities also developed in Venezuela, Guyana, and Florida. In some places, escaped slaves assimilated into indigenous communities. In Florida, for example, Africans who escaped from slavery in the Carolinas and Georgia formed an alliance with the Creek, a Native American tribe. Escaped Africans who lived among Native Americans in Florida and intermarried with them came to be known as Black Seminoles.

SLAVERY'S IMPACT ON AFRICA

As early as the 16th century, the Atlantic slave trade had brought conflict to some West African societies, such as the Kongo kingdom. Over the next two centuries, the demand for African slaves dramatically increased as the Caribbean sugar industry grew. Few West African communities escaped slavery's effects on their social, economic, and military institutions.

The Asante kingdom was one society whose leaders took part in the Atlantic slave trade. Asante was a growing power in the rain forest region of 18th-century West Africa. Asante rulers captured many prisoners as they expanded their kingdom through warfare. Before the rise of the Atlantic slave trade, some war captives would have been sent home through prisoner exchanges or redeemed for ransom. Others would have been kept as household servants and farmworkers. With the rise of the Atlantic slave trade, however, the Asante exchanged captured slaves for valuable imported goods, such as rum, cloth, and guns.

The kings of Dahomey, another West African kingdom, were more aggressive in using the slave trade to advance state interests. They traded enslaved people for guns to build a military advantage over their neighbors. Other rulers then found that they needed to conduct a similar trade for their own self-defense. They felt forced to sell Africans from neighboring societies in order to protect their own people.

This vicious cycle was reinforced by differing European and African gender preferences. Europeans preferred to buy young males, who fetched high prices because they could do hard physical labor. In contrast, West Africans preferred female slaves, who were valued as agricultural and domestic workers. In addition, female slaves could give birth to children and add to the population and labor force of a village or clan. Leaders of societies like the Asante and Dahomey could doubly benefit from the slave trade by exchanging imprisoned men for imported goods while keeping captive women for their own social and economic benefit.

Thelma Maiben-Owens, a present-day resident of Africatown, takes photos of her ancestors' graves at the Old Plateau Cemetery in Mobile, Alabama.

THE CLOTILDA

Even though the United States banned the import of enslaved Africans in 1808, plantation owners continued to make illegal slave runs to provide labor for the booming cotton industry. In 1860, an Alabama plantation owner named Timothy Meaher chartered a schooner called the Clotilda and enlisted its captain, William Foster, to sail to the kingdom of Dahomey, where Foster bought approximately 110 Africans. The Clotilda and its human cargo sailed back to Alabama, entering Mobile Bay under the cover of night. Once the slaves were unloaded, the Clotilda was taken up the Mobile River, burned, and sunk.

After being freed by Union soldiers in 1865, the Clotilda's survivors used money they had earned to buy land just north of the city of Mobile. They created a settlement called Africatown, where they formed a society based on that of their homeland. Many of the survivors' descendants still live there today and grew up hearing stories of the ship that brought their ancestors to Alabama.

In May 2019, the Alabama Historical Commission announced that a shipwreck discovered in a remote area of the Mobile River was almost certainly the Clotilda. The discovery was funded by the National Geographic Society—with Dr. Fredrik Hiebert, archaeologist-in-residence, as part of the survey team—and confirmed by archaeological analysis of the sunken vessel against existing records and registration documents.

In the spring of 2020, the U.S. government allocated money to conserve the site of the Clotilda. It remains to be determined whether the ship will be raised and restored or left at the bottom of the river as a national slave ship memorial, but its discovery has brought validation and renewal to the residents of Africatown.

The Atlantic slave trade transformed West African society, uprooting men, women, and children from their homes. The fabric of family life in Africa began to unravel as more and more people were taken away. Life became difficult and insecure as African villagers began to fear capture. The loss of population through the export of slaves harmed economic growth. Productivity suffered as Africa lost many of its young, most able workers. The amount of money gained by the sale of an enslaved person was far less than that individual may have contributed to Africa's economy over a lifetime of work. In general, the destabilization of Africa's society and economy set the stage for the entry of outside countries into the affairs of the continent.

HISTORICAL THINKING

1. **READING CHECK** In what ways did enslaved Africans resist their captivity?

2. **DRAW CONCLUSIONS** How did Asante and Dahomey doubly benefit from the Atlantic slave trade?

3. **COMPARE AND CONTRAST** How did slavery differ for male and female captives?

4. **ANALYZE CAUSE AND EFFECT** How were the economy and social structure of West African societies impacted by the Atlantic slave trade?

BACKGROUND FOR THE TEACHER

The Clotilda Even though the United States banned the import of slaves from Africa in 1808, plantation owners continued to make illegal slave runs to provide labor for the booming cotton industry. In 1860, an Alabama plantation owner named Timothy Meaher chartered a schooner called the Clotilda and enlisted its captain, William Foster, to sail to the kingdom of Dahomey, where Foster bought approximately 110 Africans. The Clotilda and its human cargo sailed back to Alabama, entering Mobile Bay under the cover of night. Once the slaves were unloaded, the Clotilda was taken up the Mobile River, burned, and sunk to conceal any evidence of illegal activity.

After being freed by Union soldiers in 1865, the Clotilda's survivors used money they earned selling vegetables and working in fields and mills to buy land just north of the city of Mobile. They created a settlement called Africatown, where they formed a society based on that of their homeland. Many of the survivors' descendants still live there today and grew up hearing stories of the ship that brought their ancestors to Alabama. Several attempts were made over the years to locate the Clotilda's remains but with no luck. Then, in May 2019, the Alabama Historical Commission made an announcement: A shipwreck discovered in a remote area of the Mobile River was almost certainly the Clotilda. The discovery was confirmed by archaeological analysis of the sunken vessel against existing records and registration documents. It is yet to be determined whether the ship will be raised and restored or left at the bottom of the river as a national slave ship memorial, but its discovery has brought validation and renewal to the residents of Africatown.

TEACH

GUIDED DISCUSSION

3. **Evaluate** How could escaped African slaves benefit from joining Native American communities? *(Possible response: These communities were established and could help Africans find food, shelter, and protection in an unfamiliar land; these communities had also been mistreated by Europeans, so they might be sympathetic to Africans.)*

4. **Analyze Cause and Effect** How did the Dahomey slaves-for-guns trade cause the slave trade in West Africa to increase? *(Other African kingdoms needed guns to protect themselves from the Dahomey, so they entered the slave trade.)*

ANALYZE VISUALS

Direct students to the photograph of the maroon community. **ASK:** What do you see in the photo that was a part of African culture during the slave era? *(Possible responses: drums and singing were part of African culture)* Why was it important for the maroons to get the British to acknowledge their freedom in a written peace treaty? *(Possible response: to ensure that the British would not try to recapture and enslave them again)*

ACTIVE OPTIONS

On Your Feet: Jigsaw Strategy Divide the class into four groups and assign each group one of the following four areas of American culture that enslaved Africans have contributed to: food and cuisine, music, language, and art. Each group should research their topic in depth. Regroup students so that each new group has at least one member from each expert group. Then have the experts take turns reporting on their topics while other students learn from their research.

| NG Learning Framework: Make a Policy Proposal
| ATTITUDE Responsibility
| SKILL Problem-Solving

Explain to students that many people have proposed that the United States should make reparations to the descendants of enslaved Africans. Have students conduct online research to learn more about reparations proposals, such as how to determine who is entitled to reparations, what benefits reparations should consist of, and how these benefits should be distributed or administered. Then students should come up with their own policy proposal for slavery reparations and back up their ideas with their research.

HISTORICAL THINKING

ANSWERS

1. While some escaped or rebelled, others coped by sending coded messages in song, slowing work, breaking farm tools, and pretending to be sick, all to harm a master's finances.

2. Possible response: They gained imported commodities in exchange for male slaves, and they used captive women for their own benefit.

3. Possible response: More males were forced to enter the overseas slave market, while most female slaves remained in Africa. This meant that more female slaves would eventually win freedom than their male counterparts. Also, male slaves were expected to do hard physical labor outside, while female slaves usually did house tasks or less demanding farm work.

4. Possible response: West Africa lost a large number of its people, productivity decreased, family life was disrupted, and Africans feared for their safety.

VOCABULARY

Match each vocabulary term with its correct definition.

1. slave narrative
2. Middle Passage
3. succession
4. maroon community
5. autonomous
6. manumission
7. triangular trade
8. abolition
9. racism

a. a trade network connecting Europe, Africa, and the Americas between the 1500s and the 1800s
b. self-governing
c. the release from slavery
d. the movement to end slavery
e. the process by which a new leader is chosen to follow an outgoing leader
f. a written account of the life of a former slave
g. the belief that a particular race of people is superior to other races
h. a self-governing group of escaped slaves
i. the journey by slave ships across the Atlantic Ocean from West Africa to the Americas

READING STRATEGY
IDENTIFY MAIN IDEAS AND DETAILS

Use a graphic organizer like the one below to identify details that support the main idea about the Atlantic slave trade. Then answer the question that follows.

Main Idea
The Atlantic slave trade had a devastating impact on family and community life in West Africa.

Detail	Detail	Detail

10. How did the Atlantic slave trade affect family and community life in West Africa?

MAIN IDEAS

Answer the following questions. Support your answers with evidence from the chapter.

11. How did Christianity spread to Central and South Africa? LESSON 1.1

12. Why were Sunni Ali and Askia Muhammad important in West Africa's history? LESSON 1.2

13. According to the slave narrative written by Olaudah Equiano, what were conditions like on the Middle Passage? LESSON 2.1

14. How did European expansion into the Americas affect Africa? LESSON 2.2

15. Why did escaped slaves band together in maroon communities? LESSON 2.4

HISTORICAL THINKING

Answer the following questions. Support your answers with evidence from the chapter.

16. COMPARE AND CONTRAST How did Africans and Europeans differ in their response to Kimpa Vita's ideas?

17. MAKE INFERENCES Why do you think cowrie shells were used as currency in West Africa?

18. SYNTHESIZE What political, social, and economic impacts did Islam have on Africa?

19. ANALYZE CAUSE AND EFFECT How did Askia Muhammad build a successful empire?

20. DRAW CONCLUSIONS Why did many slave owners react brutally to slave resistance?

21. DESCRIBE How did the treatment of enslaved people in West Africa change over time?

22. MAKE GENERALIZATIONS How did the practice of slavery conflict with religious and political principles in the United States?

23. FORM AND SUPPORT OPINIONS Do you think Olaudah Equiano's narrative is a reliable source for learning about slavery in the Americas? Support your answer with evidence.

INTERPRET VISUALS

Study the table at right and answer the questions below.

24. During what period of time were the largest number of slaves exported from Africa? Why?

25. Slavery was abolished in the United States in 1865. How does the table reflect that fact?

The Atlantic Slave Trade: Number of Enslaved People Exported from Africa, 1450–1990

Period	Number of Slaves	Percent of Total
1450–1500	81,000	0.6%
1501–1600	338,000	2.6%
1601–1700	1,876,000	14.6%
1701–1800	6,495,000	50.7%
1801–1900	4,027,000	31.4%
Total	12,817,000	100.0%

ANALYZE SOURCES

Phillis Wheatley (1753–1784) was the first African-American poet to have her work published. Born in West Africa, Wheatley was enslaved as a young girl and sold to a family of Boston Quakers who provided her with a good education. One of the enduring themes of her poetry was freedom for all. In this excerpt from her 1773 poem "To the Right Honorable William, Earl of Dartmouth" Wheatley interrupts her own desire for freedom. Read the excerpt and answer the questions that follow.

> Should you, my lord, while you peruse my song,
> Wonder from whence my love of Freedom sprung,
> Whence flow these wishes for the common good,
> By feeling hearts alone best understood,
> I, young in life, by seeming cruel fate
> Was snatch'd from Afric's fancy'd happy seat:
> What pangs excruciating must molest [disturb],
> What sorrows labor in my parent's breast?
> Steel'd was that soul and by no misery move'd
> That from a father seiz'd his babe belov'd:
> Such, such my case. And can I then but pray
> Others may never feel tyrannic sway?

26. Who is Wheatley referring to as "Steel'd was that soul and by no misery move'd"?

27. According to the poem, why does Wheatley feel uniquely qualified to argue for independence?

CONNECT TO YOUR LIFE

28. ARGUMENT Current genetic research indicates that the concept of race has no biological basis. It is merely a human construction. Do you think that knowledge of this research will put an end to racism? Write an essay stating your opinion and explaining the reasons for it.

TIPS

• Conduct responsible online research to review what genetic researchers say about the concept of race.

• Form and clearly state your opinion on the effects of this research on the existence of racism in today's society.

• Provide reasons from your research and your own experience to support your opinion.

• Write a conclusion that summarizes your argument.

Africans in the Atlantic World 531

VOCABULARY ANSWERS

1. f
2. i
3. e
4. h
5. b
6. c
7. a
8. d
9. g

READING STRATEGY ANSWER

Main Idea
The Atlantic slave trade had a devastating impact on family and community life in West Africa.

Detail	Detail	Detail
Possible response: Family and community life unraveled as people were torn from their homes and communities.	Possible response: Life became insecure as villagers lived in fear of capture.	Possible response: The loss of young, able workers hurt the economy of communities.

10. Possible response: The Atlantic slave trade devastated families and communities in West Africa. Family and community life unraveled as people were taken from their homes and communities. People became fearful and insecure. The economy of communities suffered from the loss of young, able workers.

MAIN IDEAS ANSWERS

11. Roman Catholicism spread in the Kongo kingdom of Central Africa following the conversion of King Nzinga to the religion after the arrival of the Portuguese in 1483. It was blended with African religious traditions and further spread by the Christian reformer Kimpa Vita. Dutch Calvinists and French Huguenots introduced Protestant Christianity to South Africa in the 1600s, but significant numbers of southern Africans did not convert until the 1800s.

12. Sunni Ali founded the Songhai Empire, which became an important force in West Africa. Askia Muhammad built trade relations with Muslim merchants, enabled Songhai to grow wealthy through trade, oversaw the expansion of the Songhai Empire, and established a bureaucracy based on Islamic law.

13. The Middle Passage was a scene of horror: the captives were packed and chained together in the ship's cargo so closely they could barely move, the odor was nauseating, it was hot, the chains hurt, the latrines were filthy, women were screaming, and dying people were groaning.

14. The establishment of European-controlled plantations in the Americas led to the enslavement and forced migration of Africans to work on them.

15. They needed help to survive and avoid recapture.

HISTORICAL THINKING ANSWERS

16. Kimpa Vita's ideas about the blending of religious traditions made Christianity more acceptable to the African people of the Kongo but were considered heresy by the Portuguese missionaries.

17. Possible response: They were plentiful, beautiful, relatively uniform in size, small and easy to handle, and durable.

18. Some African societies adopted Islamic law, Muslim traders brought imported goods to Africa, mosques were built in Africa, African scholars studied Islamic arts and sciences, some Africans became Muslims, and many Islamic and African traditions blended.

19. He gained wealth for Songhai by controlling the gold and salt trade passing through West Africa and used battles and conquests to strengthen Songhai's control. To oversee the growing empire, he established a bureaucracy and divided Songhai into provinces headed by loyal governors.

20. Possible response: The slave owners probably feared large-scale rebellions and wanted to maintain control through intimidation.

21. Originally, West Africans gained slaves through warfare. They used captured enemies as soldiers, workers, and servants. Some slaves had the possibility of gaining their freedom through prisoner exchanges or ransoms. Later, West Africans began selling slaves to Europeans to gain imported goods and wealth. These slaves were stripped of all rights and had little hope of escaping bondage.

22. The dominant religion was Christianity, which taught that people should treat one another with love and charity. The government was democratic and based on the principle that all people are created equal. Slavery directly contradicted these principles.

23. Possible response: Since historians have confirmed the accuracy of Equiano's account of his adult activities, that part of the book can be considered reliable. Some historians think that the part dealing with his earliest life may be based on the stories of other slaves, not his own experiences. That part could be considered a reliable secondhand source.

INTERPRET VISUALS ANSWERS

24. 1701 to 1800; There was a high labor demand and slavery wasn't abolished for another half century.

25. The table shows a large drop in the number of slaves exported in the 1800s.

ANALYZE SOURCES ANSWERS

26. Wheatley is referring to the person who took her from her family as a child.

27. Wheatley was taken from her family at a young age and knows how it feels to live under oppression.

CONNECT TO YOUR LIFE ANSWER

28. In their essays, students should demonstrate an understanding of the scientific research on the subject, clearly state an opinion, and provide supporting reasons.

The Epic Quest for a Northwest Passage

BY GREG MILLER Adapted from "These Maps Show the Epic Quest for a Northwest Passage" by Greg Miller, news.nationalgeographic.com, October 20, 2016

You've read about how the spirit of seafaring propelled European and African empires as they expanded. Had the Northwest Passage existed during this time of growth, it would have been a real game-changer.

It had to be there: an ocean at the top of the world. The ancient Greeks drew it on their maps, and for centuries, the rest of Europe did too. Since the 1800s, countless men have died trying to find a maritime shortcut across the Arctic that would open up new trade routes to Asia. Now, thanks to a warming planet, the long-sought Northwest Passage actually exists, at least for part of the year.

This 1872 map erroneously shows the Gulf Stream and other warm currents feeding an open sea around the North Pole.

The idea of a northern ocean passage dates back at least to the second century c.e. Ptolemy and other ancient Greek geographers believed Earth had four habitable zones balanced by two uninhabitable frigid zones—often thought to be water—at the top and bottom of the globe. But it wasn't until the early 16th century, after the voyages of Columbus, that the idea of a Northwest Passage really took hold among Europeans. Columbus, after all, had sailed west looking for a sea route to the East. Instead, he found a continent blocking the way. The Northwest Passage would be a way around this continent.

Maps from this period are filled with the wild imaginings of mapmakers, from nonexistent bays and islands to sea monsters. Early explorers also occasionally adjusted the facts. The Englishman Martin Frobisher made three voyages in search of the Northwest Passage in the late 1500s. He didn't find it. But he pretended to have discovered more straits than he did.

Perhaps the most famous attempt to find the Northwest Passage was the expedition led by Sir John Franklin in 1845. A British Navy officer, Franklin had led two previous expeditions to the Arctic. But this time the expedition didn't return on schedule, and Franklin's wife, Lady Jane, began pressing the British government to send a search party, which they did in 1848. Newspaper reports on the hunt for

the missing expedition gripped the British public, but all searchers found were graves of men who had died early on and a few scattered notes and relics. The two boats in the expedition had become trapped in ice, and all 129 men, including Franklin, had perished. Over 160 years later, the wreckage of the two boats, the H.M.S. *Erebus* and *Terror*, was finally located.

Unbeknownst to Franklin and other explorers, their expeditions coincided with what scientists call the Little Ice Age, a period of several centuries of unusual cold in the Arctic. As temperatures began to climb toward the end of the 19th century, the long sought Northwest Passage finally opened up.

The Norwegian explorer Roald Amundsen completed the first journey entirely by boat through the Northwest Passage in 1906. It took three years and two winters on the ice. More recently, it's been getting easier. As polar ice has melted, the route has become more accessible. In 2016, a cruise ship carrying 1,700 people became the first passenger liner to complete the passage. The melting of Arctic sea ice has raised the possibility of new trade routes and energy production, as well as the potential for territorial conflicts and environmental damage to a relatively untouched part of Earth.

For better or worse, a new chapter in the storied history of the Arctic is just beginning. ∎

Staging the Question

In this unit, you learned how and why nations sought to expand their territories and influence through trade, conquest, and the exploration of land and sea. In Africa, Asia, and Russia, land-based empires pushed their borders outward in aggressive quests to control and incorporate new lands. Meanwhile, European powers vied for supremacy over the seas in a bid to dominate trade and establish colonies in Asia and the Americas. Advances in seafaring technology tempted rulers toward plans for expansion into distant realms. How did the most successful empires use the tools at their disposal to explore new territories and expand their existing territories?

ASSIGNMENT

Choose three nations in this unit that successfully expanded their territory and influence on land and sea.

Evaluate the methods used by the nations' rulers to promote exploration and expansion.

Think about how each nation used the resources at its disposal.

Based on your analysis of the most effective strategies for expansion, create a conqueror's toolbox of items and ideas that would allow a nation to most efficiently become an empire.

Supporting Questions: Begin by developing supporting questions to guide your research. For example: What new technology can you use to support exploration and expansion of your empire? Research the answers in this unit and in other sources, both print and online. You might want to use a graphic organizer like this one to record your questions and answers.

Summative Performance Task: Use the answers to your questions to help you determine which items you will include in your conqueror's toolbox. You can include tangible items such as maps or navigation tools. To create tools for implementing ideas and strategies, write instruction sheets or manuals with text and illustrations.

Present: Share your toolbox with the class. You might consider one of these options:

CREATE A VIRTUAL TOOLBOX
Find images of the tangible items you want to put in the toolbox and assemble them on a web page. Write a caption for each item, explaining why it is an essential tool for expanding an empire. Write at least two instruction sheets for expansion strategies and link them to your web page.

HOLD AN ACADEMIC POSTER SESSION
Create a poster featuring images of the tools with captions, and print copies of your instruction sheets. Display your poster and instruction sheets alongside those of your classmates and take time to review and comment on each other's toolboxes.

Take Informed Action:

UNDERSTAND Identify and describe a country in the news today that is using tools or strategies such as the ones you described to dominate or conquer other countries.

ASSESS Examine the consequences of this country's actions and its effects on the territories it is trying to dominate.

ACT Share your concerns by researching organizations that oppose such expansions and finding out what types of support they need. Then find a way to offer your support.

NATIONAL GEOGRAPHIC CONNECTION

GUIDED DISCUSSION FOR "THE EPIC QUEST FOR A NORTHWEST PASSAGE"

1. **Identify Main Ideas and Details** What was the Northwest Passage and why was it so important? *(The Northwest Passage was a supposed sea route across the Arctic. It was important because it would allow ships to get around North America, opening up a western trade route to Asia.)*

2. **Form and Support Opinions** Do you think the increased accessibility of the Northwest Passage in the present day is a positive or a negative occurrence? Explain your reasoning. *(Answers will vary. Possible responses: The increased accessibility of the Northwest Passage is a positive occurrence because it will open new trade routes and sources of energy that will benefit the world economy. OR The increased accessibility is a negative occurrence because it has resulted from melting ice that will affect the habitat of many plant and animal species. Increased human presence in the area will also lead to additional damage to the environment.)*

History Notebook

Encourage students to complete the Unit Wrap-Up page for Unit 6 in their History Notebooks.

UNIT INQUIRY PROJECT RUBRIC

ASSESS

Use the rubric to assess each student's participation and performance.

SCORE	ASSIGNMENT	PRODUCT	PRESENTATION
3 GREAT	• Student thoroughly understands the assignment. • Student develops thoughtful supporting questions to guide research.	• Toolbox is well thought out with a variety of useful items. • Toolbox reflects all of the key elements listed in the assignment.	• Presentation is clear, concise, and logical. • Presentation is creative and engaging.
2 GOOD	• Student mostly understands the assignment. • Student develops somewhat thoughtful supporting questions to guide research.	• Toolbox is fairly well thought out with some useful items. • Toolbox reflects most of the key elements listed in the assignment.	• Presentation is fairly clear, concise, and logical. • Presentation is somewhat creative and engaging.
1 NEEDS WORK	• Student does not understand the assignment. • Student does not develop thoughtful questions to guide research.	• Toolbox is not well thought out and contains few useful items. • Toolbox reflects few or none of the key elements listed in the assignment.	• Presentation is not clear, concise, or logical. • Presentation is not creative or engaging.

INTRODUCE THE PHOTOGRAPH

L'ARC DE TRIOMPHE DE L'ÉTOILE

The Arc de Triomphe stands in the center of a main junction formerly known as the Place de l'Étoile for its star, or *étoile*, shape. Renamed the Place Charles de Gaulle after the former French president, the plaza, which boasts the 164-foot-tall, 148-foot-wide monument, was selected as a location for the monument by French architect Jean-François-Thérèse Chalgrin. Chalgrin was commissioned by Napoleon to bring his vision of a triumphal arch, dedicated to the French army, to life. Chalgrin, along with several other prominent architects, broke ground on the arch, inspired by the Roman Arch of Titus, on August 15, 1806— Napoleon's birthday. Progress on the monument was slow; it took over two years just to lay the foundation of the arch, and the death of Chalgrin in 1811 slowed construction further. Though the project was taken over by Chalgrin's colleague, Louis-Robert Goust, the abdication of Napolean as emperor in 1814 brought all progress to a halt. Nearly 10 years later, in 1823, King Louis XVIII ordered the project to continue. Architect Guillaume Abel Blouet took over and completed the development of the monument, which was opened by King Louis-Philippe, on July 29, 1836.

The massive neoclassic monument features large relief sculptures on each of its four pedestals: *The Departure of the Volunteers in 1792* by François Rude; *Napoléon's Triumph of 1810* by Jean-Pierre Cortot; and *Resistance of 1814* and *Peace of 1815* by Antoine Etex. The most famous sculpture is *The Departure of the Volunteers,* also known as *La Marseillaise,* and is significant for its depiction of France calling together its people. The arch is engraved with the names of hundreds of generals as

CRITICAL VIEWING

The French flag—also known as the Tricolor—unfurls under the Arc de Triomphe in the middle of Paris. France adopted the blue, white, and red design after the French Revolution in 1789 and again after the revolution of 1830. Emperor Napoleon commissioned the arch in 1806 to celebrate a military victory. Based on this information, what can you infer about the importance of these two symbols to the nation of France?

534

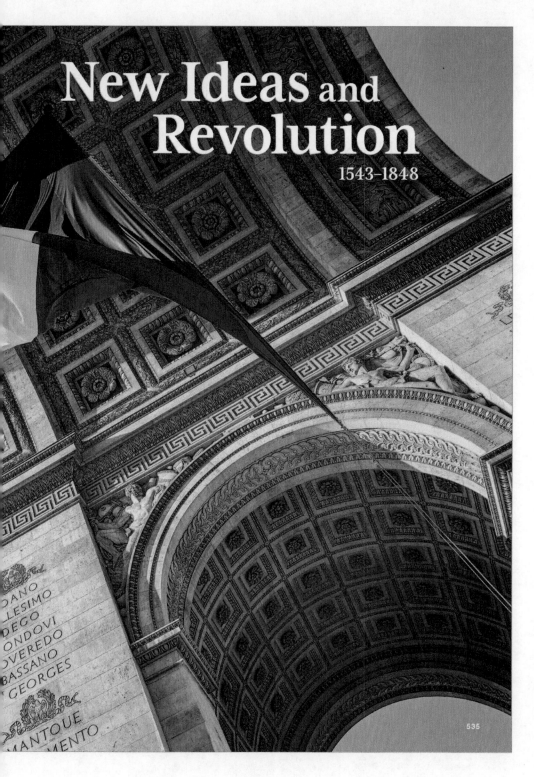

New Ideas and Revolution

1543–1848

well as revolutionary and Napoleonic battles. Stairs lead visitors to the top of the arch, where a panoramic terrace provides a full view of Paris. Beneath the arch lies France's Tomb of the Unknown Soldier along with an eternal flame of remembrance.

The Arc de Triomphe remains an iconic symbol of France. A ceremony commemorating the anniversary of the 1918 armistice that ended the First World War is held at the arch each year on November 11. On other national holidays, such as Bastille Day, the arch serves as the beginning or end of a parade route.

Direct students' attention to the photograph. **ASK:** From what location is the photograph taken? *(from below the arch)* What details can be seen in the photograph? *(Possible responses: There is a smaller arch visible on the side of the main arch; the ceilings of the arches are adorned with intricate carvings; the wall leading into the smaller arch features relief sculptures; the wall panels have words carved into them.)* What do you think the writing on the arch represents? *(Possible responses: names of battles, names of people/soldiers)* Be sure to explain that carved in the walls are the names of famous French generals and the names of revolutionary battles fought by the French.

CRITICAL VIEWING Possible response: Both are important as symbols of national pride, similar to the Stars and Stripes and the Statue of Liberty or the Washington Monument in the United States.

535

INTRODUCE TIME LINE EVENTS

IDENTIFY PATTERNS AND THEMES

Have volunteers read aloud each of the world events in the time line. **ASK:** What are some common themes or patterns that you notice with regard to these events? *(Possible response: Some common themes or patterns include political revolution, scientific development, and intellectual advancement.)* Sort the themes and patterns into categories and put them in webs like the ones shown here.

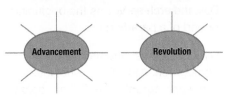

As students read the lessons for each chapter in the unit, have them add the lesson titles to the appropriate web, adding spokes or creating a new web as necessary. Advise students that they may also add or revise categories. At the end of the unit, revisit students' webs and create a final list of categories to summarize the historical themes students encountered as they read each chapter.

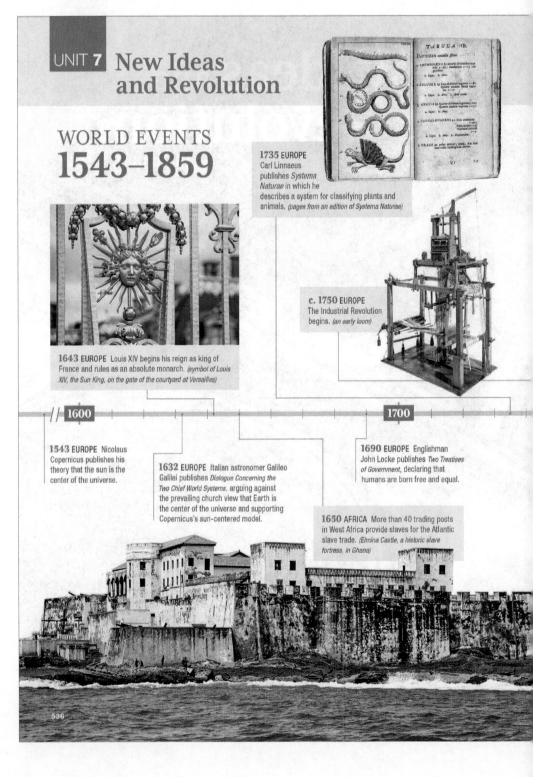

UNIT 7 New Ideas and Revolution

WORLD EVENTS 1543–1859

1735 EUROPE Carl Linnaeus publishes *Systema Naturae* in which he describes a system for classifying plants and animals. *(pages from an edition of Systema Naturae)*

c. 1750 EUROPE The Industrial Revolution begins. *(an early loom)*

1643 EUROPE Louis XIV begins his reign as king of France and rules as an absolute monarch. *(symbol of Louis XIV, the Sun King, on the gate of the courtyard at Versailles)*

1600

1700

1543 EUROPE Nicolaus Copernicus publishes his theory that the sun is the center of the universe.

1632 EUROPE Italian astronomer Galileo Galilei publishes *Dialogue Concerning the Two Chief World Systems*, arguing against the prevailing church view that Earth is the center of the universe and supporting Copernicus's sun-centered model.

1690 EUROPE Englishman John Locke publishes *Two Treatises of Government*, declaring that humans are born free and equal.

1650 AFRICA More than 40 trading posts in West Africa provide slaves for the Atlantic slave trade. *(Elmina Castle, a historic slave fortress, in Ghana)*

536

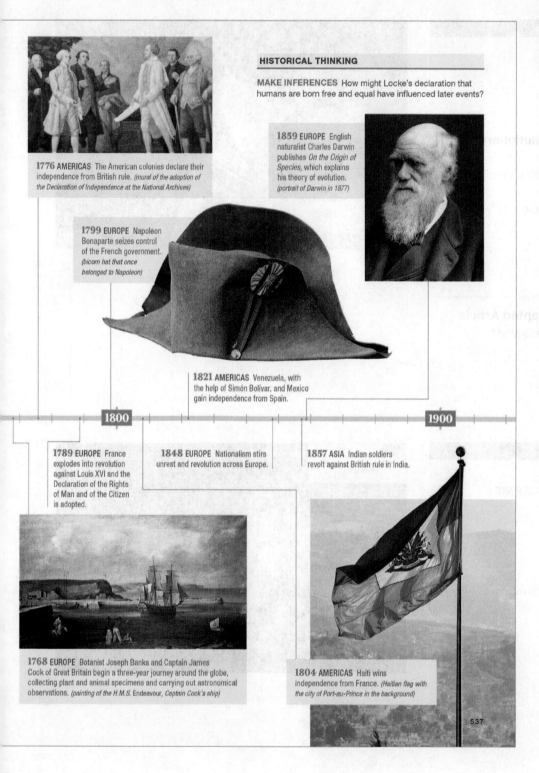

HISTORICAL THINKING

MAKE INFERENCES How might Locke's declaration that humans are born free and equal have influenced later events?

1776 AMERICAS The American colonies declare their independence from British rule. (mural of the adoption of the Declaration of Independence at the National Archives)

1859 EUROPE English naturalist Charles Darwin publishes On the Origin of Species, which explains his theory of evolution. (portrait of Darwin in 1877)

1799 EUROPE Napoleon Bonaparte seizes control of the French government. (bicorn hat that once belonged to Napoleon)

1821 AMERICAS Venezuela, with the help of Simón Bolívar, and Mexico gain independence from Spain.

1800

1900

1789 EUROPE France explodes into revolution against Louis XVI and the Declaration of the Rights of Man and of the Citizen is adopted.

1848 EUROPE Nationalism stirs unrest and revolution across Europe.

1857 ASIA Indian soldiers revolt against British rule in India.

1768 EUROPE Botanist Joseph Banks and Captain James Cook of Great Britain begin a three-year journey around the globe, collecting plant and animal specimens and carrying out astronomical observations. (painting of the H.M.S. Endeavour, Captain Cook's ship)

1804 AMERICAS Haiti wins independence from France. (Haitian flag with the city of Port-au-Prince in the background)

537

HISTORICAL THINKING

Make Inferences

Possible response: Locke's declaration may have influenced the American, French, and Haitian revolutions.

Student eEdition online

Additional content, including the unit map and Global Perspective feature, is available online.

UNIT 7 RESOURCES

UNIT INTRODUCTION

UNIT TIME LINE

UNIT MAP online

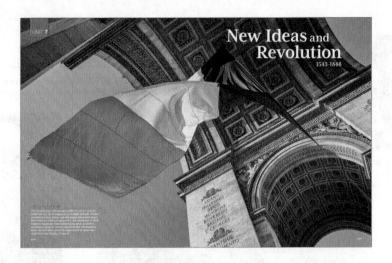

THE GLOBAL PERSPECTIVE: Revolutionary Women online

- National Geographic Explorers: Hayat Sindi, Kavita Gupta, and Peg Keiner
- On Your Feet: Turn and Talk on Topic

NG Learning Framework
Create a Web Page

UNIT WRAP-UP

National Geographic Magazine Adapted Article
- "Jane Goodall: A Revolutionary Naturalist"

Unit 7 Inquiry: Plan a Revolution

Unit 7 Formal Assessment

CHAPTER 19 RESOURCES

Available in the Teacher eEdition

TEACHER RESOURCES & ASSESSMENT

Reading and Note-Taking

Vocabulary Practice

Social Studies Skills Lessons
- Reading: Identify Problems and Solutions
- Writing: Informative

Formal Assessment
- Chapter 19 Pretest
- Chapter 19 Tests A & B
- Section Quizzes

Chapter 19 Answer Key

Cognero®

STUDENT DIGITAL RESOURCES

Available in the Student eEdition

- **eEdition** (English)
- **National Geographic Atlas**
- **Biographies**
- **Handbooks**
- **History Notebook**
- **Literature Analysis**

STRATEGY ❶

Set a Purpose for Reading

Before beginning a lesson, help students set a purpose for reading by prompting them to read the title, main idea statement, and headings. Encourage them also to look at the visuals and read the captions. Tell students to write a question they expect the lesson to answer. If needed, show them how to turn the main idea statement into a question. After they have read the lesson, instruct students to answer the question in writing.

Use with All Lessons

STRATEGY ❷

Use Reciprocal Teaching

Instruct partners to take turns reading each paragraph of the lesson aloud. At the end of the paragraph, the reading student asks the listening student questions about the paragraph. Students may ask their partners to state the main idea, identify important details that support the main idea, or summarize the paragraph in their own words.

Use with All Lessons

STRATEGY ❸

Create "What Happens" Charts

Tell students to summarize the chapter by creating two "What Happens" charts, one for the political changes that occurred in Europe and one for the scientific advances that took place during this time period. Instruct students to complete each chart with relevant information as they read the lessons. After students read independently, have pairs take turns comparing their charts and returning to the text to verify facts regarding any differences they have.

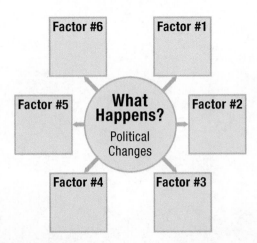

Use with All Lessons

STRATEGY ❶

Create Vocabulary Cards

Encourage students to create a vocabulary card for each boldfaced vocabulary word in a section. Students may draw a picture to illustrate each word or write a definition, synonym, and/or example. Students can work in pairs to review the words when they finish reading a section. Encourage pairs to share their cards and copy any synonyms or examples that will be helpful in remembering the meaning of the words.

Use with All Lessons

STRATEGY ❷

Describe Historical Art

Pair students who are visually impaired with students who are not. Ask the latter to read the captions and describe the historical paintings and other art, providing specific details about setting, facial expressions, gestures, and clothing, as well as giving an overall impression of the style of the painting and the feelings it evokes. Instruct visually impaired students to ask clarifying questions as necessary. Sighted students might use an Attribute Web, such as the one shown, to organize details and what the students discuss.

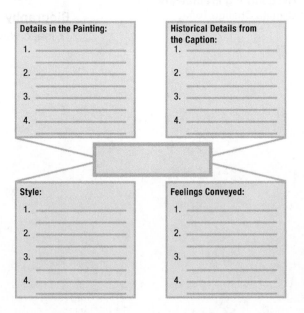

Use with Lessons 1.1, 1.2, 2.1, 2.2, and 3.1

ENGLISH LANGUAGE LEARNERS

STRATEGY 1
Order Sentence Strips

Choose a key paragraph from the lesson to read aloud while students at **All Proficiencies** follow along in their books. After reading, tell students to close their books. Provide sentence strips of the paragraph and direct students to place the strips in order. Ask students to read their paragraphs aloud.

Use with All Lessons *You may wish to ask students at the Beginning level to read the sentence strips aloud and identify meaningful words before they start placing the strips in order.*

STRATEGY 2
Develop Word Knowledge

Help students develop understanding and usage of unknown words and vocabulary words by using the words in context.

For **Beginning** level students, display sentences with choices: In an absolute monarchy, the king has limited/unlimited power. *(unlimited)*

For **Intermediate** level students, display individual sentence frames with only one blank: In a constitutional monarchy, power is _____ between a monarch and a group such as Parliament. *(balanced)*

For **Advanced** level students, display sentences with more than one blank: In an _____ monarchy, the king has _____ power. *(absolute, unlimited)*

Use with All Lessons

STRATEGY 3
Pair Partners for Dictation

After reading a lesson, ask students at **All Proficiencies** to write a sentence summarizing its main idea. Arrange students in pairs and ask them to dictate their sentences to each other. Then tell pairs to work together to check their sentences for spelling and accuracy.

Use with All Lessons *You might pair students at the Beginning level with those at the Advanced level and students at the Intermediate level with each other.*

GIFTED & TALENTED

STRATEGY 1
Compare and Contrast Two Leaders

Tell students to choose two of the political leaders presented in the lessons to compare and contrast. Encourage them to conduct research on the two leaders and organize the facts they find in a Venn diagram or a comparison chart. Have them prepare a display about the information in the graphic organizer and present the information to the class.

Use with Lessons 1.1, 1.2, and 1.3

STRATEGY 2
Portray a Scientist

Invite students to choose one of the scientists mentioned in the chapter and conduct research to create a portrayal of the person in a living wax museum. Encourage students to create a display of information, props, and a costume they can wear as they present their scientist to the class. Invite volunteers to speak as if they are the scientist and answer their classmates' questions.

Use with Lessons 2.1, 2.2, 2.3, and 3.1

PRE-AP

STRATEGY 1
Analyze Historical Accuracy

Instruct students to choose a scene from one of Shakespeare's history plays and conduct research to analyze its historical accuracy. Remind students that Shakespeare wrote during the reign of Queen Elizabeth and would have wanted her approval. Encourage students to write an essay of their analysis. Invite volunteers to share their finished essays with the class.

Use with Lesson 1.1

STRATEGY 2
Debate the Issue

Invite students to choose one of the science topics mentioned in the chapter that was controversial at its time, such as the ideas of Copernicus and Galileo versus the teachings of the Catholic Church, the dissections of human corpses that had been forbidden by ancient Roman law, or Kepler's elliptical orbits versus Aristotle's circular orbits. Encourage students to write a skit of the debate, and have pairs perform the skits for the class and prepare to answer any questions.

Use with Lessons 2.1, 2.2, 2.3, and 3.1

Europe in the
Age of Scientific
Revolution
1543–1848

HISTORICAL THINKING How can scientific advances
challenge previously accepted ideas and lead to new
knowledge?

SECTION 1 Europe's Struggle for Stability
SECTION 2 Scientific Advances
SECTION 3 Practical Science

INTRODUCE THE PHOTOGRAPH

THE MILKY WAY GALAXY VIEWED BY AN ARRAY OF RADIO TELESCOPES

Have students study the photograph of the Atacama Large Millimeter Array, or ALMA, a large radio telescope system in Chile. Explain to students that ever since humans first looked up at the night sky and saw the stars, they have been asking questions about the universe. **ASK:** What questions did the earliest scientific thinkers probably ask about the night sky? *(Possible responses: How far away from Earth are the stars? Why are some objects in the sky different colors? How many stars are in the Milky Way?)* How does the photograph illustrate the importance of technology in the quest for scientific knowledge? *(The telescope array helps humans on Earth study the stars and other objects in space. Without the telescopes, humans would know less about the universe.)* Explain to students that in this chapter they will learn about the scientific thinkers and innovators who launched the Scientific Revolution.

SHARE BACKGROUND

The Atacama Large Millimeter Array, or ALMA, is made up of 66 individual radio antenna dishes that all work together to peer into outer space. ALMA opened in 2013 and was built with the cooperation of astronomers and scientists from North America, Europe, and East Asia. (Chile, ALMA's host country, also cooperated.) ALMA is notable not only for its size and power but also for its location. Perched more than 16,000 feet above sea level in the dry Atacama Desert, ALMA does not have to look through layers of atmospheric moisture. Its clear view into space allows it to see objects that are very far away. Further, ALMA, as a radio telescope, observes wavelengths far beyond those of optical light. As a result, astronomers can observe phenomena that are usually invisible, such as the formation of planets from interstellar debris or the formation of stars from cosmic dust.

CRITICAL VIEWING Answers will vary. Possible response: There are many stars in the sky, and the Milky Way galaxy, made up of billions of stars, is so far away that it appears as a cloudy white ribbon.

HISTORICAL THINKING QUESTION
How can scientific advances challenge previously accepted ideas and lead to new knowledge?

Numbered Heads: The Tension Between Science and Religion Invite students to think about the tension that can exist between empirical science and religious beliefs. Ask them to number off within groups of four to discuss one of the following questions:

Question 1 Can the physical world, and, more broadly, life itself, be explained only with science, only with religious beliefs, or with a little of both?

Question 2 How can religious beliefs and scientific data co-exist? Discuss.

Question 3 Why is it important to sometimes challenge previously accepted ideas?

Question 4 What might the modern world be like if the great scientific thinkers of the past had not challenged the established beliefs and practices of their day?

Remind groups that each member should contribute. Call a number for students to report for the group.

KEY DATES FOR CHAPTER 19

1543	Copernicus publishes the heliocentric theory.
1611	The King James Bible is published.
1618	The Thirty Years' War begins.
1632	Galileo is arrested.
1637	Descartes publishes the deductive method.
1643	Louis XIV becomes king of France.
1660	Robert Boyle helps found the Royal Society.
1688	The Glorious Revolution occurs.
1735	Carl Linnaeus publishes *Systema Naturae*.
1768	James Cook and Joseph Banks set sail on the *Endeavour*.

INTRODUCE THE READING STRATEGY

IDENTIFY PROBLEMS AND SOLUTIONS
Explain that identifying the problems and solutions of people in the past can help students understand how the events of history unfolded. Go to the Chapter Review and preview the graphic organizer with students. As students read the chapter, have them find problems and solutions of key individuals or groups and the solutions' impacts.

INTRODUCE CHAPTER VOCABULARY

KEY VOCABULARY

SECTION 1

absolute monarchy	constitutional monarchy	orthodoxy
sovereignty		

SECTION 2

deductive approach	geocentric theory	heliocentric theory
hypothesis	inductive approach	nebula
optics	scientific method	scientific rationalism

SECTION 3

Aborigine	botany	cartography
ethnography	fauna	flora
food security	longitude	

WORD WEB
Tell students to complete a Word Web for Key Vocabulary words as they read the chapter. Direct them to write each word in the center of an oval and then look through the chapter to find examples, characteristics, and descriptive words that may be associated with the vocabulary word. After reading the chapter, ask students to share what they learned about each word. Model an example using the graphic organizer below.

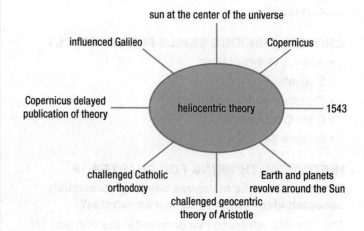

Power Struggles in France and England

If you had the power to tell people how to live and what to believe, would you do it? Louis XIV of France did just that. He amassed tremendous power, insisted on Catholicism as France's religion, and had his subjects fund his building projects and wars.

FRENCH AND ENGLISH DISCORD

The English and French monarchies had been great rivals since the Middle Ages. Though, as ambitious monarchs in both countries claimed ever greater power, their plans were complicated by religious differences within their own realms as well as conflicts with nobility who resented losing some of their own authority. In the end, both countries found paths to political stability but followed very different models of government. In France, **absolute monarchy** gave the king unquestioned and limitless power. In England, the powers of a monarch were limited by a **constitutional monarchy** that balanced power between a monarch and Parliament.

The discord between France and England was so much a part of the 16th century that English poet and playwright William Shakespeare wrote the conflict into many of his plays. In *Henry VI*, Shakespeare writes, "'Tis better using France than trusting France," and one of the characters describes the French king as "weak of courage and in judgment."

Shakespeare's plays marked the pinnacle of the English Renaissance in theater. His works depict the intrigues of kings and nobles as well as the lives of common people. English audiences, including

Queen Elizabeth and her successor King James, were captivated by Shakespeare's work. Across the English Channel, however, the French were not so pleased. Reading the plays 100 years after Shakespeare's death, the French philosopher Voltaire expressed his opinion: Shakespeare's works were "contrary to good taste" and Shakespeare was "a savage."

The Armada Portrait of Elizabeth I commemorates the great sea battle of 1588, when the English fleet defeated the Spanish Armada, which had been sent to invade England and overthrow the queen. In the painting, two windows behind Queen Elizabeth depict the outcome of the battle. In the left window, a message of Elizabeth's victory appears. In the right window, the Spanish Armada is shown sinking as the English fleet returns to shore.

QUEEN ELIZABETH

Under the major influence of **Elizabeth I**, English society entered the 17th century in relative peace and with increasing national confidence. Elizabeth supported the Church of England established by her father, Henry VIII. As you have read, Henry VIII formed the church after the pope refused to annul his marriage to his first wife. He formed the Church of England to defy the pope's authority, but he retained many Catholic rites and traditions, including powerful bishops.

When Henry's oldest daughter, Mary, took the throne before Elizabeth in 1553, she tried to return England to a Catholic state and brutally persecuted Protestants. Elizabeth brought back Protestant rule, but she was more interested in stability than in religious dogma. She worked closely with Parliament and brought peace through compromise with Catholics.

Elizabeth never married and had no children, so a relative, James Stuart, took the throne as **James I** upon her death in 1603. Unlike Elizabeth, James clashed with Parliament. He believed he had a God-given right to rule as an absolute monarch, and he was unwilling to share power with Parliament. Shortly after James became king, a group of church leaders met to request a new translation of the Bible, as existing versions had many errors. James assembled a group of about 50 translators and scholars, and in 1611 the King James Bible was the result. Even so, English Protestants, especially the English Calvinists, who were Protestant reformers known as Puritans, grew discontented with the opulent Stuart court and the luxurious lives of English bishops.

CATHOLICISM AND ABSOLUTE MONARCHY

Unlike the English, the French were predominantly Catholic. As you read earlier, however, following the murder of tens of thousands of French Protestant Huguenots in the St. Bartholomew's Day massacre of 1572, the 1598 Edict of Nantes allowed Protestants to worship in specified cities.

But **Louis XIV**, who ascended the throne as a five-year-old child in 1643, would become a monarch of legendary power over the following 72 years. He

Jean-Baptiste Colbert Presenting Members of the Royal Academy of Science to Louis XIV was painted c. 1667 and hangs in Versailles. What details in the painting convey Louis XIV's power as an absolute monarch?

emphasized the Catholic nature of his kingdom as well as his divine right to rule without limits. His motto was "One King, One Law, One Faith." As a child ruler, Louis even relied on a cardinal, a high official in the Catholic Church, to guide his kingdom. Having established the Catholic Church as the "one faith," he revoked the Edict of Nantes, triggering the exodus, or flight, of about 200,000 French Protestants to areas of Calvinist control such as Switzerland, the Netherlands, and Cape Town in South Africa.

Elsewhere in Europe, Protestants objected to Louis's treatment of the Huguenots. But Louis was the envy of all who aspired to absolute power. His huge Palace of Versailles displayed his power and wealth, and he entertained with extravagant banquets and first-rate theater and music.

HISTORICAL THINKING

1. **READING CHECK** In what ways were England and France different in terms of religion and government?

2. **ANALYZE POINTS OF VIEW** How did Shakespeare's plays reflect discord between France and England? In what ways did they show bias?

3. **EVALUATE** Which form of government do you think was most effective in leading the country to a prosperous future, Queen Elizabeth's or King Louis XIV's? Why?

PLAN: 2-PAGE LESSON

OBJECTIVE

Describe the religious and political conflicts that gripped England and France in the 16th and 17th centuries.

CRITICAL THINKING SKILLS FOR LESSON 1.1

- Analyze Points of View
- Evaluate
- Compare and Contrast
- Draw Conclusions
- Analyze Visuals

HISTORICAL THINKING FOR CHAPTER 19

How can scientific advances challenge previously accepted ideas and lead to new knowledge?

The scientific advances that occurred in the 16th and 17th centuries took place against certain political backdrops. Lesson 1.1 describes the monarchies of England and France in the 16th and 17th centuries.

Student eEdition online

Additional content for this lesson, including a photograph, is available online.

BACKGROUND FOR THE TEACHER

Louis XIV and the Nobility Known as the "Sun King," Louis XIV epitomized royal absolutism and established firm control over the French state. Though all French politics orbited around him, he still had to negotiate relations with noblemen who resented losing some of their own authority to the king's men. When Louis became king, the nobility still dominated the countryside, and they remained protective of their power. Both lords and peasants lived in a world where local affiliations and obligations were more important than national ones. As during medieval times, peasants labored on their lords' estates and were subject to manorial courts. Louis increased the number of royal officials—men who depended on royal patronage and owed their loyalty to the king—sent to the countryside and provincial cities. These officials enforced royal edicts that cut into the power of the landed nobility. Eventually the nobles gave up the fight; there were benefits to staying on the king's good side. The nobles sought their own royal patronage as they gravitated toward Louis's lavish court at Versailles.

INTRODUCE & ENGAGE

ACCESS PRIOR KNOWLEDGE

Write William Shakespeare's name on the board. Invite students to brainstorm as many Shakespeare plays as they can think of (there are 37 in total), and mark them as comedies, tragedies, or histories. Select one and lead a class discussion about its characters, plot, and theme and the treatment of politics in the play. Record their ideas on the board. Tell students that in this lesson they will learn about how Shakespeare often included the conflict between England and France in his plays.

TEACH

GUIDED DISCUSSION

1. **Compare and Contrast** What was one difference between Queen Elizabeth I and King James? *(Elizabeth got along with Parliament; James saw himself as an absolute ruler and clashed with Parliament.)*

2. **Draw Conclusions** How did King Louis XIV's motto "One King, One Law, One Faith" sum up his approach to ruling France? *(Louis XIV saw himself as a divine Catholic ruler with no limits to his power.)*

ANALYZE VISUALS

Ask students to examine closely the painting *The Armada Portrait of Elizabeth I.* **ASK:** What details in the painting tell you that Elizabeth was a powerful ruler? *(Her clothing is very opulent, and her crown is visible in the background. She has her hand on a globe, which shows she was a world leader.)* How would you compare Elizabeth to Louis XIV based on the details you identified in her portrait and details from the painting *Jean-Baptiste Colbert Presenting Members of the Royal Academy of Science to Louis XIV? (The painting of Elizabeth shows her alone, as a single, powerful leader. The painting of Louis shows other people who are being presented to him. The former conveys a solitary power; the latter conveys a far-reaching power.)*

ACTIVE OPTIONS

On Your Feet: Roundtable Organize students into teams of four. Pose the following question: How would you characterize the political differences between England and France in the 16th and 17th centuries? Tell each student to answer the question within the group and explain his or her answer based on the lesson. Allow time for groups to share the different answers with the class.

> **NG Learning Framework: Research Louis XIV**
> **ATTITUDE** Curiosity
> **KNOWLEDGE** Our Human Story

Arrange students in groups to learn more about the reign of Louis XIV. Instruct groups to investigate his politics, his patronage of the arts, and the Palace of Versailles. Invite groups to share their findings with the class and debate whether Louis was more interested in the arts or in politics.

DIFFERENTIATE

STRIVING READERS

Write a Tweet As students read the lesson, direct them to write a short tweet to summarize each paragraph's main idea in their own words. Have pairs read their tweets aloud, alternating paragraphs until they reach the end of the lesson.

GIFTED & TALENTED

Research the King James Bible
Tell students to research and present an oral report about the King James Bible. Suggest they use a graphic organizer to keep track of their research and to organize their report. Students may wish to conclude with their thoughts on why the King James Bible has endured and is still used today. Invite students to present their oral reports to the class.

See the Chapter Planner for more strategies for differentiation.

HISTORICAL THINKING

ANSWERS

1. England wavered between Catholicism and Protestantism but became predominantly Protestant during Elizabeth's reign. Elizabeth, however, compromised with Catholics, instead of persecuting them. She also shared power with Parliament. France was a Catholic kingdom with an absolute monarch. The French persecuted Protestants.

2. He wrote about their long history of rivalry. Shakespeare's bias against France was evident in the way he depicted French characters.

3. An absolute ruler, such as King Louis XIV, can bring about change quickly because he has limitless and unquestioned power. However, by working with Parliament, Queen Elizabeth might have been better able to influence lasting change. Also, by compromising with the Catholics, she brought stability to England.

War, Peace, and the Rise of Prussia

Things are seldom as simple as they seem. In the case of the Thirty Years' War, the Catholics were fighting the Protestants. Then France, a staunchly Catholic state, joined the war on the side of the Protestants.

A TIME OF WARS

You remember that James I of England had clashed with Parliament. His son, Charles I, followed a similar path. He pursued war against Spain and supported Protestant rebels in France. However, Parliament blocked his ability to finance his wars and presented a petition against him. In retaliation, Charles disbanded Parliament for 11 years. When Parliament reconvened in 1640, it sought to limit the king's power. Tensions exploded, and Charles arrested several leaders of Parliament on charges of treason, or the crime of betraying one's country. The people of London reacted with violence, and the king fled, triggering the English Civil War.

Oliver Cromwell, a Puritan and member of Parliament, organized opposition to the king's forces. He and the Puritans fought to rid the Church of England of Catholic influences, destroying statues and stained glass windows much as the followers of Ulrich Zwingli had done in Switzerland more than a century earlier. After seven years of fighting, Charles I was captured and beheaded in 1649.

While war raged in England, religious hostilities spread across other countries in Europe. In Spain, Philip II aggressively imposed Catholic **orthodoxy,** established beliefs and practices, on his subjects. He killed or expelled Spain's *moriscos,* people whose families had

converted from Islam to Catholicism during the 1492 expulsion of Jews and Muslims. As you have learned, he also waged war against the Dutch provinces, though by 1609 they had gained their independence.

In 1618, the Holy Roman Emperor, Ferdinand II, revoked a policy of tolerance toward Protestants, inciting the catastrophic **Thirty Years' War.** As you have learned, this was the final and most violent of Europe's religious wars. The Holy Roman Empire was supported by Catholic Habsburg rulers in Spain and Austria against the Protestant forces of Denmark and Sweden. France did not fit this pattern because although the kingdom was Catholic, it was competing with the Habsburgs for power and therefore sided with the Protestant coalition. Armies rampaged through German towns and countryside. Around eight million people perished. Rural communities suffered the most with losses of up to 30 percent of their population.

By 1644, all sides were exhausted and sent representatives to Westphalia in northern Germany to discuss peace. It took them four years to reach an agreement, but in 1648 the Peace of Westphalia finally brought some stability to Western Europe. The treaty redrew political and religious maps of Europe, splitting the area into separate states that, whether Catholic or Protestant, recognized one another's **sovereignty,** or right to control their own affairs. One important feature of the Peace of Westphalia was that ambassadors sent to represent one kingdom at the court of another could not be arrested or disturbed, meaning that diplomacy could continue even during times of conflict. After 1648, the era of Habsburg dominance and religious warfare had come to an end.

THE RISE OF PRUSSIA

Following the defeat of the Habsburgs in the Thirty Years' War, five kingdoms emerged to dominate the balance of power in Europe: England, France, Prussia,

Europe, c. 1715

Russia, and Austria. Spain was no longer one of Europe's great powers.

The Protestant-dominated German-speaking lands were divided into numerous territories after the war, with Prussia emerging as the strongest German state. Frederick William I made his kingdom a pioneer in military technology and organization. He used the latest cannons and muskets and developed a professional army of well-trained troops. Precision marching and constant drilling were the hallmarks of the Prussian military. The landowning rural aristocracy cooperated in taxing the peasants, which gave Frederick William and his successors the resources to expand the military and make Prussia, with its capital at Berlin, a powerful force.

The competition between France and England would go global, with competing colonial and trade interests in North America, the West Indies, and South Asia. France's Louis XV built on his father's accomplishments

and invested in both a large army and a naval force strong enough to challenge the English. However, maintaining such military forces decade after decade came at a great expense. For their part, the English used their island location to advantage with a clear focus on their navy and merchant shipping.

Austria, which had held a leading role among German states, was threatened by Prussia's rise. It sought to bolster its position through an alliance with France, while the Prussians allied themselves with Britain. By the mid-18th century, this tangle of alliances would turn local squabbles into international conflicts.

Meanwhile, as you have learned, Russia emerged as a great military power under the Romanov rulers Peter the Great and Catherine the Great. Although partly an Asian empire, Russia's huge military would make it an important player in the European balance of power as well.

HISTORICAL THINKING

1. **READING CHECK** In what ways were both England's Civil War and the Thirty Years' War about religion? In what ways were they about politics?

2. **INTERPRET MAPS** After the Thirty Years' War, which powers became dominant in Europe in 1715? Why?

3. **IDENTIFY** What types of technology did the Prussian king use to boost the state's power?

PLAN: 2-PAGE LESSON

OBJECTIVE

Summarize the causes and effects of the Thirty Years' War, including the rise of Prussia as a powerful German state.

CRITICAL THINKING SKILLS FOR LESSON 1.2

- Interpret Maps
- Identify
- Compare and Contrast
- Identify Problems and Solutions

HISTORICAL THINKING FOR CHAPTER 19

How can scientific advances challenge previously accepted ideas and lead to new knowledge?

One of the hallmarks of the Scientific Revolution is its negotiation between scientific advances and previously accepted religious ideas. Lesson 1.2 discusses the Thirty Years' War, the last great European religious war, which provides context for the Scientific Revolution.

Student eEdition online

Additional content for this lesson, including a painting, is available online.

BACKGROUND FOR THE TEACHER

The Puritans The Puritans were 17th-century reformers of the Church of England who attempted to "purify" the church of all Catholic influences. They were Calvinists who emphasized Bible reading, simplicity and modesty, and the rejection of priestly authority and elaborate rituals. The Puritans emerged out of early Protestantism. During the reign of Queen Mary, a Catholic, many Protestants fled to mainland Europe. A group went to Geneva, where they came under the influence of John Calvin. Upon the ascension of Elizabeth I to the throne, these Protestants, now called Puritans, hoped to see reforms in the establishment church, but they were disappointed. Soon Puritans experienced their own schisms, with one offshoot group, the Separatists, forming their own church. The official church, under Elizabeth's leadership, repressed them. When James I, a Calvinist, succeeded Elizabeth to the throne, again the Puritans hoped for reform; again, they were disappointed. The rule of Charles I was no better; however, the king's split with Parliament offered an opportunity for Puritan leaders to push for reform.

INTRODUCE & ENGAGE

PREVIEW USING TEXT FEATURES

Tell students to preview the lesson's introductory paragraph and Main Idea, the two headings, and the map of Europe c. 1715. **ASK:** Based on these features, what questions do you expect this lesson to answer? *(Answers will vary. Possible responses: Who was Oliver Cromwell? Who won the Thirty Years' War? How did the Thirty Years' War affect the political organization of Europe?)* Use a Five-Ws chart to categorize the questions. After students have read and discussed the lesson, ask them to add answers that they found. Urge students to research unanswered questions and report the answers to the class.

TEACH

GUIDED DISCUSSION

1. **Identify** Who was Oliver Cromwell, and what did he seek to accomplish? *(Oliver Cromwell was a Puritan and a member of Parliament. He opposed King Charles I and wanted to purge Parliament of any Catholic influence.)*

2. **Compare and Contrast** What did Prussia and Russia have in common after the Thirty Years' War? *(Both were powerful military states.)*

IDENTIFY PROBLEMS AND SOLUTIONS

Ask students to study the map of Europe c. 1715. **ASK:** In what way does the map illustrate the problem that led to the Thirty Years' War? *(Various Catholic and Protestant countries were forced to coexist on the European mainland, and many sought to expand their influence.)* In what way does the map also show a solution to the problem? *(The map's colored areas show the major European players that existed after the war ended.)*

ACTIVE OPTIONS

On Your Feet: Inside-Outside Circle Arrange students in concentric circles facing each other. Tell students in the outside circle to ask students in the inside circle a question about the lesson. After students answer, have the outside circle rotate one position to the right to create new pairings. After five questions, tell students to switch roles and continue.

> **NG Learning Framework: Sequence Events**
> **SKILLS** Collaboration, Communication
> **KNOWLEDGE** Our Human Story

Instruct students to work in pairs to discover the main events of the Thirty Years' War. Ask them to conduct online research about the war, including its major players and their alliances. Then tell them to use a sequence chain graphic organizer to organize the war's major events. Instruct students to use their research and completed graphic organizers to collaborate on a short news article reporting on the war. Then ask one student from each pair to read their news report to the class.

DIFFERENTIATE

ENGLISH LANGUAGE LEARNERS

Determine Word Meanings Explain that readers can often use context clues to figure out the meaning of unfamiliar words. Pair students at the **Beginning** level with students at the **Intermediate** or **Advanced** level. Ask pairs to use context clues to help them determine the meanings of the words *orthodoxy* and *sovereignty* and any other unfamiliar words in the lesson. Invite them to look up each word in a dictionary to verify its meaning.

PRE-AP

The Treaty of Westphalia Direct students to conduct online research to learn more about the Treaty of Westphalia and the aftermath of the Thirty Years' War. Encourage students to explore the nuances of what it meant for each country to be on the winning or losing side. They should also explore the significance of each country recognizing each other's sovereignty.

See the Chapter Planner for more strategies for differentiation.

HISTORICAL THINKING

ANSWERS

1. In the English Civil War, the Puritans were fighting King Charles partially because they believed he was leading the Church of England with too much Catholic influence. The Thirty Years' War began when Ferdinand II rejected policies of tolerance of Protestants. The English Civil War was also about King Charles's persecution of leaders in Parliament. In this way it was about power rather than religion. France joined the Thirty Years' War in favor of the Protestants although France was Catholic. They were threatened by the Habsburgs.

2. By early 1715, the dominant powers in the west were France, Britain, Austria, Russia, and Prussia.

3. the latest technology of cannons and muskets

The Houses of Parliament and Big Ben, the clock tower at the northern end, lie along the Thames River in London, England.

The Glorious Revolution

Imagine if the U.S. Congress asked Canada to help overthrow the U.S. president because they didn't like the president's religion. That's pretty much what happened in England in 1688. Parliament asked the Dutch to help them overthrow the king.

RELIGIOUS CONFLICT AND REVOLUTION

Like Prussia and France, England was a powerful force in the late 1600s. After Charles I's execution, Oliver Cromwell took power and instituted a series of radical reforms. He abolished the monarchy and the Church of England and organized a republic in which citizens were allowed to vote for representatives. But he also instituted highly unpopular reforms. For example, Puritans thought plays were sinful, so Cromwell closed all the theaters. Many Londoners resented the reforms.

After Cromwell died in 1658, Parliament invited Charles's son, Charles Stuart, home from exile to re-establish the monarchy, a time period known as the Restoration. A patron of the arts, Charles II ended the unpopular restrictions on theaters. He also founded the Royal Observatory and supported the Royal Society to promote scientific research. But the Stuarts were seen as too tolerant of Catholics—some of them even were Catholic. Terrified the Stuarts would make England a Catholic state, Parliament enlisted the support of the Dutch in what is called the Glorious Revolution of 1688. Dutch forces supported Parliament in overthrowing the last Stuart king. Protestant princess Mary and her Dutch husband William were installed as the new monarchs. The ascension of **William III and Mary II** to the English throne made permanent the Protestant character of the English monarchy and the Church of England.

William and Mary were required to approve the **English Bill of Rights**, which guaranteed a number of important freedoms, such as freedom of speech in Parliament and the right to a trial by jury. Restrictions on individual liberties remained for working people, the middle class, Catholics, and women, but the document set an important precedent for England and the world, and by the 18th century, the balance of power between king and Parliament provided a stable foundation for England.

The English Bill of Rights and its predecessor, the Magna Carta, had tremendous influence on the founders of the United States. Americans looked to the British documents as they drafted the Declaration of Independence and their own Bill of Rights. The following are some of the rights guaranteed in the English Bill of Rights, written in 1689. Do they sound familiar?

PRIMARY SOURCE

- It is the right of the subjects to petition the king, . . . prosecutions for such petitioning are illegal;
- The raising and keeping of a standing army . . . in time of peace, unless it be with consent of Parliament, is against the law;
- The subjects which are Protestant may have arms for their defense . . . as allowed by law;
- The election of members of Parliament ought to be free;
- The freedom of speech . . . in Parliament ought not to be . . . questioned . . . ;
- Excessive bail ought not to be required, nor excessive fines imposed, nor cruel and unusual punishments inflicted;
- Jurors ought to be duly impaneled [appropriately chosen] . . . ;
- All . . . fines . . . before conviction are illegal and void;
- For redress of all grievances, and for the amending, strengthening, and preserving of laws, Parliaments ought to be held frequently. . . .

THE LITTLE ICE AGE

In an age of upheaval, the English Parliament took charge to limit the monarchy's power. In England during its Civil War and in many other societies in the mid-1600s, changes in climate had brought famine, disease, and social unrest.

According to climate historian Geoffrey Parker, "An intense episode of global cooling coincided with an unparalleled spate of revolutions and state breakdowns around the world." While Europeans saw religion as the source of these clashes, Parker and other climate historians looking at the miserable harvests of the 1640s point to a more basic cause of conflict: hunger.

By the late 16th century, the climate of the northern hemisphere had become progressively colder and unpredictable. Cooler and erratic temperatures caused poor harvests and rising prices in grain. The cost of wheat doubled in some places from the beginning to the middle of the 17th century.

Glaciers in Japan and in the Alps engulfed farms and villages and closed a gold mine in Austria. Cod off the Scottish coast moved south to warmer waters. Drier conditions in North American prairies made farming difficult, and some Native Americans shifted from farming to hunting.

Many people died from malnutrition, famine, and disease. Others rebelled. Poor harvests meant diminished tax revenues in England, France, China, and the Ottoman Empire. The turmoil weakened leaders and contributed to decades of war and violence.

Then, late in the 1600s, warmer temperatures and better harvests returned. Perhaps it is not a coincidence that the end of the Little Ice Age saw the return of stability to places like England, with the success of its Glorious Revolution, and China, with the rise of the powerful Qing dynasty.

HISTORICAL THINKING

1. **READING CHECK** Why did Parliament oust the Stuart king?

2. **MAKE CONNECTIONS** Which of the rights from the English Bill of Rights are included in the U.S. Bill of Rights?

3. **ANALYZE CAUSE AND EFFECT** According to climate historians, what effect might climate have had on global turmoil in the 17th century?

PLAN: 2-PAGE LESSON

OBJECTIVE
Summarize the events of the Glorious Revolution and describe the Little Ice Age and its effects on Europe.

CRITICAL THINKING SKILLS FOR LESSON 1.3
- Make Connections
- Analyze Cause and Effect
- Make Generalizations
- Analyze Primary Sources

HISTORICAL THINKING FOR CHAPTER 19
How can scientific advances challenge previously accepted ideas and lead to new knowledge?

Some monarchs and political leaders supported scientific inquiry. Lesson 1.3 covers the reign of King Charles II of England, who founded the Royal Observatory and supported the Royal Society.

Student eEdition online
Additional content for this lesson, including an image and a graph, is available online.

BACKGROUND FOR THE TEACHER
Ousting James II The Glorious Revolution deposed a Stuart king, but it was not Charles II. The king's younger brother James began serving as duke of Albany upon Charles's restoration in 1660. In 1668 or 1669, James converted to Roman Catholicism; however, he maintained strong political allegiance to Anglican leaders in Parliament. As heir to the throne (Charles II was childless), his Catholicism was controversial. When he married a Catholic woman, plans were put into motion to prevent him from ever succeeding to the throne. Such efforts were unsuccessful, and James became king in 1685. Next, a series of pro-Catholic actions (and anti-Anglican ones) taken by the king fostered more mistrust and alienated him from Parliament. Then, in 1687, he and the queen, Mary of Modena, announced they were expecting a child. The idea of a Roman Catholic heir was a bridge too far for Protestant leaders, and in June of 1688, William of Orange and his army were invited to come to England to depose the last Stuart king.

INTRODUCE & ENGAGE

COMPLETE A WORD WEB

Write the term *U.S. Bill of Rights* in the center of a Word Web. Ask students to name as many of the 10 rights in the Bill of Rights as they can and write them on the spokes. Pick one or two rights and discuss with students how their lives might be different if those rights were not protected. Then tell students that in this lesson they will learn about the English Bill of Rights, an important predecessor to the U.S. Bill of Rights.

TEACH

GUIDED DISCUSSION

1. **Make Generalizations** In what way did Oliver Cromwell's reforms represent radical change? *(Cromwell abolished the monarchy and the Church of England, both of which had been at the center of England's political identity for many years.)*

2. **Make Connections** What was the connection between the Little Ice Age and the widespread hunger that occurred in the late 16th century and early 17th century? *(Cooler temperatures resulted in poor harvests, driving up the cost of wheat. People could not afford to buy it. As a result, people went hungry.)*

ANALYZE PRIMARY SOURCES

Instruct students to review the excerpt from the English Bill of Rights. **ASK:** In what way does the English Bill of Rights provide a balance between the monarch and Parliament? Give a specific example from the excerpt to support your thinking. *(The English Bill of Rights guarantees certain rights for members of Parliament, even as the monarch retains his or her power and legal authority. For example, the English Bill of Rights states that the monarch cannot form an army without Parliament's approval. That prevents the crown from becoming too powerful.)*

ACTIVE OPTIONS

On Your Feet: Compare Bills of Rights Direct students to locate and read the complete English Bill of Rights and the U.S. Bill of Rights. Both are widely available online. Ask students to complete a Venn diagram that compares and contrasts the content of the documents. Then encourage them to share with the class their thoughts about the importance of the bills to the development of representative and parliamentary democracies.

NG Learning Framework: Climate Change Today STEM
ATTITUDE Responsibility
KNOWLEDGE Our Living Planet

Guide students to research how climate change is impacting modern-day Europe. Encourage students to select one European country and explore how it is affected by climate change and how it is addressing it, if at all. Arrange small groups of students for a discussion of the similarities and differences between their chosen countries. Then lead a class discussion in which students compare modern climate change to the Little Ice Age of the late 16th century.

DIFFERENTIATE

INCLUSION

Describe a Graph Pair students who are visually impaired with students who are not. Ask the latter to describe the line graph (available in the Student eEdition) in detail. Encourage visually impaired students to ask clarifying questions as necessary.

GIFTED & TALENTED

Create a Multimedia Presentation Ask students to conduct online research about Charles II's patronage of science and the arts. Have them create a multimedia presentation that provides examples of his patronage and conveys his enduring influence. Tell students to use photographs, news headlines, video clips, and other media to enhance their presentation. Invite students to share their presentations with the class.

See the Chapter Planner for more strategies for differentiation.

HISTORICAL THINKING

ANSWERS

1. The Stuarts were tolerant of Catholics, and people were afraid England would become a Catholic state.

2. The U.S. Bill of Rights includes the right to freedom of speech but extends it to all people, not just Congress. It includes the right to petition the government. We have the right to bear arms, but this right is not just for Protestants. The U.S. Bill of Rights also states that people have a right to a trial by jury and should not be inflicted with excessive bail, fines, or unusual punishment.

3. Climate historians show that the 17th century was a time of unusually cold and unpredictable weather. They suggest that human suffering from the weather may have contributed to unrest and weakened governments.

Traditions of Inquiry

Generally, scientists build upon the work of others, challenging it, expanding on it, and documenting new findings. But the scientists aren't the only ones challenging scientific research. New ideas have often been resisted. And sometimes they are outright forbidden.

BEFORE THE SCIENTIFIC REVOLUTION

In the 17th century, people didn't have the scientific knowledge and historical data available to help them analyze climate change like that experienced during the Little Ice Age. For most Europeans at the time, the Christian faith, whether Catholic or Protestant, still held most of the answers to basic questions about relationships between God, humanity, and the natural world.

However, scientific pursuits are as old as the human desire to understand the world. The ancient Greek scholar Aristotle studied the heavens in the fourth century B.C.E. and concluded that Earth was the center of a universe of revolving spheres. People accepted this **geocentric theory** for hundreds of years. Many early scientists used mathematics as a basis for scientific inquiry. As you have learned, Eratosthenes used rays of sunlight and geometry to calculate the circumference of Earth as 24,427 miles. His calculations were off by less than two percent. The actual circumference is 24,857 miles.

After the collapse of the Western Roman Empire in 476, the Greek tradition of classical learning was lost in Europe, and Europeans contributed little to scientific inquiry. Greek science was still studied in the Byzantine Empire, however, and science thrived in Muslim-ruled cities like Baghdad, Cairo, and Córdoba. Here, Muslim and Jewish scholars built on Greek writings. Between the 600s and 1100s, Muslim scholars studied scientific theories from Greece and other regions of the world. They advanced mathematical understanding by adopting the decimal system, the number zero, and Hindu-Arabic numerals, as you've already read. The knowledge they gained from the study of stars led to advances in navigation and the development of more accurate calendars.

Translations of Greek texts, along with the advanced knowledge of Byzantine, Jewish, and Muslim scholars spread to Europe around 1200. Inspired in part by the work of the Muslim scientists, the Franciscan monk Roger Bacon began to study **optics**, light and vision, and astronomy during the Middle Ages. He believed that the study of science and the natural world would help people understand God. He argued for a change to the Christian calendar so that it would more accurately reflect time for religious holidays. However, the Franciscan order considered his studies to be contrary to religious tradition. Rather than encourage his research, the Roman Catholic Church imprisoned Bacon. The calendar didn't change for another 300 years.

Thomas Aquinas was more successful in adapting Greek learning to medieval Christianity. As you have learned, Aquinas combined Aristotle's writings with those of early church writers to create a philosophical foundation for the Catholic faith. For example, Aquinas determined that since both Aristotle and the early Christians agreed that Earth was the center of the solar system, the geocentric view was supported by both reason and faith.

COPERNICUS AND GALILEO

As European Christians questioned their faith during the Reformation and Renaissance, they also challenged Aquinas's understanding of the physical world. Both mathematics and observation of the natural world struck at the heart of that intellectual system, challenging the church's assumptions about the natural world.

In the 16th century, most people believed Aristotle's teachings that the sun and other planets revolved around Earth. However, in 1543, a Polish astronomer and mathematician, **Nicolaus Copernicus**, proposed the revolutionary idea that the sun was actually the center of the solar system. According to his **heliocentric theory**, Earth and other planets revolved around the sun. This theory used mathematics to propose heliocentrism as a simpler explanation for planetary movement, but it introduced a huge problem. To believe this theory, people would have to admit that Aristotle and the Catholic Church had been wrong. Knowing that his work would be controversial, Copernicus delayed publication of his book and dedicated it to the pope. He died soon after it was published.

Despite the controversy, the Italian mathematician **Galileo Galilei** took Copernicus's heliocentric theory very seriously. He invented a telescope and pointed it at the heavens, where he discovered spots on the sun, craters on the moon, and other indications that the heavens were not perfect and unchanging as the church had claimed. He contradicted Aristotle and Aquinas by observing that a body in motion would stay in motion unless acted upon by an external force. This insight would later prove essential to new understandings of planetary motion. Most importantly, Galileo confirmed Copernicus's theory that the sun was the center of the solar system. Church authorities argued that the heliocentric theory contradicted the teachings of the Bible regarding God's creation. They arrested and tried Galileo as a heretic and forced him to renounce his support for the heliocentric theory.

Galileo was placed under house arrest and forbidden from publishing scientific research, but the Scientific Revolution that he and Copernicus helped launch could not be so easily suppressed. By the 18th century, the use of scientific observation and the application of mathematics were becoming increasingly common, especially among the elite of northern Europe. Aided by royal and aristocratic patronage, they began to pursue the "new science."

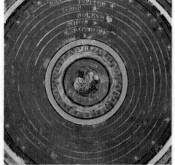

A visual representation of the Greek geocentric theory appears above (top) in a 13th-century French miniature. Below it is a visual representation of Copernicus's heliocentric theory, which shows the sun at the center of the universe.

HISTORICAL THINKING

1. **READING CHECK** What were some early scientific and mathematical discoveries in ancient Greece?

2. **DESCRIBE** What was the heliocentric theory? Why was it revolutionary?

3. **MAKE CONNECTIONS** Why were Greek and Muslim advances in mathematics essential to the development of the "new science"?

PLAN: 2-PAGE LESSON

OBJECTIVE

Describe the approach to scientific thinking in the years leading up to the Scientific Revolution.

CRITICAL THINKING SKILLS FOR LESSON 2.1

- Describe
- Make Connections
- Make Generalizations
- Analyze Cause and Effect
- Ask and Answer Questions

HISTORICAL THINKING FOR CHAPTER 19

How can scientific advances challenge previously accepted ideas and lead to new knowledge?

The early investigations into the physical world by Roger Bacon, Copernicus, and Galileo challenged established religious orthodoxy. Lesson 2.1 describes these scientific thinkers' theories.

Student eEdition online

Additional content for this lesson, including images, is available online.

BACKGROUND FOR THE TEACHER

Nicolaus Copernicus Nicolaus Copernicus was born in Poland in 1473. After his father died when Copernicus was 10 years old, he was raised by his uncle, who led young Nicolaus into a religious education. Copernicus enrolled at the University of Bologna in Italy where he pursued a degree in canon law, or Catholic studies. Copernicus's transition into astronomy was somewhat of an accident; in Bologna he lived in the same house as the university's main astronomer, Domenico Maria de Novara. Copernicus observed Novara and even assisted his work on planetary orbits and their order in the heavens. By the early 1500s, Copernicus had earned his doctorate in canon law, but his side interest in astronomy continued. Building on the planetary theories of Aristotle and Ptolemy, Copernicus eventually wrote his *Commentariolus* ("Little Commentary") in which he asserted a sun-centered universe and devised a new order of the known planets. His theory was so different from accepted norms that he chose not to publish it for many years; it finally appeared in 1543, the year he died.

INTRODUCE & ENGAGE

ACTIVATE PRIOR KNOWLEDGE

Ask students to recall what they have learned about Eratosthenes, Muslim scholars, and Thomas Aquinas. (*Eratosthenes calculated the circumference of Earth; Muslim scholars made advances in mathematics; Thomas Aquinas supported the geocentric theory of the universe with both faith and reason.*) Discuss the ways in which they were important scholars of their times. Explain that this lesson discusses scientific thinkers who advanced certain scientific and mathematical theories that challenged establishment thinking.

TEACH

GUIDED DISCUSSION

1. **Make Generalizations** What was the pursuit of scientific knowledge in Europe like before the Scientific Revolution? (*Without much scientific data, most Europeans believed religious concepts explained the relationship between God and the physical world. Greek scholars influenced the early work of Byzantine, Jewish, and Muslim thinkers.*)

2. **Analyze Cause and Effect** In what way did Copernicus anticipate the controversy of his theory of planetary movement? (*delayed publishing his theory; dedicated it to the pope, hoping that would assuage those who opposed his challenge to established teachings of Catholicism*)

ASK AND ANSWER QUESTIONS

Ask students to examine the visual representations of the geocentric theory and the heliocentric theory. **ASK:** What questions do you have about the visual representation of the geocentric theory? (*Answers will vary. Possible responses: What does the orange ring stand for? Where is the moon? How many planets were known at that time?*) What questions do you have about the visual representation of the heliocentric theory? (*Answers will vary. Possible responses: Are the positions of the planets correct? Why are astrological symbols included on the outer ring?*)

ACTIVE OPTIONS

On Your Feet: Jigsaw Strategy Organize students into "expert" groups. Assign each group one of the following scientific thinkers to research, analyze, and summarize the major scientific theories of: Roger Bacon, Nicolaus Copernicus, and Galileo Galilei. Then regroup students into new groups so that each new group has at least one member from each expert group. Students in the new groups take turns sharing the summaries from their expert groups.

| **NG Learning Framework: Design an Infographic**
| SKILL Communication
| KNOWLEDGE Our Living Planet, Our Human Story

Instruct small groups to conduct research and create an infographic that displays the differences between Aristotle's geocentric theory and Copernicus's heliocentric theory. Have students represent each thinker's main ideas visually and summarize in text how each came to discover his theory. They should also include how people reacted to both theories and how long the theories endured. Ask groups to share their infographics.

DIFFERENTIATE

STRIVING READERS

Summarize Have pairs create a Concept Cluster with the lesson title in the center oval and the section headings in the smaller ones. As students read each section, tell them to record key facts and ideas on the spokes. Then invite volunteers to summarize the lesson and the early scientific inquiries that led to the Scientific Revolution.

PRE-AP

Explore Byzantine Science Instruct students to write an essay that explores the scientific theories that developed during the Byzantine era. Tell students to conduct online and print research to find out when Byzantine-era thinkers relied on and aligned with classical Greek thought and religious thought and when they diverged. Encourage them to investigate the exchange between Byzantine and Islamic scholars and thinkers. Students should gather primary and secondary sources and cite them appropriately.

See the Chapter Planner for more strategies for differentiation.

HISTORICAL THINKING

ANSWERS

1. Aristotle studied the heavens and concluded that Earth was at the center of the solar system. Eratosthenes used rays of sunlight and geometry to calculate the circumference of Earth.

2. It proposed the idea that Earth and the other planets revolve around the sun. It was revolutionary because, previously, people had believed that the sun and planets revolved around a stationary Earth.

3. Accurate mathematics were needed to chart and record observations, and the new science relied on observation to overturn knowledge passed from Greek philosophers and the Bible.

The Scientific Method

When you think of a scientist, you probably think of someone who conducts experiments. But observations and experiments are relatively new to science. In the 16th and 17th centuries, the pursuit of truth through experimentation was revolutionary.

In this 19th-century painting, the English physician and scientist William Gilbert shows Queen Elizabeth I and her court his experiment on electricity. The first to use the term *electricity*, Dr. Gilbert established the magnetic nature of Earth.

548 CHAPTER 19

THE "MODERNS"

In the 17th century, an intellectual debate divided western European thinkers into two camps: the "ancients" and the "moderns." The ancients based their beliefs about medicine, mathematics, and astronomy on the ideas of classical authors such as Aristotle.

The moderns rejected the idea that classical authors and Christian theology were infallible. They argued that human reason provided the key to knowledge. The moderns believed that God created humans with reason so humans could observe and accurately describe God's creation.

Sir Francis Bacon was one of the moderns who applied reason and advanced an **inductive approach** to science. Inductive reasoning involves working from carefully controlled observations of natural phenomena toward larger truths. Bacon urged scientists to gather data by following specific steps. This new approach to science would become the **scientific method**, a logical procedure for developing and testing ideas.

The French scientist **René Descartes** applied reason using a **deductive approach**. This method involved moving from general principles to specific truths. Descartes argued that philosophy had to be firmly grounded in reason, and he emphasized systematic doubt as a key to knowledge. His famous saying, "I think, therefore I am," expressed his belief that his ability to reason was proof of his existence. Descartes also argued that he had to doubt the existence of God before he could prove that God did, in fact, exist.

SCIENTIFIC RATIONALISM

The ideas promoted by Bacon and Descartes became known as **scientific rationalism**. In this school of thought, observation, experimentation, and mathematical reasoning replaced ancient wisdom and church teachings as the source of scientific

THE SCIENTIFIC METHOD

The ideas of Bacon and Descartes eventually led to a new approach to scientific inquiry. "All our knowledge begins with the senses, proceeds then to the understanding, and ends with reason. There is nothing higher than reason," wrote the German philosopher Immanuel Kant. The scientific method is a logical approach to forming a **hypothesis**, an unproven theory, which might answer a question and can be tested. Generally, the steps are as follows:

Step 1: Observe and Question A scientist makes an observation, gathers information, and forms a question about a subject.

Step 2: Hypothesize The scientist proposes a hypothesis.

Step 3: Experiment The scientist designs and conducts an experiment to test the hypothesis.

Step 4: Analyze Data The scientist records and carefully examines the data from the experiment.

Step 5: Evaluate and Share Results The scientist judges whether the data do or do not support the hypothesis and publishes the results of the experiment.

truth. Scientific rationalism provided a procedure for establishing proof for scientific theories, and it laid a foundation for formulating theories on which other scientists could build.

Building upon previous research had become easier by the 17th century. After the mid-1400s, when the printing press came into wide use, books were more easily available. In fact, many people believe the 1543 publication of Copernicus's book *On the Revolution of the Heavenly Spheres* sparked the Scientific Revolution.

Along with books, universities and scientific societies played an important role in spreading ideas such as scientific rationalism. Perhaps the most important scientific society was the Royal Society of England. Many of England's greatest scientists were members.

As ideas spread, scientific rationalism extended beyond science. Bacon was a politician, so he applied the principles to government, arguing that the direction of government should be based on actual experience. As you will learn, the thinkers of the European Enlightenment were optimistic that reason would provide the key to improving human society as well.

HISTORICAL THINKING

1. **READING CHECK** What new ideas did Sir Frances Bacon and René Descartes propose?

2. **IDENTIFY SUPPORTING DETAILS** How did scientists share knowledge during the Scientific Revolution?

3. **ANALYZE CAUSE AND EFFECT** What was the effect of the Scientific Revolution on broader areas of society?

Europe in the Age of Scientific Revolution 549

PLAN: 2-PAGE LESSON

OBJECTIVE

Describe the scientific approaches of Sir Francis Bacon and René Descartes and explain the scientific method.

CRITICAL THINKING SKILLS FOR LESSON 2.2

- Identify Supporting Details
- Analyze Cause and Effect
- Compare and Contrast
- Make Connections
- Identify Problems and Solutions

HISTORICAL THINKING FOR CHAPTER 19

How can scientific advances challenge previously accepted ideas and lead to new knowledge?

The idea that scientific research should be based on observation and experimentation challenged established religious doctrine. Lesson 2.2 explains how Sir Francis Bacon and René Descartes applied reason to scientific thinking.

Student eEdition online

Additional content for this lesson, including an image, is available online.

BACKGROUND FOR THE TEACHER

Beliefs About Using the Senses The "moderns" believed that humankind was endowed by God with reason and through that reason could apprehend and accurately describe God's creation. A quote from German philosopher Immanuel Kant (1724–1804) captures this belief well: "All our knowledge begins with the senses, proceeds then to the understanding, and ends with reason. There is nothing higher than reason." In imperial China, however, the reliability of input from the senses was a point of debate among Confucian scholars. Doubt characterized the late Ming dynasty period, when the Neo-Confucianism of Wang Yangming focused on the priority of inward contemplation. The 18th century, however, saw a re-emphasis on the more empirical tradition of Confucianism during the reign of the Yongzheng emperor, when "evidential learning" led to the compilation of what was then the world's largest encyclopedia. For most Hindus and Buddhists, on the other hand, the issue was hardly debatable: the material world is illusory, and our senses are distractions from the truth, not guides toward it.

INTRODUCE & ENGAGE

SHARE REASONING EXPERIENCES

Invite students to share personal experiences about how they use reason in their daily lives. Ask them how they generally approach problems: by observing what's happening (or what has happened) and coming up with a larger truth, or by using their previous knowledge and experience to move towards a more specific truth. Lead a discussion about the merits of both approaches. Tell students that they will learn about the scientific thinkers who pioneered these approaches to scientific investigation.

TEACH

GUIDED DISCUSSION

1. **Compare and Contrast** How were "moderns" and "ancients" different? *(The scientific beliefs of "ancients" were based on religious and classical ideas. "Moderns" challenged these established views and argued that knowledge is derived from human reason.)*

2. **Make Connections** In the scientific method, how are hypothesizing and experimenting connected? *(One must begin with a hypothesis, or theory, about why some scientific phenomena has occurred; then one experiments to test the hypothesis.)*

IDENTIFY PROBLEMS AND SOLUTIONS

Ask students to study the steps of the scientific method. **ASK:** Do you think the scientific method is an effective way of finding a solution to a problem? Explain your thinking. *(The scientific method is very effective for solving problems because it relies on—and demands—observation, experimentation, and human reason. The step-by-step approach ensures that the solution to the original query is founded on actual evidence.)*

ACTIVE OPTIONS

On Your Feet: Fishbowl Arrange students in two concentric circles. Ask students in the inner circle to discuss this question: How did the ideas of Bacon and Descartes lead to the scientific method? Students in the outer circle listen to the discussion and then switch roles. Ask the new inner circle to discuss this question: What role does human reason play in the scientific method? Encourage both groups to draw conclusions about why the scientific method remains at the center of scientific inquiry today.

> **NG Learning Framework: Devise an Experiment** STEM
> **SKILL** Collaboration
> **KNOWLEDGE** New Frontiers

Explain to students that they can use the scientific method to test simple hypotheses from their daily lives. Have pairs or small groups come up with a question about a subject they are curious about and have observed. If students struggle with narrowing their search, encourage them to conduct online research for ideas, such as "does caffeine make people type faster?" Ask pairs or groups to design an experiment using the scientific method. Students should be prepared to explain their experiment and its purpose, using visual support as appropriate.

DIFFERENTIATE

ENGLISH LANGUAGE LEARNERS

Practice Pronunciation Write the following names and terms on the board: *René Descartes, inductive, deductive,* and *hypothesis.* Pronounce each word and have students repeat. Pair students at the **Beginning** level with those at the **Intermediate** or **Advanced** level, and instruct them to take turns finding passages in the lesson that contain any of the words and read the passages aloud.

GIFTED & TALENTED

Write a Dialogue Encourage pairs of students to work together to craft a script for an informal discussion between Sir Francis Bacon and René Descartes. Tell them to use information from the lesson and from online and library sources to create their dialogue. Ask students to identify what ideas the two men might talk about and any details that might illustrate their personalities. When pairs have completed their script, invite them to perform the dialogue for the class as time permits or post the script to a class blog.

See the Chapter Planner for more strategies for differentiation.

HISTORICAL THINKING

ANSWERS

1. They proposed new ways to conduct scientific research through observation and experimentation.

2. Books had become much more available since the printing press was invented, so scientists were able to publish their work in books. Also, universities and scientific societies helped to spread ideas.

3. Scientific rationalism was applied to government. Bacon believed that people's actual experience should influence how they are governed. This challenged the Church and fostered ideals that would eventually lead to democratic government.

Thinkers and Innovators

After seeing what happened to Galileo, would you be willing to stand up for science? Many people did. In fact, in 18th-century Europe studying science was all the rage. Women scientists pushed against gender norms as well as religious pressures.

THINKERS AND INNOVATORS AT WORK

During the Renaissance, the Flemish physician **Andreas Vesalius** dissected human corpses to create careful descriptions of human anatomy. Before Vesalius, people turned to the Greek physician Galen for information. Galen, who lived at the time of the Roman Empire, had dissected many birds and other animals, but dissecting a human body was forbidden by Roman law. Therefore, Galen's theories about the human body were based largely on speculation. Although many Christians objected to the dissection of dead bodies, Vesalius's books revolutionized biology and medicine.

Using a Copernican framework of the sun at the center of the solar system, **Johannes Kepler** analyzed the orbit of the planet Mars. Kepler's calculations showed that the planets move in elliptical rather than circular paths. This contrasted with Aristotle's and Christian teachings that all celestial motion was circular. Therefore, Kepler reinforced Galileo's challenge to Christian teachings. However, Kepler presented his findings as God's harmonious plan for the universe.

When French mathematician **Blaise Pascal** was a teenager, he started work on a device that would help his father calculate taxes. The Pascaline, or Arithmetic Machine, uses wheels and dials to add and subtract. Some people consider it the first digital calculator. Later, Pascal conducted experiments on atmospheric pressure and pressure applied to liquids. The Pascal principle explains that pressure applied to a confined liquid will transmit throughout the liquid, regardless of where the pressure is applied.

The Irish chemist **Robert Boyle** also studied air pressure. In 1662, he and English scientist Robert Hooke discovered that the volume of a gas decreases with increased pressure and that the inverse is also true. This finding is known as "Boyle's law."

Englishman **Isaac Newton** was one of the most important scientists of the Scientific Revolution. He followed Descartes's and Bacon's lead in using reasoning and experimentation. He used beams of light and prisms to observe how light splits into a spectrum of colors, proving that the colors were a property of light. He also used his studies of light to invent a new telescope that uses mirrors to reflect light and create a sharper image.

Newton is best known for his studies of gravity. He used deductive reasoning to propose a universal law of attraction between objects based on their mass and distance. He then used inductive reasoning in the experiments he conducted to support his theory. With this theory and his three laws of motion, Newton created a complete mechanical explanation of motion in the universe. He explained that gravity keeps planets in place as they orbit the sun. His work is the foundation of modern physics and led to scientific advances ranging from steam engines to space rockets.

By the time of Newton's death in 1727, the earlier tensions between science and Christian faith had lessened. An English poet even celebrated Newton with the lines: "Nature and Nature's laws lay hid in night / God said, 'Let Newton Be!' and all was light."

WOMEN IN SCIENCE AND MATHEMATICS

Even before **Laura Bassi** completed her doctorate, the Bologna Academy of Sciences admitted her as an honorary member for her work in physics. After she attained her degree in 1732, the University of Bologna in Italy offered her a position. She would be the first woman professor of physics, and she later became chair of experimental physics.

Fascinated by the work of Isaac Newton, Bassi based many of her lectures on Newtonian physics. She is one of the scientists credited with introducing Newton's ideas to Italy. She is also recognized for her research on electricity and its uses in medicine.

A contemporary of Bassi, another woman of Bologna, **Maria Gaetana Agnesi** was also a child prodigy. As a teenager, she participated in philosophical discussions with well-known intellectuals. However, she is best recognized for her work in mathematics. Agnesi's algebra book, *Analytical Institutions*, was translated into many languages, and it included relatively new subjects, such as integral and differential calculus. The French Academy of Sciences wrote that it was "the most complete and best made treatise." Even the pope recognized the value of her work and appointed Agnesi professor of mathematics at the University of Bologna. However, she turned down the position, choosing instead to dedicate her life to charity.

The German astronomer **Caroline Lucretia Herschel** started scanning the heavens after she and her brother William, an astronomer, moved to England. Together, they identified 2,500 new star clusters and **nebulae**, clouds of gas and dust in outer space. Herschel also made many discoveries on her own, the most famous of which were eight comets she discovered between 1786 and 1797. Because of her contributions to astronomy, Herschel received the Gold Medal of the Royal Astronomical Society and became an honorary member of the Royal Society. Many of the comets she discovered are named after her.

NATIONAL GEOGRAPHIC EXPLORER **KATHY KU**

Just the Beginning

In 2010, American college student Kathy Ku arrived in the East African nation of Uganda to teach. She became aware that both she and her host family frequently got sick because they were drinking dirty water.

One way to treat the contaminated water was to set it out in clear plastic bottles in the sun, but Ku found this method literally distasteful. "I took a swig of the water and essentially spit it back out because it tasted like burnt plastic, and it was really warm as well. It's a very effective way of treating your water, but I thought there had to be a better solution that people would actually like to use."

The problem of making unclean water drinkable lodged itself in Ku's mind and would not go away, even after she returned to college. At age 19, Ku designed a ceramic water filter. To develop her idea more fully, Ku took a year off during her junior year. Her goal was not just to bring water filters to Uganda but to have them constructed there using locally sourced clay and sawdust.

Ku's vision became a reality in 2014, the year her first water-filter factory began operating. The factory has since moved into a bigger and better space near Kampala, Uganda's capital and largest city. The new facility has the capacity to produce 10,000 water filters a month. "We have provided 100,000 people with access to clean drinking water," says Ku. "But there's still much more to do!" For more on Kathy Ku and her work, check out National Geographic's website.

HISTORICAL THINKING

1. **READING CHECK** Many scientists were devout Christians. How did they reconcile their religious and scientific ideals?

2. **FORM AND SUPPORT OPINIONS** Was the work of Bassi, Agnesi, and Herschel more important to the advancement of science or the advancement of women? Why?

3. **EVALUATE** Which of these thinkers and innovators do you think contributed most to the field of science? Why?

Europe in the Age of Scientific Revolution 551

PLAN: 2-PAGE LESSON

OBJECTIVE

Summarize the achievements of the mathematicians, scientists, and philosophers who contributed to the Scientific Revolution.

CRITICAL THINKING SKILLS FOR LESSON 2.3

- Form and Support Opinions
- Evaluate
- Identify Main Ideas and Details
- Identify Supporting Details
- Make Connections

HISTORICAL THINKING FOR CHAPTER 19

How can scientific advances challenge previously accepted ideas and lead to new knowledge?

At the height of the Scientific Revolution, mathematicians, scientists, and philosophers were challenging accepted theories about the natural world and the universe. Lesson 2.3 describes these thinkers and innovators and explains their work.

BACKGROUND FOR THE TEACHER

Later Astronomers As Copernicus and Galileo had demonstrated, astronomy was a prime example of how empirical scientists used systematic observation and the application of mathematics to unlock the secrets of a rationally ordered cosmos. Tycho Brahe (1546–1601), a Danish nobleman, also contributed to this effort. In 1573, using observations made with only the naked eye, Brahe challenged the Aristotelian concept of an eternally unchanging celestial sphere by demonstrating that a bright supernova had emerged beyond Earth's atmosphere. The German-Polish astronomer Johannes Hevelius (1611–1687) was another innovator in celestial observation and data collection, using telescopes of his own design to study lunar topography. A member of London's Royal Society, Hevelius and his second wife, Elisabeth, who came to him begging for instruction when she was just a teenager, collaborated together. After Johannes died, Elisabeth Hevelius (1647–1693) achieved independent recognition for her continued work.

Student eEdition online

Additional content for this lesson, including images, is available online.

INTRODUCE & ENGAGE

PREVIEW LESSON CONTENT

Direct students to preview the lesson title, introduction, Main Idea statement, headings, and visuals. Draw a two-column chart on the board, labeling the first column *Questions* and the second column *Answers.* Ask students what questions the lesson brings to mind. Record their questions in the chart. Later, after students have read and discussed the lesson, prompt them to answer as many of the listed questions as they can.

TEACH

GUIDED DISCUSSION

1. **Identify Main Ideas and Details** Did Kepler's theory of planetary orbits support or refute Christian beliefs? Explain. *(His theory refuted Christian beliefs. His theory showed that planets moved in elliptical orbits. Christian theory held that the planets moved in circular orbits.)*

2. **Identify Supporting Details** Why is Newton remembered as such an important figure of the Scientific Revolution? *(Newton posited theories and discoveries in numerous scientific fields: he proved that colors were a property of light; he invented a new and improved telescope; he proposed a law of universal attraction; he discovered a complete mechanical explanation of motion in the universe.)*

MAKE CONNECTIONS

Ask students to review the National Geographic Explorer sidebar on Kathy Ku. **ASK:** In what way or ways does Kathy Ku capture the spirit of the great innovators and thinkers of the Scientific Revolution? *(Kathy Ku observed a problem and set out to solve it. Her solution came from her curiosity but also her desire to help people. She likely had to experiment with different ways of developing her water filter but ultimately came to a solution that has had a wide-reaching impact.)*

ACTIVE OPTIONS

On Your Feet: Three-Step Interview Direct pairs to interview each other about women innovators of the Scientific Revolution, using the following questions: Who was Laura Bassi and what did she achieve? Why does history remember Maria Gaetana Agnesi? What were the most important contributions of Caroline Lucretia Herschel? Then have students reverse roles. Invite students to share the results of their interviews.

> **NG Learning Framework: Craft an Oral Report**
> SKILL Collaboration
> KNOWLEDGE Our Living Planet

Invite pairs to find out more about one of the thinkers or innovators they read about in the lesson. Tell partners to collaborate on an oral report that discusses the person's achievements, his or her relationship to established religious ideas of the day, and the ways in which his or her accomplishments are still felt today. When they have completed their reports, direct pairs to communicate their findings to the class.

DIFFERENTIATE

STRIVING READERS

Chart Details About Innovators and Thinkers Instruct pairs to create a three-column chart with the columns labeled with three scientific thinkers from the lesson. Have them take turns reading paragraphs of the lesson aloud to each other. Tell students to pause after each paragraph and record at least two important details about each person they selected. They can skip paragraphs that are not about their chosen scientists. Invite pairs to exchange and compare their completed charts.

GIFTED & TALENTED

Create an "Innovator and Thinker" Meme Challenge students to create a meme using a quotation from one of the scientists they learned about in the lesson. Ask students to conduct online research to find a quote that either relates to the scientist's innovation or to his or her views on religion. Tell students to add a photograph or artwork to enhance the scientific content of the quotation. Have them share their memes with the class.

See the Chapter Planner for more strategies for differentiation.

HISTORICAL THINKING

ANSWERS

1. Many scientists saw their work as religious in nature. They believed that God had granted them the ability to reason so that they would be able to understand the brilliance of God's creation.

2. Answers will vary. Possible response: Their contributions were extremely important in challenging gender norms. They showed that women have the intellectual capacity to understand and contribute to subjects that were often considered beyond their intellectual capabilities.

3. Answers will vary.

Science and Empire

Progress is good, right? Maybe not always. As British scientists applied scientific advances to agriculture, some people were winners, but many others struggled to survive.

BOTANICAL SCIENCE AND "IMPROVEMENT"

People have always studied ways to use plants for medicine as well as for food. With the rise of modern **botany**, the science of plants and plant life, scientists began to systematically collect and categorize **flora**, or plants, from around the world.

One of these scientists was **Carl Linnaeus**. In 1735, he published *Systema Naturae* in which he describes a system for organizing species into hierarchical categories. The Linnaean system classifies plants by the hierarchy of species, genus, family, order, class, phylum, and kingdom. Linnaeus also developed a two-name system of Latin names for organisms. The first name indicates the genus and the second the species.

With the support of Britain's George III, farmers derived practical economic lessons from Linnaeus's botanical work. In agriculture, this improvement meant using scientific methods to increase the productivity of existing farmland and to cultivate unused land.

By the 18th century, agricultural improvement brought about an agricultural revolution. Wealthy farmers in Great Britain invested in windmills to pump water from marshes, and they also began to rotate crops and crossbreed farm animals. Through these practices, more land was available for planting, and food production became more efficient. The resulting increase in food supply would be necessary as people began to move to cities during the Industrial Revolution.

EMPIRE AND POVERTY

This agricultural revolution brought efficiencies in production, but it led to greater inequality. Previously, English farm families had all shared common access to pastures and woodlands. But new laws, known as enclosure laws, allowed the wealthy to acquire common lands as private property. The rationale was that these landowners would farm the land more efficiently.

CRITICAL VIEWING This hand-colored engraving of a sunflower by botanical illustrator John Miller appeared in a 1777 English translation of a botanical treatise by Carl Linnaeus. Why do you think the artist paid such close attention to detail?

However, these laws meant that rural families lost access to the commons, as common lands were known, that they had once used for grazing cattle or sheep or for hunting. When they could no longer sustain themselves, many farming families went to work for the rich, while others drifted to cities or took jobs mining coal.

Therefore, what was known as improvement for some led to poverty for others. The price of bread increased and laws barred the poor from hunting wild game. As affordable food sources were taken away, rural people lost their **food security**, or their assurance that they would be able to obtain the food needed for

Originally established in 1759, Kew Gardens in London, England, housed more than 3,400 plant species by 1769. Sir Joseph Banks, whom you will learn about in the next lesson, managed the gardens from 1772 to 1819 and brought back plant specimens from all over the world.

good health. People resisted both in the cities and countryside, but laws were on the side of the upper class. The people in Parliament and the courts were from the landowning and wealthy classes. The interests of the poor were not represented.

Outside Great Britain, botany played a pivotal role in globalizing the practical application of science. British scientists brought new plant specimens from around the world to be examined, catalogued, and cultivated.

Throughout the expanding empire, British governors and commercial enterprises established botanical gardens as part of the effort to achieve improvement on a global scale. For example, when the Royal Navy needed timber for ships, British botanists identified South Asian mahogany as ideal for its height and durability. Breadfruit from Polynesia became an inexpensive yet nutritious food for slaves in the West Indies.

The British Empire used science to justify its dominance as well as to expand it. When confronted with the wealth produced by European science and technology, people in other parts of the world questioned the value of their own traditions and beliefs. In some places, such as Africa, conquest was so rapid that people had no time to make choices or to adjust. The prevailing belief among Europeans was that there was no need to take indigenous interests into account. Instead, they believed that the process of improvement gave them rights over land anywhere in the world. "Economic botany" one scientist wrote, referring to the idea that plants could be used to increase wealth, "would help to banish famine in India and win the love of the Asiatics for their British conquerors." Instead, Britain's empire was based on racial inequality, and Indians would suffer many famines under British rule.

HISTORICAL THINKING

1. **READING CHECK** What were some examples of agricultural advancements in the 18th century?

2. **IDENTIFY SUPPORTING DETAILS** How did Carl Linnaeus contribute to the science of botany?

3. **FORM AND SUPPORT OPINIONS** Who benefited and who suffered as agricultural improvement was implemented? Why?

PLAN: 2-PAGE LESSON

OBJECTIVE

Summarize the advances in botanical science that took place during and after the Scientific Revolution and how they were employed by the British Empire to mixed effect.

CRITICAL THINKING SKILLS FOR LESSON 3.1

- Identify Supporting Details
- Form and Support Opinions
- Make Generalizations
- Identify Main Ideas and Details
- Identify Problems and Solutions

HISTORICAL THINKING FOR CHAPTER 19

How can scientific advances challenge previously accepted ideas and lead to new knowledge?

Advances in scientific thinking reached the field of botany, which led to an agricultural revolution. In Lesson 3.1, students will learn how Britain used botanical science to expand its empire.

Student eEdition online

Additional content for this lesson, including a diagram, is available online.

BACKGROUND FOR THE TEACHER

Science and Museums The work of museums in the collection, analysis, classification, and preservation of natural and cultural phenomena can be traced back to the foundation of the British Museum in 1759. From the 16th century, the inquisitive thrust of the new science had an acquisitive dimension as well. Gentlemen and aristocrats competed to assemble "cabinets of curiosities"—shelves full of interesting and exotic specimens—both for their own amusement and to provoke their visitors' envy and astonishment. Then the 18th century brought a new seriousness of purpose, the rise of a more rigorous culture of evidence and classification. Sir Hans Sloane (1660–1753) pioneered this more focused approach. Sloane was a member of the Royal Society who traveled to Jamaica, collecting not only flora and fauna but also cultural artifacts characteristic of its largely African population. As Sloane's acquisitions and reputation grew, others sent him samples from their own collections, forming the basis of the donation that would found the British Museum.

INTRODUCE & ENGAGE

ACTIVATE PRIOR KNOWLEDGE

Draw a Word Web on the board and write the word *empire* in the center. Ask students to associate words and phrases with the term, drawing on their knowledge of world history and the empires built by other nations and states, such as Spain. Discuss with them the different empires they may have read or learned about. Then explain that this lesson describes how the British Empire used science, and botany in particular, to expand.

TEACH

GUIDED DISCUSSION

1. **Make Generalizations** In what way was the agricultural revolution of the 18th century truly a "revolution"? *(Scientific principles that came out of the Scientific Revolution were applied to agriculture. As a result, plants were used in many new ways.)*

2. **Identify Main Ideas and Details** What is food security, and why did it become an issue for people living in rural areas? *(the assurance that people would be able to have enough food to eat and be healthy; Rural people lost their food security when wealthy landowners took over common lands and poorer people could no longer sustain themselves.)*

IDENTIFY PROBLEMS AND SOLUTIONS

Ask students to study the diagram (available in the Student eEdition). **ASK:** In what way does the Linnaean System of Classification represent a solution to a certain scientific problem? Explain your thinking by identifying the problem and describing the effectiveness of the Linnaean System. *(Before the Linnaean System, there was no way to organize the kinds of animals in the natural world. The Linnaean System provides a hierarchical structure to the animal kingdom. It offers an effective method of classifying known animals and can be used to identify new animals.)*

ACTIVE OPTIONS

On Your Feet: True-False Quiz Tell half the class to write True-False statements based on the "Empire and Poverty" section of the lesson. Tell the other half to create response cards, with "True" written on one side and "False" on the other. As students read their statements aloud, direct the second group to respond using their "True" or "False" cards. When discrepancies occur, review the statement and the text and discuss which is correct. After all statements are assessed, have groups reverse roles.

> **NG Learning Framework: Create an Illustrated Time Line**
> SKILL Communication
> KNOWLEDGE Our Human Story

Instruct groups to use the lesson and additional research to generate an annotated and illustrated time line of botanical gardens in the British Empire, starting with Oxford's Botanic Garden (1621). Tell them to include botanic gardens from Australia and India. The illustrations should include examples of early botanic illustrations; the annotations should provide information about the botanic gardens today. Ask groups to share their time lines with the class.

DIFFERENTIATE

STRIVING READERS

Pose and Answer Questions Have pairs take turns reading paragraphs of the lesson aloud. Instruct partners to pause after each paragraph and ask one another *who, what, where, when,* or *why* questions about what they have just read. Suggest students use a Five-Ws Chart to help organize their questions and answers.

PRE-AP

Create a Diagram Have students use the diagram of the Linnaean System of Classification (available in the Student eEdition) as a model and create another version of the diagram with new examples and illustrations for each level of classification (except the *animalia* kingdom). You may wish to give students the species first and have them "work backwards" to create their diagrams.

See the Chapter Planner for more strategies for differentiation.

HISTORICAL THINKING

ANSWERS

1. windmills to pump water, rotating crops, crossbreeding farm animals, the use of plants from around the world; These practices allowed for more land use and increases in production.

2. He collected many different types of plants and developed a system for categorizing them. His two-name system for plants also helped create a common name for plants according to genus and species.

3. The wealthy benefited because they could apply new efficiencies and the laws benefited them. The poor suffered as they lost common lands for farming and laws were written to increase "improved" farmlands.

CRITICAL VIEWING Answers will vary.

Traveler: Joseph Banks
Father of Australia 1743–1820

If you had the chance to sail around the world, what would you bring home as a souvenir? The botanist Joseph Banks wasn't your everyday tourist. He brought back thousands of plant species and drawings of plants and animals.

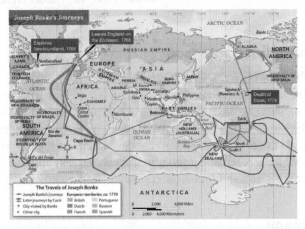

The Travels of Joseph Banks

JOSEPH BANKS AND JAMES COOK

From 1768 to 1771, botanist Joseph Banks sailed the Pacific Ocean aboard the *Endeavour* in search of flora and **fauna**, or animals. He brought back drawings and specimens of 1,400 plants and 1,000 animals previously unknown in Europe. He dried the plants between pages of books and systematically classified and catalogued his findings. His work greatly expanded European knowledge of the natural world.

Although botany was central to Banks's mission on the *Endeavour*, he was also very interested in the people he encountered. He kept careful notes of his interactions with native peoples of Tierra del Fuego (the southern tip of South America), the Polynesians of the Pacific, and the **Aborigines**, the original inhabitants of Australia.

When Banks learned that Tahitians understood the speech of the Maori of New Zealand, he realized that there was a family connection between the two peoples. Through these encounters, Banks became a pioneer of **ethnography**, the study of the linguistic and cultural relationships between peoples.

While Banks studied plants and animals and learned about the people he encountered on his travels, the *Endeavour*'s captain, James Cook, carried out important astronomical observations that helped solve the problem of identifying a ship's **longitude**, or east-west position.

Cook also used his mathematical and navigational skills to chart the oceans. He was assisted in this endeavor by a Tahitian high priest named Tupaia, who also helped Banks understand Polynesian language and culture. As you have learned, Polynesian sailors were masters at using wind, currents, and stars to find their way.

Tupaia came from a family of navigators and was able to supplement Cook's instruments and charts with a local understanding of winds and currents. By charting the Pacific Ocean, Cook facilitated future European voyages to such places as Hawaii, New Zealand, and Australia.

SCIENCE AT THE SERVICE OF EMPIRE

The *Endeavour* returned to England in 1771 after a three-year journey. The surviving crewmen were among the few at that time who had sailed around the world, and Captain Cook became an instant celebrity.

While Cook would make two more journeys, Banks never again traveled outside Europe. However, he came home dreaming of "future dominions," and he became

The Polynesian people fascinated Banks and his shipmates. In this excerpt from his journal, Banks describes a ritual they witnessed and participated in just after they stepped ashore on the island of Tahiti.

PRIMARY SOURCE

Though at first they hardly dared approach us, after a little time they became very familiar. The first who approached us came crawling almost on his hands and knees and gave us a green bough [branch]. . . . This we received and immediately each of us gathered a green bough and carried it in our hands. They marched with us about half a mile and then made a general stop, and scraping the ground clean . . . every one of them threw his bough down upon the bare place and made signs that we should do the same. . . . Each of us dropped a bough upon those that the Indians had laid down, we all followed their example and thus peace was concluded.

—from Joseph Banks's journal

an influential advocate of British settlement in Australia. In fact, he is sometimes called "the Father of Australia" for the role he played in the foundation of the colony of New South Wales.

You read about the long competition between France and Britain. Louis XIV had founded the French Academy of Sciences, and later kings also supported scientists to advance their military and empire. But the most prestigious scientific establishment of the day was Britain's Royal Society. Joseph Banks served as president of the Royal Society from 1778 to 1820. He focused on economic botany, which linked science to technological and economic development.

Through his role at the Royal Society, Banks promoted the introduction of Merino sheep to New South Wales,

where Botany Bay is named in his honor. Wool exports from these sheep strengthened the colony's economy, and the British founded new colonies across Australia. Banks believed these developments exemplified the successful outcome of applied practical science.

Unfortunately, British settlement had a devastating impact on the Aborigines. Before European contact, Aborigines lived in small bands, using their deep understanding of local environments for hunting and gathering. Many were pushed off their traditional lands as the British fenced off vast landholdings for sheep. In the 19th century, more than half of the Aboriginal population died from diseases introduced by European settlers.

HISTORICAL THINKING

1. **READING CHECK** What goals did Banks and Cook have for their voyage in the Pacific?

2. **ANALYZE POINTS OF VIEW** Some Australians call Joseph Banks the "Father of Australia." Why? What opinion do you think Aborigines might have of Banks? Why?

3. **DESCRIBE** How did the work of Banks and Cook in the Pacific further the progress of science?

4. **FORM AND SUPPORT OPINIONS** Do you think Banks's work in the Pacific was more beneficial or more devastating in the long run? Support your opinion with evidence from the text.

PLAN: 2-PAGE LESSON

OBJECTIVE

Describe what Joseph Banks and James Cook accomplished on their journey aboard the *Endeavour* and how they impacted the growth of the British Empire.

CRITICAL THINKING SKILLS FOR LESSON 3.2

- Analyze Points of View
- Describe
- Form and Support Opinions
- Explain
- Make Connections
- Analyze Primary Sources

HISTORICAL THINKING FOR CHAPTER 19

How can scientific advances challenge previously accepted ideas and lead to new knowledge?

Accepted ideas about scientific topics typically remain that way only until someone introduces new evidence. Lesson 3.2 explains how Joseph Banks expanded European knowledge of the natural world through his discovery of previously unknown flora and fauna during his travels in the Pacific Ocean with James Cook.

BACKGROUND FOR THE TEACHER

Science and Empire After Cook's and Banks's work on the *Endeavour*, science enjoyed considerable social and political support. European leaders, especially those in Britain and France, understood the connection between science and empire. In fact, the Royal Society, which had to petition King George III himself for approval, sponsored Cook's voyages. Cook's first voyage was supported by 4,000 pounds from King George III. Upon his return, Cook was promoted by the king to the rank of commander. Banks's exploration and study of the natural world, like that of the physical world undertaken by Cook, was a prelude to the more assertive European imperialism of the 19th century. So, while Polynesians were struggling to understand what they saw as the strange behavior of their British visitors, Cook was claiming their islands "for the use of his Brittanick majesty." Science and empire would remain companions for the remainder of the 19th century.

History Notebook

Encourage students to complete the Traveler page for Chapter 19 in their History Notebooks as they read.

Student eEdition online

Additional content for this lesson, including an image gallery, is available online.

INTRODUCE & ENGAGE

SHARE TRAVEL EXPERIENCES

Ask students to describe trips they have taken during which they have seen or experienced something for the first time, such as a landmark or monument, a different culture, or new foods. Invite students to discuss their motivations for travel. Ask them to compare and contrast the reasons people travel today with those of people in the past. *(Possible response: Today: leisure, business, or to aid others; Past: economic reasons or to spread culture)* Tell students that they will learn about the voyage of the *Endeavour* and the new experiences of Joseph Banks and James Cook.

TEACH

GUIDED DISCUSSION

1. **Explain** How did Tupaia help Joseph Banks and James Cook? *(Tupaia helped interpret Polynesian cultural practices and language for Banks; he shared with Cook his knowledge of local winds and ocean currents.)*

2. **Make Connections** How did Joseph Banks's botanical discoveries fuel Britain's economic development? *(Banks was familiar with Merino wool. He promoted introducing Merino sheep to New South Wales, a British colony. Wool production and sales boosted the economy.)*

ANALYZE PRIMARY SOURCES

Ask students to reread the excerpt from Joseph Banks's journal. **ASK:** How did the Polynesian people first react to Banks? *(They were cautious at first. Then, Banks writes, they "became very familiar.")* Why do you think Banks and his shipmates believed the Polynesian people were making peace? *(They got on their hands and knees, offered some green branches, and invited Banks and his shipmates to participate in a ritual.)*

ACTIVE OPTIONS

On Your Feet: Four Corners Have students examine the gallery of Parkinson's illustrations (available in the Student eEdition). Assign each question to a corner of the room: What do the illustrations have in common? How do the illustrations differ? What is striking about the flora and fauna depicted in the illustrations? What can be inferred about Sydney Parkinson from his illustrations? Students choose a corner and discuss the question. Then groups share their ideas with the class.

> **NG Learning Framework: Stage a Debate**
> **SKILLS** Communication, Collaboration
> **KNOWLEDGE** Our Human Story

Tell students to imagine they are members of Parliament debating the colonization of Australia. Divide the class into two teams, and assign each team to argue either for or against expansion of the British Empire. Team members should work together to locate information in the lesson and online about the settlement of Australia. Remind them to explore the pros and cons of the proclamation, searching for details that support their argument and any counterarguments. Be sure that students consider the impact of British settlement on Aborigines as part of their debate.

DIFFERENTIATE

INCLUSION

Understand a Map Instruct pairs to read the map legend, trace the lines showing Banks's and Cook's journeys, and study the colored areas of the map showing European territories. As they read the lesson, encourage students to use the map to trace Banks's and Cook's journeys.

GIFTED & TALENTED

Create a Digital Slideshow Instruct students to find examples online of the illustrations of flora and fauna Joseph Banks brought back from his travels by a variety of artists. Tell students to create a digital slideshow of the examples they find, with a caption on each slide. Ask students to present their slideshows.

See the Chapter Planner for more strategies for differentiation.

HISTORICAL THINKING

ANSWERS

1. Banks: study plants and animals; He also became interested in the people; Cook: chart the ocean for future travel and study the movement of Venus across the face of the sun

2. Banks supported the colonization of Australia and helped to build its economy through the export of wool. Aborigines may appreciate his effort to build the economy. However, the colonization introduced disease that devastated many indigenous people and robbed them of their lands.

3. Europeans learned about the natural world from Banks's collection of flora and fauna. He helped develop a process for categorizing the material. His notes about his travels and the people he met also provided information about other cultures. Cook's work charting the ocean facilitated future travel and his observation of Venus contributed to astronomy.

4. Answers will vary.

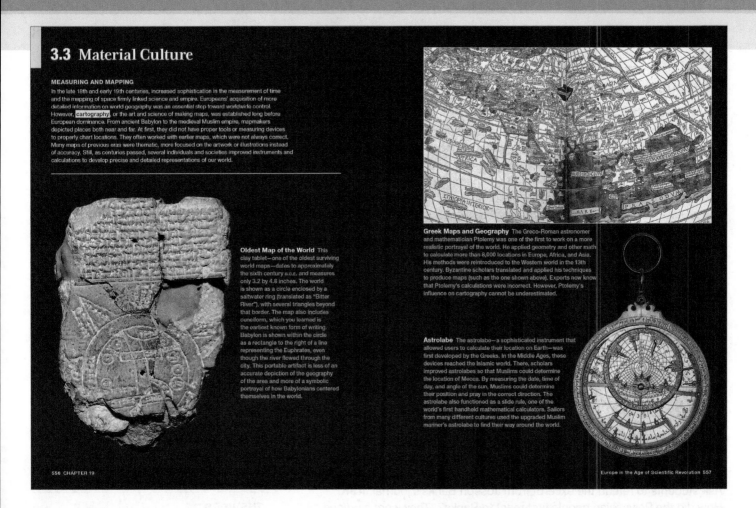

3.3 Material Culture

MEASURING AND MAPPING

In the late 18th and early 19th centuries, increased sophistication in the measurement of time and the mapping of space firmly linked science and empire. Europeans' acquisition of more detailed information on world geography was an essential step toward worldwide control. However, cartography, or the art and science of making maps, was established long before European dominance. From ancient Babylon to the medieval Muslim empire, mapmakers depicted places both near and far. At first, they did not have proper tools or measuring devices to properly chart locations. They often worked with earlier maps, which were not always correct. Many maps of previous eras were thematic, more focused on the artwork or illustrations instead of accuracy. Still, as centuries passed, several individuals and societies improved instruments and calculations to develop precise and detailed representations of our world.

Oldest Map of the World This clay tablet—one of the oldest surviving world maps—dates to approximately the sixth century B.C.E. and measures only 3.2 by 4.8 inches. The world is shown as a circle enclosed by a saltwater ring (translated as "Bitter River"), with several triangles beyond that border. The map also includes cuneiform, which you learned is the earliest known form of writing. Babylon is shown within the circle as a rectangle to the right of a line representing the Euphrates, even though the river flowed through the city. This portable artifact is less of an accurate depiction of the geography of the area and more of a symbolic portrayal of how Babylonians centered themselves in the world.

Greek Maps and Geography The Greco-Roman astronomer and mathematician Ptolemy was one of the first to work on a more realistic portrayal of the world. He applied geometry and other math to calculate more than 8,000 locations in Europe, Africa, and Asia. His methods were reintroduced to the Western world in the 13th century. Byzantine scholars translated and applied his techniques to produce maps (such as the one shown above). Experts now know that Ptolemy's calculations were incorrect. However, Ptolemy's influence on cartography cannot be underestimated.

Astrolabe The astrolabe—a sophisticated instrument that allowed users to calculate their location on Earth—was first developed by the Greeks. In the Middle Ages, these devices reached the Islamic world. There, scholars improved astrolabes so that Muslims could determine the location of Mecca. By measuring the date, time of day, and angle of the sun, Muslims could determine their position and pray in the correct direction. The astrolabe also functioned as a slide rule, one of the world's first handheld mathematical calculators. Sailors from many different cultures used the upgraded Muslim mariner's astrolabe to find their way around the world.

PLAN: 4-PAGE LESSON

OBJECTIVE

Trace the development of mapmaking and measuring instruments over time that linked science and empire and provided detailed representations of our world.

CRITICAL THINKING SKILLS FOR LESSON 3.3

- Analyze Visuals
- Make Connections
- Compare and Contrast
- Identify Problems and Solutions
- Interpret Maps

HISTORICAL THINKING FOR CHAPTER 19

How can scientific advances challenge previously accepted ideas and lead to new knowledge?

Mapmaking is an area of scientific learning that has been highly influenced by advances in technology. Lesson 3.3 shows that, over many centuries, maps became more accurate as technology became more sophisticated.

Student eEdition online

Additional content for this lesson, including a map, is available online.

BACKGROUND FOR THE TEACHER

The World's Oldest Astrolabe In 1998, a shipwreck of one of Portuguese explorer Vasco da Gama's vessels, the *Esmeralda*, was discovered off the coast of Oman in the Middle East. It is believed to be the oldest ship ever recovered and is an invaluable artifact from the Age of Exploration. Thousands of objects have been recovered from the wreck since excavations began in 2013, but none so mysterious as a small disc found in 2014. Some believed it was merely a decoration, but others thought it might be an astrolabe. In early 2019, laser scans produced a 3-D virtual model of the object. That model proved that the object was indeed an astrolabe—the world's oldest, in fact. The instrument likely belonged to Vicente Sodré, one of da Gama's two uncles who commanded a fleet of five ships along the Malbar Coast of India in 1503. That year, Sodrés sailed the fleet to the Gulf of Aden and robbed some Arab ships of their cargo. Unfortunately, a terrible storm arose, and the *Esmeralda* sank.

History Notebook

Encourage students to complete the Material Culture page for Chapter 19 in their History Notebooks as they read.

INTRODUCE & ENGAGE

PREVIEW USING VISUALS

Draw students' attention to the photograph of the clay tablet labeled "Oldest Map of the World." **ASK:** How can you tell that this object is a map? *(There is a pictorial symbol on it, and it has cuneiform writing that could explain what it means.)* How can you tell that this map is very old? *(It is carved into a piece of clay and has pieces missing.)* What would a modern map of Babylon have that this map does not have? *(Possible responses: a key or legend; dots indicating cities; blue lines indicating rivers; place markers and labels)* Tell students that in this lesson they will learn about how maps have developed throughout history.

TEACH

GUIDED DISCUSSION

1. **Compare and Contrast** What are similarities and differences between modern maps and the maps in the lesson, particularly Ptolemy's map, Kangnido, and Tabula Rogeriana? *(Possible response: They are all similar in the ways they distinguish between land and water. They also all use symbols to indicate features. However, the symbols on the maps in the lesson are not as familiar as symbols on modern maps. Modern maps are also far more accurate than the maps in the lesson.)*

2. **Identify Problems and Solutions** What problems did Muslims help solve when they improved the astrolabe? *(The improved astrolabe could determine the location of Mecca, which meant Muslims could pray in the correct direction. Also, the improved astrolabes were more accurate and helped sailors from all different cultures find their way as they traveled.)*

INTERPRET MAPS

Have students examine each of the maps that appear in the lesson. Ask volunteers to point out parts on each map that are recognizable to them (such as the Korean Peninsula and islands of Japan in the map known as Kangnido or Europe and the Mediterranean on the map based on Ptolemy's calculations). Then discuss areas that are not recognizable (such as China and the Indian subcontinent on the Kangnido map or Asia on the Tabula Rogeriana). **ASK:** Why might certain areas not be recognizable by today's standards? *(Possible response: Certain areas, such as large parts of Asia, might not be recognizable on these maps because mapmakers hadn't yet explored these areas and therefore weren't able to accurately calculate shape and distance.)*

DIFFERENTIATE

ENGLISH LANGUAGE LEARNERS

Pronunciation Before reading, preview with students of **All Proficiencies** the following words and names: *Babylon* (and *Babylonians*); *Ptolemy; Kangnido; Tabula Rogeriana; Al-Idrisi; chronometer.* Say each word slowly, and have students repeat it. You may wish also to give students the cultural origin of each word. Suggest students make word cards for each word, writing definitions and pronunciation hints for themselves.

GIFTED & TALENTED

Create a Map Encourage students to find a free online mapmaking tool (such as National Geographic's MapMaker Interactive) and then make a digital map of their own choosing. Give them a wide latitude: they could map their neighborhood or community; they could make a map using real-world data; they could make an alternate history map; or they could make a fantasy map that goes with a fictional place from a film, novel, or their own idea. Prompt them to include as many relevant details as possible, such as place names, physical landforms, historic events, or geographic data. Invite students to present their maps to the class and answer any questions.

See the Chapter Planner for more strategies for differentiation.

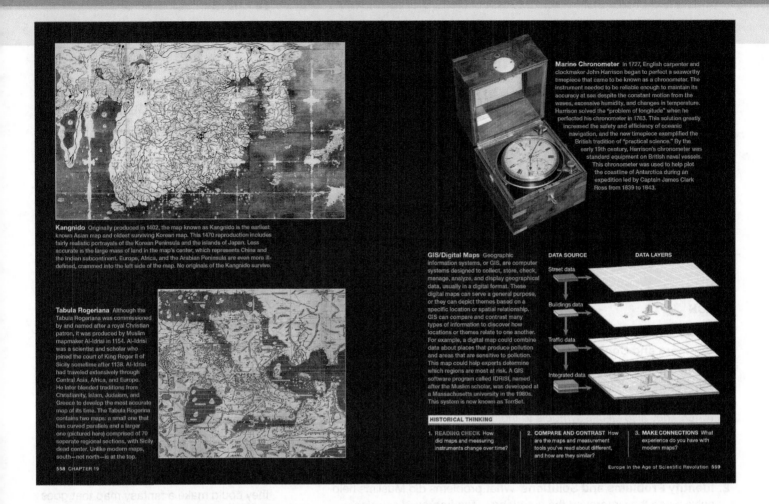

Kangnido Originally produced in 1402, the map known as Kangnido is the earliest known Asian map and oldest surviving Korean map. This 1470 reproduction includes fairly realistic portrayals of the Korean Peninsula and the islands of Japan. Less accurate is the large mass of land in the map's center, which represents China and the Indian subcontinent. Europe, Africa, and the Arabian Peninsula are even more ill-defined, crammed into the left side of the map. No originals of the Kangnido survive.

Tabula Rogeriana Although the Tabula Rogeriana was commissioned by and named after a royal Christian patron, it was produced by Muslim mapmaker Al-Idrisi in 1154. Al-Idrisi was a scientist and scholar who joined the court of King Roger II of Sicily sometime after 1138. Al-Idrisi had traveled extensively through Central Asia, Africa, and Europe. He later blended traditions from Christianity, Islam, Judaism, and Greece to develop the most accurate map of its time. The Tabula Rogerina contains two maps: a small one that has curved parallels and a larger one (pictured here) comprised of 70 separate regional sections, with Sicily dead center. Unlike modern maps, south—not north—is at the top.

Marine Chronometer In 1727, English carpenter and clockmaker John Harrison began to perfect a seaworthy timepiece that came to be known as a chronometer. The instrument needed to be reliable enough to maintain its accuracy at sea despite the constant motion from the waves, excessive humidity, and changes in temperature. Harrison solved the "problem of longitude" when he perfected his chronometer in 1763. This solution greatly increased the safety and efficiency of oceanic navigation, and the new timepiece exemplified the British tradition of "practical science." By the early 19th century, Harrison's chronometer was standard equipment on British naval vessels. This chronometer was used to help plot the coastline of Antarctica during an expedition led by Captain James Clark Ross from 1839 to 1843.

GIS/Digital Maps Geographic information systems, or GIS, are computer systems designed to collect, store, check, manage, analyze, and display geographical data, usually in a digital format. These digital maps can serve a general purpose, or they can depict themes based on a specific location or spatial relationship. GIS can compare and contrast many types of information to discover how locations or themes relate to one another. For example, a digital map could combine data about places that produce pollution and areas that are sensitive to pollution. This map could help experts determine which regions are most at risk. A GIS software program called IDRISI, named after the Muslim scholar, was developed at a Massachusetts university in the 1980s. This system is now known as TerrSet.

DATA SOURCE — Street data, Buildings data, Traffic data, Integrated data

DATA LAYERS

HISTORICAL THINKING

1. **READING CHECK** How did maps and measuring instruments change over time?

2. **COMPARE AND CONTRAST** How are the maps and measurement tools you've read about different, and how are they similar?

3. **MAKE CONNECTIONS** What experience do you have with modern maps?

BACKGROUND FOR THE TEACHER

National Geographic's MapMaker Interactive MapMaker Interactive is an online mapping tool that allows the user to explore the world using map themes, data, and tools. You can access the tool directly via a link on the home page of the Teacher or Student eEdition, and you have the ability to save maps for future reference. Following is a brief overview of features that make it easy for you and your students to visually explore and interact with our interconnected social and physical Earth systems.

1. **Base Maps:** You can choose from a variety of base maps depending on the information you want to display on your map. Examples include National Geographic style, topographic, satellite, and streets.

2. **Map Layers:** Different data layers allow you to explore different spatial phenomena, such as climate zones, population density, and gross domestic product, by adding them to your base map. You can project multiple layers at a time, arrange these layers, and change their transparency to explore spatial relationships.

3. **Drawing Tools:** You can use the drawing toolbar to add lines, rectangles, circles, polygons, and labels to your map.

4. **Customization:** Customize your maps by adding photos, videos, and descriptions to features on your map.

TEACH

GUIDED DISCUSSION

1. **Identify Problems and Solutions** What important calculation did the invention of John Harrison's chronometer allow for? *(It allowed for the calculation of a ship's longitude, which increased the safety and efficiency of navigation.)*

2. **Make Connections** What types of information might GIS be used to analyze? *(Answers will vary. Students' responses should involve a combination of data that could be used to determine something. For example a region's rate of food insecurity combined with the number of grocery stores in the area could help experts determine where new grocery stores should be located.)*

MATERIAL CULTURE

Remind students of the Historical Thinking question for this chapter: How can scientific advances challenge previously accepted ideas and lead to new knowledge? **ASK:** How do the maps and instruments presented in this lesson help you answer this question? *(Possible responses: Each map represents the known world at the time it was made. As travelers learned more about the world, old maps and ideas were discarded and new maps drawn. Cartographers used Ptolemy's measurements of latitude and longitude and other math calculations to produce maps, until experts realized his calculations were incorrect. Also, improvements made to the astrolabe and marine chronometer made sea journeys safer and led to more accurate maps of the world.)*

ACTIVE OPTION

On Your Feet: Jigsaw Strategy Organize students into "expert" groups and assign each group one of the maps from the lesson: the old clay tablet map of Babylon; Ptolemy's map of the world; Kangnido; Tabula Rogeriana; the Lewis and Clark Expedition (available in the Student eEdition). Each group should research each map and discover its history and its historical significance, especially in terms of the history of mapmaking. Then regroup students into new groups so that each new group has at least one member from each expert group. Students in the new groups take turns sharing the summaries from their expert groups.

HISTORICAL THINKING

ANSWERS

1. Maps and measuring instruments were improved over time. The first maps were drawn on clay and were of small areas. Later maps were drawn of much larger areas, sometimes using latitude and longitude calculations. The most recent maps are made using computer systems in a digital format. The astrolabe and marine chronometer also were improved to be much more accurate.

2. The maps differ in the areas of the world that they depict, the geography represented, and the accuracy of the distances depicted. They are similar in that all use symbols to help people travel through the known world at the time. The astrolabe uses the stars, whereas the marine chronometer is a timepiece. However, they are similar in that both were used to navigate the sea safely.

3. Answers will vary. Possible response: I have a maps app on my phone and in my car that gives me directions on how to get places.

REVIEW

VOCABULARY

Write one or more sentences that explains the connection between the two concepts.

1. absolute monarchy; constitutional monarchy
2. geocentric theory; heliocentric theory
3. ethnography; Aborigine
4. flora; fauna
5. scientific method; hypothesis
6. inductive approach; deductive approach
7. botany; food security

READING STRATEGY
IDENTIFY PROBLEMS AND SOLUTIONS

Identifying problems faced by individuals and nations and tracking their solutions can help you understand the way history unfolds. Complete the Problem-and-Solution Chart to analyze several problems faced during this period of European history. For example, how did England achieve religious and political stability? How did German-speaking nations resolve religious conflicts? How did British scientists solve the longitude problem? You may also choose another problem from the chapter. Then answer the question.

8. What possible problem was created by the stated solution?

MAIN IDEAS

Answer the following questions. Support your answers with evidence from the chapter.

9. What was the main source of instability in England during the 16th and 17th centuries? LESSON 1.1

10. Which countries gained power during the Thirty Years' War? Which countries lost power? LESSON 1.2

11. What were William and Mary required to accept when they became king and queen of England? LESSON 1.3

12. Why was Galileo Galilei imprisoned? LESSON 2.1

13. How did Sir Francis Bacon's approach to scientific inquiry differ from René Descartes's approach? LESSON 2.2

14. How were Vesalius, Kepler, Newton, and Bassi influenced by scientists who came before them? LESSON 2.3

15. How did the Scientific Revolution lead to expansion of the British Empire? LESSON 3.1

16. How did Joseph Banks and James Cook contribute to science through their voyage on the Endeavour? LESSON 3.2

HISTORICAL THINKING

Answer the following questions. Support your answers with evidence from the chapter.

17. IDENTIFY In what ways did monarchs and the church support the Scientific Revolution?

18. FORM AND SUPPORT OPINIONS If scientists of the 16th and 17th centuries knew more about climate change, do you think they could have prevented some of the turmoil in the world during the time of the Little Ice Age? Why or why not?

19. ANALYZE CAUSE AND EFFECT Describe how ideas from the Renaissance and Reformation led to the Scientific Revolution.

20. EXPLAIN How did scientific theories and methods of the Scientific Revolution challenge earlier beliefs and church orthodoxy?

21. IDENTIFY PROBLEMS AND SOLUTIONS What types of problems did the study of science create in the British Empire? How effective were the British solutions?

INTERPRET VISUALS

Study the time line of scientific and political events. Then answer the questions that follow.

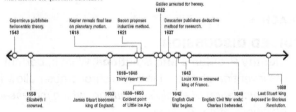

22. What was the difference in the political climate between England and France in the early 1640s?

23. What kind of weather was Europe experiencing around the time Galileo was arrested? What was happening in Germany during this same period?

ANALYZE SOURCES

English scientists believed nothing should stand in the way of scientific progress. Read the following quotation from Sir Francis Bacon about farmers in Ireland and answer the questions that follow.

> We shall reclaim them [the lands] from their [the farmers'] barbarous manners . . . populate, plant and make civil all the provinces of that kingdom.
>
> —Sir Francis Bacon

24. What practice is Sir Francis Bacon referring to in this quote? What is he suggesting should be done in the Irish provinces?

25. What attitude does this statement convey about the rural farmers of Ireland?

CONNECT TO YOUR LIFE

26. INFORMATIVE This chapter describes the effect a changing climate had on people living in Europe during the Little Ice Age. Use reliable Internet and print sources to learn about current scientific research into one aspect of climate change. Write a short essay to inform others of the measures being advocated to prevent further climate disruption.

TIPS

* Revisit the information on the Little Ice Age in this chapter. Summarize the information and use it to open your essay.

* Take notes on one aspect of present-day climate change. Consult at least three reliable sources linked to major university, museum, or research institutions.

* Be sure to attribute any quotations or ideas to the appropriate people or institutions.

* Conclude with a paragraph that sums up the current thinking on climate change and what steps should be undertaken to lessen its impact.

VOCABULARY ANSWERS

1. In an absolute monarchy, the king has unlimited power. However, in a constitutional monarchy, the king has to share power with Parliament.

2. The heliocentric theory suggests that Earth revolves around the sun. This idea challenged the traditional geocentric theory that suggested that the sun and planets revolved around Earth.

3. Because Joseph Banks was interested in ethnography, he probably found the Aborigines fascinating.

4. Joseph Banks studied the flora and fauna of the places he visited. He brought back many specimens of plants and animals.

5. When scientists use the scientific method, they ask a question, develop a hypothesis that might explain the question, and then conduct experiments to test the hypothesis.

6. Sir Francis Bacon promoted an inductive approach to science in which one starts with a test and then draws conclusions. René Descartes used a deductive approach in which he started with a general idea and used tests to prove or disprove it.

7. Scientific study of botany led to improvements in agriculture and food security.

READING STRATEGY ANSWER

8. Answers will vary. Students should describe one problem Europeans faced during the period between the mid-1500s and mid-1800s and list events that led to a solution of that problem.

MAIN IDEAS ANSWERS

9. Religious discord between Catholics and Protestants was the main source of conflict in England.

10. France and Prussia gained power. Spain lost power.

11. They had to work with Parliament and accept the English Bill of Rights.

12. His scientific studies contradicted the teachings of the Catholic Church.

13. Bacon's approach was inductive. He believed a scientist should experiment and observe carefully to create a generalization. Descartes's approach was deductive. He believed a scientist should start with a general principle and then test it to determine a specific truth.

14. Vesalius studied the work of the ancient Greek physician Galen. He then did his own work to expand on Galen's work on anatomy. Kepler studied and confirmed Copernicus's heliocentric model. Newton used the scientific method following Descartes's and Bacon's philosophies. He also expanded on the work of Kepler and Galileo. Bassi studied and taught the work of Newton.

15. Better understanding of plants helped farmers produce more food. Also, they were able to use plants and other natural resources from colonies around the world to improve the economy of the empire.

16. Joseph Banks collected plant and animal specimens from his travels. These contributed greatly to British understanding of botany and wildlife. James Cook charted the oceans, which helped future expeditions to Hawaii, Polynesia, and Australia. He participated in observing how Venus traveled across the sky. His research contributed to determining how to calculate longitude.

HISTORICAL THINKING ANSWERS

17. King Charles II founded the Royal Observatory and the Royal Society. King Frederick William pioneered military technology. Early on the Catholic Church accepted ancient Greek science, such as the work of Aristotle and Galen. Although popes objected to the work of Bacon and Galileo, later, as science became less controversial, Pope Benedict XIV recognized the work of scientists such as Maria Agnesi, offering her a professorship at the University of Bologna. King George III supported Carl Linnaeus's work in botany. British monarchs also supported scientific research as a way to justify and build the empire.

18. Answers will vary. Possible response: Even a better understanding of the climate probably wouldn't have had much effect. People didn't have the technology to warm their homes, grow crops in such cold weather, or alter the weather.

19. During the Renaissance, many people stopped blindly obeying the teachings of the Church. Instead, people started studying new ideas such as humanism. They also found inspiration in ancient Greek and Roman texts, which had been hidden away for centuries. The Reformation was also a time of questioning. People questioned the teachings of the Church and developed their own ideas. Also, ideas spread quickly through the invention of the printing press.

20. The Catholic Church had accepted the geocentric theory of the universe in which the sun and planets circled Earth. They presented this as God's perfect universe. Other classic ideas all suggested that God's creation was perfect and could not be challenged. Through mathematical calculations and observation, scientists discovered that Earth revolves around the sun and that there are imperfections in creation. The Church took these discoveries as a challenge to its authority.

21. Scientific discoveries changed the way people farmed to increase crop yields. However, many of the poorer farmers were displaced. In Australia, sheep were brought in as a way of building up the economy, but Aborigines were forced off their traditional lands. British policy makers argued that eventually these changes would benefit everyone, so they didn't work to help the poor. Instead, laws benefited the rich and the empire.

INTERPRET VISUALS ANSWERS

22. In England, the English Civil War was beginning, while in France, Louis XIV was crowned king.

23. Europe was probably experiencing very cold and erratic weather since this was the coldest era of the Little Ice Age. During this same time period, the Thirty Years' War was ravaging Germany.

ANALYZE SOURCES ANSWERS

24. Bacon is referring to "enclosure." The practice takes common lands from rural farmers and privatizes them for wealthy farmers who will use more efficient farming techniques. He is suggesting that the farms be taken from Irish farmers.

25. He is suggesting that the Irish farmers are barbarous and have no manners or education. It's an attitude of supreme superiority suggesting that the British will come in and make everything "civil."

CONNECT TO YOUR LIFE ANSWER

26. Students' informative essays will vary but should contain a thesis and develop the thesis with relevant, supporting details, including quotations or ideas from appropriate people or institutions. Students' essays should include a concluding statement that sums up the current thinking on climate change and steps to lessen its impact.

UNIT INTRODUCTION

UNIT TIME LINE

UNIT MAP online

THE GLOBAL PERSPECTIVE: Revolutionary Women online

- National Geographic Explorers: Hayat Sindi, Kavita Gupta, and Peg Keiner
- On Your Feet: Turn and Talk on Topic

| **NG Learning Framework**
Create a Web Page

UNIT WRAP-UP

National Geographic Magazine Adapted Article

- "Jane Goodall: A Revolutionary Naturalist"

Unit 7 Inquiry: Plan a Revolution

Unit 7 Formal Assessment

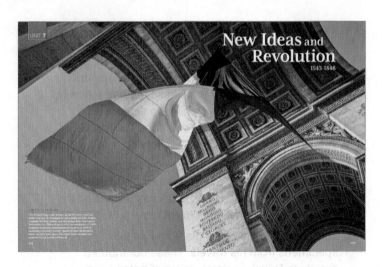

New Ideas and Revolution
1543–1848

CHAPTER 20 RESOURCES

Available in the Teacher eEdition

TEACHER RESOURCES & ASSESSMENT

Reading and Note-Taking

Vocabulary Practice

Document-Based Question Template

Social Studies Skills Lessons

- Reading: Make Inferences
- Writing: Explanatory

Formal Assessment

- Chapter 20 Pretest
- Chapter 20 Tests A & B
- Section Quizzes

Chapter 20 Answer Key

Cognero®

STUDENT DIGITAL RESOURCES

Available in the Student eEdition

20 European Enlightenment
1650–1800

- eEdition (English)
- Handbooks
- National Geographic Atlas
- History Notebook
- Biographies
- Literature Analysis

STRATEGY ❶

Use a 5Ws Summary

Display the 5Ws on the board. After reading, have students record key ideas under each heading.

Who?
What?
When?
Where?
Why?

Use with All Lessons

STRATEGY ❷

Complete a Main Ideas and Details Chart

As they read each lesson, encourage students to work in pairs to complete a Main Ideas and Details Chart. Point out the kinds of details (facts, dates, events, reasons) that support main ideas. Then ask each pair to alternate reading paragraphs aloud and writing down main ideas and details. Tell them this process will help them identify and remember the most important information in the lesson. Ask volunteers to share their completed chart with other student pairs and discuss the similarities and differences in their charts.

Main Ideas	Details

Use with All Lessons

STRATEGY ❸

Record Information

Post this heading: *What I Have Learned About the European Enlightenment*. Instruct students to copy the heading into their notebooks. After students read each lesson, challenge them to add at least three sentences under the heading. Invite volunteers to share their sentences with the class. Encourage students to add sentences from their peers to create a comprehensive list.

Use with All Lessons *Throughout the chapter, remind students to add to their lists as they read.*

STRATEGY ❶

Describe Lesson Visuals

Pair visually impaired students with students who are not impaired. Ask the latter to describe the visuals and answer any questions the visually impaired students might have.

Use with All Lessons *For example, for the photo of the palace at Versailles in Lesson 1.1, students might describe the chandeliers and gold statues.*

STRATEGY ❷

Use Echo Reading

Point out that the Main Idea statements all relate to important ideas and events that impacted European societies from about 1650 to 1800. Pair students with proficient readers who can read aloud the Main Idea statement at the beginning of each lesson. Tell the partner to "echo" the statement and then restate it in his or her own words to check comprehension.

Use with All Lessons Pairs might continue to echo read selected paragraphs or entire sections of each lesson.

STRATEGY ❶

Build Vocabulary

Help students at **All Proficiencies** learn unfamiliar words by substituting synonyms. Display difficult words paired with synonyms, such as these examples from Lesson 1.1:

sparked / started
entrenched / fixed
optimistic / hopeful
component / part
inherent / inborn

Tell students that when they encounter a confusing or difficult word, such as *entrenched*, they should try to replace it with a word they are familiar with, such as *fixed*.

Guide students to use a thesaurus to practice looking up and substituting words to find a synonym that makes sense in the context of the sentence.

Use with All Lessons *Students at the Advanced level could help students at the Beginning or Intermediate level find appropriate synonyms. Look for opportunities in all lessons to use synonyms and a thesaurus to aid comprehension.*

STRATEGY ②
Use Context Clues

Pair students at the **Beginning** level with those at the **Intermediate** or **Advanced** level. Instruct pairs to identify the context clues or textual definitions that provide the meaning of Key Vocabulary words. Then guide students in writing original sentences using the words. Have the more proficient students assist others in checking the accuracy of the sentences. Invite pairs to share their sentences and discuss different ways to use each word or term.

Use with All Lessons *For example, in Lesson 2.1, have pairs identify context clues that help them determine the meaning of the following words:* deism *(religious philosophy),* salons *(social gatherings),* bourgeoisie *(middle class).*

STRATEGY ③
Use Paired Reading

Pair students at the **Intermediate** and **Advanced** levels and tell them to read passages from the text aloud.

1. Partner 1 reads a passage. Partner 2 retells the passage in his or her own words.
2. Partner 2 reads a different passage. Partner 1 retells it.
3. Pairs repeat the process with additional passages.

Use with All Lessons

GIFTED & TALENTED

STRATEGY ①
Teach a Class

Before beginning the chapter, allow students to choose one of the lessons listed below and prepare to teach the content to the class. Give them a set amount of time in which to present their lesson. Suggest that students think about any visuals or activities they want to use when they teach.

Use with Lessons 1.1, 1.3, 2.1, and 2.3

STRATEGY ②
Write a Historical Dialogue

Tell students to write a fictional dialogue between one of the philosophers presented in the chapter and a fictional guest at a salon that conveys the philosopher's personality, philosophy, and views on Enlightenment ideas. Students may want to supplement their dialogues by conducting online research using primary and secondary sources. Encourage students to perform their completed dialogues for the class and answer any questions.

Use with Lessons 2.1 and 2.3

PRE-AP

STRATEGY ①
Use a Cubing Tool for Writing

Suggest that students look at the term *laissez-faire* from a variety of perspectives. Display the perspectives below as six sides of a cube. Direct students to choose four perspectives and write a paragraph discussing *laissez-faire* from each one.

Describe (What is it?)
Compare (What is it similar to or different from?)
Associate (What does it make you think of?)
Analyze (What are its traits or attributes?)
Apply (What can you do with the information?)
Argue (Take a stand in favor or against.)

Use with Lesson 1.3

STRATEGY ②
Use the "PERSIA" Approach

Have students write an essay explaining the significance of the Enlightenment. Tell them to consider P: political, E: economic, R: religious, S: social, I: intellectual, and A: artistic events as they write.

Use with All Lessons

HISTORICAL THINKING How were enlightened ideas a break from the past?

SECTION 1 Reason and Society
SECTION 2 Belief in Progress

CRITICAL VIEWING
The General Staff Building in St. Petersburg, Russia, was built in the early 19th century and served as the headquarters of the Russian armed forces and several ministries. A triumphal arch connects two wings of the building and is topped by a sculpture symbolizing victory. The building is an example of neoclassical architecture, a style that arose during the Enlightenment and was influenced by that movement's admiration of classical Greece and Rome. What architectural elements of the building reflect classical influence?

INTRODUCE THE PHOTOGRAPH

NEOCLASSICAL ARCHITECTURE

Invite students to examine the photograph of the General Staff Building in St. Petersburg, Russia. Read the caption aloud. Ask volunteers to identify elements of classical art from ancient Greece and Rome. Point out that the prefix *neo-* means "new" and that *neoclassical* refers to the revival of classical styles. Then discuss the answer to the Critical Viewing question in class.

SHARE BACKGROUND

The General Staff Building was designed by Italian architect Carlo Rossi and built between 1820 and 1830. Situated in St. Petersburg's Palace Square, the crescent-shaped building curves for about three-tenths of a mile along the south side of the square. It is situated directly across from the Winter Palace, the former residence of the tsars. The triumphal arch of the General Staff Building is a typical classical feature. The sculpture at the top was influenced by ancient Roman depictions of chariots and horses. Here, the sculpture commemorates Russia's military triumph over Napoleon's invading French troops in 1812. Today, the General Staff Building is part of the Hermitage Museum. It houses collections of 19th-century Russian and European art and displays works of contemporary art.

CRITICAL VIEWING Answers will vary. Possible response: the arch, columns, sculptures, symmetry

HISTORICAL THINKING QUESTION
HOW WERE ENLIGHTENED IDEAS A BREAK FROM THE PAST?

Numbered Heads: The Power of Ideas Organize the class into groups of four and have students number off within each group. Ask each group to discuss the following topic: Ideas have the power to cause a break from the past and change government and society. Following the discussion, call a number. Students with that number should report on the group's discussion.

KEY DATES FOR CHAPTER 20

1689	Locke proposes his own social contract in *Two Treatises of Government*.
1694	Mary Astell addresses the lack of women's education in *A Serious Proposal to the Ladies*.
1740	Frederick the Great begins his reign and is influenced by the Enlightenment.
1748	Montesquieu backs separation of powers in *The Spirit of Laws*.
1751	The first volume of Diderot's *Encyclopedia* is published.
1762	Rousseau advocates democracy in *The Social Contract*.
1763	Voltaire defends free inquiry in *A Treatise on Tolerance*.
1776	Adam Smith urges free markets in *The Wealth of Nations*.
1792	Mary Wollstonecraft publishes *A Vindication of the Rights of Woman*.

INTRODUCE THE READING STRATEGY
MAKE INFERENCES

Explain to students that they can make inferences by using the text and their prior knowledge to make "educated guesses" about the information in the text. Go to the Chapter Review and preview the cluster diagram with students. As they read the chapter, have students make inferences about the Enlightenment.

INTRODUCE CHAPTER VOCABULARY
KEY VOCABULARY

SECTION 1

laissez-faire	natural rights	philosophe
social contract	tyranny	

SECTION 2

bourgeoisie	deism	enlightened despot
salon		

VOCABULARY STUDY CARDS

Have students use index cards to make a study card for each Key Vocabulary word.

1. On the front of each card, have students copy and complete the Word Map shown here. They should write a vocabulary word in the center oval, a definition in their own words in the top box, and an example and similar words in the left and right boxes.

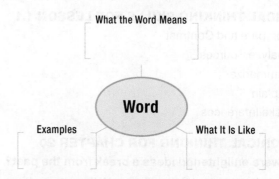

2. On the back of each card, have students note information about the word's pronunciation, synonyms and antonyms, connotation, word family, and a sample sentence.

3. Suggest that students use these study cards for review as they progress through the chapter.

The Age of Reason

Ideas can be dangerous, especially when they question long-held beliefs and the authority of leaders. But in the 17th century, some European philosophers contested established thought and used what they called the "light" of human reason to bring about change.

ROOTS OF THE ENLIGHTENMENT

As you know, the Scientific Revolution ushered in a new way of viewing the natural world. Scientists, including Galileo, Francis Bacon, and Isaac Newton, used not only observation and experimentation but also logic and reason to try to answer their questions about the universe. The Scientific Revolution helped inspire European thinkers in the mid-1600s to challenge traditional ideas about religion, government, and society. They believed people should use reason—the power of the human mind to think and understand in a logical way—to help them understand the physical world and their place in it.

CRITICAL VIEWING Louis XIV of France built his palace at Versailles to demonstrate his power as an absolute monarch. The palace's Hall of Mirrors, shown here, celebrates the king's reign and the economic prosperity of the French upper classes. How does the style of the room contrast with Enlightenment ideals?

These thinkers sparked an intellectual movement called the Enlightenment, also known as the Age of Reason. Rather than simply accept what religious and political figures had to say, Enlightenment philosophers encouraged others to use reason and experience to gain knowledge and shatter the "darkness" of ignorance. Their revolutionary political ideas challenged and often opposed traditional and entrenched institutions, beliefs, and social orders.

The Enlightenment had its deepest roots in the classical world of ancient Greece and Rome. Remember reading about the ancient Greek philosophers Plato and his student Aristotle? Their philosophical ideas differed in many respects, but they generally agreed on the evils of **tyranny**, a state of government in which rulers have unlimited power and use it unfairly. Plato called tyranny the "worst disorder of a state." He asserted that tyrants and their states lacked reason and order. The best government, Plato believed, was one led by an aristocracy of philosophers who would promote the common good. Aristotle contended that tyranny could corrupt monarchy. He wrote that powerful monarchs often acted only in their own selfish interest, not for the common good.

During the Renaissance, classical ideas and culture were revived, and these would later influence Enlightenment thinkers. The Protestant Reformation, the result of questioning the authority and practices of the Catholic Church, also had a significant impact on the movement.

THE SOCIAL CONTRACT

Two English philosophers of the 1600s, **Thomas Hobbes** and **John Locke**, helped lay the foundation of enlightened thought with the notion of a **social contract**. This was an agreement between rulers and the ruled to cooperate for mutual social benefits in pursuit of an ordered society, with clearly defined rights and responsibilities for each. But the two men came to very different conclusions about government and human nature.

Hobbes witnessed the terrible violence of the English Civil War and the Thirty Years' War and, as a result, took a dim view of people. In his 1651 work, *Leviathan*, he described humans as naturally selfish and wicked. Free to do what they liked, he wrote, people's lives would be "solitary, poor, nasty, brutish, and short." Hobbes maintained that, for the sake of peace, individuals must hand over their rights to a strong ruler.

Locke took a more optimistic view of humankind. He claimed that people had the ability to reason and learn for themselves, and they could use their acquired knowledge

to benefit society. In his 1689 book, *Two Treatises of Government*, Locke proposed his own social contract. A key component of the contract was the idea that all people are born free and equal with **natural rights**, such as life, liberty, and property. It was the duty of government to protect these rights, Locke declared. But if it failed to do so, the people had the right to overthrow the ruler and establish a new government. In fact, Locke had been involved in England's Glorious Revolution, and his ideas influenced the English Bill of Rights.

The concept of natural rights was not new, but in the late 1600s, only certain privileged classes enjoyed these inherent rights. Locke's call for natural rights was, in part, a rejection of the unlimited authority of the absolute monarchs who ruled in Europe during the 1600s and 1700s. The European king who best characterized absolute rule was Louis XIV of France, whom you've read about. He enforced his will and subdued any challenges to his authority. Still, absolute monarchs were not just found in Europe. Most states and empires in the world at that time were ruled by one leader, variously called a king, tsar, sultan, emperor, shah, or prince.

Locke's ideas greatly influenced other philosophers—especially in France. And, as you'll learn later, his ideas would have a lasting impact on political thought.

In *Politics*, a work of political philosophy, Aristotle set out to investigate the factors that comprise a good government and those that combine to form a bad one. The following excerpt from the work discusses some of these factors.

PRIMARY SOURCE

It is evident, then, that all those governments which have a common good in view are rightly established and strictly just, but those who have in view only the good of the rulers are all founded on wrong principles, and are widely different from what a government ought to be, for they are tyranny over slaves, whereas a city is a community of freemen.

—from *Politics* by Aristotle, 350 B.C.E.

HISTORICAL THINKING

1. **READING CHECK** What inspired the Enlightenment?

2. **COMPARE AND CONTRAST** How did the views of Hobbes and Locke differ with regard to rulers and the ruled?

3. **ANALYZE SOURCES** According to Aristotle, what do the ruler and the ruled become when a government focuses only on the good of the ruler?

PLAN: 2-PAGE LESSON

OBJECTIVE

Explain that the intellectual movement known as the Enlightenment arose when thinkers began to re-evaluate old ideas about society.

CRITICAL THINKING SKILLS FOR LESSON 1.1

- Compare and Contrast
- Analyze Sources
- Summarize
- Explain
- Make Inferences

HISTORICAL THINKING FOR CHAPTER 20

How were enlightened ideas a break from the past?

The Renaissance and Scientific Revolution inspired 17th-century thinkers to challenge entrenched beliefs and institutions. Lesson 1.1 discusses how European thinkers used reason to propose new ideas about religion, government, and society.

Student eEdition online

Additional content for this lesson, including an image, is available online.

BACKGROUND FOR THE TEACHER

John Locke and Education In addition to careers as a physician, diplomat, and political advisor, John Locke tutored children of the nobility for many years. He published *Some Thoughts on Education* in 1693, based on letters to a friend who sought advice on educating a gentleman's son. The work was so popular that numerous editions followed, along with translations into several European languages. As an Enlightenment thinker, Locke broke from the past view of children as miniature adults. He promoted the idea that children were rational beings, and born with different temperaments and interests that educators should respect. He emphasized children's need for free choice and play as a strategy for learning.

INTRODUCE & ENGAGE

MAKE WORD ASSOCIATIONS

Have students draw a Word Web with the word *Enlightenment* in the center circle. Ask them to write down all the associations that come to mind when they hear the word *Enlightenment*. After students have individually written their associations, invite them to share their thoughts with the class. You might want to have students revisit and revise their webs after they have read the lesson.

TEACH

GUIDED DISCUSSION

1. **Summarize** How did the Scientific Revolution influence Enlightenment thinkers to challenge traditional ideas? *(Scientists used observation and experimentation along with logic and reason. Enlightenment thinkers applied these methods to question entrenched institutions and beliefs.)*

2. **Explain** How did reason and natural rights help define the Enlightenment? *(Enlightenment thinkers used reason to help understand the world. They believed that natural rights, such as life, liberty, and property, applied to everyone.)*

MAKE INFERENCES

Encourage students to make inferences about the events that influenced the views of Thomas Hobbes and John Locke. **ASK:** What do you think Hobbes witnessed during the English Civil War and the Thirty Years' War to convince him that people were naturally selfish and wicked? *(Possible response: He witnessed people fighting over food and goods and refusing to help each other.)* How might Locke's involvement in the Glorious Revolution have affected his more positive view of humankind? *(Possible response: He saw people working together for the common good.)*

ACTIVE OPTIONS

On Your Feet: History Relay Have students form two teams on opposite sides of the room. Give students time to think of at least two questions about the lesson. Then students from each team should take turns posing their questions to a student on the opposing team. If the student answers correctly, the student who asked the question must move to the other team. If the student answers incorrectly, he or she must switch teams. If time permits, allow students to continue until everyone has had a turn asking a question. The team with more students at the end is the winner.

NG Learning Framework: Trace Influences on the Enlightenment
SKILL Collaboration
KNOWLEDGE Our Human Story

Invite students to work in small groups to trace the influences of classical Greek and Roman philosophers, Christianity, the Renaissance, the Reformation, and the Scientific Revolution on Enlightenment ideas. Ask students to share research tasks to ensure that everyone participates. On a large sheet of paper or a whiteboard, have groups pool their findings to create a Concept Cluster displaying the influences.

DIFFERENTIATE

ENGLISH LANGUAGE LEARNERS

Expand Vocabulary Ask students to write the word *tyranny* in a Word Square and then write its definition and characteristics. Have students provide examples and non-examples of the word. After students complete the Word Square, ask them to create another one for the term *natural rights*.

INCLUSION

Work in Pairs Pair students who have visual or learning disabilities with partners who are proficient readers. Have the proficient reader read the primary source excerpt aloud and pause frequently to discuss and explain Aristotle's ideas. Encourage pairs to record Aristotle's ideas on an Idea Web.

See the Chapter Planner for more strategies for differentiation.

HISTORICAL THINKING

ANSWERS

1. the ideas of ancient Greek and Roman philosophers, the Renaissance, the Reformation, and the Scientific Revolution

2. Hobbes believed people were naturally selfish and wicked, and so needed a strong ruler to keep them under control. Locke believed that people, as reasonable beings, could govern their own affairs, and he rejected absolute rule.

3. The ruler becomes a tyrant, and the people are reduced to slaves.

CRITICAL VIEWING Answers will vary. Possible response: It promotes the king, not the people; it flaunts the opulence of the king at the expense of the people; it underscores the king's power over the people.

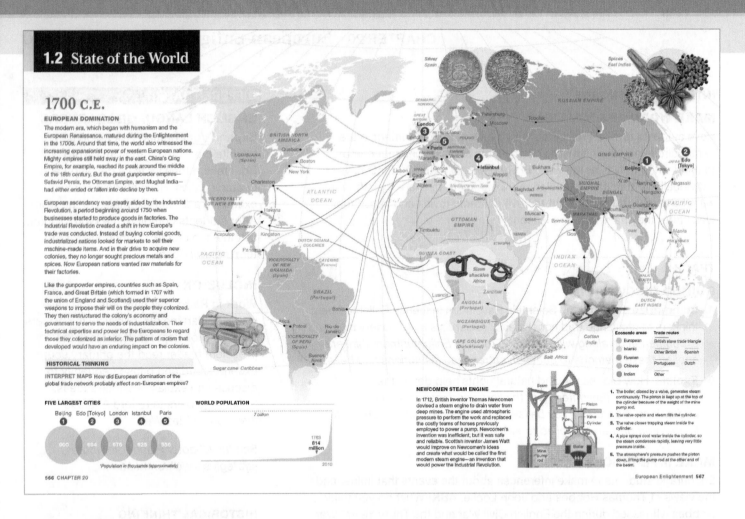

1.2 State of the World

1700 C.E.

EUROPEAN DOMINATION

The modern era, which began with humanism and the European Renaissance, matured during the Enlightenment in the 1700s. Around that time, the world also witnessed the increasing expansionist power of western European nations. Mighty empires still held sway in the east. China's Qing Empire, for example, reached its peak around the middle of the 18th century. But the great gunpowder empires—Safavid Persia, the Ottoman Empire, and Mughal India—had either ended or fallen into decline by then.

European ascendancy was greatly aided by the Industrial Revolution, a period beginning around 1750 when businesses started to produce goods in factories. The Industrial Revolution created a shift in how Europe's trade was conducted. Instead of buying colonial goods, industrialized nations looked for markets to sell their machine-made items. And in their drive to acquire new colonies, they no longer sought precious metals and spices. Now European nations wanted raw materials for their factories.

Like the gunpowder empires, countries such as Spain, France, and Great Britain (which formed in 1707 with the union of England and Scotland) used their superior weapons to impose their will on the people they colonized. They then restructured the colony's economy and government to serve the needs of industrialization. Their technical expertise and power led the Europeans to regard those they colonized as inferior. The pattern of racism that developed would have an enduring impact on the colonies.

HISTORICAL THINKING

INTERPRET MAPS How did European domination of the global trade network probably affect non-European empires?

FIVE LARGEST CITIES

Beijing	Edo [Tokyo]	London	Istanbul	Paris
①	②	③	④	⑤
900	694	676	625	556

*Population in thousands (approximately)

WORLD POPULATION

7 billion

1763
814 million

2010

NEWCOMEN STEAM ENGINE

In 1712, British inventor Thomas Newcomen devised a steam engine to drain water from deep mines. The engine used atmospheric pressure to perform the work and replaced the costly teams of horses previously employed to power a pump. Newcomen's invention was inefficient, but it was safe and reliable. Scottish inventor James Watt would improve on Newcomen's ideas and create what would be called the first modern steam engine—an invention that would power the Industrial Revolution.

1. The boiler, closed by a valve, generates steam continuously. The piston is kept up at the top of the cylinder because of the weight of the mine pump rod.
2. The valve opens and steam fills the cylinder.
3. The valve closes trapping steam inside the cylinder.
4. A pipe sprays cool water inside the cylinder, so the steam condenses rapidly, leaving very little pressure inside.
5. The atmosphere's pressure pushes the piston down, lifting the pump rod at the other end of the beam.

Economic areas

- European
- Islamic
- Russian
- Chinese
- Indian

Trade routes

- British slave trade triangle
- Other British / Spanish
- Portuguese / Dutch
- Other

566 CHAPTER 20

European Enlightenment 567

PLAN: 2-PAGE LESSON

OBJECTIVE

Describe the domination of world trade by western European nations in the 1700s.

CRITICAL THINKING SKILLS FOR LESSON 1.2

- Analyze Visuals
- Interpret Maps
- Identify Main Ideas and Details
- Analyze Cause and Effect

HISTORICAL THINKING FOR CHAPTER 20

How were enlightened ideas a break from the past?

The modern era matured during the Enlightenment movement in the 1700s. Lesson 1.2 explores the increasing power of western European nations as they increased their hold on world trade and expanded their empires.

Student eEdition online

Additional content for this lesson, including a video, is available online.

BACKGROUND FOR THE TEACHER

Istanbul In 1763, Istanbul was the fourth largest city in the world, and the capital of the Ottoman Empire. Situated between Europe and Asia, the city has been an important trade center for centuries. As a result, battles have been waged over its control throughout history. Istanbul has also been torn by natural disasters, including earthquakes, fires, and pestilence. The Golden Horn and the Bosporus separate European Istanbul from the Asian sector. In the 19th century, however, an Ottoman sultan authorized the construction of a bridge across the Golden Horn, and eventually railroads connected Istanbul with Europe. After a long decline, Ottoman rule ended in 1922, and the Turkish Republic was established the following year. While Istanbul remains Turkey's largest city, it is no longer its capital. Ankara was declared the country's capital in 1923.

History Notebook

Encourage students to complete the State of the World page for Chapter 20 in their History Notebooks as they read.

INTRODUCE & ENGAGE

PREVIEW WITH A MAP

Have students study the map showing world trade routes in 1763. Explain that the routes were largely traveled by European traders. Invite students to trace the brown-colored route. Then ask the following questions:

- Who traveled these routes? *(the Portuguese)*
- Where did the routes take these traders? *(to South America, Africa, Europe, and Asia)*
- What might they have traded in Africa? *(Possible response: gold, salt, slaves)*

Tell students that in this lesson they will learn about the European domination of world trade in the 1700s.

TEACH

GUIDED DISCUSSION

1. **Identify Main Ideas and Details** How did industrialization encourage the growing power of western European nations? *(European nations wanted new markets for their manufactured goods and colonized lands that could provide raw materials for their factories.)*

2. **Analyze Cause and Effect** Why did the Europeans consider those they colonized inferior? *(because the Europeans had greater technical expertise and power than those they colonized)*

STATE OF THE WORLD

Watch the State of the World: Global Trade in 1763 video (available in the Student eEdition) in class and discuss it with students. **ASK:** How were many of the raw materials obtained? *(through slave labor)* What machines in the video were used in the British textile mill? *(a water wheel and spinning jenny)* Then, as a class, discuss the positive and negative aspects the video reveals about global trade in the 1700s.

ACTIVE OPTION

On Your Feet: Fishbowl Have students examine the diagram of the Newcomen Steam Engine and read the text. Then organize students into two groups. Have one group sit in a small, inner circle. Have the other group sit in a larger outer circle. Ask students in the inside circle to discuss the diagram: what is its importance, how did it help power the Industrial Revolution, and explain how it works. During the discussion, students in the outer circle should listen for new information and evaluate what they hear. Then have groups reverse positions.

DIFFERENTIATE

STRIVING READERS

Make a List of Facts Tell students to reread the lesson and study its visuals. Then ask students to write down five facts they remember from the text, without looking back at the lesson. Have students meet with a partner to compare lists and consolidate the two lists into one. Encourage partners to go back into the lesson to note additional facts to make a final list.

PRE-AP

Research and Report Have students research and report on one of the five largest cities in 1763: Beijing, Edo [Tokyo], London, Istanbul, or Paris. Tell them to find out what led to the growth of the city they have chosen. Why did people want to live there in the 1700s? What resources—natural or human-made—did it boast? What positive and negative impact did the large population have on life in the city? Invite students to present their findings to the class.

See the Chapter Planner for more strategies for differentiation.

HISTORICAL THINKING

ANSWER

Answers will vary. Possible response: They probably suffered economically and politically.

Civic and Social Reformers

What problems do you think need to be fixed in American society, and how would you address them? Europe's enlightened thinkers believed they could apply reason to solve problems in government, religion, education, and economics.

Enlightened thought wasn't only spread through publications. By the late 1600s, coffeehouses had become popular places to exchange Enlightenment ideas, especially in London. For a penny, a man—and coffeehouses only admitted men—could sit by the fire, drink a cup of coffee, and join the conversation. As a result, the coffeehouses of the 17th and 18th centuries came to be known as "penny universities."

THE PHILOSOPHES

The Enlightenment reached its height in France in the mid-1700s with a group of social critics known as **philosophes** (fee-luh-ZAWFS), the French word for philosophers. A philosophe named **Charles-Louis de Secondat, Baron de Montesquieu** (mahn-tuh-SKYOO) wrote about political liberty. Like Locke, Montesquieu agreed that liberty was a natural right. During his travels in England, he had observed the English form of government and been impressed with what he called its separation of powers. As a result, Montesquieu advocated for the separation of government into three branches—executive, legislative, and judicial—in his 1748 book, *The Spirit of the Laws*. Doing so, he said, would prevent any individual or group from seizing control of all the power.

One of the most popular and influential of the philosophes was a writer who went by the pen name **Voltaire**. He used satire to poke fun at religious leaders, the wealthy, and government. His witty attacks on aristocrats at the French court sometimes landed him in trouble. Voltaire was jailed twice and exiled to England for several years. Nevertheless, he continued to fight for social reforms, including religious tolerance and freedom of speech.

Jean-Jacques Rousseau (roo-SOH) is another great philosophe whose views, though, were often at odds with many other Enlightenment thinkers. While most of the movement's philosophers believed in the power of reason and science to improve the world, Rousseau claimed that civilization had corrupted people's natural goodness and destroyed their liberty. He wrote, "Man is born free, and everywhere he is in chains." Like Hobbes and Locke, Rousseau proposed a social contract. Unlike these earlier thinkers, however, Rousseau's contract was an agreement among individuals to create their own government. In his 1762 work, *The Social Contract*, he called for a direct democracy in which people would give up some of their freedom for the common good. Under Rousseau's social contract, all people would be equal, and there would be no kings or titled nobility.

WOMEN OF THE ENLIGHTENMENT

Even though Rousseau maintained that everyone should be equal, he drew the line at granting this right to women. He supported reforming childhood education, but he believed girls should be instructed in how to be good wives and mothers. For all their progressive ideas, most of the philosophes, in fact, relegated women to their traditional societal roles.

Some women in the 1600s pushed back against this characterization of them. English philosopher, writer, and scientist **Margaret Cavendish** criticized the restrictions on women's freedom and said they resulted from nothing more than the "conceit men have of themselves." Although she had no formal schooling herself, Cavendish was a prolific, or highly productive, writer. In several of her works, she encouraged the equality and education of women. Cavendish wrote scientific treatises as well, a rare accomplishment for a woman at that time.

Another Englishwoman, **Mary Astell**, also addressed the lack of educational opportunities for women in *A Serious Proposal to the Ladies*, published in 1694. In other writings, Astell challenged the reasoning of some male Enlightenment thinkers. For example, questioning Locke's rejection of absolute rule, she wrote, "If absolute sovereignty [rule] be not necessary in a state, how comes it to be so in a family?" And to Rousseau's assertion that "man is born free," she countered, "If all men are born free, how is it that all women are born slaves?"

The most famous and outspoken female social critic of the 1700s was the English writer **Mary Wollstonecraft**. In her 1792 work, *A Vindication of the Rights of Woman*, she argued that because women have the ability to reason, they deserve the rights that men enjoy, including education. She wrote, "How many women waste life away . . . who might have practiced as physicians, regulated a farm, managed a shop, and stood erect, supported by their own industry?" Wollstonecraft also encouraged women to enter such male-dominated domains as medicine and politics.

ECONOMIC LIBERTY

Enlightenment thinkers even influenced economics. As you know, many European countries in the 1600s and 1700s based their economy on mercantilism, a system in which the government closely controlled commerce. A Scottish economist named **Adam Smith** promoted the idea of free markets in his 1776 book *The Wealth of Nations*. He believed businesses and industries should regulate their activities without government interference. This economic policy is called **laissez-faire** (LEH-say-FEHR), which is French for "let do" but, in this context, is often translated as "leave us alone."

Laissez-faire capitalism, which you learned is a system in which businesses are privately owned and exist to make profits, would create a free-market economy in which the people selling and buying products would determine what goods were needed and what price should be paid for them. Smith reasoned that this economic liberty would ensure economic progress and produce more wealth for all.

In his book, Smith supported his ideas with what he called the three natural laws of economics. The first was the law of self-interest. Smith declared that people worked for their own good: to earn money and acquire the things they needed. Competition, the second law, guaranteed that companies would try to make better products that would appeal to buyers. And these products would be regulated by the third law—the law of supply and demand. In a free-market economy, according to this law, a greater supply of goods would lower the demand for them and lower their price. Conversely, low supply and high demand would cause prices to rise.

PLAN: 4-PAGE LESSON

OBJECTIVE
Describe the efforts of Enlightenment philosophers to challenge powerful institutions and call for reform.

CRITICAL THINKING SKILLS FOR LESSON 1.3
- Compare and Contrast
- Make Inferences
- Draw Conclusions
- Describe
- Summarize
- Analyze Visuals
- Analyze Primary Sources

HISTORICAL THINKING FOR CHAPTER 20
How were enlightened ideas a break from the past?

The Enlightenment reached its height in France in the mid-1700s. Lesson 1.3 discusses key Enlightenment philosophers from France and Britain and their ideas to reform government, religion, education, and economics.

BACKGROUND FOR THE TEACHER
Enlightenment Music The Enlightenment affected the arts as well as government. Through the advent of public concerts, music became accessible to the middle class. Composers began writing for large audiences rather than for small, intimate gatherings. Composer Franz Joseph Haydn, for example, sought to keep audiences entertained with musical special effects, such as those that characterize his "Surprise" Symphony. Haydn also wrote music that was "democratic" in nature. His invention of the string quartet enabled each player to participate equally in the music.

INTRODUCE & ENGAGE

DISCUSS REFORMERS

Invite students to identify people whose ideas persuaded others to push for change. Examples might be leaders in the civil rights movement or advocates for local community reform. Encourage volunteers to suggest how these people spread their ideas. Then tell students that in this lesson they will learn about philosophers and thinkers whose ideas were designed to help bring about civic and social reform.

TEACH

GUIDED DISCUSSION

1. **Describe** What words would you use to describe Voltaire? *(Possible response: witty, charming, daring, reckless, principled, liberal)*

2. **Make Inferences** If Montesquieu had not proposed the separation of government powers, how might the government of the United States be different today? *(Possible response: The United States might not have three branches of government.)*

ANALYZE VISUALS

Direct students' attention to the images of the Enlightenment thinkers in the lesson. Ask them to study the portrayal of each one. **ASK:** How does each painting reflect the ideals or character of its subject? *(Possible response: The painting of Montesquieu presents him in the garb of an ancient Greek or Roman official, reflecting his ideals of government reform; the painting of a smiling Voltaire reflects his charm and good nature; the painting of Rousseau dressed in animal furs emphasizes his love of nature; the painting of Wollstonecraft seated at a desk with a book conveys her call for equal education for women.)*

DIFFERENTIATE

ENGLISH LANGUAGE LEARNERS

Make Key Vocabulary Cards Have students of **All Proficiencies** make and use flashcards to learn and practice the vocabulary words in this lesson. On one side of the card, have students write the key term. On the other side, have students write the term's definition and description and draw a picture that helps them recall the meaning. Encourage students to use the flashcards for review.

GIFTED & TALENTED

Create Social-Networking Profiles Ask students to research to learn more about Margaret Cavendish, Mary Astell, Adam Smith, and Denis Diderot. Then have each student select a thinker and create a social-networking profile on him or her, providing a brief summary and "photos." Invite students to share their profiles with the rest of the class. Encourage students to "friend" the Enlightenment thinkers and send them messages about the thinkers' lives and ideas.

See the Chapter Planner for more strategies for differentiation.

Enlightenment Thinkers

CHARLES-LOUIS MONTESQUIEU
Montesquieu first became famous for *Persian Letters*, a work in which he satirized Parisian society, mocked the rule—just ended—of Louis XIV, and criticized Catholicism. However, Montesquieu is best remembered for *The Spirit of the Laws*, considered one of the great works in the history of political theory. The masterpiece, consisting of 31 books, surprised most people at that time, who considered Montesquieu to be brilliant but rather superficial.

In this excerpt from *The Spirit of the Laws*, Montesquieu explains how a lack of separation of powers—specifically with regard to the judiciary power—enfringes on a person's liberty.

PRIMARY SOURCE

[T]here is no liberty, if the judiciary power be not separated from the legislative and executive. Were it joined with the legislative, the life and liberty of the subject would be exposed to arbitrary control; for the judge would be then the legislator. Were it joined to the executive power, the judge might behave with violence and oppression. There would be an end of everything, were the same man or the same body . . . to exercise those three powers, that of enacting laws, that of executing the public resolutions, and of trying the causes of individuals.

VOLTAIRE
Voltaire, portrayed here as a young man, was a prolific writer who produced poetry, prose, plays, satires, and thousands of letters. In his best-known work, *Candide*, Voltaire pokes fun at religion, government, and philosophers. However, some historians believe Voltaire's greatest contribution was introducing the ideas of Isaac Newton to France and much of Europe. The philosophe popularized the story that Newton formulated the laws of gravity when the scientist saw an apple fall from a tree.

Voltaire's *A Philosophical Dictionary* contains a series of articles, some of which are critical of religion and other institutions. In this excerpt from the dictionary, Voltaire takes aim at those theologians, or religious scholars, who tried to restrict freedom of expression.

PRIMARY SOURCE

In general, we have as natural a right to make use of our pens as our language, at our peril, risk, and fortune. I know of none which have done real evil. I know many books which fatigue, but I know of none which have done real evil. Theologians, or pretended politicians, cry: "Religion is destroyed, the government is lost, if you print certain truths or certain paradoxes [contradictory statements]. Never attempt to think, till you have demanded permission from a monk or an officer. It is against good order for a man to think for himself."

JEAN-JACQUES ROUSSEAU
While Rousseau believed people were naturally good, he didn't believe they were naturally intelligent. As a result, Rousseau suggested that people entrust a great lawgiver to develop their constitution and set of laws. To convince people to accept the laws, Rousseau said the lawgiver could claim he'd been guided by divine inspiration. Rousseau's reforms revolutionized music as well as society. He promoted freedom of expression in music and inspired such musicians as Austrian composer Wolfgang Amadeus Mozart.

A key idea of Rousseau's *Social Contract* is the concept of the "general will," which looks to the welfare of the whole and not the individual. Rousseau argues that, under the social contract, a person gains freedom by submitting to the general will.

PRIMARY SOURCE

Whatever benefits he had in the state of nature but lost in the civil state, a man gains more than enough new ones to make up for them. His capabilities are put to good use and developed; his ideas are enriched, his sentiments made more noble, and his soul elevated to the extent that—if the abuses in this new condition did not often degrade him to a condition lower that the one he left behind—he would have to keep blessing this happy moment which snatched him away from his previous state and which made an intelligent being and a man out of a stupid and very limited animal. . . .

MARY WOLLSTONECRAFT
Wollstonecraft called not only for equal educational opportunities for women but also for their social equality. She tried to live according to her beliefs. In a male-dominated world, Wollstonecraft worked as an editor, reviewer, and writer. Wollstonecraft died shortly after giving birth to a child she named Mary. Her daughter would become Mary Shelley, after marrying English poet Percy Shelley, and wrote the novel *Frankenstein*.

Wollstonecraft believed Enlightenment ideas must also apply to women. In this excerpt from *A Vindication of the Rights of Women*, she attacks Jean-Jacques Rousseau for his views on women's education—namely that women should be taught to make themselves agreeable to men.

PRIMARY SOURCE

Rousseau declares that a woman should never, for a moment, feel herself independent, that she should be governed by fear to exercise her natural cunning, and made a coquettish slave in order to render her a more alluring object of desire, a sweeter companion to man. . . . He [Rousseau] carries the arguments, which he pretends to draw from the indications of nature, still further, and insinuates that truth and fortitude, the corner stones of all human virtue, should be cultivated with certain restrictions, because, with respect to the female character, obedience is the grand lesson which ought to be impressed with unrelenting vigor. What nonsense!

Smith believed the interplay among self-interest, competition, and supply and demand would result in what he called the "invisible hand" of the market to control and regulate itself. *The Wealth of Nations* is considered by many experts to be the most influential book on market economics ever written, and Adam Smith is often called the "father of modern economics."

SPREAD OF ENLIGHTENMENT IDEAS

As you know, some of the philosophes were punished for their views. In France, it was illegal to criticize the government or the Catholic Church. But that didn't stop enlightened thinkers from publishing their beliefs. As a result, their ideas spread throughout Europe and beyond in books, magazines, newspapers, pamphlets—and letters. Voltaire wrote thousands of them, and these were often shared with an ever-expanding audience.

No publication helped spread Enlightenment ideas as much as the set of books that comprised the *Encyclopedia*, largely created by French philosophe **Denis Diderot** (DEE-duh-roh). Diderot and other Enlightenment philosophers and scholars contributed articles on topics including natural law, the history of philosophy, and social theory. The first volume of the *Encyclopedia* was published in 1751. Although the French government banned the work, Diderot continued with his project until the final volume was produced in 1772. Translations of the *Encyclopedia* into English, German, Spanish, and Italian spread Enlightenment ideas across Europe and around the world.

Women weren't invited to write for the *Encyclopedia*. But, as you'll see, some women in Paris found their own way to spread Enlightenment ideas in their homes.

HISTORICAL THINKING

1. **READING CHECK** What government reform did Montesquieu propose?

2. **COMPARE AND CONTRAST** How did Rousseau's social contract differ from John Locke's?

3. **MAKE INFERENCES** Why do you think Mary Astell used the words of male Enlightenment philosophers to make her points?

4. **DRAW CONCLUSIONS** How did Adam Smith's ideas on economics reflect enlightened thought?

BACKGROUND FOR THE TEACHER

Diderot and the *Encyclopedia* In 1746, Denis Diderot assisted with a French translation of Ephraim Chambers' *Cyclopaedia*, a dictionary of the arts and sciences. With the help of mathematician Jean Le Rond d'Alembert, Diderot turned the work into the revolutionary *Encyclopedia.* Fearing trouble, however, d'Alembert abandoned the work in 1758. The French government banned the *Encyclopedia* in 1759, but Diderot continued working on it secretly in Paris. When the final *Encyclopedia* volume was published in 1772, Diderot had no money left. Catherine the Great of Russia, an Enlightenment supporter, helped Diderot by buying his library through a contact in Paris. She asked Diderot to keep the books until his death and provided him with an ongoing salary as her librarian.

TEACH

GUIDED DISCUSSION

3. **Draw Conclusions** Why did female Enlightenment thinkers press for equal education opportunities for women? *(Possible response: Without a good education, women would remain ignorant and appear to be inferior to men.)*

4. **Summarize** How did Enlightenment philosophers spread their ideas? *(Philosophers spread their ideas through the Encyclopedia and by writing letters, books, articles in magazines and newspapers, and pamphlets. They also exchanged ideas in coffeehouses.)*

ANALYZE PRIMARY SOURCES

Invite a volunteer to read the primary source by Voltaire aloud. Have students discuss the meaning of each sentence. Then point out the humor in the excerpt's final sentence. **ASK:** What is the impact of Voltaire's use of humor here? *(Possible response: The humorous exaggeration makes those who repress free speech and expression seem ridiculous.)*

ACTIVE OPTIONS

On Your Feet: Corners Strategy Make a sign for each of these thinkers: Montesquieu, Voltaire, Rousseau, and Wollstonecraft. Place one sign in each corner of the room. Tell students to go to the corner representing the writer they think had the best or most influential ideas. Give students in each group time to discuss the reasons for their choice. Then have a representative from each group present the group's collective ideas to the class.

> **NG Learning Framework: Define the Social Contract**
> **SKILL** Communication
> **KNOWLEDGE** Our Human Story

Review with students the fundamental concepts of the social contract: 1) People are born free and equal with natural rights; 2) People consent to form a government to protect those rights; 3) People are obligated to overthrow a government that stops protecting these rights. Have students choose one of the following project options to express their understanding of the social contract.

- Write a story
- Create a visual (cartoon, multimedia display, painting)
- Compose and act out a skit

HISTORICAL THINKING

ANSWERS

1. He proposed the separation of government into three branches—executive, legislative, and judicial.

2. While Locke believed government should serve to protect people's natural rights, Rousseau said that individuals should create their own government.

3. Answers will vary. Possible response: She used their words to show them that her ideas to improve women's status were based on reason—and men's own reasoning.

4. Answers will vary. Possible response: His ideas reflected the Enlightenment philosophers' emphasis on the individual. Smith believed that individuals acting in their own self-interest would create economic growth.

Paris at the Center

Today, many people debate their ideas on social media. Enlightened thinkers probably would have enjoyed trading views online, too. But instead, they networked in person. And Paris was the best place to do it.

THE CITY OF LIGHT

In the 1700s, philosophers, artists, and scientists from all over Europe and the Americas flocked to Paris to study and discuss ideas. Because the brightest minds of the Enlightenment gathered there (and also because it was one of the first European cities to adopt street lighting), Paris earned the nickname *La Ville-Lumière*, or "The City of Light."

You've read that Enlightenment ideas were disseminated through print media, such as letters, newspapers, pamphlets, and the *Encyclopedia*. But the Enlightenment also spread by word of mouth. Ideas were intensely discussed in the drawing rooms of wealthy Parisian women who organized regular social gatherings called **salons**. There, guests debated the latest Enlightenment contributions to philosophy, science, art, and literature. The women who hosted the salons chose the topics for discussion and controlled the flow of conversation. As you know, women at this time received little formal education, so the salons served as a socially accepted substitute for learning.

One of the best-known salon hosts was Marie Thérèse Geoffrin (joh-FREHN). Her salons had theme nights. Art was the theme on Mondays. Wednesdays were reserved for literature. But Geoffrin was a strict host. She never allowed any discussion of politics or religion at her salons. A generous patron of enlightened thinkers, Geoffrin also helped finance Diderot's vast project. Another popular host, Sophie de Grouchy (grew-SHEE), promoted equal rights for women at her gatherings. And she collaborated with her husband, Nicolas de Condorcet, on his works supporting educational reform and the abolition of slavery. Condorcet supported women's rights and racial equality, arguing that prejudices against women and Africans came from ignorance and would be ended by reason.

Guests at the Parisian salons ranged from nobles and bishops to painters and politicians. Well-known philosophes, including Voltaire, Montesquieu, and Diderot, were frequent visitors. American statesman **Benjamin Franklin** also regularly attended salons when he served as America's first ambassador to France. He once came to the salon of Marie Paulze-Lavoisier (luh-vwah-see-AYE) who was an artist known for her finely detailed scientific illustrations.

FREEDOM OF THOUGHT AND SPEECH

Salons did not welcome people of the working-class majority, but high-ranking members of the **bourgeoisie** (burzh-wah-ZEE), or middle class, were often invited to attend. However, they were expected to observe upper-class rules on proper behavior. The gatherings helped break down social and intellectual barriers but only if middle-class guests remembered to flatter their hosts and address aristocrats deferentially.

Lights illuminate the Pont Neuf, the oldest standing bridge in Paris. To ensure the safety of Paris at night, Louis XIV had candle-lit lanterns hung in the streets, primarily during the winter. The city first installed gas streetlights in the 1820s.

Salon hosts and guests may have made an exception for Voltaire, who was born into the middle class. His wit, intelligence, and dazzling conversation made him a favorite. But his views, particularly on religion, sometimes scandalized his audience. For instance, Voltaire championed **deism**, a religious philosophy that supports the idea of "natural religion." Deists believe that people are either born with a certain amount of religious knowledge or can acquire it using reason. They believe God created the universe but, after doing so, had no further involvement in it, allowing the world to run according to natural laws. Deism spread through Europe and across the Atlantic, where the philosophy would influence the founders of the United States.

As a deist, Voltaire believed organized religion hindered free and rational inquiry, and many philosophes rejected the core beliefs of Christianity. Nevertheless, most of them tolerated the right of others to express their religious views and ideas. Voltaire defended a Protestant family—in Catholic France—against persecution and religious intolerance in his 1763 essay, "A Treatise on Tolerance." In the essay, he wrote, "Think for yourself and let others enjoy the privilege to do so, too." The following more famous quotation has been attributed to Voltaire, but it was actually written by a 20th-century biographer of the philosophe: "I disapprove of what you say, but I will defend to the death your right to say it." Nevertheless, it sums up Voltaire's attitude—and that of many other Enlightenment thinkers—toward free speech.

HISTORICAL THINKING

1. **READING CHECK** What occurred at Parisian salons?

2. **EVALUATE** How did salons empower the women who hosted them?

3. **MAKE CONNECTIONS** How did the beliefs of deists support Enlightenment thought?

PLAN: 2-PAGE LESSON

OBJECTIVE

Explain how 18th-century Paris became the intellectual center of the Enlightenment.

CRITICAL THINKING SKILLS FOR LESSON 2.1

- Evaluate
- Make Connections
- Make Inferences
- Analyze Primary Sources

HISTORICAL THINKING FOR CHAPTER 20

How were enlightened ideas a break from the past?

Enlightened thinkers from all over Europe flocked to Paris to discuss their ideas. Lesson 2.1 discusses the role of Parisian salons in spreading enlightened ideas, including those calling for freedom of speech and religion.

Student eEdition online

Additional content for this lesson, including a video and an image of a painting, is available online.

BACKGROUND FOR THE TEACHER

Marie Paulze-Lavoisier Marie Paulze married Antoine-Laurent Lavoisier, a nobleman and chemist, when she was 13 years old and he was 28. Lavoisier pioneered studies on oxygen, gunpowder, and the chemical composition of water. His wife played a crucial role in his work. Marie Paulze-Lavoisier managed her husband's laboratory schedule and recorded data for experiments. She also created fine drawings of the equipment her husband designed and used. Marie Paulze-Lavoisier illustrated many of her husband's published works, including his groundbreaking 1789 *Elementary Treatise of Chemistry*. She even painted a portrait of Benjamin Franklin, after he attended her salon in Paris.

INTRODUCE & ENGAGE

PREVIEW WITH VISUALS

Direct students' attention to the painting of a salon (available in the Student eEdition). Tell them that the painting depicts a salon, a gathering hosted by a woman where enlightened thinkers discussed their ideas. **ASK:** What does the number of people at the gathering suggest about the Enlightenment? *(The large number of people there suggests the importance of the movement.)* Then discuss the possible topics the people in the room may have discussed. List the topics on the board and revise the list as needed after students have read the lesson.

TEACH

GUIDED DISCUSSION

1. **Make Inferences** Why is "The City of Light" an appropriate nickname for Paris? *(Possible response: because many enlightened thinkers came to the city to work and discuss their ideas)*

2. **Evaluate** Why might Voltaire have been considered a radical thinker in his time? *(Possible response: because he espoused freedom of thought, speech, and religion and rejected the core beliefs of Christianity)*

ANALYZE PRIMARY SOURCES

Have students read the primary source excerpt. **ASK:** What skills as a host did Julie de Lespinasse possess? *(Possible response: She was able to bring together like-minded people who engaged in lively conversation.)* Why might it have been difficult to regulate the conversation at a salon? *(Possible response: Everyone might have wanted to talk at once. It would have taken an adept host to make sure each participant had the opportunity to speak.)*

ACTIVE OPTIONS

On Your Feet: Numbered Heads Organize students into groups of four and instruct members to number off within each group. Ask each group to discuss the following topic: Social media networking is today's version of the 18th-century salon. After a time, call a number and ask the student with that number to report for the group.

> **NG Learning Framework: Make Connections**
> **ATTITUDE** Empowerment
> **KNOWLEDGE** Our Human Story

Ask students to find and read Dr. Martin Luther King, Jr.'s "Letter from Birmingham Jail" online. Have them discuss in small groups how the letter reflects the ideas of the Enlightenment. Continue the discussion as a class and, as a homework assignment, have students write a brief essay on Enlightenment principles and how they are still reflected today.

DIFFERENTIATE

INCLUSION

Use Supported Reading In small groups, have students read aloud the lesson, paragraph by paragraph. Have them use sentence frames to tell about the text:

- This lesson is about _____.
- One detail is _____.
- The vocabulary word _____ means _____.
- I don't think I understand _____.

Be sure to help students with portions of the lesson they do not understand.

PRE-AP

Write a Character Sketch Direct students to conduct research to learn more about one of the salon hosts in the lesson. Then ask students to write or illustrate a character sketch that describes the host, her salon, and the guests who attended. Invite students to share their character sketches.

See the Chapter Planner for more strategies for differentiation.

HISTORICAL THINKING

ANSWERS

1. Guests debated the latest Enlightenment ideas in philosophy, science, art, and literature.

2. Possible response: In their salons, women could determine the content of discussions and influence what philosophers would write about.

3. Possible response: Deists and enlightened thinkers both believed the universe ran according to natural law and was not governed by a supernatural power.

CRITICAL VIEWING (painting available in the Student eEdition) Answers will vary. Possible response: They were included but were greatly outnumbered by the men.

2.2 Government and Natural Rights

What is the primary role of government? To keep its people safe? Provide economic regulation? Maintain services and infrastructure? The Enlightenment gave rise to the ideas that people should be the basis of government and that they create government to protect natural rights. As a result, many enlightened thinkers became civic reformers. A few even rejected the idea of monarchy and aristocracy altogether and called for popular rule through a republican form of government.

As you've read, Enlightenment philosophers claimed that natural rights, including life, liberty, and property, were inherent in human beings. Civic reformers argued that these rights should be protected by rulers through the social contract. In return, individuals would agree to cede, when necessary, some of their freedom.

These ideas arose, in part, in resistance to absolutism, the rule of absolute monarchs in Europe. Concern about the dangers of their tyranny led Charles-Louis Montesquieu to argue for a separation of powers and embrace representative governments of limited power as the ideal form of government. In his works, Denis Diderot opposed the political establishment by promoting religious tolerance and freedom of thought. Mary Wollstonecraft called for a radical reform of the national education system for the benefit of women and all society.

While Voltaire championed liberty, he didn't think democracy was the ideal form of government. He believed people were basically selfish and incapable of self-control and needed the guidance of a wise monarch. And actually, in time, a few absolute monarchs began to govern more wisely. Influenced by the Enlightenment and its philosophers, some kings and queens took a new path and became more tolerant rulers.

Voltaire is buried in the Pantheon of Paris, where many great French citizens have been laid to rest. His tomb is shown here. Voltaire's coffin is inscribed with the following: "Poet, philosopher, historian, he made the human mind to soar and prepared us to be free."

DOCUMENT ONE
Primary Source: Book
from *The Spirit of the Laws* by Charles-Louis Montesquieu, 1748

Montesquieu begins *The Spirit of the Laws* with an explanation of the laws that govern the physical world and animals. He then goes on to discuss the laws that govern humans when they live together in society. In this excerpt from his work, Montesquieu describes the laws and government best suited for societies.

CONSTRUCTED RESPONSE According to Montesquieu, what is the best form of government?

Better is it to say, that the government most conformable [similar] to nature is that which best agrees with the humor and disposition [state of mind and character] of the people in whose favor it is established. The strength of individuals cannot be united without a conjunction [joining] of all their wills. . . . Law in general is human reason, inasmuch as it governs all the inhabitants of the earth. . . . They [the laws of each nation] should be adapted in such a manner to the people for whom they are framed.

DOCUMENT TWO
Primary Source: Book
from *A Vindication of the Rights of Woman* by Mary Wollstonecraft, 1792

Mary Wollstonecraft believed women should receive the same educational opportunities as men and have the same civil and political rights as well. In *A Vindication of the Rights of Woman*, she argues that, as a result of men's subjugation, women do not live in a "natural state." Here, Wollstonecraft explains what might happen if women had equal rights.

CONSTRUCTED RESPONSE In Wollstonecraft's view, how would women benefit from achieving the same rights as men?

Asserting the rights which women in common with men ought to contend [strive] for, I have not attempted to extenuate [excuse] their [women's] faults; but to prove them to be the natural consequence of their education and station in society. If so, it is reasonable to suppose that they will change their character, and correct their vices and follies, when they are allowed to be free in a physical, moral, and civil sense. Let woman share the rights, and she will emulate [imitate] the virtues of man; for she must grow more perfect when emancipated [freed].

DOCUMENT THREE
Primary Source: Book
from *Denis Diderot: The Encyclopedia Selections* translated by Stephen Gendzier, 1967

Unlike encyclopedias today, Denis Diderot's volumes were meant not only to provide information but also to guide opinion. In fact, Diderot claimed that the aim of the work was "to change the way people think." The following excerpt from the *Encyclopedia* is drawn from the entry on government.

CONSTRUCTED RESPONSE According to the writer, what is the greatest good of the people?

[T]he good of the people must be the great purpose of the government. The governors are appointed to fulfill it; and the civil constitution that invests them with this power is bound therein by the laws of nature and by the law of reason. . . . The greatest good of the people is its liberty. Liberty is to the body of the state what health is to each individual. . . . A patriotic governor will therefore see that the right to defend and to maintain liberty is the most sacred of his duties.

SYNTHESIZE & WRITE

1. REVIEW Review what you have learned about the Enlightenment and the views of enlightened thinkers on government and natural rights.

2. RECALL On your own paper, write down the main idea expressed in each document.

3. CONSTRUCT Construct a topic sentence that answers this question: How did Enlightenment philosophers apply their ideas about natural rights to government?

4. WRITE Using evidence from this chapter and the documents, write an informative paragraph that supports your topic sentence in Step 3.

PLAN: 2-PAGE LESSON

OBJECTIVE
Analyze documents that convey how Enlightenment philosophers applied their ideas about natural rights to government.

CRITICAL THINKING SKILLS FOR LESSON 2.2
- Synthesize
- Identify
- Analyze Cause and Effect
- Evaluate

HISTORICAL THINKING FOR CHAPTER 20
How were enlightened ideas a break from the past?

Lesson 2.2 focuses on how Enlightenment writers called for civic, government, and educational reforms.

BACKGROUND FOR THE TEACHER

Olympe de Gouges Another document closely related to these primary sources was the *Declaration of the Rights of Woman and of the Female Citizen* by Frenchwoman Olympe de Gouges, written in 1791. De Gouges strongly advocated equal rights and free speech for women. She was a social reformer who supported a number of causes, including divorce and the establishment of maternity hospitals. De Gouges believed that citizens should choose their form of government, and she called for a plebiscite, or direct vote, to that end.

INTRODUCE & ENGAGE

PREPARE FOR THE DOCUMENT-BASED QUESTION

Before students start on the activity, briefly preview the three documents. Remind students that a constructed response requires full explanations in complete sentences. Emphasize that students should use what they have learned about the Enlightenment in addition to the information in the documents.

TEACH

GUIDED DISCUSSION

1. **Identify** What does Montesquieu equate "law in general" with? *(human reason)*

2. **Analyze Cause and Effect** According to Wollstonecraft, what is the cause of women's faults? *(their lack of education and low station in life)*

EVALUATE

After students have completed the Synthesize & Write activity, allow time for them to exchange paragraphs and read and comment on the work of their peers. Establish guidelines for comments prior to the activity so feedback is constructive and encouraging in nature. Comments should focus on the most significant parts that address the purpose of the activity and the audience.

ACTIVE OPTION

On Your Feet: Host a DBQ Roundtable Direct students to gather into groups of four. Hand each group a sheet of paper with the question: What basic rights do you think people should have? Instruct the first student in each group to write an answer, read it aloud, and pass the paper clockwise to the next student. The paper may circulate around the table several times. Then reconvene the class and discuss the groups' responses.

DIFFERENTIATE

STRIVING READERS

Summarize Main Ideas Arrange students in pairs to read the information presented about each document. Instruct them to pause after reading about a document and ask each other *Who? What? Where? When?* and *Why?* questions. Students may use a 5Ws chart to organize their questions and answers. Then ask them to use their responses to summarize the main ideas about each document.

GIFTED & TALENTED

Interview a Historical Figure Ask students to work in pairs to plan, write, and perform a television or radio interview with Charles-Louis Montesquieu, Mary Wollstonecraft, or Denis Diderot. Invite students to research their selected historical figure and focus on his or her actions, goals, and achievements. Encourage pairs to conduct their interviews before the class.

SYNTHESIZE & WRITE

ANSWERS

1. Answers will vary.

2. Answers will vary. Possible response: Document One: The people should have the sole power to enact or approve laws. Document Two: If women had the same rights as men, women's minds and characters would vastly improve. Document Three: The primary duty of a ruler is to defend and maintain the people's liberty.

3. Answers will vary. Possible response: Enlightenment philosophers believed that natural rights entitled people to government established in accordance with their will, gender equality, and liberty.

4. Answers will vary. Students' paragraphs should include their topic sentence from Step 3 and provide several details from the documents to support it.

CONSTRUCTED RESPONSE

Document One: one that best agrees with the state of mind and character of the people in whose favor it is established

Document Two: Their faults would lessen, and they would grow more perfect.

Document Three: its liberty

A New Sense of Confidence

Imagine you were an absolute ruler with plenty of power and wealth to spare. Would you want to give any of it up? Well, that's just what some European monarchs chose to do during the Enlightenment.

Frederick the Great was a generous patron of the arts and an accomplished musician. In this 1852 painting, *Flute Concert with Frederick the Great in Sans Souci,* he performs an evening concert at his palace. Austrian composer Wolfgang Amadeus Mozart wrote three pieces for the Prussian king.

ENLIGHTENED DESPOTS

Do you remember reading about the power of the Catholic Church during the Middle Ages? Its authority surpassed that of kings and queens. But with the decline of medieval order, monarchs began to assume more power. By 1600, as you know, some ruled as absolute monarchs, with unlimited authority and almost no legal limits. They claimed to rule by divine right, mandated, they believed, by the will of God.

At the same time, though, a growing middle class was pressing for more of a voice in government—especially in England. In 1689, the English Bill of Rights guaranteed basic rights to English subjects, and Parliament limited the king's power. (Still, many centuries would pass before most people were allowed to vote.) And, as you've read, the English philosophers John Locke and Thomas Hobbes began writing about the rights and responsibilities of rulers and the ruled, paving the way for enlightened thought.

576 CHAPTER 20

William Wilberforce, a member of the British House of Commons, worked to put an end to the slave trade. After introducing many resolutions and bills to Parliament, he finally succeeded in his struggle in 1807. In this excerpt from a speech he made to Parliament in 1789, Wilberforce explains why the British slave trade should be abolished.

PRIMARY SOURCE

As soon as ever I had arrived thus far in my investigation of the Slave Trade, I confess to you, Sir, so enormous, so dreadful, so irremediable [irreversible] did its wickedness appear, that my own mind was completely made up for the abolition. A Trade founded in iniquity [evil], and carried on as this was, must be abolished, let the Policy be what it might, let the consequences be what they would, I from this time determined that I would never rest till I had effected its abolition.

—from William Wilberforce's speech in the House of Commons, May 12, 1789

When the Enlightenment spread in the 1700s, some monarchs embraced the new ideas and made reforms in their countries. Because they never surrendered their complete authority, they became known as **enlightened despots,** absolute rulers who applied certain Enlightenment ideas. You've already read about the reign and reforms of one of these enlightened rulers: Catherine the Great of Russia. A favorite of the philosophes, Catherine exchanged letters with Voltaire and read many of the Enlightenment thinkers' latest works. However, as you know, she failed to follow through on many of her reforms, and the Enlightenment ultimately had little impact on Russia.

Frederick the Great, who ruled Prussia from 1740 to 1786, was another enlightened despot. While Louis XIV of France had declared, "I am the state," Frederick said, "I am the first servant of the state." The Prussian king introduced religious tolerance, reduced censorship of the press, and reformed the country's legal system. However, although Frederick believed serfdom was wrong, he did not take steps to abolish it because he needed the support of wealthy landowners.

Like Frederick, **Joseph II** of Austria promoted religious freedom, freedom of the press, and legal reforms during his reign from 1780 to 1790. Many of these reforms had begun under Joseph's mother, Maria Theresa. But while practical reasons guided Maria Theresa, Joseph was driven by Enlightenment ideals. Joseph also freed the serfs under his rule and had landowners pay peasants for their labor. These changes made Joseph unpopular with the aristocracy, and most of his reforms were dismantled after his death.

IMPACT OF THE ENLIGHTENMENT

The impact of the Enlightenment wasn't limited to monarchs and their reforms. New ideas also influenced ordinary people. The ideas of equality, representation, and rights inspired people because they emerged in a world dominated by hierarchy, inequality, and lack of representation and rights. The argument for a more democratic form of government, with people taking an active role in it, promoted the rise of individualism. And the claim that people should question their own religious beliefs led to a more secular outlook. Encouraged to depend less on the authority of the church and their rulers, people began to think for themselves and use reason to judge right from wrong.

Many Enlightenment thinkers also railed against injustice. While Montesquieu approved of slavery, Voltaire, Rousseau, Wollstonecraft, and others urged an end to the institution and the Atlantic slave trade. Rousseau wrote, "The words slave and *right* contradict each other, and are mutually exclusive." Wollstonecraft called the slave trade "an atrocious insult to humanity." As you've learned, France and Britain controlled much of the slave trade in the 18th century. Enlightened thinkers' opposition to slavery may have encouraged politicians and lawmakers to demand its abolition.

Philosophers of the Enlightenment advocated reform, but they lived in a world of ideas. They weren't active revolutionaries. Yet their assertion that a government should be overthrown if it failed to protect an individual's rights resonated with many people. In the 18th and 19th centuries, this notion would inspire democratic revolutions in the American colonies, France, and other parts of the world. Although the Enlightenment would not lead to a perfect world, it would give many western Europeans confidence that their lives would improve and the belief that reason could bring progress.

HISTORICAL THINKING

1. **READING CHECK** Why did some European monarchs in the 18th century come to be known as enlightened despots?

2. **MAKE INFERENCES** Why do you think many Enlightenment thinkers believed the slave trade should be abolished?

3. **SUMMARIZE** How did the Enlightenment and the social contract affect ordinary people?

PLAN: 2-PAGE LESSON

OBJECTIVE

Explain that the Enlightenment influenced some European monarchs and had a lasting impact on government, religion, and the social order.

CRITICAL THINKING SKILLS FOR LESSON 2.3

- Make Inferences
- Summarize
- Compare and Contrast
- Analyze Primary Sources

HISTORICAL THINKING FOR CHAPTER 20

How were enlightened ideas a break from the past?

Lesson 2.3 discusses the influence of the Enlightenment on several European monarchs and its impact on their governments.

Student eEdition online

Additional content for this lesson, including an image, is available online.

BACKGROUND FOR THE TEACHER

Divine Right The divine right of kings had its origin in Europe during medieval times. Just as the Christian Church asserted that its spiritual power came from God, European monarchs claimed that God granted them their political power. As a result, absolute rulers refused to be held accountable to any earthly power. By the 1600s, many rulers went so far as to claim authority over the Church as well as the state. Supporters of the doctrine believed that both the ruler's authority and person were sacred. It would take revolutions in England, America, and France to deprive the doctrine of its credibility.

INTRODUCE & ENGAGE

ACTIVATE PRIOR KNOWLEDGE

Ask students to volunteer ideas that have changed the world. Students might suggest the idea of the sun-centered solar system, evolution, human rights, and democracy. Once students have shared their thoughts, explain that this lesson will provide examples of how Enlightenment ideas led to reform in some European countries.

TEACH

GUIDED DISCUSSION

1. **Compare and Contrast** How were the reforms of Frederick the Great and Joseph II similar and different? *(Both promoted religious freedom, freedom of the press, and legal reform, but Frederick the Great did not abolish serfdom because he needed the support of wealthy landowners. In contrast, Joseph II abolished serfdom and had landowners pay peasants for their labor.)*

2. **Summarize** How did the Enlightenment inspire the rise of individualism? *(Enlightenment ideas of equality, democracy, and rights reached the common people and inspired the rise of individualism.)*

ANALYZE PRIMARY SOURCES

Tell students to read the excerpt by William Wilberforce. **ASK:** What does Wilberforce mean what he states, "let the consequences be what they would"? *(Possible response: Wilberforce realizes that the British economy may suffer if slavery is abolished.)*

ACTIVE OPTIONS

On Your Feet: Three-Step Interview Instruct students to work in pairs to interview each other about how Enlightenment ideas led to reform in Europe. Direct Student A to interview Student B, and then have them reverse roles. Finally, ask students to share information from their interviews with the class.

> **NG Learning Framework: Be a Reformer**
> ATTITUDE Responsibility
> SKILL Problem-Solving

Organize students into small groups and have them discuss social problems today that they believe need to be addressed. Encourage them to consider problems on the school, community, or national level. Then ask them to take on the role of reformers and do research to write an article that describes the problems and also suggests possible ways in which the government or individuals could solve them. Ask group representatives to read the finished articles. Then hold a class discussion in which students compare the problems and solutions they identified.

DIFFERENTIATE

ENGLISH LANGUAGE LEARNERS

Provide Sentence Frames Have students read the lesson and complete the sentences below.

- Monarchs who embraced and implemented Enlightenment ideas were called _____. *(enlightened despots)*
- The argument for a more democratic government, with people taking a more active role in it, promoted the rise of _____. *(individualism)*
- Many Enlightenment thinkers called for an end to _____. *(slavery)*

PRE-AP

Synthesize and Strategize Allow students to work in teams to discuss what they have learned and inferred about the effects of the Enlightenment. Have them compose a list of ways that the Enlightenment brought about issues that countries may still face today. Then ask them to present strategies that might help countries face these issues.

See the Chapter Planner for more strategies for differentiation.

HISTORICAL THINKING

ANSWERS

1. They were influenced by Enlightenment ideas and made reforms in their countries.

2. Answers will vary. Possible response: because the practice violated the natural rights of life and liberty

3. They promoted the rise of individualism, led to a more secular outlook, and encouraged people to think for themselves and use reason to judge right from wrong rather than depend on the authority of the Church and their rulers.

VOCABULARY

Match each vocabulary word below with its definition.

1. bourgeoisie
2. tyranny
3. philosophe
4. enlightened despot
5. natural rights
6. salon
7. laissez-faire
8. social contract

a. an absolute ruler who made reforms
b. an agreement between rulers and the ruled
c. a state of government in which rulers use unlimited power unfairly
d. an economic system opposed to government regulation of business
e. the middle class
f. a gathering at which guests discussed Enlightenment ideas
g. life, liberty, and property
h. a thinker during the Enlightenment

READING STRATEGY
MAKE INFERENCES

Use a cluster diagram like the one below to make inferences about the Enlightenment. Then answer the questions.

Facts — **Enlightenment** — Facts — Inferences

9. Why do you think the French government banned Denis Diderot's *Encyclopedia*?

10. Why did the reforms introduced by Austrian ruler Joseph II make him unpopular with the aristocracy?

MAIN IDEAS

Answer the following questions. Support your answers with evidence from the chapter.

11. According to the philosophes, who were the recipients of natural rights? LESSON 1.1

12. What did Mary Wollstonecraft and other female Enlightenment thinkers advocate for women? LESSON 1.3

13. According to Adam Smith, how would competition help control the market? LESSON 1.3

14. How did salons help spread Enlightenment ideas? LESSON 2.1

15. Who were some of the enlightened despots? LESSON 2.3

16. Why did the Enlightenment result in a more secular outlook among some people? LESSON 2.3

HISTORICAL THINKING

Answer the following questions. Support your answers with evidence from the chapter.

17. FORM AND SUPPORT OPINIONS How do you think Louis XIV of France reacted to the Enlightenment? Explain.

18. COMPARE AND CONTRAST How did Rousseau's view of civilization differ from that of other enlightened thinkers?

19. MAKE INFERENCES Why did civic reformers argue for representative governments?

20. EVALUATE Why did deism appeal to some of the enlightened thinkers?

21. ANALYZE CAUSE AND EFFECT How did salons impact the Enlightenment?

22. DRAW CONCLUSIONS How did the Enlightenment encourage people to believe that reason could improve their lives and bring progress?

23. FORM AND SUPPORT OPINIONS What is the most important legacy of the Enlightenment?

INTERPRET CHARTS

Study the chart at right, which summarizes the major ideas of Enlightenment thinkers. Then answer the questions below.

24. What form of government encompasses all of these ideas?

25. In your opinion, which is the most important Enlightenment idea? Explain your answer.

Major Ideas of Enlightenment Thinkers

Enlightenment Thinker	Idea
John Locke	Government established to protect people's natural rights: life, liberty, and property
Charles-Louis Montesquieu	Government separated into three branches: executive, legislative, judicial
Voltaire	Enforce policy of religious tolerance and freedom of expression
Jean-Jacques Rousseau	People create own government and give up some of their freedom for the common good
Mary Wollstonecraft	Grant equality and education for woman

ANALYZE SOURCES

In *An Essay Concerning Human Understanding*, published in 1690, John Locke states that people acquire knowledge through their perceptions and experiences and then use reason to form ideas. In this excerpt from the introduction to the work, Locke discusses the unwillingness of people to embrace new ideas. Read the excerpt and then answer the question that follows.

> Truth scarce ever yet carried it by vote [never was accepted by the majority of people] anywhere at its first appearance: new opinions are always suspected, and usually opposed, without any other reason but because they are not already common. But truth, like gold, is not the less so for being newly brought out of the mine. It is trial and examination must give it price, and not any antique fashion; and though it be not yet current by the public stamp, yet it may, for all that, be as old as nature, and is certainly not the less genuine.

26. Why do you think Locke compared truth to gold?

CONNECT TO YOUR LIFE

27. EXPLANATORY You have read about the lasting impact of Enlightenment ideas. Ideas about religious tolerance, representative government, and freedom of expression would result in spreading democracy around the world. Think about how these and other enlightened ideas affect your own life. Then write a short essay explaining the impact of Enlightenment ideas on your life today.

TIPS

• Review the Enlightenment thinkers and ideas discussed in this chapter.

• Choose two or three enlightened ideas that have had the greatest impact on your own life.

• Use at least two or three vocabulary words from the chapter in your essay.

• Conclude your essay by summarizing the impact of Enlightenment ideas on Americans today.

VOCABULARY ANSWERS

1. e
2. c
3. h
4. a
5. g
6. f
7. d
8. b

READING STRATEGY ANSWERS

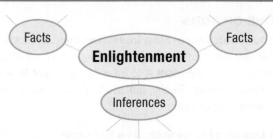

Facts — **Enlightenment** — Facts — Inferences

9. Answers will vary. Possible response: The French government feared the enlightened ideas and opinions expressed in the work might provoke rebellion.

10. Answers will vary. Possible response: Joseph's reforms to free the serfs and force landowners to pay their peasant laborers limited the aristocrats' power and forced them to part with some of their money.

MAIN IDEAS ANSWERS

11. only the privileged

12. the equality and education of women

13. Competition would guarantee that companies would try to make better products that would appeal to buyers.

14. Ideas discussed at the salons were spread to other people outside the gatherings by word of mouth.

15. Catherine the Great, Frederick the Great, and Joseph II

16. Enlightened thinkers encouraged people to question their religious beliefs.

HISTORICAL THINKING ANSWERS

17. Answers will vary. Possible response: Louis XIV probably rejected Enlightenment ideas because they threatened his power.

18. Answers will vary. Possible response: Rousseau believed that civilization corrupted people and destroyed their liberty, while many other philosophers embraced civilization but wanted to change aspects of it.

19. Answers will vary. Possible response: because a representative government best protects the people's natural rights

20. Answers will vary. Possible response: because Deism isn't bound by doctrine and practices that hinder reason and individual freedom

21. Answers will vary. Possible response: Salons brought enlightened thinkers together to discuss and debate ideas, spread Enlightenment ideas, and allowed upper-class women to learn and exercise a certain amount of power.

22. Answers will vary. Possible response: Ideas of equality led people—especially among the lower classes—to hope they would gain a voice in society and more power.

23. Answers will vary. Possible response: The Enlightenment's promotion of representative government and natural rights is its greatest legacy.

INTERPRET CHARTS ANSWERS

24. a democracy

25. Answers will vary. Possible response: Religious tolerance and freedom of expression are the most important because the policies allow individuality and are fundamental to liberty.

ANALYZE SOURCES ANSWER

26. Answers will vary. Possible response: because truth is as rare and precious as gold

CONNECT TO YOUR LIFE ANSWER

27. Essays will vary but should contain main ideas and relevant supporting details on how Enlightenment ideas have affected students' lives.

UNIT 7 RESOURCES

UNIT INTRODUCTION

UNIT TIME LINE

UNIT MAP online

THE GLOBAL PERSPECTIVE:
Revolutionary Women online

- National Geographic Explorers: Hayat Sindi, Kavita Gupta, and Peg Keiner
- On Your Feet: Turn and Talk on Topic

| **NG Learning Framework**
Create a Web Page

UNIT WRAP-UP

National Geographic **Magazine Adapted Article**
- "Jane Goodall: A Revolutionary Naturalist"

Unit 7 Inquiry: Plan a Revolution

Unit 7 Formal Assessment

New Ideas and Revolution
1543-1846

CHAPTER 21 RESOURCES

Available in the Teacher eEdition

TEACHER RESOURCES & ASSESSMENT

Reading and Note-Taking

Vocabulary Practice

Document-Based Question Template

Social Studies Skills Lessons
- Reading: Draw Conclusions
- Writing: Narrative

Formal Assessment
- Chapter 21 Pretest
- Chapter 21 Tests A & B
- Section Quizzes

Chapter 21 Answer Key

Cognero®

21 Political Revolution
1750-1830

STUDENT DIGITAL RESOURCES

Available in the Student eEdition

- **eEdition** (English)
- **National Geographic Atlas**
- **Biographies**
- **Handbooks**
- **History Notebook**
- **Literature Analysis**

STRIVING READERS

STRATEGY 1
Preview the Text

Work with students to preview each lesson in the chapter. Guide them to read each lesson's title, introduction, Main Idea statement, captions, and section headings. Then tell them to list the information they expect to find in the text. Instruct students to read the lesson and then discuss with a partner what they learned and whether or not the information matches the ideas on their list.

Use with All Lessons

STRATEGY 2
Turn Headings into Outlines

To help striving readers organize and understand lesson content, explain that headings can provide a high-level outline of the lesson. Model for students how to use the lesson title and headings to create a basic outline structure. Encourage students to take notes and flesh out their outlines as they read.

Use with All Lessons

STRATEGY 3
Clarify Information

Students may have trouble understanding and keeping track of the different revolutions in the lessons: the leaders, their supporters, their goals, and the results. To help students organize their reading and clarify information, encourage them to use a 5Ws Chart to take notes on the information for each lesson.

Use with All Lessons

INCLUSION

STRATEGY 1
Describe Artwork

To help a sight-impaired student understand details of the artwork in the chapter, pair the student with a teacher aide or another student. Have the sight-impaired student describe what he or she can see in the artwork. Instruct the teacher aide or other student to describe details that can be difficult to see, such as the expressions on people's faces and their clothing. Encourage the pair to discuss how the artwork enhances the information in the text.

Use with All Lessons

STRATEGY 2
Use a Graphic Organizer

Tell students that when they read, they will often need to analyze the evidence in the text and use their own judgment to form an idea or draw a conclusion. When they draw a conclusion, they are developing an idea as the next logical step using the information they have been given. After students read each lesson, pair them and have them use the following graphic organizer to write evidence from the text and a conclusion about the evidence.

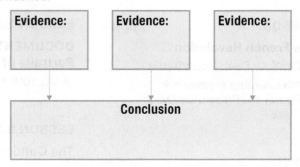

Use with All Lessons

ENGLISH LANGUAGE LEARNERS

STRATEGY 1
Activate Prior Knowledge

Display the words and terms below in a random "splash" arrangement. Tell students that all terms relate to the political revolutions from 1750 to 1830. Ask them to discuss ideas that the terms bring to mind and which terms still relate to important issues today. Then instruct pairs to write sentences using the terms. You may wish to pair students at the **Beginning** level with students at the **Intermediate** or **Advanced** level.

Use with All Lessons

STRATEGY ②

Use a Main Idea Cluster

Pair students at the **Beginning** and **Intermediate** levels with students at the **Advanced** level. Instruct pairs to use a Main Idea Cluster to check their understanding of the lesson. Tell students to take turns reading a section of the lesson. Then have them work together to record the main idea and four details. Instruct pairs to trade and compare clusters.

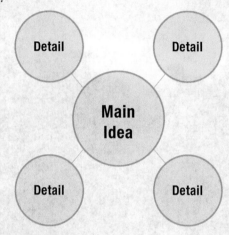

Use with All Lessons

STRATEGY ③

Summarize

Place students of **All Proficiencies** in pairs and assign partners one or more paragraphs from the lesson. Instruct students to read their assigned paragraphs and then work together to summarize each paragraph in one or two sentences. When all pairs are finished, ask them to read their summaries in the order in which the material appears in the lesson.

Use with All Lessons

GIFTED & TALENTED

STRATEGY ①

Map a Revolution

Instruct students to choose one of the revolutions presented in the chapter and conduct online research to learn more about the major battles and/or events involved in the revolution. Tell students to plot the battles/events on a map with a key that includes the dates and other information about each one. Invite students to share their maps with the class.

Use with Lessons 1.1, 1.2, 1.3, 2.1, 3.1, and 3.2

STRATEGY ②

Research and Perform a Speech

Tell students to conduct online research to find the text of one of Napoleon's speeches or Simón Bolívar's speech to the Congress of Angostura. Instruct students to choose a segment of the speech and practice it, trying to capture the speaker's emotions. Then ask students to perform their speech excerpts for the class.

Use with Lessons 2.1 and 3.1

PRE-AP

STRATEGY ①

Define a Revolution

Instruct students to research the view that the American Revolution was not a true "revolution" because it did not include "a rearrangement of social and economic power." Encourage students to agree or disagree and present an oral argument that defines a revolution and voices an opinion on whether or not the American Revolution was a true "revolution." Invite students to present their oral argument to the class.

Use with Lesson 1.1

STRATEGY ②

Write an Analysis Essay

Direct students to conduct research using online and print sources—including maps, charts, speeches, and other documents—to analyze the success or failure of one of the revolutions discussed in the chapter. Students could focus on topics such as the leaders, the goals, who influenced the revolution, and the results. Prompt students to write an essay analyzing the revolution and its impact on the world. Invite students to share their essays with the class.

Use with Lessons 1.1, 1.2, 1.3, 2.1, 3.1, and 3.2

CHAPTER
21 Political
Revolution
1750–1830

HISTORICAL THINKING What factors can lead
to revolution?

SECTION 1 Revolutions in the West
SECTION 2 Napoleon
SECTION 3 Wars for Liberation

CRITICAL VIEWING
Near the Patowmack Canal in Virginia, National Geographic
photographer Ken Garrett captures an evening reenactment
of an American Revolution skirmish. What conclusions can
you draw about warfare during the 18th and 19th centuries
based on details in this photograph?

INTRODUCE THE PHOTOGRAPH

BATTLE REENACTMENTS

Have students study the reenactment of the American
Revolution skirmish. Direct students to focus on the
weapons used and the nighttime conditions. **ASK:** How
difficult might it have been to use weapons such as the
ones shown at night during a battle of the Revolutionary
War? *(Possible response: It would have been difficult
to see the weapons and move them around at night. It
is very dark and the smoke that accumulates after the
canon is fired makes it hard to see.)* Why do you think
reenactments are done of historic battles? Explain.
*(Possible response: People enjoy living history, and
reenactments enable them to get an idea of what
happened during an event, even though some of what
they see might not be true.)* Explain that this reenactment
shows what might have happened during an American
Revolution battle and what it might have looked like
since there were no cameras or video at the time. Tell
students that in this chapter they will learn about political
revolutions around the world that were influenced by the
American Revolution.

CRITICAL VIEWING Answers will vary. Possible
responses include that warfare was difficult, confusing,
and somewhat primitive as compared to warfare today.

SHARE BACKGROUND

In the spring of 1831, after the American Revolution, Alexis
de Tocqueville traveled to America. Afterward, he wrote
Democracy in America, based on his observations of the
young country. The son of an aristocrat, de Tocqueville
traveled to the United States with Gustave de Beaumont.
The two were charged with the task of researching prisons
in the United States, both of which were experiments in
the making. As a court official in France, de Tocqueville
had studied law and had reached the conclusion that the
current state of the French government was approaching
failure. De Tocqueville penned his observations, including
interviews, in no less than 14 notebooks. He noted how
involved citizens were in policy-making and remarked that
the citizens of the United States were surprisingly equal,
which was quite the contrary in France. Even though the
equality he observed was largely based on what only free
white males enjoyed, it was a radical idea. In France, the
class system remained in place and many people were
still struggling with the transition to democracy. They did
not necessarily think that it would take hold, and France
would return to its aristocratic state. De Tocqueville's
book certainly was evidence that democracy was here
to stay in the United States and possibly one of the best
experiments undertaken. He remarked that it was truly
revolutionary.

HISTORICAL THINKING QUESTION
What factors can lead to revolution?

Four Corners: Preview Content This activity will help students preview and discuss the topics covered in the chapter. Provide a brief description and question for each section of the chapter, such as the ones shown below, and designate each of four corners as one of the main areas of revolution in the world. Divide the class into four groups and direct each group to go to one of the corners and discuss issues in their assigned country or region that could have contributed to the revolutions that broke out.

Group 1 United States: What made up what is now the United States, and who ruled it?

Group 2 France: What form of government did France have, and what was the role of its citizens?

Group 3 Haiti: Who ruled Haiti, and what rights did its citizens have?

Group 4 Latin America: Who ruled countries in Latin America, and what rights did its citizens have?

KEY DATES FOR CHAPTER 21

1775	The first skirmishes of the American Revolution begin.
1776	The U.S. Congress approves the Declaration of Independence.
1783	The American Revolution ends.
1789	The French Revolution begins.
1791	Civil wars break out in Haiti between whites and gens de couleur.
1793	The French monarchs Louis XVI and Marie Antoinette are executed.
1799	The French Revolution ends.
1804	The Haitian Revolution ends; Napoleon I crowns himself emperor of the French Empire.
1810	Led by Father Miguel Hidalgo y Costilla, Mexicans begin to fight for freedom from Spain.
1813	Simón Bolívar begins to liberate countries in South America.
1814	The Congress of Vienna restores the balances of power in Europe.
1821	Mexico wins its freedom from Spain.
1824	Simón Bolívar completes the liberation of South America.

INTRODUCE THE READING STRATEGY

DRAW CONCLUSIONS

Explain that drawing conclusions about events and individuals' actions and the effects of those events and actions can help students better understand the relationships among historical events. Turn to the Chapter Review and preview the diagram with students. As they read the chapter, encourage them to draw conclusions about the different revolutions, the individuals and events that caused these revolutions, and what the effects were.

INTRODUCE CHAPTER VOCABULARY

KEY VOCABULARY

SECTION 1

common law	constitutionalism	despotism
disenfranchised	estate	federal
guillotine	insurgent	militia
popular sovereignty		

SECTION 2

archetype	ideology	nationalism
nation-state	neoclassicism	propaganda
Romanticism	status quo	

SECTION 3

caudillo	junta

DEFINITION CHART

As they read the chapter, encourage students to complete a Definition Chart for Key Vocabulary terms. Instruct students to list the Key Vocabulary terms in the first column of the chart. They should add each term's definition in the center column as they encounter the term in the chapter and then restate the definition in their own words in the third column. Model an example on the board, using the graphic organizer shown.

Word	Definition	In My Own Words
nationalism	the belief that individuals are bound together by ties of language, culture, history, and often religion	people are united together because they have strong feelings for and love of their country

Debate and War in America

The principles of the Enlightenment spread to different parts of the world, including the Americas. Enlightenment concepts such as John Locke's call for protection of the basic rights of "life, liberty, and property" fueled the American colonists' desire for independence from Britain.

THE AMERICAN WAR FOR INDEPENDENCE

For many years, the British ruled their colonies in North America relatively peacefully. At the end of the French and Indian War, however, the colonists' joy over the British victory soured when Britain issued the Proclamation of 1763, limiting colonial westward expansion. The British wanted to avoid further conflict with French settlers and Native Americans.

Uneasiness grew as the British imposed additional taxes on the colonists to cover the costs of the war. Colonists bitterly resented these taxes because they had no representatives in Parliament who could vote in favor of or against them. Many people began to call themselves "Americans." They adopted the slogan "No taxation without representation!" and formed **militias**, or volunteer armies.

Fighting broke out in April 1775 when British soldiers marched on Concord, Massachusetts, to destroy militia supplies. Several weeks later, members of the Continental

CRITICAL VIEWING *Washington Crossing the Delaware*, painted by Emanuel Leutze in 1851, honors the moment the American general George Washington and his troops sailed across the Delaware River on the night of December 25–26, 1776, to surprise German forces on the other side. Based on this image, how do you think the artist viewed Washington and the Continental Army?

Congress met to determine future actions, one of which was to appoint **George Washington** commander of the Continental Army. On July 4, 1776, Congress approved the **Declaration of Independence** written by **Thomas Jefferson.**

The declaration built on John Locke's Enlightenment idea of a social contract. Locke believed that subjects could overthrow leaders who did not honor their side of the contract. Using Locke's logic, Jefferson argued that an American rebellion was justified. Jefferson included Locke's idea of **popular sovereignty**—the belief that government authority arises from the people themselves—as well. And Jefferson also incorporated ideas from the English Bill of Rights, which outlined the basic rights of British citizens.

Revolutionary leaders also drew upon the political philosophy of **William Blackstone,** a British attorney whose lectures on British **common law,** or laws determined by earlier court decisions, were published as *Commentaries on the Laws of England.* They cited this work as a basis for the argument that Americans were not merely subjects of the king but also British citizens with fundamental rights, and that taxation without consent was unfair.

Rebellious colonists became determined to create a republic with a government in which they had a voice. Their fight for independence during the American Revolution was long and difficult. The makeshift Continental Army was pitted against the well-equipped and well-trained British "redcoat" soldiers. A key turning point was the American victory at the Battle of Saratoga, after which France threw its support behind the colonists. In 1781, the Americans finally defeated the British army at the decisive Battle of Yorktown.

CONSEQUENCES OF THE REVOLUTION

The first attempt to form a confederation of the former colonies was unsuccessful. National leaders such as **James Madison** argued that the individual states would have to give up more of their power to a central government. In 1787, delegates met at the Constitutional Convention in Philadelphia, where they wrote the Constitution of the United States of America. Their goal was to create an American republic in which the people vote for their leaders. The delegates planned a government based on **constitutionalism,** an approach to government that strictly defines and limits its powers.

Madison and other founders incorporated ideas of the Enlightenment into the U.S. Constitution. Inspired by Montesquieu's belief in the separation of powers, they created three branches of government: executive, legislative, and judicial. Each branch could check and balance the powers of the other branches.

Compromise was the hallmark of the Constitution. For example, delegates from large and small states agreed on a two-house legislature called Congress. The House of Representatives would have representatives based on a state's population, and the Senate would have an equal number of senators for each state. The delegates also agreed to balance the powers of individual states with **federal** powers, or the shared authority of the states united in a single nation. Their resulting Constitution remains the supreme law of the United States and has lasted more than 230 years.

The issue of slavery required negotiation as well. Leaders from southern states argued that enslaved people should count in a state's population when calculating the number of representatives and electoral college votes. Northern delegates disagreed; they thought slaves should not be counted because they could not vote. The sides reached a compromise: when creating congressional districts, five enslaved African Americans would count as three free persons. Slavery remained legal, with 40 percent of southerners and many people in the North held in bondage.

Congress amended the Constitution in 1791 by adding a **Bill of Rights** that guaranteed civil liberties, such as freedom of religion, freedom of the press, and freedom of assembly. However, most states restricted the vote to white men who owned property. As in Europe, the Enlightenment idea that "all men are created equal" was not applied to everyone. Women, Native Americans, and most free black people were denied many basic rights.

Historians debate whether the American Revolution was a true "revolution" because a rearrangement of social and economic power did not take place. For the French Revolution that followed, there is no such debate.

The Declaration of Independence details the colonists' grievances and makes a stirring announcement of universal values.

PRIMARY SOURCE

We hold these truths to be self-evident, that all men are created equal, that they are endowed by their Creator with certain inalienable Rights, that among these are Life, Liberty and the pursuit of Happiness.—That to secure these rights, Governments are instituted among Men, deriving their just powers from the consent of the governed.

HISTORICAL THINKING

1. READING CHECK How did the nation's founders incorporate Enlightenment ideas as they established the United States?

2. IDENTIFY MAIN IDEAS AND DETAILS Why did the American colonists protest taxes that were imposed to cover the costs of the French and Indian War?

3. MAKE CONNECTIONS Did the phrase "all men are created equal" apply to the United States after its revolution? Explain.

PLAN: 2-PAGE LESSON

OBJECTIVE
Describe how Enlightenment ideas inspired American colonists to declare independence and establish their own republic.

CRITICAL THINKING SKILLS FOR LESSON 1.1
- Identify Main Ideas and Details
- Make Connections
- Analyze Cause and Effect
- Draw Conclusions

HISTORICAL THINKING FOR CHAPTER 21
What factors can lead to revolution?

Throughout history, people have risked their lives for worthy causes, especially when people lack basic rights and freedoms, have no voice in government, and are forced to live in abhorrent conditions. These are causes that spark a revolution. Lesson 1.1 discusses what caused the debate for independence in the British colonies in North America and how that debate led to war and a new country.

Student eEdition online
Additional content for this lesson, including a painting, is available online.

BACKGROUND FOR THE TEACHER
Revolutionary Tea At the famous "Tea Party" of May 1773, colonists threw Indian tea into Boston Harbor, protesting a new British policy intended to oblige them to buy tea directly from the East India Company. At that time, colonists were drinking 1,200,000 pounds of tea each year. The Tea Act angered local merchants who had been smuggling tea into Massachusetts, as well as consumers who anticipated that an East India Company monopoly would eventually lead to higher prices. By then, the combination of Asian tea and sugar from the West Indies had become an expected part of their daily routines. A total of 342 chests of tea were dumped into Boston Harbor. Other tea "confrontations" took place in cities throughout the colonies such as one in Charleston, South Carolina, in which tea arrived from Britain in a ship ironically called the *Magna Carta*, but none of the tea made it out of the harbor.

INTRODUCE & ENGAGE

DISCUSS THE IMPORTANCE OF TIMING

Invite students to discuss examples of when events happened "at the right time" and how this is important in understanding history. *(Possible responses might include a protest, new legislation, or new leadership.)* Tell students that in this lesson they will learn about how events in one country can influence those in another and that often movements for change and freedom can have global effects.

TEACH

GUIDED DISCUSSION

1. **Analyze Cause and Effect** What caused colonists to write the Declaration of Independence? *(They were angry about taxation without representation in government and their lack of freedom and rights.)*

2. **Identify Main Ideas and Details** What were the main debates at the Constitutional Convention, and what solution did the delegates make? *(Possible responses: They did not all agree about state representation and how enslaved people should count in a state's population. They made a compromise that involved shared state powers and federal powers, and slaves were counted as five enslaved African Americans equaling three free people.)*

DRAW CONCLUSIONS

Have students read the primary source excerpt from the Declaration of Independence. **ASK:** What beliefs about the origin and purpose of government did colonists hold? *(Possible response: The colonies acknowledged the need to name reasons for declaring independence. When a government destroys the rights, given by their Creator, of a people, the people should form a new government. People have a duty to throw off tyranny and secure their own rights and universal values.)*

ACTIVE OPTIONS

On Your Feet: Think, Pair, Share Ask the following question and then allow a few minutes for students to think about it: On what grounds did the colonists think they were entitled to gain their independence? Then tell students to choose partners and talk about the question for five minutes. After discussion time, invite students to share their ideas with the class.

> **NG Learning Framework: Research Details About the American Revolution**
> **ATTITUDE** Curiosity
> **SKILLS** Collaboration, Communication

Assign groups of students to learn more about the American Revolution, such as causes, key people on both sides, and major battles. Groups should create a chart or digital presentation of the information they have gathered, including photographs or illustrations. Invite groups to share their completed work with the class.

DIFFERENTIATE

ENGLISH LANGUAGE LEARNERS

Practice Pronunciation Preview with students the words *Enlightenment* and *independence*. Point out the root words and affixes to help students understand their meanings. Then say each word slowly, and have students repeat it. You may want to preview other words from the lesson that may be challenging to pronounce, such as *declaration, militias, proclamation, sovereignty, constitution,* and *revolution*. Suggest students make word cards for each word, writing definitions and pronunciation hints.

PRE-AP

Analyze the Success of the Continental Army Tell students to research women spies who helped the Continental Army and the revolutionary war effort. Instruct students to investigate one person in detail and write an essay that analyzes that person's impact on the Continental Army's successes. Invite students to post their essays on a class website or blog.

See the Chapter Planner for more strategies for differentiation.

HISTORICAL THINKING

ANSWERS

1. Americans built on the Enlightenment ideas of government being based on a contract between citizens and leaders, popular sovereignty, liberty, separation of powers, and checks and balances.

2. They had no representatives in British Parliament to vote for or against these taxes.

3. Possible response: No. Only white men who owned property could vote. Also, slavery was still practiced.

CRITICAL VIEWING Possible response: heroic; he shows the general, standing tall and fearless, courageously leading his troops in the surprise attack.

The French Revolution

Change can happen slowly—or it can explode suddenly and dramatically. Drastic developments quickly swept through France as its common people rebelled against the ruling classes during the French Revolution. This turning point would impact governments and societies throughout Europe and change the course of history.

RULE UNDER LOUIS XVI

Combined social and economic issues led French citizens to topple the monarchy during the French Revolution of 1789. Three distinct social classes, or **estates**, existed in France at the time. The First Estate consisted of the Catholic clergy, the Second Estate included the nobility, and the Third Estate contained everyone else.

The Third Estate included the bourgeoisie, which you learned is the middle class. The bourgeoisie in France was made up of highly educated and often property-owning professionals, such as doctors, lawyers, and merchants. However, the majority of the Third Estate were peasants who lived in rural farming villages.

The Third Estate had far fewer rights than the other classes did. The Catholic Church owned much of the property in France, so the church and its clergy enjoyed many special advantages. The nobles of the Second Estate benefited from privileges as well. Both the First Estate and the Second Estate were exempt from direct taxation, while the Third Estate was burdened with heavy taxes.

Just as the American colonists admired the Glorious Revolution and its English Bill of Rights, so did the overburdened French

middle class. Members of the French bourgeoisie also felt **disenfranchised**, or without rights or the ability to influence their government. They wanted their government to reflect the ideas of Montesquieu, Rousseau, and other Enlightenment thinkers by recognizing the French bourgeoisie's rights.

In the early 18th century, a period of prosperity had boosted birth rates and made France the most populous

CRITICAL VIEWING In this political cartoon from the 18th century, the First and Second Estates—personified by a clergyman and an aristocratic military officer, respectively—crush a man representing the Third Estate under a large stone that represents taxation. What conclusion can you draw about the three estates from this image?

country in Europe. But fighting and losing the French and Indian War had been expensive, and in the 1780s, bad harvests and higher taxes caused suffering for this vast population. Many people fled their farms for Paris and other cities, where they faced overcrowding and unemployment. Like the American colonists, they believed they were being mistreated by their king.

The absolute monarch **Louis XVI** ruled over his 24 million French subjects from his spectacular palace at Versailles, 12 miles outside Paris. Though wealthy and powerful, he was a poor decision maker, and he often relied on his wife and queen, **Marie Antoinette**, for advice. Many people believed that the queen was under the influence of her relatives in Austria, and she was known for her extravagant tastes. Much of the nobility and the Third Estate distrusted her. Some spread a rumor that when she was told the people of France had no bread, Marie Antoinette cruelly replied, "Let them eat cake!"

OVERTHROWING THE MONARCHY

Like Britain before the American Revolution, France had accumulated a lot of war debt. Funding the French and Indian War and supporting the American rebels had emptied the French treasury, and the common people were crushed by taxes.

In 1789, Louis and his ministers reluctantly convened an Estates-General to address their economic woes. Each of the three orders of French society sent representatives to the rarely held assembly. Third Estate delegates hoped to create a representative legislative body. However, each estate had only one vote on each issue; the First and Second Estates sided together, so none of the Third Estate's proposals were accepted. Furious, the Third Estate delegates formed their own National Assembly and pledged to hold meetings until a constitutional monarchy was formed. Recall that a constitutional monarchy is a government in which the monarch shares power with a parliament. Rather than give in to this demand, Louis XVI ordered 18,000 troops to defend his palace at Versailles. The French Revolution had begun.

The common people of Paris soon joined the fight for rights. Working-class men called *sans-culottes*— because they wore trousers instead of the lavish clothes of the rich—stormed the Bastille. The Bastille was a building in Paris that served as both a jail and armory, or place where government weapons are stored. Thomas

The Declaration of the Rights of Man and of the Citizen includes many statements of liberty.

PRIMARY SOURCE

Law is the expression of the general will. Every citizen has a right to participate personally, or through his representative, in its foundation. It must be the same for all, whether it protects or punishes. All citizens, being equal in the eyes of the law. . . .

Jefferson, then the U.S. minister to France, was in Paris at the time. He most likely noticed that commoners took a greater role in the French Revolution than the common people in America had during the American Revolution. In the former British colonies, the privileged and well educated led the rebellion. Jefferson described the storming of the Bastille in a letter: "They took all the arms, discharged the prisoners & such of the garrison as were not killed in the first moment of fury, carried the Governor & Lieutenant governor to the Grave (the place of public execution) cut off their heads, & sent them through the city in triumph to the Palais royal."

Louis XVI quickly recognized the National Assembly. It immediately declared equality before the law, eliminated special rights for nobles, and dismissed all feudal obligations. The assembly's **Declaration of the Rights of Man and of the Citizen** stated that "men are born and remain free and equal in rights" and "the natural and inalienable rights of man" are "liberty, property, security, and resistance to oppression." Government positions were open to all, and taxes were assigned more equally. Freedom of thought and religion were granted, and mandatory payments to the Catholic Church ended.

The National Assembly vowed to work with Louis XVI to establish a new constitutional monarchy. However, some 20,000 Parisians—mostly women—who distrusted the king and were also angry about the high price of bread advanced toward Versailles. This "March of the Women" forced the king and his family to relocate to Paris, where revolutionaries could better watch them. Farmers throughout France stormed noble estates, causing many aristocrats to flee the country.

Following the example of the Constitutional Convention in the United States, the National Assembly formed a Legislative Assembly to draft a new set of basic laws, which Louis XVI promptly rejected. He was captured and held prisoner in his Parisian palace. Although other European rulers attempted to come to Louis's aid and overthrow the revolution, French citizens thwarted an Austrian attack. The French monarchy was doomed.

OBJECTIVE

Explain how French commoners worked together to seize power from the upper classes.

CRITICAL THINKING SKILLS FOR LESSON 1.2

- Analyze Cause and Effect
- Identify Main Ideas and Details
- Sequence Events
- Compare and Contrast
- Make Inferences
- Form and Support Opinions
- Analyze Primary Sources
- Analyze Visuals

HISTORICAL THINKING FOR CHAPTER 21
What factors can lead to revolution?

Across the Atlantic Ocean, the French were struggling with similar issues as the former British colonists in America: lack of rights, the desire to have a voice in government, and high taxes to pay. Many French people, especially the largest class in society, thought that change was essential. Lesson 1.2 discusses the causes, course, and effects of the French Revolution.

BACKGROUND FOR THE TEACHER

Reflections on the French Revolution British parliamentarian Edmund Burke has been called "the father of conservatism," a reputation that came mostly from his denunciation of the excesses of the French Revolution in a letter he wrote to a French aristocrat, published as *Essays on the French Revolution*. In fact, Burke's politics were generally liberal: he upheld the rights of Parliament and limitations on those of the king, supported the American Revolution and the abolition of the slave trade, and spoke strongly against the corruption of the British East India Company. In the *Essays*— written in 1790 before the execution of Louis XVI, the bloodshed of the Reign of Terror, and the dictatorship of the Jacobins—Burke argued that the French had been mistaken in basing their case for liberty on abstract ideals such as "the rights of man." Instead, he explained how liberty was better protected with a constitution grounded on inherited cultural and political institutions.

Student eEdition online

Additional content for this lesson, including an image gallery, is available online.

INTRODUCE & ENGAGE

DISCUSS THE IMPORTANCE OF MODELS

Invite students to discuss relationships they have experienced or witnessed with role models. Encourage them to provide specific examples or share information about people they have read about. Tell students that in this lesson they will learn about how the United States and the American Revolution served as a model for France and the French Revolution.

TEACH

GUIDED DISCUSSION

1. **Compare and Contrast** How were the rights of the French middle class similar to those of American colonists? *(American colonists and the French middle class both were disenfranchised.)*

2. **Analyze Cause and Effect** Why was an Estates-General held, and why was it unsuccessful? *(Possible response: The common people had to pay a lot of taxes because of France's war debts, so it convened to address economic concerns. The Third Estate wanted a constitutional monarchy, but because it was outvoted by the other two estates, it was forced to take action on its own.)*

ANALYZE PRIMARY SOURCES

Have students read the primary source excerpt. **ASK:** How are the ideas expressed in this excerpt similar to and different from those expressed in the excerpt you read from the Declaration of Independence in Lesson 1.1? *(Possible response: Both discuss equality and that the power of the government should come from the people. However, in the Declaration of the Rights of Man and of the Citizen, it specifically says that citizens can participate in government personally or through a representative. The Declaration of Independence is not specific about the citizens' participation in government.)* Why do you think there are some distinctions in the ideas expressed between the two declarations? *(Possible response: Americans were creating a new country and a new government, while the French were changing their existing government. The French probably had a more specific vision of what that new type of government and citizen involvement would be.)*

DIFFERENTIATE

STRIVING READERS

Summarizing Using a Concept Cluster Help pairs summarize the lesson by guiding them to create a Concept Cluster with the lesson title in the center oval and the section headings in the smaller ones. As students read each section, tell them to record key facts and ideas on the spokes. After students complete the Concept Cluster, invite volunteers to summarize the lesson and explain what caused the French Revolution and its outcome.

PRE-AP

Write a Declaration Have students write a declaration that embodies the ideas expressed in the Declaration of Independence, Declaration of the Rights of Man and of the Citizen, and *The Declaration of the Rights of Women*. Students should share specific excerpts from all three documents, as well as make clear which ideas they think best express the goals of the French Revolution. Invite students to share their declarations with the class.

See the Chapter Planner for more strategies for differentiation.

French artist Jean-Pierre Houël's *Storming of the Bastille* captures the scene after commoners attacked the Paris prison on July 14, 1789.

Fearful of losing control, Robespierre sacrificed liberty in favor of **despotism**, the oppressive rule by a leader with absolute power. His Committee of Public Safety began a Reign of Terror in which more than 17,000 people were executed. More than 300,000 citizens were arrested. Some were imprisoned without trial and tortured.

The symbol of the French Revolution became the **guillotine** (gee-yuh-TEEN), a machine with a sharp blade designed to behead people. Joseph Guillotin, a doctor, devised the guillotine as a rational Enlightenment device that would make public executions less violent. Ironically, his invention was identified with the cruelty and despotism of revolutionary terror.

By July 1794, the tables had turned. Robespierre and many other Jacobins lost their own heads to the sharp blade of the guillotine. One journalist wrote, "the revolution was devouring its own children." The National Assembly reasserted its power and created a new constitution with a limited electorate and a separation of powers. Although France appeared to be on its way to a stable representative government, the nation would face years of upheaval.

The American Revolution and the French Revolution differed in several ways. Americans fought to break away from a governing country, while the French wanted internal change. Many historians believe the Americans had a clearer goal—the colonists wanted to establish a new nation. The French, instead, wanted to create a society of perfect equality. However, both revolutions inspired other people, including French colonists in what would become Haiti, to fight for liberty and independence.

The blade on this 18th century guillotine reads *Armées de la République*, which translates to "Armies of the Republic."

REVOLUTIONARY DESPOTISM

The National Assembly dissolved itself in 1791 in favor of a National Convention. This new legislative body began writing a republican constitution and ordered the execution of Louis XVI and Marie Antoinette in January 1793. The French Constitution of 1793 granted all male citizens full voting rights, even non-property-owners. In this way, it was more radical than the U.S. Constitution.

Most French revolutionaries, similar to American rebels, only recognized the rights of free men, not of women or enslaved people. However, in her *Declaration of the Rights of Women*, author Olympe de Gouges argued, "The exercise of the natural rights of women has only been limited by the perpetual tyranny that man opposes to them; these limits should be reformed by the laws of nature and reason." Some revolutionaries decreed

that enslaved people should be freed, raising hopes for freedom and equality among those held in bondage in the French Caribbean.

The **Jacobins**, a radical faction, took control of the government, ushering in a time of extreme violence. Their leader was former lawyer **Maximilien Robespierre**, who won followers because of his support of liberty and equal rights and his determination to defend France from outside attack.

Robespierre wanted to transform society into a "Republic of Virtue" in which corruption and inequality would be eliminated—through intense fear, if necessary. When the Jacobins confiscated land, however, many of the bourgeoisie resisted. And when Jacobins attacked the power and property of the Catholic Church, many conservative peasants in rural France opposed them.

HISTORICAL THINKING

1. **READING CHECK** How did the Third Estate differ from the First and Second Estates before the French Revolution?

2. **ANALYZE CAUSE AND EFFECT** What were three main causes of the French Revolution?

3. **IDENTIFY MAIN IDEAS AND DETAILS** What political reforms did the National Assembly establish in France?

4. **SEQUENCE EVENTS** In what order did the following actions take place: the meeting of the National Convention, the establishment of the National Assembly, and the adoption of a constitution?

BACKGROUND FOR THE TEACHER

The Radical Calendar When Jacobin Maximilien Robespierre rose to power, he and his supporters made great efforts to radicalize France, not just in thought but in many facets of life. Their motto could have been "out with the old and in with the new," and they wanted to secularize France, too. Starting in 1793, churches all throughout France were closed because the Jacobins believed that religion was detrimental and passé. Then the Jacobins unveiled a new calendar on October 5, to replace France's Gregorian (named for Pope Gregory XIII) calendar that had been used since the late 1500s. The revolutionary calendar effectively de-Christianized French society. Sundays were removed from the calendar. Months were renamed and based on natural and scientific terms. For example, some of their names in English were *heat, fruits, seedtime, frost,* and *meadow.* Days of the week were also renamed based on the same guidelines. Some of these renamed days included names of animals, plants, and flowers. All Christian festivals were removed from the calendar, and the first year of the calendar, year 1, marked the start of the Revolution in September 1792. Five Republican revolutionary days were added to the calendar. But like the Jacobins, their French republican calendar was short-lived. It was eventually replaced on January 1, 1806, by Napoleon I, with the Gregorian calendar.

TEACH

GUIDED DISCUSSION

3. **Make Inferences** Why do you think the Jacobins and Robespierre were unsuccessful in their attempt to maintain power? *(Possible response: They were too extreme and relied on terror to achieve their means.)*

4. **Form and Support Opinions** Why do you think that France still faced upheaval after a new constitution was written? *(Possible response: because France had just experienced a lot of change and it would take a while to gain support from the people and the government)*

ANALYZE VISUALS

Have students examine the details in the painting of the gathering of the National Assembly (available in the Student eEdition). **ASK:** Why do you think the oath that the National Assembly members took is called the "Tennis Court Oath"? Support your response with specific details from the painting. *(Possible response: It appears that the members are in an indoor court. There are stands on either side of the "court" and what appears to be a stage at the back of the court.)* Why do you think the members of the National Assembly are in such an unusual setting to take an important oath? *(Possible response: They were not welcome where the French government usually met because they were rebelling against the existing government, so they needed to find a space large enough to hold everyone.)*

ACTIVE OPTIONS

On Your Feet: Roundtable Arrange students in groups of three. Assign one student in each group the role of someone from the First Estate, Second Estate, and Third Estate. Instruct students to discuss the rights that they have from the three different perspectives, as well as the taxes they pay. Then ask students to answer the following question from their assigned perspective: Should changes be made to the current political, economic, and social systems in France or should they remain the same? Explain. Encourage students to conduct their own research and draw on information from the lesson to help them answer the question.

> **NG Learning Framework: Portray the Present-Day Middle Class**
> **SKILL** Communication
> **KNOWLEDGE** Our Human Story

Guide a discussion about the details that reinforce the burden that the Third Estate (middle class) carries in the cartoon that accompanies the lesson, such as the heavy stone, a clergyman, and an aristocratic military officer. Then direct pairs to create a piece of art or literary work, such as a painting, song, mural, or short story, that depicts the role of the middle class in present-day society. Create a space for students to display their art and provide an opportunity for students to perform or read their written work. Ask students to comment on how these pieces demonstrate the ways that the burden of the middle class is the same or if it has changed.

HISTORICAL THINKING

ANSWERS

1. The Third Estate did not have the social and political privileges of the other two classes and were required to pay the bulk of the taxes that supported the government.

2. Possible response: I believe that the French Revolution was mainly caused by the influence of Enlightenment ideas, the inequality between the French social classes that led the Third Estate to have fewer rights, and France's economic state.

3. Possible response: The National Assembly declared equality before the law, eliminated special rights for nobles, dismissed all feudal obligations, opened government positions to everyone, assigned taxes more equally, granted freedom of thought and religion, ended mandatory payments to the Catholic Church, and drafted a new set of basic laws.

4. Sequence of events: the establishment of the National Assembly, the adoption of a constitution, and the meeting of the National Convention

CRITICAL VIEWING Possible response: The three estates were not equal, and the Third Estate carried much of the burden of the other two estates.

Haiti's Revolution

For people trapped in slavery, a better life seemed impossible. However, on a French island in the Caribbean, enslaved people took action to make their dreams of liberty come true.

UPRISING IN SAINT-DOMINGUE

The colony of Saint-Domingue, which occupied the western half of the island of Hispaniola in the Caribbean Sea, was France's richest overseas possession, or territory controlled by outsiders. Tending to vast sugarcane fields, half a million enslaved Africans toiled on the colony's plantations under harsh conditions.

News of the 1789 French uprising sparked hints of revolution in Saint-Domingue. The first to call for more rights were the *gens de couleur*, free men and women of mixed race. These literate artisans and farmers were slaveholders and had some wealth. Gens de couleur sought the same rights as the white plantation owners, and by 1791 civil war broke out between the two groups.

When he was growing up, African-American artist Jacob Lawrence did not see any black heroes in textbooks. So he decided to paint some. As a young man, Lawrence created a series of 41 panels about the Haitian Revolution, which included the famous rebel general Toussaint L'Ouverture. Decades later, in the 1990s, Lawrence revisited these images. *L'Ouverture (The Opener)* epitomizes Lawrence's distinctive style.

Neither faction wanted to end slavery, but their conflict led to a large slave uprising led by a man who was called Boukman because he could read. He was a priest in the *voudon* religion, which combined West African and Roman Catholic rituals and beliefs, and he was able to summon thousands of slaves to revolt in the summer of 1791. Like the French peasants who burned the manors of aristocratic landholders, Boukman's slave army attacked the planters' estates. The **insurgents**, or rebel fighters, marched on the city of Le Cap and slaughtered many white planters and gens de couleur until planter forces captured and executed Boukman.

TOUSSAINT L'OUVERTURE AND INDEPENDENCE

In 1792, the French government sent an army to restore order, but a new Saint-Domingue commander emerged. Because he was enslaved, we know little about his family or childhood, but we do know that he received a French education during his time in a slaveholder's house. The name this man is remembered by, **Toussaint L'Ouverture** (TOO-san LOO-vuhr-tyur), refers to the "opening" he made in the enemy lines. His military, political, intellectual, and diplomatic strengths would help free the colony from the French.

Toussaint knew how to organize slaves and simultaneously form alliances with whites, gens de couleur, and foreign forces. By 1801, his army controlled most of the island. He supported a new constitution that granted rights to all and named Toussaint governor-general for life.

By this time, France's government had shifted from a republic to a dictatorship. A French military unit was dispatched to crush Toussaint's army. Toussaint fought off the threat for several months and then agreed to meet with French officers to make a peace treaty. The officers betrayed him and sent him to prison in France, where he died after harsh treatment.

After Toussaint's death, the French lost the war—and disease played an important role. People born in Saint-Domingue had built up resistance to malaria and yellow fever, tropical diseases spread by mosquitoes. Soldiers fresh from France, however, were vulnerable to these illnesses. Toussaint had been aware of this,

so he often forced the French to camp in swampy ground, where many soldiers became sick and died. To avoid additional casualties, the French removed their forces from the island. Saint-Domingue became the independent nation of Haiti in 1804.

Slaveholders in the United States were terrified of the Haitian example of the enslaved rising up to overthrow the people who had forced them into bondage. So the United States placed a trade embargo on the new country. And even though Haiti officially established itself as a black-ruled republic in 1820, the United States did not recognize Haitian independence for years to come. Britain and France also refused to accept Haiti as a free nation.

Although the rebels who spearheaded the Haitian Revolution found inspiration in the American and the French revolutions, the Haitian Revolution differed from the other two. The Haitian Revolution expressly addressed the unfairness of the colonial social hierarchy based on race. And only the Haitians immediately abolished slavery, granting liberty and basic human rights to people of all races. After their victory in 1783, Americans did not grant rights to people of African heritage, Native Americans, or women. Likewise, the French did not offer suffrage to women. However, all three revolutions resulted in a written constitution and the establishment of a republic—though France's republic would not last long.

> The following excerpts are from the 1801 Haitian constitution endorsed by Toussaint L'Ouverture.
>
> **PRIMARY SOURCE**
>
> **Art. 3**—There can be no slaves on this territory; servitude has been forever abolished. All men are born, live, and die there free and French.
>
> **Art. 4**—All men can work at all forms of employment, whatever their color.
>
> **Art. 5**—No other distinctions exist than those of virtues and talents, nor any other superiority than that granted by the law in the exercise of a public charge. The law is the same for all, whether it punishes or protects.

HISTORICAL THINKING

1. **READING CHECK** Why is Toussaint L'Ouverture considered a hero to the people of Haiti?

2. **DRAW CONCLUSIONS** Why do you think the United States failed to recognize Haiti's independence?

3. **COMPARE AND CONTRAST** Which revolution—American, French, or Haitian—had the greatest impact on its society? Explain your response.

PLAN: 2-PAGE LESSON

OBJECTIVE

Explain how enslaved people in Saint-Domingue rebelled against their bondage and won freedom as the new independent nation of Haiti.

CRITICAL THINKING SKILLS FOR LESSON 1.3

- Draw Conclusions
- Compare and Contrast
- Analyze Cause and Effect
- Form and Support Opinions
- Interpret Charts

HISTORICAL THINKING FOR CHAPTER 21

What factors can lead to revolution?

Subjected to brutal treatment and inequality under French colonialism, enslaved Africans in Saint-Domingue led an uprising, and *gens de couleur* and whites started a civil war. Lesson 1.3 discusses the causes and effects of the Haitian Revolution and Haitian independence.

Student eEdition online

Additional content for this lesson, including a chart, is available online.

BACKGROUND FOR THE TEACHER

The Role of Disease in Biological Warfare Even though diseases decimated much of the native populations of Central America and South America during the European Age of Exploration, many native peoples had built up resistance to such diseases by the time that revolutions started to break out in the Americas. Toussaint L'Ouverture and other rebels lured European troops into swampy areas knowing how effective mosquito-borne diseases such as yellow fever were in defeating the enemy. This technique became known as "guerilla warfare." Just like the French troops that Napoleon sent in to Saint-Domingue to squash the rebellion had little resistance to malaria and yellow fever, so did the British. In 1793, Britain tried to invade Saint-Domingue. More than 50 percent of the 20,000 British soldiers who went into Saint-Domingue died of yellow fever. The British were forced to withdraw by 1798. But Napoleon learned from this experience and used it to his advantage in the late 1700s during the Napoleonic Wars. During his invasion of Mantua, Italy, Napoleon ordered his army to flood the surrounding plains. The conditions were perfect for cultivating yellow fever. His plan worked. He took the city and conquered nearly all of northern Italy.

INTRODUCE & ENGAGE

DISCUSS SOCIAL HIERARCHY

Invite students to discuss the role of social hierarchy in society, including class divisions, equality, privileges, and rights. Make a list on the board as students share their ideas. Discuss examples of social hierarchy today and how it affects society. Tell students that in this lesson they will learn about how the social hierarchy created under French colonialism led to a revolution in Haiti.

TEACH

GUIDED DISCUSSION

1. **Analyze Cause and Effect** What effect do you think being literate had on the influence of the gens de couleur? *(Possible response: They probably understood rights better than if they had been illiterate. They would also have been able to learn new ideas from reading and writing, which gave them an advantage.)*

2. **Form and Support Opinions** If Haiti had not achieved independence, do you think that slavery would have been abolished earlier in the British Empire? Explain your response. *(Possible response: Yes, I think it would have been abolished earlier. The British were probably fearful that if they freed the slaves an independence movement would follow.)*

INTERPRET CHARTS

Have students look at the chart (available in the Student eEdition).
ASK: Which revolution do you think had the most positive and negative consequences? Explain. *(Possible response: Positive: Haiti because it won independence and ended slavery; Negative: France, because even though some people gained rights, there was still turmoil and no definitive resolution)* Do you think the country's goals impacted the consequences? Explain. *(Possible response: Yes, France had very lofty goals that were probably unrealistic, which led to negative consequences.)*

ACTIVE OPTIONS

On Your Feet: Think Like a Historian Extend the lesson by posing the following question to small groups: Why was Haiti's role so important in this period of revolutions, and how was it unique? Remind students that historians examine multiple causes and effects, as well as consider multiple points of view. Allow time for groups to share their different answers with the class before engaging in a class discussion.

> **NG Learning Framework: Research the Conditions Needed to Contract Yellow Fever**
> ATTITUDE Curiosity
> KNOWLEDGE Our Living Planet

Share the Background for the Teacher. Then invite small groups to research the conditions needed to contract and spread the yellow fever virus. Ask groups to find out why it is so contagious and dangerous to a population, when a vaccine was discovered, where there have been significant outbreaks of the disease today, and what steps are being taken to prevent its spread. Groups should present their findings.

DIFFERENTIATE

INCLUSION

Determine Chronology Pair students with disabilities with students without disabilities to determine the chronology of events presented in the lesson. Suggest that they scan the lesson and write the dates mentioned in chronological order in a Sequence Chain. Then ask students to read the lesson, pausing to jot down notes in their Sequence Chain about significant events that happened on various dates. When they have finished, instruct students to take turns reading their notes aloud, using transitions such as *and*, *then*, or *after that* to indicate connections between events.

PRE-AP

Create an Online Profile Tell students to write a profile about Jacob Lawrence, using multiple print and digital sources. They should include a brief biography and an overview of his art, including how and why he made it and where, if applicable, the art has been curated. Ask students to share their profiles.

See the Chapter Planner for more strategies for differentiation.

HISTORICAL THINKING

ANSWERS

1. He defied all odds to lead the people toward independence. He was largely responsible for the establishment of the first American republic controlled by former enslaved Africans.

2. Possible response: It feared that it would inspire slave revolts in their own country, strengthen calls for abolition of slavery, and negatively affect the U.S. economy.

3. Possible response: The Haitian Revolution, because it completely changed Haiti's class system by granting equal rights to all. It was a true revolution because it caused a break from the past society.

Napoleon Bonaparte

Certain individuals make extremely powerful impacts—some positive, some negative—on the world. For better or worse, the French leader Napoleon Bonaparte affected Europe so strongly that the era of his rise, rule, and collapse is sometimes called the "Age of Napoleon."

CRITICAL VIEWING *The Coronation of Napoleon* by French artist Jacques-Louis David shows the newly crowned emperor placing a crown on the head of his wife, Josephine, in front of a large crowd. The 1807 canvas is more than 20 feet high and 32 feet wide. What does the portrayal of the ceremony and the size of the painting tell you about how Napoleon viewed himself?

590 CHAPTER 21

THE RISE OF A NEW LEADER

The French Revolution quickly moved through three distinct stages. As you learned, the focus at first centered around establishing a constitutional or limited monarchy. Once that proved impossible, revolutionary leaders sought to fundamentally transform French society and turned to democratic despotism under the Jacobins. Finally, amid the turmoil, an emerging military genius would create a French empire.

Despite efforts by the National Convention, France remained sharply divided from 1795 to 1799. The new republic's executive branch, the Directory, faced conspiracies by both Jacobins and monarchists. Meanwhile, French armies collected victories under the young general **Napoleon Bonaparte**, whose troops captured northern Italy from the Austrians in 1796. Then, in 1799, two members of the Directory plotted with Napoleon to launch a successful coup, or sudden overthrow, of the French government.

Like George Washington, Napoleon looked to ancient Rome for inspiration. However, while Washington admired the Roman Republic, Napoleon followed Rome's imperial example and transformed France's republic into his empire. Most French people were proud of Napoleon's military successes and eager to emerge from the turmoil of the revolution, so they continually voted to approve Napoleon's growing power. In addition, Napoleon encouraged his political opposition to join his administration. He also restored papal authority to gain the support of Catholics, especially in the countryside. As a result, he faced little opposition when he crowned himself Emperor Napoleon I in 1804.

Napoleon appeared to be the enlightened despot Enlightenment philosophes had hoped for. (Recall that an enlightened despot was an absolute ruler who applied certain Enlightenment ideas.) To many French citizens, Napoleon embodied the **ideology**, or basic beliefs, of the French Revolution. His domestic policies brought order to France and seemed to have the interest of its people at heart. Napoleon started the Bank of France to stabilize the economy and enforced the more rational use of the metric system of weights and measures to improve trade.

Most importantly, the new emperor created the **Napoleonic Code**, a clear and organized system of laws that recognized the legal equality of all French citizens. Napoleon made sure that these laws addressed Enlightenment ideals such as personal liberty, freedom of religion for Protestants and Jews, and the rule of law. Still, the growth of executive power under Napoleon lessened the separation of powers emphasized

earlier by Montesquieu. And the Napoleonic Code reduced rights for women and reestablished slavery in French colonies.

Napoleon proved to be a master of **propaganda**, information used by a government to make people think or act in a particular way. He commissioned artwork to show himself as an infallible leader in the spirit of the Roman Empire and issued collectible medals touting his fame. He also ordered that newspapers must publish articles slanted in his favor. All such propaganda efforts were aimed at gaining the approval of the public.

FRENCH NATIONALISM

Determined to expand his empire, Napoleon led military campaigns throughout Europe. Many historians point out that these campaigns provided the French people with a national identity. A sense of **nationalism**—or belief that individuals are bound together by ties of language, culture, history, and often religion—developed in France. Previously, French nobles had refused to believe that they had any affiliation to the lower ranks of society. French peasants and commoners felt a connection to their local community but not the French state in Paris. As soldiers fighting for France, common people began to see themselves as citizens of a nation rather than merely subjects of a king. Napoleon made the most of France's growing nationalism and promised French citizens glory, if not representative government.

Bringing together the people of France enabled Napoleon to create a political structure known as a **nation-state**. A nation-state is a state mostly made up of people of one nationality, sharing common traits

In his own account of the 1799 coup, Napoleon glosses over his role as an instigator of the plot to abolish the French constitution and legislature.

PRIMARY SOURCE

The Council of Elders summoned me; I answered its appeal. A plan of general restoration had been devised by men whom the nation had been accustomed to regard as the defenders of liberty, equality, and property; this plan required an examination, calm, free, exempt from all influence and all fear. Accordingly, the Council of Elders resolved upon the removal of the Legislative Body to Saint-Cloud; it gave me the responsibility of disposing the force necessary for its independence. I believed it my duty to my fellow citizens, to the soldiers perishing in our armies, to the national glory acquired at the cost of their blood, to accept the command.

—from Napoleon's account of his role in the coup, 1799

Political Revolution 591

PLAN: 4-PAGE LESSON

OBJECTIVE

Explain how Napoleon Bonaparte restored stability to post-revolutionary France, initiated reforms, and attempted to conquer Europe before his eventual and total defeat.

CRITICAL THINKING SKILLS FOR LESSON 2.1

- Draw Conclusions
- Form and Support Opinions
- Interpret Maps
- Explain
- Make Inferences
- Sequence Events
- Analyze Primary Sources

HISTORICAL THINKING FOR CHAPTER 21

What factors can lead to revolution?

Political, economic, military, and religious conflicts can lead to revolutions. However, after the chaos of revolution, order must be restored. Lesson 2.1 discusses Napoleon's reign in France and his establishment of a French empire following the French Revolution.

BACKGROUND FOR THE TEACHER

Napoleon's Early Years Napoleon Bonaparte was born on August 15, 1769, on the island of Corsica, which had been recently conquered by France. While he and many of Corsica's citizens detested the French, his father was one who submitted to French rule and adopted French styles. His mother was harsh and punished Napoleon and his seven siblings to teach them sacrifice and discipline. At nine years old, Napoleon was sent to study in private academies in France. After being bullied for being a foreigner, Napoleon felt closer to his Corsican heritage. Once he graduated at age 16, Napoleon began training with the French army. At 23, he took a leave of absence and led a force in Corsica, fighting to keep the island as part of revolutionary France. His opponent, Paoli, wanted Corsica to be independent. Paoli won this battle and forced Napoleon and his family to flee. Napoleon returned to the French army as a major and had his first victory in battle against the English. This victory sparked a desire for greater advancement and set the stage for his military career.

Student eEdition online

Additional content for this lesson, including an illustration, is available online.

INTRODUCE & ENGAGE

BRAINSTORM STRONG LEADERS

Ask students to identify people in history who are considered strong leaders. Then work together to brainstorm a list of characteristics that strong leaders possess. Tell students that in this lesson they will learn about Napoleon Bonaparte and his role as a strong leader of France.

TEACH

GUIDED DISCUSSION

1. **Explain** How did Napoleon gain the support to crown himself Emperor Napoleon I? *(Possible response: He gained the support of the majority of the French people, who were eager to move past the chaos of the revolution, through his military successes, political compromises, and restoration of papal authority.)*

2. **Form and Support Opinions** Could nationalism be a negative concept? Explain. *(Possible responses: Yes, as people cling to the identity of their nation, they may reject other nationalities, perhaps believing the superiority of their own. No, nationalism provides a sense of belonging that is a positive thing for people.)*

ANALYZE PRIMARY SOURCES

Instruct students to read the primary source. **ASK:** Whose idea was the coup? *(the Council of Elders)* What was the plan? *(to remove the legislative body)* What does Napoleon say his reason was for accepting the request to lead the coup? *(He says he felt it was his duty to his citizens, soldiers, and the glory of his nation.)*

DIFFERENTIATE

STRIVING READERS

Use Reciprocal Teaching Tell partners to take turns reading each paragraph of the lesson aloud. At the end of the paragraph, the reading student should ask the listening student questions about the paragraph. Students may ask their partners to state the main idea, identify important details that support the main idea, or summarize the paragraph in their own words. Then tell students to work together to answer the Historical Thinking questions.

GIFTED & TALENTED

Perform a Play Encourage a group of students to learn more about the reign of Napoleon. Then challenge the group to present what they have learned about a specific event—such as a battle, Napoleon's coronation, his exile, his death—to the class in a short play. Provide the following guidelines for the group:

- Assign each member of the group a role, including that of narrator.
- Compose dialogue that moves the action along.
- Convey the personalities of Napoleon and the other characters.
- Use props, if possible, to help the audience understand the scene.
- Have the narrator or a character summarize the historical significance of the scene.

See the Chapter Planner for more strategies for differentiation.

such as language and heritage. Earlier empires such as the Roman, Ming, Mughal, and Habsburg empires always included diverse peoples. However, the unity often ended when the empire fell. In the nation-states that formed in modern times, people began to see themselves as "Dutch," "French," or "English" and maintained this identity through changes in leadership. Today, a sense of nationalism and of belonging to a nation is common around the world.

BUILDING AN EMPIRE

Napoleon's military seemed unstoppable in what became known as the Napoleonic Wars. His troops swept through Italy and Spain, which also created conditions for independence in Latin America, which you will read about later. Napoleon's forces claimed control over the Netherlands, Switzerland, Poland, and the western half of Germany, and inflicted losses on the Austrians and the Prussians. However, Napoleon experienced challenges and losses as well. In 1798, his defeat in a disastrous expedition into Egypt dashed his plans to conquer lands in Africa. In 1803, Napoleon sold a huge parcel of North American land to the United States in an exchange known as the Louisiana Purchase, quite possibly to raise money for his military efforts.

The French invasions spread nationalism through Europe. At first, many Germans hoped the French would bring the Enlightenment principles of freedom and equality. But they were treated as conquered people with limited rights. Resistance to France's domination encouraged a sense of German nationalism. Likewise, people in the diverse kingdoms of the Italian Peninsula developed a common "Italian" identity to rally against French invaders.

NAPOLEON'S DOWNFALL

In the end, Napoleon's ambition caused his demise. In 1812, he mounted an attack on Russia. Napoleon and his troops trekked thousands of miles to reach Moscow only to find it abandoned and almost burned to the ground. Forced to retreat during the harsh Russian winter, the French suffered enormous losses. Fewer than 100,000 of the 700,000 troops returned home.

Napoleonic Europe in 1810

Anti-French forces across Europe banded together to form a coalition. The united front invaded France, made Napoleon abdicate, and restored the monarchy by placing Louis XVIII on the French throne. After being banished to the Mediterranean island of Elba, Napoleon escaped. He rebuilt his army and made a dramatic return to Paris before he was overpowered by British and Prussian forces at the Battle of Waterloo in 1815. After Napoleon's final loss, France finally became a constitutional monarchy.

Napoleon died in exile, but his global impact was substantial. His grouping of small western German states into the Confederation of the Rhine paved the way for German nationalism. Eventually, German-speaking people formed a centralized German nation-state. The people of the Italian Peninsula would also unite. Across the ocean, the United States expanded to twice its size as a result of the Louisiana Purchase. In contrast, Ottoman power was reduced when Ottoman armies lost control of the Nile to an ambitious new Egyptian dynasty.

The return of Louis XVIII to the French throne was a major sign that Europe's enthusiasm for revolutions had run out of steam as European elites worked to suppress reform. A series of meetings called the **Congress of Vienna** began in 1814 and restored the balance of power among Britain, France, Austria, Prussia, and

In 1806, Napoleon commissioned a monument to be built in Paris to celebrate French victories during the Napoleonic Wars. The Arc de Triomphe de l'Étoile (Triumphal Arch of the Star)—known more simply as the Arc de Triomphe—is one of the most famous symbols of France.

Russia. The main goal of the aristocratic members of the congress was to return to a time when the upper class wielded power and to make sure that monarchies would continue as forms of government. The former French empire was taken apart and the monarchical government restored. However, no territory was taken from France itself, and the nation remained one of the great powers of Europe along with Britain, Austria, Prussia, and Russia.

The Concert of Europe was an informal agreement among the major European monarchies aimed at safeguarding peace in Europe. It was also meant to preserve the European **status quo**, or existing condition, and ensure that all the major monarchies would support and defend any monarchy threatened with upheaval. Europe enjoyed relative peace for almost a century. But demands for nationalism continued to grow stronger and stronger.

HISTORICAL THINKING

1. **READING CHECK** How did Napoleon rise to power, and what was his role in French government?

2. **DRAW CONCLUSIONS** How did growing nationalism in France help Napoleon achieve his goals?

3. **FORM AND SUPPORT OPINIONS** Do you think a European ruler today could gain the power Napoleon had? Use evidence in the text to support your answer.

4. **INTERPRET MAPS** What was the status of the cities of Bremen, Zurich, Vienna, and London during the time period shown on the map?

BACKGROUND FOR THE TEACHER

Napoleon's Rise, Fall, and Legacy As commander in chief, Napoleon transformed the Army of Italy from a group of malnourished, weak men into powerful soldiers. He believed that every man should have the same chance to rise based on his ability. However, Napoleon's leadership style turned more into a dictatorship, as he employed spies who ensured people could not express themselves in ways he would not want. He also oversaw the production of plays and ended playwrights' careers if he disapproved of their work. He controlled the press in Paris by limiting the number of newspapers from more than 60 to only 4. In Italy, Napoleon reported from the battlefield information that would increase his glory and mask the ruthlessness of his plunders. However, his tolerance, support of Jews, respect for human life, and Enlightenment ideals made him far from a Hitler- or Stalin-type dictator.

Napoleon's second exile was on a rocky island in the South Atlantic Ocean called St. Helena. Unlike his first exile on the island of Elba, Napoleon was a true prisoner. He was allowed to bring a small group of loyal followers with him, but he was guarded by 2,000 soldiers and two ships, continuously circling the island. Unable to roam freely on the island without an English soldier, Napoleon shut himself in and focused on reading French books and newspapers and writing his memoirs. His lack of activity led to a decline in his health. A stomach ailment left him bedridden for years, and he died on May 5, 1821. It wasn't until 1840 that Napoleon's legacy was realized, his remains were brought back to France, and a proper funeral was held. His administrative, judicial, financial, educational, and military reforms made a lasting impact on France and the rest of the world.

TEACH

GUIDED DISCUSSION

3. **Make Inferences** How do you think French invasions spread nationalism throughout Europe? *(Possible response: As countries were invaded by France, which did not bring the enlightenment it promised, a sense of nationalism likely grew in each country whose people likely felt that they needed to band together to resist French influence.)*

4. **Sequence Events** What was the sequence of the following events: Napoleon lost the Battle of Waterloo; Louis XVIII took the throne; Napoleon led his troops to Russia; the Congress of Vienna began; Napoleon returned from Russia with a fraction of his troops? *(Napoleon led his troops to Russia; Napoleon returned from Russia with a fraction of his troops; Louis XVIII took the throne; the Congress of Vienna began; Napoleon lost the Battle of Waterloo)*

INTERPRET MAPS

Direct students' attention to the map. **ASK:** What does the map show about Napoleon's empire and its relationship with other regions? *(Possible response: In 1810, far more territory was either part of the empire or allied with it than at war with it.)* What is a common feature of all parts of the French Empire? *(All parts of the French Empire have sea borders.)* How might the map look during a different year? *(Possible responses: In 1798, the map would show Cairo in yellow. In 1815, the map would show Prussia in yellow.)*

ACTIVE OPTIONS

On Your Feet: Evaluate the Napoleonic Code Ask a volunteer to find a copy of the Napoleonic Code online. Organize students into groups and ask each group to choose a section of the code that interests them. Then instruct the groups to create a simplified version of that section of the code. Invite groups to share their summaries with the class. Evaluate as a class whether the provisions of the code are relevant today.

> **NG Learning Framework: Napoleonic Wars Time Line**
> **ATTITUDE** Empowerment
> **SKILLS** Communication, Collaboration

Instruct pairs to conduct online research to learn more about the Napoleonic Wars. Encourage each pair to focus on a different key battle—including the Battle of the Pyramids and the Battle of Waterloo, mentioned in the lesson. Then tell each pair to summarize the battle and its significance in history and add their summary along with a visual to a time line either posted in the classroom or online. Direct students to share their summaries and visuals in chronological order.

HISTORICAL THINKING

ANSWERS

1. Napoleon rose through the ranks of the French army to become a general. He then took part in a coup d'état, after which he became a despotic leader who ruled with a firm hand. He waged battle to enlarge the French Empire, brought order to France, established a code of law, and encouraged France's people to develop a spirit of nationalism.

2. Possible response: Growing French Nationalism caused French citizens to be willing to fight in the Napoleonic Wars, follow a despot determined to bring France glory, and allow Napoleon to use despotic methods to bring order to the empire.

3. Answers will vary. Most students will likely say that that a modern European leader could not gain the power that Napoleon had. They might cite such reasons as the relative balance of power among nations in Europe, the established nationalism of countries, the number of independent nations, the emphasis on representative government in Europe, and the ongoing cooperation among European nations.

4. Bremen was part of the French Empire, Zurich was located in one of France's dependent states, Vienna was allied with France, and London was free of French control.

CRITICAL VIEWING Answers will vary. Possible response: The portrayal of the ceremony as a magnificent spectacle and the massive size of the painting show that Napoleon viewed himself with grandeur.

2.2 Portraits of Power

During the 18th and 19th centuries, political leaders in the Americas and in Europe commissioned paintings of themselves to project images of power. The portraits were meant to inform people not only of the leaders' power but also of the type of power with which they were associated.

President George Washington of the United States and Emperor Napoleon Bonaparte of France were both aware of classical Greek and Roman models that signified power. Their respective portraitists Gilbert Stuart and Jean-Auguste-Dominique Ingres knew about these examples as well. Washington identified himself with the democratic tradition of Athens and the republican period of Rome. In contrast, Napoleon emphasized the imperial Roman tradition.

No portrait of Toussaint L'Ouverture was created during his lifetime. Many portraits made after his death exaggerated Toussaint's physical features. In 1877, Haitian artist Louis Rigaud used written eyewitness descriptions to present a realistic approximation of the revolutionary's appearance. Rigaud wanted viewers to think of Toussaint as a leader who adhered to the democratic tradition.

This marble statue—*Augustus of Prima Porta*—shows an idealized image of the Roman emperor Augustus. Recall that Augustus ended the Roman Republic but brought peace to the Roman Empire. Here, the sculptor portrays Augustus as a strong young military leader addressing his troops.

ARTIFACT ONE

Primary Source: Painting
George Washington by Gilbert Stuart, 1796

CONSTRUCTED RESPONSE Why do you think Stuart included the inkstand on the table and the books below it in Washington's portrait?

The stormy sky in the background might illustrate the difficult times that Washington and his comrades weathered, while the rainbow might symbolize their ultimate victory.

Washington wears no sign of military rank, holds a sheathed sword that points down, and offers his open hand. The impression is one of a man who seeks peace.

ARTIFACT TWO

Primary Source: Painting
Napoleon on His Imperial Throne by Jean-Auguste-Dominique Ingres, 1806

CONSTRUCTED RESPONSE Why do you think Ingres shows Napoleon wearing a crown?

Napoleon holds a scepter topped by a figure of Charlemagne, the early medieval emperor who ruled over most of Europe.

Unlike Washington's open right hand, Napoleon's right fist is clenched high on his scepter, adding to the contrast between the French emperor and Washington.

ARTIFACT THREE

Primary Source: Painting
Toussaint L'Ouverture by Louis Rigaud, 1877

CONSTRUCTED RESPONSE
Why do you think Rigaud chose a simple background, without much adornment?

The portrait shows Toussaint in uniform because he is most remembered as a military leader. He was killed before he could rule Haiti in peacetime.

Rigaud references written and visual descriptions that emphasize Toussaint's good posture, determined expression, and care in dress.

SYNTHESIZE & WRITE

1. **REVIEW** Review what you have read and observed about revolutionary leaders and their portraits.

2. **RECALL** On your own paper, list two details you observed by looking at each portrait.

3. **CONSTRUCT** Construct a topic sentence that answers this question: How are the three portraits similar to and different from one another?

4. **WRITE** Using evidence from this chapter and the portraits, write an informative paragraph that supports your topic sentence in Step 3.

PLAN: 2-PAGE LESSON

OBJECTIVE

Identify and understand characteristics in revolutionary leaders that project images of power.

CRITICAL THINKING SKILLS FOR LESSON 2.2

- Synthesize
- Analyze Visuals
- Form and Support Opinions
- Evaluate

HISTORICAL THINKING FOR CHAPTER 21

What factors can lead to revolution?

Lesson 2.2 focuses on portraits of American and European revolutionary leaders that symbolize their power.

BACKGROUND FOR THE TEACHER

Becoming a Revolutionary The decision to appoint George Washington as commander of the Continental Army was advantageous. As a slaveholder from Virginia, Washington brought the largest colony into the fight and dispelled the idea that American independence was primarily the concern of rabble-rousing New Englanders. In addition, as a veteran of the French and Indian War, he was perhaps the colonies' most experienced and decorated warrior—a vital asset, considering he would be leading ill-trained bands of state militias and citizen-soldiers against the greatest military force in the world.

When Napoleon and the French were faced with a slave revolt in present-day Haiti, Toussaint was at first uncommitted. After watching rebel leaders compromise with the French, he became angry and gathered an army of his own, which he trained to use guerilla warfare. When France and Spain went to war, the Spaniards knighted Toussaint for his military ability. He became a general who attracted new recruits, and renowned warriors followed under him. Toussaint won victories in the north and south and pushed the British off of the coasts of Haiti. He then turned against Spain, slaughtering the Spaniards and forcing them out of Haiti. He became known as a decisive revolutionary leader.

INTRODUCE & ENGAGE

PREPARE FOR THE DOCUMENT-BASED QUESTION

Before students start on the activity, briefly preview the three paintings. Remind students that a constructed response requires full explanations in complete sentences. Emphasize that students should use what they have learned about George Washington, Napoleon Bonaparte, and Toussaint L'Ouverture in addition to the information in this lesson.

TEACH

GUIDED DISCUSSION

1. **Analyze Visuals** What elements in each portrait symbolize power? *(Possible responses: Washington is shown standing tall and looking confident. In the background, there are columns and rich furnishings, showing wealth or status; Napoleon is dressed as a king in a red robe adorned with gold, wearing a crown, and sitting on a throne. All of these features show power and authority; Toussaint is dressed in military attire adorned with gold, which symbolizes power and wealth, and his hair is fashioned similar to European styles of the wealthy and powerful.)*

2. **Form and Support Opinions** After reading the text and examining the portraits, which painting do you think most portrays a feeling of power similar to classical Greek and Roman models? *(Answers will vary, but students should choose one of the paintings and explain the reasons why the painting portrays a feeling of power similar to the marble statue of Augustus or other Greek or Roman models.)*

EVALUATE

After students have completed the Synthesize & Write activity, allow time for them to exchange paragraphs and read and comment on the work of their peers. Establish guidelines for comments prior to the activity so that feedback is constructive and encouraging. Comments should focus on the most significant parts that address the purpose of the activity and the audience.

ACTIVE OPTION

On Your Feet: Think, Pair, Share Ask the following question and then allow a few minutes for students to think about it: How do the clothes each man is wearing symbolize power? Then tell students to choose partners and talk about the question for five minutes. After discussion time, invite students to share their ideas with the class.

DIFFERENTIATE

STRIVING READERS

Chart Details About Revolutionary Leaders Ask pairs to create a three-column chart with the columns labeled with the revolutionary leaders from the lesson. Then direct pairs to skim through the chapter to find text about the men. When they find a section of text about one of the leaders, they should take turns reading paragraphs aloud to each other. They should pause after each paragraph and record at least five important details in their chart. Invite pairs to exchange and compare completed charts.

GIFTED & TALENTED

Create a Revolutionary Leader Meme Have students create a meme using a quotation from one of the leaders they learned about in the lesson. Ask students to conduct online research to find a quote that either relates to the leader's revolutionary ideals or provides insight about the leader's goals or ambitions. Tell students to add a photo or artwork to enhance the content of the quotation. Invite students to share their memes with the class.

SYNTHESIZE & WRITE

ANSWERS

1. Answers will vary.

2. Possible response: Washington—the emphasis on his stately black outfit and the fact that he is standing; Napoleon—the splendor of his gold, red, and white outfit and the fact that he is sitting; Toussaint—the gold and blue in his uniform and the fact that he is shown in profile.

3. Possible response: Both similarities and differences relating to backgrounds, color use, and dress can be identified among the three portraits.

4. Answers will vary. Students' paragraphs should include their topic sentence from Step 3 and provide several observations of the three portraits to support the sentence.

CONSTRUCTED RESPONSE

Artifact One: They show Washington's importance in crafting the nation's foundational documents.

Artifact Two: to emphasize his perceived connection to the royal traditions of the past; as a symbol of power.

Artifact Three: to represent the "light" that Toussaint shared as he led the enslaved people of what would become the country of Haiti out of bondage; to place the emphasis on Toussaint's profile

The Culture of Romanticism

Often, cultural movements are closely connected to historical events. The chaos of the French Revolution and the Age of Napoleon turned Europeans away from Enlightenment concepts of structure and restraint and aimed them toward the untamed wonders of nature and the imagination.

EMERGENCE OF ROMANTICISM

Writers, artists, and musicians of the Enlightenment practiced **neoclassicism**, a style based on Greek and Roman ideals. Neoclassic works usually showed symmetry and proportion, for example, in graceful images and buildings. In contrast, **Romanticism** emphasized emotions. Romantic writers, artists, and musicians introduced unpredictability into their creations, with possible surprises around every corner. Their work was subjective, or based on an individual's personal viewpoint. Nature was a way to connect to spirituality, and Romantic writers and artists addressed their topics in a sublime—or awe-inspiring—manner.

Romantics made seemingly insignificant objects appear grand or even terrifying. A simple Greek vase inspired the English poet John Keats to write "Beauty is truth, truth beauty,—that is all / Ye know on earth, and all ye need to know." Romantics believed works of true beauty

could only come from the imagination. They tackled subjects such as imagined places, unusual locations, and the supernatural. However, Romantic artists also found inspiration in folktales and myths from the Middle Ages.

LITERATURE

In Britain, writers like **William Wordsworth**—considered the first Romantic writer—sought new poetic forms, innovative word choices, and passionate appeals. Long walks in nature provided inspiration for Wordsworth and other Romantic artists, and he claimed that "all good poetry is the spontaneous overflow of powerful feelings."

In Britain, George Gordon, best known by the title **Lord Byron**, wrote Romantic poetry as well. Byron was well known for his dashing good looks and daring lifestyle, which were similar to the main characters of many

The English Romantic poet **William Blake** composed songlike lyric poems, often with spiritual and supernatural overtones. He wrote political poems as well. His works—which were sometimes accompanied by images he drew himself—contained themes of freedom, innocence, and the dangers of commercialism.

Tyger Tyger, burning bright,
In the forests of the night;
What immortal hand or eye,
Could frame thy fearful symmetry?

In what distant deeps or skies
Burnt the fire of thine eyes?
On what wings dare he aspire?
What the hand, dare seize the fire?

And what shoulder, & what art,
Could twist the sinews of thy heart?
And when thy heart began to beat,
What dread hand? & what dread feet?

What the hammer? what the chain,
In what furnace was thy brain?
What the anvil? what dread grasp,
Dare its deadly terrors clasp!

When the stars threw down their spears
And water'd heaven with their tears:
Did he smile his work to see?
Did he who made the Lamb make thee?

Tyger Tyger burning bright,
In the forests of the night:
What immortal hand or eye,
Dare frame thy fearful symmetry?

—"The Tyger" by William Blake, 1789

Romanticism vs. Neoclassicism

In painting, neoclassicism is a simple, straightforward technique that uses distinct and purposeful lines. Jacques-Louis David, a leading French neoclassic painter, created works inspired by the styles of ancient Greece and Rome as well as their values of courage and honor. However, the lush and expressive Romantic movement that emerged from the calm, rational order of neoclassicism led to a distinct change in painting and portraiture. Many of Spanish artist Francisco de Goya's works feature visible, blurred brushstrokes, which are a visual representation of Romanticism's reaction against the established values of the time.

CRITICAL VIEWING Compare and contrast de Goya's Romantic *The Clothed Maja* (below) with David's neoclassic *Portrait of Madame de Verninac* (left).

PLAN: 4-PAGE LESSON

OBJECTIVE

Describe the cultural movement of Romanticism that focuses on nature and emotion.

CRITICAL THINKING SKILLS FOR LESSON 2.3

- Analyze Cause and Effect
- Identify Main Ideas and Details
- Describe
- Compare and Contrast
- Synthesize
- Form and Support Opinions
- Analyze Primary Sources
- Analyze Visuals

HISTORICAL THINKING FOR CHAPTER 21

What factors can lead to revolution?

Influenced by the American and French revolutions, Romantic writers, artists, and musicians moved away from structure and restraint, and focused on the beauty and isolation of nature and imagination. Lesson 2.3 discusses key Romantic figures and developments in writing, art, and music during the 18th and 19th centuries.

BACKGROUND FOR THE TEACHER

The Romantic Poets Six poets embody the Romantic Age of literature: William Blake (1757–1827); William Wordsworth (1770–1850); Samuel Taylor Coleridge (1772–1834); George Gordon, or Lord Byron, (1788–1824); Percy Bysshe Shelley (1792–1822); and John Keats (1795–1821). Wordsworth and Coleridge were life-long friends who wrote poetry and discussed political philosophies together. They were inspired by the American Revolution and traveled to France to witness the French Revolution. However, both became disillusioned with revolution during the "September Massacre" in France, in which hundreds of French aristocrats were killed regardless of their political views. The pair's book, *Lyrical Ballads, with a Few Other Poems*, included Coleridge's "The Rime of the Ancient Mariner" and Wordsworth's "Lines Composed a Few Miles Above Tintern Abbey." The two poems are among the most important poems in English literature. Byron, Keats, and Shelley are considered the "young" romantic poets, not only because they were born after the revolutions, but also because each died tragically young at the height of his poetic genius.

Student eEdition online

Additional content for this lesson, including a painting, is available online.

INTRODUCE & ENGAGE

PREVIEW WITH VISUALS

Explain to students that the term *romantic* does not describe sentiment in this context but instead applies to a cynical time when people were asked to question tradition and authority in order to better imagine healthier, fairer, and happier ways to live. Direct students' attention to the art presented in the lesson. Write *Romantic Art* at the center of a Concept Cluster and ask volunteers to list traits of Romantic paintings based on their observation of the art and arrange them into groups on the cluster. At the end of the lesson, revisit the Concept Cluster and add or remove traits based on what students learned.

TEACH

GUIDED DISCUSSION

1. **Compare and Contrast** How do neoclassicism and Romanticism differ? *(Neoclassicism focuses on symmetry and proportions, while Romanticism emphasizes emotion and unpredictability and is subject to one's own viewpoint.)*

2. **Synthesize** Review the descriptions of Byron's Romantic hero and Goethe's main character Faust. **ASK:** What type of experience do the two heroes share and how does each writer represent the Romantic ideals? *(Both Byron and Goethe focus on a hero who faces tragedy. Byron's heroes, although defiant, succumb to tragic ends and Goethe's hero is not only a Romantic figure but also a tragic one. Both writers include characters who face internal struggles and external conflicts as they search for knowledge.)*

ANALYZE PRIMARY SOURCES

Discuss Blake's poem "The Tyger" that appears in the lesson. Explain that Blake wrote a book of poems called *Songs of Innocence and Experience*. "The Tyger" is from his *Songs of Experience*, but its counterpart, "The Lamb," is from the *Songs of Innocence*. "The Lamb" is filled with love, nurturing, and caring, as the lamb symbolizes the innocence and capacity a child has for simple faith and joy, before children become adults. Have students read the introductory material and the poem "The Tyger." **ASK:** What does the Tyger represent? *(Possible responses: the corruptness of an adult; industry, factories)* In the fourth stanza, with what other process is the creation of the Tyger connected? *(The Tyger is linked to the forging of iron in factories.)* What does this metaphor suggest about the Tyger? *(Possible responses: that the Tyger is not human; it is evil, and has the strength to forge iron. OR that the Tyger is not human; it is corruptness of industry and unfair conditions for factory workers.)* If the Creator of the Tyger is the same as the Creator of the Lamb, according to Blake, what contrasts exist in the world? *(Possible response: Both good and evil exist in the world.)*

DIFFERENTIATE

ENGLISH LANGUAGE LEARNERS

Dictate Sentence Summaries Pair students at the **Beginning** level with those at the **Advanced** level. After students read each section, Emergence of Romanticism, Literature, Visual Art, and Music, direct them to identify two-to-three sentences from each that contain an important idea. Then tell each student to write that idea in a summary sentence using his or her own words. Partners then take turns dictating their sentences to each other. Encourage them to work together to check each other's work for accuracy and spelling.

GIFTED & TALENTED

Evaluate Music Direct students to conduct online research to find samples of the music from one of the composers mentioned in this lesson. Have each student choose three to five music samples from her/his chosen composer to write a paragraph about the feelings and emotions the music evokes in her/him. Ask students to provide a brief recording of one of the music samples to play for the class and then ask other students to comment on the emotions they feel when listening to the music.

See the Chapter Planner for more strategies for differentiation.

literary works of the era. These fictional individuals were **archetypes**, or perfect examples, of a Romantic hero. Sometimes called a Byronic hero, this archetype was an unhappy, defiant figure who faced internal and external conflicts. Romantic heroes often came to tragic ends. One fellow aristocrat described Byron as "mad, bad, and dangerous to know."

Romanticism was not just a British cultural movement. In Germany, **Johannes Wolfgang von Goethe** (GUHR-tuh) wrote novels, plays, and poems. In his famous epic poem *Faust*, the main character signs a pact with the devil to exchange his soul for knowledge and power. Faust was presented as not only a Romantic figure but also a tragic one. Goethe was a strong supporter of both art and science. At his home, Goethe hosted a salon for the most important German artists and thinkers.

This cultural movement also included female authors from different European countries. The English writer **Mary Shelley** wrote her famous novel *Frankenstein* to address the Romantic themes of nature and human ambition. The story raised moral questions such as,

"Was Dr. Frankenstein interfering with God and Nature by bringing his monstrous creation to life?"

VISUAL ART
Painters of the 1790s and early 1800s took the medium in dramatically new directions. Romantic artists captured on canvas the raging waters of Niagara Falls, torrential storms, and imposing cliffs. The English painter **J.M.W. Turner** and German painter Casper David Friedrich showed the power of nature and instilled fear and awe in viewers. Yet some Romantic painters, such as John Constable, portrayed nature at peace.

Romanticism inspired artists to paint portraits to show what a person thought and felt rather than what that individual exactly looked like. Some painters illustrated the stories created by writers such as Lord Byron or Goethe. Recall that Blake often illustrated his own works. Nationalism, which you learned about earlier in this chapter, motivated artists to concentrate on local folklore and nature as well as victories in battle and the attainment of liberty, as demonstrated by the works of the French artist Eugène Delacroix (oo-ZHEHN deh-luh-KRWAH).

Richard Wagner drew on medieval German romances for the plot of his opera *Lohengrin*, which tells the tale of a mysterious knight in the 10th century. London's Royal Opera updated the setting to the 1930s in its 2018 production.

J.M.W. Turner's 1810 painting *The Wreck of a Transport Ship* exemplifies Romanticism's love of dramatic, emotional scenes of nature and natural events.

MUSIC
During the final years of the French Revolution, the German composer **Ludwig van Beethoven** worked on a piece of music to be titled "Bonaparte Symphony." However, he scratched out that dedication on the manuscript after Napoleon crowned himself emperor. Beethoven dedicated his Third Symphony, also called the *Eroica* Symphony, to a patron instead. First performed in 1804, this intricate symphony built on the neoclassical tradition of symmetry and proportion but added elements of surprise that provoke an emotional response. Beethoven's Ninth Symphony is often performed today to celebrate moments of human triumph over adversity.

The Austrian composer Franz Schubert blurred the line between classical and Romantic music styles like Beethoven did. Other musicians represented Romanticism more fully. The Hungarian pianist and composer Franz Liszt whipped audiences into excited

frenzies with his musical originality, experimentation, focus on nature, and revolutionary zeal. In contrast, the Polish-French musician Frédéric Chopin simply expressed his creativity and individuality through his piano concertos. The Russian composer Peter Ilych Tchaikovsky (chy-KAWF-skee) appealed to listeners' emotions, heritage, and nationalistic desires in famous symphonies as well as in ballets such as *Swan Lake* and *The Nutcracker*. As the Prussian Romantic writer and composer E.T.A. Hoffmann rejoiced, "Music is the most Romantic of the arts."

The German **Richard Wagner** was an extremely ambitious composer, writing massive operas on mythological themes. Wagner created a specifically "German art" that clearly connects the concepts of Romanticism and nationalism. His works are still performed, although critics have been disturbed by Wagner's prejudice against Jews as well as the presence of anti-Semitism in his music.

HISTORICAL THINKING

1. **READING CHECK** What universal themes are expressed in the works of Romantic writers, artists, and musicians?

2. **ANALYZE CAUSE AND EFFECT** How did the distant and recent past influence the development of Romanticism?

3. **IDENTIFY MAIN IDEAS AND DETAILS** What was William Wordsworth's contribution to Romanticism?

4. **DESCRIBE** In what ways did musical composers of the time communicate the themes of Romanticism?

BACKGROUND FOR THE TEACHER
Romanticism in Germany The word *romantic* was first used by critics Friedrich von Schlegel and August Wilhelm von Schlegel in Germany, in 1789. The literary style was known in Germany as *Strum und Drang* ("storm and stress") and was used by German writers Johann Wolfgang von Goethe and Johann Friedrich von Schiller. Germany's Ludwig van Beethoven influenced succeeding generations with his Fifth and Ninth symphonies, which emphasized a musical progression from storm and stress to triumph. Though not a Romantic himself, Beethoven became the champion of the elements that defined the Romantics who came after him. His music reached out to capture the humanist ideas of the time. Beethoven's influence on music's sonata, symphony, concerto, and quartet and his combination of using both vocals and instruments in his Ninth Symphony changed the world of music. Beethoven defined his Sixth (Pastoral) Symphony as "more an expression of emotion than painting." Beethoven, with the help of the Mannheim Orchestra, promoted rationalism to feeling in music. Although his personal life was a struggle, during which he tragically dealt with hearing loss and complete deafness for the last 10 years of his life, he continued to compose until his death. Beethoven is known as one of the greatest composers/artists who ever lived. His works influenced his German friends, including composer Robert Schumann and pianist Johann Nepomuk Hummel.

TEACH

GUIDED DISCUSSION

3. **Describe** How would you describe the emotions in J.M.W. Turner's *The Wreck of a Transport Ship*, and how does the artist convey these emotions? *(Possible response: Turner uses grays and blacks to create a sense of tragedy and emotional turmoil, showing nature's power as the sea turns the ship on its side. The artist shows fierce movement of the waves exemplifying the raw power of nature, which is a theme of Romanticism.)*

4. **Form and Support Opinions** What do you think E.T.A. Hoffmann meant by the comment "Music is the most Romantic of the arts," and do you agree? *(Answers will vary but should be supported. Possible response: As a composer and musician, Hoffman believed that Romantic musicians expressed the turbulent emotions of Romanticism better than the writers and artists of the time. Answers will vary to the second part of the question.)*

ANALYZE VISUALS

Ask students to examine the photograph of a scene from Wagner's opera *Lohengrin*. **ASK:** Knowing that the setting was updated to the 1930s, what details from the original mysterious knight scene changed? *(Possible responses: The soldiers would be holding swords, not guns. The dress of the people would reflect medieval times, not the 1930s' attire. The woman at the front of the stage would be in a long dress, not a skirt and boots.)*

ACTIVE OPTIONS

On Your Feet: Team Word Webbing Organize students into groups of three or four to discuss the themes, people, and important works of art, music, and literature during the Romantic Period. Arrange teams around a large sheet of paper and give each student a different color marker or pencil. Encourage students to add their ideas to the part of the page closest to them. On your signal, tell students to rotate the page and add new ideas to the area in front of them. When the page has rotated back to its original position, tell groups to summarize their ideas and share their webs with the class.

> **NG Learning Framework: Explore Romantic Poems and Poets**
> **ATTITUDE** Curiosity
> **KNOWLEDGE** Our Human Story

Share the Background for the Teacher information on the Romantic Poets. Invite students to conduct online research into one of the poets mentioned but not featured, such as Coleridge, Shelley, Bryon, or Keats. Have them select a poem written by the poet and analyze it in terms of what they have learned about Romantic poetry. Have volunteers read the poem to the class and describe its Romantic characteristics.

HISTORICAL THINKING

ANSWERS

1. Possible response: Universal themes related to Romanticism include appreciation of beauty, love of nature, faith, freedom, individuality, heroism, heritage and tradition, fear, desire for change, pride in one's work, and importance of self.

2. Possible response: People who had lived through the Enlightenment were tired of its restraint and order. At the same time, they were inspired by recent revolutions. They also focused some of their subject matter on folklore and folktales, myths of the Middle Ages, and past victories in battle.

3. Considered to be the first Romantic writer, Wordsworth introduced new poetic forms, innovative word choice, and appeals to emotion.

4. Possible response: Romantic composers represented their cultural movement through their interest in revolutions and nature, introduction of the unexpected, creativity and originality, and appeal to emotions, individualism, heritage, and nationalism.

CRITICAL VIEWING Possible response: Jacques-Louis David introduces a woman sitting upright, in a clean, white gown with a gold sash, and her perfectly proportioned (classical) face shows a slight smile, while Francisco de Goya shows a woman reclining in a muted white and pink gown with a pale pink sash, and her face shows more emotion. Jacques-Louis David's brushwork is precise and shows distinct lines, while Francisco de Goya's brushwork is looser and more flowing; the lines of the painting are soft and not quite as definite.

Simón Bolívar

Some people dedicate themselves to supporting causes such as helping animals, fighting injustice, or protecting the environment. History includes many individuals who took great risks for a cause they truly believed in. For Simón Bolívar, that goal was independence and unity for South America.

DEMOCRATIC IDEALS TAKE SHAPE

Simón Bolívar was born in South America in 1783, six years before the French Revolution. He was raised in a privileged household in Spanish-controlled Caracas, now the capital of Venezuela, but he witnessed firsthand the inequities in the South American social classes. Recall that the *peninsulares* (Spaniards born in Spain) dominated the affairs of church and state in the Spanish colonies. American-born Spaniards were known as *criollos* (cree-OH-yohs). Criollos were aware of Enlightenment calls for fairness and equality. They wanted more economic and political freedom, and the lack of it caused them to resent the Spanish.

As a young man, Bolívar became enthralled with the Enlightenment principles and the democratic ideals expressed during the American and French revolutions. Traveling to Madrid, Rome, and Paris during Napoleon's rule convinced Bolívar to play a part in winning liberty for South Americans. He vowed, "I swear before you, I swear by the God of my fathers, I swear on their graves. I swear by my Country that I will not rest body or soul until I have broken the chain binding us to the will of Spanish might!"

This oath changed not only Bolívar's life but also the course of South American history. Bolívar envisioned true liberation for South America. He did not want his homeland to experience a reign of terror or rule by a dictator like Napoleon. At the same time, he envied Napoleon's success and thought he could gain his own glory as a freedom fighter. Bolívar would dedicate all his time and energy to the struggle for South American independence. He wanted South America to equal or surpass the revolutionary success of the neighboring United States and Haiti.

BOLÍVAR IN ACTION

In 1808, Napoleon replaced Spain's king with his own brother. The South American elite did not believe that France had a rightful claim to South America, so its members set up **juntas** (HUN-tuhs)—military or political ruling groups who take power by force—to oversee local lands until Spain regained its authority. Bolívar, however, saw the transition to French rule as the perfect time for an attempt at independence.

Bolívar soon proved his brilliance as a military leader. To gain followers, he formed alliances and offered freedom to slaves who joined his army. He encouraged the spirit of revolution in indigenous peoples, Africans, and people of mixed descent as well. They made up the majority of Venezuela, so their support was critically needed. Bolívar gained the loyalty of his soldiers through his toughness

in battle and by enduring the same hardships. For example, he once spent a whole night immersed in a lake to avoid Spanish forces.

In 1813, Bolívar led his army to a successful takeover of Venezuela, but civil war soon broke out among Venezuela's social classes. Bolívar fled into exile. Then, in 1815, Napoleon's defeat at Waterloo resulted in the restoration of the Spanish monarchy. South Americans did not want to lose freedoms they had gained when Spain was under French control, and more and more of them lost their sense of loyalty to Spain.

Bolívar returned to Venezuela. By 1817, he made some progress and headed into Venezuela's interior to rebuild his army. Soon, the freedom fighter was recognized as the supreme commander of the various patriotic forces.

In 1819, Spain still held Caracas, but colonial delegates at the ongoing Congress of Angostura made plans for Venezuela's independence. Bolívar argued for a solid central government with effective executive powers because he thought a strong legislature would lead to instability and division. Fearing that the congress would not heed his advice, he developed a new plan. He would move his army south and attempt to liberate a larger area, where he could create a constitutional union called **Gran Colombia**. This union included present-day Venezuela, Colombia, Panama, Ecuador, and Peru.

Bolívar, sometimes called "the Liberator," started his military and political journey with high hopes founded in Enlightenment optimism, and he did help overthrow monarchical authority in South America. Still, turning independence from Spanish rule into true liberty for South Americans proved harder than he imagined. Even though he fought for freedom until his death, Bolívar never achieved his goal of a stable and united continent. His story, as one biographer explained, was one of "liberation and disappointment."

Simón Bolívar, shown here, was nicknamed "the Liberator" of South America. His birthday, July 24, is a holiday that is celebrated in many Latin American countries.

PRIMARY SOURCE

While in exile on the island of Jamaica in 1815, Simón Bolívar wrote a letter to the governor of Jamaica. It analyzes the state of the struggle for independence. In this excerpt, he explains why the people of South America desire independence.

Americans today, and perhaps to a greater extent than ever before, who live within the Spanish system occupy a position in society no better than that of serfs destined for labor. . . . Yet even this status is surrounded with galling restrictions, such as being forbidden to grow European crops, or to store products which are royal monopolies, or to establish factories of a type the Peninsula itself does not possess. . . . South Americans have made efforts to obtain liberty . . . doubtless out of that instinct to aspire to the greatest possible happiness, which common to all men, is bound to follow in civil societies founded on the principles of justice, liberty, and equality.

HISTORICAL THINKING

1. **READING CHECK** What were Simón Bolívar's goals for South America?

2. **COMPARE AND CONTRAST** How did differences in South American social classes both help and hurt the revolutionary cause?

3. **ANALYZE SOURCES** What evidence in Bolívar's letter to the governor of Jamaica suggests his belief in Enlightenment principles?

OBJECTIVE

Explain why Simón Bolívar devoted most of his life to liberating the people of South America from Spain.

CRITICAL THINKING SKILLS FOR LESSON 3.1

- Compare and Contrast
- Analyze Sources
- Form and Support Opinions
- Analyze Primary Sources

HISTORICAL THINKING FOR CHAPTER 21

What factors can lead to revolution?

Simón Bolívar saw firsthand the divisions and inequalities among social classes in South America, which were largely the result of Spanish colonization. Lesson 3.1 discusses his passion and commitment to liberating South America from Spain and unifying the continent.

Student eEdition online

Additional content for this lesson, including a photograph, is available online.

BACKGROUND FOR THE TEACHER

Travel and Influence When Simón Bolívar was born, Napoleon was a teenager, already in military school and paving a path for himself that would lead to military genius and later to become emperor of France. Bolívar grew up privileged and was profoundly influenced not by a military education like Napoleon but by his tutor Simón Rodríguez, who exposed him to Enlightenment thoughts and ideas. But it was on Bolívar's travels to Paris with Rodríguez where Bolívar met a German scientist named Alexander von Humboldt, who convinced Bolívar that the time was right for the independence of Spain's colonies. Another influence on Bolívar was the self-coronation of Napoleon in 1804. Even though Bolívar admired Napoleon and his successes, he was not impressed with Napoleon's self-righteousness and abandonment of the ideas of the French Revolution for his own grandeur. Bolívar also found inspiration in the American Revolution and its establishment of a democratic government with checks and balances. Like George Washington and other revolutionary leaders, Bolívar was a slave owner.

INTRODUCE & ENGAGE

DISCUSS DEMOCRATIC IDEALS AND GOVERNMENT

Discuss how democratic ideals, past or present, have influenced government policy, why they appeal to some governments but not to others, and how basic rights such as freedom and equality have been driving factors in revolutions over time. Ask students to consider why democratic ideals are sometimes the driving force behind a movement for change. Tell students that they will learn about how democratic ideals influenced Simón Bolívar to lead the liberation of South America.

TEACH

GUIDED DISCUSSION

1. **Compare and Contrast** How was Simón Bolívar's mission similar to and different from that of Napoleon? *(Possible response: Similar: They were both driven by Enlightenment ideas and glory. Different: Simón Bolívar wanted to liberate the people of South America from Spanish rule, whereas Napoleon wanted France to have a new government.)*

2. **Form and Support Opinions** Do you think that Simón Bolívar's goal of unifying South America was attainable? Explain your reasoning. *(Possible response: No, because different countries in South America probably wanted to have their own governments and had different influences that would have made it challenging to unite as one.)*

ANALYZE PRIMARY SOURCES

Tell students to read the primary source excerpt. **ASK:** Why do you think Simón Bolívar wrote this letter? *(Possible response: He thought he could convince the governor to support him in his mission to liberate the people of South America.)* Have students examine the details he uses to convince the governor and how those details are similar to those expressed in the American and French revolutions.

ACTIVE OPTIONS

On Your Feet: Become an Expert Assign each of four "expert" groups one of the following to research: Bolívar and Enlightenment ideas, Bolívar and Gran Colombia, Bolívar as Liberator, Bolívar and South American Unity. Regroup students so that each new group has at least one member from each expert group. Ask experts to report on their study. Then share the Background for the Teacher with the class and discuss the factors that influenced Bolívar, his successes and failures, and how the dream of liberty could be compatible with the reality of slavery.

NG Learning Framework: Trace Bolívar's Quest to Unify South America
ATTITUDE Curiosity
KNOWLEDGE Our Human Story

Explain that Bolívar led many military victories in order to liberate and unify South America. Ask small groups to research the key battles and campaigns that helped him achieve his goal. Have them create a time line of the information they find or annotate a map to show Bolívar's path of liberation and then present their work in a large-group discussion format.

DIFFERENTIATE

STRIVING READERS

List Biographical Facts Ask students to copy this heading onto a piece of paper: Five Facts About Simón Bolívar. After students read the lesson, ask them to write five sentences that each contain one fact about Bolívar's life. Invite volunteers to share their sentences with a partner.

PRE-AP

Investigate Primary Sources Prompt students to research Simón Bolívar's Proclamation of 1813, in which he appealed to Venezuelans in the city of Trujillo for support in liberating Venezuela from Spanish rule. Then ask students to write a short essay that explains Bolívar's purpose and mission and the effect of the proclamation.

See the Chapter Planner for more strategies for differentiation.

HISTORICAL THINKING

ANSWERS

1. for it to be free from European rule and united as one continent

2. Possible response: Social class differences inspired criollos to seek more rights and freedoms. These inequalities also allowed Bolívar to recruit dissatisfied members of the lower classes for his army. However, the divisions also provoked civil wars, which made the road to independence less smooth.

3. When Bolívar explains why South Americans desire freedom, he refers to the natural right of happiness and how it can be attained in a society "founded on the principles of justice, liberty, and equality."

CRITICAL VIEWING (available in the Student eEdition) Possible response: a central location in an open-air space surrounded by buildings; a public place for people to meet, relax, and converse

Latin American Wars of Independence

Almost all of Latin America—Mexico, Central America, South America, and the islands of the Caribbean—was controlled by European powers at the beginning of the 19th century. Yet the people who lived there heard the call of liberty and were eager to answer it.

CRITICAL VIEWING In 1810, Father Miguel Hidalgo y Costilla rallied the common people of Mexico, especially mestizos and native peoples, under the banner of the Virgin of Guadalupe for independence from Spain. Based on this mural painted by David Leonardo in 1999, how do you think Mexicans remember Father Hidalgo?

A CONTINUING STRUGGLE

In late 1819, Simón Bolívar led his troops south, intent on liberating South America and establishing Gran Colombia. Even though Bolívar and his troops suffered greatly as they traveled into the frigid Andean Mountains, their morale remained high. The same was not true for the Spanish soldiers who realized that their generals' skills could not match those of the Liberator. Bolívar's army quickly won territory as far south as Ecuador. At the same time, another leader, **José de San Martín**, was successfully leading the fight for independence in central and southern South America. His military prowess allowed him to win freedom for Argentina and Chile. San Martín next moved north into Peru, where he claimed the capital, Lima.

Meanwhile, Bolívar continued his march south until he met up with San Martín, who stepped aside to enable the Liberator to win the final victory. Bolívar's soldiers engaged the Spanish in the Andes in 1824 at the Battle of Ayacucho in southern Peru. Their triumph finally freed South America from Spanish control.

MEXICO, BRAZIL, AND THE CARIBBEAN

In Mexico, indigenous peoples and mestizos led the way to independence. In 1810, a priest in the parish of Dolores named **Miguel Hidalgo y Costilla** rallied the poor with his speech now known as "Grito de Dolores," or "Cry of Dolores," which implored Mexicans to fight for freedom. However, criollo soldiers supporting the Spanish status quo crushed Hidalgo's troops and killed the priest. When Spain began to enact liberal reforms, however, Mexican criollos feared such changes would cause them to lose their power. Criollo military leader Augustin de Iturbide and his elite supporters fought for and won Mexico's freedom in 1821. Wealthy hacienda owners now controlled Mexico. This independence brought neither the social nor economic reform Father Hidalgo had hoped for.

Controlled by Portugal, Brazil followed its own distinct path to independence. In 1808, the Portuguese royal family sought refuge in Brazil to escape an invasion by Napoleon. The king returned to his home country in 1821, but his son Pedro remained in Brazil. Pedro then announced that he would support the cause of Brazilian independence, which was achieved in 1822. In 1824, Pedro I became the constitutional monarch of Brazil.

Women, such as Manuela Sáenz (shown here with Simón Bolívar), played an important role in Latin America's struggle for independence. Sáenz was an Ecuadorian noblewoman who saved Bolívar's life when political rivals tried to assassinate him in 1828.

Just as in the United States, Brazil became free without toppling the elite control of society and the economy. Also, the institution of slavery continued.

Meanwhile, in the Caribbean, enslaved Jamaicans revolted in 1831 and 1832, inspired by the abolitionist movement in Britain. They wanted to be paid for their labor and to be free to leave their plantations. Plantation owners put down the uprising, but it marked the last gasp of slavery in Jamaica. Two years later, Parliament freed all enslaved people in the British Empire.

Just south of Mexico, the people of Central America gained independence with little bloodshed. This region briefly became a territory of the newly independent Mexico. Then it broke away from foreign control in 1824 to become the United Provinces of Central America. The union soon disbanded, however, and Guatemala, Honduras, Nicaragua, El Salvador, and Costa Rica became independent republics.

HISTORICAL THINKING

1. **READING CHECK** In what different ways did countries of Latin America win independence?

2. **ANALYZE CAUSE AND EFFECT** What effect did José de San Martín's military actions have on South America's history?

3. **FORM AND SUPPORT OPINIONS** Did independence make life better or worse for the Mexican people? Explain.

PLAN: 2-PAGE LESSON

OBJECTIVE

Explain how in the early 1800s, the people of Latin American and Caribbean colonies fought for and won independence from the nations in Europe that controlled them.

CRITICAL THINKING SKILLS FOR LESSON 3.2

• Analyze Cause and Effect
• Interpret Maps
• Compare and Contrast
• Make Inferences
• Analyze Visuals

HISTORICAL THINKING FOR CHAPTER 21

What factors can lead to revolution?

South America was not the only place in Latin America where people called for independence from the Spanish. Lesson 3.2 examines the independence movements in Mexico, Central America, and the Caribbean.

BACKGROUND FOR THE TEACHER

Allegiances José de San Martín was born to Spanish parents in present-day Argentina. He was loyal to the Spanish crown and a lifelong soldier like his father. When he was fighting the French in their occupation of Spain under Napoleon, he grew to detest European colonialism and rule by absolute monarchy. He resigned in 1811 and on his way to Lima (the capital of present-day Peru), he traveled to London, England, where he joined a group of Spanish revolutionaries and British supporters of an independence movement in Spanish-held territories. Then San Martín made his way to Peru where he trained an army. Even though it is unclear if he put his ambitions aside to allow Bolívar to complete the independence movement in southern South America, his ability to lead his troops through the Andean cordillera (Andes Mountains) illustrates his skill as one of the greatest military leaders.

INTRODUCE & ENGAGE

DISCUSS REVOLUTIONARY LEADERS

Point out that students have been learning about different leaders in revolutionary movements. **ASK:** What common traits and characteristics did these leaders have? *(Possible response: bravery, courage, influenced by Enlightenment ideas; Some valued glory and power over ideals.)* Which of these qualities do you think were most important, and why? *(Possible response: influence of Enlightenment ideas and military experience, because it took both to be driven to fight and to succeed in battle)*

TEACH

GUIDED DISCUSSION

1. **Compare and Contrast** How was Brazil's independence movement similar to and different from that of the United States? *(Similar: They were both colonies, gained independence without toppling the elite control of society, and kept slavery legal. Different: Brazil became a constitutional monarchy and the United States became a democratic republic.)*

2. **Make Inferences** Why do you think the abolitionist movement in Britain inspired a slave rebellion in Jamaica? *(Possible response: Slaves in Jamaica most likely saw it as an opportunity to gain their freedom since slavery was ending in Britain.)*

ANALYZE VISUALS

Have students examine the mural showing Father Hidalgo leading the fight for Mexican independence from Spain. Explain that the Virgin of Guadalupe appeared to Juan Diego, an Aztec man who became a Christian in 1531. In 1810, Father Hidalgo used the Virgin of Guadalupe as a symbol of the independence movement. Today, Our Lady of Guadalupe is one of the most important symbols in Mexico. **ASK:** Why do you think the Virgin of Guadalupe is such an important symbol in Mexico? *(Possible response: because she symbolizes nationalism and Mexican identity)*

ACTIVE OPTIONS

On Your Feet: Research Contributions to the Cause Assign each of two teams to mestizos and indigenous peoples. Instruct them to gather in separate areas of the room to research how each group contributed to the cause for independence in Latin America, positively, negatively, or both. Reconvene as a class. Have a student from each team share two or three points they discovered about the groups' contributions.

> **NG Learning Framework: Evaluate San Martín's Leadership and Actions**
> **SKILL** Communication
> **KNOWLEDGE** Our Human Story

Ask small groups to gather information from the lesson and from their own research about José de San Martín. Tell them to write an evaluation of his actions as a military leader and how he stepped aside to allow Bolívar to complete the independence movement in southern South America. Have them include specific details and support in their evaluation. Invite groups to share their evaluations with the class.

DIFFERENTIATE

ENGLISH LANGUAGE LEARNERS

Create a Time Line Have pairs of **All Proficiencies** work together to create a time line of events in the lesson. Ask guiding questions to help get students started, such as the following: When did South America gain its independence? When did Mexico gain its independence?

GIFTED & TALENTED

Trace and Annotate a Map Have students copy the map in the next lesson. They may trace it or sketch it. Then ask them to annotate the map with details about each independence movement. Students should use information from the lesson and from outside research. Then have students use their annotated maps to discuss the course of South American independence in small groups.

See the Chapter Planner for more strategies for differentiation.

HISTORICAL THINKING

ANSWERS

1. Mexico and the countries of South America won independence through warfare, while Brazil and Central American countries won freedom through more peaceful means.

2. His actions freed central and southern South America from Spanish control, helping the people of the continent gain independence.

3. Possible response: Independence made life worse for most people, specifically indigenous people and the mestizos, who might have benefited from reforms being introduced by Spain. The wealthy were the people who benefited most from independence.

CRITICAL VIEWING Possible response: as a brave and courageous leader of the people; his faith and strength attracted many people to the movement for independence

The Spread of Revolutionary Ideas

The revolutions of national independence and the search for liberty did not have the same results everywhere. Different circumstances, situations, and attitudes of the era influenced how and why successive events unfolded.

SPREAD OF DEMOCRATIC CONCEPTS

During the Enlightenment, philosophers and other educated individuals took part in what became informally known as the "republic of letters," sharing thoughts about topics such as medicine, science, religion, and government through their correspondence with one another. John Locke alone composed more than 3,000 letters.

In the revolutionary era, letters became an important way to transmit ideas and news of current events over the Atlantic Ocean. This transatlantic communication helped relay subversive ideas to other parts of the world. It also inspired people in the Americas to fight for liberty and independence. In addition to letters, visits from foreign leaders and printed books and pamphlets sowed the seeds of revolution. For example, American founder Benjamin Franklin lived in Europe for a significant amount of time and sent back letters before, during, and after the American Revolution.

REVOLUTIONARY OUTCOMES

The circulation of revolutionary ideas and experiences connected the Atlantic world. Clearly, knowledge of the struggles in the United States and France inspired the uprising in Saint-Domingue, which you know later became Haiti. Likewise, those revolutions and Haiti's success influenced Simón Bolívar's drive for South American independence. In the Americas, leaders hoped to bring liberty and equality to their people, and many succeeded in overthrowing monarchical authority. Yet by 1830, the outcomes of revolutions in Europe and the Americas proved to be vastly different.

In Europe, the excesses of French politics led to the revival of conservative ideas. Europe's revolutionary flame was quickly extinguished after the fall of Napoleon. European conservatives attempted to return to the age of strong monarchs, but they could not combat the surge of nationalism that would eventually lead regions such as Greece, Germany, and Italy to unite. In addition, many Europeans would not rest until a more equal distribution of wealth existed on their continent.

Benjamin Franklin (shown at right in a 1767 portrait) spent most of the American Revolution in France. In a 1782 letter from Paris, Franklin shares some concerns with Henry Laurens, an American who was tasked with negotiating peace with Great Britain.

PRIMARY SOURCE

I have never yet known of a Peace made that did not occasion a great deal of popular Discontent, Clamor, and Censure on both Sides. This is, perhaps, owing to the usual Management of the Ministers and Leaders of the contending Nations who, to keep up the Spirits of their People for continuing the War, generally represent the State of their own Affairs in a better Light and that of the Enemy in a worse than is consistent with the Truth, Hence the Populace on each Side expect better Terms than really can be obtained, and are apt to ascribe their Disappointment to Treachery.

In North America, the more privileged and educated had spearheaded the American Revolution. However, the doctrine of popular sovereignty required the leaders of the newly formed United States to look beyond their own self-interests to create a more just society. They increased access to political power—but only to white men with property. African Americans, Native Americans, and women did not gain any rights.

The United States set up a strong federal system based on popular sovereignty, constitutionalism, separation of powers, and checks and balances. It then focused on expansion; it doubled its size with the Louisiana Purchase in 1803 and claimed territory even farther west. European immigrants rushed to the new country, which promised opportunities for cheap land and good wages. Although the republic seemed to be flourishing, its relations with Native Americans were poor, and the institution of slavery caused division.

In Haiti, the shift from slave colony to free republic proved difficult. Former slaves fled plantations to establish small farms of their own. These changes led to a drop in crop production, which resulted in a decrease in government tax revenue. The greed of Haitian leaders and divisions between the mixed-race gens de couleur and Haitians of African heritage caused additional problems. The republic became a dictatorship that was run by corrupt leaders, and control by military dictators allied with wealthy landowners doomed democracy in the island nation.

In Latin America, Simón Bolívar's attempt at a united South America fell apart. Military commanders seized power, allying themselves with dominant landowners and church officials. By 1830, much of South

America was ruled by self-interested military rulers called **caudillos** (cow-THEE-yohs), who gained power through violence. Criollos prospered following the exodus of peninsulares, but the other classes suffered. Africans, indigenous peoples, and people of mixed races had played an important role during the fight for freedom, but they did not reap the benefits. In general, the Catholic Church still sided with the wealthy and powerful instead of those who suffered in poverty.

Rebels around the world were unable to undertake a "complete revolution," or a top-to-bottom transformation of society. However, Enlightenment concepts were now a permanent part of the political conversation in many parts of the world.

Independence in the Americas, 1804–1839

MEXICO 1821 · Gulf of Mexico · HAITI 1804 · ATLANTIC OCEAN · Caribbean Sea · GRAN COLOMBIA 1819–1830 · PERU 1824 · EMPIRE OF BRAZIL 1822 · PACIFIC OCEAN · BOLIVIA 1825 · PARAGUAY 1811 · UNITED PROVINCES OF RIO DE LA PLATA 1816 · CHILE 1818 · URUGUAY 1830 · PATAGONIA (Disputed) · 0 400 800 Miles · 0 400 800 Kilometers

HISTORICAL THINKING

1. **READING CHECK** In what ways were the consequences of the American Revolution unique compared to other revolutions that followed?

2. **IDENTIFY MAIN IDEAS AND DETAILS** What were positive and negative effects of independence for Haiti?

3. **MAKE CONNECTIONS** In what ways were the challenges faced by the rulers of newly independent nations similar?

PLAN: 2-PAGE LESSON

OBJECTIVE

Explain how Enlightenment principles inspired revolutions in the United States, France, Haiti, and Latin America, with varying and lasting effects.

CRITICAL THINKING SKILLS FOR LESSON 3.3

- Identify Main Ideas and Details
- Make Connections
- Analyze Cause and Effect
- Analyze Primary Sources

HISTORICAL THINKING FOR CHAPTER 21

What factors can lead to revolution?

Revolutionary thought, based on Enlightenment ideas, spread during the revolutionary era. Lesson 3.3 discusses the outcomes, successes, and failures of each of the revolutions discussed in the chapter.

Student eEdition online

Additional content for this lesson, including a video, is available online.

BACKGROUND FOR THE TEACHER

Spreading the News Letter-writing was an important medium of communication in the late 1700s and early 1800s, but so were newspapers. In the early 1800s, it could take as many as four days for news from London, England, to reach Brussels, Belgium. As technology improved, so did spreading the news. The French Revolution caused a rise in newspaper printing, but when Napoleon I came to power he placed limits on newspaper publishing. Napoleon I actually had his own newspaper and allowed few others to exist while he was the leader of France. By the time the American Revolution broke out, there were more than three dozen newspapers in circulation in the colonies. The movement of news was not the only challenge; translation was another one. Even when news came from abroad, it was often in a different language. One French company started translating news items in the 1830s to help solve this issue in Europe.

INTRODUCE & ENGAGE

DISCUSS SLAVERY, DEMOCRACY, AND REVOLUTION

Prompt students to think about how slavery might have been affected by the democratic ideals that drove each of the revolutions. Discuss what factors might have influenced whether or not slavery was banned in a country that experienced a revolution. Invite students to think about how economic and cultural influences could have had an impact on whether each country allowed slavery to continue even after the country had gained its freedom or experienced a revolution.

TEACH

GUIDED DISCUSSION

1. **Analyze Cause and Effect** What caused conservatism to re-emerge in France after the revolution, and how did it affect conservatism in Europe? *(Possible response: the excesses of French politics; Conservatism rose in Europe, but it was suppressed by nationalist movements that broke out and were successful.)*

2. **Make Connections** Why do you think military commanders took power in South America after the independence movements? *(Possible response: These countries did not have capable and educated leaders outside of the military because they were either suppressed through the social structure or had no experience.)*

ANALYZE PRIMARY SOURCES

Have students read carefully the excerpt from Benjamin Franklin's letter to Henry Laurens in the lesson. **ASK:** What main point does Franklin express about the state of affairs? *(Possible response: that countries often are not forthright and honest about the actual state of affairs)* Why does Franklin make this assertion? *(Possible response: He says that states do this because they want to raise the spirits of their citizens, thinking that their state is succeeding even if it is failing.)*

ACTIVE OPTIONS

On Your Feet: Fishbowl After students have viewed the video "History 101: Revolutions" (available in the Student eEdition), arrange them in a Fishbowl formation to discuss the following question: What characteristics were aspects that led to the American, French, and Latin American revolutions? After both groups have had a chance to discuss the question, ask students to exchange ideas and summarize the results of the discussions.

> **NG Learning Framework: Compare the Lasting Effects of the Revolutions**
> **ATTITUDE** Curiosity
> **KNOWLEDGE** Our Human Story

Explain that the American, French, and Latin American revolutions all had lasting effects. Ask small groups to research how these effects were similar and different and if their effects can still be seen today. Tell them to create guiding questions for their research and use graphic organizers to collect and compare information. Have groups present their findings to the class.

DIFFERENTIATE

INCLUSION

Work in Pairs Have students with disabilities partner with students who can read the lesson aloud to them. Then have pairs answer the Historical Thinking questions.

PRE-AP

Research and Write a Narrative Have students write a narrative from the perspective of someone who fought for independence in Latin America but did not reap the benefits, such as an indigenous person, African, or person of mixed heritage. Tell them to include how their lives changed or did not change after independence, including their roles and livelihoods. Students should cite their sources and ensure details are accurate. They may read their narratives to the class or post on a class blog.

See the Chapter Planner for more strategies for differentiation.

HISTORICAL THINKING

ANSWERS

1. Possible response: The United States was able to establish a long-lasting government based on democratic ideas and had times of relatively peaceful growth. Social classes that played important roles in revolution in France, Haiti, and Latin America did not benefit from it as in the United States. However, slavery, which was abolished elsewhere, continued. The basic structure of society changed little in the post-revolutionary period.

2. Enslaved people were freed; Haiti's economy suffered; Social conflicts flared; Military dictators took over; It became a republic in name only.

3. Possible response: They included how to structure government, extend liberty and equality, create economic success, and make decisions without outside influence.

VOCABULARY

Complete each of the following sentences using one of the vocabulary words from the chapter.

1. Any government that places legal limits on its powers is practicing _____.

2. The upper class in South America established violent _____ that supervised local lands.

3. Some people in France were _____ and wanted more rights.

4. Napoleon Bonaparte used _____ to manipulate French citizens to think and act in a particular way.

5. The rise of _____ gave the French a sense of their common identity.

6. The 18th-century cultural movement that emphasized emotion over reason is known as _____.

7. Rebel fighters, or _____, in Saint-Domingue followed Boukman as they fought for independence.

8. The people of Venezuela feared their _____, a powerful leader.

READING STRATEGY
DRAW CONCLUSIONS

When you draw conclusions, you make a judgment based on what you have read. You analyze the facts, make inferences, and use your own experiences to form your judgment. Use a diagram like this one to draw conclusions about why people rebelled against their governments. Then answer the question.

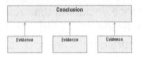

9. Why did people in Europe and the Americas rebel against their governments in the late 1700s and early 1800s?

MAIN IDEAS

Answer the following questions. Support your answers with evidence from the chapter.

10. How did Thomas Jefferson use Enlightenment ideas to justify the American colonists' break from Britain? LESSON 1.1

11. Who were the bourgeoisie in France, and what was their role in the French Revolution? LESSON 1.2

12. Why did most people in the French colony of Saint-Domingue want to rebel? LESSON 1.3

13. What actions did Napoleon take to assure that he would be well remembered throughout history? LESSON 2.1

14. What types of subject matter did Romantic writers address? LESSON 2.3

15. What led Simón Bolívar to seek independence for Latin America? LESSON 3.1

16. What was the role of Miguel Hidalgo y Costilla in Mexico's fight for freedom? LESSON 3.2

17. What new challenges did South American countries face following independence? LESSON 3.3

HISTORICAL THINKING

Answer the following questions. Support your answers with evidence from the chapter.

18. MAKE CONNECTIONS Why were American colonists so interested in John Locke's ideas of popular sovereignty and "consent of the governed"?

19. COMPARE AND CONTRAST In what ways were the American Revolution and the French Revolution similar and different?

20. ANALYZE CAUSE AND EFFECT What were the immediate effects and long-term effects of the revolution led by Toussaint L'Ouverture?

21. DETERMINE CHRONOLOGY What sequence of events illustrate the rise, rule, and fall of Napoleon Bonaparte?

22. MAKE GENERALIZATIONS Based on what you read, how important was Romanticism to society in the early 1800s?

23. FORM AND SUPPORT OPINIONS Do you agree with Simón Bolívar's viewpoint that South America needed a strong executive branch and a weak or nonexistent legislative branch? Explain.

24. ANALYZE CAUSE AND EFFECT What impact did Napoleon have on Latin America in the early 1800s?

25. DRAW CONCLUSIONS Why did European leaders want to revert to the past while American leaders preferred to focus on the future?

INTERPRET VISUALS

Caspar David Friedrich was a leading artist in the German Romantic movement. His painting *Wanderer Above the Sea of Fog* is one example of his extensive work. Study the painting and answer the question that follows.

26. In what ways does this painting represent the ideals of Romanticism?

ANALYZE SOURCES

Mercy Otis Warren was a political writer and propagandist who knew several key figures of the American Revolution. Read the following excerpt from a letter she wrote to the writer and historian Catherine Macauley in 1787 and answer the questions.

> Our situation is truly delicate and critical. On the one hand we are in need of a strong federal government founded on principles that will support the prosperity and union of the colonies. On the other hand we have struggled for liberty and made lofty sacrifices at her shrine: and there are still many of us who revere her name too much to relinquish (beyond a certain medium) the rights of man for the dignity of government.

27. What Enlightenment political idea does the excerpt best support? Explain your answer.

28. The letter was written in 1787. How did events at that time influence the message conveyed in the excerpt?

CONNECT TO YOUR LIFE

29. NARRATIVE Choose a revolutionary movement from this chapter. Imagine you are living in the time and place of this revolution. The rebellion has ended, and you are writing a letter to a friend or relative in another country describing the events that happened during and after the revolution and whether you think the movement succeeded or failed.

TIPS

* Skim the chapter and choose a revolution that interests you.

* Consider the leadership and initial goals of your chosen revolutionary movement, who participated in the revolution, expected or unexpected obstacles, and the outcomes of the revolutionary effort.

* Develop your topic by discussing ways in which your own circumstances and attitudes changed or did not change.

* Use vivid, descriptive language and two or three vocabulary terms from the chapter in your letter.

* End your letter with a brief summary of how you feel at the current time.

VOCABULARY ANSWERS

1. constitutionalism
2. juntas
3. disenfranchised
4. propaganda
5. nationalism
6. Romanticism
7. insurgents
8. caudillo

READING STRATEGY ANSWER

Conclusion
Enlightenment ideas encouraged the lower classes to fight for freedom.

Evidence	Evidence	Evidence
Monarchs and the upper classes held most of the power and wealth.	Many of the lower classes and poor had no rights.	Enlightenment ideals of equality slowly spread throughout the world.

9. People rebelled against their governments in the 1700s and 1800s because they wanted independence from European powers.

MAIN IDEAS ANSWERS

10. In the Declaration of Independence, Jefferson alluded to the Enlightenment ideas that all people have basic human rights, that unjust governments may be overthrown, and that people should hold the power of government.

11. The bourgeoisie were the educated middle class of France who had fewer rights than the upper classes did. Members of the bourgeoisie used the ideas of the Enlightenment to seek changes within the French government to improve their situation.

12. The whites of Saint-Domingue, who only numbered around 30,000, dominated the plantation economy. The gens de couleur lacked equal rights, and the enslaved Africans had no rights and were forced to work under harsh conditions.

13. Possible response: He became emperor of France, built a European empire, introduced the idea of nation-states, and caused the growth of nationalism.

14. Possible responses: the natural world, interaction between people and nature, freedom, innocence, seemingly insignificant objects made sublime, the imagined, myth, history, heroes, urban problems

15. His experience as a criollo in colonial Latin America, his knowledge of Enlightenment ideas, and his travel throughout Europe instilled a revolutionary spirit.

16. He rallied Mexico's poor to seek independence from Spain; his forces were crushed and he was killed.

17. Possible response: Military leaders took control. Criollos prospered; poor Africans, Native Americans, and people of mixed races suffered.

HISTORICAL THINKING ANSWERS

18. Possible response: The American colonies had no voice in the government. Some colonists felt that the British monarch and Parliament could do whatever they wanted. The colonists believed that they should be able to choose leaders who would represent them; they realized that popular sovereignty was the best way to achieve these goals. Through "consent of the governed," leaders and government would lose their power if they didn't represent the people.

19. Possible response: Both fought against oppressive governments and taxes without representation, wanted rights and freedoms, excluded women from equal rights, drew on Enlightenment ideas, and inspired others. Americans declared independence before the French did, were led by the privileged and well educated, wanted to establish a new nation, and experienced stability after the revolution. The French used the United States as a model, advanced their cause through the participation of common people, wanted to change their government internally, and faced years of struggle following revolution.

20. Possible response: The immediate effects were that Saint-Domingue became free from French control, ended the institution of slavery there, and formed a republic named Haiti. Long-term effects were that crop production dropped dramatically, and eventually dictators gained control of Haiti.

21. Possible events: becomes general in French army, stages coup d'état, gains power through citizens' vote, crowns himself emperor, creates Napoleonic Code, leads military campaigns, builds empire, unsuccessfully attacks Russia, abdicates throne, is banished to Elba, attempts comeback, is defeated at Waterloo, dies in exile

22. Possible response: It represented a drastic move away from order and reason; expanded people's creativity, emotional range, individuality, world view, and appreciation of the beauty of nature; spread through every artistic medium; influenced generations of writers, artists, and musicians.

23. Answers will vary. Some students may say that a strong executive branch would lead to dictatorship and loss of individual rights. Others may say that only a strong executive branch could create unity for South America and that a strong legislative branch would delay the time it took to make decisions.

24. Possible response: In some ways, Napoleon inspired Simón Bolívar to seek a path of glory as the liberator of South America. Also, the Napoleonic Wars changed the balance of power in Europe, and Napoleon's takeover of Spain provided an opportunity for Latin Americans to seek independence. In addition, Napoleon's quest to claim Portugal forced Portugal's royal family into exile in Brazil and set the stage for Brazil to become a constitutional monarchy.

25. Possible response: European leaders wanted to return to a time when they held wealth and power. They feared the spread of equality and nationalism. In contrast, American leaders had participated in the revolution to free the colonies from British control. They wanted to ensure that their new nation would survive, remain united, and grow physically and economically.

INTERPRET VISUALS ANSWER

26. Possible response: It shows the subject matter imaginatively and subjectively, and a natural setting is addressed in a sublime way. Every effort is made to appeal to the senses and to emotion. The painting portrays freedom and individualism.

ANALYZE SOURCES ANSWERS

27. Possible response: the social contract; While the excerpt also addresses liberty and equality, the main focus is the relationship between citizens and their government.

28. Possible response: It was written at the end of the revolutionary period and emphasized that the new United States must be careful as it forms a new government that has the consent of the governed.

CONNECT TO YOUR LIFE ANSWER

29. Students' letters should correctly describe their chosen revolution's leadership, participants, initial goals, expected or unexpected obstacles, and outcomes; use details from the chapter to support their explanation of how their circumstances and attitudes changed or did not change; use vivid language and two or three vocabulary terms.

Jane Goodall:
A Revolutionary Naturalist

BY TONY GERBER Adapted from "Becoming Jane" by Tony Gerber,
National Geographic, October 2017

The basic narrative of Jane Goodall's life is instantly recognizable from the many times it's been written, broadcast, or otherwise sent into the world: *A young Englishwoman conducts chimpanzee research in Africa and winds up revolutionizing primate science.* But how did it happen? How did a woman with a passion for animals but no formal background in research navigate the male-dominated worlds of science and media to make enormous discoveries in her field and become a world-famous face of the conservation movement?

While conducting research at Gombe Stream Game Reserve in present-day Tanzania, Goodall withstood all manner of natural threats: malaria, parasites, snakes, storms. But in her dealings with the wider world, the challenges often required shrewd strategy and delicate diplomacy. Early in her career, Goodall had to contend with a primarily male science establishment that didn't take her seriously and with media executives whose support hinged on her willingness to be scripted and glamorized. Through it all, Goodall's philosophy seemed the same: She would endure slights, accommodate demands, tolerate fools, make sacrifices—if it served to sustain her work.

From the start, Goodall followed her instincts for conducting research. Not knowing that the established scientific practice was to use numbers to identify animals under study, she recorded observations of the chimps by names she concocted. She saw them as individuals with distinct traits and personalities. She wrote about them as individuals with distinct traits and personalities.

At Gombe, Goodall made three discoveries that would turn established science on its head. First, she observed a chimp she named David Greybeard gnawing on the carcass of a small animal, which belied the prevailing belief that apes didn't eat meat. Her next discovery was truly game-changing. She saw the same chimp pick a blade of grass and poke it into a termite tunnel. When he pulled it out, it was covered with termites, which he slurped down. In another instance, Goodall saw David Greybeard pick a twig and strip it of leaves before using it to fish for termites.

In the early 1960s in what is now Tanzania, Jane Goodall touches chimpanzees Fifi and Flint as Flo, the chimps' mother, looks on. Physical contact with chimps in the wild is no longer deemed appropriate.

The chimp had exhibited both tool use and toolmaking—two things that previously only humans were believed capable of. In the wake of these discoveries, National Geographic gave Goodall a grant to continue her work.

But as Goodall began to publish her field research, she met with skepticism from the scientific community. In the spring of 1962, she gave a presentation at the Zoological Society of London's primate symposium. Although she impressed many people, she also faced derision. A society officer critiqued her work as making no "real contribution to science." An Associated Press report described Goodall as a "willowy blonde with more time for monkeys than men."

Over time, however, her findings sparked worldwide interest and upended conventional wisdom about humans. Since those early discoveries, Goodall has completed a Ph.D. at Cambridge University, authored dozens of books, mentored new generations of wildlife conservation, and established several sanctuaries for chimps. Today, the Jane Goodall Institute's Roots & Shoots program operates in nearly a hundred countries, training young people to be conservation leaders.

And on her way to becoming a world-renowned naturalist, Goodall forever changed the way we think about our relatives, the apes. ■

Staging the Question

In this unit, you learned about various revolutions that brought dramatic changes to Western society. The Scientific Revolution introduced a new procedure for developing and testing ideas in science. The Enlightenment spread revolutionary ideas in philosophy, government, religion, economics, education, and other fields. These new ideas helped inspire political revolutions in Europe and the Americas. All these revolutions were sparked by individuals or groups who were able to change the way an entire society thought or acted. How does an individual change the thinking or actions of a whole culture?

Supporting Questions: Begin by developing supporting questions to guide your thinking. For example: What topic are you passionate about? Perhaps you have ideas about revolutionizing education or changing social media. What changes would you like to see? How would you go about effecting those changes?

Summative Performance Task:
Use the answers to your questions to plan your revolution. Identify your goal and list specific actions to be taken to promote the changes you'd like to see. You might use a graphic organizer like this one to develop your plan.

Present: Share your toolbox with the class. You might consider one of these options:

ASSIGNMENT
Select three individuals who have initiated or contributed to revolutions in a particular field. You may choose people from this unit or from your own research.

Identify the kind of change that each person promoted and the reasons for it.

Describe the revolutions that resulted.

Based on your analysis of how individuals have sparked revolutions, plan a revolution of your own on a subject you care deeply about.

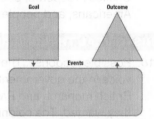

CREATE A FLYER
Write and illustrate a flyer that describes the changes you're promoting, the reasons for the changes, and their benefits. Use persuasive language or a personal story to engage readers and enlist them in your cause. Display the flyer in your classroom.

PREPARE A TALK
Record a short talk in which you promote your ideas. Include graphics, photos, or other visuals to support your ideas. You might search the Internet for an inspiring talk to serve as a model.

Take Informed Action:

UNDERSTAND Identify both the pros and the cons of your plan. Ask yourself who would be likely to oppose the plan and why.

ASSESS Revolutions seldom happen overnight; they occur over time. Assess how long it would likely take for your revolution to take hold.

ACT Choose one of the actions listed in your plan and start your revolution.

NATIONAL GEOGRAPHIC CONNECTION

GUIDED DISCUSSION FOR "JANE GOODALL: A REVOLUTIONARY NATURALIST"

1. **Identify** What discoveries did Goodall make about chimps, and why were these discoveries significant? *(Goodall discovered that chimps eat meat, make tools, and use tools. These discoveries contradicted past research about chimps, especially the belief that only humans could make and use tools. These discoveries also led to Goodall's sponsorship by National Geographic that allowed her research to continue.)*

2. **Explain** What challenges did Goodall face while breaking into the scientific community? *(Possible response: Goodall faced skepticism and criticism from the science community, having to prove herself as a researcher in a male-dominated field.)*

History Notebook
Encourage students to complete the Unit Wrap-Up page for Unit 7 in their History Notebooks.

UNIT INQUIRY PROJECT RUBRIC

ASSESS

Use the rubric to assess each student's participation and performance.

SCORE	ASSIGNMENT	PRODUCT	PRESENTATION
3 GREAT	• Student thoroughly understands the assignment. • Student develops thoughtful supporting questions to guide research.	• Plan is well thought out with a clear goal and specific actions to be taken. • Plan reflects all of the key elements listed in the assignment.	• Presentation is clear, concise, and logical. • Presentation is creative and engaging.
2 GOOD	• Student mostly understands the assignment. • Student develops somewhat thoughtful supporting questions to guide research.	• Plan is fairly well thought out with an unclear goal and actions to be taken. • Plan reflects most of the key elements listed in the assignment.	• Presentation is fairly clear, concise, and logical. • Presentation is somewhat creative and engaging.
1 NEEDS WORK	• Student does not understand the assignment. • Student does not develop thoughtful questions to guide research.	• Plan is not well thought out and does not contain a goal or actions to be taken. • Plan reflects few or none of the key elements listed in the assignment.	• Presentation is not clear, concise, or logical. • Presentation is not creative or engaging.

INTRODUCE THE PAINTING

COALBROOKDALE BY NIGHT

This painting by the English painter Philip James de Loutherbourg shows the ever-burning Bedlam Furnaces in Shropshire, England. The flames from the furnace light up the night sky as if the city were on fire. The oil painting depicts the Madeley Wood (or Bedlam) Furnaces that burned in the Coalbrookdale Company from 1776 to 1796. *Coalbrookdale by Night* symbolizes the birth of the Industrial Revolution.

Direct students' attention to the painting. **ASK:** From what location is the artist viewing the city? *(from a road leading into the city)* How do the artist's vantage point and the night sky affect his portrayal of the furnaces? *(The artist is able to view the furnace flames from a distance, which gives him a broad view of the buildings near the furnaces and shows the bright flames and orange-colored smoke against the dark backdrop of the night sky.)* Explain that Loutherbourg was known for his three-dimensional paintings. **ASK:** What 3-D elements do you see in the painting? *(Possible response: Looking down the street, the man walking, the city buildings, and the mountains in the background all add to the three-dimensional qualities of the painting.)*

PHILIP JAMES DE LOUTHERBOURG

Philip James de Loutherbourg was an early Romantic painter, illustrator, printmaker, and scenographer born in Chiswick, Middlesex, England, in 1740. His specialty was painting landscapes and battles, but he was also known for his innovative scenery designs and the special effects that he brought to theater. He originally trained under his father in Paris, and then worked as a theatrical designer at the Drury Lane Theater in London until 1785. He was the first to

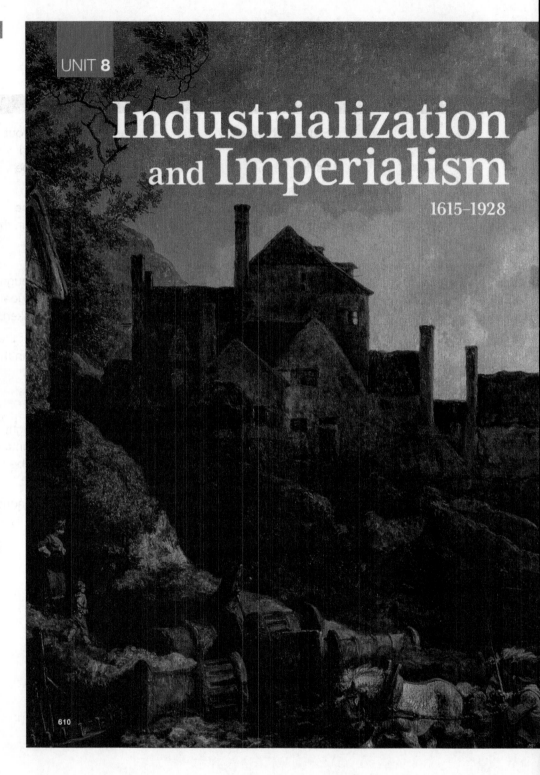

UNIT **8**

Industrialization and **Imperialism**

1615–1928

610

611

introduce scrims (gauzes that appear transparent) and three-dimensional scenery. Loutherbourg was received into the French Royal Academy of Painting and Sculpture in 1767 and was made a member of the British Royal Academy in 1780.

CRITICAL VIEWING Possible response: Life was probably difficult for the people who lived near the furnaces. They likely suffered from poor health, since they had to breathe in smoke from the furnaces, and the furnaces probably made the area hotter during the summer. There may also have been constant noise from the furnaces.

INTRODUCE TIME LINE EVENTS

IDENTIFY PATTERNS AND THEMES

Have volunteers read aloud each of the world events in the time line. **ASK:** What are some common themes or patterns that you notice with regard to these events? *(Possible responses: Some common themes or patterns include technological innovation and industrialization, colonization and conquest, and changes in work conditions and slavery.)* Sort the themes and patterns into categories and put them in a chart like the one shown here.

Innovation and Industrialization	Colonization and Conquests	Work Conditions and Slavery

As students read the lessons for each chapter in the unit, have them add the lesson titles to the appropriate column in the chart. Advise students that they may also add or revise categories as necessary. At the end of the unit, revisit students' charts and create a final list of categories to summarize the historical themes students encountered as they read each chapter.

UNIT 8 Industrialization and Imperialism

WORLD EVENTS
1765–1912

1776 EUROPE Scottish philosopher Adam Smith publishes *The Wealth of Nations*, in which the idea of capitalism is described for the first time. *(portrait of Adam Smith, 1795)*

1839–1842 ASIA The First Opium War is fought between China and Britain after the Chinese government tries to stop the trade of opium in its country. *(painting of British ships destroying an enemy fleet off the coast of China)*

1831 AMERICAS American industrialist Cyrus McCormick develops a mechanical reaper that revolutionizes wheat harvesting.

| 1750 | 1775 | 1800 | 1825 |

1765 EUROPE Scottish inventor James Watt greatly improves the efficiency of the steam engine.

1836 AFRICA The Boers, farmers of Dutch, French, and German descent, undertake their "Great Trek" through southern Africa to escape British rule.

c. 1793 AMERICAS American inventor Eli Whitney invents the cotton gin, making it easier to remove cottonseeds from cotton fiber. *(patent model of Whitney's cotton gin)*

1838 EUROPE English writer Charles Dickens publishes *Oliver Twist*, which criticizes the workhouse system and exposes the conditions of the poor in Britain. *(title page of a serialized version of Oliver Twist)*

1848 EUROPE German philosophers Karl Marx and Friedrich Engels publish the pamphlet *The Manifesto of the Communist Party*, which calls for the creation of a workers' society that does away with class struggles and abolishes private property.

HISTORICAL THINKING

ANALYZE CAUSE AND EFFECT What earlier event might have helped promote the European race for territory in Africa?

1848 EUROPE Nationalism stirs unrest and revolution across Europe. *(portrait of Italian patriot Giuseppe Garibaldi)*

1858 ASIA France begins colonizing cities in Vietnam and eventually expands its control over Cambodia and Laos. *(presidential palace in Hanoi, once the home of the French governor of Indochina)*

1884–1885 AFRICA The Berlin Conference divides Africa among European powers and triggers a race for territory on the continent.

| 1850 | 1875 | 1900 | 1925 |

1856 EUROPE English engineer Henry Bessemer invents a process to manufacture steel inexpensively.

1859 EUROPE British naturalist Charles Darwin publishes *On the Origin of Species*, which some people use to justify inequality in human society as "survival of the fittest."

1869 AFRICA The completion of the Suez Canal in Egypt separates the continents of Africa and Asia and links the Mediterranean and Red seas. *(painting of the inauguration of the Suez Canal)*

1912 ASIA Two thousand years of imperial rule in China come to an end when revolutionary forces overthrow the Qing dynasty. *(Puyi, China's last emperor, in 1910)*

613

HISTORICAL THINKING

Analyze Cause and Effect

Possible response: The completion of the Suez Canal, which allowed ships to pass from the Mediterranean Sea through to the Indian Ocean, might have triggered the European race for territory in Africa.

Student eEdition online

Additional content, including the unit map and Global Perspective feature, is available online.

UNIT 8

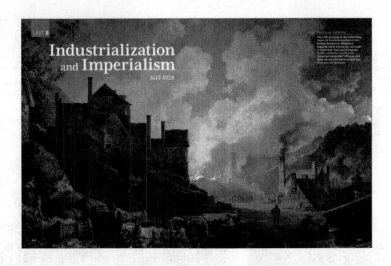

STRATEGY ❶
Analyze Main Ideas

Direct students to read aloud the Main Idea statement for each lesson. Explain that these statements identify and summarize the key idea for each lesson. As students read the lessons, encourage them to make notes about details they find in the text that connect to the Main Idea statements. Tell them this process will help them identify and remember the most important information.

Use with All Lessons

STRATEGY ❷
Make a Problem-and-Solution Chart

Instruct students to make a chart to help them understand the problems and solutions discussed in the chapter. Tell them to note in the chart the problems faced by the people of the Industrial Revolution, details related to those problems, and the eventual solutions to the problems. Tell students to read independently first, and then to work in pairs to identify one of the problems and write it in the first column. Then tell them to take turns, with one partner rereading aloud the paragraphs related to the problem, while the other listens and identifies details to list in the second column and a solution to list in the third column.

Problems	Details	Solutions

Use with All Lessons

STRATEGY ❸
List "Top Five Facts"

After students finish a lesson, direct them to write in their own words five important facts they have learned. Ask them to compare lists with a partner and consolidate their two lists into one. Then have each pair turn their facts into questions and then work with another pair, taking turns asking and answering their "Top Five" questions.

Use with All Lessons

STRATEGY ❶
Preview Using Maps

Preview maps to orient students to the lesson topic and to help them comprehend lesson text. Tell students to read the map title and legend and then place a finger on relevant information and trace arrows if present. For example, for the map of Industrialization in Continental Europe, c. 1850, in Lesson 1.1, point out the color in the legend that represents the emerging industrial areas. For the Italian and German Unification map in Lesson 2.2, encourage students to identify the German and Italian empires and identify sections that were added to each empire. For the map of Indian Railroads, 1893 (available in the Student eEdition), in Lesson 3.2, point out the color in the legend that represents the railroad tracks and tell students to trace the journey from Bombay to Lahore.

Use with Lessons 1.1, 2.2, and 3.2

STRATEGY ❷
Use Supported Reading

Have student pairs read aloud the chapter lesson by lesson. Instruct them to stop at the end of each lesson and use the sentence frames to monitor their comprehension:

- This lesson is mostly about _____ .
- Other topics in this lesson include _____ .
- One question I have about the lesson is _____ .
- I don't think I understand _____ .
- One word I do not recognize is _____ .
- It means _____ .

Use with All Lessons

STRATEGY ❶
Chart Events

To build comprehension of the issues and events surrounding the Industrial Revolution, have students of **All Proficiencies** chart these developments discussed in Lesson 1.2: types of industries, important inventions, working conditions, living conditions, and political changes. Chart globalization in Lesson 2.1: types of transportation advancements, where transportation improved, types of communication, and inventors. Chart political ideals in Lesson 2.2: political philosophy, what it is, and who or where the philosophy was practiced.

Use with Lessons 1.2, 2.1, and 2.2

STRATEGY ②
Rewrite Captions

Challenge students at the **Beginning** and **Intermediate** levels to write in their own words one-sentence captions for the visuals in Lesson 3.1. Ask students at the **Advanced** level to write captions of a few sentences or a short paragraph to accompany the visuals in the lesson. Suggest they vary the sentence structure of their captions.

Use with Lesson 3.1 *This strategy may be used with all lessons. You might pair students at the **Beginning** level with students of different proficiency levels.*

STRATEGY ③
Create a Word Wall

Work with students at the **Beginning** and **Intermediate** levels to select three words from each lesson to display in a grouping on a Word Wall. Choose words students are likely to encounter in other lessons, such as *sabotage, globalization,* and *communism.* Keep the words displayed throughout the chapter and discuss each one as it comes up during reading. Suggest that students at the **Advanced** level contribute by adding phrases or examples to each word to develop understanding.

Use with All Lessons

GIFTED & TALENTED

STRATEGY ①
Create a Podcast

Direct students to choose one lesson or part of a lesson as the basis for an episode of a history podcast. Tell students that their podcast should express a point of view so that it is both informative and entertaining. Suggest they write a script for their podcast and include sound effects and music. Have students present their episode to the class or record it on a phone or other device.

Use with All Lessons

STRATEGY ②
Extend Knowledge

Invite students to conduct online research to learn more about a person, an invention, or an event introduced in this chapter. For example, students might choose to research James Watt, Henry Bessemer, the cotton gin, pit ponies (or other exploited animals), Queen Victoria, Louis Pasteur, the Crystal Palace in Kensington Gardens, Hong Xiuquan, Empress Ci Xi, or the growth of imperialism or militarism. Invite students to present their findings in an oral report to the class or in a digital report posted on a class website or blog.

Use with All Lessons

PRE-AP

STRATEGY ①
Read a Book or Poetry Collection

Challenge students to read a biography or historical fiction novel related to the chapter, such as a book by Charles Dickens, Elizabeth Gaskell, or Emily or Charlotte Brontë, or a collection of poetry by Elizabeth Barrett Browning, William Blake, Michael Thomas Sadler, or Percy Bysshe Shelley. Establish criteria for evaluating the text, such as readability, interest, and historical accuracy. Based on the criteria, ask students to write a review to share with the class that includes quotes from the text pertaining to the Industrial Revolution.

Use with All Lessons

STRATEGY ②
Consider Both Sides

Have students write a short essay about the Industrial Revolution and its effects on daily life in Britain. Instruct students to present both positive and negative effects of the shift to a factory system, the development of widespread transportation networks, and the rise of new technologies. Tell students to conclude the essay with their opinion on whether the Industrial Revolution was more harmful or more beneficial. Have students present their essays to the class and encourage listeners to offer opposing opinions.

Use with Lesson 1.2 *Suggest that students first make a list of the pros and cons of the Industrial Revolution in Britain and refer to it as they write.*

Industrial Revolution
1615–1928

CRITICAL VIEWING
A steam-powered locomotive chugs along through a snow-covered forest in Germany. In what way is the steam-powered locomotive symbolic of the Industrial Revolution?

INTRODUCE THE PHOTOGRAPH

STEAM LOCOMOTIVES

Have students study the photograph of the steam locomotive pulling out of a railway station in Pennsylvania. **ASK:** In what ways might the steam-powered locomotive have changed life for people during this period? *(Possible response: Steam locomotives could move people and goods quickly, making travel between cities, states, countries, or far distances possible.)* Explain that though they were originally built to haul coal from mines, by 1820, steam trains were being used in European cities to move people and goods. In the United States, the first locomotives were British, but soon American inventors developed their own engines that worked better on American tracks. Tell students that in this chapter they will learn more about the inventions and other life-changing events of the Industrial Revolution.

SHARE BACKGROUND

The main inventor of the steam locomotive was George Stephenson, a British engineer. Though Stephenson went to work at an early age, he later learned how to read and write in night school. He became an expert on steam engines. His first steam engine, the *Blucher*, could pull eight loaded wagons of coal, which weighed 30 tons. He improved on this engine by developing a chimney to channel the steam and increase the draft, which burned the coal in the engine more quickly and increased the engine's speed. In 1825, Stephenson developed the first passenger train engine, the *Active*, which transported 450 people from Darlington, England, to Stockton, England, at 15 miles per hour. Four years later, he won a competition with another passenger locomotive, the *Rocket*, which could travel at a record 36 miles per hour.

CRITICAL VIEWING Answers will vary. Possible response: The steam-powered locomotive is symbolic of the Industrial Revolution because it made it possible for people and goods to travel farther and faster, thereby enabling people to spread and settle across the country. In addition, steam power as a whole revolutionized the world in many areas, not just in transportation.

HISTORICAL THINKING QUESTION

How did the Industrial Revolution transform people's lives around the world?

Roundtable Activity: Impact of the Industrial Revolution Arrange students in groups. Ask half of the groups these two questions: What are examples of technologies that have been transformative? How did they change the world in positive ways? Ask the other groups these two questions: What negative impacts do transformative technologies bring? Do the negatives outweigh the positives? Have the first student in each group write an answer to the questions on a sheet of paper and pass the paper clockwise to the next student, who answers the questions in a different way. Students should continue until they are out of ideas. As a class, compile a master list of answers for the questions. Then tell students that in Chapter 22 they will learn about the technologies of the Industrial Revolution and how they changed the world.

KEY DATES FOR CHAPTER 22

1750	India and China produce much of the world's manufactured products.
1765	Scotsman James Watt introduces a workable steam engine.
1793	American Eli Whitney invents the cotton gin.
1831	American Cyrus McCormick invents the McCormick reaper.
1838	Charles Dickens publishes *Oliver Twist*.
1848	*The Manifesto of the Communist Party* is published by Karl Marx and Friedrich Engels.
1851	*The Great Exhibition of the Works of Industry of All Nations* opens.
1856	Henry Bessemer invents a low-cost way to produce high-quality steel.
1869	An underwater telegraph cable is laid in the Atlantic Ocean.
1893	The Ferris Wheel is introduced at the Chicago World's Fair.

INTRODUCE THE READING STRATEGY

DETERMINE CHRONOLOGY

Explain to students that determining the order in which events occurred helps put events in perspective and can help determine causal relationships. Go to the Chapter Review and preview the time line with students. As they read the chapter, have students note key events in the text and add them to the time line.

INTRODUCE CHAPTER VOCABULARY

KEY VOCABULARY

SECTION 1

cottage industry	division of labor	exposition
sabotage	social criticism	

SECTION 2

communism	globalization	liberalism
proletariat	Social Darwinism	socialism

SECTION 3

extraterritoriality	militarism	sepoy
zaibatsu		

WORD MAPS

As they read the chapter, encourage students to complete a Word Map for each Key Vocabulary word. Have them write the word in the center oval, and, as they encounter the word in the chapter, complete the Word Map for that word. At the end of the chapter, ask students what they learned about each word. Model an example for students on the board, using the graphic organizer below.

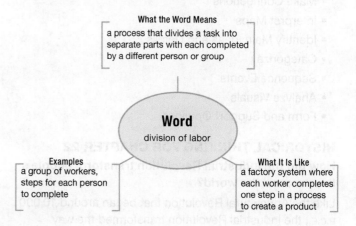

What the Word Means
a process that divides a task into separate parts with each completed by a different person or group

Word
division of labor

Examples
a group of workers, steps for each person to complete

What It Is Like
a factory system where each worker completes one step in a process to create a product

Origins of Industrialization

Look around the room. How many objects around you were manufactured by machines? Now imagine how the room would look if every object had been made by hand. The way in which things were produced is one of the changes caused by the Industrial Revolution.

COAL, STEAM, AND IRON

In 1750, India and China made over half of the world's manufactured products. By 1860, this had changed. Using revolutionary techniques to expand production, western European nations were now in the lead role.

You have learned about the "practical science" of Britain in the 1800s. Now Britain, with a strong mercantile class and an aristocracy willing to provide capital, was becoming the most powerful nation in the world. It controlled the seas, had an extensive trading network, and ruled colonies around the globe that supplied low-paying and unpaid (slave) labor while also providing access to a huge variety of raw materials. Before 1780, sugar had been the most important import, along with cotton textiles from India. Profits from the earlier trade provided the money for British businessmen to invest in new machines and systems of working. With the rise of the factory system, raw cotton became the most significant import, especially from the expanding plantation system in the southern United States.

CRITICAL VIEWING This 19th-century painting shows a pithead, which is the top of a mining pit or coal shaft. What elements in the painting illustrate the ways people worked before the Industrial Revolution? What elements illustrate innovations that changed the way people worked?

In 1765, a Scotsman named **James Watt** introduced a machine he'd invented—the world's first workable steam engine. The machine was powered by coal, which heated water into steam that moved pistons and gears. With this machine the Industrial Revolution began.

It would be difficult to exaggerate the consequences of the Industrial Revolution. There had been no bigger revolution in human society since humans first began farming 12,000 years ago. Between 1750 and 1900, total global manufacturing production rose more than 400 percent. The centers of manufacturing shifted from India and China in the east to Europe and the United States in the west. So did the profits. Europe and the United States accounted for nearly three-quarters of production output by 1900. Global population doubled in the same time period.

The Industrial Revolution was also an energy revolution. The massive use of fossil fuels began at this time, unlocking the vast stored energy of coal—and later petroleum and natural gas. Less than 90 years after the introduction of Watt's machine, Britain's coal production had increased 10 times. This huge increase in power from fossil fuels led to further innovations in technology and in ways of organizing human labor. Almost every sphere of human activity was altered.

Coal provided more than just steam for the steam engine. It also provided the ability to create mass quantities of the iron needed to build the engine itself. For thousands of years, charcoal from wood had fueled smelting furnaces, which meant iron could only be produced in small batches. British forests could never supply the amount of wood needed for an industrial breakthrough, even with imports from North America. Improvements in technology, including the use of stronger vacuum pumps to remove water from coal mines, helped the British break through that energy barrier.

Around the same time that Watt unveiled his steam engine, English inventors learned to use coal more efficiently. A purified, concentrated form of coal called "coke" made it possible to produce low-cost, high-quality iron in large amounts. In 1856, the Industrial Revolution received another boost when **Henry Bessemer** invented a way to manufacture high-quality steel more cheaply. Steel is much stronger than iron and could be turned into track for railroads and beams and girders for skyscrapers.

Meanwhile, other changes were happening in manufacturing. In his book *The Wealth of Nations*, which you read about earlier, Adam Smith argued that **division of labor**, or a process that divides a task into separate parts with each completed by a different person or group, was a key to increased productivity. For example, a single shoemaker could make an excellent pair of shoes, but not as efficiently as a group of workers who each focused on a single step in the process. Smith was describing the new factory system of production.

The Luddites Many workers protested the changes brought about by new machines. In the late 18th and early 19th centuries, artisans organized secret societies and attacked the textile machines that threatened their way of life. Factory work required less training, and these skilled artisans resented the reduced quality and lower wages that occurred as a result. Those machine smashers were called "Luddites" after a fictional figure, shown here, named Ned Ludd, or General Ludd, who supposedly organized armies of machine smashers. In response to such incidents, Parliament made industrial **sabotage**, or deliberate destruction, a capital crime, and many Luddites were executed or exiled. Over time, however, the Luddites themselves became as mythological as their fictional leader, representing the desire of many to halt or slow the changes forced by new technology. Today, you might call anyone slow to adopt new technology a "Luddite."

PLAN: 4-PAGE LESSON

OBJECTIVE

Understand how scientific advancements in energy, agriculture, and technology during the Industrial Revolution dramatically impacted human society.

CRITICAL THINKING SKILLS FOR LESSON 1.1

- Analyze Cause and Effect
- Make Connections
- Interpret Maps
- Identify Main Ideas and Details
- Categorize
- Sequence Events
- Analyze Visuals
- Form and Support Opinions

HISTORICAL THINKING FOR CHAPTER 22

How did the Industrial Revolution transform people's lives around the world?

Like the Agricultural Revolution that began around 10,000 B.C.E., the Industrial Revolution transformed the way humans lived and worked. Lesson 1.1 discusses the key inventions and developments that launched the Industrial Revolution.

BACKGROUND FOR THE TEACHER

James Watt One of the leading figures in the origins of the Industrial Revolution was James Watt. Watt, who was Scottish, decided at a young age that he wanted to be a mathematical instrument maker. He studied in Glasgow and London between ages 17 and 19. By 19, Watt had figured out how to improve existing steam engines by adding a separate condenser unit. He opened his own instrument shop in Glasgow at age 21. He took out a patent on his steam engine and worked on his invention over the next several years. Eventually, Watt's engines were in great demand, and he became a wealthy man. His steam engine was one of the most important developments of the early Industrial Revolution, and as a result, the standard unit of power, the watt, was named after him.

Student eEdition online

Additional content for this lesson, including a video and an image gallery, is available online.

INTRODUCE & ENGAGE

PREVIEW WITH VISUALS

Direct students' attention to the photograph of William Murdock's steam engine in the lesson. **ASK:** From what is this steam engine made? *(Possible response: wood, brass, pulleys)* Then lead a class discussion on what modern engines, cell phones, and other technological devices are made from today. Point out that although this engine looks like an antique, it was revolutionary at the time. Have students discuss how technology might change over the next 200 years.

TEACH

GUIDED DISCUSSION

1. **Make Connections** What economic development in Britain made funding for revolutionary machines and processes possible? *(The development of a strong mercantile class and an aristocracy willing to provide capital for new ventures made the Industrial Revolution possible.)*

2. **Identify Main Ideas and Details** What machine essentially launched the Industrial Revolution? *(the steam engine)*

ANALYZE VISUALS

Direct students' attention to the Inventions and Inventors image gallery (available in the Student eEdition). Have them view the images and read the captions. **ASK:** What was the main purpose of the inventions shown in the gallery? *(Possible response: to make work easier and faster and to eliminate some of the manual labor required)* Then discuss Henry Bessemer's invention. **ASK:** Why was the Bessemer process a key development in the Industrial Revolution? *(Possible response: The Bessemer process allowed steel, which was stronger than iron, to be made more cheaply. The steel could then be used to build skyscrapers and railroad tracks.)*

DIFFERENTIATE

ENGLISH LANGUAGE LEARNERS

Give a Thumbs Up or Thumbs Down Write a set of true-false statements about the lesson, such as "The invention of the cotton gin did not increase slave labor." Read aloud the lesson, with students following along in their books. Then have them close the books and listen as you read the true-false statements. Students should give a thumbs up if a statement is true and a thumbs down if a statement is false.

GIFTED & TALENTED

Create a Visual Prompt students to conduct research to find out more about one of the inventions of the Industrial Revolution mentioned in this lesson. Then invite them to create a drawing, photograph, cartoon, graphic, video, or other visual about the invention and how it worked. Encourage students to present their finished visuals to the class and explain how the parts and functions of the invention are represented in their work.

See the Chapter Planner for more strategies for differentiation.

TEXTILE MANUFACTURING

It was in the textile industry where division of labor and steam power combined to full potential. For a thousand years, India had been the world's largest producer of cotton textiles, and Indian calico cloth flooded the British market. This competition hurt the British wool industry, so in the early 18th century Parliament passed the Calico Acts, which limited the amount of cotton cloth that could be imported from India. The Calico Acts helped Britain's wool industry—more than a quarter of British exports for the next 80 years were woolen goods—and the British cotton cloth industry.

Prior to industrialization, British cotton textiles were a **cottage industry**. A merchant provided raw materials to a rural family. In a traditional division of labor, the women spun the cotton into thread, and the men wove the thread into cloth. These methods were slow. With the steam engine, cloth manufacturers could organize and speed up the process.

Spinning raw cotton into thread was the slowest part of the manufacturing process and was the first to be mechanized. Women were no longer needed to spin, but men still worked in their own homes to weave the thread. Within decades, though, the steam-driven loom took the entire process out of homes and into factories. As the production of cloth grew faster and more efficient, demand for raw cotton rose. Another new invention would meet that demand, shift the main source of raw cotton away from India, and change the course of U.S. history.

In the late 1700s, some observers thought that slavery was in the process of dying out in the United States. Then in 1793, the American inventor **Eli Whitney** invented the cotton gin, a machine that quickly separated seeds from cotton, a process that took a long time when done by hand. This new machine meant that cotton grown and processed through slave labor in the South could supply the growing demand for cheap cotton in Britain at a huge profit to plantation owners in North America. These profits created a powerful incentive to acquire land—at any cost—to establish cotton plantations. New and devastating policies removed native Cherokee and Creek people from the southeastern United States to Oklahoma. As plantations expanded, slavery increased in extent and barbarity, cotton production surged, and the southern United States became the largest source of cotton for British textile manufacturers. By the 1830s, cloth manufacturing was fully mechanized, and Britain was the world's leading textile manufacturer, with sources of raw cotton from India and Egypt in addition to the United States.

AGRICULTURAL AND TECHNOLOGICAL INNOVATIONS

As you read earlier, the use of scientific improvements such as crossbreeding of livestock and crop rotation provided more food in England. In addition, farmers were reclaiming land, especially marshlands in eastern England, so more was available for farming. At the same time, however, new enclosure laws passed in the 17th and 18th centuries allowed aristocrats and wealthy farmers to claim common lands as their own private property, cutting off access to the common people to grazing lands and hunting grounds. Furthermore, new inventions such as the seed drill, which planted seeds more quickly, meant fewer farm laborers were needed. The McCormick Reaper, invented by the American industrialist **Cyrus McCormick** in 1831, revolutionized wheat harvesting in England. With no access to common land and fewer jobs for farm laborers, many rural families moved to towns and cities and became the workforce for mines and factories.

In addition to new agricultural practices, there were innovations in technology, specifically in transportation and communication. Steam power and iron production created new types of transportation that shipped raw materials into and finished products out of factories at greater speeds and in greater quantities than ever before. In the 1820s, steamships began to increase the efficiency of water transport, especially regarding international trade. As important as the rise of the steamship was the advance of the railroad. As iron became easier and cheaper to produce, its price dropped, and so did the cost of railroad tracks.

Britain led the Industrial Revolution, but it was not the only nation to industrialize. Belgium had rich iron ore and coal deposits as well as a history of textile manufacturing, so it industrialized soon after Britain. France and Switzerland had fewer natural resources but became leaders in the production of specialty and luxury goods. France's industrial output came to equal Britain's. Germany and the northern United States developed later but both had the raw materials (coal and iron) needed to build powerful industrial economies. You'll read later about how North American and European industrial states turned to Africa, Asia, and Latin America as sources of raw materials and markets for manufactured goods.

Industrialization in Continental Europe, c.1850

North Sea
Kiel
Hamburg
Bremen
ENGLAND
NETHERLANDS
Amsterdam
Berlin
POLAND
Warsaw
Posen
Essen
Cologne
Kassel
Breslau
Odra
Dieppe
Lille
Brussels
Liège
BELGIUM
GERMAN CONFEDERATION
Kraków
Le Havre
Rouen
Paris
Frankfurt
Prague
Orléans
Seine
Danube
Linz
Vienna
Nantes
Loire
Munich
Buda
Pest
Mulhouse
Zürich
SWITZERLAND
AUSTRIAN EMPIRE
Le Creusot
FRANCE
Lyons
Trieste
Grenoble
Turin
Milan
Po
Vienna
Bay of Biscay
Bordeaux
Genoa
Avignon
Toulouse
Marseilles
Livorno
Florence
OTTOMAN EMPIRE
Adriatic Sea
Mediterranean Sea

— Railroads completed, ca. 1850
■ Major exposed coal deposits
○ Emerging industrial areas
⚡ Scattered ironworks

0 50 100 Miles
0 50 100 Kilometers

STEAM ENGINE This sectional model, made in 1866, shows an 18th-century beam engine, a type of steam engine, invented by William Murdock, a Scottish inventor and engineer.

HISTORICAL THINKING

1. **READING CHECK** What was the Industrial Revolution?

2. **ANALYZE CAUSE AND EFFECT** How did mechanization in agriculture change life in Britain's cities and towns?

3. **MAKE CONNECTIONS** What was the relationship between the invention of a workable steam engine and the Industrial Revolution?

4. **INTERPRET MAPS** Based on details in the map, what conclusion can be drawn about the impact railroads had on the Industrial Revolution?

BACKGROUND FOR THE TEACHER

Steamships The steam engine revolutionized transportation not only on land but also on water. Part of the success of steamship travel was due to the efforts of Robert Fulton, an American nautical engineer who developed an early steamship in Paris financed by Robert Livingston, an American diplomat in France. The successful launch of Fulton's steamship on the Seine River in Paris impressed the crowd, even though the ship eventually sank. Fulton returned to the United States with Livingston and set to work on another steamship, the *Clermont*, which successfully steamed 150 miles from New York to Albany up the Hudson River. The ship traveled up the Hudson, arriving in Albany a day and a half after its launch. A sailing ship would have taken about a week to make the same trip.

TEACH

GUIDED DISCUSSION

3. **Categorize** What mechanical advancements were made during the Industrial Revolution? *(Possible response: Industrial Revolution mechanical advancements included machinery, railroads, trains, and electric wires.)*

4. **Sequence Events** Describe the sequence of events in the industrialization of the British textile industry. *(Possible response: Initially, textiles were made in rural homes in what is known as a cottage industry. Women spun cotton into thread, and men wove the thread into cloth. Then thread spinning was mechanized, but men still wove the cloth. With the development of the mechanical loom, the textile industry moved out of rural homes altogether and into factories.)*

FORM AND SUPPORT OPINIONS

Have students read The Luddites feature. Discuss as a class the reasons for the destruction of new machines during the Industrial Revolution. **ASK:** Do you think Parliament should have made industrial sabotage a capital crime, punishable by death? *(Answers will vary, but some students may oppose a death penalty entirely, while others may say that death for the destruction of property is too harsh.)* Then lead a class discussion about people who oppose new technology today.

ACTIVE OPTIONS

On Your Feet: Team Word Webbing Divide the class into three groups. Give each group a single large piece of paper. Assign each group one of the following topics: energy, labor, or agriculture. Then have each student add facts and points of view on the part of the paper nearest to him or her. On a signal, students rotate the paper and each student adds to the nearest part again. When students have finished, ask groups to share their completed team webs with the class.

| **NG Learning Framework: Write a Profile**
| **ATTITUDE** Curiosity
| **SKILL** Collaboration

Encourage students to learn more about the people mentioned in the lesson. Instruct them to work in pairs to research an individual who interests them, focusing on how that person helped transform society. Guide students to focus on the impact of one or more of the individual's innovations rather than write a general overview. Students can publish their profiles electronically on a class blog or website or in a printed class magazine.

HISTORICAL THINKING

ANSWERS

1. The Industrial Revolution was a period that had a global impact on how goods were manufactured and how and where people worked.

2. Mechanization in agriculture led to fewer people working as farm laborers. Those people then moved to cities and towns and were available for work in factories.

3. A workable steam engine could be modified to mechanize many machines, such as looms, spinners, and ships. It was the leading force behind the Industrial Revolution.

4. Answers will vary. Possible response: Railroads supplemented rivers and canals, creating more efficient transportation and spurring industrialization in parts of Europe.

CRITICAL VIEWING Answers will vary. Possible response: The use of animals and hand-operated tools such as shovels illustrates the ways people worked before the Industrial Revolution. The large metal machines and burning smoke stack show the ways people worked after the Industrial Revolution.

Daily Life Transformed

When you think of a revolution, you might think of crowds in the streets and breaking news reports. People in Europe experienced a revolution starting in the 1700s, but most of it took place in their homes and workplaces, not in the streets.

SOCIAL CHANGE

Daily life in Britain began to change drastically and rapidly in the 1700s compared to the small, slow changes of previous centuries. People moved from rural areas to live in cities and towns. In 1801, the population of Britain was about 9.3 million. Just 40 years later, it climbed 60 percent to 15.9 million. Manchester, England, a textile manufacturing center, grew by six times between 1771 and 1831.

The rapid social change of modern times disrupted many older ways of life. For example, in a traditional English village time was flexible, measured by the tasks that needed to be done that day and by the rhythm of the seasons. Now a worker's schedule was dominated by the blast of the factory whistle and the need to keep pace with ever faster machines.

Population growth outstripped the ability of urban areas to create housing and sanitation systems. As a result, cities became crowded and filthy. Air and water were polluted by factory smokestacks and manufacturing waste. The Romantic poet William Blake wrote of the "dark, Satanic mills" that created so much smog in some cities that people had to light candles in the middle of the day in order to see. Most workers lived in small houses with no yard, little natural light, and no toilet, bathing facilities, or running water. A typical block of homes might have 40 houses with nine people living in each house, and only six toilets for the entire block.

Disease spread rapidly in such neighborhoods, becoming even more deadly after increased contact with India brought cholera to England. In London alone, thousands died from infected water supplies. Even as some suffered from poverty, filth, and disease, however, the middle class was growing and consuming the merchandise being produced in the new factories. Better-off families moved to cleaner neighborhoods.

It was typical for everyone in a working-class household, including children, to work outside the home. Employers hired children to work many jobs because they could pay children a lower wage, and children could fit into tight spaces and were easier to control. Mine owners hired adult men but also relied on young women and adolescent boys and girls. Mining was dangerous work, and even those who survived the frequent accidents were likely to die early from lung disease. But conditions in factories weren't much better. Wages were low and working conditions were hazardous. The advances of the early Industrial Revolution might have improved life for the middle and upper classes, but not for the working class and poor. Even animals suffered for Britain's industrial progress—for example, the "pit ponies" who labored in the darkness of deeper and deeper coal mines.

POLITICAL CHANGE

Early in the Industrial Revolution, workers had almost no political rights. They could not vote, and Parliament made it illegal for them to form unions to increase their bargaining power. In 1819 in the city of Manchester, the British cavalry charged a crowd of about 60,000 that was demanding parliamentary representation. At least 15 demonstrators were killed. Finally in 1832, the Great Reform Act passed through Parliament, giving more seats to growing urban areas and the right to vote to more members of the middle class.

Reforms continued during the long reign of **Queen Victoria**, who ruled from 1837 to 1901. The popular queen supported social and political reforms, and Britain saw dramatic improvements in health conditions, wages, and political rights for the working class. Her belief in modesty, thrift, and hard work, as well as personal and social responsibility, informed the character of the entire era, known today as the Victorian Era.

CRITICAL VIEWING People gather in a courtyard on the Kensington High Street, London, in this photo taken around 1895. What details in the photo show what living conditions were like in urban homes and neighborhoods?

After a movement gathered one million signatures in support of greater voting rights, finally, by the 1880s, nearly all British men could vote. (Women would not get the vote until 1928, which you will read about later.) Representation in Parliament was changed to reflect the movement of much of the population from farms to towns and cities. To a small degree, new legislation protected the needs of the working poor over the profits of the gentry. Restrictions on trade unions were eased and the bargaining power of the working class increased. Laws regulated labor conditions and put some controls on the use of child labor.

Writers such as **Charles Dickens** and **Elizabeth Barrett Browning** sought change through **social criticism**, or a type of writing that tries to improve social conditions. For example, a government report, "The Condition and Treatment of the Children" about conditions in the mines, inspired both Dickens's famous story "A Christmas Carol" and Browning's poem "The Cry of the Children," in which she imagines children escaping from urban poverty to nature. Dickens himself grew up in poverty and became the most famous English author of the period, writing about the appalling living and working conditions of the poor. He wrote *Oliver Twist* in part as a criticism of the 1834 New Poor Law, which created the workhouse system that provided lodging for the poor in return for labor. He was such a popular author that his works made people all over the world aware of the conditions of the poor.

Scientists also contributed to reforms. For example, after Louis Pasteur discovered that microorganisms cause fermentation and disease in the 1860s, he developed a heating process to make milk safe to drink. This widely used process was named *pasteurization* after him. He also developed vaccines against anthrax and rabies. Joseph Lister applied Pasteur's discoveries to hospitals and surgery. His demands for cleanliness and the use of antiseptics to prevent infection saved countless lives.

The combination of economic success and relatively peaceful political reform made many Victorians extremely confident about their nation and optimistic about its future. Elsewhere, in Ireland and on the European continent, in contrast, many societies were rocked by famine, revolution, and changing national borders.

HISTORICAL THINKING

1. **READING CHECK** How did the Industrial Revolution change British society?

2. **IDENTIFY PROBLEMS AND SOLUTIONS** What were some of the problems created by the Industrial Revolution and how were they solved?

3. **DRAW CONCLUSIONS** How did writers such as Dickens and Browning influence reform in Britain?

PLAN: 2-PAGE LESSON

OBJECTIVE

Identify how the Industrial Revolution changed the way people lived in Europe.

CRITICAL THINKING SKILLS FOR LESSON 1.2

- Identify Problems and Solutions
- Draw Conclusions
- Identify Supporting Details
- Summarize
- Analyze Visuals

HISTORICAL THINKING FOR CHAPTER 22

How did the Industrial Revolution transform people's lives around the world?

The Industrial Revolution positively changed people's lives in many ways but also caused many negative social changes. Lesson 1.2 discusses the impact of the urban population boom that resulted from industrialization and the toll it took on the lives of the working poor, many of whom were children.

Student eEdition online

Additional content for this lesson, including an illustration, is available online.

BACKGROUND FOR THE TEACHER

John Snow Before the mid-1800s, no one knew exactly what caused cholera outbreaks. One of the first scientists to study these epidemics was John Snow. Many scientists during this period believed that cholera was spread by exposure to "bad air." Snow argued that the disease was spread through contaminated water, contact with the feces of an infected person, or contact with dirty clothing. He studied the London cholera outbreak of 1853–1855 using maps and graphs to record where illness was occurring. One of his studies focused on the Broad Street water pump in Soho. Another study, called the Grand Experiment, focused on the health of people who relied on two different water supplies, one that was relatively clean and another that was often contaminated with sewage. Snow was able to prove the relationship between dirty water and disease. His work is still widely regarded by epidemiologists today.

INTRODUCE & ENGAGE

DISCUSS LIVING CONDITIONS

Divide the class into two groups, one twice as large as the other. Tell the larger group to move their desks close together. Tell the smaller group to spread out their desks slightly. Move the class trash can to the middle of the spread-out group and place a water bottle on one of their desks. Tell the class to suppose that these groups represent two neighborhoods. In one, people have plenty of space, sewers, water, and trash collectors. In the other, people live in crowded buildings without sewers or water. **ASK:** Which neighborhood will have more health problems? *(the one with the crowded buildings without water or proper sewage)* Tell the class that in this lesson they will learn how society and living conditions changed as a result of the Industrial Revolution.

TEACH

GUIDED DISCUSSION

1. **Identify Supporting Details** Why did many British cities become crowded and filthy during the Industrial Revolution? *(Many people moved to the cities to find jobs. Cities could not keep pace with the population growth. Housing and sanitation systems became overtaxed.)*

2. **Summarize** What rights did many workers gain during the mid- to late-1800s? *(British men gained the right to vote, restrictions on unions were eased, wages increased, and laws regulating working conditions were passed.)*

ANALYZE VISUALS

Have students examine the illustration from the book *Oliver Twist* (available in the Student eEdition). **ASK:** Which character do you think is Oliver? Why? *(Possible response: The character on the far right of the illustration is Oliver because he has a worried look on his face, while the others are picking the pocket of the wealthy man in tails.)*

ACTIVE OPTIONS

On Your Feet: Jigsaw Strategy Organize students into "expert" groups and assign each group one of the following topics: daily life, urban growth, working conditions, political change, or social reforms. Have students in each group study and discuss their topic in depth. Then regroup students so that each new group has at least one member from each expert group. Experts in the new groups report on their topic.

NG Learning Framework: Create an Advertisement
ATTITUDE Communication
KNOWLEDGE Our Human Story

Ask pairs of students to create an advertisement designed to recruit potential workers for a 19th-century Manchester factory. Encourage students to consider what they have learned about inventions, working conditions, and specific skills employers look for to recruit. Direct students to create and illustrate era-appropriate advertisements. Invite pairs to present each advertisement for a class discussion.

DIFFERENTIATE

INCLUSION

Facilitate Comprehension Pair students with special needs with proficient readers. Coach students with special needs to jot down headings, boldface terms, and difficult words and concepts that confuse them. Have their partners use information from the lesson to help define words and answer questions.

GIFTED & TALENTED

Analyze a Poem Have students locate a copy of Elizabeth Barrett Browning's poem "The Cry of the Children" and write an analysis of it. Tell them to analyze the themes of the poem as well as its structure, rhyme scheme, tone, and language by citing specific examples. Invite students to share their analyses with the class.

See the Chapter Planner for more strategies for differentiation.

HISTORICAL THINKING

ANSWERS

1. People moved from farms to cities to work in factories. The middle class grew. As a result of reforms, workers received better wages, and conditions improved. Both the working and middle classes gained voting rights.

2. The Industrial Revolution created problems such as overcrowding, poor sanitation, pollution, and increased disease. These problems were solved by reform efforts. Scientists' discoveries also improved health.

3. Writers brought widespread attention to the conditions of the poor, which helped spark change.

CRITICAL VIEWING Answers will vary. Possible response: The windows, bricks, and walls are uneven and broken, the living quarters are close together, and there are many people in one small courtyard.

London's Great Exhibition

Have you ever been excited to attend an exhibition of the latest comics, movies, and video games? In the mid-1800s, people were just that excited to go to an exhibition about what was new in the field of industry.

THE GREAT EXHIBITION

In 1851, Britain celebrated the Industrial Revolution with an event called the *Great Exhibition of the Works of Industry of All Nations*. Queen Victoria's husband, Prince Albert, was one of the main planners for the event. In a period of five months, over six million people—more than twice as many who lived in the city of London— came from around the world to see the Great Exhibition.

The exhibition building, called the Crystal Palace, was itself a work of art and a testament to industrial progress. A new process for manufacturing large, strong sheets of glass made this building possible and provided architects with the large panes necessary to give the building a "crystal" effect of clear walls and ceilings. The building measured 1,851 feet long (more than five football fields) and 128 feet (or about 12 stories) high. Over 10 miles of viewing space inside displayed 100,000 objects.

The main attractions were exhibits of the latest industrial technology. Queen Victoria wrote in her diary that "every conceivable invention" was on display. Visitors could examine the recently invented daguerreotype, an early type of photograph. A number of American inventions were introduced to the world at the exhibition, including Cyrus McCormick's reaper, which harvested crops more efficiently. The largest exhibit was a huge hydraulic press used for bridge building that included a series of enormous metal tubes, each weighing over 1,000 tons. A central area was the site of concerts,

circuses, and tightrope walking. The world's largest organ provided music. The exhibition also provided the world's first public toilets, first just for men, then later for women as well.

Over half the exhibit space was used to display British products, with a special section showing colonial contributions. For example, the Great Exhibition featured the arts of India, including the world's largest diamond. In these galleries, visitors learned that Britain was now a great power in Asia.

INFLUENCE OF THE EXHIBITION

When the Great Exhibition ended, it had raised enough money through admission fees to fund the creation of Britain's Victoria and Albert and Natural History museums, both of which still stand near Hyde Park in London today. It also inspired other world fairs,

This engraving shows the exterior of the Crystal Palace, as seen from Kensington Gardens in 1851. Designed by Sir Joseph Paxton, the glass-and-iron exhibition hall included more than eight miles of display tables on the ground floor and galleries for the 14,000 exhibitors who participated.

PRIMARY SOURCE

Of foreign contributions to the Exhibition, France will be the largest contributor; next to it will come the Zollverein [German states] and Austria; then Belgium. To these succeed Russia, Turkey, and Switzerland. Holland, its commercial importance considered, will occupy a very small space. The northern states of Germany not included in the Zollverein, Egypt, Spain, Portugal, the Brazils, and Mexico have confined themselves within still narrower limits; and China, Arabia, and Persia have the smallest. Of the British dependencies the East Indies claim the lion's share of room, and of the whole ground assigned to industrial products of the United Kingdom, nearly one-half has been appropriated to machinery. As far as possible, the different nations have been arranged in a manner corresponding to their distances from the equator; the products of tropical climates being brought nearest to the transept [central aisle], and those of colder regions being placed at the extremities of the building.

—Excerpt from "London Companion During the Great Exhibition" by R. Beasland, London, 1851

or **expositions**. In a time before television or the Internet, these exhibitions were ways for countries to celebrate their power and accomplishments, often through a signature structure. A major Paris exhibition in 1889 included the monumental Eiffel Tower, and the Chicago World's Fair in 1893 introduced the world to the Ferris Wheel.

Far more important, however, was the way these exhibitions spread interest in and knowledge of technological advancements. An 1878 exhibition in Paris introduced the world to the Singer sewing machine, Alexander Graham Bell's telephone, and **Thomas Edison's** microphone and phonograph. Edison

displayed his other major invention, electric lighting, at an 1881 Paris exposition and a London exposition the following year. By the Chicago exposition in 1893, electricity had advanced enough that 120,000 electric lamps lit the exhibition halls at night. Other uses of electricity at that fair included an elevated railroad, electric boats, and a moving sidewalk. The 1964 New York World's Fair introduced the world to the first picture phone and computer modem. In 2010, the Shanghai World Exposition showed off China's economic and technological advances in the 21st century. For many years, these exhibitions have inspired, educated, and shown the world the future.

HISTORICAL THINKING

1. **READING CHECK** What was the main purpose of the Great Exhibition?

2. **DRAW CONCLUSIONS** What was the most important outcome of the Great Exhibition, and why?

3. **MAKE INFERENCES** Why do you think so many exhibitions included monumental architecture, such as the Crystal Palace or the Eiffel Tower?

PLAN: 2-PAGE LESSON

OBJECTIVE

Describe Britain's 1851 exhibition, which displayed the advancements of its Industrial Revolution to the rest of the world.

CRITICAL THINKING SKILLS FOR LESSON 1.3

- Draw Conclusions
- Make Inferences
- Analyze Primary Sources

HISTORICAL THINKING FOR CHAPTER 22

How did the Industrial Revolution transform people's lives around the world?

The advancements of the Industrial Revolution were the focus of the Great Exhibition in London in 1851. Lesson 1.3 discusses the organization of the Great Exhibition and the contents of its displays.

BACKGROUND FOR THE TEACHER

The Crystal Palace Astonishingly, the Crystal Palace took only 16 months to build. It was made from prefabricated parts that were assembled on site. Sir Joseph Paxton was a greenhouse designer and used the greenhouse structure as inspiration for the Crystal Palace. The exhibition ran from May to October 1851. During that time, about 6 million people viewed the exhibits, including celebrities such as Charles Dickens and Charlotte Brontë. After the exhibition ended, the Crystal Palace was taken apart and reconstructed in southeast London. It hosted other exhibits, shows, concerts, and soccer matches, but it caught fire and burned in November 1936. The remaining towers were destroyed in 1941 because the government believed they served as a target for German bombers during World War II.

INTRODUCE & ENGAGE

DISCUSS MONUMENTAL ARCHITECTURE

Direct students to look at the drawing of the Crystal Palace that appears in the lesson. Explain to students that Sir Joseph Paxton was originally a gardener who became famous for his greenhouses. **ASK:** What elements of this structure are similar to a greenhouse? *(Possible response: the metal frame, the glass walls and roof)* Tell students that the Crystal Palace revolutionized building design, and that in this lesson they will learn about the industrial technology exhibited in it.

TEACH

GUIDED DISCUSSION

1. **Draw Conclusions** Why do you think part of the exhibition was dedicated to the British colonies? *(Possible response: Britain most likely wanted not only to honor colonial contributions to its own development but also to show off its power.)*

2. **Make Inferences** Why did other countries hold similar exhibitions after London's Great Exhibition? *(Possible response: They wanted to spread interest in and knowledge of their technological advancements.)*

ANALYZE PRIMARY SOURCES

Have students read the primary source in the lesson. **ASK:** How were the different nations organized in the exhibition? *(They were organized according to geographical location; the colder nations were on the outside edges of the building, while those closer to the equator were located toward the center.)*

ACTIVE OPTIONS

On Your Feet: Four Corners Make four signs and place one in each corner of the room: hydraulic press, public toilets, phonograph, and electric lighting. Tell students to choose the invention or advancement they feel had the greatest impact on daily life and go to the corner with that sign. Groups in each corner should then discuss the invention they chose. Have at least one student from each corner share about their corner discussion.

| **NG Learning Framework: Present an Exhibition**
| **SKILL** Communication
| **KNOWLEDGE** Our Human Story

Have student groups research the inventions and other items displayed at the Great Exhibition and then create an exhibit featuring at least 10 of them. Students may use photos or drawings of the items and should provide captions for each one, explaining its function and significance. Encourage groups to post their exhibitions in class or on a class website or blog.

DIFFERENTIATE

STRIVING READERS

Rewrite a Passage Instruct pairs to read the primary source feature. Based on context or research, have students define the following words: *corresponding* (related), *equator* (circle of the earth that divides it equally between north and south), *extremities* (farthest parts). Tell pairs to work together to write the excerpt in conversational, or informal, English. Then have them share and compare their work with other pairs.

PRE-AP

Create a Time Line Direct students to conduct research and create a time line illustrating various world fairs of technology, starting with the Great Exhibition. Tell them to add at least five events to their time lines, along with their locations and some key technological innovations on display. Invite students to share their time lines with the class.

See the Chapter Planner for more strategies for differentiation.

HISTORICAL THINKING

ANSWERS

1. The main purpose of the Great Exhibition was to highlight Britain's industrial advancements.

2. Answers will vary. Possible response: The most important outcome of the exhibition was to inform people about the advancements industry had made. This must have inspired inventors to develop even more new ideas and made visitors feel excited about the changes and innovations.

3. Answers will vary. Possible response: Exhibitions probably included a monumental work of architecture because it featured innovations in building materials and design. Also, buildings such as the Crystal Palace or Eiffel Tower would impress everyone and be remembered long after the exhibition ended.

The World Economy Accelerates

From its beginning, the Industrial Revolution was a global process. Improvements in transportation and communication created a worldwide market. However, the entire world did not profit from it.

Because of a labor shortage on the Pacific coast of the United States, Chinese immigrants performed much of the work building the Transcontinental Railroad, which was completed in 1869. This photo, part of a series taken by Alfred A. Hart between 1865 and 1869, shows a Chinese camp and construction train in Nevada.

GLOBAL DIMENSIONS OF THE INDUSTRIAL REVOLUTION

Some historians point to the Industrial Revolution as one of the first examples of globalization. Globalization refers to the development of an increasingly integrated global economy marked especially by free trade and by the free flow of capital. The Industrial Revolution created a growing world economy that tightly connected producers and consumers around the world like

never before. By the end of the 19th century, most of humankind was participating in the global commodity markets of industrial capitalism.

As the Industrial Revolution spread, steamships and railroads made the world a much smaller place. The first steam-powered crossing of the Atlantic took place in 1838 and of the Pacific in 1853. By the 1870s, steamships dramatically reduced transportation

times and shipping costs. In the United States, large waterways like the Mississippi River transported people and goods over great distances. The Suez Canal, finished in 1869, linked the Mediterranean and Red Seas and reduced the travel time from Europe to South Asia from months to weeks. These advances enabled an increased European presence in Africa and Southeast Asia and the tightening of control over existing colonies, such as British India.

By midcentury, a dense network of railroads covered western Europe, increasing both urbanization and mobility. In North America, transcontinental railroads crossed the United States and Canada, linking the coasts and creating national identities. By 1890, railroads were spreading across Russia, British India, and Mexico.

Inventions in communication also increased the pace of global interactions. After Samuel Morse invented the telegraph, information moved even more quickly than people and goods. The first long-range telegraph message was sent in 1844. In 1869, an underwater cable was laid in the Atlantic Ocean. Telegraphs allowed traders to accurately compare prices instantaneously across continents. Shipping companies used the telegraph to lower their costs and increase global trade.

All of these advances led to more powerful European (and later, U.S., Russian, and Japanese) militaries. Railroads, steamships, and increasingly sophisticated weaponry moved soldiers quickly and made them deadlier than the people they set out to conquer or subdue.

Globalization through military conquest or trade had enormous cultural and intellectual effects. European tastes and ideas gained prominence, and as their power grew, Europeans came to view customs and cultures in many other parts of the world as inferior to their own.

FACTORS IN INDUSTRIAL GROWTH

Historians are still debating why the Industrial Revolution took off in Britain and not in the more developed regions of China. By 1750, the two countries had a great deal in common. They shared a high life expectancy. They were both consumer societies, and they both traded

British inventor and entrepreneur Charles Wheatstone invented the automatic telegraph transmitter in 1858.

and had advanced national and international markets. Furthermore, they both faced the same ecological challenges, so were at the same disadvantage.

Some historians refer to the split that occurred between western Europe and Asia around 1750 as the Great Divergence. (Divergence means "a drawing apart or a separating.") Historians are still debating why it took place. Some emphasize cultural factors, such as the Protestant Reformation, which connected hard work with godliness, and the Scientific Revolution, which stimulated the spirit of invention. Other historians argue that material factors were more important. First, British coal fields lay close at hand, while in China the main coal areas were thousands of miles from the manufacturing regions. Second, the British could import timber from its colonies in North America, easing ecological limits to growth. Finally, workers' wages were higher in Britain than in China. That gave European businessmen an incentive to invest in machines to lower costs, leading to expanded markets and greater profits.

Some historians have also pointed out that a lot of British capital came from the huge profits of the Atlantic slave trade and the sugar plantations of the Caribbean. The unpaid labor of enslaved Africans was thus used to finance industry, even as the slave plantations of the southern United States provided much of the cotton for Britain's factory system.

HISTORICAL THINKING

1. **READING CHECK** How is the Industrial Revolution the first example of globalization?

2. **MAKE CONNECTIONS** Why did European tastes and ideas become more valued around the world during the Industrial Revolution?

3. **MAKE PREDICTIONS** What do you think will happen to the nations of Asia as a result of the Great Divergence?

PLAN: 2-PAGE LESSON

OBJECTIVE

Identify how the Industrial Revolution affected the world economy and led to a shift in the global balance of power.

CRITICAL THINKING SKILLS FOR LESSON 2.1

- Make Connections
- Make Predictions
- Identify
- Compare and Contrast
- Analyze Visuals

HISTORICAL THINKING FOR CHAPTER 22

How did the Industrial Revolution transform people's lives around the world?

The Industrial Revolution led to a shift in the global balance of economic power. Lesson 2.1 discusses how changes in transportation, communication, and trade during the Industrial Revolution led to globalization.

Student eEdition online

Additional content for this lesson, including an image gallery, is available online.

BACKGROUND FOR THE TEACHER

Suez Canal Today, the Suez Canal is one of the world's busiest shipping lanes. In its first 14 years of existence, however, navigation proved challenging because the canal was so narrow, shallow, and winding. More than 3,000 ships ran aground during this period. Beginning in 1876, improvements were made to widen and deepen the canal. Improvements have continued throughout much of the canal's history. The most recent major improvement was made by the Egyptian government in 2015, when it spent some $8.5 billion on modifications and added almost 18 miles to the canal's length. During its first year of operation, only 486 trips were made. In 2018, that number was more than 18,000.

INTRODUCE & ENGAGE

DISCUSS IMMIGRANT LIFE

Direct students to study the photograph of the railroad camp in the lesson. Explain that Chinese immigrants built the railroads because white workers didn't want the job. The conditions were rough—long hours, dangerous conditions, and frequent mistreatment were common. In addition, Chinese workers were paid less than white workers. **ASK:** Based on the photograph, what do you think life was like for these Chinese railroad workers? *(Possible response: Living in tents next to a railroad track would be difficult and uncomfortable. Exposure to the elements would likely pose challenges as well.)* Tell students that in this lesson they will learn how railroads helped make the world a much smaller place.

TEACH

GUIDED DISCUSSION

1. **Identify** What is globalization? *(Globalization is an integrated world economy based on free trade and the free flow of goods.)*

2. **Compare and Contrast** In 1750, what did Britain and China have in common? *(They shared a high life expectancy, were both consumer societies, traded, had advanced national and international markets, and faced similar ecological challenges.)*

ANALYZE VISUALS

Have students examine the photos in the Advances in Transportation and Communication image gallery (available in the Student eEdition) and the photo of Wheatstone's telegraph. **ASK:** What common benefit did all of these developments provide? *(Possible response: They all saved time— the canal cut down travel time, the telegraph made communication more immediate, and the steamboat was faster than other existing modes of water transport.)*

ACTIVE OPTIONS

On Your Feet: Fishbowl Group students so that part of the class sits in a close circle facing inward and the other part sits in a larger circle around them. Ask students on the inside circle to discuss why the Great Divergence took place. During the discussion, those on the outside circle should listen for new information and evaluate what is said. After the discussion is over, direct groups to reverse positions.

NG Learning Framework: Report on Railroads
ATTITUDE Empowerment
SKILLS Communication, Collaboration

Invite students to work in pairs to find out about the early history of railroads around the world. Tell partners to collaborate on an oral report that includes statistics on the countries that built early railroads and which countries had the highest number of miles of track in the world by the early 1900s. When they have completed their reports, have pairs communicate their findings to the class.

DIFFERENTIATE

INCLUSION

Work in Pairs Consider pairing students with disabilities with more proficient readers. Have the proficient reader read aloud the lesson text. After each paragraph, the listening student should briefly summarize the information or ask questions if needed to clarify the material.

GIFTED & TALENTED

Deliver a Monologue Instruct students to research the life of someone who lived during the Industrial Revolution and worked on a railroad or in a factory or mine. Then prompt them to write a monologue that focuses on a typical day of work. Ask volunteers to perform their monologues and respond to questions from their classmates.

See the Chapter Planner for more strategies for differentiation.

HISTORICAL THINKING

ANSWERS

1. Increased industrial production combined with faster transportation of raw materials and goods meant that the world was economically more tightly interconnected and interdependent than ever before.

2. Answers will vary. Possible response: The Industrial Revolution made Europe more powerful and economically successful. As a result, many people around the world emulated European tastes and values.

3. Answers will vary. Possible response: Asia will fall behind Europe economically and will therefore be subject to European domination.

Political Ideals

Is it better to focus on individual freedom or the collective good of society? Should the production of goods be controlled by the government or by the seller and consumer? The events of the Industrial Revolution led many people to ask these questions and to think and act to find answers.

PHILOSOPHY AND CHANGE

As you have read, the Industrial Revolution resulted in more efficient transportation and communication. However, it also resulted in unsanitary and unsafe working conditions, poverty, and overcrowded living spaces. Philosophers, politicians, and religious leaders looked at the changing world and began to question ideas about how humans should live. Latin Americans, Africans, and Asians, as well as Europeans, all discussed these key ideas.

In Victorian Britain, the rising ideals were those of classical **liberalism**, which stressed the virtues of freedom. Though the term has different meanings today, to 19th-century liberals, freedom of religion, freedom of trade, freedom of conscience, and freedom of expression were universal values. Following these ideals, Parliament agreed to remove restrictions on British Catholics, eliminate tariffs on imported grain, and allow workers the legal right to organize unions.

A major supporter of liberalism was the British philosopher **John Stuart Mill**. In his book *On Liberty*, Mill argued that liberty involved freedom not only from unnecessary government interference but also from "the tendency of society to impose . . . its own ideas and practices . . . on those who dissent from [disagree with] them." His emphasis on freedom from both

political oppression and social conformity led Mill to opinions that were radical for the time. For example, he thought the vote should be extended not only to working men but also to women. British liberalism was a global inspiration for people seeking freedom. For example, Mill's liberal ideas spread to East Asia after the book was translated by a Japanese reformer.

CRITICAL VIEWING In 1848, demonstrators in Paris set up barricades and demanded a republican form of government. This painting by Horace Vernet captures the uprising. What ideas and emotions are conveyed in the painting?

You've already read about capitalism, in which the means of production are owned by private individuals and the production, prices, and distribution of goods are determined by competition in a free market. This term was first used in the middle of the 19th century, but it describes an economic system that had been growing in Europe since the development of the cloth industry in the 16th and 17th centuries.

Industrialists across Europe wanted governments that supported capitalism; therefore, as industry became a more dominant force in daily life, so did capitalism. But some members of society did not benefit as much from capitalism as others. This led to the development of alternative economic philosophies, which challenged the idea of private ownership and a free market.

Debates about liberalism and capitalism became more intense in 1848 when political revolutions spread across Europe. Starting in Paris, the revolutionary spirit quickly sparked revolts in Rome, Berlin, Prague, and other capitals. By then, people were debating ideas of how industrial society might emphasize the greater good over individual interests. The most influential work resulting from the debate was *The Manifesto of the Communist Party*, published in 1848 by **Karl Marx** and **Friedrich Engels**. In the manifesto, Marx argued that economic forces—the way things are produced—shape society and that the social classes created by the economic forces come into conflict politically.

Marx believed that industrial society created two social classes in conflict: the property-owning bourgeoisie and the exploited industrial workers, whom he called the **proletariat**. He predicted that the clash between the bourgeoisie and the proletariat would inevitably lead to a violent overthrow of capitalism. At first, the workers would seize power, take property from the bourgeoisie, and use state ownership of factories to create a more equal and just society—an economic system known as **socialism**. Eventually, class divisions would disappear, and society would follow the motto "From each according to his abilities, to each according to his needs." This new economic and political system was known as **communism**.

Marx's theory wasn't the only socialist ideal. Welsh industrialist Robert Owen believed that factory owners themselves could reform the industrial system so that workers would lead better lives, with clean surroundings and education for their children. Owen tried out his ideas at New Lanark, Indiana, a utopian community built as a model to a brighter future. He lost all his money on this experiment and then became a leader in the early trade union movement.

Other socialists opposed Marx's idea of violent overthrow by arguing that liberalism and socialism could be combined. These moderate socialists argued that when workers gained the vote they could use the power of government for socialist reforms.

Apart from liberalism and socialism, the most important political philosophy of the period was nationalism. To Marx, the workers' true interests lay not with the rich and powerful who might speak the same language, but with workers across the world who share the same economic and social burdens. Nationalists, on the other hand, believed that bonds of culture and history unified people across class lines.

Germans were discussing all these ideals, and reformers hoped to combine liberalism and nationalism to create a modern, unified country. In 1848, the Frankfurt Assembly proposed to unify Germany as a constitutional monarchy. They offered the crown to the king of Prussia, but he refused to accept popular sovereignty or the separation of powers. Later, Germany would be unified not by liberalism but by the combination of military power and nationalism.

Meanwhile, in 1859, **Charles Darwin** published his groundbreaking book, *On the Origin of Species*, which put forward the theory of evolution. Some people applied Darwin's concepts of biological adaptation and natural selection to human society, with dangerous implications. **Social Darwinism** was the idea that differences in wealth and power could be explained by the superiority of some and the inferiority of others. Some Europeans and North Americans used it to justify social inequality and the idea that Europe's increasing global dominance was a natural result of racial superiority. Darwin himself did not draw such social and political conclusions, but many others did as they looked to science to justify their prejudices.

NATIONALISM AND A CHANGING EUROPE

As you have learned, 1848 was a turbulent year in Europe. For a while it seemed that the status quo of monarchs and aristocrats was coming to an end. However, in most countries conservatives won out over liberal and socialist reforms.

In early 1848, France was a constitutional monarchy, but only male property owners had the right to vote. In February, police in Paris fired on a crowd of demonstrators calling for a democratic form of government, and in response 1,500 barricades went up around the city. The king, Louis Philippe, gave up the throne and fled to England. A few weeks after the uprising in Paris, people in Vienna also took to the

---

PLAN: 4-PAGE LESSON

OBJECTIVE

Describe how the changes caused by the Industrial Revolution led to the development of various economic, political, and social philosophies.

CRITICAL THINKING SKILLS FOR LESSON 2.2

- Compare and Contrast
- Interpret Maps
- Draw Conclusions
- Explain
- Identify
- Identify Main Ideas and Details
- Describe
- Make Connections

HISTORICAL THINKING FOR CHAPTER 22

How did the Industrial Revolution transform people's lives around the world?

Though the Industrial Revolution improved means of transportation, communication, construction, and manufacturing, it also led to many changes. Lesson 2.2 discusses these changes and how some philosophers and politicians believed they should be addressed.

BACKGROUND FOR THE TEACHER

Karl Marx Karl Marx was born in Trier, Germany, and attended a high school in the city that was believed by the government to inspire liberalist thought and was thus under police surveillance. After graduation, Marx attended the University of Bonn and then the University of Berlin. Eventually, he received a doctorate degree and later wrote for a newspaper in Cologne. He became editor of another paper in 1842 and then married Jenny von Westphalen in 1843. They moved to Paris, where Marx experienced greater exposure to socialism and communism and also met Friedrich Engels. The two became lifelong collaborators.

Student eEdition online

Additional content for this lesson, including a photo and a portrait, is available online.

INTRODUCE & ENGAGE

PREVIEW LESSON CONTENT

Direct students' attention to the heading "Philosophy and Change" in the lesson. Remind students that philosophy is the study of the nature of existence, reality, and knowledge. Hold a class discussion on what might be covered by the text under the heading "Philosophy and Change." **ASK:** How might philosophy and change have been interrelated during the Industrial Revolution? *(Possible response: Many problems were associated with the changes resulting from the Industrial Revolution, and philosophers might have had ideas about how to address these problems.)*

TEACH

GUIDED DISCUSSION

1. **Explain** What did *liberalism* mean in Victorian Britain? *(It meant freedom of religious worship, freedom of trade, freedom of conscience, and freedom of expression.)*

2. **Identify** What would eliminate the differences between rich and poor, according to Marx? *(State ownership of factories would eliminate the differences.)*

MAKE CONNECTIONS

Have students read the feature The Anthropocene: A New Geological Epoch. Discuss as a class the impact that the Industrial Revolution has had on the planet. **ASK:** What is the primary characterization of the Anthropocene, according to scientists? *(the human use of fossil fuels)* How does the Industrial Revolution continue to affect Earth today? *(It has dramatically accelerated global warming.)*

streets to demand new rights from the Austrian Empire. But unlike France, Austria was a multiethnic empire. Italians, Hungarians, Germans, Czechs, Croatians, and other subjects fought for their rights, which threatened the existence of the empire itself. The uprising spread to Italy, which at the time was a group of individually governed states. There the desire was not to break up an empire, but to create a new country.

The French uprising was the only one that was immediately successful. A moderate socialist government was created, but it was not popular with the rural majority. By summer, the tide was turning away from republicanism, and people turned to nationalism. Louis Napoleon, nephew of Napoleon Bonaparte, was elected president and then organized and won a national vote making him Napoleon III, Emperor of France. He represented, in his own words, "order, authority, religion, popular welfare at home, national dignity abroad." Once again, France had gone from monarchy, to republic, to empire.

Napoleon III ruled over France's Second Empire, a period of stability, prosperity, and expanding French power that lasted from 1852–1870. The government invested in infrastructure and supported industry. Although Napoleon III had absolute power, he respected the rule of law and basic civil liberties. Like his uncle, he gained support by appealing to French nationalism and by expanding the overseas French Empire.

In Austria, the rebellions were suppressed, but over the next 20 years the empire lost northern Italy and the northern German states. Other regions were in rebellion as well. In 1867, Emperor Franz Joseph II eased tensions in Hungary by proclaiming a dual monarchy under which he would be both emperor of Austria and king of Hungary, but Hungary would control its own state institutions. However, this did not solve the many other ethnic and national grievances within the empire.

The uprising in Italy was the beginning of a 20-year effort led by Giuseppe Garibaldi to unify the peninsula under a liberal, representative government. Garibaldi was a revolutionary who was condemned to death for leading an uprising in Genoa. He fled to Brazil, took part in an uprising there, and returned to Italy to lead a revolutionary army. By 1870, the Italian Peninsula was joined in a single constitutional monarchy with a limited electorate, a relatively weak legislature, and Rome as its capital. Sharp divisions remained, however. For many, the concept of being "Italian" was still something entirely new. The north, which had been under Austrian rule, had experienced industrialization and urbanization, while the south was still largely agricultural.

Italian and German Unification, 1858–1871

Germany also unified in the 1860s. Led by chancellor **Otto von Bismarck**, Prussia—the largest and most powerful German state—united the other states, captured territory from Austria, and won wars with both Denmark and France. In 1871 a new German state was founded under the leadership of the Prussian king, Kaiser Wilhelm II. The new Germany was based on nationalism and military power. Manufacturing boomed and the new state's gross national product doubled between 1870 and 1890.

Almost immediately, Germany became an important force in world affairs and significantly altered the balance of power. It became more aggressive in challenging the British Empire, leading to a competition for colonies in Africa and Asia. This military and economic power fed a nationalism that would have far-reaching consequences in the next century.

GLOBAL LABOR

The Industrial Revolution changed how people worked. Before that time, not many people supported themselves and their families by working for wages. In most places, peasants grew their own food, while nomads tended their herds. Capitalism now brought the very different idea that people would sell their labor to an employer and be paid wages set by the marketplace.

This transition was difficult for traditional farmers. Even those who remained in the countryside were affected by the spread of commodity markets, for example by growing more crops for export. The results were especially painful in Ireland. English landlords charged high rents that could only be paid for by exporting Irish crops. Local farmers became dependent on cheap potatoes for food, and in the 1840s many starved to death when a potato blight left them with nothing to eat. This period is known as the Irish Potato Famine.

Of course, spreading markets could also mean new opportunities. In Argentina, cheaper transport meant the growth of the beef industry. In the past, cattle had to be slaughtered very near the place of consumption. Then after 1870, refrigerated steamships allowed the export of fresh meat from South America to Europe. Livestock farmers grew rich.

In Asia, mines and plantations combined foreign investment with social labor. Instead of growing their own food, some people in Vietnam and Malaysia were now working for wages on rubber plantations or in tin mines. Much of the rice came from increasing production in other parts of the region. As to be expected with globalization, economies were becoming more and more interconnected.

Just as financial investment went global, so did labor. The late 19th century saw massive movements of people in search of a better life. Migrants from the poorer parts of Europe came to the Americas looking for opportunity, joined by Chinese and Japanese immigrants crossing the Pacific. Many rural Jews left the Russian Empire to escape political oppression and poverty. Irish emigrants streamed toward the United States, Canada, and Australia. Vast new gold mines in South Africa attracted workers from across the region.

Abuses of migrant laborers were common. Many in British India were so desperate to escape village poverty that they signed up as indentured servants for very low pay and were taken to distant lands. Very often, immigrants were met with racism and discrimination. Still, these great population movements showed just how global the Industrial Revolution really was.

THE ANTHROPOCENE: A NEW GEOLOGICAL EPOCH Geologists, who study the history of Earth, employ much larger time frames than historians. In fact, most of the world history you've read about has taken place during a single geological epoch: the Holocene. This epoch extends back 11,700 years—since the end of the last ice age.

Now some geologists think it is time to insert a new benchmark: the Anthropocene ("human epoch"). They argue that the planet's physical features have been so strongly affected by the human species since 1800 that this new epoch better describes Earth systems in the very recent past. According to this view, the Anthropocene began about two centuries ago with the intensive use of fossil fuels during the Industrial Revolution.

An article published by the Royal Swedish Academy of Sciences used measurements of carbon dioxide in the atmosphere to track the impact of fossil fuels. The preindustrial level of 270–275 parts per million (ppm) had risen to 310 ppm by 1950. In 2014, carbon dioxide peaked at over 400 ppm. This "Great Acceleration," as the authors call it, "is reaching criticality. Whatever unfolds, the next few decades will surely be a tipping point in the evolution of the Anthropocene." That tipping point could mean catastrophic and irreversible global warming.

The International Union of Geological Sciences is currently considering a proposal that formally declares that the end of the Holocene was in 1800 and that the current epoch is the Anthropocene. That term, they state, "has emerged as a popular scientific term used by scientists, the scientifically engaged public, and the media to designate the period of Earth's history during which humans have had a decisive influence on the state, dynamics, and future of the Earth system."

Historians have long recognized that the Industrial Revolution was also an energy revolution. Now geologists are affirming that the global effects of those changes were even more revolutionary than previously thought.

HISTORICAL THINKING

1. **READING CHECK** What were the major political philosophies that arose as a result of the Industrial Revolution?

2. **COMPARE AND CONTRAST** What are the main differences between capitalism, communism, and socialism?

3. **INTERPRET MAPS** What do the unification of Germany and Italy have in common?

4. **DRAW CONCLUSIONS** How did nationalism influence changes in Europe during the Industrial Revolution?

BACKGROUND FOR THE TEACHER

The Great Famine Irish soil was particularly difficult to grow crops in, so Irish farmers relied on the potato because it grew well in the soil. Potatoes were also filling and nutritious. By the mid-1800s, many poor Irish farming families relied almost entirely on potatoes for food. Because farmers grew only one or two types of potato, if the crops were susceptible to a disease, then the entire harvest would be destroyed. The blight that ruined the potato harvests arrived from North America in 1845. That year's crops rotted in the fields, and so did those of subsequent years. Many Irish people starved to death. In addition, many Irish tenant farmers were evicted from their land by British landlords for unpaid bills. Between 1844 and 1851, Ireland's population dropped from around 8.4 million to just under 6.6 million due to the famine.

TEACH

GUIDED DISCUSSION

3. **Identify Main Ideas and Details** How did Social Darwinism explain the differences between rich and poor? *(Social Darwinism supported the idea that wealthy and powerful people were superior to the poor.)*

4. **Describe** How did Europeans in some countries try to change their governments and circumstances? *(They demonstrated and revolted against their governments.)*

INTERPRET MAPS

Direct students' attention to the map of Italian and German unification. Review the map legend and have students trace the outlines of unified Italy and Germany. **ASK:** What other major empires existed in Europe at that time? *(the Russian Empire and Austria-Hungary)* How might a unified Italy and Germany have affected the balance of power in Europe? *(Possible response: The two new empires may have challenged the power of Russia and Austria-Hungary.)*

ACTIVE OPTIONS

On Your Feet: Fact-Finding Bee Invite students to consider the facts they have learned in this lesson about social changes, philosophies, and revolutions during the Industrial Revolution. Arrange students into two teams, and give each a few minutes to create lists of facts. Have teams form two rows, face each other, and take turns providing a fact. Any student who makes an untrue statement or repeats a fact sits down. The team with the most facts and fewest number of students sitting wins.

> **NG Learning Framework: Research Italian States**
> **SKILL** Communication
> **KNOWLEDGE** Our Human Story

Point out that the unification of Italy brought together many different states. Ask students to refer to the map in the lesson and each choose one of the Italian states to research. Ask them to write a short report on their chosen state that covers who lived there and what type of government the state had before unification. Invite students to share their reports with the class and discuss ways in which the states differed.

HISTORICAL THINKING

ANSWERS

1. The major political philosophies of capitalism, socialism, nationalism, and communism arose as a result of the Industrial Revolution.

2. Answers will vary. Possible response: In capitalism, the means of production are privately owned. In communism, the means of production are owned by the state. In socialism, the means of production are owned by the state or by collectives, but some private property ownership is allowed.

3. In both Germany and Italy, numerous small states or principalities united to create whole new countries, redrawing the political map of Europe.

4. Answers will vary. Possible response: Nationalism led some countries to unify and some empires to fall apart.

CRITICAL VIEWING Answers will vary. Possible response: The painting conveys a sense of fearlessness on the part of the Parisians and the idea that they are willing to fight for freedom at any cost.

How To Be Modern?

Imagine having to choose between something old that feels like it defines who you are and something new that would help you achieve who you want to become. That is what societies all over the world faced during the Industrial Revolution.

Taken in 1855 during the Crimean War, this photo shows rows of caissons, or chests, holding artillery ammunition and, in the background, British military tents. Britain and France joined the Ottomans to fight against the Russians during the war.

A SHIFTING BALANCE OF POWER

As you have read, the rise of modern nation-states and economies was disruptive of Europeans' social stability and traditional values. In the 19th century, that instability spread across the entire world. For Africans and Asians, and for indigenous peoples everywhere, that meant dealing with the rising influence of Europe.

The technological and financial costs of manufacturing steam-powered battleships and more powerful weapons were difficult, if not impossible, for other countries in other parts of the world to meet. Not even the mighty Russian military was able to keep up. The Industrial Revolution had given western Europe the advantage in finance, logistics, medical science, engineering, and many other areas, elevating European social, cultural, and political systems in the rest of the world as well. The question other nations faced was how to become a modern industrial society without losing their unique cultural identity.

THE CRIMEAN WAR

In the middle of the 19th century, the Russian and Ottoman empires were in a tense rivalry. In 1853, the Russian army crossed into Ottoman territory near the Danube River and the Ottomans declared war. Britain and France, fearing a stronger Russia, allied with the Ottomans. Named the **Crimean War** because it was mainly fought on the Crimean Peninsula, the war ended in a deadlock in 1856.

While neither country won, the Crimean War helped Russian and Ottoman leaders realize that modern wars could not be won without the development of industry. But how? Should they emulate western Europe or reject foreign influences and remain true to their own traditions?

Even before the war, Ottoman leaders recognized the need to modernize and, starting in 1839, instituted the Tanzimat Reforms. These ambitious reforms reshaped

the government, as well as the Ottoman legal and educational systems, resulting in a more efficient administration, greater investment, and economic growth. But the reforms also increased divisions among more secular, European-oriented people in urban areas and more traditional, religiously oriented people in rural areas. After 1880, the traditional factions defeated liberal reformers and instituted policies based on the authority of the sultan and religious conservatives.

Russia came to reform later than the Ottomans, and even less successfully. At the time of the Crimean War, Russia had the world's largest army, a vast Eurasian empire, and yet was still overwhelmingly rural. It had a powerful aristocracy, a weak middle class, a huge underclass of serfs owned by the landowning nobility, and almost no modern industry. Serfs had so few rights that they could be traded in a game of cards. The country lacked a property-owning class willing to build factories and an urban labor force to work in them. The nobility profited from the old system, as did the government, which depended on serfs to populate Russia's huge army.

By the end of the Crimean War, **Tsar Alexander II** understood the need for change. In 1861, he attempted to reform the feudal system by freeing the serfs. But in an attempt to appease the nobility, he required serfs to pay for their own emancipation, which most could not afford. As with freed slaves in the southern United States, not much changed for most Russian serfs after their emancipation. Unpaid for their own labor, they did not have resources that would have allowed them to escape the poverty of their villages.

Alexander's efforts toward industrialization were more successful. He boosted railroad construction, which stimulated the coal and iron industries, and instituted tariffs on imports, which stimulated the establishment of some factories. As a result, by the 1880s Russian workers were living and working in the same dangerous and squalid conditions that marked the early industrial periods of western Europe.

At the same time, Russian intellectuals and artists were debating how deeply Russian society should change. Should Russia learn from and adopt western European cultural and constitutional models? If so, to what degree? "Westernizers" believed in looking to Europe, while "Slavophiles" declared that Russia should keep its own Slavic traditions. The debate produced a flowering of art in Russia, particularly in the field of music. Two composers in the Romantic tradition, represent the two sides. **Peter Ilyich Tchaikovsky** followed Western classical models to become Russia's best-known composer, while "Slavophiles" like **Nicolai Rimsky-Korsakov** emphasized Slavic and central Eurasian themes.

In 1881, Alexander II was assassinated, resulting in a backlash against reform and a crackdown on opposition. Reform initiated from above can be revoked from above, and Alexander's son and successor did just that. While the building of railroads and industrial development continued, modest steps toward representative government, even at the local level, stopped. The Westernizers lost and the Slavophile slogan "Orthodoxy, Autocracy, and Nationality" came to guide Russian policy.

FLORENCE NIGHTINGALE AND MARY SEACOLE

Great advances in nursing were one result of the Crimean War. In 1854, a British nurse named Florence Nightingale (far left) arrived to find filthy and overcrowded hospitals. She and her team secured more supplies, cleaned the wards, and greatly improved the standard of care. Another nurse named Mary Seacole (left), who was originally from Jamaica, wanted to assist but was turned down by the British government. Instead, she set up her own "hotel" behind the battle lines and tended to soldiers. While Nightingale brought modern medical science to the battlefield, Seacole added emotional support and herbal medicines to her therapy.

PLAN: 4-PAGE LESSON

OBJECTIVE

Analyze how people everywhere struggled to balance traditional values and cultures with modern technology and industry during the Industrial Revolution.

CRITICAL THINKING SKILLS FOR LESSON 3.1

- Compare and Contrast
- Make Predictions
- Make Inferences
- Identify Main Ideas and Details
- Determine Chronology
- Make Connections
- Analyze Visuals

HISTORICAL THINKING FOR CHAPTER 22

How did the Industrial Revolution transform people's lives around the world?

Lesson 3.1 discusses how the Industrial Revolution disrupted Europeans' social stability and how indigenous people everywhere dealt with the rising influence of Europe.

BACKGROUND FOR THE TEACHER

Steam-Powered Battleships From the 1820s through the 1850s, advances in steam engines and propulsion crafted by the United States and Britain made steamships practical for ocean travel. At the same time, advances in weaponry made by several European countries led to the French 6.5-inch cast-iron rifled guns used in the Crimean War. These guns were superior in range, destructive power, and accuracy. The French also developed large shells that exploded upon impact to replace the traditional solid iron cannonball. Then the U.S. Army developed a slower-burning black powder that made the large guns on ships safer to fire. Heavy wrought iron plates were built over thick wooden backing to provide protection to steam-powered battleships.

Student eEdition online

Additional content for this lesson, including a painting, is available online.

INTRODUCE & ENGAGE

DISCUSS TRADITIONAL AND MODERN ASPECTS OF LIFE

Ask students to discuss how their lives reflect both traditional and modern aspects. Examples could include traditional and modern forms of dance, dress, and food. Tell students that in this lesson they will learn about countries that had to decide how to balance traditional values with the modern technology of the Industrial Revolution.

TEACH

GUIDED DISCUSSION

1. **Identify Main Ideas and Details** How did the Industrial Revolution give Europe a technological advantage over countries in other parts of the world? *(Europe could manufacture steam-powered battleships and more powerful weapons.)*

2. **Compare and Contrast** How were Florence Nightingale and Mary Seacole similar and different? *(Same: Both were nurses during the Crimean War who wanted to improve the standard of care for soldiers. Different: Nightingale was British, Caucasian, and brought modern medical science to the battlefield; Seacole was Jamaican, of African descent, and rejected by the British government but brought emotional support and herbal medicines to the soldiers under her care.)*

ANALYZE VISUALS

Instruct students to examine the photo taken during the Crimean War. **ASK:** What tells you that this photo was taken during a time before automobiles and trucks? *(The caissons are on wagons made to be pulled by horses.)* How does the photo reflect the influence of the Industrial Revolution? *(The similarity of the caissons and of the tents suggest mass production, and the photo itself suggests the new technology of the camera during the Industrial Revolution.)*

DIFFERENTIATE

ENGLISH LANGUAGE LEARNERS

Review Transitional Words To help students summarize what they read and put events relating to the challenges of modernization in chronological order, display the following transitional words: *first, next, then, also, while, immediately, later, earlier, meanwhile, whenever, simultaneously, subsequently, during, following, before, afterwards,* and *finally.* Direct mixed pairs of students at the **Beginning** and **Intermediate** levels to write a series of sentences that state the major events in the lesson in chronological order. Encourage them to use a variety of transitional words and to vary their sentence structure.

GIFTED & TALENTED

Write a Persuasive Speech Encourage students to learn more about one of the following topics:

- the view of either the "Westernizers" or the "Slavophiles" on how Russian society should change
- Florence Nightingale's fight to clean and supply hospitals during the Crimean War
- Mary Seacole's determination to help during the Crimean War even after the British government turned her down
- Lin Zezu's opposition to the importation of opium to China

Then challenge students to write a persuasive speech that the person they have researched might have made on the topic. Invite students to present their persuasive speeches to the class.

See the Chapter Planner for more strategies for differentiation.

Given to the British after defeat in the Opium Wars, Hong Kong was returned to China on July 1, 1997. The city, which continued to exercise political autonomy after its return, had its political freedom sharply curtailed by the Chinese government in 2020 after an increase in pro-democracy protests there.

THE OPIUM WARS

As Russia and the Ottoman Empire struggled to industrialize, China faced a different problem. In the 1600s, the British discovered Chinese tea and loved it. By the late 1700s, the drink was so popular that the average Londoner spent five percent of his or her income on tea. But the old problem for European merchants was that they did not have any goods that interested the Chinese. Opium solved that problem.

In the 1770s, European countries (mainly Britain) began to smuggle the highly addictive drug from India into China to trade it for tea, silk, and other goods. To build a market for the drug, traders gave out free samples. The plan worked: Opium use in China rose and the market grew. Many in Britain knew that the trade was morally wrong and even hypocritical. At the same time that opium was being smuggled into China, the British were trying to end opium addiction at home. However, the supporters of free trade and profit got their way.

By the 1820s, opium addiction had reached epidemic proportions and was causing great harm to China's society and economy. In 1839, the Qing government decided to fight back. An official named Lin Zezu was put in charge, and he wrote to Queen Victoria informing her that any foreigners caught importing opium would be put to death. In addition, Lin dumped large amounts of opium into the sea. Britain demanded to be compensated for its lost product, but China refused and the first Opium War began.

The Chinese were stunned by Britain's advanced ships and weapons. Ironclad British steamships simply blew the Chinese ships out of the water. Unlike the Qianlong emperor who had rejected British diplomacy five decades earlier, by 1842 Qing officials knew they had lost and agreed to the humiliating terms of the Treaty of Nanjing, which opened five "treaty ports" to unrestricted foreign trade and gave Hong Kong to the British. The treaty also promised British subjects **extraterritoriality**, or exemption from local laws in the treaty ports.

This was the first in a series of unequal treaties that eroded Chinese sovereignty. The following year, France and the United States signed similar treaties with the Qing. China's loss in the second Opium War (1856–1860) led to more open ports and the creation of "international settlements" in key Chinese cities. Only Europeans were allowed to live in these settlements, and they were ruled by European law. Foreigners were also given permission to travel, work as missionaries, and establish businesses anywhere in the country.

After losing the two Opium Wars, China was forced to face the same questions as the Russian and Ottoman empires: whether and how to become a modern industrial nation that could compete with western Europe. Some government officials recognized that things needed to change. Beginning with the loss of the first Opium War in 1842, these men advocated for reform. You will read more about these "self-strengthening" policies shortly.

JAPAN AND SIAM

You have already read about Tokugawa Japan and know that Japanese society in the early 19th century was strictly hierarchical and ruled by conservative shoguns who upheld conservative Confucian values, one of which was to disrespect commerce and the Japanese merchant class. Interaction with Europeans was still limited to a single Dutch trade mission every year.

Then, in 1853, the American commodore **Matthew Perry** came to Japan. He arrived with two steamships and two sailing ships. Perry's mission was to intimidate the Tokugawa government, force it to establish diplomatic relations, and open Japanese ports to foreign trade. Edo's (now Tokyo's) harbor was poorly defended. Aware of China's loss in the first Opium War, Japanese officials saw that isolation was no longer possible and decided to negotiate.

In 1858, the Japanese signed an unequal treaty with the United States and five European powers that—like the treaties with China—granted the Europeans access to treaty ports and rights of extraterritoriality. Daimyo lords were angered by the treaty, and some rebelled against the shogun. By the early 1860s, it was not clear whether the Tokugawa government would be able to maintain power. Japan faced the same decision as other societies that had been challenged by European industrial power: develop Western-style industry or reject the West and try to maintain a traditional society. Until 1868, the traditionalists held power, but then Japan took a different course. It adopted many Western institutions and technologies, adapting them to Japanese culture and creating a modern industrial society.

Like Japan, the kingdom of Siam (present-day Thailand) adopted Western technology while maintaining its culture and political independence. Two kings,

Mongkut (MANG-koot) and Chulalongkorn (CHOO-luh-AWHN-korn), used internal reform and diplomatic engagement to achieve this balance. King Mongkut included Westerners among his advisors and opened Siam to foreign trade. His son, Chulalongkorn, who was educated by an English tutor, altered the legal system to protect private property and abolished slavery and debt peonage, expanded access to education, and encouraged development of telegraphs and railroads. At the same time, these Siamese kings balanced imported ideas with continued support for Buddhist temples and traditional artistic traditions.

Like his father, Chulalongkorn was a skilled diplomat who played Europeans off one another. Lacking a strong army, he gave up claims to parts of his empire to protect the core of his kingdom. Despite this, if the British or French had wanted to conquer Siam, they could have. But Siam sat—and served as a buffer—between the British in India and the French in the Southeast Asian region of Indochina. In 1896, the two powers agreed to recognize the independent kingdom of Siam.

CRITICAL VIEWING This Japanese woodblock print depicts the arrival of American commodore Matthew Perry to Japan in 1853. What details in the print express the point of view of the artist toward Perry's arrival?

HISTORICAL THINKING

1. **READING CHECK** How did Siam's kings balance Western ideas and local traditions?

2. **COMPARE AND CONTRAST** How were the Ottomans and Russians similar in their reactions to the Industrial Revolution?

3. **MAKE PREDICTIONS** How do you think opium addiction harmed China's economy and society?

4. **MAKE INFERENCES** Why is this lesson titled "How To Be Modern?"?

BACKGROUND FOR THE TEACHER

Hong Kong Originally, Hong Kong, which means "fragrant harbor," was a small fishing establishment. It was mountainous and visited frequently by pirates. However, when the British arrived, they quickly realized that the deep, sheltered harbor was relatively safe and was situated on the main Asian trade routes. They saw its great commercial and strategic significance and forced China to cede the island in 1842 after the first Opium War. Then in 1898, the British government forced China to lease the whole area with 235 islands to Britain for 99 years. In the mid-1980s, China and Britain began negotiating the transfer of Hong Kong back to China. The transfer occurred in July 1997 after more than 150 years of British control.

TEACH

GUIDED DISCUSSION

3. **Determine Chronology** What earlier event led British steamships to blow Chinese ships out of the water? *(Lin Zezu triggered the first Opium War by dumping large amounts of British opium into the sea and refusing to compensate Britain for the lost product.)*

4. **Make Connections** How did Japan learn from China's experiences with European powers? *(Possible response: Japan knew of China's problems with opium and the British and decided to negotiate with the United States and five European powers rather than suffer what China had gone through.)*

DETERMINE CHRONOLOGY

Direct students to compare the dates of the Crimean War, the Opium Wars, and Matthew Perry's visit to Japan. **ASK:** Which of these events came first? *(The first Opium War between China and Britain began in 1839 and ended in 1842.)* Which events occurred in 1853? *(The Crimean War began and Perry's visit to Japan both occurred in 1853.)* What date do the Crimean War and the second Opium War share? *(In 1856, the Crimean War ended and the second Opium War began.)*

ACTIVE OPTIONS

On Your Feet: Jigsaw Strategy Group students into five expert groups and assign each group one of the following five societies and determine how it tried to balance traditional values with the technological advances of the Industrial Revolution: Russia, the Ottomans, China, Japan, and Siam. When they finish their research, regroup the students so that each new group has at least one member from each expert group. The experts should then report on their study so that other students can learn more about each society.

> **NG Learning Framework: Research and Write a Newspaper Article**
> **ATTITUDE** Empowerment
> **KNOWLEDGE** Our Human Story

Tell students to imagine they are newspaper reporters covering the arrival of Commodore Perry and his gunboats in Japan in 1853. Instruct them to use a variety of online sources to research Perry's arrival. Then have students write a newspaper account from the Japanese point of view. Encourage students to use images and quotes from the Americans and Japanese in their article. Ask volunteers to share their articles with the class.

HISTORICAL THINKING

ANSWERS

1. Siam adopted western technology, was open to foreign trade, abolished slavery and debt peonage, and expanded access to education but also continued to support Buddhist temples and traditional artistic traditions.

2. Both the Russians and the Ottomans tried to become more industrial, but traditionalists eventually took power.

3. Answers will vary. Possible response: With so much of the population addicted to opium, the society was less productive and the economy suffered.

4. Answers will vary. Possible response: The lesson is about how non-European countries faced the decision about how or whether to adopt modern technology and economic systems in order to compete with Europe.

CRITICAL VIEWING Possible response: The front and back of the ship are drawn with faces that depict frowning, determined expressions. One cannon appears to be firing. These details express the point of view of a threatening power attacking.

British India and Indian Revolt

For centuries, invaders like the Mughals had crossed the Himalaya mountain passes into the Indian subcontinent. Arriving by sea, however, the British represented an entirely new threat. Starting from a base in Bengal, they would fill the power vacuum left by Mughal decline.

THE BRITISH EAST INDIA COMPANY

Unlike China and Japan, the Mughal Empire welcomed trade with Europe, and in the 17th century allowed European companies to open trading stations, or "factories." The most powerful was the British East India Company, which founded its first factory in 1615 at Surat on India's west coast. Another factory, founded by the company in 1690 in Calcutta (present-day Kolkata) in the province of Bengal, received permission in 1717 to trade tax-free, giving it a great advantage over both Indian and European competitors.

After an Iranian invasion in 1739, the Mughal Empire became less powerful. The expansion of British power in India was not planned, but the vacuum left by declining Mughal power eventually combined with greed and ambition to push British frontiers forward. The British East India Company let the Mughal emperor keep his throne while steadily extending the company's power, first by becoming the official tax collector, then by using the threat of military force to divide and conquer local rulers. Company employees abused their power and plundered Bengal and other areas. In 1769, the company's brutal treatment of Indians became crystal clear when a famine hit Bengal and killed one-third of its population. The company was accused of only feeding its own people, not even giving its surplus food to starving Bengalis while still demanding regular tax payments from them.

In an effort to end abuses such as the East India Company's actions during the famine, the British government took greater control in India with a plan to promote justice and fairness by keeping the roles of commercial traders and government officials separate. As the Mughal Empire continued to weaken, Britain expanded its control. In 1818, Britain defeated its last major resistance, the Maratha confederacy from the

west coast of India. Without an initial plan of conquest, the British had gone from coastal factories devoted to trading to complete control of the Indian subcontinent.

Britain used its newfound power to drain India of its raw materials to feed British industry. One result was Indian deindustrialization, notably in textile manufacturing. As you have read, the British had been importing Indian cotton cloth, but with the development of factories in Britain, Britain began to import only raw cotton. By 1830, millions of unemployed Indian textile workers were forced to leave factory work for farming in a reversal of the industrial British rural-to-urban migration.

Technological advancements also caused shifts in British-Indian society. In the early days of the East India Company, many British employees adopted aspects of Indian culture and married into Indian families. After steamships, telegraphs, and the Suez Canal shortened the distance between Europe and India, British men brought their families from England with them. The British began to create a separate society in India. Indians—no matter how accomplished—were excluded, except as servants. Meanwhile, the British intruded more and more into Indian customs and culture. This intrusion provoked a powerful counterreaction, especially after an increase in the number of missionaries raised both Muslim and Hindu concerns that the British wanted to convert them to Christianity.

THE REBELLION OF 1857

Indians under British rule faced a dilemma: reject British customs, embrace them, or balance them with Indian traditions. The first of those choices inspired a major rebellion in 1857.

The immediate cause of the revolt was Britain's introduction of a new, faster-loading rifle. The loading

CRITICAL VIEWING This 1784 painting is based on an actual cockfight in the city of Lucknow. The fight had been arranged as an amusement by Colonel Mordaunt, the tall standing figure dressed in white. In 1857, Lucknow became the center of a massive revolt against British authority. What differences are there in the depiction of the Europeans and Indians in this painting?

procedure required the **sepoys**, or Indian soldiers under British command, to bite off the greased ends of the guns' ammunition cartridge casings. A rumor spread among Muslim troops that the cartridges had been greased with pig fat, while many Hindus believed that fat from cattle had been used. Since contact with pork was forbidden to Muslims and cattle were sacred to Hindus, both groups suspected that the British were trying to pollute them as part of a plot to convert them to Christianity. Some soldiers refused to use the new cartridges and were arrested. In response, other soldiers rebelled and killed their British officers.

Ultimately 200,000 sepoys joined the rebellion. They marched to Delhi and rallied support for the restoration of the Mughal emperor. The revolt quickly spread across northern and western India, where the queen of Jhansi, one of the Maratha kingdoms, rode into battle with her troops. The rebellion was very violent on both sides and many were killed.

However, in less than a year, Britain regained control. The British government disbanded the East India Company, destroyed all remaining Mughal authority, and took over the rule of India itself. In 1876, Queen Victoria added "Empress of India" to her titles, and British dominance of India was complete.

Even under the Mughals, India was one of the most ethnically diverse regions of the world, with more than a dozen major languages, multiple castes, and many different religions and ethnicities. While that diversity continued, after 1857 there was also a move toward greater unity. The British built an extensive transportation and communication infrastructure throughout the country, which put India's diverse peoples and regions in closer contact than ever before. Thus, the tools of industrialization provided the foothold for Indians to overthrow their colonizers. A growing middle class began to join together and develop a clear vision of India as a single, unified nation. In 1885, they organized a new political movement called the Indian National Congress.

HISTORICAL THINKING

1. **READING CHECK** How did the East India Company expand its control over India?

2. **MAKE CONNECTIONS** How did the Industrial Revolution in Britain lead to deindustrialization in India?

3. **MAKE INFERENCES** Why did the British improve railway and communications systems in India, and what was an unintended consequence of those improvements?

PLAN: 2-PAGE LESSON

OBJECTIVE

Describe how the British slowly took control over all of India and suppressed any attempts at rebellion.

CRITICAL THINKING SKILLS FOR LESSON 3.2

- Make Connections
- Make Inferences
- Determine Chronology
- Analyze Cause and Effect
- Interpret Maps

HISTORICAL THINKING FOR CHAPTER 22

How did the Industrial Revolution transform people's lives around the world?

The consequences of the Industrial Revolution in India were the opposite of those in Britain—factories shut down and more people became farmers to meet British demands for raw materials. Lesson 3.2 discusses how society shifted in India as the British imposed their power, customs, and culture on the Indians.

Student eEdition online

Additional content for this lesson, including a map, is available online.

BACKGROUND FOR THE TEACHER

Indian National Congress The Indian National Congress first met in 1885 with the purpose of opposing British rule. One of the most significant leaders of the Congress was Mohandas Gandhi. Gandhi led protest marches, including one in 1930 called the Salt March. Its purpose was to oppose the British monopoly over the salt trade. Indian natives were prohibited from producing or selling salt and had to buy expensive imported salt that was taxed at a high rate. Gandhi began the Salt March in March with a small group of followers. Large numbers of people joined the group along the way. They marched more than 240 miles to the town of Dandi on the Arabian Sea to collect salt along the shore. More than 60,000 marchers were jailed during the protest, including Gandhi. A truce was eventually signed with the British government.

INTRODUCE & ENGAGE

DISCUSS CULTURAL DIFFERENCES

Tell students that, in this lesson, they will learn about what happened to traditional culture in India when the British government took control. **ASK:** What kinds of cultural differences might there be between a ruling power and the people of its colony? *(Possible response: Foods, social organization, religious affiliations, clothing, and housing might all be different.)* What kinds of conflicts might these differences cause? *(Possible response: People might have religious differences, and the conquering society might feel superior to the conquered.)*

TEACH

GUIDED DISCUSSION

1. **Determine Chronology** What event allowed the British to gain a strong foothold in India in 1739? *(The Mughal Empire became less powerful after an Iranian invasion in 1739.)*

2. **Analyze Cause and Effect** What was the main cause of the rebellion of 1857? *(Muslim and Hindu soldiers believed that the British were trying to convert them to Christianity and that new greased rifle cartridges violated religious prohibitions against certain types of animal products.)*

INTERPRET MAPS

Instruct students to examine the map of Indian Railroads, 1893 (available in the Student eEdition). **ASK:** Which region of the country had the fewest railroads? *(areas not under direct British control)* Why do you think that was the case? *(Possible response: The British built the railroads largely for their own use.)*

ACTIVE OPTIONS

On Your Feet: Three-Step Interview Direct students to form pairs. Ask Student A to interview Student B about the effects of British control over India. Then have pairs reverse roles. When pairs have finished, invite Student A to share with the class information from Student B. Then Student B should share information from Student A.

> **NG Learning Framework: Write Journal Entries**
> SKILL Communication
> KNOWLEDGE Our Human Story

Have students learn more about the sepoys and the causes of their rebellion in 1857. Then ask students to write several journal entries from the point of view of a sepoy. The entries should feature a time before, during, and after the rebellion. Encourage students to post their journal entries on a class website or blog.

DIFFERENTIATE

STRIVING READERS

Write a Tweet As students read the lesson, direct them to write a tweet that summarizes each paragraph's main idea in their own words. Encourage students to read their tweets aloud to a partner.

PRE-AP

Report on British Reactions Instruct students to conduct research and present an oral report about the British government's reaction to the formation of the Indian National Congress. Tell them to conclude their report by discussing the impact the Indian National Congress had on the Indian independence movement. Invite students to present their oral report.

See the Chapter Planner for more strategies for differentiation.

HISTORICAL THINKING

ANSWERS

1. The East India Company expanded its control over India by taking advantage of Mughal weakness and by slowly expanding its trading ports.

2. When Britain began to build its own mills and import only raw cotton, textile mills in India closed and Indians were forced to return to farming.

3. Answers will vary. Possible response: Britain improved railway and communications systems to make industry and the military more effective. However, these new systems also brought Indians closer together and helped them form a resistance to British rule.

CRITICAL VIEWING Answers will vary. Possible response: The British are presented as more sophisticated in dress and manner. The Indians are shown huddling or handling the roosters. The Indians' traditional dress and the cockfight would all appear exotic to someone in the West.

Rebellions in China

In the 1700s, the Qing dynasty in China was at the top of its game. But by the end of the 1800s, the empire was devastated economically, socially, and politically. How did China fall so far, so fast?

THE TAIPING REBELLION

By the mid-19th century, in addition to the devastation of opium addiction, the Opium Wars, and the growing power of the Europeans, China also faced enormous internal stresses, mainly as a result of four centuries of success.

The main issue was high population growth. Food production and government services could not keep up. Some scholars estimate that by the early 1800s, one local magistrate might be responsible for as many as 250,000 people. As a result, corruption rose and local strongmen gained power. Rural farmers became poorer as revenues went down and taxes went up, leading to peasant revolts in different regions. By far the largest and most successful was the Taiping Rebellion, which began in 1850 in Guangdong province and then spread throughout southern China.

During the Taiping Rebellion, Taiping forces break through a strategic encirclement by the Qing army in Pucheng, as shown in this finely detailed painting.

The leader of the rebellion was Hong Xiuquan (hoong shee-OH-chew-an), who proclaimed that he was the younger brother of Jesus Christ. Educated by missionaries, Hong mixed Christianity with a traditional Buddhist message of fairness and justice, which appealed to the poor and attracted hundreds of thousands of followers. Many at the center of the rebellion were, like Hong, from the Hakka ethnic group, which had been independent until the Ming era. As a result, they had not completely adopted Confucian ideas of hierarchy. Women had relatively independent roles, and Hakka men often refused to wear the long, braided ponytail (or queue) required as a sign of

subservience by the Manchu ethnic group that founded the Qing dynasty.

In late 1850, Taiping rebels captured the city of Nanjing and killed tens of thousands of Manchu, but the rebels had difficulty maintaining a functional government. Their religious beliefs went against the Confucian ideals of scholar-officials on which the imperial system had long been based. Also, landowners and educated elites, who were threatened by the rebellion's ideas about equality, successfully resisted Taiping rule. By 1853, the rebellion was in trouble, and in the 1860s European interests began to support the very dynasty they had just finished fighting in the Opium Wars. In 1864, Qing forces, supported by European soldiers and arms, took Nanjing and the Taiping Rebellion ended. A staggering 30 million people had been killed, and China's rulers were more indebted to European powers than ever before.

THE BOXER REBELLION

As you have read, in response to the loss of the Opium Wars, some Chinese began arguing for internal "Self-Strengthening" reforms. The movement's motto was "Confucian ethics, Western science," China, these reformers said, could acquire modern technology and scientific knowledge while keeping its Confucian traditions. Traditionalists, however, opposed the Self-Strengthening Movement. Like Muslim scholars who opposed reforms in the Ottoman Empire, Chinese scholar-officials got their power and prestige from training in a traditional body of knowledge. To accept foreign principles in education would give them less influence, and to emphasize military over scholarly pursuits would go against Confucianism.

The powerful regent Empress Ci Xi (kee SHEE) shared these traditional views. She resented the unequal treaties with European nations, and the arrogance of their representatives infuriated her. Ci Xi stopped funding modernization programs, such as railways and military improvements, and started funding projects like rebuilding the ruined summer palace destroyed earlier by European soldiers. She even spent from the naval budget on a marble boat to host tea parties in her garden.

This meant that China was unable to address internal crises. From 1876 to 1879, drought combined with overpopulation, resulting in one of the most brutal famines in the empire's history and claiming at least 9.5 million lives. Ten years later, another major famine hit the country, weakening it even more.

External pressures threatened China as well. From their base in Vietnam, the French had conquered most of Indochina by 1885, and the Korean Peninsula and Taiwan were lost to Japan in 1895. From 1895 to 1900, European aggression intensified. Germans seized the port city of Qingdao and claimed mineral and railway rights on its entire peninsula. The British and Russians expanded their control. Public anger toward the Qing grew in China.

In 1898, Ci Xi quickly charged some advocates of Self-Strengthening with conspiracy. Those who were not executed left the country or gave up and went silent. In the meantime, Empress Ci Xi lent her support

A court photographer took this official portrait of Empress Ci Xi, c. 1895.

to an anti-foreign secret society, the "Society of Righteous and Harmonious Fists" (also known as the Boxers), which had been gaining power and influence. In 1898, the society attacked European missionaries and Chinese Christian converts, beginning the Boxer Rebellion.

To put down the Boxers, troops from different nations, including Russia, Britain, the United States, Austria-Hungary, and Italy, marched on Beijing and occupied the Forbidden City in the summer of 1900. Most humiliating to the Chinese were the Japanese soldiers proudly flying their flag in the heart of the Chinese capital. It seemed that this invasion of "barbarians" had turned the world upside down.

The Qing were required to pay 450 million ounces of silver (twice the country's annual revenue) to the occupying forces. In addition, the Confucian examination system was abolished, and plans were made to draw up a constitution with some degree of popular representation. But it was much too late. Just a few years later, in 1912, revolutionaries overthrew the decrepit Qing dynasty.

HISTORICAL THINKING

1. **READING CHECK** Why was the 19th century a period of rebellion and unrest in China?

2. **ANALYZE CAUSE AND EFFECT** What effect did rejection of Confucian ideals have on the success of the Taiping Rebellion?

3. **DESCRIBE** How did the Qing dynasty react to attempts to adopt Western ideas and industry?

PLAN: 2-PAGE LESSON

OBJECTIVE

Explain why the Chinese began to rebel, both against their Qing rulers and against British and other European powers.

CRITICAL THINKING SKILLS FOR LESSON 3.3

- Analyze Cause and Effect
- Describe
- Summarize
- Identify
- Analyze Visuals

HISTORICAL THINKING FOR CHAPTER 22

How did the Industrial Revolution transform people's lives around the world?

In a little more than 100 years, China went from being a global powerhouse in the 1700s to being controlled by foreign powers made strong by the Industrial Revolution. Lesson 3.3 discusses the events that led the Chinese to rebel.

Student eEdition online

Additional content for this lesson, including a photo, is available online.

BACKGROUND FOR THE TEACHER

Regent Empress Ci Xi Ci Xi's son became the emperor upon his father's death. Because he was only six years old, a council ruled in his place. Ci Xi joined forces with two other court members and led a coup against the council. She was successful and ruled as regent for her young son. The regency lasted until her son was old enough to rule. However, he died before his mother, and she arranged for a three-year-old nephew to assume the throne and again ruled as regent. When the young emperor took over, some conservatives in China opposed the reforms he proposed. These people rallied around Ci Xi, who returned to the regency.

INTRODUCE & ENGAGE

PREVIEW VISUALS

Direct students to examine the painting of the Taiping Rebellion asking them to note the red uniformed British soldiers. Explain that the British were only one of the foreign groups that intervened in Chinese affairs during the late 1800s. **Ask:** How do you think the Chinese felt fighting side-by-side with foreign soldiers? *(Possible response: They probably resented the foreigners' presence and interference.)* Tell students that in this lesson they will learn about China's rebellions against foreign interference.

TEACH

GUIDED DISCUSSION

1. **Summarize** How did four centuries of success lead to enormous internal stresses in China during the mid-1800s? *(The centuries of success led to high population growth, food shortages, and corrupt government practices. Many rural farmers became poorer as their income went down and taxes went up.)*

2. **Identify** Who were the Boxers, and who supported and opposed them? *(The Boxers were members of a group called the "Society of Righteous and Harmonious Fists" that opposed foreign influence. Empress Ci Xi supported them, and troops from different nations opposed them.)*

ANALYZE VISUALS

Direct students to study the photograph of Ci Xi while you share the Background for the Teacher information with them. **ASK:** Which details in this photograph suggest that she is an empress? *(Possible response: She is wearing what appears to be an elaborate Chinese silk robe, a crown, and fine jewelry.)* What do Ci Xi's long fingernails suggest about her duties as empress? *(Possible response: She didn't do anything that required manual labor.)*

ACTIVE OPTIONS

On Your Feet: Fishbowl Arrange students so that part of the class sits in a close circle facing inward and the other part sits in a larger circle around them. Ask students on the inside circle to discuss the events that led to foreign intervention in China. During the discussion, those on the outside circle should listen for new information and evaluate what is said. After the discussion is over, direct groups to reverse positions.

> **NG Learning Framework: Stage a Debate**
> **ATTITUDE** Empowerment
> **SKILL** Communication

Prompt students to imagine they are a group of Chinese citizens discussing the policies of Empress Ci Xi. Divide the class into two teams and assign each team to argue either for or against the empress's policies. Encourage team members to work together to locate information in the lesson and online in preparation for their debate about the policies. Remind students to explore the pros and cons, searching for details that support their argument as well as any counterarguments they could make during the debate.

DIFFERENTIATE

INCLUSION

Preview and Predict Pair students with reading or perception issues with proficient readers and direct them to read the lesson title and section headings together. Then ask proficient students to describe lesson visuals and read the captions, working together to write notes predicting what the lesson will be about. After reading, ask pairs to review their notes to correct inaccuracies.

PRE-AP

Create a Multimedia Presentation Prompt students to learn more about the Boxer Rebellion, including events leading up to the rebellion. Tell students to create a multimedia presentation about the Boxers. The presentation might include maps, drawings, paintings, artifacts, and other visuals. Encourage students to post the presentation on a class website.

See the Chapter Planner for more strategies for differentiation.

HISTORICAL THINKING

ANSWERS

1. Internal stresses and foreign intervention led to rebellion and unrest.

2. The rebels had a hard time making the government work because their religious beliefs went against the Confucian ideals of scholar-officials.

3. While members of the Self-Strengthening Movement thought China could adopt western ideas and industry while maintaining Confucian ideals, the Qing government ultimately fought against it. Instead, they tried to throw the Europeans out of China entirely. It was only after they lost the Boxer Rebellion that China instituted any western-style reforms.

The Meiji Restoration

If someone tries to force you to change, how do you respond? Perhaps you think some kind of change might be a good thing. Even so, you probably want to do things *your* way, not theirs.

MEIJI REFORMS

Both Tokugawa Japan and Qing China were divided between conservatives, who rejected Western influences, and reformers, who argued for modernization to strengthen the empire. In China, it was the opponents of change who won out, but Japan was able to borrow foreign ideas and adapt them to their own culture, achieving the "self-strengthening" that Chinese reformers had not.

In 1867, the army of the Tokugawa shogun faced off against supporters of the Japanese emperor. Inspired by the slogans "Revere the Emperor!" and "Expel the Barbarians!" the emperor's armies were successful, and in 1868 the Meiji (MAY-jee) Restoration brought the Meiji ("enlightened") teenage emperor into power.

Reformers dominated the new emperor's administration, and they began to transform Japan's closed, traditional society. Mainly men from middle- and lower-class samurai families who placed a strong emphasis on scholarship, the Meiji reformers dismantled the feudal system and declared all classes in society equal. Tax collection was centralized to solidify the government's economic control, and a modern army and national education system were created.

CRITICAL VIEWING From a series of prints called *Famous Places on the Tokaido: A Record of the Process of Reform*, this print showcases the new Tokyo-Yokohama railway, built in 1872. What message about Meiji reforms does the print express?

These reforms were met with some resistance, but any rebellions were quickly put down. And while Japan adopted a constitution in 1889, like the German constitution it copied, the emperor, rather than elected representatives, had the real power.

The Meiji reformers did not believe in a free-market economy, and free-trade economic ideas were never particularly strong in Japan as compared to Britain and the United States. Japanese leaders thought that economic planning would be more likely to lead to social harmony than market competition. And the Meiji government, like Germany but even more so, gave the state control over industrial development. The government constructed railroads, harbors, and telegraph lines and made direct investments in industry as well.

Ultimately, the government did begin to open industry to private companies and sold off some of its industrial assets. After 1880, Japanese industry was dominated by **zaibatsu**, large industrial conglomerates that worked closely with the government. (Some of the 19th-century zaibatsu, like Mitsubishi, still exist today.)

As in Europe, the rewards of increased industrial productivity were not equally distributed in Meiji Japan. Landowners benefited the most from advances in agriculture. Rice output increased 30 percent between 1870 and 1895, but peasants often paid half their crop in land rent and now had to pay taxes to the central government as well. To make ends meet, many rural families sent their daughters to work in factories.

Some reformers worked to bring education to girls as the first step toward greater equality. A 20-year-old woman named Kishida Toshiko went even further, speaking powerfully for women's rights in meetings across the country. Toshiko was arrested, fined, and silenced for speaking out. The men at the top of Meiji society chose the slogan "Good Wife, Wise Mother" to reinforce tradition, defining proper women as submissive, subservient, and legally inferior.

Women work in a Japanese silk factory at the beginning of the 20th century, boiling cocoons and spinning silk.

GROWING MILITARISM

During the late 19th century like many other industrialized countries around the world, Japan was moving toward **militarism**, a policy of continuous military development and readiness for war. Many in Japan embraced Social Darwinist concepts, promoting the idea that the Japanese were racially superior to other Asians and destined to lead the continent forward.

The first place Japan showed its true intentions was on the Korean Peninsula. As you have read, Japan gained control of the peninsula and Taiwan in 1895. In addition, the Meiji government forced the Qing to grant it access to China's treaty ports and rights of extraterritoriality, similar to those of the European powers. At the same time, Japan renegotiated its own treaties with Europe, this time demanding equality. In 1910, the Meiji government formally annexed Korea.

Next, in order to solidify its influence in northeastern Asia, the Meiji government decided to challenge Russian ambitions in Manchuria and Korea. In 1905, the Japanese navy won a great military victory over the Russian fleet. Japan's victory proved that European superiority was not inevitable and that Japan had to be counted among the world's great powers.

HISTORICAL THINKING

1. **READING CHECK** What were the major reforms of the Meiji Restoration?

2. **MAKE CONNECTIONS** How did women's lives change or not change in Japan during this period?

3. **MAKE PREDICTIONS** How might increasing nationalism affect Japan in the future?

PLAN: 2-PAGE LESSON

OBJECTIVE
Describe how and why Japan industrialized and centralized state power while maintaining its social, cultural, and spiritual traditions.

CRITICAL THINKING SKILLS FOR LESSON 3.4
- Make Connections
- Make Predictions
- Compare and Contrast
- Synthesize
- Analyze Visuals

HISTORICAL THINKING FOR CHAPTER 22
How did the Industrial Revolution transform people's lives around the world?

Japanese leaders industrialized and modernized without losing Japan's traditional culture. Lesson 3.4 discusses the reforms the Japanese government put in place by borrowing foreign ideas while making its own imperialist advances.

BACKGROUND FOR THE TEACHER
Zaibatsu The word *zaibatsu* in Japanese means "wealthy clique," which is an apt description for these organizations. Essentially, a zaibatsu was a trust under which several businesses operated. Most zaibatsu included a bank to finance their operations. There were four main zaibatsu: Mitsui, Mitsubishi, Sumitomo, and Yasuda. They developed after the Meiji Restoration and grew quickly in economic power, particularly during World War I due to industrial investment in the war. After Japan's defeat in World War II, the zaibatsu were forced to disband. Though the powerful trusts no longer controlled the companies, most of the individual leadership of the member companies remained the same. As a result, many companies continued to organize loosely in groups, particularly those that had been part of the Mitsubishi, Mitsui, and Sumitomo groups. These groups were able to pool resources and thus successfully contribute to Japan's postwar growth.

INTRODUCE & ENGAGE

DISCUSS JAPANESE INDUSTRY

Help students prepare for the lesson by having them discuss Japanese industry today. Ask students to identify some of the products Japan exports to the United States and find out whether students have any of these products at home. *(televisions, DVD players, computers, cars, video games)* Point out that Japan has the third largest economy in the world after the United States and China. Tell students that in this lesson they will learn how modern industry in Japan began to develop.

TEACH

GUIDED DISCUSSION

1. **Compare and Contrast** Why was Japan more successful than China in its modernization process? *(The Japanese took foreign ideas and adapted them to their own culture, while the Chinese did not.)*

2. **Synthesize** How did Social Darwinism help encourage Japan's militarism and imperialism? *(Possible response: The Japanese believed they were racially superior to other Asians and destined to lead the continent forward.)*

ANALYZE VISUALS

Instruct students to study the print of the Tokyo-Yokohama railway. **ASK:** How does this image reflect the technological advances of the Industrial Revolution? *(Possible response: The print shows a steam-powered locomotive.)* What other details in the print suggest western influence? *(Possible response: The people shown are wearing western-style clothing.)*

ACTIVE OPTIONS

On Your Feet: Inside-Outside Circle Have students form concentric circles facing each other. Allow students time to write questions about the Meiji reforms. Then have students in the inside circle pose questions to students in the outside circle. Have students switch roles. Students may ask for help from other students in their circle if they are unable to answer a question.

NG Learning Framework: Conduct a Panel Discussion on the Japanese Military
SKILL Collaboration
KNOWLEDGE Our Human Story

Arrange students in small groups to present a panel discussion on the Japanese military buildup after the Meiji Restoration. Have them learn about the results of the buildup, including the takeover of Korea and other territory Japan had its sights on. Tell students to analyze the strengths and weaknesses of the military, the reasons for the buildup, the goals of the military, and predictions on how Japan's military buildup might affect the world in the future. If possible, direct groups to record and post their panel discussion for the class to view.

DIFFERENTIATE

STRIVING READERS

Recall and Record Facts After students have read the lesson, set a short time limit and tell them to write a list of facts they recall. Encourage them to group facts under the two section headings. Then direct them to work in pairs to compare and combine their lists.

INCLUSION

Discuss Details Pair students who are visually impaired with students who are not. Have students study the photo of the Japanese women working in a silk factory. Ask them to discuss the details in the photo, the women and their work, and the likely role of the woman in front of the workers. Encourage students to answer any questions their visually impaired partners might have.

See the Chapter Planner for more strategies for differentiation.

HISTORICAL THINKING

ANSWERS

1. They dismantled the feudal system and centralized many elements of government, including the tax system and the army. They established a national education system. The central government also controlled industry and developed infrastructure.

2. More women went to work in factories during the Meiji Restoration, but they did not gain more legal rights or an improved social position.

3. Answers will vary. Possible response: Japan will become more imperialistic and will try to gain more territory, which might lead to war.

CRITICAL VIEWING Answers will vary. Possible response: It shows a positive view of the reforms by depicting a modern-looking train station and people in western-style dress waiting for the train.

VOCABULARY

Use each of the following vocabulary words in a sentence that shows an understanding of the term's meaning.

1. division of labor
2. sabotage
3. exposition
4. globalization
5. liberalism
6. communism
7. socialism
8. extraterritoriality

READING STRATEGY
DETERMINE CHRONOLOGY

When you determine chronology, you place events in the order in which they occurred and note correlations between events. Use a time line like this one to order key events of the Industrial Revolution and analyze its impact.

	EVENTS
1750	Revolutionary uprisings across Europe
1775	Meiji Restoration
	Cotton gin
1800	Indian National Congress
1825	England controls India
	Steam engine
1850	China loses Opium War
1875	London's Great Exhibition
	Boxer Rebellion
1900	Abolition of British slave trade

9. Choose two of the events from your time line and describe the relationship between them.

MAIN IDEAS

Answer the following questions. Support your answers with evidence from the chapter.

10. What were two major changes in manufacturing that occurred as a result of the Industrial Revolution? LESSON 1.1

11. How did the Crystal Palace serve as an emblem of the advancements of the Industrial Revolution? LESSON 1.2

12. How did the Industrial Revolution lead to reform movements? LESSON 1.3

13. What do some historians mean by the term *Great Divergence*? LESSON 2.1

14. How are the Industrial Revolution and capitalism linked? LESSON 2.2

15. What were some dilemmas faced by non-Western countries in the 19th century? LESSON 3.1

16. What role did the British East India Company play in the British colonization of India? LESSON 3.2

17. What effect did the rebellions of the 19th century have on China and its development? LESSON 3.3

18. What effect did the Industrial Revolution have on Japan? LESSON 3.4

HISTORICAL THINKING

Answer the following questions. Support your answers with evidence from the chapter.

19. ANALYZE CAUSE AND EFFECT How did the Industrial Revolution affect the balance of power among the world's nations?

20. FORM AND SUPPORT OPINIONS Do you think life was better for most people before or after the Industrial Revolution? Explain.

21. IDENTIFY PROBLEMS AND SOLUTIONS What problems were communism, socialism, and utopian socialism trying to solve?

22. MAKE CONNECTIONS How did access to coal lead to the development of new technologies?

23. SUMMARIZE How did attitudes toward slavery change over the course of industrialization?

24. HYPOTHESIZE How might the world have been different if China had won the Opium Wars and decided to modernize?

25. COMPARE AND CONTRAST How did Siam and Japan react to Western power and influence?

26. DRAW CONCLUSIONS Why was the Industrial Revolution categorized as a "revolution"?

INTERPRET GRAPHS

Study the graph below, which shows the respective share of gross domestic product (GDP) among the world's most powerful countries.

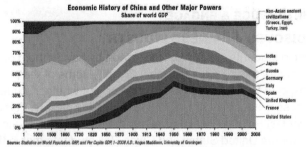

Economic History of China and Other Major Powers
Share of world GDP

Source: Statistics on World Population, GRP, and Per Capita GDP, 1–2008 A.D. Angus Maddison, University of Groningen

27. Which countries had the largest share of the world's GDP in 1700?

28. According to this graph, which countries had the largest share in 1900? Based on the text, how would you explain this change?

ANALYZE SOURCES

In 1835, Andrew Ure wrote about the growing Industrial Revolution in *The Philosophy of Manufactures*.

> Steam-engines . . . create a vast demand for fuel; they call into employment multitudes of miners, engineers, shipbuilders, and sailors, and cause the construction of canals and railways. Thus therefore, in enabling these rich fields of industry to be cultivated to the utmost, they leave thousands of fine arable fields free for the production of food to man, which must have been otherwise allotted to the food of horses.

29. What is the author's argument on the benefits of steam engines?

30. How does this excerpt relate to the population increase that resulted from the Industrial Revolution?

CONNECT TO YOUR LIFE

31. ARGUMENT The British abolitionist movement used many tactics in its efforts to end slavery in the British Empire and beyond. One of these techniques was a boycott, or refusal to buy or use, sugar because sugar was produced with the labor of enslaved people. Have you ever taken part in or considered taking part in a boycott? Why did you or did you not participate? Do you think boycotts are effective? Write a paragraph in which you make an argument for or against taking part in a boycott.

TIPS

* Describe the boycott you want to argue for or against.

* Explain the goals of the boycott you are describing.

* Evaluate how effective the boycott is likely to be or was. Think in terms of both short- and long-term effects as well as direct and indirect effects.

* Address any counterarguments.

* Conclude your argument with a sentence summarizing your position.

VOCABULARY ANSWERS

Possible responses:

1. Factories used the division of labor to make production more efficient.

2. The artisans used sabotage to destroy the machines that replaced them.

3. The Great Hall was built for the exposition in 1893.

4. Today, many people fear that globalization hurts local industry and workers.

5. The theory of liberalism in Victorian Britain emphasized the virtues of freedom.

6. Marx's theory of communism promoted the idea that equality could be achieved only through a classless society with no private property.

7. Many people in Scandinavia believe in socialism, in which the public or the state owns or controls many or most of the means of production.

8. The terms of the Treaty of Nanjing granted the British extraterritoriality, which meant they were exempt from local laws in the treaty ports.

READING STRATEGY ANSWERS

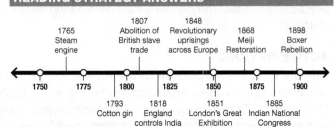

9. Possible response: The invention of the steam engine helped England control India.

MAIN IDEAS ANSWERS

10. Factories became mechanized and used steam engines. Workers performed one task over and over in a division of labor.

11. The Crystal Palace used glass made with a new manufacturing technique.

12. The early Industrial Revolution caused people to live and work in unsanitary and dangerous conditions. This sparked movements to reform those conditions.

13. *Great Divergence* is a term used to describe the split between the economic and technological advancements of Europe and Asia when Asian countries fell behind.

14. Free markets and private ownership in capitalism made the development of industry and the Industrial Revolution possible.

15. In the 19th century, non-European countries had to decide whether to modernize and, if they needed to, whether to model themselves after European capitalist societies.

16. The British East India Company established a foothold in India. It established relationships with the Mughal government, acquired territory, and gained political power.

17. The rebellions in China caused political and economic turmoil and stood in the way of any possibility that the country would modernize or industrialize on the scale necessary for it to compete with Europe.

18. The Industrial Revolution caused Japan to come out of its isolation and modernize.

HISTORICAL THINKING ANSWERS

19. The Industrial Revolution made Europe and later Japan the most powerful nations in the world. Most of the other nations were at a disadvantage. They were either colonized or had to treat European nations favorably to survive.

20. Possible response: Most people benefited from the Industrial Revolution. This is shown by the growth in population, the growth of the middle class, and the technological and scientific advancements that improved everyone's overall quality of life.

21. Possible response: Communism, socialism, and utopianism were all trying to solve issues of inequality and to improve the quality of life for the working class, both of which were caused by the early Industrial Revolution.

22. Coal was essential for making the iron needed in manufacturing new machines as well as for powering them after they were built.

23. Possible response: At the beginning of the Industrial Revolution, slavery provided many of the raw materials necessary for the factories. Later, many realized that slavery was not only wrong but that it also distorted the free market, hurt economies, and reduced the possible pool of consumers of finished products.

24. Possible response: China would have become a major world power. It would have probably colonized nations as the Europeans had, and its cultural influence would have spread around the world.

25. Possible response: Siam and Japan both maintained their independence from Europe. Both modernized while maintaining their unique cultures. Unlike Japan, Siam did not become more imperialistic as a result of modernization.

26. Possible response: Advancements in technology, the invention of new machines, changes in labor, and political and social changes led to the Industrial Revolution's categorization as a revolution.

INTERPRET GRAPHS ANSWERS

27. India and China

28. According to the graph, the United States, the United Kingdom, and Germany had the largest proportion of world GDP in 1900. This was most likely the result of industrialization in those countries.

ANALYZE SOURCES ANSWERS

29. The author is saying that the use of steam engines increases employment and leaves fields that would have to be used to feed horses open to being farmed for food for people.

30. Possible response: More food would be needed to feed the growing population that resulted from the Industrial Revolution, and the land became available because it was no longer needed to feed horses, which were replaced by steam engines.

CONNECT TO YOUR LIFE ANSWER

31. Students' arguments will vary but should explain the goals of the boycott they are arguing for or against, evaluate the effectiveness of the boycott, and address any counterarguments to the boycott. Students' arguments should include a concluding statement that summarizes their position.

UNIT 8 RESOURCES

UNIT INTRODUCTION

UNIT TIME LINE

UNIT MAP online

THE GLOBAL PERSPECTIVE: A Sense of the World: The Environment in History online

- National Geographic Explorers: Amanda Koltz, Jerry Glover, Adjany Costa
- On Your Feet: Jigsaw Strategy

UNIT WRAP-UP

National Geographic Magazine Adapted Article
- "Awash in Plastic"

Unit 8 Inquiry: Create a Sustainable Living Plan

Unit 8 Formal Assessment

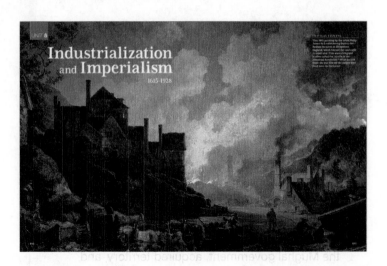

UNIT 8

Industrialization and Imperialism
1615–1928

CHAPTER 23 RESOURCES

Available in the Teacher eEdition

TEACHER RESOURCES & ASSESSMENT

Reading and Note-Taking

Vocabulary Practice

Document-Based Question Template

Social Studies Skills Lessons
- Reading: Draw Conclusions
- Writing: Informative

Formal Assessment
- Chapter 23 Pretest
- Chapter 23 Tests A & B
- Section Quizzes

Chapter 23 Answer Key

Cognero®

23 Changes in the Americas
1807–1924

HISTORICAL THINKING How did regional, cultural, and ethnic divisions shape the Americas in the 19th century?

SECTION 1 North America After Industrialization
SECTION 2 Latin America After Independence
SECTION 3 Rebellion and Reform

STUDENT DIGITAL RESOURCES

Available in the Student eEdition

- eEdition (English)
- National Geographic Atlas
- Biographies
- Handbooks
- History Notebook
- Literature Analysis

STRATEGY 1

Focus on Main Ideas

Explain that the Main Idea statements at the beginning of each lesson summarize the important ideas of the lesson and help students focus on key facts and ideas. Ask students to copy each Main Idea statement into a Main Ideas and Details List and then list details that support the statement as they read the lesson.

Use with All Lessons

STRATEGY 2

Use a TASKS Approach

Help students get information from visuals by using the following TASKS strategy:

T Look for a **title** that may provide the main idea.
A **Ask** yourself what the visual is trying to show.
S Determine how **symbols** on a map are used.
K Look for a **key** or legend on a map.
S **Summarize** what you have learned.

Use with Lessons 1.1, 1.3–1.4, 2.1, and 3.1–3.2

STRATEGY 3

Create a 3-2-1 Summary

After they read a lesson, instruct students to complete a 3-2-1 summary by writing three important ideas under the number three, two Key Vocabulary terms and their definitions under the number two, and one main idea question to ask another student under the number one.

Use with Lessons 1.1, 1.3–1.4, 2.1, and 3.1–3.2

STRATEGY 1

Pose and Answer Questions

Pair students who have reading or perception issues with more proficient readers. Have pairs read each paragraph of the lesson. Allow the student with reading difficulties to ask questions for clarification. Have the more proficient readers pose one recall question per paragraph for their partners to answer.

Use with All Lessons

STRATEGY 2

Provide Terms and Names on Audio

Decide which of the terms and names are important for mastery and ask a volunteer to record the pronunciations and a short sentence defining each word. Encourage students to listen to the recording as often as necessary.

Use with All Lessons *You might also use the recording to quiz students on the mastery of the terms. Play one definition at a time from the recording and ask students to identify the term or name described.*

STRATEGY 1

Predict Word Meanings

Before students read a lesson that has two or more Key Vocabulary terms, use a matching task like the example below to help them predict word meanings. Have them write each word next to the definition they predict is correct. After they finish reading, have students revisit their predictions and correct any mistakes.

segregation; strike; muckraker

1. _____ a work stoppage

2. _____ separation of races

3. _____ journalist who investigates corruption

Use with Lessons 1.1, 1.3–1.4, 2.1, and 3.1–3.2 *Pair students at the **Beginning** level with students at the **Intermediate** or **Advanced** levels to predict and verify meanings.*

STRATEGY 2

Use Visuals to Predict Content

Direct students at the **Beginning** and **Intermediate** levels to read the lesson title and look at the visuals. Then ask them to write a sentence predicting how each visual is related to the lesson. After students read the lesson, you may wish to have them verify their predictions and reword sentences if necessary.

Use with All Lessons

STRATEGY ③
Build a Concept Cluster

Write the Key Vocabulary word *tenement* in a Concept Cluster on the board and ask students for words, phrases, or pictures that come to mind. Have volunteers add the words and draw simple pictures to the cluster. Call on students to create sentences about the words and pictures. Then tell students to suggest questions they would like to have answered about the Key Vocabulary word.

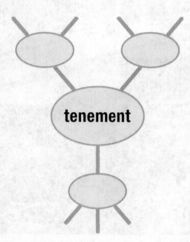

Use with Lesson 1.4 *You may wish to pair students at the **Beginning** level with students at the **Intermediate** and **Advanced** levels and have more advanced students assist less advanced students.*

STRATEGY ①
Present a Monologue

Ask students to portray a historical figure and present a monologue from that person's point of view. For example, Abraham Lincoln might discuss his decision to shift the purpose of the American Civil War to ending slavery. Benito Juárez might discuss the reforms he proposed.

Use with Lessons 1.1, 2.1, and 3.1–3.2

STRATEGY ②
Teach a Class

Before beginning the chapter, allow students to choose one of the lessons listed below and prepare to teach the content to the class. Give them a set amount of time in which to present their lesson. Suggest that students think about any visuals or activities they want to use when they teach.

Use with Lessons 1.1, 1.3–1.4, 2.1, and 3.1–3.2

STRATEGY ①
Form a Thesis

Have each student develop a thesis statement for a specific topic related to one of the lessons in the chapter. Be sure the statement makes a claim that is supportable with evidence either from the chapter or through further research. Ask students to present their thesis statements to the class.

Use with All Lessons

STRATEGY ②
Write a Summary

Remind students of the Historical Thinking question: How did regional, cultural, and ethnic divisions shape the Americas in the 19th century? Tell students to review the chapter and identify the divisions that resulted in profound change in the Americas. Then have students write a summary using the examples they identify to answer the Historical Thinking question.

Use with All Lessons *Encourage students to use a three-column chart to organize their ideas.*

CHAPTER
23 Changes in the Americas
1803–1924

HISTORICAL THINKING How did regional, cultural, and ethnic divisions shape the Americas in the 19th century?

SECTION 1 North America After Industrialization
SECTION 2 Latin America After Independence
SECTION 3 Rebellion and Reform

CRITICAL VIEWING
Many Europeans immigrated to the United States in the 19th century in search of greater economic opportunities and settled in big industrial cities, including New York, Chicago, Detroit, and Philadelphia. By the late 1800s, American cities were becoming the bustling places we know today. What modern aspects of a city do you recognize in this 1899 photo of a downtown street in New York?

642 CHAPTER 23   Changes in the Americas 643

INTRODUCE THE PHOTOGRAPH

NEW YORK CITY IN THE 19th CENTURY

Have students study the photograph of New York in the late 19th century. Read aloud the caption and have students identify items in the photo that they might see in a modern city. Point out that people arrived in this downtown area of New York by streetcar, horse-and-carriage, and by walking. Tell students that an elevated train line also provided transportation. **ASK:** How does the photo convey that commerce, transportation, and people are all interdependent? (*Possible response: Transportation is carrying people and goods to and from the city. Some people are carrying packages, suggesting they have been shopping in the stores.*)

SHARE BACKGROUND

Immigrant education was an important issue in large cities in the late 1800s. In New York and Chicago, for instance, nearly four out of five school-age children had immigrant parents, and not all immigrant parents favored educating their children. For some, it was an economic choice between having their children work to help support the family or sending them to school. For others, it was a cultural issue, as parents who had farmed in Europe were unused to sending their children to school and often were uneducated themselves. Schools, for their part, often went beyond teaching the standard curriculum and added instruction for immigrant children on citizenship, dress, hygiene, diet, patriotism, and English language skills.

CRITICAL VIEWING Answers will vary. Possible response: department stores, streetcars, tall buildings, sidewalks, streetlights, advertisements

HISTORICAL THINKING QUESTION

How did regional, cultural, and ethnic divisions shape the Americas in the 19th century?

Roundtable Activity: Divisive Factors This activity introduces students to some of the factors that divided people in the Americas in the 1800s and early 1900s: regional, cultural, and ethnic differences. Divide the class into three groups and have each group sit at a table. Assign the following questions to the groups.

Group 1 How do regional differences in the United States affect the country today?

Group 2 What are the pros and cons of a multicultural society?

Group 3 Why do some ethnic groups within a nation clash?

Ask students at each table to take turns answering the question. When they have finished their discussion, ask a representative from each table to summarize that group's answers.

KEY DATES FOR CHAPTER 23

1847–1901	The Maya fight against Mexico in the Yucatán Rebellion.
1861	Benito Juárez is elected president of Mexico.
1861–1865	The United States fights the Civil War.
1865–1877	Reconstruction attempts to integrate former slaves into the American republic.
1867	Several Canadian colonies unite to form the Confederation of Canada.
1876	Native Americans defeat American troops at the Battle of the Little Bighorn.
1884	The Seneca Falls Convention is held in New York.
1885	Indigenous people in Canada fight and lose the North-West Rebellion.
1886	The Haymarket Riot takes place in Chicago between workers and police.
1896	The U.S. Supreme Court legalizes segregation in *Plessy* v. *Ferguson*.

INTRODUCE THE READING STRATEGY

DRAW CONCLUSIONS

Explain to students that drawing conclusions involves making a judgment based on their analysis of the facts in a text and on their own experiences and background knowledge. Go to the Chapter Review and preview the cluster diagram with students. As they read the chapter, have students draw conclusions about the changes taking place in the Americas during the 1800s and early 1900s.

INTRODUCE CHAPTER VOCABULARY

KEY VOCABULARY

SECTION 1

anarchist	Confederacy	dominion
embargo	Métis	Reconstruction
secede	sectionalism	segregation
strike	tenement	

SECTION 2

debt peonage	*La Reforma*

SECTION 3

autonomy	Ghost Dance	Jim Crow Laws
monopoly	muckraker	suffrage

WORD WEB

As students read each lesson, encourage them to complete a Word Web for each Key Vocabulary term. Ask them to write each word in the center oval. Explain that they should use the smaller circles to record examples, characteristics, and descriptive words associated with the Key Vocabulary word as they encounter it in the lesson. Model an example for students on the board using the graphic organizer below.

Civil War in the United States

Do you think regional differences could cause the United States to split into two
countries today? It's happened before. In the 1860s, some states chose to break
away and form their own government. A war would decide the nation's fate.

TENSIONS BETWEEN NORTH AND SOUTH

In the years following the American Revolution, the
United States had steadily expanded westward. By
1850, the country had spread to the Pacific Ocean. But
as each new state entered the Union, the question of
whether it would allow slavery bitterly divided the nation.
Those in the North thought the new territories should
be admitted as free states, while the South called for
new slave states. Northerners didn't want to strengthen
the institution of slavery. And both sides feared that an
imbalance in free and slave states would result in more
political power for the other side. Congress tried to keep
the total of free and slave states equal, but tensions
between the two regions grew.

The North and the South began to establish separate
identities, and people came to feel strong loyalty
toward the part of the country in which they lived, a
concept called **sectionalism**. Economic differences
between the two regions helped drive sectionalism. The
Industrial Revolution had spread to the United States,
and factories sprang up in the North. Manufacturing
boosted industries that supported the factory-
based economy, including banking and improved
transportation systems—roads, canals, and railroads—
to transport goods. The South, on the other hand,
remained an agrarian, or agricultural, society. Cotton
was a major cash crop. And white plantation owners in
the South relied heavily on slave labor to grow this crop
and others.

Violent conflicts took place between proslavery and
antislavery forces. For example, violent assaults by
pro-slavery activists and armed retaliation by their
enemies in Kansas further divided the nation. In 1854,
the Republican Party was established. Its members
dedicated themselves to stopping the spread of
slavery. They opposed those in the Democratic Party,
particularly southern Democrats, who supported
slavery. The Republicans nominated **Abraham Lincoln**

as their candidate in the presidential election of 1860.
Lincoln won by carrying the western states and most of
those in the North. He didn't even appear on the ballot
in the South.

After Lincoln's election, several southern states
seceded, or withdrew, from the Union. More states
joined them and, in 1861, they established a new country
called the Confederate States of America, also referred
to as the **Confederacy**. That same year, Confederate
soldiers bombarded Union soldiers inside Fort Sumter,
a U.S. possession in South Carolina. The Union forces
surrendered, but the attack sparked the Civil War.

WAR AND ITS AFTERMATH

The Union and the Confederacy quickly mobilized
armies and prepared to fight. At the outset, the North
held an advantage in terms of overall resources,
including a more extensive system of roads and canals,
greater industrial capacity, more food, and four times
as many men eligible for military service. The South had
an initial advantage in military leadership. In addition,
Confederate soldiers were fighting to protect their
homeland and way of life.

Union and Confederate forces clashed in bloody battles
throughout the war. Advances in technology made the
fighting deadlier than ever. A new and more precise
kind of rifle replaced the muskets used in the American
Revolution, and the repeating rifle allowed soldiers to
fire several times before having to reload. During battles
at sea, ironclad ships plated with thick metal withstood
cannon and rifle fire. You have learned that, during the
Crimean War, advances in nursing improved care for
wounded soldiers. Unfortunately, medical technology
had not kept pace with weapons technology. Effective
treatments for infections, such as antibiotics, had not yet
been discovered. When the Civil War ended with a Union
victory in 1865, an estimated 620,000 men had died—
the most American lives lost in any conflict to date.

CRITICAL VIEWING Throughout
the Civil War, Mathew Brady and his
team photographed its key players
and battle scenes. Their images
of the dead and wounded on the
battlefield brought home the terrible
reality of warfare. This photo was
shot a couple of weeks after the
Union victory at the one-day Battle
of Antietam, which caused a total of
about 23,000 casualties. President
Lincoln stands in the center of the
photo and is flanked on his right
by Allan Pinkerton, the head of the
newly formed Secret Service, and
by General George McClellan on his
left. Why would Lincoln travel to a
battlefield after a victory?

At the beginning of the war, the Union fought to reunite
the nation. In 1863, however, President Lincoln shifted
the purpose to ending slavery. Just before the war
ended, Congress passed the 13th Amendment, which
abolished slavery. Over the next five years, two more
amendments were passed: the 14th, which guaranteed
citizenship and equal protection under the law to all
persons born or naturalized in the United States; and the
15th, which prohibited federal and state governments
from restricting the right to vote because of race, color,
previous condition of servitude, or slavery.

On April 11, 1865, two days after the Confederacy
surrendered, Lincoln announced a plan to rebuild
the former Confederate states and integrate former
slaves into the American republic. The plan became
known as **Reconstruction**. But just a few days after
his announcement, Lincoln was shot by an assassin's
bullet and died. Reconstruction went forward, but it
fell short of its goals. African Americans made some

advances. For instance, they took part in the political
process for the first time and had increased educational
opportunities. But white southerners resisted
Reconstruction and undermined efforts to promote
African-American equality—sometimes violently.
A secret society called the Ku Klux Klan became
particularly powerful and used terrorism to deprive
African Americans of their new constitutional rights.

Finally, in 1877, Republicans and Democrats
agreed to end Reconstruction. Discrimination
against black southerners continued in the South,
where state legislatures enacted policies that
enforced **segregation**, or the separation of races, in
public places. African Americans were also deprived
of their right to vote through violent intimidation and
through laws that made registration almost impossible.
Racial discrimination would become entrenched
throughout the nation.

HISTORICAL THINKING

1. **READING CHECK** What factors
contributed to the development of
sectionalism in the United States?

2. **DRAW CONCLUSIONS** How
did states in the South feel
about the Republican Party?

3. **MAKE INFERENCES** Why do
you think Lincoln shifted the war's
purpose to ending slavery?

PLAN: 2-PAGE LESSON

OBJECTIVE

**Explain how economic and cultural differences
between the North and South in the United States led
to a civil war that tore the country apart.**

CRITICAL THINKING SKILLS FOR LESSON 1.1

- Interpret Maps
- Make Inferences
- Analyze Cause and Effect
- Draw Conclusions
- Interpret Models

HISTORICAL THINKING FOR CHAPTER 23

**How did regional, cultural, and ethnic divisions shape
the Americas in the 19th century?**

By the 1860s, the North and South had developed
separate identities. Lesson 1.1 discusses how these
sectional differences erupted in the American Civil War.

Student eEdition online

Additional content for this lesson, including a map and a
diagram, is available online.

BACKGROUND FOR THE TEACHER

The South's Advantage At the outset of the war, the
South seemed to have the advantage in both political and
military leadership. Jefferson Davis, the president of the
Confederacy, had served in both houses of Congress and
had held the position of secretary of war under President
Franklin Pierce. Davis was a graduate of West Point, the
U.S. Military Academy, with a distinguished record of
service in the Mexican-American War. Abraham Lincoln,
on the other hand, had served one term in the House of
Representatives, and his military experience consisted of
service in the Black Hawk War, during which he did not
fight in any battles. Davis served as his own secretary
of war, whereas Lincoln struggled to find competent
advisors.

INTRODUCE & ENGAGE

ACTIVATE PRIOR KNOWLEDGE

Complete a K-W-L Chart in class to jot down what students already know about the Civil War. Ask them what led to war, who fought in it, and what happened as a result. Then elicit and record in the chart questions that students would like to have answered as they study the lesson. At the end of the lesson, provide time for a discussion to fill in the last column of the K-W-L Chart with what they have learned.

TEACH

GUIDED DISCUSSION

1. **Analyze Cause and Effect** How did Lincoln's election in 1860 precipitate the start of the Civil War? *(Lincoln was a member of the new Republican Party, whose mission was to stop the spread of slavery. His election in 1860 motivated several southern states to secede from the Union.)*

2. **Draw Conclusions** What conclusions can you draw about the effectiveness of Reconstruction? *(Possible response: Reconstruction wasn't very successful because segregation and racial discrimination continued in the South after it ended.)*

INTERPRET MODELS

Have students look at the diagram of the *Monitor* (available in the Student eEdition) and review the labels and caption. **ASK:** Where is the battleship's rotating turret located? *(on top of the ship)* Then point out that the warship carried a crew of 58 men. Invite students to discuss what life must have been like for the crew members onboard the ship.

ACTIVE OPTIONS

On Your Feet: Four Corners Post the following signs in the corners of the classroom: the North and South before the war; Abraham Lincoln and the Republican Party; the Civil War; Reconstruction. Have students gather in the corner of their choice to discuss the topic. After the discussions are finished, invite at least one student from each corner to share a couple of facts and ideas about the topic discussion.

NG Learning Framework: Commemorate a Battle
ATTITUDE Responsibility
SKILL Communication

Invite students to choose a battle from the Civil War Battles map (available in the Student eEdition) and research it to create an exhibition commemorating the battle. Have students write a brief summary describing the battle and honoring those who participated. Encourage students to enhance their summary with a map, photos, a time line, or other visuals to create an appropriate display to post in the classroom.

DIFFERENTIATE

STRIVING READERS

Use Reciprocal Reading Have partners take turns reading aloud each paragraph of the lesson and the photo caption. After reading each paragraph or the caption, the reader should ask the listener questions about it. Students may ask their partners to state the main idea, identify important details that support the main idea, or summarize the material in their own words. When partners have finished reading the lesson, have them work together to answer the Historical Thinking questions.

PRE-AP

Research Reconstruction Ask students to conduct online research to learn more about Reconstruction. Have them find information on the Freedmen's Bureau, the first African Americans in the U.S. Congress, sharecropping, and resistance in the South, including the activities of the Ku Klux Klan. Hold a panel discussion with the whole class to have students present the findings of their research.

See the Chapter Planner for more strategies for differentiation.

HISTORICAL THINKING

ANSWERS

1. economic differences between the industrial North and agrarian South and the South's reliance on slave labor

2. They did not like the Republican Party, as evidenced by the fact that Abraham Lincoln didn't even appear on the ballot in the South.

3. Answers will vary. Possible response: Ending slavery gave the war a moral purpose, which may have rallied more northerners to the Union's cause.

CRITICAL VIEWING Answers will vary. Possible response: to show support for the soldiers; to congratulate and confer with the generals

1.2 A Global Commodity: Cotton

In the 19th century, cotton was king in the southern United States. After 1793, Eli Whitney's cotton gin had greatly decreased the time required to process cotton crops. It also significantly increased the demand for enslaved people in the South. In the 1800s, southern plantations began to supply large quantities of cotton to textile industries at home and abroad—including Britain, where the manufacture of cotton cloth was its biggest industry.

After the outbreak of the American Civil War, the Confederacy tried—and failed—to pressure Britain into supporting its cause by threatening an embargo or ban, on cotton sold to British manufacturers. As a result, exports of the commodity to Britain fell dramatically, eventually triggering a "cotton famine" there. But traders at the port of Liverpool, England, where most of the cotton arrived, had been stockpiling it in the months leading up to the war. In time, the traders began a lucrative business, exporting armaments to the South in exchange for more cotton. Meanwhile, British merchants found other sources of cotton in India, Egypt, and Brazil. King Cotton still reigned, but a thread of new global industrial networks had been spun.

Today, with the advent of the fast fashion industry, cheap cotton is still in high demand—resulting in unfair labor practices (especially forced or child labor) in some of the largest cotton-producing countries in the world, including Uzbekistan, India, China, and Egypt.

Why do commodities like cotton have the power to impact war?

IN HIGH COTTON
The fluff in this Texas field may look like cotton candy, but it's not edible. These cotton balls are likely to be woven into a lacy tablecloth or sturdy denim jeans. Cotton grows fairly quickly and produces an abundant harvest. A few months after the seeds are sown, green pods, called bolls, appear on the plants. Fibers inside the boll expand until they split it apart, and soft balls of cotton pop out. The expression "in high cotton," which refers to doing well or being successful, is a nod to the time when cotton was the main cash crop in the southern United States.

648 CHAPTER 23

PLAN: 4-PAGE LESSON

OBJECTIVE
Understand the history and evolution of the cotton industry.

CRITICAL THINKING SKILLS FOR LESSON 1.2
- Analyze Visuals
- Make Connections
- Make Inferences
- Identify Main Ideas and Details
- Draw Conclusions
- Summarize

HISTORICAL THINKING FOR CHAPTER 23
How did regional, cultural, and ethnic divisions shape the Americas in the 19th century?

African Americans performed slave labor on cotton plantations in the southern United States. Lesson 1.2 discusses the cotton industry and its impact on the Civil War and the U.S. economy.

Student eEdition online
Additional content for this lesson, including photos and captions, is available online.

BACKGROUND FOR THE TEACHER
Making Cotton Seeds Edible Cotton seeds contain high levels of a toxin called *gossypol,* which in high concentrations can lead to respiratory distress, decreased immune function, and even death. However, researchers have found a way to modify the seeds by interfering with a gene that virtually eliminates gossypol. As a result, researchers hope that edible cotton seeds will soon be used to combat malnutrition in developing countries across the world by feeding between 5 and 6 million people per year. Cotton seeds could be eaten whole as a roasted and salted snack, enjoyed as a spread similar to hummus or peanut butter, or used as a flour in baked goods.

History Notebook
Encourage students to complete the Global Commodity page for Chapter 23 in their History Notebooks as they read.

INTRODUCE & ENGAGE

DISCUSS THE IMPORTANCE OF COTTON

Take an informal survey to find out how many students are wearing clothing or have purses or backpacks made from cotton. Tell them that cotton has been one of the most important fabrics in history. Ask what qualities they think contribute to cotton's usefulness and list products made from the commodity. Tell students that in this lesson they will learn about the history of the cotton industry and how it has evolved.

TEACH

GUIDED DISCUSSION

1. **Make Inferences** Why was cotton referred to as "King Cotton" in the South? *(because it was the most important crop in the economy of the southern United States)*

2. **Identify Main Ideas and Details** What happened when the Confederacy threatened an embargo on cotton sold to British manufacturers? *(Exports of cotton to Britain fell dramatically, triggering a cotton famine. But traders in Liverpool, England, had stockpiled the commodity. They began exporting armaments to the South in exchange for more cotton. Britain also found other sources of cotton.)*

A GLOBAL COMMODITY

One bale of cotton, approximately 480 pounds, can produce 215 pairs of jeans, 1,200 t-shirts, 4,300 pairs of socks, and 680,000 cotton balls. Depending on the area, 1 acre of cotton can produce between 1 and 3 bales and between 25 and 30 gallons of cottonseed oil. Cottonseed oil can be used as a cooking oil and is also found in foods such as mayonnaise, salad dressing, and baked goods as well as in cosmetics, pharmaceuticals, rubber, and plastics.

DIFFERENTIATE

ENGLISH LANGUAGE LEARNERS

Use Terms in Sentences Pair students at the **Beginning** level with those at the **Intermediate** or **Advanced** level. Ask pairs to write sentences for terms related to cotton and slavery, such as *fibers, bolls, labor, pickers,* and *plantation.* Invite pairs to share their sentences and discuss different ways to use each term.

PRE-AP

Research Unfair Labor Practices Have students research unfair labor practices in the cotton industry today (specifically child labor in Uzbekistan) and present their findings to the class.

See the Chapter Planner for more strategies for differentiation.

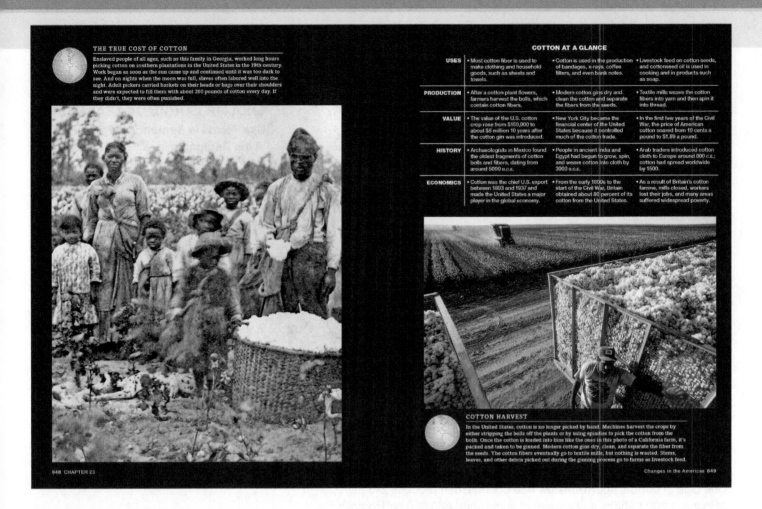

Enslaved people of all ages, such as this family in Georgia, worked long hours picking cotton on southern plantations in the United States in the 19th century. Work began as soon as the sun came up and continued until it was too dark to see. And on nights when the moon was full, slaves often labored well into the night. Adult pickers carried baskets on their heads or bags over their shoulders and were expected to fill them with about 200 pounds of cotton every day. If they didn't, they were often punished.

COTTON AT A GLANCE

USES	• Most cotton fiber is used to make clothing and household goods, such as sheets and towels.	• Cotton is used in the production of bandages, x-rays, coffee filters, and even bank notes.	• Livestock feed on cotton seeds, and cottonseed oil is used in cooking and in products such as soap.
PRODUCTION	• After a cotton plant flowers, farmers harvest the bolls, which contain cotton fibers.	• Modern cotton gins dry and clean the cotton and separate the fibers from the seeds.	• Textile mills weave the cotton fibers into yarn and then spin it into thread.
VALUE	• The value of the U.S. cotton crop rose from $150,000 to about $8 million 10 years after the cotton gin was introduced.	• New York City became the financial center of the United States because it controlled much of the cotton trade.	• In the first few years of the Civil War, the price of American cotton soared from 10 cents a pound to $1.89 a pound.
HISTORY	• Archaeologists in Mexico found the oldest fragments of cotton bolls and fibers, dating from around 5000 B.C.E.	• People in ancient India and Egypt had begun to grow, spin, and weave cotton into cloth by 3000 B.C.E.	• Arab traders introduced cotton cloth to Europe around 800 C.E.; cotton had spread worldwide by 1500.
ECONOMICS	• Cotton was the chief U.S. export between 1803 and 1937 and made the United States a major player in the global economy.	• From the early 1800s to the start of the Civil War, Britain obtained about 80 percent of its cotton from the United States.	• As a result of Britain's cotton famine, mills closed, workers lost their jobs, and many areas suffered widespread poverty.

COTTON HARVEST

In the United States, cotton is no longer picked by hand. Machines harvest the crops by either stripping the bolls off the plants or by using spindles to pick the cotton from the bolls. Once the cotton is loaded into bins like the ones in this photo of a California farm, it's packed and taken to be ginned. Modern cotton gins dry, clean, and separate the fiber from the seeds. The cotton fibers eventually go to textile mills, but nothing is wasted. Stems, leaves, and other debris picked out during the ginning process go to farms as livestock feed.

BACKGROUND FOR THE TEACHER

The Cotton Gin In 1793, American inventor Eli Whitney visited a southern plantation and observed that the system used to remove seeds from picked cotton was slow and labor intensive. To solve this problem, he invented the cotton gin, a machine fitted with teeth to grab the seeds and separate them from cotton tufts. The cotton gin greatly increased the efficiency of cotton production. A single gin could produce as many as 50 pounds of cleaned cotton fiber each day. In contrast, a person removing the seeds by hand could produce only about one pound of fiber in a day. Cotton soon became the main cash crop on many southern farms, but the cotton gin had unintended social consequences. Both the plantation system and slavery became more deeply entrenched in the South as the demand for labor to harvest the ever larger cotton crops increased.

TEACH

GUIDED DISCUSSION

3. **Draw Conclusions** Why did the price of cotton soar during the first years of the Civil War? *(Possible response: Cotton production greatly decreased as southern farmers left to fight in the war and battles were fought on farmland.)*

4. **Summarize** How is cotton harvested and woven today in the United States? *(Machines harvest the cotton crop, which is then packed and taken to be ginned. Modern cotton gins separate the fiber from seeds. The cotton fibers go to textile mills where machines weave the cotton into cloth.)*

ANALYZE VISUALS

Instruct students to study the photo of the family standing in a cotton field on a farm in Georgia. **ASK:** How do the people in the photo appear? *(Possible response: tired, dirty, dressed in ragged clothes)* What does the presence of children in the photo suggest about the farm's owners? *(Possible response: They want to maximize their profits and have no concern for the welfare of small children.)*

ACTIVE OPTION

NG Learning Framework: Explore the Modern Cotton Industry
ATTITUDE Curiosity
SKILL Collaboration

Invite groups of students to learn more about the modern cotton industry. Provide students with these questions to guide their research: Where is most cotton grown today? Why? What modern products and industries depend on cotton? What are labor conditions like? How does the industry use new technologies? Have groups collaborate to prepare a short oral report on their findings to present to the class. Encourage students to explain one or two ways in which the industry has or has not changed over time.

ANSWER

Answers will vary. Possible response: Cotton is a major industry and has many uses. Countries that produce the commodity can make a lot of money from it—and use the profits to wage or fund war.

Confederation in Canada

Canada is the second largest country in the world today—and also one of the most sparsely populated. In the late 1700s, Canada seemed to have room for its diversity of immigrants and indigenous peoples alike. But would they all get along?

PEOPLE AND PROVINCES

As you've read, Britain acquired most of New France—the French colonies in North America—in 1763 after winning the French and Indian War. Britain called the territory Quebec. Many immigrants from Great Britain settled in the province after it came under British rule. People also arrived from the American colonies. When the American Revolution began, some colonists remained loyal to Britain. About 40,000 of these mostly Protestant Loyalists settled in Quebec and Nova Scotia after the war and lived separately from the largely Catholic French.

Nevertheless, religious and cultural differences between the English and French speakers led to conflict. In an attempt to resolve these issues, Britain divided Quebec into two provinces in 1791: a predominantly English-speaking Upper Canada and a predominantly French-speaking Lower Canada. Each province had its own elected legislature. The government in Upper Canada was based on English law, while the government in Lower Canada was based on French law and Catholicism.

Some parts of Canada remain as unspoiled as they were when the confederation was formed. In 1893, the Canadian government established the Algonquin Park, shown here, in the province of Ontario to protect the territory's forests and rivers. The huge park, which covers nearly 3,000 square miles today, is the oldest provincial park in Canada and can only be explored by foot or canoe.

You might remember that the French had conducted a profitable fur trade with Native Americans in New France. The British took over this trade and, at first, traded north and west of the Great Lakes. Eventually, trading posts were established in territory as far west as the present-day province of Manitoba. British merchants traded with many First Nations groups. The **Métis**, people of mixed European and indigenous descent, also took part in the trade.

UNION AND EXPANSION

Although the people of Upper and Lower Canada had been granted some say in their governments, real power remained in the hands of British officials. In time, people began to call for political and economic reforms. In 1830, rebellions in both provinces broke out. To remedy the situation, Britain reunited Upper and Lower Canada to form the province of Canada and allowed it to largely control its domestic matters. Canada would also welcome more British immigrants. Through these reforms, the British hoped to avoid another expensive war of independence in North America.

By the mid-1800s, many Canadians believed they needed a strong central government. Britain possessed several other colonies in Canada, including Nova Scotia, Prince Edward Island, and New Brunswick. Canadian politicians wanted to unite all of the British North American colonies and form a larger, stronger territory. They feared the United States might start eyeing the lands to its north and stage an attack. Moreover, Britain was getting tired of the expense and burden of governing its far-flung Canadian colonies.

In 1867, the union, or confederation, of the colonies finally took place. Canada was divided into two new provinces—Quebec and Ontario—and these united with Nova Scotia and New Brunswick to form the Dominion of Canada. As a **dominion**, Canada was self-governing but still part of the British Empire. Canada expanded to the west, and the confederation gained many new provinces. By 1871, Canada stretched to the Pacific Ocean. To connect the vast lands, the country's first prime minister, John MacDonald, had a transcontinental railway built. It was completed in 1885.

As the century ended, the railway and the country's increasing industrialization, mining, and agricultural enterprises caused a great crisis for the First Nations when they were displaced from their traditional lands. Meanwhile, the government emphasized the idea that Canada would be a bicultural land where English and French could live in peace with mutual tolerance. Although Canadians did not always live up to that ideal, a unique national identity took shape.

PAULINE JOHNSON-TEKAHIONWAKE
A popular Canadian poet and performer in the 19th century, Pauline Johnson-Tekahionwake (da-geh-EEON-wah-geh) was born in 1861 to an English mother and a father of Mohawk and European descent. Johnson-Tekahionwake traveled throughout Canada (and sometimes in the United States), reading her poetry. She often wore traditional Mohawk dress, as shown in the photo here, while reciting poems dealing with the racism and poverty indigenous peoples faced and then changed into western clothes to read her work about nature and love. As a loyal Canadian whose Mohawk ancestors had fought alongside the British, Johnson-Tekahionwake's poetry reflected her desire to find a balance between her English and Native American roots.

HISTORICAL THINKING

1. **READING CHECK** Why did Britain divide Quebec into Upper Canada and Lower Canada?

2. **DRAW CONCLUSIONS** Why weren't indigenous people included in the Canadian national identity envisioned by the government?

3. **MAKE INFERENCES** Why did Pauline Johnson-Tekahionwake wear different styles of clothing when she recited her poems?

PLAN: 2-PAGE LESSON

OBJECTIVE
Explain how the Confederacy of Canada was forged from a diverse population.

CRITICAL THINKING SKILLS FOR LESSON 1.3
- Draw Conclusions
- Interpret Maps
- Analyze Cause and Effect
- Make Predictions

HISTORICAL THINKING FOR CHAPTER 23
How did regional, cultural, and ethnic divisions shape the Americas in the 19th century?

After Britain acquired Quebec from the French colonies in 1763, conflict between the English and French speakers erupted, forcing the British to split Quebec into two territories. Lesson 1.3 discusses how political and cultural divisions between British and French colonists in Canada led to the formation of the Confederation of Canada and shaped the country's unique national identity.

Student eEdition online
Additional content for this lesson, including a map, is available online.

BACKGROUND FOR THE TEACHER
The Seven Years' War The Seven Years' War began in 1756 and ended in 1763 with the signing of the Treaty of Paris. It was a war that crossed continents, inciting conflicts in Europe, North America, the Caribbean, the Philippines, India, and Africa. In Europe, the Seven Years' War was sparked by the attempt of the Hanovers of Austria to capture Silesia, a province that had been seized from them by Prussia. The conflict in North America, referred to as the French and Indian War, was an imperial war between Great Britain and France. Britain made enormous territorial gains during the conflict, but these gains came at a price. After the war, disputes over governance, taxation, borders, and war debt eventually led to the American Revolution.

INTRODUCE & ENGAGE

CONNECT TO TODAY

Remind students that people from different cultural, religious, and political backgrounds within the same nation don't always get along. Ask students to brainstorm some recent examples of clashes in culture, religion, or politics that they have heard about in the news or read about online. Record their responses on the board. Then have students discuss what they think are the causes of these clashes and make suggestions about how some of these conflicts could be resolved. Tell students that in this lesson they will learn how a diverse group of Canadians came together, despite their many differences, to form the Confederation of Canada.

TEACH

GUIDED DISCUSSION

1. **Analyze Cause and Effect** What caused some American colonists to migrate to Canada during and after the American Revolution? *(loyalty to Britain)*

2. **Make Predictions** How do you think the First Nations people reacted to being displaced from their traditional lands? *(Answers will vary. Possible response: They probably reacted with anger, fear, and great sadness.)*

DRAW CONCLUSIONS

Discuss with students the feature on Pauline Johnson-Tekahionwake. **ASK:** What do you think Johnson-Tekahionwake was trying to accomplish with her poetry? *(Possible response: She was trying to bring the plight of indigenous people to the attention of her listeners and to bring about change in their treatment.)*

ACTIVE OPTIONS

On Your Feet: Fishbowl Have part of the class sit in a close circle facing inward. Position the other part of the class in a larger circle around them. Pose the following question: Do you think Britain's plan to divide newly acquired territories into two independent, self-governing provinces would have worked if it had been better executed? Why or why not? Direct students in the inner circle to discuss their answers, while students in the outer circle listen and evaluate the ideas they hear. Then reverse roles and ask students in the inner circle to continue the discussion by supporting or refuting the ideas they just heard. Provide time for both groups to exchange ideas and summarize the results of their discussions.

NG Learning Framework: Research Canada's Indigenous Populations
ATTITUDE Curiosity
SKILL Communication

Organize students in pairs or small groups and assign each an indigenous population in Canada to learn more about. Instruct students to research aspects of their assigned indigenous population, such as details about its population, culture, and history. Then have students use their research to create a profile of the population. Have groups share their profiles with the rest of the class.

DIFFERENTIATE

INCLUSION

Narrate the Map Pair students who are visually challenged with students who are not visually challenged. Ask the latter to narrate the map (available in the Student eEdition) by identifying the territories shown, describing the route of the transcontinental railway, and answering any questions that arise.

GIFTED & TALENTED

Create an Advertisement Invite students to learn more about Canada's transcontinental railroad. Have them research the railway's history and its route. Instruct students to use their research to create a poster or brochure advertising the railway that would appeal to travelers in the late 1880s. Encourage students to use descriptive language and geographic details to attract prospective tourists. Work with students to create a format for sharing their creations with the class.

See the Chapter Planner for more strategies for differentiation.

HISTORICAL THINKING

ANSWERS

1. to resolve religious and cultural differences between the English and the French speakers in Quebec and to address the calls for a more representative government

2. because the indigenous peoples were viewed as inferior

3. She wore different styles of clothing to symbolize her heritage as a Mohawk and a Canadian.

The Gilded Age

All that glitters is not gold. Toward the end of the 1800s, many cities in the United States glittered with new buildings, department stores, and streetcars. But beneath the surface, poor working-class people were struggling to get by.

URBANIZATION

Between 1870 and 1900, approximately 12 million people migrated to the United States, most of them from southern and eastern Europe, Asia, and Mexico. These immigrants came in search of a better life and greater job opportunities, particularly in the cities. Many Americans also flocked to urban areas seeking work in the factories and industries that emerged as a result of the Industrial Revolution. As the country's railroad transportation hub, Chicago experienced the most dramatic growth. In 1840, it had a population of just under 4,500 citizens. By 1890, it numbered more than one million.

But cities like Chicago and New York had trouble coping with the influx of both immigrants and American citizens. Housing couldn't keep up with the increased demand. So apartment buildings called **tenements** were quickly constructed to shelter the new residents. Most tenements were six- or seven-story multi-resident buildings designed to house as many people as possible. The tiny apartments were dark and narrow, and the space between two tenement buildings was so small that people could reach out a window and touch their neighbor next door. Diseases spread quickly in the tenements because of the poor ventilation and unsanitary conditions. And the overcrowding and shoddy construction made

CRITICAL VIEWING Photographer Jacob Riis took this picture of an immigrant family crowded into a one-room apartment in New York around 1910. Riis, an immigrant from Denmark, photographed the living conditions of the urban poor in New York and published what he saw in his 1890 work *How the Other Half Lives.* How do you think the public reacted when they saw this image and others of crowded tenements?

the structures prone to fire. By contrast, wealthy city residents lived in spacious apartment buildings and townhouses.

As industry in the United States expanded over the last three decades of the 19th century, those who profited by it were mainly owners and stockholders, and they grew immensely rich. Many of them engaged in dishonest business practices to increase their wealth and power. Because of this greed and corruption, the era is called the Gilded Age. To gild something means to coat it with a thin layer of gold that can disguise what

lies underneath. The term was coined by the American writers Mark Twain and Charles Dudley Warner in their novel *The Gilded Age* to draw attention to the way in which spectacular wealth masked the greed and corruption of industrialists and politicians.

WORKERS ORGANIZE

In reaction to the inequality between the industrialists and their employees, workers began to organize into labor unions. You may recall that British workers fought to form unions. Americans first started to unionize in the 1820s to call for better pay, safer working conditions, and other benefits. The effort gathered strength after the Civil War. Most union members then sought an 8-hour workday to replace the more typical 10- to 12-hour workday. They often used **strikes**, or work stoppages, as a tactic to achieve their demands when companies refused to negotiate with them. In 1877, about 100,000 railroad workers across the country took part in what came to be known as the Great Railroad Strike. Violence broke out at one point, resulting in the deaths of about 100 people. However, the strikers eventually succeeded in convincing management to negotiate with their union representatives.

Another violent episode occurred in 1886 after a striking union member at Chicago's McCormick Works, a harvesting machine factory, was killed by police. The next day, union leaders organized a peaceful rally in the city's Haymarket Square. However, the rally became chaotic when someone threw a bomb and police responded with gunfire. Several police officers and protesters died during the **Haymarket Riot**, as it came to be called. The police arrested eight protesters, whom they claimed were **anarchists**, people willing to use force to overthrow oppression. Four of those arrested were hanged, and one was sentenced to 15 years in prison. Their guilt was

never adequately proven, however, and the remaining defendants were eventually pardoned. In much of the world, May 1, the anniversary of the Haymarket Riot, is celebrated as International Workers' Day.

In 1893, the United States suffered a severe economic depression, the worst in the nation's history up to that time. The collapse of a major railroad and a growing depression in Europe were among its causes. As panic gripped American financiers, banks closed, businesses failed, and the unemployment rate in the country climbed to about 20 percent. Many of those who remained employed were forced to take substantial pay cuts, causing workers all over the country to stage strikes and protests. The economy began to stabilize around 1897, and by 1900 the United States had become the world's largest economy. But the continuing social inequalities inspired even more people to call for workers' rights and social reforms.

CHICAGO'S COLUMBIAN EXPOSITION In 1893, Chicago hosted the World's Columbian Exposition to celebrate the 400-year anniversary of Columbus's arrival in the Americas. The fair showcased the "progress of civilization" and trumpeted the country's rapid industrialization and the strength of its industries. Visitors enjoyed a ride on the world's first Ferris wheel, which rose 264 feet in the air, and marveled at the new inventions—especially electricity, which most Americans had never seen before. Hundreds of thousands of electric lights illuminated the fair at night, creating a magical setting. Those attending the exposition bought an admission ticket like the one shown above, featuring a photo of Abraham Lincoln, to gain entry.

HISTORICAL THINKING

1. **READING CHECK** How did some cities solve the problem of housing their growing populations?

2. **MAKE INFERENCES** Why do you think the police considered those they arrested at the Haymarket Riot to be anarchists?

3. **SYNTHESIZE** How did the Columbian Exposition symbolize the Gilded Age?

PLAN: 2-PAGE LESSON

OBJECTIVE

Examine how disparity between the rich and poor in American cities in the late 19th century led many workers to demand their rights.

CRITICAL THINKING SKILLS FOR LESSON 1.4

- Make Inferences
- Synthesize
- Identify Main Ideas and Details
- Form and Support Opinions
- Analyze Visuals

HISTORICAL THINKING FOR CHAPTER 23

How did regional, cultural, and ethnic divisions shape the Americas in the 19th century?

Industrialization in the 19th century brought more economic opportunities and more people to American cities than ever before. Lesson 1.4 discusses the growing economic inequality between owners and workers and the unrest that arose as a result.

BACKGROUND FOR THE TEACHER

Jacob Riis Jacob Riis understood using the power of photography to persuade an audience, and he embraced the new technology of flash photography to enhance his work. He believed that people would respond with compassion or concern if they saw how the poor lived. He included his photographs in his books and lectures he gave to middle-class audiences across the United States. The flash lamp enabled him to capture scenes in dark, windowless rooms of tenements and in back alleys where the desperately poor and homeless spent their nights. As a strong advocate of redesigning tenements and adding parks and playgrounds for children, Riis was able to inspire many housing reforms.

INTRODUCE & ENGAGE

DISCUSS URBAN PROBLEMS

Create a Word Web with the term *urban problems* in the center. Ask students to suggest words they associate with present-day problems in cities. Then discuss solutions that have been attempted to solve the problems listed. Tell students that this lesson discusses the problems that faced American cities in the late 19th century.

TEACH

GUIDED DISCUSSION

1. **Identify Main Ideas and Details** Why are the last 30 years of the 19th century in the United States known as the Gilded Age? *(The era is referred to as the Gilded Age because wealth at this time disguised the greed and corruption of industrialists and politicians.)*

2. **Form and Support Opinions** Do you think striking is an effective way for workers to achieve their goals? Explain why or why not. *(Possible response: It is effective because the stoppage costs the owners money and demonstrates the value of the workers.)*

ANALYZE VISUALS

Direct students' attention to the admission ticket shown in the feature on Chicago's Columbian Exposition. **ASK:** Why do you think organizers of the exposition chose to feature a portrait of Lincoln on the ticket? *(Possible response: The purpose of the exposition was to show what was in store for the future of America, and Abraham Lincoln had played a key role in shaping that future only 30 years earlier by ending slavery and reuniting the country under one flag.)*

ACTIVE OPTIONS

On Your Feet: Travel Around the World Position two students in one corner of the room and one student in each of the other three corners. Ask the two students in the first corner a question about the lesson. Whoever correctly answers the question first becomes the "traveler" and moves to another corner to stand with a new partner while the first partner sits down. Repeat the process for as long as time permits. A traveler who correctly answers one question in each corner has "traveled around the world."

> **NG Learning Framework: Conduct a Legislative Hearing**
> ATTITUDE Responsibility
> KNOWLEDGE Our Human Story

Ask students to conduct a mock legislative hearing to investigate the causes and consequences of the Haymarket Riot, noting the complexity of determining the causes. Assign students the roles of state or federal legislators and testifying individuals, including union leaders, McCormick managers, and the police superintendent. Encourage students to conduct additional research to help formulate the legislators' questions and the testifiers' responses.

DIFFERENTIATE

STRIVING READERS

Use Supported Reading Assign pairs to read aloud the lesson together. At the end of each paragraph, have them use the following sentence frames to tell what they do and do not understand.

- This paragraph is about _____.
- One detail that stood out to me is _____.
- The word _____ means _____.
- One thing I would like to understand more clearly is _____.

PRE-AP

Research the Columbian Exposition Direct students to research the main exhibits at Chicago's Columbian Exposition, choosing at least one of the following main exhibit buildings: Agriculture, Electricity, Machinery, Manufactures and Liberal Arts, Mines and Mining, and Transportation. Instruct them to find out what was considered modern or state of the art in 1893 based on the exhibits in each building. Ask students to present their findings on a class website.

See the Chapter Planner for more strategies for differentiation.

HISTORICAL THINKING

ANSWERS

1. They built tenements.

2. Possible response: The police and others in authority believed the labor movement supported lawlessness and terrorism.

3. Possible response: By showcasing new inventions and opportunities, the fair presented a golden view of life in America that most people would never experience.

CRITICAL VIEWING Answers will vary. Possible response: They were appalled and angry; they wanted city officials to improve housing conditions for immigrants and the poor.

Latin America in the Industrial Age

When a country wins its independence, the people celebrate their victory. But after the confetti is swept away, they're faced with the difficult task of building a new nation. In Latin American countries, the struggle to recover economically and politically was just as hard as the struggle for independence.

CRITICAL VIEWING After rule by a series of dictators, a liberal reformer named Benito Juárez rose to power and became Mexico's president in 1861. This 1948 mural by José Clemente Orozco, *Benito Juárez and La Reforma*, represents Juárez's triumph over Mexican emperor Ferdinand Maximilian Joseph, who had overthrown the president. Maximilian's shrouded corpse is carried on the shoulders of Mexican conservatives. How does the mural's portrayal of Juárez—the monumental head in the center—contrast with that of the conservatives?

ECONOMIC DEPENDENCY

The economies of many Latin American countries didn't change after independence. Most people still worked on large farms that belonged to wealthy landowners. Workers had to use their wages to pay for the supplies they needed to do their jobs. And since wages were low and the price of the supplies was high, workers went into debt. In this system, called **debt peonage**, workers paid their debts with labor and were, in effect, reduced to the status of slaves.

Landowners, on the other hand, grew richer. Government leaders often seized lands that had belonged to native peoples or the Catholic Church and then sold them to the highest bidders. Only the wealthy could afford to buy this property, and as a result, the lands fell into the hands of a small percentage of the population. The unequal distribution of land ensured that the old rigid social order remained in place. The inequality increased when the owners of these *latifundia*, or very large farms, used their land to grow crops to sell internationally. The owners reaped the profits of global trade while rural workers lived in poverty.

After independence, Latin American countries were no longer limited to conducting trade with their colonizers. In time, Britain and the United States were among their major trading partners. However, Latin American countries produced mainly cash crops and mined raw materials and exchanged these for cheap goods, which harmed local industries. Just as in colonial times, they depended on exports from other countries to obtain manufactured goods. Consequently, landowners

CUBAN FREEDOM FIGHTER While other Latin American countries achieved sovereignty, Spain crushed Cuba's bid for independence in 1878. **José Martí**, a writer and an outspoken advocate for Cuban independence, was exiled and lived many years in New York City. While there, he helped organize an army to continue the fight and, in 1895, led his followers to Cuba to launch a second war for independence. Martí was killed early in the struggle, but the United States would eventually join Cuba's war for independence—with mixed results for the Cuban people. Today, Martí appears on Cuba's one-peso banknote.

and businesspeople had little incentive to develop manufacturing industries.

The region did benefit in some ways from the Industrial Revolution. Railroads and steamships connected it with North America and the world beyond, and Latin America's exports grew. For example, gold mines and coffee plantations stimulated Brazil's economy, leading to the growth of cities and the arrival of new immigrants. However, most of the profits went to a small minority of privileged Brazilians, and slavery remained part of society until 1888.

Debt was often a problem in Latin America. Countries often came under the power of European nations and the United States after accepting large loans to help them develop transportation and communication networks. If the countries were unable to pay their debts, their lenders sometimes seized their industries. As you'll learn in the next chapter, foreign control over Latin American economies set the stage for this practice elsewhere.

POLITICAL DIVISIONS IN MEXICO

You probably remember reading that Latin American countries also experienced political challenges

following independence. Like other countries, Mexico's government fell into the hands of caudillos. Only those from the upper and middle classes who owned property and could read were allowed to vote, and caudillos supported their interests. And after colonial rule, most Mexicans were accustomed to dictatorship.

One of Mexico's military dictators, General **Antonio López de Santa Anna**, served as president four times between 1833 and 1855. Under his presidency and military leadership, Mexico lost Texas after that territory won its war for independence in 1836. And then, when the United States annexed Texas and invaded Mexico, Santa Anna and his troops fought and lost the Mexican-American War in 1848. In exchange for $15 million, Mexico gave up its northernmost territories to the United States, including present-day California, Nevada, and Utah, as well as parts of Arizona, New Mexico, Colorado, and Wyoming.

As Santa Anna's power declined, a Zapotec from Oaxaca named **Benito Juárez** became a strong force in Mexican politics. He started a reform movement called *La Reforma*, which called for the redistribution

of lands, the separation of church and state, and greater educational opportunities for the poor. Conservatives in the country—mostly wealthy upper-class Mexicans—opposed Juárez's reforms, and a civil war erupted. The reformers won the war, and Juárez was elected president in 1861. But the conservatives in Mexico didn't give up. They enlisted the help of the French emperor Napoleon III, who overthrew Juárez. France occupied Mexico for five years but was under constant attack by those, including Juárez, who opposed French rule. Exhausted by the struggle, the French withdrew from Mexico in 1867.

Juárez was re-elected president that same year, and Mexico enjoyed a period of relative peace and progress. After his death, however, **Porfirio Díaz** came to power in 1876 and ruled as a dictator. Under his regime, railroads in Mexico expanded, the economy stabilized, and foreign investments grew. However, these measures mostly benefited wealthy landowners. The poor, meanwhile, grew poorer. Díaz remained in power until the early 1900s, when protesters called for reforms, and a revolution began to brew.

HISTORICAL THINKING

1. **READING CHECK** Why did farm workers in many Latin American countries fail to benefit economically after independence?

2. **DRAW CONCLUSIONS** What prevented Latin American countries from becoming world economic powers?

3. **MAKE INFERENCES** Why did the conservatives in Mexico oppose Juárez and his reforms?

PLAN: 2-PAGE LESSON

OBJECTIVE

Explain why many Latin Americans suffered under economic and political systems after achieving independence.

CRITICAL THINKING SKILLS FOR LESSON 2.1

- Draw Conclusions
- Make Inferences
- Summarize
- Analyze Visuals

HISTORICAL THINKING FOR CHAPTER 23

How did regional, cultural, and ethnic divisions shape the Americas in the late 19th century?

The economies of many Latin American countries didn't change after independence. Lesson 2.1 discusses the disparity between the owners of large farms and their workers and the countries' dependence on foreign exports.

Student eEdition online

Additional content for this lesson, including images, is available online.

BACKGROUND FOR THE TEACHER

Benito Juárez Benito Juárez was born to a peasant family in Oaxaca in 1806. As a Zapotec, he was Mexico's first and only indigenous president and, for his entire career, worked to restore the rights of the country's indigenous populations. His advocacy earned him the title the "Lincoln of Mexico." In 1850, when he was forced to leave the country, Abraham Lincoln sent him a message of support that called for the liberty of his government and people. Juárez had planned to become a Catholic priest before ultimately deciding to study law. He believed capitalism and an end to the monopolization of land by the wealthy would release the working class from poverty. As Minister of Justice later in life, he was responsible for the passage of the Lerdo Law, which forced the Roman Catholic Church to sell all of its property. The intent of the law was to break up large-landed estates and return the land to the people.

INTRODUCE & ENGAGE

ACTIVATE PRIOR KNOWLEDGE

Ask students to recall what they have learned about the political changes Latin American countries experienced following independence. Discuss the rule of caudillos and the inability of ordinary people to realize the ideals of liberty and equality. Then tell students that in this lesson they will learn about the continuing economic and political inequalities in Latin America.

TEACH

GUIDED DISCUSSION

1. **Summarize** Why didn't Latin American countries develop manufacturing industries of their own? (*Latin American countries produced mainly cash crops and mined raw materials and exchanged these for cheap manufactured goods made in other countries, harming local manufacturers.*)

2. **Draw Conclusions** Why do you think the emperor of France was willing to help the conservatives in Mexico overthrow Benito Juárez? (*Possible response: The emperor wanted to squash democratic forms of government because he feared that such radical ideas might spread to Europe.*)

ANALYZE VISUALS

Have students study the painting of Benito Juárez. **ASK:** Who are the soldiers shown at the top of the painting fighting for, and how are they portrayed? (*Possible response: They are fighting for Benito Juárez, and they appear to be poor and working class but strong and valiant soldiers.*) How does the corpse of Maximilian appear to be affecting those who are carrying him? (*Possible response: The corpse appears to be crushing those who are supporting him.*) How is Juárez portrayed in the painting? (*Possible response: as strong, noble, victorious*)

ACTIVE OPTIONS

On Your Feet: Think, Pair, Share Give students a few minutes to think about the following question: What advantages did European nations and the United States gain from offering large loans to Latin American countries? Then have students choose partners and discuss the question for five minutes. Finally, allow individual students to share their ideas with the class.

> **NG Learning Framework: Write a Biography**
> **ATTITUDE** Curiosity
> **KNOWLEDGE** Our Human Story

Have students write a short biography of Antonio López de Santa Anna. Instruct students to use multiple print and online resources for their research, using search terms effectively to find out about Santa Anna's life and the role he played as one of Mexico's military dictators. Remind students to paraphrase their conclusions and to cite their sources using a standard format. Students may present their biographies to the class or post them on a class blog.

DIFFERENTIATE

ENGLISH LANGUAGE LEARNERS

Use Sentence Frames Provide students with a set of sentence frames that summarize the lesson. Leave one blank per sentence for students at the **Intermediate** level and more than one blank for students at the **Advanced** level. Depending on your students' proficiency, you might wish to provide a word bank or list of answers for students to use to complete the sentences. After they complete the sentence frames individually, allow students to work in pairs to compare answers and read the sentences.

PRE-AP

Write a News Report Instruct students to conduct online research to learn more about the Battle of the Alamo. Then have them write a detailed news story about the event from the point of view of a reporter in 1836, including quotes from eyewitnesses. Invite students to publish their stories on a class blog or school website.

See the Chapter Planner for more strategies for differentiation.

HISTORICAL THINKING

ANSWERS

1. They had to use their wages to pay for the supplies they needed to do their jobs and went into debt. Workers paid off their debt with labor and were like slaves.

2. Answers will vary. Possible response: They weren't industrialized and had to depend on imported manufacturing goods from other countries.

3. Answers will vary. Possible response: He wanted to redistribute lands, which would have reduced their holdings and wealth.

CRITICAL VIEWING Answers will vary. Possible response: Juárez appears strong, healthy, and powerful, while the conservatives appear small, defeated, and pale.

2.2 Labor and Profit in Latin America

Most Latin American countries gained independence while the Industrial Revolution was taking place in Europe. And, as you know, textile production under the factory system in the 1830s led to an expansion of slavery in the southern United States. Just as in Europe and the United States, economic growth in Latin America resulted in wealth for some and hard work with little reward for many.

The growth of international trade did have positive effects, however. For example, Britain, Germany, the United States, and other countries invested capital in Latin America, where much of the money was used to build railroads. Railroads and steamships with refrigerated compartments carried goods such as beef from Argentina, silver from Mexico, and coffee from Brazil to international markets. In return, manufactured goods and luxury items flowed back to Latin America. This relationship, in which Latin America exported relatively cheap products and depended on foreign markets for more expensive imports, is called "economic dependency."

Economic dependency caused two problems. First, governments often had to borrow money to build ports and railroads to support trade. These debts meant that the governments often put the interests of foreign investors above those of their own people. Second, this type of trading system concentrated wealth in only a few hands.

In Argentina and most other Latin American countries, this wealth was concentrated in less than 10 percent of the population—upper-class landowners and middle-class professionals. The lower-class majority lived in poverty. Slavery had been abolished in most Latin American countries by the late 19th century, but those who worked on farms and in mines, as you know, were no better off than slaves. The resulting inequality between the wealthy and the poor was mirrored by growing divisions between the "haves" and "have nots" in many of these societies. As governments ignored the condition of urban laborers, the workers began to strike and organize.

By the early 1900s, Argentina had greatly prospered from trade, although only those at the very top of society enjoyed the wealth. In this photo of the Argentine capital of Buenos Aires from that period, automobiles cruised along its spacious boulevards. The modernized city became known as "The Paris of South America."

DOCUMENT ONE

Primary Source: Travel Chronicle
from *Exploration of the Valley of the Amazon, 1851–1852,* by William Lewis Herndon

In 1851, U.S. Navy commander William Lewis Herndon led an expedition from Peru to Brazil to explore the Amazon Valley. He recorded his observations in narrative form in *Exploration of the Valley of the Amazon.* In this excerpt from the book, Herndon describes a rural area after visiting Lima, the capital of Peru.

CONSTRUCTED RESPONSE How do conditions in the rural area compare with those in Lima?

To the right were the green cane and alfalfa fields . . . but ahead all was barren, grim, and forbidding. . . . It was remarkable to see such poverty and squalid wretchedness at nine miles from the great city of Lima; it was like passing in a moment from the most luxurious civilization into savage barbarity . . . from the garden to the desert. . . . [Later the] superintendent of the mines . . . received us kindly. . . . His house was comfortably heated with a stove, and the chamber furnished with a large four-post bedstead and the biggest and heaviest bureau I had ever seen.

DOCUMENT TWO

Primary Source: Letter
from "A Letter to Striking Workers" by Matías Romero, 1892

As Minister of Finance under President Porfirio Díaz, Matías Romero strongly supported foreign investment. The following is an excerpt from a letter Romero wrote to striking workers after they requested his help.

CONSTRUCTED RESPONSE What does Romero say the government can do for the striking workers?

Given the institutions that govern us, it is unfeasible [impossible] to restrict freedom of hiring or to intervene directly in the improvement of basic working conditions. No legal document authorizes this, nor do any economic interests oblige the Government to dictate salaries, or prices, or working hours. . . . The Government can only contribute to improving labor conditions by indirect means such as keeping the peace, the promotion of industry, and the investment of both national and foreign capital in native elements of the country's wealth [such as plantations and mines], and thus ensure national credit.

DOCUMENT THREE

Primary Source: Political Pamphlet
from "First Electoral Manifesto of the Argentine Socialist Worker Party," 1896

In reaction to the inequality between Argentina's lower and upper classes, many laborers united to form the Argentine Socialist Worker Party. The unions that arose in many countries were often inspired by new ideologies of socialism, particularly the concept of conflict between capitalists and laborers. In this excerpt from their manifesto, the party takes aim at the treatment of workers in Argentina.

CONSTRUCTED RESPONSE According to the manifesto, what will happen as a result of the greed of Argentina's "rich class"?

All of the parties of Argentina's rich class are of one mind when it comes to increasing profits of capital at the cost of working people, even as it stupidly compromises the country's general development. . . . [They have increased . . . the price of products and reduced wages. They have seized public lands, expelling primitive peoples, the only ones with a right to occupy them. . . . And to complete this barbaric system of exploitation [unfair treatment], they use taxes on consumption, internal taxes, and customs duties [taxes on imports] to take away a large share of what little workers earn.

SYNTHESIZE & WRITE

1. REVIEW Review what you have learned about the economic and political challenges Latin American countries faced after independence.

2. RECALL On your own paper, write down the main idea expressed in each document.

3. CONSTRUCT Construct a topic sentence that answers this question: How did the plight of workers and owners in 19th-century Latin America differ?

4. WRITE Using evidence from this chapter and the documents, write an informative paragraph that supports your topic sentence in Step 3.

PLAN: 2-PAGE LESSON

OBJECTIVE
Explain how economic growth in Latin America resulted in wealth only for upper-class landowners and middle-class professionals.

CRITICAL THINKING SKILLS FOR LESSON 2.2
- Synthesize
- Identify
- Analyze Cause and Effect
- Evaluate

HISTORICAL THINKING FOR CHAPTER 23
How did regional, cultural, and ethnic division shape the Americas in the 19th century?

Just as in Europe and the United States, Latin America experienced economic growth as a result of the Industrial Revolution. Lesson 2.2 focuses on written historical documents that reveal the inequality between the wealthy and the poor in Latin America.

BACKGROUND FOR THE TEACHER
While military men often dominated national politics in Latin American countries, rich business leaders controlled economic life. They used their international connections to profit as intermediaries between local producers and global traders. Meanwhile, economic dependency undermined peasant communities. With the transition to labor-intensive plantation crops for export, they often lost control over their own land and labor, forced by taxes, debt peonage, and sometimes direct coercion to leave their villages to work for miserable wages in mines and on plantations. Economies were growing in ways that made many people poorer, a process that one historian has called "the poverty of progress."

INTRODUCE & ENGAGE

PREPARE FOR THE DOCUMENT-BASED QUESTION

Before students start on the activity, briefly preview the three documents. Remind students that a constructed response requires full explanations in complete sentences. Emphasize that students should use what they have learned about industrialization in Latin America in addition to the information in the documents.

TEACH

GUIDED DISCUSSION

1. **Identify** What is economic dependency? *(a relationship in which a country exports relatively cheap products and depends on foreign markets for more expensive imports)*

2. **Analyze Cause and Effect** What caused urban workers to strike and organize in Latin America? *(Governments ignored the conditions under which they worked.)*

EVALUATE

After students have completed the Synthesize & Write activity, allow time for them to exchange paragraphs and read and comment on the work of their peers. Establish guidelines for comments prior to the activity so that feedback is constructive and encouraging in nature. Comments should focus on the most significant parts that address the purpose of the activity and the audience.

ACTIVE OPTION

On Your Feet: Jigsaw Strategy Organize students into "expert" groups and assign each group one of the documents to analyze and summarize its main ideas in their own words. Then regroup students into new groups so that each new group has at least one member from each expert group. Students in the new groups take turns sharing the summaries from their expert groups.

DIFFERENTIATE

ENGLISH LANGUAGE LEARNERS

Summarize Pair students at **Beginning** and **Intermediate** proficiencies and assign each pair a document to read together and summarize in a few written sentences. When all pairs are finished, call on them to read aloud their summaries. You may provide sentence frames to help students write their summaries.

INCLUSION

Highlight and Summarize Provide students with a copy of the three excerpts printed on a separate piece of paper to minimize distractions. Model for them the strategy of highlighting the most important phrases and sentences in the text. Then have them write brief summaries of each excerpt in their own words.

See the Chapter Planner for more strategies for differentiation.

SYNTHESIZE & WRITE

ANSWERS

1. Answers will vary.

2. Answers will vary. Possible response: Document One: The prosperous conditions in Lima contrast sharply with the poverty in the rural area just outside the city. Document Two: Mexico's government claims that it can do nothing to improve the plight of workers other than promote and invest in industry. Document Three: The Argentine Socialist Worker Party rebukes the country's upper class for putting their greed before workers' rights and the economic development of the country.

3. Answers will vary. Possible response: In 19th-century Latin America, workers lived in poverty, while owners grew wealthy.

4. Answers will vary. Students' paragraphs should include their topic sentence from Step 3 and several details from the documents as support.

CONSTRUCTED RESPONSE

Document One: Lima is a "luxurious civilization," while the rural area is poor and "squalid."

Document Two: He says the government can keep the peace, promote industry, and invest both national and foreign capital in the country's wealth.

Document Three: The development of the country will suffer.

Indigenous Societies Rebel

What would you do if the government seized your home and gave it to someone else? When that happened to indigenous people in North America, some of them chose to resist and fight back.

National Geographic photographer Anand Varma captured this scene overlooking a canyon in the Black Hills, a small mountain range that rises in South Dakota and extends into Wyoming. The Lakota have long considered the Black Hills their spiritual home. Ever since the U.S. government seized the mountain range from them, the Lakota have sought to get it back. Their efforts continue today, and they have refused monetary compensation for the land.

MAYA REVOLT

After the Spanish conquered Central America, many Maya continued to live on the Yucatán Peninsula where they grew maize and other crops. In 1846, Yucatán claimed **autonomy**, or independence, from Mexico and formed the Republic of Yucatán. But like Mexico, the republic was controlled by rich *peninsulares*, the descendants of Spanish-born settlers. The following year, Yucatán's government took control of Maya farms and sold them to plantation owners.

Soon, sugar plantations sprang up on former Maya cornfields in the southeastern part of the Yucatán Peninsula. Taxes also increased. In need of work, Maya farmers labored on the plantations, where they sometimes endured physical abuse. Similar to many other poor farmers in Latin America, the Maya became trapped in their jobs by debt peonage and worked to repay their employers.

Angered by their mistreatment and domination by white leaders, a group of Maya militants attacked government officials and landowners in 1847. By the spring of 1848, the Maya had taken over most of the Yucatán Peninsula in a conflict that came to be known as the **Yucatán Rebellion**. Because the rebellion was partly motivated by the Maya's resentment of the white leaders' ideology—their belief in their racial superiority—it is also called the Caste War of the Yucatán.

The Yucatán government offered to reunite with Mexico in exchange for help in putting down the rebellion. Mexico agreed. The country had extra funds due to the payment it had received from the United States for territory taken at the end of the Mexican-American War. Armed with new guns and joined by Mexican troops, the large landowners gradually regained control of the peninsula.

Scattered fighting continued until 1901, when Mexican forces overran the Maya rebels. About 50 percent of the Maya on the Yucatán Peninsula were killed during the long conflict, and many of their villages were destroyed. A group of Maya rebels retreated to the eastern part of the peninsula, where they established new villages and preserved their traditions and identity.

NATIVE AMERICAN RESISTANCE

Native Americans, such as the Creek and Choctaw, were also forced to leave their traditional lands in the southeastern United States. After gold was discovered in Georgia, southern states passed laws allowing farmers, miners, and other settlers to claim Native American lands for themselves. Then in 1830, President Andrew Jackson approved the Indian Removal Act,

Sitting Bull was imprisoned on a Dakota reservation in 1881, but he was allowed to join Buffalo Bill's Wild West Show in 1885. This traveling show used Native Americans, cowboys, sharpshooters, and bison to re-enact stories of the West—often inaccurately. Sitting Bull only appeared in the show's opening procession, but he gained international fame. He returned home after a single season and was eventually sent back to the reservation.

a law that relocated Native Americans to an area of land that includes present-day Oklahoma and parts of Kansas and Nebraska, and would be called Indian Territory. In time, the U.S. government also set aside specific areas of land for Native Americans called reservations. But some offered resistance to removal, including the Cherokee. Their forced march to Indian Territory in the late 1830s is known as the Trail of Tears.

In the Great Plains, the Lakota—part of the larger Sioux nation—had negotiated a treaty with the U.S. government that forbade white settlement in the Black Hills, which the Lakota considered sacred. The treaty was canceled, however, when gold was discovered there in 1874, and U.S. authorities demanded that all Lakota leave the Black Hills. Sitting Bull, the leader of the Lakota, refused to move, and troops arrived to force the relocation. Eventually, **Sitting Bull** moved his band to a camp in the valley of the Little Bighorn

---

PLAN: 4-PAGE LESSON

OBJECTIVE

Examine how indigenous people in North America in the 19th century fought to keep their land, culture, and identity intact.

CRITICAL THINKING SKILLS FOR LESSON 3.1

- Draw Conclusions
- Make Inferences
- Make Connections
- Analyze Cause and Effect
- Identify Main Ideas and Details
- Compare and Contrast
- Interpret Maps

HISTORICAL THINKING FOR CHAPTER 23

How did regional, cultural, and ethnic divisions shape the Americas in the 19th century?

As European settlers migrated to North America, the continent's indigenous populations found themselves in a fight for land and resources. Lesson 3.1 examines the indigenous populations that fought back.

BACKGROUND FOR THE TEACHER

The Caste War By 1850, Mexico had succeeded in pushing back the Maya. The Mexican government took control of the northwestern part of the Yucatán Peninsula, while the Maya controlled the southeastern part. The Maya might have ended their rebellion at that time, but they were inspired by a vision of the "Talking Cross." According to legend, the cross appeared to Maya leaders and told them to continue their fight. The leaders believed their gods were communicating to them through the cross. The place where the cross was said to have appeared was called *Chan Santa Cruz,* or Small Holy Cross, and became the center of Maya resistance. In addition, the Maya rebellion took on religious significance. As a result, the Caste War continued for many more years.

Student eEdition online

Additional content for this lesson, including a map, is available online.

INTRODUCE & ENGAGE

PREDICT THE OUTCOME

Read aloud the title of the lesson. Explain that in this lesson, students will learn about what happened when indigenous societies in North America rebelled. Ask students to predict what they think will happen when the indigenous peoples took this action. Write their predictions on the board. Then at the end of the lesson, review the predictions and compare them with the actual outcome.

TEACH

GUIDED DISCUSSION

1. **Draw Conclusions** Why is the Yucatán Rebellion sometimes called the Caste War of the Yucatán? *(Possible response: because the white settlers' feelings of racial superiority led them to consider the Maya as a different and inferior class, or caste)*

2. **Analyze Cause and Effect** What led southern states to pass laws allowing settlers to claim Native American lands? *(the discovery of gold in Georgia)*

INTERPRET MAPS

Have students study the map of indigenous revolts and locate Indian Territory (available in the Student eEdition). Tell them that many of the Native Americans who relocated to Indian Territory had lived in the southeastern part of the United States. **ASK:** What can you infer about the distance these Native Americans traveled? *(They traveled very long distances.)* Then instruct students to locate the Yucatán Peninsula, where the Maya revolt took place, and the battles that took place in Canada. **ASK:** What do all the battles and rebellions waged by the Maya, Native Americans, First Nations, and Métis have in common? *(Possible response: Indigenous people in all of these locations rose up to defend their long-established cultures against foreign intrusion and commercial agriculture.)*

STRIVING READERS

Make a Chart Before they begin studying the lesson, instruct student pairs to make a three-column chart titled Resistance of Americas' Indigenous Societies and label the columns Maya Revolt, Native American Resistance, and First Nations and the Métis Rebellion. After they read each section of the lesson, have pairs work together to list as many details as they can about what they have read. Remind them to include information about key events, dates, and historical figures. You might have one student read aloud each paragraph while the other student listens and records main ideas. Invite pairs to compare their lists with others in the room, adding and editing as necessary to develop the most complete chart.

GIFTED & TALENTED

Create a Podcast Tell students to prepare an episode of a history podcast relating to Sitting Bull, the Ghost Dance, or the assimilation of indigenous children. Suggest that students write a script for their podcast and include sound effects if possible. Tell them to take a point of view on the subject so that the podcast is informative, entertaining, and maybe even provocative. Then have students present their podcast to the class or record it on a phone or other device and play it for the class.

See the Chapter Planner for more strategies for differentiation.

CRITICAL VIEWING The Apache children shown in these two photos taken by John Choate were sent to the Carlisle Indian Industrial School, a boarding school in Pennsylvania, to learn white values and culture. Choate took the photo on the left in November 1886, shortly after the children's arrival at the school. The photo on the right, showing the same children, was taken four months later. What does the children's physical appearance reveal about the ways in which they were changed by the school?

River in present-day Montana. He was joined there by the Cheyenne and other Native Americans who had abandoned their reservations.

In 1876, roughly 2,000 Native Americans clashed with about 200 U.S. troops led by Colonel George Custer at Sitting Bull's encampment. The Native Americans killed nearly all of the soldiers, including Colonel Custer, in the **Battle of the Little Bighorn**. However, the U.S. Army ultimately forced the Lakota to relocate to reservations, and the United States seized the Black Hills.

By the late 1880s, most Native Americans lived on reservations, but they were still defiant. Some Native Americans, including the Lakota, practiced the **Ghost Dance**, a ceremony they believed would drive evil from the land, restore the bison, and allow them to return to lives of peace and prosperity. The U.S. government believed Sitting Bull had instigated the Ghost Dance, and authorities went to arrest him in 1890 at his reservation on Wounded Knee Creek in present-day South Dakota. Sitting Bull resisted and was fatally shot. Two weeks later, the U.S. Army confronted Lakota ghost dancers at Wounded Knee Creek and demanded they hand over their weapons. When an unknown person fired a shot, the U.S. troops opened fire in return, killing about 300 people. The **Wounded Knee Massacre** put an end to any further Native American resistance.

FIRST NATIONS AND THE MÉTIS REBELLION

Like other indigenous people in the Americas, the First Nations people in Canada endured racism and discrimination. In 1876, Canada passed the Indian Act, which aimed to assimilate, or integrate, First Nations people into the rest of Canadian society. By doing so, the Canadian government hoped to wipe out First Nations culture. The act also established reserves for First Nations people, lands set aside for their "use and benefit."

To further the assimilation process, later amendments to the act required First Nations children to attend residential, or boarding, schools. Students in these "industrial" schools wore Western-style clothing, spoke only English or French, and were pressured to convert to Christianity. Similar schools were established for Native American children in the United States. Another amendment to Canada's Indian Act outlawed certain religious ceremonies, including the potlatch, practiced by First Nations people in the Canadian province of British Columbia. The potlatch is a gift-giving feast used to mark important events and occasions.

The Métis, the people of mixed European and indigenous descent you've read about, took action to protect their culture and land rights just before Canada acquired Rupert's Land, a vast territory in northern and western Canada. The Métis, who lived in the territory, feared the Canadian government would take away their rights. As a result, they staged an uprising between 1869 and 1870 and formed a temporary government to negotiate terms for joining the Canadian Confederation.

Negotiations led to the creation of the province of Manitoba, where the Métis were granted rights to some land. The Métis also gained a new leader, **Louis Riel**, who emerged as a hero to the indigenous people. The Canadian government, however, considered him an outlaw. In 1870, British and Canadian troops marched into Manitoba, and Riel fled to the United States. Over the next decade, the Métis were increasingly pushed into the North-West Territories by European settlers from places like Germany and Sweden, and the Canadian government failed to honor its promise to protect indigenous land rights. The Métis way of life was disappearing and so were the bison, a major food source of the indigenous people.

Riel returned to Canada in 1884 to plead the Métis' case, but the government ignored his petition. The following year, Riel organized an army and formed alliances with First Nations peoples. Their goal was to establish a nation independent of the Dominion of Canada, but they were no match for the Canadian soldiers. After a series of battles, the indigenous people lost the **North-West Rebellion** within about three months. Riel was arrested, convicted of treason, and hanged.

The struggle for indigenous rights continued for decades in North America. Pauline Johnson-Tekahionwake expressed the sadness of all indigenous people in her poem "A Cry from an Indian Wife." She asks how white settlers would feel "If some great nation came from far away, / Wresting [seizing] their country from their hapless braves [unfortunate warriors], / Giving what they gave us—but war and graves."

NATIONAL GEOGRAPHIC EXPLORERS
JON WATERHOUSE AND MARY MARSHALL

Capturing Indigenous Voices

National Geographic Explorer Jon Waterhouse and photographer Mary Marshall share a remarkable mission and passion—giving voice to indigenous peoples, specifically empowering them to communicate their knowledge of the natural world. As a person of S'Klallam, Chippewa, and Cree descent, Waterhouse believes we must blend indigenous knowledge with contemporary science to fully understand our planet. In 2007, he collected scientific readings of water quality on the Yukon River while also gathering traditional knowledge about respecting and protecting the environment from people living there. Since then, Waterhouse and Marshall have partnered with people in remote regions to study their local water and environmental health and digitally record aspects of their cultures. For the explorers, environmental stewardship involves listening to native voices. As Waterhouse says, indigenous people "are witnesses to significant environmental changes from place-based people." Marshall took the above photo of Waterhouse (on the left) giving final instructions to his team before they canoed down the Tanana River in Alaska to collect water-quality data.

HISTORICAL THINKING

1. **READING CHECK** Why did the Maya who lived on the Yucatán Peninsula rebel?

2. **DRAW CONCLUSIONS** Why did the U.S. government want to put a stop to the Ghost Dance ceremony?

3. **MAKE INFERENCES** What impact do you think the residential schools in North America had on indigenous families?

4. **MAKE CONNECTIONS** How do Pauline Johnson-Tekahionwake's words reflect the experience of all indigenous peoples in the Americas?

BACKGROUND FOR THE TEACHER

The Trail of Tears After the Cherokee refused to leave their traditional land, American soldiers forced them on a march to Indian Territory. The terrible journey lasted about four months, during the fall and winter of 1838 and 1839. The Cherokee were not given adequate food, shelter, or clothing as they struggled in the rain and snow. Some soldiers even stole the few supplies that had been provided to the Native Americans. As a result, about 4,000 people died from cold, illness, and starvation on the march. Because of the suffering the Cherokee endured, the journey became known as the Trail of Tears.

TEACH

GUIDED DISCUSSION

3. **Identify Main Ideas and Details** What was the Wounded Knee Massacre, and what was its significance to Native American resistance? *(Three hundred Lakota were killed by U.S. troops at Wounded Knee Creek when the Native Americans refused to surrender their weapons. The massacre signified the end of Native American resistance.)*

4. **Compare and Contrast** How did the indigenous people of Canada and the Canadian government regard Louis Riel? *(The indigenous people regarded him as a hero, while the Canadian government considered him as an outlaw.)*

MAKE INFERENCES

Initiate a class discussion about the National Geographic Explorers feature. Invite volunteers to summarize the mission of the featured scientist and photographer. **ASK:** How is listening to and recording the voices of indigenous people both an act of environmental stewardship and scientific research? *(Possible response: Recording the voices of indigenous people is a way of protecting their cultures and preventing them from being forgotten. Making sure indigenous knowledge about the environment isn't lost may aid scientific studies as well.)* Tell students interested in this topic to research ethnography, a field in which researchers conduct systematic studies of people and their cultures.

ACTIVE OPTIONS

On Your Feet: Roundtable Divide the class into groups of four or five. Hand each group a sheet of paper with the following question: What might have happened if Louis Riel and his allies had succeeded in establishing a nation independent of the Dominion of Canada? The first student in each group should write an answer, read it aloud, and pass the paper clockwise to the next student. Have students circulate the paper until they run out of answers or time is up.

> **NG Learning Framework: Research Battles and Rebellions**
> **SKILL** Collaboration
> **KNOWLEDGE** Our Human Story

Organize students in small groups and instruct them to work together to develop a presentation about one of the battles or rebellions mentioned in the lesson's text and map. Once groups have decided on a topic, instruct group members to divide tasks among themselves. Students should research who was involved in the conflict, what spurred the clash, where it occurred, how long it lasted, what was at stake for each side, and what effects it had. Encourage students to integrate their findings into a coherent understanding of the battle or rebellion. Invite each group to share its findings with the class.

HISTORICAL THINKING

ANSWERS

1. because white leaders took away Maya lands, increased their taxes, and impoverished them

2. Answers will vary. Possible response: The government feared the ceremony would incite Native Americans to kill white settlers.

3. Answers will vary. Possible response: The residential schools broke up families and disrupted their traditional culture.

4. Answers will vary. Possible response: The people who "came from far away" killed and fought wars with indigenous peoples to take their lands and put an end to their cultures.

CRITICAL VIEWING Answers will vary. Possible response: The children's hair has been cut, they are wearing Western-style clothing, and they appear to be passive and defeated.

Inequality and Reform

Immigrants arrived in the United States full of hope, but they did not always feel welcome. Like African Americans and others outside of the white majority, they were often met with resentment and distrust.

CRITICAL VIEWING This political cartoon appeared in a humor magazine called *Puck* in February 1913. The cartoon satirizes the "separate but equal" policy enforced in the southern United States with this airplane and its segregated accommodations for white and African-American passengers. How does the cartoon convey the inherent inequality of segregated accommodations?

SEPARATE BUT EQUAL

The millions of immigrants who came to the United States in the late 19th and early 20th centuries encountered not only difficult living and working conditions but also discrimination. Asian immigrants were frequent targets of racial hostility. Anti-Chinese sentiment led the federal government to pass the **Chinese Exclusion Act** in 1882 to prevent Chinese immigrants from working in the United States. And, while many Mexican immigrants in the West and Southwest were welcomed as workers, they were often the victims of violence.

As you know, racism against African Americans continued after the Civil War and Reconstruction. Southern politicians stripped away the rights African Americans had gained by passing so-called **Jim Crow laws**, named for a form of entertainment in the early 1800s that mocked people of African descent. These laws established separate schools for African Americans and prohibited them from using the same restrooms, restaurants, theaters, and parks as white people. Since African Americans were often prevented from voting, they could not use democracy to protect their constitutional rights.

In 1891, a man named Homer Plessy, who was one-eighth African American, tested a law that separated whites and African Americans on public transportation by sitting in a railway car reserved for whites. He was arrested, and his case eventually came before the U.S. Supreme Court. His lawyers argued in *Plessy v. Ferguson* that the legalized segregation on trains

violated the 14th Amendment, which guaranteed "equal protection of the laws" to all American citizens. However, in 1896, the court upheld the segregation, stating that the accommodations on the train were the same for whites and African Americans (they weren't), even if they were separate. The ruling allowed governments, businesses, and institutions to enact "separate but equal" policies for decades to come.

MUCKRAKERS AND REFORMERS

You've read that American industrial workers formed unions to protect their rights. In 1886, a British immigrant named Samuel L. Gompers brought many small unions of skilled industrial workers together to form the **American Federation of Labor (AFL)**. The AFL did not focus on political issues but rather used collective bargaining to fight for higher wages, shorter hours, and improved working conditions for its members.

The causes championed by unions were sometimes brought to the attention of the public by journalists known as **muckrakers**, who investigated and exposed corruption and poor social and working conditions. One of the first muckrakers, **Ida Tarbell**, wrote about the secret deals and unethical practices of John D. Rockefeller, the founder of the Standard Oil Company. Largely as a result of her articles, the Supreme Court decided in 1911 that Standard Oil was an illegal **monopoly**, or a company that has complete control of an industry, and ordered it broken into 34 separate companies. Many Americans supported this antitrust legislation because they wanted to prevent such monopolies from forming again.

Muckraker **Upton Sinclair** investigated the working conditions in the meatpacking industry and wrote about what he saw in his 1906 novel *The Jungle*. Sinclair's description of the industry's unsanitary conditions led Congress to pass the Pure Food and Drug Act and the Meat Inspection Act. Like the British in the 19th century, Americans came to expect their government to play a positive role in making life better by preventing dangerous food from reaching the market or by limiting child labor and other abuses.

Private citizens such as **Jane Addams** also worked to address social problems. She founded a community center in Chicago called Hull House that provided services for immigrants in the neighborhood, including a kindergarten, day care, and classes and activities for adults. The Salvation Army and the YMCA, which spread to the United States from Britain, also supported aid for the poor. Members in both countries were motivated by their Christian faith to work with the poor and the vulnerable.

Another powerful voice for change was Emma Goldman, an immigrant who spoke only Russian and Yiddish when she arrived in New York. After working to bring medical care to immigrant women, she became a prominent public speaker, supporting the rights of working women from all backgrounds.

WOMEN'S RIGHTS

Women worked alongside men in the fight for social and political reform. They also demanded their own right to full U.S. citizenship. Women took a major step toward this goal in 1848 at the **Seneca Falls Convention** in New York, the first women's rights convention held in the United States. There, organizers Elizabeth Cady Stanton and Lucretia Mott read their "Declaration of Sentiments and Resolutions," modeled after the U.S. Declaration of Independence, and asserted that "all men and women are created equal."

One of the first programs Jane Addams set up at Hull House was a nursery school, where she often read to and taught young children. Addams also fought for women's suffrage in the late 1800s.

Daringly, Stanton and Mott even called for women's **suffrage**, or the right to vote, a demand that met with anger even by some who supported other rights for women. Later reformers would continue the fight, but women's suffrage wouldn't be granted until 1920 with the passage of the 19th Amendment. Still, some states were ahead of the federal government. Wyoming gave women the vote in 1890, and Colorado followed in 1893.

The move toward women's rights was global. In 1893, New Zealand became the first nation to give women the vote. By 1900, women in Mexico, Brazil, and Canada were also fighting to achieve legal equality and voting rights. Historians call this movement "first-wave feminism." Later in the 20th century, as you will learn, "second-wave feminism" would spread even more widely, expanding women's demands to include equal rights in education and employment.

HISTORICAL THINKING

1. **READING CHECK** How did the Supreme Court uphold the segregation of whites and African Americans on public transportation?

2. **ANALYZE CAUSE AND EFFECT** What effect did the work of the Muckrakers have on the poor business practices of the era?

3. **MAKE INFERENCES** Why do you think it took so long for women to gain the right to vote in the United States?

PLAN: 2-PAGE LESSON

OBJECTIVE

Explain that people of color in the United States often faced discrimination near the turn of the 20th century, but reformers worked to make life better for all Americans.

CRITICAL THINKING SKILLS FOR LESSON 3.2

- Analyze Cause and Effect
- Make Inferences
- Explain
- Draw Conclusions
- Analyze Visuals

HISTORICAL THINKING FOR CHAPTER 23

How did regional, cultural, and ethnic divisions shape the Americas in the 19th century?

Millions of immigrants came to the United States in the late 19th and early 20th centuries. Lesson 3.2 discusses the discrimination some of these immigrants and people of color faced and the efforts of reformers to protect Americans' rights.

BACKGROUND FOR THE TEACHER

The 14th Amendment In addition to the decision in *Plessy* v. *Ferguson*, the 14th Amendment has been applied to decisions in a wide variety of U.S. Supreme Court cases. One such case was *Lochner* v. *New York*. The case centered on John Lochner, a baker from New York who, in 1901, was convicted of violating the New York Bakeshop Act. This law stated that employees in a bakery could not work more than 60 hours in one week or more than 10 hours in one day. Lochner was convicted on a charge that he had violated the law when he permitted one of his employees to work more than 60 hours in one week. In 1905, in a 5–4 decision, the Supreme Court struck down the Bakeshop Act, ruling that it infringed on Lochner's "right to contract," or the freedom of employees to sell their labor to employers. The Court based this right on the protection offered by the due process clause in the 14th Amendment. The decision ruled that having limits to working time violated the 14th Amendment.

Student eEdition online

Additional content for this lesson, including a photograph, is available online.

INTRODUCE & ENGAGE

CONNECT TO TODAY

Write the term *equal rights* in the center of a Concept Cluster on the board. **ASK:** What do you think of when you hear that term? How does it apply to issues of equal rights in the United States today? *(Possible response: African Americans fight against discrimination, women fight for equal pay, transgender people fight for equal rights)* Tell students that in this lesson they will learn about the fight for equal rights in the late 1800s and early 1900s for African Americans, women, and workers.

TEACH

GUIDED DISCUSSION

1. **Explain** How did *Plessy* v. *Ferguson* impact African Americans for decades? *(The court case enforced a policy of "separate but equal" facilities, accommodations, and institutions for African Americans.)*

2. **Draw Conclusions** Why did many Americans want to prevent monopolies from forming? *(Possible response: Without any competition to reign them in, monopolies could inflate prices for goods and reduce pay for employees.)*

ANALYZE VISUALS

Have students study the political cartoon satirizing the "separate but equal" policy. Tell them that a political cartoon often ridicules public figures or policies and expresses the artist's point of view. Discuss the details of the cartoon in class. **ASK:** Based on this political cartoon, what is the artist's opinion of the "separate but equal" policy? *(The artist opposes the policy and believes the separate accommodations are not at all equal.)*

ACTIVE OPTIONS

On Your Feet: Three-Step Interview Tell students to think about which muckraker or reformer they believe made the greatest contribution to addressing inequality or upholding people's rights. Students must be able to support their choice with evidence from the text or other sources. Ask students to work in pairs to interview each other about their choices. Then each student should share with the class the choice and reasons expressed by the classmate he or she interviewed.

NG Learning Framework: Interpret Child Labor Laws
ATTITUDE Responsibility
SKILL Problem-Solving

Tell students that one result of reformers' efforts was a changing attitude toward child workers. Direct them to government websites to research current child labor laws in their state. Point out that the state may have separate laws for different types of work, such as work on farms or in family businesses. Ask students to write a short report to answer the following questions: Are you currently allowed to work in your state? What jobs could you get? Whose permission do you need?

DIFFERENTIATE

ENGLISH LANGUAGE LEARNERS

Create a Meaning Map Students may be confused by the word *suffrage* because of its similarity to *suffering*. Pair students at the **Beginning** level with more proficient students and have them complete a Meaning Map for *suffrage*. Tell students to use *suffrage* in a sentence and then trade sentences with another pair to check for accuracy and spelling.

GIFTED & TALENTED

Compare and Contrast Declarations Have students locate the full text of the Declaration of Sentiments and Resolutions and a copy of the Declaration of Independence. Tell them to compare and contrast the texts and then write a short essay describing the ways in which the concept of freedom differs in the two documents. Their concluding paragraphs should answer the question: How did the concept of freedom change over time?

See the Chapter Planner for more strategies for differentiation.

HISTORICAL THINKING

ANSWERS

1. It stated that the accommodations on the train were the same for whites and African Americans, even if they were separate.

2. Congress passed the Pure Food and Drug Act and the Meat Inspection Act.

3. Possible response: Most Americans believed women were inferior to and less intelligent than men.

CRITICAL VIEWING (Puck cartoon) Possible response: The African-American passengers are crowded onto a platform held up by a balloon and towed by the plane; white passengers ride in comfort and safety at the front.

(breaker boys, available in the Student eEdition) Possible response: The work is dirty, hard, and cold.

VOCABULARY

Use each of the following vocabulary words in a sentence that shows an understanding of the term's meaning.

1. secede
2. suffrage
3. tenement
4. debt peonage
5. monopoly
6. autonomy
7. segregation
8. muckraker

READING STRATEGY
DRAW CONCLUSIONS

Use a cluster diagram like the one below to draw conclusions about the changes that occurred in the Americas during the late 19th and early 20th centuries. Then answer the questions.

9. Who benefited most from industrialization in the Americas in the late 1800s and early 1900s?

10. What role did racism play in the plans of the U.S. and Canadian governments to forcibly assimilate indigenous people into their societies?

MAIN IDEAS

Answer the following questions. Support your answers with evidence from the chapter.

11. How did advances in weapons technology affect soldiers fighting the U.S. Civil War? LESSON 1.1

12. What impact did Canada's transcontinental railway have on indigenous people? LESSON 1.3

13. What tactics did union members sometimes use to achieve their demands? LESSON 1.4

14. In what ways did Latin Americans benefit from the Industrial Revolution? LESSON 2.1

15. Why did the U.S. government want the Lakota to leave the Black Hills? LESSON 3.1

16. What issues did American women fight for in the late 1800s? LESSON 3.2

HISTORICAL THINKING

Answer the following questions. Support your answers with evidence from the chapter.

17. MAKE INFERENCES Why do you think Abraham Lincoln's name didn't appear on the ballot in southern states in the U.S. presidential election of 1860?

18. EVALUATE How would you describe Canada's road to independence?

19. COMPARE AND CONTRAST How did the lives of rich industrial owners and their employees differ during the Gilded Age in the United States?

20. DRAW CONCLUSIONS After achieving independence, why did many government leaders in Latin America seize lands and sell them to the highest bidders?

21. ANALYZE CAUSE AND EFFECT What impact did the close of the Mexican War have on events in the Yucatán?

22. MAKE CONNECTIONS Why did Elizabeth Cady Stanton and Lucretia Mott assert that "all men and women are created equal" in their "Declaration of Sentiments and Resolutions"?

23. SYNTHESIZE What role did railroads play in the U.S. Civil War, the Confederation of Canada, and the economies of Latin America?

INTERPRET VISUALS

In this 1900 political cartoon called "What a Funny Little Government," Standard Oil Company founder John D. Rockefeller holds the White House in his hand and peers at it through a magnifying glass. Illustrator Horace Taylor has turned the Capitol Building and Treasury Department in the background into oil refineries, with thick smoke pouring out of their smokestacks. Study the political cartoon. Then answer the questions that follow.

24. How are the officials in the White House portrayed and what are they giving to Rockefeller?

25. What does the cartoon suggest about the relationship between industries like Rockefeller's and government?

ANALYZE SOURCES

In 1858, Abraham Lincoln ran for a U.S. Senate seat in Illinois. After accepting his party's nomination, he delivered what is known as the "House Divided" speech at the Republican Convention. In this excerpt from the speech, Lincoln uses a Bible quotation and metaphor to compare the nation to a house. Read the excerpt and then answer the following question.

"A house divided against itself cannot stand." I believe this government cannot endure permanently half slave and half free. I do not expect the Union to be dissolved; I do not expect the house to fall; but I do expect it will cease to be divided. It will become all one thing, or all the other.

26. How does the excerpt foreshadow what would occur in the country?

CONNECT TO YOUR LIFE

27. INFORMATIVE In this chapter, you've read about many groups and individuals who fought for their rights or worked to reform social problems. What right or cause would you like to champion? Perhaps you'd like to address an injustice in your school or provide a service to help the homeless in your community. Choose a problem that interests you and write a brief essay about how you would try to solve it.

TIPS

* Review what you've read about the indigenous people and reformers in this chapter who fought for themselves and for others.

* Consider how you might use their example to effect change of your own.

* Use two or three vocabulary terms from the chapter in your essay.

* Provide a concluding statement in which you compare your goals and methods with those of the fighters and reformers in the chapter.

VOCABULARY ANSWERS

Answers will vary. Possible responses:

1. After Lincoln was elected president, some southern states seceded, or withdrew, from the Union.

2. Women fought for suffrage, or the right to vote, for many years.

3. Many of those who immigrated to the United States in the late 1800s lived in crowded, poorly constructed buildings known as tenements.

4. Debt peonage reduced workers to the status of slaves because they had to buy the supplies they needed and pay off their debt with labor.

5. Under John D. Rockefeller, the Standard Oil Company eliminated its competition and gained a monopoly over the industry.

6. The Republic of Yucatán wanted to secure its autonomy, or independence, from Mexico.

7. After Reconstruction, southern politicians enacted laws that enforced segregation by calling for separate facilities for whites and African Americans.

8. Investigative journalists known as muckrakers revealed government corruption and unsafe working conditions.

READING STRATEGY ANSWERS

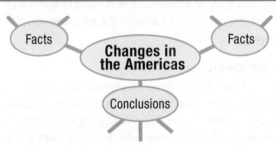

9. Answers will vary. Possible responses: the wealthy, industrial leaders, and some government officials

10. Answers will vary. Possible response: Both governments believed the cultures of the indigenous peoples were inferior to white culture and so tried to eradicate indigenous traditions.

MAIN IDEAS ANSWERS

11. The advanced weapons made the fighting deadlier.

12. The railway and the country's increasing industrialization, mining, and agricultural enterprises expanded into the traditional lands of indigenous peoples and displaced them.

13. strikes and protests

14. Railroads and steamships connected the people with the rest of North America and the world beyond, and Latin America's exports grew.

15. Gold had been discovered there.

16. They fought for the right to vote and for social and political reform.

HISTORICAL THINKING ANSWERS

17. Answers will vary. Possible response: Very few people in the South supported Lincoln's bid for the presidency.

18. Answers will vary. Possible response: It was largely peaceful.

19. Answers will vary. Possible response: Workers lived in crowded tenements and labored for long hours for little pay, while the owners lived in spacious apartment buildings and townhouses and pocketed most of their business profits.

20. Answers will vary. Possible response: After fighting long and expensive wars, the governments probably needed money to rebuild and run their countries.

21. Mexico was able to join the fight against the Maya and fund it with money the country received at the end of the war.

22. Answers will vary. Possible response: They wanted to use the words from the Declaration of Independence to make the point that their inequality under the law was unjust and un-American.

23. Answers will vary. Possible response: The North used railroads to transport soldiers and supplies in the Civil War, and a transcontinental railroad united Canada. In Latin America, railroads carried exports to the coast where they could be shipped to industrialized countries. However, railroads also displaced indigenous people.

INTERPRET VISUALS ANSWERS

24. The officials are tiny in comparison with Rockefeller, and they are offering him bags of money.

25. Answers will vary. Possible response: Industry leaders exercise a great deal of control over the government and hold them in the palms of their hands.

ANALYZE SOURCES ANSWER

26. Answers will vary. Possible response: It foreshadows the Civil War and the struggle to reunite the country—whether it would become all free or all slave.

CONNECT TO YOUR LIFE ANSWER

27. Essays will vary but should contain a plan for addressing a social or political problem.

UNIT 8 RESOURCES

UNIT INTRODUCTION

UNIT TIME LINE

UNIT MAP online

THE GLOBAL PERSPECTIVE: A Sense of the World: The Environment in History

- National Geographic Explorers: Amanda Koltz, Jerry Glover, Adjany Costa
- On Your Feet: Jigsaw Strategy

UNIT WRAP-UP

National Geographic **Magazine Adapted Article**

- "Awash in Plastic"

Unit 8 Inquiry: Create a Sustainable Living Plan

Unit 8 Formal Assessment

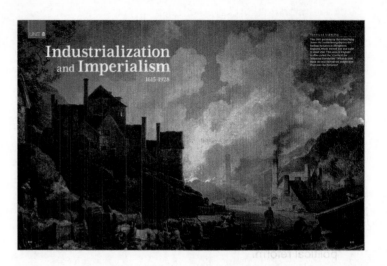

Industrialization and Imperialism
1615–1928

CHAPTER 24 RESOURCES

Available in the Teacher eEdition

TEACHER RESOURCES & ASSESSMENT

Reading and Note-Taking

Vocabulary Practice

Social Studies Skills Lessons

- Reading: Synthesize
- Writing: Explanatory

Formal Assessment

- Chapter 24 Pretest
- Chapter 24 Tests A & B
- Section Quizzes

Chapter 24 Answer Key

Cognero®

24 The New Imperialism
1850–1914

STUDENT DIGITAL RESOURCES

Available in the Student eEdition

- eEdition (English)
- Handbooks
- National Geographic Atlas
- History Notebook
- Biographies
- Literature Analysis

STRATEGY ❶

Set a Purpose for Reading

Before beginning a lesson, help students set a purpose for reading by prompting them to read the title, Main Idea statement, and headings. Encourage them also to look at the visuals and read the captions. Tell students to write a question they expect the lesson to answer. If needed, show them how to turn the Main Idea statement into a question. After they have read the lesson, instruct students to answer the question in writing.

Use with All Lessons *For example, a question for Lesson 1.1 might be: How did King Khama protect his land and his people?*

STRATEGY ❷

Use K-W-L Charts

Arrange students in pairs and provide each pair with a K-W-L Chart. Have partners brainstorm what they know about the lesson topic and add their ideas to the first column in the chart. In the second column, tell students to write at least three questions they have, such as: What was King Khama III's mission of diplomacy? What caused the South African war? Who were the guerrilla warriors, and what battles did they fight? Remind students to complete their charts as they read each lesson by answering their questions and recording what they learned in the third column.

K What Do I Know?	W What Do I Want To Learn?	L What Did I Learn?

Use with All Lessons

STRATEGY ❸

Pose and Answer Questions

Arrange students in pairs and ask them to reread the lesson together. Instruct them to pause after each paragraph and ask each other *who, what, when, where,* and *why* questions about what they have just read. Suggest students use a 5Ws Chart to help organize their questions and answers. Encourage partners to assist each other as needed.

Use with All Lessons

STRATEGY ❶

Use Visuals to Predict

Direct students to read the lesson titles and look at the visuals. Then ask them to write a sentence predicting how the visual is related to the lesson. After reading, you may wish to have students verify their predictions and reword sentences as necessary.

Use with All Lessons

STRATEGY ❷

Build a Time Line

Instruct students to identify key events in each lesson and add them to a time line on the board or a chart. You might continue to expand and extend the time line by guiding students to add to it as they progress through the chapter. Encourage students to enhance the time line with relevant graphics or photos.

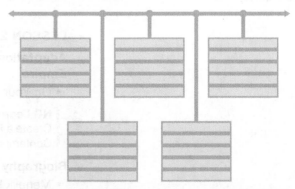

Use with All Lessons *For example, key events from Lesson 1.2 might include: discovery of quinine to protect against malaria (1840s); the French build the Suez Canal (1869); the era of New Imperialism begins (1870); Berlin Conference (1884); Battle of Omdurman (1898).*

ENGLISH LANGUAGE LEARNERS

STRATEGY ❶
Create a Word Web

To activate prior knowledge and build vocabulary, work with students at the **Intermediate** and **Advanced** levels to create two Word Webs for the words *subjugation* and *imperialism* before they read Lesson 1.1. Tell students to write one of the Key Vocabulary words in the center of each web, and then ask students to think of words they associate with the vocabulary word. If needed, have students use a thesaurus for additional synonyms and ideas.

Use with Lessons 1.2, 1.3, 2.2, and 2.4 *Encourage students to create a Word Web for each of the Key Vocabulary words in the chapter.*

STRATEGY ❷
Order Sentence Strips

Choose a key paragraph from the lesson to read aloud while students at **All Proficiencies** follow along in the student text. After reading, tell students to close the student text. Provide sentence strips of the paragraph and direct students to place the strips in order. Ask students to read their paragraphs aloud.

Use with All Lessons *You may wish to ask students at the Beginning level to read the sentence strips aloud and identify meaningful words before they start placing the strips in order.*

STRATEGY ❸
Use Paired Reading

Pair students at the **Beginning** and **Intermediate** levels to read aloud passages from the text.

1. Partner 1 reads a passage; partner 2 retells the passage in his or her own words.
2. Partner 2 reads a different passage; partner 1 retells it.
3. Pairs repeat the process, switching roles.

Use with All Lessons

GIFTED & TALENTED

STRATEGY ❶
Write an Essay

Encourage students to write an essay in which they explain the impact of imperialism on societies in Africa.

Essays should emphasize key events students have learned about in the chapter. Students may use outside sources in addition to evidence from the text to explain their ideas. Invite students to post their essays on a class website.

Use with All Lessons

STRATEGY ❷
Read Historical Biographies

Direct students to use the school or local library to locate a historical biography of an individual they encountered in the chapter. Tell students to read their chosen biography independently and then develop a profile for the person they read about. Encourage students to share their profiles with the class.

Use with All Lessons

PRE-AP

STRATEGY ❶
Analyze Impact

Explain to students that imperialist tactics were often cruel and violent takeovers that brought about the destruction of the traditional cultures of many indigenous peoples. Ask students to choose an indigenous society of Southeast Asia, the Pacific, or Austronesia, such as the Maori, and write a report analyzing how the society was changed through contact with Americans and Europeans. Encourage students to use online resources to include additional information in their reports.

Use with Lesson 2.2

STRATEGY ❷
Write a Summary

Remind students of the Historical Thinking question: How did imperialism affect the economic, political, and cultural life of subjugated peoples? Tell students to review the chapter and identify natural resources, industries, and inventions that drove imperialism and caused drastic changes to subjugated peoples. Then have students write a summary using the examples they identify to answer the Historical Thinking question.

Use with All Lessons *Encourage students to use a Three-Column Chart to organize their ideas.*

CHAPTER

24 The New
Imperialism
1850–1914

HISTORICAL THINKING How did imperialism
affect the economic, political, and cultural life of
subjugated peoples?

SECTION 1 Dividing and Dominating
SECTION 2 Targeting the Pacific

CRITICAL VIEWING
With a depth of approximately 700 feet,
the Big Hole in Kimberley, South Africa,
is the largest hand-dug excavation
in the world. More than 13.6 million
carats of diamonds were mined from
the site, which was owned by the De
Beers Mining Company, between 1871
and 1914. Today, the hole serves as a
reminder of the exploitation of Africa's
resources and people by Europeans.
Based on the details in the photograph,
how would you describe the impact of
the mining process on the land?

INTRODUCE THE PHOTOGRAPH

KIMBERLEY DIAMOND MINE

Have students examine the photograph of what is now
called the Big Hole in Kimberley, South Africa. **ASK:**
What details in the photograph show how the natural
environment is recovering after years of excavation?
*(Possible response: Trees are growing in the big hole,
and it is filled with water, which could provide an aquatic
habitat.)* How could humans intervene to help speed up
the environmental recovery of the former Kimberley mine?
*(Possible responses: Humans could set limitations on
other mining activities nearby. They could reintroduce
plants and animals that lost their habitat due to mining.)*

SHARE BACKGROUND

This chapter discusses the impact of European
economic interests on the native people of Africa and
Southeast Asia. The city of Kimberley, South Africa, in
the background of the photograph was founded by the
British in 1878 specifically as a site for diamond mining.
During the South African War, discussed in Lesson 1.3,
the Boers seized Kimberley and held the city for 126
days. The Kimberley mine was part of a trust created by
Cecil Rhodes, a government leader and diamond mogul
known for his British-supremacist views and ambitious
desire to place the entire east coast of Africa under British
rule. Today there are still several active diamond mines in
Kimberley, although the social and environmental impact
of diamond mining is under scrutiny.

CRITICAL VIEWING Answers will vary. Possible
response: The impact of the mining process on the land
might take thousands of years to reverse since the mine
has already been closed for over 100 years and the hole
is still extremely deep. Mining likely destroyed the habitat
for many native plants and animals.

HISTORICAL THINKING QUESTION

How did imperialism affect the economic, political, and cultural life of subjugated peoples?

Team Word Webbing Place students in groups of four, and provide each team with a single large piece of paper. Give each student in a group a different colored marker. Ask teams to write the Historical Thinking question in a circle in the center of the paper, and have each student add an idea to the part of the web nearest him or her. On a signal, have students rotate the paper and have each student add to the nearest part again, building upon what the previous student wrote. Encourage students to preview the chapter while they complete the word web, noting important images, vocabulary words, and headings that may help spark ideas about the Historical Thinking question.

KEY DATES FOR CHAPTER 24

1840s	Quinine is discovered as a treatment for malaria.
1884	European powers meet at the Berlin Conference to divide control of Africa among themselves.
1887	The French establish French Indochina.
1895	King Khama III begins his diplomatic mission to Britain.
1896	Ethiopia staves off an attack from Italy.
1898	The United States annexes Hawaii.
1899–1902	The British and the Boers fight the South African War.
1900	Western nations have control over most of the globe.
1906	The Maji Maji Revolt secures additional rights for native peoples in East Africa.
1910	The British and the Boers establish the Union of South Africa.

INTRODUCE THE READING STRATEGY

SYNTHESIZE

Explain to students that synthesizing can help them more deeply understand concepts and events. Go to the Chapter Review and preview the synthesis chart with students. As they read the chapter, have students synthesize evidence and explanations of how imperialism affected subjugated peoples around the world.

INTRODUCE CHAPTER VOCABULARY

KEY VOCABULARY

SECTION 1

Boer	concentration camp	genocide
guerrilla warfare	imperialism	magnate
sphere of influence	subjugation	

SECTION 2

coercion	Pan-Africanism

DEFINITION CHART

As they read the chapter, encourage students to complete a Definition Chart for Key Vocabulary terms. Instruct students to list the Key Vocabulary terms in the first column of the chart. They should add each term's definition in the center column as they encounter the term in the chapter and then restate the definition in their own words in the third column. Model an example on the board, using the graphic organizer shown.

Word	Definition	In My Own Words
Pan-Africanism	the idea that people of African descent have a common heritage and should be unified	working to ensure the rights of African people around the world and recognizing their shared history

Traveler: King Khama III
Mission of Diplomacy c. 1837–1923

Who would you go to if people were invading your country? For King Khama and his neighboring kings, the only option seemed to be to go to the home of the invaders and to appeal to their neighbors for help.

A FLOOD OF INVADERS

During his lifetime, King Khama III of the Bangwato people of southern Africa witnessed great challenges as European empires advanced. As a child, he had been familiar with the occasional European hunter or missionary crossing the kingdom. As a king, however, he decided to take drastic action to prevent the complete **subjugation**, or conquest, of his society.

In the short space of 20 years, European powers had drawn colonial boundaries on maps of Africa without the consent or knowledge of those they planned to rule. In many places, Africans resisted, but the Europeans' technological superiority was impossible to overcome.

A DIPLOMATIC MISSION

In 1895, King Khama III and two neighboring kings began a long diplomatic mission. They were in a difficult position. White settlement had already been established in South Africa, but now it was moving northward. The discovery of diamonds and gold had added momentum to that expansion. The kings hoped to convince the British government to declare the Bangwato lands as a protectorate of Great Britain. In this way, the Bangwato people would retain their farming and grazing lands and at least keep some control over their own affairs.

Khama and his companions had converted to Christianity years earlier. So they sought out evangelical groups in London and appealed to Christians' sense of morality. After hearing their appeals, many British Christians supported the kings. The colonial secretary argued in their favor, too. They even met with Queen Victoria. Thanks in large part to the kings' effort and skill, the Bechuanaland protectorate was established.

King Khama went on to establish schools and a trading company in the 20th century. Today, the people of Botswana live in a peaceful and relatively prosperous state. Because they were not ruled by South Africa, they avoided the terrible violence resulting from a system of segregation and discrimination that separated black Africans from white settlers who occupied the land.

Still, measured against the great events of the time, Khama's success was a small victory. African societies could not escape the forces taking over the continent. Technological advances and economic demand for commodities and markets powered what became known as the New Imperialism. **Imperialism** is a practice in which a country increases its power by gaining control over other areas of the world. In Africa and Southeast Asia, local leaders were able to resist only by manipulating European rivalries for their own ends. However, even the most independent states eventually succumbed to imperialism. Indigenous leaders around the world shared King Khama's predicament. But many did not achieve as positive an outcome.

PRIMARY SOURCE

At first we saw the white people pass, and we said, "They are going to hunt for elephant-tusks and ostrich-feathers, and then they will return where they came from." . . . But now when we see white men we say "Jah! Jah!" ["Oh Dear!"]. And now we think of the white people like rain, for they come down as a flood. When it rains too much, it puts a stop to us all. . . . It is not good for the black people that there should be a multitude of white men.

—King Khama III

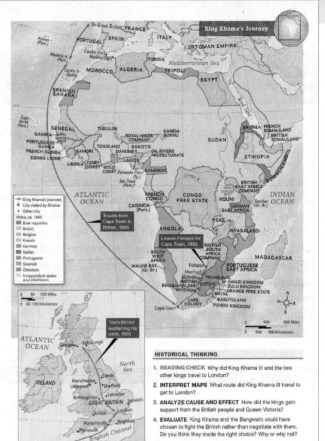

HISTORICAL THINKING

1. **READING CHECK** Why did King Khama III and the two other kings travel to London?

2. **INTERPRET MAPS** What route did King Khama III travel to get to London?

3. **ANALYZE CAUSE AND EFFECT** How did the kings gain support from the British people and Queen Victoria?

4. **EVALUATE** King Khama and the Bangwato could have chosen to fight the British rather than negotiate with them. Do you think they made the right choice? Why or why not?

PLAN: 2-PAGE LESSON

OBJECTIVE

Describe how, after Europeans flooded their lands, King Khama and neighboring kings set out on a journey to protect their land and people.

CRITICAL THINKING SKILLS FOR LESSON 1.1

- Interpret Maps
- Analyze Cause and Effect
- Evaluate
- Make Connections
- Analyze Primary Sources

HISTORICAL THINKING FOR CHAPTER 24

How did imperialism affect the economic, political, and cultural life of subjugated peoples?

As European exploration and economic interests in Africa heightened, some African nations took proactive steps to protect themselves. Lesson 1.1 explains how King Khama III negotiated with the British to secure protection for his people.

BACKGROUND FOR THE TEACHER

King Khama's Negotiation Tactics and View of the Boers In his diplomatic exchanges with the British, Khama strategically played off of Britain's rivalry with the Dutch. In a letter to the British that he wrote in 1876, Khama describes the Boers, descendants of Dutch settlers in southern Africa, as barbaric and cruel. He says that the Boers treat the African people as currency and appeals to the British for protection by referring to himself and his people as subjects of the British monarchy. Khama does not mince words and describes the Boers as violent, war-mongering drunks who have little respect for the sanctity of human life. Khama's description of the Boers was corroborated by others, including the noteworthy British explorer Dr. David Livingstone and Dutch clergy members.

History Notebook

Encourage students to complete the Traveler page for Chapter 24 in their History Notebooks as they read.

Student eEdition online

Additional content for this lesson, including an image, is available online.

INTRODUCE & ENGAGE

PREVIEW USING VISUALS

Direct students' attention to the visuals in the lesson. Draw a two-column chart on the board, labeling the first column *Questions* and the second column *Answers.* Ask students what questions these visuals bring to mind. Record their questions in the chart. After students have read and discussed the lesson, prompt them to answer as many of the listed questions as they can.

TEACH

GUIDED DISCUSSION

1. **Analyze Cause and Effect** How might King Khama's conversion to Christianity have influenced the willingness of the British to negotiate with him? *(They likely viewed King Khama as more relatable and sympathetic.)*

2. **Make Connections** How do King Khama's actions continue to benefit the people of Botswana today? *(King Khama maintained control, so Botswana has not faced the same struggles as the other African lands under European control.)*

ANALYZE PRIMARY SOURCES

Direct students to the primary source quotation from King Khama. **ASK:** What does King Khama mean when he compares white people to rain? *(Possible response: So many white people are coming to Africa that they are causing problems and threatening African peoples' way of life, just like a flood can threaten crops and food security.)* How might the feelings expressed in the quotation have guided King Khama's actions? *(Possible response: King Khama took action to secure the interests of the Bangwato people.)*

ACTIVE OPTIONS

On Your Feet: Three-Step Interview In pairs, tell one student to assume the role of King Khama III and the other student to assume the role of a journalist. Instruct the student in the journalist role to interview the student in the King Khama III role about Khama's motivations, strategies, and hopes for negotiating with the British. Then direct partners to reverse roles. After the interviews, each student should share their partners' responses with the class.

> **NG Learning Framework: Compare Political Maps of Africa**
> **ATTITUDE** Curiosity
> **SKILL** Observation

Prompt students to conduct online research to discover what political maps of Africa looked like in the 1850s, the early 1900s, the 1970s, and today. Encourage students to note which political borders have stayed the same, which have changed, and how the names of countries have changed. Instruct students to write several paragraphs describing the changes to the political landscape in Africa that they observe in the maps.

DIFFERENTIATE

INCLUSION

Understand Information in a Map Pair strong readers with students who have reading or perception difficulties. Instruct pairs to study the map of King Khama's journey. Direct them to read the legend together and to use a finger to trace King Khama's route from Botswana to Britain. Have pairs work together to determine what route King Khama traveled to get to London.

GIFTED & TALENTED

Write a Dialogue Invite students to write a dialogue that could have taken place between King Khama III, Sebele I, and Bathoen I. Before writing, direct students to conduct online research. Suggest that students consider similarities and differences between the experiences of Khama, Sebele, and Bathoen that would have affected their outlook toward negotiations. Invite students to perform their dialogue for the class.

See the Chapter Planner for more strategies for differentiation.

HISTORICAL THINKING

ANSWERS

1. They traveled to London in hopes that the British would retain their lands as a protectorate rather than allow the lands to be engulfed by South Africa.

2. He traveled south to Cape Town. Then took a ship around Africa to Portsmouth, England and on to London.

3. They used Christian morality to appeal to the British sense of justice.

4. Possible response: Although they became a British protectorate, they were allowed to retain their lands and much of their way of life. Had they fought, they probably would have lost much more against the military power of the British. And if they had become part of South Africa, they would later be forced to live in a segregated society.

A Scramble for Africa

How would you react if foreigners flooded into your community and claimed ownership over the land, the government, and even your home? This was what Africans faced as European nations scrambled to get their piece of Africa.

THE NEW IMPERIALISM

As King Khama witnessed, after 1870 Africans suddenly confronted large numbers of Europeans. The era of the New Imperialism had begun. Industrialized countries were engaged in heavy competition for African resources, and the British were determined not to lose their earlier dominance of Africa. But the newly united Germany was the fastest growing industrial economy, and Germans were eager to gain equality with Britain. The French had just been defeated by Germany, and they were itching to restore their international standing. The Americans and Japanese had also joined the imperial club and were gaining military power in Asia.

Competition was fueled by technology and industrial capitalism. Refinements for processing chemicals and metals were brought on by the Industrial Revolution. To compete economically, countries developed more sophisticated production techniques and much larger industrial corporations, which required secure access to raw materials from around the world.

As you have learned, in Latin America this search for raw materials could lead to economic growth but also to violence and inequality. The same was true in Africa, and a good example is rubber. Factories required rubber for conveyor belts, and the invention of bicycles and cars led to even greater demand. There were only two places where wild rubber grew in abundance: the Amazon region of South America and the Congo region of Central Africa. In both places, ruthless exploitation of indigenous lands and labor made a small number of outsiders very wealthy, while local peoples suffered from violence and even death.

Before that time, the interior of most of Africa had been "off-limits" to Europeans. For example, European slave traders faced death from malaria, a blood disease transmitted by mosquito bites, if they ventured far into Africa. However, the discovery of the medicine quinine in the 1840s provided protection against malaria, opening access to Africa's interior. With this medical advance, European exploration and exploitation in the tropics became possible.

Politicians used patriotic appeals to gain support for their imperialist endeavors. Leaders of the French Third Republic appealed to "national honor" in extending their colonial frontiers, and candidates of the Conservative Party in Britain used appeals to pride in global dominance to win elections. In Germany, Kaiser Wilhelm focused on military glory and imperial expansion to strengthen German unity.

Europeans also used humanitarian and religious appeals to justify imperialism. Many considered their mission to be one of "civilizing the savages." Missionaries believed they were "saving" African souls. David Livingstone, one of the most famous missionaries, believed that Africans who converted to Christianity would uplift the continent spiritually and materially. He spent the better part of his life exploring the continent and preaching Christianity. However, when the British lost contact with Livingstone, they feared he was lost in Central Africa. They sent explorer Henry Morton Stanley to find him. Unlike Livingstone, Stanley treated Africans harshly. After the British government condemned him, Stanley formed an alliance with King Leopold II of Belgium who was convinced he could gain great wealth in Africa. Joining in the imperial scramble, King Leopold declared, "I must have my share of this magnificent African cake!"

A group of men sit atop a pile of ivory tusks on the island of Zanzibar off the coast of Africa. Ivory became one of the primary materials exploited by Europeans, decimating the elephant population.

PLAN: 4-PAGE LESSON

OBJECTIVE

Explain how European competition fueled an all-out scramble for control of Africa and how many Africans resisted but could not compete with European technology.

CRITICAL THINKING SKILLS FOR LESSON 1.2

- Identify
- Interpret Maps
- Compare and Contrast
- Synthesize
- Analyze Cause and Effect
- Describe
- Analyze Visuals

HISTORICAL THINKING FOR CHAPTER 24

How did imperialism affect the economic, political, and cultural life of subjugated peoples?

As European countries became aware of the vast amount of natural resources in Africa, they took interest in profiting from African land. Lesson 1.2 discusses the many European powers that tried to take control of Africa and Africans' resistance to imperialism.

BACKGROUND FOR THE TEACHER

Quinine and Malaria Quinine, the chemical compound used as anti-malarial medicine during the onset of the 20th century, made European imperialism possible in much of Africa. Malaria is a protozoic parasite that is transferred to humans through mosquitoes. The parasite invades red blood cells and causes flu-like symptoms. The disease's severity can range from mild discomfort to death. When quinine is administered to a patient, the quinine prevents the parasite from reproducing and usually the patient's blood is parasite-free within a short time. However, even after treatment a patient can experience a malarial relapse weeks, months, or years later. The relapse is due to malarial parasites that have invaded the liver and evaded treatment in the blood. In developed countries, quinine is rarely used to combat malaria today as more advanced treatments have become available.

History Notebook

Encourage students to complete the "Diamonds" Global Commodity page for Chapter 24 in their History Notebooks as they read.

Student eEdition online

Additional content for this lesson, including a Global Commodity feature, is available online.

INTRODUCE & ENGAGE

CONSIDER POLITICAL AND CULTURAL BOUNDARIES

Invite students to consider their community, including the location of its cultural institutions, resources, businesses, outdoor spaces, and places where people live. Discuss the layout of the community and then ask students to think about how they would react if people who lived thousands of miles away suddenly decided that they were in charge and divided the community among themselves. Encourage students to think about the consequences of not having access to the places they depend on and enjoy or being cut off from family and friends. Then tell students that in this lesson they will learn about how Europeans attempted to divide the African continent among themselves with little to no regard for the African people.

TEACH

GUIDED DISCUSSION

1. **Compare and Contrast** How did the rubber trade affect local people and foreigners in the Congo? *(Local people were exploited and faced terrible violence at the hands of Europeans. A few foreigners became very wealthy.)*

2. **Synthesize** How might decisions made during the Berlin Conference still affect Africans today? *(The European powers at the Berlin Conference did not take into account the local people or their boundaries when claiming land for themselves. The arbitrary boundaries established by Europeans could still cause conflict and unrest in Africa for decades to come.)*

SYNTHESIZE

Encourage students to consider the various reasons that different European countries were interested in Africa. **ASK:** What evidence and explanations show the motivations of different European countries? *(Possible responses: David Livingstone's missionary work shows evidence of Britain's quest to convert Africans to Christianity. Germany forcing Africans to grow cotton is evidence of Germany's focus on economic gains.)* How can you synthesize your evidence and explanations to draw a conclusion about European imperialism in Africa? *(Answers will vary. Possible responses: European countries' interest in Africa was primarily self-serving, whether it was spreading one's own belief system or benefiting financially.)*

DIFFERENTIATE

ENGLISH LANGUAGE LEARNERS

Ask and Answer Questions Pair students at the **Beginning** level with those at the Intermediate level. Tell them to write several short-answer questions, such as the ones below, about people and ideas in this lesson. Then have each pair take turns asking and answering questions with another pair.

- What was a major difference between David Livingstone and Henry Morton Stanley? *(Stanley treated Africans harshly while Livingstone did not.)*
- Which African queen mother led a resistance against the British? *(Yaa Asantewaa)*
- Why was control of the Suez Canal desirable? *(The canal was a shipping route from Europe to Asia.)*

GIFTED & TALENTED

Present Information Graphically Direct students to the map at the beginning of the lesson that shows how European presence in Africa grew. Tell students to conduct online research to learn more about the influx of Europeans in Africa, such as population statistics of European colonizers from various countries. Challenge students to design a way to present the information from their research visually, such as in a simple chart or bar graph or in a more creative infographic. Invite them to display their work on a class bulletin board, website, or blog, and encourage students to compare visual representation strategies.

See the Chapter Planner for more strategies for differentiation.

Afraid that King Leopold would destabilize the balance of power, Germany's Otto von Bismarck organized the Berlin Conference in 1884. Thirteen European nations met in Berlin to divide up the continent and determine **spheres of influence**, or areas in which colonial powers recognized one another's claims to dominance. No Africans were invited to attend, nor did European representatives pay any attention to traditional ethnic or cultural boundaries. According to the rules of the conference, nations in attendance could claim any unclaimed area of Africa as long as they occupied and administered it. For Africans, this decision meant 20 years of warfare and instability as European governments launched waves of invasions to secure their claims. Millions of Africans died in this "scramble for Africa."

Some of the worst violence occurred in the Congo, which King Leopold claimed as his own personal property. While claiming to be spreading Christianity and "civilization," Leopold's agents brutalized the indigenous people, using armed force and torture to increase supplies of ivory and rubber. African women were held captive until their husbands brought enough rubber to free them. Famine spread as farmers were forced to ignore their own crops.

The Polish-English writer Joseph Conrad witnessed this brutality. In his novella *Heart of Darkness*, he tells the story of an Englishman who travels up the Congo River as he searches for a successful but mysterious European merchant. When he finally reaches the remote camp, he finds that the man has gone insane with greed. The merchant's final words, "The horror! The horror!" reflect the darkness that had come with European imperialism.

AFRICAN RESPONSES

Before 1878, European colonial presence was largely limited to coastal areas. The all-out scramble for control of Africa was something new. Telegraphs provided an important source of communication, and steamships allowed Europeans to venture farther up African rivers. The suddenness of the onslaught caught Africans off guard. Should they fight back? Seek diplomatic options? Ally themselves with the intruders? African leaders tried all of these options with little success. When Africans rose up to defend their lands and traditions, the Europeans came in with machine guns and field cannons.

The Industrial Revolution was changing the balance of power, as witnessed in the 19th-century Anglo-Asante (ah-SAHN-tee) Wars. The powerful Asante Empire in the West African forest resented British attempts to use their coastal settlement to dominate trade. In 1824, this competition led to warfare, and the Asante easily won. But by 1896, the British had much better technology, including rifles, and now easily conquered the Asante. The Asante king, known for his wealth in gold, was sent into exile.

This African salt cellar, or salt container, is carved out of an ivory elephant tusk. The carvings on the salt cellar depict European men with long hair and beards.

Many Asante people felt humiliated, and a queen mother, **Yaa Asantewaa**, spoke up to motivate her people: "[If] you the men of Asante will not go forward, then we . . . the women will. I shall call upon my fellow women. We will fight the white men. We will fight till the last of us falls in the battlefields." The British defeated the Asante. But Yaa Asantewaa's passion caused the British governors to treat the royal family and Asante traditions with greater respect.

The British were competing with the French for control in West Africa, and that is why they moved to occupy the area of today's northern Nigeria. The region had been dominated by the Sokoto (SOH-kuh-toh) caliphate, but after its leader's death, it had split into a number of separate states. The lack of a unified army made British occupation easier. Some leaders fought, but their cavalry forces on horseback were no match for machine guns, and British cannons easily blew holes in their palace walls.

The British and the Germans scrambled for territory in East Africa. The lands the Germans conquered did not have any obvious sources of wealth, however. To make their East African colony pay, the Germans forced East Africans to grow cotton. It was hard work, enforced by the whip, and cotton ruined the soil with no benefit to local farmers. As a result, in 1905 the religious prophet, Kinjeketile (kin-JEK-eh-tayl), led the Maji Maji Revolt. The Germans easily overpowered Kinjeketile's followers who believed they would be spared by bathing in a stream of *Maji Maji*, meaning "powerful water." The rebellion was not completely futile, though. After the revolt, the Germans no longer imposed such heavy restrictions on the African people under their control.

Egypt became another area of resistance. You already read that in 1869 the French designed and built the Suez Canal to create a shipping route between Europe and Asia. The Egyptian leader believed that revenue from the canal would allow Egypt to maintain its independence. However, economic hardships forced the Egyptians to sell their shares in the canal to the British. Taking control of more than the canal, the British imposed their own officers on Egypt's military. Nationalist Egyptian military officers rebelled, but the British quickly suppressed the rebellion.

THINGS FALL APART In 1958, a young Nigerian writer named Chinua Achebe imagined what the "scramble for Africa" would have felt like for his own ancestors. Achebe was an Igbo, a society with a complex culture where status came from achievement rather than inherited status. The main character in Achebe's novel, *Things Fall Apart*, is Okonkwo, a man who received nothing from his father but had a burning ambition to earn the "titles" that would mark him as a great man. Unfortunately, the British arrived and changed the rules of success. Okonkwo's community became divided between Christian converts, including his own son, and those who, like Okonkwo, stuck to the old ways. Says one character in the course of the novel, "They have put the knife on the things that held us together, and we have fallen apart." For many years, Achebe's great novel has helped readers understand the human side of this tragic period in Africa's long history.

Once in control of Egypt, the British needed to control the Upper Nile Valley as well. First in the 1880s and again in the 1890s, the British fought Sudanese resistance to take control of the Nile Valley. The Battle of Omdurman (ohm-der-MAHN) in 1898 was the bloodiest battle between European and African forces during the entire period. The Sudanese forces were fighting on behalf of a Muslim religious prophet who said he had come to declare the end of days and the victory of the righteous. The battle was one of the most lopsided in history. The British, armed with machine guns invented in 1884, lost 47 soldiers. Over 10,000 Sudanese forces were killed.

The British also faced stiff resistance in the southern African kingdom of the Ndebele (endeh-BEE-lee). The Ndebele were militarily formidable, but they were no match for the British. The Ndebele king tried to protect his people by signing a treaty granting the British mineral rights while retaining his own authority. He feared the British would not keep their promises, and sure enough, the kingdom fell to the British colony of Rhodesia (roh-DEE-zhuh) after losing two wars of resistance in the 1890s.

HISTORICAL THINKING

1. **READING CHECK** What political, economic, and social motivations influenced European imperialism in Africa?

2. **IDENTIFY** How did military technology, communications technology, and medical advancements help initiate and advance imperialism in Africa?

3. **INTERPRET MAPS** According to the information in the map, which European country's occupation was met with the most resistance movements?

BACKGROUND FOR THE TEACHER

The Ndebele and the British In their quest to take over Ndebele land, the British took note of tensions between the Ndebele and other Africans in order to use those tensions in their favor. The British stoked conflict between the Ndebele and the Mashona and then intervened in order to gain a political foothold. Linguistic differences may have exacerbated the relationship between the British and Ndebele when they signed a treaty that the Ndebele believed was granting the British mineral rights but that the British insisted gave them a right to rule Ndebele territory. After the British attacked and subsequently conquered the Ndebele, Ndansi Kumalo, an Ndebele writer, chronicled the brutality suffered by his people. Kumalo wrote that the British placed African enemies of the Ndebele in supervisory positions and that the Ndebele were forced to endure such horrific conditions that they were spurred to fight the British. According to Kumalo, the Ndebele knew that they were out-militarized by the British, but, despite this disadvantage, they decided that it would be better to fight than to endure the hardships imposed upon them.

TEACH

GUIDED DISCUSSION

3. **Analyze Cause and Effect** What effects did Yaa Asantewaa's actions have on the relationship between the Asante and the British? *(The British respected Asantewaa's actions, so they treated the Asante more humanely than they otherwise might have.)*

4. **Describe** How did the Maji Maji Revolt benefit Africans? *(The Germans eased the restrictions that they were placing on the African people.)*

ANALYZE VISUALS

Direct students to the photograph of the African salt cellar and encourage them to observe closely the way the European men are depicted and the objects they are holding or wearing. **ASK:** What do the objects held by the men carved in the salt cellar convey about how Africans viewed Europeans? *(Possible response: The men carved in the salt cellar have crosses and hold what appear to be weapons. This indicates that Africans viewed Europeans as zealous missionaries who were concerned with conquest as well as religious conversion.)* What can you infer based on the expressions on the men's faces? *(Possible response: Each man is frowning. The carvings portray the men as serious, determined, and lacking kindness.)*

ACTIVE OPTIONS

On Your Feet: Roundtable Seat students around a table in groups of four, and direct them to the sidebar about Chinua Achebe's novel *Things Fall Apart.* Ask students to consider how, based on what they have read about the motivations of European imperialism in Africa, the Igbo's achievement-based society may have clashed with British culture. Instruct group members to go around the table and take turns answering the question in a different way. If time allows, invite groups to share their answers with the class.

NG Learning Framework: Propose a Solution to Conflict Diamonds
ATTITUDE Responsibility
SKILL Problem-Solving

Direct students to the Diamonds Online Global Commodity feature (available in the Student eEdition). After students read the feature, invite them to research conflict diamonds. Encourage students to focus on the definition of a conflict diamond, the problems that arise from trading conflict diamonds, and what solutions are being implemented and proposed to put a halt to trading conflict diamonds. Then have students outline a potential solution for ending the conflict-diamond trade. Invite volunteers to share their solutions with the class and compare and contrast one another's ideas.

HISTORICAL THINKING

ANSWERS

1. European countries were in competition both politically and economically. The British had been dominant in Africa, but Germans had just united and wanted to demonstrate their power. The French had been defeated by Germany and wanted to restore their reputation. King Leopold of Belgium saw Africa as a source of personal wealth. The industrial nations needed raw materials to advance their industries, and Africa provided a source. These countries used patriotic and social appeals to garner support for colonization. They appealed to national pride and to humanitarian missions to "civilize" or "save" Africans.

2. Europeans had machine guns that outgunned African weapons, so Africans could not effectively protect themselves against colonization. The discovery of quinine allowed Europeans to advance farther into Africa without contracting malaria. Europeans also had the telegraph to help them communicate.

3. Africans resisted British occupation the most. Africans resisted British occupation in four different places on the map: Asante in 1900, Sakoto in 1900, Omdurman in 1898, and Ndebele in 1896.

The South African War

Wars usually end with one side winning and another losing, right? In South Africa, the white warring parties ended up with a compromise that benefited both sides while resulting in a brutal loss for indigenous Africans.

Boer families were placed by British soldiers in concentration camps like this one in Eshowe, Zululand, during the second Boer War.

CLASHING INTERESTS IN SOUTH AFRICA

The European presence in Africa increased greatly after 1870, but some countries had begun exploring the continent even earlier. As you have learned, the Dutch East India Company had established a trade center in Cape Town in present-day South Africa as early as 1652. Later, settlers known as **Boers**, or farmers, moved to the interior. There was no malaria here to block European movement. Also, the indigenous people were unable to resist as they were hunter-gatherers with no metal weapons and no resistance to the smallpox brought by the settlers. By the time of the New Imperialism, the Boers, who are now known as Afrikaners, had lived in the Cape area for 200 years.

On the other side of South Africa, the Boers were challenged by entirely different African societies with great herds of cattle, powerful chiefs, and iron weapons. These were the descendants of the Bantu-speaking migrants you already learned about. In the late 18th century, drought had caused these chiefdoms to compete for water resources, and one group rose to dominate the others. This was the Zulu Empire under the great warrior **King Shaka**, who grew in power as he brought the young men of conquered chiefdoms into his own regiments. Other societies abandoned their lands to escape the violence.

At the same time, the Boers were expanding. They moved into territories that had been abandoned in

the wake of Zulu warfare. However, they were unable to overpower Zulu resistance, and the Zulu and other African societies retained their sovereignty into the 1870s.

Earlier, the British had taken Cape Town from the Dutch during the wars with Napoleon. Initially, the British focused their attention on maritime trade. But when diamonds were discovered in 1868, the British looked to conquer the interior. That led to conflict with the Zulu kingdom. In 1879, British authorities demanded that the Zulu disband their regiments, but the Zulu king refused. The Zulu warriors attacked and defeated the British at the Battle of Isandhlwana (ee-san-DLWAH-nah). Enraged by their defeat, the British sacked the Zulu capital and sent the king into exile.

Meanwhile, as many Africans sought safety in the mountains, the Boers took advantage by settling much of the interior. But the republics they founded there were also challenged by the British Empire, especially after gold was discovered in 1884. The city of Johannesburg

rose almost overnight, and the clash between Boer and British aspirations led to the South African War.

WAR AND AFTERMATH

During the war, which lasted from 1899 to 1902, the British took control of towns and railway lines while Boer combatants blended into civilian populations and engaged in **guerrilla warfare**, or small-scale surprise attacks, against the British. To separate civilians from soldiers, the British sent Boer civilians to **concentration camps**, where they were confined under armed guard. Over 20,000 Boers, many of them women and children, died of illness in the camps. Though the South African War was between the British and the Boers, tens of thousands of Africans also died.

The British won the war, but less than a decade later they developed a compromise with the Boers. They created the Union of South Africa to combine British colonies with Boer republics under the British flag. This 1910 compromise secured both groups' common interest: cheap African labor for mining and agriculture.

In 1913, the all-white South African parliament passed the Native Land Act. The law limited Africans to "native reserves" that included only a tiny portion of their traditional land. The goal was to strip indigenous communities of their ability to grow their own food and to force them to work in mines and white farms at the lowest possible pay.

In response to the injustice of the Native Land Act, a group of educated African leaders banded together to form the **African National Congress (ANC)**. At first the ANC had no success challenging white domination of South Africa. But much later, as you will learn, the ANC would finally win its battle for democracy and greater racial equality.

GENOCIDE IN GERMAN SOUTHWEST AFRICA

As the British and Boers ended their war in South Africa, another chilling event was underway in neighboring German Southwest Africa (present-day Namibia). After the Germans claimed the territory, they took more and more land from the Herero people. In 1904, the Herero rebelled, but the Germans suppressed the rebellion and drove the Herero into the Kalahari Desert. Prevented from returning, tens of thousands of Herero died. Those

who survived were sent to concentration camps and forced to perform hard labor. Harsh labor conditions killed half of the people in the camps. All in all, about 75 percent of the Herero population died. This was the 20th century's first **genocide**, or attempt to destroy an entire people and their culture.

THE RHODES COLOSSUS

CECIL RHODES The main figure of the New Imperialism in southern Africa was the mining **magnate**, or wealthy and powerful businessperson, Cecil Rhodes (shown above). He dreamed of British imperial control of eastern and southern Africa "from Cape to Cairo." Combining political and economic clout, Rhodes was prime minister of the Cape Colony, owner of some of the world's richest gold and diamond mines, and head of the British South Africa Company (BSAC). Through the BSAC, Rhodes even had his own army, which he used to conquer the territory later named Rhodesia. Once Africans regained their independence, they dropped Rhodesia and proudly called their country Zimbabwe, after the great early kingdom of their ancestors.

HISTORICAL THINKING

1. **READING CHECK** What interests led the Boers and the British to fight the South African War?

2. **COMPARE AND CONTRAST** How did British colonialism differ in the Asante Kingdom and South Africa?

3. **ANALYZE CAUSE AND EFFECT** How did the compromise between the British and the Boers affect black South Africans?

PLAN: 2-PAGE LESSON

OBJECTIVE

Explain how imperial interests in South Africa led to war between European colonists.

CRITICAL THINKING SKILLS FOR LESSON 1.3

- Compare and Contrast
- Analyze Cause and Effect
- Explain
- Identify Supporting Details
- Analyze Visuals

HISTORICAL THINKING FOR CHAPTER 24

How did imperialism affect the economic, political, and cultural life of subjugated peoples?

The discovery of resources in southern Africa led to conflict between the Boers and the British. Lesson 1.3 discusses how this European conflict affected indigenous Africans and the course of South African history.

Student eEdition online

Additional content for this lesson, including a photograph, is available online.

BACKGROUND FOR THE TEACHER

Afrikaans Language Today, South Africa has 11 official languages. One of these is Afrikaans, a language that developed through the interactions of European imperialists, indigenous peoples, and South Asians who were brought by Europeans to southern Africa as slaves. Afrikaans most closely resembles Dutch, with enough overlap that some Afrikaans and Dutch speakers can understand one another. While primarily of Dutch origin, the Boers were also comprised of German settlers and French Huguenots (Protestants) who fled to southern Africa to escape persecution in France. Afrikaans has some German and French influence, attributes of the native Khoisan language, and some elements that resemble South Asian languages. In 1914, the language was adopted by some schools in South Africa and became one of the nation's official languages in 1924.

INTRODUCE & ENGAGE

DISCUSS ALLIANCES

Ask students to think of an alliance in present-day politics. Invite them to discuss the issues that created the need for the alliance and any benefits that might come from it. Explain that in this lesson students will learn about how the British and Boers first fought one another in southern Africa but then formed an alliance to create the Union of South Africa at the expense of indigenous Africans' rights, livelihood, and safety.

TEACH

GUIDED DISCUSSION

1. **Explain** How did the discovery of diamonds and gold in the interior region of southern Africa affect the relationship between the British, the Boers, and the Zulu kingdom? *(The British took interest in political and economic control of the interior, which led to conflict because the Zulu and the Boers were already living in this region.)*

2. **Identify Supporting Details** What aspects of the Native Land Act sparked the creation of the African National Congress? *(The Native Land Act stripped Africans of their land and thus their ability to grow food and support themselves without reliance on low-paying jobs in European mines and farms.)*

ANALYZE VISUALS

Direct students to the Cecil Rhodes cartoon and the sidebar. **ASK:** How does the drawing depict Rhodes's attitude toward Africa? *(Possible response: Because Rhodes straddles the entire continent and lifts his arms emphatically, he appears to view Africa as something to be conquered and dominated.)*

ACTIVE OPTIONS

On Your Feet: Fishbowl Organize the class so that part of the class sits in a close circle facing inward and the other part of the class sits in a larger circle around them. Prompt students on the inside of the circle to assume the role of members of the African National Congress and discuss European imperialism in southern Africa. Students should consider what outcomes the African National Congress would like to achieve and how they could best achieve these outcomes, such as through war or negotiations. Then tell the groups to reverse roles.

NG Learning Framework: Write Regulations to Prevent Genocide
ATTITUDE Responsibility
SKILL Communication

Instruct students to research the genocide of the Herero people in southwest Africa. After learning more about the events that led to the genocide and its devastating outcome, challenge students to propose a list of international laws that could be used to prevent genocide from happening today. Invite volunteers to share their ideas with the class.

DIFFERENTIATE

ENGLISH LANGUAGE LEARNERS

Identify Causes and Effects This lesson contains many examples of cause and effect. Have mixed proficiency pairs discuss and write about important events that occurred leading up to and in the early years of the South African War.

PRE-AP

Explore Roots of Conflict Challenge students to learn more about how the competition for resources in southern Africa and the burgeoning diamond industry led to conflict between the British, Boers, and Zulu people and to the South African War. Tell students to use their findings to create a report that connects economic factors and conflicts. Invite them to share their report orally or post it on a class blog.

See the Chapter Planner for more strategies for differentiation.

HISTORICAL THINKING

ANSWERS

1. The Boers had lost their colony to the British and probably resented that. The Boers wanted to expand and gain new land. The British discovered diamonds and gold and decided they wanted to occupy those areas for their resources.

2. The British continually attacked the Asante Kingdom, destroying its capital on several occasions, but the determination of an Asante queen led the British to respect Asante royalty and traditions. In South Africa, the British quashed the Zulu and later brutally exploited indigenous South Africans. They showed no respect for native peoples of South Africa.

3. The compromise benefited white colonizers financially. They exploited indigenous black South Africans by destroying their ability to be self-sufficient and employing them at cheap wages.

Southeast Asia and Austronesia

Have you ever heard people say they must "keep up with the Joneses"? The idiom refers to the need to compete with one's neighbors for social status. During the New Imperialism, imperialist nations were not content to just take over Africa and South America. They also swept up lands in Asia and the Pacific. After all, they had to keep up with their neighbors.

Workers in Myanmar use elephants to help them haul teak wood. Teak, which is a preferred wood for boats and furniture, has been a main export from Myanmar (once known as Burma) since the New Imperialism.

SOUTHEAST ASIA

As in Africa, Europeans competed for access to trade in Southeast Asia well before the 19th century. But the same motives that drove the New Imperialism in Africa motivated industrial powers to clamor for control of Southeast Asia and Austronesia, or the islands of the southern Pacific Ocean. By the end of the 19th century, Western domination was nearly complete.

In 1802, the French aided the Nguyen family in establishing a new dynasty in Vietnam. As a result, French missionaries were allowed to preach there. However, Nguyen tolerance toward Catholicism declined, leading to the execution of a missionary. In 1858, the French emperor Napoleon III invaded Vietnam, citing as justification the persecution of missionaries, increased interest in trade in Southeast Asia, and the belief that the British would take Vietnam if the French didn't. Finally, the besieged Nguyen ruler ceded the commercial center of Saigon to France, opened three "treaty ports" to European trade, and gave the French free passage up the Mekong River.

Adding to their territory, the French conquered the neighboring kingdom of Cambodia. An agreement with the kingdom of Siam also gave Laos to the French. In 1887, they combined the three territories into the Federation of Indochina, or simply **French Indochina**. French authorities took

over vast estates and grew rubber and rice, which they exported. The profits went almost entirely to the French.

Like the French in Indochina, the British took Burma into their empire in stages. By the 1870s, Britain controlled the south. In 1886, British forces from India invaded Burma and took Mandalay, the capital. They suppressed a number of rebellions and began building railroads. Their goal was to access the rich timber resources of the Burmese jungles.

Singapore had been Britain's most valuable possession in Southeast Asia since 1819. Initially, the British were content to control the port and grow rich on the trade between the Indian Ocean and the South China Sea. But after the completion of the Suez Canal in

Imperialism in Southeast Asia, 1910

Egypt, British merchants became anxious to exploit the rich tin resources of the Malay Peninsula.

The British started their conquest of Malaya by making alliances with local Muslim leaders. When some of those leaders refused British demands, the fighting started, and British firepower dominated. Once in control, the British expanded plantations of commercial crops such as pepper, palm oil, and rubber.

The Dutch had been the dominant European presence in the islands of Southeast Asia since the 17th century. During the 19th century, authorities asserted more and more formal control over Java and Sumatra, where individual sultans had previously been left in charge of local affairs. At the same time, the increasing presence of other European powers motivated the Dutch to seek control of hundreds of other islands. Under the New Imperialism, the Dutch significantly expanded their power over the Indonesian archipelago.

THE PACIFIC AND AUSTRONESIA

While European powers vied for control of Southeast Asia, the United States claimed a direct territorial stake in the Pacific by annexing the Hawaiian Islands in 1898. The further extension of American imperialism to the Philippines came as a result of the Spanish–American War from 1898 to 1900. That war initially centered in Cuba. It then spread to include the Philippines, which Spain had ruled since the founding of Manila in 1571.

As you have learned, British involvement in Australia and New Zealand predated the New Imperialism. By the 1870s, in fact, the Australian economy was booming as a result of wool exports and the discovery of gold. However, the boom had been at the expense of the Aborigines. White immigrants reduced them to a defeated and subservient people. In New Zealand, however, British settlers faced tough resistance from the Polynesian-speaking Maori. An 1840 treaty created the framework for British-Maori coexistence. The treaty guaranteed land rights and status as British subjects to the Maori. But by the 1860s, war had broken out. A British victory followed, and by 1890 indigenous Maori, like the people of Hawaii, had lost nearly all of their land. That was the same year as the massacre of the Lakota Sioux at Wounded Knee, which you read about earlier. By then, indigenous people had lost their sovereignty all across the world.

HISTORICAL THINKING

1. **READING CHECK** What were some of the raw materials that Europeans sought in Southeast Asia and Austronesia?

2. **INTERPRET MAPS** Who controlled the most land as colonial possessions in the Pacific?

3. **IDENTIFY SUPPORTING DETAILS** How did the United States participate in the New Imperialism in these areas of the world?

PLAN: 2-PAGE LESSON

OBJECTIVE
Describe how the continued pursuit of raw materials led European and industrial powers to take control of Southeast Asia, Austronesia, and the Pacific.

CRITICAL THINKING SKILLS FOR LESSON 2.1
- Interpret Maps
- Identify Supporting Details
- Explain
- Analyze Cause and Effect

HISTORICAL THINKING FOR CHAPTER 24
How did imperialism affect the economic, political, and cultural life of subjugated peoples?

In addition to seeking dominance over Africa, European powers set their sights on colonizing Southeast Asia and Austronesia. Lesson 2.1 discusses the various European powers invading these regions, resistance of indigenous peoples, and the motivations behind both.

Student eEdition online
Additional content for this lesson, including a photograph, is available online.

BACKGROUND FOR THE TEACHER
The Quest for Philippine Independence Spain had colonized and ruled the Philippines for several centuries until, at the end of the Spanish-American War, Spain transferred control of the Philippines to the United States. However, many Filipino people desired independence, not a transfer of colonial power. Several days after the ratification of the Treaty of Paris between the United States and Spain in 1899, fighting erupted between Filipino Nationalists and American forces in the Philippines. The war lasted for three years and had devastating consequences, including the death of more than 4,200 Americans, 20,000 Filipino military members, and 200,000 Filipino civilians. During the war, the United States government initiated and gained Filipino support for a campaign that would gradually grant the Philippines more independence over time. Some Filipino elites disagreed with the militant rebels' ideas for establishing a Philippine government, and their support of the United States' plan for gradual independence helped end the war. Eventually, the Philippines became an autonomous commonwealth in 1935 and an independent nation in 1946.

INTRODUCE & ENGAGE

CONSIDER NATURAL RESOURCES

Prompt students to identify the natural resources being used in the photo of workers in Myanmar. As a class, brainstorm a list of natural resources common to your state or region. Guide students to create categories, such as soil, forests, minerals, and water, and to consider how these resources might boost the area's economy. Ask them to list businesses and commercial trade that might evolve from such resources. Tell students that they will learn how access to natural resources in Southeast Asia and Austronesia led to the expansion of imperialism.

TEACH

GUIDED DISCUSSION

1. **Explain** What shift in the relationship between the French and the Nguyens led to Napoleon III's invasion of Vietnam? *(In the early 1800s, the French and Vietnamese worked together to establish the Nguyen dynasty. However, tolerance of the French and Catholicism decreased in Vietnam, which was one reason Napoleon III cited for invasion.)*

2. **Analyze Cause and Effect** How did the Suez Canal influence Britain's interest in Southeast Asia? *(It provided a faster shipping route between Europe and Southeast Asia, so Britain became interested in harvesting natural resources in Southeast Asia for export back to Europe.)*

INTERPRET MAPS

Direct students to the map. **ASK:** Based on the map, what are your predictions about how imperialism might further spread in the region? *(Possible responses: The French or British might invade Siam because it is adjacent to their current territory, or the Dutch might try to take control of Northern Australia due to its proximity to Indonesia.)*

ACTIVE OPTIONS

On Your Feet: Jigsaw Strategy Students form four "expert" groups to research some of the Western powers vying for control of Southeast Asia and Austronesia: the British, the French, the Dutch, and the Americans. Their research should focus on the imperialist strategies and motivations of each group. Regroup students so that each new group has at least one member from each expert group. Have experts share their research.

> **NG Learning Framework: Create a Presentation About Indigenous Resistance**
> ATTITUDE Curiosity
> KNOWLEDGE Our Human Story

Have students research resistance to European imperialism in Southeast Asia and Austronesia. They may focus on the Burmese king's attempt to regain control of northern Burma, the Maori's insistence on gaining rights under the British crown, the Vietnamese struggle against French rule, or another example of their own choosing. Tell students to create a brief presentation of their findings, present their information to the class, and compare and contrast, as a class, different resistances within the region.

DIFFERENTIATE

STRIVING READERS

Read and Recall Invite students to work in pairs. First have each student read the lesson independently. After reading, partners meet without the book and take notes as they share ideas they recall. Pairs then review the lesson together and decide what to add or change in their notes.

GIFTED & TALENTED

Create an Annotated Time Line Tell students to research the United States' annexation of Hawaii and to create an annotated time line of the history of Hawaii as a part of the United States, including events before and after its statehood up until the present day. Encourage the use of an online time line creation tool, if available. Ask students to include the date and specific details for each event and visuals if relevant. Invite students to share their completed time lines with the class.

See the Chapter Planner for more strategies for differentiation.

HISTORICAL THINKING

ANSWERS

1. The French sought rubber and rice in Indochina. The British sought lumber in Burma, tin, pepper, palm oil, and rubber in Malaya, and wool and gold in Australia.

2. The Dutch controlled the most land. They controlled much of the East Indies and Dutch New Guinea.

3. The United States annexed Hawaii and took control of the Philippines after the Spanish–American War.

Imperialist Tactics

What would you do if your country took over another country and used violent tactics to control the people there? Would you support your country, or would you try to persuade your government to change its ways? This was the situation Americans and Europeans faced when their countries took control of other lands.

IMPERIALIST TACTICS

Taking control of Southeast Asia, the Pacific, and Austronesia wasn't always easy. Guerrilla warriors took up arms against the French in Indochina. The Maori fought a war against the British in New Zealand. Farmers in the islands of Southeast Asia rebelled against Dutch demands, and Filipino revolutionaries struggled for independence from the United States. To subdue these groups, imperialists developed a series of tactics.

Resistance to foreign occupation was a constant theme in Vietnamese history, first with imperial China and then with the French. The Vietnamese people were not willing to simply hand their country over to the French. Guerrilla fighters rose up from rural villages across the country. To fight guerrilla resistance, French authorities started a campaign of "pacification." This tactic was to subdue and calm the resisters. French authorities sought to win the hearts of the Vietnamese by building roads, opening schools, and providing health care. At the same time, they forcibly suppressed rebels, killing anyone who appeared to be hostile to their control.

The British took a different tactic. In Malaya, as in Africa, the British supported a policy of "divide and conquer," creating and playing off local rivalries. British "residents" gave local Malaya rulers "advice" on the governance of their sultanates. If a sultan refused to follow their advice, the British simply recognized another ambitious man as ruler and worked through him. In this way, the British could claim that indigenous rulers remained in place, but power was squarely in the hands of Europeans.

The Dutch used **coercion**, or force. Farmers in Java had long grown rice for self-sufficiency. But in 1830, Dutch authorities forced rice farmers to convert to

Queen Liliuokalani was the last sovereign ruler of the Kamehameha dynasty of the Hawaiian kingdom.

sugar production. One Dutch official declared that "they must be taught to work, and if they were unwilling out of ignorance, they must be ordered to work." Through such coercion, the Dutch could buy sugar at low prices and then sell it for a large profit on world markets. The Europeans demanded cash taxes, but the only way local people could obtain colonial currency was by working for Europeans or by growing cash crops for export. Thus, peasants became dependent on the sale of crops like sugar and coffee. Those who resisted, such as rebels on the Hindu-ruled island of Bali, were killed or sent into exile.

Meanwhile, the tactic of the United States was occupation. Hawaii was a monarchy with a constitution that blended indigenous elements with imported ones, such as an elected legislature and limits on executive power. Americans with business interests in Hawaii such as Sanford B. Dole, a pineapple planter, worked with missionaries to lead a coup against Hawaii's **Queen Liliuokalani** (leelee-ookah-LAHNI). President Benjamin Harrison justified the overthrow of the queen saying, "It is quite evident that the monarchy had become effete [ineffective] and the Queen's Government so weak and inadequate as to be the prey of . . . unscrupulous [immoral] persons." He claimed that annexing Hawaii was "highly promotive of the best interests of the Hawaiian people" and was the only way to "adequately secure the interests of the United States." Writing from the Iolani Palace in Honolulu, where she was kept under house arrest, Queen Liliuokalani wrote: "It was the intention of the officers of the government to humiliate me by imprisoning me, but my spirit rose above that. I was a martyr to the cause of my people and was proud of it."

As you have read, the United States occupied the Philippines after the Spanish-American War. Initially, the Filipinos believed that the United States would grant them independence. However, when that did

American author Mark Twain and British author Rudyard Kipling were on opposite sides of the debate as to the motivations behind imperialism. Twain wondered what the United States' true purpose was. Kipling felt the Americans had a duty to continue the spread of "civilization."

PRIMARY SOURCE

[I] have seen that we do not intend to free, but to subjugate the people of the Philippines. We have gone there to conquer, not to redeem. . .

It should, it seems to me, be our pleasure and duty to make those people free and let them deal with their own domestic questions in their own way.

—Mark Twain, from the *New York Herald*, October 15, 1900

Take up the White Man's burden—
Send forth the best ye breed—
Go bind your sons to exile
To serve your captives' need;
To wait in heavy harness,
On fluttered folk and wild—
Your new-caught sullen peoples,
Half-devil and half-child.

—Rudyard Kipling, from "The White Man's Burden," 1899

not happen, Filipino revolutionaries led by **Emilio Aguinaldo** took up arms in a guerrilla war against the U.S. Army. Over 20,000 Filipino combatants were killed and 200,000 Filipino civilians died from violence, disease, or famine.

DEBATE OVER IMPERIAL AMBITIONS

Some Americans protested that waging war against people who were fighting for independence was contrary to American principles. The writer Mark Twain joined the Anti-Imperialist League, declaring that American involvement in the Philippines was impure and motivated by economic greed. Commenting on the Americans' use of torture against Filipinos, the American journalist and explorer George Kennan wrote: ". . . to resort to inquisitorial methods [torture], and use them without discrimination, is unworthy of us and will recoil [backfire] on us as a nation."

Observing the debate in America, the British poet Rudyard Kipling urged the United States to shoulder its imperial responsibilities after it took over the Philippines. He worried that the British Empire was in decline and that only an imperialistic United States could save the world for "Anglo-Saxon civilization."

HISTORICAL THINKING

1. **READING CHECK** Describe some of the tactics that Europeans used to suppress resistance to their control of Southeast Asia.

2. **EVALUATE** How effective do you think the French tactic of pacification was in winning support in French Indochina?

3. **ANALYZE POINTS OF VIEW** What different viewpoints did Twain and Kipling have regarding the occupation of the Philippines? How do you think the Filipinos felt about the occupation?

PLAN: 2-PAGE LESSON

OBJECTIVE
Identify how imperial powers used a number of tactics to control their colonies but not without controversy at home.

CRITICAL THINKING SKILLS FOR LESSON 2.2
- Evaluate
- Analyze Points of View
- Compare and Contrast
- Explain
- Analyze Visuals

HISTORICAL THINKING FOR CHAPTER 24
How did imperialism affect the economic, political, and cultural life of subjugated peoples?

Despite similar interests in global expansion, imperial powers utilized different control strategies in Southeast Asia. Lesson 2.2 discusses the differences between how European powers and the United States attempted to control their colonies.

BACKGROUND FOR THE TEACHER
The Anti-Imperialist League Although the majority of Americans supported American imperialism abroad, a significant minority, which included such noteworthy citizens as Mark Twain and Andrew Carnegie, were staunchly opposed to the practice. Spurred to action by the Philippine-American War in 1899, a group of Americans founded the Anti-Imperialist League, an organization dedicated to protesting American imperialism. The Anti-Imperialist League believed that the goal of imperialism was not to benefit the lands that were occupied by the United States, but rather to exploit and profit from them while impeding on the liberty of colonized people. They also stated that imperialist tactics were in direct opposition to the values that the United States was founded upon and that were solidified in the Declaration of Independence and Constitution.

Student eEdition   online
Additional content for this lesson, including a photograph, is available online.

INTRODUCE & ENGAGE

DISCUSS THE RATIONALE BEHIND IMPERIALISM

Lead students in brainstorming reasons why and how a government might try to expand its global control. Record students' responses and then prompt a discussion with the following questions: Under what circumstances might a government try to gain control over another group of people? What tactics could a government use to expand an empire? Tell students that in this lesson they will learn about the different imperial tactics used by several European powers and the United States.

TEACH

GUIDED DISCUSSION

1. **Compare and Contrast** How did the imperial tactics of the British differ from those of the Dutch? *(Possible response: The British sought to pit different native groups against one another, while the Dutch used economic means to subjugate native peoples.)*

2. **Explain** Why, as a British citizen, was Rudyard Kipling concerned about the United States' role in global imperialism? *(Kipling thought that the British Empire was in decline and that the United States should continue a fight for Anglo-Saxon global dominance.)*

ANALYZE VISUALS

Direct students to the photograph of the steam locomotive (available in the Student eEdition). **ASK:** Based on this image, what do you think the locomotive represented to the French people? *(Possible response: progress, economic success, and global expansion)* What do you think it represented to native people? *(Possible response: It represented increased access to resources but also subjugation.)*

ACTIVE OPTIONS

On Your Feet: Three-Step Interview Direct students' attention to the primary sources written by Mark Twain and Rudyard Kipling. Then organize students into pairs and tell Student A to interview Student B about Mark Twain's stance on imperialism. Then instruct partners to reverse roles, with Student B interviewing Student A about Rudyard Kipling's beliefs about imperialism. After pairs finish their interviews, invite Student A to share student B's responses with the class and Student B to share Student A's responses.

> **NG Learning Framework: Debate Imperialist Strategies**
> **ATTITUDE** Responsibility
> **SKILL** Communication

Organize students into groups of four, and assign one of the following roles to each student in each group: indigenous person, British citizen, French citizen, and Dutch citizen. Within each group, have students debate the merits and disadvantages of the three imperialist powers' approaches to colonization. Students who are in the indigenous role should focus on the ways in which these strategies affect native communities and can advocate for independence as an option. Allow students time to conduct online research before debating one another.

DIFFERENTIATE

INCLUSION

Highlight and Paraphrase Give each student with learning or perception issues a handout of the primary source excerpts. Pair these students with strong readers to highlight important words and ideas. Then ask pairs to write in their own words a sentence that summarizes each document's main idea.

PRE-AP

Write a Biographical Essay Direct students to research how Queen Liliuokalani resisted U.S. control of the Hawaiian Islands. Tell students to form a thesis and provide evidence and reasoning to support that thesis in a biographical essay about Queen Liliuokalani.

See the Chapter Planner for more strategies for differentiation.

HISTORICAL THINKING

ANSWERS

1. The French used pacification to try to win support from people while killing others who were hostile toward them. The British searched for new leaders that they could officially recognize if the existing leader of a sultanate refused to follow British guidance. This divided the people, creating rivalries. The Dutch used coercion to force farmers to grow cash crops.

2. Answers will vary.

3. Possible response: Many Americans probably supported imperialism because it would benefit the country economically, and they may have thought that the governments of the countries were too weak to control themselves. Others believed it was oppressive and greedy. Kipling suggested that it was a duty because it would save the colonized people from their "wild" ways. Filipinos must have been upset to be passed from one imperial power to the next.

2.3 A Global Commodity: Rubber

European explorers brought samples of rubber back from the Americas after marveling at the elastic balls Native American players bounced off their hips in a ritual game. The ancient Olmec of Mesoamerica—sometimes called "the rubber people"—were probably the first to make rubber using latex, a sticky, milky sap found in some plants and trees, more than 3,000 years ago. The substance was dubbed *rubber* in 1770 by British scientist Joseph Priestly after he discovered it could be used as an eraser to rub out pencil marks on paper.

In the 1840s, the American chemist Charles Goodyear found that heating rubber, in a process he called *vulcanization*, allowed it to remain elastic in extreme temperatures. His discovery helped fuel the new industrial age, with rubber in great demand for tires. So-called rubber barons in Brazil, the main source of rubber at that time, stepped up production by making indigenous peoples toil in the Amazon jungles. But Brazil's rubber boom would be short-lived. In the early 1900s, Southeast Asia, with its cheaper supplies of rubber, came to dominate the market.

How did rubber help promote imperialism?

WHERE THE RUBBER MEETS THE ROAD
From rubber bands to wetsuits to tires, rubber is an incredibly useful commodity. Natural rubber starts with latex, the white sap you can see in this photo. Workers harvest latex by cutting slits in the bark of a rubber tree and collecting the sap in cups. The chemicals in latex allow the substance to stretch and snap back. About 90 percent of natural rubber is obtained from a tree called *Hevea brasiliensis*, commonly known as the rubber tree. Other plants, including dandelions, produce latex, but you'd need to grow an awful lot of the weeds to satisfy the world's demand for rubber.

PLAN: 4-PAGE LESSON

OBJECTIVE
Explain the history of the rubber industry and its impact on subjugated peoples.

CRITICAL THINKING SKILLS FOR LESSON 2.3
- Analyze Visuals
- Make Connections
- Identify
- Compare and Contrast
- Draw Conclusions
- Interpret Charts

HISTORICAL THINKING FOR CHAPTER 24
How did imperialism affect the economic, political, and cultural life of subjugated peoples?

Imperialists often forced subjugated peoples to work on plantations, such as rubber plantations in Southeast Asia. Lesson 2.3 discusses the rubber industry and its impact on indigenous peoples.

Student eEdition online
Additional content for this lesson, including photos and captions, is available online.

BACKGROUND FOR THE TEACHER
Amazonian Rubber In the 1800s, the Brazilian government granted land concessions in the Amazon, which were controlled by wealthy rubber barons. To control their lands and reap profits, rubber barons commissioned their own private armies to acquire land and laborers. Indigenous peoples were captured and forced to collect latex in the rain forest. Thousands of men, women, and children were murdered if they failed to meet their quota or if they rebelled. Barons were known to enslave and impregnate women to build their labor force. As a result of the brutal treatment and the introduction of foreign disease, native peoples perished rapidly. Many fled to the forests to escape the violence. Despite the atrocities, rubber production soared. Although slavery had been abolished in Brazil toward the end of the 1800s and the Brazilian rubber boom came to an end, production of rubber and mistreatment of indigenous laborers persisted in South America through the mid-20th century. While no longer slaves, some laborers were indebted to landowners or bosses.

History Notebook
Encourage students to complete the "Rubber" Global Commodity page for Chapter 24 in their History Notebooks as they read.

INTRODUCE & ENGAGE

PREVIEW THE TOPIC

Write the word *rubber* on the board and invite students to provide examples of products made from rubber. Students may supply examples from the classroom, such as erasers, shoe soles, raincoats, electric cables, and rubber bands, or from outside the classroom, such as tires, surgical gloves, and balloons. Discuss what students already know about rubber, including its uses, history, and production.

TEACH

GUIDED DISCUSSION

1. **Identify** How is latex obtained? *(by cutting slits in the bark of a rubber tree and collecting the sap)*

2. **Compare and Contrast** Based on the information in the lesson and in the Student eEdition, why was rubber production in Southeast Asia more efficient than in Brazil? *(Rubber was harvested from wild trees in the rain forests in Brazil; whereas farmers in Southeast Asia raised rubber trees on plantations. Having easier access to trees on a plantation makes production more efficient.)*

A GLOBAL COMMODITY

The wide dispersion of trees in rain forests is an adaptation to protect them from diseases. Wild rubber trees are no exception. When planted close together on plantations, *Hevea* trees are at an increased susceptibility to South American leaf blight, which spreads quickly and can decimate the entire plantation. Trees in Southeast Asia and other parts of the world have no resistance to the fungus. Trees and the rubber industry are so vulnerable to leaf blight that the introduction of minuscule spores could destroy plantations and halt production for at least a decade. The risk of the disease spreading to other countries is increased with air travel between tropical regions. There is also concern that dissemination of the disease could someday be an act of biological terrorism.

DIFFERENTIATE

STRIVING READERS

Record and Compare Facts After reading the lesson, ask students to write three important facts they learned about rubber. Allow groups of students to compare and check their facts and then combine their facts into one longer list. Ask a volunteer from each group to write the most important fact from each group's list.

PRE-AP

Write a Business Plan Ask students to imagine that they are the owner of a medical-supply factory. They are currently experiencing a shortage of rubber needed to produce their supplies. Have students research both natural and synthetic rubber and decide which would be best for their products. Then have them write a brief plan describing what source they will use to obtain the rubber, why their chosen type of rubber is the best option, and how they will solve specific problems that may arise from changing suppliers. Encourage students to present their business plans to the class or share them on a class website.

See the Chapter Planner for more strategies for differentiation.

RUBBER AT A GLANCE

USES	• More than half of all natural and synthetic rubber is used in tires for cars and other vehicles	• Rubber goes into industrial parts, including tubes, hoses, belts, and gaskets.	• Consumer goods, such as toys, shoes, furniture, and medical gloves, contain rubber.
PRODUCTION	• Natural rubber is most often harvested by tapping rubber trees and extracting their latex.	• To produce commercial rubber, the latex is dried, rolled, mixed with chemicals, and vulcanized.	• To produce synthetic rubber, oil is first processed in a refinery and then treated in a rubber plant.
HISTORY	• In 1876, English explorer Henry Wickham collected thousands of rubber tree seeds in Brazil to cultivate and plant in Southeast Asia.	• In the 1890s, Leopold II of Belgium forced Africans in the Congo Free State to harvest rubber, resulting in the deaths of 10 million people.	• During World War II, the demand for rubber led scientists to develop synthetic rubber that could be produced cost-effectively.
VALUE	• Wickham was paid about $1,000 for the Brazilian rubber tree seeds he took—some say stole—from Brazil.	• The price of rubber fell sharply after the low-cost rubber from plantations in Southeast Asia flooded world markets.	• By 2017, big increases in rubber supplies caused the price of rubber to drop to less than one U.S. dollar per pound.
ECONOMICS	• During the rubber boom in the late 1800s, Manaus, Brazil, grew from a small Amazon River town to a wealthy center of commerce.	• In 1855, Brazil exported about 2,100 tons of rubber; by 1879, Brazilian exports of rubber rose to about 10,000 tons.	• Synthetic rubber came to dominate the U.S. rubber market until an oil embargo in 1973 doubled its price.

RUBBER FACTORY

Workers at a rubber factory in Africa's Ivory Coast select dried latex to use in the production of finished rubber products. The latex has been set in a heated mold, which helps vulcanize the material. Charles Goodyear named the process after Vulcan, the ancient Roman god of fire. Ivory Coast was the first African country to grow rubber and is the continent's top producer of the commodity. However, since 2011, falling natural rubber prices have sharply reduced the profits for many Ivory Coast rubber farmers.

RUBBER TIRES

Most rubber today—both natural and synthetic—is used in the production of tires. But manufacturers made tires for bicycles first. Before rubber, bike tires were wooden and covered by bands of leather or metal. Scotsman John Dunlop developed the first type of rubber tire. After World War II cut off U.S. access to most of the rubber supply from Southeast Asia, Americans held rubber drives to support the war effort. People brought items such as old tires, boots, and raincoats to the drives and received a penny per pound.

BACKGROUND FOR THE TEACHER

Forced Labor in the Congo King Leopold II of Belgium claimed a large territory in Africa—the size of the present-day Democratic Republic of the Congo—as his own. In the Congo Free State, Leopold first made a fortune from ivory, but then he discovered the value of rubber. Wild rubber grown on *Landolphia* vines was plentiful in the Central African rain forest. Leopold commissioned his 19,000-man private army into villages to lock women in cages and force men into the forests to gather a monthly quota of wild rubber. Vines were quickly drained and the men were forced to walk days or weeks to find new vines to meet the quota needed to free their wives and daughters. This search for rubber left few able-bodied adults for hunting, fishing, and farming, and millions suffered famine and increased susceptibility to disease. The tens to hundreds of thousands of people who fled in an attempt to avoid forced labor found little food and shelter in the rain forests.

Although other countries, such as France, Germany, and Portugal, used forced labor for gathering rubber with similar fatalities for more than a century, the brutality of Leopold's army made his reign the most notorious. When quotas were not met or rebellions arose, his army shot tens of thousands of people. To prove the bullets had not been wasted, Leopold's soldiers were required to produce the severed hands of their victims to their officers. To protect themselves after missing a shot or hunting, soldiers at times cut a hand from a living victim to present to their officers for any bullets expended. The hands were exchanged for cash rewards. With nearly 50 percent of the Congo population perishing and fleeing, the results of Leopold's forced labor alone were catastrophic.

TEACH

GUIDED DISCUSSION

3. **Identify** Based on information in the lesson and in the Student eEdition, what countries are the leading producers of natural rubber today? *(Thailand, Indonesia, and Malaysia)*

4. **Draw Conclusions** What items could be recycled in the event of a rubber shortage? *(Answers will vary. Possible responses from the lesson: tires, boots, raincoats, wires, rubber bands, gloves, wetsuits, balloons, erasers, tubes, hoses, belts, gaskets)*

INTERPRET CHARTS

Direct students to the chart in the lesson. **ASK:** Why was synthetic rubber developed? *(because the demand for rubber was so high and a more cost-effective method of producing it was needed)* What is necessary for the production of synthetic rubber? *(oil)* What caused the price of synthetic rubber to double? *(an oil embargo in 1973)*

ACTIVE OPTION

NG Learning Framework: Create an Infographic
ATTITUDE Curiosity
SKILLS Communication, Collaboration

Instruct partners to use information from the lesson and from additional research to create an infographic depicting the steps of processing rubber and turning it into a product, such as a tire or a glove. Direct students to work together to draw or use photos to illustrate each step and to write a detailed explanation of each step. Encourage pairs to share their infographics with the class.

Adaptation and Resistance to Empire

Would you believe a peace treaty if it were written in another language? What if it were translated to your language, too? The Ethiopians believed the Italians had accurately translated the articles of a treaty, only to learn that their translation did not match the Italian treaty.

ENDURING MONARCHIES

While European countries used their overwhelming strength to exert domination over Africa and Southeast Asia, Ethiopia and Siam retained their independence. Both countries used skillful diplomatic maneuvering to take advantage of inter-European rivalries.

You have read about the ancient Christian kingdom of Ethiopia. It first met modern European firepower in 1868 when a British relief team rescued several British subjects held hostage by the Ethiopian king. The British easily crushed the Ethiopian army but did not stay to occupy the land. The "scramble for Africa" had not yet begun.

King **Menelik II** desired to strengthen his state against further attack. He consolidated power at the imperial court, created his own standing army, and imported the latest firearms from Europe. Through military conquests, he doubled the size of Ethiopia and moved the capital to new lands in the south. He also introduced land reforms allowing males and females of any social class the right to inherit land.

In 1896, Italy attacked Ethiopia at the Battle of Adowa. Although Italy took the region of Eritrea on the Red Sea, the Ethiopians held out against the Italians. As a Christian, Menelik was able to gain diplomatic influence in Europe. He also played European powers against one another to Ethiopia's advantage. Menelik convinced Britain, the dominant power in northeastern

Africa, that Ethiopia would provide security along the Egyptian border and allow European traders free access into Ethiopia. Permitting Menelik to retain his reign was a cheaper solution than occupying Ethiopia by force. Instead, the British and the French sponsored the development of banks and railroads in Ethiopia.

Simultaneously, the kings of Siam also faced the danger of European imperialism. The British expanded from India in the west and the French threatened from Indochina in the east. But two kings whom you read about earlier, Mongkut and his son Chulalongkorn, secured Siam's independence using internal reform and diplomatic engagement.

King Menelik II used diplomacy and military reorganization to retain Ethiopian independence, defeating an Italian army at the Battle of Adowa in 1896.

You may recall that, Mongkut invited Westerners to his capital and installed them as advisors. Though he favored the British, he had French and Dutch advisors, too. He also opened Siam to foreign trade, giving merchants from various countries a stake in his system.

When Chulalongkorn came to power in 1868, he appointed Siamese advisors who understood that their independence depended on reforms and diplomacy. As you already learned, Chulalongkorn gave up Laos to the French to protect his core kingdom. This action satisfied the French and the British, who understood that Siam would continue to welcome Europeans and provide security. In 1896, the French and British agreed to recognize the independence of Siam.

IDEAS FOR AND AGAINST EMPIRE

The territorial acquisitions of the New Imperialism continued into the Pacific. Japan annexed Okinawa in 1879. Germany took New Guinea in 1899, and in the same year Samoa was divided between Germany and the United States. In 1900, the French combined their island claims in the Pacific to establish French Polynesia. By 1900, there were no more unclaimed territories on which to plant the flag of empire.

The continuation of imperialism was driven by Social Darwinism, which you learned is the idea that racial groups are naturally arranged along a hierarchy and that white people sit on top of that hierarchy. This philosophy (since rejected) had become conventional wisdom in Europe, something that people simply believed without question, fueling colonial expansion as part of the natural order of things.

Meanwhile, nationalist movements among colonized people were growing all across Africa and Asia. Wealthy, Western-educated Indians formed the **Indian National Congress** to organize for self-rule under the British Empire. Other Indian nationalists called for an end to British rule altogether.

In Africa, religion often played a role in anti-colonial resistance. As you know, in the Sahel region of West Africa, Islam was well-established. Here guerrilla leader Samori Toure (sam-or-REE too-RAY) used the doctrine of jihad—"struggle"—to organize a long resistance to French invasion. Resistance to empire

could also be found among the many Africans who converted to Christianity at this time. Some rejected European religious authority, breaking away from missionary groups and founding their own Protestant denominations, often blending African culture into their Christian worship.

Nationalist movements grew in Africa when educated and highly trained Africans were denied leading positions due to colonial racism. Some organized for greater rights within their own colonies, while others joined with people of African descent from around the word to support **Pan-Africanism**, which stressed the need for solidarity to overcome the inequalities in treatment of black people everywhere.

As anti-colonial nationalism campaigns grew, the flags of empire crowded against each other across the world. As you will read, inter-European competition led the colonial powers to turn their deadly weapons against one another, simultaneously drawing the world's peoples into their devastating conflicts.

Chulalongkorn, shown here with his son in 1890, used diplomacy to maintain the independence of Siam during the height of the European scramble for colonial territory.

HISTORICAL THINKING

1. **READING CHECK** How did Ethiopia and Siam retain their independence?

2. **COMPARE AND CONTRAST** How were the actions of Menelik II and the kings of Siam similar? How were they different?

3. **MAKE PREDICTIONS** What problems will following the ideas of Social Darwinism create for the future of the people during this time period?

PLAN: 2-PAGE LESSON

OBJECTIVE

Explain how through diplomatic skill and reform the rulers of Ethiopia and Siam were able to maintain independence while imperialist powers occupied even more areas of the world.

CRITICAL THINKING SKILLS FOR LESSON 2.4

- Compare and Contrast
- Make Predictions
- Identify Supporting Details
- Analyze Cause and Effect
- Analyze Visuals

HISTORICAL THINKING FOR CHAPTER 24

How did imperialism affect the economic, political, and cultural life of subjugated peoples?

As European imperial powers swept up lands in Africa and Asia, two significant kingdoms evaded colonization. Lesson 2.4 discusses the similarities and differences between Ethiopia's and Siam's relationships with Europeans.

BACKGROUND FOR THE TEACHER

Samori Toure Samori Toure grew up to become a trader and then, when he was in his twenties, acquired military skills with the explicit purpose of freeing his mother, who had been captured. Toure participated in military campaigns for several leaders, refining the skills he would need when he eventually founded his own kingdom in what is now Gambia. At the height of his empire in the 1880s, it extended as far north as Mali, to the southern coast of western Africa, and to the eastern border with the Sudan. When the French invaded western Africa, Toure first fought them off with his military prowess and then managed to negotiate peace treaties with the French government. However, as the French pressed on even after treaties had been reached, Toure and his people were forced to move to the east. In 1889, Toure once again fell into conflict with the French, and due to difficulties from a famine in his country, he was captured and sent into exile.

Student eEdition online

Additional content for this lesson, including a photograph, is available online.

INTRODUCE & ENGAGE

DISCUSS INDEPENDENCE AS A CONCEPT

Prompt students to discuss independence as a concept. Begin by writing the word in the center of a Concept Cluster, and add students' ideas to the cluster during the classroom discussion. Ask students to consider reasons why a person or group would want to be independent and what they would gain or lose as a consequence. Tell students that in this lesson they will learn about two societies, Ethiopia in Africa and Siam in Southeast Asia, both of which maintained their independence during the global imperialist period.

TEACH

GUIDED DISCUSSION

1. **Identify Supporting Details** How did King Menelik II strengthen Ethiopia? *(He conquered neighboring lands to increase the size of Ethiopia and expanded the ability of the Ethiopian people to own land. He also imported firearms from Europe.)*

2. **Analyze Cause and Effect** What happened when educated Africans were denied positions of authority in their own lands? *(African nationalist movements rose as Africans stood up in opposition to racism.)*

ANALYZE VISUALS

Direct students to the photograph of the first Indian National Congress (available in the Student eEdition). **ASK:** What can you infer about the congress session based on the photograph? *(Possible response: The first session was well-attended by male delegates. Women were not included in the process of organizing against British rule.)*

ACTIVE OPTIONS

On Your Feet: Roundtable Organize students in groups of four. Ask them to consider how maintaining independence from colonial rule benefited the Siamese people, both during the imperial era and up until the present day. Tell each student in the group to answer the question in a different way.

> **NG Learning Framework: Create a Presentation on Contemporary Pan-Africanism**
> **ATTITUDE** Curiosity
> **KNOWLEDGE** Our Human Story

Instruct students to conduct online research on contemporary Pan-Africanism. Encourage students to focus on the issues that Pan-Africanism seeks to improve today as well as its focus on celebrating African culture and heritage. Then direct students to use what they have learned to create a presentation that includes visuals, such as a poster or a digital multimedia presentation, and share it with the class.

DIFFERENTIATE

STRIVING READERS

Complete a Venn Diagram Tell students to take notes in a Venn diagram about the similarities and differences between Ethiopia's and Siam's successful resistance to colonialism. Then ask pairs to discuss the ways Ethiopia and Siam secured resources from Europeans, played Europeans against one another, and negotiated instead of fighting a war.

PRE-AP

Extend Knowledge Prompt students to research the philosophy of the African-American leader W.E.B. Du Bois and his support of Pan-Africanism. Ask them to quote or paraphrase and cite primary and secondary sources and share their findings in an oral or written report.

See the Chapter Planner for more strategies for differentiation.

HISTORICAL THINKING

ANSWERS

1. Ethiopia: convinced the British that they could provide protection at the Egyptian border and allow Europeans easy access through their lands; Siam: welcomed Europeans into their government as advisors, gave up Laos to France, were willing to work with Europeans, offered to be a buffer between French and British lands

2. Similar: implemented reforms and worked European powers against each other to their advantage; gave up some of their land to Europeans and presented their countries as buffers; Different: Menelik II was militarily formidable and grew his country through military conquests; kings of Siam kept their country small

3. The belief of racial superiority will become one of the greatest issues of the 20th century and continue into the 21st century. It will lead to genocide and equality movements.

24 REVIEW

VOCABULARY

Match each vocabulary word with its definition.

1. coercion
2. imperialism
3. genocide
4. magnate
5. sphere of influence
6. Boer
7. concentration camp
8. subjugation
9. guerrilla warfare
10. Pan-Africanism

a. a Dutch or French settler in South Africa

b. the practice by which a country gains control over other areas of the world

c. the idea that people of African descent should be unified

d. small-scale surprise attacks

e. the state of being under control or governance

f. a place where large numbers of people are imprisoned

g. the systematic destruction of a racial or cultural group

h. an area in which the dominance of one power is recognized above all others

i. the use of force or threats

j. a wealthy, powerful, and influential businessperson

READING STRATEGY
SYNTHESIZE

When you synthesize, you use evidence and explanations from the text along with prior knowledge to form an overall understanding. Use the chart below to help you synthesize the information presented in this chapter. Then answer the question.

The New Imperialism

| Evidence: | Supporting Explanation: | Synthesis: |

11. What were the motives that drove the New Imperialism?

MAIN IDEAS

Answer the following questions. Support your answers with evidence from the chapter.

12. What motivated King Khama and his neighboring kings to travel to London? LESSON 1.1

13. Why were Europeans so successful in colonizing Africa? LESSON 1.2

14. Which two groups of people fought in the South African War? LESSON 1.3

15. Which European countries colonized Southeast Asia? LESSON 2.1

16. What controversy did the United States face when it took control of the Philippines? LESSON 2.2

17. What skills did Emperor Menelik II and kings Mongkut and Chulalongkorn employ to keep their countries free of imperialist control? LESSON 2.4

HISTORICAL THINKING

Answer the following questions. Support your answers with evidence from the chapter.

18. ANALYZE POINT OF VIEW How did Europeans' opinions of their own cultures and religions, and those of Africa and Asia contribute to imperialism?

19. SYNTHESIZE What was the role of transportation technology in initiating and advancing imperialism in Africa, Latin America, and Southeast Asia?

20. ANALYZE CAUSE AND EFFECTS Analyze the causes of the New Imperialism and its effects on indigenous peoples.

21. MAKE PREDICTIONS What effect will imperialism have on the world into the 20th and 21st centuries?

INTERPRET VISUALS

Study the 1884 French political cartoon at right, which shows Otto von Bismarck of Germany preparing to cut into a cake. Then answer the questions that follow.

22. What event does this political cartoon depict?

23. What do the expressions of the men at the table convey about what is happening?

ANALYZE SOURCES

In 1897, the king of Ethiopia, Menelik II, wrote a letter to his neighbor, the caliph of Sudan. Read the excerpt below from that letter and answer the questions.

This is to inform you that the Europeans who are present round the White Nile with the English . . . intended to enter between my country and yours and to separate and divide us. . . . I have ordered my troops to advance towards the White Nile. . . . And you look to yourself, and do not let the Europeans enter between us. Be strong, lest if the Europeans enter our midst a great disaster befall us and our children have no rest. And if one of the Europeans comes to you as a traveler, do your utmost to send him away in peace; and do not listen to rumors against me. All my intention is to increase my friendship with you, and that our countries may be protected from enemies.

24. What is King Menelik's opinion of Europeans?

25. What is his purpose for writing this letter?

CONNECT TO YOUR LIFE

26. EXPLANATORY Nationalism, or the belief that people are bound through identification with a certain nation, was a driver of imperialism as well as of resistance to imperialism and growing independence movements. Write a short paragraph describing how you see nationalism affecting the world or a part of the world today. Do you think nationalism is a positive force? Explain why or why not.

TIPS

- List examples of nationalism you see in today's world. Do additional online research if you need to understand the causes and effects of the examples you think of.

- Decide whether the examples you've chosen have a positive or negative impact by evaluating the ways in which they affect those who are part of the nationalist movement and those who are not part of it.

- State your main idea at the beginning of the paragraph.

- Provide a concluding sentence that summarizes your views about nationalism and its impact.

VOCABULARY ANSWERS

1. i
2. b
3. g
4. j
5. h
6. a
7. f
8. e
9. d
10. c

READING STRATEGY ANSWER

The New Imperialism

Evidence:	Supporting Explanation:	Synthesis:
"agents brutalized the indigenous people" "armed force and torture" "cavalry forces on horseback were no match for machine guns and British cannons..." "Over 20,000 Filipino combatants were killed" "concentration camps" "about 75 percent of the Herero population died"	Europeans acquired land, raw materials, and labor through violence and brutality toward indigenous people.	The New Imperialism was catastrophic for indigenous peoples across the world.

11. European powers were motivated by the desire for raw materials to fuel their growing industrial economies. They were also driven by concepts of national glory and competition with other European powers (and the United States and Japan). They justified their imperial efforts with appeals to religious and humanitarian ideals that were founded on Social Darwinist beliefs that white Europeans had a superior culture and intelligence and thus were entitled to "help" others. The white Europeans also believed they were entitled to lower cultures' land and resources.

MAIN IDEAS ANSWERS

12. They hoped to convince the British that their lands should become a protectorate rather than become part of South Africa.

13. They used machine guns and new communication technologies that Africans did not yet possess.

14. The groups were Dutch and French Boers, who had settled South Africa much earlier, and the British, who were newer to the area.

15. France took control of Indochina. The Netherlands controlled Indonesia and many islands. The British controlled Burma, Singapore, and Malaya.

16. Many Americans thought it was wrong to occupy a country that was seeking independence. Others believed that becoming an imperialist power was a necessary burden.

17. They used diplomatic skills in welcoming Europeans and political skills such as reforming their own countries. They also manipulated European rivalries to their advantage.

HISTORICAL THINKING ANSWERS

18. Many Europeans saw their cultures and religions as superior to African and Asian cultures and religions. They believed that imperialism served to "civilize" or "save" the people of Africa and Asia. Imperialist countries also felt the need to flex their patriotic muscle to compete with other imperialists. They used these beliefs as justification for imperialism.

19. In Africa, the use of steamships allowed Europeans to travel deeper into Africa through rivers. Railroads in Africa and Latin America allowed for easier transportation of people and raw materials from the interiors of the continents to the coasts where they could be shipped. The Suez and Panama canals provided shipping routes through the Americas and Africa. Control of the Strait of Malacca and Singapore allowed Europeans to control shipping through Southeast Asia.

20. The Second Industrial Revolution was a major cause of the New Imperialism. Industrialized nations needed additional raw materials, including rubber and oil. Another cause was both economic and political competition among industrial powers. Germany was becoming a strong competitor for Britain, and France was feeling degraded by defeat from Germany. The effects on indigenous people were devastating. European powers took control of nearly all of Africa and Southeast Asia.

In the process, indigenous people were forced to work for low wages and to produce products for Europeans that did not help indigenous people with self-sufficiency. Europeans killed people who resisted their advances, and in some cases genocide or labor abuses killed off large sectors of the population.

21. People will seek independence. Nationalist movements will continue, and indigenous people will seek new ways of fighting, including more guerilla warfare. Some countries will become communist or socialist as a response to economic exploitation.

INTERPRET VISUALS ANSWERS

22. the Berlin Conference

23. The men represent European countries. Their expressions convey a strong interest in how Africa will be divided among the different imperialist powers.

ANALYZE SOURCES ANSWERS

24. He considers the Europeans to be enemies and a threat to both his country and Sudan.

25. He is writing to warn the caliph of Sudan of the European plan to divide and conquer. He hopes to confront the Europeans with a unified front between the two countries.

CONNECT TO YOUR LIFE ANSWER

26. Answers will vary.

Awash in Plastic

BY LAURA PARKER Adapted from "Plastic" by Laura Parker,
National Geographic, June 2018

We made it. We depend on it. Now we're drowning in it

Although plastic was invented in the late 19th century, its production really only took off around 1950. A *Life* magazine article in 1955 celebrated the dawn of "Throwaway Living," in which American housewives would be liberated from drudgery, thanks in large part to disposable plastics. While single-use plastics have brought great convenience to people around the world, they also make up a big part of the plastic waste that's now choking our oceans. The growth of plastic production has far outstripped the ability of waste management to keep up, which is why the oceans are under assault. In 2013, a group of scientists, writing in *Nature* magazine, declared that disposable plastic should be classified not as a housewife's friend but as a hazardous material.

No one knows how much unrecycled plastic waste ends up in the ocean, Earth's last sink. In 2015, Jenna Jambeck, a University of Georgia engineering professor, caught everyone's attention with a rough estimate: between 5.3 million and 14 million tons each year just from coastal regions. Most of it isn't thrown off ships, she and her colleagues say, but is dumped carelessly on land or in rivers, mostly in Asia. It's then blown or washed into the sea. Imagine five plastic grocery bags stuffed with plastic trash, Jambeck says, sitting on every foot of coastline around the world—that would correspond to about 8.8 million tons, her middle-of-the-road estimate of what the oceans gets from such an annually. It's unclear how long it will take for that plastic to completely biodegrade into its constituent molecules. Estimates range from 450 years to never.

Meanwhile, ocean plastic is estimated to kill millions of marine animals every year. Nearly 700 species, including endangered ones, are known to have been affected by it. Some are harmed visibly—strangled by abandoned fishing nets or discarded six-pack rings. Many more are probably harmed invisibly. Marine species of all sizes, from zooplankton to whales, now eat microplastics, the

A Bangladeshi family removes labels from plastic bottles, sorting green from clear ones to sell to a scrap dealer.

bits smaller than one-fifth of an inch across. On Hawaii's Big Island, on a beach that seemingly should have been pristine—no paved roads lead to it—I walked ankle-deep through microplastics. They crunched like Rice Krispies under my feet. After that, I could understand why some people see ocean plastic as a looming catastrophe, worth mentioning in the same breath as climate change.

And yet there's a key difference: Ocean plastic is not as complicated as climate change. There are no ocean trash deniers, at least so far. To do something about it, we don't have to remake our planet's entire energy system.

"This isn't a problem where we don't know what the solution is," says Ted Siegler, a Vermont resource economist who has spent more than 25 years working with developing nations on garbage. "We know how to pick up garbage. Anyone can do it. We know how to dispose of it. We know how to recycle." It's a matter of building the necessary institutions and systems, he says—ideally before the ocean turns, irretrievably and for centuries to come, into a thin soup of plastic. ∎

Staging the Question

In this unit, you learned about the widespread changes that the Industrial Revolution brought to people's lives. With the increased production and consumption of manufactured goods, the Industrial Revolution brought a higher standard of living for many people. But it also introduced a host of environmental problems, including air pollution, water pollution, habitat destruction—and eventually climate change and a massive amount of plastic waste. The long-term impact of the Industrial Revolution can be seen around the world, from our crowded cities to the most remote ocean beaches. How can individuals today reduce the negative impact of the Industrial Revolution on our planet?

Supporting Questions: Begin by developing supporting questions to guide your thinking. For example: What aspects of the way I live and act have a negative impact on the environment? What is the negative effect of each action?

Summative Performance Task: Use the answers to your questions to create a sustainable living plan that identifies at least 10 actions individuals can take to help protect the environment. Describe each action to be taken and the positive effect it will have. You might use a graphic organizer like this one to develop your plan.

Present: Share your plan with the class. You might consider one of these options:

ASSIGNMENT

Identify some current environmental problems that stem from the Industrial Revolution.

Analyze the causes of these environmental problems.

Think of ways that individuals could help solve these problems by making changes in their lifestyles.

Create a plan identifying lifestyle changes that individuals today could make to help solve serious environmental problems.

Action	Effect

DISCUSS IN GROUPS

Form small groups and share your ideas. Then compile your group's ideas with those of other groups to create a master plan. Post the composite plan in the classroom.

MAKE A PODCAST

Work with classmates to create a podcast in which everyone shares their ideas on sustainable living. You might incorporate such elements as music, interviews, research, and storytelling.

Take Informed Action:

UNDERSTAND Recognize that people act out of habit much of the time but may change their habits for important reasons.

ASSESS Think about the reasons for protecting and preserving our natural resources. Ultimately, our lives and the lives of those who come after us depend on it.

ACT Choose at least one of the actions in your plan and incorporate it into your daily life. Then gradually make other changes.

NATIONAL GEOGRAPHIC CONNECTION

GUIDED DISCUSSION FOR "AWASH IN PLASTIC"

1. **Analyze Cause and Effect** What are the effects of plastic in the ocean? (*Plastic is killing millions of marine animals every year as marine species ingest bits of plastic and is causing the destruction of beaches around the world.*)

2. **Form and Support Opinions** Do you think plastic should be classified as a "hazardous material"? Explain your reasoning. (*Answers will vary. Possible responses: Yes, plastic harms marine life and is polluting the coastlines. OR No, people are the problem, not plastic, because people should reuse and recycle plastic and dispose of it properly.*)

History Notebook

Encourage students to complete the Unit Wrap-Up page for Unit 8 in their History Notebooks.

UNIT INQUIRY PROJECT RUBRIC

ASSESS

Use the rubric to assess each student's participation and performance.

SCORE	ASSIGNMENT	PRODUCT	PRESENTATION
3 GREAT	• Student thoroughly understands the assignment. • Student develops thoughtful supporting questions to guide research.	• Actions in the plan are well thought out and offer a variety of solutions. • The plan reflects all of the key elements listed in the assignment.	• Presentation is clear, concise, and logical. • Presentation is creative and engaging.
2 GOOD	• Student mostly understands the assignment. • Student develops somewhat thoughtful supporting questions to guide research.	• Actions in the plan are fairly well thought out with a variety of useful solutions. • The plan reflects most of the key elements listed in the assignment.	• Presentation is fairly clear, concise, and logical. • Presentation is somewhat creative and engaging.
1 NEEDS WORK	• Student does not understand the assignment. • Student does not develop thoughtful questions to guide research.	• Actions in the plan are not thought out and do not contain valuable solutions. • The plan reflects few or none of the key elements listed in the assignment.	• Presentation is not clear, concise, or logical. • Presentation is not creative or engaging.

INTRODUCE THE PHOTOGRAPH

BLOOD SWEPT LANDS AND SEAS OF RED AT THE TOWER OF LONDON

The *Blood Swept Lands and Seas of Red* art installation was created by artists Paul Cummins and Tom Piper. Ceramic artist Cummins conceived the idea when he came across the will of a soldier that described the bloody war landscape as "The blood-swept lands and seas of red, where angels fear to tread." Soldiers often drafted wills and carried them in their pocketbooks so they could be recovered and presented to their families if they died. The will that inspired Cummins was never delivered to the soldier's loved ones; his name remains unknown.

Cummins's team included many artists who had family members in the military and whose lives were touched by the display. Each poppy was handmade by Cummins and his team, who worked around the clock in shifts. Over 21,600 volunteers from across the world came together to install the poppies in the dry moat around the Tower of London.

The poppies, encircling the Tower, created a place for personal reflection. Each day at sunset, visitors gathered around the moat to hear the names of fallen soldiers read aloud. The names were nominated by members of the public on a first-come, first-serve basis weekly. Five million people visited the installation during the four months that it was on display. When it was disassembled, all of the poppies were sold to members of the public. The money raised—millions of British pounds—was divided evenly and donated to six charities.

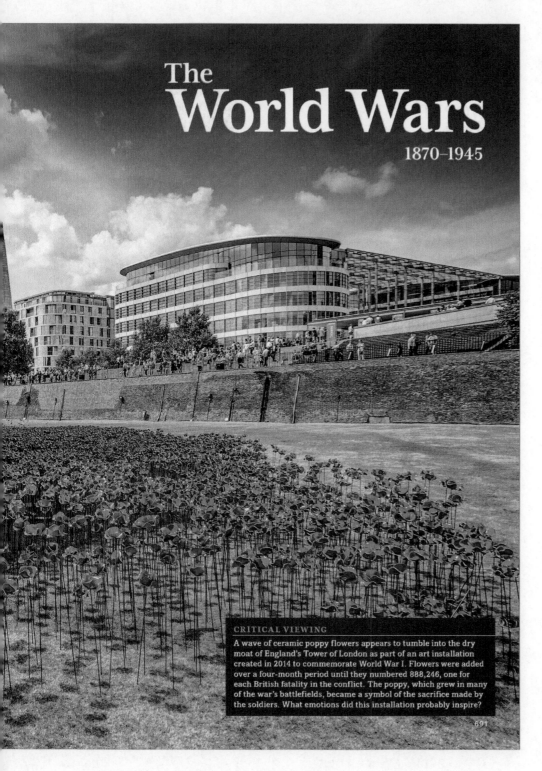

The World Wars
1870–1945

A wave of ceramic poppy flowers appears to tumble into the dry moat of England's Tower of London as part of an art installation created in 2014 to commemorate World War I. Flowers were added over a four-month period until they numbered 888,246, one for each British fatality in the conflict. The poppy, which grew in many of the war's battlefields, became a symbol of the sacrifice made by the soldiers. What emotions did this installation probably inspire?

691

Direct students' attention to the photograph. **ASK:** What illusion is created by the poppies on the trellis outside the window? *(the illusion of blood flowing)* Why is this significant? *(The display of red poppies flowing out of the window into the dried-up moat represents not only each life lost in World War I but also all of the blood that was shed during World War I.)*

CRITICAL VIEWING Possible response: The installation possibly inspired emotions such as sadness at the number of people who lost lives and gratitude toward those people who sacrificed themselves to protect their country.

IDENTIFY PATTERNS AND THEMES

Have volunteers read aloud each of the world events in the time line. **ASK:** What are some common themes or patterns that you notice with regard to these events? *(Possible responses: Some common themes or patterns include war, political conflicts, economic turmoil, and religious persecution.)* Sort the themes and patterns into categories and put them in a chart like the one shown here.

Themes and Patterns	Time Line Events	Lessons
War		
Political Conflicts		
Economic Turmoil		
Religious Persecution		

As students read the lessons for each chapter in the unit, have them add the lesson titles to the appropriate row(s) in the chart. Advise students that they may also add or revise categories as necessary. At the end of the unit, revisit students' charts and create a final list of categories to summarize the historical themes students encountered as they read each chapter.

UNIT 9 The World Wars

WORLD EVENTS
1914–1945

1914 EUROPE The assassination of Archduke Franz Ferdinand of Austria-Hungary sets off a chain of events leading directly to World War I. *(Italian newspaper artwork depicting the assassination)*

1917 EUROPE The Russian Revolution begins as revolutionaries overthrow the tsar and the Bolsheviks take control of the government. *(Soviet propaganda poster featuring Vladimir Lenin)*

1917 AMERICAS On April 6, the United States enters World War I after German U-boats sink three U.S. ships in one month.

1900 **1910** **1920**

1918 EUROPE On November 11, Germany signs the Armistice, ending World War I.

1929 AMERICAS The stock market crashes in October, marking the start of the Great Depression. *(unemployed men lined up outside a soup kitchen in Chicago in 1931)*

HISTORICAL THINKING

COMPARE AND CONTRAST What was similar about the decisions by the United States to enter the two world wars?

1945 ASIA In early August, the United States drops atomic bombs on Hiroshima and Nagasaki in Japan. *(replica of the "Little Boy" atomic bomb that dropped over Hiroshima)*

1938 EUROPE On *Kristallnacht*, Nazis destroy Jewish homes, businesses, and synagogues and force Jews into segregated ghettos. *(Jewish-owned shoe store destroyed by Nazis in Vienna, Austria)*

1939 EUROPE Germany invades Poland, causing Britain and France to declare war on Germany, beginning World War II.

1942 ASIA The United States wins an important victory over Japan at the Battle of Midway.

1945 EUROPE Germany surrenders on May 8, a day that becomes known as V-E Day. *(German military officials signing the document of surrender in Reims, France)*

1930   1940   1950

1933 EUROPE Adolf Hitler becomes chancellor of Germany.

Honolulu Star-Bulletin 1st EXTRA

WAR!
OAHU BOMBED BY JAPANESE PLANES

SIX KNOWN DEAD, 21 INJURED, AT EMERGENCY HOSPITAL

SAN FRANCISCO, Dec. 7.—President Roosevelt announced this morning that Japanese planes had attacked Manila and Pearl Harbor.

1941 AMERICAS On December 7, the Japanese attack Pearl Harbor, drawing the United States into the war. *(front page of a special edition of the Honolulu Star Bulletin on December 7, 1941)*

1944 EUROPE Germany launches its last major offensive of the war in the Battle of the Bulge but is forced to retreat.

1944 EUROPE On June 6 (D-Day), American, British, and Canadian troops storm German-occupied beaches at Normandy on the coast of France.

1945 ASIA On September 2 (V-J Day) Japan officially surrenders, ending World War II. *(people celebrating V-J Day in Times Square in New York City)*

693

HISTORICAL THINKING

Compare and Contrast

Possible response: In each case, the United States declared war after an attack was made that directly affected the nation.

Student eEdition online

Additional content, including the unit map and Global Perspective feature, is available online.

STRIVING READERS

STRATEGY ❶
Create Idea Webs
Prompt students to summarize the chapter by creating four Idea Webs with the center sections labeled as follows: *Total War and Its Causes, The Great War's Consequences, Revolutions in Russia and China,* and *Revolution in Mexico.* Instruct students to complete each web with relevant information as they read the corresponding set of lessons.

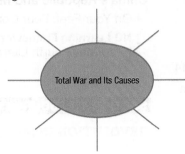

Use with All Lessons *For example, for* Total War and Its Causes, *students may add these topics to their Idea Web: Assassination starts the war; brutal trench warfare on two fronts; United States at first remains neutral but then enters the war on the side of the Allies.*

STRATEGY ❷
Analyze Main Ideas
Direct students to read aloud the Main Idea statement for each lesson. Explain that these statements identify and summarize the key idea for each lesson. As students read the lessons, encourage them to make notes about details they find in the text that connect to the Main Idea statements. Tell them this process will help them identify and remember the most important information.

Use with All Lessons

STRATEGY ❸
Clarify Information
Students may have trouble understanding the complicated alliances that led to World War I (Lessons 1.1, 1.2, 1.3, and 1.4) and the multistep peace process and redrawing of national boundaries at the end of the war (Lesson 2.1). To help them organize the information, instruct them to take notes on information under each heading in the text using a Five-Ws Chart.

Use with Lessons 1.1, 1.2, 1.3, 1.4, and 2.1

INCLUSION

STRATEGY ❶
Preview Using Maps
To help students better understand the major changes in national boundaries that resulted from World War I, direct them to preview the maps in Lessons 1.1, 1.2, and 2.1. First have students analyze the map of the Balkans in 1914. Discuss the historic rivalries of some of the great powers. Then have students use a finger to trace the territory held by the Triple Entente and its allies, the Central Powers, and the neutral nations from August 1914 through April 1917. Then have them trace the new boundaries of countries on the map of territorial changes in Europe after World War I. Explain that the areas lost by the empires were returned to populations that had been taken over by the empires.

Use with Lessons 1.1, 1.2, and 2.1

STRATEGY ❷
Describe Lesson Visuals
Pair students who are sight impaired with students who are not. Ask the latter to describe the visuals in the lesson and read all captions. Encourage students with sight impairments to ask questions to clarify anything they do not understand, and instruct partners to answer the questions. Prompt sighted partners to identify any important or dramatic details they notice.

Use with All Lessons

ENGLISH LANGUAGE LEARNERS

STRATEGY ❶
Review Transitional Words
To help students put events in chronological order and summarize what they read, write these transitional words on the board: *first, next, then, also, while, later, earlier, meanwhile, whenever, simultaneously, during, following, before, afterward,* and *finally*. Direct students at the **Beginning** and **Intermediate** levels to work together to write a series of sentences that tell what happens in each lesson. Encourage them to add transitional words to their sentences to tell about the time order of events. Prompt students at the **Advanced** level to construct a paragraph that summarizes the lesson. Encourage them to use a variety of transitional words and sentence structures.

Use with All Lessons

STRATEGY ②
Modify Vocabulary Lists

Limit the number of vocabulary words, terms, and names students at the **Beginning** level will be required to master. Direct students to write each word from your modified list on a colored sticky note and put it on the page next to where it appears in context.

Use with All Lessons

STRATEGY ③
Create a Definition Chart

Place students in mixed pairs, such as students at the **Beginning** level with those at the **Intermediate** and **Advanced** levels. Tell pairs to work together to identify at least three Key Vocabulary words from the lesson that they have had difficulty understanding. Instruct students to create a Definition Chart for those words. Then tell pairs to trade their chart with another pair and ask and answer questions about the information in the chart.

Word	Definition	In My Own Words

Use with All Lessons

GIFTED & TALENTED

STRATEGY ①
Create a Poster

Instruct students to research the images, slogans, and persuasive appeals used in propaganda posters during World War I and the Russian Revolution. Then have them create a poster in a similar style. They could use conventional art materials or a digital design program. Invite students to display their posters and explain the images, colors, and words they chose to use based on their research.

Use with Lessons 1.1 and 3.1

STRATEGY ②
Compare and Contrast Two Societies

Direct students to use the chapter text and online resources to design and prepare a museum exhibit about the experiences of soldiers and civilians during World War I, both on the home front and on the battlefields of Europe. Suggest that students look for letters, newspaper articles, photographs, and other primary source materials. Encourage students to also use secondary source documents and address bias and prejudice in historical interpretations of the subject. Invite students to display their exhibits in the classroom.

Use with Lessons 1.1, 1.2, 1.3, and 1.4

PRE-AP

STRATEGY ①
Explore Short- and Long-Term Impacts

Instruct students to conduct online research about women's roles in World War I. Tell students to select a role played by women and write a feature article about what women in this role did during the war. Prompt students to make connections between women's experiences during the war and broader social, economic, and political trends during and after the war.

Use with All Lessons *You may wish to provide examples of feature articles as a guide.*

STRATEGY ②
Analyze Long-Term Effects

Tell students to research and examine one of the following topics related to World War I:

- long-term consequences
- race and/or gender inequalities
- economic changes
- political changes

Suggest that students develop an infographic to display the results of their investigation. Encourage students to share their research projects with the class in a panel discussion.

Use with Lesson 2.1, 2.3, 2.4, and 2.5

The First World War
and 20th-Century
Revolutions

1870-1935

HISTORICAL THINKING How did the Great War affect
the world politically, socially, and economically?

SECTION 1 Total War and Its Causes

SECTION 2 The Great War's Consequences

SECTION 3 Revolutions in Russia and China

SECTION 4 Revolution in Mexico

CRITICAL VIEWING
Munitions workers inspect weapons in a storage
warehouse in Chilwell, Nottinghamshire, in 1917.
National Shell Filling Factory No. 6 was one of
the largest shell factories in Britain. What details
in this photo convey the magnitude of the war?

694 CHAPTER 25

The First World War and 20th-Century Revolutions 695

INTRODUCE THE PHOTOGRAPH

WEAPONS SHELL STORAGE WAREHOUSE

Have students study the photograph of the National Shell
Filling Factory No. 6 in Chilwell, Nottinghamshire, Britain.
Explain to students that World War I was a conflict of
unprecedented size and scope. The countries around
the world that participated—more than 100 by some
counts—mobilized troops and supported them with
massive amounts of natural and human resources. Every
country keenly felt the reality of the war in political, social,
and economic ways. **ASK:** How does the photograph
illustrate a certain economic reality for wartime Britain?
*(Manufacturing that many weapons and on that scale
had to have been expensive, including a great cost of
materials and labor. In order to be able to compete in the
war, Britain had to come up with money and resources.)*
Tell students that in this chapter they will learn about
World War I and its political, social, and economic effects
on the world.

SHARE BACKGROUND

Britain figured prominently before, during, and after
World War I. At the beginning of the 20th century, Britain
was an empire: a world power in every sense. Politically,
it maintained key European alliances (which would
ultimately draw it into the conflict). The British navy was
already legendary in terms of its size and strength, and
at the beginning of the war, Britain raised a huge army as
well. The country deployed a total force of some 9 million
troops. Economically, Britain was a powerhouse, leading
the world in trade and commerce. Once the war broke
out, it contributed mightily: the war cost Britain more
than 35 billion dollars. The human cost to Britain was
unimaginable, with more than 908,000 killed and another
2 million wounded.

CRITICAL VIEWING The factory is extremely
large, and it is filled with what looks to be thousands
of weapons. Also, many workers are tending to the
weapons. These details all support the idea that the war
was large, organized, and violent.

HISTORICAL THINKING QUESTION
How did the Great War affect the world politically, socially, and economically?

Four Corners: Preview Content This activity will help students preview and discuss the topics covered in the chapter. Provide a brief description and question for each section of the chapter, such as the ones shown below, and designate each of four corners as being "home" to one of the sections. Divide the class into four groups. Each group goes to one of the corners and discusses the topic of the section for a short time.

Group 1 Section 1 is about the causes of the war. **ASK:** What reasons might European nations have for fighting one another?

Group 2 Section 2 is about the consequences of the war. **ASK:** What are some ways that a war could end?

Group 3 Section 3 is about revolutions in Russia and China. **ASK:** What political issues might lead people to revolt against their leaders?

Group 4 Section 4 is about the Mexican revolution. **ASK:** What economic issues might cause a revolution?

Then ask each group to summarize their ideas for the class.

KEY DATES FOR CHAPTER 25

1914	World War I begins in Europe.
1915	The Armenian Genocide occurs.
1916	The Battle of Verdun begins and lasts for 10 months.
1917	The Russian Revolution occurs.
1917	The United States enters the war.
1919	The war is officially ended at the Paris Peace Conference.
1919	The Tiananmen Square demonstration occurs in China on May 4.
1919	Mexican revolutionary Emiliano Zapata is assassinated.
1920	Iraq is formed out of three former Ottoman provinces.
1922	The U.S.S.R. is formed.

INTRODUCE THE READING STRATEGY

COMPARE AND CONTRAST
Preview the chart comparing revolutions in the Chapter Review. Explain that comparing and contrasting in such a chart can help readers better understand similarities and differences among people, events, or movements in history. As they read the chapter, have students compare the Russian, Chinese, and Mexican revolutions.

INTRODUCE CHAPTER VOCABULARY

KEY VOCABULARY

SECTION 1

annex	armistice	artillery
mobilize	stalemate	total war
trench warfare		

SECTION 2

authoritarianism	countercultural	deportation
expatriate	pandemic	reparations
self-determination	shell shock	

SECTION 3

Gulag	nationalize

SECTION 4

campesino	vaquero

WORD WEB
As they read the chapter, have students complete Word Maps for Key Vocabulary terms. Tell students to make a Word Map for each term. Have them write the term in the center oval and then, as they encounter the term in the chapter, complete as much of the Word Map for that term as they can. Model an example for students on the board, using the graphic organizer below.

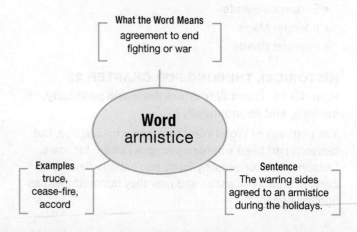

What the Word Means
agreement to end fighting or war

Word armistice

Examples
truce, cease-fire, accord

Sentence
The warring sides agreed to an armistice during the holidays.

Rivalries, Assassination, Propaganda

Over several generations, regional and global conflicts and wars increased simmering tensions throughout Europe. People of the early 20th century could not have predicted that what came to be known as World War I would be the deadliest conflict ever recorded at the time.

TURMOIL IN THE BALKANS

By the early 1900s, the dominant European nations known as the Great Powers were Britain, France, Russia, Italy, Germany, and Austria-Hungary. Britain and France presided over immense global empires. Russia led the world's largest military, and Germany had the fastest-growing industrial economy. Italy and Austria-Hungary were both eager to extend their territories. All six nations viewed one another as rivals. The competition for economic and political dominance would, in 1914, lead these powerful countries into

the Great War—later known as the First World War or World War I.

In the late 19th century, tensions between the Great Powers had found an outlet in competition for colonies outside of Europe. By 1900, however, European empires had seized large swaths of territory in Africa, Asia, and the Pacific. No unclaimed lands remained. Instead, the Great Powers chose to focus their attentions much closer to home—the Balkan Peninsula in southeastern Europe.

Archduke Francis Ferdinand and his wife, Sophie, leave City Hall in Sarajevo on June 28, 1914. The archduke was heir to the Austro-Hungarian throne. Minutes later, the couple was assassinated by a Serb nationalist, sparking the beginning of the First World War.

696 CHAPTER 25

The Balkans included Greece, Serbia, Bulgaria, and a few other states. In the early 1800s, the Ottoman Empire ruled this territory as well as areas in North Africa and Southwest Asia. By 1900, however, the Ottoman Empire was losing territory, including to an independent nationalist government in Serbia. In spite of that setback, the Ottomans managed to retain several Balkan provinces. But an alliance of Balkan states backed by Russia stripped away these lands in the First Balkan War between 1912 and 1913. A brief Second Balkan War between the Balkan allies resulted in a substantial expansion of Serbia's territory.

The powerful empire of Austria-Hungary took advantage of Ottoman weakness. In 1908, the empire **annexed**, or incorporated into its territory, Bosnia and Herzegovina, a land populated by Catholic Croatians, Orthodox Serbians, and Muslim Bosnians. Orthodox nationalists were outraged at the intrusion of rulers from Vienna and called upon Serbia and Russia for support. Bosnian Muslims with ties to the Ottoman Empire were also concerned. The stage for conflict was now set.

RISING TENSIONS

Historic rivalries created long-lasting friction between some of the Great Powers. The treaty ending the Franco-Prussian War of 1870 transferred the French territory Alsace-Lorraine to Germany. This loss created anti-German feelings among the French. Russia and Austria-Hungary both continued to compete for control of former Ottoman territories in the Balkans.

In search of greater security, some Great Powers formed alliances. In 1879, Germany and Austria-Hungary signed a treaty promising mutual support. In 1894, France and Russia pledged to assist each other if Germany ever attacked either country. This partnership made Germany nervous—now it had potential enemies to the east and west.

In the early 1900s, the alliance system solidified into two opposing blocs. France and Russia added Britain to their existing alliance to form the **Triple Entente**. Germany, Austria-Hungary, and Italy established the **Triple Alliance** in response. Treaties signed by these nations obligated each country to come to the aid of

any ally who was attacked. Members of both groups felt more secure, but the very nature of their alliances could cause a minor dispute to turn into a major conflict.

The Russian rivalry with Austria-Hungary was a prime example. The growing strength of Serbia threatened Austria-Hungary's quest to dominate the Balkans. Austria-Hungary anticipated that one day it might go to war against Serbia. Austria-Hungary and its ally Germany realized that Russian support for the Serbs could draw all of the Great Powers into conflict.

If war should break out, however, Germany was ready. In 1890, **Wilhelm II**, Germany's emperor, had dismissed his chancellor, Otto von Bismarck. Wilhelm abandoned Bismarck's cautious foreign policy and instead pursued militarism. By 1914, the German army had grown to more than 600,000 men.

The other Great Powers decided to respond in kind to Germany's aggressiveness. As imperialist nations, they already had the strong armies and navies needed to establish and maintain control of their colonial resources and markets. Now they took stock of their armed forces and made improvements where needed. Should war happen, they all intended to be prepared.

Britain, known for its centuries of seafaring prowess, boosted its construction of warships to match Germany's naval buildup. Russia, still reeling from its loss to Japan in the Russo-Japanese War of 1905,

The Balkans, 1914

Predominantly Serbs and Croats
Predominantly Romanians
GERMANS Other ethnic majority

PLAN: 4-PAGE LESSON

OBJECTIVE
Understand how certain relationships among European nations led to the outbreak of the Great War.

CRITICAL THINKING SKILLS FOR LESSON 1.1
- Make Inferences
- Draw Conclusions
- Explain
- Describe
- Sequence Events
- Interpret Maps
- Interpret Charts

HISTORICAL THINKING FOR CHAPTER 25
How did the Great War affect the world politically, socially, and economically?

The outbreak of World War I took some by surprise, but tensions had been simmering across Europe for years. Lesson 1.1 describes why European nations developed certain regional alliances and how they honored them as fighting began.

BACKGROUND FOR THE TEACHER
Alsace-Lorraine Control of Alsace-Lorraine has been a matter of dispute for much of the region's history. In the ninth century, Alsace-Lorraine was part of the Frankish empire ruled by Charlemagne. During the Holy Roman Empire, the region was controlled by Germany and stayed that way until the Thirty Years' War, when the 1648 Peace of Westphalia ceded it to France. Alsace-Lorraine remained French until 1871, when Germany reclaimed it at the end of the Franco-Prussian War. At the end of World War I, it went back to France, only to see Germany annex it again during World War II. The end of that war saw the territory returned to France, where it remains today. Interestingly, Alsace-Lorraine has tried to become an autonomous region more than once in its history. In 1905, the territory tried to become recognized within Germany, but the end of World War I stymied that attempt. Then, in the 1920s, it tried to become autonomous within France but again was unsuccessful.

INTRODUCE & ENGAGE

UNDERSTAND THE NUMBERS

Use comparisons to help students put the human toll of World War I in perspective. **ASK:** How many people do you think would fill a stadium at a professional football game? *(about 75,000)* About how many people live in the most populous U.S. city? *(about 8.5 million)* How many thousands of people are in 1 million? *(one thousand thousands)* Point out that some wars have lasted for hundreds of years and have resulted in hundreds of thousands of people killed. Explain that World War I lasted only four years, but 9 million soldiers were killed, and an additional 21 million soldiers were wounded or listed as missing. Tell students that in this lesson they will learn how World War I began.

TEACH

GUIDED DISCUSSION

1. **Describe** What was the relationship like between Germany and France in the years leading up to the outbreak of the Great War? Explain using details. *(Their relationship was tense. France had to give up its Alsace-Lorraine territory to Germany at the end of the Franco-Prussian War. Germany was uneasy about France's alliance with Russia.)*

2. **Make Inferences** How did imperialism add to tensions between European nations? *(European powers such as Great Britain, Germany, and France competed for colonies in Africa and Asia, and so they saw each other as rivals.)*

INTERPRET MAPS

Guide students to analyze the map of the Balkans in 1914. **ASK:** What does the shaded brown line around Bosnia & Herzegovina indicate? *(This is probably the area that Austria-Hungary annexed since the color of Bosnia & Herzegovina is the same color as Austria-Hungary.)* How does the map support the idea that Austria-Hungary and the Ottoman Empire competed for land in the Balkans? *(The Ottoman Empire is large and located near some Balkan states. The shaded brown line around Serbia and Bosnia & Herzegovina and the shaded red line around Romania and the Transylvanian Hungarians indicate areas that Austria-Hungary had annexed. That annexation likely caused tension with the Ottoman Empire.)*

DIFFERENTIATE

STRIVING READERS

Turn Headings into Questions To help students set a purpose for reading, tell them to read each section heading and then turn it into a question they think will be answered in the lesson, such as *Why did tensions rise in Europe?* or *How did Europe prepare for war?* Direct students to record their questions. After reading the lesson, have students write the answer to each question.

GIFTED & TALENTED

Create an Annotated Time Line Ask students to develop a list of events in the lead-up to the outbreak of World War I, including the dates in which various nations made their declarations of war. Ask students to form small groups to better divide the research, which they may conduct online. Then provide a large sheet of paper to each group and tell members to work together to create a time line and label and annotate the events. Annotations should indicate the significance of each event in relation to the simmering tensions between various nations. Direct groups to present their time lines to the class, with special emphasis on the sequence of events and how each event led to another event.

See the Chapter Planner for more strategies for differentiation.

The Great Powers of World War I			
Country	Leader	Title	Reason for Going to War
Britain	Herbert Henry Asquith	Prime Minister	To secure the freedom of Belgium and France after Germany had invaded both countries
Germany	Theobald von Bethmann Hollweg	Chancellor	To support its ally Austria-Hungary and to crush historical enemies (and neighbors) France and Russia before they built up their militaries
France	Raymond Poincaré	President	To restore French control over the region of Alsace-Lorraine, lost to German states in the Franco-Prussian War
Austria-Hungary	Franz Joseph II	Emperor	To avenge the assassination of Archduke Franz Ferdinand
Russia	Nicholas II	Tsar	To protect Serbia from the threat of invasion by Austria-Hungary
Ottoman Empire	Ismail Enver	Minister of War	To end its steady decline and strengthen itself by allying with Germany, a military powerhouse
Italy	Antonio Salandra	Prime Minister	To gain control of Austro-Hungarian and Ottoman territory it had long wanted

believed it could field some 800,000 soldiers. France set a goal of 1.3 million regular troops and reserves. Besides expanding its regular army, Austria-Hungary moved 200,000 reserves into Bosnia and Herzegovina. All allies on both sides made detailed plans for war.

The growing militarism, the rivalries between the Great Powers, and the alliance system all seemed to edge Europe closer to war. However, in 1899 and again in 1907, representatives of more than 40 countries met in the Dutch city of The Hague, Netherlands. There, they established rules for land warfare and a court for the peaceful settlement of international disputes. All Great Powers signed what became known as the Hague Convention. In 1912 and 1913, the same nations met again, this time at the London Peace Conference. They worked together to resolve disputes among the states involved in the First Balkan War. The forces of peace still seemed to hold the upper hand.

THE SPARK: ASSASSINATION

As you have read, Austria-Hungary was a multiethnic empire ruled by Franz Joseph II. Within its borders lived Germans, Magyars (Hungarians), and Slavs. Slavic groups included Czechs and Poles as well as Serbs and Croats. Even though Slavs accounted for more than 60 percent of the population, they had little power. The Germans controlled the Austrian half of the empire, and the Magyars controlled the Hungarian half.

Ethnic difficulties plagued Austria-Hungary. The Czechs, who inhabited a large area in the northwest of the empire, wanted greater self-government. Their demands awakened nationalistic feelings in the empire's other Slavic peoples, including the Serbs, Croats, and Bosnians. In the years following the annexation of Bosnia and Herzegovina in 1908, nationalist movements

in the Balkans grew stronger. Activists talked of rebelling against Austro-Hungarian rule and forming an independent Slavic state.

On June 28, 1914, Bosnian Serb nationalist Gavrilo Princip saw an opportunity to advance the Slavic cause. **Archduke Franz Ferdinand**, heir to the Austro-Hungarian throne, had traveled to Bosnia and Herzegovina on an official visit. As the archduke rode through the streets in an open car, Princip shot and killed him and his wife. This assassination kindled a series of events that drew all the Great Powers into war.

Austria-Hungary blamed its longtime rival Serbia for the assassination, and it threatened Serbia with war if Serbia did not comply with a set of humiliating demands. Serbia refused. Nobody at the time thought a war between these adversaries would affect other nations, but the alliance system soon took effect. The Serbs appealed to Russia for help, and the Germans backed Austria-Hungary. The Russian army started to **mobilize**, or assemble and prepare for war. Throughout July, many European leaders searched for a diplomatic way to end the crisis. They failed.

On July 28, Austria-Hungary declared war on Serbia. Two days later, Germany began to mobilize its army, and the next day Austria-Hungary did the same. Then, on August 1, Germany declared war on Russia. On August 3, Germany declared war on France and immediately sent soldiers toward the French border. These German troops first crossed into Belgium. A British security agreement with neutral Belgium led Britain to declare war on Germany on August 5. That same day, Austria-Hungary declared war on Russia, and a week later Britain and France officially declared war on Austria-Hungary. Any hopes for peace evaporated.

The Ottoman Empire, weak as it was, allied itself with Germany and Austria-Hungary. They became known as the **Central Powers**. After a period of indecision, Italy joined Britain, France, and Russia, and the four nations became known as the **Allies**. All the European powers plunged into war.

PREPARING FOR WAR

How did Europe find itself engulfed in this conflict? Historians believe that imperialism, militarism, ethnic unrest, and nationalism all played a role. The assassination of Archduke Franz Ferdinand provided the spark that set Europe alight, propelling the Great Powers toward full-scale war.

Whatever the causes, Europeans did not express alarm at the declarations of war. They seemed to think this contest would be quick and conclusive and that their side would win. The press created war fever to sell newspapers, and the public responded with patriotic demonstrations. Europeans simply could not conceive of the horrors of modern industrialized warfare.

The leaders of the main combatants may have known better. In addition to mobilizing their armies, they set out to rally the civilian population. Governments expected everyone to contribute to the war effort. They clarified this point through posters, songs, newspapers, and other propaganda. Both the Allies and the Central Powers sought to persuade their citizens that the war was a just war. They also used propaganda to provoke nationalistic feelings and hatred of the enemy.

As the war progressed, some nations appealed more to ideology. Britain and France encouraged their citizens to think of the war as a battle to preserve liberty, democracy, and the rule of law. Meanwhile, Germany told its people that the British and French colonial

powers were trying to deny the German nation the global stature it deserved.

This was a **total war**. It required the complete mobilization of all resources, including human resources. Men marched off to battle. Some women served as nurses in the war zones, while others joined the labor force at home. Factories had to drastically increase their production of war materials—from guns and bombs to wagons and ships. Sources of oil, coal, and iron needed to be secured. To manage all this, governments assumed controls over the economy and society that they had not had before.

Total war also required access to global reserves. European imperial powers looked to their colonies for manpower and raw materials. Because of their huge empires, Britain and France benefited more from their colonial resources than other nations engaged in the war. Their empires also ensured that the war would not be limited to Europe.

CRITICAL VIEWING The title of this German propaganda poster translates to "Who Is a Militarist?" The size of the soldiers reflects the amount of military spending in Britain, Germany, and France. What message was the German government trying to communicate with this poster?

HISTORICAL THINKING

1. READING CHECK How did ethnic conflict and nationalism lead to the assassination of Archduke Franz Ferdinand?

2. MAKE INFERENCES Why did the Ottoman Empire ally with Germany and Austria-Hungary in 1914?

3. DRAW CONCLUSIONS Do you think the Great Powers wanted to engage in a major war? Why or why not?

4. EXPLAIN How did propaganda support a nation's ability to engage in total war?

BACKGROUND FOR THE TEACHER

Gavrilo Princip and Black Hand Gavrilo Princip was not even 20 years old when he committed the act that triggered the Great War and forever changed the world. Princip, a Bosnian Serb, was born in 1894 to a poor peasant family. He developed a passion for Slavic nationalism as a youth after coming under the influence of Black Hand, a secret society that used terrorism to advance the cause of Serbian independence. Black Hand was formed in 1911 by Serbian military men who became skilled in using pro-Serb propaganda techniques. Black Hand grew in size and influence before and after the Balkan Wars and eventually came to dominate Serbia's army and its national government. With the help of Black Hand members, Princip planned the assassination of the archduke after learning that the archduke would be visiting Sarajevo in June 1914. The archduke's assassination on June 28 was actually comprised of two events. First, Princip and a small group of his fellow revolutionaries threw a bomb at the archduke's car, and the bomb exploded, wounding an Austrian official. When the archduke and his consort, Sophie, were on their way to the hospital to visit the official, Princip opened fire and shot them both to death. Princip received only 20 years in jail due to his youth. Stricken with tuberculosis during his imprisonment, Princip died in 1918. Black Hand had already met its end by that time; its leaders stood trial in 1917 in Serbia and three were executed, with hundreds more sent to prison.

TEACH

GUIDED DISCUSSION

3. **Sequence Events** What was one major event in each of the following months in 1914: June, July, and August? *(On June 28, a Bosnian Serb nationalist assassinated Archduke Franz Ferdinand, who was heir to the Austro-Hungarian throne; on July 28, Austria-Hungary declared war on Serbia; on August 5, Britain declared war on Germany.)*

4. **Draw Conclusions** In the context of looming war in the early 1900s, what might be some advantages and disadvantages of maintaining alliances and the understood agreement that an attack against one is an attack against all? *(Possible responses: Advantages: With tensions rising and war on the horizon, a nation with allies can count on other nations to come to its defense in case of attack. Alliances might prevent an attack in the first place, since an aggressive nation might think twice about attacking a small or weak nation with powerful allies. Disadvantages: A nation might be drawn into a war it doesn't want in order to defend another nation. A nation might have to cut ties with nations with which it has no quarrel.)*

INTERPRET CHARTS

Ask students to study the chart of the great powers of World War I. **ASK:** What alliance drew Britain into the war? *(Britain promised to defend Belgium from attack; Germany invaded Belgium.)* What was Italy's reason for joining the war? *(to gain control of land in Austria-Hungary and the Ottoman Empire that it had long desired)* If Serbia were on the chart, what would its reason be for going to war? *(to become its own independent Slavic state)*

ACTIVE OPTIONS

On Your Feet: Roundtable Organize students into teams of four. Pose the following question: Why do you think one particular event, the assassination of two people, led to the development of a war that spread across and beyond Europe? Have each student answer the question within the group and explain his or her answer based on what they learned in the lesson. Allow time for groups to share the different answers with the class.

NG Learning Framework: Compare and Contrast Propaganda
SKILL Observation
KNOWLEDGE Our Human Story

Prompt students to work in groups to research British and German World War I propaganda posters and develop an oral presentation based on their research. Instruct them to choose one poster from each country and then compare and contrast each poster's message and symbolism and how they interact. Ask groups to make their oral presentations to the rest of the class.

HISTORICAL THINKING

ANSWERS

1. The desire by a Bosnian Serb nationalist to create a Slavic state and overthrow Austria-Hungary led him to assassinate Franz Ferdinand.

2. Possible response: The Ottoman Empire had steadily been losing territory—including its possessions in southeastern Europe. The empire was also likely weaker economically than the rest of Europe. The Central Powers were against Russia, who had earlier taken Balkan territories from the Ottomans.

3. Possible response: Germany's militarism suggests that Germany intended to expand its territory, which may have made it more willing to engage in war. The other Great Powers seemed more reluctant to go to war.

4. Possible response: Total war required a nation mobilizing all of its resources. Through propaganda, a government could persuade its people that they should do everything they could to increase productivity and otherwise contribute to the war effort.

CRITICAL VIEWING Possible response: The German government wanted to portray Germany as the "little guy" fighting against the powerful and warmongering Britain and France.

War on Many Fronts

Hundreds of thousands of soldiers fighting in World War I were teenagers—some as young as 14. Many of them joined the army for patriotic reasons, often lying about their age, and others thought the war would be an amusing adventure. Imagine how quickly their minds changed once they leaped headfirst into a muddy hole in the ground to escape a burst of deadly machine-gun fire.

STALEMATE IN THE WEST

From the start of the war, geography put Germany in an awkward position. Germany would have to face the Russian army to the east and the French army to the west, but this position was not a surprise to the military-minded Germans. Years earlier, they had established a plan to handle a war on two fronts—zones of combat between two opposing forces. The Germans knew that the Russians, who were not fully mobilized, would be slower than the French to form an invasion force. Germany's strategy was to attack France first.

The French fully expected a German invasion; they had established defensive fortifications along the German border. After the German army's initial push through Belgium in early August 1914, French and German forces battled along France's eastern border.

In early September, the Germans broke through French defenses and moved toward Paris. The French, aided by a British force, counterattacked. Their success at the First Battle of the Marne forced the Germans to withdraw. More attacks and counterattacks followed. By the end of 1914, each side had seen hundreds of thousands of soldiers killed and even more wounded.

The First Battle of the Marne is considered a turning point in the war. After the French victory in northern France, the Western Front settled into a **stalemate**, a situation in which neither side can defeat the other. The opposing armies dug in—literally. They sought protection from opponents' gunfire by concealing themselves in trenches, or long ditches in the ground, that were fortified with barbed wire. What followed became known as **trench warfare**.

Soldiers were constantly miserable, eating and sleeping in the muddy trenches as they fought a nonstop battle

German soldiers in a trench in Ypres, Belgium, take advantage of a break during the fighting to read newspapers.

against rats and lice and suffered from boredom and disease. As the war continued, troops dug deeper trenches and linked them into networks that included supply posts, kitchens, and first-aid stations.

Battle lines established during this time in Belgium and northern France hardly shifted as the war continued, but not for lack of trying. Soldiers were regularly ordered to climb "over the top" of trenches and charge enemy positions. Their chances of breaking through the battlefront were small, and their chances of dying were high.

Charging troops faced rapid-firing machine guns and **artillery**, large field guns that fire high-explosive shells. They were also often bombarded with chemical weapons. Clouds of chlorine gas and a much deadlier chemical, phosgene, attacked victims' lungs, and mustard gas blistered people's skin. In spite of soldiers' heroic efforts, neither side made much progress.

Trench warfare had many victims. In the 19th century, cavalry units led by officers on horses were the pride of European armies. But animals had no place in industrialized warfare. Like thousands of men that they served, millions of horses were killed by barbed wire, artillery, and poison gas.

World War I, August 1914–April 1917

A GLOBAL CONFLICT

In 1914, while fighting raged on the Western Front, Austria-Hungary launched an invasion north into Russia's Polish provinces. The Russian army forced the Austro-Hungarian army to retreat and then threatened to invade Germany's heavily industrialized northeast. The Germans beat the Russian troops back. Russia lost many men in these early battles, and by the end of September 1914 it had suffered some 250,000 casualties—soldiers captured, wounded, or killed. The Eastern Front later expanded farther into Russia.

Austria-Hungary invaded Serbia in late August 1914. Their two armies clashed for months, but neither side could gain a complete victory. By the end of the year, the Serbs had driven enemy forces from their country. Warfare on the Balkan Front, however, resumed in 1915.

Other regions experienced a similar series of battles. In 1915, an Italian army invaded Austria-Hungary in hopes of seizing lands it claimed belonged to Italy. Fighting on the Italian Front would continue into 1917. Also in 1915, a British naval force opened the Southern Front by attacking the Ottoman Empire. The Ottomans had joined the Central Powers in October 1914 partly because, in the late 19th century, German banks, businesses, and manufacturers had invested heavily in the Ottoman economy. Ottoman leaders saw an alliance with Germany as protection against the French, British, and Russians. You will learn more about how the opening of this Southern Front brought the peoples of Egypt, Syria, and India into World War I.

Another alliance carried the Great War to East Asia. In 1902, Japan had sought support against Russian aggression by allying itself with Britain. After World War I began, Japan sided with the Allies and declared war against Germany. Japan, however, did not play a major role in the war beyond seizing German colonial holdings in China and occupying German islands in the Pacific.

German colonies in Africa also came under attack. In 1915, soldiers from the Union of South Africa captured German South West Africa, present-day Namibia. In East Africa, a German general led his African troops on raids against invading British forces, which were largely composed of soldiers from India. Local Africans were forced to carry loads for the European armies, and many died when famine spread in the wake of war.

Troops from Australia, New Zealand, India, Canada, and other nations with links to Britain fought for the Allies. One former British colony joined the Allies in April 1917. That nation, the United States, would play a major role in the remainder of the war.

HISTORICAL THINKING

1. **READING CHECK** Why was the Great War a worldwide struggle?

2. **MAKE INFERENCES** Based on what you have read, what can you infer about the effectiveness of trench warfare?

3. **INTERPRET MAPS** How did Germany's geographic location affect its strategy for fighting the Great War?

PLAN: 2-PAGE LESSON

OBJECTIVE

Describe the early weeks and months of the war during which the conflict took place on various fronts around the world.

CRITICAL THINKING SKILLS FOR LESSON 1.2

- Make Inferences
- Interpret Maps
- Compare and Contrast
- Identify Main Ideas and Details

HISTORICAL THINKING FOR CHAPTER 25

How did the Great War affect the world politically, socially, and economically?

It was the complexities of Europe's political alliances that triggered the Great War in the first place, and those alliances provided the theaters in which the war was fought. Lesson 1.2 describes the various fronts that saw the early fighting of the war.

Student eEdition online

Additional content for this lesson, including a diagram, is available online.

BACKGROUND FOR THE TEACHER

A Controversial Plan Count Alfred von Schlieffen, a chief of the German general staff, devised a plan to consolidate the German Empire by defeating both France and Russia in a two-front war. Schlieffen was inspired by Hannibal, a Carthaginian general whose tactics resulted in the defeat of a Roman force in 216 B.C.E. Schlieffen's plan involved four army groups and a detailed timetable. It relied on continuous forward movement of the army—a departure from German military thinking. One strategist disapproved of the plan because it required the creation of new military units, potentially weakening the regular army. The German navy objected because the plan called for land engagements rather than the building of battleships. Schlieffen first proposed his plan in 1905, but it was not put into action until World War I. At the war's end, German military leaders blamed the plan for Germany's defeat. The Schlieffen Plan was then locked in an archive at Potsdam, where it was destroyed during a British bomber attack on April 14, 1945.

INTRODUCE & ENGAGE

CONNECT TO TODAY

Ask students to imagine that the United States has declared war today. Discuss the following questions: Under what circumstances would you enlist in the military? How would you feel if you were ordered to serve? What do you think should be the minimum age for someone to serve? Explain that in this lesson students will learn about the circumstances surrounding the early part of the war and what thousands of young European soldiers were up against as the fighting began.

TEACH

GUIDED DISCUSSION

1. **Compare and Contrast** In what way were France and Germany prepared for war? *(Years before the outbreak of the war, Germany had put in place a plan to fight a two-front war against France in the west and Russia in the east. France was expecting Germany to attack them first, so they fortified their eastern border with Germany.)*

2. **Identify Main Ideas and Details** What brought Japan into the war, and how did that expand the global reach of the war? *(Japan had allied with Britain years earlier in order to keep Russia at bay. Japan joined the war on the side of the Allies. Japan was far away from Europe in East Asia, demonstrating that the war was truly a global conflict.)*

COMPARE AND CONTRAST

Ask students to study the diagram (available in the Student eEdition). **ASK:** How were communication trenches different from the parallel trenches? *(Communication trenches ran perpendicular to the parallel trenches and connected the rows of parallel trenches.)* How was No Man's Land different from the main area of each side fighting the war? *(It had barbed wire to keep enemy soldiers from advancing; soldiers stayed in the trenches on their sides, where they could move around and communicate.)*

ACTIVE OPTIONS

On Your Feet: Card Response Tell half the class to write 10 True-False statements based on the lesson. Instruct the other half to create answer cards, writing "True" on one side and "False" on the other side. Students from the first group take turns reading their statements. Students from the second group hold up their cards, showing either "True" or "False."

NG Learning Framework: Present Dramatic Monologues
ATTITUDE Curiosity
SKILL Communication

Prompt small groups to conduct research to write a set of dramatic monologues that represent the views of trench warfare from a variety of fighters—from both sides of the war, if possible. For example, monologues might portray a soldier who lived, a soldier who died, a commanding officer, and a medic. Instruct students to think about the context (World War I, early 1900s) as they consider the norms and values of the people they are portraying and avoid present-day slang. Allow groups to choose a format for presenting their dramatic monologues.

DIFFERENTIATE

INCLUSION

Use Supported Reading Prompt students to read the lesson and use these sentence frames to monitor their comprehension of the text:

- This lesson is mostly about _____.
- Other topics in this lesson are _____, _____, and _____.
- One question I have is _____.
- One of the vocabulary words is _____, and it means _____.
- One word I don't recognize is _____.

PRE-AP

Research Trench Warfare Tell students to conduct a short research project to answer specific questions about trench warfare. Ask students to generate an initial research question based on information in the lesson. As they research, encourage them to use their question as a springboard for generating additional questions for which they'd like to find answers. Prompt students to share their findings with the class in an oral or written report.

See the Chapter Planner for more strategies for differentiation.

HISTORICAL THINKING

ANSWERS

1. The Great War involved a large number of countries in Europe and also other countries around the world with ties to Europe, making it a worldwide conflict.

2. Trench warfare was not very effective because each side had many, many casualties without gaining the upper hand or area from its opponent.

3. Because Germany was located between two Allies—France to the west and Russia to the east—its military leaders had to decide which nation to fight first. They chose to attack France before battling Russia.

The Course to the End

Although industrialization brought many new and helpful technologies to Europe, it also led to the development of destructive advancements. Powerful new military weapons would add to the horror and devastation of warfare.

German sailors crowd together in the engine room of an oil-burning submarine.

WEAPONS OF WAR

During the First World War, the goal of the Allies and the Central Powers was the same: win at all costs. This contest was, after all, a total war. As a result of this approach, millions of people—soldiers and civilians—died. The weapons used in this armed conflict contributed greatly to the enormous number of killed and wounded.

Europeans dominated many areas of the world in part because of their innovations in firearms technology. Soldiers carried semiautomatic pistols that had higher rates of fire than older revolvers, and artillery pieces fired faster as well. The heavy, single-barrel machine guns used in colonial warfare during the 1890s were made lighter and more mobile by the time of World War I.

These new technologies and other improvements came into play during the Battle of Verdun, on the Western Front in France. In February 1916, the Germans attacked the fortress of Verdun with artillery and machine guns, and the French defended their positions with the same deadly weapons. The Germans also lobbed more than 100,000 shells of poison phosgene gas at their enemy, although another piece of modern technology—the gas mask—prevented mass French casualties.

To monitor the progress of its soldiers on the ground, the Germans took to the air. They employed 168 airplanes, 14 observation balloons, and 4 airships known as zeppelins. At first, the aircraft mainly tracked troop movements. Later in the conflict, German and French pilots engaged in "dogfights" over Verdun. In these close-range aerial battles, pilots often fired pistols at their opponents.

The Battle of Verdun lasted until December 1916, when the Germans had to retreat for lack of resources. After 10 months of fighting, neither side had taken much territory. Casualties were fairly equal too— 337,000 Germans killed or wounded and somewhat more for the French. Like much of the area throughout the Western Front, the environment surrounding Verdun had been pulverized. Trenches and huge craters left by artillery shells dotted the landscape. A forest of oak and chestnut trees lay shattered. At least one nearby village was completely destroyed.

In 1916, Britain introduced a new and menacing weapon: the tank. The British first used this technology in September at the Battle of the Somme in France. As one German soldier remarked, the tanks "advanced relentlessly. . . . Holes, hills, rocks, even barbed wire meant nothing." From inside the vehicle, the crew fired machine guns at enemy positions.

THE WAR AT SEA

Much of the Great War was fought at sea. Germany and Britain had engaged in a naval arms race dating from about 1900. In 1906,

THROUGH THE LENS JEFF GUSKY

The Hidden World of the Great War

Descriptions of conditions on the Western Front usually paint a picture of dejected soldiers crouched in a muddy ditch, bullets whizzing overhead. National Geographic Explorer Jeff Gusky, who is a photographer and also an emergency medicine physician, took his camera underground to document a less hostile side of trench warfare.

In northern France, deep below Earth's surface, Gusky entered a network of ancient limestone rock quarries. During the First World War, the quarries were transformed into underground cities that had electric lights, telephones, housing, offices, hospitals, and a rail line. In this hidden world, troops from both sides of the war found refuge from the mud, noise, and terror of the battlefield.

These soldiers realized that the limestone could be carved, and many of them left their names and addresses in the stone walls. Others chiseled images that represented their families, their homes, their religious views, or their states of mind. Gusky first captured these carvings in a series of black-and-white photographs, and a Smithsonian Channel 2017 documentary shows his further examinations of this underground world. According to Gusky's website, he wants "to inspire belief in a future where we find hope in the human decency and courage of ordinary people and safety in seeing human nature for what it is . . . permanently imperfect."

This underground chapel, tucked away from a French hospital in a limestone quarry, offered a place for World War I soldiers to seek solace and temporarily escape the horrors of the battle above.

PLAN: 4-PAGE LESSON

OBJECTIVE

Understand how new warfare technology and the conditions in the trenches affected soldiers fighting in World War I.

CRITICAL THINKING SKILLS FOR LESSON 1.3

- Make Generalizations
- Analyze Cause and Effect
- Form and Support Opinions
- Compare and Contrast
- Make Inferences
- Integrate Visuals

HISTORICAL THINKING FOR CHAPTER 25

How did the Great War affect the world politically, socially, and economically?

A vast array of new weapons, military theaters, and civilian participation came into being during World War I. Lesson 1.3 describes how these wartime innovations were used as the war marched toward its ultimate end, which was hastened by America's entry into the conflict.

BACKGROUND FOR THE TEACHER

The Tank Winston Churchill, who served as Britain's First Lord of the Admiralty early in the war, strongly advocated the development of "land boats," which became known as "tanks" to disguise their real purpose by suggesting they were designed to carry water. Churchill established the Landships Committee early in 1915, and by that September the first prototype was put through its paces. After refinements, British tanks appeared on the battlefield for the first time in September 1916, at the First Battle of the Somme. More improvements followed, with even greater battlefield success. France, the United States, and Italy developed tanks, too; in fact, the French ultimately produced more tanks (3,870) during the war than the British did (2,636). Germany was less sure of the value of tanks; nevertheless, Germany produced and used some 20 tanks during the war.

Student eEdition online

Additional content for this lesson, including photographs and captions, is available online.

INTRODUCE & ENGAGE

COMPARE TECHNOLOGIES

Ask students to name examples of technology used in current wars. Use a chart like the one shown here to list the examples. Invite students to suggest examples of technology that might have been invented and used during World War I. Add their suggestions to the chart. Finally, have students list examples of technology used in earlier wars around the world. Tell students to copy the chart and update it as they read about technology during World War I. If time permits, revisit the chart after students have read the lesson, and discuss how weapons technology has evolved over time.

Weapons in War Today	Weapons in World War I	Weapons in Earlier Wars

TEACH

GUIDED DISCUSSION

1. **Compare and Contrast** How was World War I weapons technology similar to and different from that used in previous wars? *(Possible response: Technology was similar in that guns continued to be used as weapons. Differences included the use of semiautomatic pistols, artillery pieces, poison gas, tanks, airplanes and zeppelins, and antiaircraft guns.)*

2. **Make Inferences** Considering the context of when World War I began, what made submarines (and the German U-boat) more lethal than traditional battleships? *(Submarines and U-boats could travel under water, which would have made them difficult for ships of that era to detect. Battleships were large and floated above the surface.)*

INTEGRATE VISUALS

Draw students' attention to the Weapons of the Great War image gallery (available in the Student eEdition). **ASK:** How could you classify the weapons by land, by sea, and by air? *(The airplanes are by air, the tank is by land, and the submarine is by sea.)* How does the photo of the machine gun inside the airplane show two types of warfare innovations? *(Not only were airplanes a new kind of warfare technology but putting a machine gun inside it was also totally new.)* What do the photos tell you about the overall lethality of the Great War? *(Possible response: The weapons demonstrate technological advances that were not used before. The gas masks in particular show how deadly poison gas could be.)*

DIFFERENTIATE

STRIVING READERS

Sequence Events Direct students to work in pairs to determine the sequence of events leading to the end of World War I. Have students use a Sequence Chain graphic organizer like the one shown. Tell students to decide on four major events leading up to the Paris Peace Conference, which will serve as the final event in their chain. Instruct them to include the date and a summary of each event. Invite students to share their Sequence Chains with other pairs and discuss any differences.

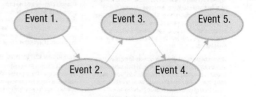

GIFTED & TALENTED

Create a Cause-and-Effect Presentation Direct students to conduct online research to learn more about the sinking of the *Lusitania* in order to create a multimedia presentation about its causes and effects. Encourage students to use a Cause-and-Effect Chart to keep track of the relationship among events. Invite students to share their cause-and-effect presentations with the class.

See the Chapter Planner for more strategies for differentiation.

the British unveiled a newly designed battleship—the H.M.S. *Dreadnought*—that was bigger, faster, and more powerful than any existing warship. By 1914, Britain had built 30 more *Dreadnought*-style ships.

The Germans were determined to keep up with the British, long considered "masters of the sea." German engineers produced their own version of the new British battleship. When World War I broke out, Germany had 13 of its own large, formidable warships. The navies of both nations were prepared for battle.

After the war was underway, the British used their superior naval resources to prevent merchant ships from entering the North Sea and German ports. Britain sharply limited German imports of food and raw materials from overseas, and Germany intended to break this blockade. In 1916, German battleships faced off against British battleships in the North Sea off Jutland, or mainland Denmark.

At the Battle of Jutland, the two fleets clashed from May 31 to June 2, their big guns blazing. Both countries lost many sailors, and their ships were heavily damaged. Even though both sides claimed victory, the blockade continued. Jutland was the last major sea battle of the war that did not include airplanes or another development in military technology: the submarine.

France designed and built the first submarines in the late 19th century. By 1914, France, Britain, Russia, and Germany each had at least three dozen submarines. The Germans had the fewest, but they saw the value of U-boats (short for *unterseeboot*, or "undersea boat") to their war effort. As the war persisted, technologically advanced German U-boats continually launched torpedo attacks against Allied merchant and military ships.

ON THE HOME FRONT

Soldiers fighting on the various military fronts relied on their home country's resources—human and material—to support them. The term *home front*, used to describe the activities of civilians in support of the troops, reflects the nature of the First World War as a total war. Everyone had to participate to keep the war machine running.

Governments expanded their powers to mobilize their economies and keep them strong. In Germany, state agencies assumed control of production, labor, wages, and prices, while other European powers established some form of national economic planning as well. As a result, the free market was restricted. To blunt opposition to their policies, governments also often limited civil liberties such as freedom of speech and freedom of assembly.

For European women, the war brought opportunities. The nursing profession expanded, and women took on greater responsibilities in factories and on family farms. However, women also paid a high price. They toiled long hours on extra shifts in factories, often in dangerous conditions, to make up for the labor shortage. They raised their children on their own, and they feared for their husbands, brothers, and sons in combat zones.

Total war also brought the violence of the battlefield to the home front. Many civilians living in or near an area of conflict were killed unintentionally, but in January 1915, for the first time, civilians were specifically targeted in war. With the Western Front at an impasse, the Germans sent two zeppelins across the North Sea to Britain. There, the airships dropped bombs on two coastal towns, killing several people.

Nations also engaged in economic warfare. Britain's blockade of the North Sea deprived Germans of food and other resources, and similar blockades had similar effects. German U-boats prowling the Mediterranean Sea regularly sunk Allied supply ships headed for the Balkan Front or the Southern Front. The French barricaded Ottoman territory in the eastern Mediterranean.

Britain managed to maintain its troop strength through volunteers. Other governments relied on conscription, which you learned is forced enrollment in the armed services. Universal military service was the rule in Germany, and every French man was expected to serve his country.

Russian conscripts were mainly peasants, and morale among them was poor; they did not want to fight and die for the tsar. Sometimes they just dropped their weapons on the battlefield and walked home. Life for Russian civilians was no better. The disruption of food production led to famine, and factories shut down for lack of capital. In March 1917, Russian revolutionaries overthrew the tsar, and a year later, Russia signed a peace treaty with Germany. You will learn more about the Russian Revolution later in this chapter.

AMERICAN ENTRY INTO THE WAR

With the Eastern Front stabilized, Germany could move its forces from Russia to the Western Front, end the stalemate there, and achieve victory. France and Britain needed help. It came from the United States.

When the Great War started in 1914, the United States had only a small army. Americans at the time tended

The New York Times. EXTRA
6:30 A.M.

LUSITANIA SUNK BY A SUBMARINE, PROBABLY 1,260 DEAD;
TWICE TORPEDOED OFF IRISH COAST; SINKS IN 15 MINUTES;
CAPT. TURNER SAVED, FROHMAN AND VANDERBILT MISSING;
WASHINGTON BELIEVES THAT A GRAVE CRISIS IS AT HAND

The May 8, 1915, edition of the *New York Times* reported details of the *Lusitania* attack on its front page.

to agree with the viewpoint that George Washington held more than a century earlier. He believed that the republic should not "entangle our peace and prosperity in the toils of European ambition." U.S. neutrality in the war had brought the nation benefits, including profitable exports to Britain and France that boosted U.S. industry without any military cost.

The United States entered the war largely in response to Germany's submarine warfare. In 1915, a German U-boat sank the R.M.S. *Lusitania*, a privately owned British passenger ship that had many Americans onboard. After U.S. president **Woodrow Wilson** protested the unprovoked action, Germany promised to stop attacking ships without warning them first.

In January 1917, Germany foreign secretary Arthur Zimmermann, a backer of unregulated submarine attacks, sent a coded telegram to the Mexican president. He proposed that, in return for financial support, Mexico ally itself with Germany and "reconquer the lost territory in Texas, New Mexico, and Arizona." Britain intercepted the **Zimmermann Telegram**, translated it, and forwarded it to the United States in February.

That same month, Germany restored its policy of unrestricted submarine warfare against all shipping by any nation and sank three U.S. ships in March. President Wilson then asked Congress to declare war, proclaiming that "the world must be made safe for democracy." Congress complied with his request on April 6, 1917. The arrival of a million-strong U.S. force in Europe was the turning point in favor of the Allied cause. On November 11, 1918, the Germans signed an **armistice**, an agreement to end hostilities. The war was over.

HISTORICAL THINKING

1. **READING CHECK** How did new technology influence the Great War?

2. **MAKE GENERALIZATIONS** How did the Battle of Verdun echo the general experience of the armies fighting on the Western Front?

3. **ANALYZE CAUSE AND EFFECT** Why do you think governments limited freedom of speech and assembly during the war?

4. **FORM AND SUPPORT OPINIONS** Do you think that the United States should have remained neutral instead of involving itself in European affairs? Explain your response.

BACKGROUND FOR THE TEACHER

Woodrow Wilson and Neutrality U.S. president Woodrow Wilson was an idealist as well as a pacifist. He envisioned a world in which nations agreed to avoid arms races and in which the United States would help negotiate peace. As a boy, Wilson had witnessed the Civil War; as president, he was determined not to send American troops into similar conditions in Europe. Even after approving the idea of loans to Britain—prompted by the sinking of the *Lusitania*—Wilson clung to his neutrality stance. Various groups, including the Women's Christian Temperance Union and the United Mine Workers, participated in anti-war rallies that supported Wilson's policy of neutrality. In his "Peace Without Victory" speech of January 22, 1917, Wilson reiterated his policy of neutrality. Ultimately, however, his stance would not be able to forestall the United States' entry into war.

While Wilson wanted to stay out of the war in Europe, his interests beyond U.S. borders revolved around the idea that exporting American goods and democratic and capitalistic ideals would be good for the United States and other countries. In a 1916 address to the Salesmanship Congress in Detroit, Michigan, Wilson said:

Lift your eyes to the horizons of business: do not look too close at the little processes with which you are concerned, but let your thoughts and your imaginations run abroad throughout the whole world, and with the inspiration of the thought that you are Americans and are meant to carry liberty and justice and the principles of humanity wherever you go, go out and sell goods that will make the world more comfortable and more happy, and convert them to the principles of America.

TEACH

GUIDED DISCUSSION

3. **Integrate Visuals** How does the May 18, 1915, headline of *The New York Times* connect the event of the *Lusitania's* sinking to larger political developments? *(Possible response: The "grave crisis" mentioned in the headline likely refers to whether Wilson was considering the death of American passengers to be an act of war against the United States. One potential political development could be the U.S. entry into the war in Europe.)*

4. **Form and Support Opinions** What do you think the main impact might have been if America had not entered the war? Explain whether and how you think the war might have gone in a different direction. *(Answers will vary. Possible response: The Allies might have lost the war—they needed America's military might, not just its supplies.)*

MAKE INFERENCES

Have students review the "Through the Lens" feature about Jeff Gusky. **ASK:** What do the carvings indicate about the soldiers and life in the trenches? *(Answers will vary. Possible response: The carvings indicate that the underground cities created in the rock quarries provided an escape from the horrors of the trenches above ground.)* Explain that soldiers in the underground cities often left inscriptions on the walls, such as their names, hometowns, and addresses. **ASK:** Considering the context in which these events unfolded, why do you think they might have wanted to leave that kind of information behind? *(Answers will vary. Possible response: The soldiers faced the possibility of dying in the war at any moment. They wanted to leave behind evidence that they were there and that their contributions to the war mattered. They wanted people to remember them.)*

ACTIVE OPTIONS

On Your Feet: Roundtable Have students sit in groups of four around a table to discuss the following question: How did World War I change the way in which war was fought? Provide each group with a large sheet of paper. Tell group members to take turns jotting down as many answers to the question as possible. Encourage them not only to include warfare technology but also to make other connections—numbers of nations, people killed, alliances, and any other response they can justify to show ways in which World War I was different from previous wars. Then call on a representative from each group to share the group's ideas. You may wish to compile a master list of responses.

NG Learning Framework: Write a Photo Caption
SKILL Observation
KNOWLEDGE Our Human Story

Have students learn more about the World War I carvings photographed by Jeff Gusky. Direct students to Gusky's website to find additional carvings that Gusky recorded with his camera. Ask each student to choose two photographs and write a caption for each that describes the soldier's story captured by the photograph. As a class, discuss why the soldiers might have chosen to carve those particular items.

HISTORICAL THINKING

ANSWERS

1. The new technology caused more people to die in the Great War than any other conflict before it. Soldiers carried semiautomatic pistols, artillery pieces fired faster than earlier weapons, and single-barrel machine guns were more mobile. The Germans deployed more than 100,000 shells of poison phosgene gas. Airplanes allowed pilots to survey what was happening on the ground. Tanks were introduced. U-boats sank enemy ships, both military and civilian.

2. After 10 months of fighting in the Battle of Verdun, hundreds of thousands of soldiers had died, but neither side had secured much new territory. This pattern of low gains for high casualties repeated throughout the war.

3. Possible response: Governments likely limited free speech to silence opposition to the war or to their policies. They limited freedom of assembly to try to keep groups from demonstrating or making plans to undermine the war effort.

4. Possible responses: Yes, the United States should have remained neutral. World War I brought misery and pain to all participating nations, and the conflicts were on the other side of the world. No, the United States should not have remained neutral. It had much in common historically and politically with the Allies, and a German victory would have posed a threat to European democracy.

Global Dimensions of Total War

In the past, historians writing about the First World War generally focused on the Western Front and on the Europeans who fought there, which left a lot of the story uncovered. They now have a better idea of the worldwide range of this conflict.

This Senegalese Sharpshooter fighting for "the greater glory of France" is most likely a West African Muslim. He wears several German helmets atop his head.

GALLIPOLI: AN EXAMPLE OF GLOBAL WAR

By the time the United States joined the Allies in 1917, the Great War was truly a world war. Battles took place in various regions of Europe, Asia, and Africa. The theaters of war—areas of land, sea, or air directly involved in military operations—also included the North Sea, Mediterranean Sea, and Atlantic and Pacific oceans.

In 1915, with the Western Front in stalemate, Allied military leaders looked for a major victory elsewhere. They decided that the Ottoman Empire, the weakest of the Central Powers, could be defeated fairly quickly. They were wrong.

The Allies' Ottoman strategy called for taking the Dardanelles. This narrow strait is part of a waterway that leads from the Mediterranean Sea to the Black Sea. The Ottoman capital, Constantinople, was located between these two bodies of water, along the Sea of Marmara. Controlling the Dardanelles and then capturing Constantinople would open up the waterway as a badly needed Allied supply route to Russia. This defeat would also likely knock the Ottoman Empire out of the war.

In February 1915, fully armed British and French battleships tried to force their way through the thin channel. Ottoman artillery, fired from the heights above the port of Gallipoli, pushed them back. The Allies shifted to a new strategy.

In April, Britain and France attacked the heavily fortified high ground. These ground troops included soldiers from Australia, New Zealand, Ireland, India, Arabia, and Senegal. The Ottomans fiercely defended their positions. The Allies resorted to trench warfare, but they were overmatched. In January 1916, having experienced 250,000 casualties, they withdrew.

706 CHAPTER 25

MOBILIZATION OF COLONIAL SUBJECTS

In the wake of their losses at Gallipoli, British leaders decided they could no longer spare men or war materials from their home islands to fight on the Southern Front. Instead, they relied on army units from their African and Asian colonies.

The British army sent Jamaican soldiers from its West Indian Regiment against the Ottomans in Palestine. The majority of troops in that theater were Egyptian soldiers under British command. Meanwhile, Indian soldiers engaged Ottoman forces in Mesopotamia. India also

supplied troops to fight on the Western Front, and by the end of the war, Britain had mobilized some 1.5 million Indians.

To help their effort against the Ottomans, the British formed an alliance with Arab leaders eager to overthrow Turkish rule. Having been promised an independent Arab kingdom after the war, Arab fighters conducted guerrilla strikes against Ottoman positions. Elsewhere, Egyptian forces helped the British take Jerusalem, and Indian troops captured Baghdad. Many of these allied soldiers were Muslims.

France, who did little fighting outside of Europe, also looked to its empire for support. At the start of the war, colonial French troops numbered around 90,000. The most famous regiment was the Senegalese Sharpshooters, who were mostly young Muslims. Of the 130,000 of these highly disciplined soldiers sent to the Western Front, around 30,000 died and many more were wounded.

When the number of volunteers from its imperial possessions in Africa did not meet wartime demand, France turned to conscription. French officials pressured local African leaders to supply troops for the French army. France ended up recruiting more than 400,000 men from its African colonies. Most of them served in Africa as laborers or as porters, carrying supplies for the army.

In Southeast Asia, the French recruited young Vietnamese men for the Indochinese Labor Corps. These young conscripts worked on the Western Front, behind the battle lines. They performed tedious tasks such as digging fortifications and maintaining roads, which allowed the French army to concentrate more troops on the front line. At the same time, rice and rubber from Indochina were exported to France to further support the war effort.

The Indians, West Africans, and Vietnamese who served as volunteers or conscripts contributed greatly to the Allied victory in the war, as did the civilians in colonial territories who produced coffee, rubber, tin, and many other goods for imperial forces. However, they received little in return. Later, anti-colonial nationalists would base their claims to greater self-government or independence on the sacrifices they made during World War I.

Members of an Indian cavalry march near the Franco-Belgian border in 1915.

The Allied troops entrenched at Gallipoli suffered through trying environmental conditions. The heat, poor sanitation, and intestinal diseases all served to sap soldiers' strength. One British soldier still remembered the flies, long after the Gallipoli campaign had ended.

PRIMARY SOURCE

One of the biggest curses was the flies. There was millions and millions and millions of flies. The whole of the side of the trench used to be one black swarming mass. Anything you opened, if you opened a tin of bully [canned beef] or went to eat a biscuit [cookie], next minute it would be swarming with flies. They were all around your mouth and on any cuts or sores that you'd got. . . . It was a curse, really, it really was.

—from an oral history by British private Harold Boughton, 1984

HISTORICAL THINKING

1. **READING CHECK** What two strategies did the Allies employ to attack the Ottoman Empire between 1915 and 1916?

2. **MAKE INFERENCES** Why do you think it was so important to the Allies to "knock the Ottoman Empire out of the war"?

3. **DRAW CONCLUSIONS** How did colonial conscripts feel about fighting for France?

The First World War and 20th-Century Revolutions 707

PLAN: 2-PAGE LESSON

OBJECTIVE

Explain how the global nature of World War I was exemplified by Britain's and France's use of resources from their colonial holdings around the world.

CRITICAL THINKING SKILLS FOR LESSON 1.4

- Make Inferences
- Draw Conclusions
- Explain
- Identify Supporting Details
- Analyze Primary Sources

HISTORICAL THINKING FOR CHAPTER 25

How did the Great War affect the world politically, socially, and economically?

At the time of World War I, Britain and France were global imperial powers with significant colonial holdings. Lesson 1.4 shows how these two empires used their colonial resources—human and otherwise—to their advantage.

BACKGROUND FOR THE TEACHER

Fighting the War in East Africa Battles between German East Africa and British-controlled Kenya also demonstrated the scope of total war. The British, like the French, Portuguese, and Germans, had colonies in Africa, and the continent's minerals, precious metals, and farmable land were highly prized. Tensions among the colonizing nations had been simmering for decades, and the Great War ignited them. Just as the war began, Britain was concerned about protecting its trade routes to and from Africa. Indeed, the first shot fired by a British soldier in the war was by an officer in present-day Togo, which was then the German colony of Togoland. Britain's African army was largely made up of Indian soldiers, and German officers led African soldiers on the other side. Germany's main goal was to tie down the Anglo-Indian forces to keep them from being redeployed to the Middle East. Germany therefore repeatedly struck and then retreated, requisitioning local food reserves and destroying what was left to deny sustenance to its opponents. Famine and disease stalked the land as total war reached even the remote interior of East Africa.

INTRODUCE & ENGAGE

USE VISUALS AS A SPRINGBOARD

Direct students' attention to the visuals in this lesson. Draw a T-Chart on the board, labeling the first column *Visuals* and the second column *Questions*. Ask students what questions these visuals bring to mind. Record their questions in the T-Chart. After students have read and discussed the lesson, prompt them to answer the listed questions.

TEACH

GUIDED DISCUSSION

1. **Explain** Why did the Allies turn their attention to defeating the Ottoman Empire in 1915? *(because the Western Front in Europe had reached a stalemate)*

2. **Identify Supporting Details** What role did the country of Vietnam play in the war? *(Vietnam was a French territory. France brought young Vietnamese men to the Western Front where they performed hard labor, such as digging fortifications and maintaining roads. The country's resources were also used; rice and rubber were exported to France during the war.)*

ANALYZE PRIMARY SOURCES

Ask students to reread the excerpt from the oral history of the British private. **ASK:** What does the soldier say was one of the main problems with so many flies? *(The flies covered anything he or his fellow soldiers tried to eat.)* What inferences about fighting the war can you draw from the excerpt? *(Possible response: The war was extremely hard on soldiers for many reasons. They were in danger of being killed by weapons; the conditions were awful; flies and ticks likely carried disease.)*

ACTIVE OPTIONS

On Your Feet: Inside-Outside Circle Arrange students in concentric circles facing each other. Direct each student in the outside circle to ask a question about the global nature of the war. Each student in the inside circle answers his or her partner's question. On a signal, students should rotate to create new partnerships. On another signal, students trade inside/outside roles.

> **NG Learning Framework: Design an Infographic Map**
> **SKILL** Communication
> **KNOWLEDGE** Our Human Story

Ask groups to summarize the global nature of World War I in an illustrated and annotated infographic map. The base image should be a world map, and students should highlight the various non-European nations they read about in the lesson that became involved in the war because of their alliances or because they were colonies of one of the major powers. Infographics should use text, visuals, and graphics (such as arrows, lines, and callout boxes) to show details such as which country was allied with which other country, what battles took place in certain places, and so forth. Groups should display their maps.

DIFFERENTIATE

ENGLISH LANGUAGE LEARNERS

Read in Pairs Pair students at the **Beginning** and **Intermediate** levels with English-proficient speakers to read the lesson together, pausing when they hear a word or sentence construction that is confusing. Have English-proficient speakers point out context clues to help their partners understand the meanings of unfamiliar terms or constructions. Ask English language learners to restate sentences in their own words.

PRE-AP

Write Diary Entries Instruct students to use online and print sources to find more primary sources from World War I soldiers like Harold Boughton. (Have them also look for firsthand war accounts from other people who served in the war, such as medics.) Tell students to then write their own war diary excerpt as if they served alongside one of the people they found in their research. They should include rich and specific details about the war. Invite students to present their diary entries.

See the Chapter Planner for more strategies for differentiation.

HISTORICAL THINKING

ANSWERS

1. They sailed battleships into the Dardanelles. Then they sent ground troops against the Ottoman forces.

2. Possible responses: Doing so would open an Allied water supply route to Russia, helping the Russian forces on the Eastern Front. The Allies would gain more control of the Mediterranean Sea and the Black Sea. Defeat of the Ottoman Empire would have been a blow to the morale of the Central Powers.

3. Possible responses: Some probably accepted it as their patriotic duty or because they earned a salary. Others probably felt no responsibility to fight for their imperialist rulers, especially if it meant becoming a casualty of war.

Postwar Treaties and Conflicts

After the First World War, the victors had an opportunity to put world affairs on a new, more stable, and peaceful path. Would their decisions ensure a better future for themselves as well as for those they defeated?

Territorial Changes in Europe After World War I

POSTWAR SETTLEMENTS

Recall that the entry of the United States into World War I tipped the balance toward the Allies, which put the United States in a position to influence the peace talks that followed the armistice. Those meetings took place in Versailles, just outside Paris, in 1919. The Central Powers were excluded from the Paris Peace Conference, as were Asians and Africans whose fates were also to be determined.

As diplomats headed to the conference, a lethal outbreak of influenza was racing around the world. Between 1918 and 1920, as many as 50 million people died from it, far more than those who had lost their lives during the war itself. This **pandemic**, or worldwide outbreak of infectious disease, further deepened the global distress resulting from the Great War. The world seemed changed in some fundamental way, leaving people uncertain about the future.

In this charged atmosphere, representatives of the Allies gathered in Versailles. They faced the enormous challenge of reincorporating a defeated Germany into Europe as well as addressing the postwar collapse of the Austro-Hungarian and Ottoman empires. Their declines left entire regions of central Europe and Southwest Asia in need of new political systems.

U.S. president Wilson presented a plan known as the Fourteen Points in a speech to Congress months before the war ended. The plan contained recommendations based on a few clear principles. Wilson called for freedom of navigation on the seas and progress toward free trade, and he spoke against treaties drawn up in secret. He supported the right of people to engage in **self-determination**—the process by which a people forms its own state and chooses its own government. He also proposed the creation of a permanent international assembly to safeguard against future wars.

The other Allies, however, had their own agendas. The British wanted to safeguard their imperial interests. The French priority was to penalize Germany. And the Italians wanted some of Austria-Hungary's territory.

In the end, the **Treaty of Versailles**, signed in June 1919, fell far short of Wilson's goals. Britain and France held to their imperialist ambitions, refusing to encourage self-determination in their colonies. France insisted on punishing Germany. The Germans had to hand over all of their colonial possessions and about 10 percent of their territory, which included the return of Alsace-Lorraine to France.

The Allies forced Germany and Austria-Hungary to take the blame for starting the war, in what is known as the "war-guilt" clause of the treaty. Germany also had to agree to provide **reparations**—money or goods paid to cover wartime damages—totaling some $33 billion. To keep Germany from starting another conflict, the Allies limited the size of its army and banned it from producing tanks, submarines, and other weapons of war.

The Allies did not ignore all of Wilson's ideas. They accepted his plan for a **League of Nations**, the assembly of sovereign states that intended to provide a permanent diplomatic forum in hopes of avoiding future conflict. However, the U.S. Senate rejected membership in the league and refused to ratify the Treaty of Versailles, thus returning to the United States' prewar position of avoiding entanglement in European affairs.

NATION-BUILDING IN EUROPE

The German Empire ended in November 1918, when Wilhelm II abdicated. In 1919, as peace talks took place in France, the German assembly established a liberal, democratic constitution and a government known as the **Weimar Republic**. The new government faced enormous challenges. At the war's end, the German people were hungry, cold, and dejected. The treaty's

huge reparation payments undermined Germany's recovery, and its military and territorial reductions wounded the people's national pride.

German centrists in the government tried to promote the liberal political culture needed to sustain a free society. Other and more radical elements opposed them, leading to uprisings, an attempt to seize power, and general instability. By 1923, the republic was struggling. It could not pay reparations. The government printed more money, but that caused inflation to spiral out of control. By 1925, the situation began to improve. International agreements eased Germany's reparations payments, the economy returned to prewar levels, and Germany was offered membership in the League of Nations.

Postwar diplomacy created new nations in eastern, central, and southeastern Europe, but nearly all of them proved to be unstable. They were prone to **authoritarianism**, a political system characterized by a powerful leader and limited individual freedoms. The complex mix of ethnic, linguistic, and religious groups in these regions made democratic government difficult, especially when leaders targeted minority groups.

The slide toward authoritarian rule arose mainly from a conflict between two ideologies. Nationalism, you may recall, stresses loyalty to the nation-state, while liberalism focuses on the rights of individuals within the state. Nationalists also had an "us versus them" view of the world. They tended to restrict the rights of minorities rather than follow the liberal philosophy of protecting the individual rights of all people, regardless of their ethnic background. The problem was particularly acute for groups such as Europe's Jews and Roma (formerly called Gypsies), neither of whom had an official state of their own to protect them.

HISTORICAL THINKING

1. **READING CHECK** What key goals kept the British and French from supporting Wilson's Fourteen Points?

2. **IDENTIFY PROBLEMS AND SOLUTIONS** Why did the representatives at the peace talks near Paris agree to form the League of Nations?

3. **MAKE INFERENCES** How did the reparations clause of the Treaty of Versailles stifle Germany's economic recovery?

PLAN: 2-PAGE LESSON

OBJECTIVE

Summarize the peace process at the end of World War I and its geopolitical implications.

CRITICAL THINKING SKILLS FOR LESSON 2.1

- Identify Problems and Solutions
- Make Inferences
- Evaluate
- Compare and Contrast
- Analyze Visuals

HISTORICAL THINKING FOR CHAPTER 25

How did the Great War affect the world politically, socially, and economically?

The negotiations that took place at the end of the Great War amounted to a wholescale geopolitical re-sorting of much of the world. Lesson 2.1 explores the settlements and conflicts that resulted from the peace process.

Student eEdition online

Additional content for this lesson, including photos and captions, is available online.

BACKGROUND FOR THE TEACHER

The League of Nations The League of Nations was established in 1920, with headquarters in Geneva, Switzerland. Its two main bodies were an Assembly of Member States and a Council made up of 5 permanent members—the United Kingdom, France, Italy, Japan, and Germany (from 1926 to 1933)—and up to 10 rotating members. The Secretariat aided in administrative matters, and a Court of International Justice met in The Hague, in the Netherlands, to rule on international disputes. The United States was not a member of the league because the U.S. Congress rejected it, much to President Woodrow Wilson's disappointment. Wilson campaigned hard in support of American membership, telling Congress, "There can be no question of our ceasing to be a world power. The only question is whether we can refuse the moral leadership that is offered us, whether we shall accept or reject the confidence of the world. . . ." Although the United States never joined, the Harding, Coolidge, and Hoover administrations were sympathetic to much of the League's work.

INTRODUCE & ENGAGE

TALK ABOUT WINNING

Prompt students to think about various instances in which one person or group faces off against another, such as a sporting event or an argument. **ASK:** What does it mean to be the victor? *(Possible responses: One side wins, proving it is stronger or better than the other. One side gets what it wants.)* If there is a winner, does there also have to be a loser? *(Possible response: No, there could be a tie, or both could win in different ways.)* Explain that before the United States entered the war, President Wilson advocated for a "Peace Without Victory." **ASK:** What do you think that phrase means? *(Possible response: It means that both sides agree to end a conflict without declaring that one side won and the other lost.)*

TEACH

GUIDED DISCUSSION

1. **Evaluate** How successful was Wilson in negotiating the Treaty of Versailles? Cite evidence to support your answer. *(moderately successful; he experienced both victories—peace was established and his idea for a League of Nations was adopted by the international community—and defeats—Congress refused to have the United States join the League of Nations or ratify the Treaty of Versailles.)*

2. **Compare and Contrast** How was Germany's condition different in 1925 than in 1923? *(In 1923, Germany was struggling. The terms of the Treaty of Versailles left it poor, humiliated, and suffering from inflation and other economic maladies. By 1925, however, its economy had recovered somewhat and it was invited to join the League of Nations.)*

ANALYZE VISUALS

Ask students to study the map. **ASK:** Which countries lost territory as a result of the war? *(the German, Russian, and Austro-Hungarian empires and Bulgaria)* Where is South Tyrol, and what was its status before and after the war? *(a small area in southern Austria; Before the war, it was part of the Austro-Hungarian Empire. After the war, it became part of Italy.)* Which countries had been part of the Russian Empire before the war? *(Finland, Estonia, Latvia, Lithuania, Poland, and Bessarabia)*

ACTIVE OPTIONS

On Your Feet: Numbered Heads Arrange students in four groups, and assign each group one of the following topics: Wilson's Fourteen Points, the Treaty of Versailles, the League of Nations, postwar Germany. Students should number off within each group; then groups should discuss the topic so that any member can report for the group. Finally, call a number and have the students with that number report for their group.

NG Learning Framework: Discuss Authoritarianism
ATTITUDE Curiosity
SKILL Collaboration

Ask small groups to discuss this question: What is authoritarianism and why did it emerge at the end of World War I? Have them generate as many responses as they can, making sure their discussion covers nationalism and liberalism. As a class, compile a master list of responses.

DIFFERENTIATE

ENGLISH LANGUAGE LEARNERS

Use Terms in Sentences Pair English language learners of mixed proficiencies. Ask the more English-proficient partner to model the exercise by using the first Key Vocabulary term in a sentence. Tell them to take turns composing sentences for each Key Vocabulary term in the lesson. Have pairs share their sentences with the class. Discuss different ways to use each word.

PRE-AP

Research the Weimar Republic Review with students that the Weimar Republic was created by Germany at the end of the Great War in an effort to establish a democratic government. Challenge students to conduct online research about the Weimar Republic. Ask them to learn about its political leaders, including the centrists and radicals who set its political agenda and who rose to power. Invite students to present their findings to the class in an oral or written report.

See the Chapter Planner for more strategies for differentiation.

HISTORICAL THINKING

ANSWERS

1. They wanted to hold on to their empires, so they did not support self-determination. The French also wanted to punish Germany.

2. Possible response: They recognized the need for an international assembly at which nations could iron out their differences before they led to armed conflict.

3. Possible response: Germany had to pay so much in reparations that it could not rebuild its economy.

CRITICAL VIEWING (available in the Student eEdition) The value of German money plunged so low that children were allowed to play with banknotes, since they were practically worthless.

2.2 The Paris Peace Conference

How would you feel if you could not determine your own future and, instead, a group of powerful people determined it for you? At the Paris Peace Conference in 1919, four countries—Britain, France, Italy, and the United States—made decisions that affected the political and economic future of much of the world.

In 1919, delegates from the victorious nations traveled to France for the Paris Peace Conference. Concerned about the outcome of those negotiations, representatives from defeated nations like Germany and spokespeople for African, Southeast Asian, and Arab societies entangled in European empires also came to Paris, but they were not allowed to participate in peace talks. They could only wait to see what the Allies would decide for them.

Syrian nationalists had sided with Britain against the Ottoman Empire during the war, and after the fighting ceased Syria wanted independence. Influenced by Woodrow Wilson's Fourteen Points, a young nationalist named Nguyen Ai Quoc (later know as Ho Chi Minh) sought greater autonomy for Vietnam. And the Pan-African Congress demanded an end to colonial rule.

W.E.B. Du Bois (doo BOYS)—an African-American scholar, journalist, and social reformer—helped organize the first formal Pan-African Congress in 1919 in Paris. Nearly 60 representatives from 15 nations joined Du Bois in France to ask the Allies and their associates to "establish a code of laws for the international protection of the natives of Africa."

DOCUMENT ONE

Primary Source: Resolution from the "Congress of Damascus Resolution" by the General Syrian Congress of Damascus, July 2, 1919

Article 22 of the Covenant, or formal agreement, of the League of Nations classified Syria as one of the territories "not yet able to stand by themselves under the strenuous conditions of the modern world." France was assigned to provide advice and assistance until Syria was "able to stand alone." The Syrian Congress passed a resolution that attempted to stop France from applying Article 22.

CONSTRUCTED RESPONSE Why would an independent Syrian government, as described in the excerpt, appeal to the expressed democratic ideals of France, Britain, and the United States?

We ask that the Government of this Syrian country should be a democratic civil constitutional Monarchy on broad decentralization principles, safeguarding the rights of minorities. . . .

Considering the fact that the Arabs inhabiting the Syrian area are not naturally less [capable] than other more advanced races . . . we protest against Article 22 of the Covenant of the League of Nations, placing us among the nations in their middle stage of development which stand in need of a mandatory power. . . .

We do not acknowledge any right claimed by the French Government in any part whatever of our Syrian country.

DOCUMENT TWO

Primary Source: Petition from "Eight Points" by Nguyen Ai Quoc, 1919

Nguyen Ai Quoc drafted and submitted an eight-point petition to the Paris Peace Conference. His demands reflected Wilson's call for self-determination as well as Thomas Jefferson's ideas about equality and rights. Nguyen aimed his requests at "the governments of the Allied Powers in general, and the French government in particular."

CONSTRUCTED RESPONSE According to the petition, did Nguyen demand independence for Vietnam? Explain your response.

1. General amnesty for all Vietnamese political prisoners.
2. Equal rights for Vietnamese and French in Indochina, suppression of the Criminal Commissions which are instruments of terrorism aimed at Vietnamese patriots.
3. Freedom of press and opinion.
4. Freedom of association and assembly.
5. Freedom to travel at home and abroad.
6. Freedom to study and the opening of technical and professional schools for natives of the colonies.
7. Substitute rule of law for government by decree.
8. Appointment of a Vietnamese delegation alongside that of the French government to settle questions related to Vietnamese interests.

DOCUMENT THREE

Primary Source: Manifesto from "To the World" by the Second Pan-African Congress, 1921

In 1921, the Second Pan-African Congress met in London, Brussels, and Paris. Delegates came from Africa, the Caribbean, Europe, and the United States. These representatives produced a manifesto in hopes of persuading the Allied powers to encourage and support self-determination in Africa and around the world.

CONSTRUCTED RESPONSE What political demands did the Second Pan-African Congress delegates make in their manifesto?

The absolute equality of races, physical, political, and social, is the founding stone of world peace and human advancement. . . . The beginning of wisdom in interracial contact is the establishment of political institutions among suppressed [conquered] peoples. The habit of democracy must be made to encircle the earth. . . . Local self-government with a minimum of help and oversight can be established tomorrow in Asia, in Africa, in America and in the Isles of the Sea.

SYNTHESIZE & WRITE

1. **REVIEW** Review what you have learned about the political desires of colonial peoples after the Great War.
2. **RECALL** On your own paper, list two details about the person or organization that produced one of the excerpts and two details about the excerpt itself.
3. **CONSTRUCT** Construct a topic sentence that answers this question: What kind of political system did colonial peoples favor?
4. **WRITE** Using evidence from the documents, write a paragraph that supports your topic sentence in Step 3.

PLAN: 2-PAGE LESSON

OBJECTIVE

Analyze written appeals to the Allied powers after the Paris Peace Conference in 1919.

CRITICAL THINKING SKILLS FOR LESSON 2.2

- Synthesize
- Form and Support Opinions
- Compare and Contrast
- Evaluate

HISTORICAL THINKING FOR CHAPTER 25

How did the Great War affect the world politically, socially, and economically?

Lesson 2.2 focuses on excerpts from political leaders in Syria, Vietnam, and Africa asking for their country's right to independence and self-determination during and after the Paris Peace Conference in 1919. These excerpts help us understand the political desires of colonial peoples after the Great War.

BACKGROUND FOR THE TEACHER

William Edward Burghardt Du Bois was born on February 23, 1868, in Great Barrington, Massachusetts. Du Bois received his Ph.D. from Harvard University in 1895. At the time, many sociologists were discussing race relations, but Du Bois focused on the conditions of blacks in the United States. He became a professor at Atlanta University and wrote 16 research monographs based on his investigations. Eventually, he came to believe that in a climate of racism, social change could only be accomplished through agitation and protest. In 1905, Du Bois founded the Niagara Movement, which led to the development of the NAACP in 1909. Du Bois became the director of research and editor of its magazine. However, his most influential achievement was his advocacy of Pan-Africanism. Du Bois was the leader of the Pan-African Conference in 1900 and brought about four more Pan-African Congresses between 1919 and 1927. Du Bois believed that all people of African descent should work together to fight for their freedoms. Through his own writing, he also cultivated the development of black literature and art throughout the world. In 1934, he left the NAACP because he believed the organization was ignoring the problems of the black masses. He returned to Atlanta University as a professor and devoted the rest of his life to teaching and writing.

INTRODUCE & ENGAGE

PREPARE FOR THE DOCUMENT-BASED QUESTION

Before students start on the activity, briefly preview the three documents. Remind students that a constructed response requires full explanations in complete sentences. Emphasize that students should use what they have learned about the Allied powers and the political desires of colonial peoples after the Great War in addition to the information in the documents.

TEACH

GUIDED DISCUSSION

1. **Form and Support Opinions** Based on Nguyen's petition, which point do you think is most important? *(Answers will vary. Students should choose one of the eight points and supply an explanation for their reasoning.)*

2. **Compare and Contrast** Direct students to compare and contrast the written appeals made to the Allied powers. **ASK:** Which excerpt do you feel is the most compelling? Explain. *(Answers will vary. Possible response: "To the World" is the most compelling because it calls for absolute equality, and I agree that equality is central for world peace and human advancement.)*

EVALUATE

After students have completed the Synthesize & Write activity, allow time for them to exchange paragraphs and read and comment on the work of their peers. Establish guidelines for comments prior to the activity so that feedback is constructive and encouraging. Comments should focus on the most significant parts that address the purpose of the activity and the audience.

ACTIVE OPTION

On Your Feet: Host a DBQ Roundtable Divide the class into groups of four. Hand each group a sheet of paper with the following question: What rights and freedoms are necessary for people to attain equality? Instruct the first student in each group to write an answer, read it aloud, and pass the paper clockwise to the next student. The paper may circulate around a group several times. Then reconvene the class and discuss the groups' responses.

DIFFERENTIATE

STRIVING READERS

Summarize Read each document aloud to students. Have two students work together, as one student rereads a document and the other student summarizes the document. After each document is summarized, read the constructed response question with all of the students to make sure all students understand it. Then have volunteers suggest responses. Complete this activity until all of the documents have been reread and summarized.

GIFTED & TALENTED

Write a News Report Assign students the role of journalists reporting on the Paris Peace Conference in 1919. Point out that news reports begin with the most important information and usually answer most or all of the questions *Who?, What?, Where?, When?, Why?,* and *How?* by the end. Invite students to post their articles on a class blog or publish them on a class or grade website.

SYNTHESIZE & WRITE

ANSWERS

1. Answers will vary.

2. Answers will vary. Possible response: Nguyen Ai Quoc was a Vietnamese nationalist; Woodrow Wilson's Fourteen Points influenced him. The "Eight Points" excerpt includes a demand for equal rights for the Vietnamese and French in Indochina; it also calls for various freedoms for the Vietnamese people.

3. Answers will vary. Possible response: After the Great War, colonial peoples favored a democratic political system.

4. Answers will vary. Students' informative paragraphs should include their topic sentence from Step 3 and provide several details from the documents to support the sentence.

CONSTRUCTED RESPONSE

Document One: Possible response: The Syrians claim that their government would be a democratic civil constitutional monarchy and that it will safeguard the rights of minorities. These liberal political ideas are similar to those found in France, Britain, and the United States.

Document Two: No, the petition does not demand independence but rather an equal share with the French in making decisions relevant to the Vietnamese people.

Document Three: The manifesto calls for the absolute equality of races, democracy, and local self-government.

The Armenian Genocide

Imagine being told by government officials that you must leave your home. They give you barely any time to sell your possessions and pack your things. Armed guards march you, your family, and all your neighbors out of your village. You have no idea where they will take you. Many Armenians faced this exact fate in the Ottoman Empire.

CRITICAL VIEWING Yepraksia Gevorgyan (seated) and her family escaped the Armenian genocide by crossing the Akhurian River, pictured in the large photographic panel behind her, in 1915. She remembers the river, now bordering Armenia and Turkey, as "red, full of blood" after the Ottomans threw dead Armenians into the water. What does the panel add to this portrait of Gevorgyan?

NATIONALISM, REBELLION, AND WAR

Anatolia (present-day Turkey) was the core territory of the Ottoman Empire. Most Armenians in the empire lived as peasant farmers in eastern Anatolia. They considered this mountainous region their homeland, although they remained a minority within it. Armenians also lived just across Anatolia's northeastern border in the Caucasus region of southern Russia.

For centuries, Armenian Christians had flourished in the Ottoman Empire. But rising Turkish nationalism made their situation less comfortable, and by the 1880s, some Armenian leaders began to call for a nation of their own. Ottoman leaders refused to listen to Armenian demands because Armenian self-determination could lead to the breakup of their empire.

During World War I, the Ottomans faced an invasion by Russia across their northeastern border. Some Armenian revolutionaries fought alongside the Russians and otherwise aided the Russian army against the Ottoman troops. Pressured by events on the Eastern Front, Russia chose to pull its forces out of Ottoman territory.

DEPORTATIONS AND DEATH

Ottoman leaders decided that because some Armenians were aiding enemy Russians, the leaders were justified in taking radical steps against them. In the first few months of 1915, government orders led to the murder of many Armenian leaders and soldiers as well as Armenian villagers thought to support Russia. These human rights violations were just the beginning of the retaliations. Mehmed Talaat Pasha (meh-MEHT tah-LAHT pah-SHAH), a top Ottoman leader, ordered a series of mass **deportations**, or removals, of Armenians from eastern Anatolia and other areas.

From the spring through the fall of 1915, entire Armenian villages were emptied. Able-bodied men were killed. Women, children, and the elderly were forced to march southward through the mountainous terrain of eastern Anatolia. Most Armenians who survived this trek ended up in camps in the Syrian Desert. Others were sent farther east into an arid, hostile region of Mesopotamia. Often left without food or shelter, many died of starvation or exposure to the desert environment.

Henry Morgenthau wrote a book at the end of the First World War. In it, he cites a conversation with Talaat Pasha in which the Ottoman leader clarifies why his government began deporting Armenians in August 1915. Talaat Pasha was assassinated in 1921 in Berlin by an Armenian nationalist.

PRIMARY SOURCE

"I have asked you to come to-day," began Talaat, "so that I can explain our position on the whole Armenian subject. We base our objections to the Armenians on three distinct grounds. In the first place, they have enriched themselves at the expense of the Turks. In the second place, they are determined to domineer over us and to establish a separate state. In the third place, they have openly encouraged our enemies. They have assisted the Russians in the Caucasus and our failure there is largely explained by their actions. We have therefore come to the irrevocable decision that we shall make them powerless before this war is ended."

—from *Ambassador Morgenthau's Story* by Henry Morgenthau, 1918

As U.S. ambassador to the Ottoman Empire from 1913 to 1916, Henry Morgenthau had access to information about the mass Armenian deportations. On July 16, 1915, he wrote a telegram to the U.S. secretary of state describing what he had learned. "Deportation of and excesses against peaceful Armenians is increasing," he explained, "and from harrowing reports of eyewitnesses it appears that a campaign of race extermination is in progress under a pretext of reprisal against rebellion." In spite of his report, the U.S. government failed to act. Since the United States had not officially declared war on the Ottoman Empire and no American rights had been violated, President Wilson did not encourage intervention.

Historians generally agree that what Morgenthau called "race extermination" amounted to an Armenian genocide. Hundreds of thousands of Armenians—perhaps as many as 1.5 million—died during the deportation period. Many others escaped into neighboring countries, where relief organizations such as the International Red Cross supplied desperately needed aid to the survivors. Most Armenians would never return to their homes. They had lost their property, their possessions, and for many, their families.

HISTORICAL THINKING

1. **READING CHECK** Why did some Armenians clash with Ottoman leadership?

2. **DRAW CONCLUSIONS** Why do you think the U.S. government did not take action to stop the deportations?

3. **ANALYZE SOURCES** What reasons did Mehmed Talat Pasha give the U.S. ambassador for the Ottoman government's deportation of the Armenians?

PLAN: 2-PAGE LESSON

OBJECTIVE

Describe the expulsion of Armenians from the Ottoman Empire that is today widely believed to have been genocide.

CRITICAL THINKING SKILLS FOR LESSON 2.3

- Draw Conclusions
- Analyze Sources
- Make Connections
- Make Inferences
- Analyze Primary Sources

HISTORICAL THINKING FOR CHAPTER 25

How did the Great War affect the world politically, socially, and economically?

The political situation before, during, and after World War I was an environment ripe for nationalism. One example was in the Ottoman Empire, where Turkish and Armenian nationalism were on the rise. Lesson 2.3 describes how, when nationalist segments of the Armenian population decided to support Russia in the war, the Ottomans used that as an excuse to completely purge their empire of Armenians.

BACKGROUND FOR THE TEACHER

The Armenian Genocide To this day, there is still disagreement around the Armenian genocide. Perhaps not surprisingly, Turkey argues that much of the story is exaggerated. For example, Armenians claim 1.5 million died in the genocide, and Turkey believes the number to be closer to 300,000. Turkey also disputes the central idea that the genocide was premeditated. Turkish officials say there was nothing systematic about the killing of Armenians—as there was, say, with Jews in Germany during the Holocaust in World War II—just that it was an extremely unfortunate side effect of mass relocation, which the Turkish do not deny doing. Armenians push back, saying that from the earliest days of the war, Armenians were persecuted, and it was deadly. They point to April 24, 1915, as the beginning of the genocide; on that day 50 Armenian leaders were arrested and later executed. Today, some countries officially refer to "genocide"; others, including the United States, do not. Who uses the term and who does not is a source of great diplomatic tension between Turkey and many nations.

Student eEdition online

Additional content for this lesson, including a photograph, is available online.

INTRODUCE & ENGAGE

PREVIEW USING VISUALS

Ask students to look at the photograph and its caption. **ASK:** Based on the photo and caption, what questions do you have about the Armenian genocide? *(Possible responses: Why did the Ottomans kill so many Armenians that the Akhurian River was "full of blood"? When did the Armenian genocide occur, before or after the Great War?)*

TEACH

GUIDED DISCUSSION

1. **Make Connections** What reason might the Ottoman Empire's Armenian population have had for aiding Russia during World War I? *(The Ottoman Empire was invaded by Russia during World War I, and some Armenian revolutionaries may have felt that if Russia were to be victorious, the Ottoman Empire would break up and Armenia would have an opportunity to become its own nation.)*

2. **Make Inferences** During the Armenian genocide, why were able-bodied men killed when women and children were deported? *(The Ottoman Empire probably regarded able-bodied men as a greater threat, thinking they could rebel or revolt. They probably thought women and children were less likely to do that, so they spared them.)*

ANALYZE PRIMARY SOURCES

Have students review the excerpt from Henry Morgenthau's book. **ASK:** What were the "three grounds" on which Talaat Pasha defended the deportation of Armenians? *(that the Armenians have enriched themselves at the expense of the Turks, want to break away and establish their own state, and sided with Russia in the Great War)* If you were in the position of the ambassador, would you think any part of Talaat Pasha's explanation was sound? Explain your reasoning. *(Answers will vary.)*

ACTIVE OPTIONS

On Your Feet: Fishbowl Arrange students in two concentric circles. Ask students in the inner circle to discuss this question: What caused the Armenian genocide? Ask students in the outer circle to listen carefully to the discussion. After a time, direct the two circles to exchange places. Ask the new inner circle to discuss this question: What actually happened during the Armenian genocide? Ask both groups to draw conclusions about why the Armenian genocide remains a controversial issue today.

> **NG Learning Framework: Write a Letter to the Editor**
> **SKILL** Communication
> **KNOWLEDGE** Our Human Story

Ask students to imagine it is 10 years or so after the end of World War I and they are assisting Ambassador Henry Morgenthau. As part of their work, they became familiar with the arguments on both sides of the Armenian genocide. Instruct students to write a letter for publication in a newspaper, expressing and supporting the view that the Armenian deportation was indeed genocide. As part of their letter, have them refute the points made by Talaat Pasha. Students may compile the letters into a classroom display or post them on a classroom website.

DIFFERENTIATE

INCLUSION

Use Clarifying Questions Allow students with disabilities to work with students who are able to read the lesson aloud to them and describe the photo. Tell partners to ask and answer clarifying questions and answer the Critical Viewing and Historical Thinking questions.

PRE-AP

Write a Report Tell students to research and write a report on the Armenian genocide, focusing on one aspect of the issue, such as Armenian nationalism or the modern geopolitical ramifications that occur when a country chooses not to use the term *genocide* when describing the event. Invite them to share their reports.

See the Chapter Planner for more strategies for differentiation.

HISTORICAL THINKING

ANSWERS

1. Armenians were a Christian minority in a land of Muslims; they wanted their own separate state. Ottoman leaders opposed this, as it would lead to the empire breaking apart.

2. Possible responses: It was a neutral country, and U.S. policy was to avoid involvement in foreign affairs. Action against the Ottoman Empire might have been viewed as taking sides.

3. Possible response: Leaders thought the Armenians became rich at the expense of the Turks; the Armenians wanted to liberate themselves and establish their own independent state; and the leaders thought the Armenians were supporting the Ottomans' main enemy in the war.

CRITICAL VIEWING The panel shows a structure that appears to have one side blown in by a bomb and the river that she crossed many years ago. This picture lends credence to the argument that the Armenian relocation was genocide.

Expanding European Imperialism

The triumphant Allied powers viewed the former colonies and provinces of the German and Ottoman empires as weak regions that needed authority figures to oversee them. This paternalistic attitude reinforced the victors' greed to exploit their new territories.

THE MANDATE SYSTEM

After the war, the fate of former German colonies and Ottoman provinces lay with the Allies. To govern those peoples, the Allies devised the **Mandate System**, which was authorized by Article 22 of the League of Nations Covenant. The covenant mandated, or empowered, "advanced nations" to rule over certain territories until the "advanced" leaders felt that the peoples in those areas were ready to govern themselves. Race was the unspoken but key factor in determining which colonies and provinces were considered capable of self-rule.

In Africa, the Mandate System allowed the French, British, Belgian, and South African governments to take over former German colonies. Britain added German East Africa (present-day Tanzania) to its assets, France expanded its West African holdings, and Belgium enlarged its Central African empire. The Mandate System required reports to the League of Nations from each European nation showing that they were furthering "native rights." Instead, European nations ruled the mandated territories like traditional colonies. They did little or nothing to prepare people in these regions for eventual self-determination.

Still, the ideal of national self-rule inspired a new generation of African nationalists. In South Africa, leaders of the African National Congress called for greater rights. In West Africa, returning war veterans promoted an awareness of Africa's role in the wider world. More African students left to study in Europe and the United States and returned to their home countries questioning the concept of colonial rule.

THE BALFOUR DECLARATION

Many of today's complications in Southwest Asia can be traced to several contradictory promises made by the British during World War I. First, to secure Arab help in defeating the Ottomans, the British pledged to support an independent Arab state. At the same time, Britain and France secretly agreed to divide Ottoman provinces—including Arab lands—between them after the war. Finally, Britain backed the Zionists, or Jewish nationalists, and their dream for a Jewish homeland.

In the **Balfour Declaration**, the British government agreed to help create a "national home" for the Jewish people in what was then Ottoman Palestine. Zionists hoped to establish their own state on the site of the ancient Hebrew kingdoms. Zionism had originated in the later 19th century among European Jews who were alarmed by persistent anti-Semitism. Zionists argued that a nation-state was necessary to the security of Jews and to represent their interests in the world.

At the end of the war, the British occupied Palestine. In 1920, they began permitting Jews to settle there. By 1922, when the League of Nations approved a British mandate in Palestine, Jewish immigration was steadily increasing. However, more than 80 percent of the people living in Palestine were Muslim or Christian Arabs. Palestine was their traditional homeland, and massive Arab demonstrations erupted. When the British responded by cutting back Jewish immigration, Zionist leaders were furious. Political tensions in the territory remained high.

SYRIA AND IRAQ

In 1920, Britain assumed a proposed mandate over three Ottoman provinces. The British stitched those provinces together into a new entity they called Iraq. In 1923, the League of Nations assigned a mandate over Syria and Lebanon to France. Lebanon, a mix of Christians and Muslims, fairly quickly accepted French oversight. Stability was far more difficult to achieve in Syria.

714 CHAPTER 25

As you have read, the Syrian Congress of Damascus refused to accept French authority over their country. In March 1920, the Syrian Congress declared Faisal al-Hashemi king of Syria. When Faisal rejected French authority, France imposed it by force. Faisal, a Sunni Muslim, then fled to Baghdad, where the British agreed to install him as king of Iraq.

Iraq was unstable at the start. An artificial creation, it was divided among the Shiite majority in the south, a Sunni minority in the center, and a Kurdish-dominated region in the north. Britain's installation of Faisal as king caused friction because Shiite Iraqis resented the Sunnis' rise to political power. Nationalist opposition to British control and a shared goal of establishing an Arab state, however, helped foster unity between the Sunni and Shiite populations.

British and French leaders viewed their mandated territories as spoils of war—profits they were entitled to as victors. Both countries assumed they would retain their global empires after the war. But the world had changed. Britain had been forced to cash in many foreign investments to pay for the war, and it also took on significant debts, especially to the United States. Western European global economic supremacy was declining. Simultaneously, the forces of anti-colonial nationalism were on the rise through Africa and Asia. The British and French could not know it, but the age of European empires would soon come to an end.

Mandates in Africa and Southwest Asia

Mandates in the Pacific Islands

HISTORICAL THINKING

1. **READING CHECK** Why did the mandated territory of Iraq suffer from instability?

2. **MAKE CONNECTIONS** Why were Britain and France the main beneficiaries of the Mandate System?

3. **INTERPRET MAPS** What do you notice about the British and French mandates in Africa and Southwest Asia?

The First World War and 20th-Century Revolutions 715

PLAN: 2-PAGE LESSON

OBJECTIVE

Explain how the Mandate System allowed Britain and France to take control of former German colonies and Ottoman provinces.

CRITICAL THINKING SKILLS FOR LESSON 2.4

- Make Connections
- Interpret Maps
- Identify Main Ideas and Details
- Draw Conclusions

HISTORICAL THINKING FOR CHAPTER 25

How did the Great War affect the world politically, socially, and economically?

At the end of World War I, one of the tasks of the League of Nations was to establish a Mandate System in which certain Allies took charge of former German colonies and Ottoman provinces. Lesson 2.4 details which parts of the world came under the rule of Allied nations as part of this system.

Student eEdition online

Additional content for this lesson, including a photograph, is available online.

BACKGROUND FOR THE TEACHER

Tanganyika Territory The east African country of Tanzania provides a good illustration of the Mandate System. Then called Tanganyika Territory, the land was given to the British to administer, and despite the racist and patronizing underpinning of the system itself, the territory did experience some benefits. First, the British made serious efforts to support local governance. Two bodies, the Native Authority Ordinance and the Native Courts Ordinance, were put in place in the late 1920s to allow for native administration of the territory's affairs—though always with the British looking over the government's shoulder. Economically, Tanganyika benefited from an extension of the Central Railway Line that the British paid for. These improvements slowed when the world was hit by the Great Depression in the 1930s. During and after World War II, Tanganyika focused on developing its ability to produce its own food and other goods. Again, this was done with British support.

INTRODUCE & ENGAGE

DEVELOP A WORD MAP

Prompt students to discuss the meaning of the word *mandate*. Begin by adding the word to the center of a Word Map, and complete the map during classroom discussion. Guide students to consider the word's etymology by using a dictionary. Revisit this activity at the end of the lesson and discuss how Britain and France felt they had a mandate to take charge of former German colonies and Ottoman provinces and how problematic that turned out to be.

TEACH

GUIDED DISCUSSION

1. **Identify Main Ideas and Details** What had the British promised the Arabs at the end of the Great War, and what happened to that promise? *(Britain had promised the Arabs that they would have their own independent state. Palestinian Arabs resented having to share their traditional homeland with Jews.)*

2. **Draw Conclusions** What evidence was there at the end of the war that the age of European empires was declining? *(Britain was carrying a lot of war debt as the economic domination of Western Europe was declining. Additionally, areas of Africa and Asia were seeing a rise in anti-colonial nationalism.)*

INTERPRET MAPS

Tell students to review the map of League of Nations mandates. **ASK:** Which country was a Belgian mandate? *(Ruanda-Urundi)* What was an Australian mandate? *(New Guinea)* What conclusion can you draw about the Japanese mandate? *(Possible response: Because the Japanese mandate encompassed a large area with many small islands, it may have been difficult to govern and, if necessary, defend.)*

ACTIVE OPTIONS

On Your Feet: Think, Pair, Share Give students a few minutes to think about this question: What was the explicit reasoning behind the Mandate System, and what was its implicit reasoning? Then have students choose partners and talk about the question for five minutes. Finally, ask volunteers to share their ideas with the class.

> **NG Learning Framework: Research the Role of Race**
> ATTITUDES Responsibility, Empowerment
> KNOWLEDGE Our Human Story

Direct students to work in groups to conduct online research related to this line from the lesson: "Race was the unspoken but key factor in determining which colonies and provinces the league considered capable of self-rule." Tell students to investigate how the Europeans' racial attitudes toward the people of the former German colonies impacted the way the Mandate System was enacted. Then have groups use their research findings to help them hold a class discussion on the role race played in the Mandate System.

DIFFERENTIATE

STRIVING READERS

Use Reciprocal Teaching Have partners read the first paragraph in the lesson silently. Instruct students to quiz each other about the paragraph, asking their partners to state the main idea, identify important details that support the main idea, and then summarize the paragraph in their own words. Partners should then complete the exercise with the remaining paragraphs.

PRE-AP

Analyze Impacts Tell students to work alone or in pairs to conduct online research into the impact of the Mandate System on one of the territories they saw on the map but did not read about in the lesson, such as French Cameroun, New Guinea, or South West Africa. Suggest that students use a graphic organizer to help organize their research. They might also display a graphic organizer to show the results of their investigation and explain their analysis to the class.

See the Chapter Planner for more strategies for differentiation.

HISTORICAL THINKING

ANSWERS

1. Iraq was unstable because it was an artificial creation that merged three provinces and because the Shiite Iraqis resented being ruled by a Sunni king.

2. Possible response: Britain and France were the most powerful Allies who were also members of the League of Nations, and both countries had experience administering territories.

3. Possible response: In Africa and in Southwest Asia, nearly all the British and French mandates border each other.

The "Lost Generation"

A thunderstorm can be a frightening thing. First comes a bright flash of lightning, followed by a loud crack of thunder. Even indoors, out of danger, the noise can be startling. Soldiers in trenches on World War I battlefields had a similar—but much more terrifying—experience with the thunderous explosions of artillery shells, which haunted them for years to come.

THE GREAT WAR'S LASTING EFFECTS

During and after the First World War, people had to adjust to the harsh realities of existence during a time of total war. Around nine million soldiers, sailors, and airmen died, leaving women without husbands, children without fathers, and parents without sons. In addition, at least five million civilian deaths can be blamed on bombings, famine, and other war-related causes.

The millions of young adults in their teens and twenties who died in the conflict comprise a "**Lost Generation**." Along with their lives, the war wiped away their potential contributions to the world—as leaders, teachers, artists,

or scientists. The term, which originally referred to a particular group of writers but is now used generally, applies not just to those who lost their lives but also to everyone who lost their faith in traditional values as a result of the war.

The Great War had a devastating effect on the environment as well. Artillery did the most damage; an array of these field guns could spray projectile bombs, or shells, over a wide expanse. The resulting explosions smashed buildings, roads, trees, and everything else in the area. By the end of the war, the Western Front was largely a wasteland.

CRITICAL VIEWING One hundred years after the Battle of the Somme, morning mist rises from the Beaumont-Hamel Newfoundland Memorial in France. The clash on these grounds began on July 1, 1916, and ended four-and-a-half months later. It is considered one of the bloodiest battles in history: more than one million people were wounded or killed. Why do you think the French chose to preserve the battlefield in this way?

716 CHAPTER 25

During the five days of the First Battle of the Marne in 1914, the opposing armies fired some 432,000 artillery shells at one another. Artillery shells easily destroyed shallow trenches, and they could also cause deeper trenches to collapse. Soldiers in the trenches could hear the "loud singing, wailing noise" of an incoming shell and knew it could mean death if the shell landed nearby. A German soldier later described how soldiers felt during the shelling: "You cower in a heap alone in a hole," he wrote, "and feel yourself the victim of a pitiless thirst for destruction."

Many who survived the unceasing barrage of rifle, machine-gun, and artillery fire experienced trembling, dizziness, confusion, loss of memory, and sleeplessness. This set of symptoms indicated a condition doctors called **shell shock**, a mental health condition that would later be referred to as combat fatigue or post-traumatic stress disorder (PTSD). Doctors in field hospitals near the front lines had limited means to treat shell-shocked troops. They could, however, save many soldiers whose physical injuries might have killed them in an earlier conflict, such as the U.S. Civil War. Advances in the understanding of infections improved survival rates. So did the use of blood transfusions—transfers of blood from healthy soldiers to patients.

The scientist **Marie Curie**, a winner of the Nobel Prize for physics in 1903 and then for chemistry in 1911, believed that radium, the element she discovered in 1898, had value as a medicine. She also promoted the use of x-rays to diagnose injuries. In France during the Great War, she rode to field hospitals in an ambulance equipped with an x-ray machine.

Soldiers returning home from the battlefield with mental or physical conditions needed care. Hospitals excelled at healing physical wounds, but doctors had no standard way to treat those suffering from severe emotional wounds. Families of shell-shocked soldiers often bore the main burden of care—one more expectation of those on the home front.

The war also disrupted the global economy. Before World War I, living standards were rising rapidly, people were free to migrate across borders, and international trade was booming. After the war, the increase in living standards slowed, nations put up barriers to migration, and tariffs blunted trade. Also, as you have read, governments expanded their powers during the war.

Ernest Hemingway served as an ambulance driver in World War I. His novels *A Farewell to Arms* and *For Whom the Bell Tolls* reflect that experience. In this brief excerpt from one of his essays, he pointedly expresses his disgust for war.

PRIMARY SOURCE

They wrote in the old days that it is sweet and fitting to die for one's country. But in modern war there is nothing sweet nor fitting in your dying. You will die a dog for no good reason.

—from "Notes on the Next War: A Serious Topical Letter" by Ernest Hemingway, 1935

Afterward, especially in Europe and the United States, they used business regulations and income taxes to continue to exert control over the economy.

THE "LOST GENERATION" IN PARIS

The American writer **Gertrude Stein** was an **expatriate**, or person who chooses to live outside his or her home country, who settled in Europe in the early 20th century. A respected art critic, she collected works by **Pablo Picasso** and other artists whose experimental paintings expanded the definition of modern art.

In the 1920s, Stein befriended American novelists **Ernest Hemingway**, F. Scott Fitzgerald, and John Dos Passos, as well as poets Hart Crane and E.E. Cummings. The First World War had left these men feeling disillusioned. They thought the social values they believed in before the war were an illusion and no longer applied to postwar society. Stein hosted a literary salon in Paris that gave them a place to share ideas. Reportedly, she was the first to call these writers the Lost Generation. The label stuck.

Like many postwar artists, the Lost Generation writers created **countercultural** art movements that challenged or rejected existing styles and traditions. Their ways of looking at the world contradicted those of mainstream society. The war, they believed, had radically changed society, and their writings reflected that change.

HISTORICAL THINKING

1. **READING CHECK** What medical advances helped doctors at the battlefront treat soldiers' physical injuries?

2. **IDENTIFY MAIN IDEAS** What was the main cause of shell shock?

3. **MAKE PREDICTIONS** How do you think older members of mainstream society might have reacted to the works of the Lost Generation writers, and why?

The First World War and 20th-Century Revolutions 717

PLAN: 2-PAGE LESSON

OBJECTIVE

Summarize the enormous impact the Great War had on people, society, and the environment.

CRITICAL THINKING SKILLS FOR LESSON 2.5

- Identify Main Ideas
- Make Predictions
- Explain
- Form and Support Opinions
- Analyze Primary Sources

HISTORICAL THINKING FOR CHAPTER 25

How did the Great War affect the world politically, socially, and economically?

After World War I ended, its effects would be felt forever. Lesson 2.5 describes how those who survived the war struggled to deal with the aftereffects of the conflict.

Student eEdition online

Additional content for this lesson, including photographs, is available online.

BACKGROUND FOR THE TEACHER

Chemical Warfare World War I is sometimes known as "the chemist's war," due to the large-scale use of chemical weapons. The French first used gas as a weapon whose purpose was not to kill but to render soldiers unable to fight. The Germans used poison gas, initially chlorine, in 1915 against the French, but the British picked up the idea quickly. However, the gas sometimes blew back into the faces of the attackers, incapacitating them as well. Later, troops used phosgene and mustard gas, which were more lethal. Mustard gas damaged lungs and raised blisters on skin. These poison gases were the most feared weapons of the war, and both sides quickly developed gas masks. Over the course of the war, gas killed about 10 percent of its victims, but it left hundreds of thousands with long-lasting damage.

INTRODUCE & ENGAGE

CONNECT TO TODAY

On the board, write the term *PTSD* in the center of a Word Web. **ASK:** What words and phrases come to mind when you hear this term, which stands for post-traumatic stress disorder? *(Possible responses: war, veterans, mental health)* Add students' ideas to the web. Explain that in this lesson they will learn about shell shock, which was what PTSD was called back in the World War I era and which afflicted many veterans.

TEACH

GUIDED DISCUSSION

1. **Explain** How does the term *shell shock* describe a condition that some soldiers suffered as a result of the war? *(Answers will vary. Possible response: For some soldiers, the experience of being shelled by the enemy resulted not in lost limbs or other physical problems but in severe mental or emotional stress, or shock.)*

2. **Form and Support Opinions** Why do you think Gertrude Stein called Fitzgerald, Cummings, and their contemporaries a "Lost Generation"? *(Possible response: Those writers had come of age believing in a certain set of social values that were completely subverted by the war. As a result, after the war, many of them felt "lost" and disillusioned.)*

ANALYZE PRIMARY SOURCES

Have students review the excerpt from the essay by Ernest Hemingway. **ASK:** In what way does the excerpt show that Hemingway could be considered a member of the "Lost Generation"? *(Answers will vary. Possible response: In the essay, Hemingway compares attitudes toward war between "the old days" and the present day. He writes that after seeing World War I and its effects, he feels there is nothing noble or sweet in dying for one's country. This disillusionment with old ideas about bravery and war is characteristic of members of the "Lost Generation.")*

ACTIVE OPTIONS

On Your Feet: Inside-Outside Circle Arrange students in concentric circles facing each other. Tell students in the outside circle to ask students in the inside circle a question about shell shock. After students answer, have the outside circle rotate one position to the right to create new pairings. After five questions, tell students to switch roles and continue.

> **NG Learning Framework: Analyze a Selection by a "Lost Generation" Writer**
> **SKILL** Communication
> **KNOWLEDGE** Our Human Story

Ask students to locate and read a selection of 1920s poems or excerpts from a work by Ernest Hemingway, F. Scott Fitzgerald, John Dos Passos, or Ezra Pound. Instruct students to select and read closely one poem or excerpt that appeals to them, considering the following question: What is the historical context of the piece, and how does the language reflect the theme of disillusionment or despair? Tell students to refer to specific words, phrases, or symbols to support their statements.

DIFFERENTIATE

ENGLISH LANGUAGE LEARNERS

Use New Words in Sentences Pair **Beginning** or **Intermediate** level students with students at the **Advanced** level. Direct the latter to pronounce and clarify the meanings of the vocabulary terms in the lesson. Have pairs compose an original sentence for each term and any other new words in the lesson.

GIFTED & TALENTED

Illustrate War Trauma Ask students to interpret visually the phrase *shell shock*, conveying what happens when minds and bodies are pushed to the limit by battlefield stress and trauma. They may create a drawing, painting, collage, or digitally altered photograph incorporating World War I scenes and metaphorical representations of psychological states. They may incorporate contemporary visuals related to veterans suffering from PTSD that indicate what has been learned about diagnosing and treating this condition since World War I. Ask them to present their artistic renderings.

See the Chapter Planner for more strategies for differentiation.

HISTORICAL THINKING

ANSWERS

1. a better understanding of infections, blood transfusions, x-ray machines

2. Possible response: the unceasing barrage of loud and deadly weapons firing on the battlefield and soldiers' fear that they were about to be killed by an artillery shell

3. Possible response: They probably reacted negatively, as the writings did not reflect traditional values.

CRITICAL VIEWING to show a contrast between the battlefield during the war (covered in bodies, environment damaged) and now (peaceful, serene, naturally beautiful); By highlighting this contrast, the battlefield serves as a message for peace.

Lenin and the Bolshevik Revolution

In 1905 and in 1917, people rebelled in Russia because of poor leadership, food shortages, and a war that would not end. The final chapter of the Russian Revolution tells the story of how a group of political radicals forced their way into power.

LENIN THE REVOLUTIONARY

In 1905, the Russian navy was reeling from its humiliating loss to Japan, and Russians had grown disillusioned with their all-powerful tsar, Nicholas II. Worker strikes, student riots, and a general uprising forced the tsar to accept a set of reforms. They included the establishment of the Duma, a representative assembly. Although Russia became, for the first time, a constitutional monarchy, Nicholas and his ministers retained most of the power over the government and the military.

The main Russian revolutionary group at the time, the Social-Democratic Workers' Party, consisted of two socialist factions with opposing plans for Russia: the Mensheviks and the Bolsheviks. The Mensheviks were traditional Marxists. Recall that Karl Marx's ultimate goal was communism, an economic and political system in which all property is public and owned by the central state and in which goods are distributed to everyone according to their needs. Mensheviks believed that a modern industrial economy would have to be built before the workers would be strong enough to seize power.

The Bolsheviks, led by **Vladimir Lenin**, were Marxists who had a more radical ideology. They argued that a small group of revolutionaries

CRITICAL VIEWING The title of this propaganda poster from 1920 translates to "Long Live the First of May." A working man stands on a globe, breaking chains and waving a flag with Vladimir Lenin's profile on it. Based on details from the poster, what inference can you make about the importance of Lenin and the Russian Revolution?

should seize power first and establish a "dictatorship of the proletariat." In communism, the proletariat is the industrial working class, or factory workers. Public outrage over the failures of Russia in the Great War as well as the lack of food and other problems would offer the Bolsheviks the chance to put their beliefs into practice.

In September 1915, a year after World War I began, Nicholas took command of the Russian army. The tsar was an incompetent general, and when the army failed to stop the German invaders, the people blamed him. By early 1917, Russian soldiers were abandoning their posts in droves. The Russian masses, angered by factory closings and the scarcity of food, rioted in the streets of the capital, Petrograd (present-day St. Petersburg). The local military unit supported the people of Petrograd in what they called the February Revolution. This was the first of two uprisings in 1917 that, together, became known as the Russian Revolution. Nicholas was forced to abdicate, which ended the monarchy in Russia.

That summer, the moderate Provisional Government that replaced Nicholas decided to continue fighting against the Central Powers. At that point, though, the Russian people were simply tired of war. Throughout the country, they had begun setting up a new form of social and political organization: the soviet (Russian for "committee"). The soviets were local councils of workers, urban residents, soldiers, and sailors, and anyone could vote for representatives to the councils. A radical form of democracy, the soviets passed laws through public discussion and agreement.

In the capital, the Petrograd Soviet challenged the authority of the Provisional Government. Leon Trotsky, a prominent Bolshevik, gave fiery speeches and organized tirelessly to advance the communist cause. By the fall of 1917, the Bolsheviks, demanding "peace, land, and bread," controlled the Petrograd Soviet.

Lenin and the Bolsheviks made their move, executing a coup and overthrowing the Provisional Government in what is called the October Revolution. Bolshevik forces faced only minimal resistance. Lenin quickly disbanded the Duma and took charge of the government. In just two days, he and the Bolsheviks successfully completed the Russian Revolution.

CIVIL WAR IN RUSSIA

For the Bolsheviks, securing the government was its first goal. In November 1917, they decreed that Russia would withdraw from the Great War. Four months later, in March 1918, the Bolsheviks signed a treaty with Germany officially ending Russian participation in the war. Russia relinquished large swaths of its western territory—including Ukraine, Poland, and Finland—to Germany. Those lands contained at least one-fourth of Russia's citizens and much of Russia's industrial, agricultural, and mineral resources. The Bolsheviks believed that a communist uprising in Germany would return all that land to them.

That same month, the Bolsheviks changed their name to the Russian Communist Party and moved the capital from Petrograd to Moscow. The communists soon found themselves contending with powerful counterrevolutionary forces. Once Russia pulled out of World War I, aristocratic generals turned their attention from fighting the Germans to undoing the revolution.

The Russian Civil War broke out by June 1918. It pitted the communist Red Army against the volunteers of the White Army, a variety of groups that united to oppose the Bolsheviks. The Reds' control of the major cities and their industries gave them an advantage, and so did their army of peasants and workers. The western Allies sent around 60,000 soldiers to help the White Army but limited Allied troops mainly to support roles away from the battlefields.

Lenin took steps to ensure the survival of his new government. In July 1918, fearing that opponents might rally around the tsar, Lenin had Nicholas and the rest of the royal family brutally murdered. In the past, the Romanovs had employed secret police and Siberian prison camps to identify and punish their enemies. Lenin and the Bolsheviks greatly expanded both systems. Through the secret police, the government weaponized terror.

In November 1920, the Russian Civil War ended with a communist victory. The Bolsheviks had already secured control of the government by expelling non-Bolshevik socialists from the soviets. The democratic nature of rule by the soviets gave way to an authoritarian, communist dictatorship with Lenin in charge.

HISTORICAL THINKING

1. **READING CHECK** How did the Mensheviks' plan for seizing power differ from the Bolsheviks' plan?

2. **SEQUENCE EVENTS** Put the following events in the order in which they occurred: February Revolution, Russian Civil War, 1905 uprising, October Revolution.

3. **DRAW CONCLUSIONS** Why do you think the communist Reds won the Russian Civil War?

PLAN: 2-PAGE LESSON

OBJECTIVE
Describe the series of events that comprised the Russian Revolution.

CRITICAL THINKING SKILLS FOR LESSON 3.1
- Sequence Events
- Draw Conclusions
- Make Inferences
- Identify Supporting Details
- Analyze Visuals

HISTORICAL THINKING FOR CHAPTER 25
How did the Great War affect the world politically, socially, and economically?

Fatigue with the Great War was one of the reasons why the Bolsheviks wanted to overthrow Tsar Nicholas II and his family. Lesson 3.1 explains the motivations behind the Russian Revolution and the rise of Vladimir Lenin.

Student eEdition online
Additional content for this lesson, including a photograph, is available online.

BACKGROUND FOR THE TEACHER
Two Calendars Today, most of the world organizes the calendar year using the Gregorian calendar; however, this has not always been the case. The Gregorian calendar is actually a reform of the Julian calendar, a dating system established by Julius Caesar in the 40s B.C.E. that established the 12-month calendar year. However, the astronomer who advised Caesar made a miscalculation, and by the 1500s, the Julian calendar was running 10 days ahead of the solar calendar, which measures how long it takes Earth to revolve around the Sun. To fix this discrepancy, Pope Gregory XIII reformed the calendar in 1582. Acceptance of the Gregorian calendar was gradual. Russia only adopted it in 1918, which is why many of the key events of the Russian Revolution in 1917 are identified with two dates. For example, Tsar Nicholas II abdicated on March 15 using the Gregorian calendar; however, at the time, the date would have been March 2, since Russia was still using the Julian calendar, which by then was 13 days off.

INTRODUCE & ENGAGE

ACTIVATE PRIOR KNOWLEDGE

Review with students the key beliefs of traditional Marxism: Industrial society created two social classes in conflict—the property-owning bourgeoisie and the exploited proletariat; The clash between the two classes would inevitably lead to a violent overthrow of capitalism; The workers would seize power and give ownership of factories to the state to create a more equal society; Class divisions would disappear and the government would share wealth and property equally among the people.

TEACH

GUIDED DISCUSSION

1. **Make Inferences** Why might food shortages lead a nation to revolution? *(Possible response: People need food for survival, and the lack of it would mobilize them to support a person who convinced them of how they could get it. Also the Russian people, exhausted by the ongoing hardships of war and widespread hunger, blamed the government and became desperate for change and reform.)*

2. **Identify Supporting Details** What happened in 1917 that made that year so significant in the history of Russia? Be specific. *(It was the year of the Russian Revolution. February: Russians rioted in the streets of Petrograd, and, with the support of the local military, forced the tsar to abdicate. Summer: the Provisional Government decided to remain in World War I, angering the Bolsheviks. October: Lenin and the Bolsheviks overthrew the Provisional Government.)*

ANALYZE VISUALS

Ask students to examine the photograph of the Romanovs (available in the Student eEdition). **ASK:** What details in the photo tell you that the Romanovs lived a "lavish, privileged lifestyle"? *(Their clothing is luxurious and opulent; the furniture looks expensive; a formal portrait would have been reserved for important people.)* How do the Romanovs in the photo compare to the man in the propaganda poster? *(Photo: well dressed, relaxed, content; Poster: plainly dressed, agitated, fiercely determined)*

ACTIVE OPTIONS

On Your Feet: Team Word Webbing Arrange students in groups of four and provide each group with a large sheet of paper. Tell group members to take turns contributing a detail to a word web with the topic *The Russian Revolution* at the center. When time for the activity has elapsed, call on a student from each group to share the group's web.

> **NG Learning Framework: Create a Biographical Infographic**
> **ATTITUDE** Empowerment
> **SKILL** Communication

Ask groups to research Vladimir Lenin's early life, his beliefs and philosophy, and his influence to create a biographical infographic. Display the infographics in the classroom or on a class blog or website. Ask students to suggest similarities among the infographics.

DIFFERENTIATE

ENGLISH LANGUAGE LEARNERS

Identify Facts Conduct a Round Robin activity to review what students of mixed proficiencies learned about the events of the Russian Revolution. Have them spend a few minutes generating facts, with all students contributing and taking notes. Ask students to share responses. Write the facts on the board.

PRE-AP

Research Russia's Exit from the War Remind students that one of the causes of the Russian Revolution was the Russian people's fatigue with World War I and the blame they put on Nicholas II. Ask students to research why Russia exited the Great War. Invite students to present their findings to the class in an oral or written report.

See the Chapter Planner for more strategies for differentiation.

HISTORICAL THINKING

ANSWERS

1. Mensheviks: believed that workers had to get stronger before trying to seize power; Bolsheviks: believed that a small group of revolutionaries should seize power first and create a "dictatorship of the proletariat"

2. 1905 uprising; February Revolution; October Revolution; Russian Civil War

3. Possible responses: The Red Army had more support from the masses of peasants and workers. The Reds controlled cities and their industries, so they could probably manufacture more weapons. The Allied military presence was not large or strong enough for the White Army to defeat the Red Army.

CRITICAL VIEWING Possible response: He must have been important, as his picture is on the banner. The Russian Revolution must have been an impactful event, as the man is standing on a globe.

Communist Policy in the New U.S.S.R.

In *The Manifesto of the Communist Party* and other writings, Karl Marx introduced the idea of a complex, revolutionary economic system that inspired Vladimir Lenin and the Bolsheviks decades later. Marx could hardly have predicted how his theory would play out in the real world.

NEW ECONOMIC POLICY

Lenin ruled with an iron hand. He made sure that all political parties and social organizations either accepted Communist Party rule or were destroyed. He expected the proletariat to demonstrate discipline, which he defined as "unity of action, freedom of discussion and criticism." Even within the Communist Party Central Committee—the core group of Bolshevik decision-makers—Lenin allowed only limited debate.

After the October Revolution, the Bolsheviks **nationalized**, or seized for the state, most privately owned industries and railroads. They established a centrally planned economy for Russia, meaning that the communist government would do the planning.

The Bolsheviks also struck a blow against large landowners and in favor of the peasants, who historically did not own the land they cultivated. In the early 1900s, new laws had allowed peasants to establish their own farms. By the time of the Russian Revolution, peasants owned much of the available farmland or rented it from large landowners. A 1918 decree broke up Russia's remaining large estates into small holdings. The government distributed these state-owned properties only to peasants willing to cultivate the land themselves.

Lenin speaks to Soviet soldiers in Sverdlov Square in Moscow in 1920. Even though this image implies that Lenin was a passionate orator, he was not as good a public speaker as Leon Trotsky, who stands to the right of the podium. A similar photograph from this speech was reproduced around the world.

During the civil war, however, Lenin took a radical step to supply the Red Army and people in the cities with food. He ordered peasants to give all their surplus grain to the government. In return, the government would provide peasants with any needed factory goods. Lenin justified this action as reflecting the socialist principle that basic resources are to be distributed equally. However, the peasants defied Lenin's order and instead grew less grain. This reaction resulted in widespread famine that led to an estimated five million deaths in 1921 and 1922. At the same time, peasant rebellions broke out in the countryside.

Lenin knew that the Communist Party could not stay in power without the support of the peasants—and the food that they produced. In 1921, in the midst of the famine, he instituted the New Economic Policy. This policy stopped forcing peasants to surrender their grain, gave them long-term leases on their land, and allowed them to sell food on the open market. It also returned small-scale businesses to private hands. However, the government maintained firm control of heavy industry, transportation, and banking.

FIRST YEARS OF THE U.S.S.R.

For the rest of the 1920s, the country experienced a period of relative peace. The New Economic Policy reenergized the peasants and stimulated the economy. Industry bounced back, and more private enterprises emerged. An improved economy helped Lenin and the Bolsheviks solidify their rule. They were able to assert their claim to power not only in Russia but also across much of the former Russian Empire. They restored to Russia the rich farmlands of Ukraine. They exerted control over Central Asia and the Caucasus to the south and the vast territory of Siberia to the east.

In 1922, Russia and the regions it controlled formed the **Union of Soviet Socialist Republics (U.S.S.R.)**, also known as the Soviet Union. Officially a federal republic, the Soviet Union was in reality a dictatorship, dominated by Russia and ruled from Moscow by the Bolsheviks. The Soviet government continued a practice employed by the Russian Empire that sent citizens to distant prison camps where they had to complete physically demanding tasks in brutal conditions. In 1923, Lenin's

Labor camp inmates haul rocks to build the Belomorkanal, or the White Sea–Baltic Canal. Between 12,000 and 24,000 workers died during its construction from 1931 to 1933.

secret police opened the first Bolshevik forced-labor camp on a remote island off the nation's northern coast.

The people sent to these remote detention locations were political prisoners—opponents of Lenin and the Bolsheviks. They worked as slave laborers at various jobs, such as logging, fishing, and construction. Besides being forced to work, prisoners were often tortured; sometimes, they were killed in mass executions. In the years that followed, many additional sites were built. The Soviets called this system of labor camps the **Gulag** (GOO-lahg).

Lenin, the founder of the Communist Party and its undisputed leader, had a stroke in 1922 that left him partially paralyzed. As a result, he began to cut back his activities. At the same time, **Joseph Stalin**—someone Lenin did not like or trust—began exerting greater influence over party matters. In January 1924, after two more strokes, Lenin died. Stalin used his position as General Secretary of the Central Committee to seize the leadership of the Soviet Union. Stalin was impatient with the New Economic Policy and began radical changes to create a highly centralized, fast-growing industrial economy.

HISTORICAL THINKING

1. **READING CHECK** How did Lenin's order to peasants to supply food for the Red Army and the urban population affect the entire nation?

2. **DRAW CONCLUSIONS** Did the New Economic Policy end the policy of nationalization? Explain your response.

3. **COMPARE AND CONTRAST** How did Soviet forced-labor camps differ from traditional prisons?

OBJECTIVE

Explain how Lenin and the Bolsheviks established a communist economic system in Russia and how the Soviet Union emerged in the 1920s.

CRITICAL THINKING SKILLS FOR LESSON 3.2

- Draw Conclusions
- Compare and Contrast
- Make Generalizations
- Analyze Cause and Effect
- Analyze Visuals

HISTORICAL THINKING FOR CHAPTER 25

How did the Great War affect the world politically, socially, and economically?

In the years following the Great War, Russia experienced great political, social, and economic change. Lesson 3.2 explains how Lenin and the Bolsheviks centralized their power via a communist economic system.

BACKGROUND FOR THE TEACHER

History, Photography, and Power When Joseph Stalin consolidated his power over the Soviet Union beginning in the late 1920s, he ordered that the history of the Russian Revolution be altered to magnify his own role. Stalin's propagandists portrayed him as having been exceptionally close to Vladimir Lenin; however, the truth was that while Lenin appreciated Stalin's discipline and loyalty, he regarded the younger man as of limited intelligence. In the 1930s, when Stalin began purging many of Lenin's closest allies from the Communist Party and executing many of the "Old Bolsheviks" who knew Lenin personally, the historical record was "adjusted" to remove many prominent revolutionists from the story. Stalin's propagandists altered the photographic record as well as the historical record of the revolution. The iconic photo of Lenin speaking in Moscow in 1920 is a good example. Beginning in the late 1920s, the version of that photo that was produced and distributed was an altered image in which two prominent Communists, Leon Trotsky and Lev Kamenev, had been erased and replaced with a set of wooden steps.

INTRODUCE & ENGAGE

K-W-L CHART

Lead students in a discussion to brainstorm what they already know about communist economic systems. Ask them to record their knowledge in the first row of a K-W-L chart. Then ask students to write questions they would like to have answered as they study Lesson 3.2. Allow time at the end of the lesson for students to complete the K-W-L Chart with what they have learned.

TEACH

GUIDED DISCUSSION

1. **Make Generalizations** In what way was the Russian economy centralized before the New Economic Policy was put in place? *(The communist government planned every aspect of the economy. It took control of industry and the railroads. It seized large estates, broke them up into smaller properties, and distributed them among peasants. It ordered peasants to give their excess grain to the government so it could be distributed among the populace.)*

2. **Analyze Cause and Effect** What impact did the New Economic Policy have on the political power of the Bolsheviks? *(Because the New Economic Policy produced positive economic results, the Bolsheviks strengthened their rule.)*

ANALYZE VISUALS

Ask students to closely examine the photograph of the Russian labor camp. **ASK:** What details in the photograph show that the labor camps were harsh environments? *(The men are dressed in filthy, shabby clothes and are working hard to haul rocks up a rather steep slope. The camp is surrounded by wooden fencing.)* What do you think the reaction of Soviet citizens might have been if such a photograph had leaked out? *(Possible response: Some citizens might have been outraged and demanded reform from the government.)*

ACTIVE OPTIONS

On Your Feet: Thumbs Up/Thumbs Down Divide the class into groups and have each group write six True-False statements about the lesson with the correct answers included. Collect the statements. Mix them up and read them aloud to the class, skipping any duplicates. Have students give a "thumbs up" for true statements and a "thumbs down" for false statements. Correct any misconceptions.

NG Learning Framework: Present an Account
SKILL Communication
KNOWLEDGE Our Human Story

Ask students to briefly search online for a firsthand account of being in a Soviet labor camp (Gulag). Once students have chosen an account, have them prepare and perform a reading of it for the class. Students should first introduce the account by telling the person's name and providing relevant background information. After each reading, invite the class to briefly discuss it before continuing with the next one.

DIFFERENTIATE

STRIVING READERS

Summarize Ask students to work in pairs to read and summarize the text and photo captions. Tell students to write at least three notes for each section. After they have completed writing notes, guide students to create a summary statement for each section and then a summary statement for the whole lesson.

GIFTED & TALENTED

Engage in a Debate Tell students they will assume the role of either a supporter of communism as an economic system or an opponent of such a system. Tell students to decide which side they will take and then conduct online research to learn more about the pros and cons of communism as an economic system. Students should take detailed notes and use their notes to practice and role-play the debate in front of their classmates.

See the Chapter Planner for more strategies for differentiation.

HISTORICAL THINKING

ANSWERS

1. The peasants refused to give their surplus grain to the government, and Russia suffered a widespread famine that lasted two years and caused 5 million deaths.

2. No; the New Economic Policy returned small-scale businesses to private hands, but the large-scale industries, transportation, and banking continued to be owned by the state.

3. Possible response: Traditional prisons hold criminals for a specific amount of time. Forced-labor camps held political prisoners, forced them to perform hard labor, often tortured them, and sometimes executed them.

A statue of young Mao Zedong towers to a height of more than 100 feet on Orange Isle in Changsha, China. The sculpture was unveiled in 2009.

China's Republic and Mao's Goals

Does your local government accomplish its goals? Efficient governments include honest and skillful leadership, sound policies and programs, and broad popular support. After the collapse of the Qing dynasty, the Chinese people struggled to establish an effective national government.

END OF THE QING DYNASTY

The Boxer Rebellion of 1899–1901 did little to halt the spread of Western and Japanese influence in Qing China. The country desperately needed a government that could unify the Chinese people and defend them against foreign aggression. Some Chinese pushed for reforms, while others argued that only a revolution would bring about the needed changes.

In October 1911, a mutiny by troops in southeastern China triggered an uprising. Frustration with Qing rule helped the insurrection spread. By the end of the year, more than a dozen provinces and numerous army units had joined the Chinese revolution. The rebels set up a provisional republic in the city of Nanjing. They chose respected revolutionary **Sun Yat-sen** to lead it.

Sun was a nationalist who envisioned a strong, unified, and modernized China. As head of a political movement known as the Revolutionary Alliance, he had spent much of his time outside China, trying to raise money and support. Now he hoped to help China take its rightful place among the world's great powers.

In February 1912, the Qing emperor—just six years old—abdicated. After more than 2,000 years of imperial rule, the Chinese empire quietly came to an end. In its place arose the Republic of China, with a new constitution and an elected assembly, in which Sun's newly formed Nationalist Party held a majority of seats.

For the sake of peace and unity, Sun yielded the presidency of the new republic to a leading military official who ruled from Beijing. But instead of governing according to the constitution, the president tried to make himself emperor, and in 1916 he was overthrown. A period of disorder followed. Local warlords reigned over large parts of the country, backed by private armies. China was no longer a unified state.

In the southern port city of Guangzhou (gwahng-joh), Sun tried to establish a government separate from the weakened government in Beijing, and a hundred or so members of the national assembly joined him there. They tried but failed to gain recognition by Western nations as the legitimate Chinese government.

During the First World War, China and Japan both supported the Allies. After the war, the Chinese expected the return of German-held territory on the Shandong Peninsula in eastern China. Instead, the Treaty of Versailles gave the territory to Japan. Japan, as you read earlier, had already acquired Taiwan and Manchuria, in northeastern China, in previous wars.

On May 4, 1919, some 3,000 university students held a demonstration in Tiananmen Square in Beijing to oppose the plan to give additional Chinese territory to Japan. They appealed to the government to restore Chinese dignity in the face of Japanese aggression. Their **May Fourth Movement** led to labor strikes, mass meetings, and a boycott of Japanese goods. As a result of these widespread protests, China refused to sign the Treaty of Versailles. Chinese nationalism was on the rise.

COMMUNISM IN CHINA

The activist spirit generated by the May Fourth Movement increased membership in Sun Yat-sen's Nationalist Party. The Western powers had no interest in helping Sun, so he turned to the new communist government in Russia for support. Lenin's Bolsheviks offered to help Sun strengthen the Nationalist Party. They told Sun that they would provide him political guidance, guns, and money if he agreed to cooperate with the Chinese communists. He conceded. He also agreed to modify his ideology with a shift from nationalism and economic security to anti-imperialism and socialism.

After Sun died in 1925, his brother-in-law Jiang Jieshi, known in the West as **Chiang Kai-shek**, gained control of the Nationalist Party. After defeating the warlords to take control of China, Chiang turned against the communists in 1927. His National Party forces killed thousands of communists in the coastal cities, forcing the survivors to flee to the countryside.

These communists were now guided by **Mao Zedong** (mow dzuh-dahng), who had participated in the May Fourth Movement while he attended university. Mao proved to be a brilliant military strategist, shifting the Chinese communist emphasis from industrial workers toward an alliance with the rural poor, the peasant class who made up the vast majority of China's population. Mao became the leader of the Chinese Communist Party in 1935.

Unlike Marx and Lenin, Mao believed it would be the peasants—not industrial workers—who would lead the way to socialism in China.

PRIMARY SOURCE

In a very short time, in China's central, southern and northern provinces, several hundred million peasants will rise like a mighty storm, like a hurricane, a force so swift and violent that no power, however great, will be able to hold it back. They will smash all the trammels [shackles; restraints] that bind them and rush forward along the road to liberation. They will sweep all the imperialists, warlords, corrupt officials, local tyrants and evil gentry into their graves.

—from "Report on an Investigation of the Peasant Movement in Hunan" by Mao Zedong, March 1927

HISTORICAL THINKING

1. **READING CHECK** What group started the May Fourth Movement, and what effects did it have on Chinese society?

2. **DRAW CONCLUSIONS** Based on what you have read earlier, why do you think warlords arose in a country like China in the early 1900s?

3. **MAKE PREDICTIONS** Who do you think will be involved in a future conflict over the right to govern China, and why?

PLAN: 2-PAGE LESSON

OBJECTIVE
Summarize the events that led to the end of the Qing dynasty and explain the rise of communism in China.

CRITICAL THINKING SKILLS FOR LESSON 3.3
- Draw Conclusions
- Make Predictions
- Identify Main Ideas and Details
- Compare and Contrast
- Analyze Primary Sources

HISTORICAL THINKING FOR CHAPTER 25
How did the Great War affect the world politically, socially, and economically?

Part of the Treaty of Versailles was its transfer of German-held territories to other nations. Lesson 3.3 describes how a revolution was triggered in China when it was not given some territory that it was expecting to receive. That revolution changed China forever.

Student eEdition online

Additional content for this lesson, including photos and captions, is available online.

BACKGROUND FOR THE TEACHER

Chiang Kai-Shek As a young man, Chiang Kai-Shek trained at a Japanese military academy and served in the Japanese army. During this time, Chiang came under the influence of Chinese republicans who were working to overthrow the Qing dynasty, and, in 1918, he connected with Sun Yat-Sen. When Sun's Nationalist Party took power in China, Chiang went to the Soviet Union to study their system. With his military background, the Red Army was of particular interest. After Sun's death in 1925, Chiang became commander in chief of the revolutionary army and served as leader of China's nationalists who were by then engaged in a fierce battle with Chinese communists for control of the country. In 1928, a nationalist government was established with Chiang as its leader. Continuing internal conflict with communists and external conflict with Japan characterized Chiang's leadership. After World War II, the communists took over, and in 1949 the People's Republic of China was established. Chiang moved to Taiwan, becoming the leader of its nationalist movement. He died in 1975.

INTRODUCE & ENGAGE

PREVIEW USING TEXT FEATURES

Have students preview the lesson's introductory paragraph, Main Idea, headings, and photo. **ASK:** Based on these features, what questions do you expect this lesson to answer? *(Answers will vary. Possible responses: How did the Qing dynasty come to an end? When did China become a communist country?)* Use a Five-Ws chart to categorize the questions. Ask students to add answers that they find while reading and to research unanswered questions and report the answers to the class.

TEACH

GUIDED DISCUSSION

1. **Identify Main Ideas and Details** How and why did the Qing dynasty come to an end? *(The Chinese were frustrated with the emperor's inability to stem Western and Japanese influence. Many wanted a unified China with a strong defense that would make it a great world power. Sun Yat-Sen led a revolutionary political movement that put pressure on the emperor, who then abdicated.)*

2. **Compare and Contrast** How was Chinese communism different after it came under the leadership of Mao Zedong? *(The base constituency shifted from industrial laborers to rural workers.)*

ANALYZE PRIMARY SOURCES

Have students review the excerpt by Mao Zedong. **ASK:** In what way does the excerpt reveal Mao's approach to communism? *(Mao describes an uprising of rural peasants, not industrial workers. That difference was at the core of his approach to communism.)* How would you characterize Mao's language in the excerpt, and how do you think peasants might respond to it? *(Possible response: descriptive, energetic, passionate; He describes them as a "mighty storm" having a "swift and violent" force. They might get excited and be motivated to join his crusade.)*

ACTIVE OPTIONS

On Your Feet: Four Corners Assign each question to a corner of the room: Who was Sun Yat-Sen, and what did he accomplish? What was the May Fourth Movement? How did communism emerge in China? Who was Mao Zedong, and in what way did he represent change? Ask students to go to the corner of their choice to discuss the question. Then hold a class discussion to share each group's ideas.

| **NG Learning Framework: Read May Fourth Literature**
| **ATTITUDE** Curiosity
| **SKILL** Observation

One aspect of the May Fourth Movement was a reform of the Chinese language in which the vernacular became more widely used. As a result, new literary traditions emerged. Ask students to locate and read a literary work from the May Fourth period by Zhou Shuren, who wrote under the pseudonym Lu Xun. Ask students to report on the work, including thoughts on its historical context and whether or not it seeks to critique any aspects of Chinese life.

DIFFERENTIATE

ENGLISH LANGUAGE LEARNERS

Practice Pronunciation Write the following names and terms on the board: *Qing dynasty, Tiananmen Square, Sun Yat-sen, Guangzhou, Chiang Kai-shek,* and *Mao Zedong.* Pronounce each word and have students repeat. Pair students at the **Beginning** level with those at the **Intermediate** or **Advanced** level. Ask them to take turns finding passages in the lesson that contain any of the words and reading the passages aloud.

GIFTED & TALENTED

Create an Online Profile Have students conduct research to write an online profile about Sun Yat-Sen, Chiang Kai-shek, or Mao Zedong. Direct students to use multiple print and digital sources and to cite both primary and secondary sources. The profile should elucidate the person's background, philosophy, motivations, and influence on early 20th-century China. Invite volunteers to post their profiles on a class or school website.

See the Chapter Planner for more strategies for differentiation.

HISTORICAL THINKING

ANSWERS

1. University students; It led to labor strikes, mass meetings, a boycott of Japanese goods, and increased nationalism.

2. Possible response: Warlords took charge when the government—either of the Qing dynasty or the Republic of China—was not strong enough to keep order in certain regions of the country.

3. Possible responses: I think Chiang Kai-shek and Mao Zedong will battle for the right to govern China. Both leaders are ambitious, and they have clashing ideologies. Mao might want revenge for Chiang's massacre of communists.

Instability and Revolt

Have you ever taken part in a public demonstration? If so, what motivated you? If not, what would it take for you to personally commit to a cause? The main force propelling the Mexican Revolution was peasants who were willing to stand up and fight for their rights.

THE MEXICAN REVOLUTION

From 1870 to 1911, Porfirio Díaz ruled Mexico for all but four years. He held the title of president, but in reality he was a dictator. He won elections, but they were rigged. By the early 1900s, many middle-class Mexicans no longer accepted Díaz's political monopoly. Mexican peasants were angry that farming policies favored wealthy landlords producing commodities for distant markets. Instead, the peasants, mainly mestizos and indigenous peoples, wanted control of their own land and labor.

Francisco Madero, son of a prosperous merchant and landowner, ran against Díaz in the presidential election of 1910. Madero's campaign slogan—"Effective Suffrage and No Re-election"—reflected the desire of many Mexicans for voting rights and an end to Díaz's six-term presidency. Díaz, fearing he might lose, had Madero arrested. He ran unopposed in June and claimed victory.

Released from prison after the election, Madero fled to Texas. There, in October 1910, he published a plan in which he proclaimed himself president of Mexico, argued for a single-term presidency, and supported land reform. He also called on Mexicans to revolt on November 20, which came and went without any unrest. Madero did, however, inspire several groups to organize against the Díaz regime. The Mexican Revolution had begun.

When Madero returned to Mexico in February 1911, he participated in some of the fighting but mainly focused on persuading Díaz to leave office. Finally, in May, Díaz resigned and went into exile in France. In new elections that June, Madero won the presidency of Mexico. However, this achievement did not mark the end of the revolution. Motivated peasants kept fighting for their land rights.

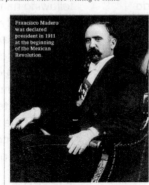

Francisco Madero was declared president in 1911 at the beginning of the Mexican Revolution.

POLITICAL DISORDER

As president, Madero failed to please either his revolutionary supporters or government officials who had retained their positions after the fall of the Díaz government. In 1913, Madero's army chief of staff, Victoriano Huerta, joined a rebellion of army soldiers and arrested Madero, who was later executed. Huerta became a military dictator—but he did not rule for long.

In 1914, rebels from the countryside led by **Venustiano Carranza**—and aided by U.S. troops—forced Huerta to flee the country. For two years, Mexico had an interim, or temporary, president. Carranza and other reformers, including **Álvaro Obregón**, gathered armies, formed alliances, and fought for control of the nation. When this civil war ended in 1917, Carranza's forces controlled all but two of Mexico's 28 states.

Carranza, a nationalist, had not wanted the U.S. Army's help in ousting Huerta from office. After he was elected president in 1917, Carranza tried to nationalize Mexico's oil industry, prompting loud protests from the United States because three-quarters of Mexico's oil wells were American-owned.

As president, Carranza helped draft a new constitution. A constitutional assembly that included a mix of conservative and liberal delegates drafted a document that gave Carranza significant powers but also included articles that responded to the demands of middle-class Mexicans and peasants. One of those articles supported land reform. All lands taken from the peasants during the Díaz regime were to be returned to them. Another article established free, compulsory education and completely separated the church from the state.

The constitution also provided for an eight-hour workday, a minimum wage, and the right of workers to strike. However, Carranza did not enforce the social reforms built into the constitution, and peasants continued to attack government positions in the north and south. The revolution moved forward.

Obregón stayed out of the fight until 1920, when Carranza threatened to use federal troops to break a strike by rail workers in Obregón's home state of Sonora. In April, Obregón joined an uprising that pushed Carranza out of office, and that November, Obregón was elected president. More realist than revolutionary, Obregón enforced constitutional reform but also encouraged Mexican capitalists. In this way, he brought a measure of peace and unity to Mexico.

The Mayo people joined Obregón's forces during the Mexican Revolution. Many of them brought bows and arrows into battles.

HISTORICAL THINKING

1. **READING CHECK** Which of the many Mexican presidents during the revolutionary era accomplished the most in terms of social reform?

2. **CATEGORIZE** Would you label Francisco Madero a revolutionary? Why or why not?

3. **MAKE INFERENCES** Why did Venustiano Carranza's presidency fail to end the revolution?

PLAN: 2-PAGE LESSON

OBJECTIVE

Describe the causes of the Mexican Revolution as well as the key figures and events that figured into it.

CRITICAL THINKING SKILLS FOR LESSON 4.1

- Categorize
- Make Inferences
- Analyze Cause and Effect
- Identify Supporting Details
- Analyze Visuals

HISTORICAL THINKING FOR CHAPTER 25

How did the Great War affect the world politically, socially, and economically?

The tumult of the Great War was a backdrop for numerous revolutions, including those in Russia, China, and Mexico. Lesson 4.1 explains how Mexicans demanded certain reforms and fought a revolution to achieve them.

Student eEdition online

Additional content for this lesson, including a photograph, is available online.

BACKGROUND FOR THE TEACHER

"Social Clauses" and Stability The Mexican Constitution of 1917 balanced moderate and radical demands. Moderates won a legal framework that protected property rights; radicals gained a set of "social clauses" that enshrined the rights of workers among other reforms. After his election as president in 1920, Álvaro Obregón tried to stabilize the country with cautious implementation of the "social clauses." His educational reforms, however, antagonized the Catholic Church and many of its supporters. Obregón was assassinated in 1928 by a member of the Cristeros movement, which opposed limits on the power and property of the Catholic Church. Stability only came to Mexico in 1929, when the formation of the Party of the Mexican Revolution brought the debates between moderates and radicals into a single political party. Party leaders then used patronage, corruption, and backroom deals to try to reconcile the nation's contending needs and interests. Some leaders had less interest in government policy than in enhancing their own wealth, status, and power. Furthermore, by institutionalizing the revolution, the party took away its energy and popular base.

INTRODUCE & ENGAGE

BRAINSTORM A LIST

Write the term *popular uprising* on the board and ask students to brainstorm a list of issues that can lead to a popular uprising. Encourage them to use their prior knowledge about popular uprisings in history as part of their brainstorm, but they should also consider what might motivate a popular uprising today. Then compile their ideas in a class list. Explain that this lesson describes the issues that Mexicans cared about in the early part of the 20th century that led to a revolution.

TEACH

GUIDED DISCUSSION

1. **Analyze Cause and Effect** What were the issues that the Mexican people were demanding action on as part of the revolution? *(farming policies, land rights, fair elections, ending the presidency of Porfirio Díaz)*

2. **Identify Supporting Details** What reforms were included in the Mexican constitution? *(the return of land to peasants, separation of church and state, establishment of free and compulsory education, an eight-hour workday, a minimum wage, the right of workers to strike)*

ANALYZE VISUALS

Direct students to the photograph of the Mayo people in the lesson. **ASK:** What do the weapons of the Mayo people tell us? *(The Mayo people did not have access to advanced weapons technology.)* How do their weapons compare with other nations in the 1920s? *(Possible response: They are not as advanced as the weapons used by European nations in World War I.)*

ACTIVE OPTIONS

On Your Feet: Inside-Outside Circle Arrange students in concentric circles facing each other. Tell students in the outside circle to ask students in the inside circle a question about the lesson. After students answer, have the outside circle rotate one position to the right to create new pairings. After five questions, tell students to switch roles and continue.

| **NG Learning Framework: Create an Illustrated Time Line**
| **SKILL** Communication
| **KNOWLEDGE** Our Human Story

Instruct students to work in groups and use facts from the lesson and from additional research to generate an illustrated time line of the events of the Mexican Revolution and the following years. Have students begin their time lines with Francisco Madero's challenge of Porfirio Díaz in the 1910 election and end with Álvaro Obregón's election in November 1920. The illustrations could be portraits of the key individuals or sketches of important events. Ask groups to share their time lines with the class.

DIFFERENTIATE

INCLUSION

Provide Terms and Names on Audio
Have a student record the pronunciations and a short sentence identifying each of the following names: Porfirio Díaz, Francisco Madero, Venustiano Carranza, and Álvaro Obregón. Invite students to listen to the recordings as often as they need. You might also use the recordings to quiz students on their mastery of the names. Play one identification sentence at a time from the recording and ask students to identify the person's name.

PRE-AP

Write a News Report Instruct students to research one of the key events of the Mexican Revolution, such as the fall of the Díaz government or the Sonoran rail workers' strike. Then have them write a detailed news story from the point of view of a Mexico-based journalist from the period, including quotes from eyewitnesses. Invite students to post their stories on a class blog or publish them on a school website.

See the Chapter Planner for more strategies for differentiation.

HISTORICAL THINKING

ANSWERS

1. Obregón enforced the social reforms called for in the 1917 constitution several years later. Madero supported land reform but did not make much progress toward it.

2. Possible responses: Yes; he fought with the revolutionaries against the Díaz government and played a lead role in overthrowing Díaz. No; he was a wealthy landowner whose policies as president did not please the peasants and other supporters.

3. Carranza refused to enforce the social reforms that were part of the 1917 constitution, which motivated the peasants to keep fighting.

The Campesinos, Zapata, and Villa

When people choose leaders, they often favor those who are like them and who they think will understand their needs. The main military leaders of the Mexican Revolution were, like most of their followers, peasants.

DEMANDING LAND REFORM

During the Mexican Revolution, the government in Mexico City changed hands a number of times. In the countryside, peasants and their leaders carried the revolution forward. Their main goals related to land reform. The most valuable farmland in the nation was located in south-central Mexico, where most Mexicans lived. Historically, the indigenous peoples of this region cultivated communal lands: lands that they held in common, not privately or individually.

Policies put forth by Porfirio Diaz established a market-based approach to land ownership. Encouraged by these protocols, wealthy landowners bought or seized more and more agricultural land and the villages linked to it. As a result, the **campesinos**—rural villagers and small farmers—lost control of their communal lands. To survive, they were forced to work for low wages on haciendas, or vast privately owned agricultural estates.

Mexico's arid and mountainous north had a much smaller population. A rural middle class of cattle ranchers controlled much of the land. They hired many **vaqueros** (vah-KEHR-ohs), or cowboys and cattle herders, to work as ranch hands on their relatively small haciendas. Other poor laborers in this region included peasants, miners, and railroad workers.

By 1910, haciendas had consumed around 80 percent of all local communities in Mexico. Two key leaders of the Mexican Revolution, **Emiliano Zapata and Pancho Villa** (VEE-yuh), organized armies

of peasants who had been evicted from their homes as well as other poor Mexicans. They engaged in guerrilla warfare against Mexican army posts. Zapata and Villa vowed to fight for the return of their followers' lost land and independent way of life.

Zapata was born into a peasant family in 1879 in the state of Morelos, just south of Mexico City. The economy of this agricultural state was based on growing and processing sugar. Expanding haciendas claimed land and water rights at the expense of peasants and others in the region. As a teenager, Zapata took part in a protest against a hacienda that sought to take over his village. In 1909, after briefly serving in the army, he led a group of villagers that reclaimed, by force, the hacienda land.

This photograph from 1915 shows Pancho Villa (left, sitting on the presidential throne in the National Palace) with Emiliano Zapata (right) at his side, Zapata's trademark hat on his knee. Forces loyal to Venustiano Carranza soon chased the two revolutionaries from Mexico.

Villa, who like Zapata was a peasant, worked on a hacienda in the state of Durango in northern Mexico. In 1894, at the age of 16, Villa shot and killed a hacienda owner who had attacked his sister. Villa fled to the mountains, where he joined and later led a group of bandits. These outlaws survived mainly by stealing cattle from wealthy ranchers.

ARMIES OF THE SOUTH AND NORTH

In February 1911, when Francisco Madero returned to Mexico, Villa and his followers joined him. Together, they gathered an army of peasants and other rural poor and fought their way toward Mexico City. In March, Zapata led a small force northward from his village. They seized a town and blockaded the road to Mexico City. The revolutionaries forced Diaz to give up the presidency. When Madero failed to support land reform as president, Zapata issued the Plan of Ayala, which declared that Madero had betrayed the revolution. Zapata vowed to "end the tyranny which oppresses us."

In the mountains of the southwest, Zapata organized a band of peasants to "sustain and carry out the promises" of the revolution. This group, which grew to number some 25,000 soldiers, became known as the Liberation Army of the South. With Zapata in command, the army quickly took control of the haciendas in his home state of Morelos and redistributed the land to peasants. These revolutionaries adopted the slogan "Justicia, Tierra, y Libertad!"—Justice, Land and Liberty!

Zapata and his Liberation Army helped overthrow Madero and Victoriano Huerta. However, his opposition to Mexico's next president, Venustiano Carranza, ended badly for Zapata. In 1919, Carranza's troops ambushed Zapata and killed him.

Meanwhile, Villa gathered and trained peasants, small ranchers, vaqueros, and railroad workers. This army became known as the Division of the North. Villa used his soldiers' skills to advantage. He and his horse-riding vaqueros made cavalry charges against federal soldiers, and his railroad workers took over trains and used them to transport men, weapons, and supplies.

In March 1916, Villa crossed into U.S. territory. His army raided Columbus, New Mexico, leaving 18 Americans—including 10 civilians—dead. Backed by machine guns, U.S. soldiers retaliated and killed more than 100 of

A *soldadera*, or female soldier, looks down the Buenavista station train platform in Mexico City.

Villa's troops. The United States, which supported Carranza over Villa in the civil war, sent a force of some 12,000 soldiers into Mexico to punish Villa, but the former bandit and his guerrillas had vanished.

Smaller revolutionary forces also emerged in Mexico. In the south, the Mayo people fought for land reform. In the north, the Yaqui and Oculla (oh-KWEE-luh) did the same. Women joined some of the revolutionary armies, and a few led their own. Margarita Neri, a former landowner, formed an army that looted haciendas in southern Mexico until she was caught and executed. Other women rose to high positions in existing armies.

Villa and his army continued guerrilla raids against haciendas and Carranza's forces in the north. Only after Carranza was driven out of the presidency in 1920 did Villa put down his weapons. The struggle for peasants' land rights would endure for more than a decade. Finally, in the late 1930s, Lázaro Cárdenas (KAHR-duh-nahs), a progressive president, redistributed land to peasants and enacted other policies that supported the goals of the Mexican Revolution.

HISTORICAL THINKING

1. **READING CHECK** Why did Emiliano Zapata and Pancho Villa focus on attacking haciendas?

2. **IDENTIFY MAIN IDEAS AND DETAILS** Why did Zapata issue the Plan of Ayala?

3. **IDENTIFY PROBLEMS AND SOLUTIONS** Why do you think Zapata and Villa joined forces to pursue change in Mexico?

PLAN: 2-PAGE LESSON

OBJECTIVE

Describe how Emiliano Zapata and Pancho Villa rallied Mexican peasants in the fight for land reform during the Mexican Revolution.

CRITICAL THINKING SKILLS FOR LESSON 4.2

- Identify Main Ideas and Details
- Identify Problems and Solutions
- Explain
- Analyze Cause and Effect
- Analyze Visuals

HISTORICAL THINKING FOR CHAPTER 25

How did the Great War affect the world politically, socially, and economically?

The revolutions that took place against the backdrop of World War I produced a number of significant figures whose impact would be felt for many decades afterward. Lesson 4.2 details the achievements of two such leaders, Emiliano Zapata and Pancho Villa.

BACKGROUND FOR THE TEACHER

Margarita Neri Margarita Neri was one of many *soldaderas*, women fighters who participated in revolutionary military campaigns. Neri was born in 1865 in Quintana Roo, a Mexican state on the Yucatan peninsula. Her mother was of Maya descent, and her father was a former Mexican military general who long opposed President Porfirio Díaz. The red-headed "La Neri" was a fierce commander of a group of 1,000 soldiers that she recruited herself. Their loyalty to her was due to her shooting and riding skills, said to have been on par with those of her soldiers. She and her troops were violent to the point of brutality; they would loot and then burn entire towns. A 1911 article in the *Los Angeles Times* reported on a "Mexican 'Joan of Arc'" who led hundreds of "Indians" against federal troops in the state of Guererro and who sustained an injury to her left arm. Historians believe that Neri was ultimately captured and executed, but it is unknown where, when, and by whom it was done.

INTRODUCE & ENGAGE

THE QUALITIES OF A LEADER

Ask students to brainstorm qualities that they would look for in a political leader, particularly during a period of national strife, conflict, or division. Prompt students' thinking with the following: How important would it be for a political leader to share your personal values? have served in the military? be from a similar socioeconomic status as you? Tell students that they will learn about two leaders of the Mexican Revolution.

TEACH

GUIDED DISCUSSION

1. **Explain** What role did the railroad play in the Mexican Revolution? *(Poor railroad workers in the north were part of the group of peasants and laborers who felt their way of life had been taken away by middle-class hacienda owners. They were also part of Pancho Villa's Division of the North, which fought President Carranza's federal army. As part of their effort, they took over federally controlled trains and used them to transport revolutionaries and their weapons and supplies.)*

2. **Analyze Cause and Effect** What event finally brought progressive reform to Mexico? *(the election of Lázaro Cárdenas as president)*

ANALYZE VISUALS

Ask students to examine the photo of Emiliano Zapata and Pancho Villa. **ASK:** In what ways do Villa and Zapata appear different? *(Villa is sitting on the presidential throne, smiling and laughing, and wearing military garb. Zapata is sitting next to him holding a traditional Mexican hat. He looks very serious or even angry.)* If you were thinking of joining their revolutionary forces and you saw this photo, do you think you would be more or less likely to join? Explain your thinking. *(Answers will vary.)*

ACTIVE OPTIONS

On Your Feet: Fishbowl Arrange students in two concentric circles. Ask students in the inner circle to discuss this question: What land reforms were Zapata, Villa, and their followers demanding? Ask students in the outer circle to listen to the discussion. After a time, direct the two circles to exchange places. Ask the new inner circle to discuss this question: What did Zapata and Villa achieve? Have both groups draw conclusions about whether the Mexican Revolution can be regarded as a success.

| NG Learning Framework: Fact Check a Historical Movie
| ATTITUDE Responsibility
| SKILLS Observation, Communication

Ask small groups to watch the 1952 film *Viva Zapata!*, record their reactions to and opinions about the movie, and then conduct fact-checking using online research, print media, and/or interviews with experts on the subject. Ask them to write a report rating the movie's accuracy, describing changes made for dramatic effect, and summarizing how what they learned from fact-checking affected their reactions to or opinions about the movie and its subject.

DIFFERENTIATE

STRIVING READERS

Write a Tweet As students read the lesson, direct them to write a tweet that summarizes each paragraph's main idea in their own words. Encourage students to read their tweets aloud to a partner, alternating paragraphs. Pairs continue the activity until they reach the end of the lesson.

PRE-AP

Explore Other Revolutionary Forces Challenge students to learn more about the smaller revolutionary forces mentioned in the lesson, such as the Mayo, the Yaqui, and the Ocuila. Ask students to conduct online research and then use their findings to create a report that makes a connection between the group's effort and the larger revolutionary movement. Encourage them to present their report to the class orally or post it on a class blog.

See the Chapter Planner for more strategies for differentiation.

HISTORICAL THINKING

ANSWERS

1. Owners of these vast estates had taken control of much of the peasants' communal farmland. By attacking the haciendas, Zapata and Villa aimed to take back that land for the peasants.

2. Zapata issued the plan because he believed Madero had betrayed the revolution, and Zapata wanted a strategy that would carry the revolution forward.

3. Possible response: Zapata and Villa likely realized that Carranza's forces were too strong for either one of them to defeat by himself.

4.3 The Revolution in Murals

How important is it for people to have a positive image of themselves, of their nation, and of their culture? The Mexican Revolution focused on the rights of peasants, mainly people of native or mixed descent. In a sense, the revolution began a period in which Mexicans incorporated their ancient, indigenous past into their present sense of who they were. Mexican artists and their murals influenced how Mexicans saw—and still see—themselves.

Mexican muralists Diego Rivera, David Alfaro Siqueiros, and José Clemente Orozco emerged in the years following the Mexican Revolution. The revolution inspired all three men, not only as a subject for their art but as motivation to examine Mexico's heritage.

Rivera took part in the Mexican Revolution as an artist, not a fighter. In 1910, at age 23, he designed a poster backing Francisco Madero's call for a peasant rebellion. In 1922, Rivera began his first mural work, mixing European and Mexican folk-art styles. He subsequently created murals in public buildings across Mexico and in major U.S. cities. His mural *History of Mexico* is in the National Palace in Mexico City, home to the executive branch of the federal government. It includes a slogan of the Zapatistas, or followers of Emiliano Zapata: "Tierra y Libertad," which means "Land and Liberty."

Siqueiros earned a scholarship to study art in Paris. There, in 1919, he met Rivera, who urged him to pursue mural painting, which Siqueiros did with a passion. At first, Siqueiros worked in the fresco style, but he later shifted to an experimental, modernist approach. He sometimes dripped or splattered paint on a wall or used an airbrush to apply it.

As a young man, Orozco had a job preparing architectural drawings. He later applied his drawing and mathematics skills to his art. In the 1920s, the Mexican government commissioned him, along with Rivera and Siqueiros, to paint murals aimed at educating and unifying the people. Orozco's murals, created using the traditional fresco technique, are known for their vivid colors.

Diego Rivera studied art for eight years in Europe, where he learned the traditional fresco technique of painting with watercolors on moist plaster that he used to create his murals.

ARTIFACT ONE

Primary Source: Mural (detail)
from *From the Dictatorship of Porfirio Diaz to the Revolution* by David Alfaro Siqueiros, 1957–1966

Siqueiros fought in the Mexican Revolution, joining the army of Venustiano Carranza at the age of 16. Siqueiros's military experience may have contributed to the emotional intensity of his murals. This detail is from a much larger work that covers several walls in Mexico's National Museum of History. The entire mural—not a fresco but acrylic paint on plywood—portrays the politicians and revolutionaries, as well as the peasants, who made history during this era. The way the soldiers are dressed suggests they are Zapatistas.

CONSTRUCTED RESPONSE What gives this image its emotional intensity?

ARTIFACT TWO

Primary Source: Mural
Zapatistas by José Clemente Orozco, 1916

At age 17, Orozco lost his left hand in a school laboratory accident, so he did not fight in the Mexican Revolution. In 1914, however, when the revolution turned into a civil war, Orozco joined the staff of a revolutionary newspaper. He worked as a political cartoonist for the paper, which supported Carranza. Unlike Rivera and Siqueiros, Orozco did not glorify the revolution in his murals; he tried to present a realistic view, one that often revealed the horrors of war. His mural *Zapatistas* offers a somber look at the lives of peasants on the march.

CONSTRUCTED RESPONSE How is Orozco's vision of the revolution in his *Zapatistas* mural similar to and different from Siqueiros's depiction in *From the Dictatorship of Porfirio Diaz to the Revolution*?

SYNTHESIZE & WRITE

1. REVIEW Review what you have learned about the three Mexican muralists, their styles, and their subjects.

2. RECALL On your own paper, list two details about one artist and two details about that artist's mural.

3. CONSTRUCT Construct a topic sentence that answers this question: Which muralist best represents the Mexican Revolution, its goals, and its participants?

4. WRITE Using evidence from this chapter and the images, write an informative paragraph that supports your topic sentence in Step 3.

PLAN: 2-PAGE LESSON

OBJECTIVE
Analyze the similarities and differences between two murals representing the Mexican Revolution.

CRITICAL THINKING SKILLS FOR LESSON 4.3
- Synthesize
- Analyze Visuals
- Make Inferences
- Evaluate

HISTORICAL THINKING FOR CHAPTER 25
How did the Great War affect the world politically, socially, and economically?

Lesson 4.3 focuses on murals painted during and after the Mexican Revolution. The murals represent the people and emotions surrounding this period in history.

BACKGROUND FOR THE TEACHER
Diego Rivera and the Fresco Technique of Painting Rivera began to formally study art at the age of 10 at the Academy of San Carlos on a government scholarship. He went on to study in Spain and in Paris, where he became friends with Pablo Picasso. After meeting Siqueiros in Europe, the two decided to return to Mexico to create a new art theme that would focus on the Mexican Revolution. After Rivera painted *Creation*, his first important mural, he was commissioned to paint the walls of the Ministry of Public Education building in Mexico City. Rivera painted large frescoes that reflected the people and culture of Mexico. The fresco technique includes mixing paint with plaster so that the art is infused into the wall, making it a permanent plaster-based art piece. Fresco painting dates back to the ancient Romans and became popular during the Renaissance. The fresco technique was used by Michelangelo in his painting of *The Creation of Adam* in the Sistine Chapel and by Raphael to paint murals in the Vatican during the early 1500s. Rivera and other Mexican muralists revived the fresco technique in the early 20th century.

INTRODUCE & ENGAGE

PREPARE FOR THE DOCUMENT-BASED QUESTION

Before students start on the activity, briefly preview the two murals. Remind students that a constructed response requires full explanations in complete sentences. Emphasize that students should use what they have learned about the Mexican Revolution in addition to the information presented in the murals to answer the questions.

TEACH

GUIDED DISCUSSION

1. **Analyze Visuals** How do the colors in these murals help represent the Mexican Revolution? *(Possible responses: The red hues in both paintings represent revolution, fighting, and blood, and the bright yellow colors and green hues add to the feelings of intense passion that is generated during a revolution.)*

2. **Make Inferences** Why do you think both artists included women in their murals? *(Possible response: Since the murals represent the people of Mexico, and women were a valued part of Mexican society, they were included to emphasize their importance. Also, some women served as* soladeras, *female soldiers who joined revolutionary armies.)*

EVALUATE

After students have completed the Synthesize & Write activity, allow time for them to exchange paragraphs and read and comment on the work of their peers. Establish guidelines for comments prior to the activity so that feedback is constructive and encouraging. Comments should focus on the most significant parts that address the purpose of the activity and the audience.

ACTIVE OPTION

On Your Feet: Jigsaw Strategy Organize students into "expert" groups and assign each group one of the artifacts to analyze and summarize its main ideas in their own words. Then regroup students into new groups so that each new group has at least one member from each expert group. Students in the new groups take turns sharing the summaries from their expert groups.

DIFFERENTIATE

INCLUSION

Explore Visuals Direct students to examine Siqueiros's mural. Pose the following questions: What are the people doing in the mural? What are the men holding? How are the men dressed? What do you think they are about to do? Direct students to examine Orozco's mural. Pose the following questions: What are the people doing in the mural? What type of hats are the men wearing? What are the men who are walking holding? What expression do the women have on their faces? What do you think the people are about to do?

PRE-AP

Explore Mexican Revolution Art Encourage students to further explore art that was created during or after the Mexican Revolution. Ask them to conduct research to find additional art depicting various aspects of Mexican culture during the decade of revolution. Tell students to create a visual presentation of the art along with a brief report about each piece and its relationship to the Mexican Revolution. Ask students to present their findings to the class.

SYNTHESIZE & WRITE

ANSWERS

1. Answers will vary.

2. Answers will vary. Students should list two details they learned about one of the authors and two details they observed about the artist's mural.

3. Answers will vary. Students' sentences should include which muralist best represents the Mexican Revolution, its goals, and its participants in their opinion.

4. Answers will vary. Students' paragraphs should include their topic sentence from Step 3 and several details from the documents as support.

CONSTRUCTED RESPONSE

Artifact One: Possible response: The soldiers, armed with rifles and wearing belts of bullets, are tightly packed together and extend back to infinity—a revolutionary mass seemingly moving forward into battle. They are supported by strong-looking peasant women.

Artifact Two: Possible response: Both show armed soldiers and women during the revolution. Orozco's painting offers a serious, realistic view of the lives of peasants on the march. Siqueiros's abstract painting offers a more positive view, suggesting an infinite mass of well-armed peasants prepared to do battle.

25 REVIEW

VOCABULARY

Complete each of the following sentences using one of the vocabulary words from the chapter.

1. Russia began to _____ its armed forces in case the country was drawn into war.

2. Many historians consider the Ottoman Empire's _____ of Armenians to be genocide.

3. After World War I, the Germans agreed to pay _____ to the Allies to cover wartime damages.

4. Many of Pancho Villa's soldiers were cowboys and cattle herders, known in Mexico as _____.

5. After the Russian Revolution, the Bolsheviks decided to _____ many industries.

6. Many _____ settled in Paris after World War I.

7. Imperialists often add to their empires by _____ smaller countries or territories.

8. The war on the Western Front settled into a _____ in which neither side could win.

READING STRATEGY
COMPARE AND CONTRAST

Making a chart can help you understand events in history. List details about the Russian, Chinese, and Mexican revolutions. Then answer the question.

Compare Revolutions

	Russian	Chinese	Mexican
Starting Date			
Goals			
Major Figures			
Significant Events			

9. Why is it difficult to identify the point at which a revolution ends?

MAIN IDEAS

Answer the following questions. Support your answers with evidence from the chapter.

10. Why is the Great War considered to have been a total war? LESSON 1.1

11. How did imperialism prepare European powers to immediately engage in battle? LESSON 1.2

12. What role did German U-boats play in the First World War? LESSON 1.3

13. What was the result of the Allies' attempt to secure the Dardanelles in 1915? LESSON 1.4

14. Which agreement from the Paris Peace Conference established new borders in Europe? LESSON 2.1

15. How did Ottoman authorities justify their decision to remove the Armenian population? LESSON 2.3

16. For which people did the Balfour Declaration create a "national home"? LESSON 2.4

17. What political party did Vladimir Lenin and the Bolsheviks establish in 1918? LESSON 3.1

18. How did the New Economic Policy help stimulate the Soviet market? LESSON 3.2

19. Why did Sun Yat-sen agree to cooperate with the Chinese communists? LESSON 3.3

20. Why did Mexican peasants dislike Porfirio Díaz's market-based land policies? LESSON 4.2

HISTORICAL THINKING

Answer the following questions. Support your answers with evidence from the chapter.

21. ANALYZE CAUSE AND EFFECT What was the main cause of the Great War? Explain.

22. EXPLAIN Why did the First World War result in so many casualties?

23. DRAW CONCLUSIONS What limited the role of airplanes in World War I?

24. MAKE INFERENCES Why do you think that the Weimar Republic failed in Germany?

25. IDENTIFY PROBLEMS AND SOLUTIONS Why did Lenin and the Bolsheviks send their political opponents to the Gulag?

26. EVALUATE Did the tactic of guerrilla warfare benefit the Mexican revolutionaries? Explain.

INTERPRET VISUALS

Study the table at right, which shows the casualties suffered by each of the main powers in the Great War. Then answer the questions that follow.

27. Which country suffered the greatest number of casualties?

28. Why are U.S. casualties so much lower than those of the other countries?

Casualties in the Great War

Country	Killed and Died	Wounded	Prisoners and Missing	Total Casualties
Allies				
Russia	1,700,000	4,950,000	2,500,000	9,150,000
France	1,357,800	4,266,000	537,000	6,160,800
Britain	908,371	2,090,212	191,652	3,190,235
Italy	947,000	650,000	600,000	2,197,000
United States	116,516	204,002	4,500	325,018
Central Powers				
Germany	1,773,700	4,216,058	1,152,800	7,142,558
Austria-Hungary	1,200,000	3,620,000	2,200,000	7,020,000
Ottoman Empire	325,000	400,000	250,000	975,000

Sources: U.S. War Department in February 1924. U.S. casualties as amended by the Statistical Services Center, Office of the Secretary of Defense, Nov. 7, 1957

ANALYZE SOURCES

In 1917, Lenin and the Bolsheviks hoped to seize power and establish a "dictatorship of the proletariat." Read the excerpt from an essay by Lenin that first appeared in a Russian magazine less than two weeks before the Bolshevik victory in the October Revolution. Then answer the question that follows.

> We have already seen the strength of the capitalists' resistance. . . . We have not yet seen, however, the strength of resistance of the proletarians and poor peasants, for this strength will become fully apparent only when power is in the hands of the proletariat, when tens of millions of people who have been crushed by want and capitalist slavery see from experience and feel that state power has passed into the hands of the oppressed classes, that the state is helping the poor to fight the landowners and capitalists, is breaking their resistance.

29. According to Lenin, what groups in Russian society are the enemies of the "proletarians and poor peasants"?

CONNECT TO YOUR LIFE

30. NARRATIVE You have read about the aftermath of the Great War and its lasting effects on ordinary citizens. Write a story in which you are a main character and explore what you may have thought or done in the aftermath of the Great War.

TIPS

* Skim the chapter for a person who appeals to you, such as a soldier, someone on the home front, a colonial subject, or a member of the Lost Generation. Use that person as a basis for your character.

* Identify when and where your story takes place and your character's thoughts and feelings about events.

* Use vivid language to describe the location of your story, what is occurring, and how your character reacts.

* Include realistic dialogue in your story.

* Use two or three vocabulary terms from the chapter in your narrative.

* End your narrative by describing what you think one or more of the characters will do in the future.

VOCABULARY ANSWERS

1. mobilize
2. deportation
3. reparations
4. vaqueros
5. nationalize
6. expatriates
7. annexing
8. stalemate

READING STRATEGY ANSWERS

Compare Revolutions

	Russian	Chinese	Mexican
Starting Date	1905	1911	1905
Goals	reform the government; overthrow the tsar; establish communism; leave the Great War	remove the emperor; establish a national government	stop a dictatorship; restore land to the peasants
Major Figures	Mensheviks; Bolsheviks; Lenin; Red Army; White Army	Sun Yat-sen; Chiang Kai-shek; Mao Zedong	Porfirio Díaz; Francisco Madero; Victoriano Huerta; Venustiano Carranza; Álvaro Obregón; Emiliano Zapata; Pancho Villa
Significant Events	establishment of the Duma; February Revolution; October Revolution; assassination of royal family; Russian Civil War	troop mutiny in southeastern China; establishment of republic; May Fourth Movement; massacre of Communists by Nationalists	Madero runs for president against Díaz; Díaz puts Madero in prison, declares himself the winner; Madero goes to Texas; Zapata and Villa help Madero; Madero wins election and is sworn in as president

9. Revolutions usually begin with a public uprising or an easily identified statement. However, the goals of revolutions are often idealistic, and different factions may continue to vie for power. It is not always possible to determine an exact end date.

MAIN IDEAS ANSWERS

10. It required the mobilization of all of a country's resources, including its human resources.

11. Imperialist powers, to protect their colonies, had developed and maintained their armed forces in peacetime.

12. Technologically advanced German U-boats, or submarines, were able to attack Allied merchant and military ships from underwater.

13. The Ottoman defenders, from their position on the high ground, kept the Allied forces from securing the Dardanelles.

14. The Treaty of Versailles redefined borders in Europe.

15. The Ottomans believed the Armenians had chosen to side with Russia and against the Ottoman Empire in the Great War.

16. The Balfour Declaration created a "national home" for the Jewish people.

17. In 1918, Lenin and the Bolsheviks established the Russian Communist Party.

18. The New Economic Policy allowed peasants to keep their grain, gave them long-term leases on their land, and allowed them to sell food on the open market. It also returned small-scale businesses to private hands.

19. Sun Yat-sen realized that his Nationalist Party could not take control of China without help from the Bolsheviks, who insisted that he cooperate with the Chinese Communists.

20. Porfirio Díaz's market-based land policies allowed wealthy landowners to buy up or seize lands that had formerly been cultivated communally, which meant most peasants had to work for low wages on haciendas.

HISTORICAL THINKING ANSWERS

21. Answers will vary. Possible responses: The alliance system—forced countries to enter the war in support of their allies. Rivalries—France and Germany fought a war in 1870; Russia and Austria-Hungary both sought control of former Ottoman territories. Militarism—Germany and other countries kept their militaries prepared for war.

22. Possible response: Advances in weapons technology—including machine guns, artillery, and poison gas—made the battlefields more dangerous and deadly.

23. Answers will vary. Possible responses: Airplanes were a new technology at the time; airplanes at the time were too small to carry a crew or a load of bombs; airplanes at the time were not designed to employ automatic weapons.

24. Possible response: Even though the Weimar Republic established a liberal, democratic constitution, Germany still suffered repercussions of the Great War, including reparations, a reduced army, a smaller region, and inflation. Germans turned from this unstable government toward authoritarianism, a controlled system with fewer personal freedoms.

25. Possible response: Lenin's Soviet Union was an authoritarian, communist dictatorship, and Lenin did not allow other points of view. Sending political opponents to the Gulag silenced them.

26. Possible response: Yes; Mexican revolutionaries' forces were generally smaller than those of the federal army, so they benefited from being able to make small-scale surprise attacks and get away before being overwhelmed.

INTERPRET VISUALS ANSWERS

27. Russia suffered the greatest number of casualties.

28. Possible response: The United States did not enter the war until April 1917, so its troops fought for about 18 months. The other countries battled one another for more than four years.

ANALYZE SOURCES ANSWER

29. Lenin implies that the landowners and capitalists are the enemies of the proletarians and peasants.

CONNECT TO YOUR LIFE ANSWER

30. Students' stories should
   • include themselves as the main character in the aftermath of the Great War;
   • describe the setting (time and place) and their character's thoughts and feelings;
   • include vivid language, realistic dialogue, and two or three vocabulary terms from the chapter;
   • conclude with character predictions;
   • be written in a formal style.

UNIT 9 RESOURCES

UNIT INTRODUCTION

UNIT TIME LINE

UNIT MAP online

THE GLOBAL PERSPECTIVE: Against Inhumanity online

- National Geographic Explorers: Natalia Ledford, Ami Vitale, and Lynn Johnson
- On Your Feet: Turn and Talk on Topic
- **NG Learning Framework**
  Curate a Photography Exhibit

UNIT WRAP-UP

National Geographic Magazine Adapted Article
- "The Science of Good and Evil"

Unit 9 Inquiry: Perform a Reenactment

Unit 9 Formal Assessment

CHAPTER 26 RESOURCES

Available in the Teacher eEdition menu

TEACHER RESOURCES & ASSESSMENT

Reading and Note-Taking

Vocabulary Practice

Document-Based Question Template

Social Studies Skills Lessons
- Reading: Compare and Contrast
- Writing: Explanatory

Formal Assessment
- Chapter 26 Pretest
- Chapter 26 Tests A & B
- Section Quizzes

Chapter 26 Answer Key

Cognero®

STUDENT DIGITAL RESOURCES

Available in the Student eEdition

- eEdition (English)
- National Geographic Atlas
- Biographies
- Handbooks
- History Notebook
- Literature Analysis

STRIVING READERS

STRATEGY ①
Turn Headings into Outlines

To help students organize and understand lesson content, explain that headings can provide a high-level outline of the lesson. Model for students how to use the lesson title and headings to create a basic outline, leaving space after each heading to take notes. Encourage students to add information to the outline after reading each section.

Use with All Lessons

STRATEGY ②
Use a Sorting Activity

Display the following terms and tell students to sort them into three groups of four related terms. Then instruct students to write a paragraph that shows how the terms in each set are related.

mass media	tariffs	radio
boycotts	unemployment	anticolonial
speculators	New Deal programs	nationalism
popular culture	nonviolence	
civil disobedience	wireless messages	

Use with Lessons 1.1, 1.3, and 3.1 *You may use this activity before and again after students study each of these lessons.*

STRATEGY ③
Summarize with Idea Webs

Prompt students to summarize the chapter by creating four Idea Webs, one for each section, and label the center sections as follows: The Twenties, Dictatorships, Nationalism and Colonial Resistance, and The Road to War. Instruct students to complete each web as they read the corresponding lesson. Encourage students to share their idea webs.

Use with All Lessons

INCLUSION

STRATEGY ①
Echo Main Ideas

Point out that the Main Idea statements all relate to important aspects of each of the four chapter sections: The Twenties, Dictatorships, Nationalism and Colonial Resistance, and The Road to War. Pair students with a proficient reader. Ask the proficient reader to read the Main Idea statement at the beginning of a lesson aloud. Tell the less proficient partner to "echo" the statement and then restate it in his or her own words. Encourage partners to discuss what they anticipate the lesson will be about. Have them continue to read together and verify the main ideas as they read.

Use with All Lessons

STRATEGY ②
Provide Alternative Ways of Assessing Knowledge

Adapt tests or quizzes for students with disabilities by having teacher aides or other students read tests and quizzes aloud to students with disabilities. Break multi-step questions into parts, so that each part is more manageable for students with disabilities to answer. Accept oral responses rather than written responses, when appropriate.

Use with All Lessons

ENGLISH LANGUAGE LEARNERS

STRATEGY ①
Pronounce Words

Before reading, preview with students at **All Proficiencies** vocabulary terms such as *innovations, propaganda, broadcasts, speculation, nationalization, nationalism, dismal, totalitarian, scapegoats,* and *sovereign.* Say each word slowly, and have students repeat, noting the pronunciation and syllable stress. Suggest students make word cards for each word, writing definitions and pronunciation hints for themselves.

Use with All Lessons

STRATEGY ❷
Develop Vocabulary

Help students at each level to develop understanding of the lesson vocabulary words. Write the words and keep them displayed throughout the chapter. Discuss each term as it comes up during reading.

Beginning Use vocabulary words in either/or questions, such as: Is a radio or an airplane a form of **mass media**? *(radio)* Do people who buy on **speculation** take huge risks or invest money wisely? *(take huge risks)*

Intermediate Use sentence frames with one blank, such as: A form of **mass media** is _____. *(radio, newspapers, magazines)* A **totalitarian** political system takes _____ control over a society. *(total)*

Advanced Use sentence frames with two blanks, such as: **Popular culture** is the _____ experiences of _____ people. *(shared/everyday)* People who buy _____ on **speculation** take _____. *(shares/huge risks)*

Use with All Lessons

STRATEGY ❸
Connect Visuals to Lesson Content

Direct students at the **Beginning** and **Intermediate** levels to read each lesson and study the visuals. Have them explain how the visuals are related to the lesson.

Use with All Lessons *Encourage students at the Beginning level to ask questions if they have trouble connecting a visual with its lesson. Suggest students at the Advanced level help students of lower proficiencies.*

GIFTED & TALENTED

STRATEGY ❶
Create a Podcast

Direct students to choose one lesson or part of a lesson as the basis for an episode of a historical podcast. Tell students that their podcast should establish a point of view that is both informative and entertaining. Suggest that they write a script for their podcast and include sound effects and music. Invite students to present their podcast live or record it with a phone or other device and play it for the class.

Use with All Lessons

STRATEGY ❷
Report on a Documentary

Invite students to watch brief segments of some of the many documentaries about one of the topics in the chapter, such as early aviation, the Great Depression, or the rise of Hitler. Then direct them to choose one documentary to research and watch in its entirety. Tell students to gather information about the documentarians and analyze their motivations, filmmaking process, and style. Instruct students to write a report about the documentary, including clips to illustrate the points they make. Ask students to share their reports with the class.

Use with All Lessons

PRE-AP

STRATEGY ❶
Compare and Contrast Political Responses

Instruct students to conduct online research about how different countries responded to World War I and the Great Depression, such as the rise of fascism in Italy, communism in Russia, or ultranationalists in Japan. Tell students to select two political responses and write a feature article comparing and contrasting the impact each event had on the countries involved.

Use with All Lessons

STRATEGY ❷
Extend Knowledge

Invite students to conduct research about a person, event, or topic introduced in the chapter and to connect their subject to larger social, economic, environmental, or political trends. For example, students might choose to investigate what forms of mass media have the greatest impact on popular culture today or how the speculation and stock market crash of the 1920s led to some of the regulations on the stock market today. Direct students to present their findings in an oral report to the class or in a digital report posted on a class blog.

Use with All Lessons

CHAPTER

26

Economic
Depression and
Authoritarian
Regimes

1908–1939

HISTORICAL THINKING Is it better to have security
or freedom?

SECTION 1 **The Twenties**
SECTION 2 **Dictatorships**
SECTION 3 **Nationalism and Colonial Resistance**
SECTION 4 **The Road to War**

CRITICAL VIEWING
In 1936, during a Nazi Party rally in Nuremberg, Germany,
soldiers in combat gear stand at attention, listening to
a speech by Adolf Hitler. Based on details in the photo,
what can you infer about the purpose of the rally? What
message do the Nazis want to convey to the world?

INTRODUCE THE PHOTOGRAPH

A NUREMBERG RALLY

Have students closely examine the photograph of the
1936 Nazi rally in Nuremberg, Germany. Explain to
students that the years between World War I and World
War II were a time of enormous political, economic, and
social uncertainty. This global unrest had numerous
effects, one of which was a rise in authoritarian regimes.
ASK: Why might people look to a strong, charismatic
leader during times of economic insecurity? *(During a
time of economic insecurity, a feeling of helplessness
and great need might lead people to follow someone—
anyone—who promised a solution or a return to better
times.)* Why might a charismatic national leader want to
build a strong military? *(A charismatic national leader
would want a strong military to demonstrate that he
or she was a strong leader. By projecting an image of
strength, the leader could maintain high popular opinion
and hold on to power. Also, a strong military would be
needed for any possible armed conflict.)*

SHARE BACKGROUND

In 1923, the Nazi Party began holding massive
propaganda rallies in which the principles of National
Socialism were displayed for all the world to see. The
earliest rallies were relatively small affairs, but their size
and scope expanded greatly over the years. By 1933,
these rallies were annual affairs that could last for up to
eight days and included fireworks, bonfires, torchlight
marches, military parades, swastika banners, and human
swastika formations. Attendees heard military-style
songs and marches accompanied by drums, as well as
the grand operatic music of Richard Wagner. The rallies
also included addresses by party leaders, including
Adolf Hitler, and would end with a presentation of Nazi
flags. Rallies were attended by hundreds of thousands
of participants and spectators, including international
journalists, who sent home word of the chilling pageantry.

CRITICAL VIEWING Answers will vary. Possible
response: Hitler used the rally to show off Germany's
military strength and to communicate to the German
public—and the entire world—that Germany was united
in its determination to achieve its goals and a force to be
reckoned with. I can infer that the purpose of the rally was
to show off the might of the Nazi army as well Germany's
widespread support for Hitler.

Is it better to have security or freedom?

Roundtable Activity: Causes of Conflict This activity introduces students to some of the ideologies and circumstances that led countries to declare war on each other. Divide the class into groups of four and have each group sit at a table. Ask groups to discuss what they have learned about other wars, such as World War I, and encourage students to consider factors that led to those wars. Assign one of the following questions to each group:

Question 1 What ideas of dictators or totalitarian leaders can lead to war?

Question 2 What leads countries to attempt to expand and acquire more land?

Question 3 How can economic hardship lead to conflict?

Ask students at each table to take turns answering the question. When they have finished their discussion, ask a representative from each table to summarize that group's answers.

KEY DATES FOR CHAPTER 26

1923	The Turkish republic is formed with Atatürk as its leader.
1927	Charles Lindbergh completes his first solo, nonstop transatlantic flight.
1928	Stalin launches his first Five-Year Plan.
1929	The New York Stock Exchange crashes; Nigerian women stage the Igbo Women's War.
1930	Mohandas Gandhi leads the Salt March in India.
1931	Japan invades and conquers Manchuria.
1933	Hitler becomes the German chancellor.
1935	Mussolini invades Ethiopia.
1936	Francisco Franco seizes power in Spain.
1937	Amelia Earhart disappears; Getúlio Vargas launches his "New State" in Brazil; Japanese troops commit the Rape of Nanjing; Picasso paints *Guernica*.
1938	The Munich Agreement is signed.
1939	Hitler invades Poland.

INTRODUCE THE READING STRATEGY

COMPARE AND CONTRAST

Explain to students that comparing and contrasting can help them more deeply understand concepts and events. Turn to the Chapter Review and preview the Venn diagram with students. As they read the chapter, have students compare and contrast the actions taken by the totalitarian leaders of Nazi Germany and the Soviet Union in the 1930s and 1940s.

INTRODUCE CHAPTER VOCABULARY

KEY VOCABULARY

SECTION 1

Great Depression	mass media	mass society
popular culture	speculation	

SECTION 2

Blackshirt	collectivization	cult of personality
fascism	Kristallnacht	kulak
totalitarian	ultranationalist	

SECTION 3

ahimsa	civil disobedience	Dalit
equatorial	Hind Swaraj	satyagraha

SECTION 4

appeasement	carpet-bombing	isolationism
nonintervention	remilitarization	sanction

DEFINITION CHART

As they read the chapter, encourage students to complete a Definition Chart. Ask them to list the Key Vocabulary terms in the left column of their charts. As students encounter each Key Vocabulary term in the chapter, they should write its definition in the center column and explain what it means, using their own words, in the right column. Model an example for students, using the graphic organizer below.

Word	Definition	In My Own Words
mass media	means of communication meant to reach many people	movies, TV shows, news, and online content that reaches everyone

Over the Air

Many people today want to get their hands on the latest smartphone or other communication technology. Likewise, in the 1920s, people were thrilled by the chance to listen to a popular radio program or the possibility of traveling by air.

AVIATION TAKES FLIGHT

The early years of the 20th century introduced the age of aviation, or the use of aircraft. **Orville and Wilbur Wright** attained a remarkable achievement when their *Flyer I* briefly rose off the ground in Kitty Hawk, North Carolina. For the first time, a powered vehicle had lifted off the ground and successfully taken flight. In 1908, the brothers brought their invention to Europe. Soon, people around the globe became captivated by air flight and the speed at which people and goods could travel.

Aviation innovations increased during World War I as fighting nations looked to use the new technology to their advantage. The first war planes were used simply to observe the position and movement of enemy forces, but later airplanes were fitted with machine guns and engaged in battle. In another military advancement, grenades were tossed from airplanes called bombers. Civilians were enthralled by tales of dogfights, or conflicts between fighter planes. The daring exploits of flying aces—such as the German Red Baron (Manfred

On the morning of December 17, 1903, Orville Wright makes the historic first powered airplane flight, as his brother Wilbur runs alongside the wingtip of *Flyer I* in Kitty Hawk, North Carolina. On this first successful flight, which lasted 12 seconds, Wright flew the airplane 120 feet.

This photo of Bessie Coleman was taken in the 1920s. Discrimination kept Coleman from entering aviation schools in the United States. However, that didn't stop her from fulfilling her dream to fly. Coleman learned French and was accepted at an aviation school in France. In 1921, she became the first American woman to receive an international pilot's license.

von Richthofen), American Eddie Rickenbacker, France's Georges Guynemer, and Britain's Albert Ball—were used as propaganda tools in the war. In reality, aircraft and air battles did not play a major role in the war's outcome, but aviation proved it could be important in future wars.

Aviation advances and enthusiasm did not stop after World War I. In 1927, pilot Charles Lindbergh impressed the world with his solo, nonstop transatlantic voyage in the airplane *Spirit of St. Louis*. Bessie Coleman, the first African-American pilot, used her aviation skills to demonstrate that the skies were open to all. Amelia Earhart served as a role model for other women

to become pilots. The achievements of such pilots help explain why the period following World War I is remembered as the "Golden Age of Flight." At this time, the first permanent commercial airports were built in such locations as the United States, Australia, France, Britain, Germany, and Thailand. The growing demand for the movement of passengers and freight caused even more aviation innovation.

TUNING INTO THE RADIO

Alexander Graham Bell's telephone had shown that spoken words could travel long distances by wire. But could words travel over the air without wires? In

---

PLAN: 4-PAGE LESSON

OBJECTIVE

Describe how the airplane and the radio impacted the world and contributed to the development of popular culture and a mass society.

CRITICAL THINKING SKILLS FOR LESSON 1.1

- Draw Conclusions
- Compare and Contrast
- Analyze Cause and Effect
- Form and Support Opinions
- Synthesize
- Explain

HISTORICAL THINKING FOR CHAPTER 26

Is it better to have security or freedom?

In the years leading up to World War II, many countries wrestled with achieving a balance between security and freedom. Security meant having a strong military; freedom meant avoiding a militaristic society. Lesson 1.1 sets the stage as technologies like the radio and the airplane transformed how the world moved and communicated.

BACKGROUND FOR THE TEACHER

WWI Impact on Aviation Just a little more than a decade passed from the Wright Brothers' first flight to the beginning of World War I. The first airplanes used in the war had open cockpits, were made of lightweight materials such as wood and canvas, and had basically no instruments. Pilots frequently got lost, often resorting to following train tracks to help them navigate to their destinations. They had no parachutes and no radio to communicate with others. Some planes carried homing pigeons in case they were shot down. Despite these early problems, the military quickly recognized the importance of the airplane. During the next four years, advancements were continually made to the more than 200,000 aircraft built during the war, with the Allied nations out-producing the Germans by nearly five to one. By the end of the war, airplane engines had been greatly improved. By the 1920s, airplanes were made of metal, were much more reliable, and were capable of flying longer distances.

INTRODUCE & ENGAGE

CONNECT WITH TODAY

Display a Concept Cluster for students. Write *Global Culture* in the center oval and label the other ovals *Music, Fashion,* and *Sports.* Ask students to suggest how music, fashion, and sports influence popular culture today. Record and discuss student responses. Tell students that in this lesson they will learn about how these areas of popular culture developed in the years following World War I.

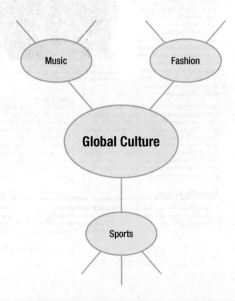

TEACH

GUIDED DISCUSSION

1. **Analyze Cause and Effect** What effect did the airplane have on World War I? *(Possible response: Aircraft did not have a huge effect on the outcome of World War I, but they allowed opponents to observe the position and movement of the enemy. Dogfights helped to keep civilians at home interested in the war and ensure that victory could be achieved. The war served as a prototype for the crucial role aircraft would play in future wars.)*

2. **Analyze Cause and Effect** What effect did the radio have on World War I? *(Possible response: Radios greatly changed how soldiers were able to react to enemy movements. Portable radios were carried by radio operators, who could warn soldiers of attacks, relay orders, and communicate locations. Radios also allowed battleships and warplanes to communicate through Morse code.)*

COMPARE AND CONTRAST

Direct students' attention to the photographs of the Wright Brothers' airplane and Bessie Coleman beside her plane. **ASK:** How are the Wright Brothers' airplane and Bessie Coleman's airplane different? *(The Wright Brothers' plane has a very wide wingspan and the wings look like they are fragile, perhaps made of paper or wood; also, the plane looks like it is gliding in the air via wind power. Coleman's plane looks more technologically sophisticated: it has a large metal propeller.)*

DIFFERENTIATE

STRIVING READERS

Ready, Set, Recall After students have read the lesson, set a short time limit and tell them to write a list of facts they learned. Direct students to work in pairs to compare and combine their lists. Then ask pairs to alternately read facts from their lists until all pairs run out of new details. Keep a tally of the number of facts each pair contributes. The pair with the most facts wins.

PRE-AP

Write an Online Profile Instruct students to use multiple sources to gather information about one of the individuals they read about in the lesson, such as the Wright Brothers, the Red Baron, Bessie Coleman, Amelia Earhart, Guglielmo Marconi, Louis Armstrong, or Josephine Baker. Tell students to examine the individual's accomplishments and consider why he or she is remembered in history. Encourage students to use words, photographs, and music clips in their profiles. Invite volunteers to share their profiles with the class.

See the Chapter Planner for more strategies for differentiation.

1902, Guglielmo Marconi showed that they could by using his new invention—the radio—to send a wireless message across the Atlantic Ocean.

As it did for aviation, World War I brought improvements and refinements to the radio. Military radio operators used the new technology to warn soldiers of attacks and relay orders. The portability of the radio provided fighters with a way to communicate no matter their location. As technology improved, the radio allowed battleships and warplanes to communicate with one another through Morse code, a series of dots and dashes that could be transcribed into letters.

After the war, the radio became an important source of entertainment for the war-weary. Listeners in the United States tuned into the news, musical presentations, political speeches, weather reports, comedy and adventure shows, and soap operas. In Europe and Asia, the radio was used at first primarily for public service purposes, such as the first broadcasts of the British Broadcasting Corporation, or BBC.

Never before had so many people had such quick and convenient access to the same information and entertainment at the same time. Radio, along with newspapers and magazines, became an early form of **mass media**, or means of communication meant to reach many people. These mass media influenced the **popular culture**, or the shared experiences and interests of everyday people. Popular culture in the United States at the time included a love of jazz, baseball, and the Charleston dance. Some people say that mass media caused the formation of a **mass society**, in which large numbers of people share the same experiences without actually having to meet.

The radio was not the only new technology that fascinated people in the world's more advanced consumer societies. They were happy to replace their old iceboxes with electric refrigerators. Movies with sound provided hours of entertainment. Where mass-produced and less-expensive automobiles were available, people could explore beyond their region and gain more freedom—especially women.

MASS SOCIETY AND GLOBAL CULTURE

New forms of communication and transportation allowed greater cultural exchange around the early 20th-century world. Both radio and early films, for example, made possible the global popularity of jazz music. Jazz originated with African-American musicians combining African rhythmic traditions with sparkling new melodies. Radio listeners from Miami to Berlin and Cape Town to Shanghai tapped their toes to jazz rhythms.

Apart from radio, new phonograph technology played a role, helping the jazz trumpeter and vocalist Louis Armstrong make his way from childhood poverty in New Orleans to international fame. The voice of Italian opera singer Enrico Caruso could be heard in living rooms around the world. Mass magazines also played a role, for example, spreading the word about the glamorous cabaret star Josephine Baker, who escaped a tough childhood in East St. Louis and found stardom in Harlem. She then left New York City for Paris, opening her own nightclub and becoming one of Europe's wealthiest performers.

Women's fashions were also affected. In cities everywhere you could find the controversial figure of the "modern girl." Whether in Dallas, Istanbul, or Mexico City, these young women pushed back against traditional ideas of how they should dress and behave, wearing elegant clothing and using cosmetics that showed cosmopolitan influences from fashion centers like Paris. Their idea of being free to express themselves as individuals and not limited to roles as daughters and wives was a very bold one at that time.

This photograph of American trumpeter and singer Louis Armstrong was taken around 1930. Armstrong, who excelled at the art of improvisation, became one of jazz's legendary greats.

Sports also showed the influence of mass society. In the United States and much of Latin America and the Caribbean, fans could now follow their team's games play-by-play, and the best players, like the Yankees' Babe Ruth, became international stars. In most of the world, football—or soccer—held center stage. The modern Olympics were first held in Athens, Greece, in 1896. Before long, millions would listen and watch as the world's best athletes represented their nations, giving people both a sense of national pride and a greater awareness of the wider world.

A German family gathers around a radio in their home in 1933. Radios became popular consumer items and offered in-home entertainment.

HISTORICAL THINKING

1. **READING CHECK** How did the inventions of the airplane and radio change people's lives?

2. **DRAW CONCLUSIONS** How do times of peace and war affect the development of technology differently?

3. **COMPARE AND CONTRAST** How did new technologies affect music and fashion around the world?

BACKGROUND FOR THE TEACHER

Technology Fuels the Popularity of Music In the 1920s, radio and phonographs overtook sheet music as a medium for the spread of music. Record sales for popular music jumped from around 25 million in 1914 to around 110 million in 1922. Big-name companies such as Columbia, Edison, and RCA Victor, as well as a host of independent producers, manufactured 78-rpm records with a single three-minute song on each side. This new technology allowed Louis Armstrong and his Hot Five and Hot Seven bands to release 65 records between 1925 and 1928. The phonograph also boosted interest in classical music. The Italian tenor Enrico Caruso made more than 200 opera recordings, most of them for the Victor Talking Machine Company, based in Camden, New Jersey, and bought by RCA in 1929. The RCA Victor recordings of another Italian, conductor Arturo Toscanini, popularized much of the standard orchestral repertoire. Though the length of many works was not always compatible with the technology of the time, his recording of Beethoven's *Third Symphony* took up 12 sides of six 12-inch records.

TEACH

GUIDED DISCUSSION

3. **Form and Support Opinions** Why might music, sports, and fashion have influenced global culture more than other topics? *(Possible response: Music, sports, and fashion have more of a universal appeal and are not as tied to language and cultural differences.)*

4. **Synthesize** Why might some people be more susceptible than others to the dissemination of mass culture brought by the radio and other technologies? *(Possible response: Certain technologies would have been expensive in their day, such as radios and phonographs. As a result, if people could not afford a radio or a phonograph, they would not be as easily exposed to certain aspects of mass culture.)*

EXPLAIN

Direct students' attention to the photographs of the German family listening to the radio and Louis Armstrong with his trumpet. **ASK:** What do both photographs convey about the development of a mass society? *(Possible response: The German family photo shows many people around a single radio, which shows that the radio had mass appeal for people of all ages and could be enjoyed by many people at once. The photo of Louis Armstrong is clearly a posed publicity photo, which shows that Armstrong was popular, and he had cultivated a certain image that was being marketed to a wide audience.)*

ACTIVE OPTIONS

On Your Feet: Inside-Outside Circle Use the Inside-Outside Circle strategy to check students' understanding. Direct students in the outer circle to pose the following question: In what ways were jazz, fashion, and sports evidence of the emergence of a global culture in the early 20th century? Direct students in the inner circle to answer the question. Then ask students to trade inside/outside roles.

> **NG Learning Framework: Explore 1920s Radio Advertising**
> **ATTITUDE** Curiosity
> **SKILL** Communication

Assign students to work with partners or in small groups to research examples of radio advertisements from the 1920s. Have groups analyze the goals and techniques of each advertisement and its contribution to building popular culture and a mass society. Have each group share its analysis in a multimedia presentation.

HISTORICAL THINKING

ANSWERS

1. The airplane provided a new and speedy way to travel, altered how people fought wars, and captured the public's imagination. The radio provided people with a way to communicate wirelessly over long distances in times of war and peace. It helped the war effort in World War I and provided people with hours of entertainment in the post-war years.

2. Possible response: During wartime, most innovations are made to help nations achieve victory and therefore are created with military purposes in mind, often emphasizing large-scale destruction and death. During times of peace, innovations are mainly made to improve life, including home, work, and leisure activities. Often, innovations of war are adapted to have peacetime applications.

3. New technologies, like the airplane, the radio, the phonograph, and motion pictures, allowed for a broader and quicker cultural exchange. Radio and the phonograph drove interest in music as people listened to jazz and other genres on records and over the airwaves. Movie stars, dressed in the latest fashions, were seen by millions on film and in magazines.

Daring to Fly

"As soon as we left the ground, I knew I myself had to fly."
—Amelia Earhart, after her first plane ride

A crowd of people enthusiastically greet Amelia Earhart after her transatlantic crossing from Newfoundland in 1932.

WHERE IS AMELIA EARHART? On July 2, 1937, Amelia Earhart and her navigator, Fred Noonan, took off from Lae, Papua New Guinea, bound for Howland Island, one of the last stops on their 29,000-mile flight around the world. They disappeared somewhere over the Pacific, spawning multiple theories about their fate.

— Flight path   --- Intended flight path

738 CHAPTER 26

MAIN IDEA Pioneer pilot Amelia Earhart set numerous aviation records and championed women's rights and abilities.

Amelia Earhart fell in love with flight on her first airplane ride in 1920, when she was just 23 years old and aviation was still in its infancy. Within a year, Earhart was flying solo. The next year, she set a record, flying at an altitude of 14,000 feet—higher than any woman had flown before. Earhart went on to set numerous aviation records, and in the process she challenged people's notions about women's limitations. Adventurous and independent from childhood on, Earhart encouraged women to dare to fly—not only in airplanes but in their personal lives as well. She challenged herself and other women to explore the frontiers of what a woman could achieve.

SETTING RECORDS

Amelia Earhart first made worldwide headlines for a flight on which she was only a passenger. In 1928, she became the first woman to cross the Atlantic Ocean in an airplane piloted by two men. Although Charles Lindbergh had completed a nonstop, solo flight from New York to Paris in 1927, transatlantic flights were still risky. Others had died trying to fly nonstop across the Atlantic Ocean. Treated to a ticker-tape parade in New York and a reception at the White House, Earhart became an international celebrity.

By 1932, Earhart was ready to attempt the transatlantic flight by herself. Piloting her red Lockheed Vega 5B, she set a record as the first woman to make a solo, nonstop flight across the Atlantic Ocean. Moreover, she overcame mechanical problems, strong winds, and icy conditions to complete the flight in record time: 14 hours, 56 minutes. She was the first person since Charles Lindbergh to accomplish the feat. The National Geographic Society awarded her its Gold Medal, given for notable geographic achievement. Earhart was the first woman to receive the prestigious medal.

In addition to "first woman" records, Earhart also set "first person" records. In 1935, she made the first solo flight from Hawaii to California, a hazardous trip that was longer in distance than the flight from the United States to Europe. Later that year, she became the first person to fly alone from Los Angeles to Mexico City.

One of the most celebrated aviators of her time, Earhart wrote three books about her flights as well as articles for *National Geographic* and other magazines. She used her fame to promote opportunities for women in aviation and other fields. She supported women's issues and encouraged women to assert their independence and gain control of their lives. Earhart described her own marriage to George Putnam, a publisher, as a "partnership" with "dual control."

THE LAST FLIGHT

In 1937, nearing the age of 40, Earhart was determined to become the first woman to fly around the world. She declared, "I have a feeling that there is just one more flight in my system." On June 1, Earhart and navigator Fred Noonan left Miami for the 29,000-mile trip. Over the next few weeks, they stopped a number of times to refuel before landing at Lae, New Guinea, on June 29. By then, they had covered 22,000 miles—more than three-fourths of the distance.

On July 2, Earhart and Noonan took off for Howland Island, located about 2,600 miles away in the Pacific Ocean. Earhart knew that the tiny island would be difficult to spot in the vast Pacific. During the flight, she maintained intermittent radio contact with a U.S. Coast Guard boat situated nearby. Late in the journey, Earhart radioed that she and Noonan must be near the island, but they couldn't see it and were running low on fuel. One more radio message arrived . . . and then silence.

In a rescue attempt, the U.S. government launched the largest air and sea search in naval history, involving 3,000 people, 10 ships, and about 65 planes. No sign of Earhart, Noonan, or their plane was discovered, and the search ended on July 19. The U.S. government concluded that Earhart's plane had run out of fuel and crashed into the Pacific.

Over the years, other theories about Earhart's fate have circulated. Many groups searched for traces of Earhart, Noonan, and the plane. In August 2019, National Geographic sponsored an expedition to the tiny island of Nikumaroro based on a theory that Earhart landed the plane there after she couldn't locate Howland Island. However, the expedition, led by National Geographic Explorer Robert Ballard, found no evidence of the plane. After nearly a century, people are still transfixed by this trailblazing woman who dared to explore the frontiers of flight.

HISTORICAL THINKING

1. **READING CHECK** What are some of the aviation records that Amelia Earhart set?

2. **EVALUATE** Why was Amelia Earhart an unusual woman for her time?

Economic Depression and Authoritarian Regimes 739

PLAN: 2-PAGE LESSON

OBJECTIVE

Examine the experiences of one of the most celebrated female aviators in the world, who promoted women's issues and strove for equality, Amelia Earhart.

CRITICAL THINKING SKILLS FOR LESSON 1.2

- Evaluate
- Draw Conclusions
- Form and Support Opinions
- Interpret Maps

HISTORICAL THINKING FOR CHAPTER 26

Is it better to have security or freedom?

Not only did Amelia Earhart set numerous aviation records, she also promoted women's issues, strove for equality, and challenged women to explore. Lesson 1.2 discusses the achievements and last flight of Amelia Earhart.

Student eEdition online

Additional content for this lesson, including a photograph, is available online.

BACKGROUND FOR THE TEACHER

Amelia Earhart After World War I, Amelia Earhart attended Columbia University in New York as a premed student until her parents asked her to live with them in California. It was there that she went on her first airplane ride. In 1921, she bought an airplane. Two years later, she earned her pilot's license and began flying solo. In 1928, she was selected to be a passenger aboard a seaplane as it crossed the Atlantic Ocean. Upon landing in Wales, Earhart became an international celebrity. She wrote and toured the United States, giving lectures about the flight. She married her publisher, George Palmer Putnam, who encouraged her to fly and handled her publicity. After her solo flight across the Atlantic, she published a book about her life and love for flying. Her fame helped Earhart encourage women to reject the social norm and to pursue their dreams. She created a women's active clothing line, championed athletic training for girls, and founded an organization for female pilots. During her last flight, Earhart sent several letters and diary entries to her husband. After her disappearance, he helped write and publish her final book, *Last Flight,* in 1937.

History Notebook

Encourage students to complete the National Geographic Explorer page for Chapter 26 in their History Notebooks as they read.

INTRODUCE & ENGAGE

CONNECT TO TODAY

Remind students that during the 1920s, women had won the right to vote and were ready to exercise their freedoms. Discuss contemporary women who have dared to challenge the norm. **ASK:** How were women's experiences in the 1920s different from and similar to those of women today? *(Possible response: Women today have more employment options than women in the 1920s did, but women are still often paid less for doing the same jobs as men. The most powerful positions are still reserved for men, often restricting women's advancement.)* With her piloting skills, Amelia Earhart proved that a woman could be as good as or better than a man at a typically male career.

TEACH

GUIDED DISCUSSION

1. **Draw Conclusions** In what way was Amelia Earhart an effective role model? *(Earhart set "first woman" records, as well as "first person" records, proving women were equal to, or better than, men.)*

2. **Form and Support Opinions** How do you think Earhart's celebrity status helped promote her aviation goals? Explain your response. *(Possible response: People wanted to see her succeed. This probably helped her receive funding for additional flights and better equipment to help her make and break aviation records.)*

INTERPRET MAPS

Direct students to the map. **ASK:** Where was Earhart supposed to land? *(Howard Island)* Why was it difficult to find Howard Island? *(It was very small. The Pacific Ocean is vast.)* Could she have landed on the wrong island? *(Yes, Nikumaroro and Marshall islands are near Howard Island.)*

ACTIVE OPTIONS

On Your Feet: Travel Around the World Position two students in one corner of the room and one student in each of the other corners. Ask the two students in the first corner a question about the lesson. Whoever correctly answers the question first becomes the "traveler" and moves to another corner to stand with a new partner, while the first partner sits down and another student takes his or her place. Repeat the process for as long as time permits. A traveler who correctly answers one question in each corner has "traveled around the world."

> **NG Learning Framework: Create a Multimedia Newscast**
> **SKILL** Collaboration
> **KNOWLEDGE** Our Human Story

Tell small groups to conduct research to find photos and newspaper articles about the aviation records achieved by Amelia Earhart. Prompt groups to write a script in the form of a contemporary newscast. Then direct students to make a video of their newscast, featuring the photos they found. Instruct groups to present their newscast to the class.

DIFFERENTIATE

STRIVING READERS

Use Sentence Starters Provide these sentence starters for students to complete after reading:

1. Earhart started flying when she was _____.

2. Her first record was _____.

3. Earhart encouraged women to _____.

4. Earhart described her marriage as _____.

5. Her last flight was an attempt to _____, but _____.

GIFTED & TALENTED

Investigate Amelia Earhart's Disappearance Challenge students to investigate Amelia Earhart's disappearance. Tell students to conduct research to find probable locations, speculate why the locations are viable, and determine whether the mystery can be solved. Encourage students to write an investigative report that includes facts, their opinions about their findings, and explanations of their speculations. Invite students to share their reports with the class.

See the Chapter Planner for more strategies for differentiation.

HISTORICAL THINKING

ANSWERS

1. Amelia Earhart set many "first woman" aviation records, including the first woman to fly solo, nonstop across the Atlantic Ocean. She also set many "first person" records, such as the first solo flight from Hawaii to California and the first solo flight from Los Angeles to Mexico City.

2. Possible response: Not only was Earhart a trailblazing aviator who set many records, she also championed women's rights and encouraged women to explore their own ambitions and abilities.

The Great Depression

The economies of countries around the world have ups and downs all the time. When a country's economy declines over a period of time, that country is experiencing a recession. If the country's economy dips far lower, then it enters into a depression, or an extremely difficult economic time. That's just what happened around the world in the 1930s.

GLOBAL IMPACT OF U.S. ECONOMIC WOES

By the mid-1920s, the global economy had recovered from World War I, and international trade and investment were once again on the rise. No one was prepared for the shock that came next. In October 1929, prices on the New York Stock Exchange plunged so low that the stock market crashed. Within two months, stocks lost half their value. Bank failures across Europe and the Americas brought about the **Great Depression**, a time of intense financial hardship that lasted throughout the 1930s. Today, historians still discuss and debate the multiple causes of the global economic depression.

Just a few years earlier, many people in the United States were living a good life, buying homes, automobiles, and shares of stock. Many people thought that investing in the stock market was the key to gaining wealth. They were so intent on becoming stockholders that they bought shares on **speculation**, or the taking of huge risks to gain great rewards. Speculators low on cash borrowed money from banks to buy shares. They falsely believed that markets would endlessly increase in value and did not realize speculation would cause problems.

Worried that their stocks were overvalued, some investors sold them. This caused other investors to panic and sell as well, sending stock prices down. Many Americans lost all their money and could not buy products, causing factories to close. By 1932, one-fourth of workers in the United States were unemployed.

The Great Depression soon revealed problems with the international financial system. Following World War I, many European governments were deeply in debt to American banks. In fact, they had acquired more debt than they could repay. Germany was particularly

People gather on Wall Street by the New York Stock Exchange on October 24, 1929.

affected because it owed $33 billion in reparations, payments to France required by the Versailles Treaty. It had turned to American banks for loans to repay these reparations. After the stock market crash, the U.S. banks called in their loans to German banks, leading to the collapse of the financial system.

The Great Depression also had a devastating effect on people in countries that depended on the export of minerals and agricultural commodities. Prices for crops fell sharply because of a drop in demand. Hard-hit farmers tried producing more, but this lowered prices even further. In Africa, a huge drop in cocoa and coffee prices meant farmers could not pay their debts or taxes to colonial governments. In Southeast Asia, a decline in automobile and bicycle production caused rubber

prices to crash and unemployment to soar. In India, desperate peasant families were forced to sell gold jewelry they were saving for their daughters' weddings. Throughout the nonindustrial world, people could no longer purchase the manufactured products industrial nations depended on them to buy.

GOVERNMENTS RESPOND

Around the world, people expected their governments to solve economic problems, no longer believing that free markets were the answer. British economist John Maynard Keynes developed a theory supporting the idea of greater government involvement. Keynes argued that during a severe downturn government should increase the money supply and borrow money for investment to stimulate the economy and lead to the return of economic growth. Once the economy was healthy again, governments should pay down the debt they had taken on.

Governments in France, Britain, and the United States took a more active role in their economies. U.S. president **Franklin Delano Roosevelt** responded to the depression by implementing his New Deal programs. Social Security, one of these programs, created a "safety net" for many of the nation's elderly. The Works Progress Administration (WPA) put many unemployed people to work on roadbuilding and construction projects and employed writers, artists, and actors in cultural programs. Price subsidies helped stabilize prices. France and Britain undertook similar measures. Sweden, Norway, and Denmark used a different approach. These nations promised to protect their citizens through comprehensive education, health care, housing subsidies, and unemployment insurance.

A WPA project, this mural was painted by Millard Owen Sheets in 1939.

One common response was economic nationalism. Many countries, including the United States, raised their tariffs. The idea was for each nation to protect its own producers from competition, but international trade declined even further as a result, making most people even poorer. In Latin America, some leaders took up economic nationalization, or the claiming of ownership of private business or industry by a government. In the late 1930s, Mexico's president, Lázaro Cárdenas, nationalized the country's petroleum industry. He argued that oil profits should benefit the Mexican people, not foreign companies.

HISTORICAL THINKING

1. **READING CHECK** How did the results of World War I contribute to the global economic collapse?

2. **ANALYZE CAUSE AND EFFECT** What were the two most important causes of the Great Depression? Explain.

3. **COMPARE AND CONTRAST** What did the economic relief efforts of various political leaders have in common?

PLAN: 2-PAGE LESSON

OBJECTIVE
Summarize the causes and effects of the global economic depression that lasted throughout the 1930s.

CRITICAL THINKING SKILLS FOR LESSON 1.3
- Analyze Cause and Effect
- Compare and Contrast
- Explain
- Identify Problems and Solutions
- Analyze Visuals

HISTORICAL THINKING FOR CHAPTER 26
Is it better to have security or freedom?

In the years leading up to World War II, national security was not the only concern for many countries. As a result of the global economic depression, economic security became a major issue. Lesson 1.3 describes the causes of the global economic depression of the 1930s and how different countries responded to the crisis.

Student eEdition online
Additional content for this lesson, including a video and a photo, is available online.

BACKGROUND FOR THE TEACHER

Making Money from the Crash The popular perception of the stock market crash of 1929 is that all investors lost all their money. In fact, some investors who understood the market actually made money before and after the crash. Before the crash, a savvy investor might have realized that a stock was overvalued, for instance, selling at $100 a share when it was really worth only $50 a share. He would then bet that this stock price would fall, not rise. This type of trade is called a short sale—a strategy still used today. When the crash began, these investors made a great deal of money when nearly all stock prices fell. After the crash, investors could buy undervalued stocks and wait for them to rise. When the market hit bottom in late 1929, cheap stocks were readily available for investors to buy.

INTRODUCE & ENGAGE

FOLLOW THE CROWD?

Present a situation to students in which people must make decisions in a crisis, such as an approaching hurricane or a company filing for bankruptcy. Discuss how people might react in that situation. Would they get swept up in the emotions of others and follow the crowd? Or would they act calmly? Talk about the reasons why one course of action might be better than another. This lesson discusses how investors got caught up in buying and selling frenzies and the effect on the economy.

TEACH

GUIDED DISCUSSION

1. **Explain** What is meant by the term *speculation* in the context of the global economic depression? *(It is the taking of huge risks to gain great rewards. During the global economic depression, this took the form of people buying large amounts of stock with borrowed money.)*

2. **Identify Problems and Solutions** Why did some leaders believe tariffs were a way of solving the problems caused by the global economic depression? *(Tariffs, or taxes on imports, were levied in order to protect a country's own producers from international competition. The hope was that it would compel consumers to buy goods produced in their home country.)*

ANALYZE VISUALS

Direct students to the video (available in the Student eEdition). **ASK:** What reasons does the video give for the unemployment that existed in the United States before the stock market crash? *(young people looking for their first jobs, seasonal workers, and workers whose jobs were replaced with machines)* In what way was unemployment a "horrible pestilence"? *(It rose suddenly and spread widely, as if a contagious disease had infected many people as in a plague or epidemic.)*

ACTIVE OPTIONS

On Your Feet: Fishbowl Direct half the class to sit in a circle facing inward and the other half to sit in a larger circle around them. Ask the inner circle to discuss this question: How did governments respond to the global economic depression? Students in the outer circle should listen to the discussion and evaluate the points made. Then ask the groups to reverse positions and continue the discussion.

| **NG Learning Framework: Write an Article**
| SKILL Problem-Solving
| KNOWLEDGE New Frontiers

Ask students to research and write an article about how economists and governments are working to prevent another global recession or depression, including what the current risks are and what fuels them. Tell students to take a particular look at the role technology will play in the next global downturn—technology companies as well as technological innovations that may be able to spot early warning signs.

DIFFERENTIATE

STRIVING READERS

Use Context Clues Model how to use context clues to unlock the meaning of a new word or phrase. Ask students to write the sentences containing the terms *Great Depression* and *speculation* on a piece of paper. Tell them to underline the context clues or textual definitions. Have them write an original sentence using each term.

PRE-AP

Compare and Contrast Programs Ask pairs to research programs that were part of the WPA, such as the Household Service Demonstration Project, the National Youth Administration, or the Federal Theater Project, to prepare a presentation in which they compare and contrast the programs. Ask them to focus on the purpose of the programs, who participated in them, and what—if anything—was created. Tell them to find out how much previous experience, training, or education was required for participants. Students should look for primary and secondary sources. Students should give their presentations to the rest of the class. Lead a class discussion synthesizing the information from the presentations and evaluating the scope and impact of the WPA.

See the Chapter Planner for more strategies for differentiation.

HISTORICAL THINKING

ANSWERS

1. Germany had acquired huge debts because it was required to pay reparations for its role in World War I. When the Great Depression hit, Germany could not repay those debts, which caused repercussions for the former Allied nations as well.

2. Answers will vary.

3. Possible response: They tried to address citizens' struggles by feeding money into the economy.

The Rise of Mussolini

You've probably heard the expression "desperate times call for desperate measures." The tough conditions of World War I, followed by the desperate times of the Great Depression, caused people in Italy and other countries to take desperate steps to reverse their dismal economies.

FASCISM GAINS MOMENTUM

Before World War I, many people saw a promising future in liberal democracy, with fair elections, protection of individual rights, and free market economies spreading around the world. During and after the war, some began to lose faith in liberal democracy. On the far political left were the communists who argued for a "dictatorship of the proletariat." On the far right were fascists who believed that the interests of the nation are more important than individual rights.

By the early 1920s, fascists in Italy and Germany were arguing that inefficient and corrupt politicians needed to be replaced by stern, disciplined leaders. The crisis of the Great Depression made this idea even more appealing. **Fascism** then developed as a way of governing based on extreme nationalism, racism, and suppression of opposition. Fascists opposed democracies that placed a high value on individual liberty and leaders who yielded to the will of the people. In contrast, they supported strong leaders who promised national greatness and put the needs of the nation as a whole over those of minority groups. To fascists, pursuing a united national purpose and the goals of the state was more important than individual rights.

Fascism, like communism, is a political philosophy that establishes a **totalitarian** political system to exert total control over a society, often violently. However, communism stressed class solidarity over national unity. Fascists and communists despised each other, but they loathed even more the compromises that marked liberal democratic governments and the limits that legislatures placed on executive power.

MUSSOLINI TAKES CONTROL OF ITALY

Uncertain times in Italy led to the rise of **Benito Mussolini**. For Mussolini, the state bound the people together: "Everything for the state, nothing against the state, no one outside the state." To kickstart his political rise, Mussolini organized military-like groups made up of former soldiers called **Blackshirts**. The main purpose of these groups was to crush those Mussolini opposed, such as socialists and communists. Soon Mussolini's supporters began calling him *Il Duce* (ihl DOO-chay), or "the leader." Mussolini proved to be an electrifying and charismatic speaker who confidently relayed his plans for solving Italy's problems. He presented a strong case for order, discipline, and unity in the form of extreme nationalism. He also advocated replacing local dialects and cultural traditions with a united Italian identity. Soon he won the financial support of landowners and industrialists, who hired the Blackshirts to attack striking automobile workers in the north and put down protests by rural tenants on large farms in the south. In return, Mussolini gained support from wealthy Italians.

In 1922, Mussolini organized dissatisfied war veterans to march on Rome. Italy's elected government tried to put down Mussolini's play for power. However, the support of the elite allowed Mussolini to bully his way into the prime minister's position. To solidify his control, he had his opponents arrested or killed and outlawed competing political parties. After 1926, Mussolini ruled as dictator, and after the economic crash of 1929, he centralized power even more.

As Italy's absolute ruler, Mussolini made changes that conflicted with democratic ideals. For example, he denied citizens the right to meet freely in groups of their own choosing. Instead, he formed "corporations" that forcibly organized all citizens who shared a similar undertaking. In this way, labor unions and youth groups came under state influence. Yet despite Mussolini's efforts, he could not gain complete control of society. Most Italians remained loyal to the church, community, and family.

In the past, Italy's parliamentary democracy had made decisions through discussion and compromise. Mussolini relied instead on theatrical politics that involved singing, flag waving, marching, propaganda, and stirring speeches. Mussolini often alluded to Rome's imperial past and promised to make Rome the center of a mighty Italian empire once again. He began his efforts by invading Ethiopia in 1935 as payback for Italy's 1896 defeat by King Menelik II's army. In May 1936, after a brutal campaign of bombing the Ethiopian people, Mussolini proudly announced his success to a crowd of 400,000 people. Rousing patriotism in the cause of empire building allowed Mussolini to firmly unite the Italian people.

Some Italians willingly traded their liberty for security and a sense of national pride. Others, especially communists, paid for their opposition to Mussolini with their lives. Most Italians did not seem to care about politics and simply went on with their lives.

Benito Mussolini, the founder of the fascist movement in Italy, speaks to a large crowd gathered at the Colosseum in Rome on November 2, 1920.

The Italian socialist writer Antonio Gramsci wrote about the situation in Italy before he was imprisoned for most of the rest of his life by fascist forces.

PRIMARY SOURCE

Indifference is actually the mainspring of history. . . . What comes to pass does so not as much because a few people want it to happen, as because the mass of citizens abdicate their responsibility and let things be.

—from *Avanti!* (an Italian newspaper), August 1916

HISTORICAL THINKING

1. **READING CHECK** What were three reasons Benito Mussolini and his fascist regime rose to power in Italy?

2. **MAKE CONNECTIONS** How did Mussolini's rise to power reflect political trends of the times?

3. **ANALYZE POINT OF VIEW** Why do you think some people opposed Mussolini's tactics while others embraced them?

PLAN: 2-PAGE LESSON

OBJECTIVE

Explain how Benito Mussolini rose to power as the fascist dictator of Italy.

CRITICAL THINKING SKILLS FOR LESSON 2.1

- Make Connections
- Analyze Point of View
- Compare and Contrast
- Identify Supporting Details
- Analyze Primary Sources

HISTORICAL THINKING FOR CHAPTER 26

Is it better to have security or freedom?

The global economic crisis contributed to a worldwide feeling of uncertainty which led many countries to consider—or reconsider—what kind of government they wanted. Lesson 2.1 describes how Italy developed into a fascist state led by the dictator Benito Mussolini.

Student eEdition online

Additional content for this lesson, including a photograph, is available online.

BACKGROUND FOR THE TEACHER

The Blackshirts The Blackshirts began their fascist acts of terror years before Mussolini formally acquired political power. In the beginning, the Blackshirts consisted of loosely organized "action squads" that popped up all over Italy with the purpose of opposing and attacking Socialists. One of their recurring targets was the office of *L'Avanti!*, Italy's daily Socialist newspaper. By 1920, these fascist squads expanded their reach to attack communists, republicans, Catholics, members of trade unions, striking workers, local politicians, and peasants living in cooperatives. Thousands were beaten, killed, or tortured; a preferred method was tying someone to a tree and forcing him to drink castor oil. The Blackshirts eventually were so organized that they held a convention in 1922. In early 1923, they were reorganized into a national militia called the Voluntary Fascist Militia for National Security. When Mussolini rose to power, he used the Blackshirts to intimidate and terrorize those who opposed him.

INTRODUCE & ENGAGE

COMPLETE A WORD WEB

Display a Word Web and write the term *fascism* in the center. Ask students to come up with names, words, and ideas related to what they already know about fascism. Explain that they will learn about Benito Mussolini and how he became a fascist dictator of Italy during the 1930s.

TEACH

GUIDED DISCUSSION

1. **Compare and Contrast** How are fascism and communism alike and different? *(Both are totalitarian political philosophies, and both appealed to people who were losing faith in liberal democracy. They are different in that communism stresses class solidarity and unifying workers, while fascism favors the interests and the goals of the state.)*

2. **Identify Supporting Details** What were the main characteristics of Mussolini's fascist dictatorship? *(Possible responses: extreme nationalism, suppression of political protestors, arrest of political opponents, outlaw of opposing political parties, violence in pursuit of unity and discipline, support from Italy's elite, denial of the right to assemble, nationalization of groups like labor unions, highly theatrical nationalist demonstrations, promises of a return to previous greatness)*

ANALYZE PRIMARY SOURCES

Ask students to reread the excerpt from *Avanti!* **ASK:** What does Gramsci say actually causes most events in history? *(indifference)* Do you agree with Gramsci's assertion? Why or why not? *(Answers will vary. Possible responses: Yes, because most of the positive changes that have happened in recent history are the result of people actively working to affect change. No, because people do not have as much political power as they believe, and history provides many examples of major events happening regardless of people's political participation.)*

ACTIVE OPTIONS

On Your Feet: Team Word Webbing Organize students into teams of four and have them record on a sheet of paper what they know about Mussolini's rise to power and the methods he used to hold on to it, developing a dictatorship in the process. Ask students to build on their teammates' entries as they pass the paper from one member to the next. Call on students to make statements about Mussolini's dictatorship.

NG Learning Framework: Create a Short Documentary
SKILL Communication
KNOWLEDGE Our Human Story

Ask small groups to prepare a short documentary about life in Italy during Mussolini's rule. Organize groups so that different aspects of Italian life are covered, such as agriculture, business, the Blackshirts, youth and youth organizations, education, women, artists, and so forth. Students can use video or another multimedia format to present their documentary. Invite students to share their documentary with the class.

DIFFERENTIATE

ENGLISH LANGUAGE LEARNERS

Clarify Vocabulary To help **Beginning** level students clarify vocabulary, provide sentence frames with one blank each. Ask **Intermediate** students to complete sentence frames with two blanks. Have **Advanced** students draw a three-column chart with the following headings: *Word/ Know/Learned.* Tell students to write an unfamiliar word under *Word,* write what they already know about the word and what the context and word parts show under *Know,* and explain what they learned about the word under *Learned.*

GIFTED & TALENTED

Research and Write Tell students to research more about people in Italy who either supported or opposed Mussolini. For example, Italian landowners and industrialists supported him; communists and other anti-fascists did not. Ask them to find primary source documents, such as interview transcripts. Have students write a dialogue between a supporter and opponent of Mussolini, clearly showing each point of view. They can set the scene and basic scenario behind the interaction.

See the Chapter Planner for more strategies for differentiation.

HISTORICAL THINKING

ANSWERS

1. Answers will vary. Reasons include Italy's struggle to regain economic strength, growing interest in fascism, dissatisfaction with democracy, Mussolini's charisma and stirring speeches, his bullying tactics, his call for nationalism and unity.

2. Possible response: a democratic government was replaced by a totalitarian government

3. Possible response: They placed popular sovereignty and human rights above national pride and the desire to improve lives at any cost.

Hitler's Scapegoats

Like the Italians, Germans suffered from the postwar settlements and the effects of the Great Depression. In spite of the democracy of the Weimar Republic, many of them became disillusioned and were ready for new solutions.

REASONS FOR HITLER'S RISE

As you've read, Germany was both humiliated and financially devastated after World War I. The Weimar Republic had brought liberal democracy to Germany in the 1920s, but the Great Depression left Germans once again desperate for solutions. Weimar leaders believed in Enlightenment ideas as a means of achieving a just and stable social order. However, for many Germans, the war had called that belief into question.

During what some historians have called an "age of anxiety," artists explored darker emotions, as with the nightmarish images painted by German Expressionists. New scholarly ideas added more uncertainty. Austrian **Sigmund Freud** introduced a new view of human psychology in his unsettling theory that powerful subconscious urges challenged the reason of the conscious mind. Meanwhile, in physics, German astrophysicist **Albert Einstein** announced his special theory of relativity. He discarded Newton's idea of a constant relationship between time and space, stating that the location of the observer could affect the relationship between these dimensions. Thus science, along with artistic modernism and psychology, reinforced the climate of uncertainty.

The Great Depression made everything worse for the German people. Into this time of uncertainty stepped **Adolf Hitler** and the National Socialist German Workers, or Nazi, Party. Hitler promised to restore greatness, confidence, and order to Germany, just as Mussolini had promised in Italy. Hitler denounced modern painting as "degenerate art" and ranted against "Jewish science." Feeling harassed, Einstein and many other Jews who were able to do so fled Germany.

Already in 1925, Hitler had written about Germany's Jews, saying that "the personification of the devil as the symbol of all evil assumes the living shape of the Jew." Needing a scapegoat to blame for the country's problems, Hitler tapped into the centuries-old practice of anti-Semitism, or hostility and discrimination against Jews. German Jews had been assimilated into the national culture, but now their differences were highlighted. Step by step, Hitler led Germans toward his "final solution": the mass murder of European Jews.

Hitler's attack on the Jews was based on his claim that people of "pure" German descent were a superior race, and that mixing with Jews threated that "purity." According to Hitler's views, which became known as Nazism, anyone who did not live up to the ideal of racial purity needed to be excluded from society. In this way, Germany could create a "master race." Apart from Jews, the Nazis targeted Germans with disabilities as "degrading" their "superior" race, performing horrible experiments and forced sterilizations in the name of "racial science."

The Nazis' other targets included communists because they divided the nation by dividing the rich and the poor. Jehovah's Witnesses were targets because they believe that only God can be worshiped, and they refused to salute Hitler or his flag. Homosexuals were hunted down and sent to concentration camps since they did not conform to the Nazi idea of the "proper family." The Nazis saw Germany's Roma minority like they did the Jews—as needing to be wiped out.

Support for the Nazi Party rose as the Great Depression increased fear and anxiety. Its share of the vote jumped from 2.6 to 37.6 percent between 1928 and 1932. By 1932, Hitler's supporters controlled more than a third of the seats in the Reichstag, or German legislature.

The nation's newly elected president needed Hitler's support to form a conservative governing coalition, supported by industrial and military leaders who feared rising support for socialists and communists on the left. Hitler agreed to join the coalition, on the condition that he be made Germany's chancellor.

HITLER'S EXTREME TACTICS FOR CONTROL

After becoming chancellor in 1933, Hitler ordered elected Communist Party legislators arrested and sent to concentration camps, where they could be brutally mistreated without ever being charged with a crime. More moderate socialist legislators saw the danger and boycotted the legislature. Then Hitler seized his chance. He said that a fire in the Reichstag building showed the communist danger, and in 1933 the remaining Reichstag members passed a "temporary" law giving Hitler dictatorial powers. He never gave those powers back.

Hitler then took command of Germany as dictator and made extreme changes to society. The state took over all responsibility for the national economy and most other aspects of life. To eliminate dissent, the Nazis outlawed other political parties and jailed their opponents. They also restricted the authority of religious leaders. Even so, most people did not speak out in protest of Hitler's policies.

The Nuremberg Laws of 1935 deprived Jews of all civil rights and forbade intermarriage with other Germans. Some Jews emigrated, but others could not bring themselves to leave their homes, businesses, friends, and extended families. Then, on November 9 and 10, 1938, the Nazis attacked Jewish homes, businesses, and synagogues across Germany and Austria during *Kristallnacht*, or "Night of Broken Glass." More Jews fled. Those who stayed were forced into segregated ghettos, their property taken over by their former neighbors.

German citizens' wish to pin their problems on others was one reason why Hitler's tactics gained traction. Another reason was the sharp drop in unemployment because of Hitler's intervention in the German economy. Huge public works projects, such as the world's first superhighways, and a large military re-armament put Germans back to work.

Leipzig Street with Electric Tram is a painting created in 1914 by Ernst Ludwig Kirchner. Kirchner was one of the founders of an artists' group called "The Bridge," which is now considered to be the birth of German Expressionism. In Kirchner's words, the Expressionists sought to express themselves "directly and authentically" in their art.

Hitler promised the return of the traditional values of courage, order, and discipline. He imposed new social hierarchies to do this. In Hitler's new social order, non-Germans fell to the bottom of society, and the roles of men and women grew further apart. To Hitler, women's highest calling was raising purebred German children. To cement their control, the Nazis held ultra-patriotic rallies, with in-step marching, flag waving, and rousing speeches. Such events gave ordinary Germans a sense of being part of something larger than themselves. Propaganda-filled radio broadcasts and films further spread excitement. Most Germans did not seem to mind new limitations on individual rights and were content with their country's order and economic success.

HISTORICAL THINKING

1. **READING CHECK** Why did Hitler and the Nazis rise to power? Why did the German people support them?

2. **FORM AND SUPPORT OPINIONS** Do you think Hitler could have risen to power if the Great Depression had not taken place? Explain your response.

3. **DRAW CONCLUSIONS** How did *Kristallnacht* gain its name?

PLAN: 2-PAGE LESSON

OBJECTIVE

Summarize the events that led to Adolf Hitler's ascent in Germany and describe how he maintained his power.

CRITICAL THINKING SKILLS FOR LESSON 2.2

- Form and Support Opinions
- Draw Conclusions
- Analyze Visuals
- Make Connections
- Analyze Primary Sources

HISTORICAL THINKING FOR CHAPTER 26

Is it better to have security or freedom?

After World War I, a totally humiliated Germany was looking for greater economic, military, and social stability. Lesson 2.2 describes how the country attained its security at the expense of others' freedoms.

Student eEdition online

Additional content for this lesson, including photographs and a primary source excerpt, is available online.

BACKGROUND FOR THE TEACHER

Hitler Becomes Chancellor German statesman Franz von Papen was a key figure in Adolf Hitler's rise to power. Papen belonged to the extreme right wing of the Catholic Centre and was relatively unknown by the German public, so when Papen was appointed chancellor in 1932, it came as a complete surprise to most German citizens. Papen's newly established authoritarian government did not have a voting majority, so he attempted to enlist the support of the second most powerful party in the German parliament, the Nazis. However, Nazi leader Adolf Hitler had no interest in supporting Papen. Eventually, Papen resigned his chancellorship and put his support behind Hitler and the Nazis. He persuaded President Carl von Hindenburg to appoint Hitler as chancellor and himself as vice chancellor. Papen hoped to grow his own power base and keep Hitler in check at the same time, but he soon found himself powerless with Hitler actively working against him.

INTRODUCE & ENGAGE

CONNECT TO THE PRESENT DAY

Ask students to imagine that the U.S. government passes a law revoking citizenship for blond Americans and making them enemies of the state. Police begin to round them up and move them to containment areas. Citizens who harbor blonds or offer assistance in any way are executed. Ask students the following questions: If you were blond, what would you do? If you were not blond, what, if anything, would you do? Display a T-Chart and record actions that students say they would take based on whether they are blond or not. Discuss their responses.

TEACH

GUIDED DISCUSSION

1. **Analyze Visuals** What details in the scene from *The Cabinet of Dr. Caligari* (available in the Student eEdition) convey the sense of anxiety and uncertainty that pervaded Germany in the years following World War I? *(Possible response: A shadowy figure carries the limp body of a woman while standing on a ledge. The ledge is narrow and elevated, conveying a sense that he might fall off, or even drop her body off, the edge. There are other shapes sticking up out of the jagged surfaces that surround him, suggesting an unfamiliar and unsafe environment.)*

2. **Make Connections** What role did mass media play in Hitler's rise to power? *(Hitler and the Nazis spread propaganda to millions of Germans via radio broadcasts and films.)*

ANALYZE PRIMARY SOURCES

Ask students to read the primary source (available in the Student eEdition). **ASK:** What rule about burning down synagogues did Heydrich make? *(They should only be burned down when there is no danger to "German lives or property.")* What was symbolic about the Nazis targeting synagogues as part of *Kristallnacht*? *(Targeting Jews' places of worship sent a message that even their most sacred spaces were not safe.)*

ACTIVE OPTIONS

On Your Feet: Four Corners Assign each question to a corner of the room: What were the core beliefs of Nazism? Why might a time of great social upheaval also be a time of great creativity in the arts and sciences? What did the Nuremberg Laws of 1935 mean for German Jews? How did scapegoating contribute to Hitler's rise? Have students choose a corner and discuss the question. As a class, discuss groups' ideas.

NG Learning Framework: Analyze Expressionist Paintings
ATTITUDE Curiosity
KNOWLEDGE Our Human Story

Invite students to pick a German expressionist painter, such as Ernst Ludwig Kirchner, Max Beckmann, Franz Marc, Otto Dix, George Grosz, or Emil Nolde, and one of their works to analyze. Have students research the artist and the work and explain how the work visually conveys darker emotions. Have them present the work and their analyses to the class.

DIFFERENTIATE

INCLUSION

Visual Partners Pair sight-impaired students with sighted students to interpret visuals. Ask sighted students to describe each of the photographs in the image gallery (available in the Student eEdition) to the sight-impaired students. Remind partners to identify details in the photographs and give particular emphasis to the qualities and traits characteristic of the Age of Anxiety and German Expressionism.

PRE-AP

Research and Analyze Photographs Instruct students to find photographs of public Nazi rallies. Explain that these rallies were staged. Ask students to analyze the photographs they choose and investigate how the rallies—and the photos of the rallies—emphasize Hitler's power. Also, have them consider how the photos express nationalism, keeping in mind that nationalism is a key driver of totalitarianism. Ask for volunteers to share their photos and analyses with the class.

See the Chapter Planner for more strategies for differentiation.

HISTORICAL THINKING

ANSWERS

1. The reasons Hitler and the Nazis rose to power include the following: economic hard times in Germany, dissatisfaction with their existing government, need for order and stability, need for scapegoats, lack of national pride, desire for a strong government. The German people supported Hitler and the Nazis because they thought they could improve their lives, strengthen their country, and restore their pride.

2. Answers will vary.

3. Possible response: On that night ("nacht") of destruction, much glass ("Kristall") was broken.

Stalin's Dictatorship and Purges

Think about how well you adapt to change. How would you feel if your country's leader was determined to alter every aspect of your life, including how and what you learn, the kind of work you do, and even what you think? Joseph Stalin attempted to do that in the Soviet Union during the later 1920s through the early 1950s.

RISE TO POWER

Following Lenin's death in 1924, **Joseph Stalin** vied for leadership with other communists, including Leon Trotsky. Trotsky believed that socialism in Russia could only be advanced through worldwide uprisings of the proletariat. In contrast, Stalin supported the idea that the Soviet Union could go it alone with a policy of "Socialism in One Country." He also thought that Soviet socialism must be built through top-down government control of every aspect of life. Even Lenin had allowed peasants to have some control over their own lives, including owning land. By 1926, Stalin had become the sole Soviet leader, had forced Trotsky into exile, and had begun totally transforming his country into a communist totalitarian state.

In 1928, Stalin launched his first **Five-Year Plan.** Stalin's goal was to catapult the backward Soviet Union into an industrial powerhouse and a true global power. Noting that Russia was far behind more advanced economies, Stalin said, "We must make good this lag in ten years . . . or we will be crushed." However, the dictator was determined to follow a state-controlled Marxist model rather than a capitalist structure. Stalin explained why the country needed to industrialize in this way: ". . . we are

This communist propaganda poster from the Soviet Union proclaims, "Long live Stalin!" A profile of Lenin appears behind the image of Stalin.

still the only country of the proletarian dictatorship and are surrounded by capitalist countries, many of which are far in advance of us technically and economically." To meet his goal, Stalin nationalized all industries and quickly made them more productive. The drive for industrialization focused on such industries as oil, steel, and electricity at the expense of consumer-oriented industries. The Soviet people were subjected to low wages and harsh working conditions in the new factories.

Stalin's methods were harsh, but they did produce results. While the capitalist economies fell into economic depression in the 1930s, the Soviet Union became the world's fastest-growing industrial economy.

Stalin next applied his policy of "Socialism in One Country" to rural areas. Unlike Lenin, Stalin rejected private ownership, requiring farmers to give up their small plots of land. He ordered **collectivization,** or the replacement of privately owned peasant farms with state-run collective farms. On a collective farm, farmers work together and do not gain individual profits. Unwilling peasants were marched at gunpoint onto the collective farms. Stalin claimed that violence was necessary to overcome the resistance of **kulaks** (koo-LAHKs), the most prosperous peasants. In fact, Stalin used the Red Army to wage war on his own people, murdering many while forcing villagers onto collective farms. A famine that resulted from the attempt at collectivization killed two million people between 1932 and 1933. The Ukrainian people were hit especially hard during this Terror Famine, as starving peasants there had to surrender to the state any food they managed to grow.

Meanwhile, industrialization of the Soviet Union continued at a frantic pace. The Communist Party bureaucracy made use of non-Russian parts of the Soviet Union mainly as a source of raw materials as if they were colonial territories. Their resources were transported into the Russian heartland for industrial use. The Soviets required all citizens to work but offered low wages so they could pour money into industry. The government established a system of Gulag labor camps

Workers on a Soviet collective farm break for lunch during the harvest of August 1936.

in the Soviet Union and Siberia. Slave labor at these camps also boosted Soviet productivity. One survivor, author Aleksandr Solzhenitsyn (sohl-zhuh-NEET-suhn), wrote about the hardships endured at a slave-labor camp in his nonfiction book *The Gulag Archipelago.*

THE GREAT PURGES

As Soviet leader, Stalin expanded the Gulag system, using it to imprison all those who opposed him, targeting Jews, leaders of non-Russian minority groups, and dissident communists. Stalin was paranoid about plots against him, which led him to initiate the **Great Purges,** the execution of those who had served under Lenin. Stalin feared these Old Bolsheviks might threaten his rule. He also ordered the rounding up of artists, intellectuals, writers, army officers, engineers, and scientists who he believed would undermine him, then staged show trials, in which the accused were forced to confess and predetermined verdicts were announced.

Stalin worked hard to achieve what is known as a **cult of personality,** presenting himself as a great person to be admired through the use of propaganda. For example, he ordered reporters to write glowing articles about him and eliminated a free press that could report on the problems of his regime. Yet Soviet citizens lived in a constant state of terror. One wrong word or glance could lead to a trip to the Gulag. As Stalin said, "The easiest way to gain control of the population is to carry out acts of terror."

HISTORICAL THINKING

1. **READING CHECK** How did Joseph Stalin transform the Soviet Union?

2. **DRAW CONCLUSIONS** Why do you think peasants in the Soviet Union objected to collectivization?

3. **MAKE INFERENCES** Why did Stalin expand the Gulag system?

PLAN: 2-PAGE LESSON

OBJECTIVE
Understand how Joseph Stalin became dictator of the Soviet Union and how he used purges to eliminate opposition to his totalitarian rule.

CRITICAL THINKING SKILLS FOR LESSON 2.3
- Draw Conclusions
- Make Inferences
- Compare and Contrast
- Explain
- Analyze Visuals

HISTORICAL THINKING FOR CHAPTER 26
Is it better to have security or freedom?

Like Italy and Germany, the Soviet Union became a totalitarian dictatorship after World War I. Lesson 2.3 explains how Joseph Stalin, the Soviet leader, held on to his power by stifling dissent and opposition, and, therefore, freedom.

BACKGROUND FOR THE TEACHER
The Great Famine of 1932–1933 By the 1920s, Ukraine was firmly under Soviet control and it suffered under Stalin's brutal imposition of collectivization. From 1932–1933, the entire Soviet Union experienced a terrible famine as a direct result of the government demanding food quotas from its collective farms. These demands were especially felt in Ukraine, which was largely rural and dotted with farming villages, but which also strongly resisted collectivization. Stalin's response was severe. He deliberately punished the Ukrainians for their resistance by setting Ukrainian food quotas at unattainably high levels. Soviet agents would forcibly enter homes and confiscate every scrap of food. Starving Ukrainians who stole food from local storehouses were summarily shot by Soviet firing squads. Five million people died during the famine, and nearly 4 million of them were Ukrainians. When Ukraine finally became an independent nation in 1991, its leaders defined the Great Famine of 1932–1933 as genocide.

INTRODUCE & ENGAGE

K-W-L CHART

Joseph Stalin is a major figure of 20th-century history. Ask students what they already know about Stalin and the Soviet Union during his rule, which ended in 1953. Use a K-W-L Chart to record their answers. Add to the chart what students would like to know. Allow time at the end of the lesson for students to complete the chart with information they learned.

TEACH

GUIDED DISCUSSION

1. **Compare and Contrast** What were the key differences between Leon Trotsky and Joseph Stalin? *(Trotsky wanted to see socialism emerge on a global scale via proletariat uprisings, where Stalin was singularly focused on socialism in the Soviet Union, believing that a top-down government system would be sufficient.)*

2. **Explain** What is meant by the term "cult of personality," and how did it apply to Stalin's rule? *(A "cult of personality" is when a totalitarian leader fosters an image of himself as a great and powerful leader. Stalin built a cult of personality by eliminating a free press and controlling how the media portrayed him.)*

ANALYZE VISUALS

Ask students to study the photograph of the Soviet collective farm. **ASK:** What details in the photograph convey a sense of collectivization? *(Possible response: The farm workers are all eating together in large groups in an organized fashion, rather than eating in small groups around various areas of the farm. This conveys a sense of order and control, as if they were commanded to eat in this manner.)*

ACTIVE OPTIONS

On Your Feet: Inside-Outside Circle Arrange students in concentric circles facing each other. Allow students time to write questions about Stalin's communist philosophy, his Five-Year Plan, collectivization, and how he used fear and violence to hold on to power. Tell students in the inside circle to pose questions to students in the outside circle. Have students switch roles. Students may ask for help from other students in their circle if they are unable to answer a question.

> **NG Learning Framework: Compare Dictatorships**
> **SKILLS** Communication, Collaboration
> **KNOWLEDGE** Our Human Story

Assign to small groups the totalitarian regimes that they have learned about: Mussolini's, Hitler's, or Stalin's. Have them review the lessons and conduct research to prepare a short presentation on the characteristics of their assigned regime, including the causes that empowered it. After all groups have presented, lead a class discussion about the commonalities among these regimes and the steps that could have been taken to prevent each dictator from coming to power.

DIFFERENTIATE

STRIVING READERS

Make a List Post this heading: Five Things I Know About Joseph Stalin and Soviet Communism. After students read the lesson, ask them to copy the posted heading and add five sentences about the topic. Invite volunteers to share their sentences with the class.

PRE-AP

Form and Support a Hypothesis Have students research the impact of Stalin's style of Communism on one of the groups mentioned in the lesson, such as one of the groups sent to Gulags. First, instruct students to develop a hypothesis regarding the predominant impact on their chosen group. Then ask them to find evidence that supports or refutes their hypothesis, using a variety of primary and secondary sources. Prompt students to write an essay based on their findings.

See the Chapter Planner for more strategies for differentiation.

HISTORICAL THINKING

ANSWERS

1. asserting totalitarian control, banning private ownership, industrializing, establishing collectivization, exploiting resources, eliminating portions of the population that objected to his policies, and creating an atmosphere of fear

2. Possible response: Peasants may have wanted to profit directly from the work that they did, may not have been willing to accept radical changes to their traditional way of life out of fear of the new technology, and might have objected to their being forced to give up their land and to losing decision-making power over their own lives.

3. Possible response: He had many enemies that he wanted removed from society; his growing industrial nation needed huge amounts of free labor to achieve success within his timeline.

Totalitarianism in Asia and Latin America

Living in a democracy, you may not understand how anyone would accept another system of government. Yet when faced with crises in the 1920s and 1930s, people in much of Asia and Latin America, as in Germany and Italy, turned to totalitarian leaders who promised relief from economic hardship and growing uncertainty.

INTENSE NATIONALISM IN JAPAN

In the 1920s, Japan had shown signs of heading in a more democratic direction. It had become a constitutional monarchy, with an emperor whose role was mainly ceremonial. Yet, Japan's large industrial businesses, the zaibatsu, exerted much power over the government and the influence of the military was increasing. Like Mussolini in Italy, Japan's military leaders emphasized national glory over individual liberty. When the emperor **Hirohito** rose to the throne in 1926, these **ultranationalists**, or extreme nationalists, saw a chance to expand their powers. After the market collapse of 1929 and the onset of the Great Depression, support

In promoting modernization, Turkish leader Mustafa Kemal launched an alphabet reform initiative. Arabic script was replaced by a new alphabet to reflect the sounds of spoken Turkish. Kemal toured the country, explaining the new writing system.

for the military grew among the many farm families whose sons made up most of the empire's armies.

The Japanese had begun to build an empire by claiming Korea, Taiwan, and China's Shandong Province across the Yellow Sea from Korea. The ultranationalists believed that Japan's only avenue for gaining economic strength was through expansion, and they wanted to make use of East and Southeast Asia's resources and cheap labor. To accomplish this, they invaded Manchuria, a province in China north of Korea, in 1931. The Japanese military blew up some railroad tracks there and then blamed Chinese nationalists. Western nations condemned the action. The Japanese people, however, became enraged by the outside criticism, feeling more enthralled with the Japanese military and increasingly supportive of imperial expansion. As imperial fever grew, elected politicians lost control of the military. As in Italy and Germany, militarization strengthened the economy, and rising employment caused the working class to rally behind the ultranationalists.

RISE OF MODERN TURKEY

Meanwhile, in Southwest Asia, the new nation of Turkey emerged from the violent collapse of the Ottoman Empire. The leadership of **Mustafa Kemal** prevented Turkey from being divided by victorious Allies after World War I. With the success of Kemal's armies, by 1923 the Great Powers agreed to recognize a sovereign Turkish republic. For his role, Kemal earned the name *Atatürk*, or "Father Turk." The new country was a result of Turkish nationalism, so the needs of other ethnic groups, such as the Armenians, Greeks, and Kurds, were largely ignored. Thousands of Greeks were forced to flee Turkey

for their homeland and many Turks were expelled from Greece in a population exchange between the two countries. Such mass movements provide evidence of how hard it can be to organize national boundaries along ethnic lines.

From the start, Atatürk made it clear that he intended to be the unchallenged ruler of Turkey. He ordered rapid modernization so that Turkey might rival the economy and military power of European countries. Atatürk believed that adopting Western ways would bring his country success, so he imposed a secular constitution with strict separation between Islam and government. His drive to remove religion from politics included laws to improve the status of women. He also granted girls the right to an education and extended suffrage to women. At the same time, he banned the wearing of veils in public.

Wanting immediate change rather than gradual reform, the totalitarian leader imposed his own will on the nation. Atatürk died in 1938, but an authoritarian government continued in Turkey with the military playing a strong role.

BRAZIL'S "NEW STATE"

Latin American nations also experienced the growth of totalitarianism to combat the economic problems brought on by the global Great Depression. Brazil came closest to following the European models of fascism. **Getúlio Vargas** (jay-TOO-lee-oh VAHR-guhs) assumed power in 1930 and soon began strengthening the economy through government involvement, such as nationalizing natural resources.

In 1937, Vargas made a bold political move by suspending the Brazilian constitution and announcing the beginning of his *Estado Novo*, or "New State." According

By 1932, the world market price for coffee had plunged so dramatically that Brazil, the world's leading producer, destroyed tens of thousands of tons of coffee by burning it or shoveling it into the sea.

to Vargas, the goal of the *Estado Novo* was to stimulate Brazil's weak economy. He swore to "crisscross the nation with railroads, highways, and airlines; to increase production; to provide for the laborer." He also pledged to bring about unity in Brazil by eliminating regional competition. His stated goal was "to organize public opinion so that there is, body and soul, one Brazilian thought." That one thought would be his own.

Brazil had something in common with Turkey, Japan, Italy, Germany, the Soviet Union, and other countries that abandoned democracy and free markets for more centralized political and economic systems. Would the values of liberal democracy—such as divided government, free enterprise, and the rule of law—be able to make a comeback?

HISTORICAL THINKING

1. **READING CHECK** What was the connection between totalitarianism and economic conditions in the 1930s?

2. **COMPARE AND CONTRAST** How was the rise of totalitarianism in Germany similar to and different from that in Japan?

3. **DRAW CONCLUSIONS** Why might someone living in Turkey have opposed Mustafa Kemal?

PLAN: 2-PAGE LESSON

OBJECTIVE

Understand how global uncertainty caused totalitarian governments to take hold in parts of Asia and Latin America.

CRITICAL THINKING SKILLS FOR LESSON 2.4

- Compare and Contrast
- Draw Conclusions
- Identify Main Ideas and Details
- Explain
- Analyze Visuals

HISTORICAL THINKING FOR CHAPTER 26

Is it better to have security or freedom?

The sense of insecurity that plagued Europe after the end of World War I also spread to parts of Asia and Latin America. Lesson 2.4 explains how Japan, Turkey, and Brazil moved towards totalitarianism during that time.

Student eEdition online

Additional content for this lesson, including a photograph, is available online.

BACKGROUND FOR THE TEACHER

Islamists and Secularists in Modern Turkey

Supporters of Mustafa Kemal's legacy of secular nationalism built a cult around his memory during the many years when they monopolized Turkish politics. But late in the 20th century, Kemalists found themselves challenged by Turks who resented having religiosity banned from public life and envisioned a greater role for religion in government. Long suppressed by the secularist military, the Islamist Justice and Development Party (JDP) scored a definitive victory in the 2002 elections. The headscarf has become symbolic of the divide between Kemalists and Islamists. Previously, women were not allowed to wear headscarves in public places. In the 2010s, however, they became increasingly common. Kemalists (and Turkish feminists) see JDP policies as rolling back Kemal's expansion of women's rights. In 2014, President Recep Tayyip Erdoğan publicly proclaimed that motherhood was every woman's calling, saying that women are "too delicate" for "manly" tasks. Such patriarchal pronouncements play well with the party's conservative base but arouse the ire of secularists.

INTRODUCE & ENGAGE

REVIEW TOTALITARIANISM

Students have so far learned about totalitarianism as it took shape in Italy, Germany, and Russia. Review the characteristics of totalitarianism by writing the term in the center of a Word Web and adding students' ideas to the spokes. Explain that in this lesson they will learn about totalitarian governments in Japan, Turkey, and Brazil.

TEACH

GUIDED DISCUSSION

1. **Identify Main Ideas and Details** In what way is Turkey a good example of how drawing national boundaries along ethnic lines can be problematic? *(When the new country of Turkey emerged after World War I, its ethnic minorities were excluded. Further, many Greeks were forced out of Turkey and many Turks were expelled from Greece.)*

2. **Explain** What did Getúlio Vargas promise Brazilians in his vision for a "New State"? *(Vargas wanted to stimulate Brazil's economy with investments in infrastructure like railroads, highways, and airlines. In so doing, production would increase and employment would rise. He also promised to eliminate economic competition from regional neighbors.)*

ANALYZE VISUALS

Direct students to the photo of Japanese soldiers on the train (available in the Student eEdition). **ASK:** What details in the photo convey a feeling of Japan's emerging ultranationalism? *(The soldiers are dressed exactly alike, in smart-looking uniforms, and they are waving Japanese flags. The train is bolted with metal rivets, which gives it a militaristic feel. Excessive patriotism and strong militarism are key components of ultranationalism.)*

ACTIVE OPTIONS

On Your Feet: Three Corners Label three corners of the room with the countries discussed in the lesson: Japan, Turkey, and Brazil. Have students move to the corner of their choice for a focused discussion that addresses how and why totalitarianism developed in their chosen country. Allow members of each group to summarize their discussions.

| **NG Learning Framework: Investigate Brazil's Coffee Industry**
| **SKILL** Problem-Solving
| **KNOWLEDGE** Our Living Planet

Explain that Brazil is the world's largest producer of coffee and coffee is central to that country's economy. Have small groups conduct online research about Brazil's modern coffee industry. They should explore the problems the industry faces (such as the cost of production, competition with other coffee-producing countries, changing tastes around the world, and the sustainability of coffee fields as a result of climate change) as well as the solutions being attempted. Ask students to divide their research: one person investigates the industry's problems, one looks for the role technology is playing in the solutions, and one looks at the role of the government in the coffee industry. Have each group prepare an oral presentation of their findings and present it to the class.

DIFFERENTIATE

ENGLISH LANGUAGE LEARNERS

Pose and Answer Questions Pair **Beginning** and **Intermediate** level students to reread the lesson, pausing after each paragraph to ask one another *who, what, when, where,* or *why* questions about what they have just read. Suggest that students use a 5Ws Chart to help organize their questions and answers.

GIFTED & TALENTED

Interview a Historical Figure Have pairs plan, write, and perform a TV interview with Mustafa Kemal (Atatürk), Emperor Hirohito, or Getúlio Vargas. Tell them to research the historical figure and focus on his motivations, actions, goals, achievements, and failures. Ask pairs to conduct their interview in front of the class.

See the Chapter Planner for more strategies for differentiation.

HISTORICAL THINKING

ANSWERS

1. Using Japan, Turkey, and Brazil as examples, the lesson shows that tough economic times or new and/or faltering economies encouraged the rise of totalitarianism. Citizens looked to strong, authoritarian leaders to solve their economic problems at the risk of losing some liberties.

2. Possible response: Both: result of the loss of faith in newly established democracies, economic decline, and the desire to build an empire and expand; Germany: coordinated by the ambitions of a single ruthless dictator; Japan: achieved by the military and ultranationalists

3. Possible response: The person may have preferred democracy, been a member of a minority ethnic group, feared the military, not supported Kemal's secular policies, or preferred traditional ways over modernization.

Gandhi and India

While nationalism in Europe led people to yield to totalitarian control, it had a different effect on people in South Asia. India had long been subjected to imperialism under British rule. Now its people were ready for change, leading to the rise of anti-colonial nationalism on the Indian subcontinent.

INDIANS CALL FOR MORE RIGHTS

India's rich natural resources and large workforce made it the "Jewel in the Crown" of the British Empire. Yet the people of India were growing discontented with their lack of rights. More than a million Indians had risked their lives for Britain in World War I, and they believed they deserved a greater voice in government in return.

CRITICAL VIEWING Mohandas Gandhi sits and spins cotton in Ceylon in November 1927. He was committed to traditional ways of making cloth in part to boycott British-made goods. What details in the photo express Gandhi's commitment to the Indian people?

At first, the Indian National Congress simply worked for reforms and better treatment, but the British only slightly increased Indian participation in government.

Then in 1919, the **Amritsar Massacre** shocked the Indian people. An unarmed crowd had gathered in a garden area for a religious ceremony, unaware that the British had banned public meetings. A British officer ordered his Indian troops to fire directly into the crowd. This horrible display of violence left 400 dead and 1,200 wounded and caused the Indian National Congress to stop cooperating with the British and confront them instead. In 1920, the Indian National Congress launched its first mass public protest to gain **Hind Swaraj,** Indian self-rule.

GANDHI AND NONVIOLENCE

At about this time, the young Western-educated lawyer **Mohandas K. Gandhi** became a leader of the Indian National Congress. To show his commitment to the Indian people, Gandhi discarded European dress for the spare clothing of a Hindu holy man. Yet his philosophy was inspired by both Western and Indian traditions. Western ideals of equality affected his view that the **Dalits,** those lowest in the Hindu caste hierarchy, were entitled to more rights. But Gandhi acquired two main moral principles from South Asian tradition. He strongly believed in **ahimsa** (uh-HIHM-sah), or absolute nonviolence, and **satyagraha** (suh-TYAH-gruh-huh)—or "soul force"—the application of nonviolence to politics. Gandhi's idea that violence should never counter violence earned him the title *Mahatma,* or "Great Soul."

Gandhi implored the Indian people to engage in **civil disobedience,** or the refusal to follow unjust laws, in a peaceful way. In 1920, the British threw Gandhi and other congress leaders in jail for encouraging dissent. Acts of violence that followed caused Gandhi

THE SALT MARCH Salt was readily available along the long ocean shores of India. However, the British required that all purchases of salt be made through them. Indians had objected to this policy for many decades because most of them could not afford the expensive, heavily taxed salt. Protesting this situation, Gandhi began his 240-mile walk to the sea that became known as the Salt March, along with several dozen supporters. Dressed in traditional Indian clothing using a walking stick, Gandhi gained the world's attention. Newspapers everywhere printed stories and published photographs of the 24-day journey.

Every day, Gandhi was joined by many more marchers, and many others gathered in crowds along the route to hear him speak. Once at the coast, Gandhi and the other marchers symbolically gathered salt deposits lying on the beach. His march had made clear the injustices that Indians faced under British rule, as people around the world saw films and photographs of Gandhi's protest.

to determine that the Indian people were not ready for self-rule through satyagraha. He then retreated to his *ashram* (AHSH-ruhm), a communal rural home, where he enjoyed the simple rural life that he believed was the ideal existence. He spent hours sitting at a wheel spinning cotton, and the gentle clicking of the wheel helped him meditate. It also symbolized the rejection of British textiles and the exploiting of the Indian workforce. Without Gandhi, a new generation of congress leaders emerged in India, including British-educated **Jawaharlal Nehru** (juh-WAH-hur-lahl NAY-roo), who would later win election as the party's president in 1929.

In 1930, Gandhi re-emerged to lead a new campaign of civil disobedience. He led strikes as well as boycotts of British products. His best-known act of mass disobedience was the Salt March to protest a British law that forbade Indians from making their own salt. The march kicked off a movement that led to the arrests of some 60,000 people for nonviolent civil disobedience by the end of 1930.

Initially, the British responded by jailing congress leaders, but then they compromised by issuing the Government of India Act of 1935. This act called for the election of semi-representative regional assemblies. The congress complained that this action was inadequate, but it took part in the elections anyway, scoring huge victories.

Gandhi and Nehru agreed that the Indian National Congress should embrace members of all faiths. This did not appease, or satisfy, leaders of the new **Muslim League** in India. They feared that under Indian self-rule they would be oppressed by the Hindu majority. Distrust grew between the two religious communities. Muslim League leaders began to call for the creation of a separate Muslim state called Pakistan. Gandhi did his best to reassure the Muslim community, and Nehru envisioned a secular nation. The British insisted that only through their continued control could the diverse people of India live in peace.

HISTORICAL THINKING

1. **READING CHECK** Why did Gandhi undertake the Salt March?

2. **MAKE PREDICTIONS** How might events have been different if the British had met the early demands of the Indian National Congress?

3. **EVALUATE** How effective was Gandhi as a leader?

PLAN: 2-PAGE LESSON

OBJECTIVE

Describe how the nonviolent protests of Mohandas K. Gandhi led to political change in India.

CRITICAL THINKING SKILLS FOR LESSON 3.1

- Make Predictions
- Evaluate
- Analyze Cause and Effect
- Analyze Visuals

HISTORICAL THINKING FOR CHAPTER 26

Is it better to have security or freedom?

As part of the British Empire, India fought bravely on the side of the Allies during World War I. Lesson 3.1 explains how, after the war ended, India wanted its freedom from British rule.

Student eEdition online

Additional content for this lesson, including a video, is available online.

BACKGROUND FOR THE TEACHER

Gandhi and Nehru Both Mohandas K. Gandhi and Jawaharlal Nehru were influenced by the time they spent in Great Britain. Gandhi sailed to Britain in 1888 to pursue a law degree, and while in London he was strongly influenced by philosophers who called into question the relentless materialism of late Victorian society. Among them were vegetarians and Theosophists, who emphasized intuition and mysticism over rationalism and formal theology. He was also influenced by the American writer Henry David Thoreau and the Russian novelist Leo Tolstoy, both of whom celebrated the simplicity of rural life. Nehru's British experience was quite different. His wealthy father sent him to study at the Harrow School and then Cambridge University. Interacting with England's elite, the young Nehru was strongly influenced by the fashionable reformist socialists who accepted the need for the economic development that came with capitalist industrialism but argued for a more equitable distribution of its proceeds. As a result, Gandhi and Nehru, though they were close friends and political allies, had very different visions of India's future.

INTRODUCE & ENGAGE

MAKE HISTORICAL CONNECTIONS

As a class, review the reasons why the original 13 American colonies wanted to declare their independence from Britain. Record, display, and discuss students' responses. Then explain that in Lesson 3.1 students will learn about India, which, 150 years after the American Revolution, found itself also wanting independence from Britain.

TEACH

GUIDED DISCUSSION

1. **Analyze Cause and Effect** What was the Amritsar Massacre, and what effect did it have on India's politics? *(A British military officer ordered his Indian troops to fire on a group of unarmed Indian citizens who were gathered for a religious ceremony. The Indian people were outraged; the massacre accelerated the drive toward Indian self-rule.)*

2. **Analyze Cause and Effect** Why was the country of Pakistan formed? *(Muslims in India, especially leaders of the Muslim League, were fearful of oppression by the Hindu majority in the Indian National Congress. As a result, they called for the creation of a separate Muslim state.)*

ANALYZE VISUALS

Direct students to the video (available in the Student eEdition). Explain that Gandhi is making comments after attending the second session of the Round Table Conference, a meeting between British and Indian officials to discuss a future Indian constitution that took place in London in 1931. **ASK:** What does Gandhi say that he and the other Indian attendees want? *(complete independence)* In what way is the video an example of mass media? *(Films were a form of mass communication that could reach people around the world.)* How might the video have rallied worldwide support for Gandhi's goals? Explain your thinking. *(Answers will vary. Possible response: It would have been seen by people who had never seen nor heard Gandhi. They might have been struck by his non-Western clothing and determination for India's complete independence.)*

ACTIVE OPTIONS

On Your Feet: Think, Pair, Share Ask students to think about whether civil disobedience is an effective method of political protest or not. Tell students to form pairs in order to discuss the topic. Once pairs have completed their discussion, invite them to share their ideas with the class.

| **NG Learning Framework: Write a Biographical Comparison**
| SKILL Observation
| KNOWLEDGE Our Human Story

Have students research additional information about Gandhi and Nehru. Instruct students to write a biographical sketch that compares and contrasts the two leaders and present it to the class. Tell students to use reliable online or print sources and to focus on life experiences and events that would help the class gain insight into each leader's actions as described in the lesson. Ask students to invite questions and comments from the class after they make their presentations.

DIFFERENTIATE

ENGLISH LANGUAGE LEARNERS

Practice Pronunciation Write these names and terms on the board: *Hind Swaraj, Mohandas K. Gandhi, Dalits, ahimsa, satyagraha, Mahatma,* and *Jawaharlal Nehru.* Pronounce each name or term and have students repeat. Pair students of mixed proficiencies to find passages in the lesson that contain any of the names or terms and read the passages aloud.

GIFTED & TALENTED

Perform a Speech Tell students to find the full text of one of Gandhi's or Nehru's speeches online. Have them prepare a dramatic reading of a section of the speech. Before performing, students should explain its context, stating when, where, and what prompted it. Tell them to be prepared to discuss the words and literary devices Gandhi or Nehru used to add to the effectiveness of the speech.

See the Chapter Planner for more strategies for differentiation.

HISTORICAL THINKING

ANSWERS

1. to nonviolently protest the British monopoly on salt and to call attention to the unfair treatment of Indians under imperialism

2. Possible response: They might have accepted India remaining part of the British Empire. Some amount of home rule might have convinced Indians to remain loyal to Britain.

3. Possible response: extremely effective; encouraged nonviolent change, united Indians of all classes, caused people around the world to be sympathetic to India's plight

CRITICAL VIEWING Possible response: He wears traditional Hindu dress; he is spinning cotton, which demonstrates that he wanted India to support itself by making its own goods.

3.2 On Progress and Civilization

Which would you prefer, living in the city and working in an office or living in the countryside and working outdoors? Your answer may depend on your past experiences and how they have shaped your way of thinking. Like other people, whether in the past or present, you have developed a frame of reference that is based at least partially on where, when, and how you live your life.

Nehru and Gandhi discuss ideas at a meeting of the Indian National Congress in 1936.

Mohandas K. Gandhi and Jawaharlal Nehru were the two most influential Indian leaders of the 20th century. Born 20 years apart, they represented different generations in the Indian National Congress. Gandhi was the main force behind Indian resistance to British colonialism in the 1920s and 1930s. In contrast, Nehru served as the first prime minister of the independent Indian republic from 1947 to 1964.

Both men were influenced by the time they spent in Britain. Living there as a law student in the late 1800s, Gandhi met British idealists and rebels who valued intuition over reason and rejected the mainstream values of an industrial society.

Nehru's British experience was quite different from Gandhi's. Nehru's wealthy background allowed him to mingle with Britain's elite. He was also strongly influenced by the reformist socialist movement of the early 1900s. These socialists accepted the economic development that came with capitalist industrialism, but they wanted fairer distribution of wealth. Gandhi and Nehru's varying experiences would shape the two leaders' visions for an independent India.

752 CHAPTER 26

DOCUMENT ONE
Primary Source: Book
from *Hind Swaraj* by Mohandas K. Gandhi, 1909

Born in 1869 in the western Indian state of Gujarat, Mohandas Gandhi grew up under modest circumstances in a deeply religious Hindu family. Gandhi's time in London for legal studies confirmed his belief that industrialism negatively affected society. Gandhi would later describe the ills of society as well as possible solutions in his book *Hind Swaraj*. Written over the course of a voyage from London to South Africa, the book is a condemnation of "modern civilization." In it, Gandhi argues that Indian self-rule will make little difference in the lives of the Indian people if the new leaders govern by the same principles and commitment to industrialization as their English oppressors. In this excerpt, Gandhi questions characteristics of "civilization" and wonders if they really do make people happier.

CONSTRUCTED RESPONSE Based on this excerpt, what are the evils of civilization?

Let us first consider what state of things is described by the word "civilization." . . . Formerly, in Europe, people ploughed their lands mainly by manual labor. Now one man can plough a vast tract by means of steam engines and can thus amass great wealth. This is called a sign of civilization. . . . Formerly, men worked in the open air only as much as they liked. Now thousands of workmen meet together and work in factories or mines. Their condition is worse than that of beasts. They are obliged to work, at the risk of their lives, at most dangerous occupations, for the sake of millionaires. Formerly, men were made slaves under physical compulsion. Now they are enslaved by temptation of money and of the luxuries that money can buy. . . . This civilization takes note neither of morality nor of religion. . . . This civilization . . . has taken such a hold on the people in Europe that those who are in it appear to be half mad. They lack real physical strength or courage. . . . They can hardly be happy in solitude.

DOCUMENT TWO
Primary Source: Book
from *Jawaharlal Nehru, An Autobiography*, 1936

The future prime minister was born into the highest class of Hindu society in 1889, making him 20 years younger than Gandhi. Nehru earned a degree from Britain's Cambridge University and then became a lawyer, but he was more interested in politics and helping India win independence than in practicing law. Nehru describes his close relationship with fellow freedom seeker Gandhi in his autobiography; however, the two men did not see eye to eye on everything. While many Indians have been strongly influenced by Gandhi's philosophy, Nehru's attitude has been much more evident in Indian government policy since the country achieved independence in 1947.

CONSTRUCTED RESPONSE According to the excerpt, why is it best to accept the existence of civilization?

Personally I dislike the praise of poverty and suffering, . . . Nor do I appreciate in the least the idealization of the "simple peasant life." I have almost a horror of it, and instead of submitting to it myself I want to drag out even the peasantry from it. . . . What is there in "The Man with the Hoe" to idealize over? Crushed and exploited for innumerable generations, he is only little removed from the animals who keep him company. . . . The desire to get away from the mind of man to primitive conditions where mind does not count, seems to me quite incomprehensible. . . . Present-day civilization is full of evils, but it is also full of good; and it has the capacity to rid itself of those evils. To destroy it root and branch is to remove that capacity from it and revert to a dull, senseless, and miserable existence. But even if that were desirable it is an impossible undertaking. We cannot stop the river of change or cut ourselves adrift from it, and psychologically we who have eaten of the apple of Eden cannot forget that taste and go back to primitiveness.

SYNTHESIZE & WRITE

1. **REVIEW** Review what you have read and observed about the two viewpoints regarding civilization.

2. **RECALL** On your own paper, list two details about the writer of one of the excerpts and two opinions expressed in the excerpt from that writer.

3. **CONSTRUCT** Construct a topic sentence that answers this question: How and why are the two leaders' opinions about civilization both similar and different?

4. **WRITE** Using evidence from this chapter and the documents, write an informative paragraph that supports your topic sentence in Step 3.

Economic Depression and Authoritarian Regimes 753

PLAN: 2-PAGE LESSON

OBJECTIVE
Analyze written documents by Mohandas K. Gandhi and Jawaharlal Nehru on the advancement of civilization.

CRITICAL THINKING SKILLS FOR LESSON 3.2
- Synthesize
- Analyze Points of View
- Form and Support Opinions
- Evaluate

HISTORICAL THINKING FOR CHAPTER 26
Is it better to have security or freedom?

As India sought independence from Britain, two leaders emerged from the Indian National Congress to shape the resistance movement. Lesson 3.2 focuses on excerpts by Mohandas Gandhi and Jawaharlal Nehru that discuss society's progress and peoples' changing freedoms.

BACKGROUND FOR THE TEACHER
Nehru's Independence Gandhi's influences swept through India and the world, making it impossible for Nehru to ignore. Nehru followed Gandhi's movement of nonviolent resistance, which appealed to the younger generation of educated Indians, and helped him rally followers to gain independence from Britain. But Nehru went a step further than Gandhi; he was a key leader at the Indian National Congress, and it was Nehru who first promoted India's place in the world community. After Nehru became India's first prime minister, he emphasized that India needed both democracy and socialism. He did not hide his differences of opinion with Gandhi on industrialization but instead geared India's first five-year plans toward heavy manufacturing. His plan to make India an important member of the international community soon succeeded. Nehru gained and maintained the support of the Congress Party throughout his term in office. His domestic policies stayed focused on the foundations of democracy, socialism, unity, and secularism. Nehru served as the prime minister of India for 17 years, until his death in 1964, and will be forever identified as a prominent leader in India's history.

INTRODUCE & ENGAGE

PREPARE FOR THE DOCUMENT-BASED QUESTION

Before students read the lesson, briefly preview the two documents. Remind students that a constructed response requires full explanations in complete sentences. Emphasize that students should use what they have learned about industrialization and society's levels of civilization advancement in addition to the information in the documents.

TEACH

GUIDED DISCUSSION

1. **Analyze Points of View** According to Gandhi, why do people "appear to be half mad"? *(because people are forced to work and risk their lives in dangerous occupations all so that others can become millionaires)*

2. **Form and Support Opinions** Which excerpt do you most agree with? Explain. *(Answers will vary. Students should choose one of the excerpts and supply an explanation for their reasoning.)*

EVALUATE

After students have completed the Synthesize & Write activity, allow time for them to exchange paragraphs and read and comment on the work of their peers. Establish guidelines for comments prior to the activity so feedback is constructive and encouraging. Comments should focus on the most significant parts that address the purpose of the activity and the audience.

ACTIVE OPTION

On Your Feet: Host a DBQ Roundtable Divide the class into groups of four. Explain that Gandhi wanted to rid civilization of the advancement of industry, calling it an evil. Hand each group a sheet of paper with the following question: Is it possible for society to rid itself of industry? Explain why or why not. Instruct the first student in each group to write an answer, read it aloud, and pass the paper clockwise to the next student. The paper may circulate around the table several times. Then reconvene the class and discuss the groups' responses.

DIFFERENTIATE

INCLUSION

Summarize Read each document aloud to students. Have two students work together, as one student rereads a document and the other student summarizes the document. After each document is summarized, read the constructed response question with the class and have volunteers suggest responses.

GIFTED & TALENTED

Make a Documentary Ask students to pose questions about the life and beliefs of Gandhi that can be answered through research. Emphasize the importance of asceticism and nonviolence that Gandhi practiced. Then have students consult print and online resources to find answers. Have them create a documentary about Gandhi, using the medium of their choice, to present to the class.

SYNTHESIZE & WRITE

ANSWERS

1. Answers will vary.

2. Possible response: Gandhi: born in 1869, thought industrialism had negative effects; excerpt: it is absurd to prefer civilization to the simple life; civilized people are not strong. Nehru: born 20 years after Gandhi, earned law degree from Cambridge; excerpt: living the simple life would be dull and meaningless; civilization has both good and evil aspects.

3. Possible response: Both Gandhi and Nehru were influenced by the years they spent in Great Britain pursuing law degrees. While Gandhi believed that civilization had no value, Nehru believed it had both good and bad aspects.

4. Answers will vary. Students should include their topic sentence from Step 3 and provide evidence to support their claim.

CONSTRUCTED RESPONSE

Document One: According to the excerpt, people are less active and less strong, forced to work long hours indoors in dangerous conditions, and required to labor so that others can profit and become wealthy.

Document Two: Nehru believes civilization allows people to overcome the environment and live more comfortable and meaningful lives. He also says that there is no turning back to earlier times before present-day civilization.

Global Resistance to Colonialism

Thinking only of one's self-interest can have devastating effects on others. That's just what happened in Africa, the Caribbean, and Southeast Asia. The people in these locations suffered at the hands of imperialist powers that profited at their expense. The oppressed people longed for self-rule.

COLONIAL RULE CONTINUES

As in South Asia, nationalist movements developed in Africa, the Caribbean, and Southeast Asia. Many colonized people believed they deserved freedom for their help in fighting World War I, but European powers continued to rule. One way they maintained control was by enlisting indigenous allies—native people who helped control and administer the colonial territory. The native workers were educated so they could perform their jobs as clerks, nurses, and primary school teachers. Along the way, however, they also learned about Western revolutions and began to envision freedom for their own nations.

Nnamdi Azikiwe smiles in response to greetings from crowds of Nigerians at Euston Station in London, where he was attending the Nigerian constitutional conference in 1958. In 1963, Azikiwe would become the first president of independent Nigeria.

French assimilation policies promised that Asians and Africans could become French in language and culture. Despite this, they would always be perceived as inferior because of the racist ideas of the colonialists. The British did not believe in assimilation, so there the distinction between the rulers and the ruled was even clearer. The British employed what they called "indirect rule," relying on "native authorities" to carry out day-to-day administrative tasks such as collecting taxes. Yet in no way were these authorities considered British.

AFRICA

In Africa, chiefs were made "native authorities," supposedly to show that the British respected local customs. In reality, the colonialists simply wanted the local leaders to work at the bottom rungs of their

administration. By the 1930s, many nationalists viewed this practice as hurtful to their cause. One such leader was Western-educated Nigerian nationalist **Nnamdi Azikiwe** (NAHM-dee ah-zee-KEE-way). He believed that Nigerians of varying backgrounds needed to join together to work for self-rule and founded the Nigerian Youth Movement as one way to achieve unity. Azikiwe also created a sports association focused on Nigerians' love of soccer to encourage nationalist feeling.

At the same time, occasional uprisings took place in response to colonial tax, trade, and land policies. In the 1929 Igbo Women's War, women in southeastern Nigeria protested colonial interference in household and village affairs. They gathered in large numbers, wore symbolic costumes, and sang songs mocking chiefs who followed British orders. The British changed their

tax system slightly after this, but the local uprising did not threaten colonial rule.

Tensions were greatest in places where Europeans came to Africa not just as rulers but also as settlers. In South Africa and Kenya, Africans not only lost their sovereignty but also their best lands. Because of this, a mass protest movement arose in Kenya in the 1920s. Again, local protest was not enough to bring immediate and major reforms, but the groundwork was being laid. While Europe prepared for yet another deadly war, young Africans such as Jomo Kenyatta studied abroad, preparing for their roles as future leaders of nationalist movements. Kenyatta's book *Facing Mt. Kenya* was one of the first to explain African history and culture from an African point of view.

THE CARIBBEAN

Mass nationalism developed more rapidly in the British West Indies than in Africa. By the 1920s, Jamaican-born **Marcus Garvey** had gained a huge following for his United Negro Improvement Association (UNIA). His "back-to-Africa" philosophy called on all people of African heritage to band together. In this way, he believed they could gain dignity and improve their economic situation. In the United States, the National Association for the Advancement of Colored People (NAACP) continued to agitate for equal rights, with W.E.B. Du Bois writing on international affairs in the NAACP journal, *The Crisis*.

Meanwhile, the Great Depression made the conditions even worse in the Caribbean as well as in African colonies. Colonial powers were desperate for cheap goods to prop up their own weak economies. In the British West Indies, falling prices and depressed wages led to unrest. Across the ocean in equatorial Africa, the French made farmers keep planting, weeding, and harvesting cotton despite falling prices. The British imposed a "grow more crops" campaign in East Africa, where peasants were required to keep growing coffee for export despite losses from doing so. This meant that farmers did not have time or land for the subsistence farming that fed their families.

SOUTHEAST ASIA

After 1929, a drop in automobile manufacturing depressed the world market for rubber. Unemployment

Many civil rights groups adopted Marcus Garvey's message that urban blacks should unite to gain political and economic power. This 1920 photo portrays the charismatic Garvey riding in a Harlem parade at what he called the "First International Convention of the Negro Peoples of the World."

jumped in the Southeast Asian lands of Malaya, Vietnam, and the Dutch West Indies. Some farmers stopped growing export crops to raise food for themselves and their families, but the French still required them to pay taxes in cash. Those who objected were forced to work on government projects and French-owned plantations.

The people of French Indochina were not organized enough to resist the colonialists, but their continued oppression would change that over time. In 1930, the Vietnam National Party was punished for a failed rebellion. The group's leader stated at his execution: "If France does not want to have increasing trouble with revolutionary movements, she should immediately modify the cruel and inhuman policy now practiced in Indochina."

Across the colonies, nationalist leaders were laying the foundation for change. Mass nationalism would emerge following the new worldwide military conflict soon to erupt.

HISTORICAL THINKING

1. **READING CHECK** What was the effect of the Great Depression on colonized peoples?

2. **EXPLAIN** Why did tensions increase between colonized peoples and European colonizers following World War I?

3. **MAKE PREDICTIONS** What might cause colonial independence movements to gain traction in the coming years?

PLAN: 2-PAGE LESSON

OBJECTIVE

Explain how peoples in Africa, the Caribbean region, and Southeast Asia began to resist colonial rule in the 1920s and 1930s.

CRITICAL THINKING SKILLS FOR LESSON 3.3

- Explain
- Make Predictions
- Compare and Contrast
- Analyze Cause and Effect

HISTORICAL THINKING FOR CHAPTER 26

Is it better to have security or freedom?

When a colonial power promises its colonies security, it often materializes as oppression. Lesson 3.3 explains how nationalist movements took hold among peoples in Africa, the Caribbean region, and Southeast Asia as they began to resist the imperial powers that dominated them.

BACKGROUND FOR THE TEACHER

Marcus Garvey and Pan-Africanism The charismatic Marcus Garvey preached the doctrine of Pan-Africanism, a movement that sought to unify people of African descent. Many of Garvey's followers hoped to establish settlements in Africa so that African Americans could move there and live together. Garvey led this back-to-Africa movement and promised to "organize the 400,000,000 Negroes of the World into a vast organization to plant the banner of freedom on the great continent of Africa." His group, the Universal Negro Improvement Association (UNIA), worked to establish such settlements in areas of Africa that were not controlled by imperialist nations. Pan-African rallies in New York and other cities often drew 25,000 people and raised funds for the UNIA. As part of his message of economic independence, Garvey started several enterprises, including a shipping company, the Black Star Line, and the Negro Factories Corporation, which provided employment and financial support for black-owned businesses, including a clothing factory, grocery stores, restaurants, and a printing press.

INTRODUCE & ENGAGE

ACTIVATE PRIOR KNOWLEDGE

Invite students to share what they already know about colonialism—how it starts, how it endures, and how it affects indigenous peoples—and the role of racism. Use a Word Web to record responses and to discuss the reasons why colonized peoples might desire self-rule. Students will learn how peoples in three regions of the world worked to achieve self-rule.

TEACH

GUIDED DISCUSSION

1. **Compare and Contrast** How was French colonial rule different from British colonial rule? *(The French believed in assimilation. Their policies encouraged Asian and African colonists to learn the French language and culture. The British did not believe in assimilation. Their directives were carried out by "native authorities," but there was no question who was superior—the British.)*

2. **Analyze Cause and Effect** What conditions fueled anti-colonial sentiments in Southeast Asia? *(When unemployment went up during the global economic depression, some Southeast Asian farmers gave up growing export crops to grow crops for themselves. This angered the French, who colonized the area and still required farmers to pay taxes in cash as well as work on French-owned plantations. This lack of autonomy fueled rebellious feelings among native peoples.)*

COMPARE AND CONTRAST

Ask students to think about the nationalist movements in the regions discussed. **ASK:** How did the organization of nationalist forces differ in Africa and Southeast Asia? *(Nigeria: Nnamdi Azikiwe founded the Nigerian Youth Movement to help organize the push for self-rule. Kenya: The movement was less organized, but the groundwork was being laid by leaders who studied in the West. Vietnam: Vietnam National Party was organized enough to stage a rebellion, though unsuccessful.)*

ACTIVE OPTIONS

On Your Feet: Turn and Talk Ask groups to discuss this topic: Western ideas influenced nationalist movements in Africa and the Caribbean. Tell them to build a paragraph by having each student contribute one sentence. Suggest that students first identify the key figures they learned about and consider which of them came under Western influence, by travel or study (or both). Have students read their sentences to present the paragraph.

NG Learning Framework: Research Non-Self-Governing Territories
SKILLS Observation, Problem-Solving
KNOWLEDGE New Frontiers

Ask small groups to research the colonies that still exist in the world. Have them choose a colony and find which country administers it, what the local politics are around the issues of colonialism, imperialism, and nationalism, and the opposing forces, if any, that exist within the colony. Groups should prepare a short oral presentation to share with the class.

DIFFERENTIATE

STRIVING READERS

Connect Details to a Main Idea Ask students to work in pairs to fill out a Main-Idea Diagram for each section of the lesson. Model the kinds of details (facts, dates, events, descriptions) that often support a main idea. Students can share their main ideas and details with other pairs when they have finished.

GIFTED & TALENTED

Create Social-Networking Profiles Tell students to research Nnamdi Azikiwe, Jomo Kenyatta, and Marcus Garvey to learn more about each man's biographical details, accomplishments, personality, philosophy, and approach to nationalism and self-rule. Then have students create social-networking profiles for each person, including photos. Invite students to share their profiles with the entire class.

See the Chapter Planner for more strategies for differentiation.

HISTORICAL THINKING

ANSWERS

1. Because of the Great Depression, imperial powers increased their economic demands on colonized people.

2. Possible response: Colonized peoples resented that they were not rewarded for their service in World War I. Western education had made them more aware of the possibility of freedom. They also resented the harsh treatment they continued to receive. They were unhappy with increased demands placed on them because of the Great Depression and how colonizers treated them as inferiors.

3. Answers will vary. Students should offer several reasons why the independence movement might gain traction.

Japanese Aggression, Italian Invasion

War does not sneak up on anyone. Usually, there are warning signs even if they are not fully recognized at the time. Prior to World War II, aggressive acts by Japan toward China and by Italy toward Ethiopia heralded a coming conflict.

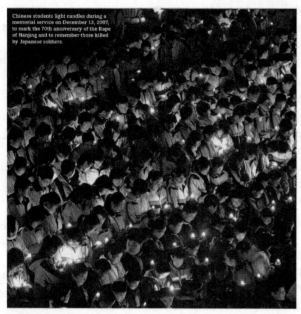

Chinese students light candles during a memorial service on December 13, 2007, to mark the 70th anniversary of the Rape of Nanjing and to remember those killed by Japanese soldiers.

JAPAN ON THE OFFENSIVE

As Japan's military attempted to expand its empire, it found China vulnerable to conquest. China was in a state of internal conflict between the nationalist government of Chiang Kai-shek and communist revolutionaries led by Mao Zedong. A nationalist attack in 1927 forced the communists to retreat to China's interior. During the Long March of 1934–1937, the communists walked about 7,500 miles across deserts and mountains to regroup in the northeast.

The Japanese had already defied the League of Nations with the occupation of Manchuria. In 1937, they launched a savage attack on coastal China in what became known as the Second Sino-Japanese War. Chiang and Mao agreed to put aside their differences to fight the common enemy, but they never combined forces or coordinated their efforts.

Convinced of their ethnic superiority, the Japanese cruelly mistreated the Chinese in their path. Japanese soldiers killed hundreds of thousands of civilians during the **Rape of Nanjing**. They viciously attacked women and disfigured children to spread terror among the population. Their complete disregard of the difference between soldiers and civilians took total war to a new level. About 300,000 noncombatants died. The Japanese then headed west and farther south through China. Other nations seemed unable or unwilling to stop Japanese aggression and atrocities.

MUSSOLINI STRIKES

Like Japanese leaders, Benito Mussolini of Italy did not listen when world leaders criticized his military aggression, and he ordered the invasion of Ethiopia in 1935. The Ethiopians put up a strong fight to defend their independent kingdom. But Mussolini was willing

Ethiopian emperor Haile Selassie addresses the League of Nations in 1936, urging members to take action to protect his country from Italian invasion: "I ask the 52 nations, who have given the Ethiopian people a promise to help them in their resistance to the aggressor, what are they willing to do for Ethiopia? . . . What reply shall I have to take back to my people?"

to bring total war to Africa, for example, by ordering Italian planes to drop poison gas on Ethiopian villagers. Such use of new, highly destructive technology gave the Ethiopians little hope.

The Ethiopian emperor **Haile Selassie** went to Geneva to beg the League of Nations for help. He warned that no small nation would ever be safe if the international community did not take action now. The League of Nations placed economic **sanctions**, or trade restrictions, on Mussolini but went no further. Italy had access to colonial resources such as Libyan oil and received aid from Germany, so the League's economic sanctions had little effect. Also, most European nations seemed uninterested in assisting African people. Little did they realize that Italy's aggressive action put the entire world at risk.

HISTORICAL THINKING

1. **READING CHECK** What made China vulnerable to Japanese attacks in the 1930s?

2. **INTERPRET MAPS** According to the map, why do you think the area of Japanese expansion had not extended much farther west by 1939?

3. **DRAW CONCLUSIONS** What did Mussolini's attack on Ethiopia reveal about the League of Nations? How did this affect the League?

PLAN: 2-PAGE LESSON

OBJECTIVE
Describe the land grabs Japan and Italy executed in the 1930s that resulted in escalated world tensions.

CRITICAL THINKING SKILLS FOR LESSON 4.1
- Interpret Maps
- Draw Conclusions
- Make Connections
- Analyze Cause and Effect

HISTORICAL THINKING FOR CHAPTER 26
Is it better to have security or freedom?

Aggressive moves by Japan and Italy contributed to the feeling of global unrest in the 1930s. Lesson 4.1 describes those actions and how they impacted the security and freedom of the people of China and Ethiopia, respectively.

Student eEdition online
Additional content for this lesson, including a map, is available online.

BACKGROUND FOR THE TEACHER
The Long March In 1930–1934, Chiang Kai-shek's nationalist forces launched a series of attacks on Mao Zedong's communists in southeastern China. The communists were overwhelmed by the well-armed nationalist. Then, in October 1934, 86,000 communist troops escaped their base and headed west, in what became known as the Long March. During the first three months of the Long March, attacks by Chiang's forces reduced the 86,000 troops by half. The survivors—both military and civilian—crossed 24 rivers and 18 mountain ranges before reaching northern Shaanxi, near the border China shared with the Soviet Union. The march solidified Mao as the Communist Party leader and moved the Chinese Communist Party's base to northwestern China. Stories of heroism from the arduous journey inspired young people to join Mao's cause. By the end of 1936, more than 30,000 troops joined the Red Army, and from their new base, they were eventually able to organize and defeat the nationalists for control of China.

INTRODUCE & ENGAGE

CONSIDER A LONG MARCH

Ask students how they would feel about joining a march that would take a year to complete. Tell them that they would have to carry all their supplies and find food along the way. Discuss the following questions: Under what circumstances would you consider participating in such a march? What hardships might you have to endure on a year-long march? Explain to students that in this lesson they will learn about a march by Chinese communists that lasted for a year.

TEACH

GUIDED DISCUSSION

1. **Make Connections** How did the concept of total war play out in the Japanese and Italian aggression of the 1930s? (*During the Rape of Nanjing, Japanese soldiers showed little care for Chinese women and children, terrorizing them at a new level of cruelty. In Ethiopia, the Italian military dropped poison gas on Ethiopian villagers.*)

2. **Analyze Cause and Effect** Why were the League of Nation's economic sanctions on Italy largely ineffective? (*Italy's colonies and European allies sustained it; Italy had access to Libyan oil and received aid from Germany.*)

INTERPRET MAPS

Have students analyze the map (available in the Student eEdition). **ASK:** What forms the northern border of Japan's land grab? (*the Amur River and the Ussuri River*) For how many years did Japan control Korea? (*35 years*) For how many years did Japan control Taiwan? (*50 years*) How does the map convey the potential conflicts (or alliances) that could play out in another world war? (*Possible response: China and the Soviet Union may be Japan's enemies, wary of further aggression or annexation. Korea may look to Japan's enemies for support in gaining independence.*)

ACTIVE OPTIONS

On Your Feet: Team Word Webbing Organize students into teams of four to record on a sheet of paper what they know about Japanese aggression in Asia. Tell students to build on their teammates' entries as they rotate the paper from one member to the next. Call on students to make statements about Japanese aggression based on their webs.

NG Learning Framework: Evaluate a Speech
SKILL Communication
KNOWLEDGE Our Human Story

Tell students to locate the speech Ethiopian emperor Hailie Selassie gave to the League of Nations in Geneva in June 1936 in which he asked member nations what they were "willing to do for Ethiopia" and "what measures" they intended "to take." Tell students to evaluate Selassie's speech for how well it describes Ethiopia's plight and how well it makes a case for international intervention. Ask a few students to recite the speech to the class before having students present their evaluations.

DIFFERENTIATE

INCLUSION

Facilitate Comprehension Pair special-needs students with proficient readers who can help them understand the main text and features in this lesson. Coach special-needs students to jot down difficult words and concepts that confuse them. Coach their partners to use information from the lesson to help define words and answer questions.

GIFTED & TALENTED STEM

Create a Website Prompt students to research the Rape of Nanjing and create an informative website that includes information about the event, the people who carried it out, the people affected by it, and the people who survived it. Ask students to find primary and secondary sources. Tell them to design a home page and then create a site map for the supporting pages. Invite students to share their website designs with the class. Some may wish to use website templates or design software to create and publish their websites.

See the Chapter Planner for more strategies for differentiation.

HISTORICAL THINKING

ANSWERS

1. internal conflicts between the nationalists and the communists

2. Possible responses: Many Chinese had become concentrated in China's interior, posing a greater resistance to Japanese forces; China was more mountainous to the west; it may have been harder for Japan to maintain its troops farther away from its homeland.

3. Possible response: that the League of Nations was ineffective and that totalitarian aggressors would ignore its sanctions; The League of Nations will continue to be ineffective to the point that it will cease to exist.

Franco and the Spanish Civil War

What sparks creativity? Often it can be the desire to bring beauty into the world. Or it can be to express an important idea or message. During a time of turbulence in Spain, artists, photographers, and writers found new ways to portray the evils of war and fascism.

FRANCO GAINS POWER

A warning bell was tolling across the world in the late 1930s. Japanese, Italian, and German aggression hinted that another war was imminent. The Paris Peace Conference that ended World War I had left a bitter taste for those penalized by it, and as you have read, the Great Depression led many to lose interest in liberal democracy and capitalism. In Europe, far-right fascism competed for influence with far-left communism. Intent on maintaining peace, liberal democracies ignored the warnings against authoritarianism.

Spain became a battleground in the struggle for power between right and left. Spain's monarchy had come to a crashing end in 1931, and a democratic government took its place. But some Spanish citizens were unhappy with the government's socialist approach to combating the Great Depression. By this time, the fascist movement had spread from Italy and Germany to Spain. Spanish conservatives, intrigued with fascism, took up arms under General **Francisco Franco** to seize power in Spain in 1936.

THE SPANISH CIVIL WAR

Francisco Franco's attempted coup divided the nation, leading to the Spanish Civil War. On one side were the conservative national forces, or Nationalists, led by Franco and backed by Germany and Italy. On the other side were the Republican forces, or the Loyalists, backed by the Soviet Union. Both sides depended on external support for war supplies. Eager to spread fascism in Europe, Germany offered Spain not only soldiers but also tanks, rifles, and airplanes. Germany

saw the conflict in Spain as a chance to try out its newest military technology. Noticeably absent from involvement in the Spanish Civil War were Britain, France, and the United States. Yet some of their citizens fought alongside the Republicans. Anti-fascist volunteers from the United States organized themselves in "Lincoln Brigades" to fight for Spanish democracy.

The Nationalists began a concentrated advance on Republican territory. Unsuccessful in capturing Madrid outright, they began a 28-month siege on the capital city. They also attacked northern Spain, home of the Basque people and a center of Republican support. Soon Nationalist troops occupied the entire northern coast of Spain. Catalonia, the last holdout, eventually fell as well. The Republicans had been largely defeated, and many fled the country. The Nationalists claimed Madrid and all government power in 1939. In all, almost one million people died as a result of the war.

Both sides committed horrendous acts, but those inflicted by the Nationalists were more deliberate and intense. One especially cruel event was the **carpet-bombing**, or dropping of a large number of bombs, of the Basque town of Guernica in 1937. The plan was to

For Whom the Bell Tolls The writer Ernest Hemingway believed that the United States should do more to stop fascism. His novel *For Whom the Bell Tolls* follows a young American volunteer in the Lincoln Brigade as he risks his life for the cause of Spanish democracy. Hemingway borrowed the title from an English poet, who had written: "No man is an Island, entire of itself . . . any man's death diminishes me, because I am involved in Mankind; and therefore never send to know for whom the bell tolls; it tolls for thee." For Hemingway, the Spanish Civil War was a warning bell for democracy everywhere.

kill as many civilians as possible rather than hit military targets. Through his painting *Guernica*, Pablo Picasso hoped to alert the world to the attack's inhumanity and sway public opinion against the fascists. Other artists and writers used the Spanish Civil War as subject matter as well. Photographers Robert Capa and Gerda Taro documented the war in their photographs. Ernest Hemingway's experiences while reporting the war led him to write the novel *For Whom the Bell Tolls*. Fellow writer George Orwell fought on the Republican side and described his experience in his *Homage to Catalonia*.

The war's end left Franco firmly in control of Spain. He then launched a campaign to eliminate or imprison any Republicans still in the country. He also imposed harsh restrictions on Spain's population, such as outlawing labor unions and curtailing the rights of the Basques. The war left Spain in rough economic shape. Franco supported the fascist cause but would not be a major player in the upcoming world conflict.

HISTORICAL THINKING

1. **READING CHECK** How did Francisco Franco become Spain's dictator?

2. **DRAW CONCLUSIONS** Why do you think the bombing of Guernica targeted civilians?

3. **FORM AND SUPPORT OPINIONS** What do you think rule under the Republicans would have been like had they been victorious in Spain? Why?

CRITICAL VIEWING After the Germans bombed Guernica, Spain, the artist Pablo Picasso created what would become one of his most famous works, *Guernica*. A powerful political statement, Picasso painted it as an immediate reaction to the inhumanity of the attack and to show the world the suffering of the Spanish people. What images in the painting help convey suffering and inhumanity?

© 2019 Estate of Pablo Picasso/Artists Right Society (ARS), New York

---

PLAN: 2-PAGE LESSON

OBJECTIVE
Explain the rise of Francisco Franco in Spain, the causes of the Spanish Civil War, and the artistic response to the war.

CRITICAL THINKING SKILLS FOR LESSON 4.2
- Draw Conclusions
- Form and Support Opinions
- Make Connections
- Describe
- Integrate Visuals

HISTORICAL THINKING FOR CHAPTER 26
Is it better to have security or freedom?

The fascist movements in Italy and Germany soon migrated to Spain, where a dictator named Francisco Franco rose to power and suppressed the freedoms of Spanish citizens. Lesson 4.2 details Franco's rise and the larger civil war that accompanied it.

Student eEdition online
Additional content for this lesson, including photographs, is available online.

BACKGROUND FOR THE TEACHER
The Abraham Lincoln Brigade The 2,800 Americans who fought on the side of the government in the Spanish Civil War did not have military backgrounds, as one might expect. Brought to Spain by the communist organization Comintern, most members of the Lincoln Brigade had never fired a rifle before. Their commander, Robert Hale Merriman, was a graduate student, and others had careers ranging from miners to acrobats, with the last surviving veteran having been a dishwasher. The brigade's numbers also included more than 80 African Americans and one woman, Marion Merriman, the wife of the brigade's commander, who worked at the brigade's headquarters in Madrid. The inexperience of the troops contributed to the overall American death rate being much higher than that of the rest of the Republican Army. During the brigade's first engagement near the Jarama River, so many Americans died that their fellow soldiers were unable to bury them all. They eventually burned the remaining dead, leaving behind a pile of rocks, helmets, skulls, and bones.

INTRODUCE & ENGAGE

PREVIEW USING VISUALS

Direct students' attention to the visuals in the lesson and Student eEdition. Call on volunteers to generate questions they would like to ask about the Spanish Civil War based on what they see in the visuals. Keep track of the suggested questions on the board. Return to the questions at the end of the lesson to see if all have been answered or if students would like to pursue answers through research.

TEACH

GUIDED DISCUSSION

1. **Make Connections** What role (or roles) did other European countries play in the Spanish Civil War and the rise of Franco? *(Fascist movements that had already taken hold in Italy and Germany spread to Spain. During the Spanish Civil War, the Nationalists, led by Franco, a fascist, were supported by Germany and Italy.)*

2. **Describe** What was Franco's rule of Spain like after his victory in the Spanish Civil War? *(After the war, Franco worked to eliminate any Republicans still in the country. He ruled with autocratic power, declaring labor unions illegal, establishing a secret police force, and suppressing the rights of the Basques, a minority group.)*

INTEGRATE VISUALS

Ask students to study the painting *Guernica* and think about what they have learned about art during wartime. **ASK:** How is *Guernica* similar to and different from the German expressionist art that emerged during Hitler's rise? *(Possible response: Both are nightmarish responses to fascism and the general sense of anxiety that pervaded the world in the 1930s. Guernica is different in that it is an immediate response to a specific event: the German carpet-bombing of the Spanish city during the Spanish Civil War.)* How might *Guernica* have impacted people's ideas about war? *(Possible response: The disturbing representations of people and horses might have awakened people to the horrors of war.)*

ACTIVE OPTIONS

On Your Feet: Three-Step Interview Direct pairs to interview each other about Franco and the Spanish Civil War, using the following questions: What was the conflict between right and left in Spain that allowed Franco to rise to power? What role did Franco play in the cause of the Spanish Civil War? Invite each student to share with the class the interview results.

> **NG Learning Framework: Investigate Wartime Technology**
> **SKILL** Observation
> **KNOWLEDGE** New Frontiers

Tell pairs or small groups to prepare a report on the military technology Germany used during the Spanish Civil War. Ask them to conduct online research about the technology and how it represented an advance from the weapons used during World War I. Ask students to conclude their reports with an analysis of the technology's impact on the Nationalists' victory. Groups should be prepared to report their findings to the class.

DIFFERENTIATE

INCLUSION

Describe and Chart Details Pair students who are sight-impaired with those who are not. Ask the latter to provide specific details about what the painting *Guernica* depicts and the style of what is depicted (realistic or abstract), read the caption, and organize details from the caption and their discussion.

GIFTED & TALENTED STEM

Create a Digital Slideshow Instruct students to find other works of art that were created in response to the Spanish Civil War, beginning their search with *The Reaper* by Joan Miró and *Mercury Fountain* by Alexander Calder. Tell them to create a digital slideshow of the works they find, with a caption on each slide that explains the image.

See the Chapter Planner for more strategies for differentiation.

HISTORICAL THINKING

ANSWERS

1. his skill as a general in the Spanish Civil War, the Spanish people's dissatisfaction with their liberal democracy and their economic position following the Great Depression, Germany's support of the Nationalists' fascist cause

2. Possible response: The Germans and Spanish Nationalists wanted to instill fear throughout Spain and encourage supporters of the Republicans to give up their cause.

3. Answers will vary.

CRITICAL VIEWING Possible response: The people are twisted into unnatural shapes with eyes displaced and mouths open, screaming in what appears to be pain and suffering. A horse is so graphically represented as to be unrecognizable, adding to the chaos and inhumanity in the painting.

The Hitler-Stalin Pact

Throughout history, people have encroached on the rights and land of others. Sometimes, the encroachment is simply accepted, but often the affected people or others step up to take immediate action. However, like in Spain, Western democracies were well aware of Adolf Hitler's escalating aggression in the 1930s, but they did little to stop it.

Growth of Nazi Germany, 1933–1939

Key:
- International boundaries, 1936
- Germany in 1933
- Remilitarized in 1936
- Annexed in 1938
- Satellite states, March 1939
- Conquered by Germany in September 1939
- Annexed by Soviet Union in September 1939

GERMAN ENCROACHMENTS
Before World War I, the Rhineland, which abutted France, had belonged to Germany. The Treaty of Versailles gave some of that land to France and also specified that the rest be demilitarized to ensure France's safety. Hitler was furious about this and other clauses in the treaty. In 1936, he built up German military forces and ordered them into the Rhineland region. This **remilitarization**, or rearming, and reoccupation of land both violated the Treaty of Versailles. The Western democracies complained but did not take any action. Their policy of **nonintervention**, or not getting involved, made Hitler even bolder.

Hitler had long declared that the Germans needed *Lebensraum* (LAY-buhns-rowm), or "living space" and that Germans in countries to the east needed to be reunited with their homeland. Hitler believed that Germans could pursue their racial destiny only by gaining more land and imagined vast eastern spaces cleared of Jews. The Slavic peoples, whom he considered inferior to Germans, would provide slave labor under German command. The Nazi leader's plan carried the Social Darwinist idea of a racial "struggle for existence" to the extreme. Joseph Stalin took Hitler's expansion threat seriously, but Western leaders were more worried about their own domestic issues. In fact, some Westerners agreed with Hitler's anti-Semitic and anti-communist views.

Encouraged by the lack of response to his remilitarization of the Rhineland, Hitler annexed neighboring Austria. Next, Hitler moved to annex the Sudetenland, a province in Czechoslovakia. One member of the British Parliament, **Winston Churchill**, urged quick action against German aggression. But Churchill, who would become Britain's great wartime leader, was unable to get the British people to take a firm stand and thus risk war.

APPEASEMENT AND ISOLATIONALISM

Instead of taking military action, British prime minister **Neville Chamberlain** flew to Munich to negotiate with Hitler through **appeasement**, or the giving of concessions to keep the peace. Chamberlain did not trust Hitler, but he was willing to appease Hitler to avoid the horrors of another total war. Still dazed from World War I, the British public largely supported Chamberlain's quest for "peace for our time." Because of this, Germany occupied the Sudetenland unchecked. Ever since, the term *appeasement* has meant the failure to stop an aggressor in time.

The lack of resolve on the part of Western nations alarmed Joseph Stalin. He came to believe that only through Western support could his Soviet army withstand a German attack. Without the promise of such support, Stalin decided to deal with Hitler directly. Even though the two leaders hated and distrusted each other, they signed a nonaggression agreement that became known as the Hitler-Stalin Pact in 1939.

British Prime Minister Neville Chamberlain returns to London in September 1938, claiming "peace for our time" after negotiating with Hitler.

A secret addition to this nonaggression agreement divided Poland and other parts of eastern Europe into Soviet and German spheres of influence. Neither man was a trustworthy negotiator, however. Hitler was merely delaying his planned attack on Russia, while Stalin was stalling for time to prepare his country for war.

Hitler's invasion of Poland on September 1, 1939, caused Britain and France to immediately declare war on Germany. However, they took no active steps to confront the German army. Meanwhile, public opinion in the United States remained opposed to getting involved in European affairs. Soon, however, peoples across Europe, Africa, Asia, and the Americas would be embroiled in total war. This world conflict would be unlike anything humanity had seen before.

HISTORICAL THINKING

1. **READING CHECK** What were two early acts of aggression by Adolf Hitler?

2. **MAKE CONNECTIONS** Why did nonintervention by Western democracies following Hitler's early aggression make the German leader bolder?

3. **ANALYZE CAUSE AND EFFECT** What event caused Great Britain to end its policy of appeasement toward Hitler? Why did this event spark Great Britain to abandon appeasement?

PLAN: 2-PAGE LESSON

OBJECTIVE
Summarize Hitler's acts of encroachment in the 1930s that led to France and Britain declaring war on Germany.

CRITICAL THINKING SKILLS FOR LESSON 4.3
- Make Connections
- Analyze Cause and Effect
- Make Inferences
- Interpret Maps

HISTORICAL THINKING FOR CHAPTER 26
Is it better to have security or freedom?

Hitler's aggression in Europe was a leading cause of World War II. Lesson 4.3 describes Hitler's invasions across the continent and how other countries either appeased him or dealt with him directly.

Student eEdition online
Additional content for this lesson, including a photo and caption, is available online.

BACKGROUND FOR THE TEACHER
The Munich Agreement The Munich Agreement was British Prime Minister Neville Chamberlain's attempt to forestall German aggression toward Czechoslovakia. However, prior to the actual agreement, which was signed by the major parties on September 30, 1938, Chamberlain had actually met with Hitler on multiple occasions to propose various alternatives. One idea was to allow the people of the Sudetenland to vote on the issue of joining Germany. Ultimately, all of these early proposals were rejected. As Hitler's demands increased, it was Chamberlain who proposed the conference that resulted in the Munich Agreement. The infamous final agreement was proposed by Mussolini but secretly written by the German Foreign Office. In the end, Czechoslovakia was given a choice: it could try to defend itself from Germany without help from its allies or submit to annexation.

INTRODUCE & ENGAGE

DECIDING WHEN TO ACT

Tell students to consider the pre-war events of WWI and other historical examples they've learned about. **ASK:** What would make national leaders stay out of a conflict even if a national figurehead was doing something illegal and abhorrent? *(Possible response: avoiding a costly and deadly war)* What kind of event might be a "red line" for a country to enter a war? *(Answers will vary. Possible response: a direct attack on one's own country or a heinous act done by a national actor to an ally)* Students will learn about Hitler's aggression in Europe and the ways in which other countries dealt with that aggression in hopes of avoiding another world war.

TEACH

GUIDED DISCUSSION

1. **Make Inferences** How did Hitler use his fascist beliefs to justify his land encroachments in Europe? *(Hitler believed that the Rhineland belonged to Germany and that it was unjustly taken away in the Treaty of Versailles, that Germans living to the east deserved to be part of the German homeland, and that Germany's destiny—which was of racial purity—could be achieved by expanding into needed Lebensraum that was cleared of Jews and other "inferior" groups.)*

2. **Make Connections** How did historical events influence Neville Chamberlain's decision to appease Hitler and the British public's support of that decision? *(The memory of World War I likely pushed Chamberlain and the British public to try to avoid war at all costs.)*

INTERPRET MAPS

Tell students to examine the map. **ASK:** What information does the map provide about the Rhineland? *(It was part of the area remilitarized by Germany in 1936.)* What area (or areas) did Germany annex in 1938? *(the Sudetenland and Austria)* After conquering western Poland in September 1939, what do you think would be Hitler's next move? Why? *(Answers will vary. Possible response: into Lithuania and Latvia to challenge Stalin)*

ACTIVE OPTIONS

On Your Feet: Inside-Outside Circle Arrange students in concentric circles facing each other. Tell students in the outside circle to ask students in the inside circle a question about the lesson. After students answer, have the outside circle rotate one position to the right to create new pairings. After five questions, tell students to switch roles and continue.

> **NG Learning Framework: Create an Annotated Time Line**
> **SKILL** Communication
> **KNOWLEDGE** Our Human Story

Have groups create a time line of Germany's encroachments and land grabs that led to the start of World War II, using the lesson and research. Each event should be annotated, indicating the significance of each event in relation to the progress toward war. As they present, groups should emphasize the sequence of events and how other nations responded.

DIFFERENTIATE

STRIVING READERS

Create Word Maps Ask students to write the word *appeasement* in the center oval of a Word Map. Then tell them to consult a dictionary or conduct online research in order to write the definition and characteristics of the word in the appropriate boxes. Guide students to identify and add examples and non-examples to their Word Maps.

PRE-AP

Report on U.S. Isolationism and Neutrality Instruct students to research and present an oral report about isolationism and neutrality in the United States in the years leading up to World War II. Encourage students to investigate the reasons why many Americans wanted to stay out of the war and why others, including President Franklin Roosevelt, believed the United States needed to become more involved. Have students present their oral reports to the class and answer questions.

See the Chapter Planner for more strategies for differentiation.

HISTORICAL THINKING

ANSWERS

1. The remilitarization of the Rhineland and the annexation of the Sudetenland were two early acts of aggression by Hitler.

2. Possible response: Nonintervention on the part of Western democracies emboldened Hitler because he believed that he could get away with anything.

3. Possible response: Germany's invasion of Poland caused Great Britain to abandon its policy of appeasement because it realized that peaceful negotiations would not stop Hitler's aggression and conquest.

26 REVIEW

VOCABULARY

Write one or more sentences that explains the connection between each pair of words.

1. mass media; popular culture
2. Great Depression; speculation
3. fascism; totalitarianism
4. collectivization; kulak
5. Hind Swaraj; civil disobedience
6. ahimsa; satyagraha
7. remilitarization; nonintervention
8. appeasement; isolationism

READING STRATEGY
COMPARE AND CONTRAST

Comparing and contrasting can help you form a deeper understanding of concepts. Complete a Venn diagram to compare and contrast the totalitarian leaders of Nazi Germany and the Soviet Union.

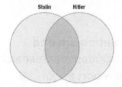

Stalin   Hitler

9. What was the greatest similarity between the two leaders? What was the greatest difference?

MAIN IDEAS

Answer the following questions. Support your answers with evidence from the chapter.

10. What made radio technology so useful during World War I? LESSON 1.1

11. What was a political cause of Germany's suffering during the Great Depression? LESSON 1.3

12. What is the main characteristic of totalitarianism? LESSON 2.1

13. Why did Hitler believe that Germans should dominate the world? LESSON 2.2

14. Why did Stalin introduce collectivization in the Soviet Union? LESSON 2.3

15. Why did the Japanese launch an invasion of the Manchurian province of China? LESSON 2.4

16. What was the goal of Gandhi's Salt March and what were the effects? LESSON 3.1

17. How did Nnamdi Azikiwe think independence could be achieved for Nigeria? LESSON 3.3

18. How did technology give the Italians an advantage over the Ethiopians? LESSON 4.1

19. What caused the Spanish Civil War, who were the opponents, and how did it end? LESSON 4.2

20. How did the political views of Winston Churchill and Neville Chamberlain differ? LESSON 4.3

HISTORICAL THINKING

Answer the following questions. Support your answers with evidence from the chapter.

21. EVALUATE How important was aviation technology to the winning of World War I?

22. ANALYZE POINT OF VIEW Why might Americans have had differing views about the government's response to the Great Depression?

23. FORM AND SUPPORT OPINIONS Do you think a leader like Mussolini could rise again? Explain.

24. DRAW CONCLUSIONS What was Hitler's rationale for excluding certain groups of people from society?

25. DESCRIBE How might you describe the government of Japan during the 1930s?

26. COMPARE AND CONTRAST How were the rise and aggression of Hitler, Mussolini, and Stalin alike and different?

INTERPRET VISUALS

Study the table, which shows unemployment rates for various countries in the years 1929–1934. Then answer the questions below.

27. Which country had the highest unemployment rate in 1929? Why do you think this was so?

28. What might have caused the sharp drop in Germany's unemployment rate in 1934?

Unemployment Rates, 1929–1934

	Great Britain	Germany	Belgium	Sweden	United States
1929	10.4	13.3	1.3	10.2	3.2
1930	16.1	22.7	3.6	11.9	8.7
1931	21.3	34.3	10.9	16.8	15.9
1932	22.1	43.8	19.0	22.4	23.6
1933	19.9	36.2	16.9	23.3	24.9
1934	16.7	20.5	18.9	18.0	21.7

Source: Walter Galenson and Arnold Zellner, "International Comparison of Unemployment Rates," *The Measurement and Behavior of Unemployment* (National Bureau of Economic Research, 1957)

ANALYZE SOURCES

In the 1930s, the Japanese began a policy of expansion to solve their overcrowding problem and improve their economy. In this excerpt from a 1939 speech, military leader Hashimoto Kingoro offers a justification for why Japan chose this path for growth. Read the excerpt and answer the question that follows.

> We are like a great crowd of people packed into a small and narrow room, and there are only three doors through which we might escape, namely emigration, advance into world markets, and expansion of territory. The first door has been barred to us by the anti-Japanese immigration policies of other countries. The second is being pushed shut by tariff barriers. . . . It is quite natural that Japan should rush upon the last remaining door . . . of territorial expansion.

29. What does the primary source tell you about why Japan concentrated on expansion to meet its needs?

CONNECT TO YOUR LIFE

30. EXPLANATORY Think about how Mahatma Gandhi's and Jawaharlal Nehru's different views made them both great leaders of India's independence movement. Then think about movements you care about today. Can you identify two leaders who exemplify

the inspirational and practical roles for this movement? Do you think one role is more important than the other, or are both roles needed? Write a short essay to express your views, using examples from movements you know of today.

TIPS

* Use a T-Chart to make notes about Gandhi's and Nehru's views and their roles. Conduct additional Internet or library research if necessary.

* Use another T-Chart to make notes about the views and roles of leaders of a movement today, again conducting additional research as necessary.

* Draft an essay describing the two leaders you've chosen, explaining their roles and evaluating the importance of those roles.

* Use two or three vocabulary terms from the chapter in your essay.

* End your essay with a generalization explaining why different types of leaders are needed in different situations.

Economic Depression and Authoritarian Regimes 763

VOCABULARY ANSWERS

1. Newspapers, radio, and other forms of mass media gave rise to popular culture, giving people across a region the same information and entertainment.

2. Borrowing money to buy stocks on speculation was a main cause of the Great Depression of the 1930s.

3. One type of totalitarian government was the fascism of the far right, which brought with it extreme nationalism.

4. Kulaks, or wealthy Russian peasants, disliked giving up private ownership of property for collectivization.

5. Mohandas Gandhi encouraged the use of civil disobedience rather than violence to achieve Hind Swaraj, or Indian self-rule.

6. Gandhi believed in two moral principles from Indian tradition: ahimsa, absolute nonviolence; satyagraha, the application of nonviolence to politics.

7. Remilitarization of the Rhineland did not cause Western democracies to abandon their policy of nonintervention and take up arms against Germany.

8. While Chamberlain thought Great Britain could contain Hitler's ambition through appeasement, the United States adopted a policy of isolationism and stayed out of European conflicts.

READING STRATEGY ANSWERS

Stalin

supported socialism through a top-down government and communism; used labor camps to imprison those who opposed him and others to increase labor productivity; wanted to industrialize Russia; ordered collectivization; executed those who served under Lenin

(overlap) totalitarian leaders; ruled as dictators; used propaganda; used violence against opponents; wanted to reorganize the economy and society

Hitler

supported Nazism; used rousing speeches, marching, flag-waving, and rallies to gain support; used concentration camps against anyone who opposed him or whom he viewed as inferior; promoted nationalism; violently opposed communism; had a goal of restoring greatness, confidence, and order; wanted to create a master race and exterminate Jews; wanted more territory

9. Possible response: Both wanted to reorganize their economies and societies, used violence toward goals. Stalin supported socialism and communism. Hitler abhorred communists, promoted Nazism.

MAIN IDEAS ANSWERS

10. the portability of the radio, the fact that messages could be sent anywhere, the distance radio messages could be sent, and the fact that people no longer had to hand deliver messages

11. Germany had to pay reparations for its role in World War I. It then suffered during the Great Depression

because American investors called in the loans they took out to pay the reparations, leading to the collapse of the German economy.

12. total control of government by a person or group

13. Hitler said that the Germans were a superior race and that only they could create a "master race."

14. He believed in socialism and thought that Soviet socialism must be built through top-down government control of every aspect of life.

15. to expand the territory under its control and to gain economic strength of Manchuria's resources and cheap labor

16. to protest a British law that forbade Indians from making their own salt; The British jailed Indian National Congress leaders. Later, they passed the Government of India Act of 1935, which called for elections that the Congress mainly won.

17. only if Nigerians of all backgrounds joined together to work for self-rule; He encouraged this by creating the Nigerian Youth Movement and a Nigerian sports association that publicized soccer.

18. They dropped poison gas out of airplanes.

19. Francisco Franco's attempted overthrow of Spain's liberal democracy; The Nationalists who supported fascism waged war against the Republicans who opposed fascism. The Nationalists won after gaining control of Republican-held land.

20. Churchill urged an immediate military reaction to German aggression. Chamberlain thought negotiation and concessions were the best policies. The German invasion of Poland convinced Chamberlain that the British must go to war against Germany.

HISTORICAL THINKING ANSWERS

21. Possible response: It was not crucial because the military was just discovering the capabilities of planes, and the aircraft used were rather primitive. Both sides were about equal in their use of aircraft. The new technology did help heighten interest in the war and showed that aircraft could be used for military purposes more extensively in the future.

22. Possible response: Many unemployed people might have welcomed Roosevelt's programs as helpful and necessary. However, some Americans may have felt that in a capitalist economy, there should be little government involvement.

23. Answers will vary. Yes; Fascism seems to rise when people are suffering hard times and desire more order and when ultranationalist feelings and strong prejudice surface. Nations in which the military

has power, and in which political dissension is not tolerated, would be most likely to accept such a leader.

24. Possible response: Hitler believed communists advocated an opposing philosophy; homosexuals and the physically and mentally handicapped were inferior; the elderly could not contribute to society because they could no longer procreate; and the Jews were not the same race as Germans and anti-Semitism made them easy targets.

25. Answers will vary. Possible responses: totalitarian, ultranationalist, militaristic, expansionist, aggressive

26. Possible response: All: totalitarian leaders, encouraged expansion, aggressive conquest, curtailed human rights, used a strong-arm group to quash enemies; Hitler and Mussolini: claimed power in Germany and Italy, fascists, main goal was national unity, governments replaced liberal democracies; Hitler and Stalin: rose up through the political ranks; Mussolini: gained control through a military role, claimed Ethiopia; Hitler: took Austria, the Sudetenland, and western Poland; Stalin: ruled parts of Eastern Europe and northern Asia (the Soviet Union), communist, a communist government was already in place, goal was class solidarity, took eastern Poland

INTERPRET VISUALS ANSWERS

27. Germany; Its economy was in shambles after its loss in World War I and the payment of reparations.

28. the institution of massive public works projects

ANALYZE SOURCES ANSWER

29. Possible response: They had limited land and resources. Japanese people were restricted on where they could immigrate and were forced to pay high tariffs, which meant that they could not make money through trade with Western powers. They thought they had no choice but to expand to acquire new land, resources, and markets for trade.

CONNECT TO YOUR LIFE ANSWER

30. Students' essays will vary but should express their views regarding the inspirational and practical roles played by leaders of a contemporary movement and include supporting examples and an evaluation of the importance of the different leadership roles.

The
World Wars
1870-1945

27 The Second
World War
1939-1945

SECTION 1 RESOURCES

THE ALLIED AND AXIS POWERS

LESSON 1.1   p. 766

Germany's Military Might
- On Your Feet: Inside-Outside Circle

| **NG Learning Framework**
Write a Profile

Biography
- Winston Churchill `online`

LESSON 1.2   p. 768

Japan's Rising Sun
- On Your Feet: Three-Step Interview

| **NG Learning Framework**
Write a Report

Biography
- Emperor Hirohito `online`

LESSON 1.3   p. 770

Allied Momentum
- On Your Feet: Fishbowl

| **NG Learning Framework**
Profile a Commander

SECTION 2 RESOURCES

TOTAL WAR

LESSON 2.1   p. 774

**TRAVELERS NANCY WAKE AND JOSEPHINE BAKER
French Resistance Fighters**
- On Your Feet: Think, Pair, Share

| **NG Learning Framework**
Write a Biography

LESSON 2.2   p. 776

Wartime Preparations and Policies
- On Your Feet: Roundtable

| **NG Learning Framework**
Explore War Propaganda

LESSON 2.3   p. 778

Civilians, Technology, and the War's Toll
- On Your Feet: Numbered Heads

| **NG Learning Framework**
Understand a Different Point of View

SECTION 3 RESOURCES

THE HOLOCAUST AND THE LEGACY OF WAR

LESSON 3.1   p. 780

"The Final Solution"
- On Your Feet: Inside-Outside Circle

| **NG Learning Framework**
Write an Article

LESSON 3.2   p. 782

The Holocaust
- On Your Feet: Think, Pair, Share

| **NG Learning Framework**
Investigate Holocaust Horrors

LESSON 3.3   p. 784

**PRESERVING CULTURAL HERITAGE
Saving the Past**

| **NG Learning Framework**
Create a Museum Website or App

LESSON 3.4   p. 786

Justice and Remembrance
- On Your Feet: Numbered Heads

| **NG Learning Framework**
Research Holocaust Heroes

CHAPTER 27 REVIEW

STRATEGY ❶
Clarify Information

Students may have trouble understanding aspects of World War II, such as how different alliances were formed, why particular battles were won or lost, and the global extent of the war. To clarify information, instruct students to use a 5Ws Chart to write questions they have on each section in the lessons. Then lead a discussion group to answer students' questions.

Use with All Lessons

STRATEGY ❷
Compare and Contrast

To help students organize and understand lesson content, instruct them to create a T-Chart and label the first column *Axis Powers* and the second column *Allied Powers*. Tell them to jot down key facts including the countries that formed each group, the leaders of those countries, the victories and defeats of each group, and the losses each group suffered as a result of the war. Encourage pairs to review their charts and compare and contrast the two sides.

Axis Powers	Allied Powers

Use with All Lessons

STRATEGY ❸
Summarize with a List of Outstanding Facts

Post this heading on the board: Outstanding Facts I Know About World War II. Ask students to copy the heading onto a sheet of paper. As they read each lesson, prompt them to write the lesson title and at least five sentences of outstanding facts, including reasons for alliances, battles, strategies, victories, and defeats. After each lesson, invite volunteers to share their sentences with the class to summarize what they have read.

Use with All Lessons

STRATEGY ❶
Preview and Predict

Pair students with reading or perception issues with proficient readers and direct them to read the lesson title and section headings together. Then ask proficient students to guide their partners in describing details in lesson visuals and reading the captions, working together to write notes predicting what the lesson will be about. After reading, ask pairs to review their notes to confirm their predictions and correct inaccuracies.

Use with All Lessons *For example, in Lesson 1.2, tell proficient students to read the title and section headings and describe the photo of the Japanese soldiers. Then have students write predictions, such as: This lesson will describe how Japan used its military might to attack other countries.*

STRATEGY ❷
Mark Up Maps

Provide students with colored markers and printouts of maps from the lessons. Direct students to read the legend for each map, and then instruct them to use one chosen color to highlight the Axis Powers and another chosen color to highlight the Allied Powers. Have students continue to mark up their maps as they read the lesson, using the map as a reference guide. Then have pairs write sentences about what the map shows in relation to the lesson.

Use with Lessons 1.1, 1.3, and 2.1 and also with Student eEdition Lessons 1.2, 2.2, and 3.2

STRATEGY ❶
Use Context Clues

Pair students at the **Beginning** level with those at the **Intermediate** or **Advanced** level. Model how to use context clues to learn the meaning of unfamiliar words. Instruct students to find the context clues or textual definitions that provide the meaning of the terms *infantry* (soldiers) and *armored divisions* (armored tanks) from Lesson 1.1. Then have students look for context clues to help them understand other unfamiliar words and write an original sentence using each word. Prompt more proficient students to assist others in checking the accuracy of their sentences. Invite pairs to share their sentences and discuss different ways to use each word.

Use with All Lessons

STRATEGY 2
Identify Word Parts

Remind students of **All Proficiencies** that two words can be combined to make a compound word and that meaningful prefixes and suffixes can be added to a word. Write the following words from Lesson 1.1 on the board: *overran, thickly, firepower, unfortunately, firefighter, nighttime,* and *headquarters.* Instruct students to copy the words and circle the word parts. Then place students in mixed-proficiency pairs and have them work together to use the word parts to define the resulting word. Invite a proficient student to identify compound words and words with prefixes and suffixes in other lessons in the chapter for the students to analyze.

Use with All Lessons

STRATEGY 3
Dictate Sentence Summaries

Pair students at the **Beginning** level with those at the **Advanced** level. After students have finished reading the lesson, direct them to identify three sentences that contain an important idea. Tell students to write that idea in a summary sentence using their own words. Partners then take turns dictating their sentences to each other. Encourage them to check each other's work for accuracy and spelling.

Use with All Lessons

GIFTED & TALENTED

STRATEGY 1
Present an Invention

Direct students to choose one of the inventions or technological advances made during World War II, such as advancements in military aircraft, battleships, code breaking, bombs, submarines, or detecting submarines. Then have them find out more about how it worked and how it impacted the war. Encourage students to incorporate diagrams, photographs, and other visuals to convey the mechanics and the importance of the item. Invite students to present their findings to the class and to answer questions about their presentations.

Use with Lessons 1.1, 1.2, 1.3, 2.2, and 2.3

STRATEGY 2
Write a Letter Home

Tell students to conduct online research about one of the battles mentioned in the chapter to better understand the location, events, and experiences of the soldiers involved in the battle. Then ask students to write a letter from the point of view of one of the soldiers to a family member or friend about their experiences and their hopes for the future of the war. Invite volunteers to read their letters to the class or post them on a class website or blog.

Use with All Lessons

PRE-AP

STRATEGY 1
Explore Impacts

Instruct students to choose one of the people or groups mentioned in the chapter and conduct research to write an essay that examines that person's or group's impact on the history of World War II. Encourage students to incorporate photographs, art, and other visuals in their essays. Invite volunteers to share their finished essays with the class and to answer questions about their essays.

Use with All Lessons *Students could research one of the following: the French Resistance, a survivor from one of the famous battles mentioned, the Tuskegee Airmen, the 442nd Regimental Combat Team, the Navajo code talkers.*

STRATEGY 2
Analyze a Speech

Invite students to conduct research about a speech given during World War II, such as Winston Churchill's speech before the House of Commons on June 4, 1940, or President Franklin Roosevelt's speech to Congress on December 8, 1941. Suggest that students analyze the speaker's choice of words, repetition of words, and tone of voice and how these impacted listeners. Remind students that people heard these speeches on the radio as there were no televisions at this time. Direct students to present their findings in an oral report to the class or in a digital report posted on a class blog.

Use with All Lessons

HISTORICAL THINKING How was World War II a
total war?

SECTION 1 **The Allied and Axis Powers**
SECTION 2 **Total War**
SECTION 3 **The Holocaust and the Legacy of War**

CRITICAL VIEWING
On June 6, 1944, Allied British, American, and Canadian
forces invaded western Europe to free the region from
German occupation during World War II. The Allies began the
operation by landing on the beaches of the French province of
Normandy. In this photo, U.S. soldiers jump off their landing
craft and prepare for battle on what came to be known as
D-Day. What might have been some of the challenges and
dangers the soldiers faced once they jumped into the water?

INTRODUCE THE PHOTOGRAPH

THE PIVOTAL ROLE OF D-DAY

Have students study the photo of the Normandy landing
by U.S. soldiers that appears at the beginning of the
chapter. Direct students to read the text that clarifies
the depicted action. **ASK:** How does the photo indicate
that more than one branch of the military achieved
the Normandy landing? *(Possible response: The navy
provided small craft, with support from warships, to
deliver foot soldiers to the beach at Normandy.)* Explain
that the Normandy landing was a pivotal event in the war
against Nazi Germany. It paved the way for Allied forces
to gain a foothold in France and advance from there. Tell
students that in this chapter they will learn about the key
events, strategies, and technologies of a war that involved
many countries around the world.

SHARE BACKGROUND

The D-Day landing required complex planning and
unprecedented international cooperation. Troops from
more than 12 countries provided support. U.S. General
Dwight D. Eisenhower led the Allied forces in a landing
strategy that included an air campaign and deception.
Thousands of airplanes bombed French bridges, roads,
and rail networks to isolate the landing area. Bombs
dropped deliberately outside the area, along with fake
radio transmissions, convinced the Germans that they
would be targeted in France but not at Normandy.

Before the landing began, under the cover of darkness,
aircraft dropped thousands of American, British, and
Canadian paratroopers behind the Germans guarding
Normandy. German antiaircraft fire forced many
paratroopers to land off course. Many drowned in flooded
fields. Similarly, many troops who stormed the beaches at
Normandy either drowned or died from German machine-
gun fire. Nonetheless, more than 1 million Allied troops
eventually liberated Paris.

CRITICAL VIEWING Answers will vary. Possible
response: The water might have been rough and difficult
to wade through; once the soldiers got to the beach, the
enemy might have been waiting to shoot at them.

HISTORICAL THINKING QUESTION
How was World War II a Total War?

Actions and Philosophies that Lead to War Arrange students in groups of four. Assign half of the groups this question: What events and actions contribute to the emergence of war? Assign the remaining groups this question: What are some of the ways a nation's or leader's philosophy and interactions with other countries lead to war? Have one student in each group write an answer to the question on a sheet of paper and pass the paper clockwise to the next student, who adds an answer, continuing until students are out of ideas. As a class, compile a master list of answers for each question. Then tell students that in Chapter 27 they will learn how numerous countries can become involved in a major war.

KEY DATES FOR CHAPTER 27

1939	The German invasion of Poland begins World War II.
1940	Japan joins Germany and Italy as Axis Powers.
1941	Japan bombs Pearl Harbor; the United States joins the Allied Powers.
1942	Nazis hold the Wannsee Conference to plan the "final solution."
1942–43	Allied forces mobilize in Europe, Africa, and the Pacific theater.
1944	Allied troops storm Normandy beaches on D-Day.
1945	Germany surrenders; the United States drops atomic bombs on Japanese cities; Japan surrenders.

INTRODUCE THE READING STRATEGY

IDENTIFY MAIN IDEAS AND DETAILS
Explain that identifying main ideas and details helps readers recognize important concepts and enables them to locate supporting evidence for answers or arguments. Ask them to turn to the Chapter Review and preview the graphic organizer with them. As they read the chapter, encourage students to identify main ideas and supporting details about topics pertaining to the Second World War.

INTRODUCE CHAPTER VOCABULARY

KEY VOCABULARY

SECTION 1

atomic bomb	blitzkrieg	D-Day
infamy	island hopping	kamikaze

SECTION 2

depth charge	napalm

SECTION 3

atrocity	crematoria	tribunal

DEFINITION CHART
As they read the chapter, encourage students to complete a Definition Chart. Ask them to use the left column of their charts to list the Key Vocabulary words or terms. As they encounter each Key Vocabulary word or term in the chapter, students should write its definition in the center column and explain what it means, using their own words, in the right column. Model an example using the graphic organizer below.

Word	Definition	In My Own Words
infamy	an extremely shameful or evil act	a horrible crime or scandal that is well known because it is so bad

Germany's Military Might

You can't always reason with a bully. Britain tried to keep the peace with Germany, but then the Nazis bullied their way into Poland. In the end, Britain and other European nations decided they had no choice but to fight.

German Advances, 1938–1941

Legend:
- Allied territory
- Axis powers
- Axis satellite
- Axis-controlled by 1940
- Soviet territory
- Neutral nation
- German troop movements
- Battle of Britain and the Blitz, 1940–1941

GERMAN OFFENSIVE

The German army was ready for war. By the time Adolf Hitler's forces invaded Poland on September 1, 1939, Germany had mobilized 100 infantry divisions, with between 12,000–25,000 soldiers in each one. The army also boasted six armored divisions, which included its superior fleet of thickly armored tanks known as panzers. In the early years of the war, German soldiers used a tactic called the **blitzkrieg** (BLIHTS-kreeg), or "lightning war." This tactic employed speed, surprise, and the combined firepower of tanks, bombers, and ground forces. All of these elements were set into motion before the enemy could organize a defense. The blitzkrieg was used to overwhelm Poland.

As you've read, Britain and France declared war on Germany after the invasion, marking the beginning of World War II. The two countries—and others that would later oppose Germany—were called the **Allied Powers.** Germany, Italy, and Japan would form the principal partners of the **Axis Powers.** After declaring war, France and Britain moved troops to the Maginot Line, a series of fortifications built after World War I along the French-German border. But for the next six months, no major battles took place. For that reason, some journalists referred to the period as the "Phony War."

Unfortunately, the war would soon become all too real. In April 1940, German forces swept through Denmark and Norway, quickly conquering both countries. Following this act of German aggression, British prime minister Neville Chamberlain resigned from office, and Winston Churchill took his place. Then in May, Germany invaded Luxembourg, the Netherlands, and Belgium. Luxembourg and the Netherlands surrendered within days. Meanwhile, Britain and France sent troops north to Belgium and fell into a trap. Germany invaded the country from the south and surrounded the British and French forces.

The Allies were cornered in the port of Dunkirk on the northern coast of France. Convinced it was his only option, Churchill ordered the evacuation of the Allied troops. While German planes bombed the port, British naval ships and even private vessels owned by British civilians came to rescue the soldiers and carry them across the English Channel. Nearly 350,000 British and French troops were saved. Although they had been driven from the European continent, the British resolve to fight was strengthened by their effort at Dunkirk.

BRITISH RESOLVE

After the evacuation, the German army swept through France, defeating the remaining French forces. The Germans entered Paris on June 14, and about a week later, France signed an armistice with Germany. Under its terms, German troops occupied northern France and a strip of western France along the Atlantic coast. Southern France remained under French control, and the town of Vichy (VIH-shee) became the capital of this unoccupied part of France. The government of Vichy France largely cooperated with the Germans. Nevertheless, some of the French continued their fight against the Nazis. French general **Charles de Gaulle**

set up headquarters in Britain to allow "Free French" forces to continue fighting as a resistance force. De Gaulle had the support of many French citizens who saw Vichy leaders as Nazi puppets, but he had few troops or bases. As a result, Britain was left largely isolated.

In control of continental Europe, Hitler targeted Britain next. Germany began the **Battle of Britain** in July, which pitted Britain's Royal Air Force (RAF) against the German air force, the Luftwaffe. While the Luftwaffe inflicted heavy damage on British cities, the RAF put up stiff resistance and eventually forced Germany's air force to retreat. The Luftwaffe then began to bomb London and other British cities in September. These air raids, known as the Blitz, continued nearly every night until May 1941. The Blitz left much of London in ruins and killed about 43,000 British civilians.

Although the United States maintained a neutral position in the war, President Franklin Roosevelt began to provide military supplies and other aid to Britain in March 1941. By doing so, Roosevelt claimed the United States would become "the arsenal of democracy." The American president also agreed to issue the **Atlantic Charter** jointly with Churchill in August. Under the eight-point charter, the two leaders agreed to such principles as freedom of the seas, greater trade among nations, and the right of people to choose the kind of government they desired. Very soon, Roosevelt would take more substantial action to protect these principles.

After the retreating Allied soldiers made it safely across the English Channel from Dunkirk, Winston Churchill spoke before the House of Commons. In this excerpt from the House of Commons speech, the prime minister seeks to rally the British to fight on against Germany.

PRIMARY SOURCE

[W]e shall not flag [tire] or fail. We shall go on to the end, we shall fight in France, we shall fight on the seas and oceans, . . . we shall defend our island, whatever the cost may be, we shall fight on the beaches, we shall fight on the landing grounds, we shall fight in the fields and in the streets, we shall fight in the hills; we shall never surrender.

—from a speech before the House of Commons by Winston Churchill, June 4, 1940

HISTORICAL THINKING

1. **READING CHECK** What made the German army a formidable fighting force?

2. **INTERPRET MAPS** Why was it important for Germany to occupy France before targeting Britain?

3. **DRAW CONCLUSIONS** How did Hitler underestimate Britain and the British people?

PLAN: 2-PAGE LESSON

OBJECTIVE

Explain how Germany overran much of western Europe in the first two years of World War II.

CRITICAL THINKING SKILLS FOR LESSON 1.1

- Interpret Maps
- Draw Conclusions
- Make Inferences
- Analyze Primary Sources

HISTORICAL THINKING FOR CHAPTER 27

How was World War II a total war?

The Nazi regime in Germany solidified its power and built its army for several years preceding World War II. Lesson 1.1 discusses the German military aggression that forced Britain and other European nations into war.

Student eEdition online

Additional content for this lesson, including photographs, is available online.

BACKGROUND FOR THE TEACHER

Nazi Allies in Europe France was not the only European nation where local allies aided Nazi rule. Fascists in Norway, Denmark, and the Netherlands accepted positions under Nazi authority. In Norway, the German administration used Nazi collaborator Vidkun Quisling as a figurehead. Quisling's past included founding the 1930s fascist National Union party. In Denmark, most companies exploited the Danish policy of collaboration with Germany. They profited from adapting industrial production to German needs. In the Netherlands, the Dutch National Socialist Movement (NSB), composed of Nazi sympathizers, collaborated with the Germans. Some 20,000 Dutch citizens joined the Nazi protection known as the SS. In the Balkans, the Germans found willing allies like the Croatian Ustaše, extreme nationalists led by the fascist Ante Pavelić. The Ustaše extended Croatian state outreach and brutally persecuted Yugoslavia's Serbs, Muslims, Jews, and Roma. With the support of fascist Italy under Benito Mussolini and the neutrality maintained by Francisco Franco's Spain, the Nazis were in command of Europe.

INTRODUCE & ENGAGE

CONSIDER GERMAN AGGRESSION

Direct students to study the map that appears at the beginning of the lesson. Invite volunteers to suggest conditions within a country that could help a powerful invader take control. *(Possible responses might include the surprise factor, a country's weak military, poor leadership, dissatisfied citizenry, or sympathizers with the invader's ideology.)* Then tell students that in this lesson they will explore how Nazi Germany gained control over most of western Europe within the first two years of war.

TEACH

GUIDED DISCUSSION

1. **Draw Conclusions** Why was the Allied situation at Dunkirk a major factor in the German occupation of France? *(France lost thousands of troops, including British allies, in the evacuation to Britain from Dunkirk. Thousands more troops surrendered at Dunkirk. The situation aided the German occupation of northern and western coastal France.)*

2. **Make Inferences** Aside from the resolve to fight, what might have helped the British prevail during the Battle of Britain? *(The British knew of German invasions in other countries. This allowed British leaders to anticipate an attack and assemble military forces.)*

ANALYZE PRIMARY SOURCES

Have students read the primary source excerpt from Winston Churchill's House of Commons speech. **ASK:** What is the main idea of Churchill's speech? *(The main idea is that the British will keep fighting and never surrender.)* Explain that Churchill was a great orator and writer who won the Nobel Prize in Literature in 1953. **ASK:** In this excerpt, how does Churchill use language to support his main idea? How do you think this language affected a British citizen listening to the speech? *(Possible response: The repetition of the phrase "We shall" is powerful and probably helped rally the people listening to Churchill's speech.)*

ACTIVE OPTIONS

On Your Feet: Inside-Outside Circle Arrange students in concentric circles facing each other. Tell students in the outside circle to pose questions about the wartime goals, military strategies, and battles discussed in the lesson, such as: How did Britain respond to German aggression? What happened to France? What was the official position of the United States? Ask students in the inner circle to answer their partner's questions. Then have students trade roles.

> **NG Learning Framework: Write a Profile**
> ATTITUDE Empowerment
> SKILL Problem-Solving

Prompt students to write a short profile of Charles de Gaulle using information from the chapter and additional source material. Suggest students focus on Charles de Gaulle's approach to French resistance during World War II. Invite students to read their profiles to the class.

DIFFERENTIATE

STRIVING READERS

Determine Strategies and Events Encourage students to work in pairs. First tell each student to read the lesson independently and take notes. Then have partners meet to identify and list the war strategies and major events discussed in the lesson for each of the following countries: Germany, Britain, France, and the United States.

PRE-AP

Atlantic Charter Feature Story Direct students to use print and online research to write a feature story about the Atlantic Charter. Ask students to include a summary and analysis of the aims, principles, and influence of the charter. Encourage students to include and assess the relationship between Franklin Roosevelt and Winston Churchill as they faced German aggression. Invite students to share their feature stories on a class blog or website.

See the Chapter Planner for more strategies for differentiation.

HISTORICAL THINKING

ANSWERS

1. Germany had mobilized 100 infantry divisions and 6 armored divisions, which included its fleet of panzers, and used the blitzkrieg to surprise and unsettle opponents.

2. By occupying the northern part of France, Germany was within close striking distance of Britain.

3. Answers will vary. Possible response: He underestimated the ingenuity, determination, and spirit of Britain and its people.

CRITICAL VIEWING Answers will vary. Possible response: It was intense and designed to cause as much damage and as many deaths as possible.

Japan's Rising Sun

On December 7, 1941, the unthinkable happened. Flying its flag, the "Rising Sun," Japan launched an unprovoked attack on the U.S. Navy, forcing the Americans to go to war.

A DAY OF INFAMY

President Franklin Roosevelt had watched Japan's aggression and expansion into China under its emperor, Hirohito, and prime minister, **Tojo Hideki**, with alarm. Tojo would go on to direct many of Japan's battles and essentially seize control of the country's government. Roosevelt's concern over Japanese expansionism increased after Japan joined Germany and Italy in the war.

In response, the president froze Japanese business assets in the United States in 1941. Roosevelt also placed an embargo on essential goods, such as oil, to Japan. A country of limited natural resources, Japan needed oil to ensure the continued growth of its industries and military. Many people believed war between the United States and Japan would erupt soon. But no one guessed the Japanese would be bold enough to strike Pearl Harbor, Hawaii, where the U.S. Pacific Fleet was headquartered.

Japan's military saw American power in the Pacific as an obstacle to its imperial designs and had planned the attack for months. On December 7, 1941, a large convoy of Japanese battleships, destroyers, aircraft carriers, and cruisers was within 200 miles of Pearl Harbor. Early that morning, Japanese bomber planes took off from the aircraft carriers. When military personnel at the U.S. naval base at Pearl Harbor detected the planes on their radar, they thought the bombers were American aircraft. And the Japanese had deliberately chosen a Sunday for their attack, when they believed security would be more relaxed.

Japanese soldiers charge into battle under the banner of the Rising Sun flag. The flag was first used by feudal Japanese warlords in the 1600s. Since Japan is often referred to as "the land of the rising sun," many Japanese view the flag as a symbol of their country.

The assault came in two waves as Japanese planes rained their bombs and bullets down on U.S. battleships and military aircraft. Nearly 20 American warships and about 200 planes were demolished or damaged. And more than 2,300 Americans were killed. The Japanese lost fewer than 100 men.

The next day, President Roosevelt addressed Congress and the American people by radio, saying, "Yesterday, December 7, 1941—a date which will live in infamy—the United States of America was suddenly and deliberately attacked by naval and air forces of the Empire of Japan." **Infamy** refers to an extremely shameful or evil act. Roosevelt called for a declaration of war, and Congress agreed. On December 8, Congress declared war on Japan. Three days later, Germany and Italy declared war on the United States. The United States joined the other Allied Powers in the fight against the Axis.

JAPANESE VICTORIES AND DEFEATS

Just hours after the attack on Pearl Harbor, Japan struck the Philippines, a U.S. territory at that time. Under the command of American general **Douglas MacArthur**, the U.S. Armed Forces in the Far East (USAFFE), which included many Filipino troops, had mobilized but were unprepared for a full-scale attack. The Japanese struck the Philippines by air and on land. By January 2, 1942, they had taken Manila, the country's capital. Unable to defend the territory, the USAFFE retreated to the jungles of the Bataan Peninsula. The crippled U.S. Navy was unable to provide backup. Eventually, 75,000 Filipino and American troops surrendered to the Japanese.

Allied soldiers captured by the Japanese were often horribly mistreated. After the USAFFE troops surrendered in the Philippines, the Japanese forced them to march about 60 miles to a prison camp with very little food or water. Those who fell, tried to escape, or stopped to drink from a puddle along the way were beaten, bayoneted, or shot. About 10,000 Filipinos and 750 Americans died in what became known as the **Bataan Death March**.

Meanwhile, Japan's imperial forces were expanding their control of the Pacific. By 1942, Japan had seized Korea, Taiwan, Hong Kong, French Indochina, Singapore, and the Dutch East Indies. The Japanese claimed they were liberating the European colonies. But economic reasons and imperialist ambitions were the real motivating factors.

In the summer of 1942, the Allies finally handed the Japanese a couple of major setbacks. Japanese forces wanted to take control of the sea route north of Australia so they could destroy U.S. naval bases along the nation's eastern coast. However, Allied code breakers had uncovered the plan and alerted U.S. officials. The Allies launched a preemptive strike and battled the Japanese by air and sea off the coast of New Guinea for several days in May during the Battle of the Coral Sea. Eventually, the Japanese fighters turned back.

Next, Japan intended to seize Midway Island, located 1,400 miles west of Hawaii, and destroy a U.S. carrier stationed there. Yet once again, code breakers discovered Japan's battle plans. The intelligence allowed the Allies to stay one step ahead of the Japanese. On June 3, U.S. bombers attacked the Japanese fleet when it was still 500 miles from Midway. Japan attacked Midway the following morning. The three-day-long **Battle of Midway** that ensued greatly reduced Japan's naval forces. The Allied victory marked a major turning point of the war in the Pacific.

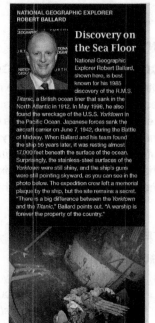

NATIONAL GEOGRAPHIC EXPLORER
ROBERT BALLARD

Discovery on the Sea Floor

National Geographic Explorer Robert Ballard, shown here, is best known for his 1985 discovery of the R.M.S. *Titanic*, a British ocean liner that sank in the North Atlantic in 1912. In May 1998, he also found the wreckage of the U.S.S. *Yorktown* in the Pacific Ocean. Japanese forces sank the aircraft carrier on June 7, 1942, during the Battle of Midway. When Ballard and his team found the ship 56 years later, it was resting almost 17,000 feet beneath the surface of the ocean. Surprisingly, the stainless-steel surfaces of the *Yorktown* were still shiny, and the ship's guns were still pointing skyward, as you can see in the photo below. The expedition crew left a memorial plaque by the ship, but the site remains a secret. "There is a big difference between the *Yorktown* and the *Titanic*," Ballard points out. "A warship is forever the property of the country."

HISTORICAL THINKING

1. **READING CHECK** What happened on December 7, 1941?

2. **MAKE PREDICTIONS** What might have happened if Allied code breakers hadn't uncovered Japan's plan to seize Midway Island?

3. **DRAW CONCLUSIONS** Why was the victory at the Battle of Midway a major turning point of the war in the Pacific?

PLAN: 2-PAGE LESSON

OBJECTIVE

Explain how Japan forced the United States to enter World War II.

CRITICAL THINKING SKILLS FOR LESSON 1.2

- Make Predictions
- Draw Conclusions
- Evaluate
- Analyze Cause and Effect
- Make Inferences

HISTORICAL THINKING FOR CHAPTER 27

How was World War II a total war?

Japan joined the Axis Powers to advance longstanding imperialist aims throughout the Pacific. Lesson 1.2 discusses the Pearl Harbor attack with a focus on efforts by U.S.-led Allied forces to halt Japan's expansion in the Pacific.

Student eEdition online

Additional content for this lesson, including a photo and a video, is available online.

BACKGROUND FOR THE TEACHER

Asia for the Asians In August 1940, Japan established the Greater East Asia Co-Prosperity Sphere. The slogan was "Asia for the Asians." The official purpose was to create a bloc of Asian nations, self-sufficient and free of Western powers. Instead, the alliance was a front for Japan's own imperialist ambitions. Japan wanted an empire such as the British had in Asia and such as Germany had begun carving out in Europe. Germany and Japan also shared similar beliefs of racial or cultural superiority over people of other nations. In November 1942, Japan established a Greater East Asia Ministry supposedly for a common good, but the aim was colonialism. Under the guise of liberating East Asia from the burden of British-American domination, and ensuring common prosperity, Japan created puppet governments. Thousands of Japanese officials traveled to East Asian nations. They oversaw local administrations and set up cultural programs slanted toward the interests of Japan. The Greater East Asia Co-Prosperity Sphere collapsed with Japan's defeat in World War II.

INTRODUCE & ENGAGE

DISCUSS NEUTRALITY

Prompt students to recall what they learned about the position of the United States as World War II began. Encourage discussion of the following questions: Could President Roosevelt aid the Allied Powers without entering the war? Should a nation remain neutral when its allies are attacked? What can force a nation to declare war? Then tell students that in this chapter they will learn how the United States joined the Allied Powers and fought against Japan in the Pacific.

TEACH

GUIDED DISCUSSION

1. **Evaluate** Why was striking the naval base at Pearl Harbor a strategic move for Japan? *(Possible response: Pearl Harbor was located in the Pacific far from the U.S. mainland and home to the U.S. Pacific Fleet. With the fleet destroyed, Japan could slow the Allied response in the Pacific.)*

2. **Analyze Cause and Effect** How did the attack on Pearl Harbor affect the results of Japan's attack on the Philippines? *(Because the Pearl Harbor attack had crippled the U.S. Pacific Fleet, the U.S. Navy was unable to provide backup to the soldiers in the Philippines. This contributed to the defeat of U.S. and Filipino troops.)*

MAKE INFERENCES

Direct students to the information about National Geographic Explorer Robert Ballard. **ASK:** Why do you think Ballard's expedition left a memorial plaque by the wreckage of the U.S.S. *Yorktown*? *(The ship contains the remains of its crew.)* What could happen if Ballard revealed the *Yorktown* site? *(Possible response: The ship could be subject to illegal salvage operations and looting.)*

ACTIVE OPTIONS

On Your Feet: Three-Step Interview Have students work in pairs to interview each other about World War II in the Pacific. Direct one student to interview the other by asking this question: What economic reasons and imperialist ambitions motivated Japan to attack Pearl Harbor? Then tell students to reverse roles, with the second student asking this question: What events enabled the Allies to turn the tide of the war against the Japanese? Finally, ask students to share information from the interviews with the class.

NG Learning Framework: Write a Report
SKILL Communication
KNOWLEDGE Our Human Story

After students watch the lesson video on Japanese soldiers, instruct them to research and write a report about the Bataan Death March using information from the chapter and additional source material such as, if available, the book *Ghost Soldiers* by Hampton Sides. Suggest that students focus on stories of Allied soldiers who survived the treatment by the Japanese soldiers. Invite students to share their reports with the class.

DIFFERENTIATE

ENGLISH LANGUAGE LEARNERS

Ask and Answer Questions Pair students at the **Beginning** level with students at the **Intermediate** or **Advanced** level and tell them to read the lesson together. Have them pause at the end of each paragraph and ask each other a *who, what, where, when,* or *why* question about what they have just read. Allow time for partners to provide answers.

PRE-AP

Investigate Historical Interpretations Explain to students that even today some historians still debate whether the United States provoked the attack on Pearl Harbor, and whether the president and other officials knew about the attack before it occurred. Ask students to conduct research to find out more about these varying historical interpretations. Then, to help flesh out the complexity of these issues, suggest that students hold a panel discussion. Encourage other students to ask questions and, as appropriate, add their views to the discussion.

See the Chapter Planner for more strategies for differentiation.

HISTORICAL THINKING

ANSWERS

1. Japan attacked Pearl Harbor, killing about 2,300 Americans and destroying or damaging about 20 American warships and 200 planes.

2. Japanese forces might have further crippled the U.S. Navy and moved closer to the mainland United States.

3. Answers will vary. Possible response: The Allied victory at Midway put a halt to Japan's plan to control the Pacific.

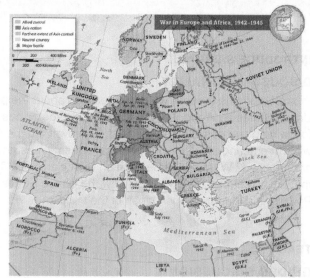

War in Europe and Africa, 1942–1945

Allied Momentum

When Napoleon invaded Russia in 1812, the campaign ended in disaster. Adolf Hitler hoped for a different outcome when his powerful German army marched into the Soviet Union. He didn't get one.

INVASION OF THE SOVIET UNION

As you've read, Adolf Hitler and Soviet leader Joseph Stalin signed a nonaggression pact in 1939. Hitler ended the pact between the two nations in June 1941, however, when his army invaded the Soviet Union. Stalin had asked the Allies to establish a front in western Europe to help his soldiers combat the Germans, but the Allies refused. The Soviet Union would bear the brunt of the German army alone.

More than three million German soldiers and 3,000 panzers plunged deep into Soviet territory at the beginning of the invasion known as Operation Barbarossa. But the Soviet forces, or Red Army, used a "scorched-earth" strategy as it retreated, destroying crops, bridges, and railroad cars. This meant that advancing German troops were left without shelter or additional food supplies as they advanced. Nonetheless, Hitler's soldiers pushed on. By mid-July, they were within a couple hundred miles of Moscow.

Over the next few months, an early and severe winter settled across the Soviet Union. Because they were running short of fuel, German commanders abandoned their plan to take Moscow and moved their troops south toward Soviet oil fields. As the German army pressed on, the troops suffered in the cold. By November 1941, about 700,000 Germans had died. Still, the German army continued to fight and managed to hold onto most of the ground it had captured earlier in the year. By the summer of 1942, Soviet casualties stood at about four million. The number of Germans who died or were wounded was high but not nearly as staggering.

The Soviets finally put an end to the German advance at the Battle of Stalingrad. (Stalingrad is now known as Volgograd.) About two million soldiers fought for nearly six months in the Soviet city. The two armies fought in the streets, causing high numbers of civilian casualties. When the German troops finally surrendered at the end of January 1943, the momentum of the entire European war shifted. Most historians regard the Battle of Stalingrad as the single most important Allied victory of World War II.

CAMPAIGNS IN NORTH AFRICA AND ITALY

While German forces were on the offensive in 1940 and 1941, Italy's Benito Mussolini was having a difficult time in the Mediterranean. Italy invaded Greece in October 1940, but the German army had to come to the aid of their fascist ally in 1941 when Greek partisans strongly resisted Italian forces. In Africa, Mussolini used his control over Libya and Ethiopia to invade British-controlled Egypt in 1940. After the British repelled that incursion, the Germans once again intervened the following year. However, the British beat the German army in Egypt at the Second Battle of El-Alamein in the fall of 1942. The victory marked the beginning of the end for the Axis Powers in North Africa and was another turning point for the Allies.

The United States now entered the North African theater when U.S. general **Dwight D. Eisenhower** led the Allied forces there in an invasion called Operation Torch in November 1942. By May 1943, American and British forces had recaptured Morocco and Algeria and defeated the German army. Vichy collaborators were replaced in North Africa by French officials loyal to Charles de Gaulle. As a result, his Free French army was now bolstered with North African recruits.

Once they were firmly established in North Africa, the Allied forces used it as a base of operations against Italy. In July 1943, the Allies began the Italian campaign by invading the island of Sicily and conquering it within about a month. As Italian troops fell back, the government in Rome arrested Mussolini. He managed to escape with German support but was eventually captured and executed by communist partisans. Fascism in Italy was over.

D-DAY AND THE BATTLE OF THE BULGE

Following these victories, the Allies were in a very strong position. At the end of 1943, Roosevelt, Churchill, and Stalin met in Tehran, Iran, to discuss plans to invade western Europe and take back France. British and Soviet troops had seized Iran in August 1941 in large part because the overland resupply routes there were critical to the war effort. After months of strategizing, General Eisenhower led an Allied invasion of the French coastal province of Normandy. On June 6, 1944, a fleet of warships and thousands of airplanes and naval vessels, called amphibious landing craft, headed toward five Normandy beaches. By sundown that day, which came to be known as **D-Day**, about 150,000 American, British, and Canadian troops had stormed the beaches.

Many troops drowned during the landing, and others were struck by German machine-gun fire as they set foot on the beaches. But Allied forces soon began to move inland. On August 19, Parisians, who were aware that the Allies would soon reach them, rose up against the occupying Germans. When the Allies arrived in Paris on August 25, the Nazis were ready to surrender.

In early September, the Allies advanced from northern France and recaptured Antwerp, Belgium. From there, they set off for the German border. But German forces had strengthened. In mid-December, more than 200,000 German soldiers advanced into southern Belgium, greatly outnumbering the Allied troops there, and broke through the Allied front line. This break in the front created a "bulge," which gave the battle its name: the **Battle of the Bulge**. Eisenhower called in reinforcements, and on December 26, the soldiers broke through German lines and captured the strategic Belgian town of Bastogne. Then in January 1945, thousands of Allied aircraft bombed the Germans and their supply lines, forcing the Nazis to withdraw.

PLAN: 4-PAGE LESSON

OBJECTIVE

Describe the Allied victories in Europe, Africa, and Asia that ended World War II.

CRITICAL THINKING SKILLS FOR LESSON 1.3

- Interpret Maps
- Identify Main Ideas and Details
- Draw Conclusions
- Evaluate
- Describe
- Make Inferences

HISTORICAL THINKING FOR CHAPTER 27

How was World War II a total war?

Axis invasions of the Soviet Union, North Africa, and the Pacific islands forced the Allies to engage in multiple battle zones. Lesson 1.3 discusses key figures, strategies, and battles in Europe and Asia that eventually ended World War II.

Student eEdition online

Additional content for this lesson, including an image and a diagram, is available online.

BACKGROUND FOR THE TEACHER

Hitler's Suicide Adolf Hitler committed suicide on April 30, 1945. Traditions of death before defeat might have been a factor. Another likely factor was an addiction to prescription drugs, which Hitler could no longer obtain. He was in his Berlin bunker as Soviet forces closed in. He had also just learned that Mussolini had been executed and his corpse put on public display and abused. To prepare for death, Hitler married his longtime companion Eva Braun and planned their joint suicide. He ordered staff to burn their bodies afterward and bury them to prevent public display. Soviet troops found the grave and identified Hitler's remains through dental records, saving the teeth. Instead of notifying the public, the Soviets fostered the belief that Hitler had escaped with help from the Americans or British. This deception linked the Allies to Nazism and led to decades of conspiracy theories that Hitler was still alive. The deception ended some 70 years later, when pathologists were allowed to examine the teeth and confirm that Hitler died in 1945.

INTRODUCE & ENGAGE

ACTIVATE PRIOR KNOWLEDGE

To help students understand the continuity of events in World War II, have them recall what they learned in the previous two lessons. Invite volunteers to identify the nations that formed the Allied and Axis powers. Ask students to discuss topics such as German aggression in Europe, Japan's motives to pursue war, and the attack that forced the United States to abandon a neutral position. Then tell students that in this lesson they will learn how Allied victories in separate parts of the world finally ended World War II.

TEACH

GUIDED DISCUSSION

1. **Evaluate** How did the outcome of Operation Torch justify the decision to invade Europe from North Africa instead of establishing a front in western Europe? *(Possible response: Britain and the United States succeeded in defeating the Germans in North Africa, securing a base from which the Allies could invade Italy.)*

2. **Describe** How did Allied and German military strategies lead to the Battle of the Bulge? *(Allied forces advanced from northern France after D-Day and recaptured Antwerp, Belgium, in early September. Then they headed for the German border. More than 200,000 German soldiers advanced into southern Belgium and attacked the Allied troops there, breaking through the Allied front line to create the "bulge.")*

INTERPRET MAPS

Direct students' attention to the map that shows areas controlled by Axis and Allied powers in Europe and North Africa. **ASK:** How does the map support the Allied strategy of staging a landing at Normandy? *(The beaches at Normandy were located approximately 150 miles from the coast of the United Kingdom, an Allied power.)*

DIFFERENTIATE

INCLUSION

Use Clarifying Questions Ask students to work with a partner who can read the lesson aloud to them. The proficient partner should interpret maps and photographs along with the reading. Encourage students to ask and answer clarifying questions about the maps, photographs, and accompanying text. Then instruct pairs to work together to answer the Historical Thinking questions.

GIFTED & TALENTED

Investigate News of the Day Instruct students to conduct online research to locate newspaper headlines, editorials, and political cartoons from the final year of the war. Have students work together to create a display of their findings. Challenge the class to make connections between the items on display and particular events mentioned in the lesson.

See the Chapter Planner for more strategies for differentiation.

Meanwhile, Soviet troops had moved across Poland toward Germany. Other Allied forces pressed east from France and Belgium, while those on the Italian Peninsula continued to push German troops north. To prepare for the ground-force invasion of Germany, the Allies intensified the aerial bombing of the country in February, targeting both industrial and civilian areas.

Soviet troops reached Berlin around mid-April. As they closed in on the underground bunker where Hitler was hiding, he committed suicide on April 30. Germany surrendered on May 8, 1945. The war in Europe was over. However, the war in the Pacific dragged on.

ISLAND HOPPING

After their victory at the Battle of Midway, the Allies went on the offensive to gain control of the Pacific. They used a two-pronged approach. Admiral Chester Nimitz of the U.S. Navy would travel west from Hawaii, and General Douglas MacArthur would travel north from Australia, both carrying out a campaign of **island hopping**. This strategy was designed to capture and control islands in the Pacific one by one. The Allies planned to establish bases on the islands to create a path to the Japanese homeland in preparation for an Allied attack on Japan.

The offensive began with an invasion of U.S. Marines on the island of Guadalcanal, where the Japanese were building an air base. By late 1942, each side had more than 20,000 troops engaged in battle on the small island. After six months of grueling combat, the Americans finally held Guadalcanal.

More Pacific victories soon followed for the Allies. By early 1944, Nimitz and MacArthur had taken control of the Marshall Islands and Guam. From there, the two commanders set their sights on the islands of Japan, only about 1,200 miles away.

By March 1945, the United States had reconquered the Philippines. The Japanese suffered heavy losses in the fighting, largely due to the use of suicide bomber pilots called **kamikaze**, meaning "divine wind." These Japanese pilots volunteered to crash their planes, loaded with explosives, into Allied ships. From October 1944 to the end of the war, the kamikaze destroyed 34 ships, but about 2,800 pilots died in the process.

The Allies were getting closer and closer to Japan. During the **Battle of Iwo Jima**, U.S. Marines were surprised by the fierce resistance of the Japanese soldiers, who fought from hidden caves and tunnels. In the American counterattack, nearly every Japanese soldier and civilian on the island perished. Fierce Japanese resistance also took place during the Battle of Okinawa, just 400 miles from Tokyo. Despite kamikaze air raids and artillery fire from Japanese troops deeply entrenched in concrete bunkers, the Allies prevailed.

VICTORY OVER JAPAN

Now Japan lay open to invasion. But an alternative plan presented itself to **Harry S. Truman**, who became president after Franklin Roosevelt's death in April 1945. Soon after taking office, Truman learned that Roosevelt had decided to have an atomic bomb built after he was advised the Nazis were building one themselves. An **atomic bomb** is a type of nuclear bomb whose violent explosion is triggered by splitting atoms and that releases intense heat and radioactivity. Truman was prepared to deploy it.

The American president warned Japan about the disaster that would befall if the nation refused to surrender. But for the Japanese, any surrender would be a great dishonor to their country. Finally, Truman decided that, although using atomic weapons would cause horrendous loss of life, it would also end the war more quickly and thereby save more lives in the long run. He had two Japanese cities bombed, Hiroshima on August 6, and Nagasaki on August 9. More than 200,000 people were killed in the bombings.

On August 15, Japan accepted the terms of surrender, and the war officially ended on September 2. The Allies occupied Japan, but Hirohito was allowed to remain in power to restore order. Tojo was not so fortunate—he was executed in 1948. World War II was over, and the Allies had won, but the human toll and destruction caused by the conflict were immense.

CRITICAL VIEWING Japanese pilots salute their commander before they take part in suicide attacks during the fighting in the Philippines. These pilots—and many others—had volunteered to crash their aircraft into enemy ships, mainly aircraft carriers. The tactic reflects the Japanese tradition of choosing death over defeat or capture. How do the pilots in the photo seem to be facing their imminent death?

An atomic bomb explodes over Nagasaki, Japan, on August 9, 1945. In addition to the deaths caused by the explosions in both Nagasaki and Hiroshima, tens of thousands more Japanese died from radiation sickness.

HISTORICAL THINKING

1. **READING CHECK** How did the Soviet army's scorched-earth strategy impact the German offensive?

2. **INTERPRET MAPS** Why was North Africa a logical choice as a base of operations against Italy?

3. **IDENTIFY MAIN IDEAS AND DETAILS** What was the ultimate goal of island hopping?

4. **DRAW CONCLUSIONS** Why did President Truman warn Japan ahead of time about the destruction the atomic bombs would cause?

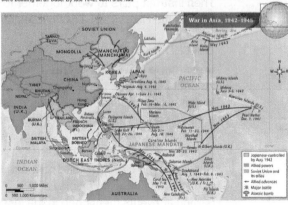

War in Asia, 1942–1945

BACKGROUND FOR THE TEACHER

The Manhattan Project In August 1939, President Franklin Roosevelt received a letter from Albert Einstein, renowned Nobel laureate. Einstein wrote at the urging of some American scientists who believed that Nazi Germany was trying to develop an atomic weapon—and Adolf Hitler would use it, Einstein warned the president. In October 1939, President Roosevelt authorized a study on the feasibility of inventing atomic weapons. Preliminary research proved that fission—atom-splitting—chain reactions could generate power. In August 1942, the Manhattan Project began as a federally funded research program to develop an atomic bomb. U.S. Army Brigadier General Leslie Groves, initially in charge, code-named the project *Manhattan* for the New York City borough where the first offices were located. Actual bomb development took place at various sites, mostly Hanford, Washington; Oak Ridge, Tennessee; and Los Alamos, New Mexico. General Groves charged J. Robert Oppenheimer, director of the Los Alamos Laboratory, with research and design. Oppenheimer has often been called the "father of the atomic bomb." Among many scientists on the project were Ernest O. Lawrence, Enrico Fermi, and Leo Szilard. Lawrence held many project positions. Fermi and Szilard had conducted preliminary research, first at Columbia University and later at the University of Chicago. Their team, which included Arthur H. Compton, developed the first self-sustaining nuclear reaction. Leo Szilard, a Hungarian physicist, left Europe when the Nazis came to power. He helped draft the Einstein letter that started the project.

TEACH

GUIDED DISCUSSION

3. **Identify Main Ideas and Details** What was the Allied two-pronged approach in the Pacific, and how was it implemented? *(U.S. Navy Admiral Nimitz would travel west from Hawaii, while U.S. General MacArthur would travel north from Australia. Their forces would capture islands in the Pacific, one by one, to establish military bases and carve out a path to Japan.)*

4. **Make Inferences** How did Japanese traditions affect the way Japan responded in later stages of the war? *(Japanese traditions called for death over defeat or capture. This explains the strategy of kamikaze air raids and fierce Japanese fighting at Iwo Jima and Okinawa. The tradition that surrender would dishonor the country and its emperor could explain Japan's refusal to heed President Truman's warning of an atomic bomb attack.)*

INTERPRET MAPS

Have students carefully study the map titled War in Asia, 1942–1945. **ASK:** How does the map help explain the fierce Japanese resistance at Iwo Jima and Okinawa? *(The two islands are located closest to the Japanese mainland. Loss of the islands would allow the Allies to establish military bases close enough to attack Japan directly.)*

ACTIVE OPTIONS

On Your Feet: Fishbowl Point out that the Allies had to mobilize for a two-front war, one in Europe and North Africa and the other in the Pacific. Arrange students in a fishbowl configuration. Assign the inner circle this question to discuss: How did the Allies fight differently on the North African European front versus on the Pacific front? Prompt students to identify the strategies and key battles as they discuss the question. Have students in the outside circle listen and take notes. After several minutes, have the circles change positions and restart the discussion.

 NG Learning Framework: Profile a Commander
 ATTITUDE Empowerment
 SKILL Problem-Solving

Instruct students to research and write a short biography or profile of Dwight D. Eisenhower using information from the chapter and additional source material. Suggest that students focus on Eisenhower's role as supreme commander of the Allied forces in World War II and his ability to solve problems facing the Allies. Invite students to share their profiles with the class.

HISTORICAL THINKING

ANSWERS

1. The Red Army destroyed crops, bridges, and railroad cars, leaving German troops without shelter and food, which impacted them negatively, especially when an early and severe winter set in on them.

2. Sicily, which is part of Italy, is only about 150 miles from North Africa's coast.

3. The ultimate goal was for the Allied forces to get close enough to Japan to stage an attack on the nation.

4. Answers will vary. Possible response: He hoped the warning would persuade the Japanese to surrender.

CRITICAL VIEWING Answers will vary. Possible response: They seem unemotional, resolute, prepared to lose their lives for Japan.

Travelers: Nancy Wake 1912–2011 and Josephine Baker 1906–1975
French Resistance Fighters

War can produce unlikely heroes. Before World War II, Nancy Wake and Josephine Baker moved to France looking for adventure, fame, and fun. After the war started, they risked their lives to spy for the Allies.

THE WHITE MOUSE

Earlier in this chapter, you read about French general Charles de Gaulle, who left German-occupied France and established a resistance force in London. From this base, de Gaulle recruited an army of volunteers to liberate France. His resistance movement and other anti-German movements that operated underground in France are often collectively referred to as the French Resistance.

Australian Nancy Wake did not set out to be a resistance fighter. As a child, she dreamed of seeing the world. When she settled in Paris as a journalist in 1934, Wake was more interested in parties than politics. However, her attitude changed during a trip to Vienna, Austria, when she witnessed Jews being publicly beaten by a group of Nazis. After that episode, she resolved to "do anything, however big or small, stupid or dangerous" to oppose the Nazi Party. In 1939, Wake married a wealthy French businessman and continued to enjoy her life in France. But she and many of her friends believed war with Germany was inevitable.

The German invasion of Poland in 1939 confirmed their fears. Six months after the invasion of France in 1940, Wake joined the resistance. She began serving as a courier, passing messages and helping resistance fighters escape from the Nazis and French collaborators, or traitors. Wake also assisted in the escape of Allied soldiers and Jewish refugees from France into neutral Spain. Nazi Germany's secret police, the Gestapo, called her "the White Mouse" for her ability to evade capture.

Nancy Wake wrote about her experiences as a resistance agent in *The Autobiography of the Woman the Gestapo Called the White Mouse*. In this excerpt from the book, Wake describes her appearance and her feelings just before she parachutes into France.

PRIMARY SOURCE

Huddled in the belly of the bomber, airsick and vomiting, I was hardly Hollywood's idea of a glamorous spy. I probably looked grotesque. Over civilian clothes, silk-stockinged and high-heeled, I wore overalls, [and] carried revolvers in the pockets. . . . Even more incongruous [odd] was the matronly handbag [a large, plain purse], full of cash and secret instructions for D-Day. . . . But I'd spent years in France working as an escape courier . . . and I was desperate to return to France and continue working against Hitler. Neither airsickness nor looking like a clumsily wrapped parcel was going to deter me.

—from *The Autobiography of the Woman the Gestapo Called the White Mouse* by Nancy Wake, 1985

As pressure from the Gestapo mounted, Wake hiked over the Pyrenees Mountains into Spain in 1943. From there she traveled to England where she was trained in special intelligence operations. In April 1944, along with other resistance agents, Wake parachuted into central France behind German lines to help with preparations for D-Day. Among other tasks, she hid weapons and ammunition dropped by parachute for the advancing Allied armies. Wake reached Paris just as Allied forces liberated the city on August 25.

After World War II ended, Wake became the most decorated woman of the war. From Britain, she received the George Medal; from France, the Legion of Honor, the Croix de Guerre (War Cross), and the Resistance Medal; and from the United States, the Medal of Freedom.

774 CHAPTER 27

Nancy Wake's and Josephine Baker's Journeys, 1942–1944

DANCER, SINGER, SOLDIER, SPY

Like Wake, American Josephine Baker moved to Paris when she was a young woman. She moved, in part, to escape the racism she had experienced as an African American. Baker was already a well-known dancer in the United States, but in 1925, she was offered twice as much money to perform in Paris. Her singing, dancing, and outrageous costumes soon made her one of the most popular entertainers in France. In 1937, she became a French citizen.

After World War II began and Germany occupied France, Baker added to her accomplishments. She worked for the Red Cross, where she aided Belgian refugees, and served as a sub-lieutenant in the French Women's Auxiliary Air Force. Baker also became a spy for the French Resistance. As a celebrity, Baker was often invited to perform at embassy parties attended by high-ranking Axis officials and diplomats. Always charming, she coaxed secret military information from the guests and then passed it along to leaders of the resistance.

Because Nazi authorities considered Baker to be a harmless entertainer, she was allowed to travel outside of France to entertain troops in its colonies in North Africa. She also traveled in other parts of Europe where she met with Allied agents and passed them notes describing Nazi activities in France. The notes were written on her sheet music—in invisible ink. Sometimes Baker also smuggled photos of German military installations out of France by pinning them to her underwear.

At the end of the war, General de Gaulle awarded Baker the Croix de Guerre and the Legion of Honor with the Resistance Medal. She was the first American-born woman to receive these honors.

HISTORICAL THINKING

1. **READING CHECK** What did Nancy Wake do soon after Germany invaded France?

2. **ANALYZE SOURCES** Why do you think Wake was wearing civilian clothes and high-heeled shoes and carrying a purse when she parachuted into France?

3. **COMPARE AND CONTRAST** How were the lives of Nancy Wake and Josephine Baker similar?

The Second World War 775

PLAN: 2-PAGE LESSON

OBJECTIVE

Describe how Nancy Wake and Josephine Baker worked as agents to free France and fight Nazi Germany.

CRITICAL THINKING SKILLS FOR LESSON 2.1

- Analyze Sources
- Compare and Contrast
- Make Inferences

HISTORICAL THINKING FOR CHAPTER 27
How was World War II a total war?

Although often less recognized than men for their service, women critically aided the Allied Powers. Lesson 2.1 focuses on the work of Nancy Wake and Josephine Baker as agents in the French resistance and spies for the Allies.

Student eEdition online

Additional content for this lesson, including a photograph, is available online.

BACKGROUND FOR THE TEACHER

Josephine Baker Freda Josephine McDonald Baker was born into poverty in St. Louis, Missouri, in 1906. She worked from childhood at odd jobs, dancing for panhandling money, waiting tables, and touring with musical groups. She moved to New York in 1921 and danced in the African-American musical *Shuffle Along*. Her move to Paris in 1925 brought her lasting acclaim in Europe. Josephine Baker performed in French theater and film before and after World War II. Rampant segregation and racist audiences thwarted her attempts to perform in the United States. She settled on her French estate and adopted children of various ethnicities, calling them her "rainbow tribe," living proof that racial differences did not matter. She continued to visit the United States to support the civil rights movement. For her vigorous activism, the National Association for the Advancement of Colored People named May 20 Josephine Baker Day. Josephine Baker performed in Paris to a sold-out audience days before she died in 1975. The French government honored her with a state funeral.

History Notebook

Encourage students to complete the Traveler page for Chapter 27 in their History Notebooks as they read.

INTRODUCE & ENGAGE

WOMEN'S WARTIME ROLES

Direct students to look at the photographs in the lesson. Prompt students to recall what they already know about the status of women in the mid-20th century. Then ask students to discuss how the women in the photographs might have challenged traditional expectations for women at that time. Tell students that in this lesson they will learn about the remarkable activities of two women who helped the Allies defeat Nazi Germany.

TEACH

GUIDED DISCUSSION

1. **Compare and Contrast** Why did the Nazis allow Josephine Baker to travel freely in their occupied territories outside of France, whereas Nancy Wake faced capture? (*The Nazis believed Josephine Baker to be a harmless entertainer, whereas the German Gestapo had identified Nancy Wake as a resistance fighter.*)

2. **Make Inferences** Why do you think Nancy Wake received the Medal of Freedom from the United States but Josephine Baker did not? (*Answers will vary. Possible response: Nancy Wake was "the White Mouse," but Josephine Baker was an African American who left the United States, which might have prevented full recognition of her service.*)

ANALYZE SOURCES

Direct students' attention to the primary source feature from Nancy Wake's autobiography. **ASK:** What point was Nancy Wake making when she wrote, "I was hardly Hollywood's idea of a glamorous spy"? (*Possible response: She was suggesting that films glamorize war and spies.*) What does the excerpt convey about Nancy Wake's expectations for women? (*Possible response: She expected women to fulfill critical roles.*)

ACTIVE OPTIONS

On Your Feet: Think, Pair, Share Give students a few minutes to think about the following question: What kinds of training prepared Nancy Wake and Josephine Baker to spy for the Allies? Then have students choose partners and talk about the topic for five minutes. Finally, allow individual students to share their ideas with the class.

| **NG Learning Framework: Write a Biography**
| **ATTITUDE** Responsibility
| **SKILL** Communication

Instruct students to research and write a short biography of Nancy Wake or Josephine Baker that reveals information not included in the lesson. Encourage them to use online and print sources. Suggest that students focus on aspects of Wake's or Baker's life that might have prepared her for the mission she set for herself and the responsibility she felt to help her country. Remind students to communicate facts correctly and without bias. Invite students to post their biographies for the class to read.

DIFFERENTIATE

STRIVING READERS

Summarize Using a Web Have pairs summarize information by creating a Concept Web for each woman discussed in the lesson. Tell them to place the name of the woman in the center. As students read each section, ask them to record key achievements on the spokes. After students complete their Webs, invite volunteers to summarize each woman's achievements.

GIFTED & TALENTED

Research and Report Instruct students to conduct online research to locate information on two additional women who spied or assisted the Allies in World War II. Have students work together to prepare a report on their findings. Suggest they include photographs or other illustrations in their report. Encourage students to compare their subjects with the women discussed in the lesson. Invite students to share their reports with the class.

See the Chapter Planner for more strategies for differentiation.

HISTORICAL THINKING

ANSWERS

1. She joined the resistance, passed messages, and helped in the escape of resistance fighters, Allied soldiers, and Jewish refugees.

2. The clothing and purse were intended to serve as a disguise so that she would look like any other French woman.

3. Answers will vary. Possible response: Both women moved to Paris when they were fairly young; both worked for the French Resistance, carrying messages; both moved in the upper circles of French society; both served as spies; both were honored for their wartime work.

Wartime Preparations and Policies

Total war demands total commitment from the people caught up in the conflict. Nations all over the world mobilized for the fight. Those on the war front as well as on the home front would contribute to the effort.

THE WAR EFFORT

World War II required a massive buildup of resources. Many of the Allied Powers drafted colonial subjects to help in the war effort. The British mobilized over two million Indian soldiers to fight the Axis Powers in Europe and Asia. But these numbers were not enough. The United States and Britain supplied the Nationalist government of China with weapons along the Burma Road in Burma, present-day Myanmar, but the supply route was seized by Japan in 1942. To launch a counterattack against the Japanese, the British recruited soldiers from their African colonies, including Nigeria and Kenya, and sent them to fight in the jungles of Burma. By defending Burma, the British were also seeking to secure the borders of nearby India. The Burma Road was finally reopened in early 1945.

As you know, France had a long history of recruiting African soldiers into its armies. When France came under the control of the Germans and the Vichy government, the first Free French outpost was established in French Equatorial Africa. After the Allies took North Africa back from Germany, African troops were once again conscripted in large numbers. In fact, almost half of the Allied soldiers who liberated France in 1943 and 1944 came from French colonies such as Morocco, Algeria, and Senegal.

Millions of men volunteered for military service in the United States, including many from minority groups. These soldiers were placed in segregated troops. Nevertheless, they served with valor and distinction. The Tuskegee Airmen, a squadron of African-American pilots, shot down a dozen Nazi planes during an invasion in Italy in 1943. The 442nd Regimental

Total war required the complete mobilization of civilian populations beyond a nation's military. Traditional gender roles were transformed as female factory workers replaced departed servicemen. In this photo, a British worker finalizes the assembly of the nose cone of a bomber in 1943.

Combat Team, a military unit that consisted entirely of Japanese Americans, fought in Europe in 1944 and rescued a regiment of Texas soldiers surrounded by German forces.

People at home also contributed to the war effort. When men in the United States and Britain left their jobs to fight in the war, for instance, women filled their places in factories and offices. And many of these women worked in the defense industries to produce airplanes, weapons, and ammunition. In the Soviet Union, women not only worked on the home front but some also took up arms to resist the Nazi invasion.

To help pay for the high cost of war, free markets were often controlled. In Britain, the government took over the economy and allocated resources for the military. Few consumer goods were produced, and a rationing system limited each family's supply of bread, milk, eggs, sugar, and meat. Still, the British largely accepted such sacrifices as a necessary price to defeat Hitler.

LIMITED FREEDOMS

You may recall that many governments put restraints on civil liberties during World War I. The same thing happened in World War II. In the United States, thousands of Japanese Americans were relocated and sent to internment camps in military zones, where they lived in prison-like surroundings until the war's end. In the Soviet Union, Joseph Stalin squashed whatever freedom his people had enjoyed before the war. Still, during the Great Patriotic Fatherland War, as they called World War II, the Soviet people banded together as never before and conferred on Stalin a near god-like status.

Britain also curtailed the freedom of local governments in colonial countries. Although Egypt had been given the basic right to govern itself, Britain still had troops stationed there. In the Suez Canal zone. The British used those forces to defend Egypt from Italian invasion. However, they did not clear these actions with the Egyptian government first. Offended Egyptian protesters filled the streets of Cairo.

The wartime situation was equally tense in India. As you've read, millions of Indian soldiers aided the Allied cause, but the Indian National Congress refused to

Indian army troops march in formation in 1942.

cooperate. As in Egypt, the British had declared war against the Axis on behalf of India without consulting Indian political leaders. Indian activist Mohandas Gandhi responded with a "Quit India" campaign, calling for the British to leave India.

In Italy and Germany, Mussolini and Hitler eliminated independent social organizations. Strict controls were placed on Catholic and Protestant churches to make sure they adhered to fascist policy. While some Christians obeyed, others remained defiant and held fast to their principles. Some European Jews owed their lives to the courageous help of their Christian neighbors.

Both Allied and Axis powers tried to control public opinion through propaganda and media censorship. Racist imagery was often used to justify military policy. Americans saw stereotypical images of the Japanese, while Japanese children were told they were racially superior to all other Asians. Nazi propaganda focused on the "decadence" of the United States and its racial diversity, which was seen as a weakness.

HISTORICAL THINKING

1. **READING CHECK** How did people in British and French colonies help the Allied war effort?

2. **MAKE INFERENCES** Why do you think Japanese Americans wanted to fight in World War II?

3. **DRAW CONCLUSIONS** Why did the Indian and Egyptian people object when Britain declared war against the Axis on their behalf without consulting their leaders?

PLAN: 2-PAGE LESSON

OBJECTIVE

Identify the war efforts of all nations that sometimes cost citizens their civil liberties.

CRITICAL THINKING SKILLS FOR LESSON 2.2

- Make Inferences
- Draw Conclusions
- Explain
- Integrate Visuals

HISTORICAL THINKING FOR CHAPTER 27

How was World War II a total war?

World War II demanded the total commitment of civilians to support military forces. Lesson 2.2 discusses the mobilization of people of all nations and ethnicities with a focus on policies that impacted civil liberties.

BACKGROUND FOR THE TEACHER

Rosie the Riveter American women joined the workforce in huge numbers during World War II, filling jobs thought to be men's domain. Women worked not only in factories and munitions plants but as code breakers and scientists on the Manhattan Project. To meet growing war demands, the U.S. government waged a campaign to recruit women. The Rosie the Riveter icon emerged from that effort. Rosie inspired a hit song of the 1940s. A popular Norman Rockwell painting portrayed Rosie as a sturdy woman on a lunch break, a rivet gun in her lap and a copy of Hitler's *Mein Kampf* placed contemptuously underfoot. The *Saturday Evening Post* published the painting on the cover of a 1943 issue. A poster by artist J. Howard Miller, displayed briefly at Westinghouse factories, showed Rosie close up wearing a red-and-white bandanna, flexing her arm and exclaiming, "We can do it!" Years after World War II ended, activists rediscovered the image. Rosie the Riveter has become a symbol of the movement for women's rights.

INTRODUCE & ENGAGE

CONSIDER THE CONSEQUENCES

Ask students to consider how fear can result in the public and government singling out certain groups for suspicion or segregation. Discuss what consequences could result for these groups of people. Record students' ideas on the board. Tell students that in this lesson they will learn about the wartime efforts of nations during World War II that sometimes resulted in discriminatory policies or the loss of civil liberties.

TEACH

GUIDED DISCUSSION

1. **Explain** What explains the mobilization of soldiers from countries that were not actual Allied Powers? *(Britain and France had colonial subjects in many areas in Africa. Britain also had colonial subjects in India.)*

2. **Draw Conclusions** Given the segregation of African-American troops, why might the Tuskegee Airmen have wanted to serve the United States with distinction? *(Answers will vary. Possible response: They were as loyal and capable as any U.S. servicemen, and they hoped their excellence would help raise public awareness of the injustices of racism and segregation.)*

INTEGRATE VISUALS

Prompt students to view the image of the British worker assembling the nose cone of a bomber. **ASK:** How does the image reflect the lesson's main idea? *(Possible response: The image confirms that civilians, including women, gave up their usual jobs and traditional roles to support their nation's military.)*

ACTIVE OPTIONS

On Your Feet: Roundtable Organize students into four groups. Tell students to imagine that they are wartime journalists working on a news story about the curtailment of civil liberties in World War II. Have groups begin the article with an attention-grabbing headline. Ask one student in each group to write the first sentence of the article. Other students can then take turns adding sentences. Groups should continue adding sentences until they feel the article is thorough. Invite groups to share the articles.

> **NG Learning Framework: Explore War Propaganda**
> **ATTITUDE** Curiosity
> **KNOWLEDGE** Our Human Story

Share the Background for the Teacher content with students. Explain that the Rosie image is an example of propaganda—forms of communication that spread information for the purpose of furthering a particular cause. Point out that both sides used propaganda of varying types during World War II. Ask students to conduct online research to locate several examples of propaganda created by each side. Have students share their findings and discuss the purpose of each example.

DIFFERENTIATE

ENGLISH LANGUAGE LEARNERS

Identify Main Ideas and Details Help students sort through the mixture of ideas and nations named in the lesson. Pair students at the **Beginning** and **Intermediate** levels with students at the **Advanced** level. Tell students to take turns reading, pausing after each paragraph to record relevant details. Then have pairs work together to write a main idea about the details. Ask pairs to share their results.

PRE-AP

Write a Report Instruct students to conduct research to learn about the experiences of a specific American of Japanese ancestry who was interned during the war. Have students use what they learn to write a report about a person that focuses on how Executive Order 9066 impacted the person's life. One group might choose to explore *Korematsu* v. *United States* and report on the particulars of the case. Invite volunteers to read their reports to the class.

See the Chapter Planner for more strategies for differentiation.

HISTORICAL THINKING

ANSWERS

1. Soldiers were drafted from these colonies to fight against the Axis Powers.

2. Answers will vary. Possible response: They wanted to show, in spite of their internment, that they were loyal Americans.

3. Answers will vary. Possible response: They objected because they wanted to assert and hold onto what little autonomy they possessed.

Civilians, Technology, and the War's Toll

Soldiers aren't the only casualties of war. Civilians, caught in the crossfire, have always died in conflicts. But World War II introduced a whole new dimension to this killing. New weapons and technology allowed both sides to inflict severe tolls on civilian populations.

In the Pacific war, the Allies used several Native American languages as wartime codes. Recruits speaking the Navajo language, like those in this photo, were the largest group of Code Talkers, as they came to be called.

TARGETING CIVILIANS

The targeting of civilians was a tactic adopted by both Axis and Allied powers. One of the worst examples was the Siege of Leningrad in the Soviet Union. Between 1941 and 1944, the German army surrounded the city and prevented supplies from reaching the starving residents. An estimated one million people died before the city was liberated.

Both Japan and Germany used slave labor. The Japanese forced hundreds of thousands of Koreans to toil in terrible conditions. In Vietnam, the Japanese occupiers worked the local population so hard and left them with so little food that as many as one million people died during a famine in 1945. Of course, the Nazis were notorious for their harsh treatment. With many of their men off to fight, they forced Poles and Russians to perform menial work.

As you know, Germany mainly targeted British civilians during the Blitz. Later on, the Allies used their bombers to attack Japanese and German cities. First, Allied bombers focused on military and industrial targets. Then in 1945, the Allies used napalm firebombs against Japan. **Napalm** is a highly flammable, jelly-like substance that sticks to targets and generates extreme heat. The first of these firebombs was dropped on Tokyo and destroyed 25 percent of the city's buildings and killed tens of thousands of its people. Around the same time, the Allies also used napalm in the firebombing of Dresden, Germany, in which an estimated 25,000–35,000 civilians died.

778 CHAPTER 27

TECHNOLOGY OF WAR

After the United States entered World War II, President Franklin Roosevelt stated, "This war is a new kind of war. . . . It is warfare in terms of every continent, every island, every sea, every air lane in the world." From the beginning, technology developed to meet the demands of the war. Soldiers used tanks, airplanes, and submarines more extensively than in World War I.

While the tanks used by the Allied and German forces in Europe and North Africa often determined the outcome of land battles, success at sea depended on new technology such as **depth charges**, underwater bombs that are programmed to explode at certain depths. By mid-1943, the German submarine threat in the Atlantic had been neutralized.

Knowledge of the enemy's position was key in battle. The Allies used radar to locate German and Japanese ships and airplanes. They also tried to decode

enemy intelligence. The Germans sent coded naval communications—on a device called the Enigma machine—about the movements of their submarines. If the Allies could understand these messages, they could direct their fleets away from German torpedoes. By 1940, a British mathematician named Alan Turing had designed a machine called the Bombe that could crack the code used in messages sent by the Enigma machine. The Bombe would help decode intercepted enemy messages for the remainder of the war.

The Allies devised codes of their own. In 1942, the U.S. Marines began using a secret code that relied on speakers of the Navajo language. Code Talkers sent and received messages rapidly over open radio channels. Enemy listeners could hear them, but they could not decode the language. In the Pacific, the Navajo Code Talkers were instrumental in several Allied victories.

THE HUMAN TOLL

Overall, historians estimate that 60 million, or three percent of the world's population, died as a result of the war. This toll includes a large casualty rate among civilians. The Soviet Union is believed to have suffered the most civilian deaths at an estimated 19 million, followed by China, with as many as 10 million. A total of about 17 million soldiers died in World War II.

The war also inflicted terrible damage on cities, particularly in Japan and Germany, where houses, factories, and transportation and communication systems were destroyed by bombs. After the war, millions of starving and homeless people were left to wander through the ruins. The financial cost of the war was immense. Economists estimate that it reached approximately $1 trillion in 1945 dollars, with the United States spending the most at about $300 billion.

As terrible as the death toll of World War II was, even more deaths remained to be discovered. Toward the close of the war, the Allies confronted murder of civilians on a scale never seen before.

COMFORT WOMEN The Japanese forced some female civilians to live under conditions of sexual slavery during the war. Known as "comfort women," these women provided sexual services to improve the morale of Japanese troops. At least 200,000 women—mostly from Korea, Taiwan, and the Philippines—were held against their will in so-called comfort stations located in Japan and all Japanese-occupied areas. Women who resisted were often beaten or murdered.

NATIONAL GEOGRAPHIC EXPLORER
ARI BESER

The Survivors' Side of the Story

National Geographic Explorer Ari Beser has a unique connection to the bombs that fell on Hiroshima and Nagasaki. His grandfather was the only U.S. serviceman to fly on both bombing missions. Beser's research began in 2011 but culminated in a 2015 Fulbright-National Geographic Storytelling Fellowship that allowed him to travel to Japan and visit with some of those who survived the bombings. The experience helped him understand that all stories have more than one point of view. Ever since, he has been sharing both American and Japanese stories of the bombings to promote reconciliation and nuclear disarmament. As Beser says, "I believe it is crucial to our understanding and our future as a functioning society that we take a step back and look objectively at each side." In the photo above, Ari Beser (far left) poses with Clifton Truman Daniel (far right), grandson of President Truman. They are joined by survivors of the bombs and their family members in Hiroshima.

HISTORICAL THINKING

1. **READING CHECK** What happened at the Siege of Leningrad?

2. **MAKE INFERENCES** Why do you think more soldiers and civilians were killed in the Soviet Union than in any other country?

3. **SYNTHESIZE** Why was the death toll so high in World War II?

The Second World War 779

PLAN: 2-PAGE LESSON

OBJECTIVE

Describe the attacks on civilians and war machinery that took a toll on the global population.

CRITICAL THINKING SKILLS FOR LESSON 2.3

• Make Inferences
• Synthesize
• Summarize
• Draw Conclusions
• Analyze Visuals

HISTORICAL THINKING FOR CHAPTER 27

How was World War II a total war?

The war proceeded with technological advances of an unprecedented kind. Lesson 2.3 discusses the new technology of war with a special focus on the impact to civilians.

Student eEdition online

Additional content for this lesson, including a photograph and a diagram, is available online.

BACKGROUND FOR THE TEACHER

Navajo Code Talkers The U.S. Marine Corps knew they needed a solution when they realized that the Japanese were intercepting and deciphering their messages. A World War I veteran named Philip Johnston had grown up on a Navajo reservation where his parents were missionaries. He suggested that the Marines develop a code based on the Navajo language. The Marines launched the project in 1942 with 29 Navajo recruits. The Navajo language is complex, tonal, and almost entirely oral, which meant that code breakers could not find written definitions for words. The code team devised a system of word substitutions in which a different Navajo word would stand for each letter of the English alphabet. To avoid spelling out every word, commonly used military terms were assigned their own Navajo words. To prepare the recruits to transmit and translate encrypted messages, the recruits underwent extensive training. They had to learn to operate communications equipment and memorize the code perfectly. The Navajo Code Talkers were unknown until 1968, when their work was declassified.

INTRODUCE & ENGAGE

BRAINSTORM MILITARY STRATEGY

Explain to students that casualties among civilian populations were unprecedented during World War II. Ask volunteers to suggest reasons for this, and whether military gains can be made without targeting civilians. *(Possible response: Most people live in cities, and cities support military forces. When bombing these sites, civilian casualties seem inevitable.)* Tell students that in this lesson they will learn about new technology that had disastrous effects not only on troops but on millions of civilians.

TEACH

GUIDED DISCUSSION

1. **Summarize** How did napalm help the Allied war effort, and where was it used? *(Napalm allowed Allied forces to firebomb and severely damage Tokyo and Dresden.)*

2. **Draw Conclusions** What did the wartime use of slave labor by Germany and Japan suggest about these countries? *(Possible response: These countries likely faced dwindling resources during the war. With many citizens off fighting, both countries had far fewer workers and Allied attacks reduced populations.)*

ANALYZE VISUALS

Direct students to examine the Antisubmarine Technology diagram (available in the Student eEdition). **ASK:** How did the invention of depth charges help neutralize the threat of German submarines? *(The depth charges damaged submarines, forcing them to rise to the water's surface where naval gunners destroyed them. This technology reduced the number of German submarines.)*

ACTIVE OPTIONS

On Your Feet: Numbered Heads Organize students into groups of four and instruct members to number off from one to four. Ask each group to think about and discuss a response to the following question: Was new technology the determining factor in the toll inflicted on global populations during World War II? After a time, call out a number and have the student with that number report for the group.

> **NG Learning Framework: Understand a Different Point of View**
> SKILL Communication
> KNOWLEDGE Our Human Story

Point out the photo of National Geographic Explorer Ari Beser and explain that two of the people pictured are the brother and nephew of Sadako Sasaki, who died of leukemia at the age of 10 in 1955 as a result of radiation from the atomic bomb dropped on Hiroshima. Have pairs of students research the life and legacy of Sadako Sasaki and/or read the book *Sadako and the Thousand Paper Cranes* by Eleanor Coerr. Then, as a class, discuss the bombing based on Sadako's point of view and how this knowledge helps students understand the bigger picture.

DIFFERENTIATE

INCLUSION

Interpret Diagrams and Photographs Pair special-needs students with proficient readers who can help them describe the diagram (available in the Student eEdition) and photographs. Encourage pairs to relate the diagram and photographs to the main text. Coach special-needs students to ask questions about words or concepts that are confusing and their partners to answer the questions.

PRE-AP

Hold a Roundtable Discussion Assign students to read National Geographic Explorer Ari Beser's book *The Nuclear Family*, which tells the stories of *hibakusha*, Japanese survivors affected by the atomic bombs and the radiation they released. Have students hold a roundtable discussion in which they discuss the bombings and whether there can ever be a resolution between the American and Japanese points of view.

See the Chapter Planner for more strategies for differentiation.

HISTORICAL THINKING

ANSWERS

1. Between 1941 and 1944, the German army surrounded the city and prevented supplies from reaching the starving population. An estimated 1 million people died.

2. Answers will vary. Possible response: Long and terrible battles were fought on Soviet soil.

3. Answers will vary. Possible response: The death toll in World War II was high because it was fought in Europe, Asia, Africa, and the Pacific. New weapons technology made the war deadlier than any before.

CRITICAL VIEWING Answers will vary. Possible response: Dresden was almost totally destroyed and reduced to rubble.

"The Final Solution"

People in the Allied nations knew about Adolf Hitler's hatred of the Jews, but few grasped the full extent of his anti-Semitic fervor. After the war in Europe was over, the world learned what the Nazis were capable of.

CRITICAL VIEWING The Nazi plan for the mass killing of Jews included imprisoning them in concentration camps. This 2004 photo shows the train tracks leading to Auschwitz, the most notorious camp. Zyklon B, the poison gas used to murder Jews, was first tested there. Why do you think the Nazis built this concentration camp in such an isolated area?

PERSECUTION OF THE JEWS

When the Allies invaded Germany and Poland in the spring of 1945, they encountered scenes of horror: concentration camps full of starving and dying prisoners. Most were Jews, but there were also non-Jewish Poles, Roma, homosexuals, Jehovah's Witnesses, and political dissidents who opposed the policies of the Nazi Party.

Europe had a long tradition of anti-Semitism. Jews had been persecuted and confined in ghettos for centuries. In the 19th century, the idea that people within a nation were bound by race and common values and characteristics took hold. Those who belonged to a different race and shared different values were often considered inferior and even subhuman. A movement called eugenics also arose in the 1800s, which promoted the idea that traits from "only the more suitable races" should be passed down to future generations.

As you've learned, Hitler believed in racial "purity" and in the superiority of what he called the Aryan race. The Jews, he asserted, belonged to an inferior race. Nazi dehumanization of the Jews and other victims began after Hitler became Germany's chancellor in 1933. On his command, the Nazis began to systematically restrict the civil and political rights of Jews. They removed Jews from German schools and universities and banned them from many public areas. Businesses were taken away from their Jewish owners, and Jewish doctors and lawyers were not allowed to practice their vocations. In time, the Jewish people lost their right to vote. Nazi persecution of the Jews escalated with Kristallnacht on November 9, 1938, when, as you have read, rioters attacked and killed about 100 Jews and destroyed Jewish shops and synagogues.

Remember reading about the Armenian genocide carried out by the Ottoman Turks during World War I? On the eve of the invasion of Poland in 1939, Hitler said to his generals, "Who, after all, speaks today of the annihilation [massacre] of the Armenians?" Numerous German military officers who had been stationed in Turkey during World War I had been aware of the Ottoman regime's plan to destroy the Armenians, and some of them even issued orders for the deportation of Armenians. A few of these officers later became leaders in the Nazi military apparatus that would carry out the systematic murder of Jews. Hitler thought that, like the Armenian genocide, the execution of Jews could be accomplished without penalty.

After the invasion of Poland, German authorities required Polish Jews over the age of 10 to wear a yellow Star of David, a symbol of Judaism. Eventually, all Jews six years of age or older in many German-occupied territories were ordered to wear the star with *Jew* written on it in the local language. The Germans also created about 1,000 ghettos in Poland, Hungary, and the Soviet Union. Huge numbers of Jews were forced to live in these ghettos, which were isolated from non-Jewish populations and surrounded by barbed wire, thick walls, and armed guards. In 1941, the Nazis rounded up others they had imprisoned as "undesirables" and sent them to the ghettos. But these enclosed districts were just holding places until the Nazis came up with a plan to solve what they called "the Jewish question."

THE WANNSEE CONFERENCE

Hitler thought the answer to the question was the extermination of the Jews. This had been his goal since at least 1919 when he wrote in a letter that the final objective of anti-Semitism "must unswervingly [without fail] be the removal of Jews altogether." "Final solution" was code for the plan to murder all the Jews in Europe—approximately 11 million in all.

In January 1942, **Reinhard Heydrich**, the head of the Gestapo, called a meeting of high-ranking Nazis in Wannsee, a suburb of Berlin. Heydrich gathered the men together at the **Wannsee Conference** to explain how the "final solution" would be carried out. Heydrich told the men that concentration camps would be constructed in eastern Europe. Jews would be sent to the camps, where those strong enough would build roads and work in factories to support Germany's economy. However, the work would be so hard that many Jews would die due to "natural reduction." Those who resisted or refused to work would be killed.

Actually, the real purpose of the camps was genocide. A major step toward this objective had been taken in 1941 when Germany invaded the Soviet Union. Special military forces known as mobile killing units accompanied the German army during the invasion. These groups were mostly composed of special officers of the SS, or *Schutzstaffel* (SHOOT-stah-fuhl), meaning "Protection Guards." The SS were the "political soldiers" of the Nazi Party. Their task in 1941 was to kill Jews, Roma, and Soviet political leaders. By 1943, they had executed an estimated one million Jews. As the war continued, it took thousands of ordinary Germans to operate the machinery of death. The German military, infrastructure, and even the economy would be mobilized to carry out the mass killings.

Jews in Germany were forced to wear a yellow badge, like this one, with the German word *Jude*, meaning "Jew," written on it. Any Jew who refused to wear the badge faced severe punishment or even death.

HISTORICAL THINKING

1. **READING CHECK** What did the Allies find when they invaded Germany and Poland in the spring of 1945?

2. **MAKE INFERENCES** Why do you think the Nazis forced Jews to wear the Star of David badges?

3. **IDENTIFY MAIN IDEAS AND DETAILS** What was the "final solution"?

PLAN: 2-PAGE LESSON

OBJECTIVE

Explain the Nazi persecution of Jews and their plan for mass killing.

CRITICAL THINKING SKILLS FOR LESSON 3.1

- Make Inferences
- Identify Main Ideas and Details
- Summarize
- Make Connections
- Analyze Visuals

HISTORICAL THINKING FOR CHAPTER 27

How was World War II a total war?

Longstanding notions of racial purity laid the foundation for the Nazi plan to murder Jews. Lesson 3.1 focuses on the Nazi subjugation of Jews and the 1942 Wannsee Conference that planned their extermination.

BACKGROUND FOR THE TEACHER

Nazi Germany's SS The *Schutzstaffel*, or SS, originated for the protection of Adolf Hitler. Its head was Heinrich Himmler, who also controlled the *Gestapo*. Himmler built the SS from some 300 members in the early 1930s to hundreds of thousands during World War II. Recruits for the SS were screened to prove they had no Jewish or "subhuman" ancestry. Unlike German soldiers fighting on the fronts, the SS specialized in finding and exterminating the Jews. Himmler established special SS killing units commanded by Reinhard Heydrich. Their methods were unusually brutal. They carried out mass shootings of Jews initially in Poland and the Soviet Union, often forcing their victims to dig their own graves first. When Himmler noticed that shootings burdened his men psychologically, he requested an improved killing method. In 1941, the SS revamped an old barracks near the Polish rail junction at Auschwitz, installing gas chambers and crematoria to conduct the mass murder of Jews. More concentration camps followed as Heydrich's plan for "the final solution" proceeded.

INTRODUCE & ENGAGE

DISCUSS THE POWER OF BELIEFS

Ask students to consider how common beliefs or prejudices can change lives, and discuss common prejudices toward people today. Ask volunteers to suggest how these beliefs or attitudes toward people might produce harmful or unintended results. Then tell students that in this lesson they will learn how anti-Semitism and the belief in racial purity resulted in the persecution and mass killing of Jews.

TEACH

GUIDED DISCUSSION

1. **Summarize** What was the "natural reduction" part of the plan conceived at the Wannsee Conference? (*Jews would be sent to concentration camps in eastern Europe where the strongest would be selected to build roads and work in factories. The work would be so hard that many would die as a result of exhaustion.*)

2. **Make Connections** What connection can you make between Hitler's goal of expansion in Europe and the extermination of Jews? (*Hitler wanted to expand the boundaries of the German state but also ensure that the populations he controlled were racially pure according to his definition.*)

ANALYZE VISUALS

Prompt students to reflect on the photograph of the train tracks leading to the Auschwitz concentration camp. **ASK:** What features of the Auschwitz exterior suggest that escape was virtually impossible? (*Possible response: The high fence, guard towers, and flat open area suggest that anyone trying to escape would be easily seen and recaptured or shot.*)

ACTIVE OPTIONS

On Your Feet: Inside-Outside Circle Arrange students in concentric circles facing each other. Tell students in the outside circle to pose questions about the persecution of Jews, its impact, and planning "the final solution," such as: What motivated the Nazi persecution of Jews? Was Hitler shortsighted in assuming that the extermination of Jews would have little impact inside or outside Germany? Ask students in the inner circle to answer their partner's question. On a signal, have students trade roles so that those in the inside circle ask questions and those in the outside circle answer them.

> **NG Learning Framework: Write an Article**
> SKILL Communication
> KNOWLEDGE Our Human Story

Direct students to write a short article explaining the similarities between the 19th-century concept of eugenics and German anti-Semitism. Encourage students to begin with information from the chapter and conduct further research online. Suggest that students focus on Hitler's beliefs. Invite students to post their articles on a class blog or website.

DIFFERENTIATE

STRIVING READERS

Recognizing Context Clues Help students use text definitions and context clues to understand challenging words. Point to the word *eugenics* and the explanation that follows in the same sentence. Pair students with a proficient reader who can identify clues that unlock the meaning of other difficult words such as *dissidents, dehumanization, genocide, natural reduction, SS,* and *mobilized.*

GIFTED & TALENTED

Prepare a Comparison Report Have students work in groups to conduct online research about the Armenian genocide in 1939. Suggest that students include informational articles and websites of survivors' testimonies. Tell students to prepare a report that compares the Armenian genocide with the Nazi plan to exterminate Jews. Students should comment on the motivations involved in each case and attempt to verify Hitler's claim that the Armenian genocide was forgotten. Ask groups to share their reports orally with the class.

See the Chapter Planner for more strategies for differentiation.

HISTORICAL THINKING

ANSWERS

1. concentration camps filled with dying prisoners, mainly Jews

2. Answers will vary. Possible response: The Nazis wanted to make the Jewish people in a region easy to identify.

3. to build concentration camps where Jews would perform hard labor and be systematically murdered

CRITICAL VIEWING Answers will vary. Possible response: They wanted to hide what they were doing from public view.

The Holocaust

Life in the ghettos was miserable. In the crowded quarters, food was scarce, and disease spread quickly. There was little the Jews could do to fight back against the Nazis. But some still tried.

WARSAW GHETTO UPRISING

Even though they risked their lives by doing so, many Jews in the ghettos put up some resistance. They smuggled in food, medicine, and weapons. Others set up secret schools or organized musical performances. And some brave ghetto dwellers even tried to escape. Those who succeeded often joined local resistance fighters who carried out surprise attacks on German army units.

The most famous example of resistance took place in the Polish ghetto of Warsaw. This ghetto in Poland's capital was the largest in the country. More than 400,000 Jews were crowded into the ghetto, which covered an area of only about 1.3 square miles. In 1942, the Nazis had begun rounding up millions of Jews all across Europe. They were then packed into trains for "deportation," or transport, to the death camps, where Jews and other enemies of the Nazis were murdered. The Germans removed about 265,000 Jews from the Warsaw ghetto for transport and killed another 35,000. Only about 60,000 Jews remained.

In 1943, most of the remaining residents decided to fight back. On April 19, SS and police units entered the ghetto and found the streets deserted. The Jews were hiding, some of them in underground bunkers they'd built in preparation for a battle with the Nazis. Suddenly, armed with weapons they had snuck into the ghetto, the Warsaw Jews fired on the Germans, forcing them to retreat. On the third day of fighting, the Germans began burning down all the buildings in the ghetto to drive the Jews from their hiding places. Jewish fighters held off the Nazis for almost a month during the **Warsaw Ghetto Uprising** but finally surrendered on May 16. About 7,000 of those in the Warsaw ghetto were shot immediately. The rest—about 50,000—were sent to the death camps.

When he was a teenager, Romanian-born Elie Wiesel was transported with his parents and sisters to Auschwitz in 1944. His mother, father, and little sister died, but Wiesel survived. After U.S. forces arrived in April 1945 at Buchenwald, the concentration camp to which Wiesel had been transferred, they photographed the survivors, including Wiesel. In the photo below, he is seventh from the left in the second row of bunks from the bottom. In 1958, Wiesel published *Night*, a memoir of his experiences in the camps. In this excerpt from the book, he describes the horrors he witnessed the day he arrived at Auschwitz.

PRIMARY SOURCE

Never shall I forget that night, the first night in camp, that turned my life into one long night seven times sealed. Never shall I forget that smoke. Never shall I forget the small faces of the children, whose bodies I saw transformed into smoke under a silent blue sky.

—from *Night* by Elie Wiesel, 1958

In 1943, the Jews in Poland's Warsaw ghetto fought back against the Nazis but were eventually forced to surrender. An SS general placed photos like this one in his report to his commanding officer. After the war ended, the report was used as evidence to convict the general of war crimes, and he was hanged.

DEATH CAMPS

The major death camps were located in Poland and included Chelmno, Treblinka, and Auschwitz (OWSH-vits), the largest of the camps. The Auschwitz complex consisted of three main camps. All were labor camps, and one included a killing center. Because Auschwitz was at a junction where several railways converged, the camp served as a convenient place for the Nazis to transport prisoners from all across Europe. In 1944, for example, Nazis transferred more than 400,000 Hungarian Jews there.

The train cars that brought the Jews to the death camps were overcrowded and hot in the summer and freezing in the winter. Passengers did not receive food or water during the journey. Some died before they reached their destination. Those who survived were inspected by a doctor upon arrival. The doctor sent certain groups of people to their death, including pregnant women, young children, the elderly, the disabled, and the ill. Most of these people were killed immediately in specially prepared gas chambers, where they were told they would simply be taking a shower. Then the victims' bodies were burned in **crematoria**, or ovens.

As you've read, those who were in good physical shape were put to work, often in factories in the area. When the laborers could no longer work due to malnutrition, illness, or exhaustion, the Nazis sent them to the gas chambers. An estimated 1.1 million Jews died at Auschwitz alone, including those who had been subjected to terrible medical "experiments" performed by the camp's chief doctor, Josef Mengele.

Even when the end of the war in Europe—and the end of Nazi Germany—was in sight, the killings at Auschwitz and other death camps continued. But as the Soviets and other Allies advanced across eastern Europe, the Nazis who ran the camps tried to destroy any evidence of what had happened there before they fled. They dismantled the barracks where prisoners had lived, burned down buildings that housed crematoria, and destroyed warehouses containing prisoners' clothing and personal items. Nonetheless, plenty of evidence remained of the murders that had taken place in the camps. In all, about six million Jews died in the Holocaust, which is what the systematic genocide carried out by the Nazis came to be called. Jews often use the word *Shoah*, a Hebrew word meaning "catastrophe," to refer to the Holocaust.

HISTORICAL THINKING

1. **READING CHECK** What happened in the Warsaw Ghetto Uprising?

2. **DRAW CONCLUSIONS** Why did the Nazis try to destroy evidence of what they'd done in the death camps?

3. **ANALYZE SOURCES** Why do you think Wiesel repeats "Never shall I forget" several times in the passage?

PLAN: 2-PAGE LESSON

OBJECTIVE

Describe the uprisings and subsequent mass killings of European Jews.

CRITICAL THINKING SKILLS FOR LESSON 3.2

- Draw Conclusions
- Analyze Sources
- Form and Support Opinions
- Evaluate
- Integrate Visuals

HISTORICAL THINKING FOR CHAPTER 27

How was World War II a total war?

German anti-Semitism finally took form in the mass confinement and killing of Jews. Lesson 3.2 describes the Jewish resistance, notably the Warsaw ghetto uprising, and provides an overview of the Nazi labor and death camps.

Student eEdition online

Additional content for this lesson, including a map, is available online.

BACKGROUND FOR THE TEACHER

Elie Wiesel Born in Romania in 1928, Elie Wiesel was 12 years old when Germany's ally Hungary annexed his hometown of Sighet. He was 15 when the Nazis invaded to identify Jews and confiscate their property. Although freed from Buchenwald at 17, he remained haunted by the horrors he experienced and witnessed. He went to France where the novelist François Mauriac encouraged him to write about his memories. Wiesel came to the United States in 1956, the year *Night* was first published, and taught at the college level. He received the Nobel Peace Prize in 1986 and the Presidential Medal of Freedom in 1992. He spoke at the dedication of the United States Holocaust Memorial Museum in 1993 and at the White House in 1999 for the Millennium Lecture Series. He ceaselessly urged his audiences to take responsibility, to let the sufferers of violence and oppression know that they are not alone, and above all to avoid the "perils of indifference." Wiesel published more than 55 books before his death in 2016.

INTRODUCE & ENGAGE

BRAINSTORM THE VALUE OF WITNESS ACCOUNTS

Direct students to read the primary source that appears in the lesson. Share the Background for the Teacher information about Elie Wiesel. Ask students to consider witness accounts they have read or heard, answering questions such as: Are witness accounts merely personal, or do they have universal value? Do they change the way people think? Are they useful as a deterrent to future crimes against humanity? Tell students that in this lesson they will learn about the confinement of Jews in ghettos, their efforts to resist, and the mass killings in Nazi death camps.

TEACH

GUIDED DISCUSSION

1. **Form and Support Opinions** Would it have been better for the Warsaw Jews if they had chosen not to fight the Nazis? Explain your answer. *(Possible response: No, it would not have been better because the Nazis would have tried to kill them in any case. The Jews thought there was a chance that their efforts would succeed.)*

2. **Evaluate** How might an earlier discovery of the death camps have changed the fate of European Jews? *(Possible response: An earlier discovery might have led to greater efforts of rescue and offers of sanctuary from the Allies and neutral nations.)*

INTEGRATE VISUALS

Prompt students to examine the photographs in the lesson and read the primary source. **ASK:** What does the quotation by Elie Wiesel suggest about the fate of the women and children in the first photograph? *(Possible response: Women and children were separated from men and most likely gassed. The smoke that Wiesel recalled came from the crematoria where the bodies were burned.)*

ACTIVE OPTIONS

On Your Feet: Think, Pair, Share Give students a few minutes to think about the following question: Why should everyone learn about the Holocaust? Then have students choose partners and discuss the question for several minutes. Finally, allow volunteers to share their ideas with the class.

> **NG Learning Framework: Investigate Holocaust Horrors**
> **ATTITUDE** Responsibility
> **KNOWLEDGE** Our Human Story

During World War II, countless numbers of Jews in Europe died of disease and starvation in Nazi camps. A famous one was Anne Frank, who died at the Bergen-Belsen camp in 1945. Her diary was found after her death. Ask students to conduct online research to learn the specifics of Anne Frank's story and develop a report to share with the class.

DIFFERENTIATE

INCLUSION

Understand Visuals Pair strong readers with special-needs students and those with perception difficulties. Instruct pairs to study the photographs and primary source. Ask stronger readers to help integrate these with main ideas in the text. Then have pairs work together to answer the Historical Thinking questions.

GIFTED & TALENTED

Create a Multimedia Presentation Direct students to create a multimedia presentation using first-person accounts of Holocaust survivors other than Elie Wiesel. Instruct students to find and use written, audio, and video testimonies collected by organizations such as the World Holocaust Remembrance Center and the United States Holocaust Memorial Museum. If possible, have students find accounts that establish what life was like before the war, in a ghetto or concentration camp during the war, and after liberation. Invite students to share finished multimedia presentations with the class.

See the Chapter Planner for more strategies for differentiation.

HISTORICAL THINKING

ANSWERS

1. Some Jewish residents rose up and fought against their captors. The Jews held the Germans off for a time, but the Nazi troops eventually overpowered them.

2. Answers will vary. Possible response: They had lost the war and knew that the murders carried out in the death camps were war crimes that could result in their execution.

3. Answers will vary. Possible response: He is emphasizing the horror of what he witnessed in Auschwitz, but he is also exhorting his readers never to forget what happened in the Holocaust as well.

3.3 Preserving Cultural Heritage

SAVING THE PAST

In 1943, President Roosevelt established the Roberts Commission to promote the preservation of cultural properties during war. This commission provided the military with lists and reports of valuable works of art, and they established the Allies' Monuments, Fine Arts, and Archives (MFAA) program.

The MFAA—or the Monuments Men—was a small corps of men and women who found and recovered priceless artwork damaged or stolen by the Nazis during World War II. The men and women who served in the MFAA were not soldiers. Most of the group consisted of historians, art conservators, architects, museum curators, archivists, and professors.

Hitler had a mission to culturally dominate the world and set out to create his own museum filled with Europe's great works of art. The Nazis stole valuable artwork from wealthy Jewish families to stockpile Hitler's collection. The Monuments Men set out to recover the countless pieces of art hidden away. With limited resources and virtually no crew, the Monuments Men used German sheepskin coats and gas masks as packing material and enlisted local prisoners to pack and load the art for safe transport.

This group of committed men and women risked their lives to recover, restore, and return approximately five million pieces of priceless art and artifacts. Without their determination and tireless action, important pieces of cultural heritage would have been erased forever.

HISTORICAL THINKING

MAKE INFERENCES Why would restoring a country's art and artifacts be important?

MONUMENTS MAN Harry Ettlinger stands in front of Rembrandt's *Self-Portrait.* The painting had been removed legally from a museum in Karlsruhe during World War II and stored in a crate in a German mine. A Jew born in Karlsruhe, Ettlinger had fled Germany with his family in 1938 and settled in the United States. Nazis prohibited Jews from entering museums. As a result, Ettlinger saw the painting for the first time when he opened the crate where it had been placed for safekeeping.

GERMANY
In this 1945 photo, an American soldier stands guard over artwork and other items stored by the Nazis in a German church during World War II. As Nazi soldiers stormed through Europe, they stole valuable paintings from private and public collections. Many pieces of art were looted from the homes of Jews who were rounded up and transported to concentration camps.

PLAN: 2-PAGE LESSON

OBJECTIVE

Explain the importance of preserving and recovering historical and cultural artwork stolen by the Nazis during World War II.

CRITICAL THINKING SKILLS FOR LESSON 3.3

- Make Connections
- Make Inferences
- Identify
- Explain

HISTORICAL THINKING FOR CHAPTER 27

How was World War II a total war?

World War II had devastating effects on people, cities, countries, and cultures. Lesson 3.3 discusses the impact of World War II on cultural and historical artwork.

Student eEdition online

Additional content for this lesson, including an image, is available online.

BACKGROUND FOR THE TEACHER

Führermuseum As a teenager, Hitler had a dream of becoming an artist and applied to Vienna's Academy of Fine Arts. Although he was not admitted and turned his sights on a political career, his passion for art never waned. Hitler's new dream was to build his Führermuseum, literally "Leader Museum," also known as Gemäldegalerie Linz, in his hometown of Linz, Austria. The museum was to be part of an art and cultural complex that would include an opera house and a library, and would bring glory to the city, which would outshine Vienna. Hitler was presented with catalogs of artwork from which he selected the pieces that would fill his museum. His final selections were compiled in a collection of 31 leather-bound Gemäldegalerie Linz Albums, many of which have been recovered and are on display in the Deutsches Historisches Museum in Berlin. The remaining albums, just as the artwork they contain, are still missing and presumed to have been destroyed.

History Notebook

Encourage students to complete the Preserving Cultural Heritage page for Chapter 27 in their History Notebooks as they read.

INTRODUCE & ENGAGE

MAKE CONNECTIONS

Ask students to describe works of art that they have seen that inspired them or were otherwise significant in their lives. Encourage students to consider the importance of art to a nation's history and culture. Discuss what would be lost if artwork was not preserved in museums. Tell students that in this lesson they will learn about the European art that was stolen during World War II and efforts to recover the pieces.

TEACH

GUIDED DISCUSSION

1. **Identify** Who were the Monuments Men? *(a group of historians, art conservators, architects, museum curators, archivists, and professors who found and recovered damaged or stolen art during and after World War II)*

2. **Explain** Why did the Nazis destroy and steal artwork? *(Hitler wanted to dominate the world culturally, so he stole certain pieces of art to display in his own museum and destroyed other works that were not significant to him.)*

PRESERVING CULTURAL HERITAGE

Artwork stolen from museums, churches, universities, and private collections was stored in thousands of buildings such as castles, monasteries, and military bunkers. The majority of items, though, were hidden inside salt, potassium, and copper mines in Austria and Germany. Many of the items recovered included paintings, sculptures, tapestries, relics, and other pieces of art. However, the mines also contained furniture, jewels, books, manuscripts, maps, sheet music, stage costumes, bags of foreign currency, gold bars worth more than $200 million, German munitions and military supplies, caskets of Prussian royalty and leaders, and the personal belongings, jewels, and gold teeth of victims of Nazi concentration camps.

ACTIVE OPTION

NG Learning Framework: Create a Museum Website or App STEM
ATTITUDE Empowerment
SKILLS Collaboration, Communication

Arrange students in groups to research the pieces of art that were stolen and destroyed during World War II. Prompt students to think about which works they would display in their own museums. Have each group member select at least one piece of art to feature in their museum and supply an image of the work, an explanation of why they find it to be significant, and background information about the piece and the artist. Instruct groups to compile the information into a single collection and display it on a museum website or app. Ask groups to name their museums and include a page on their website or app providing information about their imagined museums. Encourage groups to share their websites or apps with the class.

DIFFERENTIATE

STRIVING READERS

Write About It Tell students to imagine they are Monuments Men discovering a hidden collection of artwork during World War II. Guide them in writing short narrative paragraphs explaining this experience. Then have volunteers share their paragraphs with the class.

GIFTED & TALENTED

Create a Public Service Announcement Tell students to research items stolen during World War II that are still missing and create a PSA encouraging the general public to look at their own art collections and return any stolen pieces to their rightful owners. Students' announcements should explain why it is important to return the items, include visuals, show examples of pieces, and direct viewers to the Monuments Men Foundation website for a complete list of missing pieces. Ask students to record their PSA and play it for the class.

See the Chapter Planner for more strategies for differentiation.

HISTORICAL THINKING

ANSWER
Possible response: Restoring art and artifacts restores a country's culture and identity. It can have a healing effect on people in a war-torn city and give them some sense of normalcy and identity.

Justice and Remembrance

Following the war, the Allies had to decide how to deal with the Nazis who had carried out the most monstrous crimes, particularly in the Holocaust. Rather than simply execute them, the Allies chose to bring them to trial.

THE NUREMBERG TRIALS

The world learned about the extent of Nazi **atrocities**, or extremely cruel and shocking acts of violence, when the International Military Tribunal charged and tried former Nazi officials, military officers, industrialists, and others as war criminals. A **tribunal** is a court with authority over a specific matter. The series of trials, known as the **Nuremberg trials**, took place in Nuremberg, Germany, beginning in 1945.

The tribunal determined that defendants could be charged with any of the following: crimes against peace, for having waged a war of aggression; crimes against humanity, for having exterminated groups of people; and war crimes, for having violated common and agreed-upon laws of war. Members of the tribunal represented the United States, Britain, France, and the Soviet Union and had the authority to determine the guilt of any individual or group. As evidence, the prosecution presented Nazi propaganda films, footage taken by Allied troops at concentration camps, and ghastly artifacts taken from the camps. Survivors of the camps also described what they had witnessed and experienced.

Trials for 22 major Nazi war criminals were held in 1945 and 1946. Several of the leading figures in the party could not be tried, however. Hitler and two of his top officers, Heinrich Himmler, the head of the SS, and Joseph Goebbels, the minister of Nazi propaganda, committed suicide before they could be brought to justice. Most of those charged did not deny or apologize for their actions. In their defense, many said they were "just following orders."

On October 1, 1946, the tribunals issued their verdicts, acquitting some of those charged with war crimes and sending others to prison. They also sentenced 12 to death by hanging, including Hermann Goering, whom Hitler had designated as his successor. However, Goering evaded execution by taking poison.

NEVER AGAIN

Nazi officials weren't the only ones complicit in the Holocaust. Ordinary German citizens often turned on their Jewish neighbors. Some operated the trains that carried Jews to death camps. Others processed the documents authorizing the deportation of the Jews. Still others served as guards in the concentration camps.

Before the death camps were built, thousands of Jewish refugees fled Europe. Some were able to move to Britain or the United States, but poorer Jews were often turned away. Anti-Semitism and racially discriminatory immigration policies meant that ships full of Jewish refugees were turned back from both New York and British-controlled Palestine.

> Robert Jackson, a public prosecutor and the Chief of Counsel for the United States at Nuremberg, delivered the opening statement at the International Military Tribunal. In these first words from his statement, Jackson explains why Nazi atrocities had to be punished.
>
> **PRIMARY SOURCE**
>
> The privilege of opening the first trial in history for crimes against the peace of the world imposes a grave responsibility. The wrongs which we seek to condemn and punish have been so calculated, so malignant [evil], and so devastating, that civilization cannot tolerate their being ignored, because it cannot survive their being repeated. That four great nations, flushed with victory and stung with injury stay the hand of vengeance and voluntarily submit their captive enemies to the judgment of the law is one of the most significant tributes that Power has ever paid to Reason.
>
> —from the Opening Statement before the International Military Tribunal by Robert H. Jackson, Nuremberg, November 21, 1945

Shoes that belonged to people deported to Auschwitz are displayed at the Auschwitz-Birkenau Memorial and Museum, located in the former German death camp. The shoes in the photo number about 25,000 and were collected in one day, at the height of the gassing. This is one of several such exhibits that appear in Holocaust memorials and museums around the world.

Even Allied leaders did not do all they could to stop the genocide. In 1942, Roosevelt, Churchill, and Stalin officially recognized the mass murder of European Jews. Still, the Allies did not make bombing death camps and the railroad tracks that led to them a priority. In 1944, Roosevelt created the War Refugee Board, but by then millions of Jews had been killed.

Immediately after the war, genocide was established as a crime under international law through the development of the **United Nations**. This international organization was founded in 1945 by 51 countries committed to maintaining international peace and security and preventing future wars.

For the rest of their lives, the Jews who survived the Holocaust were haunted by their experiences, but they did not want the world to forget that the Nazis had tried to exterminate them and their culture. The phrase "never again" became a call to action when those in power threatened any group of people with destruction. Holocaust museums created after World War II document the experiences of those victimized by genocide. By telling the stories of the victims and survivors, these museums show that those affected were not numbers but real people. The museums also stress the responsibility of citizens to speak out against hatred and prejudice to help prevent genocide from happening again.

HISTORICAL THINKING

1. **READING CHECK** What was the purpose of the Nuremberg trials?

2. **ANALYZE SOURCES** Why do you think the Allies chose not to seek vengeance against the Nazis?

3. **DRAW CONCLUSIONS** How does telling the stories of victims in Holocaust museums help visitors understand that the victims were not just numbers?

PLAN: 2-PAGE LESSON

OBJECTIVE

Describe the Nazi war crime trials and international efforts to prevent future genocide.

CRITICAL THINKING SKILLS FOR LESSON 3.4

- Analyze Sources
- Draw Conclusions
- Make Inferences
- Summarize

HISTORICAL THINKING FOR CHAPTER 27

How was World War II a total war?

The full extent of Nazi atrocities became clear at the war's end. Lesson 3.4 discusses the Nuremberg trials, treatment of Jewish refugees, and steps taken to prevent future genocide.

Student eEdition online

Additional content for this lesson, including a photograph and an image gallery, is available online.

BACKGROUND FOR THE TEACHER

Raoul Wallenberg Swedish businessman and diplomat Raoul Wallenberg achieved one of the most extensive rescue efforts during World War II. He saved tens of thousands of Hungarian Jews from Nazi death camps. The U.S. War Refugee Board, set up in January 1944 by President Roosevelt, helped finance the effort. Wallenberg traveled to Nazi-occupied Hungary in July 1944, several months after German SS forces began rounding up Jews. Wallenberg set up hospitals, soup kitchens, and safe houses for the Jews in Budapest. He and his colleagues also distributed certificates of protection and Swedish passports to the Jews. During World War II, Sweden remained neutral, which meant that the Nazis could not legally harm citizens holding a Swedish passport. In violation of that immunity, Soviet forces arrested Wallenberg when he reached Budapest. The Soviet claim that Wallenberg died in prison in 1947 was never confirmed. President Ronald Reagan signed legislation in 1981 granting Wallenberg U.S. citizenship. Representative Tom Lantos backed the resolution in Congress. Lantos, a Holocaust survivor, was saved by Wallenberg.

INTRODUCE & ENGAGE

DISCUSS NATIONAL RESPONSIBILITY

Ask students to think about the question of genocide and other atrocities in the world. Invite students to respond to questions such as: Does a nation have a moral responsibility to intervene when outside populations are threatened? How should perpetrators of genocide be dealt with? Can future war crimes be prevented? Conclude by telling students that in this lesson they will learn how the Allies punished Nazi officials after World War II and how nations planned to prevent genocide.

TEACH

GUIDED DISCUSSION

1. **Make Inferences** How might the phrase "never again" help prevent future genocide? *(Answers will vary. Possible response: The phrase is associated with the Holocaust and Holocaust museums reminding people to speak out against hatred and prejudice to prevent future genocide.)*

2. **Summarize** What kinds of evidence convicted Nazi officials at Nuremberg? *(The prosecution presented Nazi propaganda films along with film footage and ghastly artifacts taken by Allied troops at concentration camps. Camp survivors also testified.)*

ANALYZE PRIMARY SOURCES

Direct students to read the primary source statement by Robert Jackson. **ASK:** Why did Jackson believe the trial was necessary? Explain in detail. *(Possible response: The trial was needed because the crimes were so malignant that civilization could not survive if they were repeated. He believed that the trial could deter future genocide.)*

ACTIVE OPTIONS

On Your Feet: Numbered Heads Organize students into small groups and have them count off within each group. Ask them to examine the photographs in the image gallery (available in the Student eEdition) and think about the following question: How can museums dedicated to the Holocaust, such as the ones pictured in the lesson and the United States Holocaust Memorial Museum, help to deter future crimes against groups of people? Instruct students to discuss the question for several minutes. Finally, call out a number and invite the student with that number to summarize the group's discussion for the class.

| **NG Learning Framework: Research Holocaust Heroes**
ATTITUDE Responsibility
KNOWLEDGE Our Human Story

During World War II, thousands of non-Jews in Europe did what they could to save Jews from the Nazis. Years later, many were honored by the Israeli Parliament for their heroic deeds. Ask students to conduct online research to learn about one of these individuals. Prompt them to share the specifics of the person's story with the class.

DIFFERENTIATE

ENGLISH LANGUAGE LEARNERS

Use Terms in Sentences Pair students at the **Beginning** level with those at the **Intermediate** or **Advanced** level. Direct partners to take turns creating sentences for the Key Vocabulary terms *atrocities* and *tribunal*. Students might expand the exercise to other words from the lesson such as *defendants, aggression, propaganda,* and *witnessed.* Encourage pairs to share their sentences and discuss different ways to use each word.

PRE-AP

Research and Report Challenge students to conduct research online and in print sources to locate additional information about the treatment of Jewish refugees during World War II. Ask students to locate sources that deepen understanding of reasons for the rejection of Jews seeking asylum. Have students also reference news stories about the refugee situation in the world today. Encourage students to prepare a list of sources they consulted. Invite students to hold a panel discussion to share their findings and the conclusions they drew. Invite questions from the class.

See the Chapter Planner for more strategies for differentiation.

HISTORICAL THINKING

ANSWERS

1. The trials tried former Nazi officials, military officers, industrialists, and others as war criminals.

2. Answers will vary. Possible response: They wanted to show the world that they, unlike the Nazis, were guided by the law and reason.

3. Answers will vary. Possible response: The stories remind visitors that the victims were real people.

REVIEW

VOCABULARY

Use each of the following vocabulary words in a sentence that shows an understanding of the term's meaning.

1. blitzkrieg
2. infamy
3. island hopping
4. kamikaze
5. tribunal

READING STRATEGY
IDENTIFY MAIN IDEAS AND DETAILS

Use a diagram like the one below to list details about the ways in which Germany mobilized its forces to carry out the Holocaust. Then answer the questions that follow.

Main Idea:
Germany mobilized all its resources to operate its machinery of death during the Holocaust.

Detail
Detail
Detail
Detail

6. How was Germany's economy mobilized to carry out the murder of the Jewish people?

7. What role did some ordinary German citizens play in the Holocaust?

MAIN IDEAS

Answer the following questions. Support your answers with evidence from the chapter.

8. What happened at Dunkirk? LESSON 1.1

9. How did code breakers help secure an Allied victory at the Battle of Midway? LESSON 1.2

10. What was the objective of the D-Day invasion? LESSON 1.3

11. What strategy finally brought an end to World War II? LESSON 1.3

12. How did both Allied and Axis powers try to control public opinion during the war? LESSON 2.2

13. Why did the Navajo language serve as an effective code? LESSON 2.3

14. How did the Nazis isolate the Jewish ghettos? LESSON 3.1

15. What were conditions like on the trains that brought the Jews to the death camps? LESSON 3.2

16. Which four Allied nations were represented at the Nuremberg trials? LESSON 3.4

HISTORICAL THINKING

Answer the following questions. Support your answers with evidence from the chapter.

17. EVALUATE What do you think President Roosevelt meant when he said that, through the Lend-Lease Act, the United States would become "the arsenal of democracy"?

18. DRAW CONCLUSIONS What were the key goals of the Axis and Allied powers?

19. SYNTHESIZE How did technology affect World War II?

20. COMPARE AND CONTRAST How did World War II's actors, goals, and strategies compare with those of World War I?

21. IDENTIFY MAIN IDEAS AND DETAILS How was the war mobilized on different fronts?

22. DESCRIBE What characteristics do you think Nancy Wake and Josephine Baker possessed to become resistance fighters?

23. DRAW CONCLUSIONS Why was it important to the Allies to take back France?

24. MAKE INFERENCES Why do you think so many German citizens were complicit in the Holocaust?

INTERPRET VISUALS

When the United States entered the war, the government mobilized its civilians to combat the Axis Powers. Americans were urged to hold metal and rubber drives to collect scrap for the war effort. Posters like the one shown here were created to stir the public to action. Study the poster. Then answer the questions below.

25. What does the poster suggest is being produced from scrap metal?

26. Why is the poster effective?

Your METAL saves our convoys

KEEP IT COMING!

ANALYZE SOURCES

President Roosevelt's annual address to Congress in January 1941, in which he discussed "four essential human freedoms," became known as the "Four Freedoms" Speech. He used his speech to frame the war as a conflict about fundamental values. This excerpt from Roosevelt's address details the four freedoms. Read the excerpt and answer the question that follows.

> The first is freedom of speech and expression—everywhere in the world.
>
> The second is freedom of every person to worship God in his own way—everywhere in the world.
>
> The third is freedom from want—which, translated into world terms, means economic understandings which will secure to every nation a healthy peacetime life for its inhabitants—everywhere in the world.
>
> The fourth is freedom from fear—which, translated into world terms, means a worldwide reduction of armaments to such a point and in such a thorough fashion that no nation will be in a position to commit an act of physical aggression against any neighbor—anywhere in the world.

27. How does Roosevelt frame his speech on both a personal and an international level?

CONNECT TO YOUR LIFE

28. INFORMATIVE Think about the causes and effects of President Truman's decision to drop the atomic bombs on Japan. Do a little research to find more information on the effects of the bombs and learn what historians say today about Truman's decision. Then consider whether Truman's actions were justified. Write an essay in which you discuss the causes and effects of the bombings and indicate whether you believe Truman's decision was the right one.

TIPS

* Review what you've learned about what led Truman to drop the bombs and what happened as a result of the bombings.

* Conduct research to find out more about the effects of the bombings, including the long-term impact of radiation in Japan.

* Study the opinions of historians today regarding Truman's decision.

* Use two or three vocabulary words from the chapter in your essay.

* Provide a concluding statement in which you explain whether you think Truman's actions were justified.

VOCABULARY ANSWERS

Answers will vary.

1. The blitzkrieg tactic, which employed speed, surprise, and the combined firepower of tanks, bombers, and ground forces, allowed the German army to quickly overwhelm Poland.

2. President Roosevelt referred to December 7, 1941, as "a date which will live in infamy" because it was the day Japan attacked Pearl Harbor.

3. The Allies carried out a campaign called island hopping to capture and control islands in the Pacific one by one.

4. Japanese kamikaze pilots volunteered to crash their planes, loaded with explosives, into Allied ships.

5. A military tribunal charged and tried former Nazi officials, military officers, industrialists, and others as war criminals during the Nuremberg trials.

READING STRATEGY ANSWERS

Main Idea:
Germany mobilized all of its resources to operate its machinery of death during the Holocaust.

The Nazis constructed concentration camps in eastern Europe.
The SS went from guarding Hitler to killing Jews, Roma, and Soviet political leaders.
The Nazis enlisted civilians to help carry out the events of the Holocaust.

6. Answers will vary. Possible response: Germany used millions of prisoners in the camps to perform slave labor in factories and support its economy.

7. Answers will vary. Possible response: Some operated the trains that carried Jews to death camps, some worked in offices that processed the documents authorizing the deportation of the Jews, and some served as guards in the concentration camps.

MAIN IDEAS ANSWERS

8. The British navy and civilians successfully evacuated 350,000 British and French troops trapped there by the Germans.

9. Code breakers discovered Japan's battle plans and alerted the Allies, allowing the Allies to stay one step ahead of the enemy and attack the Japanese fleet when it was still 500 miles from Midway.

10. The objective of the D-Day invasion was to take back France from the Nazis.

11. The United States dropped atomic bombs on the Japanese cities of Hiroshima and Nagasaki.

12. Both sides relied on propaganda and media censorships.

13. The unfamiliar language was so complex that enemy listeners could not decode it.

14. The Nazis surrounded the ghettos with barbed wire, thick walls, and armed guards and built the enclosed districts far away from non-Jewish populations.

15. The trains were overcrowded and hot in the summer and freezing in the winter, and passengers did not receive food or water during the journey. Some died before they reached the camps.

16. The United States, Great Britain, France, and the Soviet Union were represented by members of the tribunal.

HISTORICAL THINKING ANSWERS

17. Answers will vary. Possible response: He meant that the United States would provide weapons and supplies to defend democracy around the world.

18. The key goals of the Axis Powers were to expand their territory and influence around the world. The key goals of the Allied Powers were to protect democracy and the freedom of people everywhere.

19. New technology made the war deadlier than ever, particularly for civilians.

20. Answers will vary. Possible response: Both wars involved military alliances among different groups of countries; the goals of the Central Powers in World War I and the Axis Powers in World War II were to expand their empires, while the goals of the Allies in both wars were to safeguard democracy and stop German expansionism; much of World War I was fought in trenches, while the players in World War II used tanks, missiles, encryption codes, and atomic bombs.

21. World War II was fought on many islands in the Pacific, in various places along the Mediterranean, and on multiple fronts in Europe.

22. Answers will vary. Possible response: They must have been brave, daring, reckless, intelligent, patriotic, and freedom-loving.

23. Before it was conquered by Germany, France had been on the Allied side. Taking it back was both a strategic and a symbolic victory for the Allies.

24. Answers will vary. Possible response: They believed in the cause and were loyal to Hitler because he had stabilized the German economy.

INTERPRET VISUALS ANSWERS

25. The poster suggests the metal is being used to build heavy weapons to battle the enemy.

26. Answers will vary. Possible response: It appeals to Americans' patriotism and shows that their scrap metal is helping the Allies win the war.

ANALYZE SOURCES ANSWER

27. Answers will vary. Possible response: He frames the freedoms as fundamental to all individuals but also applies them to what is happening in the war. He suggests that restricting freedoms is endangering the world.

CONNECT TO YOUR LIFE ANSWER

28. Essays will vary but should discuss the causes and effects of Truman's decision to drop atomic bombs on Japan and include an opinion on whether the decision was justified.

The Science of Good and Evil

BY YUDHIJIT BHATTACHARJEE Adapted from "The Science of Good and Evil" by Yudhijit Bhattacharjee, *National Geographic*, January 2018

For centuries, the question of how good and evil originate was a matter of philosophical or religious debate. But in recent decades, researchers have made advances toward understanding the science of what drives good and evil. Both seem to be linked to empathy, an intrinsic ability of the brain to experience how another person is feeling. Researchers have found that empathy is the kindling that fires compassion, impelling us to help others in distress. Studies have traced violent, psychopathic behaviors to a lack of empathy, which appears to stem from impaired circuits in the brain.

Most individuals do not ordinarily commit violent acts against one another. And yet, there are genocides, which require the complicity and passivity of large numbers of people. Time and again, social groups organized along ethnic, national, racial, or religious lines have savaged other groups. Nazi Germany's gas chambers extinguished millions of Jews, the Communist Khmer Rouge slaughtered fellow Cambodians, and Hutu extremists in Rwanda killed several hundred thousand Tutsis and moderate Hutus. Events such as these provide evidence that evil can hold entire communities in its grip.

How the voice of conscience is silenced in a genocide can be partly understood through the prism of the well-known experiments conducted in the 1960s by the psychologist Stanley Milgram at Yale University. In those studies, subjects were asked to deliver electric shocks to a person in another room for failing to answer questions correctly, increasing the voltage with every wrong answer. At the prodding of a person who played the role of a researcher, the subjects often dialed up the shocks to dangerously high voltage levels. The shocks weren't real and the cries of pain were prerecorded, but the subjects only found that out afterward. The studies demonstrated what Milgram described as "the extreme willingness of adults to go to almost any lengths on the command of an authority."

Gregory Stanton, founder of Genocide Watch, a nonprofit that works to prevent mass murder, has identified the

stages that can lead otherwise decent people to commit murder. It starts when demagogic leaders define a target group as "the other" and claim it is a threat. Discrimination follows, and soon the leaders characterize their targets as subhuman, eroding the in-group's empathy for "the other."

Next, society becomes polarized. "Those planning the genocide say, 'You are either with us or against us,'" says Stanton. This is followed by a phase of preparation, with the architects of the genocide drawing up death lists, stocking weapons, and planning how the rank and file are to execute the killings. Members of the out-group are sometimes forced to move into ghettos or concentration camps. Then the massacres begin.

Many perpetrators show no remorse because they find ways to rationalize the killings. James Waller, a genocide scholar at Keene State College in New Hampshire, says he got a glimpse of this "incredible capacity of the human mind to make sense of and to justify the worst of actions" when he interviewed Hutu men convicted or accused of atrocities during the Rwandan genocide. Some had killed children. Their rationale, according to Waller, was: "If I didn't do this, those children would have grown up to come back to kill me. This was something that was a necessity for my people . . . to survive." ∎

Neuroscientist Kent Kiehl, shown here, has taken brain scans of more than 4,000 prison inmates to measure brain activity and size in different regions of the organ. According to Kiehl, psychopaths have impairments in the part of the brain that helps process emotions.

Staging the Question

In this unit, you learned about two world wars and a worldwide economic depression, all of which occurred in the first half of the 20th century. These events resulted in horrific suffering for people in many parts of the world and included some shocking examples of human behavior at its worst. Amid all the suffering and brutality, where did people find hope? How did people manage to maintain their human decency in the face of so much horror? What lessons can we learn from this period in history?

Supporting Questions: Begin by developing supporting questions to guide your thinking. For example: What was admirable about this person or group's actions in this situation?

Summative Performance Task: Write a letter nominating your candidate for a humanitarian award. You might use a graphic organizer like this one to explain the situation behind the person or people's heroic actions.

Present: Share your nomination letter with the class. You might consider one of the following options.

Who?	
What?	
Where?	
When?	
Why?	

ASSIGNMENT

Research primary and secondary sources to find examples of people—whether famous leaders or average citizens—who acted honorably or compassionately during these trying times. You might choose examples from this unit or from your own research.

Select one of the people or groups of people to focus on. Conduct additional research to learn as much as you can about the situation and the actions of the person or people involved.

Analyze what lessons might be learned from the actions of the person or people you've chosen.

Write a letter of recommendation nominating the person or people you have chosen for a humanitarian award. Explain the circumstances behind your candidate's actions.

DELIVER A NOMINATION SPEECH

Practice your speech before delivering it to the class. Invite the class to comment on what they can learn from the nominee's actions. Your class might compile a list of lessons gained from all the nomination speeches.

PRODUCE A NOMINATION VIDEO

Instead of delivering your speech live, you might record it as part of a nomination video. This option allows you to incorporate other media to help you present your choice for nominee.

Take Informed Action:

UNDERSTAND In one or two sentences, write the lesson to be learned from the person or people you chose.

ASSESS Think about how you might apply that lesson in your own life and who you might share it with.

ACT Share the lesson with others and implement it in your life if possible.

NATIONAL GEOGRAPHIC CONNECTION

GUIDED DISCUSSION FOR "THE SCIENCE OF GOOD AND EVIL"

1. **Make Connections** What types of people display empathy? *(Possible response: people who volunteer to help others)*

2. **Form and Support Opinions** Do you think any person can be persuaded to commit genocide? Explain your reasoning. *(Answers will vary. Possible response: Yes, the text says that there is a process that leads people to support and participate in genocide that can be imposed on anyone; OR No, truly empathetic people could not be persuaded and would rather lose their own lives trying to save people than hurt anyone.)*

History Notebook

Encourage students to complete the Unit Wrap-Up page for Unit 9 in their History Notebooks.

UNIT INQUIRY PROJECT RUBRIC

ASSESS

Use the rubric to assess each student's participation and performance.

SCORE	ASSIGNMENT	PRODUCT	PRESENTATION
3 GREAT	• Student thoroughly understands the assignment. • Student develops thoughtful supporting questions to guide thinking.	• Letter is well thought out with a lesson clearly conveyed. • Letter reflects all of the essential elements listed in the assignment.	• Speech is clear, concise, and logical. • Speech is creative and engaging.
2 GOOD	• Student mostly understands the assignment. • Student develops somewhat thoughtful supporting questions to guide thinking.	• Letter is fairly well thought out with an unclear lesson. • Letter reflects most of the essential elements listed in the assignment.	• Speech is fairly clear, concise, and logical. • Speech is somewhat creative and engaging.
1 NEEDS WORK	• Student does not understand the assignment. • Student does not develop thoughtful questions to guide thinking.	• Letter is not well thought out and contains no lesson. • Letter reflects few or none of the essential elements listed in the assignment.	• Speech is not clear, concise, or logical. • Speech is not creative or engaging.

INTRODUCE THE PHOTOGRAPH

HONG KONG AERIAL PHOTOGRAPH

Hong Kong is one of the most densely populated places in the world with nearly 7.5 million people living in a territory that is roughly 685 square miles. Famous for both its skyline and natural harbor, Hong Kong is located on the south coast of China and is surrounded by the Pearl River Delta and the South China Sea. Originally part of China, Hong Kong Island was ceded to Great Britain in 1842. The remaining territories were leased for 99 years to Great Britain for use of the harbor and for the economic advantages of the opium trade. In 1984, the Chinese-British joint declaration paved the way for Hong Kong to be returned to China.

Hong Kong officially rejoined China in 1997 and became part of the largest populated country in the world. As of 2019, China boasts a population of 1,433,783,686. It is closely followed by India, with a population total of 1,366,417,754 in 2019. In third place is the United States, with a population of 329,064,917. These three countries are also considered to be the countries with the most economic expansion. While the population in most countries is growing, there are some countries where the population is in decline, such as Japan, Italy, Ukraine, Poland, and Venezuela.

However, the population size or the landmass size of a country does not always correlate to economic prosperity. Monaco, Luxembourg, and the Cayman Islands, all countries with populations of less than 1 million people, are leaders in the financial world. Similarly, Canada, which has a small population relative to its large landmass, is also considered a top economic player.

UNIT 10

Global Challenges
1945–Present

792

CRITICAL VIEWING

Hong Kong, shown in this aerial photo, is one of the most densely populated places in the world. What details in the photo help convey the city's overcrowding?

793

Direct students' attention to the photograph. **ASK:** Based on the photograph, how would you describe the economy of Hong Kong? Explain. *(Possible response: I think Hong Kong has a high yielding economy because the buildings are very tall and stately looking; this seems to indicate wealth because it takes a lot of money to design and build tall skyscrapers.)*

CRITICAL VIEWING Possible response: The aerial view of skyscrapers crowded together helps convey the level of overcrowding in the city, along with the ratio of greenery to buildings.

INTRODUCE TIME LINE EVENTS

IDENTIFY PATTERNS AND THEMES

Have volunteers read aloud each of the world events in the time line. **ASK:** What are some common themes or patterns that you notice with regard to these events? *(Possible responses: Some common themes or patterns include conquest, reform, political revolution, space exploration, and human conflicts.)* Sort the themes and patterns into categories and put them in webs like the ones shown here.

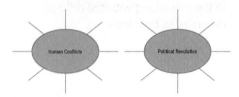

As students read the lessons for each chapter in the unit, have them add the lesson titles to the appropriate web, adding spokes or creating a new web as necessary. Advise students that they may also add or revise categories. At the end of the unit, revisit students' webs and create a final list of categories to summarize the historical themes students encountered as they read each chapter.

UNIT **10** Global Challenges

WORLD EVENTS 1945–PRESENT

1947 AMERICAS The Truman Doctrine promises U.S. support for countries threatened by communism.

1948 ASIA Israel declares independence as a Jewish state; Arab nations respond by declaring war and invading the country. *(Jewish immigrants with the flag of Israel)*

1959 AMERICAS Fidel Castro leads the Cuban Revolution, overthrowing the regime of dictator Batista and establishing a communist government in Cuba.

1961 EUROPE Soviet cosmonaut Yuri Gagarin becomes the first human to orbit Earth. *(Yuri Gagarin aboard the Soviet Vostok 1 spacecraft)*

1950   1960   1970   1980

1950 ASIA North Korea invades South Korea, starting the Korean War.

1952 AFRICA Mau Mau rebels in Kenya revolt against British rule. *(Mau Mau soldiers at their military camp)*

1949 ASIA In China, Mao Zedong and his Communist Party defeat nationalist forces and establish the People's Republic of China. *(portrait of Mao Zedong at the Forbidden City in Beijing)*

The New York Times.
U.S. IMPOSES ARMS BLOCKADE ON CUBA ON FINDING OFFENSIVE-MISSILE SITES; KENNEDY READY FOR SOVIET SHOWDOWN

1962 AMERICAS During the Cuban Missile Crisis, the United States prevents the Soviet Union from placing nuclear missiles in Cuba. *(The New York Times front page on Tuesday, October 23, 1962)*

794

2018 THE WORLD A refugee crisis occurs around the world as people flee religious persecution, war, poverty, and climate change. *(Honduran migrant caravan heading through Mexico to the United States)*

HISTORICAL THINKING

ANALYZE CAUSE AND EFFECT What effect do you think the Truman Doctrine might have had on conflicts that arose in the second half of the 20th century?

1990   2000   2010   2020

1989 EUROPE
The Berlin Wall comes down, leading to the reunification of Germany.

2008 AMERICAS The crash of the New York Stock Exchange and the housing market cause the Great Recession, which spreads across the globe.

1965 ASIA President Lyndon Johnson sends U.S. combat troops to Vietnam. *(American soldiers with transport helicopter, 1966)*

1994 AFRICA Three years after the end of apartheid, voters elect Nelson Mandela president in South Africa's first democratic election. *(Nelson Mandela's inauguration)*

1985 EUROPE Soviet leader Mikhail Gorbachev introduces reform programs called glasnost and perestroika to encourage more openness and freedom within the Soviet Union. *(Mikhail Gorbachev speaking to the press)*

HISTORICAL THINKING

Analyze Cause and Effect

Possible response: The Truman Doctrine committed the United States to aid any country that was threatened by communism, which forced the United States to involve itself in conflicts in many locations around the world.

Student eEdition online

Additional content, including the unit map and Global Perspective feature, is available online.

795

UNIT 10 RESOURCES

UNIT INTRODUCTION

UNIT TIME LINE

UNIT MAP online

THE GLOBAL PERSPECTIVE:
Who We Are: Shared Cultures and Identities

- National Geographic Explorers: Topher White, Danielle N. Lee, and Paul Salopek
- On Your Feet: Ready, Set, Recall

| **NG Learning Framework**
Explore High-Tech Forensics

UNIT WRAP-UP

National Geographic Magazine Adapted Article
- "Navigating the Anthropocene"

Unit 10 Inquiry: Create an NGO

Unit 10 Formal Assessment

CHAPTER 28 RESOURCES

Available in the Teacher eEdition

TEACHER RESOURCES & ASSESSMENT

Reading and Note-Taking

Vocabulary Practice

Social Studies Skills Lessons
- Reading: Determine Chronology
- Writing: Argument

Formal Assessment
- Chapter 28 Pretest
- Chapter 28 Tests A & B
- Section Quizzes

Chapter 28 Answer Key

Cognero®

STUDENT DIGITAL RESOURCES

Available in the Student eEdition

- eEdition (English)
- Handbooks
- National Geographic Atlas
- History Notebook
- Biographies
- Literature Analysis

STRIVING READERS

STRATEGY ❶
Outline and Take Notes

Help students develop their reading and comprehension skills by asking them to work in pairs to write an outline for each lesson. Instruct them in using an outline format, such as the one shown. Tell them to identify main ideas and then look for two details that support each one.

I. _____
   A. _____
   B. _____
II. _____
   A. _____
   B. _____
III. _____
   A. _____
   B. _____

Use with All Lessons *You might want to pair students of different proficiencies.*

STRATEGY ❷
Sequence Events

To build understanding of the critical events in a section and their relationship to one another in time, encourage students to note them in a Sequence Chain. Suggest that students use the Sequence Chain to trace the sequence of events related to the Cold War conflict between the Soviet Union and the United States.

Use with All Lessons

STRATEGY ❸
Use Reciprocal Teaching

Instruct partners to take turns reading each paragraph of the lesson aloud. At the end of the paragraph, the reading student asks the listening student questions about the paragraph. Students may ask their partners to state the main idea, identify important details that support the main idea, or summarize the paragraph in their own words.

Use with All Lessons

INCLUSION

STRATEGY ❶
Preview Using Maps

Preview maps to orient students to the lesson topic and to help them comprehend lesson text. Tell students to read the map title and legend and then place a finger on relevant information and trace arrows if present. For example, for the Division of Europe During the Cold War map in Lesson 1.2, point out the colors in the legend that represent the NATO nations and the Warsaw Pact nations, and tell students to use a finger to trace the divisions.

Use with Lessons 1.2, 2.3, 3.1, 4.1, and 4.2

STRATEGY ❷
Build a Time Line

To increase understanding of how the Cold War conflicts in the chapter built upon one another, instruct students to identify and list the conflicts and the countries involved on a time line. Each entry should include the date of the conflict and a brief summary of what happened. Encourage students to enhance their time lines with relevant graphics or photos.

Use with All Lessons

ENGLISH LANGUAGE LEARNERS

STRATEGY ❶
PREP Before Reading

Encourage students at **All Proficiencies** to use the PREP strategy to prepare for reading. Display this acrostic for students:

Preview the title.
Read the Main Idea statement.
Examine the visuals.
Predict what you will learn.

Use with All Lessons *Encourage students at the* **Beginning** *level to ask questions if they have trouble writing a prediction. Students at the* **Intermediate** *or* **Advanced** *levels may be able to help.*

STRATEGY 2
Look for Cognates

Suggest students look for words that are similar in spelling and meaning to words in their home language as they read. For each word they identify, have students of **All Proficiencies** make a vocabulary card with the English word and definition on one side and the word and definition in their home language on the other side. Encourage them to note any differences in the meanings of the two words.

Use with All Lessons *For example, in Lesson 1.1, the words* conference, enemy, alliance, cooperate, international, *and* security *have cognates in Spanish:* conferencia, enemigo, alianza, cooperar, internacional, seguridad.

STRATEGY 3
Use a Term in a Sentence

Pair English language learners at **All Proficiencies** with English-proficient students. Provide pairs with a list of important words and terms from the lesson. Then have each pair work together to use each word in a written sentence. Invite pairs to share their sentences and discuss different ways to use each word. The list might include these terms from Lesson 1.1: *control, hostile, opposing, assist, reconstruction,* and *reforms.*

Use with All Lessons *You may wish to pair students at the* **Beginning** *level with those at the* **Advanced** *level and students at the* **Intermediate** *level with one another.*

GIFTED & TALENTED

STRATEGY 1
Research and Perform a Speech

Instruct students to conduct online research to find the text and/or a video of a speech made about one of the events in the chapter, such as President Roosevelt's remarks at the Yalta Conference, President Roosevelt's report on the Yalta Conference to Congress, George C. Marshall's speech on the Marshall Plan, President Truman's speech on the Truman Doctrine, or President Kennedy's speech on the goal of landing on the moon. Ask students to choose and perform part of a speech for the class.

Use with All Lessons

STRATEGY 2
Report on a Conflict

Invite students to choose one of the many conflicts mentioned in the chapter, such as Castro in Cuba, Mao in China, an African nation struggling for independence, the conflict over the Suez Canal, or an Eastern European country's conflict with the Soviet Union. Tell students to gather information, analyze the motivations of the people on both sides of the conflict, and explain the outcome. Instruct students to write a report about the conflict, including visuals and maps. Encourage them to share their reports with the class.

Use with All Lessons

PRE-AP

STRATEGY 1
Write an Analysis Essay

Prompt students to learn more about the division of Korea or Vietnam into "north" and "south" and the factors that contributed to the war in that country. Then challenge them to research the present-day politics of the country and how it has or has not changed since the war. Instruct students to use their research to write an essay analyzing the past and present problems of the country and the United States' involvement.

Use with Lessons 4.1 and 4.2

STRATEGY 2
Form and Support a Thesis

Instruct students to consider the freedoms guaranteed to U.S. citizens by the Bill of Rights and how these rights, which we often take for granted, are denied to many people in other countries. Tell students to form and support a thesis about why the denial of one or more of these rights frequently leads to conflict and/or revolution. Direct students to use one or more countries profiled in the chapter as examples in their thesis. Have them present their research in an oral report to the class or in a digital report posted on a class blog.

Use with All Lessons

CHAPTER

28 Cold War and Global Upheavals

1945–1979

HISTORICAL THINKING How do countries maintain their independence and security?

SECTION 1 Superpowers in an Arms Race
SECTION 2 Communism
SECTION 3 Colonies Seek Independence
SECTION 4 Wars in Asia and Global Crises

CRITICAL VIEWING Antiaircraft tanks parade in Red Square in Moscow in 1958 past a portrait of Vladimir Lenin, the founder of the Russian Communist Party. What does such a parade suggest about the Soviet Union at this time?

796 CHAPTER 28

Cold War and Global Upheavals 797

INTRODUCE THE PHOTOGRAPH

SOVIET UNION MILITARY PARADE

Have students study the photograph of the military parade in Moscow and read the caption. Then direct students to examine the portrait of Vladimir Lenin. **ASK:** How do you think the Soviets perceived Lenin after his death? *(Possible response: They revered Lenin as the founder and former leader of the Soviet Union.)* What does the juxtaposition of Lenin's portrait with the military parade convey? *(Possible response: that Lenin is watching over the success and growth of the Soviet Union)* Explain that the government, both in terms of its leaders and its policies, played a strong role in Soviet life. Tell students that in this chapter they will learn about the tensions that built up between the United States and Soviet Union after World War II and how those tensions manifested in many regions throughout the world.

SHARE BACKGROUND

Vladimir Lenin, the Bolshevik revolutionary shown in the portrait, and Joseph Stalin, who became leader of the Soviet Union after Lenin's death, had distinctly different views about how the government of the Soviet Union should function. Lenin wanted the Soviet Union to exist as a loose affiliation of Soviet states, all of which maintained their autonomy. He proposed that the government of the Russian Federation remain intact, while a new, moderately powerful governing body be created for the entirety of the Soviet Union. Stalin, on the other hand, proposed expanding the government of the Russian Federation to rule the entirety of the Soviet Union, giving Russia a greater amount of control than other member states. When Lenin passed away and Stalin succeeded him as the leader of the Soviet Union, Stalin was free to pursue his plan for the Soviet government.

CRITICAL VIEWING Answers will vary. Possible responses include that the parade suggests the Soviet Union's commitment to building a strong military and spreading communism throughout the world.

HISTORICAL THINKING QUESTION
How do countries maintain their independence and security?

Team Word Webbing: Brainstorm About Communism
Divide students into teams of four, and provide each team with a single large piece of paper. Give each student a different colored marker. Instruct students to brainstorm about the term *communism*. Encourage students to think about how communist governments work, what their values are, how communism affects the daily lives of average citizens, and how the United States has reacted toward communism. Have each student add to the part of the web nearest to him or her. On a signal, have students rotate the paper and have each student add to the nearest part again, building upon what the previous student wrote.

KEY DATES FOR CHAPTER 28

1945	World War II ends and the United Nations is formed.
1947	The Truman Doctrine is established.
1949	Chinese Nationalists flee to Taiwan and Mao Zedong takes control of mainland China.
1950	The Korean War begins.
1955	Leaders from developing nations meet at the Bandung Conference.
1956	Egypt nationalizes the Suez Canal.
1957	Ghana becomes the first African nation to gain independence from European colonization.
1962	The United States and Soviet Union face off in the Cuban Missile Crisis.
1964	The United States enters the Vietnam War.
1969	Two American astronauts, Buzz Aldrin and Neil Armstrong, become the first people to walk on the moon.
1991	The Soviet Union dissolves and the Cold War ends.

INTRODUCE THE READING STRATEGY

DETERMINE CHRONOLOGY
Explain to students that determining chronology can help them more deeply understand the order in which events occurred and how past events shaped the future. Go to the Chapter Review and preview the Major Events of the Cold War time line with students. As they read the chapter, have students determine the chronology of events pertaining to the Cold War and how they impacted relations in the international community.

INTRODUCE CHAPTER VOCABULARY

KEY VOCABULARY

SECTION 1

containment policy	domino effect	insolvency
proxy war	satellite state	Soviet bloc

SECTION 2

embargo	indoctrinate	people's commune
populism	revisionist	

SECTION 3

apartheid	neocolonialism	nonalignment
partition	referendum	

SECTION 4

atheism	demilitarized zone	mujahideen
trusteeship		

WORD MAP
As students read the chapter, ask them to complete a Word Map for each Key Vocabulary word. Tell them to write the word in the oval and, as they encounter the word in the chapter, complete the Word Map. Model an example using the graphic organizer below.

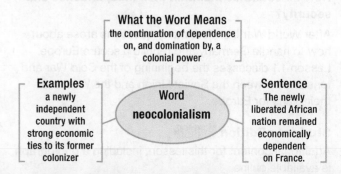

What the Word Means
the continuation of dependence on, and domination by, a colonial power

Examples
a newly independent country with strong economic ties to its former colonizer

Word
neocolonialism

Sentence
The newly liberated African nation remained economically dependent on France.

The Yalta Conference and Shifts in Power

Have you ever heard the saying "The enemy of my enemy is my friend"? The alliance between the United States and the Soviet Union during World War II was built on the basis of a common enemy. It fell apart soon after the Axis powers no longer posed a threat.

CAUSES OF THE COLD WAR

Just before the end of World War II, in February 1945, the Allied Powers met at Yalta, a Black Sea port on Ukraine's Crimean Peninsula, to plan Germany's unconditional surrender and the war's aftermath. President Franklin Roosevelt's priority for the meeting, called the Yalta Conference, was to get Joseph Stalin to cooperate in founding the United Nations (UN). Roosevelt achieved that goal.

The chief purpose of the UN was to maintain international peace and security through diplomacy. All the main bodies of the UN that exist today were established in 1945. They include the General Assembly, a policymaking body composed of all member nations, and the Security Council, a body originally composed of the major war allies: Great Britain, China, France, the Soviet Union, and the United States. Each member of the Security Council has veto power, which means that decisions can only be reached through consensus. The UN also includes the International Court of Justice, which settles legal disputes, and the Secretariat, which carries out the organization's day-to-day work. The Allies believed that the design of the UN would make it more effective than the League of Nations had been.

Another goal of the Yalta Conference was to create a plan for the countries of Eastern Europe that had been liberated from Nazi rule. The British and Americans had

At the Yalta Conference on the Crimean Peninsula in 1945, Prime Minister Winston Churchill of Great Britain, President Franklin Roosevelt of the United States, and Premier Joseph Stalin of the Soviet Union (seated left to right) met to plan the end of World War II and its aftermath.

promised that Poland would have free elections after the war. However, Stalin was not willing to give up Soviet control—he knew that any Polish government chosen through free elections would be hostile to the Soviet Union. As soon as the war was over, it became clear that Stalin would continue to occupy Poland and install a communist government there.

The Allied Powers met again six months later in Potsdam, Germany. By this time, the Soviets had occupied all of Eastern Europe, and Roosevelt had died and been replaced as U.S. president by Harry Truman. The Allies agreed to reduce the size of Germany, hold trials of Nazi war criminals in an international court, and dismantle Germany's military. They couldn't agree on

the fate of Europe, however. Truman insisted that the people of Europe had the right to free elections. Stalin responded, "Everyone imposes his own system as far as his army can reach."

In some Eastern European countries, local communists had strong political influence since they had played an important role in resisting the Nazis. In elections held in Czechoslovakia after the war, the Communist Party won enough seats in parliament to join a coalition government along with other parties. But Stalin wanted complete control and unquestioned loyalty. He used the Soviet army to establish loyal communist governments in Eastern European countries. A major reason that Stalin wanted to control Eastern Europe was to provide a buffer against any future invasion of Soviet territory from the west. Russia, after all, had just suffered its second 20th-century invasion by Germany.

By 1948, the countries of Europe had been divided into two opposing camps, one aligned with the United States and the other aligned with the Soviet Union. The United States and the Soviet Union, two superpowers, were now bitter enemies rather than allies. The Cold War division of Europe became economic as well as political and military. Countries aligned with the United States had market-based, capitalist economies. Those aligned with the Soviet Union had socialist economies with centralized government planning.

RECONSTRUCTION, NOT REPARATIONS

At both the Yalta and Potsdam conferences, the Allies discussed requiring reparations from Germany. However, Truman knew that the harsh reparations imposed on Germany following World War I had led to the rise of the Nazis. Instead, he proposed the **Marshall Plan** to assist in the rebuilding of war-ravaged countries. The plan was named after U.S. secretary of state George C. Marshall. In early 1948, the United States announced that $13 billion would be available to rebuild Europe's postwar economies and restore prosperity.

The Marshall Plan worked in conjunction with two international institutions formed earlier: the World Bank and the International Monetary Fund. The World Bank loaned money to nations in need of a jumpstart. The International Monetary Fund provided emergency loans to nations in danger of **insolvency**, or bankruptcy.

Because the Marshall Plan was designed to enhance the stability of free-market economies, the Soviet Union and its Eastern European **satellite states** refused to participate. A satellite state is a country that is formally independent but under the control or influence of another country. Instead of joining the Marshall Plan, the Soviet Union focused on rebuilding itself with resources from Eastern Europe. Entire factories were moved from eastern Germany to the Soviet Union.

Like Germany, Japan was also in need of rebuilding. After Japan surrendered, the Allies occupied the country and initiated a series of reforms. The occupation and reconstruction was completed in three phases. In Phase 1 (1945–1947), war criminals were tried in Tokyo, the Japanese army was dismantled, and military officials were banned from political leadership. In Phase 2 (1947–1950), Allied advisors drafted a new constitution to reduce the emperor's power, empower parliament, advance the rights of women, and abolish Japan's right to wage war. Economic reforms included the redistribution of land and the breakup of monopolies. In Phase 3 (1950–1951), a formal peace treaty ensured Japan's continued security while allowing the United States to keep military bases in Japan as protection against communist incursion in the area.

THE BERLIN AIRLIFT After the Potsdam Conference, collaboration between the Soviets and the Western powers broke down, and no conclusive agreement was reached on Germany's future. The Soviets occupied the eastern part of the country, and the British, Americans, and French occupied the western part. The capital city of Berlin was divided into four sections: British, American, French, and Soviet. Tensions escalated in 1948 when the Soviets cut off rail, road, and water access to Berlin. The United States and the United Kingdom responded by sending supplies to West Berlin by air. The Berlin Airlift was successful; supplies were delivered efficiently to the war-torn city and eventually the Soviets lifted the blockade. But the crisis led to the creation of two separate states: the Federal Republic of Germany (West Germany) and the German Democratic Republic (East Germany). This division became the symbolic battle line of the Cold War.

HISTORICAL THINKING

1. **READING CHECK** How did the outcome of World War II contribute to the development of the Cold War?

2. **DRAW CONCLUSIONS** At the Yalta Conference, why was Roosevelt eager to form the United Nations?

3. **COMPARE AND CONTRAST** How did the Marshall Plan in Europe compare with economic reforms in Japan?

PLAN: 2-PAGE LESSON

OBJECTIVE

Explain how, as World War II came to an end, a split developed between the United States and the Soviet Union over plans for Europe.

CRITICAL THINKING SKILLS FOR LESSON 1.1

- Draw Conclusions
- Compare and Contrast
- Evaluate
- Make Predictions
- Determine Chronology

HISTORICAL THINKING FOR CHAPTER 28

How do countries maintain their independence and security?

After World War II ended, many questions arose about how to handle Germany and rebuild a secure Europe. Lesson 1.1 discusses the beginning of the Cold War and tensions between the Soviet Union and the West over their plans for Europe.

Student eEdition online

Additional content for this lesson, including a photograph, is available online.

BACKGROUND FOR THE TEACHER

The Marshall Plan General George Marshall became Secretary of State in 1947 after a highly distinguished career in the U.S. Army. Many members of Congress initially opposed the $27 billion budget that Marshall requested for his European Recovery Program, but a reduced budget of $13 billion was passed in 1948. The economic benefits Marshall predicted soon bore fruit. As countries rebuilt their war-torn cities and economies, the standard of living began to rise, economic confidence throughout Europe grew stronger, and the United States gained more stable and wealthy trading partners for American goods. These strengthened trade markets helped fuel America's increasingly robust postwar economy. As demand for products grew at home and abroad, more Americans found work and saw their own standard of living increase.

INTRODUCE & ENGAGE

CONNECT TO EXPERIENCES WITH TEAMWORK

Have students consider times they have worked with others to accomplish a common goal, such as on a sports team, in a music or acting group, or on a school project. Then ask students to think about times they may have worked with people who had different views or opinions. Ask them to share what strategies they used to work with others when they did not agree. Tell students that in this lesson they will learn about the United States and the Soviet Union, two countries who worked together to end World War II but then struggled to resolve their differences of opinion.

TEACH

GUIDED DISCUSSION

1. **Evaluate** In what ways was the Yalta Conference a success and a failure? *(Possible responses: It was a success because the United Nations was founded. It was a failure because the Soviet Union and the United States failed to agree on a plan for Europe.)*

2. **Make Predictions** How could the Soviet Union's plan to rebuild itself with Eastern European resources make it difficult for Eastern Europe to recover from the war? *(Possible response: Eastern Europe might not have enough resources left for its own people.)*

DETERMINE CHRONOLOGY

Tell students to write the dates of important events in the lesson and examine the chronology. Ask students to list examples of how one event led to or influenced a later event. For example, less-powerful countries falling to communism caused Truman to enact the Marshall Plan, or the Allies dismantled the Japanese military in Phase 1 of reconstructing Japan so that they could reform the existing government in Phase 2.

ACTIVE OPTIONS

On Your Feet: Inside-Outside Circle Organize students into concentric circles facing each other. Designate the inside circle as the Soviet Union and the outside circle as the United States. First, instruct students in the outside circle to ask students in the inside circle questions about how they want to rebuild Europe after World War II. Then, on a signal, have students rotate to create new partnerships. On another signal, have students switch roles. Students now on the outside, playing the role of the United States, should ask the students on the inside questions about their plans for Europe. Students may ask for help from other students in their circle if they are unable to answer a question.

> **NG Learning Framework: Design a Diagram**
> **ATTITUDE** Curiosity
> **SKILL** Communication

Direct students to read the sidebar about the Berlin Airlift and instruct them to conduct additional research about what life was like for German civilians in East Berlin (the Soviet portion) and West Berlin (the British, American, and French portions). Instruct students to design a diagram that represents the similarities and differences between life in the two sides of Berlin. Invite volunteers to share their diagrams with the class.

DIFFERENTIATE

ENGLISH LANGUAGE LEARNERS

Pose and Answer Questions Pair students at the **Beginning** and **Intermediate** levels and ask them to reread the lesson together. Instruct them to pause after each paragraph, caption, or quotation and ask one another about what they have just read. Tell students at the **Intermediate** level to assist students at the **Beginning** level as needed.

GIFTED & TALENTED

Create Social-Networking Profiles Tell students to research Franklin Roosevelt, Winston Churchill, and Joseph Stalin to learn more about their character, philosophies, and thoughts about communism and democracy. Then have students create social-networking profiles for each, providing a brief summary and one or two photos. Ask students to end each profile with a statement that sums up that person's belief system. Invite students to share their profiles with the class.

See the Chapter Planner for more strategies for differentiation.

HISTORICAL THINKING

ANSWERS

1. Following WWII, the Soviet Union had different plans for Europe and Germany than the United States and Great Britain did; these differences created distrust and animosity among the former allies.

2. He hoped that the organization would help to prevent new wars and support continued diplomacy between the allied countries.

3. The Marshall Plan provided loans so that European countries could rebuild after the war. In Japan, economic reforms included the redistribution of land and the breakup of monopolies.

CRITICAL VIEWING (available in the Student eEdition) that the Soviets intended to maintain control of Berlin

American Alliances vs. the Soviet Bloc

Have you ever lined up dominoes in a row so that when you push on one at the end, the others all topple over? As the Soviet Union took control of Eastern Europe, American leaders envisioned one country after another falling to communism, just like a row of dominoes.

Division of Europe During the Cold War, 1960

NATO nation
Warsaw Pact nation
Non-aligned nation
Iron Curtain

CONTAINING THE SPREAD OF COMMUNISM
Throughout the Cold War years, the term **Iron Curtain** would be used to describe the political and military barrier created by the Soviets to keep the people of Eastern Europe and the Soviet Union from having contact with the West.

Western leaders began to fear a **domino effect**, by which one country after another would fall to communism like a row of dominoes. Hoping to stop the spread of communism, President Truman issued the **Truman Doctrine** in 1947, declaring that the United States would aid countries threatened by communism. Truman's declaration came as communists in Greece fought to establish a socialist government there. Truman promised American aid to suppress the rebellion.

> The term *Iron Curtain* originated in a speech given in 1946 by former British prime minister Winston Churchill in which he described the division of Europe into two opposing camps.
>
> **PRIMARY SOURCE**
>
> From Stettin in the Baltic to Trieste in the Adriatic, an iron curtain has descended across the Continent. Behind that line lie all the capitals of the ancient states of Central and Eastern Europe. . . . [A]nd the populations around them . . . are subject in one form or another, not only to Soviet influence but to a very high and, in many cases, increasing measure of control from Moscow.
>
> —Winston Churchill, former British prime minister, March 5, 1946

The Truman Doctrine advanced the **containment policy**, providing military and economic aid to protect countries from communist takeover. In reality, however, Stalin had already conceded Greece to Western control. And despite Truman's strong language, the United States did nothing to stop the Soviet takeover of Czechoslovakia.

SPHERES OF INFLUENCE
As hostilities increased between the Soviets and the Western powers, the United States allied with Canada and the European democracies to form the **North Atlantic Treaty Organization (NATO)**. The member nations agreed to a collective defense, stating "an armed attack against one or more of them in Europe or North America shall be considered an attack against them all." When West Germany was accepted as a member of NATO, the Soviet Union responded by forming the **Warsaw Pact**, an alliance with Eastern European nations under its sway.

Both superpowers presented themselves as champions of freedom. The Soviets identified colonialism and imperialism as the main barriers to liberation. They supported nationalists and socialists fighting European or American domination. But Moscow did not tolerate liberation movements within the **Soviet bloc**, the group of nations under its control. Secret police networks kept people from openly expressing anti-communist or anti-Soviet views. East Germany, for example, had a spy network called the *Stasi* that planted informers at all levels of society and encouraged neighbors to spy on one another. Still, in June 1953 East Germans rose up in large demonstrations to protest against low wages and bad working conditions. The communist

government violently put down the protests with the aid of Soviet tanks.

Americans were quick to point out that the Soviet Union suppressed individual freedoms. But by the 1950s, paranoia about communism led to practices that contradicted American ideals in the United States. In Congress, Senator Joseph McCarthy from Wisconsin stoked public fear by making unproven charges of communist infiltration in the government. As a result, many Americans accused of communist leanings lost their jobs and reputations.

The United States also backed authoritarian dictatorships around the world simply because they opposed communism. Guatemala was a democratic country with an elected president who wanted to redistribute land to aid the country's poor. That policy was opposed by the powerful United Fruit

Company, which convinced the U.S. government to secretly intervene to overthrow the elected government and replace it with an authoritarian one. Democracy was overthrown in Guatemala in the name of anti-communism.

THE ORGANIZATION OF AMERICAN STATES In 1948, a year before the formation of NATO, the Organization of American States (OAS) was formed at the urging of the United States to fight communism in the Americas and to maintain peace among the North and South American states. Initially, the OAS had 21 member countries, including the United States. Today, it includes all 35 independent states of the Americas. The OAS works to promote democracy, defend human rights, ensure security, and foster development and prosperity.

HISTORICAL THINKING

1. **READING CHECK** How did Western nations work together to keep the Soviets from expanding into Western Europe?

2. **IDENTIFY PROBLEMS AND SOLUTIONS** What problem did the Truman Doctrine seek to address?

3. **INTERPRET MAPS** What European countries were aligned with the Soviet Union during the Cold War?

PLAN: 2-PAGE LESSON

OBJECTIVE
Explain how, as the Soviet Union established communist governments throughout Eastern Europe, the Western powers worked together to contain the spread of communism.

CRITICAL THINKING SKILLS FOR LESSON 1.2
- Identify Problems and Solutions
- Interpret Maps
- Analyze Cause and Effect
- Evaluate

HISTORICAL THINKING FOR CHAPTER 28
How do countries maintain their independence and security?

As their alliance fell apart, the United States and the Soviet Union both scrambled to form alliances with other nations. Lesson 1.2 discusses the descent of the Iron Curtain in Europe and its effects around the globe.

Student eEdition online
Additional content for this lesson, including a photograph, is available online.

BACKGROUND FOR THE TEACHER
Soviet Control of Eastern European Countries The cost of winning World War II devastated the Soviet Union's economy. Stalin demanded that Soviet-controlled Eastern European countries provide raw materials and machinery to aid in the Soviet recovery. Stalin also used the threat of war with the West—specifically the United States—as a way to tighten economic control. Though Stalin used military force to gain power over many Eastern European nations during the war, he also promoted local communist parties so they could gain political power and maintain communist control in the region. By 1948, seven countries were controlled by communist governments. This allowed the Soviet Union to access the resources necessary to aid in Stalin's confrontation with the Western Allies.

INTRODUCE & ENGAGE

CONNECT TO TODAY

Display a Word Web with *Relations Between the United States and Russia* in the center. Remind students that present-day Russia was once part of the Soviet Union and an ally during World War II. Then ask students to suggest words they associate with the current relationship between the United States and Russia. Tell students that in this lesson they will examine how the two superpowers each sought to gain more control globally during the Cold War.

TEACH

GUIDED DISCUSSION

1. **Analyze Cause and Effect** Why did the United States, Canada, and European democracies form NATO? *(to protect one another and deter communist nations from attacking NATO nations)*

2. **Evaluate** How did U.S. opposition to communism both support and contradict American ideals? *(Possible response: U.S. opposition to communism fought against restricted freedoms within the Soviet Union but also infringed on democratic governments abroad if those governments were suspected of communist leanings.)*

INTERPRET MAPS

Direct students to the Division of Europe During the Cold War map. **ASK:** Which non-aligned nations might the United States identify as most at-risk to falling to communism? Why? *(Possible response: Yugoslavia, because it is behind the Iron Curtain, or Finland, because it shares a long border with the Soviet Union.)*

ACTIVE OPTIONS

On Your Feet: Team Word Webbing Have students read the Winston Churchill primary source about the Iron Curtain. Then organize them into teams of four, and provide each team with a single large piece of paper. Give each student a different colored marker. Assign the topic "Iron Curtain," and tell each student to write something about the Iron Curtain on the part of the web nearest to him or her. Encourage students to think about the economic, social, and cultural effects of the Iron Curtain. On a signal, students should rotate the paper and each student should add to the part nearest to him or her again.

> **NG Learning Framework: Draw a Sequence Diagram or Time Line**
> **SKILL** Communication
> **KNOWLEDGE** Our Human Story

Instruct students to read the sidebar about the Organization of American States and conduct further research about how the OAS evolved and expanded from its formation in 1948 to the present. Students should draw a sequence diagram or time line to share their research. Hang students' diagrams and time lines on the wall and encourage them to compare and contrast one another's work.

DIFFERENTIATE

ENGLISH LANGUAGE LEARNERS

Compose Captions Pair students at the **Beginning** and **Intermediate** levels with English-proficient students. Tell students to cover the caption of the photograph of President Truman addressing Congress (available in the Student eEdition) and work together to write an original and accurate caption for the photograph based on what they have learned in this lesson. Then have students uncover the original caption to compare it to theirs.

GIFTED & TALENTED

Illustrate a Metaphor Direct students' attention to the metaphor "iron curtain" used by Winston Churchill to describe the division of Europe between communism and capitalism. Invite students to draw a picture or use computer software to render the metaphor graphically in any artistic style, from realistic to impressionistic to a cartoon style. Encourage students to share their pictures with the class and explain why they chose the style and images they did.

See the Chapter Planner for more strategies for differentiation.

HISTORICAL THINKING

ANSWERS

1. The Western countries formed NATO to support each other militarily if one or more countries were attacked.

2. The Truman Doctrine was intended to contain the spread of communism and Soviet aggression.

3. East Germany, Poland, Czechoslovakia, Hungary, Romania, Bulgaria, and Albania were aligned with the Soviet Union.

The Arms and Space Races

In 1969, more than half a billion people around the world watched an awe-inspiring event on TV: American astronauts walking on the moon. They also saw a clear view of the entire Earth, maybe sensing the common destiny of all those living on that fragile sphere.

CAUSES AND EFFECTS OF THE ARMS RACE

As you've read, the United States and the Soviet Union had become bitter enemies by 1948. The two superpowers engaged in a global struggle for power, seeking to draw more countries into their orbits. But full-scale war between them never developed. The threat of nuclear weapons raised the stakes of total war too high. Fearful of nuclear annihilation, they never engaged in direct combat with each other. Instead, the Cold War turned hot in **proxy wars** around the world. In a proxy war, one or both sides are supported by, and serve the interests of, another country. The Cold War featured proxy wars in such countries as Greece, Korea, the Democratic Republic of the Congo, and Vietnam.

Seeking military superiority, the United States and the Soviet Union competed in an arms race from the late 1940s to the early 1990s. They spent billions of dollars building up their military strength and amassed nuclear weapons many times more powerful than those dropped on Hiroshima and Nagasaki. At the height of the arms race in 1986, each superpower possessed the ability to destroy the planet several times over.

People in both countries lived with the fear of a nuclear war. In the United States, school children practiced "duck and cover" drills, in which they ducked under their desks and covered their heads. Families built bomb shelters behind their homes where they hoped to hide in the event of a nuclear explosion. But most people realized that a nuclear war would result in the destruction of both countries and much of the world.

In 1972 and 1979, leaders of the two governments met to discuss how to limit nuclear weapons. These **Strategic Arms Limitation Talks (SALT)** had little success, but during the 1970s, both sides agreed to nuclear test ban treaties and limits on weapons production. Talks broke down, however, in 1979 when the Soviet Union invaded Afghanistan. By the time the Cold War ended in 1991, the cost of the arms race had overwhelmed the Soviet Union, contributing to its demise.

Both sides also expanded their intelligence operations during the Cold War. The Soviet spy agency, known as the KGB, worked through local proxy agencies, such as the East German Stasi, to maintain tight control over its satellite states while trying to infiltrate Western political, military, and intelligence communities. The United States formed the Central Intelligence Agency (CIA), which greatly expanded its operations during the 1950s to counter Soviet influence. The agency was involved in the overthrow of elected leaders in Guatemala, Iran, and the Democratic Republic of the Congo.

THE SPACE RACE

As the Soviets and Americans built rockets to transport long-range weapons, they realized that rockets could also be used to transport people into outer space. Thus began the space race, the competition between the United States and the Soviet Union to lead in space exploration. Getting to outer space first became a matter of national pride. In 1957, the Soviets launched Sputnik I, a satellite that successfully orbited Earth. Americans were humiliated and enraged that the Soviets had beat them, so the Eisenhower administration responded by creating the **National Aeronautics and Space Administration (NASA)** in 1958.

The American public eagerly followed news of the space race, and many Americans became obsessed with space exploration. The Soviet government, on the other hand, didn't announce its launches in advance. But its successes were highly publicized. The Soviets followed the launching of the first satellite in 1957 by sending the

802 CHAPTER 28

NATIONAL GEOGRAPHIC EXPLORER BUZZ ALDRIN

Astronaut Buzz Aldrin (shown here inside the Apollo 11 lunar module and above walking on the moon near a leg of the lunar module) famously described the lunar landscape as "magnificent desolation."

Beyond the Moon

On July 20, 1969, Buzz Aldrin and Neil Armstrong became the first two people to walk on the moon. Following that Apollo 11 mission, Aldrin and his fellow crew members were awarded the Presidential Medal of Freedom and the Congressional Gold Medal.

While Aldrin is most famous for the moon landing, he has had many other accomplishments. Born in 1930, Aldrin was raised in New Jersey and graduated third in his class at the United States Military Academy at West Point. He earned his doctorate in astronautics from the Massachusetts Institute of Technology (MIT) and flew a jet fighter in the Korean War. In 1963, he was selected by NASA to be a member of the third group of astronauts.

Aldrin retired from NASA in 1971, but he has dedicated his life to promoting space exploration. He has written nine books, made speeches around the world, and appeared on numerous TV shows to advance education in space research and exploration.

first dog, Laika, into space later the same year. Soviet cosmonaut Yuri Gagarin became the first man to orbit Earth in 1961, and two years later cosmonaut Valentina Tereshkova became the first woman to do so. By 1966, the Soviets had achieved the first spacewalk and had orbited the moon for the first time.

In 1961, U.S. president John F. Kennedy challenged NASA to put an American on the moon by the end of the decade. That ambitious goal became a reality in 1969 when U.S. astronaut Neil Armstrong became the first human to set foot on the moon.

HISTORICAL THINKING

1. **READING CHECK** What prevented the Soviet Union and the United States from actually fighting a war against each other?

2. **ANALYZE CAUSE AND EFFECT** How did the arms race contribute to the eventual demise of the Soviet Union?

3. **SEQUENCE EVENTS** When did the United States and the Soviet Union begin to work toward denuclearization—before or after the main events of the space race?

Cold War and Global Upheavals 803

PLAN: 2-PAGE LESSON

OBJECTIVE

Identify how rivalry between the Soviet Union and the United States contributed to competitions to build the most powerful arsenal of weapons and to lead space exploration.

CRITICAL THINKING SKILLS FOR LESSON 1.3

- Analyze Cause and Effect
- Sequence Events
- Explain
- Compare and Contrast
- Interpret Graphs

HISTORICAL THINKING FOR CHAPTER 28

How do countries maintain their independence and security?

Two primary areas of advancement emerged at the forefront of innovation during the Cold War. Lesson 1.3 discusses how the United States and the Soviet Union competed in terms of military power and space exploration.

BACKGROUND FOR THE TEACHER

Technology in the Arms and Space Races During the last years of World War II, America's aerospace industry was booming—factories were in production 24 hours a day, 6 or 7 days a week. In 1944, 96,000 planes were built. Thousands of those were sold to the Soviet Union in the effort to defeat Germany. After the war ended, the United States and the Soviet Union continued developing new aerospace weaponry. In the Soviet Union, production was controlled by the government; in the United States, inventors and designers at aerospace companies worked with the military. As the Cold War evolved and the superpowers advanced their nuclear threats, the focus turned to guided missile technology. Starting in 1950, the United States developed anti-aircraft missiles, air-launched weapons, drone bombers, and ground-to-air defense systems. Electronics technology became an important component of aerospace defense systems, with the Soviet Union and the United States competing to build the fastest and most nimble aircraft.

Student eEdition online

Additional content for this lesson, including a video, a graph, and images, is available online.

INTRODUCE & ENGAGE

CONSIDER ESCALATING TENSIONS

Prompt students to think about how and why tensions escalate between groups of people. Examples include gang rivalries, political differences among relatives, or even something as explosive as the relationships between some African-American communities and the local police. **ASK:** Why do you think conflicts between groups can easily escalate? *(Answers will vary. Possible responses: deteriorating trust between groups or competition for scarce resources)* Tell students that in this lesson they will learn more about the events that led to escalating tensions between the Soviet Union and the United States during the Cold War.

TEACH

GUIDED DISCUSSION

1. **Explain** How did the arms race lead to the demise of the Soviet Union? *(It was so costly that it crippled the Soviet Union's economy.)*

2. **Compare and Contrast** What differences were there in the publicity approaches to the space race between the Soviet Union and the United States? *(The United States publicized rocket launches to drum up public excitement. The Soviet Union did not release information about launches and only publicized its successes.)*

INTERPRET GRAPHS

Direct students to the Stockpile of U.S. and Soviet Nuclear Warheads graph (available in the Student eEdition). **ASK:** When did the number of weapons held by the Soviet Union surpass the number held by the United States? *(between 1977–1978)* How might the data shown in the graph have been different if the United States had started out with far fewer nuclear warheads? *(Possible response: If the United States had started out with fewer nuclear warheads, the Soviet Union might not have felt pressured to keep up and to steadily increase the number of nuclear warheads between 1962 and 1986.)*

ACTIVE OPTIONS

On Your Feet: Think, Pair, Share After watching the video of President Kennedy's "Moon" speech (available in the Student eEdition), give students several minutes to think about the content individually. Then instruct pairs to discuss their thoughts with one another. Finally, invite students to share information from their pair discussions with the class.

| **NG Learning Framework: Write a Personal Essay on Space Exploration**
| **ATTITUDE** Curiosity
| **KNOWLEDGE** New Frontiers

Direct students to read the National Geographic Explorer sidebar "Buzz Aldrin: Beyond the Moon." Then prompt students to contemplate whether or not, if given the opportunity, they would travel on a space exploration mission. Encourage students to examine the physical, mental, and emotional aspects of such a journey. Then instruct them to write a personal essay explaining why they would or would not embark on a space journey. Invite volunteers to share their essays with the class.

DIFFERENTIATE

STRIVING READERS

Create Word Squares Ask students to write *Arms Race* in the center oval of a Word Square and to write the definition and characteristics of the phrase in the appropriate boxes. Guide them to identify examples and non-examples.

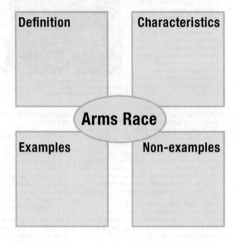

PRE-AP

Write a Report Direct students to gather information from several sources to write a report on the military-industrial complex in the United States that emerged during the Cold War. Encourage students to conclude the report with an assessment of the current state of U.S. military spending and the ease or difficulty of controlling the military-industrial complex today. Invite students to share their reports with the class.

See the Chapter Planner for more strategies for differentiation.

HISTORICAL THINKING

ANSWERS

1. They feared that the war would lead to nuclear annihilation of both countries and much of the world.

2. The cost overwhelmed the Soviet Union financially.

3. in the late 1980s, nearly two decades after the main events of the space race

Cuba and Castro

For 13 days in October 1962, people around the world waited in fear as the two superpowers hovered on the brink of nuclear war. The Americans and Soviets both stood their ground in a showdown over Cuba.

THE CUBAN REVOLUTION

In the 1950s, Cuba was an island of contrasts. Its capital, Havana, was famous for its beaches and nightclubs. But Cuba's wealthy economy, based on luxury hotels and tourism, obscured a darker underside of corruption. The American Mafia, an organization of criminals, controlled Havana's casinos, and American business interests supported the country's corrupt dictator, Fulgencio Batista (fool-HEHN-see-oh buh-TEE-stuh). Most Cubans lived in poverty, without democratic freedoms or access to good jobs, health care, or education.

Cuban revolutionary leader Fidel Castro, shown with his arm raised, and his fellow rebels enter Havana, Cuba, on January 8, 1959, after overthrowing the dictatorship of Fulgencio Batista.

An idealistic young Cuban named **Fidel Castro** renounced middle-class privilege and promoted **populism**, or support for the concerns of ordinary people, as he started the Cuban Revolution to end Batista's rule. Castro led an attack on an army barracks and was imprisoned in 1953. After his release, he fled to Mexico, where he formed a small band of rebels determined to overthrow the Cuban dictator. One of Castro's revolutionary friends was the Argentinian **Ernesto "Che" Guevara**. Guevara was in Guatemala during the U.S. overthrow of its government, fled to Mexico, and then went on to Cuba.

In 1956, when Castro and Guevara and other revolutionaries returned to Cuba, they recruited more rebels from the local population and stockpiled ammunition. They used guerrilla tactics, such as quick raids and surprise ambushes, to fight the Cuban army. On New Year's Day 1959, Batista fled to the Dominican

Republic, and Castro's forces entered Havana a few days later.

RELATIONS WITH THE SUPERPOWERS

As the new leader of Cuba, Castro sought support from the United States. But relations with the United States deteriorated after Cuba passed a law that nationalized land owned by American corporations. Soon corporate lobbyists and Cold War hawks, who supported an aggressive foreign policy, portrayed Castro as a Soviet threat. Pro-Batista forces in the United States, who were mostly Cuban exiles, lobbied for an American-backed invasion.

In the spring of 1961, a U.S.-sponsored group of Cuban exiles stormed Cuba's Bay of Pigs. Castro's forces crushed the invasion, but Castro's distrust of the United States increased. Meanwhile, the United States placed

804 CHAPTER 28

This photograph, taken by National Geographic photographer David Guttenfelder, shows people lining the streets of the town of Las Tunas, Cuba, as Fidel Castro's funeral procession passes by. Guttenfelder rented a blue 1958 Buick and followed the multi-day funeral cortege from Havana to Santiago de Cuba.

"All along the way, on the edge of the highway, with their horses in sugarcane fields, on the streets of every village and town," says Guttenfelder, "people came out to line the road—millions of people, whole communities—standing in silent attention, some weeping, to witness the end of an era."

an economic **embargo**, or trade ban, on Cuba, making diplomacy and compromise all but impossible.

Tensions between the United States and Cuba culminated in the **Cuban Missile Crisis** of 1962. Castro was convinced that the United States would never let his socialist changes in Cuba proceed in peace, so he developed closer ties with the Soviet Union. **Nikita Khrushchev** (nuh-KEE-tuh krush-AWF), the Soviet premier, took advantage of the situation and secretly shipped nuclear missiles to Cuba. When American surveillance aircraft detected the missiles, President Kennedy demanded their removal. Khrushchev refused, and Kennedy ordered a naval quarantine to prevent Soviet ships from reaching Cuba. For 13 days, the people of the world held their breath as the two countries moved closer to war. Then both sides backed down. Khrushchev removed the Soviet missiles from Cuba, and Kennedy removed U.S. missiles from Turkey and promised not to invade Cuba.

To help Cuba withstand the American embargo, the Soviets bought the island's entire sugar crop at above-market prices and provided subsidized fuel and agricultural machinery. By the mid-1960s, Cubans were

better fed and better housed than they had been before the revolution. Basic healthcare and education became free for all. But as Castro transformed Cuba into a communist country, underlying economic problems remained. Cuba depended on the Soviet Union in the same way Latin American countries had depended on colonial powers in the past, exporting agricultural products while importing higher-valued industrial goods. In time, Cuban workers complained of low wages and shortages of basic goods. Castro's government viewed all opposition to its policies as being promoted by the United States and its community of Cuban exiles in Florida. Cubans who publicly complained might be denied jobs, arrested, sent to labor camps, or even executed.

HISTORICAL THINKING

1. **READING CHECK** What conditions in Cuba motivated Fidel Castro and other rebels to start the Cuban Revolution?

2. **MAKE INFERENCES** Why did American troops invade Cuba at the Bay of Pigs?

3. **DESCRIBE** Explain what happened during the Cuban Missile Crisis.

Cold War and Global Upheavals 805

OBJECTIVE

Describe how Cold War conflicts increased in the Americas as Cuba formed ties with the Soviet Union.

CRITICAL THINKING SKILLS FOR LESSON 2.1

- Make Inferences
- Describe
- Identify
- Identify Supporting Details
- Analyze Visuals

HISTORICAL THINKING FOR CHAPTER 28

How do countries maintain their independence and security?

Economic inequality and insecurity in many countries around the world led people to communism. Lesson 2.1 discusses how Cuba transformed into a communist state under the leadership of Fidel Castro.

Student eEdition online

Additional content for this lesson, including a sidebar, is available online.

BACKGROUND FOR THE TEACHER

National Geographic Photographer David Guttenfelder David Guttenfelder is a National Geographic photographer who took the photo of Fidel Castro's funeral procession that appears in the lesson. Originally from Iowa, Guttenfelder has traveled around the world documenting geopolitics and conservation for more than 20 years. While working for the Associated Press, he spent time based in Nairobi, New Delhi, Tokyo, and North Korea, where he was part of the first Western news outpost in the historically inaccessible country. Guttenfelder's work first appeared in National Geographic in 2011, where he documented the opium wars in Afghanistan. He has taught workshops on capturing the world through smartphone photography, as well as photography programs for young adults. His accolades include a World Press Photo Award, Pictures of the Year International, and *TIME* magazine's "100 Most Influential Photographs Ever Taken."

INTRODUCE & ENGAGE

DISCUSS CONFRONTATION AND COMPROMISE

Ask students to recall a time from their own lives or from history when there was a serious argument or confrontation that ended in a compromise. Discuss the issues that were at stake, and use a Sequence Chart to diagram the steps that led to a compromise, thus resolving the situation. Tell students that in this lesson they will learn about a confrontation between the United States and Soviet Union involving Cuba that brought the world to the brink of nuclear war, until a compromise allowed both superpowers to step back.

TEACH

GUIDED DISCUSSION

1. **Identify** What role did American corporations play in the dissolution of the relationship between Cuba and the United States? *(American corporations portrayed Cuba and Castro as a Soviet threat after Castro nationalized Cuban land that had been owned by American corporations.)*

2. **Identify Supporting Details** How did Soviet intervention improve the lives of the Cuban people? *(The Soviets provided economic aid by purchasing Cuba's sugar crop at above-market prices and subsidizing necessities such as fuel and machinery.)*

ANALYZE VISUALS

Direct students to the photograph of Fidel Castro and other rebels after overthrowing the dictator Batista. **ASK:** What can you infer from Fidel Castro's body language in the photograph? *(Possible response: Fidel Castro's raised arm and straightforward gaze show that he feels victorious and excited about the road ahead.)*

ACTIVE OPTIONS

On Your Feet: Roundtable Instruct students to read the Cuba After Castro sidebar (available in the Student eEdition) and to examine the photograph of Fidel Castro's funeral procession. Seat students around a table in groups of four and ask them to contemplate how Cuba has changed over the last 70 years. Tell each student around the table to answer the question in a different way and to consider how the politics and economy of Cuba have affected daily life and culture.

> **NG Learning Framework: Write an Editorial**
> **SKILL** Observation
> **KNOWLEDGE** Our Human Story

Prompt students to conduct online research about how communism and life under Castro's rule affected the Cuban people. Suggest to students that they focus on education, medical care, access to resources, the arts, and religion. Then have students write an editorial either in favor or against communism in Cuba based on their research.

DIFFERENTIATE

STRIVING READERS

Predict Using Visuals Before reading the lesson, guide students to predict how the two photos are related to the rise and gradual decline of communism in Cuba. First, tell students to read the lesson title and Main Idea statement. Then ask them to examine the visuals and read the captions, using that information to write predictions. After reading the lesson, tell pairs to discuss what they learned and whether it matched their predictions.

PRE-AP

Engage in a Negotiation Tell students to conduct further research about the Cuban Missile Crisis and then organize into two teams, one that represents the United States and another that represents the Soviet Union. Tell the groups to negotiate an end to the Cuban Missile Crisis. Remind students to focus on the motivations and long-term goals of each country, as well as the logistics of disarmament.

See the Chapter Planner for more strategies for differentiation.

HISTORICAL THINKING

ANSWERS

1. Cuba was controlled by a dictator who was backed by American economic interests. Cubans had limited access to employment, healthcare, education, and democratic freedoms.

2. to protect their economic interests and contain the threat of communism by overthrowing Castro

3. Castro built ties with the Soviet Union; Khrushchev sent Soviet missiles to Cuba; the Americans spotted the missile site; Kennedy demanded that the missiles be removed; a standoff ensued; the two sides compromised; Khrushchev removed the missiles; the United States removed missiles from Turkey and agreed not to interfere in Cuban affairs.

2.2 Preserving Cultural Heritage

FORGOTTEN ART SCHOOLS

The Cuban Revolution brought a spirit of optimism to life in Cuba. The oppressive Batista regime was in the past, and the future seemed to hold great possibilities. In 1961, Fidel Castro and Argentine revolutionary leader Che Guevara enthusiastically proposed five tuition-free schools where students from around the world could study ballet, modern dance, music, art, and theater in a creative environment.

A trio of architects developed a different design for each of the five schools. But all the designs incorporated the natural landscape, common architectural structures, and Cuban-made bricks and terra-cotta tiles. For four years, the schools buzzed with activity as students danced through curved colonnades and construction continued on domed pavilions and concert halls.

Following the Cuban Missile Crisis in 1962, national security became Cuba's top priority and Soviet ideology took precedence over artistic endeavors. The project came to a dramatic halt in 1965. The schools' three

architects were accused of valuing material goods rather than revolutionary ideals. One architect was imprisoned; the other two fled the country. Over the next 40 years, the unfinished schools fell into ruin, though students continued to study at several of the neglected campuses.

In the 1990s, Castro invited the original architects to restore the school buildings. Cuba's National Council of Cultural Heritage recognized the schools as a national monument in 2011. Today, the National Art Schools are considered the most important architectural achievement of the Cuban Revolution.

HISTORICAL THINKING

ANALYZE VISUALS How do the photos and history of Cuba's National Art Schools reflect the country's own history?

The unifying design element of the National Art Schools was a ceiling made by a technique called *Catalan vault*. Using this technique, a builder places bricks lengthwise over parallel wooden beams to form an arch-shaped ceiling. The Catalan vaults increased the structural strength of ceilings and allowed builders to use materials readily available in Cuba.

This unfinished hallway is part of the School of Music.

HAVANA, CUBA
The National Art Schools were added to the 2016 World Monuments Watch, which lists sites around the world "that are at risk from the forces of nature and the impact of social, political, and economic change."

PLAN: 2-PAGE LESSON

OBJECTIVE

Learn about the National Art Schools in Cuba commissioned by Fidel Castro and Che Guevara during the Cuban Revolution.

CRITICAL THINKING SKILLS FOR LESSON 2.2

- Analyze Visuals
- Make Connections
- Make Inferences
- Explain

HISTORICAL THINKING FOR CHAPTER 28

How do countries maintain their independence and security?

The Cuban Revolution inspired architecture and artistic expansion. However, Cuba's freedom to artistic expression was stifled by Soviet ideology and prioritization of national security. Lesson 2.2 discusses the development and subsequent abandonment of Cuba's National Art Schools.

Student eEdition online

Additional content for this lesson, including a photo, is available online.

BACKGROUND FOR THE TEACHER

The National Art Schools Fidel Castro and Che Guevara conceived the idea of creating a space to encourage artistic and cultural expression on a golf course, deciding to transform Havana's country club, with its rolling hills, into an art campus. Cuban architect Ricardo Porro was chosen to bring the vision to life, along with Italian architects Roberto Gottardi and Vittorio Garatti. The men eagerly began the creation of the five schools commissioned by Castro: the School of Ballet, the School of Plastic Arts, the School of Dramatic Arts, the School of Music, and the School of Modern Dance. Porro favored organic architecture, with buildings in harmony with the landscape, and strong, Mediterranean-inspired domes with soft, curving lines. He included elements of Cuba's African heritage in the School of Plastic Arts, evident in its skylights and open-room design. When the project was halted, three of the five schools were left unfinished and were never utilized. However, students filled the vine-covered, partially deteriorating campus for decades.

History Notebook

Encourage students to complete the Preserving Cultural Heritage page for Chapter 28 in their History Notebooks as they read.

INTRODUCE & ENGAGE

PREVIEW WITH VISUALS

Prompt students to examine the photographs in the lesson. Encourage them to discuss the buildings' unique features and consider what the buildings may be used for. Ask students to point out features in the buildings and compare and contrast them with other buildings they have viewed in the text. Explain that the photographs depict an art school in Cuba, which they will learn about in this lesson.

TEACH

GUIDED DISCUSSION

1. **Make Inferences** Since their conception, how have the National Art Schools been "at risk from the forces of nature and the impact of social, political, and economic change"? *(Possible response: They were commissioned during a time of political upheaval, and several were not completed, so they have been at risk from the beginning. The economic and social ideals that followed the political shift only put the building complex at further risk. The unused and unpreserved buildings have been at risk from natural weathering and plant overgrowth, as well as other natural forces such as hurricanes.)*

2. **Explain** What was the fate of the architects who designed the schools? *(Possible responses: One was imprisoned and two fled the country when they were accused of valuing material goods over revolutionary ideals. They were all invited by Castro to restore the buildings in the 1990s.)*

PRESERVING CULTURAL HERITAGE

In 1991, architect and historian John Loomis visited Havana and, led by architect Roberto Gottardi, explored the complete ruins of the National Art Schools. Enthralled by their magnificence, Loomis published a book in 1999 entitled *Revolution of Forms: Cuba's Forgotten Art Schools.* The book, which made the schools famous, reached Castro and encouraged him to begin efforts to renew and preserve the buildings. The three original architects came together to begin plans to revive the schools. Over the years, the School of Plastic Arts and the School of Modern Dance were restored and the three uncompleted buildings were cleaned and stabilized.

ACTIVE OPTION

NG Learning Framework: Restore a Monument
ATTITUDE Responsibility
SKILLS Collaboration, Problem Solving

Guide students to the restoration projects on the World Monuments Fund website. Ask small groups to research a monument and create a presentation to explain the significance of the site and persuade their audience to take an active role in preserving and/or restoring the monument. They should include photographs and outline the actions the audience could take, detailed plans for the restoration, and funding either from the public or the government. Groups may present to the class or share a recording of their presentations in class or on a class website.

DIFFERENTIATE

ENGLISH LANGUAGE LEARNERS

Make Word Cards Pair students at **All Proficiencies** to make word cards for difficult or unfamiliar terms in the lesson, including *enthusiastically, Catalan vault, colonnades, pavilions, precedence, endeavors,* and *neglected.* Tell pairs to write the term on one side of a card and define it on the opposite side, either in English or in their first language. Encourage pairs to find pronunciations of the terms or seek assistance if needed. Have students quiz one another about the meaning of each term until all cards are shared.

GIFTED & TALENTED STEM

Work as an Architect Have students research the National Art Schools and find photographs, videos, and descriptions of the buildings. Challenge students to create blueprints of the complex (either drawing by hand or using computer software), or build a model of one of the buildings. Encourage students to share their blueprints or models with the class.

See the Chapter Planner for more strategies for differentiation.

HISTORICAL THINKING

ANSWER

Possible response: The creativity and beauty of the architecture reflect the utopian vision of Cuba's new leaders in the early 1960s. The buildings' ruins reflect the hardships the country endured under communism. The renewed interest and building restoration convey hope for Cuba's future.

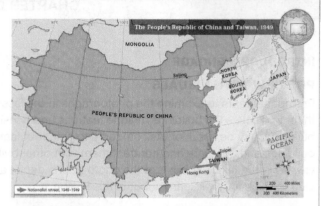

The People's Republic of China and Taiwan, 1949

Mao Zedong and the People's Republic of China

Have you ever asked your friends for their opinions, only to have them tell you something you really didn't want to hear? That's what happened in China. The leader of the Chinese Communist Party got such negative feedback that he punished all the people who spoke out, along with anybody associated with them.

THE CHINESE CIVIL WAR

As a young man, **Mao Zedong**, the future ruler of China, studied various political philosophies before embracing communism. He believed revolution in China would start with the peasants, and beginning in the 1920s, he spent many years politically organizing the peasants in China's countryside. Meanwhile, **Chiang Kai-shek** became the head of the Nationalist government in China in 1928. The Nationalists fought the Communists intermittently for years until the two groups united in 1937 to fight the Japanese, who had invaded China.

After Japan's defeat in World War II in 1945, Mao and Chiang resumed the Chinese Civil War. Chiang's Nationalists had a large army, the support of Western powers, and control of China's largest cities. But Mao had the support of Chinese peasants who had waged guerrilla warfare against the Japanese invaders. After World War II, Mao's People's Liberation Army joined with peasants in waging guerrilla warfare against the Nationalists.

In 1949, Mao Zedong and his Communist Party emerged victorious in the civil war and established the People's Republic of China on the mainland. Chiang Kai-shek and his Nationalist followers fled to the island of Taiwan, where they established the Republic of China.

Once in power, the Communists revolutionized China from the bottom up. They organized peasants into agricultural working groups called cooperatives, expanded educational opportunities, formed youth organizations, and enrolled workers in state-sponsored unions. Within the youth organizations, unions, and other groups, citizens were **indoctrinated**, or rigidly trained, in "Mao Zedong Thought." Those who expressed ideas that deviated from Mao's ideology were shamed and forced to publicly confess their "errors."

This photograph shows Chinese Communist leader Mao Zedong (far left) talking with peasants in a northern province of China. The photo dates to the time of the war between the Chinese and the Japanese that lasted from 1937 to 1945.

THE CHINESE AND SOVIETS SPLIT

Initially, the People's Republic of China followed Soviet-style economic policies of state-run industries and collective farms, which were cooperative associations of farmers who worked land owned by the government. The Chinese sent engineers and state planners to the Soviet Union for training. Mao hoped to stimulate rapid economic growth, but the results were disappointing. The growth of industrial and agricultural production was slower than Mao expected, and new leadership in the Soviet Union didn't suit Mao's ideology. Soviet Premier Khrushchev criticized his predecessor—Stalin— for fostering a cult of personality, in which a public figure is idolized. Mao had admired Stalin, and he had modeled his own cult of personality after Stalin's. Khrushchev also implemented political reforms, such as relaxing censorship and easing tensions with the West. Mao considered Khrushchev's approach weak and **revisionist**, or straying from the revolutionary spirit of Marxist doctrine. Mao continued to use strong anti-capitalist and anti-imperialist rhetoric against the West.

Mao broke ties with the Soviets and sought a solution to China's slow advancement. To inspire new ideas, he launched a program that became known as the Hundred Flowers Campaign. The program encouraged people to speak freely and offer suggestions. China's intellectuals responded with open criticism of the Communist Party and Mao's leadership. In 1957, Mao had the intellectuals arrested, imprisoned, and exiled.

After purging the intellectual "rightists," Mao began to describe the Communist Party as being divided into two factions, which he labeled "expert" and "red." According to Mao, the "experts," who managed collectivization and industrial development, were becoming a technical elite, or upper class, cut off from the "masses," or common people. Mao believed the "reds," leaders who emphasized socialist willpower rather than technical ability, would rapidly bring about socialist prosperity by unleashing the true revolutionary potential of China's peasants and workers. Basically, Mao believed people would work harder because of their deeply held socialist beliefs. In Mao's thinking, the people working collectively could literally move mountains.

HISTORICAL THINKING

1. **READING CHECK** What led Mao Zedong to break away from Soviet communism?

2. **ANALYZE CAUSES AND EFFECTS** What factors contributed to the Communists' victory in the Chinese Civil War?

3. **INTEGRATE VISUALS** How did the Republic of China, established by Chiang Kai-shek, compare in size with the People's Republic of China?

PLAN: 2-PAGE LESSON

OBJECTIVE

Describe how Mao Zedong's Communist Party took power in China in 1949 but split with the Soviet Union to create its own version of communism.

CRITICAL THINKING SKILLS FOR LESSON 2.3

- Analyze Causes and Effects
- Integrate Visuals
- Make Connections
- Draw Conclusions
- Interpret Maps

HISTORICAL THINKING FOR CHAPTER 28

How do countries maintain their independence and security?

The Soviet Union was not the only communist superpower in the East. Lesson 2.3 discusses the Chinese Civil War and the rise of communism under Mao Zedong after World War II.

BACKGROUND FOR THE TEACHER

The Marshall Plan and a Fractured China Before the Chinese Nationalists fled to Taiwan and the Chinese Communist Party took over the government of mainland China, the United States tried unsuccessfully to broker a deal between the two parties. While World War II was still winding down, Chiang Kai-shek invited Mao Zedong to negotiate rebuilding China together. In 1945, after the war had ended, American ambassador Patrick Hurley accompanied Mao to meet with Chiang in Chongqing. A verbal agreement was reached, but fighting erupted between the Communists and Nationalists before a specific plan forward could be created. George C. Marshall traveled to China in December of 1945 to bring the Communists and Nationalists back to the negotiating table. By the end of January 1946, it appeared as though an agreement had been reached. However, fighting resumed as the details and implementation strategy were still being negotiated.

INTRODUCE & ENGAGE

REVIEW AND PREVIEW

Tell students to review previous lessons concerning communism around the world, such as in the Soviet Union, Eastern Europe, and Latin America. They should then preview this lesson's photo, map, headings, and Key Vocabulary words. Suggest that students think about how this lesson might be similar to and different from previous lessons about communist regimes. Prompt them to write three things they would like to know about communism in China. If the lesson does not answer their questions, urge them to conduct independent research.

TEACH

GUIDED DISCUSSION

1. **Make Connections** In what way was the relationship between the Chinese Nationalists and the Chinese Communists similar to the relationship between the United States and the Soviet Union? *(Like the United States and Soviet Union, the Chinese Nationalists and Chinese Communists joined together to fight the Axis powers in World War II, but after World War II, the two sides disagreed over different economic ideologies.)*

2. **Draw Conclusions** What responses from intellectuals do you think Mao Zedong was hoping to achieve through the Hundred Flowers Campaign? *(Possible response: Since Mao Zedong punished those who disagreed with him, he was probably hoping for responses that would justify and support his policies.)*

INTERPRET MAPS

Direct students to the People's Republic of China and Taiwan map. **ASK:** Based on the size of the People's Republic and the size of Taiwan, what can you infer about the number of Nationalists and Communists? *(There were probably many more Communists than Nationalists.)*

ACTIVE OPTIONS

On Your Feet: Numbered Heads Tell students to number off within groups of four. Ask students to think individually about how the Chinese Communist Party differed from the Communist Party in the Soviet Union and what brought about those differences. Then instruct groups to discuss the topic so that any member of the group can report on the discussion. Call a number and have the student with that number report for the group.

NG Learning Framework: Write a Character Profile
ATTITUDE Responsibility
KNOWLEDGE Our Human Story

Instruct students to research some of the prominent intellectuals of the Hundred Flowers Campaign. Tell them to choose one person who spoke out against the Chinese Communist Party to research further. Explain that it is their responsibility to give a voice to someone who was wrongfully silenced. Students should put together a character profile of the person they choose, emphasizing his or her ideology and belief system.

DIFFERENTIATE

INCLUSION

Work in Pairs Allow students with disabilities to work with students who can make the lesson more accessible for them. The partner without disabilities should describe in detail the photograph and the map. Suggest that students use a graphic organizer to help them better understand communism in China.

PRE-AP

Write an Explanatory Essay Direct students to use primary and secondary sources to write an explanatory essay that summarizes the causes and effects of the Chinese Civil War. Guide students in looking at how different experiences and access to resources could lead the Chinese Nationalists and peasants of the Communist Party to draw very different conclusions about how China should move forward as a nation. Invite volunteers to share their essays with the class.

See the Chapter Planner for more strategies for differentiation.

HISTORICAL THINKING

ANSWERS

1. Mao split from Soviet communism after Khrushchev came to power and criticized Stalin's cult of personality. Mao admired Stalin and promoted a strong cult of personality himself. When Khrushchev began easing relations with the West and relaxing censorship, Mao considered his policies weak and revisionist.

2. They had cultivated relationships with the peasants during the Japanese invasion and had learned to use guerilla warfare. The peasants supported the communists.

3. The Republic of China was a tiny fraction of the size of the People's Republic of China.

Communes and Chaos

Mao Zedong had great faith in the common people of China, believing they had an "inexhaustible enthusiasm for socialism." Aiming to harness their revolutionary spirit, he introduced programs that tested that enthusiasm.

THE GREAT LEAP FORWARD

Hoping to harness the zeal and power of the masses, Mao launched a campaign called the **Great Leap Forward** in 1958 to stimulate rapid industrialization. The peasants were now organized into **people's communes**, which combined a number of collective farms. Unlike the former collective farms, in which people engaged exclusively in agricultural activities, the people's communes were multipurpose. The communes pooled the labor of thousands of peasants from different villages to increase agricultural production and to engage in local industrial production. Small furnaces were set up across the country to produce steel, for example.

On the communes, the people were organized into communal, or shared, living areas as well as work units. Communal kitchens replaced private kitchens, and a team of people cooked for the community, whose members ate together. Meanwhile, property rights were restricted, and peasants lost access to the small plots they had formerly relied on to feed their families. Mao directed the masses to pour all their energy and enthusiasm into communal production.

The Great Leap Forward was disastrous. The steel produced in small communal furnaces was of poor quality, and food production declined. As many as 30 million people died in the famine that followed. Recognizing the catastrophic failure of the plan, the Communist Party secretly reduced Mao's authority. But party leaders disagreed on the cause of the failure. Some claimed it was poor management and overzealous policies. Others blamed the lack of expertise and material incentives.

THE CULTURAL REVOLUTION

In an effort to reassert his authority and silence his critics, Mao launched a movement in 1966 to instill his thinking into Chinese society. In the **Cultural Revolution**, Mao organized young people into militant groups called

the Red Guard. Members of the Red Guard were taught that Mao himself was the source of all wisdom. A "little red book" of Mao's quotations became the bible of the Red Guard movement. At large public gatherings, members of the Red Guard would wave the book enthusiastically in the air to pay homage to their leader.

Mao used the Red Guard to attack his enemies within the Communist Party, the "rightists" and "experts" who had reduced Mao's power following the Great Leap Forward. The Red Guard attacked party officials and publicly humiliated schoolteachers. They destroyed cultural artifacts that linked China to its past and harassed anyone they thought needed "re-education." Educated people were sent to farms or factories to humble themselves and to absorb the revolutionary spirit of the masses. Many died.

CRITICAL VIEWING Members of the Red Guard wave the "little red book" of quotations by Mao Zedong in the air to honor their leader. What details about these Red Guard members stand out?

CRITICAL VIEWING This poster promotes the Great Leap Forward, a campaign that Mao Zedong launched in 1958 to increase industrial and agricultural production in China. What kind of image of Chinese society does the poster convey?

By 1968, the Cultural Revolution had reduced the country to chaos. Schools had closed, and the economy was at a standstill. Communist leaders who had a pragmatic, or practical, approach to politics finally convinced Mao to allow the People's Liberation Army to restore governmental authority. Now the Red Guard themselves were sent to remote villages and labor camps. Still, a bitter power struggle continued behind the scenes. A radical faction called the "Gang of Four," led by Mao's wife, Jiang Qing (jahng CHIHNG), plotted to restore the Cultural Revolution. On the other side were pragmatists like Deng Xiaoping (DEHNG shah-oh-PIHNG), an "expert" who was struggling to regain his influence. By this time, Mao was no longer in complete command, so Deng and the "expert" faction reasserted themselves.

In 1972, the pragmatists scored a victory when U.S. president Richard Nixon came to Beijing to re-establish

relations with China. Armed confrontation had recently taken place along China's border with the Soviet Union. The Chinese were worried about the Soviets and so welcomed the possibility of closer ties with the Americans. Although Nixon was a die-hard anti-communist, he hoped that better relations with China would increase his bargaining power with the Soviet Union and might help the United States get out of Vietnam, a conflict you'll read about later in this chapter.

While the shadow of the Cultural Revolution still hung over China at the time of Mao's death in 1976, the eventual victory of Deng Xiaoping over the Gang of Four carried the People's Republic of China into an entirely new, market-oriented direction. But the people of China had paid a terrible price for Mao's political adventures: the Great Leap Forward and the Cultural Revolution had killed tens of millions.

HISTORICAL THINKING

1. **READING CHECK** What were the purpose and the result of the Great Leap Forward?

2. **IDENTIFY PROBLEMS AND SOLUTIONS** What problems did the Cultural Revolution produce?

3. **EVALUATE** How effective was Mao as a leader? Support your evaluation with evidence from the text.

PLAN: 2-PAGE LESSON

OBJECTIVE

Describe how Mao Zedong initiated economic and social programs that caused massive turmoil in China.

CRITICAL THINKING SKILLS FOR LESSON 2.4

- Identify Problems and Solutions
- Evaluate
- Form and Support Opinions
- Analyze Visuals

HISTORICAL THINKING FOR CHAPTER 28

How do countries maintain their independence and security?

Mao launched movements to transform China, but his form of communism had drastic effects on the nation. Lesson 2.4 discusses how the Great Leap Forward and Cultural Revolution wreaked havoc upon China.

Student eEdition online

Additional content for this lesson, including an image, is available online.

BACKGROUND FOR THE TEACHER

The Red Guard Members of Mao's Red Guard were predominantly young people, usually high school or college-aged. Mao's intentions for the Red Guard were to oust communist leaders who did not agree with him and to have a paramilitary group to support his own agenda. While many members of the Red Guard did support Mao's vision, many others saw themselves as part of a movement to eliminate China's past history and culture completely. They wanted to destroy anything they perceived as bourgeois and targeted both intellectuals and communist party leaders who disagreed with them. Hundreds of thousands of people died at the hands of the Red Guard, and infighting became such a problem that the Communist Party eventually encouraged the disbanding of the organization. In total, the Red Guard likely had over 11 million members from its formation in 1966 to its dissolution in 1968.

INTRODUCE & ENGAGE

PREVIEW USING VISUALS

Direct students' attention to the photograph and the poster. **ASK:** What can you infer about Mao Zedong and communism in China from these visuals? *(Answers will vary. Possible response: Chinese citizens were very enthusiastic about communism, revered Mao Zedong, and viewed themselves as part of a collective whole.)* Tell students that in this lesson they will learn about some of the failures of communism in China and the disastrous effects of the Great Leap Forward and the Cultural Revolution.

TEACH

GUIDED DISCUSSION

1. **Form and Support Opinions** What were some of the benefits and drawbacks of the people's communes? *(Possible response: A sense of community and stronger relationships with others would be a benefit; a drawback would be the loss of personal property.)*

2. **Identify Problems and Solutions** Why were President Nixon and Chinese leaders both willing to examine restoring diplomatic relationships? *(Both were worried about a possible Soviet invasion and thought they could find support in one another.)*

ANALYZE VISUALS

Direct students to the poster from the Cultural Revolution (available in the Student eEdition). **ASK:** Why do you think Chairman Mao is portrayed as the sun? *(Possible response: He wanted to be seen as a shining beacon of light, bringing communism to the Chinese people.)*

ACTIVE OPTIONS

On Your Feet: Jigsaw Strategy Instruct students in four "expert" groups to research in greater depth one of the aspects of Chinese Communism: the Great Leap Forward, life in the people's communes, the Cultural Revolution, and the Red Guard. Tell each group to create a summary of their research about Chinese Communism. Regroup students into four new groups so each group has at least one person from each of the four expert groups. Invite students in the new group to take turns sharing the summary they created in their "expert" groups.

| **NG Learning Framework: Design a Poster** |
| SKILL Communication |
| KNOWLEDGE Our Human Story |

Instruct students to examine the poster from the Great Leap Forward and the poster from the Cultural Revolution (available in the Student eEdition). Then invite students to create their own poster to serve as a piece of political propaganda for one of these movements. Encourage students to think about what the Communist Party was trying to communicate through these posters. If time allows, direct students to conduct independent research on communist propaganda in China.

DIFFERENTIATE

INCLUSION

Use Supported Reading Ask pairs to read aloud each paragraph. Tell them to use these sentence frames to identify what they do and do not understand:

- This paragraph is about _____.
- One fact that stood out to me was _____.
- I had trouble understanding _____, so I figured it out by _____.

GIFTED & TALENTED

Research and Role-Play Invite students to research the relationship between Mao Zedong and Deng Xiaoping, including their agreements, disagreements, and viewpoints regarding communism in China. Ask them to craft a conversation between the two over their views for the future of China. Have students form pairs, with one student each playing the parts of Mao Zedong and Deng Xiaoping.

See the Chapter Planner for more strategies for differentiation.

HISTORICAL THINKING

ANSWERS

1. to stimulate rapid industrialization; It devastated the economy and led to a terrible famine, during which many millions of people died.

2. schools closed, the economy came to a standstill, scholars and leaders were persecuted by young people in the Red Guard, people's lives were disrupted when they were moved to remote villages and labor camps, people feared voicing their opinions, cultural artifacts were destroyed

3. Answers will vary.

CRITICAL VIEWING (Red Guard photo) waving red books, young, enthusiastic, dressed alike in khaki uniforms; (poster) prosperous, healthy, happy

Decolonization in Africa

Look at a map showing Africa in 1945, and you'll see only four self-governing countries: Egypt, Ethiopia, Liberia, and South Africa. European colonial powers controlled the rest of the continent. Three decades later, just a few colonies remained.

AFRICAN INDEPENDENCE MOVEMENTS

After supporting the Allies during World War II, Africans thought the time had come for the end of colonialism, and nationalist movements grew throughout Africa. Entering the 1950s, the French, British, and Belgians failed to recognize the change in African attitudes. Over the next three decades, however, these colonial powers would confront a wave of independence movements that would engulf the continent, creating many new nations.

The people of Ghana led the effort, gaining their independence in 1957. Their leader was **Kwame Nkrumah**, who returned to Africa after studying in the United States and Britain. He became Ghana's first prime minister and an international symbol of African liberation and Pan-Africanism. But the economic structures of colonialism remained in most nations, making true independence difficult. The new nations lacked the capital and expertise to develop their economies. They borrowed money from European nations, which led to **neocolonialism**, the continuation of dependence on, and domination by, a colonial power.

Achieving Independence in Africa, 1847–1993

Even before talk of independence, France had laid the foundations for neocolonial control of its African colonies. The French promised citizenship to educated Africans, creating an African elite that strongly identified with French culture. Appealing to these French Africans, French President Charles de Gaulle announced a **referendum** on the question of independence to be held across French Africa. A referendum is a public vote on a single political question. A "yes" vote would allow former French colonies to control their own internal affairs, while the French would retain control over their economic policy, foreign affairs, and military. A "no" vote meant complete and immediate independence, with all ties to France severed.

All but one colony voted to retain ties with France. The exception was Guinea, where the vote for complete independence prompted the French government to stop economic aid and withdraw its administrators overnight. The French ripped telephones from the walls as they vacated their offices. The result was an economic crisis and the rise of an authoritarian regime. Other African leaders heeded the French message and cooperated with France.

In some colonies, especially those in which many Europeans had settled, Africans took up arms to liberate themselves. For instance, over a million Europeans lived in Algeria, and after World War II, Algerian nationalists demanded rights equal to those of the white settlers. To gain a voice in their own governance, they began an armed struggle in 1954. It became a brutal war. Some Algerians launched terrorist attacks on French civilians, and the French military tortured Algerian resistance fighters. Over time, French public opinion soured on the violence, and in 1962, the French agreed to recognize Algerian independence.

Like Algeria, Kenya had a large population of European settlers. The Kenyan activist Jomo Kenyatta had met with other African nationalist leaders in England at a Pan-African Congress in 1946, hoping to develop a large organization to force the British into negotiations. But an impatient group of Kenyan rebels took a more militant stand. They formed a secret society, stole arms from police stations, and assassinated a chief who collaborated with the colonists. The British called the rebels the Mau Mau and depicted them as "savages."

Outgunned by colonial forces, the rebels carried on their guerrilla fight by relying on their knowledge of the forest and the support of the local population. The government moved the rural population into barbed-wire villages to cut them off from the rebels. By the late 1950s, the rebellion was contained, but publicity of British military abuses embarrassed the British, leading them to compromise with more moderate African nationalists. In 1963, Jomo Kenyatta became prime minister of an independent Kenya.

PROXY WAR IN THE CONGO

Although Britain and France negotiated independence for their African colonies without superpower intervention, Belgium did not. A former Belgian colony, the new Democratic Republic of the Congo became the site of a proxy war between the United States and the Soviet Union.

The Belgian administration did little to prepare Africans in the Congo for independence. But with the Congo caught up in the nationalist fever spreading across the continent, the Belgians made hasty plans for independence. At the independence ceremony in 1960, the Belgian king gave a patronizing speech praising his country's "civilizing mission" in Africa. **Patrice Lumumba**, the country's new prime minister, responded with a list of Belgian crimes against Africans. The speech made Lumumba a hero to African nationalists, but Belgium and the United States regarded him as a dangerous radical.

Although the Democratic Republic of the Congo was rich in natural resources, including gold, copper, diamonds, cobalt, uranium, and oil, Lumumba faced immediate challenges. African soldiers mutinied against their Belgian officers, and the mineral-rich province of Katanga seceded. The United Nations sent in peacekeeping forces, but Lumumba also turned to the Soviet Union for military aid. Branding Lumumba a "communist," the CIA cooperated in his capture and execution. Rebel armies arose in several provinces. Finally, **Joseph Mobutu**, an army officer long on the CIA payroll, seized power in late 1960. Its relationship with Mobutu allowed the United States to become the main power broker in Central Africa and to secure the mineral riches of the Congo. Some of these minerals were vital to the defense and aerospace industries.

HISTORICAL THINKING

1. **READING CHECK** Why did many newly independent African countries choose to maintain ties with their European colonizers?

2. **INTERPRET MAPS** Which two European countries had the largest number of colonies in Africa?

3. **ANALYZE CAUSE AND EFFECT** Why did the United States and the Soviet Union get involved in the Democratic Republic of the Congo?

PLAN: 2-PAGE LESSON

OBJECTIVE
Explain how, following World War II, African colonies sought independence from European rule but many remained economically tied to their former colonial rulers.

CRITICAL THINKING SKILLS FOR LESSON 3.1
- Interpret Maps
- Analyze Cause and Effect
- Explain
- Compare and Contrast

HISTORICAL THINKING FOR CHAPTER 28
How do countries maintain their independence and security?
After aiding their colonizers during World War II, many African countries desired independence from colonial rule. Lesson 3.1 discusses the rise of independence movements across Africa and how many of these countries struggled for economic security.

Student eEdition online
Additional content for this lesson, including photographs and captions, is available online.

BACKGROUND FOR THE TEACHER
Jomo Kenyatta Jomo Kenyatta adopted a rational approach to Kenyan independence. In 1928, he founded a newspaper that focused on self-improvement, and its support of Kenyan independence was subtle enough that it was accepted by the British government. Kenyatta continued to advocate for Kenya through his writing, sending a letter to *The Times* in London in 1930 that spelled out five issues that Kenyans needed resolved: land ownership, more educational opportunities, repeal of unfair taxes, African political representation, and allowing Kenyans to practice traditional customs. Despite his brief involvement with the communist party and trip to Russia in the 1930s, the United States was not as threatened by Kenyatta as it was by other African leaders that it perceived to have communist leanings after World War II. Finally, in 1962, Kenyatta was able to negotiate Kenya's independence with the British.

INTRODUCE & ENGAGE

PREVIEW USING MAPS

Direct students' attention to the map. Ask volunteers to point out the location of the European countries and the regions of Africa that they colonized. **ASK:** Why are many European countries' colonies grouped together in the same region? *(Possible response: It was probably easier for a European country to assert control over colonies in one region than across many regions.)* Why did many former European colonies break into multiple countries? *(Possible response: Each European colony encompassed people from many different ethnic groups.)* Tell students that in this lesson they will learn about the many African countries that sought independence from their European colonizers.

TEACH

GUIDED DISCUSSION

1. **Explain** How did the French maintain control of many African colonies during the African quest for independence? *(The French granted citizenship to educated Africans, indoctrinating them in French culture so that they would support continued ties with France.)*

2. **Compare and Contrast** How did the United States and African nationalists view Patrice Lumumba? *(African nationalists regarded him as a hero, but Americans regarded him as a radical.)*

INTERPRET MAPS

Direct students to the map. **ASK:** What year did most French colonies gain independence? *(1960)* Why do you think so many colonies gained independence during the same year? *(Possible response: The colonies likely were inspired by the nationalist fervor sweeping across Africa.)*

ACTIVE OPTIONS

On Your Feet: Jigsaw Strategy After students view the image gallery (available in the Student eEdition), organize them into four "expert" groups and assign each group one of the four African leaders. Instruct each group to create a summary of what they learn about the leader they research. Regroup students so each group has at least one person from each of the four expert groups. Invite students in the new groups to take turns sharing the summary they created in their "expert" groups.

NG Learning Framework: Evaluate Independence Strategies
ATTITUDE Empowerment
SKILL Problem-Solving

Prompt students to select two or three African countries that sought independence from European colonial powers after World War II. Have them research the fight for independence in those countries and write an essay comparing and contrasting different strategies for gaining independence. Tell students to form a thesis about which strategies for independence were the most successful and why. Invite volunteers to share their essays with the class.

DIFFERENTIATE

STRIVING READERS

List Details About a Topic After students read the lesson, tell pairs to create a table using the section headings: African Independence Movements and Proxy War in the Congo. Have pairs take turns rereading paragraphs aloud, while their partner listens and identifies details to add to the table.

PRE-AP

Analyze Precedents Ask students to learn more about the precedents that Ghana set for other African nations when it earned its independence in 1957. Tell them to write an essay analyzing the impact of Ghana's independence on other African nations. Invite volunteers to share their reports with the class.

See the Chapter Planner for more strategies for differentiation.

HISTORICAL THINKING

ANSWERS

1. They lacked the capital to develop their economies and had to borrow from European countries, which kept them indebted.

2. France and Great Britain

3. The United States considered Lumumba, the new leader of the Congo, to be a radical because of his deprecating statements about the Belgians, who formerly ruled the Congo. Lumumba's request for military assistance from the Soviet Union furthered the U.S. belief that he was a radical and a communist. Both the United States and the Soviet Union had interest in the country's mineral resources, many of which were vital for the development of weapons and spacecraft.

CRITICAL VIEWING (available in the Student eEdition) happy and excited

Apartheid in South Africa

After World War II, most Africans began gaining their freedom and independence from European rule. But those in South Africa were losing more of their rights. A white minority controlled the government of South Africa and refused to share power with the country's black majority.

RACIAL SEGREGATION IN SOUTH AFRICA

As you have already learned, the discovery of diamonds and gold in southern Africa in the late 1800s led to a struggle between the Dutch settlers called Boers and British imperialists for control of the region. The British won the war that resulted, known as the South African War, in 1902. The British and the Dutch then formed the Union of South Africa in 1910. They ruled together, united by their shared desire for cheap African labor. In 1961, South Africa became a republic, controlled by a white minority.

After World War II, white minority rulers in South Africa solidified their power over the African majority, as well as mixed-race South Africans known as "coloreds" and the country's Indian minority. In 1948, the older system of racial segregation grew even more extreme when the National Party came to power and instituted **apartheid** (uh-PAHR-tayt), which means "separateness." This system of racial segregation and discrimination lasted until the early 1990s. The system dictated where black and brown people could live and work, what they could and could not study, and who they could date and marry. Nonwhites were denied the right to vote and other basic rights.

Less than 10 percent of South Africa's population was white, but white people owned and controlled 90 percent of the land and resources. People classified as "black" or "colored" could not even live in the same town with white people unless they were working for a white-owned business. Their families had to live elsewhere.

RESISTANCE TO APARTHEID

During the early years of the Cold War, British and American governments overlooked the repressive policies in South Africa because the country's leaders were adamantly anti-communist. In 1952, an organization called the **African National Congress (ANC)** began a "defiance campaign" based on nonviolent resistance. Led by South African activist **Nelson Mandela**, the campaign followed Gandhi's method of drawing attention to repressive laws by having large numbers of people openly violate them. The hope was that as the police arrested lawbreakers, the prisons would overflow, forcing

TREVOR NOAH Growing up in apartheid South Africa, comedian Trevor Noah was literally "born a crime." His white European father and his Xhosa African mother were not allowed to be together. Walking in the park, Noah had to be careful not to shout "Papa" to his father—since Noah was an illegal child, police could take him away from his parents at any time. With the sacrifice and support of his mother, Noah overcame the rough street life of the segregated black townships, got a good education, and found success as an international television star.

the government to abolish the laws. However, the police responded with brutality, and instead of abolishing laws, the government intensified the repression.

In 1960, about 20,000 people assembled before a police station in the black township of Sharpeville to protest the "pass laws," which restricted the movements of black Africans. The police shot into the crowd, killing 69 protesters and wounding another 180. This event, which became known as the Sharpeville massacre, sparked international criticism of apartheid.

Mandela and the ANC then turned to a sabotage campaign, in which they deliberately bombed pass offices and other targets. Mandela and other organizers were arrested. Mandela was tried for treason, and in 1964, he was sentenced to life in prison.

With the imprisonment of Mandela, hopes for transforming South Africa were at an all-time low. The government invested heavily in defense in the 1970s to suppress domestic and outside resistance to apartheid. However, the resistance continued. The Black Consciousness Movement led by **Steve Biko** inspired young people to overcome the sense of inferiority they had been given by apartheid, to be proud and confident in themselves as Africans.

Although Biko was murdered by apartheid police, his influence was shown in 1976 when thousands of children in Soweto, a black township, rose up to protest their inferior education. As protesters marched to a rally, police shot into the crowd. The event caused a national uprising and a series of protests, during which the police killed more than 500 people. The UN Security Council voted unanimously to ban sales of arms to South Africa.

As images of police violence in South Africa spread around the world, more leaders and groups in the global community condemned apartheid. Many countries levied economic and cultural sanctions against the regime. In the 1970s, students at historically black U.S. colleges and universities such as Spelman, Morehouse, and Howard launched a series of protests. They called for their schools to divest, or remove their investments, from South Africa. Protests spread to other universities, including Occidental College in California, where a young student named Barack Obama gave his first

public speech, denouncing apartheid. Obama later became president of the United States.

Continued domestic resistance and economic sanctions made governance increasingly difficult for the ruling National Party. In 1990, South Africa's newly elected moderate president, **F.W. de Klerk**, released Nelson Mandela from prison. De Klerk legalized the ANC and prepared the way for democratic, multiracial elections. You will read more about Nelson Mandela and the changes in South Africa in the next chapter.

South Africa's system of strict racial segregation applied to public restrooms and other facilities. Bold letters in English, Afrikaans, and Tswana indicated who could use this restroom in Soweto, a township on the outskirts of Johannesburg, South Africa.

HISTORICAL THINKING

1. **READING CHECK** How did apartheid affect the lives of South Africans?

2. **ANALYZE CAUSE AND EFFECT** How did the international reaction to apartheid change over time, and what effect did it have?

3. **DESCRIBE** What were some of the successes and failures of the resistance movement in South Africa?

PLAN: 2-PAGE LESSON

OBJECTIVE

Describe how, as nationalism spread across Africa, the white minority rulers of South Africa imposed strict racial segregation and limited the rights of black South Africans.

CRITICAL THINKING SKILLS FOR LESSON 3.2

- Analyze Cause and Effect
- Describe
- Identify
- Analyze Visuals

HISTORICAL THINKING FOR CHAPTER 28

How do countries maintain their independence and security?

Tensions between people of European descent and Africans continued as decolonization spread through the African continent. Lesson 3.2 discusses how a white minority in South Africa oppressed the African majority, and how the African majority fought for and eventually gained equal rights.

BACKGROUND FOR THE TEACHER

South Africa's Population Registration Act In 1950, the South African government passed the Population Registration Act, essentially writing apartheid into law and giving all South African people an identification number. Under the Population Registration Act, all South African people had to register as a white person, a native person, or a colored person. In South Africa, the term *colored* refers to a person of mixed-race descent. The act also specified that all people registered as colored had to list the ethnic groups to which they belonged. If it was discovered that a person was misclassified, the person would be offered an opportunity to appeal the classification and then be reclassified by the government. Other identifying information was included in the registration as well, such as voter registration, a right that was granted to white people but denied to all non-white South Africans. The Population Registration Act was not repealed until 1991.

Student eEdition online

Additional content for this lesson, including a photograph, is available online.

INTRODUCE & ENGAGE

CONSIDER HUMAN RIGHTS MOVEMENTS

Display a K-W-L Chart on the board and discuss what students already know about human rights movements around the world. Ask students to consider the rights specific groups have fought for, the violations they have fought against, and the means they used to bring attention to their cause or achieve results. Ask students to list questions that they would like to have answered in this lesson, which will discuss the fight for civil rights in South Africa. Allow time at the end of the lesson for students to complete the chart using what they learned in this lesson.

TEACH

GUIDED DISCUSSION

1. **Analyze Cause and Effect** Why did Great Britain and the United States ignore racial segregation in South Africa? *(South Africa's white leaders were anti-communist, and the United States and Great Britain were more concerned about the spread of communism.)*

2. **Identify** Why was it important for Steve Biko to help young people overcome a sense of inferiority? *(Possible response: Young people growing up under apartheid constantly received messages that they were second-class citizens. In order to stand up for their rights, young people needed to believe that they mattered.)*

ANALYZE VISUALS

Direct students to the photograph of South African students protesting (available in the Student eEdition). **ASK:** What characteristics do the people in the photograph have in common? *(The protesters are all young and black.)* How might these characteristics influence their opinion of Afrikaans? *(Possible response: The protesters probably view Afrikaans as the language of oppressors and believe that they would have more opportunities for success if they could learn in English.)*

ACTIVE OPTIONS

On Your Feet: Fishbowl Organize students so that part of the class sits in a close circle facing inward and the other part of the class sits in a larger circle around them. Ask students on the inside circle to play the role of members of the African National Congress and discuss their approach to dismantling apartheid in South Africa. Students on the outside should listen for new information and evaluate the discussion. Then tell groups to reverse positions.

> **NG Learning Framework: Write a Thesis**
> **ATTITUDE** Curiosity
> **SKILL** Problem-Solving

Instruct students to find and read excerpts of Trevor Noah's memoir, *Born a Crime*. Ask them to consider Noah's approaches to problem-solving, which could include challenges he faced as a child and his accomplishments as an adult. Tell students to form a thesis about how apartheid in South Africa affected Noah's approach to life.

DIFFERENTIATE

ENGLISH LANGUAGE LEARNERS

Create a Word Web Pair **Beginning** and **Intermediate** level students with students at the **Advanced** level. Tell them to take turns reading paragraphs, noting on the spokes of a Word Web examples of apartheid and ways in which the South African people rose against racial discrimination.

GIFTED & TALENTED

Connect Past and Present Tell students to research information for an oral report connecting past and present protests against racial injustice around the world. Have them learn about how apartheid developed in South Africa and how it was eventually discontinued. Students may research the Civil Rights movement and the Black Lives Matter movement. Ask students to present their oral reports or record and post them on a class website.

See the Chapter Planner for more strategies for differentiation.

HISTORICAL THINKING

ANSWERS

1. classified them into different races, controlled where black South Africans could live and work, what blacks could study, who they could date or marry, and their ability to move freely around their country

2. It was initially overlooked because the South African government was anti-communist. As news of police brutality spread, the international community began to levy boycotts and sanctions against South Africa, contributing to government reforms and the release of Nelson Mandela.

3. Successes and failures may be associated with the defiance campaign, the sabotage campaign, the protests in Sharpeville and Soweto, domestic resistance, and international sanctions.

The Bandung Generation

Voters sometimes find it difficult to embrace either candidate in a major election because the flaws of both are obvious. That was the situation many Asian and African countries faced in the Cold War as they were pressured to align with either the United States or the Soviet Union.

THE BANDUNG CONFERENCE

In 1955, the leaders of 29 former colonial states met in Bandung, Indonesia, for the first Asian-African Conference, also called the Bandung Conference. They discussed strategies to avoid both neocolonialism and superpower intervention and to promote economic and cultural cooperation. The participating countries unanimously agreed to the following goals:

- abolish colonialism and the subjugation, domination, and exploitation of people;
- support human rights and self-determination;
- promote world peace and international cooperation;
- work to abolish nuclear weapons;
- cooperate in promoting economic development; and
- promote cultural understanding, education, and information exchange.

The Bandung Conference formed the basis of a general movement toward **nonalignment**, in which leaders of developing countries joined together in remaining neutral in the Cold War. The participants in the Bandung Conference later were called the Bandung Generation. The term **Third World** was used to describe economically developing countries that did not align with either the United States or the Soviet Union.

The United States did not participate in the Bandung Conference. American leaders were suspicious of the gathering, fearing it would issue

a general condemnation of the West. The Americans supported decolonization and self-determination in theory, but in practice they usually supported the British, Dutch, French, and Portuguese colonizers who were close allies in the fight against communism.

DIFFICULTIES WITH NONALIGNMENT

Many developing countries found it difficult to remain nonaligned with either the United States or the Soviet Union during the Cold War. The careers of two leaders at the Bandung Conference—one Indonesian and one Indian—illustrate the difficulties.

Many Muslims fled India after the British divided the Indian colony into two states based on religion in 1947. In this photograph, Muslim refugees crowd onto the roof of a train near New Delhi as they try to reach Pakistan.

In 1945, Indonesian nationalist **Ahmed Sukarno** and his party declared Indonesia's freedom from both the Dutch and the Japanese. Indonesia had been a colony of the Netherlands when the Japanese invaded during World War II. After the war, Indonesia had to fight Dutch reoccupation forces for five years. In 1950, the hundreds of diverse islands that formed the colony joined together to create the independent nation of Indonesia. Today, Indonesia is the world's fourth largest nation and the largest Muslim majority country. To unify the country's scattered islands, Sukarno sponsored the development of a common language with a simplified grammar.

Sukarno was popular at first, but he had no experience running a country. In 1963, he declared himself "president for life," and his popularity waned. A powerful communist insurgency developed. The Indonesian military suspected that Sukarno was either sympathetic to communism or too weak to fight it and so carried out a murderous crackdown in 1964.

The United States also considered Sukarno too weak to battle communism. In 1967, the United States backed a corrupt, authoritarian general named Suharto in ousting Sukarno. American leaders turned a blind eye when Suharto suspended the constitution. Having a dependable ally in the struggle against communism took precedence over the civil rights of Indonesians.

India's prime minister, Jawaharlal Nehru (whom you read about earlier), was more successful in remaining neutral in the Cold War. However, like other leaders of newly independent nations, he faced tremendous problems. In 1947, the British divided the Indian colony into two separate states based on religious differences in their populations: India, with a Hindu majority, and Pakistan, with a Muslim majority. However, a substantial Hindu minority lived in Pakistan, and an even larger Muslim minority lived in India. Fearing religious persecution, millions of people tried desperately to cross to the country of their religion after the **partition**, or division. Violence followed. As many as 10 million people were dislocated, perhaps 75,000 women were abducted, and more than 1 million people were killed.

Nehru also faced military tensions along India's borders with Pakistan and China. To maintain neutrality, Nehru purchased military equipment from both the United States and the Soviet Union. Despite India's nonalignment, the United States was concerned about its military ties to the Soviet Union. In 1958, the United States entered into a defense agreement with India's neighbor—and enemy—Pakistan. This agreement gave the United States a reliably anti-communist ally in the region and pulled South Asia into Cold War politics.

MOTHER TERESA'S WORK IN INDIA

Along with international problems, India faced the domestic challenges of poverty and illiteracy. Mother Teresa, a Catholic nun from Albania, went to India in 1929 to serve as a teacher. She taught for 17 years before she realized that her true calling was working with India's poor and sick. To fulfill her calling, she moved to the slums of Calcutta (now Kolkata), where she founded the Order of the Missionaries of Charity. The photograph above shows Mother Teresa with children at her mission in Calcutta.

Mother Teresa eventually became an Indian citizen and established a hospice for India's terminally ill, centers for blind and disabled people, and a colony for people suffering from leprosy. Mother Teresa's work later extended beyond India. Beginning in the 1960s, she opened houses for the poor in Venezuela, in Tanzania, and in communist countries, including her childhood home, Albania.

Mother Teresa was honored with numerous awards for her humanitarian work, including the Nobel Peace Prize in 1979. In 2016, nearly 20 years after her death, Mother Teresa was canonized, or declared, a saint in the Roman Catholic Church.

HISTORICAL THINKING

1. **READING CHECK** What was the purpose of the Bandung Conference?

2. **SYNTHESIZE** How did the threat of the spread of communism affect American foreign policy in Africa and Asia?

3. **IDENTIFY PROBLEMS AND SOLUTIONS** What problems did Nehru face as he formed an independent government in India?

PLAN: 2-PAGE LESSON

OBJECTIVE

Explain how many newly independent African and Asian countries tried to remain neutral as the United States and the Soviet Union pushed them to take sides in the Cold War.

CRITICAL THINKING SKILLS FOR LESSON 3.3

- Synthesize
- Identify Problems and Solutions
- Describe
- Analyze Cause and Effect
- Analyze Visuals

HISTORICAL THINKING FOR CHAPTER 28

How do countries maintain their independence and security?

The United States and the Soviet Union were both paranoid that other, smaller nations would align with one superpower or the other. Lesson 3.3 discusses how newly independent nations in Asia and Africa worked together to maintain neutrality during the Cold War.

BACKGROUND FOR THE TEACHER

The Non-Alignment Movement On the heels of the Bandung Conference, the Non-Alignment Movement was founded with the purpose of denouncing imperialism and colonialism, focusing on self-determination for developing nations, as well as maintaining neutrality in the Cold War. The Non-Alignment Movement is still active and currently comprises more than 100 member nations that collectively represent more than half of the world's population. The first meeting of the Non-Alignment Movement took place in 1961 in Belgrade. Jawaharlal Nehru (from India), Kwame Nkrumah (from Ghana), and Ahmed Sukarno (from Indonesia) were all leaders of the event, as well as Josip Broz Tito of Yugoslavia and Gamal Abdel Nasser of Egypt. Today, the Non-Alignment Movement has shifted its focus now that the Cold War has ended. The movement is primarily dedicated to expressing inequalities in the world economic order stemming from a colonial past and calling for international cooperation while maintaining the autonomy of individual nations.

Student eEdition online

Additional content for this lesson, including photographs, is available online.

INTRODUCE & ENGAGE

INTERPRET A HISTORICAL EVENT

Direct students' attention to the photograph of Jawaharlal Nehru, U Nu, and Ali Sastroamidjojo at the Bandung Conference (available in the Student eEdition). **ASK:** Based on this photograph, what can you predict about how South Asian countries will react to the Cold War and decolonization efforts in Africa? *(Possible response: South Asian countries will support decolonization efforts and independence and work together rather than taking sides in the Cold War.)* Tell students that in this lesson they will learn about how newly independent African and Asian nations sought to remain neutral during the Cold War but were often subject to pressures from the United States and Soviet Union.

TEACH

GUIDED DISCUSSION

1. **Describe** How did the United States exemplify and contradict the values established at the Bandung Conference? *(In theory, decolonization was in line with American values, but in practice, the United States formed allegiances with imperialist European countries.)*

2. **Analyze Cause and Effect** How did Nehru's attempt to maintain Cold War neutrality by purchasing weapons from both the United States and Soviet Union backfire? *(Because he purchased weapons from the Soviet Union, the United States became concerned about a possible alliance and made a defense agreement with Pakistan.)*

ANALYZE VISUALS

Direct students to the photograph of Muslims in India trying to board a train to Pakistan. **ASK:** Based on the photo, what can you infer about the desire of Muslims to move to Pakistan? *(Possible response: The Muslim refugees appear desperate to get to Pakistan because they are trying to board an already overcrowded train as if it is their only option.)*

ACTIVE OPTIONS

On Your Feet: Roundtable Seat students around a table in groups of four and instruct them to read the sidebar about Mother Teresa. Ask students to consider how Mother Teresa gained the trust of the people that she helped. Each student around the table should answer the question in a different way. Encourage students to draw upon information directly from the text and make inferences based on what they read.

| **NG Learning Framework: Write a List of Goals** |
| **ATTITUDE** Empowerment |
| **KNOWLEDGE** New Frontiers |

Direct students to the list of goals that were agreed to during the Bandung Conference. Ask students to consider the state of the world today and then develop a list of international goals for the world in the 21st century. Encourage students to conduct online research if they struggle to think of contemporary issues with a global impact. Invite volunteers to share their goals with the class.

DIFFERENTIATE

STRIVING READERS

Read and Recall Have students read the lesson independently. Then ask them to meet in groups of two or four without the book and share information they recall as one student takes notes. Groups should review the lesson and decide what to add or change in their notes.

PRE-AP

Write a Biographical Article Direct students to research one of the leaders who attended the Bandung Conference. Have students write a biographical article, including information about the attendee's childhood and background and how that affected his or her values and goals for the nations participating in the Bandung Conference. Ask students to post their articles on a class website.

See the Chapter Planner for more strategies for differentiation.

HISTORICAL THINKING

ANSWERS

1. Former colonies of Asia and Africa met at Bandung to plan how they could avoid racism, neocolonialism, and superpower intervention as they formed independent nations.

2. It led the United States to support authoritarian rulers in both areas.

3. India had been split in two, with India being a predominantly Hindu country and Pakistan being a predominantly Muslim country. Violence erupted as people desperately tried to move to the country where they felt they belonged. India's borders were unstable, and the country suffered from extreme poverty. Nehru needed military support, but he didn't want to align with either the Soviet Union or the United States, so he purchased weapons from both. However, this tactic backfired, as it led both superpowers to distrust Nehru.

The Suez Crisis

Have you ever had a trusted friend you thought would always have your back? That is what Britain thought about the United States. But when Egypt resisted Britain's attempts to retain control of the Suez Canal, the United States refused to support Britain's military aggression.

EGYPT NATIONALIZES THE SUEZ CANAL

One of the prominent leaders at the Bandung Conference in 1955 was **Gamal Abdel Nasser**, prime minister of Egypt. Nasser believed that Arabs should unite against European neocolonialism and American imperialism. Rejecting religion as a basis for politics, he embraced secular, or nonreligious, Arab nationalism. He banned the Muslim Brotherhood, a political organization that promoted Islam as a guiding philosophy for government. Instead, he elevated the military as a political force.

Nasser had plans for building a giant dam on the Nile River to provide electricity for industrialization. However, Egypt could not fund the dam's construction without aid,

Gamal Abdel Nasser became a hero in the Arab world for confronting Western powers in the Suez Crisis of 1956. Nasser served as prime minister of Egypt from 1954 to 1956 and then as president from 1956 to 1970.

The Suez Canal in Egypt, completed in 1869, provides the shortest sea route between Europe and countries bordering the Indian and Pacific oceans. This photograph shows a container ship passing through the canal in the present day.

so Nasser approached the British and the Americans for financial assistance. They agreed to provide $270 million for the first stage of the project. However, as a precondition, they insisted that Nasser join an anti-Soviet alliance. Nasser was committed to nonalignment after the Bandung Conference and so refused. Instead, he nationalized the Suez Canal, which passed through Egyptian territory. He believed that Egypt could pay for the dam by collecting tolls from ships traveling through the canal. At the time, the Suez Canal Company, a joint British-French enterprise that owned and operated the canal, made a yearly profit of approximately $31 million.

Egypt's nationalization of the canal, legal under international law, was a humiliation for the British, who saw their once great empire in rapid decline. For standing up to them, Nasser became a great hero not only to Egyptians and Arabs but to anti-colonial nationalists around the world.

INTERNATIONAL REACTION

Outraged at Egypt's action, the British secretly met with the French and Israelis on October 24, 1956, to plan an attack. The Israelis and Egyptians had been in conflict since the establishment of the state of Israel in 1948, and Egypt had blocked the Israelis from accessing the Suez Canal. The Israelis were eager to gain support in their conflict with Egypt, and they invaded Egypt's Sinai Peninsula on October 29. Under the pretext of protecting the canal from both the Egyptians and the Israelis, the French and British followed two days later. They bombed Egyptian air bases and occupied the Canal Zone.

The Egyptian military responded by blockading the canal, preventing Britain from gaining access to the Middle Eastern oil on which it depended. Meanwhile, Egyptian civilians took up arms to protect their country from the foreign invaders. The international community was critical of the occupation, and the United States quickly condemned the action.

At the time of the Suez Crisis, the Soviet Union was involved in a violent suppression of an uprising in Hungary. To distract from the Soviets' own brutality, Soviet premier Nikita Khrushchev strongly criticized the British for occupying Egypt. He threatened to use nuclear weapons against the British and French. Faced

with the threat of nuclear war, the United Nations sent an emergency peacekeeping force to Egypt on November 21. The French, British, and Israelis then withdrew all their troops.

The Suez Canal remained in the hands of the Egyptians, who formed a military alliance with the Soviet Union. The Soviets then funded the building of the Aswan Dam. True "non-alignment" was difficult to achieve.

In an address to the House of Commons, British prime minister Anthony Eden explained the reasons for the military action taken by the Israelis, French, and British in the Suez Crisis. That same day, U.S. president Dwight D. Eisenhower spoke about the Suez Crisis in a radio and television address to the American people.

PRIMARY SOURCE

It is really not tolerable that the greatest sea highway in the world, one on which our Western life so largely depends, should be subject to the dangers of an explosive situation in the Middle East, which it must be admitted has been largely created by the Egyptian government. . . . [W]e have witnessed, all of us, the growth of a specific Egyptian threat to the peace of the Middle East. Everybody knows that to be true. In the actions we have now taken, we are not concerned to stop Egypt, but to stop war. Nonetheless, it is a fact that there is no Middle Eastern problem at present which could not have been settled or bettered but for the hostile and irresponsible policies of Egypt in recent years.

—Anthony Eden, British prime minister, October 31, 1956

As it is the manifest right of any of these nations to take such decisions and actions, it is likewise our right—if our judgment so dictates—to dissent. We believe these actions to have been taken in error. For we do not accept the use of force as a wise or proper instrument for the settlement of international disputes. To say this—in this particular instance—in no way to minimize our friendship with these nations—nor our determination to maintain those friendships. . . . In the circumstances I have described, there will be no United States involvement in these present hostilities.

—Dwight D. Eisenhower, president of the United States, October 31, 1956

HISTORICAL THINKING

1. **READING CHECK** Why did Egyptian prime minister Nasser nationalize the Suez Canal?

2. **EXPLAIN** Why was the Suez Canal so important to Britain and France?

3. **DRAW CONCLUSIONS** Was the resolution of the Suez Crisis a victory for the Americans or the Soviets in the Cold War? Explain your response.

PLAN: 2-PAGE LESSON

OBJECTIVE
Explain how an international crisis occurred during the Cold War when the Egyptians seized the Suez Canal and the British, French, and Israelis responded by invading Egypt.

CRITICAL THINKING SKILLS FOR LESSON 3.4
- Interpret Maps
- Draw Conclusions
- Explain
- Form and Support Opinions

HISTORICAL THINKING FOR CHAPTER 28
How do countries maintain their independence and security?

As world superpowers, the United States and Soviet Union often got drawn into conflicts that, on the surface, did not appear to concern them. Lesson 3.4 discusses the Suez Crisis and how control of the canal brought several nations into conflict.

BACKGROUND FOR THE TEACHER

Egypt and the United States During the Cold War As decolonization played out across the world stage, the United States had several goals for developing countries that were often at odds with one another: help emerging nations reach self-determination and curb the spread of communism across the globe. Often, the United States looked at developing nations through its own Western lens, assuming, sometimes in error, that these nations shared the same ideals of building up a capitalist democracy as the United States had done. When it came to relations with Egypt after World War II, the United States made nebulous promises to Egyptian leaders. The United States pledged to help Egypt against large powers seeking to control the country. The United States interpreted this as protection from the Soviet Union, while Egypt interpreted the pledge as an offer to help the country ward off British occupation. Britain, meanwhile, depended upon the Suez Canal for its oil supply and reacted harshly to any threats to its access to the canal.

Student eEdition online
Additional content for this lesson, including a map, is available online.

INTRODUCE & ENGAGE

DISCUSS BOTH SIDES OF A CONFLICT

Ask students to consider conflicts, such as those they have recently heard about in the news or even a conflict they have had with another person. Prompt students to consider both sides of the conflict and list reasons why each side was justified in its beliefs. Then have students think about ways that third parties attempted to stay neutral during these conflicts, and if they were successful in remaining neutral or eventually got pulled to one side or the other. Tell students that in this lesson they will learn about how a conflict with Britain and France exerted pressure on Egypt to form a Cold War alliance.

TEACH

GUIDED DISCUSSION

1. **Explain** Why did nationalists around the world view Gamal Abdel Nasser as a hero? *(because he stood up to the British by nationalizing the Suez Canal)*

2. **Form and Support Opinions** Do you think Egypt should have accepted funding for the Aswan Dam from the Soviets? Why or why not? *(Possible responses: Yes, because they needed the infrastructure; No, because forming an alliance with the Soviets was not in accordance with non-alignment.)*

INTERPRET MAPS

Direct students to the map (available in the Student eEdition). **ASK:** Why do you think Israel was involved in the Suez Crisis? *(Possible responses: Israel is geographically close to the Suez Canal. Israel had had prior conflicts with Egypt. Israel was aligned with Western nations.)*

ACTIVE OPTIONS

On Your Feet: Four Corners Designate each corner of the room for focused discussion on a particular perspective of the Suez Crisis: the perspectives of Egypt, the Soviet Union, Great Britain, and the United States. Allow students time to think and write individually about the Suez Crisis before joining the group in the corner of their choice to discuss the topic. Have at least one student from each corner share their corner's discussion.

| **NG Learning Framework: Engage in a Debate**
| **ATTITUDE** Responsibility
| **SKILL** Problem-Solving

Prompt students to read the primary source excerpts from Anthony Eden and Dwight D. Eisenhower about the Suez Crisis. In pairs, have one student assume the role of Anthony Eden and the other assume the role of Dwight D. Eisenhower. The two should debate the extent to which international intervention is appropriate in the Suez Crisis. Encourage students to consider the greater context of the world, such as the Cold War, Egypt's need to fund the Aswan Dam, and Egypt's previous commitment to non-alignment.

DIFFERENTIATE

INCLUSION

Understand a Map Pair students with those who can help them understand the information presented in the map (available in the Student eEdition) and how that information relates to the Suez Crisis. Tell pairs to read the legend and trace the arrows that show the shipping route from Europe to Asia through the Suez Canal. As they read, have them refer back to the map to better understand why Britain and France were eager to maintain control of the canal.

PRE-AP

Analyze Photographs Direct students to the photograph of the Suez Canal today, and encourage them to find more contemporary photographs online of the canal in use. Tell them to analyze the content of each photograph—what they see in the canal, how it is presented, and what inferences they can make based on these observations. Students should consider how these photographs depict the importance of the Suez Canal today and think about how that relates to its importance during the time of the Suez Crisis. Invite students to share their analysis with the class in an oral report.

See the Chapter Planner for more strategies for differentiation.

HISTORICAL THINKING

ANSWERS

1. He needed money for the Aswan Dam but could not obtain it from the British or Americans, and so he decided to raise the money with tolls from the canal.

2. The Suez Canal gave Great Britain and France a much shorter route for shipping goods to and from Asia.

3. It was a victory for the Soviets because Egypt became allied with the Soviets and Western powers were criticized as being aggressors.

The Korean War

After living through the fear, pain, and horror of World War II, Americans hoped to avoid any more war in their lifetimes. But just five years later, American parents were sending their young sons to fight and die in the Korean War, the first major conflict of the Cold War.

DIVISION OF THE KOREAN PENINSULA

The Koreans are a proud people who, as you have learned, borrowed a great deal from Chinese civilization while retaining their independence. It was a great shock when, in 1910, the country was annexed by Japan. People resented the arrogance of their colonial rulers, who forced Korean schoolchildren to adopt Japanese names and sing the praises of the Japanese emperor. The peninsula suffered under Japanese control into World War II.

The Allies agreed that Korea should one day be free and independent. With that goal in mind, the Soviets attacked the Japanese from the north in

Division of Korea, 1953

CHINA

NORTH KOREA

Pyongyang
Demilitarized zone

Sea of Japan
(East Sea)

38th parallel
Seoul

Yellow Sea

SOUTH KOREA

0   50   100 Miles
0   50 100 Kilometers

JAPAN

the last year of the war, and the Americans attacked from the south. The Japanese surrendered to either the Soviets or the Americans depending on their location.

At the Potsdam Conference in 1945, the Allies agreed that Korea would be temporarily divided at the 38th parallel, or latitude 38 degrees north of the equator. The Soviets would occupy the north, and the Americans would occupy the south in a five-year **trusteeship**, in which they would have administrative control. The Allies hoped to develop a plan for unification of the peninsula over the course of the five years.

In 1947, the new United Nations took over responsibility for Korea. The UN recognized the democratic Republic of Korea, also called South Korea. Anti-communist leader Syngman Rhee became president. At the same time, communist leader **Kim Il-sung** had taken control of North Korea and began to strengthen its military. By 1950, he had built a strong military with armaments supplied by the Soviet Union. He sought to unite the two Koreas by force.

WAR BREAKS OUT

With the backing of the Soviets, North Korean soldiers invaded South Korea on June 25, 1950. South Korea's military was unprepared and poorly trained, so the United Nations came to the country's assistance. The United States provided the largest number of troops, who fought under the leadership of U.S. general Douglas MacArthur. The United States considered the Korean War an application of the Truman Doctrine, providing military aid to prevent the spread of communism.

UN troops recaptured Seoul and South Korea in September 1950. They drove the communists north in an attempt to control the entire peninsula. Kim Il-sung requested military aid from the Chinese, who feared that the United States intended to attack them as well. With

a commitment from the Soviets to provide air power, the Chinese sent in ground forces to support North Korea. With Soviet and Chinese support, North Korea pushed its enemies back below the 38th parallel.

Some military leaders urged President Truman to strike China with nuclear weapons, believing such force was necessary to win the war. President Truman refused, fearing the use of nuclear weapons would provoke a larger, more deadly war. Acting on his own, General MacArthur threatened to attack Chinese territory. Truman then replaced the general.

In July 1953, after three years and more than three million deaths, the two sides signed a truce that stopped the fighting without formally ending the war. The truce called for both sides to pull back from the

battle line. It designated the space between them along the 38th parallel as a **demilitarized zone**, an area where weapons and military forces are forbidden. This neutral area separated the communist regime in North Korea from the authoritarian regime that Rhee had established in South Korea. The stalemate between the two sides has continued into the 21st century.

> **SOUTHEAST ASIA TREATY ORGANIZATION** After the Korean War, the United States and its allies were concerned that communism might spread throughout Southeast Asia. To prevent such communist expansion, representatives from Australia, France, Great Britain, New Zealand, Pakistan, the Philippines, Thailand, and the United States came together in 1954 to form the Southeast Asia Treaty Organization (SEATO). Like NATO, SEATO was intended to provide nations in the region with advice on self-defense, to prevent or thwart subversive activities, and to promote economic and social progress. Before long, the United States would use the provisions of SEATO as justification for its involvement in Vietnam.

HISTORICAL THINKING

1. **READING CHECK** Why did the Americans, Soviets, and Chinese all get involved in the Korean War?

2. **FORM AND SUPPORT OPINIONS** In your opinion, did Truman make the right decision about the use of nuclear weapons in the Korean War? Why or why not?

3. **INTERPRET MAPS** Why do you think the 38th parallel was chosen as the dividing line between North and South Korea?

CRITICAL VIEWING
The Joint Security Area in Korea was the site of peace talks during the Korean War and has since hosted many diplomatic conferences. It is the only part of the Demilitarized Zone (DMZ) where North and South Korean forces directly face each other. This photograph shows North Korean guards standing near the blue buildings. In the background is Freedom House in South Korea. How would you describe the level of fortification in this section of the DMZ?

PLAN: 2-PAGE LESSON

OBJECTIVE

Describe how the Cold War broke out in combat when the communists of North Korea, backed by the Soviet Union, attacked South Korea, a U.S. ally.

CRITICAL THINKING SKILLS FOR LESSON 4.1

- Form and Support Opinions
- Interpret Maps
- Draw Conclusions

HISTORICAL THINKING FOR CHAPTER 28

How do countries maintain their independence and security?

As the Allies divvied up control of countries around the globe in the aftermath of World War II, some countries adopted communist leanings, while others aligned themselves with the West. Lesson 4.1 discusses the division of North and South Korea and the Korean War stalemate.

Student eEdition online

Additional content for this lesson, including a photograph, is available online.

BACKGROUND FOR THE TEACHER

Kim Il-Sung North Korean Premier Kim Il-Sung was a native son, though his family moved to Manchuria during the Japanese occupation of Korea. As a teenager, he became involved with a communist youth group, eventually serving jail time as a result of his participation. He learned guerrilla warfare tactics while fighting against Japanese rule in Korea and was sent to the Soviet Union to receive both political and military training. Kim fought during World War II as a major in the Soviet army and after the war, when Korea was divided into North and South Korea, was selected—with support from the Soviets—to be the new country's leader. Although Kim's great desire to unify Korea failed, he ruled North Korea for 46 years.

INTRODUCE & ENGAGE

MAKE A CHOICE

Ask students to consider a time when they were forced with the choice of whether or not to intervene in a conflict between two other parties. Encourage students to share examples they have experienced or witnessed and to discuss the benefits and drawbacks of intervening or remaining neutral. After discussing each example, take a class poll and have students decide whether to intervene or stay out of each dispute. Tell students that in this lesson they will learn about how the United States decided to intervene when communist North Korea attacked South Korea, an ally of the West.

TEACH

GUIDED DISCUSSION

1. **Form and Support Opinions** Do you agree with Truman's decision to replace General MacArthur? Why or why not? *(Possible responses: Yes, because General MacArthur could have caused a much greater and more devastating war with China and the Soviet Union; No, because the Korean War ended in a stalemate and it may have ended in a U.S. victory under the leadership of a strong general.)*

2. **Draw Conclusions** Why do you think the stalemate between North and South Korea lasted into the 21st century? *(Possible response: Both Koreas could function independently due to the peace established along the demilitarized zone.)*

INTERPRET MAPS

Direct students to the Division of Korea map. **ASK:** What geographic factors led to North Korea becoming communist? *(Possible response: North Korea shares a border with China and is very close to the Soviet Union.)*

ACTIVE OPTIONS

On Your Feet: Think, Pair, Share Instruct students to read the sidebar about SEATO, and ask them to think individually about how SEATO could be helpful or harmful to developing nations in Southeast Asia. Then have students choose partners and discuss the question for five minutes. Finally, allow individual students to share their opinions with the class.

> **NG Learning Framework: Review Personal Stories**
> **ATTITUDE** Curiosity
> **KNOWLEDGE** Our Human Story

Have students read and evaluate excerpts from *I Remember Korea* by Linda Granfield or *The Coldest Winter* by David Halberstam. Suggest that each student read a section of 5 to 10 pages from one of the books. Explain that the writers use personal accounts, research, and interviews to convey the experiences of soldiers and refugees involved in the Korean War. Organize students into small groups to discuss what they learned from their readings, noting what people endured during the war. Invite each group to present a summary of their findings to the class.

DIFFERENTIATE

INCLUSION

Use Clarifying Questions Pair students with disabilities with proficient students who can read the lesson aloud to them. Ask the partners to describe the map and the photograph as needed for sight-impaired students. Encourage students to ask clarifying questions as needed.

GIFTED & TALENTED

Engage in a Debate Tell students they will assume the role of either President Truman or General MacArthur and debate that person's position regarding the better military strategy for the Korean War. Students should decide which person they will play, research that person's military and diplomatic strategies, take detailed notes, and use their notes to practice and role-play the debate in front of their classmates.

See the Chapter Planner for more strategies for differentiation.

HISTORICAL THINKING

ANSWERS

1. After WWII, Korea was split into two parts, with the Soviets occupying the north and the Americans occupying the south. The Soviets supported North Korea in building their military and attacking the south, in the hope that the peninsula would unite as a communist country. The Americans were afraid that communism would spread throughout the region if they didn't contain it. The Chinese were afraid that the Americans were preparing to attack them as well.

2. Answers will vary but should provide support from the lesson.

3. The 38th parallel may have been chosen because it divides Korea roughly in half.

CRITICAL VIEWING Fortification appears almost nonexistent in this section of the DMZ.

Two Wars in Vietnam

How did an Asian country 30 times smaller than the United States become the site of the longest and "hottest" war in the Cold War? For many Vietnamese, the war was about independence from 80 years of colonialism. For many Americans, it was about containing the spread of communism.

VIETNAM FIGHTS FRENCH COLONIALISM

For most of their history, the Vietnamese had lived in the shadow of imperial China and often had to fight for their independence from their northern neighbors. Then in the 1800s, the French were a new threat when they colonized Indochina, which included Cambodia, Laos, and Vietnam.

As you have learned, during World War II the Germans conquered France and found collaborators in the French Vichy regime. The Vichy government agreed to let Japan, Germany's ally, send troops to occupy Vietnam and use its airports. **Ho Chi Minh**, a revolutionary Marxist who had sought Vietnam's independence from

France before World War II, cooperated with the Allied powers. He led military campaigns against the Japanese during the war. With the defeat of Germany and Japan in 1945, Ho Chi Minh declared an independent Democratic Republic of Vietnam, referring to the American Declaration of Independence as inspiration.

France ignored Ho's declaration and sent forces into Vietnam to re-establish colonial control. But French forces were simultaneously fighting to hold on to Algeria, France's colony in north Africa. Since Algeria was home to a million French citizens, it became the priority. In 1954, the Vietnamese defeated the French, ending 80 years of French colonial rule in Vietnam.

The U.S. military helps South Vietnamese citizens flee the capital city of Saigon during the North Vietnamese invasion in April 1975. American involvement in the Vietnam War came to an end with the fall of Saigon.

THE UNITED STATES INTERVENES

A peace agreement in 1954 called for temporarily partitioning Vietnam into northern and southern regions with a plan to reunite the country after elections there. But the United States feared that Ho Chi Minh would win the elections and communism would spread throughout Southeast Asia. To prevent such an occurrence, the United States supported the formation of a separate anti-communist government in South Vietnam.

Conflict between the two Vietnams intensified as the United States supplied the south with weapons and military training, while the communist government in the north sponsored a rebel army in the south. The rebel army was called the National Front for the Liberation of South Vietnam, or the **Vietcong**.

In 1964, U.S. president Lyndon Johnson began to escalate the war against North Vietnam. By the next year, 200,000 American troops had been deployed to Southeast Asia. Despite massive U.S. bombing attacks on North Vietnam, the Vietcong grew in strength and gained support among the Vietnamese people. American soldiers were often unable to distinguish between guerrilla soldiers and civilians. In this first "televised war," gruesome images of death and destruction were transmitted around the world. Protests against the war grew in the United States and in other countries as people witnessed the slaughter of villagers and the spread of napalm and poisonous chemicals across the Vietnamese countryside by U.S. forces. Anti-American sentiment increased in countries throughout the world.

On January 31, 1968, the Vietcong launched attacks on South Vietnam's capital of Saigon and over 100 other cities and airfields during Tet, the Lunar New Year festival in Vietnam. Television coverage of the widespread attacks, called the Tet Offensive, showed the American public that the war was not proceeding as successfully as the government had reported. Opposition to U.S. military action intensified, and anti-war protests spread across American college campuses and among young people all across the world. Church groups and American veterans joined the anti-war efforts.

Having replaced Johnson as U.S. president in 1969, Richard Nixon promised to achieve "peace with honor." He intensified the bombing of North Vietnam and began replacing American ground troops with South Vietnamese forces. But after the United States withdrew its last ground troops, communist forces overtook Saigon on April 30, 1975. They renamed it Ho Chi Minh City and reunified the country under communist rule.

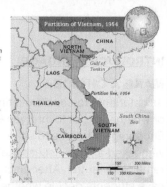

Partition of Vietnam, 1954

Ho Chi Minh led the Vietnamese nationalist movement for almost 30 years. He became president of North Vietnam in 1945. He died in 1969, before Vietnam was united under communist rule.

HISTORICAL THINKING

1. **READING CHECK** Why did the Vietnamese support Ho Chi Minh?

2. **IDENTIFY PROBLEMS AND SOLUTIONS** What were some problems the American government faced in Vietnam and at home during the years of the Vietnam War?

3. **INTERPRET MAPS** How would you describe the physical shape of Vietnam before its partition?

Cold War and Global Upheavals 823

PLAN: 2-PAGE LESSON

OBJECTIVE

Identify that Vietnamese communists fought off the Japanese, the French, and the Americans to gain independence for their country.

CRITICAL THINKING SKILLS FOR LESSON 4.2

- Identify Problems and Solutions
- Interpret Maps
- Make Connections
- Describe

HISTORICAL THINKING FOR CHAPTER 28

How do countries maintain their independence and security?

As former colonies gained their independence, the Soviet Union and United States tried to steer new nations toward their respective systems of government. Lesson 4.2 discusses Vietnam's quest for independence from colonial rule and the onset of the Vietnam War.

BACKGROUND FOR THE TEACHER

Ngo Dinh Diem The Eisenhower administration's positive view of Ngo Dinh Diem, the president of South Vietnam, was colored by American religious and cultural views of the 1950s. American supporters of Diem, including much of the media, were comforted by the fact that Diem was a Roman Catholic and assumed that meant he would favor democracy, oppose communism, and champion capitalism. At the same time, the Eisenhower administration accepted Diem's more authoritarian approach to governing because they believed that a firm hand would help the predominantly peasant population grow into democratic participation. Supporters also touted the fact that the Republic of Vietnam operated under a constitution. However, they failed to realize or simply ignored the fact that the constitution provided Diem with almost unlimited power to change laws, control the military, declare states of emergency, and suspend civil liberties.

INTRODUCE & ENGAGE

CONNECT TO TODAY

Ask students to consider contemporary protests that they have witnessed either in the news or in person. **ASK:** Why do individuals or groups protest? *(Possible responses: to bring attention to unfair or unjust practices; to inform the greater public)* Discuss the examples students cite, and ask them if they think these protests were successful. Tell students that many people in the United States and around the world protested the Vietnam War in the 1960s and 1970s. Then explain that in this lesson they will learn about the causes and eventual outcome of the Vietnam War.

TEACH

GUIDED DISCUSSION

1. **Make Connections** How did Algeria affect the fate of Vietnam? *(France had colonized both Algeria and Vietnam. As Algeria fought for its independence, France sacrificed control of Vietnam to focus its efforts on maintaining control over Algeria.)*

2. **Describe** What role did television play in the Vietnam War? *(Television showed people how gruesome the war was and that U.S. forces were not faring as well as the government claimed. This led to widespread opposition to the war.)*

INTERPRET MAPS

Direct students to the Partition of Vietnam map. **ASK:** Which portion of Vietnam, north or south, do you think was more likely to be influenced by China? *(Possible response: North Vietnam was more likely to be influenced by China because it shares a border with China.)*

ACTIVE OPTIONS

On Your Feet: Roundtable Organize students in groups of four and ask them to compare and contrast Vietnam's struggle for independence from France to the American Revolution. Encourage students to contemplate how the Declaration of Independence inspired Ho Chi Minh and what a free society looked like in the eyes of the Vietnamese as opposed to the eyes of colonial Americans. Each student in the group should answer the question in a different way.

> **NG Learning Framework: Discuss the Fall of Saigon**
> **ATTITUDE** Responsibility
> **SKILL** Collaboration

Assign small groups of students to examine the photograph of South Vietnamese fleeing Saigon and to research the withdrawal of U.S. troops and the end of the Vietnam War. Instruct groups to find out about the invasion of North Vietnamese forces, the evacuation of U.S. personnel and South Vietnamese from the city, the Vietnamese boat people, and those who were left behind at the end of the war. Once groups have finished researching, have them record their notes into a class chart or graphic organizer. Then hold a class discussion to evaluate how the United States handled the fall of Saigon.

DIFFERENTIATE

STRIVING READERS

Summarize Have students work in pairs to read and summarize the lesson text and photograph captions. Tell students to write at least three notes for each of the lesson's sections. After they have completed taking notes, guide students to create a summary statement for each section and then a summary statement for the whole lesson.

PRE-AP

Write a Letter Home Tell students to research the experiences of U.S. soldiers in Vietnam. Ask them to find actual letters from soldiers in online archives and in nonfiction books about the war. Then have students imagine themselves as soldiers who were trained to fight a conventional war but are now fighting a guerrilla war in Vietnam. Have them write a letter to a friend or family member about what they see, hear, feel, and think about the conflict. Invite volunteers to post their letters on a class blog or read them aloud to the class.

See the Chapter Planner for more strategies for differentiation.

HISTORICAL THINKING

ANSWERS

1. Ho Chi Minh had been successful in fighting the Japanese in WWII, and he promised independence for Vietnam.

2. Ho Chi Minh was popular with the Vietnamese people, and his support grew. American troops found it difficult to distinguish between guerrilla soldiers and civilians. The president faced protests from American students, veterans, and clergy who witnessed war atrocities on TV and realized that the president's account of the war wasn't quite accurate.

3. Before its partition, Vietnam was long and thin.

Strife Around the Globe

Although the armed forces of the United States and the Soviet Union never directly battled each other during the Cold War, they were busy nonetheless. Both countries sent their troops or provided military aid to other countries in attempts to control the outcome of conflicts that spanned the globe.

POLAND AND EASTERN EUROPE

Like the United States, the Soviet Union sometimes faced strong opposition to its interference in the affairs of other nations. You've read that the Soviets did not tolerate liberation movements within the Soviet bloc. Opposition to Soviet control sprang up in Poland, Hungary, and Czechoslovakia.

The predominantly Catholic people of Poland detested the policies of the pro-Moscow government imposed on them by Stalin, especially the official **atheism** of the communist state. Atheism is the belief that there is no God. In June 1956, a religious gathering attended by many Poles turned into an anti-government demonstration. Rather than cracking down on the protest, the Soviets compromised and allowed some religious freedom. However, they made it clear that any attempt to weaken Poland's ties to the Soviet Union would not be tolerated.

Later in 1956 in Hungary, students, factory workers, and middle-class professionals rose up to protest the country's Soviet-imposed communist dictatorship. The protest became known as the Hungarian Uprising. The Hungarian government collapsed. Leaders of the new provisional government feared a Soviet invasion, but they expected support from the Western democracies. While the Americans encouraged the rebellion, they did not intervene because they considered the danger of nuclear confrontation with the Soviets too great. Soviet tanks rolled in and crushed the Hungarian revolt with mass arrests and executions.

More than a decade after the Polish and Hungarian uprisings, workers and students in Czechoslovakia organized strikes and protests against Soviet-imposed communism. They forced hardline communist leaders to resign. In early 1968, political leader Alexander

Dubček became the new head of the Czechoslovak Communist Party. He promised "socialism with a human face" and granted greater freedom of speech and more market-oriented economic policies. The people of Czechoslovakia enthusiastically supported Dubček's reforms, known as the **Prague Spring**. But the Soviets, fearing the reform movement would spread, sent troops into Czechoslovakia. They believed they could remove Dubček from power and quell any resistance within a few days. But a nonviolent resistance movement rose up. For eight months, people defied curfews, moved street signs to confuse invading troops, and even set themselves on fire in protest. In the end, however, the Soviets succeeded in removing Dubček and returning hardline communists to power.

GLOBAL HOT SPOTS

From the 1950s through the 1970s, the Cold War played out in hot spots around the world. These hot spots included Iran, Haiti, Angola, Afghanistan, and Cambodia.

In the early 1950s, Iran had a parliament led by democratically elected prime minister Mohammad Mosaddegh (MOH-sah-dehk). Tensions rose in Iran when **Mohammad Reza Shah Pahlavi** (rih-ZAH shah PAH-luh-vee), the shah, or king, of Iran and an ardent anti-communist, fostered a close alliance with the administration of U.S. president Dwight Eisenhower.

Hoping that Iran could earn more money from its rich oil fields, Prime Minister Mosaddegh tried to renegotiate Iran's contracts with multinational petroleum companies. When negotiations failed, he threatened to nationalize the entire oil industry. Fearing that the Soviet Union would gain control of Iran's oil, the United States supported the Iranian military in arresting the popular prime minister and expanding Shah Pahlavi's power. Many Iranians considered the shah to be an American puppet.

In Haiti, **Francois Duvalier**, also known as "Papa Doc," was elected president in 1957. He became an authoritarian dictator. He amassed power by removing Haiti's Supreme Court, reducing the size of the military, and forming a secret army that terrorized the population. Duvalier gained U.S. aid with the claim that Haiti was likely to fall to communism unless the United States backed his presidency.

After gaining independence from Portugal in 1975, Angola became another Cold War battleground. Civil war broke out among three groups: the National Front for the Liberation of Angola (FNLA), the National Union for the Total Independence of Angola (UNITA), and the Popular Movement for the Liberation of Angola (MPLA). The United States backed both the FNLA and UNITA, the Soviet Union and Cuba supported the MPLA, and China assisted the FNLA. The Angolan civil war heightened tensions between the United States and the Soviet Union just as they were trying to improve relations through arms control and trade agreements in the late 1960s and the 1970s. The discovery of massive oil reserves made Angola even more valuable as a Cold War prize.

Perhaps the most aggressive Soviet intervention came in 1978 when the Soviet Union supported Afghan communists in seizing power. The Soviet occupation of Afghanistan faced tough resistance from Islamic guerrilla fighters known as the **mujahideen** (moo-ja-hih-DEEN). The United States and neighboring Pakistan responded by aiding the mujahideen, whose familiarity with the land and the people proved to be an advantage. As death tolls increased, the Soviets grew weary of the war, but their occupation lasted almost 10 years. The Soviets finally withdrew from Afghanistan in 1988.

In 1956, Hungarians revolted against the Soviet-imposed communist dictatorship that ruled the country. The Soviets sent tanks and troops and brutally crushed the rebellion. This photograph shows Hungarian patriots on top of a Soviet tank in Budapest during the uprising.

In Cambodia in 1975, radical communist forces called the **Khmer Rouge** replaced the existing government, which had been supported by France and the United States. The Khmer Rouge began a campaign of genocide. Hoping to create a classless society, they murdered former government officials, intellectuals, and monks. Then they emptied out cities and marched people to the countryside, where they forced them to work in what were called "the killing fields" in a film about the Khmer Rouge regime. Between 1975 and 1979, more than two million Cambodians died from mistreatment, starvation, disease, or execution. The United States refrained from getting involved, having just experienced a disastrous defeat in Vietnam. The brutal regime came to an end after the Vietnamese, backed by the Soviet Union, invaded Cambodia in 1979.

HISTORICAL THINKING

1. **READING CHECK** Why did the United States and the Soviet Union engage in conflicts around the world during the Cold War?

2. **SYNTHESIZE** Why would people in Eastern Europe have expected the United States to help them if they resisted their communist governments?

3. **EXPLAIN** Why might less powerful countries have mistrusted both the United States and the Soviet Union during the Cold War?

PLAN: 2-PAGE LESSON

OBJECTIVE
Identify the conflicts around the world that the United States and Soviet Union were involved in during the Cold War.

CRITICAL THINKING SKILLS FOR LESSON 4.3
- Synthesize
- Explain
- Compare and Contrast
- Make Connections
- Interpret Maps

HISTORICAL THINKING FOR CHAPTER 28
How do countries maintain their independence and security?

Many countries around the world experienced political upheaval in the wake of World War II. Lesson 4.3 discusses uprisings against communism and authoritarian regimes that sprouted up in all corners of the globe.

Student eEdition online
Additional content for this lesson, including a map and an image gallery, is available online.

BACKGROUND FOR THE TEACHER
Francois Duvalier Francois Duvalier, aka "Papa Doc," served as the president of Haiti for 14 years and was the longest-serving Haitian president at the time of his death. Originally trained as a doctor, he practiced medicine before entering the political world as the director general of the National Public Health Service in 1946 under President Dumarsais Estimé. When Estimé was overthrown by Paul E. Magloire, Duvalier worked in the resistance movement against the Magloire regime. When Magloire resigned, the government of Haiti was thrown into turmoil for about 10 months, culminating in Duvalier's election in 1957. Duvalier oversaw a forceful government, utilizing a group of *Tontons Macoute* to kill and terrorize anyone critical of his administration. Similar to Stalin and Mao, Duvalier ruled with a cult of personality and portrayed himself as a divine symbol of Haiti. When he died, he transferred control of the Haitian government to his son.

INTRODUCE & ENGAGE

ACTIVATE PRIOR KNOWLEDGE

Ask students to consider how the Cold War played out around the world, including how various nations reacted to, embraced, or rejected communism. Begin a class K-W-L Chart, with students providing responses for the first column. Responses might include that many developing nations tried to practice non-alignment, that the United States and Soviet Union were both concerned about nuclear war, and that communism spread in east and southeast Asia. Then ask students to list questions that they would like to have answered as they study this lesson. Allow time at the end of the lesson for a class discussion. Prompt students to use the information they learned in the lesson to complete the last column of the K-W-L Chart.

TEACH

GUIDED DISCUSSION

1. **Compare and Contrast** How does "socialism with a human face" differ from Soviet communism? *("Socialism with a human face" allowed for more personal freedoms and some market-oriented economic policies, whereas Soviet communism denied many freedoms and strictly controlled the economy.)*

2. **Make Connections** How did dictators in developing nations gain the support of the United States? *(The United States feared the spread of communism, so dictators that pledged to fight against communism often received support from the United States.)*

INTERPRET MAPS

Direct students to the map (available in the Student eEdition). **ASK:** What metaphorical boundary in Europe is demarcated by the Cold War hot spots that run from north to south through the continent? *(the iron curtain)*

ACTIVE OPTIONS

On Your Feet: Jigsaw Strategy Organize students into three "expert" groups and have them research the uprisings against communism in Poland, Hungary, and Czechoslovakia. Tell each group to create a simplified summary of what they learned from their research. Regroup students into three new groups so each group has at least one person from each expert group. Invite students in the new group to take turns sharing the simplified summary they created in their "expert" groups.

> **NG Learning Framework: Synthesize Photographic Evidence**
> ATTITUDE Curiosity
> SKILL Observation

Direct students to the image gallery (available in the Student eEdition), and instruct them to analyze the photographs of struggles in different parts of the world during the Cold War. Encourage students to focus on the people in the photographs, what they are doing, and what they might be feeling. Then have them write several sentences synthesizing the information they observed in the photographs.

DIFFERENTIATE

ENGLISH LANGUAGE LEARNERS

Make Word Cards Pair students at the **Beginning** level with students at the **Intermediate** or **Advanced** level. Instruct partners to read the sentences in the lesson containing the vocabulary words *atheism* and *mujahideen* and make a word card for each word, including the definition, pronunciation, and an original sentence using the word. Ask pairs to discuss how the words help them understand the global strife that occurred during the Cold War.

GIFTED & TALENTED

Create a Multimedia Newscast Challenge students to conduct online research to find photographs and newspaper articles about an issue of their choice from the lesson. Then prompt students to write a script in the form of a contemporary newscast, incorporating the information, images, and video clips they discovered. Instruct students to assemble their script and research materials into a multimedia newscast about the incident and present it to the class.

See the Chapter Planner for more strategies for differentiation.

HISTORICAL THINKING

ANSWERS

1. Both countries sought allies in their fight against each other. The Soviets wanted to spread communism around the world, and the United States wanted to spread capitalism and democracy.

2. The Truman Doctrine suggested that the United States would come to the aid of any country threatened by communism.

3. Both countries supported authoritarian rulers and governments that were repressive and unpopular, and both countries interfered in and tried to control the domestic affairs of other countries.

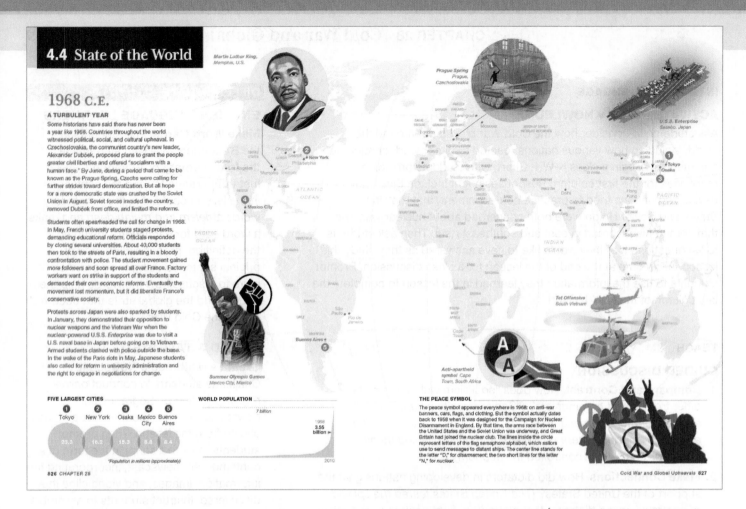

4.4 State of the World

Martin Luther King, Memphis, U.S.

Prague Spring Prague, Czechoslovakia

U.S.S. Enterprise Sasebo, Japan

1968 C.E.

A TURBULENT YEAR

Some historians have said there has never been a year like 1968. Countries throughout the world witnessed political, social, and cultural upheaval. In Czechoslovakia, the communist country's new leader, Alexander Dubček, proposed plans to grant the people greater civil liberties and offered "socialism with a human face." By June, during a period that came to be known as the Prague Spring, Czechs were calling for further strides toward democratization. But all hope for a more democratic state was crushed by the Soviet Union in August. Soviet forces invaded the country, removed Dubček from office, and limited the reforms.

Students often spearheaded the call for change in 1968. In May, French university students staged protests, demanding educational reform. Officials responded by closing several universities. About 40,000 students then took to the streets of Paris, resulting in a bloody confrontation with police. The student movement gained more followers and soon spread all over France. Factory workers went on strike in support of the students and demanded their own economic reforms. Eventually the movement lost momentum, but it did liberalize France's conservative society.

Protests across Japan were also sparked by students. In January, they demonstrated their opposition to nuclear weapons and the Vietnam War when the nuclear-powered U.S.S. *Enterprise* was due to visit a U.S. naval base in Japan before going on to Vietnam. Armed students clashed with police outside the base. In the wake of the Paris riots in May, Japanese students also called for reform in university administration and the right to engage in negotiations for change.

Summer Olympic Games Mexico City, Mexico

Tet Offensive South Vietnam

Anti-apartheid symbol Cape Town, South Africa

FIVE LARGEST CITIES

① Tokyo 23.3
② New York 16.2
③ Osaka 15.3
④ Mexico City 8.8
⑤ Buenos Aires 8.4

Population in millions (approximate)

WORLD POPULATION

7 billion

1968
3.55 billion ►

2010

THE PEACE SYMBOL

The peace symbol appeared everywhere in 1968: on anti-war banners, cars, flags, and clothing. But the symbol actually dates back to 1958 when it was designed for the Campaign for Nuclear Disarmament in England. By that time, the arms race between the United States and the Soviet Union was underway, and Great Britain had joined the nuclear club. The lines inside the circle represent letters of the flag semaphore alphabet, which sailors use to send messages to distant ships. The center line stands for the letter "D," for *disarmament*; the two short lines for the letter "N," for *nuclear*.

PLAN: 4-PAGE LESSON

OBJECTIVE
Learn about the political, social, and cultural upheavals in and around 1968 C.E.

CRITICAL THINKING SKILLS FOR LESSON 4.4
- Analyze Visuals
- Make Connections
- Interpret Visuals
- Compare and Contrast
- Analyze Cause and Effect
- Form and Support Opinions

HISTORICAL THINKING FOR CHAPTER 28

How do countries maintain their independence and security?

Many people took to the streets to protest the actions of their governments in the late 1960s. Lesson 4.4 explores a particularly tumultuous year, characterized by political, social, and cultural disturbances around the world.

Student eEdition `online`
Additional content for this lesson, including a video, is available online.

BACKGROUND FOR THE TEACHER

Chicago, 1968 History has labeled the 1968 Democratic National Convention in Chicago as a "violent and unprecedented disaster." Thousands of young protesters arriving in Chicago led the police to call in reinforcements from the Army, National Guard, and Secret Service to handle the record-breaking crowds. As the protesters marched toward the convention site on August 28, police tried to stop them with tear gas, rifles, and clubs. Chaos ensued as protesters, reporters, onlookers, doctors, and medical helpers caring for the injured were beaten and arrested. The brutality of the police was reportedly extraordinary. Reporters flashed photos as four police officers beat an unarmed man with their billy-clubs. News broadcasts across the nation showed videos of police beating unarmed protesters throughout the day and into the night as the streets "literally ran with blood." By the end of the week, more than 600 people were arrested and over 200 people suffered serious injuries. The breakdown in law and order destroyed the reputations of Chicago police, soldiers, and politicians for many years.

History Notebook
Encourage students to complete the State of the World page for Chapter 28 in their History Notebooks as they read.

INTRODUCE & ENGAGE

EXPLORE HISTORY USING VISUALS

Tell students that the photographs, map, and diagram in this lesson represent the important developments that were taking place around the world in 1968. **ASK:** What visuals on these pages intrigue you? What questions do you have about them? *(Answers will vary. Possible responses may include questions about the location of the world's most populated cities, the peace symbols, or the raised black-gloved fist.)* Write down students' questions and have students supply the answers as they read the lesson.

TEACH

GUIDED DISCUSSION

1. **Compare and Contrast** How did the student protests in France compare to the student protests in Mexico? *(Both countries experienced student protests against their governments, and the governments in France and Mexico both responded with violent military action against the students.)*

2. **Analyze Cause and Effect** What was the cause of the Prague Spring, and what effect did it have? *(The Czechs were calling for greater civil liberties and democratization, but the Soviet Union invaded the country and limited further Czechoslovakian reforms.)*

STATE OF THE WORLD

Direct students to watch the video 1968: A Turbulent Year (available in the Student eEdition). Remind students of the essential question for this chapter: How do countries maintain their independence and security? **ASK:** Based on the information presented in this lesson and in the video, how would you answer this question? *(Possible response: Some countries try to maintain security by limiting those who enter its borders, such as Kenya and Britain. Some countries use military violence to maintain security, such as France, Mexico, and the United States. Some countries seek domination, such as the Soviet Union over Czechoslovakia and the North Vietnamese over South Vietnam.)*

DIFFERENTIATE

STRIVING READERS

Create a Chart Group students in pairs and tell them to read and take notes about the turmoil and turbulences found in this lesson. Have partners compare notes and sort their details about each turmoil or turbulence into a chart.

PRE-AP

Research Cultural Influences Have students conduct research into one of these cities: Tokyo, New York, Osaka, Mexico City, or Buenos Aires. Tell them to include information about their city's main culture as well as other cultures that may have influenced it throughout history. Encourage students to present their findings to the class. Then determine as a class the similarities and differences among the cultures found in the cities.

See the Chapter Planner for more strategies for differentiation.

In Mexico City, a fight between high school students led to unrest. After the government called out the army to stop the fighting, the soldiers killed some of the students. Over the next few months, university students in the city organized protests and rallies to demonstrate against the government's use of violence. At a meeting attended by thousands of the students in October, soldiers arrived to arrest the movement's leaders. Gunfire broke out and lasted for almost two hours. An estimated 300 civilians died, and the government blamed the deaths on the students' actions.

Students challenged apartheid at the University of Cape Town in South Africa. The university had offered employment to a black lecturer but was forced to withdraw the offer by the government. Students staged a sit-in at the university's administration building but, bowing to pressure from the government and the university, ended it after 10 days.

Perhaps no country was roiled more by the turmoil of 1968 than the United States. Throughout the year, anti-war protests took place on many college campuses. And the assassination in April of civil rights leader Martin Luther King, Jr., triggered racial violence across the country. Another assassination took place in June when Robert F. Kennedy, a Democratic candidate for president was shot and killed after winning the California primary. Then in August, chaos erupted in Chicago during the Democratic National Convention as Vietnam War protesters battled police in the streets.

At the end of the year, the U.S. crew of Apollo 8, the first manned spacecraft to orbit the moon, sent a note of hope from space. On Christmas Eve, they read a message wishing everyone on Earth "good night, good luck." Still, the aftershocks of 1968 continue to be felt worldwide more than 50 years later.

HISTORICAL THINKING

INTERPRET VISUALS Based on the images and the map, what words best describe the world in 1968?

Smoke billows from the remains of the U.S. Army 8th Division headquarters in Saigon after an attack by the Vietcong on January 31.

Martin Luther King, Jr., lies at the feet of his associates on the balcony of the Lorraine Motel in Memphis, Tennessee, on April 4.

Students and workers march through the streets of Paris on May 13 to demand educational and economic reform.

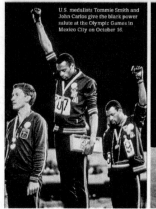

U.S. medalists Tommie Smith and John Carlos give the black power salute at the Olympic Games in Mexico City on October 16.

U.S. astronaut Bill Anders took this photo of Earth rising above the moon's surface on December 24.

BACKGROUND FOR THE TEACHER

United States, 1968 Before the violence in Chicago, there were many large protests that helped fuel the political, social, and cultural climate in the United States. On January 15, Montana congresswoman Jeanette Rankin, at age 87, led 5,000 women on a march in Washington, D.C., to protest the Vietnam War. On February 1, black sanitation workers Echol Cole and Robert Walker were crushed to death in Memphis by a malfunctioning garbage truck, but the public works facility refused to compensate their families. This incident drew the attention of the civil rights movement and Dr. Martin Luther King, Jr., which many claimed led to his assassination. On February 8, police opened fire on students protesting segregation at the South Carolina State campus. Three people were killed and 27 were wounded. The police officers were tried but acquitted of all charges, while the protest coordinator was sent to prison for seven months. On March 1–8, 15,000 Latina students walked out of classrooms to protest better education for minorities in Los Angeles. On April 4, Martin Luther King, Jr. was assassinated in Memphis. This sparked riots all over the nation, resulting in 39 people dead, 2,600 injured, and 21,000 arrested in just one week. On April 6, in Oakland, California, a 17-year-old Black Panther tried to surrender during a shoot-out but was gunned down by police. On June 19, in Washington, D.C., 50,000 people showed up for the Solidarity Day Rally for Jobs, Peace, and Freedom. On July 24, a shoot-out in Cleveland resulted in the death of three black militants and one bystander. Riots broke out for the next five days. The unrest caused by these events eventually came to a head in Chicago on August 28.

TEACH

GUIDED DISCUSSION

3. **Form and Support Opinions** Why do you think students often sparked the call for change? *(Answers will vary. Students should provide reasonable answers using examples from the lesson to support their claims.)*

4. **Make Connections** Why was the peace symbol from 1958 resurrected and used in 1968? *(The symbol originally represented people's desire for peace between the United States and the Soviet Union. It was used again in 1968 when conflicts were breaking out all over the United States and around the world, and people desired peace around the world.)*

ANALYZE VISUALS

Have students examine the Five Largest Cities diagram and the World Population map. **ASK:** Based on the map, where are two of the largest cities in the world located? *(Japan)* How many people live in the five largest cities in the world? *(72 million people)* How does the world's population in 1968 compare to its population in 2010? *(There are approximately 3.45 billion more people in 2010 than there were in 1968.)* Explain to students that the black dots on the map indicate the location of other large cities in the world in 1968, including some cities where disturbances have broken out. As a class, discuss the regions in the world that are the most and least populated. Then discuss why protests and upheavals often occur in large cities.

ACTIVE OPTIONS

On Your Feet: Research Turbulence in 1968 Instruct students to form six teams, and assign each team one of the following turbulences showcased in the lesson: Black Power salute at the Summer Olympic Games, assassination of Martin Luther King, Jr., Prague Spring invasion, Sharpeville massacre, Tet Offensive, or protest against the U.S.S. *Enterprise*. Instruct groups to gather in separate areas of the room to conduct additional research and then to discuss the information about the turmoil. Reconvene as a class and ask a volunteer from each group to share two or three additional points that were not covered in the lesson.

| **NG Learning Framework: Plan a Movement**
| ATTITUDES Responsibility, Empowerment
| SKILL Collaboration

Divide the class into small groups. Direct them to plan a peaceful protest, social media campaign, or other movement in support of a current civil rights issue. Examples could include transgender rights, issues of religious freedom, or the rights of people convicted of a crime. Have groups identify and research an issue and make a peaceful plan that includes a description of the issue, the goals of the movement, supporting arguments, the target audience, proposed solutions, and the next course of action. Ask groups to designate a group member to present the group's plan to the class.

HISTORICAL THINKING

ANSWER

Answers will vary. Possible response: The words *riots, protests, demonstrations, anger, violence, political conflicts, social and cultural disagreements*, and *assassinations* describe the world in 1968.

VOCABULARY

Match each vocabulary word below with its definition.

VOCABULARY WORDS

1. proxy war
2. populism
3. apartheid
4. indoctrinate
5. domino effect
6. neocolonialism
7. nonalignment
8. satellite state
9. nationalize

DEFINITIONS

a. a policy of not allying with other countries
b. an independent country under the control of a stronger country
c. the theory that the fall of one country to communism will result in neighboring countries falling to communism
d. a former system of racial segregation and discrimination against nonwhites in South Africa
e. to transfer from private to government ownership
f. a war in which one or both sides are serving the interests of another country
g. the domination of less-developed countries by former colonial powers
h. to train a person to accept a certain doctrine
i. political philosophy that emphasizes support for the concerns of ordinary people

READING STRATEGY
DETERMINE CHRONOLOGY

Use a time line like the one below to organize the major events of the Cold War. Include dates and notes on the events and add boxes if necessary. Then answer the question.

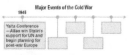

Major Events of the Cold War

1945
Yalta Conference —Allies win Stalin's support for UN and begin planning for post-war Europe

10. What was the most significant event of the Cold War? Explain your choice.

MAIN IDEAS

Answer the following questions. Support your answers with evidence from the chapter.

11. What was the purpose of the Marshall Plan? LESSON 1.1
12. How did the arms race affect direct hostility between the Soviet Union and the United States? LESSON 1.3
13. Why did Fidel Castro seek a closer relationship with the Soviet Union? LESSON 2.1
14. What were the outcomes of the Great Leap Forward and the Cultural Revolution? LESSON 2.4
15. How did France foster neocolonial control of its former African colonies? LESSON 3.1
16. What was the main result of the Bandung Conference in 1955? LESSON 3.3
17. What was the strategic importance of the Suez Canal? LESSON 3.4
18. What was the cause of the Korean War? LESSON 4.1
19. What led the United States to support the formation of South Vietnam? LESSON 4.2

HISTORICAL THINKING

Answer the following questions. Support your answers with evidence from the chapter.

20. **ANALYZE CAUSE AND EFFECT** How did power shifts resulting from World War II lead to Soviet control over Eastern Europe and economic recoveries in Germany and Japan?
21. **DESCRIBE** Explain the purpose of the UN, NATO, the Warsaw Pact, SEATO, and OAS.
22. **DRAW CONCLUSIONS** Choose one of these nationalist leaders mentioned in the chapter. What was the leader's impact on the country?
23. **COMPARE** How and why was the U.S. response to policies in South Africa similar to its response to the Democratic Republic of the Congo?

INTERPRET VISUALS

This political cartoon by Edmund Valtman entitled "This hurts me more than it hurts you!" was published in 1962 following the Cuban Missile Crisis. Study the cartoon and answer the questions that follow.

"THIS HURTS ME MORE THAN IT HURTS YOU !"

24. The man with the pliers represents Soviet premier Nikita Khrushchev. Who does the man with the open mouth represent?
25. What is Khrushchev pulling out of the man's open mouth?
26. What message does the cartoon convey about the results of the Cuban Missile Crisis?

ANALYZE SOURCES

In April 1961, President Kennedy of the United States and Premier Khrushchev of the Soviet Union exchanged letters regarding the political situation in Cuba. Read the following excerpts from their letters and answer the question that follows.

> You are under serious misapprehension in regard to events in Cuba. For months there has been evident and growing resistance to the Cuban dictatorship. More than 100,000 refugees have recently fled from Cuba into neighboring countries. . . . These are unmistakable signs that Cubans find intolerable the denial of democratic liberties. . . .
>
> —John F. Kennedy, U.S. president, letter to Nikita Khrushchev, 1961

> In the present case, apparently, the United States Government is seeking to restore to Cuba that "freedom" under which Cuba would dance to the tune of her more powerful neighbor and foreign monopolies would again be able to plunder the country's national wealth, to wax rich on the sweat and blood of the Cuban people.
>
> —Nikita Khrushchev, Soviet premier, reply to John Kennedy's letter, 1961

27. How did the two world leaders differ in their view of the political situation in Cuba?

CONNECT TO YOUR LIFE

28. **ARGUMENT** During the Vietnam War, American men between the ages of 18 and 25 were drafted to fill vacancies in the armed forces. Opposition to both the draft and the war fueled protests on college campuses. Put yourself in the place of a young college student eligible for the draft. How would you feel about being drafted to fight in a war? Would you agree to serve your nation or protest against the war? Write an essay stating your position and explaining your reasons.

TIPS

* Review the discussion of the Vietnam War in the chapter. If necessary, conduct research to learn more about the military draft. Based on what you learn, form an opinion.
* Write an introductory paragraph that provides the context for your essay and includes a topic sentence that clearly states your position on the war and the draft.
* In the body of your essay, explain the reasons for your position. If appropriate, use two or three vocabulary words from the chapter in your argument.
* Conclude your essay by summarizing your position.

VOCABULARY ANSWERS

1. f
2. i
3. d
4. h
5. c
6. g
7. a
8. b
9. e

READING STRATEGY ANSWERS

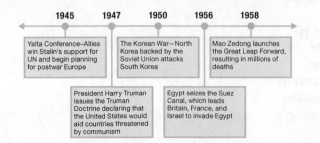

1945	1947	1950	1956	1958

Yalta Conference–Allies win Stalin's support for UN and begin planning for postwar Europe

The Korean War—North Korea backed by the Soviet Union attacks South Korea

Mao Zedong launches the Great Leap Forward, resulting in millions of deaths

President Harry Truman issues the Truman Doctrine declaring that the United States would aid countries threatened by communism

Egypt seizes the Suez Canal, which leads Britain, France, and Israel to invade Egypt

10. Answers will vary. Possible response: The Truman Doctrine was the most significant event of the Cold War because it involved the United States in affairs across the world for decades.

MAIN IDEAS ANSWERS

11. The Marshall Plan provided money to help European countries rebuild after World War II and was designed to enhance the stability of free-market economies.

12. The large number of weapons built and their power would mean mutual destruction if nuclear weapons were used in a war, so the two countries were careful not to get into a situation where they might actually use the weapons and threaten their own existence.

13. Corporate lobbyists, Cold War hawks, and pro-Batista forces in the United States opposed Castro and cast him as a communist threat, leading the United States to invade Cuba to try to overthrow Castro. The United States also placed an embargo on Cuba. To defend himself and maintain the country's economy, Castro developed closer ties with the Soviet Union.

14. The Great Leap Forward was a disaster because expertise was not valued and small-scale production units were not as efficient as large factories. In the Cultural Revolution, the country fell into chaos as schools closed and the economy stagnated. In the end, the students who had enthusiastically supported Mao were sent to labor camps themselves.

15. France promised citizenship to educated Africans, who came to identify with French culture. They held a referendum on independence, in which former French colonies could control their own internal affairs while France would retain control over their economic policy, foreign affairs, and military. All but one colony voted to retain ties with France.

16. Leaders of former colonial states in Africa and Asia agreed to remain neutral in the Cold War and to abolish colonialism and support self-determination.

17. It was the main shipping route between Europe and Asia. It was of vital importance for shipping oil.

18. After World War II, the Korean peninsula was divided, with the Soviets occupying the north and the Americans occupying the south. After the Soviets and Americans left the peninsula, a communist government headed North Korea and a democratic government headed South Korea. The war began because North Korea invaded South Korea in the hope of uniting the peninsula.

19. The United States feared Ho Chi Minh would be elected and wanted to prevent communism from spreading throughout Southeast Asia.

HISTORICAL THINKING ANSWERS

20. The Soviets occupied Eastern Europe and did not allow free elections. The Soviet Union and the United States built up their own military power, creating a power shift. To help with economic recovery, the United States developed the Marshall Plan, and the Supreme Command of Allied Powers worked to rebuild Japan. They also implemented economic reforms to promote recovery.

21. The UN was formed to promote international peace and security through diplomacy. NATO was formed to provide mutual defense, contain communism, and promote democracy. The Warsaw Pact was created in opposition to NATO. It provided mutual defense for Soviet bloc countries and strengthened the Soviet's hold over those countries. Like NATO, SEATO and OAS were formed to contain communism.

22. Answers will vary. Possible response: Fidel Castro: built up a guerrilla force and ousted the dictator; was branded a communist and was forced to seek aid from the Soviet Union; policies provided some improvements in life in Cuba but also created a dependency on the Soviet Union; in the mid-1960s, Cubans enjoyed better food and shelter, basic healthcare, and free education; over time, the economy stagnated; those who protested against his policies were sent to labor camps or executed.

23. Possible response: During the Cold War years, the United States was much more concerned with the spread of communism than with repressive governments. It overlooked repression in South Africa because the white-majority government opposed communism. In the Congo, the United States supported the removal of the country's prime minister because he was considered a communist. It supported the rise of the dictator Joseph Mobutu in the Congo because he was anti-communist and allied with the United States.

INTERPRET VISUALS ANSWERS

24. Fidel Castro

25. missiles

26. The removal of missiles from Cuba was painful for Cuba and the Soviets.

ANALYZE SOURCES ANSWER

27. Kennedy insists that the influx of Cuban refugees in neighboring countries is proof that the Cuban people are unhappy and can no longer tolerate communist rule. He claims they are escaping to countries with "democratic liberties." Khrushchev believes that the United States' intention is to exploit the Cubans. His letter implies that the people are better off under communism than they were before when the Americans plundered the country's "national wealth" and exploited the Cuban people for cheap labor.

CONNECT TO YOUR LIFE ANSWER

28. In their essays, students should clearly state a position on the Vietnam War and the draft and explain their reasons for their position.

UNIT 10 RESOURCES

UNIT INTRODUCTION

UNIT TIME LINE

UNIT MAP  online

THE GLOBAL PERSPECTIVE:
Who We Are: Shared Cultures and Identities

- National Geographic Explorers: Topher White, Danielle N. Lee, and Paul Salopek
- On Your Feet: Ready, Set, Recall

NG Learning Framework
Explore High-Tech Forensics

UNIT WRAP-UP

National Geographic Magazine Adapted Article

- "Navigating the Anthropocene"

Unit 10 Inquiry: Create an NGO

Unit 10 Formal Assessment

UNIT 10
Global Challenges
1945–Present

CRITICAL VIEWING

CHAPTER 29 RESOURCES

Available in the Teacher eEdition

TEACHER RESOURCES & ASSESSMENT

Reading and Note-Taking

Vocabulary Practice

Document-Based Question Template

Social Studies Skills Lessons
- Reading: Analyze Cause and Effect
- Writing: Informative

Formal Assessment
- Chapter 29 Pretest
- Chapter 29 Tests A & B
- Section Quizzes

Chapter 29 Answer Key

Cognero®

CHAPTER 29
Conflicts and Transformations
1947–2000

HISTORICAL THINKING: What battles and other drastic changes altered the global landscape in the last half of the 20th century?

SECTION 1 Soviet Collapse
SECTION 2 Global Democratic Possibilities
SECTION 3 The Middle East
SECTION 4 Promises and Challenges of Globalization

CRITICAL VIEWING

ACHTUNG!
SIE VERLASSEN
JETZT
WEST-BERLIN

STUDENT DIGITAL RESOURCES

Available in the Student eEdition

- eEdition (English)
- Handbooks
- National Geographic Atlas
- History Notebook
- Biographies
- Literature Analysis

STRATEGY ❶

Turn Titles into Questions

To help students set a purpose for reading, tell them to read the title of each lesson in a section and then turn that title into a question they believe will be answered in the lesson. Students can record their questions and write their own answers or they can ask each other questions.

Use with All Lessons *For example, Section 1 questions could be: How did glasnost connect to the fall of the Berlin Wall? What were some of the post-Soviet transitions? What caused unrest in Beijing?*

STRATEGY ❷

Connect Main Ideas and Details

As they read each lesson, encourage students to work in pairs to complete a Main Idea and Details Chart. Point out the kinds of details (facts, dates, events, reasons) that support main ideas. Then ask each pair to alternate reading paragraphs aloud and writing down main ideas and details. Tell them this process will help them identify and remember the most important information in the lesson. Ask volunteers to share their completed chart with other student pairs and discuss the similarities and differences in their charts.

Use with All Lessons

STRATEGY ❸

Create "What Happens" Charts

Tell students to summarize the chapter by creating two "What Happens" Charts, one for the conflicts and one for the transformations that occurred in the world during the final decades of the 20th century. Instruct students to complete each chart with relevant information as they read the lessons. After students read independently, place them in pairs and tell them to take turns comparing their charts and returning to the text to verify facts regarding any differences they have.

Use with All Lessons

STRATEGY ❶

Sequence Events

Write the main events of a lesson on index cards. There should be one event on each index card. Have the student work with another student or a teacher aide to read the lesson. Then have the student place the cards listing the events in the order in which they occurred. Use the following main events for Lesson 3.1:

- In the Balfour Declaration of 1917, Britain promised a "national home" for Jews.
- The Southwest Asian countries of Iraq, Lebanon, Syria, and Jordan gained independence before, during, or shortly after World War II.
- In 1947, Britain transferred the lands of Palestine to the United Nations.
- Zionist leader David Ben-Gurion declared the independence of Israel in 1948.
- Egypt, Lebanon, Iraq, Syria, and Jordan declared war on the new republic of Israel.
- Israelis routed the Arab armies.
- Israel won financial support from other nations, including the United States.
- Arabs and Israelis continue to quarrel.

Use with All Lessons

STRATEGY ❷

Create Vocabulary Cards

Encourage students to create a vocabulary card for each boldfaced vocabulary word in a section. Students may draw a picture to illustrate each word or write a definition, synonym, and/or example. Students can work in pairs to review the words when they finish reading a section. Encourage pairs to share their cards and copy any synonyms or examples that will be helpful in remembering the meaning of the words.

Use with All Lessons

STRATEGY ❶

Develop Word Knowledge

Help students develop their understanding and usage of unknown words and vocabulary words by using the words in context.

- For **Beginning** students, display sentences with choices: Glasnost called for restricted/unrestricted discussion of issues. *(unrestricted)*
- For **Intermediate** students, display individual sentence frames with only one blank: The policy of glasnost encouraged _____ discussion of political and social issues. *(unrestricted)*
- For **Advanced** students, display sentences with more than one blank: Through his policy of perestroika, Gorbachev wanted to _____ the Soviet _____. *(reform, economy)*

Use with All Lessons

STRATEGY ❷
Compose Captions

Pair students at the **Beginning** and **Intermediate** levels with English-proficient students, and instruct them to work together to write original captions for the photographs in each lesson of the chapter. After they have finished, ask volunteers to share their captions.

Use with All Lessons *Suggest that students first read the printed caption aloud, then cover it with a piece of paper and write their original caption on the paper. Their caption may paraphrase and expand upon the one in the text. Then lead a discussion comparing the different captions.*

STRATEGY ❸
Create a Word Wall

Work with students at the **Beginning** and **Intermediate** levels to select five terms from each lesson to display on a Word Wall. Choose terms students are likely to encounter in other lessons in the unit, such as *tensions, reforms, domination, regime,* and *fled.* Keep the words displayed throughout the chapter, adding terms for each new lesson. Discuss each term as it comes up during reading.

Use with All Lessons

GIFTED & TALENTED

STRATEGY ❶
Create a Multimedia Presentation

Instruct students to use multiple online sources to access historians' analyses of the legacy of President Carter, Reagan, Bush, or Clinton in regards to global conflicts. Tell students to focus on how the president pursued peace or conflict. Students should use an online presentation tool, relevant photographs, videos, charts, and other visuals. Invite students to share their presentations with the class and answer questions.

Use with Lessons 1.1, 2.1, 3.2, 3.3, and 4.4

STRATEGY ❷
Teach a Class

Before beginning the chapter, allow students to choose one of the lessons and prepare to teach the content to the class. Give them a set amount of time in which to present their lesson. Suggest that students think about any visuals or activities they will want to use when they teach.

Use with All Lessons

PRE-AP

STRATEGY ❶
Write an Editorial

Encourage students to write an editorial in which they comment on a connection between an event in this chapter and a current or recent event in world affairs. Students could connect China's economic transformation with U.S. economic concerns or connect the lesson on Latin American struggles with immigration concerns today. Tell students to locate present-day statistics and expert opinions to reference in their editorials. Instruct students to post their editorials on a school website and to submit them to local newspapers for publication.

Use with All Lessons

STRATEGY ❷
Explore Long-term Consequences

Direct students to research and evaluate various historians' analyses of the consequences of past U.S.-Israeli policies. Tell students to use the analyses to write an essay on the long-term impacts of U.S. support of Israel, focusing on the relationship between the two nations and how this relationship has impacted U.S.-Arab relationships. Instruct students to conclude their essay with what they consider to be the most important lessons learned. Invite students to share their essays with the class.

Use with Lessons 3.1, 3.2, and 3.3

HISTORICAL THINKING What battles and other drastic changes altered the global landscape in the last half of the 20th century?

SECTION 1 Soviet Collapse

SECTION 2 Global Democratic Possibilities

SECTION 3 The Middle East

SECTION 4 Promises and Challenges of Globalization

CRITICAL VIEWING In East Germany, people gather at the Berlin Wall near the Brandenburg Gate after it was opened in November 1989. The sign translates to "Caution! You are now leaving West Berlin" in English. Why was the collapse of this structure such an important moment?

ACHTUNG!
SIE VERLASSEN
JETZT
WEST BERLIN

INTRODUCE THE PHOTOGRAPH

THE BERLIN WALL

Have students examine the photograph of people standing at the Berlin Wall shortly after the gate was opened. **ASK:** Why do you think these people are gathering at the wall? *(Possible responses: Now that the gate is open, they want to cross to the other side, or they are gathering to demonstrate support for or opposition against something.)* Explain that the Berlin Wall was erected in 1961 to limit the passage of people and goods between the West and the Soviet bloc and that it cut off families and friends as well as access to economic opportunities. The Berlin Wall was not torn down until 1989. Tell students that in this chapter they will learn about how the fall of the Soviet Union, including the dismantling of the Berlin Wall, led to revolutions and nation-building around the world.

SHARE BACKGROUND

From 1949 to 1961, 2.5 million East Germans, many of whom were skilled workers and members of the professional class, fled to West Germany. The loss of these workers greatly threatened East Germany's economic future. The Berlin Wall was part of East Germany's strategy to stave off economic disaster. The barrier was 15 feet high, built of concrete, surrounded by live mines, and guarded by armed sentinels. These measures failed to keep East Germans from attempting to reach West Berlin, and over the years nearly 5,000 people made it to West Germany. Another 5,000 were captured, and close to 200 were killed as they tried to escape East Berlin. The Berlin Wall fell in 1989 along with the hardline communist government of East Germany as democratic sentiment began to reach a critical mass throughout Eastern Europe. For the first time in decades, free movement between East Germany and West Germany was possible.

CRITICAL VIEWING Answers will vary. Possible response: The collapse of the Berlin Wall symbolized the collapse of the Soviet Union, which led to battles for freedom and leaps forward in technology that connected people globally in ways that had never been seen before.

HISTORICAL THINKING QUESTION

What battles and other drastic changes altered the global landscape in the last half of the 20th century?

Team Word Webbing This activity will help students preview and discuss the topics covered in the chapter. Divide the class into groups of four and provide each group with a blank Word Web on a single large piece of paper. Give each student in the group a different colored marker. Ask students to consider the primary forces affecting the world in the latter half of the 20th century. Remind students that these forces can be political, economic, technological, or cultural. Have each student add to the part of the web nearest him or her. On a signal, students rotate the paper and each student adds to the nearest part again. Have group members present their web to the rest of the class, and lead a class discussion about the main events/issues affecting the world in the latter half of the 20th century.

KEY DATES FOR CHAPTER 29

1948	The United Nations approves the Universal Declaration of Human Rights; Israel is established as a nation.
1973	OPEC is founded.
1985	Gorbachev introduces glasnost and perestroika.
1987	Palestinians begin the first intifada.
1989	The Berlin Wall falls; Chinese students protest in Tiananmen Square.
1991	The CIS is established.
1993	Yitzhak Rabin and Yasir Arafat unsuccessfully try to negotiate peace between Israel and Palestine.
1994	Nelson Mandela is elected president of South Africa.

INTRODUCE THE READING STRATEGY

ANALYZE CAUSE AND EFFECT

Explain to students that analyzing causes and effects can help them more deeply understand concepts and events. Go to the Chapter Review and preview the Cause and Effect diagram with students. As they read the chapter, have students list the causes and effects of events pertaining to the restructuring of the world in the years following the collapse of the Soviet Union.

INTRODUCE CHAPTER VOCABULARY

KEY VOCABULARY

SECTION 1

détente	glasnost	perestroika

SECTION 2

leftist	nation-building	passive resistance

SECTION 3

fundamentalism	intifada	preempt
two-state solution		

SECTION 4

cost-benefit analysis	multinational corporation	neoliberalism
nongovernmental organization	outsourcing	pacifist

WORD WEB

As they read the chapter, encourage students to complete a Word Web for selected Key Vocabulary terms. Ask them to write each word in the center of an oval. Have them look through the chapter to find examples, characteristics, and descriptive words that may be associated with the Key Vocabulary term. At the end of the chapter, ask students what they learned about each term. Model an example for students on the board.

Glasnost to the Fall of the Berlin Wall

Imagine a crack in a dam splitting open as the pent-up water rushes through. During the 1980s, cracks began to appear in the political structure of the Soviet Union. Borders opened, a wall fell, and many people who had suffered under Soviet rule for decades rushed toward freedom.

GORBACHEV'S REFORMS

By 1980, after the communist victory in Vietnam, the Soviet Union was seen as advancing on the world stage, while the United States was in retreat. An earlier policy of eased tensions between the two countries, known as **détente**, had also come to an end with the Soviet invasion of Afghanistan in 1979.

The new U.S. president, **Ronald Reagan**, set out to restore America's global power and influence. During his first term in office (1981–1985), he sharply increased defense spending to strengthen the U.S. military and modernize its nuclear arsenal. Calling the Soviet Union

an "evil empire," he vowed to destroy communism. **Margaret Thatcher**, Britain's prime minister from 1979 to 1990, fully supported Reagan's anti-communist stance and arms buildup.

In 1985, a new leader emerged in the Soviet Union. **Mikhail Gorbachev** (mih-KYL GOR-buh-chof), unlike previous Soviet leaders, was a reformer. He believed the Soviet system needed major changes to better serve the Soviet people and to achieve the economic success of the United States and the rest of the Western world. Gorbachev introduced two major reforms: **glasnost**, or "openness," and **perestroika** (pehr-uh-STROY-kuh), or economic restructuring.

A Soviet woman waiting in line displays a ration coupon for sugar in a state-owned store in St. Petersburg.

Through his policy of glasnost, Gorbachev encouraged an unrestricted discussion of political and social issues and greater freedom of the press. Honesty, he promised, would replace the lies and cover-ups that marked earlier Soviet administrations. For the first time since the earliest days of the Russian Revolution, the Soviet people were free to speak their minds and publish their opinions without repercussions.

Gorbachev's new openness was soon put to the test. In April 1986, Soviet officials tried to cover up a disastrous explosion at the Chernobyl nuclear power plant in Ukraine. It was the worst nuclear accident in history up to that time, and it contaminated a wide area around the plant. Three weeks after the explosion, Gorbachev gave a speech explaining how the accident had happened and what Soviet officials were doing to protect people. He also took the opportunity to call for a ban on nuclear weapons testing.

Through his policy of perestroika, Gorbachev sought to reform the Soviet economy. The state would still dominate, but industry would respond to market signals rather than economic commands issued by government planners. However, perestroika did not have the hoped-for effect on the economy. Soviet citizens still faced their dreary daily routine of standing in long lines for basic staples like milk, bread, and eggs. The only difference was that citizens were free to voice their displeasure about the lack of food and other goods.

Gorbachev recognized that massive military spending was a drain on the struggling Soviet economy. The arms race with the United States and the ongoing war in Afghanistan were both major drains on the Soviet treasury. Meeting with Reagan in 1988, Gorbachev agreed to an arms-control treaty eliminating many land-based missiles. In 1989, he withdrew Soviet troops from Afghanistan.

MARGARET THATCHER Margaret Thatcher (shown here with U.S. president Ronald Reagan at the White House in 1983) served as Britain's first woman prime minister from 1979 to 1990. She advocated for the independence of the individual from the state and less government interference in the economy. Her conservative approach focused on privatization and deregulation. During her first term, unemployment increased dramatically and inflation doubled in just over one year, drastically reducing her popularity. This unpopularity would have guaranteed her defeat in the 1983 election but for two factors: the Falkland Islands War and division within the opposing Labour Party. Her leadership during the Falkland Islands War in 1982 led to Britain reclaiming the islands, which rallied much of the British population around her. Thatcher also made gains in international relationships, condemning communism and supporting NATO. However, against much opposition, she also reduced Britain's contribution to the European Community's (EC's) budget. This action instigated discord in her traditionally pro-Europe party. Her implementation of a poll tax in 1989 met with public disapproval and alarmed her already divided Conservative Party. Without majority support from her party, Thatcher announced her resignation in November 1990.

The effectiveness of glasnost was not all positive for the Soviet Union. The policy allowed discontented ethnic groups to publicly vent their negative feelings about Russian domination of the U.S.S.R. In the late 1980s, those objections expanded into outbursts of nationalism in several non-Russian Soviet republics. For example, demonstrators in Georgia demanded greater self-government. Each Baltic state—Latvia, Lithuania, and Estonia—replaced Russian with its home language as the official "state language."

Rising Russian nationalism also undermined Soviet unity. After glasnost increased free speech, old prejudices reappeared, including anti-Semitism and negative stereotypes of ethnic groups from the largely Muslim regions to the south.

PLAN: 4-PAGE LESSON

OBJECTIVE

Describe how liberal reform policies in the Soviet Union triggered nationalist movements and calls for more freedom and self-government in the Soviet bloc.

CRITICAL THINKING SKILLS FOR LESSON 1.1

- Identify Main Ideas and Details
- Analyze Cause and Effect
- Make Connections
- Draw Conclusions
- Describe
- Interpret Maps

HISTORICAL THINKING FOR CHAPTER 29

What battles and other drastic changes altered the global landscape in the last half of the 20th century?

As the Soviet Union made gradual reforms, satellite states in the Soviet bloc began to demand freedom, democracy, and representation. Lesson 1.1 discusses how many countries in Eastern Europe gained their independence in the years leading up to the fall of the U.S.S.R.

BACKGROUND FOR THE TEACHER

Opening the Gates of the Berlin Wall In the months leading up to the dismantling of the Berlin Wall, many East Germans were already finding a route to the West. Hungary had opened its border with Austria, and many East Germans were traveling through Hungary into Austria. Others traveled to Prague and sought asylum in the West German embassy there. On November 9, 1989, an East German official mistakenly communicated via a televised broadcast that East Germans could pursue passage to the West. The intention was to communicate that East Germans could apply for visas over the course of several months, but the statements were interpreted by the public as the immediate opening of the Berlin Wall. Citizens crowded the wall on both sides, and without a plan in place to handle such crowds, the border guards opened the gates.

Student eEdition online

Additional content for this lesson, including an image gallery, is available online.

INTRODUCE & ENGAGE

CONSIDER EXAMPLES OF NATIONALISM

As a class, have students list examples of nationalism that they have learned about throughout world history or that they have observed occurring in the world today. **ASK:** What have been some negative effects of nationalist movements? *(Possible response: Nationalist movements have sometimes led to prejudice and discrimination against minorities.)* What have been some positive effects of nationalist movements? *(Possible response: People involved in nationalist movements have fought for freedom from oppressors and for political autonomy.)* Tell students that in this lesson they will learn about the beginning of the end of the Soviet Union and how nationalist movements in Eastern Europe played a part in the dissolution of the Iron Curtain.

TEACH

GUIDED DISCUSSION

1. **Make Connections** How was Gorbachev's handling of the nuclear explosion at Chernobyl an example of glasnost? *(Gorbachev spoke openly about the causes of the explosion and what the Soviet government was going to do to help people after the accident.)*

2. **Draw Conclusions** Considering that the Communist government generally supported an atheist view, why might Pope John Paul II have joined Solidarity? *(Possible response: Pope John Paul II might have seen a challenge to communism as a path to eventually re-establishing religion and Catholicism in his home country of Poland.)*

ANALYZE CAUSE AND EFFECT

Ask students to consider the perspective of a Soviet family planning their weekly meals and groceries. **ASK:** What effects might perestroika have had on a family's meal planning? *(Possible responses: If perestroika were successful in shifting production to follow market demands, a family might have increased access to foods that they want, rather than whatever foods are produced and rationed out by the government; or, because perestroika was not completely efficient in following market demands, citizens would have seen little change in their weekly grocery options.)*

DIFFERENTIATE

ENGLISH LANGUAGE LEARNERS

Pose and Answer Questions Arrange students at the **Beginning** and **Intermediate** levels in mixed pairs and ask them to reread the text together. Instruct them to pause after each paragraph and ask one another *who, what, when, where,* or *why* questions and provide answers. Ask students at the **Intermediate** level to assist students at the **Beginning** level as needed.

GIFTED & TALENTED

Perform a Dramatic Reading Have students find online text and video of Reagan's speech at the Berlin Wall in 1987. Then challenge students to prepare a dramatic reading of one or more excerpts from the speech. Encourage them to imitate Reagan's delivery style. After they have practiced, invite students to perform their dramatic reading in front of the class. Ask the class to discuss how the reading affected their interpretation and understanding of the speech and its impact on the United States, the Soviet Union, West Germany, and East Germany.

See the Chapter Planner for more strategies for differentiation.

W SAMO POŁUDNIE
4 CZERWCA 1989

CRITICAL VIEWING A Solidarity movement poster shows actor Gary Cooper in his role as a U.S. marshal in the western film *High Noon*. The artist added a Solidarity badge on Cooper's chest and ballot in his hand. The text translates to "High Noon, June 4, 1989" in English. Why do you think members of Solidarity chose this image and slogan for their 1989 campaign?

REVOLUTIONS IN EASTERN EUROPE

In Poland, discontent with the communist regime led to radical political change. In 1980, Polish workers led by Lech Wałęsa (LEHK vuh-WEHN-suh) formed **Solidarity**, the first independent trade union in the Soviet bloc. In a direct challenge to the authority of the Communist Party, nearly one-third of Poland's population joined Solidarity. Pope **John Paul II**, a native of Poland, supported Wałęsa, helped keep Solidarity a nonviolent movement, and discussed relevant issues with Soviet and Polish Communist officials. Meanwhile, in 1988, the Polish people demanded greater self-government. Faced with increasing unrest and nationwide strikes, the government agreed to hold free elections in August 1989. Solidarity won a huge victory and took control of the government, and a year later, Wałęsa became Poland's first directly elected president.

Challenges to Soviet domination also occurred elsewhere in Eastern Europe. In January 1989, Hungary's parliament voted to allow noncommunist political parties. Soviet control was further weakened

when, in September, Hungary opened its border with the democratic republic of Austria. East Germans by the tens of thousands fled into Hungary, crossed the open border into Austria, and moved from there into West Germany—and to freedom.

The imaginary Iron Curtain surrounding the Soviet empire had begun showing its cracks. But in Berlin, Germany, a very real wall was about to crumble.

THE WALL: A SYMBOL OF OPPRESSION

Berlin, a city divided between West and East, was located completely inside communist East Germany. Residents of East Berlin could cross fairly easily into West Berlin—and they did, by the thousands each month. After World War II, many East Berliners left their communist-controlled city for the freedom in West Berlin and beyond. Worried about the large numbers of skilled and educated workers moving west for higher pay, East German and Soviet leaders vowed to block the flow of escaping citizens. In 1961, with Soviet backing, East Germany built a tall wall of brick and concrete that separated East Berlin from West Berlin and also sealed off the rest of West Berlin with walls and fences. Workers placed minefields and guard towers along the border. For the next 28 years, few East Germans managed to escape to the West.

In 1987, President Reagan visited West Berlin. Standing before the Berlin Wall, he spoke in general terms about Gorbachev's liberal policies, expressing hope that the Soviet system was becoming more open and

Berlin, 1961

EAST GERMANY

WEST GERMANY

EAST BERLIN

WEST BERLIN

free. However, Reagan suggested that the wall was a barrier to tolerance and independence. Partway through his speech, he challenged the Soviet leader. "Mr. Gorbachev," he called out, "tear down this wall!"

After Hungary opened its border to Austria in September 1989, East German demonstrators pressured their government to allow freer transit to the West. On November 9, as huge crowds gathered at the wall, a single gate unexpectedly opened, and a flood of East Berliners streamed through into West Berlin. Soon, jubilant residents of East Berlin and West Berlin began demolishing the wall. The fall of the Berlin Wall, the most visible symbol of communist oppression, signaled the coming collapse of the entire Soviet empire.

MORE POLITICAL UPRISINGS

In the days and weeks that followed, the Soviet bloc continued to splinter. On November 10, a communist reform politician ousted Bulgaria's authoritarian party

leader. On December 3, the East German government resigned. Three weeks later, Nicolae Ceaușescu (NIHK-oh-ly chow-SHEHS-koo), Romania's hated leader, ordered troops to fire on antigovernment demonstrators. Instead, the troops joined the protesters, overthrew Ceaușescu, and executed him.

The revolution in Czechoslovakia happened less violently. Anti-communist reformers had long pushed for a new constitution. Nationwide demonstrations starting in mid-November 1989 brought a police crackdown, but this time—unlike during the Prague Spring of 1968—no Soviet forces arrived to support them. The reformers in Czechoslovakia, like those in much of Eastern Europe, triumphed. The Czech people elected a noncommunist government on December 10, and on December 25, **Václav Havel** (VAHT-slav HAH-vehl) became the first democratically elected president of the country. Communism's fall went so smoothly in Czechoslovakia that it has been called the "Velvet Revolution."

During the revolution in Romania, some protesters cut out the communist symbol in the center of the Romanian national flag.

HISTORICAL THINKING

1. READING CHECK How did Gorbachev's policies change Soviet economic, social, and cultural life?

2. IDENTIFY MAIN IDEAS AND DETAILS What factors helped Margaret Thatcher keep her position as British prime minister in 1983?

3. ANALYZE CAUSE AND EFFECT Why did so many citizens of East Germany want to flee to the West?

4. MAKE CONNECTIONS How did Poland's Solidarity movement connect with the series of political revolutions that took place in the Soviet bloc?

BACKGROUND FOR THE TEACHER

The Velvet Divorce While the revolution in Czechoslovakia is often referred to as the *Velvet Revolution* due to its nonviolent nature and fracturing of Czechoslovakia into two independent countries, Slovakia and the Czech Republic, it is sometimes called the *Velvet Divorce* because it was also a peaceful separation. Czechoslovakia first became a unified country in 1918 after the fall of the Austro-Hungarian Empire. The country was formed from several different provinces encompassing three primary ethnic groups: Bohemians, Moravians, and Slovaks. Before the onset of World War II, Czechoslovakia was one of the most prosperous countries in Eastern Europe. After the Velvet Revolution in 1989, the newly established government focused on privatizing formerly government-run businesses and fostering economic growth. However, the economic drivers of different regions within Czechoslovakia were quite different, and in 1993 the country peacefully split into Slovakia and the Czech Republic.

TEACH

GUIDED DISCUSSION

3. **Describe** How was the fall of the Berlin Wall a symbol of the collapse of communism? *(Possible response: The Berlin Wall was a physical barrier between the Soviet bloc and the West, and its fall represented the dissolution of cultural and economic barriers between the two.)*

4. **Analyze Cause and Effect** How did a lack of Soviet forces affect the outcome of the revolution in Czechoslovakia? *(Because there were no Soviet forces to fight the Czech reformers, the revolution in Czechoslovakia had little violence.)*

INTERPRET MAPS

Direct students to the map of Berlin in 1961. **ASK:** Why did the Soviets construct a barricade around the entire city of West Berlin? *(Possible response: Because West Berlin was completely surrounded by East Germany, East Germans could escape to West Berlin from all directions.)* What physical geographic factors would the Soviets need to address in their blockade of West Berlin? *(Possible response: The Soviets would need to block access to West Berlin's rivers so that the rivers could not be used to transport people or supplies.)*

ACTIVE OPTIONS

On Your Feet: Jigsaw Strategy Direct students to the European Revolutions image gallery (available in the Student eEdition). Group students evenly into five "expert" groups, and assign each group one of the following topics to study in depth: the Solidarity campaign in Poland, the opening of the border between Austria and Hungary, movement between East and West Germany after the fall of the Berlin Wall, the Romanian Revolution, and the Velvet Revolution in Czechoslovakia. After students have completed their research, regroup students into groups of five so that each new group has at least one member from each expert group. Have experts take turns reporting on their topic while other students in the group learn from the experts.

NG Learning Framework: Compare and Contrast Leadership Styles
ATTUTUDE Responsibility
SKILL Communication

Instruct students to read the sidebar about Margaret Thatcher and to view the photo of Thatcher with U.S. President Ronald Reagan. Then have students conduct online research to learn more about the leadership styles of Thatcher and Reagan, including where they converged in opposition to communism and in favor of fiscal conservatism as well as any areas of divergence. Have students determine a means to share their research with the class, such as through a diagram comparing and contrasting the two leaders or by writing several paragraphs analyzing their leadership styles and priorities while in office.

HISTORICAL THINKING

ANSWERS

1. Gorbachev's glasnost policy encouraged openness and honesty in communication, and his perestroika policy brought an end to massive economic centralization. This was an enormous shift from the Soviet standards of covering up controversial or differing issues and strict government economic control.

2. Thatcher's leadership during the Falkland Islands War in 1982 leading to Britain reclaiming the islands and division within the opposing Labour Party led to her re-election.

3. Possible response: Some East Germans likely wanted to live in a free, democratic society. Other East Germans may have wanted greater economic or social opportunities.

4. Possible response: Poland's Solidarity movement won an early victory for democratic rule, which likely encouraged others in the Soviet bloc to challenge communist authority. However, Gorbachev's glasnost policy also had an important role in bringing dormant anticommunist discontent to the surface.

CRITICAL VIEWING Possible response: U.S. westerns usually included a lawman who obeyed the rules and upheld laws that protected every citizen. The United States also had a free, democratic society, something the Solidarity movement wanted for Poland.

1.2 Through The Lens

GERD LUDWIG

National Geographic photographer Gerd Ludwig has covered a variety of subjects related to the post–Cold War era, including the reunification of Germany in 1990 and the changes that occurred in the former Soviet Union after its dissolution in 1991. He is best known for his photos of the aftermath of the Chernobyl nuclear disaster, which he turned into an award-winning book, *The Long Shadow of Chernobyl*, in 2014.

In 2015, Ludwig shot a series of photos of Berlin to accompany a *National Geographic* magazine story about how the city had transformed itself after the fall of the Berlin Wall over 25 years earlier. Growing up in Germany during the Cold War, Ludwig had a personal connection to the assignment, which he says always helps shape his approach: "As a documentary photographer I have the obligation to show what is out there, but I also show it from a very personal point of view. And that personal point of view is determined by my life experience."

How do the buildings and monuments shown in these images reflect both Germany's past and present?

BERLIN, GERMANY

A Slovakian street artist (above) poses as an East German border guard in front of the Brandenburg Gate. Once a symbol of Cold War oppression, Berlin is now a city of opportunity that attracts people from all over the world. The face of Dieter Weckeiser (top, opposite page), who was killed in 1968 while attempting to swim to freedom across the Spree River to West Berlin, forms part of a memorial where a stretch of the wall has been preserved. Young professionals (opposite page, bottom) go about their daily business outside the St. Oberholz cafe. Located in a 19th-century building that once housed a restaurant for the working class, the cafe provides specialty coffee and trendy coworking spaces. The sign on the wall of the cafe reads: "Das Leben ist kein Ponyhof"—life isn't easy.

838 CHAPTER 29

PLAN: 2-PAGE LESSON

OBJECTIVE

Describe how the details in the photographs of Berlin reflect both Germany's past and present.

CRITICAL THINKING SKILLS FOR LESSON 1.2

- Analyze Visuals
- Make Connections
- Identify
- Form and Support Opinions

HISTORICAL THINKING FOR CHAPTER 29

What battles and other drastic changes altered the global landscape in the last half of the 20th century?

The reunification of Germany in 1990 was one of the changes that altered the global landscape. Lesson 1.2 uses detailed photographs by National Geographic photographer Gerd Ludwig to show how the city of Berlin has transformed itself since the fall of the Berlin Wall.

History Notebook

Encourage students to complete the Through the Lens page for Chapter 29 in their History Notebooks as they read.

BACKGROUND FOR THE TEACHER

Gerd Ludwig Gerd Ludwig was born in Alsfeld, Germany, in 1947. He left his university studies of literature and political science to travel through Scandinavia and North America. He worked a variety of jobs to support himself as he traveled, including bricklayer, sailor, gardener, and dishwasher. Perhaps these experiences inspired him to capture people and the world through photographs because he returned to Germany and studied photography for five years, graduating in 1972. Over the next two decades, he worked for several major international publications and relocated to New York in 1984. In the early 1990s, he became a contract photographer for *National Geographic* magazine. His photographs of the social changes in Germany and Eastern Europe became a book, *Broken Empire: After the Fall of the U.S.S.R.*, a 10-year retrospective published by National Geographic. His photographs combine a full scale of emotion with strong composition and journalistic style. He has won several awards including the 2006 Lucie Award for International Photographer of the Year. He lectures at universities and photography workshops throughout the world.

INTRODUCE & ENGAGE

DISCUSS A QUOTATION

Invite students to consider what a documentary photographer does. Discuss the quotation at the beginning of the lesson. Ask students what they think the "obligation" of a documentary photographer is. Discuss the perspective of the opening photograph and why Ludwig may have purposely included the street artist holding his modern cell phone while portraying a border guard from the mid-20th century.

TEACH

GUIDED DISCUSSION

1. **Identify** What are two sets of documentary photographs taken by Gerd Ludwig? *(photos of the aftermath of the Chernobyl nuclear disaster and of Berlin 25 years after the fall of the Berlin Wall)*

2. **Form and Support Opinions** Should a documentary photographer let a personal point of view affect the photographs he or she takes? Explain your opinion. *(Possible responses: Yes, a documentary photographer should let a personal point of view affect his or her photographs because the personal point of view makes the photographs stronger and more meaningful; or No, the photographer should not let a personal point of view affect his or her photographs because a personal point of view could insert bias into the documentary, which should be objective.)*

THROUGH THE LENS

Share the Background for the Teacher information with students. Then have them study the photographs. **ASK:** How does the second photo commemorate a loss of life? *(Possible response: Ludwig photographs the Berlin Wall with a faded person overlay to represent the people lost.)* In the third photo, why do you think Ludwig made sure he included the sign that reads in German "Life isn't easy" while framing the image with the two poles covered with advertisements? *(Possible response: The advertisements on the poles show that the young professionals in the photo are bombarded with information while pursuing a hectic lifestyle, which isn't easy.)*

ACTIVE OPTION

NG Learning Framework: Photos Capture Reality
ATTITUDE Responsibility
SKILL Communication

From Background for the Teacher, share the information about how Ludwig combines a full scale of emotion with strong composition and journalistic style. Discuss why writers and photographers have a responsibility to treat a documentary subject with respect. Have students research other photographs by Gerd Ludwig, choose one or two, and write a description of what the photos communicate and how they combine emotion with strong composition and journalistic style.

DIFFERENTIATE

ENGLISH LANGUAGE LEARNERS

Photograph Vocabulary Guide **Beginning** level students in understanding and using appropriate vocabulary to discuss and write about the photographs in the lesson. Explain that a *street artist* dresses and acts like another person, a *professional* is a business person, a *memorial* is a collection of objects to remember a person or a group of people, and an *intersection* is a place where two streets meet. Point to and name any details in the photographs that students are unsure of, and have students repeat each word. Then guide them in using the word in a simple sentence. Provide **Intermediate** level students with sentence frames to help them describe the photographs, such as: The people look _____. The memorial is _____. The intersection looks _____.

PRE-AP

Write a Profile Tell students to write a profile of photographer Gerd Ludwig and his photography for National Geographic. Ask them to conduct online research and draw on primary and secondary sources to supplement information from the text. Invite students to post their completed profiles on a class blog or school website or read them to the class.

See the Chapter Planner for more strategies for differentiation.

ANSWERS

Possible response: Each place shown in the images had a past significance that is now merged with a new, modern Berlin—for instance the café/co-working space is located in an old, historic restaurant building, and the redeveloped Rosenthaler Platz stands on land once bisected by the Berlin Wall.

Post-Soviet Transitions

Changing a lifelong habit is rarely easy, even if you know it will improve your life. Trying to get others to change is even more challenging. When Mikhail Gorbachev set out to reshape the Soviet political system, he discovered just how difficult the process of change can be.

TURMOIL IN THE SOVIET UNION

As Soviet power over its empire eroded in the fall of 1989, Mikhail Gorbachev continued moving the U.S.S.R. closer to representative democracy. In February 1990, the Congress of People's Deputies, or Soviet parliament, accepted Gorbachev's plan to eliminate the Communist Party's monopoly on political power and allow the formation of competing political parties. The parliament also elected Gorbachev president of the Soviet Union.

Gorbachev's ongoing reforms provided further challenges to Soviet domination. In March 1990, Lithuania declared its independence. Gorbachev initially threatened military action, but he decided against it. Two months later, the other two Baltic republics—Latvia and Estonia—also declared independence. As Poland, Hungary, and Czechoslovakia continued toward democratic rule, Gorbachev quietly accepted their noncommunist governments.

The future of East Germany, however, had not yet been settled. Gorbachev wanted to keep East Germany within the Soviet bloc, at least for a while, but pressure for the speedy restoration of a united Germany came from the West German government as well as from vocal groups within East Germany. Gorbachev finally conceded. East Germany and West Germany were officially reunified as Germany in October 1990.

Dissolution of the Soviet Union and Aligned Nations

RUSSIA

KAZAKHSTAN

KYRGYZSTAN

Commonwealth of Independent States
Baltic states
Nations formerly under Soviet influence

0 300 600 Miles
0 300 600 Kilometers

By the summer of 1991, Soviet-bloc countries and individual republics were steadily moving beyond the control of the U.S.S.R. In July, Warsaw Pact leaders canceled their mutual-defense treaty, and Gorbachev began to withdraw Soviet troops from Eastern Europe. It was clear that the Soviet communist system was breaking down.

However, a group of communist hard-liners—people who remained stubbornly loyal to Soviet ideology—would not give up. In August, this group launched a coup to try to restore central control and remove Gorbachev from power. In Moscow, the popular president of the Russian Republic, **Boris Yeltsin**, led protests against the coup, which ended when the army refused to attack the Russian parliament building.

840 CHAPTER 29

COMMONWEALTH OF INDEPENDENT STATES

After the coup attempt, Gorbachev left the Communist Party. Then he banned the party completely. In September 1991, he and leaders of 10 of the republics agreed to shift their authority to an emergency State Council.

In December, Russia, Ukraine, and Belarus formed a loose association of equals known as the **Commonwealth of Independent States (CIS)**. Eight additional republics soon joined the CIS. Each member of the commonwealth participated as a sovereign nation. The Soviet Union was dissolved, and Gorbachev resigned his presidency.

Boris Yeltsin (left) stands on top of a tank, rallying the people of Moscow in defense of their new democratic institutions. This image was shown on state television and became a uniting point for further defense of democracy.

STRUGGLES FOR PROSPERITY AND DEMOCRACY

The failure of the coup and Gorbachev's resignation put Russian president Yeltsin in a position to define a new path for his country—by far the strongest state in the CIS. U.S. economists advised him that free markets would bring prosperity. Following their advice, Yeltsin instituted bold economic reforms.

The immediate results were disappointing. The transition to a market economy caused many Russians to suffer. The Soviet system had provided free education and health care, guaranteed jobs, and old-age pensions. The new market system did not instantly make up for these losses. Stores filled with imported consumer products, but few Russians had the means to purchase them. By the end of the 1990s, too many Russians were hungry and cold.

The former Central Asian republics faced equally difficult transitions. Kazakhstan and Uzbekistan were typical, run by former Communist officials who paid lip service to democracy, holding tight to power and exploiting the region's plentiful natural resources.

In 1999, an ailing Yeltsin handed power to **Vladimir Putin**, a former intelligence officer for the KGB, the

Soviet spy agency. Putin won the presidency of Russia in 2000 by appealing to voters eager for a strong leader. As president, he reined in capitalism by reestablishing state authority over the economy and the media, and he used his control of oil revenues and television as bases of power. He stood up to the United States on the global stage and restored order at home. Putin managed to achieve stability at the expense of democracy and civil rights.

In general, the countries of Eastern Europe enjoyed a smoother transition to liberal governance and market economics than Russia did. Poland and Estonia made steady political and economic progress in the 1990s, with the formation of the free associations that characterize a democratic society. Czechoslovakia split peacefully into the Czech Republic and Slovakia in 1993. Yugoslavia, as you will learn, was a different story, with ethnic differences tearing the nation apart.

The reunification of Germany proved difficult as well. East Germans were much poorer than West Germans, and many East Germans lacked competitive job skills. They gained freedom and opportunity but also faced unemployment and insecurity. Still, a unified Germany became a global leader in science, technology, and manufacturing.

HISTORICAL THINKING

1. **READING CHECK** Why was the reunification of Germany such a challenge?

2. **DRAW CONCLUSIONS** Do you think Gorbachev planned to dissolve the Soviet Union? Explain.

3. **COMPARE AND CONTRAST** How did the Commonwealth of Independent States differ from the Soviet Union?

Conflicts and Transformations 841

PLAN: 2-PAGE LESSON

OBJECTIVE
Explain how the weakening and eventual collapse of the Soviet Union resulted in the formation of many new countries.

CRITICAL THINKING SKILLS FOR LESSON 1.3
- Draw Conclusions
- Compare and Contrast
- Form and Support Opinions
- Interpret Maps

HISTORICAL THINKING FOR CHAPTER 29
What battles and other drastic changes altered the global landscape in the last half of the 20th century?

As former members of the U.S.S.R. formed new nations, they worked to re-establish their governments and build their economies. Lesson 1.3 discusses the challenges and triumphs of nations that gained independence when the U.S.S.R. fell.

BACKGROUND FOR THE TEACHER
Integrating the Militaries of East and West Germany
When Germany was reunified, there was no need to absorb the entire East German army into a reunified German army, and the question became what to do with 170,000 East German soldiers. As plans moved forward for Germany's reunification, part of the problem solved itself when many of the 92,500 East German army conscripts simply blended into the crowd after the border was opened. However, high-ranking officers in the East German army, all of whom had been members of the Communist Party, were not considered fit for duty in the new German military. East German soldiers age 25 or younger, on the other hand, were regarded as the best candidates for continued military service under the new German government.

INTRODUCE & ENGAGE

REBUILD A GOVERNMENT

Discuss with students what they think happens when a government collapses. **ASK:** What factors might lead to a government collapse? *(Possible responses: economic depression, protests for freedom and civil rights, too much government control)* Have students brainstorm the consequences of a government collapse. **ASK:** How might citizens work to rebuild a government after it collapses? *(Possible responses: restructuring international agreements, stimulating economic growth)* Tell students that in this lesson they will learn about the fall of the Soviet Union and how Russia and other former U.S.S.R. countries worked to rebuild their governments and economies.

TEACH

GUIDED DISCUSSION

1. **Form and Support Opinions** Why do you think Gorbachev initially wanted to keep East Germany under Soviet control while other nations within the Soviet bloc gained their independence? *(Possible response: Gorbachev might have been concerned that a unified Germany could pose a threat or that without East Germany, the Soviet Union would not be able to survive.)*

2. **Compare and Contrast** What similarities did Russians and East Germans experience as their countries transitioned to market economies? *(Both relied on state-provided resources. Without these resources many Russians and East Germans suffered in poverty.)*

INTERPRET MAPS

Direct students to the Dissolution of the Soviet Union and Aligned Nations map. **ASK:** Based on the map, why do you think Latvia and Estonia quickly declared independence after Lithuania did? *(Possible response: Because these nations are next to one another, people in Latvia and Estonia likely witnessed and were inspired by Lithuanian independence.)*

ACTIVE OPTIONS

On Your Feet: Fishbowl Have part of the class sit in a close circle facing inward and the other part of the class sit in a larger circle around them. Have students on the inside discuss ways to successfully transition a formerly communist country to a market economy and democratic system of government. Encourage students to list examples from the lesson. Students in the outside should evaluate how well they think the transitional strategies will work. Then have groups reverse positions.

NG Learning Framework: Write a Persuasive Essay
ATTITUDE Responsibility
SKILL Problem-Solving

Have students conduct online research about Vladimir Putin's policies and leadership style in Russia. Then have them analyze the benefits and drawbacks of Putin's administration. Encourage students to consider how the government regulations put in place by Putin could affect daily life for Russians. Instruct students to write a brief persuasive essay in which they argue for or against a policy of their choice from Putin's presidency.

DIFFERENTIATE

STRIVING READERS

Preview and Review the Text Have students preview the lesson by reading the title and introductory text and examining the map and photograph. Instruct them to write questions about the photograph that might be answered in the caption. Then have them read the caption. After students read the lesson, have them discuss what they learned.

PRE-AP

Analyze a Leader's Role Have students gather information in order to write an essay about one of the leaders who played an important role in ending the Cold War. Instruct students to use multiple reputable online sources and to cite both primary and secondary sources in their essay. Encourage them to elucidate the key communications and events, as well as the individual's personality, in analyzing the leader's role in ending the Cold War. Invite volunteers to share their essays with the class.

See the Chapter Planner for more strategies for differentiation.

HISTORICAL THINKING

ANSWERS

1. East Germans were generally poorer than West Germans and lacked competitive job skills.

2. Possible response: No; Gorbachev sought to reform the Soviet Union, not dissolve it. The process of moving the Soviet Union's government closer to a representative democracy triggered unforeseen events that led to the dissolution of the country.

3. The Commonwealth of Independent States consisted of a loose association of sovereign states, all of which were equal. The Soviet Union was made up of republics that were controlled by the central government and dominated by Russia.

This photograph was taken with a long-range lens from a Beijing hotel room. The lone figure trying to stop a line of surging tanks (which eventually went around him) along the Avenue of Eternal Peace in Beijing sums up both the heroism and the futility of the Tiananmen protests. This individual has never been identified.

Unrest in Beijing

Like the Soviet Union, China struggled to make its communist economic and political systems work. When Chinese students and workers gathered peacefully in a public square to protest against their government, leaders ordered the Red Army to attack.

CHINA'S ECONOMIC REBOUND

In 1800, China produced one-third of the world's manufactured goods. But the Industrial Revolution bypassed China, and Europe dominated the world's economy. By 1949, the country produced just three percent of the world's total industrial output, and the following years under communist rule saw little improvement. Recall that in 1958, Mao Zedong aimed to fix the economy with his Great Leap Forward. As you learned, it proved to be a disaster.

By the last two decades of the 20th century, however, China was experiencing astonishing economic growth. More people were lifted out of poverty than at any previous stage in human history. That turnabout resulted from the policies of Deng Xiaoping, who rose to power in the late 1970s, after Mao's death. (You first read about Deng in the previous strike.)

Deng put China on a new economic path by adopting market incentives. His first step was to grant peasants their own farm plots for private cultivation, and Deng allowed them to sell their surplus crops in free markets. Food production surged. Deng became a hero to millions of Chinese farming families, who could now afford small luxuries for the first time. When asked how he, a lifelong communist, justified adopting capitalist principles, Deng replied, "It does not matter whether the cat is black or white, as long as she catches mice." He added, "To get rich is glorious."

The second stage in Deng's reforms was development of China's industrial sector. Deng invited foreign investors to build manufacturing plants in Guangzhou (gwahng-joh), a region of southern China near the British-controlled territory of Hong Kong. Deng's embrace of international capitalism would have been unthinkable under Mao. Cheap Chinese labor drew many corporations to Guangzhou.

As manufacturing spread from Guangzhou throughout eastern and central China, a vast stream of finished goods crossed the Pacific to reach American markets. China's cities experienced a huge construction boom, attracting millions of rural migrants. The coastal city of Shanghai became a glittering cosmopolitan center, with soaring skyscrapers and a rapid-transit system.

By the 1990s, China's economic transformation was generating challenges for the government. Environmental problems multiplied. The gap between rich and poor increased, as did imbalances between wealthier coastal regions and China's interior. Money brought corruption, which triggered protests among the same rural population that Mao had made the center of his revolution. Still, Deng's economic policies raised the standard of living, linked the nation to the global economy, and allowed China to achieve the status of a great world power. Many Chinese believed their country had returned to its proper place after two centuries of humiliation by Western imperialists and Japan.

PROTESTS IN TIANANMEN SQUARE

A big test of Deng's leadership came in the spring of 1989. University students organized an anti-government rally in Tiananmen Square, a large public plaza in the center of Beijing. They called for liberal political reforms—including freedom of speech and assembly—to match the economic reforms established in the preceding decade. They also criticized corruption among officials and the widening income gap.

The first student protests at Tiananmen Square took place on April 17. Word spread quickly. On April 22, tens of thousands of students gathered in Beijing as well as in other cities all over China. The government began to notice. On April 26, a front-page editorial in the *People's Daily*, the Beijing newspaper controlled by the Chinese Communist Party, accused student activists of causing turmoil and undermining political stability.

Peaceful protests of varying sizes continued for the next few weeks. In mid-May, some participants began a weeklong hunger strike. Around the same time, student leaders presented their demands at a meeting with officials and later with China's premier, Li Peng. But the talks failed to end the demonstrations. Thousands of protesters remained in Tiananmen Square through the end of May, their spirits raised after art students built the 33-foot-high statue that became known as the Goddess of Democracy out of foam, papier mâché, and plaster. While the statue began as the figure of a man holding a pole, during construction it was transformed into a woman holding a torch.

During this time, government and party officials debated how they should respond. Some advocated negotiating with the students, but hard-liners argued in favor of crushing the demonstrations. They were aware of how Gorbachev's glasnost policy was undermining Soviet power, and they did not intend to make the same mistake. Ultimately, the decision was up to Deng, who remembered the chaos caused by student rebels during the Cultural Revolution, which you read about earlier. On the night of June 3–4, 1989, tanks and armored personnel carriers rolled into Tiananmen Square, and troops opened fire on the demonstrators. Hundreds, perhaps thousands, of student activists were killed in the **Tiananmen Square Massacre**. Thousands more were wounded. A widespread crackdown on dissidents led to thousands of arrests.

A year and a half after the bloodshed at Tiananmen Square, Chai Ling, one of the main leaders of the pro-democracy movement, recalled why students protested. "The key issue for the demonstrators," she told a reporter for the *New York Times*, "was that people were used to being treated like slaves, and the people naturally wanted to become human beings, have equality, dignity, and freedom."

HISTORICAL THINKING

1. READING CHECK What policy put in place by Deng Xiaoping led to a surge in food production?

2. IDENTIFY MAIN IDEAS AND DETAILS What allowed for the growing presence of corporations in China?

3. MAKE CONNECTIONS Were the Tiananmen Square demonstrators influenced by the political ideals of the United States? Explain.

842 CHAPTER 29

Conflicts and Transformations 843

PLAN: 2-PAGE LESSON

OBJECTIVE

Explain how pro-democracy demonstrations in Beijing, China, in which students demanded political freedoms to match growing economic freedoms, ended in a massacre.

CRITICAL THINKING SKILLS FOR LESSON 1.4

- Identify Main Ideas and Details
- Make Connections
- Make Generalizations
- Identify
- Analyze Visuals

HISTORICAL THINKING FOR CHAPTER 29

What battles and other drastic changes altered the global landscape in the last half of the 20th century?

Economic reforms in China led many citizens to demand further political reforms. Lesson 1.4 discusses the causes and effects of a large-scale government protest in China's Tiananmen Square.

Student eEdition online

Additional content for this lesson, including a photograph, is available online.

BACKGROUND FOR THE TEACHER

U.S. Reaction to Tiananmen Square The massacre of protesters in Tiananmen Square shook the world. In the United States, the administration of President George H.W. Bush shifted U.S. policy toward China after the event. The United States halted the sale of military equipment to China, and many members of Congress suggested more stringent economic sanctions against China. To show their commitment to the safety and welfare of the Chinese people, some United States government officials met personally with Chinese students studying in the United States. President Bush issued an executive order and passed the Chinese Student Protection Act in 1992 that granted all Chinese students residing in the United States at the time of the Tiananmen massacre the right to remain in the country. Around 41,000 Chinese nationals became permanent residents of the United States in the year following the order, and around 54,000 more gained permanent resident status throughout the rest of the 1990s and 2000s.

INTRODUCE & ENGAGE

DISCUSS WHY PEOPLE PROTEST

Ask students to consider examples of large protests, either that they have studied or that they have observed in their lifetimes. **ASK:** What are some reasons that people protest? *(Answers will vary. Possible responses: civil rights, government reforms, or a company's or organization's policies)* What do you think makes a protest effective? *(Answers will vary. Possible responses: the number of people participating in the protest, the rationale behind the protestors' demands)* Tell students that in this lesson they will learn about a massive protest that took place in China as the country transitioned from communism to a more market-driven economy.

TEACH

GUIDED DISCUSSION

1. **Make Generalizations** How did China's increasing industrialization affect population trends? *(Many people moved to the coastal cities, where wealth, power, and economic opportunity were concentrated.)*

2. **Identify** What two factors influenced Deng Xiaoping's decision to use military force against student protesters? *(glasnost and the Cultural Revolution)*

ANALYZE VISUALS

Direct students to the photograph of the man standing in front of a line of tanks at Tiananmen Square, and tell them that this photograph influenced how the United States and other nations thought of China. **ASK:** Why do you think this photograph had a profound affect on how the world viewed China? *(Possible response: The tanks have so much power and the person appears determined to stand up for his rights, which made the Chinese government appear extremely oppressive.)*

ACTIVE OPTIONS

On Your Feet: Roundtable Seat students around a table in groups of four, then ask them to consider the factors that led to the student protests in Tiananmen Square. Encourage students to consider how the Chinese government, economy, and culture were evolving in the years before the protest took place. Each student around the table should answer the question in a different way.

> **NG Learning Framework: Report on Tiananmen Square**
> **SKILL** Observation
> **KNOWLEDGE** Our Human Story

Organize students into pairs to research the student protest at Tiananmen Square in 1989 to create a news report. Have half of the pairs write the report from the perspective of a Chinese journalist in 1989 communist China. The other half will prepare a news report from the perspective of a U.S. journalist today. Invite pairs to present their news reports to the class. Ask the class to compare the past account of the event with the present account, evaluating the consequences and determining lessons learned from the event.

DIFFERENTIATE

INCLUSION

Predict Using Photographs and Captions Pair special needs students with students who can assist in making the text more accessible. Ask pairs to look at each photograph and take turns reading its caption. Instruct students to predict what they will learn based on what they read and see.

PRE-AP

Extend Knowledge Instruct students to gather information from a variety of sources to write an essay about the many ways in which the Chinese economy improved under the leadership of Deng Xiaoping. Tell students to explain the reasons behind the various improvements and their impacts on the lives of average Chinese citizens.

See the Chapter Planner for more strategies for differentiation.

HISTORICAL THINKING

ANSWERS

1. Deng granted peasants their own farm plots and allowed them to sell their surplus crops in free markets, which increased food production.

2. Possible response: Deng developed China's industrial sector by inviting foreign investors to build manufacturing plants in Guangzhou and embracing international capitalism.

3. Possible responses: Yes. The demonstrators' demands for freedom of speech and assembly reflected First Amendment rights of Americans.

CRITICAL VIEWING (available in the Student eEdition) Possible response: Chinese protesters chose the Goddess of Democracy as their symbol because it was similar to the U.S. Statue of Liberty, a known symbol of freedom.

Toward Democracy in Latin America

After a rough period, a fresh start can be quite welcome. That was Latin America after the Cold War, which had promoted divisions and justified dictatorships. Though challenges remained, many Latin Americans were on the path toward democracy.

POLITICS IN SOUTH AMERICA AND MEXICO

By the late 1990s, military rule and dictatorships were disappearing throughout Latin America as trends moved toward democracy and civilian rule. The end of the Cold War opened the door to new democratic possibilities. In Argentina, defeat in 1982's Falklands War against Britain showed the incompetence of Argentine generals and brought about calls for change. Elections swept the military from power in Brazil as well. Even in Chile, where the Pinochet regime was deeply entrenched, pressures mounted for a free election. In 1988, Chilean voters turned down Pinochet's continued dictatorship.

The democratization of Latin American nations paralleled the liberation of Eastern Europe. But where countries like Poland had escaped from Soviet domination, nations like Chile had freed themselves from dictatorships allied with the United States.

In Mexico, the problem was neither military governments nor Cold War alignments but the political monopoly of the Institutional Revolutionary Party (PRI). The PRI had ruled Mexico since 1929—when the party brought peace and stability to the country after the chaos of the Mexican Revolution. After World War II, Mexico prospered thanks in part to a flourishing oil industry. But because the PRI had a political monopoly, elections were little more than a joke. Economic growth mostly benefited PRI's leadership, and corruption was everywhere. Lacking opportunity at home, many Mexicans crossed into the United States in search of a better life.

By the 1990s, Mexicans grew tired of the PRI's corruption and incompetence. Helped by PRI-backed electoral reforms, opposition parties began to win elections at the local, state, and national levels. In 2000, the National Action Party (PAN) finally broke the PRI's 71-year grip on power when its candidate won the presidency. Mexico—like much of Latin America—does not have many liberal institutions, but it is still working toward establishing a strong democratic culture.

CRITICAL VIEWING Salvadorans participate in a commemorative march 38 years after Archbishop Oscar Romero's assassination in 1980. Which details in the banner connect to Romero and what he represents?

CONFLICT IN CENTRAL AMERICA

A key goal for the United States during the Cold War was to contain the Soviet Union and block its efforts to spread communism around the world. In the 1970s and 1980s, Central America was a principal battleground between leftist rebels and military forces backed by the United States. (Leftists generally fight for radical economic and social changes, including an end to inequality and poverty.)

Nicaragua had long been ruled by members of the Somoza family, dictators whose anti-communism brought them strong U.S. support, even though they stole millions of dollars earmarked for relief aid. Resistance to the Somoza dictatorship was organized by the Sandinista National Liberation Front. The Sandinistas ousted the regime in 1979. The newly formed government seized the Somoza family's landholdings and nationalized major industries.

Soldiers loyal to Somoza leadership aimed to take back political control. These counterrevolutionaries—known as contras—received support from U.S. president Reagan after he took office in 1981. Reagan illegally evaded a congressional ban on military aid to the contras by selling arms to Iran. He then used the resulting funds to finance the contras. The Sandinistas relied on support from the Soviet Union and Cuba and clamped down on civil liberties.

The end of the Cold War brought a solution. The collapse of the Soviet Union led Mikhail Gorbachev to sharply reduce aid to Cuba, Cuba could no longer support the Sandinistas, and U.S. leaders no longer saw the contras as necessary allies. Nicaragua held free elections in 1989. The defeated Sandinistas handed over power peacefully, a major step forward.

Violence also marred Guatemalan society in the 1980s. Semiofficial "death squads" linked to the military government targeted villagers, mostly indigenous Maya people, suspected of aiding rebel guerrillas. As many as one million Guatemalans fled from their mountain homes to the cities or across the border to Mexico.

After the Cold War, the United States helped work out a peace deal in Guatemala. In 1996, the rebels laid down their arms in exchange for land. Guatemalans voted in free elections for the first time since 1952. In 1999,

Nicaragua's Sandinistas modeled themselves on Cuban revolutionary heroes; the soldier on the right wears a red-starred beret like that of Che Guevara.

a special commission determined that the army had committed the majority of the human-rights abuses during the long civil war.

These conflict resolutions allowed the people of Nicaragua and Guatemala to begin the process of nation-building—establishing order and a functioning government in a country that has been plagued by violence and instability.

Latin America was largely Roman Catholic, and the church played an influential role in everyday society. In El Salvador, where the military had seized power, the Catholic Church suffered two major tragedies in 1980. In March, Archbishop Oscar Romero, long a voice for poor Salvadorans, was assassinated while offering Mass. Later that year, El Salvador's National Guard murdered three American nuns and a lay missionary who worked with the poor.

Although El Salvador held elections in 1992 after the end of its 12-year civil war, trading drugs for guns easily available in the United States. Threatened by both poverty and gang violence, many Salvadorans left their homes in search of a better life for themselves and their children.

HISTORICAL THINKING

1. **READING CHECK** Why did the United States support military dictatorships in Latin America during the Cold War?

2. **DRAW CONCLUSIONS** Under what circumstances would an election be free but not fair?

3. **MAKE CONNECTIONS** What effect do you think the end of the Cold War had on the level of conflict in Central America? Explain.

PLAN: 2-PAGE LESSON

OBJECTIVE

Identify how, when faced with economic challenges and some dictatorships, many Latin Americans experienced increased prosperity and freedom by the end of the 20th century.

CRITICAL THINKING SKILLS FOR LESSON 2.1

- Draw Conclusions
- Make Connections
- Form and Support Opinions
- Compare and Contrast
- Analyze Visuals

HISTORICAL THINKING FOR CHAPTER 29

What battles and other drastic changes altered the global landscape in the last half of the 20th century?

As the Cold War came to an end, countries where the Soviet Union and United States had vied for control began to gain their independence. Lesson 2.1 discusses the quest for democracy in Latin America.

BACKGROUND FOR THE TEACHER

The Iran-Contra Scandal The Iran-Contra scandal violated the Boland Amendment, which restricted assistance to Nicaragua from the CIA and Department of Defense. The Reagan administration found a way around the amendment to continue supplying the Contras with aid by setting up an illegal deal with Iran. In 1985, Iranian terrorists were holding seven Americans hostage. When Iran made a secret request to buy weapons from the United States, despite an arms embargo, Reagan agreed to an arms-for-hostages exchange. Iran had received more than 1,500 missiles by the time the sales were discovered, but only three hostages had been released. The initial investigation revealed that only some of the money paid by Iran was received. Lieutenant Colonel Oliver North had been redirecting the funds to the Contras, with the knowledge of the national security advisor, Admiral John Poindexter. Following an eight-year investigation, 14 people were charged with involvement in the Iran-Contra scandal.

INTRODUCE & ENGAGE

COMPOSE A CAPTION

Direct students to the photograph of the march commemorating Archbishop Oscar Romero. Before reading the caption, challenge students to compose a one-sentence caption that expresses the feelings inspired by the photograph. Invite students to share their captions. Then ask the class to categorize the captions as expressions of awe, respect, passion, determination, or other feelings. Tell students that in this lesson they will learn about nation-building in Latin America as the Cold War came to an end. Point out that the people of Latin America likely experienced a wide range of feelings during this tumultuous period.

TEACH

GUIDED DISCUSSION

1. **Form and Support Opinions** Do you think Nicaraguans would have been better off under the leadership of the Somoza family or under the leadership of the Sandinistas? Why? *(Answers will vary. Possible response: Nicaraguans would have been better off with the Sandinistas because they redistributed resources to the poor; or, Nicaraguans would have been better off under the Somoza family because the Sandinistas limited civil liberties.)*

2. **Compare and Contrast** How was the end of the Cold War similar and different for Eastern Europe and Latin America? *(Countries in both regions began to gain their independence. Eastern Europe gained independence from Soviet control; Latin America gained independence from U.S.-backed dictatorships.)*

ANALYZE VISUALS

Direct students to the photograph of the Sandinistas. **ASK:** Based on this photograph, what can you deduce about how the Sandinistas' living conditions may have influenced them? *(Possible response: The Sandinistas' living conditions were fairly sparse. This may have compelled them to fight against the Somoza family.)*

ACTIVE OPTIONS

On Your Feet: Team Word Webbing Organize students into teams of four, and provide each team with a single large piece of paper. Give each student a different colored marker. Assign the vocabulary term *nation-building* as the topic for the word web. Have each student add to the part of the web nearest to him or her. On a signal, students should rotate the paper and each student should add to the nearest part again.

NG Learning Framework: Diagram the Roles of Nations
SKILL Communication
KNOWLEDGE Our Human Story

Have students examine the relationship between Guatemala, Cuba, the Soviet Union, and the United States. Students should review the text and may wish to conduct additional research. Then have them design a diagram to visually represent the complicated relationship between these four countries. Invite volunteers to share their diagrams with the class.

DIFFERENTIATE

STRIVING READERS

Summarize Direct students to work in pairs to read and summarize the text and photograph captions. Tell students to write at least two notes for each. Then guide students to create a summary statement for each section followed by a summary statement for the whole lesson.

PRE-AP

Analyze How the Past Affects the Present Have students analyze how the political climate in Guatemala and Nicaragua in the 1980s and 1990s has influenced life in those countries today. Challenge students to consider how events several decades ago led to immigration patterns that they can observe today. Students should conduct research, then write an essay that makes a claim about how politics in the past affects Latin America today. Invite volunteers to share their essays with the class.

See the Chapter Planner for more strategies for differentiation.

HISTORICAL THINKING

ANSWERS

1. The United States relied on military regimes to prevent communism from taking hold in Latin America.

2. Possible response: In a free election, all citizens who qualify to vote would be allowed to vote. But if the ruling party cheated, the election would not be fair.

3. Possible response: The end decreased the level of conflict in Central America because it brought an end to Soviet support for leftist rebellions and U.S. support for military rulers.

CRITICAL VIEWING The image connects to the Catholic belief in helping the poor, which Romero and others in the "liberation theology" movement did.

Traveler: Nelson Mandela
Anti-Apartheid Activist 1918–2013

Nelson Mandela devoted his life to fighting South Africa's apartheid policies. He paid a price for his activism—27 years in prison. But in the end, he led the way to the destruction of one of the world's most oppressive governments.

FIGHTING FOR DEMOCRACY AND FREEDOM

You've read that apartheid was a system in South Africa that separated black Africans from their white rulers. Throughout the 1950s, Nelson Mandela campaigned against apartheid in South Africa. As a leader of the African National Congress (ANC), he sought racial justice and democracy. Forced underground in 1961 when the South African government banned the ANC, Mandela traveled across Africa seeking support for a guerrilla army. After returning to South Africa in 1962, he was captured and charged with treason. In 1964, he was sentenced to life in prison.

Finally, in early 1990, after decades of repression and violence in South Africa, the nation's white leaders responded to massive South African protests and international calls for Mandela's release. A few hours after Mandela walked through the prison gates, he spoke before a large crowd in Cape Town and before a global television audience.

RISE TO THE PRESIDENCY

Mandela was born and grew up in the Transkei region of eastern South Africa. As a youth, he received an education in the history of his own Tembu people and in the protocols of the chief's court. He also attended an English-language primary school, where Mandela's teacher changed his name to Nelson, a "proper" English name. Before that, Mandela was called Rolihlahla ("pulling the branch of a tree" or "troublemaker"). He would live up to his African name.

To avoid an arranged marriage, Mandela fled to Johannesburg in 1941. There, he earned his college degree, studied law, and became one of South Africa's few black lawyers. He combined his practice of law with a passion for politics. In 1942, he joined the ANC—the

PRIMARY SOURCE

Today, the majority of South Africans, black and white, recognize that apartheid has no future. . . . Negotiations on the dismantling of apartheid will have to address the overwhelming demands of our people for a democratic, nonracial, and unitary South Africa. There must be an end to white monopoly on political power, and a fundamental restructuring of our political and economic systems to ensure that the inequalities of apartheid are addressed and our society thoroughly democratized. . . . I wish to quote my own words during my trial in 1964. They are as true today as they were then: "I have fought against white domination and I have fought against black domination. I have cherished the ideal of a democratic and free society in which all persons live together in harmony and with equal opportunities. It is an ideal which I hope to live for and to achieve. But, if needs be, it is an ideal for which I am prepared to die."

—from "Nelson Mandela's Address to Rally in Cape Town on His Release from Prison," February 11, 1990

political party that had worked for racial equality in South Africa since 1912—and soon rose to a leadership position.

During World War II, many Africans supported the Allies and applauded ideals expressed by Franklin Roosevelt and Winston Churchill in the Atlantic Charter: freedom and national self-determination. Members of the ANC invoked the Atlantic Charter in their call to end racial segregation and discrimination. Mandela praised the British and U.S. political systems. He later cited as additional influences the Magna Carta, the British Petition of Right, and the Bill of Rights.

As you have read, in the early 1950s, the ANC began to organize nonviolent demonstrations against South Africa's apartheid policies. Its program of passive resistance, or nonviolent opposition to authority,

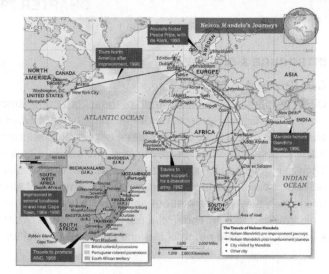

included refusing to obey unjust laws, such as one that required African men to carry passes that restricted their freedom of movement. Passive resistance also involved strikes and boycotts. But after the brutal police response to what became known as the Sharpeville Massacre in 1960, Mandela and the ANC began using sabotage, or the intentional destruction of property or disruption of transportation, communication, or government systems. After Mandela was imprisoned in 1964, South Africans from several racial groups continued the struggle against apartheid.

One of them, the Anglican archbishop Desmond Tutu, also promoted nonviolent protest and encouraged the United States and other countries to impose sanctions, or economic restrictions, on South Africa. In 1984, Tutu won the Nobel Peace Prize for his efforts. Mandela was released from prison in 1990, and by 1991, South Africa had gradually dismantled its apartheid policies. In 1993, Mandela was awarded the Nobel Peace Prize for his accomplishments.

Mandela ran for president in the 1994 election, the first election in which all South African citizens age 18 or older could vote. He won easily, and the ANC became the dominant political force in a new South Africa. True to the words he had spoken at his trial in 1964, Mandela emphasized inclusiveness in his government. He also worked to resolve the lingering tensions and anger of the apartheid era. Without Nelson Mandela, it is doubtful whether South Africa could have navigated the post-apartheid era as safely and successfully as it did.

HISTORICAL THINKING

1. **READING CHECK** How did the Sharpeville Massacre change the ANC's tactics?

2. **MAKE INFERENCES** How did Mandela "live up to his African name"?

3. **DRAW CONCLUSIONS** What did Mandela's election victory suggest about black South Africans' readiness to participate in political life?

PLAN: 2-PAGE LESSON

OBJECTIVE

Describe how Nelson Mandela's courageous struggle to end discrimination and segregation in South Africa ended with his election to the presidency.

CRITICAL THINKING SKILLS FOR LESSON 2.2

- Make Inferences
- Draw Conclusions
- Interpret Maps
- Analyze Primary Sources

HISTORICAL THINKING FOR CHAPTER 29

What battles and other drastic changes altered the global landscape in the last half of the 20th century?

Even after decolonization, racial tensions in South Africa remained high for many decades. Lesson 2.2 explains one man's journey to unite South Africans of all races.

Student eEdition online

Additional content for this lesson, including a photograph, is available online.

BACKGROUND FOR THE TEACHER

Apartheid *Apartheid* is an Afrikaans word whose literal meaning is "separateness." As a political structure, apartheid was meant to keep races rigidly separated. The Group Areas Act, passed in 1950 by the South African government, created residential and business areas based solely on race. Individuals from another race were barred from owning land or having a residence or business in an area designated for a specific race. As a direct result of the Group Areas Act, 80 percent of South Africa's land was designated as "white," even though whites were a minority.

Laws passed later restricted social contact between races, created separate educational standards, segregated jobs along racial lines, and prevented nonwhites from participating in government. Individuals who ventured into restricted areas were required to carry documents authorizing their presence or face arrest. In 1959, the Promotion of Bantu Self-Government Act created 10 African homelands, all of which were politically and economically dependent on South Africa.

History Notebook

Encourage students to complete the Traveler page for Chapter 29 in their History Notebooks as they read.

INTRODUCE & ENGAGE

PREVIEW USING VISUALS

Direct students to the map of Nelson Mandela's Journeys and have students read the entries. Point out the entry that shows Mandela was imprisoned from 1964–1990. **ASK:** What can you infer about the political climate of South Africa based on this information? *(Possible responses: The political climate was quite turbulent; the government imprisoned people who tried to oppose their leadership.)* Tell students that in this lesson they will learn about how Nelson Mandela fought tirelessly for freedom and equality in post-colonial South Africa.

TEACH

GUIDED DISCUSSION

1. **Interpret Maps** How did Mandela's journeys to promote the ANC differ from his travels to gain support for an army? *(Possible response: Mandela's trips for the ANC were limited to South Africa. His later journeys to raise support for a liberation army took him all over Africa and to Europe.)*

2. **Make Inferences** How do you think Mandela felt when his teacher changed his name? *(Answers will vary. Possible response: Mandela felt offended because he was proud of his African heritage.)*

ANALYZE PRIMARY SOURCES

Have students read the primary source excerpt from Nelson Mandela's address to the rally in Cape Town after his release from prison. **ASK:** Based on Mandela's discussion about race in South Africa, what can you infer about the racial makeup of the rally? *(Possible response: Because Mandela speaks about racial unity and does not disparage white South Africans' oppression of other races, the crowd likely included people of many different races, and Mandela wanted to build a united society going forward.)*

ACTIVE OPTIONS

On Your Feet: Think, Pair, Share Divide the class into pairs and ask them to think individually about Nelson Mandela's original commitment to nonviolent protest and his later transition to a strategy of sabotage. Encourage students to consider how the context of the political climate in South Africa influenced Mandela's actions. Have pairs discuss the topic, then have students individually share information with the class.

| **NG Learning Framework: Encourage Voter Turnout** |
| ATTITUDE Responsibility |
| SKILL Problem-Solving |

Have students view the photograph of South Africans standing in line to vote (available in the Student eEdition). Then have them research voter turnout in South Africa as well as voter turnout in the United States and compare the data they find as well as information on the attitudes of voters in South Africa and voters in the United States. Based on their findings, have students come up with a campaign to increase voter turnout in the United States.

DIFFERENTIATE

INCLUSION

Map Comprehension Pair inclusion students with partners who can aid in making the text accessible. More proficient students might assist their partners by explaining the map legend, by pointing out political boundaries, or by explaining the routes shown by the arrows.

PRE-AP

Analyze Leadership Style Have students conduct additional research to integrate with information from the text about Nelson Mandela's approach to leadership over the years. Encourage students to consider different ways in which Mandela was a leader, such as through his actions, through his communications, and through his ideas. Then have students write an essay in which they analyze Mandela's leadership style and evaluate which aspects were the most successful.

See the Chapter Planner for more strategies for differentiation.

HISTORICAL THINKING

ANSWERS

1. After Sharpeville, the ANC shifted from promoting nonviolent strikes and boycotts to a policy of disruptive sabotage.

2. Possible response: As a member of the ANC, Mandela was considered a troublemaker by the South African government for his activities opposing apartheid.

3. Possible response: Black South Africans must have voted in great numbers to elect Mandela, which suggests they were ready and eager to take part in political life.

Nationalist Conflicts

Until fairly recently in human history, people thought of themselves as belonging to large extended families—or perhaps to territories. The notion of a nation is only a few centuries old, and nationalism has allowed large and diverse groups of people to live together successfully. But at the same time, nationalism has been the source of many conflicts, some of which continue to this day.

NORTHERN IRELAND

The island of Ireland contains the Republic of Ireland and, to the far northeast, Northern Ireland. The Republic of Ireland is largely Roman Catholic. The people of Northern Ireland—part of the United Kingdom, which includes Britain—are a fairly even mix of Protestants and Catholics. Historically, however, Protestants have dominated Northern Ireland politically.

Since 1922, Protestant unionists (who want to remain in the United Kingdom) and Catholic nationalists (who want to join the Republic of Ireland instead) have regularly clashed. The level of conflict escalated in 1968, when Catholics marching in protest against discrimination were confronted by Protestant counterprotesters. In the 30 years that followed, during a period known as the "Troubles," British security forces tried to keep the peace between violent nationalist and unionist paramilitary forces. But armed battles and bombings continued, resulting in more than 3,600 deaths.

In 1985, Britain and the Republic of Ireland reached an agreement by which Irish government officials would serve as advisors in Northern Ireland. Paramilitary groups on both sides largely rejected this agreement. But by the 1990s, the adversaries began to realize that nobody could win this struggle militarily. In 1998,

Local residents of Derry, Northern Ireland, watch as troops from the British Army dismantle barricades that had been erected against the unionists during what became known as the Battle of the Bogside. During this conflict, Catholic nationalists clashed with Protestants from August 12–14, 1969. The three-day riot led to similar violent outbreaks in other parts of Northern Ireland.

all sides signed the Good Friday Agreement, which stated that Northern Ireland would remain in the United Kingdom unless majorities in Ireland and Northern Ireland voted otherwise. Twenty years later, the agreement was still in place.

YUGOSLAVIA AND ETHNIC CLEANSING

You learned about religious and ethnic conflict in the Balkans region prior to World War I and similar hostilities during Nazi rule. After 1945, Yugoslavia finally became stable under the leadership of Josip Bro, commonly known as Marshal Tito. Although he was an authoritarian communist, Tito remained independent

Bosnian Muslims in a UN refugee camp watch the trial of former Yugoslavian president Slobodan Milosevic on television in 2002. Milosevic was charged with crimes against humanity and genocide in the ethnic wars that broke out in the former Yugoslavia in the 1990s.

from the Soviet Union and treated all Yugoslavs equally. The successful Winter Olympics in 1984 showcased Yugoslavia as a modern, prosperous European republic.

After Tito's death and instability in the Soviet Union, Serbian nationalists were inspired to fight for their vision of a "Greater Serbia." Because the populations were so mixed, Serbian commanders ordered campaigns of "ethnic cleansing." The leaders' intention was to drive Catholic Croatians and Muslim Bosnians out of villages where they had formerly lived with Orthodox Serbs. During the Srebrenica massacre in the summer of 1995, more than 8,000 Bosnian Muslims were systematically murdered by Serbian militiamen. Ethnic cleansing became another term for genocide.

Fortunately, Western leaders were able to use international institutions to end the conflict. Through the North Atlantic Treaty Organization (NATO), the United States and its European allies launched a military intervention and then sponsored negotiations that led to the breakup of Yugoslavia. The former nation was divided into six republics and two provinces.

KASHMIR

Across Tibet's western border lies Kashmir, a mountainous territory claimed by India and Pakistan, which were separated into two nations in 1947. India declared that an Indian prince transferred the region to India as part of this partition. Pakistan based its case on Kashmir's large Muslim population. Soon after the split, India and Pakistan went to war to gain control of Kashmir.

The United Nations negotiated a cease-fire in January 1949 but could not persuade both sides to withdraw their troops from Kashmir. Later that year, India and Pakistan established a temporary cease-fire line. It ended up being a permanent boundary that split control of the territory between the two countries. Hostilities continued, with armed conflict breaking out in 1965 and again in 1971.

Starting in the late 1980s, pro-independence groups from the Pakistani side of the cease-fire line launched attacks against Indian troops. In 1999, their actions led to yet another war between Pakistan and India,

---

PLAN: 4-PAGE LESSON

OBJECTIVE

Describe how, in several parts of the modern world, nationalists and their opponents have engaged in decades of conflict.

CRITICAL THINKING SKILLS FOR LESSON 2.3

- Make Connections
- Analyze Cause and Effect
- Form and Support Opinions
- Compare and Contrast
- Identify Main Ideas and Details
- Analyze Visuals
- Make Inferences

HISTORICAL THINKING FOR CHAPTER 29

What battles and other drastic changes altered the global landscape in the last half of the 20th century?

At the height of decolonization and the Cold War, power shifts were happening all over the globe. Lesson 2.3 discusses nationalist conflicts occurring in five different regions, some of which have been resolved and others of which are ongoing today.

BACKGROUND FOR THE TEACHER

Josip Tito and Nonalignment in Yugoslavia Although Yugoslavia was technically a communist country, President Josip Tito was a staunch believer in nonalignment with the Soviet Union. Tito clashed with Stalin, and subsequently Yugoslavia received aid from the West. However, his dictatorial policies were at conflict with Western values. After Stalin's death in 1953, Tito was faced with the option of growing his relationship with the West while relinquishing some of his power or reconciling with the Soviet Union. Witnessing problems between the Soviet Union and other European countries—notably the conflicts in Hungary and Poland—Tito took inspiration from the leaders of other developing nations and became a strong player in the nonalignment movement, sponsoring the first meeting of nonaligned states in Belgrade in 1961.

INTRODUCE & ENGAGE

CONSIDER SOCIAL DIVISIONS

Guide students to suggest some issues that divide society today, such as health care and climate change. Encourage students to consider how cultural, regional, and religious differences may play a role in differing opinions on these issues. **ASK:** Why do you think people have such different beliefs? *(Answers will vary. Students might point out that people who have grown up in certain environments may have different levels of exposure to information and ideas surrounding these issues, or that peoples' values are influenced by their cultural and religious backgrounds.)* Tell students that in this lesson they will learn about five regions in the world that have experienced nationalist conflicts, many of which stem from differing political and religious beliefs.

TEACH

GUIDED DISCUSSION

1. **Compare and Contrast** What major difference between various groups led to conflict in both Northern Ireland and Yugoslavia? *(religious differences)*

2. **Identify Main Ideas and Details** How did India stake its claim on Kashmir, and how did Pakistan respond? *(India declared that an Indian prince transferred Kashmir to India when India and Pakistan were separated into two nations in 1947. Pakistan based its case on Kashmir's large Muslim population.)*

ANALYZE VISUALS

Direct students to the photograph of British troops dismantling barricades in Northern Ireland and discuss the caption as a class. **ASK:** How do you think the unionists felt toward the British troops? *(Possible response: Because the unionists were Protestants and wanted to remain a part of the United Kingdom, they likely felt allied with and protected by the British troops.)*

DIFFERENTIATE

STRIVING READERS

Use Reciprocal Teaching Have partners read each paragraph silently. After reading, instruct students to quiz each other about the paragraph, asking their partners to state the main idea, identify important details that support the main idea, and then summarize the paragraph in their own words.

GIFTED & TALENTED

Write an Interview Working with a partner, have students write and perform an interview with the Dalai Lama. Tell students to create a list of questions that will allow the Dalai Lama to reflect on significant events between Tibet and China. Then instruct students to conduct online research about Tibetan Buddhism and the Dalai Lama's political and spiritual beliefs. When students have completed writing and rehearsing their interview, invite pairs to perform it for the class.

See the Chapter Planner for more strategies for differentiation.

two states with nuclear weapons. Ongoing violence, including renewed attacks by Pakistani nationalists as well as Indian assaults on Pakistani demonstrators, have kept tensions high in Kashmir well into the 21st century. Peace talks continue as well, but there is still little hope of settling the dispute.

CYPRUS

Greeks first immigrated to Cyprus, a large island in the eastern Mediterranean Sea, during the 1200s B.C.E. A number of Mediterranean empires controlled the island during the centuries that followed. In the 1570s C.E., the Ottoman Empire seized the island, beginning 300 years of Turkish rule. By the 20th century, the island's population consisted mainly of Greeks and Turks.

During World War I, Britain annexed the island, and in 1925, Cyprus officially became a British colony. The Greek Cypriots, or Greek inhabitants of Cyprus, demanded that Cyprus become part of Greece. But Britain and Greece could not agree on how to

accomplish that task. In 1955, Greek Cypriot nationalists launched a campaign for unification with Greece that included the bombing of government buildings. Turkish Cypriots staunchly opposed union with Greece. Armed conflict began between the two Cypriot communities.

In 1960, prodded by Greece, Turkey, and Britain, Greek and Turkish Cypriots agreed to the creation of an independent republic of Cyprus. The two communities would share the governing, although the Greek Cypriots, by far the majority of the population, were to have greater political representation. After fighting erupted again, Turkish Cypriots largely withdrew to the northern third of the island, and Greek Cypriots took control of the rest.

Not much changed in the decades that followed. In 1981, the Turkish Republic of Northern Cyprus proclaimed its independence, but it did not receive international recognition. UN-sponsored talks aimed at reuniting the two Cypriot communities had, as late as 2017, all failed.

In the Kashmir Himalaya, a Changpa nomad and her herd of goats cross a stream. The area is claimed by both India and Pakistan.

The Dalai Lama speaks to a crowd in Central Park in New York City on September 21, 2003. This Tibetan religious leader continues to speak against Chinese dominion over his home region, where he has not lived for decades.

TIBET

Tibet is a region in Central Asia located largely on a plateau that averages 16,500 feet above sea level. The Himalaya form its western and southern borders, and the Kunlun Mountains rise to the north. For these reasons, Tibet is often called "the roof of the world."

From the late 1400s until the 1950s, Tibet was ruled by a Buddhist holy man known as the **Dalai Lama**. In 1950, a communist Chinese force invaded eastern Tibet and swiftly subdued Tibetan troops. Chinese emperors had long claimed the right to station troops in Tibet and oversee its politics. In reality, however, Tibetans had mostly looked after their own affairs. The Chinese communists in the 1950s wanted to expand their authority, and their invasion stirred Tibetan nationalism.

In 1959, Chinese troops quickly put down an anti-Chinese uprising centered in the Tibetan capital of Lhasa, and the reigning Dalai Lama fled to India. In 1965, China

officially revoked Tibet's independent status, making Tibet an autonomous, or self-governing, region of China. In the years that followed, China's Cultural Revolution—which you read about earlier—led to the repression of Tibetans and attacks on their Buddhist culture.

Economic growth after the 1980s put even greater pressure on Tibet. Tibetan resources helped build the Chinese economy and increased immigration by Han Chinese onto the plateau. Government promises of autonomy were contradicted by authoritarian policies coming from Beijing.

Some Tibetan nationalists will settle only for complete independence. Others are willing to compromise in the direction of true "autonomy," in which Tibetan language and cultural rights, freedom of religious worship, and the development of the economy to meet Tibetan needs will be guaranteed. The Dalai Lama continues his nonviolent campaign for Tibetan rights. Like Desmond Tutu and Nelson Mandela, he too won the Nobel Peace Prize.

HISTORICAL THINKING

1. **READING CHECK** What action played a major role in most of these nationalist conflicts?

2. **MAKE CONNECTIONS** How did the "ethnic cleansing" in Yugoslavia in the 1990s build on pre-World War I conflicts in the Balkans?

3. **ANALYZE CAUSE AND EFFECT** How did China's rapid economic growth affect the fate of Tibet?

4. **FORM AND SUPPORT OPINIONS** Which region do you think has the best prospect for lasting peace? Why?

Conflicts and Transformations 851

BACKGROUND FOR THE TEACHER

Cyprus at the Crossroads The third-largest island in the Mediterranean Sea, Cyprus sits at a junction near Europe, Asia, and Africa. This strategic location made it readily susceptible to the influence of several major empires over the centuries. About 500 years after the Greeks immigrated to Cyprus, the Assyrian kingdom held minimal power over Cypriots for roughly 50 years, after which the island-dwellers experienced 100 years of independence before they were under Egyptian rule. The next kingdom to dominate Cyprus was the Persian Empire, followed by (among others) Egypt—again—under Ptolemy, the Roman Republic, the Byzantine Empire, the Caliphate, the Genoese, and the Venetians, who fortified towns to repel the Ottoman Turks. All these cultures impacted the island, creating a diverse tapestry of traditions unique to Cyprus.

TEACH

GUIDED DISCUSSION

3. **Make Connections** How do many centuries of history play a part in the conflict in Cyprus that persists today? *(Cyprus has been under both Greek and Turkish control at different points in its history, leading to a large Greek population and a significant minority Turkish population, which are still at odds with one another.)*

4. **Make Inferences** What does the photograph of the Dalai Lama speaking at Central Park imply about his status? *(Possible response: The Dalai Lama is an important international figure because he can draw large crowds in a country that he isn't originally from.)*

MORE INFORMATION

The Dalai Lama in Exile After his escape from Tibet, the Dalai Lama lived in Dharamsala in northern India, which is also home to Tibet's government-in-exile. With his assistance, the Central Tibetan Administration was fully democratized in May 1990; members of the Cabinet had previously been appointed by the Dalai Lama. In September 2001, the Tibetan people were allowed to elect their leaders for the first time. And in March 2011, the holy man retired as head of state, although he remains a revered figure around the world. He has visited more than 67 countries during his lifetime. Speaking of his role in a democratic, secular government-in-exile, he said, "Personally, I feel the institution of the Dalai Lama has served its purpose." **ASK:** Do you think that the democratization of Tibet's government-in-exile helps or hurts its chances for complete independence? Explain. *(Possible responses: Democratization helps Tibet's chance for complete independence because it is no longer a country ruled by a religious leader. Democratization hurts Tibet's chance for complete independence because China, a nondemocratic country, would not want to lose territory.)*

ACTIVE OPTIONS

On Your Feet: Corners Designate five areas of the classroom for focused discussion on conflict in one of the following regions: Northern Ireland, Cyprus, Kashmir, Tibet, or Yugoslavia. Students should individually write about nationalism in one of these regions for a short time. Then have students go to the designated area of their choice to discuss conflict in one of the regions from this lesson. Have at least one student from each group share his or her group's discussion with the class.

> **NG Learning Framework: Make a Claim about the United Nations**
> **ATTITUDE** Responsibility
> **KNOWLEDGE** Our Human Story

Have students work in pairs to conduct further research on the role of the United Nations in resolving the nationalist conflicts discussed in this lesson. Based on their research, students should make a claim about how well the United Nations is fulfilling its mission to maintain international peace and security. Students should present their claim, along with several details to back it up, to the class.

HISTORICAL THINKING

ANSWERS

1. State or territorial division played a role in the nationalist conflicts in Kashmir, Cyprus, and Northern Ireland. The conflict in Tibet arose from an invasion of the country by the Chinese.

2. Religious and ethnic conflict in the Balkans helped ignite World War I. After the war, much of the region was united as the new nation of Yugoslavia, creating mixed ethnic and religious populations. In the 1990s, Serbian commanders ordered campaigns of "ethnic cleansing" to drive Catholic Croatians and Muslim Bosnians out of villages where they had formerly lived with Orthodox Serbs.

3. China's rapid economic growth increased the country's need for Tibetan resources, which led to increased immigration of Chinese citizens to Tibet and less autonomy for Tibetans.

4. Possible responses: Northern Ireland—the Good Friday Agreement seems to have put Northern Ireland on the road to peace. Tibet—the Dalai Lama's pursuit of a nonviolent campaign against China has a chance of keeping peace in the region.

The State of Israel

Since the late 1800s, Jews around the world have felt inspired to make Aliyah, to immigrate to Israel. Following World War II and the Holocaust, many Jewish people moved to Palestine for safety and to work for the creation of an independent Israel.

CALLS FOR A JEWISH STATE

You learned that in the Balfour Declaration of 1917, Britain promised Jewish independence and a "national home" for Jews on the lands of the ancient Hebrew kingdoms. This area, known at the time as Palestine, consisted of what is now Jordan, Israel, the West Bank,

and the Gaza Strip. At first, the British allowed Jews to settle in Palestine freely. However, Britain also faced competing pleas from Arabs to protect the Arab majority of Palestine. Growing Arab protests caused Britain to limit Jewish immigration to Palestine. But many Jews still found ways to enter what they believed to be their promised land.

In June 1969, Israeli prime minister Golda Meir (center) meets with politicians—including British prime minister Harold Wilson (left) and West German minister for foreign affairs Willy Brandt (right)—at a Socialist International Congress meeting in Eastbourne, England.

852 CHAPTER 29

By 1945, more than 660,000 Jews lived in Palestine, and Zionists—people who supported the formation of a Jewish nation—increased calls for independence. Other Southwest Asian countries, including Iraq, Lebanon, Syria, and Jordan, had all gained independence before, during, or shortly after World War II. The horrors of the Holocaust had also convinced many people of the need for a Jewish state. Jews who had survived the Holocaust moved to Palestine, and other Zionists from around the world who wanted to help build a Jewish nation joined them.

Frustrated by the growing conflicts between Arabs and Jews, Britain gave up its mandate in 1947 and transferred the land to the fledgling United Nations. The UN planned to partition Palestine into separate Jewish and Arab states. But when fighting broke out between Arabs and Jews, UN plans for a **two-state solution** were dashed.

ISRAELI INDEPENDENCE

In 1948, the Zionist leader **David Ben-Gurion** declared the independence of Israel. Ben-Gurion, a Polish immigrant, would become the new nation's first prime minister. Egypt, Lebanon, Iraq, Syria, Jordan, and Iraq immediately declared war, intending a quick end to the newly declared republic. During the 1948 conflict, at least 600,000 Arab refugees and perhaps as many as one million people fled the fighting in an event known as *al-nakbah*, or "the catastrophe," by Palestinians. Israelis routed the Arab armies and then expanded Israel's borders beyond what the UN planners had envisioned. Meanwhile, Egypt claimed the Gaza Strip, and Jordan occupied the West Bank and East Jerusalem. Arabs were angry that many Palestinian Arabs had been displaced and that a Palestinian state was never established. To this day, the quarrel between Arabs and Israelis has had a major effect on world affairs.

NATAN SHARANSKY Natan Sharansky (shown here) was born in Soviet-controlled Ukraine not long after Israel gained independence. As a young man, Sharansky spoke out against Soviet human-rights violations against the Jewish people. In 1973, he sought permission to emigrate to Israel, but the government would not let him leave. Sharansky voiced his opposition to the unfair treatment he and other *refuseniks*, as Soviet dissidents were called, received. The Soviet government accused him of treason and imprisoned him in a labor camp in Siberia in 1977. In time, the pleas of his wife prompted international protests. The Soviets finally released Sharansky in 1986, and he left the Soviet Union to make a new home in Israel. In 2018, he was awarded an Israel Prize—the highest award given annually by the Israeli government to those who make significant contributions to Israeli culture—for his efforts to guarantee human rights to all.

Following the war, Israeli leaders created a government, including a legislative body eventually known as the Knesset. One of these leaders was Golda Meir. Born in Kiev, Ukraine, Meir immigrated to Milwaukee, Wisconsin, with her family when she was a young girl. After she graduated from college, she moved with her husband to what was then Palestine in 1921. During World War II, she became a powerful spokesperson for the Zionist cause. She signed Israel's independence declaration in 1948 and served Israel as minister of labor (1949–1956), as foreign minister (1956–1966), and ultimately as its first woman prime minister (1969–1974). Meir died in 1978 after a 12-year battle with leukemia.

Israel won financial support from other nations, such as the United States and West Germany. Its leaders looked for ways to blend Jews of different ethnic backgrounds into one culture. The use of Hebrew helped unify Jews who arrived in Israel speaking different languages. Today, Israel is an economically successful and predominantly secular state. It is plagued, however, by pockets of religious extremism and the unresolved conflicts with Palestinians. You will learn more about these disputes in the next lesson.

HISTORICAL THINKING

1. **READING CHECK** What events led to the declaration of Israeli independence?

2. **DRAW CONCLUSIONS** Why do you think Jews around the world supported the establishment of an independent Israel even if they did not plan to live there?

3. **ANALYZE CAUSE AND EFFECT** Why did Israel's declaration of independence cause neighboring countries to immediately declare war?

Conflicts and Transformations 853

PLAN: 2-PAGE LESSON

OBJECTIVE

Explain how, in 1947, a group of Jewish people living in what was then Palestine declared the establishment of an independent state: Israel.

CRITICAL THINKING SKILLS FOR LESSON 3.1

- Draw Conclusions
- Analyze Cause and Effect
- Analyze Points of View
- Form and Support Opinions
- Interpret Graphs

HISTORICAL THINKING FOR CHAPTER 29

What battles and other drastic changes altered the global landscape in the last half of the 20th century?

After the horrors of the Holocaust, many leaders around the world believed that Jewish people needed a nation to call their home. Lesson 3.1 discusses the formation of that nation: the state of Israel.

Student eEdition online

Additional content for this lesson, including a graph and a photograph, is available online.

BACKGROUND FOR THE TEACHER

The UN Partition Plan Palestine had been ruled by Great Britain since 1922, so after World War II ended, Britain assumed the authority of granting the United Nations the duty of carving an Israeli state out of Palestine. The UN originally drafted two proposals: one that would create two separate states and another that would create one state made of two autonomous areas. The first proposal was accepted by the Jews but denied by the Arabs and then passed by the UN in 1947. However, the map of the partition plan did not divide the region evenly down the center. Instead, it divvied up several portions of land and designated some for Arabs and some for Jews, with the city of Jerusalem set aside to be governed by an international entity. However, violence erupted soon after the passage of the two-state solution, preventing it from being fully realized.

INTRODUCE & ENGAGE

PREVIEW VOCABULARY

Write *two-state solution* on the board. Tell students that this was the UN plan to temper Arab-Israeli conflict. **ASK:** What do you think this phrase implies? *(Possible response: that the UN would create a country for Jews and a country for Arabs)* What might be some potential challenges to this plan? *(Possible response: Arabs and Israelis might have different opinions about which group is entitled to which parcel of land.)* Tell students that in this lesson they will learn about the formation of Israel, a Jewish state, and the resulting conflicts that ensued.

TEACH

GUIDED DISCUSSION

1. **Analyze Points of View** Why do you believe the Arab people did not want to accept a two-state solution? *(Possible response: The Arab people may have thought that Arabs had a right to all the land, that the Jewish people were intruding on their land, that they were being singled out to give up their land when a Jewish state could be established elsewhere, and that the claim that the Jewish people were entitled to Palestine because it was their "promised land" should be disputed.)*

2. **Form and Support Opinions** Why do you think Israel sought to blend Jews from different ethnic backgrounds into one culture? *(Possible responses: to create a strong, unified Jewish state; to celebrate the commonalities of the Jewish experience)*

INTERPRET GRAPHS STEM

Direct students to the Jewish Immigration to Israel graph (available in the Student eEdition). **ASK:** Roughly how many Jewish people immigrated to Israel between 1948 and 1952? *(approximately 725,000)*

ACTIVE OPTIONS

On Your Feet: Inside-Outside Circle Organize students into concentric circles facing each other. Have students in the outside circle ask questions about the complex relationship between the Israelis and the Palestinians and the formation of the nation of Israel. Students on the inside of the circle should answer the questions. Encourage students to consider the political climate in the region and Israel's relationship with the Palestinians. On a signal, have students rotate to create new partnerships. On another signal, have students trade inside/outside roles.

| NG Learning Framework: Create an Annotated Time Line
| ATTITUDE Empowerment
| SKILL Collaboration

Direct students to read about Natan Sharansky. Instruct them to work in pairs to conduct further research on Jewish *refuseniks* in the Soviet Union. Encourage students to focus on what the *refuseniks* wanted to accomplish, why the Soviet government tried to silence them, and the persecution they faced. With their partners, students should create an annotated time line that showcases the history of the *refusenik* movement.

DIFFERENTIATE

INCLUSION

Use Clarifying Questions Allow students with disabilities to work with students who are able to read the lesson aloud to them. Encourage partners to ask and answer clarifying questions. Ask the partner without disabilities to describe the photograph of Golda Meir with other world leaders. Then prompt partners to answer the Historical Thinking questions.

PRE-AP

Analyze Impacts Tell students to conduct online research about Great Britain's occupation of Palestine from 1922 until shortly after World War II. Based on their research, ask them to analyze how British colonial rule of Palestine might have affected the attitudes of Palestinians toward the formation of Israel. Suggest that students develop a graphic organizer and write an essay based on their research. Their thesis should state how British colonial rule of Palestine affected the attitudes of the Palestinians.

See the Chapter Planner for more strategies for differentiation.

HISTORICAL THINKING

ANSWERS

1. After WWII there were enough Jewish people in Palestine to consider establishing a nation; the Balfour Declaration promised a Jewish state; the UN was planning to partition Palestine; and attacks by Arabs led Zionists to declare an independent state.

2. Possible response: The Holocaust made Jewish people desire a safe haven and many wanted to fulfill the biblical vow of a return to the "promised land."

3. The neighboring countries were Arab countries and were upset about the displacement of Arab Palestinians.

Arab-Israeli Conflicts

Close proximity can bring about cooperation, conflict, or both. For example, people might decide to share resources with an ally or to wage battle against a foe. In Southwest Asia and North Africa, confrontations over contested territory seemed to be the rule.

THE SIX-DAY WAR AND AFTERMATH

Arab states neighboring Israel remained bitter about Israeli independence. Hundreds of thousands of Palestinians remained displaced, with the majority relocating to the West Bank. As many as 800,000 Jews left Muslim countries to resettle in Israel or elsewhere. Unlike the Jewish people, however, the Palestinians had not gained their own independent state. Although Jews from all nations have a right to settle in Israel, Palestinian families that became refugees in the war of 1948 are prevented from returning.

In 1967, Israel learned that Egyptian president Gamal Abdel Nasser was preparing for battle. Israel decided to **preempt**—or prevent from happening—Arab strikes by attacking Egypt first in what became known as the **Six-Day War**. Israeli planes eliminated much of the Egyptian air force and then occupied Egypt's Sinai Desert and Gaza, Syria's Golan Heights, and Jordan's West Bank and East Jerusalem. After the Arab League, a regional organization of Arab states in North Africa and Southwest Asia, made it clear it would never accept Israel's existence, Israel pledged to hold these lands as a security measure. When the conservative Likud Party gained power in Israel's Knesset, its members went further, claiming that the captured Arab lands were part of Israel itself. The Likud government sponsored Jewish settlements on the West Bank, in violation of international laws that prevent the colonization of land taken in war.

The Palestine Liberation Organization (PLO) headed by **Yasir Arafat** (YAH-ser AHR-uh-faht) dedicated itself to regaining lost Palestinian land and creating a Palestinian state. It used a variety of tactics, including terrorist attacks on civilians. Groups such as the Iranian-supported Hezbollah and the Palestinian Hamas also

Arab-Israeli Conflicts, 1947–1967

- Jewish state after UN partition of Palestine, 1947
- Israel after War of 1948–1949
- Area controlled by Israel after Six-Day War, 1967

This 1993 handshake between Israeli prime minister Yitzhak Rabin and PLO leader Yasir Arafat gave the world hope for peace in the Middle East. However, negotiations for a peace accord mediated by U.S. president Bill Clinton proved unsuccessful.

pursued the cause of a Palestinian state, though not always in agreement with one another.

Meanwhile, U.S. president **Jimmy Carter** encouraged Israeli prime minister **Menachem Begin** and Egyptian president **Anwar Sadat** to hold peace talks. The Camp David Accords of 1978 led to the Israel-Egypt Peace Treaty. Israel returned the Sinai Peninsula to Egypt in exchange for Egypt's acknowledgement of Israel's right to exist. Both Begin and Sadat were awarded the Nobel Peace Prize for their contributions to the agreements.

In 1997, Palestinians began the first **intifada**, or "ceaseless struggle," against Israeli occupation of Gaza and the West Bank. Israel responded by restricting the movement of Palestinians. However, while tensions increased on the ground, acts of diplomacy were also bearing fruit.

THE OSLO ACCORDS

In 1991, the United States and several European nations arranged for Israeli and Palestinian diplomats to meet. In 1993, the two sides signed the Oslo Accords. This peace agreement laid out a "road map" for peace based on the idea of two separate and secure nations side by side. U.S. president **Bill Clinton** invited Arafat and Israeli prime minister **Yitzhak Rabin** (YIHT-shak rah-BEEN) to Washington. But the talks soon broke down. Arafat refused to accept a land-for-peace offer more generous than any previous proposal. Israel still would not allow Palestinian refugees to return to their former homes. Also, the two sides could not agree on the status of Jerusalem, which both Israelis and Palestinians claim as their capital. The so-called road map had led nowhere. Rabin was later assassinated by an Israeli extremist angry with the prime minister's peaceful approach.

HISTORICAL THINKING

1. **READING CHECK** Following the Six-Day War, what did each side in the Arab-Israeli conflict want?

2. **DRAW CONCLUSIONS** Why was it difficult for the Israelis to give up occupied territory?

3. **INTERPRET MAPS** What impact did Israel's location have on Israel in the 20th century?

PLAN: 2-PAGE LESSON

OBJECTIVE

Identify how territorial disputes in Southwest Asia and North Africa led to continuing conflicts between Israelis and Palestinians and their Arab allies during the mid- to late-20th century.

CRITICAL THINKING SKILLS FOR LESSON 3.2

- Draw Conclusions
- Interpret Maps
- Identify Supporting Details
- Form and Support Opinions

HISTORICAL THINKING FOR CHAPTER 29

What battles and other drastic changes altered the global landscape in the last half of the 20th century?

The lack of a Palestinian state led to ongoing conflict in Southwest Asia and North Africa. Lesson 3.2 discusses conflicts and negotiations between Israel and its Arab neighbors.

Student eEdition online

Additional content for this lesson, including a photograph, a video, and a time line, is available online.

BACKGROUND FOR THE TEACHER

U.S. Intervention in the Yom Kippur War The Yom Kippur War—which resulted in tense relationships and boundary disputes between Israel and its neighbors—provided the United States with an opportunity to negotiate peace in the region. While President Nixon was preoccupied with matters at home, Secretary of State Henry Kissinger embarked on multiple short trips among capitals in Southwest Asia and North Africa (a technique dubbed "shuttle diplomacy") in an attempt to broker a deal between Egypt, Syria, and Israel. Quickly, the U.S. secretary of state successfully negotiated an agreement between Egypt and Israel. However, finding common ground between Israel and Syria proved much more difficult. Separate pre-negotiation meetings with both sides took place in Washington for several weeks. Then Kissinger traveled to Israel for almost a month of tense negotiations before Syria and Israel finally signed an agreement. In the end, shuttle diplomacy had established a reasonable stability among Israel and its neighbors.

INTRODUCE & ENGAGE

CONSIDER CONFLICT RESOLUTION

Ask students to consider times when they have had to negotiate with someone to reach a mutual agreement, such as determining who would accomplish a chore or how to divvy up the work of a group project. Have them also consider whether any intermediaries were involved, such as a teacher, another peer, or a parent. **ASK:** How did you approach this negotiation? *(Answers will vary. Possible responses: I thought of my needs as well as the needs of the other party; I tried to be equitable in distributing work or resources.)* Tell students that in this lesson they will learn about negotiations between Israeli and Palestinian leaders in an attempt to reach peace.

TEACH

GUIDED DISCUSSION

1. **Identify Supporting Details** From the perspective of Israel, what was the cause of the conflict with Egypt? *(Egypt did not recognize Israel's right to exist.)*

2. **Form and Support Opinions** Was it right for Israel to restrict the movement of Palestinians? Why or why not? *(Possible responses: No. Restricting movement was an infringement upon Palestinians' civil rights; Yes. The intifada caused a threat to the safety of Israelis.)*

INTERPRET MAPS

Direct students to the Arab-Israeli Conflicts map. **ASK:** What do all the areas that became part of Israel after the War of 1948–1949 have in common? *(These areas are all adjacent to Palestinian-controlled lands.)*

ACTIVE OPTIONS

On Your Feet: Three-Step Interview Divide the class into pairs. Have Student A assume the role of Yassir Arafat, and have Student B interview Student A about the goals of the PLO. Then have partners reverse roles. Student A will share information with the class from Student B, then Student B will share information with the class from Student A.

| **NG Learning Framework: Negotiate Peace in the Middle East**
| **ATTITUDE** Responsibility
| **SKILLS** Problem-Solving, Collaboration

Have students watch the Six-Day War video (available in the Student eEdition), then conduct additional research on the perspectives of Israel and the Arab League. Divide the class into groups of four, and have two students in each group represent Israel and the other two students represent the Arab League. Instruct students to negotiate a peace agreement between the two sides, and encourage them to find an agreement that is mutually beneficial and meets the needs of all.

DIFFERENTIATE

ENGLISH LANGUAGE LEARNERS

Use Meaning Maps Pair students at the **Beginning** level with students at the **Intermediate** or **Advanced** levels. Instruct students to use the text as well as a dictionary and print or online sources to complete Meaning Maps for the terms *preempt* and *intifada*. Pairs should also discuss how the terms help them understand the lesson content.

GIFTED & TALENTED

Write a Historical Dialogue Instruct students to conduct online research to learn more about the peace negotiations that President Carter facilitated between Anwar Sadat and Menachem Begin at Camp David in 1978. Students should use what they learn to write dialogues that could have taken place between the leaders. The dialogues might include establishing diplomatic relations in Southwest Asia/North Africa; Israel's capture or withdrawal from territories; or the right of Israelis and Palestinians to exist as independent nations. Challenge students to rehearse and perform their dialogues for the class.

See the Chapter Planner for more strategies for differentiation.

HISTORICAL THINKING

ANSWERS

1. The Palestinians wanted a return of lost land to form a Palestinian state. Israel wanted peace and acknowledgement of its right to exist.

2. Possible response: Returning the occupied territory was difficult for the Israelis because they had built Jewish settlements and they worried about aggression from Arab nations.

3. Possible response: Israel's location gave it access to trade opportunities, but placed it among Arab nations that were likely to attack.

Revolution and Turmoil

The Israelis and the Palestinians were not the only groups feuding in Southwest Asia in the mid-to-late 20th century. Other ethnic and religious rivalries also created divisions. By the 1970s, the strategic importance of the region as a source of oil added more turmoil.

Iranian nationalists, suspicious of both the United States and the Soviet Union, flocked to the banner of Ayatollah Khomeini to establish an Islamic republic in 1979. Khomeini returned from exile in France as their spiritual and political leader.

IRAN VERSUS IRAQ

The uneven distribution of oil has been a continuing source of worldwide conflict. Many nations depend on Southwest Asia's oil. In the 1960s, oil-producing nations such as Iran, Iraq, Kuwait, and Saudi Arabia formed the **Organization of the Petroleum Exporting Countries (OPEC)**. They banded together to topple the control Western oil companies had on oil prices. In 1973, OPEC suspended oil exports to the United States because of U.S. military aid to Israel. Increased oil and energy prices and a global economic slowdown followed.

In 1979, the world focused its attention on the Iranian Revolution. For the first time, a modern state would be expressly ruled by sharia, which you learned is Islamic law. Recall that Sunni and Shiite Muslims had many ideological differences. Yet both groups were increasingly influenced by Islamists who believe that laws and constitutions should be guided by Islamic principles and that religious authorities should be directly involved in the government. Islamists promised social and economic success by returning to the core religious values of Islam.

Islamism threatened secular Arab nations such as Egypt, Syria, Iraq, and Jordan, which were all ruled by secular, nationalist regimes. The United States had long supported Iran's authoritarian shah, Mohammed Reza Pahlavi. Pahlavi industrialized Iran and granted new freedoms to women, but he repressed any opposition. Conservative religious leaders claimed the shah supported decadent Western values. Spreading demonstrations against him led Pahlavi to flee to the United States in 1979.

Religious leader **Ayatollah Khomeini** gained control of Shiite-dominated Iran. He promised to reject Western influences and introduce more religious authority to his Islamic republic. For example, he wanted women to return to their earlier, more traditional roles. A growing sense of nationalism caused many Iranians to support the new government.

In neighboring Iraq, a Sunni minority ruled over a Shiite majority, and Iraqi leader **Saddam Hussein** felt threatened by the Iranian revolution. His brutal invasion of Iran in 1980 lead to more than one million deaths. Iranians suffered terribly from the Iraqi army's use of chemical weapons, and the war ended eight years later in a stalemate.

Then, in 1990, Hussein invaded Kuwait, a small oil-rich state on the Persian Gulf. In response, U.S. president **George H.W. Bush** formed an international coalition against Iraq. The **Persian Gulf War** began in 1991 with the devastating U.S. bombing of Baghdad and quickly concluded with liberation for Kuwait. To maintain a balance of power between Iraq and Iran—and between Sunnis and Shiites—Bush decided not to oust Hussein from his position as president. Hussein then brutally crushed a rebellion in Iraq's Shiite south.

AFGHANISTAN AND SAUDI ARABIA

In 1993, U.S. president Clinton turned his attention toward Afghanistan. After the Soviet Union withdrew its forces, Afghanistan fell under the control of the **Taliban**. This group of Sunni Islamists supported **fundamentalism**, or the belief that laws and social practices should be guided by strict principles, often religious ones. Women's freedoms were severely curtailed under Taliban control, and education for girls was eliminated.

The mujahedeen, guerrilla fighters backed by the United States in the war to drive out the Soviets, supported the Taliban. Among them was **Osama bin Laden**, a son of a wealthy Saudi Arabian builder. He despised the United States for its aid to Israel and claimed that the United States supported corrupt regimes. Bin Laden and his followers in the terrorist group **al Qaeda** (ahl KY-dah) carried out truck bomb attacks on U.S. embassies in Africa in 1998.

Meanwhile, the United States maintained a close relationship with Saudi Arabia. It exchanged military aid for the right to import oil from Saudi Arabia's vast oil fields. The wealth derived from oil sales allowed the Saudis to improve their system of education, modernize industries, and expand urban centers. Yet many other nations were dismayed by Saudi Arabia's denial of rights to women, its suppression of opposing viewpoints, and the role that the Saudis played in sponsoring radical religious fundamentalism across Asia and Africa.

Members of the Taliban pose on top of a tank in Kabul, Afghanistan.

HISTORICAL THINKING

1. **READING CHECK** In what important way are nations of Southwest Asia vital to the interconnected world economy?

2. **ANALYZE CAUSE AND EFFECT** Why did radical Islamic fundamentalism develop in Southwest Asia, and what effect did it have?

3. **MAKE INFERENCES** Why is the Persian Gulf critical to the exportation of oil in Southwest Asia?

OBJECTIVE

Explain how the desire for the resource of oil and differing religious viewpoints caused clashes among the diverse nations in Southwest Asia.

CRITICAL THINKING SKILLS FOR LESSON 3.3

- Analyze Cause and Effect
- Interpret Maps
- Identify
- Explain

HISTORICAL THINKING FOR CHAPTER 29

What battles and other drastic changes altered the global landscape in the last half of the 20th century?

Southwest Asia is composed of many small nations of varying religious and political belief systems. Lesson 3.3 discusses how access to oil and ideological differences caused conflict throughout the region.

Student eEdition online

Additional content for this lesson, including a map, is available online.

BACKGROUND FOR THE TEACHER

The United States and Iran In 1953, U.S. president Eisenhower approved a CIA operation to return the shah of Iran, Reza Shah Pahlavi, to power by overthrowing the democratically-elected prime minister Mohammed Mossadegh. Many Iranians resented the United States for directly interfering with their government, and the restoration of the shah's power contributed to the onset of the Iranian Revolution in 1979. In October of that year, U.S. president Carter allowed the deposed shah to enter the United States to receive cancer treatments. This decision, which Carter viewed as a humanitarian gesture, angered many Iranians. In November 1979, militant Iranians took 66 Americans hostage at the American embassy in Iran. The world watched as the blindfolded prisoners were paraded before television cameras. The militants demanded that the United States return the shah to Iran for trial in exchange for the release of the hostages. Ultimately, some of the hostages were held for 444 days.

INTRODUCE & ENGAGE

DISCUSS OIL DEPENDENCE

Ask students to consider the many ways in which they depend on oil. If necessary, probe students to think about means of transportation that they use, ways goods they consume are transported, and ways other goods they use may contain petroleum products. **ASK:** How do you use oil in your everyday life? *(Answers will vary. Possible responses: I travel by a car or bus that runs on gasoline; I eat foods that have been transported to the store on a vehicle that utilizes gasoline; oil is used to make some plastics.)* How might life become difficult if access to oil were limited? *(Possible responses: I might not be able to travel efficiently; I might have limited access to some goods that I typically use.)* Tell students that in this lesson they will learn about how oil is a crucial resource in Southwest Asia, and that access to oil has led to conflict in the region.

TEACH

GUIDED DISCUSSION

1. **Identify** In what way was the formation of OPEC a reaction to the West? *(One reason OPEC was founded was to combat the West's control of oil prices.)*

2. **Explain** Why does the United States maintain a close relationship with Saudi Arabia? *(The United States is reliant on oil imports from Saudi Arabia.)*

INTERPRET MAPS

Direct students to the Middle East Oil map (available in the Student eEdition). **ASK:** Which two countries share a border in an oil-rich region, and how might this lead to conflict? *(Possible response: Iraq and Iran have many oil fields along their border. Iraq and Iran have already had conflicts over ideological values, which could escalate to conflict over resources.)*

ACTIVE OPTIONS

On Your Feet: Roundtable Seat students around a table in groups of four. Ask them to consider the following question: How did the Cold War affect the relationship between the United States and Afghanistan for decades to come? If time allows, encourage students to conduct additional research on the relationship between the United States and Afghanistan. Have each student around the table answer the question in a different way.

> **NG Learning Framework: Connect Past and Present**
> ATTITUDE Curiosity
> KNOWLEDGE Our Human Story

Divide the class into three groups to gather facts about Iran's government under Reza Shah Pahlavi, the government under Ayatollah Ruhollah Khomeini, and the current relationship between the United States and Iran. Invite each group to choose an appropriate means of sharing information with the class. Then discuss how the content of the three presentations is related, focusing specifically on how events of the past influence current realities.

DIFFERENTIATE

STRIVING READERS

Summarize Direct students to work in pairs to read and summarize the text and photograph captions. Tell students to write at least two notes for each section. Then guide students to create a summary statement for each section followed by a summary statement for the lesson.

PRE-AP

Write a Comparison-Contrast Essay Instruct students to conduct online research to learn more about the Persian Gulf War in 1991 and the War in Iraq in the early 2000s. Encourage students to use a Venn diagram or Comparison Chart to note the similarities and differences between the two conflicts. Instruct students to use their research to write a compare-and-contrast essay and to share their essays with the class.

See the Chapter Planner for more strategies for differentiation.

HISTORICAL THINKING

ANSWERS

1. The nations are vital to the world's economy because they provide the majority of the world's oil supply.

2. Possible response: Radical Islamic fundamentalism developed in Southwest Asia because some Muslims rejected Western ways. Fundamentalism led to the removal of rights for women, the rise of Osama bin Laden, and an increase in terrorist acts.

3. Possible response: The Persian Gulf is critical to the exportation of oil in Southwest Asia because most oil fields lie along its coast, making it easier to transport oil after it has been processed.

Global Human Rights

The horrors of the Holocaust and devastation caused by other wars pushed the issue of human rights into the global spotlight. The fascist affronts to humanity during World War II had been stopped. But the now closely connected global population knew action was needed to halt human rights abuses throughout the world.

HUMAN RIGHTS AND THE UNITED NATIONS

As you learned, 51 of the world's nations formed the United Nations in 1945. This international organization was established as a forum, or public meeting place, to maintain worldwide peace and security and prevent future wars. Protecting human rights across the globe was a top priority.

In 1946, the UN formed the Commission on Human Rights, which sought to protect all people. Former U.S. first lady Eleanor Roosevelt led the commission in the creation of a set of international standards for ensuring people's basic rights called the **Universal Declaration of Human Rights.** This document was approved by the UN in 1948. The standards include "all the rights and freedoms set forth . . . without distinction of any kind, such as race, color, sex, language, religion, political or other opinion, national or social origin, property, birth or other status." When **Kofi Annan** of Ghana became UN secretary general in 1997, he worked to widen awareness of war crimes, genocide, and crimes against humanity.

In 1979, a UN women's convention, or treaty, declared that women are entitled to voting rights, fair employment, and protection from sex trafficking. The 1989 UN Convention on the Rights of the Child declared that children should be protected from physical abuse and poor health. Yet as industrialized nations turned to developing nations for cheap labor, children faced dangerous working conditions in factories, farms, and mines. Sadly, children in some regions are forced to traffic drugs or serve as soldiers.

More than 15 years later, the UN established the Human Rights Council, a group of 47 countries elected for three-year terms. This council has been criticized, however, for its perceived unfair treatment of Israel as well as its inclusion of nations said to abuse human rights. Even so, most people around the world seem pledged to continue to protest human rights violations.

HUMAN RIGHTS AROUND THE WORLD

Some **nongovernmental organizations** (NGOs), nonprofit groups that support a particular cause, specialize in protecting human rights. NGOs

PRIMARY SOURCE

Article 4: No one shall be held in slavery or servitude; slavery and the slave trade shall be prohibited in all their forms.

Article 5: No one shall be subjected to torture or to cruel, inhuman or degrading treatment or punishment. . . .

Article 8: Everyone has the right to an effective remedy by the competent national tribunals for acts violating the fundamental rights granted him by the constitution or by law. . . .

Article 15: (1) Everyone has the right to a nationality. (2) No one shall be arbitrarily deprived of his nationality nor denied the right to change his nationality. . . .

Article 25: (1) Everyone has the right to a standard of living adequate for the health and well-being of himself and of his family, including food, clothing, housing and medical care and necessary social services, and the right to security in the event of unemployment, sickness, disability, widowhood, old age or other lack of livelihood in circumstances beyond his control. . . .

Article 26: (1) Everyone has the right to education. Education shall be free, at least in the elementary and fundamental stages. Elementary education shall be compulsory. Technical and professional education shall be made generally available and higher education shall be equally accessible to all on the basis of merit. . . .

—from the Universal Declaration of Human Rights by the United Nations,1948

858 CHAPTER 29

Members of the United Nations Human Rights Council listen to a report presented by the Commission of Inquiry on Syria, on March 13, 2018 in Geneva, Switzerland.

with this mission include Amnesty International, Human Rights Watch, Freedom House, and Médecins Sans Frontières (Doctors Without Borders). Others, such as the Human Rights Education Associates (HREA), provide educational material about humanitarian law.

Improved communications technology, such as satellite broadcasting and videos recorded on smartphones, made it more difficult to hide human rights abuses. Cold War tensions also played a part in exposing mistreatment. Western democracies criticized the Soviet Union for its cruelties, and many nations began to consider human rights when developing their foreign policy. However, NGOs also pointed to issues in Western nations, such as overcrowding in prisons and the use of the death penalty.

In the late 20th century, many countries employed diplomatic pressure and sanctions to convince South Africa to abandon apartheid. In the 1990s, indignation at ethnic cleansing in Bosnia led to a 1999 UN war crimes

tribunal. The 1990s also saw the genocide of Rwanda's Tutsi people at the hands of the rival Hutu until growing world outrage brought an end to the slaughter and the guilty were put on trial.

THE INTERNATIONAL CRIMINAL COURT

Today, some of the most blatant cases of human rights abuses are tried at the International Criminal Court (ICC) at The Hague in the Netherlands. The ICC was founded in 1998 by the Rome Statute—an international treaty—and established in 2002 after 60 states ratified the agreement. The court works closely with the United Nations but is independent from it. The ICC prosecutes individuals, not nations or organizations, for genocide, war crimes, and crimes against humanity. In 2019, 123 nations have ratified the Rome Statute. The United States, Russia, Israel, and China are among the countries that do not recognize the ICC.

HISTORICAL THINKING

1. **READING CHECK** How did globalization affect human rights both positively and negatively in the 20th century?

2. **DRAW CONCLUSIONS** Why do racial- and ethnic-based human rights abuses take place, and why might other nations be slow or quick to try to stop them?

3. **FORM AND SUPPORT OPINIONS** Do you think some nations were right to criticize the UN's Human Rights Council? Explain.

Conflicts and Transformations 859

PLAN: 2-PAGE LESSON

OBJECTIVE

Describe how the second half of the 20th century saw increased concern for human rights on the part of governments and organizations—even as abuses continued.

CRITICAL THINKING SKILLS FOR LESSON 4.1

- Draw Conclusions
- Form and Support Opinions
- Evaluate
- Analyze Cause and Effect
- Analyze Visuals

HISTORICAL THINKING FOR CHAPTER 29

What battles and other drastic changes altered the global landscape in the last half of the 20th century?

The events of the 20th century raised concerns across the globe about human rights. Lesson 4.1 discusses how the UN and other organizations work to ensure that the basic human rights of all people are met.

Student eEdition online

Additional content for this lesson, including a photograph, is available online.

BACKGROUND FOR THE TEACHER

Convention on the Rights of the Child The Convention on the Rights of the Child is the most widely-ratified human rights treaty in world history. By 2015, 196 countries had ratified the Convention—with the exception of the United States. However, the United States has signed the convention, signaling to the world that it does support the Convention's content. Many parties with differing areas of expertise had input in drafting the convention over the course of a 10-year period. These experts included lawyers, healthcare specialists, educators, child development experts, religious leaders, human rights advocates, governments, and nongovernmental organizations. The Convention on the Rights of the Child defines "child" as any person under 18 years of age and focuses on the varying developmental needs of children throughout their adolescence, assuring that they are not treated as the property of their parents but as human beings and individuals.

INTRODUCE & ENGAGE

CONSIDER BASIC HUMAN RIGHTS

Ask students to think about what human rights are essential for their safety and security. Encourage students to think about their physical and mental health, ability to achieve success, access to resources, and freedom to express their ideas. Make a list of students' responses on the board, and, as a class, edit the list to create a document that lists rights that the class believes every person on the planet should be entitled to. Explain that in this lesson students will learn about how human rights abuses caused concern throughout the world and resulted in actions by the UN to address the rights of all global citizens.

TEACH

GUIDED DISCUSSION

1. **Evaluate** How was the UN's declaration of children's rights in contrast to the economic motivations of industrialized nations? *(When industrialized nations outsourced production to developing nations, sometimes children were forced to work in dangerous conditions.)*

2. **Analyze Cause and Effect** How did technology focus the world's attention on human rights abuses? *(Increased broadcasting and communications technology exposed human rights abuses.)*

ANALYZE VISUALS

Direct students to examine the photograph of the meeting of the United Nations Human Rights Council. **ASK:** How does the design of this meeting space complement the purpose of the Council? *(Possible response: The room is round, like a globe, which positions all attendees to participate in the conversation and has connotations of world unity.)*

ACTIVE OPTIONS

On Your Feet: Numbered Heads Instruct students to read the Universal Declaration of Human Rights primary source. Then divide the class into groups of four and have them number off within each group. Provide students with an article in the Declaration of Human Rights that corresponds with their number: Article 8 with 1, Article 15 with 2, Article 25 with 3, and Article 26 with 4. Have each student think individually about the article assigned to their number, paying particular attention to what global events may have been the impetus for that article's inclusion and the desired effects of the article. Then have groups discuss all four articles together.

| **NG Learning Framework: Present an Analysis of the ICC**
| ATTITUDE Responsibility
| SKILL Communication

Have students conduct additional research to learn more about why the United States, Russia, Israel, and China have not ratified the Rome Statute. Then have students compile their research into an oral report to share with the class. As a class, discuss the merits of the ICC and the potential drawbacks that caused these nations to refrain from ratifying the Rome Statute.

DIFFERENTIATE

STRIVING READERS

Read and Recall Arrange students in mixed-proficiency pairs. After students have read the lesson, tell them to close the text and share ideas and facts from the lesson. Then invite pairs to re-open the text to create a master list of ideas and facts about the lesson.

GIFTED & TALENTED

Examine the U.S. Approach to the Convention Have students conduct online research to determine why the United States has not ratified the Convention on the Rights of the Child. Then have students write a paragraph about whether or not the United States should ratify the Convention.

See the Chapter Planner for more strategies for differentiation.

HISTORICAL THINKING

ANSWERS

1. Positively by bringing the issue to the world's attention, by joining together to solve human rights problems, and by making it difficult to hide human rights abuses. Negatively by increasing economic dependency of developing nations on industrialized nations, by increasing the demand for cheap labor, and by not caring how work gets done.

2. Possible response: Human rights abuses might take place because of prejudice, racism, economic competition related to available resources, past conflicts, or lack of a fair government. Other nations might be slow because they want to stay out of the affairs of other countries or have a strong economic or political tie to an offending country. Other nations might be quick to take action if they believe the act of abuse is horrendous.

3. Answers will vary.

DOCUMENT-BASED QUESTION
On Nonviolence

You probably know several methods of nonviolent conflict resolution. Until the middle of the 20th century, most people assumed that the most successful way to overcome oppression and settle conflict was through violence. However, as the century progressed, people began to realize that peaceful methods often worked better than physical aggression in achieving their goals.

CRITICAL VIEWING Images can often allow viewers to see the concern or anguish as well as the actions of the participants. What tools of nonviolent protest are the female protesters at Plaza de Mayo using in this photograph?

You have already learned that Mohandas K. Gandhi showed the world the effectiveness of nonviolent protest. His actions inspired **Dr. Martin Luther King, Jr.,** to organize African Americans in nonaggressive acts to gain civil rights in the United States. King's methods included boycotts and protest marches. Gandhi, King, and other participants of nonviolent direct action have motivated many other people around the world, including **pacifists,** people with a religious or philosophical objection to violence.

In 1977, Argentinian mothers, or *madres,* began weekly nonviolent demonstrations near Buenos Aires's Presidential Palace. They became known as Las Madres de la Plaza de Mayo, named for the place where they gathered every Thursday in silent protest. They sought information about the fate of their missing children: union-affiliated workers, intellectuals, and dissidents. These offspring had been made to "disappear" by the

right-wing authoritarian government of Argentina in the late 1970s and early 1980s.

But Argentina led the way toward democracy in 1982, when its generals were overthrown and replaced by an elected government. Other nations followed that example over the next ten years, as corrupt dictatorships and authoritarian governments were pushed aside in countries such as Czechoslovakia, South Korea, East Germany, and Chile.

For decades, it seemed as if there were only two choices for deposing bad rulers: either a bloody revolution—as in Russia, Mexico, China, and Cuba—or the military replacing a corrupt government. But in the 1980s, the new option of "people's power" spread around the world. Demonstrators flooded the streets, stood up to tyrants and dictators, and demanded fundamental change. Their successes increased optimism about the future of democracy.

DOCUMENT ONE
Primary Source: Article
from "Guidelines on Christian Conduct during Elections" by Cardinal Jaime Sin, 1986

The leader of the Catholic Church in Manila, Cardinal Jaime Sin, played a central role in guiding the Philippines toward nonviolent, democratic change. Sin was instrumental in the 1986 People Power Revolution that overthrew the corrupt regime of Ferdinand Marcos and elected Corazon Aquino president.

CONSTRUCTED RESPONSE Based on this excerpt, how does the cardinal urge Christians to conduct themselves during the elections, and why?

We all know how important these elections are. They are so decisive that their failure may plunge our country into even greater instability and violence. It is thus of the utmost importance that every voting Filipino does all in his power; 1) to vote in this election; 2) to assure that it is peaceful and honest in its conduct; and 3) to ensure that it becomes really an expression of the people's sovereign will. . . . By our vigilance and Christian involvement in the February 7 elections, let us prove . . . that there is an effective nonviolent way to change the structure in our society. May the Lord God of history lead us all to a better future through the expression of, and respect for, the people's sovereign will.

DOCUMENT TWO
Primary Source: Letter
from "Letter from the Gdańsk Prison" by Adam Michnik, 1985

In the 1980s, activist journalist Adam Michnik was jailed for his reform activities in communist Poland. While in prison, he wrote letters and articles about the situation in Poland and Solidarity's belief in nonviolence. Since Poland's independence, Michnik has continued his work as a journalist and has won a number of awards for his writing.

CONSTRUCTED RESPONSE According to the excerpt, what would be the consequence of Solidarity taking up arms?

Why did Solidarity renounce violence? . . . People who claim that the use of force in the struggle for freedom is necessary must first prove that, in a given situation, it will be effective, and that force, when it is used, will not transform the idea of liberty into its opposite.

No one in Poland is able to prove today that violence will help us to dislodge Soviet troops from Poland and to remove Communists from power. The U.S.S.R. has such enormous military power that confrontation is simply unthinkable. In other words: we have no guns.

DOCUMENT THREE
Primary Source: Article
from "Purple Reign" by Alison Ozinsky, 1989

In September 1988, local leaders in Cape Town organized massive protests against elections in which blacks could not vote. Police sprayed the demonstrators with purple dye so that authorities would be able to identify and arrest the protesters. Instead, the purple stains became a rallying symbol for further resistance.

CONSTRUCTED RESPONSE Based on this excerpt, how were these nonviolent actions effective?

The marchers brace themselves. Somewhere a critical button is pushed and a sharp jet of water bursts forth, changing in mid-stream to lurid purple. Some are hit head on, full in the face. Some are knocked off their knees. . . . Then it stops. A lone protester has climbed on top of the truck and is diverting the nozzle away from the people. . . . The crowd stares for a moment in disbelief—then goes wild, cheering, shouting, and leaping in the air with delight for this brave young man. . . . By Monday morning an efficient graffiti artist has said it all for all of us. "The purple shall govern," I can believe it.

SYNTHESIZE & WRITE

1. **REVIEW** Review what you have read and observed about the three viewpoints about nonviolence in the 20th century.

2. **RECALL** On your own paper, list two details about the writer of one of the excerpts and two details about the excerpt from that writer.

3. **CONSTRUCT** Construct a topic sentence that answers this question: How, why, and when was nonviolent protest used in the 20th century?

4. **WRITE** Using evidence from this chapter and the documents, write an informative paragraph that supports your topic sentence in Step 3.

PLAN: 2-PAGE LESSON

OBJECTIVE
Analyze how peaceful methods of nonviolence often brought about change better than violent actions did.

CRITICAL THINKING SKILLS FOR LESSON 4.2
- Synthesize
- Compare and Contrast
- Form and Support Opinions
- Evaluate

HISTORICAL THINKING FOR CHAPTER 29
What battles and other drastic changes altered the global landscape in the last half of the 20th century?

The last half of the 20th century saw global changes, many of which were accomplished without physical aggression. Lesson 4.2 focuses on leaders who rose up during the 1980s to encourage people to take nonviolent action to bring about reform in countries around the world.

BACKGROUND FOR THE TEACHER
"Purple Reign" Aftermath When activist Alison Ozinsky arrived in Greenmarket Square at 11 a.m. on Saturday, September 2, 1989, near the center of Cape Town, she did not know what to expect as she was ushered into a nearby church. She felt fear but was soon caught up in the march. After the "brave young man" Philip Ivey turned the spray nozzle away from the protesters, security officials retaliated with tear gas. Soon marchers and policemen were all choking on the fumes, creating a war-like atmosphere. This provided time for the protesters to take off or change out of the now purple-colored clothing; however, 500 people were arrested. The aftermath demonstrated that the people of the city had chosen unity in a nonviolent, peaceful protest, which included Cape Town's mayor, Gordon Oliver, as one of the march participants, and most protesters were soon released. On September 13, more than 20,000 anti-government protesters gathered in a "march for peace." The protest was orderly and without incident, opening the door to a dialogue about a new constitution in which nonwhites would gain political rights.

INTRODUCE & ENGAGE

PREPARE FOR THE DOCUMENT-BASED QUESTION

Before students start on the activity, briefly preview the three documents. Remind students that a constructed response requires full explanations in complete sentences. Emphasize that students should use what they have learned about nonviolent protests in other lessons in addition to the information in the documents.

TEACH

GUIDED DISCUSSION

1. **Compare and Contrast** What commonality do all three nonviolent activists want to gain? *(All three activists are calling for reform in their respective government's leadership; in the first two documents, the activists are calling for democratic elections, and in the third document the activist is calling for equal voting rights.)*

2. **Form and Support Opinions** After reading the documents, which of the three documents did you find most effective? *(Answers will vary, but students should choose one of the documents and should explain why it was effective by providing evidence from the document to support all claims.)*

EVALUATE

After students have completed the Synthesize & Write activity, allow time for them to exchange paragraphs and read and comment on the work of their peers. Establish guidelines for comments prior to the activity so feedback is constructive and encouraging. Comments should focus on the most significant parts that address the purpose of the activity and the audience.

ACTIVE OPTION

On Your Feet: Jigsaw Strategy Organize students into "expert" groups and assign each group one of the documents to analyze and summarize its main ideas in their own words. Then regroup students into new groups so that each new group has at least one member from each expert group. Students in the new groups take turns sharing the summaries from their expert groups.

DIFFERENTIATE

STRIVING READERS

Summarize Have two students work together as one student rereads a document and the other student summarizes the document. Encourage students to discuss difficult words or to seek definitions for the words. After each document is summarized, read the constructed response question to make sure all students understand it. Then have volunteers suggest responses.

GIFTED & TALENTED

Interview a Historical Figure Ask students to work in pairs to plan, write, and perform a television or radio interview with Cardinal Jaime Sin, Adam Michnik, or Alison Ozinsky. Invite students to research their selected historical figure and focus on his or her actions, goals, and achievements. Encourage pairs to record or conduct their interviews in front of the class.

SYNTHESIZE & WRITE

ANSWERS

1. Answers will vary.

2. Answers will vary. Possible response: Cardinal Jaime Sin was leader of the Catholic Church in Manila, Philippines. He played a central role in guiding the nation toward nonviolent, democratic change.

3. Answers will vary. Possible response: In the late 20th century, nonviolent actions began to show their effectiveness compared to physical aggression.

4. Answers will vary. Students' paragraphs should include their topic sentence from Step 3 and provide several details to support the sentence.

CONSTRUCTED RESPONSE

Document One: Cardinal Jaime Sin wants Christians to vote peacefully to prove "that there is an effective non-violent way to change the structures in our society."

Document Two: Michnik claims that if Solidarity took up arms, the Soviet Union would crush Poland, and the Polish people would have even fewer liberties.

Document Three: The authorities sprayed protesters with identifying purple dye until one individual moved the nozzle, which boosted the morale of the nonviolent crowd. The dye also turned a negative into a positive with the motto, "The purple shall govern."

CRITICAL VIEWING Protesters hold up signs of their children or relatives that have "disappeared" and the look of anguish alerts reporters and others of the crisis.

Economic Challenges

In the late 20th century, extensive financial integration moved front and center on the world stage. Expanding global trade led to unprecedented growth and international fiscal connections for many nations.

Development of the European Union

Founding member state, 1957–1967 (European Economic Community)
Countries added 1957–1991 (European Community)
Countries added 1991–2013 (European Union)
Countries leaving EU, 2020

GLOBALIZATION AND ECONOMIC CHANGE

At the end of the 20th century, countries once at conflict partnered to boost their economies. **Neoliberalism**—an economic approach that emphasizes free markets and international trade—was adopted by many governments. **Multinational corporations**, or companies with ownership and management teams from more than one nation, flourished with branches located in various countries.

International organizations formed after World War II played a greater role in the global economy. The World Bank and the International Monetary Fund, for example, loaned money to developing nations. In 1947, many nations signed the General Agreement on Tariffs and Trade (GATT), which encouraged free trade. In 1995, the World Trade Organization (WTO) replaced GATT. It established rules for international trade, with an emphasis on lowering tariffs and other barriers to the free movement of goods.

Economic globalization was not a new concept. But in the 1970s, new communications technology enabled rapid transmission of financial data and funds throughout the world. Lower transportation costs led to increased movement of goods. Advertisers could promote products worldwide. Radio and television commercials encouraged a homogenized world culture.

Asian economies in particular surged after World War II. Production of high-quality and well-priced products allowed Japan to rebuild its economy. However, by 1989 the bubble had burst. In contrast, China's economy soared in the last two decades of the 20th century because of the policies of its leader Deng Xiaoping.

FREE TRADE BLOCS

In the 1990s, neoliberalism led to the creation of free trade blocs. In 1992, the creation of the **European Union (EU)** increased the economic clout of Western European nations. It limited the debt new members could hold, created a European Central Bank to set monetary policy, and established the euro as the common currency. The EU accounted for more than 18 percent of global exports by the century's end.

In 1994, Canada, the United States, and Mexico created the **North American Free Trade Agreement**

(NAFTA) to increase North American trade. NAFTA was controversial from the start. Critics in the United States warned that NAFTA might mean the loss of high-paying jobs as manufacturers seeking to pay lower wages moved south of the U.S. border. Some Mexican farmers worried about whether they could compete with U.S. farmers, who received government subsidies.

Debate still rages about whether free trade helps or hurts an economy. It leads to loss of high-paying factory jobs, and companies may be unable to compete on pricing. Consumers benefit because of increased purchasing power. Export companies may make gains as well, since they can expand their markets. Individual companies can see how free trade affects them by conducting a **cost-benefit analysis**, or comparison of the positive and negative effects, of free trade on their business. Free trade affected people in different ways, creating opportunity for some and insecurity for others.

Economic globalization brought greater financial security to much of the world, but it also increased inequality. More money flowed into the hands of business owners than into the pockets of workers. Foreign business owners increased profits by paying workers in developing nations low wages. The policy of **outsourcing**, or the use of people in lower-wage countries to do work once carried out in industrialized nations, means greater unemployment among former high-wage workers.

No matter if the expansion of free trade was cheered or jeered, one thing seemed certain: capitalism became the main player in the global economy.

"ASIAN TIGERS" The economies of other Asian nations grew enormously over the last half of the 20th century as well. South Korea, Taiwan, and Singapore were known as the "Asian Tigers." South Korea succeeded financially because of the close relationships between its government and large companies such as Samsung and Hyundai. Taiwan owed the growth of its trade to the now market-oriented Chinese mainland. Singapore's wealth soared because of its government's single-minded determination to attract foreign investment and build a world-class economy.

HISTORICAL THINKING

1. **READING CHECK** What was the impact of economic globalization in the late 20th century?

2. **MAKE PREDICTIONS** How do you think increased economic globalization will affect life in the early 21st century? in the next 30 years?

3. **INTERPRET MAPS** Study the map. Which nations were the original members of what became the European Union?

Conflicts and Transformations 863

PLAN: 2-PAGE LESSON

OBJECTIVE

Describe how increased economic globalization following World War II had enormous effects on the world's people, nations, and capital.

CRITICAL THINKING SKILLS FOR LESSON 4.3

- Make Predictions
- Interpret Maps
- Evaluate
- Analyze Cause and Effect

HISTORICAL THINKING FOR CHAPTER 29

What battles and other drastic changes altered the global landscape in the last half of the 20th century?

As technology allowed nations across the globe to become more connected, the economies of different nations became increasingly linked. Lesson 4.3 discusses the forces affecting 20th-century globalization and globalization's impacts on life around the world.

Student eEdition online

Additional content for this lesson, including a photograph, is available online.

BACKGROUND FOR THE TEACHER

Effects of NAFTA in Mexico Critics note that the North American Free Trade Agreement hurt Mexican workers. Before NAFTA, all of Mexico's maquiladoras (plants located in export-processing zones) were located along the border. NAFTA enabled foreign companies to open free-enterprise zone factories in other areas of Mexico as easily as they could along the border. This led to the growth of maquiladoras since NAFTA is fueled, in part, by low wages. Mexican workers' hourly wages have stagnated, while wages in countries like China have risen; China's average hourly wage topped Mexico's in 2011, and today those wages are as much as 40 percent higher. Wages are particularly low for maquiladora workers along the border. Critics argue that low wages, long hours, and poor working conditions encourage Mexican workers to cross the U.S. border to find better opportunities.

INTRODUCE & ENGAGE

DISCUSS GLOBALIZATION

Ask students to consider how their lives are affected by globalization. Encourage students to think about how they directly and indirectly benefit from goods and culture imported from overseas, as well as how outsourcing jobs in the United States may indirectly affect them through the overall impact on the economy. *(Answers will vary but may include students enjoying media created in other countries, using products that were manufactured abroad, or parents' and other community members' jobs being affected by outsourcing.)* Tell students that in this lesson they will learn about how globalization took force over the latter half of the 20th century and the positive and negative outcomes of an increasingly connected world.

TEACH

GUIDED DISCUSSION

1. **Evaluate** In what ways do you think the World Bank and International Monetary Fund helped and hindered developing nations? *(Possible response: These organizations helped developing nations by giving them access to capital but may have hindered them by restricting the services their governments could provide.)*

2. **Analyze Cause and Effect** Why do you think Denmark, Sweden, and the United Kingdom did not adopt the euro? *(Possible response: These countries already had strong currencies that were worth more than the euro.)*

INTERPRET MAPS

Direct students to the Development of the European Union map. **ASK:** Besides Sweden and Finland, what do many countries that joined the European Union after 1991 have in common? *(Many of these countries were formerly part of the Soviet bloc.)*

ACTIVE OPTIONS

On Your Feet: Roundtable Seat students around a table in groups of four and have them consider the effects of economic inequality that have resulted from globalization. Encourage students to think about examples of economic inequality that they may have witnessed in the United States as well as examples from abroad. Ask them to evaluate how a global society should approach economic inequality going forward. Each student around the table should answer the question in a different way.

NG Learning Framework: Evaluate Rules on Trade
ATTITUDE Responsibility
SKILL Collaboration

In pairs, have students conduct further research on the World Trade Organization's rules for international trade. Students should create a list of all of the rules they encounter and write a brief synopsis of how each rule affects the economies of both developed and developing nations. Invite volunteers to share their synopsis with the class and discuss any areas of disagreement between groups.

DIFFERENTIATE

ENGLISH LANGUAGE LEARNERS

Preview and Review the Text Prompt students to preview the lesson. First have them read the title, Main Idea, headings, captions, and questions. Then ask them to write questions that they expect to be answered in the text. After students read the lesson, have them work with a partner to discuss answers to their questions.

GIFTED & TALENTED

Interpret a Slogan Explain to students that the day NAFTA went into effect, a group called the Zapatistas staged a rebellion in Chiapas, a region in southern Mexico. Tell students that the Zapatistas' slogan translates to: "For everyone, everything. For us, nothing." (You may ask Spanish-speaking students to consider the slogan in its original language: *Para todos todo, para nosotros nada.*) Challenge students to interpret the slogan artistically—in a painting, drawing, or other art form. Invite students to display their interpretations and answer classmates' questions.

See the Chapter Planner for more strategies for differentiation.

HISTORICAL THINKING

ANSWERS

1. Globalization caused the world's economies to be interconnected and helped many succeed, but globalization also increased the disparity of wealth among nations.

2. Answers will vary. Accept all reasonable responses. Students may say that nations will continue to benefit from free trade and form more trade blocs. Students may also mention that protests against free trade will grow and some countries will announce tariffs.

3. Belgium, West Germany, France, Italy, Luxembourg, and the Netherlands

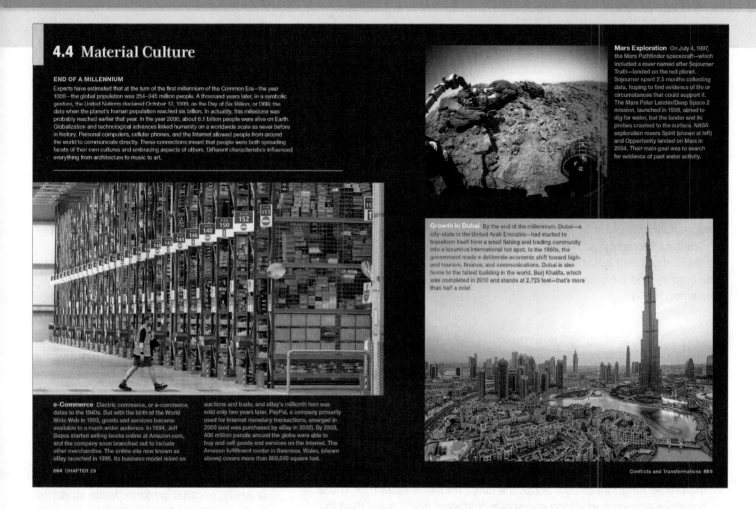

4.4 Material Culture

END OF A MILLENNIUM

Experts have estimated that at the turn of the first millennium of the Common Era—the year 1000—the global population was 254–345 million people. A thousand years later, in a symbolic gesture, the United Nations declared October 12, 1999, as the Day of Six Billion, or D6B; the date when the planet's human population reached six billion. In actuality, this milestone was probably reached earlier that year. In the year 2000, about 6.1 billion people were alive on Earth. Globalization and technological advances linked humanity on a worldwide scale as never before in history. Personal computers, cellular phones, and the Internet allowed people from around the world to communicate directly. These connections meant that people were both spreading facets of their own cultures and embracing aspects of others. Different characteristics influenced everything from architecture to music to art.

Mars Exploration On July 4, 1997, the Mars Pathfinder spacecraft—which included a rover named after Sojourner Truth—landed on the red planet. Sojourner spent 2.5 months collecting data, hoping to find evidence of life or circumstances that could support it. The Mars Polar Lander/Deep Space 2 mission, launched in 1999, aimed to dig for water, but the lander and its probes crashed to the surface. NASA exploration rovers Spirit (shown at left) and Opportunity landed on Mars in 2004. Their main goal was to search for evidence of past water activity.

Growth in Dubai By the end of the millennium, Dubai—a city-state in the United Arab Emirates—had started to transform itself from a small fishing and trading community into a luxurious international hot spot. In the 1980s, the government made a deliberate economic shift toward high-end tourism, finance, and communications. Dubai is also home to the tallest building in the world, Burj Khalifa, which was completed in 2010 and stands at 2,723 feet—that's more than half a mile!

e-Commerce Electric commerce, or e-commerce, dates to the 1940s. But with the birth of the World Wide Web in 1993, goods and services became available to a much wider audience. In 1994, Jeff Bezos started selling books online at Amazon.com, and the company soon branched out to include other merchandise. The online site now known as eBay launched in 1995. Its business model relied on auctions and trade, and eBay's millionth item was sold only two years later. PayPal, a company primarily used for Internet monetary transactions, emerged in 2000 (and was purchased by eBay in 2002). By 2000, 400 million people around the globe were able to buy and sell goods and services on the Internet. The Amazon fulfillment center in Swansea, Wales, (shown above) covers more than 800,000 square feet.

864 CHAPTER 29

Conflicts and Transformations 865

PLAN: 4-PAGE LESSON

OBJECTIVE

Explore technological innovations and the spread of cultures around the world by the year 2000.

CRITICAL THINKING SKILLS FOR LESSON 4.4

- Analyze Visuals
- Make Connections
- Compare and Contrast
- Make Predictions
- Identify

HISTORICAL THINKING FOR CHAPTER 29

What battles and other drastic changes altered the global landscape in the last half of the 20th century?

Many global changes occurred in the last half of the 20th century. Lesson 4.4 explores the technological innovations and spread of cultures around the world by the year 2000.

History Notebook
Encourage students to complete the Material Culture page for Chapter 29 in their History Notebooks as they read.

BACKGROUND FOR THE TEACHER

e-Commerce Since 2000, e-commerce has grown exponentially. It has impacted advertising, leading to the development of Google AdWords in 2000 and Facebook advertising in 2011. It has also led to the development of elite memberships with benefits such as free shipping, as seen with the launch of Amazon Prime in 2005. In addition, e-commerce has led to the creation of new marketplaces, such as Etsy in 2005 and Jet.com in 2014, and new digital payment methods, such as Google Wallet in 2011 and Apple Pay in 2014. Ninety-six percent of Americans with Internet access have made an online purchase at some point in their lives and 80 percent have made an online purchase within the last month. Today, 51 percent of Americans prefer online over in-store shopping. However, omni-channel shoppers, or consumers who shop both in stores and online, spend two to three times as much as single-channel shoppers. E-commerce sellers are able to target very specific groups and provide customized experiences. Consumers are most strongly inclined to purchase a physical or digital product by friends, peers, and trusted influencers on social networks such as Facebook, Instagram, and Twitter. E-commerce sellers are able to reach anyone, anywhere in the world, *from* anywhere in the world, 24/7.

INTRODUCE & ENGAGE

BRAINSTORM

Brainstorm as a class what daily life would be like if personal computers, the Internet, and cell phones had not been invented. Tell students to think about how the technologies have evolved since their original conception, and discuss how they may be improved upon or replaced in the future.

TEACH

GUIDED DISCUSSION

1. **Make Connections** Based on the Technology at the End of the Millennium image gallery (available in the Student eEdition), how have mobile phones and personal computers evolved? *(Possible response: They have all gotten much smaller, lighter, cheaper, and easier to use and have many more functions and capabilities.)*

2. **Identify** What have been the goals of rovers on Mars? *(The goals of rovers on Mars have been to find any evidence of life or circumstances that could support it and to find water or evidence of past water activity.)*

MATERIAL CULTURE

Encourage students to look at this lesson in the Student eEdition, which contains additional images not shown here. Prompt students to consider how all the images connect to one another. **ASK:** What themes are prevalent in the lesson? *(Possible response: innovation, architecture, culture, and art)* How do these themes connect? *(Possible response: They all influence one another.)*

Ask students to think about the following question: What influences have these elements had on one another? Then, as a class, discuss the following information:

- Technological innovations have launched e-commerce and space exploration.
- Advances in technology, in addition to elements of culture, have inspired and facilitated architecture, such as in Dubai, Bilbao, and Yugoslavia. These creations are works of art, but they also have inspired other cultures to adopt some of their methods, thus blending styles across regions.
- Technology has aided in the spread of hip-hop and Latin music and culture and has both inspired and helped disseminate Afrofuturism.
- Jean-Michel Basquiat used his background and culture to celebrate black heroes and created his own artistic style by blending street art with traditional art, which inspired other artists.

ENGLISH LANGUAGE LEARNERS

Explore the Cultural Impact of Music Direct students of **All Proficiencies** to the Hip-Hop and The Latin Explosion sections of the lesson. Explain that music can transcend cultures and languages. Ask students to find classroom-appropriate songs in their home languages that blend two languages, just as the Latin explosion blends Spanish and English, or that have been influenced by hip-hop. Encourage students to share their songs with the class and explain their influence. Students may work with partners or in small groups if necessary.

GIFTED & TALENTED

Report on Mars Exploration Ask students to research Mars exploration and write a detailed report from the perspective of an astronaut exploring the planet. Students' reports should provide detailed descriptions of the journey to Mars and of the planet, including what is seen, heard, felt, and so on. Encourage students to include visuals and to share their reports with the class.

See the Chapter Planner for more strategies for differentiation.

Afrofuturism In the early 1990s, academic Mark Dery coined the term *Afrofuturism* in the essay "Black to the Future." The concept had already been around for decades, but Dery gave a name to the intersection of black culture, including the African Diaspora, with technology and science fiction. He asked, "Can a community whose past has been deliberately rubbed out, and whose energies have subsequently been consumed by the search for legible traces of its history, imagine possible futures?"

Afrofuturism reached the global mainstream more recently in 2018's blockbuster film *Black Panther*. It was the highest-grossing movie that year. The fictional, never-colonized African nation of Wakanda disguises itself—and hides its highly advanced technology—to the rest of the world. But its new king, T'Challa, wonders if he should open up Wakanda's borders. Production designer Hannah Beachler and costume designer Ruth E. Carter both won Academy Awards for their work on the movie. They also made history by being the first African Americans to receive Oscars in their respective categories. Carter researched many cultures in Africa and then put her own modern twist on the clothing she produced. "This futuristic African film that's based on indigenous tribes connects the beginning and the future," she says.

Black Panther first appeared in a July 1966 comic book but was then sidelined. In 1998, Christopher Priest—the first black writer and editor in comics—reintroduced the character in a series.

▲ **Hip-Hop** Hip-hop—which includes deejaying, rapping, painting graffiti, and dancing—moved to the center of the U.S. stage in the 1980s and 1990s. Run D.M.C. (above) were the first rappers to have a gold album and the first to have a video air on MTV. Other notable hip-hop artists of the era were Public Enemy, Queen Latifah, N.W.A., Salt-N-Pepa, Notorious B.I.G., and Tupac Shakur. By the late 1990s, hip hop was the largest selling genre of music in the United States, and its style and influence began to dominate global pop culture.

▶ **The Latin Explosion** At the 1999 Grammy Awards, Puerto Rican Ricky Martin kicked off what later became known as "The Latin Explosion." Singing in English—and then in Spanish—Martin's dynamic performance of "La Copa de la Vida" (The Cup of Life) led to his mainstream success. Other Latino artists, including Marc Anthony, Enrique Iglesias, and Jennifer Lopez, followed. Lopez had portrayed Tejano singer Selena (right) in a biopic, bringing her story to a wider audience. Selena, who sang in Spanish but was working on an English album, was shot and killed by a former employee in 1995.

According to *Black Panther* costume designer Ruth E. Carter, the spy Nakia's traditional costume (shown above) "is inspired by the Surma and the Suri people of Africa." Carter used a green color palate to connect all of the character's many outfits.

HISTORICAL THINKING

1. **READING CHECK** What two innovations linked people at the end of the second millennium on a scale never before seen in history?

2. **COMPARE AND CONTRAST** How do the examples of Afrofuturism you've read about differ, and how are they alike?

3. **MAKE PREDICTIONS** How do you think Afrofuturism will evolve in the future?

BACKGROUND FOR THE TEACHER

Afrocentrism Another art form that represented the African community was Afrocentrism. Jean-Micheal Basquiat gained fame for his depictions of social injustices and stereotypes against the African community. He was inspired by the cultural movement of Afrocentrism, which values traditional African culture over the dominant European culture. Afrocentrism argues that nonwhite cultures have been suppressed—and nonwhite people have been oppressed—by Europeans and European descendants for millennia, and stresses the need for the attention and appreciation of African history, culture, and values. It also emphasizes the spread of contemporary African-American culture in language, music, dance, cuisine, and clothing.

Elements of Afrocentric art include African cultural and ethnic symbols and details, such as masks that symbolize war and male dominance. Basquiat used these elements to express the connection between African men and African-American men and how his heritage molded him as an artist. He used self-portraits as a representation of others' perceptions of young black men and to evoke emotions such as sadness and frustration for the oppressed. In his 1982 painting *Self Portrait as a Heel*, Basquiat's face is portrayed as an African mask, fearful and angry. His shirt shows that he is just another number, possibly alluding to the African slave trade or the mass incarceration of young black men in the United States. To illustrate the oppression he feels, Basquiat's portrait features restraints depicting bars and shackles around his neck. Although he faced pressure and criticism, he never wavered from his goal of challenging people's perceptions and encouraging people to put themselves in the shoes of an oppressed individual who has been viewed in a negative light and considered an antagonist, or a *heel*.

TEACH

GUIDED DISCUSSION

3. **Compare and Contrast** How do hip-hop and Latin music today compare with the same music from the 1990s? Explain. *(Possible response: They are extremely similar. Hip-hop artists continue to address serious social issues, and Latin artists continue to blend English and Spanish in different genres. However, they also seem to be blending in the musical styles of artists such as Pitbull.)*

4. **Identify** What elements in the Black Panther image depicts Afrofuturism? *(Possible responses: the characters' costumes, the vibranium-powered gauntlets)*

ANALYZE VISUALS

Prompt students to analyze the Black Panther comic book covers.
ASK: What do you see on the covers? *(Possible response: the image of the Black Panther as a super-hero perhaps fighting a villain)* Ask volunteers to share what they know about the Black Panther based on the information in the lesson and from their prior knowledge. Then share the second Background for the Teacher information about Afrocentrism.
ASK: How are Afrofuturism and Afrocentrism the same? How do they differ? *(Answers will vary. Possible response: Afrofuturism focuses on the African community and culture as portrayed in the future. Afrocentrism is a traditional African cultural movement. Both focus on African culture, but one concentrates on traditional aspects and the other portrays futuristic concepts.)*

ACTIVE OPTION

On Your Feet: Write an Architecture Profile Direct students' attention to the Burj Khalifa in Dubai. In pairs or small groups, have students conduct research to write a profile of the work and its architect, who commissioned it, and other details relevant to its history. Tell students to find additional visuals to include in their profiles. Encourage students to share their profiles with the class or on a class website.

HISTORICAL THINKING

ANSWERS

1. Personal computers, cellular phones, and the Internet linked people at the end of the second millennium on a scale never before seen in history.

2. Answers will vary. Accept all reasonable responses. Students may point out that all of the examples of Afrofuturism are very modern and celebrate black culture—be it either traditional styles or black heroes. Differences may include the fact that Basquiat's style is more abstract than the detailed art of the Black Panther comics.

3. Answers will vary. Accept all reasonable responses. Students might comment on the commercial success of the film *Black Panther* and predict that Afrofuturism will become even more mainstream and celebrated as it attracts a wide variety of audiences.

29 REVIEW

VOCABULARY

Complete each of the following sentences using one of the vocabulary words from the chapter.

1. Sit-ins, protest marches, and boycotts are all examples of _____.

2. Through his policy of _____, Mikhail Gorbachev encouraged an open discussion of political issues.

3. Several nonprofit groups, or _____, work to protect human rights all over the world.

4. A formerly unstable country begins the process of _____ to establish a functioning government.

5. The embrace of _____ led to the formation of many free-trade blocs.

6. In 1987, Palestinians began a multiyear _____ to protest Israel's presence in Gaza and the West Bank.

7. Companies that have ownership and management teams in more than one country are _____.

8. Moving a U.S. company's technology helpdesk to India is an example of _____.

READING STRATEGY
ANALYZE CAUSE AND EFFECT

When you identify causes and effects, you can examine and determine what different events might have in common. Complete the following chart to identify causes and effects related to major political transformations of the late 20th century. Then answer the question that follows.

Causes	Effects
	Fall of the Berlin Wall
	Deng Xiaoping's economic policies
	End of South Africa's apartheid system

9. Describe ways in which ordinary people, as opposed to government officials, brought about one or more of the major transformations listed in the chart.

MAIN IDEAS

Answer the following questions. Support your answers with evidence from the chapter.

10. What changes in the late 1980s weakened Soviet control in Hungary? LESSON 1.1

11. What role did Boris Yeltsin play in the coup launched against Gorbachev? LESSON 1.3

12. What challenges did China's economic transformation present to the Chinese government? LESSON 1.4

13. Why were elections considered unfair during the period in which the Institutional Revolutionary Party (PRI) ruled Mexico? LESSON 2.1

14. Which two nations both claim Kashmir as their territory? LESSON 2.3

15. Which events from the 20th century explain the ongoing conflict between Palestinians and Israelis? LESSON 3.2

16. What role did Osama bin Laden play in the development of radical Islamic fundamentalism? LESSON 3.3

17. What are three ways in which the United Nations helped the cause of human rights in the 20th century? LESSON 4.1

HISTORICAL THINKING

Answer the following questions. Support your answers with evidence from the chapter.

18. IDENTIFY SUPPORTING DETAILS How did Ronald Reagan put pressure on the Soviet Union?

19. DRAW CONCLUSIONS When Lithuania declared its independence, why did Gorbachev decline to take military action against the new republic?

20. MAKE CONNECTIONS How did the United States apply Harry Truman's policy of containment in Central America?

21. SUMMARIZE How did Golda Meir influence the world in the 20th century?

22. COMPARE AND CONTRAST How was life in Iran different under Shah Mohammed Reza Pahlavi than under Ayatollah Khomeini?

23. FORM AND SUPPORT OPINIONS Do you think children in developing countries benefited more or suffered more because of 20th century globalization? Explain.

INTERPRET MAPS

Study the map below, which shows the the British Isles and the countries on each island.

The British Isles

24. Northern Ireland is a part of what country?

25. How did geography contribute to the political conflict that plagued Northern Ireland?

ANALYZE SOURCES

Boutros Boutros-Ghali served as secretary-general of the United Nations from 1992 to 1996. In this excerpt from a 1996 speech, he describes the benefits and costs of economic globalization. Read the excerpt and answer the question that follows.

> The global economy is now a fact of life. In the economic field, large companies are feeling the impact of technological progress and new production methods. . . . Globalization brings progress. It should be encouraged. But dangers remain. The global economy can be hard on those unable to benefit from its opportunities. Traditional ties of community and solidarity can be undermined. Whole countries and regions can become marginalized. So the gap between rich and poor grows even wider.

26. Based on the excerpt, what are the advantages and disadvantages of globalization?

CONNECT TO YOUR LIFE

27. INFORMATIVE The costs and benefits of NAFTA depended on one's role. Write a short speech that you would deliver to a U.S. congressional hearing on this trade agreement. Choose the perspective of an American, Canadian, or Mexican business owner, farmer, or industrial worker.

TIPS

* Review the section about NAFTA in the text, taking note of who benefited and who lost ground under NAFTA.

* Decide which role you want to take. Make a list of ways in which NAFTA benefited you and ways in which it hurt you. Remember that NAFTA may affect the same person in different ways. For example, workers are also consumers.

* Prepare your speech. Be sure to identify your role. Use language appropriate to a hearing before the U.S. Congress.

* Use key vocabulary from the chapter in your speech.

* Conclude your speech with a clear statement that summarizes the costs and benefits.

VOCABULARY ANSWERS

1. passive resistance
2. glasnost
3. nongovernmental organizations
4. nation-building
5. neoliberalism
6. intifada
7. multinational corporations
8. outsourcing

READING STRATEGY ANSWERS

Causes	Effects
Policy of glasnost and opening of Hungarian borders	Fall of the Berlin Wall
Years under communist rule and failure of the Great Leap Forward	Deng Xiaoping's economic policies
Passive resistance, boycotts, strikes, and sanctions against South Africa	End of South Africa's apartheid system

9. Answers will vary but may include descriptions of the role of ordinary Eastern Europeans in protesting and resisting Soviet domination and of East Germans gathering at the wall and exiting through an open gate of the Berlin Wall and then dismantling the structure, or of ongoing and sustained protests within South Africa and by people in other countries who pressured institutions, governments, and businesses to withdraw investments and stop doing business with the apartheid regime.

MAIN IDEAS ANSWERS

10. Hungary's parliament voted to allow non-communist political parties, and Hungary opened its border with the democratic republic of Austria.

11. Yeltsin led protests against the coup plotters.

12. China's environmental problems multiplied, the gap between rich and poor increased, and money brought corruption, which triggered protests.

13. The PRI held a monopoly on political power, often listing only the PRI candidate's name on ballots.

14. India and Pakistan both claim Kashmir as their territory.

15. In the early 20th century, many Jews moved to what was then Palestine alongside Arabs already living there and began to press for their own homeland. The Palestinians and other Arabs objected to the idea of two states—one Jewish and one Arab—and waged war to prevent this. Attempts at establishing peace failed throughout the 20th century, so the conflict continues.

16. Osama bin Laden led the terrorist group al Qaeda, which attacked nations that stood in the way of the integration of Islam into all aspects of life.

17. The United Nations helped the cause of human rights in the 20th century by providing a forum to help solve world problems; by creating the Commission on Human Rights; by creating the Universal Declaration of Human Rights; by ensuring human dignity for all people; by making the world aware of war crimes, genocide, and crimes against humanity; and by issuing conventions for the protection of the rights of both women and children.

HISTORICAL THINKING ANSWERS

18. Possible responses: Reagan increased defense spending, which pressured the Soviet Union to spend more to keep up with the United States. Reagan also pressured Gorbachev to tear down the Berlin Wall.

19. Possible response: Gorbachev realized that military action against Lithuania would only incite further rebellion. He could not stop the movement toward democratic freedoms among members of the Soviet bloc.

20. Possible response: To contain the Soviet Union during the Cold War, the United States supported anticommunist regimes in Central America.

21. Possible response: Golda Meir was a leader in the establishment of Israel as a nation and later served as its prime minister.

22. Possible response: The shah advocated a modern secular Iran and the adoption of aspects of Western culture and ideologies, while the Ayatollah promised a purely Islamic state steeped in tradition and devoid of Western influences. Under the shah, women had been granted new freedoms that were later eliminated under the Ayatollah.

23. Answers will vary. Some students will say that children benefited more from globalization because the world learned more about their plight and that UN conventions served to protect the children. Others will say that children suffered more because of increased economic pressures placed on the children's home nation.

INTERPRET MAPS ANSWERS

24. Northern Ireland is a part of the United Kingdom.

25. Possible response: Northern Ireland was located on the island of Ireland, which tied it geographically with the Republic of Ireland, rather than with the United Kingdom. Its location ensured that many citizens of Northern Ireland were Irish and identified with the Irish republic.

ANALYZE SOURCES ANSWER

26. Possible response: Advantages of globalization are technological progress and new production methods. Disadvantages of globalization are the weakening of traditional community ties and solidarity as well as the marginalization of entire countries and regions.

CONNECT TO YOUR LIFE ANSWER

27. Students' speeches should include who benefited and who lost ground under NAFTA, have a clearly defined role and a list that includes ways in which NAFTA benefited and cost them, use language appropriate to a hearing before the U.S. Congress as well as key vocabulary from the chapter, and a conclusion statement that summarizes the costs and benefits of NAFTA.

UNIT 10 RESOURCES

UNIT INTRODUCTION

UNIT TIME LINE

UNIT MAP online

THE GLOBAL PERSPECTIVE: Who We Are: Shared Cultures and Identities

- National Geographic Explorers: Topher White, Danielle N. Lee, and Paul Salopek
- On Your Feet: Ready, Set, Recall

| NG Learning Framework
Explore High-Tech Forensics

UNIT WRAP-UP

***National Geographic* Magazine Adapted Article**

- "Navigating the Anthropocene"

Unit 10 Inquiry: Create an NGO

Unit 10 Formal Assessment

CHAPTER 30 RESOURCES

Available in the Teacher eEdition

TEACHER RESOURCES & ASSESSMENT

Reading and Note-Taking

Vocabulary Practice

Document-Based Question Template

Social Studies Skills Lessons

- Reading: Make Inferences
- Writing: Informative

Formal Assessment

- Chapter 30 Pretest
- Chapter 30 Tests A & B
- Section Quizzes

Chapter 30 Answer Key

Cognero®

STUDENT DIGITAL RESOURCES

Available in the Student eEdition

- eEdition (English)
- Handbooks
- National Geographic Atlas
- History Notebook
- Biographies
- Literature Analysis

STRATEGY ❶

Use K-W-L Charts

Arrange students in pairs and provide each with a K-W-L Chart. Tell partners to brainstorm what they know about the lesson topic and add their ideas to the chart. In the second column, tell students to use the lesson title, section headings, and visuals to write at least three questions they have about the lesson topic. After they have read the lesson, remind students to write the answers to their questions and other information they learned in the third column. Encourage them to keep their charts for each lesson to help them review the entire chapter.

Use with All Lessons

STRATEGY ❷

Make a Chart

Instruct students to make a chart to help them understand the problems and solutions discussed in the chapter. Tell them to note in the chart the problems people are facing in the 21st century and possible solutions to the problems. Tell students to read independently first and then to work in pairs to identify one of the problems and write it in the first column. Then tell them to take turns, with one partner rereading paragraphs related to the problem aloud, while the other listens and identifies details to list in the second column and a solution to list in the third column.

Use with All Lessons

STRATEGY ❸

Summarize a Lesson

Instruct pairs of students to read each paragraph silently and write a sentence to summarize what they read. Tell partners to trade sentences and then work together to clarify the meaning of each paragraph. Point out to students that, taken together, the summary sentences represent a summary of the whole lesson.

Use with All Lessons

STRATEGY ❶

Echo Main Ideas

Point out that the Main Idea statements all relate to important aspects of the world in the 21st century. Pair students with a proficient reader. Ask the proficient reader to read the Main Idea statement at the beginning of a lesson aloud. Tell the less proficient partner to "echo" the statement and then restate it in his or her own words. Encourage partners to agree on what they anticipate the lesson to be about. Have them continue to read together and verify the main ideas as they read.

Use with All Lessons

STRATEGY ❷

Use Supported Reading

Ask students to read the chapter aloud lesson by lesson. Instruct them to stop at the end of each lesson and use these sentence frames to monitor their comprehension of the text:

- This lesson is mostly about _____.
- Other topics in this lesson are _____ and _____.
- One question I have is _____.
- One of the vocabulary words is _____, and it means _____.
- One word I don't recognize is _____.

Use with All Lessons

STRATEGY ❶

Use Terms in a Sentence

Pair students at the **Beginning** level with students at the **Intermediate** or **Advanced** level. Instruct pairs to work together to compose a sentence using selected Key Vocabulary words and terms. Ask the more proficient students to assist their partners in checking the accuracy of the sentences. Invite pairs to share their sentences and discuss different ways to use each word or term.

Use with All Lessons

STRATEGY ❷
Build Vocabulary

Help students at **All Proficiencies** learn unfamiliar words by introducing synonyms they might know. Display difficult words paired with more familiar words, as with these examples from Lesson 1.1:

conflict / fighting
coalition / team
oust / remove
assail / attack
executed / killed
quell / stop

Tell students that when they encounter a difficult word, such as *coalition*, they should try to replace it with a word they may be familiar with, such as *team*. Guide students to use a thesaurus to practice looking up and substituting words, encouraging them to look among the synonyms to find one that makes sense in context.

Use with All Lessons *Students at the **Advanced** level could help students at the **Beginning** and **Intermediate** levels find appropriate synonyms.*

STRATEGY ❸
Summarize Main Ideas

After reading a lesson, ask students at **All Proficiencies** to write a sentence summarizing its main idea. Arrange students in pairs and ask them to dictate their sentences to each other. Then tell partners to work together to check the sentences for spelling and accuracy.

Use with All Lessons *You may wish to pair students at the **Beginning** level with those at the **Advanced** level and students at the **Intermediate** level with one another.*

GIFTED & TALENTED

STRATEGY ❶
Design an Infographic

Direct students to create an infographic that presents information about a specific event discussed in the chapter, such as the Arab Spring or the 2008 recession. Guide them to conduct research to learn more about their chosen topic and collect interesting visual information before designing their infographic. Invite students to share their infographics with the class.

Use with All Lessons

STRATEGY ❷
Debate Views

Direct pairs of students to choose opposing sides of a global issue to research and develop an argument about, such as the bailout of financial institutions in 2008 or providing stimulus money to strengthen an economy or save a country from debt. Invite students to present their debate in front of the class.

Use with All Lessons

PRE-AP

STRATEGY ❶
Make a Prediction

Encourage students to conduct further research on an event or situation in this chapter and its global impact on the future, such as the growth of China's economy and the fact that it is poised to be the world's largest economy by 2050. Tell students to locate present-day statistics and expert opinions to use to make a prediction about how this event or situation will play out in the future and how students their age could impact these future results. Instruct students to post their predictions on a school website.

Use with All Lessons

STRATEGY ❷
Write an Editorial

Encourage students to write an editorial in which they comment on a connection between an event or issue discussed in this chapter and their own lives. Possible events or issues might include increased globalization, gender rights, the 2008 recession, climate change, increased connectivity, health care, or food security. Tell students to include personal experiences in their editorials. Instruct students to post their editorials on a school website or in the student newspaper.

Use with All Lessons

CHAPTER
30 A Global
21st Century
2000–Present

HISTORICAL THINKING What challenges does the world face in the 21st century?

SECTION 1 The Political Picture
SECTION 2 The Economic Picture
SECTION 3 Science and Technology
SECTION 4 Visions for the Future

CRITICAL VIEWING
Double-decker buses, taxis, shoppers, and tourists are a constant presence in London's Piccadilly Square. With a population of 8.8 million, London isn't the largest city in the world—that honor goes to Shanghai, China—but it is one of the most ethnically diverse. What challenges might a city like London face on a daily basis?

870 CHAPTER 30

A Global 21st Century 871

INTRODUCE THE PHOTOGRAPH

LONDON'S PICCADILLY SQUARE

Have students study the photograph of London's Piccadilly Square that appears at the beginning of the chapter. Have them focus on details that indicate what life is like in a major city. **ASK:** What does the photograph suggest about conditions in cities? *(Possible response: It suggests that cities are overcrowded, congested with traffic, and lacking in areas of grass or trees.)* Explain that Piccadilly Square, also known as Piccadilly Circus, is located in an old, established area of shops and nightclubs in the heart of London. It is a much-visited part of London that exemplifies the challenges faced by cities today. Tell students that in this chapter they will learn about different kinds of challenges, some local and some global. These challenges include political conflicts, financial crises, climate change, human rights issues, and even situations that threaten the lives of whole populations.

SHARE BACKGROUND

Estimates indicate that half the people globally live in cities and that two-thirds will occupy urban areas by 2050. Cities are challenged to find solutions to problems of traffic congestion, air and water pollution, rising housing costs, poverty, and environmental degradation. The city of London is no exception. London is a global city of 9 million people and continues to expand largely through immigration.

After he was elected mayor of London in 2016, Sadiq Khan embraced the global National Park City idea proposed by National Geographic Explorer Daniel Raven-Ellison. The intent is to make cities greener, healthier places to live. On July 22, 2019, Mayor Khan signed a charter making London the world's first National Park City. He set a goal to make London 50 percent green by 2050 and has gained widespread support. Residents are planting gardens and growing plants on balconies and in yards.

CRITICAL VIEWING Possible response: The city might face some difficulty in terms of accommodating such a diverse population whose needs and wants might be different. London might also face problems with infrastructure and housing due to its large population.

HISTORICAL THINKING QUESTION
What challenges does the world face in the 21st century?

Roundtable This activity will help students preview some of the chapter content. Tell students that the chapter covers numerous topics of concern today. Arrange students in small groups. Ask groups to discuss what they know about current events. If students need help coming up with ideas, invite them to consider these questions:

- Is terrorism an ongoing problem?
- What conflicts exist among nations?
- Have the Internet and social media had positive or negative effects?
- How important is climate change?

At the end of the activity, have groups share the ideas they discussed.

KEY DATES FOR CHAPTER 30

2000	The Human Genome Project maps DNA.
2001	Al Qaeda terrorists attack targets in the United States.
2003	U.S. and British forces invade Iraq to locate WMDs.
2008	The global Great Recession begins.
2010	A Tunisian produce seller starts the Arab Spring.
2011	U.S. forces kill al Qaeda leader Osama bin Laden.
2016	The Paris Agreement on climate change is ratified.
2016	Voters in the United Kingdom approve Brexit.
2017	The United States withdraws from the Paris Agreement.
2018	U.S. president Trump meets North Korea's Kim Jong-un.
2020	The emergence of a new coronavirus, SARS-CoV-2, causes a worldwide pandemic.

INTRODUCE THE READING STRATEGY

MAKE INFERENCES
Explain to students that they can use the text and their prior knowledge to make inferences, or "educated guesses," about the information in the text. Go to the Chapter Review and preview the Reading Strategy chart with students. As they read the chapter, have students make inferences about key events pertaining to the impact of globalization in the 21st century.

INTRODUCE CHAPTER VOCABULARY

KEY VOCABULARY

SECTION 1

asylum	civil liberties	displaced
drone	extremist	religiosity
social justice	surveillance	weapons of mass destruction
xenophobia		

SECTION 2

bailout	fiscal austerity	recession
stimulus	subprime mortgage	

SECTION 3

climate change	connectivity	conservation
cryptography	fracking	geothermal energy
green building	hacker	sustainable
troll		

SECTION 4

biotechnology	longevity

DEFINITION CHART
As they read the chapter, encourage students to complete a Definition Chart for Key Vocabulary terms. Instruct students to list the Key Vocabulary terms in the first column of the chart. They should add each term's definition in the center column as they encounter the term in the chapter and then restate the definition in their own words in the third column. Model an example on the board, using the graphic organizer shown.

Word	Definition	In My Own Words
stimulus	an incentive	a reason or motive to do something

September 11 and Aftermath

Most people never forget tragic events that took place in their lifetimes. Events such as the assassination of President John F. Kennedy or the explosion of the space shuttle *Challenger* were etched into the minds of people of the times. Relatives older than you likely remember exactly what they were doing when terrorists struck on September 11, 2001.

Firefighters walk among the smoldering rubble of the World Trade Center following the September 11 terrorist attack.

A TRAGIC DAY

As the 21st century dawned, dreams that peace could finally triumph over conflict quickly ended on September 11, 2001. Nineteen **extremists**, people with radical views, hijacked four airplanes in the United States. They then turned them into weapons of destruction.

The terrorists crashed two planes into the twin towers of the World Trade Center—the tallest buildings in New York City. A third plane hit the Pentagon just outside Washington, D.C., while the fourth crashed into a Pennsylvania field. In all, almost 3,000 civilians were killed. The terrorist group al Qaeda had planned the attack. As you have already learned, one of the leaders of al Qaeda was Osama bin Laden, a former U.S. ally in the fight against the Soviet Union in Afghanistan. Embittered by U.S. support for "moderate" Arab regimes and Israel and seeking revenge for the oppression they thought was faced by Muslims across the world, bin Laden and al Qaeda intended the attack as a warning to the United States.

A "WAR ON TERROR"

In response to the September 11 attacks, U.S. president George W. Bush declared a "war on terror." In October 2001, he sent U.S. forces to Afghanistan to defeat the Taliban, who had aided al Qaeda. An international coalition joined in the attack. Though battered, al Qaeda and Taliban fighters avoided capture. Since then, the Taliban has continued its fight to oust Afghanistan's internationally recognized government. Bin Laden continued to assail Western ideas, staging terrorist attacks in Yemen, Kenya, Saudi Arabia, Spain, and Britain. His reign of terror would end with his capture and killing by U.S. Navy Seals in 2011.

In 2003, President Bush carried his fight against terrorism to Saddam Hussein's Iraq, claiming that Hussein had stockpiled **weapons of mass destruction** (WMDs) that could destroy large areas. But many people believed that Iraq had no connection to al Qaeda or the events of September 11, and the WMDs were never found. With the British as their only ally, U.S. forces removed Saddam Hussein from power. The despotic leader was later tried and executed by the Iraqi people in 2006. The war in Iraq continued until 2011 as U.S. and British forces tried to quell insurgents in revolt against the new Iraqi republic. They faced Shiite militias funded by neighboring Iran as well as Sunni terrorists backed by al Qaeda. The United States had shifted the balance between Sunni and Shiite Muslims in the region by removing the Sunni leader of Iraq and allowing greater Shiite influence in the region, strengthening Iran. Meanwhile, in the north, Kurdish forces tried to establish their own autonomous area.

To combat terrorism, the United States and other nations strengthened airport security. The United States also created a new cabinet department called the Department of Homeland Security. In addition, nations refined their intelligence-gathering operations to prevent terrorist acts. In doing so, they made greater use of **surveillance**, methods for observing and tracking a person or group, a practice that many believe violates the right to privacy.

CRITICAL VIEWING Iraqis attempt to pull down a statue of Saddam Hussein in central Baghdad in April 2003. Why might citizens want to take down statues of their former leader?

THE RISE OF ISIS

By 2014, the U.S. withdrawal from Iraq left a power vacuum that the extremist group **Islamic State of Iraq and Syria (ISIS)**, also known as the Islamic State of Iraq and the Levant (ISIL), attempted to fill. It took advantage of instability in the region to try to create a new caliphate, a global center for Sunni Muslim power like the old Abbasid caliphate centered in Baghdad, which you learned about in an earlier chapter. ISIS fighters set to work gaining strongholds in parts of Iraq. The United States was reluctant to return troops to Iraq to halt their advance.

Terrorism continued to spread. Al Qaeda-backed gunmen killed 67 people in a siege on a Kenyan mall in 2013. Then in 2015, two gunmen shouting *"Allahu Akbar!"* (God is Great!) struck Paris. They opened fire in the offices of a French satire magazine, killing 12 people and wounding 11 others. The magazine had published cartoons of the Prophet Muhammad mocking Islamic terrorists. As of early 2019, ISIS had been driven out of many of its prior strongholds in Syria, but military intelligence indicates that many fighters simply fled to other parts of Syria, Turkey, and Iraq.

HISTORICAL THINKING

1. **READING CHECK** What action did the United States take to respond to the September 11 terrorist attack?

2. **FORM AND SUPPORT OPINIONS** Was George W. Bush's decision to invade Iraq in 2003 helpful or hurtful to the war on terrorism? Explain your response.

3. **DRAW CONCLUSIONS** What are the main stumbling blocks preventing the formation of a stable and democratic Iraqi government?

OBJECTIVE

Describe the September 11 attacks and U.S. action against terrorism that greatly affected Afghanistan and Iraq.

CRITICAL THINKING SKILLS FOR LESSON 1.1

- Form and Support Opinions
- Draw Conclusions
- Make Connections
- Identify
- Analyze Visuals

HISTORICAL THINKING FOR CHAPTER 30

What challenges does the world face in the 21st century?

The 21st century had just dawned when terrorism changed the course of world events. Lesson 1.1 discusses the September 11 attacks on U.S. targets, President Bush's war on terror, and the military action that had a severe impact on Iraq and Afghanistan.

Student eEdition online

Additional content for this lesson, including photographs, is available online.

BACKGROUND FOR THE TEACHER

September 11 Heroes More than 400 police officers and firefighters died at the World Trade Center. They had rushed into the burning towers to rescue the people inside. Workers within the towers did their best to help others escape. One worker was Rick Rescorla, security chief of banking company Morgan Stanley Dean Witter, located in the south tower. Rescorla was in the World Trade Center when it was bombed in 1993. The bomb did little damage, but Rescorla realized that the towers were vulnerable to an attack. He warned bank management and began holding escape drills by having company employees practice walking as quickly as possible down the long tower stairs. As a result, everyone knew what to do when the second plane struck the south tower. Rescorla escorted 21 floors of bank employees out of the tower, singing patriotic songs to keep them calm. He then went back in to search for stragglers and died when the tower collapsed. His remarkable foresight and discipline saved 2,700 lives that day.

INTRODUCE & ENGAGE

ACTIVATE PRIOR KNOWLEDGE

Have students recall and comment on what they learned about the attack on Pearl Harbor. *(Possible response: Japan suddenly attacked the U.S. fleet at Pearl Harbor, forcing the United States to declare war against Japan and join the Allies in World War II.)* Then tell students that they will learn about another sudden attack. This lesson discusses the September 11, 2001, terrorist attacks in New York City, President Bush's war on terror, and the military action that followed in Afghanistan and Iraq.

TEACH

GUIDED DISCUSSION

1. **Make Connections** What message might the attackers have intended to send by targeting major U.S. centers of business and government? *(Possible response: The attackers might have wanted to show that the United States, despite its economic and political strengths, was vulnerable to a small, dedicated force.)*

2. **Identify** What methods did nations develop to combat terrorism after the World Trade Center attack? *(The United States and other nations strengthened airport security and made greater use of surveillance methods to track individuals and groups. The United States created a Department of Homeland Security.)*

ANALYZE VISUALS

Have students view the photograph of firefighters in the rubble of the World Trade Center. **ASK:** Why might the physical details and firefighter images provoke strong feelings in viewers? *(Possible response: The rubble and smoking ruins emphasize the complete destruction and certain loss of life. Viewers might feel great sorrow by assuming the firefighters are conducting a fruitless search for survivors.)*

ACTIVE OPTIONS

On Your Feet: Inside-Outside Circle Arrange students into concentric circles facing each other. Tell students in the outside circle to pose questions about the aftermath of the September 11 attack, such as the following: How did the attack affect other nations? Ask students in the inner circle to answer their partner's questions. Then have students trade roles so that those in the inside circle ask questions and those in the outside circle answer them.

> **NG Learning Framework: Research the Iraq War**
> SKILLS Observation, Communication
> KNOWLEDGE Our Human Story

Have groups investigate the war with Iraq initiated in 2003. Suggest students find out about U.S.-Iraqi relations before 2003 and locate additional details about events in Iraq after 2003. Encourage students to explore the effect on Iraqi citizens of the overthrow of Saddam Hussein. Invite students to share with the class what they learned.

DIFFERENTIATE

STRIVING READERS

Sequence Events Tell students to note critical events and their relationships in a Sequence Chain. Pair students and ask them to tell their partner about each event, why it is important, and how it affected other events in the chain.

GIFTED & TALENTED

Perform a Speech Have students find online the text of President Bush's "September 22, 2001: Address on the U.S. Response to the Attacks of September 11." Instruct them to select a segment that they find particularly meaningful. Have students perform their selections for the class. Invite listeners to discuss how the speech suggests that President Bush viewed the attacks as a global concern.

See the Chapter Planner for more strategies for differentiation.

HISTORICAL THINKING

ANSWERS

1. George W. Bush declared a war on terror, first sending troops into Afghanistan and then into Iraq.

2. Answers will vary. Some students may say it was helpful because it overthrew a tyrant opposed to democracy and prevented him from developing weapons of mass destruction to aid terrorists. Others may say it was hurtful because it caused terrorist groups to gain more of a presence in Iraq and did little to stabilize the region.

3. Possible response: the emergence of ISIS; support by countries opposed to democracy and the United States; and internal conflicts among Sunnis; Shiites, and Kurds

CRITICAL VIEWING Possible response: to symbolize freedom from the former leader's repressive policies

A Kurdish refugee mother and her son walk beside their tent in a refugee camp on the Turkish-Syrian border in 2014. Many Syrian Kurds fled to Turkey to escape ISIS militants during the ongoing civil war in Syria.

Arab Spring, Syrian Crisis

In the 21st century, social media plays a major role in connecting people around the world. In 2011, it even contributed to a time of revolution across the Arab world.

AN ARAB SPRING

Citizen outrage at autocratic leadership was slow to come to Muslim countries in Asia and Africa. However, in 2009 Iranians took to the streets of Tehran to protest a presidential election they considered fixed. Then in December 2010, a frustrated produce seller in rural Tunisia publicly set himself on fire in protest of harsh police action against him. This individual action inspired citizens throughout Tunisia to gather in mass protest against its government. Less than a month later, before the end of January 2011, Tunisia's president of 23 years resigned.

The success in Tunisia ignited citizen revolutions known as the **Arab Spring** across North Africa and Southwest Asia. The protesters, many of them young, turned out to agitate for **social justice**, or equal rights for all under the law. In Egypt, throngs of protesters in Cairo's Tahrir Square rose up against President Hosni Mubarak, eventually gaining the support of the military. A revolt by the citizens of Libya against their totalitarian leader, Muammar Qaddafi, led to armed conflict. In both cases, the end result was the overthrow of an autocratic leader. Other countries such as Yemen, Bahrain, and Syria also saw protests against authoritarian rulers.

Internet-based social media was a driving force in the Arab Spring. Young Arab bloggers spread news of injustices committed by repressive governments. Organizers spread word on Twitter of when and where

Egyptians rally in Cairo's Tahrir Square in February 2011 in hopes of pressuring President Hosni Mubarak to step down.

protests would take place. Activists posted cell-phone images and videos of mass demonstrations and of violence against protesters on social media.

Yet revolutions are not completed overnight, as you have seen in earlier efforts, and the optimism of the Arab Spring turned to disappointment. In Egypt, military and political elites regained control of the nation. In Libya, citizens continue to suffer as rival militias battle it out. Syria also remains mired in conflict.

PROBLEMS IN SYRIA

Despite calls for his resignation by hundreds of thousands of protesters, Syrian president **Bashir Al-Assad** refused to step down. Rebel groups formed to

battle with Assad and his Syria Arab Army in a civil war. ISIS fighters also joined the fray, as did Kurdish fighters who hoped for independence. By 2018, more than 400,000 Syrians had died in the fighting. Assad has been accused of using chemical weapons against rebels and civilians. Other charges against him include the targeting of civilians, torture, and the turning away of humanitarian assistance. The civil war entered a new phase with the use of **drones**, pilotless aircraft, to bomb enemy sites.

Syria's conflict has created tensions around the world. Rebel forces have the support of the United States, Britain, and France. Turkey, Saudi Arabia, and Jordan also support the rebel cause. Russia and Iran, on the other hand, back Assad financially and militarily. Yet Russia has joined with Western nations to force ISIS from the region. The militant group Hezbollah has provided military help to the Syrian government.

The war has caused many Syrian civilians to be **displaced**, or forced from their homes. More than

six million refugees, mostly women and children, have moved elsewhere in Syria. Another nearly five million have sought refuge in other countries. Some of these now make their homes in refugee camps in countries such as Turkey and Jordan.

A stream of refugees from Syria and other troubled countries have sought **asylum**, or a place of safety, in Europe. While some countries have opened their borders to refugees, others have closed them. Hungary even erected a razor wire fence on much of its southern border to prevent refugees from crossing through the country on their way to Germany, which had a much more welcoming policy. In some countries, people fear that refugees may put a strain on their resources. **Xenophobia**, or fear of foreigners, also encourages anti-immigrant propaganda and support for far-right politicians and candidates who would deny human rights to refugees. Far-right politicians have won seats in the legislatures of such countries as Italy, Poland, Denmark, and Hungary.

HISTORICAL THINKING

1. **READING CHECK** How are the Arab Spring and the Syrian crisis related?

2. **EVALUATE** Explain how you would rate the success of the Arab Spring.

3. **MAKE PREDICTIONS** What do you think the situation will be like in Syria in five years? Explain your answer.

PLAN: 2-PAGE LESSON

OBJECTIVE

Describe the Arab Spring democratic reform movements and the few advances achieved.

CRITICAL THINKING SKILLS FOR LESSON 1.2

- Evaluate
- Make Predictions
- Identify Main Ideas and Details
- Form and Support Opinions
- Interpret Charts

HISTORICAL THINKING FOR CHAPTER 30

What challenges does the world face in the 21st century?

Less than a decade after terrorists targeted the United States, Arab citizens staged protests against autocratic rule. Lesson 1.2 discusses the Arab Spring revolutions across North Africa and Southwest Asia with a focus on the Syrian conflict and its global impact.

Student eEdition online

Additional content for this lesson, including a chart, is available online.

BACKGROUND FOR THE TEACHER

Anti-Immigration Policies in Europe A number of European countries have enacted legislation in response to the increased immigration of people fleeing violence in Southwest Asia and North Africa. Policies in Denmark are among the toughest in Europe thanks to the Danish People's Party, which exploited public concerns about the influence of Islam. Danish police can seize the property of migrants to pay for their upkeep. Italy's League party approved policies such as erecting fences and turning away rescue ships carrying immigrants to Italian ports. Parties in Germany, Spain, Finland, and Estonia won votes by advocating against immigration. The anti-immigrant prime minister of Hungary, Viktor Orbán, said, "We don't see these people as Muslim refugees. We see them as Muslim invaders." In 2016, the European Union agreed to pay Turkey to prevent migrants from entering Europe. Turkey eventually hosted some 3.6 million Syrian refugees and planned to create a "safe zone" for them. However, Turkey's president Erdogan claimed in 2019 that the European Union had not paid in full. He warned that he would "open the gates" to let a flood of migrants into Europe.

INTRODUCE & ENGAGE

CONNECT TO GLOBAL ISSUES

Have students think about the word *refugee*. Write the word *refugee* at the center of a Concept Cluster and ask volunteers to offer words and phrases that come to mind when they hear this word. Tell students that in this lesson they will learn about protests for democratic reform in Arab countries and the ensuing Syrian civil war that created millions of refugees.

TEACH

GUIDED DISCUSSION

1. **Identify Main Ideas and Details** Why did Syrian refugees find that some countries would not take them in? *(Some countries feared that refugees would strain their resources. The fear of foreigners in some places encouraged support for anti-immigration politicians.)*

2. **Form and Support Opinions** Do you think the Arab Spring could have happened without modern cell phone technology? Why or why not? *(Possible responses: Yes—even without modern cell phone technology, protests would be publicized in the news media and spread by word of mouth; no—the protesters were living under repressive governments that likely controlled the media and other avenues of communication.)*

INTERPRET CHARTS

Have students study the chart of the destination countries for displaced Syrians (available in the Student eEdition). **ASK:** Based on the chart, where did most displaced Syrians go? *(They remained within Syrian territory.)* Which European countries were willing to receive immigrants? *(Germany and Sweden)*

ACTIVE OPTIONS

On Your Feet: Three-Step Interview Direct pairs to interview each other about the Arab Spring. Ask the first student to ask the other this question: How would you describe the Arab Spring protests? Encourage the first student to ask follow-up questions based on the response. Then tell students to switch roles, with the second student asking this question: What problems has Syria created for its citizens and the world? Ask students to share information from the interviews with the class.

> **NG Learning Framework: Explore the Syrian Refugee Crisis**
> **ATTITUDE** Responsibility
> **SKILL** Communication

Have students conduct online research to learn more about the experiences of Syrian refugees who fled the civil war. Groups might focus on different topics, such as when and why particular individuals and families decided to flee, hardships of the journey, making a home in a foreign land, obstacles to immigration, or discrimination in their new surroundings. Invite students to discuss their findings as a class.

DIFFERENTIATE

ENGLISH LANGUAGE LEARNERS

Use Paired Reading Pair students at the **Intermediate** and **Advanced** levels to read passages from the text aloud.

1. Partner 1 reads a passage. Partner 2 retells the passage.
2. Partner 2 reads a different passage. Partner 1 retells it.
3. Pairs continue the process.

PRE-AP

Write an Analysis Have students conduct research for an essay about President Bashir Al-Assad and his role in Syria's ongoing crisis. Encourage them to elucidate Al-Assad's role in key events and include information about his personality. Invite volunteers to share their essays with the class.

See the Chapter Planner for more strategies for differentiation.

HISTORICAL THINKING

ANSWERS

1. Syrian citizen protests during the Arab Spring led to the use of force against them.

2. Answers will vary. Few students will argue its success. Some might argue for limited success because it met immediate goals to displace leaders and claim rights. Many will rate it unsuccessful, as few rights were gained, few countries are democratic, and conflicts have flourished.

3. Answers will vary. Some students might foresee continuing conflict because of Assad's intransigence, outside support of new rebel forces, and terrorist influences. Others might argue the war's end because of rising support for the rebel cause, increased military support from outside, Assad's death or exile, one side's increased use of advanced weapons, or world pressure for peace.

The Future of Southwest Asia

"The cradle of civilization," "the birthplace of three religions," "a trading crossroads" . . . Southwest Asia has long been a source of opportunity—and challenges. With ongoing conflicts and transitions throughout the region, the world watches to see what the future will bring.

DEFINING THE MIDDLE EAST

You have probably heard the region of Southwest Asia more commonly referred to as the "Middle East." However, people who live there do not call it that. That terminology is a Western construct that came about after World War I. Prior to the First World War, most of Southwest Asia was part of the Ottoman Empire. After the war and the decline of the empire, many people in that region hoped for their own independent states. Instead, as you may recall, Britain and France divided the area into states that they controlled, which they then called the Middle East. After the end of British and French colonialism, Westerners continued to use the term.

There is also no standard definition of the Middle East—though it is generally considered to consist of the countries of the Arabian Peninsula, Cyprus, Egypt, Iraq, Iran, Israel, Jordan, Lebanon, the Palestinian territories, Syria, and Turkey. At times, Afghanistan, Pakistan, and North African nations west of Egypt are also included.

As you've learned, this area has a rich history of trade and culture that continues to the present day. Two-thirds of the world's oil supply comes from this region, and nations that are the largest consumers of oil depend on that supply. The demand for oil brings wealth and power—as well as conflict—to the countries

The Middle East

that produce it. But oil is not the only source of discord. Claims over disputed territory, ethnic and religious differences, and competition over other resources continue to create conflict in the region.

PRESERVING THE PAST TO BUILD THE FUTURE

According to the United Nations, the preservation of cultural heritage and identity is key to promoting stability in the Middle East. As you have seen in some of the Preserving Cultural Heritage lessons in this text,

violent extremists often target sites of cultural importance along with human lives to destroy anything that doesn't fit within their system of beliefs. In addition to destruction by terrorism or extremism, cultural heritage sites are also falling victim to companies that want to extract valuable resources from their locations.

What does the future hold for this region? While no one can know for sure, many people are striving for peace and stability and working to preserve its culture for future generations. National Geographic is working with some of those people— educators, paleoanthropologists, archaeologists, peace activists— toward a brighter future.

BUILDING BRIDGES

As the Israeli-Palestinian conflict continues, we often hear stories of destruction and loss. However, there are also positive tales. And National Geographic Explorer Aziz Abu Sarah is helping people tell them. A cultural educator and peace activist, Abu Sarah works to help people find common ground through personal stories and cross-cultural learning in an attempt to bring peace to the region.

As a Palestinian and a native of Jerusalem, Abu Sarah has experienced firsthand the devastating damage from disputes in the region. When he was a young boy, his older brother, Tayseer, was arrested for suspicion of throwing stones. While in custody, Tayseer was beaten and later died from his injuries. Angered by Tayseer's death, Abu Sarah wanted revenge and was motivated to strike back. He became politically active, and by age 16 he was leading and organizing protests and writing political articles.

After high school, he realized that to live in Jerusalem he needed to learn Hebrew, something he had refused to do growing up. He went to an Israeli school to study the language. For the first time, he met Israelis who were not soldiers. As the only Palestinian in the class,

NATIONAL GEOGRAPHIC EXPLORER AZIZ ABU SARAH

Connecting Cultures

Palestinian Aziz Abu Sarah spent several years in the resistance movement against Israel. But he is now committed to fostering mutual understanding and improving relationships between people from different backgrounds. "I decided to dedicate my life to bringing down the walls that separate people," explains Abu Sarah.

he kept to himself at first but soon started talking to the other students. And at this point, things changed for Abu Sarah.

Through his conversations with Jewish classmates, Abu Sarah became aware of things that they had in common, such as a love of country music. He realized that what separates people isn't politics or the land but an emotional wall—a wall built of anger, fear, and ignorance. As he got to know his fellow students, those fearful preconceptions disappeared. "When that wall goes away, it's amazing how you can come together," says Abu Sarah.

PLAN: 6-PAGE LESSON

OBJECTIVE

Identify efforts by National Geographic Explorers to bring peace and stability to Southwest Asia.

CRITICAL THINKING SKILLS FOR LESSON 1.3

- Evaluate
- Form and Support Opinions
- Explain
- Make Connections
- Compare and Contrast
- Make Inferences
- Identify Problems and Solutions
- Interpret Maps
- Analyze Visuals

HISTORICAL THINKING FOR CHAPTER 30

What challenges does the world face in the 21st century?

Conflict and instability in Southwest Asia have continued into the 21st century. Lesson 1.3 discusses the efforts of several National Geographic Explorers to bring peace to the region by focusing on cultural preservation.

BACKGROUND FOR THE TEACHER

Aziz Abu Sarah In a TED Radio Hour interview, Abu Sarah recalled his hatred of Israelis. His mother gave him an onion to carry to school every morning. She said that cutting an onion, putting it close to his nose, and inhaling it would keep him from passing out if he was shot with tear gas. Later, after his positive experiences attending a Hebrew class, Abu Sarah explored the horrors endured by Jews by visiting Yad Vashem, Israel's Holocaust memorial museum. He had the idea that tourism could resolve conflict. Mejdi Tours was founded to inspire visitors to have compassion for a place. Abu Sarah has received awards for his work, among them the European Parliament's Silver Rose Award, the Eisenhower Medallion, and the Goldberg IIE Prize for Peace in the Middle East. He won the Faith Travel Association's Inspire Award for greatly advancing the faith-based travel market. Mejdi is partnered with National Geographic to present the Holy Land in a way that is respectful to Israelis and Palestinians, as well as Jews, Muslims, and Christians.

History Notebook

Encourage students to complete the "Future of Southwest Asia" page for Chapter 30 in their History Notebooks as they read.

INTRODUCE & ENGAGE

DISCUSS CULTURAL PRESERVATION

Direct students to think about the value of museum collections or historic sites. Invite volunteers to name the museums or historic sites they know about or have visited. **ASK:** Why would preservation of the culture of a particular country be of value for present or future generations? *(Possible responses: Cultural preservation might encourage pride in the art or other achievements of the past. The visual record might help prevent future generations from repeating the wrongs of the past.)* Tell students that in this lesson they will learn how several National Geographic Explorers are using cultural preservation to transform Southwest Asian conflict zones. Their work conforms to the perspective of the United Nations that the preservation of cultural heritage and identity can bring stability.

TEACH

GUIDED DISCUSSION

1. **Explain** What factors create conflict in Southwest Asia? *(The demand for oil brings wealth, power, and conflict. The countries also dispute territory, compete over other resources, and clash over ethnic and religious differences.)*

2. **Explain** How does Aziz Abu Sarah define the wall that separates people, and what could eliminate it? *(Abu Sarah believes people are separated by an emotional wall of anger, fear, and ignorance. He creates opportunities for dialogue among people on conflicting sides as an aid to peace. His Mejdi Tours company brings tourists to Jerusalem with two guides, one Jewish and one Palestinian, who provide different perspectives.)*

INTERPRET MAPS

Direct students to locate the Palestinian territories on the map of the Middle East. Explain that the Palestinian territories are generally considered as consisting of the West Bank, which includes East Jerusalem, and the Gaza Strip. Then have students review the text about Aziz Abu Sarah, view his photograph, and read the caption. **ASK:** How does the map aid understanding of the Israeli-Palestinian conflict and Abu Sarah's mission? *(Answers will vary. Possible response: The map shows that the Palestinians occupy territories within or largely surrounded by Israel. The Palestinians and Israelis have many opportunities to interact because they live in very close proximity. Mutual respect and understanding of each other's differences could further peace.)*

DIFFERENTIATE

INCLUSION

Describe Lesson Visuals Pair students who are visually impaired or have special needs with students who do not. Ask the latter to describe the visuals in the lesson and read the captions. Have them work with their partner to link the visuals with ideas in the related lesson text. Ask pairs to focus special attention on the map. Encourage proficient students to point out countries on the map and point out the specific countries of individuals discussed in the lesson. Invite proficient students to answer any questions their partner might have.

See the Chapter Planner for more strategies for differentiation.

From that point, he decided to take a different form of action. Instead of protesting, Abu Sarah committed himself to creating cracks in the metaphorical walls that divide Israelis and Palestinians. Today, he creates opportunities for dialogue among people on opposite sides of the conflict through education, tours, and personal narratives. He started a company called Mejdi Tours to foster peace by bringing tourists to Jerusalem with two guides—one Jewish and one Palestinian—so that people can learn about the history and narrative of the city from different perspectives.

And Abu Sarah isn't stopping with the Israelis and Palestinians; he has added tours to Iran, Turkey, and other regions with cultural and political struggles. His goal is international conflict resolution.

BRINGING LIGHT INTO THE DARK
Science and comedy may not seem like they go together. But to paleoanthropologist and archaeologist—and stand-up comic—Ella Al-Shamahi, comedy is a great tool for presenting scientific research. Al-Shamahi specializes in Neanderthals, studying their evolution and migration. She's searching for the origins of humanity. (You read that a Neanderthal is a member of an extinct species of early humans.)

Al-Shamahi is passionate about Neanderthals, and it's her mission to change our impressions of them. As the host and producer of the BBC/PBS two-part documentary, *Neanderthals: Meet Your Ancestors*, she worked with actor Andy Serkis to shed light on just what kind of people these early humans were. Even though the title of the series names Neanderthals as our "ancestors," modern-day people are not directly descended from this species. But recall that some individuals who have some European or Asian ancestry may have inherited Neanderthal DNA.

Al-Shamahi's work has taken her into conflict zones in Yemen and Iraq, underexplored areas that have much to offer in terms of early human history and culture.

In Yemen, her search for fossils is to test a theory that early humans may have migrated out of Africa via land bridges between East Africa and Yemen. Yemen has been in a state of civil war since 2015, so Al-Shamahi had to cut back her fieldwork there. The fighting has destroyed many cultural sites, including UNESCO World Heritage Sites. Today, along with digging for fossils, Al-Shamahi is trying to bring awareness to the destruction of Yemeni heritage and is working to preserve these historic sites.

Working in unstable places can take its toll, however, so Al-Shamahi uses comedy to brighten dark situations. She notes, "I'm the stereotype of the comic who does comedy because she needs to laugh." She also finds that comedy provides a way to engage people in science. When she's not excavating ancient remains or safeguarding cultural treasures, she's performing her comedy in London and internationally.

NATIONAL GEOGRAPHIC EXPLORER **ELLA AL-SHAMAHI**

Funny Bones
Ella Al-Shamahi contemplates a cast of a Neanderthal skull in her lab at the Anthropology Department of University College London. She uses humor to relieve stress, as her work often takes her to dangerous areas torn by strife. Al-Shamahi believes that these places "deserve narratives of hope, and science and exploration can be a part of that."

As the war continues in Yemen, the country's future seems dim. But Al-Shamahi believes preservation of Yemen's historic sites provides some hope. She says that Yemenis are proud of their heritage and know the importance of protecting those cultural places. "When you see devastation to our sites, you see Yemenis kick up a fuss about it." By giving its people the tools and solutions to preserve their culture, Yemen can gain strength.

SAVING OUR HERITAGE
As you have already learned, war causes destruction and robs a country of its heritage. Since the war began in Syria in 2011, countless historic sites and treasures have been destroyed. About 90 percent of Syria's cultural sites are located in areas of fighting and civil unrest. Syrian-born archaeologist Salam Al Kuntar has made it her mission to preserve not only the past but also the future of her war-torn homeland's heritage.

Before the war, Al Kuntar lived in Damascus and worked as the codirector of excavations at the Chalcolithic/Bronze Age site of Hamoukar. But the constant threat of bombings during the war meant she would not be safe doing her work in that area. So Al Kuntar accepted a position as a research scholar at the Penn Museum of the University of Pennsylvania.

Her work with Syria didn't end after she arrived in the United States. In response to the destruction of archaeological sites in her homeland, she helped design and implement a training program for the emergency preservation of Syrian artifacts. Collaborating with the Smithsonian Institution and a network of Syrian scholars in Europe along with a group of heritage professionals inside Syria, she and her colleagues have been able to provide much-needed emergency preservation work and conservation materials and training to salvage damaged collections and sites during the conflict.

Today, Al Kuntar is an assistant professor of archaeology at Rutgers University in New Jersey and a cofounder and board member of Syrians for Heritage

NATIONAL GEOGRAPHIC EXPLORER **SALAM AL KUNTAR**

Protecting Traditions
Salam Al Kuntar wants to make sure that Syrian customs and items will survive a brutal war that has been raging in the country since 2011. The unrest caused her to move to the United States, where she continues to advocate for the preservation of valuable sites and artifacts. "For me," Al Kuntar says, "keeping that connection alive and building on it to preserve the spirit of the people is important."

(SIMAT), an organization striving to preserve Syrian heritage for all Syrians and for the rest of the world.

PHOTOGRAPHING SHARBAT GULA
For more than 30 years, National Geographic photographer Steve McCurry has been capturing the spirit of human struggle and joy all over the world with his compelling color photography. In 1984, he documented the plight of Afghan refugees who fled Afghanistan during the Soviet invasion. His work took him to a refugee tent camp in Pakistan, where he took pictures of young students in the school tent. The last photo he took was of a 12-year-old girl with piercing sea green eyes. This single haunting look came to represent the story of millions of refugees—and the tragedy of war.

The iconic photograph of the Afghan girl, as the photo came to be known, ran on the June 1985 cover of *National Geographic* magazine and became one of the

BACKGROUND FOR THE TEACHER
Cultural Heritage Preservation Ella Al-Shamahi believes that Yemen is virtually untouched territory, scientifically speaking. She traveled to the island of Socotra in 2018, three years after a Saudi-led coalition conducted airstrikes to help Yemen fight Houthi rebels in the area. Socotra contains many species that exist nowhere else, and Al-Shamahi wanted to verify that they remained safe. Socotra is among several of Yemen's UNESCO World Heritage Sites. Others include Sanaa, the 2,500-year-old capital city of Yemen; the walled city of Shibam, one of the oldest examples of urban planning; and Zabid, a former capital known for its Islamic university. Armed conflict in the region has caused severe damage to these Yemeni sites. Airstrikes also damaged Yemen's Great Dam of Marib, considered a marvel of technical engineering and an important cultural heritage site for the entire Arabian Peninsula.

Threatened World Heritage Sites in Syria include the ancient city of Aleppo, located at the crossroads of several trade routes; Bosra, a stopover on the ancient caravan route to Mecca; and Damascus, inhabited as early as 8000 to 10,000 B.C.E. Conflict between rebels and the Syrian army destroyed the ancient Umayyad Mosque in 2013. The World Monuments Fund points out that such historic sites are often used as military bases by conflicting forces. Looters also are a significant threat. UNESCO has repeatedly condemned the destruction and partnered with agencies to monitor damage to heritage sites via satellite imagery. The UNESCO Assistant Director of Culture emphasizes that respect for cultural diversity and a sense of community ownership aids recovery from the trauma of war. Salam Al Kuntar says that if a country loses its sense of place, people might as well be anywhere.

TEACH

GUIDED DISCUSSION

3. **Make Connections** How does Ella Al-Shamahi tie her study of Neanderthals to Yemen? *(Al-Shamahi studies Neanderthals to understand the origins of humanity and the theory that early humans might have used land bridges to migrate between East Africa and Yemen. If proved, this would become a part of Yemen's heritage.)*

4. **Compare and Contrast** How are Ella Al-Shamahi and Salam Al Kuntar similar and different in the pursuit of their goals and approach to science? *(Both actively pursue a common goal of preserving the historic sites and cultural treasures of their respective war-torn countries. Al-Shamahi differs by her background in research about Neanderthals and her belief that comedy can engage people in science. Al Kuntar is a research scholar who designed and implemented a training program for the preservation of Syrian artifacts. She collaborates with scholars inside and outside Syria to provide preservation work, conservation materials, and training to salvage damaged collections and sites.)*

ANALYZE VISUALS

Direct students to view the photographs of Ella Al-Shamahi and Salam Al Kuntar and read the captions. **ASK:** How would you interpret and compare the quotations within each caption? *(Possible response: Al-Shahami believes that people in strife-torn areas deserve hope, which she feels science and exploration can help provide; Al Kuntar connects sites and artifacts with a people's spirit, and she believes it is important to keep that connection alive and build on it.)*

DIFFERENTIATE

PRE-AP

Evaluate and Discuss Share the Background for the Teacher information about Mes Aynak with students. Have students use that information and the lesson text about Mes Aynak as a starting point to research this question: Is cultural preservation more valuable to a struggling nation than the need for economic development? Ask students to conduct online research to locate details that will help them form an opinion on the question. Then invite students to present and support their opinions in a panel discussion. Encourage other class members to ask questions or comment.

See the Chapter Planner for more strategies for differentiation.

Solving A Mystery

The identity of the refugee in Steve McCurry's famous image was unknown for nearly two decades. McCurry found her in 2002 and was able to add a name to the face: Sharbat Gula. "She's as striking as the young girl I photographed 17 years ago," says McCurry.

most widely recognized photographs in the world. And although the photograph was well known, the young girl's name was not.

In 2002, after 17 years, National Geographic and McCurry returned to the same refugee camp in Pakistan to search for her. A local man recognized her photograph, and McCurry tracked her down in a small village in the mountains of the Afghanistan-Pakistan border. McCurry instantly knew the woman he met was her—she had the same eyes. And at long last, McCurry learned her name: Sharbat Gula.

For more than 30 years, Gula lived in Pakistan, surviving the wars and refugee camps. But in 2016, as an unregistered refugee, she was forced to return to Afghanistan. The Afghan government welcomed her

back with a deed to her own home. Gula is one of the small percentage of women homeowners in the country. As someone recognized around the world, she has become a symbol again for the hundreds of thousands of refugees returning to Afghanistan.

RESCUING MES AYNAK

Conflict and war aren't the only threats to preserving Southwest Asia's cultural heritage. Mes Aynak, a 5,000-year-old Buddhist city in Afghanistan, is home to one of the most important archaeological finds in the region. It's also home to a large supply of copper ore that promises to bring a lot of business to a country greatly in need of an economic boost.

In 2007, the Afghan government granted China permission to extract copper from the site on a 30-

year lease. China bid three billion dollars and promised to provide infrastructure for the undeveloped region. Afghanistan would not only have much-needed revenue but better roads, railways, and electric grids.

While there were several challenges to getting the copper, the main issue was the preservation of many treasures and artifacts found at Mes Aynak. In a nation torn apart by successive wars, preserving any remnants of the rich history there is critical. Cultural heritage advocates lobbied to excavate the site's treasures and record them before any mining began—which was no easy task.

With time running out before the mining project began, archaeologists and conservationists worked to collect the artifacts before they disappeared. They also faced the risk of land mines left by the Soviets in the 1980s, explosive devices left by al Qaeda, and rocket attacks by the Taliban in 2012 and 2013.

Then the archaeologists got a lucky break. Scheduled to start in 2012, the mining project was suspended, due to logistical challenges. A lack of water and the lack of a railroad to transport the copper out of the region created major obstacles.

The delay wasn't good for business, but it gave the archaeologists more time to excavate. Today, decisions are still being made as to whether to allow the copper extraction to continue, which leaves the fate of Mes Aynak undetermined.

An Afghan worker walks through an ancient monastery at the Mes Aynak site in Afghanistan in this 2010 photo.

HISTORICAL THINKING

1. **READING CHECK** What is the current state of Southwest Asia?

2. **EVALUATE** What are the greatest challenges facing the region?

3. **FORM AND SUPPORT OPINIONS** What do you think are the best ways to preserve a culture and build for its future? Explain your response.

4. **EXPLAIN** Which of the explorers featured in the lesson do you find most interesting? Why?

BACKGROUND FOR THE TEACHER

Mes Aynak A team of Afghan and international archaeologists began work at Mes Aynak in 2009. The team has unearthed entire Buddhist monastery complexes along with thousands of statues, coins, wall paintings, manuscripts, and stupas—mound-shaped monuments containing sacred relics. One manuscript mentions troops led by Alexander the Great, who marched through Afghanistan in 330 B.C.E. The copper ore lies directly below the ruins and extends into the Baba Wali mountain. Deposits of blue, purple, and green slag—the solidified residue from smelting—spill down the mountain slopes. These are evidence that the ancient monks made their wealth from copper and produced it on an almost industrial scale. The name *Mes Aynak* means "little copper well" in Dari, an Afghan dialect of Persian. Preservationists believe that Mes Aynak is a key to information about the ancient Buddhist economic system. They claim that the artwork and manuscripts could be crucial to understanding Mes Aynak's historical role in trade along the Silk Roads. They argue also that Mes Aynak belongs to the world and that Afghan citizens will gain nothing from Chinese mining. Mes Aynak has potential as a tourist attraction that would enrich Afghanistan, a very poor country. Advocates of the opposite view include the World Bank, which supports copper mining as a source of wealth and recovery for Afghanistan. However, mining development must surmount the obstacles of Afghanistan's lack of infrastructure, political corruption, and dangers from the Taliban or terrorists. Al Qaeda used Mes Aynak as a training camp in the 1990s. Four of the hijackers who took part in the 2001 attacks on New York City and Washington, D.C., trained there.

TEACH

GUIDED DISCUSSION

5. **Make Inferences** Based on the information about Sharbat Gula, how typical is she of returning Afghan refugees? *(Possible response: The fact that she is one of a small percentage of women homeowners indicates that her experience is not typical of returning Afghan refugees.)*

6. **Identify Problems and Solutions** What problems did China promise to solve for the undeveloped Mes Aynak region, and how would these problems be resolved? *(The region needs infrastructure in the form of railways, improved roads, and electric grids. China promised to provide this infrastructure in return for the permission to extract copper.)*

ANALYZE VISUALS

Direct students to view the photograph of Steve McCurry and his photos of Sharbat Gula. Have students read the caption. **ASK:** How would you describe the expression of Sharbat Gula in each photo? *(Possible response: As a child, her eyes show fear. As an adult, she seems fearless and determined.)* Why might Steve McCurry be considered a National Geographic Explorer as well as a National Geographic Photographer? *(Answers will vary. Possible response: He investigates important issues and brings them to the attention of the public as an explorer does, except that he uses a camera to document situations and raise awareness.)*

ACTIVE OPTIONS

On Your Feet: Roundtable Organize students in small groups. Tell students to imagine that they are journalists working on a feature article about a Southwest Asian conflict zone and the efforts to bring peace and stability to that zone. The article will appear in a weekly current affairs magazine. Have students assume that their goal is to sell a lot of magazines. Instruct groups to begin the article with an attention-grabbing headline. Ask one student in each group to write the first sentence of the article. Other students can then take turns adding sentences. Groups should continue adding sentences until they feel the article is thorough. Encourage students to add notes advising the magazine editor about illustrations that should accompany the article. Finally, invite groups to share their articles.

> **NG Learning Framework: Explore the Israeli-Palestinian Conflict**
> **ATTITUDE** Responsibility
> **SKILLS** Observation, Communication

Have small groups of students conduct research about the Israeli-Palestinian conflict. Direct them to include research on the history of Israeli-Palestinian relations, but tell them to focus mainly on the conflict in its recent and current stages. Encourage students to find news stories, opinion pieces, or articles that describe the issues involved and that depict the conflict from more than one perspective. Ask students to keep a record of the sources they consult. Finally, invite volunteers from each group to share their findings and sources with the class.

HISTORICAL THINKING

ANSWERS

1. Ongoing conflicts threaten the stability of the region as well as historic sites.

2. Answers will vary. Some students might say that establishing and maintaining peace is the greatest challenge. Others might say that preserving the culture and rebuilding cities will be the greatest challenge.

3. Answers will vary. Some students might say that protecting historic sites and treasures is the most important way to preserve the culture and build for the future by encouraging tourism to help the region's economy. Others might say that building industries and cultivating natural resources for export, such as Mes Aynak copper, can best preserve the culture and build for the future because the region will have money to support its people and infrastructure.

4. Students' responses will vary. Students should choose one of the explorers mentioned in the lesson and provide evidence to support their choice.

Breakdowns and Breakthroughs

Up to now, you've read about the distant and recent past. But events of today become history tomorrow. This lesson presents some of the history that has taken place during your lifetime.

Unmarked soldiers in full body armor and armed with assault rifles march away from a besieged Ukrainian military base in Crimea. The Russian government claimed the soldiers were members of locally organized self-defense groups protecting the residents of Crimea instead of Russian forces deployed to occupy the region.

ENDURING CONFLICTS AND RESOLUTION

Conflicts that stem from events long ago still present challenges in different parts of the world, but there has also been progress toward peace. For much of the 20th century, Ukraine was a part of the U.S.S.R. It gained independence as a democratic republic following the breakup of the Soviet Union. In 2013, as the fledgling democracy prepared to form an association with the European Union, the Russian-speaking minority backed a president whose plan was to align the country with Russia instead. Pro-democracy protesters thronged the Ukrainian capital of Kiev, eventually winning the corrupt president's ouster. Almost immediately, the eastern Ukrainian province of Crimea announced its secession, and Russia quickly annexed it. Fighting intensified between pro-Russian separatists and Ukrainian soldiers. A 2015 ceasefire did little to end the conflict. To date, the death toll has exceeded 10,000 people, many of whom were civilians not involved in the war. Then, in May 2019, the Ukrainians surprised the world by electing Volodymyr Zelensky president. Zelensky, a young comedian of Jewish heritage, had no ties to the old political system. By electing an outsider, the Ukrainians were gambling on a fresh start.

With the exception of the conflict between Russia and Ukraine, 21st-century foreign relations demonstrate that the Cold War is over for many countries. A number of former Soviet-satellite nations are members of the European Union, including Bulgaria, Estonia, Hungary, Lithuania, and Poland. Cuba began to reestablish economic ties with the United States in 2014. Vietnam, which remains communist, is on good diplomatic terms with Western countries. North Korea, however, is not part of this trend. For much of his time in office, North Korean leader **Kim Jong-un** has been belligerent toward democratic nations, and he has done little to ensure human rights or remove nuclear threats. In 2018, Kim Jong-un met with U.S. president Donald Trump and South Korean president Moon Jae-in, but future plans for closer ties seem uncertain.

Elsewhere in Asia, the Indian subcontinent's disputed region of Kashmir reflects the lasting effects of colonialism. As you have read, the question of who should control this far-northern region arose in 1947 when Britain partitioned its colony between India and Pakistan. After fighting for control of Kashmir, the two countries agreed to divide it. Since then, simmering tensions have periodically led to violence. Both nations have nuclear capabilities, so future war could be catastrophic. China's claim to parts of northern Kashmir also puts the region in peril. Given a choice, most Kashmir residents would prefer independence. However, in 2019, the Indian government revoked the region's decades-long special status as an autonomous region, creating a new conflict with Pakistan.

Continuing ethnic conflicts on the African continent also stem from European colonialism. You've already learned about the end of apartheid in South Africa and the Rwandan genocide at the end of the 20th century. In Sudan, civil war between the government and southern rebels carried over into the 21st century until a 2005 peace agreement led to the independence of South Sudan in 2011. But competition for oil meant that border skirmishes continued. Meanwhile, the world was shocked by another genocide, this time in Sudan's western region of **Darfur**. Sudan's longtime president, **Omar al-Bashir**, was indicted by the International Criminal Court for crimes against humanity, but he remained in power until ousted by a popular uprising in 2019. Elsewhere in Africa, Nigeria's Islamist militant group Boko Haram has ruthlessly fought for control of much of the countryside. Civil wars rage in Libya, Somalia, and the Central African Republic, and the International Criminal Court has launched an investigation into crimes against humanity in Burundi.

CHALLENGES TO DEMOCRACY

In the 20th century, millions of people worldwide yearned for democracy, but far fewer seem to be working toward this goal in the 21st century. This reality has caused the democratic system of government to become fragile. Often, citizens are unwilling or unable to prevent autocrats from usurping their rights. In Thailand, General Prayuth Chan-ocha and his military junta keep tight control of the government but promise a return to democracy. In Venezuela, the autocratic government of Nicolas Maduro has done little to solve such problems as crime, poverty, and a lack of food and electricity, and now there is a growing effort by opposition leaders to unseat him. This is unlikely as long as Maduro retains the support of the military. Myanmar's military government seemed to be improving its record on human rights, but in 2017 it began committing atrocities against a minority ethnic group, the Rohingya Muslims.

While Pakistan officially became an Islamic republic in 1956, it has alternated between civilian and military rule over the years. In 2001, ruling Pakistani general Pervez Musharraf claimed the presidency of his country. Shortly afterwards, Pakistan was drawn into the "War on Terror" launched by President George W. Bush in response to the 9/11 attacks. Hoping to maintain ties to the United States, Pakistan pledged to hunt out members of the Taliban and al Qaeda. However, Islamist sentiment remained strong in northwestern Pakistan near Afghanistan. The 2007 assassination of former prime minister Benazir Bhutto showed the extent of contention in Pakistani politics. Today, the country faces poverty, an unstable economy, internal ethnic conflicts, political corruption, terrorist attacks, and a tense political situation. Yet history was made in Pakistan in 2018 when a Hindu candidate defeated Muslim candidates for a seat in the previously all-Muslim legislature.

Turkey had long been a secular representative democracy, but the military frequently staged coups to gain control of government. In 2003, **Recep Tayyip Erdogan** (reh-JEHP ty-YEHP UR-doh-wahn) won election as Turkey's prime minister. As prime minister, he supported greater integration of Islam into government at the cost of secularism. Over time, Erdogan became more authoritarian in his rule, crushing opposition and limiting human rights. However, in 2010, he supported the passage of 26 constitutional amendments favoring democracy in a successful attempt to gain Turkey's entry into the European Union. Term limits on the office of prime minister led Erdogan to become Turkey's president, a less important office, in 2014. Two years later, he conducted a major purge of government following an unsuccessful coup attempt. In 2018, constitutional amendments strengthened the role of president.

Vladimir Putin has dominated Russia's politics for the entire 21st century, serving as president most of that time. Putin supported the U.S. "War on Terror" but otherwise has had a strained relationship with the United States and other democratic nations. In 2013, Putin angered the United States by providing refuge to classified document leaker Edward Snowden. To the dismay of many, he also initiated harsh laws against gays and lesbians and ordered cruel treatment of dissidents. Assistance to Iran, the Syrian government, and Crimean separatists have also placed Russia under fire. A U.S. investigation took place to determine whether Putin and other Russians interfered in the 2016 U.S. presidential elections. In 2018, Russian voters elected him to a fourth term as president, and in early 2020 he backed a proposed constitutional amendment that would allow him to run for two additional terms.

One beacon of democracy is Ethiopia, where the early 2000s saw rapid economic growth under an authoritarian government. Hopes for a more liberal political direction were raised in 2018 when a new prime minister, Abiy Ahmed, released imprisoned journalists, formed a government with more balanced regional representation, appointed women to more than half of

---

PLAN: 4-PAGE LESSON

OBJECTIVE

Explain the influence of conflicts, authoritarian leaders, and opposing viewpoints on 21st-century events.

CRITICAL THINKING SKILLS FOR LESSON 1.4

- Draw Conclusions
- Make Predictions
- Analyze Cause and Effect
- Identify
- Describe
- Analyze Visuals

HISTORICAL THINKING FOR CHAPTER 30

What challenges does the world face in the 21st century?

Many challenges faced by the world today developed in the previous century. Lesson 1.4 discusses ongoing conflicts in Ukraine, Asia, and Africa; support for populism and authoritarian leaders; the effects of globalization; and specific challenges to democracy and nation-states.

BACKGROUND FOR THE TEACHER

The Rohingya The United Nations calls the situation of hundreds of thousands of Rohingya the world's fastest growing refugee crisis. The vast majority of Myanmar's Rohingya are Muslim, whereas Mynamar—formerly British-controlled Burma—is a predominantly Buddhist country. The Rohingya have been denied citizenship although they claim to be descendants of people who resided in Myanmar for centuries. The situation worsened in August 2017 after a faction of Rohingya militants attacked police posts. Government troops and Buddhist mobs retaliated by burning Rohingya villages and killing civilians. It is estimated that some 6,700, including children, died within a month and close to 290 villages were partly or entirely burned in Myanmar's Rakhine state. Most refugees have fled to Bangladesh, where they arrive traumatized. They are in dire need of water, food, adequate shelter, and healthcare. The United Nations and World Bank have urged the international community to help. Countries have responded with aid for refugees but have been hesitant to discuss placing sanctions on Myanmar.

Student eEdition online

Additional content for this lesson, including image galleries, is available online.

INTRODUCE & ENGAGE

BRAINSTORM IDEAS

Ask students to discuss whether it is better for a nation to isolate itself from world problems or to work with other nations to find solutions. Have a volunteer record ideas on the board. Encourage students to reach a class consensus. Then tell them that in this lesson they will learn about ongoing conflicts, the effects of globalization that include isolationist ideas, and challenges to democracy and nation-states worldwide.

TEACH

GUIDED DISCUSSION

1. **Draw Conclusions** Why might the election of Volodymyr Zelensky in 2019 have represented the hope of ending conflict in Ukraine? *(Zelensky had no ties to the old political system. This suggested that he could end the conflict with Russia in eastern Ukraine because he was not bound to respect entrenched political forces on either side.)*

2. **Analyze Cause and Effect** What was the initial cause of ethnic conflicts and civil wars in many African countries, and how have Ethiopia and Eritrea addressed the problem? *(The initial cause of African ethnic conflicts was European colonialism. Ethiopia and Eritrea agreed in 2018 to work toward peace.)*

ANALYZE VISUALS

Have students view the image galleries titled "Enduring Conflicts in the 21st Century" and "Challenges to Democracy in the 21st Century" (available in the Student eEdition). Tell students to read the captions. Then direct attention specifically to the photographs with captions headed "Darfur" and "Myanmar." **ASK:** What can you infer from these photographs and captions about the similarity of responses to conflicts and nondemocratic governments? Explain your answer. *(Answers will vary. Possible response: The responses in common are the displacement of some groups of people who become refugees. People flee to escape dangerous conflicts and to be free from governments that repress or discriminate against them.)*

DIFFERENTIATE

INCLUSION

Work in Pairs Pair students with disabilities with students who can review the image galleries (available in the Student eEdition) with them. Have the partner without disabilities describe the photographs and read the captions. Encourage the pairs to discuss how the information is related to the lesson texts. Invite pairs to work together to answer any questions.

PRE-AP

Evaluate Foreign Policy Invite students to become journalists for a current affairs magazine. Direct them to conduct online research to locate information about the meetings between U.S. president Trump and Kim Jong-un of North Korea. Tell students to focus their research on details and analyses of U.S. foreign policy toward North Korea and President Trump's goals for a relationship with Kim Jong-un. Ask students to use factual information in their articles to assess the prospects for achieving a meaningful relationship with North Korea. Encourage inclusion of comments about the leadership qualities of Kim Jong-un. Have students post their articles for the class to review.

See the Chapter Planner for more strategies for differentiation.

Rohingya refugees arrive on homemade rafts at an island off the coast of Bangladesh. Nearly 700,000 refugees have fled from Myanmar to neighboring Bangladesh since August 2017.

his cabinet positions, and extended a peace initiative to the country's long-time rival, neighboring Eritrea. Progress for Ethiopia, a U.S. ally with the largest military in Africa, will be a positive sign for the entire region.

You may wonder why democracy has become so fragile. Some experts point to 2008's Great Recession as a turning point for losing faith in democracy. (You will learn more about the causes and effects of this recession in the next lesson.) Others say that people began to believe that economic success is not contingent on democracy, citing China as proof.

RESPONSES TO GLOBALIZATION

As you have already learned, nation-states were created to unite people who share a language, culture, and religion. A unified government gave citizens a sense of identity and a source for solving conflicts and better meeting economic needs. Today, however, globalization has created challenges for nation-states. Issues such as protecting the environment or avoiding nuclear war cannot be solved by any one country alone. So organizations such as the United Nations have emerged, but they are not governments. This means there is no clear decision-maker for solving international problems. Nation-states are also challenged by non-state actors such as multinational corporations, offshore banks, and NGOs usually working on the ground to help poor communities. These private entities may have more influence on a nation's people than the nation itself.

Another problem is ethnic rivalry in a country that might tear it apart. The refugee crisis has also lessened loyalty to nation-states. In addition, mass media, especially social media, now unite people beyond their nation-states. For these reasons, nation-states no longer enjoy the autonomy they once had.

Perhaps as a response to increasing globalization, the early 2000s saw the rise of populism, which you learned is a movement that claims to represent the ordinary people over the established elite. In Europe and the United States. People have voted in favor of nationalism and expressed distrust for international groups. For example, citizens of the United Kingdom have voted for **Brexit**, or a British exit from the European Union. Populists generally oppose mass immigration; some are motivated by racism. Populist voters are often willing to accept authoritarian leaders who promise employment and economic growth at the expense of **civil liberties**, or basic freedoms, and authoritarian leaders try to build support with propaganda about the opposition and condemnations of the free press. Some fear that such politicians herald a return to fascism.

In 2016, **Donald Trump**, running as a Republican on a populist platform, surprised much of the world with his victory over Democrat Hillary Clinton to become the 45th president of the United States. Clinton received almost three million votes more than Trump, but Trump won the Electoral College vote 306 to 232. Trump had

promised to "Make America Great Again" by cutting taxes, renegotiating trade deals, curtailing Muslim immigration, and removing all illegal immigrants. He also pledged to reshape the U.S. Supreme Court, and so far he has had the opportunity to appoint two conservative justices. The passage of a Congressional tax package in 2017, that many say favors the rich, met an important economic goal. His administration has faced criticism for many actions, including its 2018 decision to separate newly arrived immigrant children from their parents. It is too early to tell whether Trump's 2018 trade tariffs on imports from other countries will positively or negatively affect the U.S. economy.

Trump's plan for a renegotiation of NAFTA, which opened Mexico to globalization, is one of many factors affecting the United States' neighbor to the south. Illegal immigration of Mexicans and refugees fleeing from Central America through Mexico to get to the United States is also an area of concern. Mexicans are pushed from their country for such reasons as unemployment, poverty, crime, and poor health care. They are pulled to the United States because of the perceived availability of jobs, the desire to reunite with family, and educational opportunities. Trump has promised his supporters that he will build a border wall to stop illegal entry.

Another problem for Mexico is the drug trade, which not only encourages violence but also government corruption. Extreme poverty is also a major issue in some Mexican states, such as Chiapas. Yet, starting in 2009, the number of Mexicans leaving the United States was greater than the number entering the country. The reasons for this shift may include a worsening U.S. economy and stricter border enforcement. In the meantime, however, the number of immigrants from Honduras, Guatemala, and El Salvador has increased, with those applying for refugee status citing widespread violence as a push factor and jobs as a pull factor in their decision to immigrate to the United States.

Another challenge to nation-states is a rebound of **religiosity**, or strong religious belief, in the 21st century. Religion now flourishes in Eastern Europe's formerly communist countries where atheism was once the rule. India was formed as a secular nation, but under the premiership of **Narendra Modi** the government has emphasized the country's essentially Hindu nature.

Western Europe and China may seem to be exceptions to the trend toward increased religiosity. But in many European countries, even many non-religious populists claim that their anti-immigration proposals are a defense of "Christian Europe." In China, attacks on religion have greatly increased in recent years. Christian churches have been closed, and in the far west as many as one million Muslims have been forced into concentration camps.

In many countries, debates rage between the religiously orthodox and secularists. In both Istanbul and Paris, people debate the issue of allowing women to wear headscarves. People in the United States are divided about the extent to which laws should be guided by conservative Christian beliefs." In Israel, ultra-orthodox rabbis work to impose their strict rules on more secular Jews. It is clear that religious belief will play a role in shaping political action in the coming years.

Supporters throw flower petals as Narendra Modi, leader of India's Bharativa Janata Party (BJP), in 2014. The BJP, which has historically reflected Hindu nationalist positions, was part of a coalition that won a majority of seats in India's general election in 2014. Modi subsequently became prime minister.

HISTORICAL THINKING

1. **READING CHECK** What issues have caused problems for people throughout the world in the 21st century?

2. **DRAW CONCLUSIONS** Why is it important that such countries as Bulgaria, Estonia, Hungary, Lithuania, and Poland have joined the EU?

3. **MAKE PREDICTIONS** How do you think people will be united in the future?

BACKGROUND FOR THE TEACHER

Turkey Under Erdogan Recep Tayyip Erdogan helped form the Justice and Development Party (AKP) in Turkey in 2001. His Islamist-rooted AKP party won parliamentary elections in 2007. In 2013, during Erdogan's third term as prime minister, Istanbul police violently broke up a small protest to preserve a public park. This led to demonstrations across Turkey against growing authoritarianism. In 2016, Erdogan survived a coup attempt by plotters who accused Erdogan and his AKP of undermining democracy and the rule of law. The government retaliated by removing tens of thousands of soldiers, journalists, lawyers, police officers, academics, and civil servants from their jobs and arresting others for supposed support of the coup. Erdogan's intervention in the legal system caused an international coalition of lawyers to petition the United Nations Human Rights Council to help protect the right of every Turkish citizen to legal representation and a fair trial. In another area of human rights, Erdogan said that men and women cannot be treated equally. He claimed that women who choose careers over motherhood are "half persons." He approved lifting a decades-old ban on wearing headscarves—a sign of Islam—at state institutions and became an advocate of separate universities for men and women. In March 2019, police fired tear gas at women gathered in Istanbul for a march to celebrate International Women's Day. However, municipal elections held the same month led to a defeat for the AKP in Turkey's three biggest cities, including Istanbul—a blow to Erdogan who once was mayor. The opposition candidate, Ekrem Imamoglu, was considered a representative of hope for an inclusive Turkey and freedom from the corruption of 25 years of authoritarian rule. The opposition forces celebrated the win as evidence that Turkish democracy is still alive.

TEACH

GUIDED DISCUSSION

3. **Identify** What is the significance of Brexit as a challenge to globalization? *(Brexit involves an exit from the European Union. It represents British voters' distrust for international groups and the economic isolation of Britain.)*

4. **Describe** How would you describe U.S. president Trump's approach to immigration? *(President Trump's policies include curtailing Muslim immigration, removing all illegal immigrants, and building a southern border wall to stop illegal entry by Mexicans and immigrants from Latin American countries.)*

ANALYZE VISUALS

Have students view the image gallery titled "Effects of Globalization in the 21st Century" (available in the Student eEdition). Then focus attention on the photograph and caption titled "United Kingdom." **ASK:** Based on the situation portrayed, what can happen as a result of globalization? *(Possible response: Conflicts can arise because some citizens want to maintain contact with allied nations, while others fear change and want to keep foreign influences out.)*

ACTIVE OPTIONS

On Your Feet: Numbered Heads Arrange students in groups of four. Ask group members to number off from one to four. Instruct groups to think about and discuss the following question: Which challenges to democracy do you think are the most threatening and important to resolve? Tell students to cite evidence from the text or other reliable sources to support their responses. Then call out a number and have students with that number summarize their group's discussion.

> **NG Learning Framework: Write a Report**
> **ATTITUDES** Responsibility, Empowerment
> **SKILL** Collaboration

Have small groups of students use the lesson information and online research to investigate Russian interference in U.S. interests. Suggest students focus on the protection of Edward Snowden and efforts to skew election results. Tell students to take notes as they conduct their research and use them to prepare a written report of their findings. Ask groups to share and compare their reports.

HISTORICAL THINKING

ANSWERS

1. Possible responses: ethnic differences, authoritarian leaders, genocide, the economy, populism, white supremacy, religious differences, increased religiosity, terrorism by fundamentalists, aggression by nations, human rights abuses

2. Possible response: Their membership shows that the countries have aligned closely with other democratic nations, found ways to strengthen the economies, and prefer cooperation to conflict.

3. Answers will vary. Accept all reasonable answers. Students might say that smaller "kingdom-like" governments could form, that nations will merge into super-nations, or that little change will occur in the size and function of nation-states. Others might say that people could be united remotely by similar interests, perhaps even choosing which government suits them. A few might predict an international government.

Global Financial Crisis

Imagine scrimping and saving money for your future only to find that your savings are suddenly worth much less than you thought. Millions of people experienced this unfortunate situation during a major economic recession that began in 2008.

Two employees of Christie's Auction House in London transport a corporate sign of Lehman Brothers, an investment bank. Lehman Brothers filed for the largest bankruptcy in U.S. history in September 2008, causing a ripple effect through global financial markets.

A TIME OF RECESSION

The interconnected world financial markets that resulted from globalization seemed strong as the 21st century began. In the United States, consumers eagerly bought new houses, and banks readily offered mortgages that kept payments low. **Subprime mortgages**, or loans to people with poor credit, encouraged people to buy more expensive homes even as the price of real estate increased due to all this activity. When home prices fell, many homeowners found they owed more than the value of their houses. The faltering economy left many people unemployed, and they could not pay their mortgages. Banks foreclosed, or took possession of these homes, leaving people with huge debts and nowhere to live. An economic domino effect caused stock exchanges around the world to drop. The New York Stock Exchange lost 22 percent of its value in a single week.

This period became known as the **Great Recession**. A **recession** is a period of reduced economic activity. Not since the Great Depression had the economy seen such a crisis. Panic spread across world financial markets as people faced the possibility of a collapse of the interconnected global banking and stock market systems. Banks and other financial institutions began to close.

Economists and world leaders decided that government intervention was needed to save more financial institutions from bankruptcy. U.S. president George W. Bush proposed a program that made $700 billion available to help financial institutions in the belief that they were "too big to fail"—in other words, their failure would bring down the whole economy. The United Kingdom organized a similar recovery operation. Some citizens voiced objection to the **bailout**, or financial rescue, of companies that made risky business

decisions, but the infusion of cash kept many banks and investment houses in business.

Still, the world felt the effects of the recession. The United States and Europe faced high unemployment, and global markets shrank. The countries of the world had to make tough decisions. To recover, they could incur debt by borrowing money and cutting taxes. Or they could practice **fiscal austerity**, a debt-avoidance measure, by cutting spending and raising taxes.

GOVERNMENTS RESPOND

Under newly elected president Barack Obama, the United States provided a $787 billion **stimulus**, or incentive, package to strengthen the economy, an approach that had been advocated by British economist John Maynard Keynes during the Great Depression. The United Kingdom, by contrast, slashed spending and cut government services to avoid high debt. France offered a modest stimulus, and Ireland made harsh spending cuts. Greece was already deeply in debt, and a default on its debt would negatively affect all of Europe. Amid controversy, European Union members agreed to loan Greece money if it made deep spending cuts. Later, the EU would provide money to other struggling nations such as Spain and Italy. Meanwhile, members of the eurozone, EU nations using the euro, struggled to strengthen their currency.

The Great Recession had a huge effect on developing countries because they were highly dependent on imports for income. Financial disaster struck both Ireland and Iceland hard, leading to the failure of major banks. But Iceland emerged in better financial shape for several reasons. First, Ireland bailed out its banks, while Iceland let its banks collapse. Second, having its own currency (the króna) helped Iceland. The króna lost more value than Ireland's euro did, so Iceland gained

more purchasing power. Because of the devalued króna, Icelandic companies that chose to keep salaries the same actually lowered their employees' wages. However, this decision allowed the island nation to avoid the rising unemployment that affected other areas.

The financial crisis was not limited to North America and Western Europe. China was drawn into the recession because its exports to affected countries dropped severely. Highly dependent on trade with the West, Japan's economy sank dramatically as well. Developing countries found that their export products now sold for lower prices.

At the same time, the tremendous financial reserves that China had built up since the 1980s helped stabilize a global economy that now had multiple points of growth in Asia and Latin America. Though there was plenty of

pain, there was no complete breakdown of international markets like the world had seen in the 1930s.

By 2015, the economic crisis had eased in some parts of the world. Europe, though, remained in a critical situation. Some displaced Europeans sought changes in government to address the situation. For example, Greek people were unhappy with the austerity measures foisted on them and voted out their government. The youth unemployment rate in Europe, especially in the southern part of the continent, remained high; in Italy, it was almost 32 percent in 2018. Throughout the world, a shift in wealth has taken place since the financial crisis. Today, the richest 1 percent of the world's population controls close to 50 percent of its wealth, and in 2017 the world's eight wealthiest families owned as much as the bottom 50 percent of the human population.

HISTORICAL THINKING

1. **READING CHECK** What did the 2008 financial crisis reveal about the world's economies?

2. **MAKE GENERALIZATIONS** Why did Europeans have such varied opinions about how to handle the financial crisis?

3. **CATEGORIZE** Why might the 2008 financial crisis not only be categorized as an economic challenge but also as a political challenge and a social challenge?

PLAN: 2-PAGE LESSON

OBJECTIVE

Explain how economic globalization led to a worldwide recession beginning in 2008.

CRITICAL THINKING SKILLS FOR LESSON 2.1

- Make Generalizations
- Categorize
- Describe
- Make Connections
- Analyze Visuals

HISTORICAL THINKING FOR CHAPTER 30

What challenges does the world face in the 21st century?

Globalization has connected financial markets worldwide since before the 21st century began. Lesson 2.1 discusses the global financial crisis called the Great Recession and the measures taken by various countries in response.

Student eEdition online

Additional content for this lesson, including a photograph, is available online.

BACKGROUND FOR THE TEACHER

Bailout of Automakers The U.S. auto industry was on the brink of collapse by late 2008. The financial crisis had nearly frozen access to credit for vehicle loans, and auto sales had plummeted by close to 40 percent. Congress authorized the Troubled Asset Relief Program (TARP) in October 2008 to stabilize the country's financial system. The program authorized billions of taxpayer dollars to be loaned or invested in major corporations and banks. Major automakers General Motors Company (GM) and Chrysler LLC asked Congress for help similar to the bailout offered to banks. The U.S. Department of the Treasury provided GM and Chrysler with bailouts that eventually totaled some $80 billion. Ford Motor Company was in a better situation but asked to be included. Ford did not receive TARP funds, but it did receive government loans that were critical because banks were not lending. The bailout helped create several hundred thousand jobs over time, including auto parts manufacturing jobs, and led to improved practices in the auto industry.

INTRODUCE & ENGAGE

ACTIVATE PRIOR KNOWLEDGE

Ask students to recall what they learned about the Great Depression of the 1930s. Invite students to name some of its causes and effects. *(It was an economic downturn caused by a stock market crash in the United States. It lasted for years.)* Tell students that in this lesson they will learn about the global Great Recession that began in 2008 and the measures taken by governments in response. Explain that the recession is considered to be the longest period of economic decline since the Great Depression.

TEACH

GUIDED DISCUSSION

1. **Describe** How did falling home prices in the United States lead to a drop in stock markets worldwide? *(Homeowners owed more on mortgages than their houses were worth. The economy faltered, leaving many people unemployed and unable to make payments. Banks foreclosed, leaving people with huge debts. The economic domino effect caused stock markets to drop worldwide because of globalization.)*

2. **Make Connections** Why were China and Japan affected by the Great Recession that occurred in North America and Western Europe? *(China and Japan traded with the West. Their economies were affected by the loss of trade and by lower prices of export products.)*

ANALYZE VISUALS

Have students view the photo of taxis at the Athens airport (available in the Student eEdition) and read the caption. **ASK:** What can you infer about the impact of the Great Recession on ordinary citizens? *(Possible response: Ordinary citizens suffered financially and, as in Greece, sometimes had to endure harsh policies designed to restore economic strength.)*

ACTIVE OPTIONS

On Your Feet: Inside-Outside Circle Arrange students into two concentric circles facing each other. Have students in the outside circle pose questions such as the following: How did subprime mortgages affect the economy? What program did George W. Bush propose? How did the European Union respond to the recession? Tell students in the inner circle to answer the questions. Then ask students to trade inside/outside roles for another round of questions.

NG Learning Framework: Write a Profile
SKILLS Observation, Problem-Solving
KNOWLEDGE Our Human Story

Have students write a short profile of the state of the economy in Greece, Italy, Spain, Ireland, or Iceland today. Have them begin with information in the lesson and then conduct online research to locate news about the topic. Encourage students to focus on problems that impacted the economy and possible solutions. Invite students to share their profiles and discuss the topic as a class.

DIFFERENTIATE

ENGLISH LANGUAGE LEARNERS

Use Financial Terms Write the following words on the board: *subprime mortgages, foreclosed, recession, bailout, fiscal austerity, stimulus, eurozone.* Read each term aloud. Then pair students at the **Beginning** or **Intermediate** level with those at the **Advanced** level. Have partners create word cards and use them to check each other's understanding.

PRE-AP

Compare Financial Crises Direct students to work individually or in pairs to conduct research and write a report comparing the Great Recession of 2008 with the Great Depression of the 1930s. Tell students to explore the cause of the financial crisis and the worldwide impact of each. Ask them to draw comparisons based on their findings. Invite students to share their reports with the class.

See the Chapter Planner for more strategies for differentiation.

HISTORICAL THINKING

ANSWERS

1. It revealed that the world's economies were so closely connected because of globalization that one country's economic downturn affected the entire world.

2. Possible response: The different countries looked first at how to address the financial crisis based on their own situation. Countries with a greater level of debt faced a harsher reality than less debt-ridden countries, so the level of distress determined the action each took. Opinions of the various leaders also caused variances in proposed solutions.

3. Possible response: Political: It caused the downfall of some political leaders and their governments; Social: It had a negative effect on the lives of many people.

The Impact of Globalization

For much of modern history, European countries and then the United States dominated the world's economy. Now the "rise of the rest" is leading to a world with multiple centers of economic power, such as in Asia.

EMERGING ECONOMIC PLAYERS

Despite the economic downturn that began in 2008, the global economic growth rate is now about three percent a year. Globalization has not only increased the world's overall wealth but also shifted it. Economic power is now more diversified, or balanced among countries.

The world economic shift stems from changes in world demographics. As the population soars in Asia, China—the world's most populous country, with over 1.4 billion people in 2018—is poised to have the largest economy of any nation by 2050. The market-oriented policies initiated by Deng Xiaoping have led China's economy to grow at nearly 10 percent a year. Yet this growth has come at the cost of damage to the environment and the spread of corruption. Thirty years after the Tiananmen Square Massacre, it was still unclear whether economic growth might lead to more liberal policies in China, but in the short run, the communist state was becoming more repressive than ever.

India's population of 1.35 billion in 2018 may well overtake China's by the early 2020s. India has used its huge present-day labor force to grow its economy through the production of high-tech and domestic goods. Add in modest growth in established economies, such as Japan, South Korea, and Taiwan, and dynamic growth in emerging economies, such as Vietnam, Malaysia, and Indonesia, and the future of Asia as an economic giant seems clear. Less certain is whether China's authoritarian government or India's democracy will be more successful.

The United States remains the world's economic leader but faces problems maintaining this position.

Its aging population, shrinking workforce, and welfare and social security programs may stress its economy. Also, wage inequality, budgetary and trade deficits, and large amounts of money owed to foreign investors have all increased. Yet after the shock of 2008, the country's economy recovered, with GDP growing and unemployment falling by over half from 2012 to 2018.

By then, global trade had regained momentum lost through the economic recession. But problems loomed because of issues such as Brexit, a possible renegotiation of NAFTA, and the threat of tariffs—situations that might cause trade wars that would have a negative effect on economic growth. In the 21st century, it is growing more difficult to predict future winners in the race for economic success. Changes in leadership, loss of trade partners, and strikes or natural disasters can quickly turn an economy upside down.

ISSUES RELATED TO GLOBALIZATION

You have learned that globalization has affected the world in both positive and negative ways. Many people credit it with modernizing societies, but others say it has stripped them of their traditional cultures. Globalization

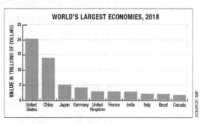

WORLD'S LARGEST ECONOMIES, 2018

has led to transnational organizations such as Amnesty International and Greenpeace that work to better the world. But it has also allowed the growth of both criminal and terrorist groups that want to advance their own interests at the expense of the rest of the world. International crimes include the illegal transport of drugs and weapons, human trafficking, and unlawful Internet activities. Terrorist groups commit violent acts against symbolic targets around the globe and use social media to gain new followers worldwide. However, Internet cooperation can also help prevent terrorist attacks.

People also disagree about the costs and benefits of multinational corporations. On the plus side, corporations bring jobs to various parts of the world. For example, workers in the United States, China, Taiwan, South Korea, and other nations contribute

to manufacturing cell phones. People in developing countries may learn new skills in careers they never imagined. Their countries benefit from the infusion of money. In all these ways, the standard of living in developing nations improves.

On the minus side, many people claim that the corporations exploit the workers and natural resources of developing countries. These critics say that the corporations are more concerned about profits than about environmental deterioration and human rights abuses in the countries in which they do business. They also claim that foreign workers must adapt to the home country of multinational corporations. For example, workers in India might have to work through the night to be at their desks at the same time as their American counterparts.

CRITICAL VIEWING A woman sews garments in Dhaka, the largest city and capital of Bangladesh. What can you infer about the job and its working conditions based on the details in the photograph?

HISTORICAL THINKING

1. **READING CHECK** What evidence supports the prediction that Asia will become an economic powerhouse by the mid-21st century?

2. **DRAW CONCLUSIONS** Why might U.S. budgetary and trade deficits become problems for the economy of the United States?

3. **FORM AND SUPPORT OPINIONS** Which country do you think has the best chance of solving such problems as violence, corruption, and instability—China or India? Explain your response.

PLAN: 2-PAGE LESSON

OBJECTIVE

Identify positive and negative effects of globalization on people, nations, and capital.

CRITICAL THINKING SKILLS FOR LESSON 2.2

- Draw Conclusions
- Form and Support Opinions
- Analyze Cause and Effect
- Make Predictions
- Interpret Charts

HISTORICAL THINKING FOR CHAPTER 30

What challenges does the world face in the 21st century?

The effects of globalization became increasingly apparent after the 21st century began. Lesson 2.2 discusses the shift in wealth among nations since 2000, emerging economies, and the pros and cons of issues related to globalization.

Student eEdition online

Additional content for this lesson, including a photograph, is available online.

BACKGROUND FOR THE TEACHER

Globalization and Terrorism U.S. president George W. Bush spoke about terrorism days after the September 11, 2001, attacks. He urged a global approach: "An attack on one is an attack on all." He asked for help from police forces, intelligence services, and banking systems worldwide. Writing in *The Washington Post*, James Stavridis, former NATO supreme allied commander, warned in 2013 about terrorist exploitation, especially in the cyber-world, of sophisticated trafficking routes used by drug cartels and other criminals to move illicit goods. He called this the "dark side" of globalization. In an October 2018 policy paper, President Donald Trump's White House urged basically the strategy of President Bush but fine-tuned it for the present situation. The paper warned that terrorists are more geographically dispersed and their tactics more diversified. It also stated that an increasing number are exploiting global trends, including the emergence of more secure modes of communication and the expansion of social and mass media. The White House advocated enhanced information-sharing with allies and across public and private sectors to prevent terrorists' abuse of global financial systems.

INTRODUCE & ENGAGE

THINK ABOUT GLOBALIZATION

Invite volunteers to recall what they learned about the global impact of financial crises. Ask students to think about other ways in which globalization has affected modern life and to discuss the impact of social media, the spread of terrorist networks, and the effects of outsourcing jobs. Then explain that in this lesson students will learn about the impact of globalization on the worldwide distribution of economic power along with the positive and negative effects of globalization on people and nations.

TEACH

GUIDED DISCUSSION

1. **Analyze Cause and Effect** Has globalization advanced or slowed the progress of terrorism? *(Globalization has done both. It has advanced terrorism by making it possible for terrorist groups to recruit followers worldwide via the Internet and social media. At the same time, Internet cooperation has made it easier to prevent terrorist attacks.)*

2. **Make Predictions** How might bringing jobs to developing countries affect the workforce in developed countries? *(Answers will vary. Possible responses: It could make certain types of jobs less available in developed countries. It could affect wages, possibly in negative ways because of a larger pool of workers and because workers in developing countries earn less.)*

INTERPRET CHARTS

Have students study the chart titled "World's Largest Economies, 2018." **ASK:** Based on the chart, how much greater in approximate value is the economy of China than the combined economies of Japan and Germany? *(approximately 5 trillion dollars greater)* How does the economy of China compare with the economy of the United States? *(China's economy is valued at approximately 6-to-7 trillion dollars less.)*

ACTIVE OPTIONS

On Your Feet: Think, Pair, Share Give students a few minutes to think about the following topic: How might the United States maintain its position as the world's economic leader? Then have students choose partners and talk about the topic for five minutes. Finally, allow individual students to share their ideas with the class.

NG Learning Framework: Write an Essay
ATTITUDES Curiosity, Responsibility
SKILL Communication

Have students write a short essay that explores the topic of U.S. trade deficits and tariffs. Encourage students to start with information in the lesson and conduct online research to locate additional information, including information from current news stories. Students' essays should draw conclusions based on their research. Invite students to read their essays aloud to the class.

DIFFERENTIATE

STRIVING READERS

Read and Recall Have students read the lesson independently. Then tell pairs to meet without the lesson text and take notes as they share the ideas they recall. Ask pairs to reread the lesson together and decide whether they should revise their notes.

PRE-AP

Deliver a Report Have students research and prepare an oral report about the features of multinational corporations and the reasons corporations become global. Tell them to focus on a particular multinational corporation and to share their reports.

See the Chapter Planner for more strategies for differentiation.

HISTORICAL THINKING

ANSWERS

1. economic growth in China and India, along with modest to dynamic growth in other Asian countries

2. Possible response: Budgetary deficits might limit how much the United States can invest to continue economic growth. Trade deficits could mean that it will not bring in enough money to grow the economy and its debt will increase. Rising debt could mean that it must pay more on interest and less on citizen services.

3. Answers will vary. Some students will say that an authoritarian government might solve the problems through force or harsh laws. Others will say that it would exacerbate the problems and only a democratic government can truly enact reform.

CRITICAL VIEWING The woman seems uncomfortably positioned and appears to be the primary worker. The child beside her indicates that childcare is unavailable. The clutter and lack of a clear exit would make evacuation difficult if a fire started.

2.3 Income Inequality

A trip to India can provide a crash course on income inequality. In the large city of Mumbai, you can marvel at how an emphasis on high technology has transformed the country economically. For example, many Indians use electric trains to get to their information processing jobs. Yet you will see a stark contrast between the wealthy and the poor. High walls protect glistening new suburbs from the noise and filth of overcrowded slums. And in rural areas, hundreds of millions of Indians live without clean water or basic sanitation.

Globalization has generated economic growth, but it has also caused rising income inequality. Money and goods move freely around the world, but workers do not have a similar mobility. They must try to eke out a living wherever they are, which is often where they were born. Many companies based in industrialized countries have moved their manufacturing plants to developing nations. These business decisions mean that some jobs are exported at a cost to workers in the industrialized nations. And workers in the developing countries have few choices but to accept the low wages offered. In many cases, children have to work to help their families survive.

You may have heard the expression "The rich get richer and the poor get poorer." The French economist Thomas Piketty concludes that structures of capitalism trend toward increasing inequality over time, which supports the saying. In his book *Capital in the Twenty-First Century*, he says that people with inherited money and property will always earn more income than people who can only offer labor and that market economies result in a gap between the "haves" and "have-nots" that grows bigger over time. So without corrective action, a disparity between rich and poor will continue within and among countries.

890 CHAPTER 30

DOCUMENT ONE
Primary Source: Chart
Richest and Poorest Countries by Income

The extent of income inequality among nations is determined by examining various factors, including the use of economic measurement tools. One measure is the GDP (gross domestic product) per capita of a nation, which tells how much an individual would earn if the GDP of a country was divided evenly among everyone who lived in the country. Of course, people do not share equally in a nation's wealth, but comparing different countries' GDP per capita informs people of the extent of income inequality between nations.

CONSTRUCTED RESPONSE Based on the chart, what generalizations can you make about the countries with the lowest GDPs per capita?

Sampling of Richest and Poorest Countries by Income

HIGH GDP PER CAPITA		LOW GDP PER CAPITA	
Country	GDP Per Capita	Country	GDP Per Capita
Qatar	$124,500	Burundi	$700
Monaco	$115,700	Mozambique	$1,200
Singapore	$93,900	Malawi	$1,200
Brunei	$78,200	Yemen	$1,300
Norway	$71,800	South Sudan	$1,500
United States	$59,500	North Korea	$1,700
Saudi Arabia	$54,800	Afghanistan	$2,000
Germany	$50,400	Rwanda	$2,100
Australia	$50,300	Uganda	$2,400
Japan	$42,800	Kenya	$3,500

Latest available year per country Source: https://www.cia.gov/library/publications/the-world-factbook/rankorder/2004rank.html

DOCUMENT TWO
Primary Source: Chart
Greatest and Least Income Inequality Within a Country

The Gini coefficient (named for the Italian social scientist who invented it) examines the extent of income inequality within a country. This tool measures the distribution of income within a country by comparing the country's income distribution to that of an imagined country with equal income distribution. The result is a ratio that is often represented as a percentage, such as 59.7 percent. The higher the ratio (or percentage), the greater the income inequality in a country. Note, however, that even a country with little income inequality isn't necessarily wealthy. It may have a low GDP per capita, which means nearly everyone in the country has very little income.

CONSTRUCTED RESPONSE According to the chart, how does the income inequality of Guatemala compare to that of Botswana and Slovenia?

Greatest and Least Income Inequality Within a Country

GREATEST INCOME INEQUALITY		LEAST INCOME INEQUALITY	
Country	Gini Ratio	Country	Gini Ratio
Lesotho	63.2	Kosovo	23.2
South Africa	62.5	Slovakia	23.7
Micronesia	61.1	Slovenia	24.4
Haiti	60.8	Sweden	24.9
Botswana	60.5	Ukraine	25.5
Namibia	59.7	Belgium	25.9
Zambia	57.5	Kazakhstan	26.3
Comoros	55.9	Belarus	26.5
Guatemala	53	Norway	26.8
Paraguay	51.7	Moldova	26.8

Latest available year per country
Source: https://www.cia.gov/library/publications/the-world-factbook/rankorder/2172rank.html

DOCUMENT THREE
Primary Source: Chart
Countries with Highest and Lowest Happiness Index

Have you ever heard the expression, "Money can't buy happiness"? The Happiness Index is a tool that measures the extent of happiness within countries. It averages the responses of citizens in various countries to how they would rank the quality of their life on a scale from 0 to 10. And indeed, the countries with the happiest people are not necessarily the wealthiest. Experts on the topic find that the keys to happiness are livable income, healthy life expectancy, adequate social support, freedom, trust, and generosity. Causes for unhappiness include unfair treatment by the government, poverty, conflict in region, and prevalence of disease.

CONSTRUCTED RESPONSE What do most of the countries listed in the Low column of the chart have in common?

Countries with Highest and Lowest Happiness Index

HIGH HAPPINESS INDEX		LOW HAPPINESS INDEX	
Country	Happiness Index	Country	Happiness Index
Finland	7.632	Malawi	3.587
Norway	7.594	Haiti	3.582
Denmark	7.555	Liberia	3.495
Iceland	7.495	Syria	3.462
Switzerland	7.487	Rwanda	3.408
Netherlands	7.441	Yemen	3.355
Canada	7.328	Tanzania	3.303
New Zealand	7.324	South Sudan	3.254
Sweden	7.328	Central African Republic	3.083
Australia	7.272	Burundi	2.905

Latest available year per country
Source: https://countryeconomy.com/demography/world-happiness-index

SYNTHESIZE & WRITE

1. REVIEW Review what you have read and observed about income inequality in the 21st century.

2. RECALL On your own paper, list two details about one of the measurement tools and two details about the chart relating to it.

3. CONSTRUCT Construct a topic sentence that answers this question: How are people around the world affected differently by income inequality?

4. WRITE Using evidence from this chapter and the documents, write an informative paragraph that supports your topic sentence in Step 3.

A Global 21st Century 891

PLAN: 2-PAGE LESSON

OBJECTIVE
Analyze information from three documents that rank different types of economic indicators for various countries around the world.

CRITICAL THINKING SKILLS FOR LESSON 2.3
- Synthesize
- Make Inferences
- Compare and Contrast
- Evaluate

HISTORICAL THINKING FOR CHAPTER 30
What challenges does the world face in the 21st century?

Globalization has promoted economic growth in many countries, but it has also resulted in larger income inequality within and between countries. Lesson 2.3 focuses on income inequality between countries as presented in three economic measurement tools.

Student eEdition online
Additional content for this lesson, including a photo and caption, is available online.

BACKGROUND FOR THE TEACHER
Thomas Piketty Born in Clichy, France, Thomas Piketty earned a Ph.D. in economics in 1993 for his theory on the redistribution of wealth. He taught at the Massachusetts Institute of Technology in the United States but then returned to France as a research fellow and professor. After writing numerous books and articles and as the compiler of the World Top Incomes Database, he became famous in 2014, after writing the book *Capital in the Twenty-first Century*. The publication started a debate between liberals and conservatives over the economic inequalities in the distribution of wealth between the rich and poor. Piketty based his conclusion on 200 years of tax records from the United States and Europe, which he collected himself with the help of two other colleagues. His claim concludes that inherited wealth will grow faster than earned wealth, leading to further economic inequality that could threaten democracy and lead to "patrimonial capitalism" (wealth that is acquired through marriage rather than labor). Therefore, Piketty called for changes to taxation policies. The *Financial Times* investigated his data and found that, in some instances, Piketty had made errors. He conceded that not all data sources on wealth inequality are systematic; however, his findings continue to generate the debate about wealth and income inequality.

INTRODUCE & ENGAGE

PREPARE FOR THE DOCUMENT-BASED QUESTION

Before students start on the activity, briefly preview the three GDP documents. Remind students that a constructed response requires full explanations in complete sentences. Emphasize that students should use what they have learned about economic challenges that many countries are facing in addition to the income inequality information in the charts.

TEACH

GUIDED DISCUSSION

1. **Make Inferences** Based on the information related to Norway in all three charts, what is the quality of life for people in Norway? *(Possible response: Norway has a high GDP per capita, is among the countries with the least amount of income inequality, and is toward the top of the happiness index. Based on these statistics, I believe that people in Norway have an elevated quality of life.)*

2. **Compare and Contrast** Based on the charts, what comparisons can be made between the countries of Yemen and Rwanda? *(Possible response: Both countries have a low GDP per capita and rank amongst the lowest in happiness levels.)*

EVALUATE

After students have completed the Synthesize & Write activity, allow time for them to exchange paragraphs and read and comment on the work of their peers. Establish guidelines for comments prior to the activity so that feedback is constructive and encouraging. Comments should focus on the most significant parts that address the purpose of the activity and the audience.

ACTIVE OPTION

On Your Feet: Jigsaw Strategy Organize students into "expert" groups and assign each group one of the charts to analyze and summarize its elements into a paragraph. Then regroup students into new groups so that each group has at least one member from each expert group. Students in the new groups take turns sharing the summaries from their expert groups.

DIFFERENTIATE

ENGLISH LANGUAGE LEARNERS

Summarize Assign pairs of students at **Beginning** and **Intermediate** proficiencies a document. Instruct them to read the document together and then write a few sentences to summarize it. When all pairs are finished, call on them to read their summaries aloud in the order in which the material appears to provide an overview of the entire lesson. You may provide sentence frames to help students write an effective summary for each document.

PRE-AP

Create a GDP Chart Instruct students to research GDP inequalities between cities or regions within the United States. Have them analyze the similarities and differences found within the country to create a GDP index chart of their own, showing their findings. Remind students to use reliable sources as they gather data. Then ask students to share their charts in an oral presentation to the class.

See the Chapter Planner for more strategies for differentiation.

SYNTHESIZE & WRITE

ANSWERS

1. Answers will vary.

2. Possible response: The Gini Coefficient measures income inequality within a nation. A high Gini ratio means that much income inequality exists in a country. Lesotho has the highest income inequality at 63.2 percent while Moldova and Norway have the lowest at 26.8 percent.

3. Possible response: Income inequality appears to be stronger in developing nations than in industrialized nations but is only one factor affecting happiness.

4. Answers will vary. Students should include their topic sentence from Step 3 and evidence from the lesson information and charts and from information learned in earlier chapters to support their claim.

CONSTRUCTED RESPONSE

Document One: All the countries with the lowest GDPs per capita are developing nations. The majority of the countries with the lowest GDPs per capita are in Africa.

Document Two: Guatemala's income inequality is greater than that of Slovenia but less than that of Botswana.

Document Three: Most of the countries listed in the Low column are experiencing or have recently experienced war or conflict between ethnic groups.

New and Old Energy Sources

What's the best source of energy for the world's growing population? Decades ago, there weren't many choices. But today, we consider issues like pollution, climate change, environmental impact, cost, and safety as the world tries to meet its energy needs.

A floating solar energy farm in the village of Chunjiangyuan in China's Zhejiang province provides 20 million kilowatt-hours each year through a power station. Though nearly two-thirds of the country's electricity still comes from burning air-polluting coal, demand for solar power is growing.

SEARCHING FOR ENERGY SOLUTIONS

You learned that scientists now use the term *Anthropocene* to describe the changed global ecology of the past 200 years—since the Industrial Revolution brought about the large-scale use of fossil fuels. Today, widely used fossil fuels such as oil and coal raise concerns about environmental harm.

Fossil fuels can not only cause air pollution when burned but also water and soil pollution when spilled during transport or drilling. In 2010, a huge spill fouled the Gulf of Mexico following an explosion on the Deepwater Horizon oil rig. **Fracking**, the process of drilling into the earth and applying water pressure to force out natural gases by breaking up rock, is also harmful to the environment.

Fossil fuels are nonrenewable resources. Once depleted they are gone forever. Nonrenewable resources do not provide a **sustainable**, or unceasing, source of energy. This fact has led companies and governments to explore renewable resources as sources of energy. Wind farms, some containing thousands of wind turbines, have become an important source for renewable energy.

The Gansu Wind Farm in China is huge, with 7,000 turbines, but an even bigger offshore wind farm is planned for the United Kingdom. At more than 150 square miles, this wind farm, slated for completion in 2022, will provide power to one million homes. While wind farms harness a renewable resource, they take up a lot of land, are expensive, and cause harm to birds.

Solar energy uses heat from the sun's rays to generate electricity. But it too faces hurdles in becoming a widely used energy source. Problems include resistance from fossil fuel suppliers, toxic materials in solar cells, the cost of switching to solar panels, and flaws in reliability. In some cases, governments have been slow to encourage the use of solar energy. In some areas, governments offer tax incentives to producers

of solar panels and tax credits to individuals who install them. Governments can also stimulate use by allowing consumers to sell excess solar energy back to utilities.

Geothermal energy, derived from Earth's heat, is another source of sustainable energy. Renewable and clean, geothermal energy is ideal for heating and cooling. Hot water or steam from underground sources can also be used to turn turbines to create electricity. Large thermal power plants are located in California as well as in Italy, Mexico, Iceland, and Indonesia.

The most immediate alternative to fossil fuels is nuclear power. Nuclear power plants in 30 different countries produce more than 10 percent of the world's electricity. However, many people remain wary of its health and environmental consequences.

In 2011, an earthquake in Japan caused a tsunami that led to the release of radiation from the Fukushima electricity plant. The death toll was more than a thousand, but the deaths resulted from the evacuation process rather than radiation exposure. Even so, several nuclear reactors were damaged beyond use, and the vast majority of the area's former residents have decided not to return home. This disaster contributed to Germany's decision to shut down its nuclear energy program. However, France has decided to maintain its nuclear program, which provides 75 percent of the country's electricity.

Developing countries face special challenges in providing energy. China and India depend on burning coal for economic growth. They believe that this is the only way to fully develop their economies. Their leaders also realize the damage that fossil fuels inflict on people's health as the air becomes almost unbreathable in cities such as Beijing and New Delhi. Still, the challenge remains since more than one billion people worldwide do not have electricity.

CONSERVING RESOURCES

Consumption of natural resources has increased since the Industrial Revolution. Environmentalists encourage the **conservation**, or careful protection, of natural resources. They stress reducing, reusing, and recycling. They also encourage **green building**, or designing and building structures with the environment in mind. Green builders make efficient use of natural resources such as water, minerals, and fuel sources to create buildings that are safe for humans and the environment. Examples of green buildings are Shanghai Tower in China and the Manitoba Hydro Place in Canada.

Obtaining food and water for survival can be hard in developing nations. The "green revolution" of the mid-20th century transformed the way in which rice, wheat, and other grains were grown and harvested. New seed varieties, advanced farm equipment, and chemical fertilizers allowed commercial farms to produce more crops and charge lower prices for them. However, the increased use of fertilizers and pesticides raised concerns about costs and environmental and human effects. In addition, some farmers could not afford the fertilizers and pesticides, so they did not obtain

the promised results. Even so, the new methods are estimated to have saved as many as one billion people from starvation.

The challenge is great, but the story of the ozone layer provides hope that environmental progress is possible. In the 1980s, scientists became concerned that the ozone layer, which shields us from the sun's ultraviolet radiation, was disappearing. They traced the cause to the use of chemical compounds called chlorofluorocarbons (CFCs) in aerosol sprays. Since those compounds were banned by international agreement, the hole in the ozone layer has been steadily shrinking.

HISTORICAL THINKING

1. **READING CHECK** Classify the energy resources in this lesson as old energy or new energy, and then list important distinctions between the two types.

2. **FORM AND SUPPORT OPINIONS** Which new energy source do you think has the most potential for use in homes, and what roadblocks stand in the way? Explain your response.

3. **IDENTIFY** How does green building protect the environment?

PLAN: 2-PAGE LESSON

OBJECTIVE

Identify alternative energy sources and the consequences of using fossil fuels.

CRITICAL THINKING SKILLS FOR LESSON 3.1

- Form and Support Opinions
- Identify
- Draw Conclusions
- Make Connections

HISTORICAL THINKING FOR CHAPTER 30

What challenges does the world face in the 21st century?

Problems connected with using fossil fuels were apparent well before the 21st century began. Lesson 3.1 discusses fossil fuels, alternative energy sources to replace them, and current efforts to protect natural resources.

Student eEdition online

Additional content for this lesson, including a Global Commodity feature and a photograph, is available online.

BACKGROUND FOR THE TEACHER

Deforestation National Geographic reported in 2019 that about 30 percent of Earth's land area consists of forests that are disappearing. According to the World Bank, Earth lost 502,000 square miles of forest between 1990 and 2016. That represents an area larger than South Africa and a loss equivalent to 1,000 football fields every hour. Farming, livestock grazing, mining, and logging are among the major reasons for deforestation. Forests are leveled in Malaysia and Indonesia to permit the production of palm oil, used in all sorts of products. Cattle ranching and farming, especially soy plantations, cause deforestation in the Amazon. According to the World Resources Institute, it will be almost impossible to achieve the climate goals of the 2015 Paris Agreement unless tropical forests are protected. Trees are essential to absorb carbon dioxide and the heat-trapping greenhouse gases emitted by human activities. Environmental activists are working to preserve existing forests and restore lost tree cover.

History Notebook

Encourage students to complete the "Oil" Global Commodity page for Chapter 30 in their History Notebooks as they read.

INTRODUCE & ENGAGE

ACTIVATE PRIOR KNOWLEDGE

Write two terms on the board: *fossil fuels* and *alternative energy sources*. Ask students to name different energy sources and ask which term describes the source. Have students explain the different types of energy sources they have read or learned about. Ask what they know about the advantages and disadvantages of each type. Then tell students that in this lesson they will learn about nonrenewable and renewable energy sources, along with efforts to conserve natural resources that include what is labeled *green building*.

TEACH

GUIDED DISCUSSION

1. **Draw Conclusions** Why would consumers be likely to prefer wind, solar, or geothermal energy over nuclear power? *(Many people are wary of the health and environmental impacts of nuclear power, especially in the wake of the disasters that occurred at the Chernobyl and Fukushima nuclear power plants.)*

2. **Identify** Why do China and India continue to rely on energy from coal in spite of the harmful effects? *(Their leaders believe that this is the only way to achieve economic growth.)*

MAKE CONNECTIONS

Have students read the Global Commodity feature on oil (available in the Student eEdition), and then ask students to answer the section question: Based on the reading, how do the factors of price and supply affect resources? *(When a resource is in short supply, the price can rise considerably. The need for a resource, possible shortages, and higher prices can lead to a search for alternate resources.)* **ASK:** What could limit the production of oil even when reserves are available? *(Countries could limit production for political or economic gain.)*

ACTIVE OPTIONS

On Your Feet: Fishbowl Arrange students in concentric circles. Direct the inner circle to discuss the consequences of using fossil fuels for energy and the advantages of developing alternative energy sources. The outer circle listens to this discussion and then the groups are signaled to reverse positions. Ask the new inner circle to continue the discussion, including what the positive and negative consequences might be of using alternative energy sources.

> **NG Learning Framework: Profile a Green Building**
> **ATTITUDES** Curiosity, Responsibility
> **KNOWLEDGE** Our Living Planet

Have students write a profile of a green building, referencing one named in the lesson or in an additional source. Suggest students focus research on how the construction helps protect the environment by efficient use of natural resources. Invite students to read their profiles to the class.

DIFFERENTIATE

STRIVING READERS

Create Lists Pair students to create a list of facts about renewable energy resources. Tell pairs to create a separate list of facts about green building and the "green revolution." Invite pairs to answer the Historical Thinking questions.

GIFTED & TALENTED STEM

Create a Poster Presentation Direct students to research the use of wind energy in different countries. Ask them to present the information in a poster that also explains how a wind turbine works. Posters should include photos or diagrams. Have students present their completed posters to the class. Invite feedback about the use of wind power.

See the Chapter Planner for more strategies for differentiation.

HISTORICAL THINKING

ANSWERS

1. New: wind, solar, and geothermal energy; Old: fossil fuels such as oil, gas, and coal; Generally, the old energy sources are nonrenewable and cause air, water, and soil pollution.

2. Possible response: Solar energy has potential because the sun's rays are abundant in most locations and solar panels can be installed on homes. Roadblocks include the cost of replacing an old energy source, consumers believing that the savings are not enough, and fossil-fuel producers' resistance to solar energy gaining acceptance.

3. Possible response: It protects Earth and the health of people within structures by limiting the use and type of resources in construction.

CRITICAL VIEWING (available in the Student eEdition) Possible response: Plants produce oxygen that helps reduce air pollution and its effects.

Reinventing Clean Energy

"I think I can save the world with nuclear power."
—Leslie Dewan

CRITICAL VIEWING Leslie Dewan is determined to use nuclear power to provide energy for people all over the world. "I'm doing this because I think nuclear power is the best way of producing large amounts of carbon-free electricity," she says.

"The idea of an energy source that never turns off, and the concept of volcanoes leading us into a green energy future, blew my mind and became my passion." –Andrés Ruzo

Even with green energy projects, there is a responsible way and an irresponsible way of doing things. When he started his Ph.D. research, Andrés Ruzo's dream was to find a powerful geothermal feature to harness, and, by doing so, help Peru establish its first geothermal power plant. However, when Ruzo came face-to-face with the sacred Boiling River of the Amazon, it was clear to him that this place should not be developed and deserves legal protection.

894 CHAPTER 30

Scores of scientific studies tell us that the primary cause of climate change on Earth is the burning of fossil fuels for energy. Scientists know it is of the utmost importance to protect our resources and develop clean energy options that are commercially viable, economically sustainable, and safe. Two visionary explorers are making clean energy their business.

MAIN IDEA National Geographic Explorers Leslie Dewan and Andrés Ruzo analyze how clean energy sources can be economically sustainable.

SAFER, MORE EFFICIENT NUCLEAR REACTORS

Nuclear engineer Leslie Dewan is determined to develop a cleaner, more efficient form of nuclear power that will reinvent the definition of clean energy. She believes that with safer nuclear reactors that produce less waste, we can power the entire world with carbon-free energy.

One concern about nuclear power is the disposal of nuclear waste. Compared to the amount of waste created by fossil fuel plants, the amount of nuclear waste generated by nuclear power plants is small. However, spent nuclear fuel is highly radioactive and must be permanently stored somewhere safe and secure, usually deep underground.

That's where Dewan comes in. She and her colleague Mark Massie developed a new design for a molten salt reactor as a more secure, more economical alternative to today's nuclear reactors. In 2011, Dewan and Massie established Transatomic Power, intending to develop their reactor on a commercial scale.

They initially thought that their reactor would be able to consume nuclear waste directly, which would have helped solve one of the biggest problems with nuclear power. However, as they continued to develop their design and talked with other scientists about their work, they realized this was not possible with their reactor. Their design still has benefits—it uses half the fuel and produces less than half the waste of a conventional nuclear power plant—but it can't solve the nuclear waste problem on its own.

Dewan shut down her company in late 2018. At the same time, she made the decision to open-source its patents, reactor plans, and design. "We wanted to bring it out into the world," she says, "so that everyone could use it." She firmly believes in collaboration in the scientific community.

Dewan thinks that other new nuclear reactor designs will be able to consume nuclear waste. She is currently advising other companies that are developing these designs. Dewan also works with other experts at National Geographic Labs to use "satellite imagery to monitor nuclear facilities worldwide to make sure that they are safe and are not hurting the environment," continuing her aims of nuclear safety and scientific cooperation.

AN UNSTOPPABLE SOURCE OF CLEAN ENERGY

As a child growing up in Peru, geoscientist Andrés Ruzo played among fumaroles, the steaming openings found in or near volcanoes that emit hot, sulfurous gases. He also heard legends of a boiling river deep in the Peruvian Amazon. These experiences ignited a passion in Ruzo, and he pursued it by studying geologic wonders around the world. His fieldwork in the United States involved improving mapping methods to highlight geothermal energy potential within the country. In Peru, Ruzo proved the existence of the Boiling River of the Peruvian Amazon. "It's an anomalously large geothermal feature, which basically means it's freaking big," Ruzo explains. And although it is located far from any active volcano, the river can reach a temperature of more than 200°F.

As Ruzo solves this mystery, he continues to explore geothermal regions. Naturally, he visited Iceland, a geothermal paradise that provides a successful example of geothermal energy's commercial success. Ruzo applies what he learns to his own business-related work, which focuses on building maintainable economic systems to promote conservation and clean energy.

As a geothermal scientist, conservationist, science communicator, and educator, Ruzo anchors the many things that he does on the belief that environmentalism and economic prosperity can work together. And his enthusiasm for what he does is contagious. His oral and written storytelling inspires people to explore our world and consider how we can integrate clean energy and conservation into our lives.

HISTORICAL THINKING

1. **READING CHECK** What problems is Dewan attempting to solve with her development of new nuclear reactor technology?

2. **ANALYZE POINT OF VIEW** Why does Ruzo think geothermal activity could lead to a green energy future, and how is he trying to apply that belief?

3. **DRAW CONCLUSIONS** How might successful clean energy businesses help reduce the number of businesses that burn fossil fuels?

A Global 21st Century **895**

PLAN: 2-PAGE LESSON

OBJECTIVE
Examine how National Geographic Explorers Leslie Dewan and Andrés Ruzo analyze how clean energy sources can be economically sustainable.

CRITICAL THINKING SKILLS FOR LESSON 3.2
- Analyze Point of View
- Draw Conclusions
- Explain
- Identify
- Analyze Visuals

HISTORICAL THINKING FOR CHAPTER 30
What challenges does the world face in the 21st century?

The world continues to face the challenge of converting to clean energy sources. Lesson 3.2 discusses the efforts of two National Geographic Explorers in developing economically sustainable clean energy sources.

BACKGROUND FOR THE TEACHER
Andrés Ruzo and the Boiling River The Boiling River Project is a nonprofit that strives to understand, protect, and bring value to the Boiling River and turn it into a mecca for scientific investigation. The Boiling River is the largest geothermal river in the world. The lower four miles of the five-and-a-half-mile system are almost 100 feet wide, 15 feet deep at most, and reach temperatures high enough to kill anyone who falls in, boiling them alive. Andrés Ruzo, the founder and director of the nonprofit project, was the first geoscientist to study the unique feature, earning the blessing of the shamanic communities along the river to explore. He has played an active role in indigenous and local empowerment work in the Central Peruvian Amazon by creating educational and sustainable economic initiatives. His research includes the fields of geoscience, biology, microbiology, botany, anthropology, linguistics, ethno-history, shamanism, conservation economics, wildlife trafficking, and sustainable tourism.

History Notebook
Encourage students to complete the National Geographic Explorer page for Chapter 30 in their History Notebooks as they read.

INTRODUCE & ENGAGE

PREVIEW NUCLEAR AND GEOTHERMAL POWER

Display a T-Chart on the board and record what students know about nuclear power in one column and geothermal power in the other column. Encourage students to add to the T-Chart as they read the lesson. Tell students that in this lesson they will learn about the efforts of National Geographic Explorers Leslie Dewan and Andrés Ruzo in developing economically sustainable clean energy sources.

TEACH

GUIDED DISCUSSION

1. **Explain** What did Leslie Dewan and Mark Massie discover about their molten salt reactor? *(Dewan and Massie discovered the limitations of their reactor and that it could not consume nuclear waste directly as they had believed.)*

2. **Identify** How is Andrés Ruzo a catalyst for environmental responsibility? *(Ruzo believes that it is possible to protect the environment while also realizing economic prosperity. He believes that the two practices don't have to be in opposition to each other.)*

ANALYZE VISUALS

Have students look at the photographs in the lesson. **ASK:** What are the differences between the photographs, and how do they show the differences between Dewan and Ruzo? *(Possible response: Dewan is photographed with an industrial background, while Ruzo is out in nature. This shows that Dewan's work takes a more mechanized approach, while Ruzo works directly with Earth and its natural resources.)*

ACTIVE OPTIONS

On Your Feet: Class Debate Invite students to engage in a class debate. Direct half the class to argue in favor of nuclear power and the other half in favor of geothermal power. Instruct groups to research the benefits of their type of power to support their opinion. After the debate, lead a class discussion in which students determine the strongest arguments presented by each side.

NG Learning Framework: Design an Infographic **STEM**
ATTITUDE Curiosity
SKILL Observation

Have students research the machines or tools involved in each type of power and select one to examine further. Ask them to use their research to create an infographic with a drawing or photographs of the tool, how it works, what it does, its parts, and its significance. Have them present their infographics to the class.

DIFFERENTIATE

ENGLISH LANGUAGE LEARNERS

Complete Sentence Frames Use sentence frames such as those below to help students demonstrate understanding of difficult words and ideas in the lesson. You may wish to allow students to choose words from a list on the board.

- An option that is **viable** is (unreasonable, practical). *(practical)*
- An **anomalously** large geothermal feature is (typical, unusual). *(unusual)*

PRE-AP

Analyze Impacts Tell students to conduct research into the impacts of using clean energy. Ask them to analyze the connection between energy sources and climate change. Students might use a graphic organizer to show the results of their investigation as they explain their analysis to the class.

See the Chapter Planner for more strategies for differentiation.

HISTORICAL THINKING

ANSWERS

1. Dewan is attempting to make nuclear reactors safer and more efficient. She is also attempting to make reactors that can recycle nuclear fuel, which would reduce nuclear waste.

2. Ruzo believes that Earth's geothermal activity, such as volcanoes, is plentiful and constant, so it could be a leading source of green energy. He travels to learn about geothermal activity around the world, shares what he learns, and inspires others to consider how green energy can work in their location on the planet.

3. Successful clean energy businesses will support economies, making it easier for energy businesses not to rely on fossil fuels to make a profit.

3.3 A Global Commodity: Conflict Minerals

Computers and handheld gadgets have revolutionized how people connect with each other and access information, but the technology has exacted a high price. Some of the commodities needed to produce these electronic devices, including gold, tin, tungsten, and tantalum, a hard, blue-gray metal that resists corrosion, are plentiful in the eastern regions of the Democratic Republic of the Congo (DRC). The sale of these natural resources—known as conflict minerals and often referred to as 3TG—have helped fund the fierce fighting that has embroiled the eastern DRC since the 1990s and killed an estimated six million people.

Armed militias have gained control of many of the DRC's rich mineral mines and employed local men and children to work them. Laborers use shovels and their bare hands to extract minerals that will be exchanged for weapons and ammunition. In 2010, Congress passed the Dodd-Frank Act, which included legislation requiring companies to disclose their sources of conflict minerals. Opponents of the law claimed it would result in the loss of mining jobs. Congress sought to repeal the conflict minerals rule in 2017, but the law's fate remains unclear.

In addition to conflict minerals, what other commodities traded throughout history have raised ethical issues?

GOLD
Congolese gold miners dig in an open pit and use a human chain to remove the red mud. Most of the gold produced by small-scale mines like this one is smuggled out of the Congo. And armed groups supervise about half of these artisanal mines. Miners are only paid when they find gold. Any amount found is usually so small that it is weighed against a matchstick.

898 CHAPTER 30

A Global 21st Century 897

PLAN: 2-PAGE LESSON

OBJECTIVE
Understand the global impact of using conflict minerals.

CRITICAL THINKING SKILLS FOR LESSON 3.3
- Analyze Visuals
- Make Connections
- Describe
- Explain

HISTORICAL THINKING FOR CHAPTER 30
What challenges does the world face in the 21st century?

The materials needed to produce our electronic devices are often controlled by groups who use profits to fund warfare and terrorism. Lesson 3.3 discusses the impact of these conflict minerals.

Student eEdition online
Additional content for this lesson, including photos and captions, is available online.

BACKGROUND FOR THE TEACHER
Conflict in the DRC The Rwandan genocide in 1994 resulted in a flood of refugees seeking asylum in nearby regions. The Hutu fled to the Democratic Republic of the Congo to form armed groups, and the Tutsi formed rebel groups. The Congolese government was unable to quell armed groups who threatened neighboring countries, and a war broke out. The Second Congo War was fought between the government, with the support of Angola, Namibia, and Zimbabwe, and the rebels, with the support of Rwanda and Uganda. The war resulted in about 3 million deaths between 1998 and 2003, and rebel groups continued to terrorize citizens. Armed groups continue to subject civilians in the eastern DRC to human rights violations, sexual violence, and poverty. It is believed that weak governance and institutions as well as corruption are responsible for the inability to suppress the more than 100 violent regimes, despite efforts by the UN, African Union, and neighboring countries. UN estimates cite 4.5 million people are displaced within the DRC and there are more than 800,000 refugees in other nations.

History Notebook
Encourage students to complete the "Conflict Minerals" Global Commodity page for Chapter 30 in their History Notebooks as they read.

INTRODUCE & ENGAGE

PREVIEW CONFLICT MINERALS

Explain that conflict minerals are materials used in common, everyday products that produce revenue for oppressive regimes throughout the world. These regimes may be involved in military conflicts or participate in human rights abuses, slavery, or even genocide. Explain that the main conflict minerals are known as 3TG—tantalum, tungsten, tin, and gold, and write the words on the board. Invite students to supply examples of products that contain these minerals and list any details about the minerals. Have students add to the list as they read the lesson. When they've finished reading, encourage students to research the minerals and add information to the list as a class.

TEACH

GUIDED DISCUSSION

1. **Describe** What is tantalum (discussed in the Student eEdition), and why is it a conflict mineral? *(Tantalum is a hard, blue-gray metal that resists corrosion. It is considered a conflict mineral because it has helped fund decades of fierce fighting in the DRC that has killed approximately 6 million people.)*

2. **Explain** Why are conflict minerals unable to be replaced, despite electronic manufacturers' pledges to stop using them? *(There are not enough conflict-free mineral producers to meet the world's demand for electronics, therefore the minerals remain in demand.)*

A GLOBAL COMMODITY

Congo's estimated $24 trillion in untapped mineral resources encourages terrorist regimes who try to profit from the sale of the minerals. Around $28 billion worth of gold lies beneath Congo's soil. To acquire the greatest profits, foreign companies operate illegally in Congo by providing weapons to terrorist groups, taxing workers, and supplying large machines to dredge riverbeds for gold. They smuggle the gold and tax revenue out of the country without paying taxes to the Congolese government. Although the illegal companies and armed militias profit from these gold rushes, the workers and residents of the towns are left in extreme poverty without roads, electricity, or running water.

ACTIVE OPTION

NG Learning Framework: Research Electronic Devices
ATTITUDE Responsibility
SKILL Collaboration

Divide the class into small groups and assign an electronic device to each, such as different types of cell phones, laptop computers, tablets, fitness trackers, and music devices. Have groups research the materials used to manufacture their assigned device, compile a list of the materials, and identify which materials are conflict minerals. Then have groups compare their lists with other groups and identify which device uses the most conflict minerals.

DIFFERENTIATE

ENGLISH LANGUAGE LEARNERS

Identify Facts Divide the class into small groups and have the groups conduct a round-robin activity to review what they have learned in the lesson. Ask groups to generate facts for about three to five minutes, with all students contributing. Finally, invite one student from each group to share his or her group's responses. Write all the facts on the board.

PRE-AP

Report on Conflict Mineral Provisions
Have students research the Dodd-Frank Act as well as steps other countries around the world have taken to avoid the use of conflict minerals. Ask them to investigate the opinions of opponents and proponents of these measures and report on their findings. Encourage students to state their position on any provisions.

See the Chapter Planner for more strategies for differentiation.

ANSWER

Possible response: Other commodities traded throughout history that have raised ethical issues include humans (as in the slave trade) and commodities that have either been strongly tied to the slave trade, such as cotton and sugar, or that have come from industries that exploit their workers and the environment, such as rubber, gold, and diamonds.

The Digital Era in the Balance

By definition, a revolution results in drastic change, and many times this change is positive. It is certainly true that the technology revolution of the late 20th and early 21st centuries has enhanced the modern world economy and society. But this transformation has also created new challenges.

A 2019 study suggests that the glacial ice sheet that covers Greenland is melting four times faster than scientists originally thought, with the loss of approximately 280 billion tons of ice per year between 2002 and 2016.

REVOLUTIONS IN TECHNOLOGY

The 20th-century invention of computers and later the microchip that increased their speed and reduced their size and cost transformed the way the world works, communicates, and transports goods and people. New technology has improved world **connectivity**, the state of being connected to others. People today use computers to manage their finances, buy products and services, keep up with the news, and do their jobs from different places. These activities are accomplished via the Internet with the help of artificial satellites, which can also use Global Positioning Systems (GPS) to find exact locations. You use advanced technology every time you post a photo or an emoji on social media. Astronauts and physicists use some of this technology in modern space exploration, including the International Space Station, planet rovers, and space probes.

Advanced technology has given us new capabilities, but it has also created never-before-dreamed-of problems. The Internet allows quick transmission of information, but many people, businesses, and even governments want access to that information for personal gain or control. Cloud computing, or the storage of information through the Internet, has increased the risk of information falling into the wrong hands. **Hackers** are individuals who illegally gain access to electronic information. Some commit cybercrimes, or illegal activity committed online. For example, Russian hackers have been accused of using technology to interfere with the 2016 U.S. presidential election. Other hacking crimes include phishing, which is a type of Internet scam that tricks people into providing personal information, and the use of malware, software that makes computers unusable.

Other cyber criminals commit electronic espionage, or spying to gain information from businesses or government. The posting of classified U.S. documents

by the group WikiLeaks raised debate about the concept of treason versus free speech. Electronic sabotage—or destruction of property such as a company, political party, or government website—is a crime, too. Computer engineers continue to explore the use of **cryptography**, secret codes and scrambling of data, to keep electronic information safe. Other problems include lack of privacy, addiction to the Internet, and disrespectful social network messages. Those who post offensive or threatening messages are known as **trolls**. People also wonder whether workers will lose their jobs to robotic equipment in the near future.

ENVIRONMENTAL CHALLENGES

Today, Earth is warming at an alarming rate as a result of **climate change**, or changes to global weather patterns. Melting polar ice caps may cause extreme flooding in some places. For example, 55 million people living in Bangladesh's coastal lands would be displaced by a slight rise in sea levels. Elsewhere, global warming causes severe droughts. Most scientists believe current climate change is the effect of burning carbon-emitting

fossil fuels, which create greenhouse gases. These gases trap heat in the atmosphere and speed global warming.

Climate change can disrupt economies and governments. You read about the theory that food shortages due to climate change contributed to wars and other hostilities around the world during the 17th century. Both floods and droughts may cause food shortages, which lead to higher food prices. Regional conflicts might erupt due to scarcity not only of food but also of water. Human migration patterns might change as people in affected locations try to move to safer places, causing overpopulation or tension over immigration policies. And disease flourishes in areas hit by natural disasters.

Some nations have made significant investments in renewable energy sources to replace fossil fuels. Germany plans to rely primarily on renewable fuel sources by 2020. A 2015 meeting resulted in the UN-sponsored Paris Agreement on climate change, in which 195 nations pledged to limit greenhouse gas emissions. However in 2017, President Donald Trump announced that the United States would withdraw from the accord.

Selected Breakthroughs in Computer Technology

1946	ENIAC, the first programmable general-purpose electronic digital computer, is completed in Philadelphia, Pennsylvania. It takes up a 1,500-square-foot room.
1969	ARPANET—a forerunner of the Internet—is established as the first computer network.
1971	Intel introduces its first microchip, for memory storage, and microprocessor, for computation.
1972	The release of PONG jumpstarts the new industry of arcade video games.
1976	Steve Wozniak joins with partner Steve Jobs to market his Apple-1 computer.
1981	The market for personal computers booms after IBM introduces its PC with its MS-DOS operating system. The PC is widely cloned by companies such as Compaq.
1984	Apple introduces the Macintosh, developing a reputation not just for computer strength but also for innovative design.
1990	Microsoft introduces the Windows 3.0 operating system, bundling it with Word and Excel software programs.
1991	The U.S. Congress passes the High Performance Computing and Communication Act, providing massive financial support for Internet connectivity.
1998	Google launches its search engine.
2000	The camera phone, the USB flash drive, and Sony's PlayStation 2 are introduced to the market.
2003	MySpace is founded, spreading the popularity of social networks, followed by Facebook in 2004.
2006	Amazon introduces cloud-based computing services.
2007	Apple releases the iPhone, ushering in the age of the smartphone.
2011	Netflix transitions from a DVD-by-mail service to a streaming video service.
2015	Apple releases the Apple Watch.

HISTORICAL THINKING

1. **READING CHECK** What are three benefits of communication technology?

2. **FORM AND SUPPORT OPINIONS** Which event from the time line of computer history do you think had the greatest impact on society? Explain.

3. **MAKE CONNECTIONS** How might climate change affect the region where you live?

PLAN: 2-PAGE LESSON

OBJECTIVE
Explain the improvements created by advanced technology and the consequent problems.

CRITICAL THINKING SKILLS FOR LESSON 3.4
- Form and Support Opinions
- Make Connections
- Summarize
- Identify
- Interpret Charts

HISTORICAL THINKING FOR CHAPTER 30
What challenges does the world face in the 21st century?

Developments in computer technology began by the mid-20th century, and climate change was evident long before then. Lesson 3.4 discusses the improvements created by advanced technology as well as consequent challenges and focuses briefly on environmental challenges.

Student eEdition online
Additional content for this lesson, including a photograph, is available online.

BACKGROUND FOR THE TEACHER
WikiLeaks Its website describes WikiLeaks as a multinational media organization specializing in the publication of censored and restricted official materials. Julian Assange, an Australian computer programmer and hacker, created the website in 2006. He defined WikiLeaks in *Der Spiegel* as "a giant library of the world's most persecuted documents." Based on his philosophy of opposition to "authoritarian" governments, among which he included the United States, Assange, through WikiLeaks, has published millions of classified and secret documents from sources and hackers worldwide. In May 2019, the U.S. Department of Justice, based on the Espionage Act, issued an 18-count superseding indictment against Assange for his role in publishing hundreds of thousands of secret military and diplomatic documents. The indictment alleged that beginning in late 2009, Assange was complicit with Chelsea Manning, then a U.S. Army intelligence analyst, to obtain and reveal the documents. Manning was convicted of espionage and theft in 2013. Assange was arrested in April 2019 in the United Kingdom and imprisoned pending extradition to the United States.

INTRODUCE & ENGAGE

TAKE A POLL

Poll students about their views on current issues. Ask students if their use of the Internet and social media has had positive or negative effects. Discuss student responses. Next ask students how worried they are about climate change and whether they believe world governments can work toward a solution. Again, discuss responses. Then tell students that this lesson will discuss the improvements and challenges created by advanced technology, along with challenges related to the environment.

TEACH

GUIDED DISCUSSION

1. **Summarize** Which type of cybercrime allows hackers to make purchases on other people's credit cards, and how does it work? *(Hackers engage in phishing, which is an Internet scam that tricks people into providing their personal information. The hackers use that information to make purchases for themselves.)*

2. **Identify** What computer technology can protect electronic information, and how is it defined? *(Cryptography can protect electronic information using secret codes and scrambling data.)*

INTERPRET CHARTS

Allow time for students to read and examine the table of breakthroughs in computer technology. **ASK:** In which year did the marketing of a personal computer begin, and which brand was first marketed? *(Marketing began with the Apple brand in 1976.)* Which company introduced the Windows operating system, and in which year? *(Microsoft introduced Windows in 1990.)*

ACTIVE OPTIONS

On Your Feet: Think, Pair, Share Give students a few minutes to think about the following topic: Democratic governments should regulate social media companies to eliminate fake news, hate speech, and other harmful content. Then have students choose partners and talk about the topic for five minutes. Finally, allow individual students to share their ideas with the class.

> **NG Learning Framework: Write a Report**
> ATTITUDES Responsibility, Empowerment
> KNOWLEDGE Our Living Planet

Direct students to conduct research to learn more about the Paris Agreement, such as what the pact says, which countries signed it, and its goals. Then ask students to explain in a brief report the impact of and reasoning behind President Trump's withdrawal from the pact, including possible tensions between the United States and its allies. Invite volunteers to present their reports to the class.

DIFFERENTIATE

STRIVING READERS

Interpret a Chart Pair students with proficient readers who can help them understand the time line of computer technology history. Tell pairs to read the table together. As they read, have the proficient partner point out what might be the more significant breakthroughs. Then have them work together to answer Historical Thinking questions 1 and 2.

PRE-AP

Analyze a Paradox Share the Background for the Teacher information. Explain that the case of Julian Assange has caused some news analysts to raise this question: Did Assange act as a cybercriminal or as a journalist whose investigative reporting falls under the protection of First Amendment rights of a free press? Direct students to research the question and write an argumentative essay to support their opinion. Invite them to share their essays with the class.

See the Chapter Planner for more strategies for differentiation.

HISTORICAL THINKING

ANSWERS

1. Answers will vary but might include sharing information, quickly learning about world news, enabling working from home, finding locations through GPS, increasing purchasing options, communicating easily among people.

2. Answers will vary. Possible response: the invention of ARPANET, because it led to development of the Internet, which revolutionized communication and commerce

3. Answers will vary but might focus on flooding or drought conditions, food and water shortages, changes in economic activity, migration to and from certain places, stronger restrictions on burning fossil fuels, and increased wildfires.

Traveler: Ai Weiwei
A Creative Force in China B. 1957

Chinese artist Ai Weiwei uses his art to challenge the status quo, forcing us to take a critical look at the world around us. His works transcend the present day to convey universal themes, such as individuals in society. His conceptual art can make us uncomfortable, forcing us to think rather than merely consume.

HIS LIFE
Ai Weiwei grew up in poverty in the desert camp where his father, once a famous poet, was sent during one of Mao Zedong's purges. But he persisted in his quest to be an artist. As a young man, he traveled to New York City with a camera but almost no money. In 1993, he returned to China, finding success and impressing the world with his design for Beijing's Bird's Nest Stadium for the 2008 Summer Olympics.

However, Ai's work was often subversive of government authority, as when he investigated the 2008 Sichuan earthquake and exposed government lies by using his

Remembering (top right): This installation commemorates the children lost in a 2008 Sichuan earthquake because poorly constructed buildings collapsed. The Chinese government tried to keep this information secret, but Ai wanted the world to know.
Forever Bicycles (right): This dazzling installation of more than 1,200 Chinese bikes went on display in Austin, Texas, in 2017. Ai's work laments that bikes—a long-time important means of transportation for the Chinese people—are being replaced by cars.

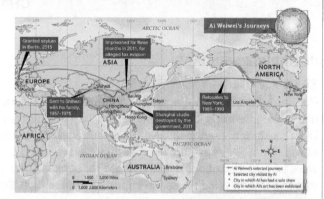

website to publish the names of all the children who were killed. To silence him, the Chinese government shut down his blog, put him under police surveillance, severely damaged his Shanghai studio, detained him for several months, and placed him under house arrest. When the government confiscated Ai's passport, his response was characteristically creative. As he explained, "Every morning I am putting a bouquet of flowers in the basket of a bicycle outside the front door." No longer allowed to post on his blog, he turned to Twitter to relay messages. Although he was allowed to travel again in 2015, China's harassment of Ai continues. His studio was destroyed again in 2018. Even so, he is determined not to give up his rights to freedom of expression and freedom of speech.

HIS WORK
Ai Weiwei mainly expresses himself through sculpture and art installations, which consist of many items made with mixed media displayed in a large area. Even when Ai was not allowed to travel, his exhibitions could. In 2014, an exhibit exploring the theme of incarceration went on display at the former Alcatraz Prison in San Francisco. In 2017, Ai created a documentary film called *Human Flow*, described as "a heartbreaking exploration into the global refugee crisis." At about the same time, his New York City public art project *Good Fences Make Good Neighbors* invited immigrants to share their own stories and those of their families.

On August 3, 2018, without warning, Chinese authorities began demolishing Ai Weiwei's studio in Beijing to make room for redevelopment. Ai's staff scrambled to remove artworks before they were destroyed. In the following excerpt from an interview with National Public Radio, Ai discusses the status of the art community in China.

PRIMARY SOURCE

Free speech and free expression have simply never existed in China or in its artist communities. Those who do not belong to the establishment, including artists, are always the first to be discriminated against and sacrificed. Often, the authorities face no consequences in doing so.

—Ai Weiwei, 2018

HISTORICAL THINKING

1. **READING CHECK** What three issues are important to Ai Weiwei?

2. **INTERPRET MAPS** Where has Ai's art been exhibited the most? Why?

3. **MAKE INFERENCES** What was the significance of Ai's putting flowers in a bicycle basket daily while he was denied his passport?

4. **ANALYZE VISUALS** Choose one of Ai's works. What universal themes are addressed in this work?

PLAN: 2-PAGE LESSON

OBJECTIVE
Understand how artist Ai Weiwei has used his art to critique China's corrupt and authoritarian bureaucracy, provoking a backlash from the government.

CRITICAL THINKING SKILLS FOR LESSON 4.1
- Interpret Maps
- Make Inferences
- Analyze Visuals
- Synthesize
- Explain
- Analyze Primary Sources

HISTORICAL THINKING FOR CHAPTER 30
What challenges does the world face in the 21st century?

The world continues to face challenges in the realms of human rights, freedom of speech and expression, rights of prisoners, responsibility of government, and preservation of cultural heritage. Lesson 4.1 discusses Chinese artist Ai Weiwei's expression of these social and political issues.

BACKGROUND FOR THE TEACHER

Early Years Ai Weiwei's father, Ai Qing, was one of China's leading poets, having traveled to Paris in the 1920s. He joined the Communist Party, was imprisoned by the Nationalist Party, and achieved fame in the 1950s before Mao launched an "anti-rightist" campaign and sent Ai Qing with his family into exile near the Gobi Desert. For 20 years his poetry was forbidden while he cleaned toilets at a "re-education" camp. Even the thaw that came with Mao's death, and the return of his father to official favor, did not create the space Ai Weiwei needed for his art. In 1981, at age 24, he fled to New York. Menial labor and financial hardship were part of Ai Weiwei's New York experience but so was the freedom to explore, energized by the East Village artist scene. When his father fell ill in 1993, Ai Weiwei returned home to replicate that type of artist community in Beijing, rising rapidly to international success and then being repressed by the communist rule.

📝 History Notebook
Encourage students to complete the Traveler page for Chapter 30 in their History Notebooks as they read.

Student eEdition online
Additional content for this lesson, including an image gallery, is available online.

INTRODUCE & ENGAGE

DISCUSS PROTESTS

Ask students to think about ways people protest social and political issues. Explain that art is one way in which people express their concerns and protest repressive governments. Tell students that they will learn about how one Chinese artist uses art to protest the Chinese government.

TEACH

GUIDED DISCUSSION

1. **Synthesize** How do the experiences of Ai Weiwei exemplify some of the best and some of the worst aspects of contemporary China? *(Possible response: Ai has found success and impressed the world with his art. However, he has faced repression, harassment, violence, imprisonment, and vandalism at the hands of the Chinese government.)*

2. **Explain** Why does the Chinese government continue to harass Ai Weiwei? *(Possible response: because he remains determined to criticize its actions through his art)*

ANALYZE PRIMARY SOURCES

Ask students to examine the primary source. **ASK:** How does Ai describe the art community in China? *(without free speech and free expression, first to be discriminated against and sacrificed)* How is this discrimination evident? *(Without warning or consequences, authorities demolished Ai's studio.)* How would the situation have been different if Chinese authorities allowed freedom of expression? *(Possible response: They would have worked with Ai on a solution rather than demolish his studio.)*

ACTIVE OPTIONS

On Your Feet: Jigsaw Strategy Have students form "expert" groups to research each art piece in the lesson and in the image gallery (available in the Student eEdition). Tell them to research the public opinion of each piece. Regroup students so that each group has at least one member from each expert group. Students report on their findings and discuss their impressions of each piece in comparison to the public's opinion.

NG Learning Framework: Analyze Ai Weiwei's Works
ATTITUDE Empowerment
SKILL Observation

Ai Weiwei practices conceptual art, with a predominant idea underlying his artistic execution and materials and aesthetics embodying his driving concept. It is always relevant to ask: What does it mean? Assign groups the following works: *Dropping a Han Dynasty Urn, Study of Perspective, Sunflower Seeds,* and *Straight.* After they examine each work online, have them consider the following questions: What thoughts and feelings might Ai be intending to provoke? What concept underlies these images? What might be Ai's rationale behind this piece? What does it mean? Tell groups to discuss their ideas and any information they found about the piece to create a brief presentation for the class. As a class, discuss the similarities and differences between Ai's works and their meanings.

DIFFERENTIATE

STRIVING READERS

Preview Text Preview the lesson title, main idea, headings, photos, map, and primary source. Ask students what they think the lesson will be about, referring to the information gained from the features. As students read, help them confirm their understandings of each paragraph and feature before moving on to the next.

PRE-AP

Analyze a Documentary Ask students to view the documentary film *Ai Weiwei: Never Sorry.* Note that the film is R-rated; if students are unable to watch it, tell them to research the film, read reviews, and watch the trailer. Have them write a report on the film, analyzing its purpose, its effectiveness in achieving its goal, and the filmmaker's perspective toward Ai and his work. They should include their thoughts on the film and the reasons they would or would not recommend it to others.

See the Chapter Planner for more strategies for differentiation.

HISTORICAL THINKING

ANSWERS

1. Important issues: calling out human rights abuses, protection of human rights, responsibility of government, rights of prisoners, protection of freedom of speech and expression, preserving cultural heritage

2. The United States and Western Europe; those areas include democratic nations that allow freedom of speech and expression.

3. Answers will vary but may include: to continue to bring beauty and color to the world, to remind people daily of his predicament, to protest in a lighthearted and creative way.

4. Answers will vary.

Women's Leadership and Gender Rights

History has had no lack of powerful and notable women leaders, from Cleopatra VII to Elizabeth I. But while "women hold up half the sky," they are still less likely than men to hold positions of leadership and power.

WOMEN LEADING NATIONS AND CORPORATIONS

You have already learned about three influential women leaders in the 20th century—Indira Gandhi of India, Golda Meir of Israel, and Margaret Thatcher of the United Kingdom. Since their time in office, the number of women heads of state has grown—albeit slowly. According to the United Nations, as of January 2019 there are 10 women currently serving as head of state and 10 women serving as head of government.

The most recent of these leaders is **Sahle-Work Zewde** of Ethiopia, who was elected as the country's first female president in October 2018. While the role of president is traditionally a ceremonial role, her election was part of a larger movement to appoint more women to influential positions in the Ethiopian government by Prime Minister Abiy Ahmed. As you've already learned, half of the prime minister's cabinet is composed of women.

The world's youngest female head of government is **Jacinda Ardern** of New Zealand. She became prime minister in 2017 at the age of 37. In addition to promoting the progressive agenda of her Labour Party, including the passage of housing affordability measures and tax credits for new parents and vulnerable families, Ardern also gave birth to her first child, becoming the first leader of a country in nearly 30 years to give birth while in office.

CRITICAL VIEWING New Zealand prime minister Jacinda Ardern consoles members of the Muslim community at a refugee center the day after a right-wing extremist terrorized two mosques in the city of Christchurch, killing 50 worshipers. Based on the details in the photo, how would you characterize Ardern as a leader?

In March 2019, attacks on two mosques in New Zealand left 50 dead and approximately 50 injured. Ardern was praised around the world for her response to the tragedy. Calling the assaults a "terrorist attack" and one of the "darkest days" in her country's history, she led the charge for changes to New Zealand's gun laws while showing empathy toward the victims and denouncing white nationalism. In 2020, Ardern was also praised for her response to the COVID-19 pandemic.

In addition to government and politics, women have also made strides as leaders of large corporations and international organizations. One of the most powerful women in the financial world is France's **Christine Lagarde**, who has served as managing director of the International Monetary Fund (IMF) since 2011—the first woman to do so. As a strong advocate of female economic empowerment, Lagarde believes it is key to the strength of the world economy. She also believes a greater presence of women in senior leadership positions in the financial industry would lead to less risk and speculation. After the 2008 financial crisis, she noted that "if it had been Lehman Sisters rather than Lehman Brothers, the world might well look a lot different today."

The "civilizing" presence of women in leadership positions also holds true in the corporate world. As CEO of PepsiCo, Indian-born **Indra Nooyi** guided the company through the Great Recession, creating a rise in shareholder returns and a growth in net revenue. She also steered the company toward selling more nutritious options such as hummus, juices, and kombucha. PepsiCo celebrated Nooyi as a new type of business leader who tried to "do well by doing good."

Even with these successes, there is still a long way to go. When Nooyi stepped down as CEO in 2018, she was replaced by a man. Today, the percentage of women CEOs at Fortune 500 companies is 6.6 percent. In government, only 24 percent of all national legislative bodies around the world are women. And even though 39 percent of the global workforce consists of women, as of 2018, women are still paid only 68 percent of what men earn for the same jobs.

Malala Yousafzai gives a speech as she unveils her official portrait at the Barbar Institute of Fine Arts in Birmingham, England, in 2018. The event occurred three years after she was shot and seriously wounded by Taliban fighters for speaking out against restrictions to women's education.

WOMEN LEADING CAUSES

Women's leadership isn't limited to political or business roles. Women have led social movements, taking a stand and improving not only women's rights but also human rights. From the fight for the right to vote to access to education to the fight for basic freedoms, women around the world have led the way in causes for social and economic advancement. The path has not been easy and those who have fought for women's rights have done so at great risk. Even so, their commitment and courage is unwavering.

In 2011, the Nobel Committee awarded the Nobel Peace Prize to Yemeni activist **Tawakkol Karman**, founder of Women Journalists Without Chains—an organization dedicated to women's rights, civil rights, and freedom of expression. She also became a leader of the Arab Spring in Yemen, organizing peaceful protests for which she was arrested and imprisoned several times. Today, she continues to speak out against the ongoing civil conflict that is tearing her country apart and creating a humanitarian crisis.

Another Nobel Laureate (2014), **Malala Yousafzai** of Pakistan, has led the way for young girls to demand equal education. When she was 11 years old, she began blogging about life under the Islamist Taliban, whose severe form of Islamic law restricted education for

---

PLAN: 6-PAGE LESSON

OBJECTIVE

Evaluate progress made in the areas of women's leadership and gender rights in the 21st century.

CRITICAL THINKING SKILLS FOR LESSON 4.2

- Make Inferences
- Analyze Language Use
- Draw Conclusions
- Evaluate
- Make Generalizations
- Compare and Contrast
- Summarize
- Explain
- Analyze Visuals

HISTORICAL THINKING FOR CHAPTER 30

What challenges does the world face in the 21st century?

Gender equality remained an important issue as the 21st century began. Lesson 4.2 focuses on key figures and developments in women's leadership and gender rights and assesses the progress made by the LGBTQ community.

BACKGROUND FOR THE TEACHER

Jacinda Ardern New Zealand prime minister Jacinda Ardern grew up on the country's North Island. After receiving a degree in communication studies in 2001, she worked in the offices of Prime Minister Helen Clark and, in England, Prime Minister Tony Blair. Ardern entered New Zealand's Parliament in 2008. She became Labor Party leader in August 2017 and prime minister the following October. She is an advocate of child poverty reduction and a strong opponent of racism. Although raised a Mormon, Ardern left the church because of its discriminatory policies toward same-sex marriage and the LGBTQ community. She has become a feminist icon for her promotion of gender equality. Ardern advocated global women's rights in a speech to the United Nations. "Me Too must become We Too," she said. Ardern advocated optimism at the Climate Action Summit of the United Nations in September 2019. She outlined methods in trading relationships that could contribute to a solution, and pointed out that 80 percent of New Zealand's electricity already comes from hydroelectric and wind power.

Student eEdition online

Additional content for this lesson, including photographs and captions, is available online.

INTRODUCE & ENGAGE

PREVIEW WITH VISUALS

Direct students' attention to the photo of Jacinda Ardern. Have students respond to the Critical Viewing question and discuss the responses as a class. Challenge students to compose a one- or two-sentence caption for the photo that characterizes Jacinda Ardern as a leader. Then tell students that in this lesson they will learn about women in leadership positions along with gains in gender rights and progress for the LGBTQ community.

TEACH

GUIDED DISCUSSION

1. **Evaluate** How might Indra Nooyi exemplify the idea expressed by Christine Lagarde that women's leadership can result in economic strength and lead to less risk and speculation? *(Possible response: Nooyi demonstrated the kind of wise financial management Lagarde's remarks imply. Nooyi guided PepsiCo through the Great Recession. She was able to create a rise in shareholder returns and grow net revenue.)*

2. **Make Generalizations** How would you characterize women's abilities from the examples of women in corporate and government leadership positions? *(Answers will vary. Possible response: Women are equal to men in the ability to lead and can bring a new perspective to the role of leadership.)*

ANALYZE VISUALS

Have students read the information about Tawakkol Karman and view the photograph and accompanying caption in the Student eEdition. **ASK:** How does the information about Karman indicate that the Arab Spring failed in Yemen? *(Karman was arrested and imprisoned for organizing peaceful protests, which indicates that women's rights and civil liberties are still harshly repressed in Yemen.)*

DIFFERENTIATE

GIFTED & TALENTED

Create a Photo Essay Direct students to conduct online research to find five additional women who are leaders in government, the corporate world, or public life as advocates of social causes. Ask students to use online and print sources to locate photos of the women they choose. Then have students create a photo essay. Remind them to cite the sources of the photographs and to write a brief caption about each woman as a leader. Suggest students include a brief overview to begin the photo essay. Ask students to present their photo essays to the class.

See the Chapter Planner for more strategies for differentiation.

girls. As Yousafzai spoke out against the restrictions, she gained international prominence but also incited revenge from the Taliban. On her way home from school one day in 2012, Taliban fighters stopped her school bus and shot her in the head. After undergoing surgery and rehabilitation in Britain, Yousafzai launched the Malala Fund, an organization that supports leadership and learning for girls.

In Saudi Arabia, women have been fighting for decades for their rights, including their right to drive. In 2018, the country lifted the ban on women driving, but that progress came with a price. Weeks prior to the end of the ban, the Saudi government arrested several women's rights activists who challenged the driving ban and made peaceful calls for reform. Charged with harming national interests, the women were held in prison for nearly a year without a trial. In early 2019, some women faced trial and some women were released, but others remain in prison, where they have undergone torture and harassment.

GENDER RIGHTS FOR LGBTQ PEOPLE

In June 2015, the U.S. Supreme Court ruled that same-sex couples could marry nationwide. The court's ruling was a long-awaited step forward for the gay community. These rights aren't limited to the United States. In May 2019, Taiwan also made history by becoming the first country in Asia to legalize same-sex marriage. As of 2019, more than 25 countries in the world have laws protecting the right of same-sex couples to marry.

As support for LGBTQ (lesbian, gay, bisexual, transgender, and questioning or queer) rights seems to be increasing around the world, gender rights continue to be an issue. Many LGBTQ people have suffered from discrimination and violence because of their sexual orientation or gender identity. Many countries still criminalize same-sex relations—with some even applying the death penalty as punishment. In Russia, a 2013 law defined advocating for the human rights of LGBTQ people as "propaganda" and stated that anyone supporting LGBTQ rights could be arrested. In 2019 in

Supporters of same-sex marriage participate in a rally outside the parliament building in Taipei, Taiwan, as lawmakers discuss three different draft bills of a same-sex marriage law.

NATIONAL GEOGRAPHIC EXPLORER **KAKENYA NTAIYA**

Empowering Kenya's Girls

Kakenya Ntaiya (shown here with her students) grew up in Enoosaen, Kenya, a rural community about 250 miles from Nairobi. Engaged to a neighbor boy at the age of five, Ntaiya was expected to marry him when she turned 12. Tradition required her to drop out of school at this time, but Ntaiya bargained with her father to let her finish high school and remain unmarried. He agreed. Ntaiya bucked tradition again when she won a scholarship to a U.S. college. The village elders eventually agreed to support her education after she promised to return to Kenya. Her dream? To build a school for girls. Ntaiya established the Kakenya Center for Excellence boarding school in Kenya in 2009 with 30 students, and today, it boasts several hundred success stories. "We've created a model for rural communities to empower and create leaders," Ntaiya says. "The goal is to plant women in leadership positions so they can make a difference." The families of girls who attend the school must promise that their children will remain unmarried while in school. "In the process, I learned something much bigger," Ntaiya notes. "When you empower a girl, you transform a community. School is just a start."

response to a global backlash, however, the government of Brunei backtracked on enforcing laws that would have made same-sex relationships punishable by stoning to death.

Progress has also been made related to transgender rights in some countries. Denmark became the first European nation to allow for legal documents reflecting the gender identity of transgender people. In 2014, India's Supreme Court officially recognized transgender people as a legal third gender. Third gender is a category for individuals defined by either themselves or by society as neither man nor woman. It is a category in societies that recognize three or more genders.

In 2017, *National Geographic* magazine dedicated an entire issue to the topic of gender. One of the topics covered in the issue was the complexity of gender and how it is an amalgamation of several elements, including chromosomes, anatomy, hormones, psychology, and culture. The magazine also profiled cultures where a third gender is the norm, such as the *fa'afafine* of Samoa.

With each step forward for gender rights for LGBTQ and third gender people, pioneering activists and lawmakers around the world are slowly making progress and creating hope for the future.

HISTORICAL THINKING

1. **READING CHECK** What are some key issues that women's rights activists around the world are fighting for?

2. **MAKE INFERENCES** Why do you think the growth in the number of women in political leadership positions has been slow to progress?

3. **ANALYZE LANGUAGE USE** What do you think Christine Lagarde meant when she said, "If it had been Lehman Sisters rather than Lehman Brothers, the world might well look a lot different today"?

4. **DRAW CONCLUSIONS** What conclusions can you draw about the attitude of groups like the Taliban and the government of Saudi Arabia toward women?

BACKGROUND FOR THE TEACHER

Kakenya Ntaiya No girl from Kakenya Ntaiya's village had ever left to attend college in the United States. Ntaiya received a scholarship to attend Randolph College (formerly Randolph-Macon Woman's College) in Virginia. Although she grew up in a home without electricity, Ntaiya soon learned to compose her papers on computers. Ntaiya became the first youth advisor to the United Nations Population Fund and traveled worldwide to advocate for girls' education. She went on to receive her doctorate in education from the University of Pittsburgh in 2011. She is a strong advocate of the right of girls to reject mutilation and childhood marriage. She believes that educating a girl also educates the fathers, boys, and everybody in the girl's circle. In that way, the community can learn to respect the rights of girls and women. Ntaiya looks toward a world in which boys and girls are treated equally. She is the founder of Kakenya's Dream, an international nonprofit organization formed to motivate girls to become leaders and agents of change. "We are powerful," Ntaiya said in a Harvard Voices of Leadership interview. "We are the change makers. And we are the future." Her numerous awards include a Vital Voices Global Leadership Award and the Global Women's Rights Award by the Feminist Majority Foundation. She was named one of *Newsweek's* "150 Women Who Shake the World" in 2011 and a Top Ten CNN Hero in 2013.

TEACH

GUIDED DISCUSSION

3. **Compare and Contrast** How would you compare expectations for girls in Pakistan and Kenya based on the experiences of Malala Yousafzai and Kakenya Ntaiya? *(In both countries, girls are minimally educated and expected to marry young. In Pakistan, the Taliban Islamists severely restrict learning for girls. Taliban fighters shot Yousafzai for advocating education. In Kenya, girls leave school at age 12 and marry. However, Ntaiya was able to bargain with her father and village elders to become educated and found a girls' school.)*

4. **Summarize** What gains has the LGBTQ community experienced in the 21st century? *(In 2015, the U.S. Supreme Court ruled that same-sex couples could marry nationwide. In 2019, Taiwan legalized same-sex marriage. As of 2019, more than 25 countries legally protect same-sex marriage. Denmark allows legal documents to reflect the gender identity of transgender people. In 2014, India recognized transgender people as a legal third gender.)*

MORE INFORMATION

Loujain al-Hathloul A prominent Saudi Arabian women's rights defender, Loujain al-Hathloul was arrested in May 2018, along with a number of other women activists. Their crime was "attempting to destabilize the kingdom" due to their challenge of the country's ban on women driving and other guardianship laws that give Saudi men almost complete control over the lives of women. Even though the driving ban was overturned in 2019 and the government has eased some of the guardianship restrictions, al-Hathloul has not been released from prison. Instead, she has been subjected to torture, sexual harassment, and threats of execution and rape. According to her brother, al-Hathloul was offered a release if she signed a document and appeared on television denying accusations of torture. She refused. Her trial, which was supposed to begin in March 2020 was indefinitely postponed due to the COVID-19 pandemic. The detention of al-Hathloul and other activists has tainted the reputation of Saudi Crown Prince Muhammad bin Salman, heir to the throne, who has tried to bill himself as a reformer.

DIFFERENTIATE

INCLUSION

Predict Using Photographs and Captions Pair special needs students with students who can assist in making the text more accessible. Ask pairs to look at each photograph and take turns reading its caption, including the photos and captions in the Student eEdition. Ask students to predict what they will learn based on what they read and see. Encourage students who are assisting to aid in taking notes.

See the Chapter Planner for more strategies for differentiation.

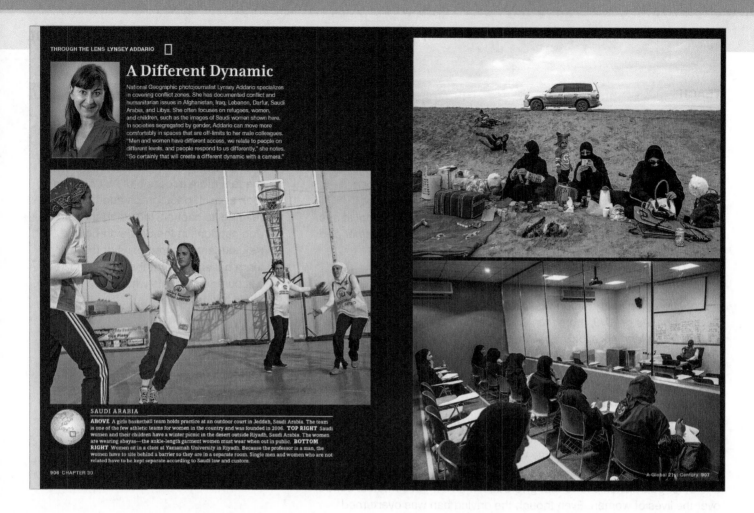

A Different Dynamic

National Geographic photojournalist Lynsey Addario specializes in covering conflict zones. She has documented conflict and humanitarian issues in Afghanistan, Iraq, Lebanon, Darfur, Saudi Arabia, and Libya. She often focuses on refugees, women, and children, such as the images of Saudi women shown here. In societies segregated by gender, Addario can move more comfortably in spaces that are off-limits to her male colleagues. "Men and women have different access, we relate to people on different levels, and people respond to us differently," she notes. "So certainly that will create a different dynamic with a camera."

SAUDI ARABIA

ABOVE A girls basketball team holds practice at an outdoor court in Jeddah, Saudi Arabia. The team is one of the few athletic teams for women in the country and was founded in 2006. **TOP RIGHT** Saudi women and their children have a winter picnic in the desert outside Riyadh, Saudi Arabia. The women are wearing abayas—the ankle-length garment women must wear when out in public. **BOTTOM RIGHT** Women sit in a class at Yamamah University in Riyadh. Because the professor is a man, the women have to site behind a barrier so they are in a separate room. Single men and women who are not related have to be kept separate according to Saudi law and custom.

BACKGROUND FOR THE TEACHER

Lynsey Addario After studying international relations, National Geographic photographer Lynsey Addario had a thought: photojournalism could be a marriage between international relations and art, telling stories with pictures. Fast-forward a few years, and Addario is one of National Geographic's most accomplished conflict photographers. Refugees and the contemporary effects of migration are a primary focus of her work. "My philosophy has always been that I'm there for the people I'm covering," says Addario. "I'm just a messenger documenting whatever is going on and bringing their message to people in power who may be able to do something about it."

Addario's journalism uncovers how location affects human experiences. In addition to documenting forced migration and refugees, Addario exposes life and conflict in Afghanistan since the fall of the Taliban, stark reality in sub-Saharan Africa, and the often hidden experiences of women in Southwest Asia. Yet even after winning numerous prestigious awards—including a Pulitzer Prize—Addario confesses she still panics before a new assignment, concerned that her photographs won't capture the story. Even so, Addario believes she understands how to photograph people better than she did when she started. For one thing, she's learned how important it is to form a deep connection with people before she turns her lens toward them.

TEACH

GUIDED DISCUSSION

5. **Compare and Contrast** Study Lynsey Addario's photo of the picnic scene in the desert. How does it resemble a picnic you might see in your hometown? How is it different? *(Possible response: The picnic is similar to something I might see in my hometown in that it is a group of mothers and children spending time socializing together in nature, away from the city. The picnic is different because the women are dressed to cover themselves while the children are not. There is also no indication that fathers or other adult males are part of the picnic.)*

6. **Explain** According to Addario, how is it easier for her to document the lives of women in societies that are segregated by gender? *(Because she is also a woman, Addario can gain access to places that men cannot. Women in these societies are also probably more comfortable around her than they would be around a male photographer, so Addario can get a more accurate glimpse into everyday life.)*

THROUGH THE LENS

Draw attention to the Through the Lens feature. Briefly discuss Lynsey Addario's perspective on a woman's ability to function in societies segregated by gender. Then have students view the photographs and read the captions. **ASK:** What message does Addario convey through her images of women in Saudi Arabia? *(Possible response: Saudi women lack full equality. They cannot mingle with men in public and must wear ankle-length black garments and headscarves. However, although kept separated from a male professor, women may attend university classes. They may join one of the few women's athletic teams and enter the workforce.)*

ACTIVE OPTIONS

On Your Feet: Numbered Heads Arrange students in small groups and have members of each group number off. Ask students to think about the following question: What are the prospects for full equality for women worldwide based on the information in the lesson? Then tell groups to discuss the topic for several minutes. Finally, call out a number and have the student with that number summarize the group's discussion.

> **NG Learning Framework: Prepare a Comparative Report**
> **ATTITUDE** Empowerment
> **KNOWLEDGE** Our Human Story

Have students work in groups to conduct online research about the different expectations for women around the world today. Ask students to use information in the lesson as a starting point, including their response to Historical Thinking question 4. Ask groups to use their research to prepare a report in which they compare the rights of women in as many as three countries in various locations. Countries might include Saudi Arabia, Yemen, China, the United States, or the United Kingdom. Invite students to present and discuss their reports as a class.

HISTORICAL THINKING

ANSWERS

1. Key issues include the rights to an education and basic freedoms, such as the right to drive a car.

2. Answers will vary. Students might say that fewer women than men run for office or that women have fewer opportunities than men who have been in politics for a long time.

3. Possible response: Lagarde meant that if more women had been involved in the financial industry, the 2008 financial crisis might not have occurred.

4. Possible response: These groups are fearful of women having the same rights and power as men. They might also think that women are inferior to men.

CRITICAL VIEWING Ardern wears a headscarf to show her respect for the traditional style of Muslim women. She holds a woman's hand in both of hers, which indicates compassion, and her expression conveys a willingness to listen attentively.

The State of Global Health

Throughout history, the movement of diseases has accompanied the movement of people. At the end of 2019, a novel, or new, coronavirus was identified in Wuhan, China. The virus, which causes a serious respiratory illness called COVID-19, quickly spread around the world, leading to unprecedented social and economic disruptions as countries raced to contain outbreaks.

TODAY'S HEALTH CONCERNS

As you have witnessed with COVID-19, international mobility has increased the risk of pandemics around the world. Related illnesses, such as MERS and SARS, spread among countries through contact with infected foreign visitors. New strains of malaria hop from continent to continent by way of mosquito hosts carried on airplanes. Another species of mosquito spreads the Zika virus in a similar manner. And an overreliance on antibiotics has allowed the growth of new strains of bacteria that are resistant to treatment. Such developments overtax health care systems around the world.

Students return to class at a school in Hebei Province, China, for the first time in five months after schools were closed due to the COVID-19 pandemic.

Over the years, more than 35 million people worldwide have lost their lives to HIV/AIDS, which spreads through human contact. About 37 million people—two-thirds of them in Africa—currently live with the disease. It strikes people at the prime of their productive and reproductive lives, so it can have devastating effects on society. Infection rates have stabilized in wealthier nations but not in developing ones. In India, where hundreds of millions of people lack basic health care, the number of people with HIV/AIDS has soared past 2.5 million.

The social and economic impacts of pandemics can be catastrophic. Infected people are removed from the workforce, causing economic setbacks. Social interaction becomes limited as individuals avoid public places for fear of contracting the disease. Businesses may be forced to close for weeks or even months, creating a dip in a nation's revenue. A decline in tourism can cause monetary loss as well. Also, countries with pandemics must devote large sums to fighting them that might otherwise go to infrastructure improvements.

Diseases and health-related fatalities are more common among some populations than others. In high-poverty areas, people cannot afford medical attention, and any they receive may be inadequate. Proper health care may be unavailable in places torn apart by war, experiencing a natural disaster, lacking electricity, or located far from a city. The shortage of medical facilities in such places prevents adequate disease surveillance. Even in a country with advanced medical facilities, such as the United States, poorer people often suffer from medical conditions that might easily be treated.

Other causes for the spread of disease include food scarcity, overcrowding, and poor sanitary conditions. Groups such as the World Health Organization (WHO) work to solve health challenges. So do NGOs such as Doctors Without Borders, Partners in Health, and Project HOPE. These NGOs supply health resources such as medicines, vaccines, and dietary guidance.

While much of the work of NGOs is geared toward solving health problems in high-poverty nations, more affluent nations are not exempt from experiencing health issues. In this case, one crisis may be linked to too much food rather than too little. In wealthier countries, obesity and inactivity lead to heart disease, type 2 diabetes, and other deadly conditions.

HEALTH ADVANCES

Despite increasing the spread of disease, globalization has contributed to improved health throughout the world. Breakthroughs have led to positive advances worldwide. Surgeon Charles R. Drew developed a way to store blood plasma in blood banks for future transfusion: an innovation that saved many lives worldwide. Mass vaccination resulted in the eradication of smallpox and has mostly eliminated polio. However, a recent increase in vaccine hesitancy has led to a resurgence of diseases that were once considered extinct around the world, such as measles and whooping cough. Later innovations included open-heart surgery, organ transplants, and the pacemaker. All these medical advances have helped many people survive.

By the year 2000, a breakthrough had been made in knowledge of the genome—the Human Genome Project had successfully mapped DNA. Solving this puzzle paved the way for new medical improvements. Also, the new century witnessed many innovations ranging from bionic prosthetics to targeted disease therapy. Many breakthroughs have been made in the field of **biotechnology**, the use of biological organisms or processes to create new products that improve life. One result is increased **longevity**, or increased lifespan, of individuals around the globe.

HISTORICAL THINKING

1. **READING CHECK** What causes diseases to spread from their point of origin to other places around the world?

2. **DRAW CONCLUSIONS** Why might a country like Syria be prone to pandemics?

3. **POSE AND ANSWER QUESTIONS** What three questions would you ask a scientist about biotechnology and the world's food supply?

NATIONAL GEOGRAPHIC EXPLORER
HAYAT SINDI

A Paper Medical Lab

For a girl growing up in Saudi Arabia, a country in which it was recently illegal for women to drive, becoming an expert in biotechnology seemed almost impossible. But Hayat Sindi beat the odds. A National Geographic Explorer, doctor, and scientist, she sums up her exciting career in one sentence: "My mission is to find simple, inexpensive ways to monitor health that are specifically designed for remote places and harsh conditions." And Sindi did just that when she created a low-cost disease detector from a small piece of paper. An individual only has to spit on the chemical-laced paper. Almost instantly, a dot on the paper changes color to reveal any liver damage in the patient. Sindi's invention allows people in remote rural areas to receive the medical attention they need to survive.

NATIONAL GEOGRAPHIC EXPLORER
JACK ANDRAKA

A Science Fair Discovery

In 2012, 15-year-old Jack Andraka was grieving for a friend he had lost to pancreatic cancer. He was also thinking about what to do for a science fair project. Andraka ended up creating a blood-test strip that costs just pennies to produce but accurately identifies signs of pancreatic cancer. For his efforts, Andraka won the top prize at the 2012 Intel International Science and Engineering Fair. The youthful innovator majored in electrical engineering and anthropology at Stanford University and founded his own company. His dream is to find solutions to health-care deficiencies in the developing world.

OBJECTIVE

Explain the influence of globalism on the growth of pandemics and treatment of diseases.

CRITICAL THINKING SKILLS FOR LESSON 4.3

- Draw Conclusions
- Pose and Answer Questions
- Summarize
- Compare and Contrast

HISTORICAL THINKING FOR CHAPTER 30

What challenges does the world face in the 21st century?

Medical advances and challenges continued into the new century. Lesson 4.3 discusses ongoing health concerns and the risk of pandemics with a focus on medical breakthroughs and technological innovations since the year 2000.

Student eEdition online

Additional content for this lesson, including photos and captions, is available online.

BACKGROUND FOR THE TEACHER

Global Malnutrition According to a 2018 Global Nutrition Report, malnutrition is unacceptably high and affects every country in the world. Malnutrition has various forms. The World Health Organization (WHO), a United Nations agency, indicates that malnutrition can cause a low height or weight for age, micronutrient deficiencies, obesity, and diet-related diseases such as heart disease, diabetes, and cancer. The WHO estimated in 2018 that 1.9 billion adults globally are overweight or obese and 462 million are underweight. An estimated 41 million children below the age of 5 years are overweight or obese, 155 million have a low height for their age, and 69 million are underweight. Approximately 45 percent of deaths among children under the age of 5 years are linked to under-nutrition. Many families cannot afford or obtain nutritious foods such as fruits, vegetables, meat, and milk, whereas foods high in fat, sugar, and salt are cheaper and easier to access. Malnutrition has serious social and economic consequences for countries. Progress in combating global malnutrition has been slow, but it is taking place.

INTRODUCE & ENGAGE

DISCUSS MEDICAL ADVANCES

Invite students to share what they know about the spread of diseases worldwide and their own experiences during the 2020 coronavirus pandemic. Ask students if they have heard or read about any recent discoveries in health care and discuss their answers. Tell students that in this lesson they will learn about the effect of globalism on pandemics, the health concerns of today, and the medical breakthroughs of the 21st century.

TEACH

GUIDED DISCUSSION

1. **Summarize** What are the possible economic impacts of a pandemic? *(Infected people leave the workforce, possibly forcing businesses to close for weeks with a consequent dip in tax revenue. Financial loss could occur from the decline of tourism. Fighting a pandemic diverts a country's funds away from infrastructure improvements that grow the economy.)*

2. **Draw Conclusions** Why might people in developed or affluent nations experience serious medical problems despite available healthcare? *(Obesity, inactivity, and too much food can cause medical conditions such as heart disease and type 2 diabetes. Distrust of being vaccinated could cause the resurgence of a disease that was once considered extinct.)*

COMPARE AND CONTRAST

Have students read and think about the National Geographic Explorer features on Hayat Sindi and Jack Andraka that appear in the lesson. **ASK:** How do the goals of Hayat Sindi and Jack Andraka compare? *(Possible response: Both are dedicated to finding inexpensive ways to detect illnesses so that healthcare can be improved among people in remote or developing parts of the world.)*

ACTIVE OPTIONS

On Your Feet: Inside-Outside Circle Arrange students in concentric circles facing each other. Tell students in the outside circle to pose questions about global health concerns and the impact of pandemics, such as the following: How can diseases spread worldwide? Ask students in the inner circle to answer their partner's question. On a signal, have students in the inside circle ask questions and those in the outside circle answer them.

| **NG Learning Framework: Research and Report**
ATTITUDES Curiosity, Responsibility
SKILL Problem-Solving

Instruct students to conduct research online and in print sources to answer the questions they developed in their response to Historical Thinking question 3 at the end of the lesson. Tell students to take notes as they conduct their research and summarize their findings in a report. Invite students to present their reports orally for class discussion.

DIFFERENTIATE

STRIVING READERS

Use Reciprocal Teaching Have pairs read each paragraph silently. Tell them to quiz each other about the paragraph, asking their partners to state the main idea, identify important details that support the main idea, and summarize the paragraph in their own words.

PRE-AP

Write an Article Have students research the Human Genome Project. Tell them to take notes as they conduct their research and maintain a record of the sources they consult. Encourage students to find information that explains the project, its goals, and its significance in the diagnosis and cure of disease. Ask students to write an article based on their findings and cite their sources. Invite students to share their articles on a class blog or website.

See the Chapter Planner for more strategies for differentiation.

HISTORICAL THINKING

ANSWERS

1. the movement of animal hosts and people already infected with the diseases

2. Possible response: Syria might be prone to pandemics because it has been completely disrupted by war. Also, because many Syrians have been forced to leave familiar areas, they might not have health resources available or not know where such resources are located.

3. Questions will vary but might include the following: How can biotechnology positively affect the world's food supply? What are genetically engineered crops, and how are they different from other crops? What possible dangers might biotechnology pose to the world's food supply?

Food Security

When you see an image of a vast field in Iowa or Nebraska—America's famed "amber waves of grain"—it probably doesn't occur to you that you're looking at the planet's largest ecosystem. Worldwide, agriculture covers more land than any other type of ecosystem. And yet, in many parts of the world, people struggle to get enough to eat.

A WORLD OF MOUTHS TO FEED

Food security means more than obtaining the minimum number of calories needed to stay alive. In the *Economist's* annual report on the state of global food security, the magazine defines it as "the state in which people at all times have physical, social and economic access to sufficient and nutritious food that meets their dietary needs for a healthy and active life."

Achieving food security is not simply a matter of quantity. When evaluating a region's food security, experts look at the availability of food, but they also consider affordability, quality, and safety. The Irish Potato Famine of 1845–1849 illustrates several of these issues. Irish people were starving because their diet relied on a potato crop that failed repeatedly, while Ireland under British rule was growing enough other crops to export. Food was being produced, but it was not available to a large part of the population. Or, when accessible, it was not affordable. Ireland's famine also illustrates a dimension of food security that many researchers are studying today—resilience in the face of shocks such as drought or natural disasters. Around one million people died because the potatoes they relied on for most of their nutrition were wiped out by a single disease.

Members of the Venezuelan military under the authority of President Nicolás Maduro guard the border between Venezuela and Colombia in an attempt to block humanitarian aid requested by opposition leader Juan Guaidó. The conflict between the two leaders had caused widespread food insecurity within the country.

Food security benefits not only individuals but society in general. You read that malnutrition contributes to rates of disease in a region. It also leads to stunted growth in children and can harm brain development. One study has found that undernutrition depresses the global gross domestic product of Asia and Africa by 11 percent.

THREATS TO FOOD SECURITY

Lack of food security remains a clear and persistent threat. A 2016 study estimated that 795 million people faced hunger every day. Additionally, more than two billion people were lacking nutrients such as zinc, iron, and vitamin A, which are essential to health and proper growth.

The origins of hunger are complex and varied. As you have learned, key forces such as globalization, technology, power, and conflict have been at work throughout human history, and food security is braided through all of them. For example, one theory claims that food shortages contributed to the French Revolution. Power and conflict also played a defining role in the Irish Potato Famine, as the British government prevented the Irish people from accessing other food sources. In the present day, the efforts of Venezuela's rulers to stay in power have led to profound food insecurity and open conflict in that nation.

In recent times, globalization and technology have supported advances in food security, making it easier to export food to regions experiencing hunger and helping make agricultural lands more productive. However, globalization becomes a disadvantage when prices rise and a region that relies on food imports can no longer afford them. Technology has also caused problems at times. In parts of India, for example, crops developed in labs to combat hunger eventually dried out and depleted the soil in which they were planted.

Looking to the future, many researchers view population growth and climate change as the greatest threats to food security. According to one estimate, if current population trends continue, farmers will need 120 percent more water and 42 percent more cropland to meet humanity's needs in 2050. It is highly doubtful that the planet can provide these resources.

Climate change, meanwhile, has already begun affecting food production. Rising temperatures have disrupted the regular climate patterns across Earth. Destructive events such as intense droughts, powerful storms, and cold snaps are becoming more common. Ironically, agriculture itself is part of the problem. It has been estimated that food production is responsible for one-third of all greenhouse gas emissions.

CRITICAL VIEWING Small, individually owned farms border a giant corporate-owned banana farm outside the city of Maputo in the sub-Saharan African country of Mozambique. Once torn apart by civil war, the country is now a major producer of agricultural exports. How might the increased presence of corporate farms impact the owners of smaller farms?

PLAN: 6-PAGE LESSON

OBJECTIVE

Describe efforts to secure access to nutritious food for millions of people worldwide.

CRITICAL THINKING SKILLS FOR LESSON 4.4

- Make Connections
- Compare and Contrast
- Analyze Cause and Effect
- Explain
- Identify Problems and Solutions
- Draw Conclusions
- Analyze Visuals
- Identify Supporting Details

HISTORICAL THINKING FOR CHAPTER 30

What challenges does the world face in the 21st century?

The recognition that world peoples are interconnected underlies current efforts to solve global problems of health and nutrition. Lesson 4.4 discusses global food security with a focus on the work of scientists who are National Geographic Explorers.

BACKGROUND FOR THE TEACHER

Agriculture and Food Security According to the U.S. Agency for International Development (USAID), more than 800 million people worldwide go to bed hungry at night. Most are smallholder farmers who rely on agriculture for their income, and many are women. The U.S. Department of Agriculture (USDA) estimates that as many as 870 million people worldwide do not have access to a sufficient supply of nutritious, safe food. Taking into account population growth and rising incomes, the USDA estimates that the demand for food will rise by 70 to 100 percent by the year 2050. A United Nations estimate suggests that production in developing countries will need to be almost double. The USDA has aligned programs since 2010 with Feed the Future, a USAID initiative, to support agricultural development in countries and regions where help is needed, including Africa and Central America. In addition, the Food and Agriculture Organization (FAO) of the United Nations is active in more than 130 countries to work toward global security and high-quality food for all.

Student eEdition online

Additional content for this lesson, including a photo and caption, is available online.

INTRODUCE & ENGAGE

PREVIEW LESSON VISUALS

Direct students' attention to the photos and captions presented in the lesson. Ask students what these suggest about problems to be solved in the 21st century. Encourage volunteers to respond with information they recall from previous lessons that could be related to the topics depicted in the photos. Then tell students that in this lesson they will learn about threats to global food security and the work of two National Geographic Explorers who have been finding solutions.

TEACH

GUIDED DISCUSSION

1. **Make Connections** How is food security beneficial to the economy and the health of individuals and regions? *(A study has shown that undernutrition can depress the global gross domestic product by 11 percent. Malnutrition contributes to a region's rate of disease. It leads to stunted growth in children and hinders brain development.)*

2. **Analyze Cause and Effect** How has climate change added to the complexity of the problem of future food security? *(Rising temperatures have disrupted climate patterns and affected food production while droughts, powerful storms, and cold snaps are becoming more common. Agricultural production itself is a factor in climate change because it is estimated to amount to one-third of all greenhouse gas emissions.)*

ANALYZE VISUALS

Direct students to view the first two photographs in the lesson and to read the captions about farms in Mozambique and the conflict in Venezuela. Have students consider the Critical Viewing question together with the following question. **ASK:** How do these photos depict situations that could disrupt food security in a region? *(Owners of the large corporate farm could ignore local needs and export their agricultural products to other nations for better profits. Regional conflicts could disrupt local farming and prevent residents from receiving food from outside sources.)*

History Notebook

Encourage students to complete the "Food Security" page for Chapter 30 in their History Notebooks as they read.

DIFFERENTIATE

STRIVING READERS

Analyze Main Ideas and Details Direct students to read the Main Idea statement, captions, and lesson's headings. Then assign student pairs to read alternating paragraphs aloud. After students read each paragraph, encourage them to make notes about details that connect to the Main Idea statement. Tell them this process will help them remember the important information.

See the Chapter Planner for more strategies for differentiation.

National Geographic Explorer T.H. Culhane stands in front of solar panels that help power his home in Florida.

NATIONAL GEOGRAPHIC EXPLORER T.H. CULHANE

Living Off the Grid

Being "off the grid" means generating one's own power rather than buying it from an electric or gas company. In many places where T.H. Culhane has lived and worked, people have no choice but to live off the grid, either because electricity is not available or because they cannot afford it. At his southern Florida home, Culhane can access electricity that he is able to pay for. And yet, he is living off the grid.

"After years of exploring ways to live off-grid around the world," he explains, "we've finally brought it all back to our home . . . without sacrificing any comforts at all." Indeed, he and his wife, Enas, live in a comfortable trailer home with familiar modern appliances, including a microwave, a dishwasher, a refrigerator, a big-screen TV, and computers. The electricity to operate these devices comes mainly from solar panels and biodigesters, which Culhane describes as "domestic fire-breathing dragons that turn all our food and toilet waste . . . into clean fuel and fertilizer." The fertilizer then feeds extensive gardens that grow a variety of produce.

What's the point of living like this when electricity is freely available and reasonably priced? Culhane believes in "life testing" the solutions he offers to other people, showing that his ideas work in the real world—and that the necessary technology is not difficult to build or buy. By living off the grid, he is showing the world that sustainable food and energy production is within everyone's reach.

Culhane demonstrates the effectiveness of using biogas to fuel a cookstove at the Mukuru Arts and Crafts Academy in Nairobi, Kenya. The school's cook (on the left) is amazed by how clean and odorless the fuel is.

Not all the food security news is bad, however. The *Economist* noted progress in several nations in its annual reports for 2015, 2016, and 2018. Some of these advances result from the hard work of researchers who use both global and local approaches to tackling problems surrounding food production. National Geographic Explorers T.H. Culhane and Jerry Glover are among the scientists working not only in labs and universities but also with groups and individuals worldwide to ensure a reliable, nutritious food supply for everyone.

THINK LOCAL . . .

T.H. Culhane travels the world with a garbage disposal in his suitcase. In Culhane's hands, however, a noisy machine that normally grinds up unwanted food and flushes it away becomes a tool for recycling resources and improving a community's food security. In places as diverse as Portugal and Florida, he has used an everyday disposal unit to shred all manner of waste. He then lets nature take over, watching as worms and bugs turn garbage into fertile soil. Giving people the tools to use all of their available resources is at the core of Culhane's mission.

Culhane's enlightened ideas about garbage were inspired in part by his work with the Zabaleen people in Cairo, Egypt, when he was earning his Ph.D. The name *Zabaleen* translates literally as "garbage people," and the Zabaleen make their living collecting and recycling the city's waste. "The Zabaleen view everything around them as useful for something," Culhane remarks. Building on this ethic, he introduced the Zabaleen to biogas digesters. These units convert kitchen scraps and other waste into gas that can be used for heating or generating electricity. He also helped families create roof gardens that allow them to grow their own food without using soil. Since his time in Egypt, Culhane has helped communities implement similar systems in Tanzania, Kenya, Brazil, and even refugee camps in Palestine.

These projects are possible, Culhane emphasizes, because they do not rely on advanced technology and are all based locally. Community members build their gardens and energy generators using basic plumbing supplies and easily available materials. More importantly, they bring their ingenuity and their hard-won knowledge of what works in their own environments. "The poor aren't a class of weak victims," Culhane insists. "They're millions of creative individuals."

When it comes to food security, Culhane sees opportunities in some of the most unlikely places. He points out, "Cities have not necessarily eliminated agricultural land. Instead, they've elevated it." In his view, building roofs and walls can be converted into productive spaces for growing food using techniques that do not require soil.

Cities as a whole have yet to take on the challenge of converting themselves into vertical, urban farm fields, but Culhane has faith in the power of individuals to create solutions for their own communities. And the best ideas, when they have been tested and shown to work, will make their way out into the world.

. . . THEN GO GLOBAL

When he's not on the road helping communities build energy and food solutions, Culhane lives in southern Florida. He is the Director of Climate Change and Sustainability at the University of South Florida's Patel College of Global Sustainability. He is also the founder of Solar CITIES, an organization that trains members of poor communities around the world to build biodigesters and food-growing systems. In addition, he is a founding member of the Rosebud Continuum, which serves as a testing ground for sustainable energy and food solutions. Rosebud invites students and community members to visit, learn, enjoy themselves, and—most enthusiastically—"try this at home."

While much of his focus is on intensely local, relatively low-tech projects, Culhane does not dismiss the advantages of globalization and advanced technology. At Rosebud, he has been experimenting with augmented and virtual reality to help visitors immerse themselves in a world of sustainable possibilities. Participants are encouraged to use this technology to advance their knowledge and spark their own ideas about producing food and energy. T.H. Culhane believes that all people can contribute to sustainable food security and that the globalization of good ideas benefits everyone.

ONE SIZE DOES NOT FIT ALL

Some commentators have remarked that Earth is capable of producing enough food for everyone. Jerry Glover is not so sure. "A good global food supply does not solve regional problems," he counters. An exceptional wheat harvest in Argentina does not translate to food security for a village in Malawi where farmers struggle with nutrient-poor soil. That's why Glover, like T.H Culhane, advocates for food security solutions that focus on local needs and conditions.

Jerry Glover is an agricultural ecologist who works with farming communities around the world to improve crop yields and local food security. His projects have taken him to parts of Africa where untold generations of

BACKGROUND FOR THE TEACHER

Dr. Thomas H. Culhane, Teacher According to his Solar C3ITIES "blogspot," Culhane was a high school science teacher from 1989 into the 21st century. He worked in inner-city schools in connection with NASA's Challenger Center, the Office of Naval Research, and the Junior ROTC to create STEAM, the integration of STEM with art and music—Science, Technology, Engineering, the Arts, and Math. He left the United States in 2003 to work overseas at problem solving and improving science education. Culhane helped build and direct the Wadi Environmental Science Center in Egypt to train Arab youth in problem solving. He recognized from spending time in a Cairo slum that the wood and charcoal people used for water heating and cooking caused dangerous indoor air pollution. He has taught the use of biogas since then, which he calls the "missing piece of the sustainable development puzzle." Other renewable energy forms are problematic, he points out—the sun does not always shine, rain does not always fall, and the wind does not always blow. Culhane believes that teaching what he calls "applied microbiology to meet sustainable development goals"—the basis of biogas fuel—is easy to do, safe, and accessible; and it meets many STEM and STEAM goals. "We teach a new generation to explore, to experiment, to create, to solve problems," he affirms. "We are science teachers. The world is in good hands when we work with our students to make a better world."

TEACH

GUIDED DISCUSSION

3. Compare and Contrast What similar idea forms the basis of T.H. Culhane's projects of using biogas digesters and creating rooftop gardens? *(Both projects build on the same idea of recycling and using garbage and other kinds of waste to create biogas for fuel as well as a soilless medium for rooftop gardening.)*

4. Explain Why does Culhane believe that his projects can contribute to food security worldwide? *(Culhane emphasizes that his projects do not rely on technology and are locally based. People, especially the poor, can apply his ideas for food production by using their ingenuity and knowledge of what works in their environments.)*

IDENTIFY SUPPORTING DETAILS

Direct students to view the photographs of T.H. Culhane in the lesson and in the Student eEdition and to read the captions. Have them also read the section titled "Living Off the Grid." **ASK:** What evidence suggests that Culhane is as concerned about the environment as he is about food security? *(Culhane tells a resident of Nairobi that burning corncobs still creates air pollution, although it lessens the demand for charcoal that destroys trees and wildlife. Culhane lives off the grid to show that sustainable energy, as well as food production, is accessible to everyone. A Nairobi school's cook is amazed that Culhane is showing her how to use fuel that is clean and odorless.)*

ACTIVE OPTION

On Your Feet: Roundtable Display the Food Security and Climate Change map that appears at the beginning of the unit or ensure that students have copies. Allow a few minutes for students to study the map. Then seat students around a table in small groups. Provide each group with several questions about the map to discuss and answer, such as the following:

- Which continent has the largest percentage of undernourished people?
- Which regions are less likely to be affected by climate change?
- Where are populations most likely to experience hunger due to climate change?
- Where in South America might farmers want to raise their crops?

Then have a volunteer from each group report the questions and the group's answers. Tell students they may point to a location on the map to support their answer. Conclude with a class discussion summarizing the information depicted on the map.

DIFFERENTIATE

GIFTED & TALENTED

Create a Multimedia Presentation Have students conduct online research about women and food security. Ask them to learn about the experiences of individual women in less developed regions who are succeeding in securing food for their families. As needed, guide students to use the FAO website along with the USAID website, where they can locate the "gender equality and women's empowerment" section and access "Frontlines" articles as well. Then direct students to combine their findings with those of other students to create a multimedia presentation that includes sources and photos. Invite them to share the presentation with the rest of the class.

See the Chapter Planner for more strategies for differentiation.

Women and Food Security

Often, the most effective way to introduce new farming techniques is to talk with women who live and work in the community. In Malawi and elsewhere in Africa, Jerry Glover noticed that training women in perennial planting techniques resulted in increased yields, greater nutrition for families, and crops that are better equipped to survive in harsh weather. Data supports these personal observations. A study by the University of Queensland, Australia, found that one of the surest predictors of crop yield was the level of education of the women in the household.

As Glover explains, agriculture is not simply a matter of food production. It is entwined with both the economics and culture of a community. Therefore, before approaching the women—or the men—in a village, it is important to understand their deeply ingrained traditions. "I've been in places where women were only allowed to speak to me through the men," he reports. The time and effort taken to understand the cultural dynamics and women's roles in a community reap an ample payoff when crops increase and families eat well.

In 2015, photographer Jim Richardson teamed up with National Geographic Explorer and agricultural ecologist Jerry Glover to create striking photographs of perennial prairie plants' deep roots.

farming have dried out the soil and depleted its nutrients. There, people often struggle to coax enough crops from their land to feed their families.

One strategy Glover uses to help farmers boost their yields is to introduce perennial plants into their fields. Perennials are plants that survive from year to year, in contrast to annual crops that are pulled from the ground after a growing season. Glover helped some farmers in Malawi plant "fertilizer trees" in their maize fields. The trees' roots draw water and nutrients from deep within the soil. When the trees drop their leaves, the leaves return the nutrients to the shallower layer of soil where the maize has its roots. One farmer in Malawi who planted fertilizer trees increased his yield by ten times in six years.

Glover and his colleagues are also attempting to cultivate perennial versions of familiar foods. These crops would be more resilient in the face of shocks related to climate change, and their deep roots would help stabilize the soil. They could also be bred so that they are adapted to local conditions. Promising perennial wheat and rice plants have been developed, but they have not yet been put into broader cultivation.

When working with farmers, Glover is mindful of their individual needs and concerns. Global solutions imposed by governments or large agricultural companies are doomed to fail, he says, because they ignore local conditions. "Farmers are not fools," he notes. "They make their decisions for logical reasons" based on their experiences, their culture, and the materials they have at hand. Successfully introducing new ideas means understanding where the old ones come from. It also means empowering farmers to make their own logical decisions based on the evidence presented to them.

Workers maneuver a boat around rows of algae that are being cultivated off the coast of the Philippines. This particular algae, known as carrageen, is used in both the food and pharmaceutical industries.

THE FUTURE OF FOOD

While Glover believes that improvements in agriculture can help feed today's hungry world, he sees the future of food security in new and different sources of nourishment. "We're working off a 19th-century vision of agriculture, trying to improve efficiency but still relying on the same group of crops we've had for years," he says.

Glover and many others believe that food producers need to explore new staples to put on our menu, including insects, algae, and meat grown in labs. With modern food-processing technology, these substances can be made into familiar dishes with no shock to the taste buds. "I've had pasta made from insects," he says, "and it tasted just like regular pasta." In fact, several food manufacturers have started to experiment with alternative ingredients. Crickets, for example, are high in protein and can be used to make chips, protein bars, and smoothie powders. At least two companies are already marketing popular burgers that taste remarkably like beef but are made from grains and vegetables, which take much fewer resources to grow than beef. Perhaps in the not-so-distant future, everyone will be joining Jerry Glover in a tasty meal made from sources we never imagined.

The pulled "pork" in this sandwich is actually jackfruit, a fruit that grows in the tropical areas of Southeast Asia, Brazil, and Africa. The fruit has the consistency of chicken or pork and is a popular meat replacement.

HISTORICAL THINKING

1. **READING CHECK** What factors contribute to food security?

2. **MAKE CONNECTIONS** How might efforts to slow climate change affect food security?

3. **COMPARE AND CONTRAST** How would you compare and contrast T.H. Culhane's and Jerry Glover's approaches to food security?

BACKGROUND FOR THE TEACHER

Women and Food Security A September 2019 USAID press release about the Feed the Future initiative displayed a headline that contained these words: "Women Are Key To Ending Hunger." The 2019 Annual Report published by Feed the Future indicated that women make up nearly half the agricultural labor force in developing countries. According to the report, women own one-third of small- and medium-sized businesses in emerging markets, but the number is growing. The success of economically empowered women leads to better nutrition and health—and less hunger. Data indicated that in areas where Feed the Future worked for more than three years, 2.6 million more women gained access to credit, 3.3 million more had reasonable workloads, and 3.7 million more had greater input into decisions on what to plant. Since 2018, Feed the Future has helped nearly 3 million women producers use new technologies and modern farming methods. Feed the Future also provided training on nutrition to more than 420,000 women. According to USAID, gender equality and women's empowerment are critical. When women farmers have the same access as men to land, new technologies, and capital, crop yields can increase by as much as 30 percent, helping to feed a growing population.

TEACH

GUIDED DISCUSSION

5. **Identify Problems and Solutions** What are "fertilizer trees," and how does Jerry Glover expect them to solve the problem of food security? *(Fertilizer trees can revitalize dried-out and nutrient-depleted soil. They draw water and nutrients from deep within the soil. When the trees drop their leaves, the nutrients fall in the shallower layer of soil where maize has its roots. Glover expects the trees to increase maize yields for Malawian farmers.)*

6. **Draw Conclusions** Why does Glover believe that "a 19th-century vision of agriculture" is inadequate for food security in the future? *(Glover believes that current global solutions are based on traditional agricultural methods. He advocates a focus on local conditions, including climate change and individual needs and concerns. He sees future food production in terms of exploring new and different sources of nourishment, such as insects, algae, and meat grown in labs using modern food-processing technology.)*

EXPLAIN

Direct students to view the photograph of Jerry Glover and to read the caption. Ask students to read the section titled "Women and Food Security." **ASK:** Why does Glover believe his work includes understanding a community's cultural dynamics and women's roles? *(Glover can more effectively introduce farming techniques such as perennial planting by teaching them to women, and he has found that he must approach women according to community traditions.)* What is the importance of the study by the University of Queensland? *(The study indicates that the level of education of women in the household is one of the surest predictors of crop yield.)*

ACTIVE OPTIONS

NG Learning Framework: Write an Article STEM
ATTITUDES Responsibility, Empowerment
KNOWLEDGE Our Human Story, Our Living Planet

Ask students to use information in the lesson and from other sources to write an article about biodigesters. Encourage students to focus on these questions: What is biogas? How is it formed? How does a biodigester work? How can biodigesters be used for large and small applications? Suggest that students conclude the article with a sentence or two about the value of biodigesters in solving problems of food security and environmental protection. Invite volunteers to read their articles to the class.

HISTORICAL THINKING

ANSWERS

1. Food security depends on the availability, affordability, quality, and safety of food items.

2. Slowing climate change could keep temperatures from rising and disrupting climate patterns, which could affect crop outputs. It might also decrease the number of destructive weather events that affect food security.

3. Answers will vary. Possible response: T.H. Culhane concentrates on helping people develop their own technology and solutions locally with whatever resources are at hand. Jerry Glover focuses on cultivating more perennial plants and looking for different sources of nourishment, such as insects or algae.

CRITICAL VIEWING Possible response: Owners of small farms have much less land, so they have smaller yields and make less money. They could find it hard to compete with corporations that can spend money for farm equipment to increase production. Owners of small farms might have to supplement their farm incomes with other work or sell their land because they cannot afford to stay in business.

VOCABULARY

Use each of the following vocabulary words in a sentence that shows an understanding of the term's meaning.

1. religiosity
2. displaced
3. xenophobia
4. bailout
5. conservation
6. connectivity
7. hacker
8. biotechnology

READING STRATEGY
MAKE INFERENCES

Use a chart like the one below to make inferences about the impact of globalization. Then answer the question.

Key Events	Impact	Inferences

9. How has globalization increased international cooperation? How has it increased international conflict? Offer one example of international cooperation and one of international conflict and explain your responses.

MAIN IDEAS

Answer the following questions. Support your answers with evidence from the chapter.

10. What event led to the rise of ISIS? LESSON 1.1

11. Why did citizens of many Arab nations participate in the Arab Spring protests? LESSON 1.2

12. How do foreign relations policies differ for the communist countries of Vietnam and North Korea? LESSON 1.4

13. Which banking policies caused the financial crisis that began in 2008? LESSON 2.1

14. How has globalization affected the world's wealth? LESSON 2.2

15. How are nonrenewable resources and renewable resources different? Provide an example of each. LESSON 3.1

16. How did Ai Weiwei resist the Chinese government's efforts to silence him? LESSON 4.1

17. How might you explain the term *biotechnology* to a younger student? LESSON 4.3

HISTORICAL THINKING

Answer the following questions. Support your answers with evidence from the chapter.

18. DRAW CONCLUSIONS Why do you think the September 11 terrorists picked the World Trade Center towers and the Pentagon as their targets?

19. ANALYZE CAUSE AND EFFECT How has civil war in Syria affected other countries?

20. MAKE CONNECTIONS How does a fast-growing population affect a nation's economy in positive and negative ways?

21. FORM AND SUPPORT OPINIONS Do you think the positive effects of multinational corporations outweigh the negative effects? Explain your response.

22. MAKE PREDICTIONS Is another world financial crisis likely in the next five years? Explain your response.

23. SUMMARIZE How has Ai Weiwei made a difference in the world?

24. EVALUATE Which 21st-century health advancement do think is most important? Why?

INTERPRET GRAPHS

Study the graph at right, which shows the range of carbon dioxide levels through the centuries. Then answer the questions below.

25. By about how much has the carbon dioxide level risen since 1950?

26. This graph shows the naturally occurring ups and downs in carbon dioxide levels over many centuries. Why does this data alarm many scientists?

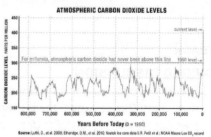

ATMOSPHERIC CARBON DIOXIDE LEVELS

Source: Luthi, D., et al. 2008; Etheridge, D.M., et al. 2010; Vostok ice core data/J.R. Petit et al.; NOAA Mauna Loa CO₂ record

ANALYZE SOURCES

Some of the largest and most successful emerging economies—Brazil, Russia, India, China, and South Africa—have formed an economic bloc that is commonly referred to as BRICS. The bloc's main goal is to cooperate so that each member can continue to enjoy economic success. This excerpt is from a declaration issued at the 2017 BRICS Science, Technology & Innovation (STI) ministerial meeting. Read it and answer the question that follows.

> [We] agree to promote entrepreneurship and build platforms in BRICS countries and mainly collaborate in technology cooperation, technology transfer and translation, science and technology parks, youth innovation and entrepreneurship and in fostering strategic and long-term university-industry partnerships so as to build sound ecosystems for innovation and entrepreneurship.

27. What evidence in the excerpt shows that BRICS is looking to the future?

CONNECT TO YOUR LIFE

28. INFORMATIVE Talk to family members or other adults you know about the global refugee crisis. Ask them what they know about it and what they think should be done. Share your own views of the situation, including the ways in which an influx of refugees could change a country. Then write an essay about your conversation, describing ways in which you and the person or people you spoke with agreed and disagreed. Did anyone change their minds during the conversation? Explain why or why not.

TIPS

* Use information from the chapter to craft your questions before you conduct your interviews.

* Ask the people you interview for concrete details as they discuss what they know and what they think should be done.

* Maintain an open, curious, and respectful tone in your interview. Seek areas of agreement before you move to areas of disagreement.

* Be sure to thank people you interview for being willing to share their thoughts with you on an important topic.

* In writing about the views of others, try to find the logic in their position and also look for the emotional perspective. Ask yourself whether people are expressing fear, anger, compassion, or some other emotion in their response to the situation.

* Try to step outside your own position to see how it might appear to someone else. In writing your essay, assess areas of agreement and disagreement. Consider the ways in which your conversation might reflect areas of agreement or disagreement within the larger society.

VOCABULARY ANSWERS

1. Possible response: Increased religiosity has led some people to seek a closer connection between their spiritual beliefs and the laws they live under.

2. Possible response: Civil war in a country may displace many citizens and force them to become refugees who seek shelter in other countries.

3. Possible response: People's xenophobia may cause them to support candidates who denounce immigration.

4. Possible response: The bailout of banks following the 2008 financial crisis helped stabilize the U.S. economy.

5. Possible response: Conservation of natural resources will help ensure the well-being of future generations.

6. Possible response: Global connectivity allows immigrants to a new country to instantaneously learn news from their homeland.

7. Possible response: Unfortunately, a hacker accessed the small business's online bank account and depleted the company's funds.

8. Possible response: A scientist specializing in the field of biotechnology may search for ways to make crops more disease resistant.

READING STRATEGY ANSWERS

Key Events	Impact	Inferences
Creation of transnational organizations Growth of criminal and terrorist groups Creation of multinational corporations	Transnational organizations work to better the world. International criminals and terrorist groups commit violent crimes with the support of the Internet. Multinational corporations bring jobs to various parts of the world; however, they also exploit workers and natural resources in developing countries.	The impact of globalization can be both positive and negative for people and businesses around the world.

9. Answers will vary but might include examples such as international cooperation to combat climate change, expand trade, and improve world health. Examples of conflict might include the refugee crisis resulting from the Syrian civil war and economic inequality.

MAIN IDEAS ANSWERS

10. The U.S. withdrawal from Iraq left a power vacuum that led to the rise of ISIS.

11. Citizens of many Arab countries joined together during the Arab Spring to protest unjust governments and the lack of social justice in the region.

12. Vietnam is on good terms with Western nations while North Korea is antagonistic toward them.

13. Banks offered mortgages to people who could not afford them or were bad risks.

14. Globalization has increased the world's wealth and shifted it so that more nations share in it.

15. Nonrenewable resources, such as oil, can be depleted while renewable resources, such as the wind, do not run out.

16. Ai Weiwei utilized such tools as Twitter to communicate, sent his work throughout the world, and continued to create works that brought the misdeeds of the Chinese government to light.

17. Possible response: Biotechnology is the way scientists use plant and animal material to create new foods, medicines, and devices to help people.

HISTORICAL THINKING ANSWERS

18. Possible response: The September 11 terrorists picked their targets to create the greatest impact on the American people and disrupt business and government in the United States.

19. Possible response: The Syrian war has caused other nations to take sides, send military or financial aid, make tough decisions about whether to accept refugees, re-evaluate economic policies based on growing xenophobia, support anti-immigration leaders, and step up anti-terrorism strategies as new terrorist groups have formed.

20. Answers will vary. Some students may say that a fast-growing population strengthens the workforce while others may say that it places too much stress on resources and the budget.

21. Some students may say that the benefits outweigh the negative effects because the creation of new jobs and the infusion of money will eventually allow people to rise out of poverty and build their economy. Others will say that the negative effects outweigh the benefits because the self-interest of the companies will cause developing nations to lose their national identity and remain mired in poverty.

22. Answers will vary. Some students will say that another financial crisis is unlikely because of lessons learned and precautions that have been put in place. Others may predict that another financial crisis is possible because housing prices in the United States have risen, some financial policies have been relaxed, and some countries are highly in debt.

23. Possible response: Ai Weiwei has enriched the world with his art, challenged it to address important societal issues, and questioned China's record on human-rights abuses.

24. Students' choices for most important advancement will vary. Accept all answers that are convincingly supported. Possible response: The Human Genome Project is most important because it is a huge step toward eradicating disease.

INTERPRET GRAPHS ANSWERS

25. The level of carbon dioxide has increased by over 100 parts per million since 1950.

26. Possible response: Scientists are alarmed by the large increase in carbon dioxide levels since 1950, with higher levels than ever before. They believe that this change is not caused by nature but by human activity since it came about so quickly and does not follow the pattern of the past.

ANALYZE SOURCES ANSWER

27. The fact that there is an emphasis on youth innovation and long-term university partnerships is evidence that BRICS is looking to the future, focusing on the next generation that will one day be in power.

CONNECT TO YOUR LIFE ANSWER

28. Student essays should be based on an interview with at least one person and describe ways in which the person or people and the student agreed and disagreed. They should also show an effort on the part of the student to understand the logic in positions that are different than their own and should reflect how the conversation mirrors that within the larger society.

Navigating the Anthropocene

BY OWEN GAFFNEY Adapted from "Walking the Anthropocene" by Owen Gaffney.
Out of Eden Walk post, March 16, 2015

Throughout human history, major geological events have punctuated our journey. Just 11,700 years ago, a slight shift in Earth's orbit around the sun brought our planet out of a deep ice age. Earth's systems—ocean currents, ice sheets, biodiversity, and climate—settled into a new equilibrium, and we entered the epoch called the Holocene.

The Holocene was a "goldilocks" period for *Homo sapiens*: not too hot, not too cold. Preceded by an ice age, the Holocene's climate allowed agriculture to develop and flourish independently in the Middle East, China, and elsewhere. More complex social structures such as towns and cities arose, followed much more recently by enormous population growth and development. The Holocene is the only known epoch capable of supporting 7.2 billion people.

But what if Earth has moved out of the Holocene? What if the ship on which we sail has grown so large that its insatiable appetite and increasing effluence have radically altered all around it? Many of the world's top Earth-system scientists believe we have entered a new geological epoch shaped by people, called the Anthropocene. They debate when this new epoch began, however. Some argue that the Anthropocene began around 1800, with the Industrial Revolution.

Many others point to about 1950, when humanity's effect on Earth crossed a tipping point. Post–World War II production and consumption slipped into overdrive. We, the producers and consumers, moved onto a new, almost exponential trajectory fueled by use of Earth's natural resources. Incredibly, in a single human lifetime, changes in major planetary indicators started moving in accord with social and economic indicators of change, one force seemingly driving the other. A single species, ours, had come to dominate Earth's natural cycles.

Today we use an area the size of South America to grow our crops and an area the size of Africa to graze our livestock. We move more sediment and rock annually than all natural processes combined. And we are in the midst of Earth's sixth mass extinction, a result of human activity.

This nighttime image of Asia and Australia was assembled from data acquired by a satellite in 2012 and shows the regions' city lights. Scientists use images like this to track urban and suburban growth.

As we leave the Holocene behind, the human impact on the planet is growing, in what a team of Earth-system scientists has called the "Great Acceleration." To continue on this trajectory risks the stability of Earth's natural systems.

Two indicators of stability provide reason for hope, however. Following a ban on chlorofluorocarbons, the Antarctic ozone hole visibly stabilized. We also are on track for Earth's human population to stabilize soon.

But other indicators are worrisome. Marine fish captures are leveling off as we run out of fish to catch. Consumption and production continue to rise. From deforestation to fossil-fuel use, consumption is driving the most significant changes. With every passing year, we are degrading the only known safe operating space for our species.

While we—*Homo sapiens*—have traveled far, we did not travel together, nor take the same route. But we're all in the same boat now. ∎

918 UNIT 10

UNIT INQUIRY
UNIT 10 Create an NGO

Staging the Question

In this unit, you learned about global challenges in the 20th and 21st centuries. Some, such as war and prejudice, are as old as humanity. Others, like human-caused climate change, are relatively recent. Still other forces, such as globalization and the digital revolution, remain ambiguous—do they hold the solutions to our problems, or will they ultimately cause more harm than good? In Units 9 and 10, you have also read about some NGOs (nongovernmental organizations) that confront today's challenges using both ages-old and cutting-edge methods. Which problem of today is the most urgent, and how can global citizens organize to solve it?

Supporting Questions: Begin by developing supporting questions to guide your thinking. For example: How have problems like this one been solved in the past? What resources can I use that did not exist in the past? Research the answers in this unit and in other sources. You might want to use a graphic organizer like this one to help you organize your ideas.

Summative Performance Task: Use the answers to your questions to help you envision a plan for an NGO that would work to overcome the challenge. Include a mission statement and specific actions for meeting your NGO's goals. For inspiration, you might research the websites of existing NGOs.

Present: Share your NGO plan with the class. You might consider one of the following options:

ASSIGNMENT

Identify the present-day global challenges described in this unit.

Choose the challenge you believe is the most urgent or that you feel most strongly about.

Analyze the problem and make a list of actions that individuals or organizations could take to help solve it.

Based on your analysis, make a plan for an NGO that focuses on the challenge you chose. You may work together with others who selected the same issue.

Problem

Step 1

Step 2

Step 3

CREATE A WEBSITE

Include pages that describe your NGO's message, mission, and goals. You may model your site on that of an existing organization. Include a page that tells readers what they can do to help.

MAKE A FUNDING PITCH

Present your NGO to the board of a company (your classmates) that is considering a big donation. Use presentation software to explain your NGO's goals and methods and to tell how you will effectively confront the challenge.

Take Informed Action:

UNDERSTAND Research existing NGOs that are working to solve the problem you chose.

ASSESS Compare and contrast the NGOs and choose the one you believe is the most effective and in line with your own beliefs.

ACT Contact the NGO and choose the way to participate in its activities that best suits you. Share with classmates why you support this organization.

Global Challenges 919

GUIDED DISCUSSION FOR "NAVIGATING THE ANTHROPOCENE"

1. **Describe** What caused the Holocene, and what changes did it bring about? (*A slight shift in Earth's orbit caused the Holocene, which changed Earth's systems. These changes took the planet out of an ice age and created a climate that is favorable for humans, agriculture, and the creation of towns and settlements.*)

2. **Compare and Contrast** What is the Anthropocene, and how is it similar to or different from the Holocene? (*Possible response: The Anthropocene is what many scientists are calling the new geological epoch of Earth's system changes. The Holocene and the Anthropocene differ because the Holocene was caused by a shift in Earth's orbit, while the Anthropocene is caused by people. Also, the effects of the Holocene on Earth's systems are continuing, while the Anthropocene seems to show that some of the effects of humans on Earth's natural systems are stabilizing and others are rapidly depleting/altering Earth's natural systems.*)

History Notebook

Encourage students to complete the Unit Wrap-Up page for Unit 10 in their History Notebooks.

UNIT INQUIRY PROJECT RUBRIC

ASSESS

Use the rubric to assess each student's participation and performance.

SCORE	ASSIGNMENT	PRODUCT	PRESENTATION
3 GREAT	• Student thoroughly understands the assignment. • Student develops thoughtful supporting questions to guide research.	• NGO plan is well thought out and includes many specific details and advantages for each side. • NGO plan reflects all of the key elements listed in the assignment.	• Presentation has a focused mission statement and clearly lays out specific actions for meeting NGO goals. • Presentation is concise, logical, and engaging.
2 GOOD	• Student mostly understands the assignment. • Student develops somewhat thoughtful supporting questions to guide research.	• NGO plan is fairly well thought out and includes some specific details and advantages for each side. • NGO plan reflects most of the key elements listed in the assignment.	• Presentation has a mission statement that is fairly clear and lays out some actions for meeting a few NGO goals. • Presentation is fairly concise, logical, and engaging.
1 NEEDS WORK	• Student does not understand the assignment. • Student does not develop thoughtful questions to guide research.	• NGO plan is not well thought out and includes few specific details and advantages for each side. • NGO plan reflects few or none of the key elements listed in the assignment.	• Presentation is missing a mission statement and does not clearly lay out actions for meeting NGO goals. • Presentation is not logical or engaging.

STUDENT REFERENCES

AVAILABLE IN THE STUDENT eEDITION
Geography and the Environment Handbook
Primary and Secondary Source Handbook
Skills Handbook
Economics and Government Handbook
World Religions Handbook
National Geographic Atlas

GLOSSARY

A

abdicate *(AB-dih-kayt) v.* to formally give up something, such as a throne (page 203)

abolition *(a-buh-LIH-shuhn) n.* the movement to end slavery (page 519)

Aborigine *(a-buh-RIH-juh-nee) n.* an original inhabitant of Australia (page 554)

absolute monarchy *(AB-suh-loot MAH-nur-kee) n.* a government in which the monarch has unlimited authority (page 540)

adapt *(uh-DAPT) v.* to develop characteristics that aid in survival (page 14)

agora *(A-guh-ruh) n.* an open-air marketplace in a Greek city-state (page 128)

agriculture *(A-grih-kuhl-chur) n.* the cultivation of plant foods and domestication of animals (page 22)

ahimsa *(uh-HIHM-sah) n.* the Indian concept of absolute nonviolence (page 750)

alliance *(uh-LY-uhns) n.* a partnership (page 40)

alphabet *(AL-fuh-beht) n.* the group of letters that form the individual elements of a writing system (page 126)

amphitheater *(AM-fuh-thee-uh-tur) n.* a large, open-air theater (page 163)

amphora *(AM-fuh-ruh) n.* a large two-handled ceramic jar with a narrow neck (page 161)

anarchist *(A-nur-kihst) n.* a person who is willing to use force to overthrow authoritarian oppression (page 653)

anatomy *(uh-NA-tuh-mee) n.* the study of the interior and exterior structures of living things (page 418)

ancestor worship *(AN-sehs-tur WUR-shuhp) n.* the practice of contacting dead ancestors with the belief that they can intercede in human events on behalf of the living (page 83)

annex *(A-nehks) v.* to incorporate territory into an existing state (page 697)

anti-Semitism *(an-tee-SEH-meh-tih-zuhm) n.* hostility toward and discrimination against Jews (page 294)

apartheid *(uh-PAHR-tayt) n.* a system of racial segregation and discrimination against nonwhite South Africans that lasted until the early 1990s (page 814)

appeasement *(uh-PEEZ-muhnt) n.* the giving of concessions to keep the peace (page 761)

aqueduct *(A-kwuh-duhkt) n.* a stone channel that carried clean water from hilltops to cities (page 163)

arabesque *(a-ruh-BEHSK) n.* an abstract design made up of repeating patterns or flowers, leaves, vines, or geometric shapes (page 258)

archetype *(AHR-kih-typ) n.* a perfect example of something (page 598)

archipelago *(ahr-kuh-PEH-luh-goh) n.* a chain of islands (page 208)

archon *(AHR-kawn) n.* a chief ruler in ancient Athens (page 130)

aristocrat *(uh-RIHS-tuh-krat) n.* a person of wealth and high social rank (page 130)

armistice *(AHR-muh-stuhs) n.* an agreement between opposing sides to end hostilities (page 705)

artifact *(AHR-tih-fakt) n.* an object of historical value made by human beings (page 8)

artillery *(ahr-TIH-lur-ee) n.* large field guns that fire high-explosive shells (page 701)

ascetic *(uh-SEH-tihk) n.* one who chooses a life of poverty (page 72)

assimilate *(uh-SIH-muh-layt) v.* to merge into another culture (page 273)

astrolabe *(AS-truh-layb) n.* a sophisticated instrument that allowed users to calculate their location on Earth (page 259)

asylum *(uh-SY-luhm) n.* a place of safety (page 875)

atheism *(AY-thee-ih-zuhm) n.* the belief that God does not exist (page 824)

atomic bomb *(uh-TAH-mihk bahm) n.* a type of nuclear bomb whose violent explosion is triggered by splitting atoms and releases intense heat and radioactivity (page 773)

atrocity *(uh-TRAH-suh-tee) n.* an extremely cruel and shocking act of violence (page 786)

authoritarianism *(aw-thahr-uh-TEHR-ee-uh-nih-zuhm) n.* a political system characterized by a powerful leader and limited individual freedoms (page 709)

autonomous *(aw-TAH-nuh-muhs) adj.* self-governing (page 527)

autonomy *(aw-TAH-nuh-mee) n.* independence to self-govern (page 659)

B

bailout *(BAYL-owt) n.* a rescue from financial distress (page 886)

bioarchaeologist *(by-oh-AHR-kee-ah-luh-jihst) n.* a person who studies human remains to learn about archaeology (page 205)

biotechnology *(by-oh-tehk-NAH-luh-jee) n.* the use of biological organisms or processes to create new products that improve life (page 909)

Blackshirt *(blak-shurt) n.* a member of a militant group that attacked Mussolini's opponents (page 743)

blitzkrieg *(BLIHTS-kreeg) n.* a German battle tactic that used speed, surprise, and the combined firepower of tanks, bombers, and ground forces (page 766)

Boer *(bawr) n.* a Dutch or French settler in South Africa, also called an Afrikaner (page 674)

botany *(BAH-tuh-nee) n.* the study of plants and plant life (page 552)

bourgeoisie *(burzh-wah-ZEE) n.* the middle class (page 572)

bronze *(brahnz) n.* a mixture of the metals tin and copper (page 35)

bureaucracy *(byu-RAH-kruh-see) n.* a group of administrative government officials (page 88)

C

caliph *(KAY-luhf) n.* the title of a Muslim leader who was a successor of Muhammad (page 247)

calligraphy *(ka-LIH-gra-fee) n.* a form of elegant handwriting (page 258)

campesino *(kam-puh-SEE-noh) n.* a rural villager or small farmer in Latin America (page 726)

canonize *(KA-nuh-nyz) v.* to make someone a saint in the Catholic Church (page 441)

capital *(KA-puh-tuhl) n.* money or other assets that can be used to invest in business (page 277)

capitalism *(KA-puh-tuh-lihz-uhm) n.* a free-market economic system in which businesses are privately owned and exist for the purpose of making profits (page 492)

caravan *(KAIR-uh-van) n.* a group of people who travel together (page 367)

caravel *(KEHR-uh-vehl) n.* a small, fast ship used by Portuguese and Spanish explorers (page 482)

carpet-bombing *(KAHR-puht-bah-mihng) n.* the dropping of a large number of bombs on a designated area (page 726)

cartography *(kahr-TAH-gruh-fee) n.* the science or art of making maps (page 556)

caste system *(kast SIH-stuhm) n.* a rigid social hierarchy in ancient India that divided people into hereditary classes (page 71)

catacomb *(KA-tuh-kohm) n.* a hidden underground chamber where early Christians buried their dead (page 175)

cataract *(KA-tuh-rakt) n.* a steep, unnavigable rapid along the course of a river (page 42)

cathedral *(kuh-THEE-druhl) n.* the principal church of a district administered by a bishop (page 279)

caudillo *(cow-THEE-yoh) n.* a Latin American military dictator who gained power through violence (page 605)

cavalry *(KA-vuhl-ree) n.* a group of soldiers mounted on horseback (page 55)

celibate *(SEH-luh-buht) v.* to remain unmarried (page 204)

cenote *(sih-NOH-tee) n.* a large natural pool or open cave (page 391)

census *(SEHNT-suhs) n.* an official count of the population (page 204)

chinampa *(chuh-NAM-puh) n.* an artificial island created to raise crops (page 395)

chronicle *(KRAH-nih-kuhl) n.* a factual account or record (page 199)

circumnavigate *(sur-kuhm-NA-vuh-gayt) v.* to travel completely around the world (page 484)

city-state *(SIH-tee-STAYT) n.* a city whose ruler governs both the city and the surrounding countryside (page 37)

civil disobedience *(SIH-vuhl dihs-uh-BEE-dee-uhnts) n.* the refusal to follow unjust laws (page 750)

civil liberties *(SIH-vuhl LIH-bur-teez) n.* basic freedoms that cannot be regulated by the government, such as freedom of speech (page 884)

civilization *sih-vuh-luh-ZAY-shuhn n.* an advanced and complex society (page 34)

clan *(klan) n.* a group of people with a common ancestor (page 208)

clergy *(KLUR-jee) n.* people appointed to religious service by the church (page 278)

climate change *(KLY-muht chaynj) n.* changes to global weather patterns (page 899)

Clovis point *(KLOH-vuhs point) n.* a type of stone spear point used by prehistoric residents of North America (page 384)

coalition *(koh-uh-LIH-shuhn) n.* a temporary alliance (page 139)

codex *(KOH-dehks) n.* a folded book made of tree-bark paper (page 389)

coercion *(koh-UR-zhuhn) n.* the use of force or threats (page 678)

collectivization *(kuh-lehk-tih-vuh-ZAY-shuhn) n.* the replacement of privately owned peasant farms with state-run collective farms (page 747)

Columbian Exchange *(kuh-LUHM-bee-uhn ihks-CHAYNJ) n.* the exchange of plants, animals, microbes, people, and ideas between Europe and the Americas, following Columbus's first voyage to the Western Hemisphere (page 488)

commerce *(KAH-muhrs) n.* the large-scale buying and selling of goods (page 277)

commission *(kuh-MIH-shuhn) n.* a request for a specific art or design project, usually from the nobility (page 417)

commodity *(kuh-MAH-duh-tee) n.* a valuable trade good (page 134)

common law *(KAH-muhn law) n.* a set of laws determined by earlier court decisions (page 583)

communism *(KAHM-yuh-nih-zuhm) n.* an economic and political system where all property is public, owned by the central state, and goods are distributed to everyone according to their needs (page 627)

compulsory education *(kuhm-PUHLS-ree eh-juh-KAY-shuhn) n.* education required by law (page 395)

concentration camp *(kahnt-suhn-TRAY-shuhn kamp) n.* a place where large numbers of people are imprisoned under armed guard; especially the camps created by the Nazis to hold Jews and other prisoners during World War II (page 675)

Confederacy *(kuhn-FEH-duh-ruh-see) n.* the 11 southern states that seceded from the Union to form their own nation (page 644)

connectivity *(kah-nehk-TIH-vuh-tee) n.* the state of being connected to others, especially through a computer system (page 898)

conquistador *(kahn-KEE-stuh-dawr) n.* a Spanish explorer who conquered lands in the Americas (page 484)

conscription *(kuhn-SKRIHP-shuhn) n.* forced enrollment in the military (page 475)

conservation *(kahnt-sur-VAY-shuhn) n.* the careful protection and preservation of something (page 893)

consolidate *(kuhn-SAH-luh-dayt) v.* to unify and strengthen (page 299)

constitutional monarchy *(kahnt-stuh-TOO-shnuhl MAH-nur-kee) n.* a government in which the monarch's power is limited by a constitution (page 540)

constitutionalism *(kahnt-stuh-TOO-shuh-nuh-lih-zuhm) n.* the concept of governing based on a set of basic principles or laws called a constitution (page 583)

consumption *(kuhn-SUHMP-shuhn) n.* spending (page 468)

containment policy *(kuhn-TAYN-muhnt PAH-luh-see) n.* a U.S. Cold War policy of providing military and economic aid to protect countries from communist takeover (page 800)

GLOSSARY

cosmopolitan *(kahz-muh-PAH-luh-tuhn) adj.* diverse and having familiarity with people, ideas, and objects from many parts of the world (page 205)

cost-benefit analysis *(KAWST-BEH-nuh-fiht uh-NA-luh-suhs) n.* the process in which good and bad points are compared to see whether the benefits of something outweigh its cost (page 863)

cottage industry *(KAH-tihj IHN-duh-stree) n.* a type of industry in which a family unit or individual creates a product at home with their own equipment (page 618)

countercultural *(kown-tur-KUHLCH-ruhl) adj.* relating to styles and traditions that run counter to those of mainstream society (page 717)

coup *(koo) n.* a sudden overthrow of government (page 110)

covenant *(KUHV-nuhnt) n.* a religious agreement (page 59)

crematoria *(kree-muh-TAWR-ee-uh) n.* ovens, especially those used by the Nazis in World War II to burn the bodies of those they murdered (page 783)

Crusade *(kroo-SAYD) n.* a Christian military expedition to recover the land of Palestine from Muslim rule (page 290)

cryptography *(krihp-TAH-gruh-fee) n.* secret codes and scrambling of data to keep electronic information safe (page 899)

cult of personality *(kuhlt uhv pur-suh-NA-luh-tee) n.* the promotion of a public figure as a person to be revered (page 747)

cultural diffusion *(KUHLCH-ruhl dih-FYOO-zhuhn) n.* the process by which cultures interact and ideas spread from one area to another (page 81)

cultural heritage *(KUHLCH-ruhl HEHR-uh-tihj) n.* the attributes of a group or society inherited from past generations (page 56)

cuneiform *(kyoo-NEE-uh-fawrm) n.* the earliest form of writing, developed by the Sumerians (page 39)

currency *(KUR-uhnt-see) n.* money in circulation (page 311)

D

D-Day *(DEE-day) n.* a term used to refer to the Allied invasion of Normandy, France, during World War II (page 771)

daimyo *(DY-mee-oh) n.* a wealthy landowner in feudal Japan (page 317)

Dalit *(DAL-iht) n.* a member of the lowest Hindu caste in traditional Indian society (page 750)

debt peonage *(deht PEE-uh-nihj) n.* a system in which workers pay off their debt with labor (page 654)

deductive approach *(dih-DUHK-tihv uh-PROHCH) n.* an approach to scientific inquiry that involves moving from general principles to specific truths (page 549)

deism *(DEE-ih-zuhm) n.* a religious philosophy that supports the idea of natural religion, in which God does not interfere with natural laws (page 573)

deity *(DEE-uh-tee) n.* a god or goddess (page 133)

delegation *(deh-lih-GAY-shuhn) n.* a group of people chosen to represent others (page 198)

delta *(DEHL-tuh) n.* a triangular-shaped area of low, flat land at the mouth of a river (page 42)

demilitarized zone *(dee-MIH-luh-tuh-ryzd zohn) n.* an area where weapons and military forces are forbidden (page 821)

democracy *(dih-MAH-kruh-see) n.* a form of government in which common citizens have a voice in making decisions and choosing leaders (page 130)

demographics *(deh-muh-GRA-fihks) n.* the characteristics of a particular population (page 309)

deportation *(dee-pawr-TAY-shuhn) n.* the removal of a person from a nation (page 713)

depose *(dih-POHZ) v.* to remove from power (page 207)

depth charge *(dehpth chahrj) n.* an underwater bomb that is programmed to explode at a certain depth (page 778)

despotic *(dehs-PAH-tihk) adj.* tyrannical, having absolute power (page 340)

despotism *(DEHS-puh-tih-zuhm) n.* the oppressive rule by a leader with absolute power (page 587)

détente *(day-TAHNT) n.* the easing of tensions and an improvement in relations between nations (page 834)

dharma *(DUR-muh) n.* a Sanskrit term meaning the way of righteous conduct (page 71)

dhimmitude *(DIH-muh-tood) n.* the protected status of certain non-Muslims in the Muslim world (page 251)

dhow *(dow) n.* an early type of ship that carried trade goods across the Indian Ocean (page 375)

dialect *(DY-uh-lehkt) n.* a regional variation in language (page 309)

diaspora *(dy-AS-puh-ruh) n.* the migration of people from an ancestral homeland (page 17)

dictator *(DIHK-tay-tuhr) n.* a person who rules with total authority (page 153)

diplomacy *(duh-PLOH-muh-see) n.* negotiation between governments (page 48)

disenfranchised *(dihs-ihn-FRAN-chyzd) adj.* lacking rights or the ability to influence a government (page 584)

displaced *(dihs-PLAYST) adj.* forced from a place or home (page 875)

dissident *(DIH-sih-duhnt) n.* a person who is at odds with an established practice, such as a particular religion (page 442)

division of labor *(duh-VIH-zhuhn uhv LAY-bur) n.* a system in which people perform different jobs to meet the needs of a society; a process that divides a task into separate parts with each completed by a different person or group (pages 34 and 617)

doctrine *(DAHK-truhn) n.* an official belief (page 289)

domestication *(duh-mehs-tih-KAY-shuhn) n.* the taming of wild animals (page 23)

dominion *(duh-MIH-nyuhn) n.* a self-governing commonwealth within an empire (page 651)

domino effect *(DAH-muh-noh ih-FEHKT) n.* the belief that if one country becomes communist, its neighbors will fall to communism like a row of dominoes (page 800)

dowry *(DOW-ree) n.* property that a woman brings to her marriage (page 458)

drone *(drohn) n.* a pilotless airplane run by remote control (page 875)

duchy *(DUH-chee) n.* a territory ruled by a duke or duchess (page 271)

dynastic cycle *(dy-NAS-tihk SY-kuhl) n.* the pattern of the rise and fall of dynasties in ancient and early China (page 84)

dynasty *(DY-nuh-stee) n.* a series of rulers from the same family (page 44)

E

earthwork (URTH-wurk) n. a construction of soil and rocks (page 392)

economy (ih-KAH-nuh-mee) n. the system for producing and obtaining goods and services (page 24)

edict (EE-dihkt) n. an official proclamation (page 159)

embargo (ihm-BAHR-goh) n. a ban on engaging in commerce with specified countries (pages 646 and 805)

embellish (ihm-BEH-lihsh) v. to decorate with ornamental details (page 455)

empire (EHM-pyr) n. a group of nations or peoples ruled by a single person or government (page 39)

encomienda (ehn-koh-mee-EHN-duh) n. a legal system that allowed each settler in the Spanish Americas to exact tribute, mainly in labor, from a certain number of Native Americans (page 497)

enlightened despot (ihn-LY-tuhnd DEHS-puht) n. an absolute ruler who applied certain Enlightenment ideas (page 577)

enlightenment (ihn-LY-tuhn-muhnt) n. a state when someone obtains a deep understanding and sense of clarity (page 72)

entrepreneur (ahn-truh-pruh-NUR) n. a person who organizes and operates a business (page 465)

envoy (EHN-voy) n. a diplomatic representative (page 339)

epic (EH-pihk) n. a long narrative poem that relates the adventures of a legendary or historical hero (page 37)

epistle (ih-PIH-suhl) n. a letter (page 175)

equatorial (ee-kwuh-TAWR-ee-uhl) adj. located at or near the equator (page 755)

estate (ih-STAYT) n. one of three distinct social classes in prerevolutionary France—the First Estate (clergy); the Second Estate (nobility); and the Third Estate (commoners) (page 584)

ethnography (ehth-NAH-gruh-fee) n. the study of the linguistic and cultural relationships between peoples (page 554)

excommunication (ehk-skuh-myoo-nuh-KAY-shuhn) n. explusion from the Christian Church (page 275)

exile (EHG-zyl) n. the forced removal from one's homeland (page 61)

expatriate (ehk-SPAY-tree-uht) n. a person who chooses to live outside of his or her home country (page 717)

exposition (ehk-spuh-ZIH-shuhn) n. a world fair or exhibition (page 623)

extraterritoriality (ehk-struh-tair-uh-tawr-ee-A-luh-tee) n. exemption from local law (page 632)

extremist (ihk-STREE-mihst) n. a person with a radical view (page 872)

F

famine (FA-muhn) n. an extreme shortage of food in a country or large geographic area (page 296)

fascism (FA-shih-zuhm) n. a way of governing based on extreme nationalism, racism, and suppression of opposition (page 742)

fauna (FAW-nuh) n. the animals of a specific place (page 554)

federal (FEH-duh-ruhl) adj. relating to a government where power is shared between the central, national government and that of states or provinces (page 583)

feudalism (FYOO-duh-lih-zuhm) n. a name given to the legal and social system in medieval Europe in which serfs worked the land and vassals performed military service for their lords in return for protection (page 276)

figurehead (FIH-gyur-hehd) n. a leader in name only (page 257)

filial piety (FIH-lee-uhl PY-uh-tee) n. respect for one's parents (page 86)

fiscal austerity (FIH-skuhl aw-STEHR-uh-tee) n. any measure to avoid debt, such as cutting spending or raising taxes (page 886)

flora (FLAWR-uh) n. the plants of a specific place (page 552)

food security (food sih-KYOOR-uh-tee) n. the assurance that food will be available to maintain health (page 552)

fracking (FRA-kihng) n. the process of drilling into the earth and applying water pressure to force out natural gases by breaking up rock (page 892)

fresco (FREH-skoh) n. a painting drawn on wet plaster (page 124)

fundamentalism (fuhn-duh-MEHN-tuh-lih-zuhm) n. a strict adherence to a set of basic principles, often relating to political or religious beliefs (page 857)

G

garrison town (GAIR-uh-suhn town) n. a town where soldiers of an empire were based (page 203)

genocide
genocide (JEH-nuh-syd) n. the systematic destruction of a racial or cultural group (page 675)

geocentric theory (jee-oh-SEHN-trihk THEE-uh-ree) n. the theory that the sun and planets revolve around Earth (page 546)

geoglyph (JEE-uh-glihf) n. a large geometric design or shape drawn on the ground, created by scraping away dark surface dirt and rocks to reveal lighter-colored soil (page 396)

geothermal energy (jee-oh-THUR-muhl EH-nur-jee) n. energy derived from heat released by Earth's interior (page 892)

ger (gur) n. a portable felt tent used by Mongol nomads (page 326)

ghazi (GAH-zee) n. a warrior for Islam (page 344)

ghetto (GEH-toh) n. a separate section of a city in which minority groups are forced to live (page 294)

Ghost Dance (gohst dahnts) n. a ceremonial dance performed by some Native Americans who believed the dance would summon a deliverer who would restore their world (page 680)

gladiator (GLA-dee-ay-tur) n. a man who battled wild animals or other men to entertain spectators (page 163)

glasnost (GLAZ-nohst) n. a government policy of open communication in the former Soviet Union (page 834)

globalization (gloh-buh-luh-ZAY-shuhn) n. the development of an increasingly integrated global economy marked especially by free trade, free flow of capital, and the tapping of cheaper foreign labor markets (page 624)

Great Depression (grayt dih-PREH-shuhn) n. a time of intense financial hardship that lasted throughout the 1930s (page 740)

green building (green BIHL-dihng) n. the act of designing and building structures with the environment in mind (page 893)

griot (GREE-oh) n. a West African storyteller who relates stories through the oral tradition (page 361)

guerrilla warfare (guh-RIH-luh WAWR-fair) n. small-scale surprise attacks (page 675)

guild (gihld) n. an association formed by artisans or merchants to improve their business (page 277)

guillotine (gee-yuh-TEEN) n. a machine with a sharp blade designed for beheading people (page 587)

GLOSSARY

Gulag *(GOO-lahg) n.* the Soviet system of forced-labor camps (page 721)

H

habeas corpus *(HAY-bee-uhs KAWR-puhs) n.* a legal procedure that prevents the government from holding a person indefinitely, without coming before a judge (page 283)

hacienda *(hah-see-EHN-duh) n.* a large plantation in a Spanish-speaking colony (page 497)

hacker *(HA-kur) n.* an individual who illegally gains access to electronic information (page 898)

hajj *(haj) n.* a Muslim pilgrimage to the holy city of Mecca (page 245)

heliocentric theory *(hee-lee-oh-SEHN-trihk THEE-uh-ree) n.* the theory that Earth and other planets revolve around the sun (page 547)

Hellenization *(hehl-luh-nuh-ZAY-shuhn) n.* the process by which Greek culture was spread throughout the Persian Empire (page 140)

helot *(HEH-luht) n.* a state-owned slave in ancient Sparta (page 129)

heretic *(HEHR-uh-tihk) n.* a church member who holds religious views contrary to official doctrine (page 294)

hieroglyph *(HY-ruh-glihf) n.* a picture representing an object, sound, or idea that was part of the ancient Egyptian writing system (page 46)

Hind Swaraj *(hihnd swuh-RAHJ) n.* the idea of self-rule in India (page 750)

Hindu-Arabic numerals *(HIHN-doo-ehr-uh-bihk NOOM-ruhlz) n.* the numerals 1, 2, 3 . . . etc. originally from India and brought to the West through Arab traders (page 195)

historiography *(hih-stawr-ee-AH-gruh-fee) n.* the art and science of creating a reliable and useful story from bits of information about the past (page 8)

holy war *(HOH-lee wawr) n.* warfare in defense of a religious faith (page 290)

hoplite *(HAWP-lyt) n.* a heavily armed soldier of ancient Greece (page 129)

human record *(HYOO-muhn REH-kurd) n.* the story of human life on Earth over the centuries (page 56)

humanism *(HYOO-muh-nih-zuhm) n.* an intellectual movement based on the works of classical Greek and Roman thinkers (page 424)

hunter-gatherer *(HUHN-tuhr-GA-thur-ur) n.* a person who survives by hunting game and gathering wild plants (page 13)

hypothesis *(hy-PAH-thuh-suhs) n.* an unproven theory that might answer a question and can be tested (page 549)

I

icon *(EYE-kahn) n.* a sacred or religious image (page 234)

iconoclast *(eye-KAH-nuh-klast) n.* a member of Byzantine society opposed to the use of icons; literally means "image breaker" (page 235)

ideology *(eye-dee-AH-luh-jee) n.* a system of ideas expressing a social or political philosophy about the world (page 591)

imperialism *(ihm-PIHR-ee-uh-lih-zuhm) n.* the practice by which a country increases its power by gaining control over other areas of the world (page 668)

indentured servant *(ihn-DEHN-churd SUR-vuhnt) n.* a person under contract to work, usually without pay, in exchange for free passage to the colonies (page 505)

indigenous *(ihn-DIH-juh-nuhs) adj.* native to a particular place (page 15)

indoctrinate *(ihn-DAHK-truh-nayt) v.* to rigidly train in a theory or doctrine (page 808)

inductive approach *(ihn-DUHK-tihv uh-PROHCH) n.* an approach to scientific research that involves working from carefully controlled observations to larger truths (page 549)

indulgence *(ihn-DUHL-juhnts) n.* a special prayer that could be purchased from the Roman Catholic Church to save a person's soul (page 434)

infamy *(IHN-fuh-mee) n.* an extremely shameful or evil act (page 768)

inflation *(ihn-FLAY-shuhn) n.* an increase in the price of goods and services compared to the value of money (page 455)

infrastructure *(IHN-fruh-struhk-chur) n.* networks for transportation, water, and other utilities (page 315)

Inquisition *(ihn-kwuh-ZIH-shun) n.* a special court formed by the Roman Catholic Church to hear charges against accused heretics (page 294)

insolvency *(ihn-SAWL-vuhnt-see) n.* the inability to pay debts; bankruptcy (page 799)

institution *(ihn-stuh-TOO-shuhn) n.* an organization that is established for a specific purpose and continues over time (page 35)

insurgent *(in-SUR-juhnt) n.* a rebel fighter (page 589)

intermediary *(ihn-tur-MEE-dee-air-ee) n.* a person who serves as a go-between in an exchange involving two other parties (page 362)

intifada *(ihn-tuh-FAH-duh) n.* a Palestinian uprising against Israel's occupation of the West Bank and Gaza (page 855)

iron *(EYE-urn) n.* a heavy metal that is used to make steel (page 54)

irrigation *(ihr-uh-GAY-shuhn) n.* a human-made system to transport water where it is needed (page 35)

Islamist *(ihs-LAH-mihst) n.* a Muslim who believes that laws and constitutions should be guided by Islamic principles and that religious authorities should be directly involved in the government (page 515)

island hopping *(EYE-luhnd HAH-ping) n.* a strategy designed by the Allies in World War II to capture and control islands in the Pacific one by one (page 772)

isolationism *(eye-suh-LAY-shuh-nih-zuhm) n.* a policy in which a nation refrains from alliances and other international political relations (page 761)

J

janissary *(JA-nuh-sair-ee) n.* a highly trained and disciplined soldier and slave in the Ottoman army (page 450)

Jim Crow Laws *(jihm kroh lawz) n.* laws established after Reconstruction that enforced racial segregation across the southern United States (page 662)

joint-stock company *(joynt-stahk KUHM-puh-nee) n.* a business enterprise funded by the sale of shares to multiple investors (page 492)

junta *(HUN-tuh) n.* a military or political ruling group who often take power by force (page 600)

K

kamikaze *(kah-mih-KAH-zee) n.* a Japanese suicide bomber pilot during World War II (page 772)

karma *(KAHR-muh) n.* the sum of a person's actions in life that determines his or her rebirth in the next life (page 71)

khanate *(KAH-nayt) n.* an area of the Mongol Empire ruled by a khan (page 328)

knight *(nyt) n.* a horse-riding warrior who served as a lord's vassal (page 276)

Kristallnacht *(KRIH-stuhl-nahkt) n.* the destruction of Jewish homes, businesses, and synagogues by the Nazis on the night of November 9, 1938 (page 745)

kulak *(KOO-lak) n.* a wealthy peasant in the Soviet Union of the early 20th century (page 747)

L

La Reforma *(lah reh-FAWRM-uh) n.* a reform movement in Mexico that called for the redistribution of land, the separation of church and state, and greater educational opportunities for the poor (page 655)

laissez-faire *(LEH-say-FEHR) n.* an economic system in which businesses and industries regulate their activities without government interference (page 569)

laity *(LAY-uh-tee) n.* members of the church who are not clergy (page 288)

lar *(lahr) n.* a Roman household god (page 157)

leftist *(LEHF-tihst) n.* a person who supports radical economic and social changes (page 845)

legionary *(LEE-juh-nehr-ee) n.* a paid professional soldier in the Roman army (page 162)

liberalism *(LIH-buh-ruh-lih-zuhm) n.* a belief system that argues that the liberty of the individual is the main concern of politics (page 626)

lineage *(lih-NEE-ihj) n.* a group of descendants from a common ancestor (page 361)

Linear B *(LIH-nee-ur bee) n.* the Mycenaean writing system, believed to be an early form of the Greek language (page 125)

linear perspective *(LIH-nee-ur pur-SPEHK-tihv) n.* an artistic technique in which the artist uses the placement and size of figures on a flat plane to make a scene appear three-dimensional (page 426)

liturgy *(LIH-tur-jee) n.* a form of worship (page 437)

loess *(lehs) n.* a type of fine, fertile, yellow silt that floats through the waters of the Huang He in China (page 83)

longevity *(lahn-JEH-vuh-tee) n.* an increased lifespan (page 909)

longitude *(LAHN-juh-tood) n.* an object's east-west position measured in degrees or difference in time (page 554)

M

magnate *(MAG-nayt) n.* a wealthy, powerful, and influential businessperson (page 675)

maize *(mayz) n.* a grain similar to corn (page 386)

Mandate of Heaven *(MAN-dayt uhv HEH-vuhn) n.* the ancient Chinese belief that Heaven, the generalized forces of the cosmos, chooses the rightful ruler who rules as long as Heaven believes he is worthy (page 84)

manorialism *(muh-NAWR-uh-lih-zuhm) n.* a medieval economic, social, and political system in which agricultural laborers were tied to the land they farmed and to the lord who owned the land (page 276)

mansa *(MAHNT-suh) n.* a West African king (page 362)

manumission *(man-yuh-MIH-shuhn) n.* the release of a person from slavery (page 518)

maritime *(MEHR-uh-tym) adj.* relating to the sea (page 200)

maroon community *(muh-ROON kuh-MYOO-nuh-tee) n.* one of the self-governing groups of escaped slaves common in the Caribbean and coastal areas of Central and South America beginning in the 1500s (page 527)

mass media *(mas MEE-dee-uh) n.* means of communication meant to reach many people (page 736)

mass society *(mas suh-SY-uh-tee) n.* a society in which large numbers of people share the same experience without actually having to meet (page 736)

mausoleum *(maw-suh-LEE-uhm) n.* a large tomb (page 459)

medieval *(mee-DEE-vuhl) adj.* referring to a period in European history from about 500 to 1500 C.E. (page 227)

mercantilism *(MUR-kuhn-tuh-lih-zuhm) n.* a system in which government protects and encourages trade, based on the theory that such businesses create wealth (page 483)

mercenary *(MUHR-suh-nehr-ee) n.* a soldier who is paid to fight (page 154)

meritocracy *(mehr-uh-TAH-kruh-see) n.* a system in which qualified people are chosen and promoted on the basis of their achievement rather than social position (page 88)

mestizo *(mehs-TEE-zoh) n.* person of mixed Spanish and Native American ancestry (page 497)

metallurgy *(MEH-tuhl-uhr-jee) n.* the science or technology of working with metals (page 195)

Métis *(may-TEES) n.* people of mixed European and indigenous descent (page 651)

Middle Passage *(MIH-duhl PA-sihj) n.* the journey by slave ships across the Atlantic from West Africa to the Americas (page 518)

migrate *(MY-grayt) v.* to move from one region to another (page 11)

militarism *(MIH-luh-tuh-rih-zuhm) n.* a government policy of continuous military development and readiness for war (page 639)

militia *(muh-LIH-shuh) n.* a volunteer army (page 582)

minaret *(mih-nuh-REHT) n.* a tall tower from which specially trained Muslims issue the call to prayer (page 252)

missionary *(MIH-shuh-nehr-ee) n.* a person sent out to convert others to a religion (page 175)

mitochondrial Eve *(my-tuh-KAHN-dree-uhl EEV) n.* a single human female ancestor common to all human beings (page 8)

mobilize *(MOH-buh-lyz) v.* to assemble and prepare for war (page 698)

monarchy *(MAH-nur-kee) n.* a government ruled by a single person, such as a king (page 44)

monastery *(MAH-nuh-stehr-ee) n.* a Christian religious community and center of learning, work, and worship (page 271)

monopoly *(muh-NAH-puh-lee) n.* sole control over something; the complete and exclusive control of an industry by one company (pages 362 and 663)

monotheism *(MAH-nuh-thee-ih-zuhm) n.* the belief in one God (page 59)

monsoon *(mahn-SOON) n.* a strong seasonal wind in South and Southeast Asia (page 81)

mosaic *(moh-ZAY-ihk) n.* a group of tiny colored stone cubes set in mortar to create a picture or design (page 239)

mosque *(mahsk) n.* a Muslim place of worship (page 247)

mother culture *(MUH-thur KUHL-chur)* *n.* a civilization that greatly influences other civilizations (page 387)

movable type *(MOO-vuh-buhl typ) n.* individual clay tablets that could be arranged to form text in an early form of printing (page 310)

muckraker *(MUHK-ray-kur) n.* an investigative journalist of the early 1900s who exposed misconduct by powerful organizations and people (page 663)

mujahideen *(moo-ja-hih-DEEN) n.* Islamic guerilla fighters (page 825)

multinational corporation *(muhl-tee-NASH-nuhl kawr-puh-RAY-shuhn) n.* a company with locations around the world that is owned and managed by teams from more than one nation (page 863)

mummy *(MUH-mee) n.* the preserved body of a pharaoh or other person in ancient Egypt (page 45)

mystic *(MIHS-tihk) n.* a person who seeks knowledge of God through devotion or meditation (page 279)

N

napalm *(NAY-pahm) n.* a highly flammable, jelly-like substance that sticks to targets and generates extreme heat (page 778)

nation-building *(NAY-shuhn BIHL-dihng) n.* the establishment of order and a functioning government in a country that has been plagued by violence and instability (page 845)

nation-state *(NAY-shuhn-STAYT) n.* a state made up of people of one nationality, sharing common traits (page 591)

nationalism *(NASH-nuh-lih-zuhm) n.* the belief that individuals are bound together by ties of language, culture, history, and often religion (page 591)

nationalize *(NASH-nuh-lyz) v.* to bring a private business or industry under the control of the national government (page 720)

nativism *(NAY-tih-vih-zuhm) n.* the practice of favoring ideas of the home country rather than those of immigrants or foreign countries (page 469)

natural rights *(NA-chuh-ruhl ryts) n.* inherent rights, such as life, liberty, and property (page 565)

naturalism *(NA-chuh-ruh-lih-zuhm) n.* an artistic style that strove for accurate depictions of people or the natural world (page 418)

Neanderthal *(nee-AN-dur-tawl) n.* a member of an extinct species of early humans (page 15)

nebula *(NEH-byuh-luh) n.* a cloud of gas and dust in outer space (page 551)

neoclassicism *(nee-oh-KLA-suh-sih-zuhm) n.* a creative style based on Greek and Roman ideals (page 596)

neocolonialism *(nee-oh-kuh-LOHN-yuh-lih-zuhm) n.* the continuation of dependence on, and domination by, a colonial power (page 812)

neoliberalism *(nee-oh-LIH-bruh-lih-zuhm) n.* an economic approach that emphasizes free markets and wide international trade (page 863)

Neolithic *(nee-uh-LIH-thihk) adj.* the term to describe people who use stone tools and practice agriculture; means "new stone age" (page 22)

nirvana *(nihr-VAH-nuh) n.* a state of blissful escape from suffering caused by the cycle of life and rebirth (page 72)

nomad *(NOH-mad) n.* a person who migrates from place to place (page 69)

nonalignment *(nahn-uh-LYN-muhnt) n.* a policy of not allying with other countries, specifically with either the communist or noncommunist countries during the Cold War (page 816)

nongovernmental organization (NGO) *(nahn-guh-vurn-MEHN-tuhl awr-guh-nuh-ZAY-shuhn) n.* a nonprofit group that supports a particular cause (page 858)

nonintervention *(nahn-ihn-tur-VEHNT-shuhn) n.* the policy of not getting involved in the affairs of other countries (page 760)

Northwest Passage *(nawrth-WEHST PA-sihj) n.* a sea route from the Atlantic Ocean to the Pacific along the northern coast of North America (page 493)

O

oasis *(oh-AY-suhs) n.* an isolated place in the desert with water where plants can grow (page 244)

oligarchy *(AW-luh-gawr-kee) n.* a form of government ruled by a few powerful citizens (page 129)

omnipotence *(ahm-NIH-puh-tuhnts) n.* unlimited power (pages 192 and 341)

optics *(AHP-tiks) n.* the study of light and vision (page 546)

oracle bone *(AWR-uh-kuhl bohn) n.* a bone used in ancient China to consult ancestors about the future; now known to be China's earliest surviving written records (page 83)

oral tradition *(AW-ruhl truh-DIH-shuhn) n.* a group of stories that take a standard form and are passed down through generations by people talking with one another (page 125)

oratory *(AWR-uh-tawr-ee) n.* the art of public speaking (page 184)

orthodoxy *(AWR-thuh-dahk-see) n.* established beliefs and practices (page 542)

outsourcing *(OWT-sawr-sihng) n.* the practice of sending work once done internally at a company to be done by people outside the company, usually for lower wages (page 863)

P

pacifist *(PA-suh-fihst) n.* a person with a religious or philosophical objection to violence (page 860)

Pan-Africanism *(pan-A-frih-kuh-nih-zuhm) n.* the idea that people of African descent have a common heritage and should be unified (page 685)

pandemic *(pan-DEH-mihk) n.* a worldwide outbreak of infectious disease (page 708)

pantheon *(PAN-thee-ahn) n.* a group of officially recognized gods and goddesses (page 157)

papyrus *(puh-PY-ruhs) n.* a paperlike material made from reeds (page 46)

Parliament *(PAHR-luh-muhnt) n.* the lawmaking body in England (page 283)

partition *(pahr-TIH-shuhn) n.* the division of a country (page 817)

passive resistance *(PA-sihv rih-ZIH-stuhnts) n.* nonviolent opposition to authority (page 846)

patriarchy *(PAY-tree-ahr-kee) n.* a society in which men have all the power (page 156)

patrician *(puh-TRIH-shuhn) n.* a wealthy landowner in Roman society (page 153)

patron *(PAY-truhn) n.* a person who gives artists financial support (page 415)

people's commune *(PEE-puhlz KAHM-yoon) n.* in China, a grouping of collective farms in which people lived and worked together to produce both crops and industrial goods (page 810)

perestroika *(pehr-uh-STROY-kuh) n.* a government policy of economic and government reform in the former Soviet Union (page 834)

petition *(puh-TIH-shuhn) n.* a formal written request (page 476)

phalanx *(FAY-langks) n.* a body of soldiers moving in close formation (page 114)

pharaoh *(FEHR-oh) n.* a king of ancient Egypt (page 43)

philosophe *(fee-luh-ZAWF) n.* one of the writers and thinkers of the European Enlightenment (page 568)

physiography *(fih-zee-AH-gruh-fee) n.* the physical geography of a place (page 316)

piety *(PY-uh-tee) n.* a strong belief in religion shown through worship (page 441)

pilgrimage *(PIHL-gruh-mihj) n.* a journey to a holy place (page 176)

plague *(playg) n.* a deadly epidemic disease (page 226)

plebeian *(plih-BEE-uhn) n.* a commoner in Rome (page 153)

pogrom *(puh-GRAHM) n.* an organized attack upon or massacre of a minority group (page 294)

polis *(PAW-luhs) n.* a Greek city-state (page 128)

polytheism *(PAH-lee-thee-ih-zuhm) n.* the belief in many gods (page 38)

popular culture *(PAH-pyuh-lur KUHL-chur) n.* the shared experiences and interests of everyday people (page 736)

popular sovereignty *(PAH-pyuh-lur SAH-vuh-ruhn-tee) n.* the belief that government arises from the people themselves (page 583)

populism *(PAH-pyuh-lih-zuhm) n.* a political movement that claims to support the concerns of common people (page 804)

preempt *(pree-EHMPT) v.* to prevent from happening (page 854)

principate *(PRIHN-suh-payt) n.* a type of monarchy in which some republican ideals are upheld (page 159)

proletariat *(proh-luh-TEHR-ee-uht) n.* the working class (page 627)

propaganda *(prah-puh-GAN-duh) n.* information used by a government to make people think or act in a particular way (page 591)

Protestant *(PRAH-tuh-stuhnt) n.* a person who protested against the Catholic Church and became part of a reformed church (page 436)

proxy war *(PRAHK-see WAWR) n.* a war in which one or both sides are supported by, and serve the interests of, another country (page 802)

public works *(PUH-blihk wurks) n.* government construction projects that benefit a community (page 40)

pull factor *(pul FAK-tur) n.* a factor or incentive that attracts people to move to a new country (page 477)

push factor *(push FAK-tur) n.* a factor or condition that causes people to leave their home countries (page 477)

pyramid *(PIHR-uh-mihd) n.* a large, four-sided monument built in ancient Egypt as a tomb for a pharaoh (page 44)

Q

qadi *(KAH-dee) n.* a Muslim judge (page 256)

quipu *(KEE-poo) n.* a series of knotted strings the Inca used to keep records (page 399)

quorum *(KWAWR-uhm) n.* a minimum number of people who must be present to conduct a group's business (page 131)

R

racism *(RAY-sih-zuhm) n.* the belief that the color of a person's skin makes them superior or inferior (page 521)

recession *(rih-SEH-shuhn) n.* a period of reduced economic activity (page 886)

Reconstruction *(ree-kuhn-STRUHK-shuhn) n.* the effort to rebuild and reunite the United States after the Civil War (page 645)

redistributive economy *(ree-duh-STRIH-byoo-tihv ih-KAH-nuh-mee) n.* a type of economy in which produce and other goods are stored in a central place and are then sorted and distributed to the population (page 124)

referendum *(reh-fuh-REHN-duhm) n.* a public vote on a single political question (page 813)

refugee *(reh-fyoo-JEE) n.* a person who is forced to leave his or her homeland because of war, persecution, or natural disaster (page 61)

regent *(ree-juhnt) n.* a person who rules when a monarch or emperor is unable to do so (page 209)

reincarnation *(ree-ihn-kahr-NAY-shuhn) n.* the rebirth of a soul in a different body over different life cycles (page 71)

relief *(rih-LEEF) n.* a type of sculpture in which three-dimensional elements rise from a flat background (page 56)

religiosity *(rih-lih-jee-AH-suh-tee) n.* a strong religious belief (page 885)

religious syncretism *(rih-LIH-juhs SING-kruh-tih-zuhm) n.* the blending of different belief systems (page 443)

religious tolerance *(rih-LIH-juhs TAH-luh-ruhnts) n.* the acceptance of the beliefs and practices of others (page 253)

remilitarization *(ree-mih-luh-tuh-ruh-ZAY-shuhn) n.* the process of rearming (page 760)

reparations *(reh-puh-RAY-shuhnz) n.* money or goods paid to cover wartime damages (page 708)

republic *(rih-PUH-blihk) n.* a form of government in which people choose officials to represent them instead of voting directly on laws and policies (page 153)

revenue *(REH-vuh-noo) n.* income for the government, such as taxes (page 458)

revisionist *(rih-VIH-zhuh-nihst) adj.* straying from the revolutionary spirit of Marxist doctrine (page 809)

Romanticism *(roh-MAN-tuh-sih-zuhm) n.* a cultural movement originating in the 18th century that emphasized emotions over reason (page 596)

S

sabotage *(SA-buh-tahzh) n.* a deliberate destruction (page 617)

Sahel *(SA-hihl) n.* a semidesert region south of the Sahara (page 360)

salon *(suh-LAHN) n.* a social gathering organized by Parisian women to discuss Enlightenment ideas (page 572)

sanction *(SANGK-shuhn) n.* a trade or financial restriction placed by one nation on another (page 757)

Sanskrit *(SAN-skriht) n.* a classical Indo-European language spoken by Indo-Aryan migrants to northern India around 1500–1000 B.C.E. (page 69)

satellite state *(SA-tuh-lyt STAYT) n.* a country that is formally independent but under the control or influence of another country (page 799)

satire *(SA-tyr) n.* humor and sarcasm used to expose or ridicule human foolishness or weakness (pages 133 and 425)

satrap *(SAY-trap) n.* a provincial governor (page 104)

satyagraha *(suh-TYAH-gruh-huh) n.* the application of nonviolence to politics, according to Indian belief (page 750)

GLOSSARY

savanna *(suh-VA-nuh) n.* an area of lush tropical grasslands (page 360)

scientific method *(sy-uhn-TIH-fihk MEH-thuhd) n.* a logical procedure for developing and testing scientific ideas (page 549)

scientific rationalism *(sy-uhn-TIH-fihk RASH-nuh-lih-zuhm) n.* a school of thought in which observation, experimentation, and mathematical reasoning replace ancient wisdom and church teachings as the source of scientific truths (page 549)

scribe *(skryb) n.* a professional writer who recorded official information in ancient societies (page 46)

script *(skrihpt) n.* a form of writing (page 153)

secede *(sih-SEED) v.* to formally withdraw from a nation (page 644)

sectionalism *(SEHK-shuh-nuh-lih-zuhm) n.* a loyalty to whichever section or region of the country one is from, rather than to the nation as a whole (page 644)

secular *(SEH-kyuh-lur) adj.* not belonging to a religious order (page 288)

segregation *(seh-grih-GAY-shuhn) n.* the separation of different groups of people, usually based on race (page 645)

self-determination *(sehlf-dih-tur-muh-NAY-shuhn) n.* the process by which a people forms its own state and chooses its own government (page 708)

Senate *(SEH-nuht) n.* the governing body in ancient Rome that advised the consuls and was initially made up of wealthy landowners (page 153)

sepoy *(SEE-poy) n.* an Indian soldier under British command (page 635)

serf *(suhrf) n.* a medieval agricultural worker who was tied to the land (page 276)

shah *(shaw) n.* a king in Iran (page 452)

sharia *(shuh-REE-uh) n.* Islamic law covering all aspects of life (page 246)

sheikh *(sheek) n.* the leader of a Bedouin clan (page 244)

shell shock *(shehl shahk) n.* a mental health condition resulting from exposure to warfare (page 717)

shogun *(SHOH-guhn) n.* a Japanese general who is the military ruler of the country (page 317)

silt *(silt) n.* especially fine and fertile soil (page 35)

slash-and-burn agriculture *(slash-uhnd-burn A-grih-kuhl-chur) n.* a method of clearing fields for planting (page 388)

slave narrative *(slayv NAIR-uh-tihv) n.* a written account of the life of a fugitive or former slave (page 518)

social class *(SOH-shuhl klas) n.* a system in which people are grouped according to rank and power (page 35)

social contract *(SOH-shuhl KAHN-trakt) n.* an agreement between rulers and the ruled to cooperate for mutual social benefits in pursuit of an ordered society, with clearly defined rights and responsibilities for each (page 565)

social criticism *(SOH-shuhl KRIH-tuh-sih-zuhm) n.* a type of writing that tries to improve social conditions (page 617)

Social Darwinism *(SOH-shuhl DAHR-wuh-nih-zuhm) n.* the idea that racial groups are naturally arranged along a hierarchy (page 627)

social justice *(SOH-shuhl JUH-stuhs) n.* equal rights for all under the law (page 874)

socialism *(SOH-shuh-lih-zuhm) n.* an economic system in which industry is collectively owned, private property is allowed, and people are paid based on their contribution to production (page 627)

sovereignty *(SAH-vuh-ruhn-tee) n.* freedom from external control (page 542)

Soviet bloc *(SOH-vee-eht BLAHK) n.* a group of nations under the control of the Soviet Union (page 800)

speculation *(speh-kyuh-LAY-shuhn) n.* the taking of huge risks to gain great rewards (page 740)

sphere of influence *(sfihr uhv IHN-floo-uhnts) n.* an area in which the dominance of one colonial power is recognized above all others (page 672)

stagnation *(stag-NAY-shuhn) n.* a lack of growth and development (page 227)

stalemate *(STAYL-mayt) n.* a situation in which neither side can defeat the other (page 700)

status quo *(STAY-tuhs-KWOH) n.* an existing condition (page 593)

stela *(STEE-luh) n.* a stone pillar used for the purpose of commemorating an important event or accomplishment (page 41)

steppe *(stehp) n.* a vast, grassy plain (page 326)

stimulus *(STIHM-yuh-luhs) n.* an incentive (page 886)

strike *(stryk) n.* a work stoppage used as a labor union tactic (page 653)

subjugation *(suhb-jih-GAY-shuhn) n.* the state of being under control or governance (page 668)

subprime mortgage *(SUHB-prym MAWR-gihj) n.* a home loan given to someone with poor credit (page 886)

succession *(suhk-SEH-shuhn) n.* the process by which a new leader is chosen to follow an outgoing leader (page 512)

suffrage *(SUH-frihj) n.* the right to vote (page 663)

sultan *(SUHL-tuhn) n.* a ruler of a Muslim state (page 345)

surplus *(SUR-pluhs) n.* a supply of goods and labor not needed for short-term survival (page 28)

surveillance *(sur-VAY-luhnts) n.* the act of watching over a person or group (page 873)

sustainable *(suh-STAY-nuh-buhl) adj.* unceasing, especially relating to a way of using a resource so it is not depleted (page 892)

synagogue *(SIH-nuh-gahg) n.* a Jewish house of worship (page 61)

T

taiga *(TY-guh) n.* land covered with scattered evergreen trees in the far north or subarctic area (page 470)

technology *(tehk-NAH-luh-jee) n.* the practical application of knowledge; any tool or technique that helps people accomplish tasks (page 35)

tenement *(TEH-nuh-muhnt) n.* a large apartment building that is usually overcrowded and badly maintained (page 652)

terrace *(TAIR-uhs) n.* a stepped platform (page 387)

tetrarchy *(TEH-trahr-kee) n.* a structure of government in which four persons rule jointly (page 180)

theocracy *(thee-AH-kruh-see) n.* a form of government in which the legal system is based on religious law (page 61)

tithe *(tyth) n.* ten percent of a person's income to be paid to the church (page 288)

total war *(TOH-tuhl wawr) n.* a war that requires assembling and preparing all national resources and engaging civilians as well as the military (page 699)

totalitarian *(toh-ta-luh-TAIR-ee-uhn) adj.* relating to a political system that exerts total control over a society often through violent means (page 743)

trans-Saharan trade network *(tran-suh-HAIR-uhn trayd NEHT-wurk) n.* a group of overland trade routes that carried goods between North Africa and sub-Saharan Africa (page 368)

treason *(TREE-zuhn) n.* the crime of betraying one's government or country (page 199)

trench warfare *(trehnch WAWR-fair) n.* a type of warfare in which soldiers fight from long ditches that are fortified by barbed wire (page 700)

triangular trade *(try-ANG-gyuh-lur trayd) n.* the transatlantic trade network connecting Europe, West Africa, and the Americas between the 1500s and the 1800s (page 520)

tribe *(tryb) n.* an extended family unit (page 60)

tribunal *(try-BYOO-nuhl) n.* a court with authority over a specific matter (page 786)

tribune *(TRIH-byoon) n.* an elected representative who protected the rights of ordinary citizens in Rome (page 153)

tribute *(TRIH-byoot) n.* a tax required of conquered people (page 194)

trireme *(try-REEM) n.* an ancient Greek warship with three banks of oars (page 115)

troll *(trohl) n.* a person who purposely posts offensive or threatening messages on the Internet (page 899)

truce *(troos) n.* a temporary halt of warfare (page 290)

trusteeship *(truh-STEE-shihp) n.* the administrative control over a territory by one or more countries (page 820)

tsar *(zahr) n.* the ruler of imperial Russia (page 471)

tundra *(TUHN-druh) n.* treeless arctic plains (page 470)

two-state solution *(too-stayt suh-LOO-shuhn) n.* a solution to the Israeli-Palestinian conflict that calls for an independent state of Palestine alongside the state of Israel (page 853)

tyranny *(TIHR-uh-nee) n.* a state of government in which rulers have unlimited power and use it unfairly (page 565)

U

ultranationalist *(uhl-truh-NASH-nuh-lihst) n.* an extreme nationalist (page 748)

V

vaquero *(vah-KEHR-oh) n.* a cowboy or cattle herder (page 726)

varna *(VAHR-nuh) n.* the four major social groups of ancient Indian society, ranked in order of purity (page 71)

vassal *(VA-suhl) n.* in medieval Europe, a person who gave military service and pledged loyalty to a lord in exchange for protection and land to live on (page 276)

Vedic *(VAY-dihk) adj.* associated with the society or religion of the Indo-Aryan migrants (page 70)

venerate *(VEH-nuh-rayt) v.* to honor or adore (page 234)

vernacular *(vuhr-NA-kyuh-lur) n.* the everyday language spoken by people (page 281)

veto *(VEE-toh) v.* to vote against (page 129)

viceroy *(VYS-roy) n.* a representative of the king in the Spanish Americas (page 497)

viceroyalty *(VYS-roy-uhl-tee) n.* a colony (page 497)

W

weapons of mass destruction *(WEH-puhnz uhv mas dih-STRUHK-shuhn) n.* weapons that can cause extreme destruction over a wide area (page 873)

X

xenophobia *(zeh-nuh-FOH-bee-uh) n.* a fear of foreigners (page 875)

Z

zaibatsu *(zy-BAHT-soo) n.* a powerful financial and industrial Japanese conglomerate (page 639)

ziggurat *(ZIH-gur-rat) n.* a large, stepped structure in a Sumerian temple (page 39)

GLOSARIO

A

abdicar *v.* renunciar formalmente a algo, como a la soberanía del trono (página 203)

abolición *s.* movimiento para acabar con la esclavitud (página 519)

aborigen *s.* habitante originario de Australia (página 554)

acueducto *s.* canal de piedra que transportaba agua limpia desde las colinas hasta las ciudades (página 163)

adaptarse *v.* desarrollar características que contribuyen a la supervivencia (página 14)

adoctrinar *v.* entrenar rígidamente en una teoría o doctrina (página 808)

adoración de los ancestros *s.* práctica de contactar a los antepasados muertos con la creencia de que pueden interceder en eventos humanos en nombre de los vivos (página 83)

ágora *s.* mercado al aire libre en una ciudad-estado griega (página 128)

agricultura *s.* cultivo de alimentos vegetales y la domesticación de animales (página 22)

agricultura de tala y quema *s.* método para despejar campos para plantar (página 388)

ahimsa *s.* concepto indio de la no violencia absoluta (página 750)

aislacionismo *s.* política en la que una nación se abstiene de alianzas y otras relaciones políticas internacionales (página 761)

alfabeto *s.* grupo de letras que forman los elementos individuales de un sistema de escritura (página 126)

alianza *s.* asociación (página 40)

alminar *s.* torre alta desde la cual musulmanes especialmente entrenados emiten el llamado a la oración (página 252)

análisis costo-beneficio *s.* proceso en el que se comparan los puntos buenos y malos para ver si los beneficios de algo superan su costo (página 863)

anarquista *s.* persona que está dispuesta a usar la fuerza para derrocar la opresión autoritaria (página 653)

anatomía *s.* estudio de las estructuras interiores y exteriores de los seres vivos (página 418)

anexar *v.* incorporar territorio a un estado existente (página 697)

anfiteatro *s.* teatro grande al aire libre (página 163)

ánfora *s.* gran jarrón de cerámica de dos asas con un cuello estrecho (página 161)

antisemitismo *s.* hostilidad y discriminación contra los judíos (página 294)

apaciguamiento *s.* proveer concesiones para mantener la paz (página 761)

apartheid *s.* sistema de segregación racial y discriminación contra sudafricanos no blancos que duró hasta principios de los años noventa. (página 814)

arabesco *s.* diseño abstracto compuesto por patrones repetitivos o flores, hojas, enredaderas o formas geométricas (página 258)

archipiélago *s.* cadena de islas (página 208)

arconte *s.* gobernante de importancia en la antigua Atenas (página 130)

aristócrata *s.* persona de riqueza y alto rango social (página 130)

armas de destrucción masiva *s.* armas que pueden causar destrucción extrema en un área amplia (página 873)

armisticio *s.* acuerdo entre las partes opuestas para poner fin a las hostilidades (página 705)

arquetipo *s.* ejemplo perfecto de algo (página 598)

artefacto *s.* objeto de valor histórico hecho por los seres humanos (página 8)

artillería *s.* grandes cañones de campaña que disparan proyectiles altamente explosivos (página 701)

asceta *s.* persona que elige una vida de pobreza (página 72)

asilo *s.* lugar seguro (página 875)

asimilar *v.* fusionarse con otra cultura (página 273)

astrolabio *s.* instrumento sofisticado que permitía a los usuarios calcular su ubicación en la Tierra (página 259)

ateísmo *s.* creencia de que Dios no existe (página 824)

atrocidad *s.* acto de violencia extremadamente cruel e impactante (página 786)

austeridad fiscal *s.* cualquier medida para evitar deudas, como recortar gastos o aumentar los impuestos (página 886)

autodeterminación *s.* proceso mediante el cual un pueblo forma su propio estado y elige a su propio gobierno (página 708)

autonomía *s.* independencia para autogobernarse (página 659)

autónomo *adj.* que se autogobierna (página 527)

autoritarismo *s.* sistema político caracterizado por un líder poderoso y libertades individuales limitadas (página 709)

B

bioarqueólogo *s.* persona que estudia restos humanos para aprender sobre arqueología (página 205)

biotecnología *s.* uso de organismos o procesos biológicos para crear nuevos productos que mejoren la vida (página 909)

Bloque soviético *s.* grupo de naciones bajo el control de la Unión Soviética (página 800)

bóer *s.* colono holandés o francés en Sudáfrica, también llamado Afrikaner (página 674)

bomba atómica *s.* tipo de bomba nuclear cuya explosión violenta se desencadena al dividir átomos y libera calor intenso y radiactividad (página 773)

bombardeo de saturación *s.* caída de una gran cantidad de bombas en un área designada (página 759)

botánica *s.* estudio de las plantas y la vida vegetal (página 552)

bronce *s.* mezcla de los metales estaño y cobre (página 35)

burguesía *s.* clase media (página 572)

burocracia *s.* grupo de funcionarios administrativos del gobierno (página 88)

C

caballería *s.* grupo de soldados montados a caballo (página 55)

caballero *s.* guerrero a caballo que servía como vasallo de un señor (página 276)

califa *s.* título de un líder musulmán que fue sucesor de Mahoma (página 247)

caligrafía *s.* forma de escritura elegante (página 258)

cambio climático *s.* cambios en los patrones climáticos globales (página 899)

Camisas negras *s.* miembros de un grupo militante que atacó a los oponentes de Mussolini (página 743)

campesino *s.* aldeano rural o agricultor menor en América Latina (página 726)

campo de concentración *s.* lugar donde un gran número de personas están encarceladas bajo una guardia armada; especialmente los campos creados por los nazis para retener a los judíos y a otros prisioneros durante la Segunda Guerra Mundial (página 675)

canonizar *v.* hacer de alguien un santo en la Iglesia Católica (página 441)

capital *s.* dinero u otros recursos que pueden usarse para invertir en negocios (página 277)

capitalismo *s.* sistema económico de libre mercado en el que las empresas son de propiedad privada y existen con el fin de obtener ganancias (página 492)

carabela *s.* barco pequeño y rápido utilizado por exploradores portugueses y españoles (página 482)

caravana *s.* grupo de personas que viajan juntas (página 367)

carga de profundidad *s.* bomba submarina que está programada para explotar a cierta profundidad (página 778)

cartografía *s.* la ciencia o el arte de hacer mapas (página 556)

catacumba *s.* cámara subterránea escondida donde los primeros cristianos enterraban a sus muertos (página 175)

catarata *s.* rápido empinado y no navegable a lo largo del curso de un río (página 42)

catedral *s.* iglesia principal de un distrito administrado por un obispo (página 279)

caudillo *s.* dictador militar latinoamericano que ganó poder a través de la violencia (página 605)

cazador-recolector *s.* persona que sobrevive mediante la caza de animales y la recolección de plantas silvestres (página 13)

celibato *s.* acto de permanecer soltero (página 204)

cenote *s.* piscina natural de gran tamaño o cueva abierta (página 391)

censo *s.* recuento oficial de la población. (página 204)

cha *s.* rey en Irán (página 452)

chinampa *s.* isla artificial creada para cultivar (página 395)

ciclo dinástico *s.* patrón del auge y caída de las dinastías en la antigua y temprana China (página 84)

cipayo *s.* soldado indio bajo mando británico (página 635)

circunnavegar *v.* viajar alrededor de todo el mundo (página 484)

ciudad de la guarnición *s.* ciudad donde se asentaban los soldados de un imperio (página 203)

ciudad-estado *s.* ciudad cuyo gobernador rige tanto la ciudad como las áreas circundantes (página 37)

civilización *s.* sociedad avanzada y compleja (página 34)

clan *s.* grupo de personas con un ancestro común (página 208)

clase social *s.* sistema en el que las personas se agrupan de acuerdo con el rango y el poder (página 35)

clero *s.* personas designadas para el servicio religioso por la iglesia (página 278)

coalición *s.* alianza temporal (página 139)

códice *s.* libro doblado hecho de papel de corteza de árbol (página 389)

coerción *s.* uso de la fuerza o amenazas (página 678)

colectivización *s.* reemplazo de granjas campesinas privadas con granjas colectivas estatales (página 747)

comercio *s.* compra y venta de bienes a gran escala (página 277)

comercio triangular *s.* red comercial transatlántica que conectaba Europa, África Occidental y América entre los años 1500 y 1800 (página 520)

comisión *s.* solicitud de un proyecto de arte o diseño específico, generalmente de la nobleza (página 417)

comuna popular *s.* en China, una agrupación de granjas colectivas en las que las personas vivían y trabajaban juntas para producir cultivos y bienes industriales (página 810)

comunidad granate *s.* uno de los grupos autónomos de esclavos que escaparon, común en el Caribe y las zonas costeras de América Central y del Sur a partir del siglo XVI (página 527)

comunismo *s.* sistema económico y político donde todas las propiedades son públicas, pertenecientes al estado central, y los bienes se distribuyen a todos de acuerdo con sus necesidades (página 627)

conectividad *s.* estado de estar conectado a otros, especialmente a través de un sistema informático (página 898)

Confederación *s.* los 11 estados del sur que se separaron de la Unión para formar su propia nación (página 644)

conquistador *s.* explorador español que conquistó tierras en las Américas (página 484)

conservación *s.* protección y preservación cuidadosa de algo (página 893)

consolidar *v.* unificar y fortalecer (página 299)

constitucionalismo *s.* concepto de gobernar basado en un conjunto de principios básicos o leyes llamadas constitución (página 583)

construcción nacional *s.* establecimiento del orden y de un gobierno en funcionamiento en un país que ha estado plagado de violencia e inestabilidad (página 845)

consumo *s.* gasto (página 468)

contracultural *adj.* relacionado con estilos y tradiciones que van en contra de los de la sociedad dominante (página 717)

contrato social *s.* acuerdo entre gobernantes y gobernados para cooperar en beneficio social mutuo en la búsqueda de una sociedad ordenada, con derechos y responsabilidades claramente definidos para cada uno (página 565)

conventillo *s.* edificio grande de apartamentos que generalmente está abarrotado y mal mantenido (página 652)

corporación multinacional *s.* empresa con ubicaciones en todo el mundo que es propiedad de y está administrada por equipos de más de una nación (página 863)

cosmopolita *adj.* diverso y familiarizado con personas, ideas y objetos de muchas partes del mundo (página 205)

crematorios *s.* hornos, especialmente aquellos utilizados por los nazis durante la Segunda Guerra Mundial para quemar los cuerpos de los asesinados (página 783)

criptografía *s.* códigos secretos y codificación de datos para mantener segura la información electrónica (página 899)

crítica social *s.* tipo de escrito que intenta mejorar las condiciones sociales (página 621)

crónica *s.* recuento o registro de hechos (página 199)

GLOSARIO

Cruzada s. expedición militar cristiana para recuperar la tierra de Palestina del dominio musulmán (página 290)

culto de personalidad s. promoción de una figura pública como persona que debe ser venerada (página 747)

cultura madre s. civilización que influye mucho en otras civilizaciones (página 387)

cultura popular s. experiencias e intereses compartidos de la gente común (página 736)

cuneiforme s. primera forma de escritura, desarrollada por los sumerios (página 39)

D

daimyo s. terrateniente rico en el Japón feudal (página 317)

Dalit s. miembro de la casta hindú más baja en la sociedad india tradicional (página 750)

Danza fantasma s. danza ceremonial realizada por ciertos pueblos nativoamericanos, quienes creían que la danza convocaría a un ente que restauraría su mundo (página 660)

Darwinismo social s. Idea de que los grupos raciales están naturalmente organizados a lo largo de una jerarquía. (página 627)

deidad s. dios o diosa (página 133)

deísmo s. filosofía religiosa que apoya la idea de la religión natural, en la que Dios no interfiere con las leyes naturales (página 573)

delegación s. grupo de personas elegidas para representar a otros (página 198)

delta s. área triangular de tierra baja y plana en la desembocadura de un río (página 42)

democracia s. forma de gobierno en la que los ciudadanos comunes tienen voz para tomar decisiones y elegir a sus líderes (página 130)

demografía s. características de una población particular (página 309)

deponer v. sacar del poder (página 207)

deportación s. remoción de una persona de una nación (página 713)

derechos naturales s. derechos inherentes, como la vida, la libertad y la propiedad (página 565)

desobediencia civil s. negativa a seguir leyes injustas (página 750)

déspota adj. tiránico, que tiene poder absoluto (página 340)

déspota ilustrado s. gobernante absoluto que aplicaba ciertas ideas de la Ilustración (página 577)

despotismo s. gobierno opresivo de un líder con poder absoluto (página 587)

desterrado adj. forzado a abandonar un lugar u hogar (página 875)

dharma s. término del sánscrito que significa el camino de la conducta justa (página 71)

dhimmitude s. estado protegido de ciertas personas no musulmanas en el mundo musulmán (página 251)

dhow s. primer tipo de barco que transportaba mercancías comerciales a través del océano Índico (página 375)

Día D s. término utilizado para referirse a la invasión aliada de Normandía, Francia, durante la Segunda Guerra Mundial (página 771)

dialecto s. variación regional de un idioma (página 309)

diáspora s. migración de personas desde su patria ancestral (página 17)

dictador s. persona que gobierna con total autoridad (página 153)

diezmo s. diez por ciento de los ingresos de una persona que se pagan a la iglesia (página 288)

difusión cultural s. el proceso mediante el cual las culturas interactúan y las ideas se difunden de un área a otra (página 81)

dinastía s. serie de gobernantes provenientes de una misma familia (página 44)

diplomacia s. negociación entre gobiernos (página 48)

director s. tipo de monarquía en la que se mantienen algunos ideales republicanos (página 159)

disidente s. persona que está en desacuerdo con una práctica establecida, como una religión en particular (página 442)

distensión s. el alivio de las tensiones y la mejora de las relaciones entre las naciones (página 834)

división del trabajo s. sistema en el que las personas realizan diferentes trabajos para satisfacer las necesidades de una sociedad (página 34)

división del trabajo s. proceso que divide una tarea en partes separadas, cada una completada por una persona o grupo diferente (página 617)

doctrina s. creencia oficial (página 289)

domesticación s. acción de domesticar animales salvajes (página 23)

dominio s. comunidad autónoma dentro de un imperio (página 651)

dote s. propiedad que una mujer aporta a su matrimonio (página 458)

dron s. avión sin piloto operado por control remoto (página 875)

ducado s. territorio gobernado por un duque o duquesa (página 271)

E

economía s. sistema para producir y obtener bienes y servicios (página 24)

economía redistributiva s. tipo de economía en la que los productos y otros bienes se almacenan en un lugar central y luego se clasifican y distribuyen a la población (página 124)

ecuatorial s. ubicado en o cerca del ecuador (página 755)

edicto s. proclamación oficial (página 159)

edificio verde s. acto de diseñar y construir estructuras teniendo en cuenta el medio ambiente.(página 893)

educación obligatoria s. educación requerida por ley (página 395)

efecto dominó s. creencia de que, si un país se vuelve comunista, sus vecinos sucumbirán al comunismo como una hilera de fichas de dominó (página 800)

embargo s. prohibición de participar en el comercio con países específicos (páginas 646 y 805)

embellecer v. decorar con detalles ornamentales (página 455)

empresario s. persona que organiza y opera un negocio (página 465)

encomienda s. sistema legal que permitió a cada colono en las Américas españolas extraer tributo, principalmente en trabajo, de un cierto número de indígenas americanos (página 497)

energía geotérmica s. energía derivada del calor liberado por el interior de la Tierra (página 892)

enfoque deductivo s. enfoque de la investigación científica que implica pasar de principios generales a verdades específicas (página 549)

enfoque inductivo *s.* enfoque para la investigación científica que implica trabajar desde observaciones cuidadosamente controladas hasta verdades más amplias (página 549)

enviado *s.* representante diplomático (página 339)

epístola *s.* carta (página 175)

escriba *s.* escritor profesional que registraba la información oficial en las sociedades antiguas (página 46)

esfera de influencia *s.* área en la que el dominio de una potencia colonial se reconoce por encima de todas las demás (página 672)

especulación *s.* asumir grandes riesgos para obtener grandes recompensas (página 740)

estado *s.* una de las tres clases sociales distintas en la Francia prerrevolucionaria: el primer estado (clero); el segundo estado (nobleza); y el tercer estado (plebeyos) (página 584)

estado satelital *s.* país que es formalmente independiente, pero que está bajo el control o influencia de otro país (página 799)

estancamiento *s.* falta de crecimiento y desarrollo (página 227)

estancamiento militar *s.* situación en la que ninguna de las partes puede vencer a la otra (página 700)

estela *s.* pilar de piedra utilizado para conmemorar un evento o logro importante (página 41)

estepa *s.* vasta llanura cubierta de hierba (página 326)

estímulo *s.* incentivo (página 886)

etnografía *s.* estudio de las relaciones lingüísticas y culturales entre los pueblos (página 554)

Eva mitocondrial *s.* un solo ancestro femenino humano común a todos los seres humanos (página 8)

excomunión *s.* expulsión de la Iglesia cristiana (página 275)

exilio *s.* expulsión forzada de la patria (página 61)

expatriado *s.* persona que elige vivir fuera de su país de origes (página 717)

exposición *s.* feria o exposición mundial (página 623)

extraterritorialidad *s.* exención de la ley local (página 632)

extremista *s.* persona con una visión radical (página 872)

F

faccionalismo *s.* lealtad a cualquier sección o región del país de la que provenga, en lugar de a la nación en su conjunto (página 644)

factor de atracción *s.* factor o incentivo que atrae a las personas a mudarse a un nuevo paí. (página 477)

factor de empuje *s.* factor o condición que hace que las personas abandonen sus países de origen (página 477)

falange *s.* cuerpo de soldados que avanzan en formación contigua (página 114)

faraón *s.* rey del antiguo Egipto (página 43)

fascismo *s.* forma de gobernar basada en el nacionalismo extremo, el racismo y la represión de la oposición (página 742)

fauna *s.* animales de un lugar específico (página 554)

federal *adj.* Relacionado con un gobierno donde el poder es compartido entre el gobierno central, nacional y el de los estados o provincias. (página 583)

feudalismo *s.* nombre dado al sistema legal y social en la Europa medieval en el que los siervos trabajaban la tierra y los vasallos realizaban el servicio militar para sus señores a cambio de protección (página 276)

fideicomiso *s.* control administrativo sobre un territorio por uno o más países (página 820)

figura insigne *s.* líder, pero solo de nombre (página 257)

filósofos *s.* escritores y pensadores de la Ilustración europea (página 568)

fisiografía *s.* geografía física de un lugar (página 316)

flora *s.* plantas de un lugar específico (página 552)

fracking *s.* roceso de perforar la tierra y aplicar presión de agua para liberar los gases naturales al romper la roca (página 892)

fresco *s.* pintura dibujada sobre yeso mojado (página 124)

fundamentalismo *s.* estricta adhesión a un conjunto de principios básicos, a menudo relacionados con creencias políticas o religiosas (página 857)

G

genocidio *s.* destrucción sistemática de un grupo racial o cultural (página 675)

geoglifo *s.* gran diseño geométrico o figura dibujada en el suelo, creada al rayar la tierra y las rocas de la superficie oscura para revelar un suelo de color más claro (página 396)

ger *s.* tienda de fieltro portátil utilizada por nómadas mongoles (página 326)

ghazi *s.* guerrero por el islam (página 344)

ghetto *s.* sección separada de una ciudad en la que los grupos minoritarios se ven obligados a vivir (página 294)

gladiador *s.* hombre que luchaba con animales salvajes u otros hombres para entretener a los espectadores (página 163)

glasnost *s.* política gubernamental de comunicación abierta en la antigua Unión Soviética (página 834)

globalización *s.* desarrollo de una economía global cada vez más integrada, marcada especialmente por el libre comercio, el libre flujo de capital y el aprovechamiento de mercados laborales extranjeros más baratos (página 624)

golpe *s.* derrocamiento repentino del gobierno (página 110)

Gran Depresión *s.* época de intensas dificultades financieras que duró toda la década de 1930 (página 740)

gremio *s.* asociación formada por artesanos o comerciantes para mejorar sus negocios (página 277)

griot *s.* narrador de historias de África Occidental que cuenta historias a través de la tradición oral (página 361)

guerra de guerrillas *s.* ataques sorpresa a pequeña escala (página 675)

guerra de poder *s.* guerra en la que uno o ambos bandos son apoyados y sirven a los intereses de otro país (página 802)

guerra de trincheras *s.* tipo de guerra en la que los soldados luchan desde largas zanjas fortificadas con alambre de púas (página 700)

guerra relámpago *s.* táctica de batalla alemana que usaba la velocidad, la sorpresa y la potencia combinada de fuego de tanques, bombarderos y fuerzas terrestres. (página 766)

guerra santa *s.* guerra en defensa de una fe religiosa (página 290)

guerra total *s.* guerra que requiere reunir y preparar todos los recursos nacionales e involucrar tanto a los civiles como a los militares (página 699)

GLOSARIO

guillotina *s.* máquina con una cuchilla afilada diseñada para decapitar personas (página 587)

guion *s.* forma de escritura (página 153)

Gulag *s.* sistema soviético de campos de trabajos forzados (página 721)

H

habeas corpus *s.* procedimiento legal que impide que el gobierno detenga a una persona indefinidamente sin presentarse ante un juez (página 283)

hacienda *s.* plantación de gran tamaño en una colonia de habla hispana (página 497)

hacker *s.* individuo que ilegalmente obtiene acceso a información electrónica (página 898)

hajj *s.* peregrinación musulmana a la ciudad sagrada de La Meca (página 245)

hambruna *s.* escasez extrema de alimentos en un país o área geográfica grande (página 296)

Helenización *s.* proceso mediante el cual la cultura griega se extendió por todo el Imperio persa (página 140)

hereje *s.* miembro de la iglesia que tiene opiniones religiosas contrarias a la doctrina oficial (página 294)

hierro *s.* metal pesado que se usa para fabricar acero (página 54)

Hind Swaraj *s.* idea del autogobierno en la india (página 750)

hipotecas de alto riesgo *s.* préstamo hipotecario otorgado a alguien con mal crédito (página 886)

hipótesis *s.* teoría no probada que puede responder una pregunta y puede ser probada (página 549)

historiografía *s.* el arte y la ciencia de crear una historia confiable y útil a partir de fragmentos de información sobre el pasado (página 8)

hoplita *s.* soldado poderosamente armado de la antigua Grecia (página 129)

huelga *s.* paro laboral utilizado como táctica sindical (página 653)

hueso oracular *s.* hueso usado en la antigua China para consultar a los antepasados sobre el futuro; ahora se sabe que son los primeros registros escritos que sobrevivieron en China (página 83)

humanismo *s.* movimiento intelectual basado en las obras de pensadores clásicos griegos y romanos (página 424)

I

ícono *s.* imagen sagrada o religiosa (página 234)

iconoclasta *s.* miembro de la sociedad bizantina opuesta al culto de íconos religiosos; literalmente significa "rompedor de imágenes" (página 235)

ideología *s.* sistema de ideas que expresan una filosofía social o política sobre el mundo (página 591)

ilota *s.* esclavo poseído por el estado en la antigua Esparta (página 129)

iluminación *s.* estado en el que alguien obtiene una comprensión profunda y un sentido de claridad (página 72)

imperialismo *s.* práctica mediante la cual un país aumenta su poder al obtener el control sobre otras áreas del mundo (página 668)

imperio *s.* grupo de naciones o pueblos gobernados por una sola persona o gobierno (página 39)

indemnización *s.* dinero o bienes pagados para cubrir los daños causados en tiempos de guerra (página 708)

indígena *adj.* que es originario de un lugar en particular (página 15)

indulgencia *s.* oración especial que se podía comprar de la Iglesia Católica Romana para salvar el alma de una persona (página 434)

industria artesanal *s.* tipo de industria en la que una unidad familiar o un individuo crea un producto en casa con sus propios equipos (página 618)

infamia *s.* acto extremadamente vergonzoso o malvado (página 768)

inflación *s.* aumento en el precio de los bienes y servicios en comparación con el valor del dinero (página 455)

infraestructura *s.* redes para el transporte, el agua y otros servicios públicos (página 315)

ingresos públicos *s.* entradas para el gobierno como, por ejemplo, los impuestos (página 458)

Inquisición *s.* tribunal especial formado por la Iglesia Católica Romana para escuchar los cargos contra los herejes acusados (página 294)

insolvencia *s.* incapacidad de pagar deudas; bancarrota (página 799)

institución *s.* organización establecida para un propósito específico y que continúa a lo largo del tiempo (página 35)

insurgente *s.* luchador rebelde (página 589)

intercambio colombino *s.* intercambio de plantas, animales, microbios, personas e ideas entre Europa y las Américas, luego del primer viaje de Colón al hemisferio occidental (página 488)

intermediario *s.* persona que sirve de interceptor en un intercambio que involucra a otras dos partes (página 362)

intifada *s.* levantamiento palestino contra la ocupación israelí de Cisjordania y Gaza (página 855)

irrigación *s.* sistema hecho por el hombre para transportar el agua hacia donde se necesita (página 35)

islamista *s.* musulmán que cree que las leyes y las constituciones deben guiarse por los principios islámicos y que las autoridades religiosas deben participar directamente en el gobierno (página 515)

izquierdista *s.* persona que apoya cambios económicos y sociales radicales (página 845)

J

jenízaro *s.* soldado y esclavo altamente entrenado y disciplinado en el ejército otomano (página 450)

jeque *s.* líder de un clan beduino (página 244)

jeroglífico *s.* imagen que representa un objeto, sonido o idea y que era parte del antiguo sistema de escritura egipcio (página 46)

junta *s.* grupo militar o político que a menudo toma el poder por la fuerza (página 600)

justicia social *s.* igualdad de derechos para todos bajo la ley (página 874)

K

kamikaze *s.* piloto suicida japonés durante la Segunda Guerra Mundial (página 772)

kanato *s.* área del Imperio mongol gobernada por un khan (página 328)

karma *s.* suma de las acciones de una persona en la vida que determina su renacer en una próxima vida (página 71)

Kristallnacht *s.* destrucción de hogares, negocios y sinagogas judías por los nazis en la noche del 9 de noviembre de 1938 (página 745)

kulak s. campesino rico de la Unión Soviética de principios del siglo XX (página 747)

L

La Reforma s. movimiento de reforma en México que pidió la redistribución de las tierras, la separación de la iglesia y el estado, y mayores oportunidades educativas para los pobres (página 655)

laicado s. miembros de la iglesia que no son clérigos (página 288)

laissez-faire s. sistema económico en el que las empresas y las industrias regulan sus actividades sin interferencia del gobierno (página 569)

lar s. dios de la casa romana (página 157)

legionario s. soldado profesional pagado del ejército romano (página 162)

ley común s. conjunto de leyes determinadas por decisiones judiciales anteriores (página 583)

Leyes de Jim Crow s. leyes establecidas después de la Reconstrucción que impusieron la segregación racial en todo el sur de los Estados Unidos (página 662)

liberalismo s. sistema de creencias que argumenta que la libertad del individuo es la principal preocupación de la política (página 626)

libertades civiles s. libertades básicas que no pueden ser reguladas por el gobierno, como la libertad de expresión (página 884)

limo s. suelo esencialmente fino y fértil (página 35)

linaje s. grupo de descendientes con un antepasado en común (página 361)

Lineal B s. sistema de escritura micénica, que se cree que es una forma temprana de la lengua griega (página 125)

liturgia s. forma de adoración (página 437)

loess s. tipo de limo fino, fértil y amarillo que flota a través de las aguas del Huang He en China. (página 83)

longevidad s. tener una larga vida útil (página 909)

longitud s. posición este-oeste de un objeto medida en grados o diferencia de tiempo (página 554)

M

magnate s. empresario rico, poderoso e influyente (página 675)

maíz indígena s. grano similar al maíz actual (página 386)

Mandato celestial s. la antigua creencia china de que el Cielo, las fuerzas generalizadas del cosmos, elige al gobernante legítimo que manda siempre y cuando el Cielo crea que es digno de hacerlo (página 84)

manorialismo s. sistema económico, social y político medieval en el que los trabajadores agrícolas estaban ligados a la tierra que cultivaban y al señor que poseía dicha tierra (página 276)

mansa s. rey de África occidental (página 362)

manumisión s. liberación de una persona de la esclavitud (página 518)

marítimo *adj.* relacionado con el mar (página 200)

mausoleo s. tumba de gran tamaño (página 459)

medieval *adj.* que se refiere a un período en la historia europea de aproximadamente 500 a 1500 E.C. (página 227)

medios de comunicación masivos s. medios de comunicación destinados a llegar a muchas personas (página 736)

mercancía s. bien comercial valioso (página 134)

mercantilismo s. sistema en el que el gobierno protege y fomenta el comercio, basado en la teoría de que tales negocios crean riqueza (página 483)

mercenario s. soldado al que se le paga por luchar (página 154)

meritocracia s. sistema en el que las personas calificadas son elegidas y promovidas en función de sus logros en lugar de su posición social (página 88)

mestizo s. persona de ascendencia mixta española y nativoamericana (página 497)

metalurgia s. ciencia o tecnología de trabajar con metales (página 195)

Métis s. personas de ascendencia mixta europea e indígena (página 651)

método científico s. procedimiento lógico para desarrollar y probar ideas científicas (página 549)

mezquita s. lugar de culto musulmán (página 247)

migrar *v.* mudarse de una región a otra (página 11)

milicia s. ejército voluntario (página 582)

militarismo s. política gubernamental de desarrollo militar continuo y preparación para la guerra (página 639)

misionero s. persona enviada para convertir a otros a una religión (página 175)

místico s. persona que busca el conocimiento de Dios a través de la devoción o la meditación (página 279)

momia s. cuerpo preservado de un faraón o de otra persona en el antiguo Egipto (página 45)

monarquía s. gobierno presidido por una sola persona como, por ejemplo, un rey (página 44)

monarquía absoluta s. gobierno en el que el monarca tiene autoridad ilimitada (página 540)

monarquía constitucional s. gobierno en el que el poder del monarca está limitado por una constitución (página 540)

monasterio s. comunidad religiosa cristiana y centro de aprendizaje, trabajo y adoración (página 271)

moneda s. dinero en circulación (página 311)

monopolio s. control exclusivo sobre algo; control completo y exclusivo de una industria por una sola empresa (páginas 362 y 663)

monoteísmo s. creencia en un Dios (página 59)

monzón s. fuertes vientos estacionales en el sur y sureste de Asia (página 81)

mosaico s. grupo de pequeños cubos de piedra de colores colocados en un mortero para crear una imagen o diseño (página 239)

movilizar *v.* armarse y prepararse para la guerra (página 698)

muckraker s. periodista de investigación de principios de 1900 que expuso la mala conducta de organizaciones y personas poderosas (página 663)

mujahideen s. guerrilleros islámicos (página 825)

N

nación-estado s. estado formado por personas de una nacionalidad, que comparten rasgos comunes (página 591)

nacionalismo s. creencia de que los individuos están unidos por lazos de idioma, cultura, historia y, a menudo, religión (página 591)

nacionalizar *v.* poner una empresa o industria privada bajo el control del gobierno nacional (página 720)

GLOSARIO

napalm *s.* sustancia gelatinosa altamente inflamable que se adhiere a los objetivos y genera calor extremo (página 778)

narrativa de esclavos *s.* relato escrito de la vida de un esclavo fugitivo o de un exesclavo (página 518)

nativismo *s.* la práctica de favorecer las ideas del país de origen en lugar de las de los inmigrantes o países extranjeros (página 469)

naturalismo *s.* estilo artístico que buscaba realizar representaciones precisas de personas o del mundo natural (página 418)

Neanderthal *s.* miembro de una especie extinta de humanos primitivos (página 15)

nebulosa *s.* nube de gas y polvo en el espacio exterior (página 551)

neoclasicismo *s.* estilo creativo basado en ideales griegos y romanos (página 596)

neocolonialismo *s.* continuación de la dependencia y el dominio de un poder colonial. (página 812)

neoliberalismo *s.* enfoque económico que enfatiza los mercados libres y el amplio comercio internacional (página 863)

Neolítico *adj.* término empleado para describir a las personas que usaban herramientas de piedra y practicaban la agricultura; significa "nueva edad de piedra" (página 22)

neurosis de guerra *s.* condición de salud mental resultante de la exposición a la guerra (página 717)

nirvana *s.* estado de gozoso escape del sufrimiento causado por el ciclo de la vida y el renacimiento (página 72)

no alineamiento *s.* política de no aliarse con otros países, específicamente con los países comunistas o no comunistas durante la Guerra Fría (página 816)

no intervención *s.* política de no involucrarse en los asuntos de otros países (página 760)

nómada *s.* persona que migra de un lugar a otro (página 69)

números hindúes-árabes *s.* los números 1, 2, 3 . . . etc., originarios de la India y traídos a Occidente a través de comerciantes árabes (página 195)

O

oasis *s.* lugar aislado en el desierto y con agua donde las plantas pueden crecer (página 244)

oligarquía *s.* forma de gobierno liderada por unos pocos ciudadanos poderosos (página 129)

omnipotencia *s.* poder ilimitado (páginas 192 y 341)

óptica *s.* estudio de la luz y la visión (página 546)

oratoria *s.* arte de hablar en público (página 184)

organización no gubernamental (ONG) *s.* grupo sin fines de lucro que apoya una causa particular (página 858)

ortodoxia *s.* creencias y prácticas establecidas (página 542)

outsourcing *s.* práctica de enviar trabajo una vez realizado internamente en una empresa a cargo de personas ajenas a la empresa, generalmente por salarios más bajos (página 863)

P

pacifista *s.* persona con una objeción religiosa o filosófica a la violencia (página 860)

pacto *s.* acuerdo religioso (página 59)

panafricanismo *s.* idea de que las personas de ascendencia africana tienen un patrimonio común y que deberían unificarse (página 685)

pandemia *s.* brote mundial de una enfermedad infecciosa (página 708)

panteón *s.* grupo de dioses y diosas oficialmente reconocidos (página 157)

papiro *s.* material hecho de cañas, parecido al papel (página 46)

Parlamento *s.* cuerpo legislativo en Inglaterra (página 283)

partición *v.* división de un país (página 817)

Pasaje del noroeste *s.* ruta marítima desde el océano Atlántico hasta el Pacífico a lo largo de la costa norte de América del Norte (página 493)

Pasaje Medio *s.* viaje en barco de esclavos a través del Atlántico desde África occidental hasta las Américas (página 518)

patriarcado *s.* sociedad en la cual los hombres tienen todo el poder (página 156)

patricio *s.* terrateniente rico en la sociedad romana (página 153)

patrimonio cultural *s.* atributos de un grupo o sociedad heredados de generaciones pasadas (página 56)

patrocinador *s.* persona que brinda apoyo financiero a artistas (página 415)

peonaje de la deuda *s.* sistema en el que los trabajadores pagan su deuda con la mano de obra (página 654)

peregrinaje *s.* viaje a un lugar sagrado (página 176)

perestroika *s.* política gubernamental de reforma económica y gubernamental en la antigua Unión Soviética (página 834)

perspectiva lineal *s.* técnica artística en la que el artista utiliza la colocación y el tamaño de las figuras en un plano para hacer que una escena parezca tridimensional (página 426)

petición *s.* solicitud formal por escrito (página 476)

piedad *s.* fuerte creencia en la religión que se muestra a través de la adoración (página 441)

piedad filial *s.* respeto por los propios padres (página 86)

pirámide *s.* gran monumento de cuatro lados construido en el antiguo Egipto como una tumba para un faraón (página 44)

plaga *s.* enfermedad epidémica mortal (página 226)

plebeyo *s.* persona que no era noble en Roma (página 153)

poema épico *s.* largo poema narrativo que relata las aventuras de un héroe legendario o histórico (página 37)

pogrom *s.* ataque organizado o masacre de un grupo minoritario. (página 294)

polis *s.* ciudad-estado griega (página 128)

politeísmo *s.* creencia en varios dioses (página 38)

política de contención *s.* política de la Guerra Fría de los Estados Unidos de proporcionar ayuda militar y económica para proteger a los países de la toma de poder comunista (página 800)

populismo *s.* movimiento político que apoya las preocupaciones de la gente común. (página 804)

prevenir *s.* evitar que algo suceda (página 854)

privado de sus derechos *adj.* despojado de sus derechos o de la capacidad de influir en un gobierno (página 584)

proletariado *s.* clase obrera (página 627)

propaganda *s.* información utilizada por un gobierno para hacer que las personas piensen o actúen de una manera particular (página 591)

protestante *s.* persona que protestó contra la Iglesia Católica y se convirtió en parte de una iglesia reformada (página 436)

Punto de Clovis *s.* tipo de punta de lanza de piedra utilizada por los habitantes prehistóricos de América del Norte (página 384)

Q

qadi s. juez musulmán (página 256)

quipu *s.* serie de cuerdas anudadas que los incas usaban para llevar registros (página 399)

quórum *s.* número mínimo de personas que deben estar presentes para llevar a cabo los negocios de un grupo (página 131)

R

racionalismo científico *s.* escuela de pensamiento en la que la observación, la experimentación y el razonamiento matemático reemplazan la sabiduría antigua y las enseñanzas de la iglesia como fuente de verdades científicas. (página 549)

racismo *s.* creencia de que el color de la piel de una persona la hace superior o inferior (página 521)

recesión *s.* período de actividad económica reducida (página 886)

reclutamiento *s.* inscripción forzada en el ejército (página 475)

Reconstrucción *s.* esfuerzo por reconstruir y reunir a los Estados Unidos después de la Guerra Civil (página 645)

red comercial transahariana *s.* grupo de rutas comerciales terrestres a través de las cuales se transportaban mercancías entre el norte de África y el África subsahariana (página 368)

reencarnación *s.* renacimiento de un alma en un cuerpo diferente a lo largo de diferentes ciclos de vida (página 71)

referéndum *s.* votación pública sobre una sola cuestión política (página 813)

refugiado *s.* persona que se ve obligada a abandonar su tierra natal debido a la guerra, la persecución o un desastre natural (página 61)

regente *s.* persona que gobierna cuando un monarca o emperador no puede hacerlo (página 209)

registro humano *s.* historia de la vida humana en la Tierra a lo largo de los siglos (página 56)

relieve *s.* tipo de escultura en la que elementos tridimensionales se elevan desde un fondo plano (página 56)

religiosidad *s.* fuerte creencia religiosa (página 885)

remilitarización *s.* proceso de rearme (página 760)

república *s.* forma de gobierno en la que las personas eligen a los funcionarios para que los representen en lugar de votar directamente sobre las leyes y políticas (página 153)

rescate financiero *s.* rescate de dificultades financieras (página 886)

resistencia pasiva *s.* oposición no violenta a la autoridad (página 846)

revisionista *adj.* que se desvía del espíritu revolucionario de la doctrina marxista (página 809)

Romanticismo *s.* movimiento cultural originario del siglo XVIII que enfatizaba las emociones sobre la razón (página 596)

S

sabana *s.* área de exuberantes praderas tropicales (página 360)

sabotaje *s.* destrucción deliberada (página 617)

Sáhel *s.* región semidesértica al sur del Sahara (página 360)

salón *s.* reunión social organizada por mujeres parisinas para discutir ideas de la Ilustración (página 572)

saltar entre islas *s.* estrategia diseñada por los Aliados durante la Segunda Guerra Mundial para capturar y controlar islas en el Pacífico una por una (página 772)

sanción *s.* restricción comercial o financiera impuesta por una nación a otra (página 757)

sánscrito *s.* idioma indoeuropeo clásico hablado por inmigrantes indoarios hacia el norte de la India alrededor de 1500–1000 A.E.C. (página 69)

sátira *s.* humor y sarcasmo utilizados para exponer o ridiculizar la tontería o debilidad humana (páginas 133 y 425)

sátrapa *s.* gobernador provincial (página 104)

satyagraha *s.* aplicación de la no violencia a la política, según la creencia india (página 750)

secular *s.* no perteneciente a una orden religiosa (página 288)

segregación *s.* separación de diferentes grupos de personas, generalmente basada en la raza (página 645)

seguridad alimentaria *s.* garantía de que habrá alimentos disponibles para mantener la salud (página 552)

Senado *s.* cuerpo gobernante en la antigua Roma que asesoraba a los cónsules y que inicialmente estaba compuesto por terratenientes ricos (página 153)

separarse *v.* retirarse formalmente de una nación (página 644)

sharia *s.* ley islámica que cubre todos los aspectos de la vida (página 246)

shogun *s.* general japonés que es el gobernante militar del país (página 317)

siervo *s.* trabajador agrícola medieval que estaba atado a una tierra (página 276)

sinagoga *s.* edificio dedicado al culto de la religión judía (página 61)

sincretismo religioso *s.* mezcla de diferentes sistemas de creencias (página 443)

sirviente por contrato *s.* persona bajo contrato para trabajar, generalmente sin paga, a cambio de un pasaje gratuito a las colonias (página 505)

sistema de castas *s.* rígida jerarquía social en la India antigua que dividía a las personas en clases hereditarias (página 71)

soberanía *s.* libertad del control externo (página 542)

soberanía popular *s.* creencia de que el gobierno surge de la gente misma (página 583)

socialismo *s.* sistema económico en el que la industria es de propiedad colectiva, se permite la propiedad privada y se paga a las personas en función de su contribución a la producción (página 627)

sociedad anónima *s.* empresa comercial financiada por la venta de acciones a múltiples inversores (página 492)

sociedad de masas *s.* sociedad en la que un gran número de personas comparten la misma experiencia sin tener que reunirse (página 736)

solución de dos estados *s.* solución al conflicto israelí-palestino que exige un estado independiente de Palestina junto con el estado de Israel (página 853)

GLOSARIO

sostenible *v.* incesante, especialmente en relación con una forma de utilizar un recurso para que no se agote (página 892)

status quo *s.* condición ya existente (página 593)

subyugación *s.* estado de estar bajo control o gobierno (página 668)

sucesión *s.* proceso mediante el cual se elige a un nuevo líder para suceder a un líder que deja su puesto (página 512)

sufragio *s.* derecho a votar (página 663)

sultán *s.* gobernante de un estado musulmán (página 345)

superávit *s.* oferta de bienes y mano de obra que no se necesita para la supervivencia a corto plazo (página 28)

T

taiga *s.* tierra cubierta de árboles de hoja perenne dispersos en el extremo norte o área subártica (página 470)

tecnología *s.* aplicación práctica del conocimiento; cualquier herramienta o técnica que ayuda a las personas a realizar tareas (página 35)

teocracia *s.* forma de gobierno en la que el sistema legal se basa en la ley religiosa (página 61)

teoría geocéntrica *s.* teoría que indica que el Sol y los planetas giran alrededor de la Tierra (página 546)

teoría heliocéntrica *s.* teoría que indica que la Tierra y otros planetas giran alrededor del Sol (página 547)

terraplén *s.* construcción de tierra y rocas (página 392)

terraza *s.* plataforma escalonada (página 387)

tetrarquía *s.* estructura de gobierno en la que cuatro personas gobiernan conjuntamente (página 180)

tipos móviles *s.* tabletas de arcilla individuales que podían organizarse para crear textos en una forma temprana de impresión (página 310)

tiranía *s.* estado de gobierno en el que los gobernantes tienen un poder ilimitado y lo usan injustamente (página 565)

tolerancia religiosa *s.* aceptación de las creencias y prácticas religiosas de los demás (página 253)

totalitario *adj.* relacionado con un sistema político que ejerce un control total sobre una sociedad, a menudo a través de medios violentos (página 743)

trabajos públicos *s.* proyectos de construcción impulsados por el gobierno que benefician a una comunidad (página 40)

tradición oral *s.* grupo de historias que toman una forma estándar y que son transmitidas de generación en generación por personas que se comunican entre sí (página 125)

traición *s.* delito de traicionar al gobierno o al propio país (página 199)

tregua *s.* alto temporal de la guerra (página 290)

tribu *s.* unidad familiar extendida (página 60)

tribuna *s.* representante electo que protegió los derechos de los ciudadanos comunes en Roma (página 153)

tribunal *s.* tribunal con autoridad sobre un asunto específico (página 786)

tributo *s.* impuesto requerido de los pueblos conquistados (página 194)

trirreme *s.* antiguo buque de guerra griego con tres bancos de remos (página 115)

troll *s.* persona que deliberadamente publica mensajes ofensivos o amenazantes en la Internet (página 899)

tundra *s.* llanuras árticas sin árboles (página 470)

U

ultranacionalista *s.* nacionalista extremo (página 748)

V

vaquero *s.* jinete o pastor de ganado (página 726)

varna *s.* los cuatro principales grupos sociales de la antigua sociedad india, clasificados en orden de pureza (página 71)

vasallo *s.* en la Europa medieval, una persona que prestaba servicios militares y prometía lealtad a un señor a cambio de protección y tierra para vivir (página 276)

védico *adj.* asociado con la sociedad o la religión de los inmigrantes indoarios (página 70)

venerar *v.* honrar o adorar (página 234)

vernáculo *s.* lenguaje cotidiano que hablan las personas (página 281)

vetar *v.* votar en contra de algo (página 129)

vigilancia *s.* acto de velar por una persona o grupo (página 873)

virreinato *s.* colonia (página 497)

virrey *s.* representante del rey en las Américas españolas (página 497)

X

xenofobia *s.* miedo a los extranjeros (página 875)

Z

zaibatsu *s.* poderoso conglomerado financiero e industrial japonés (página 639)

zar *s.* gobernante de la Rusia imperial (página 471)

zigurat *s.* gran estructura escalonada en un templo sumerio (página 39)

zona desmilitarizada *s.* área donde las armas y las fuerzas militares están prohibidas (página 821)

INDEX

INDEX

INDEX

SKILLS INDEX

A

Analyze, 199
Analyze Cause and Effect, 11, 41, 99, 109, 115, 118, 123, 129, 165, 188, 195, 197, 212, 214, 240, 245, 259, 260, 297, 299, 304, 311, 315, 317, 333, 339, 349, 350, 380, 389, 391, 399, 417, 423, 435, 437, 443, 444, 445, 453, 459, 469, 478, 483, 491, 493, 497, 503, 505, 506, 515, 529, 530, 545, 549, 560, 578, 587, 599, 603, 606, 607, 613, 619, 637, 640, 663, 664, 669, 675, 686, 705, 730, 741, 761, 795, 803, 809, 813, 815, 830, 837, 851, 853, 857, 916
Analyze Language Use, 475, 905
Analyze Perspective, 49
Analyze Point of View, 89, 235, 449, 541, 555, 679, 686, 743, 762, 895
Analyze Sources, 103, 349, 485, 565, 601, 713, 775, 783, 787
Analyze Visuals, 53, 56, 77, 806, 901
Ask and Answer Questions, 273, 365, 449

C

Categorize, 253, 380, 725, 887
Compare and Contrast, 27, 41, 43, 92, 113, 125, 129, 155, 157, 161, 177, 181, 188, 193, 203, 214, 221, 239, 260, 271, 275, 279, 295, 303, 317, 321, 323, 345, 363, 385, 393, 404, 433, 441, 445, 475, 477, 478, 485, 493, 506, 511, 519, 529, 530, 559, 565, 571, 578, 589, 601, 606, 629, 633, 640, 664, 675, 685, 693, 721, 737, 741, 749, 762, 775, 788, 799, 830, 841, 867, 869, 915

D

Describe, 11, 30, 69, 71, 83, 87, 92, 175, 193, 205, 277, 449, 459, 471, 478, 516, 530, 547, 555, 599, 637, 762, 788, 805, 815, 830
Determine Chronology, 205, 411, 606
Distinguish Fact and Opinion, 260

Draw Conclusions, 11, 24, 30, 47, 49, 73, 79, 81, 92, 105, 113, 118, 125, 127, 133, 153, 163, 165, 183, 187, 188, 207, 225, 233, 239, 240, 245, 251, 260, 267, 277, 283, 289, 293, 304, 322, 329, 350, 357, 363, 375, 376, 380, 387, 395, 404, 415, 417, 425, 441, 444, 487, 489, 506, 529, 530, 571, 578, 589, 593, 607, 621, 623, 629, 640, 645, 651, 655, 661, 664, 699, 707, 713, 719, 721, 723, 730, 737, 745, 747, 749, 757, 759, 762, 767, 769, 773, 777, 783, 787, 788, 799, 819, 830, 841, 845, 847, 853, 855, 859, 868, 873, 885, 889, 895, 905, 909, 916

E

Evaluate, 55, 65, 79, 117, 118, 187, 188, 197, 227, 240, 257, 260, 293, 350, 367, 380, 389, 463, 541, 551, 573, 578, 664, 669, 730, 739, 751, 762, 788, 811, 875, 881, 916
Explain, 69, 214, 240, 380, 515, 560, 699, 730, 755, 819, 825, 881

F

Form and Support Opinions, 30, 55, 65, 92, 117, 118, 131, 139, 147, 148, 173, 188, 199, 214, 230, 240, 245, 259, 304, 322, 350, 380, 404, 489, 506, 530, 551, 553, 555, 560, 578, 593, 603, 607, 640, 705, 745, 759, 762, 821, 851, 859, 869, 873, 881, 889, 893, 899, 916

H

Hypothesize, 640

I

Identify, 11, 15, 39, 61, 89, 131, 315, 369, 404, 423, 477, 543, 560, 673, 893
Identify Main Ideas, 511, 717
Identify Main Ideas and Details, 15, 29, 37, 73, 83, 199, 247, 253, 260, 273, 283, 421, 439, 583, 587, 599, 605, 727, 773, 781, 788, 837, 843
Identify Problems and Solutions, 13, 37, 61, 159, 214, 227, 237, 260, 309, 404, 415, 439, 469, 560, 621, 640, 709, 727, 730, 801, 811, 817, 823

Identify Supporting Details, 233, 451, 471, 549, 553, 677, 868
Integrate Visuals, 286, 809
Interpret Charts, 195
Interpret Maps, 24, 37, 43, 81, 103, 111, 115, 127, 141, 155, 161, 166, 175, 177, 183, 201, 203, 209, 225, 237, 251, 254, 257, 271, 275, 293, 297, 329, 333, 343, 345, 346, 361, 367, 387, 393, 399, 403, 443, 451, 453, 465, 483, 491, 497, 505, 515, 519, 521, 543, 566, 593, 619, 629, 669, 673, 677, 701, 715, 757, 767, 773, 801, 813, 821, 823, 855, 863, 901
Interpret Visuals, 426, 828

M

Make Connections, 27, 61, 87, 143, 148, 309, 321, 350, 395, 404, 433, 545, 547, 559, 573, 583, 605, 606, 619, 625, 635, 639, 640, 661, 664, 715, 743, 761, 837, 843, 845, 851, 868, 899, 915, 916
Make Generalizations, 30, 47, 64, 133, 148, 240, 304, 367, 444, 455, 530, 607, 705, 887
Make Inferences, 24, 39, 47, 64, 71, 77, 85, 92, 105, 111, 118, 139, 147, 148, 153, 157, 159, 163, 181, 187, 188, 201, 209, 235, 260, 279, 283, 303, 304, 343, 350, 361, 365, 369, 375, 380, 385, 421, 435, 437, 455, 459, 465, 487, 503, 506, 521, 530, 537, 571, 577, 578, 623, 633, 635, 645, 651, 653, 655, 661, 663, 664, 699, 701, 707, 709, 725, 730, 747, 777, 779, 781, 784, 788, 805, 847, 857, 901, 905
Make Predictions, 148, 188, 289, 329, 343, 404, 475, 625, 633, 639, 685, 686, 717, 723, 751, 755, 769, 863, 867, 875, 885, 916

P

Pose and Answer Questions, 909

S

Sequence Events, 207, 295, 299, 304, 323, 587, 719, 803
Summarize, 30, 577, 640, 868, 916
Synthesize, 64, 85, 118, 141, 147, 188, 311, 322, 339, 350, 403, 404, 426, 478, 506, 530, 653, 664, 686, 779, 788, 817, 825

ACKNOWLEDGMENTS

National Geographic Learning gratefully acknowledges the contributions of the following National Geographic Explorers and affiliates to our program:

Sam Abell, National Geographic Photographer
Lynsey Addario, National Geographic Photographer
Robert Ballard, National Geographic Explorer-in-Residence
Ari Beser, Fulbright-National Geographic Fellow
Jimmy Chin, National Geographic Photographer
Kevin Crisman, National Geographic Explorer
Jason De León, National Geographic Explorer
Leslie Dewan, National Geographic Explorer
Jeffrey Gusky, National Geographic Photographer
David Guttenfelder, National Geographic Photographer
Kevin Hand, National Geographic Explorer
Fredrik Hiebert, National Geographic Archaeologist-in-Residence
Kathryn Keane, Vice President, National Geographic Exhibitions
Bill Kelso, National Geographic Explorer
Michael Nichols, National Geographic Photographer
Paul Nicklen, National Geographic Photographer
Sarah Parcak, National Geographic Fellow
William Parkinson, National Geographic Explorer
Sandra Postel, National Geographic Freshwater Fellow (2009–2015)
Robert Reid, National Geographic Digital Nomad
Andrés Ruzo, National Geographic Explorer
Tristram Stuart, National Geographic Explorer

PHOTOGRAPHIC CREDITS

Illustration: All illustrations are owned by © Cengage.

Cover Atakorn/iStock/Getty Images, Marco Bicci/Alamy Stock Photo, kathykonkle/DigitalVision Vectors/Getty Images, coolbiere photograph/Getty Images; **i** Atakorn/iStock/Getty Images; **iii** (tl) Victoria Sanchez, California State University, Long Beach, (cl) Mary Lynne Ashley Photography/Cengage, (bl) Mark Thiessen/National Geographic Image Collection; **iv** (tl1) Dan Westergren/National Geographic Image Collection, (tl2) © Lynsey Addario, (tc1) (tc2) Sora Devore/National Geographic Image Collection, (tc3) White House/Zuma Wire/Shutterstock.com, (tr1) Alexandra Verville/National Geographic Image Collection, (tr2) Bryan Bedder/Getty Images Entertainment/Getty Images, (cl1) National Geographic Image Collection, (cl2) Courtesy of Ari Beser, (cl3) Jimmy Chin/National Geographic Image Collection, (c) Robert Clark/National Geographic Image Collection, (cr1) © Kara Kooney, (cr2) Shutterstock.com, (cr3) (cr3) Randall Scott/National Geographic Image Collection, (cl1) Mark Thiessen/National Geographic Image Collection, (cl2) © Guillermo de Anda, (cl3) Courtesy of Leslie Dewan, (c) Universal History Archive/Universal Images Group/Getty Images, (cr1) Paul Morigi/Getty Images Entertainment/Getty Images, (cr2) Steven Ellis/National Geographic Image Collection, (bl1) © George Ohrstrom, (bl2) Courtney Rader/National Geographic Image Collection, (bl3) Courtesy of Kavita Gupta, (bc) © Jeff Gusky, (br1) David Guttenfelder/National Geographic Image Collection, (br2) Mark Thiessen/National Geographic Image Collection, (br3) Courtesy of Patrick Hunt; **v** (tl1) (cl1) Courtesy of Terry Hunt, (tl2) (tc) (tr2) (bl2) Randall Scott/National Geographic Image Collection, (tl3) Mark Thiessen and Rebecca Hale/National Geographic Image Collection, (tr1) KMK/National Geographic Image Collection, (tr2) © Peg Keiner, (tr3) © Amanda Koltz, (tl1) Kathy Ku/National Geographic Image Collection, (tl2) Sora Devore/National Geographic Image Collection, (tl3) (tr3) (bc) Mark Thiessen/National Geographic Image Collection, (tc) © Emmanuel Habimana, (tr1) Mark Thiessen/National Geographic Image Collection, (cl2) Gerd Ludwig/National Geographic Image Collection, (cl3) © Jim Haberman, (c) O. Louis Mazzatenta/National Geographic Image Collection, (cr1) Felix Hörhager/picture alliance/Getty Images, (cr2) Sharon Farmer/National Geographic Image Collection, (cr3) Courtesy of Kakenya Ntaiya, (cl1) © Freddie Claire, (cl2) Alan Parente/National Geographic Image Collection, (cl3) Brian Nehlson/National Geographic Image Collection, (c) Courtesy of Matt Piscitelli, (cr1) © Kristin Romey, (cr2) Scott Degraw/National Geographic Image Collection, (cr3) Courtesy of Andrés Ruzo, (bl1) Damon Winter/The New York Times/Redux, (bl2) (bl3) (br2) Rebecca Hale/National Geographic Image Collection, (br1) Nora Shawki/National Geographic Image Collection, (br3) Mauricio Handler/National Geographic Image Collection, (bl1) © Jen Shook, (bl3) Colby Bishop/National Geographic Image Collection, (bc) © Bruno Calendini, (br1) Dillon von Petzinger/National Geographic Image Collection, (br2) Sora Devore/National Geographic Image Collection, (br3) © Allegra Boverman/MIT News; **vi** George Steinmetz/Corbis Documentary/Getty Images; **vii** (tl) John Stanmeyer/National Geographic Image Collection, (tr1) Ender Bayindir/iStock/Getty Images, (tr2) marcos alvarado/Alamy Stock Photo; **viii** Reynold Mainse/Design Pics/Shutterstock Offset; **ix** (tl) Menahem Kahana/AFP/Getty Images, (tr) China: A sleepy cameleer resting on his Bactrian camel, Tang Dynasty, c.7th-9th century CE/Pictures from History/Bridgeman Images; **x** Lars Schreiber/Robert Harding; **xi** (tl) Emad Aljumah/Moment/Getty Images, (tr) Ivy Close Images/Alamy Stock Photo, (c) Merghoub Zakaria/Shutterstock.com; **xii** Fighting between samurai, detail byobu (screen) scenes from war Gempei 12th century, Japan Tosa School, Edo Period, early 17th century/De Agostini Editore/Bridgeman Images; **xiii** (tl) © Freddie Claire, (tr) © The Metropolitan Museum of Art, (c) zhangshuang/Moment/Getty Images; **xiv** Henry Georgi/Aurora/Getty Images; **xv** (tl) © The Metropolitan Museum of Art, (tr) Paul Nicklen/National Geographic Image Collection, (cl) Ariadne Van Zandbergen/Alamy Stock Photo; **xvi** View of Naples/Wittel, Gaspar van (Gaspare Vanvitelli) (1653-1736)/Fratelli Alinari S.P.A./Palatine Gallery, Pitti Palace, Florence/Bridgeman Images; **xvii** (tl) Dave Yoder/National Geographic Image Collection, (tr) Marco Ferrarin/Moment Unreleased/Getty Images; **xviii** Martial Colomb/Photographer's Choice RF/Getty Images; **xix** (t) Testelin, Henri (1616-95), "Jean-Baptiste Colbert (1619-1683) Presenting the Members of the Royal Academy of Science to Louis XIV (1638-1715)". c.1667. Oil on Canvas. Chateau de Versailles, France, Lauros. Giraudon/The Bridgeman Art Library, (cl) John Kellerman/Alamy Stock Photo, (cr) Julian Elliott/Robert Harding; **xx** Coalbrookdale by Night, 1801 (oil on canvas)/Loutherbourg, Philip James (Jacques) de (1740-1812)/Science and Society Picture Library/Science Museum, London, UK/Bridgeman Images; **xxi** (t) Gavin Hellier/Robert Harding, (cl) Everett Collection, (cr) Biosphoto/Alamy Stock Photo; **xxii** ED/CM/Richard Lea-Hair/Camera Press/Redux; **xxiii** (tl) © Jeff Gusky, (tr) Keystone Features/Hulton Archive/Getty Images; **xxiv** pa_Yon/Moment/Getty Images; **xxv** Steve Winter/National Geographic Image Collection; **xxvi** Robert Clark/National Geographic Image Collection; **xxxii** CLempe/National Geographic/Kobal/Shutterstock.com; **T4** Cory Richards/National Geographic Image Collection; **T5** KMK/National Geographic Learning; **T6** © George Ohrstrom/Kenneth Garrett Photography; **T10** Victoria Sanchez, California State University, Long Beach; **T12** © Mary Lynne Ashley Photography/Cengage; **1** CLempe/National Geographic/Kobal/Shutterstock.com; **2-3** (spread) George Steinmetz/Corbis Documentary/Getty Images; **4** (tl) Mohammed Kamal/United Press International (UPI)/Jebel Irhoud/Morocco/Newscom, (tr) Nancy Brown/Photolibrary/Getty Images, (bl) Nathan Benn/Corbis Historical/Getty Images, (br) Chris McGrath/Getty Images News/Getty Images; **5** (tl) © The Metropolitan Museum of Art, 66.173, (tr) (bl) Dea Picture Library/De Agostini/Getty Images, (br) kaetana/Shutterstock.com; **6-7** (spread) Emad Aljumah/Moment/Getty Images; **9** (t) Kenneth Garrett/National Geographic Image Collection, (bl) Marc Steinmetz/Visum für Geo/R edux; **12** National Geographic Television/National Geographic Image Collection; **14** Zoonar GmbH/Michal Bednarek/Alamy Stock Photo; **15** Ian S Foulk/National Geographic Image Collection; **16** John Stanmeyer/National Geographic Image Collection; **19** (t) (b) John Stanmeyer/National Geographic Image Collection; **20** © Dillon von Petzinger; **21** (tr) Ferrero-Labat/ard/AGE Fotostock, (cr) Beth Wald/Aurora Photos, (br) HomoCosmicos/iStock/Getty Images; **22** Erich Lessing/Art Resource, NY; **23** (t) Yadid Levy/Aurora Photos, (br) Christophel Fine Art/Universal Images Group/Getty Images; **24** Dea/G. Dagli Orti/De Agostini/Getty Images; **26** (cr) The Lady and the Unicorn: 'Sight' (tapestry) (detail of 172864)/French School, (15th century)/Musee National du Moyen Age et des Thermes de Cluny, Paris/Bridgeman Images, (bl) Head of an animal with a human head in the open jaws, found at Tula, Hidalgo, Mexico, Early Post-Classic (900-1250) (pottery with mother-of-pearl mosaic)/Toltec/Museo Nacional de Antropologia, Mexico City, Mexico/Bridgeman Images; **27** (tl) oversnap/E+/Getty Images, (cr) Cyril Ruoso/Minden Pictures, (bl) Jayne Russell/Alamy Stock Photo; **29** Vincent J. Musi/National Geographic Image Collection Magazines/Getty Images; **32-33** (spread) Nick Brundle Photography/Moment/Getty Images; **35** Bronze Axes, Bronze Age (bronze)/Bronze Age (2000-600 BC)/AISA/Museo Episcopal de Vic, Osona, Catalonia, Spain/Bridgeman Images; **36** (tl) Balage Balogh/Art Resource, NY, (tr) Tablet from Jamdat Nasr in Iraq, listing quantities of various commodities in archaic Sumerian (early cuneiform script) c.3200-3000 BC (clay) (recto, for verso see 113701)/Ashmolean Museum, University of Oxford, UK/Bridgeman Images, (c) The Picture Art Collection/Alamy Stock Photo, (bl) Erich Lessing/Art Resource, NY, (bc) Dea/G. Dagli Orti/De Agostini Picture Library/Getty Images, (br) Werner Forman/Universal Images Group/Getty Images; **38** The Trustees of the British Museum/Art Resource, NY; **39** Cuneiform tablet, c.2300 BC (clay)/The Trustees of the

Warburton-Lee/Danita Delimont Stock Photography; **283** Heritage Image Partnership Ltd/Alamy Stock Photo; **284-285** (spread) Gilles Rolle/Rea/Redux; **286** Julien Fromentin/Moment/Getty Images; **287** Godong/Universal Images Group/Getty Images; **288** Luca Antonio Lorenzelli/Alamy Stock Photo; **289** St. Francis of Assisi preaching to the birds (oil on panel)/Giotto di Bondone (c.1266-1337)/Louvre, Paris, France/Bridgeman Images; **291** Siege of Antioch in Turkey during the 1st Crusade in 1098, manuscript/Tallandier (RDA)/Bridgeman Images; **293** AGE Fotostock/Alamy Stock Photo; **295** Ferdinand II of Aragon and Isabella I of Castile (oil on panel)/Spanish School, (15th century)/Jurgens Osteuropa-Photo/Convento Agustinas, Madrigal, Avila/Bridgeman Images; **296** The Triumph of Death, c.1562 (oil on panel)/Bruegel, Pieter the Elder (c.1525-69)/Prado, Madrid, Spain/Bridgeman Images; **299** Ms 6 f.221v Battle of Poitiers - the King of France surrenders to the Black Prince, 1356, from 'St. Alban's Chronicle' (vellum)/English School, (15th century)/Lambeth Palace Library/Lambeth Palace Library, London, UK/Bridgeman Images; **300** nikonaft/iStock/Getty Images; **301** (tl) De Agostini Picture Library/De Agostini/Getty Images, (tr) Centre Historique des Archives Nationales, Paris, France/Bridgeman Images, (bl) Sylvain Sonnet/Corbis Documentary/Getty Images, (br) alxpin/iStock/Getty Images; **302** (tl) Musee des Beaux-Arts, Rouen, France/Bridgeman Images, (tr) Joan of Arc's Death at the Stake, 1843 (oil on canvas)/Stilke, Hermann Anton (1803-60)/State Hermitage Museum, St. Petersburg, Russia/Bridgeman Images, (br) Joan of Arc, 1879 (oil on canvas)/Bastien-Lepage, Jules (1848-84)/Superstack Inc./Private Collection/Bridgeman Images; **303** (tl) Herbert Dorfman/Corbis Historical/Getty Images, (tr) Universal History Archive/Universal Images Group/Getty Images, (br) 'The Suffragette', 1912 (colour litho)/English School, (20th century)/Museum of London/Museum of London, UK/Bridgeman Images; **306-307** (spread) February/Moment/Getty Images; **308** zhangshuang/Moment/Getty Images; **311** China: A palace examination at Kaifeng. Song Dynasty painting (960-1279 CE)/Pictures from History/Bridgeman Images; **312** Antonio Zanghì/Moment/Getty Images; **315** Eye Ubiquitous/Universal Images Group/AGE Fotostock; **316** JTB Photo/UIG/AGE Fotostock; **318** Robert Harding Picture LIbrary; **319** (tl) Westend61/Getty Images, (cr) Japan: 'A Young Woman Practicing the Kanji', Meiji Period woodblock print by Toyohara Chikanobu (1838-1912), 1897/Pictures from History/Bridgeman Images, (bl) The Trustees of the British Museum/Art Resource, NY; **320** (t) Jason Langley/Robert Harding, (b) The Thunder God Raijin (left) and the Wind God Fujin (right), four panel folding screen, c.1700 (colour on gold leafed paper)/Korin, Ogata (1658-1716)/Pictures from History/Tokyo National Museum, Japan/Bridgeman Images; **321** (tr) Erich Lessing/Art Resource, NY, (cl) © The Jack and Belle Linsky Collection, 1982; **324-325** (spread) Jose Fuste Raga/AGE Fotostock; **326** Egmont Strigl/Robert Harding; **327** Jon Arnold/Danita Delimont; **329** Ben Horton/National Geographic Image Collection; **330** Battle between Mongolians and Egyptians, miniature from manuscript 1113, folio 236, Persia, 14th century/De Agostini Editore/Bridgeman Images; **333** Universal History Archive/Universal Images Group/Getty Images; **334-337** John Stanmeyer/National Geographic Image Collection; **338** Mel Longhurst/AGE Fotostock; **339** © The Metropolitan Museum of Art; **340** © Purchase, Sir Joseph Hotung and The Vincent Astor Foundation Gifts, 2001; **342** National Geographic Maps/National Geographic Image Collection; **345** Interfoto/Alamy Stock Photo; **348** Erich Lessing/Art Resource, NY; **351** Dennis Cox/Alamy Stock Photo; **354-355** (spread) Henry Georgi/Aurora/Getty Images; **356** (tl) Richard Hewitt Stewart/National Geographic Image Collection, (tr) Ira Block/National Geographic Image Collection, (bl) Mayan/Getty Images, (br) gift of Mr. and Mrs. Meredith Long/Tonto style jar (olla) with checkerboard and sun designs, Ancestral Pueblo, c.1300 (earthenware with slip)/Anasazi School (1100-1300)/Museum of Fine Arts, Houston/Museum of Fine Arts, Houston, Texas, USA/Bridgeman Images; **357** (tc) Candlestick, Mamluk dynasty, mid 14th century (brass)/Egyptian School (14th century AD)/Cincinnati Art Museum/Cincinnati Art Museum, Ohio, USA/Bridgeman Images, (tr) GL Archive/Alamy Stock Photo, (bl) Denny Allen/Gallo Images/Getty Images, (br) DEA/De Agostini/Getty Images; **358-359** (spread) Jim Keir/Alamy Stock Photo; **361** (tc) Spani Arnaud/hemis.fr/Getty Images, (tr) Spani Arnaud/hemis.fr/Getty Images; **363** George Steinmetz/Corbis Documentary/Getty Images; **364** Christopher Scott/Alamy Stock Photo; **365** Simon Colmer/Alamy Stock Photo; **368** Abraham Cresques/Art Images/Getty Images; **369** © The Metropolitan Museum of Art; **370-371** (spread) Yannick Tylle/Corbis Documentary/Getty Images; **372-373** (spread) Finbarr O'Reilly/Reuters; **374** Ulrich Doering/Robert Harding; **375** Bridgeman-Giraudon/Art Resource, NY; **376** Andrew McConnell/Robert Harding; **377** WitR/Shutterstock.com; **378** Ariadne Van Zandbergen/Alamy Stock Photo; **382-383** (spread) John Coletti/Photolibrary/Getty Images; **385** Phil Degginger/Alamy Stock Photo; **387** Courtesy of Matt Piscitelli; **388** AKG Images; **390** Paul Nicklen/National Geographic Image Collection; **391** © Karla Ortega; **393** Michael Runkel/Robert Harding; **395** PHAS/Universal Images Group/Getty Images; **396** AGE Fotostock/Alamy Stock Photo; **398-399** (spread) Sean Caffrey/Lonely Planet

Images/Getty Images; **401** (t) © Terry Hunt and Carl Lipo, (cl) (bl) Courtesy of Terry Hunt; **402** Stephen Alvarez/National Geographic Image Collection; **403** (tr) © Jago Cooper, (cr) Shutterstock.com; **405** (tr1) Gavin Hellier/Robert Harding, (tr2) Nick Brundle Photography/Moment/Getty Images; **406** Randy Olson/National Geographic Image Collection; **408-409** (spread) View of Naples/Wittel, Gaspar van (Gaspare Vanvitelli) (1653-1736)/Fratelli Alinari S.P.A./Palatine Gallery, Pitti Palace, Florence/Bridgeman Images; **410** (tl) 1763 copy by Mo Yi Tongof a map of the world drawn by Zheng He (1371-1433) chinese explorer c. 1421. On r is America, so Zheng He may have discovered America before Christopher Colombus during on of his travels ordered by chinese emperor Zhu Di/PVDE (RDA)/Bridgeman Images, (tr) AGE Fotostock/Alamy Stock Photo, (bl) San Giorgio, marble, detail/Donatello, (c.1386-1466)/Fratelli Alinari S.P.A./Museo Nazionale del Bargello, Florence, Tuscany, Italy/Bridgeman Images, (br) The Trustees of the British Museum/Art Resource, NY; **410** (tl) Album/Alamy Stock Photo, (tr) Robert Clark/National Geographic Image Collection, (bl) A figure of a lion on rockwork (cloisonne enamel)/Chinese School, Qing Dynasty (1644-1912)/Paul Freeman/Private Collection/Bridgeman Images, (br) Art Directors & Trip/Alamy Stock Photo, (c) Mughal Coin from Agra, 1556-1605 (silver)/Mughal School/Ashmolean Museum/Ashmolean Museum, University of Oxford, UK/Bridgeman Images; **412-413** (spread) Mondadori Portfolio/Hulton Fine Art Collection/Getty Images; **415** (tr) Fernando G. Baptista/National Geographic Image Collection, (br) Lorenzo Mattei/Robert harding; **416** Fratelli Alinari Idea S.p.A./Corbis Historical/Getty Images; **417** © The Gutenberg Bible, digitised by the HUMI Project, Keio University and National Library of Scotland; **419** (t) Mondadori Portfolio/Hulton Fine Art Collection/Getty Images, (bl) Art Collection 2/Alamy Stock Photo; **420** The Picture Art Collection/Alamy Stock Photo; **421** (tl) Peter Willi/SuperStock/Getty Images, (tr) Fine Art/Corbis Historical/Getty Images; **422** Dave Yoder/National Geographic Image Collection; **424** Stock Montage/Archive Photos/Getty Images; **425** Portrait of a Young Woman as a Sibyl, c.1620 (oil on canvas)/Gentileschi, Orazio (1565-1647)/Museum of Fine Arts, Houston, Texas, USA/Bridgeman Images; **426** Heritage Images/Hulton Archive/Getty Images; **427** Heritage Images/Hulton Archive/Getty Images; **428** Courtesy National Gallery of Art; **430** (tl) Man with traditional Japanese Irezumi tattoo, c.1880 (hand coloured albumen photo) (detail of 398090)/Japanese Photographer, (19th century)/Prismatic Pictures/Private Collection/Bridgeman Images, (cr) Ira Block/National Geographic Image Collection, (bl) Jorge Fernández/LightRocket/Getty Images; **431** (tl) Chuck Place/Alamy Stock Photo, (tr) Courtesy Charles S. King, (bl) De Agostini Picture Library/De Agostini/Getty Images; **432** (tl) Vanni Archive/Art Resource, NY, (cr1) (cr2) © Thomas Walsh, (bl) Museum Associates/Lacma/Art Resource, NY; **433** (tr) Mario Carrieri/Mondadori Portfolio/Getty Images, (bl) Everett Collection Inc/Alamy Stock Photo, (br) Interfoto/Alamy Stock Photo; **434** Cranach, Lucas, the Elder (1472-1553)/Bridgeman Images; **437** (tl) DEA/S. Gutierrez/De Agostini/Getty Images, (tr) David Lyons/Alamy Stock Photo; **439** Philip II and Mary I, 1558/Eworth or Ewoutsz, Hans (fl.1520-74)/Russell Ash Limited/Trustees of the Bedford Estate, Woburn Abbey, UK/Bridgeman Images; **440** Hulton Archive/Getty Images; **441** Dea Picture Library/De Agostini/Getty Images; **443** TAO Images Limited/Alamy Stock Photo; **447-448** (spread) Foofa Jearanaisil/Shutterstock.com; **450** Sultan Suleiman Khan I, 10th Sultan of the Ottoman Empire, 1815 (colour litho)/Young, John (1755-1825)/Stapleton Collection/Private Collection/Bridgeman Images; **453** Marco Ferrarin/Moment Unreleased/Getty Images; **454** Scala/Art Resource, NY; **455** A prayer arch of red satin, embroidered in gilt and silver threads and applique with brocades (satin, giland silver thread)/Turkish School, (19th century)/Christies Images/Private Collection/Bridgeman Images; **456-457** (spread) Education Images/UIG/AGE Fotostock; **458** bpk Bildagentur/Museum fuer Islamische Kunst, Staatliche Museen, Berlin, Germany/Hans Kraeftner/Art Resource; **459** Emperor Akbar conversing with Jesuit missionaries, Indian School, (16th century)/Private Collection/De Agostini Picture Library/Bridgeman Images; **460-461** (spread) Jean-Baptiste Rabouan/laif/Redux; **462-463** (spread) © Atul Loke/The New York Times; **465** The Metropolitan Museum of Art/Art Resource; **466** Ch'ien-Lung, Chinese School/Private Collection/Peter Newark Pictures/Bridgeman Images; **469** Japan: Winter: Atagoshita and Yabu Lane. Image 112 of '100 Famous Views of Edo'. Utagawa Hiroshige (first published 1856-59)/Pictures from History/Bridgeman Images; **470** Thomas L. Kelly/Media Bakery; **471** Tsar Ivan IV Vasilyevich 'the Terrible' (1530-84) 1897 (oil on canvas) (detail of 89327)/Vasnetsov, Victor Mikhailovich (1848-1926)/Tretyakov Gallery, Moscow, Russia/Bridgeman Images; **473** Igor Sinitsyn/Robert Harding; **474** Jose Fuste Raga/Corbis Documentary/Getty Images; **475** Dirk Renckhoff/imageBroker/AGE Fotostock; **477** Portrait of Catherine II, also known as Catherine the Great (Stettin, 1729-Pushkin, 1796), Empress consort of Peter III of Russia (1728-1762), c.1770/Rokotov, Fedor Stepanovich (c.1735-1808)/De Agostini Editore/Museum of History, Moscow, Russia/Bridgeman Images; **480-481** (spread) Jean Paul Villegas/iStock/Getty Images; **483** © Architect of

Camera Press/Redux; **692** (tl) Stefano Bianchetti/Corbis Historical/Getty Images, (tr) Universal History Archive/Universal Images Group/Getty Images, (b) © NARA; **693** (tl) Austria: A Jewish-owned shoe store that was destroyed by the Nazis on Kristallnacht, Vienna, 10 November, 1938 (b/w photo)/Pictures from History/Bridgeman Images, (tr1) XM Collection/Alamy Stock Photo, (tr2) Keystone/Hulton Archive/Getty Images, (bl) Ted Small/Alamy Stock Photo, (br) Universal History Archive/Universal Images Group/Getty Images; **694-695** (spread) IWM/Getty Images/Imperial War Museums/Getty Images; **696** ullstein bild Dtl./ullstein bild/Getty Images; **699** Universal History Archive/UIG/Shutterstock.com; **700** Bettmann/Getty Images; **702** Everett Collection Historical/Alamy Stock Photo; **703** (tc) (br) © Jeff Gusky; **705** John Frost Newspapers/Alamy Stock Photo; **706** Postcard depicting a Senegalese soldier, 1915 (coloured photo), French School (20th century)/Private Collection/Archives Charmet/Bridgeman Images; **707** Historical Images Archive/Alamy Stock Photo; **710** Library of Congress, Prints & Photographs Division, Reproduction number LC-DIG-ppmsca-38818 (digital file from original item) LC-USZ62-16767 (b&w film copy neg.); **712** Diana Markosian/Magnum Photos; **716** Christopher Furlong/Getty Images News/Getty Images; **718** Shawshots/Alamy Stock Photo; **720** IanDagnall Computing/Alamy Stock Photo; **721** Laski Diffusion/Hulton Archive/Getty Images; **723** Chumphon_TH/Shutterstock.com; **724** ART Collection/Alamy Stock Photo; **725** Library of Congress, Prints & Photographs Division, Reproduction number LC-DIG-ppmsca-38284 (digital file from original item) LC-USZ62-30693 (b&w film copy neg.); **726** Gianni Dagli Orti/Shutterstock.com; **727** AKG Images; **728** Victor De Palma/The Life Images Collection/Getty Images; **729** (tr) 2019 Artists Rights Society (ARS), New York/Somaap, Mexico City; Schalkwijk/Art Resource, NY; **732-733** (spread) Bettmann/Getty Images; **734** The Wright Flyer I makes its first flight of 120 feet in 12 seconds, at Kitty Hawk, North Carolina, 10.35am, 17 December 1903 (b/w photo)/Daniels, John T. (1884-1948)/Ken Welsh/Private Collection/Bridgeman Images; **735** Michael Ochs Archives/Getty Images; **736** ullstein bild Dtl./Universal Images Group/Getty Images; **737** Science History Images/Alamy Stock Photo; **738** (t) Keystone-France/Gamma-Keystone/Getty Images, (b) Clare Trainor/National Geographic Image Collection; **740** ullstein bild Dtl./Getty Images; **741** Library of Congress, Prints & Photographs Division, Reproduction number LC-DIG-highsm-24732 (original digital file); **742** Oscar Manello/Hulton Archive/Getty Images; **745** Leipzig Street with Electric Tram, 1914 (oil on canvas)/Kirchner, Ernst Ludwig (1880-1938)/Marlborough Fine Art/Museum Folkwang, Essen, Germany/Bridgeman Images; **746** Fine Art Images/Heritage Images/Hulton Archive/Getty Images; **747** Bettmann/Getty Images; **748** Sueddeutsche Zeitung Photo/Alamy Stock Photo; **749** ullstein bild Dtl./ullstein bild/Getty Images; **750** AKG Images; **751** Popperfoto/Getty Images; **752** AKG Images; **754** AP Images; **755** George Rinhart/Corbis Historical/Getty Images; **756** LIU JIN/AFP/Getty Images; **757** Bettmann/Getty Images; **758-759** (spread) Guernica, 1937 (oil on canvas)/Picasso, Pablo (1881-1973)/Museo Nacional Centro de Arte Reina Sofia, Madrid, Spain/Bridgeman Images; **761** Popperfoto/Getty Images; **764-765** (spread) Everett Collection; **768** Album/Alamy Stock Photo; **769** (tc) Bryan Bedder/Getty Images Entertainment/Getty Images, (br) David Doubilet/National Geographic Image Collection; **773** (tr) The Asahi Shimbun/Getty Images, (br) Schultz Reinhard/Prisma/Superstock; **774** UtCon Collection/Alamy Stock Photo; **775** Keystone/Corbis Historical/Getty Images; **776** Keystone Features/Hulton Archive/Getty Images; **777** Wallace/ANL/Shutterstock.com; **778** Bettmann/Getty Images; **779** Kimimasa Mayama/EPA/Newscom; **780** Scott Barbour/Getty Images News/Getty Images; **781** Arno Burgi/picture alliance/Getty Images; **782** H. Miller/Hulton Archive/Getty Images; **783** Roger Viollet Collection/Roger Viollet/Getty Images; **784** Uli Deck/picture alliance/Getty Images; **784-785** (spread) © The National Archives; **787** James L. Stanfield/National Geographic Image Collection; **789** John Parrot/Stocktrek Images/Getty Images; **798** TASS/Getty Images; **790** Lynn Johnson/National Geographic Image Collection; **792-793** (spread) pa_Yon/Moment/Getty Images; **794** (tl) Dmitri Kessel/The Life Picture Collection/Getty Images, (tr) Sovfoto/Universal Images Group/Getty Images, (cr) Hulton Deutsch/Corbis Historical/Getty Images, (bl) Education Images/Universal Images Group/Getty Images, (br) John Frost Newspapers/Alamy Stock Photo; **795** (t) Guillermo Arias/AFP/Getty Images, (bl) PhotoQuest/Archive Photos/Getty Images, (bc) Peter Turnley/Corbis Historical/Getty Images, (br) Louise Gubb/Corbis Historical/Getty Images; **798** TASS/Getty Images ; **803** (t) (c) NASA; **804** Everett Collection Historical/Alamy Stock Photo; **805** David Guttenfelder/National Geographic Image Collection; **807-808** (spread) © World Monuments Fund; **807** (tl) woodspiral/Alamy Stock Photo, (tr) © World Monuments Fund; **809** Sovfoto/Universal Images Group/Getty Images; **810** VCG/Getty Images; **811** China: Follow the Road to Cooperativisation! A poster from the time of the Great Leap Forward (1958-1961)/Pictures from History/Bridgeman Images; **814** Kevin Mazur/Getty Images; **815** Bettmann/Getty Images; **816** AP Images/Uncredited; **817** Tim Graham/Corbis Historical/Getty Images; **818** (cr) Rolls Press/

Popperfoto/Getty Images, (b) Tim Martin/Robert Harding; **821** David Guttenfelder/National Geographic Image Collection; **822** Dirck Halstead/Hulton Archive/Getty Images; **823** Sovfoto/Universal Images Group/Shutterstock.com; **825** Laszlo Almasi/Reuters; **828** (tr) tim page/Corbis Historical/Getty Images, (br) Everett Collection Historical/Alamy Stock Photo; **829** (t) Melet Georges/Paris Match Archive/Getty Images, (bl) Rolls Press/Popperfoto/Getty Images, (br) NASA; **831** Library of Congress, Prints & Photographs Division, drawing by Edmund S. Valtman, LC-DIG-ppmsc-07978; **832-833** (spread) Peter Timm/ullstein bild/Getty Images; **834** AP Images/Anatoly Maltsev; **836** mpworks/Alamy Stock Photo; **837** mark reinstein/Shutterstock.com; **838** (tl) (c) Gerd Ludwig/National Geographic Image Collection; **839** (t) (b) Gerd Ludwig/National Geographic Image Collection; **841** AP Images; **843** AP Images/Jeff Widener; **844** Marvin Recinos/AFP/Getty Images; **846** Alain BUU/Gamma-Rapho/Getty Images; **848** Independent News and Media/Hulton Archive/Getty Images; **850** Manish Lakhani/Alamy Stock Photo; **851** Stephen Chernin/Getty Images News/Getty Images; **852** Rolls Press/Popperfoto/Getty Images; **853** Terry Ashe/The Life Images Collection/Getty Images; **855** Cynthia Johnson/The Life Images Collection/Getty Images; **856** Stringer/AFP/Getty Images; **857** Robert Nickelsberg/The Life Images Collection/Getty Images; **859** Fabrice Coffrini/AFP/Getty Images; **860** Alejandro Pagni/AFP/Getty Images; **864** Matthew Horwood/Getty Images News/Getty Images; **865** (tl) NASA, (b) Andrew Madali/500px Prime/Getty Images; **866** (t) Frank Micelotta Archive/Hulton Archive/Getty Images, (br) Arlene Richie/Media Sources/Getty Images; **867** (tr) Creative Stock/Alamy Stock Photo, (b) Walt Disney Studios Motion Pictures/Everett Collection; **870-871** (spread) Daniela White Images/Moment/Getty Images; **872** Porter Gifford/Corbis Historical/Getty Images; **873** Gilles Bassignac/Gamma-Rapho/Getty Images; **874** Linda Davidson/The Washington Post/Getty Images; **875** Gokhan Sahin/Getty Images News/Getty Images; **877** Randal Scott/National Geographic Image Collection; **878** Elizabeth Dalziel/National Geographic Image Collection; **879** Jon Benz/National Geographic Image Collection; **880** Ulrich Perrey/DPA/Getty Images; **881** Shah Marai/AFP/Getty Images; **882** NurPhoto/Corbis News/Getty Images; **884** John Stanmeyer/National Geographic Image Collection; **885** Kevin Frayer/Getty Images News/Getty Images; **887** Oli Scarff/Getty Images News/Getty Images; **889** Larry Towell/Magnum Photos; **893** AP Images/Liang zhen; **894** (t) Lynn Johnson/National Geographic Image Collection, (bl) Steve Winter/National Geographic Image Collection; **896-897** (spread) Finbarr O'Reilly/Reuters; **899** Joe Raedle/Getty Images News/Getty Images; **900** (tl) Carl Court/Getty Images News/Getty Images, (cr) imageBroker/Superstock, (br) AP Images/Anthony Devlin; **902** Marty Melville/AFP/Getty Images; **903** Richard Stonehouse/Getty Images Entertainment/Getty Images; **904** Kate Cummings/National Geographic Image Collection; **905** Tyrone Siu/Reuters/Newscom; **906** (tl) © Lynsey Addario, (c) Lynsey Addario/Reportage Archive/Getty Images; **907** (t) (b) Lynsey Addario/Reportage Archive/Getty Images; **908** Li Xiaoguo Xinhua/eyevine/Redux; **909** (tc) Courtesy of Hayat Sindi, (bc) Alexandra Verville/National Geographic Image Collection; **910** Robin Hammond/National Geographic Image Collection; **911** Manuel Hernández/Vizzor Image/Getty Images News/Getty Images; **912** (t) T.H. Culhane/National Geographic Image Collection, (bl) Courtesy of TH Culhane; **914** Jim Richardson/National Geographic Image Collection; **915** (t) Patrick Aventurier/Getty Images News/Getty Images, (cr) Westend61 GmbH/Alamy Stock Photo; **918** NASA Earth Observatory image by Robert Simmon.

TEXT CREDITS

031 (top right) Yuval Noah Harari, "Why humans run the world" | TED2015.; **037** (top right) Source: Epic of Gilgamesh, translated by Maureen Gallery Kovacs, electronic edition by Wolf Carnahan, 1998.; **041** (top left) Source: Hammurabi's Code, translated by L. W. King.; **059** (top right) Source: Ten Commandments By rabbi ronald h. Isaacs.; **062** (top left) Source: Genesis Chapter 7 In the beginning by Mechon Mamre.; **063** (top left) Source: The Epic of Gilgamesh, translated by Benjamin R. Foster, 2001.; **063** (center left) Source: The Mahabharata of Krishna-Dwaipayana Vyasa, translated by Kisari Mohan Ganguli, 1883-1896; **065** (top right) Source: Book of the Dead in Ancient Near Eastern Texts Relating to the Old Testament, edited by James B. Pritchard, Third Edition, 1969.; **071** (center left) Source: "The Triumphant Wife," from the Rig Veda, translated by Wendy Doniger.; **079** (top left) Source: Asoka and the Decline of the Mauras, ed. By Romila Thapar, 1973, pp. 251-252.; **086** (bottom left) Source: Confucius, Analects: With Selections from Traditional Commentaries translated by Edward Slingerland; **092** (center left) Source: Confucius, Analects: With Selections from Traditional Commentaries translated by Edward Slingerland; **094** (center) Source: Paul Salopek, "Cities of Silence"; **103** (top right) Source: Herodotus: The Histories, translated by Aubrey de Selincourt.; **107** (top left) Source: From the Cyrus Cylinder, New translation by Irving Finkel, Curator of Cuneiform Collections at the British Museum.; **107** (bottom left) Source: Holy Bible, Revised Standard Version, The Book of Ezra, 1:1–3; **111** (center left) Source: Herodotus, The Histories, translated by Aubrey de Sélincourt.; **117** (center right) Source: Herodotus, The Histories, translated by Aubrey de Sélincourt.; **119** (center left) Source: Herodotus, The Histories, translated by Aubrey de Sélincourt.; **131** (center right) Source: JSTOR, Early Journal Content, New York Latin Leaflet, vol. 1, "The Funeral Oration of Pericles" by David H. Holmes, 1901.; **146** (bottom left) Source: Plato, Book V of The Republic, c. 380, translated by Benjamin Jowett.; **153** (center right) Source: From The Twelve Tables, Table VII. Naphtal Lewis and Meyer Reinhold, editors, Roman Civilization, The Republic and the Augustan Age, Volume 1; **175** (bottom right) Source: Holy Bible, Revised Standard Edition, The Gospel According to Luke 10:30-34.; **176** (bottom left) Source: Letters of Egeria, John Wilkinson, Egeria's Travels, Liverpool University Press, 1999; **179** (top left) Source: The Annals by Tacitus, Translated by Alfred John Church and William Jackson Brodribb; **179** (center left) Source: R. Knipfing, John, Edict of Toleration, Belgian review of philology and history, issued by Emperor Galerius.; **189** (bottom left) Source: Holy Bible, Revised Standard Edition, The Gospel According to Matthew 5:10-11; **195** (bottom right) Source: Ramayana, from a retelling by William Buck.; **198** (bottom left) Source: Ssu-ma Ch'ien, Grand Historian of China, by Burton Watson.; **209** (bottom right) Source: The Tale of Genji, by Murasaki Shikibu, edited and translated by Royall Tyler.; **215** (bottom left) Source: Lessons for Women, by Ban Zhao, Pan Chao: Foremost Woman Scholar of China, by Nancy Lee Swann, New York: American Historical Associate, 1932, pp. 84-85; **216** (center) Source: Nadia Drake, "How 'The Land of the Stars' Shaped Astronomy (and Me)"; **227** (top right) Source: The Institutes of Justinian; **233** (center right) Source: From "The Wars of Justinian" by Procopius, History of the Wars, 7 Vols., trans.

H. B. Dewing, Loeb Library of the Greek and Roman Classics, (Cambridge, Mass.: Harvard University Press, 1914), Vol. I, pp. 451-473; **241** (bottom left) Source: S. G. Mercati, "Sull'epitafio di Basilio II Bulgaroctonos," Bessarione 25 (1921), 137-42; "L'epitafio di Basilio Bulgaroctonos secondo il codice modenese greco 324," Bessarione 26 (1922), 220-2; both reprinted in: S. G. Mercati, Collectanea Byzantina , II (Bari, 1970), 226-31, 232-4; **261** (bottom left) Source: The Uthmanis, by Al-Jahiz; **262** (center) Source: Gabe Bullard, "The World's Newest Major Religion: No Religion"; **281** (top right) Source: The Project Gutenberg EBook of Chaucer's Works, Volume 4 (of 7) — The Canterbury Tales by Geoffrey Chaucer (Middle English version) pp. 85-86; **292** (bottom right) Source: Alexiad, by Anna Comnena, Book I, Chapter XIV, ca. 1148. Edited and translated by Elizabeth A. Dawes. London: Routledge, Kegan, Paul, 1928.; **305** (center left) Source: Rosemary Horrox, trans. and ed., "The Persecution of the Jews," in The Black Death (Manchester, U.K.: Manchester University Press, 1994), p. 208; **310** (center left) Source: Patricia Buckley Ebrey, "The Women in Liu Kezhuang's Family", Modern China 10, no. 4, 1984; citation pn p. 437.; **313** (top left) Source: Friedrich Hirth and W.W. Rockhill, Chau Ju-Kua: His Work on the Chinese and Arab Trade in the Twelfth and Thirteenth Centuries, Entitled Chu-fan-chi (St. Petersburg: Imperial Academy of Sciences, 1911), pp. 149, 153–154, 162–163; **313** (center left) Source: Friedrich Hirth and W.W. Rockhill, Chau Ju-Kua: His Work on the Chinese and Arab Trade in the Twelfth and Thirteenth Centuries, Entitled Chu-fan-chi (St. Petersburg: Imperial Academy of Sciences, 1911), pp. 149, 153–154, 162–163; **313** (bottom left) Source: Friedrich Hirth and W.W. Rockhill, Chau Ju-Kua: His Work on the Chinese and Arab Trade in the Twelfth and Thirteenth Centuries, Entitled Chu-fan-chi (St. Petersburg: Imperial Academy of Sciences, 1911), pp. 149, 153–154, 162–163; **313** (bottom left) Source: Allen, Terry "Byzantine Sources for the Jami' al-tawarikh of Rashid al-Din." Ars Orientalis 15 (1985), pp. 121–36.; **323** (top right) Surce: Ono no Komachi, ca. 833-857, translated by Michael R. Burch Watching wan moonlight illuminate tree limbs, my heart also brims, overflowing with autumn.; **331** (top left) Source: The Complete History, by Ibn al-Athir, Edward G. Browne, A Literary History of Persia, (Cambridge: Cambridge University Press, 1902), Vol. II, pp. 427-431.; **331** (center left) Source: The History of the World-Conqueror by Ala-ad-Din Ata-Malik Juvaini, translated from the text of Mirza Muhammad Qazvini by John Andrew Boyle, Ph.D., Volume 1 (Manchester: Manchester University Press, 1958), p. 33.; **349** (top right) Source: History of Mehmed the Conqueror by Kritovoulos, Charles T. Riggs, translator, History of Mehmed the Conqueror, Praeger, 1954.; **351** (bottom left) Source: The Travels of Marco Polo, by Marco Polo and Latham, Penguin Classics, 1958; **352** (center) Source: Christopher Shea, "Did the Vikings Get a Bum Rap?"; **362** (top right) Source: The History of Africa: The Quest for Eternal Harmony, Molefi Kete Asante, Routledge, pages 130–131. Quoted material is from Sundiata: An Epic of Old Mali, Djibril Tamsir Niane, London: Longmans, 1965.; **365** (top left) Source: The History of Africa: The Quest for Eternal Harmony, Molefi Kete Asante, Routledge, page 154. Original source is quoted as "Mallows 1984, 39, 41,56.; **366** (center right) Source: From H. A. R. Gibb, The Travels of Ibn Battuta A.D. 1325–1354, The Hakluyt Society, pp. 918, 144.; **367** (bottom right) Source: Travels by Ibn Battuta, The Story of

Swahili, John M. Mugane, Ohio University Press, 2015, page 23. Note in book: Ibn Battuta, quoted in Freeman-Grenville (1975, 29–30).; **379** (top left) Source: Kingdom of Ghana, Al-Bakri, The Book of Routes and Realms, cited in Levitzion and Hopkins, Corpus of Early Arabic Sources for West African History, (Cambridge University Press, 1981) pp. 79-81.; **379** (center left) Source: Dames, Mansel Longworth, trans. The Book of Duarte Barbosa, Volume 1 (London: Bedford Press, 1918, pp. 17–18).; **379** (bottom left) Source: Leo Africanus, A Geographical Historie of Africa, Paul Brians, et al. Reading About the World, vol. 2, 3rd ed. (Harcourt Brace College Custom Books), 1999; **405** (bottom left) Source: Popol Vuh. Translated into English by Delia Goetz and Sylvanus Griswold Morley from Adrian Recino's translation from Quiche into Spanish. Plantin Press, Los Angeles, 1954, p. 86.; **406** (center) Source: Brook Larmer, "The Real Price of Gold"; **429** (top left) Source: Cassandra Fedele, "An Oration . . . in Praise of Letters", Letters and Orations, edited and translated by Diana Robin, University of Chicago Press, 2000.; **429** (center left) Source: The Prince by Niccoló Machiavelli, translated and edited by Angelo M. Codevilla, Yale University Press, 1997.; **429** (bottom left) Source: Utopia by Thomas More, introduction by Jenny Mezciems, Random House, 1992.; **435** (top right) Source: Martin Luther, "Against the Robbing and Murdering Hordes of Peasants", E.G. Rupp and Benjamin Drewery, Martin Luther, Documents of Modern History (London: Edward Arnold, 1970), pp. 121-6.; **445** (center left) Source: Literacy Rate in Europe, Our World in Data.; **445** (top right) Source: "Account of Michelangelo", Ascanio Condivi, The Life of Michelangelo, translated by Alice Wohl (1976).; **449** (top right) Source: Robert Dankoff and Sooyong Kim, translation and commentary, An Ottoman Traveller: Selections from the Book of Travels of Evliya Çelebi (London: Eland Publishing, 2010).; **449** (bottom right) Source: Robert Dankoff and Sooyong Kim, translation and commentary, An Ottoman Traveller: Selections from the Book of Travels of Evliya Çelebi (London: Eland Publishing, 2010).; **467** (top left) Source: Letter from Voltaire to Frederick the Great, Bronson, Bennet, and Chiumei Ho, Splendors of China's Forbidden City: The Glorious Reign of Emperor Qianlong, Merrell Publishers Limited in association with the Field Museum, 2004, p. 274; **467** (center left) Source: Letter from Voltaire to Marquis de Condorcet, Voltaire in His Letters: Being a Selection from His Correspondence, by Voltaire, translated by S.G. Tallentyre, pseud. Evelyn Beatrice Hall. G.P. Putnam's Sons, New York, 1919. pp. 242-243; **467** (bottom left) Source: Letter from Qianlong to King George III, Backhouse, E. and J.O.P. Bland, Annals and Memoirs of the Court of Peking, Houghton Mifflin, Boston, 1914. pp. 322-331; **479** (center left) Source: "Frog Haiku" by Matsuo Basho, loose translation by Michael R. Burch; **485** (top left) Source: General History of the Things of New Spain by Bernardino de Sahagun, Stuart B. Schwartz, Victors and Vanquished: Spanish and Nahua View of the Conquest of Mexico, New York, Bedfore/St. Martin's, 2000.; **491** (top right) Source: Book of Useful Information on the Principles and Rules of Navigation by Ahmad Ibn Majid, cited in Aramco World (July/August 2005; vol. 56, no. 4), "The Navigator Ahmad Ibn Majid"; **495** (top left) Source: Sejarah Melayu (Malay Annals) by Tun Sri Lanang, Aran MacKinnon and Elaine MacKinnon, editors, Places of Encounters: Time, Place, and Connectivity in World History, Volume 1, Westview Press, 2012.; **495** (center left) Source:

Travels in Persia 1673-1677 by Jean Chardin, Sir John Chardin, Travels in Persia 1673-1677, London, Argonaut Press, 1927.; **495** (bottom left) Source: The Ship of Sulaimān by Muhammad Rabī ibn Muhammad Ibrāham, Translated by John O'Kane, Columbia University Press, 1972; **507** (bottom left) Source: A Brief Account of the Destruction of the Indies by Bartolome de las Casas, Project Gutenberg, epub format, p. 12.; **515** (bottom left) Source: Leo Africanus, History and Description of Africa, trans. J. Pory and ed. R. Brown, London, 1896, Vol. III, pp. 824–7, and quoted in E.W. Bovill, The Gold Trade of the Moor, OUP, Oxford, 1968, pp. 147–50), History of Africa, Kevin Shillington, Palgrave/Macmillan, page 112.; **518** (bottom right) Source: Olaudah Equiano, The Interesting Narrative of the Life of Olaudah Equiano, or Gustavus Vassa, the African; **518** (bottom left) Source as listed in Voyages, p.568: Olaudah Equiano, The Interesting Narrative of the Life of Olaudah Equiano, or Gustavus Vassa, ed. Vincent Carretta, 2d ed. (New York: Penguin, 2003), pp. 105–109)); **521** (center) Source: Greg Miller, "These Maps Show the Epic Quest for a Northwest Passage"; **527** (bottom right) Source: Sarah H. Bradford, Harriet: The Moses of Her People, copyright by Sarah H. Bradford, 1886; **531** (bottom left) Source: William Cowper, "Pity for Poor Africans", Yale University.; **542** (bottom left) Source: The Trial of Charles I (1649): Selected Links & Bibliography by Lawrence MacLachlan (http://law2.umkc.edu/faculty/projects/ftrials/charlesIlinks.html); **544** (top right) Source: The English Bill of Rights, 1689; **554** (bottom right) Source: Joseph Banks, The Endeavour Journal of Joseph Banks, J.C. Beaglehole, ed., 2nd edition, Vol.1 (Sydney: Halstead Press, 1962, p. 252).; **561** (bottom left) Source: Sir Francis Bacon, quotation, Nature's Government: Science, Imperial Britain, and the "Improvement" of the World, by Richard Drayton. (New Haven: Yale University Press, 2000, pp. 55, 118); **565** (bottom right) Source: Politics by Aristotle, Project Gutenberg, Ebook of Politics, A Treatise on Government, Book III, Chapter VI, translated by William Ellis, A.M. London & Toronto Published By J M Dent & Sons Ltd. & In New York By E. P. Dutton &. Co. First Issue Of This Edition 1912 Reprinted 1919, 1923, 1928.; **570** (center right) Source: A Philosophical Dictionary by Voltaire, University of Adelaide, entry no. 308, "Liberty of the Press".; **571** (top right) Source: "Jean-Jacques Rousseau, Emile, 1762," Liberty, Equality, Fraternity; **572** (top right) Source: Memoirs of Jean François Marmontel by Jean François Marmontel, vol. 2, p. 36, Boston, Houghton, Osgood, 1878.; **572** (top left) Source: The Spirit of Laws by Charles-Louis Montesquieu, Online Library of Liberty, Book 1, Chapter 3. Charles Louis de Secondat, Baron de Montesquieu, The Complete Works of M. de Montesquieu, Volume 1. London: T. Evans and W. Davis, 1777.; **572** (center left) Source: "A Vindication of the Rights of Woman by Mary Wollstonecraft/With Strictures on Political and Moral Subjects.", Project Gutenberg.; **572** (bottom left) Source: The Encyclopedia by Denis Diderot, Edited and translated by Stephen Gendzier, The Encyclopedia Selections, Harper Torchbooks, 1967.; **579** (bottom left) Source: An Essay Concerning Human Understanding by John Locke, Project Gutenberg, Volume 1 / MDCXC, Based on the 2nd Edition.; **583** (bottom right) Source: Thomas Jefferson, Declaration of Independence; **585** (top right) Source: The National Assembly, Declaration of the Rights of Man and of the Citizen, The Avalon Project, Lillian Goldman Law Library, Yale Law School; **589** (bottom right)

Source: The L'Ouverture Project (https://thelouvertureproject.org/index.php?title=Haitian_Constitution_of_1801_(English)); **591** (top right) Source: Napoleon's Account of His Coup d'État (10 September 1799), A Documentary Survey of the French Revolution. John Hall Stewart. New York: Macmillan, 1951, 763-765. Excerpted in Liberty, Equality, Fraternity: Exploring the French Revolution, Jack R. Censer and Lynn Hunt, eds. American Social History Productions, 2001.; **596** (bottom right) Source: William Blake, "The Tyger", Plate 42 from Songs of Innocence. William Blake. 1789. Copy Z, printed around 1826, is currently held by the Library of Congress; **600** (bottom right) Source: Simón Bolívar, letter to governor of Jamaica, September 1815, Translated by Lewis Bertrand in Selected Writings of Bolivar (New York: The Colonial Press Inc., 1951).; **604** (bottom right) Source: Benjamin Franklin, letter to to Henry Laurens, 25 May 1782, The National Historical Publications and Records Commission, the National Archives.; **607** (top right) Source: Mercy Otis Warren, letter to Catherine Macauley, September 17, 1787; **608** (center) Source: Tony Gerber, "Becoming Jane"; **622** (bottom right) Source: R. Beasland, extract from "London companion during the Great Exhibition"; **641** (center) Source: Statistics on World Population, GRP, and Per Capita GDP, 1–2008 A.D., Angus Maddison, University of Groningen; **641** (center left) Source: Andrew Ure, The Philosophy of Manufacturers, 1835; **657** (top left) Source: Exploration of the Valley of the Amazon by William Lewis Herndon; **657** (center left) Source: Voyages A-16; Mexican History: A Primary Source Reader, edited by Nora E. Jaffary, Edward W. Osowski, Susie S. Porter, Westview Press 2010, Boulder, CO, p. 257; **657** (bottom left) Source: "First Electoral Manifesto of the Argentine Socialist Worker Party"; **661** (bottom left) Source: "A Cry from an Indian Wife" by Pauline Johnson-Tekahionwake; **665** (bottom left) Source: "House Divided" speech by Abraham Lincoln; **668** (bottom right) Source: King Khama of the Bangwato, quoted in Neil Parsons, King Khama, Emperor Joe and the Great White Queen: Victorian Britain Through African Eyes (Chicago: University of Chicago Press, 1998), p. 103.; **679** (top left) Source: D.R. SarDesai, Souitheast Asia Past and Present, 4th ed. (Boulder: Westview, 1997), p. 92; **679** (top right) Source: Mark Twain, from the New York Herald, October 15, 1900; **679** (top right) Source: Rudyard Kipling, Rudyard Kipling's Verse Inclusive Edition (New York: Doubleday, Page, & Company, 1919), p. 371; **687** (bottom left) Source: G.N. Sanderson, "The Foreign Policy of Negua Menelik" in the Journal of African History, Vol. 5, 1964. Reprinted in Voyages p. 805A.; **689** (center) Source: Laura Parker, "Plastic"; **707** (bottom right) Source: British private Harold Boughton, 1984, "Voices of the First World War: Gallipoli," Imperial War Museum; **711** (top left) Source: General Syrian Congress, "Congress of Damascus Resolution," July 2, 1919, Sources of Global History Since 1900, 2d ed. James H. Overfield (New York: Wadsworth/Cengage, 2012), pp. 102-103.; **711** (center left) Source: "Eight Points," by Nguyen Ai Quoc, 1919, Rhetoric of Revolt: Ho Chi Minh's Discourse for Revolution. Peter Anthony DeCaro. Westport, CT: Greenwood, 2003, Appendix A, p. 101.; **711** (bottom left) Source: Second Pan-African Congress, "To the World," 1921; **713** (top right) Source: Henry Morgenthau, Ambassador Morgenthau's Story, Chapter XXV, "Talaat Tells Why He Deports the Armenians"; **717** (top right) Source: Ernest Hemingway, "Notes on the Next War: A Serious Topical Letter," 1935,

Hemingway on War, edited by Séan Hemingway. New York: Scribner, 2003, p. 304; **723** (bottom right) Mao Zedong, "Report on an Investigation of the Peasant Movement in Hunan" March 1927; **731** (bottom left) Source: Vladimir Lenin, "Can the Bolsheviks Retain State Power?"; **743** (bottom right) Source: Antonio Gramsci, from Avanti!, Political Writings 1910-1920 (London: Lawrence and Wishart, 1977), p. 17.; **745** (bottom right) Source: Official Kristallnacht Order, 1938; **763** (bottom left) Source: Sources of Japanese Tradition, ed. William Theodore de Bary, vol 2 (New York: Columbia university Press, 1958) p. 289; **763** (top right) Source: Walter Galenson and Arnold Zeliner, "International Comparison of Unemployment Rates," The Measurement and Behavior of Unemployment (National Bureau of Economic Research, 1957); **767** (bottom right) Source: Winston Churchill, speech before the House of Commons, June 4, 1940; **775** (top right) Source: Nancy Wake, The Autobiography of the Woman the Gestapo Called the White Mouse; **783** (top right) Source: Elie Wiesel, Night, Translated by Marion Wiesel, Hill and Wang, 2006; **787** (bottom right) Source: Robert H. Jackson, Opening Statement before the International Tribunal, Nuremberg, Germany, November 21, 1945; **789** (top left) Source: President Franklin D. Roosevelt, Annual Address to Congress, January 6, 1941, the "Four Freedoms" speech; **791** (center) Source: Yudhijit Bhattacharjee, "The Science of Good and Evil"; **800** (bottom left) Source: Westminster College, Fulton, Missouri, "The Sinews of Peace ('Iron Curtain Speech')", The International Churchill Society, March 5, 1946.; **803** (top left) Source: Bulletin of the Atomic Scientists; **819** (top right) Source: Anthony Eden, address to House of Commons on Suez Crisis, October 31, 1956; **819** (bottom right) Source: Dwight D. Eisenhower, speech on Suez Crisis,; **831** (bottom left) Source: John F. Kennedy, letter to Nikita Krushchev, state.gov,1961.; **831** (bottom left) Source: Nikita Krushchev, letter to John Kennedy, state.gov, 1961; **847** (top right) Source: "Nelson Mandela's Address to Rally in Cape Town on His Release from Prison," 1990; **852** (bottom right) Source: Jewish Virtual Library; **859** (top right) Source: United Nations, Universal Declaration of Human Rights; **861** (top left) Source: Jaime L. Sin, "Guidelines on Christian Conduct During Elections," in The Philippine Revolution and the Involvement of the Church, ed. Fausto Gomez (Manila: UST Social Research Center, 1986), pp. 40-44; **861** (center left) Source: Adam Michnik, "Letter from the Gdansk Prison," University of California Press, 1987, p86; **861** (bottom left) Source: Alison Ozinsky, "Purple Reign," Upfront, November, 1989. Reprinted in The Purple Shall Govern: A South African A to Z of Nonviolent Action, ed. Dene Smuts and Shauna Westcott (Cape Town: Oxford University Press, 1991), 13-15; **869** (top right) Source: Boutros Boutros-Ghali, "Inaugural Address," Ninth Session of the United Nations Conference on Trade and Development; **889** (center) Source: International Monetary Fund; **891** (top right) Source: CIA World Factbook; **891** (center right) Source: CIA World Factbook; **891** (bottom right) Source: countryeconomy.com; **901** (bottom right) Source: Ai Weiwei Responds To Chinese Authorities Destroying His Beijing Studio; **917** (center left) Source: Hangzhou Declaration from the 5th BRICS Science, Technology & Innovation (STI) Ministerial Meeting, Hangzhou, China, July 18, 2017.; **917** (top right) Source: Luthi, D., et al. 2008; Etheridge, D.M., et al. 2010; Vostok ice core data / J.R. Petit et al.; NOAA Mauna Loa CO2 record.